Guide to
Getting
2007
Financial Aid

Guide to Getting Financial Aid 2007

First Edition

The College Board, New York

The College Board: Connecting Students to College Success

The College Board is a not-for-profit membership association whose mission is to connect students to college success and opportunity. Founded in 1900, the association is composed of more than 5,000 schools, colleges, universities, and other educational organizations. Each year, the College Board serves seven million students and their parents, 23,000 high schools, and 3,500 colleges through major programs and services in college admissions, guidance, assessment, financial aid, enrollment, and teaching and learning. Among its best-known programs are the SAT®, the PSAT/NMSQT®, and the Advanced Placement Program® (AP®). The College Board is committed to the principles of excellence and equity, and that commitment is embodied in all of its programs, services, activities, and concerns.

Visit the College Board on the Web: www.collegeboard.com.

Editorial inquiries concerning this book should be directed to College Planning Services, College Board, 45 Columbus Avenue, New York, NY 10023-6992; or telephone 212 713-8000.

Copies of this book are available from your local bookseller or may be ordered from College Board Publications, P.O. Box 869010, Plano, TX 75074-0998. The book may also be ordered online through the College Board Store at www.collegeboard.com. The price is $19.95.

© 2006 The College Board. All rights reserved. College Board, Advanced Placement Program, AP, CLEP, CollegeCredit, College-Level Examination Program, College Scholarship Service, CSS, CSS/Financial Aid PROFILE, SAT, and the acorn logo are registered trademarks of the College Board. connect to college success, SAT Preparation Booklet, SAT Reasoning Test, SAT Subject Tests, The Official SAT Online Course, The Official SAT Study Guide, and The Official Study Guide for all SAT Subject Tests are trademarks owned by the College Board. PSAT/NMSQT is a registered trademark of the College Board and National Merit Scholarship Corporation. All other products and services may be trademarks of their respective owners.

Library of Congress Control Number: 2006903734

ISBN-13: 978-0-87447-766-5

ISBN-10: 0-87447-766-2

Printed in the United States of America

Dear Friends,

The College Board is dedicated to connecting students to college success and opportunity. We believe in the principles of excellence and equity in education and try to promote them in all that we do. With the College Board's Handbook series, we hope to put an authoritative source of college information at your fingertips to help connect you to a college education.

College is a dream worth working hard to achieve. I've been a businessman, a governor, and now the president of the College Board, but nothing makes me prouder than to say that I am a college graduate. With perseverance, anyone who desires a college education can attain one. College Board publications can help you get there.

My best wishes on your journey to success.

Gaston Caperton

Gaston Caperton
President
The College Board

Contents

Preface ix
How to Use This Book xi

Part I: Financial Aid Step by Step

    Yes, You Can Afford College 3
    Step 1: Let's Go Over the Basics 9
    Step 2: Estimate How Financial Aid Will Work for *You* 15
    Step 3: Choosing Colleges, Thinking Costs 23
    Step 4: Get Ready for the Forms 35
    Step 5: Fill Out the FAFSA 43
    Step 6: Fill Out the PROFILE 55
    Step 7: Fill Out Any Other Required Forms 69
    Step 8: Make Your Special Circumstances Known 75
    Step 9: Look for Other Sources of Money 83
    Step 10: Weigh the Offers 91
    Step 11: Consider Your Out-of-Pocket Options 99
    Once You're In College 113

Part II: Tables and Worksheets

    Worksheet 1: Meet Your Application Deadlines 121
    Worksheet 2: Scholarship Application Planner 122
    Worksheet 3: Compare Your Awards 123
    Two Sample Financial Aid Award Letters 124
    2006-07 FAFSA On the Web Worksheet 126
    Worksheet 4: Estimate Your EFC 134
    Contact Information for State Programs 139
    Contact Information for State 529 Plans 141

Part III: Financial Aid College by College

    State-by-state descriptions of colleges 147

Part IV: Scholarship Lists

    Academic scholarships 905
    Art scholarships 913
    Athletic scholarships 917
    Music/drama scholarships 953
    ROTC scholarships 957

Glossary 965
Alphabetical index 977

List of Figures

Fig. 1.	Average Total College Price by Institution Type	4
Fig. 2.	Average Annual Earnings by Education Level	5
Fig. 3.	Estimated Cumulative Earnings Minus College Costs	6
Fig. 4.	Total Financial Aid Available by Source (in billions)	13
Fig. 5.	Sample EFC Illustration	21
Fig. 6.	Distribution of Full-Time Undergraduates at Four-Year Institutions by Tuition and Fee Charges	26
Fig. 7.	FAFSA PIN Site	41
Fig. 8.	FAFSA on the Web	45
Fig. 9.	Finding a College's Federal Code	52
Fig. 10.	CSS/Financial Aid PROFILE Online	56
Fig. 11.	Finding a College's CSS Code	59
Fig. 12.	collegeboard.com's Scholarship Search	85
Fig. 13.	Sample Financial Aid Award Letter 1	124
Fig. 14.	Sample Financial Aid Award Letter 2	125

List of Tables

Table 1.	Sample Average Undergraduate Budgets, 2005-06	28
Table 2.	State Aid Deadlines	72
Table 3.	Comparison of Education Savings Options	102
Table 4.	Calculating Your Monthly Loan Payment	106
Table 5.	Effects of Letting Interest Accrue While You're In College	107
Table 6.	Comparison of Education Loan Options	108
Table 7.	Federal Income Tax Benefits for Higher Education	111
Table 8.	Federal EFC Allowances for State Taxes	136
Table 9.	Federal EFC Allowances for FICA and Employment	137
Table 10.	Federal EFC Income Protection Allowance for Parents	137
Table 11.	Federal EFC Adjusted Net Worth of a Business or Farm	137
Table 12.	Federal EFC Education Savings and Asset Protection Allowance for Parents	138
Table 13.	Federal EFC Parents' Contribution from Adjusted Available Income (AAI)	138

List of Worksheets

Worksheet 1.	Meet Your Application Deadlines	121
Worksheet 2.	Scholarship Application Planner	122
Worksheet 3.	Compare Your Awards	123
Worksheet 4A.	Estimate a Dependent Student's Expected Contribution	134
Worksheet 4B.	Estimate the Parents' Expected Contribution	135

Preface

Financial aid is a great equalizer. In 2005, over $120 billion in aid was awarded from government and private sources. Coupled with the wide range of lower-cost college options available, financial aid should make a college education affordable for just about everyone.

Yet a recent study by the American Council on Education shows that hundreds of thousands of students who are eligible for this boon don't even apply for it. We assume these students are either unaware of the possibility of aid, or mistakenly believe financial aid is not for them.

And many parents and students who apply for financial aid find the process to be confusing, even intimidating. Like the tax code, the forms and guidelines appear to be full of exceptions, convolutions, and incomprehensible terms.

But it doesn't have to be that way. A central aim of this book is to take the confusion and intimidation out of the process by giving clear and direct explanations of what financial aid is all about and simple, step-by-step directions for how to get it. By combining these explanations and directions with costs and financial aid facts for every accredited college that reports this data, we hope this book will achieve our ultimate goal of connecting students to colleges that match both their needs and their means.

Acknowledgments

We gratefully acknowledge the contributions of the many individuals who helped bring this book into being. George Ochoa, our writer for Part I of this book, "Financial Aid, Step by Step," transformed a complicated and intricate subject into clear and simple prose. Without his talent, the purpose of this guide could not have been achieved.

Renee Gernand provided leadership and editorial guidance throughout the project. Kathie Little and Jack Joyce, our resident experts on financial aid, reviewed the content and kept our course true, as did Cindy Bailey. Kate Crane copyedited the manuscript, and Betty Keim proofread the finished book.

While we had the advantage of many "in house" resources, we also relied upon the knowledge and advice of seven financial aid officers who took time from their busy schedules to give us interviews: Vincent Amoroso of the University of North Carolina at Chapel Hill, Bonnie Lee Behm of Villanova University, Elizabeth Bickford of the University of Oregon, Joe Paul Case of Amherst College, Mary San Agustin of Palomar College, Mike Scott of Texas Christian University, and Forrest Stuart of Rhodes College. We hope you will find their insight and advice, quoted throughout Part I, as illuminating as we did.

The descriptions of colleges presented in Part III, "Financial Aid, College by College," were compiled from the College Board's Annual Survey of Colleges. A team of editors, led by Stan Bernstein, edited, verified, and double-checked the data with the colleges. A team of programmers and composers at Thomas Technology Solutions converted the database into readable pages.

Finally, we would like to thank the Creative Services team who, under Kathryn Diminnie's direction, turned the manuscript into a finished book, especially John Ulicny, Kevin Iwano, Caitlin McClure, Alessandra Baldi, and Kiki Black.

Tom Vanderberg, Senior Editor,
Database Publications

Kevin Troy, Assistant Editor

How to Use This Book

Part I: Financial Aid, Step by Step

The first chapter, "Yes, You Can Afford College," establishes our central point: a college can be found to fit any budget. If you are skeptical about that, please start here—we think we make a strong case.

Steps 1 through 11 provide easy-to-follow directions on how to get financial aid, including what you need to know, what you need to do, and when you need to do it.

These "steps" are presented in a logical sequence. But depending upon your own circumstances—where you are in the college application process, your family's finances, what kinds of colleges you're applying to, and the policies of those individual colleges—you may need to take the steps in a slightly different order, skip some steps, or do some steps simultaneously. To keep track of what should be done when, consult the planning calendar on the inside front cover.

Financial aid officers and the forms you need to fill out often use jargon that can at times seem vague or confusing. Terms like "need" and "cost of attendance" have specific meanings that might not be the same as what you would assume. Throughout Part I, you'll find key terms defined in "Know the Lingo" sidebars (you'll also find a detailed, comprehensive glossary at the end of this book). Other sidebars emphasize or illustrate the main points of each step.

Throughout Part I, you'll find graphs and charts that also illustrate key points, and tables that summarize information and let you compare different financial aid options. You'll also find checklists and prefilled sample worksheets that will help you plan and keep track of your applications. Blank copies of those worksheets for you to fill in are in Part II.

Part II: Tables and Worksheets

One of the worksheets that you'll find in Part II will help you compare the financial aid award letters that you'll receive from colleges. To drive home the point that no two award letters are alike, we've included two samples in Part II, immediately after the comparison worksheet. These are actual award letters that were sent to the same aid applicant by two different universities, the names of which we've changed.

Part II also includes a series of worksheets that you can use to estimate how much the federal government will say you should pay for college out-of-pocket—that's your "expected family contribution" (EFC) used by colleges to award financial aid. (You'll learn more about the EFC and how it's calculated in Part I.) These worksheets are designed for dependent students and their parents. If you are an independent student, you can do the same thing with the online tools at the collegeboard.com Web site. In addition to worksheets, Part II includes a sample of the preapplication worksheet for the Free Application for Federal Student Aid (FAFSA). This worksheet shows all of the questions included on *last year's* FAFSA; it may be that some questions will change somewhat in the year you fill this out. Finally, in Part II you'll find lists of state aid programs, state-sponsored 529 college savings plans, and other useful places to find more information.

Part III: Financial Aid College by College

This is where we help you get the "financial aid picture" at specific colleges, including scholarships the colleges offer to entering students, and required forms and deadlines. To place this picture in context, we give you brief facts about the kind of college it is, and its basic costs. This information can help you compare the colleges you are considering and find colleges that look affordable. But keep in mind that the financial aid figures are mostly based on averages, meaning many students will be above or below these benchmarks.

The college descriptions in Part III are arranged alphabetically by state or territory. Running headers at the top of each page will help you orient yourself and find schools quickly. An alphabetical index of all the colleges in the book appears in Part IV.

Every college described in this book is accredited by an agency recognized by the U.S. Department of Education. Accreditation is a process in which an outside agency ensures that a college meets certain basic standards—it's a stamp of approval on the college's teaching, facilities, and administration. For financial aid purposes, accreditation by a federally recognized agency means that federal student aid dollars can be used to attend the institution.

The *College Board College Handbook* also includes full descriptions of the colleges in this book, going beyond the cost and financial aid details presented here to include information about admissions requirements, academics, housing, student life, athletics, and more.

Where the College Information Comes From

The information in the college descriptions comes from the College Board's most recent Annual Survey of Colleges, which was conducted in the spring of 2006. Every college reported its own cost and financial aid information to us. Where possible, our staff of editors verified the information by consulting third-party sources, including public university system or district offices, state education departments, and the federal government's Integrated Postsecondary Educational Database System (IPEDS). The information presented was current at the time this book went to press in May 2006—but be warned that it may have changed by the time you're reading this. Once you have narrowed down a list of colleges that you're interested in, you should confirm critical information, such as financial aid application deadlines and requirements, by visiting the colleges' Web sites or contacting their financial aid offices.

What's in the College Descriptions

Each college description begins with a shaded box that contains the name of the college, the city or town it's located in, and its Web site address. For every college, its six-digit "federal code"—the code you will need in order to have your FAFSA information sent to the college—appears in this box. If a college requires the College Board's CSS/Financial Aid PROFILE®, its four-digit CSS® code also appears in this box. (The CSS code is the same code you use to send SAT® and ACT scores and AP® Exam grades to a college; the federal code is only used for the FAFSA.)

Below the college name box you'll find a brief summary of what type of college it is—whether it's a four-year private university, a two-year community college, or a four-year culinary school run on a for-profit basis. (Definitions of all the different types of schools you might find here are in the glossary.) You'll also find information about the number of students who were enrolled in the 2005-06 school year, and the relative difficulty of obtaining admission to the college.

BASIC COSTS

"Basic Costs" lists the tuition, fees, room, and board charged by the college. The date indicates the school year for which these numbers apply—if the college was unable to report final or projected figures for the upcoming school year, last year's figures are given. If the college combines tuition, fees, and room and board expenses, that single figure is given as a comprehensive fee.

It's important to note that these figures do not include other out-of-pocket costs, such as books, supplies, transportation, and personal expenses. These costs can be substantial, depending upon where and how you live, and what you study. But since these costs vary widely from student to student, we felt it would be misleading to display average amounts.

FINANCIAL AID PICTURE

The core of each college's description is the information about the financial aid it offers. Again, the date indicates the school year for which the college reported numbers—either the current year or the prior year. Depending on the aid programs offered by the college and the figures they reported, you may see one or several of these elements of the financial aid picture:

- **Students with Need.** This shows how financial aid was given to students who could not afford the full cost of attending the college on their own (a full explanation of how "need" is determined is found in Part I, Step 1). The focus is on the entering freshman class but, if a college was unable to provide that breakdown, the numbers are for all undergraduates. Most colleges disclosed the average percentage of need met by financial aid packages, and the relative proportion of aid given as scholarships and grants as opposed to loans or work-study jobs. Use this data to get a sense of how likely a college is to meet your full need, and how much aid will probably come in the form of loans.

- **Students Without Need.** Even though a student does not need financial aid, it's still possible that a college will provide aid based on merit or other criteria, such as alumni affiliation or minority status. That's what is shown here. If a college has a policy of only awarding aid to students who have need, this is also stated here.

- **Scholarships Offered.** This gives details on merit scholarships offered by the college and their criteria for being awarded. Here you can get a sense of whether your GPA or SAT scores put you in the right ballpark for a merit-based grant. You'll also find information about the number of student-athletes who were given a scholarship by the college, and the average award.

- **Cumulative Student Debt.** This tells you how many students borrowed money to pay for college and how much they owed, on average, when they graduated. This is another way for you to measure how much of a college's aid will be loan based. The numbers here only include student loans taken out through the college—not PLUS loans, private education loans, or other borrowing done through a third-party lender.

FINANCIAL AID PROCEDURES

The financial aid application forms required by the college, and the priority date and/or deadlines that the financial aid office has set, appear here. This section also includes information about notification—that is, when you can expect to hear back from the financial aid office after applying, and by when they will need your final answer about whether you'll be attending. Unless otherwise noted, all dates given in this section are for applicants who intend to enroll in the fall of 2007. If you plan to apply for admission to the spring 2008 term, contact the college's financial aid office to find out about their policies and deadlines.

CONTACT

The final section of each college description lists the mailing address of the school's financial aid office.

Part IV: Scholarship Lists

If you want to zero in on colleges that offer scholarships for your particular talents and interests, the lists in Part IV will help you do that. Arranged alphabetically by state, these lists will point you to colleges that offer scholarships for a variety of achievements. Please note that, in many cases, merit is not the only criterion used by the college when awarding aid: it may require recipients to also demonstrate financial need by submitting the FAFSA or another financial aid form.

At some colleges, every applicant is automatically considered for merit scholarships. At others, you have to specifically apply for a given scholarship. And in some cases, a scholarship is only open to you if you've been recommended by your principal, school counselor, or teacher.

What's in the College Lists

Each list points to colleges that offer aid for a specific talent or area of interest.

Academics. This list names colleges that offer merit aid for academic achievement. Typical criteria include the classes you've taken, your GPA, and your standardized test scores.

Art. This list includes colleges that offer merit aid for artistic ability, as reflected by grades in art classes, teacher recommendations, and/or a portfolio you submit to the college.

Athletics. If a college offers scholarships for a certain sport, it will be listed here. The letters "M" and "W" indicate whether the scholarship is available to men, women, or both. Please note that, at most colleges, only a very few athletes receive significant scholarships. No one should rely on athletic achievements alone to get into college or to pay for it. Instead, make sure your academic record is solid, and be sure to apply for need-based financial aid by submitting the FAFSA and any other required forms.

Music/Drama. This list includes colleges and conservatories that offer merit aid for talent in the performing arts, as reflected by grades in music, dance, or drama classes; teacher recommendations; and/or an audition or a submitted tape.

ROTC. Three lists are included here, one each for the Air Force, Army, and Naval Reserve Officers Training Corps. (Marine Corps ROTC is included in Naval ROTC; the Coast Guard and Merchant Marine do not have ROTC programs.) The schools listed may not necessarily have all their ROTC programs on campus; they may have a sponsorship agreement with a neighboring college or university instead. If you enroll in ROTC, you will need to apply separately for the actual ROTC scholarship from the service branch you've chosen—the money doesn't come automatically. (For information on how much money is awarded and how to apply, consult *The College Board Scholarship Handbook*, or visit your local recruiting station.) Some colleges offer additional institutional scholarships for ROTC candidates from their own funds, beyond what's awarded by the Department of Defense.

Part I

Financial Aid Step by Step

Yes, You Can Afford College

Yes, you can afford college. How do we know? Because most colleges are not as expensive as you think. Because if a college wants you as a student, it will try to help you with financial aid. Because most students get financial aid. And because there are ways to reduce the amount you have to pay now, including working part-time and taking out loans.

This is not what everyone will tell you. You may hear discouraging words like, "Most colleges are expensive" and "You won't qualify for financial aid." People may hint that college is not worth all the trouble. The financial aid forms may look complicated and confusing.

We will show you how to get past these doubts. You *can* afford college, and we will show you how. College is worth the expense; you should apply for financial aid. With our step-by-step guide through the process, you'll sidestep confusion and be able to focus on the important decisions in front of you.

This book will help you if you have already saved some money for college—and also if you have not. It will help if you are a student, or a parent of a student. It will help if you have already decided what colleges to apply to, and also if you are not sure where you'd like to go. You may be the first in your family to consider college, or the latest in a family tradition. You might think your family doesn't make enough money to afford college, or that it makes too much to be awarded financial aid. You may have an expensive "dream college" you hope to attend, or you may be looking only for the best buy. You may plan to work or not to work, commute or live on campus, rely on your parents' money or pay your own way. No matter what your situation, you can afford college and we will help you do it.

Why You Can Afford College

Despite media hype about pricey colleges and the soaring cost of higher education, most colleges are not as expensive as you might think. In addition, the published prices of many colleges, though high, are not the whole story. If a college wants you as a student, and if you and your parents don't have enough money, the college will usually offer help so you can attend. That help is financial aid—and because of it, a college's published tuition and fees are not what most people pay.

Financial aid is a great equalizer, and most students benefit from it. Currently 62 percent of full-time college students receive gifts of money to help them foot the bill. Those gifts, known as grants, come either from the government, the college, or both, and grants do not have to be paid back. Many students also receive other forms of help, including federal tax credits and deductions that allow their families to keep more of their money at tax time. Thanks to all this assistance, full-time college students pay, on average, much less than the advertised price of their education. In 2005-06, for example, students at four-year private colleges paid an average net price of $11,600 in tuition and fees instead of the published price of $21,235. Students at four-year public universities received a proportionally similar discount.

Even expensive colleges are less costly than you might think because they offer more financial aid. Since a high-priced college often awards more assistance than a low-priced one, a particular student might end up paying the same out-of-pocket cost at both. That's why you shouldn't rule out your "dream college" as too expensive until you find out if it wants you and what kind of financial aid package it will give you.

That said, there are great deals to be found. At a public college—one supported by a state or local government—the average tuition and fees in 2005-06 were $5,500 a year. That's a 74 percent saving over the $21,235 a year charged by private colleges. Another way to save money is to spend your first two years at a community college, which is a public college that specializes in two-year education programs. Published tuition and fees at community colleges averaged less than $2,200 a year—a 60 percent saving over the average at a public four-year college.

Here's one last reason you can afford college: you don't have to pay every penny up front. You can borrow money at a low interest rate and pay it back after your studies are over. There are also ways to reduce the amount you have to pay now. (See Step 11 for more on these "out-of-pocket" options).

> **MYTH/FACT**
>
> **Myth:** Most colleges are expensive.
>
> **Fact:** The most expensive colleges get the most media attention, which creates the illusion that all colleges are expensive. The truth is that colleges vary greatly in price, and most are much more affordable than people think, especially once financial aid is factored in.

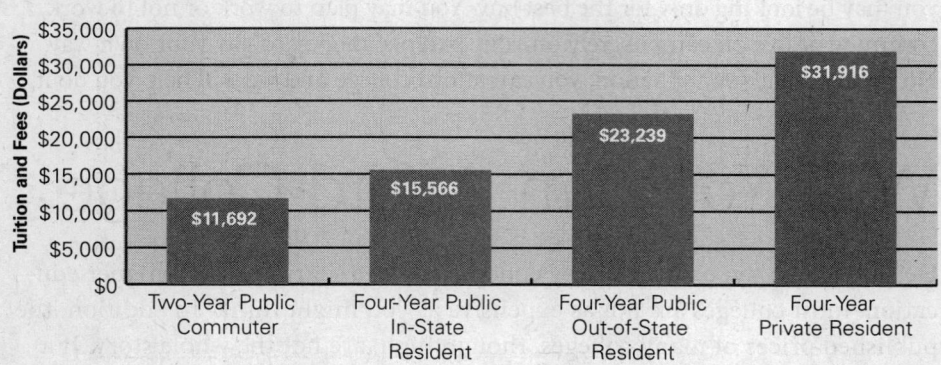

Figure 1:
Average Total College Price by Institution Type

Prices given here are for the total cost of attendance: tuition, fees, room, board, books and supplies, transportation, and personal expenses. See Step 3 for more about the components of college costs.

Is College Worth It?

Even if you can afford college, is it a good idea? No matter how much financial aid you get, college will still require a sacrifice of money, time, and effort. Kids who go straight to work after high school have more spending money sooner. Does college give enough bang for the buck?

The answer is yes, for three reasons: money, job insurance, and intangibles.

In terms of money, college clearly pays. The difference in earnings between college graduates and high school graduates has increased sharply over the past three decades. The typical male college graduate now earns 60 percent more than the typical male high school graduate; for women, the difference is 69 percent. College graduates earn an average of $1 million more over their careers than high school graduates. Even if you borrow to pay for part of your education, it's worth it. Provided you borrow intelligently, your increased earnings will help you pay back the loan (see Step 11).

You might think that the increased earnings from your college education won't make up for the total costs and the years that you won't be in the work force. But Figure 3 on the next page shows otherwise. The grey line shows the cumulative earnings at each age for the average high school graduate who enters the workforce full-time at the age of 18. The black line shows the cumulative earnings at each age for the average college graduate who enters

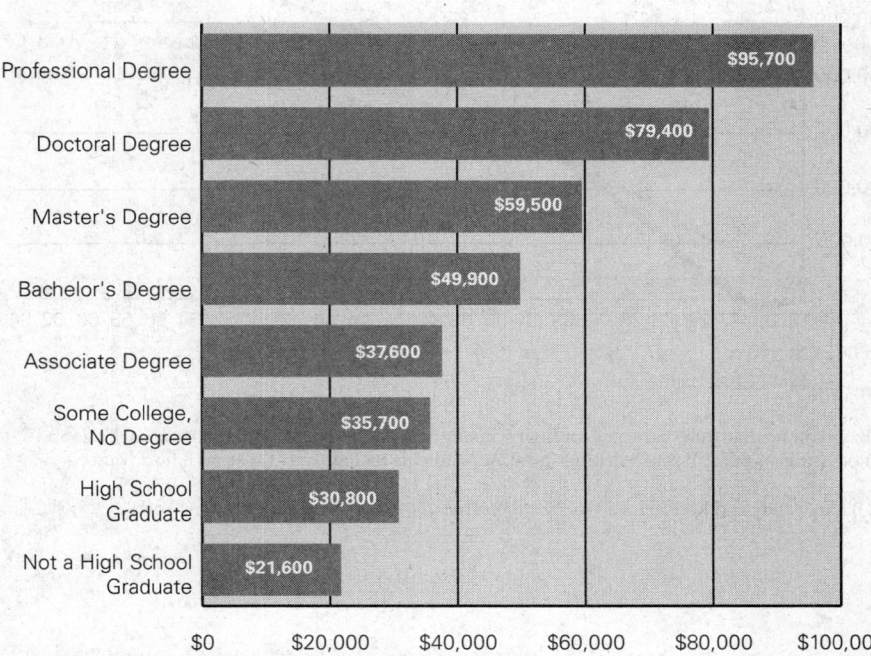

Figure 2:
Average Annual Earnings by Education Level

Note: Includes full-time, year-round workers age 25 and older.
Sources: U.S. Census Bureau, 2004a, PINC-03; Internal Revenue Service, 2004, Table 3; McIntyre, et al., 2003; calculations by the authors.

the workforce at age 22, after subtracting average tuition and fees paid over four years at a public college or university. As you can see, by age 32 the lines intersect. From that point on, the investment in college pays off.

College also provides job insurance in a world whose economy is constantly changing. As new industries develop and many jobs are outsourced to foreign countries, you can compete better with a college degree. A college degree teaches you how to acquire knowledge and put it to use no matter what the circumstances. In fact, some higher-education credential—at least an associate degree—is a minimum to stay employed in the "knowledge economy" of the twenty-first century. A mere high school diploma is obsolete; college helps to ensure employment.

But the value of college can't be reduced to dollars alone. It involves intangibles, things you can't touch directly: how you value yourself, your dreams, and your ambitions. If you are an artist, a musician, a writer, a scientist, or a thinker, college will help you cultivate those talents. If you are hoping to find yourself, meet people who are more like you, and meet people who are different and interesting, college can contribute to that search too.

On every front, as a matter of value for dollars, college is a good buy. You can afford college—and it is worth the price.

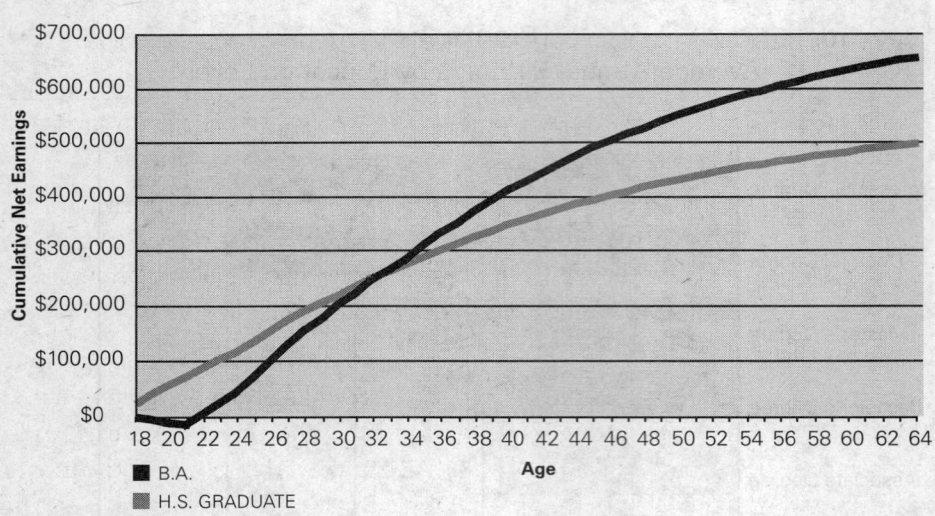

Figure 3:
Estimated Cumulative Earnings Minus College Costs

Notes: Based on median 2003 earnings for high school graduates and college graduates at each age and discounted using a 5 percent rate. Earnings for B.A. recipients include only those with no advanced degree.
Source: Baum, Sandy and Kathleen Payea, *Education Pays 2004*, The College Board, New York.

How This Book Will Help You

Through this book, you will learn how to make college affordable for you. You'll find out exactly what you need to know so you can apply for financial aid, choose an affordable college, and control costs while at college. In Part I, we will walk you step-by-step through the process. There are 11 steps in all:

- **Step 1:** you'll find out the key facts about financial aid.
- **Step 2:** you'll get an idea of how much financial aid you can get.
- **Step 3:** you'll see how and why college costs vary.
- **Step 4:** you'll figure out which forms you need to fill out, and when.
- **Step 5:** you'll learn how to fill out the Free Application for Federal Student Aid (FAFSA).
- **Step 6:** you'll find out how to complete the CSS/Financial Aid PROFILE® form (called the PROFILE for short), if your colleges require it.
- **Step 7:** you'll learn how to fill out any other forms a particular college might require.
- **Step 8:** if your family has special circumstances, you'll find out the best way to explain them to colleges.
- **Step 9:** you'll learn about scholarships and other aid you can get from sources outside of a college.
- **Step 10:** you'll learn how to compare award letters from colleges and decide which offer is best for you.
- **Step 11:** you'll learn how to pay your share of the cost of college through work, loans, and other means.

In Part II of the book, tables and worksheets will help you make informed decisions and stay in control of the financial aid process. Part III will paint a clear picture of the financial facts about each college you might want to investigate. That includes its costs and its approach to financial aid.

No one will tell you that paying for college is fun. But what you're getting—a college education—is worth it and is within reach. College is a big-ticket purchase that requires careful thought and preparation, like a house or a car. And it shouldn't be done in the dark. This book will guide you into one of the most important purchases you'll ever make—with your eyes wide open.

KEEP IN MIND

Don't approach the chronology of this book too rigidly—**not all steps have to come in this order.** For example, Step 9, "Look for Other Sources of Money," can be done at any time. Since outside scholarships aren't tied to a particular college, you can start researching and applying for them before you've even made a short list of schools. In fact, this is a good idea since the application deadline for these scholarships may be as early as November 1, before most college admissions applications are due.

Step 1: Let's Go Over the Basics

QUICK OVERVIEW

The first step to getting financial aid is to understand the basic facts about it. In this step we will explain what financial aid is (money to help you pay for college), what types there are (the kind that comes free and the kind that doesn't), who gets it, and where it comes from.

The most important point: almost everyone qualifies for at least one form of financial aid. As long as you apply, the chances are excellent that you will get some.

Just What Is Financial Aid?

Financial aid is money given or loaned to you to help you pay for college. Different forms have different rules. The vast majority of aid comes from the federal government, and most of it consists of loans that you must pay back. However, some aid does not require repayment—which makes it the best kind of aid to get.

If you qualify for financial aid, your college will put together an aid "package," usually with different types of aid bundled together. You and your parents will almost certainly still have to pay something, but the aid package will help. Most students qualify for some form of financial aid, so it makes sense to apply for it.

You'll apply for financial aid either at the same time or soon after you apply for admission. You may have to fill out more than one application. At the very least you will fill out the FAFSA, or federal government form. You may also fill out another form, the PROFILE, which many colleges require. And some colleges and state aid agencies require their own financial aid forms, too. The colleges to which you apply will use the forms to figure out what your family can afford to pay and what your "need" is—that is, the difference between what you can pay and what the college actually costs. If the school wants you as a student but sees that you can't handle the whole bill, it will make you a financial aid offer to help you meet your need. If you accept, that financial aid package is your award.

You will need to apply for financial aid every year that you are in college, mainly because your family's financial situation changes yearly. As a result, your financial aid package will probably be somewhat different from year to year.

Financial aid is a helping hand, not a free pass. In the United States, everyone has a right to a free public school education, but not to a free college education. The federal government and most colleges agree that students and their parents are the ones most responsible for paying for college. "The primary responsibility of paying for the student's education lies with the student and his or her parents," says Forrest M. Stuart, the director of financial aid at Rhodes College in Memphis, Tennessee. "Financial aid comes in to fill that gap, if you will, between what they can afford and what the college costs." Even so, financial aid can be the deciding factor in whether or not a student attends college.

Types of Aid

Financial aid may come in many forms. However, all forms can be grouped into two major categories: gift aid and self-help aid.

GIFT AID

Gift aid is free money, money that you don't have to pay back or work for. Naturally, this is the kind of aid most people want. It can take the form of grants or scholarships.

The terms "grant" and "scholarship" are often used interchangeably to mean free money. But here's the difference. A grant is usually given only on the basis of need, or your family's inability to pay the full cost of college. Scholarships are usually awarded only to those who have "merit," such as proven ability in academics, the arts, or athletics. Once you're in college, you may have to maintain a minimum GPA or take certain courses to continue receiving a scholarship.

SELF-HELP AID

Self-help aid is money that requires a contribution from you. That can mean paying back the money (if the aid is a loan) or working for the money (if the aid is a work-study job).

The most common form of self-help aid is also the most common of any form of financial aid: the loan. A loan is money that you have to pay back with interest. In light of that, you might not consider this aid at all. But it is—a loan means you don't have to pay the full price of college all at once: you can stretch the payments over time, as you would when buying a house or a car. Furthermore, some student loans are subsidized by the federal government. With these loans, you don't have to pay the interest that comes due while you're in college. The federal government subsidizes, or helps to pay, the loan by paying that interest while you're enrolled and for the first few months after you graduate.

EXPERT ADVICE

"One of the **most important things for students** to understand is what loans are about, and what indebtedness means, so that they don't stumble through four years of college having signed promissory notes blindly, and then come to the end of their senior year and say, I really owe that much money? They should know that they have to pay loans back, and they should **think about their total indebtedness** in relation to what their prospective income is and how it might affect some life choices."

—Joe Paul Case, dean and director of financial aid, Amherst College, Amherst, Massachusetts

KNOW THE LINGO

Grant—money that is given away for free, usually on the basis of who needs it

Merit scholarship—money that is given away for free on the basis of academic qualifications or special talents

Subsidized loan—money that you have to pay back with interest; however, the federal government pays the interest for you while you are in college

Work-study—a program in which you take a part-time job to earn money for your education; the federal government pays part of your salary

---

Subsidized loans, which are awarded based on need and administered by the college, are the best kind. But you can also take out unsubsidized student loans and parent loans, which are not packaged by most colleges. However, be careful not to take on more debt than necessary. No matter what kind of loan you take out, you will have to pay it back.

Another form of self-help is work-study. This is financial aid in the form of a job. Since you earn the money through your work, this too may not seem like aid. But it is, because the federal work-study program pays most of your wages. And work-study jobs are usually available right on campus, with limits on your hours so that you won't be unduly distracted from studying.

Aid can also come in the form of tax cuts—income tax deductions and credits for education. But colleges don't award this variety, and you don't apply for it in the same way as you would loans or grants, so we will discuss it separately, in Step 11.

Who Gets Aid?

Grants and loans are not just for the poorest of the poor, nor are scholarships only for the smartest of the smart. The truth about who gets financial aid is somewhat different from what many people think.

Those Who Need It

Most financial aid is based on need, not merit. There is money for merit, but since the 1950s most colleges in the United States have focused their financial aid packages on meeting financial need.

However, there is a lot of confusion about what need means. Many people think it means a state of dire poverty, so that no working-class or middle-class student need apply. "A lot of people think that they either have to be on welfare or Social Security—really 'dirt poor'—to get financial aid, and that's not correct," says Mary San Agustin, director of financial aid and scholarships at Palomar College in San Marcos, California. On the other hand, some rich families mistakenly think they are needy because their high living expenses leave them little money for college. "It's this expectation of, I pay my taxes, so my kid should be entitled to some federal financial aid regardless of how much money I make," says Ms. San Agustin.

Need simply means that your family can't afford to pay the full cost of a particular college. The *amount* of your need will vary from college to college, because it depends on the cost of attending an individual college. Whether your family has need is determined not by whether you think you are rich or poor, but by the financial aid forms you fill out.

Just fill out the forms. If you do have need, you will be considered for financial aid.

Those Who Don't

Despite the overall emphasis on need, many colleges do give away money on the basis of merit. They do this to attract the students they want most, and they may award this money even if it is more than the student needs. However, in many cases, the student both needs the money and has earned it on the basis of merit.

Don't think that only geniuses get merit aid. At many colleges a "B"-average GPA can put you in the running for merit money. Sometimes a separate application for merit aid is required to put you into consideration; sometimes your application for admission is enough. In either case, don't count yourself out by not applying; apply and let the college decide.

Grants are sometimes awarded based on neither need nor merit. For example, you may get a grant if you are in a certain field of study, are a resident of the state, or are a student from the same town as the college. For more information, see Step 9, "Look for Other Sources of Money."

Part-Time Students

Some kinds of aid are only available to students enrolled in college full-time—usually 12 or more credit hours of courses per semester. But part-time students are eligible for some financial aid. For example, federal loan programs require only that students be enrolled at least half-time. Also, some employers offer tuition reimbursement benefits to students who work full-time and go to college part-time.

> **KNOW THE LINGO**
>
> **Merit aid**—aid awarded on the basis of academics, character, or talent
>
> **Need-based aid**—aid awarded on the basis of a family's inability to pay the cost of attending a particular college
>
> **Non-need-based aid**—aid awarded on some basis other than need or merit, such as grants with eligibility requirements related to field of study or state residence

Where the Money Comes From

Financial aid comes from three basic sources: governments (both federal and state), colleges, and outside benefactors.

From the Government

The lion's share of total financial aid awarded in this country comes from the federal government. Fully 68 percent of all student aid is sent from Washington. The largest chunk of that consists of federal loans, which total $61 billion a year and represent 51 percent of all student aid. The loans take multiple shapes. Perkins loans are subsidized, with the lowest interest rate of any educational loan. Stafford loans may be subsidized or unsubsidized. Both Perkins and Stafford loans are for students, but parents may take out a PLUS loan, which is not subsidized, to help pay for their children's educations.

The federal government also funds several grants: the Pell Grant, the Supplemental Educational Opportunity Grant (SEOG), the Academic Competitiveness Grant, and the SMART Grant. The Pell and SEOG are strictly need-based, while the last two are based on both need and academic criteria. The government also funds the federal work-study program.

A much smaller piece of the financial aid pie (5 percent) comes from individual state governments. This is available in the form of grants, scholarships, and loans. Most of this aid is for use only at colleges within the state, though a few states offer "portable" aid, which state residents can take with them to a college in another state.

From the College

A great deal of financial aid comes from individual colleges. In fact, colleges award nearly half of all grants. Many, though not all, award merit scholarships as well as need-based grants. They may also offer on-campus job opportunities and loans.

Private colleges give more financial aid than public ones, but their tuition is usually higher as well. Public colleges award less aid, but taxpayer support keeps their tuition lower.

Outside Grants and Scholarships

Outside grants and scholarships come from sources other than the government or the college. These sources may include corporations like Coca-Cola or community groups like the Elks Club. Some are well known, such as the National Merit Scholarship Awards, but altogether they are the smallest piece of the financial aid pie: only 7 percent of all student aid comes from this source. Pursue them, but don't expect them to outweigh the other aid you will get.

Bear in mind also that your outside scholarship is unlikely to expand the total aid you receive. Most colleges will use an outside scholarship to substitute for some other piece of aid rather than increase the total aid package. Think of your financial aid package as a barrel: when the barrel is full, no more can be added unless something is taken away. The last thing colleges will take away is whatever sum of money your family is expected to contribute. However, at many colleges, the first thing taken away is self-help aid such

Figure 4:
Total Financial Aid Available by Source (in billions)

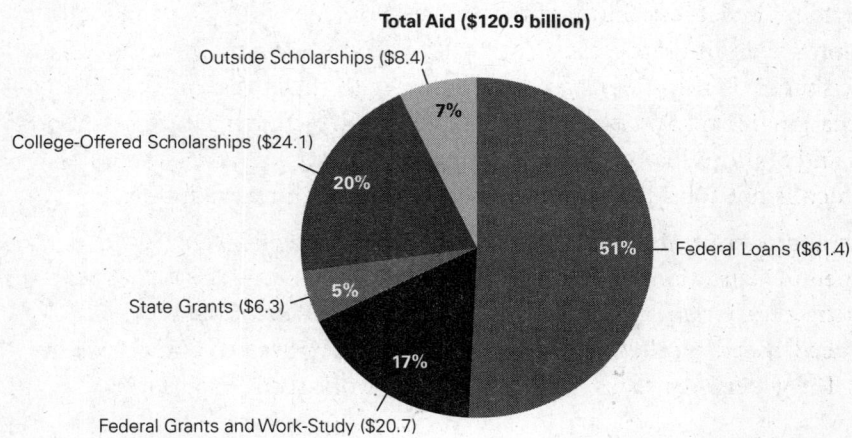

as loans. Since that could reduce the total amount you will have to pay back later, it is worth applying for outside scholarships. For more on these sources of aid, see Step 9.

There is a lot of financial aid out there, in many forms. Apply for it—there is a good chance you will get some. These are the main things to know about financial aid:

- It is money to help you pay for college.
- It may come in the form of a gift (grants and scholarships) or in the form of self-help (loans and work-study).
- Most people get it because they need it, though some get it solely because of merit.
- The federal government funds most of it, but states, colleges, and outside sources also help.

QUICK RECAP

Step 2: Estimate How Financial Aid Will Work for You

QUICK OVERVIEW

Only rarely does a student get a "free ride" scholarship. You and your parents will have to contribute some money to your education—the precise amount will be determined by the college's analysis of financial aid forms you'll fill out. But even before you fill out the forms, you can estimate your share of the cost and begin planning for how to pay it.

Don't Count Yourself Out

Most college students get some financial aid, but few receive exactly the same financial aid package. Financial aid packages are as individual as the financial circumstances of the students who apply. One family makes $50,000 a year and has two children, a house, and a savings account; another makes $50,000 a year but has only one child, a rented apartment, and no savings. What financial aid package will each family receive? The answer: you can't tell. Families must first submit their applications for consideration by the colleges.

"Probably the question I'm most often asked is, 'is there a cutoff?'" says Joe Paul Case, the dean and director of financial aid at Amherst College in Amherst, Massachusetts. Financial aid officers agree that there is no single salary cutoff for financial aid—no one income figure that will definitely exclude a student from receiving financial aid. Income is only one criterion for giving out aid: colleges also consider such factors as family size, number of children in college, and savings. Many students who would be eligible for financial aid fail to apply because they don't realize this.

"I always tell families, don't cut yourself off from the application process," says Bonnie Lee Behm, the director of financial assistance at Villanova University in Villanova, Pennsylvania. "Apply and let it work through the system."

Even if you feel absolutely sure that your family doesn't qualify for financial aid, fill out the forms. Your family circumstances might change suddenly—a lost job, health problems, a new child. Then you may need financial aid, and it will help to be in the system already. A college can assist you faster if your financial aid application is on file.

EXPERT ADVICE

"We always encourage students to **go ahead and apply** for financial aid even though you may not qualify for anything but a student loan. **At least get the paperwork in**, because if something happens in the middle of the year, we already have the financial aid data we need to make adjustments."

—Forrest M. Stuart, director of financial aid, Rhodes College, Memphis, Tennessee

What "Expected Family Contribution" Means

Even though you probably will qualify for some financial aid, it's very unlikely that you will get the fabled "full ride." Colleges do sometimes award full tuition—or even full room and board—to a student they greatly want to attract, but that is rare. Almost always, the family is expected to contribute some money. The exact dollar amount will be based on the family's ability to pay. That dollar amount is the expected family contribution, or EFC.

The EFC is carefully calculated to be your "fair share." It is what you can afford to pay based on your financial circumstances—no more and no less. The methodologies that the federal government and colleges use to calculate EFC are ultimately intended to make sure that the EFC is fair.

In some ways, the concept of EFC works in your favor. No matter what a college costs, so long as it awards you the full financial aid you need you won't have to pay more than your EFC—the amount your family is able to pay. Say your EFC is $8,000. At a college with a total cost of attendance of $11,000, you could get up to $3,000 in financial aid. At a college where the total cost is $25,000, you could get up to $17,000 in aid. Because of financial aid, any college is at least worth considering; no college should be ruled out in advance as too expensive.

On the other hand, even though the expected family contribution is based on ability to pay, that does not simply mean how much the family would like to pay. For any purchase, most people would *like* to pay zero dollars. But what they are *able* to pay is how much money they have minus how much they need to keep for other things, such as food, rent, heat, and retirement. When colleges award financial aid, they calculate your ability to pay by looking at your income and financial assets as you lay them out in your financial aid application. Using what are called need-analysis formulas, they analyze your data to see how much of the college costs you are able to pay (your EFC) and how much you are unable to pay (your need). How much you would like to pay is not part of the calculation.

Costs – EFC = Need

Your expected family contribution is your family's share of college costs. Any cost greater than that is your need. Need varies from college to college because it depends on the cost of the individual college. It's simple arithmetic: college costs minus your EFC equals your need. At colleges that award enough financial aid to meet your need, the aid package will equal the amount of your need. Costs minus aid equals what you pay.

Unmet Need (a.k.a. "Gap")

Unfortunately, not all colleges will award enough aid to meet your full need. Some colleges may "gap" your package—that is, not meet your full need. Economics plays a part here. While some colleges may have enough aid dollars available to meet every student's full need, some colleges lack such funds. If your college cannot meet your full need, costs minus aid will still equal what you pay. But what you pay will be more than your EFC. Step 11 has information on loans and other ways to help fill such a gap.

If you do encounter a "gap" in your award, compare the package with the ones you've gotten from other schools, and consider your priorities. Do you want to go to that college, no matter the cost? Or does cost matter more? For more on this topic, see Step 10.

It Depends on the College

The amount of aid you get—along with the kind of aid you get, whether gift or self-help—ultimately depends on the college. Formulas and forms are important, but so is the professional judgment of the financial aid officer. And so is the desire of the college to attract you to its campus.

How Your Case Will Be Figured

Once you've submitted your financial aid forms, the college will analyze them to see how much you can afford to pay (your EFC) and how much you can't (your need). The college will have different buckets of money to distribute based on its judgment of which students need it most. One bucket is federal money, subject to federal rules. Some of it is the college's own "institutional" money. The method they use to figure out what you can afford is called a need analysis methodology.

There are two main methodologies. One is the Federal Methodology, or "FM." The federal government and most state governments use this to calculate your eligibility for the aid they award. Most public universities and many private colleges use it to award their own institutional funds as well. The Federal Methodology calculations are based on the data about your family's finances that you submit on the FAFSA, the federal financial aid form.

Some private colleges and scholarship programs use a different approach, the Institutional Methodology, or "IM." While they use the Federal Methodology to award federal and state money, they use the Institutional Methodology to determine your eligibility for their own grant and scholarship funds. The IM is based on the data gathered about your family's finances in the PROFILE form (more formally known as the College Board's CSS/Financial Aid PROFILE application) and/or the college's own financial aid application form.

KEEP IN MIND

If a college offers you a financial aid award that doesn't meet your full need, you may be able to fill the "gap" in your package with an **outside scholarship**. For more on outside scholarships, see Step 9.

The Federal and Institutional methodologies have several things in common. Both base their calculations on your family's total income in the calendar year before the one in which you will enroll in college. That includes the income of both student and parents, from wages to interest, dividends, Social Security, and child support. Neither methodology intends to leave your family stretched: both assume that some of your income will be needed for basic living expenses such as housing, clothing, and food. Both make allowances for family size, recognizing that bigger families have bigger expenses. But both assess, or charge, you a portion of whatever income is left after such expenses. The rate of assessment gets higher as the parents' income gets higher. In the Federal Methodology, the assessment of parents' income ranges from 22 percent to 47 percent, after allowances are subtracted.

Both methodologies consider the assets as well as the income of student and parents, but assess them at a much lower rate. They review not just how much your family makes every year (income), but how much money you have or property you own (assets), whether it takes the form of savings, stocks and bonds, or real estate. They figure that a family with greater assets will have more ability than a family with smaller assets to dip into its resources. Yet both methodologies count income more heavily than assets. On the assumption that the bulk of your assets are being saved for emergencies, retirement, and other nondiscretionary uses, these methodologies examine assets at a much lower rate than income.

Both methodologies require students to contribute a larger percentage of their own income and assets than their parents. This is based on the assumption that students will benefit directly from college and have fewer financial responsibilities than their parents.

Despite all the similarities, there are differences between the FM and IM. These differences are worth knowing about so you get a better idea of what your college will expect you to pay.

Federal Methodology vs. Institutional Methodology: The Differences

Colleges that require the Institutional Methodology do so because they think it presents a fuller picture of your family's financial situation. "I just think it does a much better job of measuring ability to pay," says Forrest M. Stuart, whose institution, Rhodes College, requires the PROFILE.

Does that mean you will pay more under one methodology than the other? It depends. Some of the differences tend to make your expected family contribution lower under the Federal Methodology; others tend to reduce it under the Institutional Methodology.

For example, if your parents own a home, they probably have a certain amount of home equity—the market value of the property minus the amount they still owe on the mortgage. The Federal Methodology doesn't count home

> **KNOW THE LINGO**
>
> **EFC (Expected Family Contribution)**—How much money a family is expected to pay for college.
>
> **FM (Federal Methodology)**—The formula that federal and state governments, and most colleges, use to calculate your eligibility for federal aid and most kinds of state aid.
>
> **IM (Institutional Methodology)**—The formula that some colleges and scholarship programs use to calculate your eligibility for their own nonfederal grant and scholarship funds.

equity as an asset, while the Institutional Methodology does. This tends to make the institutional calculation of your EFC higher than the federal one.

Here are some other reasons your EFC might be lower under the Federal Methodology. It allows you to reduce your declared income by including business and other losses; the Institutional Methodology doesn't. If a family has two children in college at the same time, the FM lets the family split their EFC equally between the students, while the IM requires them to pay 60 percent of the EFC for each student. The Federal Methodology does not assess the first $2,550 of student income, while the Institutional Methodology does.

On the other hand, there are ways in which the Institutional Methodology might work in your favor. In most states, the IM protects more of your income to pay for state income and sales taxes than the FM does. The Institutional Methodology sets aside a bigger allowance for family living expenses. Overall, the IM has a lower assessment rate for assets. Finally, the Institutional Methodology makes allowances for parents to save for younger siblings' college educations, while the Federal Methodology doesn't.

At one time, the Institutional Methodology tended to result in higher expected family contributions than the Federal Methodology, but more recently it has tended to result in lower ones. How it shakes out in your case, however, will depend on your individual family circumstances.

Will College Savings Count Against You?

While some families save diligently for their children's college educations, others think this is a mistake. They worry that having a lot of savings will keep colleges from awarding financial aid. But savings do not count against you, and here is why.

First, your family will be expected to contribute something to college costs and, if you have savings, you have the pot from which you can draw that contribution. The alternative is to pay it out of your monthly earnings or borrow it—both of which are less appealing choices than using savings. "If I were preparing to send a son or daughter off to school, I would want to have as much savings available to me as I realistically could," says Vincent Amoroso, deputy director of the Office of Scholarships and Student Aid at the University of North Carolina at Chapel Hill. "The reason is because, just like in other situations, money equates to flexibility and independence for me to make choices that are good for myself and my son or daughter."

A second reason why savings do not count against you: All savings are not created equal. Both the Federal Methodology and the Institutional Methodology look at family funds differently depending on whether they are discretionary or nondiscretionary. Discretionary money can be used any way you want—to splurge on a vacation, redecorate the house, and so on. Nondiscretionary money is reserved for necessities, such as food and medical emergencies.

To distinguish the two, the methodologies include what they call an "asset protection allowance." This is the amount of money considered reasonable to set aside for educational savings and emergencies. These "free" savings are not assessed at all. The federal asset protection allowance varies based on the age of the oldest parent, and it can be several tens of thousands of dollars for a married couple in their 40s or 50s. These savings are clearly worth having, since they aren't included when calculating your EFC. (To get an estimate of what your parents' asset protection allowance is, see Table 12 on page 138.)

Even if your family does have significant discretionary assets, they are assessed at a maximum rate of only 5.6 percent. This is better than discretionary income, which, in the Federal Methodology, is assessed from 22 percent to 47 percent. So even if 5.6 percent of your discretionary savings count "against" you when it comes to federal need determination, 94.4 percent count "for" you. You can use them to meet your expected contribution, whatever it turns out to be.

Responsibilities Within the Family

Who should pay for college? Is it entirely the parents' duty, or should the student be responsible? If both, which combination of both? There is no single right answer to questions like these. But families need to discuss the topic, and the sooner the better. Your college will expect someone in the family to make a contribution, and you and your parents should figure out who that is before the bill comes due.

"Families should discuss college costs, family budget, financial aid, and financing options at the beginning of the college application process, not at the end," says Carlene Riccelli, a college adviser at Amherst Regional High School in Amherst, Massachusetts. Try to reach decisions that are as specific as possible, so that you each know what's expected of you. Try to make the decisions fair, so that no one feels used. What portion of your summer job income should go toward college? If your family takes out loans, should they be in your name, your parents' name, or both? Don't forget to discuss ways of keeping costs down, such as living at home and taking community college courses.

If your family is nontraditional, the discussion should include all adults involved in your care. When considering the financial need of students with divorced parents, for example, some colleges that use the Institutional Methodology will assess the income and assets of both natural parents. It will be up to the family to decide how to pay the expected family contribution, but part of that contribution will be based on the income and assets of the parent without custody. (See Step 8 for more information.)

While it's important to talk about money, your family also needs to talk about other aspects of choosing a college, such as its academic and social environment. Some of the discussion will have nothing to do with money, but others will have financial aspects: for example, going away to an expensive college versus staying home and commuting to a cheaper one. Step 3 will further explore how to think about these issues. But the important thing is to start having the discussions—financial and otherwise—as early as possible.

Crunch Some Numbers

If you want a sneak peek at what your expected family contribution will be, crunch some numbers. Part II contains worksheets and tables that you can use to calculate the EFC of a "typical" family under the Federal Methodology. Use the worksheets to add up your income, then subtract deductions and allowances. Total up your assets, too. Apply the formulas in the worksheets to calculate the contribution that is expected from you as a student. Then use the next set of worksheets and tables to calculate your parents' expected contribution. When you're finished, you will have your estimated EFC.

The figure you come up with will only be an estimate. Your actual EFC may be higher or lower, depending on the exact data you ultimately submit and the particular college's financial aid policies. But at least this exercise will give you a ballpark figure for what you can expect to pay.

Online Calculators

If you'd prefer to estimate your EFC online, there are several Web sites with special calculators. They include:

- **collegeboard.com**—Our Financial Aid EasyPlanner lets you "Do the Math" not only on EFC but on college costs, savings, and loans.
- **finaid.org**—Their interactive calculators include one for EFC.
- **College and university Web sites**—These sites sometimes include calculators geared to their individual financial aid policies.

Figure 5:
Sample EFC Illustration

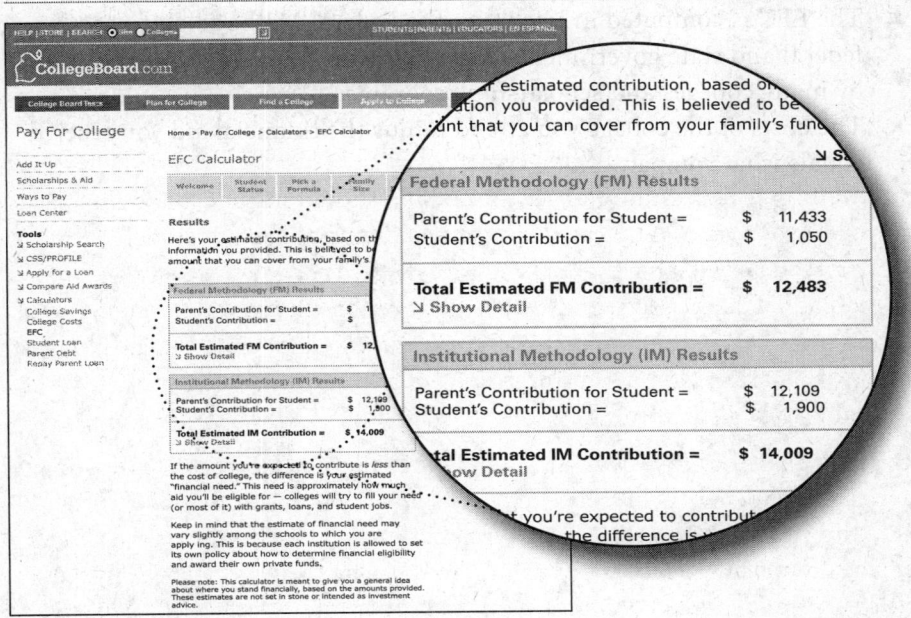

Online calculators like the one at www.collgeboard.com can help you estimate your expected family contribution.

Your Unique Situation Counts Too

Colleges expect families to contribute some money toward students' education, and the amount they expect is your EFC. But colleges are not just faceless buildings of stone, and your EFC is not fixed in cement. The financial aid officer in charge of distributing a college's financial aid is a human being, and he or she does have some room to adjust how the EFC calculations are made based on your individual circumstances.

Step 8 will go into greater detail on how to notify your college about changes in your family's financial situation, such as a lost job. And Step 10 will discuss how to appeal if you think the college hasn't taken all your circumstances into account. Generally, financial aid officers are sympathetic if you are struggling with problems such as caring for an elderly parent or sending money to your family overseas. They will be less sympathetic if it seems that you've chosen your financial problems—such as buying a new motorcycle with money that could have gone to pay your college bill. Still, financial aid officers are not heartless, and they will try to help when there is genuine distress.

QUICK RECAP

The American education system expects families to bear as much responsibility for the costs of higher education as they can, but not more. Your family will have to contribute to your college costs, but will also receive help.

- Your family will be required to pay an expected family contribution, or EFC.
- The EFC is computed in two ways: the Federal Methodology, used by federal and state governments; and the Institutional Methodology, used by many colleges and scholarship programs.
- The costs of the college you attend minus the financial aid you receive equals what you pay.

Step 3: Choosing Colleges, Thinking Costs

QUICK OVERVIEW

Thanks to financial aid, cost doesn't need to be the most important factor in deciding where to apply for college. What matters more is how the college will fit you academically and socially. Still, cost is a factor to consider. This step shows you how to think about cost when choosing a college. You'll see why you shouldn't exclude any college from consideration just because of its price. You'll learn what your different college expenses will be, from tuition to pizza money; how costs can vary from college to college; and how to factor in the financial aid package the college is likely to give.

How to Think About College Costs

When you're thinking about where to apply for college, cost should not be the main consideration. Because financial aid will probably be available to help meet your need, even a college that appears exorbitant may in fact be within reach. A college's published costs are only one part of the equation when it comes to what you'll actually pay. Until you've applied for and received an offer of financial aid, you won't know the real cost to your family.

Remember that financial aid works like this: Total cost of attendance *minus* your family's expected family contribution (EFC) *equals* your financial need. As long as the college meets your need, the amount you pay stays the same whatever the price of the college. "I don't think college cost really should be a factor to where students apply for admission," says Vincent Amoroso of the University of North Carolina. "I say that because your family contribution, in theory, is the same whether you apply to a school that costs $4,000 or to a school that costs $40,000."

In practice, your expected family contribution may actually vary somewhat from college to college. As noted in Step 2, a college using the Federal Methodology to assess your ability to pay might calculate a higher or lower EFC than a college that uses the Institutional Methodology. Even two institutions using the same methodology might calculate slightly different EFCs, depending on how they have treated any special circumstances that may apply to your family. (See Step 8 for more on special circumstances.) But, in general, the principle holds that your EFC will be constant from college to college, while your need will vary depending on the price of each college.

The main thing to consider when applying for college is whether you and that school will be a good fit. Look for the academic and social aspects that are likely to make you happy and successful there. Are you artistic? Are you mathematical? Do you love to learn for learning's sake? Do you have strong career ambitions in a particular field? Do you long to get away and see the world? Or does it matter more to stay near your family and the place where you grew up? "Students should not just look at a school because it's affordable," says Bonnie Lee Behm of Villanova University. "They should look at a school because it's the right fit for them academically, socially, spiritually, and physically. Is cost an important part? Yes. It's a consideration, but only one among many." And remember—you can find a good fit at more than one college.

To discover what specific colleges have to offer, research them. You can find a lot of information about majors offered, the composition of the student body, academic policies, and extracurricular and athletic offerings in the *College Board College Handbook*. You can also learn more on the College Search engine on collegeboard.com, and from college guidebooks and Web sites. If you know people who have gone to the colleges you're considering, talk to them and get their opinions.

So, when deciding which colleges to apply to, don't focus too much on cost. But do be aware of what the costs are; cost may become a factor depending on what financial aid packages you are ultimately offered. Even though your EFC should in principle be the same at all colleges, not all schools always meet full need. And even those that do may meet it with different packages—some with more loans, others with more grants. It makes sense to know what kinds of packages a particular school is likely to give.

By using Part III of this book as a guide, and also by contacting the admissions and financial aid offices of the colleges you're considering, gather as much information as you can about the costs of the school and the type of aid they offer. The rest of Step 3 suggests the kinds of information you should be seeking from each school.

Choosing Colleges

Both you and your parents should be involved in the discussion about where to apply for college. You will share the responsibility for paying for college, so you should all have a voice. Furthermore, your parents can give you good advice about what colleges to consider based on their life experiences, their knowledge of you, and their understanding of the family finances—even if they themselves have never been to college. The deciding vote, however, should be yours. You are the one who will have to start and finish college, and you are more likely to do so successfully if you have chosen the college yourself. "Only the student knows the fit that he or she will have at a particular

> **EXPERT ADVICE**
>
> "For the most part, if a family presents a case on their financial aid forms, it's going to be **read essentially the same way** by each of the institutions, whether it be a two-year community college, or a four-year public or a four-year private, or a for-profit trade school."
>
> —Joe Paul Case, dean and director of financial aid, Amherst College, Amherst, Massachusetts

institution academically, socially, and financially as well," says Forrest Stuart of Rhodes College.

When you begin choosing where to apply, don't exclude any college. Let every college be on the table, even if it seems too difficult academically or financially. Aim high. Shop around. The best colleges for you may not be the ones that occur to you first.

If a college is a good fit for you, there is probably a way to make it work financially. "Apply to those colleges that you think, okay, maybe we could afford these, but also apply above that level, because some schools may be much more manageable than you expect," says Bonnie Lee Behm of Villanova University.

Do Consider a "Financial Safety"

Even though all colleges should be on the drawing board, you should also consider applying to a financial "safety" school—one that is a good academic fit and that you feel fairly confident you can afford. Your financial safety school is one you would be happy attending and that has either low published costs or will almost certainly offer enough grant money to make attendance affordable. A public university in your state, a local community college, or a private university where you are highly likely to win a merit scholarship might all be financial safeties.

A financial safety is a good idea because your top choices may not give you as much financial aid as you want. "We know students who are really strong academically, but they're not at the top of their class, and they apply to the college of their dreams," says Elizabeth Bickford, director of the Office of Student Financial Aid and Scholarships at the University of Oregon in Eugene. Despite their hopes for a full merit scholarship, such students may find that they can enroll only if they are willing to take out a large amount in unsubsidized loans—something their family may not be willing to do.

In these and other situations, a financial safety is a good backup. For example, if you accept admission to a far-off university, but find that you can't get used to it and want to come back to the financial safety school near home, it will be easier to transfer if you've already applied and been admitted. Still, Elizabeth Bickford says she encourages students to "dream large, because it's your one opportunity. When you go from high school to that first year in college, that's where most of the scholarships are—for entering freshmen. It's your opportunity to make that big step away from home."

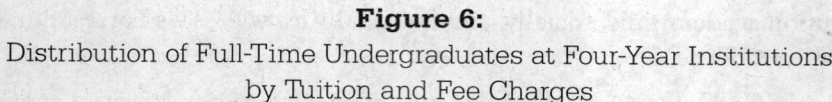

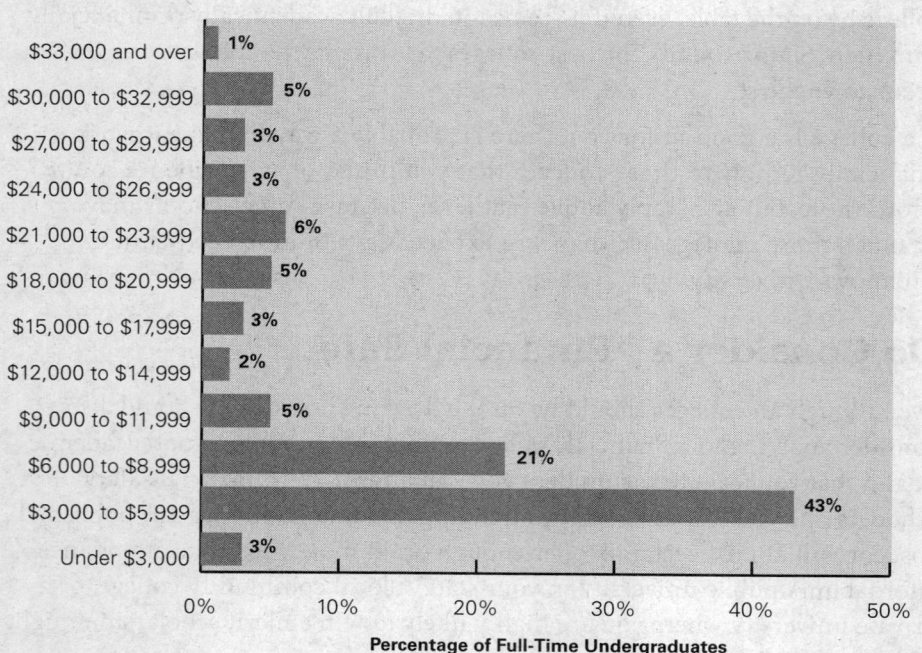

Forty-six percent of full-time undergraduates attend colleges with published tuition and fee charges of less than $6,000. After financial aid, many of those students pay an even lower "net price" for tuition.

Source: *Annual Survey of Colleges,* The College Board, New York, NY.

Components of College Costs

The price of a college education has several parts. The most obvious is tuition, the cost of taking courses. Tuition varies depending on how many courses you take, but full-time students pay a flat rate for a full schedule of courses. If you attend part-time, you will likely pay by credit hours, a measure of how long each class is. Most courses are three credit hours apiece, which usually translates to three one-hour classes each week. Most full-time students take an average of four or five courses per semester, for a total of 12 to 15 credit hours per semester for a full load.

Fees are another component of college costs. Fees are usually billed to all students as funding for the college's general expenses, such as the library or student activities. But there may be additional special fees for students enrolled in certain classes or activities. A chemistry student may pay lab fees, for example.

Tuition and fees are just one part of what you'll pay for college, and often not even half. Another large component is room and board. "Room" is the cost of housing you, and "board" is the cost of food. You may live in a dorm on campus, or off campus—in an apartment or a house with other students, or at home with your parents. You may be on a meal plan where all your meals are prepared for you for one price, or you may fend for yourself, buying groceries and cooking meals. Either way, these basic living expenses are your room and board.

Taken together, tuition, fees, room, and board are the largest chunk of college costs. On average, at four-year public colleges across the nation, these elements together make up 78 percent of what students pay for college—tuition and fees 35 percent, room and board 43 percent. Yet there is still another 22 percent of costs to be accounted for. These include:

- Books and supplies—class expenses that are not covered by tuition and will vary depending on the courses you take.
- Transportation expenses—for on-campus students, this is the cost of trips home during holidays; for commuters, this is the cost of either mass transit or a car. Car costs include parking, gas, insurance, and maintenance.
- Computer equipment costs—if required by the college. Some colleges may insist that you buy a certain model of computer, or bring your own computer but have special hardware and software installed to make it work on the campus network.
- Personal expenses—everything from snacks outside the meal plan to newspaper subscriptions to haircuts and toothpaste to membership fees for student groups.

How Costs Can Vary

Each college has different price tags for each of the cost components. For example, on average, books and supplies cost $750 for the first year at Montana State University, but $1,200 at St. Leo University in Florida. Table 1 on page 28 shows national averages for cost components.

To get specifics for a particular college that you're considering, check its Web site and look for the school's published estimate of what the average student spends on the different expense categories. The college will use these averages as part of the calculation of your "total cost of attendance," which will partly determine how much aid you're awarded. You can also consult Part III of this book for a school-by-school summary of costs.

However, remember that these average costs are only averages. You are an individual, and you may pay more or less than average, depending on your individual circumstances. For example, if you attend college in California but your family lives in New York, you will pay more for traveling to and from home than if your family is also in California.

Textbook and supply costs can also vary widely depending on your major. If you are an architecture or drafting student, you might have to buy an expensive computer-aided design program that your English major friends won't need. Science students might need to buy a statistical-modeling software package; studio artists a graphic-design suite. At least software like this only has to be bought once and is then used to do work for several classes; furthermore, educational discounts may be available for such purchases. In some programs, students might have to buy supplies that frequently get used up and must be replenished, such as brushes and paints for art students.

Rooming costs will vary a little between different dorm complexes on campus—for example, newer dorms may cost more, and a single room is always more expensive than one shared with a roommate. There will also be differences between various off-campus rooming locations.

Finally, your personal expenses may be higher or lower than average depending on lifestyle factors—but they will almost always be higher than you think. As James Schembari wrote in the *New York Times*, there is always a need for "pizza money"—money to buy pizza, go on a road trip, or hang out at the student union. Books, supplies, travel, and everyday expenses "can add $3,000 or more a year, depending on parents' generosity and where their child goes to college," wrote Mr. Schembari.

Table 1:
Sample Average Undergraduate Budgets, 2005-06
(Enrollment-Weighted Averages)

SECTOR	TUITION AND FEES	BOOKS AND SUPPLIES	ROOM AND BOARD	TRANSPORTATION	OTHER EXPENSES	TOTAL** EXPENSES
Two-Year Public						
Resident	$2,191	$801	*	*	*	*
Commuter	$2,191	$801	$5,909	$1,175	$1,616	$11,692
Four-Year Public						
Resident	$5,491	$894	$6,636	$852	$1,693	$15,566
Commuter	$5,491	$894	$6,476	$1,168	$1,962	$15,991
Out-of-State	$13,164	$894	$6,636	$852	$1,693	$23,239
Four-Year Private						
Resident	$21,235	$904	$7,791	$691	$1,295	$31,916
Commuter	$21,235	$904	$7,249	$1,060	$1,622	$32,070

Enrollment-weighted tuition and fees are derived by weighting the price charged by each institution by the number of full-time students enrolled. Room and board charges are weighted by the number of students residing on campus.

* Sample too small to provide meaningful information.
** Average total expenses include room and board costs for commuter students, which are average estimated living expenses for students living off campus but not with parents. These are estimated average student expenses as reported by institutions in the *Annual Survey of Colleges*.
Note: Four-year public resident and commuter tuition and fee levels are based on in-state charges only.
Source: *Annual Survey of Colleges*, The College Board, New York, NY.

Ways to Save

There are a few time-tested ways of saving money on some of the major cost components of college. To save money on tuition and fees, many students have attended public colleges and community colleges. To save money on room and board, many have commuted rather than roomed on campus. Here are the pros and cons for these money-saving techniques.

Public vs. Private, In-State vs. Out-of-State

Attending a public college in your own state is an excellent way to save money on tuition and fees. Public colleges are subsidized by state taxes, so their tuition and fees for state residents are usually much less than at private colleges—74 percent less, on average. Depending on the school, the quality of education may be as good or even better than what you would get at a private college.

On the other hand, the true cost picture is more complicated than it looks. Even though private colleges charge more for tuition and fees, most of them also give more scholarships and grants than public colleges do, which helps to even out the costs. "There's an adage that the more expensive the school, the more money they give away," says Mike Scott of Texas Christian University, a private institution.

Cost isn't everything. If a particular private school has some valuable characteristic that you want—smaller classes, professors you want to study with—it may be worth the extra tuition money. But cost is a factor to consider. If a certain state school can give you all that you want from college, why not go there and save some money?

If you would like to study at a public college or university in another state, be aware that most public schools charge higher tuition to students from out of state than they do to in-state students. On average, public colleges currently charge $5,491 in tuition and fees to a state resident, but $13,164 to an out-of-state student. The in- and out-of-state rates for specific public colleges and universities are listed in Part III.

PAYING IN-STATE RATES IN ANOTHER STATE

It is sometimes possible to get the in-state tuition rate, or at least a lowered tuition rate, even if you are an out-of-state student. For example, some state universities have "reciprocity agreements" with neighboring states. Minnesota residents pay their in-state tuition rate at most University of Wisconsin campuses, and vice versa. There are also discipline-based "consortiums" of public colleges that let you get the in-state tuition rate at another state's public college if your desired major is not available at any public college in your own state.

Your school counselor and state board of education Web site can give you more information about programs for paying in-state rates in another state.

Community Colleges

Community colleges are another great way of saving money on tuition and fees. A community college is a two-year school subsidized by a local government, such as a county or city. Its cost for tuition and fees is usually much lower than that of a four-year institution—60 percent lower, on average, than a public four-year college. Community colleges often charge tuition in three tiers—in district, in state, and out of state—with the lowest price for those who live in the local district. Though community colleges do not offer a four-year bachelor's degree (B.A. or B.S.), they do provide courses whose credits can be transferred toward a bachelor's degree at another college. Because those courses cost much less, this can be a way to save money in your first two years of college—money you can use to help pay for the last two years. Four out of 10 college-bound high school graduates start their college education this way.

There are other reasons to attend a community college besides saving money. If you aren't sure whether you want to go to a four-year college, a community college will give you a sense of what the college experience is like. If you don't know what kind of program you want to pursue—science, art, business, or something else—you can explore different subject areas at a community college before committing to a program. And if you need to be able to work, perhaps to support a family, you can work out a more flexible schedule at a community college, where many students work full-time.

A community college is also a golden opportunity for students who didn't do well enough in high school to win admission to the college of their choice. Community colleges are open to everyone, and some have agreements with four-year colleges that guarantee admission in the third year for students who have maintained good grades. This is the case in California, according to Mary San Agustin of Palomar College, a community college. If students, she says, "have their heart set in going, let's say, to Stanford or U.C. Berkeley, we have an excellent articulation program that allows them to take the two-year required courses and get guaranteed admissions in their junior year at those schools that they prefer to go to." In this way, a community college can open the door to a four-year college for you.

There are advantages to entering a four-year college as a freshman rather than two years later as a transfer from a community college. Socially and academically, you may enjoy a fuller college experience. You will be part of a graduating class from the beginning, and will benefit from the teaching of faculty who may be at the leading edge of research in their field. "It's all the things that you can't quite name," says Elizabeth Bickford of the University of Oregon. "There is something that you do lose in that transition as an 18- or 19-year-old." But those factors have to be balanced against financial realities, as Ms. Bickford found when she was making her own college decisions. "I'm a community college transfer to a four-year myself. So is my husband. We wouldn't have financially been able to make it if we hadn't done it that way. I think it's a good way to make it if all the support isn't there."

Living Away from Home vs. Commuting

A good way to save money on room and board is to commute. Instead of paying for campus housing and meals—an average cost of $7,791 a year for private colleges—you continue to live at home. There your housing and meal costs remain whatever they have been, and you commute to campus daily by train, bus, car, or other means. This will probably be more inconvenient than living on campus, where you would only have to walk a few steps from your dorm to the classroom. But you will almost certainly save a lot of money.

However, commuting has hidden costs. You will have transportation expenses that you wouldn't have if you lived on campus. If you use mass transit, these costs will probably be low enough to make economic sense. But they might not if you have to buy a car and insure it just to save money on room and board. If you're thinking of relying on a family member for rides to and from campus, remember that their schedules may not overlap with yours. Your own schedule may change day to day and semester to semester, depending on your classes and activities. You probably will need your own car if mass transit isn't available.

Also, don't forget that you cost money at home, too. You're still eating and using utilities at home, and you'll inevitably add pick-up meals on campus to those costs. Financial aid packages usually offer help in paying for room and board as well as tuition and fees, so your actual cost for living on campus would probably not be as high as the published price. Commuting is usually a bargain, but it isn't always as big a bargain as it might first appear.

Financial costs aside, there may be intangible costs to commuting. By not living on campus, you may miss opportunities to make friends and form lifelong connections. And you may miss a chance to mature and become independent more quickly.

If you don't want to commute but still want to save money on room and board, you'll find that the costs of room and board vary widely. One college might offer a better deal than another. By residing near campus in an apartment that you share with classmates, you may be able to live more cheaply than you could in the dorms. But be sure to check the college's policies—many do not allow freshmen to live off campus if they're under 21 and not living with their parents.

How to Factor in Financial Aid

Every college publishes an average price for the various cost components, but that published price is probably not the price you will end up paying. Your financial aid package will reduce your actual costs. Yet financial aid packages vary from college to college as much as costs do. In thinking about where you will apply, you need to find out some financial aid basics about each college on your short list. How great a percentage of need does it usually meet? How much aid does it award in grants and how much in loans? Does the college offer any merit scholarships or other forms of aid not based on need?

Part III of this book, "Financial Aid College by College," gives you these financial aid basics, along with a number of other essential facts. These include:

- the school's Web address
- what type of school it is, such as public or private
- how many students are enrolled
- how selective the school is
- basic costs, including tuition, fees, room, and board
- financial aid application procedures, including deadlines and required forms
- contact information for the financial aid office

In addition, the "Financial Aid Picture" section of each college's profile tells you how much aid is being distributed to how many students and in what form. This information is useful, but note that it only shows averages. Since few families are "average," the numbers in the financial aid profile shouldn't be considered a guarantee of what you'll get or how much you'll have to pay. For example, in-state students at public colleges usually borrow much less than the average debt per student listed in the profiles, while out-of-state students usually borrow more. What you can use the profiles for is to compare colleges: This college meets a greater percentage of need than most; this college awards a relatively large portion of aid in grants.

Check with the Financial Aid Office Before You Apply

Before you apply for financial aid, check with the financial aid offices of the colleges to which you're planning to apply for admission—by simply visiting their Web site, or by talking to them on the phone or in person. Confirm which forms you need to complete and the deadlines. Better to get these details right before you get started than to find out after the fact that you filed too late or didn't file the proper form.

Bear in mind also that each college has its own financial aid policies, such as how outside scholarships are treated and whether or not aid awards can be appealed. When you contact the office, whether long distance or in a campus visit, find out as much as you can about these policies, along with facts about costs and the financial aid process. If possible, schedule an interview with a member of the financial aid staff. They'll give you a lot of information, but don't expect them to offer you aid until they've seen your forms.

KNOW THE LINGO

Need-blind admissions—If a college has a "need-blind admissions" policy, this means that it will admit a student solely on the basis of their academic merit or other characteristics not related to financial status. However, just because a college practices need-blind admissions does not mean it guarantees to meet full need. It may admit a student but be unable to offer a financial aid package equal to his or her need.

Questions to Ask Colleges

Here are some questions worth asking the aid office:

✔ What are your average costs for the first year for:
- tuition and fees
- room and board
- books and supplies
- transportation
- other personal expenses

✔ What is the range of costs for:
- rooms (single, double)
- board (different meal plans)
- tuition rates (flat rate, per credit, etc.)

✔ By how much will total costs increase each year?

✔ How much have tuition and fees and room and board increased over the past three to five years?

✔ Does financial need have an impact on admissions decisions?

✔ Does the school offer both need-based and merit-based financial aid?

✔ Do I need to file a separate application for merit-based scholarships?

✔ If the financial aid package isn't enough, under what conditions, if any, will the aid office reconsider the offer?

✔ How will the aid package change from year to year?

✔ What will happen if my family's financial situation changes?

✔ What are the terms and conditions of your aid programs? For example, what are the academic requirements or other conditions for renewing financial aid from year to year?

✔ When can we expect to receive bills from the college? Is there an option to spread the yearly payment over equal monthly installments?

QUICK RECAP

When deciding where to apply to college, cost is not the most important factor, but it is a factor. Don't exclude any college from consideration because of cost, but do be aware of cost.

- Each school has different costs and financial aid policies.
- Your costs might vary from the published averages.
- You might be able to save money at a public college or community college or by commuting—but there are pros and cons to all those strategies.
- Research the colleges you're considering and contact their financial aid offices early.

Step 4: Get Ready for the Forms

QUICK OVERVIEW

Depending on where you'll apply, you may need to file up to three kinds of forms to get financial aid: the FAFSA, the CSS/Financial Aid PROFILE, and forms for individual colleges or states. Step 4 gets you ready for those forms. There are two main things to remember. First, file before the deadlines. The early bird—or at least the timely bird—gets the worm. Second, don't be intimidated. The forms are easier to fill out than they look.

Forms You'll Fill Out

Applying for financial aid is basically a matter of filling out a few financial aid forms on time. The forms may look complicated and be hard to face, but they are simpler than they look, and millions of people fill them out every year. We will guide you through them so they make sense.

The three steps that follow this one walk you through the forms you may need to complete: the FAFSA (Step 5), the PROFILE (Step 6), and whatever forms your individual colleges may require (Step 7). This step will help you create a timeline of which colleges require which forms when.

You may not need to fill out all the forms we describe. Most colleges require only one form, the FAFSA. If you do need to fill out more than one form, take heart. Most of the other forms ask for information similar to what the FAFSA requests. Repeating that information may be annoying, but it isn't hard.

FAFSA: The Federal Form

This is the big one. The FAFSA, or Free Application for Federal Student Aid, must be completed by everyone who wants federal government aid. Just about every college financial aid program requires it, even if they also require other forms. Most schools and states use nothing but the FAFSA to determine eligibility for aid.

There is no charge for completing the FAFSA. You can mail in your form on paper, but the easiest way to fill it out is online (see "Paper or Online?" on page 40). Copies of the paper form are widely available in high school guidance offices, college financial aid offices, and public libraries, usually in the late fall. You can

KEEP IN MIND

Even though this book presents the financial aid forms in order of FAFSA, PROFILE, and institutional forms, bear in mind that you may need to submit them in a different order depending on the financial aid deadlines of your colleges. In some cases, you may have to file PROFILE a few weeks before FAFSA, or the institutional form on the same day as FAFSA.

also download the FAFSA from www.fafsa.ed.gov. You cannot file the FAFSA before January 1 of the year for which you're seeking aid. For example, if you start school in September 2007, you cannot file the FAFSA before January 1, 2007. If you want a head start, visit the FAFSA Web site earlier so you can familiarize yourself with the form and start working on your application as soon after January 1 as possible. If you don't have all your tax documents together before you need to file, you can estimate your tax information using your end-of-year pay stubs and last year's income tax return (see "Get Your Stuff Together" on page 41).

Once it's January 1, get ready to file as soon as possible. Most college deadlines for financial aid are in February or March, and they need the government to send them your FAFSA information before they can calculate your award. The window of time between January 1 and the financial aid deadlines, some of which fall as early as February 1, isn't big. So, come January, the earlier that you start working on the FAFSA, the better. Don't worry about filing your tax return first: you can work from an unsubmitted draft of the return, or—if you can't complete a draft before you need to file—you can estimate the figures and, if necessary, update them later. The most important thing is to leave time for your FAFSA to be processed. If you're filing on paper, leave at least four weeks before your earliest college or state deadline. If you're filing online, you can wait until only a week before the earliest deadline.

The FAFSA may seem complicated, but it's a lot easier than it looks. Detailed information on how to complete the FAFSA is available on the Web, by phone, and in Step 5.

On the FAFSA, you'll provide financial information about yourself and also about your parents, if you're a dependent student. The information will be based on your income tax returns plus your own reporting of your financial assets, such as bank accounts and savings bonds. The federal government will use that data to calculate your Expected Family Contribution, or EFC. That will be used by each college to determine your financial need and how much federal aid you can get. Most colleges also use this data to figure out how much aid they'll give you from their own funds. However, some use the PROFILE or their own forms for that.

Soon after you've submitted the FAFSA, you'll receive the Student Aid Report (SAR). This lists the information you reported on your FAFSA and tells you what your EFC is. This report is important. Check it over as soon as possible and, if necessary, update it with your family's latest tax return information. Don't sit on the SAR: keep the process moving quickly.

PROFILE

The FAFSA is the only form you can use to obtain federal aid. But in addition, some colleges and scholarship programs also require that you fill out the CSS/Financial Aid PROFILE to award their own nonfederal funds. They believe this form gives a more complete picture of students' financial circumstances, allowing them to allocate money as fairly as possible. PROFILE is

---

GOOD TO KNOW

If you're **filing both the PROFILE and the FAFSA**, it might help to **do the PROFILE first**. One feature of the PROFILE Web site is that once you've completed your application, it will create a worksheet you can use to fill out the FAFSA.

administered by the College Board, though the College Board itself does not give out any need-based scholarships.

A few colleges require PROFILE only if you're applying for early decision or early action. Others require it for all applicants. If your college requires it and you're applying early, it is often the first form to fill out—ahead of even FAFSA. To find out if your colleges require PROFILE, see Part III or contact your colleges' financial aid offices.

PROFILE is online only; there are no paper forms. You can register for PROFILE at www.collegeboard.com beginning October 1 of the year before you intend to start college. Once you register, you can either complete your application then and there or return to it at a later time. It's best if you submit it at least one week before your earliest college financial aid deadline. You can use the same application for multiple colleges, and you'll receive an online acknowledgment confirming which schools you're sending the information to.

There is a $23 fee to register for PROFILE and send your information to one college, plus a fee of $18 for each additional institution. However, depending on the information you submit, you may qualify for a fee waiver. Automatically awarded to low-income, first-time applicants, the fee waiver covers the costs of the PROFILE registration and up to six school reports.

College Forms

Some colleges—most of them private—require you to complete their own financial aid form as well as the FAFSA. Usually the forms are not complicated, and filling them out is not a big deal. Mike Scott of Texas Christian University says, "We have a very simple online form, where we just ask a couple of extra questions." Some of the questions are about projected enrollment: "Are they going to be full-time or part-time? When do they think they're going to graduate?" Others are aimed at matching students to outside sources of aid.

Find out if your colleges require you to file their own form, and if they do, file them on time.

State Forms

Most states offer need-based financial aid to students who live there. Ask your school counselor for information on what form you need to complete to apply for state scholarship or grant programs. In many states, the FAFSA alone is enough to establish eligibility—but some states require their own form. If your state does, find out the deadline and add it to your master timeline for applying for aid. Ask your school counselor for information about your state's required forms. In states that have a separate form, most colleges require you to apply for state aid as part of the financial aid application process. A table showing the deadlines for state aid, and which forms each state requires, appears on page 72 of this book.

KNOW THE LINGO

FAFSA (Free Application for Federal Student Aid)—The form that must be completed by everyone applying for federal government aid.

PROFILE (CSS/Financial Aid PROFILE)—A Web-based form offered by the College Board and used by some colleges and scholarship programs to award their own financial aid.

PIN (Personal Identification Number)—A number that serves as your electronic signature for filing FAFSA on the Web.

SAR (Student Aid Report)—A report based on the information you provided in your FAFSA that reports your federally calculated EFC. The SAR is sent to every student who files a FAFSA.

Know the Deadlines!

Deadlines count. If you're on time, the colleges to which you've applied will have more money to give you; if you're late, they will have less money—or even none. Late means less money, so be on time! That means knowing and keeping track of all the financial aid deadlines you have to meet.

This can be tricky, because the deadlines are not all the same. Many schools and states may require you to fill out their own financial aid forms, and those forms may have deadlines that differ from those of the FAFSA or PROFILE. And keep in mind that a college's due date for financial aid applications is typically different from its due date for admissions applications.

Many colleges have no firm deadline or closing date for applying for financial aid; rather, they have a "priority" date. Often falling in February or March, the priority date is the date by which the school needs to receive your application to make its most attractive aid offer. After that date, funds may be limited or used up, and you may not get as much aid as you need. "I urge my students to apply for aid by the priority date," says Lauri Benton, a counselor at Columbia High School in Decatur, Georgia. "They are more likely to get the aid they need early in the process, when the colleges have ample money to award."

Some colleges accept financial aid applications on a "rolling" basis. This means that applications are reviewed as they come in on a first-come, first-reviewed basis. Applicants are notified—that is, sent a financial aid award letter—a few weeks after they submit their forms. Most colleges that have a priority date will review late applications on a rolling basis. If you're applying to a rolling-applications college that doesn't have any set deadlines or priority dates, you're best off applying by mid-February or early March, when they will probably still have enough money available to meet your need.

Part III of this book, "Financial Aid College by College," lists deadlines and priority dates for colleges, along with their required forms. But it is worth confirming this information with the schools to which you're applying—at least by visiting their Web sites in November or December. Remember: time is money. To get the most aid available, apply by the priority date. (See also "Do You Get More Money If You Apply Early?" on page 40.)

Creating a Timeline for Aid Applications

There are a lot of dates to remember as you apply for financial aid, but they don't have to be overwhelming. You can stay on top of them by making a timeline.

When you've found out the priority dates of the colleges and scholarship programs to which you're applying, as well as those of your state financial aid agency, list them in chronological order. Make that list part of a month-by-month timeline. Don't worry about the past; start the timeline with whatever month you're in now. The chart on the opposite page is an example of the sort of timeline you might construct. A blank copy of this chart for you to fill in appears in Part II on page 121.

EXPERT ADVICE

"If you **meet our priority date**, we're going to guarantee you a full package here. You'll get 100 percent of need if you meet that priority deadline. If you don't, then it's what's left over, if we have money left over. And we typically do—but we don't have enough to meet 100 percent of the need of every late applicant."

—Vincent Amoroso, deputy director, Office of Scholarships and Student Aid, University of North Carolina at Chapel Hill

WORKSHEET 1:
Meet Your Application Deadlines

		COLLEGE 1: *1st Choice Univ.*	COLLEGE 2: *Private Univ.*	COLLEGE 3: *Financial Safety*
FORMS REQUIRED	FAFSA	Yes	Yes	Yes
	PROFILE	For ED (by 11/1)	Yes	No
	State form	Yes	No	Yes
	Institutional form	No	Laptop loaner	Yes
	Tax returns	Verification only	Verification only	Yes
	Other			
SCHOOL CODES	Federal code	999999	888888	777777
	CSS code	999Z	999X	
PRIORITY DATE		3/1 (FAFSA, State Form)	2/1	3/15
CLOSING DATE		None	2/15	None
AFTER APPLYING	Need to send letter?			
	Documentation required?			
COMPARE AWARDS	Notification date	12/15	4/1	2 weeks after applying
	Reply-by date	Immediately (if accepted ED)	5/1	4 weeks after notification

For a blank version of this worksheet that you can photocopy for your own use, see page 121.

Throughout the period that you're applying for aid, keep your timeline where you can see it, check off what you've done, and remind yourself of what to do next. This will put the deadlines in your control. (See the inside front cover of this book for a calendar of general dates.)

Do You Get More Money If You Apply Early?

No. If you apply for financial aid Tuesday and another student applies Wednesday, you don't get more money than that student—so long as both of you apply by the deadline (or the priority date). However, when it comes to the college's own funds, and certain "campus-based" federal student aid programs (such as federal work-study), aid is distributed first-come, first-served once that date has passed. If you don't apply for aid until later than the deadline, the pool of funds may be used up. So always apply on time.

WHAT ABOUT EARLY DECISION?

Many schools allow students to apply for admission under early-decision or early-action programs. Whether early acceptance to a school affects the student's financial aid package varies from school to school. Depending on the college, the student accepted early may get more financial aid, less, or the same.

If you are considering early-decision programs, ask each school's financial aid officer: How is financial aid affected if I apply early decision? You may not know exactly what aid you'll get until after you accept. Don't panic: The rules of early decision allow you to turn down the college's acceptance offer if it doesn't offer you enough aid.

Paper or Online?

With the FAFSA, you have the choice of filing on paper or online. Filing online saves a lot of time and is usually easier. It can cut processing time by one to two weeks—essential if you're running late. It can also reduce delays due to errors because the site edits your information before you submit it, allowing you to correct it before submitting. Also, once you have submitted the form online, you will instantly get your EFC back from the Web site, which reduces some of the anxiety in the process. The FAFSA Web site gives lots of help in completing the form.

Important: If you do file online, save and print out a hard copy of the confirmation you'll receive after submitting your application. If you file a paper form, make a photocopy for your records.

PROFILE is only available online. If you don't have a computer at home, find out if one of your parents can use a computer at work, or use a computer at your school's guidance office or the library. You can print out the PROFILE Preapplication Worksheet to help you gather the information you'll need, then complete the application online.

KEEP IN MIND

If you fill out the FAFSA online, both you and one of your parents need to ask for a U.S. Department of Education PIN, or **Personal Identification Number**. This is important: the PIN will allow you to sign your FAFSA electronically when submitting it online, which will cut down your processing time. **You and one of your parents must each request a PIN** at www.pin.ed.gov. You should register for your PINs **before you fill out the FAFSA**, because they will snail mail them to you, and that can take a week. A good time to ask for your PINs is November of your senior year. Remember your PIN and write it down in a safe place: if you forget it, the government can't "remind" you of it later on.

Figure 7:
FAFSA PIN Site

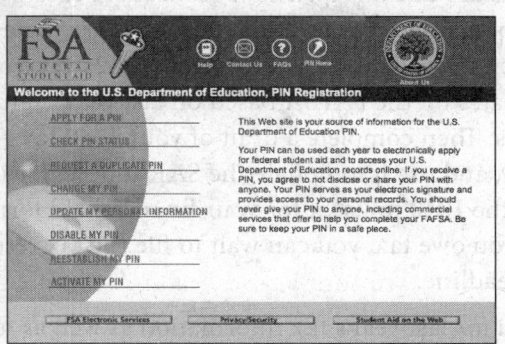

Get Your Stuff Together

For maximum efficiency, gather all the records you need to complete the forms before you sit down to work on them. That will save you a lot of time getting up, hunting around, and forgetting where you left off. For both you and your parents, you'll probably need tax returns and related documents (such as W-2 forms) for the year that just ended, as well as end-of-year pay stubs, bank statements, and other financial records. If you're filling out the PROFILE, you will also need tax documents from the previous year. If your parents own their home, you will need current mortgage information to fill out the PROFILE.

The FAFSA and PROFILE preapplication worksheets are basically a way to help you gather your information before filling out the actual application. Use them that way. Add a list of all the records you need to assemble. It should be comprehensive and indicate which records are for all forms and which are for PROFILE only.

Establish Eligibility

To be eligible for federal financial aid, among other requirements, you'll have to:

- be a U.S. citizen or eligible noncitizen
- have a valid Social Security Number
- not have been convicted of sale or possession of drugs
- if male and at least 18 years old, be registered with the Selective Service (in most cases)

Most of these requirements will not require extra work for most students. But two of them may. If you don't have a Social Security Number, get one as soon as possible (go to www.ssa.gov to learn how), and certainly before you file your FAFSA. And if you are male, you can register for the Selective Service through the FAFSA application if you haven't already. If you do have a drug conviction, you may still be able to establish eligibility by completing a treatment program.

EXPERT ADVICE

If, like many students, you've never filed a tax return, you'll probably find it helpful to **get a blank copy of IRS Form 1040EZ** and the instructions that come with it. This is the simplest tax return form there is, and most high school and college students use it to report their summer and after-school job earnings. If your parents have filed for you in past years, **ask them to walk you through your return** for the last year.

Tax Forms and Other Records

Income tax returns are due on April 15, but most colleges want your financial aid forms much sooner. Don't wait until your taxes are done to file your financial aid forms. Even if you haven't received your W-2s yet, you can still file the FAFSA. Use estimates on the FAFSA based on last year's return and your current-year pay stubs. Then complete a draft of your 1040 tax return as soon as possible afterward, and use it to update the SAR if necessary. You don't necessarily have to file the 1040 to use it for your financial aid forms; you just need to complete it. If you owe tax, you can wait to file the tax return until closer to the April 15 tax deadline.

PROFILE asks you for last year's tax information as well as for this year's. For this year, it asks you whether the figures are estimated or final. It also asks for estimated income for next year, which you can base on this year's information.

QUICK RECAP

You'll have to file some forms to get financial aid, but they aren't as difficult as they might look. The main forms are FAFSA and PROFILE, plus whatever other forms your colleges or state may require.

- File on time.
- File your FAFSA online to save time. Get a PIN for yourself and for one of your parents early.
- Make a timeline to keep track of your deadlines, including college priority dates.
- As early as possible, check with your colleges to be sure you know what forms they each require.
- Gather together the records you need to fill out the forms.
- If you don't have one already, get a Social Security Number.

Step 5: Fill Out the FAFSA

QUICK OVERVIEW

The FAFSA may look intimidating, but it's actually pretty easy to fill out. We'll walk you through the seven steps of this key financial aid form. The questions mainly concern your income and assets and those of your parents, but they also touch on other matters, such as your citizenship status and the schools to which you want the FAFSA to be sent. You'll find tips about how to avoid delays, such as by filing electronically and making sure the name on your FAFSA matches the name on your Social Security card. Above all: file on time!

General Advice

Nobody likes to fill out forms, with their cramped boxes and unfamiliar terms. And no one enjoys having to share information about family finances. But the potential result—money to help you pay for college—is well worth it. And you will see in this step that the FAFSA is really pretty simple. In fact, the form has only seven sections, one of which is, essentially, "sign here."

Again, remember that you don't have to do the steps in this book in exactly the order presented. If the colleges require you to submit the PROFILE before the FAFSA, then do the PROFILE first, even though we present the FAFSA first. In fact, one nice thing about the PROFILE is that, after you've submitted it, you'll receive a worksheet that you can use to fill out the FAFSA, making this step much easier.

Help is available by phone and online if you have questions about FAFSA (see the "Good to Know" sidebar on page 45). And don't be afraid to call the financial aid offices of the colleges to which you're applying. If you're confused about this or any other aspect of the financial aid process, these offices can help. "Our job is to get students through this maze," said Bonnie Lee Behm of Villanova University. "You'd call a mechanic if your car is broken. Well, why not call us if you have a question about financial aid applications? That is our job—to get you through the process."

EXPERT ADVICE

"People look at the FAFSA and/or the PROFILE, and they find it a bit overwhelming initially, particularly if they're not very financially savvy or they're not number crunchers themselves. So they come to us seeking guidance and reassurance on how to get through the application process. We tell them **it's not as overwhelming or as complicated as it looks** initially."

—Vincent Amoroso, deputy director, Office of Scholarships and Student Aid, University of North Carolina at Chapel Hill

Apply on Time

You can't file your FAFSA before January 1 of the year you're applying for aid. Most college deadlines for financial aid are in March, and some fall as early as February, so the window for filing is narrow. You have to leave time for your FAFSA to be processed. If you're filing on paper, allow at least four weeks before your earliest college or state deadline. If you're filing online, leave at least one week before the earliest deadline.

Don't wait until the April 15 tax deadline to file your FAFSA. Most priority dates will be long over by then. If your earliest deadline doesn't fall until March, you can wait for W-2s, 1099s, and other official tax documents to arrive from employers and banks and then complete draft income tax returns. You don't have to file those draft returns with the IRS, but you can use the information from them on your FAFSA. The advantage of using draft tax returns this way is that you probably won't have to correct your FAFSA after you've submitted it, and it will be easier to answer the questions on the form that refer directly to lines on the 1040.

If your earliest deadline falls in February, however, you should have a backup plan in case W-2s don't arrive in time. The best thing to do in this case is to use end-of-year pay stubs, quarterly bank statements, and similar records to estimate your and your parents' income. You can also use 1040 forms for the previous year as a frame of reference, but don't just plug in the information from last year's returns into the FAFSA—you really do need to estimate the current information, not duplicate old information. (Also, be warned that the numbers assigned to each line of the 1040 tend to change whenever the IRS adds new credits or deductions, so the references on the FAFSA you're filling out may not match old 1040s.)

No matter how you derive the numbers, remember this above all: get the FAFSA in on time.

Read Instructions Carefully; Fill Out the Form Accurately

With the FAFSA as with all financial aid forms, accuracy is vital. Read the directions. Understand the terms that are being used. Many terms, such as "date of birth," are straightforward, but others, such as "investments," require you to read the instructions carefully so you know what they mean in this context. Even the term "parent," as discussed below, has a special meaning on the FAFSA.

Be as complete and accurate as you can about your financial circumstances. If you submit incorrect data or leave out requested information, your forms will probably end up having to be corrected, and this will create delays that could endanger your aid. By avoiding errors, you will increase your chances of getting all the aid for which you are eligible.

KNOW THE LINGO

If you've never filed an income tax return before—or if your parents file for you—you may not be familiar with these IRS forms:

1040—the main form of your tax return, this is a summary of all the taxable income you or your parents made last year, possible deductions from that income, the tax owed on that income, and credits that give some of that tax back.

W-2—a tax form prepared by the employer stating how much taxable income they paid you last year, as well as untaxed benefits you or your parents received from them. Information on this form is used on both the 1040 and the FAFSA.

1099—a form similar to the W-2 that shows income you received from anyone other than an employer. For example, if one of your parents is an independent contractor, he or she may receive a 1099-MISC showing the nonemployee compensation a client paid them.

1098—a tax form showing payments for which you can take a deduction or credit. For example, if you take out a student loan, once you begin repaying it you will receive a 1098-E from your lender every year showing how much interest you paid on the loan.

File Electronically, If Possible

You can submit a paper FAFSA, but it's easier and faster to submit your FAFSA online at www.fafsa.ed.gov. Filing the FAFSA on the Web can reduce processing time by a couple of weeks. It also reduces delays due to errors: the site edits your information before you submit it, so if you made errors or left out information, you can correct it before submitting it.

As an added convenience, you don't have to complete the FAFSA on the Web in one sitting. At the start, you'll supply a password that will allow you to leave the application before completing it and to return later, so long as you come back within 45 days. But make sure you write down the password and keep it in a safe place where you can find it again. Unlike most Web sites, the FAFSA site provides no hint or reminder to aid your memory. If you forget the password, there will be no way to retrieve your data, and you'll have to start over.

If you file online, get PINs ahead of time for both yourself and for one of your parents so you can sign the form electronically. The PINs can be ordered at www.pin.ed.gov. You should do this in advance because it will take a week to get the PINs—a delay you may not be able to afford later in the process. Write down the PIN in a safe place; if you forget it, that could make you miss your deadline.

> **GOOD TO KNOW**
>
> Detailed information on how to complete the paper FAFSA is available on the Web at **www.studentaid.ed.gov/completefafsa**. If you're filing the FAFSA online at **www.fafsa.ed.gov**, that same site offers help screens for each question and live, one-on-one online help with a customer service representative. Click the "help" icon to access that feature. For help over the phone with either the paper or online FAFSA, call **1 800 4-FED-AID (1 800 433-3243)**.
>
> Avoid any Web site that offers to help you file the FAFSA for a fee. The federal government offers its help for free and does not endorse any site that charges money for assistance.

Figure 8:
FAFSA on the Web

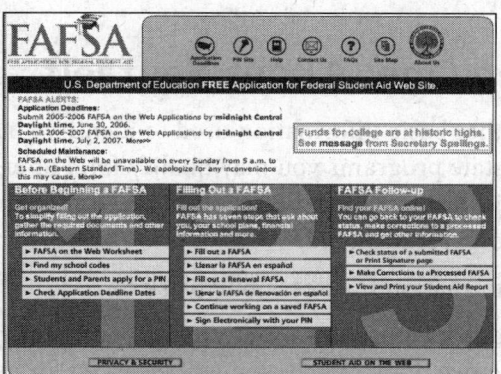

Let's Walk Through It

The FAFSA consists of seven sections, or "steps," each of which contains a number of questions with a common theme. The exact questions change from year to year (last year's preapplication worksheet is in Part II), but the substance remains more or less the same. The point never changes: to provide information about yourself and your family that colleges will use to figure out how much federal student aid you qualify for.

There are a few general tips to keep in mind while filling out the FAFSA:

- The word "you" always means you, the student.
- The word "college" means a college, university, community college, or any other school beyond high school.
- The phrase "net worth" means the current value of an asset (such as a business) minus the amount of debt owed on it.
- Questions about income are for the previous year; questions about assets ask for their value as of the day you fill out the form.
- When entering dollar figures, round to the nearest dollar and don't use commas or decimal points.
- If you submit on paper, don't enclose written notes or letters with your FAFSA—they'll be thrown out. If you have special financial circumstances you want to explain, write to your colleges directly (see this book's Step 8, "Make Your Special Circumstances Known").

Here is a step-by-step walk through the key questions of the FAFSA. The version used here is the paper version, which presents the seven steps in full detail one after another. The electronic version has similar content, but because it is interactive, it will automatically skip over some questions or sections depending on how you answer. For example, if you say that you're not married, you won't be asked questions about your spouse. Worksheets are included in a paper form with the paper FAFSA, and in an electronic form with the online FAFSA.

FAFSA Step One: About Yourself

These questions gather basic information used to identify you and determine which federal and state programs you may qualify for. For example, the question about your citizenship is there because only U.S. citizens (or eligible non-citizens) can get federal student aid.

Here's the main information this section will ask for:

Your name. Put down your name exactly as it appears on your Social Security card. If the two don't match, you will be asked for more documentation through the mail, slowing down the whole process.

Where you live. Use a permanent home mailing address here, not a school or office address.

Your Social Security Number (SSN). As noted in Step 4, you need to have an SSN to apply for federal aid. If you submit the form without one, it will be returned to you unprocessed.

Your date of birth.

Your permanent telephone number. Use a permanent home telephone number, not a school or office number.

Your driver's license number (if any).

Your e-mail address. This is optional, but if you provide it, the government can send you your Student Aid Report (SAR) by e-mail instead of snail mail, so it will reach you faster.

Whether you're single, married, divorced, widowed, or separated.

Whether you are a citizen or an eligible noncitizen. You are a citizen if you were born in this country or became a citizen through the naturalization process. An eligible noncitizen is someone such as a U.S. permanent resident, a person holding a green card (Permanent Resident Card) who is allowed to live permanently in the United States. It is not someone visiting on a student visa. If you're an eligible noncitizen, you'll have to fill in your Alien Registration Number. If you're neither a citizen nor an eligible noncitizen, you can't get federal aid, but you may be eligible for state or college aid.

The state in which you legally reside. Your answer will determine whether you're eligible for scholarships and grants from your state . It's also used to estimate how much state income tax you pay. In some cases, your state of legal residence—where you officially live—might be different from the state where you're actually living at the time you fill out the FAFSA. This might be the case if you've recently moved or one of your parents is in the military.

Whether you're male. If you are and you haven't registered with the Selective Service yet, you'll have the option of registering now via the FAFSA. To get federal aid, male students 18 years or older must be registered with the Selective Service, the agency responsible for providing drafted men to the armed forces in an emergency.

What level of education you've reached. This question determines which aid programs you qualify for. For example, the SMART grant is only available to students in their junior or senior year of college.

Whether you're interested in loans and work-study. Always say yes to both! Preserve your options. It doesn't matter if you aren't sure. Answer yes. Answering no won't make colleges more likely to give you grants, but it might keep you from getting loan and work-study aid if you change your mind later. By the time you change your mind, all the funds might be gone.

The highest level of education completed by your father and mother. This won't affect your federal aid, but some states use this information to award scholarships to students who are the first in their family to attend college.

Whether you've ever been convicted of possessing or selling illegal drugs. Don't leave this blank or you won't be able to get federal aid. If you have a conviction, say so—but don't be discouraged. You might still qualify. The government will send you a worksheet to determine whether the conviction affects your eligibility for federal student aid. (If you're filling out the FAFSA online, the worksheet will automatically appear once you've completed this question.) Even if your federal eligibility is revoked, you might still be eligible for state or college aid.

FAFSA Step Two: Your Income and Assets

These questions ask about *your* income and assets—the student's. Income is how much money you made last year; assets are what you own and the savings you have. If you are married, they also want to know about your spouse's income and assets. They won't ask about your parents' income and assets until later.

These are the main things that this section asks for:

Whether you've completed a tax return for the past year. This means the return that is due the coming April 15, not the one you filed a year ago. If you have filed a return or plan to file one, they will ask what form you're using, for example, the 1040 or 1040A. If you're not going to file any tax return, they will still ask how much you (and, if you have one, your spouse) earned from working.

Whether you're eligible to file the 1040A or 1040EZ tax form. The instructions on the FAFSA explain who can file these forms. Most students can. If you can, say yes.

What income and tax information you and your spouse will report on your tax returns. As discussed at the beginning of this chapter, these questions are easy to answer if you've already completed a draft of your tax return. For example, if you used IRS Form 1040, the FAFSA will ask you for the adjusted gross income you reported on that form, and will even tell you the line number where you will find it. All you have to do is read it off that line and enter it in the box on the FAFSA. If you haven't completed your tax return yet, your job is a little harder. You can estimate what the information on the completed return will be and update the information later if necessary. Use pay stubs and, if you have one, your prior-year tax return to make the income estimates. Just don't put off filing the FAFSA because you haven't done your taxes yet. You're not required to file your tax return before completing the FAFSA.

What your untaxed income and benefits are. These are items like earned income credits, welfare benefits, Social Security benefits, child support, and other money that came to you without being taxed. If you're filing online, you will be asked about these in a series of questions on one screen. If you are filling out the paper FAFSA, you should use the worksheets that come with the form to add them all up, then fill in the totals on your FAFSA. Don't submit the worksheets, but keep copies of them on file. (If you're filing online, the worksheets will appear as part of the confirmation you receive after submitting the application.) A financial aid office may want those details later.

Veteran's noneducation benefits. If you are a veteran, the untaxed-income worksheets will ask you to list your noneducation benefits. But if you're receiving veteran's education benefits (for example, GI Bill funds) that are paid directly to a college, do not report those as income in this section (you'll report them a little later in a separate question). Do report any military pensions, health benefits, or the like.

What your assets are. This question is meant to provide the government with a snapshot of your assets, the money or property you currently own. Using current banking statements and investment records, say how much cash and savings you have, as well the total value of any stocks, other investments, or investment properties that you own. (An investment property is a residence or farm that you finance to make a profit, not one you live in or on.) If you're still in high school, chances are that you only have a small savings or checking account, which you should report on the line asking for "cash, savings accounts, and checking accounts." You may also have some government savings bonds, certificates of deposit (CDs), or a few shares of stock; those should be reported on the line asking about "investments."

Veterans' education benefits. Here you do report any education benefits you get as a veteran, such as GI Bill funds. (Be sure to report the monthly benefit amount, not the annual amount.) These are not used in calculating your EFC, but colleges take them into account when putting together an aid package, as described in Step 9 of this book.

FAFSA Step Three: Are You Independent?

The questions in this step determine whether or not you're an independent student. To be considered independent for the purpose of federal student aid eligibility, it is not enough to feel independent, have a job, or even to have moved away from your parents. For that matter, it has nothing to do with whether your parents claim you as a dependent on their tax return. You will be classified as a dependent unless you can truthfully answer "yes" to at least one of the questions in this section. If you answer "yes" to even one of the questions, you will be considered independent.

If you are independent, the main difference is that you can skip Step Four, which asks about your parents' income and assets. But there are certain cases where a college financial aid office will want to know about your parents' finances even if you are an independent. If you do meet one of the criteria on the list below, it's a good idea to ask the colleges to which you're applying whether they'll consider you fully independent for the purpose of awarding their own institutional funds. If one or more of them won't, you should fill out FAFSA Step Four. (If you're filing online, the application will ask you whether you want to fill it out or skip it.)

The things that would classify you as independent are:

- You turn age 24 or older in the year you start college.
- You'll be enrolled in a graduate degree program in the year for which you're seeking aid.
- You're married.
- You have children who get more than half of their support from you.
- You have dependents other than your children or spouse who live with you and get more than half their support from you.

> **GOOD TO KNOW**
>
> Most students are eligible to file IRS Form 1040EZ or 1040A as their tax return. Some parents can, too. (The rules determining whether you can are explained in the FAFSA instructions.) **If both you and your parents are eligible to file the 1040A or 1040EZ**, you may qualify for a "simplified needs analysis," wherein only your income (not your assets) will be assessed when calculating your expected family contribution.

- You're an orphan, or you've been a ward/dependent of the court.
- You're currently serving in, or are a veteran of, the active-duty U.S. armed forces. (If you served only as a reservist and were never activated for reasons other than training, answer "no.")

FAFSA Step Four: Your Parents' Income and Assets

These questions are about your parents' income and assets. If you're a dependent student, you have to answer these questions even if you don't live with your parents. You have to name your parent(s) and give their Social Security Number(s). (If neither of your parents has a SSN, fill this question in with nine zeroes.) It isn't enough to fill out your parents' income and asset information while leaving the SSN question blank—if you do, your application will be rejected. When you're ready to submit the application, you will also need one of your parents to sign it, either on the paper form or by using a PIN on the electronic version.

Modern family life can make the definition of "parent" complicated. But the FAFSA definitions are fairly clear:

- If both your parents are living and married to each other, answer the questions about both of them.
- If only one of your parents is living, answer the questions about him or her.
- If your widowed parent remarried, answer the questions about your stepparent too.
- If you were raised by a single parent, answer the questions about him or her.
- If your parents are divorced or separated, answer the questions about the parent you lived with the most during the past 12 months.
- If that parent remarried, answer the questions about your stepparent, too.
- Don't provide information about grandparents, legal guardians, or foster parents. FAFSA doesn't consider them your parents unless they have legally adopted you.

Step Four also asks about the number of people in your parents' household, including you and your parents, and the number who will be in college during the next year, including you. These questions affect how much money your parents will be expected to contribute to your education.

Beyond that, this section is mostly a repeat of FAFSA Step Two, with the difference that the questions are about your parents' finances instead of yours. Just as it asked of you earlier, the FAFSA now asks of your parents:

Whether they've completed a tax return for the past year.

Whether they're eligible to file the 1040A or 1040EZ tax form. Once again, they should answer yes if they're eligible to file this form. If they would normally file the 1040A but filed the full 1040 only to take advantage of an education tax benefit relating to a child already in college, they can still check this box.

What income and tax information they reported on their tax return. Once again, these questions are easier to answer if your parents already completed their tax return. Most likely they have not, but don't let that delay filing the FAFSA; it's acceptable to estimate the figures and correct them after your parents have filed their return. It's far more important to meet your financial aid deadlines and priority dates than to report on the FAFSA exactly what your parents will eventually report to the IRS. As discussed above in "FAFSA Step Two," pay stubs and the prior-year tax return can be used for estimates.

What their untaxed income and benefits are. Once again, this includes items like earned income credits, welfare benefits, Social Security benefits, child support, and other money that didn't get taxed. It also includes any contributions your parents made for the last tax year to Individual Retirement Accounts (IRAs) or employer-sponsored retirement plans such as 401(k)s or 403(b)s. Again, add this up on worksheets and fill in the totals on the FAFSA. Keep the worksheets on file in case a financial aid administrator asks about them later. If you're filling out the worksheets online, the information will appear on the confirmation page you'll see after submitting, which you should print out.

What their assets are. Again, this includes the value of all cash, savings, stocks or other investments (including real estate investment properties), and large businesses or investment farms owned by your parents. It *doesn't* include the home where they live, a family-owned and controlled small business, or a family farm that they live on and operate. However, if your parents own more than one home—a summer cottage, for example, or an investment property—they also should report their equity in that home on the "investments" line. If they own a farm that they don't live on, they also should report the value of that farm as an investment. Another thing your parents do not need to include here is any money they have in tax-advantaged retirement accounts, such as IRAs, 401(k)s, 403(b)s, and the like.

FAFSA Step Five: Independent Students' Household Information

This section is only for independent students—those who answered "yes" to any question in Step Three. It collects information about the number of people in their household and the number of those who will be in college this year. If you are a dependent student, ignore this section.

EXPERT ADVICE

"**Some people overthink the FAFSA** questions. They'll get to what we would see as straightforward questions: 'How many are in your household?' And then 'How many in your household go to college?' Well, some families will list every person who's ever lived in the household and then every member who has ever attended college. And actually **what we want to know** is, how many are living in your household now, and how many of them are in college now."

—Elizabeth Bickford, director, Office of Student Financial Aid and Scholarships, University of Oregon, Eugene

FAFSA Step Six: College Codes

Now you're in the home stretch. There are no more questions about your family's finances or personal life. All this section of the FAFSA asks is which colleges should receive your information. You list the colleges, and the government will send the processed information to them. List up to six. Identify the colleges by federal school code. You can get the federal school code from Part III of this book (see Figure 9). You can also get it from www.fafsa.ed.gov or the colleges' financial aid Web sites.

For each college, you have to say whether you plan to live on campus, off campus, or with your parents. Your answer will affect the housing costs that the school will estimate for you, and therefore your financial need. If you haven't made a decision yet, assume you'll live on campus.

If you're applying for admission to more than six schools, you'll need to choose six to send the information to first, then add the additional schools later. You'll have an opportunity to do that when you get your Student Aid Report (SAR) (see page 53). The same "six only" rule will apply if you send in corrections to your SAR. In choosing the first six, choose the colleges whose financial aid deadlines come first.

You don't need to request that your information be sent to the state agency; the government will automatically send your processed information to the agency of your state government that administers financial aid programs for state residents, whether scholarships, grants, or loans. Do be aware, however, that some states require an additional financial aid form, as discussed in Step 7 of this book.

> **GOOD TO KNOW**
>
> The FAFSA asks both you and your parents to report the amount of income tax you will have to pay on last year's income. The **amount they want here is only the federal income tax amount**—don't include Social Security, Medicare, or any of the taxes that are reported in the "other taxes" section of Form 1040. If you or one of your parents is self-employed or has to self-report tip income from a restaurant job, you should keep this in mind.

Figure 9:
Finding a College's Federal Code

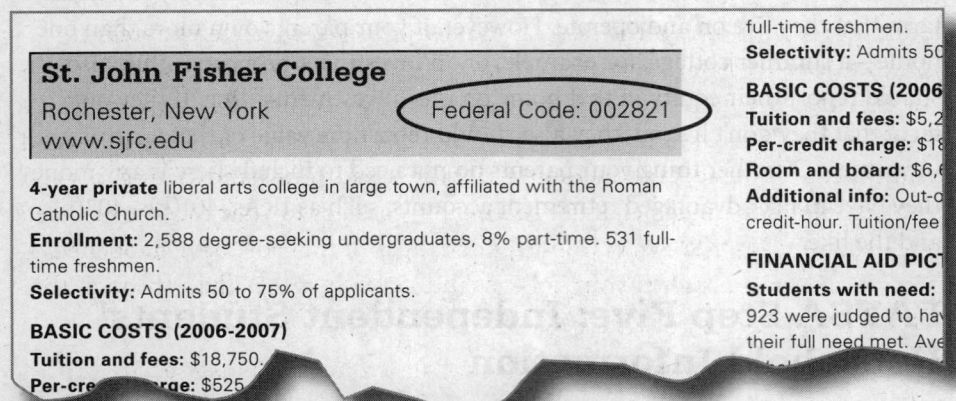

The Federal Code for each college in this book can be found in its college description.

FAFSA Step Seven: Sign Here, Please

Now you're at the last step. This is where you sign and date the form. If your parents provided financial information in Step Four, one of them also needs to sign.

If you file using the paper form, make a photocopy of it before mailing it, and keep that photocopy together with the worksheets you filled out and all the records you used.

If you apply online, you and a parent both sign electronically using your PINs. Be sure to keep clicking on "next" until you get to the confirmation page! Your FAFSA is not truly submitted until then. Be sure to print that confirmation page, and save it as an electronic file to your hard drive as well.

Check Your Student Aid Report!

After you submit your FAFSA, you'll receive your Student Aid Report, or SAR. How long it will take for you to receive it, and in what form, will depend on how you filed the FAFSA. If you filed a paper FAFSA and did not provide an e-mail address, you'll receive a paper SAR within about four weeks. If you filed FAFSA on the Web, signed it with your PIN, and provided an e-mail address, you'll receive an e-mail link to your online SAR information much faster—within one to three days.

In whatever form the SAR reaches you, check it over carefully. It will include a summary detailing the information you supplied on the FAFSA. Make sure this information is correct. If not, make the necessary changes: on paper or online, there will be space for you to do so.

Make corrections only if the data on the SAR doesn't accurately represent your family's financial situation at the time the FAFSA was originally filed. For example, if you estimated the previous year's income but have since filed a tax return with exact figures, substitute those figures now. Or if you mistyped a number, or if the federal data-entry clerk misread your handwriting, correct that. But don't make changes that reflect changes to your income or assets since you filed the FAFSA. If important changes of that sort have happened—such as a lost job—inform your colleges individually rather than through the FAFSA (see Step 8).

In the upper-right part of the SAR's front page, you should also see an estimate of your EFC: the amount of money your family is expected to contribute toward college costs. The only reason you won't see it is if your SAR has been rejected because you didn't provide required signatures, valid Social Security Numbers, or enough data to calculate the EFC. If that happens to you, submit the necessary corrections and you'll get your EFC estimate. The actual EFC calculated by a given college may be different than what you'll see here, especially if that college uses the Institutional Methodology, or if its financial aid office has adjusted your EFC based on special circumstances that you brought to the college's attention.

You can submit corrections on paper or online through Corrections on the Web at www.fafsa.ed.gov. Online submission of corrections is faster and easier—and you can do it even if you submitted your original FAFSA on paper, as long as you have a PIN. Some college financial aid offices can transmit corrections electronically for you if you ask them to do so.

The colleges you requested to receive your FAFSA information will automatically get your SAR. At the corrections stage, you'll have an opportunity to add up to six more colleges to receive your FAFSA information. You can also give a school permission to add itself to the list. Just provide the college with the Data Release Number (DRN) at the bottom-left corner of the first page of the SAR. The school will use your DRN to access your application record.

The SAR gives you an estimate of how much money your family is expected to pay for college, but not how much financial aid you'll receive. You'll find that out when your individual colleges send you their award letters. Even so, by filing your FAFSA, you've taken a big step toward getting those letters.

If the expected family contribution (EFC) indicated on the SAR looks too high for your family to afford, you should talk to your parents and discuss other financing options with them (see Step 11). It could also mean that you need to explain some special financial circumstances to the colleges to which you've applied to (see Step 8).

> **KEEP IN MIND**
>
> Eligibility for **federal student aid does not automatically continue** from one year to the next. You have to reapply every year that you're in college. Do that by filling out a **Renewal FAFSA**. This is a partially preformatted version of the FAFSA that you can use so long as you applied for federal aid the previous year.

QUICK RECAP

The FAFSA is easier than it looks. Most of it is about your income and assets, and that of your parents. It's organized in seven steps. Remember:

- File on time. Send in your FAFSA as soon as possible, beginning January 1 of the year you'll start college.
- It helps to have your tax return finished first, but don't let that delay you. You can estimate your figures and correct them later.
- Read instructions.
- Be accurate.
- A paper FAFSA is all right, but filing electronically will save time and reduce error.
- Reapply every year.

Step 6: Fill out the PROFILE (If Required)

QUICK OVERVIEW

Whether you have to fill out the CSS/Financial Aid PROFILE depends on the colleges to which you're applying. If you do, you'll find it mainly asks for "more of the same"—information about your family's income, expenses, and assets—rather than something completely new. The online form is customized to your situation, so you won't be presented with too many questions that don't apply to you. However, the application does take time to fill out, so leave yourself plenty of time to submit it before your colleges' deadlines.

General Advice

Step 6 is to fill out the CSS/Financial Aid PROFILE—but only if you need to. If the schools to which you're applying don't require this financial aid form, you don't have to complete it. Find out if they require it by checking Part III of this book or the colleges' Web sites.

The PROFILE is administered by the College Board, a not-for-profit association of schools and colleges (and the publisher of this book). It is available online only: you can't file on paper. The upside of this is that PROFILE is available 24 hours a day, seven days a week. Furthermore, its system of online edits alerts you to missing or incorrect information before you submit the application, eliminating a potential source of delays. Firewall protection and data encryption protect the information you submit about your family and its finances. The downside is that if you don't have a computer with Internet access at home, you will have to use one at your school, a library, or a parent's workplace.

The PROFILE doesn't replace the FAFSA: you still need to complete that, too, because that's the form required for federal student aid, which any college will expect you to seek before they give away their own institutional funds. The schools that require the PROFILE do so because they believe it gives a more complete account of your financial situation to guide them in awarding their own funds. The College Board provides the colleges with your PROFILE information, and the colleges use it to calculate your expected family contribution and your need.

Colleges that use PROFILE generally follow the Institutional Methodology (IM) for calculating students' need, an approach that differs in several ways from the Federal Methodology (FM) followed by FAFSA (see Step 2 for a guide to the differences). Since the IM is meant to give a more complete picture of your finances, it is not surprising that the PROFILE is longer than the FAFSA. It's the same general concept, but you'll need to gather more records to answer all the questions, and it will take more time to fill out.

Figure 10:
CSS/Financial Aid PROFILE Online

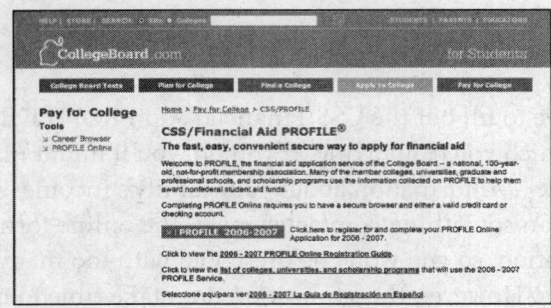

> **EXPERT ADVICE**
>
> "Chapel Hill is no different than most schools that require the PROFILE and use it when they're investing a lot of their own institutional dollars into need-based programs. We use it because **the PROFILE gives us an added, more in-depth look** at a family's financial strength. Our ultimate goal is to give the right dollars to the right students at the right time, and this PROFILE application helps us do that."
>
> —Vincent Amoroso, deputy director, Office of Scholarships and Student Aid, University of North Carolina, Chapel Hill

Register and File Early

Because the PROFILE form is more involved, and because colleges may ask for additional information even after the form is filed (such as data on a family-owned farm or store), register well before your colleges' deadlines and leave yourself lots of time to fill out the application. The College Board usually processes your PROFILE information and transmits it to colleges within two business days, but delays can happen—especially in late January and early February. Also, don't assume it can all be completed in one session; you may need to gather additional information to complete the form (especially if a college asks for additional information in section Q). Fortunately, you can go back and forth to your application online, rather than having to finish it in one sitting.

It's best to submit the PROFILE at least one week before your earliest financial aid priority date. Remember, colleges use PROFILE information to determine who gets their limited grant dollars. If you file late, you will have to make do with whatever funds, if any, are left over.

You may need to submit the PROFILE ahead of the FAFSA, depending on the deadlines your colleges set. In fact, some of the colleges that require the PROFILE will ask you to submit it before you submit your FAFSA. This is especially likely if you're applying early decision or early action for admission to the college. If a college requires the PROFILE before January 1, you can submit a PROFILE with estimated income figures for this year based on your year-to-date pay stubs and your previous year's tax return, then send corrections to the college later if necessary.

GOOD TO KNOW

Help is available to get you through the PROFILE application. If you're not sure about how to answer any question, **check the online Help Desk** that's built into the online application. If you can't find an answer to your question there, contact the PROFILE help line, either by e-mail (**help@cssprofile.org**) or by phone (**305 829-9793**). From October to April, PROFILE customer service hours are Monday through Friday, 8 a.m. to 10 p.m. Eastern Time.

You can also contact the financial aid office at the college to which you're applying. In addition, your high school counselor may be able to answer your questions.

Even if college deadlines don't require the PROFILE first, it may save you time to complete it before the FAFSA. The PROFILE collects all the information asked for by the FAFSA, and when you complete the application, PROFILE will generate a worksheet that you can print out and use to complete the FAFSA.

Preparing for the PROFILE

You can get ready to complete the PROFILE with the Preapplication Worksheet, available from the PROFILE site at www.collegeboard.com. You can also download and print out the PROFILE Registration Guide and Application Instructions from the same site. All of these materials are available in both English and Spanish.

The Preapplication Worksheet can save you a lot of time by helping you gather all your necessary family financial information before starting the application. Filling it out on paper can also speed your way if you have to file the application on a computer where your log-in time is limited, such as at school or a library.

Whether you're filling out the Preapplication Worksheet or the PROFILE itself, you'll need to gather more records to fill out the PROFILE than you will for the FAFSA. For example, in addition to asking about your parents' income for the year before you plan to enter college, the PROFILE asks about their income the year before that, as well as their projected income in the year to come. There are also questions about your projected summer and school-year earnings during your first year in college. The purpose of this is to give financial aid officers a better idea of whether last year's income was typical or unusually low or high. But it also means that you must collect more documents, such as tax returns for the prior year, and you'll need to estimate future income.

Documents You'll Need Before You Fill Out Your PROFILE

It's a good idea to gather the necessary records before you start and have them handy as you work on the PROFILE. You'll need records for both yourself and your parents.

- ✔ U.S. income tax return for the year before you start college, if completed, or pay stubs and other income-related records for estimates
- ✔ U.S. income tax return for the year before that
- ✔ W-2 forms and other records of money earned the year before you start college
- ✔ Records of untaxed income for those two years
- ✔ Current bank statements and mortgage information
- ✔ Records of stocks, bonds, trusts, and other investments

As with the FAFSA, it's easiest if you've already completed your tax return for the most recent tax year before you start filling out the PROFILE. But don't let that hold you up. Estimate your tax return information if you haven't completed your return by the time you need to file the PROFILE. (There are tools on the PROFILE site to help you and your parents estimate this information.) You can correct PROFILE information, if necessary, directly with the colleges after filing your return.

How to Register/File on the Web

Just like registering ahead of time for a FAFSA PIN, it's best to register for the PROFILE well before the first college's deadline. Since the PROFILE is entirely Web based, you do this online at www.collegeboard.com. You'll need to create a collegeboard.com account (with a username and password) before you can file; setting up the account is free. (If you previously registered online for the SAT, you already have this account: it's the same one you used then.) If you don't have Internet access at home, ask your school counselor or librarian if you can use one of the school's computers.

It's smart to register for PROFILE as soon as you're sure about where you'll be applying for aid, but in any case at least one week before the earliest financial aid filing date you need to meet. Registrations are accepted beginning October 1 of the year before you intend to start college. Once you register, you can either complete your application then and there or return to it at a later time. Your PROFILE application will be customized to your circumstances based on the information you give when you register.

Most families will have to pay a fee of $23 to register for the PROFILE and to have their information sent to one college, plus $18 for each additional college. The fee can be paid with most major credit cards, some bank debit cards, or by an electronic withdrawal from your checking account. Low-income families applying for the first time may qualify for a fee waiver (see sidebar).

Registration will involve providing some preliminary information such as your date of birth; mailing address; the year in school for which you're seeking aid; whether you are a U.S. citizen, a veteran, or an orphan; whether you have dependents or have separated or divorced parents; and whether your parents own a home, or all or part of a business or farm. The questions usually won't involve looking up documents; just answer them straightforwardly. Some of them (such as the questions about date of birth and being a veteran) are intended to clarify whether you're a dependent or independent student.

> **GOOD TO KNOW**
>
> If your family's income and assets are very low, and you are applying for financial aid for the first time, **you may be eligible for a fee waiver** covering registration costs and up to six school reports. Whether you qualify will be determined based on the information that you provide in the PROFILE form itself. **You will automatically get the waiver if you qualify—** you don't have to apply for it separately.

Figure 11:
Finding a College's CSS code

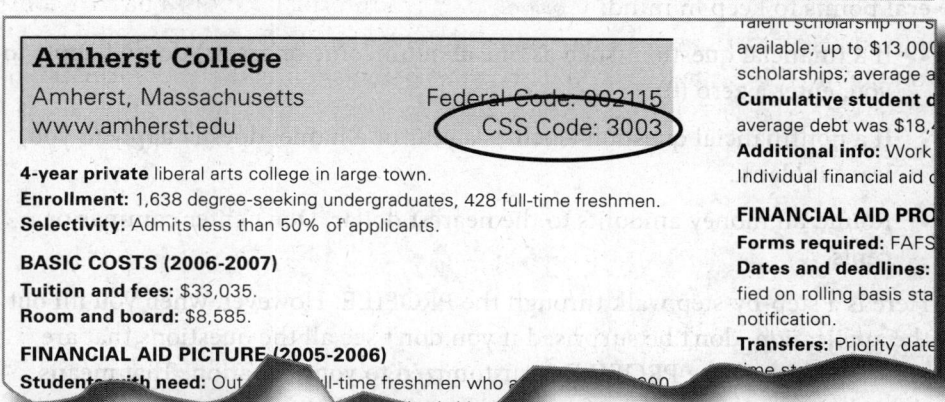

The College Scholarship Service® (CSS®) Code for each college in this book can be found in its college description.

During registration you will also be asked a few very basic questions about your family's finances; these determine whether you will be asked certain questions that usually don't apply to low-income families. For example, if your parents rent their house, they won't be asked about home equity in Section L.

You will also have to select the colleges or scholarship programs to which you would like to have your PROFILE report sent. You'll need to give their CSS codes, which you can find in Part III of this book, the PROFILE Registration Guide, or on collegeboard.com. You can add more colleges to this list after you register, or even after filing your application (see "After Submitting Your PROFILE" on page 66).

Let's Walk Through It

The PROFILE application has 17 sections, lettered from A to Q. The application includes questions about you and your finances (mostly in sections A through E) and questions about your parents and their finances (mostly in sections F through N). There is a place for you to explain in writing any special financial circumstances (section O) and a place for any additional questions that may be required by one or more of the schools to which you're applying (section Q). In addition, if your parents are divorced or separated, your noncustodial parent might need to complete an online Noncustodial PROFILE. If your family owns a business or farm, they might need to fill out a Business/Farm Supplement. That supplement cannot be filed online; the form has to be downloaded, printed, and mailed in.

To help you fill out the PROFILE, there are instructions online that you can follow, along with other avenues for help (see sidebar on page 57). A few general points to keep in mind:

- If a financial question (such as one about income or assets) doesn't apply to you, enter a zero (0).
- If a nonfinancial question (such as a year or a name) doesn't apply to you, leave it blank.
- Round all money amounts to the nearest dollar. Don't enter commas or cents.

Here is a step-by-step walk through the PROFILE. However, when you fill out the application, don't be surprised if you don't see all the questions that are mentioned here. The PROFILE is customized to your situation. That means that when you complete the form, any questions that are known not to apply to you won't even be presented. For example, if your parents are married, you won't be shown any questions that assume you have a noncustodial parent.

Section A: Student's Information

This is the beginning of the part of PROFILE that focuses on you, the student applying for aid. In Section A, you provide some basic information about yourself. Much like on the FAFSA, you'll be asked to name your current legal state of residence, which may not be the same as the state you're actually living in now (see page 47).

If you're an independent student, you'll be asked about your spouse, children, and any other dependents. These questions are asked because you may have greater financial need if other people depend on you for financial support.

Section B: Student's Income and Benefits for the Previous Year

This section asks about your income and benefits in the year before you intend to start college.

If you have a completed tax return for that year, this section is mostly a matter of copying the amounts from the correct lines, such as the adjusted gross income and income tax paid. If you haven't filed a return but plan to do so later, you'll have to fill in estimates. If you don't plan to file a return but you did make some money last year, you'll have to report it. Untaxed income and benefits, such as Social Security benefits, also go in this section. A worksheet is available for you to tally it up.

Section C: Student's Expected Summer/School-Year Resources for the Coming School Year

Here you're asked to state your expected resources for this coming summer and this coming school year. You're also asked about scholarships you expect to get from sources other than the colleges to which you're applying and how much money your parents think they'll be able to pay for your college expenses.

This may seem like a strange series of questions, especially if you don't know yet where you'll be going to college next year, or where (even if) you'll be working. But colleges that use the Institutional Methodology want to have as clear a picture as possible of your future resources, not just your past ones. For example, if you currently have an after-school job but will leave that job when you graduate, the financial aid offices need to know that the income from that job won't be available to you anymore once you've started college.

Do the best you can to estimate these figures. If you're not sure how to answer in your particular case, check the PROFILE help online or contact the financial aid office at the college to which you're applying.

Section D: Student's Assets

This section asks about your assets—the money or property you, the student, currently own. These too affect your ability to pay for college. You need to list any cash you have and any checking or savings accounts in your name. Give their value as of the day you're filling out the application. You should also include any investments, such as certificates of deposit, savings bonds, stocks, or real estate that you own. If you have any Individual Retirement Accounts (IRAs) or other tax-advantaged retirement accounts, you should also list them here.

If you're an independent student, then any money you have in 529 prepaid tuition or college savings plans or Coverdell savings accounts should be included here. If you're a dependent, those will be considered your parents' assets, and the information about them should go in Section H.

This section will also ask you to answer questions about any trust accounts your parents or other relatives may have established for you. A trust account is money that is held for you by somebody else until you reach a certain age, at which point it becomes yours. Colleges want to know about this because if you have a trust, that money will eventually reach your hands, lowering your ultimate financial need. If you have any trust accounts, list their value here and answer the questions about them. But don't include money in Section 529 prepaid tuition plans; those aren't the same as trusts.

Section E: Student's Expenses for the Previous Year

You only need to answer these questions if you're an independent student. If so, you'll be asked about any child support you or your spouse paid to a former spouse and any medical and dental expenses you had last year that weren't covered by insurance. Most colleges will consider these expenses in determining your financial need.

Section F: Parents' Information

Now the PROFILE application switches away from its focus on you, the student, and starts asking questions about your parents. The term "parents" as PROFILE understands it might need some defining. It basically means your custodial parents, the people with whom you live. If both your parents are living, married to each other, and have custody of you, answer the questions about both of them. But if that isn't the case, follow these rules:

- If your birth parents are divorced, separated, or were never married, then you only need to provide information about the parent with whom you live. If you lived with both equally in the past 12 months, answer the questions about the parent who provided most of your financial support.

- If you have a widowed or single parent or a legal guardian, answer the questions only about that person.

- If your parent (as defined above) has married or remarried, include information about your stepparent too.

Your parents should use section F to provide information about themselves, including name, date of birth, employment status, and whether they themselves are in college or graduate school. Some of these questions have to do with clarifying financial strength—for example, the question about what kind of retirement plans your parents have. Some are just matters of housekeeping, such as their preferred daytime telephone number in case they need to be contacted.

Section G: Parents' Household Information

Here your parents give basic information about their household, such as how many members are in their household and how many of them will be in college. The more dependents your parents have, and the more college educations they have to pay for, the less they will be expected to contribute to your own college education.

Section H: Family Member Listing

This section asks questions about dependent members of your household other than your parents. If you're an independent student, the household in question here is the one you described in Section A; if you're a dependent, it's your parents' household as described in Section G.

The questions in Section H ask for more information about these household members: their names, how they're related to you, their ages, and to what extent you or your parents are required to pay for their school or college education last year and next year. The reason for these questions is that if household members other than you are enrolled in college, and your family is paying heavily to fund those educations, the colleges will take this into account when they determine the expected family contribution (EFC) to your own education. If there are younger children in the family, the colleges will assume that a certain portion of the household's income and assets need to be saved for their college educations, which will also affect your EFC.

Section I: Parents' Income and Benefits for the Previous Year

In this section, your parents report their income and benefits for the year before you intend to start college. Just as with the section about your income, this is important in establishing the resources they have available to pay for college.

This section is essentially a longer version of Section B, which asked about your income. Again, if your parents have a completed tax return, filling in this section is mostly a matter of copying from the right lines. If they haven't filed a return but will do so later, they'll need to estimate the amounts. If they don't plan to file a return, they still have to report income. Again they have to list untaxed income and benefits, such as Social Security benefits, child support, or the earned income credit.

Section J: Parents' Income and Benefits for the Year Before Last

Here your parents are asked to give information about income and benefits not for the year before you intend to start college, but the year before that year. Together with sections K and L, this is meant to give the PROFILE colleges more of a long-term view of your family's finances in order to clarify whether or not last year was typical. This section is fairly easy to fill out: for most of the questions—e.g., adjusted gross income, income taxes, and itemized deductions—your family has only to look up their tax return for that year. You also have to calculate any untaxed income and benefits, using a worksheet that's provided.

Section K: Parents' Expected Income and Benefits for This Year

Here your parents have to estimate how much they expect to receive in income and benefits during the year in which you start college. Again, the idea is to establish as clear a picture as possible about your family's finances in the long term, and to show whether the year before you started college was typical or not. Your parents will have to estimate work income, other taxable income, and untaxed income and benefits. In Section O, explain any unusual increases or decreases in income and benefits (10 percent or more) from last year.

Section L: Parents' Assets

This section asks about your parents' assets because these are resources that can help them finance college. There are questions about cash and savings and checking accounts (with their value as of the day you fill out the form). If they own their home, there are questions about home equity, the difference between the current market value of their home and the outstanding mortgage debt.

There are also questions about the current market value of any other assets they own, including investments, businesses, farms, other real estate, and the value of any of their retirement accounts, such as IRAs, 401(k)s, or 403(b)s. They also need to include educational savings accounts, such as 529 prepaid tuition or college savings plans or Coverdell savings accounts that they've opened for you or one of your siblings.

Section M: Parents' Expenses

This section asks about certain special expenses your parents might have. These are not just any expenses, such as grocery bills or vacation airfare, but specific costs that might legitimately affect their ability to pay for college. Included here are child support payments, certain educational costs, and medical and dental expenses not covered by insurance.

Section N: Information About a Noncustodial Parent

If your parents are divorced or separated, this section asks for information about the parent who doesn't have custody of you. But it should be filled out by your custodial parent. If for any reason you can't get sufficient information about the noncustodial parent, explain why in Section O. Many colleges want this information because they believe it is the responsibility of both your biological or adoptive parents to pay for your college costs, even if they no longer live together, and even if the parent who does have custody of you has remarried. That's why, after you've filled out this section and submitted your

PROFILE, they may request that the noncustodial parent fill out a supplemental form, the Noncustodial PROFILE (see "After Submitting Your PROFILE" on page 66). The section you're filling out here is not that supplemental form; the noncustodial parent will fill out that form if it's required.

Section O: Explanations/ Special Circumstances

This is the one free-form part of the PROFILE, where you write rather than fill in boxes. This section gives you a chance to explain anything unusual in your application or any special circumstances that affect your family's ability to pay for college. You can mention, for example, reasons for unusually high medical or dental expenses, steep rises or falls in income from year to year, or loss of employment. You should also give information about any outside scholarships you've been awarded. This allows the PROFILE colleges to better understand your financial picture.

In addition to telling the colleges about anything you think it's important that they know about, you should also use this section to expand on your answers to certain questions in previous sections, per the instructions that you'll find on the PROFILE Web site. For example, if there are more than six dependent members of your household, you won't be able to list them all in section H. The instructions will tell you to list the additional members here.

You're limited to 27 lines of information in this section. If you need more space, send the information on paper directly to your colleges, including your name and Social Security number on all correspondence. See Step 8 for tips on how to let your college know about your special circumstances.

Section P: PLUS Loan Preapplication

This section gives your parents the opportunity to have the College Board evaluate their credit record and let them know if they're preapproved for a College Board–sponsored PLUS loan, a type of federal loan that is not subsidized and is taken out in the parents' name. If your parents don't want to authorize the College Board to make this evaluation, just say no: this section is entirely optional. If they do authorize it, it doesn't commit your parents to taking out a PLUS loan from the College Board (or anyone else). All they'll get is information about their eligibility for such a loan. The fact that your parents have expressed interest in a PLUS loan—or any other information from this section of the PROFILE, for that matter—is not shared with the colleges to which you're applying, and will not affect your eligibility for need-based financial aid.

Section Q: Supplemental Information

Section Q may not be included in your application. You will only see it if one or more of the colleges to which you're applying requires more information. In that case, you'll see additional questions here. Your answers to these questions will be used only by the colleges that ask for them. Some of the questions colleges ask here are used to determine your eligibility for purely need-based financial aid; others are used to determine if you're eligible for scholarships that have non-need-based criteria.

Here are some examples of the types of questions you might see:

- What is the year, make, and model of the family's primary car?
- Do you or either of your parents receive free food or housing as a job benefit?
- What is your family's religious denomination? (This information will be used to determine scholarship eligibility.)
- What field of study do you plan to major in?

After Submitting Your PROFILE

After you complete your PROFILE, you'll receive an online PROFILE acknowledgment that confirms the colleges to which you're sending the information and gives you the opportunity to correct any data you submitted. You should print the acknowledgment, which includes the list of colleges and the data you entered on the form. Once you submit your PROFILE, you can't revise your information online. Use the printed acknowledgment to make changes, if necessary, to the PROFILE information, and send those corrections directly to your colleges.

The College Board analyzes your data and reports it to the colleges to which you're applying. The schools then apply their own need-analysis formulas, usually based on the Institutional Methodology, to figure out your expected family contribution (EFC). From this analysis, they determine how great your need is and how much institutional financial aid to give you.

You can delete colleges from your list of schools only before you submit the application. After that, all the listed colleges will get your information. But you can add colleges whenever you want, even after you submit the application. Just go to the PROFILE Web site and click on "Add Colleges to Submitted Application." The fee is $18 for each additional college or program to which you want your information sent.

Some colleges require supplemental information that's not on the main PROFILE application. For example, one college might require information about a farm or small business owned by your parents, while another might not. If that happens, the PROFILE Web site will instruct you during the reg-

GOOD TO KNOW

If only one of your birth parents has custody of you, your college may still require information from both parents. If that happens, the main PROFILE application collects information from one parent, and the noncustodial parent PROFILE collects information from the other. After the information is processed, the college will complete the EFC calculation. How to divide up payment of the EFC among you and your parents is a family decision.

istration process to download the Business/Farm Supplement form, print it, fill it out, and send it to the college that wants it. Or a college may require a Noncustodial PROFILE if you don't live with both of your birth parents. When you register for the PROFILE and indicate that your biological or adoptive parents are not married, you will receive an e-mail with instructions, a temporary password, and a link to forward to your noncustodial parent for him or her to complete. This form can be completed only by the noncustodial parent.

Don't be surprised, then, if after you submit the PROFILE you get a follow-up message instructing you to fill out a supplemental form. Don't panic, either: this is not an audit, but a normal part of the process that sometimes happens. However, be aware that these follow-ups take additional time. All the more reason to leave yourself plenty of time to file the PROFILE before your college financial aid deadlines.

QUICK RECAP

The PROFILE form is longer but otherwise not very different from the FAFSA. The main difference is that it tries to get a more complete picture of your family's finances. A few points to keep in mind:

- File early.
- The PROFILE is online only, so you have to submit it on a computer.
- Prepare using the Preapplication Worksheet.
- There are fees, but low-income students may qualify for a fee waiver.
- After you submit your PROFILE, you'll get an online acknowledgment confirming that you submitted it. To make corrections to your information, you should write your colleges directly.
- Depending on your circumstances, you or one of your parents may have to submit a supplemental form to one or more of your colleges.

Step 7: Fill Out Any Other Required Forms

QUICK OVERVIEW

The FAFSA and PROFILE are the big ones, but don't forget to file any other forms that may be required by your state or by the colleges to which you're applying. You don't want to have your application for financial aid marked "incomplete" because you didn't file a one-page form. The particulars of these forms vary widely from college to college, and from state to state. For example, they may be trying to get more information about your finances, or to find out if you're a member of a particular group that is eligible for a special scholarship or grant.

Some Colleges Have Their Own Financial Aid Application

Some colleges have their own forms that you have to submit in addition to the FAFSA and the PROFILE. If a college requires such a form from all first-time applicants, its description in Part III of the book will say "institutional form required" under the "application procedures" section. Contact the financial aid office at your colleges to find out more.

The good news is that these forms are generally not long or complicated—they are usually just a page or two in length. They manage to stay short because they are intended not to duplicate the FAFSA or PROFILE forms but to supplement them and help the financial aid office keep track of applications. Such a "one pager" might, for example, ask for basic identifying information, some demographic facts, and whether you are interested in loans and work-study. This kind of form is typical at community colleges and most four-year public colleges. "It's almost like an update form," Mary San Agustin says of the institutional form currently in use at her institution, Palomar College. "It's basically just a supplemental form in case any changes occurred since the time the student applied for admission or completed the FAFSA."

Sometimes a college might require a longer form that asks questions about your finances that are about as broad and deep as the FAFSA or PROFILE. Usually this only happens with colleges that practice their own institutional methodology to calculate need, but choose not to use the PROFILE to help them with it.

Another reason a college might require its own financial aid form is if it requires every student to have a computer on campus. Such schools sometimes have a supplemental form that qualifies needy applicants for a stipend to buy a computer, or places them in a "loaner" program so they can borrow one. The University of Virginia has two forms that deal with computers. One form is for its "laptop loaner" program, and a different form is for a "one-time computer expense" that allows students who want to buy a laptop to add the purchase price to their cost of attendance; that way their aid package may cover the cost.

Still another kind of institutional form is one for early-decision applicants. Such a form works as a sort of "pre-read" meant to help students get an early estimate of their expected family contribution and the financial aid package they will receive if they accept an early-decision offer. (The rules of early decision require them to accept the offer if the college offers enough financial aid for them to attend.) Some schools offer a similar pre-read form for student athletes who are being recruited by a coach.

Scholarship and Grant Forms

Some colleges require a separate form for students applying for merit scholarships. This isn't always the case: at many schools, every student who applies for admission is automatically considered for merit scholarships. But at some schools, you must file a separate application for merit scholarships. The rules may even differ from department to department, depending on your major. "Theater majors may have to audition," says Bonnie Lee Behm of Villanova University. "Or a film major may need to send in a tape." Contact the financial aid office at your colleges for more details, and check with the department in which you're interested in majoring.

Some institutional forms ask questions to find out if you qualify for financial aid funds set aside for students with particular characteristics. For example, the college might offer grants that are only available to children of alumni or descendants of the town's founding families. At most colleges, these grants are part of the need-based aid program, so you have to demonstrate need through the FAFSA along with proving you have the right characteristics for the grant.

Verification of Your Tax Return

Some colleges require you to send copies of your family's federal or state tax returns. They may tell you to mail them with your initial application, or they may require them for only a few applicants who have been selected for verification.

"Verification" doesn't mean that you did something wrong. It's not like an IRS audit, where only suspicious tax returns are selected for special scrutiny. Since colleges disburse federal money—in the form of grants, work-study, and loans—they are required by law to check the information that a certain percentage of financial aid applicants has submitted. Some colleges exceed this minimum requirement and, for the sake of safety and fairness, verify all applications.

If you are selected for verification by one or more colleges, you'll have to submit tax documents: for example, the 1040 and any attached schedules, along with the W-2s or 1099s you received from employers and banks. Usually you'll also have to fill out a form that allows colleges to confirm details, like how many of your siblings are enrolled in college. The college may ask you to send your documents directly to the financial aid office, or it might ask you to send them to the College Board's institutional documentation (IDOC) service.

Some colleges will request verification if the data you submitted on the FAFSA looks unusual. As an extreme example, people who reported that they had no income last year may be asked how they supported themselves.

State Forms

Most states rely on the FAFSA to award their need-based grants and loans to students. But a few states have their own financial aid forms. For example, New York State has an application for its Tuition Assistance Program (TAP) that is sent to eligible students who submit a FAFSA. See Table 2 on the next page for a list of states that require their own forms; the list gives the name of each form and the program's Web site and mailing address.

Even though the thought of filling out yet another form may seem burdensome, and you feel sure that you won't qualify for the state aid program, fill it out. If you don't, your application might be marked "incomplete" at your colleges. These state forms are usually short and don't take long to fill out, especially once you do the prep work of filling out the FAFSA. If you file the FAFSA online, you'll be automatically directed to your state's form. If you file the FAFSA paper form, you'll usually have to send away for a paper copy of your state form.

Step 7: Fill Out Any Other Required Forms

Table 2:
State Aid Deadlines

STATE	FORM(S) REQUIRED	DEADLINE	NOTES
Alaska	FAFSA	4/15	
Arizona	FAFSA	6/30	
Arkansas	FAFSA	4/1	
California	FAFSA, state form	3/2	Initial awards
		9/2	Additional community college awards
Delaware	FAFSA	4/15	
District of Columbia	FAFSA, DC form	6/28	
Florida	FAFSA	5/15	
Illinois	FAFSA	9/30	First-time applicants
		8/15	Continuing applicants
Indiana	FAFSA	3/10	
Iowa	FAFSA	7/1	
Kansas	FAFSA, state form	4/1	
Kentucky	FAFSA	3/15	
Louisiana	FAFSA	5/1	Priority date
		7/1	Closing date
Maine	FAFSA	5/1	
Maryland	FAFSA	3/1	
Massachusetts	FAFSA	5/1	
Michigan	FAFSA	3/1	
Minnesota	FAFSA	30 days after start of term	
Missouri	FAFSA	4/1	
Montana	FAFSA	3/1	
New Hampshire	FAFSA	5/1	
New Jersey	FAFSA	6/1	Tuition Aid Grant applicants
		10/1	All other applicants
		3/1	Spring-term applicants only
New York	FAFSA, state form	5/1	
North Carolina	FAFSA	3/15	
North Dakota	FAFSA	3/15	
Ohio	FAFSA	10/1	
Oklahoma	FAFSA	4/30	Priority date
		6/30	Closing date
Pennsylvania	FAFSA, state form	5/1	Degree program candidates
		8/1	Other applicants
Rhode Island	FAFSA	3/1	
South Carolina	FAFSA	6/30	
Tennessee	FAFSA	5/1	
West Virginia	FAFSA, state form	3/1	

Residents of states not listed in this table should contact their state aid office directly. See page 139 for a list of addresses, phone numbers, and Web sites for each state's aid office.

QUICK RECAP

In addition to the FAFSA and PROFILE, some states and colleges have financial aid forms of their own. Here's what to know about them:

- They're usually short.
- Their questions vary from school to school and from state to state.
- They may determine if you're eligible for special grants.
- They may help verify your financial information, perhaps through questions about your tax returns.
- If state aid is available, apply for it, or your colleges might consider your financial aid application incomplete.
- If one of your colleges requires an institutional application, fill it out, or you'll disqualify yourself from financial aid.

Step 8: Make Your Special Circumstances Known

QUICK OVERVIEW — If something in your family's financial life can't be explained on the financial aid forms, make sure your colleges know about it. These "special circumstances" may include a lost job, high medical expenses, or supporting an extended family. Colleges are willing to listen and, if you make your case, may be able to improve your financial aid package by taking those circumstances into account. This step is about how to prepare your case.

Be a Person, Not Just a Form

Sometimes the financial aid forms you fill out don't tell the whole story. They may not show that your family sends money every month to support relatives in another country. Since the forms are based on last year's tax forms, they may not reveal this year's events: how one of your parents just lost a job, or will be shifting from full-time to half-time work. When the forms don't adequately report a special circumstance that affects your family's ability to pay for college, let your college know—it may change how much financial aid you get!

Even if you're not sure your circumstance qualifies as special, speak up. The financial aid office will let you know whether it qualifies. Don't think you're limited to communicating with your college only through the financial aid forms. If there's any doubt in your mind about whether those forms give a true picture of your family's situation, feel free to go beyond the form and contact the financial aid office. Be a person, not just a form. There are two reasons to do this: it guarantees that the college knows how much you are able to pay, and it shows that you're interested in the college—which may affect the lengths to which they'll go to help you.

Using the Financial Aid Forms

In some cases, you can inform your colleges of special circumstances through the financial aid forms themselves—the FAFSA, PROFILE, and institutional forms (Steps 5, 6, and 7, respectively, of this book). If you're supporting children, if you've been in the military, or if your parents are divorced, your FAFSA form will make that clear. For colleges requiring PROFILE, you can use Section O of that form to describe special financial circumstances. Elsewhere on the PROFILE form, you can list special family expenses, such as your family's medical and dental expenses, or any private school tuition that your parents might pay for your younger siblings. While forms may serve well enough, it may still be a good idea to write a letter or schedule a visit. If there's any doubt in your mind about whether forms convey your situation, definitely contact the college.

You can communicate certain kinds of information just by correcting the forms. This is the case if you submitted data that was mistaken—for example, if you checked the wrong box or made an incorrect estimate about your income or expenses. FAFSA has a process for submitting corrections when you receive your Student Aid Report (SAR), and PROFILE sends you a Data Confirmation Report that allows you to send corrections to your colleges. Some schools routinely use their own financial aid form to allow students to update the school about any changes that happened since they applied for financial aid.

Going Beyond the Forms

You may have special circumstances that aren't covered by the forms. Or financially significant events may happen after you submit the forms—events that may be too complicated to explain in a simple correction. If that happens, communicate with the aid office as soon as possible after you realize you have special circumstances or after any financial hardships arise. The sooner you act, the sooner the college can adjust your award—and the more likely they are to still have the funds available to do so.

Even after you start college, if a financial emergency occurs, let the school know. The financial aid director can often help needy students with unusual expenses, such as medical costs, emergency trips home, or funding to allow them to take an unpaid internship in the summer instead of working for money.

How to Contact the College

A letter to the financial aid office explaining your circumstances is often the best way to state your case. Some schools have a form specifically for explaining special circumstances; it's worth asking your colleges what they prefer. The more closely you follow their procedures, the more likely you are to be heard.

No matter how you communicate with your college, be polite, clear, and specific. There's no need for a despairing or bullying tone. Remember, you're trying to put a face to the form, so make it a friendly one. You'll get further by calmly presenting your situation and giving as many relevant specifics as possible. A school will want to know not only that a parent got laid off, but what the prospects for reemployment might be, whether the parent has filed for unemployment benefits and, if so, the amount of the benefit payments awarded to the parent. Don't be surprised or offended if the college responds to you with a request for documentation, such as a copy of your tax return or a recent pay stub.

The Special Circumstances Form

Some colleges have a form through which you can let them know about special circumstances. At Rhodes College, it's called the Special Financial Circumstances Form, and it is available on the school's Web site. "The purpose of the form is not to make everybody jump through a hoop," says Forrest Stuart, the director of financial aid at Rhodes. "It's to help the parents and the student put on paper all the information we need to help them out."

The form asks the student for the specific data—such as about changes in income and expenses—that the financial aid office will need to reach a decision about their case. It helps the school treat students equally, and it prevents the vagueness that might be found in a letter. "A lot of time we'll just get letters—I've lost my job, I need more aid," says Stuart. "Well, that doesn't tell me a whole lot. But if I can see some concrete information, then that gives me an idea of how I can help this student."

Communicating by Letter

With many schools, the best way to contact the aid office is in a letter. Often, it can strengthen your case to enclose photocopies of supporting documentation with the letter—for example, a paper showing your parent was laid off. The aid officer may also ask you for specific documentation.

After sending your letter, follow up with the financial aid office a week or two later to make sure they received it and to see if they have any questions. You can do this by e-mail or telephone. If you live close by, or have scheduled a campus visit, you should also visit the aid office, but call first to make an appointment.

E-Mail

Some colleges prefer to have you contact them by e-mail. At the University of Oregon, applicants can communicate their special financial circumstances through the school's Web site, where they can find an e-mail address for the financial aid office. "That way, they can do it whenever they think about it," says Elizabeth Bickford, the financial aid director.

EXPERT ADVICE

"**We must have documentation**, and what we really like too is a nice **letter explaining the situation**. But on top of that, we also like to have a phone call or, if the student's already on campus, to have them come in and talk to us. That way, we can have a **dialogue about the situation** and give them some direction on what to provide to us and how to provide it."

—Vincent Amoroso, deputy director, Office of Scholarships and Student Aid, University of North Carolina, Chapel Hill

Examples of Special Situations

Many circumstances can affect your family's ability to pay for college. They may include a change in your financial situation from what was reported in the financial aid forms, such as a lost job, emergency expenses, health problems, or even a windfall that misrepresents your usual level of income.

Family ties can also have financial implications, such as supporting an extended family or going through a divorce. And if you've served in the military, there are some special instructions you need to follow on the financial aid forms.

Change in Financial Situation

Financial aid officers want to know not only that your financial aid situation changed, but why it changed. Certain types of changes are more likely than others to persuade them to give you more financial aid. Generally, aid officers will look more kindly on circumstances that are beyond your control, rather than the result of poor planning. For example, if your father gets laid off because his company has fallen on hard times, that is more likely to get attention than if he retires early to spend more time golfing. And the college is more likely to turn a sympathetic eye to necessary roof repairs than a loan to install a backyard Jacuzzi.

LOST JOB OR LOST INCOME

If you or your parents had a job when you filled out the FAFSA, and now you don't, that will clearly affect your ability to pay. Even if you receive a severance package or collect unemployment benefits, your long-term ability to pay will still be reduced. This is information your financial aid office needs to know. For Palomar College, you would fill out a form that allows the financial aid office to override the FAFSA data with the new data. "You have to still report 2006," according to Palomar's Mary San Agustin, "but we override it with the current-year income."

Equally important are changes in other sources of income besides wages and salaries. For example, suppose a student's mother becomes disabled in August and has to stop working, and her employer's disability insurance plan gives her a large percentage of her salary for the first six months (through February), but a much lower percentage afterward. The FAFSA will show a larger income than she will be receiving once the student arrives in college. This change in disability benefits, like a lost job, needs to be communicated to the college.

> **GOOD TO KNOW**
>
> If you're explaining your special financial circumstances by letter, it's best to send it to the financial aid office via mail or fax, so that it can be **easily incorporated into your file**. Write and format it as a standard business letter. **Put your name and Social Security Number** in the first paragraph, so the financial aid office won't have trouble matching the letter to your file.

EMERGENCY SAVINGS DRAWDOWN

An emergency may force your family to spend some of the savings that you reported on the financial aid forms. For example, suppose your house is damaged by a fire the day after you submit the FAFSA. Your family needs to spend a large amount of money to pay for the repairs. Depending on where the money comes from—regular savings, a retirement account, borrowing through a home-equity loan—this will have different effects on your need calculation. But no matter what the emergency or the source of the money you wind up spending is, you should tell the aid office.

Sometimes one crisis will have several different effects. Hurricane Katrina in 2005 might not only have destroyed an applicant's home in Louisiana, but put the family breadwinners temporarily out of work. In such a case, make sure the aid office knows about all the different effects on your financial situation.

HEALTH PROBLEMS

A serious health problem in your family can have financial as well as medical effects. It may involve both an emergency savings drawdown to pay for medical expenses, and loss of income if the patient is too sick to work. If someone in your family has recently become disabled, developed a chronic illness, or had major surgery, this has a clear impact on your family's ability to pay for college. Your college's financial aid office should be able to help.

A letter, or the school's own "special circumstances" form (if they have one), is a good way to let a college know about your family's medical problem. But the financial aid forms provide some paths as well. The PROFILE form allows you to list medical expenses that weren't covered by insurance last year, and estimate the same for this year. You can also explain high medical expenses in the "Explanations/Special Circumstances" box (Section O). The FAFSA, on the other hand doesn't ask specifically about medical expenses. If your college only uses the FAFSA, and you have unusually high medical expenses, a letter to the college makes sense.

WINDFALL

In financial terms, a windfall is a sum of money you didn't expect to get, which is normally a good thing—but even a windfall can have its downside. On your financial aid forms, if you received a windfall last year, that makes your annual income look higher than it normally is, which will tend to raise your expected family contribution (EFC).

Some windfalls are better than others. A windfall is usually understood as a genuine, one-time boost to your finances. It might be an inheritance from an aunt you never knew or an unusually high year-end bonus from your job. If you get such a windfall, inform the aid office that your income was higher than usual last year, and that they shouldn't expect a repeat performance next year.

But some windfalls not only make your annual income look bigger than it is, but represent an overall loss to your financial position. Examples include a severance package on losing your job, or an early withdrawal from a retirement plan, such as an IRA, to cover an emergency. In both situations, your records for that year show a boost in income, but that apparent good news conceals bad financial news—that you lost your job, in one case, and suffered a massive hit to your retirement savings in the other. If you experience this kind of windfall, explain the reality to your aid office.

Family Ties

Not every family has two parents married to each other. And some families have stronger ties to grandparents, uncles, aunts, and cousins than others. Different families live in different ways. The way your family lives may have financial implications that your financial aid office should recognize.

SUPPORTING EXTENDED FAMILY

The financial aid forms tell the colleges about how many people live in your household, including you, your parents, and your siblings. But many families give financial support to an extended family of relatives who live outside the household. Immigrant families, for example, often send money regularly to grandparents, aunts, or uncles in another country. Since that decreases the amount you have available to pay for college, make sure the financial aid office knows about it.

DIVORCED OR SEPARATED PARENTS

If your parents have divorced or separated, make sure the colleges know how that has affected your ability to pay. To do this, follow the rules on the financial aid forms. For the FAFSA, provide only the information on the parent you lived with more during the past 12 months (your custodial parent)—and, if that parent has remarried, your stepparent. For the PROFILE, provide not only that data but also information on your other parent, the one who does not have custody of you—your noncustodial parent. That information goes in Section N of the PROFILE.

Some colleges that use PROFILE will also want your noncustodial parent to submit information separately on the Noncustodial PROFILE. That information will be confidential; you and your custodial parent won't be able to see the data the other parent provides, nor will that parent see yours. However, the information submitted by your noncustodial parent will affect the college's calculation of your total expected family contribution (EFC). If you don't think it will be possible to get your noncustodial parent to fill out the form, let the college know. However, the school isn't likely to waive its requirement for the form for anything less than a significant reason.

In the parent-income section of either the FAFSA or PROFILE, a custodial parent who is receiving alimony or child support payments should report only what he or she received, not what he or she was supposed to receive. In certain circumstances, documented evidence that your noncustodial parent is behind in payments could help support your case if you appeal your award.

Military Service

If you're currently serving in the active-duty military or the reserves, or if you are a veteran, don't assume that your military benefits alone will meet your full financial need. At most institutions, they no longer will. Benefits or not, you should apply for financial aid by submitting the FAFSA and any other required forms.

When filling out these forms, there are a few points to remember. Read the instructions carefully to make sure you qualify as a veteran for purposes of federal student aid. You should report housing allowances, subsistence allowances, and untaxed combat pay as income. But don't include veterans' education benefits or ROTC scholarships when answering the questions about your untaxed income. The colleges consider them outside resources to be reported separately. (For more information on outside resources, see Step 9.)

Veterans are as liable as anyone to the special situations discussed earlier, from lost jobs to medical crises. That includes windfalls. For example, if you received a lot of combat pay last year but have now been discharged and won't receive it again, you should explain that to the colleges.

For more information on the intricacies of how veterans' benefits affect the FAFSA, see the FinAid.org Web site at www.finaid.org/military.

QUICK RECAP

If there are special circumstances that affect your ability to pay for college, let your college know.

- Tell the college financial aid office as soon as you know about your special circumstances—either before you get your award or afterward.
- Use the FAFSA and PROFILE forms to tell your story, but if they aren't enough, use the college's special form, write a letter, e-mail, call, or visit.
- Explain your situation clearly, documenting it where appropriate.
- The situations that may affect your ability to pay range from a lost job or high medical bills to status as a veteran or an undocumented immigrant.

Step 9: Look for Other Sources of Money

QUICK OVERVIEW — It's worth it to look for financial aid beyond what you'll get from colleges and federal student aid programs. This "outside money" probably won't amount to a "full ride," but it can help. Begin your search for outside scholarships around the time you start looking for a college because many scholarships have early deadlines.

Scholarships Colleges Give You vs. Scholarships You Get on Your Own

KNOW THE LINGO

Outside money—Grants and scholarships that come from sources other than colleges or the federal government, such as states and private organizations.

Portable money—Grants and scholarships that you can take with you to whichever college you attend.

College-offered money—Grants and scholarships that colleges award from their own funds.

Financial aid doesn't come only from the government and colleges. It also comes in the form of scholarships from outside sources, including states and private donors. This money doesn't come looking for you: you have to find the programs that fit you and apply. You will have to qualify for the scholarship in some way, whether through academic merit, artistic talent, or fitting some set of criteria, such as being a person of Japanese descent living in either Connecticut, New York, or New Jersey. Very few outside scholarships offer anything close to full tuition, fees, room, and board. But they're worth the search because every little bit helps.

The scholarships you can get from outside sources are not exactly like the scholarships you might get from your college. These are the basic facts to know about each type.

College-Offered Scholarships

In most cases, you don't have to apply separately for the scholarships that colleges award. You're automatically considered for them when you apply to the school. If you qualify, the college will include the scholarship in your financial aid package as they see fit. However, some colleges have merit-based scholarships for which you must apply separately.

To find out what the rules are for scholarship aid at your colleges, contact the schools or look at their Web sites, which usually describe the process for applying for scholarships under "admissions" and then under "financial aid." Be sure to do this research *before* you submit your application for admission. At some colleges, you have to indicate on your admissions application that you are applying for a special scholarship; for example, this is true of Boston University's Trustee Scholar Program. At others, you don't have to apply for special scholarships until after you've submitted your application for admission.

Many college merit scholarships have to be renewed from year to year. To make sure yours is renewed, know the school's criteria for keeping it—for example, maintaining a certain GPA. Different scholarships will have different criteria at each college.

Outside Scholarships: State Sources

Almost every state offers scholarships to their residents. These scholarships are usually available only for state residents attending colleges within the state, though a few states offer "portable" aid that a state resident can take to a college in another state.

Take the time to research scholarships and grants in your state. Almost every state has a department of education Web site that describes state scholarships and how to apply for them. These are usually separate from the state-sponsored, need-based financial aid programs that you apply for through the FAFSA or the state's own financial aid form, such as the Tuition Assistance Program (TAP) in New York State. An example of a state-sponsored, merit-based scholarship program with a separate application process is Florida's Merit Scholars Award, for which applicants must show high academic achievement.

Outside Scholarships: Private Sources

Private scholarships are offered by many sources, including foundations, corporations, civic groups, religious organizations, veterans' associations, and the military. The Society of Women Engineers offers the Bechtel Corporation Scholarship to high-achieving female students of engineering. United Methodist Scholarships are available to students who belong to that Christian denomination. The Senator George J. Mitchell Scholarship Research Institute offers awards to Maine residents studying in state.

Don't assume you have to be a genius to get a private scholarship. Although many scholarship programs consider academic merit, a range of conditions may qualify you for a scholarship, including interests, ethnic background, and community work. The Los Padres Foundation grants scholarships to low-income Latino students. California students pursuing a career in agriculture are eligible for a California Farm Bureau Scholarship.

Most scholarships come with limits. Though a few programs will pay full tuition, the amount of most awards is much smaller, as little as $500 or $1,000.

MYTH/FACT

Myth: "Untold millions" of scholarship dollars are available for use every year.

Fact: Private scholarships are only a small segment of the overall money available for college—just 7 percent. True, that share amounts to $8.4 million a year, but that's dwarfed by the $120.5 million paid out by other sources. Money from federal, college-granted, and state funds, in that order, are likely to be much more important in your overall financial aid package. It's worth looking for private scholarships, but don't count on them as your sole source of funding.

Many awards are limited to the freshman year of study. Fortunately, other scholarships are only for later years. The Bechtel Corporation Scholarship, for example, is just for women in their sophomore, junior, or senior year of study. And once you've declared a major you may find yourself eligible for a scholarship that is aimed only at students in your academic discipline.

Searching for Scholarships

Searching for private scholarships takes effort. But there are a number of Web-based scholarship search engines, like the ones on collegeboard.com and fastweb.com, that can help you zero in on scholarships for which you may qualify. If you like using this *Guide to Getting Financial Aid*, you might prefer to search for scholarships using the *College Board Scholarship Handbook*. It describes more than 2,100 outside scholarships, internships, and loan programs, and is indexed by eligibility requirements—such as minority status, religious affiliation, and state of residence—to help you match yourself to the programs.

Beware of commercial scholarship search companies that offer to help you find scholarships for a fee. Some do a responsible job, but many charge exorbitant fees and make fraudulent claims. For example, if they "guarantee" you a scholarship or promise to "do all the work for you," they are probably lying. Getting a scholarship is never guaranteed and, no matter what, you are going to have to do some work to apply.

Your school counselor may be of more help. Many private scholarships send application forms directly to school counselors. Tell your counselor in your junior year or early in your senior year that you are interested in applying for private scholarships.

Figure 12:
collegeboard.com's Scholarship Search

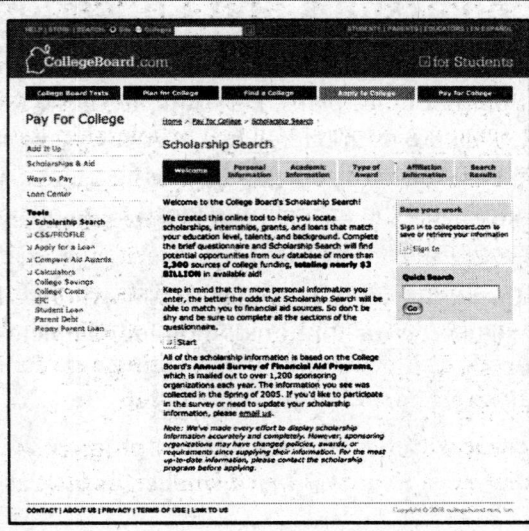

Start researching options as soon as possible. You'll need time to learn about scholarships, request information and application materials, and complete your application. Some programs, such as the Discover Card Tribute Award Scholarship Program (see sidebar on page 89), are looking only for students in their junior year of high school. Even if you're past that point, look as soon as you can—in the summer before your senior year, or by October or November of that year.

Look Locally

The national and state programs that you'll find on Web-based scholarship search engines and in print directories are good sources of scholarship aid. But don't forget to look even closer to home: your own county, city, town, employer, or church. When looking for scholarships, it pays to look locally.

The fact is, you are more likely to obtain a scholarship from a local organization than from a state or national one. On the local level, you will be competing with a smaller pool of applicants and are more likely to have characteristics that interest the donors. Again, your school counselor can help. The counseling office will have a file of local scholarships—from banks, the Kiwanis, the local garden club, and other groups. Let your counselor know you are looking for scholarships; stop by the counseling office regularly to read the scholarship files or check the scholarship bulletin board. The office may also use Internet announcements, e-mail postings, or newsletters to spread the word about scholarship programs to interested students.

Employers can also be a source of scholarship money. If you have a part-time job after school or a summer job, check to see if the company that employs you has a scholarship program or offers tuition assistance. For example, Chick-fil-A has a well-known scholarship program for its employees. Some companies provide their employees with a dependent tuition-assistance benefit. That means one of your parents might be able to get his or her employer to pay some of your tuition.

Military Scholarships and Education Benefits

In return for military service, the armed forces offer a variety of college scholarships and education-assistance plans. For example, in the Reserve Officer Training Corps (ROTC) program offered by the Army, Navy, and Air Force, you get scholarship assistance for college while being trained as a military officer. When you graduate, you are commissioned as an officer in the reserves and begin your term of military service.

Educational assistance for veterans is available in most states. If you're a veteran, contact your state veterans' administration for complete information and application forms.

Applying for Scholarships

Once you find the programs for which you qualify, you have to apply. This may mean not only another form to fill out, but compiling supporting documents, such as transcripts, recommendations, and an essay. Depending on the program, you may have to provide evidence of leadership, patriotism, depth of character, desire to serve, or financial need. Get to know the requirements of each scholarship as early as possible, so you can do any necessary extra work on time.

A few pointers to remember:

Apply early! Apply as early as possible to scholarship programs. If you can, do it in the fall of your senior year, even if the deadlines aren't until February or March. Very often, scholarship programs will have awarded all their funds for the year on a first-come, first-served basis before their stated deadline.

Follow directions. Read instructions carefully and do what they say. Scholarship programs receive hundreds and even thousands of applications. Don't lose out because of failure to submit a typewritten essay versus a handwritten one if required, or to provide appropriate recommendations. If you have a question about your eligibility for a particular scholarship or how to complete the application, contact the scholarship sponsors.

Be organized. It's a good idea to create a separate file for each scholarship and sort them by their due dates. Track application deadlines and requirements using Worksheet 2 (a blank copy of this worksheet appears on page 122). In one place, store the different supporting documents you may need, such as transcripts, standardized test scores, and letters of recommendation.

Check your work. Proofread your applications for spelling or grammatical errors, fill in all blanks, and make sure your handwriting is legible.

Keep copies of everything. If application materials get lost, having copies on file will make it easier to resend the application quickly.

Reapply. Some programs only offer money for the first year of college, but others can be renewed each subsequent year. If your program is one of them, it pays to reapply once you're in college.

WORKSHEET 2:
Scholarship Application Planner

	PROGRAM 1	PROGRAM 2	PROGRAM 3
PROGRAM/SPONSOR	National Merit Scholarship	Young Epidemiology Scholars	First Bank
ELIGIBILITY REQUIREMENTS	Academic merit	Academic merit	Need, local residency
TYPE OF AWARD	Scholarship	Scholarship	Internship
AMOUNT OF AWARD	$2,500	$1,000 or more	$2,500
CAN BE USED FOR	Tuition/fees	Any expense	Any expense
CAN BE USED AT	First-choice college	Any college	In-state colleges
DEADLINE	October 1 (give essay to English teacher for review)	February 1	April 1st
FORMS REQUIRED	NMSC application	Web form	Application (includes need analysis)
TEST SCORES REQUIRED	PSAT/NMSQT (already took), SAT (by December)	None	SAT
ESSAY OR ACADEMIC SAMPLE	Personal statement, academic transcript	Essay, research project	None required
RECOMMENDATIONS	Principal	None	One teacher (Mr. Filmer), Local branch manager
NOTIFICATION BEGINS	February	Not sure	May 15th
REQUIREMENTS TO KEEP AFTER FRESHMAN YEAR	One-time payment only	One-time payment only	Based on performance during internship

For a blank version of this worksheet that you can photocopy for your own use, see page 122.

Effect on Financial Aid Package

SCHOLARSHIP PROFILE

The **Discover Card Tribute Award Scholarship** is one example of the many sources of private scholarship aid. Run by Discover Financial Services, Inc., and the American Association of School Administrators, this national program issues more than 400 awards each year ranging in size from $2,500 to $25,000. To be eligible, you must be a high school junior who demonstrates achievement in three of four areas: special talents, leadership, community service, and obstacles overcome. You also need a minimum cumulative GPA of 2.75 for the ninth and tenth grades.

If a college to which you're applying hasn't met your full need—that is, if there's a "gap" in your financial aid award—outside scholarships can be used to fill that gap. That will make the college much more affordable and give you more choices when it comes time to decide which college you want to attend.

If, on the other hand, a college is already meeting your full need, it works a little differently. It would be nice if your outside scholarship were added on top of all your other financial aid to make your total aid package even bigger. But it probably won't be. Following federal policy, your college will most likely count any outside scholarship or tuition assistance you receive as an "outside resource" that decreases your aid package dollar for dollar. So the total amount of your financial aid package will be exactly the same.

You might think this is unfair: this is money you found and, in the case of employer tuition assistance and veteran's benefits, money you earned. On the other hand, it is money that's available to pay for your education without your having to dip into your income and assets. The philosophy behind financial aid is that everyone should pay what they can out of income and assets (your expected family contribution, or EFC), and then financial aid, including any outside resources, makes up the difference. The only way you can pay less than your EFC is if you get so many outside scholarships that they exceed your financial need. This is highly unlikely.

However, it is still worth getting outside scholarships. For one thing, it increases your freedom to choose a college regardless of cost. "If I'm a student, the more money that I can bring to the table for myself, the better position I'm going to be in to exercise choices that I might want to make," says Vincent Amoroso of the University of North Carolina at Chapel Hill. For another thing, many colleges will use your outside scholarship money to reduce the self-help part of your aid package first—loans and work-study. This can significantly reduce the amount of money you'll owe after college or the time you'll need to spend working during college.

At some colleges, your outside scholarships will not be used to reduce your gift aid (grants and scholarships) unless the amount exceeds your self-help aid. Others use a formula in which at least a portion of your outside money will be used to decrease loans. For example, the first $500 in outside scholarships might be used to reduce your loans, then any funds remaining would be split 50/50 between reducing loans and cutting grants. Colleges that don't meet your full financial need may first apply outside scholarships toward filling the gap. Most colleges decide these issues on a case-by-case basis, but a few have stated policies that they publish on their financial aid Web page or will share with you if asked.

No matter what their policies, colleges welcome outside scholarships because they may reduce the amounts of college funds that have to be spent. Indeed, some schools encourage students to look for outside scholarships. According to Vincent Amoroso, the institutional financial aid form at his college asks students for data related to outside sources of financial aid, including global foundations, to "help us know [if] the student might match up to one of these other foundations that's awarding money."

In making admissions decisions, admissions offices are likely to look on outside scholarships favorably. Students who have searched for and found outside scholarships on their own will probably be seen as students with initiative and a sense of responsibility. That makes the student a stronger candidate for admission.

If you win a scholarship after you've already submitted your FAFSA and/or PROFILE, tell the colleges to which you've applied. Many schools have a special form specifically designed for you to submit this information. If you don't tell the colleges about a scholarship, it could jeopardize your eligibility for federal aid.

Tax Effects

Your outside scholarship may be taxed as income—this depends on the use for which it's designated by the program that awards the scholarship. Generally, scholarship dollars used for costs that are purely educational, such as tuition and fees, will be tax-free. But money used for living expenses, transportation, or books will be taxed as unearned income. The scholarship program will let you know how much (if any) of your award is taxable, and will send you a copy of the IRS's Form 1098 at the end of each tax year.

Employer tuition assistance is tax free up to $5,250 dollars a year. After that amount, it's taxable.

It takes work to hunt down and apply for outside scholarships, but it's worth it. Just remember:

- Outside scholarships will probably provide only a small part of the money you need for college, but every little bit helps.
- There are national and statewide scholarships programs, but look locally too.
- Web sites, books, and your school counselor can help you match outside scholarships to your qualifications.
- Search and apply early, and follow instructions.
- Your outside scholarship may affect the financial aid package awarded by your college, and it may be taxable as income.

QUICK RECAP

Step 10: Weigh the Offers

QUICK OVERVIEW

After you've submitted all the financial aid forms, you'll receive offers of financial aid from the colleges that have accepted you. This step will help you weigh these award letters and make an informed decision based on an "apples to apples" comparison of the packages. If an award leaves you with a larger out-of-pocket share than you think your family can handle, you can appeal.

Comparing Award Letters from Colleges

Sometime after a college accepts you for admission, it will send you a financial aid award letter. The letter will detail your award—the financial aid package the college is offering you. It will contain an outline of the expected costs you will incur during a year at the college, your expected family contribution (EFC) toward those costs, and the types and amounts of financial aid the college is offering to make up the difference between the costs and the EFC.

The letter will also contain instructions on how to accept the aid package and how to contact the aid office if you have any questions or want to appeal the award. Often, the award letter will come with a thick packet of supplementary documents, including promissory notes for any loans offered and information about work-study jobs, if you've been offered those.

It's best to wait until you have the award letters from all the different colleges that have accepted you before deciding which one to accept. If you have questions, wait until you've gotten answers from all the financial aid offices involved before you decide.

The offers in your award letters will differ. The amount and type of aid given will vary, and the letters may also differ in format, especially in how they itemize costs. In weighing the offers, the important thing is to compare apples to apples and not apples to oranges. For example, just because School A offers $10,000 in financial aid while School B only offers $8,000 doesn't necessarily mean School A has the better deal. If School A's aid package has $3,000 in

KNOW THE LINGO

Aid package—The total amount of all financial aid being offered to a student by a college.

Award letter—A document that a college sends to a student detailing the financial aid package. It indicates the type and amount of each scholarship, grant, loan, or work-study opportunity being offered.

Appeal—A request that a college reconsider its financial aid package.

WORKSHEET 3:
Compare Your Awards

	COLLEGE 1	COLLEGE 2	COLLEGE 3
Step 1. List the name of each college you want to consider attending, the award deadline, and the total cost of attendance. This figure should be in your award letter. If not, refer to the college catalog or contact the college financial aid office.			
Name of college	Private Univ.	Small College	Regional State
Award deadline date	5/1	5/1	4 weeks
Total cost of attendance	$31,825	$33,410	$15,566
Step 2. List the financial aid awards each school is offering. Don't forget that grants, scholarships, and work-study do not have to be repaid, while all loans must be repaid.			
Grants and scholarships			
• Pell Grant (federal)			
• SEOG (federal)			
• State	can't use	$2,000	$2,000
• College	$12,700	$13,785	$941
• Other			
Total grants/scholarships	$12,700	$15,785	$2,941
Percentage of package that is grant/scholarship	60%	74%	53%
Work-study opportunities	$2,000	$1,000	
Loans			
• Stafford-Direct (federal)	$2,625	$2,625	$2,625
• Perkins (federal)	$4,000	$2,000	
• Other			
Total loans	$6,625	$4,625	$2,625
Percentage of package that is work or loans	40%	26%	47%
Total financial aid award	$21,325	$21,410	$5,566
Grants and scholarships + work-study + loans			
Step 3. Calculate what it will cost you to attend each college you are considering. For each college, enter the total cost of attendance. Then, subtract the total financial aid award from the total cost of attendance. That number is the net cost, or what it will cost you to attend that college.			
a) Total cost of attendance	$31,825	$33,410	$15,566
b) Total financial aid award	$21,325	$21,410	$5,566
c) Net cost to attend (a minus b)	$10,500	$12,000	$10,000

For a blank version of this worksheet that you can photocopy for your own use, see page 123.

EXPERT ADVICE

"It's **not simply the dollar amount of the grant or scholarship** that families should focus on. They need to **lay out, side by side, the full picture**. What's the cost of attendance, including out-of-pocket expenses? What's the family contribution? What are the elements of aid? What's going to happen with loans, with work?"

—Joe Paul Case, dean and director of financial aid, Amherst College, Amherst, Massachusetts

grants and $7,000 in loans, but School B has $6,000 in grants and $2,000 in loans, School B is offering you more free money (grants) than School A.

There is another reason why a financial aid package may not be as big as it seems: higher costs. If one school's costs are higher than another's, you may be left with a higher out-of-pocket expense even after subtracting a "bigger" aid package. Don't be dazzled by a large award. Instead, look for the bottom line: your net cost to attend the school.

Collegeboard.com has an online "Compare Your Aid Awards" tool that lets you do this kind of side-by-side comparison of your awards. You can also use Worksheet 3 to break out the different components of costs and aid packages and compare them side by side (a blank copy of this worksheet appears in Part II). When doing this analysis, keep an eye out for both quantity and quality. On the quantity side, for example, the "Family Share of Costs" figure tells you the amount of money your family will be expected to contribute. Your family will need to decide whether this amount is affordable. Look especially for evidence of "gapping," the practice of leaving a gap between the cost of attendance and the money accounted for by aid and EFC. You will be expected to fill that gap—in effect increasing your EFC.

On the quality side, consider the figures for "% of Award That Is Gift Aid" and "% of Award That Is Loan." The higher the proportion of gift aid (grant or scholarships) to loans, the better the award.

Loans vs. Grants

All other things being equal, it's better to receive a grant or scholarship than a loan. For that reason, a financial aid package with a high percentage of gift aid is more attractive, on the face of it, than one with a high percentage of loans. But there are circumstances where you might take the award that offers more loans and less gift aid: for example, if that college is a better fit for you overall.

In any event, don't be surprised if your award includes loans. Most aid packages contain them. Loans are optional; you don't have to take them out. But if offered as part of a need-based aid package, they can be an excellent way to help finance your education. The alternative—taking only grant aid and trying to pay the costs that the loans would cover out-of-pocket—could put your family under much more financial stress than the loan would.

It's usually in your best interest to accept subsidized Stafford and Perkins loans that are part of the aid package: the repayment terms are good and the government pays the interest while you're in school. Unsubsidized loans—such as unsubsidized Stafford, PLUS loan, and private loans from a bank—should be studied more carefully to make sure the terms are acceptable. You should understand the specific terms of each loan, including its interest rate, the origination fee, the term of the loan, and the grace period before repayment begins. You should also realize that unsubsidized loans are not need based and are typically used to help your families pay their EFC. If a college offers them as part of your aid package, consider them as an option, but don't weigh them equally with subsidized loans in the package.

KEEP IN MIND

Just because you're awarded a loan to pay part of your college costs **doesn't mean you have to accept it**. If your family has funds available in savings or current income, you can use these funds if you prefer. The downside is that you'll have less money available now, which could put your family under financial stress. The upside is that you won't have to pay the money back later with interest.

Work-study jobs are also optional, but if you're offered one and you can manage the time, take it. Having a job on campus brings in income, expands your social networks, allows you to make contacts with professors and administrators, and gives you experience that can improve your résumé.

Questions to Ask About Your Award

These are some questions to ask your college financial aid office if you're awarded gift aid:

✔ What do I have to do to keep my scholarship?
✔ Do I have to do anything more than maintain satisfactory academic progress?
✔ Is there a minimum GPA or other condition?
✔ Is the scholarship renewable in subsequent years?
✔ If I win an outside scholarship, what happens to my aid?

Questions to ask if you're awarded a loan:

✔ What are the terms of my loan?
✔ What is the interest rate, and when do I start repayment?
✔ How much will I owe by the time I graduate?
✔ What will my monthly repayment be?
✔ By how much will my loan increase after my first year?

Questions to ask if you're awarded work-study:

✔ Do I have a "guaranteed" job, or will I have to find one?
✔ How are jobs assigned?
✔ How many hours per week will I be expected to work?
✔ What is the hourly wage?
✔ How often will I be paid?
✔ Will I be paid directly, or will my student account get credited?

Appealing Your Award

Even though your award letters are printed in black and white, they aren't necessarily the last word. It is possible to appeal the awards: to ask the colleges to reconsider their aid packages. There is no guarantee that they will grant your request, but there are circumstances where it's worth trying.

One reason you might appeal a package is if it has a lot of unsubsidized loans. However, bear in the mind that the college probably offered those loans because there wasn't enough gift aid to go around. Another reason to appeal is if you don't think you can afford the expected family contribution. You will need to have evidence to make that case. The college based its calculation of your EFC on the financial information you submitted. If you think this calculation was wrong, ask the financial aid office how it was made and see if you can find out if a mistake occurred. It will help if you have special circumstances that weren't communicated in your financial aid forms, such as a recent layoff; situations like this will clearly demonstrate why your family would have difficulty paying its EFC. (See Step 8, "Make Your Special Circumstances Known.")

"I've changed financial aid packages on appeal if somebody can demonstrate why they can't afford it," says Forrest Stuart of Rhodes College. "It may be the need analysis just didn't take some things into account. If they can show me where there's a real problem, even to the point where they show me their monthly budget, I might say, 'Man, you are right. You've got these medical expenses or you've got this and that. Let me see if I can help you.' I am not perfect, and the need analysis is not perfect, and we'll sometimes overlook something."

Still another reason for appealing an award is if you have better offers from other colleges, and would like to see if this college can match them. Some aid offices will consider matching a better offer from another college. But most will only hear an appeal that's based on your family's financial circumstances. "We don't bargain," says Mike Scott of Texas Christian University. "We just don't want to play that game of, 'Well, we'll give you more money simply because another school gave you more money.'"

You might see the entire appeal process as essentially negotiation or bargaining—trying to get as much as possible from the school you'd like to attend. However, most financial aid officers loathe the term "negotiate." Your appeal will have a better chance of success if it appears not a matter of haggling but of providing information not previously available to the financial aid office.

It will also help your cause if you are obviously doing your part to fund your education. A student who accepts the self-help components of a school's financial aid package will be more likely to get extra help than one who declined them. "If the student is not willing to somehow contribute, either by working or taking out a student loan, then we are very unlikely to give them any extra money," says Mike Scott.

KNOW THE LINGO

There are three types of federal loans for educational expenses:

Stafford—Loan to students. May be subsidized (if student demonstrates need) or unsubsidized. If subsidized, the government pays the interest on the loan while the student is in college.

PLUS—Loan to parents. Not subsidized.

Perkins—Subsidized loan to students with exceptional need. Perkins-loan debt may be forgiven if the borrower enters a career in the public service.

EXPERT ADVICE

"I tell families **not to use the word 'negotiate.'** If an aid package is much lower than what's being offered by similar institutions, families should call and ask if there is additional information that may make a difference."

—Carlene Riccelli, college adviser, Amherst Regional High School, Amherst, Massachusetts

A phone call is a good way to start the appeal process, even though most colleges will want you to put your reasons for an appeal in writing. Some have a specific form for appeals; others would like for you to state your case in a letter. Find out the college's preferred procedure by calling or checking their Web site. No matter how you file your appeal, your case will be stronger if you can provide data to back it up. A few days after filing your appeal, follow up with a phone call or, if possible, by visiting the aid office. Within a short time, the college will let you know its decision.

If you receive a revised award, take the new award letter and compare it to your other aid packages. It's best not to decide where to enroll until you've received the final offer from each college. But keep in mind the deadline set by each college for acceptance of its award. If you miss the deadline, you could lose the package. If you do need more time, try asking the college for an extension.

Follow Up: Accepting an Award

Once you've compared all the awards and any appeals have been ruled upon, you and your family will have to decide on a college. Many factors, including costs and financial aid, will be in play. If your first-choice college has accepted you but not given as much aid as you'd hoped, the choice may be difficult. Do you go to your first-choice college even though it's a financial risk for your family, or to a second-choice college your family can safely afford? In the end, your own preferences should have the greatest weight. Most of the loan debt, payable after graduation, will be on your shoulders. And your personal happiness at the school will have a major influence on whether you graduate successfully. If your family can put together a sensible financial plan to pay the costs, the best choice is the one that fits you best academically and personally.

Once you've decided which offer to accept, it's polite to send a note declining the offers of the colleges you're rejecting. That way any funds they offered you can be made available to other students. As for the offer you're accepting, follow whatever instructions came in the award packet. If you're being asked for more information, send it. Complete any forms that came with the award letter. Sign the letter and return it by the due date.

Step 10: Weigh the Offers

QUICK RECAP

When you receive your award letters from colleges, you'll have to decide which offer to accept.

- Compare apples to apples, analyzing the awards to see what the real costs and financial aid elements are.
- Just because loans are offered, you don't have to accept them. But they're worth considering, especially if they're subsidized loans.
- If you appeal an award, you'll be on stronger ground if you can demonstrate circumstances that weren't previously made clear to the school.
- Your decision about which offer to accept should be based not just on cost but on how well the college fits you academically, socially, and personally.

Step 11: Consider Your Out-of-Pocket Options

QUICK OVERVIEW — Financial aid is intended to cover the difference between your expected family contribution (EFC) and the total cost of college. However, you still have to pay your EFC and whatever gap there might be between the aid you received and your financial need. This step is about ways to meet those out-of-pocket costs.

Making Up the Difference

For almost every family, college is going to cost money. Even a generous financial aid package will usually leave you with some bills to pay. Some packages will meet less than your full need and leave you spending more than your EFC. You can afford to make up this difference between the total cost of attendance and the aid you're receiving if you take advantage of the various resources available to you. Most families use a combination of savings, current income, and loans to pay their out-of-pocket costs. You'll have to decide how to do that in a way that fits your own particular situation. But you'll have help, because there are a number of programs and strategies that can help you save, pay, or borrow for college.

Save for It

You shouldn't spend your entire family savings on college: you need to leave some for other uses, such as retirement and emergency medical costs. But it makes sense to use some of your savings for college.

Don't worry if your family doesn't already have a huge sum of money saved for college. Every little bit helps, and it's never too late to start saving. Even while you're applying to college, your family can start saving. Try to save as much as you can from summer and after-school jobs, and encourage your parents to set aside some money from every paycheck. Talk with your parents about how much money you and they already have saved for your college costs, and discuss how your family can afford the rest of the bill.

Don't believe anyone who says you shouldn't save for college because it will reduce your chances of getting financial aid. As noted in Step 2, savings are worth having so you can pay out-of-pocket costs without having to borrow. Very little, if any, of your parents' savings are counted against you when your financial need is determined. "Parents should not avoid saving because, frankly, a family that has saved has a resource to draw on, whereas a family that hasn't is totally dependent on current income and loans," says Joe Paul Case, dean and director of financial aid at Amherst College in Amherst, Massachusetts.

There are a number of places families can put their savings. The most traditional is a regular bank savings account, which pays a little interest and offers freedom to withdraw and deposit money at any time. A certificate of deposit (CD) has stricter rules about when you can withdraw money, but it usually pays higher interest than a savings account. Both of these options are good for short-term, flexible savings. But neither has any tax incentives—tax breaks that make them especially attractive for college savings.

The following savings vehicles do come with tax breaks. For more details, see Table 3 on page 102:

529 college savings plan. Also known as the QTP (Qualified Tuition Program), these are tax-advantaged accounts sponsored by the various states. Interest earned in these plans is not taxed as income, and some states also offer a state income-tax deduction for contributions their residents make to the state's plan. There are no income restrictions, and contribution limits are high. Grandparents, uncles, and aunts are also allowed to contribute to the plan, even if they don't live in the same state as you and your parents—in fact, you don't have to be a resident of a state to contribute to its plan, and you can withdraw funds from a state's plan to pay for expenses at a college in another state. Most plans offer a few different investment types, such as a fund that invests in stocks or one that invests in bonds.

Coverdell Education Savings Account. These tax-free trust or custodial accounts are similar to 529s, but they're sponsored by banks and brokerage houses instead of states, and therefore offer a greater range of investment choices. They can be used to pay private elementary and high school costs as well as college costs, unlike 529s, which can only be used for college costs. Total contributions for the student can't be more than $2,000 in a given year, and your family income has to be less than $110,000 (for single filers) or $220,000 (for joint filers). You can contribute to both a 529 and a Coverdell in the same year for the same student.

529 prepaid tuition plan. Like the 529 college savings plans, these are sponsored by the states, but they work differently. A 529 prepaid tuition plan lets a family make advance tuition payments years before their children will enter college. That allows them to "lock in" today's tuition rates instead of paying the higher rates likely to prevail years from now. Provided the student is admitted, the plans are guaranteed to be honored by public universities and some private colleges in the state that sponsors the plan. However, these plans have drawbacks. They can only be used for tuition and fees, not for room, board, or other supplemental costs. When that's combined with the fact that funds in the plan can't be used at out-of-state colleges, most parents prefer the more flexible 529 savings plans.

Independent 529 prepaid tuition plan. This is a special 529 prepaid tuition plan sponsored by a group of private colleges and universities and administered by TIAA-CREF. For more information, visit www.independent529plan.org.

U.S. savings bonds. If your parents pay for some of your college costs by cashing in U.S. government savings bonds, the interest that has accumulated on the bond may be tax exempt. That means the interest won't be taxed as income and your tax bill will be smaller. There's a penalty if you cash in the bonds less than five years after the date of issue, and there are some restrictions on the tax exemption. The bond must be issued after 1989 and your parent must have been age 24 or older when the bond was issued. This deduction can't overlap with any other education tax break. You can't use two different tax breaks to pay for the same expense. The family income must be less than $76,200 (for single filers) or $121,850 (for joint filers).

Uniform Gifts to Minors Act (UGMA) or Uniform Transfers to Minors Act (UTMA) account. These accounts allow parents to put money in the child's name so it will receive preferential tax treatment. Much of the earnings are taxed at the child's rate rather than the parent's rate. Such accounts were popular in the 1980s, but the advent of tax-free 529s and Coverdells has made them nearly obsolete as a college-savings vehicle.

Individual Retirement Account (IRA). Generally, it's not a good idea to raid the family retirement funds, such as IRAs, to pay for college. "We tell parents all the time, you can borrow money to pay for your kid's education. You cannot borrow money to retire with," says Mike Scott of Texas Christian University. It's usually better to take out a PLUS loan than to diminish retirement assets. Still, if your family does need to go into an IRA to pay college expenses, the government doesn't charge the 10 percent additional tax you would ordinarily have to pay for breaking open an IRA before age 59 1/2.

Table 3:
Comparison of Education Savings Options

	COVERDELL EDUCATION SAVINGS ACCOUNT	529 COLLEGE SAVINGS PLAN	529 PREPAID TUITION PLAN	U.S. GOVERNMENT SAVINGS BONDS	UNIFORM GIFTS TO MINORS ACT ACCOUNT	INDIVIDUAL RETIREMENT ACCOUNT
Tax advantages	Earnings in account not taxed as income	Earnings in account not taxed as income Some states allow residents to deduct contributions for state income tax purposes	Earnings in account not taxed as income Some states allow residents to deduct contributions for state income tax purposes	Interest earned is not taxed if used for qualified expenses	Interest earned is taxed at child's rate	Exception to the 10% early withdrawal penalty rule
Expenses that qualify	• Tuition & fees • Books & supplies • Room & board (if half-time) • Expenses for special needs services • K–12 education expenses	• Tuition & fees • Books & supplies • Room & board (if half-time)	Tuition & fees	• Tuition & fees • Contributions to a Coverdell or 529	Any expense (not limited to education)	• Tuition & fees • Books & supplies • Room & board (if half-time)
Contribution limits	$2,000 per year	None	None	None	None	$5,000 per year ($5,500 if over 50)
Income phaseout for benefits	$95,000–$110,000 (single filers) $190,000–$220,000 (joint filers)	None	None	$61,200–$76,200 (single filers) $91,850–$121,850 (joint filers)	None	Varies by type of account
Other limitations	Assets must be distributed by age 30 Must pay 10% penalty if distributions not used for qualified expenses	Must pay 10% penalty if distributions not used for qualified expenses	Benefits may only be used at colleges that participate in the plan Must pay 10% penalty if distributions not used for qualified expenses	Applies only to Series EE or Series I bonds issued after 1989 and purchased after owner turned 24	Counted as student asset for financial aid purposes	Interest earned will still be taxed at your regular rate

Work for It

Besides a summer job, you might also want to consider working during the school year to help meet expenses. There are two basic approaches. You can go to college full-time while working part-time, or you can hold a full-time job while attending college part-time.

Full-Time Student, Part-Time Job

If you're offered a work-study job as part of your financial aid package, the earnings from that job will go toward your college costs. Even if you're not offered work-study, you may still be able to find a part-time job on or near campus. You can also work during the summer to make money to put toward college.

Work has benefits beyond the extra income it generates. It can help you structure your time, which can make you a more disciplined student. Studies have shown that students who work part-time get better grades and are more likely to finish college than those who don't work at all. If the job is on campus, it enhances the college experience by connecting students more closely with the school and giving them a chance to meet people they wouldn't meet in classes.

On the other hand, don't work so many hours that you jeopardize your ability to get through college. If you're going to college full-time, the recommended workload is about 10 to 15 hours a week. If you work more than 20 hours a week, you're likely to get overloaded and put yourself at risk of dropping out. If you take fewer courses to make time for work, you may drop below full-time status, which could make you ineligible for many grants and scholarships. If your financial situation makes you feel that you have to work more hours, it might be better to borrow more money so you don't have to work so much.

Part-Time Student, Full-Time Job

A different (and much more difficult) way of approaching work is to be a full-time worker who goes to college part-time. This is possible as long as you don't take too many credits in one semester. If you try for more than six credits while working full-time, you'll probably have trouble getting everything done. On the other hand, if you take fewer than six credits a semester, you won't be eligible for need-based subsidized Stafford or Perkins loans.

Working full-time while going to school part-time is an especially attractive way to pay for an associate degree or a vocational certificate. Most community colleges cater to working students and offer classes at night to meet their needs. If you take six credits per semester, you can probably earn an associate degree in four or five years.

If you're planning on earning a bachelor's degree, however, you should strongly consider attending college full-time and borrowing money to replace the income that you won't be earning through a job. Why? If you take only six credits a semester, it will take ten years to earn a bachelor's! You will probably

> **EXPERT ADVICE**
>
> "**Work gives students structure.** First, they have to be somewhere. They have to be doing something at certain times of the week, which helps them manage their time. Second, if the job is on campus, they get involved with an office or a department or a faculty member, and that helps to **strengthen that student's connection with that school**, which always enhances the academic experience."
>
> —Vincent Amoroso, deputy director, Office of Scholarships and Student Aid, University of North Carolina, Chapel Hill

earn more money in the long run if you get that bachelor's in the usual four or five years, and concentrate on your career after you've earned that degree.

Some employers offer tuition assistance or scholarship money to employees who are attending college. Check to see if your employer is one of them. For a typical educational assistance program, up to $5,250 of those benefits will be tax free each year.

Co-op and Internship Programs

Many colleges sponsor internships or "co-op" (cooperative) programs with local employers. Some interns and almost all co-op participants receive payment from their employers along with academic credit. In co-op programs, you may be able to alternate periods of full-time work and full-time study. Often the business at which you intern end ups hiring you after graduation, or at least recommending you to others. Internship and co-op programs can help you make money, get academic credit, gain job experience, and make contacts with potential employers.

Promising to Work Later

Holding a job during college is not the only way of using work to pay your college costs. There are several programs that allow you to commit to work in public service after graduation in exchange for either a non-need-based scholarship while in college or a stipend that can be used to repay student loans after college. The ROTC program is an example of the former, and AmeriCorps is an example of the latter.

ROTC

In return for military service, the armed forces offer career training and a number of educational benefits to help pay for college, including full college scholarships and education assistance plans. If you're interested in training to be a military officer during college in return for educational benefits, check with the Reserve Officers Training Corps (ROTC) office at your high school or on your college campus. Each branch of the military offers ROTC training. Part IV of this book contains lists of colleges that offer ROTC programs for each service branch.

OTHER SERVICE PROGRAMS

AmeriCorps is a network of national service programs for which you can work as a volunteer, full- or part-time for up to a year. After completing a term of service with AmeriCorps, you're eligible for an education award, which can be used either to repay student loans or to pay for college tuition. The amount of the award depends on how long you worked for the program, and for how many hours each week. (Currently, completion of one year's full-time service earns an award of $4,750.) For more information, go to www.americorps.org.

Another type of program is one that hinges on your financial aid package and the profession you choose after college. If you received a Perkins loan as part of your package, the loan may be forgiven if you enter certain professions serving the public, such as teaching, nursing, or law enforcement.

> **KEEP IN MIND**
>
> As noted in Step 2, you will be **expected to contribute** a larger percentage of your **work income to college costs** than your parents will. This is because it is expected that you have fewer financial responsibilities and will benefit more from college than your parents will. In general, you will be expected to pay about 50 percent of your earnings toward the EFC.

Borrow It

To borrow money is to spend today what you'll earn in the future. You will have to pay the loan back, with interest, when you start earning money after college. A loan can be intimidating because it assumes you'll have the money for repayment, and you may not feel sure of that. But rest assured that college will increase your earning power, which will make it possible to repay your loans.

There are many forms of "bad debt" in our society, such as credit card debt, where you borrow money on unfavorable terms to buy consumer goods that will have little or no value in a year. By comparison, an education loan is a "good debt." You are borrowing money on favorable terms to achieve an outcome—higher lifetime earnings—that will more than pay back the loan.

Subsidized Stafford loans, Perkins loans, and need-based state loans all have excellent terms that make them worth considering. Some institutions also offer their own need-based loans to qualified students. However, these loans are intended as financial aid to cover your need. In general, you won't be able to use them towards your expected family contribution.

However, loans are available that are not based on need and that your family can use to borrow money to meet their EFC. The terms are not as favorable as the need-based loans, but the loans may be helpful just the same. The most common types are the unsubsidized Stafford and the PLUS loan, both of which are guaranteed by the federal government, but there are also state and private sources.

How Much Should You Borrow?

If your family decides to borrow money to pay for college, they should consider the total debt that you will carry after graduation. That total debt includes any subsidized, need-meeting loans that you accept as part of the college's aid package as well as any non-need-based loans your family takes out to meet the EFC. When you pay back that debt, you'll do so in the form of monthly payments, and those payments should be reasonable ones that you can afford to pay from the income you're likely to have. The total monthly payment will usually be similar to a car payment—$200 to $300 a month. But the amount will vary with the amount borrowed and interest rate offered. See Table 4 on the next page for help in determining what your monthly payment will be. It shows monthly repayment over 10 years for various loan amounts and interest rates. To calculate a monthly payment for a loan amount not listed on the table, multiply the amount borrowed by the repayment factor for your interest rate. For example, if you borrowed $12,500 at 7.5 percent, your monthly payment would be $148.46 ($12,500 × .0118770).

There are some ways to make your repayment burden lighter after college. Many lenders will offer to cut your interest rate a bit if you make your first 12 monthly payments on time. If you borrow from multiple federal loan programs, such as the Perkins, subsidized Stafford, and unsubsidized Stafford, you can consolidate these loans after graduation, which will simplify things by allowing you

---

GOOD TO KNOW

To apply for EFC-meeting loans, shop around on the Internet. The FinAid Web site (www.finaid.com) maintains lists of lenders. Your college financial aid office may also be able to recommend their "preferred" lenders. Three of the most popular lenders are the College Board, The Educational Resources Institute (TERI), and SallieMae.

KNOW THE LINGO

Principal—the portion of debt that is left over from the amount you originally borrowed.

Interest—the portion of debt that has been charged to you by the lender as a fee for loaning you the principal.

to make only one payment a month. Consolidation also gives you the option of "re-amortizing" your loans—that means stretching your payments over a longer period of time than you would normally have left to repay the debt. If you re-amortize when you consolidate, you will usually have a lower monthly payment, but will pay more interest over the total life of all the loans.

Table 4:
Calculating Your Monthly Loan Payment

AMOUNT OF LOAN	INTEREST RATE	REPAYMENT FACTOR	MONTHLY PAYMENT
$10,000	4.00%	.010125	$101.25
	4.50%	.010364	$103.64
	5.00%	.010607	$106.07
	5.50%	.010853	$108.53
	6.00%	.011102	$111.02
	6.50%	.011355	$113.55
	7.00%	.011611	$116.11
	7.50%	.011870	$118.70
	8.00%	.012133	$121.33
	8.50%	.012399	$123.99

> **GOOD TO KNOW**
>
> When you start paying back your educational loan, remember that the **interest is tax deductible**. To a maximum of $2,500 per year, you can deduct the interest you pay from your income, which will lower your tax bite. In effect, the government will be subsidizing your loan. This is true for every kind of loan used to pay for postsecondary education, including PLUS loans.

Types of Non-Need-Based Loans

There are three basic types of loans you can use to pay your out-of-pocket costs: federal, state, and private.

FEDERAL LOANS

Federal loans have relatively low interest rates and are guaranteed by the federal government. This means that if you don't pay your loan back to the lender (though, of course, you should), the federal government will. That encourages lenders to lend you money even if you're a student with no credit history and little employment record.

Two basic kinds of federal loans are used for paying an EFC, one for students, one for parents:

- **Student Loans (Unsubsidized Stafford).** With an unsubsidized Stafford loan, you borrow money through participating colleges or directly from a bank or other lender. You'll be charged only interest while you're in school, and can either pay it while you're in school or let it accrue (accumulate) for payment after school. If you let the interest accrue, the bank will "capitalize" it into the principal of the loan when you start sending them payments after graduation. Table 5 shows the effects of interest accrual. The calculations on the table are for example only—they assume that you borrow $3,500 at the beginning of your freshman year and don't borrow any more to fund subsequent years of education. With this amount and the interest rate shown, letting the interest accrue saves you a $20 monthly payment while you're in college, but it ends up costing you about $407 more over the life of the loan. Whether or not you let interest accrue, six months after leaving school (your grace period), you have to begin paying back both the principal and the interest. To apply for an unsubsidized Stafford loan, ask your college financial aid office; they will refer you to lenders.

Table 5:
Effects of Letting Interest Accrue While You're In College

	INTEREST RATE IN COLLEGE	MONTHLY PAYMENT IN COLLEGE	DEBT REMAINING AFTER COLLEGE	INTEREST RATE AFTER COLLEGE	MONTHLY PAYMENT AFTER COLLEGE	TOTAL INTEREST PAID OVER LIFE OF THE LOAN
Subsidized Stafford	0%	$0	$3,500.00	6.8%	$40.28	$1,333.28
Unsubsidized Stafford (no interest accrual)	6.8%	$19.83	$3,500.00	6.8%	$40.28	$2,404.60
Unsubsidized Stafford (interest accrual option)	6.8%	$0	$4,571.00	6.8%	$52.60	$2,812.00

- **Parent Loans (PLUS).** With a PLUS loan, your parents borrow money to pay for your education either through the school or a third-party lender. They can borrow any amount up to the student's total cost of attendance minus the financial aid you receive. To get a PLUS loan, your parents have to fill out an application and pass a credit review. They will have to start making payments on the entire debt—both the principal and the interest—as soon as the loan money is disbursed to the school.

If you take out a federal loan, you'll receive a loan repayment schedule that spells out when your first payment is due and the number, frequency, and amounts of the payments. You'll have to pay back the loan on schedule or go into default, an official state of failure to repay a loan. That would hurt your credit rating—your ability to borrow more money later.

Under certain circumstances, such as economic hardship, you can postpone repayment of a federal student loan by applying for a deferment (during which no interest accumulates) or forbearance (during which it does). Under exceptional circumstances, such as total disability or teaching in a designated low-income school, some borrowers get a loan discharge, or cancellation of the debt. These rules apply to all federal student loans, but not to PLUS loans.

STATE LOANS

Some states sponsor loan programs for students and parents in their state. These loans are usually neither subsidized nor based on need. Check with your state financial aid agency to find out more.

PRIVATE LOANS

Many banks, credit unions, and other organizations offer their own education loans. These usually have slightly higher interest rates than federal loans, but they have lower interest rates than other consumer borrowing options, and may have attractive features, such as deferred repayment while in school. The borrowers—usually parents—have to prove their creditworthiness to get these loans.

HOME-EQUITY LOANS

Many parents consider taking out a loan against their home equity to pay for their children's higher education. While this may be an attractive option for your family, you should keep in mind that, unlike PLUS loans and other education loans, home-equity loans do come with the condition that if you can't pay back the loan, the bank can foreclose on your house.

Table 6:
Comparison of Education Loan Options

	SUBSIDIZED STAFFORD	PERKINS	UNSUBSIDIZED STAFFORD	PLUS	PRIVATE/ ALTERNATIVE EDUCATION LOAN	HOME EQUITY LOAN OR LINE OF CREDIT
BORROWING LIMIT	$3,500 first year $4,500 second year $5,500 third and fourth years Higher limits for independent students and for graduate study	$4,000/year $20,000 undergraduate maximum	Same as for Subsidized Stafford Students whose parents have been turned down for a PLUS Loan may borrow more.	Maximum is difference between total cost of attendance and financial aid awarded	Depends on credit check Maximum is difference between total cost of attendance and financial aid awarded	Depends on credit check and home equity
INTEREST RATES FOR 2006-2007	In school: 0% In repayment: 6.8% (fixed)	In school: 0% In repayment: 5% (fixed)	In school: 6.8% (fixed) In repayment: 6.8% (fixed)	8.5% (fixed)	Depends on lender and credit check; range from 7% to 12%; may be fixed or variable	Depends on lender and credit check; may be fixed or variable
PROS	Interest that accumulates while you're in college paid by federal government	No origination fee Interest that accumulates while you're in college paid by federal government Debt may be forgiven if you enter a career in the public service	Option of not making payments during college and "capitalizing" accrued interest into the loan upon graduation Same deferment, and forbearance rules as subsidized loans	No collateral required	Available for nondegree programs and adult continuing education Repayment term may be longer than for federal loans	Can use money for non-educational purposes Repayment term may be longer than for federal loans
CONS	Only available to students with financial need 4% origination fee (may be discounted by lender)	Only available to students with financial need Amount of loan you're offered subject to college financial aid office's discretion	4% origination fee (may be discounted by lender)	Parents must pass credit check to take out loan Parents must begin paying interest immediately 4% origination fee	Student must pass credit check Parents may have to co-sign promissory note May have high origination fees	Home used as collateral for loan Can take several months to secure loan; may need to have house appraised

Cut It

In addition to spending past, present, and future resources to pay your college bill, you can also take steps to make that bill smaller. This is an especially smart move if it looks like college won't be affordable otherwise, even when you contribute all you can from savings, current income, and loans. But some strategies to cut college costs are worth using even if your family is financially comfortable.

Tuition "On the Cheap"

Tuition, the cost of taking classes, is usually high at four-year colleges. But you can get a reduced rate on those classes by taking them ahead of time at your own high school or a community college. By doing this, you may also be able to reduce the number of semesters you have to spend in college, which will cut not only your tuition costs but all other costs, such as room and board. Some colleges offer accelerated programs that will help you do that.

AP®/CLEP® OUT

Several programs let you earn college-level credit or advanced placement. They include the Advanced Placement Program (AP) and the College-Level Examination Program® (CLEP®) which are sponsored by the College Board; and the International Baccalaureate (IB) program. The programs differ in various ways. For example, students take AP and IB courses as part of their high school curriculum, but they can prepare to take the CLEP examinations by any number of means—in school, on the job, or just reading books in their spare time. These programs are similar, however, in that you earn credit by taking an examination and receiving a score that your college accepts.

Colleges differ as to which programs, courses, and scores they accept and how much credit they grant. But every credit you receive means a credit you don't have to pay for in college. Depending on your exam scores and your college's policies, you may be able to graduate a semester or even a year early if you've taken enough AP or IB exams.

CLEP exams can often be taken on campus or at a nearby campus, and can be used to "CLEP out" of introductory-level courses. For more information see collegeboard.com/clep. To find out about your college's policy on AP credit, go to collegeboard.com and use the AP Credit Policy Info tool.

TAKE COMMUNITY COLLEGE CLASSES OVER THE SUMMER

Courses at a community college usually cost much less than at a four-year college. Find out if there are courses you can take at a local community college in the summers and transfer to your four-year college. For example, if you don't have the knowledge of a certain subject that you need to pass a CLEP exam, you may still be able to take that course at a community college over the summer and transfer the credit to your four-year college.

OTHER ACCELERATED PROGRAMS

Some colleges offer an "accelerated program" designed for students who want to graduate in three years. These programs require a lot of work and dedication, but they will cut your college costs substantially by eliminating an entire year of expenses. It's possible to get through these programs if you're determined. An index of colleges with accelerated programs appears in the *College Board's Book of Majors*.

Cutting Other Expenses

Tuition is not the only college cost you can cut. Room, board, books, supplies, transportation—all of these add substantially to your total college bill. (Most people are shocked at what college textbooks cost these days.) Here are some suggestions to reduce these expenses:

BOOKS
- ✔ Buy used textbooks instead of new ones.
- ✔ Comparison shop for textbooks online.
- ✔ Sell your textbooks at the end of the semester.

ROOM AND BOARD
- ✔ Live off campus in a house or apartment that you share with classmates. That can be cheaper than a college dorm. (But check the policy at the college you want to attend—many require freshmen to live on campus.)
- ✔ If you live off campus, take turns cooking meals with your roommates. That can be cheaper than the meal plan.
- ✔ If you plan to live in a dorm in your sophomore year and beyond, try to get a position as a resident adviser and the free room and board that comes with it.

TRANSPORTATION
- ✔ If you're commuting to school, carpool with a classmate from your area.

Education Tax Breaks

Federal student aid isn't the only way that Uncle Sam can help you pay for college. There are also tax breaks available for higher-education costs. By reducing the amount your family has to pay the government at tax time, these programs amount to federal subsidies for out-of-pocket costs. Some of them take the form of tax credits, which cut your taxes dollar for dollar: that is, a $1 tax credit would make your tax bill $1 smaller. Others take the form of tax deductions,

> **GOOD TO KNOW**
>
> The information about higher-education tax breaks printed here is current as of early 2006. **To make sure you qualify for a deduction or credit** before you file, download IRS Publication 970, "Tax Breaks for Higher Education," from www.irs.gov.

which lower the amount of your income that is subject to tax, indirectly lowering your tax bill.

There are two federal income tax credits for higher-education expenses: the Hope tax credit and the Lifetime Learning tax credit. Both of these benefits let your family reduce the tax they pay by a fraction of their out-of-pocket costs, but the criteria for eligibility are different. The Hope tax credit, which is worth up to $1,500 per student per year, is available to families that have a first- or second-year student enrolled at least half-time in an undergraduate degree program. To be eligible for the Lifetime Learning tax credit, you don't have to be enrolled half-time or even be in a degree program. It's available for almost any kind of postsecondary education and training. The Lifetime Learning tax credit is equal to 20 percent of your family's tuition expenses, up to a $2,000 credit for $10,000 in tuition. Unlike the Hope Scholarship Credit, the Lifetime Learning Credit is calculated on a per-family, not a per-student, basis, so the maximum credit has to be shared among all students in the family.

Your family can't use both of these credits for the same student in the same year, though they can use both credits if they're applied to separate students. For either tax credit, the amount depends in part on your family's income, as calculated according to a formula called modified adjusted gross income. The more your family makes, the less money they'll be eligible for. Past a certain level of income ($53,000 for single filers; $107,000 for joint filers), your family won't be eligible at all. Still, for many people, the tax credits are a big help in paying the tuition bills.

Interest paid on student loans is tax deductible to a maximum of $2,500 per year. This benefit applies to all loans used to pay for college, including PLUS loans. To be eligible for this deduction, your income has to be lower than

Table 7:
Federal Income Tax Benefits for Higher Education

	HOPE EDUCATION CREDIT	LIFETIME LEARNING CREDIT	STUDENT LOAN INTEREST DEDUCTION
AVAILABLE FOR	Tuition and fees only 1st two years of undergraduate study only Associate and bachelor's degree programs only	Tuition and fees only All years of study Any degree program, also nondegree courses to acquire job skills	Any higher education cost All years of study Any degree program
MAXIMUM VALUE	$1,500 credit per student	$2,000 credit per family	$2,500 deduction from taxable income
INCOME RANGE FOR BENEFIT PHASE OUT	$43,000–$53,000 (single filers) $87,000–$107,000 (joint filers)		$50,000–$65,000 (single filers) $105,000–$135,000 (joint filers)
CONDITIONS	Student must be enrolled at least half-time Student may not have felony drug conviction(s) Can be claimed for only two tax years for each student	Cannot claim both Lifetime Learning and Hope credits for same student in same year	Student must have been enrolled at least half-time May not claim if married and filing singly

$65,000 (for single filers) or $135,000 (for joint filers). The tax break is only for interest—the amount you pay the lender as the price for borrowing a sum of money, rather than the starting sum itself (the principal). If you take out a student loan, the lender will send a 1098 form to you at the end of each tax year telling you how much of your payments went to interest that year.

Some states also allow you to take tax credits or deductions off your state income taxes. Find out about yours from your state government.

> **QUICK RECAP**
>
> To deal with out-of-pocket college costs, you have several options. You can draw on savings or current income to pay, or you can borrow some portion of the total bill. And you can cut the costs.
>
> - Several savings options, including U.S. savings bonds, 529s, and Coverdell accounts, have tax benefits that can also help.
> - You can work during college or promise to work later through programs like ROTC or AmeriCorps.
> - You can borrow through student or parent loans.
> - You can reduce your costs by such means as taking college-level courses for credit before you enter college.
> - Tax breaks can help you meet college costs.

Once You're in College

QUICK OVERVIEW

Once you're in college, you shouldn't be preoccupied with paying for it. Academics, extracurricular activities, and making friends are more important. But there are some things you need to do to stay on target financially. This chapter will tell you what they are.

Stay on Track

The first thing to keep in mind if you've been awarded federal student aid is maintaining eligibility for that aid. To stay eligible, stay in school at least half-time, and avoid illegal drugs. A drug-related conviction can lead to suspension or revocation of your federal-aid eligibility.

To maintain federal eligibility, you don't have to maintain a particular GPA (though you do have to meet your individual school's standards for "satisfactory academic progress"). But the financial aid your college gives you, such as scholarships, may have specific academic requirements. Do your best in all your classes and stay on track academically, not only because it will help you get the most out of college but because it will help you keep your financial aid. To maintain or establish eligibility for academic scholarships, an on-campus job as a teaching or research assistant, or a "co-op" program between your department and a local employer, you'll need to be in good academic standing.

Maintain Grades

To keep up your grades, you'll have to make decisions about how to spend your time. It's important to build social relationships, pursue extracurricular activities, and earn money through work, but balance those against the need to maintain a good academic record. If you have a job, don't work so hard at it that you jeopardize your aid eligibility (see "Expert Advice" sidebar).

EXPERT ADVICE

"There are students who tell me that the reason they didn't pass their class was they're **too busy working**, because they need the money to support themselves. And I tell them, you need to determine your priorities. There's a limit of how much financial aid I can give you to help offset that."

—Mary San Agustin, director of financial aid and scholarships, Palomar College, San Marcos, California

Don't Stay Too Long (Pick a Major, Any Major)

Did you know that only about one-third of all students who enter a four-year college graduate in four years? Most take six or more years to earn a bachelor's degree. Obviously, the longer you stay in college, the more it's going to cost you—not only in tuition, fees, room, board, and other expenses, but also in lost earnings from a delayed career.

Make it a goal to graduate on time. Make sure you are on track to complete your college's core requirements, as well as the core requirements for your major.

Speaking of majors, don't feel that you need to rush into choosing one. Except for some very specialized career and technical institutes, most colleges and universities allow you to take time during your first two years to take classes in different fields and make sure you know enough to choose a major that fits your interests and abilities. On the other hand, don't wait so long that you neglect to take the courses that are requirements for a major. You don't want to have to pay for an extra semester to get your biology degree because you didn't take that required organic chemistry course your sophomore year.

Community College Students

If you're going to a community college, and plan to transfer to a four-year college, make sure you know all the transfer requirements—including whatever courses are needed for the major you intend to declare. It helps if your community college has an articulation agreement with the four-year college specifying exactly what courses are required for transfer. Almost all community colleges have a transfer adviser on staff who can help you make sure you're on track. Get to know your adviser and check in with him or her regularly.

Watch Your Personal Expenses

The purpose of financial aid is to give you the money you need to pay for college costs. But that aid can quickly become too little if you spend too much. To avoid overspending, live within your means and don't run up frivolous debt. That means sticking to a budget and avoiding credit cards.

Student Budgeting

To live within your means, all you have to do is not spend more than you receive in income. The best way to do that is to create a budget at the beginning of each semester and stick to it. Your budget should list the funds you will receive (such as money from parents, savings, work, grants, and loans), subtract how much money you plan to spend on given items (such as tuition,

> **MYTH/FACT**
>
> **Myth:** Only certain majors will lead to high earnings after graduation.
>
> **Fact:** Don't be fooled. If you're not drawn to the major, you probably won't like the work and will leave that field before you ever reach the high earnings. Instead, choose a major based on your interests and talents, not on someone else's predictions of industrial trends. And remember that many of today's highest paying fields—such as marketing and software engineering—require critical thinking skills that you will acquire in courses like anthropology and philosophy. To learn more about specific academic fields and what it's like to major in them, read the College Board's *Book of Majors*.

fees, room, board, books, clothes, and recreation), and calculate the difference—the bottom line. If the bottom line is a negative number—that is, if your expenses exceed your income—you're overspending. Once you have a budget where your income is equal to or greater than your expenses, follow it, and you'll be living within your means.

To create a budget, first examine what you have actually been spending, then set priorities if you're spending too much. That alone can help you to spend less, as you realize you can make do with one latte a day instead of two. "You start making conscious decisions about what it is that you want to do," says Elizabeth Bickford of the University of Oregon at Eugene. "You're actually just taking control over your financial spending."

By all means have fun, but don't spend too much money on nonessential items like CDs, DVDs, high-end clothes, or trips to the beach. Some of your friends at college may have more money than you, but don't let social pressure push you into trying to spend like they do. Learn to suggest ordering pizza from the local hangout instead of driving to an expensive restaurant.

Save money wherever you can—for example, limit your cell phone use to free times. Comparison shop for groceries and supplies. And don't visit the ATM too often: it's too easy to withdraw money and overspend. See collegeboard.com for more advice on budgeting and financial planning.

Credit Card Debt

Be especially careful with your credit cards. They can be convenient for paying for big-ticket items like textbooks and airplane tickets, if you use them sparingly and pay off the entire amount when you get the bill. But if you abuse them, they can land you in a world of trouble.

A credit card is essentially a high-interest loan with an annual fee just for having the card. Pulling it out at a cash register to make an impulse purchase may give you a feeling of freedom, but you won't feel free once you get the bill—especially when you're still paying interest on that impulse purchase months or years later. If you let the debt accumulate, it may swell so much that you won't be able to pay down the debt. This can affect your future academic career. If you miss payments on your credit cards, or if your credit card debt is high, you can hurt your credit rating. A bad credit rating can harm your chances of getting student loans to pay for graduate school, or a car loan when you start working. It can even prevent you from getting a job with certain security-conscious employers, such as banks or government agencies.

Use credit cards only when you know you can repay the debt promptly. Save them for emergencies. (A spring-break vacation is not an emergency.) Think through each credit card purchase before you spend. If you do get in over your head with credit card use, cut your expenses and talk to your family and financial aid administrator for more guidance.

Saving for Future Needs

While you're trying to live within your means, it's also wise to save for the future. Savings will give you greater freedom to cope with college and personal costs to come. If at all possible, make sure your budget includes money set aside for future needs. Your parents, of course, should do the same.

Try to save what you can from the jobs you have during the school year and in the summer. Think about the following as goals for your savings:

Students Should Think About…

- ✔ Next year's college expenses
- ✔ Application fees and tuition for graduate school
- ✔ A vacation with friends after you graduate
- ✔ Moving to another city after you graduate
- ✔ The unexpected (such as traveling to a friend's wedding or a family funeral)

Parents Should Think About…

- ✔ Next year's college expenses
- ✔ College expenses for younger children (if any)
- ✔ Retirement
- ✔ The unexpected (such as making it through a layoff or paying for a child's wedding)

Reapply for Aid Each Year!

Don't forget to reapply to renew your aid package every year! Check at your financial aid office to make sure you have the right forms and know what the deadlines are. Most colleges have a renewal deadline for financial aid that's a week or two later than the deadline for new applicants.

When you renew, don't expect your aid package to stay exactly the same. It may become more loan heavy each year, with more money in subsidized loans. The borrowing limits on the subsidized Stafford loan are higher for sophomores than for freshmen, and even higher for juniors and seniors. Also, keep in mind that some scholarships and grants are for freshmen only.

While you're reapplying for the financial aid you already have, keep an eye out for new opportunities. As you move on to higher grades and declare a major, you may become eligible for outside scholarships that weren't open to you in the past. Follow the guidelines in Step 9 to look for outside sources of money.

Final Thoughts

Once you're in college, you may sometimes wonder if it's worth it. Can your family afford the expense? Will you be able to repay your student loans? If you've made reasonable choices along the way, the answer is yes. If you ever have doubts, visit your school's career center and do some research into the fields of work you might enter. Find out how much money you're likely to be earning when you first graduate, and how much five years later. A light might go on for you, as Elizabeth Bickford has often observed with other students. "When they see that relationship, many students say, 'Oh, wait a second, I can do that.'"

You will be able to pay back your student loans. College is a sound investment. You can afford college!

QUICK RECAP

Once you're in college, make sure you stay on track financially.

- Maintain your federal eligibility by staying in school the right number of hours and avoiding illegal drugs.
- Keep up your grades. Don't let them get derailed by too much time spent on work or other nonacademic activities.
- Declare a major at a suitable time.
- Make a budget and stick to it.
- Be wary of credit cards.
- Save for future expenses.
- Reapply for aid every year.
- Keep an eye out for new sources of outside scholarships.
- Remember that college is worth it!

Part II

Tables and Worksheets

WORKSHEET 1:
Meet Your Application Deadlines

		COLLEGE 1:	COLLEGE 2:	COLLEGE 3:
FORMS REQUIRED	FAFSA			
	PROFILE			
	State form			
	Institutional form			
	Tax returns			
	Other			
SCHOOL CODES	Federal code			
	CSS code			
PRIORITY DATE				
CLOSING DATE				
AFTER APPLYING	Need to send letter?			
	Documentation required?			
COMPARE AWARDS	Notification date			
	Reply-by date			

WORKSHEET 2:
Scholarship Application Planner

	PROGRAM 1	PROGRAM 2	PROGRAM 3
PROGRAM/SPONSOR			
ELIGIBILITY REQUIREMENTS			
TYPE OF AWARD			
AMOUNT OF AWARD			
CAN BE USED FOR			
CAN BE USED AT			
DEADLINE			
FORMS REQUIRED			
TEST SCORES REQUIRED			
ESSAY OR ACADEMIC SAMPLE			
RECOMMENDATIONS			
NOTIFICATION BEGINS			
REQUIREMENTS TO KEEP AFTER FRESHMAN YEAR			

WORKSHEET 3:
Compare Your Awards

	COLLEGE 1	COLLEGE 2	COLLEGE 3
Step 1. List the name of each college you want to consider attending, the award deadline, and the total cost of attendance. This figure should be in your award letter. If not, refer to the college catalog or contact the college financial aid office.			
Name of college			
Award deadline date			
Total cost of attendance			
Step 2. List the financial aid awards each school is offering. Don't forget that grants, scholarships, and work-study do not have to be repaid, while all loans must be repaid.			
Grants and scholarships			
• Pell Grant (federal)			
• SEOG (federal)			
• State			
• College			
• Other			
Total grants/scholarships			
Percentage of package that is grant/scholarship			
Work-study opportunities			
Loans			
• Stafford-Direct (federal)			
• Perkins (federal)			
• Other			
Total loans			
Percentage of package that is work or loans			
Total financial aid award			
Grants and scholarships + work-study + loans			
Step 3. Calculate what it will cost you to attend each college you are considering. For each college, enter the total cost of attendance. Then, subtract the total financial aid award from the total cost of attendance. That number is the net cost, or what it will cost you to attend that college.			
a) Total cost of attendance			
b) Total financial aid award			
c) Net cost to attend (a minus b)			

Figure 13:
Sample Financial Aid Award Letter 1

Blue University   Cost of Attendance: $ 28,706.00

CLASS: 01

March 22, 2006

TENTATIVE
FINANCIAL AWARD NOTIFICATION FOR 2006-2007

Based on the information that you submitted on your FAFSA and to our office, **Blue University** can offer you the following TENTATIVE awards.

This package is based on an award period from 09/10/06 to 06/06/07.

AID AWARD	ACCEPT AWARD		OFFERED AMOUNT
	Yes	NO	
FEDERAL PERKINS LOAN	_____	_____	$1,143
STATE WORK-STUDY	_____	_____	$2,400
BLUE EDUCATIONAL GRANT	_____	_____	$3,538
UNIVERSITY SCHOLARSHIP	_____	_____	$2,000
RESIDENCE HALL GRANT	_____	_____	$2,000
FEDERAL STAFFORD LOAN – SUB.	_____	_____	$2,625

Finalize your financial aid award as soon as possible by forwarding to our office the forms listed on the Missing Documents Form included with this letter.

Please read the important information pamphlet! Indicate your intent by checking whether or not you accept each aid award, then sign and return this letter in order to reserve your award(s).

Please refer to the Cost Worksheet to help determine your expenses for the academic year.

If direct loan amounts desired are less than above, please indicate below:

    Requested Federal Stafford Loan (Sub.) $ _____
    Requested Federal Perkins Loan $ _____

I acknowledge that I have read and will comply with all the supporting information in the Important Information Pamphlet. Furthermore, if I receive any financial assistance not included in this award letter, including tuition waivers or employer reimbursement, I will notify your office immediately.

Signature _____   Date _____

Figure 14:
Sample Financial Aid Award Letter 2

Green University | Office of Student Financial Planning

Cost of Attendance: $ 26,005.00

March 1, 2006

Step 1. Circle A for Accept or D for Decline for each individual award where indicated below:

	Fall 2006	Spring 2007	Total	A / D
Presidential Freshman Scholarship	$3,250	$3,250	$6,500	A / D
Green University Grant	$705	$705	$1,410	A / D
Total Grants and Scholarships			**$7,910**	
Federal Unsubsidized Stafford Loan	$1,313	$1,312	$2,625	A / D
Total Student Loans			**$2,625**	
Federal College Work-Study	$330	$330	$660	A / D
Federal PLUS Loan and/or Green Partnership Loan	$7,405	$7,405	$14,810	

Step 2. Please note the following:

Your awards are based on full-time enrollment for the fall and spring terms and residence hall occupancy for the fall and spring terms (for financial aid purposes, full-time is defined as 12 credits or more per term).

You have been offered loan(s) that require separate loan materials.

The amount of your Green University Grant was based upon residence hall occupancy for the fall and spring terms. A change in housing status may result in a reduction of this award.

Step 3. Please list other financial assistance, scholarships, or loans you will receive not indicated above. List the scholarship/donor name and the expected amount (example: Elks Club $100).

Name	Amount

Step 4. Attention: Your awards are not final until you complete the items on the ACTION REQUESTED page.

2006-2007 FAFSA ON THE WEB WORKSHEET
WWW.FAFSA.ED.GOV

DO NOT MAIL THIS WORKSHEET.

You must complete and submit a *Free Application for Federal Student Aid* (FAFSA) to apply for federal student financial aid and to apply for most state and college aid. Applying online with *FAFSA on the Web* at www.fafsa.ed.gov is faster and easier than using a paper FAFSA.

For state or college aid, the deadline may be as early as January 2006. See the table to the right for state deadlines. Check with your high school counselor or your college's financial aid administrator about other deadlines.

- Complete this Worksheet only if you plan to use *FAFSA on the Web* to apply for student financial aid.
- Sections in grey require parent information.
- Submit your FAFSA early, but not before January 1, 2006.

Apply Faster—Sign your FAFSA with a U.S. Department of Education PIN. If you do not have a PIN, you can apply for one at www.pin.ed.gov before beginning *FAFSA on the Web*. You will receive your PIN within a few days, and then you can electronically sign your FAFSA when you submit your information. If you are providing parent information, one parent must sign your FAFSA. To sign electronically, your parent can also apply for a PIN at www.pin.ed.gov.

You will need the following information to complete this Worksheet:

- ❑ Your Social Security Number and your parents' Social Security Numbers if you are providing parent information;
- ❑ Your driver's license number if you have one;
- ❑ Your Alien Registration Number if you are not a U.S. citizen;
- ❑ 2005 federal tax information or tax returns (including IRS W-2 information) for yourself and spouse if you are married, and for your parents if you are providing parent information. If you have not yet filed a 2005 income tax return, you can still submit your FAFSA but you must provide income and tax information.
- ❑ Records of untaxed income, such as Social Security benefits, welfare benefits (e.g., TANF), and veterans benefits, for yourself, and your parents if you are providing parent information; and
- ❑ Information on savings, investments, and business and farm assets for yourself, and your parents if you are providing parent information.

WARNING!	**NOTE:**
Be wary of organizations that charge a fee to submit your application or to find you money for school. In general, the help you pay for can be obtained for free from your school or from the U.S. Department of Education.	If you or your family has unusual circumstances (such as loss of employment), complete FAFSA on the Web to the extent you can, then submit the application and consult the financial aid office at the college you plan to attend.

STATE AID DEADLINES

	AK	April 15, 2006 *(date received)*
	AR	For Academic Challenge - June 1, 2006 *(date received)*. For Workforce Grant - check with your financial aid administrator
	AZ	June 30, 2007 *(date received)*
*	CA	For initial awards - March 2, 2006 For additional community college awards - September 2, 2006 *(date postmarked)*
*	DC	June 30, 2006 *(date received by state)*
	DE	April 15, 2006 *(date received)*
	FL	May 15, 2006 *(date processed)*
	IA	July 1, 2006 *(date received)*
#	IL	First-time applicants - September 30, 2006 Continuing applicants - August 15, 2006 *(date received)*
	IN	March 10, 2006 *(date received)*
#*	KS	April 1, 2006 *(date received)*
#	KY	March 15, 2006 *(date received)*
#	LA	May 1, 2006 Final deadline - July 1, 2006 *(date received)*
#	MA	May 1, 2006 *(date received)*
	MD	March 1, 2006 *(date received)*
	ME	May 1, 2006 *(date received)*
	MI	March 1, 2006 *(date received)*
	MN	30 days after term starts *(date received)*
	MO	April 1, 2006 *(date received)*
#	MT	March 1, 2006 *(date received)*
	NC	March 15, 2006 *(date received)*
	ND	March 15, 2006 *(date received)*
	NH	May 1, 2006 *(date received)*
	NJ	June 1, 2006, if you received a Tuition Aid Grant in 2005-2006 All other applicants - October 1, 2006, for fall and spring terms; March 1, 2007, for spring term only *(date received)*
*	NY	May 1, 2007 *(date received)*
	OH	October 1, 2006 *(date received)*
#	OK	April 15, 2006 Final deadline - June 30, 2006 *(date received)*
#	OR	March 1, 2006 *(date received)*. Final deadline - contact your financial aid administrator
*	PA	All 2005-2006 State Grant recipients & all non-2005-2006 State Grant recipients in degree programs – May 1, 2006 All other applicants – August 1, 2006 *(date received)*
#	RI	March 1, 2006 *(date received)*
	SC	June 30, 2006 *(date received)*
	TN	For State Grant - May 1, 2006 For State Lottery–September 1, 2006 *(date received)*
*	WV	March 1, 2006 *(date received)*

For priority consideration, submit application by date specified.
* Additional form may be required.

Check with the school's financial aid administrator for these states and territories: AL, *AS, CO, *CT, *FM, GA, *GU, *HI, ID, *MH, *MP, MS, *NE, *NM, *NV, PR, *PW, *SD, *TX, UT, *VA, *VI, *VT, WA, WI, and *WY

2006-2007 FAFSA on the Web Worksheet **127**

SECTION 1 – STUDENT INFORMATION

- *Use of this Worksheet is optional. It should not be submitted to the U.S. Department of Education or to your school.*
- *Not all of the questions from FAFSA on the Web appear in this Worksheet, but questions are generally ordered as they appear online.*
- *Once you are online, you may be able to skip some questions based on your answers to earlier questions.*

Your last name

Your state of legal residence

Your Social Security Number

Your driver's license number (optional)

Are you a U.S. citizen?

If you are neither a citizen nor an eligible noncitizen, you are not eligible for federal student aid. However, you should still complete the application, because you may be eligible for state or college aid.

If you are in the U.S. on an F1 or F2 student visa, or a J1 or J2 exchange visitor visa, or a G series visa (pertaining to international organizations), you must answer "Neither citizen nor eligible noncitizen."

❏ U.S. citizen

❏ Eligible noncitizen

Generally you are an eligible noncitizen if you are:
- A U.S. permanent resident with a Permanent Resident Card (I-551);
- A conditional permanent resident (I-551C); or
- The holder of an Arrival-Departure Record (I-94) from the Department of Homeland Security showing any of the following designations: "Refugee," "Asylum Granted," "Parolee" (I-94 confirms paroled for a minimum of one year and status has not expired), or "Cuban-Haitian Entrant."

❏ Neither citizen nor eligible noncitizen

Your Alien Registration Number

If you are an eligible noncitizen, enter your eight- or nine-digit Alien Registration Number.

A [ ][ ][ ][ ][ ][ ][ ][ ][ ]

Your marital status as of today

"As of today" refers to the day that you complete your FAFSA online.

❏ Single, divorced, or widowed
❏ Married/remarried   ❏ Separated

Month and year you were married, separated, divorced or widowed
(Example: Month and year: 05/1995)

M M Y Y Y Y

Did you become a legal resident of your state before January 1, 2001?

❏ Yes   ❏ No

If "No," when did you become a legal resident of your state?
(Example: Month and year: 05/1995)

M M Y Y Y Y

Most male students must register with the Selective Service System to get federal aid. If you are a male between the ages of 18 and 25 and **NOT** already registered with Selective Service, answer "Yes" and Selective Service will register you.

❏ Yes   ❏ No

What degree or certificate will you be working on during 2006-2007?

❏ 1st bachelor's degree
❏ 2nd bachelor's degree
❏ Associate degree—occupational/technical program
❏ Associate degree—general education or transfer program
❏ Certificate or diploma for completing an occupational, technical, or educational program of less than two years
❏ Certificate or diploma for completing an occupational, technical, or educational program of at least two years
❏ Teaching credential—nondegree program
❏ Graduate or professional degree
❏ Other/Undecided

What will be your grade level when you begin the 2006-2007 school year?

❏ 1st year/never attended college
❏ 1st year/attended college before
❏ 2nd year/sophomore
❏ 3rd year/junior
❏ 4th year/senior
❏ 5th year/other undergraduate
❏ 1st year graduate/professional
❏ Continuing graduate/professional or beyond

PART II: TABLES AND WORKSHEETS

SECTION 1 (CONTINUED) – STUDENT INFORMATION

Will you have your first bachelor's degree by July 1, 2006?	❏ Yes ❏ No
In addition to grants, would you like to be considered for student loans, which you must pay back?	❏ Yes ❏ No
Are you interested in work-study employment that is arranged or sponsored by the school you plan to attend?	❏ Yes ❏ No
Highest school your father completed Some states and schools offer aid based upon the level of schooling your parents have completed.	❏ Middle school/Jr. High ❏ High school ❏ College or beyond ❏ Other/unknown
Highest school your mother completed Some states and schools offer aid based upon the level of schooling your parents have completed.	❏ Middle school/Jr. High ❏ High school ❏ College or beyond ❏ Other/unknown
Have you ever been convicted of possessing or selling illegal drugs? A federal law suspends eligibility for some students with drug convictions. Answer "No" if you have no convictions. Also answer "No" if you have a conviction that was not a federal or state conviction. Do not count convictions that have been removed from your record, or that occurred before you turned 18 years old unless you were tried as an adult. If "Yes," you can complete an interactive worksheet when you complete the FAFSA online, or you can print a worksheet at www.fafsa.ed.gov/q31wksht67.pdf. Based on the worksheet questions, you will be able to answer whether you are eligible for federal aid when you complete your FAFSA online.	❏ Yes If you have a conviction for possessing or selling illegal drugs, you should submit your FAFSA anyway. You may be eligible for non-federal student aid from state or private sources. ❏ No

SECTION 2 – STUDENT STATUS

For federal student aid purposes, you must provide parent information if you answer "NO" to ALL of the following questions. If you answer "YES" to ANY of the following questions, you do not have to provide parent information.

Were you born before January 1, 1983?	❏ Yes ❏ No
At the beginning of the 2006-2007 school year, will you be working on a master's or doctorate program (such as an MA, MBA, MD, JD, PhD, EdD, or graduate certificate, etc.)?	❏ Yes ❏ No
As of today, are you married? (Answer "Yes" if you are separated but not divorced.) "As of today" refers to the day that you complete your FAFSA online.	❏ Yes ❏ No
Do you have children who receive more than half of their support from you?	❏ Yes ❏ No
Do you have dependents other than your children/spouse who live with you and who receive more than half of their support from you, now and through June 30, 2007?	❏ Yes ❏ No
Are (a) both of your parents deceased, or (b) are you (or were you until age 18) a ward/dependent of the court?	❏ Yes ❏ No
Are you a veteran of the U.S. Armed Forces? Answer "No," you are not a veteran, if you (1) have never engaged in active duty in the U.S. Armed Forces, (2) are currently an ROTC student or a cadet or midshipman at a service academy, or (3) are a National Guard or Reserves enlistee activated only for training. Also answer "No" if you are currently serving in the U.S. Armed Forces and will continue to serve through June 30, 2007. Answer "Yes," you are a veteran, if you (1) have engaged in active duty in the U.S. Armed Forces (Army, Navy, Air Force, Marines, or Coast Guard) or are a National Guard or Reserves enlistee who was called to active duty for purposes other than training, or were a cadet or midshipman at one of the service academies, and (2) were released under a condition other than dishonorable. Also answer "Yes" if you are not a veteran now but will be by June 30, 2007.	❏ Yes ❏ No

SECTION 3 – STUDENT FINANCES

- *Answer these questions as of the date you will submit your FAFSA.*
- *This section asks about your income. Refer to your IRS tax return when necessary.*
- *If you filed a foreign tax return, convert all figures to U.S. dollars, using the exchange rate. To view the daily exchange rates, go to www.federalreserve.gov/releases/h10/update.*
- *If you are married as of today, report your and your spouse's income, even if you were not married in 2005. Ignore references to spouse if you are single, divorced, separated or widowed.*

Have you completed a 2005 IRS income tax return or other income tax return?	❑ Already completed ❑ Will file ❑ Will not file
What income tax return did you file or will you file for 2005?	❑ IRS 1040 ❑ IRS 1040A or 1040EZ ❑ A foreign tax return ❑ A tax return for a U.S. Territory or a Freely Associated State
If you filed or will file a 1040, were you eligible to file a 1040A or 1040EZ? In general, you are eligible to file a 1040A or 1040EZ if you make less than $100,000, do not itemize deductions, do not receive income from your business or farm, and do not receive alimony. You are not eligible if you itemize deductions, receive self-employment income or alimony, or are required to file Schedule D for capital gains. If you filed a 1040 only to claim Hope or Lifetime Learning tax credits, and you would otherwise have been eligible for a 1040A or 1040EZ, you should answer "Yes."	❑ Yes ❑ No ❑ Don't know

If you are providing parent information, you will see several parent questions on the Web at this point. Then you will be asked the following questions.

What was your (and your spouse's) adjusted gross income for 2005? Adjusted gross income is on IRS Form 1040—line 37; 1040A—line 21; or 1040EZ—line 4.	$
What was your (and your spouse's) income tax for 2005? Income tax amount is on IRS Form 1040—line 57; 1040A—line 36; or 1040EZ—line 10.	$
Enter your (and your spouse's) exemptions for 2005. Exemptions are on IRS Form 1040—line 6d or 1040A—line 6d. On the 1040EZ, if a person checked either the "you" or "spouse" box on line 5, use EZ worksheet line E to determine the number of exemptions ($3,200 equals one exemption). If a person didn't check either box on line 5, enter 01 if he or she is single, or 02 if he or she is married.	
How much did you (and your spouse) earn from working (wages, salaries, tips, combat pay, etc.) in 2005? Answer this question whether or not you filed a tax return. This information may be on your W-2 forms or on IRS Form 1040—lines 7+12+18; 1040A—line 7; or 1040EZ—line 1.	Student $ Spouse $

SECTION 4 – STUDENT HOUSEHOLD

- *If you answered "NO" to ALL the questions in Section 2, skip this section and go to Section 5.*
- *If you answered "YES" to ANY question in Section 2, complete this section and then go to Section 6.*

How many people are in your household?
Include in your household: (1) yourself (and your spouse, if you are married), (2) your children, if you will provide more than half of their support from July 1, 2006 through June 30, 2007, and (3) other people if they now live with you, you provide more than half of their support, and you will continue to provide more than half of their support from July 1, 2006 through June 30, 2007.

How many people in the question above will be college students in 2006-2007?
Always count yourself. Do not include your parents. Include others only if they will attend college at least half time in 2006-2007 in a program that leads to a college degree or certificate.

SECTION 5 – PARENT FINANCES

- If you answered "YES" to ANY question in Section 2, skip this section and go to Section 6.
- If you answered "NO" to all the questions in Section 2, you must complete this section even if you do not live with your parents. Refer to your parents' IRS tax return when necessary.
  - Answer these questions as of the date you will submit your FAFSA.
  - Grandparents, legal guardians, and foster parents are not considered parents for this section.
  - If both of your parents are living and married to each other, answer the questions about them.
  - If your parent is widowed or single, answer the questions about that parent. If your widowed parent is remarried as of today, answer the questions about that parent and the person to whom your parent is married (your stepparent).
  - If your parents are divorced or separated, answer the questions about the parent you lived with more during the past 12 months. If you did not live with one parent more than the other, give answers about the parent who provided more financial support during the past 12 months, or during the most recent year that you actually received support from a parent. If this parent is remarried as of today, answer the questions about that parent and the person to whom your parent is married (your stepparent).

What is your parents' marital status as of today?
"As of today" refers to the day that you submit your FAFSA online.

❏ Married/remarried
❏ Single
❏ Divorced/separated
❏ Widowed

Month and year your parents were married, separated, divorced, or widowed
(Example: Month and year: 05/1995)

| M | M | Y | Y | Y | Y |

Have your parents completed a 2005 IRS income tax return or other income tax return?

❏ Already completed
❏ Will file
❏ Will not file

What income tax return did your parents file or will they file for 2005?

❏ IRS 1040
❏ IRS 1040A, 1040EZ
❏ A foreign tax return
❏ A tax return for a U.S. Territory or a Freely Associated State

If your parents have filed or will file a 1040, were they eligible to file a 1040A or 1040EZ?

In general, a person is eligible to file a 1040A or 1040EZ if he or she makes less than $100,000, does not itemize deductions, does not receive income from his or her business or farm, and does not receive alimony. You are not eligible if you itemize deductions, receive self-employment income or alimony, or are required to file Schedule D for capital gains. If you filed a 1040 only to claim Hope or Lifetime Learning tax credits, and would have otherwise been eligible for a 1040A or 1040EZ, you should answer "Yes."

❏ Yes
❏ No
❏ Don't know

What was your parents' adjusted gross income for 2005?
Adjusted gross income is on IRS form 1040—line 37; 1040A—line 21; or 1040EZ—line 4.

$ _____

How much did your parents earn from working (wages, salaries, tips, combat pay etc.) in 2005? Answer this question whether or not your parents filed a tax return. This information may be on their W-2 forms, or on IRS Form 1040—lines 7+12+18; 1040A—line 7; or 1040EZ—line 1.

Father/Stepfather $ _____
Mother/Stepmother $ _____

SECTION 6 – STUDENT FAFSA WORKSHEETS A, B AND C

Complete the Worksheets on page 8 to answer the questions below.

Your amount from FAFSA Worksheet A $ _____
Your amount from FAFSA Worksheet B $ _____
Your amount from FAFSA Worksheet C $ _____

SECTION 6 (CONTINUED) – STUDENT ASSETS AND VETERANS' BENEFITS

- *Answer these questions as of the date you will submit your FAFSA.*
- *Investments include real estate (do not include the home you live in), trust funds, money market funds, mutual funds, certificates of deposit, stocks, stock options, bonds, other securities, Coverdell savings accounts, college savings plans, installment and land sale contracts (including mortgages held), commodities, etc. Investment value includes the market value of these investments as of today. Investment debt means only those debts that are related to the investments.*
- *Investments do not include the home you live in; the value of life insurance, retirement plans (pension funds, annuities, noneducation IRAs, Keogh plans, etc.), and prepaid tuition plans; or cash, savings, and checking accounts.*
- *Business and/or investment farm value includes the market value of land, buildings, machinery, equipment, inventory, etc. Business and/or investment farm debt means only those debts for which the business or investment farm was used as collateral.*

As of today, what is your (and your spouse's) total current balance of cash, savings and checking accounts?	$
As of today, what is the net worth of your (and your spouse's) investments, including real estate (not your home)? Net worth means current value minus debt.	$
As of today, what is the net worth of your (and your spouse's) business and/or investment farms? Do not include a farm that a student lives on and operates. Net worth means current value minus debt.	$
If you receive veterans' education benefits, for how many months from July 1, 2006 through June 30, 2007 will you receive these benefits? Use 01 to 12.	
What is the amount of your monthly veterans' education benefits?	$

SECTION 7 – PARENT INFORMATION

- If you answered "NO" to ALL the questions in Section 2, complete this section and then go to Section 8.
- If you answered "YES" to ANY of the questions in Section 2, skip this section and go on to Section 8.

What is your parents' e-mail address? (optional)	
What is your father's (or stepfather's) Social Security Number?	
What is your father's (or stepfather's) last name?	
What is your father's (or stepfather's) date of birth? (Example: Month, day and year: 05/07/1959)	M M D D Y Y Y Y
What is your mother's (or stepmother's) Social Security Number?	
What is your mother's (or stepmother's) last name?	
What is your mother's (or stepmother's) date of birth? (Example: Month, day and year: 05/07/1959)	M M D D Y Y Y Y
How many people are in your parents' household? Include in your parents' household: (1) your parents and yourself, even if you don't live with your parents, (2) your parents' other children if (a) your parents will provide more than half of their support from July 1, 2006 through June 30, 2007, or (b) the children could answer "No" to every question in Section 2 of this worksheet, and (3) include other people only if they live with your parents, your parents provide more than half of their support, and your parents will continue to provide more than half of their support from July 1, 2006 through June 30, 2007.	
How many people in the question above will be college students in 2006-2007? Always count yourself. **Do not include your parents.** Include others only if they will attend college at least half time in 2006-2007 in a program that leads to a college degree or certificate.	

SECTION 7 (CONTINUED) – PARENT INFORMATION

What is your parents' state of legal residence?

Did your parents become legal residents of the state before January 1, 2001? ☐ Yes ☐ No

If "No," give month and year legal residency began for the parent who has lived in the state the longest. (Example: Month and year: 05/1995)

M M Y Y Y Y

What was the amount your parents paid in income tax for 2005?
Income tax amount is on IRS Form 1040—line 57; 1040A—line 36; or 1040EZ—line 10.

$

Enter your parents' exemptions for 2005.
Exemptions are on IRS Form 1040—line 6d or 1040A—line 6d. On the 1040EZ, if a person checked either the "you" or "spouse" box on line 5, use EZ worksheet line E to determine the number of exemptions ($3,200 equals one exemption). If a person didn't check either box on line 5, enter 01 if he or she is single, or 02 if he or she is married.

Parent FAFSA Worksheets A, B and C. Complete the Worksheets on page 8 to answer the questions below.

Your parents' amount from FAFSA Worksheet A — $
Your parents' amount from FAFSA Worksheet B — $
Your parents' amount from FAFSA Worksheet C — $

Parent Asset Information (See instructions on reporting assets, top of page 6)

As of today, what is your parents' total current balance in cash, savings, and checking accounts? — $

As of today, what is the net worth of your parents' investments, including real estate (not their home)? Net worth means current value minus debt. — $

As of today, what is the net worth of your parents' business and/or investment farms? Do not include a farm that your parents live on and operate. Net worth means current value minus debt. — $

SECTION 8 – SCHOOLS TO RECEIVE INFORMATION

	1st school code	2nd school code	3rd school code	4th school code	5th school code	6th school code
Federal School Codes If you do not know the school code, write the school's name. You will have a chance online to search for the school code.						
For each school code, indicate the corresponding housing plan.	1st school code ☐ on campus ☐ off campus ☐ with parent	2nd school code ☐ on campus ☐ off campus ☐ with parent	3rd school code ☐ on campus ☐ off campus ☐ with parent	4th school code ☐ on campus ☐ off campus ☐ with parent	5th school code ☐ on campus ☐ off campus ☐ with parent	6th school code ☐ on campus ☐ off campus ☐ with parent

For the 2006-2007 academic year, please report your expected enrollment status (Enrollment definitions refer to undergraduate study).

☐ Full time—at least 12 credit hours in a term or 24 clock hours per week
☐ 3/4 time—at least 9 credit hours in a term or 18 clock hours per week
☐ Half time—at least 6 credit hours in a term or 12 clock hours per week
☐ Less than half time--fewer than 6 credit hours in a term or less than 12 clock hours per week
☐ Not sure

Go to www.fafsa.ed.gov and enter the information from this Worksheet.
Remember to apply for a PIN at www.pin.ed.gov.
Additional help is available online or you can call 1-800-4-FED-AID. TTY users may call 1-800-730-8913.
Visit www.studentaid.ed.gov for more information on federal student aid.
Talk with your school's financial aid office about other types of aid.

DO NOT MAIL THIS WORKSHEET.

FAFSA WORKSHEETS – CALENDAR YEAR 2005

These worksheets are solely for completing the FAFSA Worksheet questions,
on page 5 for the student and, on page 7 for the student's parents.

FAFSA Worksheet A—Report Annual Amounts

Student/Spouse For Page 5		Parents For Page 7
$	Earned income credit from IRS Form 1040—line 66a; 1040A—line 41a; or 1040EZ—line 8a	$
$	Additional child tax credit from IRS Form 1040—line 68 or 1040A—line 42	$
$	Welfare benefits, including Temporary Assistance for Needy Families (TANF). Do not include food stamps or subsidized housing.	$
$	Social Security benefits received, for all household members as reported in student's household size (or parents' household size), that were not taxed (such as SSI). Report benefits paid to parents in the parents' column, and benefits paid directly to student in the student/spouse column.	$
$ Enter in Worksheet A question on Page 5.		Enter in Worksheet A question on Page 7. $

FAFSA Worksheet B—Report Annual Amounts

Student/Spouse For Page 5		Parents For Page 7
$	Payments to tax-deferred pension and savings plans (paid directly or withheld from earnings), including, but not limited to, amounts reported on the W-2 Form in Boxes 12a through 12d, codes D, E, F, G, H, and S.	$
$	IRA deductions and payments to self-employed SEP, SIMPLE, and Keogh and other qualified plans from IRS Form 1040—line 28 + line 32 or 1040A—line 17	$
$	Child support you received for all children. Don't include foster care or adoption payments.	$
$	Tax exempt interest income from IRS Form 1040—line 8b or 1040A—line 8b	$
$	Foreign income exclusion from IRS Form 2555—line 43 or 2555EZ—line 18	$
$	Untaxed portions of IRA distributions from IRS Form 1040—lines (15a minus 15b) or 1040A—lines (11a minus 11b). Exclude rollovers. If negative, enter a zero here.	$
$	Untaxed portions of pensions from IRS Form 1040—lines (16a minus 16b) or 1040A—lines (12a minus 12b). Exclude rollovers. If negative, enter a zero here.	$
$	Credit for federal tax on special fuels from IRS Form 4136—line 15—nonfarmers only	$
$	Housing, food, and other living allowances paid to members of the military, clergy, and others (including cash payments and cash value of benefits)	$
$	Veterans' noneducation benefits such as Disability, Death Pension, or Dependency & Indemnity Compensation (DIC), and/or VA Educational Work-Study allowances	$
$	Other untaxed income not reported elsewhere on Worksheets A and B, such as workers' compensation, untaxed portions of railroad retirement benefits, Black Lung Benefits, disability, etc. Tax filers only: report combat pay not included in adjusted gross income. Don't include student aid, Workforce Investment Act educational benefits, combat pay if you are not a tax filer, or benefits from flexible spending arrangements, e.g., cafeteria plans.	$
$	Money received, or paid on your behalf (e.g., bills), not reported elsewhere on this form	XXXXXXXX
$ Enter in Worksheet B question on Page 5.		Enter in Worksheet B question on Page 7. $

FAFSA Worksheet C—Report Annual Amounts

Student/Spouse For Page 5		Parents For Page 7
$	Education credits (Hope and Lifetime Learning tax credits) from IRS Form 1040—line 50 or 1040A—line 31	$
$	Child support you paid because of divorce or separation or as a result of a legal requirement. Don't include support for children in your (or your parents') household.	$
$	Taxable earnings from need-based employment programs, such as Federal Work-Study and need-based employment portions of fellowships and assistantships.	$
$	Student grant and scholarship aid reported to the IRS in your (or your parents') adjusted gross income. Includes AmeriCorps benefits (awards, living allowances, and interest accrual payments), as well as grant or scholarship portions of fellowships and assistantships.	$
$ Enter in Worksheet C question on Page 5.		Enter in Worksheet C question on Page 7. $

Estimate Your EFC Under Federal Methodology

WORKSHEET 4A:
Estimate a Dependent Student's Expected Contribution

STUDENT'S INCOME	
1. Taxable income ("adjusted gross income" from IRS Form 1040)	$
2. Untaxed income/benefits	+
3. Taxable student aid	-
4. Total student's income (sum of lines 1 and 2, minus line 3)	=
Allowances	
5. U.S. income tax paid (from IRS Form 1040)	
6. State taxes paid (% from Table 8 x line 4)	+
7. F.I.C.A. (Table 2)	+
8. Income protection allowance	$2,550
9. Parents' negative available income offset (line 11 of parents' worksheet, if negative)	+
10. Total allowances (sum of lines 5–9)	=
11. Available income (line 4 minus line 10)	=
12. Available income assessment rate	x 0.50
13. Contribution from income (line 11 x line 12; if negative, enter $0)	=
Student's Assets*	
14. Cash, savings, and checking accounts	
15. Other real estate/investment equity	+
16. Business/nonfamily farm equity	+
17. Net assets (sum of lines 14–16)	=
18. Asset assessment rate	x 0.35
19. Contribution from assets (line 17 x line 18; if simple needs test or negative, enter $0)	=
Contribution**	
20. Total Student Contribution (sum of lines 13 and 19)	=

* For parents and students who file or are eligible to file an IRS 1040A or 1040EZ form or who are not required to file, no assets are included in the methodology if parents' taxable income is less than $50,000.

** Federal need analysis provides a variant for families with parent's AGI of $15,000 or less who file or who are eligible to file an IRS 1040A or 1040EZ form, or who are not required to file. In such cases, no contribution is expected.

WORKSHEET 4B:
Estimate the Parents' Expected Contribution

Parents' Income	
1. Taxable income ("adjusted gross income" from IRS Form 1040)	$
2. Untaxed income/benefits	+
3. Income exclusions (child support paid + education tax credits)	-
4. Total parents' income (sum of lines 1 and 2, minus line 3)	=
Allowances	
5. U.S. income tax paid (from IRS Form 1040)	
6. State taxes paid (% from Table 8 × line 4)	+
7. F.I.C.A. paid (Table 9)	+
8. Employment allowance (Table 9)	+
9. Income protection allowance (Table 10)	+
10. Total allowances (sum of lines 5–9)	=
11. Available income (line 4 minus line 10)	=
Parents' Assets*	
12. Cash, savings, and checking accounts	
13. Other real estate/investment equity	+
14. Adjusted business/nonfamily farm equity (Table 11)	+
15. Net worth (sum of lines 12–14)	=
16. Education Savings and Asset protection allowance (Table 12)	-
17. Discretionary net worth (line 15 minus line 16)	=
18. Conversion percentage	× 12%
19. Contribution from assets (line 17 × line 18; if simple needs test or negative, enter $0)	=
20. Adjusted available income (sum of line 11 and line 19)	=
Contribution**	
21. Total contribution (calculate using line 20 and Table 13)	=
22. Number of dependent children in college at least half-time	÷
23. Parents' contribution for student (line 21 divided by line 22; if negative, enter $0)	=

* For parents and students who file or are eligible to file an IRS 1040A or 1040EZ form or who are not required to file, no assets are included in the methodology if parents' taxable income is less than $50,000.

** Federal need-analysis provisions provide a variant for families with parent's AGI of $15,000 or less who file or who are eligible to file an IRS 1040A or 1040EZ form, or who are not required to file. In such cases, no contribution is expected.

Worksheet 4: Estimate Your EFC Under Federal Methodology

TABLE 8: Federal EFC Allowances for State Taxes

	Parents TOTAL INCOME		Student TOTAL INCOME		Parents TOTAL INCOME		Student TOTAL INCOME
	$ 0–15,000	$15,001 or more	Any amount		$ 0–15,000	$15,001 or more	Any amount
Alabama*(AL)	3%	2%	2%	North Dakota*(ND)	2	1	1
Alaska*(AK)	2	1	0	Northern Mariana Islands*(MP)	3	2	2
American Samoa (AS)	3	2	2	Ohio*(OH)	6	5	4
Arizona*(AZ)	4	3	2	Oklahoma*(OK)	4	3	3
Arkansas*(AR)	3	2	3	Oregon*(OR)	7	6	5
California*(CA)	7	6	5	Palau*(PW)	3	2	2
Canada*(CN)	3	2	2	Pennsylvania*(PA)	5	4	3
Colorado*(CO)	4	3	3	Puerto Rico*(PR)	3	2	2
Connecticut*(CT)	7	6	4	Rhode Island*(RI)	7	6	4
Delaware*(DE)	4	3	3	South Carolina*(SC)	5	4	3
District of Columbia*(DC)	7	6	6	South Dakota*(SD)	1	0	0
Federated States of Micronesia*(FM)	3	2	2	Tennessee*(TN)	1	0	0
Florida*(FL)	2	1	0	Texas*(TX)	2	1	0
Georgia*(GA)	5	4	3	Utah*(UT)	5	4	4
Guam*(GU)	3	2	2	Vermont*(VT)	6	5	3
Hawaii*(HI)	4	3	4	Virgin Islands*(VI)	3	2	2
Idaho*(ID)	5	4	3	Virginia*(VA)	5	4	3
Illinois*(IL)	5	4	2	Washington*(WA)	2	1	0
Indiana*(IN)	4	3	3	West Virginia*(WV)	3	2	2
Iowa*(IA)	5	4	3	Wisconsin*(WI)	7	6	4
Kansas*(KS)	5	4	3	Wyoming*(WY)	1	0	0
Kentucky*(KY)	5	4	4	Not Reported*(NR)	3	2	2
Louisiana*(LA)	2	1	2				
Maine*(ME)	6	5	4				
Marshall Islands*(MH)	3	2	2				
Maryland*(MD)	7	6	5				
Massachusetts*(MA)	6	5	4				
Mexico*(MX)	3	2	2				
Michigan*(MI)	5	4	3				
Minnesota*(MN)	6	5	4				
Mississippi	3	2	2				
Missouri*(MO)	4	3	3				
Montana*(MT)	5	4	3				
Nebraska*(NE)	5	4	3				
Nevada*(NV)	2	1	1				
New Hampshire*(NH)	4	3	1				
New Jersey*(NJ)	8	7	4				
New Mexico*(NM)	4	3	3				
New York*(NY)	8	7	5				
North Carolina*(NC)	6	5	4				

PART II: TABLES AND WORKSHEETS

Worksheet 4: Estimate Your EFC Under Federal Methodology

TABLE 9. Federal EFC Allowances for FICA and Employment

FICA: WAGES

$1 to $90,000	7.65% of income earned by each wage earner (maximum $6,885.00 per person)
$90,001 or more	$6,885.00+ 1.45% of income earned above $90,900 by each wage earner
EMPLOYMENT ALLOWANCE	35% of lesser earned income to a maximum $3,100 (single parent: 35% of earned income to a maximum of $3,100)

TABLE 10. Federal EFC Income Protection Allowance for Parents

Family Size* (including student)	Number in College**				
	1	2	3	4	5
2	$ 14,430	$ 11,960			
3	17,970	15,520	$ 13,050		
4	22,200	19,730	17,270	$ 14,800	
5	26,190	23,720	21,270	18,800	$ 16,340
6	30,640	28,170	25,710	23,240	20,790

*For each additional family member, add $3,460.
**For each additional college student, subtract $2,460.

TABLE 11. Federal EFC Adjusted Net Worth of a Business or Farm

NET WORTH	ADJUSTED NET WORTH		
Less than $1	$ 0		
$1 to 105,000	$ 0	+	40% of net worth
$105,001 to 310,000	$ 42,000	+	50% of net worth over $105,000
$310,001 to 515,000	$ 144,500	+	60% of net worth over $310,000
$515,001 or more	$ 267,500	+	100% of net worth over $515,000

TABLE 12. Federal EFC Education Savings and Asset Protection Allowance for Parents

AGE OF OLDER PARENT OR STUDENT	COUPLE/ MARRIED	UNMARRIED/ SINGLE
25 or under	$0	$0
26	2,600	1,200
27	5,200	2,400
28	7,800	3,600
29	10,500	4,800
30	13,100	6,000
31	15,700	7,200
32	18,300	8,400
33	20,900	9,600
34	23,500	10,800
35	26,100	12,000
36	28,700	13,200
37	31,400	14,400
38	34,000	15,600
39	36,600	16,800
40	39,200	18,000
41	40,200	18,400
42	41,200	18,800
43	42,200	19,200
44	43,200	19,700
45	44,300	20,100
46	45,400	20,600
47	46,600	21,000
48	47,700	21,500
49	48,900	22,100
50	50,100	22,600
51	51,600	23,000
52	52,900	23,600
53	54,500	24,100
54	55,800	24,800
55	57,500	25,400
56	58,900	26,000
57	60,600	26,600
58	62,400	27,400
59	64,200	28,000
60	66,100	28,800
61	68,000	29,500
62	70,000	30,300
63	72,300	31,100
64	74,400	32,000
65 or over	76,900	32,900

TABLE 13. Federal EFC Parents' Contribution from Adjusted Available Income (AAI)

ADJUSTED AVAILABLE INCOME (AAI)	TOTAL CONTRIBUTIONS FROM INCOME
Less than $-3,409 (3,409)	$ -750
$(3,409) to 12,900	22% of AI
$12,901 to 16,200	$2,838 + 25% of AI over $12,900
$16,201 to 19,500	$3,663 + 29% of AI over $16,200
$19,501 to 22,800	$4,620 + 34% of AI over $19,500
$22,801 to 26,100	$5,742 + 40% of AI over $22,800
$26,101 or more	$7,062 + 47% of AI over $26,100

Contact Information for State Aid Programs

ALABAMA
Alabama Commission on Higher Education
P.O. Box 302000
100 North Union Street
Montgomery, AL 36130-2000
334 242-1998
www.ache.state.al.us

ALASKA
Alaska Commission on Postsecondary Education
3030 Vintage Boulevard
Juneau, AK 99801-7100
800 441-2962
www.state.ak.us/acpe

ARIZONA
Arizona Department of Education
1535 W. Jefferson Street
Phoenix, AZ 85007
800 352-4558
www.ade.state.az.us

ARKANSAS
Arkansas Department of Higher Education
114 East Capitol
Little Rock, AR 72201
501 371-2000
www.arkansashighered.com

CALIFORNIA
California Student Aid Commission
P.O. Box 419027
Rancho Cordova, CA 95741-9026
888 224-7268
www.csac.ca.gov

COLORADO
Colorado Department of Education
201 East Colfax Avenue
Denver, CO 80203-1799
303 866-6600
www.cde.state.co.us

CONNECTICUT
Connecticut Department of Higher Education
61 Woodland Street
Hartford, CT 06105-2326
860 947-1800
www.ctdhe.org

DELAWARE
Delaware Higher Education Commission
820 North French Street
Wilmington, DE 19801
800 292-7935
www.doe.state.de.us/high-ed

DISTRICT OF COLUMBIA
State Education Office
1350 Pennsylvania Avenue NW
Washington, DC 20004
202 698-2400
www.seo.dc.gov

FLORIDA
Florida Department of Education
Office of Student Financial Assistance
1940 N. Monroe Street, Suite 70
Tallahassee, FL 32303-4759
888 827-2004
www.firn.edu/doe

GEORGIA
Georgia Student Finance Commission
2082 East Exchange Place
Tucker, GA 30084
800 505-4732
www.gsfc.org

HAWAII
Hawaii State Department of Education
P.O. Box 2360
Honolulu, HI 96804
808 586-3230
www.doe.k12.hi.us

IDAHO
Idaho State Department of Education
P.O. Box 83720
650 West State Street
Boise, ID 83720-0027
208 332-6800
www.sde.state.id.us

ILLINOIS
Illinois Student Assistance Commission
1755 Lake Cook Road
Deerfield, IL 60015-5209
800 899-4722
www.collegezone.com

INDIANA
State Student Assistance Commission of Indiana
150 W. Market Street, Suite 500
Indianapolis, IN 46204
888 528-4719
www.in.gov/ssaci

IOWA
Iowa College Student Aid Commission
200 10th Street, Fourth Floor
Des Moines, IA 50309-2036
515 242-3344
www.iowacollegeaid.org

KANSAS
Kansas Board of Regents
1000 SW Jackson Street, Suite 520
Topeka, KS 66612-1368
785 296-3421
www.kansasregents.org

KENTUCKY
KHEAA Student Aid Branch
1050 U.S. 127 South
P.O. Box 798
Frankfort, KY 40602
800 928-8926
www.kheaa.com

LOUISIANA
Louisiana Office of Student Financial Assistance
P.O. Box 91202
Baton Rouge, LA 70821-9202
800 259-5626
www.osfa.state.la.us

MAINE
Finance Authority of Maine
Education Assistance Division
P.O. Box 949
5 Community Drive
Augusta, ME 04332
800 228-3734
www.famemaine.com

MARYLAND
Maryland Higher Education Commission
Office of Student Financial Assistance
839 Bestgate Road, Suite 400
Annapolis, MD 21401
800 974-0203
www.mhec.state.md.us

MASSACHUSETTS
Massachusetts Board of Higher Education
Office of Student Financial Assistance
454 Broadway, Suite 200
Revere, MA 02151-3034
617 727-9420
www.mass.edu

MICHIGAN
Michigan Higher Education Assistance Authority
Office of Scholarships and Grants
P.O. Box 30462
Lansing, MI 48909-7547
517 373-3394
www.michigan.gov/mistudentaid

MINNESOTA
Minnesota Higher Education Services Office
1450 Energy Park Drive, Suite 350
St. Paul, MN 55108-5227
651 642-0533
www.mheso.state.mn.us

MISSISSIPPI
Mississippi Office of State Student Financial Aid
3825 Ridgewood Road
Jackson, MS 39211-6453
800 327-2980
www.ihl.state.ms.us

MISSOURI
Missouri Department of Higher Education
3515 Amazonas Drive
Jefferson City, MO 65109-5717
573 751-2361
www.dhe.mo.gov

MONTANA
Montana Board of Regents
P.O. Box 203101
2500 Broadway
Helena, MT 59620-3101
406 444-6570
www.montana.edu/wwwbor

NEBRASKA
Nebraska Coordination Commission for
Postsecondary Education
P.O. Box 95005
Lincoln, NE 68509-5005
402 471-2847
www.ccpe.state.ne.us

NEVADA
Nevada Department of Education
Attn: Wendy Skibinski
700 East 5th Street
Carson City, NV 89701
775 687-9228
e-mail: wskibinski@doe.nv.gov

NEW HAMPSHIRE
New Hampshire Postsecondary Education Commission
3 Barrell Court, Suite 300
Concord, NH 03301-8543
603 271-2555
www.state.nh.us/postsecondary

NEW JERSEY
New Jersey Higher Education Student Assistance Authority
4 Quakerbridge Plaza
P.O. Box 540
Trenton, NJ 08625
800 792-8670
www.hesaa.org

NEW MEXICO
New Mexico Commission on Higher Education
1068 Cerillos Road
Santa Fe, NM 87505
505 476-6500
www.nmche.org

NEW YORK
New York State Higher Education Services Corporation
99 Washington Avenue
Albany, NY 12255
888 697-4372
www.hesc.state.ny.us

NORTH CAROLINA
North Carolina State Education Assistance Authority
P.O. Box 14103
Research Triangle Park, NC 27709
919 549-8614
www.ncseaa.edu

NORTH DAKOTA
North Dakota University System
600 East Boulevard, Dept. 215
Bismarck, ND 58505-0230
701 328-2960
www.ndus.nodak.edu

OHIO
Ohio Board of Regents
State Grants and Scholarships Department
P.O. Box 182452
Columbus, OH 43218
888 833-1133
www.regents.state.oh.us/sgs

OKLAHOMA
Oklahoma State Regents for Higher Education
Tuition Aid Grant Program
655 Research Parkway, Suite 200
Oklahoma City, OK 73104
405 225-9100
www.okhighered.org

OREGON
Oregon Student Assistance Commission
1500 Valley River Drive, Suite 100
Eugene, OR 97401
800 452-8807
www.ossc.state.or.us

PENNSYLVANIA
Pennsylvania Higher Education Assistance Agency
1200 N. Seventh Street
Harrisburg, PA 17102
800 692-7392
www.pheaa.org

PUERTO RICO
Departmento de Educacion
P.O. Box 190759
San Juan, PR 00919-0759
787 759-2000
www.de.gobierno.pr

RHODE ISLAND
Rhode Island Higher Education Assistance Authority
560 Jefferson Boulevard
Warwick, RI 02886
401 736-1100
www.riheaa.org

SOUTH CAROLINA
South Carolina Commission on Higher Education
1333 Main Street, Suite 200
Columbia, SC 29201
803 737-2260
www.che400.state.sc.us

SOUTH DAKOTA
South Dakota Department of Education
Office of Finance and Management
700 Governors Drive
Pierre, SD 57501
605 773-3248
www.state.sd.us/deca

TENNESSEE
Tennessee Student Assistance Corporation
404 James Robertson Parkway, Suite 1950
Nashville, TN 37243-0820
615 741-1346
www.state.tn.us/tsac

TEXAS
Texas Higher Education Coordinating Board
Division of Student Services
P.O. Box 12788, Capital Station
Austin, TX 78711
512 427-6101
www.collegefortexans.com

UTAH
Utah Higher Education Assistance Authority
Board of Regents Building, The Gateway
60 South 400 West
Salt Lake City, UT 84101-1284
801 321-7200
www.uheaa.org

VERMONT
Vermont Student Assistance Corporation
P.O. Box 2000
Winooski, VT 05404
802 655-9602
www.vsac.org

VIRGINIA
State Council of Higher Education for Virginia
101 North 14th Street
Richmond, VA 23219
804 225-2600
www.schev.edu

WASHINGTON
Washington Higher Education Coordination Board
917 Lakeridge Way
P.O. Box 43430
Olympia, WA 98504-3430
360 753-7800
www.hecb.wa.gov

WEST VIRGINIA
West Virginia Higher Education Policy Commission
Central Office, Higher Education Grant Program
1018 Kanawha Boulevard East, Suite 700
Charleston, WV 25301-2800
304 558-2101
www.hepc.wvnet.edu

WISCONSIN
Wisconsin Higher Educational Aids Board
131 West Wilson, Suite 902
Madison, WI 53707
608 267-2206
www.heab.state.wi.us

WYOMING
Wyoming Department of Education
2300 Capitol Avenue
Hathaway Building, Second Floor
Cheyenne, WY 82002
307 777-7673
www.k12.wy.us

GUAM
University of Guam
Student Financial Aid Office
UOG Station
Mangilao, GU 96923
671 735-2287
www.uog.edu

VIRGIN ISLANDS
Financial Aid Office, Virgin Islands Board of Education
P.O. Box 11900
St. Thomas, VI 00801
340 774-4546

Contact Information for State 529 Plans

STATE	PROGRAM NAME	CONTACT INFORMATION	PLAN TYPE
AK	University of Alaska College Savings Plan	University of Alaska 866 277-1005 http://www.uacollegesavings.com	Savings
	John Hancock, Inc.	https: www.johnhancockfreedom529.com	Savings
AL	Prepaid Affordable Tuition Plan (PACT)	State Treasurer 334 242-7500	Prepaid
	Van Kampen Investments	866 529-2228 http://www.treasury.state.al.us	Savings
AZ	Arizona Family College Savings Programs (AFCSP)	http://www.azhighered.org/college	Savings
	Arizona Family College Savings Programs	Securities Management and Research, Inc. 888 667-3239 http://www.smrinvest.com/College/default.asp	Savings
	InvestEd	Waddell & Reed's InvestEd Plan 888 923-3355 http://www2.waddell.com	Savings
AR	GIFT College Investing Plan	Franklin Templeton Investments/Mercury Advisors 877 615-4116 http://www.thegiftplan.com	Savings
CA	Golden State ScholarShare College Savings Trust	Golden State ScholarShare 877 728-4338 http://www.scholarshare.com	Savings
CO	CollegeInvest—Stable Value Plus College Savings Program	CollegeInvest 800 265-5343 http://www.collegeinvest.org	Savings
	CollegeInvest—Scholars Choice College Savings	Scholars Choice 888 265-5343 http://www.collegeinvest.org or http://www.scholars-choice.com	Savings
CT	Connecticut Higher Education Trust (CHET)	Connecticut's 529 College Savings Program 888 799-2438 http://www.aboutchet.com	Savings
DC	DC College Savings Plan	800 368-2745 or 800 987-4859 — D.C. residents http://www.dccollegesavings.com	Savings
DE	Delaware College Investment Plan	800 544-1655 http://www.fidelity.com/delaware	Savings
FL	Florida Prepaid College Program	Florida Prepaid College Program Board 800 552-4723 http://www.florida529plans.com	Prepaid
	Florida College Investment Plan	Florida Prepaid College Program Board 800 552-4723 http://www.florida529plans.com	Savings
GA	Georgia Higher Education Savings Plan	877 424-4377 http://www.gacollegesavings.com	Savings
HI	TuitionEDGE	Delaware Investments TuitionEDGE Plan 866 529-3343 http://www.tuitionedge.com	Savings
IA	College Savings Iowa	Iowa State Treasurer's Office 888 672-9116 http://www.collegesavingsiowa.com	Savings
ID	Idaho College Savings Program (IDeal)	866 433-2533 http://www.idsaves.org	Savings
IL	College Illinois!	877 877-3724 http://www.collegeillinois.com	Prepaid
	Bright Start Savings	877 432-7444 http://www.brightstartsavings.com	Savings
IN	CollegeChoice 529 Investment Plan	One Group Investments 866 400-7526 http://www.collegechoiceplan.com	Savings
KS	Kansas Learning Quest Education Savings	American Century 800 579-2203 http://www.learningquestsavings.com	Savings
KY	Kentucky's Affordable Prepaid Tuition (KAPT)	Kentucky Higher Education Assistance Authority 888 919-5278 http://www.getKAPT.com	Prepaid
	Kentucky Education Savings Plan Trust	Kentucky Higher Education Assistance Authority 877 598-7878 http://www.kentuckytrust.org	Savings
LA	Student Tuition Assistance and Revenue Trust (START)	Louisiana Office of Student Financial Assistance 800 259-5626 (x1012) http://www.osfa.state.la.us/START	Savings

STATE	PROGRAM NAME	CONTACT INFORMATION	PLAN TYPE
MA	The U Plan	Massachusetts Educational Finance Authority 800 449-6332 http://www.mefa.org	Prepaid
	The U Fund	Massachusetts Educational Finance Authority 800 449-6332 http://www.mefa.org	Savings
MD	Prepaid College Trust	College Savings Plans of Maryland 888 463-4723 http://www.collegesavingsmd.org	Prepaid
	College Investment Plan	College Savings Plans of Maryland 888 463-4723 http://www.collegesavingsmd.org	Savings
ME	NextGen College Investing Plan	Merrill Lynch 877 463-9843 http://www.nextgenplan.com	Savings
MI	Michigan Education Trust (MET)	Michigan Department of Treasury 800 638-4543 http://www.michigan.gov/treasury	Prepaid
	Michigan Education Savings Program (MESP)	Michigan Department of Treasury 877 861-6377 http://www.misaves.com	Savings
MN	Minnesota College Savings Plan	877 338-4646 http://www.mnsaves.org	Savings
MO	Missouri Savings for Tuition (MO$T)	888 414-6678 http://www.missourimost.org	Savings
MS	Mississippi Prepaid Affordable College Tuition Program (MPACT)	Mississippi State Treasury Department 800 987-4450 http://www.treasury.state.ms.us/mpact.htm	Prepaid
	Mississippi Affordable College Savings (MACS)	800 486-3670 http://www.collegesavingsms.com	Savings
MT	Montana Family Education Savings Program	http://montana.collegesavings.com	Savings
	CollegeSure 529	Montana Commission for Higher Education 800 888-2723 http://montana.collegesavings.com	Prepaid
	529 College Savings Plan	Pacific Funds 800 722-2333 http://www.pacificlife.com	Savings
NC	North Carolina's National College Savings Program	College Foundation of North Carolina 800 600-3453 http://www.cfnc.org/savings	Savings
	National College Savings Program	J. & W. Seligman & Co. Incorporated 800 221-7844 http://www.seligman529.com	Savings
ND	Morgan Stanley	866 728-3529 http://www.collegesave4U.com	Savings
NE	College Savings Plan of Nebraska	Nebraska State Treasurer 888 993-3746 http://www.planforcollegenow.com	Savings
	The AIM College Savings Plan	Nebraska State Treasurer 888 993-3746 or AIM College Savings Plan 866 246-0529 http://www.aiminvestments.com/home	Savings
	TD Waterhouse 529 College Savings Plan	877 408-4644 http://www.tdwaterhouse.com/planning/college	Savings
NH	Unique College Investing Plan	Fidelity Investments 800 544-1914 http://www.state.nh.us/treasury or http://www.fidelity.com/uniquex	Savings
NJ	New Jersey Better Educational Savings Trust (NJBEST)	Higher Education Student Assistance Authority 877 465-2378 http://www.njbest.com	Savings
NM	The Education Plan's College Savings Program	The Education Plan of New Mexico 800 499-7581 http://www.tepnm.com/education	Savings
	Scholar'sEdge	866 529-7283 http://www.scholarsedge529.com	Savings
	CollegeSense	866 529-7367 http://www.collegesense.com	Savings
	Arrive Education Savings Plan	877 277-4838 http://www.arrive529.com	Savings
NV	Prepaid Tuition Program	Nevada State Treasurer 888 477-2667 http://www.nevadatreasurer.com/college	Prepaid
	USAA College Savings Plan	800 292-8825 http://www.lc.usaa.com	Savings
	Vanguard 529 Savings Plan	866 734-4530 http://www.vanguard.com	Savings
NY	New York's 529 College Savings Program	Comptroller & Higher Ed. Services Corp. 877 697-2837 http://www.nysaves.uii.upromise.com	Savings

STATE	PROGRAM NAME	CONTACT INFORMATION	PLAN TYPE
OH	CollegeAdvantage Savings Plan	Ohio Tuition Trust Authority 800 233-6734 http://www.collegeadvantage.com	Savings
	Putnam CollegeAdvantage	Putnam Investments 800 225-1581 http://www.putnaminvestments.com/individual/index_529.html	Savings
OK	Oklahoma College Savings Plan	877 654-7284 http://www.ok4savings.org	Savings
OR	Oregon College Savings Plan	Oregon Qualified Tuition Savings Board 866 772-8464 http://www.oregoncollegesavings.com	Savings
PA	Tuition Account Program (TAP 529) – Guaranteed Savings Plan	Pennsylvania State Treasury 800 440-4000 http://www.patap.org	
	Tuition Account Program (TAP 529) – Investment Plan	Pennsylvania State Treasury 800 440-4000 http://www.patap.org	Savings
RI	CollegeBound Fund	AllianceBernstein 800 251-0539 http://www.collegeboundfund.com	Savings
SC	South Carolina Tuition Prepayment Program (SCTPP)	South Carolina Office of State Treasurer 888 772-4723 http://www.scgrad.org	Prepaid
	FUTURE Scholar	Nations Funds 888 244-5674 http://www.futurescholar.com	Savings
SD	CollegeAccess 529	Pimco Funds 866 529-7462 http://www.collegeaccess529.com	Savings
	Legg Mason Core4College 529 Plan	800 822-5544 http://www.leggmason.com	Savings
TN	BEST Prepaid College Tuition Plan	State of Tennessee Treasury Department 888 486-2378 www.treasury.state.tn.us/best	Savings
	BEST Savings Plan	State of Tennessee Treasury Department 888 486-2378 http://www.tnbest.org	Savings
TX	Texas Guaranteed Tuition Plan	Texas Comptroller of Public Accounts 800 445-4723 http://www.tgtp.org	Prepaid
	Tomorrow's College Investment Plan	Texas Comptroller of Public Accounts 800 445-4723 http://www.enterprise529.com	Savings
UT	Utah Educational Savings Plan Trust (UESP)	Utah State Board of Regents 800 418-2551 http://www.uesp.org	Savings
VA	Virginia Prepaid Education Program (VPEP)	Virginia College Savings Plan 888 567-0540 http://www.virginia529.com	Prepaid
	Virginia Education Savings Trust (VEST)	Virginia College Savings Plan 888 567-0540 http://www.virginia529.com	Savings
	CollegeAmerica	American Funds 800 421-4120 http://www.americanfunds.com	Savings
VT	Vermont Higher Education Investment Plan	Vermont Student Assistance Corporation 800 637-5860 http://www.vsac.org	Savings
WA	Guaranteed Education Tuition Program (GET)	Committee on Advanced Tuition Payment 877 438-8848 http://www.get.wa.gov	Prepaid
WI	EdVest	EdVest College Savings Program 888 338-3789 http://www.edvest.com	Savings
	Tomorrow's Scholar	Wells Fargo 866 677-6933 http://wellsfargoadvantage.com	Savings
WV	SMART529—College Savings Option	Hartford Life Insurance Co. 866 574-3542 http://www.smart529.com	Savings
WY	The 529 College Achievement Plan	Mercury Asset Management 877 529-2655 http://www.collegeachievementplan.com	Savings

Part III

Financial Aid College by College

Alabama

Alabama Agricultural and Mechanical University
Huntsville, Alabama
www.aamu.edu Federal Code: 001002

4-year public university and agricultural college in small city.
Enrollment: 5,047 undergrads, 8% part-time. 1,088 full-time freshmen.
Selectivity: GED not accepted.

BASIC COSTS (2005-2006)
Tuition and fees: $4,940; out-of-state residents $8,840.
Per-credit charge: $188; out-of-state residents $331.
Room and board: $3,592.
Additional info: Part-time student required fees are $350. Tuition/fee waivers available for minority students.

FINANCIAL AID PICTURE
Students with need: Need-based aid available for full-time and part-time students. Work study available weekends and for part-time students.
Students without need: No-need awards available for athletics, minority status.
Scholarships offered: Presidential scholarship for students with 4.0 GPA, pays tuition and fees.

FINANCIAL AID PROCEDURES
Forms required: FAFSA, institutional form.
Dates and Deadlines: Applicants notified on a rolling basis; must reply within 2 week(s) of notification.

CONTACT
Carlos Clark, Director of Financial Aid
Box 908, Normal, AL 35762
(256) 851-5400

Alabama State University
Montgomery, Alabama
www.alasu.edu Federal Code: 001005

4-year public university in small city.
Enrollment: 4,455 undergrads, 11% part-time. 1,213 full-time freshmen.
Selectivity: Admits 50 to 75% of applicants.

BASIC COSTS (2006-2007)
Tuition and fees: $4,008; out-of-state residents $8,016.
Per-credit charge: $167; out-of-state residents $334.
Room and board: $3,600.

FINANCIAL AID PICTURE (2005-2006)
Students with need: Out of 1,101 full-time freshmen who applied for aid, 1,016 were judged to have need. Of these, 981 received aid, and 130 had their full need met. Average financial aid package met 63% of need; average scholarship/grant was $3,644; average loan was $2,589. For part-time students, average financial aid package was $6,356.
Students without need: 21 full-time freshmen who did not demonstrate need for aid received scholarships/grants; average award was $4,751. No-need awards available for academics, art, athletics, minority status, music/drama, ROTC.
Scholarships offered: 45 full-time freshmen received athletic scholarships; average amount $8,980.
Cumulative student debt: 13% of graduating class had student loans; average debt was $21,150.

FINANCIAL AID PROCEDURES
Forms required: FAFSA.
Dates and Deadlines: Priority date 5/1; no closing date. Applicants notified on a rolling basis starting 6/1.
Transfers: Applicants notified on a rolling basis starting 5/1.

CONTACT
Dorenda Adams, Director of Financial Aid
PO Box 271, Montgomery, AL 36101-0271
(334) 229-4323

Athens State University
Athens, Alabama
www.athens.edu Federal Code: 001008

Upper-division public business and teachers college in large town.
Enrollment: 2,496 undergrads.

BASIC COSTS (2005-2006)
Tuition and fees: $3,870; out-of-state residents $7,200.
Per-credit charge: $111; out-of-state residents $222.

FINANCIAL AID PICTURE (2004-2005)
Students with need: 21% of average financial aid package awarded as scholarships/grants, 79% awarded as loans/jobs. Need-based aid available for part-time students. Work study available nights, weekends, and for part-time students.
Students without need: No-need awards available for academics, alumni affiliation, art, athletics, leadership, minority status.

FINANCIAL AID PROCEDURES
Forms required: FAFSA.
Dates and Deadlines: No deadline. Applicants notified on a rolling basis starting 6/1; must reply within 3 week(s) of notification.

CONTACT
Sarah McAbee, Director, Student Financial Services
300 North Beaty Street, Athens, AL 35611
(256) 233-8122

Auburn University
Auburn, Alabama
www.auburn.edu Federal Code: 001009

4-year public university in large town.
Enrollment: 19,222 undergrads, 8% part-time. 3,564 full-time freshmen.
Selectivity: Admits over 75% of applicants.

BASIC COSTS (2005-2006)
Tuition and fees: $5,278; out-of-state residents $14,878.
Room and board: $6,952.

FINANCIAL AID PICTURE (2004-2005)
Students with need: Out of 1,757 full-time freshmen who applied for aid, 1,212 were judged to have need. Of these, 1,124 received aid, and 187 had their full need met. Average financial aid package met 46% of need; average scholarship/grant was $4,417; average loan was $2,935. For part-time students, average financial aid package was $5,998.
Students without need: 302 full-time freshmen who did not demonstrate need for aid received scholarships/grants; average award was $3,047.
Scholarships offered: *Merit:* Entering Freshmen Academic Scholarship requires minimum 29 ACT or 1280 SAT and 3.5 GPA; up to full tuition awarded. National Merit and National Achievement Finalists, renewable with maintenance of 3.0 GPA; full tuition plus $750-$2,000. General and departmental scholarships, minimum 27 ACT or 1200 SAT and 3.5 GPA required for freshmen, 3.5 GPA for transfers, 3.0 GPA for other students, financial need con-

Alabama Auburn University

sidered. SAT scores exclusive of Writing. **Athletic:** 62 full-time freshmen received athletic scholarships; average amount $13,084.
Cumulative student debt: 65% of graduating class had student loans; average debt was $19,423.
Additional info: State of Alabama has pre-paid college tuition plan for residents.

FINANCIAL AID PROCEDURES
Forms required: FAFSA, institutional form.
Dates and Deadlines: Priority date 3/1; no closing date. Applicants notified on a rolling basis starting 5/1; must reply within 2 week(s) of notification.

CONTACT
Mike Reynolds, Director of Student Financial Aid
108 Mary Martin Hall, Auburn, AL 36849

Auburn University at Montgomery
Montgomery, Alabama
www.aum.edu   Federal Code: 008310

4-year public university in small city.
Enrollment: 4,118 undergrads, 35% part-time. 605 full-time freshmen.
Selectivity: Admits over 75% of applicants.

BASIC COSTS (2005-2006)
Tuition and fees: $4,720; out-of-state residents $13,690.
Per-credit charge: $147; out-of-state residents $446.
Room and board: $4,890.

FINANCIAL AID PICTURE (2004-2005)
Students with need: Out of 382 full-time freshmen who applied for aid, 374 were judged to have need. Of these, 291 received aid, and 61 had their full need met. For part-time students, average financial aid package was $7,580.
Students without need: No-need awards available for academics, alumni affiliation, art, athletics, job skills, leadership, minority status, music/drama, state/district residency.

FINANCIAL AID PROCEDURES
Forms required: FAFSA, institutional form.
Dates and Deadlines: Priority date 3/1; no closing date. Applicants notified on a rolling basis; must reply within 2 week(s) of notification.
Transfers: Aid awarded based on need and the availability of funds.

CONTACT
Daniel Miller, Director of Financial Aid
7400 East Drive, Montgomery, AL 36124-4023
(334) 244-3571

Birmingham-Southern College
Birmingham, Alabama
www.bsc.edu   Federal Code: 001012

4-year private liberal arts college in very large city, affiliated with United Methodist Church.
Enrollment: 1,356 undergrads, 2% part-time. 367 full-time freshmen.
Selectivity: Admits over 75% of applicants.

BASIC COSTS (2005-2006)
Tuition and fees: $21,450.
Per-credit charge: $851.
Room and board: $7,230.

FINANCIAL AID PICTURE (2005-2006)
Students with need: Out of 272 full-time freshmen who applied for aid, 187 were judged to have need. Of these, 187 received aid, and 56 had their full need met. Average financial aid package met 78% of need; average scholarship/grant was $12,222; average loan was $3,736. For part-time students, average financial aid package was $7,800.
Students without need: 166 full-time freshmen who did not demonstrate need for aid received scholarships/grants; average award was $9,894. No-need awards available for academics, alumni affiliation, art, athletics, job skills, leadership, minority status, music/drama, religious affiliation, ROTC, state/district residency.
Scholarships offered: Merit: McWane Honors Award; full tuition plus $11,000 per year stipend; based on academic achievement; 1 awarded. Neal and Anne Berte Scholarship; full tuition; academic achievement; 1 awarded. Blount-Monaghan/Vulcan Materials Company Scholarship; full tuition; academic achievement; 1 awarded. William Jones and Elizabeth Perry Rushton Scholarship; full tuition; based on academic achievement; 1 awarded. Phi Beta Kappa; full tuition; based on academic achievement. United Methodist Scholarship; $1,000-$2,500; awarded to United Methodist with recommendation from senior United Methodist Minister. **Athletic:** 50 full-time freshmen received athletic scholarships; average amount $17,518.
Additional info: Auditions required for music, theater, dance applicants seeking scholarships. Portfolios required for art applicants seeking scholarships, and essays recommended for all applicants seeking scholarships.

FINANCIAL AID PROCEDURES
Dates and Deadlines: Priority date 3/1; closing date 8/1. Applicants notified on a rolling basis starting 3/30.

CONTACT
Ron Day, Director of Financial Aid
900 Arkadelphia Road, Birmingham, AL 35254
(205) 226-4688

Bishop State Community College
Mobile, Alabama
www.bishop.edu   Federal Code: 001030

2-year public community college in small city.
Enrollment: 4,887 undergrads.
Selectivity: Open admission; but selective for some programs.

BASIC COSTS (2005-2006)
Tuition and fees: $2,700; out-of-state residents $4,800.
Per-credit charge: $72; out-of-state residents $144.

FINANCIAL AID PICTURE (2004-2005)
Students with need: 90% of average financial aid package awarded as scholarships/grants, 10% awarded as loans/jobs.
Students without need: No-need awards available for academics, athletics.

FINANCIAL AID PROCEDURES
Forms required: FAFSA, institutional form.
Dates and Deadlines: Priority date 4/1; no closing date. Applicants notified on a rolling basis; must reply within 2 week(s) of notification.

CONTACT
Charles Holloway, Manager of Student Financial Aid and Veterans Services
351 North Broad Street, Mobile, AL 36603-5898
(251) 690-6458

Chattahoochee Valley Community College
Phenix City, Alabama
www.cv.edu					Federal Code: 012182

2-year public community and junior college in large town.
Enrollment: 2,031 undergrads.
Selectivity: Open admission; but selective for some programs.

BASIC COSTS (2005-2006)
Tuition and fees: $2,700; out-of-state residents $4,830.
Per-credit charge: $71; out-of-state residents $142.

FINANCIAL AID PICTURE (2004-2005)
Students with need: 98% of average financial aid package awarded as scholarships/grants, 2% awarded as loans/jobs. Need-based aid available for part-time students. Work study available nights, weekends, and for part-time students.
Students without need: No-need awards available for academics, art, athletics, leadership, music/drama.

FINANCIAL AID PROCEDURES
Forms required: FAFSA.
Dates and Deadlines: Priority date 7/1; no closing date. Applicants notified on a rolling basis; must reply within 1 week(s) of notification.

CONTACT
Joan Waters, Director of Financial Aid
2602 College Drive, Phenix City, AL 36869
(334) 291-4915

Concordia College
Selma, Alabama
www.concordiaselma.edu			Federal Code: 010554
						CSS Code: 1989

4-year private liberal arts college in large town, affiliated with Lutheran Church - Missouri Synod.
Enrollment: 850 undergrads.
Selectivity: Open admission.

BASIC COSTS (2005-2006)
Tuition and fees: $6,167.
Room and board: $3,600.
Additional info: Tuition/fee waivers available for adults.

FINANCIAL AID PICTURE (2005-2006)
Students with need: Need-based aid available for part-time students.
Students without need: This college only awards aid to students with need.

FINANCIAL AID PROCEDURES
Forms required: FAFSA, CSS PROFILE, state aid form, institutional form.
Dates and Deadlines: Priority date 4/1; no closing date. Applicants notified on a rolling basis starting 6/15; must reply within 2 week(s) of notification.

CONTACT
Director of Financial Aid
1804 Green Street, Selma, AL 36701
(334) 847-5700 ext. 160

Faulkner University
Montgomery, Alabama
www.faulkner.edu				Federal Code: 001003

4-year private university and liberal arts college in small city, affiliated with Church of Christ.
Enrollment: 2,144 undergrads, 27% part-time. 185 full-time freshmen.
Selectivity: Admits less than 50% of applicants.

BASIC COSTS (2006-2007)
Tuition and fees: $11,565.
Per-credit charge: $400.
Room and board: $5,400.
Additional info: Tuition/fee waivers available for adults, minority students, unemployed or children of unemployed.

FINANCIAL AID PICTURE (2004-2005)
Students with need: Out of 170 full-time freshmen who applied for aid, 136 were judged to have need. Of these, 136 received aid, and 14 had their full need met. Average financial aid package met 60% of need; average scholarship/grant was $2,450; average loan was $2,625. For part-time students, average financial aid package was $3,650.
Students without need: 9 full-time freshmen who did not demonstrate need for aid received scholarships/grants; average award was $1,650. No-need awards available for academics, alumni affiliation, art, athletics, leadership, music/drama, religious affiliation, ROTC, state/district residency.
Scholarships offered: 22 full-time freshmen received athletic scholarships; average amount $4,650.
Cumulative student debt: 85% of graduating class had student loans; average debt was $18,800.

FINANCIAL AID PROCEDURES
Forms required: FAFSA, state aid form, institutional form.
Dates and Deadlines: Priority date 5/1; no closing date. Applicants notified on a rolling basis starting 6/1; must reply within 3 week(s) of notification.

CONTACT
William Jackson, Director of Financial Aid
5345 Atlanta Highway, Montgomery, AL 36109-3398
(334) 386-7195

Gadsden State Community College
Gadsden, Alabama
www.gadsdenstate.edu			Federal Code: 001017

2-year public community college in large town.
Enrollment: 5,426 undergrads, 45% part-time. 1,184 full-time freshmen.
Selectivity: Open admission; but selective for some programs.

BASIC COSTS (2005-2006)
Tuition and fees: $2,700; out-of-state residents $4,830.
Per-credit charge: $71; out-of-state residents $142.
Room only: $2,800.
Additional info: Tuition/fee waivers available for unemployed or children of unemployed.

FINANCIAL AID PICTURE (2005-2006)
Students with need: Need-based aid available for part-time students.
Students without need: No-need awards available for academics, athletics, state/district residency.

FINANCIAL AID PROCEDURES
Forms required: FAFSA, institutional form.
Dates and Deadlines: Priority date 4/15; no closing date. Applicants notified on a rolling basis starting 6/10; must reply within 2 week(s) of notification.

CONTACT
Kim Carter, Director of Financial Aid
1001 George Wallace Drive, Gadsden, AL 35902-0227
(256) 549-8267 ext. 8267

Heritage Christian University
Florence, Alabama
www.hcu.edu   Federal Code: 015370

4-year private Bible college in large town, affiliated with Church of Christ.
Enrollment: 97 undergrads, 56% part-time. 6 full-time freshmen.
Selectivity: Open admission.

BASIC COSTS (2005-2006)
Tuition and fees: $8,940.
Per-credit charge: $278.
Room only: $1,650.

FINANCIAL AID PICTURE (2004-2005)
Students with need: Out of 2 full-time freshmen who applied for aid, 2 were judged to have need. Of these, 2 received aid. Average financial aid package met 63% of need; average loan was $2,625. For part-time students, average financial aid package was $4,092.
Students without need: 4 full-time freshmen who did not demonstrate need for aid received scholarships/grants; average award was $1,510.
Cumulative student debt: 38% of graduating class had student loans; average debt was $21,048.

FINANCIAL AID PROCEDURES
Forms required: FAFSA.
Dates and Deadlines: Priority date 6/1; no closing date. Applicants notified on a rolling basis starting 6/1; must reply within 2 week(s) of notification.
Transfers: No deadline.

CONTACT
Angie Horton, Financial Aid Counselor
3625 Helton Drive, Florence, AL 35630
(256) 766-6610 ext. 224

Herzing College
Birmingham, Alabama
www.herzing.edu   Federal Code: 010193

4-year for-profit business and technical college in very large city.
Enrollment: 430 undergrads.

BASIC COSTS (2005-2006)
Additional info: Per-credit-hour charge ranges from $255 to $300 depending on program.

FINANCIAL AID PICTURE
Students with need: Need-based aid available for full-time students.
Students without need: This college only awards aid to students with need.

FINANCIAL AID PROCEDURES
Forms required: FAFSA.

CONTACT
Kentray Sims, Director of Financial Services
280 West Valley Avenue, Birmingham, AL 35209
(205) 916-2800

Huntingdon College
Montgomery, Alabama
www.huntingdon.edu   Federal Code: 001019

4-year private liberal arts college in small city, affiliated with United Methodist Church.
Enrollment: 750 undergrads.
Selectivity: Admits 50 to 75% of applicants.

BASIC COSTS (2006-2007)
Tuition and fees: $16,690.
Room and board: $6,400.
Additional info: Tuition at time of enrollment locked for 4 years.

FINANCIAL AID PICTURE
Students with need: Need-based aid available for full-time and part-time students. Work study available nights, weekends, and for part-time students.
Students without need: No-need awards available for academics, alumni affiliation, art, leadership, music/drama, religious affiliation, ROTC, state/district residency.
Scholarships offered: Academic achievement scholarships range from $3,000 to full tuition. Special grants awarded in recognition of visual or performing arts talent.

FINANCIAL AID PROCEDURES
Forms required: FAFSA, state aid form, institutional form.
Dates and Deadlines: Priority date 4/15; no closing date. Applicants notified on a rolling basis starting 3/1; must reply by 5/1 or within 4 week(s) of notification.

CONTACT
Belinda Duett, Director of Financial Aid
1500 East Fairview Avenue, Montgomery, AL 36106-2148
(334) 833-4428

J. F. Drake State Technical College
Huntsville, Alabama
www.drakestate.edu   Federal Code: 00526

2-year public technical college in small city.
Enrollment: 759 undergrads, 40% part-time.
Selectivity: Open admission; but selective for some programs.

BASIC COSTS (2005-2006)
Tuition and fees: $2,700; out-of-state residents $4,830.
Per-credit charge: $72; out-of-state residents $144.

FINANCIAL AID PICTURE (2005-2006)
Students with need: Need-based aid available for full-time and part-time students.
Students without need: No-need awards available for academics, state/district residency.

FINANCIAL AID PROCEDURES
Forms required: FAFSA.
Dates and Deadlines: Priority date 7/1; no closing date. Applicants notified on a rolling basis.

CONTACT
Joylyn Trotman, Financial Aid Officer
3421 Meridian Street North, Huntsville, AL 35811
(256) 551-3127

Jacksonville State University
Jacksonville, Alabama
www.jsu.edu Federal Code: 001020

4-year public university in small town.
Enrollment: 6,937 undergrads, 18% part-time. 1,111 full-time freshmen.
Selectivity: Admits over 75% of applicants.

BASIC COSTS (2005-2006)
Tuition and fees: $4,040; out-of-state residents $8,080.
Per-credit charge: $169; out-of-state residents $338.
Room and board: $4,094.

FINANCIAL AID PICTURE (2005-2006)
Students with need: 95% of average financial aid package awarded as scholarships/grants, 5% awarded as loans/jobs. Need-based aid available for part-time students. Work study available nights, weekends, and for part-time students.
Students without need: No-need awards available for academics, alumni affiliation, art, athletics, music/drama, ROTC.
Scholarships offered: Entering freshmen from Alabama with ACT 28 or SAT 1230 can apply for 4-year tuition scholarship.

FINANCIAL AID PROCEDURES
Forms required: FAFSA, institutional form.
Dates and Deadlines: Priority date 3/15; no closing date. Applicants notified on a rolling basis starting 5/15; must reply within 2 week(s) of notification.

CONTACT
Vickie Adams, Director of Financial Aid
700 Pelham Road North, Jacksonville, AL 36265-1602
(256) 782-5006

Jefferson State Community College
Birmingham, Alabama
www.jeffstateonline.com Federal Code: 001022

2-year public community college in large city.
Enrollment: 5,660 undergrads, 54% part-time. 810 full-time freshmen.
Selectivity: Open admission; but selective for some programs.

BASIC COSTS (2005-2006)
Tuition and fees: $3,060; out-of-state residents $5,190.
Per-credit charge: $71; out-of-state residents $142.

FINANCIAL AID PICTURE
Students with need: Need-based aid available for full-time and part-time students. Work study available nights.
Students without need: No-need awards available for academics, art, athletics, leadership, music/drama.
Additional info: Any Alabama resident over age 60 may attend classes tuition free.

FINANCIAL AID PROCEDURES
Forms required: FAFSA, institutional form.
Dates and Deadlines: Priority date 5/1; no closing date. Applicants notified on a rolling basis starting 6/1.
Transfers: Transfer students not eligible for academic scholarships until 12 hours have been completed on campus.

CONTACT
Tracy Adams, Director, Financial Aid
2601 Carson Road, Birmingham, AL 35215-3098
(205) 856-7704

Judson College
Marion, Alabama
www.judson.edu Federal Code: 001023

4-year private liberal arts college for women in small town, affiliated with Baptist faith.
Enrollment: 331 undergrads, 22% part-time. 79 full-time freshmen.
Selectivity: Admits over 75% of applicants.

BASIC COSTS (2006-2007)
Tuition and fees: $10,670.
Per-credit charge: $322.
Room and board: $7,190.

FINANCIAL AID PICTURE (2004-2005)
Students with need: Out of 79 full-time freshmen who applied for aid, 66 were judged to have need. Of these, 66 received aid, and 10 had their full need met. Average financial aid package met 77% of need; average scholarship/grant was $7,376; average loan was $2,611. For part-time students, average financial aid package was $1,283.
Students without need: 13 full-time freshmen who did not demonstrate need for aid received scholarships/grants; average award was $5,903. No-need awards available for academics, art, athletics, leadership, music/drama, religious affiliation, state/district residency.
Scholarships offered: Garner-Webb Honors Scholarship; full tuition; up to 5 given to applicants who are National Merit Finalists or have ACT of 30 or above. Lockhart Competitive Scholarships; 1 full tuition, 2 for $2,500, 3 for $2,000; awarded based on exam scores. Music scholarships; $1,500; awarded based on audition.
Cumulative student debt: 72% of graduating class had student loans; average debt was $15,690.

FINANCIAL AID PROCEDURES
Forms required: FAFSA, state aid form, institutional form.
Dates and Deadlines: Priority date 3/15; no closing date. Applicants notified on a rolling basis starting 3/15; must reply within 2 week(s) of notification.

CONTACT
Doris Wilson, Financial Aid Officer
302 Bibb Street, Marion, AL 36756
(334) 683-5157

Lawson State Community College
Birmingham, Alabama
www.lawsonstate.edu Federal Code: 001059

2-year public community college in small city.
Enrollment: 3,370 undergrads, 48% part-time. 643 full-time freshmen.
Selectivity: Open admission; but selective for some programs.

BASIC COSTS (2005-2006)
Tuition and fees: $2,700; out-of-state residents $4,830.
Per-credit charge: $72; out-of-state residents $144.

FINANCIAL AID PICTURE (2005-2006)
Students with need: Average financial aid package met 40% of need; average scholarship/grant was $465. Need-based aid available for part-time students.
Students without need: This college only awards aid to students with need.

FINANCIAL AID PROCEDURES
Forms required: FAFSA.
Dates and Deadlines: Priority date 6/1; no closing date. Applicants notified on a rolling basis starting 8/1; must reply within 2 week(s) of notification.

Alabama Lawson State Community College

CONTACT
Cassandra Matthews, Director of Financial Aid
3060 Wilson Road SW, Birmingham, AL 35221-1717
(205) 929-6380

Marion Military Institute
Marion, Alabama
www.marionmilitary.edu   Federal Code: 001026

2-year private junior and military college in small town.
Enrollment: 175 undergrads.

BASIC COSTS (2006-2007)
Tuition and fees: $775; out-of-state residents $13,955.
Room and board: $3,180.
Additional info: Additional $1600 for uniforms. Tuition at time of enrollment locked for 2 years.

FINANCIAL AID PICTURE (2004-2005)
Students with need: 52% of average financial aid package awarded as scholarships/grants, 48% awarded as loans/jobs. Need-based aid available for part-time students.
Students without need: No-need awards available for academics, alumni affiliation, athletics, leadership, music/drama, ROTC.

FINANCIAL AID PROCEDURES
Forms required: FAFSA.
Dates and Deadlines: No deadline. Applicants notified on a rolling basis starting 6/15; must reply within 6 week(s) of notification.
Transfers: Priority date 5/15.

CONTACT
Kimberly Stewart, Director of Financial Aid
1101 Washington Street, Marion, AL 36756-0420
(334) 683-2309

Miles College
Birmingham, Alabama
www.miles.edu   Federal Code: 001028

4-year private liberal arts college in very large city, affiliated with Christian Methodist Episcopal Church.
Enrollment: 1,758 undergrads.
Selectivity: Open admission; but selective for some programs.

BASIC COSTS (2006-2007)
Tuition and fees: $6,410.
Room and board: $4,222.

FINANCIAL AID PICTURE
Students with need: Need-based aid available for full-time and part-time students.
Students without need: This college only awards aid to students with need.

FINANCIAL AID PROCEDURES
Forms required: FAFSA.
Dates and Deadlines: Priority date 4/15; no closing date. Applicants notified on a rolling basis starting 7/15; must reply within 2 week(s) of notification.

CONTACT
Percy Lanier, Financial Aid Administrator
5500 Myron-Massey Boulevard, Fairfield, AL 35064
(205) 929-1665

Northeast Alabama Community College
Rainsville, Alabama
www.nacc.edu   Federal Code: 001031

2-year public community college in rural community.
Enrollment: 1,710 undergrads.
Selectivity: Open admission; but selective for some programs.

BASIC COSTS (2005-2006)
Tuition and fees: $2,700; out-of-state residents $4,830.
Per-credit charge: $71; out-of-state residents $142.
Additional info: In-state costs apply to on-campus or distance-learning courses. Out-of-state distance-learning students pay $5,400 for academic year (or $180 per-credit-hour).

FINANCIAL AID PICTURE (2004-2005)
Students with need: 78% of average financial aid package awarded as scholarships/grants, 22% awarded as loans/jobs. Need-based aid available for part-time students.
Students without need: No-need awards available for academics, art, leadership, minority status, music/drama.

FINANCIAL AID PROCEDURES
Forms required: FAFSA.
Dates and Deadlines: No deadline. Applicants notified on a rolling basis.

CONTACT
Harold Brookshire, Director of Financial Aid
Admissions Office, NACC, Rainsville, AL 35986-0159
(256) 228-6001 ext. 227

Northwest-Shoals Community College
Muscle Shoals, Alabama
www.nwscc.edu   Federal Code: 005697

2-year public community and technical college in large town.
Enrollment: 3,380 undergrads, 37% part-time. 473 full-time freshmen.
Selectivity: Open admission; but selective for some programs.

BASIC COSTS (2005-2006)
Tuition and fees: $2,700; out-of-state residents $4,830.
Per-credit charge: $71; out-of-state residents $142.
Room only: $1,600.
Additional info: Tuition at time of enrollment locked for 2 years; tuition/fee waivers available for minority students, unemployed or children of unemployed.

FINANCIAL AID PICTURE (2005-2006)
Students with need: 53% of average financial aid package awarded as scholarships/grants, 47% awarded as loans/jobs. Need-based aid available for part-time students. Work study available nights, weekends, and for part-time students.
Students without need: No-need awards available for academics, art, athletics, leadership, minority status, music/drama.
Cumulative student debt: 30% of graduating class had student loans; average debt was $3,704.

FINANCIAL AID PROCEDURES
Forms required: FAFSA, institutional form.
Dates and Deadlines: Priority date 4/1; no closing date. Applicants notified on a rolling basis; must reply within 2 week(s) of notification.
Transfers: No deadline. Applicants notified on a rolling basis; must reply within 2 week(s) of notification. Students without 1-year Alabama residency before fall term ineligible for state grant.

CONTACT
Joel Parris, Director of Student Financial Aid Services
PO Box 2545, Muscle Shoals, AL 35662
(256) 331-5368

Oakwood College
Huntsville, Alabama
www.oakwood.edu   Federal Code: 001033

4-year private liberal arts college in small city, affiliated with Seventh-day Adventists.
Enrollment: 1,751 undergrads, 11% part-time. 406 full-time freshmen.

BASIC COSTS (2005-2006)
Tuition and fees: $11,722.
Per-credit charge: $476.
Room and board: $6,630.

FINANCIAL AID PICTURE
Students with need: Need-based aid available for full-time students.
Students without need: No-need awards available for academics, leadership, religious affiliation, state/district residency.

FINANCIAL AID PROCEDURES
Forms required: FAFSA, state aid form.
Dates and Deadlines: Priority date 3/31; no closing date. Applicants notified on a rolling basis starting 4/1.

CONTACT
Fred Stennis, Director of Financial Aid
7000 Adventist Boulevard, NW, Huntsville, AL 35896
(256) 726-7208

Prince Institute of Professional Studies
Montgomery, Alabama
www.princeinstitute.edu   Federal Code: 022960

2-year for-profit technical college in large city.
Enrollment: 38 undergrads, 39% part-time. 5 full-time freshmen.
Selectivity: Open admission.

BASIC COSTS (2005-2006)
Tuition and fees: $6,131.
Additional info: Additional required fees vary per program.

FINANCIAL AID PICTURE
Students with need: Need-based aid available for full-time and part-time students.
Students without need: This college only awards aid to students with need.

FINANCIAL AID PROCEDURES
Forms required: FAFSA.
Dates and Deadlines: No deadline.

CONTACT
Mark Prince, Financial Aid Administrator
7735 Atlanta Highway, Montgomery, AL 36117-4231
(334) 271-1670

Remington College: Mobile
Mobile, Alabama
www.educationamerica.com

2-year private technical college in large city.
Enrollment: 300 undergrads.
Selectivity: Open admission.

BASIC COSTS (2005-2006)
Additional info: Bachelor programs $28,890. Associate programs $31,490. Diploma programs (allied health) $11,730. Cost includes tuition, fees and books.

FINANCIAL AID PICTURE
Students with need: Need-based aid available for full-time students. Work study available nights.
Students without need: This college only awards aid to students with need.

FINANCIAL AID PROCEDURES
Forms required: FAFSA.

CONTACT
Linda Calvanese, Financial Aid Director
828 Downtowner Loop West, Mobile, AL 36609-5404
(251) 343-8200

Samford University
Birmingham, Alabama
www.samford.edu   Federal Code: 001036

4-year private university in very large city, affiliated with Southern Baptist Convention.
Enrollment: 2,879 undergrads, 5% part-time. 667 full-time freshmen.
Selectivity: Admits over 75% of applicants.

BASIC COSTS (2006-2007)
Tuition and fees: $16,000.
Room and board: $6,060.

FINANCIAL AID PICTURE (2004-2005)
Students with need: Out of 457 full-time freshmen who applied for aid, 276 were judged to have need. Of these, 271 received aid, and 74 had their full need met. Average financial aid package met 76% of need; average scholarship/grant was $8,149; average loan was $3,169. For part-time students, average financial aid package was $5,779.
Students without need: 151 full-time freshmen who did not demonstrate need for aid received scholarships/grants; average award was $3,664. No-need awards available for academics, athletics, leadership, music/drama, religious affiliation, ROTC, state/district residency.
Scholarships offered: 51 full-time freshmen received athletic scholarships; average amount $10,898.
Cumulative student debt: 46% of graduating class had student loans; average debt was $17,532.
Additional info: Consideration for merit scholarships automatically given to students with admission files completed by December 15.

FINANCIAL AID PROCEDURES
Forms required: FAFSA.
Dates and Deadlines: Priority date 3/1; no closing date. Applicants notified on a rolling basis starting 5/1.

CONTACT
Lissa Burleson, Director of Financial Aid
800 Lakeshore Drive, Birmingham, AL 35229
(205) 726-2905

Shelton State Community College
Tuscaloosa, Alabama
www.sheltonstate.edu   Federal Code: 005691

2-year public community and technical college in small city.
Enrollment: 4,622 undergrads, 35% part-time. 1,187 full-time freshmen.

Selectivity: Open admission.
BASIC COSTS (2005-2006)
Tuition and fees: $2,730; out-of-state residents $4,890.
Per-credit charge: $72; out-of-state residents $144.
FINANCIAL AID PICTURE
Students with need: Need-based aid available for full-time and part-time students. Work study available nights.
Students without need: This college only awards aid to students with need.
FINANCIAL AID PROCEDURES
Forms required: FAFSA.
Dates and Deadlines: Priority date 6/30; no closing date. Applicants notified on a rolling basis starting 7/30.
CONTACT
JoeAnn Cousette, Financial Aid Coordinator
9500 Old Greensboro Road, Tuscaloosa, AL 35405-8522
(205) 391-2376

Snead State Community College
Boaz, Alabama
www.snead.edu   Federal Code: 001038

2-year public community college in small town.
Enrollment: 1,695 undergrads.
Selectivity: Open admission; but selective for some programs.
BASIC COSTS (2005-2006)
Tuition and fees: $2,820; out-of-state residents $4,950.
Per-credit charge: $71; out-of-state residents $142.
Room and board: $2,474.
FINANCIAL AID PICTURE
Students with need: Need-based aid available for full-time and part-time students. Work study available nights.
Students without need: No-need awards available for academics, alumni affiliation, art, athletics, leadership, music/drama.
FINANCIAL AID PROCEDURES
Forms required: FAFSA.
Dates and Deadlines: Priority date 4/15; no closing date. Applicants notified on a rolling basis starting 4/15.
CONTACT
Kelly D'Eath, Financial Aid Officer
PO Box 734, Boaz, AL 35957-0734
(256) 840-4127

South University
Montgomery, Alabama
www.southuniversity.edu   Federal Code: 004463

4-year for-profit business and health science college in small city.
Enrollment: 408 undergrads, 43% part-time. 97 full-time freshmen.
Selectivity: Admits over 75% of applicants.
BASIC COSTS (2006-2007)
Tuition and fees: $11,850.
FINANCIAL AID PICTURE (2004-2005)
Students with need: 22% of average financial aid package awarded as scholarships/grants, 78% awarded as loans/jobs. Need-based aid available for part-time students.
Students without need: This college only awards aid to students with need.

Cumulative student debt: 95% of graduating class had student loans; average debt was $9,800.
FINANCIAL AID PROCEDURES
Forms required: FAFSA.
Dates and Deadlines: No deadline. Applicants notified on a rolling basis starting 6/1.
Transfers: No deadline. Applicants notified on a rolling basis.
CONTACT
James Berry, Director of Financial Aid
5355 Vaughn Road, Montgomery, AL 36116-1120
(334) 395-8800

Southeastern Bible College
Birmingham, Alabama
www.sebc.edu   Federal Code: 013857

4-year private Bible college in very large city, affiliated with interdenominational tradition.
Enrollment: 232 undergrads.
Selectivity: Admits 50 to 75% of applicants.
BASIC COSTS (2005-2006)
Tuition and fees: $9,015.
Per-credit charge: $295.
Room and board: $4,300.
FINANCIAL AID PICTURE
Students with need: Need-based aid available for full-time and part-time students.
Students without need: No-need awards available for academics.
FINANCIAL AID PROCEDURES
Forms required: FAFSA, state aid form, institutional form.
Dates and Deadlines: Priority date 5/1; closing date 8/15. Applicants notified by 7/15; must reply within 2 week(s) of notification.
CONTACT
Joanne Belin, Financial Aid Officer
2545 Valleydale Road, Birmingham, AL 35244
(205) 970-9215

Southern Christian University
Montgomery, Alabama
www.southernchristian.edu   Federal Code: 016885

4-year private university and seminary college in small city, affiliated with Church of Christ.
Enrollment: 371 undergrads, 15% part-time.
Selectivity: Open admission; but selective for some programs.
BASIC COSTS (2005-2006)
Tuition and fees: $10,400.
Per-credit charge: $400.
Additional info: Undergraduates taking a minimum of 12 hours in a given semester receive scholarships in the amount of $2,400 per student.
FINANCIAL AID PICTURE (2004-2005)
Students with need: 2% of average financial aid package awarded as scholarships/grants, 98% awarded as loans/jobs. Need-based aid available for part-time students.
Students without need: No-need awards available for academics, leadership.
Additional info: Scholarships based on need and grades. Half-tuition scholarship is available for full-time undergraduate students.

FINANCIAL AID PROCEDURES
Forms required: FAFSA, institutional form.
Dates and Deadlines: Priority date 5/1; closing date 6/30. Applicants notified by 6/30; must reply by 8/15 or within 2 week(s) of notification.
Transfers: No deadline.

CONTACT
Rosemary Kennington, Financial Aid Director
1200 Taylor Road, Montgomery, AL 36117-3553
(800) 351-4040 ext. 7527

Southern Union State Community College
Wadley, Alabama
suscc.edu   Federal Code: 001040

2-year public community and technical college in small city.
Enrollment: 4,560 undergrads.
Selectivity: Open admission; but selective for some programs.

BASIC COSTS (2005-2006)
Tuition and fees: $2,700; out-of-state residents $4,830.
Per-credit charge: $71; out-of-state residents $142.
Room and board: $2,400.

FINANCIAL AID PICTURE
Students with need: Need-based aid available for full-time and part-time students.

FINANCIAL AID PROCEDURES
Forms required: FAFSA.
Dates and Deadlines: No deadline. Applicants notified on a rolling basis.

CONTACT
Pam Jones, Director of Financial Aid
750 Roberts Street, Wadley, AL 36276
(256) 395-2215

Spring Hill College
Mobile, Alabama
www.shc.edu   Federal Code: 001041

4-year private liberal arts college in large city, affiliated with Roman Catholic Church.
Enrollment: 1,174 undergrads, 9% part-time. 274 full-time freshmen.
Selectivity: Admits over 75% of applicants.

BASIC COSTS (2006-2007)
Tuition and fees: $22,000.
Per-credit charge: $773.
Room and board: $8,120.

FINANCIAL AID PICTURE (2005-2006)
Students with need: Out of 228 full-time freshmen who applied for aid, 188 were judged to have need. Of these, 188 received aid, and 44 had their full need met. Average financial aid package met 83% of need; average scholarship/grant was $14,874; average loan was $3,583. For part-time students, average financial aid package was $5,613.
Students without need: 73 full-time freshmen who did not demonstrate need for aid received scholarships/grants; average award was $10,788. No-need awards available for academics, alumni affiliation, athletics, job skills, leadership, state/district residency.
Scholarships offered: *Merit:* Spring Hill Scholars scholarships: $30,000 annually for 4 years; awarded to incoming freshmen who have demonstrated academic excellence, leadership, and service; 3.5 high school GPA and 28 ACT or 1230 SAT. Trustee Honors Scholarship: $20,000 annually; 3.5 high school GPA and 28 ACT or 1230 SAT. Presidential Honors Scholarship: $10,000-$14,000 annually; awarded on the basis of grades, test scores, and leadership potential. Faculty Honors Scholarship; $8,000-$13,000 annually; awarded on the basis of grades, test scores, and leadership potential. Academic Honors Scholarship: $7,000-$12,000 annually; awarded on the basis of grades, test scores, and leadership potential. *Athletic:* 33 full-time freshmen received athletic scholarships; average amount $4,303.
Cumulative student debt: 80% of graduating class had student loans; average debt was $14,074.

FINANCIAL AID PROCEDURES
Forms required: FAFSA, state aid form, institutional form.
Dates and Deadlines: Priority date 3/1; no closing date. Applicants notified on a rolling basis starting 2/15; must reply by 5/1 or within 2 week(s) of notification.
Transfers: No deadline. Applicants notified on a rolling basis starting 2/1; must reply within 2 week(s) of notification. Transfer scholarships are awarded to students transferring to Spring Hill from an accredited college or university with a minimum cumulative grade point average of 3.0. These scholarships range from $3,000 to $6,000 annually and are renewable with a 2.5 GPA. Transfer students who are members of Phi Theta Kappa and transfer students who plan to pursue a degree in nursing may receive additional scholarship funding.

CONTACT
Ellen Foster, Director of Financial Aid
4000 Dauphin Street, Mobile, AL 36608-1791
(251) 380-3460

Stillman College
Tuscaloosa, Alabama
www.stillman.edu   Federal Code: 001044

4-year private liberal arts college in small city, affiliated with Presbyterian Church (USA).
Enrollment: 850 undergrads.

BASIC COSTS (2005-2006)
Tuition and fees: $11,605.
Per-credit charge: $438.
Room and board: $5,500.

FINANCIAL AID PICTURE
Students with need: Need-based aid available for full-time and part-time students.
Students without need: This college only awards aid to students with need.

FINANCIAL AID PROCEDURES
Forms required: FAFSA, institutional form.
Dates and Deadlines: Priority date 6/1; no closing date. Applicants notified on a rolling basis; must reply within 4 week(s) of notification.

CONTACT
Jacqueline Morris, Director of Financial Aid
3600 Stillman Boulevard, Tuscaloosa, AL 35403
(205) 366-8950

Talladega College
Talladega, Alabama
www.talladega.edu   Federal Code: 001046
                                CSS Code: 1800

4-year private liberal arts college in large town, affiliated with United Church of Christ.
Enrollment: 368 undergrads, 8% part-time. 313 full-time freshmen.
Selectivity: Admits less than 50% of applicants.

Alabama Talladega College

BASIC COSTS (2005-2006)
Tuition and fees: $7,128.
Per-credit charge: $280.
Room and board: $4,420.

FINANCIAL AID PICTURE (2004-2005)
Students with need: Out of 235 full-time freshmen who applied for aid, 235 were judged to have need. Of these, 235 received aid, and 72 had their full need met. Average financial aid package met 75% of need; average loan was $2,625. For part-time students, average financial aid package was $8,328.
Students without need: This college only awards aid to students with need.

FINANCIAL AID PROCEDURES
Forms required: FAFSA, CSS PROFILE, state aid form, institutional form.
Dates and Deadlines: Priority date 4/15; no closing date. Applicants notified on a rolling basis; must reply within 2 week(s) of notification.

CONTACT
Michael Francois, Director of Financial Aid
627 West Battle Street, Talladega, AL 35160
(256) 761-6256

Trenholm State Technical College
Montgomery, Alabama
www.trenholmtech.cc.al.us   Federal Code: 005734

2-year public technical college in large city.
Enrollment: 1,379 undergrads, 48% part-time. 432 full-time freshmen.
Selectivity: Open admission; but selective for some programs.

BASIC COSTS (2005-2006)
Tuition and fees: $2,700; out-of-state residents $4,860.
Per-credit charge: $71; out-of-state residents $142.

FINANCIAL AID PICTURE (2004-2005)
Students with need: Out of 432 full-time freshmen who applied for aid, 194 were judged to have need. Of these, 194 received aid. Average financial aid package met .81% of need; average scholarship/grant was $1,816. For part-time students, average financial aid package was $1,183.
Students without need: 26 full-time freshmen who did not demonstrate need for aid received scholarships/grants; average award was $2,304. No-need awards available for academics, leadership, state/district residency.
Scholarships offered: Institutional Scholarships - $3,240 annually.

FINANCIAL AID PROCEDURES
Forms required: FAFSA, state aid form.
Dates and Deadlines: No deadline. Applicants notified on a rolling basis.

CONTACT
Betty Edwards, Director of Financial Aid
1225 Air Base Boulevard, Montgomery, AL 36108
(334) 420-4322

Troy University
Troy, Alabama
www.troy.edu   Federal Code: 001047

4-year public university in large town.
Enrollment: 18,501 undergrads, 55% part-time. 1,434 full-time freshmen.

BASIC COSTS (2005-2006)
Tuition and fees: $4,678; out-of-state residents $8,682.
Per-credit charge: $170; out-of-state residents $340.
Room and board: $5,157.

FINANCIAL AID PICTURE (2005-2006)
Students with need: Out of 888 full-time freshmen who applied for aid, 759 were judged to have need. Of these, 759 received aid. For part-time students, average financial aid package was $3,761.
Students without need: 457 full-time freshmen who did not demonstrate need for aid received scholarships/grants; average award was $2,407. No-need awards available for academics, athletics, ROTC.
Scholarships offered: 59 full-time freshmen received athletic scholarships; average amount $4,447.

FINANCIAL AID PROCEDURES
Forms required: FAFSA, institutional form.
Dates and Deadlines: Closing date 5/1. Applicants notified on a rolling basis starting 5/1; must reply within 2 week(s) of notification.

CONTACT
Carol Supri, Director of Financial Aid
University Avenue, Adams Administration 111, Troy, AL 36082
(334) 670-3186

Tuskegee University
Tuskegee, Alabama   Federal Code: 001050
www.tuskegee.edu   CSS Code: 1813

4-year private university and liberal arts college in small town.
Enrollment: 2,510 undergrads, 5% part-time. 730 full-time freshmen.
Selectivity: Admits over 75% of applicants.

BASIC COSTS (2006-2007)
Tuition and fees: $12,985.
Per-credit charge: $510.
Room and board: $7,110.

FINANCIAL AID PICTURE (2005-2006)
Students with need: Out of 664 full-time freshmen who applied for aid, 564 were judged to have need. Of these, 479 received aid, and 281 had their full need met. Average financial aid package met 85% of need; average scholarship/grant was $8,000; average loan was $5,625. Need-based aid available for part-time students.
Students without need: 212 full-time freshmen who did not demonstrate need for aid received scholarships/grants; average award was $6,000. No-need awards available for academics, athletics, ROTC, state/district residency.
Scholarships offered: 58 full-time freshmen received athletic scholarships; average amount $10,641.

FINANCIAL AID PROCEDURES
Forms required: FAFSA, CSS PROFILE, institutional form.
Dates and Deadlines: Closing date 3/31. Applicants notified on a rolling basis starting 5/15; must reply within 2 week(s) of notification.

CONTACT
Leslie Porter, Vice President for Business and Fiscal Affairs
102 Old Administration Building, Tuskegee, AL 36088
(334) 727-8201

University of Alabama
Tuscaloosa, Alabama
www.ua.edu   Federal Code: 001051

4-year public university in small city.
Enrollment: 17,374 undergrads, 9% part-time. 3,345 full-time freshmen.
Selectivity: Admits 50 to 75% of applicants.

BASIC COSTS (2005-2006)
Tuition and fees: $4,864; out-of-state residents $13,516.
Room and board: $5,024.

FINANCIAL AID PICTURE (2004-2005)
Students with need: Out of 2,547 full-time freshmen who applied for aid, 1,210 were judged to have need. Of these, 1,191 received aid, and 405 had their full need met. Average financial aid package met 67% of need; average scholarship/grant was $3,847; average loan was $3,367. For part-time students, average financial aid package was $5,327.
Students without need: 1,200 full-time freshmen who did not demonstrate need for aid received scholarships/grants; average award was $5,431. No-need awards available for academics, alumni affiliation, art, athletics, leadership, minority status, music/drama, ROTC, state/district residency.
Cumulative student debt: 50% of graduating class had student loans; average debt was $18,545.

FINANCIAL AID PROCEDURES
Forms required: FAFSA.
Dates and Deadlines: Priority date 3/1; no closing date. Applicants notified on a rolling basis starting 4/1; must reply within 3 week(s) of notification.
Transfers: Scholarship opportunities for transfer students.

CONTACT
Roger Thompson, Assistant Vice President for Enrollment Management
Box 870132, Tuscaloosa, AL 35487-0132
(205) 348-5666

University of Alabama at Birmingham
Birmingham, Alabama
www.uab.edu   Federal Code: 001052

4-year public university in very large city.
Enrollment: 11,060 undergrads, 28% part-time. 1,543 full-time freshmen.
Selectivity: Admits over 75% of applicants.

BASIC COSTS (2005-2006)
Tuition and fees: $4,792; out-of-state residents $10,732.
Per-credit charge: $132; out-of-state residents $330.
Room and board: $4,490.

FINANCIAL AID PICTURE (2004-2005)
Students with need: Out of 1,226 full-time freshmen who applied for aid, 813 were judged to have need. Of these, 804 received aid, and 103 had their full need met. Average financial aid package met 39% of need; average scholarship/grant was $3,204; average loan was $2,962. For part-time students, average financial aid package was $5,553.
Students without need: 345 full-time freshmen who did not demonstrate need for aid received scholarships/grants; average award was $7,335. No-need awards available for academics, alumni affiliation, art, athletics, leadership, minority status, music/drama, ROTC.
Scholarships offered: 39 full-time freshmen received athletic scholarships; average amount $10,048.
Cumulative student debt: 54% of graduating class had student loans; average debt was $17,594.

FINANCIAL AID PROCEDURES
Forms required: FAFSA, institutional form.
Dates and Deadlines: Priority date 4/1; no closing date. Applicants notified on a rolling basis starting 4/1; must reply within 4 week(s) of notification.

CONTACT
Jan May, Director of Financial Aid
260 HUC, 1530 3rd Avenue South, Birmingham, AL 35294-1150
(205) 934-8223

University of Alabama in Huntsville
Huntsville, Alabama
www.uah.edu   Federal Code: 001055

4-year public university in small city.
Enrollment: 5,232 undergrads, 26% part-time. 654 full-time freshmen.
Selectivity: Admits over 75% of applicants.

BASIC COSTS (2005-2006)
Tuition and fees: $4,688; out-of-state residents $9,886.
Per-credit charge: $176; out-of-state residents $370.
Room and board: $5,320.

FINANCIAL AID PICTURE (2004-2005)
Students with need: Out of 590 full-time freshmen who applied for aid, 265 were judged to have need. Of these, 257 received aid, and 40 had their full need met. Average financial aid package met 51% of need; average scholarship/grant was $2,866; average loan was $2,247. For part-time students, average financial aid package was $4,306.
Students without need: 254 full-time freshmen who did not demonstrate need for aid received scholarships/grants; average award was $2,647. No-need awards available for academics, art, athletics, leadership, minority status, music/drama, ROTC.
Scholarships offered: 54 full-time freshmen received athletic scholarships; average amount $3,662.
Cumulative student debt: 52% of graduating class had student loans; average debt was $17,272.
Additional info: Application deadline for institutional scholarships is February 1.

FINANCIAL AID PROCEDURES
Forms required: FAFSA, institutional form.
Dates and Deadlines: Priority date 4/1; closing date 7/31. Applicants notified on a rolling basis starting 4/1; must reply within 2 week(s) of notification.

CONTACT
Andy Weaver, Director of Student Financial Services
301 Sparkman Drive, Huntsville, AL 35899
(256) 824-6241

University of Mobile
Mobile, Alabama
www.umobile.edu   Federal Code: 001029

4-year private university and liberal arts college in small city, affiliated with Alabama Baptist Convention.
Enrollment: 1,549 undergrads, 18% part-time. 262 full-time freshmen.
Selectivity: Admits 50 to 75% of applicants.

BASIC COSTS (2006-2007)
Tuition and fees: $12,330.
Per-credit charge: $420.
Room and board: $6,680.

FINANCIAL AID PICTURE (2005-2006)
Students with need: Out of 248 full-time freshmen who applied for aid, 248 were judged to have need. Of these, 248 received aid. Average financial aid package met 64% of need; average scholarship/grant was $4,283; average loan was $2,625. For part-time students, average financial aid package was $4,200.
Students without need: 80 full-time freshmen who did not demonstrate need for aid received scholarships/grants; average award was $5,823. No-need awards available for academics, alumni affiliation, art, athletics, job skills, leadership, minority status, music/drama, religious affiliation, ROTC, state/district residency.

158   Alabama University of Mobile

FINANCIAL AID PROCEDURES
Forms required: FAFSA, state aid form, institutional form.
Dates and Deadlines: Priority date 3/31; no closing date. Applicants notified on a rolling basis; must reply within 2 week(s) of notification.

CONTACT
Marie Thomas, Director of Financial Aid
5735 College Parkway, Mobile, AL 36613-2842
(251) 442-2252

University of Montevallo
Montevallo, Alabama
www.montevallo.edu   Federal Code: 001004

4-year public university and liberal arts college in small town.
Enrollment: 2,557 undergrads, 9% part-time. 526 full-time freshmen.
Selectivity: Admits 50 to 75% of applicants.

BASIC COSTS (2005-2006)
Tuition and fees: $5,664; out-of-state residents $11,124.
Per-credit charge: $182; out-of-state residents $364.
Room and board: $3,966.

FINANCIAL AID PICTURE (2004-2005)
Students with need: Out of 420 full-time freshmen who applied for aid, 312 were judged to have need. Of these, 309 received aid, and 119 had their full need met. Average financial aid package met 46% of need; average scholarship/grant was $4,511; average loan was $1,653. For part-time students, average financial aid package was $5,759.
Students without need: 103 full-time freshmen who did not demonstrate need for aid received scholarships/grants; average award was $3,774. No-need awards available for academics, art, athletics, leadership, minority status, music/drama, ROTC.
Scholarships offered: 15 full-time freshmen received athletic scholarships; average amount $8,339.

FINANCIAL AID PROCEDURES
Forms required: FAFSA.
Dates and Deadlines: Priority date 4/15; no closing date. Applicants notified by 6/1; must reply within 2 week(s) of notification.

CONTACT
Maria Parker, Director of Financial Aid
Station 6030, Montevallo, AL 35115-6030
(205) 665-6050

University of North Alabama
Florence, Alabama
www.una.edu   Federal Code: 001016

4-year public university in large town.
Enrollment: 5,016 undergrads, 12% part-time. 825 full-time freshmen.
Selectivity: Admits over 75% of applicants.

BASIC COSTS (2005-2006)
Tuition and fees: $4,282; out-of-state residents $7,930.
Room and board: $4,710.

FINANCIAL AID PICTURE (2004-2005)
Students with need: Out of 549 full-time freshmen who applied for aid, 412 were judged to have need. Of these, 389 received aid, and 83 had their full need met. Average financial aid package met 35% of need; average scholarship/grant was $3,297; average loan was $2,983. Need-based aid available for part-time students.
Students without need: No-need awards available for academics, art, athletics, leadership, minority status, music/drama, ROTC, state/district residency.
Scholarships offered: 38 full-time freshmen received athletic scholarships; average amount $6,961.

FINANCIAL AID PROCEDURES
Forms required: FAFSA.
Dates and Deadlines: Priority date 4/1; no closing date. Applicants notified on a rolling basis starting 5/31; must reply within 2 week(s) of notification.

CONTACT
Ben Baker, Director of Student Financial Services
UNA - Box 5011, Florence, AL 35632-0001
(256) 765-4590

University of South Alabama
Mobile, Alabama
www.southalabama.edu   Federal Code: 001057

4-year public university in small city.
Enrollment: 9,957 undergrads, 25% part-time. 1,198 full-time freshmen.
Selectivity: Admits over 75% of applicants.

BASIC COSTS (2005-2006)
Tuition and fees: $4,502; out-of-state residents $8,312.
Per-credit charge: $127; out-of-state residents $254.
Room and board: $4,648.
Additional info: Tuition/fee waivers available for minority students.

FINANCIAL AID PICTURE (2005-2006)
Students with need: Average financial aid package met 23% of need; average scholarship/grant was $1,702; average loan was $1,301. Need-based aid available for part-time students.
Students without need: No-need awards available for academics, alumni affiliation, art, athletics, minority status, music/drama, ROTC, state/district residency.

FINANCIAL AID PROCEDURES
Forms required: FAFSA, institutional form.
Dates and Deadlines: Priority date 5/1; no closing date. Applicants notified on a rolling basis starting 5/15.

CONTACT
Emily Johnston, Director of Financial Aid
182 Administration Building, Mobile, AL 36688-0002
(251) 460-6231

University of West Alabama
Livingston, Alabama
www.uwa.edu   Federal Code: 001024

4-year public university in small town.
Enrollment: 1,645 undergrads, 8% part-time. 359 full-time freshmen.
Selectivity: Admits over 75% of applicants.

BASIC COSTS (2005-2006)
Tuition and fees: $4,778; out-of-state residents $8,616.
Per-credit charge: $162; out-of-state residents $324.
Room and board: $3,318.

FINANCIAL AID PICTURE (2005-2006)
Students with need: Average financial aid package for all full-time undergraduates was $10,765. 24% awarded as scholarships/grants, 76% awarded as loans/jobs. Need-based aid available for part-time students. Work study available nights, weekends, and for part-time students.

Students without need: No-need awards available for academics, alumni affiliation, athletics, leadership, music/drama, state/district residency.
Cumulative student debt: 62% of graduating class had student loans; average debt was $16,043.

FINANCIAL AID PROCEDURES
Forms required: FAFSA.
Dates and Deadlines: Priority date 4/1; no closing date. Applicants notified on a rolling basis starting 6/1; must reply within 2 week(s) of notification.

CONTACT
Don Rainer, Director of Financial Aid
Station 4, Livingston, AL 35470
(205) 652-3576

Virginia College at Huntsville
Huntsville, Alabama
www.vc.edu   Federal Code: 030106

4-year for-profit business and technical college in small city.
Enrollment: 760 undergrads.
Selectivity: Open admission.

BASIC COSTS (2005-2006)
Additional info: Tuition varies by program. Per-credit-hour charge ranges from $255 to $285.

FINANCIAL AID PICTURE
Students with need: Need-based aid available for full-time and part-time students.

FINANCIAL AID PROCEDURES
Forms required: FAFSA, institutional form.
Dates and Deadlines: No deadline. Applicants notified on a rolling basis.

CONTACT
Samantha Williams, Student Finance Director
2800 Bob Wallace Avenue, Huntsville, AL 35805
(256) 533-7387

Wallace State Community College at Hanceville
Hanceville, Alabama
www.wallacestate.edu   Federal Code: 007871

2-year public health science and community college in rural community.
Enrollment: 4,871 undergrads.
Selectivity: Open admission; but selective for some programs.

BASIC COSTS (2005-2006)
Tuition and fees: $2,700; out-of-state residents $4,830.
Per-credit charge: $71; out-of-state residents $142.
Room only: $1,450.

FINANCIAL AID PICTURE (2004-2005)
Students with need: Need-based aid available for part-time students. Work study available nights.
Students without need: This college only awards aid to students with need.

FINANCIAL AID PROCEDURES
Forms required: FAFSA.
Dates and Deadlines: Priority date 5/1; no closing date. Applicants notified on a rolling basis starting 7/15; must reply within 2 week(s) of notification.
Transfers: No deadline.

CONTACT
Becky Graves, Director of Student Financial Aid
P. O. Box 2000, Hanceville, AL 35077-2000
(256) 352-8182

Alaska

Alaska Bible College
Glennallen, Alaska
www.akbible.edu   Federal Code: 014325

4-year private Bible college in rural community, affiliated with nondenominational tradition.
Enrollment: 43 undergrads.
Selectivity: Open admission; but selective for some programs.

BASIC COSTS (2006-2007)
Tuition and fees: $5,950.
Per-credit charge: $260.
Room and board: $4,750.

FINANCIAL AID PICTURE (2005-2006)
Students with need: 31% of average financial aid package awarded as scholarships/grants, 69% awarded as loans/jobs. Work study available nights, weekends, and for part-time students.
Students without need: This college only awards aid to students with need.

FINANCIAL AID PROCEDURES
Forms required: institutional form.
Dates and Deadlines: Priority date 4/30; closing date 8/1. Applicants notified on a rolling basis; must reply within 2 week(s) of notification.

CONTACT
Kevin Newman, Financial Aid Officer
Box 289, Glennallen, AK 99588-0289
(907) 822-3201

Alaska Pacific University
Anchorage, Alaska
www.alaskapacific.edu   Federal Code: 001061

4-year private university and liberal arts college in large city.
Enrollment: 471 undergrads, 37% part-time. 39 full-time freshmen.
Selectivity: Admits less than 50% of applicants.

BASIC COSTS (2006-2007)
Tuition and fees: $19,610.
Per-credit charge: $760.
Room and board: $6,800.
Additional info: Tuition at time of enrollment locked for 4 years.

FINANCIAL AID PICTURE (2005-2006)
Students with need: Out of 36 full-time freshmen who applied for aid, 33 were judged to have need. Of these, 33 received aid, and 12 had their full need met. Average financial aid package met 86% of need; average scholarship/grant was $2,945; average loan was $2,625. For part-time students, average financial aid package was $6,305.
Students without need: 3 full-time freshmen who did not demonstrate need for aid received scholarships/grants; average award was $6,665. No-need awards available for academics, alumni affiliation, leadership, religious affiliation, state/district residency.
Cumulative student debt: 66% of graduating class had student loans; average debt was $39,463.

Alaska — Alaska Pacific University

FINANCIAL AID PROCEDURES
Forms required: FAFSA.
Dates and Deadlines: Priority date 4/15; no closing date. Applicants notified on a rolling basis starting 2/1; must reply within 4 week(s) of notification.

CONTACT
Peter Miller, Director of Student Financial Services
4101 University Drive, Anchorage, AK 99508
(907) 564-8341

Charter College
Anchorage, Alaska
www.chartercollege.edu   Federal Code: 017377

4-year private junior and technical college in large city.
Enrollment: 475 undergrads.
Selectivity: Open admission.

BASIC COSTS (2005-2006)
Additional info: Tuition ranges from $19,000 to $23,000 for associates and from $38,000 to $44,000 for bachelors depending on program; includes books and supplies.

FINANCIAL AID PICTURE
Students with need: Need-based aid available for full-time and part-time students.

FINANCIAL AID PROCEDURES
Forms required: FAFSA.
Dates and Deadlines: No deadline. Applicants notified on a rolling basis; must reply within 5 week(s) of notification.

CONTACT
Janell McIntyre, Director of Student Services
2221 East Northern Lights Boulevard, Suite 120, Anchorage, AK 99508
(907) 777-1314

Prince William Sound Community College
Valdez, Alaska
www.pwscc.edu   Federal Code: 011462

2-year public community college in small town.
Enrollment: 105 undergrads, 28% part-time. 56 full-time freshmen.
Selectivity: Open admission.

BASIC COSTS (2005-2006)
Tuition and fees: $3,060.
Per-credit charge: $94.
Room only: $3,634.

FINANCIAL AID PICTURE
Students with need: Need-based aid available for full-time and part-time students.
Students without need: No-need awards available for state/district residency.

FINANCIAL AID PROCEDURES
Forms required: FAFSA.
Dates and Deadlines: Priority date 6/30; no closing date. Applicants notified on a rolling basis.
Transfers: Priority date 4/1; closing date 5/1.

CONTACT
Douglas Desorcie, Registrar
Box 97, Valdez, AK 99686
(907) 834-1666

Sheldon Jackson College
Sitka, Alaska
www.sj-alaska.edu   Federal Code: 001062

4-year private liberal arts and teachers college in small town, affiliated with Presbyterian Church (USA).
Enrollment: 122 undergrads.
Selectivity: Open admission.

BASIC COSTS (2005-2006)
Tuition and fees: $11,300.
Room and board: $7,300.

FINANCIAL AID PICTURE
Students with need: Need-based aid available for full-time students.
Additional info: Financial aid available from Bureau of Indian Affairs and Alaska State Loan Program.

FINANCIAL AID PROCEDURES
Forms required: FAFSA.
Dates and Deadlines: Priority date 3/15; no closing date. Applicants notified on a rolling basis starting 4/1; must reply within 3 week(s) of notification.

CONTACT
Louise Driver, Financial Aid Director and Director of Admissions
801 Lincoln Street, Sitka, AK 99835
(907) 747-5211

University of Alaska Anchorage
Anchorage, Alaska
www.uaa.alaska.edu   Federal Code: 011462

4-year public university in large city.
Enrollment: 11,398 undergrads. 1,153 full-time freshmen.
Selectivity: Admits 50 to 75% of applicants.

BASIC COSTS (2005-2006)
Tuition and fees: $3,734; out-of-state residents $11,354.
Per-credit charge: $109; out-of-state residents $363.
Room and board: $6,730.

FINANCIAL AID PICTURE (2005-2006)
Students with need: Out of 842 full-time freshmen who applied for aid, 402 were judged to have need. Of these, 371 received aid, and 108 had their full need met. Average financial aid package met 66% of need; average scholarship/grant was $3,906; average loan was $5,460. Need-based aid available for part-time students.
Students without need: 157 full-time freshmen who did not demonstrate need for aid received scholarships/grants; average award was $2,755. No-need awards available for academics, athletics.
Scholarships offered: 20 full-time freshmen received athletic scholarships.

FINANCIAL AID PROCEDURES
Forms required: FAFSA, institutional form.
Dates and Deadlines: Priority date 4/1; closing date 8/1. Applicants notified on a rolling basis starting 3/15; must reply within 4 week(s) of notification.
Transfers: Closing date 8/30.

CONTACT
Ted Malone, Director of Financial Aid
3211 Providence Drive, #158, Anchorage, AK 99508-8046
(907) 786-1586

University of Alaska Fairbanks
Fairbanks, Alaska
www.uaf.edu   Federal Code: 001063

4-year public university in small city.
Enrollment: 4,862 undergrads, 32% part-time. 806 full-time freshmen.
Selectivity: Admits over 75% of applicants. GED not accepted.

BASIC COSTS (2005-2006)
Tuition and fees: $3,946; out-of-state residents $11,566.
Per-credit charge: $109; out-of-state residents $363.
Room and board: $5,580.

FINANCIAL AID PICTURE (2005-2006)
Students with need: Out of 729 full-time freshmen who applied for aid, 302 were judged to have need. Of these, 280 received aid, and 78 had their full need met. Average financial aid package met 62% of need; average scholarship/grant was $3,768; average loan was $5,690. For part-time students, average financial aid package was $6,843.
Students without need: 120 full-time freshmen who did not demonstrate need for aid received scholarships/grants; average award was $2,557. No-need awards available for academics, art, athletics, job skills, ROTC, state/district residency.
Scholarships offered: 17 full-time freshmen received athletic scholarships; average amount $9,816.
Cumulative student debt: 49% of graduating class had student loans; average debt was $23,994.

FINANCIAL AID PROCEDURES
Forms required: FAFSA.
Dates and Deadlines: Priority date 7/1; no closing date. Applicants notified on a rolling basis starting 3/1; must reply within 2 week(s) of notification.

CONTACT
Deanna Dieringer, Co-Director of Financial Aid
PO Box 757480, Fairbanks, AK 99775-7480
(907) 474-7256

University of Alaska Southeast
Juneau, Alaska
www.uas.alaska.edu   Federal Code: 001065

4-year public university in large town.
Enrollment: 1,280 undergrads, 43% part-time. 158 full-time freshmen.
Selectivity: Admits 50 to 75% of applicants.

BASIC COSTS (2005-2006)
Tuition and fees: $3,798; out-of-state residents $11,418.
Per-credit charge: $109; out-of-state residents $363.
Room and board: $5,780.

FINANCIAL AID PICTURE (2005-2006)
Students with need: 40% of average financial aid package awarded as scholarships/grants, 60% awarded as loans/jobs. Need-based aid available for part-time students. Work study available nights, weekends, and for part-time students.
Students without need: No-need awards available for academics, leadership.
Cumulative student debt: 43% of graduating class had student loans; average debt was $19,982.
Additional info: Transfer, continuing, and freshman scholarship deadline March 1.

FINANCIAL AID PROCEDURES
Forms required: FAFSA.
Dates and Deadlines: Priority date 6/1; no closing date. Applicants notified on a rolling basis starting 2/15; must reply within 3 week(s) of notification.

CONTACT
Barbara Burnett, Manager of Financial Aid
11120 Glacier Highway, Juneau, AK 99801-8681
(907) 796-6255

Arizona

Arizona State University
Tempe, Arizona
www.asu.edu   Federal Code: 001081

4-year public university in small city.
Enrollment: 39,649 undergrads, 17% part-time. 6,917 full-time freshmen.
Selectivity: Admits over 75% of applicants.

BASIC COSTS (2005-2006)
Tuition and fees: $4,407; out-of-state residents $15,095.
Per-credit charge: $225; out-of-state residents $625.
Room and board: $7,150.

FINANCIAL AID PICTURE (2004-2005)
Students with need: Out of 3,851 full-time freshmen who applied for aid, 2,628 were judged to have need. Of these, 2,628 received aid, and 524 had their full need met. Average financial aid package met 64% of need; average scholarship/grant was $5,946; average loan was $2,729. For part-time students, average financial aid package was $6,137.
Students without need: 1,488 full-time freshmen who did not demonstrate need for aid received scholarships/grants; average award was $5,463. No-need awards available for academics, art, athletics, leadership, music/drama, ROTC.
Scholarships offered: 62 full-time freshmen received athletic scholarships; average amount $11,868.
Cumulative student debt: 51% of graduating class had student loans; average debt was $17,016.

FINANCIAL AID PROCEDURES
Forms required: FAFSA.
Dates and Deadlines: Priority date 3/1; no closing date. Applicants notified on a rolling basis.

CONTACT
Craig Fennell, Director of Student Financial Assistance
Box 870112, Tempe, AZ 85287-0112
(480) 965-3355

Arizona State University West
Phoenix, Arizona
www.west.asu.edu   Federal Code: 001081

4-year public university in small city.
Enrollment: 5,551 undergrads, 27% part-time. 372 full-time freshmen.
Selectivity: Admits 50 to 75% of applicants.

BASIC COSTS (2005-2006)
Tuition and fees: $4,343; out-of-state residents $15,092.
Per-credit charge: $221; out-of-state residents $625.

FINANCIAL AID PICTURE (2004-2005)
Students with need: Out of 239 full-time freshmen who applied for aid, 184 were judged to have need. Of these, 184 received aid, and 20 had their full need met. Average financial aid package met 63% of need; average scholarship/grant was $5,776; average loan was $2,447. For part-time students, average financial aid package was $6,123.

Students without need: 63 full-time freshmen who did not demonstrate need for aid received scholarships/grants; average award was $3,842. No-need awards available for academics.

FINANCIAL AID PROCEDURES
Forms required: FAFSA.
Dates and Deadlines: Closing date 3/1. Applicants notified on a rolling basis starting 3/15; must reply within 4 week(s) of notification.

CONTACT
Leah Samudio, Financial Aid Manager
PO Box 37100 MC 0250, Phoenix, AZ 85069-7100
(602) 543-8178

Arizona Western College
Yuma, Arizona
www.azwestern.edu   Federal Code: 001071

2-year public community college in small city.
Enrollment: 5,602 undergrads, 69% part-time. 519 full-time freshmen.
Selectivity: Open admission; but selective for some programs.

BASIC COSTS (2006-2007)
Tuition and fees: $1,200; out-of-state residents $5,760.
Per-credit charge: $40; out-of-state residents $46.
Room and board: $4,468.

FINANCIAL AID PICTURE
Students with need: Need-based aid available for full-time and part-time students. Work study available nights, weekends, and for part-time students.
Students without need: No-need awards available for academics, athletics.

FINANCIAL AID PROCEDURES
Forms required: FAFSA, institutional form.
Dates and Deadlines: Priority date 4/1; no closing date. Applicants notified on a rolling basis starting 5/1.

CONTACT
Luis Barajas, Director of Financial Aid
P.O. Box 929, Yuma, AZ 85366-0929
(928) 344-7634

Art Center Design College
Tucson, Arizona
www.theartcenter.edu   Federal Code: 024915

3-year for-profit visual arts college in very large city.
Enrollment: 578 undergrads.

BASIC COSTS (2006-2007)
Tuition and fees: $13,680.
Per-credit charge: $570.

FINANCIAL AID PICTURE
Students with need: Need-based aid available for full-time and part-time students.
Students without need: This college only awards aid to students with need.

FINANCIAL AID PROCEDURES
Forms required: FAFSA.
Dates and Deadlines: No deadline.

CONTACT
Amy Woods, Education Finance Advisor
2525 North Country Club Road, Tucson, AZ 85716
(520) 325-0123

Central Arizona College
Coolidge, Arizona
www.centralaz.edu   Federal Code: 007283

2-year public community college in rural community.
Enrollment: 4,155 undergrads, 58% part-time. 597 full-time freshmen.
Selectivity: Open admission; but selective for some programs.

BASIC COSTS (2006-2007)
Tuition and fees: $1,348; out-of-state residents $6,388.
Per-credit charge: $47; out-of-state residents $94.
Room and board: $4,200.

FINANCIAL AID PICTURE
Students with need: Need-based aid available for full-time and part-time students. Work study available nights, weekends, and for part-time students.

FINANCIAL AID PROCEDURES
Forms required: FAFSA.
Dates and Deadlines: Priority date 5/1; closing date 7/15. Applicants notified by 5/30; must reply within 3 week(s) of notification.

CONTACT
Elisa Juarez, Director of Student Financial Aid
8470 North Overfield Road, Coolidge, AZ 85228-9778
(520) 426-4230

Chandler-Gilbert Community College: Pecos
Chandler, Arizona
www.cgc.maricopa.edu   Federal Code: 030722

2-year public community college in small town.
Enrollment: 987 full-time undergrads.
Selectivity: Open admission.

BASIC COSTS (2005-2006)
Tuition and fees: $1,810; out-of-state residents $7,750.
Per-credit charge: $60; out-of-state residents $258.

FINANCIAL AID PICTURE (2005-2006)
Students with need: 52% of average financial aid package awarded as scholarships/grants, 48% awarded as loans/jobs.

CONTACT
Doug Bullock, Director of Financial Aid
2626 East Pecos Road, Chandler, AZ 85225

Cochise College
Douglas, Arizona
www.cochise.edu   Federal Code: 001072

2-year public community college in large town.
Enrollment: 3,289 undergrads.
Selectivity: Open admission; but selective for some programs.

BASIC COSTS (2006-2007)
Tuition and fees: $1,440; out-of-state residents $6,360.
Room and board: $4,392.

FINANCIAL AID PICTURE (2004-2005)
Students with need: 97% of average financial aid package awarded as scholarships/grants, 3% awarded as loans/jobs. Need-based aid available for part-time students.

FINANCIAL AID PROCEDURES
Forms required: FAFSA.

Dates and Deadlines: Closing date 4/15. Applicants notified on a rolling basis starting 6/15; must reply within 2 week(s) of notification.

CONTACT
Dartle Atherton, Director of Financial Aid
4190 West Highway 80, Douglas, AZ 85607-6190
(520) 515-5417

Coconino County Community College
Flagstaff, Arizona
www.coconino.edu   Federal Code: 031004

2-year public community college in small city.
Enrollment: 1,574 undergrads.
Selectivity: Open admission; but selective for some programs.

BASIC COSTS (2006-2007)
Tuition and fees: $1,464; out-of-state residents $7,320.
Per-credit charge: $61; out-of-state residents $305.

FINANCIAL AID PICTURE (2004-2005)
Students with need: 95% of average financial aid package awarded as scholarships/grants, 5% awarded as loans/jobs.

FINANCIAL AID PROCEDURES
Dates and Deadlines: Priority date 4/15; closing date 6/30.

CONTACT
Patt Sprengeler, Director for Student Support Services and Financial Assistance
2800 S Lone Tree Road, Flagstaff, AZ 86001
(928) 226-4219

DeVry University: Phoenix
Phoenix, Arizona
www.devry-phx.edu   Federal Code: 008322

4-year for-profit university in large city.
Enrollment: 1,164 undergrads, 34% part-time. 508 full-time freshmen.

BASIC COSTS (2005-2006)
Tuition and fees: $12,140.
Per-credit charge: $440.

FINANCIAL AID PICTURE (2004-2005)
Students with need: Out of 317 full-time freshmen who applied for aid, 296 were judged to have need. Of these, 290 received aid, and 11 had their full need met. Average financial aid package met 37% of need; average scholarship/grant was $5,256; average loan was $4,662. For part-time students, average financial aid package was $8,129.
Students without need: This college only awards aid to students with need.

FINANCIAL AID PROCEDURES
Forms required: FAFSA.
Dates and Deadlines: No deadline. Applicants notified on a rolling basis.

CONTACT
Kathy Wyse, Dean of Student Finances
2149 West Dunlap Avenue, Phoenix, AZ 85021-2995
(602) 870-9229

Dine College
Tsaile, Arizona
www.dinecollege.edu   Federal Code: 008246

2-year public community college in rural community.
Enrollment: 1,753 undergrads, 52% part-time. 236 full-time freshmen.
Selectivity: Open admission.

BASIC COSTS (2006-2007)
Tuition and fees: $850.
Per-credit charge: $30.
Room and board: $3,764.

FINANCIAL AID PICTURE (2004-2005)
Students with need: Out of 46 full-time freshmen who applied for aid, 43 were judged to have need. Of these, 43 received aid, and 10 had their full need met. Average financial aid package met 4% of need; average scholarship/grant was $4,025. For part-time students, average financial aid package was $4,025.
Students without need: 3 full-time freshmen who did not demonstrate need for aid received scholarships/grants; average award was $250.

FINANCIAL AID PROCEDURES
Forms required: FAFSA, institutional form.
Dates and Deadlines: Priority date 4/15; no closing date. Applicants notified on a rolling basis starting 5/1; must reply within 4 week(s) of notification.

CONTACT
Gary Segay, Director of Financial Aid
Box 67, Tsaile, AZ 86556
(928) 724-6737

Eastern Arizona College
Thatcher, Arizona
www.eac.edu   Federal Code: 001073

2-year public community college in large town.
Enrollment: 2,758 undergrads, 53% part-time. 614 full-time freshmen.
Selectivity: Open admission; but selective for some programs.

BASIC COSTS (2006-2007)
Tuition and fees: $1,220; out-of-state residents $6,460.
Per-credit charge: $50; out-of-state residents $100.
Room and board: $4,320.

FINANCIAL AID PICTURE (2005-2006)
Students with need: Out of 387 full-time freshmen who applied for aid, 298 were judged to have need. Of these, 250 received aid, and 17 had their full need met. Average financial aid package met 45% of need; average scholarship/grant was $3,978. For part-time students, average financial aid package was $2,431.
Students without need: 178 full-time freshmen who did not demonstrate need for aid received scholarships/grants; average award was $2,580. No-need awards available for academics, art, athletics, leadership, music/drama, state/district residency.
Scholarships offered: Merit: Departmental Scholarships; in-state tuition, based on 2.5 minimum GPA. Academic Scholarships; in-state tuition, based on 3.0 minimum GPA. Performing Arts Scholarships; amounts vary, based on 2.5 minimum GPA, audition. **Athletic:** 37 full-time freshmen received athletic scholarships; average amount $3,689.
Additional info: Limited number of tuition waivers for New Mexico residents. Unlimited number of waivers for those meeting WUE requirements.

FINANCIAL AID PROCEDURES
Forms required: FAFSA, institutional form.
Dates and Deadlines: Priority date 3/1; no closing date. Applicants notified on a rolling basis starting 3/15.

164 Arizona Eastern Arizona College

Transfers: No deadline. Applicants notified on a rolling basis starting 3/15.
CONTACT
Geraldine Covert, Director of Financial Aid
615 North Stadium Avenue, Thatcher, AZ 85552-0769
(928) 428-8287

Embry-Riddle Aeronautical University: Prescott Campus
Prescott, Arizona
www.embryriddle.edu   Federal Code: 014797

4-year private university in large town.
Enrollment: 1,644 undergrads, 11% part-time. 358 full-time freshmen.
Selectivity: Admits over 75% of applicants.
BASIC COSTS (2006-2007)
Tuition and fees: $25,120.
Per-credit charge: $1,020.
Room and board: $7,070.
FINANCIAL AID PICTURE (2005-2006)
Students with need: Out of 319 full-time freshmen who applied for aid, 252 were judged to have need. Of these, 252 received aid. For part-time students, average financial aid package was $10,256.
Students without need: No-need awards available for academics, alumni affiliation, athletics, leadership, ROTC.
Cumulative student debt: 73% of graduating class had student loans; average debt was $49,532.
FINANCIAL AID PROCEDURES
Forms required: FAFSA.
Dates and Deadlines: No deadline. Applicants notified on a rolling basis starting 3/1; must reply within 4 week(s) of notification.
CONTACT
Daniel Lupin, Director of Financial Aid
3700 North Willow Creek Road, Prescott, AZ 86301-3720
(928) 777-3765

Estrella Mountain Community College
Avondale, Arizona
www.emc.maricopa.edu   Federal Code: 031563

2-year public community college in small city.
Enrollment: 1,870 undergrads.
Selectivity: Open admission.
BASIC COSTS (2005-2006)
Tuition and fees: $1,810; out-of-state residents $7,750.
Per-credit charge: $60; out-of-state residents $258.
FINANCIAL AID PICTURE (2004-2005)
Students with need: 67% of average financial aid package awarded as scholarships/grants, 33% awarded as loans/jobs. Need-based aid available for part-time students. Work study available nights.
Students without need: No-need awards available for leadership.
FINANCIAL AID PROCEDURES
Dates and Deadlines: Priority date 4/1; no closing date. Applicants notified on a rolling basis starting 4/15.
CONTACT
Rosanna Short, Director, Financial Aid
3000 North Dysart Road, Avondale, AZ 85323
(623) 935-8940

Gateway Community College
Phoenix, Arizona
www.gwc.maricopa.edu   Federal Code: 008303

2-year public community and technical college in very large city.
Enrollment: 8,500 undergrads.
Selectivity: Open admission; but selective for some programs.
BASIC COSTS (2005-2006)
Tuition and fees: $1,810; out-of-state residents $7,750.
Per-credit charge: $60; out-of-state residents $258.
FINANCIAL AID PICTURE
Students with need: Need-based aid available for full-time and part-time students. Work study available nights, weekends, and for part-time students.
Students without need: No-need awards available for athletics.
FINANCIAL AID PROCEDURES
Forms required: FAFSA, institutional form.
Dates and Deadlines: Priority date 4/15; no closing date. Applicants notified on a rolling basis starting 7/1; must reply within 4 week(s) of notification.
CONTACT
Bradley Honius, Director of Financial Aid
108 North 40th Street, Phoenix, AZ 85034
(602) 286-8115

Glendale Community College
Glendale, Arizona
www.gc.maricopa.edu   Federal Code: 001076

2-year public community college in small city.
Enrollment: 4,431 undergrads, 60% part-time.
Selectivity: Open admission; but selective for some programs.
BASIC COSTS (2005-2006)
Tuition and fees: $1,810; out-of-state residents $7,750.
Per-credit charge: $60; out-of-state residents $258.
FINANCIAL AID PICTURE
Students with need: Need-based aid available for full-time and part-time students. Work study available nights, weekends, and for part-time students.
FINANCIAL AID PROCEDURES
Forms required: FAFSA.
Dates and Deadlines: Priority date 4/30; closing date 8/1. Applicants notified on a rolling basis starting 6/1.
CONTACT
Ellen Neel, Director of Financial Aid
6000 West Olive Avenue, Glendale, AZ 85302
(623) 845-3366

Grand Canyon University
Phoenix, Arizona
www.gcu.net   Federal Code: 001074

4-year for-profit university in very large city.
Enrollment: 1,700 undergrads.
Selectivity: Open admission; but selective for some programs.
BASIC COSTS (2006-2007)
Tuition and fees: $12,500.
Room and board: $7,194.
FINANCIAL AID PICTURE
Students with need: Need-based aid available for full-time students.

Students without need: No-need awards available for academics, alumni affiliation, art, athletics, leadership, minority status, music/drama, religious affiliation.

FINANCIAL AID PROCEDURES
Forms required: FAFSA.
Dates and Deadlines: No deadline. Applicants notified on a rolling basis.

CONTACT
Joyce Hatch, Director of Finance
3300 West Camelback Road, Phoenix, AZ 85017
(800) 800-9776

High-Tech Institute
Phoenix, Arizona
www.hightechinstitute.edu   Federal Code: 022631

2-year for-profit technical college in very large city.
Enrollment: 2,044 undergrads. 576 full-time freshmen.
Selectivity: Open admission.

BASIC COSTS (2005-2006)
Additional info: Total costs of associate degrees vary by program and range from $18,450 to $25,850. Total costs of diplomas vary by program and range from $8,850 to $16,250.

FINANCIAL AID PICTURE
Students with need: Need-based aid available for full-time students.
Students without need: This college only awards aid to students with need.

FINANCIAL AID PROCEDURES
Dates and Deadlines: No deadline.

CONTACT
Alma Cleveland, Financial Director
1515 East Indian School Road, Phoenix, AZ 85014-4901
(602) 279-9700

International Institute of the Americas: Phoenix
Phoenix, Arizona
www.iia.edu   Federal Code: 022188

2-year private business and health science college in very large city.
Enrollment: 450 undergrads. 228 full-time freshmen.
Selectivity: Open admission.

BASIC COSTS (2006-2007)
Tuition and fees: $10,050.
Additional info: Tuition and fees may vary by program.

FINANCIAL AID PICTURE
Students with need: Need-based aid available for full-time students.
Students without need: This college only awards aid to students with need.

FINANCIAL AID PROCEDURES
Forms required: FAFSA, institutional form.
Dates and Deadlines: No deadline.

CONTACT
Melba Moore, Financial Aid Director
6049 North 43rd Avenue, Phoenix, AZ 85019
(623) 849-7830

International Institute of the Americas: Tucson
Tucson, Arizona
www.iia.edu   Federal Code: 022188

4-year private business and health science college in very large city.
Enrollment: 500 undergrads. 298 full-time freshmen.
Selectivity: Open admission.

BASIC COSTS (2006-2007)
Tuition and fees: $10,050.
Additional info: Tuition and fees may vary by program.

FINANCIAL AID PICTURE
Students with need: Need-based aid available for full-time and part-time students.
Students without need: This college only awards aid to students with need.

FINANCIAL AID PROCEDURES
Forms required: FAFSA, institutional form.
Dates and Deadlines: No deadline.

CONTACT
Melba Moore, Financial Aid Director
5441 East 22nd Street, Suite 125, Tucson, AZ 85711
(623) 849-7830

Lamson College
Tempe, Arizona
www.lamsoncollege.com   Federal Code: 005186

2-year for-profit junior and technical college in very large city.
Enrollment: 300 undergrads.
Selectivity: Open admission.

BASIC COSTS (2005-2006)
Additional info: Tuition at time of enrollment locked for 2 years.

FINANCIAL AID PICTURE
Students with need: Need-based aid available for full-time and part-time students.

FINANCIAL AID PROCEDURES
Forms required: FAFSA.
Dates and Deadlines: No deadline. Applicants notified on a rolling basis.

CONTACT
1126 North Scottsdale Road, Suite 17, Tempe, AZ 85281-1700
(480) 898-7000

Mohave Community College
Kingman, Arizona
www.mohave.edu   Federal Code: 011864

2-year public community college in large town.
Enrollment: 2,690 undergrads, 54% part-time. 236 full-time freshmen.
Selectivity: Open admission; but selective for some programs.

BASIC COSTS (2006-2007)
Tuition and fees: $1,500; out-of-state residents $4,500.
Per-credit charge: $50; out-of-state residents $150.

FINANCIAL AID PICTURE
Students with need: Need-based aid available for full-time and part-time students. Work study available nights.

FINANCIAL AID PROCEDURES
Forms required: FAFSA, institutional form.
Dates and Deadlines: Priority date 4/15; no closing date. Applicants notified on a rolling basis starting 5/1; must reply within 2 week(s) of notification.

CONTACT
Joseph Heinley, Director of Financial Aid
1971 Jagerson Avenue, Kingman, AZ 86409
(866) 664-2832

Northcentral University
Prescott, Arizona
www.ncu.edu   Federal Code: 038133

4-year for-profit virtual university in large town.
Enrollment: 128 undergrads.

BASIC COSTS (2005-2006)
Per-credit charge: $375.
Additional info: Students pay $375 per semester credit. Tuition/fee waivers available for adults.

FINANCIAL AID PICTURE (2005-2006)
Students with need: Average financial aid package met 48% of need; average loan was $3,912. For part-time students, average financial aid package was $500.

FINANCIAL AID PROCEDURES
Dates and Deadlines: No deadline. Must reply within 4 week(s) of notification.

CONTACT
Jane Hersh, Director of Financial Aid
505 West Whipple Street, Prescott, AZ 86301-1747
(928) 541-7777 ext. 8080

Northern Arizona University
Flagstaff, Arizona
www.nau.edu   Federal Code: 001082

4-year public university in small city.
Enrollment: 13,116 undergrads, 14% part-time. 2,277 full-time freshmen.
Selectivity: Admits over 75% of applicants.

BASIC COSTS (2005-2006)
Tuition and fees: $4,393; out-of-state residents $13,023.
Per-credit charge: $221; out-of-state residents $536.
Room and board: $5,960.

FINANCIAL AID PICTURE (2004-2005)
Students with need: Out of 1,720 full-time freshmen who applied for aid, 1,102 were judged to have need. Of these, 1,078 received aid, and 204 had their full need met. Average financial aid package met 62% of need; average scholarship/grant was $4,199; average loan was $2,465. For part-time students, average financial aid package was $6,140.
Students without need: 578 full-time freshmen who did not demonstrate need for aid received scholarships/grants; average award was $3,124. No-need awards available for academics, alumni affiliation, art, athletics, music/drama, ROTC.
Scholarships offered: 34 full-time freshmen received athletic scholarships; average amount $9,767.
Cumulative student debt: 60% of graduating class had student loans; average debt was $16,473.

FINANCIAL AID PROCEDURES
Forms required: FAFSA.
Dates and Deadlines: Priority date 2/14; no closing date. Applicants notified on a rolling basis starting 3/15.

CONTACT
Director of Financial Aid
Box 4084, Flagstaff, AZ 86011-4084
(928) 523-4951

Northland Pioneer College
Holbrook, Arizona
www.npc.edu   Federal Code: 011862

2-year public community college in small town.
Enrollment: 1,500 undergrads.
Selectivity: Open admission; but selective for some programs.

BASIC COSTS (2005-2006)
Tuition and fees: $1,008; out-of-state residents $6,600.
Per-credit charge: $42; out-of-state residents $72.
Room only: $2,000.

FINANCIAL AID PICTURE
Students with need: Need-based aid available for full-time and part-time students. Work study available nights, weekends, and for part-time students.
Students without need: No-need awards available for academics, art, job skills, leadership, minority status, music/drama, state/district residency.

FINANCIAL AID PROCEDURES
Forms required: FAFSA, institutional form.
Dates and Deadlines: Priority date 6/1; no closing date. Applicants notified on a rolling basis starting 5/15; must reply within 2 week(s) of notification.

CONTACT
Beaulah Bob-Pennypacker, Financial Aid Coordinator
PO Box 610, Holbrook, AZ 86025-0610
(928) 524-7470

Paradise Valley Community College
Phoenix, Arizona
www.pvc.maricopa.edu   Federal Code: 026236

2-year public community college in very large city.
Enrollment: 2,862 undergrads, 61% part-time.
Selectivity: Open admission.

BASIC COSTS (2005-2006)
Tuition and fees: $1,810; out-of-state residents $7,750.
Per-credit charge: $60; out-of-state residents $258.

FINANCIAL AID PICTURE
Students with need: Need-based aid available for full-time and part-time students.

FINANCIAL AID PROCEDURES
Forms required: FAFSA.
Dates and Deadlines: No deadline. Applicants notified on a rolling basis starting 6/1.

CONTACT
JoAnn Caufield, Director, Financial Aid
18401 North 32nd Street, Phoenix, AZ 85032
(602) 787-7100

Phoenix College
Phoenix, Arizona
www.pc.maricopa.edu   Federal Code: 001078

2-year public community college in very large city.
Enrollment: 12,200 undergrads.
Selectivity: Open admission; but selective for some programs.

BASIC COSTS (2006-2007)
Tuition and fees: $1,980; out-of-state residents $7,770.
Per-credit charge: $65; out-of-state residents $280.

FINANCIAL AID PICTURE
Students with need: Work study available weekends and for part-time students.

FINANCIAL AID PROCEDURES
Forms required: FAFSA.
Dates and Deadlines: Priority date 6/30; no closing date. Applicants notified on a rolling basis starting 5/1.

CONTACT
Genevieve Watson, Director of Financial Aid
1202 West Thomas Road, Phoenix, AZ 85013
(602) 285-7404

Pima Community College
Tucson, Arizona
www.pima.edu   Federal Code: 007266

2-year public community and technical college in very large city.
Enrollment: 25,145 undergrads, 67% part-time. 2,318 full-time freshmen.
Selectivity: Open admission; but selective for some programs.

BASIC COSTS (2005-2006)
Tuition and fees: $1,405; out-of-state residents $6,565.
Per-credit charge: $44; out-of-state residents $74.

FINANCIAL AID PICTURE
Students with need: Need-based aid available for full-time and part-time students.
Students without need: No-need awards available for academics, alumni affiliation, art, athletics, minority status, music/drama.

FINANCIAL AID PROCEDURES
Forms required: FAFSA.
Dates and Deadlines: Priority date 3/15; no closing date. Applicants notified on a rolling basis starting 7/1; must reply within 2 week(s) of notification.

CONTACT
Ramanjot Chowhan, Acting Director of Financial Aid
4905B East Broadway, Tucson, AZ 85709-1120
(520) 206-4950

Prescott College
Prescott, Arizona
www.prescott.edu   Federal Code: 013659

4-year private liberal arts college in large town.
Enrollment: 752 undergrads, 9% part-time. 41 full-time freshmen.
Selectivity: Admits over 75% of applicants.

BASIC COSTS (2006-2007)
Tuition and fees: $18,661.

FINANCIAL AID PICTURE (2004-2005)
Students with need: Out of 25 full-time freshmen who applied for aid, 23 were judged to have need. Of these, 23 received aid. Average financial aid package met 35% of need; average scholarship/grant was $4,627; average loan was $2,501. For part-time students, average financial aid package was $7,818.
Students without need: No-need awards available for academics, alumni affiliation, minority status, state/district residency.
Cumulative student debt: 68% of graduating class had student loans; average debt was $18,235.

FINANCIAL AID PROCEDURES
Forms required: FAFSA, institutional form.
Dates and Deadlines: Priority date 4/1; no closing date. Applicants notified on a rolling basis starting 3/15; must reply within 3 week(s) of notification.

CONTACT
Heather Lester, Director of Financial Aid
220 Grove Avenue, Prescott, AZ 86301
(928) 778-2090

Rio Salado College
Tempe, Arizona
www.riosalado.edu   Federal Code: 014483

2-year public virtual community college in very large city.
Enrollment: 16,604 undergrads.
Selectivity: Open admission; but selective for some programs.

BASIC COSTS (2006-2007)
Tuition and fees: $1,810; out-of-state residents $7,750.
Per-credit charge: $60; out-of-state residents $258.

FINANCIAL AID PICTURE (2004-2005)
Students with need: 32% of average financial aid package awarded as scholarships/grants, 68% awarded as loans/jobs. Need-based aid available for part-time students.
Students without need: This college only awards aid to students with need.

FINANCIAL AID PROCEDURES
Forms required: FAFSA, institutional form.
Dates and Deadlines: Priority date 6/30; no closing date. Applicants notified on a rolling basis starting 6/30.

CONTACT
Linda Ross, Director of Financial Aid
2323 West 14th Street, Tempe, AZ 85281
(480) 517-8310

Scottsdale Community College
Scottsdale, Arizona
www.sc.maricopa.edu   Federal Code: 008304

2-year public community college in small city.
Enrollment: 3,168 undergrads.
Selectivity: Open admission.

BASIC COSTS (2006-2007)
Tuition and fees: $2,010; out-of-state residents $8,460.
Per-credit charge: $65; out-of-state residents $280.
Additional info: Tuition/fee waivers available for adults, minority students.

FINANCIAL AID PICTURE (2004-2005)
Students with need: 35% of average financial aid package awarded as scholarships/grants, 65% awarded as loans/jobs.
Students without need: No-need awards available for academics, athletics.

Additional info: Athletic scholarships offered in rodeo. All athletic scholarships limited to county residents.

FINANCIAL AID PROCEDURES
Forms required: FAFSA, institutional form.
Dates and Deadlines: Priority date 6/30; no closing date. Applicants notified on a rolling basis starting 4/1; must reply by 7/15 or within 3 week(s) of notification.

CONTACT
Dee Shipley, Director of Placement and Financial Aid
9000 East Chaparral Road, Scottsdale, AZ 85256-2626
(480) 423-6549

South Mountain Community College
Phoenix, Arizona
www.smc.maricopa.edu   Federal Code: 015001

2-year public community college in very large city.
Enrollment: 4,295 undergrads.
Selectivity: Open admission.

BASIC COSTS (2006-2007)
Tuition and fees: $1,980; out-of-state residents $6,480.
Per-credit charge: $65; out-of-state residents $215.

FINANCIAL AID PICTURE
Students with need: Need-based aid available for full-time and part-time students. Work study available nights, weekends, and for part-time students.
Students without need: No-need awards available for academics, athletics, minority status, music/drama.

FINANCIAL AID PROCEDURES
Forms required: FAFSA.
Dates and Deadlines: Priority date 5/1; no closing date. Applicants notified on a rolling basis starting 5/15; must reply within 3 week(s) of notification.

CONTACT
Inez Moreno-Weinert, Director of Financial Aid and Placement
7050 South 24th Street, Phoenix, AZ 85042
(602) 243-8300

Southwestern College
Phoenix, Arizona
www.swcaz.edu   Federal Code: 007113

4-year private Bible college in very large city, affiliated with Baptist faith.
Enrollment: 281 undergrads, 10% part-time. 49 full-time freshmen.
Selectivity: Admits 50 to 75% of applicants.

BASIC COSTS (2005-2006)
Tuition and fees: $11,560.
Per-credit charge: $464.
Room and board: $4,360.

FINANCIAL AID PICTURE
Students with need: Need-based aid available for full-time and part-time students.
Students without need: No-need awards available for academics, alumni affiliation, leadership, music/drama, religious affiliation.

FINANCIAL AID PROCEDURES
Forms required: FAFSA.
Dates and Deadlines: Priority date 3/15; closing date 8/31. Applicants notified on a rolling basis.

CONTACT
Cheryl Hansen, Director of Financial Aid
2625 East Cactus Road, Phoenix, AZ 85032-7042
(602) 992-6101 ext. 115

Tohono O'odham Community College
Sells, Arizona
www.tocc.cc.az.us   Federal Code: 037844

2-year public community college in rural community.
Enrollment: 52 undergrads. 11 full-time freshmen.
Selectivity: Open admission.

BASIC COSTS (2006-2007)
Tuition and fees: $1,270; out-of-state residents $6,340.
Per-credit charge: $42; out-of-state residents $72.

FINANCIAL AID PICTURE (2004-2005)
Students with need: Out of 11 full-time freshmen who applied for aid, 11 were judged to have need. Of these, 11 received aid. Need-based aid available for part-time students.
Students without need: This college only awards aid to students with need.

FINANCIAL AID PROCEDURES
Forms required: FAFSA, institutional form.
Dates and Deadlines: No deadline. Applicants notified on a rolling basis.

CONTACT
Alvaro Rivera, Financial Aid Director
P.O. Box 3129, Sells, AZ 85634-3129
(520) 383-8401 ext. 41

University of Advancing Technology
Tempe, Arizona
www.uat.edu   Federal Code: 017188

4-year for-profit university and technical college in very large city.
Enrollment: 1,172 undergrads. 259 full-time freshmen.

BASIC COSTS (2006-2007)
Tuition and fees: $15,500.
Additional info: Tuition at time of enrollment locked for 4 years.

FINANCIAL AID PICTURE (2004-2005)
Students with need: Out of 213 full-time freshmen who applied for aid, 189 were judged to have need. Of these, 189 received aid. Average financial aid package met 24% of need; average scholarship/grant was $2,550; average loan was $2,625. Need-based aid available for part-time students.
Cumulative student debt: 70% of graduating class had student loans; average debt was $42,679.

FINANCIAL AID PROCEDURES
Forms required: FAFSA.
Dates and Deadlines: Priority date 4/15; no closing date. Applicants notified on a rolling basis; must reply within 2 week(s) of notification.
Transfers: No deadline. Must reply within 2 week(s) of notification. Loan periods may not overlap.

CONTACT
Katherine Christie, Senior Financial Aid Administrator
2625 West Baseline Road, Tempe, AZ 85283-1056
(602) 383-8218

University of Arizona
Tucson, Arizona
www.arizona.edu   Federal Code: 001083

4-year public university in very large city.
Enrollment: 28,023 undergrads, 12% part-time. 5,780 full-time freshmen.
Selectivity: Admits over 75% of applicants.

BASIC COSTS (2005-2006)
Tuition and fees: $4,487; out-of-state residents $13,671.
Per-credit charge: $230; out-of-state residents $583.
Room and board: $7,460.
Additional info: Tuition/fee waivers available for minority students.

FINANCIAL AID PICTURE (2004-2005)
Students with need: Out of 3,446 full-time freshmen who applied for aid, 2,231 were judged to have need. Of these, 2,041 received aid, and 403 had their full need met. Average financial aid package met 66% of need; average scholarship/grant was $5,488; average loan was $2,468. For part-time students, average financial aid package was $5,572.
Students without need: 3,883 full-time freshmen who did not demonstrate need for aid received scholarships/grants; average award was $5,021. No-need awards available for academics, art, athletics, leadership, minority status, music/drama, ROTC, state/district residency.
Scholarships offered: *Merit:* Over $3 million in merit scholarships available to freshmen. National Merit scholarship packages range from $6,000 - $10,000 a year. *Athletic:* 995 full-time freshmen received athletic scholarships.

FINANCIAL AID PROCEDURES
Forms required: FAFSA.
Dates and Deadlines: Priority date 3/1; no closing date. Applicants notified on a rolling basis starting 4/1; must reply within 3 week(s) of notification.
Transfers: Some waivers available for Arizona Community College transfer students with 3.2 GPA who are Arizona residents.

CONTACT
Phyllis Bannister, Executive Director of Student Financial Aid
Robert L. Nugent Building, Tucson, AZ 85721-0040
(520) 621-1858

Yavapai College
Prescott, Arizona
www.yc.edu   Federal Code: 001079

2-year public community college in large town.
Enrollment: 4,035 undergrads, 69% part-time. 295 full-time freshmen.
Selectivity: Open admission; but selective for some programs.

BASIC COSTS (2005-2006)
Tuition and fees: $1,320; out-of-state residents $7,120.
Per-credit charge: $44; out-of-state residents $237.
Room and board: $4,940.

FINANCIAL AID PICTURE
Students with need: Need-based aid available for full-time and part-time students.
Students without need: No-need awards available for academics, athletics.

FINANCIAL AID PROCEDURES
Forms required: FAFSA.
Dates and Deadlines: Priority date 4/15; no closing date. Applicants notified on a rolling basis.

CONTACT
Vikki Gill, Director of Financial Aid
1100 East Sheldon Street, Prescott, AZ 86301
(928) 776-2152

Arkansas

Arkansas Baptist College
Little Rock, Arkansas
www.arbaptcol.edu   Federal Code: 001087

4-year private liberal arts college in large city, affiliated with American Baptist Churches in the USA.
Enrollment: 320 undergrads.

BASIC COSTS (2005-2006)
Tuition and fees: $5,074.
Per-credit charge: $157.
Room and board: $6,826.

FINANCIAL AID PICTURE
Students with need: Need-based aid available for full-time and part-time students.
Students without need: This college only awards aid to students with need.

FINANCIAL AID PROCEDURES
Forms required: FAFSA.
Dates and Deadlines: Closing date 5/1. Applicants notified on a rolling basis starting 6/15.

CONTACT
Jamesetta Ballard, Director of Admissions and Financial Aid
1600 Bishop Street, Little Rock, AR 72202
(501) 374-0804

Arkansas Northeastern College
Blytheville, Arkansas
www.anc.edu   Federal Code: 012860

2-year public community college in large town.
Enrollment: 1,559 undergrads, 41% part-time. 336 full-time freshmen.
Selectivity: Open admission; but selective for some programs.

BASIC COSTS (2005-2006)
Tuition and fees: $1,610; out-of-district residents $1,910; out-of-state residents $3,410.
Per-credit charge: $47; out-of-district residents $57; out-of-state residents $107.

FINANCIAL AID PICTURE (2005-2006)
Students with need: Out of 290 full-time freshmen who applied for aid, 267 were judged to have need. Of these, 253 received aid, and 1 had their full need met. Average financial aid package met 40% of need; average scholarship/grant was $1,889; average loan was $1,589. For part-time students, average financial aid package was $3,892.
Students without need: 18 full-time freshmen who did not demonstrate need for aid received scholarships/grants; average award was $633. No-need awards available for academics, minority status, music/drama, state/district residency.

FINANCIAL AID PROCEDURES
Forms required: FAFSA, institutional form.
Dates and Deadlines: Priority date 4/15; no closing date. Applicants notified on a rolling basis starting 5/1; must reply within 2 week(s) of notification.

CONTACT
Laura Yarbrough, Director of Financial Aid
Box 1109, Blytheville, AR 72316-1109
(870) 762-1020 ext. 1160

Arkansas State University
State University, Arkansas
www.astate.edu   Federal Code: 001090

4-year public university in small city.
Enrollment: 8,650 undergrads, 18% part-time. 1,499 full-time freshmen.
Selectivity: Admits 50 to 75% of applicants.

BASIC COSTS (2005-2006)
Tuition and fees: $5,440; out-of-state residents $12,145.
Per-credit charge: $142; out-of-state residents $366.
Room and board: $4,540.

FINANCIAL AID PICTURE (2005-2006)
Students with need: Average financial aid package met 67% of need; average scholarship/grant was $5,900; average loan was $3,100. Need-based aid available for part-time students.
Students without need: No-need awards available for academics, alumni affiliation, art, athletics, leadership, minority status, music/drama, ROTC, state/district residency.
Cumulative student debt: 68% of graduating class had student loans; average debt was $18,500.

FINANCIAL AID PROCEDURES
Forms required: FAFSA, institutional form.
Dates and Deadlines: Priority date 2/15; closing date 7/1. Applicants notified on a rolling basis starting 6/1; must reply within 2 week(s) of notification.

CONTACT
Gregory Thornburg, Dean Of Enrollment Services/Director of Financial Aid
PO Box 1630, State University, AR 72467
(870) 972-2310

Arkansas State University: Beebe
Beebe, Arkansas
www.asub.edu   Federal Code: 001090

2-year public branch campus and community college in small town.
Enrollment: 3,200 undergrads.
Selectivity: Open admission.

BASIC COSTS (2005-2006)
Tuition and fees: $2,280; out-of-state residents $3,750.
Per-credit charge: $68; out-of-state residents $117.
Room and board: $2,480.

FINANCIAL AID PICTURE
Students with need: Need-based aid available for full-time and part-time students. Work study available nights, weekends, and for part-time students.
Students without need: No-need awards available for academics, leadership, minority status, music/drama.

FINANCIAL AID PROCEDURES
Forms required: FAFSA, institutional form.
Dates and Deadlines: Priority date 7/1; no closing date. Applicants notified on a rolling basis starting 6/1; must reply within 2 week(s) of notification.

CONTACT
Dena Prior, Director of Student Aid
PO Box 1000, Beebe, AR 72012-1000
(501) 882-8245

Arkansas State University: Mountain Home
Mountain Home, Arkansas
www.asumh.edu   Federal Code: 001090

2-year public community and technical college in large town.
Enrollment: 1,031 undergrads, 39% part-time. 229 full-time freshmen.
Selectivity: Open admission; but selective for some programs.

BASIC COSTS (2006-2007)
Tuition and fees: $2,370; out-of-state residents $3,900.
Per-credit charge: $71; out-of-state residents $122.

FINANCIAL AID PICTURE
Students with need: Need-based aid available for full-time and part-time students.
Students without need: No-need awards available for academics, state/district residency.

FINANCIAL AID PROCEDURES
Forms required: FAFSA, institutional form.
Dates and Deadlines: Priority date 7/1; no closing date. Applicants notified on a rolling basis starting 5/1; must reply within 2 week(s) of notification.

CONTACT
Lyndle McCurley, Vice Chancellor Administrative Affairs
1600 South College Street, Mountain Home, AR 72653
(870) 508-6195

Arkansas State University: Newport
Newport, Arkansas
www.asun.edu

2-year public community and liberal arts college in small town.
Enrollment: 1,217 undergrads.
Selectivity: Open admission.

BASIC COSTS (2005-2006)
Tuition and fees: $2,190; out-of-state residents $3,660.
Per-credit charge: $68; out-of-state residents $117.

FINANCIAL AID PICTURE (2004-2005)
Students with need: 70% of average financial aid package awarded as scholarships/grants, 30% awarded as loans/jobs.

CONTACT
Deana Tims, Director of Financial Aid
7648 Victory Boulevard, Newport, AR 72112
(870) 512-7812

Arkansas Tech University
Russellville, Arkansas
www.atu.edu   Federal Code: 001089

4-year public university and liberal arts college in large town.
Enrollment: 6,162 undergrads, 13% part-time. 1,403 full-time freshmen.
Selectivity: Admits less than 50% of applicants.

BASIC COSTS (2005-2006)
Tuition and fees: $4,700; out-of-state residents $8,990.
Per-credit charge: $143; out-of-state residents $286.
Room and board: $4,556.

FINANCIAL AID PICTURE (2004-2005)
Students with need: Out of 1,075 full-time freshmen who applied for aid, 899 were judged to have need. Of these, 887 received aid, and 245 had their full need met. Average financial aid package met 37% of need; average scholarship/grant was $2,516; average loan was $843. For part-time students, average financial aid package was $3,873.
Students without need: 347 full-time freshmen who did not demonstrate need for aid received scholarships/grants; average award was $5,655. No-need awards available for academics, art, athletics, leadership, minority status, music/drama, ROTC.
Scholarships offered: 51 full-time freshmen received athletic scholarships; average amount $2,500.
Cumulative student debt: 53% of graduating class had student loans; average debt was $17,064.

FINANCIAL AID PROCEDURES
Forms required: FAFSA.
Dates and Deadlines: Priority date 4/15; no closing date. Applicants notified on a rolling basis starting 5/1; must reply within 2 week(s) of notification.

CONTACT
Shirley Goines, Director of Student Financial Aid
Doc Bryan Student Services Building, Russellville, AR 72801-2222
(479) 968-0399

Central Baptist College
Conway, Arkansas
www.cbc.edu   Federal Code: 001093

4-year private Bible and junior college in large town, affiliated with Baptist faith.
Enrollment: 392 undergrads.
Selectivity: Admits over 75% of applicants.

BASIC COSTS (2005-2006)
Tuition and fees: $8,450.
Room and board: $4,960.

FINANCIAL AID PICTURE
Students with need: Need-based aid available for full-time students.
Students without need: No-need awards available for academics, state/district residency.

FINANCIAL AID PROCEDURES
Forms required: FAFSA.
Dates and Deadlines: Priority date 7/1; closing date 8/1. Applicants notified on a rolling basis starting 4/1.
Transfers: No deadline.

CONTACT
Christi Bell, Director of Financial Aid
1501 College Avenue, Conway, AR 72034
(501) 329-6872 ext. 185

Cossatot Community College of the University of Arkansas
De Queen, Arkansas
http://cccua.edu   Federal Code: 012432

2-year public community college in small town.
Enrollment: 633 undergrads, 46% part-time. 72 full-time freshmen.
Selectivity: Open admission; but selective for some programs.

BASIC COSTS (2006-2007)
Tuition and fees: $1,546; out-of-district residents $1,846; out-of-state residents $5,146.
Per-credit charge: $45; out-of-district residents $55; out-of-state residents $165.
Additional info: Residents of bordering out-of-state counties may qualify for in-state tuition.

FINANCIAL AID PICTURE (2004-2005)
Students with need: Out of 61 full-time freshmen who applied for aid, 60 were judged to have need. Of these, 60 received aid, and 1 had their full need met. For part-time students, average financial aid package was $1,754.
Additional info: Active or honorably discharged military and their dependents receive tuition discounts.

FINANCIAL AID PROCEDURES
Forms required: FAFSA, institutional form.
Dates and Deadlines: Priority date 5/1; no closing date. Applicants notified on a rolling basis starting 3/1.
Transfers: Applicants notified on a rolling basis starting 3/1.

CONTACT
Denise Hammond, Director of Financial Aid
183 Highway 399, De Queen, AR 71832
(870) 584-4471

Crowley's Ridge College
Paragould, Arkansas
www.crowleysridgecollege.edu   Federal Code: 001095

2-year private junior college in large town, affiliated with Church of Christ.
Enrollment: 165 undergrads.
Selectivity: Open admission.

BASIC COSTS (2006-2007)
Tuition and fees: $7,700.
Per-credit charge: $240.
Room and board: $4,700.
Additional info: Technology fee for non-resident students is $75 per semester. Tuition/fee waivers available for adults.

FINANCIAL AID PICTURE
Students with need: Work study available nights, weekends, and for part-time students.
Students without need: No-need awards available for academics, leadership, music/drama.

FINANCIAL AID PROCEDURES
Forms required: FAFSA.

CONTACT
David Goff
100 College Drive, Paragould, AR 72450
(870) 236-6901

East Arkansas Community College
Forrest City, Arkansas
www.eacc.edu   Federal Code: 012260

2-year public community college in large town.
Enrollment: 1,267 undergrads, 41% part-time. 231 full-time freshmen.
Selectivity: Open admission.

BASIC COSTS (2005-2006)
Tuition and fees: $1,620; out-of-district residents $1,860; out-of-state residents $2,220.
Per-credit charge: $49; out-of-district residents $57; out-of-state residents $69.

Arkansas — East Arkansas Community College

FINANCIAL AID PICTURE
Students with need: Need-based aid available for full-time and part-time students.
Students without need: This college only awards aid to students with need.

FINANCIAL AID PROCEDURES
Forms required: FAFSA.
Dates and Deadlines: Priority date 3/1; closing date 7/1. Applicants notified on a rolling basis starting 5/15; must reply within 2 week(s) of notification.

CONTACT
Alvin Coleman, Director of Financial Aid
1700 Newcastle Road, Forrest City, AR 72335-9598
(870) 633-4480 ext. 225

Ecclesia College
Springdale, Arkansas
www.ecollege.edu   Federal Code: 038553

4-year private Christian college emphasizing Biblical higher education in large town, affiliated with interdenominational tradition.
Enrollment: 35 undergrads.
Selectivity: Open admission; but selective for some programs.

BASIC COSTS (2006-2007)
Tuition and fees: $12,520.
Per-credit charge: $395.
Room and board: $4,500.
Additional info: Full-time nonresidents pay additional fee: $545. Tuition/fee waivers available for adults.

FINANCIAL AID PICTURE
Students with need: Need-based aid available for full-time and part-time students. Work study available nights, weekends, and for part-time students.
Students without need: No-need awards available for academics, athletics, leadership, music/drama.

FINANCIAL AID PROCEDURES
Forms required: FAFSA.
Dates and Deadlines: No deadline.

CONTACT
Jesse Wadkins, Financial Aid Officer
9653 Nations Drive, Springdale, AR 72762
(479) 248-7236 ext. 108

Harding University
Searcy, Arkansas
www.harding.edu   Federal Code: 001097

4-year private university in large town, affiliated with Church of Christ.
Enrollment: 4,092 undergrads, 5% part-time. 969 full-time freshmen.
Selectivity: Admits 50 to 75% of applicants.

BASIC COSTS (2006-2007)
Tuition and fees: $11,650.
Per-credit charge: $375.
Room and board: $5,442.
Additional info: Additional $142 required fees for campus residents.

FINANCIAL AID PICTURE (2004-2005)
Students with need: Out of 890 full-time freshmen who applied for aid, 238 were judged to have need. Of these, 238 received aid, and 68 had their full need met. Average financial aid package met 69% of need; average scholarship/grant was $5,100; average loan was $3,892. Need-based aid available for part-time students.
Students without need: 272 full-time freshmen who did not demonstrate need for aid received scholarships/grants; average award was $4,700. No-need awards available for academics, art, athletics, music/drama, religious affiliation, ROTC, state/district residency.
Cumulative student debt: 70% of graduating class had student loans; average debt was $18,200.
Additional info: Music scholarships available, audition required.

FINANCIAL AID PROCEDURES
Forms required: FAFSA, institutional form.
Dates and Deadlines: Priority date 4/1; no closing date. Applicants notified on a rolling basis starting 2/15; must reply within 2 week(s) of notification.
Transfers: No deadline.

CONTACT
Jon Roberts, Director of Financial Aid
900 East Center, Searcy, AR 72149-0001
(501) 279-4257

Henderson State University
Arkadelphia, Arkansas
www.getreddie.com   Federal Code: 001098

4-year public university and liberal arts college in large town.
Enrollment: 2,728 undergrads, 12% part-time. 602 full-time freshmen.
Selectivity: Admits 50 to 75% of applicants.

BASIC COSTS (2005-2006)
Tuition and fees: $4,645; out-of-state residents $8,695.
Per-credit charge: $135; out-of-state residents $270.

FINANCIAL AID PICTURE (2004-2005)
Students with need: Out of 410 full-time freshmen who applied for aid, 384 were judged to have need. Of these, 296 received aid, and 241 had their full need met. Average financial aid package met 83% of need; average scholarship/grant was $4,400; average loan was $2,699. For part-time students, average financial aid package was $1,801.
Students without need: 102 full-time freshmen who did not demonstrate need for aid received scholarships/grants; average award was $4,135. No-need awards available for academics, alumni affiliation, art, athletics, leadership, minority status, music/drama, state/district residency.
Cumulative student debt: 34% of graduating class had student loans; average debt was $17,800.

FINANCIAL AID PROCEDURES
Forms required: FAFSA.
Dates and Deadlines: Priority date 6/1; no closing date. Applicants notified on a rolling basis starting 4/1; must reply within 2 week(s) of notification.

CONTACT
Jo Holland, Director of Financial Aid
1100 Henderson Street, Arkadelphia, AR 71999-0001
(870) 230-5094

Hendrix College
Conway, Arkansas
www.hendrix.edu   Federal Code: 001099

4-year private liberal arts college in small city, affiliated with United Methodist Church.
Enrollment: 1,010 undergrads, 1% part-time. 280 full-time freshmen.
Selectivity: Admits over 75% of applicants.

BASIC COSTS (2006-2007)
Tuition and fees: $22,916.
Per-credit charge: $853.

Room and board: $6,738.

FINANCIAL AID PICTURE (2005-2006)

Students with need: Out of 229 full-time freshmen who applied for aid, 157 were judged to have need. Of these, 157 received aid, and 56 had their full need met. Average financial aid package met 84% of need; average scholarship/grant was $13,129; average loan was $3,798. For part-time students, average financial aid package was $3,103.

Students without need: 120 full-time freshmen who did not demonstrate need for aid received scholarships/grants; average award was $18,999. No-need awards available for academics, art, leadership, music/drama, religious affiliation.

Scholarships offered: Hays Memorial Scholarship; full tuition, room, board, mandatory fees; based on academic excellence. Visual and Performing Arts Scholarships (music, theatre, art); $1,000 to $5,000 per year; auditions/portfolios required. Leadership and United Methodist (UMYF) scholarships; $1,000 to $3,500.

Cumulative student debt: 78% of graduating class had student loans; average debt was $16,122.

FINANCIAL AID PROCEDURES

Forms required: FAFSA, state aid form.

Dates and Deadlines: Priority date 2/15; no closing date. Applicants notified on a rolling basis starting 3/1; must reply by 5/1 or within 2 week(s) of notification.

CONTACT

Mark Bandre, Director of Financial Aid
1600 Washington Avenue, Conway, AR 72032-3080
(501) 450-1368

John Brown University
Siloam Springs, Arkansas
www.jbu.edu   Federal Code: 001100

4-year private liberal arts college in large town, affiliated with interdenominational tradition.

Enrollment: 1,608 undergrads, 2% part-time. 262 full-time freshmen.
Selectivity: Admits 50 to 75% of applicants.

BASIC COSTS (2006-2007)

Tuition and fees: $16,158.
Per-credit charge: $644.
Room and board: $5,956.
Additional info: Tuition/fee waivers available for adults.

FINANCIAL AID PICTURE (2005-2006)

Students with need: Out of 221 full-time freshmen who applied for aid, 182 were judged to have need. Of these, 182 received aid, and 29 had their full need met. Average financial aid package met 50% of need; average scholarship/grant was $5,030; average loan was $3,573. For part-time students, average financial aid package was $2,868.

Students without need: 62 full-time freshmen who did not demonstrate need for aid received scholarships/grants; average award was $3,868. No-need awards available for academics, alumni affiliation, art, athletics, leadership, music/drama, ROTC.

Scholarships offered: 10 full-time freshmen received athletic scholarships; average amount $9,333.

Cumulative student debt: 60% of graduating class had student loans; average debt was $19,262.

FINANCIAL AID PROCEDURES

Forms required: FAFSA, institutional form.

Dates and Deadlines: Priority date 3/1; no closing date. Applicants notified on a rolling basis starting 3/1; must reply by 5/1 or within 4 week(s) of notification.

CONTACT

Kim Eldridge, Director of Financial Aid
2000 West University Street, Siloam Springs, AR 72761-2121
(877) 528-4636

Lyon College
Batesville, Arkansas
www.lyon.edu   Federal Code: 001088

4-year private liberal arts college in small town, affiliated with Presbyterian Church (USA).

Enrollment: 484 undergrads, 5% part-time. 110 full-time freshmen.
Selectivity: Admits 50 to 75% of applicants.

BASIC COSTS (2006-2007)

Tuition and fees: $14,860.
Per-credit charge: $600.
Room and board: $6,270.

FINANCIAL AID PICTURE (2005-2006)

Students with need: Out of 87 full-time freshmen who applied for aid, 65 were judged to have need. Of these, 65 received aid, and 27 had their full need met. Average financial aid package met 85% of need; average scholarship/grant was $10,531; average loan was $3,464. For part-time students, average financial aid package was $8,167.

Students without need: 37 full-time freshmen who did not demonstrate need for aid received scholarships/grants; average award was $11,096. No-need awards available for academics, art, athletics, leadership, minority status, music/drama, religious affiliation, state/district residency.

Scholarships offered: *Merit:* Brown Scholarship; tuition, room, board, mandatory fees and books; based on high school record, standardized test scores; 4 awarded. Anderson Scholarship; tuition, mandatory fees and books; based on high school record, test scores; 4 awarded. Lyon Fellowship; $10,000; based on high school record, test scores, with a preference for students with a career interest in business or public service or a strong academic interest in computer science or the fine arts; up to 8 awarded. *Athletic:* 21 full-time freshmen received athletic scholarships; average amount $4,957.

Cumulative student debt: 92% of graduating class had student loans; average debt was $15,956.

FINANCIAL AID PROCEDURES

Forms required: FAFSA.

Dates and Deadlines: Priority date 3/15; no closing date. Applicants notified on a rolling basis starting 3/1; must reply by 8/15.

CONTACT

Louise Strauser, Assistant Director of Student Financial Assistance
PO Box 2317, Batesville, AR 72503-2317
(870) 698-4257

Mid-South Community College
West Memphis, Arkansas
www.midsouthcc.edu   Federal Code: 015862

2-year public community and junior college in large town.
Enrollment: 965 undergrads, 55% part-time. 128 full-time freshmen.
Selectivity: Open admission.

BASIC COSTS (2006-2007)

Tuition and fees: $1,620; out-of-district residents $1,950; out-of-state residents $3,360.
Per-credit charge: $47; out-of-district residents $58; out-of-state residents $105.

Arkansas Mid-South Community College

FINANCIAL AID PICTURE
Students with need: Need-based aid available for full-time and part-time students. Work study available nights.
Students without need: No-need awards available for academics, state/district residency.

FINANCIAL AID PROCEDURES
Forms required: FAFSA, institutional form.
Dates and Deadlines: No deadline. Applicants notified on a rolling basis starting 6/1; must reply within 2 week(s) of notification.

CONTACT
Jackie Brubaker, Director of Financial Aid
2000 West Broadway, West Memphis, AR 72301
(870) 733-6741

National Park Community College
Hot Springs, Arkansas
www.npcc.edu   Federal Code: 012105

2-year public community college in large town.
Enrollment: 2,200 undergrads.
Selectivity: Open admission; but selective for some programs.

BASIC COSTS (2005-2006)
Tuition and fees: $1,230; out-of-district residents $1,470; out-of-state residents $3,030.
Per-credit charge: $50; out-of-district residents $60; out-of-state residents $125.

FINANCIAL AID PICTURE
Students with need: Need-based aid available for full-time and part-time students. Work study available nights, weekends, and for part-time students.
Students without need: No-need awards available for academics, minority status, music/drama, state/district residency.

FINANCIAL AID PROCEDURES
Forms required: FAFSA, institutional form.
Dates and Deadlines: Priority date 7/1; no closing date. Applicants notified on a rolling basis starting 3/1.
Transfers: Transfer applicants must furnish evidence of good standing at previous institution to qualify for financial aid.

CONTACT
Lisa Hopper, Counselor and Financial Aid Adviser
101 College Drive, Hot Springs, AR 71913
(501) 760-4235

North Arkansas College
Harrison, Arkansas
www.northark.edu   Federal Code: 012261

2-year public community and technical college in large town.
Enrollment: 1,715 undergrads, 35% part-time. 382 full-time freshmen.
Selectivity: Open admission; but selective for some programs.

BASIC COSTS (2005-2006)
Tuition and fees: $1,590; out-of-district residents $2,130; out-of-state residents $4,110.
Per-credit charge: $53; out-of-district residents $71; out-of-state residents $137.

FINANCIAL AID PICTURE (2005-2006)
Students with need: Out of 297 full-time freshmen who applied for aid, 277 were judged to have need. Of these, 263 received aid, and 19 had their full need met. Average financial aid package met 49% of need; average scholarship/grant was $3,958; average loan was $2,517. For part-time students, average financial aid package was $5,273.
Students without need: 22 full-time freshmen who did not demonstrate need for aid received scholarships/grants; average award was $1,919. No-need awards available for academics, athletics, state/district residency.
Scholarships offered: 1 full-time freshmen received athletic scholarships; average amount $820.
Cumulative student debt: 34% of graduating class had student loans; average debt was $7,246.

FINANCIAL AID PROCEDURES
Forms required: FAFSA, institutional form.
Dates and Deadlines: Priority date 5/1; no closing date. Applicants notified on a rolling basis starting 5/1.
Transfers: No deadline. Applicants notified on a rolling basis starting 5/1.

CONTACT
Nancy Fountain, Director of Financial Aid
1515 Pioneer Drive, Harrison, AR 72601
(870) 391-3266

Northwest Arkansas Community College
Bentonville, Arkansas
www.nwacc.edu   Federal Code: 030633

2-year public community college in large town.
Enrollment: 4,753 undergrads, 61% part-time. 516 full-time freshmen.
Selectivity: Open admission; but selective for some programs.

BASIC COSTS (2005-2006)
Tuition and fees: $1,878; out-of-district residents $2,868; out-of-state residents $3,918.
Per-credit charge: $55; out-of-district residents $88; out-of-state residents $123.

FINANCIAL AID PICTURE
Students with need: Need-based aid available for full-time and part-time students. Work study available nights, weekends, and for part-time students.
Students without need: No-need awards available for academics, leadership, music/drama, state/district residency.

FINANCIAL AID PROCEDURES
Forms required: FAFSA, institutional form.
Dates and Deadlines: Priority date 4/1; no closing date. Applicants notified on a rolling basis starting 4/1; must reply within 2 week(s) of notification.

CONTACT
Michelle Cordell, Financial Aid Director
One College Drive, Bentonville, AR 72712
(479) 619-4129

Ouachita Baptist University
Arkadelphia, Arkansas
www.obu.edu   Federal Code: 001102

4-year private liberal arts college in large town, affiliated with Southern Baptist Convention.
Enrollment: 1,420 undergrads, 1% part-time. 368 full-time freshmen.
Selectivity: Admits 50 to 75% of applicants.

BASIC COSTS (2006-2007)
Tuition and fees: $16,990.
Per-credit charge: $460.
Room and board: $5,000.
Additional info: Tuition at time of enrollment locked for 4 years.

FINANCIAL AID PICTURE (2005-2006)
Students with need: For part-time students, average financial aid package was $11,833.
Students without need: No-need awards available for academics, athletics, job skills, leadership, minority status, music/drama, religious affiliation, ROTC, state/district residency.

FINANCIAL AID PROCEDURES
Forms required: institutional form.
Dates and Deadlines: Priority date 2/15; closing date 6/1. Applicants notified on a rolling basis starting 3/31; must reply by 5/1.

CONTACT
Lane Smith, Director of Financial Aid
OBU Box 3776, Arkadelphia, AR 71998-0001
(870) 245-5570

Ouachita Technical College
Malvern, Arkansas
www.otcweb.edu   Federal Code: 009976

2-year public community and technical college in large town.
Enrollment: 1,591 undergrads.
Selectivity: Open admission; but selective for some programs.

BASIC COSTS (2006-2007)
Tuition and fees: $1,950; out-of-state residents $3,510.
Per-credit charge: $52; out-of-state residents $104.

FINANCIAL AID PICTURE
Students with need: Need-based aid available for full-time and part-time students. Work study available nights.

FINANCIAL AID PROCEDURES
Forms required: FAFSA.
Dates and Deadlines: Closing date 6/30. Applicants notified on a rolling basis starting 7/1; must reply within 6 week(s) of notification.

CONTACT
Teresa Avery, Director of Financial Aid
One College Circle, Malvern, AR 72104
(501) 337-5000 ext. 1122

Ozarka College
Melbourne, Arkansas
www.ozarka.edu   Federal Code: 013217

2-year public community and technical college in rural community.
Enrollment: 765 undergrads.
Selectivity: Open admission; but selective for some programs.

BASIC COSTS (2006-2007)
Tuition and fees: $2,285; out-of-state residents $5,375.
Per-credit charge: $65; out-of-state residents $168.

FINANCIAL AID PICTURE
Students with need: Need-based aid available for full-time and part-time students.

FINANCIAL AID PROCEDURES
Forms required: FAFSA.

Dates and Deadlines: No deadline. Applicants notified on a rolling basis; must reply within 2 week(s) of notification.

CONTACT
Joyce Goff, Financial Aid Officer
218 College Drive, Melbourne, AR 72556-0010
(870) 368-7371 ext. 2010

Philander Smith College
Little Rock, Arkansas
www.philander.edu   Federal Code: 001103

4-year private liberal arts college in small city, affiliated with United Methodist Church.
Enrollment: 670 full-time undergrads.
Selectivity: Open admission.

BASIC COSTS (2005-2006)
Tuition and fees: $7,766.
Per-credit charge: $495.
Room and board: $5,090.

FINANCIAL AID PICTURE (2004-2005)
Students with need: 34% of average financial aid package awarded as scholarships/grants, 66% awarded as loans/jobs. Need-based aid available for part-time students.
Students without need: This college only awards aid to students with need.

FINANCIAL AID PROCEDURES
Forms required: FAFSA, institutional form.
Dates and Deadlines: Priority date 5/1; no closing date. Applicants notified on a rolling basis starting 5/1; must reply within 2 week(s) of notification.
Transfers: Priority date 3/1; closing date 6/30.

CONTACT
Director of Financial Aid
One Trudie Kibbe Reed Drive, Little Rock, AR 72202-3718
(501) 370-5350

Phillips Community College of the University of Arkansas
Helena, Arkansas
www.pccua.edu   Federal Code: 001104

2-year public community college in large town.
Enrollment: 1,600 undergrads. 199 full-time freshmen.
Selectivity: Open admission; but selective for some programs.

BASIC COSTS (2005-2006)
Tuition and fees: $1,760; out-of-district residents $2,030; out-of-state residents $3,170.
Per-credit charge: $50; out-of-district residents $59; out-of-state residents $97.

FINANCIAL AID PICTURE
Students with need: Need-based aid available for full-time and part-time students. Work study available nights.
Students without need: This college only awards aid to students with need.

FINANCIAL AID PROCEDURES
Forms required: FAFSA.
Dates and Deadlines: Priority date 4/1; closing date 5/1. Applicants notified on a rolling basis starting 4/1; must reply within 2 week(s) of notification.

CONTACT
Barbra Stevenson, Director of Financial Aid
1000 Campus Drive, Helena, AR 72342
(870) 338-6474 ext. 1160

Pulaski Technical College
North Little Rock, Arkansas
www.pulaskitech.edu   Federal Code: 014167

2-year public community and technical college in small city.
Enrollment: 6,740 undergrads.
Selectivity: Open admission; but selective for some programs.

BASIC COSTS (2005-2006)
Tuition and fees: $2,340; out-of-state residents $3,660.
Per-credit charge: $68; out-of-state residents $112.

FINANCIAL AID PICTURE (2005-2006)
Students with need: 35% of average financial aid package awarded as scholarships/grants, 65% awarded as loans/jobs. Need-based aid available for part-time students.

FINANCIAL AID PROCEDURES
Forms required: FAFSA, institutional form.
Dates and Deadlines: Priority date 5/15; no closing date. Applicants notified on a rolling basis starting 5/1; must reply within 2 week(s) of notification.

CONTACT
Kris Buford, Director Financial Aid
3000 West Scenic Drive, North Little Rock, AR 72118
(501) 812-2289

Rich Mountain Community College
Mena, Arkansas
www.rmcc.edu   Federal Code: 012435

2-year public community college in small town.
Enrollment: 550 undergrads.
Selectivity: Open admission; but selective for some programs.

BASIC COSTS (2005-2006)
Tuition and fees: $1,290; out-of-district residents $1,890; out-of-state residents $4,590.
Per-credit charge: $40; out-of-district residents $50; out-of-state residents $150.

FINANCIAL AID PICTURE (2005-2006)
Students with need: Need-based aid available for part-time students.
Students without need: No-need awards available for academics.

FINANCIAL AID PROCEDURES
Forms required: FAFSA, institutional form.
Dates and Deadlines: Priority date 7/1; no closing date. Applicants notified on a rolling basis starting 6/1; must reply within 2 week(s) of notification.

CONTACT
Mary Stenderfer, Director of Financial Aid
1100 College Drive, Mena, AR 71953
(479) 394-7622 ext. 1420

South Arkansas Community College
El Dorado, Arkansas
www.southark.edu   Federal Code: 013858

2-year public community and junior college in large town.
Enrollment: 1,400 undergrads.
Selectivity: Open admission.

BASIC COSTS (2005-2006)
Tuition and fees: $1,900; out-of-district residents $2,140; out-of-state residents $3,790.
Per-credit charge: $57; out-of-district residents $65; out-of-state residents $120.
Additional info: $25 lab fee for most courses.

FINANCIAL AID PICTURE
Students with need: Need-based aid available for full-time and part-time students.

FINANCIAL AID PROCEDURES
Forms required: FAFSA, institutional form.
Dates and Deadlines: Priority date 7/1; no closing date. Applicants notified on a rolling basis starting 7/1; must reply within 2 week(s) of notification.

CONTACT
Veronda Tatum, Director of Financial Aid
Box 7010, El Dorado, AR 71731-7010
(870) 864-7133

Southeast Arkansas College
Pine Bluff, Arkansas
www.seark.edu   Federal Code: 005707

2-year public community and technical college in small city.
Enrollment: 1,560 undergrads.
Selectivity: Open admission; but selective for some programs.

BASIC COSTS (2006-2007)
Tuition and fees: $1,720; out-of-state residents $3,220.
Per-credit charge: $50; out-of-state residents $100.
Additional info: $5 per credit hour technology fee. $5 assessment fee. $2 per hour services fee.

FINANCIAL AID PICTURE
Students with need: Need-based aid available for full-time and part-time students. Work study available nights, weekends, and for part-time students.
Students without need: No-need awards available for academics, leadership, state/district residency.

FINANCIAL AID PROCEDURES
Forms required: FAFSA.
Dates and Deadlines: Priority date 6/1; no closing date. Applicants notified on a rolling basis starting 5/1; must reply within 2 week(s) of notification.

CONTACT
Donna Cox, Director of Financial Aid
1900 Hazel Street, Pine Bluff, AR 71603
(870) 543-5968

Southern Arkansas University
Magnolia, Arkansas
www.saumag.edu   Federal Code: 001107

4-year public university in large town.
Enrollment: 2,683 undergrads, 10% part-time. 534 full-time freshmen.
Selectivity: Admits over 75% of applicants.

BASIC COSTS (2005-2006)
Tuition and fees: $4,310; out-of-state residents $6,320.
Per-credit charge: $130; out-of-state residents $197.
Room and board: $3,790.

FINANCIAL AID PICTURE (2004-2005)
Students with need: 50% of average financial aid package awarded as scholarships/grants, 50% awarded as loans/jobs. Need-based aid available for part-time students. Work study available nights, weekends, and for part-time students.
Students without need: No-need awards available for academics, alumni affiliation, art, athletics, leadership, minority status, music/drama, state/district residency.

FINANCIAL AID PROCEDURES
Forms required: FAFSA.
Dates and Deadlines: Priority date 7/1; no closing date. Applicants notified on a rolling basis starting 4/15; must reply within 2 week(s) of notification.

CONTACT
Bronwyn Sneed, Director of Financial Aid
Box 9382, Magnolia, AR 71754-9382
(870) 235-4023

Southern Arkansas University Tech
Camden, Arkansas
www.sautech.edu   Federal Code: 007738

2-year public junior and technical college in large town.
Enrollment: 757 undergrads, 36% part-time. 144 full-time freshmen.
Selectivity: Open admission; but selective for some programs.

BASIC COSTS (2006-2007)
Tuition and fees: $2,106; out-of-state residents $2,626.
Per-credit charge: $60; out-of-state residents $80.

FINANCIAL AID PICTURE
Students with need: Need-based aid available for full-time and part-time students.
Students without need: No-need awards available for academics, state/district residency.

FINANCIAL AID PROCEDURES
Forms required: FAFSA.
Dates and Deadlines: Priority date 6/1; no closing date. Applicants notified on a rolling basis starting 5/1.
Transfers: Priority date 4/15; closing date 6/1. Applicants notified on a rolling basis starting 5/1.

CONTACT
Vicki Taylor, Director of Financial Aid
P.O. Box 3499, East Camden, AR 71711-1599
(870) 574-4511

University of Arkansas
Fayetteville, Arkansas
www.uark.edu   Federal Code: 001108

4-year public university in small city.
Enrollment: 13,654 undergrads, 15% part-time. 2,457 full-time freshmen.
Selectivity: Admits over 75% of applicants.

BASIC COSTS (2005-2006)
Tuition and fees: $5,495; out-of-state residents $13,222.
Per-credit charge: $145; out-of-state residents $403.
Room and board: $6,365.

FINANCIAL AID PICTURE (2004-2005)
Students with need: Out of 1,391 full-time freshmen who applied for aid, 1,014 were judged to have need. Of these, 922 received aid, and 271 had their full need met. Average financial aid package met 71% of need; average scholarship/grant was $4,003; average loan was $2,592. For part-time students, average financial aid package was $6,046.
Students without need: 543 full-time freshmen who did not demonstrate need for aid received scholarships/grants; average award was $7,144. No-need awards available for academics, alumni affiliation, art, athletics, leadership, minority status, music/drama, ROTC, state/district residency.
Scholarships offered: *Merit:* Sturgis Fellowship; $11,500, based on exceptional academic performance, 10 awards available to arts and sciences majors. Bodenhamer Fellowship; $11,000, based on strong academic performance and leadership. Chancellor's Scholarships; tuition, fees, room and board. University Scholarships; $4,000, based on rank in top 5-10% of high school class. Non-resident Tuition Award; non-resident tuition, for entering freshmen from neighboring states, based on minimum ACT score of 24 or SAT of 1090 (exclusive of writing) and 3.0 high school GPA. *Athletic:* 98 full-time freshmen received athletic scholarships; average amount $9,031.
Cumulative student debt: 57% of graduating class had student loans; average debt was $18,734.

FINANCIAL AID PROCEDURES
Forms required: FAFSA.
Dates and Deadlines: Priority date 3/15; no closing date. Applicants notified on a rolling basis starting 4/1.

CONTACT
Ed Schroeder, Director of Student Financial Services
232 Silas Hunt Hall, Fayetteville, AR 72701
(479) 575-3806

University of Arkansas at Fort Smith
Fort Smith, Arkansas
www.uafortsmith.edu   Federal Code: 001110

4-year public university in small city.
Enrollment: 5,914 undergrads, 35% part-time. 1,149 full-time freshmen.
Selectivity: Open admission; but selective for some programs.

BASIC COSTS (2005-2006)
Tuition and fees: $2,830; out-of-state residents $7,720.
Per-credit charge: $72; out-of-state residents $235.

FINANCIAL AID PICTURE (2004-2005)
Students with need: Out of 829 full-time freshmen who applied for aid, 679 were judged to have need. Of these, 643 received aid, and 79 had their full need met. Average financial aid package met 66% of need; average scholarship/grant was $3,447; average loan was $2,239. For part-time students, average financial aid package was $4,367.
Students without need: 166 full-time freshmen who did not demonstrate need for aid received scholarships/grants; average award was $2,792. No-need awards available for academics, athletics, job skills, leadership, music/drama.
Scholarships offered: 34 full-time freshmen received athletic scholarships; average amount $3,456.
Cumulative student debt: 37% of graduating class had student loans; average debt was $8,956.

FINANCIAL AID PROCEDURES
Forms required: FAFSA.
Dates and Deadlines: Priority date 4/1; no closing date. Applicants notified on a rolling basis starting 3/1; must reply within 4 week(s) of notification.
Transfers: No deadline. Applicants notified on a rolling basis starting 3/1; must reply within 4 week(s) of notification.

Arkansas University of Arkansas at Fort Smith

CONTACT
Scott Medlin, Director of Financial Aid
P O Box 3649, Fort Smith, AR 72913-3649
(479) 788-7090

University of Arkansas at Little Rock
Little Rock, Arkansas
www.ualr.edu   Federal Code: 001161

4-year public university in small city.
Enrollment: 9,349 undergrads.

BASIC COSTS (2005-2006)
Tuition and fees: $5,213; out-of-state residents $12,083.
Per-credit charge: $141; out-of-state residents $370.
Room only: $2,950.
Additional info: Fees vary depending on student's field of study.

FINANCIAL AID PICTURE
Students with need: Need-based aid available for full-time and part-time students.

FINANCIAL AID PROCEDURES
Forms required: FAFSA.
Dates and Deadlines: Closing date 8/1. Applicants notified on a rolling basis starting 5/1.

CONTACT
John Noah, Director of Admissions and Financial Aid
208 Administration South, Little Rock, AR 72204
(501) 569-3035

University of Arkansas at Monticello
Monticello, Arkansas
www.uamont.edu   Federal Code: 001085

4-year public university and technical college in small town.
Enrollment: 2,915 undergrads.
Selectivity: Open admission.

BASIC COSTS (2005-2006)
Tuition and fees: $3,910; out-of-state residents $7,660.
Per-credit charge: $100; out-of-state residents $125.
Room and board: $3,640.

FINANCIAL AID PICTURE
Students with need: Need-based aid available for full-time and part-time students. Work study available nights, weekends, and for part-time students.
Students without need: No-need awards available for academics, athletics, job skills, leadership, music/drama, state/district residency.

FINANCIAL AID PROCEDURES
Forms required: FAFSA, institutional form.
Dates and Deadlines: No deadline. Applicants notified on a rolling basis starting 4/1; must reply within 2 week(s) of notification.

CONTACT
Susan Brewer, Director of Financial Aid
Box 3600, Monticello, AR 71656
(870) 460-1050

University of Arkansas at Pine Bluff
Pine Bluff, Arkansas
www.uapb.edu   Federal Code: 001086

4-year public university in small city.
Enrollment: 3,100 undergrads, 9% part-time. 714 full-time freshmen.

BASIC COSTS (2005-2006)
Tuition and fees: $4,254; out-of-state residents $8,439.
Per-credit charge: $105; out-of-state residents $245.
Room and board: $5,940.
Additional info: Tuition/fee waivers available for minority students.

FINANCIAL AID PICTURE
Students with need: Need-based aid available for full-time and part-time students. Work study available weekends and for part-time students.
Students without need: No-need awards available for academics, alumni affiliation, art, athletics, leadership, minority status, music/drama, religious affiliation, ROTC, state/district residency.

FINANCIAL AID PROCEDURES
Forms required: FAFSA.
Dates and Deadlines: Priority date 4/15; no closing date. Applicants notified on a rolling basis starting 3/1.
Transfers: Must supply financial aid transcript from prior college or university.

CONTACT
Caroline Iverson, Director of Financial Aid
1200 North University Drive, Mail Slot 4981, Pine Bluff, AR 71601-2799
(870) 575-8302

University of Arkansas for Medical Sciences
Little Rock, Arkansas
www.uams.edu   Federal Code: 001109

4-year public university and health science college in large city.
Enrollment: 820 undergrads.

BASIC COSTS (2005-2006)
Tuition and fees: $5,215; out-of-state residents $11,515.
Per-credit charge: $162; out-of-state residents $372.
Room only: $1,620.
Additional info: Reported tuition and fees are for Health Related Professions Program and majors in dental hygiene, diagnostic medical sonography, nuclear medicine imaging sciences, and radiologic imaging sciences. Tuition and fees vary by program.

FINANCIAL AID PICTURE
Students with need: Need-based aid available for full-time and part-time students.

FINANCIAL AID PROCEDURES
Forms required: FAFSA.
Dates and Deadlines: No deadline. Applicants notified on a rolling basis starting 5/1; must reply within 2 week(s) of notification.

CONTACT
Paul Carter, Assistant Dean for Graduate Studies
4301 West Markham Street, Little Rock, AR 72205
(501) 686-5454

University of Arkansas: Community College at Batesville
Batesville, Arkansas
www.uaccb.edu   Federal Code: 020735

2-year public community college in small town.
Enrollment: 1,007 undergrads.
Selectivity: Open admission; but selective for some programs.

BASIC COSTS (2006-2007)
Tuition and fees: $1,900; out-of-district residents $2,200; out-of-state residents $4,000.
Per-credit charge: $50; out-of-district residents $60; out-of-state residents $120.

FINANCIAL AID PICTURE
Students with need: Need-based aid available for full-time students. Work study available nights, weekends, and for part-time students.
Students without need: This college only awards aid to students with need.

FINANCIAL AID PROCEDURES
Forms required: FAFSA.
Dates and Deadlines: No deadline. Applicants notified on a rolling basis starting 3/1; must reply within 2 week(s) of notification.

CONTACT
John Lewis, Director of Financial Aid
Box 3350, Batesville, AR 72503
(870) 612-2036

University of Arkansas: Community College at Hope
Hope, Arkansas
www.uacch.edu   Federal Code: 005732

2-year public community and technical college in small town.
Enrollment: 923 undergrads, 39% part-time. 187 full-time freshmen.
Selectivity: Open admission; but selective for some programs.

BASIC COSTS (2006-2007)
Tuition and fees: $1,790; out-of-district residents $1,940; out-of-state residents $3,620.
Per-credit charge: $54; out-of-district residents $59; out-of-state residents $115.

FINANCIAL AID PICTURE (2004-2005)
Students with need: 89% of average financial aid package awarded as scholarships/grants, 11% awarded as loans/jobs. Need-based aid available for part-time students. Work study available nights.
Students without need: No-need awards available for academics.

FINANCIAL AID PROCEDURES
Forms required: FAFSA, institutional form.
Dates and Deadlines: Priority date 7/6; no closing date. Applicants notified on a rolling basis starting 1/1; must reply within 4 week(s) of notification.

CONTACT
Jerald Barber, Vice Chancellor for Finance
2500 South Main, Hope, AR 71802-0140
(870) 722-8264

University of Central Arkansas
Conway, Arkansas
www.uca.edu   Federal Code: 001092

4-year public university and liberal arts college in large town.
Enrollment: 9,909 undergrads, 8% part-time. 2,429 full-time freshmen.
Selectivity: Admits 50 to 75% of applicants.

BASIC COSTS (2005-2006)
Tuition and fees: $5,682; out-of-state residents $10,182.
Per-credit charge: $150; out-of-state residents $300.
Room and board: $4,320.

FINANCIAL AID PICTURE (2004-2005)
Students with need: 39% of average financial aid package awarded as scholarships/grants, 61% awarded as loans/jobs. Work study available nights, weekends, and for part-time students.
Students without need: No-need awards available for academics, athletics, music/drama, ROTC, state/district residency.
Additional info: Room and board may be paid monthly.

FINANCIAL AID PROCEDURES
Forms required: FAFSA.
Dates and Deadlines: Priority date 2/15; no closing date. Applicants notified on a rolling basis starting 5/4.

CONTACT
Cheryl Lyons, Director of Student Financial Aid
201 Donaghey Avenue, Conway, AR 72035-0001
(501) 450-3140

University of the Ozarks
Clarksville, Arkansas
www.ozarks.edu   Federal Code: 001094

4-year private university and liberal arts college in small town, affiliated with Presbyterian Church (USA).
Enrollment: 597 undergrads.
Selectivity: Admits over 75% of applicants.

BASIC COSTS (2006-2007)
Tuition and fees: $14,950.
Per-credit charge: $605.
Room and board: $5,260.
Additional info: Tuition/fee waivers available for minority students.

FINANCIAL AID PICTURE (2005-2006)
Students with need: Need-based aid available for part-time students. Work study available nights, weekends, and for part-time students.
Students without need: No-need awards available for academics, alumni affiliation, art, leadership, minority status, music/drama, religious affiliation.
Additional info: Walton International Scholarship Program provides full scholarships to selected Central American and Mexican residents.

FINANCIAL AID PROCEDURES
Forms required: FAFSA.
Dates and Deadlines: Priority date 2/15; no closing date. Applicants notified on a rolling basis starting 3/15; must reply within 2 week(s) of notification.

CONTACT
Jana Hart, Dean of Admissions and Financial Aid
415 College Avenue, Clarksville, AR 72830
(479) 979-1221

Williams Baptist College
Walnut Ridge, Arkansas
www.wbcoll.edu
Federal Code: 001106

4-year private liberal arts college in small town, affiliated with Southern Baptist Convention.
Enrollment: 512 undergrads, 4% part-time. 142 full-time freshmen.
Selectivity: Admits 50 to 75% of applicants.

BASIC COSTS (2006-2007)
Tuition and fees: $9,850.
Room and board: $4,400.

FINANCIAL AID PICTURE (2004-2005)
Students with need: Out of 133 full-time freshmen who applied for aid, 96 were judged to have need. Of these, 96 received aid. For part-time students, average financial aid package was $4,174.
Students without need: 42 full-time freshmen who did not demonstrate need for aid received scholarships/grants; average award was $3,730. No-need awards available for academics, art, athletics, leadership, minority status, music/drama, religious affiliation, state/district residency.
Scholarships offered: *Merit:* Trustee's Scholarship; up to full tuition and room and board; based on minimum composite score of 30 on enhanced ACT and minimum 3.5 high school cumulative GPA; 1 awarded; deadline March 1, renewable for 4 years with 3.5 minimum cumulative GPA on at least 15 credit hours per semester. *Athletic:* 39 full-time freshmen received athletic scholarships; average amount $3,055.
Cumulative student debt: 81% of graduating class had student loans; average debt was $14,768.
Additional info: Art scholarship applicants must submit portfolio.

FINANCIAL AID PROCEDURES
Forms required: FAFSA.
Dates and Deadlines: Priority date 5/1; no closing date. Applicants notified on a rolling basis starting 4/1; must reply within 2 week(s) of notification.
Transfers: Priority date 4/1; no deadline. Applicants notified on a rolling basis starting 4/1; must reply within 2 week(s) of notification.

CONTACT
Barbara Turner, Director of Financial Aid
PO Box 3665, Walnut Ridge, AR 72476
(870) 759-4112

California

Academy of Art University
San Francisco, California
www.academyart.edu
Federal Code: 007531

4-year for-profit university and visual arts college in very large city.
Enrollment: 6,596 undergrads, 37% part-time. 762 full-time freshmen.
Selectivity: Open admission.

BASIC COSTS (2006-2007)
Tuition and fees: $18,280.
Per-credit charge: $600.
Room and board: $12,600.

FINANCIAL AID PICTURE (2004-2005)
Students with need: Out of 328 full-time freshmen who applied for aid, 279 were judged to have need. Of these, 240 received aid. Average financial aid package met 25% of need; average scholarship/grant was $4,144; average loan was $2,555. For part-time students, average financial aid package was $10,665.
Students without need: No-need awards available for academics, art.

Additional info: Numerous summer grant programs available.

FINANCIAL AID PROCEDURES
Forms required: FAFSA, institutional form.
Dates and Deadlines: Priority date 7/10; no closing date. Applicants notified on a rolling basis.
Transfers: Priority date 3/1; no deadline. Applicants notified on a rolling basis starting 4/15.

CONTACT
Joe Vollaro, Executive Vice President for Financial Aid/Compliance
79 New Montgomery Street, San Francisco, CA 94105-3410
(415) 274-2223

Allan Hancock College
Santa Maria, California
www.hancockcollege.edu
Federal Code: 001111

2-year public community college in small city.
Enrollment: 6,446 undergrads.
Selectivity: Open admission; but selective for some programs.

BASIC COSTS (2005-2006)
Tuition and fees: $818; out-of-state residents $5,348.
Per-credit charge: $26; out-of-state residents $177.

FINANCIAL AID PICTURE
Students with need: Need-based aid available for full-time and part-time students.
Students without need: This college only awards aid to students with need.

FINANCIAL AID PROCEDURES
Forms required: FAFSA.
Dates and Deadlines: Priority date 5/1; no closing date. Applicants notified on a rolling basis starting 6/1.

CONTACT
Robert Parisi, Financial Aid Director
800 South College Drive, Santa Maria, CA 93454-6399
(805) 922-6966 ext. 3200

Alliant International University
San Diego, California
www.alliant.edu
Federal Code: 011117

Upper-division private university in very large city.
Enrollment: 307 undergrads.

BASIC COSTS (2005-2006)
Tuition and fees: $19,350.
Per-credit charge: $695.
Room and board: $7,800.
Additional info: Tuition/fee waivers available for minority students.

FINANCIAL AID PICTURE (2005-2006)
Students with need: 44% of average financial aid package awarded as scholarships/grants, 56% awarded as loans/jobs. Need-based aid available for part-time students. Work study available nights, weekends, and for part-time students.
Students without need: No-need awards available for academics, alumni affiliation, athletics, leadership.
Scholarships offered: Grants and scholarships available based on GPA and SAT/ACT scores.
Cumulative student debt: 44% of graduating class had student loans; average debt was $19,000.

FINANCIAL AID PROCEDURES
Forms required: FAFSA.
Dates and Deadlines: Priority date 3/2; no closing date. Applicants notified on a rolling basis starting 2/1; must reply within 3 week(s) of notification.

CONTACT
Deborah Spindler, Director of Financial Aid
10455 Pomerado Road, San Diego, CA 92131-1799
(858) 635-4559

American Academy of Dramatic Arts: West
Los Angeles, California
www.aada.org
Federal Code: 014801

2-year private performing arts college in very large city.
Enrollment: 258 undergrads. 119 full-time freshmen.
Selectivity: Admits less than 50% of applicants.

BASIC COSTS (2006-2007)
Tuition and fees: $17,450.

FINANCIAL AID PICTURE (2004-2005)
Students with need: 48% of average financial aid package awarded as scholarships/grants, 52% awarded as loans/jobs.
Students without need: No-need awards available for academics, music/drama.

FINANCIAL AID PROCEDURES
Forms required: institutional form.
Dates and Deadlines: Priority date 7/1; no closing date. Applicants notified on a rolling basis starting 6/1; must reply within 3 week(s) of notification.

CONTACT
Marguerite Artura, President
1336 N. La Brea Avenue, Los Angeles, CA 90028
(323) 464-2777 ext. 105

American River College
Sacramento, California
www.arc.losrios.edu
Federal Code: 001232

2-year public community college in large city.
Enrollment: 32,241 undergrads.
Selectivity: Open admission; but selective for some programs.

BASIC COSTS (2005-2006)
Tuition and fees: $812; out-of-state residents $5,342.
Per-credit charge: $26; out-of-state residents $177.
Additional info: International students pay additional $50 application fee. Tuition/fee waivers available for minority students.

FINANCIAL AID PICTURE
Students with need: Need-based aid available for full-time and part-time students.
Students without need: This college only awards aid to students with need.

FINANCIAL AID PROCEDURES
Forms required: FAFSA.
Dates and Deadlines: Priority date 3/2; no closing date. Applicants notified on a rolling basis starting 7/1; must reply within 2 week(s) of notification.

CONTACT
Roy Beckhorn, Financial Aid Supervisor
4700 College Oak Drive, Sacramento, CA 95841
(916) 484-8437

Antelope Valley College
Lancaster, California
www.avc.edu
Federal Code: 001113

2-year public community college in large city.
Enrollment: 7,450 undergrads.
Selectivity: Open admission; but selective for some programs.

BASIC COSTS (2005-2006)
Tuition and fees: $782; out-of-state residents $5,312.
Per-credit charge: $26; out-of-state residents $177.

FINANCIAL AID PICTURE
Students with need: Need-based aid available for full-time and part-time students.

FINANCIAL AID PROCEDURES
Forms required: FAFSA, state aid form, institutional form.
Dates and Deadlines: Priority date 3/2; no closing date. Applicants notified on a rolling basis starting 7/15; must reply within 2 week(s) of notification.

CONTACT
Sherrie Padilla, Director of Financial Aid
3041 West Avenue K, Lancaster, CA 93536-5426
(661) 722-6336

Antioch University Santa Barbara
Santa Barbara, California
www.antiochsb.edu
Federal Code: 003010

Upper-division private university and liberal arts college in small city.
Enrollment: 97 undergrads.

BASIC COSTS (2005-2006)
Tuition and fees: $13,188.
Per-credit charge: $440.

FINANCIAL AID PICTURE (2004-2005)
Students with need: 16% of average financial aid package awarded as scholarships/grants, 84% awarded as loans/jobs. Need-based aid available for part-time students. Work study available nights, weekends, and for part-time students.

FINANCIAL AID PROCEDURES
Forms required: FAFSA, institutional form.
Dates and Deadlines: Priority date 4/15; no closing date. Applicants notified on a rolling basis; must reply within 4 week(s) of notification.
Transfers: Priority date 4/1; no deadline.

CONTACT
Cecilia Schneider, Financial Aid Director
801 Garden Street, Santa Barbara, CA 93101-1581
(805) 962-8179 ext. 108

Art Center College of Design
Pasadena, California
www.artcenter.edu
Federal Code: 001116

4-year private visual arts college in small city.
Enrollment: 1,512 undergrads, 14% part-time. 89 full-time freshmen.
Selectivity: Admits 50 to 75% of applicants.

BASIC COSTS (2006-2007)
Tuition and fees: $26,370.

California — Art Center College of Design

FINANCIAL AID PICTURE (2005-2006)
Students with need: 28% of average financial aid package awarded as scholarships/grants, 72% awarded as loans/jobs.
Students without need: This college only awards aid to students with need.
Additional info: Students may apply for scholarships after they enroll while progressing through the program.

FINANCIAL AID PROCEDURES
Forms required: FAFSA.
Dates and Deadlines: Priority date 3/1; no closing date. Applicants notified on a rolling basis starting 5/15; must reply within 4 week(s) of notification.

CONTACT
Clema McKenzie, Director of Financial Aid
1700 Lida Street, Pasadena, CA 91103
(626) 396-2215

Art Institute of California: Los Angeles
Santa Monica, California
www.aila.artinstitutes.edu   Federal Code: 007470

2-year for-profit visual arts college in small city.
Enrollment: 2,102 undergrads.

BASIC COSTS (2006-2007)
Tuition and fees: $19,874.
Room only: $9,594.
Additional info: Tuition at time of enrollment locked for 2 years.

FINANCIAL AID PICTURE (2005-2006)
Students with need: 52% of average financial aid package awarded as scholarships/grants, 48% awarded as loans/jobs. Need-based aid available for part-time students. Work study available nights, weekends, and for part-time students.
Students without need: No-need awards available for academics.

FINANCIAL AID PROCEDURES
Forms required: FAFSA.
Dates and Deadlines: No deadline. Applicants notified on a rolling basis.

CONTACT
Kathleen Harris, Director of Student Financial Services
2900 31st Street, Santa Monica, CA 90405-3035
(310) 751-4700

Art Institute of California: Orange County
Santa Ana, California
www.aicaoc.artinstitutes.edu   Federal Code: 007236

3-year for-profit culinary school and visual arts college in very large city.
Enrollment: 1,835 undergrads, 12% part-time. 387 full-time freshmen.
Selectivity: Admits less than 50% of applicants.

BASIC COSTS (2006-2007)
Tuition and fees: $18,135.
Per-credit charge: $403.
Additional info: Typical full-time load 16 credit hours per quarter. Housing costs $2,450-$3,300 per quarter. Culinary lab fee $315 per quarter, online fee $100 per class per quarter.

FINANCIAL AID PICTURE
Students with need: Need-based aid available for full-time and part-time students. Work study available nights, weekends, and for part-time students.
Students without need: No-need awards available for academics, art, minority status.

FINANCIAL AID PROCEDURES
Forms required: FAFSA, state aid form.
Dates and Deadlines: Priority date 3/2; no closing date. Applicants notified on a rolling basis starting 2/1; must reply within 2 week(s) of notification.

CONTACT
Jennifer Olevson, Director of Student Financial Services
3601 West Sunflower Avenue, Santa Ana, CA 92704-9888
(714) 830-0202

Art Institute of California: San Francisco
San Francisco, California
www.aicasf.aii.edu   Federal Code: 007236

4-year for-profit visual arts college in very large city.
Enrollment: 1,570 undergrads.

BASIC COSTS (2005-2006)
Tuition and fees: $17,685.
Per-credit charge: $393.
Additional info: Starter kits additional $600 to $675 for all programs.

FINANCIAL AID PICTURE (2005-2006)
Students with need: 44% of average financial aid package awarded as scholarships/grants, 56% awarded as loans/jobs.
Scholarships offered: The Art Institutes and Americans for the Arts Poster Design Competition: $2,000-$3,000 locally, up to $25,000 nationally; 2 awarded per Art Institute location, 10 awarded nationally. Evelyn Keedy Memorial Scholarship: $30,000; 1 awarded nationally.

FINANCIAL AID PROCEDURES
Forms required: FAFSA.
Dates and Deadlines: No deadline. Applicants notified on a rolling basis.

CONTACT
Maria Juravic, Director of Student Financial Services
1170 Market Street, San Francisco, CA 94102
(415) 865-0198

Azusa Pacific University
Azusa, California
www.apu.edu   Federal Code: 001117

4-year private university in small city, affiliated with interdenominational tradition.
Enrollment: 4,602 undergrads, 14% part-time. 897 full-time freshmen.
Selectivity: Admits 50 to 75% of applicants.

BASIC COSTS (2006-2007)
Tuition and fees: $23,750.
Per-credit charge: $960.
Room and board: $7,328.
Additional info: Tuition/fee waivers available for minority students.

FINANCIAL AID PICTURE (2004-2005)
Students with need: Out of 897 full-time freshmen who applied for aid, 567 were judged to have need. Of these, 567 received aid, and 89 had their full need met. Average financial aid package met 70.4% of need; average scholarship/grant was $9,499; average loan was $3,706. For part-time students, average financial aid package was $11,811.
Students without need: 266 full-time freshmen who did not demonstrate need for aid received scholarships/grants; average award was $3,794. No-need awards available for academics, athletics, leadership, minority status, music/drama, religious affiliation, ROTC.
Scholarships offered: 15 full-time freshmen received athletic scholarships; average amount $10,748.

Cumulative student debt: 49% of graduating class had student loans; average debt was $19,487.

FINANCIAL AID PROCEDURES
Forms required: FAFSA, institutional form.
Dates and Deadlines: Closing date 3/2. Applicants notified on a rolling basis starting 3/1; must reply within 3 week(s) of notification.
Transfers: Cal Grants not available to first time applicants who are seniors.

CONTACT
Todd Ross, Director of Student Financial Services
901 East Alosta Avenue, Azusa, CA 91702-7000
(626) 812-3009

Barstow College
Barstow, California
www.barstow.edu   Federal Code: 001119

2-year public community college in large town.
Enrollment: 2,175 undergrads.
Selectivity: Open admission.

BASIC COSTS (2005-2006)
Tuition and fees: $780; out-of-state residents $5,190.
Per-credit charge: $26; out-of-state residents $173.
Additional info: Tuition/fee waivers available for adults, unemployed or children of unemployed.

FINANCIAL AID PICTURE
Students with need: Need-based aid available for full-time and part-time students.
Students without need: This college only awards aid to students with need.

FINANCIAL AID PROCEDURES
Forms required: FAFSA.
Dates and Deadlines: Closing date 5/22. Applicants notified on a rolling basis starting 7/1.

CONTACT
Lillian Justice, Financial Aid Coordinator
2700 Barstow Road, Barstow, CA 92311-9984
(760) 252-2411

Bethany University
Scotts Valley, California
www.bethany.edu   Federal Code: 001121

4-year private Bible and liberal arts college in small town, affiliated with Assemblies of God.
Enrollment: 461 undergrads, 17% part-time. 81 full-time freshmen.
Selectivity: Admits 50 to 75% of applicants.

BASIC COSTS (2006-2007)
Tuition and fees: $16,330.
Room and board: $6,750.

FINANCIAL AID PICTURE (2005-2006)
Students with need: 43% of average financial aid package awarded as scholarships/grants, 57% awarded as loans/jobs. Need-based aid available for part-time students. Work study available nights, weekends, and for part-time students.
Students without need: No-need awards available for academics, alumni affiliation, athletics, leadership, minority status, music/drama, religious affiliation.

FINANCIAL AID PROCEDURES
Forms required: FAFSA, institutional form.
Dates and Deadlines: Priority date 3/2; no closing date. Applicants notified on a rolling basis starting 4/15; must reply within 2 week(s) of notification.

CONTACT
Niki Santo, Dean of Enrollment Management
800 Bethany Drive, Scotts Valley, CA 95066-2898
(831) 438-3800 ext. 147

Bethesda Christian University
Anaheim, California
www.bcu.edu   Federal Code: 032663

4-year private university and Bible college in large city, affiliated with Christian Church.
Enrollment: 171 undergrads.
Selectivity: Open admission.

BASIC COSTS (2006-2007)
Tuition and fees: $6,420.

FINANCIAL AID PICTURE (2004-2005)
Students with need: 52% of average financial aid package awarded as scholarships/grants, 48% awarded as loans/jobs. Need-based aid available for part-time students.
Students without need: This college only awards aid to students with need.

FINANCIAL AID PROCEDURES
Forms required: FAFSA, institutional form.
Dates and Deadlines: Closing date 6/30. Applicants notified on a rolling basis starting 6/30.
Transfers: No deadline.

CONTACT
Soo Min
730 North Euclid Street, Anaheim, CA 92801
(714) 517-1945

Biola University
La Mirada, California
www.biola.edu   Federal Code: 001122

4-year private university and Bible college in large town, affiliated with interdenominational tradition.
Enrollment: 3,240 undergrads, 3% part-time. 688 full-time freshmen.
Selectivity: Admits over 75% of applicants.

BASIC COSTS (2006-2007)
Tuition and fees: $23,782.
Per-credit charge: $991.
Room and board: $7,116.

FINANCIAL AID PICTURE (2004-2005)
Students with need: Out of 565 full-time freshmen who applied for aid, 469 were judged to have need. Of these, 469 received aid, and 58 had their full need met. Average financial aid package met 67% of need; average scholarship/grant was $9,134; average loan was $2,479. For part-time students, average financial aid package was $9,588.
Students without need: 108 full-time freshmen who did not demonstrate need for aid received scholarships/grants; average award was $10,381. No-need awards available for academics, alumni affiliation, art, athletics, leadership, minority status, music/drama, ROTC.
Scholarships offered: *Merit:* Scholarships for Underrepresented Groups of Ethnicity: up to $6,500; based on GPA and ethnicity. Community Service

Scholarship: $2,700; based on demonstration of outstanding spiritual leadership. Alumni Dependent Scholarship: $500; given to students whose parents completed 30 units of coursework at Biola University. **Athletic:** 18 full-time freshmen received athletic scholarships; average amount $2,121.
Cumulative student debt: 74% of graduating class had student loans; average debt was $28,007.

FINANCIAL AID PROCEDURES
Forms required: FAFSA, state aid form.
Dates and Deadlines: Priority date 1/1; closing date 3/1. Applicants notified on a rolling basis starting 3/1.

CONTACT
Jonathan Choy, Director of Financial Aid
13800 Biola Avenue, La Mirada, CA 90639-0001
(562) 903-4742

California Baptist University
Riverside, California
www.calbaptist.edu   Federal Code: 001125

4-year private university and liberal arts college in large city, affiliated with Southern Baptist Convention.
Enrollment: 2,392 undergrads, 17% part-time. 317 full-time freshmen.
Selectivity: Admits 50 to 75% of applicants.

BASIC COSTS (2005-2006)
Tuition and fees: $17,470.
Per-credit charge: $625.
Room and board: $6,810.

FINANCIAL AID PICTURE (2004-2005)
Students with need: Out of 311 full-time freshmen who applied for aid, 298 were judged to have need. Of these, 298 received aid, and 67 had their full need met. Average financial aid package met 70% of need; average scholarship/grant was $7,700; average loan was $2,430. For part-time students, average financial aid package was $6,250.
Students without need: 12 full-time freshmen who did not demonstrate need for aid received scholarships/grants; average award was $5,150. No-need awards available for academics, art, athletics, leadership, music/drama, religious affiliation, ROTC.
Scholarships offered: 36 full-time freshmen received athletic scholarships; average amount $6,520.
Cumulative student debt: 87% of graduating class had student loans; average debt was $21,700.

FINANCIAL AID PROCEDURES
Forms required: FAFSA, state aid form.
Dates and Deadlines: Priority date 3/2; no closing date. Applicants notified on a rolling basis starting 3/2; must reply by 5/1 or within 3 week(s) of notification.
Transfers: No deadline. Applicants notified on a rolling basis starting 12/15.

CONTACT
Eileen Terry, Director, Financial Aid
8432 Magnolia Avenue, Riverside, CA 92504-3297
(951) 343-4236

California College of the Arts
San Francisco, California
www.cca.edu   Federal Code: 001127

4-year private visual arts college in very large city.
Enrollment: 1,312 undergrads, 6% part-time. 181 full-time freshmen.
Selectivity: Admits over 75% of applicants.

BASIC COSTS (2006-2007)
Tuition and fees: $27,914.
Per-credit charge: $1,151.
Room only: $6,200.

FINANCIAL AID PICTURE (2005-2006)
Students with need: Out of 134 full-time freshmen who applied for aid, 116 were judged to have need. Of these, 116 received aid, and 10 had their full need met. Average financial aid package met 61% of need; average scholarship/grant was $12,663; average loan was $2,798. For part-time students, average financial aid package was $9,283.
Students without need: 29 full-time freshmen who did not demonstrate need for aid received scholarships/grants; average award was $5,431. No-need awards available for academics, art, minority status.
Scholarships offered: Creative Achievement Scholarship; $3,500-$14,000; renewable; based on academic achievement and strength of admissions portfolios.
Cumulative student debt: 62% of graduating class had student loans; average debt was $28,549.
Additional info: Application deadline for merit scholarships February 15.

FINANCIAL AID PROCEDURES
Forms required: FAFSA.
Dates and Deadlines: Priority date 3/1; no closing date. Applicants notified on a rolling basis starting 4/1; must reply by 5/1 or within 3 week(s) of notification.
Transfers: Scholarships available for community college transfer students.

CONTACT
Don Crewell, Director of Financial Aid
1111 Eighth Street, San Francisco, CA 94107-2247
(415) 703-9528

California Culinary Academy
San Francisco, California
www.caculinary.edu   Federal Code: 015698

2-year for-profit culinary school in very large city.
Enrollment: 1,030 undergrads.

FINANCIAL AID PICTURE
Students with need: Need-based aid available for full-time students.
Additional info: Financial aid forms due 60 days prior to first day of classes.

FINANCIAL AID PROCEDURES
Forms required: FAFSA, state aid form.
Dates and Deadlines: No deadline. Applicants notified on a rolling basis; must reply within 1 week(s) of notification.

CONTACT
625 Polk Street, San Francisco, CA 94102
(415) 771-3500

California Institute of Technology
Pasadena, California
www.caltech.edu   Federal Code: 001131
                              CSS Code: 4034

4-year private university in small city.
Enrollment: 913 undergrads. 233 full-time freshmen.
Selectivity: Admits less than 50% of applicants.

BASIC COSTS (2006-2007)
Tuition and fees: $31,410.
Per-credit charge: $792.
Room and board: $9,102.

FINANCIAL AID PICTURE (2005-2006)
Students with need: Out of 179 full-time freshmen who applied for aid, 124 were judged to have need. Of these, 124 received aid, and 124 had their full need met. Average financial aid package met 100% of need; average scholarship/grant was $26,303; average loan was $1,503.
Students without need: 14 full-time freshmen who did not demonstrate need for aid received scholarships/grants; average award was $29,399. No-need awards available for academics.
Scholarships offered: Merit scholarships available up to full tuition and room and board. Special application not required.
Cumulative student debt: 45% of graduating class had student loans; average debt was $5,395.

FINANCIAL AID PROCEDURES
Forms required: FAFSA, CSS PROFILE, state aid form.
Dates and Deadlines: Closing date 1/15. Applicants notified by 4/15; must reply by 5/1 or within 2 week(s) of notification.
Transfers: Priority date 3/2; no deadline.

CONTACT
David Levy, Director of Financial Aid
1200 East California Boulevard, Pasadena, CA 91125
(626) 395-6280

California Institute of the Arts
Valencia, California
www.calarts.edu   Federal Code: 001132

4-year private visual arts and performing arts college in small city.
Enrollment: 803 undergrads, 1% part-time. 138 full-time freshmen.
Selectivity: Admits less than 50% of applicants.

BASIC COSTS (2006-2007)
Tuition and fees: $30,075.
Room and board: $7,700.

FINANCIAL AID PICTURE (2005-2006)
Students with need: Out of 108 full-time freshmen who applied for aid, 78 were judged to have need. Of these, 77 received aid, and 9 had their full need met. Average financial aid package met 86% of need; average scholarship/grant was $9,746; average loan was $3,586. Need-based aid available for part-time students.
Students without need: 19 full-time freshmen who did not demonstrate need for aid received scholarships/grants; average award was $3,978. No-need awards available for academics, art, minority status, music/drama.
Cumulative student debt: 76% of graduating class had student loans; average debt was $34,602.

FINANCIAL AID PROCEDURES
Forms required: FAFSA.
Dates and Deadlines: Priority date 3/1; no closing date. Applicants notified on a rolling basis starting 4/15; must reply within 3 week(s) of notification.

CONTACT
Bobbi Heuer, Financial Aid Director
24700 McBean Parkway, Valencia, CA 91355
(661) 255-1050

California Lutheran University
Thousand Oaks, California
www.clunet.edu   Federal Code: 001133

4-year private university and liberal arts college in small city, affiliated with Evangelical Lutheran Church in America.
Enrollment: 2,087 undergrads, 10% part-time. 402 full-time freshmen.
Selectivity: Admits 50 to 75% of applicants.

BASIC COSTS (2006-2007)
Tuition and fees: $24,530.
Per-credit charge: $785.
Room and board: $8,740.

FINANCIAL AID PICTURE (2004-2005)
Students with need: Out of 350 full-time freshmen who applied for aid, 285 were judged to have need. Of these, 284 received aid, and 148 had their full need met. Average financial aid package met 86% of need; average scholarship/grant was $16,616; average loan was $2,099. For part-time students, average financial aid package was $8,061.
Students without need: 117 full-time freshmen who did not demonstrate need for aid received scholarships/grants; average award was $8,484. No-need awards available for academics, alumni affiliation, art, music/drama, religious affiliation.
Cumulative student debt: 86% of graduating class had student loans; average debt was $21,140.

FINANCIAL AID PROCEDURES
Forms required: FAFSA.
Dates and Deadlines: Priority date 3/2; no closing date. Applicants notified on a rolling basis starting 3/20; must reply within 2 week(s) of notification.

CONTACT
Matt Ward, Dean of Enrollment
60 West Olsen Road #1350, Thousand Oaks, CA 91360-2787
(805) 493-3115

California Maritime Academy
Vallejo, California
www.csum.edu   Federal Code: 001134

4-year public university and maritime college in small city.
Enrollment: 750 undergrads.
Selectivity: Admits 50 to 75% of applicants.

BASIC COSTS (2005-2006)
Tuition and fees: $3,446; out-of-state residents $13,616.
Room and board: $7,030.
Additional info: Mandatory cruise fee for freshmen $3,100; uniform costs for freshman $1,550.

FINANCIAL AID PICTURE
Students with need: Need-based aid available for full-time and part-time students.
Students without need: This college only awards aid to students with need.
Additional info: US Maritime Administration provides annual incentive payment of $3,000 per student, with certain conditions. Tuition waiver for children of deceased or disabled California veterans.

FINANCIAL AID PROCEDURES
Forms required: FAFSA.
Dates and Deadlines: Priority date 3/2; no closing date. Applicants notified on a rolling basis starting 4/1.

CONTACT
Ken Walsh, Director of Financial Aid
200 Maritime Academy Drive, Vallejo, CA 94590
(707) 654-1275

California Polytechnic State University: San Luis Obispo
San Luis Obispo, California
www.calpoly.edu   Federal Code: 001143

4-year public university in large town.
Enrollment: 17,385 undergrads, 5% part-time. 2,898 full-time freshmen.
Selectivity: Admits less than 50% of applicants.

BASIC COSTS (2005-2006)
Tuition and fees: $4,246; out-of-state residents $14,416.
Room and board: $8,145.
Additional info: Required fees vary by program.

FINANCIAL AID PICTURE (2004-2005)
Students with need: Out of 1,942 full-time freshmen who applied for aid, 998 were judged to have need. Of these, 911 received aid, and 49 had their full need met. Average financial aid package met 64% of need; average scholarship/grant was $1,459; average loan was $2,466. For part-time students, average financial aid package was $5,981.
Students without need: No-need awards available for academics, alumni affiliation, art, athletics, job skills, leadership, music/drama, ROTC, state/district residency.
Cumulative student debt: 35% of graduating class had student loans; average debt was $13,788.

FINANCIAL AID PROCEDURES
Forms required: FAFSA, institutional form.
Dates and Deadlines: Priority date 3/1; closing date 6/30. Applicants notified on a rolling basis starting 4/15; must reply within 8 week(s) of notification.

CONTACT
Lois Kelly, Director, Financial Aid
Admissions Office, Cal Poly, San Luis Obispo, CA 93407
(805) 756-2927

California School of Culinary Arts
Pasadena, California
www.csca.edu   Federal Code: 032103

2-year for-profit culinary school in very large city.
Enrollment: 1,686 undergrads. 896 full-time freshmen.
Selectivity: Open admission.

FINANCIAL AID PICTURE (2004-2005)
Students with need: Average financial aid package for all full-time undergraduates was $14,000. 26% awarded as scholarships/grants, 74% awarded as loans/jobs. Need-based aid available for part-time students. Work study available nights, weekends, and for part-time students.
Cumulative student debt: 85% of graduating class had student loans; average debt was $20,443.

FINANCIAL AID PROCEDURES
Forms required: FAFSA.
Dates and Deadlines: No deadline. Applicants notified on a rolling basis.
Transfers: No deadline.

CONTACT
Sandra Fay, Director of Student Finance
521 East Green Street, Pasadena, CA 91101
(626) 229-1300

California State Polytechnic University: Pomona
Pomona, California
www.csupomona.edu   Federal Code: 001144

4-year public university in small city.
Enrollment: 17,306 undergrads, 16% part-time. 1,865 full-time freshmen.
Selectivity: Admits less than 50% of applicants.

BASIC COSTS (2005-2006)
Tuition and fees: $3,018; out-of-state residents $13,188.
Room and board: $8,478.

FINANCIAL AID PICTURE (2005-2006)
Students with need: Out of 1,352 full-time freshmen who applied for aid, 919 were judged to have need. Of these, 813 received aid, and 203 had their full need met. Average financial aid package met 84% of need; average scholarship/grant was $5,099; average loan was $6,804. For part-time students, average financial aid package was $8,298.
Students without need: 94 full-time freshmen who did not demonstrate need for aid received scholarships/grants; average award was $3,074. No-need awards available for academics, alumni affiliation, art, athletics, leadership, music/drama, state/district residency.
Scholarships offered: 34 full-time freshmen received athletic scholarships; average amount $3,302.

FINANCIAL AID PROCEDURES
Forms required: FAFSA.
Dates and Deadlines: Priority date 3/2; no closing date. Applicants notified on a rolling basis starting 4/1.

CONTACT
Diana Minor, Director of Financial Aid
3801 West Temple Avenue, Pomona, CA 91768-4019
(909) 869-3700

California State University: Bakersfield
Bakersfield, California
www.csub.edu   Federal Code: 007993

4-year public university and liberal arts college in small city.
Enrollment: 4,825 full-time undergrads.
Selectivity: Admits less than 50% of applicants.

BASIC COSTS (2005-2006)
Tuition and fees: $3,268; out-of-state residents $13,438.
Room and board: $5,946.

FINANCIAL AID PICTURE
Students with need: Need-based aid available for full-time and part-time students.
Students without need: This college only awards aid to students with need.

FINANCIAL AID PROCEDURES
Forms required: FAFSA.
Dates and Deadlines: Priority date 3/2; closing date 4/1. Applicants notified on a rolling basis; must reply within 2 week(s) of notification.

CONTACT
Clifford Smith, Associate Dean of Financial Aid
9001 Stockdale Highway, Bakersfield, CA 93311-1099
(661) 664-2011

California State University: Chico
Chico, California
www.csuchico.edu   Federal Code: 001146

4-year public university and liberal arts college in small city.
Enrollment: 14,526 undergrads, 10% part-time. 2,300 full-time freshmen.
Selectivity: Admits over 75% of applicants.

BASIC COSTS (2005-2006)
Tuition and fees: $3,370; out-of-state residents $13,540.
Room and board: $8,312.

FINANCIAL AID PICTURE (2005-2006)
Students with need: Out of 1,432 full-time freshmen who applied for aid, 871 were judged to have need. Of these, 856 received aid, and 90 had their full need met. Average financial aid package met 79% of need; average scholarship/grant was $5,735; average loan was $2,361. For part-time students, average financial aid package was $8,070.
Students without need: 86 full-time freshmen who did not demonstrate need for aid received scholarships/grants; average award was $1,465. No-need awards available for academics, art, athletics, leadership, minority status, music/drama, religious affiliation.
Scholarships offered: *Merit:* President's Scholar Award; 10 awards at $12,000 each and 12 awards at $1,000 each. *Athletic:* 28 full-time freshmen received athletic scholarships; average amount $3,634.

FINANCIAL AID PROCEDURES
Forms required: FAFSA.
Dates and Deadlines: Priority date 3/2; no closing date. Applicants notified on a rolling basis starting 2/15.

CONTACT
Meredith Kelley, Director of Financial Aid
400 West First Street, Chico, CA 95929-0722
(530) 898-6451

California State University: Dominguez Hills
Carson, California
www.csudh.edu   Federal Code: 001141
                 CSS Code: 4098

4-year public university in small city.
Enrollment: 8,943 undergrads, 40% part-time. 705 full-time freshmen.
Selectivity: Admits less than 50% of applicants.

BASIC COSTS (2005-2006)
Tuition and fees: $2,991; out-of-state residents $13,161.
Room and board: $7,770.
Additional info: Tuition/fee waivers available for adults.

FINANCIAL AID PICTURE
Students with need: Need-based aid available for full-time students.
Students without need: No-need awards available for academics, minority status.

FINANCIAL AID PROCEDURES
Forms required: FAFSA, CSS PROFILE.
Dates and Deadlines: Priority date 4/15; no closing date. Applicants notified on a rolling basis starting 2/15; must reply within 4 week(s) of notification.

CONTACT
Dolores Lee, Director of Financial Aid
1000 East Victoria Street, Carson, CA 90747
(310) 243-3696

California State University: East Bay
Hayward, California
www.csueastbay.edu   Federal Code: 001138

4-year public university in small city.
Enrollment: 8,476 undergrads, 21% part-time. 704 full-time freshmen.

BASIC COSTS (2005-2006)
Tuition and fees: $2,916; out-of-state residents $13,086.
Room and board: $6,796.

FINANCIAL AID PICTURE (2005-2006)
Students with need: Out of 275 full-time freshmen who applied for aid, 247 were judged to have need. Of these, 240 received aid, and 26 had their full need met. Average financial aid package met 68% of need; average scholarship/grant was $7,128; average loan was $2,668. For part-time students, average financial aid package was $5,388.
Cumulative student debt: 37% of graduating class had student loans; average debt was $12,312.

FINANCIAL AID PROCEDURES
Forms required: FAFSA.
Dates and Deadlines: Priority date 3/2; no closing date. Applicants notified on a rolling basis; must reply within 3 week(s) of notification.

CONTACT
Anita Patino, Financial Aid Department
25800 Carlos Bee Boulevard, Hayward, CA 94542-3095
(510) 885-3616

California State University: Fresno
Fresno, California
www.csufresno.edu   Federal Code: 001147

4-year public university in very large city.
Enrollment: 17,428 undergrads, 15% part-time. 2,218 full-time freshmen.
Selectivity: Admits 50 to 75% of applicants.

BASIC COSTS (2005-2006)
Tuition and fees: $2,933; out-of-state residents $13,103.
Room and board: $7,416.

FINANCIAL AID PICTURE (2004-2005)
Students with need: Out of 1,952 full-time freshmen who applied for aid, 1,648 were judged to have need. Of these, 1,014 received aid, and 301 had their full need met. Average financial aid package met 70% of need; average scholarship/grant was $4,334; average loan was $2,302. For part-time students, average financial aid package was $4,439.
Students without need: 49 full-time freshmen who did not demonstrate need for aid received scholarships/grants; average award was $1,431. No-need awards available for academics, alumni affiliation, athletics, leadership, music/drama, state/district residency.
Scholarships offered: 58 full-time freshmen received athletic scholarships; average amount $7,309.
Cumulative student debt: 39% of graduating class had student loans; average debt was $11,457.

FINANCIAL AID PROCEDURES
Forms required: FAFSA.
Dates and Deadlines: Priority date 3/1; no closing date. Applicants notified on a rolling basis starting 4/1; must reply within 3 week(s) of notification.

CONTACT
Maria Hernandez, Director of Financial Aid
5150 North Maple Avenue, M/S JA 57, Fresno, CA 93740-8026
(559) 278-2182

California State University: Fullerton
Fullerton, California
www.fullerton.edu
Federal Code: 001137

4-year public university in small city.
Enrollment: 27,917 undergrads, 24% part-time. 3,820 full-time freshmen.
Selectivity: Admits 50 to 75% of applicants.

BASIC COSTS (2005-2006)
Tuition and fees: $2,990; out-of-state residents $13,160.
Room and board: $7,174.

FINANCIAL AID PICTURE (2005-2006)
Students with need: Out of 2,781 full-time freshmen who applied for aid, 1,904 were judged to have need. Of these, 1,211 received aid, and 39 had their full need met. Average financial aid package met 64% of need; average scholarship/grant was $6,956; average loan was $2,492. For part-time students, average financial aid package was $5,916.
Students without need: 360 full-time freshmen who did not demonstrate need for aid received scholarships/grants; average award was $3,692. No-need awards available for academics.
Scholarships offered: 30 full-time freshmen received athletic scholarships; average amount $4,296.
Cumulative student debt: 37% of graduating class had student loans; average debt was $14,482.
Additional info: Fee waiver for children of veterans killed in action or with service-connected disability whose annual income is $5,000 or less.

FINANCIAL AID PROCEDURES
Forms required: FAFSA.
Dates and Deadlines: Priority date 3/2; closing date 5/30. Applicants notified on a rolling basis starting 4/2; must reply within 3 week(s) of notification.
Transfers: No deadline. Applicants notified on a rolling basis starting 4/2; must reply within 3 week(s) of notification.

CONTACT
Deborah McCracken, Director of Financial Aid
Box 6900, Fullerton, CA 92834-6900
(714) 278-3125

California State University: Long Beach
Long Beach, California
www.csulb.edu
Federal Code: 001139

4-year public university in large city.
Enrollment: 28,514 undergrads, 21% part-time. 3,935 full-time freshmen.
Selectivity: Admits 50 to 75% of applicants.

BASIC COSTS (2006-2007)
Tuition and fees: $2,864; out-of-state residents $13,034.
Room and board: $6,648.

FINANCIAL AID PICTURE (2005-2006)
Students with need: Out of 2,933 full-time freshmen who applied for aid, 2,088 were judged to have need. Of these, 1,835 received aid, and 1,361 had their full need met. Average financial aid package met 78% of need; average scholarship/grant was $3,550; average loan was $2,258. For part-time students, average financial aid package was $6,250.
Students without need: 271 full-time freshmen who did not demonstrate need for aid received scholarships/grants; average award was $1,610. No-need awards available for academics, alumni affiliation, art, athletics, music/drama.
Scholarships offered: President's Scholar Award; full tuition and fees, campus housing, books.
Cumulative student debt: 31% of graduating class had student loans; average debt was $10,842.

FINANCIAL AID PROCEDURES
Forms required: FAFSA.
Dates and Deadlines: Priority date 3/2; no closing date. Applicants notified on a rolling basis starting 4/1; must reply within 3 week(s) of notification.
Transfers: Community college EOPS students may apply as EOP students and thus be eligible for an EOP Grant.

CONTACT
Dean Kulju, Director of Financial Aid
1250 Bellflower Boulevard, Long Beach, CA 90840-0106
(562) 985-4641

California State University: Los Angeles
Los Angeles, California
www.calstatela.edu
Federal Code: 001140

4-year public university in very large city.
Enrollment: 14,955 undergrads, 27% part-time. 1,253 full-time freshmen.
Selectivity: Admits 50 to 75% of applicants.

BASIC COSTS (2005-2006)
Tuition and fees: $3,035; out-of-state residents $13,205.
Room and board: $7,353.

FINANCIAL AID PICTURE
Students with need: Need-based aid available for full-time and part-time students.

FINANCIAL AID PROCEDURES
Forms required: FAFSA.
Dates and Deadlines: Priority date 3/1; no closing date. Applicants notified on a rolling basis starting 4/1; must reply within 3 week(s) of notification.

CONTACT
Lindy Fong, Director of Center for Student Financial Aid
5151 State University Drive SA101, Los Angeles, CA 90032
(323) 343-1784

California State University: Monterey Bay
Seaside, California
www.csumb.edu
Federal Code: 032603

4-year public liberal arts and teachers college in large town.
Enrollment: 3,407 undergrads. 414 full-time freshmen.
Selectivity: Admits 50 to 75% of applicants.

BASIC COSTS (2005-2006)
Tuition and fees: $3,036; out-of-state residents $13,206.
Room and board: $8,880.
Additional info: Tuition/fee waivers available for unemployed or children of unemployed.

FINANCIAL AID PICTURE (2004-2005)
Students with need: Out of 338 full-time freshmen who applied for aid, 232 were judged to have need. Of these, 220 received aid, and 20 had their full need met. Average financial aid package met 65% of need; average scholarship/grant was $4,312; average loan was $1,327. For part-time students, average financial aid package was $5,022.
Students without need: This college only awards aid to students with need.
Scholarships offered: 5 full-time freshmen received athletic scholarships; average amount $1,540.

FINANCIAL AID PROCEDURES
Forms required: FAFSA, state aid form.
Dates and Deadlines: Priority date 3/2; no closing date. Applicants notified on a rolling basis starting 4/1.

CONTACT
Audren Morris, Director of Financial Aid
100 Campus Center, Building 47, Seaside, CA 93955-8001
(831) 582-4074

California State University: Northridge
Northridge, California
www.csun.edu   Federal Code: 001153

4-year public university in very large city.
Enrollment: 26,854 undergrads, 23% part-time. 2,855 full-time freshmen.
Selectivity: Admits 50 to 75% of applicants.

BASIC COSTS (2005-2006)
Tuition and fees: $3,036; out-of-state residents $13,206.
Room and board: $8,880.

FINANCIAL AID PICTURE (2005-2006)
Students with need: Need-based aid available for part-time students.
Students without need: No-need awards available for academics, athletics, state/district residency.

FINANCIAL AID PROCEDURES
Forms required: FAFSA.
Dates and Deadlines: Priority date 3/1; no closing date. Applicants notified on a rolling basis starting 5/1.

CONTACT
Diane Ryan, Director of Financial Aid
18111 Nordhoff Street, Northridge, CA 91328-8207
(818) 677-4085

California State University: Sacramento
Sacramento, California
www.csus.edu   Federal Code: 001233

4-year public university in very large city.
Enrollment: 23,028 undergrads, 22% part-time. 2,051 full-time freshmen.
Selectivity: Admits less than 50% of applicants.

BASIC COSTS (2005-2006)
Tuition and fees: $3,072; out-of-state residents $13,242.
Room and board: $8,392.

FINANCIAL AID PICTURE (2004-2005)
Students with need: Out of 1,488 full-time freshmen who applied for aid, 1,138 were judged to have need. Of these, 1,029 received aid, and 46 had their full need met. Average financial aid package met 68% of need; average scholarship/grant was $2,129; average loan was $2,498. For part-time students, average financial aid package was $6,444.
Students without need: 112 full-time freshmen who did not demonstrate need for aid received scholarships/grants; average award was $5,797.

FINANCIAL AID PROCEDURES
Forms required: FAFSA.
Dates and Deadlines: Priority date 3/2; no closing date. Applicants notified on a rolling basis starting 4/1; must reply within 4 week(s) of notification.

CONTACT
Linda Clemons, Financial Aid Director
6000 J Street, Sacramento, CA 95819-6048
(916) 278-6554

California State University: San Bernardino
San Bernardino, California
www.csusb.edu   Federal Code: 001142

4-year public university and liberal arts college in small city.
Enrollment: 12,464 undergrads, 17% part-time. 1,635 full-time freshmen.
Selectivity: Admits less than 50% of applicants.

BASIC COSTS (2005-2006)
Tuition and fees: $3,092; out-of-state residents $13,262.
Room and board: $9,072.

FINANCIAL AID PICTURE
Students with need: Need-based aid available for full-time students.

FINANCIAL AID PROCEDURES
Forms required: FAFSA.
Dates and Deadlines: Priority date 3/2; no closing date. Applicants notified on a rolling basis starting 4/1.

CONTACT
Lois Madsen, Director of Financial Aid
5500 University Parkway, San Bernardino, CA 92407-2397
(909) 880-7800

California State University: San Marcos
San Marcos, California
www.csusm.edu   Federal Code: 030113

4-year public university in large town.
Enrollment: 6,276 undergrads, 26% part-time. 680 full-time freshmen.
Selectivity: Admits less than 50% of applicants.

BASIC COSTS (2005-2006)
Tuition and fees: $3,062; out-of-state residents $13,232.
Room and board: $8,616.

FINANCIAL AID PICTURE (2005-2006)
Students with need: Average financial aid package for all full-time undergraduates was $6,946; for part-time $5,750. 61% awarded as scholarships/grants, 39% awarded as loans/jobs.
Scholarships offered: Fenstermaker scholarships of up to $6,000 a year; awarded to outstanding chemistry, biology, or computer science majors; renewable.
Cumulative student debt: 40% of graduating class had student loans; average debt was $13,112.

FINANCIAL AID PROCEDURES
Forms required: FAFSA.
Dates and Deadlines: Priority date 3/2; no closing date. Applicants notified on a rolling basis starting 4/15.

CONTACT
Cecilia Schouwe, Director of Financial Aid
333 S. Twin Oaks Valley Road, San Marcos, CA 92096-0001
(760) 750-4850

California State University: Stanislaus
Turlock, California
www.csustan.edu   Federal Code: 001157

4-year public business and liberal arts college in small city.
Enrollment: 6,434 undergrads, 31% part-time. 741 full-time freshmen.
Selectivity: Admits 50 to 75% of applicants.

California State University: Stanislaus

BASIC COSTS (2005-2006)
Tuition and fees: $3,080; out-of-state residents $13,250.
Room and board: $8,253.
Additional info: Tuition/fee waivers available for adults.

FINANCIAL AID PICTURE (2005-2006)
Students with need: Out of 662 full-time freshmen who applied for aid, 494 were judged to have need. Of these, 453 received aid, and 10 had their full need met. Average financial aid package met 66% of need; average scholarship/grant was $4,361; average loan was $2,654. For part-time students, average financial aid package was $6,189.
Students without need: 29 full-time freshmen who did not demonstrate need for aid received scholarships/grants; average award was $1,501. No-need awards available for academics, alumni affiliation, art, athletics, leadership, minority status, music/drama, state/district residency.
Scholarships offered: *Merit:* Valedictorian Scholarships; $2,500; renewable for up to 4 years; 10 available. Leadership Awards; $1,000; for student body presidents; renewable for up to 2 years; five available. International Baccalaureate Scholarships; $1,000; for candidates whose high schools have International Baccalaureate Program; 3 available. Achievement Awards; $2,000; for community college transfers; renewable for up to 2 years; 10 available. *Athletic:* 34 full-time freshmen received athletic scholarships; average amount $2,094.
Cumulative student debt: 18% of graduating class had student loans; average debt was $15,500.

FINANCIAL AID PROCEDURES
Forms required: FAFSA.
Dates and Deadlines: Priority date 3/2; no closing date. Applicants notified on a rolling basis starting 3/15; must reply within 3 week(s) of notification.

CONTACT
David Gomes, Interim Director
801 West Monte Vista Avenue, Turlock, CA 95382-0256
(209) 667-3336

Cerro Coso Community College
Ridgecrest, California
www.cerrocoso.edu   Federal Code: 010111

2-year public community college in large town.
Enrollment: 560 full-time undergrads. 130 full-time freshmen.
Selectivity: Open admission.

BASIC COSTS (2005-2006)
Tuition and fees: $780; out-of-state residents $5,790.
Per-credit charge: $26; out-of-state residents $191.

FINANCIAL AID PICTURE
Students with need: Need-based aid available for full-time and part-time students. Work study available nights.

FINANCIAL AID PROCEDURES
Forms required: FAFSA.
Dates and Deadlines: Priority date 5/15; no closing date. Applicants notified on a rolling basis starting 6/1; must reply within 2 week(s) of notification.

CONTACT
Jill Board, Vice President
3000 College Heights Boulevard, Ridgecrest, CA 93555-7777
(760) 384-6221

Chabot College
Hayward, California
www.chabotcollege.edu   Federal Code: 001162

2-year public community college in large city.
Enrollment: 7,313 undergrads, 62% part-time. 550 full-time freshmen.
Selectivity: Open admission.

BASIC COSTS (2005-2006)
Tuition and fees: $808; out-of-state residents $5,488.
Per-credit charge: $26; out-of-state residents $182.

FINANCIAL AID PICTURE
Students with need: Work study available nights, weekends, and for part-time students.
Additional info: Tuition and/or fee waivers for low-income students.

FINANCIAL AID PROCEDURES
Forms required: FAFSA, institutional form.
Dates and Deadlines: Priority date 8/1; no closing date. Applicants notified on a rolling basis.

CONTACT
Kathryn Linzmeyer, Director of Financial Aid
25555 Hesperian Boulevard, Hayward, CA 94545
(510) 723-6746

Chaffey College
Rancho Cucamonga, California
www.chaffey.edu   Federal Code: 001163

2-year public community college in small city.
Enrollment: 5,776 full-time undergrads.
Selectivity: Open admission.

BASIC COSTS (2005-2006)
Tuition and fees: $802; out-of-state residents $5,332.
Per-credit charge: $26; out-of-state residents $177.
Additional info: Tuition/fee waivers available for adults.

FINANCIAL AID PICTURE
Students with need: Need-based aid available for full-time and part-time students.
Students without need: No-need awards available for academics.
Additional info: State of California Board of Governors fee waivers to qualified state residents. Criteria for eligibility: households which receive public assistance, meet state's low income guidelines, and demonstrate need as defined by Title IV programs.

FINANCIAL AID PROCEDURES
Forms required: FAFSA.
Dates and Deadlines: No deadline. Applicants notified on a rolling basis starting 7/15; must reply within 2 week(s) of notification.

CONTACT
Karen Sanders, Financial Aid Supervisor
5885 Haven Avenue, Rancho Cucamonga, CA 91701-3002
(909) 941-2194

Chapman University
Orange, California
www.chapman.edu   Federal Code: 001164

4-year private university and liberal arts college in very large city, affiliated with Christian Church (Disciples of Christ).
Enrollment: 3,839 undergrads, 5% part-time. 754 full-time freshmen.

Selectivity: Admits 50 to 75% of applicants.

BASIC COSTS (2006-2007)
Tuition and fees: $30,748.
Per-credit charge: $920.
Room and board: $10,500.
Additional info: Tuition/fee waivers available for minority students.

FINANCIAL AID PICTURE (2004-2005)
Students with need: Out of 661 full-time freshmen who applied for aid, 474 were judged to have need. Of these, 473 received aid, and 473 had their full need met. Average financial aid package met 100% of need; average scholarship/grant was $19,640; average loan was $3,557. For part-time students, average financial aid package was $13,648.
Students without need: 99 full-time freshmen who did not demonstrate need for aid received scholarships/grants; average award was $16,440. No-need awards available for academics, alumni affiliation, art, music/drama, religious affiliation, ROTC.
Cumulative student debt: 64% of graduating class had student loans; average debt was $19,237.

FINANCIAL AID PROCEDURES
Forms required: FAFSA, state aid form.
Dates and Deadlines: Priority date 3/2; no closing date. Applicants notified on a rolling basis starting 3/15; must reply within 3 week(s) of notification.
Transfers: No deadline. Applicants notified on a rolling basis starting 3/15; must reply within 3 week(s) of notification.

CONTACT
Gregory Ball, Director of Financial Aid
One University Drive, Orange, CA 92866
(714) 997-6815

Citrus College
Glendora, California
www.citruscollege.edu   Federal Code: 001166

2-year public community college in large town.
Enrollment: 9,909 undergrads.
Selectivity: Open admission.

BASIC COSTS (2005-2006)
Tuition and fees: $808; out-of-state residents $5,338.
Per-credit charge: $26; out-of-state residents $177.

FINANCIAL AID PICTURE (2005-2006)
Students with need: 3% of average financial aid package awarded as scholarships/grants, 97% awarded as loans/jobs. Need-based aid available for part-time students. Work study available nights, weekends, and for part-time students.

FINANCIAL AID PROCEDURES
Forms required: FAFSA.
Dates and Deadlines: Priority date 3/1; no closing date. Applicants notified on a rolling basis; must reply within 2 week(s) of notification.

CONTACT
Lilia Medina, Director of Financial Aid
1000 West Foothill Boulevard, Glendora, CA 91741-1899
(626) 914-8592

City College of San Francisco
San Francisco, California
www.ccsf.edu   Federal Code: 001167

2-year public community college in very large city.
Enrollment: 12,391 undergrads.
Selectivity: Open admission.

BASIC COSTS (2005-2006)
Tuition and fees: $806; out-of-state residents $5,126.
Per-credit charge: $26; out-of-state residents $170.
Additional info: Tuition/fee waivers available for adults, unemployed or children of unemployed.

FINANCIAL AID PICTURE
Students with need: Work study available nights, weekends, and for part-time students.

FINANCIAL AID PROCEDURES
Forms required: FAFSA.
Dates and Deadlines: Priority date 3/1; no closing date. Applicants notified on a rolling basis starting 7/1.

CONTACT
Jorge Bell, Dean, Financial Aid
50 Phelan Avenue, San Francisco, CA 94112
(415) 239-3576

Claremont McKenna College
Claremont, California
www.claremontmckenna.edu   Federal Code: 001170
                               CSS Code: 4054

4-year private liberal arts college in large town.
Enrollment: 1,140 undergrads. 271 full-time freshmen.
Selectivity: Admits less than 50% of applicants.

BASIC COSTS (2006-2007)
Tuition and fees: $33,210.
Room and board: $10,740.

FINANCIAL AID PICTURE (2005-2006)
Students with need: Out of 164 full-time freshmen who applied for aid, 127 were judged to have need. Of these, 127 received aid, and 127 had their full need met. Average financial aid package met 100% of need; average scholarship/grant was $23,460; average loan was $2,991. Need-based aid available for part-time students.
Students without need: This college only awards aid to students with need.
Scholarships offered: McKenna Achievement Award: $5,000; based on strong academic record and outstanding leadership and involvement; 30 awarded, renewable for total of 4 years.
Cumulative student debt: 51% of graduating class had student loans; average debt was $10,518.

FINANCIAL AID PROCEDURES
Forms required: FAFSA, CSS PROFILE, state aid form.
Dates and Deadlines: Closing date 2/1. Applicants notified by 4/1; must reply by 5/1.
Transfers: Closing date 3/2. Applicants notified by 5/15.

CONTACT
Georgette DeVeres, Director of Financial Aid
890 Columbia Avenue, Claremont, CA 91711-6425
(909) 621-8088

Coastline Community College
Fountain Valley, California
www.coastline.cccd.edu   Federal Code: 013536

2-year public community college in small city.
Enrollment: 5,167 undergrads.
Selectivity: Open admission.

California Coastline Community College

BASIC COSTS (2005-2006)
Tuition and fees: $806; out-of-state residents $5,366.
Per-credit charge: $26; out-of-state residents $178.
Additional info: Tuition/fee waivers available for unemployed or children of unemployed.

FINANCIAL AID PICTURE (2004-2005)
Students with need: Need-based aid available for part-time students.
Students without need: This college only awards aid to students with need.
Additional info: Board of Governor's Grant: statewide fee waiver program for students or dependents receiving HFOL/TANF, SSI, General Relief, or whose income meets set standards or who are considered eligible through Federal needs analysis.

FINANCIAL AID PROCEDURES
Forms required: FAFSA, institutional form.
Dates and Deadlines: Priority date 3/2; no closing date. Applicants notified on a rolling basis starting 8/1; must reply within 2 week(s) of notification.

CONTACT
Cynthia Pienkowski, Director of Financial Aid
11460 Warner Avenue, Fountain Valley, CA 92708
(714) 241-6239

Cogswell Polytechnical College
Sunnyvale, California
www.cogswell.edu   Federal Code: 001177

4-year private visual arts and engineering college in small city.
Enrollment: 282 undergrads, 52% part-time. 33 full-time freshmen.
Selectivity: Admits over 75% of applicants.

BASIC COSTS (2005-2006)
Tuition and fees: $13,720.
Per-credit charge: $570.

FINANCIAL AID PICTURE (2004-2005)
Students with need: 43% of average financial aid package awarded as scholarships/grants, 57% awarded as loans/jobs.

FINANCIAL AID PROCEDURES
Forms required: FAFSA, institutional form.
Dates and Deadlines: Priority date 3/2; no closing date. Applicants notified on a rolling basis starting 4/30; must reply within 4 week(s) of notification.
Transfers: No closing date for financial aid application. However, tuition and fees are due upon registration for portion not covered by completed financial aid.

CONTACT
Jeff Roush, Director of Financial Aid
1175 Bordeaux Drive, Sunnyvale, CA 94089-1299
(408) 541-0100

College of Marin: Kentfield
Kentfield, California
www.marin.cc.ca.us   Federal Code: 001178

2-year public community college in small town.
Enrollment: 2,903 undergrads.
Selectivity: Open admission; but selective for some programs.

BASIC COSTS (2005-2006)
Tuition and fees: $808; out-of-state residents $5,938.
Per-credit charge: $26; out-of-state residents $197.

FINANCIAL AID PICTURE
Students with need: Need-based aid available for full-time and part-time students.

FINANCIAL AID PROCEDURES
Forms required: FAFSA.
Dates and Deadlines: Priority date 3/1; no closing date. Applicants notified on a rolling basis starting 5/15.

CONTACT
David Cook, Director of Financial Aid
835 College Avenue, Kentfield, CA 94904
(415) 457-8811

College of Oceaneering
Wilmington, California
www.natpoly.edu   Federal Code: 011696

2-year for-profit technical and maritime college in small city.
Enrollment: 485 full-time undergrads.

BASIC COSTS (2006-2007)
Tuition and fees: $16,430.
Per-credit charge: $265.

FINANCIAL AID PICTURE
Students with need: Need-based aid available for full-time students.

FINANCIAL AID PROCEDURES
Forms required: FAFSA, institutional form.
Dates and Deadlines: No deadline. Applicants notified on a rolling basis; must reply within 3 week(s) of notification.

CONTACT
Lida Castillo, Financial Aid Officer
272 South Fries Avenue, Wilmington, CA 90744
(310) 834-2501

College of the Canyons
Santa Clarita, California
www.canyons.edu   Federal Code: 008903

2-year public community college in small city.
Enrollment: 4,512 full-time undergrads.
Selectivity: Open admission; but selective for some programs.

BASIC COSTS (2005-2006)
Tuition and fees: $816; out-of-state residents $5,166.
Per-credit charge: $26; out-of-state residents $171.

FINANCIAL AID PICTURE
Students with need: Need-based aid available for full-time and part-time students. Work study available nights.
Students without need: No-need awards available for academics, alumni affiliation, art, athletics, leadership, music/drama, state/district residency.
Additional info: Enrollment fees waived for students enrolled concurrently in high school and COC. School has own payment plan.

FINANCIAL AID PROCEDURES
Forms required: FAFSA, state aid form.
Dates and Deadlines: Closing date 3/2. Applicants notified on a rolling basis starting 6/1; must reply within 4 week(s) of notification.
Transfers: No deadline.

CONTACT
Beth Asmus, Director, Financial Aid
26455 Rockwell Canyon Road, Santa Clarita, CA 91355
(661) 362-3242

College of the Desert
Palm Desert, California
www.collegeofthedesert.edu Federal Code: 001182

2-year public community college in large town.
Enrollment: 5,156 undergrads, 59% part-time. 598 full-time freshmen.
Selectivity: Open admission; but selective for some programs.

BASIC COSTS (2005-2006)
Tuition and fees: $814; out-of-state residents $5,344.
Per-credit charge: $26; out-of-state residents $177.
Additional info: Tuition/fee waivers available for adults, minority students, unemployed or children of unemployed.

FINANCIAL AID PICTURE (2004-2005)
Students with need: 91% of average financial aid package awarded as scholarships/grants, 9% awarded as loans/jobs. Need-based aid available for part-time students. Work study available weekends and for part-time students.
Students without need: This college only awards aid to students with need.
Cumulative student debt: 1% of graduating class had student loans; average debt was $6,500.

FINANCIAL AID PROCEDURES
Forms required: FAFSA, institutional form.
Dates and Deadlines: Priority date 3/2; no closing date. Applicants notified on a rolling basis starting 7/1.

CONTACT
Heidi Granger, Director of Financial Aid
43-500 Monterey Avenue, Palm Desert, CA 92260
(760) 773-2532

College of the Redwoods
Eureka, California
www.redwoods.edu Federal Code: 001185

2-year public community college in large town.
Enrollment: 4,677 undergrads.
Selectivity: Open admission; but selective for some programs.

BASIC COSTS (2005-2006)
Tuition and fees: $806; out-of-state residents $6,296.
Per-credit charge: $26; out-of-state residents $209.
Room and board: $5,700.

FINANCIAL AID PICTURE
Students with need: Need-based aid available for full-time and part-time students.

FINANCIAL AID PROCEDURES
Forms required: FAFSA, institutional form.
Dates and Deadlines: Priority date 4/15; no closing date. Applicants notified on a rolling basis starting 5/1; must reply within 6 week(s) of notification.

CONTACT
Lynn Thiesen, Director of Financial Aid
7351 Tompkins Hill Road, Eureka, CA 95501-9300
(707) 476-4182

College of the Siskiyous
Weed, California
www.siskiyous.edu Federal Code: 001187

2-year public community and junior college in small town.
Enrollment: 920 full-time undergrads.
Selectivity: Open admission.

BASIC COSTS (2005-2006)
Tuition and fees: $806; out-of-state residents $6,026.
Per-credit charge: $26; out-of-state residents $200.
Room and board: $6,350.

FINANCIAL AID PICTURE
Students with need: Need-based aid available for full-time and part-time students. Work study available nights, weekends, and for part-time students.
Students without need: This college only awards aid to students with need.

FINANCIAL AID PROCEDURES
Forms required: FAFSA.
Dates and Deadlines: Priority date 4/30; no closing date. Applicants notified on a rolling basis starting 6/1; must reply within 2 week(s) of notification.
Transfers: Academic transcripts required.

CONTACT
Vicki Wrobel, Director of Financial Aid
800 College Avenue, Weed, CA 96094
(530) 938-5209

Columbia College
Sonora, California
www.gocolumbia.org Federal Code: 007707

2-year public community college in small town.
Enrollment: 988 undergrads.
Selectivity: Open admission.

BASIC COSTS (2005-2006)
Tuition and fees: $818; out-of-state residents $5,348.
Per-credit charge: $26; out-of-state residents $177.

FINANCIAL AID PICTURE
Students with need: Need-based aid available for full-time and part-time students.
Students without need: No-need awards available for academics.

FINANCIAL AID PROCEDURES
Forms required: FAFSA, state aid form, institutional form.
Dates and Deadlines: Priority date 3/2; closing date 12/15. Applicants notified on a rolling basis starting 6/15; must reply within 2 week(s) of notification.

CONTACT
Cass Larkin, Financial Aid Officer
11600 Columbia College Drive, Sonora, CA 95370
(209) 588-5105

Concordia University
Irvine, California
www.cui.edu Federal Code: 013885

4-year private university and liberal arts college in small city, affiliated with Lutheran Church - Missouri Synod.
Enrollment: 1,357 undergrads, 4% part-time. 277 full-time freshmen.
Selectivity: Admits 50 to 75% of applicants.

California — Concordia University

BASIC COSTS (2006-2007)
Tuition and fees: $21,130.
Per-credit charge: $600.
Room and board: $7,270.
Additional info: Tuition/fee waivers available for minority students.

FINANCIAL AID PICTURE (2004-2005)
Students with need: Out of 273 full-time freshmen who applied for aid, 200 were judged to have need. Of these, 200 received aid, and 46 had their full need met. Average financial aid package met 70% of need; average scholarship/grant was $10,657; average loan was $2,583. For part-time students, average financial aid package was $12,619.
Students without need: 50 full-time freshmen who did not demonstrate need for aid received scholarships/grants; average award was $6,333. No-need awards available for academics, alumni affiliation, art, athletics, leadership, music/drama, religious affiliation.
Scholarships offered: Merit: Honors Scholarship: $5,000 and up; based on 3.9-4.0 GPA; only new freshmen eligible. Regent's Scholarship: $8,000 max; based on 3.8 and higher GPA. Dean's Scholarship: $3,000 max; based on 3.2 to 3.49 GPA. Various other academic, music, theater, athletic scholarships: amounts vary from $1,500 to $4,000. **Athletic:** 8 full-time freshmen received athletic scholarships; average amount $8,250.
Cumulative student debt: 74% of graduating class had student loans; average debt was $19,200.

FINANCIAL AID PROCEDURES
Forms required: FAFSA, institutional form.
Dates and Deadlines: Priority date 3/2; closing date 4/1. Applicants notified on a rolling basis starting 2/1; must reply within 4 week(s) of notification.

CONTACT
Lori McDonald, Executive Director, Enrollment Services
1530 Concordia West, Irvine, CA 92612-3299
(949) 854-8002 ext. 1136

Copper Mountain College
Joshua Tree, California
www.cmccd.edu
Federal Code: 035424

2-year public community college in small town.
Enrollment: 1,018 undergrads. 151 full-time freshmen.
Selectivity: Open admission.

BASIC COSTS (2005-2006)
Tuition and fees: $780; out-of-state residents $5,310.
Per-credit charge: $26; out-of-state residents $177.

FINANCIAL AID PICTURE (2004-2005)
Students with need: Out of 115 full-time freshmen who applied for aid, 105 were judged to have need. Of these, 100 received aid, and 2 had their full need met. Average financial aid package met 37% of need; average scholarship/grant was $2,954; average loan was $2,423. For part-time students, average financial aid package was $2,948.
Students without need: 4 full-time freshmen who did not demonstrate need for aid received scholarships/grants; average award was $300.

FINANCIAL AID PROCEDURES
Forms required: FAFSA.
Dates and Deadlines: Priority date 3/2; no closing date.

CONTACT
Kathryn Verseman, Director of Financial Aid
6162 Rotary Way, Joshua Tree, CA 92252
(760) 366-3791 ext. 4235

Crafton Hills College
Yucaipa, California
www.craftonhills.edu
Federal Code: 009272

2-year public community college in large town.
Enrollment: 3,257 undergrads.
Selectivity: Open admission.

BASIC COSTS (2005-2006)
Tuition and fees: $818; out-of-state residents $5,348.
Per-credit charge: $26; out-of-state residents $177.
Additional info: Tuition/fee waivers available for adults, minority students, unemployed or children of unemployed.

FINANCIAL AID PICTURE
Students with need: Need-based aid available for full-time and part-time students. Work study available nights.
Students without need: This college only awards aid to students with need.

FINANCIAL AID PROCEDURES
Forms required: FAFSA, institutional form.
Dates and Deadlines: Priority date 4/15; closing date 6/2. Applicants notified on a rolling basis starting 7/31; must reply within 2 week(s) of notification.
Transfers: Priority date 1/2; closing date 3/2.

CONTACT
John Muskavitch, Director of Financial Aid
11711 Sand Canyon Road, Yucaipa, CA 92399-1799
(909) 794-2161 ext. 3242

Cuyamaca College
El Cajon, California
www.cuyamaca.net
Federal Code: 014435

2-year public community college in small city.
Enrollment: 1,217 undergrads.
Selectivity: Open admission.

BASIC COSTS (2005-2006)
Tuition and fees: $818; out-of-state residents $5,348.
Per-credit charge: $26; out-of-state residents $177.

FINANCIAL AID PICTURE
Students with need: Work study available nights, weekends, and for part-time students.

FINANCIAL AID PROCEDURES
Forms required: FAFSA.
Dates and Deadlines: Priority date 7/21; no closing date. Applicants notified on a rolling basis; must reply within 2 week(s) of notification.

CONTACT
Morones Gene, Interim Dean of Special Funds Projects
900 Rancho San Diego Parkway, El Cajon, CA 92019-4304
(619) 660-4201

De Anza College
Cupertino, California
www.deanza.edu
Federal Code: 004480

2-year public community college in large town.
Enrollment: 14,880 undergrads.
Selectivity: Open admission; but selective for some programs.

BASIC COSTS (2005-2006)
Tuition and fees: $798; out-of-state residents $5,343.
Per-credit charge: $17; out-of-state residents $118.

FINANCIAL AID PICTURE
Students with need: Need-based aid available for full-time and part-time students.
Students without need: This college only awards aid to students with need.

FINANCIAL AID PROCEDURES
Forms required: FAFSA.
Dates and Deadlines: Priority date 3/2; no closing date. Applicants notified on a rolling basis starting 5/15; must reply within 2 week(s) of notification.

CONTACT
Cindy Castillo, Director of Financial Aid
21250 Stevens Creek Boulevard, Cupertino, CA 95014
(408) 864-8718

Deep Springs College
Dyer, Nevada
www.deepsprings.edu   Federal Code: 015483

2-year private liberal arts college for men in rural community.
Enrollment: 27 undergrads.
Selectivity: Admits less than 50% of applicants.

BASIC COSTS (2006-2007)
Additional info: All students receive full scholarship (typically renewed for second year) covering tuition, room, and board. Tuition at time of enrollment locked for 2 years.

FINANCIAL AID PICTURE
Students with need: Work study available nights, weekends, and for part-time students.
Students without need: No-need awards available for academics.

FINANCIAL AID PROCEDURES
Dates and Deadlines: No deadline.

CONTACT
F. Ross Peterson, President
HC 72, Box 45001, Dyer, NV 89010-9803
(760) 872-2000

DeVry University: Fremont
Fremont, California
www.devry.edu   Federal Code: 008322

4-year for-profit university in small city.
Enrollment: 1,446 undergrads, 35% part-time. 341 full-time freshmen.

BASIC COSTS (2005-2006)
Tuition and fees: $13,410.
Per-credit charge: $475.

FINANCIAL AID PICTURE (2004-2005)
Students with need: Out of 264 full-time freshmen who applied for aid, 255 were judged to have need. Of these, 231 received aid, and 13 had their full need met. Average financial aid package met 41% of need; average scholarship/grant was $6,702; average loan was $6,752. For part-time students, average financial aid package was $8,756.
Students without need: This college only awards aid to students with need.

FINANCIAL AID PROCEDURES
Forms required: FAFSA.
Dates and Deadlines: No deadline. Applicants notified on a rolling basis.

CONTACT
Kim Kane, Director of Financial Aid
6600 Dumbarton Circle, Fremont, CA 94555-3615
(510) 574-1120

DeVry University: Long Beach
Long Beach, California
www.devry.edu   Federal Code: 023329

4-year for-profit university in large town.
Enrollment: 1,022 undergrads, 40% part-time. 395 full-time freshmen.

BASIC COSTS (2005-2006)
Tuition and fees: $12,800.
Per-credit charge: $460.

FINANCIAL AID PICTURE (2004-2005)
Students with need: Out of 244 full-time freshmen who applied for aid, 230 were judged to have need. Of these, 224 received aid, and 8 had their full need met. Average financial aid package met 38% of need; average scholarship/grant was $5,906; average loan was $4,615. For part-time students, average financial aid package was $7,265.
Students without need: This college only awards aid to students with need.

FINANCIAL AID PROCEDURES
Forms required: FAFSA, state aid form.
Dates and Deadlines: No deadline. Applicants notified on a rolling basis.

CONTACT
Brenda Woods, Associate Director of Student Finance
3880 Kilroy Airport Way, Long Beach, CA 90806
(562) 427-0861

DeVry University: Pomona
Pomona, California
www.devry.edu   Federal Code: 023329

4-year for-profit university in small city.
Enrollment: 1,720 undergrads, 44% part-time. 481 full-time freshmen.

BASIC COSTS (2005-2006)
Tuition and fees: $12,800.
Per-credit charge: $460.

FINANCIAL AID PICTURE (2004-2005)
Students with need: Out of 313 full-time freshmen who applied for aid, 295 were judged to have need. Of these, 292 received aid, and 12 had their full need met. Average financial aid package met 39% of need; average scholarship/grant was $5,259; average loan was $5,182. For part-time students, average financial aid package was $7,561.
Students without need: This college only awards aid to students with need.

FINANCIAL AID PROCEDURES
Forms required: FAFSA.
Dates and Deadlines: No deadline. Applicants notified on a rolling basis.

CONTACT
Kathy Odom, Director of Financial Aid
901 Corporate Center Drive, Pomona, CA 91768-2642

DeVry University: West Hills
West Hills, California
www.devry.edu Federal Code: 016219

4-year for-profit university in large city.
Enrollment: 670 undergrads, 51% part-time. 195 full-time freshmen.

BASIC COSTS (2005-2006)
Tuition and fees: $12,800.
Per-credit charge: $460.

FINANCIAL AID PICTURE (2004-2005)
Students with need: Out of 101 full-time freshmen who applied for aid, 90 were judged to have need. Of these, 89 received aid, and 4 had their full need met. Average financial aid package met 38% of need; average scholarship/grant was $5,981; average loan was $4,302. For part-time students, average financial aid package was $7,342.
Students without need: This college only awards aid to students with need.

FINANCIAL AID PROCEDURES
Forms required: FAFSA.
Dates and Deadlines: No deadline. Applicants notified on a rolling basis.

CONTACT
Lou LaSota, Director of Financial Aid
22801 Roscoe Boulevard, West Hills, CA 91304-3200
(818) 932-3111

Diablo Valley College
Pleasant Hill, California
www.dvc.edu Federal Code: 001191

2-year public community college in large town.
Enrollment: 7,536 full-time undergrads.
Selectivity: Open admission.

BASIC COSTS (2005-2006)
Tuition and fees: $790; out-of-state residents $5,320.
Per-credit charge: $26; out-of-state residents $177.

FINANCIAL AID PICTURE
Students with need: Need-based aid available for full-time and part-time students.

FINANCIAL AID PROCEDURES
Forms required: FAFSA, state aid form, institutional form.
Dates and Deadlines: Priority date 3/2; closing date 5/1. Applicants notified on a rolling basis starting 6/1; must reply within 2 week(s) of notification.

CONTACT
Brenda Jerez, Financial Aid Director
321 Golf Club Road, Pleasant Hill, CA 94523
(925) 685-1230 ext. 2290

Dominican School of Philosophy and Theology
Berkeley, California
www.dspt.edu Federal Code: 016673

Upper-division private seminary college in small city, affiliated with Roman Catholic Church.
Enrollment: 10 undergrads.

BASIC COSTS (2005-2006)
Tuition and fees: $13,250.
Per-credit charge: $440.
Additional info: Required medical insurance for otherwise uninsured students costs approximately $610 per semester.

FINANCIAL AID PICTURE
Students with need: Need-based aid available for full-time and part-time students.
Students without need: This college only awards aid to students with need.
Additional info: Limited financial aid. Support available from religious orders.

FINANCIAL AID PROCEDURES
Forms required: FAFSA, institutional form.
Dates and Deadlines: Priority date 3/15; no closing date. Applicants notified on a rolling basis starting 5/15.
Transfers: Closing date 4/1.

CONTACT
Carlos Perez, Director of Financial Aid
2301 Vine Street, Berkeley, CA 94708
(510) 649-2469

Dominican University of California
San Rafael, California
www.dominican.edu Federal Code: 001196

4-year private university and nursing college in small city, affiliated with Roman Catholic Church.
Enrollment: 1,363 undergrads, 20% part-time. 225 full-time freshmen.
Selectivity: Admits 50 to 75% of applicants.

BASIC COSTS (2005-2006)
Tuition and fees: $26,150.
Room and board: $10,888.

FINANCIAL AID PICTURE (2005-2006)
Students with need: Out of 193 full-time freshmen who applied for aid, 157 were judged to have need. Of these, 156 received aid, and 20 had their full need met. Average financial aid package met 67% of need; average scholarship/grant was $14,371; average loan was $2,785. For part-time students, average financial aid package was $6,876.
Students without need: 26 full-time freshmen who did not demonstrate need for aid received scholarships/grants; average award was $8,940. No-need awards available for academics, athletics, minority status, music/drama.
Additional info: 4-year guarantee program.

FINANCIAL AID PROCEDURES
Forms required: FAFSA, institutional form.
Dates and Deadlines: Priority date 3/2; no closing date. Applicants notified on a rolling basis starting 3/15; must reply within 2 week(s) of notification.

CONTACT
Audrey Tanner, Director of Financial Aid
50 Acacia Avenue, San Rafael, CA 94901-2298
(415) 257-1350

East Los Angeles College
Monterey Park, California
www.elac.edu Federal Code: 001222

2-year public community college in small city.
Enrollment: 4,807 full-time undergrads.
Selectivity: Open admission; but selective for some programs.

BASIC COSTS (2005-2006)
Tuition and fees: $804; out-of-state residents $5,424.
Per-credit charge: $26; out-of-state residents $180.
FINANCIAL AID PICTURE
Students with need: Need-based aid available for full-time and part-time students.
Students without need: No-need awards available for academics.
Additional info: Need-based enrollment fee waivers available through a state aid program.
FINANCIAL AID PROCEDURES
Forms required: FAFSA.
Dates and Deadlines: Closing date 3/2. Applicants notified on a rolling basis; must reply within 2 week(s) of notification.
Transfers: No deadline.
CONTACT
Robert Zuniga, Director of Financial Aid
1301 Avenida Cesar Chavez, Monterey Park, CA 91754
(323) 265-8738

Empire College
Santa Rosa, California
www.empcol.edu   Federal Code: 009032

2-year for-profit business college in small city.
Enrollment: 644 undergrads, 3% part-time. 147 full-time freshmen.
Selectivity: Open admission.
FINANCIAL AID PICTURE (2005-2006)
Students with need: Average financial aid package met 55% of need; average scholarship/grant was $4,000; average loan was $2,625.
Students without need: This college only awards aid to students with need.
Scholarships offered: Dean's Scholarship for high school seniors; 10 awarded; range from $250-$1,500. Dean's Scholarships for Empire College students; 7 awarded; range from $250-$1,000. Based on academic achievement, letter of intent, extracurricular activities and letter of recommendation.
FINANCIAL AID PROCEDURES
Forms required: FAFSA.
Dates and Deadlines: No deadline. Applicants notified on a rolling basis.
CONTACT
Carol Worden, Financial Aid Officer
3035 Cleveland Avenue, Santa Rosa, CA 95403-2100
(707) 546-4000

Feather River College
Quincy, California
www.frc.edu   Federal Code: 008597

2-year public community and liberal arts college in small town.
Enrollment: 634 undergrads, 34% part-time. 124 full-time freshmen.
Selectivity: Open admission.
BASIC COSTS (2005-2006)
Tuition and fees: $836; out-of-state residents $6,086.
Per-credit charge: $26; out-of-state residents $201.
Room only: $3,825.
Additional info: Costs for Nevada residents: $42 per unit with good neighbor policy. Tuition/fee waivers available for adults, unemployed or children of unemployed.

FINANCIAL AID PICTURE (2005-2006)
Students with need: Need-based aid available for full-time and part-time students. Work study available nights, weekends, and for part-time students.
FINANCIAL AID PROCEDURES
Forms required: FAFSA.
Dates and Deadlines: No deadline. Applicants notified on a rolling basis starting 7/30; must reply within 3 week(s) of notification.
CONTACT
Mary Spady, Financial Aid Director
570 Golden Eagle Avenue, Quincy, CA 95971
(530) 283-0202 ext. 296

Foothill College
Los Altos Hills, California
www.foothill.edu   Federal Code: 001199

2-year public community college in large town.
Enrollment: 6,437 undergrads.
Selectivity: Open admission; but selective for some programs.
BASIC COSTS (2005-2006)
Tuition and fees: $798; out-of-state residents $5,343.
Per-credit charge: $17; out-of-state residents $118.
FINANCIAL AID PICTURE
Students with need: Need-based aid available for full-time and part-time students.
Students without need: This college only awards aid to students with need.
Scholarships offered: Chancellor's Scholarship for first-time freshmen who graduate in the top 20 percent of high school class as Chancellor's Scholar; $1,200 for two years.
FINANCIAL AID PROCEDURES
Forms required: FAFSA, institutional form.
Dates and Deadlines: Priority date 3/30; no closing date. Applicants notified on a rolling basis; must reply within 2 week(s) of notification.
Transfers: Application required for CDL grants, March 2 due date for CAL grant application.
CONTACT
Frances Gusman, Dean, Financial Aid & Student Services
12345 El Monte Road, Los Altos Hills, CA 94022
(650) 949-7245

Fresno City College
Fresno, California
www.fresnocitycollege.edu   Federal Code: 001307

2-year public community college in large city.
Enrollment: 12,610 undergrads.
Selectivity: Open admission; but selective for some programs.
BASIC COSTS (2005-2006)
Tuition and fees: $808; out-of-state residents $5,338.
Per-credit charge: $26; out-of-state residents $177.
Additional info: Tuition/fee waivers available for adults, minority students, unemployed or children of unemployed.
FINANCIAL AID PICTURE
Students with need: Need-based aid available for full-time and part-time students.
Students without need: This college only awards aid to students with need.

Additional info: Board of Governors Grant Program to offset enrollment fees based on untaxed income, low income, or calculated need. Students qualifying for program also automatically exempt from health fees. March 2 application deadline for California grants.

FINANCIAL AID PROCEDURES
Forms required: FAFSA, state aid form.
Dates and Deadlines: Priority date 4/15; no closing date. Applicants notified on a rolling basis starting 4/1.

CONTACT
Joaquin Jimenez, Associate Dean of Students
1101 East University Avenue, Fresno, CA 93741
(559) 442-8279

Fresno Pacific University
Fresno, California
www.fresno.edu
Federal Code: 001253

4-year private university and liberal arts college in large city, affiliated with Mennonite Brethren Church.
Enrollment: 1,399 undergrads, 11% part-time. 179 full-time freshmen.
Selectivity: Admits 50 to 75% of applicants.

BASIC COSTS (2006-2007)
Tuition and fees: $20,790.
Per-credit charge: $735.
Room and board: $5,990.

FINANCIAL AID PICTURE (2004-2005)
Students with need: Out of 148 full-time freshmen who applied for aid, 130 were judged to have need. Of these, 130 received aid, and 24 had their full need met. Average financial aid package met 81% of need; average scholarship/grant was $12,814; average loan was $2,726. For part-time students, average financial aid package was $13,839.
Students without need: 14 full-time freshmen who did not demonstrate need for aid received scholarships/grants; average award was $2,028. No-need awards available for academics, athletics, music/drama.
Scholarships offered: *Merit:* Paragon Scholarship: 2 awarded; full tuition; requires 3.65 GPA, demonstrated Christian leadership, SAT 1150 or higher. President's Scholarship: 40 awarded; $6,500-$9,500; requires 3.65 GPA, demonstrated Christian leadership, SAT 1150 or higher. Provost Scholarship: 20 awarded; $4,000-$8,000; for transfer students with 3.5 GPA and demonstrated Christian leadership. SAT scores exclusive of Writing. *Athletic:* 23 full-time freshmen received athletic scholarships; average amount $9,637.
Cumulative student debt: 50% of graduating class had student loans; average debt was $13,334.

FINANCIAL AID PROCEDURES
Forms required: FAFSA, institutional form.
Dates and Deadlines: Priority date 3/2; no closing date. Applicants notified on a rolling basis starting 3/2; must reply by 7/30 or within 3 week(s) of notification.
Transfers: No deadline.

CONTACT
Korey Compaan, Director of Student Financial Services
1717 South Chestnut Avenue, Fresno, CA 93702
(559) 453-2041

Glendale Community College
Glendale, California
www.glendale.edu
Federal Code: 001203

2-year public community college in small city.
Enrollment: 7,640 undergrads, 61% part-time. 724 full-time freshmen.
Selectivity: Open admission; but selective for some programs.

BASIC COSTS (2005-2006)
Tuition and fees: $808; out-of-state residents $5,308.
Per-credit charge: $26; out-of-state residents $176.

FINANCIAL AID PICTURE
Students with need: Need-based aid available for full-time and part-time students. Work study available nights, weekends, and for part-time students.
Students without need: This college only awards aid to students with need.

FINANCIAL AID PROCEDURES
Forms required: FAFSA, institutional form.
Dates and Deadlines: Priority date 4/15; no closing date. Applicants notified on a rolling basis starting 6/15; must reply within 2 week(s) of notification.
Transfers: No deadline.

CONTACT
Patricia Hurley, Director of Financial Aid
1500 North Verdugo Road, Glendale, CA 91208-2809
(818) 240-1000 ext. 5916

Grossmont Community College
El Cajon, California
www.grossmont.edu
Federal Code: 001208

2-year public community college in small city.
Enrollment: 16,450 undergrads.
Selectivity: Open admission; but selective for some programs.

BASIC COSTS (2005-2006)
Tuition and fees: $818; out-of-state residents $5,348.
Per-credit charge: $26; out-of-state residents $177.

FINANCIAL AID PICTURE
Students with need: Need-based aid available for full-time and part-time students. Work study available nights, weekends, and for part-time students.
Students without need: This college only awards aid to students with need.

FINANCIAL AID PROCEDURES
Forms required: FAFSA.
Dates and Deadlines: Priority date 2/1; no closing date. Applicants notified on a rolling basis starting 7/15; must reply within 2 week(s) of notification.

CONTACT
Michael Copenhauer, Director of Financial Aid
8800 Grossmont College Drive, El Cajon, CA 92020
(619) 644-7129

Harvey Mudd College
Claremont, California
www.hmc.edu
Federal Code: 001171
CSS Code: 4341

4-year private engineering and liberal arts college in small city.
Enrollment: 743 undergrads.
Selectivity: Admits less than 50% of applicants.

BASIC COSTS (2006-2007)
Tuition and fees: $33,325.
Per-credit charge: $1,035.
Room and board: $10,933.

FINANCIAL AID PICTURE (2004-2005)
Students with need: 87% of average financial aid package awarded as scholarships/grants, 13% awarded as loans/jobs. Need-based aid available for part-time students. Work study available nights, weekends, and for part-time students.
Students without need: No-need awards available for academics.
Scholarships offered: Harvey S. Mudd Scholarship: for first-time freshmen in science and technology programs; $10,000 annually for 4 years; must maintain minimum 2.75 GPA. Harvey Mudd College-sponsored National Merit Scholarships: from $750 to $2,000 based on need.

FINANCIAL AID PROCEDURES
Forms required: FAFSA, CSS PROFILE, state aid form.
Dates and Deadlines: Closing date 2/1. Applicants notified on a rolling basis starting 4/1; must reply by 5/1 or within 2 week(s) of notification.
Transfers: Priority date 3/15; no deadline.

CONTACT
Gilma Lopez, Director of Financial Aid
Kingston Hall, 301 Platt Boulevard, Claremont, CA 91711-5901
(909) 621-8055

Heald College: Concord
Concord, California
www.heald.edu   Federal Code: 030693

2-year private business college in small city.
Enrollment: 648 undergrads.

BASIC COSTS (2006-2007)
Tuition and fees: $9,900.

FINANCIAL AID PICTURE
Students with need: Need-based aid available for full-time and part-time students. Work study available nights, weekends, and for part-time students.
Students without need: This college only awards aid to students with need.

FINANCIAL AID PROCEDURES
Forms required: FAFSA.
Dates and Deadlines: No deadline. Applicants notified on a rolling basis.

CONTACT
Shelly Picinich, Director of Financial Aid
5130 Commercial Circle, Concord, CA 94520
(925) 288-5800

Heald College: Hayward
Hayward, California
www.heald.edu   Federal Code: 008532

2-year private technical college in small city.
Enrollment: 865 undergrads.

BASIC COSTS (2006-2007)
Tuition and fees: $9,900.

FINANCIAL AID PICTURE
Students with need: Need-based aid available for full-time and part-time students. Work study available nights, weekends, and for part-time students.
Students without need: This college only awards aid to students with need.

FINANCIAL AID PROCEDURES
Forms required: FAFSA.

CONTACT
Belinda Alcid, Director of Financial Aid
25500 Industrial Boulevard, Hayward, CA 94545
(510) 783-2100

Heald College: Rancho Cordova
Rancho Cordova, California
www.heald.edu   Federal Code: 025931

2-year private technical college in large city.
Enrollment: 471 undergrads.

BASIC COSTS (2006-2007)
Tuition and fees: $9,900.

FINANCIAL AID PICTURE
Students with need: Need-based aid available for full-time and part-time students. Work study available nights, weekends, and for part-time students.
Students without need: This college only awards aid to students with need.

FINANCIAL AID PROCEDURES
Forms required: FAFSA.

CONTACT
Rhonda Shaw, Director of Financial Aid
2910 Prospect Park Drive, Rancho Cordova, CA 95670
(916) 638-1616

Heald College: Roseville
Roseville, California
www.heald.edu

2-year private business and junior college in small city.
Enrollment: 528 undergrads.

BASIC COSTS (2006-2007)
Tuition and fees: $9,900.

FINANCIAL AID PICTURE
Students with need: Need-based aid available for full-time and part-time students. Work study available nights, weekends, and for part-time students.
Students without need: This college only awards aid to students with need.

FINANCIAL AID PROCEDURES
Forms required: FAFSA.

CONTACT
Rhonda Shaw, Director of Financial Aid
7 Sierra Gate Plaza, Roseville, CA 95678
(916) 789-8600

Heald College: Salinas
Salinas, California
www.heald.edu   Federal Code: 030340

2-year private business college in small city.
Enrollment: 414 undergrads.

BASIC COSTS (2006-2007)
Tuition and fees: $9,900.

FINANCIAL AID PICTURE
Students with need: Need-based aid available for full-time and part-time students. Work study available nights, weekends, and for part-time students.

Students without need: This college only awards aid to students with need.

FINANCIAL AID PROCEDURES
Forms required: FAFSA.

CONTACT
Susan Volwiler, Director of Financial Aid
1450 North Main Street, Salinas, CA 93906
(831) 443-1700

Heald College: San Francisco
San Francisco, California
www.heald.edu   Federal Code: 007234

2-year private business college in very large city.
Enrollment: 389 undergrads.

BASIC COSTS (2006-2007)
Tuition and fees: $9,900.

FINANCIAL AID PICTURE
Students with need: Need-based aid available for full-time and part-time students. Work study available nights, weekends, and for part-time students.
Students without need: This college only awards aid to students with need.

FINANCIAL AID PROCEDURES
Forms required: FAFSA.
Dates and Deadlines: No deadline.

CONTACT
Amalia Cota, Director of Financial Aid
350 Mission Street, San Francisco, CA 94103
(415) 808-3000

Heald College: San Jose
Milpitas, California
www.heald.edu   Federal Code: 025932

2-year private business college in very large city.
Enrollment: 639 undergrads.

BASIC COSTS (2006-2007)
Tuition and fees: $9,900.

FINANCIAL AID PICTURE
Students with need: Need-based aid available for full-time and part-time students. Work study available nights, weekends, and for part-time students.
Students without need: This college only awards aid to students with need.

FINANCIAL AID PROCEDURES
Forms required: FAFSA.
Dates and Deadlines: Priority date 6/1; no closing date. Applicants notified on a rolling basis starting 6/15; must reply within 2 week(s) of notification.

CONTACT
Theresa Tang, Director of Financial Aid
341 Great Mall Parkway, Milpitas, CA 95035
(408) 934-4900

Heald College: Stockton
Stockton, California
www.heald.edu   Federal Code: 025933

2-year private business college in large city.
Enrollment: 530 undergrads.
Selectivity: Open admission.

BASIC COSTS (2006-2007)
Tuition and fees: $9,900.

FINANCIAL AID PICTURE
Students with need: Need-based aid available for full-time students.

FINANCIAL AID PROCEDURES
Forms required: FAFSA.

CONTACT
Karen Bowers, Director of Financial Aid
1605 East March Lane, Stockton, CA 95210
(209) 473-5200

Holy Names University
Oakland, California
www.hnu.edu   Federal Code: 001183

4-year private university in large city, affiliated with Roman Catholic Church.
Enrollment: 657 undergrads, 33% part-time. 89 full-time freshmen.
Selectivity: Admits over 75% of applicants.

BASIC COSTS (2006-2007)
Tuition and fees: $22,710.

FINANCIAL AID PICTURE (2005-2006)
Students with need: Out of 89 full-time freshmen who applied for aid, 83 were judged to have need. Of these, 78 received aid, and 15 had their full need met. Average financial aid package met 67% of need; average scholarship/grant was $8,558; average loan was $2,842. For part-time students, average financial aid package was $10,788.
Students without need: 12 full-time freshmen who did not demonstrate need for aid received scholarships/grants; average award was $18,958. No-need awards available for academics, athletics, leadership, music/drama, religious affiliation.
Scholarships offered: *Merit:* Aspiring Leadership Grant: $5,500 annually, based on 2.70-2.99 GPA. Honors Scholarship: $8,500 annually, based on 3.00-3.29 GPA. Dean's Scholarship: $9,500 annually, based on 3.30-3.49 GPA; President's Scholarship: $11,000 annually, based on 3.50-3.74 GPA. Regent's Scholarship: $12,000 annually, based on 3.75+ GPA. Durocher Scholarship: full tuition, campus residency required; based on evidence of leadership, contributions to school and/or community and academic achievement, minimum GPA 3.75, minimum SAT 1100 (exclusive of writing); 1 awarded per year.
Athletic: 24 full-time freshmen received athletic scholarships; average amount $8,484.
Cumulative student debt: 94% of graduating class had student loans; average debt was $7,229.

FINANCIAL AID PROCEDURES
Forms required: FAFSA, state aid form.
Dates and Deadlines: Priority date 3/2; closing date 6/30. Applicants notified on a rolling basis starting 9/1; must reply by 5/1 or within 2 week(s) of notification.
Transfers: Applicants notified on a rolling basis starting 9/1; must reply by 5/1 or within 2 week(s) of notification.

CONTACT
Christina Miller, Director of Financial Aid
3500 Mountain Boulevard, Oakland, CA 94619-1699
(510) 436-1327

Hope International University
Fullerton, California
www.hiu.edu   Federal Code: 001252

4-year private university and liberal arts college in small city, affiliated with Christian Churches and Churches of Christ.
Enrollment: 825 undergrads, 21% part-time. 119 full-time freshmen.
Selectivity: Admits over 75% of applicants.

BASIC COSTS (2006-2007)
Tuition and fees: $18,700.
Room and board: $7,250.

FINANCIAL AID PICTURE (2005-2006)
Students with need: Average financial aid package met 30% of need; average scholarship/grant was $7,365; average loan was $2,365. For part-time students, average financial aid package was $8,075.
Students without need: No-need awards available for academics, alumni affiliation, athletics, leadership, music/drama, religious affiliation.

FINANCIAL AID PROCEDURES
Forms required: FAFSA, institutional form.
Dates and Deadlines: Priority date 3/2; no closing date. Applicants notified on a rolling basis starting 3/15; must reply within 2 week(s) of notification.

CONTACT
Director of Student Financial Aid
2500 East Nutwood Avenue, Fullerton, CA 92831-3199
(714) 879-3901 ext. 2207

Humboldt State University
Arcata, California
www.humboldt.edu   Federal Code: 001149

4-year public university in large town.
Enrollment: 6,245 undergrads, 9% part-time. 799 full-time freshmen.
Selectivity: Admits 50 to 75% of applicants.

BASIC COSTS (2005-2006)
Tuition and fees: $3,079; out-of-state residents $13,249.
Room and board: $7,906.

FINANCIAL AID PICTURE
Students with need: Need-based aid available for full-time and part-time students.
Students without need: No-need awards available for academics.

FINANCIAL AID PROCEDURES
Forms required: FAFSA.
Dates and Deadlines: No deadline. Applicants notified on a rolling basis starting 3/1; must reply within 6 week(s) of notification.
Transfers: Need is most salient factor for some programs.

CONTACT
Kim Coughlin-Lamphear, Director of Financial Aid Arcata, CA 95521-8299
(707) 826-4321

Humphreys College
Stockton, California
www.humphreys.edu   Federal Code: 001212

4-year private business and liberal arts college in large city.
Enrollment: 893 undergrads, 38% part-time. 87 full-time freshmen.
Selectivity: Open admission.

BASIC COSTS (2005-2006)
Tuition and fees: $9,900.
Per-credit charge: $220.
Room only: $3,150.
Additional info: School-controlled apartment housing cost quoted, not including utilities.

FINANCIAL AID PICTURE (2005-2006)
Students with need: Out of 65 full-time freshmen who applied for aid, 60 were judged to have need. Of these, 60 received aid, and 58 had their full need met. Average financial aid package met 75% of need; average scholarship/grant was $4. For part-time students, average financial aid package was $8,650.
Students without need: No-need awards available for academics.
Cumulative student debt: 96% of graduating class had student loans; average debt was $32,000.

FINANCIAL AID PROCEDURES
Forms required: FAFSA.
Dates and Deadlines: Closing date 6/30. Applicants notified on a rolling basis; must reply within 2 week(s) of notification.

CONTACT
Judi Johnston, Director of Financial Aid
6650 Inglewood Avenue, Stockton, CA 95207-3896
(209) 478-0800 ext. 122

Irvine Valley College
Irvine, California
www.ivc.edu   Federal Code: 025395

2-year public community college in small city.
Enrollment: 5,133 undergrads.
Selectivity: Open admission.

BASIC COSTS (2005-2006)
Tuition and fees: $806; out-of-state residents $5,336.
Per-credit charge: $26; out-of-state residents $177.
Additional info: Tuition/fee waivers available for minority students.

FINANCIAL AID PICTURE (2004-2005)
Students with need: 65% of average financial aid package awarded as scholarships/grants, 35% awarded as loans/jobs. Need-based aid available for part-time students. Work study available nights.
Students without need: This college only awards aid to students with need.

FINANCIAL AID PROCEDURES
Forms required: FAFSA, state aid form, institutional form.
Dates and Deadlines: No deadline. Applicants notified on a rolling basis starting 4/30.

CONTACT
Darryl Cox, Director of Financial Aid
5500 Irvine Center Drive, Irvine, CA 92618-4399
(949) 451-5287

John F. Kennedy University
Pleasant Hill, California
www.jfku.edu
Federal Code: 004484

4-year private business and liberal arts college in large town.
Enrollment: 222 undergrads.

BASIC COSTS (2005-2006)
Tuition and fees: $14,325.
Per-credit charge: $315.

FINANCIAL AID PICTURE (2004-2005)
Students with need: Need-based aid available for part-time students.
Students without need: This college only awards aid to students with need.

FINANCIAL AID PROCEDURES
Forms required: FAFSA, institutional form.
Dates and Deadlines: Priority date 3/2; no closing date. Applicants notified on a rolling basis; must reply within 4 week(s) of notification.
Transfers: Priority date 4/1.

CONTACT
Mindy Bergeron
100 Ellinwood Way, Pleasant Hill, CA 94523-4817
(925) 969-3385

King's College and Seminary
Los Angeles, California
www.kingscollege.edu

4-year private Bible and seminary college in very large city, affiliated with non-denominational tradition.
Enrollment: 631 undergrads.
Selectivity: Admits over 75% of applicants.

BASIC COSTS (2006-2007)
Tuition and fees: $7,485.
Per-credit charge: $160.
Additional info: Seminary students pay $175 per credit hour.

FINANCIAL AID PICTURE
Students with need: Need-based aid available for full-time and part-time students. Work study available nights, weekends, and for part-time students.
Students without need: No-need awards available for academics, leadership.
Additional info: Specific scholarships may require specific essays.

FINANCIAL AID PROCEDURES
Forms required: FAFSA.
Dates and Deadlines: No deadline. Applicants notified on a rolling basis.

CONTACT
Norm Stoppenbrink, Financial Aid Officer
14800 Sherman Way, Los Angeles, CA 91405-2233
(818) 779-8271

La Sierra University
Riverside, California
www.lasierra.edu
Federal Code: 001215

4-year private university in large city, affiliated with Seventh-day Adventists.
Enrollment: 1,586 undergrads, 9% part-time. 350 full-time freshmen.
Selectivity: Admits less than 50% of applicants.

BASIC COSTS (2006-2007)
Tuition and fees: $20,633.
Per-credit charge: $553.
Room and board: $5,873.

FINANCIAL AID PICTURE (2004-2005)
Students with need: Out of 296 full-time freshmen who applied for aid, 264 were judged to have need. Of these, 262 received aid, and 39 had their full need met. Average financial aid package met 71% of need; average scholarship/grant was $12,940; average loan was $2,995. For part-time students, average financial aid package was $10,079.
Students without need: 86 full-time freshmen who did not demonstrate need for aid received scholarships/grants; average award was $6,776. No-need awards available for academics, leadership, music/drama, religious affiliation.
Cumulative student debt: 70% of graduating class had student loans; average debt was $24,680.

FINANCIAL AID PROCEDURES
Forms required: FAFSA, state aid form.
Dates and Deadlines: Priority date 3/2; no closing date. Applicants notified on a rolling basis starting 4/15; must reply by 9/1.
Transfers: No deadline. Applicants notified on a rolling basis.

CONTACT
William Chunestudy, Director of Student Financial Services
4500 Riverwalk Parkway, Riverside, CA 92515-8247
(951) 785-2175

Las Positas College
Livermore, California
www.laspositas.cc.ca.us
Federal Code: 030357

2-year public community college in small city.
Enrollment: 2,392 full-time undergrads.
Selectivity: Open admission.

BASIC COSTS (2005-2006)
Tuition and fees: $808; out-of-state residents $5,488.
Per-credit charge: $26; out-of-state residents $182.
Additional info: Tuition/fee waivers available for unemployed or children of unemployed.

FINANCIAL AID PICTURE
Students with need: Need-based aid available for full-time students.

FINANCIAL AID PROCEDURES
Forms required: institutional form.
Dates and Deadlines: Priority date 5/1; no closing date. Applicants notified on a rolling basis starting 7/1; must reply within 2 week(s) of notification.

CONTACT
Andi Schreibman, Financial Aid Officer
3033 Collier Canyon Road, Livermore, CA 94551
(925) 373-5800

LIFE Pacific College
San Dimas, California
www.lifepacific.edu
Federal Code: 016029

4-year private Bible college in large town, affiliated with International Church of the Foursquare Gospel.
Enrollment: 475 undergrads. 70 full-time freshmen.
Selectivity: Admits over 75% of applicants.

BASIC COSTS (2006-2007)
Tuition and fees: $10,100.
Per-credit charge: $325.
Room and board: $5,000.

FINANCIAL AID PICTURE (2004-2005)
Students with need: Out of 57 full-time freshmen who applied for aid, 46 were judged to have need. Of these, 42 received aid, and 1 had their full need met. Average financial aid package met 31% of need; average scholarship/grant was $2,680; average loan was $2,297. For part-time students, average financial aid package was $2,833.
Students without need: No-need awards available for academics, alumni affiliation.

FINANCIAL AID PROCEDURES
Forms required: FAFSA.
Dates and Deadlines: Closing date 7/1. Applicants notified on a rolling basis starting 6/1.

CONTACT
Ken Lira, Director of Financial Aid
1100 Covina Boulevard, San Dimas, CA 91773
(909) 599-5433 ext. 322

Loma Linda University
Loma Linda, California
www.llu.edu   Federal Code: 001218

Upper-division private health science and nursing college in large town, affiliated with Seventh-day Adventists.
Enrollment: 1,119 undergrads.

BASIC COSTS (2005-2006)
Tuition and fees: $23,514.
Room only: $2,232.
Additional info: Tuition quoted for nursing program. Full-time tuition for dental hygiene program: $18,895. For allied health program $465 per credit hour for first 8 credits, $279 per credit hour after 8 credits. Application fee may vary by program.

FINANCIAL AID PICTURE
Students with need: Need-based aid available for full-time and part-time students.

FINANCIAL AID PROCEDURES
Forms required: FAFSA.
Dates and Deadlines: Applicants notified on a rolling basis.

CONTACT
Verdell Schaefer, Director of Financial Aid Loma Linda, CA 92350
(909) 558-4509

Long Beach City College
Long Beach, California
www.lbcc.edu   Federal Code: 001219

2-year public community college in large city.
Enrollment: 11,226 undergrads.
Selectivity: Open admission.

BASIC COSTS (2005-2006)
Tuition and fees: $806; out-of-state residents $5,336.
Per-credit charge: $26; out-of-state residents $177.

FINANCIAL AID PICTURE
Students with need: Need-based aid available for full-time and part-time students.

Students without need: This college only awards aid to students with need.

FINANCIAL AID PROCEDURES
Forms required: FAFSA, institutional form.
Dates and Deadlines: Priority date 5/6; no closing date. Applicants notified on a rolling basis starting 7/6; must reply within 2 week(s) of notification.

CONTACT
Toni Dubois, Director of Financial Aid and Veterans Affairs
4901 East Carson Street, Long Beach, CA 90808
(562) 938-4257

Los Angeles City College
Los Angeles, California
www.lacitycollege.edu   Federal Code: 001223

2-year public community college in very large city.
Enrollment: 5,544 full-time undergrads.
Selectivity: Open admission.

BASIC COSTS (2005-2006)
Tuition and fees: $804; out-of-state residents $5,424.
Per-credit charge: $26; out-of-state residents $180.

FINANCIAL AID PICTURE (2004-2005)
Students with need: 89% of average financial aid package awarded as scholarships/grants, 11% awarded as loans/jobs.
Additional info: Fee waivers available for public assistance and Social Security insurance recipients; fee credits available for low income families.

FINANCIAL AID PROCEDURES
Forms required: FAFSA.
Dates and Deadlines: Priority date 3/2; no closing date. Applicants notified on a rolling basis; must reply within 2 week(s) of notification.

CONTACT
Jeremy Villar, Dean of Student Services
855 North Vermont Avenue, Los Angeles, CA 90029-3589
(323) 953-4441

Los Angeles Harbor College
Wilmington, California
www.lahc.edu   Federal Code: 001224

2-year public community college in small city.
Enrollment: 2,467 full-time undergrads.
Selectivity: Open admission; but selective for some programs.

BASIC COSTS (2005-2006)
Tuition and fees: $804; out-of-state residents $5,424.
Per-credit charge: $26; out-of-state residents $180.

FINANCIAL AID PICTURE
Students with need: Need-based aid available for full-time and part-time students. Work study available nights, weekends, and for part-time students.
Students without need: This college only awards aid to students with need.

FINANCIAL AID PROCEDURES
Forms required: FAFSA, institutional form.
Dates and Deadlines: Priority date 3/2; no closing date. Applicants notified on a rolling basis; must reply within 2 week(s) of notification.
Transfers: Closing date 5/15.

CONTACT
Sheila Millman, Financial Aid Manager
1111 Figueroa Place, Wilmington, CA 90744-2397
(310) 233-4320

Los Angeles Pierce College
Woodland Hills, California
www.piercecollege.edu
Federal Code: 001226

2-year public community college in very large city.
Enrollment: 4,731 full-time undergrads.
Selectivity: Open admission; but selective for some programs.

BASIC COSTS (2005-2006)
Tuition and fees: $804; out-of-state residents $5,424.
Per-credit charge: $26; out-of-state residents $180.

FINANCIAL AID PICTURE
Students with need: Need-based aid available for full-time and part-time students.
Students without need: This college only awards aid to students with need.

FINANCIAL AID PROCEDURES
Forms required: FAFSA, institutional form.
Dates and Deadlines: Priority date 5/1; no closing date. Applicants notified on a rolling basis starting 8/1.

CONTACT
Jeremy Villar, Manager of Financial Aid
6201 Winnetka Avenue, Woodland Hills, CA 91371
(818) 719-6428

Los Angeles Southwest College
Los Angeles, California
www.lasc.cc.ca.us
Federal Code: 007047

2-year public community college in very large city.
Enrollment: 1,436 full-time undergrads.
Selectivity: Open admission; but selective for some programs.

BASIC COSTS (2005-2006)
Tuition and fees: $804; out-of-state residents $5,424.
Per-credit charge: $26; out-of-state residents $180.

FINANCIAL AID PICTURE
Students with need: Need-based aid available for full-time and part-time students.
Additional info: Board of Governors Enrollment Fee Waiver available to students receiving AFDC, SSI/SSP, or General Assistance. May also qualify on basis of income.

FINANCIAL AID PROCEDURES
Forms required: FAFSA.
Dates and Deadlines: No deadline. Applicants notified on a rolling basis; must reply within 2 week(s) of notification.

CONTACT
Marilyn Moy, Associate Dean, Student Services
1600 West Imperial Highway, Los Angeles, CA 90047
(323) 241-5225

Los Angeles Trade and Technical College
Los Angeles, California
www.lattc.edu
Federal Code: 001227

2-year public community and technical college in very large city.
Enrollment: 3,300 full-time undergrads.
Selectivity: Open admission; but selective for some programs.

BASIC COSTS (2005-2006)
Tuition and fees: $804; out-of-state residents $5,424.
Per-credit charge: $26; out-of-state residents $180.

FINANCIAL AID PICTURE
Students with need: Need-based aid available for full-time and part-time students. Work study available nights, weekends, and for part-time students.
Students without need: This college only awards aid to students with need.

FINANCIAL AID PROCEDURES
Forms required: FAFSA.
Dates and Deadlines: Priority date 5/1; no closing date. Applicants notified on a rolling basis.
Transfers: No deadline.

CONTACT
Leann Roque, Financial Aid Manager
400 West Washington Boulevard, Los Angeles, CA 90015-4181
(213) 744-9016

Los Angeles Valley College
Valley Glen, California
www.lavc.edu
Federal Code: 001228

2-year public community college in very large city.
Enrollment: 4,731 full-time undergrads.
Selectivity: Open admission; but selective for some programs.

BASIC COSTS (2005-2006)
Tuition and fees: $804; out-of-state residents $5,424.
Per-credit charge: $26; out-of-state residents $180.

FINANCIAL AID PICTURE
Students with need: Need-based aid available for full-time and part-time students.
Students without need: This college only awards aid to students with need.

FINANCIAL AID PROCEDURES
Forms required: FAFSA.
Dates and Deadlines: Priority date 6/12; no closing date. Applicants notified on a rolling basis.

CONTACT
Ruth Siegel, Coordinator of Financial Aid
5800 Fulton Avenue, Valley Glen, CA 91401-4096
(818) 947-2412

Loyola Marymount University
Los Angeles, California
www.lmu.edu
Federal Code: 001234
CSS Code: 4403

4-year private university in very large city, affiliated with Roman Catholic Church.
Enrollment: 5,419 undergrads, 3% part-time. 1,346 full-time freshmen.
Selectivity: Admits 50 to 75% of applicants.

BASIC COSTS (2006-2007)
Tuition and fees: $29,834.
Per-credit charge: $1,216.
Room and board: $12,640.

FINANCIAL AID PICTURE (2005-2006)
Students with need: Out of 1,086 full-time freshmen who applied for aid, 801 were judged to have need. Of these, 732 received aid, and 649 had their full need met. Average financial aid package met 88% of need; average scholarship/grant was $17,331; average loan was $3,332. Need-based aid available for part-time students.
Students without need: 37 full-time freshmen who did not demonstrate need for aid received scholarships/grants; average award was $11,527. No-need awards available for academics, alumni affiliation, athletics, leadership, music/drama.
Scholarships offered: 11 full-time freshmen received athletic scholarships; average amount $13,256.
Cumulative student debt: 59% of graduating class had student loans; average debt was $27,144.

FINANCIAL AID PROCEDURES
Forms required: FAFSA, CSS PROFILE, state aid form.
Dates and Deadlines: Closing date 3/2. Applicants notified on a rolling basis starting 3/15; must reply by 5/1 or within 4 week(s) of notification.

CONTACT
Catherine Kasakoff, Director of Financial Aid
Admissions, 1 LMU Drive, Los Angeles, CA 90045-8350
(310) 338-2700

Maric College: Panorama City
Panorama City, California
www.mariccollege.edu
Federal Code: 030445

2-year for-profit junior and technical college in very large city.
Enrollment: 89 undergrads.
Selectivity: Open admission.

BASIC COSTS (2006-2007)
Tuition and fees: $11,385.

FINANCIAL AID PICTURE (2005-2006)
Students with need: 56% of average financial aid package awarded as scholarships/grants, 44% awarded as loans/jobs. Work study available nights.
Students without need: This college only awards aid to students with need.

FINANCIAL AID PROCEDURES
Forms required: FAFSA, institutional form.
Dates and Deadlines: No deadline.
Transfers: No deadline.

CONTACT
Cynthia Arevalo
14355 Roscoe Boulevard, Panorama City, CA 91402
(818) 672-8907

Marymount College
Rancho Palos Verdes, California
www.marymountpv.edu
Federal Code: 010474

2-year private junior and liberal arts college in large town, affiliated with Roman Catholic Church.
Enrollment: 726 undergrads, 2% part-time. 363 full-time freshmen.
Selectivity: Admits 50 to 75% of applicants.

BASIC COSTS (2006-2007)
Tuition and fees: $19,485.
Room and board: $9,700.

FINANCIAL AID PICTURE
Students with need: Need-based aid available for full-time students.
Students without need: No-need awards available for academics, athletics, leadership.

FINANCIAL AID PROCEDURES
Forms required: FAFSA, institutional form.
Dates and Deadlines: Priority date 3/2; no closing date. Applicants notified on a rolling basis starting 4/30; must reply by 5/1 or within 2 week(s) of notification.
Transfers: No deadline. Financial aid transcripts from previous institutions required for midyear transfers.

CONTACT
David Carnevale, Director of Financial Aid
30800 Palos Verdes Drive East, Rancho Palos Verdes, CA 90275-6299
(310) 303-7217

Master's College
Santa Clarita, California
www.masters.edu
Federal Code: 001220

4-year private liberal arts and seminary college in small city, affiliated with Christian, Protestant, Conservative Evangelical.
Enrollment: 1,125 undergrads, 15% part-time. 260 full-time freshmen.
Selectivity: Admits over 75% of applicants.

BASIC COSTS (2006-2007)
Tuition and fees: $27,670.
Per-credit charge: $870.
Room and board: $7,150.

FINANCIAL AID PICTURE (2004-2005)
Students with need: Out of 153 full-time freshmen who applied for aid, 123 were judged to have need. Of these, 121 received aid, and 26 had their full need met. Average financial aid package met 68% of need; average scholarship/grant was $9,316; average loan was $2,776. For part-time students, average financial aid package was $7,718.
Students without need: 56 full-time freshmen who did not demonstrate need for aid received scholarships/grants; average award was $9,838. No-need awards available for academics, alumni affiliation, art, athletics, leadership, music/drama.
Scholarships offered: 20 full-time freshmen received athletic scholarships; average amount $8,912.
Cumulative student debt: 54% of graduating class had student loans; average debt was $16,987.

FINANCIAL AID PROCEDURES
Forms required: FAFSA, state aid form, institutional form.
Dates and Deadlines: Priority date 3/2; no closing date. Applicants notified on a rolling basis starting 2/18; must reply by 5/1 or within 2 week(s) of notification.
Transfers: Closing date 3/1.

CONTACT
Gary Edwards, Director of Financial Aid
21726 Placerita Canyon Road, Santa Clarita, CA 91321-1200
(661) 259-3540 ext. 3391

Mendocino College
Ukiah, California
www.mendocino.edu   Federal Code: 011672

2-year public community college in large town.
Enrollment: 1,134 full-time undergrads.
Selectivity: Open admission.

BASIC COSTS (2005-2006)
Tuition and fees: $799; out-of-state residents $6,049.
Per-credit charge: $26; out-of-state residents $201.

FINANCIAL AID PICTURE
Students with need: Need-based aid available for full-time and part-time students.

FINANCIAL AID PROCEDURES
Forms required: FAFSA.
Dates and Deadlines: Priority date 5/31; no closing date. Applicants notified on a rolling basis starting 7/1; must reply within 2 week(s) of notification.

CONTACT
Jacqueline Bradley, Director of Financial Aid
1000 Hensley Creek/Box 3000, Ukiah, CA 95482
(707) 468-3110

Menlo College
Atherton, California
www.menlo.edu   Federal Code: 001236

4-year private business and liberal arts college in small city.
Enrollment: 769 undergrads, 13% part-time. 183 full-time freshmen.
Selectivity: Admits 50 to 75% of applicants.

BASIC COSTS (2006-2007)
Tuition and fees: $26,220.
Per-credit charge: $1,080.
Room and board: $9,800.

FINANCIAL AID PICTURE (2005-2006)
Students with need: Out of 127 full-time freshmen who applied for aid, 114 were judged to have need. Of these, 114 received aid, and 14 had their full need met. Average financial aid package met 75% of need; average scholarship/grant was $17,676; average loan was $3,414. For part-time students, average financial aid package was $7,250.
Students without need: 52 full-time freshmen who did not demonstrate need for aid received scholarships/grants; average award was $10,664. No-need awards available for academics.
Scholarships offered: President's Scholarship: $12,000 annually; students with 3.5 GPA or higher. Dean's Scholarship: $11,000 annually; students with 3.1-3.49 GPA. Leadership Scholarship: $8,500 annually; students with 2.8-3.09 GPA.
Cumulative student debt: 67% of graduating class had student loans; average debt was $21,905.

FINANCIAL AID PROCEDURES
Forms required: FAFSA, state aid form.
Dates and Deadlines: Priority date 3/2; closing date 8/1. Applicants notified on a rolling basis starting 12/15; must reply by 5/1 or within 2 week(s) of notification.
Transfers: No deadline. Must reply by 5/1 or within 2 week(s) of notification.

CONTACT
Elinore Burkhardt, Director of Financial Aid
1000 El Camino Real, Atherton, CA 94027
(650) 543-3880

Merritt College
Oakland, California
www.merritt.edu   Federal Code: 001267

2-year public community college in large city.
Enrollment: 7,301 undergrads.
Selectivity: Open admission.

BASIC COSTS (2005-2006)
Tuition and fees: $784; out-of-state residents $5,704.
Per-credit charge: $26; out-of-state residents $190.
Additional info: Tuition/fee waivers available for unemployed or children of unemployed.

FINANCIAL AID PICTURE
Students with need: Need-based aid available for full-time and part-time students.

FINANCIAL AID PROCEDURES
Forms required: FAFSA, institutional form.
Dates and Deadlines: Priority date 4/1; closing date 6/30. Applicants notified on a rolling basis starting 6/1.

CONTACT
Alice Freeman, Financial Aid Coordinator
12500 Campus Drive, Oakland, CA 94619
(510) 436-2465

Mills College
Oakland, California
www.mills.edu   Federal Code: 001238

4-year private liberal arts college for women in large city.
Enrollment: 881 undergrads, 4% part-time. 135 full-time freshmen.
Selectivity: Admits over 75% of applicants.

BASIC COSTS (2006-2007)
Tuition and fees: $31,190.
Room and board: $10,290.

FINANCIAL AID PICTURE (2005-2006)
Students with need: Out of 121 full-time freshmen who applied for aid, 104 were judged to have need. Of these, 104 received aid, and 70 had their full need met. Average financial aid package met 94% of need; average scholarship/grant was $20,108; average loan was $3,885. For part-time students, average financial aid package was $8,020.
Students without need: 30 full-time freshmen who did not demonstrate need for aid received scholarships/grants; average award was $9,876. No-need awards available for academics.
Scholarships offered: Trustee Scholarship; full tuition; for entering freshmen with strong academic records. Presidential Scholarships; $5,000-$11,500 annually; for entering freshmen with strong academic records. Regional Scholarships; $5,000-$11,500 annually; for entering freshmen with strong academic records. Donner Scholarship in Music; $5,000 annually; for entering freshmen with strong talent in music. Barbara Hazelton Floyd Scholarship in Music; $5,000 annually; for entering freshmen with strong talent in piano music. Scheffler Premedical Science Scholarships; $2,500 annually; for entering freshmen and transfers with strong academic records and an interest in attending medical school; 5 awarded. Arthur Vining Davis Science Scholarship; $2,500 annually; for entering freshmen and transfers with strong academic records and an interest in science, math, or computer science. Dean's Scholarship; $4,000-$10,000 annually; for entering transfers with strong academic records. Osher Scholarships; $2,500-$10,000 annually; for entering transfers students 23 years old or older with demonstrated leadership ability; 4-8 awarded.

FINANCIAL AID PROCEDURES
Forms required: FAFSA, state aid form, institutional form.
Dates and Deadlines: Priority date 2/1; closing date 2/15. Applicants notified by 4/1; must reply by 5/1 or within 2 week(s) of notification.
Transfers: Priority date 3/2. Applications by March 2 for California residents, April 1 for out-of-state students.

CONTACT
David Gin, Director of Student Administrative Services
5000 MacArthur Boulevard, Oakland, CA 94613
(510) 430-2000

MiraCosta College
Oceanside, California
www.miracosta.edu   Federal Code: 001239

2-year public community college in large city.
Enrollment: 6,085 undergrads, 59% part-time. 672 full-time freshmen.
Selectivity: Open admission.

BASIC COSTS (2005-2006)
Tuition and fees: $816; out-of-state residents $5,346.
Per-credit charge: $26; out-of-state residents $177.

FINANCIAL AID PICTURE (2004-2005)
Students with need: 79% of average financial aid package awarded as scholarships/grants, 21% awarded as loans/jobs. Need-based aid available for part-time students.
Additional info: Waiver of in-state fees for eligible low-income students.

FINANCIAL AID PROCEDURES
Forms required: FAFSA, state aid form.
Dates and Deadlines: Priority date 3/3; no closing date. Applicants notified on a rolling basis.

CONTACT
JoAnn Bernard, Financial Aid Director
One Barnard Drive, Oceanside, CA 92056-3899
(760) 795-6711

Modesto Junior College
Modesto, California
www.mjc.edu   Federal Code: 001240

2-year public community college in small city.
Enrollment: 11,385 undergrads.
Selectivity: Open admission; but selective for some programs.

BASIC COSTS (2005-2006)
Tuition and fees: $818; out-of-state residents $5,348.
Per-credit charge: $26; out-of-state residents $177.

FINANCIAL AID PICTURE (2004-2005)
Students with need: 96% of average financial aid package awarded as scholarships/grants, 4% awarded as loans/jobs. Need-based aid available for part-time students. Work study available nights, weekends, and for part-time students.
Students without need: This college only awards aid to students with need.
Additional info: Modesto Junior College scholarship priority deadline 12/15.

FINANCIAL AID PROCEDURES
Forms required: FAFSA, state aid form, institutional form.
Dates and Deadlines: Priority date 3/2; no closing date. Applicants notified on a rolling basis starting 5/1; must reply within 2 week(s) of notification.

CONTACT
Myra Rush, Director Financial Aid, Scholarships
435 College Avenue, Modesto, CA 95350-5800
(209) 575-6023

Monterey Peninsula College
Monterey, California
www.mpc.edu   Federal Code: 001242

2-year public community college in large town.
Enrollment: 1,808 full-time undergrads.
Selectivity: Open admission; but selective for some programs.

BASIC COSTS (2005-2006)
Tuition and fees: $826; out-of-state residents $5,356.
Per-credit charge: $26; out-of-state residents $177.
Additional info: Tuition/fee waivers available for adults, minority students, unemployed or children of unemployed.

FINANCIAL AID PICTURE
Students with need: Need-based aid available for full-time and part-time students.

FINANCIAL AID PROCEDURES
Forms required: FAFSA, institutional form.
Dates and Deadlines: Priority date 3/2; no closing date. Applicants notified on a rolling basis starting 6/1.

CONTACT
Claudia Martin, Director of Financial Aid
980 Fremont Street, Monterey, CA 93940-4799
(831) 646-4000

Mount St. Mary's College
Los Angeles, California
www.msmc.la.edu   Federal Code: 001243

4-year private liberal arts college for women in very large city, affiliated with Roman Catholic Church.
Enrollment: 1,971 undergrads, 25% part-time. 178 full-time freshmen.
Selectivity: Admits over 75% of applicants.

BASIC COSTS (2006-2007)
Tuition and fees: $24,150.
Per-credit charge: $900.
Room and board: $8,747.

FINANCIAL AID PICTURE (2004-2005)
Students with need: Out of 168 full-time freshmen who applied for aid, 152 were judged to have need. Of these, 152 received aid, and 19 had their full need met. Average financial aid package met 79% of need; average scholarship/grant was $7,425; average loan was $2,485. For part-time students, average financial aid package was $8,615.
Students without need: 26 full-time freshmen who did not demonstrate need for aid received scholarships/grants; average award was $10,760. No-need awards available for academics, alumni affiliation, art, leadership, music/drama.

FINANCIAL AID PROCEDURES
Forms required: FAFSA, institutional form.
Dates and Deadlines: Priority date 3/1; no closing date. Applicants notified on a rolling basis starting 2/1; must reply by 5/1.
Transfers: No deadline.

California Mount St. Mary's College

CONTACT
La Royce Dodd, Director of Financial Aid
12001 Chalon Road, Los Angeles, CA 90049
(310) 954-4195

Mount San Antonio College
Walnut, California
www.mtsac.edu   Federal Code: 001245

2-year public community college in small city.
Enrollment: 20,587 undergrads.
Selectivity: Open admission.

BASIC COSTS (2005-2006)
Tuition and fees: $806; out-of-state residents $5,336.
Per-credit charge: $26; out-of-state residents $177.

FINANCIAL AID PICTURE
Students with need: Need-based aid available for full-time and part-time students.
Students without need: This college only awards aid to students with need.

FINANCIAL AID PROCEDURES
Forms required: FAFSA, institutional form.
Dates and Deadlines: No deadline. Applicants notified on a rolling basis starting 6/1; must reply within 4 week(s) of notification.

CONTACT
Susanna Jones, Director Financial Aid
1100 North Grand Avenue, Walnut, CA 91789
(909) 594-5611

Mount San Jacinto College
San Jacinto, California
www.msjc.edu   Federal Code: 001246

2-year public community college in small city.
Enrollment: 5,717 undergrads.
Selectivity: Open admission; but selective for some programs.

BASIC COSTS (2005-2006)
Tuition and fees: $780; out-of-state residents $5,310.
Per-credit charge: $26; out-of-state residents $177.

FINANCIAL AID PICTURE
Students with need: Need-based aid available for full-time and part-time students. Work study available nights.
Students without need: This college only awards aid to students with need.
Additional info: Board of Governors Grant Program for state residents to defray cost of enrollment fee.

FINANCIAL AID PROCEDURES
Forms required: FAFSA, institutional form.
Dates and Deadlines: Priority date 3/2; no closing date. Applicants notified on a rolling basis starting 5/1; must reply within 3 week(s) of notification.
Transfers: No deadline.

CONTACT
Mary Ellen Muehring, Financial Aid Director
1499 North State Street, San Jacinto, CA 92583
(951) 487-6752 ext. 1432

MTI College
Sacramento, California
www.mticollege.edu   Federal Code: 012912

2-year for-profit business and technical college in large city.
Enrollment: 396 undergrads. 261 full-time freshmen.

BASIC COSTS (2005-2006)
Tuition and fees: $9,050.

FINANCIAL AID PICTURE
Students with need: Need-based aid available for full-time students. Work study available nights.

CONTACT
Paula Perez, Director of Financial Aid
5221 Madison Avenue, Sacramento, CA 95841
(916) 339-1500

National University
La Jolla, California
www.nu.edu   Federal Code: 011460

4-year private university in very large city.
Enrollment: 6,186 undergrads, 74% part-time. 23 full-time freshmen.
Selectivity: Open admission; but selective for some programs.

BASIC COSTS (2005-2006)
Tuition and fees: $8,352.

FINANCIAL AID PICTURE (2004-2005)
Students with need: 37% of average financial aid package awarded as scholarships/grants, 63% awarded as loans/jobs. Need-based aid available for part-time students.

FINANCIAL AID PROCEDURES
Forms required: FAFSA, state aid form, institutional form.
Dates and Deadlines: No deadline. Applicants notified on a rolling basis.
Transfers: No deadline.

CONTACT
Marc Berman, Director of Financial Aid
11255 North Torrey Pines Road, La Jolla, CA 92037-1011
(858) 642-8500

NewSchool of Architecture & Design
San Diego, California
www.newschoolarch.edu   Federal Code: 030439

5-year for-profit visual arts and liberal arts college in very large city.
Enrollment: 175 full-time undergrads.
Selectivity: Admits over 75% of applicants.

FINANCIAL AID PICTURE
Students with need: Work study available nights.
Students without need: No-need awards available for academics.
Scholarships offered: Presidential Scholarship for incoming freshmen based on GPA, activity, recommendations, portfolio; $5,000 annually for 2 years, 15 recipients.

FINANCIAL AID PROCEDURES
Forms required: FAFSA.
Dates and Deadlines: Priority date 3/2; no closing date. Applicants notified on a rolling basis.
Transfers: Priority date 4/1; no deadline.

CONTACT
Michelle Chatelain, Director of Financial Aid
1249 F Street, San Diego, CA 92101
(619) 235-4100 ext. 206

Notre Dame de Namur University
Belmont, California
www.ndnu.edu   Federal Code: 001179

4-year private liberal arts college in large town, affiliated with Roman Catholic Church.
Enrollment: 886 undergrads.
Selectivity: Admits over 75% of applicants.

BASIC COSTS (2006-2007)
Tuition and fees: $23,850.
Per-credit charge: $545.
Room and board: $10,380.

FINANCIAL AID PICTURE
Students with need: Need-based aid available for full-time and part-time students. Work study available nights, weekends, and for part-time students.
Students without need: No-need awards available for academics, alumni affiliation, athletics, leadership, music/drama.
Scholarships offered: Presidential Scholarships; up to $7,500; based on academic merit and leadership; variable number available. Honors at Entrance/Transfer Honors; $3,000; both based on academic qualifications; unlimited number available. Regents Scholarships; up to $5,000; based on academic merit and leadership or service; 6 available. International Honors; $3,000; based on TOEFL score greater than 500 and academic record; unlimited number available. Toso Alumni Scholarship; $2,000; consideration given to those with CND graduate as a parent, grandparent, or sibling; unlimited number available. Bay Area Catholic High School; up to $7,500 per year to one student from each of Bay Area Catholic high schools in their freshman year at CND. Sealbearer Scholarships; up to $500 per year if student is a lifetime member of CSF.

FINANCIAL AID PROCEDURES
Forms required: FAFSA. CSS/ PROFILE accepted but not required.
Dates and Deadlines: Priority date 3/2; no closing date. Applicants notified on a rolling basis starting 1/15.

CONTACT
Susan Pace, Director of Financial Aid
1500 Ralston Avenue, Belmont, CA 94002-1997
(650) 508-3509

Occidental College
Los Angeles, California
www.oxy.edu   Federal Code: 001249
                                          CSS Code: 4581

4-year private liberal arts college in very large city, affiliated with nondenominational tradition.
Enrollment: 1,814 undergrads, 1% part-time. 461 full-time freshmen.
Selectivity: Admits less than 50% of applicants.

BASIC COSTS (2006-2007)
Tuition and fees: $33,644.
Per-credit charge: $1,367.
Room and board: $9,552.

FINANCIAL AID PICTURE (2005-2006)
Students with need: Out of 272 full-time freshmen who applied for aid, 207 were judged to have need. Of these, 206 received aid, and 90 had their full need met. Average financial aid package met 90% of need; average scholarship/grant was $21,416; average loan was $4,812. For part-time students, average financial aid package was $14,074.
Students without need: 142 full-time freshmen who did not demonstrate need for aid received scholarships/grants; average award was $13,633. No-need awards available for academics, leadership.
Scholarships offered: Margaret Bundy Scott Scholarship: $17,500. President's Scholarship: $12,500; awarded to top 10-15% of incoming class based on academic achievement, leadership, and citizenship.
Cumulative student debt: 61% of graduating class had student loans; average debt was $20,641.

FINANCIAL AID PROCEDURES
Forms required: FAFSA, CSS PROFILE, state aid form.
Dates and Deadlines: Priority date 11/15; closing date 2/1. Applicants notified by 3/24; must reply by 5/1.
Transfers: California residents must apply for Cal Grant by completing FAFSA and CSAC's GPA verification form by March 2.

CONTACT
Maureen McRae Levy, Director of Financial Aid
1600 Campus Road, Los Angeles, CA 90041
(323) 259-2548

Ohlone College
Fremont, California
www.ohlone.cc.ca.us   Federal Code: 004481

2-year public community college in large city.
Enrollment: 2,261 undergrads.
Selectivity: Open admission; but selective for some programs.

BASIC COSTS (2005-2006)
Tuition and fees: $816; out-of-state residents $5,346.
Per-credit charge: $26; out-of-state residents $177.
Additional info: Tuition/fee waivers available for adults, minority students, unemployed or children of unemployed.

FINANCIAL AID PICTURE
Students with need: Need-based aid available for full-time and part-time students.
Students without need: No-need awards available for academics.

FINANCIAL AID PROCEDURES
Forms required: FAFSA, state aid form, institutional form.
Dates and Deadlines: Priority date 7/1; no closing date. Applicants notified on a rolling basis starting 7/30; must reply within 2 week(s) of notification.

CONTACT
Debra Griffin, Financial Aid Director
43600 Mission Boulevard, Fremont, CA 94539-0390
(510) 659-6150

Orange Coast College
Costa Mesa, California
www.orangecoastcollege.edu   Federal Code: 001250

2-year public community college in small city.
Enrollment: 17,411 undergrads, 53% part-time. 1,881 full-time freshmen.
Selectivity: Open admission.

California Orange Coast College

BASIC COSTS (2005-2006)
Tuition and fees: $806; out-of-state residents $5,366.
Per-credit charge: $26; out-of-state residents $178.
Additional info: Tuition/fee waivers available for adults, minority students, unemployed or children of unemployed.

FINANCIAL AID PICTURE (2005-2006)
Students with need: 76% of average financial aid package awarded as scholarships/grants, 24% awarded as loans/jobs. Need-based aid available for part-time students.
Students without need: No-need awards available for academics.

FINANCIAL AID PROCEDURES
Forms required: FAFSA, institutional form.
Dates and Deadlines: Priority date 3/2; closing date 5/31. Applicants notified on a rolling basis; must reply within 2 week(s) of notification.

CONTACT
Melissa Moser, Financial Aid Director
2701 Fairview Road, Costa Mesa, CA 92628-5005
(714) 432-5508

Otis College of Art and Design
Los Angeles, California
www.otis.edu   Federal Code: 001251

4-year private visual arts college in very large city.
Enrollment: 1,023 undergrads.
Selectivity: Admits 50 to 75% of applicants.

BASIC COSTS (2006-2007)
Tuition and fees: $27,596.
Per-credit charge: $900.

FINANCIAL AID PICTURE (2004-2005)
Students with need: 72% of average financial aid package awarded as scholarships/grants, 28% awarded as loans/jobs. Need-based aid available for part-time students. Work study available nights, weekends, and for part-time students.
Students without need: No-need awards available for academics, art.

FINANCIAL AID PROCEDURES
Forms required: FAFSA, state aid form.
Dates and Deadlines: Priority date 2/15; no closing date. Applicants notified on a rolling basis starting 3/1; must reply within 2 week(s) of notification.

CONTACT
Ji Choi, Director of Financial Aid
9045 Lincoln Boulevard, Los Angeles, CA 90045-9785
(310) 665-6880

Pacific Oaks College
Pasadena, California
www.pacificoaks.edu   Federal Code: 001255

Upper-division private teachers college in small city.
Enrollment: 245 undergrads.

BASIC COSTS (2006-2007)
Tuition and fees: $22,050.
Per-credit charge: $735.

FINANCIAL AID PICTURE (2004-2005)
Students with need: Average financial aid package for all full-time undergraduates was $15,000; for part-time $7,000. 33% awarded as scholarships/grants, 67% awarded as loans/jobs. Work study available nights, weekends, and for part-time students.
Students without need: This college only awards aid to students with need.

FINANCIAL AID PROCEDURES
Forms required: FAFSA, state aid form, institutional form.
Dates and Deadlines: Closing date 4/15. Applicants notified on a rolling basis starting 5/1; must reply by 5/15 or within 4 week(s) of notification.

CONTACT
Deb Kuntz, Associate Dean, Financial Aid
5 Westmoreland Place, Pasadena, CA 91103
(626) 397-1350

Pacific States University
Los Angeles, California
www.psuca.edu   Federal Code: 031633

4-year private university in very large city.
Enrollment: 19 undergrads.
Selectivity: Open admission.

BASIC COSTS (2006-2007)
Tuition and fees: $11,040.
Per-credit charge: $195.

FINANCIAL AID PICTURE
Students with need: Need-based aid available for full-time and part-time students.
Students without need: This college only awards aid to students with need.

FINANCIAL AID PROCEDURES
Forms required: FAFSA.
Dates and Deadlines: No deadline.

CONTACT
Min Kim, Financial Aid Officer
1516 South Western Avenue, Los Angeles, CA 90006
(323) 731-2383 ext. 14

Pacific Union College
Angwin, California
www.puc.edu   Federal Code: 001258

4-year private liberal arts college in small town, affiliated with Seventh-day Adventists.
Enrollment: 1,420 undergrads, 9% part-time. 318 full-time freshmen.

BASIC COSTS (2006-2007)
Tuition and fees: $20,265.
Per-credit charge: $584.
Room and board: $5,652.

FINANCIAL AID PICTURE (2005-2006)
Students with need: 73% of average financial aid package awarded as scholarships/grants, 27% awarded as loans/jobs. Need-based aid available for part-time students.
Students without need: This college only awards aid to students with need.

FINANCIAL AID PROCEDURES
Forms required: FAFSA, state aid form, institutional form.
Dates and Deadlines: No deadline. Applicants notified on a rolling basis; must reply within 3 week(s) of notification.

CONTACT
Glen Bobst, Director of Student Financial Services
Enrollment Services, Angwin, CA 94508
(707) 965-7200

Palo Verde College
Blythe, California
www.paloverde.edu　　　　　Federal Code: 001259

2-year public community college in large town.
Enrollment: 1,027 undergrads, 50% part-time. 100 full-time freshmen.
Selectivity: Open admission; but selective for some programs.

BASIC COSTS (2005-2006)
Tuition and fees: $780; out-of-state residents $5,310.
Per-credit charge: $26; out-of-state residents $177.

FINANCIAL AID PICTURE (2004-2005)
Students with need: 98% of average financial aid package awarded as scholarships/grants, 2% awarded as loans/jobs. Need-based aid available for part-time students. Work study available nights.
Students without need: This college only awards aid to students with need.

FINANCIAL AID PROCEDURES
Forms required: FAFSA, institutional form.
Dates and Deadlines: No deadline. Applicants notified on a rolling basis starting 7/1; must reply within 4 week(s) of notification.

CONTACT
Linda Pratt, Director of Financial Aid
One College Drive, Blythe, CA 92225
(760) 921-5410

Palomar College
San Marcos, California
www.palomar.edu　　　　　Federal Code: 001260

2-year public community college in large town.
Enrollment: 14,693 undergrads.
Selectivity: Open admission; but selective for some programs.

BASIC COSTS (2005-2006)
Tuition and fees: $814; out-of-state residents $5,344.
Per-credit charge: $26; out-of-state residents $177.

FINANCIAL AID PICTURE
Students with need: Need-based aid available for full-time and part-time students. Work study available nights.
Students without need: This college only awards aid to students with need.

FINANCIAL AID PROCEDURES
Forms required: FAFSA, institutional form.
Dates and Deadlines: Priority date 4/1; no closing date. Applicants notified on a rolling basis starting 6/1.
Transfers: No deadline.

CONTACT
Mary San Agustin, Financial Aid Director
1140 West Mission Road, San Marcos, CA 92069
(760) 744-1150

Patten University
Oakland, California
www.patten.edu　　　　　Federal Code: 004490

4-year private Bible and liberal arts college in very large city, affiliated with interdenominational tradition.
Enrollment: 545 undergrads.

BASIC COSTS (2006-2007)
Tuition and fees: $11,880.
Per-credit charge: $495.
Room and board: $6,250.

FINANCIAL AID PICTURE
Students with need: Need-based aid available for full-time and part-time students.
Students without need: No-need awards available for academics, athletics, state/district residency.

FINANCIAL AID PROCEDURES
Forms required: FAFSA, institutional form.
Dates and Deadlines: Priority date 3/31; no closing date. Applicants notified on a rolling basis starting 5/31.
Transfers: No deadline.

CONTACT
Dennis Clark, Financial Aid Director
2433 Coolidge Avenue, Oakland, CA 94601-2699
(510) 261-8500 ext. 7747

Pepperdine University
Malibu, California
www.pepperdine.edu　　　　　Federal Code: 001264

4-year private university and liberal arts college in small city, affiliated with Church of Christ.
Enrollment: 3,169 undergrads, 14% part-time. 723 full-time freshmen.
Selectivity: Admits less than 50% of applicants.

BASIC COSTS (2006-2007)
Tuition and fees: $32,740.
Per-credit charge: $1,010.
Room and board: $9,500.

FINANCIAL AID PICTURE (2005-2006)
Students with need: Out of 499 full-time freshmen who applied for aid, 418 were judged to have need. Of these, 410 received aid, and 181 had their full need met. Average financial aid package met 90% of need; average scholarship/grant was $19,996; average loan was $6,114. For part-time students, average financial aid package was $10,142.
Students without need: 52 full-time freshmen who did not demonstrate need for aid received scholarships/grants; average award was $21,569. No-need awards available for academics, art, athletics, minority status, music/drama, religious affiliation.
Scholarships offered: 31 full-time freshmen received athletic scholarships; average amount $25,477.

FINANCIAL AID PROCEDURES
Forms required: FAFSA, institutional form.
Dates and Deadlines: Closing date 2/15. Applicants notified by 4/15; must reply within 2 week(s) of notification.

CONTACT
Cathy Marcus, Director of Financial Aid
24255 Pacific Coast Highway, Malibu, CA 90263-4392
(310) 506-4301

Pitzer College
Claremont, California
www.pitzer.edu
Federal Code: 001172
CSS Code: 4619

4-year private liberal arts college in large town.
Enrollment: 963 undergrads, 5% part-time. 239 full-time freshmen.
Selectivity: Admits less than 50% of applicants.

BASIC COSTS (2006-2007)
Tuition and fees: $34,038.
Room and board: $9,670.

FINANCIAL AID PICTURE (2005-2006)
Students with need: Out of 110 full-time freshmen who applied for aid, 94 were judged to have need. Of these, 94 received aid, and 94 had their full need met. Average financial aid package met 100% of need; average scholarship/grant was $24,317; average loan was $2,801. For part-time students, average financial aid package was $13,662.
Students without need: This college only awards aid to students with need.
Scholarships offered: Trustee Community Scholar Award: $10,000 per year; 20 awarded; based on extraordinary academic achievement, outstanding leadership or exceptional community service.
Cumulative student debt: 60% of graduating class had student loans; average debt was $20,900.

FINANCIAL AID PROCEDURES
Forms required: FAFSA, CSS PROFILE, state aid form.
Dates and Deadlines: Closing date 2/1. Applicants notified by 4/1; must reply by 5/1.
Transfers: Closing date 3/1. Applicants notified by 6/1.

CONTACT
Margaret Carothers, Director of Financial Aid
1050 North Mills Avenue, Claremont, CA 91711-6101
(909) 621-8208

Platt College: Cerritos
Cerritos, California
www.westerncollegesocal.com
Federal Code: 030399

2-year for-profit visual arts and business college in very large city.
Enrollment: 150 undergrads.
Selectivity: Admits over 75% of applicants.

BASIC COSTS (2006-2007)
Additional info: $18,000 for 18-month Paralegal program; $12,000 for Massage Therapy program. Tuition at time of enrollment locked for 2 years.

FINANCIAL AID PICTURE
Students with need: Need-based aid available for full-time students.
Students without need: This college only awards aid to students with need.

FINANCIAL AID PROCEDURES
Forms required: FAFSA, institutional form.

CONTACT
Deborah Rogers, Director of Financial Aid
10900 East 183rd Street, Suite 290, Cerritos, CA 90703-5342
(562) 809-5100

Platt College: Los Angeles
Alhambra, California
www.plattcollege.edu
Federal Code: 030627

2-year for-profit visual arts and technical college in very large city.
Enrollment: 125 undergrads.

BASIC COSTS (2006-2007)
Additional info: Varies by program: associate degree cost range $26,780 (paralegal) to $28,370 (information technology). Tuition at time of enrollment locked for 2 years.

FINANCIAL AID PICTURE
Students with need: Need-based aid available for full-time and part-time students. Work study available nights.

FINANCIAL AID PROCEDURES
Forms required: FAFSA, institutional form.
Dates and Deadlines: Priority date 3/2; no closing date. Applicants notified on a rolling basis starting 1/1.

CONTACT
Remie Pascual, Financial Aid Coordinator
1000 South Fremont Avenue A9W, Alhambra, CA 91803
(626) 300-5444

Platt College: Newport Beach
Huntington Beach, California
www.plattcollege.edu
Federal Code: 026203

2-year for-profit visual arts and technical college in large city.
Enrollment: 122 undergrads.

BASIC COSTS (2005-2006)
Additional info: Full academic program tuition ranges from $8,300 to $22,000. Tuition at time of enrollment locked for 2 years.

FINANCIAL AID PICTURE
Students with need: Need-based aid available for full-time and part-time students. Work study available nights.

FINANCIAL AID PROCEDURES
Forms required: FAFSA, institutional form.
Dates and Deadlines: Priority date 3/2; no closing date. Applicants notified on a rolling basis starting 1/1.

CONTACT
Colleen Atchison
7755 Center Avenue, Suite 400, Huntington Beach, CA 92647
(949) 833-2300

Platt College: Ontario
Ontario, California
www.plattcollege.edu
Federal Code: 030627

4-year for-profit branch campus and technical college in small city.
Enrollment: 400 undergrads.
Selectivity: Admits over 75% of applicants.

BASIC COSTS (2006-2007)
Additional info: Annual tuition varies by program: $10,300–$14,230. Tuition at time of enrollment locked for 4 years.

FINANCIAL AID PICTURE
Students with need: Need-based aid available for full-time and part-time students. Work study available nights.

Scholarships offered: Presidential Scholarship, CAPPS Scholarship, Imagine America Scholarship: $1,000 each; based on application and essay; approximately 100 plus available per calendar year.

FINANCIAL AID PROCEDURES
Forms required: FAFSA, institutional form.
Dates and Deadlines: Priority date 3/2; no closing date. Applicants notified on a rolling basis starting 1/1.
Transfers: No deadline.

CONTACT
Rosemarie Young, Regional Director of Compliance and Civil Rights
3700 Inland Empire Boulevard, Ontario, CA 91764
(909) 941-9410

Platt College: San Diego
San Diego, California
www.platt.edu   Federal Code: 023043

4-year for-profit visual arts and technical college in very large city.
Enrollment: 252 undergrads. 184 full-time freshmen.
Selectivity: Open admission; but selective for some programs and for out-of-state students.

BASIC COSTS (2006-2007)
Additional info: Total program cost ranges from $13,900 to $25,400 for diploma programs; associate's and bachelor's degree program costs vary. Tuition at time of enrollment locked for 4 years.

FINANCIAL AID PICTURE
Students with need: Need-based aid available for full-time and part-time students.

FINANCIAL AID PROCEDURES
Forms required: FAFSA, state aid form, institutional form.
Dates and Deadlines: Closing date 3/2. Applicants notified on a rolling basis; must reply within 1 week(s) of notification.

CONTACT
Opel Oliver, Director of Financial Aid
6250 El Cajon Boulevard, San Diego, CA 92115
(619) 265-0107

Point Loma Nazarene University
San Diego, California
www.ptloma.edu   Federal Code: 001262

4-year private university and liberal arts college in very large city, affiliated with Church of the Nazarene.
Enrollment: 2,360 undergrads, 3% part-time. 2,159 full-time freshmen.
Selectivity: Admits 50 to 75% of applicants.

BASIC COSTS (2006-2007)
Tuition and fees: $22,150.
Room and board: $7,160.

FINANCIAL AID PICTURE (2004-2005)
Students with need: Out of 1,992 full-time freshmen who applied for aid, 995 were judged to have need. Of these, 632 received aid, and 76 had their full need met. Average financial aid package met 28% of need; average scholarship/grant was $9,044; average loan was $3,502. For part-time students, average financial aid package was $7,983.
Students without need: 88 full-time freshmen who did not demonstrate need for aid received scholarships/grants; average award was $10,264. No-need awards available for academics, alumni affiliation, art, athletics, leadership, music/drama, religious affiliation, state/district residency.
Cumulative student debt: 79% of graduating class had student loans; average debt was $18,415.

FINANCIAL AID PROCEDURES
Forms required: FAFSA, institutional form.
Dates and Deadlines: Priority date 3/2; no closing date. Applicants notified on a rolling basis starting 3/1; must reply within 4 week(s) of notification.
Transfers: No deadline. Must reply within 4 week(s) of notification.

CONTACT
Matt Wickstrom, Director of Student Financial Services
3900 Lomaland Drive, San Diego, CA 92106-2899
(619) 849-2200

Pomona College
Claremont, California
www.pomona.edu   Federal Code: 001173
    CSS Code: 4607

4-year private liberal arts college in large town.
Enrollment: 1,529 undergrads. 394 full-time freshmen.
Selectivity: Admits less than 50% of applicants.

BASIC COSTS (2006-2007)
Tuition and fees: $31,865.
Room and board: $11,291.

FINANCIAL AID PICTURE (2004-2005)
Students with need: Out of 263 full-time freshmen who applied for aid, 224 were judged to have need. Of these, 224 received aid, and 224 had their full need met. Average financial aid package met 100% of need; average scholarship/grant was $24,400; average loan was $2,500. Need-based aid available for part-time students.
Students without need: This college only awards aid to students with need.
Cumulative student debt: 55% of graduating class had student loans; average debt was $15,000.

FINANCIAL AID PROCEDURES
Forms required: FAFSA, CSS PROFILE, state aid form.
Dates and Deadlines: Closing date 2/1. Applicants notified by 4/10; must reply by 5/1.
Transfers: Closing date 3/1. Candidates required to submit finanical aid transcript from previous institution directly to the college.

CONTACT
Patricia Coye, Director of Financial Aid
333 North College Way, Claremont, CA 91711-6312
(909) 621-8205

Reedley College
Reedley, California
www.reedleycollege.edu   Federal Code: 001308

2-year public community college in large town.
Enrollment: 4,812 undergrads, 61% part-time. 623 full-time freshmen.
Selectivity: Open admission.

BASIC COSTS (2005-2006)
Tuition and fees: $808; out-of-state residents $5,338.
Per-credit charge: $26; out-of-state residents $177.
Room and board: $4,520.
Additional info: Tuition/fee waivers available for adults, minority students, unemployed or children of unemployed.

FINANCIAL AID PICTURE
Students with need: Need-based aid available for full-time and part-time students.

Students without need: This college only awards aid to students with need.
Additional info: Board of Governors fee waiver available for low-income students. Book voucher available for EOPS students.

FINANCIAL AID PROCEDURES
Forms required: FAFSA, state aid form.
Dates and Deadlines: Priority date 3/2; no closing date. Applicants notified on a rolling basis starting 3/2; must reply within 3 week(s) of notification.
Transfers: Priority date 4/15. March 2 deadline for California grants.

CONTACT
Christina Cortes, Director, Financial Aid
995 North Reed Avenue, Reedley, CA 93654
(559) 638-3641

Riverside Community College
Riverside, California
www.rcc.edu   Federal Code: 001270

2-year public community college in large city.
Enrollment: 32,228 undergrads.
Selectivity: Open admission; but selective for some programs.

BASIC COSTS (2005-2006)
Tuition and fees: $820; out-of-state residents $5,350.
Per-credit charge: $26; out-of-state residents $177.
Additional info: Tuition/fee waivers available for adults, unemployed or children of unemployed.

FINANCIAL AID PICTURE (2004-2005)
Students with need: 88% of average financial aid package awarded as scholarships/grants, 12% awarded as loans/jobs. Need-based aid available for part-time students. Work study available nights, weekends, and for part-time students.
Students without need: No-need awards available for academics, alumni affiliation, art, leadership, minority status, music/drama, state/district residency.

FINANCIAL AID PROCEDURES
Forms required: FAFSA, institutional form.
Dates and Deadlines: Priority date 3/2; no closing date. Applicants notified on a rolling basis starting 7/1.
Transfers: Students who received financial aid at another institution and earned less than 2.0 GPA ineligible for aid during first semester. Students must complete 6 units and earn 2.0 GPA to be eligible.

CONTACT
Eugenia Vincent, District Dean of Student Financial Services
4800 Magnolia Avenue, Riverside, CA 92506
(951) 222-8709

Sacramento City College
Sacramento, California
www.scc.losrios.edu   Federal Code: 001233

2-year public community college in large city.
Enrollment: 13,710 undergrads.
Selectivity: Open admission.

BASIC COSTS (2005-2006)
Tuition and fees: $812; out-of-state residents $5,342.
Per-credit charge: $26; out-of-state residents $177.

FINANCIAL AID PICTURE
Students with need: Need-based aid available for full-time and part-time students. Work study available nights, weekends, and for part-time students.

FINANCIAL AID PROCEDURES
Forms required: FAFSA, state aid form.
Dates and Deadlines: Priority date 3/2; no closing date. Applicants notified on a rolling basis starting 7/1; must reply within 2 week(s) of notification.
Transfers: Priority date 5/30.

CONTACT
Pat Maga, Financial Aid Supervisor
3835 Freeport Boulevard, Sacramento, CA 95822
(916) 558-2546

Saddleback College
Mission Viejo, California
www.saddleback.edu   Federal Code: 008918

2-year public community college in small city.
Enrollment: 9,879 undergrads.
Selectivity: Open admission; but selective for some programs.

BASIC COSTS (2005-2006)
Tuition and fees: $806; out-of-state residents $5,336.
Per-credit charge: $26; out-of-state residents $177.

FINANCIAL AID PICTURE
Students with need: Need-based aid available for full-time and part-time students.
Students without need: This college only awards aid to students with need.

FINANCIAL AID PROCEDURES
Forms required: FAFSA.
Dates and Deadlines: Closing date 5/1. Applicants notified on a rolling basis; must reply within 2 week(s) of notification.

CONTACT
Mary Hall, Director, Financial Aid
28000 Marguerite Parkway, Mission Viejo, CA 92692
(949) 582-4860

St. Mary's College of California
Moraga, California
www.stmarys-ca.edu   Federal Code: 001302

4-year private liberal arts college in large town, affiliated with Roman Catholic Church.
Enrollment: 3,291 undergrads, 24% part-time. 664 full-time freshmen.
Selectivity: Admits over 75% of applicants.

BASIC COSTS (2006-2007)
Tuition and fees: $29,050.
Room and board: $10,566.

FINANCIAL AID PICTURE (2005-2006)
Students with need: Out of 513 full-time freshmen who applied for aid, 428 were judged to have need. Of these, 428 received aid, and 35 had their full need met. Average financial aid package met 71% of need; average scholarship/grant was $16,812; average loan was $2,986. For part-time students, average financial aid package was $6,948.
Students without need: 22 full-time freshmen who did not demonstrate need for aid received scholarships/grants; average award was $8,591. No-need awards available for academics, alumni affiliation, athletics.
Scholarships offered: *Merit:* Honors at Entrance Scholarship Awards awarded automatically for freshmen with a 3.7 GPA or higher and a combined SAT score of at least 1200, or transfers with over 30 semester units or the equivalent and a 3.5 GPA; for fall term applicants must be admitted by March 1; $6,000 annually. Presidential Scholars Scholarship for freshmen

with a 3.8 GPA or higher and a combined SAT score of at least 1350 (exclusive of writing). **Athletic:** 58 full-time freshmen received athletic scholarships; average amount $16,409.
Cumulative student debt: 62% of graduating class had student loans; average debt was $21,892.

FINANCIAL AID PROCEDURES
Forms required: FAFSA.
Dates and Deadlines: Closing date 3/2. Applicants notified on a rolling basis starting 3/30; must reply by 5/1 or within 2 week(s) of notification.
Transfers: To receive consideration for all types of financial aid, transfer students must be admitted by March 1 prior to enrolling in the following fall term.

CONTACT
Linda Judge, Director of Financial Aid
Box 4800, Moraga, CA 94575-4800
(925) 631-4370

Samuel Merritt College
Oakland, California
www.samuelmerritt.edu   Federal Code: 007012

Upper-division private health science and nursing college in large city.
Enrollment: 353 undergrads, 14% part-time.
Selectivity: GED not accepted.

BASIC COSTS (2006-2007)
Tuition and fees: $29,590.
Per-credit charge: $1,214.
Room only: $4,427.

FINANCIAL AID PICTURE (2005-2006)
Students with need: Average financial aid package for all full-time undergraduates was $29,750; for part-time $25,752. 56% awarded as scholarships/grants, 44% awarded as loans/jobs. Work study available nights, weekends, and for part-time students.
Students without need: No-need awards available for academics.
Cumulative student debt: 98% of graduating class had student loans; average debt was $34,135.
Additional info: Ongoing private scholarships available. Students eligible to work in Medical Center (associated with college).

FINANCIAL AID PROCEDURES
Dates and Deadlines: No deadline.
Transfers: Priority date 3/1; no deadline. Applicants notified on a rolling basis; must reply within 3 week(s) of notification.

CONTACT
Mary Robinson, Director of Financial Aid
370 Hawthorne Avenue, Oakland, CA 94609-9954
(510) 869-6511

San Diego Christian College
El Cajon, California
www.sdcc.edu   Federal Code: 012031

4-year private liberal arts college in small city, affiliated with nondenominational tradition.
Enrollment: 550 undergrads.
Selectivity: Admits 50 to 75% of applicants.

BASIC COSTS (2006-2007)
Tuition and fees: $16,992.
Per-credit charge: $570.
Room and board: $7,180.

FINANCIAL AID PICTURE
Students with need: Need-based aid available for full-time and part-time students.
Students without need: No-need awards available for academics, athletics, leadership, music/drama, religious affiliation.

FINANCIAL AID PROCEDURES
Forms required: FAFSA.
Dates and Deadlines: Priority date 3/2; closing date 7/15. Applicants notified on a rolling basis starting 4/1; must reply by 5/1 or within 4 week(s) of notification.

CONTACT
Nancy Demars, Financial Aid Director
2100 Greenfield Drive, El Cajon, CA 92019-1157
(619) 590-1786

San Diego City College
San Diego, California
www.sdccd.edu   Federal Code: 001273

2-year public community college in very large city.
Enrollment: 7,822 undergrads.
Selectivity: Open admission.

BASIC COSTS (2005-2006)
Tuition and fees: $806; out-of-state residents $5,606.
Per-credit charge: $26; out-of-state residents $186.
Additional info: Tuition/fee waivers available for unemployed or children of unemployed.

FINANCIAL AID PICTURE (2004-2005)
Students with need: 81% of average financial aid package awarded as scholarships/grants, 19% awarded as loans/jobs. Need-based aid available for part-time students.
Students without need: This college only awards aid to students with need.

FINANCIAL AID PROCEDURES
Forms required: FAFSA.
Dates and Deadlines: Priority date 4/1; no closing date. Applicants notified on a rolling basis starting 7/1; must reply within 4 week(s) of notification.
Transfers: No deadline. Aid is limited to remaining eligibility based on receipt of aid from previous college.

CONTACT
Greg Sanchez, Financial Aid Manager
1313 Park Boulevard, San Diego, CA 92101-4787
(619) 388-3501

San Diego Miramar College
San Diego, California
www.miramarcollege.net   Federal Code: 014172

2-year public community college in very large city.
Enrollment: 1,404 full-time undergrads.
Selectivity: Open admission.

BASIC COSTS (2005-2006)
Tuition and fees: $806; out-of-state residents $5,606.
Per-credit charge: $26; out-of-state residents $186.
Additional info: Tuition/fee waivers available for unemployed or children of unemployed.

FINANCIAL AID PICTURE
Students with need: Need-based aid available for full-time and part-time students.

Additional info: Private scholarships available.

FINANCIAL AID PROCEDURES
Forms required: FAFSA.
Dates and Deadlines: Priority date 3/2; no closing date. Applicants notified on a rolling basis; must reply within 3 week(s) of notification.
Transfers: No deadline. Transfers advised to apply early.

CONTACT
Ruthy Ofina, Financial Aid Officer
10440 Black Mountain Road, San Diego, CA 92126-2999
(619) 388-7865

San Diego State University
San Diego, California
www.sdsu.edu   Federal Code: 001151

4-year public university in very large city.
Enrollment: 26,690 undergrads, 18% part-time. 3,439 full-time freshmen.
Selectivity: Admits less than 50% of applicants.

BASIC COSTS (2005-2006)
Tuition and fees: $3,122; out-of-state residents $13,292.
Room and board: $9,849.

FINANCIAL AID PICTURE (2005-2006)
Students with need: Average financial aid package met 66% of need; average scholarship/grant was $5,600; average loan was $2,300. For part-time students, average financial aid package was $7,000.
Students without need: 50 full-time freshmen who did not demonstrate need for aid received scholarships/grants; average award was $2,500. No-need awards available for academics, alumni affiliation, art, athletics, leadership, music/drama, ROTC, state/district residency.
Scholarships offered: *Merit:* First Time Freshman Awards; $1,250 per semester for 4 years; based on 3.5 overall GPA; 8-10 awarded. Grant Trust Scholarship Award; includes costs of campus housing, fees, and books; based on incoming freshman status, intended biology major with 3.5 overall GPA; 2 awarded. Field Family Scholarship; includes costs of campus housing, fees and books for up to 5 years; based on maintenance of satisfactory student performance; 2 awarded every 2 years. Conrad Klement Memorial Scholarship; $2,500 - $10,000 per year; must be a permanent resident of San Diego County, parents and students must be US citizens at birth, 3.0 GPA; 2-6 awarded. *Athletic:* 70 full-time freshmen received athletic scholarships; average amount $9,900.
Cumulative student debt: 49% of graduating class had student loans; average debt was $14,500.

FINANCIAL AID PROCEDURES
Forms required: FAFSA, state aid form.
Dates and Deadlines: Priority date 3/2; no closing date. Applicants notified on a rolling basis starting 2/14.

CONTACT
Chrys Dutton, Director of Financial Aid
5500 Campanile Drive, San Diego, CA 92182-7455
(619) 594-6323

San Francisco Art Institute
San Francisco, California
www.sfai.edu   Federal Code: 003948

4-year private visual arts college in very large city.
Enrollment: 354 undergrads.

BASIC COSTS (2005-2006)
Tuition and fees: $25,670.
Per-credit charge: $1,100.
Additional info: Room charge $6,540 for 12-month contract.

FINANCIAL AID PICTURE
Students with need: Need-based aid available for full-time and part-time students.
Students without need: No-need awards available for art.
Scholarships offered: Several awards based on portfolio reviews during application for admissions process.

FINANCIAL AID PROCEDURES
Forms required: FAFSA.
Dates and Deadlines: Priority date 3/1; closing date 9/1. Applicants notified on a rolling basis starting 4/15; must reply within 3 week(s) of notification.
Transfers: Priority date 4/1; no deadline.

CONTACT
Annita Alldredge, Director of Financial Aid
800 Chestnut Street, San Francisco, CA 94133-2299
(415) 749-4520

San Francisco Conservatory of Music
San Francisco, California
www.sfcm.edu   Federal Code: 001278

4-year private music college in very large city.
Enrollment: 173 undergrads.
Selectivity: Admits less than 50% of applicants.

BASIC COSTS (2006-2007)
Tuition and fees: $28,280.
Per-credit charge: $1,240.

FINANCIAL AID PICTURE
Students with need: Need-based aid available for full-time and part-time students.
Students without need: This college only awards aid to students with need.

FINANCIAL AID PROCEDURES
Forms required: FAFSA, institutional form.
Dates and Deadlines: Priority date 3/1; no closing date. Applicants notified on a rolling basis starting 3/15; must reply by 5/1 or within 2 week(s) of notification.
Transfers: Priority date 2/1; closing date 4/1.

CONTACT
Doris Howard, Financial Aid Officer
1201 Ortega Street, San Francisco, CA 94122-4498
(415) 759-3414

San Francisco State University
San Francisco, California
www.sfsu.edu   Federal Code: 001154

4-year public university in very large city.
Enrollment: 23,074 undergrads, 22% part-time. 2,999 full-time freshmen.
Selectivity: Admits 50 to 75% of applicants.

BASIC COSTS (2005-2006)
Tuition and fees: $3,128; out-of-state residents $13,298.
Room and board: $10,458.

FINANCIAL AID PICTURE (2005-2006)
Students with need: Out of 2,582 full-time freshmen who applied for aid, 2,004 were judged to have need. Of these, 1,853 received aid, and 154 had their full need met. Average financial aid package met 62% of need; average scholarship/grant was $6,341; average loan was $1,715. For part-time students, average financial aid package was $7,466.
Students without need: This college only awards aid to students with need.
Scholarships offered: *Merit:* Presidential Scholarship; 3.8 GPA and California residency required. *Athletic:* 27 full-time freshmen received athletic scholarships; average amount $1,643.
Cumulative student debt: 46% of graduating class had student loans; average debt was $15,376.

FINANCIAL AID PROCEDURES
Forms required: FAFSA.
Dates and Deadlines: Priority date 3/1; no closing date. Applicants notified on a rolling basis starting 1/15; must reply within 2 week(s) of notification.

CONTACT
Barbara Hubler, Director of Financial Aid
1600 Holloway Avenue, San Francisco, CA 94132
(415) 338-1111

San Joaquin Delta College
Stockton, California
www.deltacollege.edu   Federal Code: 001280

2-year public community college in large city.
Enrollment: 6,839 full-time undergrads. 4,336 full-time freshmen.
Selectivity: Open admission; but selective for some programs.

BASIC COSTS (2005-2006)
Tuition and fees: $780; out-of-state residents $5,310.
Per-credit charge: $26; out-of-state residents $177.

FINANCIAL AID PICTURE (2004-2005)
Students with need: Out of 4,328 full-time freshmen who applied for aid, 3,182 were judged to have need. Of these, 2,693 received aid, and 11 had their full need met. Average financial aid package met 32% of need; average scholarship/grant was $3,453; average loan was $1,389. For part-time students, average financial aid package was $3,957.
Students without need: 2 full-time freshmen who did not demonstrate need for aid received scholarships/grants; average award was $1,812. No-need awards available for academics, athletics.
Cumulative student debt: 91% of graduating class had student loans; average debt was $5,472.
Additional info: Enrollment fee waivers available for low-income California residents.

FINANCIAL AID PROCEDURES
Forms required: FAFSA, institutional form.
Dates and Deadlines: Priority date 4/15; no closing date. Applicants notified on a rolling basis starting 5/1; must reply within 3 week(s) of notification.
Transfers: No deadline.

CONTACT
Ena Hull, Director of Financial Aid
5151 Pacific Avenue, Stockton, CA 95207-6370
(209) 954-5115

San Joaquin Valley College Inc.
Visalia, California
www.sjvc.edu   Federal Code: 021207

2-year for-profit junior college in small city.
Enrollment: 875 undergrads.
Selectivity: Open admission; but selective for some programs.

BASIC COSTS (2005-2006)
Tuition and fees: $10,753.
Per-credit charge: $348.
Additional info: Costs may vary with program, annual tuition includes textbooks and supplies.

FINANCIAL AID PICTURE
Students with need: Need-based aid available for full-time students.

FINANCIAL AID PROCEDURES
Forms required: FAFSA, state aid form, institutional form.
Dates and Deadlines: No deadline.

CONTACT
Kevin Robinson, Vice President of Student Financial Services
8400 West Mineral King Avenue, Visalia, CA 93291-9283
(559) 651-2500

San Jose State University
San Jose, California
www.sjsu.edu   Federal Code: 001155

4-year public university and liberal arts college in very large city.
Enrollment: 22,733 undergrads, 25% part-time. 2,436 full-time freshmen.
Selectivity: Admits 50 to 75% of applicants.

BASIC COSTS (2005-2006)
Tuition and fees: $3,292; out-of-state residents $13,462.
Room and board: $8,718.

FINANCIAL AID PICTURE
Students with need: Need-based aid available for full-time and part-time students. Work study available nights, weekends, and for part-time students.
Students without need: This college only awards aid to students with need.

FINANCIAL AID PROCEDURES
Forms required: FAFSA.
Dates and Deadlines: Priority date 3/2; no closing date. Applicants notified on a rolling basis starting 4/30; must reply within 2 week(s) of notification.

CONTACT
Colleen Brown, Director of Financial Aid
One Washington Square, San Jose, CA 95192-0011
(408) 283-7500

Santa Barbara City College
Santa Barbara, California
www.sbcc.edu   Federal Code: 001285

2-year public community college in small city.
Enrollment: 7,655 undergrads, 44% part-time. 1,311 full-time freshmen.
Selectivity: Open admission; but selective for some programs.

BASIC COSTS (2005-2006)
Tuition and fees: $831; out-of-state residents $5,361.
Per-credit charge: $26; out-of-state residents $177.

Additional info: Tuition/fee waivers available for unemployed or children of unemployed.

FINANCIAL AID PICTURE
Students with need: Need-based aid available for full-time and part-time students.
Additional info: California residents may qualify for Board of Governor's Financial Assistance Program, which will allow institutions to waive enrollment fee.

FINANCIAL AID PROCEDURES
Forms required: FAFSA.
Dates and Deadlines: No deadline. Applicants notified on a rolling basis starting 5/1; must reply within 2 week(s) of notification.

CONTACT
Brad Hardison, Director, Financial Aid
721 Cliff Drive, Santa Barbara, CA 93109-2394
(805) 965-0581 ext. 2716

Santa Clara University
Santa Clara, California   Federal Code: 001326
www.scu.edu   CSS Code: 4851

4-year private university in small city, affiliated with Roman Catholic Church.
Enrollment: 4,552 undergrads, 2% part-time. 1,197 full-time freshmen.
Selectivity: Admits 50 to 75% of applicants. GED not accepted.

BASIC COSTS (2006-2007)
Tuition and fees: $30,900.
Per-credit charge: $1,030.
Room and board: $10,380.

FINANCIAL AID PICTURE (2005-2006)
Students with need: Out of 735 full-time freshmen who applied for aid, 457 were judged to have need. Of these, 447 received aid, and 298 had their full need met. Average financial aid package met 71% of need; average scholarship/grant was $14,253; average loan was $3,622. Need-based aid available for part-time students.
Students without need: 248 full-time freshmen who did not demonstrate need for aid received scholarships/grants; average award was $10,595. No-need awards available for academics, alumni affiliation, athletics, music/drama, ROTC.
Scholarships offered: Merit: Dean's Scholarship: $5,000; to students admitted with distinction. Ignation Scholarship: $7,500; to 1 student from each of the 5 western province Jesuit high schools. Bannan Merit Scholarship: $1,000; based on high academic achievement. Jesuit Scholars Award: $1,000 to $5,000, based on being in top 50 outstanding Jesuit High School graduates. **Athletic:** 43 full-time freshmen received athletic scholarships; average amount $19,722.
Cumulative student debt: 50% of graduating class had student loans; average debt was $17,620.

FINANCIAL AID PROCEDURES
Forms required: FAFSA, CSS PROFILE.
Dates and Deadlines: Priority date 2/1; no closing date. Applicants notified on a rolling basis starting 4/1; must reply by 5/1 or within 2 week(s) of notification.
Transfers: No deadline. Applicants notified on a rolling basis starting 4/1; must reply by 5/1 or within 2 week(s) of notification.

CONTACT
Chas Mercurio, Director, Financial Aid
500 El Camino Real, Santa Clara, CA 95053
(408) 554-4505

Santa Monica College
Santa Monica, California
www.smc.edu   Federal Code: 001286

2-year public community college in small city.
Enrollment: 16,751 undergrads.
Selectivity: Open admission; but selective for some programs.

BASIC COSTS (2005-2006)
Tuition and fees: $804; out-of-state residents $5,454.
Per-credit charge: $26; out-of-state residents $181.
Additional info: Students may also pay annual $16 identity card fee, $20 associated student fee.

FINANCIAL AID PICTURE (2004-2005)
Students with need: 93% of average financial aid package awarded as scholarships/grants, 7% awarded as loans/jobs. Need-based aid available for part-time students.

FINANCIAL AID PROCEDURES
Forms required: FAFSA, institutional form.
Dates and Deadlines: No deadline. Applicants notified on a rolling basis starting 7/1; must reply within 2 week(s) of notification.
Transfers: No deadline.

CONTACT
Steve Myrow, Director of Financial Aid
1900 Pico Boulevard, Santa Monica, CA 90405-1628
(310) 434-4871

Santa Rosa Junior College
Santa Rosa, California
www.santarosa.edu   Federal Code: 001287

2-year public community college in small city.
Enrollment: 16,510 undergrads.
Selectivity: Open admission.

BASIC COSTS (2005-2006)
Tuition and fees: $808; out-of-state residents $6,118.
Per-credit charge: $26; out-of-state residents $203.

FINANCIAL AID PICTURE
Students with need: Need-based aid available for full-time and part-time students. Work study available nights, weekends, and for part-time students.
Students without need: No-need awards available for academics, art, music/drama.
Additional info: California's Board of Governors Program (BOG) provides fee waivers for applicants with need, welfare recipients, and families with low income.

FINANCIAL AID PROCEDURES
Forms required: FAFSA.
Dates and Deadlines: Priority date 3/1; no closing date. Applicants notified on a rolling basis starting 3/28; must reply within 4 week(s) of notification.

CONTACT
Kristin Shear, Director of Financial Aid
1501 Mendocino Avenue, Santa Rosa, CA 95401
(707) 527-4478

Santiago Canyon College
Orange, California
www.sccollege.edu

2-year public community college in large city.
Enrollment: 5,269 undergrads, 51% part-time. 681 full-time freshmen.
Selectivity: Open admission.

BASIC COSTS (2005-2006)
Tuition and fees: $808; out-of-state residents $5,338.
Per-credit charge: $26; out-of-state residents $177.

FINANCIAL AID PICTURE (2004-2005)
Students with need: 80% of average financial aid package awarded as scholarships/grants, 20% awarded as loans/jobs.

CONTACT
Syed Rizvi, Financial Aid Coordinator
8045 East Chapman Avenue, Orange, CA 92869
(714) 628-4876

Scripps College
Claremont, California
www.scrippscollege.edu
Federal Code: 001174
CSS Code: 4693

4-year private liberal arts college for women in large town.
Enrollment: 879 undergrads, 1% part-time. 234 full-time freshmen.
Selectivity: Admits less than 50% of applicants.

BASIC COSTS (2006-2007)
Tuition and fees: $33,700.
Room and board: $10,100.

FINANCIAL AID PICTURE (2005-2006)
Students with need: Out of 142 full-time freshmen who applied for aid, 100 were judged to have need. Of these, 100 received aid, and 100 had their full need met. Average financial aid package met 100% of need; average scholarship/grant was $22,305; average loan was $2,573. For part-time students, average financial aid package was $1,916.
Students without need: 21 full-time freshmen who did not demonstrate need for aid received scholarships/grants; average award was $13,626. No-need awards available for academics, leadership.
Scholarships offered: James E. Scripps Scholarship: variable amount, most recently up to half-tuition, renewable; for distinguished young women whose intellectual and personal promise can be developed with a Scripps education; 40 most recent awards; financial aid available to recipients exhibiting further need.
Cumulative student debt: 49% of graduating class had student loans; average debt was $12,907.

FINANCIAL AID PROCEDURES
Forms required: FAFSA, CSS PROFILE.
Dates and Deadlines: Priority date 2/1; no closing date. Applicants notified by 4/1; must reply by 5/1 or within 2 week(s) of notification.
Transfers: Priority date 4/1; no deadline. Applicants notified by 5/1; must reply by 6/1 or within 2 week(s) of notification. Students applying for admission as a transfer student should be aware that financial aid may be limited or unavailable.

CONTACT
Sean Smith, Director of Financial Aid
1030 North Columbia Avenue, Claremont, CA 91711
(909) 621-8275

Shasta College
Redding, California
www.shastacollege.edu
Federal Code: 001289

2-year public community college in small city.
Enrollment: 3,540 undergrads.
Selectivity: Open admission; but selective for some programs.

BASIC COSTS (2005-2006)
Tuition and fees: $847; out-of-state residents $5,977.
Per-credit charge: $26; out-of-state residents $197.
Room only: $2,525.

FINANCIAL AID PICTURE
Students with need: Need-based aid available for full-time and part-time students.
Students without need: This college only awards aid to students with need.

FINANCIAL AID PROCEDURES
Forms required: FAFSA, institutional form.
Dates and Deadlines: Priority date 3/2; no closing date. Applicants notified on a rolling basis starting 7/1.

CONTACT
Benna Starrett, Financial Aid Office Manager
Box 496006, Redding, CA 96049-6006
(530) 225-4735

Sierra College
Rocklin, California
www.sierracollege.edu
Federal Code: 001290

2-year public community college in large town.
Enrollment: 9,934 undergrads.
Selectivity: Open admission.

BASIC COSTS (2005-2006)
Tuition and fees: $816; out-of-state residents $5,346.
Per-credit charge: $26; out-of-state residents $177.
Room and board: $6,890.
Additional info: Tuition/fee waivers available for unemployed or children of unemployed.

FINANCIAL AID PICTURE (2004-2005)
Students with need: 76% of average financial aid package awarded as scholarships/grants, 24% awarded as loans/jobs. Need-based aid available for part-time students. Work study available nights, weekends, and for part-time students.

FINANCIAL AID PROCEDURES
Forms required: FAFSA.
Dates and Deadlines: Priority date 3/1; closing date 4/22. Applicants notified on a rolling basis starting 4/15.
Transfers: No deadline.

CONTACT
Craig Yamamoto, Financial Services Program Manager
5000 Rocklin Road, Rocklin, CA 95677
(916) 781-0568

Simpson University
Redding, California
www.simpsonuniversity.edu Federal Code: 001291

4-year private liberal arts college in small city, affiliated with Christian and Missionary Alliance.
Enrollment: 922 undergrads, 2% part-time. 193 full-time freshmen.
Selectivity: Admits 50 to 75% of applicants.

BASIC COSTS (2006-2007)
Tuition and fees: $17,800.
Per-credit charge: $750.
Room and board: $6,200.
Additional info: Tuition/fee waivers available for minority students.

FINANCIAL AID PICTURE (2004-2005)
Students with need: Out of 187 full-time freshmen who applied for aid, 165 were judged to have need. Of these, 165 received aid, and 11 had their full need met. Average financial aid package met 71% of need; average scholarship/grant was $4,600; average loan was $2,625. Need-based aid available for part-time students.
Students without need: 20 full-time freshmen who did not demonstrate need for aid received scholarships/grants; average award was $5,400. No-need awards available for academics, alumni affiliation, leadership, minority status, music/drama, religious affiliation, state/district residency.
Scholarships offered: Academic awards: up to $5,000 for 4.0 GPA and 1200 minimum SAT (exclusive of writing).
Cumulative student debt: 88% of graduating class had student loans; average debt was $17,600.
Additional info: Work-study programs available.

FINANCIAL AID PROCEDURES
Forms required: FAFSA, institutional form.
Dates and Deadlines: Priority date 3/2; no closing date. Applicants notified on a rolling basis starting 3/16; must reply within 3 week(s) of notification.
Transfers: No deadline. Must reply within 3 week(s) of notification.

CONTACT
James Herberger, Director of Student Financial Services
2211 College View Drive, Redding, CA 96003-8606
(530) 226-4606

Skyline College
San Bruno, California
skylinecollege.net Federal Code: 007713

2-year public community college in small city.
Enrollment: 5,290 undergrads.
Selectivity: Open admission; but selective for some programs.

BASIC COSTS (2005-2006)
Tuition and fees: $806; out-of-state residents $5,876.
Per-credit charge: $26; out-of-state residents $195.

FINANCIAL AID PICTURE
Students with need: Need-based aid available for full-time and part-time students.

FINANCIAL AID PROCEDURES
Forms required: FAFSA, institutional form.
Dates and Deadlines: Priority date 3/2; no closing date. Applicants notified on a rolling basis starting 5/1; must reply within 2 week(s) of notification.

CONTACT
Maria Escobar, Director of Financial Aid
3300 College Drive, San Bruno, CA 94066
(650) 738-4236

Sonoma State University
Rohnert Park, California
www.sonoma.edu Federal Code: 001156

4-year public university and liberal arts college in large town.
Enrollment: 6,481 undergrads, 13% part-time. 1,173 full-time freshmen.
Selectivity: Admits 50 to 75% of applicants.

BASIC COSTS (2005-2006)
Tuition and fees: $3,624; out-of-state residents $13,794.
Room and board: $8,820.

FINANCIAL AID PICTURE (2004-2005)
Students with need: Out of 671 full-time freshmen who applied for aid, 369 were judged to have need. Of these, 249 received aid, and 199 had their full need met. Average financial aid package met 80% of need; average scholarship/grant was $6,329; average loan was $2,574. For part-time students, average financial aid package was $6,240.
Students without need: 36 full-time freshmen who did not demonstrate need for aid received scholarships/grants; average award was $2,371. No-need awards available for academics, alumni affiliation, art, athletics, leadership, minority status, music/drama, state/district residency.
Scholarships offered: 5 full-time freshmen received athletic scholarships; average amount $950.
Cumulative student debt: 71% of graduating class had student loans; average debt was $5,030.

FINANCIAL AID PROCEDURES
Forms required: FAFSA.
Dates and Deadlines: Priority date 1/31; no closing date. Applicants notified on a rolling basis starting 3/15; must reply within 4 week(s) of notification.

CONTACT
Susan Gutierrez, Director, Financial Aid
1801 East Cotati Avenue, Rohnert Park, CA 94928
(707) 664-2389

Southwestern College
Chula Vista, California
www.swc.cc.ca.us Federal Code: 001294

2-year public community college in small city.
Enrollment: 10,226 undergrads, 60% part-time.
Selectivity: Open admission; but selective for some programs.

BASIC COSTS (2005-2006)
Tuition and fees: $816; out-of-state residents $5,346.
Per-credit charge: $26; out-of-state residents $177.

FINANCIAL AID PICTURE
Students with need: Need-based aid available for full-time and part-time students. Work study available nights, weekends, and for part-time students.

FINANCIAL AID PROCEDURES
Forms required: FAFSA, state aid form.
Dates and Deadlines: Closing date 3/2. Applicants notified on a rolling basis starting 7/1.

CONTACT
Arthur Lopez, Director of Financial Aid
900 Otay Lakes Road, Chula Vista, CA 91910-7297
(619) 482-6357

Stanford University
Stanford, California
www.stanford.edu
Federal Code: 001305
CSS Code: 4704

4-year private university in small city.
Enrollment: 6,491 undergrads. 1,633 full-time freshmen.
Selectivity: Admits less than 50% of applicants.

BASIC COSTS (2006-2007)
Tuition and fees: $32,994.
Room and board: $10,367.

FINANCIAL AID PICTURE (2004-2005)
Students with need: Out of 958 full-time freshmen who applied for aid, 690 were judged to have need. Of these, 683 received aid, and 608 had their full need met. Average financial aid package met 100% of need; average scholarship/grant was $24,631; average loan was $2,569. Need-based aid available for part-time students.
Students without need: This college only awards aid to students with need.
Scholarships offered: 81 full-time freshmen received athletic scholarships; average amount $30,144.
Cumulative student debt: 45% of graduating class had student loans; average debt was $15,172.

FINANCIAL AID PROCEDURES
Forms required: FAFSA, CSS PROFILE.
Dates and Deadlines: Priority date 2/1; no closing date. Applicants notified on a rolling basis starting 4/3; must reply by 5/1.
Transfers: Closing date 3/15.

CONTACT
Karen Cooper, Director, Financial Aid
Bakewell Building, Stanford, CA 94305-3020
(650) 723-3058

Taft College
Taft, California
www.taft.cc.ca.us
Federal Code: 001309

2-year public community college in small town.
Enrollment: 803 full-time undergrads.
Selectivity: Open admission.

BASIC COSTS (2005-2006)
Tuition and fees: $780; out-of-state residents $5,310.
Per-credit charge: $26; out-of-state residents $177.
Room and board: $3,148.

FINANCIAL AID PICTURE (2004-2005)
Students with need: 81% of average financial aid package awarded as scholarships/grants, 19% awarded as loans/jobs. Need-based aid available for part-time students. Work study available nights.
Students without need: No-need awards available for academics.
Scholarships offered: Taft College Merit Awards; $250; available for 2 years; based on GPA of 3.0 or higher; for students from local high schools. Taft College High School Merit Award; $600; for students from local high schools. Taft College Nonresident Awards; $4,230; available for 1 year; based on GPA of 3.0 or higher and is applied to nonresident tuition.

FINANCIAL AID PROCEDURES
Forms required: FAFSA, institutional form.
Dates and Deadlines: No deadline. Applicants notified on a rolling basis; must reply within 4 week(s) of notification.
Transfers: No deadline.

CONTACT
Gayle Roberts, Director of Financial Aid and Admissions
29 Emmons Park Drive, Taft, CA 93268
(661) 763-7762

Thomas Aquinas College
Santa Paula, California
www.thomasaquinas.edu
Federal Code: 023580

4-year private liberal arts college in large town, affiliated with Roman Catholic Church.
Enrollment: 359 undergrads. 102 full-time freshmen.
Selectivity: Admits over 75% of applicants.

BASIC COSTS (2006-2007)
Tuition and fees: $19,300.
Room and board: $6,000.

FINANCIAL AID PICTURE (2005-2006)
Students with need: Out of 81 full-time freshmen who applied for aid, 77 were judged to have need. Of these, 77 received aid, and 77 had their full need met. Average financial aid package met 100% of need; average scholarship/grant was $11,949; average loan was $2,519.
Students without need: This college only awards aid to students with need.
Cumulative student debt: 85% of graduating class had student loans; average debt was $14,000.

FINANCIAL AID PROCEDURES
Forms required: FAFSA, state aid form, institutional form.
Dates and Deadlines: Closing date 3/2. Applicants notified on a rolling basis starting 1/1; must reply by 5/1 or within 2 week(s) of notification.

CONTACT
Gregory Becher, Director of Financial Aid
10,000 North Ojai Road, Santa Paula, CA 93060-9621
(800) 634-9797

University of California: Berkeley
Berkeley, California
www.berkeley.edu
Federal Code: 001312

4-year public university in small city.
Enrollment: 23,447 undergrads. 4,059 full-time freshmen.
Selectivity: Admits less than 50% of applicants.

BASIC COSTS (2006-2007)
Tuition and fees: $6,558; out-of-state residents $25,242.
Room and board: $13,074.

FINANCIAL AID PICTURE (2005-2006)
Students with need: Out of 3,168 full-time freshmen who applied for aid, 1,994 were judged to have need. Of these, 1,934 received aid, and 995 had their full need met. Average financial aid package met 90% of need; average scholarship/grant was $12,021; average loan was $4,254. For part-time students, average financial aid package was $13,674.
Students without need: 352 full-time freshmen who did not demonstrate need for aid received scholarships/grants; average award was $2,958. No-need awards available for academics.
Scholarships offered: *Merit:* University Scholarship, President's Undergraduate Fellowships, Regents and Chancellor's Scholarships, Alumni Scholarships, Institutional National Merit Scholarships. *Athletic:* 72 full-time freshmen received athletic scholarships; average amount $16,264.
Cumulative student debt: 47% of graduating class had student loans; average debt was $13,171.

FINANCIAL AID PROCEDURES
Forms required: FAFSA, state aid form.
Dates and Deadlines: Closing date 3/2. Applicants notified by 4/15.
Transfers: Closing date 3/2. Applicants notified by 4/15.

CONTACT
Cheryl Resh, Director, Financial Aid
110 Sproul Hall, #5800, Berkeley, CA 94720-5800
(510) 642-6000

University of California: Davis
Davis, California
www.ucdavis.edu   Federal Code: 001313

4-year public university in small city.
Enrollment: 22,618 undergrads, 1% part-time. 4,381 full-time freshmen.
Selectivity: Admits 50 to 75% of applicants.

BASIC COSTS (2005-2006)
Tuition and fees: $7,457; out-of-state residents $25,277.
Room and board: $10,791.

FINANCIAL AID PICTURE (2005-2006)
Students with need: Average financial aid package met 73% of need; average scholarship/grant was $9,655; average loan was $4,425. For part-time students, average financial aid package was $12,652.
Students without need: This college only awards aid to students with need.
Cumulative student debt: 50% of graduating class had student loans; average debt was $12,701.

FINANCIAL AID PROCEDURES
Forms required: FAFSA, state aid form.
Dates and Deadlines: Priority date 3/2; no closing date. Applicants notified on a rolling basis starting 3/15.

CONTACT
Lora Bossio, Director, Financial Aid
178 Mrak Hall, Davis, CA 95616
(530) 752-2390

University of California: Irvine
Irvine, California
www.uci.edu   Federal Code: 001314

4-year public university in small city.
Enrollment: 19,930 undergrads, 3% part-time. 3,610 full-time freshmen.
Selectivity: Admits 50 to 75% of applicants.

BASIC COSTS (2005-2006)
Tuition and fees: $6,770; out-of-state residents $24,590.
Room and board: $9,202.

FINANCIAL AID PICTURE (2004-2005)
Students with need: Out of 2,745 full-time freshmen who applied for aid, 1,833 were judged to have need. Of these, 1,691 received aid, and 586 had their full need met. Average financial aid package met 85% of need; average scholarship/grant was $9,236; average loan was $5,130. For part-time students, average financial aid package was $9,804.
Students without need: 134 full-time freshmen who did not demonstrate need for aid received scholarships/grants; average award was $7,657. No-need awards available for academics, athletics, state/district residency.
Scholarships offered: 37 full-time freshmen received athletic scholarships; average amount $11,343.
Cumulative student debt: 55% of graduating class had student loans; average debt was $13,226.

FINANCIAL AID PROCEDURES
Forms required: FAFSA, state aid form.
Dates and Deadlines: Closing date 3/1. Applicants notified by 4/1; must reply by 5/1.

CONTACT
Brent Yunek, Director of Financial Aid
204 Administration Building, Irvine, CA 92697-1075
(949) 824-8262

University of California: Los Angeles
Los Angeles, California
www.ucla.edu   Federal Code: 001315

4-year public university in very large city.
Enrollment: 24,811 undergrads, 4% part-time. 3,700 full-time freshmen.
Selectivity: Admits less than 50% of applicants.

BASIC COSTS (2005-2006)
Tuition and fees: $6,504; out-of-state residents $24,324.
Room and board: $11,928.

FINANCIAL AID PICTURE (2005-2006)
Students with need: Out of 2,371 full-time freshmen who applied for aid, 1,842 were judged to have need. Of these, 1,824 received aid, and 879 had their full need met. Average financial aid package met 86% of need; average scholarship/grant was $11,316; average loan was $4,402. For part-time students, average financial aid package was $10,161.
Students without need: 220 full-time freshmen who did not demonstrate need for aid received scholarships/grants; average award was $6,778. No-need awards available for academics, athletics, ROTC.
Scholarships offered: 69 full-time freshmen received athletic scholarships; average amount $10,672.

FINANCIAL AID PROCEDURES
Forms required: FAFSA.
Dates and Deadlines: Priority date 3/2; no closing date. Applicants notified on a rolling basis starting 3/15; must reply within 3 week(s) of notification.

CONTACT
Ronald Johnson, Director, Financial Aid Office
1147 Murphy Hall, Los Angeles, CA 90095-1436
(310) 825-4321

University of California: Merced
Merced, California
www.ucmerced.edu   Federal Code: 001313

4-year public university in small city.
Enrollment: 835 undergrads. 705 full-time freshmen.
Selectivity: Admits over 75% of applicants.

BASIC COSTS (2005-2006)
Tuition and fees: $6,653; out-of-state residents $24,473.
Room and board: $9,112.

FINANCIAL AID PICTURE
Students with need: Need-based aid available for full-time and part-time students. Work study available nights, weekends, and for part-time students.
Students without need: No-need awards available for academics.
Scholarships offered: Regents Scholarships; based on strength and breadth of academic program, grades, personal statement, extracurricular activities, community activities, first-generation attendance, other indicators of academic excellence and promise.

FINANCIAL AID PROCEDURES
Forms required: FAFSA, state aid form.

Dates and Deadlines: Priority date 3/2; no closing date. Applicants notified by 4/1; must reply by 5/1.
Transfers: Must reply by 6/1.
CONTACT
Diana Ralls, Director of Financial Aid & Scholarships
PO Box 2039, Merced, CA 95344
(209) 724-4384

University of California: Riverside
Riverside, California
www.ucr.edu
Federal Code: 001316

4-year public university in large city.
Enrollment: 14,555 undergrads, 3% part-time. 2,967 full-time freshmen.
Selectivity: Admits over 75% of applicants.

BASIC COSTS (2005-2006)
Tuition and fees: $6,590; out-of-state residents $24,410.
Room and board: $10,200.

FINANCIAL AID PICTURE (2005-2006)
Students with need: Out of 2,411 full-time freshmen who applied for aid, 1,890 were judged to have need. Of these, 1,829 received aid, and 1,016 had their full need met. Average financial aid package met 89% of need; average scholarship/grant was $11,013; average loan was $4,596. For part-time students, average financial aid package was $9,256.
Students without need: 79 full-time freshmen who did not demonstrate need for aid received scholarships/grants; average award was $5,386. No-need awards available for academics, art, athletics, leadership, music/drama.
Scholarships offered: 30 full-time freshmen received athletic scholarships; average amount $12,364.
Cumulative student debt: 65% of graduating class had student loans; average debt was $14,814.

FINANCIAL AID PROCEDURES
Forms required: FAFSA, state aid form.
Dates and Deadlines: Closing date 3/2. Applicants notified on a rolling basis starting 3/1; must reply by 5/1 or within 3 week(s) of notification.
CONTACT
Sheryl Hayes, Director of Financial Aid
1120 Hinderaker Hall, Riverside, CA 92521
(951) 827-3878

University of California: San Diego
La Jolla, California
www.ucsd.edu
Federal Code: 001317

4-year public university in large town.
Enrollment: 20,339 undergrads, 1% part-time. 3,874 full-time freshmen.
Selectivity: Admits less than 50% of applicants.

BASIC COSTS (2005-2006)
Tuition and fees: $6,681; out-of-state residents $24,501.
Room and board: $9,421.

FINANCIAL AID PICTURE (2005-2006)
Students with need: 61% of average financial aid package awarded as scholarships/grants, 39% awarded as loans/jobs. Need-based aid available for part-time students.
Students without need: No-need awards available for academics, art, leadership, music/drama.

FINANCIAL AID PROCEDURES
Forms required: FAFSA, state aid form.

Dates and Deadlines: Priority date 3/2; closing date 6/1. Applicants notified on a rolling basis starting 3/15; must reply within 3 week(s) of notification.
CONTACT
Vincent De Anda, Director of Financial Aid Office
9500 Gilman Drive, 0021, La Jolla, CA 92093-0021
(858) 534-3800

University of California: Santa Barbara
Santa Barbara, California
www.ucsb.edu
Federal Code: 001320

4-year public university in small city.
Enrollment: 18,058 undergrads, 3% part-time. 3,876 full-time freshmen.
Selectivity: Admits 50 to 75% of applicants.

BASIC COSTS (2005-2006)
Tuition and fees: $6,993; out-of-state residents $24,813.
Room and board: $10,577.

FINANCIAL AID PICTURE (2004-2005)
Students with need: Out of 2,846 full-time freshmen who applied for aid, 2,002 were judged to have need. Of these, 1,782 received aid, and 899 had their full need met. Average financial aid package met 83% of need; average scholarship/grant was $10,641; average loan was $5,621. For part-time students, average financial aid package was $11,799.
Students without need: 66 full-time freshmen who did not demonstrate need for aid received scholarships/grants; average award was $5,365.
Scholarships offered: 36 full-time freshmen received athletic scholarships; average amount $10,427.

FINANCIAL AID PROCEDURES
Forms required: FAFSA.
Dates and Deadlines: Priority date 3/2; closing date 5/31. Applicants notified on a rolling basis starting 3/15; must reply within 2 week(s) of notification.
Transfers: California residents must apply for a CAL grant from the California Student Aid Commission; must complete and submit FAFSA by March 2.
CONTACT
Ron Andrade, Director of Financial Aid
1234 Cheadle Hall, Santa Barbara, CA 93106-2014
(805) 893-2432

University of California: Santa Cruz
Santa Cruz, California
www.ucsc.edu
Federal Code: 001321

4-year public university in small city.
Enrollment: 13,588 undergrads, 4% part-time. 3,037 full-time freshmen.
Selectivity: Admits over 75% of applicants.

BASIC COSTS (2005-2006)
Tuition and fees: $6,949; out-of-state residents $24,769.
Room and board: $11,571.
Additional info: Tuition/fee waivers available for unemployed or children of unemployed.

FINANCIAL AID PICTURE (2004-2005)
Students with need: Out of 1,799 full-time freshmen who applied for aid, 1,679 were judged to have need. Of these, 1,605 received aid, and 529 had their full need met. Average financial aid package met 84% of need; average scholarship/grant was $8,889; average loan was $4,196. For part-time students, average financial aid package was $9,814.
Students without need: 14 full-time freshmen who did not demonstrate need for aid received scholarships/grants; average award was $5,648. No-

need awards available for academics, alumni affiliation, art, leadership, music/drama.
Cumulative student debt: 53% of graduating class had student loans; average debt was $13,419.

FINANCIAL AID PROCEDURES
Forms required: FAFSA, state aid form.
Dates and Deadlines: Closing date 3/2. Applicants notified on a rolling basis starting 4/1; must reply within 4 week(s) of notification.

CONTACT
Ann Draper, Director of Financial Aid
Cook House, 1156 High Street, Santa Cruz, CA 95064
(831) 459-2963

University of Judaism
Bel Air, California
www.uj.edu   Federal Code: 002741

4-year private university and liberal arts college in very large city, affiliated with Jewish faith.
Enrollment: 150 undergrads.
Selectivity: Admits over 75% of applicants.

BASIC COSTS (2006-2007)
Tuition and fees: $20,290.
Room and board: $10,800.

FINANCIAL AID PICTURE
Students with need: Need-based aid available for full-time and part-time students. Work study available nights, weekends, and for part-time students.
Students without need: No-need awards available for academics, leadership.
Scholarships offered: President's scholarship based on leadership, GPA, community involvement.

FINANCIAL AID PROCEDURES
Forms required: FAFSA, state aid form, institutional form.
Dates and Deadlines: Priority date 3/1; no closing date. Applicants notified on a rolling basis starting 3/15; must reply within 3 week(s) of notification.

CONTACT
Larisa Zadoyen, Director of Financial Aid
15600 Mulholland Drive, Bel Air, CA 90077
(310) 476-9777 ext. 252

University of La Verne
La Verne, California
www.ulv.edu   Federal Code: 001216

4-year private university and liberal arts college in large town.
Enrollment: 1,666 undergrads, 5% part-time. 332 full-time freshmen.
Selectivity: Admits 50 to 75% of applicants.

BASIC COSTS (2006-2007)
Tuition and fees: $24,260.
Per-credit charge: $685.
Room and board: $9,210.

FINANCIAL AID PICTURE (2005-2006)
Students with need: Out of 308 full-time freshmen who applied for aid, 282 were judged to have need. Of these, 282 received aid, and 1 had their full need met. For part-time students, average financial aid package was $13,384.
Students without need: 42 full-time freshmen who did not demonstrate need for aid received scholarships/grants; average award was $8,988. No-need awards available for academics, alumni affiliation, art, leadership, minority status, music/drama, religious affiliation.
Scholarships offered: *Merit:* Trustee Award; $12,000. Founders Award; $10,000. 1891 Award; $9,000. Leo Award; $6,000. *Athletic:* 271 full-time freshmen received athletic scholarships; average amount $9,352.

FINANCIAL AID PROCEDURES
Forms required: FAFSA, state aid form.
Dates and Deadlines: Priority date 3/2; no closing date. Applicants notified on a rolling basis starting 3/3; must reply within 1 week(s) of notification.
Transfers: No deadline. Award amounts for transfer students are: Trustee Award - $7,000; Founders Award - $5,000; 1891 Award - $3000.

CONTACT
Leatha Webster, Director of Financial Aid
1950 Third Street, La Verne, CA 91750
(800) 649-0160

University of Redlands
Redlands, California
www.redlands.edu   Federal Code: 001322

4-year private university and liberal arts college in small city.
Enrollment: 2,358 undergrads, 1% part-time. 612 full-time freshmen.
Selectivity: Admits 50 to 75% of applicants.

BASIC COSTS (2006-2007)
Tuition and fees: $28,776.
Per-credit charge: $890.
Room and board: $9,360.

FINANCIAL AID PICTURE (2005-2006)
Students with need: Out of 514 full-time freshmen who applied for aid, 400 were judged to have need. Of these, 400 received aid, and 215 had their full need met. Average financial aid package met 91% of need; average scholarship/grant was $19,703; average loan was $4,770. For part-time students, average financial aid package was $23,148.
Students without need: 131 full-time freshmen who did not demonstrate need for aid received scholarships/grants; average award was $11,187. No-need awards available for academics, art, music/drama.

FINANCIAL AID PROCEDURES
Forms required: FAFSA, state aid form.
Dates and Deadlines: Priority date 2/15; no closing date. Applicants notified on a rolling basis starting 2/28; must reply by 5/1.
Transfers: No deadline.

CONTACT
Craig Slaughter, Director of Financial Aid
1200 East Colton Avenue, Redlands, CA 92373-0999
(909) 793-2121

University of San Diego
San Diego, California
www.sandiego.edu   Federal Code: 010395

4-year private university in very large city, affiliated with Roman Catholic Church.
Enrollment: 4,959 undergrads, 3% part-time. 1,174 full-time freshmen.
Selectivity: Admits 50 to 75% of applicants.

BASIC COSTS (2006-2007)
Tuition and fees: $30,704.
Per-credit charge: $1,050.
Room and board: $10,960.

FINANCIAL AID PICTURE (2004-2005)
Students with need: Out of 781 full-time freshmen who applied for aid, 553 were judged to have need. Of these, 553 received aid, and 203 had their full need met. Average financial aid package met 62% of need; average scholarship/grant was $13,137; average loan was $3,997. For part-time students, average financial aid package was $9,504.
Students without need: 115 full-time freshmen who did not demonstrate need for aid received scholarships/grants; average award was $7,000. No-need awards available for academics, athletics, music/drama, religious affiliation, ROTC.
Scholarships offered: *Merit:* Available for freshmen only. *Athletic:* 46 full-time freshmen received athletic scholarships; average amount $15,724.
Cumulative student debt: 43% of graduating class had student loans; average debt was $27,722.

FINANCIAL AID PROCEDURES
Forms required: FAFSA.
Dates and Deadlines: Closing date 2/20. Applicants notified on a rolling basis starting 3/1; must reply within 3 week(s) of notification.
Transfers: No deadline. Entering transfer students not eligible for institutional merit-based scholarships.

CONTACT
Judith Lewis Logue, Director of Financial Aid Services
5998 Alcala Park, San Diego, CA 92110
(619) 260-4514

University of San Francisco
San Francisco, California
www.usfca.edu   Federal Code: 001325

4-year private university in very large city, affiliated with Roman Catholic Church.
Enrollment: 4,451 undergrads, 3% part-time. 930 full-time freshmen.
Selectivity: Admits 50 to 75% of applicants.

BASIC COSTS (2006-2007)
Tuition and fees: $28,580.
Per-credit charge: $1,015.
Room and board: $10,580.

FINANCIAL AID PICTURE (2005-2006)
Students with need: Out of 667 full-time freshmen who applied for aid, 569 were judged to have need. Of these, 548 received aid, and 75 had their full need met. Average financial aid package met 70% of need; average scholarship/grant was $16,227; average loan was $3,693. For part-time students, average financial aid package was $7,330.
Students without need: 58 full-time freshmen who did not demonstrate need for aid received scholarships/grants; average award was $13,751. No-need awards available for academics, athletics, ROTC.
Scholarships offered: *Merit:* University Scholars Program: $16,000 per year for 4 years; must have 3.8 weighted GPA and combined SAT of 1320 on Critical Reading and Math sections or ACT composite of 30. Applicants must apply for admission by November 15. *Athletic:* 48 full-time freshmen received athletic scholarships; average amount $19,093.
Additional info: Individualized installment plans available.

FINANCIAL AID PROCEDURES
Forms required: FAFSA.
Dates and Deadlines: Priority date 2/1; no closing date. Applicants notified on a rolling basis starting 4/1; must reply within 4 week(s) of notification.

CONTACT
Susan Murphy, Senior Associate Dean, Director, Enrollment and Financial Services
2130 Fulton Street, San Francisco, CA 94117-1046
(415) 422-6303

University of Southern California
Los Angeles, California
www.usc.edu   Federal Code: 001328
    CSS Code: 4852

4-year private university in very large city.
Enrollment: 16,428 undergrads, 3% part-time. 2,769 full-time freshmen.
Selectivity: Admits less than 50% of applicants. GED not accepted.

BASIC COSTS (2006-2007)
Tuition and fees: $33,888.
Per-credit charge: $1,121.
Room and board: $10,144.

FINANCIAL AID PICTURE (2004-2005)
Students with need: Out of 1,805 full-time freshmen who applied for aid, 1,210 were judged to have need. Of these, 1,210 received aid, and 1,147 had their full need met. Average financial aid package met 99% of need; average scholarship/grant was $18,919; average loan was $3,767. For part-time students, average financial aid package was $13,951.
Students without need: 658 full-time freshmen who did not demonstrate need for aid received scholarships/grants; average award was $12,134. No-need awards available for academics, alumni affiliation, art, athletics, leadership, music/drama, ROTC.
Scholarships offered: 70 full-time freshmen received athletic scholarships; average amount $28,715.
Cumulative student debt: 48% of graduating class had student loans; average debt was $19,131.

FINANCIAL AID PROCEDURES
Forms required: FAFSA, CSS PROFILE.
Dates and Deadlines: Closing date 1/20. Applicants notified on a rolling basis starting 3/15; must reply by 5/1.
Transfers: Priority date 1/20; closing date 2/1. Applicants notified by 5/1; must reply by 6/1.

CONTACT
Catherine Thomas, Associate Dean/Director of Financial Aid
University of Southern California, Los Angeles, CA 90089-1158
(213) 740-1111

University of the Pacific
Stockton, California
www.pacific.edu   Federal Code: 001329

4-year private university in large city.
Enrollment: 3,436 undergrads, 3% part-time. 797 full-time freshmen.
Selectivity: Admits 50 to 75% of applicants.

BASIC COSTS (2006-2007)
Tuition and fees: $27,350.
Per-credit charge: $930.
Room and board: $8,700.

FINANCIAL AID PICTURE (2005-2006)
Students with need: Out of 657 full-time freshmen who applied for aid, 656 were judged to have need. Of these, 537 received aid, and 157 had their full need met. Need-based aid available for part-time students.
Students without need: 152 full-time freshmen who did not demonstrate need for aid received scholarships/grants; average award was $8,388. No-need awards available for academics, athletics, leadership, music/drama, religious affiliation.
Scholarships offered: 32 full-time freshmen received athletic scholarships; average amount $16,025.

FINANCIAL AID PROCEDURES
Forms required: FAFSA.

Dates and Deadlines: Priority date 2/15; no closing date. Applicants notified on a rolling basis starting 3/15.

CONTACT
Lynn Fox, Director of Financial Aid
3601 Pacific Avenue, Stockton, CA 95211-0197
(209) 946-2011

Vanguard University of Southern California
Costa Mesa, California
www.vanguard.edu   Federal Code: 001293

4-year private university and liberal arts college in small city, affiliated with Assemblies of God.
Enrollment: 1,814 undergrads, 18% part-time. 352 full-time freshmen.
Selectivity: Admits over 75% of applicants.

BASIC COSTS (2006-2007)
Tuition and fees: $21,524.
Room and board: $7,058.

FINANCIAL AID PICTURE (2004-2005)
Students with need: Out of 336 full-time freshmen who applied for aid, 302 were judged to have need. Of these, 302 received aid, and 91 had their full need met. Average financial aid package met 78% of need; average scholarship/grant was $13,567; average loan was $3,686. Need-based aid available for part-time students.
Students without need: 62 full-time freshmen who did not demonstrate need for aid received scholarships/grants; average award was $4,563. No-need awards available for academics, athletics, music/drama.
Scholarships offered: 32 full-time freshmen received athletic scholarships; average amount $10,042.
Cumulative student debt: 31% of graduating class had student loans; average debt was $19,476.

FINANCIAL AID PROCEDURES
Forms required: FAFSA, state aid form.
Dates and Deadlines: Priority date 3/2; no closing date. Applicants notified on a rolling basis starting 4/1.
Transfers: Applicants notified on a rolling basis.

CONTACT
Robyn Fournier, Director of Financial Aid
55 Fair Drive, Costa Mesa, CA 92626-9601
(714) 556-3610 ext. 355

Victor Valley College
Victorville, California
www.vvc.edu   Federal Code: 001335
    CSS Code: 4932

2-year public community college in small city.
Enrollment: 6,946 undergrads.
Selectivity: Open admission; but selective for some programs.

BASIC COSTS (2005-2006)
Tuition and fees: $790; out-of-state residents $5,500.
Per-credit charge: $26; out-of-state residents $183.
Additional info: Nevada residents pay $49 per credit hour.

FINANCIAL AID PICTURE
Students with need: Need-based aid available for full-time and part-time students.
Additional info: Board of Governors grant pays enrollment fee in full for low-income students.

FINANCIAL AID PROCEDURES
Forms required: FAFSA, CSS PROFILE, state aid form, institutional form.
Dates and Deadlines: Priority date 3/2; no closing date. Applicants notified on a rolling basis starting 8/1; must reply within 4 week(s) of notification.

CONTACT
Sharon Groom, Financial Aid
18422 Bear Valley Road, Victorville, CA 92392-5849
(760) 245-4271 ext. 2277

Vista Community College
Berkeley, California
www.peralta.cc.ca.us   Federal Code: 014311

2-year public community college in small city.
Enrollment: 1,530 undergrads.
Selectivity: Open admission.

BASIC COSTS (2005-2006)
Tuition and fees: $784; out-of-state residents $5,704.
Per-credit charge: $26; out-of-state residents $190.

FINANCIAL AID PICTURE
Students with need: Need-based aid available for full-time and part-time students.
Students without need: This college only awards aid to students with need.

FINANCIAL AID PROCEDURES
Dates and Deadlines: No deadline. Applicants notified on a rolling basis.

CONTACT
Robert Vergas, Financial Aid Coordinator
2020 Milvia Street, Berkeley, CA 94704-1183
(510) 981-2800

West Hills Community College
Coalinga, California
www.westhillscollege.com   Federal Code: 001176

2-year public community college in small town.
Enrollment: 4,545 undergrads.
Selectivity: Open admission.

BASIC COSTS (2005-2006)
Tuition and fees: $780; out-of-state residents $5,310.
Per-credit charge: $26; out-of-state residents $177.
Room and board: $4,010.
Additional info: Additional housing fee for cable, computer access and other services: $185.50/semester. Tuition/fee waivers available for unemployed or children of unemployed.

FINANCIAL AID PICTURE
Students with need: Need-based aid available for full-time and part-time students.

FINANCIAL AID PROCEDURES
Dates and Deadlines: Priority date 3/2; no closing date. Applicants notified on a rolling basis starting 6/1.

CONTACT
Jana Cox, District Director, Financial Aid
300 Cherry Lane, Coalinga, CA 93210
(559) 934-2000 ext. 2316

West Los Angeles College
Culver City, California
www.wlac.edu   Federal Code: 008596

2-year public community college in large town.
Enrollment: 1,746 full-time undergrads.
Selectivity: Open admission.

BASIC COSTS (2005-2006)
Tuition and fees: $804; out-of-state residents $5,424.
Per-credit charge: $26; out-of-state residents $180.
Additional info: Tuition/fee waivers available for unemployed or children of unemployed.

FINANCIAL AID PICTURE (2005-2006)
Students with need: 22% of average financial aid package awarded as scholarships/grants, 78% awarded as loans/jobs. Need-based aid available for part-time students.
Students without need: This college only awards aid to students with need.
Additional info: California residents may qualify for Board of Governor's Grant Program.

FINANCIAL AID PROCEDURES
Forms required: FAFSA.
Dates and Deadlines: No deadline. Applicants notified on a rolling basis; must reply within 4 week(s) of notification.
Transfers: No deadline.

CONTACT
Glenn Schenk, Financial Aid Manager
9000 Overland Ave, Culver City, CA 90230
(310) 287-4533

West Valley College
Saratoga, California
www.westvalley.edu   Federal Code: 001338

2-year public community college in large town.
Enrollment: 3,500 undergrads.
Selectivity: Open admission.

BASIC COSTS (2005-2006)
Tuition and fees: $830; out-of-state residents $5,360.
Per-credit charge: $26; out-of-state residents $177.
Additional info: Tuition/fee waivers available for unemployed or children of unemployed.

FINANCIAL AID PICTURE
Students with need: Need-based aid available for full-time and part-time students.
Students without need: This college only awards aid to students with need.

FINANCIAL AID PROCEDURES
Forms required: FAFSA.
Dates and Deadlines: Priority date 5/31; no closing date. Applicants notified on a rolling basis starting 7/1.

CONTACT
Maureen Kent, Financial Aid Coordinator
14000 Fruitvale Avenue, Saratoga, CA 95070-5698
(408) 867-2200

Western Career College: Emeryville
Emeryville, California
www.siliconvalley.edu

4-year for-profit technical college.
Enrollment: 300 undergrads.
Selectivity: Open admission.

FINANCIAL AID PICTURE
Students with need: Need-based aid available for full-time students.

FINANCIAL AID PROCEDURES
Forms required: FAFSA.
Dates and Deadlines: Applicants notified on a rolling basis.

CONTACT
1400 65th Street, Suite 200, Emeryville, CA 94608
(510) 601-0133

Westmont College
Santa Barbara, California
www.westmont.edu   Federal Code: 001341

4-year private liberal arts college in small city, affiliated with interdenominational tradition.
Enrollment: 1,358 undergrads. 334 full-time freshmen.
Selectivity: Admits 50 to 75% of applicants.

BASIC COSTS (2006-2007)
Tuition and fees: $29,470.
Room and board: $9,232.

FINANCIAL AID PICTURE (2005-2006)
Students with need: Out of 256 full-time freshmen who applied for aid, 197 were judged to have need. Of these, 197 received aid, and 21 had their full need met. Average financial aid package met 64% of need; average scholarship/grant was $12,941; average loan was $3,928.
Students without need: 106 full-time freshmen who did not demonstrate need for aid received scholarships/grants; average award was $11,168. No-need awards available for academics, art, athletics, leadership, minority status, music/drama.
Scholarships offered: *Merit:* Scholarships automatically awarded to entering students based on high school GPA and SAT or ACT scores (first-year students) or college academic GPA (transfers); renewable annually; unlimited number awarded until class is full. First-year scholarships: Presidential; $11,000; must maintain 3.25 GPA. Provost: $9,000; must maintain 3.0 GPA. Dean's: $7,000; must maintain 2.75 GPA. Transfer scholarships: Presidential; $5,000; must have 3.75 GPA and 24 or more transferable credits. Provost; $4,000; must have 3.35 GPA and 24 or more transferable credits. *Athletic:* 7 full-time freshmen received athletic scholarships; average amount $6,866.
Cumulative student debt: 74% of graduating class had student loans; average debt was $16,999.

FINANCIAL AID PROCEDURES
Forms required: FAFSA.
Dates and Deadlines: Closing date 3/1. Applicants notified by 4/1; must reply by 5/1 or within 2 week(s) of notification.
Transfers: Students may qualify for academic merit scholarships.

CONTACT
Diane Horvath, Director of Financial Aid
955 La Paz Road, Santa Barbara, CA 93108-1089
(888) 963-4624

Westwood College of Technology: Inland Empire
Upland, California
www.westwood.edu   Federal Code: 007548

3-year for-profit business and technical college in small city.
Enrollment: 1,145 undergrads. 294 full-time freshmen.

BASIC COSTS (2005-2006)
Tuition and fees: $11,745.

FINANCIAL AID PICTURE (2004-2005)
Students with need: Out of 293 full-time freshmen who applied for aid, 293 were judged to have need. Of these, 177 received aid, and 102 had their full need met. Average financial aid package met 95% of need; average scholarship/grant was $2,700; average loan was $2,700. For part-time students, average financial aid package was $2,850.
Students without need: No-need awards available for academics.

FINANCIAL AID PROCEDURES
Forms required: FAFSA, institutional form.
Dates and Deadlines: No deadline. Must reply within 1 week(s) of notification.
Transfers: No deadline.

CONTACT
Alison Lee, Director of Financial Aid
20 West Seventh Street, Upland, CA 91786
(909) 931-7599

Whittier College
Whittier, California
www.whittier.edu   Federal Code: 001342
                    CSS Code: 4952

4-year private liberal arts college in small city.
Enrollment: 1,325 undergrads, 2% part-time. 351 full-time freshmen.
Selectivity: Admits over 75% of applicants.

BASIC COSTS (2006-2007)
Tuition and fees: $28,206.
Per-credit charge: $1,075.
Room and board: $8,542.

FINANCIAL AID PICTURE (2004-2005)
Students with need: Out of 351 full-time freshmen who applied for aid, 254 were judged to have need. Of these, 254 received aid, and 79 had their full need met. Average financial aid package met 91% of need; average scholarship/grant was $12,535; average loan was $6,296. For part-time students, average financial aid package was $6,948.
Students without need: 38 full-time freshmen who did not demonstrate need for aid received scholarships/grants; average award was $7,480. No-need awards available for academics, alumni affiliation, art, music/drama.
Cumulative student debt: 78% of graduating class had student loans; average debt was $27,335.
Additional info: Auditions required for talent scholarship applicants.

FINANCIAL AID PROCEDURES
Forms required: FAFSA, CSS PROFILE.
Dates and Deadlines: Priority date 3/1; no closing date. Applicants notified on a rolling basis starting 2/1; must reply within 2 week(s) of notification.
Transfers: Priority date 2/1.

CONTACT
Vernon Bridges, Director of Student Financing
13406 East Philadelphia Street, Whittier, CA 90608-0634
(562) 907-4285

William Jessup University
Rocklin, California
www.jessup.edu   Federal Code: 001281

4-year private Bible and liberal arts college in small city, affiliated with interdenominational tradition.
Enrollment: 428 undergrads, 31% part-time. 67 full-time freshmen.
Selectivity: Admits 50 to 75% of applicants.

BASIC COSTS (2006-2007)
Tuition and fees: $17,238.
Per-credit charge: $730.
Room and board: $6,680.

FINANCIAL AID PICTURE
Students with need: Need-based aid available for full-time students. Work study available nights, weekends, and for part-time students.
Students without need: No-need awards available for academics, athletics, music/drama.

FINANCIAL AID PROCEDURES
Forms required: FAFSA.
Dates and Deadlines: Priority date 3/1; closing date 8/1. Applicants notified on a rolling basis starting 3/1; must reply by 5/1 or within 2 week(s) of notification.

CONTACT
333 Sunset Boulevard, Rocklin, CA 95765
(916) 577-2200

Woodbury University
Burbank, California
www.woodbury.edu   Federal Code: 001343

4-year private university in very large city.
Enrollment: 1,258 undergrads, 18% part-time. 131 full-time freshmen.
Selectivity: Admits over 75% of applicants.

BASIC COSTS (2006-2007)
Tuition and fees: $23,474.
Per-credit charge: $758.
Room and board: $8,463.

FINANCIAL AID PICTURE (2005-2006)
Students with need: Average financial aid package met 62% of need; average scholarship/grant was $15,470; average loan was $2,649. For part-time students, average financial aid package was $8,382.
Students without need: No-need awards available for academics.
Cumulative student debt: 91% of graduating class had student loans; average debt was $20,134.

FINANCIAL AID PROCEDURES
Forms required: FAFSA, institutional form.
Dates and Deadlines: Priority date 3/2; no closing date. Applicants notified on a rolling basis starting 3/15; must reply by 5/1 or within 2 week(s) of notification.
Transfers: No deadline. Applicants notified on a rolling basis starting 3/15; must reply by 5/1 or within 2 week(s) of notification.

CONTACT
Celeastia Williams, Director of Enrollment Services
7500 Glenoaks Boulevard, Burbank, CA 91510-7846
(818) 767-0888 ext. 220

Yuba Community College District
Marysville, California
www.yccd.edu Federal Code: 001344

2-year public community college in small city.
Enrollment: 5,156 undergrads.
Selectivity: Open admission; but selective for some programs.

BASIC COSTS (2005-2006)
Tuition and fees: $792; out-of-state residents $5,322.
Per-credit charge: $26; out-of-state residents $177.
Additional info: Tuition/fee waivers available for adults.

FINANCIAL AID PICTURE
Students with need: Need-based aid available for full-time and part-time students.
Students without need: No-need awards available for academics, athletics, job skills, minority status, music/drama.
Additional info: Tuition fee waiver based on Board of Governors Grant.

FINANCIAL AID PROCEDURES
Forms required: FAFSA.
Dates and Deadlines: Closing date 3/1. Applicants notified on a rolling basis starting 4/1.

CONTACT
Marisela Arce, Associate Dean for EOP&S and Financial Aid
2088 North Beale Road, Marysville, CA 95901
(530) 741-6781

Colorado

Adams State College
Alamosa, Colorado
www.adams.edu Federal Code: 001345

4-year public liberal arts college in small town.
Enrollment: 2,142 undergrads, 17% part-time. 484 full-time freshmen.
Selectivity: Admits 50 to 75% of applicants.

BASIC COSTS (2005-2006)
Tuition and fees: $2,853; out-of-state residents $9,123.
Room and board: $6,140.

FINANCIAL AID PICTURE (2004-2005)
Students with need: For part-time students, average financial aid package was $2,684.
Students without need: No-need awards available for academics, alumni affiliation, art, athletics, leadership, minority status, music/drama, state/district residency.
Cumulative student debt: 68% of graduating class had student loans; average debt was $15,332.

FINANCIAL AID PROCEDURES
Forms required: FAFSA.
Dates and Deadlines: Priority date 3/1; closing date 4/15. Applicants notified on a rolling basis starting 4/30; must reply within 4 week(s) of notification.

CONTACT
Phil Schroeder, Director of Financial Aid
208 Edgemont Boulevard, Alamosa, CO 81102
(719) 587-7306

Aims Community College
Greeley, Colorado
www.aims.edu Federal Code: 007582

2-year public community college in small city.
Enrollment: 3,750 undergrads.
Selectivity: Open admission; but selective for some programs.

BASIC COSTS (2005-2006)
Tuition and fees: $1,890; out-of-district residents $2,970; out-of-state residents $9,390.
Per-credit charge: $50; out-of-district residents $86; out-of-state residents $300.
Additional info: Tuition/fee waivers available for adults.

FINANCIAL AID PICTURE
Students with need: Need-based aid available for full-time students.

FINANCIAL AID PROCEDURES
Forms required: FAFSA.
Dates and Deadlines: Priority date 4/1; closing date 4/15. Applicants notified on a rolling basis starting 6/1.

CONTACT
Lynn Suppes, Financial Aid Director
5401 West 20th Street PO Box 69, Greeley, CO 80632
(970) 330-8008 ext. 6304

Arapahoe Community College
Littleton, Colorado
www.arapahoe.edu Federal Code: 001346

2-year public community college in small city.
Enrollment: 4,707 undergrads.
Selectivity: Open admission; but selective for some programs.

BASIC COSTS (2005-2006)
Tuition and fees: $2,351; out-of-state residents $10,523.
Per-credit charge: $73; out-of-state residents $345.
Additional info: In-state tuition based upon assumption of Colorado Opportunity Fund waiver of $80 per-credit-hour.

FINANCIAL AID PICTURE
Students with need: Need-based aid available for full-time and part-time students. Work study available nights, weekends, and for part-time students.
Students without need: No-need awards available for academics, athletics, leadership, state/district residency.
Scholarships offered: President's Scholarship; based on minimum 3.0 GPA, references. College Bound Scholarship; based on high GED score. All awards $750 for full-time students, $375 for half-time, $563 for three-quarters time. Awards made on first-come first-served basis.

FINANCIAL AID PROCEDURES
Forms required: FAFSA, institutional form.
Dates and Deadlines: Priority date 5/1; closing date 6/1. Applicants notified on a rolling basis starting 5/1; must reply within 3 week(s) of notification.

CONTACT
Anne Allen, Director of Financial Aid
PO Box 9002, Littleton, CO 80160-9002
(303) 797-5661

Art Institute of Colorado
Denver, Colorado
www.aic.artinstitutes.edu Federal Code: 013961

4-year for-profit visual arts and technical college in very large city.
Enrollment: 2,350 undergrads.

BASIC COSTS (2006-2007)
Tuition and fees: $18,240.
Per-credit charge: $402.
Additional info: Supply kit $530-$2,155 depending on program. Tuition at time of enrollment locked for 4 years.

FINANCIAL AID PICTURE
Students with need: Need-based aid available for full-time and part-time students. Work study available nights, weekends, and for part-time students.
Additional info: Tuition at time of first enrollment guaranteed to students for 4 years providing student maintains continuous attendance and completes program within 150% of program length.

FINANCIAL AID PROCEDURES
Forms required: FAFSA, institutional form.
Dates and Deadlines: No deadline. Applicants notified on a rolling basis.
Transfers: No deadline.

CONTACT
Shannon May, Director of Student Financial Services
1200 Lincoln Street, Denver, CO 80203
(303) 824-4757

Bel-Rea Institute of Animal Technology
Denver, Colorado
www.bel-rea.com Federal Code: 012670

2-year for-profit technical college in very large city.
Enrollment: 600 undergrads.
Selectivity: Admits 50 to 75% of applicants.

BASIC COSTS (2006-2007)
Additional info: Tuition for full associate program $20,750 including fees. Tuition at time of enrollment locked for 2 years.

FINANCIAL AID PICTURE
Students with need: Need-based aid available for full-time students.
Students without need: This college only awards aid to students with need.

FINANCIAL AID PROCEDURES
Forms required: FAFSA.
Dates and Deadlines: Priority date 8/31; no closing date. Applicants notified on a rolling basis starting 8/15.
Transfers: No deadline.

CONTACT
Stasi Botinelli, Financial Aid Director
1681 South Dayton Street, Denver, CO 80247
(303) 751-8700

Blair College
Colorado Springs, Colorado
www.cci.edu Federal Code: 004503

2-year for-profit business and junior college in large city.
Enrollment: 700 undergrads.
Selectivity: Open admission.

BASIC COSTS (2005-2006)
Additional info: For linear programs: $260 per credit hour for all other linear programs; $25 registration fee and tech fee. For modular programs: (Medical Administrative Assistant; 8 modules, 47 credits) - tuition: $9765 plus $900 for text/materials; (Homeland Security Specialist; 7 modules, 48 credits) - tuition: $8451, plus $1500 for text/matrials and uniform; (Medical Insurance Billing & Coding; 6 modules, 35 credits) - tuition: $8657, plus $900 for text/materials. Tuition at time of enrollment locked for 2 years.

FINANCIAL AID PICTURE
Students with need: Need-based aid available for full-time and part-time students. Work study available nights.

FINANCIAL AID PROCEDURES
Forms required: FAFSA, institutional form.
Dates and Deadlines: No deadline. Applicants notified on a rolling basis starting 7/1.
Transfers: No deadline.

CONTACT
Sarah Yanez, Student Financial Director
1815 Jet Wing Drive, Colorado Springs, CO 80916
(719) 638-6580

Boulder College of Massage Therapy
Boulder, Colorado
www.bcmt.org Federal Code: 030131

1-year private health science and community college in small city.
Enrollment: 220 undergrads.
Selectivity: Open admission; but selective for some programs.

BASIC COSTS (2006-2007)
Additional info: Programs range from $13,160-$16,450.

FINANCIAL AID PICTURE
Students with need: Need-based aid available for full-time and part-time students.
Students without need: This college only awards aid to students with need.

FINANCIAL AID PROCEDURES
Forms required: FAFSA.
Dates and Deadlines: No deadline.

CONTACT
Debbie Clarke, Director of Financial Aid
6255 Longbow Drive, Boulder, CO 80301
(303) 530-2100 ext. 106

Cambridge College
Aurora, Colorado
www.hightechschools.edu Federal Code: 021829

2-year for-profit technical college in small city.
Enrollment: 415 undergrads.

BASIC COSTS (2005-2006)
Additional info: Tuition for full associate degree programs ranges from $16,550 to $24,500 depending on program; tuition for diploma programs ranges from $7,950 to $10,150. Books and supplies included. Housing provided by private company.

FINANCIAL AID PICTURE
Students with need: Need-based aid available for full-time students.
Students without need: This college only awards aid to students with need.

FINANCIAL AID PROCEDURES
Forms required: FAFSA, institutional form.
Dates and Deadlines: No deadline. Applicants notified on a rolling basis.
CONTACT
Gerry Major, Director of Financial Aid
350 Blackhawk Street, Aurora, CO 80011
(720) 859-7900

CollegeAmerica-Denver
Denver, Colorado
www.collegeamerica.com   Federal Code: 025943

2-year for-profit technical college in very large city.
Enrollment: 439 undergrads. 74 full-time freshmen.
Selectivity: Open admission.
BASIC COSTS (2006-2007)
Additional info: Tuition, fees, books, and supplies: $29,950 for Associate degree programs; $54,900 for Bachelor's degree programs. Tuition at time of enrollment locked for 2 years.
FINANCIAL AID PICTURE (2005-2006)
Students with need: Out of 74 full-time freshmen who applied for aid, 74 were judged to have need. Of these, 74 received aid. Average financial aid package met 50% of need; average loan was $8,100.
Students without need: This college only awards aid to students with need.
Scholarships offered: High School Academic Scholarship.
Cumulative student debt: 99% of graduating class had student loans; average debt was $22,930.
FINANCIAL AID PROCEDURES
Forms required: FAFSA, institutional form.
Dates and Deadlines: No deadline. Applicants notified on a rolling basis; must reply within 4 week(s) of notification.
Transfers: No deadline. Applicants notified on a rolling basis.
CONTACT
Ruby Rowe, Corporate Director of Financial Aid
1385 South Colorado Boulevard, Suite A512, Denver, CO 80222-1912
(303) 691-9756

Colorado Christian University
Lakewood, Colorado
www.ccu.edu   Federal Code: 009401

4-year private university and liberal arts college in large city, affiliated with nondenominational tradition.
Enrollment: 1,772 undergrads, 41% part-time. 206 full-time freshmen.
Selectivity: Admits over 75% of applicants.
BASIC COSTS (2006-2007)
Tuition and fees: $17,530.
Per-credit charge: $750.
Room and board: $7,250.
FINANCIAL AID PICTURE
Students with need: Need-based aid available for full-time and part-time students. Work study available nights, weekends, and for part-time students.
Students without need: No-need awards available for academics, athletics, leadership, music/drama.
FINANCIAL AID PROCEDURES
Forms required: FAFSA.

Dates and Deadlines: Priority date 3/15; no closing date. Applicants notified on a rolling basis starting 4/1; must reply by 5/1 or within 4 week(s) of notification.
CONTACT
Stacy Udden, Associate Director Financial Aid
8787 West Alameda Avenue, Lakewood, CO 80226
(303) 963-3230

Colorado College
Colorado Springs, Colorado
www.coloradocollege.edu   Federal Code: 001347
    CSS Code: 4072

4-year private liberal arts college in large city.
Enrollment: 1,928 undergrads. 469 full-time freshmen.
Selectivity: Admits less than 50% of applicants.
BASIC COSTS (2006-2007)
Tuition and fees: $32,124.
Room and board: $8,052.
FINANCIAL AID PICTURE (2005-2006)
Students with need: Average financial aid package met 98% of need; average scholarship/grant was $24,621; average loan was $3,521. Need-based aid available for part-time students.
Students without need: No-need awards available for academics, athletics, state/district residency.
Scholarships offered: Barnes Scholarship; full tuition; available in all natural sciences; 4 or 5 awarded in chemistry, 4 available in remaining natural sciences. Trustee Scholarship; $7,000; based on highly rated entering students; 10 awarded. Merit Awards; up to $2,000; for National Merit finalists. Men's Ice Hockey and Women's Soccer merit awards. Colorado College Scholars; 10 merit awards for highly rated entering students from Colorado.
Additional info: Need-based financial aid available only to students enrolled half-time or more.
FINANCIAL AID PROCEDURES
Forms required: FAFSA, CSS PROFILE.
Dates and Deadlines: Closing date 2/15. Applicants notified by 3/20; must reply by 5/1.
Transfers: Closing date 4/1. Transfer students might not receive full-need package during first year.
CONTACT
James Swanson, Director of Financial Aid
14 East Cache La Poudre, Colorado Springs, CO 80903
(719) 389-6651

Colorado Mountain College: Alpine Campus
Steamboat Springs, Colorado
www.coloradomtn.edu   Federal Code: 004506

2-year public community and liberal arts college in small town.
Enrollment: 750 undergrads.
Selectivity: Open admission.
BASIC COSTS (2005-2006)
Tuition and fees: $1,490; out-of-district residents $2,360; out-of-state residents $7,130.
Per-credit charge: $43; out-of-district residents $72; out-of-state residents $231.
Room and board: $6,392.

FINANCIAL AID PICTURE
Students with need: Need-based aid available for full-time and part-time students. Work study available nights, weekends, and for part-time students.
Students without need: No-need awards available for academics, athletics, state/district residency.

FINANCIAL AID PROCEDURES
Forms required: FAFSA.
Dates and Deadlines: Priority date 3/31; no closing date. Applicants notified on a rolling basis starting 5/15; must reply within 4 week(s) of notification.
Transfers: No deadline. Transfer scholarships available to Colorado residents with 3.0 GPA and minimum 20 credits from prior institution.

CONTACT
Gary Lewis, Director of Financial Aid
1330 Bob Adams Drive, Steamboat Springs, CO 80487
(970) 870-4444

Colorado Mountain College: Spring Valley Campus
Glenwood Springs, Colorado
www.coloradomtn.edu   Federal Code: 004506

2-year public community and liberal arts college in small town.
Enrollment: 3,737 undergrads.
Selectivity: Open admission; but selective for some programs.

BASIC COSTS (2005-2006)
Tuition and fees: $1,490; out-of-district residents $2,360; out-of-state residents $7,130.
Per-credit charge: $43; out-of-district residents $72; out-of-state residents $231.
Room and board: $6,392.

FINANCIAL AID PICTURE
Students with need: Need-based aid available for full-time and part-time students. Work study available nights, weekends, and for part-time students.
Students without need: This college only awards aid to students with need.

FINANCIAL AID PROCEDURES
Forms required: FAFSA.
Dates and Deadlines: Priority date 3/31; no closing date. Applicants notified on a rolling basis starting 5/15; must reply within 4 week(s) of notification.
Transfers: Transfer scholarships available for Colorado residents with 3.0 GPA and minimum 20 credit hours from previous schools.

CONTACT
Gary Lewis, Director of Student Financial Aid
3000 County Road 114, Department CB, Glenwood Springs, CO 81601
(970) 947-8277

Colorado Mountain College: Timberline Campus
Leadville, Colorado
www.coloradomtn.edu   Federal Code: 004506

2-year public community and liberal arts college in small town.
Enrollment: 400 undergrads.
Selectivity: Open admission.

BASIC COSTS (2005-2006)
Tuition and fees: $1,490; out-of-district residents $2,360; out-of-state residents $7,130.
Per-credit charge: $43; out-of-district residents $72; out-of-state residents $231.
Room and board: $6,392.

FINANCIAL AID PICTURE
Students with need: Work study available nights, weekends, and for part-time students.
Students without need: No-need awards available for academics, athletics, state/district residency.

FINANCIAL AID PROCEDURES
Forms required: FAFSA.
Dates and Deadlines: Priority date 3/31; no closing date. Applicants notified on a rolling basis starting 5/15; must reply within 4 week(s) of notification.
Transfers: Transfer scholarships available for Colorado residents with 3.0 GPA and at least 20 credits from previous colleges.

CONTACT
Gary Lewis, Director of Financial Aid
901 South Highway 24, Dept. CB, Leadville, CO 80461
(719) 486-4293

Colorado Northwestern Community College
Rangely, Colorado
www.cncc.edu   Federal Code: 001359

2-year public community college in small town.
Enrollment: 701 undergrads, 40% part-time. 84 full-time freshmen.
Selectivity: Open admission; but selective for some programs.

BASIC COSTS (2005-2006)
Tuition and fees: $2,373; out-of-state residents $8,473.
Per-credit charge: $73; out-of-state residents $276.
Room and board: $5,650.
Additional info: In-state tuition based upon assumption of Colorado Oppurtunity Fund waiver of $80 per-credit-hour.

FINANCIAL AID PICTURE
Students with need: Need-based aid available for full-time and part-time students. Work study available nights, weekends, and for part-time students.
Students without need: No-need awards available for academics, athletics, state/district residency.
Scholarships offered: Academic Scholarships; $200-$1,000; for Colorado residents, based on grades, specific talent, area of study; requires application, essay, informal interview, minimum 2.5 GPA.

FINANCIAL AID PROCEDURES
Forms required: FAFSA, institutional form.
Dates and Deadlines: Priority date 4/15; no closing date. Applicants notified on a rolling basis starting 5/15; must reply within 4 week(s) of notification.

CONTACT
Teresa England, Director of Financial Aid
500 Kennedy Drive, Rangely, CO 81648
(970) 675-3204

Colorado School of Healing Arts
Lakewood, Colorado
www.csha.net   Federal Code: 035844

2-year for-profit health science college in small city.
Enrollment: 256 undergrads.
Selectivity: Open admission.

BASIC COSTS (2005-2006)
Additional info: Costs range from 9433 to 15,000 for entire programs, depending on program.

FINANCIAL AID PICTURE (2004-2005)
Students with need: 39% of average financial aid package awarded as scholarships/grants, 61% awarded as loans/jobs. Need-based aid available for part-time students.
Students without need: This college only awards aid to students with need.
Cumulative student debt: 90% of graduating class had student loans; average debt was $7,500.
FINANCIAL AID PROCEDURES
Forms required: FAFSA.
Dates and Deadlines: No deadline.
CONTACT
Gina Simpson, Director of Financial Aid
7655 West Mississippi, Suite 100, Lakewood, CO 80226
(303) 986-2320

Colorado School of Mines
Golden, Colorado
www.mines.edu   Federal Code: 001348

4-year public university and engineering college in large town.
Enrollment: 3,098 undergrads, 6% part-time. 852 full-time freshmen.
Selectivity: Admits over 75% of applicants.
BASIC COSTS (2005-2006)
Tuition and fees: $8,143; out-of-state residents $20,725.
Room and board: $6,750.
FINANCIAL AID PICTURE (2005-2006)
Students with need: Out of 639 full-time freshmen who applied for aid, 554 were judged to have need. Of these, 554 received aid, and 410 had their full need met. Average financial aid package met 92% of need; average scholarship/grant was $5,589; average loan was $3,700. Need-based aid available for part-time students.
Students without need: 92 full-time freshmen who did not demonstrate need for aid received scholarships/grants; average award was $4,900. No-need awards available for academics, alumni affiliation, athletics, music/drama, ROTC, state/district residency.
Scholarships offered: 75 full-time freshmen received athletic scholarships; average amount $2,950.
Cumulative student debt: 70% of graduating class had student loans; average debt was $18,500.
FINANCIAL AID PROCEDURES
Forms required: FAFSA.
Dates and Deadlines: Priority date 2/15; no closing date. Applicants notified on a rolling basis starting 3/15; must reply by 5/1 or within 2 week(s) of notification.
Transfers: Federal aid only (Pell grant and Stafford loan) available for second undergraduate degree candidates.
CONTACT
Roger Koester, Director of Financial Aid
Undergraduate Admissions, Golden, CO 80401
(303) 273-3301

Colorado State University
Fort Collins, Colorado
www.colostate.edu   Federal Code: 001350

4-year public university in small city.
Enrollment: 20,584 undergrads, 8% part-time. 4,023 full-time freshmen.
Selectivity: Admits over 75% of applicants.
BASIC COSTS (2005-2006)
Tuition and fees: $4,562; out-of-state residents $15,524.
Room and board: $6,316.
FINANCIAL AID PICTURE (2004-2005)
Students with need: Out of 2,328 full-time freshmen who applied for aid, 1,448 were judged to have need. Of these, 1,448 received aid, and 628 had their full need met. Average financial aid package met 87% of need; average scholarship/grant was $5,707; average loan was $3,318. For part-time students, average financial aid package was $5,987.
Students without need: 287 full-time freshmen who did not demonstrate need for aid received scholarships/grants; average award was $2,599. No-need awards available for academics, art, athletics, leadership, music/drama, ROTC, state/district residency.
Scholarships offered: 61 full-time freshmen received athletic scholarships; average amount $11,722.
FINANCIAL AID PROCEDURES
Forms required: FAFSA.
Dates and Deadlines: Priority date 3/1; no closing date. Applicants notified on a rolling basis starting 3/1.
CONTACT
Sandra Calhoun, Director of Financial Aid
Spruce Hall, Fort Collins, CO 80523-0015
(970) 491-6321

Colorado State University: Pueblo
Pueblo, Colorado
www.colostate-pueblo.edu   Federal Code: 001365

4-year public university in small city.
Enrollment: 4,241 undergrads, 23% part-time. 653 full-time freshmen.
BASIC COSTS (2005-2006)
Tuition and fees: $4,118; out-of-state residents $14,758.
Room and board: $6,088.
Additional info: Students from Alaska, Arizona, Hawaii, Idaho, Montana, Nevada, Oregon, South Dakota, North Dakota, Utah, New Mexico, and Wyoming pay $210 per credit hour and $6279 full time. Differential rate for Business, Nursing, Computer Information Systems, and Engineering courses is $15 more per credit hour.
FINANCIAL AID PICTURE
Students with need: Need-based aid available for full-time and part-time students. Work study available nights, weekends, and for part-time students.
Students without need: This college only awards aid to students with need.
FINANCIAL AID PROCEDURES
Forms required: FAFSA.
Dates and Deadlines: Priority date 3/1; no closing date. Applicants notified on a rolling basis starting 3/1; must reply within 3 week(s) of notification.
Transfers: No deadline.
CONTACT
Ofelia Morales, Director of Student Financial Services
2200 Bonforte Boulevard, Pueblo, CO 81001-4901
(719) 549-2753

Colorado Technical University
Colorado Springs, Colorado
www.coloradotech.edu   Federal Code: 010148

4-year for-profit university and technical college in large city.
Enrollment: 2,000 undergrads.

Colorado Technical University (continued)

BASIC COSTS (2005-2006)
Additional info: Lab fees $30 per lab class.

FINANCIAL AID PICTURE
Students with need: Need-based aid available for full-time and part-time students. Work study available nights, weekends, and for part-time students.
Students without need: No-need awards available for academics, ROTC.

FINANCIAL AID PROCEDURES
Forms required: FAFSA.
Dates and Deadlines: No deadline. Applicants notified on a rolling basis starting 6/30.
Transfers: No deadline.

CONTACT
Mary Heidrick, Director, Financial Aid
4435 North Chestnut Street, Colorado Springs, CO 80907
(719) 598-0200

Community College of Aurora
Aurora, Colorado
www.ccaurora.edu
Federal Code: 016058

2-year public community college in large city.
Enrollment: 2,650 undergrads.
Selectivity: Open admission.

BASIC COSTS (2005-2006)
Tuition and fees: $2,309; out-of-state residents $10,481.
Per-credit charge: $73; out-of-state residents $345.
Additional info: In-state tuition based upon assumption of Colorado Oppurtunity Fund waiver of $80 per-credit-hour.

FINANCIAL AID PICTURE
Students with need: Need-based aid available for full-time and part-time students. Work study available nights.

FINANCIAL AID PROCEDURES
Forms required: FAFSA, institutional form.
Dates and Deadlines: Priority date 6/1; no closing date. Applicants notified on a rolling basis starting 7/15.

CONTACT
Terry Campbell-Caron, Executive Director, Financial Aid
16000 East CentreTech Parkway, Aurora, CO 80011-9036
(303) 360-4709

Community College of Denver
Denver, Colorado
http://ccd.rightchoice.org
Federal Code: 009542

2-year public community college in very large city.
Enrollment: 1,922 full-time undergrads.
Selectivity: Open admission; but selective for some programs.

BASIC COSTS (2005-2006)
Tuition and fees: $2,795; out-of-state residents $10,967.
Additional info: In-state tuition based upon assumption of Colorado Oppurtunity Fund waiver of $80 per-credit-hour.

FINANCIAL AID PICTURE
Students with need: Need-based aid available for full-time and part-time students.

FINANCIAL AID PROCEDURES
Forms required: FAFSA, institutional form.
Dates and Deadlines: Priority date 1/1; no closing date. Applicants notified on a rolling basis starting 5/15; must reply within 3 week(s) of notification.

CONTACT
Carol Linsley, Director of Financial Aid
Campus Box 201, PO Box 173363, Denver, CO 80217-3363
(303) 556-2420

DeVry University: Colorado Springs
Colorado Springs, Colorado
www.cs.devry.edu
Federal Code: 007648

4-year for-profit university in large city.
Enrollment: 215 undergrads, 59% part-time. 12 full-time freshmen.

BASIC COSTS (2005-2006)
Tuition and fees: $12,800.
Per-credit charge: $460.

FINANCIAL AID PICTURE
Students with need: Need-based aid available for full-time and part-time students.
Students without need: This college only awards aid to students with need.

FINANCIAL AID PROCEDURES
Forms required: FAFSA.
Dates and Deadlines: No deadline. Applicants notified on a rolling basis starting 7/1.
Transfers: No deadline.

CONTACT
Carol Oppman, Director of Financial Aid
225 South Union Boulevard, Colorado Springs, CO 80910-3124
(719) 632-6750

DeVry University: Westminster
Westminster, Colorado
www.den.devry.edu
Federal Code: 014831

4-year for-profit university in very large city.
Enrollment: 616 undergrads, 35% part-time. 225 full-time freshmen.

BASIC COSTS (2005-2006)
Tuition and fees: $12,800.
Per-credit charge: $460.

FINANCIAL AID PICTURE (2004-2005)
Students with need: Out of 161 full-time freshmen who applied for aid, 151 were judged to have need. Of these, 150 received aid, and 7 had their full need met. Average financial aid package met 39% of need; average scholarship/grant was $4,455; average loan was $6,051. For part-time students, average financial aid package was $7,425.
Students without need: This college only awards aid to students with need.

FINANCIAL AID PROCEDURES
Forms required: FAFSA.
Dates and Deadlines: No deadline. Applicants notified on a rolling basis.

CONTACT
Terry Bargas, Director of Financial Aid
1870 West 122 Avenue, Westminster, CO 80234-2010
(303) 329-3340

Fort Lewis College
Durango, Colorado
www.fortlewis.edu   Federal Code: 001353

4-year public liberal arts college in large town.
Enrollment: 3,829 undergrads, 7% part-time. 959 full-time freshmen.
Selectivity: Admits 50 to 75% of applicants.

BASIC COSTS (2005-2006)
Tuition and fees: $3,298; out-of-state residents $13,704.
Room and board: $6,524.
Additional info: Tuition/fee waivers available for minority students.

FINANCIAL AID PICTURE (2004-2005)
Students with need: Out of 599 full-time freshmen who applied for aid, 415 were judged to have need. Of these, 408 received aid, and 65 had their full need met. Average financial aid package met 64% of need; average scholarship/grant was $3,192; average loan was $2,140. For part-time students, average financial aid package was $4,983.
Students without need: 74 full-time freshmen who did not demonstrate need for aid received scholarships/grants; average award was $1,547. No-need awards available for academics, alumni affiliation, art, athletics, leadership, minority status, music/drama, state/district residency.
Scholarships offered: 30 full-time freshmen received athletic scholarships; average amount $1,400.
Cumulative student debt: 60% of graduating class had student loans; average debt was $16,966.
Additional info: Tuition waived for Native Americans of federally recognized tribes; census number and CIB (Certificate of Indian Blood) must accompany application.

FINANCIAL AID PROCEDURES
Forms required: FAFSA.
Dates and Deadlines: Priority date 2/15; no closing date. Applicants notified on a rolling basis starting 4/1; must reply within 2 week(s) of notification.
Transfers: Closing date 2/15.

CONTACT
Elaine Redwine, Director of Financial Aid
1000 Rim Drive, Durango, CO 81301-3999
(970) 247-7142

Front Range Community College
Westminster, Colorado
www.frcc.cc.co.us   Federal Code: 007933

2-year public community college in large city.
Enrollment: 12,685 undergrads.
Selectivity: Open admission.

BASIC COSTS (2005-2006)
Tuition and fees: $2,452; out-of-state residents $10,624.
Per-credit charge: $73; out-of-state residents $345.
Additional info: In-state tuition based upon assumption of Colorado Oppurtunity Fund waiver of $80 per-credit-hour.

FINANCIAL AID PICTURE (2004-2005)
Students with need: 47% of average financial aid package awarded as scholarships/grants, 53% awarded as loans/jobs. Need-based aid available for part-time students. Work study available nights, weekends, and for part-time students.
Students without need: No-need awards available for academics, job skills, leadership, state/district residency.

FINANCIAL AID PROCEDURES
Forms required: FAFSA, institutional form.
Dates and Deadlines: Priority date 5/1; no closing date. Applicants notified on a rolling basis starting 7/1; must reply within 3 week(s) of notification.

CONTACT
Teri Dorchuck, Director of Financial Aid
3645 West 112th Avenue, Westminster, CO 80031
(303) 439-9454

Heritage College
Denver, Colorado
www.heritage-education.com   Federal Code: 026110

2-year for-profit health science college in very large city.
Enrollment: 480 undergrads.
Selectivity: Open admission; but selective for some programs.

FINANCIAL AID PICTURE
Students with need: Need-based aid available for full-time students. Work study available nights, weekends, and for part-time students.
Students without need: This college only awards aid to students with need.

FINANCIAL AID PROCEDURES
Forms required: FAFSA.
Dates and Deadlines: No deadline. Applicants notified on a rolling basis.

CONTACT
Anne Manning, Director of Financial Aid
12 Lakeside Lane, Denver, CO 80212-7413
(720) 855-6014

IntelliTec College: Grand Junction
Grand Junction, Colorado
www.intelliteccollege.com   Federal Code: 030669

2-year for-profit technical college in small city.
Enrollment: 243 undergrads.
Selectivity: Open admission.

BASIC COSTS (2005-2006)
Additional info: Lab fees vary per program; average $242. Tuition at time of enrollment locked for 2 years.

FINANCIAL AID PICTURE
Students with need: Need-based aid available for full-time students.
Students without need: This college only awards aid to students with need.

FINANCIAL AID PROCEDURES
Forms required: FAFSA.
Dates and Deadlines: No deadline. Applicants notified on a rolling basis.
Transfers: No deadline.

CONTACT
Sherry Martin, Financial Services Representative
772 Horizon Drive, Grand Junction, CO 81506
(970) 245-8101

Johnson & Wales University
Denver, Colorado
www.jwu.edu   Federal Code: 003404

4-year for-profit university in large city.
Enrollment: 1,544 undergrads, 1% part-time. 385 full-time freshmen.
Selectivity: Admits over 75% of applicants.

Colorado Johnson & Wales University

BASIC COSTS (2006-2007)
Tuition and fees: $20,826.
Per-credit charge: $368.
Room and board: $8,300.

FINANCIAL AID PICTURE (2005-2006)
Students with need: Out of 343 full-time freshmen who applied for aid, 298 were judged to have need. Of these, 297 received aid, and 9 had their full need met. Average financial aid package met 65% of need; average scholarship/grant was $5,180; average loan was $6,255. For part-time students, average financial aid package was $7,915.
Students without need: 56 full-time freshmen who did not demonstrate need for aid received scholarships/grants; average award was $5,015. No-need awards available for academics, leadership.
Cumulative student debt: 74% of graduating class had student loans; average debt was $14,799.

FINANCIAL AID PROCEDURES
Forms required: FAFSA.
Dates and Deadlines: No deadline. Applicants notified on a rolling basis starting 3/1; must reply within 2 week(s) of notification.

CONTACT
Lynn Robinson, Chief Financial Aid Officer
7150 Montview Boulevard, Denver, CO 80220
(800) 342-5598 ext. 4648

Mesa State College
Grand Junction, Colorado
www.mesastate.edu   Federal Code: 001358

4-year public community and liberal arts college in large town.
Enrollment: 5,499 undergrads, 19% part-time. 1,149 full-time freshmen.
Selectivity: Admits over 75% of applicants.

BASIC COSTS (2005-2006)
Tuition and fees: $3,080; out-of-state residents $10,267.
Per-credit charge: $140; out-of-state residents $439.
Room and board: $7,050.

FINANCIAL AID PICTURE (2004-2005)
Students with need: Out of 828 full-time freshmen who applied for aid, 609 were judged to have need. Of these, 609 received aid, and 131 had their full need met. Average financial aid package met 57% of need; average scholarship/grant was $3,126; average loan was $2,288. For part-time students, average financial aid package was $3,552.
Students without need: 59 full-time freshmen who did not demonstrate need for aid received scholarships/grants; average award was $1,887. No-need awards available for academics, art, athletics, leadership, music/drama.
Scholarships offered: 56 full-time freshmen received athletic scholarships; average amount $2,211.
Cumulative student debt: 53% of graduating class had student loans; average debt was $17,634.

FINANCIAL AID PROCEDURES
Forms required: FAFSA.
Dates and Deadlines: Priority date 3/1; no closing date. Applicants notified on a rolling basis starting 4/1; must reply within 5 week(s) of notification.

CONTACT
Curt Martin, Director of Financial Aid Grand Junction, CO 81501
(970) 248-1396

Metropolitan State College of Denver
Denver, Colorado
www.mscd.edu   Federal Code: 001360

4-year public liberal arts college in very large city.
Enrollment: 20,010 undergrads. 1,978 full-time freshmen.

BASIC COSTS (2005-2006)
Tuition and fees: $2,941; out-of-state residents $10,720.
Per-credit charge: $91; out-of-state residents $393.

FINANCIAL AID PICTURE (2005-2006)
Students with need: Out of 1,174 full-time freshmen who applied for aid, 868 were judged to have need. Of these, 753 received aid, and 2 had their full need met. Average financial aid package met 62% of need; average scholarship/grant was $1,902; average loan was $1,371. For part-time students, average financial aid package was $2,417.
Students without need: 48 full-time freshmen who did not demonstrate need for aid received scholarships/grants; average award was $549. No-need awards available for academics, art, athletics, job skills, music/drama, state/district residency.
Scholarships offered: 14 full-time freshmen received athletic scholarships; average amount $3,256.

FINANCIAL AID PROCEDURES
Forms required: FAFSA.
Dates and Deadlines: Priority date 3/1; no closing date. Applicants notified on a rolling basis starting 3/1.
Transfers: No deadline.

CONTACT
Cindy Hejl, Director of Financial Aid
Campus Box 16, Denver, CO 80217
(303) 873-2660

Morgan Community College
Fort Morgan, Colorado
www.morgancc.edu   Federal Code: 009981

2-year public community college in large town.
Enrollment: 360 full-time undergrads.
Selectivity: Open admission; but selective for some programs.

BASIC COSTS (2005-2006)
Tuition and fees: $2,359; out-of-state residents $10,531.
Per-credit charge: $73; out-of-state residents $345.
Additional info: In-state tuition based upon assumption of Colorado Oppurtunity Fund waiver of $80 per-credit-hour.

FINANCIAL AID PICTURE
Students with need: Need-based aid available for full-time and part-time students. Work study available nights, weekends, and for part-time students.
Students without need: No-need awards available for academics, state/district residency.

FINANCIAL AID PROCEDURES
Forms required: FAFSA.
Dates and Deadlines: Priority date 6/1; no closing date. Applicants notified on a rolling basis.

CONTACT
Kent Bauer, Director of Financial Aid
920 Barlow Road, Fort Morgan, CO 80701
(970) 542-3100

Naropa University
Boulder, Colorado
www.naropa.edu   Federal Code: 014652

4-year private liberal arts college in small city.
Enrollment: 451 undergrads, 11% part-time. 37 full-time freshmen.
Selectivity: Admits over 75% of applicants.

BASIC COSTS (2005-2006)
Tuition and fees: $18,500.
Per-credit charge: $600.
Room and board: $6,590.

FINANCIAL AID PICTURE (2005-2006)
Students with need: Out of 21 full-time freshmen who applied for aid, 20 were judged to have need. Of these, 20 received aid, and 4 had their full need met. Average financial aid package met 58% of need; average scholarship/grant was $12,267; average loan was $3,215. For part-time students, average financial aid package was $9,666.
Students without need: This college only awards aid to students with need.
Cumulative student debt: 50% of graduating class had student loans; average debt was $21,203.

FINANCIAL AID PROCEDURES
Forms required: FAFSA.
Dates and Deadlines: Priority date 3/1; no closing date. Applicants notified on a rolling basis starting 3/1; must reply within 4 week(s) of notification.
Transfers: No deadline. Applicants notified on a rolling basis starting 3/1.

CONTACT
Cheryl Barbour, Assistant Vice President of Student Administrative Services
2130 Arapahoe Avenue, Boulder, CO 80302
(303) 546-3534

Nazarene Bible College
Colorado Springs, Colorado
www.nbc.edu   Federal Code: 013007

4-year private Bible college in very large city, affiliated with Church of the Nazarene.
Enrollment: 537 undergrads, 67% part-time.
Selectivity: Open admission; but selective for some programs.

BASIC COSTS (2006-2007)
Tuition and fees: $7,350.
Per-credit charge: $250.

FINANCIAL AID PICTURE
Students with need: Need-based aid available for full-time and part-time students.
Students without need: No-need awards available for religious affiliation.
Additional info: Tuition waiver available to students serving as student body officers.

FINANCIAL AID PROCEDURES
Forms required: FAFSA.
Dates and Deadlines: Priority date 6/1; no closing date. Applicants notified on a rolling basis starting 6/15; must reply within 2 week(s) of notification.

CONTACT
Mal Britton, Director of Financial Aid
1111 Academy Park Loop, Colorado Springs, CO 80910-3717
(719) 884-5050 ext. 5050

Northeastern Junior College
Sterling, Colorado
www.njc.edu   Federal Code: 001361

2-year public junior college in large town.
Enrollment: 1,095 undergrads.
Selectivity: Open admission; but selective for some programs.

BASIC COSTS (2005-2006)
Tuition and fees: $2,776; out-of-state residents $8,876.
Per-credit charge: $73; out-of-state residents $345.
Room and board: $5,162.
Additional info: In-state tuition based upon assumption of Colorado Oppurtunity Fund waiver of $80 per-credit-hour. Tuition/fee waivers available for adults, minority students.

FINANCIAL AID PICTURE
Students with need: Need-based aid available for full-time and part-time students.
Students without need: No-need awards available for academics, athletics.
Scholarships offered: Institutional and foundation awards available.
Additional info: Need-based financial aid available to part-time students taking 6 credits or more per semester.

FINANCIAL AID PROCEDURES
Forms required: FAFSA, institutional form.
Dates and Deadlines: Priority date 3/1; no closing date. Applicants notified on a rolling basis starting 4/15; must reply within 4 week(s) of notification.

CONTACT
Alice Weingandt, Financial Aid Director
100 College Avenue, Sterling, CO 80751
(970) 521-6800

Otero Junior College
La Junta, Colorado
www.ojc.edu   Federal Code: 001362

2-year public community and junior college in small town.
Enrollment: 1,120 undergrads.
Selectivity: Open admission; but selective for some programs.

BASIC COSTS (2005-2006)
Tuition and fees: $2,354; out-of-state residents $8,454.
Per-credit charge: $73; out-of-state residents $276.
Room and board: $4,302.
Additional info: In-state tuition based upon assumption of Colorado Oppurtunity Fund waiver of $80 per-credit-hour.

FINANCIAL AID PICTURE
Students with need: Need-based aid available for full-time and part-time students.
Students without need: No-need awards available for academics, athletics, state/district residency.

FINANCIAL AID PROCEDURES
Forms required: FAFSA.
Dates and Deadlines: Priority date 4/15; no closing date. Applicants notified on a rolling basis; must reply within 2 week(s) of notification.

CONTACT
Jeff Paolucci, Director of Financial Aid
1802 Colorado Avenue, La Junta, CO 81050
(719) 384-6834

Parks College
Denver, Colorado
www.cci.edu
Federal Code: 004507

2-year for-profit junior college in large town.
Enrollment: 719 undergrads.

FINANCIAL AID PICTURE
Students with need: Need-based aid available for full-time and part-time students.

FINANCIAL AID PROCEDURES
Forms required: FAFSA, institutional form.
Dates and Deadlines: No deadline. Applicants notified on a rolling basis starting 8/1.

CONTACT
Randy Hanson, Director of Financial Services
9065 Grant Street, Denver, CO 80229

Parks College: Aurora
Aurora, Colorado
www.cci.edu
Federal Code: 004507

2-year for-profit branch campus and technical college in large city.
Enrollment: 332 undergrads.
Selectivity: Open admission.

BASIC COSTS (2005-2006)
Additional info: Tuition for homeland security program (48 credit hours) - $8048; tuition for medical administrative assistant/medical assistant (47 credit hours) - $9300; tuition for medical insurance billing and coding (35 credit hours) - $8244.

FINANCIAL AID PICTURE (2004-2005)
Students with need: Average financial aid package met 48% of need; average scholarship/grant was $1,532; average loan was $4,560. Need-based aid available for part-time students.
Students without need: This college only awards aid to students with need.

FINANCIAL AID PROCEDURES
Forms required: FAFSA, state aid form, institutional form.
Dates and Deadlines: No deadline. Applicants notified on a rolling basis; must reply within 4 week(s) of notification.
Transfers: $4,500 limitation on Colorado State Grant per award year.

CONTACT
Kim Martinez, Finance Director
14280 East Jewell Suite 100, Aurora, CO 80012
(303) 745-6244 ext. 104

Pikes Peak Community College
Colorado Springs, Colorado
www.ppcc.edu
Federal Code: 008896

2-year public community college in large city.
Enrollment: 9,300 undergrads.
Selectivity: Open admission; but selective for some programs.

BASIC COSTS (2005-2006)
Tuition and fees: $2,339; out-of-state residents $10,511.
Per-credit charge: $73; out-of-state residents $345.
Additional info: In-state tuition based upon assumption of Colorado Oppurtunity Fund waiver of $80 per-credit-hour.

FINANCIAL AID PICTURE
Students with need: Need-based aid available for full-time and part-time students.
Students without need: No-need awards available for state/district residency.

FINANCIAL AID PROCEDURES
Forms required: FAFSA.
Dates and Deadlines: Priority date 7/1; no closing date. Applicants notified on a rolling basis starting 8/1; must reply within 2 week(s) of notification.

CONTACT
Sherri McCullough, Assistant Director of Financial Aid
5675 South Academy Boulevard, Colorado Springs, CO 80906-5498
(719) 540-7089

Pueblo Community College
Pueblo, Colorado
www.pueblocc.edu
Federal Code: 014829

2-year public community college in small city.
Enrollment: 4,600 undergrads.
Selectivity: Open admission; but selective for some programs.

BASIC COSTS (2005-2006)
Tuition and fees: $2,408; out-of-state residents $10,580.
Per-credit charge: $83; out-of-state residents $345.
Additional info: In-state tuition based upon assumption of Colorado Oppurtunity Fund waiver of $80 per-credit-hour.

FINANCIAL AID PICTURE
Students with need: Need-based aid available for full-time and part-time students.
Students without need: No-need awards available for academics, state/district residency.

FINANCIAL AID PROCEDURES
Forms required: FAFSA, institutional form.
Dates and Deadlines: Priority date 3/15; no closing date. Applicants notified on a rolling basis starting 4/15.

CONTACT
Audrey Osswald, Director of Financial Aid
900 West Orman Avenue, Pueblo, CO 81004-1499
(719) 549-3020

Red Rocks Community College
Lakewood, Colorado
www.rrcc.cccoes.edu
Federal Code: 009543

2-year public community college in large city.
Enrollment: 4,510 undergrads.
Selectivity: Open admission.

BASIC COSTS (2005-2006)
Tuition and fees: $2,398; out-of-state residents $10,580.
Per-credit charge: $73; out-of-state residents $345.
Additional info: In-state tuition based upon assumption of Colorado Oppurtunity Fund waiver of $80 per-credit-hour.

FINANCIAL AID PICTURE
Students with need: Need-based aid available for full-time and part-time students. Work study available nights, weekends, and for part-time students.

FINANCIAL AID PROCEDURES
Forms required: FAFSA, institutional form.

Dates and Deadlines: Priority date 4/1; no closing date. Applicants notified on a rolling basis starting 6/1; must reply within 2 week(s) of notification.

CONTACT
Linda Crook, Director of Financial Aid
13300 West Sixth Avenue, Lakewood, CO 80228-1255
(303) 914-6256

Regis University
Denver, Colorado
www.regis.edu Federal Code: 001363

4-year private university and liberal arts college in very large city, affiliated with Roman Catholic Church.
Enrollment: 1,581 undergrads, 5% part-time. 372 full-time freshmen.
Selectivity: Admits over 75% of applicants.

BASIC COSTS (2006-2007)
Tuition and fees: $25,200.
Room and board: $8,190.

FINANCIAL AID PICTURE (2004-2005)
Students with need: Out of 368 full-time freshmen who applied for aid, 366 were judged to have need. Of these, 249 received aid, and 184 had their full need met. For part-time students, average financial aid package was $14,349.
Students without need: 94 full-time freshmen who did not demonstrate need for aid received scholarships/grants; average award was $6,488. No-need awards available for academics, athletics, leadership, minority status, religious affiliation, ROTC, state/district residency.
Scholarships offered: 30 full-time freshmen received athletic scholarships; average amount $6,466.
Additional info: Tuition free for any student maintaining the required amount of credit hours who does not graduate in four years.

FINANCIAL AID PROCEDURES
Forms required: FAFSA.
Dates and Deadlines: Priority date 3/1; no closing date. Applicants notified on a rolling basis starting 3/15.

CONTACT
Ellie Miller, Director of Financial Aid
3333 Regis Boulevard, Mail Code A12, Denver, CO 80221-1099
(800) 388-2366 ext. 4126

Remington College: Colorado Springs
Colorado Springs, Colorado
www.remingtoncollege.com Federal Code: 030121

2-year for-profit branch campus and technical college in very large city.
Enrollment: 186 undergrads. 166 full-time freshmen.
Selectivity: Open admission; but selective for some programs.

BASIC COSTS (2005-2006)
Additional info: $30,480 for all 2-year associate programs. Tuition covers costs of all books, lab fees, laptop computer. Tuition at time of enrollment locked for 2 years.

FINANCIAL AID PICTURE (2005-2006)
Students with need: Average financial aid package for all full-time undergraduates was $5,681. 35% awarded as scholarships/grants, 65% awarded as loans/jobs. Need-based aid available for part-time students. Work study available nights.
Students without need: This college only awards aid to students with need.

Cumulative student debt: 90% of graduating class had student loans; average debt was $13,116.

FINANCIAL AID PROCEDURES
Forms required: FAFSA.
Dates and Deadlines: No deadline. Applicants notified on a rolling basis; must reply within 3 week(s) of notification.
Transfers: No deadline. Applicants notified on a rolling basis.

CONTACT
Shirley McCray, Director of Financial Services
6050 Erin Park Drive, Colorado Springs, CO 80918
(719) 532-1234 ext. 228

Rocky Mountain College of Art & Design
Lakewood, Colorado
www.rmcad.edu Federal Code: 013991

4-year for-profit visual arts college in very large city.
Enrollment: 446 undergrads, 18% part-time. 58 full-time freshmen.
Selectivity: Admits over 75% of applicants.

BASIC COSTS (2006-2007)
Tuition and fees: $18,984.
Per-credit charge: $791.
Room and board: $5,427.

FINANCIAL AID PICTURE (2004-2005)
Students with need: 34% of average financial aid package awarded as scholarships/grants, 66% awarded as loans/jobs. Need-based aid available for part-time students. Work study available nights, weekends, and for part-time students.
Students without need: No-need awards available for academics, art, state/district residency.
Cumulative student debt: 80% of graduating class had student loans; average debt was $16,500.

FINANCIAL AID PROCEDURES
Forms required: FAFSA, state aid form, institutional form.
Dates and Deadlines: Priority date 3/15; no closing date. Applicants notified on a rolling basis starting 4/15; must reply within 2 week(s) of notification.

CONTACT
David Nelson, Director of Financial Aid
1600 Pierce Street, Lakewood, CO 80214
(303) 753-6046

Teikyo Loretto Heights University
Denver, Colorado
www.tlhu.edu Federal Code: 032893

4-year private business and liberal arts college in very large city.
Enrollment: 234 undergrads.

BASIC COSTS (2006-2007)
Tuition and fees: $13,600.
Per-credit charge: $445.
Room and board: $7,300.

FINANCIAL AID PICTURE
Students with need: Need-based aid available for full-time and part-time students. Work study available nights.

FINANCIAL AID PROCEDURES
Forms required: FAFSA.

240 Colorado Teikyo Loretto Heights University

CONTACT
Eric Clinkscales
3001 South Federal Boulevard, Denver, CO 80236
(303) 937-4280

Trinidad State Junior College
Trinidad, Colorado
www.trinidadstate.edu   Federal Code: 001368

2-year public community and junior college in small town.
Enrollment: 1,327 undergrads, 42% part-time. 310 full-time freshmen.
Selectivity: Open admission; but selective for some programs.

BASIC COSTS (2005-2006)
Tuition and fees: $2,733; out-of-state residents $8,833.
Per-credit charge: $73; out-of-state residents $276.
Room and board: $4,248.
Additional info: In-state tuition based upon assumption of Colorado Oppurtunity Fund waiver of $80 per-credit-hour.

FINANCIAL AID PICTURE
Students with need: Need-based aid available for full-time and part-time students. Work study available nights.
Students without need: No-need awards available for academics, athletics, state/district residency.

FINANCIAL AID PROCEDURES
Forms required: FAFSA, institutional form.
Dates and Deadlines: Priority date 5/1; no closing date. Applicants notified on a rolling basis starting 6/15.

CONTACT
Gary Fresquez, Financial Aid Director
600 Prospect Street, Trinidad, CO 81082
(719) 846-5553

United States Air Force Academy
USAF Academy, Colorado
www.usafa.edu   Federal Code: 001369

4-year public university and military college in large city.
Enrollment: 4,397 undergrads.
Selectivity: Admits less than 50% of applicants. GED not accepted.

BASIC COSTS (2006-2007)
Additional info: Tuition, room, board, medical and dental care paid by U.S. Government. Each cadet receives monthly salary to pay for uniforms, supplies and personal expenses. A government loan is advanced to each member of the freshman class.

CONTACT
HQ USAF/RRS, 2304 Cadet Drive, Suite 200, USAF Academy, CO 80840

University of Colorado at Boulder
Boulder, Colorado
www.colorado.edu   Federal Code: 001370

4-year public university in small city.
Enrollment: 25,205 undergrads, 7% part-time. 5,115 full-time freshmen.
Selectivity: Admits over 75% of applicants.

BASIC COSTS (2005-2006)
Tuition and fees: $5,372; out-of-state residents $22,826.
Per-credit charge: $268.
Room and board: $7,980.

FINANCIAL AID PICTURE (2004-2005)
Students with need: Out of 3,364 full-time freshmen who applied for aid, 1,999 were judged to have need. Of these, 1,953 received aid, and 999 had their full need met. Average financial aid package met 91% of need; average scholarship/grant was $5,256; average loan was $3,490. For part-time students, average financial aid package was $8,858.
Students without need: 1,022 full-time freshmen who did not demonstrate need for aid received scholarships/grants; average award was $3,792. No-need awards available for academics, alumni affiliation, art, athletics, leadership, music/drama, ROTC, state/district residency.
Scholarships offered: *Merit:* Chancellor's Achievement Scholarship; $15,000 over 4 years; entering non-resident freshmen in the top 25 percent of class, based on high school GPA and test scores. Must maintain 2.75 CU GPA for renewal. Parents Association Scholarship, $1,000, 15-30 awarded annually based on full-time entering freshman status with 3.5 GPA, academic excellence and extracurricular activities, nonrenewable. Norlin Scholars Program, $2,000, based on excellent academic or creative ability, 20 awards, renewable for 2 or 4 years contingent upon academic progress. First Generation Scholarship, up to $2,000, entering Colorado resident freshmen whose parents do not have college, occupational, or technical training, must demonstrate financial need and submit FAFSA, number of awards vary. *Athletic:* 38 full-time freshmen received athletic scholarships; average amount $12,632.
Cumulative student debt: 44% of graduating class had student loans; average debt was $16,348.

FINANCIAL AID PROCEDURES
Forms required: FAFSA.
Dates and Deadlines: Priority date 4/1; no closing date. Applicants notified on a rolling basis starting 2/1; must reply within 3 week(s) of notification.
Transfers: Some financial aid programs available exclusively to transfer students.

CONTACT
Gwen Eberhard, Director of Financial Aid
552 UCB, Boulder, CO 80309-0552
(303) 492-5091

University of Colorado at Colorado Springs
Colorado Springs, Colorado
www.uccs.edu   Federal Code: 004509

4-year public university in large city.
Enrollment: 6,077 undergrads, 21% part-time. 853 full-time freshmen.
Selectivity: Admits over 75% of applicants.

BASIC COSTS (2005-2006)
Tuition and fees: $4,888; out-of-state residents $16,182.
Per-credit charge: $195; out-of-state residents $830.
Room and board: $6,418.

FINANCIAL AID PICTURE (2005-2006)
Students with need: Average financial aid package met 59% of need; average scholarship/grant was $4,749; average loan was $2,619. For part-time students, average financial aid package was $5,290.
Students without need: No-need awards available for academics, athletics, leadership, state/district residency.
Scholarships offered: College Opportunity Fund for in-state undergraduates.
Cumulative student debt: 53% of graduating class had student loans; average debt was $11,347.

FINANCIAL AID PROCEDURES
Forms required: FAFSA.
Dates and Deadlines: Priority date 4/1; no closing date. Applicants notified on a rolling basis starting 4/15.

CONTACT
Lee Noble, Director of Financial Aid
PO Box 7150, Colorado Springs, CO 80933-7150
(719) 262-3460

University of Colorado at Denver and Health Sciences Center
Denver, Colorado
www.ucdhsc.edu   Federal Code: 006740

4-year public university in very large city.
Enrollment: 7,780 undergrads, 27% part-time. 687 full-time freshmen.
Selectivity: Admits 50 to 75% of applicants.

BASIC COSTS (2005-2006)
Tuition and fees: $5,021; out-of-state residents $16,191.
Per-credit charge: $225; out-of-state residents $925.
Additional info: Tuition varies by program.

FINANCIAL AID PICTURE (2004-2005)
Students with need: Out of 451 full-time freshmen who applied for aid, 322 were judged to have need. Of these, 285 received aid, and 25 had their full need met. Average financial aid package met 61% of need; average scholarship/grant was $4,296; average loan was $2,264. For part-time students, average financial aid package was $5,704.
Students without need: 20 full-time freshmen who did not demonstrate need for aid received scholarships/grants; average award was $1,733. No-need awards available for academics, art, leadership, music/drama.
Cumulative student debt: 41% of graduating class had student loans; average debt was $16,933.

FINANCIAL AID PROCEDURES
Forms required: FAFSA, institutional form.
Dates and Deadlines: Closing date 4/1. Applicants notified on a rolling basis starting 5/1.

CONTACT
Patrick McTee, Director of Financial Aid
Box 173364, Campus Box 167, Denver, CO 80217-3364
(303) 556-2886

University of Denver
Denver, Colorado
http://www.du.edu/   Federal Code: 001371

4-year private university in very large city, affiliated with United Methodist Church.
Enrollment: 4,813 undergrads, 9% part-time. 1,012 full-time freshmen.
Selectivity: Admits over 75% of applicants.

BASIC COSTS (2006-2007)
Tuition and fees: $30,372.
Per-credit charge: $823.
Room and board: $8,351.

FINANCIAL AID PICTURE (2004-2005)
Students with need: Out of 612 full-time freshmen who applied for aid, 458 were judged to have need. Of these, 458 received aid. Average financial aid package met 75% of need; average scholarship/grant was $14,582; average loan was $3,581. For part-time students, average financial aid package was $6,897.
Students without need: 307 full-time freshmen who did not demonstrate need for aid received scholarships/grants; average award was $9,182. No-need awards available for academics, alumni affiliation, art, athletics, leadership, minority status, music/drama.
Scholarships offered: 45 full-time freshmen received athletic scholarships; average amount $21,475.

FINANCIAL AID PROCEDURES
Forms required: FAFSA.
Dates and Deadlines: Priority date 2/15; no closing date. Applicants notified by 4/1; must reply within 3 week(s) of notification.

CONTACT
Barbara McFall, Interim Director of Financial Aid
2197 South University Boulevard, Denver, CO 80208
(303) 871-2337

University of Northern Colorado
Greeley, Colorado
www.unco.edu   Federal Code: 001349

4-year public university in small city.
Enrollment: 10,407 undergrads, 7% part-time. 2,431 full-time freshmen.
Selectivity: Admits over 75% of applicants.

BASIC COSTS (2005-2006)
Tuition and fees: $3,837; out-of-state residents $12,381.
Room and board: $6,744.

FINANCIAL AID PICTURE (2004-2005)
Students with need: Out of 2,003 full-time freshmen who applied for aid, 1,058 were judged to have need. Of these, 1,048 received aid, and 487 had their full need met. Average financial aid package met 95% of need; average scholarship/grant was $3,379; average loan was $3,134. For part-time students, average financial aid package was $9,007.
Students without need: 261 full-time freshmen who did not demonstrate need for aid received scholarships/grants; average award was $2,395. No-need awards available for academics, athletics, music/drama.
Scholarships offered: 16 full-time freshmen received athletic scholarships; average amount $5,063.

FINANCIAL AID PROCEDURES
Forms required: FAFSA.
Dates and Deadlines: Priority date 3/1; no closing date. Applicants notified on a rolling basis starting 4/15; must reply within 4 week(s) of notification.

CONTACT
Donni Clark, Director of Student Financial Resources
Campus Box 10, Greeley, CO 80639
(970) 351-2502

Western State College of Colorado
Gunnison, Colorado
www.western.edu   Federal Code: 001372

4-year public liberal arts college in small town.
Enrollment: 2,277 undergrads. 492 full-time freshmen.

BASIC COSTS (2005-2006)
Tuition and fees: $3,138; out-of-state residents $11,754.
Per-credit charge: $98; out-of-state residents $457.
Room and board: $6,804.
Additional info: Tuition/fee waivers available for unemployed or children of unemployed.

FINANCIAL AID PICTURE (2005-2006)
Students with need: Out of 368 full-time freshmen who applied for aid, 294 were judged to have need. Of these, 249 received aid, and 37 had their full need met. Average financial aid package met 45% of need; average scholarship/grant was $2,500; average loan was $2,625. For part-time students, average financial aid package was $5,000.
Students without need: 147 full-time freshmen who did not demonstrate need for aid received scholarships/grants; average award was $1,000. No-

need awards available for academics, alumni affiliation, art, athletics, leadership, music/drama.

Scholarships offered: *Merit:* Academic Excellence Award; $1,000; minimum 3.0 GPA and 20 ACT or 950 SAT. Non-resident Leadership Award, $2,500; 3.2 GPA, 990 SAT, leadership activities. SAT scores exclusive of Writing. *Athletic:* 50 full-time freshmen received athletic scholarships; average amount $500.

FINANCIAL AID PROCEDURES
Forms required: FAFSA.
Dates and Deadlines: Priority date 4/15; no closing date. Applicants notified on a rolling basis starting 4/15; must reply within 3 week(s) of notification.

CONTACT
Marty Somero, Director of Financial Aid
600 North Adams Street, Gunnison, CO 81231
(970) 943-3085

Westwood College of Technology
Denver, Colorado
www.westwood.edu   Federal Code: 007548

3-year for-profit technical college in very large city.
Enrollment: 932 undergrads.

BASIC COSTS (2005-2006)
Additional info: One-time tool charge ranges from $35 to $3,300. Required fees $150. Lab fees vary by program from $600 to $925 per year.

FINANCIAL AID PICTURE
Students with need: Need-based aid available for full-time and part-time students. Work study available nights.
Students without need: No-need awards available for academics, state/district residency.

FINANCIAL AID PROCEDURES
Forms required: FAFSA, state aid form, institutional form.
Dates and Deadlines: No deadline. Applicants notified on a rolling basis starting 1/1; must reply within 2 week(s) of notification.
Transfers: No deadline.

CONTACT
Amy Argyris, Director, Financial Aid
7350 North Broadway, Denver, CO 80221
(303) 426-7000

Westwood College of Technology: South
Denver, Colorado
www.westwood.edu   Federal Code: 007548

4-year for-profit technical college in very large city.
Enrollment: 363 undergrads, 15% part-time. 99 full-time freshmen.
Selectivity: Admits 50 to 75% of applicants.

BASIC COSTS (2005-2006)
Tuition and fees: $20,425.

FINANCIAL AID PICTURE
Students with need: Need-based aid available for full-time and part-time students. Work study available nights.

FINANCIAL AID PROCEDURES
Forms required: FAFSA, state aid form, institutional form.
Dates and Deadlines: No deadline. Applicants notified on a rolling basis; must reply within 2 week(s) of notification.

CONTACT
Meghann Rutledge, Assistant Director of Financial Aid
3150 South Sheridan Boulevard, Denver, CO 80227-5507
(303) 934-1122

Connecticut

Albertus Magnus College
New Haven, Connecticut
www.albertus.edu   Federal Code: 001374

4-year private liberal arts college in small city, affiliated with Roman Catholic Church.
Enrollment: 1,695 undergrads. 186 full-time freshmen.
Selectivity: Admits over 75% of applicants.

BASIC COSTS (2006-2007)
Tuition and fees: $19,390.
Per-credit charge: $778.
Room and board: $8,403.

FINANCIAL AID PICTURE (2004-2005)
Students with need: Average financial aid package met 46% of need; average scholarship/grant was $6,720; average loan was $3,550. Need-based aid available for part-time students.
Students without need: No-need awards available for academics, art, athletics, leadership, music/drama, religious affiliation, state/district residency.

FINANCIAL AID PROCEDURES
Forms required: FAFSA, institutional form.
Dates and Deadlines: Priority date 2/28; closing date 8/15. Applicants notified on a rolling basis starting 3/1; must reply within 2 week(s) of notification.
Transfers: No deadline. Must reply within 2 week(s) of notification.

CONTACT
Andrew Foster, Director of Financial Aid
700 Prospect Street, New Haven, CT 06511-1189
(203) 773-8508

Asnuntuck Community College
Enfield, Connecticut
www.acc.commnet.edu   Federal Code: 011150

2-year public community and technical college in large town.
Enrollment: 918 undergrads, 52% part-time. 145 full-time freshmen.
Selectivity: Open admission.

BASIC COSTS (2005-2006)
Tuition and fees: $2,536; out-of-state residents $7,872.
Per-credit charge: $93; out-of-state residents $279.
Additional info: New England Regional Student Program: $3,998 annual tuition/fees, $231.50 per credit-hour.

FINANCIAL AID PICTURE
Students with need: Need-based aid available for full-time and part-time students. Work study available nights, weekends, and for part-time students.
Students without need: This college only awards aid to students with need.

FINANCIAL AID PROCEDURES
Forms required: FAFSA, institutional form.
Dates and Deadlines: Priority date 6/1; no closing date. Applicants notified on a rolling basis starting 7/1; must reply within 2 week(s) of notification.
Transfers: Financial Aid Transcript required.

CONTACT
Donna Jones-Searle, Director of Financial Aid
170 Elm Street, Enfield, CT 06082
(860) 253-3030

Briarwood College
Southington, Connecticut
www.briarwood.edu   Federal Code: 009407

4-year for-profit junior college in large town.
Enrollment: 600 undergrads.
Selectivity: Open admission; but selective for some programs.

BASIC COSTS (2006-2007)
Tuition and fees: $16,335.
Per-credit charge: $520.
Room only: $3,500.
Additional info: Tuition at time of enrollment locked for 4 years.

FINANCIAL AID PICTURE
Students with need: Need-based aid available for full-time and part-time students. Work study available nights, weekends, and for part-time students.
Students without need: No-need awards available for academics, alumni affiliation, leadership.

FINANCIAL AID PROCEDURES
Forms required: FAFSA.
Dates and Deadlines: Priority date 4/30; no closing date. Applicants notified on a rolling basis starting 3/15; must reply within 2 week(s) of notification.
Transfers: Priority date 4/15.

CONTACT
Deborah Flinn, Director of Financial Aid
2279 Mount Vernon Road, Southington, CT 06489-1057
(860) 628-4751 ext. 129

Capital Community College
Hartford, Connecticut
www.ccc.commnet.edu   Federal Code: 007635

2-year public community and technical college in small city.
Enrollment: 2,912 undergrads, 70% part-time. 341 full-time freshmen.
Selectivity: Open admission; but selective for some programs.

BASIC COSTS (2005-2006)
Tuition and fees: $2,536; out-of-state residents $7,568.
Per-credit charge: $93; out-of-state residents $279.
Additional info: Out-of-state tuition includes an additional $568 in required fees. New England Regional Student Program: $5,286 annual tuition/fees, $220 per credit-hour. Tuition/fee waivers available for minority students.

FINANCIAL AID PICTURE
Students with need: Need-based aid available for full-time and part-time students. Work study available nights.
Students without need: This college only awards aid to students with need.

FINANCIAL AID PROCEDURES
Forms required: FAFSA.
Dates and Deadlines: Closing date 7/15. Applicants notified on a rolling basis starting 7/15; must reply within 2 week(s) of notification.
Transfers: Closing date 7/1.

CONTACT
Margaret Wolf, Director of Financial Aid
950 Main Street, Hartford, CT 06103-1207
(860) 906-5090

Central Connecticut State University
New Britain, Connecticut
www.ccsu.edu   Federal Code: 001378

4-year public university in small city.
Enrollment: 9,143 undergrads, 19% part-time. 1,334 full-time freshmen.
Selectivity: Admits 50 to 75% of applicants.

BASIC COSTS (2005-2006)
Tuition and fees: $6,163; out-of-state residents $14,102.
Room and board: $7,456.

FINANCIAL AID PICTURE (2004-2005)
Students with need: Average financial aid package met 77% of need; average scholarship/grant was $5,077; average loan was $2,734. For part-time students, average financial aid package was $5,782.
Students without need: This college only awards aid to students with need.
Cumulative student debt: 50% of graduating class had student loans; average debt was $13,000.

FINANCIAL AID PROCEDURES
Forms required: FAFSA.
Dates and Deadlines: Priority date 2/15; closing date 9/15. Applicants notified on a rolling basis starting 3/15; must reply within 2 week(s) of notification.

CONTACT
Richard Bishop, Director of Financial Aid
1615 Stanley Street, New Britain, CT 06050
(860) 832-2200

Charter Oak State College
New Britain, Connecticut
www.charteroak.edu   Federal Code: 032343

4-year public virtual liberal arts college in small city.
Enrollment: 1,902 undergrads, 100% part-time.

BASIC COSTS (2006-2007)
Per-credit charge: $165; out-of-state residents $235.
Additional info: In-state matriculation fee: $985; out-of-state fees: $1300. Since our students do not have to take our courses, the cost of their education varies.

FINANCIAL AID PICTURE (2004-2005)
Students with need: 32% of average financial aid package awarded as scholarships/grants, 68% awarded as loans/jobs.
Students without need: This college only awards aid to students with need.

FINANCIAL AID PROCEDURES
Forms required: FAFSA, institutional form.
Dates and Deadlines: No deadline. Applicants notified on a rolling basis starting 8/23.

CONTACT
Velma Walters, Director of Financial Aid
55 Paul Manafort Drive, New Britain, CT 06053-2142
(860) 832-3872

Connecticut College
New London, Connecticut
www.conncoll.edu
Federal Code: 001379
CSS Code: 3284

4-year private liberal arts college in large town.
Enrollment: 1,778 undergrads, 1% part-time. 492 full-time freshmen.
Selectivity: Admits less than 50% of applicants.

BASIC COSTS (2006-2007)
Comprehensive fee: $44,240.

FINANCIAL AID PICTURE (2005-2006)
Students with need: Out of 246 full-time freshmen who applied for aid, 201 were judged to have need. Of these, 201 received aid, and 201 had their full need met. Average financial aid package met 100% of need; average scholarship/grant was $24,997; average loan was $2,865. For part-time students, average financial aid package was $6,643.
Students without need: This college only awards aid to students with need.
Cumulative student debt: 44% of graduating class had student loans; average debt was $22,524.

FINANCIAL AID PROCEDURES
Forms required: FAFSA, CSS PROFILE.
Dates and Deadlines: Priority date 11/15; closing date 1/15. Applicants notified by 4/1; must reply by 5/1.
Transfers: Closing date 4/1.

CONTACT
Elaine Solinga, Director of Financial Aid
270 Mohegan Avenue, New London, CT 06320-4196
(860) 439-2058

Eastern Connecticut State University
Willimantic, Connecticut
www.easternct.edu
Federal Code: 001425

4-year public university and liberal arts college in large town.
Enrollment: 4,606 undergrads, 19% part-time. 841 full-time freshmen.
Selectivity: Admits 50 to 75% of applicants.

BASIC COSTS (2005-2006)
Tuition and fees: $5,964; out-of-state residents $13,902.
Room and board: $7,590.

FINANCIAL AID PICTURE (2004-2005)
Students with need: Out of 630 full-time freshmen who applied for aid, 504 were judged to have need. Of these, 418 received aid, and 352 had their full need met. Average financial aid package met 59% of need; average scholarship/grant was $4,730; average loan was $3,035. For part-time students, average financial aid package was $7,341.
Students without need: 72 full-time freshmen who did not demonstrate need for aid received scholarships/grants; average award was $2,885. No-need awards available for academics.
Cumulative student debt: 64% of graduating class had student loans; average debt was $14,995.
Additional info: Tuition waiver for veterans and members of National Guard.

FINANCIAL AID PROCEDURES
Forms required: FAFSA, institutional form.
Dates and Deadlines: Priority date 3/15; no closing date. Applicants notified on a rolling basis starting 2/15; must reply within 2 week(s) of notification.
Transfers: Must reply within 2 week(s) of notification.

CONTACT
Richard Savage, Director of Financial Aid
83 Windham Street, Willimantic, CT 06226-2295
(860) 465-5205

Fairfield University
Fairfield, Connecticut
www.fairfield.edu
Federal Code: 001385
CSS Code: 3390

4-year private university in small city, affiliated with Roman Catholic Church.
Enrollment: 3,688 undergrads, 7% part-time. 940 full-time freshmen.
Selectivity: Admits 50 to 75% of applicants. GED not accepted.

BASIC COSTS (2005-2006)
Tuition and fees: $30,235.
Room and board: $9,600.

FINANCIAL AID PICTURE (2005-2006)
Students with need: Out of 673 full-time freshmen who applied for aid, 501 were judged to have need. Of these, 497 received aid, and 150 had their full need met. Average financial aid package met 69% of need; average scholarship/grant was $13,151; average loan was $3,484. For part-time students, average financial aid package was $6,093.
Students without need: 61 full-time freshmen who did not demonstrate need for aid received scholarships/grants; average award was $11,803. No-need awards available for academics, alumni affiliation, art, athletics, leadership, music/drama.
Scholarships offered: *Merit:* University Fellow Scholarship; $15,000 annual grant/computer/research stipend; awarded to students in top 5% of class with high SAT scores; admission application with writing sample required by December 1. Presidential Scholarship; $12,000 annual grant/research stipend; awarded to students in top 10% of class and with high SAT scores. Dean's Scholarship; $10,000 annual grant; for students in top 20% of class. Approximately 100-160 total scholarships available. *Athletic:* 40 full-time freshmen received athletic scholarships; average amount $18,979.
Cumulative student debt: 63% of graduating class had student loans; average debt was $25,081.

FINANCIAL AID PROCEDURES
Forms required: FAFSA, CSS PROFILE.
Dates and Deadlines: Closing date 2/15. Applicants notified on a rolling basis starting 4/1; must reply by 5/1 or within 2 week(s) of notification.
Transfers: Closing date 3/15. Applicants notified on a rolling basis starting 5/1; must reply within 4 week(s) of notification. Students eligible for federal aid during first academic year of enrollment and may receive university and federal aid thereafter. Scholarships available for Phi Theta Kappa members.

CONTACT
Erin Chiaro, Director of Financial Aid
1073 North Benson Road, Fairfield, CT 06824-5195
(203) 254-4125

Gateway Community College
New Haven, Connecticut
www.gwcc.commnet.edu
Federal Code: 008303

2-year public community college in small city.
Enrollment: 4,487 undergrads, 62% part-time. 771 full-time freshmen.
Selectivity: Open admission; but selective for some programs.

BASIC COSTS (2005-2006)
Tuition and fees: $2,536; out-of-state residents $7,568.
Per-credit charge: $93; out-of-state residents $279.

Additional info: Out-of-state tuition includes additional $920 in required fees. New England Regional Student Program: $3998.00 annual tuition/fees, $231.50 per credit-hour.

FINANCIAL AID PICTURE
Students with need: Need-based aid available for full-time and part-time students. Work study available nights, weekends, and for part-time students.
Students without need: This college only awards aid to students with need.

FINANCIAL AID PROCEDURES
Forms required: FAFSA, institutional form.
Dates and Deadlines: No deadline. Applicants notified on a rolling basis; must reply within 2 week(s) of notification.

CONTACT
Raymond Zeek, Acting Director of Financial Aid
60 Sargent Drive, New Haven, CT 06511-5970
(203) 285-2032

Holy Apostles College and Seminary
Cromwell, Connecticut
www.holyapostles.edu   Federal Code: 001389

4-year private liberal arts and seminary college in small town, affiliated with Roman Catholic Church.
Enrollment: 21 undergrads, 57% part-time.

BASIC COSTS (2005-2006)
Tuition and fees: $9,350.
Per-credit charge: $230.
Room and board: $7,550.

FINANCIAL AID PICTURE (2004-2005)
Students with need: Average financial aid package for all full-time undergraduates was $5,500. 40% awarded as scholarships/grants, 60% awarded as loans/jobs. Need-based aid available for part-time students.
Students without need: This college only awards aid to students with need.
Cumulative student debt: 3% of graduating class had student loans; average debt was $11,625.

FINANCIAL AID PROCEDURES
Forms required: FAFSA, institutional form.
Dates and Deadlines: No deadline. Applicants notified on a rolling basis starting 9/15.
Transfers: No deadline.

CONTACT
Henry Miller, Financial Aid Director
33 Prospect Hill Road, Cromwell, CT 06416-2005
(860) 632-8120

Housatonic Community College
Bridgeport, Connecticut
www.hcc.commnet.edu   Federal Code: 004513

2-year public community college in small city.
Enrollment: 3,738 undergrads.
Selectivity: Open admission; but selective for some programs.

BASIC COSTS (2005-2006)
Tuition and fees: $2,536; out-of-state residents $7,568.
Per-credit charge: $93; out-of-state residents $279.
Additional info: Out-of-state tuition includes additional $568 in required fees. New England Regional Student Program: $5,286 annual tuition/fees, $220 per credit-hour.

FINANCIAL AID PICTURE (2004-2005)
Students with need: 90% of average financial aid package awarded as scholarships/grants, 10% awarded as loans/jobs. Need-based aid available for part-time students.
Students without need: This college only awards aid to students with need.

FINANCIAL AID PROCEDURES
Forms required: FAFSA.
Dates and Deadlines: Priority date 11/1; closing date 5/1. Applicants notified on a rolling basis starting 6/1.

CONTACT
Barbara Surowiec, Director of Financial Aid
900 Lafayette Boulevard, Bridgeport, CT 06604-4704
(203) 332-5047

International College of Hospitality Management
Suffield, Connecticut
www.ichm.edu

2-year for-profit culinary school and business college in small town.
Enrollment: 76 undergrads.

BASIC COSTS (2006-2007)
Tuition and fees: $17,800.
Room and board: $4,978.
Additional info: International students who have no health insurance are required to purchase it for $62 per month.

FINANCIAL AID PICTURE
Students with need: Need-based aid available for full-time and part-time students. Work study available nights, weekends, and for part-time students.
Students without need: No-need awards available for academics.

FINANCIAL AID PROCEDURES
Dates and Deadlines: No deadline. Applicants notified on a rolling basis starting 1/1.

CONTACT
Nancy Molinari, Director of Financial Aid
1760 Mapleton Avenue, Suffield, CT 06078
(860) 688-3353

Lyme Academy College of Fine Arts
Old Lyme, Connecticut   Federal Code: 030794
www.lymeacademy.edu   CSS Code: 1791

4-year private visual arts college in small town.
Enrollment: 96 undergrads, 17% part-time. 12 full-time freshmen.
Selectivity: Admits over 75% of applicants.

BASIC COSTS (2006-2007)
Tuition and fees: $18,168.
Per-credit charge: $732.

FINANCIAL AID PICTURE (2005-2006)
Students with need: Out of 9 full-time freshmen who applied for aid, 9 were judged to have need. Of these, 9 received aid. Need-based aid available for part-time students.
Students without need: No-need awards available for academics, art.

FINANCIAL AID PROCEDURES
Forms required: FAFSA, institutional form. CSS PROFILE required of all new students.

Dates and Deadlines: Closing date 2/15. Applicants notified on a rolling basis; must reply within 2 week(s) of notification.
Transfers: Priority date 2/15; no deadline. Applicants notified on a rolling basis; must reply by 5/1.
CONTACT
Jim Falconer, Director of Financial Aid
84 Lyme Street, Old Lyme, CT 06371
(860) 434-5232 ext. 114

Manchester Community College
Manchester, Connecticut
www.mcc.commnet.edu   Federal Code: 001392

2-year public community college in small city.
Enrollment: 4,995 undergrads.
Selectivity: Open admission; but selective for some programs.
BASIC COSTS (2005-2006)
Tuition and fees: $2,536; out-of-state residents $7,568.
Per-credit charge: $93; out-of-state residents $279.
Additional info: Out-of-state tuition includes additional $568 in required fees. New England Regional Student Program: $5,286 annual tuition/fees, $220 per credit-hour.
FINANCIAL AID PICTURE
Students with need: Need-based aid available for full-time and part-time students.
FINANCIAL AID PROCEDURES
Forms required: FAFSA.
Dates and Deadlines: Priority date 5/15; no closing date. Applicants notified on a rolling basis starting 5/1; must reply within 2 week(s) of notification.
CONTACT
Ivette Rivera-Dreyer, Director of Financial Aid
Great Path PO Box 1046, MS 12, Manchester, CT 06040-1046
(860) 512-3380

Middlesex Community College
Middletown, Connecticut
www.mxcc.commnet.edu   Federal Code: 008038

2-year public community college in large town.
Enrollment: 1,562 undergrads, 52% part-time. 305 full-time freshmen.
Selectivity: Open admission; but selective for some programs.
BASIC COSTS (2005-2006)
Tuition and fees: $2,536; out-of-state residents $7,568.
Per-credit charge: $93; out-of-state residents $279.
Additional info: Out-of-state students pay additional $568 required fees. New England Regional Student Program: $3,794 annual tuition/fees, $139.50 per credit-hour.
FINANCIAL AID PICTURE
Students with need: Need-based aid available for full-time and part-time students.
Students without need: This college only awards aid to students with need.
Additional info: Tuition and/or fee waiver for veterans.
FINANCIAL AID PROCEDURES
Forms required: FAFSA, institutional form.
Dates and Deadlines: Priority date 6/1; no closing date. Applicants notified on a rolling basis starting 7/1; must reply within 2 week(s) of notification.
Transfers: Closing date 9/1.

CONTACT
Gladys Colon, Director of Financial Aid
100 Training Hill Road, Middletown, CT 06457
(860) 343-5741

Mitchell College
New London, Connecticut
www.mitchell.edu   Federal Code: 001393

4-year private liberal arts college in small city.
Enrollment: 704 undergrads, 9% part-time. 239 full-time freshmen.
Selectivity: Admits 50 to 75% of applicants.
BASIC COSTS (2006-2007)
Tuition and fees: $21,737.
Per-credit charge: $275.
Room and board: $9,795.
Additional info: $6,500 additional fee for students in comprehensive program at learning center for learning disabilities.
FINANCIAL AID PICTURE
Students with need: Need-based aid available for full-time and part-time students. Work study available nights, weekends, and for part-time students.
Students without need: No-need awards available for academics, alumni affiliation, athletics, leadership.
FINANCIAL AID PROCEDURES
Forms required: FAFSA.
Dates and Deadlines: Priority date 3/1; no closing date. Applicants notified on a rolling basis starting 2/15; must reply within 2 week(s) of notification.
CONTACT
Jacklyn Stoltz, Director of Financial Aid
437 Pequot Avenue, New London, CT 06320-4498
(860) 701-5040

Naugatuck Valley Community College
Waterbury, Connecticut
www.nvcc.commnet.edu   Federal Code: 006982

2-year public community and technical college in small city.
Enrollment: 4,685 undergrads, 56% part-time. 814 full-time freshmen.
Selectivity: Open admission; but selective for some programs.
BASIC COSTS (2005-2006)
Tuition and fees: $2,536; out-of-state residents $7,568.
Per-credit charge: $93; out-of-state residents $279.
FINANCIAL AID PICTURE (2004-2005)
Students with need: Average financial aid package for all full-time undergraduates was $2,520; for part-time $1,260. 92% awarded as scholarships/grants, 8% awarded as loans/jobs.
Students without need: This college only awards aid to students with need.
FINANCIAL AID PROCEDURES
Forms required: FAFSA.
Dates and Deadlines: Priority date 4/1; no closing date. Applicants notified on a rolling basis starting 6/1.
Transfers: Financial aid transcripts from all previous schools attended.
CONTACT
Rodney Butler, Director of Financial Aid Services
750 Chase Parkway, Waterbury, CT 06708-3089
(203) 575-8006

Norwalk Community College
Norwalk, Connecticut
www.ncc.commnet.edu   Federal Code: 001399

2-year public community and technical college in small city.
Enrollment: 6,036 undergrads.
Selectivity: Open admission; but selective for some programs.

BASIC COSTS (2005-2006)
Tuition and fees: $2,536; out-of-state residents $7,568.
Per-credit charge: $93; out-of-state residents $279.
Additional info: Out-of-state tuition includes additional $568 required fees. New England Regional Student Program: $5,286 annual tuition/fees, $220 per credit-hour.

FINANCIAL AID PICTURE
Students with need: Need-based aid available for full-time and part-time students.
Students without need: No-need awards available for academics, alumni affiliation.

FINANCIAL AID PROCEDURES
Forms required: FAFSA, institutional form.
Dates and Deadlines: Priority date 4/1; no closing date. Applicants notified on a rolling basis starting 7/1; must reply within 2 week(s) of notification.

CONTACT
Norma McNerney, Director of Financial Aid
188 Richards Avenue, Norwalk, CT 06854-1655
(203) 857-7023

Paier College of Art
Hamden, Connecticut
www.paiercollegeofart.edu   Federal Code: 007459

4-year for-profit visual arts college in small city.
Enrollment: 248 undergrads, 23% part-time. 33 full-time freshmen.
Selectivity: Admits over 75% of applicants.

BASIC COSTS (2005-2006)
Tuition and fees: $11,565.
Per-credit charge: $360.

FINANCIAL AID PICTURE (2004-2005)
Students with need: Out of 24 full-time freshmen who applied for aid, 21 were judged to have need. Of these, 20 received aid, and 2 had their full need met. Average financial aid package met 58% of need; average scholarship/grant was $4,417; average loan was $2,444. For part-time students, average financial aid package was $4,259.
Cumulative student debt: 51% of graduating class had student loans; average debt was $16,069.

FINANCIAL AID PROCEDURES
Forms required: FAFSA.
Dates and Deadlines: Priority date 4/15; no closing date. Applicants notified on a rolling basis starting 6/1; must reply within 3 week(s) of notification.

CONTACT
John DeRose, Director of Financial Aid
20 Gorham Avenue, Hamden, CT 06514-3902
(203) 287-3034

Post University
Waterbury, Connecticut
www.post.edu   Federal Code: 001401

4-year for-profit university and business college in small city.
Enrollment: 1,100 undergrads.
Selectivity: Admits 50 to 75% of applicants.

BASIC COSTS (2005-2006)
Tuition and fees: $20,200.
Per-credit charge: $650.
Room and board: $8,300.

FINANCIAL AID PICTURE
Students with need: Need-based aid available for full-time and part-time students. Work study available nights, weekends, and for part-time students.
Additional info: Academic merit scholarships available based on GPA and test scores. Renewable contingent upon maintaining specific GPA.

FINANCIAL AID PROCEDURES
Forms required: FAFSA.
Dates and Deadlines: Priority date 3/15; no closing date. Applicants notified on a rolling basis starting 4/15; must reply by 5/1 or within 3 week(s) of notification.

CONTACT
Patricia Del Buono, Associate Director of Financial Aid
800 Country Club Road, Waterbury, CT 06723-2540
(203) 596-4527

Quinebaug Valley Community College
Danielson, Connecticut
www.qvcc.commnet.edu   Federal Code: 010530

2-year public community and technical college in large town.
Enrollment: 1,473 undergrads, 58% part-time. 213 full-time freshmen.
Selectivity: Open admission.

BASIC COSTS (2005-2006)
Tuition and fees: $2,536; out-of-state residents $7,568.
Per-credit charge: $93; out-of-state residents $279.
Additional info: Out-of-state tution includes additional $568 required fees. New England Regional Student Program: $5,286 annual tuition/fees, $220 per credit-hour.

FINANCIAL AID PICTURE (2005-2006)
Students with need: 99% of average financial aid package awarded as scholarships/grants, 1% awarded as loans/jobs. Need-based aid available for part-time students. Work study available nights, weekends, and for part-time students.
Students without need: This college only awards aid to students with need.

FINANCIAL AID PROCEDURES
Forms required: FAFSA.
Dates and Deadlines: Closing date 10/1. Applicants notified on a rolling basis starting 5/1.

CONTACT
Alfred Williams, Director of Financial Aid
742 Upper Maple Street, Danielson, CT 06239-1440
(860) 774-1164

Quinnipiac University
Hamden, Connecticut
www.quinnipiac.edu
Federal Code: 001402

4-year private university in small city.
Enrollment: 5,542 undergrads, 5% part-time. 1,358 full-time freshmen.
Selectivity: Admits 50 to 75% of applicants.

BASIC COSTS (2006-2007)
Tuition and fees: $26,280.
Per-credit charge: $610.
Room and board: $10,700.

FINANCIAL AID PICTURE (2005-2006)
Students with need: Out of 1,057 full-time freshmen who applied for aid, 799 were judged to have need. Of these, 796 received aid, and 98 had their full need met. Average financial aid package met 65% of need; average scholarship/grant was $10,537; average loan was $2,856. For part-time students, average financial aid package was $6,596.
Students without need: 154 full-time freshmen who did not demonstrate need for aid received scholarships/grants; average award was $7,888. No-need awards available for academics, athletics.
Scholarships offered: *Merit:* Scholarships range from $4,000 - $15,000 per year; based on high school class rank and SAT or ACT scores; renewable provided students maintain full-time status and a minimum 3.0 GPA. *Athletic:* 43 full-time freshmen received athletic scholarships; average amount $24,177.
Cumulative student debt: 70% of graduating class had student loans; average debt was $25,794.

FINANCIAL AID PROCEDURES
Forms required: FAFSA.
Dates and Deadlines: Priority date 3/1; no closing date. Applicants notified on a rolling basis starting 2/15; must reply by 5/1 or within 2 week(s) of notification.
Transfers: Priority date 6/1. Applicants notified on a rolling basis starting 3/1; must reply by 5/1 or within 2 week(s) of notification.

CONTACT
Dominic Yoia, Director of Financial Aid
275 Mount Carmel Avenue, Hamden, CT 06518-1908
(800) 462-1944

Sacred Heart University
Fairfield, Connecticut
www.sacredheart.edu
Federal Code: 001403
CSS Code: 3780

4-year private university and liberal arts college in large town, affiliated with Roman Catholic Church.
Enrollment: 4,045 undergrads, 20% part-time. 886 full-time freshmen.
Selectivity: Admits 50 to 75% of applicants.

BASIC COSTS (2005-2006)
Tuition and fees: $23,750.
Room and board: $9,654.
Additional info: Tuition/fee waivers available for minority students.

FINANCIAL AID PICTURE (2005-2006)
Students with need: Out of 812 full-time freshmen who applied for aid, 636 were judged to have need. Of these, 623 received aid, and 182 had their full need met. Average financial aid package met 66% of need; average scholarship/grant was $9,266; average loan was $5,051. For part-time students, average financial aid package was $7,463.
Students without need: 217 full-time freshmen who did not demonstrate need for aid received scholarships/grants; average award was $10,743. No-need awards available for academics, alumni affiliation, art, athletics, leadership, minority status, music/drama, ROTC.
Scholarships offered: 49 full-time freshmen received athletic scholarships; average amount $16,934.
Cumulative student debt: 93% of graduating class had student loans; average debt was $19,926.

FINANCIAL AID PROCEDURES
Forms required: FAFSA, CSS PROFILE.
Dates and Deadlines: Priority date 2/15; no closing date. Applicants notified on a rolling basis starting 3/1; must reply within 2 week(s) of notification.
Transfers: Priority date 5/1; no deadline. Applicants notified on a rolling basis.

CONTACT
Julie Savino, Dean of University Financial Assistance
5151 Park Avenue, Fairfield, CT 06825
(203) 371-7980

St. Joseph College
West Hartford, Connecticut
www.sjc.edu
Federal Code: 001409

4-year private liberal arts college for women in large town, affiliated with Roman Catholic Church.
Enrollment: 1,125 undergrads, 23% part-time. 206 full-time freshmen.
Selectivity: Admits 50 to 75% of applicants.

BASIC COSTS (2006-2007)
Tuition and fees: $23,490.
Per-credit charge: $530.
Room and board: $11,000.

FINANCIAL AID PICTURE (2005-2006)
Students with need: For part-time students, average financial aid package was $9,802.
Students without need: No-need awards available for academics, leadership.
Cumulative student debt: 97% of graduating class had student loans; average debt was $30,602.

FINANCIAL AID PROCEDURES
Forms required: FAFSA.
Dates and Deadlines: Priority date 2/15; closing date 6/30. Applicants notified on a rolling basis starting 2/1; must reply within 2 week(s) of notification.
Transfers: Applicants notified on a rolling basis; must reply within 2 week(s) of notification.

CONTACT
Amanda Cicciarella, Director of Student Financial Services
1678 Asylum Avenue, West Hartford, CT 06117-2791
(860) 231-5223

Southern Connecticut State University
New Haven, Connecticut
www.southernct.edu
Federal Code: 001406

4-year public university in small city.
Enrollment: 8,309 undergrads, 19% part-time. 1,396 full-time freshmen.
Selectivity: Admits 50 to 75% of applicants.

BASIC COSTS (2005-2006)
Tuition and fees: $5,814; out-of-state residents $13,752.
Room and board: $7,698.

FINANCIAL AID PICTURE (2004-2005)

Students with need: Out of 1,142 full-time freshmen who applied for aid, 696 were judged to have need. Of these, 661 received aid, and 166 had their full need met. Average financial aid package met 81% of need; average scholarship/grant was $4,937; average loan was $2,613. For part-time students, average financial aid package was $3,898.

Students without need: 81 full-time freshmen who did not demonstrate need for aid received scholarships/grants; average award was $2,631. No-need awards available for academics, alumni affiliation, athletics, ROTC.

Scholarships offered: *Merit:* General Academic Achievement Awards; 90 awarded. Presidential Scholarships. Trustees Scholarships. *Athletic:* 15 full-time freshmen received athletic scholarships; average amount $8,253.

FINANCIAL AID PROCEDURES

Forms required: FAFSA.
Dates and Deadlines: Closing date 3/10. Applicants notified on a rolling basis; must reply within 2 week(s) of notification.
Transfers: Applicants notified on a rolling basis starting 6/15; must reply within 2 week(s) of notification.

CONTACT

Avon Dennis, Director, Financial Aid & Scholarships
131 Farnham Avenue, New Haven, CT 06515-1202
(203) 392-5222

Three Rivers Community College
Norwich, Connecticut
www.trcc.commnet.edu   Federal Code: 009765

2-year public community and technical college in large town.
Enrollment: 3,253 undergrads. 444 full-time freshmen.
Selectivity: Open admission; but selective for some programs.

BASIC COSTS (2005-2006)

Tuition and fees: $2,536; out-of-state residents $7,568.
Per-credit charge: $93; out-of-state residents $279.
Additional info: Out-of-state tuition includes additional $568 required fees. New England Regional Student Program: $5,286 annual tuition/fees, $220 per credit hour.

FINANCIAL AID PICTURE (2005-2006)

Students with need: Out of 252 full-time freshmen who applied for aid, 144 were judged to have need. Of these, 144 received aid. Average financial aid package met 64% of need; average scholarship/grant was $1,963; average loan was $1,540. For part-time students, average financial aid package was $1,245.
Students without need: This college only awards aid to students with need.
Scholarships offered: Available for continuing students; ranging from $75 to $500.

FINANCIAL AID PROCEDURES

Forms required: FAFSA.
Dates and Deadlines: Priority date 7/15; no closing date. Applicants notified on a rolling basis; must reply within 2 week(s) of notification.

CONTACT

Dan Zaneski, Financial Aid Director
7 Mahan Drive, Norwich, CT 06360-2479
(860) 823-2870

Trinity College
Hartford, Connecticut
www.trincoll.edu   Federal Code: 001414
                     CSS Code: 3899

4-year private liberal arts college in large city.
Enrollment: 2,181 undergrads, 2% part-time. 573 full-time freshmen.
Selectivity: Admits less than 50% of applicants.

BASIC COSTS (2005-2006)

Tuition and fees: $33,630.
Room and board: $8,590.
Additional info: Tuition/fee waivers available for adults.

FINANCIAL AID PICTURE (2005-2006)

Students with need: Out of 195 full-time freshmen who applied for aid, 160 were judged to have need. Of these, 160 received aid, and 160 had their full need met. Average financial aid package met 100% of need; average scholarship/grant was $25,464; average loan was $2,688. For part-time students, average financial aid package was $31,036.
Students without need: This college only awards aid to students with need.
Cumulative student debt: 46% of graduating class had student loans; average debt was $19,969.

FINANCIAL AID PROCEDURES

Forms required: FAFSA, CSS PROFILE.
Dates and Deadlines: Closing date 2/1. Applicants notified by 4/1; must reply by 5/1 or within 2 week(s) of notification.
Transfers: Closing date 4/1.

CONTACT

Kelly O'Brien, Director of Financial Aid
300 Summit Street, Hartford, CT 06106
(860) 297-2046

Tunxis Community College
Farmington, Connecticut
www.tunxis.commnet.edu   Federal Code: 009764

2-year public community college in large town.
Enrollment: 2,774 undergrads, 52% part-time. 444 full-time freshmen.
Selectivity: Open admission; but selective for some programs.

BASIC COSTS (2005-2006)

Tuition and fees: $2,536; out-of-state residents $7,568.
Per-credit charge: $93; out-of-state residents $279.
Additional info: Out-of-state tuition includes additional $568 required fees. New England Regional Student Program: $5,286 annual tuition/fees, $220 per credit hour.

FINANCIAL AID PICTURE (2004-2005)

Students with need: 84% of average financial aid package awarded as scholarships/grants, 16% awarded as loans/jobs. Need-based aid available for part-time students. Work study available nights, weekends, and for part-time students.
Students without need: No-need awards available for academics, leadership.
Additional info: Financial aid available to all students showing need. Part-time students encouraged to apply.

FINANCIAL AID PROCEDURES

Forms required: FAFSA.
Dates and Deadlines: Priority date 6/1; no closing date. Applicants notified on a rolling basis starting 3/1.

CONTACT
David Welsh, Director of Financial Aid
271 Scott Swamp Road, Farmington, CT 06032-3187
(860) 679-9558

United States Coast Guard Academy
New London, Connecticut
www.cga.edu   Federal Code: 001415

4-year public engineering and military college in small city.
Enrollment: 1,012 undergrads. 274 full-time freshmen.
Selectivity: Admits less than 50% of applicants.

BASIC COSTS (2006-2007)
Additional info: All tuition, room and board paid for by U.S. government. Students make one-time entrance deposit of $3,000 to help defray cost of uniforms, books, supplies and personal computer. All students paid monthly stipend of $734.

CONTACT
31 Mohegan Avenue, New London, CT 06320
(860) 444-8309

University of Bridgeport
Bridgeport, Connecticut
www.bridgeport.edu   Federal Code: 001416

4-year private university in small city.
Enrollment: 1,676 undergrads, 26% part-time. 359 full-time freshmen.
Selectivity: Admits 50 to 75% of applicants.

BASIC COSTS (2005-2006)
Tuition and fees: $20,595.
Per-credit charge: $640.
Room and board: $9,000.

FINANCIAL AID PICTURE
Students with need: Need-based aid available for full-time and part-time students. Work study available nights, weekends, and for part-time students.
Students without need: No-need awards available for academics, athletics, state/district residency.
Scholarships offered: Academic Excellence and Leadership Scholarship; up to full tuition, room, and board; for students ranking in the top quarter of high school class with SAT score greater than 1200. Academic Scholarship; up to full tuition; for students in the top quarter of class and SAT score greater than 1100. Academic Grant; up to half of tuition costs; for students in top half of class and SAT greater than 1100. Challenge Grant; $3,000; for students in the top half of class and SAT greater than 1000. All SAT scores exclusive of writing.

FINANCIAL AID PROCEDURES
Forms required: FAFSA, institutional form.
Dates and Deadlines: Priority date 4/1; no closing date. Applicants notified on a rolling basis starting 4/1; must reply within 4 week(s) of notification.

CONTACT
Kathleen Gailor, Director of Financial Aid
126 Park Avenue, Bridgeport, CT 06604
(203) 576-4568

University of Connecticut
Storrs, Connecticut
www.uconn.edu   Federal Code: 007997

4-year public university in large town.
Enrollment: 15,709 undergrads, 3% part-time. 3,243 full-time freshmen.
Selectivity: Admits 50 to 75% of applicants.

BASIC COSTS (2006-2007)
Tuition and fees: $8,359; out-of-state residents $21,559.
Per-credit charge: $269; out-of-state residents $819.
Room and board: $8,266.
Additional info: Out-of-state New England residents pay 150% of in-state tuition rate for programs of study not offered at their home state university.

FINANCIAL AID PICTURE (2005-2006)
Students with need: Out of 2,628 full-time freshmen who applied for aid, 1,627 were judged to have need. Of these, 1,560 received aid, and 237 had their full need met. Average financial aid package met 70% of need; average scholarship/grant was $6,393; average loan was $4,219. For part-time students, average financial aid package was $5,496.
Students without need: 274 full-time freshmen who did not demonstrate need for aid received scholarships/grants; average award was $5,118. No-need awards available for academics, art, athletics, leadership, minority status, music/drama.
Scholarships offered: 98 full-time freshmen received athletic scholarships; average amount $19,994.
Cumulative student debt: 60% of graduating class had student loans; average debt was $19,410.
Additional info: Institution offers variety of need-based financial aid programs. Financial assistance packages may include grants, loans and work-study awards.

FINANCIAL AID PROCEDURES
Forms required: FAFSA.
Dates and Deadlines: Priority date 3/1; no closing date. Applicants notified on a rolling basis starting 3/1; must reply within 4 week(s) of notification.

CONTACT
Jean Main, Director of Financial Aid
2131 Hillside Road, Unit 3088, Storrs, CT 06269-3088
(860) 486-2819

University of Hartford
West Hartford, Connecticut
www.hartford.edu   Federal Code: 001422

4-year private university in small city.
Enrollment: 5,289 undergrads, 12% part-time. 1,318 full-time freshmen.
Selectivity: Admits 50 to 75% of applicants.

BASIC COSTS (2006-2007)
Tuition and fees: $25,766.
Per-credit charge: $360.
Room and board: $9,922.
Additional info: Tuition/fee waivers available for minority students.

FINANCIAL AID PICTURE (2004-2005)
Students with need: Out of 991 full-time freshmen who applied for aid, 865 were judged to have need. Of these, 863 received aid, and 169 had their full need met. Average financial aid package met 60% of need; average scholarship/grant was $11,833; average loan was $3,061. For part-time students, average financial aid package was $5,542.
Students without need: 386 full-time freshmen who did not demonstrate need for aid received scholarships/grants; average award was $6,557. No-need awards available for academics, art, athletics, music/drama.

Scholarships offered: 28 full-time freshmen received athletic scholarships; average amount $30,192.
Cumulative student debt: 66% of graduating class had student loans; average debt was $25,553.

FINANCIAL AID PROCEDURES
Forms required: FAFSA, institutional form.
Dates and Deadlines: Priority date 2/1; no closing date. Applicants notified on a rolling basis starting 3/1; must reply by 5/1.

CONTACT
Suzanne Peters, Director of Student Financial Assistance
Bates House, West Hartford, CT 06117-1599
(860) 768-4296

University of New Haven
West Haven, Connecticut
www.newhaven.edu   Federal Code: 001397

4-year private university in small city.
Enrollment: 2,744 undergrads, 16% part-time. 653 full-time freshmen.
Selectivity: Admits 50 to 75% of applicants.

BASIC COSTS (2006-2007)
Tuition and fees: $24,645.
Per-credit charge: $800.
Room and board: $10,130.

FINANCIAL AID PICTURE (2005-2006)
Students with need: Out of 577 full-time freshmen who applied for aid, 505 were judged to have need. Of these, 505 received aid, and 84 had their full need met. Average financial aid package met 68% of need; average scholarship/grant was $12,317; average loan was $3,320. For part-time students, average financial aid package was $4,938.
Students without need: 108 full-time freshmen who did not demonstrate need for aid received scholarships/grants; average award was $15,049. No-need awards available for academics, athletics.
Scholarships offered: Merit: Presidential Scholarship; half-tuition; for applicants in top 15% of class with 1200 SAT (exclusive of Writing) or ACT equivalent. Academic Achievement Awards available. **Athletic:** 13 full-time freshmen received athletic scholarships; average amount $17,656.
Cumulative student debt: 62% of graduating class had student loans; average debt was $30,399.

FINANCIAL AID PROCEDURES
Forms required: FAFSA, institutional form.
Dates and Deadlines: Closing date 3/1. Applicants notified on a rolling basis starting 3/15; must reply by 5/1 or within 2 week(s) of notification.

CONTACT
Karen Flynn, Director of Financial Aid
300 Boston Post Road, West Haven, CT 06516
(203) 932-7315

Wesleyan University
Middletown, Connecticut   Federal Code: 001424
www.wesleyan.edu   CSS Code: 3959

4-year private university and liberal arts college in large town.
Enrollment: 2,737 undergrads. 728 full-time freshmen.
Selectivity: Admits less than 50% of applicants. GED not accepted.

BASIC COSTS (2006-2007)
Tuition and fees: $35,144.
Room and board: $9,540.

FINANCIAL AID PICTURE (2004-2005)
Students with need: Out of 403 full-time freshmen who applied for aid, 327 were judged to have need. Of these, 327 received aid, and 327 had their full need met. Average financial aid package met 100% of need; average scholarship/grant was $23,568; average loan was $2,595. Need-based aid available for part-time students.
Students without need: This college only awards aid to students with need.
Cumulative student debt: 41% of graduating class had student loans; average debt was $22,395.

FINANCIAL AID PROCEDURES
Forms required: FAFSA, CSS PROFILE, state aid form, institutional form.
Dates and Deadlines: Closing date 2/15. Applicants notified by 4/1; must reply by 5/1 or within 2 week(s) of notification.
Transfers: Priority date 2/15; closing date 3/15. No financial aid available for international transfer candidates.

CONTACT
Jennifer Lawton, Director of Financial Aid
70 Wyllys Avenue, Middletown, CT 06459-0260
(860) 685-2800

Western Connecticut State University
Danbury, Connecticut
www.wcsu.edu   Federal Code: 001380

4-year public university in small city.
Enrollment: 4,720 undergrads, 16% part-time. 773 full-time freshmen.
Selectivity: Admits 50 to 75% of applicants.

BASIC COSTS (2005-2006)
Tuition and fees: $5,800; out-of-state residents $13,739.
Room and board: $7,353.

FINANCIAL AID PICTURE (2004-2005)
Students with need: 43% of average financial aid package awarded as scholarships/grants, 57% awarded as loans/jobs. Need-based aid available for part-time students. Work study available nights, weekends, and for part-time students.
Students without need: No-need awards available for academics.

FINANCIAL AID PROCEDURES
Forms required: FAFSA, institutional form.
Dates and Deadlines: Priority date 3/15; closing date 4/15. Applicants notified on a rolling basis starting 3/15; must reply by 5/1 or within 2 week(s) of notification.

CONTACT
William Hawkins, Director, Financial Aid/Veterans Affairs
181 White Street, Danbury, CT 06810
(203) 837-8580

Yale University
New Haven, Connecticut   Federal Code: 001426
www.yale.edu   CSS Code: 3987

4-year private university in small city.
Enrollment: 5,349 undergrads. 1,308 full-time freshmen.
Selectivity: Admits less than 50% of applicants.

BASIC COSTS (2006-2007)
Tuition and fees: $33,030.
Room and board: $10,020.

252 Connecticut Yale University

FINANCIAL AID PICTURE (2004-2005)
Students with need: Out of 802 full-time freshmen who applied for aid, 578 were judged to have need. Of these, 578 received aid, and 578 had their full need met. Average financial aid package met 100% of need; average scholarship/grant was $25,415; average loan was $1,447. Need-based aid available for part-time students.
Students without need: This college only awards aid to students with need.
Cumulative student debt: 40% of graduating class had student loans; average debt was $14,882.
Additional info: All scholarships based on demonstrated need.

FINANCIAL AID PROCEDURES
Forms required: FAFSA, CSS PROFILE, state aid form.
Dates and Deadlines: Closing date 3/1. Applicants notified by 4/1; must reply by 5/1 or within 1 week(s) of notification.

CONTACT
Caesar Storlazzi, Director of University Financial Aid
Box 208234, New Haven, CT 06520-8234
(203) 432-2700

Delaware

Delaware State University
Dover, Delaware
www.desu.edu Federal Code: 001428

4-year public university and liberal arts college in large town.
Enrollment: 3,440 undergrads, 14% part-time. 885 full-time freshmen.
Selectivity: Admits 50 to 75% of applicants.

BASIC COSTS (2005-2006)
Tuition and fees: $5,480; out-of-state residents $11,704.
Per-credit charge: $213; out-of-state residents $472.
Room and board: $7,642.

FINANCIAL AID PICTURE (2005-2006)
Students with need: 33% of average financial aid package awarded as scholarships/grants, 67% awarded as loans/jobs. Need-based aid available for part-time students.
Students without need: This college only awards aid to students with need.

FINANCIAL AID PROCEDURES
Forms required: FAFSA.
Dates and Deadlines: Priority date 3/1; closing date 4/17. Applicants notified on a rolling basis starting 4/1.
Transfers: Closing date 2/15.

CONTACT
Carylin Brinkley, Director of Financial Aid
1200 North DuPont Highway, Dover, DE 19901
(302) 857-6250

Delaware Technical and Community College: Stanton/Wilmington Campus
Newark, Delaware
www.dtcc.edu Federal Code: 021449

2-year public community and technical college in small city.
Enrollment: 2,779 full-time undergrads.
Selectivity: Open admission; but selective for some programs and for out-of-state students.

BASIC COSTS (2005-2006)
Tuition and fees: $2,166; out-of-state residents $5,100.
Per-credit charge: $82; out-of-state residents $204.

FINANCIAL AID PICTURE
Students with need: Need-based aid available for full-time and part-time students.
Students without need: No-need awards available for academics, athletics.
Additional info: Male Delaware residents must be registered for Selective Service to be eligible for state financial aid.

FINANCIAL AID PROCEDURES
Forms required: FAFSA, institutional form.
Dates and Deadlines: Priority date 7/1; no closing date. Applicants notified on a rolling basis; must reply within 2 week(s) of notification.
Transfers: Priority date 11/15.

CONTACT
Debra McCain, Student Financial Aid Officer
400 Stanton-Christiana Road, Newark, DE 19713
(302) 571-5380

Delaware Technical and Community College: Terry Campus
Dover, Delaware
www.dtcc.edu Federal Code: 011727

2-year public community and technical college in large town.
Enrollment: 874 full-time undergrads.
Selectivity: Open admission; but selective for some programs.

BASIC COSTS (2005-2006)
Tuition and fees: $2,166; out-of-state residents $5,100.
Per-credit charge: $82; out-of-state residents $204.

FINANCIAL AID PICTURE
Students with need: Need-based aid available for full-time and part-time students.

FINANCIAL AID PROCEDURES
Forms required: FAFSA.
Dates and Deadlines: No deadline. Applicants notified on a rolling basis starting 7/1; must reply within 2 week(s) of notification.

CONTACT
Jennifer Grunden, Financial Aid Director
100 Campus Drive, Dover, DE 19901
(302) 857-1040

Goldey-Beacom College
Wilmington, Delaware
www.gbc.edu Federal Code: 001429

4-year private business college in small city.
Enrollment: 450 full-time undergrads.

BASIC COSTS (2005-2006)
Tuition and fees: $13,736.
Per-credit charge: $395.
Room only: $4,240.

FINANCIAL AID PICTURE
Students with need: Need-based aid available for full-time and part-time students.
Students without need: This college only awards aid to students with need.
Additional info: Essays required for scholarship applicants.

FINANCIAL AID PROCEDURES
Forms required: FAFSA.
Dates and Deadlines: Priority date 4/1; no closing date. Applicants notified on a rolling basis starting 2/15; must reply within 2 week(s) of notification.

CONTACT
Jane Lysle, Dean of Enrollment Management
4701 Limestone Road, Wilmington, DE 19808
(302) 225-6265

University of Delaware
Newark, Delaware
www.udel.edu   Federal Code: 001431

4-year public university in large town.
Enrollment: 15,742 undergrads, 5% part-time. 3,515 full-time freshmen.
Selectivity: Admits less than 50% of applicants.

BASIC COSTS (2005-2006)
Tuition and fees: $7,318; out-of-state residents $17,474.
Room and board: $6,824.

FINANCIAL AID PICTURE (2005-2006)
Students with need: Out of 2,597 full-time freshmen who applied for aid, 1,391 were judged to have need. Of these, 1,391 received aid, and 671 had their full need met. Average financial aid package met 77% of need; average scholarship/grant was $6,600; average loan was $4,000. For part-time students, average financial aid package was $7,000.
Students without need: This college only awards aid to students with need.
Scholarships offered: Merit: All freshman applicants evaluated for a wide range of merit scholarships ranging from $1,000 to full cost of education.
Athletic: 63 full-time freshmen received athletic scholarships; average amount $13,200.
Cumulative student debt: 40% of graduating class had student loans; average debt was $15,200.
Additional info: December 15 application deadline to receive scholarship consideration. Sibling/parent tuition credit plan. Senior citizen tuition credit for state residents over 60.

FINANCIAL AID PROCEDURES
Forms required: FAFSA.
Dates and Deadlines: Priority date 2/1; closing date 3/15. Applicants notified on a rolling basis starting 3/15; must reply by 5/1 or within 3 week(s) of notification.
Transfers: No deadline. Aid usualy limited to federal and state programs.

CONTACT
Johnie Burton, Director of Financial Aid
116 Hullihen Hall, Newark, DE 19716
(302) 831-8761

Wesley College
Dover, Delaware
www.wesley.edu   Federal Code: 001433

4-year private liberal arts college in large town, affiliated with United Methodist Church.
Enrollment: 1,864 undergrads. 487 full-time freshmen.
Selectivity: Admits 50 to 75% of applicants.

BASIC COSTS (2006-2007)
Tuition and fees: $16,579.
Per-credit charge: $610.
Room and board: $7,450.

FINANCIAL AID PICTURE (2005-2006)
Students with need: Out of 466 full-time freshmen who applied for aid, 389 were judged to have need. Of these, 389 received aid. Average financial aid package met 85% of need; average scholarship/grant was $5,500; average loan was $2,200. For part-time students, average financial aid package was $3,800.
Students without need: This college only awards aid to students with need.

FINANCIAL AID PROCEDURES
Forms required: FAFSA, institutional form.
Dates and Deadlines: Priority date 4/15; no closing date. Applicants notified on a rolling basis starting 3/15; must reply within 2 week(s) of notification.

CONTACT
James Marks, Director of Student Financial Planning
120 North State Street, Dover, DE 19901-3875
(302) 736-2334

Wilmington College
New Castle, Delaware
www.wilmcoll.edu   Federal Code: 007948

4-year private liberal arts college in large town.
Enrollment: 4,220 undergrads.
Selectivity: Open admission.

BASIC COSTS (2005-2006)
Tuition and fees: $7,670.
Per-credit charge: $254.

FINANCIAL AID PICTURE (2005-2006)
Students with need: 10% of average financial aid package awarded as scholarships/grants, 90% awarded as loans/jobs. Need-based aid available for part-time students. Work study available nights, weekends, and for part-time students.
Students without need: No-need awards available for academics, athletics.

FINANCIAL AID PROCEDURES
Forms required: FAFSA.
Dates and Deadlines: Priority date 4/30; no closing date. Applicants notified on a rolling basis starting 8/5; must reply within 2 week(s) of notification.

CONTACT
Trudy Yingling, Director of Student Financial Services
320 Dupont Highway, New Castle, DE 19720
(302) 328-9401 ext. 107

District of Columbia

American University
Washington, District of Columbia
www.american.edu   Federal Code: 001434

4-year private university in very large city, affiliated with United Methodist Church.
Enrollment: 5,788 undergrads, 4% part-time. 1,223 full-time freshmen.
Selectivity: Admits 50 to 75% of applicants.

BASIC COSTS (2006-2007)
Tuition and fees: $29,673.
Per-credit charge: $973.
Room and board: $11,240.

District of Columbia — American University

FINANCIAL AID PICTURE (2005-2006)
Students with need: Out of 911 full-time freshmen who applied for aid, 630 were judged to have need. Of these, 629 received aid, and 309 had their full need met. Average financial aid package met 68% of need; average scholarship/grant was $13,745; average loan was $5,784. For part-time students, average financial aid package was $12,755.
Students without need: This college only awards aid to students with need.
Scholarships offered: *Merit:* United Methodist scholarship; supplemental application required. Phi Theta Kappa scholarship (for transfer students only). *Athletic:* 44 full-time freshmen received athletic scholarships; average amount $17,398.
Cumulative student debt: 50% of graduating class had student loans; average debt was $19,766.
Additional info: Early decision applicants must submit estimated AU Institutional financial aid application by 11/15 and a FASFA as soon as possible after Jan 1.

FINANCIAL AID PROCEDURES
Forms required: FAFSA, institutional form.
Dates and Deadlines: Closing date 2/15. Applicants notified by 4/1; must reply by 5/1 or within 4 week(s) of notification.
Transfers: Priority date 3/1.

CONTACT
Brian Lee-Sang, Director of Financial Aid
4400 Massachusetts Avenue NW, Washington, DC 20016-8001
(202) 885-6100

Catholic University of America
Washington, District of Columbia
www.cua.edu   Federal Code: 001437

4-year private university in very large city, affiliated with Roman Catholic Church.
Enrollment: 3,007 undergrads, 8% part-time. 786 full-time freshmen.
Selectivity: Admits over 75% of applicants. GED not accepted.

BASIC COSTS (2006-2007)
Tuition and fees: $27,440.
Per-credit charge: $990.
Room and board: $10,330.
Additional info: Full-time tuition for the School of Engineering is $26,400. Full-time tuition for the School of Architecture is $26,800. Part-time tuition for the School of Architecture is $1,000 per-credit-hour. Tuition/fee waivers available for adults.

FINANCIAL AID PICTURE (2005-2006)
Students with need: Out of 587 full-time freshmen who applied for aid, 448 were judged to have need. Of these, 447 received aid, and 231 had their full need met. Average financial aid package met 84% of need; average scholarship/grant was $13,234; average loan was $3,730. For part-time students, average financial aid package was $5,752.
Students without need: 319 full-time freshmen who did not demonstrate need for aid received scholarships/grants; average award was $8,224. No-need awards available for academics, alumni affiliation, leadership, music/drama, religious affiliation, state/district residency.

FINANCIAL AID PROCEDURES
Forms required: FAFSA.
Dates and Deadlines: Priority date 2/1; closing date 4/15. Applicants notified on a rolling basis starting 4/1; must reply by 5/1 or within 2 week(s) of notification.
Transfers: No deadline. Applicants notified on a rolling basis starting 4/1; must reply by 5/1 or within 2 week(s) of notification.

CONTACT
Doris Torosian, Director of Financial Aid
Office of Undergraduate Admissions, Washington, DC 20064
(202) 319-5307

Corcoran College of Art and Design
Washington, District of Columbia
www.corcoran.edu   Federal Code: 011950

4-year private visual arts college in very large city.
Enrollment: 393 undergrads, 13% part-time. 77 full-time freshmen.
Selectivity: Admits 50 to 75% of applicants.

BASIC COSTS (2005-2006)
Tuition and fees: $22,800.
Room only: $8,150.

FINANCIAL AID PICTURE (2004-2005)
Students with need: Out of 67 full-time freshmen who applied for aid, 67 were judged to have need. Of these, 67 received aid. Average financial aid package met 42% of need; average scholarship/grant was $4,640; average loan was $3,506. For part-time students, average financial aid package was $2,600.
Students without need: 9 full-time freshmen who did not demonstrate need for aid received scholarships/grants; average award was $9,390. No-need awards available for academics, art.
Scholarships offered: Dean's Merit Scholarship; $500-$3,000 for first year of study; based on art portfolio and academics. Academic Achievement and President's Awards; $1,000-$8,000 per year; four-year renewable. Faculty Chair Grants; full and half tuition awards.
Cumulative student debt: 73% of graduating class had student loans; average debt was $34,153.

FINANCIAL AID PROCEDURES
Forms required: FAFSA, institutional form.
Dates and Deadlines: Priority date 4/15; no closing date. Applicants notified on a rolling basis starting 4/15; must reply by 5/1 or within 2 week(s) of notification.

CONTACT
Diane Morris, Director of Financial Aid
500 17th Street, N.W., Washington, DC 20006-4804
(202) 639-1818

Gallaudet University
Washington, District of Columbia
www.gallaudet.edu   Federal Code: 001443

4-year private university and liberal arts college in very large city.
Enrollment: 1,213 undergrads.
Selectivity: Admits over 75% of applicants.

BASIC COSTS (2005-2006)
Tuition and fees: $10,150.
Per-credit charge: $496.
Room and board: $8,650.
Additional info: Non-resident alien tuition reduction to $14,445 for students in developing countries, if approved.

FINANCIAL AID PICTURE (2005-2006)
Students with need: 84% of average financial aid package awarded as scholarships/grants, 16% awarded as loans/jobs. Need-based aid available for part-time students.
Students without need: No-need awards available for academics.
Additional info: Institution receives substantial aid from state vocational rehabilitation agencies, supplemented by institutional grants when needed.

FINANCIAL AID PROCEDURES
Forms required: FAFSA, institutional form.
Dates and Deadlines: Priority date 7/1; no closing date. Applicants notified on a rolling basis starting 4/1; must reply within 4 week(s) of notification.

CONTACT
Nancy Goodman, Director of Financial Aid
800 Florida Avenue, NE, Washington, DC 20002
(202) 651-5290

George Washington University
Washington, District of Columbia Federal Code: 001444
www.gwu.edu CSS Code: 5246

4-year private university in very large city.
Enrollment: 10,394 undergrads, 7% part-time. 2,623 full-time freshmen.
Selectivity: Admits less than 50% of applicants. GED not accepted.

BASIC COSTS (2006-2007)
Tuition and fees: $37,820.
Per-credit charge: $1,050.
Room and board: $11,000.
Additional info: Tuition stays fixed until student graduates, for a maximum of five years.

FINANCIAL AID PICTURE (2004-2005)
Students with need: Out of 1,605 full-time freshmen who applied for aid, 1,072 were judged to have need. Of these, 1,060 received aid, and 820 had their full need met. Average financial aid package met 93% of need; average scholarship/grant was $19,024; average loan was $5,340. For part-time students, average financial aid package was $17,743.
Students without need: 495 full-time freshmen who did not demonstrate need for aid received scholarships/grants; average award was $13,805. No-need awards available for academics, art, athletics, music/drama, ROTC.
Scholarships offered: 50 full-time freshmen received athletic scholarships; average amount $18,796.
Cumulative student debt: 50% of graduating class had student loans; average debt was $27,041.
Additional info: Auditions required for performing arts scholarships.

FINANCIAL AID PROCEDURES
Forms required: FAFSA, CSS PROFILE.
Dates and Deadlines: Closing date 2/1. Applicants notified on a rolling basis starting 3/24; must reply by 5/1.
Transfers: Priority date 4/1; closing date 5/1.

CONTACT
Daniel Small, Director of Student Financial Assistance
2121 I Street NW, Suite 201, Washington, DC 20052
(202) 994-6620

Georgetown University
Washington, District of Columbia Federal Code: 001445
www.georgetown.edu CSS Code: 5244

4-year private university in very large city, affiliated with Roman Catholic Church.
Enrollment: 6,395 undergrads, 2% part-time. 1,530 full-time freshmen.
Selectivity: Admits less than 50% of applicants.

BASIC COSTS (2006-2007)
Tuition and fees: $33,934.
Room and board: $11,210.

FINANCIAL AID PICTURE (2005-2006)
Students with need: Out of 862 full-time freshmen who applied for aid, 646 were judged to have need. Of these, 642 received aid, and 642 had their full need met. Average financial aid package met 100% of need; average scholarship/grant was $23,000; average loan was $1,800. Need-based aid available for part-time students.
Students without need: No-need awards available for athletics.
Scholarships offered: 44 full-time freshmen received athletic scholarships; average amount $18,000.
Cumulative student debt: 45% of graduating class had student loans; average debt was $23,724.

FINANCIAL AID PROCEDURES
Forms required: FAFSA, CSS PROFILE.
Dates and Deadlines: Closing date 2/1. Applicants notified by 4/1; must reply by 5/1 or within 2 week(s) of notification.
Transfers: Priority date 3/1. Applicants notified by 5/15; must reply by 5/30 or within 2 week(s) of notification.

CONTACT
Patricia McWade, Dean of Student Financial Services
103 White-Gravenor, Washington, DC 20057-1002
(202) 687-4547

Howard University
Washington, District of Columbia
www.howard.edu Federal Code: 001448

4-year private university in very large city.
Enrollment: 7,164 undergrads, 6% part-time. 1,410 full-time freshmen.
Selectivity: Admits less than 50% of applicants.

BASIC COSTS (2006-2007)
Tuition and fees: $12,985.
Per-credit charge: $508.
Room and board: $6,522.

FINANCIAL AID PICTURE (2004-2005)
Students with need: 5% of average financial aid package awarded as scholarships/grants, 95% awarded as loans/jobs. Need-based aid available for part-time students.
Students without need: This college only awards aid to students with need.

FINANCIAL AID PROCEDURES
Forms required: FAFSA, institutional form.
Dates and Deadlines: Priority date 2/15; closing date 8/15. Applicants notified by 4/1; must reply by 8/1 or within 4 week(s) of notification.

CONTACT
Steven Johnson, Dean of Financial Aid and Scholarship
2400 Sixth Street Northwest, Washington, DC 20059
(202) 806-2820

Potomac College
Washington, District of Columbia
www.potomac.edu Federal Code: 032183

3-year for-profit business and technical college in very large city.
Enrollment: 210 full-time undergrads.

BASIC COSTS (2005-2006)
Tuition and fees: $17,220.
Per-credit charge: $410.

256   **District of Columbia**   Potomac College

FINANCIAL AID PICTURE
Students with need: Need-based aid available for full-time and part-time students.

FINANCIAL AID PROCEDURES
Forms required: FAFSA, institutional form.
Dates and Deadlines: No deadline. Applicants notified on a rolling basis; must reply within 4 week(s) of notification.

CONTACT
Phyllis Crews, Financial Aid Officer
4000 Chesapeake Street NW, Washington, DC 20016
(202) 686-0876

Southeastern University
Washington, District of Columbia
www.seu.edu   Federal Code: 001456

4-year private university and business college in very large city.
Enrollment: 651 undergrads.
Selectivity: Open admission.

BASIC COSTS (2005-2006)
Tuition and fees: $12,525.
Per-credit charge: $255.
Additional info: Reduction in fees available for early registration. Online programs: $305 per credit hour.

FINANCIAL AID PICTURE
Students with need: Need-based aid available for full-time and part-time students.
Students without need: No-need awards available for academics, state/district residency.

FINANCIAL AID PROCEDURES
Forms required: FAFSA, institutional form.
Dates and Deadlines: Closing date 8/15. Applicants notified on a rolling basis; must reply within 2 week(s) of notification.

CONTACT
Peter Canine, Director of Financial Aid
501 I Street Southwest, Washington, DC 20024
(202) 478-8214 ext. 276

Trinity University
Washington, District of Columbia
www.trinitydc.edu   Federal Code: 001460

4-year private liberal arts college for women in very large city, affiliated with Roman Catholic Church.
Enrollment: 948 undergrads.
Selectivity: Admits over 75% of applicants.

BASIC COSTS (2006-2007)
Tuition and fees: $17,715.
Per-credit charge: $570.
Room and board: $7,800.

FINANCIAL AID PICTURE (2005-2006)
Students with need: 3% of average financial aid package awarded as scholarships/grants, 97% awarded as loans/jobs. Need-based aid available for part-time students.
Students without need: No-need awards available for academics, alumni affiliation, leadership.

FINANCIAL AID PROCEDURES
Forms required: FAFSA.
Dates and Deadlines: Priority date 3/1; no closing date. Applicants notified on a rolling basis starting 2/1; must reply within 2 week(s) of notification.

CONTACT
Linda Weippert, Director of Financial Aid
125 Michigan Avenue, NE, Washington, DC 20017
(202) 884-9530

University of the District of Columbia
Washington, District of Columbia
www.udc.edu   Federal Code: 007015

4-year public university and liberal arts college in very large city.
Enrollment: 5,170 undergrads, 62% part-time. 498 full-time freshmen.
Selectivity: Open admission; but selective for some programs.

BASIC COSTS (2005-2006)
Tuition and fees: $2,520; out-of-state residents $4,710.
Per-credit charge: $75; out-of-state residents $185.

FINANCIAL AID PICTURE
Students with need: Need-based aid available for full-time and part-time students. Work study available nights, weekends, and for part-time students.
Students without need: This college only awards aid to students with need.

FINANCIAL AID PROCEDURES
Forms required: FAFSA.
Dates and Deadlines: Priority date 3/15; no closing date. Applicants notified on a rolling basis starting 5/1; must reply within 2 week(s) of notification.

CONTACT
Henry Anderson, Director of Financial Aid
4200 Connecticut Avenue NW, Washington, DC 20008
(202) 274-5060

Florida

Art Institute of Fort Lauderdale
Ft. Lauderdale, Florida
www.artinstitute.edu   Federal Code: 010195

4-year for-profit visual arts and technical college in large city.
Enrollment: 2,893 undergrads, 48% part-time. 399 full-time freshmen.

BASIC COSTS (2005-2006)
Tuition and fees: $17,325.
Per-credit charge: $385.
Additional info: Tuition at time of enrollment locked for 4 years.

FINANCIAL AID PICTURE (2004-2005)
Students with need: Need-based aid available for part-time students. Work study available nights, weekends, and for part-time students.
Students without need: This college only awards aid to students with need.
Scholarships offered: Art Institutes International Excellence Award; $200-300 per quarter; based on GPA.
Additional info: Internal scholarships available. Financial planning program allows personalized service to budget and meet college costs through individualized payment plans.

FINANCIAL AID PROCEDURES
Forms required: FAFSA.
Dates and Deadlines: No deadline.

CONTACT
Joy Cummings, Director of Student Financial Service
1799 Southeast 17th Street, Fort Lauderdale, FL 33316
(954) 308-2165

Baptist College of Florida
Graceville, Florida
www.baptistcollege.edu   Federal Code: 013001

4-year private Bible and teachers college in small town, affiliated with Southern Baptist Convention.
Enrollment: 593 undergrads, 28% part-time. 62 full-time freshmen.
Selectivity: Admits over 75% of applicants.

BASIC COSTS (2006-2007)
Tuition and fees: $7,550.
Per-credit charge: $240.
Room and board: $3,736.

FINANCIAL AID PICTURE (2004-2005)
Students with need: Out of 51 full-time freshmen who applied for aid, 42 were judged to have need. Of these, 42 received aid, and 3 had their full need met. Average financial aid package met 50% of need; average loan was $1,551. Need-based aid available for part-time students.
Students without need: 20 full-time freshmen who did not demonstrate need for aid received scholarships/grants; average award was $600. No-need awards available for academics, minority status, music/drama, religious affiliation.

FINANCIAL AID PROCEDURES
Forms required: FAFSA, state aid form, institutional form.
Dates and Deadlines: Priority date 4/1; closing date 4/15. Applicants notified on a rolling basis starting 6/15; must reply within 4 week(s) of notification.
Transfers: No deadline.

CONTACT
Angela Rathel, Director of Financial Aid
5400 College Drive, Graceville, FL 32440-3306
(850) 263-3261 ext. 461

Barry University
Miami Shores, Florida
www.barry.edu   Federal Code: 001466

4-year private university in large town, affiliated with Roman Catholic Church.
Enrollment: 5,677 undergrads, 20% part-time. 563 full-time freshmen.
Selectivity: Admits 50 to 75% of applicants.

BASIC COSTS (2006-2007)
Tuition and fees: $24,000.
Per-credit charge: $705.
Room and board: $7,850.

FINANCIAL AID PICTURE (2005-2006)
Students with need: Average financial aid package met 70% of need; average scholarship/grant was $9,215; average loan was $2,664. For part-time students, average financial aid package was $5,615.
Students without need: No-need awards available for academics, art, athletics, music/drama.
Cumulative student debt: 72% of graduating class had student loans; average debt was $24,091.

FINANCIAL AID PROCEDURES
Forms required: FAFSA.
Dates and Deadlines: No deadline. Applicants notified on a rolling basis starting 1/25.

CONTACT
H. Dart Humeston, Director of Financial Aid
11300 Northeast Second Avenue, Miami Shores, FL 33161-6695
(305) 899-3673

Beacon College
Leesburg, Florida
www.beaconcollege.edu   Federal Code: 033733

4-year private liberal arts college in large town.
Enrollment: 99 undergrads. 3 full-time freshmen.
Selectivity: Admits 50 to 75% of applicants.

BASIC COSTS (2005-2006)
Tuition and fees: $23,000.
Room and board: $6,860.
Additional info: Tuition/fee waivers available for minority students, unemployed or children of unemployed.

FINANCIAL AID PICTURE (2004-2005)
Students with need: Out of 3 full-time freshmen who applied for aid, 3 were judged to have need. Of these, 3 received aid. Average financial aid package met 80% of need; average scholarship/grant was $7,000; average loan was $2,625. Need-based aid available for part-time students.
Students without need: No-need awards available for academics.
Scholarships offered: Paul and Dorothy Heim Civic Award; $500; awarded annually. Ehil E. Brodbeck Book Scholarship; pays complete book costs for one semester; awarded annually based on merit or financial need.
Additional info: Work-study programs offered based on financial need.

FINANCIAL AID PROCEDURES
Forms required: FAFSA, state aid form, institutional form.
Dates and Deadlines: Priority date 4/1; no closing date. Applicants notified on a rolling basis starting 4/1; must reply within 2 week(s) of notification.
Transfers: No deadline. Applicants notified on a rolling basis starting 4/1; must reply within 2 week(s) of notification.

CONTACT
Kimberly Padget, Financial Aid Coordinator
105 East Main Street, Leesburg, FL 34748
(352) 787-7660

Bethune-Cookman College
Daytona Beach, Florida
www.bethune.cookman.edu   Federal Code: 001467

4-year private liberal arts college in small city, affiliated with United Methodist Church.
Enrollment: 3,090 undergrads, 10% part-time. 913 full-time freshmen.
Selectivity: Admits 50 to 75% of applicants.

BASIC COSTS (2006-2007)
Tuition and fees: $11,230.
Per-credit charge: $464.
Room and board: $6,692.

FINANCIAL AID PICTURE (2005-2006)
Students with need: Out of 905 full-time freshmen who applied for aid, 893 were judged to have need. Of these, 887 received aid, and 255 had their full need met. Average financial aid package met 69% of need; average scholarship/grant was $6,150; average loan was $2,604. For part-time students, average financial aid package was $9,132.
Students without need: This college only awards aid to students with need.
Scholarships offered: 74 full-time freshmen received athletic scholarships; average amount $13,550.

Cumulative student debt: 83% of graduating class had student loans; average debt was $26,740.

FINANCIAL AID PROCEDURES
Forms required: FAFSA.
Dates and Deadlines: Priority date 4/1; no closing date. Applicants notified on a rolling basis starting 4/1; must reply within 3 week(s) of notification.

CONTACT
Joseph Coleman, Director of Financial Aid
Dr. Mary McLeod Bethune Boulevard, Daytona Beach, FL 32114-3099
(800) 553-9369

Brevard Community College
Cocoa, Florida
www.brevard.cc.fl.us   Federal Code: 001470

2-year public community college in large town.
Enrollment: 12,985 undergrads.
Selectivity: Open admission; but selective for some programs.

BASIC COSTS (2005-2006)
Tuition and fees: $1,927; out-of-state residents $6,755.
Per-credit charge: $53; out-of-state residents $214.

FINANCIAL AID PICTURE (2004-2005)
Students with need: Need-based aid available for part-time students.
Students without need: No-need awards available for academics, athletics.

FINANCIAL AID PROCEDURES
Forms required: FAFSA.
Dates and Deadlines: Priority date 4/15; closing date 6/30. Applicants notified on a rolling basis starting 6/1; must reply within 2 week(s) of notification.
Transfers: Transfer students must complete at least 15 credit hours with 3.5 GPA to be considered for merit scholarship.

CONTACT
Joan Buchanan, Dean of Financial Aid/Veteran Affairs
1519 Clearlake Road Building #12, Cocoa, FL 32922-9987
(321) 632-1111

Broward Community College
Ft. Lauderdale, Florida
www.broward.edu   Federal Code: 001500

2-year public community college in small city.
Enrollment: 25,513 undergrads, 65% part-time. 2,387 full-time freshmen.
Selectivity: Open admission; but selective for some programs.

BASIC COSTS (2005-2006)
Tuition and fees: $1,892; out-of-state residents $6,857.
Per-credit charge: $52; out-of-state residents $218.
Additional info: Tuition/fee waivers available for adults, minority students.

FINANCIAL AID PICTURE (2004-2005)
Students with need: 70% of average financial aid package awarded as scholarships/grants, 30% awarded as loans/jobs. Need-based aid available for part-time students. Work study available nights, weekends, and for part-time students.
Students without need: No-need awards available for academics, athletics, leadership, state/district residency.

FINANCIAL AID PROCEDURES
Forms required: FAFSA, institutional form.
Dates and Deadlines: Priority date 4/15; closing date 7/1. Applicants notified on a rolling basis starting 7/15.
Transfers: No deadline.

CONTACT
Marcia Conliffe, Student Success and Enrollment Management Services
225 East Las Olas Boulevard, Fort Lauderdale, FL 33301
(954) 201-7635

Carlos Albizu University
Miami, Florida
www.albizu.edu   Federal Code: 010724

4-year private university and branch campus college in very large city.
Enrollment: 457 undergrads.
Selectivity: Open admission.

BASIC COSTS (2005-2006)
Tuition and fees: $7,406.
Per-credit charge: $360.
Additional info: Reported tuition, fees and per-credit-hour charge are for Bachelor's degree program in business. Other programs individually priced.

FINANCIAL AID PICTURE
Students with need: Need-based aid available for full-time and part-time students. Work study available nights.
Students without need: This college only awards aid to students with need.

FINANCIAL AID PROCEDURES
Forms required: FAFSA, institutional form.
Dates and Deadlines: Priority date 6/1; no closing date. Applicants notified on a rolling basis starting 2/1.

CONTACT
Ramona Morales, Financial Aid Director
2173 NW 99th Avenue, Miami, FL 33172
(305) 593-1223 ext. 153

Central Florida College
Winter Park, Florida
www.centralfloridacollege.edu   Federal Code: 022455

2-year for-profit technical college in very large city.
Enrollment: 349 undergrads. 254 full-time freshmen.
Selectivity: Open admission.

BASIC COSTS (2006-2007)
Additional info: Certificate and Diploma programs range fron $4,995 to $12,995. Associate of Science Degrees range from $19,995 to $22,995; including books.

FINANCIAL AID PICTURE
Students with need: Need-based aid available for full-time students.
Students without need: This college only awards aid to students with need.

FINANCIAL AID PROCEDURES
Forms required: FAFSA.
Dates and Deadlines: No deadline.

CONTACT
Cathy Lane, Corporate Finance Director
1573 West Fairbanks Avenue, Winter Park, FL 32789
(407) 843-3984

Central Florida Community College
Ocala, Florida
www.gocfcc.com   Federal Code: 001471

2-year public community college in small city.
Enrollment: 5,199 undergrads, 55% part-time. 626 full-time freshmen.
Selectivity: Open admission; but selective for some programs.

BASIC COSTS (2005-2006)
Tuition and fees: $1,843; out-of-state residents $6,015.
Per-credit charge: $54; out-of-state residents $228.
Additional info: Tuition/fee waivers available for minority students.

FINANCIAL AID PICTURE
Students with need: Need-based aid available for full-time and part-time students.
Students without need: No-need awards available for academics, athletics, minority status, music/drama, state/district residency.

FINANCIAL AID PROCEDURES
Forms required: FAFSA.
Dates and Deadlines: No deadline.

CONTACT
Maureen McFarlane, Director, Financial Aid
3001 SW College Road, Ocala, FL 34478
(352) 873-5803

Chipola College
Marianna, Florida
www.chipola.edu   Federal Code: 001472

4-year public community and junior college in small town.
Enrollment: 1,527 undergrads, 40% part-time. 208 full-time freshmen.
Selectivity: Open admission; but selective for some programs.

BASIC COSTS (2005-2006)
Tuition and fees: $1,920; out-of-state residents $5,790.
Per-credit charge: $52; out-of-state residents $181.

FINANCIAL AID PICTURE (2005-2006)
Students with need: 92% of average financial aid package awarded as scholarships/grants, 8% awarded as loans/jobs. Need-based aid available for part-time students. Work study available nights.
Students without need: No-need awards available for academics, alumni affiliation, art, athletics, job skills, leadership, minority status, music/drama.

FINANCIAL AID PROCEDURES
Forms required: FAFSA, institutional form.
Dates and Deadlines: Priority date 5/1; no closing date. Applicants notified on a rolling basis starting 1/2; must reply within 2 week(s) of notification.

CONTACT
Sybil Cloud, Director of Financial Aid
3094 Indian Circle, Marianna, FL 32446
(850) 718-2223

City College: Miami
Miami, Florida
www.citycollege.edu   Federal Code: 025154

2-year for-profit business and health science college in large city.
Enrollment: 280 undergrads.

BASIC COSTS (2005-2006)
Tuition and fees: $8,100.
Per-credit charge: $165.

FINANCIAL AID PICTURE
Students with need: Need-based aid available for full-time and part-time students.
Students without need: This college only awards aid to students with need.

FINANCIAL AID PROCEDURES
Forms required: FAFSA, institutional form.
Dates and Deadlines: No deadline. Applicants notified on a rolling basis.

CONTACT
C Fike, Director of Financial Aid
9300 South Dadeland Boulevard, Miami, FL 33156
(305) 666-9242

Clearwater Christian College
Clearwater, Florida
www.clearwater.edu   Federal Code: 015025

4-year private liberal arts college in small city, affiliated with nondenominational tradition.
Enrollment: 564 undergrads.
Selectivity: Admits over 75% of applicants.

BASIC COSTS (2006-2007)
Tuition and fees: $12,500.
Per-credit charge: $460.
Room and board: $5,330.

FINANCIAL AID PICTURE (2005-2006)
Students with need: 47% of average financial aid package awarded as scholarships/grants, 53% awarded as loans/jobs. Need-based aid available for part-time students. Work study available nights, weekends, and for part-time students.
Students without need: No-need awards available for academics, music/drama, religious affiliation.
Additional info: Special consideration for financial aid given to children of Christian service workers.

FINANCIAL AID PROCEDURES
Forms required: FAFSA, state aid form, institutional form.
Dates and Deadlines: Priority date 3/15; no closing date. Applicants notified on a rolling basis starting 4/15; must reply within 2 week(s) of notification.
Transfers: Transfer academic scholarship of $750 per semester awarded to sophomore or junior transfer with at least 3.25 cumulative GPA. After transferring, student must maintain 3.5 GPA.

CONTACT
Ruth Strum, Director of Financial Aid
3400 Gulf-to-Bay Boulevard, Clearwater, FL 33759-4595
(727) 726-1153 ext. 214

Daytona Beach Community College
Daytona Beach, Florida
www.dbcc.edu   Federal Code: 001475

2-year public community and technical college in large city.
Enrollment: 10,469 undergrads, 51% part-time. 1,275 full-time freshmen.
Selectivity: Open admission; but selective for some programs.

BASIC COSTS (2005-2006)
Tuition and fees: $2,003; out-of-state residents $7,760.
Per-credit charge: $53; out-of-state residents $245.

FINANCIAL AID PICTURE
Students with need: Need-based aid available for full-time and part-time students.
Students without need: No-need awards available for athletics, leadership, music/drama.

FINANCIAL AID PROCEDURES
Forms required: FAFSA.
Dates and Deadlines: No deadline. Applicants notified on a rolling basis starting 2/15.

CONTACT
Elly Will, Director of Financial Aid
DBCC Admissions Office, Daytona Beach, FL 32114
(386) 506-3000 ext. 3015

DeVry University: Miramar
Miramar, Florida
www.mir.devry.edu

4-year for-profit university in large town.
Enrollment: 969 undergrads, 33% part-time. 206 full-time freshmen.

BASIC COSTS (2005-2006)
Tuition and fees: $12,800.
Per-credit charge: $460.

FINANCIAL AID PICTURE (2004-2005)
Students with need: Out of 106 full-time freshmen who applied for aid, 101 were judged to have need. Of these, 97 received aid, and 6 had their full need met. Average financial aid package met 44% of need; average scholarship/grant was $5,299; average loan was $5,065. For part-time students, average financial aid package was $5,767.
Students without need: This college only awards aid to students with need.

FINANCIAL AID PROCEDURES
Forms required: FAFSA.
Dates and Deadlines: No deadline. Applicants notified on a rolling basis.

CONTACT
Scott Howard, Assistant Director of Student Finance
2300 Southwest 145th Avenue, Miramar, FL 33027
(954) 499-9700

DeVry University: Orlando
Orlando, Florida
www.orl.devry.edu   Federal Code: 022966

4-year for-profit university in very large city.
Enrollment: 1,048 undergrads, 33% part-time. 229 full-time freshmen.

BASIC COSTS (2005-2006)
Tuition and fees: $12,800.
Per-credit charge: $460.

FINANCIAL AID PICTURE (2004-2005)
Students with need: Out of 131 full-time freshmen who applied for aid, 125 were judged to have need. Of these, 125 received aid, and 5 had their full need met. Average financial aid package met 41% of need; average scholarship/grant was $4,432; average loan was $5,684. For part-time students, average financial aid package was $6,861.
Students without need: This college only awards aid to students with need.

FINANCIAL AID PROCEDURES
Forms required: FAFSA.

Dates and Deadlines: No deadline. Applicants notified on a rolling basis starting 7/2.

CONTACT
Estrella Velasquez Domenech, Director of Student Finance
4000 Millennia Boulevard, Orlando, FL 32839-2426
(407) 345-2800

Eckerd College
St. Petersburg, Florida
www.eckerd.edu   Federal Code: 001487

4-year private liberal arts college in large city, affiliated with Presbyterian Church (USA).
Enrollment: 1,756 undergrads, 1% part-time. 470 full-time freshmen.
Selectivity: Admits 50 to 75% of applicants.

BASIC COSTS (2006-2007)
Tuition and fees: $27,624.
Per-credit charge: $943.
Room and board: $7,868.

FINANCIAL AID PICTURE (2005-2006)
Students with need: Out of 347 full-time freshmen who applied for aid, 273 were judged to have need. Of these, 273 received aid, and 74 had their full need met. Average financial aid package met 87% of need; average scholarship/grant was $17,956; average loan was $2,204.
Students without need: 93 full-time freshmen who did not demonstrate need for aid received scholarships/grants; average award was $9,250. No-need awards available for academics, alumni affiliation, art, athletics, leadership, minority status, music/drama, religious affiliation, ROTC, state/district residency.
Scholarships offered: *Merit:* Academic scholarships; ranging from $7,000 to $10,000 per year; available to entering freshmen regardless of financial need. Additional Trustee, Presidential, and Dean's Scholarships range from $13,000 to $25,000 awarded to outstanding freshmen with strong scholastic records and leadership potential. A limited number of Artistic Achievement Awards in music, theatre, visual art and creative writing are also available through a separate application process. *Athletic:* 4 full-time freshmen received athletic scholarships; average amount $24,292.

FINANCIAL AID PROCEDURES
Forms required: FAFSA.
Dates and Deadlines: Priority date 2/15; no closing date. Applicants notified on a rolling basis starting 2/1.

CONTACT
Patricia Watkins, Director of Financial Aid
4200 54th Avenue South, St. Petersburg, FL 33711-4700
(727) 864-8334

Edison College
Fort Myers, Florida
www.edison.edu   Federal Code: 001477

2-year public community college in very large city.
Enrollment: 4,210 undergrads.
Selectivity: Open admission; but selective for some programs.

BASIC COSTS (2005-2006)
Tuition and fees: $1,983; out-of-state residents $6,611.
Per-credit charge: $55; out-of-state residents $209.

FINANCIAL AID PICTURE
Students with need: Need-based aid available for full-time and part-time students. Work study available nights, weekends, and for part-time students.

Students without need: No-need awards available for art, music/drama.

FINANCIAL AID PROCEDURES
Forms required: FAFSA.
Dates and Deadlines: Priority date 5/1; no closing date. Applicants notified on a rolling basis starting 6/1; must reply within 2 week(s) of notification.

CONTACT
Cindy Lewis, District Director of Financial Aid
Box 60210, Fort Myers, FL 33906-6210
(239) 489-9346

Edward Waters College
Jacksonville, Florida
www.ewc.edu
Federal Code: 001478

4-year private liberal arts college in very large city, affiliated with African Methodist Episcopal Church.
Enrollment: 837 undergrads, 2% part-time. 206 full-time freshmen.
Selectivity: Open admission.

BASIC COSTS (2005-2006)
Tuition and fees: $9,176.
Per-credit charge: $382.
Room and board: $6,474.

FINANCIAL AID PICTURE
Students with need: Need-based aid available for full-time and part-time students. Work study available nights, weekends, and for part-time students.
Students without need: No-need awards available for academics, athletics, minority status, state/district residency.

FINANCIAL AID PROCEDURES
Forms required: FAFSA, state aid form, institutional form.
Dates and Deadlines: Closing date 4/15. Applicants notified on a rolling basis starting 5/1; must reply within 2 week(s) of notification.

CONTACT
Landi Myrick, Director of Financial Aid
1658 Kings Road, Jacksonville, FL 32209
(904) 470-8190

Embry-Riddle Aeronautical University
Daytona Beach, Florida
www.embryriddle.edu
Federal Code: 001479

4-year private university in small city.
Enrollment: 4,352 undergrads, 6% part-time. 976 full-time freshmen.
Selectivity: Admits over 75% of applicants.

BASIC COSTS (2006-2007)
Tuition and fees: $25,490.
Per-credit charge: $1,020.
Room and board: $7,070.

FINANCIAL AID PICTURE (2005-2006)
Students with need: Out of 806 full-time freshmen who applied for aid, 667 were judged to have need. Of these, 667 received aid. For part-time students, average financial aid package was $12,133.
Students without need: No-need awards available for academics, alumni affiliation, athletics, leadership, ROTC.
Cumulative student debt: 68% of graduating class had student loans; average debt was $52,276.

FINANCIAL AID PROCEDURES
Forms required: FAFSA.
Dates and Deadlines: No deadline. Applicants notified on a rolling basis starting 3/1; must reply within 4 week(s) of notification.

CONTACT
Maria Shaulis, Director of Financial Aid
600 South Clyde Morris Boulevard, Daytona Beach, FL 32114-3900
(386) 226-6300

Embry-Riddle Aeronautical University: Extended Campus
Daytona Beach, Florida
www.embryriddle.edu
Federal Code: 001479

4-year private university in small city.
Enrollment: 10,776 undergrads, 81% part-time. 70 full-time freshmen.

BASIC COSTS (2005-2006)
Additional info: Per credit hour charges range from $176 to $274.

FINANCIAL AID PICTURE (2005-2006)
Students with need: Out of 18 full-time freshmen who applied for aid, 16 were judged to have need. Of these, 16 received aid. For part-time students, average financial aid package was $4,268.
Students without need: No-need awards available for academics.
Cumulative student debt: 18% of graduating class had student loans; average debt was $11,565.

FINANCIAL AID PROCEDURES
Forms required: FAFSA.
Dates and Deadlines: Priority date 4/15; no closing date. Applicants notified on a rolling basis starting 3/1; must reply within 4 week(s) of notification.

CONTACT
Maria Shaulis, Director of Financial Aid
600 South Clyde Morris Boulevard, Daytona Beach, FL 32114-3900
(386) 226-6300

Everglades University
Boca Raton, Florida
www.evergladesuniversity.edu
Federal Code: 031085

4-year private university in large city.
Enrollment: 360 undergrads.

BASIC COSTS (2005-2006)
Tuition and fees: $12,500.
Per-credit charge: $390.

FINANCIAL AID PICTURE
Students with need: Need-based aid available for full-time students.
Additional info: Federal Pell Grant, Federal Direct Stafford Student Loan, Federal Family Education Loan (Stafford Student Loan), Unsubsidized Federal Direct and FFEL Stafford Loans and Federal Plus Loans offered.

FINANCIAL AID PROCEDURES
Forms required: FAFSA.
Dates and Deadlines: No deadline. Applicants notified on a rolling basis.

CONTACT
Seeta Singh-Moonilall, Director of Financial Aid
5002 T-REX Avenue, Suite 100, Boca Raton, FL 33431
(561) 912-1211

Flagler College
St. Augustine, Florida
www.flagler.edu Federal Code: 007893

4-year private liberal arts college in large town.
Enrollment: 2,157 undergrads, 3% part-time. 459 full-time freshmen.

BASIC COSTS (2006-2007)
Tuition and fees: $9,450.
Per-credit charge: $315.
Room and board: $5,760.

FINANCIAL AID PICTURE (2005-2006)
Students with need: Out of 333 full-time freshmen who applied for aid, 209 were judged to have need. Of these, 206 received aid, and 63 had their full need met. Average financial aid package met 75% of need; average scholarship/grant was $3,152; average loan was $2,721. For part-time students, average financial aid package was $5,356.
Students without need: 7 full-time freshmen who did not demonstrate need for aid received scholarships/grants; average award was $7,869. No-need awards available for academics, art, athletics, job skills, leadership, minority status, music/drama, state/district residency.
Scholarships offered: *Merit:* Lewis-Wiley Scholarship for freshmen who demonstrate exceptional leadership and academic achievement; 4 awarded; tuition, fees, room and board for 4 years. *Athletic:* 31 full-time freshmen received athletic scholarships; average amount $3,739.
Cumulative student debt: 55% of graduating class had student loans; average debt was $15,037.

FINANCIAL AID PROCEDURES
Forms required: FAFSA, state aid form, institutional form.
Dates and Deadlines: Priority date 4/1; no closing date. Applicants notified on a rolling basis starting 3/1; must reply within 2 week(s) of notification.
Transfers: Transfer students receiving Florida-sponsored aid must notify Florida Office of Student Financial Assistance (OSFA) of their transfer.

CONTACT
Christopher Haffner, Director of Financial Aid
74 King Street, St. Augustine, FL 32084
(800) 304-4208

Florida Agricultural and Mechanical University
Tallahassee, Florida
www.famu.edu Federal Code: 001480

4-year public university in small city.
Enrollment: 10,372 undergrads.
Selectivity: Admits 50 to 75% of applicants.

BASIC COSTS (2005-2006)
Tuition and fees: $3,188; out-of-state residents $15,177.
Per-credit charge: $99; out-of-state residents $498.
Room and board: $5,667.

FINANCIAL AID PICTURE (2005-2006)
Students with need: 56% of average financial aid package awarded as scholarships/grants, 44% awarded as loans/jobs. Need-based aid available for part-time students.
Students without need: No-need awards available for academics, art, leadership.

FINANCIAL AID PROCEDURES
Forms required: FAFSA.
Dates and Deadlines: Priority date 3/1; closing date 6/30. Applicants notified on a rolling basis starting 3/1; must reply within 2 week(s) of notification.

CONTACT
Bryan Davis, Director of Financial Aid
FHAC, G-9, Tallahassee, FL 32307-3200
(850) 599-3730

Florida Atlantic University
Boca Raton, Florida
www.fau.edu Federal Code: 001481

4-year public university in small city.
Enrollment: 19,951 undergrads, 41% part-time. 2,215 full-time freshmen.
Selectivity: Admits 50 to 75% of applicants.

BASIC COSTS (2005-2006)
Tuition and fees: $3,259; out-of-state residents $15,765.
Per-credit charge: $72; out-of-state residents $488.
Room and board: $6,783.
Additional info: Additional $625 in fees for out-of-state students.

FINANCIAL AID PICTURE (2005-2006)
Students with need: Out of 1,793 full-time freshmen who applied for aid, 1,007 were judged to have need. Of these, 966 received aid, and 166 had their full need met. Average financial aid package met 82% of need; average scholarship/grant was $5,768; average loan was $2,345. For part-time students, average financial aid package was $4,914.
Students without need: 70 full-time freshmen who did not demonstrate need for aid received scholarships/grants; average award was $2,028. No-need awards available for academics, athletics, state/district residency.
Scholarships offered: 44 full-time freshmen received athletic scholarships; average amount $7,600.

FINANCIAL AID PROCEDURES
Forms required: FAFSA.
Dates and Deadlines: Priority date 3/1; no closing date. Applicants notified on a rolling basis starting 5/1; must reply within 3 week(s) of notification.
Transfers: Scholarships available.

CONTACT
Carol Pfeilsticker, Director of Financial Aid
777 Glades Road, Boca Raton, FL 33431
(561) 297-2738

Florida Christian College
Kissimmee, Florida
www.fcc.edu Federal Code: 015192

4-year private Bible and teachers college in small city, affiliated with Independent Christian Church and Church of Christ.
Enrollment: 278 undergrads. 90 full-time freshmen.
Selectivity: Admits 50 to 75% of applicants.

BASIC COSTS (2006-2007)
Tuition and fees: $9,990.
Per-credit charge: $318.
Room only: $2,350.
Additional info: Tuition at time of enrollment locked for 4 years.

FINANCIAL AID PICTURE (2004-2005)
Students with need: Out of 71 full-time freshmen who applied for aid, 60 were judged to have need. Of these, 58 received aid. For part-time students, average financial aid package was $4,537.
Students without need: 17 full-time freshmen who did not demonstrate need for aid received scholarships/grants; average award was $1,553. No-need awards available for academics, alumni affiliation, leadership, music/drama, religious affiliation, state/district residency.

Cumulative student debt: 70% of graduating class had student loans; average debt was $16,241.

FINANCIAL AID PROCEDURES
Forms required: FAFSA, institutional form.
Dates and Deadlines: Priority date 5/1; closing date 7/15. Applicants notified on a rolling basis starting 3/1.
Transfers: Available only if funding remains.

CONTACT
Sandra Peppard, Director of Student Financial Aid
1011 Bill Beck Boulevard, Kissimmee, FL 34744-4402
(407) 569-1163

Florida College
Temple Terrace, Florida
www.floridacollege.edu   Federal Code: 001482

4-year private liberal arts college in large town.
Enrollment: 456 undergrads, 4% part-time. 221 full-time freshmen.
Selectivity: Admits 50 to 75% of applicants.

BASIC COSTS (2006-2007)
Tuition and fees: $11,380.
Per-credit charge: $430.
Room and board: $5,460.

FINANCIAL AID PICTURE (2004-2005)
Students with need: Out of 141 full-time freshmen who applied for aid, 60 were judged to have need. Of these, 60 received aid, and 19 had their full need met. Average financial aid package met 40% of need; average scholarship/grant was $3,316; average loan was $1,789. For part-time students, average financial aid package was $9,495.
Students without need: 38 full-time freshmen who did not demonstrate need for aid received scholarships/grants; average award was $839. No-need awards available for academics, athletics, state/district residency.
Scholarships offered: 24 full-time freshmen received athletic scholarships; average amount $3,456.
Cumulative student debt: 15% of graduating class had student loans; average debt was $6,835.
Additional info: Music and forensic scholarships available. Audition required for music scholarships.

FINANCIAL AID PROCEDURES
Forms required: FAFSA, state aid form, institutional form.
Dates and Deadlines: Priority date 4/1; closing date 6/1. Applicants notified on a rolling basis starting 3/1; must reply within 2 week(s) of notification.
Transfers: No deadline.

CONTACT
Karla Nicholas, Financial Aid Director
119 North Glen Arven Avenue, Temple Terrace, FL 33617
(813) 899-6774

Florida College of Natural Health
Pompano Beach, Florida
www.fcnh.com   Federal Code: 030086

2-year for-profit junior college in very large city.
Enrollment: 114 undergrads.
Selectivity: Open admission; but selective for some programs.

BASIC COSTS (2005-2006)
Additional info: Tuition varies per program.

FINANCIAL AID PICTURE
Students with need: Need-based aid available for full-time students.
Students without need: This college only awards aid to students with need.

FINANCIAL AID PROCEDURES
Forms required: FAFSA.
Dates and Deadlines: No deadline. Applicants notified on a rolling basis.

CONTACT
Jorge Villasante, Director of Financial Aid
2001 West Sample Road, Suite 100, Pompano Beach, FL 33064
(954) 975-6400

Florida College of Natural Health: Bradenton
Bradenton, Florida
www.fcnh.com

2-year for-profit health science college in large town.
Enrollment: 88 undergrads.
Selectivity: Open admission; but selective for some programs.

BASIC COSTS (2005-2006)
Additional info: 3 degree programs with $236 per-credit-hour charge. 2 diploma programs with flat rate: therapeutic massage 6-month training program, $6100; skincare 4 to 5-month training program, $3250.

FINANCIAL AID PICTURE
Students with need: Need-based aid available for full-time students.
Students without need: This college only awards aid to students with need.

FINANCIAL AID PROCEDURES
Forms required: FAFSA.
Dates and Deadlines: No deadline. Applicants notified on a rolling basis.

CONTACT
Jorge Villasante, Director of Financial Aid
616 67th Street Circle East, Bradenton, FL 34208
(954) 975-6400

Florida College of Natural Health: Maitland
Maitland, Florida
www.fcnh.com   Federal Code: 030086

2-year for-profit health science and junior college in large town.
Enrollment: 177 undergrads.

BASIC COSTS (2006-2007)
Additional info: Tuition for paramedical skin care program: $18,600. 5-month therapeutic massage training diploma program: $8,100.

FINANCIAL AID PICTURE
Students with need: Need-based aid available for full-time students.
Students without need: This college only awards aid to students with need.

FINANCIAL AID PROCEDURES
Forms required: FAFSA.
Dates and Deadlines: No deadline. Applicants notified on a rolling basis.

CONTACT
Jorge Villasante, Director of Financial Aid
2600 Lake Lucien Drive; Suite 140, Maitland, FL 32751
(954) 975-6400

Florida College of Natural Health: Miami
Miami, Florida
www.fcnh.com
Federal Code: 030086

2-year for-profit branch campus and community college in very large city.
Enrollment: 114 undergrads.

BASIC COSTS (2006-2007)
Additional info: Tuition for paramedical skin care program: $18,600. 5-month therapeutic massage training diploma program: $8,100.

FINANCIAL AID PICTURE
Students with need: Need-based aid available for full-time students.
Students without need: This college only awards aid to students with need.

FINANCIAL AID PROCEDURES
Forms required: FAFSA.
Dates and Deadlines: No deadline. Applicants notified on a rolling basis.

CONTACT
Jorge Villasante, Director of Financial Aid
7925 Northwest 12th Street, Suite 201, Miami, FL 33126
(954) 975-6400

Florida Community College at Jacksonville
Jacksonville, Florida
www.fccj.org
Federal Code: 001484

2-year public community college in very large city.
Enrollment: 4,974 undergrads, 73% part-time. 209 full-time freshmen.
Selectivity: Open admission; but selective for some programs.

BASIC COSTS (2005-2006)
Tuition and fees: $1,897; out-of-state residents $7,176.
Per-credit charge: $55; out-of-state residents $231.

FINANCIAL AID PICTURE (2004-2005)
Students with need: 54% of average financial aid package awarded as scholarships/grants, 46% awarded as loans/jobs. Need-based aid available for part-time students. Work study available nights, weekends, and for part-time students.
Students without need: No-need awards available for academics, alumni affiliation, art, athletics, job skills, leadership, minority status, music/drama.

FINANCIAL AID PROCEDURES
Forms required: FAFSA, institutional form.
Dates and Deadlines: Priority date 8/1; no closing date.

CONTACT
Joel Friedman, Director of Student Aid
501 West State Street, Jacksonville, FL 32202
(904) 632-3352164

Florida Gulf Coast University
Ft. Myers, Florida
www.fgcu.edu
Federal Code: 032553

4-year public university in small city.
Enrollment: 5,974 undergrads, 23% part-time. 924 full-time freshmen.
Selectivity: Admits over 75% of applicants.

BASIC COSTS (2005-2006)
Tuition and fees: $3,191; out-of-state residents $15,287.
Per-credit charge: $102; out-of-state residents $505.
Room and board: $7,460.

FINANCIAL AID PICTURE (2004-2005)
Students with need: Out of 760 full-time freshmen who applied for aid, 339 were judged to have need. Of these, 339 received aid, and 69 had their full need met. Average financial aid package met 66% of need; average scholarship/grant was $3,044; average loan was $2,351. For part-time students, average financial aid package was $5,734.
Students without need: 387 full-time freshmen who did not demonstrate need for aid received scholarships/grants; average award was $1,550. No-need awards available for academics, athletics, leadership, minority status, music/drama, state/district residency.
Scholarships offered: 16 full-time freshmen received athletic scholarships; average amount $4,054.
Cumulative student debt: 47% of graduating class had student loans; average debt was $13,245.

FINANCIAL AID PROCEDURES
Forms required: FAFSA, institutional form.
Dates and Deadlines: Priority date 2/1; closing date 3/15. Applicants notified on a rolling basis starting 2/15.
Transfers: Applicants notified on a rolling basis.

CONTACT
Kevin McGowan, Director, Student Financial Aid
10501 FGCU Boulevard South, Ft. Myers, FL 33965-6565
(239) 590-7920

Florida Hospital College of Health Sciences
Orlando, Florida
www.fhchs.edu
Federal Code: 031155

4-year private health science and nursing college in large city, affiliated with Seventh-day Adventists.
Enrollment: 1,943 undergrads.

BASIC COSTS (2006-2007)
Tuition and fees: $7,470.
Per-credit charge: $240.
Room only: $2,800.

FINANCIAL AID PICTURE
Students with need: Need-based aid available for full-time and part-time students. Work study available nights, weekends, and for part-time students.

FINANCIAL AID PROCEDURES
Forms required: FAFSA, institutional form.
Dates and Deadlines: Priority date 4/12; no closing date. Applicants notified on a rolling basis starting 3/1.

CONTACT
Starr Bender, Director of Financial Aid
800 Lake Estelle Drive, Orlando, FL 32803
(407) 303-6963

Florida Institute of Technology
Melbourne, Florida
www.fit.edu
Federal Code: 001469

4-year private university in small city.
Enrollment: 2,337 undergrads, 3% part-time. 604 full-time freshmen.
Selectivity: Admits over 75% of applicants.

BASIC COSTS (2006-2007)
Tuition and fees: $27,540.
Per-credit charge: $835.

Room and board: $7,400.
Additional info: Tuition $25,100 for aeronautics, business, psychology, and humanities programs.

FINANCIAL AID PICTURE (2005-2006)
Students with need: Out of 525 full-time freshmen who applied for aid, 437 were judged to have need. Of these, 437 received aid, and 145 had their full need met. Average financial aid package met 86% of need; average scholarship/grant was $15,091; average loan was $3,927. For part-time students, average financial aid package was $9,050.
Students without need: 156 full-time freshmen who did not demonstrate need for aid received scholarships/grants; average award was $8,473. No-need awards available for academics, alumni affiliation, athletics, leadership, ROTC.
Scholarships offered: 5 full-time freshmen received athletic scholarships; average amount $17,390.
Cumulative student debt: 54% of graduating class had student loans; average debt was $24,535.

FINANCIAL AID PROCEDURES
Forms required: FAFSA, state aid form.
Dates and Deadlines: Priority date 3/15; no closing date. Applicants notified on a rolling basis starting 2/15; must reply by 5/1 or within 4 week(s) of notification.
Transfers: No deadline. Applicants notified on a rolling basis starting 2/15; must reply within 4 week(s) of notification.

CONTACT
Jay Lally, Director of Financial Aid
150 West University Boulevard, Melbourne, FL 32901-6975
(321) 674-8070

Florida International University
Miami, Florida
www.fiu.edu   Federal Code: 009635

4-year public university in very large city.
Enrollment: 28,405 undergrads, 36% part-time. 2,747 full-time freshmen.
Selectivity: Admits less than 50% of applicants.

BASIC COSTS (2005-2006)
Tuition and fees: $3,210; out-of-state residents $15,609.
Per-credit charge: $102; out-of-state residents $515.
Room and board: $9,480.
Additional info: Tuition/fee waivers available for minority students.

FINANCIAL AID PICTURE
Students with need: Need-based aid available for full-time and part-time students.
Students without need: No-need awards available for academics, art, athletics, minority status, music/drama, state/district residency.

FINANCIAL AID PROCEDURES
Forms required: FAFSA.
Dates and Deadlines: Priority date 3/1; no closing date. Applicants notified on a rolling basis starting 4/15; must reply within 4 week(s) of notification.

CONTACT
Ana Sarasti, Director of Financial Aid
University Park Campus, PC 140, Miami, FL 33199
(305) 348-7272

Florida Keys Community College
Key West, Florida
www.fkcc.edu   Federal Code: 001485

2-year public community college in large town.
Enrollment: 832 undergrads.
Selectivity: Open admission; but selective for some programs.

BASIC COSTS (2005-2006)
Tuition and fees: $2,016; out-of-state residents $7,864.
Per-credit charge: $53; out-of-state residents $248.
Additional info: Tuition/fee waivers available for minority students, unemployed or children of unemployed.

FINANCIAL AID PICTURE
Students with need: Need-based aid available for full-time and part-time students. Work study available nights.
Students without need: No-need awards available for academics, art, leadership, minority status.

FINANCIAL AID PROCEDURES
Forms required: FAFSA, institutional form.
Dates and Deadlines: Priority date 5/1; no closing date. Applicants notified on a rolling basis starting 6/15; must reply within 2 week(s) of notification.
Transfers: Closing date 5/1. Florida Student Assistance Grant available to students paying Florida resident tuition.

CONTACT
Cary Trantham, Financial Aid Director
5901 College Road, Key West, FL 33040
(305) 809-3323

Florida Memorial University
Miami, Florida
www.fmuniv.edu   Federal Code: 001486

4-year private liberal arts college in very large city, affiliated with American Baptist Churches in the USA.
Enrollment: 1,945 undergrads, 9% part-time. 400 full-time freshmen.

BASIC COSTS (2006-2007)
Tuition and fees: $12,186.
Room and board: $5,134.

FINANCIAL AID PICTURE
Students with need: Need-based aid available for full-time and part-time students.
Additional info: Need-based financial aid available to part-time students taking 6 credits or more per semester.

FINANCIAL AID PROCEDURES
Dates and Deadlines: Priority date 4/15; no closing date. Applicants notified on a rolling basis; must reply within 2 week(s) of notification.
Transfers: Priority date 3/15; closing date 4/15.

CONTACT
Brian Phillip, Director of Financial Aid
15800 Northwest 42 Avenue, Miami, FL 33054
(305) 430-1168

Florida Metropolitan University: Brandon Campus
Tampa, Florida
www.fmu.edu
Federal Code: 001534

4-year for-profit university and business college in very large city.
Enrollment: 907 undergrads, 59% part-time.

BASIC COSTS (2005-2006)
Tuition and fees: $12,615.
Per-credit charge: $275.

FINANCIAL AID PICTURE
Students with need: Need-based aid available for full-time and part-time students.
Students without need: This college only awards aid to students with need.

FINANCIAL AID PROCEDURES
Forms required: FAFSA, institutional form.
Dates and Deadlines: No deadline. Applicants notified on a rolling basis; must reply within 2 week(s) of notification.

CONTACT
Diane Maloney, Director of Financial Aid
3924 Coconut Palm Drive, Tampa, FL 33619
(813) 621-0041

Florida Metropolitan University: Melbourne Campus
Melbourne, Florida
www.cci.edu
Federal Code: 001499

4-year for-profit business college in small city.
Enrollment: 950 undergrads.
Selectivity: Admits over 75% of applicants.

BASIC COSTS (2006-2007)
Tuition and fees: $10,440.
Per-credit charge: $285.

FINANCIAL AID PICTURE
Students with need: Need-based aid available for full-time and part-time students. Work study available nights.
Students without need: No-need awards available for academics.

FINANCIAL AID PROCEDURES
Forms required: FAFSA.
Dates and Deadlines: No deadline. Applicants notified on a rolling basis; must reply within 3 week(s) of notification.

CONTACT
Rhonda Landolfi, Director of Student Finance Office
2401 North Harbor City Boulevard, Melbourne, FL 32935
(321) 253-2929 ext. 140

Florida Metropolitan University: Orlando College North
Orlando, Florida
www.cci.edu
Federal Code: 001499

4-year for-profit business college in very large city.
Enrollment: 1,257 undergrads.

BASIC COSTS (2006-2007)
Tuition and fees: $10,440.
Per-credit charge: $285.

FINANCIAL AID PICTURE
Students with need: Need-based aid available for full-time and part-time students.

FINANCIAL AID PROCEDURES
Forms required: FAFSA.
Dates and Deadlines: No deadline. Applicants notified on a rolling basis starting 6/1.

CONTACT
Linda Kaisrlik, Senior Financial Aid Administrator
5421 Diplomat Circle, Orlando, FL 32810
(407) 628-5870 ext. 118

Florida Metropolitan University: Pinellas
Clearwater, Florida
www.fmu.edu
Federal Code: 025998

5-year for-profit university and business college in large city.
Enrollment: 924 undergrads.

BASIC COSTS (2006-2007)
Tuition and fees: $10,440.
Per-credit charge: $285.

FINANCIAL AID PICTURE
Students with need: Need-based aid available for full-time and part-time students. Work study available nights.

FINANCIAL AID PROCEDURES
Forms required: FAFSA, institutional form.
Dates and Deadlines: No deadline. Applicants notified on a rolling basis.

CONTACT
David Destrooper, Director of Financial aid
2471 McMullen Booth Road, Suite 200, Clearwater, FL 33759
(727) 725-2688

Florida Metropolitan University: Pompano Beach
Pompano Beach, Florida
www.fmu.edu
Federal Code: 008146

4-year for-profit business college in small city.
Enrollment: 1,500 undergrads.

BASIC COSTS (2006-2007)
Tuition and fees: $10,440.
Per-credit charge: $285.
Additional info: Tuition may vary by program.

FINANCIAL AID PICTURE
Students with need: Need-based aid available for full-time and part-time students.

FINANCIAL AID PROCEDURES
Forms required: FAFSA, institutional form.
Dates and Deadlines: No deadline. Applicants notified on a rolling basis starting 6/1.

CONTACT
Sharon Scheible, Director of Financial Aid
225 North Federal Highway, Pompano Beach, FL 33062
(954) 783-7339

Florida Metropolitan University: Tampa College
Tampa, Florida
www.fmu.edu   Federal Code: 001534

4-year for-profit university and business college in large city.
Enrollment: 1,398 undergrads.
Selectivity: Open admission.

BASIC COSTS (2006-2007)
Tuition and fees: $10,440.
Per-credit charge: $285.
Additional info: Cost of tuition may vary with program.

FINANCIAL AID PICTURE
Students with need: Need-based aid available for full-time and part-time students.
Students without need: This college only awards aid to students with need.

FINANCIAL AID PROCEDURES
Forms required: FAFSA.
Dates and Deadlines: No deadline. Applicants notified on a rolling basis.

CONTACT
Rod Kirkwood, Director of Financial Aid
3319 West Hillsborough Avenue, Tampa, FL 33614
(813) 879-6000 ext. 145

Florida Metropolitan University: Tampa College Lakeland
Lakeland, Florida
www.cci.edu   Federal Code: 025998

4-year private university and branch campus college in small city.
Enrollment: 716 undergrads.

BASIC COSTS (2005-2006)
Tuition and fees: $12,375.
Per-credit charge: $270.

FINANCIAL AID PICTURE
Students with need: Need-based aid available for full-time and part-time students.
Students without need: This college only awards aid to students with need.

FINANCIAL AID PROCEDURES
Dates and Deadlines: No deadline.

CONTACT
Linda Wagner
995 East Memorial Boulevard, Suite 110, Lakeland, FL 33801-1919
(863) 686-1449 ext. 101

Florida National College
Hialeah, Florida
www.fnc.edu   Federal Code: 017069

2-year for-profit community and junior college in very large city.
Enrollment: 2,000 undergrads.
Selectivity: Open admission.

BASIC COSTS (2006-2007)
Tuition and fees: $10,616.
Per-credit charge: $340.

FINANCIAL AID PICTURE (2005-2006)
Students with need: 37% of average financial aid package awarded as scholarships/grants, 63% awarded as loans/jobs. Need-based aid available for part-time students.
Students without need: This college only awards aid to students with need.

FINANCIAL AID PROCEDURES
Forms required: FAFSA, institutional form.
Dates and Deadlines: No deadline.

CONTACT
Omar Sanchez, Vice President for Planning and Research
4425 West 20th Avenue, Hialeah, FL 33012
(305) 821-3333 ext. 1003

Florida Southern College
Lakeland, Florida
www.flsouthern.edu   Federal Code: 001488

4-year private liberal arts college in small city, affiliated with United Methodist Church.
Enrollment: 1,816 undergrads, 3% part-time. 464 full-time freshmen.
Selectivity: Admits 50 to 75% of applicants.

BASIC COSTS (2006-2007)
Tuition and fees: $20,175.
Room and board: $7,140.

FINANCIAL AID PICTURE (2005-2006)
Students with need: Out of 395 full-time freshmen who applied for aid, 310 were judged to have need. Of these, 309 received aid, and 129 had their full need met. Average financial aid package met 72% of need; average scholarship/grant was $14,611; average loan was $4,331. For part-time students, average financial aid package was $5,672.
Students without need: 84 full-time freshmen who did not demonstrate need for aid received scholarships/grants; average award was $13,388. No-need awards available for academics, alumni affiliation, art, athletics, job skills, leadership, minority status, music/drama, religious affiliation, ROTC, state/district residency.
Scholarships offered: 12 full-time freshmen received athletic scholarships; average amount $5,527.
Cumulative student debt: 67% of graduating class had student loans; average debt was $16,072.

FINANCIAL AID PROCEDURES
Forms required: FAFSA, institutional form.
Dates and Deadlines: Priority date 4/1; closing date 8/1. Applicants notified on a rolling basis starting 3/15.

CONTACT
David Bodwell, Director of Financial Aid
111 Lake Hollingsworth Drive, Lakeland, FL 33801-5698
(863) 680-4140

Florida State University
Tallahassee, Florida
www.fsu.edu   Federal Code: 001489

4-year public university in small city.
Enrollment: 30,206 undergrads, 10% part-time. 6,021 full-time freshmen.
Selectivity: Admits 50 to 75% of applicants.

BASIC COSTS (2005-2006)
Tuition and fees: $3,208; out-of-state residents $16,340.
Per-credit charge: $101; out-of-state residents $539.

Florida Florida State University

Room and board: $6,778.

FINANCIAL AID PICTURE (2005-2006)
Students with need: Out of 3,835 full-time freshmen who applied for aid, 2,019 were judged to have need. Of these, 2,107 received aid, and 1,464 had their full need met. Average financial aid package met 65% of need; average scholarship/grant was $2,817; average loan was $2,160. For part-time students, average financial aid package was $7,056.
Students without need: 403 full-time freshmen who did not demonstrate need for aid received scholarships/grants; average award was $1,946. No-need awards available for academics, athletics, state/district residency.
Scholarships offered: *Merit:* National Merit/Achievement Scholarship: $6,000 per year; renewable for four years; based on select number of finalist who name FSU as their first choice institution. National Hispanic Scholarship: $6,000 per year; renewable for four years; awarded to a select number of scholars. University Scholarship for Freshmen: $9,600 over 4 years; based on high school grades and test scores. Incentive Scholarship: $8,000 over 4 years; based on high school grades and test scores. 21st Century Scholarship for Freshmen: $4,200 over 4 years; based on grades and test scores.
Athletic: 363 full-time freshmen received athletic scholarships; average amount $271.
Cumulative student debt: 52% of graduating class had student loans; average debt was $16,597.
Additional info: Out-of-state tuition costs waived for National Merit and National Achievement students and National Hispanic Scholars, and some southwest Georgia residents.

FINANCIAL AID PROCEDURES
Forms required: FAFSA.
Dates and Deadlines: Priority date 2/15; no closing date. Applicants notified on a rolling basis starting 3/15; must reply within 2 week(s) of notification.

CONTACT
Darryl Marshall, Director of Financial Aid
A2500 University Center, Tallahassee, FL 32306-2400
(850) 644-0539

Florida Technical College: Deland
Deland, Florida
www.flatech.edu

2-year for-profit junior and technical college in small city.
Enrollment: 258 undergrads.
Selectivity: Open admission.

BASIC COSTS (2006-2007)
Additional info: $4,347 tuition per quarter for paralegal, medical assistant, business, computer drafting & design, electronics/computer technology; $4,713 tuition per quarter for network hardware, network administration/programming, e-commerce, web-design and graphics design. $3650 per quarter for Criminal Justice and $3667 per quarter for Network Administration/Hardware with Wirelss technology. Required fees $100. Tuition includes cost of books and supplies.

FINANCIAL AID PICTURE
Students with need: Need-based aid available for full-time and part-time students. Work study available nights.
Students without need: This college only awards aid to students with need.

FINANCIAL AID PROCEDURES
Forms required: FAFSA.
Dates and Deadlines: No deadline. Applicants notified on a rolling basis.

CONTACT
Sandra Follmar, Director of Financial Aid
1199 South Woodland Boulevard, Deland, FL 32720
(386) 734-3303

Full Sail Real World Education
Winter Park, Florida
www.fullsail.com
Federal Code: 016812

2-year for-profit visual arts and technical college in very large city.
Enrollment: 5,060 undergrads.
Selectivity: Open admission; but selective for some programs.

BASIC COSTS (2005-2006)
Additional info: Tuition for associate degree programs range between $40,005 to $41,660. Tuition for bachelor degree programs range between $61,775 and $69,460. Books and supplies included in tuition.

FINANCIAL AID PICTURE
Students with need: Need-based aid available for full-time students. Work study available nights, weekends, and for part-time students.

FINANCIAL AID PROCEDURES
Forms required: FAFSA.
Dates and Deadlines: No deadline. Applicants notified on a rolling basis; must reply within 2 week(s) of notification.

CONTACT
Debbie Magruder
3300 University Boulevard, Winter Park, FL 32792-7429
(407) 679-0100 ext. 2300

Gulf Coast Community College
Panama City, Florida
www.gulfcoast.edu
Federal Code: 001490

2-year public community college in small city.
Enrollment: 7,223 undergrads, 70% part-time.
Selectivity: Open admission; but selective for some programs.

BASIC COSTS (2005-2006)
Tuition and fees: $1,871; out-of-state residents $6,489.
Per-credit charge: $51; out-of-state residents $205.

FINANCIAL AID PICTURE
Students with need: Need-based aid available for full-time and part-time students. Work study available nights, weekends, and for part-time students.
Students without need: No-need awards available for academics, athletics, job skills, leadership, minority status, music/drama, state/district residency.
Scholarships offered: GCCC Foundation scholarships based on academic performance, financial need and other criteria; more than $350,000 total annually.

FINANCIAL AID PROCEDURES
Forms required: FAFSA.
Dates and Deadlines: Priority date 4/1; closing date 7/1. Applicants notified on a rolling basis starting 7/1.
Transfers: Priority date 11/1; no deadline.

CONTACT
Herman Martin, Director of Financial Aid
5230 West Highway 98, Panama City, FL 32401-1041
(850) 872-3845

Hillsborough Community College
Tampa, Florida
www.hccfl.edu
Federal Code: 007870

2-year public community college in large city.
Enrollment: 22,125 undergrads.
Selectivity: Open admission.

BASIC COSTS (2005-2006)
Tuition and fees: $1,983; out-of-state residents $6,924.
Per-credit charge: $55; out-of-state residents $220.

FINANCIAL AID PICTURE (2004-2005)
Students with need: 60% of average financial aid package awarded as scholarships/grants, 40% awarded as loans/jobs. Work study available nights, weekends, and for part-time students.

FINANCIAL AID PROCEDURES
Forms required: FAFSA.
Dates and Deadlines: Closing date 6/30. Applicants notified on a rolling basis starting 7/1; must reply within 2 week(s) of notification.
Transfers: No deadline. Transfer students must submit academic transcripts prior to obtaining student loans at sophomore level.

CONTACT
Charlotte Johns, Director - Financial Aid
Box 31127, Tampa, FL 33631-3127
(813) 253-7235

Hobe Sound Bible College
Hobe Sound, Florida
www.hsbc.edu   Federal Code: 015463

4-year private Bible college in small town, affiliated with interdenominational tradition.
Enrollment: 133 undergrads.
Selectivity: Admits less than 50% of applicants.

BASIC COSTS (2005-2006)
Tuition and fees: $4,320.
Per-credit charge: $155.
Room and board: $3,240.

FINANCIAL AID PICTURE (2005-2006)
Students with need: Need-based aid available for part-time students.
Students without need: No-need awards available for academics, leadership.

FINANCIAL AID PROCEDURES
Dates and Deadlines: Closing date 8/1.

CONTACT
John Churchill, Director of Financial Aid
Box 1065, Hobe Sound, FL 33475
(772) 546-5534 ext. 1003

Indian River Community College
Fort Pierce, Florida
www.ircc.edu   Federal Code: 001493

2-year public community college in small city.
Enrollment: 6,862 undergrads.
Selectivity: Open admission; but selective for some programs.

BASIC COSTS (2005-2006)
Tuition and fees: $1,872; out-of-state residents $6,990.
Per-credit charge: $52; out-of-state residents $223.

FINANCIAL AID PICTURE (2004-2005)
Students with need: 77% of average financial aid package awarded as scholarships/grants, 23% awarded as loans/jobs. Need-based aid available for part-time students.
Students without need: No-need awards available for academics, athletics, minority status, music/drama, state/district residency.

FINANCIAL AID PROCEDURES
Forms required: FAFSA, institutional form.
Dates and Deadlines: Priority date 7/18; no closing date. Applicants notified on a rolling basis starting 5/15.

CONTACT
Mary Lewis, Director of Financial Aid
3209 Virginia Avenue, Fort Pierce, FL 34981-5596
(772) 462-7450

International Academy of Design and Technology: Orlando
Orlando, Florida
www.iadt.edu   Federal Code: 030314

4-year for-profit technical college in very large city.
Enrollment: 1,022 undergrads.
Selectivity: Open admission.

BASIC COSTS (2006-2007)
Tuition and fees: $15,936.
Per-credit charge: $332.

FINANCIAL AID PICTURE (2005-2006)
Students with need: 30% of average financial aid package awarded as scholarships/grants, 70% awarded as loans/jobs.

FINANCIAL AID PROCEDURES
Forms required: FAFSA.
Dates and Deadlines: No deadline.

CONTACT
Daisy Tabachow, Director of Finanacial Aid
5959 Lake Ellenor Drive, Orlando, FL 32809
(407) 857-2300

International Academy of Design and Technology: Tampa
Tampa, Florida
www.academy.edu   Federal Code: 030314

4-year for-profit visual arts and technical college in very large city.
Enrollment: 2,400 undergrads.

BASIC COSTS (2006-2007)
Tuition and fees: $17,625.
Per-credit charge: $385.

FINANCIAL AID PICTURE
Students with need: Need-based aid available for full-time and part-time students. Work study available nights, weekends, and for part-time students.
Students without need: No-need awards available for academics.

FINANCIAL AID PROCEDURES
Forms required: FAFSA.
Dates and Deadlines: No deadline.

CONTACT
Steve Wood, Financial Aid Director
5104 Eisenhower Boulevard, Tampa, FL 33634
(813) 881-0007 ext. 8054

International College
Naples, Florida
www.internationalcollege.edu
Federal Code: 030375

4-year private business college in small city.
Enrollment: 1,452 undergrads, 25% part-time. 108 full-time freshmen.
Selectivity: Open admission.

BASIC COSTS (2006-2007)
Tuition and fees: $12,530.
Per-credit charge: $405.

FINANCIAL AID PICTURE
Students with need: Need-based aid available for full-time and part-time students. Work study available nights, weekends, and for part-time students.
Students without need: No-need awards available for academics, leadership, state/district residency.

FINANCIAL AID PROCEDURES
Forms required: FAFSA.
Dates and Deadlines: No deadline. Applicants notified on a rolling basis.

CONTACT
Joe Gilchrist, Vice President of Student Financial Assistance
2655 Northbrooke Drive, Naples, FL 34119
(239) 513-1122

Jacksonville University
Jacksonville, Florida
www.jacksonville.edu
Federal Code: 001495

4-year private university and liberal arts college in very large city.
Enrollment: 2,113 undergrads, 10% part-time. 531 full-time freshmen.
Selectivity: Admits 50 to 75% of applicants.

BASIC COSTS (2006-2007)
Tuition and fees: $21,200.
Per-credit charge: $706.
Room and board: $6,600.
Additional info: $540 mandatory health insurance fee charged unless proof of other coverage is provided.

FINANCIAL AID PICTURE (2005-2006)
Students with need: Out of 439 full-time freshmen who applied for aid, 382 were judged to have need. Of these, 382 received aid, and 77 had their full need met. Average financial aid package met 81% of need; average scholarship/grant was $7,103; average loan was $4,291. For part-time students, average financial aid package was $5,680.
Students without need: 67 full-time freshmen who did not demonstrate need for aid received scholarships/grants; average award was $5,355. No-need awards available for academics, art, athletics, job skills, music/drama, ROTC, state/district residency.
Scholarships offered: 9 full-time freshmen received athletic scholarships; average amount $6,929.
Cumulative student debt: 53% of graduating class had student loans; average debt was $21,483.

FINANCIAL AID PROCEDURES
Forms required: FAFSA.
Dates and Deadlines: Priority date 2/1; closing date 3/15. Applicants notified on a rolling basis starting 2/1; must reply by 5/1 or within 3 week(s) of notification.
Transfers: No deadline. Applicants notified on a rolling basis.

CONTACT
Catherine Huntress, Financial Aid Director
2800 University Boulevard North, Jacksonville, FL 32211-3394
(904) 256-7060

Johnson & Wales University
North Miami, Florida
www.jwu.edu/florida
Federal Code: 003404

4-year private university in large city.
Enrollment: 2,452 undergrads, 6% part-time. 704 full-time freshmen.
Selectivity: Admits 50 to 75% of applicants.

BASIC COSTS (2006-2007)
Tuition and fees: $20,826.
Room and board: $9,300.
Additional info: Weekend meal plan is optional for $954.

FINANCIAL AID PICTURE (2005-2006)
Students with need: Out of 622 full-time freshmen who applied for aid, 590 were judged to have need. Of these, 581 received aid, and 7 had their full need met. Average financial aid package met 65% of need; average scholarship/grant was $6,734; average loan was $6,857. For part-time students, average financial aid package was $9,443.
Students without need: 64 full-time freshmen who did not demonstrate need for aid received scholarships/grants; average award was $4,670. No-need awards available for academics, alumni affiliation, job skills, leadership, state/district residency.
Cumulative student debt: 75% of graduating class had student loans; average debt was $18,634.

FINANCIAL AID PROCEDURES
Forms required: FAFSA.
Dates and Deadlines: No deadline. Applicants notified on a rolling basis starting 3/1; must reply within 2 week(s) of notification.

CONTACT
Lynn Robinson, Director, Financial Aid
1701 Northeast 127th Street, North Miami, FL 33181
(800) 342-5598

Jones College
Jacksonville, Florida
www.jones.edu
Federal Code: 001497

4-year private business college in very large city.
Enrollment: 652 undergrads, 76% part-time. 6 full-time freshmen.
Selectivity: Open admission.

BASIC COSTS (2006-2007)
Tuition and fees: $8,340.
Per-credit charge: $275.

FINANCIAL AID PICTURE
Students with need: Need-based aid available for full-time and part-time students. Work study available nights, weekends, and for part-time students.
Students without need: This college only awards aid to students with need.

FINANCIAL AID PROCEDURES
Forms required: FAFSA.
Dates and Deadlines: No deadline. Applicants notified on a rolling basis.

CONTACT
Becky Davis, Financial Assistance Director
5353 Arlington Expressway, Jacksonville, FL 32211
(904) 743-1122 ext. 100

Key College
Dania Beach, Florida
www.keycollege.edu
Federal Code: 015191

2-year for-profit business and technical college in very large city.
Enrollment: 187 undergrads.
Selectivity: Admits over 75% of applicants.

BASIC COSTS (2006-2007)
Tuition and fees: $9,220.

FINANCIAL AID PICTURE
Students with need: Work study available nights.
Additional info: Federal Supplemental Educational Opportunities Grant (FSEOG), PELL grant, FFEL (federal loan program) available; direct loans offered.

FINANCIAL AID PROCEDURES
Dates and Deadlines: No deadline.

CONTACT
McGrath Jo, Director of Financial Services
225 Dania Beach Boulevard, Dania Beach, FL 33004
(954) 923-4440

Lake City Community College
Lake City, Florida
www.lakecitycc.edu
Federal Code: 001501

2-year public community college in large town.
Enrollment: 2,736 undergrads.
Selectivity: Open admission; but selective for some programs.

BASIC COSTS (2005-2006)
Tuition and fees: $1,887; out-of-state residents $7,050.
Per-credit charge: $51; out-of-state residents $223.
Additional info: Tuition/fee waivers available for minority students.

FINANCIAL AID PICTURE (2004-2005)
Students with need: 79% of average financial aid package awarded as scholarships/grants, 21% awarded as loans/jobs. Need-based aid available for part-time students.
Students without need: No-need awards available for academics, athletics.

FINANCIAL AID PROCEDURES
Forms required: FAFSA, institutional form.
Dates and Deadlines: Priority date 6/1; no closing date. Applicants notified on a rolling basis starting 6/1; must reply within 2 week(s) of notification.

CONTACT
Debberin Tunsil, Director of Financial Aid
149 SE College Place, Lake City, FL 32025-8703
(386) 754-4282

Lake-Sumter Community College
Leesburg, Florida
www.lscc.edu
Federal Code: 001502

2-year public community college in small city.
Enrollment: 2,773 undergrads, 60% part-time. 351 full-time freshmen.
Selectivity: Open admission; but selective for some programs.

BASIC COSTS (2005-2006)
Tuition and fees: $1,932; out-of-state residents $7,108.
Per-credit charge: $52; out-of-state residents $225.

FINANCIAL AID PICTURE (2004-2005)
Students with need: 3% of average financial aid package awarded as scholarships/grants, 97% awarded as loans/jobs. Need-based aid available for part-time students. Work study available nights, weekends, and for part-time students.
Students without need: No-need awards available for academics, art, athletics, leadership, minority status, music/drama.

FINANCIAL AID PROCEDURES
Forms required: FAFSA, institutional form.
Dates and Deadlines: Priority date 4/15; no closing date. Applicants notified on a rolling basis starting 7/1.

CONTACT
Audrey Maxwell, Director - Financial Aid
9501 U.S. Highway 441, Leesburg, FL 34788-8751
(352) 365-3512

Lynn University
Boca Raton, Florida
www.lynn.edu
Federal Code: 001505

4-year private university in small city.
Enrollment: 2,281 undergrads, 14% part-time. 730 full-time freshmen.
Selectivity: Admits over 75% of applicants.

BASIC COSTS (2006-2007)
Tuition and fees: $27,350.
Per-credit charge: $873.
Room and board: $9,650.

FINANCIAL AID PICTURE (2005-2006)
Students with need: Out of 273 full-time freshmen who applied for aid, 212 were judged to have need. Of these, 209 received aid, and 20 had their full need met. Average financial aid package met 51% of need; average scholarship/grant was $11,591; average loan was $3,084.
Students without need: 230 full-time freshmen who did not demonstrate need for aid received scholarships/grants; average award was $12,376. No-need awards available for academics, art, athletics, leadership, music/drama, religious affiliation.
Scholarships offered: 47 full-time freshmen received athletic scholarships; average amount $20,523.

FINANCIAL AID PROCEDURES
Forms required: FAFSA, institutional form.
Dates and Deadlines: Priority date 3/1; no closing date. Applicants notified on a rolling basis starting 2/1; must reply within 2 week(s) of notification.
Transfers: Scholarships and grants available.

CONTACT
William Healy, Director of Financial Services
3601 North Military Trail, Boca Raton, FL 33431-5598
(561) 237-7185

Manatee Community College
Bradenton, Florida
www.mccfl.edu
Federal Code: 001504

2-year public community college in small city.
Enrollment: 8,984 undergrads, 58% part-time. 942 full-time freshmen.
Selectivity: Open admission; but selective for some programs.

BASIC COSTS (2005-2006)
Tuition and fees: $1,983; out-of-state residents $7,352.
Per-credit charge: $55; out-of-state residents $234.

FINANCIAL AID PICTURE

Students with need: Need-based aid available for full-time and part-time students. Work study available nights, weekends, and for part-time students.
Students without need: No-need awards available for academics, art, athletics, music/drama, state/district residency.

FINANCIAL AID PROCEDURES

Forms required: FAFSA.
Dates and Deadlines: Priority date 6/1; no closing date. Applicants notified on a rolling basis starting 3/15.

CONTACT

Anders Nilsen, Director of Financial Aid
Box 1849, Bradenton, FL 34206-1849
(941) 752-5309

Miami Dade College
Miami, Florida
www.mdc.edu   Federal Code: 001506

2-year public community college in very large city.
Enrollment: 47,878 undergrads, 63% part-time. 4,678 full-time freshmen.
Selectivity: Open admission; but selective for some programs.

BASIC COSTS (2005-2006)

Tuition and fees: $1,921; out-of-state residents $6,298.
Per-credit charge: $54; out-of-state residents $200.
Additional info: Additional fees of $290 are required for Out-of-State students.

FINANCIAL AID PICTURE (2005-2006)

Students with need: Average financial aid package met 68% of need; average scholarship/grant was $3,245; average loan was $1,074. For part-time students, average financial aid package was $1,742.
Students without need: No-need awards available for academics, art, athletics, music/drama, state/district residency.

FINANCIAL AID PROCEDURES

Forms required: FAFSA.
Dates and Deadlines: Priority date 3/15; no closing date. Applicants notified on a rolling basis starting 5/15.

CONTACT

Ana Sarasti, Collegewide Director of Financial Aid
11011 Southwest 104th Street, Miami, FL 33176
(305) 237-2122

New College of Florida
Sarasota, Florida
www.ncf.edu   Federal Code: 001537

4-year public liberal arts college in small city.
Enrollment: 761 undergrads. 218 full-time freshmen.
Selectivity: Admits 50 to 75% of applicants.

BASIC COSTS (2005-2006)

Tuition and fees: $3,013; out-of-state residents $15,520.
Per-credit charge: $72; out-of-state residents $488.
Room and board: $6,330.
Additional info: Additional $625 required fees for out-of-state students.

FINANCIAL AID PICTURE (2005-2006)

Students with need: Out of 144 full-time freshmen who applied for aid, 76 were judged to have need. Of these, 76 received aid, and 55 had their full need met. Average financial aid package met 96% of need; average scholarship/grant was $8,439; average loan was $2,215.

Students without need: 141 full-time freshmen who did not demonstrate need for aid received scholarships/grants; average award was $3,885. No-need awards available for academics, leadership, state/district residency.
Cumulative student debt: 38% of graduating class had student loans; average debt was $12,252.

FINANCIAL AID PROCEDURES

Forms required: FAFSA.
Dates and Deadlines: Priority date 3/1; no closing date. Applicants notified on a rolling basis starting 1/1; must reply by 5/1 or within 4 week(s) of notification.
Transfers: No deadline. Applicants notified on a rolling basis starting 1/1; must reply by 5/1 or within 4 week(s) of notification.

CONTACT

Monica Mattscheck, Director of Financial Aid
5700 North Tamiami Trail, Sarasota, FL 34243-2197
(941) 359-4255

New England Institute of Technology
West Palm Beach, Florida
www.newenglandtech.com   Federal Code: 016095

2-year for-profit technical college in small city.
Enrollment: 1,300 undergrads.
Selectivity: Open admission.

BASIC COSTS (2005-2006)

Additional info: Tuition and lab fees range from $11,700 to $36,900. Registration fee $125. Tuition at time of enrollment locked for 2 years.

FINANCIAL AID PICTURE (2004-2005)

Students with need: 52% of average financial aid package awarded as scholarships/grants, 48% awarded as loans/jobs. Work study available nights, weekends, and for part-time students.

FINANCIAL AID PROCEDURES

Forms required: FAFSA, institutional form.
Dates and Deadlines: No deadline. Applicants notified on a rolling basis.

CONTACT

Elizabeth Layton, Director of Student Financial Services
2410 Metrocentre Boulevard, West Palm Beach, FL 33407
(561) 842-8324

North Florida Community College
Madison, Florida
www.nfcc.edu   Federal Code: 001508

2-year public community college in small town.
Enrollment: 1,443 undergrads.
Selectivity: Open admission; but selective for some programs.

BASIC COSTS (2005-2006)

Tuition and fees: $1,860; out-of-state residents $4,920.
Per-credit charge: $51; out-of-state residents $153.
Additional info: $510 required fees for out-of-state students.

FINANCIAL AID PICTURE (2004-2005)

Students with need: 98% of average financial aid package awarded as scholarships/grants, 2% awarded as loans/jobs. Need-based aid available for part-time students. Work study available nights, weekends, and for part-time students.
Students without need: This college only awards aid to students with need.

FINANCIAL AID PROCEDURES
Forms required: FAFSA.
Dates and Deadlines: Priority date 5/15; no closing date. Applicants notified on a rolling basis starting 6/20; must reply within 2 week(s) of notification.

CONTACT
Amelia Mulkey, Director of Financial Aid
325 NW Turner Davis Drive, Madison, FL 32340
(850) 973-1621

Northwood University: Florida Campus
West Palm Beach, Florida
www.northwood.edu   Federal Code: 013040

4-year private university and business college in small city.
Enrollment: 721 undergrads, 4% part-time. 143 full-time freshmen.
Selectivity: Admits 50 to 75% of applicants.

BASIC COSTS (2006-2007)
Tuition and fees: $15,801.
Per-credit charge: $317.
Room and board: $7,752.

FINANCIAL AID PICTURE (2005-2006)
Students with need: Out of 97 full-time freshmen who applied for aid, 89 were judged to have need. Of these, 89 received aid, and 14 had their full need met. Average financial aid package met 67% of need; average scholarship/grant was $6,092; average loan was $2,555. For part-time students, average financial aid package was $12,697.
Students without need: 23 full-time freshmen who did not demonstrate need for aid received scholarships/grants; average award was $5,376. No-need awards available for academics, alumni affiliation, athletics, leadership, minority status, state/district residency.
Scholarships offered: Merit: $4,000-$9,000; based on test scores and GPA; unlimited number awarded. **Athletic:** 16 full-time freshmen received athletic scholarships; average amount $6,043.
Cumulative student debt: 45% of graduating class had student loans; average debt was $15,704.

FINANCIAL AID PROCEDURES
Forms required: FAFSA.
Dates and Deadlines: No deadline. Applicants notified on a rolling basis starting 3/1.

CONTACT
Teresa Palmer, Director of Financial Aid
2600 North Military Trail, West Palm Beach, FL 33409-2911
(561) 478-5590

Nova Southeastern University
Fort Lauderdale, Florida
www.nova.edu   Federal Code: 001509

4-year private university in small city.
Enrollment: 5,275 undergrads, 36% part-time. 317 full-time freshmen.
Selectivity: Admits 50 to 75% of applicants.

BASIC COSTS (2006-2007)
Tuition and fees: $18,650.
Per-credit charge: $605.
Room and board: $6,684.

FINANCIAL AID PICTURE (2004-2005)
Students with need: Out of 317 full-time freshmen who applied for aid, 288 were judged to have need. Of these, 288 received aid, and 35 had their full need met. For part-time students, average financial aid package was $9,980.
Students without need: 29 full-time freshmen who did not demonstrate need for aid received scholarships/grants; average award was $9,647. No-need awards available for academics, athletics, leadership.
Scholarships offered: 5 full-time freshmen received athletic scholarships; average amount $6,032.
Cumulative student debt: 62% of graduating class had student loans; average debt was $26,658.

FINANCIAL AID PROCEDURES
Forms required: FAFSA, institutional form.
Dates and Deadlines: Priority date 4/15; no closing date. Applicants notified on a rolling basis starting 3/15.

CONTACT
Peggy Loewy-Wellisch, Associate Vice President, Student Financial Services and Registration
3301 College Avenue, Fort Lauderdale, FL 33314
(954) 262-3380

Okaloosa-Walton College
Niceville, Florida
www.owc.edu   Federal Code: 001510

4-year public business and community college in large town.
Enrollment: 4,134 undergrads.
Selectivity: Open admission.

BASIC COSTS (2005-2006)
Tuition and fees: $1,745; out-of-state residents $6,326.
Per-credit charge: $51; out-of-state residents $203.
Additional info: Tuition/fee waivers available for minority students.

FINANCIAL AID PICTURE
Students with need: Need-based aid available for full-time and part-time students. Work study available nights.
Students without need: No-need awards available for academics, art, athletics, leadership, minority status, music/drama.

FINANCIAL AID PROCEDURES
Forms required: FAFSA, institutional form.
Dates and Deadlines: Priority date 4/1; no closing date. Applicants notified on a rolling basis starting 2/1; must reply within 2 week(s) of notification.
Transfers: Academic transcript evaluated to determine student eligibility for financial aid.

CONTACT
Pat Bennett, Director of Financial Aid
100 College Boulevard, Niceville, FL 32578-1295
(850) 678-5111

Palm Beach Atlantic University
West Palm Beach, Florida
www.pba.edu   Federal Code: 008849

4-year private university and liberal arts college in large city, affiliated with non-denominational tradition.
Enrollment: 2,461 undergrads, 7% part-time. 437 full-time freshmen.
Selectivity: Admits less than 50% of applicants.

BASIC COSTS (2006-2007)
Tuition and fees: $18,740.
Room and board: $7,100.
Additional info: Per-credit-hour charge ranges from $395 to $760 depending on the number of credits.

FINANCIAL AID PICTURE (2004-2005)
Students with need: Out of 371 full-time freshmen who applied for aid, 283 were judged to have need. Of these, 283 received aid, and 74 had their full need met. Average financial aid package met 64% of need; average scholarship/grant was $3,568; average loan was $2,462. For part-time students, average financial aid package was $3,893.
Students without need: No-need awards available for academics, alumni affiliation, athletics, minority status, music/drama, state/district residency.
Scholarships offered: 1 full-time freshmen received athletic scholarships; average amount $5,000.
Cumulative student debt: 80% of graduating class had student loans; average debt was $24,393.

FINANCIAL AID PROCEDURES
Forms required: FAFSA, state aid form.
Dates and Deadlines: Priority date 2/1; no closing date. Applicants notified on a rolling basis starting 2/15; must reply within 1 week(s) of notification.
Transfers: Applicants notified on a rolling basis starting 2/15; must reply within 1 week(s) of notification. Florida residential undergraduate students are eligible for a grant from the state if they are enrolled on a full-time basis.

CONTACT
Margherite Powell, Dean, Student Services
PO Box 24708, West Palm Beach, FL 33416-4708
(561) 803-2126

Palm Beach Community College
Lake Worth, Florida
www.pbcc.edu   Federal Code: 001512

2-year public community college in large town.
Enrollment: 13,683 undergrads, 59% part-time. 1,370 full-time freshmen.
Selectivity: Open admission; but selective for some programs.

BASIC COSTS (2005-2006)
Tuition and fees: $1,890; out-of-state residents $6,614.
Per-credit charge: $52; out-of-state residents $210.
Additional info: $279 in required fees for out-of-state students.

FINANCIAL AID PICTURE (2005-2006)
Students with need: 74% of average financial aid package awarded as scholarships/grants, 26% awarded as loans/jobs. Work study available nights, weekends, and for part-time students.
Students without need: No-need awards available for academics, alumni affiliation, athletics, leadership, state/district residency.

FINANCIAL AID PROCEDURES
Forms required: FAFSA, institutional form.
Dates and Deadlines: Priority date 7/1; no closing date. Applicants notified on a rolling basis; must reply within 2 week(s) of notification.

CONTACT
Director of Student Financial Aid
4200 Congress Avenue, Lake Worth, FL 33461
(561) 868-3330

Pasco-Hernando Community College
New Port Richey, Florida
www.phcc.edu   Federal Code: 010652

2-year public community college in large town.
Enrollment: 7,346 undergrads, 64% part-time. 683 full-time freshmen.
Selectivity: Open admission; but selective for some programs.

BASIC COSTS (2005-2006)
Tuition and fees: $1,872; out-of-state residents $7,222.
Per-credit charge: $50; out-of-state residents $199.
Additional info: $863 required fees for out-of-state students.

FINANCIAL AID PICTURE
Students with need: Need-based aid available for full-time and part-time students. Work study available nights, weekends, and for part-time students.
Students without need: No-need awards available for academics, athletics, minority status.
Additional info: Childcare assistance grants available to eligible students.

FINANCIAL AID PROCEDURES
Forms required: FAFSA.
Dates and Deadlines: Priority date 4/1; no closing date. Applicants notified on a rolling basis starting 3/1.
Transfers: Priority date 3/1.

CONTACT
Rebecca Shanafelt, Director of Financial Aid/Veterans Services
10230 Ridge Road, New Port Richey, FL 34654-5199
(727) 816-3463

Polk Community College
Winter Haven, Florida
www.polk.edu   Federal Code: 001514

2-year public community college in large town.
Enrollment: 6,018 undergrads, 68% part-time. 586 full-time freshmen.
Selectivity: Open admission; but selective for some programs.

BASIC COSTS (2005-2006)
Tuition and fees: $1,841; out-of-state residents $7,043.
Per-credit charge: $52; out-of-state residents $210.

FINANCIAL AID PICTURE (2004-2005)
Students with need: 79% of average financial aid package awarded as scholarships/grants, 21% awarded as loans/jobs. Need-based aid available for part-time students. Work study available nights, weekends, and for part-time students.
Students without need: No-need awards available for academics, athletics, leadership, state/district residency.
Cumulative student debt: 60% of graduating class had student loans; average debt was $6,000.

FINANCIAL AID PROCEDURES
Forms required: FAFSA.
Dates and Deadlines: Priority date 5/15; no closing date. Applicants notified on a rolling basis.

CONTACT
Olivia Maultsby, Director of Financial Aid
999 Avenue H NE, Winter Haven, FL 33881-4299
(863) 297-1004

Remington College: Jacksonville
Jacksonville, Florida
www.remingtoncollege.edu   Federal Code: E01175

4-year for-profit technical college in small city.
Enrollment: 310 undergrads.
Selectivity: Open admission; but selective for some programs.

FINANCIAL AID PICTURE
Students with need: Need-based aid available for full-time students.
Additional info: Participates in the Title IV Federal Financial Aid program. Financial aid is available to those who qualify. Approved for program participa-

tion by the Veterans Administration and certain other government-sponsored student assistance programs.

FINANCIAL AID PROCEDURES
Forms required: FAFSA.
Dates and Deadlines: No deadline.

CONTACT
7011 AC Skinner Parkway, Suite 140, Jacksonville, FL 32256-6954
(904) 296-3435

Remington College: Tampa
Tampa, Florida
www.remingtoncollege.edu   Federal Code: 007586

4-year for-profit technical college in very large city.
Enrollment: 586 undergrads. 463 full-time freshmen.
Selectivity: Admits 50 to 75% of applicants.

BASIC COSTS (2005-2006)
Tuition and fees: $12,711.
Per-credit charge: $302.
Additional info: Tuition includes cost of books. Some programs have additional fees that cover cost of a laptop computer.

FINANCIAL AID PICTURE
Students with need: Need-based aid available for full-time students.
Students without need: This college only awards aid to students with need.

FINANCIAL AID PROCEDURES
Forms required: FAFSA, institutional form.
Dates and Deadlines: No deadline.

CONTACT
Director of Student Financial Services
2410 East Busch Boulevard, Tampa, FL 33612
(813) 935-5700 ext. 217

Ringling School of Art and Design
Sarasota, Florida
www.ringling.edu   Federal Code: 012574

4-year private visual arts college in small city.
Enrollment: 1,088 undergrads, 3% part-time. 217 full-time freshmen.

BASIC COSTS (2006-2007)
Tuition and fees: $23,125.
Per-credit charge: $1,070.
Room and board: $9,224.

FINANCIAL AID PICTURE (2005-2006)
Students with need: Out of 165 full-time freshmen who applied for aid, 139 were judged to have need. Of these, 138 received aid, and 7 had their full need met. Average financial aid package met 30% of need; average scholarship/grant was $6,897; average loan was $2,426. For part-time students, average financial aid package was $8,608.
Students without need: This college only awards aid to students with need.
Scholarships offered: Presidential Scholarship: 1 award; up to total cost of tuition and fees; based on merit of applicant's portfolio.
Cumulative student debt: 99% of graduating class had student loans; average debt was $44,550.

FINANCIAL AID PROCEDURES
Forms required: FAFSA.
Dates and Deadlines: Priority date 3/1; no closing date. Applicants notified on a rolling basis starting 5/1; must reply by 8/1.

CONTACT
Kurt Wolf, Director of Financial Aid
2700 North Tamiami Trail, Sarasota, FL 34234
(941) 359-7534

Rollins College
Winter Park, Florida
www.rollins.edu   Federal Code: 001515

4-year private liberal arts college in large town.
Enrollment: 1,719 undergrads. 464 full-time freshmen.
Selectivity: Admits 50 to 75% of applicants.

BASIC COSTS (2006-2007)
Tuition and fees: $30,860.
Room and board: $9,626.

FINANCIAL AID PICTURE (2005-2006)
Students with need: Out of 249 full-time freshmen who applied for aid, 209 were judged to have need. Of these, 209 received aid, and 60 had their full need met. Average financial aid package met 90% of need; average scholarship/grant was $24,085; average loan was $3,739.
Students without need: 58 full-time freshmen who did not demonstrate need for aid received scholarships/grants; average award was $12,897. No-need awards available for academics, art, athletics, leadership, music/drama, state/district residency.
Scholarships offered: *Merit:* Presidential, Alonzo Rollins; $4,000-$15,000 per year; based on academic record; 130 available per year. Donald Cram; $3,000-$5,000 per year; based on academic record, science major; 10 available per year. Crosby & Cornell Leadership; $10,000-$20,000 per year; based on leadership record; 6 available per year. *Athletic:* 15 full-time freshmen received athletic scholarships; average amount $18,633.
Cumulative student debt: 50% of graduating class had student loans; average debt was $15,438.
Additional info: Audition required for theater arts and music scholarship applicants. Portfolio required for art scholarships.

FINANCIAL AID PROCEDURES
Forms required: FAFSA, institutional form.
Dates and Deadlines: Priority date 2/15; closing date 3/1. Applicants notified on a rolling basis starting 3/1.
Transfers: Priority date 4/15; no deadline.

CONTACT
Phil Asbury, Director of Financial Aid
1000 Holt Avenue, Winter Park, FL 32789
(407) 646-2395

St. Johns River Community College
Palatka, Florida
www.sjrcc.cc.fl.us   Federal Code: 001523

2-year public community college in large town.
Enrollment: 3,268 undergrads.
Selectivity: Open admission; but selective for some programs.

BASIC COSTS (2005-2006)
Tuition and fees: $2,006; out-of-state residents $6,920.
Per-credit charge: $55; out-of-state residents $218.
Additional info: $614 required fees for out-of-state students.

FINANCIAL AID PICTURE (2005-2006)
Students with need: 70% of average financial aid package awarded as scholarships/grants, 30% awarded as loans/jobs. Need-based aid available for part-time students.
FINANCIAL AID PROCEDURES
Forms required: FAFSA.
Dates and Deadlines: Priority date 5/15; no closing date. Applicants notified on a rolling basis.
CONTACT
Wayne Bodiford, Director of Financial Aid
5001 St. Johns Avenue, Palatka, FL 32177-3897
(386) 312-4040

St. Leo University
Saint Leo, Florida
www.saintleo.edu   Federal Code: 001526

4-year private university in rural community, affiliated with Roman Catholic Church.
Enrollment: 1,382 undergrads, 3% part-time. 451 full-time freshmen.
Selectivity: Admits less than 50% of applicants.
BASIC COSTS (2006-2007)
Tuition and fees: $15,226.
Room and board: $7,810.
FINANCIAL AID PICTURE (2005-2006)
Students with need: Out of 398 full-time freshmen who applied for aid, 297 were judged to have need. Of these, 296 received aid, and 104 had their full need met. Average financial aid package met 85% of need; average scholarship/grant was $10,787; average loan was $2,740. For part-time students, average financial aid package was $14,259.
Students without need: 6 full-time freshmen who did not demonstrate need for aid received scholarships/grants; average award was $10,014. No-need awards available for academics, alumni affiliation, athletics, leadership, minority status, music/drama, religious affiliation, state/district residency.
Scholarships offered: 10 full-time freshmen received athletic scholarships; average amount $8,818.
Cumulative student debt: 67% of graduating class had student loans; average debt was $15,300.
FINANCIAL AID PROCEDURES
Forms required: FAFSA.
Dates and Deadlines: Priority date 4/1; no closing date. Applicants notified on a rolling basis starting 1/31.
CONTACT
Jon Walsh, Assistant Vice President, Student Financial Services
Office of Admission, Saint Leo, FL 33574-6665
(800) 240-7658

St. Petersburg College
St. Petersburg, Florida
www.spcollege.edu   Federal Code: 001528

2-year public community college in large city.
Enrollment: 19,822 undergrads, 65% part-time. 1,697 full-time freshmen.
Selectivity: Open admission; but selective for some programs.
BASIC COSTS (2005-2006)
Tuition and fees: $1,983; out-of-state residents $6,924.
Per-credit charge: $55; out-of-state residents $219.
FINANCIAL AID PICTURE
Students with need: Need-based aid available for full-time and part-time students. Work study available nights.
Students without need: No-need awards available for academics, art, athletics, minority status, music/drama.
FINANCIAL AID PROCEDURES
Forms required: FAFSA, institutional form.
Dates and Deadlines: Priority date 4/15; no closing date. Applicants notified on a rolling basis starting 5/15; must reply within 2 week(s) of notification.
CONTACT
Marcia McConnell, Director of Financial Aid
Box 13489, St. Petersburg, FL 33733
(727) 791-2443

St. Thomas University
Miami Gardens, Florida
www.stu.edu   Federal Code: 001468

4-year private university in very large city, affiliated with Roman Catholic Church.
Enrollment: 1,158 undergrads, 5% part-time. 206 full-time freshmen.
Selectivity: Admits over 75% of applicants.
BASIC COSTS (2006-2007)
Tuition and fees: $18,750.
Per-credit charge: $625.
Room and board: $5,912.
FINANCIAL AID PICTURE (2005-2006)
Students with need: Out of 189 full-time freshmen who applied for aid, 177 were judged to have need. Of these, 177 received aid, and 70 had their full need met.
Students without need: 23 full-time freshmen who did not demonstrate need for aid received scholarships/grants; average award was $6,644. No-need awards available for academics, athletics, leadership, music/drama, state/district residency.
Scholarships offered: 17 full-time freshmen received athletic scholarships; average amount $8,812.
FINANCIAL AID PROCEDURES
Forms required: FAFSA, state aid form.
Dates and Deadlines: Priority date 4/1; no closing date. Applicants notified on a rolling basis starting 3/1.
Transfers: Priority date 4/15.
CONTACT
Ahn Do, Director of Financial Aid
16401 Northwest 37th Avenue, Miami Gardens, FL 33054-6459
(305) 628-6547

Santa Fe Community College
Gainesville, Florida
www.santafe.sfcc.edu   Federal Code: 001519

2-year public community college in small city.
Enrollment: 6,880 undergrads.
Selectivity: Open admission; but selective for some programs.
BASIC COSTS (2005-2006)
Tuition and fees: $1,900; out-of-state residents $7,041.
Per-credit charge: $52; out-of-state residents $210.
Additional info: Tuition/fee waivers available for minority students.
FINANCIAL AID PICTURE
Students with need: Need-based aid available for full-time and part-time students.
Students without need: No-need awards available for academics, art, athletics, leadership, minority status, music/drama, state/district residency.

FINANCIAL AID PROCEDURES
Forms required: FAFSA.
Dates and Deadlines: Priority date 3/15; closing date 6/30. Applicants notified by 8/1.
Transfers: Must have minimum 2.0 GPA to be eligible for financial aid.

CONTACT
Steven Fisher, Director of Financial Aid
3000 NW 83rd Street, Gainesville, FL 32606
(352) 395-5480

Schiller International University
Dunedin, Florida
www.schiller.edu   Federal Code: 023141

4-year for-profit university in large town.
Enrollment: 81 undergrads, 9% part-time.
Selectivity: Open admission.

BASIC COSTS (2006-2007)
Tuition and fees: $17,650.
Per-credit charge: $470.
Room and board: $7,600.

FINANCIAL AID PICTURE
Students with need: Need-based aid available for full-time and part-time students. Work study available nights, weekends, and for part-time students.
Students without need: No-need awards available for academics, alumni affiliation, leadership, minority status, state/district residency.
Additional info: Special scholarship program for U.S. college students studying abroad at European campuses of Schiller. Work-study available to students taking 2 or more courses.

FINANCIAL AID PROCEDURES
Forms required: FAFSA, state aid form, institutional form.
Dates and Deadlines: Closing date 4/1. Applicants notified on a rolling basis starting 5/1; must reply within 3 week(s) of notification.

CONTACT
Doris Chomba, Financial Aid Officer
453 Edgewater Drive, Dunedin, FL 34698
(727) 736-5082 ext. 253

Seminole Community College
Sanford, Florida
www.scc-fl.edu   Federal Code: 001520

2-year public community college in large town.
Enrollment: 9,951 undergrads, 59% part-time. 1,254 full-time freshmen.
Selectivity: Open admission; but selective for some programs.

BASIC COSTS (2005-2006)
Tuition and fees: $2,080; out-of-state residents $7,351.
Per-credit charge: $53; out-of-state residents $214.

FINANCIAL AID PICTURE (2004-2005)
Students with need: 54% of average financial aid package awarded as scholarships/grants, 46% awarded as loans/jobs. Need-based aid available for part-time students.
Students without need: No-need awards available for academics, art, athletics, leadership, minority status, music/drama, state/district residency.

FINANCIAL AID PROCEDURES
Forms required: FAFSA.
Dates and Deadlines: No deadline. Applicants notified on a rolling basis starting 4/1.
Transfers: No deadline. Applicants notified on a rolling basis starting 4/1.

CONTACT
Robert Lynn, Director of Financial Aid
100 Weldon Boulevard, Sanford, FL 32773-6199
(407) 708-4722 ext. 3422

South Florida Community College
Avon Park, Florida
www.southflorida.edu   Federal Code: 001522

2-year public community and technical college in small town.
Enrollment: 1,689 undergrads, 65% part-time. 96 full-time freshmen.
Selectivity: Open admission.

BASIC COSTS (2005-2006)
Tuition and fees: $1,933; out-of-state residents $7,257.
Per-credit charge: $52; out-of-state residents $210.
Room and board: $2,654.
Additional info: $ 660 required fees for out-of-state students. Tuition/fee waivers available for minority students.

FINANCIAL AID PICTURE
Students with need: Need-based aid available for full-time and part-time students.
Students without need: No-need awards available for academics, athletics, leadership, minority status, music/drama, state/district residency.

FINANCIAL AID PROCEDURES
Forms required: FAFSA.
Dates and Deadlines: Priority date 3/15; no closing date. Applicants notified on a rolling basis starting 4/1.
Transfers: Students must maintain satisfactory academic progress.

CONTACT
Susie Johnson, Director of Financial Aid
600 West College Drive, Avon Park, FL 33825
(863) 453-6661 ext. 7254

South University: West Palm Beach Campus
West Palm Beach, Florida
www.southuniversity.edu

4-year for-profit business and health science college in large city.
Enrollment: 502 undergrads, 31% part-time. 47 full-time freshmen.
Selectivity: Admits 50 to 75% of applicants.

BASIC COSTS (2005-2006)
Tuition and fees: $11,085.

FINANCIAL AID PICTURE
Students with need: Need-based aid available for full-time and part-time students. Work study available nights.
Students without need: No-need awards available for academics.

FINANCIAL AID PROCEDURES
Forms required: FAFSA, institutional form.
Dates and Deadlines: No deadline. Applicants notified on a rolling basis; must reply within 2 week(s) of notification.

CONTACT
Sharon Scheible, Director of Financial Aid
1760 North Congress Avenue, West Palm Beach, FL 33409-5178
(561) 697-9200

Southeastern College of the Assemblies of God
Lakeland, Florida
www.seuniversity.edu Federal Code: 001521

4-year private liberal arts and teachers college in small city, affiliated with Assemblies of God.
Enrollment: 2,297 undergrads, 5% part-time. 518 full-time freshmen.
Selectivity: Open admission; but selective for some programs.

BASIC COSTS (2006-2007)
Tuition and fees: $12,280.
Per-credit charge: $493.
Room and board: $6,028.

FINANCIAL AID PICTURE (2005-2006)
Students with need: 47% of average financial aid package awarded as scholarships/grants, 53% awarded as loans/jobs.
Students without need: No-need awards available for academics, leadership, music/drama.

FINANCIAL AID PROCEDURES
Forms required: FAFSA, state aid form, institutional form.
Dates and Deadlines: Priority date 5/15; no closing date. Applicants notified on a rolling basis starting 5/10; must reply within 3 week(s) of notification.

CONTACT
Carol Bradley, Financial Aid Director
1000 Longfellow Boulevard, Lakeland, FL 33801
(863) 667-5000

Southwest Florida College
Ft. Myers, Florida
www.swfc.edu Federal Code: 016068

2-year private junior college in small city.
Enrollment: 1,198 undergrads, 36% part-time. 121 full-time freshmen.
Selectivity: Open admission; but selective for some programs.

BASIC COSTS (2005-2006)
Additional info: Expenses vary with programs.

FINANCIAL AID PICTURE
Students with need: Need-based aid available for full-time and part-time students. Work study available nights.

FINANCIAL AID PROCEDURES
Forms required: FAFSA.
Dates and Deadlines: Priority date 4/15; no closing date. Applicants notified on a rolling basis.

CONTACT
Teresa Beckta, Director of Financial Aid
1685 Medical Lane, Ft. Myers, FL 33907-1108
(239) 939-4766

Stetson University
DeLand, Florida
www.stetson.edu Federal Code: 001531

4-year private university in large town.
Enrollment: 2,199 undergrads, 3% part-time. 598 full-time freshmen.
Selectivity: Admits 50 to 75% of applicants.

BASIC COSTS (2005-2006)
Tuition and fees: $25,450.
Per-credit charge: $760.
Room and board: $7,275.

FINANCIAL AID PICTURE (2004-2005)
Students with need: Out of 428 full-time freshmen who applied for aid, 345 were judged to have need. Of these, 345 received aid, and 124 had their full need met. Average financial aid package met 87% of need; average scholarship/grant was $17,501; average loan was $4,087. For part-time students, average financial aid package was $10,816.
Students without need: 234 full-time freshmen who did not demonstrate need for aid received scholarships/grants; average award was $10,354. No-need awards available for academics, alumni affiliation, art, athletics, leadership, minority status, music/drama, religious affiliation, ROTC, state/district residency.
Scholarships offered: 32 full-time freshmen received athletic scholarships; average amount $12,508.
Cumulative student debt: 55% of graduating class had student loans; average debt was $21,500.

FINANCIAL AID PROCEDURES
Forms required: FAFSA, institutional form.
Dates and Deadlines: Priority date 3/15; no closing date. Applicants notified on a rolling basis.

CONTACT
Terry Whittum, Dean of Admissions and Financial Aid
Campus Box 8378, DeLand, FL 32723
(386) 822-7120

Tallahassee Community College
Tallahassee, Florida
www.tcc.fl.edu Federal Code: 001533

2-year public community college in small city.
Enrollment: 12,348 undergrads, 63% part-time. 1,319 full-time freshmen.
Selectivity: Open admission; but selective for some programs.

BASIC COSTS (2005-2006)
Tuition and fees: $1,680; out-of-state residents $6,330.
Per-credit charge: $48; out-of-state residents $195.

FINANCIAL AID PICTURE
Students with need: Need-based aid available for full-time and part-time students.
Students without need: No-need awards available for academics, art, athletics, leadership, music/drama, state/district residency.

FINANCIAL AID PROCEDURES
Forms required: FAFSA, institutional form.
Dates and Deadlines: Priority date 5/1; no closing date. Applicants notified on a rolling basis starting 5/15.

CONTACT
William Spiers, Director of Financial Aid
444 Appleyard Drive, Tallahassee, FL 32304
(850) 201-8399

Trinity College of Florida
Trinity, Florida
www.trinitycollege.edu Federal Code: 030282

4-year private Bible college in small city, affiliated with interdenominational tradition.
Enrollment: 160 undergrads.

Selectivity: Admits less than 50% of applicants.

BASIC COSTS (2005-2006)
Tuition and fees: $8,474.
Room and board: $4,970.

FINANCIAL AID PICTURE (2005-2006)
Students with need: Need-based aid available for full-time and part-time students. Work study available nights, weekends, and for part-time students.
Students without need: This college only awards aid to students with need.

FINANCIAL AID PROCEDURES
Forms required: FAFSA, institutional form.
Dates and Deadlines: Closing date 8/2. Applicants notified on a rolling basis.

CONTACT
Sue Wayne, Financial Aid Director
2430 Welbilt Boulevard, Trinity, FL 34655
(727) 569-1413

University of Central Florida
Orlando, Florida
www.ucf.edu   Federal Code: 003954

4-year public university in very large city.
Enrollment: 37,568 undergrads, 24% part-time. 5,761 full-time freshmen.
Selectivity: Admits 50 to 75% of applicants.

BASIC COSTS (2005-2006)
Tuition and fees: $3,359; out-of-state residents $16,491.
Per-credit charge: $105; out-of-state residents $542.
Room and board: $7,529.

FINANCIAL AID PICTURE (2004-2005)
Students with need: Out of 3,860 full-time freshmen who applied for aid, 3,597 were judged to have need. Of these, 3,506 received aid, and 635 had their full need met. Average financial aid package met 70% of need; average scholarship/grant was $3,215; average loan was $2,621. For part-time students, average financial aid package was $4,223.
Students without need: 1,231 full-time freshmen who did not demonstrate need for aid received scholarships/grants; average award was $1,808. No-need awards available for academics, alumni affiliation, athletics, leadership, ROTC, state/district residency.
Scholarships offered: *Merit:* Academic scholarships, $2,000-$24,000 over 4-year period. Freshmen automatically considered. *Athletic:* 50 full-time freshmen received athletic scholarships; average amount $5,752.
Cumulative student debt: 44% of graduating class had student loans; average debt was $13,095.

FINANCIAL AID PROCEDURES
Forms required: FAFSA.
Dates and Deadlines: Priority date 3/1; closing date 6/30. Applicants notified on a rolling basis starting 3/15; must reply within 3 week(s) of notification.

CONTACT
Mary McKinney, Executive Director of Financial Aid
Box 160111, Orlando, FL 32816-0111
(407) 823-2827

University of Florida
Gainesville, Florida
www.ufl.edu   Federal Code: 001535

4-year public university in small city.
Enrollment: 34,088 undergrads, 7% part-time. 6,599 full-time freshmen.
Selectivity: Admits 50 to 75% of applicants.

BASIC COSTS (2005-2006)
Tuition and fees: $3,094; out-of-state residents $16,579.
Per-credit charge: $72; out-of-state residents $521.
Room and board: $6,260.
Additional info: Additional $643 in required fees for out-of-state students. Tuition/fee waivers available for minority students.

FINANCIAL AID PICTURE (2004-2005)
Students with need: Out of 4,144 full-time freshmen who applied for aid, 2,498 were judged to have need. Of these, 2,485 received aid, and 819 had their full need met. Average financial aid package met 84% of need; average scholarship/grant was $4,335; average loan was $2,668. Need-based aid available for part-time students.
Students without need: 3,640 full-time freshmen who did not demonstrate need for aid received scholarships/grants; average award was $4,156. No-need awards available for academics, art, athletics, leadership, minority status, music/drama, ROTC, state/district residency.
Scholarships offered: 64 full-time freshmen received athletic scholarships; average amount $8,047.
Cumulative student debt: 31% of graduating class had student loans; average debt was $13,744.

FINANCIAL AID PROCEDURES
Forms required: FAFSA.
Dates and Deadlines: Priority date 3/15; no closing date. Applicants notified on a rolling basis starting 4/1.

CONTACT
Karen Fooks, Director of Student Financial Aid
201 Criser Hall, Gainesville, FL 32611-4000
(352) 392-1275

University of Miami
Coral Gables, Florida
www.miami.edu   Federal Code: 001536

4-year private university in small city.
Enrollment: 10,132 undergrads, 5% part-time. 2,261 full-time freshmen.
Selectivity: Admits less than 50% of applicants.

BASIC COSTS (2006-2007)
Tuition and fees: $31,288.
Per-credit charge: $1,280.
Room and board: $9,334.

FINANCIAL AID PICTURE (2004-2005)
Students with need: Out of 1,496 full-time freshmen who applied for aid, 1,171 were judged to have need. Of these, 1,171 received aid, and 402 had their full need met. Average financial aid package met 80% of need; average scholarship/grant was $17,512; average loan was $3,534. For part-time students, average financial aid package was $15,203.
Students without need: 502 full-time freshmen who did not demonstrate need for aid received scholarships/grants; average award was $14,846. No-need awards available for academics, athletics, music/drama.
Scholarships offered: *Merit:* Isaac Bashevis Singer Scholarship: full tuition; based on minimum 1500 SAT or 34 ACT, A+ average, rank in top 1% of high school graduating class. Bowman Foster Ashe Scholarship: three-quarters tuition; based on minimum 1400 SAT or 32 ACT, A average, class rank in top 5%. Henry King Stanford Scholarship: half-tuition; renewable; based on minimum SAT score of 1350 or 31 ACT, A average, class rank in top 7%. George E. Merrick Scholarship: one-third tuition; 1300 SAT or 30 ACT, A- average, class rank in top 10%. Jay F.W. Pearson Scholarship: one-quarter tuition; top 10% in high school class, A- average, 1280 SAT or 28 ACT. All SAT scores exclusive of Writing. Golden Drum Ronald M. Hammond Scholarships: full tuition; renewable; for exceptionally well-qualified graduating high school seniors of black/African-American descent who are Florida residents. Music scholarships: based on performance ability, academic achievement and finan-

Florida — University of Miami

cial need. National Merit Scholarships: $750-$2,000; for National Merit finalist. **Athletic:** 47 full-time freshmen received athletic scholarships; average amount $23,653.
Cumulative student debt: 56% of graduating class had student loans; average debt was $19,140.

FINANCIAL AID PROCEDURES
Forms required: FAFSA.
Dates and Deadlines: Priority date 2/15; no closing date. Applicants notified on a rolling basis starting 3/1.
Transfers: Priority date 3/1; no deadline.

CONTACT
James Bauer, Assisstant Dean of Enrollment Management and Director of Financial Assistance Services
132 Ashe Building, Coral Gables, FL 33124-4616
(305) 284-5212

University of North Florida
Jacksonville, Florida
www.unf.edu
Federal Code: 009841

4-year public university in very large city.
Enrollment: 13,065 undergrads, 28% part-time. 2,234 full-time freshmen.
Selectivity: Admits 50 to 75% of applicants.

BASIC COSTS (2005-2006)
Tuition and fees: $3,268; out-of-state residents $14,356.
Per-credit charge: $72; out-of-state residents $441.
Room and board: $7,030.
Additional info: Additional $554 required fees for out-of-state students.

FINANCIAL AID PICTURE (2005-2006)
Students with need: Out of 1,328 full-time freshmen who applied for aid, 329 were judged to have need. Of these, 326 received aid, and 128 had their full need met. Average financial aid package met 89% of need; average scholarship/grant was $1,018; average loan was $778. For part-time students, average financial aid package was $15,836.
Students without need: 225 full-time freshmen who did not demonstrate need for aid received scholarships/grants; average award was $1,356. No-need awards available for academics, athletics, leadership, minority status, music/drama, state/district residency.
Scholarships offered: 43 full-time freshmen received athletic scholarships; average amount $2,516.
Cumulative student debt: 46% of graduating class had student loans; average debt was $16,707.

FINANCIAL AID PROCEDURES
Forms required: FAFSA.
Dates and Deadlines: Priority date 4/1; no closing date. Applicants notified on a rolling basis starting 3/15; must reply within 2 week(s) of notification.

CONTACT
Janice Nowak, Financial Aid Director
4567 St. Johns Bluff Road, South, Jacksonville, FL 32224-2645
(904) 620-2604

University of South Florida
Tampa, Florida
www.usf.edu
Federal Code: 001537

4-year public university in very large city.
Enrollment: 32,898 undergrads, 28% part-time. 4,307 full-time freshmen.
Selectivity: Admits 50 to 75% of applicants.

BASIC COSTS (2005-2006)
Tuition and fees: $3,236; out-of-state residents $15,045.
Per-credit charge: $95; out-of-state residents $488.
Room and board: $6,900.
Additional info: Some additional required fees for out-of-state students. Tuition/fee waivers available for unemployed or children of unemployed.

FINANCIAL AID PICTURE (2004-2005)
Students with need: Out of 2,554 full-time freshmen who applied for aid, 1,873 were judged to have need. Of these, 1,856 received aid, and 95 had their full need met. Average financial aid package met 31% of need; average scholarship/grant was $4,020; average loan was $2,440. For part-time students, average financial aid package was $8,019.
Students without need: 634 full-time freshmen who did not demonstrate need for aid received scholarships/grants; average award was $4,038. No-need awards available for academics, art, athletics, leadership, minority status, music/drama.
Scholarships offered: 74 full-time freshmen received athletic scholarships; average amount $3,804.
Cumulative student debt: 54% of graduating class had student loans; average debt was $17,434.
Additional info: Deferred tuition payment plan available for late financial aid recipients.

FINANCIAL AID PROCEDURES
Forms required: FAFSA.
Dates and Deadlines: Priority date 3/1; no closing date. Applicants notified on a rolling basis starting 3/15; must reply within 4 week(s) of notification.

CONTACT
Leonard Gude, Director, Student Financial Aid
4202 East Fowler Avenue, SVC 1036, Tampa, FL 33620-9951
(813) 974-4700

University of Tampa
Tampa, Florida
www.ut.edu
Federal Code: 001538

4-year private university and liberal arts college in large city.
Enrollment: 4,602 undergrads, 9% part-time. 1,003 full-time freshmen.
Selectivity: Admits 50 to 75% of applicants.

BASIC COSTS (2006-2007)
Tuition and fees: $19,628.
Per-credit charge: $398.
Room and board: $7,254.

FINANCIAL AID PICTURE (2005-2006)
Students with need: Out of 699 full-time freshmen who applied for aid, 547 were judged to have need. Of these, 547 received aid, and 120 had their full need met. Average financial aid package met 82% of need; average scholarship/grant was $7,185; average loan was $3,612. For part-time students, average financial aid package was $5,340.
Students without need: 126 full-time freshmen who did not demonstrate need for aid received scholarships/grants; average award was $6,283. No-need awards available for academics, alumni affiliation, art, athletics, leadership, music/drama, ROTC, state/district residency.
Scholarships offered: *Merit:* Presidential Scholarships; up to $7,500; 3.5 GPA. Dean's Scholarships; up to $7,000; 3.0 GPA. Departmental scholarships and athletic scholarships also awarded. **Athletic:** 2 full-time freshmen received athletic scholarships; average amount $3,500.
Cumulative student debt: 71% of graduating class had student loans; average debt was $23,051.
Additional info: Early aid estimator service.

FINANCIAL AID PROCEDURES
Forms required: FAFSA, state aid form.

Dates and Deadlines: No deadline. Applicants notified on a rolling basis starting 2/1; must reply within 3 week(s) of notification.
Transfers: No deadline. Must reply within 3 week(s) of notification. Transfer scholarships available; Phi Theta Kappa Scholarships.

CONTACT
John Marsh, Director of Financial Aid
401 West Kennedy Boulevard, Tampa, FL 33606-1490
(813) 253-6239

University of West Florida
Pensacola, Florida
www.uwf.edu   Federal Code: 003955

4-year public university in small city.
Enrollment: 7,783 undergrads, 28% part-time. 828 full-time freshmen.
Selectivity: Admits 50 to 75% of applicants.

BASIC COSTS (2005-2006)
Tuition and fees: $3,198; out-of-state residents $15,704.
Per-credit charge: $72; out-of-state residents $488.
Room and board: $6,528.

FINANCIAL AID PICTURE (2004-2005)
Students with need: 46% of average financial aid package awarded as scholarships/grants, 54% awarded as loans/jobs. Need-based aid available for part-time students. Work study available nights, weekends, and for part-time students.
Students without need: No-need awards available for academics, alumni affiliation, art, athletics, minority status, music/drama, ROTC.
Scholarships offered: John C. Pace Scholars: $16,000; based on high school record and leadership; 8 awards. John C. Pace Honors and Presidential Scholarships: $4,000; based on high school record. Both available to Florida residents only. Non-Florida tuition reduction scholarships available to non-residents.

FINANCIAL AID PROCEDURES
Forms required: FAFSA, institutional form.
Dates and Deadlines: Priority date 3/1; no closing date. Applicants notified on a rolling basis starting 2/1.

CONTACT
Cathy Brown, Director of Student Financial Aid
11000 University Parkway, Pensacola, FL 32514
(850) 474-2400

Valencia Community College
Orlando, Florida
www.valenciacc.edu   Federal Code: 006750

2-year public community college in very large city.
Enrollment: 23,865 undergrads, 55% part-time. 3,216 full-time freshmen.
Selectivity: Open admission; but selective for some programs.

BASIC COSTS (2005-2006)
Tuition and fees: $1,983; out-of-state residents $7,441.
Per-credit charge: $55; out-of-state residents $219.
Additional info: $854 required fees for out-of-state students.

FINANCIAL AID PICTURE
Students with need: Need-based aid available for full-time and part-time students. Work study available nights.

FINANCIAL AID PROCEDURES
Forms required: FAFSA, institutional form.
Dates and Deadlines: Closing date 5/15. Applicants notified on a rolling basis starting 4/2; must reply within 2 week(s) of notification.

Transfers: No deadline.

CONTACT
Linda Downing, Director of Financial Aid
PO Box 3028, Orlando, FL 32802-3028
(407) 299-5000

Warner Southern College
Lake Wales, Florida
www.warner.edu   Federal Code: 008848

4-year private liberal arts college in small town, affiliated with Church of God.
Enrollment: 903 undergrads, 14% part-time. 43 full-time freshmen.
Selectivity: Admits 50 to 75% of applicants.

BASIC COSTS (2006-2007)
Tuition and fees: $13,210.
Per-credit charge: $320.
Room and board: $6,196.
Additional info: One-time $50 security deposit for incoming freshmen living on campus.

FINANCIAL AID PICTURE (2004-2005)
Students with need: Out of 43 full-time freshmen who applied for aid, 36 were judged to have need. Of these, 36 received aid. For part-time students, average financial aid package was $6,825.
Students without need: 3 full-time freshmen who did not demonstrate need for aid received scholarships/grants; average award was $1,005. No-need awards available for academics, alumni affiliation, art, athletics, leadership, music/drama, religious affiliation, state/district residency.
Scholarships offered: 25 full-time freshmen received athletic scholarships; average amount $4,342.
Cumulative student debt: 42% of graduating class had student loans; average debt was $7,869.

FINANCIAL AID PROCEDURES
Forms required: FAFSA, state aid form.
Dates and Deadlines: Priority date 5/1; no closing date. Applicants notified on a rolling basis starting 3/15; must reply within 2 week(s) of notification.
Transfers: Priority date 10/1; closing date 5/15. Applicants notified on a rolling basis.

CONTACT
Lorrie White, Financial Aid Director
13895 Hwy. 27, Lake Wales, FL 33859
(863) 638-7202

Webber International University
Babson Park, Florida
www.webber.edu   Federal Code: 001540

4-year private university and business college in rural community.
Enrollment: 556 undergrads, 9% part-time. 135 full-time freshmen.

BASIC COSTS (2006-2007)
Tuition and fees: $15,900.
Per-credit charge: $275.
Room and board: $4,990.
Additional info: Tuition/fee waivers available for adults.

FINANCIAL AID PICTURE (2005-2006)
Students with need: Out of 85 full-time freshmen who applied for aid, 74 were judged to have need. Of these, 74 received aid, and 14 had their full need met. Average financial aid package met 62% of need; average scholarship/grant was $8,504; average loan was $2,556. For part-time students, average financial aid package was $4,162.

Students without need: 56 full-time freshmen who did not demonstrate need for aid received scholarships/grants; average award was $4,637. No-need awards available for academics, alumni affiliation, athletics, leadership, state/district residency.
Scholarships offered: 38 full-time freshmen received athletic scholarships; average amount $4,707.

FINANCIAL AID PROCEDURES
Forms required: FAFSA, state aid form.
Dates and Deadlines: Priority date 5/1; no closing date. Applicants notified on a rolling basis starting 3/15; must reply within 4 week(s) of notification.
Transfers: Closing date 8/1. Eligibility for academic scholarships predicated on 12 hours of transferable credit.

CONTACT
Kathleen Wilson, Registrar/Director of Financial Aid
1201 North Scenic Highway, Babson Park, FL 33827-0096
(863) 638-2929

Webster College
Ocala, Florida
www.webstercollege.edu   Federal Code: 008501

4-year for-profit business college in small city.
Enrollment: 345 undergrads.
Selectivity: Open admission.

FINANCIAL AID PICTURE
Students with need: Need-based aid available for full-time and part-time students.

FINANCIAL AID PROCEDURES
Forms required: institutional form.
Dates and Deadlines: Applicants notified on a rolling basis; must reply within 1 week(s) of notification.

CONTACT
2221 Southwest 19th Avenue Road, Ocala, FL 34474-7051
(352) 629-1941 ext. 109

Webster College: Holiday
Holiday, Florida
www.webstercollege.edu   Federal Code: 008501

4-year for-profit business college in small city.
Enrollment: 225 undergrads.
Selectivity: Open admission.

FINANCIAL AID PICTURE
Students with need: Need-based aid available for full-time and part-time students.
Students without need: This college only awards aid to students with need.

FINANCIAL AID PROCEDURES
Forms required: FAFSA, institutional form.
Dates and Deadlines: No deadline.

CONTACT
Tina Fisher, Financial Aid Director
2127 Grand Boulevard, Holiday, FL 34691
(727) 942-0069

Georgia

Agnes Scott College
Decatur, Georgia   Federal Code: 001542
www.agnesscott.edu   CSS Code: 5002

4-year private liberal arts college for women in very large city, affiliated with Presbyterian Church (USA).
Enrollment: 875 undergrads, 3% part-time. 229 full-time freshmen.
Selectivity: Admits 50 to 75% of applicants.

BASIC COSTS (2006-2007)
Tuition and fees: $25,410.
Per-credit charge: $1,046.
Room and board: $8,990.

FINANCIAL AID PICTURE (2005-2006)
Students with need: Out of 193 full-time freshmen who applied for aid, 151 were judged to have need. Of these, 151 received aid, and 105 had their full need met. Average financial aid package met 96% of need; average scholarship/grant was $17,390; average loan was $2,606. For part-time students, average financial aid package was $15,002.
Students without need: 75 full-time freshmen who did not demonstrate need for aid received scholarships/grants; average award was $13,438. No-need awards available for academics, leadership, music/drama, religious affiliation, state/district residency.
Scholarships offered: Presidential and Honor Scholarships; $8,750 to full tuition, room and board. College will match HOPE Scholarship for HOPE-eligible Georgia residents who meet college admission criteria. Leadership and community service awards also available.
Cumulative student debt: 71% of graduating class had student loans; average debt was $22,018.
Additional info: Middle Income Assistance Grants available. Auditions required for music scholarship applicants.

FINANCIAL AID PROCEDURES
Forms required: FAFSA, CSS PROFILE, institutional form.
Dates and Deadlines: Priority date 2/15; closing date 5/1. Applicants notified on a rolling basis starting 3/1; must reply by 5/1 or within 2 week(s) of notification.
Transfers: Must reply by 5/1 or within 2 week(s) of notification. Merit Scholarships available.

CONTACT
Karen Smith, Director of Financial Aid
141 East College Avenue, Decatur, GA 30030-3797
(404) 471-6395

Albany State University
Albany, Georgia
www.asuweb.asurams.edu   Federal Code: 001544

4-year public liberal arts college in small city.
Enrollment: 3,228 undergrads.
Selectivity: Admits over 75% of applicants.

BASIC COSTS (2005-2006)
Tuition and fees: $3,022; out-of-state residents $10,338.
Per-credit charge: $102; out-of-state residents $407.
Room and board: $4,064.

FINANCIAL AID PICTURE (2004-2005)
Students with need: 46% of average financial aid package awarded as scholarships/grants, 54% awarded as loans/jobs. Need-based aid available for part-time students.
Students without need: No-need awards available for academics, athletics, ROTC, state/district residency.
Scholarships offered: State of Georgia Hope Scholarship Award.

FINANCIAL AID PROCEDURES
Forms required: FAFSA, institutional form.
Dates and Deadlines: Closing date 4/15. Applicants notified on a rolling basis starting 7/1; must reply within 2 week(s) of notification.
Transfers: Closing date 7/1.

CONTACT
Kathleen Caldwell, Director of Financial Aid
504 College Drive, Albany, GA 31705-2796
(229) 430-4650

Albany Technical College
Albany, Georgia
www.albanytech.edu   Federal Code: 005601

2-year public technical college in small city.
Enrollment: 2,543 undergrads, 47% part-time. 365 full-time freshmen.
Selectivity: Open admission.

BASIC COSTS (2005-2006)
Tuition and fees: $1,359; out-of-state residents $2,475.
Per-credit charge: $31; out-of-state residents $62.

FINANCIAL AID PICTURE (2004-2005)
Students with need: Average financial aid package for all full-time undergraduates was $5,924. 96% awarded as scholarships/grants, 4% awarded as loans/jobs. Need-based aid available for part-time students. Work study available nights.
Students without need: No-need awards available for academics, state/district residency.

FINANCIAL AID PROCEDURES
Forms required: FAFSA, state aid form.
Dates and Deadlines: No deadline. Applicants notified on a rolling basis starting 5/1.

CONTACT
Kenneth Wilson, Financial Aid Director
1704 South Slappy Boulevard, Albany, GA 31701-3514
(229) 430-3521

Andrew College
Cuthbert, Georgia
www.andrewcollege.edu   Federal Code: 001545

2-year private junior and liberal arts college in small town, affiliated with United Methodist Church.
Enrollment: 307 undergrads.

BASIC COSTS (2006-2007)
Tuition and fees: $9,814.
Room and board: $6,166.

FINANCIAL AID PICTURE
Students with need: Need-based aid available for full-time and part-time students.
Students without need: No-need awards available for academics, art, athletics, leadership, music/drama, religious affiliation, state/district residency.

FINANCIAL AID PROCEDURES
Forms required: FAFSA, state aid form, institutional form.
Dates and Deadlines: Priority date 4/1; closing date 8/1. Applicants notified on a rolling basis starting 4/15.

CONTACT
Amy Thompson, Financial Aid Administrator
413 College Street, Cuthbert, GA 39840-1395
(229) 732-5938

Armstrong Atlantic State University
Savannah, Georgia
www.armstrong.edu   Federal Code: 001546

4-year public university in small city.
Enrollment: 5,878 undergrads, 38% part-time. 680 full-time freshmen.
Selectivity: Admits over 75% of applicants.

BASIC COSTS (2005-2006)
Tuition and fees: $2,924; out-of-state residents $10,240.
Per-credit charge: $102; out-of-state residents $407.
Room only: $4,500.

FINANCIAL AID PICTURE (2004-2005)
Students with need: Average financial aid package met 90% of need; average scholarship/grant was $2,668; average loan was $2,184. Need-based aid available for part-time students.
Students without need: No-need awards available for academics, athletics, ROTC, state/district residency.
Cumulative student debt: 40% of graduating class had student loans; average debt was $5,500.

FINANCIAL AID PROCEDURES
Forms required: FAFSA.
Dates and Deadlines: Priority date 3/15; no closing date. Applicants notified on a rolling basis starting 2/1; must reply within 2 week(s) of notification.

CONTACT
Lee Ann Kirkland, Financial Aid Director
11935 Abercorn Street, Savannah, GA 31419-1997
(912) 927-5272

Athens Technical College
Athens, Georgia
www.athenstech.edu   Federal Code: 005600

2-year public technical college in small city.
Enrollment: 2,721 undergrads. 94 full-time freshmen.
Selectivity: Open admission; but selective for some programs.

BASIC COSTS (2006-2007)
Tuition and fees: $1,359; out-of-state residents $2,475.
Per-credit charge: $31; out-of-state residents $62.

FINANCIAL AID PICTURE (2004-2005)
Students with need: Out of 60 full-time freshmen who applied for aid, 39 were judged to have need. Of these, 38 received aid. Average financial aid package met 9% of need; average scholarship/grant was $869. For part-time students, average financial aid package was $387.
Students without need: No-need awards available for academics, leadership.

FINANCIAL AID PROCEDURES
Forms required: FAFSA.
Dates and Deadlines: No deadline. Applicants notified on a rolling basis starting 6/15; must reply within 2 week(s) of notification.

CONTACT
Courtney Ray, Director of Financial Aid
800 U.S. Highway 29 North, Athens, GA 30601-1500
(706) 355-5009

Atlanta Christian College
East Point, Georgia
www.acc.edu						Federal Code: 001547

4-year private Bible and liberal arts college in small city, affiliated with Christian Church.
Enrollment: 415 undergrads. 99 full-time freshmen.
Selectivity: Admits less than 50% of applicants.

BASIC COSTS (2006-2007)
Tuition and fees: $13,040.
Room and board: $5,160.

FINANCIAL AID PICTURE
Students with need: Need-based aid available for full-time and part-time students.

FINANCIAL AID PROCEDURES
Forms required: FAFSA.
Dates and Deadlines: Priority date 6/1; closing date 8/1. Applicants notified on a rolling basis starting 3/1; must reply within 3 week(s) of notification.

CONTACT
Blair Walker, Director Financial Aid
2605 Ben Hill Road, East Point, GA 30344
(404) 669-2062

Atlanta Metropolitan College
Atlanta, Georgia
www.atlm.edu						Federal Code: 012165

2-year public junior college in very large city.
Enrollment: 1,689 undergrads.
Selectivity: Admits 50 to 75% of applicants.

BASIC COSTS (2005-2006)
Tuition and fees: $1,772; out-of-state residents $6,396.
Per-credit charge: $65; out-of-state residents $257.

FINANCIAL AID PICTURE (2004-2005)
Students with need: Average financial aid package met 31% of need; average scholarship/grant was $3,322; average loan was $2,051. For part-time students, average financial aid package was $3,065.
Students without need: This college only awards aid to students with need.

FINANCIAL AID PROCEDURES
Forms required: FAFSA, state aid form.
Dates and Deadlines: Closing date 6/1. Applicants notified on a rolling basis.

CONTACT
Vera Brooks, Director
1630 Metropolitan Parkway, SW, Atlanta, GA 30310-4498
(404) 756-4002

Augusta State University
Augusta, Georgia
www.aug.edu						Federal Code: 001552

4-year public liberal arts college in small city.
Enrollment: 5,386 undergrads, 32% part-time. 790 full-time freshmen.
Selectivity: Admits 50 to 75% of applicants.

BASIC COSTS (2005-2006)
Tuition and fees: $2,920; out-of-state residents $10,236.
Per-credit charge: $102; out-of-state residents $407.

FINANCIAL AID PICTURE (2004-2005)
Students with need: Out of 727 full-time freshmen who applied for aid, 542 were judged to have need. Of these, 525 received aid, and 11 had their full need met. Average financial aid package met 70% of need; average scholarship/grant was $6,991; average loan was $5,353. For part-time students, average financial aid package was $4,903.
Students without need: 221 full-time freshmen who did not demonstrate need for aid received scholarships/grants; average award was $502. No-need awards available for academics, art, athletics, leadership, minority status, music/drama, ROTC, state/district residency.
Scholarships offered: 18 full-time freshmen received athletic scholarships; average amount $1,367.
Cumulative student debt: 64% of graduating class had student loans; average debt was $16,092.

FINANCIAL AID PROCEDURES
Forms required: FAFSA, institutional form.
Dates and Deadlines: Closing date 6/1. Applicants notified on a rolling basis starting 3/1; must reply within 4 week(s) of notification.

CONTACT
Willene Holmes, Director of Financial Aid
2500 Walton Way, Augusta, GA 30904-2200
(706) 737-1431

Bainbridge College
Bainbridge, Georgia
www.bainbridge.edu					Federal Code: 011074

2-year public community and technical college in large town.
Enrollment: 2,475 undergrads, 61% part-time. 404 full-time freshmen.
Selectivity: Open admission; but selective for some programs.

BASIC COSTS (2005-2006)
Tuition and fees: $1,670; out-of-state residents $6,294.
Per-credit charge: $65; out-of-state residents $257.

FINANCIAL AID PICTURE (2005-2006)
Students with need: 43% of average financial aid package awarded as scholarships/grants, 57% awarded as loans/jobs. Need-based aid available for part-time students.
Students without need: This college only awards aid to students with need.
Scholarships offered: Small number of merit scholarships available.
Additional info: 30-day loans available for tuition and fees.

FINANCIAL AID PROCEDURES
Forms required: FAFSA, institutional form.
Dates and Deadlines: Priority date 6/1; closing date 8/1. Applicants notified on a rolling basis starting 6/1; must reply within 2 week(s) of notification.
Transfers: Priority date 6/11.

CONTACT
Horace Taylor, Director of Financial Aid
2500 East Shotwell Street, Bainbridge, GA 39818-0990
(229) 248-2505

Bauder College
Atlanta, Georgia
www.bauder.edu   Federal Code: 011574

4-year for-profit college of fashion, design, criminal justice, business, and technology in very large city.
Enrollment: 794 undergrads.
Selectivity: Open admission.

BASIC COSTS (2005-2006)
Additional info: Cost of tuition for design majors in 18-21 month associate degree program is $25,632; books $2,300; $50 administrative fee, $350 student activity fee; $250 technology fee; $250 graduation fee. Tuition only for the associate degree programs varies from $21,498 -$25,632. Tuition for newly instituted bachelor of science in business program is $42,996.

FINANCIAL AID PICTURE
Students with need: Need-based aid available for full-time and part-time students. Work study available nights, weekends, and for part-time students.
Students without need: This college only awards aid to students with need.

FINANCIAL AID PROCEDURES
Forms required: FAFSA, institutional form.
Dates and Deadlines: No deadline. Applicants notified on a rolling basis starting 7/15.

CONTACT
Bela Akbasheva, Director of Financial Aid
384 Northyards Boulevard NW, Ste 190, Atlanta, GA 30313
(404) 237-7573

Berry College
Mount Berry, Georgia
www.berry.edu   Federal Code: 001554

4-year private liberal arts college in large town.
Enrollment: 1,855 undergrads, 2% part-time. 510 full-time freshmen.
Selectivity: Admits over 75% of applicants.

BASIC COSTS (2006-2007)
Tuition and fees: $18,950.
Per-credit charge: $630.
Room and board: $7,164.
Additional info: Tuition/fee waivers available for adults, minority students.

FINANCIAL AID PICTURE (2005-2006)
Students with need: Out of 406 full-time freshmen who applied for aid, 300 were judged to have need. Of these, 300 received aid, and 104 had their full need met. Average financial aid package met 82% of need; average scholarship/grant was $11,582; average loan was $2,694. For part-time students, average financial aid package was $5,313.
Students without need: 208 full-time freshmen who did not demonstrate need for aid received scholarships/grants; average award was $15,263. No-need awards available for academics, art, athletics, minority status, music/drama.
Scholarships offered: Merit: HOPE Scholarship; $3,000 annually; for entering freshmen based on legal residence in Georgia and graduation from eligible high school with at least a B average in college preparatory coursework.
Athletic: 26 full-time freshmen received athletic scholarships; average amount $7,559.
Cumulative student debt: 50% of graduating class had student loans; average debt was $12,084.
Additional info: All students are encouraged to work on-campus up to 20 hours per week. Jobs available in over 100 different areas.

FINANCIAL AID PROCEDURES
Forms required: institutional form.
Dates and Deadlines: Priority date 4/1; no closing date. Applicants notified on a rolling basis starting 3/15; must reply by 5/1 or within 4 week(s) of notification.
Transfers: No deadline. Applicants notified on a rolling basis starting 4/1; must reply by 5/1 or within 4 week(s) of notification.

CONTACT
Timothy Tarpley, Director of Student Financial Aid
PO Box 490159, Mount Berry, GA 30149-0159
(706) 236-1714

Brenau University
Gainesville, Georgia
www.brenau.edu   Federal Code: 001556

4-year private liberal arts college for women in small city.
Enrollment: 696 undergrads, 4% part-time. 172 full-time freshmen.
Selectivity: Admits less than 50% of applicants.

BASIC COSTS (2006-2007)
Tuition and fees: $16,590.
Per-credit charge: $548.
Room and board: $8,550.

FINANCIAL AID PICTURE (2005-2006)
Students with need: 83% of average financial aid package awarded as scholarships/grants, 17% awarded as loans/jobs. Need-based aid available for part-time students.
Students without need: No-need awards available for academics, art, athletics, leadership, music/drama.

FINANCIAL AID PROCEDURES
Forms required: FAFSA, state aid form.
Dates and Deadlines: Priority date 3/15; no closing date. Applicants notified on a rolling basis starting 3/1.

CONTACT
Pam Barrett, Director of Scholarships and Financial Assistance
500 Washington Street SE, Gainesville, GA 30501
(770) 534-6152

Brewton-Parker College
Mount Vernon, Georgia
www.bpc.edu   Federal Code: 001557

4-year private liberal arts college in small town, affiliated with Southern Baptist Convention.
Enrollment: 1,094 undergrads, 23% part-time. 209 full-time freshmen.
Selectivity: Admits over 75% of applicants.

BASIC COSTS (2006-2007)
Tuition and fees: $13,330.
Per-credit charge: $380.
Room and board: $5,510.
Additional info: $130 per-credit fee for applied music surcharge.

FINANCIAL AID PICTURE (2005-2006)
Students with need: Average financial aid package met 62% of need; average scholarship/grant was $6,851; average loan was $2,250. Need-based aid available for part-time students.
Students without need: No-need awards available for academics, art, athletics, leadership, music/drama, religious affiliation, state/district residency.

Scholarships offered: Scholarships available for academic achievement and SAT scores for incoming freshman transfer students, ranging from $1,500-$3,000 per academic year, available for four years.
Cumulative student debt: 83% of graduating class had student loans; average debt was $19,230.

FINANCIAL AID PROCEDURES
Forms required: FAFSA, state aid form.
Dates and Deadlines: Priority date 4/1; no closing date. Applicants notified on a rolling basis starting 2/27.

CONTACT
Ione Maze, Director of Financial Aid
PO Box 197, #2011, Mount Vernon, GA 30445-0197
(912) 583-3209

Central Georgia Technical College
Macon, Georgia
www.cgtcollege.org   Federal Code: 005763

2-year public community and technical college in small city.
Enrollment: 5,530 undergrads.
Selectivity: Open admission; but selective for some programs.

BASIC COSTS (2005-2006)
Tuition and fees: $1,359; out-of-state residents $2,475.
Per-credit charge: $31; out-of-state residents $62.

FINANCIAL AID PICTURE (2004-2005)
Students with need: Need-based aid available for part-time students.

FINANCIAL AID PROCEDURES
Forms required: FAFSA, state aid form, institutional form.
Dates and Deadlines: Closing date 7/14.

CONTACT
Pennie Strong, Director, Financial Aid
3300 Macon Tech Drive, Macon, GA 31206
(478) 757-3422

Chattahoochee Technical College
Marietta, Georgia
www.chattcollege.com   Federal Code: 005620

2-year public technical college in large city.
Enrollment: 5,060 undergrads.
Selectivity: Open admission; but selective for some programs.

BASIC COSTS (2005-2006)
Tuition and fees: $1,380; out-of-state residents $2,496.
Per-credit charge: $31; out-of-state residents $62.

FINANCIAL AID PICTURE
Students with need: Need-based aid available for full-time and part-time students. Work study available nights, weekends, and for part-time students.
Students without need: No-need awards available for state/district residency.

FINANCIAL AID PROCEDURES
Forms required: FAFSA, institutional form.
Dates and Deadlines: Priority date 7/15; no closing date. Applicants notified on a rolling basis starting 6/15.

CONTACT
Lori Burnette, Director of Financial Aid
980 South Cobb Drive, Marietta, GA 30060
(770) 528-4531

Clark Atlanta University
Atlanta, Georgia
www.cau.edu   Federal Code: 001559

4-year private university in very large city, affiliated with United Methodist Church.
Enrollment: 3,253 undergrads, 5% part-time. 863 full-time freshmen.
Selectivity: Admits less than 50% of applicants.

BASIC COSTS (2005-2006)
Tuition and fees: $14,522.
Per-credit charge: $582.
Room and board: $7,415.
Additional info: Tuition at time of enrollment locked for 4 years.

FINANCIAL AID PICTURE (2005-2006)
Students with need: Average financial aid package met 7% of need; average scholarship/grant was $3,618; average loan was $2,905. For part-time students, average financial aid package was $5,465.
Students without need: No-need awards available for academics, alumni affiliation, art, athletics, job skills, leadership, minority status, music/drama, religious affiliation, ROTC, state/district residency.

FINANCIAL AID PROCEDURES
Forms required: FAFSA, state aid form.
Dates and Deadlines: Priority date 3/1; closing date 4/1. Applicants notified on a rolling basis starting 2/1; must reply within 2 week(s) of notification.

CONTACT
Dolores Davis, Director of Financial Aid
223 James P. Brawley Drive, SW, Atlanta, GA 30314
(404) 880-6018

Clayton State University
Morrow, Georgia
www.clayton.edu   Federal Code: 008976

4-year public liberal arts and technical college in small city.
Enrollment: 6,212 undergrads.
Selectivity: Admits less than 50% of applicants.

BASIC COSTS (2005-2006)
Tuition and fees: $2,962; out-of-state residents $10,278.
Per-credit charge: $102; out-of-state residents $407.

FINANCIAL AID PICTURE (2005-2006)
Students with need: 38% of average financial aid package awarded as scholarships/grants, 62% awarded as loans/jobs. Need-based aid available for part-time students.
Students without need: No-need awards available for academics.

FINANCIAL AID PROCEDURES
Forms required: FAFSA, state aid form.
Dates and Deadlines: Priority date 7/18; no closing date. Applicants notified on a rolling basis starting 3/12.

CONTACT
Melody Hodge, Director of Financial Aid
5900 North Lee Street, Morrow, GA 30260-0285
(770) 961-3551

Coastal Georgia Community College
Brunswick, Georgia
www.cgcc.edu   Federal Code: 001558

2-year public community college in large town.
Enrollment: 2,144 full-time undergrads.

Selectivity: Open admission; but selective for some programs.

BASIC COSTS (2005-2006)
Tuition and fees: $1,754; out-of-state residents $6,378.
Per-credit charge: $65; out-of-state residents $257.

FINANCIAL AID PICTURE
Students with need: Need-based aid available for full-time students.
Students without need: No-need awards available for academics, leadership, state/district residency.

FINANCIAL AID PROCEDURES
Forms required: FAFSA.
Dates and Deadlines: Priority date 5/1; no closing date. Applicants notified on a rolling basis starting 7/1.

CONTACT
Betty Coen, Financial Aid Director
3700 Altama Avenue, Brunswick, GA 31520

Columbus State University
Columbus, Georgia
www.colstate.edu   Federal Code: 001561

4-year public university and liberal arts college in large city.
Enrollment: 6,543 undergrads, 33% part-time. 1,033 full-time freshmen.
Selectivity: Admits 50 to 75% of applicants. GED not accepted.

BASIC COSTS (2005-2006)
Tuition and fees: $2,944; out-of-state residents $10,260.
Per-credit charge: $102; out-of-state residents $407.
Room and board: $5,720.

FINANCIAL AID PICTURE (2005-2006)
Students with need: Out of 680 full-time freshmen who applied for aid, 496 were judged to have need. Of these, 430 received aid, and 285 had their full need met. Average financial aid package met 58% of need; average scholarship/grant was $2,491; average loan was $2,620. For part-time students, average financial aid package was $2,847.
Students without need: 349 full-time freshmen who did not demonstrate need for aid received scholarships/grants; average award was $1,638. No-need awards available for academics, alumni affiliation, art, athletics, job skills, leadership, music/drama, ROTC.
Scholarships offered: 16 full-time freshmen received athletic scholarships; average amount $2,236.
Cumulative student debt: 71% of graduating class had student loans; average debt was $24,675.

FINANCIAL AID PROCEDURES
Forms required: FAFSA.
Dates and Deadlines: Priority date 5/1; no closing date. Applicants notified on a rolling basis starting 2/1; must reply within 4 week(s) of notification.

CONTACT
Janis Bowles, Director of Financial Aid
4225 University Avenue, Columbus, GA 31907-5645
(706) 568-2036

Columbus Technical College
Columbus, Georgia
www.columbustech.org   Federal Code: 005624

2-year public technical college in small city.
Enrollment: 3,450 undergrads.
Selectivity: Open admission; but selective for some programs.

BASIC COSTS (2006-2007)
Tuition and fees: $1,807; out-of-state residents $3,295.
Per-credit charge: $31; out-of-state residents $62.

FINANCIAL AID PICTURE
Students with need: Need-based aid available for full-time and part-time students.

FINANCIAL AID PROCEDURES
Forms required: FAFSA.
Dates and Deadlines: No deadline. Applicants notified on a rolling basis.

CONTACT
Shirley Walton, Director, Financial Aid
928 Manchester Expressway, Columbus, GA 31904-6572
(706) 649-1859 ext. 1859

Covenant College
Lookout Mountain, Georgia
www.covenant.edu   Federal Code: 003484

4-year private liberal arts college in small city, affiliated with Presbyterian Church in America.
Enrollment: 902 undergrads, 3% part-time. 261 full-time freshmen.
Selectivity: Admits 50 to 75% of applicants.

BASIC COSTS (2006-2007)
Tuition and fees: $21,740.
Per-credit charge: $880.
Room and board: $6,180.

FINANCIAL AID PICTURE
Students with need: Need-based aid available for full-time and part-time students. Work study available nights, weekends, and for part-time students.
Students without need: No-need awards available for academics, alumni affiliation, art, athletics, leadership, minority status, music/drama, religious affiliation, state/district residency.
Scholarships offered: Maclellan Scholars Program; minimum SAT 1200 (exclusive of Writing) or ACT 27, high school GPA 3.3. Presidential Scholarship; based on GPA, leadership, Christian commitment, extracurricular activities, work experience, references.

FINANCIAL AID PROCEDURES
Forms required: FAFSA, state aid form, institutional form.
Dates and Deadlines: Priority date 3/1; closing date 3/31. Applicants notified on a rolling basis starting 4/15; must reply within 3 week(s) of notification.
Transfers: Some scholarships may be depleted for mid-semester transfers, such as athletic, diversity or music.

CONTACT
Brenda Rapier, Director of Financial Aid
14049 Scenic Highway, Lookout Mountain, GA 30750
(706) 419-1126

Dalton State College
Dalton, Georgia
www.daltonstate.edu   Federal Code: 003956

4-year public liberal arts and technical college in large town.
Enrollment: 4,267 undergrads, 55% part-time. 574 full-time freshmen.
Selectivity: Admits 50 to 75% of applicants.

BASIC COSTS (2005-2006)
Tuition and fees: $1,666; out-of-state residents $6,290.
Per-credit charge: $65; out-of-state residents $257.

FINANCIAL AID PICTURE (2004-2005)
Students with need: 96% of average financial aid package awarded as scholarships/grants, 4% awarded as loans/jobs. Need-based aid available for part-time students.
Students without need: No-need awards available for academics, minority status, state/district residency.

FINANCIAL AID PROCEDURES
Forms required: FAFSA, state aid form, institutional form.
Dates and Deadlines: Priority date 7/1; no closing date. Applicants notified on a rolling basis starting 7/1.
Transfers: Priority date 6/1. Applicants notified on a rolling basis.

CONTACT
Jodi Johnson, Vice President for Enrollment Services
650 College Drive, Dalton, GA 30720
(706) 272-4545

Darton College
Albany, Georgia
www.darton.edu
Federal Code: 001543

2-year public community college in small city.
Enrollment: 4,578 undergrads.

BASIC COSTS (2005-2006)
Tuition and fees: $1,842; out-of-state residents $6,466.
Per-credit charge: $65; out-of-state residents $257.

FINANCIAL AID PICTURE
Students with need: Need-based aid available for full-time and part-time students. Work study available nights, weekends, and for part-time students.
Students without need: No-need awards available for academics, alumni affiliation, art, athletics, music/drama, state/district residency.
Additional info: Auditions, portfolios, essays, extracurricular activities impact scholarship decisions.

FINANCIAL AID PROCEDURES
Forms required: FAFSA, state aid form, institutional form.
Dates and Deadlines: No deadline. Applicants notified on a rolling basis; must reply within 3 week(s) of notification.

CONTACT
Martha Whittle, Director of Financial Aid
2400 Gillionville Road, Albany, GA 31707-3098
(229) 430-6746

DeKalb Technical College
Clarkston, Georgia
www.dekalbtech.edu
Federal Code: 016582

2-year public technical college in large city.
Enrollment: 4,063 undergrads, 65% part-time. 456 full-time freshmen.
Selectivity: Open admission; but selective for some programs.

BASIC COSTS (2005-2006)
Tuition and fees: $1,407; out-of-state residents $2,523.
Per-credit charge: $31; out-of-state residents $62.

FINANCIAL AID PICTURE (2005-2006)
Students with need: Out of 342 full-time freshmen who applied for aid, 280 were judged to have need. Of these, 257 received aid. Average financial aid package met 43% of need; average scholarship/grant was $3,048. For part-time students, average financial aid package was $3,048.

FINANCIAL AID PROCEDURES
Forms required: FAFSA.
Dates and Deadlines: Priority date 7/15; closing date 8/20. Applicants notified on a rolling basis starting 6/1.
Transfers: No deadline.

CONTACT
John Gottardy, Director of Financial Aid
495 North Indian Creek Drive, Clarkston, GA 30021-2397
(404) 297-9522 ext. 1166

DeVry University: Alpharetta
Alpharetta, Georgia
www.atl.devry.edu
Federal Code: 009224

4-year for-profit university in large town.
Enrollment: 848 undergrads, 47% part-time. 256 full-time freshmen.

BASIC COSTS (2005-2006)
Tuition and fees: $12,140.
Per-credit charge: $440.

FINANCIAL AID PICTURE (2004-2005)
Students with need: Out of 130 full-time freshmen who applied for aid, 120 were judged to have need. Of these, 120 received aid, and 11 had their full need met. Average financial aid package met 45% of need; average scholarship/grant was $4,931; average loan was $5,348. For part-time students, average financial aid package was $6,692.
Students without need: This college only awards aid to students with need.

FINANCIAL AID PROCEDURES
Forms required: FAFSA.
Dates and Deadlines: No deadline. Applicants notified on a rolling basis.

CONTACT
David Pickett, Assistant Director of Financial Aid
2555 Northwinds Parkway, Alpharetta, GA 30004
(770) 521-4900

DeVry University: Decatur
Decatur, Georgia
www.atl.devry.edu
Federal Code: 009224

4-year for-profit university in large town.
Enrollment: 1,865 undergrads, 48% part-time. 209 full-time freshmen.

BASIC COSTS (2005-2006)
Tuition and fees: $12,140.
Per-credit charge: $440.

FINANCIAL AID PICTURE
Students with need: Need-based aid available for full-time and part-time students.
Students without need: This college only awards aid to students with need.

FINANCIAL AID PROCEDURES
Forms required: FAFSA.
Dates and Deadlines: No deadline. Applicants notified on a rolling basis.

CONTACT
Robin Winston, Director of Financial Aid
250 North Arcadia Avenue, Decatur, GA 30030-2198
(404) 292-7900

East Georgia College
Swainsboro, Georgia
www.ega.edu   Federal Code: 010997

2-year public community and junior college in small town.
Enrollment: 1,511 undergrads.

BASIC COSTS (2005-2006)
Tuition and fees: $1,674; out-of-state residents $6,298.
Per-credit charge: $65; out-of-state residents $257.

FINANCIAL AID PICTURE
Students with need: Need-based aid available for full-time and part-time students.
Students without need: No-need awards available for academics, leadership, state/district residency.

FINANCIAL AID PROCEDURES
Forms required: FAFSA, institutional form.
Dates and Deadlines: Priority date 6/15; no closing date. Applicants notified on a rolling basis starting 6/15; must reply within 2 week(s) of notification.

CONTACT
Barbara Green, Director of Financial Aid
131 College Circle, Swainsboro, GA 30401-2699
(478) 289-2009

Emmanuel College
Franklin Springs, Georgia
www.emmanuelcollege.edu   Federal Code: 001563

4-year private liberal arts college in rural community, affiliated with Pentecostal Holiness Church.
Enrollment: 707 undergrads, 16% part-time. 139 full-time freshmen.
Selectivity: Admits less than 50% of applicants.

BASIC COSTS (2006-2007)
Tuition and fees: $10,650.
Per-credit charge: $429.
Room and board: $4,970.
Additional info: Tuition/fee waivers available for adults.

FINANCIAL AID PICTURE (2004-2005)
Students with need: Out of 120 full-time freshmen who applied for aid, 103 were judged to have need. Of these, 103 received aid, and 19 had their full need met. Average financial aid package met 35% of need; average scholarship/grant was $3,273; average loan was $2,421. For part-time students, average financial aid package was $4,385.
Students without need: 28 full-time freshmen who did not demonstrate need for aid received scholarships/grants; average award was $4,263. No-need awards available for academics, art, athletics, leadership, music/drama, religious affiliation, state/district residency.
Scholarships offered: 6 full-time freshmen received athletic scholarships; average amount $5,634.

FINANCIAL AID PROCEDURES
Forms required: FAFSA, state aid form, institutional form.
Dates and Deadlines: Priority date 5/1; no closing date. Applicants notified on a rolling basis starting 3/1; must reply within 2 week(s) of notification.
Transfers: Students on probation at previous institution may be accepted and funded for one semester. Continued funding dependent on satisfactory performance.

CONTACT
Donna Quick, Financial Aid Director
181 Spring Street, Franklin Springs, GA 30639-0129
(706) 245-7226

Emory University
Atlanta, Georgia
www.emory.edu   Federal Code: 001564
                                      CSS Code: 5187

4-year private university in very large city, affiliated with United Methodist Church.
Enrollment: 6,378 undergrads, 1% part-time. 1,635 full-time freshmen.
Selectivity: Admits less than 50% of applicants. GED not accepted.

BASIC COSTS (2006-2007)
Tuition and fees: $32,506.
Per-credit charge: $1,338.
Room and board: $9,938.

FINANCIAL AID PICTURE (2005-2006)
Students with need: Out of 832 full-time freshmen who applied for aid, 629 were judged to have need. Of these, 629 received aid, and 629 had their full need met. Average financial aid package met 100% of need; average scholarship/grant was $21,616; average loan was $3,529. For part-time students, average financial aid package was $11,785.
Students without need: 74 full-time freshmen who did not demonstrate need for aid received scholarships/grants; average award was $16,047. No-need awards available for academics, art, leadership, music/drama, religious affiliation, state/district residency.
Scholarships offered: Emory Scholars program; two-thirds tuition to full-cost, renewable for four years of undergraduate study; based on academic merit of incoming first-year students; requires nomination by appropriate high school official by November 1st of senior year.
Cumulative student debt: 40% of graduating class had student loans; average debt was $22,175.
Additional info: Private Emory loan programs assist families in financing tuition. Fixed tuition program also available.

FINANCIAL AID PROCEDURES
Forms required: FAFSA. All applicants wishing to be considered for institutionally funded need-based grant aid must file the CSS PROFILE.
Dates and Deadlines: Priority date 2/15; closing date 4/1. Applicants notified by 4/15; must reply by 5/1 or within 4 week(s) of notification.
Transfers: No deadline. Applicants notified on a rolling basis. Limitations on aid available to transfer students. Financial aid filing deadline for transfers is 30 days following transfer student admission date.

CONTACT
Julia Perreault, Director of Financial Aid
200 Boisfeuillet Jones Center, Atlanta, GA 30322
(800) 727-6039

Fort Valley State University
Fort Valley, Georgia
www.fvsu.edu   Federal Code: 001566

4-year public liberal arts and teachers college in small town.
Enrollment: 1,943 undergrads, 13% part-time. 317 full-time freshmen.
Selectivity: Admits less than 50% of applicants.

BASIC COSTS (2005-2006)
Tuition and fees: $3,044; out-of-state residents $10,360.
Per-credit charge: $102; out-of-state residents $407.
Room and board: $4,496.

FINANCIAL AID PICTURE
Students with need: Average financial aid package met 90% of need; average scholarship/grant was $3,040; average loan was $1,200. For part-time students, average financial aid package was $3,223.
Students without need: No-need awards available for academics, athletics, ROTC, state/district residency.

Georgia — Fort Valley State University

FINANCIAL AID PROCEDURES
Forms required: FAFSA, institutional form.
Dates and Deadlines: Priority date 4/1; no closing date. Applicants notified by 6/15; must reply within 1 week(s) of notification.
Transfers: Financial aid transcripts must be received from former institutions before application for aid will be considered complete and reviewed for awards.

CONTACT
Russell Keese, Director of Financial Aid
1005 State University Drive, Fort Valley, GA 31030-4313
(478) 825-6351

Gainesville State College
Gainesville, Georgia
www.gsc.edu   Federal Code: 001567

2-year public community and junior college in large town.
Enrollment: 4,985 undergrads.
Selectivity: Admits over 75% of applicants.

BASIC COSTS (2005-2006)
Tuition and fees: $1,686; out-of-state residents $6,310.
Per-credit charge: $65; out-of-state residents $257.
Additional info: Tuition/fee waivers available for minority students.

FINANCIAL AID PICTURE (2004-2005)
Students with need: Average financial aid package met 22% of need; average scholarship/grant was $2,760; average loan was $2,154. For part-time students, average financial aid package was $2,784.
Students without need: No-need awards available for academics, art, leadership, music/drama.

FINANCIAL AID PROCEDURES
Forms required: FAFSA.
Dates and Deadlines: Priority date 6/1; no closing date. Applicants notified on a rolling basis starting 5/1; must reply within 2 week(s) of notification.
Transfers: No deadline. Applicants notified on a rolling basis starting 5/1; must reply within 2 week(s) of notification. Must have minimum 2.0 GPA to be eligible for financial aid.

CONTACT
Susan Smith, Financial Aid Director
PO Box 1358, Gainesville, GA 30503
(770) 718-3642

Georgia College and State University
Milledgeville, Georgia
www.gcsu.edu   Federal Code: 001602

4-year public university and liberal arts college in large town.
Enrollment: 4,782 undergrads, 11% part-time. 915 full-time freshmen.
Selectivity: Admits 50 to 75% of applicants.

BASIC COSTS (2005-2006)
Tuition and fees: $4,142; out-of-state residents $14,354.
Per-credit charge: $142; out-of-state residents $568.
Room and board: $6,878.

FINANCIAL AID PICTURE (2004-2005)
Students with need: Out of 885 full-time freshmen who applied for aid, 309 were judged to have need. Of these, 307 received aid, and 8 had their full need met. Average financial aid package met 71% of need; average scholarship/grant was $2,620; average loan was $2,630. For part-time students, average financial aid package was $4,282.
Students without need: 32 full-time freshmen who did not demonstrate need for aid received scholarships/grants; average award was $1,365. No-need awards available for academics, alumni affiliation, art, athletics, job skills, leadership, minority status, music/drama, religious affiliation, ROTC, state/district residency.
Scholarships offered: Merit: Presidential Scholarship; renewable $4,000 per year; 1250 SAT or equivalent ACT, 3.5 high school GPA. Exceptional Student; one-time award of $2,000; 1350 SAT or 29 ACT, 3.2 high school GPA. Academic Excellence Scholarship; one-time award of $1500; 1300 SAT or 29 ACT and 3.0 GPA. Academic Achievement Scholarship; one-time award of $1200; 1200 SAT or 26 ACT, 3.0 high school GPA. All SAT scores exclusive of Writing. **Athletic:** 31 full-time freshmen received athletic scholarships; average amount $2,128.
Cumulative student debt: 44% of graduating class had student loans; average debt was $15,286.

FINANCIAL AID PROCEDURES
Forms required: FAFSA.
Dates and Deadlines: Priority date 3/1; no closing date. Applicants notified on a rolling basis starting 3/1; must reply within 2 week(s) of notification.
Transfers: No deadline. Applicants notified on a rolling basis starting 3/1; must reply within 2 week(s) of notification.

CONTACT
Suzanne Pittman, Assistant Vice President for Enrollment Management and Director of Financial Aid & Scholarships
Campus Box 23, Milledgeville, GA 31061-0490
(478) 445-5149

Georgia Highlands College
Rome, Georgia
www.highlands.edu   Federal Code: 009507

2-year public community and liberal arts college in small city.
Enrollment: 3,666 undergrads, 44% part-time. 833 full-time freshmen.

BASIC COSTS (2005-2006)
Tuition and fees: $1,740; out-of-state residents $6,364.
Per-credit charge: $65; out-of-state residents $257.

FINANCIAL AID PICTURE
Students with need: Work study available nights.
Students without need: No-need awards available for academics, art.

FINANCIAL AID PROCEDURES
Forms required: FAFSA.
Dates and Deadlines: Closing date 4/1. Applicants notified on a rolling basis starting 4/1; must reply within 2 week(s) of notification.

CONTACT
Kelly Gribble, Director of Financial Aid
3175 Cedartown Highway, SE, Rome, GA 30161
(706) 295-6311

Georgia Institute of Technology
Atlanta, Georgia
www.gatech.edu   Federal Code: 001569

4-year public university in very large city.
Enrollment: 11,624 undergrads, 6% part-time. 2,419 full-time freshmen.
Selectivity: Admits 50 to 75% of applicants.

BASIC COSTS (2005-2006)
Tuition and fees: $4,648; out-of-state residents $18,990.
Per-credit charge: $152; out-of-state residents $750.
Room and board: $6,802.

FINANCIAL AID PICTURE (2005-2006)
Students with need: Out of 1,855 full-time freshmen who applied for aid, 742 were judged to have need. Of these, 730 received aid, and 322 had their full need met. Average financial aid package met 76% of need; average scholarship/grant was $5,224; average loan was $3,504. For part-time students, average financial aid package was $6,360.
Students without need: 227 full-time freshmen who did not demonstrate need for aid received scholarships/grants; average award was $2,511. No-need awards available for academics, alumni affiliation, athletics, job skills, leadership, music/drama, ROTC, state/district residency.
Scholarships offered: *Merit:* President's Scholarship Program: 4-year awards range from half to full tuition; for freshmen with outstanding academic/leadership qualities. *Athletic:* 54 full-time freshmen received athletic scholarships; average amount $13,873.
Cumulative student debt: 48% of graduating class had student loans; average debt was $15,961.

FINANCIAL AID PROCEDURES
Forms required: FAFSA, institutional form.
Dates and Deadlines: Closing date 3/1. Applicants notified on a rolling basis starting 4/1; must reply by 5/1.
Transfers: Closing date 5/1. Applicants notified on a rolling basis starting 6/1; must reply within 4 week(s) of notification. Student must be officially admitted, all final transcripts must be received, and transcripts must be articulated.

CONTACT
Marie Mons, Director of Student Financial Planning and Services
225 North Avenue NW, Atlanta, GA 30332-0320
(404) 894-4160

Georgia Military College
Milledgeville, Georgia
www.gmc.cc.ga.us   Federal Code: 001571

2-year public junior and military college in large town.
Enrollment: 4,724 undergrads, 37% part-time. 903 full-time freshmen.
Selectivity: Open admission; but selective for some programs.

BASIC COSTS (2006-2007)
Tuition and fees: $13,214.
Room and board: $3,840.
Additional info: Quoted full-time tuition and fees are for cadet students. Additional $1,150 for uniforms.

FINANCIAL AID PICTURE (2004-2005)
Students with need: For part-time students, average financial aid package was $2,554.
Students without need: No-need awards available for athletics, leadership, ROTC, state/district residency.
Additional info: Institutional aid offered to those enrolled in Cadet Corps who reside on campus.

FINANCIAL AID PROCEDURES
Forms required: FAFSA, state aid form.
Dates and Deadlines: No deadline. Applicants notified on a rolling basis starting 3/1.

CONTACT
Alisa Stephens, Director of Financial Aid
201 East Greene Street, Milledgeville, GA 31061
(478) 445-0840

Georgia Perimeter College
Clarkston, Georgia
www.gpc.edu   Federal Code: 001562

2-year public junior and liberal arts college in very large city.
Enrollment: 20,461 undergrads, 55% part-time. 2,563 full-time freshmen.
Selectivity: Admits 50 to 75% of applicants.

BASIC COSTS (2005-2006)
Tuition and fees: $1,822; out-of-state residents $6,446.
Per-credit charge: $65; out-of-state residents $257.

FINANCIAL AID PICTURE (2004-2005)
Students with need: 77% of average financial aid package awarded as scholarships/grants, 23% awarded as loans/jobs. Need-based aid available for part-time students. Work study available nights, weekends, and for part-time students.

FINANCIAL AID PROCEDURES
Forms required: FAFSA.
Dates and Deadlines: Closing date 6/1. Applicants notified on a rolling basis; must reply within 3 week(s) of notification.
Transfers: Priority date 6/1; no deadline.

CONTACT
Ron Carruth, Director of Financial Aid
555 North Indian Creek Drive, Clarkston, GA 30021-2361
(678) 891-3400

Georgia Southern University
Statesboro, Georgia
www.georgiasouthern.edu   Federal Code: 001572

4-year public university in large town.
Enrollment: 13,975 undergrads, 7% part-time. 2,983 full-time freshmen.
Selectivity: Admits 50 to 75% of applicants. GED not accepted.

BASIC COSTS (2005-2006)
Tuition and fees: $3,462; out-of-state residents $10,778.
Per-credit charge: $102; out-of-state residents $407.
Room and board: $6,300.

FINANCIAL AID PICTURE (2004-2005)
Students with need: Out of 2,812 full-time freshmen who applied for aid, 1,465 were judged to have need. Of these, 1,441 received aid, and 281 had their full need met. Average financial aid package met 66% of need; average scholarship/grant was $4,871; average loan was $3,414. For part-time students, average financial aid package was $5,225.
Students without need: 82 full-time freshmen who did not demonstrate need for aid received scholarships/grants; average award was $1,348. No-need awards available for academics, alumni affiliation, art, athletics, leadership, minority status, music/drama, ROTC, state/district residency.
Scholarships offered: 44 full-time freshmen received athletic scholarships; average amount $4,677.
Cumulative student debt: 70% of graduating class had student loans; average debt was $17,913.
Additional info: The majority of scholarships available are need-blind.

FINANCIAL AID PROCEDURES
Forms required: FAFSA.
Dates and Deadlines: Priority date 3/31; no closing date. Applicants notified on a rolling basis starting 4/15.
Transfers: No deadline. Applicants notified on a rolling basis starting 4/15.

Georgia Southern University

CONTACT
Connie Murphey, Director of Financial Aid
PO Box 8024, Statesboro, GA 30460
(912) 681-5413

Georgia Southwestern State University
Americus, Georgia
www.gsw.edu
Federal Code: 001573

4-year public university and liberal arts college in large town.
Enrollment: 2,183 undergrads, 22% part-time. 357 full-time freshmen.
Selectivity: Admits 50 to 75% of applicants.

BASIC COSTS (2005-2006)
Tuition and fees: $3,034; out-of-state residents $10,350.
Per-credit charge: $102; out-of-state residents $407.
Room and board: $4,810.

FINANCIAL AID PICTURE
Students with need: Need-based aid available for full-time and part-time students.
Students without need: No-need awards available for academics, athletics, leadership.
Scholarships offered: Wheatley Scholarship; $2,000-2,500; 3.0 in college preparatory course and either 1100 SAT (exclusive of Writing) or 24 ACT; 40-50 available each year.

FINANCIAL AID PROCEDURES
Forms required: FAFSA, institutional form.
Dates and Deadlines: Priority date 4/1; closing date 6/1. Applicants notified on a rolling basis starting 3/1.

CONTACT
Freida Jones, Director of Financial Aid
800 Georgia Southwestern State University Drive, Americus, GA 31709-9957
(229) 928-1378

Georgia State University
Atlanta, Georgia
www.gsu.edu
Federal Code: 001574

4-year public university in very large city.
Enrollment: 18,480 undergrads, 26% part-time. 2,291 full-time freshmen.
Selectivity: Admits less than 50% of applicants. GED not accepted.

BASIC COSTS (2005-2006)
Tuition and fees: $4,464; out-of-state residents $15,378.
Per-credit charge: $152; out-of-state residents $607.
Room and board: $6,980.

FINANCIAL AID PICTURE (2005-2006)
Students with need: Out of 2,157 full-time freshmen who applied for aid, 1,330 were judged to have need. Of these, 1,330 received aid, and 234 had their full need met. Average financial aid package met 24% of need; average scholarship/grant was $3,227; average loan was $2,650. For part-time students, average financial aid package was $7,454.
Students without need: This college only awards aid to students with need.
Scholarships offered: 10 full-time freshmen received athletic scholarships; average amount $2,222.
Cumulative student debt: 34% of graduating class had student loans; average debt was $10,235.

FINANCIAL AID PROCEDURES
Forms required: FAFSA.
Dates and Deadlines: Priority date 4/1; closing date 11/1. Applicants notified on a rolling basis starting 3/30; must reply within 2 week(s) of notification.

CONTACT
David Bledsoe, Director of Student Financial Aid
Box 4009, Atlanta, GA 30302-4009
(404) 651-2227

Gordon College
Barnesville, Georgia
www.gdn.edu
Federal Code: 001575

2-year public junior college in small town.
Enrollment: 3,473 undergrads, 33% part-time. 1,118 full-time freshmen.
Selectivity: Admits over 75% of applicants.

BASIC COSTS (2005-2006)
Tuition and fees: $1,742; out-of-state residents $6,366.
Per-credit charge: $65; out-of-state residents $257.
Room and board: $3,990.

FINANCIAL AID PICTURE (2004-2005)
Students with need: 98% of average financial aid package awarded as scholarships/grants, 2% awarded as loans/jobs. Need-based aid available for part-time students. Work study available nights, weekends, and for part-time students.
Students without need: No-need awards available for academics, athletics, music/drama, state/district residency.

FINANCIAL AID PROCEDURES
Forms required: institutional form.
Dates and Deadlines: Priority date 5/1; no closing date. Applicants notified on a rolling basis starting 5/1.

CONTACT
Larry Micham, Director of Financial Aid
419 College Drive, Barnesville, GA 30204
(770) 358-5059

Gupton Jones College of Funeral Service
Decatur, Georgia
www.gupton-jones.edu
Federal Code: 010771

2-year private technical college in very large city.
Enrollment: 185 undergrads.
Selectivity: Open admission.

BASIC COSTS (2005-2006)
Tuition and fees: $7,550.
Per-credit charge: $175.

FINANCIAL AID PICTURE
Students with need: Need-based aid available for full-time and part-time students.
Students without need: This college only awards aid to students with need.

FINANCIAL AID PROCEDURES
Forms required: FAFSA.
Dates and Deadlines: No deadline. Applicants notified on a rolling basis.

CONTACT
James Hinz, Dean
5141 Snapfinger Woods Drive, Decatur, GA 30035
(770) 593-2257

Gwinnett College
Lilburn, Georgia
www.gwinnettcollege.edu   Federal Code: 025830

2-year for-profit junior college in large city.
Enrollment: 245 undergrads.
Selectivity: Open admission; but selective for some programs.

BASIC COSTS (2005-2006)
Additional info: 2005 Tuition is $475 per class. Required number of classes varies by program. No out-of-state tuition applicable.

FINANCIAL AID PICTURE
Students with need: Need-based aid available for full-time and part-time students.

FINANCIAL AID PROCEDURES
Forms required: FAFSA.

CONTACT
4230 Highway 29, Lilburn, GA 30047
(770) 381-7200

Gwinnett Technical College
Lawrenceville, Georgia
www.gwinnetttech.edu   Federal Code: 016139

2-year public technical college in large town.
Enrollment: 1,663 undergrads.

BASIC COSTS (2005-2006)
Tuition and fees: $1,425; out-of-state residents $2,541.
Per-credit charge: $31; out-of-state residents $62.

FINANCIAL AID PICTURE
Students with need: Need-based aid available for full-time and part-time students.

FINANCIAL AID PROCEDURES
Forms required: FAFSA.
Dates and Deadlines: Closing date 7/1.
Transfers: Priority date 7/1; no deadline.

CONTACT
Vincent Walters, Director of Financial Aid
5150 Sugarloaf Parkway, Lawrenceville, GA 30243
(770) 962-7580 ext. 6637

Kennesaw State University
Kennesaw, Georgia
www.kennesaw.edu   Federal Code: 001577

4-year public university in large town.
Enrollment: 16,599 undergrads, 32% part-time. 2,083 full-time freshmen.
Selectivity: Admits 50 to 75% of applicants. GED not accepted.

BASIC COSTS (2005-2006)
Tuition and fees: $3,044; out-of-state residents $10,360.
Per-credit charge: $102; out-of-state residents $407.
Room only: $4,900.

FINANCIAL AID PICTURE (2005-2006)
Students with need: Out of 1,836 full-time freshmen who applied for aid, 710 were judged to have need. Of these, 710 received aid, and 109 had their full need met. Average financial aid package met 19% of need; average scholarship/grant was $2,698; average loan was $2,366. For part-time students, average financial aid package was $9,241.
Students without need: 1,062 full-time freshmen who did not demonstrate need for aid received scholarships/grants; average award was $1,636. No-need awards available for academics, alumni affiliation, art, athletics, job skills, leadership, minority status, music/drama, state/district residency.
Scholarships offered: 25 full-time freshmen received athletic scholarships; average amount $3,052.
Cumulative student debt: 66% of graduating class had student loans; average debt was $14,025.

FINANCIAL AID PROCEDURES
Forms required: FAFSA.
Dates and Deadlines: Priority date 4/1; closing date 7/1. Applicants notified on a rolling basis starting 5/15.

CONTACT
Michael Roberts, Director of Financial Aid
1000 Chastain Road, Kennesaw, GA 30144-5591
(770) 423-6074

LaGrange College
LaGrange, Georgia
www.lagrange.edu   Federal Code: 001578

4-year private liberal arts college in large town, affiliated with United Methodist Church.
Enrollment: 986 undergrads, 9% part-time. 221 full-time freshmen.
Selectivity: Admits less than 50% of applicants.

BASIC COSTS (2006-2007)
Tuition and fees: $17,252.
Per-credit charge: $711.
Room and board: $7,358.

FINANCIAL AID PICTURE (2004-2005)
Students with need: Out of 194 full-time freshmen who applied for aid, 164 were judged to have need. Of these, 164 received aid, and 70 had their full need met. Average financial aid package met 86% of need; average scholarship/grant was $12,796; average loan was $2,717. For part-time students, average financial aid package was $8,450.
Students without need: 47 full-time freshmen who did not demonstrate need for aid received scholarships/grants; average award was $6,735. No-need awards available for academics, art, leadership, minority status, music/drama, religious affiliation, state/district residency.
Scholarships offered: Presidential Scholarship; competitive; full tuition. Cunningham Scholarship; competitive; $3,500 per year. Academic Achievement Awards; minimum GPA 3.0; $1,000-$4,500. Methodist Scholarship; minimum of 2 of the following criteria: 3.2 GPA, 1100 SAT (exclusive of Writing), 24 ACT; up to $1,000.
Cumulative student debt: 79% of graduating class had student loans; average debt was $17,074.

FINANCIAL AID PROCEDURES
Forms required: FAFSA, state aid form, institutional form.
Dates and Deadlines: Closing date 3/15. Applicants notified on a rolling basis starting 3/1; must reply by 8/15 or within 2 week(s) of notification.

CONTACT
Sylvia Smith, Director of Financial Aid
601 Broad Street, LaGrange, GA 30240-2999
(706) 880-8241

Life University
Marietta, Georgia
www.life.edu Federal Code: 014170

4-year private university in large city.
Enrollment: 476 undergrads. 120 full-time freshmen.
Selectivity: Open admission; but selective for some programs.

BASIC COSTS (2006-2007)
Tuition and fees: $6,975.
Per-credit charge: $148.

FINANCIAL AID PICTURE (2004-2005)
Students with need: Out of 78 full-time freshmen who applied for aid, 71 were judged to have need. Of these, 68 received aid, and 27 had their full need met. Average financial aid package met 38% of need; average scholarship/grant was $4,200; average loan was $3,100. For part-time students, average financial aid package was $6,000.
Students without need: No-need awards available for academics.
Scholarships offered: 2 full-time freshmen received athletic scholarships; average amount $3,460.
Cumulative student debt: 69% of graduating class had student loans; average debt was $13,000.

FINANCIAL AID PROCEDURES
Forms required: FAFSA, state aid form, institutional form.
Dates and Deadlines: Priority date 3/1; no closing date. Applicants notified on a rolling basis.

CONTACT
Diane Clark, Director of Financial Aid
1269 Barclay Circle, Marietta, GA 30060
(770) 426-2901

Macon State College
Macon, Georgia
www.maconstate.edu Federal Code: 007728

4-year public business and health science college in small city.
Enrollment: 5,894 undergrads, 53% part-time. 857 full-time freshmen.
Selectivity: Admits over 75% of applicants.

BASIC COSTS (2005-2006)
Tuition and fees: $1,730; out-of-state residents $6,354.
Per-credit charge: $65; out-of-state residents $257.

FINANCIAL AID PICTURE (2004-2005)
Students with need: For part-time students, average financial aid package was $4,912.
Students without need: This college only awards aid to students with need.

FINANCIAL AID PROCEDURES
Forms required: FAFSA.
Dates and Deadlines: Priority date 4/1; no closing date. Applicants notified on a rolling basis starting 4/15; must reply within 2 week(s) of notification.

CONTACT
Pat Simmons, Director of Financial Aid
100 College Station Drive, Macon, GA 31206-5145
(912) 471-2717

Medical College of Georgia
Augusta, Georgia
www.mcg.edu Federal Code: 001579

Upper-division public health science college in large city.
Enrollment: 717 undergrads, 8% part-time.

BASIC COSTS (2005-2006)
Tuition and fees: $4,224; out-of-state residents $15,138.
Per-credit charge: $152; out-of-state residents $607.
Room only: $2,586.

FINANCIAL AID PICTURE (2005-2006)
Students with need: Average financial aid package for all full-time undergraduates was $8,776; for part-time $9,462. 30% awarded as scholarships/grants, 70% awarded as loans/jobs. Work study available nights, weekends, and for part-time students.
Students without need: No-need awards available for academics, state/district residency.
Additional info: State Hope scholarships only available to Georgia residents.

FINANCIAL AID PROCEDURES
Dates and Deadlines: No deadline. Must reply within 2 week(s) of notification.
Transfers: Priority date 3/31; closing date 5/30.

CONTACT
Cynthia Parks, Director of Financial Aid
Office of Academic Admissions, Room 170 Kelly Building, Augusta, GA 30912-7310
(706) 721-4901

Mercer University
Macon, Georgia
www.mercer.edu Federal Code: 001580

4-year private university in small city, affiliated with Baptist faith.
Enrollment: 2,355 undergrads, 2% part-time. 616 full-time freshmen.
Selectivity: Admits over 75% of applicants. GED not accepted.

BASIC COSTS (2006-2007)
Tuition and fees: $25,256.
Per-credit charge: $835.
Room and board: $7,710.

FINANCIAL AID PICTURE (2005-2006)
Students with need: Out of 537 full-time freshmen who applied for aid, 418 were judged to have need. Of these, 417 received aid, and 240 had their full need met. Average financial aid package met 93% of need; average scholarship/grant was $15,670; average loan was $5,006. For part-time students, average financial aid package was $12,112.
Students without need: 193 full-time freshmen who did not demonstrate need for aid received scholarships/grants; average award was $17,027. No-need awards available for academics, art, athletics, job skills, leadership, music/drama, religious affiliation, ROTC, state/district residency.
Scholarships offered: *Merit:* Various scholarships; primarily based on high school GPA, SAT/ACT scores, and personal interview (for some); early applications given highest consideration. National Merit finalists and semi-finalists guaranteed full-tuition scholarships. *Athletic:* 31 full-time freshmen received athletic scholarships; average amount $13,651.
Cumulative student debt: 63% of graduating class had student loans; average debt was $1,107.

FINANCIAL AID PROCEDURES
Forms required: FAFSA, state aid form, institutional form.
Dates and Deadlines: Priority date 4/1; no closing date. Applicants notified on a rolling basis starting 3/15; must reply within 2 week(s) of notification.

Transfers: Priority date 6/1; no deadline.
CONTACT
Carol Williams, Associate Vice President, Student Financial Planning
1400 Coleman Avenue, Macon, GA 31207-0001
(478) 301-2670

Middle Georgia College
Cochran, Georgia
www.mgc.edu   Federal Code: 001581

2-year public junior college in small town.
Enrollment: 2,677 undergrads, 32% part-time. 755 full-time freshmen.
Selectivity: Admits over 75% of applicants.

BASIC COSTS (2005-2006)
Tuition and fees: $1,966; out-of-state residents $6,590.
Per-credit charge: $65; out-of-state residents $257.
Room and board: $4,200.

FINANCIAL AID PICTURE (2004-2005)
Students with need: Average financial aid package met 95% of need; average scholarship/grant was $2,904; average loan was $1,923. For part-time students, average financial aid package was $3,735.
Students without need: No-need awards available for academics, alumni affiliation, art, athletics, job skills, leadership, minority status, music/drama, state/district residency.

FINANCIAL AID PROCEDURES
Forms required: FAFSA.
Dates and Deadlines: Priority date 4/1; no closing date. Applicants notified on a rolling basis starting 5/1.

CONTACT
Charlene Morgan, Director of Financial Aid
1100 Second Street SE, Cochran, GA 31014
(478) 934-3133

Morehouse College
Atlanta, Georgia
www.morehouse.edu   Federal Code: 001582
                               CSS Code: 5415

4-year private liberal arts college for men in very large city.
Enrollment: 3,029 undergrads, 6% part-time. 674 full-time freshmen.
Selectivity: Admits 50 to 75% of applicants.

BASIC COSTS (2005-2006)
Tuition and fees: $16,684.
Per-credit charge: $632.
Room and board: $9,066.

FINANCIAL AID PICTURE (2005-2006)
Students with need: Average financial aid package met 58% of need; average scholarship/grant was $3,819; average loan was $2,625. Need-based aid available for part-time students.
Students without need: No-need awards available for academics, alumni affiliation, art, athletics, leadership, music/drama, ROTC, state/district residency.
Cumulative student debt: 90% of graduating class had student loans; average debt was $22,625.

FINANCIAL AID PROCEDURES
Forms required: FAFSA, CSS PROFILE, state aid form, institutional form.
Dates and Deadlines: Closing date 4/1. Applicants notified by 5/1.

CONTACT
James Stotts, Director of Financial Aid
830 Westview Drive SW, Atlanta, GA 30314
(404) 215-2638

North Georgia College & State University
Dahlonega, Georgia
www.ngcsu.edu   Federal Code: 001585

4-year public comprehensive state university with military college in small town.
Enrollment: 4,144 undergrads, 19% part-time. 719 full-time freshmen.
Selectivity: Admits 50 to 75% of applicants.

BASIC COSTS (2005-2006)
Tuition and fees: $3,044; out-of-state residents $10,360.
Per-credit charge: $102; out-of-state residents $407.
Room and board: $4,596.

FINANCIAL AID PICTURE (2004-2005)
Students with need: Out of 214 full-time freshmen who applied for aid, 214 were judged to have need. Of these, 214 received aid, and 113 had their full need met. Average financial aid package met 35% of need; average scholarship/grant was $2,562; average loan was $2,009. For part-time students, average financial aid package was $4,708.
Students without need: 422 full-time freshmen who did not demonstrate need for aid received scholarships/grants; average award was $3,482. No-need awards available for academics, alumni affiliation, art, athletics, leadership, music/drama, ROTC, state/district residency.
Scholarships offered: *Merit:* ROTC grant available to Georgia residents; $1,500 a year. Out-of-state tuition waiver; $5,628 per year. *Athletic:* 32 full-time freshmen received athletic scholarships; average amount $2,464.
Additional info: Aid to international students limited to fee waiver for cadets.

FINANCIAL AID PROCEDURES
Forms required: FAFSA, institutional form.
Dates and Deadlines: Priority date 5/1; no closing date. Applicants notified on a rolling basis starting 5/15; must reply within 3 week(s) of notification.

CONTACT
Deborah Barbone, Director of Financial Aid
82 College Circle, Dahlonega, GA 30597
(706) 864-1412

Northwestern Technical College
Rock Spring, Georgia
www.nwtcollege.org   Federal Code: 005257

2-year public technical college in small town.
Enrollment: 1,550 undergrads.
Selectivity: Open admission; but selective for some programs.

BASIC COSTS (2005-2006)
Tuition and fees: $1,359; out-of-state residents $2,475.
Per-credit charge: $31; out-of-state residents $62.

FINANCIAL AID PICTURE
Students with need: Need-based aid available for full-time and part-time students.

FINANCIAL AID PROCEDURES
Forms required: FAFSA, institutional form.
Dates and Deadlines: No deadline.

CONTACT
Sara Twiggs, Director of Financial Aid
265 Bicentennial Trail, Rock Spring, GA 30739
(706) 764-3575

Oglethorpe University
Atlanta, Georgia
www.oglethorpe.edu   Federal Code: 001586

4-year private university and liberal arts college in very large city.
Enrollment: 975 undergrads, 12% part-time. 231 full-time freshmen.
Selectivity: Admits 50 to 75% of applicants.

BASIC COSTS (2006-2007)
Tuition and fees: $23,510.
Room and board: $8,870.

FINANCIAL AID PICTURE
Students with need: Need-based aid available for full-time students.
Students without need: No-need awards available for academics, art, leadership, music/drama.

FINANCIAL AID PROCEDURES
Forms required: FAFSA, state aid form, institutional form.
Dates and Deadlines: No deadline. Applicants notified on a rolling basis starting 3/1; must reply within 3 week(s) of notification.
Transfers: No deadline.

CONTACT
Patrick Bonones, Director of Financial Aid
4484 Peachtree Road NE, Atlanta, GA 30319-2797
(404) 364-8356

Oxford College of Emory University
Oxford, Georgia   Federal Code: 001565
www.emory.edu/OXFORD   CSS Code: 5186

2-year private branch campus and liberal arts college in large town, affiliated with United Methodist Church.
Enrollment: 680 undergrads.

BASIC COSTS (2006-2007)
Tuition and fees: $24,970.
Per-credit charge: $1,025.
Room and board: $7,436.

FINANCIAL AID PICTURE (2004-2005)
Students with need: 81% of average financial aid package awarded as scholarships/grants, 19% awarded as loans/jobs. Need-based aid available for part-time students. Work study available nights, weekends, and for part-time students.
Students without need: No-need awards available for academics, leadership, religious affiliation, state/district residency.
Scholarships offered: Woodruff Scholarships; full tuition, room and board for 4 years. Dean's Scholarships; full tuition for 4 years. Faculty Scholarships; half tuition for 4 years. 2-year scholarships which range from $5,000 to $6,500 a year are also awarded.
Additional info: Deadline of November 15 to apply for Oxford College Scholars Program.

FINANCIAL AID PROCEDURES
Forms required: FAFSA, CSS PROFILE.
Dates and Deadlines: Priority date 2/15; closing date 4/1. Applicants notified by 4/1; must reply by 5/1 or within 2 week(s) of notification.

CONTACT
Jennifer Taylor, Associate Dean of Admission and Financial Aid
100 Hamill Street, Oxford, GA 30054-1418
(770) 784-8303

Paine College
Augusta, Georgia
www.paine.edu   Federal Code: 001587

4-year private liberal arts college in large city, affiliated with Christian Methodist Episcopal Church and United Methodist Church.
Enrollment: 812 undergrads, 7% part-time. 197 full-time freshmen.
Selectivity: Admits less than 50% of applicants.

BASIC COSTS (2005-2006)
Tuition and fees: $9,690.
Per-credit charge: $373.
Room and board: $4,728.

FINANCIAL AID PICTURE (2005-2006)
Students with need: Average financial aid package met 57% of need; average scholarship/grant was $6,775; average loan was $2,228. For part-time students, average financial aid package was $5,265.
Students without need: No-need awards available for academics, alumni affiliation, athletics, music/drama, religious affiliation, ROTC.
Cumulative student debt: 82% of graduating class had student loans; average debt was $18,338.

FINANCIAL AID PROCEDURES
Forms required: FAFSA, institutional form.
Dates and Deadlines: Priority date 3/1; no closing date. Applicants notified on a rolling basis starting 5/1; must reply within 2 week(s) of notification.

CONTACT
Gerri Bogan, Director of Financial Aid
1235 15th Street, Augusta, GA 30901-3182
(706) 821-8262

Piedmont College
Demorest, Georgia
www.piedmont.edu   Federal Code: 001588

4-year private liberal arts and teachers college in rural community, affiliated with Congregational Christian Churches of America.
Enrollment: 939 undergrads, 10% part-time. 157 full-time freshmen.
Selectivity: Admits 50 to 75% of applicants.

BASIC COSTS (2006-2007)
Tuition and fees: $15,500.
Per-credit charge: $646.
Room and board: $5,000.

FINANCIAL AID PICTURE (2005-2006)
Students with need: Out of 144 full-time freshmen who applied for aid, 106 were judged to have need. Of these, 106 received aid, and 67 had their full need met. Average financial aid package met 61% of need; average scholarship/grant was $2,097; average loan was $2,034. For part-time students, average financial aid package was $2,553.
Students without need: 29 full-time freshmen who did not demonstrate need for aid received scholarships/grants; average award was $2,962. No-need awards available for academics, art, leadership, music/drama, religious affiliation, state/district residency.
Scholarships offered: Each year high school seniors superior in academics, leadership, and extracurricular activities are invited to campus for an overnight scholarship competition.

Cumulative student debt: 66% of graduating class had student loans; average debt was $14,408.
Additional info: College meets 100% of unmet direct financial need for early applicants through grants, scholarships, and loan programs.

FINANCIAL AID PROCEDURES
Forms required: FAFSA, state aid form, institutional form.
Dates and Deadlines: Priority date 5/1; no closing date. Applicants notified on a rolling basis; must reply within 2 week(s) of notification.
Transfers: Priority date 5/5.

CONTACT
Kimberly Lovell, Director of Financial Aid
165 Central Avenue, Demorest, GA 30535-0010
(706) 776-0114

Reinhardt College
Waleska, Georgia
www.reinhardt.edu   Federal Code: 001589

4-year private business and teachers college in rural community, affiliated with United Methodist Church.
Enrollment: 1,008 undergrads, 12% part-time. 269 full-time freshmen.
Selectivity: Open admission; but selective for some programs.

BASIC COSTS (2005-2006)
Tuition and fees: $13,090.
Per-credit charge: $434.
Room and board: $5,900.

FINANCIAL AID PICTURE (2005-2006)
Students with need: Out of 227 full-time freshmen who applied for aid, 162 were judged to have need. Of these, 162 received aid, and 41 had their full need met. Average financial aid package met 39% of need; average scholarship/grant was $949; average loan was $2,090. For part-time students, average financial aid package was $942.
Students without need: 34 full-time freshmen who did not demonstrate need for aid received scholarships/grants; average award was $2,200. No-need awards available for academics, alumni affiliation, art, athletics.
Scholarships offered: 29 full-time freshmen received athletic scholarships; average amount $3,200.

FINANCIAL AID PROCEDURES
Forms required: FAFSA, state aid form, institutional form.
Dates and Deadlines: Priority date 5/1; no closing date. Applicants notified on a rolling basis starting 4/1; must reply within 2 week(s) of notification.

CONTACT
Robert Gregory, Director of Financial Aid
7300 Reinhardt College Circle, Waleska, GA 30183
(770) 720-5667

Savannah College of Art and Design
Savannah, Georgia
www.scad.edu   Federal Code: 015022

4-year private visual arts college in small city.
Enrollment: 6,062 undergrads, 9% part-time. 1,373 full-time freshmen.
Selectivity: Admits 50 to 75% of applicants.

BASIC COSTS (2006-2007)
Tuition and fees: $22,950.
Per-credit charge: $510.
Room and board: $9,600.
Additional info: A one-time matriculation fee of $500 is required of all students.

FINANCIAL AID PICTURE (2005-2006)
Students with need: Out of 990 full-time freshmen who applied for aid, 762 were judged to have need. Of these, 747 received aid, and 343 had their full need met. Average financial aid package met 10% of need; average scholarship/grant was $3,220; average loan was $2,590. For part-time students, average financial aid package was $8,317.
Students without need: 433 full-time freshmen who did not demonstrate need for aid received scholarships/grants; average award was $5,103. No-need awards available for academics, art, music/drama.
Scholarships offered: 44 full-time freshmen received athletic scholarships; average amount $15,290.
Additional info: Degree-seeking students may be awarded maximum of one scholarship from college, but may receive additional scholarships from other sources, as well as additional forms of financial aid. Scholarships based on academic achievement are awarded through admission office.

FINANCIAL AID PROCEDURES
Forms required: FAFSA, state aid form, institutional form.
Dates and Deadlines: Priority date 2/15; no closing date. Applicants notified on a rolling basis starting 6/1; must reply within 4 week(s) of notification.
Transfers: Transfer students eligible to apply for academic and portfolio scholarships.

CONTACT
Cindy Bradley, Director of Financial Aid
Admission Department, Savannah, GA 31402-2072
(912) 525-6109

Savannah Technical College
Savannah, Georgia
www.savannahtech.edu   Federal Code: 005618

2-year public technical college in small city.
Enrollment: 3,867 undergrads, 60% part-time. 583 full-time freshmen.
Selectivity: Open admission.

BASIC COSTS (2005-2006)
Tuition and fees: $1,359; out-of-state residents $2,475.
Per-credit charge: $31; out-of-state residents $62.

FINANCIAL AID PICTURE (2004-2005)
Students with need: 98% of average financial aid package awarded as scholarships/grants, 2% awarded as loans/jobs. Need-based aid available for part-time students.
Students without need: No-need awards available for academics, leadership, minority status, state/district residency.

FINANCIAL AID PROCEDURES
Forms required: FAFSA.
Dates and Deadlines: No deadline. Applicants notified on a rolling basis.

CONTACT
Timothy Cranford, Financial Aid Director
5717 White Bluff Road, Savannah, GA 31405
(912) 443-5705

Shorter College
Rome, Georgia
www.shorter.edu   Federal Code: 001591

4-year private liberal arts college in large town, affiliated with Southern Baptist Convention.
Enrollment: 948 undergrads, 3% part-time. 291 full-time freshmen.
Selectivity: Admits 50 to 75% of applicants.

BASIC COSTS (2006-2007)
Tuition and fees: $14,300.
Room and board: $6,600.

FINANCIAL AID PICTURE (2004-2005)
Students with need: Out of 260 full-time freshmen who applied for aid, 215 were judged to have need. Of these, 215 received aid, and 48 had their full need met. Average financial aid package met 66% of need; average scholarship/grant was $9,685; average loan was $2,470. For part-time students, average financial aid package was $6,655.
Students without need: 86 full-time freshmen who did not demonstrate need for aid received scholarships/grants; average award was $8,579. No-need awards available for academics, alumni affiliation, art, athletics, leadership, minority status, music/drama, religious affiliation, state/district residency.
Scholarships offered: 40 full-time freshmen received athletic scholarships; average amount $5,483.
Cumulative student debt: 59% of graduating class had student loans; average debt was $16,193.
Additional info: Cost is reduced for all in-state students by state tuition equalization grant program. College matches for out-of-state full-time students.

FINANCIAL AID PROCEDURES
Forms required: FAFSA, state aid form, institutional form.
Dates and Deadlines: Priority date 4/1; no closing date. Applicants notified on a rolling basis starting 3/1; must reply within 2 week(s) of notification.

CONTACT
Philip Hawkins, Assistant Vice President for Financial Aid
315 Shorter Avenue, Rome, GA 30165
(706) 233-7227

South Georgia College
Douglas, Georgia
www.sga.edu   Federal Code: 001592

2-year public community and junior college in large town.
Enrollment: 1,500 undergrads.

BASIC COSTS (2005-2006)
Tuition and fees: $1,840; out-of-state residents $6,464.
Per-credit charge: $65; out-of-state residents $257.
Room only: $2,550.

FINANCIAL AID PICTURE
Students with need: Need-based aid available for full-time and part-time students.
Students without need: No-need awards available for academics.

FINANCIAL AID PROCEDURES
Forms required: FAFSA, institutional form.
Dates and Deadlines: Priority date 6/1; no closing date. Applicants notified on a rolling basis starting 7/6; must reply within 2 week(s) of notification.

CONTACT
Gregory Fowler, Director of Financial Aid
100 West College Park Drive, Douglas, GA 31533-5098
(912) 389-4510

Southern Polytechnic State University
Marietta, Georgia
www.spsu.edu   Federal Code: 001570

4-year public university and engineering college in large city.
Enrollment: 3,299 undergrads, 34% part-time. 432 full-time freshmen.
Selectivity: Admits 50 to 75% of applicants. GED not accepted.

BASIC COSTS (2005-2006)
Tuition and fees: $3,174; out-of-state residents $11,038.
Per-credit charge: $110; out-of-state residents $437.
Room and board: $5,490.

FINANCIAL AID PICTURE (2005-2006)
Students with need: Average financial aid package met 68% of need; average scholarship/grant was $2,364; average loan was $2,531. For part-time students, average financial aid package was $2,463.
Students without need: No-need awards available for academics, athletics.
Cumulative student debt: 89% of graduating class had student loans; average debt was $4,063.

FINANCIAL AID PROCEDURES
Forms required: FAFSA.
Dates and Deadlines: Priority date 4/15; no closing date. Applicants notified on a rolling basis starting 6/1.

CONTACT
Gary Bush, Director of Financial Aid
1100 South Marietta Parkway, Marietta, GA 30060-2896
(678) 915-7290

Southwest Georgia Technical College
Thomasville, Georgia
www.southwestgatech.edu   Federal Code: 005615

2-year public technical college in large town.
Enrollment: 1,419 undergrads.
Selectivity: Open admission; but selective for some programs.

BASIC COSTS (2005-2006)
Tuition and fees: $1,359; out-of-state residents $2,475.
Per-credit charge: $31; out-of-state residents $62.

FINANCIAL AID PICTURE (2004-2005)
Students with need: Need-based aid available for part-time students. Work study available nights.
Students without need: No-need awards available for state/district residency.
Scholarships offered: Hope Scholarship; full tuition; available to GA residents with 3.0 minimum GPA.

FINANCIAL AID PROCEDURES
Forms required: FAFSA, institutional form.
Dates and Deadlines: No deadline. Applicants notified on a rolling basis starting 7/1.

CONTACT
Michael Rayburn, Director of Financial Aid
15689 US Highway 19N, Thomasville, GA 31792
(229) 225-5221

Spelman College
Atlanta, Georgia
www.spelman.edu   Federal Code: 001594
                           CSS Code: 5628

4-year private liberal arts college for women in very large city.
Enrollment: 2,229 undergrads, 4% part-time. 531 full-time freshmen.
Selectivity: Admits less than 50% of applicants.

BASIC COSTS (2005-2006)
Tuition and fees: $16,195.
Per-credit charge: $565.
Room and board: $8,455.

FINANCIAL AID PICTURE (2005-2006)
Students with need: Out of 488 full-time freshmen who applied for aid, 435 were judged to have need. Of these, 435 received aid, and 6 had their full need met. Average financial aid package met 67% of need; average scholarship/grant was $2,500; average loan was $2,625. For part-time students, average financial aid package was $3,500.
Students without need: 2 full-time freshmen who did not demonstrate need for aid received scholarships/grants; average award was $24,000. No-need awards available for academics, alumni affiliation, music/drama, state/district residency.
Cumulative student debt: 75% of graduating class had student loans; average debt was $23,500.

FINANCIAL AID PROCEDURES
Forms required: FAFSA, CSS PROFILE, state aid form, institutional form.
Dates and Deadlines: Priority date 3/1; no closing date. Applicants notified on a rolling basis starting 2/15; must reply within 2 week(s) of notification.
Transfers: Closing date 10/1. No special aid for transfer students for the first year.

CONTACT
Lenora Jackson, Director of Student Financial Services
350 Spelman Lane Southwest Campus Box 277, Atlanta, GA 30314
(404) 270-5212

Thomas University
Thomasville, Georgia
www.thomasu.edu   Federal Code: 001555

4-year private university and liberal arts college in large town.
Enrollment: 607 undergrads. 67 full-time freshmen.
Selectivity: Open admission; but selective for some programs.

BASIC COSTS (2006-2007)
Tuition and fees: $10,570.
Per-credit charge: $395.
Room only: $2,500.

FINANCIAL AID PICTURE (2004-2005)
Students with need: 25% of average financial aid package awarded as scholarships/grants, 75% awarded as loans/jobs. Need-based aid available for part-time students.
Students without need: No-need awards available for academics, athletics, ROTC, state/district residency.
Scholarships offered: Presidential Scholarships: tuition, fees, housing, $600 in meals, $500 for books (after all federal and state grants are applied); awarded to incoming freshmen in the top 10 percent of graduating class with minimum 1100 SAT (exclusive of writing) or 22 ACT, involved in extracurricular activities, with 2 high school teacher recommendations.

FINANCIAL AID PROCEDURES
Forms required: FAFSA, state aid form, institutional form.
Dates and Deadlines: Priority date 7/1; no closing date. Applicants notified on a rolling basis.
Transfers: Previous college attended must submit academic transcripts. Financial aid received during current academic year from previous school will be verified through NSLDS.

CONTACT
Angela Keys, Director of Financial Aid
1501 Millpond Road, Thomasville, GA 31792-7499
(229) 227-6931 ext. 158

Toccoa Falls College
Toccoa Falls, Georgia
www.tfc.edu   Federal Code: 001596

4-year private Bible and liberal arts college in large town, affiliated with Christian and Missionary Alliance.
Enrollment: 910 undergrads, 5% part-time. 259 full-time freshmen.
Selectivity: Admits 50 to 75% of applicants.

BASIC COSTS (2006-2007)
Tuition and fees: $13,025.
Per-credit charge: $538.
Room and board: $4,800.

FINANCIAL AID PICTURE (2005-2006)
Students with need: Average financial aid package met 61% of need; average scholarship/grant was $6,920; average loan was $2,085. For part-time students, average financial aid package was $4,654.
Students without need: No-need awards available for academics, alumni affiliation, leadership, music/drama, religious affiliation, state/district residency.
Scholarships offered: Honors scholarships; up to full tuition, renewable yearly; for students with qualifying ACT/SAT scores who maintain a GPA of at least 3.3. Music, leadership, and scholarships for high school valedictorians also available.
Cumulative student debt: 71% of graduating class had student loans; average debt was $17,273.

FINANCIAL AID PROCEDURES
Forms required: FAFSA.
Dates and Deadlines: Priority date 5/1; no closing date. Applicants notified on a rolling basis starting 3/1; must reply within 2 week(s) of notification.
Transfers: Need based aid awarded to students based on documented need reflected in information submitted to the federal government.

CONTACT
Vince Welch, Financial Aid Director
Office of Admissions, Toccoa Falls, GA 30598-0368
(706) 886-6831 ext. 5234

Truett-McConnell College
Cleveland, Georgia
www.truett.edu   Federal Code: 001597

4-year private liberal arts college in rural community, affiliated with Southern Baptist Convention.
Enrollment: 353 undergrads, 4% part-time. 170 full-time freshmen.
Selectivity: Admits less than 50% of applicants.

BASIC COSTS (2006-2007)
Tuition and fees: $12,450.
Per-credit charge: $398.
Room and board: $5,000.

FINANCIAL AID PICTURE
Students with need: Need-based aid available for full-time and part-time students.
Students without need: No-need awards available for academics, athletics, music/drama, religious affiliation, state/district residency.
Additional info: Installment plan available through AMS.

FINANCIAL AID PROCEDURES
Forms required: FAFSA, state aid form, institutional form.
Dates and Deadlines: Priority date 6/1; no closing date. Applicants notified on a rolling basis starting 4/1; must reply within 2 week(s) of notification.

CONTACT
Wendell Vonier, Director of Financial Aid
100 Alumni Drive, Cleveland, GA 30528
(800) 226-8621

University of Georgia
Athens, Georgia
www.uga.edu   Federal Code: 001598

4-year public university in small city.
Enrollment: 24,791 undergrads, 9% part-time. 4,662 full-time freshmen.
Selectivity: Admits 50 to 75% of applicants.

BASIC COSTS (2005-2006)
Tuition and fees: $4,628; out-of-state residents $16,848.
Per-credit charge: $152; out-of-state residents $661.
Room and board: $6,376.

FINANCIAL AID PICTURE (2005-2006)
Students with need: Out of 2,836 full-time freshmen who applied for aid, 1,275 were judged to have need. Of these, 1,261 received aid, and 496 had their full need met. Average financial aid package met 81% of need; average scholarship/grant was $6,148; average loan was $2,558. For part-time students, average financial aid package was $5,944.
Students without need: 378 full-time freshmen who did not demonstrate need for aid received scholarships/grants; average award was $1,656. No-need awards available for academics, athletics, ROTC, state/district residency.
Scholarships offered: 81 full-time freshmen received athletic scholarships; average amount $9,762.
Cumulative student debt: 43% of graduating class had student loans; average debt was $13,422.

FINANCIAL AID PROCEDURES
Forms required: FAFSA.
Dates and Deadlines: Priority date 3/1; no closing date. Applicants notified on a rolling basis starting 5/15; must reply within 2 week(s) of notification.

CONTACT
Susan Little, Director, Student Financial Aid
Office of Undergraduate Admissions, Athens, GA 30602-1633
(706) 542-6147

University of West Georgia
Carrollton, Georgia
www.westga.edu   Federal Code: 001601

4-year public university and liberal arts college in large town.
Enrollment: 8,346 undergrads, 17% part-time. 1,853 full-time freshmen.
Selectivity: Admits 50 to 75% of applicants. GED not accepted.

BASIC COSTS (2005-2006)
Tuition and fees: $3,270; out-of-state residents $10,586.
Per-credit charge: $102; out-of-state residents $407.
Room and board: $5,568.
Additional info: Tuition/fee waivers available for adults, minority students.

FINANCIAL AID PICTURE (2005-2006)
Students with need: Average financial aid package met 66% of need; average scholarship/grant was $4,348; average loan was $2,121. For part-time students, average financial aid package was $5,329.
Students without need: No-need awards available for academics, alumni affiliation, art, athletics, leadership, music/drama.
Cumulative student debt: 55% of graduating class had student loans; average debt was $12,249.

FINANCIAL AID PROCEDURES
Forms required: FAFSA.
Dates and Deadlines: Priority date 4/1; no closing date. Applicants notified on a rolling basis starting 3/1; must reply by 5/1.

CONTACT
Kimberly Jordan, Director of Financial Aid
1601 Maple Street, Carrollton, GA 30118-0001
(678) 839-6421

Valdosta State University
Valdosta, Georgia
www.valdosta.edu   Federal Code: 001599

4-year public university in small city.
Enrollment: 9,015 undergrads, 17% part-time. 1,716 full-time freshmen.
Selectivity: Admits 50 to 75% of applicants. GED not accepted.

BASIC COSTS (2005-2006)
Tuition and fees: $3,278; out-of-state residents $10,594.
Per-credit charge: $102; out-of-state residents $407.
Room and board: $5,524.

FINANCIAL AID PICTURE (2004-2005)
Students with need: Out of 1,681 full-time freshmen who applied for aid, 941 were judged to have need. Of these, 941 received aid, and 785 had their full need met. Average financial aid package met 82% of need; average scholarship/grant was $4,413; average loan was $2,176. For part-time students, average financial aid package was $8,921.
Students without need: 122 full-time freshmen who did not demonstrate need for aid received scholarships/grants; average award was $1,843. No-need awards available for academics, art, athletics, leadership, music/drama, ROTC, state/district residency.
Scholarships offered: 45 full-time freshmen received athletic scholarships; average amount $2,806.
Cumulative student debt: 61% of graduating class had student loans; average debt was $16,220.

FINANCIAL AID PROCEDURES
Forms required: FAFSA.
Dates and Deadlines: Priority date 5/1; no closing date. Applicants notified on a rolling basis starting 5/15.
Transfers: No deadline. Applicants notified on a rolling basis starting 5/15.

CONTACT
Doug Tanner, Director of Financial Aid
1500 North Patterson Street, Valdosta, GA 31698
(229) 333-5935

Waycross College
Waycross, Georgia
www.waycross.edu   Federal Code: 013537

2-year public community and liberal arts college in small town.
Enrollment: 754 undergrads.

BASIC COSTS (2005-2006)
Tuition and fees: $1,696; out-of-state residents $6,320.
Per-credit charge: $65; out-of-state residents $257.
Additional info: Tuition/fee waivers available for adults.

FINANCIAL AID PICTURE
Students with need: Work study available nights, weekends, and for part-time students.
Students without need: No-need awards available for academics, alumni affiliation, leadership.

FINANCIAL AID PROCEDURES
Forms required: FAFSA, institutional form.
Dates and Deadlines: Priority date 5/1; no closing date. Applicants notified on a rolling basis; must reply within 2 week(s) of notification.

CONTACT
Debbie Howard, Assistant Director of Financial Aid
2001 South Georgia Parkway, Waycross, GA 31503
(912) 285-6035

Wesleyan College
Macon, Georgia
www.wesleyancollege.edu   Federal Code: 001600

4-year private liberal arts college for women in small city, affiliated with United Methodist Church.
Enrollment: 530 undergrads, 26% part-time. 83 full-time freshmen.
Selectivity: Admits 50 to 75% of applicants.

BASIC COSTS (2006-2007)
Tuition and fees: $14,500.
Per-credit charge: $365.
Room and board: $7,500.
Additional info: Tuition/fee waivers available for adults.

FINANCIAL AID PICTURE (2004-2005)
Students with need: Out of 59 full-time freshmen who applied for aid, 46 were judged to have need. Of these, 46 received aid, and 13 had their full need met. Average financial aid package met 81% of need; average scholarship/grant was $7,469; average loan was $2,302. For part-time students, average financial aid package was $5,999.
Students without need: 30 full-time freshmen who did not demonstrate need for aid received scholarships/grants; average award was $13,262. No-need awards available for academics, alumni affiliation, art, job skills, leadership, minority status, music/drama, religious affiliation, state/district residency.
Scholarships offered: Academic Scholarships: range in value from $1,000 to $10,000 ; based on minimum 1100 SAT or 25 ACT and 3.75 GPA, or 1200 SAT/27 ACT and 3.5 GPA. SAT scores exclusive of Writing. Leadership Awards and scholarships for music, art and theater: range from $1,000-$3,000.
Cumulative student debt: 78% of graduating class had student loans; average debt was $13,824.
Additional info: Fellowships available based on number of hours and cumulative GPA transferred in, with minimum 30 semester or 45 quarter hours and 3.0 GPA required.

FINANCIAL AID PROCEDURES
Forms required: FAFSA, state aid form, institutional form.
Dates and Deadlines: Priority date 4/1; no closing date. Applicants notified on a rolling basis starting 3/1; must reply by 5/1 or within 3 week(s) of notification.

CONTACT
Patricia Gibbs, Director of Financial Aid
4760 Forsyth Road, Macon, GA 31210-4462
(478) 757-5205

West Georgia Technical College
LaGrange, Georgia
www.westgatech.org   Federal Code: 005614

2-year public technical college in small city.
Enrollment: 1,834 undergrads, 59% part-time. 3,268 full-time freshmen.
Selectivity: Open admission; but selective for some programs.

BASIC COSTS (2005-2006)
Tuition and fees: $1,359; out-of-state residents $2,475.
Per-credit charge: $31; out-of-state residents $62.
Additional info: Tuition reciprocity with bordering states. CDL program is $2012. Basic welding and EMT programs are $37 per-credit-hour.

FINANCIAL AID PICTURE (2004-2005)
Students with need: Out of 1,228 full-time freshmen who applied for aid, 954 were judged to have need. Of these, 954 received aid, and 238 had their full need met. Average financial aid package met 75% of need; average scholarship/grant was $535. Need-based aid available for part-time students.
Students without need: No-need awards available for state/district residency.

FINANCIAL AID PROCEDURES
Forms required: FAFSA, state aid form, institutional form.
Dates and Deadlines: No deadline. Applicants notified on a rolling basis; must reply within 1 week(s) of notification.
Transfers: Aid must be in order or cash paid at registration for classes.

CONTACT
Dorothy Cantor, Financial Aid Coordinator
303 Fort Drive, LaGrange, GA 30240
(706) 845-4323

Young Harris College
Young Harris, Georgia
www.yhc.edu   Federal Code: 001604

2-year private junior and liberal arts college in rural community, affiliated with United Methodist Church.
Enrollment: 532 undergrads, 5% part-time. 278 full-time freshmen.
Selectivity: Admits 50 to 75% of applicants.

BASIC COSTS (2006-2007)
Tuition and fees: $14,690.
Per-credit charge: $500.
Room and board: $4,780.

FINANCIAL AID PICTURE (2004-2005)
Students with need: 82% of average financial aid package awarded as scholarships/grants, 18% awarded as loans/jobs. Need-based aid available for part-time students. Work study available nights.
Students without need: No-need awards available for academics, art, athletics, job skills, music/drama, state/district residency.
Scholarships offered: Academic Scholarships: $5,000-$8,000; based on index including GPA and SAT/ACT; additional awards to a percentage of recipients range from additional $1,000 to full tuition, room and board.

FINANCIAL AID PROCEDURES
Forms required: FAFSA, state aid form, institutional form.
Dates and Deadlines: Priority date 4/1; no closing date. Applicants notified on a rolling basis starting 3/1; must reply within 2 week(s) of notification.

CONTACT
Clinton Hobbs, Vice President for Enrollment Management
PO Box 116, Young Harris, GA 30582-0116
(706) 379-3111 ext. 5117

Hawaii

Brigham Young University-Hawaii
Laie, Hawaii
www.byuh.edu   Federal Code: 001606

4-year private university and liberal arts college in small town, affiliated with Church of Jesus Christ of Latter-day Saints.
Enrollment: 2,398 undergrads, 7% part-time. 206 full-time freshmen.
Selectivity: Admits less than 50% of applicants. GED not accepted.

BASIC COSTS (2006-2007)
Tuition and fees: $3,040.
Per-credit charge: $190.
Room and board: $5,170.
Additional info: 100% higher tuition and per-credit-hour charges for students who are not members of The Church of Jesus Christ of Latter-day Saints.

FINANCIAL AID PICTURE
Students with need: Need-based aid available for full-time and part-time students.
Students without need: No-need awards available for academics, art, athletics, leadership, music/drama, state/district residency.
Additional info: Closing date for scholarship applications May 1.

FINANCIAL AID PROCEDURES
Forms required: FAFSA.
Dates and Deadlines: Closing date 5/30. Applicants notified by 5/1; must reply by 8/31.
Transfers: Closing date 3/15.

CONTACT
Wes Duke, Director of Financial Aid
55-220 Kulanui Street, #1973, Laie, HI 96762-1294
(808) 293-3530

Chaminade University of Honolulu
Honolulu, Hawaii
www.chaminade.edu   Federal Code: 001605

4-year private university in large city, affiliated with Roman Catholic Church.
Enrollment: 1,079 undergrads, 4% part-time. 248 full-time freshmen.
Selectivity: Admits over 75% of applicants.

BASIC COSTS (2006-2007)
Tuition and fees: $14,960.
Per-credit charge: $494.
Room and board: $9,210.

FINANCIAL AID PICTURE (2004-2005)
Students with need: Out of 202 full-time freshmen who applied for aid, 167 were judged to have need. Of these, 167 received aid, and 21 had their full need met. Average financial aid package met 65% of need; average scholarship/grant was $8,258; average loan was $2,879. For part-time students, average financial aid package was $7,547.
Students without need: 35 full-time freshmen who did not demonstrate need for aid received scholarships/grants; average award was $4,994. No-need awards available for academics, art, athletics, leadership, religious affiliation, ROTC, state/district residency.
Scholarships offered: 3 full-time freshmen received athletic scholarships; average amount $4,000.
Cumulative student debt: 65% of graduating class had student loans; average debt was $29,770.

Additional info: For students whose eligibility for federal and institutional aid does not meet entire costs, alternative student loans may be secured for eligible applicants.

FINANCIAL AID PROCEDURES
Forms required: FAFSA.
Dates and Deadlines: Priority date 2/15; no closing date. Applicants notified on a rolling basis starting 2/15; must reply within 4 week(s) of notification.

CONTACT
Eric Nemoto, Associate Dean of Enrollment Management
3140 Waialae Avenue, Honolulu, HI 96816
(808) 735-4780

Hawaii Business College
Honolulu, Hawaii
www.hbc.edu   Federal Code: 013615

2-year for-profit business and health science college in large city.
Enrollment: 350 undergrads.
Selectivity: Open admission.

FINANCIAL AID PICTURE
Students with need: Need-based aid available for full-time and part-time students. Work study available nights, weekends, and for part-time students.
Students without need: This college only awards aid to students with need.

FINANCIAL AID PROCEDURES
Forms required: FAFSA.
Dates and Deadlines: No deadline. Applicants notified on a rolling basis; must reply within 3 week(s) of notification.

CONTACT
Roxann Bedia, Director of Financial Aid
33 South King Street, 4th Floor, Honolulu, HI 96813
(808) 524-4014

Hawaii Pacific University
Honolulu, Hawaii
www.hpu.edu   Federal Code: 007279

4-year private university and liberal arts college in large city.
Enrollment: 6,296 undergrads, 36% part-time. 656 full-time freshmen.
Selectivity: Admits over 75% of applicants.

BASIC COSTS (2006-2007)
Tuition and fees: $12,312.
Per-credit charge: $510.
Room and board: $9,840.

FINANCIAL AID PICTURE (2005-2006)
Students with need: Out of 518 full-time freshmen who applied for aid, 299 were judged to have need. Of these, 280 received aid, and 49 had their full need met. Average financial aid package met 80% of need; average scholarship/grant was $4,033; average loan was $3,109. For part-time students, average financial aid package was $8,717.
Students without need: 178 full-time freshmen who did not demonstrate need for aid received scholarships/grants; average award was $7,618. No-need awards available for academics, athletics, job skills, leadership, music/drama, religious affiliation, ROTC.
Scholarships offered: *Merit:* Makana Scholarship; $2,000; 3.5 GPA or higher. Phi Theta Kappa Scholarship; $5,411 for member of Phi Theta Kappa. *Athletic:* 27 full-time freshmen received athletic scholarships; average amount $8,013.

FINANCIAL AID PROCEDURES
Forms required: FAFSA.
Dates and Deadlines: Priority date 3/1; no closing date. Applicants notified on a rolling basis starting 4/1; must reply within 3 week(s) of notification.

CONTACT
Adam Hatch, Director of Financial Aid
1164 Bishop Street, Honolulu, HI 96813
(808) 544-0253

Heald College: Honolulu
Honolulu, Hawaii
www.heald.edu   Federal Code: E00886

2-year private business and technical college in very large city.
Enrollment: 807 undergrads.
Selectivity: Open admission.

BASIC COSTS (2006-2007)
Tuition and fees: $9,900.

FINANCIAL AID PICTURE
Students with need: Need-based aid available for full-time and part-time students. Work study available nights, weekends, and for part-time students.
Students without need: This college only awards aid to students with need.

FINANCIAL AID PROCEDURES
Forms required: FAFSA.
Dates and Deadlines: No deadline.

CONTACT
Maria Buccat, Director of Financial Aid
1500 Kapiolani Boulevard, Honolulu, HI 96814-3715
(808) 955-1500

Remington College: Honolulu
Honolulu, Hawaii
www.remingtoncollege.edu   Federal Code: 030121

2-year for-profit branch campus college in very large city.
Enrollment: 538 undergrads.

BASIC COSTS (2005-2006)
Per-credit charge: $334.
Additional info: Associate degree program $32,010; Computer Networking Technology program $32,810; Bachelor programs $29,070. Tuition at time of enrollment locked for 2 years.

FINANCIAL AID PICTURE
Students with need: Need-based aid available for full-time students.
Students without need: This college only awards aid to students with need.

FINANCIAL AID PROCEDURES
Forms required: FAFSA.
Dates and Deadlines: No deadline. Applicants notified on a rolling basis.

CONTACT
Erwin Ramello, Director of Financial Services
1111 Bishop Street, Suite 400, Honolulu, HI 96813-2811

University of Hawaii at Hilo
Hilo, Hawaii
www.uhh.hawaii.edu   Federal Code: 001611

4-year public university in large town.
Enrollment: 3,363 undergrads.

BASIC COSTS (2005-2006)
Tuition and fees: $2,603; out-of-state residents $8,171.
Per-credit charge: $103; out-of-state residents $335.
Room and board: $5,472.
Additional info: Tuition at time of enrollment locked for 4 years.

FINANCIAL AID PICTURE
Students with need: Need-based aid available for full-time and part-time students. Work study available nights, weekends, and for part-time students.
Additional info: Hawaii student incentive grants and tuition waivers (merit and need-based) available to Hawaii residents at participating institutions.

FINANCIAL AID PROCEDURES
Forms required: FAFSA.
Dates and Deadlines: Priority date 3/1; no closing date. Applicants notified on a rolling basis starting 4/15; must reply within 2 week(s) of notification.

CONTACT
Jeff Schofield, Financial Aid Director
200 West Kawili Street, Hilo, HI 96720-4091
(808) 974-7324

University of Hawaii at Manoa
Honolulu, Hawaii
www.manoa.hawaii.edu   Federal Code: 001610

4-year public university in very large city.
Enrollment: 13,831 undergrads, 17% part-time. 1,884 full-time freshmen.
Selectivity: Admits 50 to 75% of applicants.

BASIC COSTS (2005-2006)
Tuition and fees: $3,697; out-of-state residents $10,177.
Per-credit charge: $146; out-of-state residents $416.
Room and board: $6,717.
Additional info: Tuition/fee waivers available for minority students.

FINANCIAL AID PICTURE (2004-2005)
Students with need: Out of 1,264 full-time freshmen who applied for aid, 686 were judged to have need. Of these, 626 received aid, and 137 had their full need met. Average financial aid package met 62% of need; average scholarship/grant was $3,516; average loan was $2,575. For part-time students, average financial aid package was $5,068.
Students without need: 219 full-time freshmen who did not demonstrate need for aid received scholarships/grants; average award was $2,574. No-need awards available for academics, alumni affiliation, art, athletics, job skills, leadership, minority status, music/drama, religious affiliation, ROTC, state/district residency.
Scholarships offered: 38 full-time freshmen received athletic scholarships; average amount $11,359.
Cumulative student debt: 29% of graduating class had student loans; average debt was $9,280.
Additional info: Hawaii student incentive grants and tuition waivers (merit and need-based) available to Hawaii residents at participating institutions.

FINANCIAL AID PROCEDURES
Forms required: FAFSA.
Dates and Deadlines: Priority date 3/1; no closing date. Applicants notified on a rolling basis starting 3/15; must reply within 4 week(s) of notification.
Transfers: No deadline. Applicants notified on a rolling basis starting 3/15; must reply within 4 week(s) of notification.

Hawaii University of Hawaii at Manoa

CONTACT
Jamie Uyehara, Director of Financial Aid
2600 Campus Road, QLC Rm 001, Honolulu, HI 96822
(808) 956-7251

University of Hawaii: Hawaii Community College
Hilo, Hawaii
www.hawcc.hawaii.edu   Federal Code: 005258

2-year public community college in small city.
Enrollment: 2,440 undergrads.
Selectivity: Open admission.

BASIC COSTS (2005-2006)
Tuition and fees: $1,594; out-of-state residents $7,384.
Per-credit charge: $49; out-of-state residents $242.

FINANCIAL AID PICTURE
Students with need: Need-based aid available for full-time and part-time students.
Students without need: This college only awards aid to students with need.
Additional info: Hawaii student incentive grants and tuition waivers (merit and need-based) available to Hawaii residents.

FINANCIAL AID PROCEDURES
Forms required: FAFSA.
Dates and Deadlines: Priority date 4/1; no closing date. Applicants notified on a rolling basis starting 5/1; must reply within 2 week(s) of notification.
Transfers: Residents of Guam, Federated States of Micronesia, Palau, Marianas Islands and certain other island nations considered residents for tuition purpose.

CONTACT
Sheryl Lundberg-Sprague, Financial Aid Officer
200 West Kawili Street, Hilo, HI 96720-4091
(808) 974-7663

University of Hawaii: Honolulu Community College
Honolulu, Hawaii
www.hcc.hawaii.edu   Federal Code: 001612

2-year public community and technical college in very large city.
Enrollment: 3,307 undergrads.
Selectivity: Open admission; but selective for out-of-state students.

BASIC COSTS (2005-2006)
Tuition and fees: $1,500; out-of-state residents $7,290.
Per-credit charge: $49; out-of-state residents $242.

FINANCIAL AID PICTURE
Students with need: Need-based aid available for full-time and part-time students.
Students without need: No-need awards available for academics, state/district residency.
Additional info: Hawaii student incentive grants and tuition waivers (merit and need-based) available to Hawaii residents at participating institutions.

FINANCIAL AID PROCEDURES
Forms required: FAFSA.
Dates and Deadlines: Priority date 4/1; no closing date. Applicants notified on a rolling basis starting 7/1; must reply within 3 week(s) of notification.

CONTACT
Jannine Oyama, Financial Aid Officer
874 Dillingham Boulevard, Honolulu, HI 96817
(808) 845-9116

University of Hawaii: Kapiolani Community College
Honolulu, Hawaii
www.kcc.hawaii.edu   Federal Code: 001613

2-year public community college in very large city.
Enrollment: 4,341 undergrads.
Selectivity: Open admission; but selective for some programs.

BASIC COSTS (2005-2006)
Tuition and fees: $1,555; out-of-state residents $7,320.
Per-credit charge: $49; out-of-state residents $242.

FINANCIAL AID PICTURE
Students with need: Need-based aid available for full-time and part-time students.
Students without need: This college only awards aid to students with need.
Additional info: Hawaii student incentive grants and tuition waivers (merit and need-based) available to Hawaii residents.

FINANCIAL AID PROCEDURES
Forms required: FAFSA.
Dates and Deadlines: Priority date 4/1; no closing date. Applicants notified on a rolling basis; must reply within 2 week(s) of notification.

CONTACT
Coleen Oshiro, Financial Aid Officer
4303 Diamond Head Road, Honolulu, HI 96816
(808) 734-9555

University of Hawaii: Kauai Community College
Lihue, Hawaii
www.kauai.hawaii.edu   Federal Code: 001614

2-year public community college in large town.
Enrollment: 1,059 undergrads.
Selectivity: Open admission; but selective for out-of-state students.

BASIC COSTS (2005-2006)
Tuition and fees: $1,500; out-of-state residents $7,290.
Per-credit charge: $49; out-of-state residents $242.

FINANCIAL AID PICTURE
Students with need: Work study available nights.
Additional info: Hawaii student incentive grants and tuition waivers (merit and need-based) available to Hawaii residents.

FINANCIAL AID PROCEDURES
Forms required: FAFSA, institutional form.
Dates and Deadlines: Priority date 3/1; closing date 5/1. Applicants notified on a rolling basis starting 5/1.
Transfers: Academic transcript evaluation by end of first semester is required.

CONTACT
Frances Dinnan, Financial Aid Officer
3-1901 Kaumualii Highway, Lihue, HI 96766-9500
(808) 245-8236

University of Hawaii: Leeward Community College
Pearl City, Hawaii
www.lcc.hawaii.edu Federal Code: 004549

2-year public community college in large town.
Enrollment: 4,598 undergrads.
Selectivity: Open admission.

BASIC COSTS (2005-2006)
Tuition and fees: $1,495; out-of-state residents $7,285.
Per-credit charge: $49; out-of-state residents $242.

FINANCIAL AID PICTURE
Students with need: Need-based aid available for full-time and part-time students.
Additional info: Leveraging Educational Assistance Partnership (LEAP) funds or tuition waivers available to students with financial need.

FINANCIAL AID PROCEDURES
Forms required: FAFSA.
Dates and Deadlines: Priority date 4/15; no closing date. Applicants notified on a rolling basis starting 6/1; must reply within 2 week(s) of notification.

CONTACT
Valerie Chun, Financial Aid Officer
96-045 Ala Ike, Pearl City, HI 96782
(808) 455-0606

University of Hawaii: Maui Community College
Kahului, Hawaii
www.maui.hawaii.edu

2-year public community college in small city.
Enrollment: 2,368 undergrads.
Selectivity: Open admission; but selective for some programs.

BASIC COSTS (2005-2006)
Tuition and fees: $1,508; out-of-state residents $7,298.
Per-credit charge: $49; out-of-state residents $242.
Additional info: Tuition/fee waivers available for minority students.

FINANCIAL AID PICTURE (2004-2005)
Students with need: 48% of average financial aid package awarded as scholarships/grants, 52% awarded as loans/jobs. Need-based aid available for part-time students. Work study available nights.

FINANCIAL AID PROCEDURES
Forms required: FAFSA, institutional form.
Dates and Deadlines: Priority date 4/1; no closing date. Must reply within 4 week(s) of notification.

CONTACT
310 West Kaahumanu Avenue, Kahului, HI 96732-1617
(808) 984-3277

University of Hawaii: West Oahu
Pearl City, Hawaii
www.uhwo.hawaii.edu Federal Code: 014315

Upper-division public liberal arts college in large town.
Enrollment: 838 undergrads, 66% part-time.

BASIC COSTS (2005-2006)
Tuition and fees: $2,266; out-of-state residents $7,402.
Per-credit charge: $94; out-of-state residents $308.
Additional info: Foreign students pay out-of-state tuition rates, except for applicants from countries with reciprocity agreements.

FINANCIAL AID PICTURE (2004-2005)
Students with need: 54% of average financial aid package awarded as scholarships/grants, 46% awarded as loans/jobs. Need-based aid available for part-time students.
Students without need: No-need awards available for academics, leadership, state/district residency.
Additional info: Tuition waivers (merit and need-based) available to Hawaii residents.

FINANCIAL AID PROCEDURES
Transfers: Priority date 4/1; no deadline. Applicants notified by 7/1.

CONTACT
Jennifer Bradley, Student Services Specialist
96-129 Ala Ike, Pearl City, HI 96782
(808) 454-4700

University of Hawaii: Windward Community College
Kaneohe, Hawaii
www.wcc.hawaii.edu Federal Code: 010390

2-year public community college in small city.
Enrollment: 1,357 undergrads.
Selectivity: Open admission.

BASIC COSTS (2005-2006)
Tuition and fees: $1,510; out-of-state residents $7,300.
Per-credit charge: $49; out-of-state residents $242.
Additional info: Tuition/fee waivers available for minority students.

FINANCIAL AID PICTURE (2005-2006)
Students with need: 72% of average financial aid package awarded as scholarships/grants, 28% awarded as loans/jobs. Need-based aid available for part-time students.
Additional info: Hawaii student incentive grants and tuition waivers (merit and need-based) available to Hawaii residents.

FINANCIAL AID PROCEDURES
Forms required: FAFSA.
Dates and Deadlines: Priority date 4/1; no closing date. Applicants notified on a rolling basis starting 3/15; must reply within 2 week(s) of notification.

CONTACT
Steven Chigawa, Financial Aid Officer
45-720 Keaahala Road, Kaneohe, HI 96744
(808) 235-7449

Idaho

Albertson College of Idaho
Caldwell, Idaho
www.albertson.edu Federal Code: 001617

4-year private liberal arts college in large town.
Enrollment: 788 undergrads, 3% part-time. 192 full-time freshmen.
Selectivity: Admits over 75% of applicants.

Albertson College of Idaho

BASIC COSTS (2006-2007)
Tuition and fees: $16,625.
Per-credit charge: $670.
Room and board: $6,191.
Additional info: Tuition/fee waivers available for adults.

FINANCIAL AID PICTURE (2005-2006)
Students with need: Out of 157 full-time freshmen who applied for aid, 139 were judged to have need. Of these, 139 received aid, and 29 had their full need met. Average financial aid package met 89% of need; average scholarship/grant was $3,737; average loan was $3,515. For part-time students, average financial aid package was $9,803.
Students without need: 55 full-time freshmen who did not demonstrate need for aid received scholarships/grants; average award was $8,667. No-need awards available for academics, alumni affiliation, art, athletics, job skills, leadership, minority status, music/drama, religious affiliation.
Scholarships offered: *Merit:* Albertson Heritage Scholarship: full tuition; minimum 3.8-4.0 GPA and 31-33 ACT or 1380-1470 SAT. Presidential Scholarship: $6,000/year; requirements range from 3.1 GPA and 36 ACT or 1600 SAT to 4.3 GPA and 25 ACT or 1140 SAT. Trustee Scholarship: $4,000/year; requirements range from 2.55 GPA and 35 ACT or 1580 SAT to 4.3 GPA and 19 ACT or 910 SAT. Albertson College Grant: $1,000/year; requirements range from 2.5 GPA and 30-35 ACT or 1340-1580 SAT to 4.1 GPA and 15 ACT or 740 SAT. All SAT scores exclusive of Writing. *Athletic:* 55 full-time freshmen received athletic scholarships; average amount $3,415.
Cumulative student debt: 94% of graduating class had student loans; average debt was $25,343.

FINANCIAL AID PROCEDURES
Forms required: FAFSA, institutional form.
Dates and Deadlines: Priority date 2/15; no closing date. Applicants notified on a rolling basis starting 3/1; must reply within 3 week(s) of notification.

CONTACT
Juanita Pearson, Director of Student Financial Services
2112 Cleveland Boulevard, Caldwell, ID 83605
(208) 459-5308

Boise Bible College
Boise, Idaho
www.boisebible.edu
Federal Code: 015783

4-year private Bible college in small city, affiliated with nondenominational tradition.
Enrollment: 171 undergrads.
Selectivity: Admits over 75% of applicants.

BASIC COSTS (2006-2007)
Tuition and fees: $7,016.
Per-credit charge: $288.
Room and board: $4,800.

FINANCIAL AID PICTURE
Students with need: Need-based aid available for full-time and part-time students.
Students without need: No-need awards available for academics, leadership, music/drama, religious affiliation.

FINANCIAL AID PROCEDURES
Forms required: FAFSA, institutional form.
Dates and Deadlines: Priority date 5/1; no closing date. Applicants notified on a rolling basis starting 5/2; must reply by 8/1 or within 2 week(s) of notification.
Transfers: Financial aid and academic transcripts must be on file before federal aid is awarded.

CONTACT
Joyce Anderson, Financial Aid Officer
8695 Marigold Street, Boise, ID 83714-1220
(800) 893-7755

Boise State University
Boise, Idaho
www.boisestate.edu
Federal Code: 001616

4-year public university and technical college in small city.
Enrollment: 15,676 undergrads, 31% part-time. 2,017 full-time freshmen.
Selectivity: Admits over 75% of applicants.

BASIC COSTS (2005-2006)
Tuition and fees: $3,872; out-of-state residents $11,280.
Per-credit charge: $195.
Room and board: $4,908.
Additional info: Out-of-state students (undergraduate and graduate) taking less than 8 credit hours pay in-state rate.

FINANCIAL AID PICTURE (2005-2006)
Students with need: Average financial aid package met 60% of need; average scholarship/grant was $2,934; average loan was $2,685. For part-time students, average financial aid package was $6,807.
Students without need: No-need awards available for academics, athletics, music/drama, ROTC, state/district residency.

FINANCIAL AID PROCEDURES
Forms required: FAFSA.
Dates and Deadlines: Priority date 4/1; no closing date. Applicants notified on a rolling basis starting 6/1; must reply within 2 week(s) of notification.
Transfers: Financial aid transcripts required from all postsecondary schools attended whether or not financial aid was received.

CONTACT
David Tolman, Director of Financial Aid
1910 University Drive, Boise, ID 83725
(208) 426-1664

Brigham Young University-Idaho
Rexburg, Idaho
www.byui.edu
Federal Code: 001625

4-year private university in large town, affiliated with Church of Jesus Christ of Latter-day Saints.
Enrollment: 12,295 undergrads, 9% part-time. 2,530 full-time freshmen.
Selectivity: Admits 50 to 75% of applicants.

BASIC COSTS (2005-2006)
Tuition and fees: $3,170.
Per-credit charge: $115.
Room and board: $5,500.
Additional info: Tuition for students who are not members of The Church of Jesus Christ of Latter-day Saints is $4,130 per academic year, $172 per credit hour.

FINANCIAL AID PICTURE
Students with need: Need-based aid available for full-time and part-time students.
Students without need: No-need awards available for academics, athletics, leadership.
Additional info: Application deadline for merit scholarships 3/1.

FINANCIAL AID PROCEDURES
Forms required: FAFSA.

Dates and Deadlines: Priority date 5/1; no closing date. Applicants notified on a rolling basis starting 2/1.

CONTACT
Dan Gulbransen, Director of Financial Aid
120 Kimball Building, Rexburg, ID 83460-1615
(208) 496-1013

College of Southern Idaho
Twin Falls, Idaho
www.csi.edu   Federal Code: 001619

2-year public community and junior college in large town.
Enrollment: 5,145 undergrads.
Selectivity: Open admission; but selective for some programs.

BASIC COSTS (2005-2006)
Tuition and fees: $1,900; out-of-state residents $5,300.
Per-credit charge: $95; out-of-state residents $265.
Room and board: $4,300.

FINANCIAL AID PICTURE (2004-2005)
Students with need: 59% of average financial aid package awarded as scholarships/grants, 41% awarded as loans/jobs. Need-based aid available for part-time students.
Additional info: Out-of-state tuition waivers based on GPA and activities.

FINANCIAL AID PROCEDURES
Forms required: FAFSA.
Dates and Deadlines: Priority date 3/1; no closing date. Applicants notified on a rolling basis starting 4/30; must reply within 3 week(s) of notification.

CONTACT
Colin Randolph, Director of Student Financial Aid
Box 1238, Twin Falls, ID 83303-1238
(208) 732-6273

Eastern Idaho Technical College
Idaho Falls, Idaho
www.eitc.edu   Federal Code: 011133

2-year public technical college in large town.
Enrollment: 638 undergrads, 65% part-time. 98 full-time freshmen.
Selectivity: Open admission; but selective for some programs.

BASIC COSTS (2005-2006)
Tuition and fees: $1,646; out-of-state residents $5,730.
Per-credit charge: $76; out-of-state residents $152.
Additional info: Fees may vary according to the program of study.

FINANCIAL AID PICTURE (2004-2005)
Students with need: 48% of average financial aid package awarded as scholarships/grants, 52% awarded as loans/jobs. Need-based aid available for part-time students.
Students without need: No-need awards available for academics, job skills, state/district residency.

FINANCIAL AID PROCEDURES
Forms required: FAFSA, institutional form.
Dates and Deadlines: Priority date 6/1; no closing date. Applicants notified on a rolling basis starting 6/6; must reply within 4 week(s) of notification.

CONTACT
Tony Siebers, Financial Aid Officer
1600 South 25th East, Idaho Falls, ID 83404-5788
(208) 524-3000 ext. 3311

Idaho State University
Pocatello, Idaho
www.isu.edu   Federal Code: 001620

4-year public university in small city.
Enrollment: 10,376 undergrads, 25% part-time. 1,470 full-time freshmen.
Selectivity: Admits over 75% of applicants.

BASIC COSTS (2005-2006)
Tuition and fees: $4,000; out-of-state residents $11,700.
Per-credit charge: $202; out-of-state residents $312.
Room and board: $4,870.
Additional info: Refundable $330 per semester or $660 per year charge for health insurance.

FINANCIAL AID PICTURE (2005-2006)
Students with need: Average financial aid package met 57% of need; average scholarship/grant was $2,503; average loan was $2,065. For part-time students, average financial aid package was $3,788.
Students without need: No-need awards available for academics, alumni affiliation, art, athletics, leadership, minority status, music/drama, ROTC, state/district residency.
Cumulative student debt: 71% of graduating class had student loans; average debt was $19,299.

FINANCIAL AID PROCEDURES
Forms required: FAFSA.
Dates and Deadlines: Priority date 2/20; no closing date. Applicants notified on a rolling basis starting 4/1.

CONTACT
Doug Severs, Director of Financial Aid
PO Box 8270, Museum Natural History 319, Pocatello, ID 83209-8270
(208) 282-2756

Lewis-Clark State College
Lewiston, Idaho
www.lcsc.edu   Federal Code: 001621

4-year public liberal arts and technical college in small city.
Enrollment: 2,944 undergrads, 23% part-time. 456 full-time freshmen.
Selectivity: Admits less than 50% of applicants.

BASIC COSTS (2005-2006)
Tuition and fees: $3,714; out-of-state residents $10,266.
Per-credit charge: $185.
Room and board: $5,400.

FINANCIAL AID PICTURE (2004-2005)
Students with need: Out of 393 full-time freshmen who applied for aid, 338 were judged to have need. Of these, 332 received aid, and 24 had their full need met. Average financial aid package met 7% of need; average scholarship/grant was $3,018; average loan was $2,203. For part-time students, average financial aid package was $4,420.
Students without need: 59 full-time freshmen who did not demonstrate need for aid received scholarships/grants; average award was $2,221. No-need awards available for academics, alumni affiliation, art, athletics, leadership, minority status, music/drama.
Scholarships offered: 29 full-time freshmen received athletic scholarships; average amount $5,445.

FINANCIAL AID PROCEDURES
Forms required: FAFSA.
Dates and Deadlines: Priority date 3/1; no closing date. Applicants notified on a rolling basis starting 4/15; must reply within 2 week(s) of notification.

Idaho — Lewis-Clark State College

CONTACT
Laura Hughes, Director of Financial Aid
500 Eighth Avenue, Lewiston, ID 83501-2698
(208) 792-2224

North Idaho College
Coeur d'Alene, Idaho
www.nic.edu   Federal Code: 001623

2-year public community college in large town.
Enrollment: 3,853 undergrads, 36% part-time. 790 full-time freshmen.
Selectivity: Open admission; but selective for some programs.

BASIC COSTS (2006-2007)
Tuition and fees: $1,992; out-of-district residents $2,992; out-of-state residents $6,544.
Per-credit charge: $123; out-of-district residents $186; out-of-state residents $408.
Room and board: $5,560.
Additional info: Tuition/fee waivers available for minority students.

FINANCIAL AID PICTURE (2004-2005)
Students with need: 57% of average financial aid package awarded as scholarships/grants, 43% awarded as loans/jobs. Need-based aid available for part-time students. Work study available weekends and for part-time students.
Students without need: No-need awards available for academics, art, athletics, leadership, minority status, music/drama, state/district residency.

FINANCIAL AID PROCEDURES
Forms required: FAFSA, institutional form.
Dates and Deadlines: Priority date 3/15; no closing date. Applicants notified on a rolling basis starting 4/1; must reply within 2 week(s) of notification.

CONTACT
Connie Dawson, Director of Financial Aid
1000 West Garden Avenue, Coeur d'Alene, ID 83814-2199
(208) 769-3368

Northwest Nazarene University
Nampa, Idaho
www.nnu.edu   Federal Code: 001624

4-year private university in small city, affiliated with Church of the Nazarene.
Enrollment: 1,128 undergrads, 6% part-time. 273 full-time freshmen.
Selectivity: Admits 50 to 75% of applicants.

BASIC COSTS (2006-2007)
Tuition and fees: $18,770.
Per-credit charge: $798.
Room and board: $5,010.

FINANCIAL AID PICTURE (2005-2006)
Students with need: Average financial aid package met 75% of need; average scholarship/grant was $2,524; average loan was $3,742. For part-time students, average financial aid package was $8,500.
Students without need: No-need awards available for academics, alumni affiliation, art, athletics, leadership, music/drama, religious affiliation, ROTC, state/district residency.
Scholarships offered: Merit scholarships for freshmen based primarily on cumulative high school GPA and ACT test scores.
Cumulative student debt: 94% of graduating class had student loans; average debt was $24,405.

FINANCIAL AID PROCEDURES
Forms required: FAFSA, institutional form.
Dates and Deadlines: Priority date 3/1; no closing date. Applicants notified on a rolling basis starting 4/1; must reply within 3 week(s) of notification.

CONTACT
Wes Maggard, Director of Financial Aid
623 Holly Street, Nampa, ID 83686-5897
(208) 467-8347

University of Idaho
Moscow, Idaho
www.uidaho.edu   Federal Code: 001626

4-year public university in large town.
Enrollment: 8,978 undergrads, 8% part-time. 1,666 full-time freshmen.
Selectivity: Admits over 75% of applicants.

BASIC COSTS (2005-2006)
Tuition and fees: $3,968; out-of-state residents $12,738.
Per-credit charge: $190; out-of-state residents $320.
Room and board: $5,888.
Additional info: Tuition/fee waivers available for minority students.

FINANCIAL AID PICTURE (2004-2005)
Students with need: Out of 1,303 full-time freshmen who applied for aid, 947 were judged to have need. Of these, 940 received aid, and 287 had their full need met. Average financial aid package met 80% of need; average scholarship/grant was $3,263; average loan was $3,337. For part-time students, average financial aid package was $7,497.
Students without need: 622 full-time freshmen who did not demonstrate need for aid received scholarships/grants; average award was $3,286. No-need awards available for academics, alumni affiliation, leadership, minority status, music/drama, ROTC, state/district residency.
Scholarships offered: 71 full-time freshmen received athletic scholarships; average amount $12,442.
Cumulative student debt: 69% of graduating class had student loans; average debt was $20,002.

FINANCIAL AID PROCEDURES
Forms required: FAFSA.
Dates and Deadlines: Priority date 2/15; no closing date. Applicants notified on a rolling basis starting 3/30; must reply within 3 week(s) of notification.

CONTACT
Dan Davenport, Director of Admissions and Financial Aid
PO Box 444264, Moscow, ID 83844-4264
(208) 885-6312

Illinois

American Academy of Art
Chicago, Illinois
www.aaart.edu   Federal Code: 001628

4-year for-profit visual arts college in very large city.
Enrollment: 410 undergrads.
Selectivity: Open admission; but selective for some programs.

BASIC COSTS (2005-2006)
Tuition and fees: $19,805.
Per-credit charge: $416.
Additional info: Fees vary by program.

FINANCIAL AID PICTURE
Students with need: Work study available nights.
Students without need: No-need awards available for art.

FINANCIAL AID PROCEDURES
Forms required: FAFSA, institutional form.
Dates and Deadlines: No deadline. Applicants notified on a rolling basis.
Transfers: Financial aid transcript from previously attended college required.

CONTACT
Ione Fitzgerald, Financial Aid Director
332 South Michigan Avenue, Suite 300, Chicago, IL 60604-4302
(312) 461-0600

Augustana College
Rock Island, Illinois
www.augustana.edu   Federal Code: 001633

4-year private liberal arts college in large city, affiliated with Evangelical Lutheran Church in America.
Enrollment: 2,364 undergrads, 1% part-time. 671 full-time freshmen.
Selectivity: Admits over 75% of applicants.

BASIC COSTS (2006-2007)
Tuition and fees: $24,924.
Per-credit charge: $1,020.
Room and board: $6,807.
Additional info: Tuition at time of enrollment locked for 4 years.

FINANCIAL AID PICTURE (2005-2006)
Students with need: Out of 579 full-time freshmen who applied for aid, 455 were judged to have need. Of these, 453 received aid, and 127 had their full need met. Average financial aid package met 88% of need; average scholarship/grant was $12,816; average loan was $3,801.
Students without need: 124 full-time freshmen who did not demonstrate need for aid received scholarships/grants; average award was $9,230. No-need awards available for academics, alumni affiliation, art, leadership, music/drama, religious affiliation.
Scholarships offered: Presidential Scholarship; $10,000 to full tuition; 28 ACT composite score (1260 combined SAT score in critical reading and mathematics) and rank in the top ten percent of high school class. Dean's Scholarship; $7,750-$9,000; 25 ACT composite score or above (1140 combined SAT score in critical reading and mathematics) and rank in the top 20 percent of their high school class. Founders Scholarship; $5,000-$7,500; must plan to enroll full-time at Augustana College. Transfer Scholarship; $3,000-$6,000; demonstrated outstanding academic performance in previous college studies.
Cumulative student debt: 71% of graduating class had student loans; average debt was $18,098.

FINANCIAL AID PROCEDURES
Forms required: FAFSA, institutional form.
Dates and Deadlines: Priority date 4/1; no closing date. Applicants notified on a rolling basis; must reply by 5/11.
Transfers: Priority date 5/1. Financial aid transcripts from previous institutions required.

CONTACT
Sue Standley, Director of Financial Aid
639 38th Street, Rock Island, IL 61201-2296
(309) 794-7207

Aurora University
Aurora, Illinois
www.aurora.edu   Federal Code: 001634

4-year private university in small city.
Enrollment: 1,897 undergrads, 11% part-time. 383 full-time freshmen.
Selectivity: Admits 50 to 75% of applicants.

BASIC COSTS (2006-2007)
Tuition and fees: $16,190.
Per-credit charge: $495.
Room and board: $6,814.

FINANCIAL AID PICTURE (2005-2006)
Students with need: Out of 383 full-time freshmen who applied for aid, 318 were judged to have need. Of these, 318 received aid, and 127 had their full need met. Average financial aid package met 90% of need; average scholarship/grant was $6,095; average loan was $2,455. For part-time students, average financial aid package was $8,674.
Students without need: 62 full-time freshmen who did not demonstrate need for aid received scholarships/grants; average award was $9,959. No-need awards available for academics, alumni affiliation, art, religious affiliation, state/district residency.
Scholarships offered: Board of Trustees scholarships: $8,000; James E. Crimi Presidential Scholarships: $6,500; Dean's scholarships: $6,000; Aurora University Opportunity Grants: $3,000-$5,000.
Cumulative student debt: 74% of graduating class had student loans; average debt was $18,374.

FINANCIAL AID PROCEDURES
Forms required: FAFSA.
Dates and Deadlines: Priority date 4/15; no closing date. Applicants notified on a rolling basis starting 3/1; must reply by 5/1 or within 3 week(s) of notification.

CONTACT
Heather Gutierrez, Dean of Student Financial Services
347 South Gladstone Avenue, Aurora, IL 60506-4892
(630) 844-5533

Benedictine University
Lisle, Illinois
www.ben.edu   Federal Code: 001767

4-year private university and liberal arts college in large town, affiliated with Roman Catholic Church.
Enrollment: 2,213 undergrads, 32% part-time. 302 full-time freshmen.
Selectivity: Admits over 75% of applicants.

BASIC COSTS (2005-2006)
Tuition and fees: $19,720.
Per-credit charge: $630.
Room and board: $6,770.
Additional info: Tuition/fee waivers available for adults.

FINANCIAL AID PICTURE (2005-2006)
Students with need: Out of 235 full-time freshmen who applied for aid, 234 were judged to have need. Of these, 232 received aid, and 100 had their full need met. Average financial aid package met 86% of need; average scholarship/grant was $6,118; average loan was $3,617. Need-based aid available for part-time students.
Students without need: 63 full-time freshmen who did not demonstrate need for aid received scholarships/grants; average award was $5,365. No-need awards available for academics, alumni affiliation, minority status, music/drama, ROTC.
Additional info: Need-based financial aid available to part-time students who are enrolled at least half-time.

FINANCIAL AID PROCEDURES
Forms required: FAFSA, institutional form.
Dates and Deadlines: Priority date 4/15; no closing date. Applicants notified on a rolling basis starting 2/15; must reply within 2 week(s) of notification.
Transfers: No deadline.

CONTACT
Diane Battistella, Associate Dean
5700 College Road, Lisle, IL 60532
(630) 829-6100

Black Hawk College
Moline, Illinois
www.bhc.edu   Federal Code: 001638

2-year public community college in large town.
Enrollment: 5,246 undergrads, 46% part-time. 670 full-time freshmen.
Selectivity: Open admission; but selective for some programs.

BASIC COSTS (2005-2006)
Tuition and fees: $2,070; out-of-district residents $4,410; out-of-state residents $7,980.
Per-credit charge: $62; out-of-district residents $140; out-of-state residents $259.
Additional info: Agreement with 5 contiguous Iowa counties for special tuition rate of $100 per credit plus required fees.

FINANCIAL AID PICTURE (2004-2005)
Students with need: Out of 390 full-time freshmen who applied for aid, 367 were judged to have need. Of these, 343 received aid, and 80 had their full need met. Average financial aid package met 69% of need; average scholarship/grant was $3,160; average loan was $1,740. For part-time students, average financial aid package was $2,400.
Students without need: 48 full-time freshmen who did not demonstrate need for aid received scholarships/grants; average award was $940. No-need awards available for academics, art, athletics, leadership, music/drama, state/district residency.
Scholarships offered: Merit: Scholarship program funded by college foundations and community donors; based on need and/or merit. Tuition awards; recent high school graduates who graduate in the top 105 of their class. **Athletic:** 55 full-time freshmen received athletic scholarships; average amount $2,339.
Cumulative student debt: 24% of graduating class had student loans; average debt was $4,094.
Additional info: Application deadlines for scholarships: 5/15 fall semester, 12/1 spring semester.

FINANCIAL AID PROCEDURES
Forms required: FAFSA.
Dates and Deadlines: Priority date 5/15; no closing date. Applicants notified on a rolling basis starting 5/1.

CONTACT
Robert Bopp, Director, Financial Aid
6600 34th Avenue, Moline, IL 61265-5899
(309) 796-5400

Blackburn College
Carlinville, Illinois
www.blackburn.edu   Federal Code: 001639

4-year private liberal arts college in small town, affiliated with Presbyterian Church (USA).
Enrollment: 598 undergrads, 2% part-time. 176 full-time freshmen.
Selectivity: Admits 50 to 75% of applicants.

BASIC COSTS (2006-2007)
Tuition and fees: $15,700.
Per-credit charge: $526.
Room and board: $3,880.

Additional info: All on-campus students participate in a work program which reduces net tuition costs.

FINANCIAL AID PICTURE (2004-2005)
Students with need: Out of 169 full-time freshmen who applied for aid, 152 were judged to have need. Of these, 152 received aid, and 66 had their full need met. Average financial aid package met 91% of need; average scholarship/grant was $8,802; average loan was $1,779. For part-time students, average financial aid package was $6,322.
Students without need: 21 full-time freshmen who did not demonstrate need for aid received scholarships/grants; average award was $4,969. No-need awards available for academics, state/district residency.
Cumulative student debt: 82% of graduating class had student loans; average debt was $15,553.
Additional info: Each resident student works 160 hours per semester.

FINANCIAL AID PROCEDURES
Forms required: FAFSA.
Dates and Deadlines: Priority date 4/1; no closing date. Applicants notified on a rolling basis starting 3/1; must reply within 4 week(s) of notification.

CONTACT
Jane Kelsey, Financial Aid Director
700 College Avenue, Carlinville, IL 62626

Blessing-Reiman College of Nursing
Quincy, Illinois
www.brcn.edu   Federal Code: 006214

4-year private nursing college in large town.
Enrollment: 211 undergrads, 9% part-time. 27 full-time freshmen.

BASIC COSTS (2005-2006)
Per-credit charge: $304.
Additional info: Partnered with Quincy University and Culver-Stockton College. Freshmen and sophomores pay partnering school's tuition rate: $17,800 at Quincy, $14,250 at Culver-Stockton.

FINANCIAL AID PICTURE (2004-2005)
Students with need: 35% of average financial aid package awarded as scholarships/grants, 65% awarded as loans/jobs. Need-based aid available for part-time students.
Cumulative student debt: 95% of graduating class had student loans; average debt was $20,000.
Additional info: Financial aid for freshmen and sophomores administered by Culver-Stockton College and Quincy University.

FINANCIAL AID PROCEDURES
Forms required: FAFSA.
Dates and Deadlines: Priority date 3/1; no closing date. Applicants notified on a rolling basis starting 7/1.

CONTACT
Sara Brehm, Financial Aid Officer
PO Box 7005, Quincy, IL 62305-7005
(217) 228-5520 ext. 6993

Bradley University
Peoria, Illinois
www.bradley.edu   Federal Code: 001641

4-year private university and engineering college in large city.
Enrollment: 5,343 undergrads, 5% part-time. 1,037 full-time freshmen.
Selectivity: Admits over 75% of applicants.

BASIC COSTS (2006-2007)
Tuition and fees: $20,078.
Room and board: $6,750.

FINANCIAL AID PICTURE (2004-2005)
Students with need: Out of 931 full-time freshmen who applied for aid, 679 were judged to have need. Of these, 679 received aid, and 347 had their full need met. Average financial aid package met 81.96% of need; average scholarship/grant was $10,648; average loan was $3,699. Need-based aid available for part-time students.
Students without need: 237 full-time freshmen who did not demonstrate need for aid received scholarships/grants; average award was $9,581. No-need awards available for academics, alumni affiliation, art, athletics, leadership, music/drama, state/district residency.
Scholarships offered: 15 full-time freshmen received athletic scholarships; average amount $11,381.
Cumulative student debt: 74% of graduating class had student loans; average debt was $15,079.

FINANCIAL AID PROCEDURES
Forms required: FAFSA.
Dates and Deadlines: Priority date 3/1; no closing date. Applicants notified on a rolling basis starting 2/15.

CONTACT
Dave Pardieck, Financial Assistance Director
1501 West Bradley Avenue, Peoria, IL 61625
(309) 677-3089

Carl Sandburg College
Galesburg, Illinois
www.sandburg.edu   Federal Code: 007265

2-year public community college in large town.
Enrollment: 3,400 undergrads.
Selectivity: Open admission; but selective for some programs.

BASIC COSTS (2005-2006)
Tuition and fees: $2,595; out-of-district residents $3,915; out-of-state residents $4,335.
Per-credit charge: $72; out-of-district residents $116; out-of-state residents $130.

FINANCIAL AID PICTURE
Students with need: Need-based aid available for full-time students.
Students without need: No-need awards available for academics, art, athletics.

FINANCIAL AID PROCEDURES
Forms required: FAFSA, institutional form.
Dates and Deadlines: Priority date 5/1; no closing date. Applicants notified on a rolling basis starting 6/15; must reply within 2 week(s) of notification.

CONTACT
Lisa Hanson, Director of Financial Aid
2400 Tom L. Wilson Boulevard, Galesburg, IL 61401
(309) 341-5283

City Colleges of Chicago: Harold Washington College
Chicago, Illinois
www.ccc.edu   Federal Code: 001652

2-year public community college in very large city.
Enrollment: 6,830 undergrads.
Selectivity: Open admission; but selective for some programs.

BASIC COSTS (2005-2006)
Tuition and fees: $2,260; out-of-district residents $5,130; out-of-state residents $8,236.
Per-credit charge: $67; out-of-district residents $163; out-of-state residents $266.

FINANCIAL AID PICTURE
Students with need: Need-based aid available for full-time and part-time students. Work study available nights.
Students without need: This college only awards aid to students with need.

FINANCIAL AID PROCEDURES
Forms required: FAFSA.
Dates and Deadlines: Priority date 5/1; closing date 6/30. Applicants notified on a rolling basis starting 7/1; must reply within 2 week(s) of notification.

CONTACT
Francois Hasouk, Director of Financial Aid
30 East Lake Street, Chicago, IL 60601
(312) 553-6041

City Colleges of Chicago: Harry S. Truman College
Chicago, Illinois
www.ccc.edu   Federal Code: 001648

2-year public community college in very large city.
Enrollment: 4,884 undergrads.
Selectivity: Open admission; but selective for some programs.

BASIC COSTS (2005-2006)
Tuition and fees: $2,260; out-of-district residents $5,130; out-of-state residents $8,236.
Per-credit charge: $67; out-of-district residents $163; out-of-state residents $266.

FINANCIAL AID PICTURE
Students with need: Need-based aid available for full-time and part-time students. Work study available nights, weekends, and for part-time students.
Students without need: This college only awards aid to students with need.

FINANCIAL AID PROCEDURES
Forms required: FAFSA.
Dates and Deadlines: No deadline. Applicants notified on a rolling basis starting 7/1; must reply within 3 week(s) of notification.

CONTACT
1145 West Wilson Avenue, Chicago, IL 60640
(773) 907-4810

City Colleges of Chicago: Kennedy-King College
Chicago, Illinois
www.ccc.edu   Federal Code: 001654

2-year public community college in very large city.
Enrollment: 3,355 undergrads.
Selectivity: Open admission.

BASIC COSTS (2005-2006)
Tuition and fees: $2,260; out-of-district residents $5,130; out-of-state residents $8,236.
Per-credit charge: $67; out-of-district residents $163; out-of-state residents $266.

Additional info: Lab fees for technical and vocational courses.

FINANCIAL AID PICTURE
Students with need: Need-based aid available for full-time and part-time students.
Students without need: This college only awards aid to students with need.

FINANCIAL AID PROCEDURES
Forms required: FAFSA.
Dates and Deadlines: Priority date 8/1; no closing date. Applicants notified on a rolling basis starting 8/15; must reply within 2 week(s) of notification.

CONTACT
Alicia Williams, Financial Aid Supervisor
6800 South Wentworth Avenue, Chicago, IL 60621
(773) 602-5133

City Colleges of Chicago: Malcolm X College
Chicago, Illinois
malcolmx.ccc.edu   Federal Code: 001650

2-year public community and junior college in very large city.
Enrollment: 3,830 undergrads.
Selectivity: Open admission; but selective for some programs.

BASIC COSTS (2005-2006)
Tuition and fees: $2,260; out-of-district residents $5,130; out-of-state residents $8,236.
Per-credit charge: $67; out-of-district residents $163; out-of-state residents $266.
Additional info: Some courses require a $20 lab fee.

FINANCIAL AID PICTURE
Students with need: Need-based aid available for full-time and part-time students. Work study available nights, weekends, and for part-time students.
Students without need: This college only awards aid to students with need.

FINANCIAL AID PROCEDURES
Forms required: FAFSA, institutional form.
Dates and Deadlines: Priority date 7/1; no closing date. Applicants notified on a rolling basis starting 7/1; must reply within 2 week(s) of notification.

CONTACT
Patricia Burke, Director, Financial Aid
1900 West Van Buren Street, Chicago, IL 60612
(312) 850-7146

City Colleges of Chicago: Olive-Harvey College
Chicago, Illinois
www.ccc.edu   Federal Code: 009767

2-year public community college in very large city.
Enrollment: 2,718 undergrads.
Selectivity: Open admission; but selective for some programs.

BASIC COSTS (2005-2006)
Tuition and fees: $2,260; out-of-district residents $5,130; out-of-state residents $8,236.
Per-credit charge: $67; out-of-district residents $163; out-of-state residents $266.

FINANCIAL AID PICTURE
Students with need: Need-based aid available for full-time and part-time students.

FINANCIAL AID PROCEDURES
Forms required: FAFSA.
Dates and Deadlines: Priority date 8/15; no closing date. Applicants notified on a rolling basis; must reply within 3 week(s) of notification.

CONTACT
Michael Shields, Director of Financial Aid
10001 South Woodlawn Avenue, Chicago, IL 60628
(773) 291-6391

City Colleges of Chicago: Richard J. Daley College
Chicago, Illinois
daley.ccc.edu   Federal Code: 001649

2-year public community college in very large city.
Enrollment: 4,566 undergrads.
Selectivity: Open admission; but selective for some programs.

BASIC COSTS (2005-2006)
Tuition and fees: $2,260; out-of-district residents $5,130; out-of-state residents $8,236.
Per-credit charge: $67; out-of-district residents $163; out-of-state residents $266.

FINANCIAL AID PICTURE
Students with need: Need-based aid available for full-time students.

FINANCIAL AID PROCEDURES
Forms required: FAFSA.
Dates and Deadlines: No deadline. Applicants notified on a rolling basis.
Transfers: College workstudy jobs and Federal Supplemental Educational Opportunity Grant (SEOG) may not be available to transfers.

CONTACT
Thelma Barnes, Dean of Student Services
7500 South Pulaski Road, Chicago, IL 60652
(773) 838-7579

City Colleges of Chicago: Wright College
Chicago, Illinois
www.ccc.edu   Federal Code: 001655

2-year public community college in very large city.
Enrollment: 6,798 undergrads.
Selectivity: Open admission.

BASIC COSTS (2005-2006)
Tuition and fees: $2,260; out-of-district residents $5,130; out-of-state residents $8,236.
Per-credit charge: $67; out-of-district residents $163; out-of-state residents $266.
Additional info: Tuition at time of enrollment locked for 2 years.

FINANCIAL AID PICTURE
Students with need: Need-based aid available for full-time and part-time students. Work study available nights, weekends, and for part-time students.

FINANCIAL AID PROCEDURES
Forms required: FAFSA, institutional form.
Dates and Deadlines: Priority date 6/1; no closing date. Applicants notified on a rolling basis starting 7/15.

CONTACT
Marco Sepulveda, Financial Aid Director
4300 N. Narragansett Avenue, Chicago, IL 60634-4276
(773) 481-8100

College of DuPage
Glen Ellyn, Illinois
www.cod.edu   Federal Code: 006656

2-year public community college in large town.
Enrollment: 22,582 undergrads, 63% part-time. 2,356 full-time freshmen.
Selectivity: Open admission; but selective for some programs.

BASIC COSTS (2006-2007)
Tuition and fees: $2,881; out-of-district residents $6,691; out-of-state residents $8,401.
Per-credit charge: $75; out-of-district residents $231; out-of-state residents $265.

FINANCIAL AID PICTURE (2004-2005)
Students with need: Out of 763 full-time freshmen who applied for aid, 553 were judged to have need. Of these, 485 received aid, and 52 had their full need met. Average financial aid package met 56% of need; average scholarship/grant was $3,477; average loan was $2,132. For part-time students, average financial aid package was $4,746.
Students without need: 101 full-time freshmen who did not demonstrate need for aid received scholarships/grants; average award was $1,103. No-need awards available for academics, art, leadership, minority status, music/drama, state/district residency.
Cumulative student debt: 5% of graduating class had student loans; average debt was $8,124.

FINANCIAL AID PROCEDURES
Forms required: FAFSA, institutional form.
Dates and Deadlines: Priority date 4/8; no closing date. Applicants notified on a rolling basis starting 6/1; must reply within 2 week(s) of notification.
Transfers: No deadline. Applicants notified on a rolling basis; must reply within 2 week(s) of notification. Must have financial aid application on file indicating previous institutions attended.

CONTACT
Mark Holysz, Director of Student Financial Aid
425 Fawell Boulevard, Glen Ellyn, IL 60137-6599
(630) 942-2251

College of Lake County
Grayslake, Illinois
www.clcillinois.edu   Federal Code: 007694

2-year public community college in large town.
Enrollment: 12,431 undergrads, 66% part-time. 1,192 full-time freshmen.
Selectivity: Admits over 75% of applicants.

BASIC COSTS (2006-2007)
Tuition and fees: $2,400; out-of-district residents $6,150; out-of-state residents $8,280.
Per-credit charge: $71; out-of-district residents $196; out-of-state residents $267.
Additional info: Tuition/fee waivers available for minority students.

FINANCIAL AID PICTURE (2004-2005)
Students with need: 88% of average financial aid package awarded as scholarships/grants, 12% awarded as loans/jobs. Need-based aid available for part-time students. Work study available nights.
Students without need: No-need awards available for academics, alumni affiliation, art, athletics, leadership, minority status, music/drama.
Scholarships offered: Academic Achievement Scholarship: based on GPA and student essay; tuition and fees.

FINANCIAL AID PROCEDURES
Forms required: FAFSA.
Dates and Deadlines: Priority date 6/5; no closing date. Applicants notified on a rolling basis starting 6/15; must reply within 2 week(s) of notification.

CONTACT
Augustine Dominguez, Chief Financial Aid Officer.
19351 West Washington Street, Grayslake, IL 60030-1198
(847) 543-2062

College of Office Technology
Chicago, Illinois
www.cot.edu   Federal Code: 017378

2-year for-profit business college in very large city.
Enrollment: 388 undergrads.
Selectivity: Open admission.

BASIC COSTS (2005-2006)
Tuition and fees: $15,705.

FINANCIAL AID PICTURE (2004-2005)
Students with need: 38% of average financial aid package awarded as scholarships/grants, 62% awarded as loans/jobs. Need-based aid available for part-time students.
Students without need: This college only awards aid to students with need.

FINANCIAL AID PROCEDURES
Forms required: FAFSA.
Dates and Deadlines: No deadline. Applicants notified on a rolling basis.

CONTACT
Paula Terronez, Educational Operations and Financial Aid Director
1520 West Division Street, Chicago, IL 60622-3312
(773) 278-0042

Columbia College Chicago
Chicago, Illinois
www.colum.edu   Federal Code: 001665

4-year private visual arts and liberal arts college in very large city.
Enrollment: 10,039 undergrads, 13% part-time. 1,757 full-time freshmen.
Selectivity: Open admission; but selective for some programs.

BASIC COSTS (2006-2007)
Tuition and fees: $16,788.
Per-credit charge: $565.
Room and board: $10,900.

FINANCIAL AID PICTURE (2004-2005)
Students with need: 34% of average financial aid package awarded as scholarships/grants, 66% awarded as loans/jobs. Need-based aid available for part-time students.
Students without need: No-need awards available for academics, art, leadership, music/drama, state/district residency.

FINANCIAL AID PROCEDURES
Forms required: FAFSA, institutional form.
Dates and Deadlines: Priority date 7/1; no closing date. Applicants notified on a rolling basis.

CONTACT
Timothy Bauhs, Executive Director of Student Financial Services
600 South Michigan Avenue, Chicago, IL 60605-1996
(866) 705-0200

Concordia University
River Forest, Illinois
www.curf.edu   Federal Code: 001666

4-year private university and teachers college in large town, affiliated with Lutheran Church - Missouri Synod.
Enrollment: 961 undergrads.
Selectivity: Admits 50 to 75% of applicants.
BASIC COSTS (2006-2007)
Tuition and fees: $20,400.
Per-credit charge: $610.
Room and board: $6,600.
FINANCIAL AID PICTURE
Students with need: Need-based aid available for full-time students.
Students without need: No-need awards available for academics, alumni affiliation, minority status, music/drama.
FINANCIAL AID PROCEDURES
Forms required: FAFSA, institutional form.
Dates and Deadlines: Closing date 4/1. Applicants notified on a rolling basis; must reply within 4 week(s) of notification.
Transfers: No deadline.
CONTACT
Deborah Ness, Director of Student Financial Planning
7400 Augusta Street, River Forest, IL 60305-1499
(708) 209-3113

Danville Area Community College
Danville, Illinois
www.dacc.cc.il.us   Federal Code: 001669

2-year public community college in large town.
Enrollment: 2,575 undergrads.
Selectivity: Open admission.
BASIC COSTS (2005-2006)
Tuition and fees: $1,920; out-of-state residents $4,680.
Per-credit charge: $58; out-of-state residents $150.
FINANCIAL AID PICTURE (2004-2005)
Students with need: 96% of average financial aid package awarded as scholarships/grants, 4% awarded as loans/jobs. Need-based aid available for part-time students. Work study available nights, weekends, and for part-time students.
Students without need: No-need awards available for academics, athletics, minority status.
FINANCIAL AID PROCEDURES
Forms required: FAFSA, institutional form.
Dates and Deadlines: Priority date 7/1; no closing date. Applicants notified on a rolling basis starting 6/1.
Transfers: NSLDS reviewed before aid disbursed.
CONTACT
Janet Ingargiola, Director of Financial Aid
2000 East Main Street, Danville, IL 61832
(217) 443-8891

DePaul University
Chicago, Illinois
www.depaul.edu   Federal Code: 001671

4-year private university in very large city, affiliated with Roman Catholic Church.
Enrollment: 14,277 undergrads, 21% part-time. 2,392 full-time freshmen.
Selectivity: Admits 50 to 75% of applicants.
BASIC COSTS (2005-2006)
Tuition and fees: $21,100.
Per-credit charge: $384.
Room and board: $9,656.
FINANCIAL AID PICTURE (2005-2006)
Students with need: Out of 1,826 full-time freshmen who applied for aid, 1,509 were judged to have need. Of these, 1,442 received aid, and 98 had their full need met. Average financial aid package met 69% of need; average scholarship/grant was $11,853; average loan was $3,248. For part-time students, average financial aid package was $9,717.
Students without need: 267 full-time freshmen who did not demonstrate need for aid received scholarships/grants; average award was $8,899. No-need awards available for academics, art, athletics, leadership, minority status, music/drama.
Scholarships offered: Merit: Various scholarships: based on top 10% of class, 1100 SAT (exclusive of writing) or 26 ACT, and active in student/community organizations. **Athletic:** 41 full-time freshmen received athletic scholarships; average amount $16,882.
Cumulative student debt: 65% of graduating class had student loans; average debt was $21,061.
FINANCIAL AID PROCEDURES
Forms required: FAFSA.
Dates and Deadlines: Closing date 5/1. Applicants notified on a rolling basis starting 2/15; must reply by 5/1 or within 4 week(s) of notification.
Transfers: Closing date 4/1. Applicants notified by 6/1. 5 different scholarships awarded to fall incoming transfer students who have been admitted, and have submitted scholarship application, by April 1. Scholarships range from $3,000-$7,000, and vary based on competitiveness of pool and student's qualifications.
CONTACT
Paula Luff, Director of Financial Aid
One East Jackson Boulevard, Chicago, IL 60604-2287
(312) 362-8091

DeVry University: Addison
Addison, Illinois
www.dpg.devry.edu   Federal Code: 016219

4-year for-profit university in large town.
Enrollment: 1,574 undergrads, 28% part-time. 605 full-time freshmen.
BASIC COSTS (2005-2006)
Tuition and fees: $12,240.
Per-credit charge: $445.
FINANCIAL AID PICTURE (2004-2005)
Students with need: Out of 333 full-time freshmen who applied for aid, 297 were judged to have need. Of these, 293 received aid, and 25 had their full need met. Average financial aid package met 48% of need; average scholarship/grant was $6,193; average loan was $4,825. For part-time students, average financial aid package was $6,906.
Students without need: This college only awards aid to students with need.

FINANCIAL AID PROCEDURES
Forms required: FAFSA.
Dates and Deadlines: No deadline. Applicants notified on a rolling basis.

CONTACT
Sajel Anin, Director of Student Finance
1221 North Swift Road, Addison, IL 60101-6106
(630) 953-1300

DeVry University: Chicago
Chicago, Illinois
www.chi.devry.edu   Federal Code: 010727

4-year for-profit university in very large city.
Enrollment: 2,042 undergrads, 37% part-time. 570 full-time freshmen.

BASIC COSTS (2005-2006)
Tuition and fees: $12,240.
Per-credit charge: $445.

FINANCIAL AID PICTURE (2004-2005)
Students with need: Out of 279 full-time freshmen who applied for aid, 268 were judged to have need. Of these, 262 received aid, and 6 had their full need met. Average financial aid package met 48% of need; average scholarship/grant was $7,316; average loan was $4,169. For part-time students, average financial aid package was $8,579.
Students without need: This college only awards aid to students with need.

FINANCIAL AID PROCEDURES
Forms required: FAFSA.
Dates and Deadlines: No deadline. Applicants notified on a rolling basis.

CONTACT
Milena Dobrina, Director of Financial Aid
3300 North Campbell Avenue, Chicago, IL 60618-5994
(773) 929-8509

DeVry University: Tinley Park
Tinley Park, Illinois
www.tp.devry.edu   Federal Code: 022966

4-year for-profit university in large town.
Enrollment: 1,047 undergrads, 33% part-time. 277 full-time freshmen.

BASIC COSTS (2005-2006)
Tuition and fees: $12,240.
Per-credit charge: $445.

FINANCIAL AID PICTURE (2004-2005)
Students with need: Out of 179 full-time freshmen who applied for aid, 162 were judged to have need. Of these, 158 received aid, and 17 had their full need met. Average financial aid package met 48% of need; average scholarship/grant was $6,298; average loan was $4,681. For part-time students, average financial aid package was $7,578.
Students without need: This college only awards aid to students with need.

FINANCIAL AID PROCEDURES
Forms required: FAFSA.
Dates and Deadlines: No deadline. Applicants notified on a rolling basis.

CONTACT
Sejal Amin, Director of Student Finance
18624 West Creek Drive, Tinley Park, IL 60477-6243
(708) 342-3219

Dominican University
River Forest, Illinois
www.dom.edu   Federal Code: 001750

4-year private university and liberal arts college in large town, affiliated with Roman Catholic Church.
Enrollment: 1,273 undergrads, 11% part-time. 267 full-time freshmen.
Selectivity: Admits over 75% of applicants.

BASIC COSTS (2006-2007)
Tuition and fees: $21,250.
Per-credit charge: $705.
Room and board: $6,620.

FINANCIAL AID PICTURE (2005-2006)
Students with need: 68% of average financial aid package awarded as scholarships/grants, 32% awarded as loans/jobs. Need-based aid available for part-time students. Work study available nights, weekends, and for part-time students.
Students without need: No-need awards available for academics, alumni affiliation, leadership.
Scholarships offered: Presidential Scholarships; $10,000. Honor Scholarships; $8,500. Achievement Scholarships; $6,500. All based on ACT/SAT scores and class rank. Ida Brechtel Scholarships; $5,000 up to full tuition; for students majoring in chemistry or biology/chemistry.

FINANCIAL AID PROCEDURES
Forms required: FAFSA.
Dates and Deadlines: Priority date 6/1; no closing date. Applicants notified on a rolling basis starting 2/15; must reply within 2 week(s) of notification.
Transfers: Merit scholarships available to full-time students with GPA of 3.3 from previous institution. Phi Theta Kappa scholarships available to PTK members.

CONTACT
Michael Shields, Director of Financial Aid
7900 West Division Street, River Forest, IL 60305-1099
(708) 524-6809

East-West University
Chicago, Illinois
www.eastwest.edu   Federal Code: 015310

4-year private university in very large city.
Enrollment: 1,035 undergrads.
Selectivity: Open admission.

BASIC COSTS (2006-2007)
Tuition and fees: $12,045.
Per-credit charge: $385.

FINANCIAL AID PICTURE
Students with need: Need-based aid available for full-time and part-time students.
Students without need: No-need awards available for academics.
Additional info: Foreign students eligible for institutional scholarship.

FINANCIAL AID PROCEDURES
Forms required: FAFSA.
Dates and Deadlines: No deadline. Applicants notified on a rolling basis starting 1/4; must reply within 4 week(s) of notification.
Transfers: Closing date 4/1.

CONTACT
Elizabeth Guzman, Director of Financial Aid
816 South Michigan Avenue, Chicago, IL 60605
(312) 939-0111

Eastern Illinois University
Charleston, Illinois
www.eiu.edu   Federal Code: 001674

4-year public university and teachers college in large town.
Enrollment: 10,243 undergrads, 11% part-time. 1,708 full-time freshmen.
Selectivity: Admits over 75% of applicants.

BASIC COSTS (2005-2006)
Tuition and fees: $6,373; out-of-state residents $15,631.
Per-credit charge: $154; out-of-state residents $463.
Room and board: $6,196.
Additional info: New students will have a guaranteed tuition rate for 4 years. Tuition at time of enrollment locked for 4 years.

FINANCIAL AID PICTURE (2005-2006)
Students with need: Out of 1,306 full-time freshmen who applied for aid, 944 were judged to have need. Of these, 837 received aid, and 606 had their full need met. For part-time students, average financial aid package was $9,983.
Students without need: 86 full-time freshmen who did not demonstrate need for aid received scholarships/grants; average award was $5,967. No-need awards available for academics, art, athletics, music/drama.
Scholarships offered: 4 full-time freshmen received athletic scholarships; average amount $5,198.
Cumulative student debt: 63% of graduating class had student loans; average debt was $15,538.

FINANCIAL AID PROCEDURES
Forms required: FAFSA.
Dates and Deadlines: Priority date 3/1; no closing date. Applicants notified on a rolling basis starting 3/1; must reply within 2 week(s) of notification.

CONTACT
Jone Zieren, Director of Financial Aid
600 Lincoln Avenue, Charleston, IL 61920-3099
(217) 581-3714

Elgin Community College
Elgin, Illinois
www.elgin.edu   Federal Code: 001675

2-year public community college in small city.
Enrollment: 8,315 undergrads, 61% part-time. 642 full-time freshmen.
Selectivity: Open admission; but selective for some programs.

BASIC COSTS (2005-2006)
Tuition and fees: $2,260; out-of-district residents $7,676; out-of-state residents $9,957.
Per-credit charge: $75; out-of-district residents $256; out-of-state residents $332.

FINANCIAL AID PICTURE
Students with need: Need-based aid available for full-time and part-time students. Work study available nights, weekends, and for part-time students.
Students without need: No-need awards available for academics, alumni affiliation, art, athletics, job skills, leadership, minority status, music/drama, religious affiliation, ROTC, state/district residency.

FINANCIAL AID PROCEDURES
Forms required: FAFSA, institutional form.
Dates and Deadlines: Priority date 5/15; no closing date. Applicants notified on a rolling basis starting 4/7; must reply within 3 week(s) of notification.

CONTACT
Robert Laws, Associate Dean of Financial Aid and Records
1700 Spartan Drive, Elgin, IL 60123-7193
(847) 214-7360

Elmhurst College
Elmhurst, Illinois
www.elmhurst.edu   Federal Code: 001676

4-year private liberal arts college in large town, affiliated with United Church of Christ.
Enrollment: 2,601 undergrads, 10% part-time. 466 full-time freshmen.
Selectivity: Admits over 75% of applicants.

BASIC COSTS (2006-2007)
Tuition and fees: $23,260.
Per-credit charge: $657.
Room and board: $7,730.

FINANCIAL AID PICTURE (2005-2006)
Students with need: Out of 395 full-time freshmen who applied for aid, 325 were judged to have need. Of these, 325 received aid, and 126 had their full need met. Average financial aid package met 93% of need; average scholarship/grant was $14,284; average loan was $3,500. For part-time students, average financial aid package was $10,338.
Students without need: 91 full-time freshmen who did not demonstrate need for aid received scholarships/grants; average award was $9,976. No-need awards available for academics, art, minority status, music/drama, religious affiliation.
Scholarships offered: Presidential Scholarship, $11,000 - $16,000; 115 awarded. Dean's Scholarship, $7,000 - $11,000, 99 awarded. Founder's Scholarship, $4,000 - $7,000, 46 awarded. Students qualify through a combination of class rank, test scores, and GPA; must be admitted to the college by 1/15 to be considered.
Cumulative student debt: 75% of graduating class had student loans; average debt was $16,080.

FINANCIAL AID PROCEDURES
Forms required: FAFSA.
Dates and Deadlines: Priority date 4/15; no closing date. Applicants notified on a rolling basis starting 3/1; must reply within 3 week(s) of notification.

CONTACT
Ruth Pusich, Director of Financial Aid
190 South Prospect Avenue, Elmhurst, IL 60126-3296
(630) 617-3075

Eureka College
Eureka, Illinois
www.eureka.edu   Federal Code: 001678

4-year private liberal arts college in small town, affiliated with Christian Church (Disciples of Christ).
Enrollment: 538 undergrads. 138 full-time freshmen.

BASIC COSTS (2006-2007)
Tuition and fees: $14,230.
Per-credit charge: $395.
Room and board: $6,220.

FINANCIAL AID PICTURE (2005-2006)
Students with need: Average financial aid package met 80% of need; average scholarship/grant was $11,896; average loan was $1,906. Need-based aid available for part-time students.
Students without need: No-need awards available for academics, alumni affiliation, art, leadership, music/drama, religious affiliation.

Scholarships offered: Reagan Fellows Program: full tuition; 5 awarded. Sandifer Mentorships: fully paid mentorship anywhere in the world at end of sophomore year; all freshmen eligible. Eureka College Ministry Fellowship: full tuition scholarships; 2 available each year.
Cumulative student debt: 89% of graduating class had student loans; average debt was $15,352.

FINANCIAL AID PROCEDURES
Forms required: FAFSA.
Dates and Deadlines: Priority date 4/15; no closing date. Applicants notified on a rolling basis starting 2/15; must reply by 5/1 or within 3 week(s) of notification.
Transfers: No deadline. Applicants notified on a rolling basis; must reply within 2 week(s) of notification.

CONTACT
Ellen Rigsby, Director of Financial Aid
300 East College Avenue, Eureka, IL 61530-1500
(309) 467-6311

Governors State University
University Park, Illinois
www.govst.edu   Federal Code: 009145

Upper-division public university in large town.
Enrollment: 2,632 undergrads, 67% part-time.
Selectivity: Open admission; but selective for some programs.

BASIC COSTS (2006-2007)
Tuition and fees: $5,230; out-of-state residents $14,530.
Per-credit charge: $155; out-of-state residents $465.
Additional info: Tuition/fee waivers available for minority students.

FINANCIAL AID PICTURE
Students with need: Need-based aid available for full-time and part-time students. Work study available nights, weekends, and for part-time students.
Students without need: No-need awards available for academics, ROTC, state/district residency.

FINANCIAL AID PROCEDURES
Forms required: FAFSA.
Dates and Deadlines: Priority date 5/1; closing date 10/1. Applicants notified on a rolling basis.
Transfers: No aid for second bachelor's or second master's degree.

CONTACT
Freda Whisenton-Comer, Office of Financial Aid
One University Parkway, University Park, IL 60466
(708) 534-4480

Greenville College
Greenville, Illinois
www.greenville.edu   Federal Code: 001684

4-year private liberal arts college in small town, affiliated with Free Methodist Church of North America.
Enrollment: 1,197 undergrads, 2% part-time. 252 full-time freshmen.
Selectivity: Admits over 75% of applicants.

BASIC COSTS (2006-2007)
Tuition and fees: $17,932.
Per-credit charge: $375.
Room and board: $6,136.
Additional info: Per-credit-hour charges vary between $375 and $750 according to number of credits taken.

FINANCIAL AID PICTURE (2004-2005)
Students with need: Average financial aid package met 81% of need; average scholarship/grant was $10,483; average loan was $3,385. For part-time students, average financial aid package was $7,250.
Students without need: No-need awards available for academics, alumni affiliation, art, leadership, minority status, music/drama, religious affiliation, state/district residency.
Scholarships offered: President's Scholarships; $8,000; requiring cumulative GPA of 3.0, ACT of 27 or SAT of 1210, and leadership qualities. Dean's Scholarship; $6,000; for GPA of 3.0, ACT of 22 or SAT of 1020, and leadership qualities. Leadership Scholarships; $500-$4,000; for GPA of 2.5, ACT of 18 or SAT 860, and leadership qualities. (All SAT scores are exclusive of Writing.).
Cumulative student debt: 86% of graduating class had student loans; average debt was $17,897.

FINANCIAL AID PROCEDURES
Forms required: FAFSA.
Dates and Deadlines: Priority date 5/1; no closing date. Applicants notified on a rolling basis starting 3/15; must reply within 3 week(s) of notification.
Transfers: No deadline. Applicants notified on a rolling basis; must reply within 3 week(s) of notification.

CONTACT
Karl Somerville, Director of Financial Aid
315 East College Avenue, Greenville, IL 62246-0159
(618) 664-7111

Harrington College of Design
Chicago, Illinois
www.harringtoncollege.com   Federal Code: 013601

4-year for-profit visual arts college in very large city.
Enrollment: 1,563 undergrads.
Selectivity: Open admission.

BASIC COSTS (2006-2007)
Tuition and fees: $17,960.
Per-credit charge: $575.
Additional info: Required fees vary from $250 to $500, depending on program.

FINANCIAL AID PICTURE
Students with need: Need-based aid available for full-time and part-time students.
Students without need: This college only awards aid to students with need.

FINANCIAL AID PROCEDURES
Forms required: FAFSA.
Dates and Deadlines: Closing date 7/15. Applicants notified on a rolling basis; must reply within 2 week(s) of notification.
Transfers: No deadline.

CONTACT
Renee Darosky, Director of Financial Aid
200 West Madison Avenue, Chicago, IL 60606
(877) 939-4975

Heartland Community College
Normal, Illinois
www.heartland.edu   Federal Code: 030838

2-year public community college in small city.
Enrollment: 4,628 undergrads, 58% part-time. 1,221 full-time freshmen.
Selectivity: Open admission; but selective for some programs.

BASIC COSTS (2005-2006)
Tuition and fees: $1,890; out-of-district residents $3,780; out-of-state residents $5,670.
Per-credit charge: $63; out-of-district residents $126; out-of-state residents $189.

FINANCIAL AID PICTURE
Students with need: Need-based aid available for full-time and part-time students. Work study available nights, weekends, and for part-time students.
Students without need: This college only awards aid to students with need.

FINANCIAL AID PROCEDURES
Forms required: FAFSA, institutional form.
Dates and Deadlines: No deadline.

CONTACT
Cheryl Schaffer, Financial Aid Director
1500 West Raab Road, Normal, IL 61761
(309) 268-8020

Highland Community College
Freeport, Illinois
www.highland.edu   Federal Code: 001681

2-year public community college in large town.
Enrollment: 1,899 undergrads, 44% part-time. 362 full-time freshmen.
Selectivity: Open admission; but selective for some programs.

BASIC COSTS (2005-2006)
Tuition and fees: $2,010; out-of-district residents $3,480; out-of-state residents $3,480.
Per-credit charge: $62; out-of-district residents $111; out-of-state residents $111.

FINANCIAL AID PICTURE (2004-2005)
Students with need: 81% of average financial aid package awarded as scholarships/grants, 19% awarded as loans/jobs. Need-based aid available for part-time students. Work study available nights.
Students without need: No-need awards available for academics, athletics.

FINANCIAL AID PROCEDURES
Forms required: FAFSA, institutional form.
Dates and Deadlines: No deadline. Applicants notified on a rolling basis starting 8/1; must reply within 2 week(s) of notification.
Transfers: No deadline. Applicants notified on a rolling basis starting 4/1.

CONTACT
2998 West Pearl City Road, Freeport, IL 61032-9341
(815) 599-3448

Illinois College
Jacksonville, Illinois
www.ic.edu   Federal Code: 001688

4-year private liberal arts college in large town; affiliated with United Church of Christ and Presbyterian Church (USA).
Enrollment: 1,019 undergrads, 1% part-time. 256 full-time freshmen.
Selectivity: Admits 50 to 75% of applicants.

BASIC COSTS (2005-2006)
Tuition and fees: $15,500.
Per-credit charge: $650.
Room and board: $6,400.
Additional info: Tuition at time of enrollment locked for 4 years; tuition/fee waivers available for minority students.

FINANCIAL AID PICTURE (2005-2006)
Students with need: Out of 241 full-time freshmen who applied for aid, 197 were judged to have need. Of these, 197 received aid, and 72 had their full need met. Average financial aid package met 82% of need; average scholarship/grant was $6,176; average loan was $3,556. For part-time students, average financial aid package was $3,570.
Students without need: 48 full-time freshmen who did not demonstrate need for aid received scholarships/grants; average award was $6,489. No-need awards available for academics, art, leadership, minority status, music/drama.
Cumulative student debt: 95% of graduating class had student loans; average debt was $11,105.

FINANCIAL AID PROCEDURES
Forms required: FAFSA.
Dates and Deadlines: Priority date 3/1; no closing date. Applicants notified on a rolling basis starting 3/1; must reply within 2 week(s) of notification.
Transfers: Applicants notified on a rolling basis starting 6/1; must reply within 2 week(s) of notification. College transfer scholarship available with 12 transferable credit hours and minimum 3.0 GPA.

CONTACT
Katherine Taylor, Director of Financial Aid
1101 West College Avenue, Jacksonville, IL 62650
(217) 245-3035

Illinois Eastern Community Colleges: Frontier Community College
Fairfield, Illinois
www.iecc.edu/fcc   Federal Code: 014090

2-year public community college in small town.
Enrollment: 1,169 undergrads.
Selectivity: Open admission.

BASIC COSTS (2005-2006)
Tuition and fees: $1,680; out-of-district residents $5,629; out-of-state residents $6,947.
Per-credit charge: $53; out-of-district residents $185; out-of-state residents $229.
Additional info: Students in qualifying Indiana districts pay per-credit-hour rate of $96.

FINANCIAL AID PICTURE
Students with need: Need-based aid available for full-time and part-time students.
Students without need: No-need awards available for academics, state/district residency.

FINANCIAL AID PROCEDURES
Forms required: FAFSA, institutional form.
Dates and Deadlines: No deadline. Applicants notified on a rolling basis starting 8/1; must reply within 2 week(s) of notification.

CONTACT
Carroll Hilliard, Director of Financial Assistance and Community Services
Frontier Drive, Fairfield, IL 62837-9801
(618) 842-3711

Illinois Eastern Community Colleges: Lincoln Trail College
Robinson, Illinois
www.iecc.edu/ltc   Federal Code: 009786

2-year public community college in small town.
Enrollment: 1,002 undergrads.
Selectivity: Open admission.

BASIC COSTS (2005-2006)
Tuition and fees: $1,680; out-of-district residents $5,629; out-of-state residents $6,947.
Per-credit charge: $53; out-of-district residents $185; out-of-state residents $229.
Additional info: Students in qualifying Indiana districts pay per-credit-hour rate of $96.

FINANCIAL AID PICTURE
Students with need: Need-based aid available for full-time and part-time students.
Students without need: No-need awards available for academics, athletics, state/district residency.

FINANCIAL AID PROCEDURES
Forms required: FAFSA, institutional form.
Dates and Deadlines: No deadline. Applicants notified on a rolling basis starting 8/1; must reply within 2 week(s) of notification.

CONTACT
Deborah Kull, Director of Financial Aid
11220 State Highway 1, Robinson, IL 62454-5707
(618) 544-8657

Illinois Eastern Community Colleges: Olney Central College
Olney, Illinois
www.iecc.edu/occ   Federal Code: 001742

2-year public community college in small town.
Enrollment: 1,022 undergrads, 31% part-time. 96 full-time freshmen.
Selectivity: Open admission; but selective for some programs.

BASIC COSTS (2005-2006)
Tuition and fees: $1,680; out-of-district residents $5,629; out-of-state residents $6,947.
Per-credit charge: $53; out-of-district residents $185; out-of-state residents $229.
Additional info: Students in qualifying Indiana districts pay per-credit-hour rate of $96.

FINANCIAL AID PICTURE
Students with need: Need-based aid available for full-time and part-time students.
Students without need: No-need awards available for academics, athletics, state/district residency.

FINANCIAL AID PROCEDURES
Forms required: FAFSA, institutional form.
Dates and Deadlines: No deadline. Applicants notified on a rolling basis starting 8/1; must reply within 2 week(s) of notification.

CONTACT
Vicki Stuckey, Financial Aid Coordinator
305 North West Street, Olney, IL 62450
(618) 395-7777

Illinois Eastern Community Colleges: Wabash Valley College
Mount Carmel, Illinois
www.iecc.edu/wvc   Federal Code: 001779

2-year public community college in small town.
Enrollment: 631 undergrads.
Selectivity: Open admission.

BASIC COSTS (2005-2006)
Tuition and fees: $1,680; out-of-district residents $5,629; out-of-state residents $6,947.
Per-credit charge: $53; out-of-district residents $185; out-of-state residents $229.
Additional info: Students in qualifying Indiana districts pay per-credit-hour rate of $96.

FINANCIAL AID PICTURE
Students with need: Need-based aid available for full-time and part-time students.
Students without need: No-need awards available for academics, athletics, state/district residency.

FINANCIAL AID PROCEDURES
Forms required: FAFSA, institutional form.
Dates and Deadlines: No deadline. Applicants notified on a rolling basis starting 8/1; must reply within 2 week(s) of notification.

CONTACT
Melinda Silvernale, Financial Aid Coordinator
2200 College Drive, Mount Carmel, IL 62863-2657
(618) 262-8641

Illinois Institute of Art-Schaumburg
Schaumburg, Illinois
www.ilis.aii.edu   Federal Code: 012584

4-year for-profit visual arts college in small city.
Enrollment: 290 full-time undergrads.

BASIC COSTS (2005-2006)
Tuition and fees: $17,100.
Per-credit charge: $380.
Room and board: $6,000.
Additional info: Tuition at time of enrollment locked for 4 years.

FINANCIAL AID PICTURE
Students with need: Need-based aid available for full-time and part-time students. Work study available nights, weekends, and for part-time students.
Students without need: No-need awards available for art.
Additional info: Merit scholarships based on GPA; talent-based scholarships.

FINANCIAL AID PROCEDURES
Forms required: FAFSA.
Dates and Deadlines: No deadline.

CONTACT
Joe Payne, Director of Student Financial Services
1000 North Plaza Drive, Schaumburg, IL 60173
(800) 314-3450

Illinois Institute of Technology
Chicago, Illinois
www.iit.edu
Federal Code: 001691

4-year private university and engineering college in very large city.
Enrollment: 2,156 undergrads, 8% part-time. 397 full-time freshmen.
Selectivity: Admits 50 to 75% of applicants. GED not accepted.

BASIC COSTS (2005-2006)
Tuition and fees: $22,982.
Per-credit charge: $692.
Room and board: $7,520.
Additional info: Tuition and fees cover unlimited number of courses during academic year and include library and computer usage fees.

FINANCIAL AID PICTURE (2004-2005)
Students with need: Out of 339 full-time freshmen who applied for aid, 290 were judged to have need. Of these, 288 received aid, and 81 had their full need met. Average financial aid package met 89% of need; average scholarship/grant was $13,991; average loan was $4,456. For part-time students, average financial aid package was $6,789.
Students without need: 106 full-time freshmen who did not demonstrate need for aid received scholarships/grants; average award was $11,390. No-need awards available for academics, alumni affiliation, athletics, leadership, minority status, ROTC.
Scholarships offered: *Merit:* Henry Heald Scholarship; $3,000-$15,000; based on ACT/SAT scores. Camras/Next Scholarship; $13,000, full tuition and room. Cyrus Tang and Chinese American Service League (CASL) Scholarship; $4,500; based on community service, essay, GPA and test scores; only open to Chinese Americans. *Athletic:* 17 full-time freshmen received athletic scholarships; average amount $3,972.

FINANCIAL AID PROCEDURES
Forms required: FAFSA.
Dates and Deadlines: Priority date 4/15; no closing date. Applicants notified on a rolling basis starting 3/1; must reply by 5/1 or within 2 week(s) of notification.
Transfers: Closing date 4/15.

CONTACT
Virginia Foster, Director for Student Finance Center
10 West 33rd Street, Chicago, IL 60616
(312) 567-7219

Illinois State University
Normal, Illinois
www.ilstu.edu
Federal Code: 001692

4-year public university in small city.
Enrollment: 17,795 undergrads, 7% part-time. 3,170 full-time freshmen.
Selectivity: Admits over 75% of applicants.

BASIC COSTS (2005-2006)
Tuition and fees: $7,091; out-of-state residents $12,971.
Per-credit charge: $180; out-of-state residents $376.
Room and board: $5,762.
Additional info: Tuition for incoming freshmen is guaranteed for 4 years. Tuition at time of enrollment locked for 4 years.

FINANCIAL AID PICTURE (2005-2006)
Students with need: Out of 2,421 full-time freshmen who applied for aid, 1,378 were judged to have need. Of these, 1,339 received aid, and 572 had their full need met. Average financial aid package met 79% of need; average scholarship/grant was $6,496; average loan was $3,988. For part-time students, average financial aid package was $9,739.
Students without need: 46 full-time freshmen who did not demonstrate need for aid received scholarships/grants; average award was $3,318. No-need awards available for academics, art, athletics, leadership, music/drama.
Scholarships offered: *Merit:* Various non-need based merit scholarships available, including Presidential Scholars' Program, Provost's Scholarship, and Dean's Scholarship. *Athletic:* 52 full-time freshmen received athletic scholarships; average amount $9,282.
Cumulative student debt: 59% of graduating class had student loans; average debt was $15,616.

FINANCIAL AID PROCEDURES
Forms required: FAFSA.
Dates and Deadlines: Priority date 3/1; no closing date. Applicants notified on a rolling basis starting 4/1; must reply within 2 week(s) of notification.

CONTACT
Charles Boudreau, Director of Financial Aid
Campus Box 2200, Normal, IL 61790-2200
(309) 438-2231

Illinois Wesleyan University
Bloomington, Illinois
www.iwu.edu
Federal Code: 001696

4-year private university and liberal arts college in small city, affiliated with United Methodist Church.
Enrollment: 2,139 undergrads. 565 full-time freshmen.
Selectivity: Admits 50 to 75% of applicants.

BASIC COSTS (2006-2007)
Tuition and fees: $29,136.
Per-credit charge: $906.
Room and board: $6,714.
Additional info: Additional expense-based fees are charged for the University's semester abroad programs in London and Madrid.

FINANCIAL AID PICTURE (2005-2006)
Students with need: Out of 429 full-time freshmen who applied for aid, 337 were judged to have need. Of these, 336 received aid, and 193 had their full need met. Average financial aid package met 91% of need; average scholarship/grant was $14,847; average loan was $4,197.
Students without need: 156 full-time freshmen who did not demonstrate need for aid received scholarships/grants; average award was $8,062. No-need awards available for academics, art, music/drama.
Scholarships offered: Academic scholarships: $5,000-16,000; based on high school academic performance, recommendations, and testing. Talent awards: $6,500-$11,000; available in music, art, theatre, and music theatre. Limited number of full tuition awards in music.
Cumulative student debt: 67% of graduating class had student loans; average debt was $21,846.

FINANCIAL AID PROCEDURES
Forms required: FAFSA, institutional form.
Dates and Deadlines: Closing date 3/1. Applicants notified on a rolling basis starting 2/1; must reply by 5/1 or within 3 week(s) of notification.
Transfers: No deadline. Applicants notified on a rolling basis.

CONTACT
Lynn Nichelson, Director of Financial Aid
PO Box 2900, Bloomington, IL 61702-2900
(309) 556-3096

International Academy of Design and Technology: Chicago
Chicago, Illinois
www.iadtchicago.edu
Federal Code: 021603

4-year for-profit visual arts and technical college in very large city.
Enrollment: 2,768 undergrads, 13% part-time.
Selectivity: Open admission; but selective for some programs.

BASIC COSTS (2006-2007)
Tuition and fees: $17,250.

FINANCIAL AID PICTURE (2004-2005)
Students with need: 20% of average financial aid package awarded as scholarships/grants, 80% awarded as loans/jobs. Need-based aid available for part-time students.
Students without need: This college only awards aid to students with need.
Additional info: College work study programs available to day and evening students.

FINANCIAL AID PROCEDURES
Forms required: FAFSA, institutional form.
Dates and Deadlines: No deadline. Applicants notified on a rolling basis starting 1/6; must reply within 2 week(s) of notification.
Transfers: No deadline. Applicants notified on a rolling basis; must reply within 2 week(s) of notification.

CONTACT
Andrea Watkins, Associate Director of Financial Aid
One North State Street, Suite 500, Chicago, IL 60602
(312) 980-9200

John A. Logan College
Carterville, Illinois
www.jalc.edu
Federal Code: 008076

2-year public community college in small town.
Enrollment: 2,632 full-time undergrads.
Selectivity: Open admission; but selective for some programs.

BASIC COSTS (2005-2006)
Tuition and fees: $1,830.
Per-credit charge: $61.

FINANCIAL AID PICTURE
Students with need: Need-based aid available for full-time and part-time students.
Students without need: This college only awards aid to students with need.

FINANCIAL AID PROCEDURES
Forms required: FAFSA, institutional form.
Dates and Deadlines: Priority date 5/1; no closing date. Applicants notified on a rolling basis starting 5/1.

CONTACT
Stacy Holloway, Director for Student Financial Assistance
700 Logan College Road, Carterville, IL 62918
(618) 985-3741 ext. 8308

John Wood Community College
Quincy, Illinois
www.jwcc.edu
Federal Code: 012813

2-year public community college in large town.
Enrollment: 1,845 undergrads, 41% part-time. 450 full-time freshmen.
Selectivity: Open admission; but selective for some programs.

BASIC COSTS (2005-2006)
Tuition and fees: $2,430; out-of-state residents $5,430.
Per-credit charge: $76; out-of-state residents $176.

FINANCIAL AID PICTURE
Students with need: Need-based aid available for full-time and part-time students. Work study available nights, weekends, and for part-time students.

FINANCIAL AID PROCEDURES
Forms required: FAFSA.
Dates and Deadlines: No deadline. Applicants notified on a rolling basis starting 3/1.

CONTACT
Bonnie Scranton, Dean of Enrollment Services
1301 South 48th Street, Quincy, IL 62305-8736
(217) 641-4336

Joliet Junior College
Joliet, Illinois
www.jjc.cc.il.us
Federal Code: 001699

2-year public community college in small city.
Enrollment: 13,022 undergrads.
Selectivity: Open admission; but selective for some programs and for out-of-state students.

BASIC COSTS (2005-2006)
Tuition and fees: $2,130; out-of-district residents $6,210; out-of-state residents $7,140.
Per-credit charge: $56; out-of-district residents $194; out-of-state residents $225.
Additional info: Additional course fees range from $3 to $90.

FINANCIAL AID PICTURE
Students with need: Need-based aid available for full-time and part-time students. Work study available nights, weekends, and for part-time students.
Students without need: No-need awards available for academics.

FINANCIAL AID PROCEDURES
Forms required: FAFSA, institutional form.
Dates and Deadlines: Priority date 6/1; no closing date. Applicants notified on a rolling basis starting 5/15.

CONTACT
Jennifer Kloberdanz, Director of Financial Aid
1215 Houbolt Road, Joliet, IL 60431-8938
(815) 729-9020 ext. 2414

Judson College
Elgin, Illinois
www.judsoncollege.edu
Federal Code: 001700

4-year private liberal arts college in small city, affiliated with American Baptist Churches in the USA.
Enrollment: 1,125 undergrads, 20% part-time. 125 full-time freshmen.
Selectivity: Admits over 75% of applicants.

BASIC COSTS (2006-2007)
Tuition and fees: $19,450.
Per-credit charge: $640.
Room and board: $6,900.

FINANCIAL AID PICTURE (2004-2005)
Students with need: Out of 115 full-time freshmen who applied for aid, 100 were judged to have need. Of these, 100 received aid, and 9 had their full need met. Average financial aid package met 40% of need; average scholarship/grant was $7,212; average loan was $2,569. For part-time students, average financial aid package was $3,573.
Students without need: 11 full-time freshmen who did not demonstrate need for aid received scholarships/grants; average award was $3,628. No-need awards available for academics, athletics, music/drama.
Scholarships offered: 24 full-time freshmen received athletic scholarships; average amount $8,999.
Cumulative student debt: 92% of graduating class had student loans; average debt was $19,216.

FINANCIAL AID PROCEDURES
Forms required: FAFSA.
Dates and Deadlines: Priority date 3/1; no closing date. Applicants notified on a rolling basis starting 3/1; must reply within 4 week(s) of notification.
Transfers: No deadline. Applicants notified on a rolling basis starting 3/1.

CONTACT
Michael Davis, Director of Financial Aid
1151 North State Street, Elgin, IL 60123-1404
(800) 879-5376

Kankakee Community College
Kankakee, Illinois
www.kcc.edu
Federal Code: 007690

2-year public community college in large town.
Enrollment: 2,488 undergrads.
Selectivity: Open admission; but selective for some programs.

BASIC COSTS (2005-2006)
Tuition and fees: $1,800; out-of-district residents $4,312; out-of-state residents $9,697.
Per-credit charge: $55; out-of-district residents $139; out-of-state residents $318.

FINANCIAL AID PICTURE
Students with need: Need-based aid available for full-time and part-time students.
Students without need: No-need awards available for athletics.

FINANCIAL AID PROCEDURES
Forms required: FAFSA, institutional form.
Dates and Deadlines: Priority date 7/1; no closing date. Applicants notified on a rolling basis; must reply within 4 week(s) of notification.

CONTACT
Al Widhalm, Director of Financial Aid
PO Box 888, Kankakee, IL 60901
(815) 802-8550

Kaskaskia College
Centralia, Illinois
www.kaskaskia.edu
Federal Code: 001701

2-year public community college in large town.
Enrollment: 3,371 undergrads, 44% part-time. 379 full-time freshmen.
Selectivity: Open admission; but selective for some programs.

BASIC COSTS (2005-2006)
Tuition and fees: $1,800; out-of-district residents $3,240; out-of-state residents $7,260.
Per-credit charge: $53; out-of-district residents $101; out-of-state residents $235.

FINANCIAL AID PICTURE (2004-2005)
Students with need: Average financial aid package for all full-time undergraduates was $2,870. 88% awarded as scholarships/grants, 12% awarded as loans/jobs. Need-based aid available for part-time students.
Students without need: No-need awards available for academics, athletics, state/district residency.

FINANCIAL AID PROCEDURES
Forms required: FAFSA.
Dates and Deadlines: Priority date 5/15; no closing date. Applicants notified on a rolling basis starting 4/1; must reply within 2 week(s) of notification.

CONTACT
Sherry Summary, Director of Financial Aid
27210 College Road, Centralia, IL 62801
(618) 545-3080

Kendall College
Chicago, Illinois
www.kendall.edu
Federal Code: 001703

4-year private culinary school and business college in very large city, affiliated with United Methodist Church.
Enrollment: 780 undergrads, 36% part-time.
Selectivity: Admits less than 50% of applicants.

BASIC COSTS (2005-2006)
Per-credit charge: $475.
Room and board: $9,000.
Additional info: Tuition costs range from $15,750 to $25,400 per academic year. Required fees: $470.

FINANCIAL AID PICTURE
Students with need: Need-based aid available for full-time and part-time students. Work study available nights, weekends, and for part-time students.
Students without need: No-need awards available for academics, athletics, religious affiliation.

FINANCIAL AID PROCEDURES
Forms required: FAFSA.
Dates and Deadlines: Priority date 6/1; no closing date. Applicants notified on a rolling basis starting 4/1; must reply within 2 week(s) of notification.

CONTACT
Cynthia Sabo, Director of Financial Aid
900 North Branch Street North, Chicago, IL 60622-4278
(877) 588-8860

Kishwaukee College
Malta, Illinois
www.kishwaukeecollege.edu
Federal Code: 007684

2-year public community college in rural community.
Enrollment: 3,258 undergrads.
Selectivity: Open admission; but selective for some programs.

BASIC COSTS (2005-2006)
Tuition and fees: $2,100; out-of-district residents $6,750; out-of-state residents $7,590.
Per-credit charge: $63; out-of-district residents $218; out-of-state residents $246.

FINANCIAL AID PICTURE
Students with need: Need-based aid available for full-time and part-time students. Work study available nights, weekends, and for part-time students.
Students without need: No-need awards available for academics, athletics, leadership, music/drama, state/district residency.

FINANCIAL AID PROCEDURES
Forms required: FAFSA, institutional form.
Dates and Deadlines: Priority date 5/1; no closing date. Applicants notified on a rolling basis starting 5/1; must reply within 2 week(s) of notification.
Transfers: Must reply within 2 week(s) of notification. Some state programs not available to sophomore status students.

CONTACT
Pamela Wagener, Coordinator of Financial Aid
21193 Malta Road, Malta, IL 60150-9699
(815) 825-2086

Knox College
Galesburg, Illinois
www.knox.edu
Federal Code: 001704

4-year private liberal arts college in large town.
Enrollment: 1,205 undergrads. 325 full-time freshmen.
Selectivity: Admits over 75% of applicants.

BASIC COSTS (2006-2007)
Tuition and fees: $27,900.
Room and board: $5,925.

FINANCIAL AID PICTURE (2005-2006)
Students with need: Out of 271 full-time freshmen who applied for aid, 216 were judged to have need. Of these, 216 received aid, and 102 had their full need met. Average financial aid package met 95% of need; average scholarship/grant was $16,474; average loan was $4,424. Need-based aid available for part-time students.
Students without need: 98 full-time freshmen who did not demonstrate need for aid received scholarships/grants; average award was $9,869. No-need awards available for academics, art, music/drama.
Scholarships offered: Academic scholarship: up to $15,000; based on high school academic performance and class rank. Visual and performing arts scholarships (in music, art, theater, dance, writing): up to $3,500; based on auditions or submission of portfolios. Social Concerns Scholarships: up to $3,500; based on community service activity.
Cumulative student debt: 68% of graduating class had student loans; average debt was $19,642.

FINANCIAL AID PROCEDURES
Forms required: FAFSA, institutional form.
Dates and Deadlines: Priority date 2/15; no closing date. Applicants notified on a rolling basis starting 3/15; must reply by 5/1 or within 2 week(s) of notification.
Transfers: Priority date 4/1.

CONTACT
Teresa Jackson, Director of Financial Aid
Campus Box 148, Galesburg, IL 61401-4999
(309) 341-7149

Lake Forest College
Lake Forest, Illinois
www.lakeforest.edu
Federal Code: 001706

4-year private liberal arts college in large town, affiliated with Presbyterian Church (USA).
Enrollment: 1,383 undergrads, 1% part-time. 358 full-time freshmen.
Selectivity: Admits 50 to 75% of applicants.

BASIC COSTS (2006-2007)
Tuition and fees: $29,034.
Per-credit charge: $897.
Room and board: $6,960.

FINANCIAL AID PICTURE (2005-2006)
Students with need: Out of 329 full-time freshmen who applied for aid, 292 were judged to have need. Of these, 292 received aid, and 292 had their full need met. Average financial aid package met 100% of need; average scholarship/grant was $18,006; average loan was $4,159.
Students without need: 34 full-time freshmen who did not demonstrate need for aid received scholarships/grants; average award was $9,544. No-need awards available for academics, alumni affiliation, art, leadership, music/drama.
Scholarships offered: Trustee Scholarship; awards up to full tuition without regard to financial need. Forester Scholarships; awarded in art, foreign language, leadership, music, science, theater, and writing without regard to financial need. Awards range from $1,000-$3,000.
Cumulative student debt: 53% of graduating class had student loans; average debt was $18,306.

FINANCIAL AID PROCEDURES
Forms required: FAFSA.
Dates and Deadlines: Priority date 2/15; no closing date. Applicants notified on a rolling basis starting 2/15; must reply by 5/1 or within 3 week(s) of notification.
Transfers: Closing date 6/1.

CONTACT
Gerard Cebrzynski, Director of Financial Aid
555 North Sheridan Road, Lake Forest, IL 60045-2399
(847) 735-5103

Lake Land College
Mattoon, Illinois
www.lakelandcollege.edu
Federal Code: 007644

2-year public community college in large town.
Enrollment: 5,277 undergrads.
Selectivity: Open admission; but selective for some programs.

BASIC COSTS (2005-2006)
Tuition and fees: $1,919; out-of-district residents $4,015; out-of-state residents $7,927.
Per-credit charge: $54; out-of-district residents $120; out-of-state residents $252.

FINANCIAL AID PICTURE (2004-2005)
Students with need: 76% of average financial aid package awarded as scholarships/grants, 24% awarded as loans/jobs. Need-based aid available for part-time students. Work study available nights, weekends, and for part-time students.
Students without need: No-need awards available for academics, athletics.

FINANCIAL AID PROCEDURES
Forms required: FAFSA, institutional form.
Dates and Deadlines: Closing date 5/1. Applicants notified on a rolling basis starting 6/1; must reply within 2 week(s) of notification.
Transfers: No deadline.

CONTACT
Paula Carpenter, Director of Financial Aid and Veteran Services
5001 Lake Land Boulevard, Mattoon, IL 61938-9366
(217) 234-5231

Lakeview College of Nursing
Danville, Illinois
www.lakeviewcol.edu
Federal Code: 010501

Upper-division private nursing college in large town.
Enrollment: 235 undergrads.

BASIC COSTS (2005-2006)
Tuition and fees: $10,650.
Per-credit charge: $355.

FINANCIAL AID PICTURE
Students with need: Need-based aid available for full-time and part-time students.
Students without need: This college only awards aid to students with need.

FINANCIAL AID PROCEDURES
Forms required: FAFSA, institutional form.
Dates and Deadlines: Closing date 4/15.
Transfers: Priority date 4/15; no deadline.

CONTACT
Janet Ingargiola, Financial Aid Officer
903 North Logan Avenue, Danville, IL 61832
(217) 554-6887

Lewis and Clark Community College
Godfrey, Illinois
www.lc.edu
Federal Code: 010020

2-year public community college in large town.
Enrollment: 5,222 undergrads.
Selectivity: Open admission; but selective for some programs.

BASIC COSTS (2005-2006)
Tuition and fees: $2,220; out-of-district residents $6,120; out-of-state residents $8,070.
Per-credit charge: $65; out-of-district residents $195; out-of-state residents $260.
Additional info: Out-of-state, out-of-district on-line tuition is $95 per credit including fees.

FINANCIAL AID PICTURE
Students with need: Need-based aid available for full-time and part-time students.

FINANCIAL AID PROCEDURES
Forms required: FAFSA.
Dates and Deadlines: Priority date 6/1; no closing date. Applicants notified on a rolling basis starting 8/1; must reply within 3 week(s) of notification.

CONTACT
Angela Weaver, Director, Financial Aid
5800 Godfrey Road, Godfrey, IL 62035-2466
(618) 468-2223

Lewis University
Romeoville, Illinois
www.lewisu.edu
Federal Code: 001707

4-year private university in large town, affiliated with Roman Catholic Church.
Enrollment: 3,543 undergrads, 25% part-time. 561 full-time freshmen.
Selectivity: Admits 50 to 75% of applicants.

BASIC COSTS (2006-2007)
Tuition and fees: $19,285.
Per-credit charge: $620.
Room and board: $7,500.
Additional info: Tuition/fee waivers available for adults.

FINANCIAL AID PICTURE (2005-2006)
Students with need: Out of 488 full-time freshmen who applied for aid, 387 were judged to have need. Of these, 387 received aid, and 186 had their full need met. Average financial aid package met 77% of need; average scholarship/grant was $6,818; average loan was $2,195. For part-time students, average financial aid package was $5,867.
Students without need: 91 full-time freshmen who did not demonstrate need for aid received scholarships/grants; average award was $7,417. No-need awards available for academics, alumni affiliation, art, athletics, leadership, music/drama, ROTC.
Scholarships offered: 56 full-time freshmen received athletic scholarships; average amount $6,818.
Cumulative student debt: 71% of graduating class had student loans; average debt was $14,328.

FINANCIAL AID PROCEDURES
Forms required: FAFSA.
Dates and Deadlines: Priority date 5/1; no closing date. Applicants notified on a rolling basis starting 2/15; must reply by 5/1 or within 2 week(s) of notification.
Transfers: No deadline. Applicants notified on a rolling basis; must reply by 8/1 or within 2 week(s) of notification.

CONTACT
Janeen Decharinte, Director of Financial Aid
One University Parkway, Romeoville, IL 60446-2200
(815) 836-5262

Lexington College
Chicago, Illinois
www.lexingtoncollege.edu
Federal Code: 016942

4-year private hospitality management college for women in very large city, affiliated with Roman Catholic Church.
Enrollment: 56 undergrads.
Selectivity: Admits 50 to 75% of applicants.

BASIC COSTS (2006-2007)
Tuition and fees: $17,700.
Per-credit charge: $591.
Room and board: $8,000.

FINANCIAL AID PICTURE
Students with need: Need-based aid available for full-time and part-time students.
Students without need: This college only awards aid to students with need.
Additional info: Work-study is available.

FINANCIAL AID PROCEDURES
Forms required: FAFSA.
Dates and Deadlines: Priority date 5/15; no closing date. Applicants notified on a rolling basis starting 7/1; must reply within 2 week(s) of notification.
Transfers: Closing date 5/15. Can only receive Illinois state aid at one institution per academic year if student enrolls and then withdraws to transfer to another college within term.

CONTACT
Maria LeBron, Director of Financial Aid
310 South Peoria Street, Suite 512, Chicago, IL 60607-3534
(312) 226-6294 ext. 227

Lincoln Christian College and Seminary
Lincoln, Illinois
www.lccs.edu Federal Code: 001708

4-year private Bible and seminary college in large town, affiliated with Christian Church.
Enrollment: 696 undergrads, 12% part-time. 180 full-time freshmen.
Selectivity: Admits over 75% of applicants.

BASIC COSTS (2006-2007)
Tuition and fees: $11,100.
Per-credit charge: $370.
Room and board: $4,580.

FINANCIAL AID PICTURE
Students with need: Need-based aid available for full-time and part-time students. Work study available nights, weekends, and for part-time students.

FINANCIAL AID PROCEDURES
Forms required: FAFSA.
Dates and Deadlines: Priority date 8/10; no closing date. Applicants notified on a rolling basis starting 3/1; must reply within 2 week(s) of notification.

CONTACT
Nancy Siddens, Director of Student Financial Aid
100 Campus View Drive, Lincoln, IL 62656
(217) 732-3168 ext. 2226

Lincoln Land Community College
Springfield, Illinois
www.llcc.edu Federal Code: 007170

2-year public community and junior college in small city.
Enrollment: 5,235 undergrads, 58% part-time. 482 full-time freshmen.
Selectivity: Open admission; but selective for some programs.

BASIC COSTS (2005-2006)
Tuition and fees: $1,986; out-of-district residents $8,104; out-of-state residents $9,687.
Per-credit charge: $63; out-of-district residents $266; out-of-state residents $317.
Additional info: Tuition/fee waivers available for minority students.

FINANCIAL AID PICTURE (2004-2005)
Students with need: 77% of average financial aid package awarded as scholarships/grants, 23% awarded as loans/jobs. Need-based aid available for part-time students. Work study available nights.
Students without need: No-need awards available for academics, athletics, minority status, state/district residency.

FINANCIAL AID PROCEDURES
Forms required: FAFSA, institutional form.
Dates and Deadlines: Priority date 5/1; no closing date. Applicants notified on a rolling basis starting 4/15; must reply within 2 week(s) of notification.

CONTACT
Lee Bursi, Director of Financial Aid
5250 Shepherd Road, Springfield, IL 62794-9256
(217) 786-2237

Loyola University of Chicago
Chicago, Illinois
www.luc.edu Federal Code: 001710

4-year private university in very large city, affiliated with Roman Catholic Church.
Enrollment: 8,616 undergrads, 7% part-time. 2,071 full-time freshmen.
Selectivity: Admits over 75% of applicants.

BASIC COSTS (2006-2007)
Tuition and fees: $26,886.
Per-credit charge: $530.
Room and board: $9,614.

FINANCIAL AID PICTURE (2005-2006)
Students with need: Out of 1,807 full-time freshmen who applied for aid, 1,531 were judged to have need. Of these, 1,526 received aid, and 177 had their full need met. Average financial aid package met 80% of need; average scholarship/grant was $12,434; average loan was $2,739. For part-time students, average financial aid package was $7,980.
Students without need: 213 full-time freshmen who did not demonstrate need for aid received scholarships/grants; average award was $6,553. No-need awards available for academics, athletics, leadership, music/drama.
Scholarships offered: 11 full-time freshmen received athletic scholarships; average amount $18,962.
Cumulative student debt: 68% of graduating class had student loans; average debt was $24,299.

FINANCIAL AID PROCEDURES
Forms required: FAFSA.
Dates and Deadlines: Priority date 3/1; no closing date. Applicants notified on a rolling basis starting 2/15; must reply within 3 week(s) of notification.
Transfers: FAFSA must be filed by July 1 to receive Illinois map grant.

CONTACT
Eric Weems, Director, Student Financial Assistance
820 North Michigan Avenue, Chicago, IL 60611-9810
(773) 508-3155

MacMurray College
Jacksonville, Illinois
www.mac.edu Federal Code: 001717

4-year private liberal arts college in large town, affiliated with United Methodist Church.
Enrollment: 683 undergrads, 6% part-time. 167 full-time freshmen.
Selectivity: Admits 50 to 75% of applicants.

BASIC COSTS (2006-2007)
Tuition and fees: $15,750.
Per-credit charge: $250.
Room and board: $5,928.

FINANCIAL AID PICTURE (2005-2006)
Students with need: Out of 167 full-time freshmen who applied for aid, 150 were judged to have need. Of these, 150 received aid, and 20 had their full need met. Average financial aid package met 72% of need; average scholarship/grant was $10,204; average loan was $3,111. For part-time students, average financial aid package was $5,018.
Students without need: 17 full-time freshmen who did not demonstrate need for aid received scholarships/grants; average award was $15,033. No-need awards available for academics, alumni affiliation, art, leadership, minority status, music/drama, religious affiliation.
Scholarships offered: Academic scholarships; $500-$1,4000; based on merit. Music performance and art competition scholarships available. Transfer scholarships; to $10,000; based on academic merit. Leadership scholarships; available based on committee selection.
Cumulative student debt: 92% of graduating class had student loans; average debt was $16,921.
Additional info: Merit scholarships for accepted, enrolled freshman based on academic record. Need-based program meets 100% of direct tuition charges after family contribution and financial aid.

FINANCIAL AID PROCEDURES
Forms required: FAFSA.

Dates and Deadlines: Priority date 5/1; closing date 8/1. Applicants notified on a rolling basis starting 3/1; must reply by 5/1 or within 4 week(s) of notification.
Transfers: No deadline.
CONTACT
Dena Dobson, Director of Financial Aid
447 East College Avenue, Jacksonville, IL 62650-2590
(217) 479-7041

McHenry County College
Crystal Lake, Illinois
www.mchenry.edu   Federal Code: 007691

2-year public community college in large town.
Enrollment: 5,416 undergrads, 62% part-time. 518 full-time freshmen.
Selectivity: Open admission.

BASIC COSTS (2005-2006)
Tuition and fees: $2,174; out-of-district residents $7,885; out-of-state residents $9,236.
Per-credit charge: $63; out-of-district residents $253; out-of-state residents $298.

FINANCIAL AID PICTURE
Students with need: Need-based aid available for full-time and part-time students. Work study available nights, weekends, and for part-time students.
Students without need: No-need awards available for academics, athletics, leadership, music/drama, state/district residency.
Scholarships offered: President's Scholarship; full tuition for two years; based on talent in academic areas; students must complete portfolio and have 3.0 GPA. Founding Faculty Scholarship; full tuition for 2 years; based on GPA and essay.
Additional info: Students can apply throughout the award year for federal and state aid. Students with physical handicaps or learning disabilities may apply for special needs scholarship.

FINANCIAL AID PROCEDURES
Forms required: FAFSA, institutional form.
Dates and Deadlines: Priority date 6/1; no closing date. Applicants notified on a rolling basis starting 5/1.

CONTACT
Marianne Devenny, Director, Office of Financial Aid and Records
8900 U.S. Highway 14, Crystal Lake, IL 60012-2761
(815) 455-8761

McKendree College
Lebanon, Illinois
www.mckendree.edu   Federal Code: 001722

4-year private liberal arts college in small town, affiliated with United Methodist Church.
Enrollment: 2,218 undergrads, 27% part-time. 261 full-time freshmen.
Selectivity: Admits 50 to 75% of applicants.

BASIC COSTS (2005-2006)
Tuition and fees: $17,800.
Per-credit charge: $590.
Room and board: $7,000.

FINANCIAL AID PICTURE (2005-2006)
Students with need: Out of 238 full-time freshmen who applied for aid, 207 were judged to have need. Of these, 207 received aid, and 50 had their full need met. Average financial aid package met 86% of need; average scholarship/grant was $14,846; average loan was $2,323. For part-time students, average financial aid package was $8,895.
Students without need: 53 full-time freshmen who did not demonstrate need for aid received scholarships/grants; average award was $13,940. No-need awards available for academics, art, athletics, leadership, minority status, music/drama, religious affiliation.
Scholarships offered: *Merit:* Academic Scholarships; $1,000 to full tuition; based on interview and at least 1 of following criteria: 25 ACT, 3.4 GPA, rank in upper 20% of class; unlimited number awarded. *Athletic:* 38 full-time freshmen received athletic scholarships; average amount $4,940.
Cumulative student debt: 57% of graduating class had student loans; average debt was $16,322.

FINANCIAL AID PROCEDURES
Forms required: FAFSA.
Dates and Deadlines: Priority date 5/31; no closing date. Applicants notified on a rolling basis starting 3/1; must reply within 4 week(s) of notification.

CONTACT
Mark Campbell, Vice President for Enrollment Management
701 College Road, Lebanon, IL 62254
(618) 537-6829

Millikin University
Decatur, Illinois
www.millikin.edu   Federal Code: 001724

4-year private university in small city, affiliated with Presbyterian Church (USA).
Enrollment: 2,597 undergrads.
Selectivity: Admits 50 to 75% of applicants.

BASIC COSTS (2006-2007)
Tuition and fees: $22,069.
Per-credit charge: $717.
Room and board: $6,773.

FINANCIAL AID PICTURE (2005-2006)
Students with need: 66% of average financial aid package awarded as scholarships/grants, 34% awarded as loans/jobs. Need-based aid available for part-time students. Work study available nights, weekends, and for part-time students.
Students without need: No-need awards available for academics, art, leadership, music/drama, state/district residency.
Scholarships offered: Freshman Honors Scholar Program; at least $10,000, may qualify for more based on financial aid.

FINANCIAL AID PROCEDURES
Forms required: FAFSA.
Dates and Deadlines: Priority date 4/1; closing date 6/1. Applicants notified on a rolling basis starting 3/1; must reply within 4 week(s) of notification.

CONTACT
Stacey Hubbard, Director, Student Service Center
1184 West Main Street, Decatur, IL 62522-2084
(217) 424-6317

Monmouth College
Monmouth, Illinois
www.monm.edu Federal Code: 001725

4-year private liberal arts college in large town, affiliated with Presbyterian Church (USA).
Enrollment: 1,336 undergrads.
Selectivity: Admits over 75% of applicants.

BASIC COSTS (2006-2007)
Tuition and fees: $21,150.
Per-credit charge: $700.
Room and board: $6,150.

FINANCIAL AID PICTURE (2004-2005)
Students with need: 77% of average financial aid package awarded as scholarships/grants, 23% awarded as loans/jobs. Work study available nights, weekends, and for part-time students.
Students without need: No-need awards available for academics, art, music/drama, state/district residency.

FINANCIAL AID PROCEDURES
Forms required: FAFSA.
Dates and Deadlines: Priority date 3/1; no closing date. Applicants notified on a rolling basis starting 2/15; must reply by 8/1.

CONTACT
Jayne Whiteside, Director of Financial Aid
700 East Broadway, Monmouth, IL 61462-9989
(309) 457-2129

Moody Bible Institute
Chicago, Illinois
www.moody.edu Federal Code: 001727

4-year private Bible college in very large city, affiliated with interdenominational tradition.
Enrollment: 1,634 undergrads, 7% part-time. 196 full-time freshmen.

BASIC COSTS (2005-2006)
Additional info: Undergraduates are not charged tuition because it is paid from external funding. Students must pay fees of $2,468 and room and board costs of $7030. Tuition at time of enrollment locked for 4 years.

FINANCIAL AID PICTURE
Students with need: Need-based aid available for full-time students.
Students without need: This college only awards aid to students with need.
Additional info: Aid available to upperclassmen is based on private and not federal/state sources.

FINANCIAL AID PROCEDURES
Dates and Deadlines: No deadline.
Transfers: Students should complete two semesters of study in residence before applying for aid.

CONTACT
Daniel Ward, Financial Aid Coordinator
820 North La Salle Boulevard, Chicago, IL 60610
(312) 329-4178

Moraine Valley Community College
Palos Hills, Illinois
www.morainevalley.edu Federal Code: 007692

2-year public community college in large town.
Enrollment: 10,738 undergrads, 48% part-time. 1,524 full-time freshmen.
Selectivity: Open admission; but selective for some programs.

BASIC COSTS (2006-2007)
Tuition and fees: $2,070; out-of-district residents $6,120; out-of-state residents $7,410.
Per-credit charge: $64; out-of-district residents $199; out-of-state residents $242.

FINANCIAL AID PICTURE (2004-2005)
Students with need: 89% of average financial aid package awarded as scholarships/grants, 11% awarded as loans/jobs. Need-based aid available for part-time students. Work study available nights.
Students without need: No-need awards available for academics, athletics, leadership.

FINANCIAL AID PROCEDURES
Forms required: FAFSA, institutional form.
Dates and Deadlines: Priority date 5/1; no closing date. Applicants notified on a rolling basis starting 3/1; must reply within 4 week(s) of notification.

CONTACT
Laurie Anema, Director of Financial Aid
9000 West College Parkway, Palos Hills, IL 60465-0937
(708) 974-5726

Morrison Institute of Technology
Morrison, Illinois
www.morrison.tec.il.us Federal Code: 008880

2-year private junior and technical college in small town.
Enrollment: 125 undergrads. 68 full-time freshmen.
Selectivity: Open admission.

BASIC COSTS (2006-2007)
Tuition and fees: $12,380.
Per-credit charge: $504.
Room only: $2,600.

FINANCIAL AID PICTURE (2004-2005)
Students with need: Need-based aid available for part-time students. Work study available nights, weekends, and for part-time students.
Students without need: No-need awards available for academics.

FINANCIAL AID PROCEDURES
Forms required: FAFSA, institutional form.
Dates and Deadlines: No deadline. Applicants notified on a rolling basis; must reply within 2 week(s) of notification.

CONTACT
Julie Damhoff, Financial Aid Officer
701 Portland Avenue, Morrison, IL 61270-2959
(815) 772-7218

Morton College
Cicero, Illinois
www.morton.edu Federal Code: 001728

2-year public community college in small city.
Enrollment: 2,310 undergrads, 59% part-time. 226 full-time freshmen.

Selectivity: Open admission; but selective for some programs and for out-of-state students.

BASIC COSTS (2005-2006)
Tuition and fees: $2,090; out-of-district residents $5,570; out-of-state residents $7,310.
Per-credit charge: $58; out-of-district residents $174; out-of-state residents $232.

FINANCIAL AID PICTURE
Students with need: Need-based aid available for full-time and part-time students. Work study available nights, weekends, and for part-time students.

FINANCIAL AID PROCEDURES
Forms required: FAFSA, institutional form.
Dates and Deadlines: Priority date 6/1; no closing date. Applicants notified on a rolling basis starting 8/1.

CONTACT
Nicole Smith, Coordinator of Financial Aid
3801 South Central Avenue, Cicero, IL 60804
(708) 656-8000 ext. 428

North Central College
Naperville, Illinois
www.northcentralcollege.edu   Federal Code: 001734

4-year private liberal arts college in small city, affiliated with United Methodist Church.
Enrollment: 2,045 undergrads, 7% part-time. 422 full-time freshmen.
Selectivity: Admits 50 to 75% of applicants.

BASIC COSTS (2006-2007)
Tuition and fees: $23,115.
Per-credit charge: $570.
Room and board: $7,440.

FINANCIAL AID PICTURE (2005-2006)
Students with need: Out of 369 full-time freshmen who applied for aid, 288 were judged to have need. Of these, 288 received aid, and 113 had their full need met. Average financial aid package met 89% of need; average scholarship/grant was $13,890; average loan was $5,167. For part-time students, average financial aid package was $10,795.
Students without need: 108 full-time freshmen who did not demonstrate need for aid received scholarships/grants; average award was $9,439. No-need awards available for academics, art, music/drama, religious affiliation.
Scholarships offered: Numerous merit and talent scholarship opportunities available.
Cumulative student debt: 70% of graduating class had student loans; average debt was $14,608.
Additional info: Part-time students, non-degree-seeking students, and degree-seeking students primarily attending night or weekend classes may apply for special student status at discounted rate.

FINANCIAL AID PROCEDURES
Forms required: FAFSA, institutional form.
Dates and Deadlines: Priority date 4/1; no closing date. Applicants notified on a rolling basis starting 3/1; must reply within 4 week(s) of notification.

CONTACT
Marty Rossman, Director of Financial Aid
Office of Admissions, Naperville, IL 60566-7063
(630) 637-5600

North Park University
Chicago, Illinois
www.northpark.edu   Federal Code: 001735

4-year private university and liberal arts college in very large city, affiliated with Evangelical Covenant Church of America.
Enrollment: 1,850 undergrads, 16% part-time. 349 full-time freshmen.
Selectivity: Admits 50 to 75% of applicants.

BASIC COSTS (2006-2007)
Tuition and fees: $14,900.
Room and board: $7,110.

FINANCIAL AID PICTURE (2004-2005)
Students with need: Out of 299 full-time freshmen who applied for aid, 254 were judged to have need. Of these, 254 received aid, and 85 had their full need met. Average financial aid package met 73% of need; average scholarship/grant was $4,600; average loan was $2,720. Need-based aid available for part-time students.
Students without need: 58 full-time freshmen who did not demonstrate need for aid received scholarships/grants; average award was $1,919. No-need awards available for academics, art, music/drama, religious affiliation.
Cumulative student debt: 68% of graduating class had student loans; average debt was $18,224.

FINANCIAL AID PROCEDURES
Forms required: FAFSA.
Dates and Deadlines: Priority date 5/1; closing date 8/1. Applicants notified on a rolling basis starting 3/10; must reply by 5/1 or within 3 week(s) of notification.

CONTACT
Lucy Shaker, Director of Financial Aid
3225 West Foster Avenue, Chicago, IL 60625-4895
(773) 244-5525

Northeastern Illinois University
Chicago, Illinois
www.neiu.edu   Federal Code: 001693

4-year public university in very large city.
Enrollment: 9,166 undergrads, 44% part-time. 960 full-time freshmen.
Selectivity: Admits 50 to 75% of applicants.

BASIC COSTS (2005-2006)
Tuition and fees: $5,646; out-of-state residents $10,446.
Per-credit charge: $160; out-of-state residents $320.

FINANCIAL AID PICTURE (2005-2006)
Students with need: Out of 704 full-time freshmen who applied for aid, 495 were judged to have need. Of these, 488 received aid, and 31 had their full need met. Average financial aid package met 62% of need; average scholarship/grant was $5,674; average loan was $2,447. For part-time students, average financial aid package was $4,913.
Students without need: 17 full-time freshmen who did not demonstrate need for aid received scholarships/grants; average award was $1,655. No-need awards available for academics, art, leadership, music/drama.
Cumulative student debt: 34% of graduating class had student loans; average debt was $12,284.

FINANCIAL AID PROCEDURES
Forms required: FAFSA, institutional form.
Dates and Deadlines: Priority date 3/1; no closing date. Applicants notified on a rolling basis starting 4/1; must reply within 3 week(s) of notification.

CONTACT
J. Jennings, Director of Financial Aid
5500 North St. Louis Avenue, Chicago, IL 60625
(773) 442-5000

Northwestern Business College
Chicago, Illinois
northwesternbc.edu   Federal Code: 012362

2-year for-profit technical college in very large city.
Enrollment: 1,922 undergrads, 59% part-time. 296 full-time freshmen.

BASIC COSTS (2006-2007)
Tuition and fees: $16,340.
Per-credit charge: $330.
Additional info: Tuition may be higher for some classes.

FINANCIAL AID PICTURE (2004-2005)
Students with need: 44% of average financial aid package awarded as scholarships/grants, 56% awarded as loans/jobs. Need-based aid available for part-time students. Work study available nights.
Students without need: This college only awards aid to students with need.
Scholarships offered: President's Scholarship; $400 per quarter, up to $2,400. Dean's Scholarship; $300 per quarter, up to $1,800. Early bird scholarships; $750 first year, $1,500 sophomore year; must enroll by May 31 for fall quarter, must be full time.
Additional info: State grant programs for Illinois residents and alternative loans offered.

FINANCIAL AID PROCEDURES
Forms required: FAFSA, institutional form.
Dates and Deadlines: Priority date 6/30; no closing date. Applicants notified on a rolling basis starting 8/15; must reply within 4 week(s) of notification.

CONTACT
Amy Perrin, Director of Financial Assistance
4839 North Milwaukee Avenue, Chicago, IL 60630
(708) 237-5000

Northwestern University
Evanston, Illinois   Federal Code: 001739
www.northwestern.edu   CSS Code: 1565

4-year private university in small city.
Enrollment: 7,902 undergrads, 1% part-time. 1,952 full-time freshmen.
Selectivity: Admits less than 50% of applicants.

BASIC COSTS (2006-2007)
Tuition and fees: $33,559.
Room and board: $10,266.

FINANCIAL AID PICTURE (2005-2006)
Students with need: Out of 1,065 full-time freshmen who applied for aid, 903 were judged to have need. Of these, 903 received aid, and 903 had their full need met. Average financial aid package met 100% of need; average scholarship/grant was $21,691; average loan was $3,284.
Students without need: This college only awards aid to students with need.
Scholarships offered: 93 full-time freshmen received athletic scholarships; average amount $24,459.
Cumulative student debt: 46% of graduating class had student loans; average debt was $18,362.

FINANCIAL AID PROCEDURES
Forms required: FAFSA, CSS PROFILE.
Dates and Deadlines: Closing date 2/1. Applicants notified by 4/15; must reply by 5/1 or within 2 week(s) of notification.
Transfers: Closing date 6/1. Transfer student aid limited for first year.

CONTACT
Carolyn Lindley, Director of University Financial Aid
1801 Hinman Avenue, Evanston, IL 60204-3060
(847) 491-7400

Oakton Community College
Des Plaines, Illinois
www.oakton.edu   Federal Code: 009896

2-year public community college in small city.
Enrollment: 4,895 undergrads.
Selectivity: Open admission; but selective for some programs.

BASIC COSTS (2006-2007)
Tuition and fees: $2,085; out-of-district residents $6,159; out-of-state residents $7,920.

FINANCIAL AID PICTURE (2004-2005)
Students with need: Average financial aid package for all full-time undergraduates was $2,121. 92% awarded as scholarships/grants, 8% awarded as loans/jobs. Need-based aid available for part-time students. Work study available nights, weekends, and for part-time students.
Students without need: No-need awards available for academics, art, leadership, minority status, music/drama, state/district residency.
Cumulative student debt: 2% of graduating class had student loans; average debt was $2,705.
Additional info: Foundation Scholarships application available January through mid-March.

FINANCIAL AID PROCEDURES
Forms required: FAFSA, institutional form.
Dates and Deadlines: Closing date 5/1. Applicants notified on a rolling basis starting 6/1; must reply within 2 week(s) of notification.

CONTACT
Cheryl Warmann, Director of Financial Aid
1600 East Golf Road, Des Plaines, IL 60016
(847) 635-1708

Olivet Nazarene University
Bourbonnais, Illinois
www.olivet.edu   Federal Code: 001741

4-year private university and liberal arts college in small city, affiliated with Church of the Nazarene.
Enrollment: 2,897 undergrads.
Selectivity: Admits over 75% of applicants.

BASIC COSTS (2006-2007)
Tuition and fees: $17,590.
Per-credit charge: $698.
Room and board: $6,800.

FINANCIAL AID PICTURE (2004-2005)
Students with need: 42% of average financial aid package awarded as scholarships/grants, 58% awarded as loans/jobs. Need-based aid available for part-time students. Work study available nights, weekends, and for part-time students.
Students without need: No-need awards available for academics, art, athletics, leadership, music/drama, religious affiliation, ROTC, state/district residency.

330 Illinois Olivet Nazarene University

FINANCIAL AID PROCEDURES
Forms required: FAFSA, institutional form.
Dates and Deadlines: Priority date 3/1; no closing date. Applicants notified on a rolling basis starting 1/15; must reply within 2 week(s) of notification.

CONTACT
Greg Bruner, Director of Financial Aid
One University Avenue, Bourbonnais, IL 60914
(815) 939-5249

Parkland College
Champaign, Illinois
www.parkland.edu
Federal Code: 007118

2-year public community college in small city.
Enrollment: 9,552 undergrads, 53% part-time. 853 full-time freshmen.
Selectivity: Open admission; but selective for some programs.

BASIC COSTS (2006-2007)
Tuition and fees: $2,220; out-of-district residents $6,360; out-of-state residents $9,450.
Per-credit charge: $72; out-of-district residents $212; out-of-state residents $315.
Additional info: For Internet classes, in-district students pay $72 per credit hour; all others pay $112 per credit hour.

FINANCIAL AID PICTURE (2004-2005)
Students with need: Out of 437 full-time freshmen who applied for aid, 389 were judged to have need. Of these, 389 received aid. Average financial aid package met 62% of need; average scholarship/grant was $3,594. For part-time students, average financial aid package was $3,926.
Students without need: No-need awards available for academics, art, athletics, leadership, minority status, music/drama, state/district residency.
Scholarships offered: 33 full-time freshmen received athletic scholarships; average amount $1,344.
Cumulative student debt: 33% of graduating class had student loans; average debt was $5,264.

FINANCIAL AID PROCEDURES
Forms required: FAFSA, institutional form.
Dates and Deadlines: Priority date 3/1; no closing date. Applicants notified on a rolling basis starting 6/1; must reply within 2 week(s) of notification.

CONTACT
Jack Lyons, Director of Financial Aid and Veterans Affairs
2400 West Bradley Avenue, Champaign, IL 61821-1899
(217) 351-2276

Prairie State College
Chicago Heights, Illinois
www.prairiestate.edu
Federal Code: 001640

2-year public community college in large town.
Enrollment: 5,083 undergrads.
Selectivity: Open admission; but selective for some programs.

BASIC COSTS (2005-2006)
Tuition and fees: $2,300; out-of-district residents $6,620; out-of-state residents $9,020.
Per-credit charge: $76; out-of-district residents $220; out-of-state residents $300.

FINANCIAL AID PICTURE
Students with need: Need-based aid available for full-time and part-time students. Work study available nights, weekends, and for part-time students.

FINANCIAL AID PROCEDURES
Forms required: FAFSA, institutional form.
Dates and Deadlines: Priority date 7/1; no closing date. Applicants notified on a rolling basis; must reply within 2 week(s) of notification.

CONTACT
Alice Garcia, Director of Financial Aid
202 South Halsted Street, Chicago Heights, IL 60411
(708) 709-3523

Principia College
Elsah, Illinois
www.prin.edu
Federal Code: 001744
CSS Code: 1630

4-year private liberal arts college in rural community, affiliated with Christian Science (unaffiliated with Christian Science Church).
Enrollment: 542 undergrads, 1% part-time. 143 full-time freshmen.
Selectivity: Admits over 75% of applicants.

BASIC COSTS (2006-2007)
Tuition and fees: $21,450.
Per-credit charge: $470.
Room and board: $7,896.

FINANCIAL AID PICTURE (2005-2006)
Students with need: Out of 93 full-time freshmen who applied for aid, 89 were judged to have need. Of these, 89 received aid, and 59 had their full need met. Average financial aid package met 95% of need; average scholarship/grant was $13,410; average loan was $4,111. Need-based aid available for part-time students.
Students without need: 40 full-time freshmen who did not demonstrate need for aid received scholarships/grants; average award was $10,081. No-need awards available for academics, alumni affiliation.
Scholarships offered: Trustee Scholarship; full tuition; Chairman's Scholarship, 3/4 tuition; Presidential Scholarship; 1/2 tuition. Dean's Scholarship; 1/4 tuition; Arthur Schulz, Jr. Alumni Scholarship; $4,500. 4-year scholarships based on high school GPA and test scores. Dean's and Arthur Schulz Scholarships available for transfer students who meet the above criteria with a minimum 3.5 GPA. Children and grandchildren of alumni eligible for 4-year scholarships based on high school or transfer GPA.
Additional info: Need-based tuition reduction work plan combines job with grant.

FINANCIAL AID PROCEDURES
Forms required: CSS PROFILE, institutional form.
Dates and Deadlines: Closing date 3/1. Applicants notified by 4/1.
Transfers: Priority date 3/1.

CONTACT
Sarah McGuigan, Director of Financial Aid
One Maybeck Place, Elsah, IL 62028-9799
(800) 277-4648 ext. 2813

Quincy University
Quincy, Illinois
www.quincy.edu
Federal Code: 001745

4-year private university and liberal arts college in large town, affiliated with Roman Catholic Church.
Enrollment: 1,000 undergrads, 7% part-time. 202 full-time freshmen.
Selectivity: Admits over 75% of applicants.

BASIC COSTS (2006-2007)
Tuition and fees: $19,010.
Room and board: $6,980.

FINANCIAL AID PICTURE (2004-2005)
Students with need: 71% of average financial aid package awarded as scholarships/grants, 29% awarded as loans/jobs. Need-based aid available for part-time students. Work study available nights, weekends, and for part-time students.
Students without need: No-need awards available for academics, art, athletics, music/drama.
Scholarships offered: Academic scholarships: $2,500-$10,000 per year; based on ACT and high school GPA; unlimited number awarded.
Cumulative student debt: 72% of graduating class had student loans; average debt was $18,714.

FINANCIAL AID PROCEDURES
Forms required: FAFSA.
Dates and Deadlines: Priority date 4/15; no closing date. Applicants notified on a rolling basis starting 2/15; must reply by 5/1 or within 2 week(s) of notification.

CONTACT
Shann Doerr, Director of Financial Aid
1800 College Avenue, Quincy, IL 62301-2699
(217) 228-5260

Rend Lake College
Ina, Illinois
www.rlc.edu   Federal Code: 007119

2-year public community college in rural community.
Enrollment: 4,913 undergrads.
Selectivity: Open admission; but selective for some programs.

BASIC COSTS (2005-2006)
Tuition and fees: $1,860; out-of-district residents $2,880; out-of-state residents $4,500.
Per-credit charge: $62; out-of-district residents $96; out-of-state residents $150.

FINANCIAL AID PICTURE (2004-2005)
Students with need: Need-based aid available for part-time students.
Students without need: No-need awards available for academics, art, athletics, leadership, music/drama, state/district residency.

FINANCIAL AID PROCEDURES
Forms required: FAFSA.
Dates and Deadlines: No deadline. Applicants notified on a rolling basis starting 3/15; must reply within 4 week(s) of notification.

CONTACT
Doug Carlson, Director of Financial Aid
468 North Ken Gray Parkway, Ina, IL 62846
(618) 437-5321 ext. 1385

Richland Community College
Decatur, Illinois
www.richland.edu   Federal Code: 010879

2-year public community college in small city.
Enrollment: 3,034 undergrads. 209 full-time freshmen.
Selectivity: Open admission; but selective for some programs.

BASIC COSTS (2005-2006)
Tuition and fees: $1,870; out-of-district residents $6,551; out-of-state residents $8,642.
Per-credit charge: $58; out-of-district residents $214; out-of-state residents $341.

FINANCIAL AID PICTURE (2004-2005)
Students with need: Out of 125 full-time freshmen who applied for aid, 79 were judged to have need. Of these, 66 received aid, and 1 had their full need met. Average financial aid package met 59% of need; average scholarship/grant was $3,336; average loan was $2,288. For part-time students, average financial aid package was $2,822.
Students without need: 5 full-time freshmen who did not demonstrate need for aid received scholarships/grants; average award was $790. No-need awards available for academics.

FINANCIAL AID PROCEDURES
Forms required: FAFSA.
Dates and Deadlines: No deadline. Applicants notified on a rolling basis starting 3/20.

CONTACT
Karen Zalkin, Director of Financial Aid
One College Park, Decatur, IL 62521
(217) 875-7200 ext. 271

Robert Morris College: Chicago
Chicago, Illinois
www.robertmorris.edu   Federal Code: 001746

4-year private business and technical college in very large city.
Enrollment: 4,847 undergrads, 3% part-time. 977 full-time freshmen.
Selectivity: Open admission; but selective for some programs.

BASIC COSTS (2006-2007)
Tuition and fees: $15,900.
Additional info: Lab fees vary by program.

FINANCIAL AID PICTURE (2005-2006)
Students with need: Out of 867 full-time freshmen who applied for aid, 839 were judged to have need. Of these, 827 received aid, and 35 had their full need met. Average financial aid package met 50% of need; average scholarship/grant was $8,318; average loan was $2,511. Need-based aid available for part-time students.
Students without need: 23 full-time freshmen who did not demonstrate need for aid received scholarships/grants; average award was $12,523. No-need awards available for academics, art, athletics, state/district residency.
Scholarships offered: 11 full-time freshmen received athletic scholarships; average amount $6,632.
Cumulative student debt: 93% of graduating class had student loans; average debt was $18,479.

FINANCIAL AID PROCEDURES
Forms required: FAFSA.
Dates and Deadlines: No deadline. Applicants notified on a rolling basis.
Transfers: No deadline. Applicants notified on a rolling basis.

CONTACT
Karen LeVeque, Director of Financial Services
401 South State Street, Chicago, IL 60605
(312) 935-4075

Rock Valley College
Rockford, Illinois
www.rockvalleycollege.edu

2-year public community college in small city.
Enrollment: 2,959 undergrads. 650 full-time freshmen.
Selectivity: Open admission; but selective for some programs.

BASIC COSTS (2006-2007)
Tuition and fees: $2,012; out-of-district residents $6,122; out-of-state residents $8,972.
Per-credit charge: $54; out-of-district residents $194; out-of-state residents $417.
Additional info: Costs vary by program.

FINANCIAL AID PICTURE
Students with need: Need-based aid available for full-time and part-time students. Work study available nights.
Students without need: No-need awards available for academics, ROTC.

FINANCIAL AID PROCEDURES
Forms required: FAFSA.
Dates and Deadlines: No deadline. Applicants notified on a rolling basis starting 4/1; must reply within 2 week(s) of notification.

CONTACT
Sue Ullrick, Coordinator of Financial Aid/Scholarships
3301 North Mulford Road, Rockford, IL 61114-5699
(815) 921-4102

Rockford Business College
Rockford, Illinois
www.rbcsuccess.com　　　　　Federal Code: 008545

2-year for-profit business and technical college in small city.
Enrollment: 471 undergrads.

BASIC COSTS (2006-2007)
Tuition and fees: $7,200.
Per-credit charge: $160.
Additional info: Per-credit-hour charge for computer courses is $285.

FINANCIAL AID PICTURE
Students with need: Need-based aid available for full-time and part-time students. Work study available nights.

FINANCIAL AID PROCEDURES
Forms required: FAFSA.
Dates and Deadlines: No deadline. Applicants notified on a rolling basis.

CONTACT
Chad Wick, Director of Student Finance Solutions
730 North Church Street, Rockford, IL 61103
(815) 967-7311

Rockford College
Rockford, Illinois
www.rockford.edu　　　　　Federal Code: 001748

4-year private liberal arts college in small city.
Enrollment: 852 undergrads, 14% part-time. 157 full-time freshmen.

BASIC COSTS (2006-2007)
Tuition and fees: $22,460.
Per-credit charge: $595.
Room and board: $7,190.

FINANCIAL AID PICTURE
Students with need: Need-based aid available for full-time and part-time students. Work study available nights, weekends, and for part-time students.
Students without need: No-need awards available for academics, alumni affiliation.
Additional info: Will attempt to meet 100% of student's demonstrated financial need. Full tuition scholarships available, separate application and interview process required.

FINANCIAL AID PROCEDURES
Forms required: FAFSA, institutional form.
Dates and Deadlines: Priority date 4/15; no closing date. Applicants notified on a rolling basis starting 4/15; must reply within 3 week(s) of notification.

CONTACT
Todd Free, Director of Student Administrative Services
5050 East State Street, Rockford, IL 61108-2393
(815) 226-3383

Roosevelt University
Chicago, Illinois
www.roosevelt.edu　　　　　Federal Code: 001749

4-year private university in very large city.
Enrollment: 3,907 undergrads, 48% part-time. 238 full-time freshmen.
Selectivity: Admits 50 to 75% of applicants.

BASIC COSTS (2006-2007)
Tuition and fees: $15,564.
Room and board: $10,366.
Additional info: Tuition for Chicago College of the Performing Arts is $21,590 per year.

FINANCIAL AID PICTURE (2004-2005)
Students with need: Out of 218 full-time freshmen who applied for aid, 190 were judged to have need. Of these, 178 received aid, and 28 had their full need met. Average financial aid package met 75% of need; average scholarship/grant was $5,740. For part-time students, average financial aid package was $8,542.
Students without need: 25 full-time freshmen who did not demonstrate need for aid received scholarships/grants; average award was $4,420. No-need awards available for academics, alumni affiliation, leadership, minority status, music/drama, state/district residency.
Scholarships offered: Presidential Award based on GPA, SAT or ACT test scores, and involvement; 5 awarded; full tuition. Honors Program for 3.5 GPA, ACT of 23, and involvement; 20-30 awarded; $14,000-$42,000 over 4 years. Recognition Award for transfers and freshmen; 60 awarded; $1,500-$6,000 annually. Music and Theater Scholarships for transfers and freshmen based on talent; approximately 90 awarded; tuition and housing.

FINANCIAL AID PROCEDURES
Forms required: FAFSA, institutional form.
Dates and Deadlines: Priority date 4/1; no closing date. Applicants notified on a rolling basis starting 3/15; must reply within 2 week(s) of notification.

CONTACT
Walter O'Neill, Director of Financial Aid
430 South Michigan Avenue, Chicago, IL 60605-1394
(312) 341-3565

Rosalind Franklin University of Medicine and Science
North Chicago, Illinois
www.rosalindfranklin.edu　　　　　Federal Code: 001659

Upper-division private university and health science college in large town.
Enrollment: 9 undergrads, 11% part-time.

BASIC COSTS (2005-2006)
Tuition and fees: $14,118.
Per-credit charge: $392.

FINANCIAL AID PICTURE
Students with need: Need-based aid available for full-time and part-time students.

Students without need: This college only awards aid to students with need.

FINANCIAL AID PROCEDURES
Forms required: FAFSA, institutional form.
Dates and Deadlines: No deadline. Applicants notified on a rolling basis.

CONTACT
Maryann DeCaire, Executive Director Admissions, Records & Financial Aid
Graduate Admissions Office, North Chicago, IL 60064-3095
(847) 578-3217

Rush University
Chicago, Illinois
www.rushu.rush.edu   Federal Code: 009800

Upper-division private health professions university in very large city.
Enrollment: 240 undergrads, 4% part-time.

BASIC COSTS (2005-2006)
Tuition and fees: $18,195.
Per-credit charge: $525.
Room only: $7,704.
Additional info: Tuition costs vary by program.

FINANCIAL AID PICTURE (2004-2005)
Students with need: 33% of average financial aid package awarded as scholarships/grants, 67% awarded as loans/jobs. Need-based aid available for part-time students. Work study available nights, weekends, and for part-time students.
Scholarships offered: Nursing Service Scholarship; full tuition-for-service scholarship; minimum service and cumulative GPA of 2.75 for BSN program, must work for medical center as nurse in area of need for 28 months.
Cumulative student debt: 80% of graduating class had student loans; average debt was $25,790.

FINANCIAL AID PROCEDURES
Forms required: FAFSA, institutional form.
Dates and Deadlines: Priority date 5/1; no closing date. Applicants notified on a rolling basis starting 4/1; must reply within 4 week(s) of notification.

CONTACT
Robert Dame, Director of Student Financial Aid
College Admissions, Chicago, IL 60612
(312) 942-6256

Saint Anthony College of Nursing
Rockford, Illinois
www.sacn.edu   Federal Code: 009987

Upper-division private nursing college in large city, affiliated with Roman Catholic Church.
Enrollment: 124 undergrads, 13% part-time.

BASIC COSTS (2006-2007)
Tuition and fees: $16,282.
Per-credit charge: $506.
Additional info: Required fees vary from $112-$262.

FINANCIAL AID PICTURE (2004-2005)
Students with need: Average financial aid package for all full-time undergraduates was $11,000. 28% awarded as scholarships/grants, 72% awarded as loans/jobs. Need-based aid available for part-time students.
Students without need: No-need awards available for academics, leadership, state/district residency.
Cumulative student debt: 85% of graduating class had student loans; average debt was $17,000.

FINANCIAL AID PROCEDURES
Forms required: FAFSA.
Dates and Deadlines: Priority date 4/15; no closing date.
Transfers: No deadline. Applicants notified on a rolling basis starting 8/18.

CONTACT
Lisa Ruch, Financial Aid Officer
5658 East State Street, Rockford, IL 61108-2468
(815) 395-5089

St. Francis Medical Center College of Nursing
Peoria, Illinois
www.sfmccon.edu   Federal Code: 006240

Upper-division private nursing college in small city, affiliated with Roman Catholic Church.
Enrollment: 223 undergrads, 16% part-time.

BASIC COSTS (2006-2007)
Per-credit charge: $440.
Room only: $1,880.
Additional info: Students enter at the junior level. Cost for 2006/2007 academic year: $13,200 (tuition), $220 (required fees).

FINANCIAL AID PICTURE (2004-2005)
Students with need: Average financial aid package for all full-time undergraduates was $12,653; for part-time $8,527. 63% awarded as scholarships/grants, 37% awarded as loans/jobs.
Students without need: No-need awards available for academics, alumni affiliation.
Cumulative student debt: 74% of graduating class had student loans; average debt was $10,969.
Additional info: Modified Education Employment Program available to full-time students on a limited basis. Tuition waiver program for hospital employees available.

FINANCIAL AID PROCEDURES
Forms required: FAFSA, institutional form.
Dates and Deadlines: Priority date 6/1; no closing date. Applicants notified by 10/30; must reply within 4 week(s) of notification.
Transfers: No deadline. Applicants notified on a rolling basis starting 5/15; must reply within 2 week(s) of notification.

CONTACT
Kathy Casey, Assistant Dean, Support Services
511 NE Greenleaf Street, Peoria, IL 61603-3783
(309) 655-2291

St. Xavier University
Chicago, Illinois
www.sxu.edu   Federal Code: 001768

4-year private university in very large city, affiliated with Roman Catholic Church.
Enrollment: 3,131 undergrads, 24% part-time. 414 full-time freshmen.
Selectivity: Admits 50 to 75% of applicants.

BASIC COSTS (2006-2007)
Tuition and fees: $19,860.
Per-credit charge: $658.
Room and board: $7,414.

FINANCIAL AID PICTURE (2004-2005)
Students with need: Out of 385 full-time freshmen who applied for aid, 340 were judged to have need. Of these, 340 received aid, and 71 had their full need met. Average financial aid package met 88% of need; average scholarship/grant was $10,853; average loan was $2,714. Need-based aid available for part-time students.
Students without need: 65 full-time freshmen who did not demonstrate need for aid received scholarships/grants; average award was $6,041. No-need awards available for academics, athletics, music/drama.
Cumulative student debt: 72% of graduating class had student loans; average debt was $19,134.

FINANCIAL AID PROCEDURES
Forms required: FAFSA.
Dates and Deadlines: Priority date 3/1; no closing date. Applicants notified on a rolling basis starting 2/1; must reply by 5/1 or within 2 week(s) of notification.

CONTACT
Susan Swisher, Director of Financial Aid
3700 West 103rd Street, Chicago, IL 60655
(773) 298-3070

Sauk Valley Community College
Dixon, Illinois
www.svcc.edu   Federal Code: 001752

2-year public community college in large town.
Enrollment: 2,085 undergrads. 299 full-time freshmen.
Selectivity: Open admission; but selective for some programs.

BASIC COSTS (2005-2006)
Tuition and fees: $2,190; out-of-district residents $7,740; out-of-state residents $8,760.
Per-credit charge: $71; out-of-district residents $256; out-of-state residents $290.

FINANCIAL AID PICTURE (2005-2006)
Students with need: Out of 201 full-time freshmen who applied for aid, 90 were judged to have need. Of these, 90 received aid, and 6 had their full need met. Average financial aid package met 81% of need; average scholarship/grant was $4,313; average loan was $2,540. For part-time students, average financial aid package was $3,067.
Students without need: 14 full-time freshmen who did not demonstrate need for aid received scholarships/grants; average award was $1,131. No-need awards available for academics, athletics, leadership, minority status, state/district residency.
Scholarships offered: 33 full-time freshmen received athletic scholarships; average amount $2,120.
Cumulative student debt: 15% of graduating class had student loans; average debt was $5,257.

FINANCIAL AID PROCEDURES
Forms required: FAFSA, institutional form.
Dates and Deadlines: Priority date 3/1; no closing date. Applicants notified on a rolling basis starting 5/1.
Transfers: No deadline. Applicants notified on a rolling basis starting 3/1.

CONTACT
Debra Stiefel, Coordinator of Financial Aid
173 Illinois Route 2, Dixon, IL 61021-9110
(815) 288-5511 ext. 339

School of the Art Institute of Chicago
Chicago, Illinois
www.artic.edu/saic   Federal Code: 001753

4-year private visual arts college in very large city.
Enrollment: 2,008 undergrads, 6% part-time. 356 full-time freshmen.
Selectivity: Admits over 75% of applicants.

BASIC COSTS (2006-2007)
Tuition and fees: $29,220.
Per-credit charge: $965.
Room only: $8,200.
Additional info: Students will be required to purchase a laptop through SAIC. Costs range from $2,000 to $2,200.

FINANCIAL AID PICTURE (2005-2006)
Students with need: Out of 268 full-time freshmen who applied for aid, 179 were judged to have need. Of these, 178 received aid. For part-time students, average financial aid package was $14,773.
Students without need: 124 full-time freshmen who did not demonstrate need for aid received scholarships/grants; average award was $5,390. No-need awards available for academics, art.
Scholarships offered: Merit scholarships; $3,000, $6,000, $12,000 and full tuition; renewable annually.
Cumulative student debt: 63% of graduating class had student loans; average debt was $28,959.

FINANCIAL AID PROCEDURES
Forms required: FAFSA.
Dates and Deadlines: Priority date 3/15; no closing date. Applicants notified on a rolling basis starting 3/1.

CONTACT
Patrick James, Director of Financial Aid
37 South Wabash Avenue, Chicago, IL 60603
(312) 899-5106

Shimer College
Waukegan, Illinois
www.shimer.edu   Federal Code: 001756

4-year private liberal arts college in small city.
Enrollment: 107 undergrads.
Selectivity: Admits over 75% of applicants.

BASIC COSTS (2005-2006)
Tuition and fees: $19,450.
Per-credit charge: $775.
Room only: $3,000.
Additional info: Tuition/fee waivers available for adults.

FINANCIAL AID PICTURE
Students with need: Need-based aid available for full-time and part-time students.
Students without need: No-need awards available for academics.

FINANCIAL AID PROCEDURES
Forms required: FAFSA.
Dates and Deadlines: Priority date 4/15; closing date 7/31. Applicants notified on a rolling basis; must reply by 8/1.
Transfers: Closing date 8/1. Applicants notified on a rolling basis.

CONTACT
Janet Henthorn, Director of Financial Aid
414 North Sheridan Road, Waukegan, IL 60085
(847) 249-7180

South Suburban College of Cook County
South Holland, Illinois
www.southsuburbancollege.edu   Federal Code: 001769

2-year public community college in large town.
Enrollment: 6,625 undergrads.
Selectivity: Open admission; but selective for some programs.

BASIC COSTS (2006-2007)
Tuition and fees: $2,880; out-of-district residents $7,890; out-of-state residents $9,540.
Per-credit charge: $87; out-of-district residents $254; out-of-state residents $309.
Additional info: Some students in nearby states may qualify for tuition rate of $99 per credit hour under regional tuition plan. Tuition/fee waivers available for adults.

FINANCIAL AID PICTURE
Students with need: Need-based aid available for full-time and part-time students. Work study available nights.
Students without need: No-need awards available for academics, art, athletics, music/drama, state/district residency.

FINANCIAL AID PROCEDURES
Forms required: FAFSA.
Dates and Deadlines: Priority date 6/1; no closing date. Applicants notified on a rolling basis starting 7/1.
Transfers: No deadline. Applicants notified on a rolling basis.

CONTACT
John Semple, Director of Financial Aid
15800 South State Street, South Holland, IL 60473
(708) 596-2000 ext. 2321

Southeastern Illinois College
Harrisburg, Illinois
www.sic.edu   Federal Code: 001757

2-year public community college in small town.
Enrollment: 1,207 undergrads.
Selectivity: Open admission; but selective for some programs.

BASIC COSTS (2005-2006)
Tuition and fees: $1,920; out-of-district residents $2,790; out-of-state residents $3,210.
Per-credit charge: $64; out-of-district residents $93; out-of-state residents $107.

FINANCIAL AID PICTURE (2004-2005)
Students with need: Need-based aid available for part-time students.
Students without need: No-need awards available for academics, alumni affiliation, art, athletics, music/drama.

FINANCIAL AID PROCEDURES
Forms required: FAFSA.
Dates and Deadlines: No deadline. Applicants notified on a rolling basis starting 4/15; must reply within 2 week(s) of notification.

CONTACT
Kelli Mahoney, Director of Financial Aid
3575 College Road, Harrisburg, IL 62946
(618) 252-5400 ext. 2450

Southern Illinois University Carbondale
Carbondale, Illinois
www.siuc.edu   Federal Code: 001758

4-year public university in large town.
Enrollment: 16,617 undergrads, 10% part-time. 2,451 full-time freshmen.
Selectivity: Admits over 75% of applicants.

BASIC COSTS (2005-2006)
Tuition and fees: $6,831; out-of-state residents $14,796.
Per-credit charge: $177; out-of-state residents $443.
Room and board: $5,560.
Additional info: Tuition at time of enrollment locked for 4 years.

FINANCIAL AID PICTURE (2005-2006)
Students with need: Out of 1,948 full-time freshmen who applied for aid, 1,413 were judged to have need. Of these, 1,390 received aid, and 1,241 had their full need met. Average financial aid package met 97% of need; average scholarship/grant was $6,609; average loan was $3,439. For part-time students, average financial aid package was $8,306.
Students without need: 131 full-time freshmen who did not demonstrate need for aid received scholarships/grants; average award was $3,418. No-need awards available for academics, alumni affiliation, art, athletics, job skills, leadership, minority status, music/drama, ROTC, state/district residency.
Scholarships offered: 35 full-time freshmen received athletic scholarships; average amount $11,671.
Cumulative student debt: 39% of graduating class had student loans; average debt was $14,708.
Additional info: Need-based financial aid available to part-time students enrolled in minimum of 6 semester hours.

FINANCIAL AID PROCEDURES
Forms required: FAFSA.
Dates and Deadlines: Priority date 4/1; no closing date. Applicants notified on a rolling basis starting 3/15; must reply within 3 week(s) of notification.

CONTACT
Donna Williams, Director of Financial Aid
Mailcode 4701, Carbondale, IL 62901-4701
(618) 453-4334

Southern Illinois University Edwardsville
Edwardsville, Illinois
www.siue.edu   Federal Code: 001759

4-year public university in very large city.
Enrollment: 10,855 undergrads, 15% part-time. 1,721 full-time freshmen.
Selectivity: Admits over 75% of applicants.

BASIC COSTS (2005-2006)
Tuition and fees: $5,209; out-of-state residents $11,734.
Per-credit charge: $145; out-of-state residents $363.
Room and board: $5,790.
Additional info: Required fees include book rental. Tuition at time of enrollment locked for 4 years.

FINANCIAL AID PICTURE (2004-2005)
Students with need: Out of 1,249 full-time freshmen who applied for aid, 850 were judged to have need. Of these, 806 received aid, and 188 had their full need met. Average financial aid package met 76% of need; average scholarship/grant was $5,573; average loan was $2,369. For part-time students, average financial aid package was $6,737.
Students without need: This college only awards aid to students with need.

Scholarships offered: 17 full-time freshmen received athletic scholarships; average amount $2,597.

FINANCIAL AID PROCEDURES
Forms required: FAFSA.
Dates and Deadlines: Priority date 3/1; closing date 6/1. Applicants notified on a rolling basis starting 3/15; must reply within 4 week(s) of notification.

CONTACT
Sharon Berry, Director of Student Financial Aid
Campus Box 1600, Rendleman Hall, Rm 2120, Edwardsville, IL 62026-1600
(618) 650-3880

Southwestern Illinois College
Belleville, Illinois
www.swic.edu
Federal Code: 001636

2-year public community college in large town.
Enrollment: 8,841 undergrads.
Selectivity: Open admission; but selective for some programs.

BASIC COSTS (2005-2006)
Tuition and fees: $1,740; out-of-district residents $4,710; out-of-state residents $7,470.
Per-credit charge: $58; out-of-district residents $157; out-of-state residents $249.
Additional info: Required fees vary by courses taken. Those 60 and over pay a reduced rate of $50 per-credit-hour.

FINANCIAL AID PICTURE (2004-2005)
Students with need: 80% of average financial aid package awarded as scholarships/grants, 20% awarded as loans/jobs. Need-based aid available for part-time students.
Students without need: No-need awards available for academics, athletics.

FINANCIAL AID PROCEDURES
Forms required: FAFSA.
Dates and Deadlines: Priority date 5/31; no closing date. Applicants notified on a rolling basis starting 7/1; must reply within 2 week(s) of notification.

CONTACT
Robert Clement, Director of Financial Aid
2500 Carlyle Avenue, Belleville, IL 62221-9989
(618) 235-2700 ext. 5288

Springfield College in Illinois
Springfield, Illinois
www.sci.edu
Federal Code: 001761

2-year private junior and liberal arts college in small city, affiliated with Roman Catholic Church.
Enrollment: 551 undergrads, 51% part-time. 117 full-time freshmen.
Selectivity: Admits over 75% of applicants.

BASIC COSTS (2005-2006)
Tuition and fees: $7,844.
Per-credit charge: $312.
Room only: $2,650.

FINANCIAL AID PICTURE
Students with need: Need-based aid available for full-time and part-time students. Work study available nights, weekends, and for part-time students.
Students without need: No-need awards available for academics, art, athletics, leadership, religious affiliation.

FINANCIAL AID PROCEDURES
Forms required: FAFSA, institutional form.
Dates and Deadlines: Priority date 3/1; no closing date. Applicants notified on a rolling basis starting 3/15; must reply within 2 week(s) of notification.

CONTACT
Josephine Negro, Director of Financial Aid
1500 North Fifth Street, Springfield, IL 62702-2694
(217) 525-1420 ext. 244

Taylor Business Institute
Chicago, Illinois
www.tbiil.org
Federal Code: 011810

2-year for-profit business college in very large city.
Enrollment: 225 undergrads.
Selectivity: Open admission.

BASIC COSTS (2005-2006)
Additional info: Costs vary by program. Tuition for non-degree programs is $15,425-$18,325; associate degree programs are $23,725-$18,325. Fees and book estimates are included in tuition charges.

FINANCIAL AID PICTURE
Students with need: Need-based aid available for full-time students. Work study available nights.

FINANCIAL AID PROCEDURES
Forms required: FAFSA, state aid form, institutional form.

CONTACT
Florence Davis, Financial Aid Director
200 North Michigan Avenue, Suite 301, Chicago, IL 60601
(312) 658-5100

Trinity Christian College
Palos Heights, Illinois
www.trnty.edu
Federal Code: 001771

4-year private liberal arts college in very large city, affiliated with Reformed (unaffiliated).
Enrollment: 1,148 undergrads, 14% part-time. 215 full-time freshmen.
Selectivity: Admits over 75% of applicants.

BASIC COSTS (2006-2007)
Tuition and fees: $18,115.
Per-credit charge: $600.
Room and board: $6,810.

FINANCIAL AID PICTURE (2004-2005)
Students with need: Out of 196 full-time freshmen who applied for aid, 163 were judged to have need. Of these, 163 received aid, and 11 had their full need met. Average financial aid package met 8% of need; average scholarship/grant was $3,995; average loan was $2,994. Need-based aid available for part-time students.
Students without need: 13 full-time freshmen who did not demonstrate need for aid received scholarships/grants; average award was $2,232. No-need awards available for academics, art, athletics, leadership, minority status, music/drama, religious affiliation.
Scholarships offered: 36 full-time freshmen received athletic scholarships; average amount $3,805.
Cumulative student debt: 75% of graduating class had student loans; average debt was $14,000.
Additional info: High school transcripts and ACT or SAT scores required for merit scholarships.

FINANCIAL AID PROCEDURES
Forms required: FAFSA, institutional form.

Dates and Deadlines: Priority date 2/15; closing date 4/15. Applicants notified by 2/28; must reply by 5/1 or within 2 week(s) of notification.
Transfers: Applicants notified by 2/28; must reply by 5/1 or within 2 week(s) of notification.

CONTACT
Denise Coleman, Financial Aid Officer
6601 West College Drive, Palos Heights, IL 60463
(708) 239-4706

Trinity International University
Deerfield, Illinois
www.tiu.edu   Federal Code: 001772

4-year private university and liberal arts college in large town, affiliated with Evangelical Free Church of America.
Enrollment: 1,249 undergrads, 13% part-time. 202 full-time freshmen.
Selectivity: Admits over 75% of applicants.

BASIC COSTS (2006-2007)
Tuition and fees: $20,106.
Per-credit charge: $820.
Room and board: $6,550.
Additional info: Tuition/fee waivers available for minority students.

FINANCIAL AID PICTURE (2005-2006)
Students with need: Out of 183 full-time freshmen who applied for aid, 153 were judged to have need. Of these, 153 received aid, and 8 had their full need met. Average financial aid package met 16% of need; average scholarship/grant was $5,897; average loan was $3,121. For part-time students, average financial aid package was $7,315.
Students without need: 16 full-time freshmen who did not demonstrate need for aid received scholarships/grants; average award was $3,469. No-need awards available for academics, alumni affiliation, athletics, minority status, music/drama, religious affiliation.
Scholarships offered: 63 full-time freshmen received athletic scholarships; average amount $8,334.
Cumulative student debt: 78% of graduating class had student loans; average debt was $17,129.

FINANCIAL AID PROCEDURES
Forms required: FAFSA.
Dates and Deadlines: Priority date 4/1; no closing date. Applicants notified on a rolling basis starting 2/15; must reply within 4 week(s) of notification.
Transfers: No deadline. Applicants notified on a rolling basis; must reply within 4 week(s) of notification.

CONTACT
Ron Campbell, Director of Financial Aid
2065 Half Day Road, Deerfield, IL 60015
(847) 317-8060

Triton College
River Grove, Illinois
www.triton.edu   Federal Code: 001773

2-year public community and junior college in large town.
Enrollment: 9,754 undergrads, 64% part-time. 1,052 full-time freshmen.
Selectivity: Open admission; but selective for some programs.

BASIC COSTS (2006-2007)
Tuition and fees: $1,980; out-of-district residents $5,550; out-of-state residents $6,960.
Per-credit charge: $56; out-of-district residents $175; out-of-state residents $222.

FINANCIAL AID PICTURE (2004-2005)
Students with need: 81% of average financial aid package awarded as scholarships/grants, 19% awarded as loans/jobs. Need-based aid available for part-time students. Work study available nights, weekends, and for part-time students.
Students without need: No-need awards available for academics, athletics.
Scholarships offered: Board of Trustees Honor Scholarship; covers tuition and fees; for in-district high school students in top 10% of graduating class.

FINANCIAL AID PROCEDURES
Forms required: FAFSA, institutional form.
Dates and Deadlines: Priority date 4/15; no closing date. Applicants notified on a rolling basis starting 4/1; must reply within 2 week(s) of notification.

CONTACT
Patty Williamson, Director of Financial Aid
2000 North Fifth Avenue, River Grove, IL 60171
(708) 456-0300 ext. 3441

University of Chicago
Chicago, Illinois
www.uchicago.edu   Federal Code: 001774
                            CSS Code: 1832

4-year private university and liberal arts college in very large city.
Enrollment: 4,638 undergrads, 1% part-time. 1,203 full-time freshmen.
Selectivity: Admits less than 50% of applicants.

BASIC COSTS (2005-2006)
Tuition and fees: $32,265.
Room and board: $10,104.

FINANCIAL AID PICTURE (2004-2005)
Students with need: 78% of average financial aid package awarded as scholarships/grants, 22% awarded as loans/jobs. Work study available nights, weekends, and for part-time students.
Students without need: No-need awards available for academics, leadership.

FINANCIAL AID PROCEDURES
Forms required: FAFSA, CSS PROFILE, institutional form.
Dates and Deadlines: Closing date 2/1. Applicants notified by 4/5; must reply by 5/1.
Transfers: Closing date 3/1. Applicants notified on a rolling basis starting 4/15; must reply by 6/1.

CONTACT
Alicia Reyes, Director of Financial Aid
1101 East 58th Street, Chicago, IL 60637
(773) 702-8666

University of Illinois at Chicago
Chicago, Illinois
www.uic.edu   Federal Code: 001776

4-year public university in very large city.
Enrollment: 15,029 undergrads, 9% part-time. 2,756 full-time freshmen.
Selectivity: Admits 50 to 75% of applicants.

BASIC COSTS (2005-2006)
Tuition and fees: $8,302; out-of-state residents $20,692.
Room and board: $7,954.
Additional info: Tuition at time of enrollment locked for 4 years; tuition/fee waivers available for minority students.

338 Illinois University of Illinois at Chicago

FINANCIAL AID PICTURE (2004-2005)
Students with need: Out of 2,181 full-time freshmen who applied for aid, 1,594 were judged to have need. Of these, 1,584 received aid, and 1,051 had their full need met. Average financial aid package met 94% of need; average scholarship/grant was $8,860; average loan was $2,822. For part-time students, average financial aid package was $3,809.
Students without need: 232 full-time freshmen who did not demonstrate need for aid received scholarships/grants. No-need awards available for academics, art, athletics, music/drama, ROTC, state/district residency.
Scholarships offered: 45 full-time freshmen received athletic scholarships; average amount $11,117.
Cumulative student debt: 46% of graduating class had student loans; average debt was $18,800.

FINANCIAL AID PROCEDURES
Forms required: FAFSA.
Dates and Deadlines: Priority date 3/1; no closing date. Applicants notified on a rolling basis starting 4/15; must reply within 2 week(s) of notification.

CONTACT
Marsha Weiss, Director of the Office of Student Financial Aid
PO Box 5220, Chicago, IL 60680
(312) 996-5563

University of Illinois at Urbana-Champaign
Champaign, Illinois
www.uiuc.edu   Federal Code: 001775

4-year public university in small city.
Enrollment: 30,251 undergrads, 2% part-time. 7,570 full-time freshmen.
Selectivity: Admits over 75% of applicants.

BASIC COSTS (2005-2006)
Tuition and fees: $8,688; out-of-state residents $22,774.
Room and board: $7,176.
Additional info: Tuition at time of enrollment locked for 4 years.

FINANCIAL AID PICTURE (2004-2005)
Students with need: Out of 4,994 full-time freshmen who applied for aid, 3,084 were judged to have need. Of these, 2,927 received aid, and 1,483 had their full need met. Average financial aid package met 90% of need; average scholarship/grant was $6,680; average loan was $3,290. For part-time students, average financial aid package was $6,170.
Students without need: 2,021 full-time freshmen who did not demonstrate need for aid received scholarships/grants; average award was $2,706. No-need awards available for academics, alumni affiliation, art, athletics, leadership, music/drama, ROTC, state/district residency.
Scholarships offered: *Merit:* President's Award Program: $1,000 - $3,000 for 4 years; based on status as member of historically underrepresented group, must have ACT composite of at least 24 or combined verbal and quantitative SAT score of at least 1060 (exclusive of Writing); approximately 500 available. Academic Achievement Scholarship: $3,000; criteria set by each college; 50 available. Matthews Scholars: $2,000 per year, renewable for 4 years if GPA of at least 3.3 is maintained; criteria includes academic achievement, leadership skills, commitment to campus and community efforts, good sponsor relations, diversity of college gender and ethnicity; approximately 150 available. FMC Award of Excellence: $1,000 a year, non-renewable; for incoming freshmen or incoming students in a particular college that requires a year or more of undergraduate work for admission; criteria set by individual colleges; 20 available. *Athletic:* 82 full-time freshmen received athletic scholarships; average amount $18,838.
Cumulative student debt: 46% of graduating class had student loans; average debt was $15,526.

FINANCIAL AID PROCEDURES
Forms required: FAFSA.
Dates and Deadlines: Priority date 3/15; no closing date. Applicants notified on a rolling basis starting 3/15.

CONTACT
Daniel Mann, Director of Student Financial Aid
901 West Illinois, Urbana, IL 61801-3028
(217) 333-0100

University of Illinois: Springfield
Springfield, Illinois
www.uis.edu   Federal Code: 009333

4-year public university and liberal arts college in small city.
Enrollment: 2,446 undergrads, 38% part-time. 90 full-time freshmen.
Selectivity: Admits 50 to 75% of applicants.

BASIC COSTS (2005-2006)
Tuition and fees: $5,375; out-of-state residents $14,525.
Per-credit charge: $153; out-of-state residents $458.
Room and board: $6,960.
Additional info: Tuition at time of enrollment locked for 4 years.

FINANCIAL AID PICTURE (2004-2005)
Students with need: Out of 87 full-time freshmen who applied for aid, 55 were judged to have need. Of these, 55 received aid, and 34 had their full need met. Average financial aid package met 88% of need; average scholarship/grant was $4,719; average loan was $2,361. For part-time students, average financial aid package was $5,039.
Students without need: 34 full-time freshmen who did not demonstrate need for aid received scholarships/grants; average award was $4,188. No-need awards available for academics, alumni affiliation, art, athletics, job skills, leadership, minority status, music/drama, state/district residency.
Scholarships offered: 9 full-time freshmen received athletic scholarships; average amount $7,542.
Cumulative student debt: 47% of graduating class had student loans; average debt was $11,069.

FINANCIAL AID PROCEDURES
Forms required: FAFSA.
Dates and Deadlines: Priority date 4/1; closing date 11/15. Applicants notified on a rolling basis starting 1/1; must reply within 3 week(s) of notification.
Transfers: No deadline.

CONTACT
Gerard Joseph, Director of Financial Aid
One University Plaza, MS UHB 1080, Springfield, IL 62703
(217) 206-6724

University of St. Francis
Joliet, Illinois
www.stfrancis.edu   Federal Code: 001664

4-year private university and liberal arts college in small city, affiliated with Roman Catholic Church.
Enrollment: 1,249 undergrads, 9% part-time. 190 full-time freshmen.
Selectivity: Admits 50 to 75% of applicants.

BASIC COSTS (2006-2007)
Tuition and fees: $19,540.
Per-credit charge: $625.
Room and board: $7,280.

FINANCIAL AID PICTURE (2005-2006)
Students with need: Out of 175 full-time freshmen who applied for aid, 144 were judged to have need. Of these, 144 received aid, and 132 had their full need met. Average financial aid package met 91% of need; average scholarship/grant was $7,030; average loan was $2,692. For part-time students, average financial aid package was $7,494.
Students without need: 30 full-time freshmen who did not demonstrate need for aid received scholarships/grants; average award was $6,098. No-need awards available for academics, alumni affiliation, art, athletics, leadership, music/drama, religious affiliation, state/district residency.
Scholarships offered: 15 full-time freshmen received athletic scholarships; average amount $8,704.
Cumulative student debt: 88% of graduating class had student loans; average debt was $14,650.

FINANCIAL AID PROCEDURES
Forms required: FAFSA, institutional form.
Dates and Deadlines: Priority date 4/1; no closing date. Applicants notified on a rolling basis starting 2/15.
Transfers: Applicants notified on a rolling basis starting 2/15.

CONTACT
Mary Shaw, Director of Financial Aid Services
500 Wilcox Street, Joliet, IL 60435
(866) 890-8331

VanderCook College of Music
Chicago, Illinois
www.vandercook.edu   Federal Code: 001778

4-year private music and teachers college in very large city.
Enrollment: 110 undergrads, 5% part-time. 22 full-time freshmen.
Selectivity: Admits 50 to 75% of applicants.

BASIC COSTS (2006-2007)
Tuition and fees: $17,890.
Per-credit charge: $720.
Room and board: $8,250.

FINANCIAL AID PICTURE (2004-2005)
Students with need: 46% of average financial aid package awarded as scholarships/grants, 54% awarded as loans/jobs.
Students without need: No-need awards available for academics, alumni affiliation, leadership, minority status, music/drama, state/district residency.
Additional info: Musical talent considered for partial tuition waiver.

FINANCIAL AID PROCEDURES
Forms required: FAFSA.
Dates and Deadlines: Priority date 3/1; closing date 4/30. Applicants notified on a rolling basis starting 5/15; must reply within 2 week(s) of notification.
Transfers: No deadline. Title IV funding prorated by semester.

CONTACT
Susan Frost, Financial Aid Administrator
3140 South Federal Street, Chicago, IL 60616-3731
(312) 225-6288

Waubonsee Community College
Sugar Grove, Illinois
www.waubonsee.edu   Federal Code: 006931

2-year public community college in small town.
Enrollment: 6,014 undergrads, 58% part-time. 596 full-time freshmen.
Selectivity: Open admission; but selective for some programs.

BASIC COSTS (2006-2007)
Tuition and fees: $1,920; out-of-district residents $6,360; out-of-state residents $7,170.
Per-credit charge: $62; out-of-district residents $210; out-of-state residents $237.

FINANCIAL AID PICTURE (2004-2005)
Students with need: 81% of average financial aid package awarded as scholarships/grants, 19% awarded as loans/jobs. Need-based aid available for part-time students. Work study available nights.
Students without need: No-need awards available for academics, art, athletics, leadership, minority status, music/drama.
Scholarships offered: Gustafson Scholarship; cost of 64 semester hours; awarded to selected local high school graduates.

FINANCIAL AID PROCEDURES
Forms required: FAFSA, institutional form.
Dates and Deadlines: Closing date 12/2. Applicants notified on a rolling basis starting 5/1.
Transfers: Closing date 4/1.

CONTACT
Laura Somerlot, Financial Aid Manager
Route 47 at Waubonsee Drive, Sugar Grove, IL 60554-9454
(630) 466-7900 ext. 5774

West Suburban College of Nursing
Oak Park, Illinois
www.wscn.edu   Federal Code: 022141

Upper-division private nursing college in very large city, affiliated with Roman Catholic Church.
Enrollment: 136 undergrads, 21% part-time.

BASIC COSTS (2005-2006)
Tuition and fees: $19,034.
Per-credit charge: $630.
Additional info: 16 month fast track nursing program available for $30,628.

FINANCIAL AID PICTURE
Students with need: Need-based aid available for full-time and part-time students.
Additional info: Financial aid administered through Concordia University.

FINANCIAL AID PROCEDURES
Forms required: FAFSA.
Dates and Deadlines: Applicants notified on a rolling basis.

CONTACT
Thomas Lambert, Financial Aid Officer
3 Erie Court, Oak Park, IL 60302
(708) 763-1426

Western Illinois University
Macomb, Illinois
www.wiu.edu   Federal Code: 001780

4-year public university in large town.
Enrollment: 11,276 undergrads, 9% part-time. 1,812 full-time freshmen.
Selectivity: Admits 50 to 75% of applicants.

BASIC COSTS (2005-2006)
Tuition and fees: $6,411; out-of-state residents $8,895.
Per-credit charge: $166; out-of-state residents $248.
Room and board: $6,143.
Additional info: Residents of nearby counties in Iowa and Missouri pay in-state tuition during first year. Incoming freshmen guaranteed the first year

tuition rate for their entire 4 years, provided they are continually enrolled. Tuition at time of enrollment locked for 4 years.

FINANCIAL AID PICTURE (2005-2006)
Students with need: Out of 1,341 full-time freshmen who applied for aid, 990 were judged to have need. Of these, 951 received aid, and 318 had their full need met. Average financial aid package met 63% of need; average scholarship/grant was $6,423; average loan was $2,517. For part-time students, average financial aid package was $5,566.
Students without need: 104 full-time freshmen who did not demonstrate need for aid received scholarships/grants; average award was $3,039. No-need awards available for academics, alumni affiliation, art, athletics, leadership, minority status, music/drama, ROTC.
Scholarships offered: 68 full-time freshmen received athletic scholarships; average amount $6,585.
Cumulative student debt: 62% of graduating class had student loans; average debt was $14,850.

FINANCIAL AID PROCEDURES
Forms required: FAFSA.
Dates and Deadlines: Priority date 2/15; no closing date. Applicants notified on a rolling basis starting 1/15.

CONTACT
William Bushaw, Director of Financial Aid
One University Circle, Macomb, IL 61455-1390
(309) 298-2446

Westwood College - DuPage
Woodridge, Illinois
www.westwood.edu

4-year for-profit technical college in large city.
Enrollment: 581 undergrads.

BASIC COSTS (2006-2007)
Comprehensive fee: $27,047.

FINANCIAL AID PICTURE (2004-2005)
Students with need: 56% of average financial aid package awarded as scholarships/grants, 44% awarded as loans/jobs.

CONTACT
Silvia Hurtado, Director of Financial Aid
7155 Janes Avenue, Woodridge, IL 60517

Wheaton College
Wheaton, Illinois
www.wheaton.edu   Federal Code: 001781

4-year private liberal arts college in small city, affiliated with nondenominational tradition.
Enrollment: 2,392 undergrads, 2% part-time. 578 full-time freshmen.
Selectivity: Admits 50 to 75% of applicants.

BASIC COSTS (2006-2007)
Tuition and fees: $22,450.
Per-credit charge: $935.
Room and board: $7,040.

FINANCIAL AID PICTURE (2005-2006)
Students with need: Out of 461 full-time freshmen who applied for aid, 287 were judged to have need. Of these, 282 received aid, and 76 had their full need met. Average financial aid package met 87% of need; average scholarship/grant was $13,546; average loan was $4,808. For part-time students, average financial aid package was $14,533.
Students without need: 149 full-time freshmen who did not demonstrate need for aid received scholarships/grants; average award was $3,251. No-need awards available for academics, alumni affiliation, art, minority status, music/drama, ROTC.
Cumulative student debt: 55% of graduating class had student loans; average debt was $17,936.

FINANCIAL AID PROCEDURES
Forms required: FAFSA, institutional form.
Dates and Deadlines: Priority date 2/15; no closing date. Applicants notified on a rolling basis starting 3/1.
Transfers: Priority date 3/1; no deadline.

CONTACT
Donna Peltz, Director of Financial Aid
501 College Avenue, Wheaton, IL 60187-5593
(630) 752-5021

William Rainey Harper College
Palatine, Illinois
www.harpercollege.edu   Federal Code: 003961

2-year public community college in small city.
Enrollment: 13,421 undergrads, 55% part-time. 1,840 full-time freshmen.
Selectivity: Open admission; but selective for some programs.

BASIC COSTS (2006-2007)
Tuition and fees: $2,868; out-of-district residents $9,048; out-of-state residents $11,180.
Per-credit charge: $77; out-of-district residents $284; out-of-state residents $354.
Additional info: In-district tuition rates available to employees of in-district companies who reside outside college district. Rates based on 30 credit hours per academic year. Full-time is considered to be 12 credit hours per semester.

FINANCIAL AID PICTURE (2004-2005)
Students with need: 66% of average financial aid package awarded as scholarships/grants, 34% awarded as loans/jobs. Need-based aid available for part-time students. Work study available nights, weekends, and for part-time students.
Students without need: No-need awards available for academics, art, leadership, minority status, music/drama, state/district residency.
Scholarships offered: Distinguished Scholar Award: full tuition and fees; available to full-time students during regular academic year who graduate in top 10% of class from district high school; renewable for second year.

FINANCIAL AID PROCEDURES
Forms required: FAFSA, institutional form.
Dates and Deadlines: Priority date 5/1; no closing date. Applicants notified on a rolling basis starting 3/1; must reply within 2 week(s) of notification.
Transfers: No deadline. Applicants notified on a rolling basis starting 3/1.

CONTACT
Bruce Foote, Director, Scholarships and Financial Assistance
1200 West Algonquin Road, Palatine, IL 60067-7398
(847) 925-6248

Indiana

Ancilla College
Donaldson, Indiana
www.ancilla.edu					Federal Code: 001784

2-year private community and liberal arts college in rural community, affiliated with Roman Catholic Church.
Enrollment: 600 undergrads.
Selectivity: Open admission; but selective for some programs.
BASIC COSTS (2005-2006)
Tuition and fees: $9,830.
Per-credit charge: $320.
FINANCIAL AID PICTURE
Students with need: Need-based aid available for full-time and part-time students.
Students without need: No-need awards available for academics, athletics, job skills, leadership.
FINANCIAL AID PROCEDURES
Forms required: FAFSA, institutional form.
Dates and Deadlines: Closing date 3/1. Applicants notified on a rolling basis starting 3/1; must reply within 2 week(s) of notification.
CONTACT
Michael Schmaltz, Director of Financial Aid
9001 Union Road, Donaldson, IN 46513
(574) 936-8898 ext. 307

Anderson University
Anderson, Indiana
www.anderson.edu					Federal Code: 001785

4-year private liberal arts college in small city, affiliated with Church of God.
Enrollment: 2,329 undergrads, 8% part-time. 566 full-time freshmen.
Selectivity: Admits over 75% of applicants. GED not accepted.
BASIC COSTS (2006-2007)
Tuition and fees: $19,990.
Per-credit charge: $833.
Room and board: $6,460.
Additional info: Tuition/fee waivers available for adults.
FINANCIAL AID PICTURE
Students with need: Need-based aid available for full-time and part-time students. Work study available nights, weekends, and for part-time students.
Students without need: No-need awards available for academics, leadership, minority status, music/drama, state/district residency.
FINANCIAL AID PROCEDURES
Forms required: FAFSA.
Dates and Deadlines: Priority date 3/1; no closing date. Applicants notified on a rolling basis starting 3/1.
CONTACT
Kenneth Nieman, Director of Financial Aid
1100 East Fifth, Anderson, IN 46012
(765) 641-4182

Ball State University
Muncie, Indiana
www.bsu.edu					Federal Code: 001786

4-year public university in small city.
Enrollment: 17,269 undergrads, 7% part-time. 3,668 full-time freshmen.
Selectivity: Admits over 75% of applicants.
BASIC COSTS (2005-2006)
Tuition and fees: $6,458; out-of-state residents $16,218.
Room and board: $6,680.
FINANCIAL AID PICTURE (2005-2006)
Students with need: Out of 3,113 full-time freshmen who applied for aid, 2,143 were judged to have need. Of these, 2,117 received aid, and 639 had their full need met. Average financial aid package met 61% of need; average scholarship/grant was $4,522; average loan was $2,794. For part-time students, average financial aid package was $5,809.
Students without need: 718 full-time freshmen who did not demonstrate need for aid received scholarships/grants; average award was $3,256. No-need awards available for academics, athletics, leadership, minority status, music/drama, ROTC, state/district residency.
Scholarships offered: 69 full-time freshmen received athletic scholarships; average amount $12,346.
Cumulative student debt: 62% of graduating class had student loans; average debt was $17,418.
FINANCIAL AID PROCEDURES
Forms required: FAFSA.
Dates and Deadlines: Priority date 3/10; no closing date. Applicants notified on a rolling basis starting 4/1.
Transfers: No deadline.
CONTACT
Robert Zellers, Director of Scholarships/Financial Aid
2000 University Avenue, Muncie, IN 47306-1022
(765) 285-5600

Bethel College
Mishawaka, Indiana
www.bethelcollege.edu			Federal Code: 001787
						CSS Code: 1079

4-year private liberal arts college in large town, affiliated with Missionary Church.
Enrollment: 1,930 undergrads.
BASIC COSTS (2005-2006)
Tuition and fees: $16,396.
Room and board: $5,330.
Additional info: All first-time, full-time students must pay a one-time fee of $600. Tuition/fee waivers available for adults, minority students.
FINANCIAL AID PICTURE
Students with need: Need-based aid available for full-time and part-time students.
Students without need: No-need awards available for academics, art, athletics, minority status, music/drama, ROTC, state/district residency.
FINANCIAL AID PROCEDURES
Forms required: CSS PROFILE, institutional form.
Dates and Deadlines: Priority date 3/1; no closing date. Applicants notified on a rolling basis starting 2/15; must reply within 2 week(s) of notification.
CONTACT
Guy Fisher, Director of Financial Aid
1001 West McKinley Avenue, Mishawaka, IN 46545
(574) 257-3316

Butler University
Indianapolis, Indiana
www.butler.edu
Federal Code: 001788

4-year private university in very large city.
Enrollment: 3,635 undergrads, 2% part-time. 865 full-time freshmen.
Selectivity: Admits 50 to 75% of applicants.

BASIC COSTS (2005-2006)
Tuition and fees: $23,774.
Per-credit charge: $980.
Room and board: $7,920.

FINANCIAL AID PICTURE (2005-2006)
Students with need: Out of 801 full-time freshmen who applied for aid, 541 were judged to have need. Of these, 541 received aid, and 136 had their full need met. Average financial aid package met 81% of need; average scholarship/grant was $13,800; average loan was $3,590. Need-based aid available for part-time students.
Students without need: 221 full-time freshmen who did not demonstrate need for aid received scholarships/grants; average award was $8,500. No-need awards available for academics, athletics, music/drama.
Scholarships offered: 30 full-time freshmen received athletic scholarships; average amount $16,500.

FINANCIAL AID PROCEDURES
Forms required: FAFSA.
Dates and Deadlines: Priority date 3/1; closing date 8/1. Applicants notified on a rolling basis starting 3/15; must reply within 3 week(s) of notification.
Transfers: Priority date 3/15; no deadline.

CONTACT
Richard Bellows, Director of Financial Aid
4600 Sunset Avenue, Indianapolis, IN 46208
(317) 940-8200

Calumet College of St. Joseph
Whiting, Indiana
www.ccsj.edu
Federal Code: 001834

4-year private liberal arts college in small city, affiliated with Roman Catholic Church.
Enrollment: 1,125 undergrads, 58% part-time. 107 full-time freshmen.

BASIC COSTS (2006-2007)
Tuition and fees: $10,575.
Per-credit charge: $350.

FINANCIAL AID PICTURE (2004-2005)
Students with need: Out of 104 full-time freshmen who applied for aid, 91 were judged to have need. Of these, 91 received aid. Need-based aid available for part-time students.
Students without need: No-need awards available for academics, alumni affiliation, religious affiliation.
Additional info: Immediate computerized estimate of financial aid eligibility available to students applying in person.

FINANCIAL AID PROCEDURES
Forms required: FAFSA.
Dates and Deadlines: Priority date 3/1; no closing date. Applicants notified on a rolling basis; must reply within 2 week(s) of notification.

CONTACT
Chuck Walz, Director of Financial Aid
2400 New York Avenue, Whiting, IN 46394-2195
(219) 473-4296

DePauw University
Greencastle, Indiana
www.depauw.edu
Federal Code: 001792

4-year private music and liberal arts college in small town, affiliated with United Methodist Church.
Enrollment: 2,345 undergrads. 661 full-time freshmen.
Selectivity: Admits 50 to 75% of applicants.

BASIC COSTS (2006-2007)
Tuition and fees: $27,780.
Per-credit charge: $856.
Room and board: $7,800.

FINANCIAL AID PICTURE (2005-2006)
Students with need: Out of 463 full-time freshmen who applied for aid, 355 were judged to have need. Of these, 355 received aid, and 304 had their full need met. Average financial aid package met 98% of need; average scholarship/grant was $13,514; average loan was $3,550. Need-based aid available for part-time students.
Students without need: 291 full-time freshmen who did not demonstrate need for aid received scholarships/grants; average award was $11,051. No-need awards available for academics, alumni affiliation, leadership, minority status, music/drama, ROTC.
Scholarships offered: Holton Scholarships recognizing exceptional leadership and/or service, ranging from $1,000 to full tuition, 50 awarded.

FINANCIAL AID PROCEDURES
Forms required: FAFSA, institutional form.
Dates and Deadlines: Closing date 2/15. Applicants notified by 3/27; must reply by 5/1.

CONTACT
Anna Sinnet, Director of Financial Aid
101 East Seminary Street, Greencastle, IN 46135-1611
(765) 658-4030

Earlham College
Richmond, Indiana
www.earlham.edu
Federal Code: 001793

4-year private liberal arts and seminary college in large town, affiliated with Society of Friends (Quaker).
Enrollment: 1,185 undergrads, 1% part-time. 334 full-time freshmen.
Selectivity: Admits 50 to 75% of applicants.

BASIC COSTS (2006-2007)
Tuition and fees: $29,320.
Per-credit charge: $953.
Room and board: $6,200.

FINANCIAL AID PICTURE (2004-2005)
Students with need: Out of 236 full-time freshmen who applied for aid, 197 were judged to have need. Of these, 197 received aid, and 23 had their full need met. Average financial aid package met 85% of need; average scholarship/grant was $12,422; average loan was $3,257. Need-based aid available for part-time students.
Students without need: 81 full-time freshmen who did not demonstrate need for aid received scholarships/grants; average award was $6,150. No-need awards available for academics, minority status, religious affiliation.
Scholarships offered: Wilkinson Scholarships for Quaker applicants; Cunningham Scholarships for selected minority applicants; C.B. Edwards Scholarship for Chemistry; Presidential Honors Scholarship available.
Cumulative student debt: 69% of graduating class had student loans; average debt was $18,900.

FINANCIAL AID PROCEDURES

Forms required: FAFSA, institutional form.
Dates and Deadlines: Closing date 3/1. Applicants notified on a rolling basis starting 3/1.
Transfers: Priority date 3/1; no deadline. Deadline for State of Indiana Grants, 3/1 (FAFSA date).

CONTACT

Robert Arnold, Director of Financial Aid
801 National Road West, Richmond, IN 47374-4095
(765) 983-1217

Franklin College
Franklin, Indiana
www.franklincollege.edu   Federal Code: 001798

4-year private liberal arts college in large town, affiliated with American Baptist Churches in the USA.
Enrollment: 1,003 undergrads, 6% part-time. 297 full-time freshmen.
Selectivity: Admits over 75% of applicants.

BASIC COSTS (2006-2007)
Tuition and fees: $20,325.
Room and board: $5,750.

FINANCIAL AID PICTURE (2004-2005)

Students with need: Out of 281 full-time freshmen who applied for aid, 246 were judged to have need. Of these, 245 received aid, and 49 had their full need met. Average financial aid package met 87% of need; average scholarship/grant was $11,507; average loan was $3,730. For part-time students, average financial aid package was $7,824.
Students without need: 51 full-time freshmen who did not demonstrate need for aid received scholarships/grants; average award was $7,895. No-need awards available for academics, alumni affiliation, leadership, minority status, religious affiliation, state/district residency.
Cumulative student debt: 90% of graduating class had student loans; average debt was $21,263.

FINANCIAL AID PROCEDURES

Forms required: FAFSA, institutional form.
Dates and Deadlines: Closing date 3/1. Applicants notified by 4/1; must reply by 5/1 or within 4 week(s) of notification.
Transfers: Must reply by 5/1 or within 2 week(s) of notification.

CONTACT

Elizabeth Sappenfield, Director of Financial Aid
101 Branigin Boulevard, Franklin, IN 46131-2623
(317) 738-8075

Goshen College
Goshen, Indiana
www.goshen.edu   Federal Code: 001799

4-year private liberal arts college in large town, affiliated with Mennonite Church.
Enrollment: 899 undergrads, 8% part-time. 195 full-time freshmen.
Selectivity: Admits over 75% of applicants.

BASIC COSTS (2006-2007)
Tuition and fees: $20,300.
Per-credit charge: $800.
Room and board: $6,700.

FINANCIAL AID PICTURE (2004-2005)

Students with need: Out of 195 full-time freshmen who applied for aid, 147 were judged to have need. Of these, 147 received aid, and 49 had their full need met. Average financial aid package met 88% of need; average scholarship/grant was $12,537; average loan was $3,558. For part-time students, average financial aid package was $5,627.
Students without need: 26 full-time freshmen who did not demonstrate need for aid received scholarships/grants; average award was $8,495. No-need awards available for academics, athletics, state/district residency.
Scholarships offered: *Merit:* Yoder Honors Scholarship; $4,000; predicted college GPA of 3.2 to 3.39 or 1110 SAT or 24 ACT or top 15% of class, renews at 3.0 GPA. Menno Simons Scholarship; $7,000; predicted college GPA of 3.6 or greater or 1270 SAT or 29 ACT or top 5% of class, renews at 3.2 GPA. President's Leadership Award; $10,000; must meet 2 of the following: predicted college GPA 3.8, 1270 SAT, 28 ACT, top 5% of class, must be a National Merit finalist, 10 awarded, renews at 3.2 or higher GPA. Wens Honors Scholarship; $4,500; predicted college GPA of 3.4 to 3.59, unlimited, renewable with 3.0 GPA. Grebel Scholarship; $2,500; predicted college GPA of 3.0 to 3.19, renewable with 3.0 GPA. All SAT scores listed are exclusive of the writing portion. *Athletic:* 3 full-time freshmen received athletic scholarships; average amount $6,000.
Cumulative student debt: 70% of graduating class had student loans; average debt was $12,933.

FINANCIAL AID PROCEDURES

Forms required: FAFSA, institutional form.
Dates and Deadlines: Priority date 2/11; no closing date. Applicants notified by 3/1; must reply by 5/1 or within 2 week(s) of notification.
Transfers: No deadline. Applicants notified by 3/1; must reply by 5/1 or within 2 week(s) of notification.

CONTACT

Judy Moore, Director of Student Financial Aid
1700 South Main Street, Goshen, IN 46526
(574) 535-7525

Grace College
Winona Lake, Indiana
www.grace.edu   Federal Code: 001800

4-year private Bible and liberal arts college in small town, affiliated with Brethren Church.
Enrollment: 1,062 undergrads, 8% part-time. 211 full-time freshmen.
Selectivity: Admits 50 to 75% of applicants.

BASIC COSTS (2006-2007)
Tuition and fees: $17,350.
Per-credit charge: $320.
Room and board: $6,360.

FINANCIAL AID PICTURE (2005-2006)

Students with need: Out of 198 full-time freshmen who applied for aid, 170 were judged to have need. Of these, 170 received aid, and 59 had their full need met. Average financial aid package met 80% of need; average scholarship/grant was $7,932; average loan was $4,381. For part-time students, average financial aid package was $6,681.
Students without need: 40 full-time freshmen who did not demonstrate need for aid received scholarships/grants; average award was $15,464. No-need awards available for academics, art, athletics, leadership, music/drama.
Scholarships offered: 25 full-time freshmen received athletic scholarships; average amount $4,427.
Cumulative student debt: 62% of graduating class had student loans; average debt was $13,104.

FINANCIAL AID PROCEDURES

Forms required: FAFSA.

Dates and Deadlines: Priority date 3/10; no closing date. Applicants notified on a rolling basis starting 3/1.

CONTACT
Sherry Shockey, Director of Financial Aid Services
200 Seminary Drive, Winona Lake, IN 46590
(574) 327-5100 ext. 6162

Hanover College
Hanover, Indiana
www.hanover.edu   Federal Code: 001801

4-year private liberal arts college in rural community, affiliated with Presbyterian Church (USA).
Enrollment: 999 undergrads. 380 full-time freshmen.
Selectivity: Admits 50 to 75% of applicants. GED not accepted.

BASIC COSTS (2006-2007)
Tuition and fees: $22,700.
Per-credit charge: $617.
Room and board: $6,800.

FINANCIAL AID PICTURE (2004-2005)
Students with need: Out of 354 full-time freshmen who applied for aid, 303 were judged to have need. Of these, 303 received aid, and 105 had their full need met. Average financial aid package met 77% of need; average scholarship/grant was $14,421; average loan was $2,765. For part-time students, average financial aid package was $8,547.
Students without need: 67 full-time freshmen who did not demonstrate need for aid received scholarships/grants; average award was $14,452. No-need awards available for academics, alumni affiliation, leadership, minority status, music/drama, religious affiliation, state/district residency.
Cumulative student debt: 63% of graduating class had student loans; average debt was $16,514.

FINANCIAL AID PROCEDURES
Forms required: FAFSA.
Dates and Deadlines: Priority date 3/1; no closing date. Applicants notified on a rolling basis starting 3/1; must reply by 5/1.
Transfers: No deadline. Applicants notified on a rolling basis starting 3/1; must reply by 5/1 or within 2 week(s) of notification.

CONTACT
Jon Riester, Associate Dean of Financial Assistance and Admission
PO Box 108, Hanover, IN 47243-0108
(812) 866-7030

Holy Cross College
Notre Dame, Indiana
www.hcc-nd.edu   Federal Code: 007263

4-year private liberal arts college in small city, affiliated with Roman Catholic Church.
Enrollment: 440 undergrads.

BASIC COSTS (2005-2006)
Tuition and fees: $11,000.
Per-credit charge: $360.
Room and board: $8,050.

FINANCIAL AID PICTURE
Students with need: Need-based aid available for full-time and part-time students. Work study available nights, weekends, and for part-time students.
Students without need: No-need awards available for academics, leadership.

FINANCIAL AID PROCEDURES
Forms required: FAFSA.
Dates and Deadlines: Priority date 3/1; no closing date. Applicants notified on a rolling basis starting 5/1; must reply within 2 week(s) of notification.

CONTACT
Doug Irving, Director of Financial Aid
54515 State Road 933N, Notre Dame, IN 46556-0308
(574) 239-8400

Huntington University
Huntington, Indiana
www.huntington.edu   Federal Code: 001803

4-year private university and liberal arts college in large town, affiliated with United Brethren in Christ.
Enrollment: 908 undergrads, 9% part-time. 224 full-time freshmen.
Selectivity: Admits over 75% of applicants.

BASIC COSTS (2006-2007)
Tuition and fees: $18,860.
Per-credit charge: $530.
Room and board: $6,530.

FINANCIAL AID PICTURE (2005-2006)
Students with need: Out of 203 full-time freshmen who applied for aid, 173 were judged to have need. Of these, 173 received aid, and 37 had their full need met. Average financial aid package met 77% of need; average scholarship/grant was $11,883; average loan was $3,067. For part-time students, average financial aid package was $7,530.
Students without need: 44 full-time freshmen who did not demonstrate need for aid received scholarships/grants; average award was $7,171. No-need awards available for academics, alumni affiliation, art, athletics, leadership, music/drama, religious affiliation.
Scholarships offered: 12 full-time freshmen received athletic scholarships; average amount $6,252.
Cumulative student debt: 62% of graduating class had student loans; average debt was $18,290.

FINANCIAL AID PROCEDURES
Forms required: FAFSA.
Dates and Deadlines: Priority date 3/1; no closing date. Applicants notified on a rolling basis starting 3/1; must reply by 5/1 or within 2 week(s) of notification.

CONTACT
Sharon Woods, Financial Aid Director
2303 College Avenue, Huntington, IN 46750-1237
(260) 359-4015

Indiana Business College
Indianapolis, Indiana
www.ibcschools.edu

2-year for-profit business and health science college in very large city.
Enrollment: 670 undergrads.

BASIC COSTS (2006-2007)
Additional info: Tuition and fees vary by program: $173 to $247 per credit hour.

FINANCIAL AID PICTURE
Students with need: Need-based aid available for full-time and part-time students.
Additional info: Work-study programs are available.

FINANCIAL AID PROCEDURES
Forms required: FAFSA.
Dates and Deadlines: Applicants notified on a rolling basis.

CONTACT
550 East Washington Street, Indianapolis, IN 46204
(800) 422-4723

Indiana Business College: Anderson
Anderson, Indiana
www.ibcschools.edu

2-year for-profit business and health science college in small city.
Enrollment: 235 undergrads.

FINANCIAL AID PICTURE
Students with need: Need-based aid available for full-time and part-time students.
Additional info: Work-study programs available.

FINANCIAL AID PROCEDURES
Forms required: FAFSA.
Dates and Deadlines: Applicants notified on a rolling basis.

CONTACT
140 East 53rd Street, Anderson, IN 46013
(800) 422-4723

Indiana Business College: Columbus
Columbus, Indiana
www.ibcschools.edu

2-year for-profit business and health science college in small city.
Enrollment: 273 undergrads.

FINANCIAL AID PICTURE
Students with need: Need-based aid available for full-time and part-time students.
Additional info: Work-study programs are available.

FINANCIAL AID PROCEDURES
Forms required: FAFSA.
Dates and Deadlines: Applicants notified on a rolling basis.

CONTACT
2222 Poshard Drive, Columbus, IN 47203
(800) 422-4723

Indiana Business College: Evansville
Evansville, Indiana
www.ibcschools.edu

2-year for-profit business and health science college in small city.
Enrollment: 295 undergrads.

FINANCIAL AID PICTURE
Students with need: Need-based aid available for full-time and part-time students.
Additional info: Work-study programs are available.

FINANCIAL AID PROCEDURES
Forms required: FAFSA.
Dates and Deadlines: Applicants notified on a rolling basis.

CONTACT
4601 Theater Drive, Evansville, IN 47715
(800) 422-4723

Indiana Business College: Fort Wayne
Fort Wayne, Indiana
www.ibcschools.edu

2-year for-profit business and health science college in large city.
Enrollment: 384 undergrads.

FINANCIAL AID PICTURE
Students with need: Need-based aid available for full-time and part-time students.
Additional info: Work-Study programs are available.

FINANCIAL AID PROCEDURES
Forms required: FAFSA.
Transfers: Applicants notified on a rolling basis.

CONTACT
6413 North Clinton St., Fort Wayne, IN 46825
(800) 422-4723

Indiana Business College: Lafayette
Lafayette, Indiana
www.ibcschools.edu

2-year for-profit business and health science college in small city.
Enrollment: 215 undergrads.

FINANCIAL AID PICTURE
Students with need: Need-based aid available for full-time and part-time students.
Additional info: Work-Study Programs are available.

FINANCIAL AID PROCEDURES
Forms required: FAFSA.
Dates and Deadlines: Applicants notified on a rolling basis.
Transfers: Applicants notified on a rolling basis.

CONTACT
4705 Meijer Court, Lafayette, IN 47905
(800) 422-4723

Indiana Business College: Marion
Marion, Indiana
www.ibcschools.edu

2-year for-profit business and health science college in large town.
Enrollment: 120 undergrads.

FINANCIAL AID PICTURE
Students with need: Need-based aid available for full-time and part-time students.
Additional info: Work-Study Programs are available.

FINANCIAL AID PROCEDURES
Forms required: FAFSA.
Dates and Deadlines: Applicants notified on a rolling basis.

CONTACT
830 North Miller Avenue, Marion, IN 46952
(800) 422-4723

Indiana Business College: Medical
Indianapolis, Indiana
www.ibcschools.edu

2-year for-profit health science college in very large city.
Enrollment: 584 undergrads.

FINANCIAL AID PICTURE
Students with need: Need-based aid available for full-time and part-time students.
Additional info: Work-study programs are available.

FINANCIAL AID PROCEDURES
Forms required: FAFSA.
Dates and Deadlines: Applicants notified on a rolling basis.
Transfers: Applicants notified on a rolling basis.

CONTACT
8150 Brookville Road, Indianapolis, IN 46239
(800) 422-4723

Indiana Business College: Muncie
Muncie, Indiana
www.ibcschools.edu

2-year for-profit business and health science college in small city.
Enrollment: 310 undergrads.

FINANCIAL AID PICTURE
Students with need: Need-based aid available for full-time and part-time students.
Additional info: Work-Study Programs are available.

FINANCIAL AID PROCEDURES
Forms required: FAFSA.
Dates and Deadlines: Applicants notified on a rolling basis.
Transfers: Applicants notified on a rolling basis.

CONTACT
411 West Riggin Road, Muncie, IN 47303
(800) 422-4723

Indiana Business College: Terre Haute
Terre Haute, Indiana
www.ibcschools.edu

2-year for-profit business and health science college in small city.
Enrollment: 220 undergrads.

FINANCIAL AID PICTURE
Students with need: Need-based aid available for full-time and part-time students.
Additional info: Work-study programs are available.

FINANCIAL AID PROCEDURES
Forms required: FAFSA.
Dates and Deadlines: Applicants notified on a rolling basis.
Transfers: Applicants notified on a rolling basis.

CONTACT
3175 South Third Place, Terre Haute, IN 47802
(812) 232-4458

Indiana Institute of Technology
Fort Wayne, Indiana
www.indianatech.edu   Federal Code: 001805

4-year private business and engineering college in large city.
Enrollment: 2,828 undergrads, 44% part-time. 327 full-time freshmen.
Selectivity: Admits 50 to 75% of applicants.

BASIC COSTS (2006-2007)
Tuition and fees: $18,560.
Per-credit charge: $610.
Room and board: $7,088.
Additional info: Tuition/fee waivers available for adults.

FINANCIAL AID PICTURE (2005-2006)
Students with need: Average financial aid package met 71% of need; average scholarship/grant was $8,828; average loan was $3,251. For part-time students, average financial aid package was $3,806.
Students without need: No-need awards available for academics, alumni affiliation, athletics, leadership, minority status, music/drama, state/district residency.
Cumulative student debt: 77% of graduating class had student loans; average debt was $16,893.

FINANCIAL AID PROCEDURES
Forms required: FAFSA, institutional form.
Dates and Deadlines: Closing date 3/10. Applicants notified on a rolling basis starting 2/2; must reply within 2 week(s) of notification.
Transfers: Priority date 3/10; no deadline. Applicants notified on a rolling basis starting 2/2; must reply within 2 week(s) of notification.

CONTACT
Judy Roy, Vice President of Finance and Administration
1600 East Washington Boulevard, Fort Wayne, IN 46803-1297
(260) 422-5561 ext. 2208

Indiana State University
Terre Haute, Indiana
www.indstate.edu   Federal Code: 001807

4-year public university in small city.
Enrollment: 8,531 undergrads, 11% part-time. 1,815 full-time freshmen.
Selectivity: Admits over 75% of applicants.

BASIC COSTS (2005-2006)
Tuition and fees: $5,864; out-of-state residents $12,860.
Room and board: $5,615.

FINANCIAL AID PICTURE (2004-2005)
Students with need: Out of 1,575 full-time freshmen who applied for aid, 1,245 were judged to have need. Of these, 1,159 received aid, and 167 had their full need met. Average financial aid package met 72% of need; average scholarship/grant was $4,790; average loan was $2,615. For part-time students, average financial aid package was $4,560.
Students without need: This college only awards aid to students with need.
Scholarships offered: 51 full-time freshmen received athletic scholarships; average amount $7,838.
Cumulative student debt: 61% of graduating class had student loans; average debt was $11,331.
Additional info: Financial aid application deadline March 1 for Indiana residents applying for state grant.

FINANCIAL AID PROCEDURES
Forms required: FAFSA.
Dates and Deadlines: Priority date 3/1; no closing date. Applicants notified on a rolling basis starting 4/15.

CONTACT
Thomas Ratliff, Director of Student Financial Aid
Office of Admissions, Tirey Hall 134, Terre Haute, IN 47809-9989
(812) 237-2215

Indiana University Bloomington
Bloomington, Indiana
www.iub.edu   Federal Code: 001809

4-year public university in small city.
Enrollment: 29,120 undergrads, 4% part-time. 6,747 full-time freshmen.
Selectivity: Admits over 75% of applicants.

BASIC COSTS (2005-2006)
Tuition and fees: $7,112; out-of-state residents $19,508.
Per-credit charge: $197; out-of-state residents $584.
Room and board: $6,240.

FINANCIAL AID PICTURE (2004-2005)
Students with need: Out of 5,460 full-time freshmen who applied for aid, 2,919 were judged to have need. Of these, 2,833 received aid, and 253 had their full need met. Average financial aid package met 66% of need; average scholarship/grant was $4,964; average loan was $3,076. For part-time students, average financial aid package was $5,926.
Students without need: 1,453 full-time freshmen who did not demonstrate need for aid received scholarships/grants; average award was $3,858. No-need awards available for academics, art, athletics, leadership, minority status, music/drama, religious affiliation, state/district residency.
Scholarships offered: Merit: Wells Scholarship; all costs for 4 years; individual schools nominate students; 25 students selected each year. Honors College Scholarship; $1,000-$6,000; 1300 SAT (30 ACT), top 10% class rank. Hudson & Holland; $4,000-$7,000; 1000 SAT (25 ACT), top 20% class rank, minimum 3.0 GPA, based on African, Hispanic, Native American ethnicity. Mathematics and Science Scholarship; $5,000-$6,000; 1000 SAT (25 ACT), top 20% class rank, minimum 3.0 GPA. E.W. Kelley Scholars Program; tuition, room and board, books (overseas study funding, if requested); business major, 1300 SAT (30 ACT), top 10% class rank. School of Music Dean's Award; competitive awards, varying in amount; exceptional talent displayed in audition. Residence Scholarship (via Honors College); $1,500; 1100 SAT (27 ACT), top 10% class rank. Faculty Scholarship; competitive awards, varying in amount; out-of-state residence; superior test scores and class rank. Valedictorian Award; $1,000; Indiana residence, highest ranking in high school class. 21st Century Scholars Award; in-state instructional fees; Indiana residence, fulfilled terms of pledged in eighth grade, filed FAFSA before March 1 of senior year. Army and Air Force ROTC Scholarships; tuition, fees, books, $200 monthly; Army: 850 SAT (19 ACT), Air Force: 1030 SAT (22 ACT). All SAT scores listed are exclusive of the writing portion. **Athletic:** 63 full-time freshmen received athletic scholarships; average amount $15,450.
Cumulative student debt: 48% of graduating class had student loans; average debt was $18,423.
Additional info: Majority of institutional gift aid merit-based. Some need-based grants go to merit winners with financial need.

FINANCIAL AID PROCEDURES
Forms required: FAFSA.
Dates and Deadlines: Priority date 3/1; no closing date. Applicants notified on a rolling basis starting 4/1.
Transfers: Except for school of music, no merit-based aid for transfer students.

CONTACT
Susan Pugh, Director of Student Financial Assistance
300 North Jordan Avenue, Bloomington, IN 47405
(812) 855-0321

Indiana University East
Richmond, Indiana
www.iue.edu   Federal Code: 001811

4-year public university and branch campus college in large town.
Enrollment: 2,128 undergrads, 40% part-time. 319 full-time freshmen.
Selectivity: Admits over 75% of applicants.

BASIC COSTS (2005-2006)
Tuition and fees: $4,806; out-of-state residents $11,484.
Per-credit charge: $149; out-of-state residents $372.

FINANCIAL AID PICTURE (2004-2005)
Students with need: Out of 280 full-time freshmen who applied for aid, 216 were judged to have need. Of these, 194 received aid, and 12 had their full need met. Average financial aid package met 55% of need; average scholarship/grant was $4,408; average loan was $2,351. For part-time students, average financial aid package was $3,402.
Students without need: 13 full-time freshmen who did not demonstrate need for aid received scholarships/grants; average award was $898. No-need awards available for academics, alumni affiliation, minority status.
Cumulative student debt: 63% of graduating class had student loans; average debt was $17,547.

FINANCIAL AID PROCEDURES
Forms required: FAFSA, institutional form.
Dates and Deadlines: Priority date 3/1; no closing date. Applicants notified on a rolling basis starting 5/1; must reply within 2 week(s) of notification.

CONTACT
James Bland, Director of Financial Aid
2325 Chester Boulevard, Richmond, IN 47374-1289
(765) 973-8206

Indiana University Kokomo
Kokomo, Indiana
www.iuk.edu   Federal Code: 001814

4-year public university in large town.
Enrollment: 2,525 undergrads, 44% part-time. 383 full-time freshmen.
Selectivity: Admits over 75% of applicants.

BASIC COSTS (2005-2006)
Tuition and fees: $4,835; out-of-state residents $11,513.
Per-credit charge: $149; out-of-state residents $372.

FINANCIAL AID PICTURE (2004-2005)
Students with need: Out of 244 full-time freshmen who applied for aid, 164 were judged to have need. Of these, 155 received aid, and 12 had their full need met. Average financial aid package met 68% of need; average scholarship/grant was $4,476; average loan was $2,283. For part-time students, average financial aid package was $4,017.
Students without need: 22 full-time freshmen who did not demonstrate need for aid received scholarships/grants; average award was $984. No-need awards available for academics.
Cumulative student debt: 55% of graduating class had student loans; average debt was $11,681.

FINANCIAL AID PROCEDURES
Forms required: FAFSA, institutional form.
Dates and Deadlines: Closing date 3/1. Applicants notified on a rolling basis starting 5/1; must reply within 4 week(s) of notification.

CONTACT
Jackie Kennedy-Fletcher, Director of Financial Aid
Box 9003, KC 230A, Kokomo, IN 46904-9003
(765) 455-9216

Indiana University Northwest
Gary, Indiana
www.iun.edu   Federal Code: 001815

4-year public university in small city.
Enrollment: 4,042 undergrads, 40% part-time. 606 full-time freshmen.
Selectivity: Admits 50 to 75% of applicants.

BASIC COSTS (2005-2006)
Tuition and fees: $4,902.
Per-credit charge: $149; out-of-state residents $372.

FINANCIAL AID PICTURE (2004-2005)
Students with need: Out of 486 full-time freshmen who applied for aid, 392 were judged to have need. Of these, 352 received aid, and 58 had their full need met. Average financial aid package met 65.8% of need; average scholarship/grant was $4,170; average loan was $2,352. For part-time students, average financial aid package was $4,434.
Students without need: 6 full-time freshmen who did not demonstrate need for aid received scholarships/grants; average award was $1,922. No-need awards available for academics, athletics.
Scholarships offered: 4 full-time freshmen received athletic scholarships; average amount $1,075.
Cumulative student debt: 47% of graduating class had student loans; average debt was $18,338.

FINANCIAL AID PROCEDURES
Forms required: FAFSA, institutional form.
Dates and Deadlines: Priority date 3/1; no closing date. Applicants notified on a rolling basis starting 5/1; must reply within 2 week(s) of notification.

CONTACT
Charles Carothers, Financial Aid Director
3400 Broadway, Gary, IN 46408
(219) 981-4271

Indiana University South Bend
South Bend, Indiana
www.iusb.edu   Federal Code: 001816

4-year public university in small city.
Enrollment: 5,818 undergrads, 38% part-time. 690 full-time freshmen.
Selectivity: Admits over 75% of applicants.

BASIC COSTS (2005-2006)
Tuition and fees: $4,989; out-of-state residents $12,408.
Per-credit charge: $153; out-of-state residents $400.

FINANCIAL AID PICTURE (2004-2005)
Students with need: Out of 563 full-time freshmen who applied for aid, 461 were judged to have need. Of these, 400 received aid, and 14 had their full need met. Average financial aid package met 48% of need; average scholarship/grant was $3,978; average loan was $2,275. For part-time students, average financial aid package was $3,892.
Students without need: 28 full-time freshmen who did not demonstrate need for aid received scholarships/grants; average award was $1,122. No-need awards available for academics, athletics.
Scholarships offered: *Merit:* Honors Scholarship; $1,200 per academic year (full-time); entering freshman, 1200 or more SAT (exclusive of Writing) or 27 ACT; rank top 10 percent, 3.5 GPA; renewable up to 8 semesters. Alumni Scholarship; $3,500 freshman year; first-time freshman from Northern Indiana, meet Honors Scholarship criteria, submit essay and 3 letters of recommendation. *Athletic:* 6 full-time freshmen received athletic scholarships; average amount $4,833.
Cumulative student debt: 48% of graduating class had student loans; average debt was $20,227.

FINANCIAL AID PROCEDURES
Forms required: FAFSA, institutional form.
Dates and Deadlines: Closing date 3/1. Applicants notified on a rolling basis starting 5/1.
Transfers: No deadline.

CONTACT
Beverly Cooper, Director of Financial Aid
1700 Mishawaka Avenue, South Bend, IN 46634-7111
(574) 520-4357

Indiana University Southeast
New Albany, Indiana
www.ius.edu   Federal Code: 001817

4-year public university in large town.
Enrollment: 5,079 undergrads, 37% part-time. 715 full-time freshmen.
Selectivity: Admits over 75% of applicants.

BASIC COSTS (2005-2006)
Tuition and fees: $4,880; out-of-state residents $11,558.
Per-credit charge: $149; out-of-state residents $372.

FINANCIAL AID PICTURE (2004-2005)
Students with need: Out of 586 full-time freshmen who applied for aid, 450 were judged to have need. Of these, 423 received aid, and 22 had their full need met. Average financial aid package met 55% of need; average scholarship/grant was $3,972; average loan was $2,166. For part-time students, average financial aid package was $3,965.
Students without need: 59 full-time freshmen who did not demonstrate need for aid received scholarships/grants; average award was $1,798. No-need awards available for academics, art, athletics, leadership, minority status, music/drama.
Scholarships offered: 13 full-time freshmen received athletic scholarships; average amount $756.
Cumulative student debt: 40% of graduating class had student loans; average debt was $16,597.

FINANCIAL AID PROCEDURES
Forms required: FAFSA.
Dates and Deadlines: Priority date 3/1; no closing date. Applicants notified on a rolling basis starting 5/1; must reply within 3 week(s) of notification.

CONTACT
Michael Barlow, Director of Scholarships and Financial Aid
4201 Grant Line Road, New Albany, IN 47150-6405
(812) 941-2246 ext. 2260

Indiana University-Purdue University Fort Wayne
Fort Wayne, Indiana
www.ipfw.edu   Federal Code: 001828

4-year public university and branch campus college in small city.
Enrollment: 10,694 undergrads, 37% part-time. 1,610 full-time freshmen.
Selectivity: Admits over 75% of applicants.

BASIC COSTS (2005-2006)
Tuition and fees: $5,630; out-of-state residents $12,984.
Per-credit charge: $168; out-of-state residents $413.
Room only: $4,750.

FINANCIAL AID PICTURE (2004-2005)
Students with need: Out of 1,296 full-time freshmen who applied for aid, 984 were judged to have need. Of these, 914 received aid, and 56 had their full need met. Average financial aid package met 69% of need; average scholarship/grant was $3,786; average loan was $2,333. For part-time students, average financial aid package was $3,824.
Students without need: 160 full-time freshmen who did not demonstrate need for aid received scholarships/grants; average award was $2,134. No-need awards available for academics, athletics, state/district residency.
Scholarships offered: 31 full-time freshmen received athletic scholarships; average amount $5,052.
Cumulative student debt: 60% of graduating class had student loans; average debt was $16,395.

FINANCIAL AID PROCEDURES
Forms required: FAFSA.
Dates and Deadlines: Priority date 3/10; no closing date. Applicants notified on a rolling basis starting 5/15; must reply within 3 week(s) of notification.
Transfers: Must reply within 3 week(s) of notification.

CONTACT
Mark Franke, Director of Financial Aid
2101 East Coliseum Boulevard, Fort Wayne, IN 46805-1499
(260) 481-6820

Indiana University-Purdue University Indianapolis
Indianapolis, Indiana
www.iupui.edu   Federal Code: 001813

4-year public university in very large city.
Enrollment: 20,537 undergrads, 34% part-time. 2,344 full-time freshmen.
Selectivity: Admits 50 to 75% of applicants.

BASIC COSTS (2005-2006)
Tuition and fees: $6,219; out-of-state residents $16,547.
Per-credit charge: $188; out-of-state residents $532.
Room and board: $4,740.

FINANCIAL AID PICTURE (2004-2005)
Students with need: Out of 1,683 full-time freshmen who applied for aid, 1,358 were judged to have need. Of these, 1,192 received aid, and 20 had their full need met. Average financial aid package met 41% of need; average scholarship/grant was $4,984; average loan was $2,449. For part-time students, average financial aid package was $4,112.
Students without need: 229 full-time freshmen who did not demonstrate need for aid received scholarships/grants; average award was $1,645. No-need awards available for academics.
Scholarships offered: 36 full-time freshmen received athletic scholarships; average amount $2,822.
Cumulative student debt: 58% of graduating class had student loans; average debt was $19,660.

FINANCIAL AID PROCEDURES
Forms required: FAFSA.
Dates and Deadlines: Priority date 3/1; no closing date. Applicants notified on a rolling basis starting 4/1.

CONTACT
Kathy Purvis, Director of Scholarships and Financial Aid
425 North University Boulevard, Cavanaugh Hall R129, Indianapolis, IN 46202-5143
(317) 274-4162

Indiana Wesleyan University
Marion, Indiana
www.indwes.edu   Federal Code: 001822

4-year private university and liberal arts college in large town, affiliated with Wesleyan Church.
Enrollment: 8,447 undergrads, 7% part-time. 1,417 full-time freshmen.
Selectivity: Admits over 75% of applicants.

BASIC COSTS (2006-2007)
Tuition and fees: $17,164.
Per-credit charge: $365.
Room and board: $6,124.
Additional info: Required fees vary by program but are minimal.

FINANCIAL AID PICTURE (2005-2006)
Students with need: Need-based aid available for part-time students. Work study available nights, weekends, and for part-time students.
Students without need: No-need awards available for academics, alumni affiliation, art, athletics, music/drama, ROTC.
Scholarships offered: Academic Scholarships with awards ranging from $750 to $6,000, 3.2 GPA and 1050 SAT (exclusive of Writing) or 23 ACT.

FINANCIAL AID PROCEDURES
Forms required: FAFSA.
Dates and Deadlines: Closing date 3/1. Applicants notified by 4/1.

CONTACT
Robert Sommers, Executive Director of Financial Aid CAS
4201 South Washington Street, Marion, IN 46953-4999
(765) 677-2116

Ivy Tech Community College: Bloomington
Bloomington, Indiana
www.ivytech.edu   Federal Code: 035213

2-year public community college in small city.
Enrollment: 3,204 undergrads, 51% part-time. 415 full-time freshmen.
Selectivity: Open admission; but selective for some programs.

BASIC COSTS (2006-2007)
Tuition and fees: $2,713; out-of-state residents $5,435.
Per-credit charge: $88; out-of-state residents $179.

FINANCIAL AID PICTURE (2004-2005)
Students with need: 50% of average financial aid package awarded as scholarships/grants, 50% awarded as loans/jobs. Need-based aid available for part-time students. Work study available nights.

FINANCIAL AID PROCEDURES
Forms required: FAFSA.
Dates and Deadlines: Priority date 3/1; no closing date. Applicants notified on a rolling basis starting 7/1.

CONTACT
Sue Allmon, Director of Financial Aid
200 Daniels Way, Bloomington, IN 47404-1511
(812) 332-1559

Ivy Tech Community College: Central Indiana
Indianapolis, Indiana
www.ivytech.edu   Federal Code: 009917

2-year public community college in very large city.
Enrollment: 10,266 undergrads, 68% part-time. 866 full-time freshmen.
Selectivity: Open admission; but selective for some programs.

BASIC COSTS (2005-2006)
Tuition and fees: $2,590; out-of-state residents $5,178.
Per-credit charge: $84; out-of-state residents $170.

FINANCIAL AID PICTURE (2004-2005)
Students with need: 51% of average financial aid package awarded as scholarships/grants, 49% awarded as loans/jobs. Need-based aid available for part-time students. Work study available nights, weekends, and for part-time students.

FINANCIAL AID PROCEDURES
Forms required: FAFSA.
Dates and Deadlines: Priority date 3/1; no closing date. Applicants notified on a rolling basis starting 7/1.

CONTACT
Mildrid Williamson, Director of Financial Aid
50 West Fall Creek Parkway North Drive, Indianapolis, IN 46208-5752
(317) 921-4777

Ivy Tech Community College: Columbus
Columbus, Indiana
www.ivytech.edu   Federal Code: 010038

2-year public community college in large town.
Enrollment: 1,887 undergrads, 61% part-time. 146 full-time freshmen.
Selectivity: Open admission; but selective for some programs.

BASIC COSTS (2005-2006)
Tuition and fees: $2,590; out-of-state residents $5,178.
Per-credit charge: $84; out-of-state residents $170.

FINANCIAL AID PICTURE (2004-2005)
Students with need: 61% of average financial aid package awarded as scholarships/grants, 39% awarded as loans/jobs. Need-based aid available for part-time students. Work study available nights.

FINANCIAL AID PROCEDURES
Forms required: FAFSA.
Dates and Deadlines: Priority date 3/1; no closing date. Applicants notified on a rolling basis starting 7/1.

CONTACT
Donna Bentz, Director of Financial Aid
4475 Central Avenue, Columbus, IN 47203-1868
(812) 372-9925

Ivy Tech Community College: East Central
Muncie, Indiana
www.ivytech.edu   Federal Code: 009924

2-year public community college in small city.
Enrollment: 5,460 undergrads, 55% part-time. 537 full-time freshmen.
Selectivity: Open admission; but selective for some programs.

BASIC COSTS (2005-2006)
Tuition and fees: $2,590; out-of-state residents $5,178.
Per-credit charge: $84; out-of-state residents $170.

FINANCIAL AID PICTURE (2004-2005)
Students with need: 62% of average financial aid package awarded as scholarships/grants, 38% awarded as loans/jobs. Need-based aid available for part-time students. Work study available nights.
Additional info: Higher Education Aid (HEA), Child of Disabled/Deceased Veterans (CDV), Ivy Tech Scholarships (IVTC) and grants, vocational rehabilitation and veteran's assistance available. None require repayment.

FINANCIAL AID PROCEDURES
Forms required: FAFSA.
Dates and Deadlines: Priority date 3/1; no closing date. Applicants notified on a rolling basis starting 7/1.

CONTACT
Sylvia Bogle, Director of Financial Aid
4301 South Cowan Road, Muncie, IN 47302-9448
(765) 289-2291 ext. 386

Ivy Tech Community College: Kokomo
Kokomo, Indiana
www.ivytech.edu   Federal Code: 010041

2-year public community college in large town.
Enrollment: 2,701 undergrads, 63% part-time. 273 full-time freshmen.
Selectivity: Open admission; but selective for some programs.

BASIC COSTS (2005-2006)
Tuition and fees: $2,590; out-of-state residents $5,178.
Per-credit charge: $84; out-of-state residents $170.

FINANCIAL AID PICTURE (2004-2005)
Students with need: 55% of average financial aid package awarded as scholarships/grants, 45% awarded as loans/jobs. Need-based aid available for part-time students. Work study available nights.

FINANCIAL AID PROCEDURES
Forms required: FAFSA.
Dates and Deadlines: Priority date 3/1; no closing date. Applicants notified on a rolling basis starting 7/1.

CONTACT
Christina Coon, Director of Financial Aid
1815 East Morgan Street, Kokomo, IN 46903-1373
(765) 459-0561 ext. 308

Ivy Tech Community College: Lafayette
Lafayette, Indiana
www.ivytech.edu   Federal Code: 010039

2-year public community college in large town.
Enrollment: 4,359 undergrads, 50% part-time. 511 full-time freshmen.
Selectivity: Open admission; but selective for some programs.

BASIC COSTS (2005-2006)
Tuition and fees: $2,590; out-of-state residents $5,178.
Per-credit charge: $84; out-of-state residents $170.

FINANCIAL AID PICTURE (2004-2005)
Students with need: 44% of average financial aid package awarded as scholarships/grants, 56% awarded as loans/jobs. Need-based aid available for part-time students. Work study available nights.

FINANCIAL AID PROCEDURES
Forms required: FAFSA.

Dates and Deadlines: Priority date 3/1; no closing date. Applicants notified on a rolling basis starting 7/1.

CONTACT
Kirsten Reynolds, Director of Financial Aid
3101 South Creasy Lane, Lafayette, IN 47905-6299
(765) 772-9111

Ivy Tech Community College: North Central
South Bend, Indiana
www.ivytech.edu   Federal Code: 008423

2-year public community college in small city.
Enrollment: 4,404 undergrads, 74% part-time. 298 full-time freshmen.
Selectivity: Open admission; but selective for some programs.

BASIC COSTS (2006-2007)
Tuition and fees: $2,713; out-of-state residents $5,435.
Per-credit charge: $88; out-of-state residents $179.

FINANCIAL AID PICTURE (2005-2006)
Students with need: 58% of average financial aid package awarded as scholarships/grants, 42% awarded as loans/jobs. Need-based aid available for part-time students. Work study available nights.

FINANCIAL AID PROCEDURES
Forms required: FAFSA.
Dates and Deadlines: Priority date 3/1; no closing date. Applicants notified on a rolling basis starting 7/1.

CONTACT
Jeff Fisher, Director of Financial Aid
220 Dean Johnson Boulevard, South Bend, IN 46601-3415
(219) 289-7001

Ivy Tech Community College: Northeast
Fort Wayne, Indiana
www.ivytech.edu   Federal Code: 009926

2-year public community college in small city.
Enrollment: 4,733 undergrads, 62% part-time. 356 full-time freshmen.
Selectivity: Open admission; but selective for some programs.

BASIC COSTS (2005-2006)
Tuition and fees: $2,590; out-of-state residents $5,178.
Per-credit charge: $84; out-of-state residents $170.

FINANCIAL AID PICTURE (2004-2005)
Students with need: 46% of average financial aid package awarded as scholarships/grants, 54% awarded as loans/jobs. Need-based aid available for part-time students. Work study available nights.

FINANCIAL AID PROCEDURES
Forms required: FAFSA.
Dates and Deadlines: Priority date 3/1; no closing date. Applicants notified on a rolling basis starting 7/1.

CONTACT
Tom Liggett, Director of Financial Aid
3800 North Anthony Boulevard, Fort Wayne, IN 46805-1489
(260) 482-9171

Ivy Tech Community College: Northwest
Gary, Indiana
www.ivytech.edu   Federal Code: 010040

2-year public community college in small city.
Enrollment: 4,024 undergrads, 66% part-time. 225 full-time freshmen.
Selectivity: Open admission; but selective for some programs.

BASIC COSTS (2005-2006)
Tuition and fees: $2,590; out-of-state residents $5,178.
Per-credit charge: $84; out-of-state residents $170.

FINANCIAL AID PICTURE (2004-2005)
Students with need: 78% of average financial aid package awarded as scholarships/grants, 22% awarded as loans/jobs. Need-based aid available for part-time students. Work study available nights.

FINANCIAL AID PROCEDURES
Forms required: FAFSA.
Dates and Deadlines: Priority date 3/1; no closing date. Applicants notified on a rolling basis starting 7/1.

CONTACT
Barb Jerzyk, Director of Financial Aid
1440 East 35th Avenue, Gary, IN 46409-1499
(219) 981-4417

Ivy Tech Community College: South Central
Sellersburg, Indiana
www.ivytech.edu   Federal Code: 010109

2-year public community college in small town.
Enrollment: 2,783 undergrads, 69% part-time. 190 full-time freshmen.
Selectivity: Open admission; but selective for some programs.

BASIC COSTS (2005-2006)
Tuition and fees: $2,590; out-of-state residents $5,178.
Per-credit charge: $84; out-of-state residents $170.

FINANCIAL AID PICTURE (2004-2005)
Students with need: 62% of average financial aid package awarded as scholarships/grants, 38% awarded as loans/jobs. Need-based aid available for part-time students. Work study available nights.

FINANCIAL AID PROCEDURES
Forms required: FAFSA.
Dates and Deadlines: Priority date 3/1; no closing date. Applicants notified on a rolling basis starting 7/1.

CONTACT
Gary Cottrill, Director of Financial Aid
8204 Highway 311, Sellersburg, IN 47172-1897
(812) 246-3301

Ivy Tech Community College: Southeast
Madison, Indiana
www.ivytech.edu   Federal Code: 009923

2-year public community college in large town.
Enrollment: 1,520 undergrads, 59% part-time. 155 full-time freshmen.
Selectivity: Open admission; but selective for some programs.

BASIC COSTS (2005-2006)
Tuition and fees: $2,590; out-of-state residents $5,178.
Per-credit charge: $84; out-of-state residents $170.

FINANCIAL AID PICTURE (2004-2005)
Students with need: 55% of average financial aid package awarded as scholarships/grants, 45% awarded as loans/jobs. Need-based aid available for part-time students. Work study available nights.

FINANCIAL AID PROCEDURES
Forms required: FAFSA.
Dates and Deadlines: Priority date 3/1; no closing date. Applicants notified on a rolling basis starting 7/1.

CONTACT
Richard Hill, Director of Financial Aid
590 Ivy Tech Drive, Madison, IN 47250-1881
(812) 265-2580 ext. 4148

Ivy Tech Community College: Southwest
Evansville, Indiana
www.ivytech.edu   Federal Code: 009925

2-year public community college in small city.
Enrollment: 4,095 undergrads, 64% part-time. 297 full-time freshmen.
Selectivity: Open admission; but selective for some programs.

BASIC COSTS (2005-2006)
Tuition and fees: $2,590; out-of-state residents $5,178.
Per-credit charge: $84; out-of-state residents $170.

FINANCIAL AID PICTURE (2004-2005)
Students with need: 52% of average financial aid package awarded as scholarships/grants, 48% awarded as loans/jobs. Need-based aid available for part-time students. Work study available nights.

FINANCIAL AID PROCEDURES
Forms required: FAFSA.
Dates and Deadlines: Priority date 3/1; no closing date. Applicants notified on a rolling basis starting 7/1.

CONTACT
Kim Heldt, Director of Financial Aid
3501 First Avenue, Evansville, IN 47710-3398
(812) 426-2865

Ivy Tech Community College: Wabash Valley
Terre Haute, Indiana
www.ivytech.edu   Federal Code: 008547

2-year public community college in small city.
Enrollment: 4,148 undergrads, 50% part-time. 504 full-time freshmen.
Selectivity: Open admission; but selective for some programs.

BASIC COSTS (2005-2006)
Tuition and fees: $2,590; out-of-state residents $5,178.
Per-credit charge: $84; out-of-state residents $170.

FINANCIAL AID PICTURE (2004-2005)
Students with need: 46% of average financial aid package awarded as scholarships/grants, 54% awarded as loans/jobs. Need-based aid available for part-time students. Work study available nights.

FINANCIAL AID PROCEDURES
Forms required: FAFSA.
Dates and Deadlines: Priority date 3/1; no closing date. Applicants notified on a rolling basis starting 7/1.

CONTACT
Julie Wonderlin, Director of Financial Aid
7999 US Highway 41 South, Terre Haute, IN 47802-4898
(812) 299-1121

Ivy Tech Community College: Whitewater
Richmond, Indiana
www.ivytech.edu   Federal Code: 010037

2-year public community college in large town.
Enrollment: 1,588 undergrads, 65% part-time. 105 full-time freshmen.
Selectivity: Open admission; but selective for some programs.

BASIC COSTS (2005-2006)
Tuition and fees: $2,590; out-of-state residents $5,178.
Per-credit charge: $84; out-of-state residents $170.

FINANCIAL AID PICTURE (2004-2005)
Students with need: 52% of average financial aid package awarded as scholarships/grants, 48% awarded as loans/jobs. Need-based aid available for part-time students. Work study available nights.

FINANCIAL AID PROCEDURES
Forms required: FAFSA.
Dates and Deadlines: Priority date 3/1; no closing date. Applicants notified on a rolling basis starting 7/1.

CONTACT
Ann Franzen-Roha, Director of Financial Aid
2325 Chester Boulevard, Richmond, IN 47374-1298
(765) 966-2656 ext. 308

Manchester College
North Manchester, Indiana
www.manchester.edu   Federal Code: 001820

4-year private liberal arts college in small town, affiliated with Church of the Brethren.
Enrollment: 1,058 undergrads, 1% part-time. 330 full-time freshmen.
Selectivity: Admits 50 to 75% of applicants.

BASIC COSTS (2006-2007)
Tuition and fees: $20,500.
Per-credit charge: $670.
Room and board: $7,260.

FINANCIAL AID PICTURE (2005-2006)
Students with need: Out of 318 full-time freshmen who applied for aid, 283 were judged to have need. Of these, 283 received aid, and 127 had their full need met. Average financial aid package met 93% of need; average scholarship/grant was $15,334; average loan was $2,213. For part-time students, average financial aid package was $8,079.
Students without need: 30 full-time freshmen who did not demonstrate need for aid received scholarships/grants; average award was $8,667. No-need awards available for academics, alumni affiliation, art, leadership, minority status, music/drama, religious affiliation.
Scholarships offered: Honors Fellowships; full tuition; based on academics; 2 awarded. Presidential Leadership Awards; $2,500 travel grant; 3 awarded. Trustee Scholarships; $12,000; based on merit; 40 awarded to each incoming class. Presidential Scholarships; $9,000; based on merit. Arts, service, modern language scholarships; $9,000; based on merit/ability.
Additional info: Students are automatically considered for all scholarship programs.

FINANCIAL AID PROCEDURES
Forms required: FAFSA.

Dates and Deadlines: Priority date 3/1; no closing date. Applicants notified on a rolling basis starting 2/15.
Transfers: Aid eligibility remaining determined by reviewing total credit hours transferred and financial aid transcripts.

CONTACT
Gina Voelz, Director of Financial Aid
604 East College Avenue, North Manchester, IN 46962-0365
(260) 982-5066

Marian College
Indianapolis, Indiana
www.marian.edu   Federal Code: 001821

4-year private liberal arts college in very large city, affiliated with Roman Catholic Church.
Enrollment: 1,573 undergrads, 31% part-time. 231 full-time freshmen.
Selectivity: Admits over 75% of applicants.

BASIC COSTS (2005-2006)
Tuition and fees: $19,060.
Per-credit charge: $780.
Room and board: $6,300.

FINANCIAL AID PICTURE (2004-2005)
Students with need: Out of 215 full-time freshmen who applied for aid, 191 were judged to have need. Of these, 191 received aid, and 115 had their full need met. Need-based aid available for part-time students.
Students without need: No-need awards available for academics, alumni affiliation, art, athletics, leadership, minority status, music/drama, religious affiliation.

FINANCIAL AID PROCEDURES
Forms required: FAFSA, institutional form.
Dates and Deadlines: Priority date 3/10; no closing date. Applicants notified on a rolling basis starting 3/15; must reply within 3 week(s) of notification.
Transfers: No deadline. Applicants notified on a rolling basis starting 3/15; must reply within 3 week(s) of notification.

CONTACT
John Shelton, Assistant Dean for Financial Aid
3200 Cold Spring Road, Indianapolis, IN 46222-1960
(317) 955-6040

Oakland City University
Oakland City, Indiana
www.oak.edu   Federal Code: 001824

4-year private university in small town, affiliated with General Association of General Baptists.
Enrollment: 1,566 undergrads, 19% part-time. 251 full-time freshmen.
Selectivity: Open admission; but selective for some programs.

BASIC COSTS (2006-2007)
Tuition and fees: $14,220.
Per-credit charge: $462.
Room and board: $5,400.
Additional info: Tuition/fee waivers available for minority students, unemployed or children of unemployed.

FINANCIAL AID PICTURE (2005-2006)
Students with need: 68% of average financial aid package awarded as scholarships/grants, 32% awarded as loans/jobs. Need-based aid available for part-time students. Work study available nights, weekends, and for part-time students.
Students without need: No-need awards available for academics, alumni affiliation, art, athletics, minority status, music/drama, religious affiliation.

FINANCIAL AID PROCEDURES
Forms required: FAFSA.
Dates and Deadlines: Closing date 3/1. Applicants notified on a rolling basis starting 6/1.

CONTACT
Caren Richeson, Director of Financial Aid
138 North Lucretia Street, Oakland City, IN 47660
(812) 749-1224

Professional Careers Institute
Indianapolis, Indiana
www.pcicareers.com   Federal Code: 009777

2-year for-profit business and health science college in very large city.
Enrollment: 600 undergrads.

BASIC COSTS (2006-2007)
Tuition and fees: $9,900.

FINANCIAL AID PICTURE
Students with need: Need-based aid available for full-time students.
Students without need: This college only awards aid to students with need.

CONTACT
Phyllis Robbins, Financial Aid Administrator
7302 Woodland Drive, Indianapolis, IN 46278-1736
(317) 293-6503

Purdue University
West Lafayette, Indiana
www.purdue.edu   Federal Code: 001825

4-year public university in small city.
Enrollment: 30,545 undergrads, 5% part-time. 7,091 full-time freshmen.
Selectivity: Admits over 75% of applicants.

BASIC COSTS (2005-2006)
Tuition and fees: $6,458; out-of-state residents $19,824.
Per-credit charge: $232; out-of-state residents $658.
Room and board: $7,160.
Additional info: Engineering students pay additional $564 fee per year. Technology students pay $137.60 fee per year. Management students pay $882.00 fee per year.

FINANCIAL AID PICTURE (2005-2006)
Students with need: Out of 5,161 full-time freshmen who applied for aid, 3,089 were judged to have need. Of these, 3,083 received aid, and 1,002 had their full need met. Average financial aid package met 92% of need; average scholarship/grant was $9,745; average loan was $3,072. For part-time students, average financial aid package was $7,707.
Students without need: 1,307 full-time freshmen who did not demonstrate need for aid received scholarships/grants; average award was $14,306. No-need awards available for academics, athletics, leadership, minority status, music/drama, ROTC, state/district residency.
Scholarships offered: 82 full-time freshmen received athletic scholarships; average amount $15,827.
Cumulative student debt: 49% of graduating class had student loans; average debt was $18,978.
Additional info: Cooperative work for credit available in many programs.

FINANCIAL AID PROCEDURES
Forms required: FAFSA.

Dates and Deadlines: Priority date 3/1; no closing date. Applicants notified by 4/15.

CONTACT
Joyce Hall, Director of Financial Aid
475 Stadium Mall Dr., West Lafayette, IN 47907-2050
(765) 494-5050

Purdue University: Calumet
Hammond, Indiana
www.calumet.purdue.edu   Federal Code: 001827

4-year public university and branch campus college in small city.
Enrollment: 7,879 undergrads, 36% part-time. 1,052 full-time freshmen.
Selectivity: Admits over 75% of applicants.

BASIC COSTS (2005-2006)
Tuition and fees: $5,071; out-of-state residents $11,371.
Per-credit charge: $156; out-of-state residents $366.

FINANCIAL AID PICTURE (2004-2005)
Students with need: Out of 777 full-time freshmen who applied for aid, 528 were judged to have need. Of these, 476 received aid. Average financial aid package met 18% of need; average scholarship/grant was $5,748; average loan was $2,763. For part-time students, average financial aid package was $4,560.
Students without need: 30 full-time freshmen who did not demonstrate need for aid received scholarships/grants; average award was $1,189. No-need awards available for academics, athletics.
Scholarships offered: 7 full-time freshmen received athletic scholarships; average amount $2,500.

FINANCIAL AID PROCEDURES
Forms required: FAFSA.
Dates and Deadlines: Priority date 3/10; closing date 6/30. Applicants notified on a rolling basis starting 5/1; must reply within 2 week(s) of notification.

CONTACT
Carol Zencka, Director of Financial Aid and Student Accounts
2200 169th Street, Hammond, IN 46323-2094
(219) 989-2301

Purdue University: North Central Campus
Westville, Indiana
www.pnc.edu   Federal Code: 001826

4-year public branch campus college in rural community.
Enrollment: 3,450 undergrads.

BASIC COSTS (2005-2006)
Tuition and fees: $5,195; out-of-state residents $12,215.
Per-credit charge: $158; out-of-state residents $392.
Additional info: Additional $50 per course fee for classes at Valparaiso Academic Center. Tuition/fee waivers available for minority students.

FINANCIAL AID PICTURE
Students with need: Need-based aid available for full-time and part-time students.
Students without need: This college only awards aid to students with need.

FINANCIAL AID PROCEDURES
Forms required: FAFSA.
Dates and Deadlines: Priority date 3/1; no closing date. Applicants notified on a rolling basis starting 5/31; must reply within 2 week(s) of notification.
Transfers: Transfer students not considered for campus-based financial aid.

CONTACT
Gerald Lewis, Director of Financial Aid
1401 South US Highway 421, Westville, IN 46391-9528
(219) 785-5278

Rose-Hulman Institute of Technology
Terre Haute, Indiana
www.rose-hulman.edu   Federal Code: 001830

4-year private engineering college in small city.
Enrollment: 1,768 undergrads. 448 full-time freshmen.
Selectivity: Admits 50 to 75% of applicants. GED not accepted.

BASIC COSTS (2006-2007)
Tuition and fees: $29,040.
Per-credit charge: $831.
Room and board: $7,869.
Additional info: Laptop computer $3,200.

FINANCIAL AID PICTURE (2005-2006)
Students with need: Out of 401 full-time freshmen who applied for aid, 320 were judged to have need. Of these, 320 received aid, and 29 had their full need met. Average financial aid package met 83% of need; average scholarship/grant was $15,300; average loan was $8,104. Need-based aid available for part-time students.
Students without need: 107 full-time freshmen who did not demonstrate need for aid received scholarships/grants; average award was $5,673. No-need awards available for academics, minority status, ROTC.
Cumulative student debt: 79% of graduating class had student loans; average debt was $33,105.

FINANCIAL AID PROCEDURES
Forms required: FAFSA.
Dates and Deadlines: Priority date 3/1; no closing date. Applicants notified on a rolling basis starting 3/10.

CONTACT
Melinda Middleton, Director of Financial Aid
Office of Admissions, Terre Haute, IN 47803-3999
(800) 248-7448

St. Joseph's College
Rensselaer, Indiana
www.saintjoe.edu   Federal Code: 001833

4-year private liberal arts college in small town, affiliated with Roman Catholic Church.
Enrollment: 991 undergrads, 11% part-time. 207 full-time freshmen.
Selectivity: Admits over 75% of applicants.

BASIC COSTS (2006-2007)
Tuition and fees: $20,960.
Per-credit charge: $700.
Room and board: $6,720.
Additional info: Tuition/fee waivers available for minority students.

FINANCIAL AID PICTURE (2004-2005)
Students with need: Out of 203 full-time freshmen who applied for aid, 165 were judged to have need. Of these, 165 received aid, and 41 had their full need met. Average financial aid package met 80% of need; average scholarship/grant was $12,307; average loan was $3,269. For part-time students, average financial aid package was $3,526.
Students without need: 31 full-time freshmen who did not demonstrate need for aid received scholarships/grants; average award was $10,128. No-need awards available for academics, alumni affiliation, athletics, minority status, music/drama.

Scholarships offered: 15 full-time freshmen received athletic scholarships; average amount $8,668.
Cumulative student debt: 74% of graduating class had student loans; average debt was $23,417.

FINANCIAL AID PROCEDURES
Forms required: FAFSA.
Dates and Deadlines: Priority date 3/1; no closing date. Applicants notified on a rolling basis starting 3/1; must reply by 5/1 or within 2 week(s) of notification.
Transfers: Must reply by 5/1 or within 2 week(s) of notification. Limited institutional academic scholarship.

CONTACT
Debra Sizemore, Director of Student Financial Services
Box 890, Rensselaer, IN 47978
(219) 866-6163

St. Mary-of-the-Woods College
St. Mary-of-the-Woods, Indiana
www.smwc.edu   Federal Code: 001835

4-year private liberal arts college for women in small city, affiliated with Roman Catholic Church.
Enrollment: 1,595 undergrads, 68% part-time. 76 full-time freshmen.
Selectivity: Admits 50 to 75% of applicants.

BASIC COSTS (2006-2007)
Tuition and fees: $19,380.
Per-credit charge: $780.
Room and board: $7,096.
Additional info: $356 per credit hour for external degree program. Tuition/fee waivers available for minority students.

FINANCIAL AID PICTURE (2004-2005)
Students with need: 50% of average financial aid package awarded as scholarships/grants, 50% awarded as loans/jobs. Need-based aid available for part-time students. Work study available nights, weekends, and for part-time students.
Students without need: No-need awards available for academics, alumni affiliation, art, athletics, leadership, minority status, music/drama, state/district residency.
Additional info: Portfolio or audition required of applicants who wish to be considered for Creative Arts Scholarship.

FINANCIAL AID PROCEDURES
Forms required: FAFSA.
Dates and Deadlines: Priority date 3/1; no closing date. Applicants notified on a rolling basis starting 12/1; must reply within 6 week(s) of notification.
Transfers: Priority date 7/1. Must reply within 8 week(s) of notification.

CONTACT
Ruby Robinson, Director of Financial Aid
Guerin Hall, SMWC, St. Mary-of-the-Woods, IN 47876
(812) 535-5109

Saint Mary's College
Notre Dame, Indiana   Federal Code: 001836
www.saintmarys.edu   CSS Code: 1702

4-year private liberal arts college for women in small city, affiliated with Roman Catholic Church.
Enrollment: 1,366 undergrads. 377 full-time freshmen.
Selectivity: Admits over 75% of applicants.

BASIC COSTS (2006-2007)
Tuition and fees: $25,580.
Per-credit charge: $989.
Room and board: $8,425.

FINANCIAL AID PICTURE (2005-2006)
Students with need: Out of 306 full-time freshmen who applied for aid, 262 were judged to have need. Of these, 262 received aid, and 67 had their full need met. Average financial aid package met 80% of need; average scholarship/grant was $9,557; average loan was $2,436. Need-based aid available for part-time students.
Students without need: 89 full-time freshmen who did not demonstrate need for aid received scholarships/grants; average award was $8,055. No-need awards available for academics, ROTC.
Cumulative student debt: 68% of graduating class had student loans; average debt was $24,617.

FINANCIAL AID PROCEDURES
Forms required: FAFSA, CSS PROFILE.
Dates and Deadlines: Priority date 3/1; no closing date. Applicants notified on a rolling basis starting 12/15; must reply by 5/1.
Transfers: Priority date 5/15. To meet Indiana grant deadlines, Indiana residents must submit FAFSA by March 1.

CONTACT
Dan Meyer, Director of Financial Aid
Admission Office, Notre Dame, IN 46556-5001
(574) 284-4557

Sawyer College: Merrillville
Merrillville, Indiana
www.sawyercollege.edu   Federal Code: 022018

2-year for-profit technical college in large town.
Enrollment: 375 undergrads.

BASIC COSTS (2005-2006)
Additional info: Program costs: $21,100 for 2-year programs, $12,100 for 9-month certificate programs.

FINANCIAL AID PICTURE
Students with need: Need-based aid available for full-time and part-time students.

FINANCIAL AID PROCEDURES
Forms required: FAFSA.
Dates and Deadlines: No deadline. Applicants notified on a rolling basis.

CONTACT
Lisa Coff, Director of Financial Aid
3803 East Lincoln Highway, Merrillville, IN 46410
(219) 736-0436

Taylor University
Upland, Indiana
www.taylor.edu   Federal Code: 001838

4-year private liberal arts college in small town, affiliated with interdenominational tradition.
Enrollment: 1,829 undergrads, 2% part-time. 458 full-time freshmen.
Selectivity: Admits over 75% of applicants.

BASIC COSTS (2006-2007)
Tuition and fees: $22,028.
Per-credit charge: $334.
Room and board: $5,867.

Indiana — Taylor University

FINANCIAL AID PICTURE (2005-2006)
Students with need: Out of 361 full-time freshmen who applied for aid, 268 were judged to have need. Of these, 268 received aid, and 69 had their full need met. Average financial aid package met 74% of need; average scholarship/grant was $10,644; average loan was $4,260. For part-time students, average financial aid package was $9,350.
Students without need: 112 full-time freshmen who did not demonstrate need for aid received scholarships/grants; average award was $4,078. No-need awards available for academics, alumni affiliation, art, athletics, leadership, minority status, music/drama, religious affiliation, state/district residency.
Scholarships offered: *Merit:* Dean's Scholarship for minimum SAT of 1200 or minimum ACT of 27 and top 15% of class; unlimited number awarded; 10-15% of tuition. President's Scholarship for SAT 1300 or ACT 29 and top 10% of class; unlimited number awarded; 15-25% of tuition. Ethnic Student Scholarship based on Christian commitment, leadership potential, willingness to contribute to the Taylor community; 10 awarded; 25% of tuition. Christian Leadership Scholarship based on leadership characteristics as determined by application and interview; 20 awarded; 25% of tuition. All SAT scores listed are exclusive of the writing portion. *Athletic:* 10 full-time freshmen received athletic scholarships; average amount $8,434.
Cumulative student debt: 60% of graduating class had student loans; average debt was $17,910.
Additional info: Reduced rates for high school students during academic year. Tuition waivers for children of alumni during summer session.

FINANCIAL AID PROCEDURES
Forms required: FAFSA, institutional form.
Dates and Deadlines: Closing date 3/10. Applicants notified on a rolling basis starting 3/1; must reply by 5/1.

CONTACT
Tim Nace, Director of Financial Aid
236 West Reade Avenue, Upland, IN 46989-1001
(765) 998-5358

Taylor University: Fort Wayne
Fort Wayne, Indiana
http://fw.taylor.edu
Federal Code: 001838

4-year private liberal arts college in large city, affiliated with Christian interdenominational tradition.
Enrollment: 408 undergrads, 17% part-time. 73 full-time freshmen.
Selectivity: Admits over 75% of applicants.

BASIC COSTS (2006-2007)
Tuition and fees: $19,056.
Room and board: $5,180.

FINANCIAL AID PICTURE (2005-2006)
Students with need: Out of 59 full-time freshmen who applied for aid, 53 were judged to have need. Of these, 53 received aid, and 22 had their full need met. Average financial aid package met 86% of need; average scholarship/grant was $11,573; average loan was $4,083. For part-time students, average financial aid package was $4,187.
Students without need: 10 full-time freshmen who did not demonstrate need for aid received scholarships/grants; average award was $4,552. No-need awards available for academics, alumni affiliation, athletics, leadership, religious affiliation, state/district residency.

FINANCIAL AID PROCEDURES
Forms required: FAFSA, institutional form.
Dates and Deadlines: Closing date 3/1. Applicants notified on a rolling basis starting 3/1; must reply by 5/1 or within 2 week(s) of notification.

CONTACT
Paul Johnston, Director of Financial Aid
1025 West Rudisill Boulevard, Fort Wayne, IN 46807
(800) 233-3922

Tri-State University
Angola, Indiana
www.tristate.edu
Federal Code: 001839

4-year private university in small town.
Enrollment: 1,126 undergrads, 12% part-time. 288 full-time freshmen.
Selectivity: Admits 50 to 75% of applicants.

BASIC COSTS (2006-2007)
Tuition and fees: $21,210.
Per-credit charge: $663.
Room and board: $6,240.

FINANCIAL AID PICTURE (2005-2006)
Students with need: Out of 271 full-time freshmen who applied for aid, 271 were judged to have need. Of these, 271 received aid, and 242 had their full need met. Average financial aid package met 58% of need; average scholarship/grant was $3,600; average loan was $2,682.
Students without need: 12 full-time freshmen who did not demonstrate need for aid received scholarships/grants; average award was $4,415. No-need awards available for academics.

FINANCIAL AID PROCEDURES
Forms required: FAFSA.
Dates and Deadlines: Closing date 3/10. Applicants notified on a rolling basis starting 2/1; must reply by 5/1 or within 2 week(s) of notification.
Transfers: No deadline.

CONTACT
Kim Bennett, Associate Director of Admission and Financial Aid
One University Avenue, Angola, IN 46703
(260) 665-4116

University of Evansville
Evansville, Indiana
www.evansville.edu
Federal Code: 001795

4-year private university and liberal arts college in small city, affiliated with United Methodist Church.
Enrollment: 2,552 undergrads, 5% part-time. 670 full-time freshmen.
Selectivity: Admits over 75% of applicants.

BASIC COSTS (2006-2007)
Tuition and fees: $22,980.
Per-credit charge: $615.
Room and board: $7,120.

FINANCIAL AID PICTURE (2005-2006)
Students with need: Out of 580 full-time freshmen who applied for aid, 491 were judged to have need. Of these, 491 received aid, and 173 had their full need met. Average financial aid package met 96% of need; average scholarship/grant was $16,730; average loan was $3,835. For part-time students, average financial aid package was $6,232.
Students without need: 150 full-time freshmen who did not demonstrate need for aid received scholarships/grants; average award was $9,757. No-need awards available for academics, alumni affiliation, art, athletics, leadership, minority status, music/drama, religious affiliation.
Scholarships offered: 21 full-time freshmen received athletic scholarships; average amount $22,701.
Cumulative student debt: 67% of graduating class had student loans; average debt was $21,142.

Additional info: Early financial planning service allows prospective students to get free estimate of available aid.

FINANCIAL AID PROCEDURES
Forms required: FAFSA. CSS PROFILE accepted but not required.
Dates and Deadlines: Priority date 3/10; no closing date. Applicants notified on a rolling basis starting 3/21.
Transfers: Must reply by 6/1. Indiana state aid is available for a total of 8 semesters.

CONTACT
JoAnn Laugel, Director of Financial Aid
1800 Lincoln Avenue, Evansville, IN 47722
(812) 488-2364

University of Indianapolis
Indianapolis, Indiana
www.uindy.edu   Federal Code: 001804

4-year private university and liberal arts college in very large city, affiliated with United Methodist Church.
Enrollment: 3,317 undergrads, 28% part-time. 731 full-time freshmen.
Selectivity: Admits over 75% of applicants.

BASIC COSTS (2006-2007)
Tuition and fees: $18,850.
Per-credit charge: $780.
Room and board: $7,380.

FINANCIAL AID PICTURE (2004-2005)
Students with need: Average financial aid package met 82% of need; average scholarship/grant was $7,850; average loan was $3,003. For part-time students, average financial aid package was $6,207.
Students without need: No-need awards available for academics, alumni affiliation, art, athletics, job skills, leadership, music/drama, religious affiliation, state/district residency.
Scholarships offered: Presidential Scholarship; upper 5% of class, 1270 SAT/29 ACT, strong college prep; full tuition. Dean's Scholarship; upper 7% of class, 1270 SAT/29 ACT, demonstrated leadership, strong college prep; 50% tuition. Alumni Scholarship; upper 15% of class, 1100 SAT/24 ACT, alumnus connection to school; 30% tuition. Service Award; demonstrated commitment to community volunteerism; $2,500. United Methodist Award; demonstrated commitment to church, activities; $2,500. SAT scores listed are exclusive of the writing portion.
Cumulative student debt: 75% of graduating class had student loans; average debt was $24,651.

FINANCIAL AID PROCEDURES
Forms required: FAFSA, institutional form.
Dates and Deadlines: Closing date 3/1. Applicants notified on a rolling basis starting 3/1; must reply within 3 week(s) of notification.
Transfers: Priority date 3/10; no deadline. Applicants notified on a rolling basis starting 3/1.

CONTACT
Linda Handy, Director of Financial Aid
1400 East Hanna Avenue, Indianapolis, IN 46227-3697
(317) 788-3217

University of Notre Dame
Notre Dame, Indiana   Federal Code: 001840
www.nd.edu   CSS Code: 1841

4-year private university in small city, affiliated with Roman Catholic Church.
Enrollment: 8,266 undergrads. 1,985 full-time freshmen.
Selectivity: Admits less than 50% of applicants. GED not accepted.

BASIC COSTS (2006-2007)
Tuition and fees: $33,407.
Per-credit charge: $1,371.
Room and board: $8,730.

FINANCIAL AID PICTURE (2005-2006)
Students with need: Out of 1,381 full-time freshmen who applied for aid, 1,050 were judged to have need. Of these, 1,050 received aid, and 878 had their full need met. Average financial aid package met 100% of need; average scholarship/grant was $19,058; average loan was $3,603. Need-based aid available for part-time students.
Students without need: 23 full-time freshmen who did not demonstrate need for aid received scholarships/grants; average award was $5,433. No-need awards available for athletics, ROTC.
Scholarships offered: 76 full-time freshmen received athletic scholarships; average amount $26,908.
Additional info: ROTC scholarships and athletic grants are available to qualified applicants on competitive basis.

FINANCIAL AID PROCEDURES
Forms required: FAFSA, CSS PROFILE.
Dates and Deadlines: Closing date 2/15. Applicants notified on a rolling basis starting 3/15; must reply by 5/1.
Transfers: Priority date 2/15.

CONTACT
Joseph Russo, Director of Financial Aid
220 Main Building, Notre Dame, IN 46556
(574) 631-6436

University of St. Francis
Fort Wayne, Indiana
www.sf.edu   Federal Code: 001832

4-year private university and liberal arts college in small city, affiliated with Roman Catholic Church.
Enrollment: 1,736 undergrads, 23% part-time. 291 full-time freshmen.
Selectivity: Admits 50 to 75% of applicants.

BASIC COSTS (2006-2007)
Tuition and fees: $18,478.
Per-credit charge: $560.
Room and board: $5,834.
Additional info: Tuition/fee waivers available for adults.

FINANCIAL AID PICTURE (2004-2005)
Students with need: Out of 280 full-time freshmen who applied for aid, 242 were judged to have need. Of these, 242 received aid, and 72 had their full need met. Average financial aid package met 75% of need; average scholarship/grant was $9,470; average loan was $2,354. For part-time students, average financial aid package was $8,687.
Students without need: 41 full-time freshmen who did not demonstrate need for aid received scholarships/grants; average award was $9,848. No-need awards available for academics, alumni affiliation, art, athletics, music/drama.
Scholarships offered: 33 full-time freshmen received athletic scholarships; average amount $4,537.
Cumulative student debt: 85% of graduating class had student loans; average debt was $22,709.

FINANCIAL AID PROCEDURES
Forms required: FAFSA.
Dates and Deadlines: Priority date 3/10; no closing date. Applicants notified on a rolling basis starting 3/1.

Indiana University of St. Francis

CONTACT
Jamie McGrath, Director of Financial Aid
2701 Spring Street, Fort Wayne, IN 46808
(260) 434-3283

University of Southern Indiana
Evansville, Indiana
www.usi.edu   Federal Code: 001808

4-year public university and liberal arts college in small city.
Enrollment: 8,977 undergrads, 17% part-time. 2,042 full-time freshmen.
Selectivity: Admits over 75% of applicants.

BASIC COSTS (2005-2006)
Tuition and fees: $4,379; out-of-state residents $10,253.
Per-credit charge: $141; out-of-state residents $337.
Room and board: $6,368.

FINANCIAL AID PICTURE (2005-2006)
Students with need: Out of 1,772 full-time freshmen who applied for aid, 1,217 were judged to have need. Of these, 1,096 received aid, and 151 had their full need met. Average financial aid package met 54% of need; average scholarship/grant was $4,506; average loan was $2,412. For part-time students, average financial aid package was $3,385.
Students without need: 211 full-time freshmen who did not demonstrate need for aid received scholarships/grants; average award was $1,994. No-need awards available for academics, alumni affiliation, art, athletics, job skills, leadership, music/drama, state/district residency.
Scholarships offered: 13 full-time freshmen received athletic scholarships; average amount $2,950.
Cumulative student debt: 60% of graduating class had student loans; average debt was $15,724.

FINANCIAL AID PROCEDURES
Forms required: FAFSA, institutional form.
Dates and Deadlines: Closing date 3/1. Applicants notified on a rolling basis starting 4/15.

CONTACT
James Patton, Director of Student Financial Assistance
8600 University Boulevard, Evansville, IN 47712
(812) 464-1767

Valparaiso University
Valparaiso, Indiana
www.valpo.edu   Federal Code: 001842

4-year private university in large town, affiliated with Lutheran Church.
Enrollment: 2,918 undergrads, 4% part-time. 673 full-time freshmen.
Selectivity: Admits over 75% of applicants.

BASIC COSTS (2006-2007)
Tuition and fees: $24,000.
Per-credit charge: $570.
Room and board: $6,640.
Additional info: College of Engineering sophomores, juniors, and seniors: engineering fee - $690; Nursing lab and test fee: beginning of sophomore year - $430; Nursing lab and test fee: beginning of sophomore year: $430; General fee for part-time students: $130. Tuition/fee waivers available for minority students.

FINANCIAL AID PICTURE (2005-2006)
Students with need: Out of 599 full-time freshmen who applied for aid, 482 were judged to have need. Of these, 482 received aid, and 128 had their full need met. Average financial aid package met 92% of need; average scholarship/grant was $13,799; average loan was $4,660. For part-time students, average financial aid package was $7,252.
Students without need: 169 full-time freshmen who did not demonstrate need for aid received scholarships/grants; average award was $7,145. No-need awards available for academics, alumni affiliation, art, athletics, leadership, music/drama, religious affiliation, ROTC.
Scholarships offered: 14 full-time freshmen received athletic scholarships; average amount $19,110.
Cumulative student debt: 71% of graduating class had student loans; average debt was $23,853.
Additional info: Financial assistance based on need, academic record, talent, etc., available through university.

FINANCIAL AID PROCEDURES
Forms required: FAFSA.
Dates and Deadlines: Priority date 3/1; no closing date. Applicants notified on a rolling basis starting 3/1.
Transfers: Transfer students are eligible for scholarships based on previous college work. Scholarship amounts vary depending on the cumulative grade point average at the previous institutions.

CONTACT
David Fevig, Director of Financial Aid
Kretzmann Hall, 1700 Chapel Drive, Valparaiso, IN 46383-6493
(219) 464-5015

Vincennes University
Vincennes, Indiana
www.vinu.edu   Federal Code: 001843

2-year public junior and technical college in large town.
Enrollment: 4,700 undergrads.
Selectivity: Open admission; but selective for some programs.

BASIC COSTS (2005-2006)
Tuition and fees: $3,376; out-of-state residents $8,200.
Per-credit charge: $108; out-of-state residents $268.
Room and board: $6,402.
Additional info: Students from Crawford, Richland, Lawrence and Wabash counties in Illinois pay tuition of $5131, $171 per credit.

FINANCIAL AID PICTURE
Students with need: Need-based aid available for full-time and part-time students. Work study available nights, weekends, and for part-time students.
Students without need: No-need awards available for academics, art, athletics, leadership, music/drama, state/district residency.
Scholarships offered: Presidential Scholarship for 1100 SAT and rank in upper 10% of class; 10 awarded; $2,000 annually. Blue & Gold Scholarship for 1010 SAT and rank in upper half of class; 40 awarded; $1,100 annually. Indiana Academic Honors Diploma, $900 annually. Walters Scholarship for candidates in good standing; tuition and room and board. Education Scholarship for education majors based on SAT scores and rank in upper 10% of class; 1 awarded. Validictorian/Salutatorian scholarships.

FINANCIAL AID PROCEDURES
Forms required: FAFSA.
Dates and Deadlines: Priority date 3/1; closing date 5/1. Applicants notified on a rolling basis starting 5/1; must reply by 8/24.
Transfers: Transfer students must notify state student assistance commission within 30 days of start of term.

CONTACT
Stanley Werne, Director of Financial Aid
1002 North First Street, Vincennes, IN 47591
(812) 888-4361

Wabash College
Crawfordsville, Indiana Federal Code: 001844
www.wabash.edu CSS Code: 1895

4-year private liberal arts college for men in large town.
Enrollment: 869 undergrads. 249 full-time freshmen.
Selectivity: Admits 50 to 75% of applicants.

BASIC COSTS (2006-2007)
Tuition and fees: $24,792.
Room and board: $7,776.

FINANCIAL AID PICTURE (2004-2005)
Students with need: Out of 217 full-time freshmen who applied for aid, 179 were judged to have need. Of these, 179 received aid, and 179 had their full need met. Average financial aid package met 100% of need; average scholarship/grant was $17,396; average loan was $1,506. Need-based aid available for part-time students.
Students without need: 58 full-time freshmen who did not demonstrate need for aid received scholarships/grants; average award was $12,915. No-need awards available for academics, art, leadership, minority status, music/drama, state/district residency.
Scholarships offered: Lilly Awards Program; covers full tuition, room, board, fees, and travel stipend; recognizes outstanding personal achievement and potential for leadership. Fine Arts Fellows; awards ranging up to $12,000; based on creativity/ability; approximately 16 awarded each year. Honor Scholars; awards ranging up to $12,000; based on competitive exams; approximately 40 awarded each year.
Cumulative student debt: 65% of graduating class had student loans; average debt was $17,328.
Additional info: Unlimited President's Scholarships based on class rank, SAT scores. Extensive merit awards including Leadership Scholarships, Fine Arts Fellowships, Lilly Awards.

FINANCIAL AID PROCEDURES
Forms required: FAFSA, CSS PROFILE.
Dates and Deadlines: Priority date 2/15; closing date 3/1. Applicants notified by 4/1; must reply by 5/1 or within 2 week(s) of notification.
Transfers: No deadline.

CONTACT
Clint Gasaway, Director of Financial Aid
PO Box 352, Crawfordsville, IN 47933
(800) 718-9746

Iowa

AIB College of Business
Des Moines, Iowa
www.aib.edu Federal Code: 003963

2-year private business and junior college in large city.
Enrollment: 811 undergrads.

BASIC COSTS (2005-2006)
Tuition and fees: $11,889.
Per-credit charge: $330.
Room and board: $3,957.

FINANCIAL AID PICTURE
Students with need: Need-based aid available for full-time and part-time students. Work study available nights, weekends, and for part-time students.
Students without need: No-need awards available for academics, alumni affiliation, leadership.
Scholarships offered: Founder's Tuition Scholarship: full tuition; awarded to students in the top 15% of their high school graduating class.

FINANCIAL AID PROCEDURES
Forms required: FAFSA, institutional form.
Dates and Deadlines: Closing date 4/1. Applicants notified on a rolling basis starting 3/1; must reply within 3 week(s) of notification.
Transfers: No deadline. Prior aid from previous institutions taken into consideration.

CONTACT
Connie Jensen, Financial Aid Director
2500 Fleur Drive, Des Moines, IA 50321-1799
(515) 244-4221

Allen College
Waterloo, Iowa
www.allencollege.edu Federal Code: 030691

4-year private health science and nursing college in small city.
Enrollment: 374 undergrads, 15% part-time. 33 full-time freshmen.
Selectivity: Admits 50 to 75% of applicants.

BASIC COSTS (2006-2007)
Tuition and fees: $13,928.
Per-credit charge: $415.
Room and board: $5,712.

FINANCIAL AID PICTURE (2004-2005)
Students with need: Out of 33 full-time freshmen who applied for aid, 24 were judged to have need. Of these, 24 received aid. Average financial aid package met 58% of need; average scholarship/grant was $3,113; average loan was $1,849. For part-time students, average financial aid package was $5,837.
Students without need: 6 full-time freshmen who did not demonstrate need for aid received scholarships/grants; average award was $397. No-need awards available for academics, leadership, minority status, ROTC.
Cumulative student debt: 86% of graduating class had student loans; average debt was $16,338.

FINANCIAL AID PROCEDURES
Forms required: FAFSA, institutional form.
Dates and Deadlines: Priority date 6/1; no closing date. Applicants notified on a rolling basis starting 4/1; must reply within 2 week(s) of notification.

CONTACT
Kathie Walters, Financial Aid Director
1825 Logan Avenue, Waterloo, IA 50703
(319) 226-2003

Ashford University
Clinton, Iowa
www.ashford.edu Federal Code: 001881

4-year for-profit university in large town, affiliated with Roman Catholic Church.
Enrollment: 376 undergrads.
Selectivity: Admits 50 to 75% of applicants.

BASIC COSTS (2006-2007)
Tuition and fees: $13,920.
Per-credit charge: $407.

Additional info: Tuition/fee waivers available for minority students, unemployed or children of unemployed.

FINANCIAL AID PICTURE (2005-2006)
Students with need: Need-based aid available for part-time students. Work study available nights, weekends, and for part-time students.
Students without need: No-need awards available for academics, alumni affiliation, art, athletics, leadership, minority status, music/drama, religious affiliation.
Scholarships offered: Divisional Awards; high school GPA of at least 3.2 and ACT score between 23 and 26; up to full tuition. Presidential Scholarships; rank in top 20% of high school class, or ACT composite of 26 or higher, or have GPA of at least 3.2; $1,500-$5,000. Departmental Awards; competitive exams in various departments; maximum $1,500. Leadership Awards; extra-curricular activities and GPA of at least 2.3; maximum $1,000. St. Francis Awards; GPA of at least 2.3 and involvement in parish activities; $500. Counselor's Choice Awards; recommendation from high school guidance counselor, GPA between 2.50 and 3.19, ACT composite between 19 and 25, and at least one extracurricular activity; $500.

FINANCIAL AID PROCEDURES
Forms required: FAFSA.
Dates and Deadlines: Priority date 3/1; closing date 8/1. Applicants notified on a rolling basis starting 3/15; must reply within 3 week(s) of notification.
Transfers: Students with GPA of 3.0 or higher eligible for Presidential Scholarship.

CONTACT
Lisa Kramer, Director of Financial Aid
400 North Bluff Boulevard, Clinton, IA 52733-2967
(563) 242-4023 ext. 1242

Briar Cliff University
Sioux City, Iowa
www.briarcliff.edu
Federal Code: 001846

4-year private liberal arts college in small city, affiliated with Roman Catholic Church.
Enrollment: 1,081 undergrads, 10% part-time. 251 full-time freshmen.
Selectivity: Admits over 75% of applicants.

BASIC COSTS (2006-2007)
Tuition and fees: $19,239.
Per-credit charge: $624.
Room and board: $5,709.

FINANCIAL AID PICTURE (2005-2006)
Students with need: Out of 251 full-time freshmen who applied for aid, 203 were judged to have need. Of these, 203 received aid, and 202 had their full need met. Average financial aid package met 98% of need; average scholarship/grant was $9,177; average loan was $3,150. Need-based aid available for part-time students.
Students without need: 251 full-time freshmen who did not demonstrate need for aid received scholarships/grants; average award was $3,950. No-need awards available for academics, alumni affiliation, art, athletics, leadership, music/drama, religious affiliation, state/district residency.
Scholarships offered: *Merit:* 3-5 Presidential Scholarships: awarded each year; achievement and demonstrated leadership, based on application and on-campus interview. Scholarships are also given for academic achievement, outstanding fine arts and athletic ability, and for leadership development. Special scholarships recognize transfer students, siblings, alumni children, and high school students from parishes in the Diocese of Sioux City. *Athletic:* 251 full-time freshmen received athletic scholarships; average amount $3,400.
Cumulative student debt: 85% of graduating class had student loans; average debt was $19,125.
Additional info: 97% of Briar Cliff's student body receive some sort of aid.

FINANCIAL AID PROCEDURES
Forms required: FAFSA.
Dates and Deadlines: Priority date 3/15; no closing date. Applicants notified on a rolling basis starting 3/15; must reply by 5/1 or within 2 week(s) of notification.
Transfers: Priority date 4/1.

CONTACT
Robert Piechota, Director of Financial Aid
3303 Rebecca Street, Sioux City, IA 51104-2100
(712) 279-5200

Buena Vista University
Storm Lake, Iowa
www.bvu.edu
Federal Code: 001847

4-year private liberal arts college in large town, affiliated with Presbyterian Church (USA).
Enrollment: 1,198 undergrads. 287 full-time freshmen.
Selectivity: Admits over 75% of applicants.

BASIC COSTS (2006-2007)
Tuition and fees: $22,556.
Per-credit charge: $758.
Room and board: $6,296.

FINANCIAL AID PICTURE (2005-2006)
Students with need: Out of 282 full-time freshmen who applied for aid, 265 were judged to have need. Of these, 265 received aid, and 38 had their full need met. Average financial aid package met 90% of need; average scholarship/grant was $7,463; average loan was $4,149. For part-time students, average financial aid package was $4,456.
Students without need: 18 full-time freshmen who did not demonstrate need for aid received scholarships/grants; average award was $8,842. No-need awards available for academics, art, leadership, minority status, music/drama, religious affiliation, state/district residency.
Cumulative student debt: 92% of graduating class had student loans; average debt was $29,059.
Additional info: Portfolio required of art scholarship applicants, audition required of music and drama scholarship applicants.

FINANCIAL AID PROCEDURES
Forms required: FAFSA.
Dates and Deadlines: Priority date 6/1; no closing date. Applicants notified on a rolling basis starting 2/20; must reply by 5/1 or within 2 week(s) of notification.

CONTACT
Leanne Valentine, Director of Financial Aid
610 West Fourth Street, Storm Lake, IA 50588
(714) 749-2164

Central College
Pella, Iowa
www.central.edu
Federal Code: 001850

4-year private liberal arts college in large town, affiliated with Reformed Church in America.
Enrollment: 1,502 undergrads, 1% part-time. 365 full-time freshmen.
Selectivity: Admits over 75% of applicants.

BASIC COSTS (2006-2007)
Tuition and fees: $21,222.
Per-credit charge: $728.
Room and board: $7,224.

Additional info: Costs provided are for main campus only. International location costs may vary by program location.

FINANCIAL AID PICTURE
Students with need: Need-based aid available for full-time and part-time students. Work study available nights, weekends, and for part-time students.
Students without need: No-need awards available for academics, alumni affiliation, art, leadership, minority status, music/drama, religious affiliation, state/district residency.
Additional info: Institutional parent loan program and interest-earning, tuition prepayment savings account available. Auditions required for music and theater scholarships, portfolios required for art scholarships. Monthly payment plan available.

FINANCIAL AID PROCEDURES
Forms required: FAFSA.
Dates and Deadlines: Priority date 3/1; no closing date. Applicants notified on a rolling basis starting 3/10; must reply by 5/1 or within 2 week(s) of notification.
Transfers: Transfers only eligible for total of 4 years of state funds.

CONTACT
Jean Vander Wert, Financial Aid Director
812 University Street, Pella, IA 50219-1999
(641) 628-5336

Clarke College
Dubuque, Iowa
www.clarke.edu   Federal Code: 001852

4-year private liberal arts college in small city, affiliated with Roman Catholic Church.
Enrollment: 982 undergrads, 13% part-time. 159 full-time freshmen.
Selectivity: Admits 50 to 75% of applicants.

BASIC COSTS (2006-2007)
Tuition and fees: $20,297.
Per-credit charge: $498.
Room and board: $6,574.

FINANCIAL AID PICTURE (2005-2006)
Students with need: Out of 155 full-time freshmen who applied for aid, 148 were judged to have need. Of these, 148 received aid, and 38 had their full need met. Average financial aid package met 100% of need; average scholarship/grant was $16,125; average loan was $2,776. For part-time students, average financial aid package was $7,154.
Students without need: 10 full-time freshmen who did not demonstrate need for aid received scholarships/grants; average award was $12,525. No-need awards available for academics, alumni affiliation, art, leadership, music/drama.
Cumulative student debt: 75% of graduating class had student loans; average debt was $18,000.
Additional info: Reduced tuition for family members of BVMs.

FINANCIAL AID PROCEDURES
Forms required: FAFSA.
Dates and Deadlines: Priority date 4/15; no closing date. Applicants notified on a rolling basis starting 3/15; must reply by 5/1 or within 2 week(s) of notification.

CONTACT
Ann Heisler, Director of Financial Aid
1550 Clarke Drive, Dubuque, IA 52001-3198
(563) 588-6327

Coe College
Cedar Rapids, Iowa
www.coe.edu   Federal Code: 001854

4-year private liberal arts college in small city, affiliated with Presbyterian Church (USA).
Enrollment: 1,331 undergrads, 6% part-time. 316 full-time freshmen.
Selectivity: Admits 50 to 75% of applicants.

BASIC COSTS (2006-2007)
Tuition and fees: $25,120.
Room and board: $6,550.
Additional info: Cost per course for part-time students (fewer than 3.0 course credits) is $3,200. Tuition/fee waivers available for adults.

FINANCIAL AID PICTURE (2005-2006)
Students with need: Out of 283 full-time freshmen who applied for aid, 253 were judged to have need. Of these, 253 received aid, and 69 had their full need met. Average financial aid package met 96% of need; average scholarship/grant was $16,012; average loan was $4,727. Need-based aid available for part-time students.
Students without need: 67 full-time freshmen who did not demonstrate need for aid received scholarships/grants; average award was $13,496. No-need awards available for academics, alumni affiliation, art, leadership, music/drama, ROTC.
Scholarships offered: Scholarships for business/economics, music, art, theater, writing, foreign language, science: based on portfolio or audition; available for non-majors except in science and business/economics. Academic Awards: $6,000-$19,000; based on high school achievement.
Cumulative student debt: 76% of graduating class had student loans; average debt was $20,237.

FINANCIAL AID PROCEDURES
Forms required: FAFSA.
Dates and Deadlines: Priority date 3/1; no closing date. Applicants notified on a rolling basis starting 3/15; must reply by 5/1 or within 2 week(s) of notification.

CONTACT
Barb Hoffman, Director of Financial Aid
1220 First Avenue, NE, Cedar Rapids, IA 52402
(319) 399-8540

Cornell College
Mount Vernon, Iowa
www.cornellcollege.edu   Federal Code: 001856

4-year private liberal arts college in small town, affiliated with United Methodist Church.
Enrollment: 1,171 undergrads, 1% part-time. 319 full-time freshmen.
Selectivity: Admits 50 to 75% of applicants.

BASIC COSTS (2006-2007)
Tuition and fees: $24,800.
Per-credit charge: $769.
Room and board: $6,660.
Additional info: Tuition/fee waivers available for adults.

FINANCIAL AID PICTURE (2005-2006)
Students with need: Out of 268 full-time freshmen who applied for aid, 222 were judged to have need. Of these, 222 received aid, and 116 had their full need met. Average financial aid package met 100% of need; average scholarship/grant was $17,905; average loan was $3,155. For part-time students, average financial aid package was $10,310.
Students without need: 85 full-time freshmen who did not demonstrate need for aid received scholarships/grants; average award was $10,950. No-

need awards available for academics, art, leadership, music/drama, religious affiliation, state/district residency.
Cumulative student debt: 78% of graduating class had student loans; average debt was $23,185.
Additional info: Portfolio required for art scholarship applicants. Audition required for music scholarship applicants.

FINANCIAL AID PROCEDURES
Forms required: FAFSA, institutional form.
Dates and Deadlines: Closing date 3/1. Applicants notified on a rolling basis starting 3/1; must reply by 5/1 or within 2 week(s) of notification.
Transfers: No deadline.

CONTACT
Cindi Reints, Director of Financial Assistance
600 First Street, SW, Mount Vernon, IA 52314-1098
(319) 895-4216

Des Moines Area Community College
Ankeny, Iowa
www.dmacc.edu   Federal Code: 004589

2-year public community college in large town.
Enrollment: 16,046 undergrads, 60% part-time. 1,259 full-time freshmen.
Selectivity: Open admission; but selective for some programs.

BASIC COSTS (2005-2006)
Tuition and fees: $2,850; out-of-state residents $5,700.
Per-credit charge: $95; out-of-state residents $190.

FINANCIAL AID PICTURE
Students with need: Need-based aid available for full-time and part-time students. Work study available nights, weekends, and for part-time students.
Students without need: No-need awards available for academics, athletics, state/district residency.
Scholarships offered: DMACC Foundation Freshmen Scholar Award; full tuition, fees and books for first year at DMACC for maximum of 15 credit hours per semester; based on available funds, offered fall term; open to all high school seniors in top 10% of graduating class.

FINANCIAL AID PROCEDURES
Forms required: FAFSA.
Dates and Deadlines: Priority date 4/1; no closing date. Applicants notified on a rolling basis starting 4/1; must reply within 2 week(s) of notification.

CONTACT
DeLores Hawkins, Director of Financial Aid
2006 South Ankeny Boulevard, Ankeny, IA 50021
(515) 964-6282

Divine Word College
Epworth, Iowa
www.dwci.edu   Federal Code: 001858

4-year private liberal arts and seminary college for men in rural community, affiliated with Roman Catholic Church.
Enrollment: 54 undergrads.
Selectivity: Admits over 75% of applicants.

BASIC COSTS (2006-2007)
Tuition and fees: $9,825.
Per-credit charge: $320.
Room and board: $2,400.

FINANCIAL AID PICTURE (2004-2005)
Students with need: 69% of average financial aid package awarded as scholarships/grants, 31% awarded as loans/jobs.

FINANCIAL AID PROCEDURES
Dates and Deadlines: Priority date 8/31; no closing date. Applicants notified on a rolling basis starting 8/1.

CONTACT
Carolyn Waechter, Director of Student Financial Aid
102 Jacoby Drive Southwest, Epworth, IA 52045
(563) 876-3057 ext. 220

Dordt College
Sioux Center, Iowa
www.dordt.edu   Federal Code: 001859

4-year private liberal arts college in small town, affiliated with Christian Reformed Church.
Enrollment: 1,233 undergrads, 3% part-time. 355 full-time freshmen.
Selectivity: Admits over 75% of applicants.

BASIC COSTS (2006-2007)
Tuition and fees: $18,660.
Per-credit charge: $770.
Room and board: $5,160.
Additional info: Tuition/fee waivers available for adults.

FINANCIAL AID PICTURE (2004-2005)
Students with need: Out of 320 full-time freshmen who applied for aid, 278 were judged to have need. Of these, 278 received aid, and 42 had their full need met. For part-time students, average financial aid package was $3,434.
Students without need: 75 full-time freshmen who did not demonstrate need for aid received scholarships/grants; average award was $8,277. No-need awards available for academics, alumni affiliation, art, athletics, leadership, minority status, music/drama, religious affiliation, state/district residency.
Scholarships offered: 17 full-time freshmen received athletic scholarships; average amount $3,386.
Cumulative student debt: 80% of graduating class had student loans; average debt was $16,900.

FINANCIAL AID PROCEDURES
Forms required: FAFSA, institutional form.
Dates and Deadlines: Priority date 4/1; no closing date. Applicants notified on a rolling basis starting 3/15; must reply within 3 week(s) of notification.

CONTACT
Michael Epema, Director of Financial Aid
498 Fourth Avenue, NE, Sioux Center, IA 51250
(712) 722-6087

Drake University
Des Moines, Iowa
www.drake.edu   Federal Code: 001860

4-year private university in large city.
Enrollment: 3,015 undergrads, 5% part-time. 809 full-time freshmen.
Selectivity: Admits over 75% of applicants.

BASIC COSTS (2006-2007)
Tuition and fees: $22,682.
Per-credit charge: $430.
Room and board: $6,500.

FINANCIAL AID PICTURE (2004-2005)
Students with need: Out of 691 full-time freshmen who applied for aid, 532 were judged to have need. Of these, 532 received aid, and 175 had their full need met. Average financial aid package met 88% of need; average scholarship/grant was $11,768; average loan was $4,783. For part-time students, average financial aid package was $7,016.
Students without need: 241 full-time freshmen who did not demonstrate need for aid received scholarships/grants; average award was $9,638. No-need awards available for academics, alumni affiliation, art, athletics, music/drama, ROTC, state/district residency.
Scholarships offered: *Merit:* Drake University Presidential Scholarship; $5,000-$9,000; based on academic merit and awards; unlimited available. National Alumni Scholarship Competition; 6 full-time tuition, room and board and 10 full-time tuition scholarships; available to top students. *Athletic:* 20 full-time freshmen received athletic scholarships; average amount $18,167.

FINANCIAL AID PROCEDURES
Forms required: FAFSA.
Dates and Deadlines: Priority date 3/1; no closing date. Applicants notified on a rolling basis starting 3/1; must reply by 5/1 or within 3 week(s) of notification.
Transfers: Must reply by 5/1 or within 2 week(s) of notification. FAFSA must be filed by July 1 for Iowa Tuition Grant deadline.

CONTACT
Susan Ladd, Director of Student Financial Planning
2507 University Avenue, Des Moines, IA 50311-4505
(515) 271-2905

Ellsworth Community College
Iowa Falls, Iowa
www.ellsworthcollege.edu   Federal Code: 001862

2-year public community college in small town.
Enrollment: 1,000 undergrads.
Selectivity: Open admission; but selective for some programs.

BASIC COSTS (2005-2006)
Tuition and fees: $3,705; out-of-state residents $4,455.
Per-credit charge: $101; out-of-state residents $126.
Additional info: Tuition/fee waivers available for adults.

FINANCIAL AID PICTURE (2004-2005)
Students with need: 39% of average financial aid package awarded as scholarships/grants, 61% awarded as loans/jobs. Need-based aid available for part-time students. Work study available nights, weekends, and for part-time students.
Students without need: No-need awards available for academics, art, athletics, leadership, minority status, music/drama.
Scholarships offered: Academic scholarships based upon ACT score and GPA; unlimited number offered; $500-$1,800. Directors Scholarship: 1st or 2nd in class; $2,300; unlimited number offered. For freshman and sophomore years.

FINANCIAL AID PROCEDURES
Forms required: FAFSA, institutional form.
Dates and Deadlines: Priority date 4/1; no closing date. Applicants notified on a rolling basis starting 2/15; must reply within 4 week(s) of notification.
Transfers: Priority date 4/15.

CONTACT
Tara Miller, Financial Aid Administrator
1100 College Avenue, Iowa Falls, IA 50126
(641) 648-4611 ext. 432

Emmaus Bible College
Dubuque, Iowa
www.emmaus.edu   Federal Code: 016487

4-year private Bible college in small city, affiliated with Brethren Church.
Enrollment: 251 undergrads, 8% part-time. 78 full-time freshmen.

BASIC COSTS (2005-2006)
Tuition and fees: $8,210.
Per-credit charge: $342.
Room and board: $4,162.

FINANCIAL AID PICTURE
Students with need: Need-based aid available for full-time and part-time students.
Students without need: No-need awards available for academics, music/drama.

FINANCIAL AID PROCEDURES
Forms required: FAFSA, institutional form.
Dates and Deadlines: Priority date 5/15; closing date 7/1. Applicants notified on a rolling basis starting 3/1; must reply within 2 week(s) of notification.

CONTACT
Joel Laos, Financial Aid Director
2570 Asbury Road, Dubuque, IA 52001
(563) 588-8000 ext. 1309

Faith Baptist Bible College and Theological Seminary
Ankeny, Iowa
www.faith.edu   Federal Code: 007121

4-year private Bible and seminary college in large town, affiliated with General Association of Regular Baptist Churches.
Enrollment: 324 undergrads, 11% part-time. 84 full-time freshmen.
Selectivity: Open admission; but selective for some programs.

BASIC COSTS (2006-2007)
Tuition and fees: $12,176.
Per-credit charge: $430.
Room and board: $4,794.

FINANCIAL AID PICTURE (2004-2005)
Students with need: 62% of average financial aid package awarded as scholarships/grants, 38% awarded as loans/jobs. Need-based aid available for part-time students.
Students without need: No-need awards available for academics, leadership, music/drama.

FINANCIAL AID PROCEDURES
Forms required: FAFSA.
Dates and Deadlines: Priority date 4/1; no closing date. Applicants notified on a rolling basis starting 3/15.

CONTACT
Breck Appell, Financial Assistance Director
1900 NW Fourth Street, Ankeny, IA 50023
(515) 964-0601 ext. 216

Graceland University
Lamoni, Iowa
www.graceland.edu
Federal Code: 001866

4-year private university and liberal arts college in rural community, affiliated with Community of Christ.
Enrollment: 1,916 undergrads, 25% part-time. 264 full-time freshmen.
Selectivity: Admits 50 to 75% of applicants.

BASIC COSTS (2006-2007)
Tuition and fees: $17,050.
Per-credit charge: $530.
Room and board: $5,650.

FINANCIAL AID PICTURE (2004-2005)
Students with need: Out of 214 full-time freshmen who applied for aid, 181 were judged to have need. Of these, 179 received aid, and 63 had their full need met. Average financial aid package met 88% of need; average scholarship/grant was $12,468; average loan was $4,489. For part-time students, average financial aid package was $6,490.
Students without need: 52 full-time freshmen who did not demonstrate need for aid received scholarships/grants; average award was $8,574. No-need awards available for academics, alumni affiliation, art, athletics, job skills, leadership, music/drama, religious affiliation.
Scholarships offered: 44 full-time freshmen received athletic scholarships; average amount $3,501.
Cumulative student debt: 78% of graduating class had student loans; average debt was $23,198.

FINANCIAL AID PROCEDURES
Forms required: FAFSA.
Dates and Deadlines: Priority date 3/1; no closing date. Applicants notified on a rolling basis starting 2/1; must reply within 2 week(s) of notification.

CONTACT
Sharon Mesle-Morain, Director of Student Finance
One University Place, Lamoni, IA 50140
(641) 784-5140

Grand View College
Des Moines, Iowa
www.gvc.edu
Federal Code: 001867

4-year private liberal arts college in large city, affiliated with Evangelical Lutheran Church in America.
Enrollment: 1,709 undergrads, 20% part-time. 221 full-time freshmen.
Selectivity: Admits over 75% of applicants.

BASIC COSTS (2005-2006)
Tuition and fees: $16,060.
Per-credit charge: $425.
Room and board: $5,422.

FINANCIAL AID PICTURE (2005-2006)
Students with need: Out of 202 full-time freshmen who applied for aid, 165 were judged to have need. Of these, 163 received aid, and 26 had their full need met. Average financial aid package met 80% of need; average scholarship/grant was $10,895; average loan was $3,000. For part-time students, average financial aid package was $6,193.
Students without need: 52 full-time freshmen who did not demonstrate need for aid received scholarships/grants; average award was $12,735. No-need awards available for academics, alumni affiliation, art, athletics, leadership, music/drama, religious affiliation.
Scholarships offered: *Merit:* Presidential Scholarship; $8,000. Honors Scholarship; $7,000. Viking Incentive Program; $6,500. All for first-time, full-time freshmen. *Athletic:* 19 full-time freshmen received athletic scholarships; average amount $3,071.
Cumulative student debt: 94% of graduating class had student loans; average debt was $18,463.

FINANCIAL AID PROCEDURES
Forms required: FAFSA.
Dates and Deadlines: Priority date 3/1; no closing date. Applicants notified on a rolling basis starting 3/1; must reply by 5/1 or within 4 week(s) of notification.

CONTACT
Michele Dunne, Director of Financial Aid
1200 Grandview Avenue, Des Moines, IA 50316-1599
(515) 263-2963

Grinnell College
Grinnell, Iowa
www.grinnell.edu
Federal Code: 001868

4-year private liberal arts college in small town.
Enrollment: 1,546 undergrads. 387 full-time freshmen.
Selectivity: Admits less than 50% of applicants.

BASIC COSTS (2006-2007)
Tuition and fees: $29,030.
Room and board: $7,700.

FINANCIAL AID PICTURE (2005-2006)
Students with need: Out of 310 full-time freshmen who applied for aid, 236 were judged to have need. Of these, 236 received aid, and 236 had their full need met. Average financial aid package met 100% of need; average scholarship/grant was $18,952; average loan was $4,384. For part-time students, average financial aid package was $4,750.
Students without need: 130 full-time freshmen who did not demonstrate need for aid received scholarships/grants; average award was $10,888. No-need awards available for academics.
Cumulative student debt: 61% of graduating class had student loans; average debt was $16,744.
Additional info: Students may apply financial aid to off-campus study programs.

FINANCIAL AID PROCEDURES
Forms required: FAFSA, institutional form.
Dates and Deadlines: Closing date 2/1. Applicants notified by 4/1; must reply by 5/1.

CONTACT
Arnold Woods, Director of Student Financial Aid
1103 Park Street, Grinnell, IA 50112-1690
(641) 269-3250

Hamilton College
Urbandale, Iowa
www.hamiltonia.edu
Federal Code: 004220

4-year for-profit business and technical college in large city.
Enrollment: 865 undergrads.

BASIC COSTS (2005-2006)
Tuition and fees: $16,000.
Per-credit charge: $292.
Additional info: Tuition includes books and fees.

FINANCIAL AID PICTURE
Students with need: Need-based aid available for full-time and part-time students. Work study available nights, weekends, and for part-time students.

Students without need: This college only awards aid to students with need.

FINANCIAL AID PROCEDURES
Forms required: FAFSA, institutional form.
Dates and Deadlines: No deadline.

CONTACT
Director of Student Finance
4655 121st Street, Urbandale, IA 50323
(515) 727-2100

Hamilton College: Cedar Falls
Cedar Falls, Iowa
www.hamiltoncf.com   Federal Code: 004220

4-year for-profit business and technical college in large town.
Enrollment: 679 undergrads, 20% part-time. 78 full-time freshmen.
Selectivity: Open admission; but selective for some programs.

BASIC COSTS (2005-2006)
Additional info: Costs vary by program.

FINANCIAL AID PICTURE (2004-2005)
Students with need: 39% of average financial aid package awarded as scholarships/grants, 61% awarded as loans/jobs. Need-based aid available for part-time students.
Students without need: This college only awards aid to students with need.
Cumulative student debt: 90% of graduating class had student loans; average debt was $3,148.
Additional info: Freshman deadline for filing required financial aid forms is 30 days after start of classes.

FINANCIAL AID PROCEDURES
Forms required: FAFSA, institutional form.
Dates and Deadlines: No deadline.

CONTACT
Brenda Biersner, Director of Finance
7009 Nordic Drive, Cedar Falls, IA 50613
(319) 277-0220

Hamilton College: Cedar Rapids
Cedar Rapids, Iowa
www.hamiltonia.edu   Federal Code: 004220

4-year for-profit business college in small city.
Enrollment: 706 undergrads, 19% part-time. 275 full-time freshmen.
Selectivity: Open admission; but selective for some programs.

FINANCIAL AID PICTURE (2004-2005)
Students with need: Out of 253 full-time freshmen who applied for aid, 250 were judged to have need. Of these, 207 received aid. Need-based aid available for part-time students.
Students without need: No-need awards available for academics.

FINANCIAL AID PROCEDURES
Forms required: FAFSA, institutional form.
Dates and Deadlines: Priority date 6/30; no closing date. Applicants notified on a rolling basis.

CONTACT
Susan Spivey, President
3165 Edgewood Parkway SW, Cedar Rapids, IA 52404
(319) 363-0481

Hawkeye Community College
Waterloo, Iowa
www.hawkeyecollege.edu   Federal Code: 004595

2-year public community and technical college in small city.
Enrollment: 4,822 undergrads.
Selectivity: Open admission; but selective for some programs.

BASIC COSTS (2005-2006)
Tuition and fees: $3,255; out-of-state residents $6,195.
Per-credit charge: $98; out-of-state residents $196.

FINANCIAL AID PICTURE (2004-2005)
Students with need: 32% of average financial aid package awarded as scholarships/grants, 68% awarded as loans/jobs. Work study available nights, weekends, and for part-time students.
Students without need: No-need awards available for academics, state/district residency.

FINANCIAL AID PROCEDURES
Forms required: FAFSA, institutional form.
Dates and Deadlines: Priority date 3/15; no closing date. Applicants notified on a rolling basis starting 4/25; must reply within 2 week(s) of notification.

CONTACT
Brian Will, Director of Financial Aid
Box 8015, Waterloo, IA 50704-8015
(319) 296-4020

Indian Hills Community College
Ottumwa, Iowa
www.indianhills.edu   Federal Code: 008298

2-year public community college in large town.
Enrollment: 3,007 undergrads, 24% part-time. 765 full-time freshmen.
Selectivity: Open admission; but selective for some programs.

BASIC COSTS (2006-2007)
Tuition and fees: $3,195; out-of-state residents $4,755.
Per-credit charge: $104; out-of-state residents $156.
Room and board: $4,300.

FINANCIAL AID PICTURE (2004-2005)
Students with need: 55% of average financial aid package awarded as scholarships/grants, 45% awarded as loans/jobs. Need-based aid available for part-time students.
Students without need: No-need awards available for athletics, state/district residency.

FINANCIAL AID PROCEDURES
Forms required: FAFSA, institutional form.
Dates and Deadlines: Priority date 4/1; no closing date. Applicants notified on a rolling basis starting 6/1; must reply within 2 week(s) of notification.

CONTACT
Jo Altheide, Financial Aid
623 Indian Hills Drive, Building 12, Ottumwa, IA 52501

Iowa Central Community College
Fort Dodge, Iowa
www.iccc.cc.ia.us   Federal Code: 004597

2-year public community college in large town.
Enrollment: 5,352 undergrads.
Selectivity: Open admission; but selective for some programs.

BASIC COSTS (2005-2006)
Tuition and fees: $3,090; out-of-state residents $4,485.
Per-credit charge: $93; out-of-state residents $140.
Room and board: $4,400.

FINANCIAL AID PICTURE
Students with need: Need-based aid available for full-time and part-time students. Work study available nights, weekends, and for part-time students.
Students without need: This college only awards aid to students with need.

FINANCIAL AID PROCEDURES
Forms required: FAFSA.
Dates and Deadlines: No deadline. Applicants notified on a rolling basis starting 4/15; must reply within 2 week(s) of notification.

CONTACT
Angie Martin, Director of Financial Aid
330 Avenue M, Fort Dodge, IA 50501

Iowa Lakes Community College
Estherville, Iowa
www.iowalakes.edu   Federal Code: 001864

2-year public community college in small town.
Enrollment: 3,046 undergrads.
Selectivity: Open admission; but selective for some programs.

BASIC COSTS (2005-2006)
Tuition and fees: $3,522; out-of-state residents $3,582.
Per-credit charge: $103; out-of-state residents $105.
Room and board: $4,120.

FINANCIAL AID PICTURE
Students with need: Need-based aid available for full-time students.

FINANCIAL AID PROCEDURES
Forms required: FAFSA, institutional form.
Dates and Deadlines: Priority date 4/22; no closing date. Applicants notified on a rolling basis starting 4/15.

CONTACT
John Beneke, Director of Financial Aid
300 South 18th Street, Estherville, IA 51334-2725
(712) 362-7917

Iowa State University
Ames, Iowa
www.iastate.edu   Federal Code: 001869

4-year public university in small city.
Enrollment: 20,364 undergrads, 5% part-time. 3,713 full-time freshmen.
Selectivity: Admits over 75% of applicants.

BASIC COSTS (2005-2006)
Tuition and fees: $5,634; out-of-state residents $15,724.
Room and board: $6,197.
Additional info: Additional $224 in fees for engineering program; additional $138 in fees for computer science and management information systems.

FINANCIAL AID PICTURE (2005-2006)
Students with need: Out of 3,046 full-time freshmen who applied for aid, 1,907 were judged to have need. Of these, 1,877 received aid, and 779 had their full need met. Average financial aid package met 76% of need; average scholarship/grant was $3,399; average loan was $3,403. For part-time students, average financial aid package was $5,674.
Students without need: 1,000 full-time freshmen who did not demonstrate need for aid received scholarships/grants; average award was $3,527. No-need awards available for academics, art, athletics, leadership, minority status, music/drama, ROTC, state/district residency.
Scholarships offered: 59 full-time freshmen received athletic scholarships; average amount $13,672.
Cumulative student debt: 67% of graduating class had student loans; average debt was $25,851.
Additional info: Short-term loan program available to meet unplanned needs. Financial counseling clinic provides budget and credit education assistance.

FINANCIAL AID PROCEDURES
Forms required: FAFSA.
Dates and Deadlines: Priority date 3/1; no closing date. Applicants notified on a rolling basis starting 4/1; must reply by 5/1.
Transfers: Priority date 2/15.

CONTACT
Roberta Johnson, Director of Student Financial Aid
100 Alumni Hall, Ames, IA 50011-2011
(515) 294-0066

Iowa Wesleyan College
Mount Pleasant, Iowa
www.iwc.edu   Federal Code: 001871

4-year private liberal arts college in small town, affiliated with United Methodist Church.
Enrollment: 844 undergrads, 28% part-time. 135 full-time freshmen.
Selectivity: Admits 50 to 75% of applicants.

BASIC COSTS (2006-2007)
Tuition and fees: $17,800.
Per-credit charge: $439.
Room and board: $5,530.
Additional info: Tuition/fee waivers available for minority students.

FINANCIAL AID PICTURE
Students with need: Need-based aid available for full-time and part-time students. Work study available nights, weekends, and for part-time students.
Students without need: No-need awards available for academics, alumni affiliation, art, athletics, job skills, leadership, minority status, music/drama, religious affiliation, state/district residency.
Scholarships offered: Goodell Scholarship for music majors: $1,000-$6,000; based on audition. Academic Achievement: up to $4,000 to $12,000; based on 3.0 GPA or 22 ACT. Academic Grant: up to $2,000; based on 2.75-2.99 GPA or 20 or above ACT. Leadership Award: up to $4,000; based on envolvement in extra-curricular activities. Athletic Scholarship: up to $5,000; based on coaches' recommendations. Music Performance Award: $1,000-$2,000; based on participation by nonmusic majors. Jericho Scholarships: (2 out of 3 requirements), 3.6 GPA, top 5% of class, 30 ACT/1310 SAT and personal interview. Presidential Scholarships: 100% tuition; 30 ACT/1310 SAT, 3.6 GPA and personal interview. SAT scores listed are exclusive of the writing portion.

FINANCIAL AID PROCEDURES
Forms required: FAFSA.
Dates and Deadlines: Priority date 4/1; no closing date. Applicants notified on a rolling basis starting 3/1; must reply within 2 week(s) of notification.

CONTACT
Melissa Kilbride, Director of Financial Aid
601 North Main Street, Mount Pleasant, IA 52641-1398
(319) 385-6242

Iowa Western Community College
Council Bluffs, Iowa
www.iwcc.edu Federal Code: 004598

2-year public community and technical college in small city.
Enrollment: 5,092 undergrads.
Selectivity: Open admission; but selective for some programs.

BASIC COSTS (2005-2006)
Tuition and fees: $3,620; out-of-state residents $5,270.
Room and board: $5,490.

FINANCIAL AID PICTURE
Students with need: Need-based aid available for full-time and part-time students.
Students without need: No-need awards available for athletics, music/drama.

FINANCIAL AID PROCEDURES
Forms required: FAFSA.
Dates and Deadlines: Priority date 5/1; no closing date. Applicants notified on a rolling basis starting 3/1; must reply within 3 week(s) of notification.

CONTACT
Blaine Duistermars, Director of Financial Aid
2700 College Road, Council Bluffs, IA 51502-3004
(800) 432-5852 ext. 292

Kaplan University
Davenport, Iowa
www.kaplan.edu/ku Federal Code: 004586

4-year for-profit university in large city.
Enrollment: 19,953 undergrads, 74% part-time. 275 full-time freshmen.
Selectivity: Open admission.

BASIC COSTS (2005-2006)
Tuition and fees: $12,000.
Additional info: Tuition figure includes fees and books.

FINANCIAL AID PICTURE
Students with need: Need-based aid available for full-time and part-time students. Work study available nights.
Students without need: No-need awards available for academics.

FINANCIAL AID PROCEDURES
Forms required: FAFSA, institutional form.
Dates and Deadlines: Priority date 5/15; no closing date. Applicants notified on a rolling basis starting 3/4; must reply by 6/15 or within 2 week(s) of notification.
Transfers: Priority date 6/15.

CONTACT
Sue McCabe, Director of Financial Aid
1801 East Kimberly Road, Suite 1, Davenport, IA 52807-2095
(563) 355-3500

Kirkwood Community College
Cedar Rapids, Iowa
www.kirkwood.cc.ia.us Federal Code: 004076

2-year public community college in small city.
Enrollment: 14,700 undergrads.
Selectivity: Open admission; but selective for some programs.

BASIC COSTS (2005-2006)
Tuition and fees: $2,850; out-of-state residents $5,700.
Per-credit charge: $95; out-of-state residents $190.

FINANCIAL AID PICTURE
Students with need: Need-based aid available for full-time and part-time students. Work study available nights, weekends, and for part-time students.
Students without need: No-need awards available for art, athletics, leadership, music/drama.

FINANCIAL AID PROCEDURES
Forms required: FAFSA.
Dates and Deadlines: Priority date 7/1; no closing date. Applicants notified on a rolling basis starting 4/1.

CONTACT
Peg Julius, Director of Financial Aid
6301 Kirkwood Boulevard SW, Cedar Rapids, IA 52406
(319) 398-1274

Loras College
Dubuque, Iowa
www.loras.edu Federal Code: 001873

4-year private liberal arts college in small city, affiliated with Roman Catholic Church.
Enrollment: 1,565 undergrads, 3% part-time. 364 full-time freshmen.
Selectivity: Admits over 75% of applicants.

BASIC COSTS (2006-2007)
Tuition and fees: $22,053.
Per-credit charge: $425.
Room and board: $6,305.

FINANCIAL AID PICTURE (2005-2006)
Students with need: Out of 342 full-time freshmen who applied for aid, 328 were judged to have need. Of these, 328 received aid, and 105 had their full need met. Average financial aid package met 85% of need; average scholarship/grant was $8,192; average loan was $4,242. For part-time students, average financial aid package was $6,728.
Students without need: 36 full-time freshmen who did not demonstrate need for aid received scholarships/grants; average award was $6,467. No-need awards available for academics, alumni affiliation, music/drama.
Cumulative student debt: 94% of graduating class had student loans; average debt was $24,320.
Additional info: Audition or portfolio recommended for music and art financial aid applicants.

FINANCIAL AID PROCEDURES
Forms required: FAFSA.
Dates and Deadlines: Priority date 4/15; no closing date. Applicants notified on a rolling basis starting 3/1; must reply within 3 week(s) of notification.

CONTACT
Julie Dunn, Director of Financial Planning
1450 Alta Vista Street, Dubuque, IA 52004-0178
(563) 588-7136

Luther College
Decorah, Iowa
www.luther.edu Federal Code: 001874

4-year private liberal arts college in small town, affiliated with Evangelical Lutheran Church in America.
Enrollment: 2,466 undergrads, 1% part-time. 630 full-time freshmen.
Selectivity: Admits over 75% of applicants.

BASIC COSTS (2006-2007)
Tuition and fees: $26,380.
Per-credit charge: $924.
Room and board: $4,290.

FINANCIAL AID PICTURE (2005-2006)
Students with need: Out of 564 full-time freshmen who applied for aid, 458 were judged to have need. Of these, 458 received aid, and 182 had their full need met. Average financial aid package met 90% of need; average scholarship/grant was $18,463; average loan was $4,640. For part-time students, average financial aid package was $8,483.
Students without need: 147 full-time freshmen who did not demonstrate need for aid received scholarships/grants; average award was $8,563. No-need awards available for academics, alumni affiliation, art, minority status, music/drama.
Scholarships offered: Academic scholarship; $4,000-$14,000; based on class rank and SAT/ACT. National Merit Scholarship; $1,000-$2,000; depending on qualification. Diversity Enrichment Scholarship; $3,000-$5,000 awarded to students with broadly diverse and distinctive backgrounds. Church Matching Scholarship; up to $750; for students from member churches. Music scholarship; $1,000-$4,000, plus one scholarship that covers one credit hour of private instruction. Legacy Award; $1,000 for children of Luther College alumni. Competitive Nursing scholarship; $750-$1,000; determined by nursing faculty and strength of admission file. Modest art scholarship; $150-$500; determined by evaluation of portfolio.
Cumulative student debt: 76% of graduating class had student loans; average debt was $18,504.

FINANCIAL AID PROCEDURES
Forms required: FAFSA, institutional form.
Dates and Deadlines: Priority date 3/1; no closing date. Applicants notified on a rolling basis starting 3/15.

CONTACT
Janice Cordell, Director of Student Financial Planning
700 College Drive, Decorah, IA 52101-1042
(563) 387-1018

Maharishi University of Management
Fairfield, Iowa
www.mum.edu
Federal Code: 011113

4-year private university and liberal arts college in small town.
Enrollment: 218 undergrads, 6% part-time. 31 full-time freshmen.
Selectivity: Admits 50 to 75% of applicants.

BASIC COSTS (2006-2007)
Tuition and fees: $24,430.
Per-credit charge: $550.
Room and board: $6,000.

FINANCIAL AID PICTURE
Students with need: Average financial aid package for all full-time undergraduates was $29,630. Need-based aid available for part-time students.
Students without need: No-need awards available for academics, alumni affiliation, music/drama, state/district residency.
Scholarships offered: Shelley Hoffman Scholarship: $500-$900; based on creative writing and/or cerebral palsy; 7 awarded. National Merit Scholarship: full tuition; for NMS finalists; 4 awarded. Ray Prat Scholarship: $500-$1,750; for musically-talented undergraduates; 4 awarded. Girl Scout Gold Award Scholarship: $1,500 renewable; for GS Gold Award recipients; 5 awarded. DeRoy D. Thomas Scholarship: $3,000 each; open to outstanding African American; 1 awarded.
Additional info: Students may earn scholarships through volunteer staff program.

FINANCIAL AID PROCEDURES
Forms required: FAFSA.
Dates and Deadlines: Priority date 4/15; no closing date. Applicants notified on a rolling basis starting 3/1; must reply within 4 week(s) of notification.

CONTACT
Bill Christensen, Director of Financial Aid Fairfield, IA 52557
(641) 472-1156

Marshalltown Community College
Marshalltown, Iowa
www.marshalltowncommunitycollege.com
Federal Code: 001875

2-year public community college in large town.
Enrollment: 1,610 undergrads.
Selectivity: Open admission; but selective for some programs.

BASIC COSTS (2006-2007)
Tuition and fees: $3,810.
Per-credit charge: $105.
Room and board: $3,400.

FINANCIAL AID PICTURE (2005-2006)
Students with need: 57% of average financial aid package awarded as scholarships/grants, 43% awarded as loans/jobs.

FINANCIAL AID PROCEDURES
Forms required: institutional form.
Dates and Deadlines: Priority date 3/1; no closing date. Applicants notified on a rolling basis starting 6/1; must reply within 2 week(s) of notification.

CONTACT
Chloe Webb, Chief Financial Aid Officer
3700 South Center Street, Marshalltown, IA 50158
(641) 752-7106

Mercy College of Health Sciences
Des Moines, Iowa
www.mchs.edu
Federal Code: 006273

4-year for-profit health science college in small city, affiliated with Roman Catholic Church.
Enrollment: 656 undergrads.
Selectivity: Admits 50 to 75% of applicants.

BASIC COSTS (2005-2006)
Tuition and fees: $11,700.
Per-credit charge: $395.

FINANCIAL AID PICTURE
Students with need: Need-based aid available for full-time and part-time students. Work study available nights.
Students without need: No-need awards available for academics.

FINANCIAL AID PROCEDURES
Forms required: FAFSA.
Dates and Deadlines: Closing date 7/1.
Transfers: Students must submit information by 7/1 to be eligible for Iowa Tuition Grant.

CONTACT
Wayne Dille, Financial Aid Coordinator
928 Sixth Avenue, Des Moines, IA 50309
(515) 643-6611

Morningside College
Sioux City, Iowa
www.morningside.edu Federal Code: 001879

4-year private liberal arts college in small city, affiliated with United Methodist Church.
Enrollment: 1,101 undergrads, 4% part-time. 316 full-time freshmen.
Selectivity: Admits over 75% of applicants.

BASIC COSTS (2006-2007)
Tuition and fees: $18,940.
Room and board: $5,930.
Additional info: Tuition/fee waivers available for adults.

FINANCIAL AID PICTURE (2005-2006)
Students with need: Out of 307 full-time freshmen who applied for aid, 280 were judged to have need. Of these, 278 received aid, and 156 had their full need met. Average financial aid package met 83% of need; average scholarship/grant was $5,850; average loan was $3,676. For part-time students, average financial aid package was $7,775.
Students without need: 35 full-time freshmen who did not demonstrate need for aid received scholarships/grants; average award was $6,528. No-need awards available for academics, alumni affiliation, art, athletics, job skills, leadership, music/drama, religious affiliation, ROTC, state/district residency.
Scholarships offered: *Merit:* President's Scholarship: $6,000 to $10,000; ACT 29 and top 10% of class. Dean's Scholarship: $3,000 to $6,000; ACT 23 or top 20% of class. Mustang Co-Curricular Award: up to $3,000; based on leadership and involvement. National Merit: full. Talent Awards: up to $4,000; based on talents in the areas of art, mass communications, music, and/or theatre. *Athletic:* 191 full-time freshmen received athletic scholarships; average amount $2,686.

FINANCIAL AID PROCEDURES
Forms required: FAFSA.
Dates and Deadlines: Priority date 3/1; no closing date. Applicants notified on a rolling basis starting 3/31.

CONTACT
Karen Gagnon, Director Student Financial Planning
1501 Morningside Avenue, Sioux City, IA 51106
(712) 274-5159

Mount Mercy College
Cedar Rapids, Iowa
www.mtmercy.edu Federal Code: 001880

4-year private liberal arts college in small city, affiliated with Roman Catholic Church.
Enrollment: 1,490 undergrads. 181 full-time freshmen.
Selectivity: Admits over 75% of applicants.

BASIC COSTS (2005-2006)
Tuition and fees: $18,030.
Per-credit charge: $500.
Room and board: $5,680.

FINANCIAL AID PICTURE (2005-2006)
Students with need: Out of 176 full-time freshmen who applied for aid, 151 were judged to have need. Of these, 151 received aid, and 71 had their full need met. Average financial aid package met 87% of need; average scholarship/grant was $11,614; average loan was $4,738. Need-based aid available for part-time students.
Students without need: 30 full-time freshmen who did not demonstrate need for aid received scholarships/grants; average award was $13,461. No-need awards available for academics, art, leadership, music/drama.

FINANCIAL AID PROCEDURES
Forms required: FAFSA.
Dates and Deadlines: Priority date 3/1; no closing date. Applicants notified on a rolling basis starting 3/15; must reply by 5/1 or within 3 week(s) of notification.
Transfers: No deadline. Applicants notified on a rolling basis starting 3/15; must reply within 4 week(s) of notification.

CONTACT
Lois Mulbrook, Director of Financial Aid
1330 Elmhurst Drive NE, Cedar Rapids, IA 52402-4797
(319) 368-6467

North Iowa Area Community College
Mason City, Iowa
www.niacc.edu Federal Code: 001877

2-year public community college in large town.
Enrollment: 2,515 undergrads, 32% part-time. 616 full-time freshmen.
Selectivity: Open admission; but selective for some programs.

BASIC COSTS (2005-2006)
Tuition and fees: $3,138; out-of-state residents $4,533.
Per-credit charge: $93; out-of-state residents $140.
Room and board: $3,920.

FINANCIAL AID PICTURE (2004-2005)
Students with need: 54% of average financial aid package awarded as scholarships/grants, 46% awarded as loans/jobs. Need-based aid available for part-time students. Work study available nights.
Students without need: No-need awards available for academics, alumni affiliation, art, athletics, leadership, music/drama.

FINANCIAL AID PROCEDURES
Forms required: FAFSA, institutional form.
Dates and Deadlines: Priority date 3/1; no closing date. Applicants notified on a rolling basis starting 4/1; must reply within 2 week(s) of notification.

CONTACT
Mary Bloomingdale, Director of Financial Aid
500 College Drive, Mason City, IA 50401
(641) 422-4351

Northeast Iowa Community College
Calmar, Iowa
www.nicc.edu Federal Code: 004587

2-year public community college in rural community.
Enrollment: 1,914 undergrads, 34% part-time. 213 full-time freshmen.
Selectivity: Open admission.

BASIC COSTS (2006-2007)
Tuition and fees: $3,894.

FINANCIAL AID PICTURE
Students with need: Need-based aid available for full-time and part-time students. Work study available nights.
Students without need: No-need awards available for academics, leadership.

FINANCIAL AID PROCEDURES
Forms required: FAFSA.
Dates and Deadlines: Priority date 7/1; no closing date. Applicants notified on a rolling basis starting 5/1.

Iowa Northeast Iowa Community College

CONTACT
Kim Baumler, Financial Aid Officer
Box 400, Calmar, IA 52132
(563) 556-5110 ext. 401

Northwest Iowa Community College
Sheldon, Iowa
www.nwicc.edu   Federal Code: 004600

2-year public community college in small town.
Enrollment: 780 undergrads.
Selectivity: Open admission; but selective for some programs.

BASIC COSTS (2005-2006)
Tuition and fees: $3,630; out-of-state residents $5,115.
Per-credit charge: $99; out-of-state residents $148.
Room only: $1,900.

FINANCIAL AID PICTURE
Students with need: Need-based aid available for full-time and part-time students.

FINANCIAL AID PROCEDURES
Forms required: FAFSA, institutional form.
Dates and Deadlines: Priority date 4/1; no closing date. Applicants notified on a rolling basis starting 5/1.

CONTACT
Karna Hofmeyer, Financial Aid Director
603 West Park Street, Sheldon, IA 51201
(712) 324-5061 ext. 138

Northwestern College
Orange City, Iowa
www.nwciowa.edu   Federal Code: 001883

4-year private liberal arts college in small town, affiliated with Reformed Church in America.
Enrollment: 1,247 undergrads, 2% part-time. 357 full-time freshmen.
Selectivity: Admits over 75% of applicants.

BASIC COSTS (2006-2007)
Tuition and fees: $18,296.
Room and board: $5,210.
Additional info: 1-4 credits, $390 per credit hour; 5-8 credits, $580 per credit hour; 9-11 credits, $770 per credit hour. Tuition/fee waivers available for adults.

FINANCIAL AID PICTURE (2004-2005)
Students with need: Out of 341 full-time freshmen who applied for aid, 289 were judged to have need. Of these, 289 received aid, and 125 had their full need met. Average financial aid package met 95% of need; average scholarship/grant was $4,931; average loan was $3,414. For part-time students, average financial aid package was $5,506.
Students without need: 65 full-time freshmen who did not demonstrate need for aid received scholarships/grants; average award was $4,473. No-need awards available for academics, art, athletics, music/drama, religious affiliation, state/district residency.
Scholarships offered: 131 full-time freshmen received athletic scholarships; average amount $2,231.
Cumulative student debt: 85% of graduating class had student loans; average debt was $22,286.

FINANCIAL AID PROCEDURES
Forms required: FAFSA.
Dates and Deadlines: Priority date 4/1; closing date 6/30. Applicants notified on a rolling basis starting 3/15; must reply within 3 week(s) of notification.
Transfers: No deadline.

CONTACT
Gerry Korver, Director of Financial Aid
101 7th Street, SW, Orange City, IA 51041
(712) 707-7131

St. Ambrose University
Davenport, Iowa
www.sau.edu   Federal Code: 001889

4-year private university and liberal arts college in small city, affiliated with Roman Catholic Church.
Enrollment: 2,634 undergrads, 17% part-time. 470 full-time freshmen.
Selectivity: Admits over 75% of applicants.

BASIC COSTS (2006-2007)
Tuition and fees: $19,460.
Per-credit charge: $605.
Room and board: $7,240.
Additional info: Tuition/fee waivers available for adults, minority students.

FINANCIAL AID PICTURE (2005-2006)
Students with need: Out of 468 full-time freshmen who applied for aid, 403 were judged to have need. Of these, 403 received aid, and 205 had their full need met. Average financial aid package met 21% of need; average scholarship/grant was $9,150; average loan was $2,742. For part-time students, average financial aid package was $7,296.
Students without need: 65 full-time freshmen who did not demonstrate need for aid received scholarships/grants; average award was $6,815. No-need awards available for academics, alumni affiliation, art, athletics, job skills, music/drama.
Scholarships offered: *Merit:* Ambrose Scholarship: 4.0 GPA and 30 ACT or 1320 SAT score required. Presidential Scholarship: 3.8 GPA and ACT 26-29 or SAT 1170-1319 required. SAT scores listed are exclusive of Writing. *Athletic:* 18 full-time freshmen received athletic scholarships; average amount $3,042.
Cumulative student debt: 79% of graduating class had student loans; average debt was $24,728.
Additional info: Iowa applicants must apply for financial aid by July 1. Audition required for music, drama scholarship applicants.

FINANCIAL AID PROCEDURES
Forms required: FAFSA.
Dates and Deadlines: Priority date 3/15; no closing date. Applicants notified on a rolling basis starting 2/1; must reply within 2 week(s) of notification.

CONTACT
Julie Haack, Director of Financial Aid
518 West Locust Street, Davenport, IA 52803-2898
(563) 333-6314

St. Luke's College
Sioux City, Iowa
www.stlukes.org   Federal Code: 007291

2-year private health science and nursing college in small city, affiliated with Lutheran and Methodist churches.
Enrollment: 155 undergrads, 15% part-time. 18 full-time freshmen.
Selectivity: Admits less than 50% of applicants.

BASIC COSTS (2006-2007)
Tuition and fees: $12,500.
Per-credit charge: $340.
Additional info: Summer general fee: $125.

FINANCIAL AID PICTURE (2004-2005)
Students with need: Out of 18 full-time freshmen who applied for aid, 16 were judged to have need. Of these, 16 received aid. For part-time students, average financial aid package was $1,504.
Students without need: 1 full-time freshmen who did not demonstrate need for aid received scholarships/grants; average award was $1,500. No-need awards available for academics, job skills, leadership.
Cumulative student debt: 99% of graduating class had student loans; average debt was $14,117.

FINANCIAL AID PROCEDURES
Forms required: FAFSA.
Dates and Deadlines: Priority date 3/1; no closing date. Applicants notified on a rolling basis starting 4/1; must reply within 2 week(s) of notification.

CONTACT
Danelle Johannsen, Coordinator, Financial Aid/Registrar
2720 Stone Park Boulevard, Sioux City, IA 51104
(712) 279-3377

Simpson College
Indianola, Iowa
www.simpson.edu   Federal Code: 001887

4-year private liberal arts college in large town, affiliated with United Methodist Church.
Enrollment: 1,899 undergrads, 22% part-time. 336 full-time freshmen.
Selectivity: Admits over 75% of applicants.

BASIC COSTS (2006-2007)
Tuition and fees: $22,266.
Per-credit charge: $245.
Room and board: $6,278.
Additional info: Tuition/fee waivers available for adults, minority students.

FINANCIAL AID PICTURE (2004-2005)
Students with need: Out of 336 full-time freshmen who applied for aid, 290 were judged to have need. Of these, 290 received aid, and 65 had their full need met. Average financial aid package met 87% of need; average scholarship/grant was $13,935; average loan was $3,208. For part-time students, average financial aid package was $5,438.
Students without need: 46 full-time freshmen who did not demonstrate need for aid received scholarships/grants; average award was $8,874. No-need awards available for academics, alumni affiliation, art, leadership, minority status, music/drama, religious affiliation, state/district residency.
Cumulative student debt: 87% of graduating class had student loans; average debt was $24,403.
Additional info: Music and theater scholarships based on audition. Art scholarships based on portfolio.

FINANCIAL AID PROCEDURES
Forms required: FAFSA.
Dates and Deadlines: Priority date 4/1; no closing date. Applicants notified on a rolling basis starting 3/15; must reply by 5/1 or within 3 week(s) of notification.

CONTACT
Tracie Pavon, Director of Financial Assistance
701 North C Street, Indianola, IA 50125
(515) 961-1630

Southeastern Community College: North Campus
West Burlington, Iowa
www.scciowa.edu   Federal Code: 004603

2-year public community and junior college in large town.
Enrollment: 4,115 undergrads.
Selectivity: Open admission; but selective for some programs.

BASIC COSTS (2005-2006)
Tuition and fees: $2,910; out-of-state residents $3,270.
Per-credit charge: $97; out-of-state residents $109.

FINANCIAL AID PICTURE
Students with need: Need-based aid available for full-time and part-time students.
Students without need: This college only awards aid to students with need.

FINANCIAL AID PROCEDURES
Forms required: FAFSA, institutional form.
Dates and Deadlines: Priority date 6/5; no closing date. Applicants notified on a rolling basis starting 6/5; must reply within 4 week(s) of notification.

CONTACT
Gwen Scholer, Financial Aid Director
1500 West Agency Road, West Burlington, IA 52655-0605
(319) 752-2731 ext. 8156

Southwestern Community College
Creston, Iowa
www.swcciowa.edu   Federal Code: 001857

2-year public community college in small town.
Enrollment: 860 undergrads.
Selectivity: Open admission; but selective for some programs.

BASIC COSTS (2006-2007)
Tuition and fees: $3,420.
Room and board: $3,800.

FINANCIAL AID PICTURE (2004-2005)
Students with need: 51% of average financial aid package awarded as scholarships/grants, 49% awarded as loans/jobs. Work study available nights, weekends, and for part-time students.
Students without need: No-need awards available for academics, athletics, leadership, music/drama, state/district residency.

FINANCIAL AID PROCEDURES
Forms required: FAFSA, institutional form.
Dates and Deadlines: Priority date 7/1; no closing date. Applicants notified on a rolling basis starting 6/1; must reply within 2 week(s) of notification.

CONTACT
Tracy Sleep, Financial Aid Officer
1501 West Townline Street, Creston, IA 50801
(641) 782-1333

University of Dubuque
Dubuque, Iowa
www.dbq.edu   Federal Code: 001891

4-year private university and seminary college in small city, affiliated with Presbyterian Church (USA).
Enrollment: 1,175 undergrads, 4% part-time. 296 full-time freshmen.

Selectivity: Admits over 75% of applicants.

BASIC COSTS (2006-2007)
Tuition and fees: $18,260.
Per-credit charge: $405.
Room and board: $6,200.

FINANCIAL AID PICTURE (2005-2006)
Students with need: Out of 290 full-time freshmen who applied for aid, 266 were judged to have need. Of these, 264 received aid, and 128 had their full need met. Average financial aid package met 87% of need; average scholarship/grant was $9,189; average loan was $9,302. For part-time students, average financial aid package was $5,479.
Students without need: 28 full-time freshmen who did not demonstrate need for aid received scholarships/grants; average award was $15,297. No-need awards available for academics, alumni affiliation, music/drama, ROTC.
Scholarships offered: Presidential Scholarship; $6,000 per annum for 4 years; top 20% of high school graduation class and top 20% of ACT. Honors Scholarship; top 20% of high school class, or top 20% of ACT/SAT, or 3.5 GPA or greater.
Cumulative student debt: 92% of graduating class had student loans; average debt was $30,963.

FINANCIAL AID PROCEDURES
Forms required: FAFSA.
Dates and Deadlines: Priority date 4/1; no closing date. Applicants notified on a rolling basis starting 3/1; must reply within 3 week(s) of notification.
Transfers: No deadline. Applicants notified on a rolling basis starting 3/1; must reply within 3 week(s) of notification. Iowa Tuition Grant available to Iowa residents.

CONTACT
Timothy Kremer, Dean of Student Financial Planning and Scholarships
2000 University Avenue, Dubuque, IA 52001-5099
(563) 589-3396

University of Iowa
Iowa City, Iowa
www.uiowa.edu
Federal Code: 001892

4-year public university in small city.
Enrollment: 19,566 undergrads, 7% part-time. 3,818 full-time freshmen.
Selectivity: Admits over 75% of applicants.

BASIC COSTS (2005-2006)
Tuition and fees: $5,612; out-of-state residents $16,998.
Room and board: $6,073.

FINANCIAL AID PICTURE
Students with need: Need-based aid available for full-time and part-time students. Work study available nights, weekends, and for part-time students.
Students without need: No-need awards available for academics, athletics, leadership, minority status, music/drama.
Scholarships offered: Presidential Scholarship: $40,000, based on ACT/SAT, GPA, essay; 20 awarded. Old Gold Scholarship: $12,000; awarded to runners-up for Presidential Scholarship; 350 awarded. Opportunity at Iowa: $20,000; members of underrepresented groups (African-American, Hispanic/Latin, Native American, Alaskan Native) with ACT of 25 and 3.5 GPA automatically considered. National Scholars Award: $10,000; for non-residents based on admission index. Iowa Scholars Award: $2,650; to residents in top 15% of class.

FINANCIAL AID PROCEDURES
Forms required: FAFSA, institutional form.
Dates and Deadlines: Priority date 1/1; no closing date. Applicants notified on a rolling basis starting 3/1.

CONTACT
Mark Warner, Assistant Provost for Enrollment Services and Director of Financial Aid
107 Calvin Hall, Iowa City, IA 52242
(319) 335-1450

University of Northern Iowa
Cedar Falls, Iowa
www.uni.edu
Federal Code: 001890

4-year public university in small city.
Enrollment: 10,734 undergrads, 10% part-time. 1,702 full-time freshmen.
Selectivity: Admits over 75% of applicants.

BASIC COSTS (2005-2006)
Tuition and fees: $5,602; out-of-state residents $13,214.
Room and board: $5,531.

FINANCIAL AID PICTURE (2005-2006)
Students with need: Out of 1,460 full-time freshmen who applied for aid, 949 were judged to have need. Of these, 913 received aid, and 209 had their full need met. Average financial aid package met 65% of need; average scholarship/grant was $2,556; average loan was $2,701. For part-time students, average financial aid package was $6,922.
Students without need: 296 full-time freshmen who did not demonstrate need for aid received scholarships/grants; average award was $2,331. No-need awards available for academics, alumni affiliation, art, athletics, leadership, minority status, music/drama, ROTC, state/district residency.
Scholarships offered: *Merit:* Presidential Scholarship; $7,000; for rank in upper 10% of high school class or rank in top 5 of class of 50 or less, ACT composite of 29 or above, academic excellence, extracurricular achievements, leadership and demonstrated potential for making a significant contribution to society; 20 awards available. Provost Scholarship; $2,000 per year for four years; same criteria as Presidential Scholarship; 30 available. *Athletic:* 60 full-time freshmen received athletic scholarships; average amount $8,202.
Cumulative student debt: 77% of graduating class had student loans; average debt was $20,239.

FINANCIAL AID PROCEDURES
Forms required: FAFSA.
Dates and Deadlines: No deadline. Applicants notified on a rolling basis starting 3/1.

CONTACT
Roland Carrillo, Director Financial Aid and Student Employment
120 Gilchrist Hall, Cedar Falls, IA 50614-0018
(319) 273-2700

Upper Iowa University
Fayette, Iowa
www.uiu.edu
Federal Code: 001893

4-year private university in rural community.
Enrollment: 691 undergrads.
Selectivity: Open admission; but selective for some programs.

BASIC COSTS (2006-2007)
Tuition and fees: $18,778.
Room and board: $5,815.

FINANCIAL AID PICTURE (2004-2005)
Students with need: 38% of average financial aid package awarded as scholarships/grants, 62% awarded as loans/jobs. Need-based aid available for part-time students.
Students without need: No-need awards available for academics.

FINANCIAL AID PROCEDURES
Forms required: FAFSA.
Dates and Deadlines: Priority date 6/1; no closing date. Applicants notified on a rolling basis starting 4/1.

CONTACT
Jobyna Johnston, Director of Financial Aid
Parker Fox Hall, Fayette, IA 52142
(800) 553-4150 ext. 3

Vatterott College
Des Moines, Iowa
www.vatterott-college.edu   Federal Code: 026092

2-year for-profit health science and technical college in large city.
Enrollment: 172 undergrads.
Selectivity: Open admission.

BASIC COSTS (2005-2006)
Additional info: Tuition ranges from $8,569 to $11,135. Costs vary depending on program for each campus. Fees included in costs. Tuition at time of enrollment locked for 2 years.

FINANCIAL AID PICTURE
Students with need: Need-based aid available for full-time students.
Students without need: This college only awards aid to students with need.
Scholarships offered: Make the Grade Scholarship available to high school graduates for 1 year after high school graduation. Based on final semester grades; maximum of $1,000 per student.

FINANCIAL AID PROCEDURES
Forms required: FAFSA.
Dates and Deadlines: No deadline. Applicants notified on a rolling basis.

CONTACT
Matt Edwards, Financial Aid Administrator
6100 Thornton, Suite 290, Des Moines, IA 50321
(515) 309-9000

Vennard College
University Park, Iowa
www.vennard.edu   Federal Code: 001894

4-year private Bible college in large town, affiliated with interdenominational tradition.
Enrollment: 77 undergrads, 9% part-time. 20 full-time freshmen.
Selectivity: Admits 50 to 75% of applicants.

BASIC COSTS (2006-2007)
Tuition and fees: $9,240.
Room and board: $4,600.

FINANCIAL AID PICTURE (2004-2005)
Students with need: 42% of average financial aid package awarded as scholarships/grants, 58% awarded as loans/jobs. Need-based aid available for part-time students.

FINANCIAL AID PROCEDURES
Forms required: FAFSA.
Dates and Deadlines: Priority date 7/1; no closing date. Applicants notified on a rolling basis starting 8/29; must reply within 1 week(s) of notification.
Transfers: Academic scholarships available to full-time new transfer students. 3.5 minimum college GPA for 2 consecutive semesters of credit work in degree granting program required.

CONTACT
Kevin Klucas, Financial Aid Director
Box 29, University Park, IA 52595-0029
(641) 673-8391 ext. 218

Waldorf College
Forest City, Iowa
www.waldorf.edu   Federal Code: 001895

4-year private liberal arts college in small town, affiliated with Evangelical Lutheran Church in America.
Enrollment: 581 undergrads, 2% part-time. 200 full-time freshmen.
Selectivity: Admits 50 to 75% of applicants.

BASIC COSTS (2006-2007)
Tuition and fees: $16,670.
Room and board: $5,120.

FINANCIAL AID PICTURE (2004-2005)
Students with need: Out of 168 full-time freshmen who applied for aid, 153 were judged to have need. Of these, 152 received aid, and 49 had their full need met. Average financial aid package met 85% of need; average scholarship/grant was $9,126; average loan was $3,421. For part-time students, average financial aid package was $8,490.
Students without need: 37 full-time freshmen who did not demonstrate need for aid received scholarships/grants; average award was $8,358. No-need awards available for academics, alumni affiliation, athletics, job skills, leadership, music/drama, religious affiliation, state/district residency.
Scholarships offered: 24 full-time freshmen received athletic scholarships; average amount $2,157.
Cumulative student debt: 63% of graduating class had student loans; average debt was $14,782.

FINANCIAL AID PROCEDURES
Forms required: FAFSA.
Dates and Deadlines: Priority date 3/1; no closing date. Applicants notified on a rolling basis starting 3/1; must reply within 2 week(s) of notification.
Transfers: Applicants notified on a rolling basis starting 3/1.

CONTACT
Duane Polsdofer, Director of Student Financial Aid
106 South Sixth Street, Forest City, IA 50436-1713
(641) 585-8120

Wartburg College
Waverly, Iowa
www.wartburg.edu   Federal Code: 001896

4-year private liberal arts college in small town, affiliated with Evangelical Lutheran Church in America.
Enrollment: 1,768 undergrads, 2% part-time. 518 full-time freshmen.
Selectivity: Admits over 75% of applicants.

BASIC COSTS (2006-2007)
Tuition and fees: $22,410.
Room and board: $6,715.

FINANCIAL AID PICTURE (2005-2006)
Students with need: Out of 464 full-time freshmen who applied for aid, 398 were judged to have need. Of these, 398 received aid, and 142 had their full need met. Average financial aid package met 90% of need; average scholarship/grant was $13,851; average loan was $3,966. For part-time students, average financial aid package was $5,715.
Students without need: 113 full-time freshmen who did not demonstrate need for aid received scholarships/grants; average award was $14,105. No-

need awards available for academics, alumni affiliation, job skills, music/drama, religious affiliation, state/district residency.
Scholarships offered: Regents scholarship: up to full tuition, fees, room and board; minimum ACT score of 28, (1240 SAT, exclusive of Writing) or rank in top 10 percent of class; renewable for 4 years, based on maintaining 3.0 cumulative GPA. Students who participate in Regents Scholarship competition not eligible for Presidential scholarship. Presidential scholarship: up to $6,000 per year, renewable for 4 years, based on maintaining 2.7 cumulative GPA.; minimum ACT score of 25 (1140 SAT, exclusive of Writing) or rank in top 20 percent of class or cumulative GPA of 3.5 or above.
Cumulative student debt: 84% of graduating class had student loans; average debt was $22,122.

FINANCIAL AID PROCEDURES
Forms required: FAFSA.
Dates and Deadlines: Priority date 3/1; no closing date. Applicants notified on a rolling basis starting 3/21; must reply within 2 week(s) of notification.

CONTACT
Jennifer Sassman, Director of Financial Aid
100 Wartburg Boulevard, PO Box 1003, Waverly, IA 50677-0903
(319) 352-8262

Western Iowa Tech Community College
Sioux City, Iowa
www.witcc.com   Federal Code: 004590

2-year public community college in small city.
Enrollment: 2,481 undergrads.
Selectivity: Open admission; but selective for some programs.

BASIC COSTS (2005-2006)
Tuition and fees: $3,240; out-of-state residents $4,440.
Per-credit charge: $93; out-of-state residents $133.
Room only: $2,655.

FINANCIAL AID PICTURE (2004-2005)
Students with need: Need-based aid available for part-time students. Work study available nights, weekends, and for part-time students.
Students without need: No-need awards available for academics, leadership.

FINANCIAL AID PROCEDURES
Forms required: FAFSA.
Dates and Deadlines: No deadline. Applicants notified on a rolling basis starting 4/1.

CONTACT
Donald Duzik, Director of Financial Aid
Box 5199, Sioux City, IA 51102-5199
(712) 274-6402

William Penn University
Oskaloosa, Iowa
www.wmpenn.edu   Federal Code: 001900

4-year private liberal arts college in large town, affiliated with Society of Friends (Quaker).
Enrollment: 1,795 undergrads.
Selectivity: Admits less than 50% of applicants.

BASIC COSTS (2005-2006)
Tuition and fees: $15,334.
Per-credit charge: $215.
Room and board: $4,896.

FINANCIAL AID PICTURE (2004-2005)
Students with need: 61% of average financial aid package awarded as scholarships/grants, 39% awarded as loans/jobs. Need-based aid available for part-time students. Work study available nights, weekends, and for part-time students.
Students without need: No-need awards available for academics, alumni affiliation, athletics, leadership, music/drama, religious affiliation.
Scholarships offered: Participation awards: up to $3,000 per year for music, drama, media, cheerleading, dance, religious leadership. Academic scholarships: based on high school GPA, ACT or SAT, class rank.

FINANCIAL AID PROCEDURES
Forms required: FAFSA.
Dates and Deadlines: Priority date 7/1; no closing date. Applicants notified on a rolling basis starting 1/1; must reply within 2 week(s) of notification.
Transfers: Priority date 4/1.

CONTACT
Cyndi Peiffer, Director of Financial Aid
201 Trueblood Avenue, Oskaloosa, IA 52577
(641) 673-1060

Kansas

Allen County Community College
Iola, Kansas
www.allencc.edu   Federal Code: 001901

2-year public community college in small town.
Enrollment: 2,800 undergrads.
Selectivity: Open admission.

BASIC COSTS (2005-2006)
Tuition and fees: $1,530; out-of-district residents $1,620; out-of-state residents $1,620.
Per-credit charge: $35; out-of-district residents $38; out-of-state residents $38.
Room and board: $3,500.

FINANCIAL AID PICTURE (2004-2005)
Students with need: 66% of average financial aid package awarded as scholarships/grants, 34% awarded as loans/jobs. Need-based aid available for part-time students. Work study available nights, weekends, and for part-time students.
Students without need: No-need awards available for academics, art, athletics, music/drama, state/district residency.
Additional info: Scholarships for livestock judging, cheerleading, choir, dance, drama, art, academic challenge, and student ambassadors.

FINANCIAL AID PROCEDURES
Forms required: FAFSA.
Dates and Deadlines: Priority date 6/1; closing date 8/1. Applicants notified on a rolling basis starting 6/1; must reply within 2 week(s) of notification.

CONTACT
Barbara Leavitt, Director of Financial Aid/Registrar
1801 North Cottonwood, Iola, KS 66749
(620) 365-5116 ext. 221

Baker University
Baldwin City, Kansas
www.bakeru.edu   Federal Code: 001903

4-year private liberal arts college in small town, affiliated with United Methodist Church.
Enrollment: 870 undergrads, 2% part-time. 239 full-time freshmen.
Selectivity: Admits 50 to 75% of applicants.

BASIC COSTS (2006-2007)
Tuition and fees: $17,580.
Per-credit charge: $515.
Room and board: $5,850.

FINANCIAL AID PICTURE (2005-2006)
Students with need: Out of 222 full-time freshmen who applied for aid, 183 were judged to have need. Of these, 183 received aid. Average financial aid package met 85% of need; average scholarship/grant was $7,981; average loan was $3,052. For part-time students, average financial aid package was $4,993.
Students without need: 52 full-time freshmen who did not demonstrate need for aid received scholarships/grants; average award was $6,901. No-need awards available for academics, alumni affiliation, art, athletics, leadership, music/drama, religious affiliation, ROTC.
Scholarships offered: *Merit:* Freshmen must meet two of the three criteria listed. Harter Scholarship; full tuition. Presidential Scholarship; 30 ACT or 1340 SAT, 3.85 GPA, top 5% class rank. Presidential Scholarships; $7,000; 28 ACT or 1260 SAT, 3.70 GPA, top 10% class rank. Faculty Merit Scholarships; $6,000; 25 ACT or 1140 SAT, 3.40 GPA, top 25% class rank. University Scholarships; $5,000; 22 ACT or 1030 SAT, 3.10 GPA, top 50% class rank. Academic Leadership Scholarships. $1,000; 22 ACT or 1030 SAT, 3.10 GPA, top 50% class rank. SAT scores listed are exclusive of the writing portion.
Athletic: 52 full-time freshmen received athletic scholarships; average amount $1,812.
Cumulative student debt: 86% of graduating class had student loans; average debt was $19,602.

FINANCIAL AID PROCEDURES
Forms required: FAFSA, institutional form.
Dates and Deadlines: Priority date 3/1; no closing date. Applicants notified on a rolling basis starting 3/1; must reply by 5/1 or within 6 week(s) of notification.
Transfers: No deadline. Applicants notified on a rolling basis starting 3/1; must reply within 6 week(s) of notification.

CONTACT
Jeanne Mott, Director of Financial Aid
618 Eighth Street, Baldwin City, KS 66006-0065
(785) 594-4595

Barclay College
Haviland, Kansas
www.barclaycollege.edu   Federal Code: 001917

4-year private Bible college in rural community, affiliated with Evangelical Friends Alliance and Friends United Meeting.
Enrollment: 122 undergrads, 26% part-time. 22 full-time freshmen.
Selectivity: Admits over 75% of applicants.

BASIC COSTS (2006-2007)
Tuition and fees: $12,730.
Per-credit charge: $390.
Room and board: $5,100.

FINANCIAL AID PICTURE (2005-2006)
Students with need: 41% of average financial aid package awarded as scholarships/grants, 59% awarded as loans/jobs. Need-based aid available for part-time students. Work study available nights, weekends, and for part-time students.
Students without need: No-need awards available for academics, alumni affiliation, leadership, music/drama, state/district residency.
Scholarships offered: President's Academic Award; $2,600; for 3.8 GPA or ACT score of 30. Dean's Academic Award; $2,000; for 3.6 GPA or ACT scores of 27-29. Trustees Academic Award; $1,600; for 3.4 GPA or ACT scores of 25-26.

FINANCIAL AID PROCEDURES
Forms required: FAFSA, institutional form.
Dates and Deadlines: Priority date 5/31; closing date 7/15. Applicants notified on a rolling basis starting 1/1; must reply within 4 week(s) of notification.

CONTACT
Michael Belasco, Director of Student Financial Services
607 North Kingman, Haviland, KS 67059
(620) 862-5252 ext. 14

Barton County Community College
Great Bend, Kansas
www.bartonccc.edu   Federal Code: 004608

2-year public community college in large town.
Enrollment: 3,258 undergrads, 71% part-time. 417 full-time freshmen.
Selectivity: Open admission; but selective for some programs.

BASIC COSTS (2005-2006)
Tuition and fees: $1,950; out-of-state residents $2,580.
Per-credit charge: $47; out-of-state residents $68.
Room and board: $3,619.

FINANCIAL AID PICTURE (2004-2005)
Students with need: 64% of average financial aid package awarded as scholarships/grants, 36% awarded as loans/jobs. Need-based aid available for part-time students.
Students without need: No-need awards available for academics, athletics.

FINANCIAL AID PROCEDURES
Forms required: FAFSA, state aid form.
Dates and Deadlines: Priority date 3/1; no closing date. Applicants notified on a rolling basis starting 6/1; must reply within 4 week(s) of notification.

CONTACT
Myrna Perkins, Director of Financial Aid
245 NE 30th Road, Great Bend, KS 67530-9283
(620) 792-9270

Benedictine College
Atchison, Kansas
www.benedictine.edu   Federal Code: 010256

4-year private liberal arts college in large town, affiliated with Roman Catholic Church.
Enrollment: 1,176 undergrads. 313 full-time freshmen.

BASIC COSTS (2005-2006)
Tuition and fees: $15,760.
Per-credit charge: $450.
Room and board: $6,478.

Kansas Benedictine College

FINANCIAL AID PICTURE (2005-2006)
Students with need: Out of 313 full-time freshmen who applied for aid, 243 were judged to have need. Of these, 243 received aid, and 40 had their full need met. Average financial aid package met 74% of need; average scholarship/grant was $8,883; average loan was $3,855. For part-time students, average financial aid package was $9,237.
Students without need: 21 full-time freshmen who did not demonstrate need for aid received scholarships/grants; average award was $6,777. No-need awards available for academics, alumni affiliation, art, athletics, job skills, leadership, minority status, music/drama, religious affiliation, ROTC.
Scholarships offered: *Merit:* Presidential Scholarship; full tuition. Dean's Scholarship; partial tuition. Both renewable every year, 5 recipients each, must maintain 3.5 GPA. Students must be admitted by Jan. 31. Academic Scholarships; renewable every year; ranges from $2,500-$7,500 depending on ACT scores; unlimited number. *Athletic:* 6 full-time freshmen received athletic scholarships; average amount $96.

FINANCIAL AID PROCEDURES
Forms required: FAFSA.
Dates and Deadlines: Priority date 3/15; no closing date. Applicants notified on a rolling basis starting 2/1; must reply within 2 week(s) of notification.
Transfers: Scholarship available for students transferring 2.0 cumulative GPA.

CONTACT
Keith Jaloma, Director of Student Financial Aid
1020 North Second Street, Atchison, KS 66002-1499
(913) 367-5340 ext. 2484

Bethany College
Lindsborg, Kansas
www.bethanylb.edu   Federal Code: 001904

4-year private liberal arts college in small town, affiliated with Evangelical Lutheran Church in America.
Enrollment: 563 undergrads, 2% part-time. 148 full-time freshmen.
Selectivity: Admits 50 to 75% of applicants.

BASIC COSTS (2006-2007)
Tuition and fees: $16,210.
Per-credit charge: $300.
Room and board: $5,250.

FINANCIAL AID PICTURE (2005-2006)
Students with need: Out of 143 full-time freshmen who applied for aid, 116 were judged to have need. Of these, 116 received aid, and 52 had their full need met. Average financial aid package met 97% of need; average scholarship/grant was $4,942; average loan was $4,430. For part-time students, average financial aid package was $8,005.
Students without need: 11 full-time freshmen who did not demonstrate need for aid received scholarships/grants; average award was $4,750. No-need awards available for academics, alumni affiliation, art, athletics, leadership, music/drama, religious affiliation.
Scholarships offered: 15 full-time freshmen received athletic scholarships; average amount $4,580.
Cumulative student debt: 82% of graduating class had student loans; average debt was $16,925.
Additional info: State financial aid deadline March 15.

FINANCIAL AID PROCEDURES
Forms required: FAFSA.
Dates and Deadlines: Priority date 3/15; no closing date. Applicants notified on a rolling basis starting 2/1; must reply within 3 week(s) of notification.

CONTACT
Brenda Meagher, Director of Financial Aid
421 North First Street, Lindsborg, KS 67456-1897
(785) 227-3311 ext. 8114

Bethel College
North Newton, Kansas
www.bethelks.edu   Federal Code: 001905

4-year private liberal arts college in large town, affiliated with Mennonite Church.
Enrollment: 514 undergrads, 7% part-time. 116 full-time freshmen.
Selectivity: Admits 50 to 75% of applicants.

BASIC COSTS (2006-2007)
Tuition and fees: $16,700.
Per-credit charge: $590.
Room and board: $6,100.

FINANCIAL AID PICTURE (2004-2005)
Students with need: Out of 106 full-time freshmen who applied for aid, 100 were judged to have need. Of these, 100 received aid, and 38 had their full need met. Average financial aid package met 90% of need; average scholarship/grant was $4,464; average loan was $3,817. For part-time students, average financial aid package was $10,594.
Students without need: 14 full-time freshmen who did not demonstrate need for aid received scholarships/grants; average award was $7,797. No-need awards available for academics, alumni affiliation, art, athletics, minority status, music/drama, religious affiliation, state/district residency.
Scholarships offered: *Merit:* Scholarships for academically talented students, ranging from 16%-50% of tuition. *Athletic:* 60 full-time freshmen received athletic scholarships; average amount $2,623.
Cumulative student debt: 84% of graduating class had student loans; average debt was $19,122.

FINANCIAL AID PROCEDURES
Forms required: FAFSA, state aid form.
Dates and Deadlines: Priority date 4/1; no closing date. Applicants notified on a rolling basis starting 2/15; must reply within 2 week(s) of notification.

CONTACT
Tony Graber, Director of Financial Aid
300 E 27th Street, North Newton, KS 67117-0531
(800) 522-1887 ext. 232

Butler County Community College
El Dorado, Kansas
www.butlercc.edu   Federal Code: 001906

2-year public community college in large town.
Enrollment: 5,859 undergrads, 51% part-time. 992 full-time freshmen.
Selectivity: Open admission; but selective for some programs.

BASIC COSTS (2005-2006)
Tuition and fees: $1,770; out-of-district residents $2,070; out-of-state residents $3,390.
Per-credit charge: $45; out-of-district residents $55; out-of-state residents $99.
Room and board: $4,335.
Additional info: Tuition/fee waivers available for unemployed or children of unemployed.

FINANCIAL AID PICTURE
Students with need: Need-based aid available for full-time and part-time students. Work study available nights, weekends, and for part-time students.
Students without need: No-need awards available for academics, athletics.

FINANCIAL AID PROCEDURES
Forms required: FAFSA, institutional form.
Dates and Deadlines: Priority date 4/1; no closing date. Applicants notified on a rolling basis starting 5/1; must reply within 2 week(s) of notification.
Transfers: Students with 90 hours or more must have classes validated by degree-granting 4-year institution.

CONTACT
Susie Edwards, Director of Financial Aid
901 South Haverhill Road, El Dorado, KS 67042-3280
(316) 322-3121

Central Christian College of Kansas
McPherson, Kansas
www.centralchristian.edu   Federal Code: 001908

4-year private liberal arts college in large town, affiliated with Free Methodist Church of North America.
Enrollment: 314 undergrads. 97 full-time freshmen.
Selectivity: Admits less than 50% of applicants.

BASIC COSTS (2006-2007)
Tuition and fees: $15,000.
Per-credit charge: $405.
Room and board: $5,000.

FINANCIAL AID PICTURE (2005-2006)
Students with need: Out of 90 full-time freshmen who applied for aid, 82 were judged to have need. Of these, 82 received aid. Average financial aid package met 62% of need; average scholarship/grant was $3,888; average loan was $3,929. Need-based aid available for part-time students.
Students without need: 8 full-time freshmen who did not demonstrate need for aid received scholarships/grants; average award was $5,899. No-need awards available for academics, alumni affiliation, athletics, leadership, music/drama, religious affiliation.
Scholarships offered: *Merit:* National Merit Scholarship; full tuition; National Merit semifinalists. Trustees Scholarship; 2/3 tuition; minimum score of 30 on ACT/1340 on SAT and minimum 3.5 high school GPA. Valedictorian Scholarship; half tuition; for students who are first in their class, with minimum 27 ACT/1220 SAT and 3.5 GPA. SAT scores listed are exclusive of the writing portion. *Athletic:* 50 full-time freshmen received athletic scholarships; average amount $1,263.
Cumulative student debt: 73% of graduating class had student loans; average debt was $20,000.

FINANCIAL AID PROCEDURES
Forms required: FAFSA.
Dates and Deadlines: Priority date 3/1; no closing date. Applicants notified on a rolling basis starting 3/1; must reply within 4 week(s) of notification.
Transfers: No deadline. Applicants notified on a rolling basis starting 3/1; must reply within 4 week(s) of notification.

CONTACT
Mike Reimer, Director of Financial Aid
1200 South Main, McPherson, KS 67460-5740
(620) 241-0723 ext. 333

Cloud County Community College
Concordia, Kansas
www.cloud.edu   Federal Code: 001909

2-year public community college in small town.
Enrollment: 1,543 undergrads.
Selectivity: Open admission.

BASIC COSTS (2005-2006)
Tuition and fees: $2,100; out-of-state residents $4,110.
Per-credit charge: $52; out-of-state residents $119.
Room and board: $3,780.

FINANCIAL AID PICTURE
Students with need: Need-based aid available for full-time and part-time students. Work study available nights, weekends, and for part-time students.

FINANCIAL AID PROCEDURES
Forms required: FAFSA.
Dates and Deadlines: Priority date 4/1; no closing date. Applicants notified on a rolling basis starting 5/1; must reply within 4 week(s) of notification.

CONTACT
Sherry Campbell, Director of Student Financial Aid
2221 Campus Drive, Concordia, KS 66901-1002
(785) 243-1435 ext. 280

Coffeyville Community College
Coffeyville, Kansas
www.coffeyville.edu   Federal Code: 001910

2-year public community college in large town.
Enrollment: 2,035 undergrads.
Selectivity: Open admission.

BASIC COSTS (2005-2006)
Tuition and fees: $1,500; out-of-state residents $2,700.
Per-credit charge: $25; out-of-state residents $65.
Room and board: $3,380.
Additional info: Oklahoma border county resident tuition: $32.50 per-credit-hour, $975 full-time. International students pay $2,610 in required fees.

FINANCIAL AID PICTURE (2005-2006)
Students with need: 89% of average financial aid package awarded as scholarships/grants, 11% awarded as loans/jobs. Need-based aid available for part-time students. Work study available nights, weekends, and for part-time students.
Students without need: No-need awards available for academics, alumni affiliation, art, athletics, leadership, music/drama.
Additional info: Provide aid to unemployed women.

FINANCIAL AID PROCEDURES
Forms required: FAFSA.
Dates and Deadlines: No deadline. Applicants notified on a rolling basis starting 6/20.

CONTACT
Rhonda Baker, Director of Financial Aid
400 West 11th Street, Coffeyville, KS 67337-5064
(620) 252-7357

Colby Community College
Colby, Kansas
www.colbycc.edu   Federal Code: 001911

2-year public community college in small town.
Enrollment: 1,175 undergrads.
Selectivity: Open admission; but selective for some programs.

BASIC COSTS (2005-2006)
Tuition and fees: $2,100; out-of-state residents $3,270.
Per-credit charge: $43; out-of-state residents $82.
Room and board: $3,542.
Additional info: Nebraska and Colorado border county residents pay $53 per-credit-hour.

FINANCIAL AID PICTURE
Students with need: Need-based aid available for full-time and part-time students. Work study available nights, weekends, and for part-time students.
Students without need: No-need awards available for academics, athletics, music/drama.

FINANCIAL AID PROCEDURES
Forms required: FAFSA, state aid form.

Dates and Deadlines: Priority date 6/1; no closing date. Applicants notified on a rolling basis starting 5/1.

CONTACT
Paula Halvorson, Director of Financial Aid
1255 South Range Avenue, Colby, KS 67701
(785) 460-4695

Cowley County Community College
Arkansas City, Kansas
www.cowley.edu   Federal Code: 001902

2-year public community and technical college in large town.
Enrollment: 3,272 undergrads, 36% part-time. 569 full-time freshmen.
Selectivity: Open admission; but selective for some programs.

BASIC COSTS (2005-2006)
Tuition and fees: $1,800; out-of-district residents $1,950; out-of-state residents $3,510.
Per-credit charge: $42; out-of-district residents $47; out-of-state residents $99.
Room and board: $3,450.
Additional info: Oklahoma border county resident tuition: $47 per-credit-hour.

FINANCIAL AID PICTURE (2005-2006)
Students with need: Out of 413 full-time freshmen who applied for aid, 413 were judged to have need. Of these, 413 received aid, and 413 had their full need met. Average financial aid package met 100% of need; average scholarship/grant was $1,407; average loan was $1,193. For part-time students, average financial aid package was $1,203.
Students without need: 140 full-time freshmen who did not demonstrate need for aid received scholarships/grants; average award was $352. No-need awards available for academics, athletics.
Scholarships offered: 51 full-time freshmen received athletic scholarships; average amount $999.

FINANCIAL AID PROCEDURES
Forms required: FAFSA, institutional form.
Dates and Deadlines: Priority date 4/15; no closing date. Applicants notified on a rolling basis starting 1/15; must reply within 2 week(s) of notification.

CONTACT
Sally Palmer, Director of Financial Aid
Box 1147, Arkansas City, KS 67005-1147
(620) 442-0430 ext. 5248

Dodge City Community College
Dodge City, Kansas
www.dccc.cc.ks.us   Federal Code: 001913

2-year public community and technical college in large town.
Enrollment: 1,805 undergrads.
Selectivity: Open admission; but selective for some programs.

BASIC COSTS (2005-2006)
Tuition and fees: $1,740; out-of-state residents $1,950.
Per-credit charge: $35; out-of-state residents $35.
Room and board: $4,060.

FINANCIAL AID PICTURE
Students with need: Need-based aid available for full-time and part-time students. Work study available nights, weekends, and for part-time students.
Students without need: No-need awards available for academics, athletics, state/district residency.

FINANCIAL AID PROCEDURES
Forms required: FAFSA, institutional form.
Dates and Deadlines: Priority date 6/1; no closing date. Applicants notified on a rolling basis; must reply within 2 week(s) of notification.

CONTACT
Dean Lyons, Director of Financial Assistance
2501 North 14th Avenue, Dodge City, KS 67801-2399
(620) 227-9336

Donnelly College
Kansas City, Kansas
www.donnelly.edu   Federal Code: 001914

2-year private community and liberal arts college in large city, affiliated with Roman Catholic Church.
Enrollment: 462 undergrads, 40% part-time. 65 full-time freshmen.
Selectivity: Open admission.

BASIC COSTS (2005-2006)
Tuition and fees: $4,536.
Per-credit charge: $162.

FINANCIAL AID PICTURE (2004-2005)
Students with need: Out of 65 full-time freshmen who applied for aid, 58 were judged to have need. Of these, 58 received aid, and 1 had their full need met. Average financial aid package met 28% of need; average scholarship/grant was $2,518; average loan was $1,784. For part-time students, average financial aid package was $1,118.
Students without need: 1 full-time freshmen who did not demonstrate need for aid received scholarships/grants; average award was $1,935. No-need awards available for academics.

FINANCIAL AID PROCEDURES
Forms required: FAFSA.
Dates and Deadlines: Priority date 6/1; no closing date. Applicants notified on a rolling basis starting 7/1.

CONTACT
Paul Gordon, Director of Financial Aid
608 North 18th Street, Kansas City, KS 66102-4210
(913) 621-8741

Emporia State University
Emporia, Kansas
www.emporia.edu   Federal Code: 001927

4-year public university and teachers college in large town.
Enrollment: 4,159 undergrads, 9% part-time. 718 full-time freshmen.
Selectivity: Admits over 75% of applicants.

BASIC COSTS (2005-2006)
Tuition and fees: $3,306; out-of-state residents $10,658.
Per-credit charge: $88; out-of-state residents $333.
Room and board: $4,787.

FINANCIAL AID PICTURE (2004-2005)
Students with need: Out of 665 full-time freshmen who applied for aid, 427 were judged to have need. Of these, 427 received aid, and 128 had their full need met. Average financial aid package met 63% of need; average scholarship/grant was $1,474; average loan was $2,135. For part-time students, average financial aid package was $4,219.
Students without need: 111 full-time freshmen who did not demonstrate need for aid received scholarships/grants; average award was $799. No-need awards available for academics, alumni affiliation, art, athletics, job skills,

leadership, minority status, music/drama, religious affiliation, state/district residency.

Scholarships offered: *Merit:* Presidential Academic Awards; $800 to $1,200; unlimited number. Challenge Awards; $500; unlimited number. Transfer President's Academic Award; $500 to $1,000; based on cumulative GPA or Phi Theta Kappa membership. Guaranteed GPA Scholarship; $500 to $1,200; based on GPA for continuing full-time undergraduates. *Athletic:* 19 full-time freshmen received athletic scholarships; average amount $1,812.

Cumulative student debt: 72% of graduating class had student loans; average debt was $16,197.

Additional info: Institution's own payment plan is available.

FINANCIAL AID PROCEDURES
Forms required: FAFSA, state aid form.
Dates and Deadlines: Priority date 3/15; no closing date. Applicants notified on a rolling basis starting 2/2; must reply within 2 week(s) of notification.

CONTACT
M. Henrie, Director of Financial Aid
1200 Commercial, Campus Box 4034, Emporia, KS 66801-5087
(620) 341-5457

Fort Hays State University
Hays, Kansas
www.fhsu.edu   Federal Code: 001915

4-year public university in large town.
Enrollment: 7,614 undergrads, 44% part-time. 781 full-time freshmen.

BASIC COSTS (2005-2006)
Tuition and fees: $3,053; out-of-state residents $9,576.
Per-credit charge: $79; out-of-state residents $296.
Room and board: $5,314.

FINANCIAL AID PICTURE (2004-2005)
Students with need: Out of 597 full-time freshmen who applied for aid, 471 were judged to have need. Of these, 461 received aid, and 100 had their full need met. Average financial aid package met 64% of need; average scholarship/grant was $3,401; average loan was $2,394. For part-time students, average financial aid package was $5,513.
Students without need: 295 full-time freshmen who did not demonstrate need for aid received scholarships/grants; average award was $2,030.
Scholarships offered: 47 full-time freshmen received athletic scholarships; average amount $2,042.
Cumulative student debt: 43% of graduating class had student loans; average debt was $15,007.

FINANCIAL AID PROCEDURES
Forms required: FAFSA.
Dates and Deadlines: Priority date 3/15; closing date 5/30. Applicants notified on a rolling basis starting 3/15; must reply within 3 week(s) of notification.
Transfers: No deadline. Applicants notified on a rolling basis starting 3/15; must reply within 3 week(s) of notification.

CONTACT
Craig Karlin, Director of Student Financial Aid
600 Park Street, Hays, KS 67601
(785) 628-4408

Friends University
Wichita, Kansas
www.friends.edu   Federal Code: 001918

4-year private business and liberal arts college in large city, affiliated with nondenominational tradition.
Enrollment: 2,166 undergrads.

BASIC COSTS (2005-2006)
Tuition and fees: $15,270.
Per-credit charge: $505.
Room and board: $4,920.

FINANCIAL AID PICTURE (2005-2006)
Students with need: 40% of average financial aid package awarded as scholarships/grants, 60% awarded as loans/jobs. Need-based aid available for part-time students.
Additional info: Scholarships for clergy/family of clergy available.

FINANCIAL AID PROCEDURES
Forms required: FAFSA, institutional form.
Dates and Deadlines: Priority date 3/15; no closing date. Applicants notified on a rolling basis; must reply within 3 week(s) of notification.

CONTACT
Myra Pfannenstiel, Director of Financial Aid
2100 University, Wichita, KS 67213
(316) 295-5200

Garden City Community College
Garden City, Kansas
www.gcccks.edu   Federal Code: 001919

2-year public community college in large town.
Enrollment: 2,257 undergrads, 56% part-time.
Selectivity: Open admission; but selective for some programs.

BASIC COSTS (2005-2006)
Tuition and fees: $1,800; out-of-state residents $2,580.
Per-credit charge: $39; out-of-state residents $65.
Room and board: $4,050.

FINANCIAL AID PICTURE (2005-2006)
Students with need: 65% of average financial aid package awarded as scholarships/grants, 35% awarded as loans/jobs. Need-based aid available for part-time students. Work study available nights, weekends, and for part-time students.
Students without need: No-need awards available for academics, art, athletics, leadership, minority status, music/drama, state/district residency.

FINANCIAL AID PROCEDURES
Forms required: FAFSA, institutional form.
Dates and Deadlines: Priority date 4/1; no closing date. Applicants notified on a rolling basis starting 4/15; must reply within 2 week(s) of notification.

CONTACT
Kathleen Blau, Director of Financial Aid
801 Campus Drive, Garden City, KS 67846-6333
(620) 276-9519

Haskell Indian Nations University
Lawrence, Kansas
www.haskell.edu   Federal Code: 010438

4-year public university in small city.
Enrollment: 900 undergrads.

Kansas Haskell Indian Nations University

BASIC COSTS (2005-2006)
Additional info: Federally subsidized college for Native Americans: no tuition; required fees $420, room and board $140.

FINANCIAL AID PICTURE
Students with need: Need-based aid available for full-time and part-time students. Work study available nights, weekends, and for part-time students.
Additional info: Some personal expenses may be offset by Bureau of Indian Affairs grants. Most students qualify for only minimum Pell grant.

FINANCIAL AID PROCEDURES
Forms required: FAFSA.
Dates and Deadlines: Priority date 5/15; no closing date. Applicants notified on a rolling basis starting 3/15; must reply within 9 week(s) of notification.
Transfers: Priority date 11/8; closing date 4/15.

CONTACT
Reta Beaver, Financial Aid Officer
155 Indian Avenue #5031, Lawrence, KS 66046-4800
(785) 830-2718

Hesston College
Hesston, Kansas
www.hesston.edu   Federal Code: 001920

2-year private junior college in small town, affiliated with Mennonite Church.
Enrollment: 456 undergrads, 9% part-time. 195 full-time freshmen.
Selectivity: Open admission; but selective for some programs.

BASIC COSTS (2006-2007)
Tuition and fees: $16,496.
Room and board: $5,858.
Additional info: $338 per-credit-hour charge for 1-5 credits; $676 per-credit-hour charge for 6-11 credits; special rates apply for high school students and senior citizens.

FINANCIAL AID PICTURE (2004-2005)
Students with need: Out of 183 full-time freshmen who applied for aid, 163 were judged to have need. Of these, 163 received aid, and 20 had their full need met. Average financial aid package met 80% of need; average scholarship/grant was $8,760; average loan was $5,495. Need-based aid available for part-time students.
Students without need: 32 full-time freshmen who did not demonstrate need for aid received scholarships/grants; average award was $1,500. No-need awards available for academics, alumni affiliation, athletics, job skills, music/drama.
Scholarships offered: 10 full-time freshmen received athletic scholarships; average amount $1,000.
Cumulative student debt: 85% of graduating class had student loans; average debt was $6,500.

FINANCIAL AID PROCEDURES
Forms required: FAFSA.
Dates and Deadlines: Priority date 4/1; no closing date. Applicants notified on a rolling basis starting 2/1; must reply within 4 week(s) of notification.

CONTACT
Marcia Mendez, Financial Aid Director
Box 3000, Hesston, KS 67062-2093
(800) 995-2757

Highland Community College
Highland, Kansas
www.highlandcc.edu   Federal Code: 001921

2-year public community college in rural community.
Enrollment: 2,821 undergrads.
Selectivity: Open admission; but selective for out-of-state students.

BASIC COSTS (2005-2006)
Tuition and fees: $1,830; out-of-district residents $2,070; out-of-state residents $3,570.
Per-credit charge: $37; out-of-district residents $45; out-of-state residents $95.
Room and board: $3,986.
Additional info: Out-of-state within 150 miles: $57 per-credit-hour.

FINANCIAL AID PICTURE
Students with need: Work study available nights, weekends, and for part-time students.
Students without need: No-need awards available for academics, alumni affiliation, art, athletics, leadership, minority status, music/drama.
Additional info: Auditions and portfolios important for certain scholarship candidates.

FINANCIAL AID PROCEDURES
Forms required: FAFSA.
Dates and Deadlines: Priority date 4/1; no closing date. Applicants notified on a rolling basis starting 4/15.

CONTACT
Kelly Twombly, Director of Student Financial Aid
606 West Main Street, Highland, KS 66035-0068
(785) 442-6023

Hutchinson Community College
Hutchinson, Kansas
www.hutchcc.edu   Federal Code: 001923

2-year public community college in large town.
Enrollment: 3,480 undergrads, 44% part-time. 814 full-time freshmen.
Selectivity: Open admission; but selective for some programs.

BASIC COSTS (2005-2006)
Tuition and fees: $1,950; out-of-state residents $3,090.
Per-credit charge: $50; out-of-state residents $88.
Room and board: $4,020.
Additional info: International students pay $750 required fees for academic year.

FINANCIAL AID PICTURE (2004-2005)
Students with need: Out of 570 full-time freshmen who applied for aid, 424 were judged to have need. Of these, 401 received aid, and 89 had their full need met. Average financial aid package met 31% of need; average scholarship/grant was $1,423; average loan was $1,016. For part-time students, average financial aid package was $1,418.
Students without need: 104 full-time freshmen who did not demonstrate need for aid received scholarships/grants; average award was $813. No-need awards available for academics, athletics, minority status, state/district residency.
Scholarships offered: 359 full-time freshmen received athletic scholarships; average amount $848.

FINANCIAL AID PROCEDURES
Forms required: FAFSA, institutional form.
Dates and Deadlines: Priority date 2/1; no closing date. Applicants notified on a rolling basis starting 4/1; must reply within 2 week(s) of notification.

CONTACT
Ron Menefee, Financial Aid Director
1300 North Plum, Hutchinson, KS 67501
(620) 665-3400

Johnson County Community College
Overland Park, Kansas
www.jccc.edu   Federal Code: 008244

2-year public community college in large city.
Enrollment: 6,231 full-time undergrads.
Selectivity: Open admission; but selective for some programs.

BASIC COSTS (2005-2006)
Tuition and fees: $1,920; out-of-district residents $2,370; out-of-state residents $4,350.
Per-credit charge: $50; out-of-district residents $65; out-of-state residents $131.

FINANCIAL AID PICTURE (2005-2006)
Students with need: Need-based aid available for part-time students.
Students without need: No-need awards available for academics.

FINANCIAL AID PROCEDURES
Forms required: FAFSA, state aid form.
Dates and Deadlines: Priority date 4/1; no closing date. Applicants notified on a rolling basis starting 4/15; must reply within 2 week(s) of notification.

CONTACT
Julie Cooper, Program Director for Student Financial Aid
12345 College Boulevard, Overland Park, KS 66210-1299
(913) 469-3840

Kansas City Kansas Community College
Kansas City, Kansas
www.kckcc.edu   Federal Code: 001925

2-year public community and junior college in very large city.
Enrollment: 3,933 undergrads, 58% part-time. 389 full-time freshmen.
Selectivity: Open admission; but selective for some programs.

BASIC COSTS (2005-2006)
Tuition and fees: $1,770; out-of-state residents $4,710.
Per-credit charge: $49; out-of-state residents $147.
Additional info: Fees vary by program.

FINANCIAL AID PICTURE (2004-2005)
Students with need: 55% of average financial aid package awarded as scholarships/grants, 45% awarded as loans/jobs. Need-based aid available for part-time students. Work study available nights, weekends, and for part-time students.
Students without need: No-need awards available for academics, art, athletics, music/drama.

FINANCIAL AID PROCEDURES
Forms required: FAFSA.
Dates and Deadlines: Priority date 4/15; no closing date. Applicants notified on a rolling basis starting 5/1; must reply within 4 week(s) of notification.

CONTACT
Mary Dorr, Director of Financial Aid
7250 State Avenue, Kansas City, KS 66112
(913) 288-7697

Kansas State University
Manhattan, Kansas
www.ksu.edu   Federal Code: 001928

4-year public university and technical college in large town.
Enrollment: 18,605 undergrads, 11% part-time. 3,283 full-time freshmen.
Selectivity: Admits 50 to 75% of applicants.

BASIC COSTS (2005-2006)
Tuition and fees: $5,124; out-of-state residents $14,454.
Per-credit charge: $152; out-of-state residents $463.
Room and board: $5,772.

FINANCIAL AID PICTURE (2004-2005)
Students with need: Out of 2,404 full-time freshmen who applied for aid, 1,678 were judged to have need. Of these, 1,665 received aid, and 203 had their full need met. Average financial aid package met 63% of need; average scholarship/grant was $3,034; average loan was $2,862. For part-time students, average financial aid package was $4,812.
Students without need: 379 full-time freshmen who did not demonstrate need for aid received scholarships/grants; average award was $2,297. No-need awards available for academics, alumni affiliation, art, athletics, leadership, music/drama, ROTC.
Scholarships offered: 148 full-time freshmen received athletic scholarships; average amount $4,592.
Cumulative student debt: 55% of graduating class had student loans; average debt was $19,000.

FINANCIAL AID PROCEDURES
Forms required: FAFSA.
Dates and Deadlines: Priority date 3/1; no closing date. Applicants notified on a rolling basis starting 3/15; must reply within 2 week(s) of notification.

CONTACT
Larry Moeder, Director of Student Financial Assistance
119 Anderson Hall, Manhattan, KS 66506
(785) 532-6420

Kansas Wesleyan University
Salina, Kansas
www.kwu.edu   Federal Code: 001929

4-year private liberal arts college in large town, affiliated with United Methodist Church.
Enrollment: 897 undergrads.

BASIC COSTS (2005-2006)
Tuition and fees: $15,800.
Room and board: $5,600.
Additional info: $200 per-credit-hour charge for 1-5 credit hours; $1,800 per semester for 6-8 credit hours; $3,600 per semester for 9-11 credit hours. Tuition/fee waivers available for adults.

FINANCIAL AID PICTURE
Students with need: Need-based aid available for full-time and part-time students.
Students without need: No-need awards available for academics, alumni affiliation, art, athletics, music/drama, state/district residency.
Additional info: Awards available for residence hall students: minimum $7,000 for 3.0 GPA plus ACT score of 22 or SAT of 950 (exclusive of Writing); minimum $8,000 for 3.5 GPA plus ACT score of 22 or SAT score of 1030 (exclusive of Writing); minimum $9,000 for 3.75 GPA plus ACT score of 25 or SAT score of 1140 (exclusive of Writing). Application deadline March 15.

FINANCIAL AID PROCEDURES
Forms required: FAFSA.

Dates and Deadlines: Closing date 3/15. Applicants notified on a rolling basis starting 1/1; must reply by 8/1 or within 3 week(s) of notification.
Transfers: Academic scholarships based upon cumulative GPA of transferring credit hours.

CONTACT
Glenna Alexander, Director of Financial Assistance
100 East Claflin Avenue, Salina, KS 67401-6196
(785) 827-5541 ext. 1130

Labette Community College
Parsons, Kansas
www.labette.edu
Federal Code: 001930

2-year public community college in large town.
Enrollment: 915 undergrads.
Selectivity: Open admission; but selective for some programs.

BASIC COSTS (2005-2006)
Tuition and fees: $2,070; out-of-state residents $3,690.
Per-credit charge: $41; out-of-state residents $95.
Additional info: Residents of neighboring states (MO, AR, OK) pay per-credit-hour rate of $62. Tuition/fee waivers available for adults, minority students, unemployed or children of unemployed.

FINANCIAL AID PICTURE
Students with need: Need-based aid available for full-time and part-time students. Work study available nights.
Students without need: No-need awards available for academics, leadership.
Scholarships offered: Foundation Scholarships.

FINANCIAL AID PROCEDURES
Forms required: FAFSA.
Dates and Deadlines: No deadline. Applicants notified on a rolling basis starting 4/4; must reply within 2 week(s) of notification.

CONTACT
Wayne Hatcher, Dean of Student Services
200 South 14th Street, Parsons, KS 67357
(620) 820-1219

Manhattan Area Technical College
Manhattan, Kansas
www.matc.net
Federal Code: 005500

2-year public technical college in large town.
Enrollment: 386 undergrads, 16% part-time. 107 full-time freshmen.
Selectivity: Open admission; but selective for some programs.

BASIC COSTS (2006-2007)
Tuition and fees: $2,100.
Per-credit charge: $60.

FINANCIAL AID PICTURE (2004-2005)
Students with need: 10% of average financial aid package awarded as scholarships/grants, 90% awarded as loans/jobs. Need-based aid available for part-time students.
Students without need: No-need awards available for academics, leadership.

FINANCIAL AID PROCEDURES
Forms required: FAFSA, institutional form.
Dates and Deadlines: No deadline. Applicants notified on a rolling basis.

CONTACT
Kelly Hoggatt, Director of Financial Aid/Registrar
3136 Dickens Avenue, Manhattan, KS 66503-2499
(785) 587-2800 ext. 105

Manhattan Christian College
Manhattan, Kansas
www.mccks.edu
Federal Code: 001931

4-year private Bible college in large town, affiliated with Christian Church.
Enrollment: 305 undergrads.

BASIC COSTS (2005-2006)
Tuition and fees: $9,494.
Per-credit charge: $389.
Room and board: $5,590.
Additional info: Additional $6 required fee per-credit-hour, up to $72; $140 per-credit-hour charge for part-time, non-degree-seeking students.

FINANCIAL AID PICTURE
Students with need: Need-based aid available for full-time and part-time students.
Students without need: No-need awards available for academics, leadership, music/drama.

FINANCIAL AID PROCEDURES
Forms required: FAFSA.
Dates and Deadlines: Priority date 4/1; no closing date. Applicants notified on a rolling basis starting 5/1; must reply within 2 week(s) of notification.

CONTACT
Margaret Carlisle, Director of Financial Aid
1415 Anderson Avenue, Manhattan, KS 66502
(785) 539-3571

McPherson College
McPherson, Kansas
www.mcpherson.edu
Federal Code: 001933

4-year private liberal arts college in large town, affiliated with Church of the Brethren.
Enrollment: 466 undergrads, 9% part-time. 108 full-time freshmen.
Selectivity: Admits over 75% of applicants.

BASIC COSTS (2005-2006)
Tuition and fees: $15,160.
Room and board: $5,850.

FINANCIAL AID PICTURE (2005-2006)
Students with need: Out of 105 full-time freshmen who applied for aid, 93 were judged to have need. Of these, 93 received aid, and 27 had their full need met. Average financial aid package met 88% of need; average scholarship/grant was $5,246; average loan was $4,384. For part-time students, average financial aid package was $9,066.
Students without need: 12 full-time freshmen who did not demonstrate need for aid received scholarships/grants; average award was $7,833. No-need awards available for academics, art, athletics, religious affiliation, ROTC, state/district residency.
Scholarships offered: Presidential Scholarship; $10,000 each year of attendance for four years; competition in fall and spring; 10 awards given per year.
Cumulative student debt: 83% of graduating class had student loans; average debt was $18,010.

FINANCIAL AID PROCEDURES
Forms required: FAFSA.

Dates and Deadlines: Priority date 3/1; no closing date. Applicants notified on a rolling basis starting 3/1; must reply within 3 week(s) of notification.

CONTACT
Carol Williams, Director of Admissions and Financial Aid
1600 East Euclid Street, McPherson, KS 67460-1402
(620) 241-0731 ext. 1271

MidAmerica Nazarene University
Olathe, Kansas
www.mnu.edu   Federal Code: 007032

4-year private university and liberal arts college in small city, affiliated with Church of the Nazarene.
Enrollment: 1,338 undergrads, 11% part-time. 215 full-time freshmen.
Selectivity: Admits 50 to 75% of applicants.

BASIC COSTS (2006-2007)
Tuition and fees: $15,968.
Per-credit charge: $500.
Room and board: $5,830.

FINANCIAL AID PICTURE (2005-2006)
Students with need: Out of 196 full-time freshmen who applied for aid, 166 were judged to have need. Of these, 166 received aid, and 4 had their full need met. Average financial aid package met 62% of need; average scholarship/grant was $7,247; average loan was $4,149. For part-time students, average financial aid package was $5,904.
Students without need: 40 full-time freshmen who did not demonstrate need for aid received scholarships/grants; average award was $2,695. No-need awards available for academics, art, athletics, leadership, music/drama, religious affiliation, ROTC.
Scholarships offered: 21 full-time freshmen received athletic scholarships; average amount $5,334.
Cumulative student debt: 80% of graduating class had student loans; average debt was $19,222.

FINANCIAL AID PROCEDURES
Forms required: FAFSA, institutional form.
Dates and Deadlines: Priority date 3/1; no closing date. Applicants notified on a rolling basis starting 3/30; must reply within 2 week(s) of notification.

CONTACT
Rhonda Cole, Director of Student Financial Services
2030 East College Way, Olathe, KS 66062-1899
(913) 791-3298

Neosho County Community College
Chanute, Kansas
www.neosho.cc.ks.us   Federal Code: 001936

2-year public community college in small town.
Enrollment: 1,019 undergrads.
Selectivity: Open admission; but selective for some programs.

BASIC COSTS (2005-2006)
Tuition and fees: $1,710; out-of-district residents $2,010; out-of-state residents $2,460.
Per-credit charge: $37; out-of-district residents $37; out-of-state residents $37.
Room and board: $3,800.

FINANCIAL AID PICTURE
Students with need: Need-based aid available for full-time and part-time students.
Students without need: No-need awards available for academics, art, athletics, music/drama.
Scholarships offered: Visual and performing arts, Academic Challenge stipends, industrial engineering and business scholarship.

FINANCIAL AID PROCEDURES
Forms required: FAFSA.
Dates and Deadlines: Priority date 7/15; no closing date. Applicants notified on a rolling basis; must reply within 4 week(s) of notification.
Transfers: All academic transcripts and financial aid transcripts must be on file before aid will be awarded.

CONTACT
800 West 14th Street, Chanute, KS 66720
(620) 431-2820 ext. 278

Newman University
Wichita, Kansas
www.newmanu.edu   Federal Code: 001939

4-year private university and liberal arts college in large city, affiliated with Roman Catholic Church.
Enrollment: 1,301 undergrads, 14% part-time. 168 full-time freshmen.

BASIC COSTS (2006-2007)
Tuition and fees: $17,308.
Per-credit charge: $567.
Room and board: $5,372.
Additional info: Tuition/fee waivers available for adults.

FINANCIAL AID PICTURE (2005-2006)
Students with need: 41% of average financial aid package awarded as scholarships/grants, 59% awarded as loans/jobs. Need-based aid available for part-time students. Work study available nights, weekends, and for part-time students.
Students without need: No-need awards available for academics, alumni affiliation, athletics, leadership, minority status, music/drama, religious affiliation.
Scholarships offered: Full tuition to any National Merit Finalist.

FINANCIAL AID PROCEDURES
Forms required: FAFSA, institutional form.
Dates and Deadlines: Priority date 3/1; no closing date. Applicants notified on a rolling basis starting 2/1.

CONTACT
Kelli Hartman, Director of Financial Aid
3100 McCormick Avenue, Wichita, KS 67213-2097
(316) 942-4291

North Central Kansas Technical College
Beloit, Kansas
www.ncktc.tec.ks.us

2-year public technical college in small town.
Enrollment: 135 undergrads.
Selectivity: Open admission.

BASIC COSTS (2005-2006)
Additional info: Tool expenses $350-$4,000 depending on program.

FINANCIAL AID PICTURE
Students with need: Need-based aid available for full-time and part-time students. Work study available nights.
Students without need: This college only awards aid to students with need.

FINANCIAL AID PROCEDURES
Forms required: FAFSA, state aid form.

CONTACT
Gary Odle, Financial Aid Director
P.O. Box 507, Beloit, KS 67420
(800) 658-4655

Ottawa University
Ottawa, Kansas
www.ottawa.edu   Federal Code: 001937

4-year private liberal arts college in large town, affiliated with American Baptist Churches in the USA.
Enrollment: 416 undergrads, 6% part-time. 113 full-time freshmen.

BASIC COSTS (2006-2007)
Tuition and fees: $15,850.
Per-credit charge: $515.
Room and board: $5,800.

FINANCIAL AID PICTURE (2005-2006)
Students with need: Average financial aid package met 90% of need; average scholarship/grant was $10,266; average loan was $3,652. For part-time students, average financial aid package was $10,191.
Students without need: No-need awards available for academics, alumni affiliation, athletics, music/drama, religious affiliation.
Cumulative student debt: 82% of graduating class had student loans; average debt was $21,612.

FINANCIAL AID PROCEDURES
Forms required: FAFSA.
Dates and Deadlines: Priority date 3/15; no closing date. Applicants notified on a rolling basis starting 2/1; must reply within 4 week(s) of notification.
Transfers: No deadline.

CONTACT
Gary Bateman, Financial Aid Administrator
1001 South Cedar Street, #17, Ottawa, KS 66067-3399
(785) 242-5200 ext. 5571

Pittsburg State University
Pittsburg, Kansas
www.pittstate.edu   Federal Code: 001926

4-year public university in large town.
Enrollment: 5,357 undergrads, 5% part-time. 979 full-time freshmen.
Selectivity: Admits over 75% of applicants.

BASIC COSTS (2005-2006)
Tuition and fees: $3,562; out-of-state residents $10,444.
Per-credit charge: $95; out-of-state residents $324.
Room and board: $4,550.
Additional info: The College of Technology assesses $14 per credit hour for technology courses with a cap of $140 per semester.

FINANCIAL AID PICTURE (2005-2006)
Students with need: Out of 739 full-time freshmen who applied for aid, 525 were judged to have need. Of these, 513 received aid, and 84 had their full need met. Average financial aid package met 89% of need; average scholarship/grant was $3,770; average loan was $2,658. For part-time students, average financial aid package was $4,150.
Students without need: 205 full-time freshmen who did not demonstrate need for aid received scholarships/grants; average award was $1,642. No-need awards available for academics, alumni affiliation, art, athletics, leadership, music/drama, ROTC.

Scholarships offered: 35 full-time freshmen received athletic scholarships; average amount $3,400.

FINANCIAL AID PROCEDURES
Forms required: FAFSA, state aid form, institutional form.
Dates and Deadlines: Priority date 3/1; no closing date. Applicants notified on a rolling basis; must reply within 2 week(s) of notification.
Transfers: Transfer student scholarships available.

CONTACT
Marilyn Haverly, Director of Student Financial Assistance
1701 South Broadway, Pittsburg, KS 66762
(620) 235-4240

Pratt Community College
Pratt, Kansas
www.prattcc.edu   Federal Code: 001938

2-year public community and technical college in small town.
Enrollment: 662 undergrads, 20% part-time. 247 full-time freshmen.
Selectivity: Open admission; but selective for some programs.

BASIC COSTS (2005-2006)
Tuition and fees: $2,070; out-of-state residents $2,070.
Per-credit charge: $40; out-of-state residents $40.
Room and board: $4,168.
Additional info: Out-of-district Kansas residents have additional fee of $100; out-of-state $200, and international students $300 for the year.

FINANCIAL AID PICTURE (2004-2005)
Students with need: 59% of average financial aid package awarded as scholarships/grants, 41% awarded as loans/jobs. Need-based aid available for part-time students.
Students without need: No-need awards available for academics, art, athletics, leadership, music/drama, state/district residency.

FINANCIAL AID PROCEDURES
Forms required: FAFSA, institutional form.
Dates and Deadlines: Priority date 5/1; closing date 8/1. Applicants notified on a rolling basis starting 2/1; must reply within 2 week(s) of notification.

CONTACT
Debbie Boley, Director of Financial Aid
348 NE SR 61, Pratt, KS 67124-8317
(620) 672-9800 ext. 248

Seward County Community College
Liberal, Kansas
www.sccc.edu   Federal Code: 008228

2-year public community college in large town.
Enrollment: 1,912 undergrads.
Selectivity: Open admission; but selective for some programs and for out-of-state students.

BASIC COSTS (2005-2006)
Tuition and fees: $1,860; out-of-state residents $2,550.
Per-credit charge: $40; out-of-state residents $63.
Room and board: $3,900.
Additional info: Residents of neighboring counties in OK, TX and CO pay per-credit-hour rate of $50.

FINANCIAL AID PICTURE
Students with need: Need-based aid available for full-time and part-time students.
Students without need: No-need awards available for academics, athletics.

FINANCIAL AID PROCEDURES
Forms required: FAFSA, institutional form.
Dates and Deadlines: Priority date 5/1; no closing date. Applicants notified on a rolling basis starting 6/15; must reply within 4 week(s) of notification.

CONTACT
Bea Rosales, Financial Aid Director
1801 North Kansas Avenue, Liberal, KS 67905-1137
(620) 629-2618

Southwestern College
Winfield, Kansas
www.sckans.edu   Federal Code: 001940

4-year private liberal arts college in large town, affiliated with United Methodist Church.
Enrollment: 1,213 undergrads, 53% part-time. 136 full-time freshmen.

BASIC COSTS (2006-2007)
Tuition and fees: $16,800.
Per-credit charge: $700.
Room and board: $5,438.

FINANCIAL AID PICTURE (2005-2006)
Students with need: Out of 123 full-time freshmen who applied for aid, 102 were judged to have need. Of these, 102 received aid, and 100 had their full need met. Average financial aid package met 82% of need; average scholarship/grant was $10,183; average loan was $4,258. For part-time students, average financial aid package was $7,089.
Students without need: 33 full-time freshmen who did not demonstrate need for aid received scholarships/grants; average award was $6,982. No-need awards available for academics, alumni affiliation, athletics, leadership, minority status, music/drama, religious affiliation, state/district residency.
Scholarships offered: *Merit:* Presidential Scholarship based on GPA, SAT/ACT scores, essay, resume, leadership, community service; full tuition. Scholarships for major based on GPA, SAT scores, essay, interview; 3 awarded. *Athletic:* 17 full-time freshmen received athletic scholarships; average amount $2,912.
Additional info: Academic and activity grants available.

FINANCIAL AID PROCEDURES
Forms required: FAFSA, institutional form.
Dates and Deadlines: Priority date 4/1; no closing date. Applicants notified on a rolling basis starting 2/1; must reply within 4 week(s) of notification.
Transfers: Activity grants and scholarships, except for presidential scholarship and premier scholarships, available to transfer students. Phi Theta Kappa scholarship available for transfer students who are members.

CONTACT
Brenda Hicks, Director of Financial Aid
100 College Street, Winfield, KS 67156
(620) 229-6215

Sterling College
Sterling, Kansas
www.sterling.edu   Federal Code: 001945

4-year private liberal arts college in rural community, affiliated with Presbyterian Church (USA).
Enrollment: 442 undergrads, 3% part-time. 136 full-time freshmen.
Selectivity: Admits 50 to 75% of applicants.

BASIC COSTS (2005-2006)
Tuition and fees: $13,906.
Room and board: $6,086.
Additional info: $275 per-credit-hour charge for 1-6 credits.

FINANCIAL AID PICTURE (2004-2005)
Students with need: Out of 112 full-time freshmen who applied for aid, 98 were judged to have need. Of these, 98 received aid, and 37 had their full need met. Average financial aid package met 92% of need; average scholarship/grant was $7,789; average loan was $3,736. For part-time students, average financial aid package was $4,854.
Students without need: 14 full-time freshmen who did not demonstrate need for aid received scholarships/grants; average award was $3,969. No-need awards available for academics, alumni affiliation, art, athletics, leadership, minority status, music/drama, religious affiliation, state/district residency.
Scholarships offered: 11 full-time freshmen received athletic scholarships; average amount $5,880.
Cumulative student debt: 79% of graduating class had student loans; average debt was $16,251.
Additional info: Twins enrolled at institution pay single tuition.

FINANCIAL AID PROCEDURES
Forms required: FAFSA.
Dates and Deadlines: Priority date 4/1; no closing date. Applicants notified on a rolling basis starting 1/1; must reply within 3 week(s) of notification.

CONTACT
Jodi Lightner, Financial Aid Coordinator
125 West Cooper, Sterling, KS 67579
(620) 278-4207

Tabor College
Hillsboro, Kansas
www.tabor.edu   Federal Code: 001946

4-year private liberal arts college in small town, affiliated with Mennonite Brethren Church.
Enrollment: 593 undergrads, 19% part-time. 123 full-time freshmen.
Selectivity: Admits over 75% of applicants.

BASIC COSTS (2005-2006)
Tuition and fees: $15,944.
Per-credit charge: $650.
Room and board: $5,670.
Additional info: Tuition/fee waivers available for adults.

FINANCIAL AID PICTURE (2005-2006)
Students with need: Out of 121 full-time freshmen who applied for aid, 98 were judged to have need. Of these, 98 received aid, and 24 had their full need met. Average financial aid package met 88% of need; average scholarship/grant was $3,855; average loan was $5,722. For part-time students, average financial aid package was $7,034.
Students without need: 25 full-time freshmen who did not demonstrate need for aid received scholarships/grants; average award was $4,961. No-need awards available for academics, alumni affiliation, art, athletics, music/drama, religious affiliation, state/district residency.
Scholarships offered: 78 full-time freshmen received athletic scholarships; average amount $3,564.
Cumulative student debt: 81% of graduating class had student loans; average debt was $19,377.

FINANCIAL AID PROCEDURES
Forms required: FAFSA, state aid form.
Dates and Deadlines: Priority date 3/1; closing date 8/15. Applicants notified on a rolling basis starting 3/15; must reply within 4 week(s) of notification.
Transfers: Transfer students not eligible for Presidential, National Merit or Dean's scholarships.

Kansas Tabor College

CONTACT
Bruce Jost, Director of Student Financial Assistance
400 South Jefferson, Hillsboro, KS 67063-1799
(620) 947-3121 ext. 1726

University of Kansas
Lawrence, Kansas
www.ku.edu
Federal Code: 001948

4-year public university in small city.
Enrollment: 20,652 undergrads, 11% part-time. 4,193 full-time freshmen.
Selectivity: Admits 50 to 75% of applicants.

BASIC COSTS (2005-2006)
Tuition and fees: $5,413; out-of-state residents $13,866.
Per-credit charge: $152; out-of-state residents $463.
Room and board: $5,852.

FINANCIAL AID PICTURE (2004-2005)
Students with need: Out of 2,598 full-time freshmen who applied for aid, 1,594 were judged to have need. Of these, 1,509 received aid, and 345 had their full need met. Average financial aid package met 62% of need; average scholarship/grant was $3,752; average loan was $2,607. For part-time students, average financial aid package was $5,465.
Students without need: 434 full-time freshmen who did not demonstrate need for aid received scholarships/grants; average award was $2,538. No-need awards available for academics, alumni affiliation, art, athletics, leadership, minority status, music/drama, ROTC, state/district residency.
Scholarships offered: 33 full-time freshmen received athletic scholarships; average amount $12,057.
Cumulative student debt: 42% of graduating class had student loans; average debt was $17,243.
Additional info: Work study available weekdays.

FINANCIAL AID PROCEDURES
Forms required: FAFSA.
Dates and Deadlines: Priority date 3/1; no closing date. Applicants notified on a rolling basis starting 4/1; must reply within 2 week(s) of notification.

CONTACT
Brenda Maigaard, Director of Student Financial Aid
1502 Iowa Street, Lawrence, KS 66045-7576
(785) 864-4700

University of Kansas Medical Center
Kansas City, Kansas
www.kumc.edu
Federal Code: 004605

Upper-division public university and health science college in very large city.
Enrollment: 479 undergrads, 23% part-time.
Selectivity: Open admission; but selective for some programs.

BASIC COSTS (2005-2006)
Tuition and fees: $5,413; out-of-state residents $13,866.
Per-credit charge: $152; out-of-state residents $463.
Additional info: Annual tuition for medical students: $18,919 (residents) and $34,674 (nonresidents); required fees are $418.

FINANCIAL AID PICTURE (2004-2005)
Students with need: Average financial aid package for all full-time undergraduates was $9,300; for part-time $6,260. 37% awarded as scholarships/grants, 63% awarded as loans/jobs. Work study available nights, weekends, and for part-time students.
Students without need: No-need awards available for academics, leadership, minority status, state/district residency.

Cumulative student debt: 57% of graduating class had student loans; average debt was $14,136.

FINANCIAL AID PROCEDURES
Forms required: FAFSA, institutional form.
Dates and Deadlines: Priority date 2/14; no closing date. Applicants notified on a rolling basis starting 4/1; must reply within 8 week(s) of notification.

CONTACT
Lisa Erwin, Director of Student Financial Aid
3901 Rainbow Boulevard, Kansas City, KS 66160-7116
(913) 588-5170

University of St. Mary
Leavenworth, Kansas
www.stmary.edu
Federal Code: 001943

4-year private university in large town, affiliated with Roman Catholic Church.
Enrollment: 435 undergrads, 14% part-time. 83 full-time freshmen.
Selectivity: Admits less than 50% of applicants.

BASIC COSTS (2005-2006)
Tuition and fees: $15,590.
Per-credit charge: $500.
Room and board: $5,850.

FINANCIAL AID PICTURE (2005-2006)
Students with need: Out of 75 full-time freshmen who applied for aid, 64 were judged to have need. Of these, 63 received aid, and 9 had their full need met. Average financial aid package met 65% of need; average scholarship/grant was $7,914; average loan was $3,838. For part-time students, average financial aid package was $4,376.
Students without need: 18 full-time freshmen who did not demonstrate need for aid received scholarships/grants; average award was $10,891. No-need awards available for academics, art, athletics, leadership, music/drama, ROTC.
Scholarships offered: 38 full-time freshmen received athletic scholarships; average amount $2,217.
Additional info: Essays may be required for scholarship applicants. Auditions recommended for music and drama scholarship applicants. Portfolio reviews for art award applicants.

FINANCIAL AID PROCEDURES
Forms required: FAFSA.
Dates and Deadlines: Priority date 4/1; no closing date. Applicants notified on a rolling basis starting 2/6; must reply within 2 week(s) of notification.

CONTACT
Judy Wiedower, Director of Financial Aid
4100 South Fourth Street Trafficway, Leavenworth, KS 66048
(913) 682-5151 ext. 6450

Washburn University of Topeka
Topeka, Kansas
www.washburn.edu
Federal Code: 001949

4-year public university in small city.
Enrollment: 5,943 undergrads, 31% part-time. 726 full-time freshmen.
Selectivity: Open admission; but selective for some programs.

BASIC COSTS (2005-2006)
Tuition and fees: $4,982; out-of-state residents $11,192.
Per-credit charge: $164; out-of-state residents $371.
Room and board: $4,752.

FINANCIAL AID PICTURE (2005-2006)
Students with need: Out of 620 full-time freshmen who applied for aid, 512 were judged to have need. Of these, 511 received aid, and 79 had their full need met. Average financial aid package met 30% of need; average scholarship/grant was $3,056; average loan was $2,526. For part-time students, average financial aid package was $5,779.
Students without need: 148 full-time freshmen who did not demonstrate need for aid received scholarships/grants; average award was $1,659. No-need awards available for academics, alumni affiliation, art, athletics, job skills, leadership, minority status, music/drama, religious affiliation, ROTC, state/district residency.
Scholarships offered: 21 full-time freshmen received athletic scholarships; average amount $6,355.
Cumulative student debt: 60% of graduating class had student loans; average debt was $13,125.

FINANCIAL AID PROCEDURES
Forms required: FAFSA.
Dates and Deadlines: Priority date 2/15; no closing date. Applicants notified on a rolling basis starting 3/15; must reply within 4 week(s) of notification.
Transfers: No deadline. Applicants notified on a rolling basis starting 3/15; must reply within 4 week(s) of notification.

CONTACT
Annita Huff, Director of Financial Aid
1700 Southwest College, Morgan 114, Topeka, KS 66621
(785) 670-1151

Wichita State University
Wichita, Kansas
www.wichita.edu
Federal Code: 001950

4-year public university in large city.
Enrollment: 9,974 undergrads, 29% part-time. 1,316 full-time freshmen.
Selectivity: Admits over 75% of applicants.

BASIC COSTS (2005-2006)
Tuition and fees: $4,232; out-of-state residents $11,685.
Per-credit charge: $114; out-of-state residents $363.
Room and board: $5,070.

FINANCIAL AID PICTURE (2004-2005)
Students with need: Out of 902 full-time freshmen who applied for aid, 887 were judged to have need. Of these, 751 received aid, and 93 had their full need met. Average financial aid package met 43% of need; average scholarship/grant was $2,897; average loan was $2,183. For part-time students, average financial aid package was $4,545.
Students without need: 263 full-time freshmen who did not demonstrate need for aid received scholarships/grants; average award was $2,150. No-need awards available for academics, alumni affiliation, art, athletics, leadership, music/drama.
Scholarships offered: 42 full-time freshmen received athletic scholarships; average amount $6,419.
Cumulative student debt: 55% of graduating class had student loans; average debt was $18,840.
Additional info: Top freshman applicants admitted by October 1 invited to university scholarship competition.

FINANCIAL AID PROCEDURES
Forms required: FAFSA.
Dates and Deadlines: Closing date 3/15. Applicants notified on a rolling basis starting 3/15; must reply within 2 week(s) of notification.

CONTACT
Deborah Byers, Director of Financial Aid
1845 Fairmount Box 124, Wichita, KS 67260-0124
(316) 978-3430

Kentucky

Alice Lloyd College
Pippa Passes, Kentucky
www.alc.edu
Federal Code: 001951

4-year private liberal arts college in rural community.
Enrollment: 612 undergrads, 4% part-time. 175 full-time freshmen.
Selectivity: Admits 50 to 75% of applicants.

BASIC COSTS (2005-2006)
Tuition and fees: $7,510.
Per-credit charge: $212.
Room and board: $3,750.
Additional info: Guaranteed tuition for students from 108-county central Appalachian service area in Kentucky, West Virginia, Virginia, Tennessee, and Ohio. Tuition/fee waivers available for minority students.

FINANCIAL AID PICTURE (2004-2005)
Students with need: Out of 175 full-time freshmen who applied for aid, 136 were judged to have need. Of these, 136 received aid, and 39 had their full need met. Average financial aid package met 78% of need; average scholarship/grant was $7,053; average loan was $228. Need-based aid available for part-time students.
Students without need: 38 full-time freshmen who did not demonstrate need for aid received scholarships/grants; average award was $7,795. No-need awards available for athletics, minority status, state/district residency.
Scholarships offered: Merit: Students meeting admissions criteria from one of 108 counties in West Virginia, Virginia, Tennessee, Ohio and Kentucky guaranteed free tuition of up to $3,180 per semester: chosen based on admission application; no limit on awards given to qualified students. Minority scholarships offered to students from 108 service areas: cover cost for tuition, room, and board. Alice Lloyd Scholars Program: awarded to up to 3 freshmen a year; covers all expenses for tuition, room, board, fees, and books. **Athletic:** 15 full-time freshmen received athletic scholarships; average amount $7,057.
Cumulative student debt: 44% of graduating class had student loans; average debt was $6,034.
Additional info: All students receive financial aid through student work program. No student denied admission because of inability to pay. All full-time students required to work minimum of 10 hours per week.

FINANCIAL AID PROCEDURES
Forms required: FAFSA.
Dates and Deadlines: Priority date 3/15; no closing date. Applicants notified on a rolling basis starting 4/1; must reply within 6 week(s) of notification.
Transfers: Closing date 3/15. Tuition guarantee only for total of 10 semesters of course work from all schools attended.

CONTACT
Nancy Melton, Director of Financial Aid
100 Purpose Road, Pippa Passes, KY 41844
(606) 368-6059

Asbury College
Wilmore, Kentucky
www.asbury.edu
Federal Code: 001952

4-year private liberal arts college in small town, affiliated with interdenominational tradition.
Enrollment: 1,139 undergrads, 2% part-time. 276 full-time freshmen.
Selectivity: Admits 50 to 75% of applicants.

Asbury College (continued)

BASIC COSTS (2006-2007)
Tuition and fees: $20,184.
Per-credit charge: $770.
Room and board: $4,974.
Additional info: Tuition/fee waivers available for minority students.

FINANCIAL AID PICTURE (2005-2006)
Students with need: Out of 253 full-time freshmen who applied for aid, 214 were judged to have need. Of these, 213 received aid, and 62 had their full need met. Average financial aid package met 81% of need; average scholarship/grant was $8,273; average loan was $2,696. For part-time students, average financial aid package was $7,933.
Students without need: 35 full-time freshmen who did not demonstrate need for aid received scholarships/grants; average award was $10,951. No-need awards available for academics, athletics, leadership, music/drama, ROTC.
Cumulative student debt: 69% of graduating class had student loans; average debt was $22,016.

FINANCIAL AID PROCEDURES
Forms required: FAFSA, institutional form.
Dates and Deadlines: Priority date 3/1; no closing date. Applicants notified on a rolling basis starting 2/15; must reply within 4 week(s) of notification.

CONTACT
Ronald Anderson, Director of Financial Aid
One Macklem Drive, Wilmore, KY 40390-1198
(859) 858-3511 ext. 2195

Beckfield College
Florence, Kentucky
www.beckfield.edu
Federal Code: 016726

4-year for-profit business and nursing college in large town.
Enrollment: 485 undergrads, 35% part-time. 70 full-time freshmen.
Selectivity: Open admission; but selective for some programs.

BASIC COSTS (2005-2006)
Tuition and fees: $10,000.
Per-credit charge: $220.
Additional info: Technology fee, where applicable, varies with program.

FINANCIAL AID PICTURE
Students with need: Need-based aid available for full-time and part-time students.
Students without need: This college only awards aid to students with need.
Scholarships offered: High School scholarship: tuition for one course per quarter for maximum of 8 quarters. Must achieve and maintain 3.0 GPA, be enrolled full-time and enter college in July or October following graduation from high school. Merit: $100 per quarter, must maintain 4.0 GPA, perfect attendance and carry at least 8 quarter credit hours.
Additional info: Deadline for filing of financial aid forms is end of first week of classes.

FINANCIAL AID PROCEDURES
Forms required: FAFSA.
Dates and Deadlines: Applicants notified on a rolling basis.

CONTACT
Robert Beck, President
16 Spiral Drive, Florence, KY 41042
(859) 371-9393

Bellarmine University
Louisville, Kentucky
www.bellarmine.edu
Federal Code: 001954

4-year private university and liberal arts college in very large city, affiliated with Roman Catholic Church.
Enrollment: 2,004 undergrads. 390 full-time freshmen.
Selectivity: Admits 50 to 75% of applicants.

BASIC COSTS (2006-2007)
Tuition and fees: $24,150.
Per-credit charge: $550.
Room and board: $6,920.

FINANCIAL AID PICTURE (2004-2005)
Students with need: Out of 326 full-time freshmen who applied for aid, 269 were judged to have need. Of these, 269 received aid, and 87 had their full need met. Average financial aid package met 89% of need; average scholarship/grant was $13,242; average loan was $2,719. For part-time students, average financial aid package was $6,186.
Students without need: 121 full-time freshmen who did not demonstrate need for aid received scholarships/grants; average award was $9,921. No-need awards available for academics, alumni affiliation, art, athletics, leadership, minority status, music/drama, religious affiliation, ROTC, state/district residency.
Scholarships offered: *Merit:* Merit Awards available to all applicants meeting academic requirements; ranging from $4,000 to full-tuition annually. *Athletic:* 77 full-time freshmen received athletic scholarships; average amount $3,814.
Cumulative student debt: 68% of graduating class had student loans; average debt was $12,263.

FINANCIAL AID PROCEDURES
Forms required: FAFSA.
Dates and Deadlines: Priority date 3/1; no closing date. Applicants notified on a rolling basis starting 4/15; must reply by 5/1 or within 3 week(s) of notification.

CONTACT
Heather Boutell, Director of Financial Aid
2001 Newburg Road, Louisville, KY 40205
(502) 452-8124

Berea College
Berea, Kentucky
www.berea.edu
Federal Code: 001955

4-year private liberal arts college in small town.
Enrollment: 1,523 undergrads. 378 full-time freshmen.
Selectivity: Admits less than 50% of applicants.

BASIC COSTS (2006-2007)
Tuition and fees: $22,116.
Room and board: $4,980.
Additional info: Only those with financial need admitted. All students receive 4-year full tuition scholarship. Students required to earn a portion of their expenses by working a minimum of 10 hours per week on campus.

FINANCIAL AID PICTURE (2005-2006)
Students with need: Out of 378 full-time freshmen who applied for aid, 378 were judged to have need. Of these, 378 received aid, and 126 had their full need met. Average financial aid package met 93% of need; average scholarship/grant was $26,190; average loan was $91.
Students without need: This college only awards aid to students with need.

Cumulative student debt: 79% of graduating class had student loans; average debt was $7,299.

FINANCIAL AID PROCEDURES
Forms required: FAFSA.
Dates and Deadlines: No deadline. Applicants notified on a rolling basis starting 4/1.
Transfers: Financial aid transcript from previous school(s) must be received before awarding aid.

CONTACT
Bryan Erslan, Director of Student Financial Aid Services
CPO 2220, Berea, KY 40404
(859) 985-3310

Big Sandy Community and Technical College
Prestonsburg, Kentucky
www.bigsandy.kctcs.edu   Federal Code: 001996

2-year public community and technical college in small town.
Enrollment: 3,589 undergrads.
Selectivity: Open admission; but selective for some programs.

BASIC COSTS (2005-2006)
Tuition and fees: $2,940; out-of-state residents $8,820.
Per-credit charge: $98; out-of-state residents $294.

FINANCIAL AID PICTURE
Students with need: Need-based aid available for full-time and part-time students.
Students without need: No-need awards available for academics.

FINANCIAL AID PROCEDURES
Forms required: FAFSA, institutional form.
Dates and Deadlines: Priority date 4/1; no closing date. Applicants notified on a rolling basis; must reply within 2 week(s) of notification.
Transfers: Kentucky State Grant must be transferred by August 1 for fall semester, December 1 for spring semester.

CONTACT
Denise Trusty, Director of Financial Aid
One Bert T. Combs Drive, Prestonsburg, KY 41653
(606) 886-3863 ext. 67255

Bluegrass Community and Technical College
Lexington, Kentucky
www.bluegrass.kctcs.edu   Federal Code: 009707

2-year public community and technical college in large city.
Enrollment: 10,128 undergrads.
Selectivity: Open admission; but selective for some programs.

BASIC COSTS (2005-2006)
Tuition and fees: $3,002; out-of-state residents $7,706.
Per-credit charge: $114; out-of-state residents $310.
Room and board: $5,840.

FINANCIAL AID PICTURE (2004-2005)
Students with need: 39% of average financial aid package awarded as scholarships/grants, 61% awarded as loans/jobs. Need-based aid available for part-time students. Work study available nights.
Students without need: No-need awards available for academics, minority status, state/district residency.

FINANCIAL AID PROCEDURES
Forms required: FAFSA, institutional form.
Dates and Deadlines: Priority date 4/15; no closing date. Applicants notified on a rolling basis starting 6/5; must reply within 3 week(s) of notification.

CONTACT
Michael Barlow, Director of Financial Aid
200 Oswald Building, Cooper Drive, Lexington, KY 40506-0235
(859) 246-6300

Brescia University
Owensboro, Kentucky
www.brescia.edu   Federal Code: 001958

4-year private university and liberal arts college in small city, affiliated with Roman Catholic Church.
Enrollment: 467 undergrads, 12% part-time. 53 full-time freshmen.
Selectivity: Admits 50 to 75% of applicants.

BASIC COSTS (2005-2006)
Tuition and fees: $12,400.
Per-credit charge: $395.
Room and board: $5,480.
Additional info: Technology fee: $10/credit hour to maximum of $60 per semester.

FINANCIAL AID PICTURE (2005-2006)
Students with need: 96% of average financial aid package awarded as scholarships/grants, 4% awarded as loans/jobs. Need-based aid available for part-time students. Work study available nights, weekends, and for part-time students.
Students without need: No-need awards available for academics, alumni affiliation, art, athletics, minority status, music/drama, religious affiliation, state/district residency.

FINANCIAL AID PROCEDURES
Forms required: FAFSA.
Dates and Deadlines: Priority date 8/1; no closing date. Applicants notified on a rolling basis starting 3/1; must reply within 3 week(s) of notification.

CONTACT
Martie Ruxer-Boyken, Director of Financial Aid
717 Frederica Street, Owensboro, KY 42301-3023
(270) 686-4290

Brown Mackie College: Hopkinsville
Hopkinsville, Kentucky
www.brownmackie.edu   Federal Code: 014493

2-year for-profit business and junior college in large town.
Enrollment: 180 undergrads.
Selectivity: Open admission.

BASIC COSTS (2005-2006)
Tuition and fees: $6,444.
Additional info: Required fees are $40 per class.

FINANCIAL AID PICTURE
Students with need: Need-based aid available for full-time students.

FINANCIAL AID PROCEDURES
Forms required: FAFSA.
Dates and Deadlines: No deadline. Applicants notified on a rolling basis.

CONTACT
Pat Bailey, Director of Financial Aid
4001 Fort Campbell Boulevard, Hopkinsville, KY 42240
(800) 359-4753

Campbellsville University
Campbellsville, Kentucky
www.campbellsville.edu Federal Code: 001959

4-year private university in large town, affiliated with Baptist faith.
Enrollment: 1,379 undergrads, 8% part-time. 394 full-time freshmen.
Selectivity: Admits 50 to 75% of applicants.

BASIC COSTS (2006-2007)
Tuition and fees: $16,340.
Per-credit charge: $665.
Room and board: $5,932.
Additional info: Tuition/fee waivers available for adults.

FINANCIAL AID PICTURE (2004-2005)
Students with need: Out of 387 full-time freshmen who applied for aid, 346 were judged to have need. Of these, 344 received aid, and 99 had their full need met. Average financial aid package met 75% of need; average scholarship/grant was $9,632; average loan was $2,779. For part-time students, average financial aid package was $9,080.
Students without need: 88 full-time freshmen who did not demonstrate need for aid received scholarships/grants; average award was $6,583.
Scholarships offered: 39 full-time freshmen received athletic scholarships; average amount $6,370.
Cumulative student debt: 80% of graduating class had student loans; average debt was $18,437.
Additional info: Matching scholarships available for students whose church contributes $200 annually. Performance grants available to members of marching band.

FINANCIAL AID PROCEDURES
Forms required: FAFSA.
Dates and Deadlines: Priority date 4/1; no closing date. Applicants notified on a rolling basis starting 5/15.

CONTACT
Chris Tolson, Director of Financial Aid
1 University Drive, Campbellsville, KY 42718-2799
(270) 789-5013

Centre College
Danville, Kentucky
www.centre.edu Federal Code: 001961

4-year private liberal arts college in large town, affiliated with Presbyterian Church (USA).
Enrollment: 1,122 undergrads. 317 full-time freshmen.
Selectivity: Admits 50 to 75% of applicants.

BASIC COSTS (2006-2007)
Comprehensive fee: $33,000.
Additional info: Students wishing to live off-campus must annually seek approval from the Dean of Students; in such cases, a reduced comprehensive fee may be available.

FINANCIAL AID PICTURE (2005-2006)
Students with need: Out of 252 full-time freshmen who applied for aid, 182 were judged to have need. Of these, 182 received aid, and 77 had their full need met. Average financial aid package met 90% of need; average scholarship/grant was $17,281; average loan was $2,716.
Students without need: 124 full-time freshmen who did not demonstrate need for aid received scholarships/grants; average award was $11,224. No-need awards available for academics, alumni affiliation, minority status, music/drama, ROTC.
Scholarships offered: Institutional Merit Award: ranging from $6,500 to full tuition; applications must be on file by February 1; renewable. Program of Music and Drama Scholarships: $5,000; minimum award available to Centre Fellows and Kentucky Governor's Scholars.
Cumulative student debt: 59% of graduating class had student loans; average debt was $13,700.

FINANCIAL AID PROCEDURES
Forms required: FAFSA, institutional form.
Dates and Deadlines: Priority date 2/15; closing date 3/1. Applicants notified by 3/25; must reply by 5/1 or within 2 week(s) of notification.
Transfers: Priority date 3/1; no deadline. Applicants notified on a rolling basis starting 3/1; must reply within 2 week(s) of notification. Financial aid transcript required.

CONTACT
Elaine Larson, Director of Student Financial Planning
600 West Walnut Street, Danville, KY 40422-1394
(859) 238-5365

Clear Creek Baptist Bible College
Pineville, Kentucky
www.ccbbc.edu Federal Code: 017044

4-year private Bible and seminary college in small town, affiliated with Southern Baptist Convention.
Enrollment: 190 undergrads, 18% part-time. 22 full-time freshmen.
Selectivity: Open admission.

BASIC COSTS (2006-2007)
Tuition and fees: $4,870.
Per-credit charge: $205.
Room and board: $3,310.
Additional info: Room and board fee given for single student. Married student housing fees vary from $160 to $325 per month.

FINANCIAL AID PICTURE (2004-2005)
Students with need: Out of 21 full-time freshmen who applied for aid, 13 were judged to have need. Of these, 13 received aid. Average financial aid package met 38% of need. For part-time students, average financial aid package was $1,150.
Students without need: 5 full-time freshmen who did not demonstrate need for aid received scholarships/grants; average award was $680. No-need awards available for academics.

FINANCIAL AID PROCEDURES
Forms required: FAFSA, institutional form.
Dates and Deadlines: Priority date 6/30; no closing date. Applicants notified on a rolling basis; must reply by 8/1.
Transfers: Priority date 5/5; no deadline. Applicants notified on a rolling basis starting 5/5.

CONTACT
Sam Risner, Director of Financial Aid
300 Clear Creek Road, Pineville, KY 40977-9754
(606) 337-3196 ext. 142

Daymar College
Owensboro, Kentucky
www.daymarcollege.edu   Federal Code: 009313

2-year for-profit business and junior college in small city.
Enrollment: 289 undergrads, 37% part-time. 182 full-time freshmen.
Selectivity: Open admission.

BASIC COSTS (2005-2006)
Additional info: Tuition at time of enrollment locked for 2 years.

FINANCIAL AID PICTURE
Students with need: Need-based aid available for full-time and part-time students.
Students without need: This college only awards aid to students with need.

FINANCIAL AID PROCEDURES
Forms required: FAFSA.
Dates and Deadlines: No deadline. Applicants notified on a rolling basis.

CONTACT
Trisha Dukes, Financial Aid Officer
3361 Buckland Square, Owensboro, KY 42301
(270) 926-4040

Draughons Junior College
Bowling Green, Kentucky
www.draughons.org   Federal Code: 004934

2-year for-profit branch campus and junior college in large town.
Enrollment: 515 undergrads.
Selectivity: Open admission.

FINANCIAL AID PICTURE
Students with need: Need-based aid available for full-time and part-time students. Work study available nights.
Students without need: This college only awards aid to students with need.

FINANCIAL AID PROCEDURES
Forms required: FAFSA.
Dates and Deadlines: No deadline.

CONTACT
Mary Hood, Financial aid Officer
2421 Fitzgerald Industrial Drive, Bowling Green, KY 42101
(615) 361-7555

Eastern Kentucky University
Richmond, Kentucky
www.eku.edu   Federal Code: 001963

4-year public university in large town.
Enrollment: 13,000 undergrads. 2,455 full-time freshmen.
Selectivity: Admits 50 to 75% of applicants.

BASIC COSTS (2005-2006)
Tuition and fees: $4,660; out-of-state residents $13,070.
Per-credit charge: $194; out-of-state residents $545.
Room and board: $4,708.

FINANCIAL AID PICTURE (2005-2006)
Students with need: Out of 1,990 full-time freshmen who applied for aid, 1,448 were judged to have need. Of these, 1,429 received aid, and 609 had their full need met. Average financial aid package met 90% of need; average scholarship/grant was $4,235; average loan was $2,069. For part-time students, average financial aid package was $5,633.
Students without need: 808 full-time freshmen who did not demonstrate need for aid received scholarships/grants; average award was $1,825. No-need awards available for academics, alumni affiliation, art, athletics, job skills, leadership, minority status, music/drama, ROTC.
Scholarships offered: 60 full-time freshmen received athletic scholarships; average amount $6,405.

FINANCIAL AID PROCEDURES
Forms required: FAFSA.
Dates and Deadlines: Priority date 4/1; no closing date. Applicants notified on a rolling basis starting 4/1.

CONTACT
Shelley Park, Director of Financial Aid
SSB CPO 54, 521 Lancaster Avenue, Richmond, KY 40475-3102

Elizabethtown Community and Technical College
Elizabethtown, Kentucky
www.elizabethtown.kctcs.edu   Federal Code: 001991

2-year public community and technical college in large town.
Enrollment: 3,130 undergrads.
Selectivity: Open admission; but selective for some programs.

BASIC COSTS (2005-2006)
Tuition and fees: $2,940; out-of-state residents $8,820.
Per-credit charge: $98; out-of-state residents $294.

FINANCIAL AID PICTURE
Students with need: Need-based aid available for full-time and part-time students. Work study available nights, weekends, and for part-time students.
Students without need: This college only awards aid to students with need.

FINANCIAL AID PROCEDURES
Forms required: FAFSA.
Dates and Deadlines: Priority date 4/1; no closing date. Applicants notified on a rolling basis starting 6/1; must reply within 2 week(s) of notification.
Transfers: Must reply within 2 week(s) of notification.

CONTACT
Kathy Hodges, Director of Financial Aid
600 College Street Road, Elizabethtown, KY 42701
(270) 769-2371 ext. 68614

Georgetown College
Georgetown, Kentucky
www.georgetowncollege.edu   Federal Code: 001964

4-year private liberal arts college in large town, affiliated with Southern Baptist Convention.
Enrollment: 1,364 undergrads, 4% part-time. 416 full-time freshmen.
Selectivity: Admits over 75% of applicants.

BASIC COSTS (2006-2007)
Tuition and fees: $20,700.
Per-credit charge: $860.
Room and board: $6,070.
Additional info: Per-credit-hour charge for only one course is $630.

FINANCIAL AID PICTURE (2005-2006)
Students with need: Out of 353 full-time freshmen who applied for aid, 268 were judged to have need. Of these, 268 received aid, and 158 had their full need met. Average financial aid package met 91% of need; average scholarship/grant was $14,359; average loan was $3,284.
Students without need: 144 full-time freshmen who did not demonstrate need for aid received scholarships/grants; average award was $9,139. No-need awards available for academics, art, athletics, leadership, minority status, music/drama, religious affiliation, ROTC.
Scholarships offered: 35 full-time freshmen received athletic scholarships; average amount $5,704.
Cumulative student debt: 69% of graduating class had student loans; average debt was $15,018.

FINANCIAL AID PROCEDURES
Forms required: FAFSA, institutional form.
Dates and Deadlines: Priority date 2/15; no closing date. Applicants notified on a rolling basis starting 3/1.

CONTACT
Rhyan Conyers, Director of Student Financial Planning
400 East College Street, Georgetown, KY 40324
(502) 863-8027

Hazard Community College
Hazard, Kentucky
www.hazard.kctcs.edu   Federal Code: 006962

2-year public community college in small town.
Enrollment: 3,885 undergrads.
Selectivity: Open admission; but selective for some programs.

BASIC COSTS (2005-2006)
Tuition and fees: $2,940; out-of-state residents $8,820.
Per-credit charge: $98; out-of-state residents $294.

FINANCIAL AID PICTURE
Students with need: Need-based aid available for full-time and part-time students.
Students without need: This college only awards aid to students with need.

FINANCIAL AID PROCEDURES
Forms required: FAFSA.
Dates and Deadlines: Priority date 4/1; no closing date. Applicants notified on a rolling basis starting 6/15; must reply within 2 week(s) of notification.

CONTACT
Chuck Anderson, Financial Aid Director
One Community College Drive, Hazard, KY 41701
(606) 487-3061

Hopkinsville Community College
Hopkinsville, Kentucky
www.hopkinsville.kctcs.edu   Federal Code: 001994

2-year public community college in small city.
Enrollment: 2,980 undergrads.
Selectivity: Open admission.

BASIC COSTS (2005-2006)
Tuition and fees: $2,940; out-of-state residents $8,820.
Per-credit charge: $98; out-of-state residents $294.

FINANCIAL AID PICTURE
Students with need: Need-based aid available for full-time and part-time students.
Students without need: No-need awards available for academics, leadership, minority status, state/district residency.
Additional info: ACT required for academic scholarships.

FINANCIAL AID PROCEDURES
Forms required: FAFSA.
Dates and Deadlines: No deadline. Applicants notified on a rolling basis starting 7/1.

CONTACT
Vincent Shykes, Director
PO Box 2100, Hopkinsville, KY 42241
(270) 886-3921 ext. 6190

Jefferson Community College
Louisville, Kentucky
www.jefferson.kctcs.edu   Federal Code: 006961

2-year public community and technical college in large city.
Enrollment: 10,600 undergrads.
Selectivity: Open admission; but selective for some programs.

BASIC COSTS (2005-2006)
Tuition and fees: $2,940; out-of-state residents $8,820.
Per-credit charge: $98; out-of-state residents $294.

FINANCIAL AID PICTURE
Students with need: Need-based aid available for full-time and part-time students.
Students without need: No-need awards available for academics, art, minority status.

FINANCIAL AID PROCEDURES
Forms required: FAFSA, institutional form.
Dates and Deadlines: Priority date 3/15; no closing date. Applicants notified on a rolling basis starting 6/15; must reply within 3 week(s) of notification.

CONTACT
Lisa Schrenger, Financial Aid Officer
109 East Broadway, Louisville, KY 40202
(502) 213-2137

Kentucky Christian University
Grayson, Kentucky
www.kcu.edu   Federal Code: 001965

4-year private Bible and liberal arts college in small town, affiliated with Christian Church/Church of Christ.
Enrollment: 550 undergrads.
Selectivity: Admits 50 to 75% of applicants.

BASIC COSTS (2005-2006)
Tuition and fees: $10,950.
Per-credit charge: $360.
Room and board: $4,514.

FINANCIAL AID PICTURE
Students with need: Need-based aid available for full-time and part-time students.
Students without need: No-need awards available for academics, alumni affiliation, leadership, music/drama, religious affiliation.

FINANCIAL AID PROCEDURES
Forms required: FAFSA.
Dates and Deadlines: Priority date 4/1; no closing date. Applicants notified on a rolling basis starting 3/15; must reply within 2 week(s) of notification.

CONTACT
Jennie Bender, Director of Financial Aid
100 Academic Parkway, Grayson, KY 41143-2205
(606) 474-3226

Kentucky Mountain Bible College
Vancleve, Kentucky
www.kmbc.edu   Federal Code: 030021

4-year private Bible college in small town, affiliated with Kentucky Mountain Holiness Association.
Enrollment: 59 undergrads.

BASIC COSTS (2006-2007)
Tuition and fees: $5,260.
Per-credit charge: $160.
Room and board: $3,200.

FINANCIAL AID PICTURE (2005-2006)
Students with need: Need-based aid available for full-time students.
Students without need: This college only awards aid to students with need.

FINANCIAL AID PROCEDURES
Forms required: FAFSA.
Dates and Deadlines: Priority date 4/1; closing date 6/30. Applicants notified on a rolling basis; must reply by 7/1.
Transfers: No deadline.

CONTACT
Sara Klopping, Director of Financial Aid
Box 10, Vancleve, KY 41385
(606) 693-5000 ext. 176

Kentucky State University
Frankfort, Kentucky
www.kysu.edu   Federal Code: 001968

4-year public university in large town.
Enrollment: 1,908 undergrads, 16% part-time. 409 full-time freshmen.

BASIC COSTS (2005-2006)
Tuition and fees: $4,170; out-of-state residents $10,612.
Per-credit charge: $148; out-of-state residents $419.
Room and board: $5,688.
Additional info: Tuition/fee waivers available for adults.

FINANCIAL AID PICTURE
Students with need: Need-based aid available for full-time and part-time students. Work study available nights, weekends, and for part-time students.
Students without need: This college only awards aid to students with need.

FINANCIAL AID PROCEDURES
Forms required: FAFSA, state aid form, institutional form.
Dates and Deadlines: Priority date 4/15; closing date 5/31. Applicants notified by 7/1; must reply by 7/15.

CONTACT
Carmella Conner, Director of Financial Aid
400 East Main Street, ASB13, Frankfort, KY 40601
(502) 597-5960

Kentucky Wesleyan College
Owensboro, Kentucky
www.kwc.edu   Federal Code: 001969

4-year private liberal arts college in small city, affiliated with United Methodist Church.
Enrollment: 734 undergrads, 2% part-time. 216 full-time freshmen.
Selectivity: Admits over 75% of applicants.

BASIC COSTS (2005-2006)
Tuition and fees: $13,115.
Per-credit charge: $390.
Room and board: $5,600.

FINANCIAL AID PICTURE (2004-2005)
Students with need: Out of 211 full-time freshmen who applied for aid, 184 were judged to have need. Of these, 183 received aid, and 42 had their full need met. Average financial aid package met 75% of need; average scholarship/grant was $10,420; average loan was $2,339. For part-time students, average financial aid package was $7,429.
Students without need: 32 full-time freshmen who did not demonstrate need for aid received scholarships/grants; average award was $9,617. No-need awards available for academics, alumni affiliation, art, athletics, leadership, music/drama, religious affiliation, state/district residency.
Scholarships offered: Scholarships range from $1,000 to full tuition. Students compete in on-campus scholarship competitions.
Cumulative student debt: 75% of graduating class had student loans; average debt was $19,990.

FINANCIAL AID PROCEDURES
Forms required: FAFSA.
Dates and Deadlines: Priority date 3/15; no closing date. Applicants notified on a rolling basis starting 2/15; must reply within 2 week(s) of notification.

CONTACT
Kurt Osborne, Financial Aid Officer
3000 Frederica Street, Owensboro, KY 42302-1039
(800) 999-0592

Lindsey Wilson College
Columbia, Kentucky
www.lindsey.edu   Federal Code: 001972

4-year private liberal arts college in small town, affiliated with United Methodist Church.
Enrollment: 1,611 undergrads, 10% part-time. 406 full-time freshmen.
Selectivity: Admits over 75% of applicants.

BASIC COSTS (2006-2007)
Tuition and fees: $14,438.
Per-credit charge: $592.
Room and board: $6,163.

FINANCIAL AID PICTURE (2004-2005)
Students with need: Out of 405 full-time freshmen who applied for aid, 382 were judged to have need. Of these, 382 received aid, and 6 had their full need met. For part-time students, average financial aid package was $1,996.
Students without need: This college only awards aid to students with need.

FINANCIAL AID PROCEDURES
Forms required: FAFSA, institutional form.
Dates and Deadlines: Priority date 4/15; no closing date. Applicants notified on a rolling basis starting 5/1; must reply within 2 week(s) of notification.

CONTACT
Marilyn Radford, Director of Financial Aid
210 Lindsey Wilson Street, Columbia, KY 42728
(270) 384-8022

Louisville Technical Institute
Louisville, Kentucky
www.louisvilletech.edu   Federal Code: 012088

2-year for-profit technical college in very large city.
Enrollment: 611 undergrads.
Selectivity: Admits over 75% of applicants.

BASIC COSTS (2005-2006)
Tuition and fees: $16,584.
Room only: $3,690.
Additional info: Computer graphic design program tuition: $12,285; fees: $1,400. Tuition at time of enrollment locked for 2 years; tuition/fee waivers available for adults.

FINANCIAL AID PICTURE
Students with need: Need-based aid available for full-time and part-time students. Work study available nights.
Students without need: No-need awards available for academics, art, job skills.
Scholarships offered: Academic Scholarships: based on class rank, high school GPA, essay; up to $4,000. Scholarship Day Competition: based upon testing scores; up to $2,000. Skills Competition: based upon open competition in electronics, drafting, interior design, computer networking and art skills; up to $4,000.

FINANCIAL AID PROCEDURES
Forms required: FAFSA.
Dates and Deadlines: No deadline. Applicants notified on a rolling basis; must reply within 2 week(s) of notification.
Transfers: No deadline. Applicants notified on a rolling basis.

CONTACT
Lisa Wright, Financial Planning Director
3901 Atkinson Square Drive, Louisville, KY 40218-4524
(502) 456-6509

Madisonville Community College
Madisonville, Kentucky
www.madisonville.kctcs.edu   Federal Code: 009010

2-year public community college in large town.
Enrollment: 3,720 undergrads.
Selectivity: Open admission; but selective for some programs.

BASIC COSTS (2005-2006)
Tuition and fees: $2,940; out-of-state residents $8,820.
Per-credit charge: $98; out-of-state residents $294.
Additional info: Tuition/fee waivers available for minority students, unemployed or children of unemployed.

FINANCIAL AID PICTURE
Students with need: Need-based aid available for full-time and part-time students. Work study available nights, weekends, and for part-time students.
Students without need: No-need awards available for minority status.

FINANCIAL AID PROCEDURES
Forms required: FAFSA, institutional form.
Dates and Deadlines: Priority date 3/15; no closing date. Applicants notified on a rolling basis; must reply within 3 week(s) of notification.

CONTACT
Caroline Clayton, Director of Financial Aid
2000 College Drive, Madisonville, KY 42431
(270) 821-6514

Maysville Community College
Maysville, Kentucky
www.maysville.kctcs.edu   Federal Code: 006960

2-year public community and technical college in small town.
Enrollment: 1,636 undergrads.
Selectivity: Open admission; but selective for some programs.

BASIC COSTS (2005-2006)
Tuition and fees: $2,940; out-of-state residents $8,820.
Per-credit charge: $98; out-of-state residents $294.

FINANCIAL AID PICTURE (2004-2005)
Students with need: 81% of average financial aid package awarded as scholarships/grants, 19% awarded as loans/jobs. Need-based aid available for part-time students. Work study available nights.
Students without need: No-need awards available for academics.

FINANCIAL AID PROCEDURES
Forms required: FAFSA, institutional form.
Dates and Deadlines: Priority date 4/1; no closing date. Applicants notified on a rolling basis starting 3/1; must reply within 3 week(s) of notification.

CONTACT
Leslie McCord, Financial Aid Coordinator
1755 US 68, Maysville, KY 41056
(606) 759-7141 ext. 6179

Mid-Continent University
Mayfield, Kentucky
www.midcontinent.edu   Federal Code: 025762

4-year private Bible and liberal arts college in large town, affiliated with Southern Baptist Convention.
Enrollment: 972 undergrads, 16% part-time. 85 full-time freshmen.

BASIC COSTS (2005-2006)
Tuition and fees: $10,100.
Per-credit charge: $295.
Room and board: $5,700.

FINANCIAL AID PICTURE (2005-2006)
Students with need: Out of 76 full-time freshmen who applied for aid, 64 were judged to have need. Of these, 64 received aid, and 11 had their full need met. Average financial aid package met 60% of need; average scholarship/grant was $4,270; average loan was $1,953. Need-based aid available for part-time students.
Students without need: 34 full-time freshmen who did not demonstrate need for aid received scholarships/grants; average award was $5,938. No-need awards available for academics.

FINANCIAL AID PROCEDURES
Forms required: FAFSA, institutional form.
Dates and Deadlines: Priority date 3/15; closing date 5/30. Applicants notified on a rolling basis starting 4/1.
Transfers: No deadline.

CONTACT
Andy Stratton, Vice President for Business Operations
99 Powell Road East, Mayfield, KY 42066-0357
(270) 247-8521 ext. 260

Midway College
Midway, Kentucky
www.midway.edu Federal Code: 001975

4-year private liberal arts college for women in small town, affiliated with Christian Church (Disciples of Christ).
Enrollment: 1,230 undergrads, 29% part-time. 129 full-time freshmen.
Selectivity: Open admission; but selective for some programs.

BASIC COSTS (2005-2006)
Tuition and fees: $13,800.
Per-credit charge: $460.
Room and board: $6,200.

FINANCIAL AID PICTURE (2005-2006)
Students with need: Out of 116 full-time freshmen who applied for aid, 105 were judged to have need. Of these, 105 received aid, and 22 had their full need met. Average financial aid package met 57% of need; average scholarship/grant was $6,530; average loan was $2,475. For part-time students, average financial aid package was $7,619.
Students without need: 3 full-time freshmen who did not demonstrate need for aid received scholarships/grants; average award was $2,417. No-need awards available for academics, alumni affiliation, art, athletics, leadership, minority status, music/drama, religious affiliation.
Cumulative student debt: 80% of graduating class had student loans; average debt was $15,407.
Additional info: Audition required of applicants for music scholarships. Portfolio required for art scholarships.

FINANCIAL AID PROCEDURES
Forms required: FAFSA, institutional form.
Dates and Deadlines: Priority date 4/1; closing date 8/1. Applicants notified on a rolling basis; must reply within 4 week(s) of notification.

CONTACT
Katie Valentine, Director of Financial Aid
512 East Stephen Street, Midway, KY 40347-1120
(859) 846-5410

Morehead State University
Morehead, Kentucky
www.moreheadstate.edu Federal Code: 001976

4-year public university in small town.
Enrollment: 6,971 undergrads, 15% part-time. 1,277 full-time freshmen.
Selectivity: Admits 50 to 75% of applicants.

BASIC COSTS (2005-2006)
Tuition and fees: $4,320; out-of-state residents $11,480.
Per-credit charge: $180; out-of-state residents $480.
Room and board: $4,798.

FINANCIAL AID PICTURE (2005-2006)
Students with need: Out of 1,137 full-time freshmen who applied for aid, 877 were judged to have need. Of these, 869 received aid, and 311 had their full need met. Average financial aid package met 88% of need; average scholarship/grant was $4,339; average loan was $2,570. For part-time students, average financial aid package was $5,572.
Students without need: 329 full-time freshmen who did not demonstrate need for aid received scholarships/grants; average award was $4,054. No-need awards available for academics, alumni affiliation, art, athletics, leadership, minority status, music/drama, ROTC, state/district residency.
Scholarships offered: 39 full-time freshmen received athletic scholarships; average amount $5,907.
Cumulative student debt: 59% of graduating class had student loans; average debt was $16,995.

FINANCIAL AID PROCEDURES
Forms required: FAFSA, institutional form.
Dates and Deadlines: Priority date 3/15; no closing date. Applicants notified on a rolling basis.
Transfers: Transfer scholarships available.

CONTACT
Carol Becker, Director of Financial Aid
Admissions Center, Morehead, KY 40351
(606) 783-2011

Murray State University
Murray, Kentucky
www.murraystate.edu Federal Code: 001977

4-year public university in large town.
Enrollment: 7,937 undergrads, 11% part-time. 1,417 full-time freshmen.
Selectivity: Admits 50 to 75% of applicants.

BASIC COSTS (2005-2006)
Tuition and fees: $4,428; out-of-state residents $12,036.
Per-credit charge: $185; out-of-state residents $502.
Room and board: $4,890.
Additional info: Tuition/fee waivers available for minority students.

FINANCIAL AID PICTURE (2004-2005)
Students with need: Out of 1,134 full-time freshmen who applied for aid, 680 were judged to have need. Of these, 639 received aid, and 601 had their full need met. Average financial aid package met 94% of need; average scholarship/grant was $2,257; average loan was $1,850. For part-time students, average financial aid package was $4,021.
Students without need: 510 full-time freshmen who did not demonstrate need for aid received scholarships/grants; average award was $2,517. No-need awards available for academics, alumni affiliation, art, athletics, job skills, leadership, minority status, music/drama, ROTC, state/district residency.
Scholarships offered: *Merit:* Tuition discount for children and grandchildren of out-of-state alumni: $7,608. Regional tuition for students from certain counties in Illinois, Tennessee, Missouri, and Indiana who meet admission requirements. *Athletic:* 55 full-time freshmen received athletic scholarships; average amount $7,310.
Cumulative student debt: 54% of graduating class had student loans; average debt was $14,488.

FINANCIAL AID PROCEDURES
Forms required: FAFSA, institutional form.
Dates and Deadlines: Priority date 4/1; no closing date. Applicants notified on a rolling basis starting 4/15.

CONTACT
Charles Vinson, Director of Financial Aid
113 Sparks Hall, Murray, KY 42071
(270) 762-2546

National College of Business & Technology: Danville
Danville, Kentucky
www.ncbt.edu Federal Code: 010489

2-year for-profit business college in large town.
Enrollment: 311 undergrads.
Selectivity: Open admission.

BASIC COSTS (2006-2007)
Tuition and fees: $8,976.
Per-credit charge: $187.

Kentucky — National College of Business & Technology: Danville

FINANCIAL AID PICTURE

Students with need: Need-based aid available for full-time and part-time students.

Students without need: This college only awards aid to students with need.

FINANCIAL AID PROCEDURES

Forms required: FAFSA.

Dates and Deadlines: No deadline. Applicants notified on a rolling basis.

CONTACT

Pamela Cotton, Director of Financial Aid and Compliance Officer
PO Box 6400, Roanoke, VA 24017
(540) 986-1800

National College of Business & Technology: Florence
Florence, Kentucky
www.ncbt.edu   Federal Code: 010489

2-year for-profit business college in large town.
Enrollment: 237 undergrads.
Selectivity: Open admission.

BASIC COSTS (2006-2007)

Tuition and fees: $8,976.
Per-credit charge: $187.

FINANCIAL AID PICTURE

Students with need: Need-based aid available for full-time and part-time students.

Students without need: This college only awards aid to students with need.

FINANCIAL AID PROCEDURES

Forms required: FAFSA.

Dates and Deadlines: No deadline. Applicants notified on a rolling basis.

CONTACT

Pamela Cotton, Director of Financial Aid and Compliance Officer
PO Box 6400, Roanoke, VA 24017
(540) 986-1800

National College of Business & Technology: Lexington
Lexington, Kentucky
www.ncbt.edu   Federal Code: 010489

2-year for-profit business and junior college in small city.
Enrollment: 369 undergrads.
Selectivity: Open admission.

BASIC COSTS (2006-2007)

Tuition and fees: $8,976.
Per-credit charge: $187.

FINANCIAL AID PICTURE

Students with need: Need-based aid available for full-time and part-time students.

Students without need: This college only awards aid to students with need.

FINANCIAL AID PROCEDURES

Forms required: FAFSA.

Dates and Deadlines: No deadline. Applicants notified on a rolling basis.

CONTACT

Pamela Cotton, Director of Financial Aid and Compliance Officer
PO Box 6400, Roanoke, VA 24017
(859) 255-0621

National College of Business & Technology: Louisville
Louisville, Kentucky
www.ncbt.edu   Federal Code: 010489

2-year for-profit business college in large city.
Enrollment: 771 undergrads.
Selectivity: Open admission.

BASIC COSTS (2006-2007)

Tuition and fees: $8,976.
Per-credit charge: $187.

FINANCIAL AID PICTURE

Students with need: Need-based aid available for full-time and part-time students.

Students without need: This college only awards aid to students with need.

FINANCIAL AID PROCEDURES

Forms required: FAFSA.

Dates and Deadlines: No deadline. Applicants notified on a rolling basis.

CONTACT

Pamela Cotton, Director of Financial Aid and Compliance Officer
PO Box 6400, Roanoke, VA 24017
(540) 986-1800

National College of Business & Technology: Pikeville
Pikeville, Kentucky
www.ncbt.edu   Federal Code: 010489

2-year for-profit business college in large town.
Enrollment: 194 undergrads.
Selectivity: Open admission.

BASIC COSTS (2006-2007)

Tuition and fees: $8,976.
Per-credit charge: $187.

FINANCIAL AID PICTURE

Students with need: Need-based aid available for full-time and part-time students.

Students without need: This college only awards aid to students with need.

FINANCIAL AID PROCEDURES

Forms required: FAFSA.

Dates and Deadlines: No deadline.

CONTACT

Pamela Cotton, Director of Financial Aid and Compliance Officer
PO Box 6400, Roanoke, VA 24017
(540) 986-1800

National College of Business & Technology: Richmond
Richmond, Kentucky
www.ncbt.edu   Federal Code: 010489

2-year for-profit business college in large town.
Enrollment: 312 undergrads.
Selectivity: Open admission.

BASIC COSTS (2006-2007)
Tuition and fees: $8,976.
Per-credit charge: $187.

FINANCIAL AID PICTURE
Students with need: Need-based aid available for full-time and part-time students.
Students without need: This college only awards aid to students with need.

FINANCIAL AID PROCEDURES
Forms required: FAFSA.
Dates and Deadlines: No deadline. Applicants notified on a rolling basis.

CONTACT
Pamela Cotton, Director of Financial Aid and Compliance Officer
PO Box 6400, Roanoke, VA 24017
(540) 986-1800

Northern Kentucky University
Highland Heights, Kentucky
www.nku.edu   Federal Code: 009275

4-year public university in large city.
Enrollment: 11,611 undergrads, 22% part-time. 1,702 full-time freshmen.
Selectivity: Open admission; but selective for some programs.

BASIC COSTS (2005-2006)
Tuition and fees: $4,968; out-of-state residents $9,696.
Per-credit charge: $207; out-of-state residents $404.
Room and board: $5,358.

FINANCIAL AID PICTURE (2004-2005)
Students with need: Out of 1,616 full-time freshmen who applied for aid, 1,293 were judged to have need. Of these, 1,293 received aid. Average financial aid package met 90% of need; average scholarship/grant was $4,214; average loan was $2,601. Need-based aid available for part-time students.
Students without need: 322 full-time freshmen who did not demonstrate need for aid received scholarships/grants; average award was $3,076. No-need awards available for academics, alumni affiliation, art, athletics, job skills, leadership, minority status, music/drama, state/district residency.
Scholarships offered: 23 full-time freshmen received athletic scholarships; average amount $4,716.
Cumulative student debt: 32% of graduating class had student loans; average debt was $21,727.

FINANCIAL AID PROCEDURES
Forms required: FAFSA.
Dates and Deadlines: Priority date 3/1; no closing date. Applicants notified on a rolling basis starting 4/1; must reply within 3 week(s) of notification.

CONTACT
Leah Stewart, Director of Financial Assistance
Administrative Center 401, Northern Kentucky University, Highland Heights, KY 41099
(859) 572-5143

Owensboro Community College
Owensboro, Kentucky
www.octc.kctcs.edu   Federal Code: 030345

2-year public community college in small city.
Enrollment: 4,084 undergrads.
Selectivity: Open admission; but selective for some programs.

BASIC COSTS (2005-2006)
Tuition and fees: $2,940; out-of-state residents $8,820.
Per-credit charge: $98; out-of-state residents $294.

FINANCIAL AID PICTURE (2004-2005)
Students with need: 83% of average financial aid package awarded as scholarships/grants, 17% awarded as loans/jobs. Need-based aid available for part-time students.
Students without need: No-need awards available for academics, state/district residency.

FINANCIAL AID PROCEDURES
Forms required: FAFSA.
Dates and Deadlines: Priority date 3/16; no closing date. Applicants notified by 6/1; must reply within 2 week(s) of notification.
Transfers: Must have financial aid transcripts from previous institutions.

CONTACT
Bernice Ayer, Financial Aid Officer
4800 New Hartford Road, Owensboro, KY 42303-1899
(270) 686-4464

Paducah Technical College
Paducah, Kentucky   Federal Code: 013661
www.paducahtech.edu   CSS Code: 0669

2-year for-profit technical college in small city.
Enrollment: 150 undergrads.
Selectivity: Open admission.

BASIC COSTS (2005-2006)
Additional info: $18,975 for 3-year program includes books, fees, tools. Tuition at time of enrollment locked for 2 years.

FINANCIAL AID PICTURE
Students with need: Need-based aid available for full-time students.

FINANCIAL AID PROCEDURES
Forms required: FAFSA, CSS PROFILE.
Dates and Deadlines: No deadline. Applicants notified on a rolling basis; must reply within 3 week(s) of notification.

CONTACT
Priscilla Meyenburg, Financial Aid Officer
509 South 30th Street, Paducah, KY 42001
(270) 444-9676

Pikeville College
Pikeville, Kentucky
www.pc.edu   Federal Code: 001980

4-year private liberal arts college in small town, affiliated with Presbyterian Church (USA).
Enrollment: 830 undergrads, 6% part-time. 206 full-time freshmen.
Selectivity: Open admission; but selective for some programs.

BASIC COSTS (2005-2006)
Tuition and fees: $11,500.
Room and board: $5,000.

FINANCIAL AID PICTURE (2005-2006)
Students with need: Out of 200 full-time freshmen who applied for aid, 200 were judged to have need. Of these, 200 received aid, and 130 had their full need met. Average financial aid package met 90% of need; average scholarship/grant was $10,040; average loan was $2,530. For part-time students, average financial aid package was $5,854.
Students without need: This college only awards aid to students with need.
Cumulative student debt: 73% of graduating class had student loans; average debt was $15,208.

FINANCIAL AID PROCEDURES
Forms required: FAFSA, institutional form.
Dates and Deadlines: Priority date 3/15; no closing date. Applicants notified on a rolling basis starting 1/15; must reply by 5/1 or within 2 week(s) of notification.
Transfers: No deadline. Must reply within 2 week(s) of notification.

CONTACT
Judy Bradley, Financial Aid Director
147 Sycamore Street, Pikeville, KY 41501-1194
(606) 218-5253

St. Catharine College
St. Catharine, Kentucky
www.sccky.edu   Federal Code: 001983

4-year private health science and liberal arts college in large town, affiliated with Roman Catholic Church.
Enrollment: 682 undergrads.
Selectivity: Open admission.

BASIC COSTS (2006-2007)
Tuition and fees: $11,900.
Per-credit charge: $435.
Room and board: $5,970.

FINANCIAL AID PICTURE
Students with need: Need-based aid available for full-time and part-time students.
Students without need: This college only awards aid to students with need.

FINANCIAL AID PROCEDURES
Forms required: FAFSA, institutional form.
Dates and Deadlines: Priority date 3/15; no closing date. Applicants notified on a rolling basis; must reply by 8/15.

CONTACT
Jane Corbett, Financial Aid Director
2735 Bardstown Road, St. Catharine, KY 40061
(502) 336-5082

Somerset Community College
Somerset, Kentucky
www.somerset.kctcs.edu   Federal Code: 001997

2-year public community and technical college in large town.
Enrollment: 4,100 undergrads.
Selectivity: Open admission; but selective for some programs.

BASIC COSTS (2005-2006)
Tuition and fees: $2,940; out-of-state residents $8,820.
Per-credit charge: $98; out-of-state residents $294.
Additional info: Tuition/fee waivers available for minority students.

FINANCIAL AID PICTURE (2005-2006)
Students with need: 80% of average financial aid package awarded as scholarships/grants, 20% awarded as loans/jobs. Need-based aid available for part-time students. Work study available nights.
Students without need: This college only awards aid to students with need.

FINANCIAL AID PROCEDURES
Forms required: FAFSA.
Dates and Deadlines: Priority date 3/1; no closing date. Applicants notified on a rolling basis starting 6/30; must reply within 2 week(s) of notification.
Transfers: Priority date 3/15; closing date 8/15.

CONTACT
Shawn Anderson, Chief Financial Aid Officer
808 Monticello Street, Somerset, KY 42501
(606) 679-8501

Southeast Kentucky Community and Technical College
Cumberland, Kentucky
www.secc.kctcs.net   Federal Code: 001998

2-year public community college in small town.
Enrollment: 1,700 undergrads.
Selectivity: Open admission; but selective for some programs.

BASIC COSTS (2005-2006)
Tuition and fees: $2,940; out-of-state residents $8,820.
Per-credit charge: $98; out-of-state residents $294.

FINANCIAL AID PICTURE
Students with need: Need-based aid available for full-time and part-time students.
Students without need: This college only awards aid to students with need.
Additional info: March 15 deadline for state financial aid.

FINANCIAL AID PROCEDURES
Forms required: FAFSA.
Dates and Deadlines: Priority date 3/15; no closing date. Applicants notified by 6/15; must reply within 2 week(s) of notification.

CONTACT
Charles Sellars, Dean of Student Affairs/Director Financial Aid
700 College Road, Cumberland, KY 40823
(606) 589-2145

Spalding University
Louisville, Kentucky
www.spalding.edu   Federal Code: 001960

4-year private university in very large city, affiliated with Roman Catholic Church.
Enrollment: 1,660 undergrads.
Selectivity: Open admission; but selective for some programs.

BASIC COSTS (2005-2006)
Tuition and fees: $14,400.
Per-credit charge: $480.
Room and board: $3,882.

FINANCIAL AID PICTURE
Students with need: Need-based aid available for full-time and part-time students. Work study available nights, weekends, and for part-time students.
Students without need: No-need awards available for academics, athletics, religious affiliation, ROTC.
Scholarships offered: Angela Garcia Residence Hall Scholarship: covers cost of a double room on campus; up to 12 awards per year; awarded to students who demonstrate leadership in campus activites, especially in residence halls.

FINANCIAL AID PROCEDURES
Forms required: FAFSA.
Dates and Deadlines: Priority date 3/1; no closing date. Applicants notified on a rolling basis starting 3/31; must reply within 2 week(s) of notification.

CONTACT
Gina Kuzoka, Director of Financial Aid
851 South Fourth Street, Louisville, KY 40203
(502) 588-7185

Spencerian College: Lexington
Lexington, Kentucky
www.spencerian.edu
Federal Code: 004618

2-year for-profit branch campus and technical college in small city.
Enrollment: 400 undergrads, 28% part-time. 530 full-time freshmen.
Selectivity: Open admission.

BASIC COSTS (2006-2007)
Tuition and fees: $14,415.
Room only: $3,960.
Additional info: Tuition at time of enrollment locked for 2 years.

FINANCIAL AID PICTURE (2005-2006)
Students with need: Average financial aid package met 100% of need; average scholarship/grant was $1,500; average loan was $5,000. Need-based aid available for part-time students.
Students without need: This college only awards aid to students with need.
Cumulative student debt: 97% of graduating class had student loans; average debt was $23,000.

FINANCIAL AID PROCEDURES
Forms required: FAFSA, state aid form, institutional form.
Dates and Deadlines: No deadline. Applicants notified on a rolling basis starting 1/1.
Transfers: No deadline. Applicants notified on a rolling basis.

CONTACT
Brian Highley, Director of Financial Planning
1575 Winchester Rd., Lexington, KY 40505
(859) 223-9608 ext. 5421

Sullivan University
Louisville, Kentucky
www.sullivan.edu
Federal Code: 004619

4-year for-profit university and culinary school and business college in large city.
Enrollment: 4,500 undergrads.

BASIC COSTS (2005-2006)
Additional info: Tuition, fees and per-credit-hour charges vary by program. Tuition costs range from $11,760 to $12,750 per academic year. Required fees are $415. Tuition at time of enrollment locked for 4 years.

FINANCIAL AID PICTURE
Students with need: Need-based aid available for full-time and part-time students.
Students without need: This college only awards aid to students with need.

FINANCIAL AID PROCEDURES
Forms required: FAFSA.
Dates and Deadlines: No deadline. Applicants notified on a rolling basis starting 1/2.

CONTACT
Caren Stewart, Financial Aid Director
3101 Bardstown Road, Louisville, KY 40205
(502) 456-6504

Thomas More College
Crestview Hills, Kentucky
www.thomasmore.edu
Federal Code: 002001

4-year private liberal arts college in small town, affiliated with Roman Catholic Church.
Enrollment: 1,343 undergrads. 176 full-time freshmen.
Selectivity: Admits 50 to 75% of applicants.

BASIC COSTS (2006-2007)
Tuition and fees: $20,220.
Per-credit charge: $480.
Room and board: $6,250.
Additional info: Tuition/fee waivers available for minority students.

FINANCIAL AID PICTURE (2004-2005)
Students with need: Out of 167 full-time freshmen who applied for aid, 167 were judged to have need. Of these, 167 received aid, and 167 had their full need met. Need-based aid available for part-time students.
Students without need: 15 full-time freshmen who did not demonstrate need for aid received scholarships/grants; average award was $5,012. No-need awards available for academics, alumni affiliation, art, job skills, leadership, minority status, music/drama, religious affiliation, ROTC, state/district residency.
Cumulative student debt: 67% of graduating class had student loans; average debt was $17,125.

FINANCIAL AID PROCEDURES
Forms required: FAFSA, institutional form.
Dates and Deadlines: Priority date 3/15; no closing date. Applicants notified on a rolling basis; must reply within 4 week(s) of notification.
Transfers: No deadline. Applicants notified on a rolling basis; must reply within 4 week(s) of notification.

CONTACT
Linda Hayes, Director of Financial Aid
333 Thomas More Parkway, Crestview Hills, KY 41017-3495
(859) 344-4043

Transylvania University
Lexington, Kentucky
www.transy.edu
Federal Code: 001987

4-year private liberal arts college in small city, affiliated with Christian Church (Disciples of Christ).
Enrollment: 1,143 undergrads, 1% part-time. 333 full-time freshmen.
Selectivity: Admits over 75% of applicants.

Kentucky — Transylvania University

BASIC COSTS (2006-2007)
Tuition and fees: $20,950.
Room and board: $6,850.
Additional info: Tuition/fee waivers available for minority students.

FINANCIAL AID PICTURE (2005-2006)
Students with need: Out of 275 full-time freshmen who applied for aid, 222 were judged to have need. Of these, 221 received aid, and 68 had their full need met. Average financial aid package met 88% of need; average scholarship/grant was $12,719; average loan was $3,080. For part-time students, average financial aid package was $5,481.
Students without need: 111 full-time freshmen who did not demonstrate need for aid received scholarships/grants; average award was $11,890. No-need awards available for academics, art, leadership, minority status, music/drama, religious affiliation, ROTC, state/district residency.
Scholarships offered: William T. Young Merit Scholarships: 25 awarded; tuition and fees.
Cumulative student debt: 59% of graduating class had student loans; average debt was $15,673.
Additional info: Auditions and portfolios required for music and art scholarships respectively. Essays required for other scholarship programs. Applications for William T. Young scholarships must be received by December 1.

FINANCIAL AID PROCEDURES
Forms required: FAFSA.
Dates and Deadlines: Priority date 3/1; no closing date. Applicants notified on a rolling basis starting 3/15; must reply by 5/1 or within 2 week(s) of notification.
Transfers: No deadline. Applicants notified on a rolling basis starting 3/15; must reply by 8/6.

CONTACT
David Cecil, Director of Financial Aid
300 North Broadway, Lexington, KY 40508-1797
(859) 233-8239

Union College
Barbourville, Kentucky
www.unionky.edu
Federal Code: 001988

4-year private liberal arts college in small town, affiliated with United Methodist Church.
Enrollment: 602 undergrads, 8% part-time. 177 full-time freshmen.
Selectivity: Open admission; but selective for some programs.

BASIC COSTS (2006-2007)
Tuition and fees: $15,290.
Per-credit charge: $250.
Room and board: $4,600.

FINANCIAL AID PICTURE (2005-2006)
Students with need: Average financial aid package met 78% of need; average scholarship/grant was $10,454; average loan was $3,570. For part-time students, average financial aid package was $5,470.
Students without need: No-need awards available for academics, athletics, leadership, minority status, music/drama, religious affiliation, state/district residency.

FINANCIAL AID PROCEDURES
Forms required: FAFSA.
Dates and Deadlines: Priority date 3/15; no closing date. Applicants notified on a rolling basis starting 4/1; must reply within 2 week(s) of notification.

CONTACT
Sue Buttery, Associate Dean for Financial Aid
310 College Street, Barbourville, KY 40906
(606) 546-1618

University of Kentucky
Lexington, Kentucky
www.uky.edu
Federal Code: 001989

4-year public university in large city.
Enrollment: 18,416 undergrads, 8% part-time. 3,825 full-time freshmen.
Selectivity: Admits over 75% of applicants.

BASIC COSTS (2005-2006)
Tuition and fees: $5,812; out-of-state residents $12,798.
Per-credit charge: $232; out-of-state residents $523.
Room and board: $5,229.
Additional info: Tuition charges include fees. Upper division tuition is $5980, in-state; $12,970, out-of-state. Tuition/fee waivers available for adults, minority students.

FINANCIAL AID PICTURE (2005-2006)
Students with need: Out of 2,387 full-time freshmen who applied for aid, 1,530 were judged to have need. Of these, 1,519 received aid, and 688 had their full need met. Average financial aid package met 79% of need; average scholarship/grant was $5,743; average loan was $2,599. For part-time students, average financial aid package was $5,470.
Students without need: 355 full-time freshmen who did not demonstrate need for aid received scholarships/grants; average award was $3,225. No-need awards available for academics, alumni affiliation, art, athletics, job skills, leadership, minority status, music/drama, ROTC, state/district residency.
Scholarships offered: 90 full-time freshmen received athletic scholarships; average amount $11,112.
Cumulative student debt: 68% of graduating class had student loans; average debt was $17,692.

FINANCIAL AID PROCEDURES
Forms required: FAFSA.
Dates and Deadlines: Priority date 2/15; no closing date. Applicants notified on a rolling basis starting 4/1; must reply within 3 week(s) of notification.
Transfers: Priority date 4/1.

CONTACT
Lynda George, Director of Student Financial Aid
100 W.D. Funkhouser Building, Lexington, KY 40506-0054
(859) 257-3172

University of Louisville
Louisville, Kentucky
www.louisville.edu
Federal Code: 001999

4-year public university in very large city.
Enrollment: 13,893 undergrads, 19% part-time. 2,264 full-time freshmen.
Selectivity: Admits over 75% of applicants.

BASIC COSTS (2005-2006)
Tuition and fees: $5,532; out-of-state residents $15,092.
Per-credit charge: $231; out-of-state residents $629.
Room and board: $4,868.

FINANCIAL AID PICTURE (2005-2006)
Students with need: Out of 1,564 full-time freshmen who applied for aid, 1,277 were judged to have need. Of these, 1,261 received aid, and 214 had their full need met. Average financial aid package met 56% of need; average scholarship/grant was $5,876; average loan was $2,618. For part-time students, average financial aid package was $5,963.
Students without need: 507 full-time freshmen who did not demonstrate need for aid received scholarships/grants; average award was $5,541. No-need awards available for academics, art, athletics, leadership, minority status, music/drama, ROTC.

Scholarships offered: 62 full-time freshmen received athletic scholarships; average amount $12,264.
Cumulative student debt: 42% of graduating class had student loans; average debt was $15,128.

FINANCIAL AID PROCEDURES
Forms required: FAFSA.
Dates and Deadlines: Priority date 3/15; no closing date. Applicants notified on a rolling basis starting 4/1; must reply by 5/1.
Transfers: Priority date 3/1.

CONTACT
Patricia Arauz, Director of Student Financial Aid
2211 South Brook Street, Louisville, KY 40292
(502) 852-5511

University of the Cumberlands
Williamsburg, Kentucky
www.ucumberlands.edu
Federal Code: 001962

4-year private liberal arts college in small town, affiliated with Baptist faith.
Enrollment: 1,456 undergrads, 3% part-time. 424 full-time freshmen.
Selectivity: Admits over 75% of applicants.

BASIC COSTS (2006-2007)
Tuition and fees: $13,658.
Room and board: $6,326.

FINANCIAL AID PICTURE (2005-2006)
Students with need: Out of 402 full-time freshmen who applied for aid, 353 were judged to have need. Of these, 353 received aid, and 209 had their full need met. Average financial aid package met 93% of need; average scholarship/grant was $6,538; average loan was $3,319. For part-time students, average financial aid package was $7,135.
Students without need: 21 full-time freshmen who did not demonstrate need for aid received scholarships/grants; average award was $5,989. No-need awards available for academics, alumni affiliation, art, athletics, leadership, music/drama, religious affiliation, ROTC, state/district residency.
Scholarships offered: 27 full-time freshmen received athletic scholarships; average amount $4,756.
Cumulative student debt: 58% of graduating class had student loans; average debt was $16,083.

FINANCIAL AID PROCEDURES
Forms required: FAFSA.
Dates and Deadlines: Priority date 3/1; no closing date. Applicants notified on a rolling basis starting 4/1; must reply within 2 week(s) of notification.

CONTACT
Steve Allen, Director of Financial Planning
6178 College Station Drive, Williamsburg, KY 40769
(800) 532-0828

West Kentucky Community and Technical College
Paducah, Kentucky
www.pccky.com
Federal Code: 001979

2-year public community college in large town.
Enrollment: 6,726 undergrads.
Selectivity: Open admission; but selective for some programs.

BASIC COSTS (2005-2006)
Tuition and fees: $2,940; out-of-state residents $8,820.
Per-credit charge: $98; out-of-state residents $294.

FINANCIAL AID PICTURE
Students with need: Need-based aid available for full-time and part-time students.

FINANCIAL AID PROCEDURES
Forms required: FAFSA.
Dates and Deadlines: Priority date 4/1; no closing date. Applicants notified on a rolling basis starting 7/15; must reply within 4 week(s) of notification.

CONTACT
Sandy Barlow, Financial Aid Officer
4810 Alben Barkley Drive, Paducah, KY 42002
(270) 554-9200

Western Kentucky University
Bowling Green, Kentucky
www.wku.edu
Federal Code: 002002

4-year public university in small city.
Enrollment: 15,341 undergrads, 15% part-time. 2,865 full-time freshmen.
Selectivity: Open admission; but selective for some programs.

BASIC COSTS (2005-2006)
Tuition and fees: $5,316; out-of-state residents $12,732.
Per-credit charge: $215; out-of-state residents $524.
Room and board: $5,220.

FINANCIAL AID PICTURE (2004-2005)
Students with need: Out of 2,265 full-time freshmen who applied for aid, 1,680 were judged to have need. Of these, 1,644 received aid, and 481 had their full need met. Average financial aid package met 29% of need; average scholarship/grant was $3,650; average loan was $2,330. For part-time students, average financial aid package was $5,014.
Students without need: 889 full-time freshmen who did not demonstrate need for aid received scholarships/grants; average award was $2,296. No-need awards available for academics, alumni affiliation, art, athletics, job skills, leadership, minority status, music/drama, religious affiliation, ROTC, state/district residency.
Scholarships offered: *Merit:* Academic scholarships; from $200 to full tuition; for first-time freshmen; number awarded varies per year. *Athletic:* 67 full-time freshmen received athletic scholarships; average amount $7,387.
Cumulative student debt: 53% of graduating class had student loans; average debt was $12,250.

FINANCIAL AID PROCEDURES
Forms required: FAFSA.
Dates and Deadlines: Priority date 4/1; no closing date. Applicants notified on a rolling basis starting 3/1.
Transfers: Transfer students receiving CAP Grant must notify the state agency by December 1 of each year.

CONTACT
Cindy Burnette, Director of Financial Assistance
1906 College Heights Boulevard, Bowling Green, KY 42101
(270) 745-2755

Louisiana

Baton Rouge Community College
Baton Rouge, Louisiana
www.mybr.cc
Federal Code: 037303

2-year public community college in large city.
Enrollment: 4,291 undergrads.

Selectivity: Open admission.

BASIC COSTS (2005-2006)
Tuition and fees: $1,776; out-of-state residents $4,584.

FINANCIAL AID PICTURE (2004-2005)
Students with need: 96% of average financial aid package awarded as scholarships/grants, 4% awarded as loans/jobs.

FINANCIAL AID PROCEDURES
Dates and Deadlines: Priority date 4/15; no closing date.

CONTACT
Keith Thomas, Director of Financial Aid
5310 Florida Boulevard, Baton Rouge, LA 70806
(225) 216-8005

Bossier Parish Community College
Bossier City, Louisiana
www.bpcc.edu   Federal Code: 012033

2-year public community college in small city.
Enrollment: 4,008 undergrads, 43% part-time. 735 full-time freshmen.
Selectivity: Open admission; but selective for out-of-state students.

BASIC COSTS (2005-2006)
Tuition and fees: $1,720; out-of-state residents $3,860.

FINANCIAL AID PICTURE (2005-2006)
Students with need: Out of 603 full-time freshmen who applied for aid, 489 were judged to have need. Of these, 454 received aid. Average financial aid package met 25% of need; average scholarship/grant was $3,428; average loan was $1,226. For part-time students, average financial aid package was $3,212.
Students without need: 84 full-time freshmen who did not demonstrate need for aid received scholarships/grants; average award was $1,272. No-need awards available for academics, alumni affiliation, athletics, minority status, music/drama.
Scholarships offered: 35 full-time freshmen received athletic scholarships; average amount $1,183.
Cumulative student debt: 46% of graduating class had student loans; average debt was $11,012.

FINANCIAL AID PROCEDURES
Forms required: FAFSA.
Dates and Deadlines: Closing date 7/1. Applicants notified on a rolling basis.
Transfers: Priority date 6/1; no deadline.

CONTACT
Vickie Temple, Financial Aid Director
6220 East Texas Street, Bossier City, LA 71111-6922
(318) 678-6026

Centenary College of Louisiana
Shreveport, Louisiana
www.centenary.edu   Federal Code: 002003

4-year private liberal arts college in small city, affiliated with United Methodist Church.
Enrollment: 880 undergrads, 1% part-time. 233 full-time freshmen.
Selectivity: Admits 50 to 75% of applicants.

BASIC COSTS (2006-2007)
Tuition and fees: $19,760.
Per-credit charge: $630.
Room and board: $6,990.

FINANCIAL AID PICTURE (2004-2005)
Students with need: Out of 205 full-time freshmen who applied for aid, 149 were judged to have need. Of these, 149 received aid, and 62 had their full need met. Average financial aid package met 71% of need; average scholarship/grant was $11,168; average loan was $2,702. For part-time students, average financial aid package was $6,875.
Students without need: 58 full-time freshmen who did not demonstrate need for aid received scholarships/grants; average award was $9,639. No-need awards available for academics, art, athletics, leadership, music/drama, religious affiliation, state/district residency.
Scholarships offered: 64 full-time freshmen received athletic scholarships; average amount $10,469.
Cumulative student debt: 53% of graduating class had student loans; average debt was $17,300.

FINANCIAL AID PROCEDURES
Forms required: FAFSA, institutional form.
Dates and Deadlines: Priority date 2/15; no closing date. Applicants notified by 3/15; must reply by 5/1.

CONTACT
Mary Sue Rix, Director of Financial Aid
Box 41188, Shreveport, LA 71134-1188
(318) 869-5137

Delgado Community College
New Orleans, Louisiana
www.dcc.edu   Federal Code: 004626

2-year public community college in very large city.
Enrollment: 15,539 undergrads. 1,695 full-time freshmen.
Selectivity: Open admission; but selective for some programs.

BASIC COSTS (2005-2006)
Tuition and fees: $1,757; out-of-state residents $4,737.

FINANCIAL AID PICTURE (2004-2005)
Students with need: Out of 935 full-time freshmen who applied for aid, 780 were judged to have need. Of these, 758 received aid, and 60 had their full need met. Average financial aid package met 54% of need; average scholarship/grant was $3,405; average loan was $2,404. For part-time students, average financial aid package was $3,877.
Students without need: 52 full-time freshmen who did not demonstrate need for aid received scholarships/grants; average award was $2,158. No-need awards available for academics, athletics, leadership, music/drama, state/district residency.
Scholarships offered: 16 full-time freshmen received athletic scholarships; average amount $2,104.

FINANCIAL AID PROCEDURES
Forms required: FAFSA, institutional form.
Dates and Deadlines: Priority date 5/1; closing date 7/15. Applicants notified on a rolling basis starting 4/1; must reply within 2 week(s) of notification.

CONTACT
Diane Jackson, Director of Student Financial Assistance
615 City Park Avenue, New Orleans, LA 70119

Dillard University
New Orleans, Louisiana
www.dillard.edu   Federal Code: 002004

4-year private university and liberal arts college in very large city, affiliated with United Church of Christ and United Methodist Church.
Enrollment: 2,155 undergrads.

BASIC COSTS (2005-2006)
Tuition and fees: $12,240.
Room and board: $7,070.

FINANCIAL AID PICTURE (2005-2006)
Students with need: Average financial aid package met 85% of need; average scholarship/grant was $3,834; average loan was $2,511. For part-time students, average financial aid package was $6,859.
Students without need: This college only awards aid to students with need.

FINANCIAL AID PROCEDURES
Forms required: FAFSA, institutional form.
Dates and Deadlines: Priority date 3/1; closing date 5/1. Applicants notified on a rolling basis starting 3/1; must reply by 5/1 or within 2 week(s) of notification.

CONTACT
Cynthia Thornton, Director of Financial Aid
2601 Gentilly Boulevard, New Orleans, LA 70122-3097
(800) 216-8094

Grambling State University
Grambling, Louisiana
www.gram.edu   Federal Code: 002006

4-year public university in small town.
Enrollment: 4,574 undergrads, 9% part-time. 1,132 full-time freshmen.
Selectivity: Open admission; but selective for out-of-state students.

BASIC COSTS (2005-2006)
Tuition and fees: $3,506; out-of-state residents $8,856.
Room and board: $4,034.
Additional info: Tuition/fee waivers available for minority students.

FINANCIAL AID PICTURE (2005-2006)
Students with need: Out of 1,085 full-time freshmen who applied for aid, 975 were judged to have need. Of these, 956 received aid, and 43 had their full need met. Average financial aid package met 90% of need; average scholarship/grant was $2,765; average loan was $2,563. For part-time students, average financial aid package was $3,130.
Students without need: 44 full-time freshmen who did not demonstrate need for aid received scholarships/grants; average award was $1,778. No-need awards available for academics, athletics, leadership, minority status, music/drama, ROTC, state/district residency.
Scholarships offered: 33 full-time freshmen received athletic scholarships; average amount $5,823.
Cumulative student debt: 90% of graduating class had student loans; average debt was $30,000.

FINANCIAL AID PROCEDURES
Forms required: FAFSA, institutional form.
Dates and Deadlines: Priority date 4/1; closing date 6/1. Applicants notified on a rolling basis starting 3/1; must reply within 2 week(s) of notification.

CONTACT
Anne Rugege, Acting Director of Student Financial Aid
PO Box 864, Grambling, LA 71245-0864

ITI Technical College
Baton Rouge, Louisiana
www.iticollege.edu   Federal Code: 015270

2-year for-profit technical college in large city.
Enrollment: 349 undergrads. 253 full-time freshmen.
Selectivity: Open admission.

BASIC COSTS (2006-2007)
Additional info: Tuition varies by program from $5,000 to $22,000.

FINANCIAL AID PICTURE (2004-2005)
Students with need: Out of 227 full-time freshmen who applied for aid, 202 were judged to have need. Of these, 202 received aid. Average financial aid package met 42% of need; average scholarship/grant was $1,950; average loan was $2,526. For part-time students, average financial aid package was $6,500.
Students without need: This college only awards aid to students with need.

FINANCIAL AID PROCEDURES
Forms required: FAFSA.
Dates and Deadlines: No deadline.

CONTACT
13944 Airline Highway, Baton Rouge, LA 70817-5998
(800) 635-8426

Louisiana State University and Agricultural and Mechanical College
Baton Rouge, Louisiana
www.lsu.edu   Federal Code: 002010

4-year public university and agricultural college in large city.
Enrollment: 25,301 undergrads, 7% part-time. 5,366 full-time freshmen.
Selectivity: Admits 50 to 75% of applicants.

BASIC COSTS (2005-2006)
Tuition and fees: $4,515; out-of-state residents $12,815.
Room and board: $6,330.

FINANCIAL AID PICTURE (2004-2005)
Students with need: Out of 4,835 full-time freshmen who applied for aid, 2,465 were judged to have need. Of these, 2,419 received aid, and 440 had their full need met. Average financial aid package met 65% of need; average scholarship/grant was $4,460; average loan was $2,366. For part-time students, average financial aid package was $5,068.
Students without need: 2,486 full-time freshmen who did not demonstrate need for aid received scholarships/grants; average award was $3,680. No-need awards available for academics, alumni affiliation, art, athletics, leadership, music/drama, ROTC, state/district residency.
Scholarships offered: 91 full-time freshmen received athletic scholarships; average amount $10,094.

FINANCIAL AID PROCEDURES
Forms required: FAFSA, institutional form.
Dates and Deadlines: No deadline. Applicants notified on a rolling basis starting 3/1; must reply within 3 week(s) of notification.

CONTACT
Mary Parker, Director of Student Aid and Scholarships
110 Thomas Boyd Hall, Baton Rouge, LA 70803-2750
(225) 578-3103

Louisiana State University at Alexandria
Alexandria, Louisiana
www.lsua.edu   Federal Code: 002011

4-year public university in small city.
Enrollment: 2,940 undergrads, 47% part-time. 385 full-time freshmen.
Selectivity: Open admission.

BASIC COSTS (2005-2006)
Tuition and fees: $3,387; out-of-state residents $6,054.

FINANCIAL AID PICTURE
Students with need: Need-based aid available for full-time and part-time students. Work study available nights.
Students without need: No-need awards available for academics, state/district residency.

FINANCIAL AID PROCEDURES
Forms required: FAFSA, institutional form.
Dates and Deadlines: Priority date 4/1; no closing date. Applicants notified on a rolling basis starting 4/20; must reply within 3 week(s) of notification.

CONTACT
Kenn Posey, Director of Student Aid and Scholarships
8100 Highway 71 South, Alexandria, LA 71302-9121
(318) 473-6423

Louisiana State University Health Sciences Center
New Orleans, Louisiana
www.lsuhsc.edu   Federal Code: 002014

Upper-division public health science and nursing college in very large city.
Enrollment: 615 undergrads.

BASIC COSTS (2005-2006)
Tuition and fees: $3,978; out-of-state residents $7,110.
Room only: $2,210.

FINANCIAL AID PICTURE (2005-2006)
Students with need: 4% of average financial aid package awarded as scholarships/grants, 96% awarded as loans/jobs. Need-based aid available for part-time students. Work study available nights, weekends, and for part-time students.
Students without need: No-need awards available for academics.

FINANCIAL AID PROCEDURES
Forms required: FAFSA, institutional form.
Dates and Deadlines: Priority date 4/15; no closing date. Applicants notified on a rolling basis starting 7/1.
Transfers: Priority date 4/15.

CONTACT
Patrick Gorman, Director of Financial Aid
433 Bolivar Street, New Orleans, LA 70112-2223
(504) 568-4820

Louisiana State University in Shreveport
Shreveport, Louisiana
www.lsus.edu   Federal Code: 002013

4-year public university in large city.
Enrollment: 3,764 undergrads, 32% part-time. 415 full-time freshmen.

BASIC COSTS (2005-2006)
Tuition and fees: $3,270; out-of-state residents $7,600.
Room only: $3,510.

FINANCIAL AID PICTURE
Students with need: Need-based aid available for full-time and part-time students. Work study available nights, weekends, and for part-time students.

FINANCIAL AID PROCEDURES
Dates and Deadlines: No deadline. Applicants notified on a rolling basis.

CONTACT
Betty McCrary, Director of Student Financial Aid
One University Place, Shreveport, LA 71115-2399
(318) 797-5363

Louisiana Tech University
Ruston, Louisiana
www.latech.edu   Federal Code: 002008

4-year public university in large town.
Enrollment: 8,892 undergrads.
Selectivity: Admits over 75% of applicants.

BASIC COSTS (2005-2006)
Tuition and fees: $4,131; out-of-state residents $10,131.
Room and board: $4,056.

FINANCIAL AID PICTURE (2005-2006)
Students with need: Average financial aid package met 53% of need; average scholarship/grant was $4,271; average loan was $2,048. For part-time students, average financial aid package was $5,623.
Students without need: No-need awards available for academics, art, athletics, leadership, music/drama, ROTC.
Cumulative student debt: 82% of graduating class had student loans; average debt was $15,860.

FINANCIAL AID PROCEDURES
Forms required: FAFSA, institutional form.
Dates and Deadlines: Priority date 4/15; no closing date. Applicants notified on a rolling basis starting 3/18; must reply within 4 week(s) of notification.
Transfers: Priority date 8/1; no deadline. Applicants notified on a rolling basis starting 8/20; must reply within 2 week(s) of notification.

CONTACT
Roger Vick, Director of Student Financial Aid
Box 3178, Ruston, LA 71272
(318) 257-2641

Loyola University New Orleans
New Orleans, Louisiana
www.loyno.edu   Federal Code: 002016

4-year private university and liberal arts college in large city, affiliated with Roman Catholic Church.
Enrollment: 3,618 undergrads. 815 full-time freshmen.
Selectivity: Admits 50 to 75% of applicants.

BASIC COSTS (2005-2006)
Tuition and fees: $25,246.
Per-credit charge: $696.
Room and board: $8,312.

FINANCIAL AID PICTURE (2005-2006)
Students with need: Out of 612 full-time freshmen who applied for aid, 481 were judged to have need. Of these, 481 received aid, and 207 had their full need met. Average financial aid package met 86% of need; average scholarship/grant was $14,770; average loan was $4,730. For part-time students, average financial aid package was $8,042.
Students without need: 203 full-time freshmen who did not demonstrate need for aid received scholarships/grants; average award was $10,642. No-need awards available for academics, alumni affiliation, art, minority status, ROTC.
Scholarships offered: *Merit:* Interview recommended of scholarship applicants. *Athletic:* 6 full-time freshmen received athletic scholarships; average amount $15,565.

FINANCIAL AID PROCEDURES
Forms required: FAFSA.
Dates and Deadlines: Priority date 2/15; no closing date. Applicants notified on a rolling basis starting 3/1; must reply by 5/1 or within 2 week(s) of notification.

Transfers: Priority date 3/1; closing date 5/1. Transfer scholarship deadline June 1.

CONTACT
Catherine Simoneaux, Director of Scholarships and Financial Aid
6363 St. Charles Avenue, New Orleans, LA 70118-6195
(504) 865-3231

New Orleans School of Urban Missions
Gretna, Louisiana
www.sumonline.org   Federal Code: 037524

2-year private Bible college in very large city, affiliated with Assemblies of God, Church of God in Christ.
Enrollment: 129 undergrads, 73% part-time. 24 full-time freshmen.

BASIC COSTS (2006-2007)
Additional info: Average tuition is $6000 per trimester, but most students receive scholarships/grants/student loans/church donations; thus, out-of-pocket costs range from $600 to $1,400 per trimester.

FINANCIAL AID PICTURE (2004-2005)
Students with need: Need-based aid available for part-time students.
Students without need: No-need awards available for academics, leadership, religious affiliation.

FINANCIAL AID PROCEDURES
Forms required: FAFSA, institutional form.
Dates and Deadlines: No deadline.

CONTACT
Bob Hornick, Business Administrator
511 Westbank Expressway, Gretna, LA 70053

Nicholls State University
Thibodaux, Louisiana
www.nicholls.edu   Federal Code: 002005

4-year public university in large town.
Enrollment: 6,861 undergrads, 20% part-time. 1,583 full-time freshmen.
Selectivity: Admits 50 to 75% of applicants.

BASIC COSTS (2005-2006)
Tuition and fees: $3,390; out-of-state residents $8,838.
Room and board: $3,720.

FINANCIAL AID PICTURE (2004-2005)
Students with need: Out of 1,442 full-time freshmen who applied for aid, 924 were judged to have need. Of these, 911 received aid, and 592 had their full need met. Average financial aid package met 87% of need; average scholarship/grant was $3,094; average loan was $2,263. For part-time students, average financial aid package was $3,660.
Students without need: 62 full-time freshmen who did not demonstrate need for aid received scholarships/grants; average award was $2,730. No-need awards available for academics, athletics, state/district residency.
Scholarships offered: 32 full-time freshmen received athletic scholarships; average amount $3,449.

FINANCIAL AID PROCEDURES
Forms required: FAFSA, state aid form, institutional form.
Dates and Deadlines: Priority date 4/17; no closing date. Applicants notified on a rolling basis; must reply within 2 week(s) of notification.
Transfers: Priority date 5/1; no deadline. Applicants notified on a rolling basis.

CONTACT
Colette Lagarde, Director of Financial Aid
PO Box 2004-NSU, Thibodaux, LA 70310
(985) 448-4048

Northwestern State University
Natchitoches, Louisiana
www.nsula.edu   Federal Code: 002021

4-year public university in large town.
Enrollment: 8,559 undergrads, 25% part-time. 1,797 full-time freshmen.
Selectivity: Admits over 75% of applicants.

BASIC COSTS (2005-2006)
Tuition and fees: $3,423; out-of-state residents $9,501.
Room and board: $3,750.

FINANCIAL AID PICTURE (2004-2005)
Students with need: Out of 1,490 full-time freshmen who applied for aid, 1,049 were judged to have need. Of these, 1,049 received aid. Average financial aid package met 34% of need; average scholarship/grant was $7,199; average loan was $3,628. For part-time students, average financial aid package was $4,161.
Students without need: 456 full-time freshmen who did not demonstrate need for aid received scholarships/grants; average award was $3,753. No-need awards available for academics, alumni affiliation, art, athletics, job skills, leadership, minority status, music/drama, religious affiliation, ROTC, state/district residency.
Scholarships offered: *Merit:* A variety of talent, athletic, and academic scholarships offered to incoming freshmen. Students are urged to apply for financial aid and to apply for scholarships through the NSU Foundation. *Athletic:* 35 full-time freshmen received athletic scholarships; average amount $6,754.
Cumulative student debt: 68% of graduating class had student loans; average debt was $17,442.

FINANCIAL AID PROCEDURES
Forms required: FAFSA, institutional form.
Dates and Deadlines: Priority date 5/1; no closing date. Applicants notified on a rolling basis starting 5/1; must reply within 4 week(s) of notification.

CONTACT
Misti Chelette, Director of Financial Aid
Roy Hall, Room 209, Natchitoches, LA 71497
(318) 357-5488

Nunez Community College
Chalmette, Louisiana
www.nunez.edu   Federal Code: 015130

2-year public community and technical college in large town.
Enrollment: 1,960 undergrads.
Selectivity: Open admission; but selective for some programs.

BASIC COSTS (2005-2006)
Tuition and fees: $1,770; out-of-state residents $4,290.

FINANCIAL AID PICTURE (2005-2006)
Students with need: For part-time students, average financial aid package was $2,842.
Additional info: Pell Grants, Stafford Loans, campus workstudy, and tuition waiver scholarships available. Louisiana National Guard tuition exemption, teacher tuition exemption, dependents of injured fire-police tuition waivers.

FINANCIAL AID PROCEDURES
Forms required: FAFSA, institutional form.

Dates and Deadlines: Priority date 4/1; closing date 7/1. Applicants notified by 8/1; must reply by 8/15.
Transfers: Applicant must supply academic transcripts from every postsecondary school attended.

CONTACT
John Whisnant, Financial Aid Officer
3710 Paris Road, Chalmette, LA 70043
(504) 680-2428

Our Lady of Holy Cross College
New Orleans, Louisiana
www.olhcc.edu   Federal Code: 002023

4-year private liberal arts college in very large city, affiliated with Roman Catholic Church.
Enrollment: 1,316 undergrads.

BASIC COSTS (2005-2006)
Tuition and fees: $8,110.
Per-credit charge: $247.

FINANCIAL AID PICTURE
Students with need: Need-based aid available for full-time and part-time students. Work study available nights, weekends, and for part-time students.
Students without need: No-need awards available for academics, state/district residency.

FINANCIAL AID PROCEDURES
Forms required: FAFSA, institutional form.
Dates and Deadlines: Priority date 4/15; no closing date. Applicants notified on a rolling basis starting 5/15; must reply within 2 week(s) of notification.

CONTACT
Johnell Armer, Director of Financial Aid
4123 Woodland Drive, New Orleans, LA 70131-7399
(504) 394-7744

Our Lady of the Lake College
Baton Rouge, Louisiana
www.ololcollege.edu   Federal Code: 031062

4-year private nursing and liberal arts college in large city, affiliated with Roman Catholic Church.
Enrollment: 2,043 undergrads. 70 full-time freshmen.
Selectivity: Open admission; but selective for some programs.

BASIC COSTS (2005-2006)
Tuition and fees: $7,430.
Per-credit charge: $226.

FINANCIAL AID PICTURE (2004-2005)
Students with need: Need-based aid available for full-time students.
Cumulative student debt: 85% of graduating class had student loans; average debt was $10,000.

FINANCIAL AID PROCEDURES
Forms required: FAFSA.

CONTACT
Sharon Butler, Director of Financial Aid
7434 Perkins Road, Baton Rouge, LA 70808
(225) 768-1714

Remington College: Lafayette
Lafayette, Louisiana
www.educationamerica.com   Federal Code: 005203

2-year for-profit junior college in small city.
Enrollment: 400 undergrads.

BASIC COSTS (2005-2006)
Tuition and fees: $15,745.

FINANCIAL AID PICTURE
Students with need: Need-based aid available for full-time students. Work study available nights.
Students without need: This college only awards aid to students with need.

FINANCIAL AID PROCEDURES
Forms required: FAFSA, institutional form.
Dates and Deadlines: No deadline.

CONTACT
JoAnn Boudreaux, Director of Financial Aid
303 Rue Louis XIV, Lafayette, LA 70508
(337) 981-4010

St. Joseph Seminary College
St. Benedict, Louisiana
www.sjasc.edu   Federal Code: 002027

4-year private liberal arts and seminary college for men in rural community, affiliated with Roman Catholic Church.
Enrollment: 67 undergrads.

BASIC COSTS (2005-2006)
Tuition and fees: $13,685.
Room and board: $7,415.
Additional info: St. Joseph Abbey subsidizes $2400 per student per year (subject to change).

FINANCIAL AID PICTURE
Students with need: Need-based aid available for full-time and part-time students.
Students without need: No-need awards available for academics, leadership.

FINANCIAL AID PROCEDURES
Forms required: FAFSA.
Dates and Deadlines: Priority date 3/15; no closing date. Applicants notified on a rolling basis starting 7/1; must reply within 4 week(s) of notification.
Transfers: Closing date 5/1.

CONTACT
George Binder, Director of Student Financial Aid
75376 River Road, St. Benedict, LA 70457-9990
(985) 867-2229

Southeastern Louisiana University
Hammond, Louisiana
www.selu.edu   Federal Code: 002024

4-year public university in large town.
Enrollment: 14,334 undergrads, 19% part-time. 2,142 full-time freshmen.
Selectivity: Admits over 75% of applicants.

BASIC COSTS (2005-2006)
Tuition and fees: $3,121; out-of-state residents $8,449.
Room and board: $5,180.

FINANCIAL AID PICTURE (2004-2005)
Students with need: Out of 1,900 full-time freshmen who applied for aid, 1,382 were judged to have need. Of these, 1,216 received aid. For part-time students, average financial aid package was $4,163.
Students without need: 85 full-time freshmen who did not demonstrate need for aid received scholarships/grants; average award was $1,113. No-need awards available for academics, athletics, job skills, leadership, music/drama, state/district residency.
Scholarships offered: *Merit:* Any student admitted with a 24 or higher ACT and a minimum 3.0 cumulative GPA on a seven-semester transcript qualifies for a scholarship. All scholarships are awarded for eight semesters, with annual awards ranging from $500 to $3,500. In addition, all students with a 30 or higher ACT and a 3.5 minimum GPA qualify for the resident's Excellence Award covering tuition and fees, books, commuter meal plan and housing. *Athletic:* 7 full-time freshmen received athletic scholarships; average amount $2,088.
Cumulative student debt: 61% of graduating class had student loans; average debt was $15,793.

FINANCIAL AID PROCEDURES
Forms required: FAFSA, institutional form.
Dates and Deadlines: Priority date 5/1; no closing date. Applicants notified on a rolling basis starting 3/1; must reply within 2 week(s) of notification.
Transfers: Applicants notified on a rolling basis starting 3/1; must reply within 2 week(s) of notification. Financial aid is available for transfer students, including those admitted on probation.

CONTACT
Rosie Toney, Director of Financial Aid
SLU 10752, Hammond, LA 70402
(985) 549-2244

Southern University and Agricultural and Mechanical College
Baton Rouge, Louisiana
www.subr.edu   Federal Code: 002025

4-year public university in large city.
Enrollment: 8,493 undergrads, 9% part-time. 1,477 full-time freshmen.
Selectivity: Admits 50 to 75% of applicants.

BASIC COSTS (2005-2006)
Tuition and fees: $3,592; out-of-state residents $9,384.
Room and board: $4,646.

FINANCIAL AID PICTURE (2005-2006)
Students with need: Average financial aid package met 79% of need; average scholarship/grant was $1,778; average loan was $2,405. For part-time students, average financial aid package was $6,820.
Students without need: No-need awards available for academics, athletics, ROTC.
Cumulative student debt: 90% of graduating class had student loans; average debt was $25,000.

FINANCIAL AID PROCEDURES
Forms required: FAFSA, institutional form.
Dates and Deadlines: Closing date 3/31. Applicants notified on a rolling basis starting 6/30; must reply within 3 week(s) of notification.
Transfers: Priority date 5/31.

CONTACT
Phillip Rodgers, Director of Financial Aid
T.H. Harris Hall, Baton Rouge, LA 70813
(225) 771-2790

Southern University at New Orleans
New Orleans, Louisiana
www.suno.edu   Federal Code: 002026

4-year public university in very large city.
Enrollment: 3,282 undergrads.
Selectivity: Open admission.

BASIC COSTS (2005-2006)
Tuition and fees: $2,958; out-of-state residents $6,696.

FINANCIAL AID PICTURE
Students with need: Need-based aid available for full-time and part-time students.
Students without need: This college only awards aid to students with need.

FINANCIAL AID PROCEDURES
Forms required: FAFSA.
Dates and Deadlines: Closing date 4/1. Applicants notified by 5/15; must reply within 1 week(s) of notification.

CONTACT
Ursula Shorty, Director of Financial Aid
6400 Press Drive, New Orleans, LA 70126
(504) 286-5263

Tulane University
New Orleans, Louisiana
www.tulane.edu   Federal Code: 002029
                            CSS Code: 6832

4-year private university in very large city.
Enrollment: 7,954 undergrads. 1,600 full-time freshmen.
Selectivity: Admits less than 50% of applicants.

BASIC COSTS (2005-2006)
Tuition and fees: $32,946.
Per-credit charge: $1,264.
Room and board: $8,152.

FINANCIAL AID PICTURE (2004-2005)
Students with need: Out of 1,082 full-time freshmen who applied for aid, 769 were judged to have need. Of these, 768 received aid, and 486 had their full need met. Average financial aid package met 92% of need; average scholarship/grant was $17,764; average loan was $4,783. For part-time students, average financial aid package was $7,473.
Students without need: 470 full-time freshmen who did not demonstrate need for aid received scholarships/grants; average award was $16,491. No-need awards available for academics, athletics, ROTC.
Scholarships offered: *Merit:* Dean's Honor Scholarship: full tuition. Distinguished Scholars Award: up to $18,000. Founders Scholarship: up to $16,000. Urban Scholars Award: full tuition. *Athletic:* 41 full-time freshmen received athletic scholarships; average amount $24,377.
Additional info: Application deadline for merit scholarships December 1.

FINANCIAL AID PROCEDURES
Forms required: FAFSA, CSS PROFILE.
Dates and Deadlines: Priority date 1/15; closing date 2/1. Applicants notified on a rolling basis starting 2/1; must reply by 5/1 or within 2 week(s) of notification.

Transfers: Applicants notified on a rolling basis starting 2/1; must reply by 5/1 or within 2 week(s) of notification.

CONTACT
Kathryn Hill, Interim Director of Financial Aid
6823 St. Charles Avenue, New Orleans, LA 70118-5680
(504) 865-5723

University of Louisiana at Lafayette
Lafayette, Louisiana
www.louisiana.edu   Federal Code: 002031

4-year public university in small city.
Enrollment: 15,093 undergrads, 14% part-time. 2,830 full-time freshmen.
Selectivity: Admits over 75% of applicants.

BASIC COSTS (2005-2006)
Tuition and fees: $3,324; out-of-state residents $9,504.
Room and board: $3,478.

FINANCIAL AID PICTURE
Students with need: Need-based aid available for full-time and part-time students. Work study available nights, weekends, and for part-time students.
Students without need: This college only awards aid to students with need.

FINANCIAL AID PROCEDURES
Forms required: FAFSA, institutional form.
Dates and Deadlines: Priority date 5/1; no closing date. Applicants notified on a rolling basis starting 4/1; must reply within 2 week(s) of notification.

CONTACT
Cindy Perez, Director, Student Financial Aid
Box 41210, Lafayette, LA 70504-1210
(337) 482-6506

University of Louisiana at Monroe
Monroe, Louisiana
www.ulm.edu   Federal Code: 002020

4-year public university in small city.
Enrollment: 7,894 undergrads, 19% part-time. 1,505 full-time freshmen.
Selectivity: Admits over 75% of applicants.

BASIC COSTS (2005-2006)
Tuition and fees: $3,353; out-of-state residents $9,305.
Room and board: $6,140.

FINANCIAL AID PICTURE (2004-2005)
Students with need: Need-based aid available for part-time students.
Students without need: No-need awards available for academics, alumni affiliation, art, athletics, job skills, leadership, minority status, music/drama, religious affiliation, ROTC, state/district residency.

FINANCIAL AID PROCEDURES
Forms required: FAFSA.
Dates and Deadlines: Priority date 4/1; no closing date. Applicants notified on a rolling basis starting 6/1; must reply within 2 week(s) of notification.

CONTACT
Judith Cramer, Director of Financial Aid
700 University Avenue, Monroe, LA 71209-1160
(318) 342-5320

University of New Orleans
New Orleans, Louisiana
www.uno.edu   Federal Code: 002015

4-year public university in very large city.
Enrollment: 13,225 undergrads. 1,962 full-time freshmen.
Selectivity: Admits 50 to 75% of applicants.

BASIC COSTS (2005-2006)
Tuition and fees: $3,814; out-of-state residents $10,854.
Room only: $3,690.
Additional info: Tuition/fee waivers available for adults.

FINANCIAL AID PICTURE (2004-2005)
Students with need: Out of 1,767 full-time freshmen who applied for aid, 1,766 were judged to have need. Of these, 1,271 received aid, and 143 had their full need met. Average financial aid package met 64% of need; average scholarship/grant was $3,231; average loan was $2,477. For part-time students, average financial aid package was $4,276.
Students without need: 111 full-time freshmen who did not demonstrate need for aid received scholarships/grants; average award was $1,471. No-need awards available for academics, athletics.
Scholarships offered: 21 full-time freshmen received athletic scholarships; average amount $6,697.
Additional info: Students in good academic and financial standing eligible to participate in Extended Payment Plan option.

FINANCIAL AID PROCEDURES
Forms required: FAFSA, institutional form.
Dates and Deadlines: Priority date 5/15; no closing date. Applicants notified on a rolling basis starting 4/20; must reply within 4 week(s) of notification.
Transfers: Mid-year transfers must submit financial aid transcript from all post-secondary schools attended. Others submit NSLDS.

CONTACT
Emily London, Director of Student Financial Aid
Administrative Building Room 103, New Orleans, LA 70148
(504) 280-6603

Xavier University of Louisiana
New Orleans, Louisiana
www.xula.edu   Federal Code: 002032

4-year private university in very large city, affiliated with Roman Catholic Church.
Enrollment: 3,224 undergrads. 999 full-time freshmen.
Selectivity: Admits over 75% of applicants.

BASIC COSTS (2005-2006)
Tuition and fees: $12,900.
Per-credit charge: $500.
Room and board: $6,200.

FINANCIAL AID PICTURE (2005-2006)
Students with need: Out of 947 full-time freshmen who applied for aid, 792 were judged to have need. Of these, 791 received aid, and 4 had their full need met. Average financial aid package met 74% of need; average loan was $2,340. For part-time students, average financial aid package was $3,648.
Students without need: 68 full-time freshmen who did not demonstrate need for aid received scholarships/grants; average award was $3,215. No-need awards available for academics, art, athletics, music/drama, religious affiliation.
Scholarships offered: 15 full-time freshmen received athletic scholarships; average amount $6,181.

FINANCIAL AID PROCEDURES
Forms required: FAFSA.

Dates and Deadlines: Closing date 1/1. Applicants notified on a rolling basis starting 4/1; must reply within 2 week(s) of notification.

CONTACT
Mildred Higgins, Director of Financial Aid
One Drexel Drive, New Orleans, LA 70125-1098
(504) 520-7517

Maine

Bates College
Lewiston, Maine
www.bates.edu
Federal Code: 002036
CSS Code: 3076

4-year private liberal arts college in large town.
Enrollment: 1,684 undergrads. 490 full-time freshmen.
Selectivity: Admits less than 50% of applicants. GED not accepted.

BASIC COSTS (2006-2007)
Comprehensive fee: $44,350.

FINANCIAL AID PICTURE (2005-2006)
Students with need: Out of 239 full-time freshmen who applied for aid, 208 were judged to have need. Of these, 182 received aid, and 177 had their full need met. Average financial aid package met 100% of need; average scholarship/grant was $24,369; average loan was $3,282.
Students without need: This college only awards aid to students with need.
Cumulative student debt: 46% of graduating class had student loans; average debt was $13,636.
Additional info: Priority date for filing required financial aid forms for early decision students is 11/15.

FINANCIAL AID PROCEDURES
Forms required: FAFSA, CSS PROFILE.
Dates and Deadlines: Closing date 2/1. Applicants notified by 4/1; must reply by 5/1.

CONTACT
Catherine Ganung, Director of Student Financial Services
Lindholm House, 23 Campus Avenue, Lewiston, ME 04240-9917
(207) 786-6096

Bowdoin College
Brunswick, Maine
www.bowdoin.edu
Federal Code: 002038
CSS Code: 3089

4-year private liberal arts college in large town.
Enrollment: 1,660 undergrads. 470 full-time freshmen.
Selectivity: Admits less than 50% of applicants. GED not accepted.

BASIC COSTS (2005-2006)
Tuition and fees: $32,990.
Room and board: $8,670.

FINANCIAL AID PICTURE (2004-2005)
Students with need: Out of 258 full-time freshmen who applied for aid, 203 were judged to have need. Of these, 203 received aid, and 203 had their full need met. Average financial aid package met 100% of need; average scholarship/grant was $23,702; average loan was $3,268.
Students without need: 16 full-time freshmen who did not demonstrate need for aid received scholarships/grants; average award was $1,000. No-need awards available for academics, leadership.
Scholarships offered: National Merit Scholarships average $1,000 per year.

Cumulative student debt: 54% of graduating class had student loans; average debt was $15,300.
Additional info: Regardless of financial circumstances, students admitted will receive money they need to attend. International students for regular admission must submit their financial aid applications by January 1st.

FINANCIAL AID PROCEDURES
Forms required: FAFSA, CSS PROFILE, institutional form.
Dates and Deadlines: Closing date 2/15. Applicants notified by 4/5; must reply by 5/1 or within 1 week(s) of notification.
Transfers: Closing date 3/1. Applicants notified by 4/5; must reply by 5/1 or within 1 week(s) of notification. Financial aid is usually not available for transfer students. Early Decision applicants must submit their financial aid applications by November 15th (ED I) and January 1st (ED II).

CONTACT
Stephen Joyce, Director of Student Aid
5000 College Station, Brunswick, ME 04011-8441
(207) 725-3273

Central Maine Community College
Auburn, Maine
www.cmcc.edu
Federal Code: 005276

2-year public community and technical college in small city.
Enrollment: 1,644 undergrads. 606 full-time freshmen.
Selectivity: Open admission; but selective for some programs.

BASIC COSTS (2005-2006)
Tuition and fees: $3,096; out-of-state residents $5,556.
Per-credit charge: $74; out-of-state residents $156.
Room and board: $5,050.
Additional info: New England Regional tuition: $111 per- credit-hour. Tuition/fee waivers available for minority students.

FINANCIAL AID PICTURE (2004-2005)
Students with need: Out of 606 full-time freshmen who applied for aid, 514 were judged to have need. Of these, 382 received aid, and 53 had their full need met. Average financial aid package met 56% of need; average scholarship/grant was $2,639; average loan was $1,396. For part-time students, average financial aid package was $3,463.
Students without need: This college only awards aid to students with need.
Cumulative student debt: 66% of graduating class had student loans; average debt was $4,747.
Additional info: Tuition and/or fee waivers may be available to orphans, Native Americans, fire fighters, police, disabled veterans, dependents or survivors of veterans killed in line of duty.

FINANCIAL AID PROCEDURES
Forms required: FAFSA, institutional form.
Dates and Deadlines: Priority date 5/1; no closing date. Applicants notified on a rolling basis starting 3/15; must reply within 2 week(s) of notification.

CONTACT
Michael Roy, Financial Aid Director
1250 Turner Street, Auburn, ME 04210
(207) 755-5269

Central Maine Medical Center School of Nursing
Lewiston, Maine
www.cmmcson.edu
Federal Code: 006305

2-year private nursing college in large town.
Enrollment: 124 undergrads, 85% part-time. 99 full-time freshmen.

Selectivity: Admits less than 50% of applicants.

BASIC COSTS (2005-2006)
Tuition and fees: $5,345.
Per-credit charge: $138.
Room and board: $3,350.

FINANCIAL AID PICTURE (2004-2005)
Students with need: Out of 89 full-time freshmen who applied for aid, 89 were judged to have need. Of these, 89 received aid. Average financial aid package met 34% of need; average scholarship/grant was $3,400; average loan was $2,625. Need-based aid available for part-time students.
Students without need: This college only awards aid to students with need.
Cumulative student debt: 78% of graduating class had student loans; average debt was $14,125.

FINANCIAL AID PROCEDURES
Forms required: FAFSA, institutional form.
Dates and Deadlines: Priority date 5/1; closing date 7/1. Applicants notified on a rolling basis starting 4/1; must reply within 2 week(s) of notification.

CONTACT
Keith Bourgault, Financial Aid Director
70 Middle Street, Lewiston, ME 04240
(207) 795-2270

Colby College
Waterville, Maine
www.colby.edu   Federal Code: 002039

4-year private liberal arts college in large town.
Enrollment: 1,868 undergrads. 511 full-time freshmen.
Selectivity: Admits less than 50% of applicants.

BASIC COSTS (2006-2007)
Comprehensive fee: $44,080.

FINANCIAL AID PICTURE (2005-2006)
Students with need: Out of 267 full-time freshmen who applied for aid, 213 were judged to have need. Of these, 213 received aid, and 213 had their full need met. Average financial aid package met 100% of need; average scholarship/grant was $27,190; average loan was $3,043.
Students without need: This college only awards aid to students with need.
Cumulative student debt: 43% of graduating class had student loans; average debt was $18,479.

FINANCIAL AID PROCEDURES
Forms required: FAFSA.
Dates and Deadlines: Closing date 2/1. Applicants notified by 4/1; must reply by 5/1.
Transfers: Priority date 2/1; closing date 3/1.

CONTACT
Lucia Whittelsey, Director of Financial Aid
4800 Mayflower Hill, Waterville, ME 04901-8848
(800) 723-3032

College of the Atlantic
Bar Harbor, Maine
www.coa.edu   Federal Code: 011385

4-year private liberal arts college in small town.
Enrollment: 295 undergrads, 2% part-time. 84 full-time freshmen.
Selectivity: Admits 50 to 75% of applicants.

BASIC COSTS (2006-2007)
Tuition and fees: $28,140.
Room and board: $7,710.

FINANCIAL AID PICTURE (2005-2006)
Students with need: Out of 79 full-time freshmen who applied for aid, 76 were judged to have need. Of these, 76 received aid, and 74 had their full need met. Average financial aid package met 98% of need; average scholarship/grant was $20,017; average loan was $2,977. For part-time students, average financial aid package was $13,500.
Students without need: 6 full-time freshmen who did not demonstrate need for aid received scholarships/grants; average award was $5,250. No-need awards available for academics, leadership.
Scholarships offered: Students may be nominated during the admission process as a Presidential Scholar that may provide travel and/or research stipend and or grant money.
Cumulative student debt: 71% of graduating class had student loans; average debt was $16,706.

FINANCIAL AID PROCEDURES
Forms required: FAFSA, institutional form.
Dates and Deadlines: Closing date 2/15. Applicants notified by 4/1; must reply by 5/1.
Transfers: Priority date 2/15. Applicants notified by 4/1; must reply by 5/1. FAFSA must be filed by 5/1 for Maine residents to be eligible for Maine state grant.

CONTACT
Bruce Hazam, Director of Financial Aid
105 Eden Street, Bar Harbor, ME 04609
(207) 288-5015 ext. 232

Eastern Maine Community College
Bangor, Maine
www.emcc.edu   Federal Code: 005277

2-year public community and technical college in large town.
Enrollment: 1,458 undergrads, 34% part-time. 434 full-time freshmen.
Selectivity: Open admission; but selective for some programs.

BASIC COSTS (2005-2006)
Tuition and fees: $2,730; out-of-state residents $5,190.
Per-credit charge: $74; out-of-state residents $156.
Room and board: $5,588.
Additional info: New England Regional tuition: $110 per credit hour. Laboratory and technology fees vary with program. Tuition/fee waivers available for minority students.

FINANCIAL AID PICTURE (2004-2005)
Students with need: 66% of average financial aid package awarded as scholarships/grants, 34% awarded as loans/jobs. Need-based aid available for part-time students. Work study available nights, weekends, and for part-time students.
Students without need: This college only awards aid to students with need.

FINANCIAL AID PROCEDURES
Forms required: FAFSA, institutional form.
Dates and Deadlines: Priority date 5/1; no closing date. Applicants notified on a rolling basis starting 5/1; must reply within 3 week(s) of notification.

CONTACT
Candace Ward, Registrar/Financial Aid Director
354 Hogan Road, Bangor, ME 04401
(207) 974-4625

Husson College
Bangor, Maine
www.husson.edu   Federal Code: 002043

4-year private business and health science college in large town.
Enrollment: 1,877 undergrads, 16% part-time. 334 full-time freshmen.
Selectivity: Admits over 75% of applicants.

BASIC COSTS (2006-2007)
Tuition and fees: $11,770.
Per-credit charge: $384.
Room and board: $6,240.

FINANCIAL AID PICTURE (2005-2006)
Students with need: Average financial aid package met 75% of need; average scholarship/grant was $6,038; average loan was $2,304. For part-time students, average financial aid package was $5,816.
Students without need: No-need awards available for academics, leadership.
Scholarships offered: Scholarships awarded based on academics and leadership, ranging from $1,000 to full tuition. Number available varies year to year. Also offer full-tuition scholarships to graduates ranked 1st or 2nd in their senior class at public comprehensive or public academic high schools in Maine.
Cumulative student debt: 80% of graduating class had student loans; average debt was $18,625.

FINANCIAL AID PROCEDURES
Forms required: FAFSA.
Dates and Deadlines: Priority date 4/15; no closing date. Applicants notified on a rolling basis starting 4/1; must reply by 5/1 or within 2 week(s) of notification.
Transfers: No deadline. Applicants notified on a rolling basis starting 2/20.

CONTACT
Linda Conant, Director of Financial Aid
One College Circle, Bangor, ME 04401
(207) 941-7156

Kennebec Valley Community College
Fairfield, Maine
www.kvcc.me.edu   Federal Code: 009826

2-year public community and technical college in small town.
Enrollment: 1,316 undergrads, 60% part-time. 165 full-time freshmen.
Selectivity: Open admission; but selective for some programs.

BASIC COSTS (2005-2006)
Tuition and fees: $2,595; out-of-state residents $5,055.
Per-credit charge: $74; out-of-state residents $156.
Additional info: New England Regional tuition: $3,060 full-time, $102 per credit hour. Health insurance required if student does not have own insurance. Lab fees vary depending on course.

FINANCIAL AID PICTURE
Students with need: Need-based aid available for full-time and part-time students.

FINANCIAL AID PROCEDURES
Forms required: FAFSA, institutional form.
Dates and Deadlines: Priority date 3/1; no closing date. Applicants notified on a rolling basis starting 5/1.

CONTACT
Anne Connors, Director of Financial Aid
92 Western Avenue, Fairfield, ME 04937-1367
(207) 453-5121

Maine College of Art
Portland, Maine
www.meca.edu   Federal Code: 011673

4-year private visual arts college in small city.
Enrollment: 449 undergrads.

BASIC COSTS (2005-2006)
Tuition and fees: $24,030.
Per-credit charge: $975.
Room and board: $8,692.
Additional info: Studio fees vary per class.

FINANCIAL AID PICTURE (2005-2006)
Students with need: Average financial aid package met 57% of need; average scholarship/grant was $11,023; average loan was $3,468. For part-time students, average financial aid package was $7,830.
Students without need: No-need awards available for academics, art.

FINANCIAL AID PROCEDURES
Forms required: FAFSA.
Dates and Deadlines: Priority date 3/15; closing date 4/15. Applicants notified on a rolling basis starting 2/15; must reply within 2 week(s) of notification.

CONTACT
Michelle LeClerc, Director of Financial Aid
97 Spring Street, Portland, ME 04101
(207) 879-5742 ext. 374

Maine Maritime Academy
Castine, Maine
www.mainemaritime.edu   Federal Code: 002044

4-year public engineering and technical and maritime college in rural community.
Enrollment: 846 undergrads, 12% part-time. 241 full-time freshmen.

BASIC COSTS (2005-2006)
Tuition and fees: $7,620; out-of-district residents $10,810; out-of-state residents $13,550.
Per-credit charge: $230; out-of-district residents $345; out-of-state residents $410.
Room and board: $6,720.
Additional info: Cruise fee of $2,600 for U.S. Coast Guard Licensing Program.

FINANCIAL AID PICTURE (2005-2006)
Students with need: Need-based aid available for part-time students. Work study available nights, weekends, and for part-time students.
Students without need: No-need awards available for academics, leadership, state/district residency.

FINANCIAL AID PROCEDURES
Forms required: FAFSA, institutional form.
Dates and Deadlines: Priority date 4/15; no closing date. Applicants notified on a rolling basis starting 3/1; must reply within 4 week(s) of notification.
Transfers: Priority date 6/1.

CONTACT
Kathey Heath, Financial Aid Officer
66 Pleasant Street, Castine, ME 04420
(207) 326-2339

New England School of Communications
Bangor, Maine
www.nescom.edu   Federal Code: 023471

4-year private college of communications in small city.
Enrollment: 305 undergrads, 3% part-time. 112 full-time freshmen.
Selectivity: Admits 50 to 75% of applicants.

BASIC COSTS (2005-2006)
Tuition and fees: $9,440.
Room and board: $6,030.

FINANCIAL AID PICTURE (2005-2006)
Students with need: Average financial aid package met 94% of need; average scholarship/grant was $1,400; average loan was $2,625. For part-time students, average financial aid package was $2,000.
Students without need: No-need awards available for academics, leadership.
Scholarships offered: Scholarships are merit based for second semester.
Cumulative student debt: 19% of graduating class had student loans; average debt was $17,125.

FINANCIAL AID PROCEDURES
Forms required: FAFSA, institutional form.
Dates and Deadlines: Priority date 4/15; no closing date. Applicants notified on a rolling basis starting 2/1; must reply by 8/15.
Transfers: No deadline. Applicants notified on a rolling basis starting 2/15; must reply within 4 week(s) of notification.

CONTACT
Nicole Rediker, Director of Financial Aid
One College Circle, Bangor, ME 04401
(207) 941-7176

Northern Maine Community College
Presque Isle, Maine
www.nmcc.edu   Federal Code: 005760

2-year public technical college in small town.
Enrollment: 839 undergrads.

BASIC COSTS (2005-2006)
Tuition and fees: $2,582; out-of-state residents $5,042.
Per-credit charge: $74; out-of-state residents $156.
Room and board: $4,490.
Additional info: New England Regional Student Program tuition: $3,060 full-time, $102 per credit hour. Tuition/fee waivers available for minority students.

FINANCIAL AID PICTURE
Students with need: Need-based aid available for full-time and part-time students.

FINANCIAL AID PROCEDURES
Forms required: FAFSA, institutional form.
Dates and Deadlines: Priority date 5/1; no closing date. Applicants notified on a rolling basis starting 4/15; must reply within 2 week(s) of notification.

CONTACT
Norma Smith, Assistant Financial Aid Director
33 Edgemont Drive, Presque Isle, ME 04769
(207) 768-2790

St. Joseph's College
Standish, Maine
www.sjcme.edu   Federal Code: 002051

4-year private liberal arts college in small town, affiliated with Roman Catholic Church.
Enrollment: 944 undergrads, 2% part-time. 266 full-time freshmen.
Selectivity: Admits over 75% of applicants.

BASIC COSTS (2006-2007)
Tuition and fees: $21,550.
Per-credit charge: $350.
Room and board: $8,980.

FINANCIAL AID PICTURE (2005-2006)
Students with need: 62% of average financial aid package awarded as scholarships/grants, 38% awarded as loans/jobs. Need-based aid available for part-time students. Work study available nights, weekends, and for part-time students.
Students without need: No-need awards available for academics, leadership.

FINANCIAL AID PROCEDURES
Forms required: FAFSA, institutional form.
Dates and Deadlines: Priority date 3/1; no closing date. Applicants notified on a rolling basis starting 3/1; must reply within 3 week(s) of notification.

CONTACT
Andrea Cross, Associate Dean for Financial Aid
278 Whites Bridge Road, Standish, ME 04084
(207) 892-6612

Southern Maine Community College
South Portland, Maine
www.smccme.edu   Federal Code: 005525

2-year public community and technical college in large town.
Enrollment: 3,720 undergrads, 40% part-time.
Selectivity: Open admission; but selective for some programs.

BASIC COSTS (2005-2006)
Tuition and fees: $2,870; out-of-state residents $5,330.
Per-credit charge: $74; out-of-state residents $156.
Room and board: $5,824.

FINANCIAL AID PICTURE
Students with need: Need-based aid available for full-time and part-time students. Work study available nights, weekends, and for part-time students.
Students without need: This college only awards aid to students with need.

FINANCIAL AID PROCEDURES
Forms required: FAFSA.
Dates and Deadlines: Priority date 3/30; no closing date. Applicants notified on a rolling basis; must reply by 5/1 or within 2 week(s) of notification.

CONTACT
Scott MacDonald, Director of Financial Aid, Transfer and Employment Services
2 Fort Road, South Portland, ME 04106
(207) 741-5518

Thomas College
Waterville, Maine
www.thomas.edu   Federal Code: 002052

4-year private business and liberal arts college in large town.
Enrollment: 700 undergrads, 15% part-time. 193 full-time freshmen.
Selectivity: Admits 50 to 75% of applicants.

BASIC COSTS (2006-2007)
Tuition and fees: $17,730.
Per-credit charge: $720.
Room and board: $7,430.

FINANCIAL AID PICTURE (2005-2006)
Students with need: Out of 183 full-time freshmen who applied for aid, 165 were judged to have need. Of these, 165 received aid, and 31 had their full need met. Average financial aid package met 85% of need; average scholarship/grant was $11,129; average loan was $3,405. For part-time students, average financial aid package was $3,950.
Students without need: 41 full-time freshmen who did not demonstrate need for aid received scholarships/grants; average award was $4,060. No-need awards available for academics, leadership, state/district residency.
Cumulative student debt: 78% of graduating class had student loans; average debt was $19,125.

FINANCIAL AID PROCEDURES
Forms required: FAFSA.
Dates and Deadlines: Priority date 2/15; no closing date. Applicants notified on a rolling basis starting 3/15; must reply within 2 week(s) of notification.

CONTACT
Jeannine Bosse, Associate Director of Student Financial Services
180 West River Road, Waterville, ME 04901
(207) 859-1105

Unity College
Unity, Maine
www.unity.edu   Federal Code: 006858

4-year private liberal arts college in rural community.
Enrollment: 518 undergrads.

BASIC COSTS (2006-2007)
Tuition and fees: $18,530.
Per-credit charge: $660.
Room and board: $6,970.

FINANCIAL AID PICTURE
Students with need: Need-based aid available for full-time and part-time students. Work study available nights, weekends, and for part-time students.
Students without need: No-need awards available for academics, leadership, minority status.

FINANCIAL AID PROCEDURES
Forms required: FAFSA.
Dates and Deadlines: Priority date 3/1; no closing date. Applicants notified on a rolling basis starting 2/15.

CONTACT
Rand Newell, Director of Financial Aid
90 Quaker Hill Road, Unity, ME 04988-0532
(207) 948-3131 ext. 201

University of Maine
Orono, Maine
www.umaine.edu   Federal Code: 002053

4-year public university in large town.
Enrollment: 8,496 undergrads, 11% part-time. 1,736 full-time freshmen.
Selectivity: Admits over 75% of applicants.

BASIC COSTS (2005-2006)
Tuition and fees: $6,910; out-of-state residents $17,050.
Per-credit charge: $184; out-of-state residents $522.
Room and board: $6,722.
Additional info: New England Regional Student Program tuition is 150% of public in-district tuition.

FINANCIAL AID PICTURE (2005-2006)
Students with need: Average financial aid package met 82% of need; average scholarship/grant was $5,909; average loan was $3,202. For part-time students, average financial aid package was $7,310.
Students without need: No-need awards available for academics, alumni affiliation, art, athletics, job skills, leadership, minority status, music/drama, religious affiliation, ROTC, state/district residency.
Scholarships offered: Academic merit scholarships range in value from $1,000 to full tuition. All awards are renewable for up to eight (8) consecutive semesters, based upon academic performance. Top Scholar Awards and Tuition Scholarships pay full resident tuition or full nonresident differential per semester each academic year.
Cumulative student debt: 75% of graduating class had student loans; average debt was $20,930.
Additional info: Financial aid is available for students entering in the spring.

FINANCIAL AID PROCEDURES
Forms required: FAFSA.
Dates and Deadlines: Priority date 3/1; no closing date. Applicants notified on a rolling basis starting 3/15; must reply by 5/1 or within 2 week(s) of notification.

CONTACT
Peggy Crawford, Director of Student Financial Aid
5713 Chadbourne Hall, Orono, ME 04469-5713
(207) 581-1324

University of Maine at Augusta
Augusta, Maine
www.uma.maine.edu   Federal Code: 006760

4-year public university and community college in large town.
Enrollment: 4,362 undergrads, 66% part-time. 301 full-time freshmen.
Selectivity: Open admission; but selective for some programs.

BASIC COSTS (2005-2006)
Tuition and fees: $5,025; out-of-state residents $11,115.
Per-credit charge: $143; out-of-state residents $346.
Additional info: New England Regional Student Program tuition is 150% of public in-district tuition.

FINANCIAL AID PICTURE (2005-2006)
Students with need: Out of 301 full-time freshmen who applied for aid, 277 were judged to have need. Of these, 264 received aid, and 37 had their full need met. Average financial aid package met 64% of need; average scholarship/grant was $4,128; average loan was $2,689. For part-time students, average financial aid package was $4,198.
Students without need: 29 full-time freshmen who did not demonstrate need for aid received scholarships/grants; average award was $3,400. No-need awards available for academics, athletics, leadership, music/drama, state/district residency.

Scholarships offered: 1 full-time freshmen received athletic scholarships; average amount $1,750.
Cumulative student debt: 62% of graduating class had student loans; average debt was $12,861.

FINANCIAL AID PROCEDURES
Forms required: FAFSA.
Dates and Deadlines: Priority date 3/1; no closing date. Applicants notified on a rolling basis starting 3/15; must reply within 2 week(s) of notification.

CONTACT
Leslie McCormick, Coordinator of Student Financial Aid
46 University Drive, Augusta, ME 04330
(207) 621-3455

University of Maine at Farmington
Farmington, Maine
www.umf.maine.edu   Federal Code: 002040

4-year public liberal arts and teachers college in small town.
Enrollment: 2,278 undergrads, 8% part-time. 510 full-time freshmen.
Selectivity: Admits 50 to 75% of applicants.

BASIC COSTS (2005-2006)
Tuition and fees: $5,541; out-of-state residents $12,771.
Per-credit charge: $167; out-of-state residents $408.
Room and board: $5,984.
Additional info: New England Regional Student Program tuition is 150% of public in-district tuition. Tuition/fee waivers available for minority students.

FINANCIAL AID PICTURE (2004-2005)
Students with need: Out of 473 full-time freshmen who applied for aid, 358 were judged to have need. Of these, 357 received aid, and 44 had their full need met. Average financial aid package met 69% of need; average scholarship/grant was $4,496; average loan was $2,849. For part-time students, average financial aid package was $6,883.
Students without need: 18 full-time freshmen who did not demonstrate need for aid received scholarships/grants; average award was $2,855. No-need awards available for academics, leadership, minority status, state/district residency.
Scholarships offered: Presidential Scholarships; $2,000 renewable annually; for non-residents graduating in top half of high school class.
Cumulative student debt: 78% of graduating class had student loans; average debt was $17,482.
Additional info: FAFSA must arrive at Federal processor by 3/1.

FINANCIAL AID PROCEDURES
Forms required: FAFSA.
Dates and Deadlines: Priority date 3/1; no closing date. Applicants notified on a rolling basis starting 3/15; must reply within 2 week(s) of notification.

CONTACT
Ronald Milliken, Director of Financial Aid
246 Main Street, Farmington, ME 04938-1994
(207) 778-7100

University of Maine at Fort Kent
Fort Kent, Maine
www.umfk.maine.edu   Federal Code: 002041

4-year public university in small town.
Enrollment: 869 undergrads, 15% part-time. 129 full-time freshmen.
Selectivity: Open admission; but selective for some programs.

BASIC COSTS (2005-2006)
Tuition and fees: $4,844; out-of-state residents $10,934.
Per-credit charge: $143; out-of-state residents $346.
Room and board: $5,984.
Additional info: New England Regional tuition is 150% of public in-district tuition.

FINANCIAL AID PICTURE (2005-2006)
Students with need: Average financial aid package met 70% of need; average scholarship/grant was $3,218; average loan was $2,647. Need-based aid available for part-time students.
Students without need: No-need awards available for academics.
Cumulative student debt: 59% of graduating class had student loans; average debt was $12,207.

FINANCIAL AID PROCEDURES
Forms required: FAFSA.
Dates and Deadlines: Priority date 3/1; no closing date. Applicants notified on a rolling basis starting 3/15; must reply within 2 week(s) of notification.

CONTACT
Ellen Cost, Director of Financial Aid
23 University Drive, Fort Kent, ME 04743
(207) 834-7607

University of Maine at Machias
Machias, Maine
www.umm.maine.edu   Federal Code: 002055

4-year public university and liberal arts college in rural community.
Enrollment: 578 undergrads, 21% part-time. 82 full-time freshmen.
Selectivity: Admits over 75% of applicants.

BASIC COSTS (2005-2006)
Tuition and fees: $4,845; out-of-state residents $12,195.
Per-credit charge: $143; out-of-state residents $388.
Room and board: $5,678.
Additional info: New England Regional Student Program tuition is 150% of public in-district tuition. Tuition/fee waivers available for minority students.

FINANCIAL AID PICTURE (2005-2006)
Students with need: Out of 76 full-time freshmen who applied for aid, 67 were judged to have need. Of these, 67 received aid, and 13 had their full need met. Average financial aid package met 79% of need; average scholarship/grant was $5,030; average loan was $2,990. For part-time students, average financial aid package was $5,853.
Students without need: 4 full-time freshmen who did not demonstrate need for aid received scholarships/grants; average award was $9,805. No-need awards available for academics, alumni affiliation, art, job skills, leadership, minority status, music/drama, state/district residency.

FINANCIAL AID PROCEDURES
Forms required: FAFSA.
Dates and Deadlines: Priority date 3/1; no closing date. Applicants notified on a rolling basis starting 2/15; must reply within 2 week(s) of notification.

CONTACT
Stephanie Larrabee, Director of Financial Aid
9 O'Brien Avenue, Machias, ME 04654
(207) 255-1203

University of Maine at Presque Isle
Presque Isle, Maine
www.umpi.maine.edu   Federal Code: 002033

4-year public university in small town.
Enrollment: 1,325 undergrads, 17% part-time. 188 full-time freshmen.
Selectivity: Admits over 75% of applicants.

BASIC COSTS (2005-2006)
Tuition and fees: $4,820; out-of-state residents $11,210.
Per-credit charge: $143; out-of-state residents $356.
Room and board: $5,246.
Additional info: Tuition/fee waivers available for minority students.

FINANCIAL AID PICTURE (2005-2006)
Students with need: Out of 187 full-time freshmen who applied for aid, 160 were judged to have need. Of these, 138 received aid, and 56 had their full need met. Average financial aid package met 89% of need; average scholarship/grant was $5,288; average loan was $2,499. For part-time students, average financial aid package was $4,678.
Students without need: 19 full-time freshmen who did not demonstrate need for aid received scholarships/grants; average award was $4,390. No-need awards available for academics, alumni affiliation, art, job skills, leadership, minority status, music/drama, state/district residency.
Cumulative student debt: 33% of graduating class had student loans; average debt was $11,181.

FINANCIAL AID PROCEDURES
Forms required: FAFSA.
Dates and Deadlines: Priority date 4/1; no closing date. Applicants notified on a rolling basis starting 3/1; must reply within 2 week(s) of notification.

CONTACT
Barbara Bridges, Director of Financial Aid
181 Main Street, Presque Isle, ME 04769
(207) 768-9510

University of New England
Biddeford, Maine
www.une.edu   Federal Code: 002050

4-year private university in small city.
Enrollment: 1,599 undergrads, 7% part-time. 464 full-time freshmen.
Selectivity: Admits over 75% of applicants.

BASIC COSTS (2006-2007)
Tuition and fees: $23,790.
Per-credit charge: $825.
Room and board: $9,255.

FINANCIAL AID PICTURE (2005-2006)
Students with need: Out of 440 full-time freshmen who applied for aid, 387 were judged to have need. Of these, 387 received aid, and 82 had their full need met. Average financial aid package met 76% of need; average scholarship/grant was $11,382; average loan was $4,294. For part-time students, average financial aid package was $13,159.
Students without need: 76 full-time freshmen who did not demonstrate need for aid received scholarships/grants; average award was $8,169. No-need awards available for academics, alumni affiliation, leadership.
Scholarships offered: UNE Scholarships and UNE Departmental Award; award amounts range from $1,000 to $12,000; non-need, based on academic qualifications as determined from GPA and SAT/ACT scores, must be a full-time undergraduate student and maintain a 2.5 GPA.
Cumulative student debt: 88% of graduating class had student loans; average debt was $37,507.

FINANCIAL AID PROCEDURES
Forms required: FAFSA.
Dates and Deadlines: Priority date 5/1; no closing date. Applicants notified on a rolling basis starting 1/25.

CONTACT
John Bowie, Director of Financial Aid
Hills Beach Road, Biddeford, ME 04005
(207) 283-0170 ext. 2342

University of Southern Maine
Gorham, Maine
www.usm.maine.edu   Federal Code: 009762

4-year public university and liberal arts college in small city.
Enrollment: 6,895 undergrads, 32% part-time. 914 full-time freshmen.
Selectivity: Admits over 75% of applicants.

BASIC COSTS (2005-2006)
Tuition and fees: $5,695; out-of-state residents $14,515.
Per-credit charge: $166; out-of-state residents $460.
Room and board: $6,689.
Additional info: New England Regional Student Program tuition is 150% of public in-district tuition. Tuition/fee waivers available for minority students.

FINANCIAL AID PICTURE (2005-2006)
Students with need: Out of 707 full-time freshmen who applied for aid, 555 were judged to have need. Of these, 531 received aid, and 100 had their full need met. Average financial aid package met 71% of need; average scholarship/grant was $4194.31; average loan was $2,988. For part-time students, average financial aid package was $6,530.
Students without need: 113 full-time freshmen who did not demonstrate need for aid received scholarships/grants; average award was $3,379. No-need awards available for academics, music/drama.
Scholarships offered: $1,500 in-state, $3,500 and $5,500 out-of-state; based on academic record, school/community leadership, and potential for intellectual/social contribution.
Cumulative student debt: 50% of graduating class had student loans; average debt was $21,800.

FINANCIAL AID PROCEDURES
Forms required: FAFSA.
Dates and Deadlines: Priority date 2/15; no closing date. Applicants notified on a rolling basis starting 3/15; must reply by 5/1 or within 2 week(s) of notification.

CONTACT
Keith Dubois, Director of Financial Aid Office
37 College Avenue, Gorham, ME 04038
(207) 780-5250

Washington County Community College
Calais, Maine
www.wccc.me.edu   Federal Code: 009231

2-year public community and technical college in small town.
Enrollment: 400 undergrads.
Selectivity: Open admission; but selective for some programs.

BASIC COSTS (2005-2006)
Tuition and fees: $2,745; out-of-state residents $5,205.
Per-credit charge: $74; out-of-state residents $156.
Room only: $2,216.
Additional info: New England Regional Student Program tuition: $111 per-credit-hour.

Maine Washington County Community College

FINANCIAL AID PICTURE
Students with need: Need-based aid available for full-time and part-time students.
Students without need: No-need awards available for academics.

FINANCIAL AID PROCEDURES
Forms required: FAFSA, institutional form.
Dates and Deadlines: Priority date 5/1; no closing date. Applicants notified on a rolling basis starting 6/1; must reply within 2 week(s) of notification.

CONTACT
Joyce Maker, Director of Financial Aid
One College Drive, Calais, ME 04619
(207) 454-1033

York County Community College
Wells, Maine
www.yccc.edu   Federal Code: 031229

2-year public community and technical college in small town.
Enrollment: 670 undergrads. 78 full-time freshmen.
Selectivity: Open admission.

BASIC COSTS (2005-2006)
Tuition and fees: $2,760; out-of-state residents $5,220.
Per-credit charge: $74; out-of-state residents $156.
Additional info: New England Regional tuition:$111 per credit hour. Lecture and lab fees may vary per class. Tuition/fee waivers available for minority students.

FINANCIAL AID PICTURE (2004-2005)
Students with need: Out of 78 full-time freshmen who applied for aid, 61 were judged to have need. Of these, 61 received aid, and 6 had their full need met. Average financial aid package met 62% of need; average scholarship/grant was $3,101; average loan was $1,629. For part-time students, average financial aid package was $2,932.
Students without need: 9 full-time freshmen who did not demonstrate need for aid received scholarships/grants; average award was $2,285. No-need awards available for academics, art, leadership.
Cumulative student debt: 54% of graduating class had student loans; average debt was $7,129.

FINANCIAL AID PROCEDURES
Forms required: FAFSA.
Dates and Deadlines: Priority date 5/1; no closing date. Applicants notified by 3/1; must reply within 2 week(s) of notification.

CONTACT
David Daigle, Director of Financial Aid
112 College Drive, Wells, ME 04090
(207) 646-9282 ext. 309

Maryland

Allegany College of Maryland
Cumberland, Maryland
www.allegany.edu   Federal Code: 002057

2-year public community college in large town.
Enrollment: 2,903 undergrads, 29% part-time. 711 full-time freshmen.
Selectivity: Open admission; but selective for some programs.

BASIC COSTS (2005-2006)
Tuition and fees: $3,005; out-of-district residents $5,465; out-of-state residents $6,365.
Per-credit charge: $90; out-of-district residents $172; out-of-state residents $202.

FINANCIAL AID PICTURE (2004-2005)
Students with need: Out of 661 full-time freshmen who applied for aid, 510 were judged to have need. Of these, 493 received aid, and 41 had their full need met. Average financial aid package met 65% of need; average scholarship/grant was $3,266; average loan was $2,135. For part-time students, average financial aid package was $3,045.
Students without need: 151 full-time freshmen who did not demonstrate need for aid received scholarships/grants; average award was $2,388. No-need awards available for academics, athletics, leadership, state/district residency.
Cumulative student debt: 55% of graduating class had student loans; average debt was $7,113.

FINANCIAL AID PROCEDURES
Forms required: FAFSA.
Dates and Deadlines: Priority date 3/15; no closing date. Applicants notified on a rolling basis starting 5/15; must reply within 2 week(s) of notification.

CONTACT
Cynthia Harbel, Director of Financial Aid
12401 Willowbrook Road, SE, Cumberland, MD 21502
(301) 784-5213

Anne Arundel Community College
Arnold, Maryland
www.aacc.edu   Federal Code: 002058

2-year public community college in large town.
Enrollment: 10,793 undergrads, 57% part-time. 1,724 full-time freshmen.
Selectivity: Open admission; but selective for some programs.

BASIC COSTS (2006-2007)
Tuition and fees: $2,860; out-of-district residents $5,200; out-of-state residents $8,980.
Per-credit charge: $86; out-of-district residents $164; out-of-state residents $290.

FINANCIAL AID PICTURE (2004-2005)
Students with need: 42% of average financial aid package awarded as scholarships/grants, 58% awarded as loans/jobs. Need-based aid available for part-time students. Work study available nights, weekends, and for part-time students.

FINANCIAL AID PROCEDURES
Forms required: FAFSA, institutional form.
Dates and Deadlines: Priority date 5/15; no closing date. Applicants notified on a rolling basis starting 7/1; must reply within 2 week(s) of notification.

CONTACT
Rich Heath, Director of Student Financial Services
101 College Parkway, Arnold, MD 21012-1895
(410) 777-2203

Baltimore City Community College
Baltimore, Maryland
www.bccc.edu   Federal Code: 002061

2-year public community college in very large city.
Enrollment: 7,160 undergrads, 63% part-time. 732 full-time freshmen.
Selectivity: Open admission; but selective for some programs.

BASIC COSTS (2005-2006)
Tuition and fees: $2,575; out-of-state residents $5,275.
Per-credit charge: $78; out-of-state residents $168.

FINANCIAL AID PICTURE
Students with need: Need-based aid available for full-time and part-time students. Work study available nights, weekends, and for part-time students.
Students without need: This college only awards aid to students with need.

FINANCIAL AID PROCEDURES
Forms required: FAFSA, state aid form, institutional form.
Dates and Deadlines: Priority date 6/1; no closing date. Applicants notified on a rolling basis starting 7/1; must reply within 2 week(s) of notification.

CONTACT
Ronald Smith, Director of Financial Aid
2901 Liberty Heights Avenue, Baltimore, MD 21215-7893
(410) 462-8500

Baltimore Hebrew University
Baltimore, Maryland
www.bhu.edu   Federal Code: 002060

4-year private university and teachers college in very large city.
Enrollment: 6 undergrads.

BASIC COSTS (2006-2007)
Tuition and fees: $13,550.
Per-credit charge: $450.

FINANCIAL AID PICTURE (2004-2005)
Students with need: 25% of average financial aid package awarded as scholarships/grants, 75% awarded as loans/jobs. Need-based aid available for part-time students.
Students without need: No-need awards available for academics.
Scholarships offered: 25% tuition subsidy for teachers employed at any Jewish congregational day school, nursery or kindergarten; 50% tuition subsidy for teachers employed at a school affiliated with Center for Jewish Education; 25% tuition discount for full-time employees of the Associated Jewish Community Federation of Baltimore.

FINANCIAL AID PROCEDURES
Forms required: FAFSA, institutional form.
Dates and Deadlines: Priority date 4/15; closing date 6/1. Applicants notified on a rolling basis starting 7/15; must reply by 9/9.
Transfers: No deadline.

CONTACT
Ellen Taksel, Financial Aid Counselor
5800 Park Heights Avenue, Baltimore, MD 21215
(410) 578-6913

Baltimore International College
Baltimore, Maryland
www.bic.edu   Federal Code: 016376

4-year private culinary school and business college in very large city.
Enrollment: 516 undergrads, 6% part-time. 135 full-time freshmen.
Selectivity: Admits over 75% of applicants.

BASIC COSTS (2006-2007)
Tuition and fees: $22,040.
Room and board: $6,938.
Additional info: Fees shown are for culinary school and include use of computer, culinary supplies, upgrading and maintenance of kitchen equipment and facilities. Day students provided one full meal daily. Business program students pay lower fees. Tuition at time of enrollment locked for 4 years.

FINANCIAL AID PICTURE (2004-2005)
Students with need: Average financial aid package for all full-time undergraduates was $12,175. 51% awarded as scholarships/grants, 49% awarded as loans/jobs. Work study available nights, weekends, and for part-time students.
Students without need: No-need awards available for academics, alumni affiliation, athletics, job skills, leadership, state/district residency.

FINANCIAL AID PROCEDURES
Forms required: FAFSA, institutional form.
Dates and Deadlines: Priority date 3/1; no closing date. Applicants notified on a rolling basis; must reply within 2 week(s) of notification.
Transfers: Priority date 7/1.

CONTACT
Kim Wittler, Director of Student Financial Planning
17 Commerce Street, Baltimore, MD 21202-3230
(410) 752-0490

Bowie State University
Bowie, Maryland
www.bowiestate.edu   Federal Code: 002062

4-year public university in small city.
Enrollment: 4,023 undergrads, 18% part-time. 647 full-time freshmen.
Selectivity: Admits less than 50% of applicants.

BASIC COSTS (2005-2006)
Tuition and fees: $5,481; out-of-state residents $14,786.
Per-credit charge: $189; out-of-state residents $572.
Room and board: $5,837.

FINANCIAL AID PICTURE (2004-2005)
Students with need: Out of 521 full-time freshmen who applied for aid, 499 were judged to have need. Of these, 499 received aid, and 129 had their full need met. Average financial aid package met 72% of need; average scholarship/grant was $4,839; average loan was $2,875. For part-time students, average financial aid package was $7,831.
Students without need: 7 full-time freshmen who did not demonstrate need for aid received scholarships/grants; average award was $10,201. No-need awards available for academics, alumni affiliation, art, athletics, leadership, music/drama, ROTC, state/district residency.
Scholarships offered: 1 full-time freshmen received athletic scholarships; average amount $4,000.
Cumulative student debt: 86% of graduating class had student loans; average debt was $15,019.

FINANCIAL AID PROCEDURES
Forms required: FAFSA.
Dates and Deadlines: Closing date 3/1. Applicants notified on a rolling basis starting 4/1; must reply within 10 week(s) of notification.
Transfers: Financial aid transcripts required from previous institutions.

CONTACT
Veronica Pickett, Director of Financial Aid
14000 Jericho Park Road, Bowie, MD 20715
(301) 860-3540

Carroll Community College
Westminster, Maryland
www.carrollcc.edu   Federal Code: 031007

2-year public community college in large town.
Enrollment: 3,102 undergrads, 57% part-time. 493 full-time freshmen.
Selectivity: Open admission; but selective for some programs.

Maryland Carroll Community College

BASIC COSTS (2005-2006)
Tuition and fees: $3,234; out-of-district residents $4,476; out-of-state residents $6,788.
Per-credit charge: $92; out-of-district residents $128; out-of-state residents $195.

FINANCIAL AID PICTURE (2004-2005)
Students with need: 96% of average financial aid package awarded as scholarships/grants, 4% awarded as loans/jobs. Need-based aid available for part-time students. Work study available nights, weekends, and for part-time students.
Students without need: No-need awards available for academics.

FINANCIAL AID PROCEDURES
Forms required: FAFSA.
Dates and Deadlines: Priority date 3/1; no closing date. Applicants notified by 6/1; must reply within 2 week(s) of notification.

CONTACT
Lori Henri, Director of Financial Aid
1601 Washington Road, Westminster, MD 21157
(410) 386-8437

Cecil Community College
North East, Maryland
www.cecilcc.edu
Federal Code: 008308

2-year public community college in small town.
Enrollment: 1,729 undergrads, 63% part-time. 195 full-time freshmen.
Selectivity: Open admission; but selective for some programs.

BASIC COSTS (2006-2007)
Tuition and fees: $2,895; out-of-district residents $5,595; out-of-state residents $6,945.
Per-credit charge: $85; out-of-district residents $175; out-of-state residents $220.
Additional info: Tuition at time of enrollment locked for 2 years.

FINANCIAL AID PICTURE (2004-2005)
Students with need: 62% of average financial aid package awarded as scholarships/grants, 38% awarded as loans/jobs.
Students without need: No-need awards available for academics, alumni affiliation, athletics, job skills, state/district residency.

FINANCIAL AID PROCEDURES
Forms required: FAFSA.
Dates and Deadlines: Priority date 8/1; no closing date. Applicants notified on a rolling basis; must reply within 2 week(s) of notification.

CONTACT
Kate Lockhart, Director of Financial Aid
One Seahawk Drive, North East, MD 21901
(410) 287-1003

Chesapeake College
Wye Mills, Maryland
www.chesapeake.edu
Federal Code: 004650

2-year public community college in rural community.
Enrollment: 1,895 undergrads.
Selectivity: Open admission; but selective for some programs.

BASIC COSTS (2005-2006)
Tuition and fees: $2,924; out-of-district residents $4,814; out-of-state residents $6,974.
Per-credit charge: $84; out-of-district residents $147; out-of-state residents $219.
Additional info: Additional capital improvement fee per semester is $10 in-district and $25 out-of-district.

FINANCIAL AID PICTURE
Students with need: Need-based aid available for full-time and part-time students.
Students without need: No-need awards available for academics, art, athletics, state/district residency.

FINANCIAL AID PROCEDURES
Forms required: FAFSA, institutional form.
Dates and Deadlines: Priority date 5/1; no closing date. Applicants notified on a rolling basis starting 5/1; must reply within 2 week(s) of notification.

CONTACT
Mindy Schaffer, Director of Financial Aid
PO Box 8, Wye Mills, MD 21679-0008
(410) 822-5400 ext. 252

College of Notre Dame of Maryland
Baltimore, Maryland
www.ndm.edu
Federal Code: 002065

4-year private liberal arts college for women in very large city, affiliated with Roman Catholic Church.
Enrollment: 1,444 undergrads.
Selectivity: Admits over 75% of applicants.

BASIC COSTS (2006-2007)
Tuition and fees: $23,000.
Per-credit charge: $360.
Room and board: $8,300.

FINANCIAL AID PICTURE (2004-2005)
Students with need: 56% of average financial aid package awarded as scholarships/grants, 44% awarded as loans/jobs. Need-based aid available for part-time students.
Students without need: No-need awards available for academics, alumni affiliation, art, leadership, music/drama, ROTC.
Scholarships offered: Academic/achievement awards; $5,000 to full tuition. Endowed scholarships; $1,000 to $8,000; variable criteria; usually 20-35 awards.
Additional info: Maximum consideration for financial aid if application received by February 15. Auditions and portfolios in areas of art, music and writing considered for scholarships.

FINANCIAL AID PROCEDURES
Forms required: FAFSA.
Dates and Deadlines: Priority date 2/15; no closing date. Applicants notified on a rolling basis starting 3/15; must reply by 5/1 or within 2 week(s) of notification.
Transfers: Specific non-need based merit scholarships available for transfer students. Transfer scholarships; range from $6,000 to full tuition.

CONTACT
Rick Staisloff, Vice President, Financial Affairs
4701 North Charles Street, Baltimore, MD 21210
(410) 532-5369

College of Southern Maryland
La Plata, Maryland
www.csmd.edu
Federal Code: 002064

2-year public community college in large town.
Enrollment: 5,987 undergrads.
Selectivity: Open admission; but selective for some programs.

BASIC COSTS (2005-2006)
Tuition and fees: $3,312; out-of-district residents $5,352; out-of-state residents $6,582.
Per-credit charge: $92; out-of-district residents $160; out-of-state residents $201.
Additional info: In-state, out-of-district fees, $960; out-of-state, $1206.

FINANCIAL AID PICTURE (2004-2005)
Students with need: 94% of average financial aid package awarded as scholarships/grants, 6% awarded as loans/jobs. Need-based aid available for part-time students. Work study available nights, weekends, and for part-time students.
Students without need: No-need awards available for academics, athletics, state/district residency.

FINANCIAL AID PROCEDURES
Forms required: FAFSA.
Dates and Deadlines: Priority date 3/1; no closing date. Applicants notified on a rolling basis starting 5/15; must reply within 2 week(s) of notification.

CONTACT
Chad Norcross, Director of Financial Assistance
8730 Mitchell Road, La Plata, MD 20646-0910
(301) 934-7533

Columbia Union College
Takoma Park, Maryland
www.cuc.edu   Federal Code: 002067

4-year private liberal arts college in large town, affiliated with Seventh-day Adventists.
Enrollment: 992 undergrads, 27% part-time. 208 full-time freshmen.
Selectivity: Admits less than 50% of applicants.

BASIC COSTS (2006-2007)
Tuition and fees: $18,439.
Per-credit charge: $725.
Room and board: $6,247.

FINANCIAL AID PICTURE (2004-2005)
Students with need: Out of 203 full-time freshmen who applied for aid, 203 were judged to have need. Of these, 203 received aid. Need-based aid available for part-time students.
Students without need: No-need awards available for academics, athletics, leadership, music/drama, state/district residency.

FINANCIAL AID PROCEDURES
Forms required: FAFSA.
Dates and Deadlines: Closing date 3/31. Applicants notified on a rolling basis starting 5/31; must reply within 4 week(s) of notification.

CONTACT
Elaine Oliver, Director of Financial Aid
7600 Flower Avenue, Takoma Park, MD 20912
(301) 891-4005

Community College of Baltimore County
Baltimore, Maryland
www.ccbcmd.edu   Federal Code: 002063

2-year public community college in very large city.
Enrollment: 17,051 undergrads, 61% part-time. 2,018 full-time freshmen.
Selectivity: Open admission; but selective for some programs.

BASIC COSTS (2005-2006)
Tuition and fees: $2,925; out-of-district residents $4,815; out-of-state residents $6,465.
Per-credit charge: $87; out-of-district residents $150; out-of-state residents $205.

FINANCIAL AID PICTURE
Students with need: Need-based aid available for full-time and part-time students.
Additional info: On-campus employment typically available.

FINANCIAL AID PROCEDURES
Forms required: FAFSA.
Dates and Deadlines: Priority date 4/15; no closing date. Applicants notified on a rolling basis starting 7/1; must reply within 2 week(s) of notification.

CONTACT
Jerome Lovick, Director of Financial Aid
800 South Rolling Road, Baltimore, MD 21228
(410) 455-4170

Coppin State University
Baltimore, Maryland
www.coppin.edu   Federal Code: 002068

4-year public liberal arts college in very large city.
Enrollment: 3,380 undergrads.

BASIC COSTS (2005-2006)
Tuition and fees: $4,714; out-of-state residents $11,235.
Per-credit charge: $151; out-of-state residents $347.
Room and board: $6,239.

FINANCIAL AID PICTURE
Students with need: Need-based aid available for full-time and part-time students.
Students without need: No-need awards available for academics, alumni affiliation, athletics, ROTC, state/district residency.
Scholarships offered: Gold Freshman Merit Award; $1,200 per year; awarded to freshmen with 950 combined SAT and 2.5 high school GPA. Gold Transfer Merit Award; $1,200 per year; awarded to Maryland Community College transfer students with 2.8 GPA and successful completion of 56 credits. Blue Freshman Merit Award; $800 per year; awarded to freshman with 900 combined SAT and 2.5 GPA. Blue Transfer Merit Award; $600 per year; awarded to Maryland Community College transfer students with 2.5 GPA and successful completion of 25 credits. SAT scores exclusive of Writing.
Additional info: Funds allocated by State of Maryland for minority students enrolled for at least 6 credits who are Maryland residents and U.S. citizens (Other Race Grant).

FINANCIAL AID PROCEDURES
Forms required: FAFSA.
Dates and Deadlines: Priority date 3/1; no closing date. Applicants notified on a rolling basis starting 4/15; must reply within 2 week(s) of notification.

CONTACT
Lady Jenkins, Director of Financial Aid
2500 West North Avenue, Baltimore, MD 21216
(410) 951-3636

Frederick Community College
Frederick, Maryland
www.frederick.edu   Federal Code: 002071

2-year public community college in small city.
Enrollment: 3,922 undergrads, 55% part-time. 701 full-time freshmen.
Selectivity: Open admission; but selective for some programs.

Maryland — Frederick Community College

BASIC COSTS (2005-2006)
Tuition and fees: $2,889; out-of-district residents $5,949; out-of-state residents $7,959.
Per-credit charge: $85; out-of-district residents $187; out-of-state residents $254.

FINANCIAL AID PICTURE
Students with need: Need-based aid available for full-time and part-time students.
Students without need: No-need awards available for academics, athletics, state/district residency.

FINANCIAL AID PROCEDURES
Forms required: FAFSA, institutional form.
Dates and Deadlines: Priority date 6/15; no closing date. Applicants notified on a rolling basis starting 5/15; must reply within 2 week(s) of notification.
Transfers: Priority date 6/1. Applicants notified on a rolling basis starting 6/1. Financial aid transcripts from prior institutions must be submitted before awards are made.

CONTACT
Brenda Dayhoff, Director, Financial Aid
7932 Opossumtown Pike, Frederick, MD 21702
(301) 846-2480

Frostburg State University
Frostburg, Maryland
www.frostburg.edu   Federal Code: 002072

4-year public university and business and liberal arts and teachers college in small town.
Enrollment: 4,246 undergrads, 5% part-time. 966 full-time freshmen.
Selectivity: Admits over 75% of applicants.

BASIC COSTS (2005-2006)
Tuition and fees: $6,230; out-of-state residents $14,480.
Per-credit charge: $207; out-of-state residents $374.
Room and board: $6,442.

FINANCIAL AID PICTURE (2005-2006)
Students with need: Out of 742 full-time freshmen who applied for aid, 506 were judged to have need. Of these, 506 received aid, and 112 had their full need met. Average financial aid package met 66% of need; average scholarship/grant was $4,439; average loan was $2,237. For part-time students, average financial aid package was $4,541.
Students without need: 141 full-time freshmen who did not demonstrate need for aid received scholarships/grants; average award was $2,142. No-need awards available for academics, leadership, minority status.
Cumulative student debt: 61% of graduating class had student loans; average debt was $15,678.

FINANCIAL AID PROCEDURES
Forms required: FAFSA.
Dates and Deadlines: Priority date 3/1; no closing date. Applicants notified on a rolling basis starting 3/15; must reply within 3 week(s) of notification.

CONTACT
Angela Hovatter, Director of Financial Aid
101 Braddock Road, Frostburg, MD 21532-1099
(301) 687-4301

Garrett College
McHenry, Maryland
www.garrettcollege.edu   Federal Code: 010014

2-year public community college in rural community.
Enrollment: 509 undergrads.
Selectivity: Open admission.

BASIC COSTS (2006-2007)
Tuition and fees: $2,970; out-of-district residents $6,180; out-of-state residents $7,260.
Per-credit charge: $78; out-of-district residents $185; out-of-state residents $221.
Room and board: $4,000.

FINANCIAL AID PICTURE (2005-2006)
Students with need: Need-based aid available for part-time students.
Students without need: No-need awards available for academics, athletics, leadership.
Additional info: Many local scholarships both merit and need based.

FINANCIAL AID PROCEDURES
Forms required: FAFSA.
Dates and Deadlines: Priority date 3/1; no closing date. Applicants notified on a rolling basis starting 5/15; must reply within 2 week(s) of notification.

CONTACT
Alan Batchelor, Director of Financial Aid
687 Mosser Road, McHenry, MD 21541
(301) 387-3057

Goucher College
Baltimore, Maryland
www.goucher.edu   Federal Code: 002073
                         CSS Code: 5257

4-year private liberal arts college in small city.
Enrollment: 1,325 undergrads, 2% part-time. 401 full-time freshmen.
Selectivity: Admits 50 to 75% of applicants.

BASIC COSTS (2006-2007)
Tuition and fees: $29,325.
Per-credit charge: $1,000.
Room and board: $9,225.

FINANCIAL AID PICTURE (2004-2005)
Students with need: Out of 293 full-time freshmen who applied for aid, 229 were judged to have need. Of these, 229 received aid, and 87 had their full need met. Average financial aid package met 81% of need; average scholarship/grant was $13,722; average loan was $3,607. For part-time students, average financial aid package was $8,215.
Students without need: 82 full-time freshmen who did not demonstrate need for aid received scholarships/grants; average award was $9,420. No-need awards available for academics, art, leadership, music/drama.
Scholarships offered: $5000-full tuition; based on academic achievement, artistic talent, leadership; 3.0 high school GPA and SAT scores of 1100 or above (exclusive of Writing).

FINANCIAL AID PROCEDURES
Forms required: FAFSA, CSS PROFILE.
Dates and Deadlines: Closing date 2/15. Applicants notified by 4/1; must reply by 5/1 or within 2 week(s) of notification.

CONTACT
Sharon Hassan, Director of Financial Aid
1021 Dulaney Valley Road, Baltimore, MD 21204-2753
(410) 337-6500

Hagerstown Business College
Hagerstown, Maryland
www.hagerstownbusinesscol.org   Federal Code: 007946

2-year for-profit business and junior college in large town.
Enrollment: 850 undergrads.
Selectivity: Open admission; but selective for some programs.

BASIC COSTS (2005-2006)
Room only: $3,360.
Additional info: Tuition and fees vary from $10,608-$26,391 for entire program.

FINANCIAL AID PICTURE
Students with need: Need-based aid available for full-time and part-time students.

FINANCIAL AID PROCEDURES
Forms required: FAFSA, institutional form.
Dates and Deadlines: No deadline. Applicants notified on a rolling basis starting 6/1; must reply within 2 week(s) of notification.

CONTACT
Kim Crites, Director of Financial Aid
18618 Crestwood Drive, Hagerstown, MD 21742
(301) 739-2670

Hagerstown Community College
Hagerstown, Maryland
www.hagerstowncc.edu   Federal Code: 002074

2-year public community college in small city.
Enrollment: 3,018 undergrads, 62% part-time. 418 full-time freshmen.
Selectivity: Open admission; but selective for some programs.

BASIC COSTS (2006-2007)
Tuition and fees: $3,120; out-of-district residents $4,770; out-of-state residents $6,180.
Per-credit charge: $93; out-of-district residents $148; out-of-state residents $195.

FINANCIAL AID PICTURE
Students with need: Need-based aid available for full-time and part-time students. Work study available nights, weekends, and for part-time students.
Students without need: This college only awards aid to students with need.

FINANCIAL AID PROCEDURES
Forms required: FAFSA.
Dates and Deadlines: No deadline. Applicants notified on a rolling basis starting 5/1.
Transfers: No deadline.

CONTACT
Carolyn Cox, Director of Financial Aid
11400 Robinwood Drive, Hagerstown, MD 21742-6590
(301) 790-2800 ext. 473

Hood College
Frederick, Maryland
www.hood.edu   Federal Code: 002076

4-year private liberal arts college in small city.
Enrollment: 1,136 undergrads, 12% part-time. 237 full-time freshmen.
Selectivity: Admits 50 to 75% of applicants.

BASIC COSTS (2006-2007)
Tuition and fees: $23,655.
Per-credit charge: $670.
Room and board: $8,135.

FINANCIAL AID PICTURE (2005-2006)
Students with need: Out of 213 full-time freshmen who applied for aid, 184 were judged to have need. Of these, 182 received aid, and 73 had their full need met. Average financial aid package met 86% of need; average scholarship/grant was $16,092; average loan was $3,819. For part-time students, average financial aid package was $5,286.
Students without need: 53 full-time freshmen who did not demonstrate need for aid received scholarships/grants; average award was $14,517. No-need awards available for academics, alumni affiliation, leadership, minority status, music/drama, ROTC.
Scholarships offered: Hood Trust Academic Scholarship; amount varies. Hodson Scholarship; amount varies. Project Excellence Scholarship; up to full tuition. Presidential Scholarship; $10,000-$13,000. Trustee Scholarship; $8,000-$10,000.
Cumulative student debt: 74% of graduating class had student loans; average debt was $16,295.

FINANCIAL AID PROCEDURES
Forms required: FAFSA.
Dates and Deadlines: Priority date 2/15; no closing date. Applicants notified on a rolling basis starting 3/1; must reply by 5/1 or within 3 week(s) of notification.

CONTACT
Ron Shunk, Director of Financial Aid
401 Rosemont Avenue, Frederick, MD 21701-8575
(301) 696-3411

Howard Community College
Columbia, Maryland
www.howardcc.edu   Federal Code: 008175

2-year public community college in small city.
Enrollment: 5,932 undergrads, 57% part-time. 910 full-time freshmen.
Selectivity: Open admission; but selective for some programs.

BASIC COSTS (2006-2007)
Tuition and fees: $3,853; out-of-district residents $6,343; out-of-state residents $7,693.
Per-credit charge: $110; out-of-district residents $193; out-of-state residents $238.

FINANCIAL AID PICTURE (2004-2005)
Students with need: 74% of average financial aid package awarded as scholarships/grants, 26% awarded as loans/jobs. Need-based aid available for part-time students. Work study available nights.

FINANCIAL AID PROCEDURES
Forms required: FAFSA, institutional form.
Dates and Deadlines: Priority date 3/1; no closing date. Applicants notified on a rolling basis starting 4/1.

CONTACT
Katherine Allen, Director of Financial Aid
10901 Little Patuxent Parkway, Columbia, MD 21044-3197
(410) 772-4604

Johns Hopkins University
Baltimore, Maryland
www.jhu.edu
Federal Code: 002077
CSS Code: 5332

4-year private university in very large city.
Enrollment: 4,306 undergrads. 1,154 full-time freshmen.
Selectivity: Admits less than 50% of applicants.

BASIC COSTS (2006-2007)
Tuition and fees: $34,400.
Per-credit charge: $1,130.
Room and board: $10,622.

FINANCIAL AID PICTURE (2005-2006)
Students with need: Out of 746 full-time freshmen who applied for aid, 572 were judged to have need. Of these, 558 received aid, and 558 had their full need met. Average financial aid package met 99% of need; average scholarship/grant was $23,713; average loan was $2,715.
Students without need: 6 full-time freshmen who did not demonstrate need for aid received scholarships/grants; average award was $23,379. No-need awards available for academics, athletics, leadership, ROTC, state/district residency.
Scholarships offered: *Merit:* Hodson Trust Scholarship; $23,000 annually for 4 years; 20 awards. Westgate Scholarship for engineering freshmen; tuition plus $1,000 for 4 years; academic excellence, leadership, demonstrated research experience required; 2 offered per year per class. Wilson Research grants; $10,000. Baltimore Scholars Program; full tuition scholarship for US citizens or permanent residents who have attended a Baltimore City public school for at least 10th, 11th, and 12th grades and meet a residency requirement. *Athletic:* 6 full-time freshmen received athletic scholarships; average amount $21,645.
Cumulative student debt: 52% of graduating class had student loans; average debt was $14,000.
Additional info: Selected students receive aid packages without loan expectation, grants to full need. Private merit aid does not reduce Hopkins grant.

FINANCIAL AID PROCEDURES
Forms required: FAFSA, CSS PROFILE.
Dates and Deadlines: Priority date 2/1; closing date 2/15. Applicants notified by 4/1; must reply by 5/1 or within 2 week(s) of notification.
Transfers: Closing date 3/15. Aid on funds-available basis.

CONTACT
Ellen Frishberg, University Director of Student Financial Services
3400 North Charles Street, 140 Garland Hall, Baltimore, MD 21218
(410) 516-8028

Johns Hopkins University: Peabody Conservatory of Music
Baltimore, Maryland
www.peabody.jhu.edu
Federal Code: E00233

4-year private music college in very large city.
Enrollment: 330 undergrads, 3% part-time. 76 full-time freshmen.

BASIC COSTS (2006-2007)
Tuition and fees: $30,690.
Per-credit charge: $840.
Room and board: $9,500.

FINANCIAL AID PICTURE
Students with need: Need-based aid available for full-time and part-time students.
Students without need: No-need awards available for academics, music/drama.

FINANCIAL AID PROCEDURES
Forms required: FAFSA, institutional form.
Dates and Deadlines: Closing date 2/1. Applicants notified by 4/7; must reply by 5/1 or within 2 week(s) of notification.

CONTACT
Anita Goodwin, Director of Financial Aid
One East Mount Vernon Place, Baltimore, MD 21202
(410) 659-8100 ext. 3023

Loyola College in Maryland
Baltimore, Maryland
www.loyola.edu
Federal Code: 002078
CSS Code: 5370

4-year private business and liberal arts college in very large city, affiliated with Roman Catholic Church.
Enrollment: 3,533 undergrads, 1% part-time. 898 full-time freshmen.
Selectivity: Admits less than 50% of applicants.

BASIC COSTS (2005-2006)
Tuition and fees: $30,500.
Per-credit charge: $486.
Room and board: $9,215.

FINANCIAL AID PICTURE (2005-2006)
Students with need: Out of 635 full-time freshmen who applied for aid, 445 were judged to have need. Of these, 445 received aid, and 434 had their full need met. Average financial aid package met 97% of need; average scholarship/grant was $13,545; average loan was $5,880.
Students without need: 85 full-time freshmen who did not demonstrate need for aid received scholarships/grants; average award was $10,076. No-need awards available for academics, athletics, minority status, ROTC.
Scholarships offered: 40 full-time freshmen received athletic scholarships; average amount $21,705.
Cumulative student debt: 74% of graduating class had student loans; average debt was $15,680.

FINANCIAL AID PROCEDURES
Forms required: FAFSA, CSS PROFILE.
Dates and Deadlines: Closing date 2/15. Applicants notified by 4/1; must reply by 5/1.
Transfers: Academic (merit-based) scholarships not available to transfer students.

CONTACT
Mark Lindenmeyer, Director of Financial Aid
4501 North Charles Street, Baltimore, MD 21210-2699
(410) 617-2576

Maryland Institute College of Art
Baltimore, Maryland
www.mica.edu
Federal Code: 002080

4-year private visual arts college in very large city.
Enrollment: 1,497 undergrads, 1% part-time. 385 full-time freshmen.
Selectivity: Admits less than 50% of applicants.

BASIC COSTS (2006-2007)
Tuition and fees: $28,670.
Per-credit charge: $1,160.
Room and board: $7,910.

FINANCIAL AID PICTURE (2005-2006)
Students with need: Out of 309 full-time freshmen who applied for aid, 229 were judged to have need. Of these, 229 received aid, and 79 had their full need met. Average financial aid package met 68% of need; average scholarship/grant was $9,640; average loan was $2,877. For part-time students, average financial aid package was $8,002.
Students without need: 92 full-time freshmen who did not demonstrate need for aid received scholarships/grants; average award was $6,139. No-need awards available for academics, art.

FINANCIAL AID PROCEDURES
Forms required: FAFSA, institutional form.
Dates and Deadlines: Closing date 3/1. Applicants notified by 4/15; must reply by 5/2.
Transfers: Applicants notified by 4/20; must reply by 5/20.

CONTACT
Diane Prengaman, Associate Vice President for Financial Aid
1300 Mount Royal Avenue, Baltimore, MD 21217-4134
(410) 225-2285

McDaniel College
Westminster, Maryland
www.mcdaniel.edu   Federal Code: 002109

4-year private liberal arts college in large town.
Enrollment: 1,645 undergrads, 2% part-time. 449 full-time freshmen.
Selectivity: Admits over 75% of applicants.

BASIC COSTS (2006-2007)
Tuition and fees: $27,280.
Per-credit charge: $843.
Room and board: $5,900.
Additional info: Tuition/fee waivers available for adults.

FINANCIAL AID PICTURE (2005-2006)
Students with need: Out of 369 full-time freshmen who applied for aid, 284 were judged to have need. Of these, 283 received aid, and 85 had their full need met. Average financial aid package met 95% of need; average scholarship/grant was $9,330; average loan was $3,892. For part-time students, average financial aid package was $4,872.
Students without need: 283 full-time freshmen who did not demonstrate need for aid received scholarships/grants; average award was $10,562. No-need awards available for academics, ROTC.
Cumulative student debt: 60% of graduating class had student loans; average debt was $21,416.

FINANCIAL AID PROCEDURES
Forms required: FAFSA, institutional form.
Dates and Deadlines: Priority date 3/1; no closing date. Applicants notified on a rolling basis starting 3/1; must reply by 5/1 or within 2 week(s) of notification.
Transfers: Academic transfer scholarships and nontraditional student reduced tuition grants available.

CONTACT
Patricia Williams, Director of Financial Aid
Two College Hill, Westminster, MD 21157-4390
(410) 857-2233

Montgomery College
Rockville, Maryland
www.montgomerycollege.edu   Federal Code: 006911

2-year public community college in very large city.
Enrollment: 16,412 undergrads, 59% part-time. 1,700 full-time freshmen.
Selectivity: Open admission; but selective for some programs.

BASIC COSTS (2005-2006)
Tuition and fees: $3,708; out-of-district residents $7,236; out-of-state residents $9,612.
Per-credit charge: $93; out-of-district residents $191; out-of-state residents $257.

FINANCIAL AID PICTURE (2004-2005)
Students with need: 76% of average financial aid package awarded as scholarships/grants, 24% awarded as loans/jobs. Need-based aid available for part-time students. Work study available nights, weekends, and for part-time students.
Students without need: No-need awards available for academics, alumni affiliation, art, music/drama, state/district residency.
Scholarships offered: Board of Trustees Academic Potential Scholarship; first year of tuition; based on GPA and high school nominations; 125 awards available.

FINANCIAL AID PROCEDURES
Forms required: FAFSA, institutional form.
Dates and Deadlines: Priority date 5/15; no closing date. Applicants notified on a rolling basis starting 5/30.

CONTACT
Melissa Gregory, Director of Financial Aid
51 Mannakee Street, Room 105, Rockville, MD 20850
(301) 279-5100

Morgan State University
Baltimore, Maryland
www.morgan.edu   Federal Code: 002083

4-year public university and liberal arts college in very large city.
Enrollment: 5,676 undergrads, 10% part-time. 760 full-time freshmen.
Selectivity: Admits less than 50% of applicants.

BASIC COSTS (2006-2007)
Tuition and fees: $6,204; out-of-state residents $13,964.
Per-credit charge: $194; out-of-state residents $458.
Room and board: $7,330.
Additional info: Tuition/fee waivers available for minority students.

FINANCIAL AID PICTURE
Students with need: Need-based aid available for full-time and part-time students.

FINANCIAL AID PROCEDURES
Forms required: FAFSA.
Dates and Deadlines: Priority date 4/1; no closing date. Applicants notified on a rolling basis starting 6/1; must reply within 2 week(s) of notification.

CONTACT
Lillian Mitchell, Assistant Director
1700 East Coldspring Lane, Baltimore, MD 21251
(443) 885-3170

Mount St. Mary's University
Emmitsburg, Maryland
www.msmary.edu   Federal Code: 002086

4-year private university and liberal arts college in rural community, affiliated with Roman Catholic Church.
Enrollment: 1,656 undergrads, 10% part-time. 439 full-time freshmen.
Selectivity: Admits over 75% of applicants.

Maryland — Mount St. Mary's University

BASIC COSTS (2006-2007)
Tuition and fees: $24,030.
Per-credit charge: $790.
Room and board: $8,690.

FINANCIAL AID PICTURE (2005-2006)
Students with need: Out of 378 full-time freshmen who applied for aid, 288 were judged to have need. Of these, 288 received aid, and 81 had their full need met. Average financial aid package met 80% of need; average scholarship/grant was $12,877; average loan was $3,359. For part-time students, average financial aid package was $2,840.
Students without need: 139 full-time freshmen who did not demonstrate need for aid received scholarships/grants; average award was $15,043. No-need awards available for academics, athletics, leadership, minority status, music/drama, ROTC.
Scholarships offered: Merit: Kuderer Scholarship; full-tuition scholarship for 4 years; based on competitive examinations, strong academic records and SAT scores of 1200 or higher (exclusive of writing); 3 awards. **Athletic:** 26 full-time freshmen received athletic scholarships; average amount $8,511.
Cumulative student debt: 75% of graduating class had student loans; average debt was $15,964.

FINANCIAL AID PROCEDURES
Forms required: FAFSA, institutional form.
Dates and Deadlines: Closing date 2/15. Applicants notified on a rolling basis starting 2/15; must reply by 5/1.
Transfers: Scholarships available based on GPA at previous institution.

CONTACT
David Reeder, Director of Financial Aid
16300 Old Emmitsburg Road, Emmitsburg, MD 21727
(800) 448-4347

Prince George's Community College
Largo, Maryland
www.pgcc.edu
Federal Code: 002089

2-year public community college in very large city.
Enrollment: 11,011 undergrads, 73% part-time. 945 full-time freshmen.
Selectivity: Open admission; but selective for some programs.

BASIC COSTS (2005-2006)
Tuition and fees: $3,710; out-of-district residents $5,840; out-of-state residents $8,480.
Per-credit charge: $94; out-of-district residents $165; out-of-state residents $263.
Additional info: Instructional services fees range from $22 to $32 per credit depending on course.

FINANCIAL AID PICTURE
Students with need: Need-based aid available for full-time and part-time students.
Students without need: This college only awards aid to students with need.

FINANCIAL AID PROCEDURES
Forms required: FAFSA, institutional form.
Dates and Deadlines: Priority date 6/1; no closing date. Applicants notified on a rolling basis starting 6/1; must reply within 2 week(s) of notification.

CONTACT
Nancy-Pat Weaver, Director of Financial Aid
301 Largo Road, Largo, MD 20774
(301) 322-0822

St. John's College
Annapolis, Maryland
www.stjohnscollege.edu
Federal Code: 002092
CSS Code: 5598

4-year private liberal arts college in large town.
Enrollment: 474 undergrads. 147 full-time freshmen.
Selectivity: Admits over 75% of applicants.

BASIC COSTS (2006-2007)
Tuition and fees: $34,506.
Room and board: $8,270.

FINANCIAL AID PICTURE (2005-2006)
Students with need: Average financial aid package met 99% of need; average scholarship/grant was $19,949; average loan was $3,967. Need-based aid available for part-time students.
Students without need: This college only awards aid to students with need.

FINANCIAL AID PROCEDURES
Forms required: FAFSA, CSS PROFILE.
Dates and Deadlines: Priority date 2/15; no closing date. Applicants notified on a rolling basis starting 1/15; must reply by 5/1.

CONTACT
Paula Abernethy, Director of Financial Aid
PO Box 2800, Annapolis, MD 21404
(410) 626-2502

St. Mary's College of Maryland
St. Mary's City, Maryland
www.smcm.edu
Federal Code: 002095

4-year public liberal arts college in rural community.
Enrollment: 1,879 undergrads, 3% part-time. 488 full-time freshmen.
Selectivity: Admits 50 to 75% of applicants.

BASIC COSTS (2006-2007)
Tuition and fees: $11,710; out-of-state residents $21,280.
Per-credit charge: $160.
Room and board: $8,505.

FINANCIAL AID PICTURE (2005-2006)
Students with need: Out of 344 full-time freshmen who applied for aid, 221 were judged to have need. Of these, 221 received aid. Average financial aid package met 59% of need; average scholarship/grant was $3,000; average loan was $2,625. For part-time students, average financial aid package was $3,500.
Students without need: 157 full-time freshmen who did not demonstrate need for aid received scholarships/grants; average award was $3,000. No-need awards available for academics, art, leadership, music/drama.
Cumulative student debt: 69% of graduating class had student loans; average debt was $17,125.

FINANCIAL AID PROCEDURES
Forms required: FAFSA.
Dates and Deadlines: Closing date 3/1. Applicants notified by 4/1.
Transfers: Priority date 3/1; closing date 6/1. All financial aid recipients must have GED or high school diploma. Financial aid transcript required from previous colleges attended.

CONTACT
Timothy Wolfe, Director of Financial Aid
18952 East Fisher Road, St. Mary's City, MD 20686-3001
(240) 895-3000

Salisbury University
Salisbury, Maryland
www.salisbury.edu   Federal Code: 002091

4-year public university and liberal arts college in large town.
Enrollment: 6,141 undergrads, 6% part-time. 986 full-time freshmen.
Selectivity: Admits 50 to 75% of applicants.

BASIC COSTS (2005-2006)
Tuition and fees: $6,376; out-of-state residents $14,054.
Per-credit charge: $200; out-of-state residents $520.
Room and board: $6,932.

FINANCIAL AID PICTURE (2004-2005)
Students with need: Out of 752 full-time freshmen who applied for aid, 374 were judged to have need. Of these, 374 received aid, and 66 had their full need met. Average financial aid package met 53% of need; average scholarship/grant was $4,754; average loan was $2,020. For part-time students, average financial aid package was $3,406.
Students without need: 182 full-time freshmen who did not demonstrate need for aid received scholarships/grants; average award was $2,787. No-need awards available for academics, alumni affiliation, art, leadership, state/district residency.
Scholarships offered: Scholarships based on outstanding scholastic achievement, extra-curricular activities, geographic residence, degree program and additional factors; over 20 awarded.
Cumulative student debt: 63% of graduating class had student loans; average debt was $15,831.
Additional info: Job opportunities provided for almost 30% of full-time undergraduate students (over 900 jobs). Students can expect to earn $1500 per academic year by working 10 to 15 hours per week.

FINANCIAL AID PROCEDURES
Forms required: FAFSA.
Dates and Deadlines: Priority date 2/1; closing date 3/1. Applicants notified on a rolling basis starting 4/1; must reply by 5/1 or within 2 week(s) of notification.
Transfers: No deadline. Financial aid transcripts from previous schools required.

CONTACT
Beverly Horner, Director of Financial Aid
1200 Camden Avenue, Salisbury, MD 21801-6862
(410) 543-6165

Sojourner-Douglass College
Baltimore, Maryland
www.sdc.edu   Federal Code: 021279

4-year private liberal arts college in very large city.
Enrollment: 1,000 full-time undergrads.

BASIC COSTS (2005-2006)
Tuition and fees: $6,190.
Per-credit charge: $333.

FINANCIAL AID PICTURE
Students with need: Need-based aid available for full-time and part-time students.

FINANCIAL AID PROCEDURES
Forms required: FAFSA, institutional form.
Dates and Deadlines: Priority date 3/1; no closing date. Applicants notified on a rolling basis; must reply within 2 week(s) of notification.

CONTACT
Rebecca Chalk, Financial Aid Administrator
500 North Caroline Street, Baltimore, MD 21205
(410) 276-0306 ext. 260

Towson University
Towson, Maryland
www.towson.edu   Federal Code: 002099

4-year public university in large city.
Enrollment: 13,969 undergrads, 10% part-time. 2,318 full-time freshmen.
Selectivity: Admits 50 to 75% of applicants.

BASIC COSTS (2005-2006)
Tuition and fees: $7,096; out-of-state residents $16,030.
Per-credit charge: $225; out-of-state residents $528.
Room and board: $7,286.

FINANCIAL AID PICTURE (2005-2006)
Students with need: Average financial aid package met 62% of need; average scholarship/grant was $4,122; average loan was $2,472. For part-time students, average financial aid package was $2,525.
Students without need: No-need awards available for academics, alumni affiliation, art, athletics, job skills, leadership, music/drama, ROTC, state/district residency.
Scholarships offered: Towson Scholar Award; full tuition, fees, room and board. Presidential Scholarship; full tuition and fees. University Scholarship; full tuition. Provost Scholarship; $1,000-$6,000. Selection based on GPA and combined SAT score.
Cumulative student debt: 53% of graduating class had student loans; average debt was $14,808.

FINANCIAL AID PROCEDURES
Forms required: FAFSA.
Dates and Deadlines: Priority date 1/31; no closing date. Applicants notified on a rolling basis starting 3/21; must reply within 2 week(s) of notification.
Transfers: Priority date 3/1.

CONTACT
Vincent Pecora, Director of Financial Aid
8000 York Road, Towson, MD 21252-0001
(410) 704-4236

United States Naval Academy
Annapolis, Maryland
www.usna.edu   Federal Code: 002101

4-year public military college in large town.
Enrollment: 4,422 undergrads. 1,179 full-time freshmen.
Selectivity: Admits less than 50% of applicants.

BASIC COSTS (2006-2007)
Additional info: First-year students pay deposit of $2,200 for initial outfitting of uniforms and other supplies. Tuition, room and board, and medical and dental care provided by United States Government. Each midshipman receives monthly salary of about $849 to cover costs of books, supplies, uniforms, laundry, and equipment, including microcomputer.

CONTACT
117 Decatur Road, Annapolis, MD 21402-5018

University of Baltimore
Baltimore, Maryland
www.ubalt.edu   Federal Code: 002102

Upper-division public university in very large city.
Enrollment: 2,096 undergrads.

BASIC COSTS (2005-2006)
Tuition and fees: $6,794; out-of-state residents $18,373.
Per-credit charge: $243; out-of-state residents $704.

FINANCIAL AID PICTURE
Students with need: Need-based aid available for full-time and part-time students.
Additional info: Full need met for dependent students only.

FINANCIAL AID PROCEDURES
Forms required: FAFSA, institutional form.
Dates and Deadlines: No deadline. Applicants notified on a rolling basis.
Transfers: Priority date 4/1. Scholarship application deadline, March 1.

CONTACT
Barbara Miller, Director, Financial Aid
1420 North Charles Street, Baltimore, MD 21201-5779
(410) 837-4763

University of Maryland: Baltimore
Baltimore, Maryland
www.umaryland.edu   Federal Code: 002104

Upper-division public university and health science college in very large city.
Enrollment: 846 undergrads, 27% part-time.

BASIC COSTS (2005-2006)
Tuition and fees: $7,579; out-of-state residents $18,649.
Per-credit charge: $301; out-of-state residents $461.

FINANCIAL AID PICTURE (2004-2005)
Students with need: 28% of average financial aid package awarded as scholarships/grants, 72% awarded as loans/jobs. Need-based aid available for part-time students. Work study available nights, weekends, and for part-time students.
Students without need: No-need awards available for ROTC.
Additional info: Maryland state deadline 3/1.

FINANCIAL AID PROCEDURES
Forms required: FAFSA, state aid form.
Dates and Deadlines: Priority date 3/15; no closing date. Applicants notified on a rolling basis starting 4/15; must reply within 2 week(s) of notification.

CONTACT
Terra Jones, Director of Financial Aid
Office of Records and Registration, Baltimore, MD 21201-1575
(410) 706-7347

University of Maryland: Baltimore County
Baltimore, Maryland
www.umbc.edu   Federal Code: 002105

4-year public university in large city.
Enrollment: 9,244 undergrads, 14% part-time. 1,403 full-time freshmen.
Selectivity: Admits 50 to 75% of applicants.

BASIC COSTS (2005-2006)
Tuition and fees: $8,520; out-of-state residents $16,596.
Per-credit charge: $270; out-of-state residents $606.
Room and board: $8,090.

FINANCIAL AID PICTURE (2004-2005)
Students with need: Out of 925 full-time freshmen who applied for aid, 630 were judged to have need. Of these, 630 received aid, and 172 had their full need met. Average financial aid package met 77% of need; average scholarship/grant was $4,761; average loan was $3,060. For part-time students, average financial aid package was $7,713.
Students without need: 287 full-time freshmen who did not demonstrate need for aid received scholarships/grants; average award was $3,839. No-need awards available for academics, art, athletics, music/drama, ROTC.
Scholarships offered: *Merit:* University Scholarships, Honors College Fellowships; tuition, fees, room and board. President's Fellowships; $5,000 per year. UMBC Merit Awards; $500-$2,500 per year. Scholastic Achievement Awards President's Scholarships; $3,500 per year. Honors College Scholarships; $1,000 per year. Scholars Programs; tuition, fees, room and board. These programs include: Center for Women and Information Technology (CWIT) Scholars Program, Humanities Scholars Program, Linehan Artist Scholars Program, Meyerhoff Scholars Program (Sciences and Engineering), Sondheim Public Affairs Scholars Program. *Athletic:* 125 full-time freshmen received athletic scholarships; average amount $3,524.
Cumulative student debt: 48% of graduating class had student loans; average debt was $19,018.

FINANCIAL AID PROCEDURES
Forms required: FAFSA.
Dates and Deadlines: Priority date 2/15; no closing date. Applicants notified on a rolling basis starting 3/30; must reply within 2 week(s) of notification.
Transfers: Two-year merit scholarships available for transfer students from community colleges.

CONTACT
Stephanie Johnson, Director, Financial Aid
1000 Hilltop Circle, Baltimore, MD 21250
(410) 455-2387

University of Maryland: College Park
College Park, Maryland
www.maryland.edu   Federal Code: 002103

4-year public university in large town.
Enrollment: 24,876 undergrads, 7% part-time. 4,178 full-time freshmen.
Selectivity: Admits less than 50% of applicants.

BASIC COSTS (2005-2006)
Tuition and fees: $7,821; out-of-state residents $20,145.
Per-credit charge: $273; out-of-state residents $787.
Room and board: $8,075.

FINANCIAL AID PICTURE (2004-2005)
Students with need: Out of 3,412 full-time freshmen who applied for aid, 1,822 were judged to have need. Of these, 1,651 received aid, and 507 had their full need met. Average financial aid package met 69% of need; average scholarship/grant was $5,885; average loan was $2,390. For part-time students, average financial aid package was $8,641.
Students without need: 935 full-time freshmen who did not demonstrate need for aid received scholarships/grants; average award was $4,876. No-need awards available for academics, art, athletics, music/drama.
Scholarships offered: 119 full-time freshmen received athletic scholarships; average amount $2,975.
Cumulative student debt: 27% of graduating class had student loans; average debt was $19,687.
Additional info: Prepaid tuition plans available through state.

FINANCIAL AID PROCEDURES
Forms required: FAFSA.

Dates and Deadlines: Priority date 2/15; no closing date. Applicants notified on a rolling basis starting 4/1.

CONTACT
Sarah Bauder, Director of Student Financial Aid
Mitchell Building, College Park, MD 20742-5235
(301) 314-9000

University of Maryland: Eastern Shore
Princess Anne, Maryland
www.umes.edu   Federal Code: 002106

4-year public university in rural community.
Enrollment: 3,448 undergrads, 8% part-time. 952 full-time freshmen.
Selectivity: Admits 50 to 75% of applicants.

BASIC COSTS (2005-2006)
Tuition and fees: $5,808; out-of-state residents $11,964.
Per-credit charge: $171; out-of-state residents $371.
Room and board: $6,010.

FINANCIAL AID PICTURE (2004-2005)
Students with need: Out of 762 full-time freshmen who applied for aid, 625 were judged to have need. Of these, 625 received aid, and 138 had their full need met. Average financial aid package met 73% of need; average scholarship/grant was $6,225; average loan was $2,600. For part-time students, average financial aid package was $5,270.
Students without need: 78 full-time freshmen who did not demonstrate need for aid received scholarships/grants; average award was $2,465. No-need awards available for academics, alumni affiliation, art, athletics, leadership, music/drama, ROTC, state/district residency.
Scholarships offered: 9 full-time freshmen received athletic scholarships; average amount $15,000.
Cumulative student debt: 82% of graduating class had student loans; average debt was $16,200.

FINANCIAL AID PROCEDURES
Forms required: FAFSA, institutional form.
Dates and Deadlines: Priority date 3/1; closing date 4/1. Applicants notified on a rolling basis starting 4/1.

CONTACT
James Kellam, Director of Financial Aid
Bird Hall, Princess Anne, MD 21853
(410) 651-6172

University of Maryland: University College
Adelphi, Maryland
www.umuc.edu   Federal Code: 011644

4-year public university in large town.
Enrollment: 17,749 undergrads, 85% part-time. 69 full-time freshmen.
Selectivity: Open admission.

BASIC COSTS (2005-2006)
Tuition and fees: $5,670; out-of-state residents $10,302.
Per-credit charge: $230; out-of-state residents $423.

FINANCIAL AID PICTURE (2004-2005)
Students with need: Out of 49 full-time freshmen who applied for aid, 48 were judged to have need. Of these, 33 received aid, and 2 had their full need met. Average financial aid package met 18% of need; average scholarship/grant was $1,639; average loan was $1,284. For part-time students, average financial aid package was $3,758.
Students without need: No-need awards available for academics, leadership.

FINANCIAL AID PROCEDURES
Forms required: FAFSA, institutional form.
Dates and Deadlines: Priority date 6/1; no closing date. Applicants notified on a rolling basis starting 5/1; must reply within 2 week(s) of notification.

CONTACT
Dawn Mosisa, Associate Vice President, Student Financial Services
3501 University Boulevard East, Adelphi, MD 20783
(301) 985-7000

Villa Julie College
Stevenson, Maryland
www.vjc.edu   Federal Code: 002107

4-year private liberal arts college in very large city.
Enrollment: 2,764 undergrads, 17% part-time. 558 full-time freshmen.
Selectivity: Admits 50 to 75% of applicants.

BASIC COSTS (2006-2007)
Tuition and fees: $16,770.
Per-credit charge: $425.
Room and board: $9,188.

FINANCIAL AID PICTURE (2004-2005)
Students with need: Out of 436 full-time freshmen who applied for aid, 347 were judged to have need. Of these, 343 received aid, and 81 had their full need met. Average financial aid package met 68% of need; average scholarship/grant was $7,806; average loan was $2,420. For part-time students, average financial aid package was $5,143.
Students without need: 143 full-time freshmen who did not demonstrate need for aid received scholarships/grants; average award was $6,206. No-need awards available for academics, art, leadership, music/drama, ROTC.
Cumulative student debt: 38% of graduating class had student loans; average debt was $15,679.
Additional info: Cooperative Education Program allows students to work in their field of study with area corporations.

FINANCIAL AID PROCEDURES
Forms required: FAFSA.
Dates and Deadlines: Priority date 2/15; no closing date. Applicants notified on a rolling basis starting 3/15; must reply by 5/1 or within 2 week(s) of notification.

CONTACT
Debra Bottoms, Director of Student Financial Aid
1525 Greenspring Valley Road, Stevenson, MD 21153-0641
(443) 334-2559

Washington Bible College
Lanham, Maryland
www.bible.edu   Federal Code: 001462

4-year private Bible and seminary college in large town, affiliated with nondenominational tradition.
Enrollment: 340 undergrads.
Selectivity: Admits 50 to 75% of applicants.

BASIC COSTS (2006-2007)
Tuition and fees: $11,150.
Per-credit charge: $360.
Room and board: $5,840.

Maryland — Washington Bible College

FINANCIAL AID PICTURE (2004-2005)
Students with need: 52% of average financial aid package awarded as scholarships/grants, 48% awarded as loans/jobs. Need-based aid available for part-time students.
Students without need: No-need awards available for academics, leadership.

FINANCIAL AID PROCEDURES
Forms required: FAFSA, institutional form.
Dates and Deadlines: Priority date 3/1; closing date 6/1. Applicants notified on a rolling basis starting 7/1; must reply within 2 week(s) of notification.

CONTACT
Diane Marineau, Administrator of Financial Aid
6511 Princess Garden Parkway, Lanham, MD 20706-3599
(301) 552-1400

Washington College
Chestertown, Maryland
www.washcoll.edu
Federal Code: 002108

4-year private liberal arts college in small town.
Enrollment: 1,292 undergrads. 343 full-time freshmen.
Selectivity: Admits 50 to 75% of applicants.

BASIC COSTS (2006-2007)
Tuition and fees: $30,200.
Per-credit charge: $1,235.
Room and board: $6,450.

FINANCIAL AID PICTURE (2004-2005)
Students with need: 77% of average financial aid package awarded as scholarships/grants, 23% awarded as loans/jobs. Need-based aid available for part-time students. Work study available nights, weekends, and for part-time students.
Students without need: No-need awards available for academics.
Scholarships offered: National Honor Society Scholarship; $40,000 over 4 years; applicant must be member of National Honor Society.

FINANCIAL AID PROCEDURES
Forms required: FAFSA, institutional form.
Dates and Deadlines: Closing date 2/15. Applicants notified on a rolling basis starting 3/1; must reply by 5/1.

CONTACT
Jean Narcum, Director of Financial Aid
300 Washington Avenue, Chestertown, MD 21620-1197
(410) 778-7214

Wor-Wic Community College
Salisbury, Maryland
www.worwic.edu
Federal Code: 013842

2-year public community college in large town.
Enrollment: 2,785 undergrads, 67% part-time. 361 full-time freshmen.
Selectivity: Open admission; but selective for some programs.

BASIC COSTS (2006-2007)
Tuition and fees: $2,336; out-of-district residents $5,816; out-of-state residents $6,776.
Per-credit charge: $76; out-of-district residents $192; out-of-state residents $224.

FINANCIAL AID PICTURE (2005-2006)
Students with need: Out of 203 full-time freshmen who applied for aid, 184 were judged to have need. Of these, 148 received aid, and 1 had their full need met. Average financial aid package met 19% of need; average scholarship/grant was $1,953; average loan was $1,173. For part-time students, average financial aid package was $1,143.
Students without need: No-need awards available for academics, state/district residency.

FINANCIAL AID PROCEDURES
Forms required: FAFSA, institutional form.
Dates and Deadlines: Priority date 6/1; no closing date. Applicants notified on a rolling basis starting 4/1.

CONTACT
Deborah Jenkins, Director of Financial Aid
32000 Campus Drive, Salisbury, MD 21804
(410) 334-2905

Massachusetts

American International College
Springfield, Massachusetts
www.aic.edu
Federal Code: 002114

4-year private liberal arts college in small city.
Enrollment: 1,398 undergrads, 13% part-time. 331 full-time freshmen.
Selectivity: Admits over 75% of applicants.

BASIC COSTS (2006-2007)
Tuition and fees: $21,000.
Per-credit charge: $445.
Room and board: $9,270.

FINANCIAL AID PICTURE (2005-2006)
Students with need: Out of 331 full-time freshmen who applied for aid, 327 were judged to have need. Of these, 327 received aid, and 55 had their full need met. Average financial aid package met 85% of need; average scholarship/grant was $12,821; average loan was $3,758.
Students without need: 44 full-time freshmen who did not demonstrate need for aid received scholarships/grants; average award was $7,499. No-need awards available for academics, athletics.
Scholarships offered: *Merit:* Presidential, Provost, Opportunity Scholarships; $5,000 to $11,000; based on class rank, SAT scores, GPA. *Athletic:* 44 full-time freshmen received athletic scholarships; average amount $14,013.
Cumulative student debt: 87% of graduating class had student loans; average debt was $29,700.

FINANCIAL AID PROCEDURES
Forms required: FAFSA.
Dates and Deadlines: Priority date 5/1; no closing date. Applicants notified on a rolling basis starting 3/15; must reply by 5/1 or within 2 week(s) of notification.

CONTACT
Irene Martin, Director of Financial Aid
1000 State Street, Springfield, MA 01109
(413) 205-3259

Amherst College
Amherst, Massachusetts
www.amherst.edu
Federal Code: 002115
CSS Code: 3003

4-year private liberal arts college in large town.
Enrollment: 1,612 undergrads. 417 full-time freshmen.
Selectivity: Admits less than 50% of applicants.

BASIC COSTS (2006-2007)
Tuition and fees: $34,890.
Room and board: $9,080.

FINANCIAL AID PICTURE (2005-2006)
Students with need: Out of 247 full-time freshmen who applied for aid, 199 were judged to have need. Of these, 199 received aid, and 199 had their full need met. Average financial aid package met 100% of need; average scholarship/grant was $29,373; average loan was $1,620.
Students without need: This college only awards aid to students with need.
Cumulative student debt: 47% of graduating class had student loans; average debt was $12,109.

FINANCIAL AID PROCEDURES
Forms required: FAFSA, CSS PROFILE.
Dates and Deadlines: Priority date 2/15; no closing date. Applicants notified by 4/1; must reply by 5/1.

CONTACT
Joe Case, Dean of Financial Aid
PO Box 5000, Amherst, MA 01002-5000
(413) 542-2296

Anna Maria College
Paxton, Massachusetts
www.annamaria.edu
Federal Code: 002117

4-year private liberal arts college in small town, affiliated with Roman Catholic Church.
Enrollment: 713 undergrads, 24% part-time. 161 full-time freshmen.
Selectivity: Admits over 75% of applicants.

BASIC COSTS (2005-2006)
Tuition and fees: $21,880.
Room and board: $7,935.
Additional info: Additional tuition for music program.

FINANCIAL AID PICTURE (2005-2006)
Students with need: Out of 142 full-time freshmen who applied for aid, 129 were judged to have need. Of these, 129 received aid, and 30 had their full need met. Average financial aid package met 78% of need; average scholarship/grant was $11,071; average loan was $2,843. For part-time students, average financial aid package was $5,682.
Students without need: 18 full-time freshmen who did not demonstrate need for aid received scholarships/grants; average award was $8,226. No-need awards available for academics, alumni affiliation, music/drama, religious affiliation, state/district residency.
Cumulative student debt: 86% of graduating class had student loans; average debt was $23,513.

FINANCIAL AID PROCEDURES
Forms required: FAFSA.
Dates and Deadlines: Priority date 3/1; no closing date. Applicants notified on a rolling basis starting 4/1; must reply within 4 week(s) of notification.
Transfers: No deadline. Applicants notified on a rolling basis starting 4/1; must reply within 4 week(s) of notification. Deadline May 1 for state aid.

CONTACT
Nicole Brennan, Director of Financial Aid
50 Sunset Lane, Box O, Paxton, MA 01612-1198
(508) 849-3366

Art Institute of Boston at Lesley University
Boston, Massachusetts
www.aiboston.edu
Federal Code: 002160

4-year private visual arts and liberal arts college in very large city.
Enrollment: 565 undergrads. 249 full-time freshmen.
Selectivity: Admits 50 to 75% of applicants.

BASIC COSTS (2006-2007)
Tuition and fees: $22,225.
Per-credit charge: $905.
Room and board: $10,500.

FINANCIAL AID PICTURE (2005-2006)
Students with need: Out of 234 full-time freshmen who applied for aid, 189 were judged to have need. Of these, 189 received aid, and 18 had their full need met. Average financial aid package met 70% of need; average scholarship/grant was $12,741; average loan was $3,507. For part-time students, average financial aid package was $9,860.
Students without need: 40 full-time freshmen who did not demonstrate need for aid received scholarships/grants; average award was $5,938. No-need awards available for academics, art, leadership, minority status.
Scholarships offered: Freshmen academic scholarships; $6,500 annually; 1100 SAT (exclusive of Writing) and 2.8 GPA required. Freshmen academic scholarships; $4,500 annually; 3.0 GPA required. Portfolio scholarships; top portfolios awarded $6,500 annually; other qualified portfolios awarded $4,500 annually. Presidential Scholarship; full tuition; based on portfolio, academic grades, SAT/ACT, interview, cocurricular activity; renewed annually. Access Scholarships; $12,000; awarded for portfolio, academics, interview, cocurricular activity, ethnic, geographic or economic diversity. AIB transfers students scholarship; $3,000 annually; based on college grades, portfolio, interview.
Cumulative student debt: 90% of graduating class had student loans; average debt was $13,650.

FINANCIAL AID PROCEDURES
Forms required: FAFSA, institutional form.
Dates and Deadlines: Priority date 3/1; no closing date. Applicants notified on a rolling basis starting 3/15; must reply within 2 week(s) of notification.
Transfers: Priority date 3/18.

CONTACT
Paul Henderson, Director of Financial Aid
700 Beacon Street, Boston, MA 02215-2598
(617) 349-8710

Assumption College
Worcester, Massachusetts
www.assumption.edu
Federal Code: 002118

4-year private liberal arts college in small city, affiliated with Roman Catholic Church.
Enrollment: 2,105 undergrads. 565 full-time freshmen.
Selectivity: Admits over 75% of applicants.

BASIC COSTS (2006-2007)
Tuition and fees: $26,060.
Per-credit charge: $863.
Room and board: $9,170.

FINANCIAL AID PICTURE (2005-2006)
Students with need: Out of 483 full-time freshmen who applied for aid, 394 were judged to have need. Of these, 394 received aid, and 69 had their full need met. Average financial aid package met 70% of need; average scholarship/grant was $12,018; average loan was $3,000. For part-time students, average financial aid package was $13,119.
Students without need: 128 full-time freshmen who did not demonstrate need for aid received scholarships/grants; average award was $15,059. No-need awards available for academics, athletics.
Scholarships offered: *Merit:* Scholar program: $9,000 to $16,000; renewable. *Athletic:* 4 full-time freshmen received athletic scholarships; average amount $33,588.
Cumulative student debt: 76% of graduating class had student loans; average debt was $21,773.

FINANCIAL AID PROCEDURES
Forms required: FAFSA.
Dates and Deadlines: Closing date 2/1. Applicants notified on a rolling basis starting 2/15; must reply by 5/1.
Transfers: Closing date 4/1. Applicants notified on a rolling basis starting 5/1.

CONTACT
Karen Puntillo, Director of Financial Aid
500 Salisbury Street, Worcester, MA 01609-1296
(508) 767-7158

Atlantic Union College
South Lancaster, Massachusetts
www.atlanticuc.edu   Federal Code: 002119

4-year private liberal arts college in small town, affiliated with Seventh-day Adventists.
Enrollment: 470 undergrads.

BASIC COSTS (2006-2007)
Tuition and fees: $14,380.
Per-credit charge: $550.
Room and board: $5,300.
Additional info: Additional fees for nursing program. Tuition/fee waivers available for adults.

FINANCIAL AID PICTURE
Students with need: Need-based aid available for full-time and part-time students. Work study available nights, weekends, and for part-time students.
Students without need: No-need awards available for academics, athletics, job skills, leadership, music/drama.

FINANCIAL AID PROCEDURES
Forms required: FAFSA, institutional form.
Dates and Deadlines: Priority date 4/1; no closing date. Applicants notified on a rolling basis starting 4/1; must reply within 2 week(s) of notification.

CONTACT
Sandra Boucher, Financial Aid Director
Main Street, South Lancaster, MA 01561
(978) 368-2275

Babson College
Babson Park, Massachusetts   Federal Code: 002121
www.babson.edu   CSS Code: 3075

4-year private business college in large town.
Enrollment: 1,725 undergrads.
Selectivity: Admits less than 50% of applicants.

BASIC COSTS (2006-2007)
Tuition and fees: $32,256.
Per-credit charge: $953.
Room and board: $11,222.

FINANCIAL AID PICTURE (2005-2006)
Students with need: 83% of average financial aid package awarded as scholarships/grants, 17% awarded as loans/jobs. Work study available nights, weekends, and for part-time students.
Students without need: No-need awards available for academics, leadership, minority status.
Scholarships offered: Presidential Scholarship; half tuition; based on high school record, cocurricular achievements, demonstrated leadership, writing skills, standardized test scores; approximately 40 awarded each year. Women's Leadership Award; one quarter tuition; based on demonstrated leadership experience, future leadership potential, and academic achievement. Diversity Leadership Award; either full or half tuition; awarded to students with the greatest potential for leadership in creating a diverse Babson community.

FINANCIAL AID PROCEDURES
Forms required: FAFSA, CSS PROFILE.
Dates and Deadlines: Closing date 2/15. Applicants notified by 4/1; must reply by 5/1.
Transfers: Closing date 4/15.

CONTACT
Melissa Shaak, Director, Student Financial Services
Lunder Undergraduate Admission Center, Babson Park, MA 02457-0310
(781) 239-4219

Bay Path College
Longmeadow, Massachusetts
www.baypath.edu   Federal Code: 002122

4-year private business and liberal arts college for women in large town.
Enrollment: 1,343 undergrads, 17% part-time. 168 full-time freshmen.
Selectivity: Admits 50 to 75% of applicants.

BASIC COSTS (2005-2006)
Tuition and fees: $20,606.
Per-credit charge: $440.
Room and board: $8,756.

FINANCIAL AID PICTURE (2005-2006)
Students with need: Average financial aid package met 74% of need; average scholarship/grant was $10,653; average loan was $3,976. For part-time students, average financial aid package was $2,719.
Students without need: No-need awards available for academics, state/district residency.
Cumulative student debt: 64% of graduating class had student loans; average debt was $21,312.

FINANCIAL AID PROCEDURES
Forms required: FAFSA, institutional form.
Dates and Deadlines: Priority date 3/15; no closing date. Applicants notified on a rolling basis starting 3/1; must reply within 2 week(s) of notification.

CONTACT
Stephanie King, Director of Financial Aid
588 Longmeadow Street, Longmeadow, MA 01106
(413) 565-1000 ext. 345

Bay State College
Boston, Massachusetts
www.baystate.edu   Federal Code: 003965

2-year private junior college in very large city.
Enrollment: 938 undergrads.
BASIC COSTS (2005-2006)
Tuition and fees: $15,650.
Per-credit charge: $510.
Room and board: $9,825.
FINANCIAL AID PICTURE
Students with need: Need-based aid available for full-time and part-time students. Work study available nights, weekends, and for part-time students.
Scholarships offered: Scholarship Day award; $1,000-$5,000; based on examination held on last Saturday of January; amount of award determined by score.
FINANCIAL AID PROCEDURES
Forms required: FAFSA, institutional form.
Dates and Deadlines: Closing date 4/15. Applicants notified on a rolling basis starting 3/15; must reply within 3 week(s) of notification.
CONTACT
122 Commonwealth Avenue, Boston, MA 02116
(617) 236-8038

Becker College
Worcester, Massachusetts
www.beckercollege.edu   Federal Code: 002123

4-year private liberal arts college in small city.
Enrollment: 1,739 undergrads, 36% part-time. 286 full-time freshmen.
Selectivity: Admits 50 to 75% of applicants.
BASIC COSTS (2006-2007)
Tuition and fees: $21,080.
Per-credit charge: $855.
Room and board: $8,500.
Additional info: Additional one time charge of $250 for nursing program.
FINANCIAL AID PICTURE (2004-2005)
Students with need: Out of 282 full-time freshmen who applied for aid, 270 were judged to have need. Of these, 267 received aid, and 2 had their full need met. Average financial aid package met 33% of need; average scholarship/grant was $6,355; average loan was $25. For part-time students, average financial aid package was $1,751.
Students without need: 14 full-time freshmen who did not demonstrate need for aid received scholarships/grants; average award was $16,222. No-need awards available for academics.
Cumulative student debt: 100% of graduating class had student loans; average debt was $12,656.
FINANCIAL AID PROCEDURES
Forms required: FAFSA.
Dates and Deadlines: Priority date 3/1; no closing date. Applicants notified on a rolling basis starting 2/1; must reply within 2 week(s) of notification.
CONTACT
Denise Lawrie, Director of Student Financial Services
61 Sever Street, Worcester, MA 01609
(508) 791-9241 ext. 242

Benjamin Franklin Institute of Technology
Boston, Massachusetts
www.bfit.edu   Federal Code: 002151

2-year private technical college in very large city.
Enrollment: 380 undergrads.
BASIC COSTS (2005-2006)
Tuition and fees: $12,500.
Per-credit charge: $521.
FINANCIAL AID PICTURE (2004-2005)
Students with need: Need-based aid available for part-time students.
Students without need: No-need awards available for academics.
FINANCIAL AID PROCEDURES
Forms required: FAFSA.
Dates and Deadlines: Priority date 4/1; no closing date. Applicants notified on a rolling basis starting 3/1; must reply within 4 week(s) of notification.
CONTACT
Kevin Sullivan, Director of Financial Aid
41 Berkeley Street, Boston, MA 02116
(617) 423-4630

Bentley College
Waltham, Massachusetts   Federal Code: 002124
www.bentley.edu   CSS Code: 3096

4-year private business college in small city.
Enrollment: 4,220 undergrads, 7% part-time. 931 full-time freshmen.
Selectivity: Admits less than 50% of applicants.
BASIC COSTS (2006-2007)
Tuition and fees: $30,044.
Room and board: $10,530.
FINANCIAL AID PICTURE (2004-2005)
Students with need: Out of 737 full-time freshmen who applied for aid, 511 were judged to have need. Of these, 511 received aid, and 122 had their full need met. Average financial aid package met 91% of need; average scholarship/grant was $16,755; average loan was $3,940. For part-time students, average financial aid package was $4,285.
Students without need: 92 full-time freshmen who did not demonstrate need for aid received scholarships/grants; average award was $11,409. No-need awards available for academics, athletics, leadership, minority status.
Scholarships offered: *Merit:* Trustee Scholarships: full tuition; based on superior record of academic accomplishment. President's Scholarships: half or one-third tuition; based on excellent academic record. Bentley's Service Learning Scholarships: $5,000; for students with excellent academic records who have demonstrated commitment to service learning. *Athletic:* 4 full-time freshmen received athletic scholarships; average amount $32,478.
Cumulative student debt: 65% of graduating class had student loans; average debt was $27,132.
Additional info: Deadlines for receipt of CSS PROFILE: early decision 12/15, early action and regular decision 2/1.
FINANCIAL AID PROCEDURES
Forms required: FAFSA, CSS PROFILE.
Dates and Deadlines: Closing date 2/1. Applicants notified on a rolling basis starting 3/25.
Transfers: Priority date 3/1; no deadline.

Massachusetts Bentley College

CONTACT
Donna Kendall, Director of Financial Assistance
175 Forest Street, Waltham, MA 02452-4705
(781) 891-3441

Berklee College of Music
Boston, Massachusetts
www.berklee.edu   Federal Code: 002126

4-year private music college in very large city.
Enrollment: 3,164 undergrads. 861 full-time freshmen.
Selectivity: Admits 50 to 75% of applicants.

BASIC COSTS (2006-2007)
Tuition and fees: $26,750.
Per-credit charge: $1,125.
Room and board: $12,550.
Additional info: Required fees include one time charge for purchase of laptop.

FINANCIAL AID PICTURE (2004-2005)
Students with need: Out of 623 full-time freshmen who applied for aid, 413 were judged to have need. Of these, 413 received aid, and 412 had their full need met. For part-time students, average financial aid package was $19,066.
Students without need: This college only awards aid to students with need.
Scholarships offered: Berklee Entering Student Talent (BEST) Awards; based on evaluation of audition tape.

FINANCIAL AID PROCEDURES
Forms required: FAFSA, institutional form.
Dates and Deadlines: Priority date 3/1; no closing date. Applicants notified on a rolling basis starting 4/1; must reply within 3 week(s) of notification.
Transfers: Financial aid transcripts required from all colleges previously attended.

CONTACT
Julie Poorman, Director of Financial Aid
1140 Boylston Street, Boston, MA 02215
(800) 538-3844

Berkshire Community College
Pittsfield, Massachusetts
www.berkshirecc.edu   Federal Code: 002167

2-year public community college in small city.
Enrollment: 1,772 undergrads, 50% part-time. 299 full-time freshmen.
Selectivity: Open admission; but selective for some programs.

BASIC COSTS (2005-2006)
Tuition and fees: $3,600; out-of-state residents $10,620.
Per-credit charge: $26; out-of-state residents $260.
Additional info: $133 per-credit-hour (tuition/fees): New England Regional tuition, New York residents. All part-time students pay $120 per-credit-hour.

FINANCIAL AID PICTURE (2004-2005)
Students with need: Average financial aid package for all full-time undergraduates was $3,602. 77% awarded as scholarships/grants, 23% awarded as loans/jobs. Need-based aid available for part-time students. Work study available nights, weekends, and for part-time students.
Cumulative student debt: 70% of graduating class had student loans; average debt was $2,200.
Additional info: Tuition waivers available to students who are Massachusetts residents and fall into one of the following categories: adopted or foster children, Massachusetts Rehabilitation Commission clients, high-scoring MCAS students, National Guard members, Native Americans, state employees and their dependents, and veterans.

FINANCIAL AID PROCEDURES
Forms required: FAFSA.
Dates and Deadlines: Priority date 5/1; no closing date. Applicants notified on a rolling basis starting 6/1; must reply within 2 week(s) of notification.

CONTACT
Anne Moore, Director of Financial Aid
1350 West Street, Pittsfield, MA 01201-5786
(413) 499-4660 ext. 279

Boston Architectural Center
Boston, Massachusetts
www.the-bac.edu   Federal Code: 003966

6-year private school of architecture, design studies and interior design in very large city.
Enrollment: 513 undergrads, 3% part-time. 75 full-time freshmen.
Selectivity: Open admission.

BASIC COSTS (2005-2006)
Tuition and fees: $8,624.
Per-credit charge: $717.

FINANCIAL AID PICTURE (2005-2006)
Students with need: Average financial aid package met 41% of need; average scholarship/grant was $4,410; average loan was $2,625. For part-time students, average financial aid package was $4,250.
Students without need: No-need awards available for academics, art, leadership.

FINANCIAL AID PROCEDURES
Forms required: FAFSA.
Dates and Deadlines: Priority date 4/15; no closing date. Applicants notified on a rolling basis starting 3/1; must reply within 2 week(s) of notification.
Transfers: Applicants notified on a rolling basis starting 3/1; must reply within 2 week(s) of notification.

CONTACT
Anne Downey, Director of Financial Aid
320 Newbury Street, Boston, MA 02115-2795
(617) 585-0125

Boston College
Chestnut Hill, Massachusetts
www.bc.edu   Federal Code: 002128
                      CSS Code: 3083

4-year private university in small city, affiliated with Roman Catholic Church.
Enrollment: 9,019 undergrads. 2,309 full-time freshmen.
Selectivity: Admits less than 50% of applicants.

BASIC COSTS (2006-2007)
Tuition and fees: $33,506.
Room and board: $10,720.

FINANCIAL AID PICTURE (2004-2005)
Students with need: Out of 1,441 full-time freshmen who applied for aid, 967 were judged to have need. Of these, 967 received aid, and 967 had their full need met. Average financial aid package met 100% of need; average scholarship/grant was $19,072; average loan was $3,707. Need-based aid available for part-time students.
Students without need: 17 full-time freshmen who did not demonstrate need for aid received scholarships/grants; average award was $10,085. No-need awards available for academics, athletics, leadership, ROTC.

Scholarships offered: 60 full-time freshmen received athletic scholarships; average amount $29,130.

FINANCIAL AID PROCEDURES
Forms required: FAFSA, CSS PROFILE.
Dates and Deadlines: Priority date 2/1; no closing date. Applicants notified by 4/1; must reply by 5/1.
Transfers: Priority date 3/15. Must reply within 2 week(s) of notification.

CONTACT
Melissa Metcalf, Manager, Student Financial Services
140 Commonwealth Avenue, Devlin Hall 208, Chestnut Hill, MA 02467-3809
(617) 552-3300

Boston Conservatory
Boston, Massachusetts
www.bostonconservatory.edu   Federal Code: 002129

4-year private music college in very large city.
Enrollment: 409 undergrads.
Selectivity: Admits less than 50% of applicants.

BASIC COSTS (2005-2006)
Tuition and fees: $26,005.
Room and board: $13,780.

FINANCIAL AID PICTURE
Students with need: Need-based aid available for full-time and part-time students.
Students without need: No-need awards available for music/drama.

FINANCIAL AID PROCEDURES
Forms required: FAFSA, institutional form.
Dates and Deadlines: Closing date 2/1. Applicants notified by 4/1; must reply by 5/1.

CONTACT
James Bynum, Director of Financial Aid
8 The Fenway, Boston, MA 02215
(617) 912-9147

Boston University
Boston, Massachusetts
www.bu.edu   Federal Code: 002130   CSS Code: 3087

4-year private university in very large city.
Enrollment: 16,538 undergrads, 2% part-time. 4,209 full-time freshmen.
Selectivity: Admits 50 to 75% of applicants.

BASIC COSTS (2006-2007)
Tuition and fees: $33,792.
Per-credit charge: $1,042.
Room and board: $10,480.

FINANCIAL AID PICTURE (2005-2006)
Students with need: Out of 2,708 full-time freshmen who applied for aid, 2,163 were judged to have need. Of these, 2,156 received aid, and 1,179 had their full need met. Average financial aid package met 90% of need; average scholarship/grant was $19,149; average loan was $3,593. For part-time students, average financial aid package was $15,463.
Students without need: 461 full-time freshmen who did not demonstrate need for aid received scholarships/grants; average award was $15,849. No-need awards available for academics, alumni affiliation, art, athletics, leadership, music/drama, religious affiliation, ROTC, state/district residency.
Scholarships offered: *Merit:* Trustee Scholar Program; full tuition and fees (renewable); candidates nominated by high school principals, headmasters, or students. University Scholarships; half tuition (renewable); based on exceptionally strong high school academic record. Dean's Scholarships; $10,000 (renewable); based on strong academic credentials; for students who have applied for need-based financial aid but have financial resources which exceed cost of attendance. Dr. Martin Luther King, Jr. Scholarship; full tuition; for academically gifted students with proven leadership abilities and strong commitment to social justice and community involvement. *Athletic:* 53 full-time freshmen received athletic scholarships; average amount $32,554.
Cumulative student debt: 57% of graduating class had student loans; average debt was $21,196.
Additional info: Financial aid deadline for early decision applicants: 11/01; notification date: 2/15.

FINANCIAL AID PROCEDURES
Forms required: FAFSA, CSS PROFILE, state aid form.
Dates and Deadlines: Closing date 2/15. Applicants notified on a rolling basis starting 3/15; must reply by 5/1 or within 2 week(s) of notification.
Transfers: Priority date 4/1. Transfer students cannot receive duplicate disbursements simultaneously from different institutions.

CONTACT
Christine McGuire, Director of Financial Assistance
121 Bay State Road, Boston, MA 02215
(617) 353-2965

Brandeis University
Waltham, Massachusetts
www.brandeis.edu   Federal Code: 002133   CSS Code: 3092

4-year private university in small city.
Enrollment: 3,215 undergrads. 739 full-time freshmen.
Selectivity: Admits less than 50% of applicants.

BASIC COSTS (2006-2007)
Tuition and fees: $34,035.
Room and board: $9,463.

FINANCIAL AID PICTURE (2005-2006)
Students with need: Out of 581 full-time freshmen who applied for aid, 401 were judged to have need. Of these, 401 received aid, and 120 had their full need met. Average financial aid package met 83% of need; average scholarship/grant was $19,252; average loan was $3,826. Need-based aid available for part-time students.
Students without need: 583 full-time freshmen who did not demonstrate need for aid received scholarships/grants; average award was $18,159. No-need awards available for academics.
Scholarships offered: Justice Brandeis Scholarships; full tuition. Martin Luther King scholarships; tuition and room and board. SERP Scholarships; $20,000; based on musical ability. Presidential scholarships; $20,000. Dean's Awards; $15,000. Waltham High School scholarships; full tuition.
Cumulative student debt: 61% of graduating class had student loans; average debt was $21,437.

FINANCIAL AID PROCEDURES
Forms required: FAFSA, CSS PROFILE.
Dates and Deadlines: Priority date 1/15; no closing date. Applicants notified on a rolling basis starting 4/1.
Transfers: Priority date 4/1. International transfer students seeking scholarship or need-based financial assistance must apply by 2/01.

CONTACT
Peter Giumette, Director of Financial Aid
Office of Admissions, Waltham, MA 02454-9110
(781) 736-3700

Bridgewater State College
Bridgewater, Massachusetts
www.bridgew.edu   Federal Code: 002183

4-year public liberal arts and teachers college in large town.
Enrollment: 7,467 undergrads, 15% part-time. 1,217 full-time freshmen.
Selectivity: Admits over 75% of applicants.

BASIC COSTS (2005-2006)
Tuition and fees: $5,506; out-of-state residents $11,646.
Per-credit charge: $38; out-of-state residents $294.
Room and board: $6,614.
Additional info: Tuition/fee waivers available for unemployed or children of unemployed.

FINANCIAL AID PICTURE (2005-2006)
Students with need: Out of 1,012 full-time freshmen who applied for aid, 709 were judged to have need. Of these, 706 received aid. Average financial aid package met 51% of need; average scholarship/grant was $2,356; average loan was $2,688. For part-time students, average financial aid package was $3,878.
Students without need: 28 full-time freshmen who did not demonstrate need for aid received scholarships/grants; average award was $3,069. No-need awards available for academics, leadership, minority status, state/district residency.
Cumulative student debt: 32% of graduating class had student loans; average debt was $15,065.

FINANCIAL AID PROCEDURES
Forms required: FAFSA.
Dates and Deadlines: Priority date 3/1; no closing date. Applicants notified on a rolling basis starting 4/1.

CONTACT
Janet Gumbris, Director of Financial Aid
Gates House, Bridgewater, MA 02325
(508) 531-1341

Bristol Community College
Fall River, Massachusetts
www.bristolcommunitycollege.edu   Federal Code: 002176

2-year public community college in small city.
Enrollment: 5,608 undergrads, 49% part-time. 1,104 full-time freshmen.
Selectivity: Open admission; but selective for some programs.

BASIC COSTS (2005-2006)
Tuition and fees: $3,720; out-of-state residents $9,900.
Per-credit charge: $24; out-of-state residents $230.
Additional info: Tuition/fee waivers available for unemployed or children of unemployed.

FINANCIAL AID PICTURE
Students with need: Need-based aid available for full-time and part-time students. Work study available nights, weekends, and for part-time students.
Students without need: No-need awards available for academics, art, leadership, minority status, music/drama.

FINANCIAL AID PROCEDURES
Forms required: FAFSA, state aid form, institutional form.
Dates and Deadlines: Priority date 5/1; no closing date. Applicants notified on a rolling basis starting 5/1; must reply within 2 week(s) of notification.

CONTACT
David Allen, Director of Financial Aid
777 Elsbree Street, Fall River, MA 02720-7395
(508) 678-2811 ext. 2513

Bunker Hill Community College
Boston, Massachusetts
www.bhcc.mass.edu   Federal Code: 011210

2-year public community college in very large city.
Enrollment: 5,723 undergrads, 62% part-time. 642 full-time freshmen.
Selectivity: Open admission; but selective for some programs.

BASIC COSTS (2005-2006)
Tuition and fees: $3,000; out-of-state residents $9,180.
Per-credit charge: $24; out-of-state residents $230.
Additional info: New England Regional Tuition: $112 per-credit-hour. Tuition/fee waivers available for minority students.

FINANCIAL AID PICTURE (2004-2005)
Students with need: 88% of average financial aid package awarded as scholarships/grants, 12% awarded as loans/jobs. Need-based aid available for part-time students.
Students without need: No-need awards available for academics.

FINANCIAL AID PROCEDURES
Forms required: FAFSA.
Dates and Deadlines: Priority date 4/15; no closing date. Applicants notified on a rolling basis starting 6/1; must reply within 2 week(s) of notification.
Transfers: No deadline. Applicants notified on a rolling basis; must reply within 2 week(s) of notification.

CONTACT
Susan Sullivan, Director of Financial Aid
250 New Rutherford Avenue, Boston, MA 02129-2925
(617) 228-2275

Cambridge College
Cambridge, Massachusetts
www.cambridgecollege.edu

4-year private liberal arts college in very large city.
Enrollment: 909 undergrads, 75% part-time. 25 full-time freshmen.
Selectivity: Open admission.

BASIC COSTS (2005-2006)
Tuition and fees: $9,750.
Per-credit charge: $325.

FINANCIAL AID PICTURE (2005-2006)
Students with need: For part-time students, average financial aid package was $8,630.

FINANCIAL AID PROCEDURES
Forms required: FAFSA, institutional form.
Dates and Deadlines: No deadline.

CONTACT
Gerri Major, Director of Financial Aid
1000 Massachusetts Avenue, Cambridge, MA 02138
(617) 868-1000

Cape Cod Community College
West Barnstable, Massachusetts
www.capecod.edu   Federal Code: 002168

2-year public community college in small town.
Enrollment: 3,209 undergrads. 324 full-time freshmen.
Selectivity: Open admission; but selective for some programs.

BASIC COSTS (2005-2006)
Tuition and fees: $3,660; out-of-state residents $9,840.
Per-credit charge: $24; out-of-state residents $230.
Additional info: Tuition/fee waivers available for minority students.

FINANCIAL AID PICTURE (2004-2005)
Students with need: Out of 203 full-time freshmen who applied for aid, 139 were judged to have need. Of these, 132 received aid, and 11 had their full need met. Average financial aid package met 55% of need; average scholarship/grant was $3,252; average loan was $1,549. For part-time students, average financial aid package was $2,978.
Students without need: 27 full-time freshmen who did not demonstrate need for aid received scholarships/grants; average award was $1,860. No-need awards available for academics, art, job skills, leadership, music/drama, state/district residency.

FINANCIAL AID PROCEDURES
Forms required: FAFSA.
Dates and Deadlines: Priority date 4/1; no closing date. Applicants notified on a rolling basis starting 5/1.

CONTACT
Sherry Andersen, Director of Financial Aid
2240 Iyanough Road, West Barnstable, MA 02668-1599
(508) 362-2131 ext. 4393

Clark University
Worcester, Massachusetts   Federal Code: 002139
www.clarku.edu   CSS Code: 3279

4-year private university and liberal arts college in small city.
Enrollment: 2,142 undergrads, 3% part-time. 557 full-time freshmen.
Selectivity: Admits 50 to 75% of applicants.

BASIC COSTS (2006-2007)
Tuition and fees: $31,465.
Per-credit charge: $975.
Room and board: $5,900.
Additional info: New student contingency fee: $50. Fifth-year tuition waived for eligible undergraduates admitted to accelerated bachelor's/master's programs.

FINANCIAL AID PICTURE (2005-2006)
Students with need: Out of 408 full-time freshmen who applied for aid, 309 were judged to have need. Of these, 302 received aid, and 204 had their full need met. Average financial aid package met 93% of need; average scholarship/grant was $17,645; average loan was $3,208. Need-based aid available for part-time students.
Students without need: 145 full-time freshmen who did not demonstrate need for aid received scholarships/grants; average award was $11,591. No-need awards available for academics, leadership.
Scholarships offered: Scholarships; $8,000-$16,000; based on superior academic achievement or community service involvement.
Cumulative student debt: 88% of graduating class had student loans; average debt was $18,990.

FINANCIAL AID PROCEDURES
Forms required: FAFSA, CSS PROFILE.
Dates and Deadlines: Closing date 2/1. Applicants notified by 3/31; must reply by 5/1 or within 2 week(s) of notification.
Transfers: Priority date 4/1; no deadline. Financial aid transcript from previous institution(s) attended required.

CONTACT
Mary Ellen Severance, Director of Financial Aid and Student Employment
950 Main Street, Worcester, MA 01610-1477
(508) 793-7478

College of the Holy Cross
Worcester, Massachusetts   Federal Code: 002141
www.holycross.edu   CSS Code: 3282

4-year private liberal arts college in small city, affiliated with Roman Catholic Church.
Enrollment: 2,777 undergrads. 721 full-time freshmen.
Selectivity: Admits less than 50% of applicants.

BASIC COSTS (2006-2007)
Tuition and fees: $33,313.
Room and board: $9,580.

FINANCIAL AID PICTURE (2005-2006)
Students with need: Out of 522 full-time freshmen who applied for aid, 437 were judged to have need. Of these, 421 received aid, and 421 had their full need met. Average financial aid package met 100% of need; average scholarship/grant was $20,573; average loan was $3,513.
Students without need: 41 full-time freshmen who did not demonstrate need for aid received scholarships/grants; average award was $17,930. No-need awards available for academics, athletics, ROTC.
Scholarships offered: 7 full-time freshmen received athletic scholarships; average amount $41,089.
Cumulative student debt: 52% of graduating class had student loans; average debt was $19,390.

FINANCIAL AID PROCEDURES
Forms required: FAFSA. CSS PROFILE required of all students applying for institutional aid.
Dates and Deadlines: Closing date 2/1. Applicants notified by 3/30; must reply by 5/1.
Transfers: Priority date 4/15.

CONTACT
Lynne Myers, Director of Financial Aid
One College Street, Worcester, MA 01610-2395
(508) 793-2265

Curry College
Milton, Massachusetts
www.curry.edu   Federal Code: 002143

4-year private nursing and liberal arts college in large town.
Enrollment: 2,503 undergrads, 22% part-time. 531 full-time freshmen.
Selectivity: Admits 50 to 75% of applicants.

BASIC COSTS (2006-2007)
Tuition and fees: $24,140.
Per-credit charge: $780.
Room and board: $9,770.
Additional info: PAL (Program for Advancement of Learning) students pay an additional program participation fee of up to $4,960.

FINANCIAL AID PICTURE (2004-2005)
Students with need: Out of 392 full-time freshmen who applied for aid, 390 were judged to have need. Of these, 389 received aid, and 9 had their full need met. Average financial aid package met 67% of need; average scholarship/grant was $10,839; average loan was $2,668. For part-time students, average financial aid package was $4,810.
Students without need: 8 full-time freshmen who did not demonstrate need for aid received scholarships/grants; average award was $3,510. No-need awards available for academics, leadership.
Cumulative student debt: 53% of graduating class had student loans; average debt was $25,604.

FINANCIAL AID PROCEDURES
Forms required: FAFSA.

Dates and Deadlines: Priority date 3/1; no closing date. Applicants notified on a rolling basis starting 3/10; must reply by 5/1 or within 2 week(s) of notification.

CONTACT
Stephanny Elias, Director, Student Financial Services
1071 Blue Hill Avenue, Milton, MA 02186-9984
(617) 333-2146

Dean College
Franklin, Massachusetts
www.dean.edu   Federal Code: 002144

2-year private junior and liberal arts college in large town.
Enrollment: 1,249 undergrads.
Selectivity: Admits 50 to 75% of applicants.

BASIC COSTS (2006-2007)
Tuition and fees: $23,783.
Per-credit charge: $452.
Room and board: $10,253.

FINANCIAL AID PICTURE (2005-2006)
Students with need: 65% of average financial aid package awarded as scholarships/grants, 35% awarded as loans/jobs. Need-based aid available for part-time students.
Students without need: No-need awards available for academics, athletics, leadership, music/drama.
Scholarships offered: Trustee's Scholarship; $10,000 - $12,000 per year; decision based on outstanding academic accomplishments or potential. President's Leadership Scholarship; $8,000 - $12,000 per year; given to students with leadership positions during their high school careers. Performing Arts Scholarship; $5,000 - $11,000 per year; achievement in dance or theatre.

FINANCIAL AID PROCEDURES
Forms required: FAFSA.
Dates and Deadlines: Priority date 3/1; no closing date. Applicants notified on a rolling basis starting 4/1; must reply within 3 week(s) of notification.

CONTACT
Jenny Aguiar, Director of Financial Aid
99 Main Street, Franklin, MA 02038-1994
(508) 541-1518

Eastern Nazarene College
Quincy, Massachusetts
www.enc.edu   Federal Code: 002145

4-year private liberal arts college in small city, affiliated with Church of the Nazarene.
Enrollment: 1,060 undergrads.

BASIC COSTS (2005-2006)
Tuition and fees: $18,310.
Per-credit charge: $715.
Room and board: $6,590.
Additional info: Tuition/fee waivers available for minority students.

FINANCIAL AID PICTURE (2005-2006)
Students with need: 76% of average financial aid package awarded as scholarships/grants, 24% awarded as loans/jobs. Need-based aid available for part-time students. Work study available nights, weekends, and for part-time students.
Students without need: No-need awards available for academics, alumni affiliation, leadership, music/drama, religious affiliation, state/district residency.
Scholarships offered: Activities Scholarship; up to $1,500 per year; competitive based on documented school, community, and church activities; up to 25 awarded.
Additional info: Participant in Massachusetts University pre-payment plan.

FINANCIAL AID PROCEDURES
Forms required: FAFSA, institutional form.
Dates and Deadlines: Priority date 2/28; no closing date. Applicants notified on a rolling basis starting 3/15; must reply within 2 week(s) of notification.
Transfers: Aid limited to amount eligible minus what students received at prior institution. Pell grant may also vary, depending on cost of attendance versus other school's cost and student's enrollment status.

CONTACT
Doug Fish, Director of Financial Aid
23 East Elm Avenue, Quincy, MA 02170-2999
(617) 745-3712

Elms College
Chicopee, Massachusetts
www.elms.edu   Federal Code: 002140

4-year private liberal arts college in small city, affiliated with Roman Catholic Church.
Enrollment: 825 undergrads.
Selectivity: Admits over 75% of applicants.

BASIC COSTS (2006-2007)
Tuition and fees: $21,585.
Per-credit charge: $440.
Room and board: $8,400.

FINANCIAL AID PICTURE
Students with need: Need-based aid available for full-time and part-time students. Work study available nights, weekends, and for part-time students.
Students without need: No-need awards available for academics, alumni affiliation, leadership, state/district residency.

FINANCIAL AID PROCEDURES
Forms required: FAFSA, institutional form.
Dates and Deadlines: Priority date 3/1; no closing date. Applicants notified on a rolling basis starting 2/15; must reply by 5/1 or within 2 week(s) of notification.

CONTACT
Troy Davis, Director of Student Financial Aid Services
291 Springfield Street, Chicopee, MA 01013
(413) 592-3189

Emerson College
Boston, Massachusetts   Federal Code: 002146
www.emerson.edu   CSS Code: 3367

4-year private college of communication and the arts in very large city.
Enrollment: 3,165 undergrads, 3% part-time. 721 full-time freshmen.
Selectivity: Admits less than 50% of applicants.

BASIC COSTS (2006-2007)
Tuition and fees: $25,718.
Per-credit charge: $789.
Room and board: $10,870.

FINANCIAL AID PICTURE (2004-2005)
Students with need: Out of 539 full-time freshmen who applied for aid, 397 were judged to have need. Of these, 397 received aid, and 302 had their full need met. Average financial aid package met 76% of need; average scholarship/grant was $11,814; average loan was $3,545. For part-time students, average financial aid package was $11,463.
Students without need: 151 full-time freshmen who did not demonstrate need for aid received scholarships/grants; average award was $9,590. No-need awards available for academics, music/drama.
Scholarships offered: Trustee's Scholarships (Honors Program); half tuition. Dean's Scholarships; $8,000. Emerson Stage Scholarships; vary, based on performing arts audition and academic merit.
Cumulative student debt: 55% of graduating class had student loans; average debt was $16,222.
Additional info: Massachusetts Loan Plan available for parents of dependent undergraduates.

FINANCIAL AID PROCEDURES
Forms required: FAFSA, CSS PROFILE.
Dates and Deadlines: Priority date 3/1; no closing date. Applicants notified on a rolling basis starting 4/1; must reply by 5/1 or within 3 week(s) of notification.
Transfers: Priority date 4/1.

CONTACT
Michelle Smith, Director of Student Financial Services
120 Boylston Street, Boston, MA 02116-4624
(617) 824-8655

Emmanuel College
Boston, Massachusetts
www.emmanuel.edu   Federal Code: 002147

4-year private liberal arts college in very large city, affiliated with Roman Catholic Church.
Enrollment: 2,000 undergrads, 25% part-time. 432 full-time freshmen.
Selectivity: Admits 50 to 75% of applicants.

BASIC COSTS (2006-2007)
Tuition and fees: $24,200.
Per-credit charge: $744.
Room and board: $10,400.

FINANCIAL AID PICTURE (2005-2006)
Students with need: Out of 387 full-time freshmen who applied for aid, 332 were judged to have need. Of these, 332 received aid, and 103 had their full need met. Average financial aid package met 68% of need; average scholarship/grant was $10,057; average loan was $3,449. For part-time students, average financial aid package was $7,315.
Students without need: 47 full-time freshmen who did not demonstrate need for aid received scholarships/grants; average award was $11,641. No-need awards available for academics, alumni affiliation, art, leadership.
Cumulative student debt: 74% of graduating class had student loans; average debt was $17,759.

FINANCIAL AID PROCEDURES
Forms required: FAFSA, institutional form.
Dates and Deadlines: Priority date 4/1; no closing date. Applicants notified on a rolling basis starting 3/15; must reply by 5/1.

CONTACT
Jennifer Porter, Assistant Vice President for Student Financial Services
400 The Fenway, Boston, MA 02115
(617) 735-9938

Endicott College
Beverly, Massachusetts
www.endicott.edu   Federal Code: 002148

4-year private liberal arts college in large town.
Enrollment: 2,038 undergrads, 9% part-time. 500 full-time freshmen.
Selectivity: Admits less than 50% of applicants.

BASIC COSTS (2006-2007)
Tuition and fees: $21,374.
Per-credit charge: $646.
Room and board: $10,254.

FINANCIAL AID PICTURE (2005-2006)
Students with need: Out of 359 full-time freshmen who applied for aid, 272 were judged to have need. Of these, 271 received aid, and 29 had their full need met. Average financial aid package met 55% of need; average scholarship/grant was $6,359; average loan was $2,851. For part-time students, average financial aid package was $5,856.
Students without need: 62 full-time freshmen who did not demonstrate need for aid received scholarships/grants; average award was $4,469. No-need awards available for academics, alumni affiliation, art, leadership, ROTC, state/district residency.
Cumulative student debt: 62% of graduating class had student loans; average debt was $18,000.

FINANCIAL AID PROCEDURES
Forms required: FAFSA, institutional form.
Dates and Deadlines: Closing date 3/15. Applicants notified on a rolling basis starting 3/15; must reply within 2 week(s) of notification.

CONTACT
Marcia Toomey, Director of Financial Aid
376 Hale Street, Beverly, MA 01915-9985
(978) 232-2060

Fisher College
Boston, Massachusetts
www.fisher.edu   Federal Code: 002150

2-year private liberal arts college in very large city.
Enrollment: 507 undergrads, 1% part-time. 219 full-time freshmen.
Selectivity: Admits 50 to 75% of applicants.

BASIC COSTS (2005-2006)
Tuition and fees: $18,450.
Room and board: $11,210.

FINANCIAL AID PICTURE (2005-2006)
Students with need: Average financial aid package met 44% of need; average scholarship/grant was $9,046; average loan was $2,959. For part-time students, average financial aid package was $6,285.
Students without need: No-need awards available for academics, alumni affiliation, state/district residency.
Scholarships offered: Fisher Honor Scholarship; $2,500 (renewable with 3.0 GPA); based on outstanding academic and personal achievement, contribution to school and community. Business Administration and Computer Technology Scholarship; $1,500 for 2.5-2.99 GPA, $3,000 for minimum 3.0 GPA; renewable; for students enrolling in associate programs in business administration or computer technology.
Cumulative student debt: 80% of graduating class had student loans; average debt was $7,100.

FINANCIAL AID PROCEDURES
Forms required: FAFSA.
Dates and Deadlines: Priority date 3/1; no closing date. Applicants notified on a rolling basis starting 3/1; must reply within 2 week(s) of notification.

Massachusetts Fisher College

CONTACT
Frank Lauder, Director of Financial Aid
118 Beacon Street, Boston, MA 02116
(617) 236-4418

Fitchburg State College
Fitchburg, Massachusetts
www.fsc.edu   Federal Code: 002184

4-year public liberal arts and teachers college in large town.
Enrollment: 3,411 undergrads, 14% part-time. 599 full-time freshmen.
Selectivity: Admits 50 to 75% of applicants.

BASIC COSTS (2005-2006)
Tuition and fees: $5,002; out-of-state residents $11,082.
Room and board: $6,104.

FINANCIAL AID PICTURE
Students with need: Need-based aid available for full-time and part-time students. Work study available nights, weekends, and for part-time students.
Students without need: No-need awards available for academics, alumni affiliation, leadership, state/district residency.
Scholarships offered: Renewable scholarships awarded on basis of high school record and test scores.

FINANCIAL AID PROCEDURES
Forms required: FAFSA, institutional form.
Dates and Deadlines: Priority date 3/1; no closing date. Applicants notified on a rolling basis starting 3/15; must reply within 2 week(s) of notification.

CONTACT
Pamela McCafferty, Dean of Enrollment Management
160 Pearl Street, Fitchburg, MA 01420-2697
(978) 665-3156

Framingham State College
Framingham, Massachusetts
www.framingham.edu   Federal Code: 002185

4-year public liberal arts and teachers college in small city.
Enrollment: 3,460 undergrads, 13% part-time. 642 full-time freshmen.
Selectivity: Admits 50 to 75% of applicants.

BASIC COSTS (2005-2006)
Tuition and fees: $4,999; out-of-state residents $11,079.
Per-credit charge: $40; out-of-state residents $294.
Room and board: $6,157.
Additional info: Fees include mandatory laptop purchase by new students. New England Regional tuition rate $1456.

FINANCIAL AID PICTURE (2004-2005)
Students with need: Out of 495 full-time freshmen who applied for aid, 345 were judged to have need. Of these, 345 received aid, and 228 had their full need met. Average financial aid package met 80% of need; average scholarship/grant was $3,512; average loan was $2,112. For part-time students, average financial aid package was $5,498.
Students without need: 29 full-time freshmen who did not demonstrate need for aid received scholarships/grants; average award was $1,867. No-need awards available for academics.
Scholarships offered: Senator Paul E. Tsongas Scholarship; full tuition and fees; available to Massachusetts residents; based on 3.75 high school GPA and test scores; 5 awarded. Merit scholarships available to students majoring in education, natural or physical sciences; based on GPA and test scores.
Cumulative student debt: 70% of graduating class had student loans; average debt was $12,500.

FINANCIAL AID PROCEDURES
Forms required: FAFSA.
Dates and Deadlines: Priority date 3/1; no closing date. Applicants notified on a rolling basis starting 4/15; must reply by 5/1 or within 2 week(s) of notification.
Transfers: Priority date 11/1; no deadline. Applicants notified on a rolling basis; must reply within 2 week(s) of notification.

CONTACT
Susan Lanzillo, Director of Financial Aid
100 State Street, Framingham, MA 01701-9101
(508) 626-4534

Franklin W. Olin College of Engineering
Needham, Massachusetts
www.olin.edu

4-year private engineering college in large town.
Enrollment: 279 undergrads. 76 full-time freshmen.
Selectivity: Admits less than 50% of applicants.

BASIC COSTS (2005-2006)
Tuition and fees: $150.
Room and board: $10,870.
Additional info: Every admitted student receives 4-year full-tuition scholarship.

FINANCIAL AID PICTURE (2005-2006)
Students with need: 81% of average financial aid package awarded as scholarships/grants, 19% awarded as loans/jobs.
Students without need: No-need awards available for academics, leadership.
Scholarships offered: All students receive full tuition scholarships.
Additional info: No financial aid forms necessary.

FINANCIAL AID PROCEDURES
Forms required: FAFSA.
Dates and Deadlines: Closing date 4/16. Applicants notified by 3/1; must reply by 5/1.

CONTACT
Duncan Murdoch, Dean of Admission
Olin Way, Needham, MA 02492-1245
(781) 292-2222

Gibbs College
Boston, Massachusetts
www.gibbsboston.edu   Federal Code: 007481

2-year for-profit junior college in very large city.
Enrollment: 900 undergrads.
Selectivity: Open admission.

BASIC COSTS (2005-2006)
Tuition and fees: $15,000.

FINANCIAL AID PICTURE
Students with need: Need-based aid available for full-time and part-time students.
Students without need: This college only awards aid to students with need.

FINANCIAL AID PROCEDURES
Forms required: FAFSA, institutional form.
Dates and Deadlines: No deadline. Applicants notified on a rolling basis.

CONTACT
Lisa Sander, Director of Financial Planning
126 Newbury Street, Boston, MA 02116
(617) 578-7100

Gordon College
Wenham, Massachusetts   Federal Code: 002153
www.gordon.edu   CSS Code: 3417

4-year private liberal arts college in small town, affiliated with nondenominational tradition.
Enrollment: 1,584 undergrads, 2% part-time. 414 full-time freshmen.
Selectivity: Admits over 75% of applicants.

BASIC COSTS (2006-2007)
Tuition and fees: $24,278.
Per-credit charge: $1,642.
Room and board: $6,640.

FINANCIAL AID PICTURE (2005-2006)
Students with need: Average financial aid package met 71% of need; average scholarship/grant was $10,938; average loan was $3,057. For part-time students, average financial aid package was $12,069.
Students without need: No-need awards available for academics, alumni affiliation, leadership, minority status, music/drama, religious affiliation.
Scholarships offered: A.J. Gordon Scholarship; $12,000; renewable annually; based on academic achievement and leadership. Dean's Scholarships; $8,000; renewable; based on academic record. Challenge Scholarships; $6,000; renewable; based on academic record. Choral Scholars Program; $6,000; renewable; for students with excellent ability/academic performance seeking career in vocal music field.
Cumulative student debt: 55% of graduating class had student loans; average debt was $19,125.

FINANCIAL AID PROCEDURES
Forms required: FAFSA, CSS PROFILE, state aid form.
Dates and Deadlines: Closing date 3/1. Applicants notified on a rolling basis starting 4/15; must reply by 5/1 or within 2 week(s) of notification.

CONTACT
Barbara Layne, Associate Vice President, Student Financial Services
255 Grapevine Road, Wenham, MA 01984-1813
(800) 343-1379

Greenfield Community College
Greenfield, Massachusetts
www.gcc.mass.edu   Federal Code: 002169

2-year public community college in large town.
Enrollment: 1,958 undergrads, 51% part-time. 229 full-time freshmen.
Selectivity: Open admission; but selective for some programs.

BASIC COSTS (2005-2006)
Tuition and fees: $4,007; out-of-state residents $11,657.
Per-credit charge: $26; out-of-state residents $260.
Additional info: Tuition/fee waivers available for adults.

FINANCIAL AID PICTURE
Students with need: Need-based aid available for full-time and part-time students. Work study available nights, weekends, and for part-time students.
Students without need: This college only awards aid to students with need.

FINANCIAL AID PROCEDURES
Forms required: FAFSA, institutional form.

Dates and Deadlines: Priority date 4/15; no closing date. Applicants notified on a rolling basis starting 5/1; must reply within 2 week(s) of notification.

CONTACT
Jane Abbott, Director of Financial Aid
One College Drive, Greenfield, MA 01301
(413) 775-1109

Hampshire College
Amherst, Massachusetts   Federal Code: 004661
www.hampshire.edu   CSS Code: 3447

4-year private liberal arts college in large town.
Enrollment: 1,362 undergrads. 399 full-time freshmen.
Selectivity: Admits 50 to 75% of applicants.

BASIC COSTS (2006-2007)
Tuition and fees: $34,605.
Room and board: $9,030.

FINANCIAL AID PICTURE (2005-2006)
Students with need: Out of 242 full-time freshmen who applied for aid, 209 were judged to have need. Of these, 208 received aid, and 161 had their full need met. Average financial aid package met 87% of need; average scholarship/grant was $21,000; average loan was $2,625.
Students without need: 69 full-time freshmen who did not demonstrate need for aid received scholarships/grants; average award was $4,375. No-need awards available for academics, leadership, minority status.
Cumulative student debt: 52% of graduating class had student loans; average debt was $19,400.

FINANCIAL AID PROCEDURES
Forms required: FAFSA, CSS PROFILE, institutional form.
Dates and Deadlines: Closing date 2/1. Applicants notified by 4/1; must reply by 5/1.

CONTACT
Kathleen Methot, Director of Financial Aid
893 West Street, Amherst, MA 01002-9988
(413) 559-5484

Harvard College
Cambridge, Massachusetts   Federal Code: 002155
www.college.harvard.edu   CSS Code: 3434

4-year private university in small city.
Enrollment: 6,613 undergrads. 1,650 full-time freshmen.
Selectivity: Admits less than 50% of applicants.

BASIC COSTS (2006-2007)
Tuition and fees: $33,709.
Room and board: $9,946.

FINANCIAL AID PICTURE (2005-2006)
Students with need: Out of 1,034 full-time freshmen who applied for aid, 852 were judged to have need. Of these, 852 received aid, and 852 had their full need met. Average financial aid package met 100% of need; average scholarship/grant was $30,162; average loan was $1,560.
Students without need: This college only awards aid to students with need.
Cumulative student debt: 49% of graduating class had student loans; average debt was $8,769.
Additional info: Institution meets full need of all admitted students.

FINANCIAL AID PROCEDURES
Forms required: FAFSA, CSS PROFILE.

Dates and Deadlines: Closing date 2/1. Applicants notified by 4/1; must reply by 5/1 or within 2 week(s) of notification.
Transfers: Closing date 2/15.
CONTACT
Sally Donahue, Director of Financial Aid
Byerly Hall, 8 Garden Street, Cambridge, MA 02138
(617) 495-1581

Hebrew College
Newton Centre, Massachusetts
www.hebrewcollege.edu   Federal Code: 002157

4-year private rabbinical college in small city, affiliated with Jewish faith.
Enrollment: 4 undergrads, 25% part-time. 2 full-time freshmen.
Selectivity: Admits 50 to 75% of applicants.
BASIC COSTS (2006-2007)
Tuition and fees: $24,500.
Per-credit charge: $810.
FINANCIAL AID PICTURE
Students with need: Need-based aid available for full-time and part-time students.
Students without need: No-need awards available for academics.
FINANCIAL AID PROCEDURES
Forms required: FAFSA, institutional form.
Dates and Deadlines: Priority date 5/1; no closing date. Applicants notified on a rolling basis starting 7/1; must reply within 3 week(s) of notification.
Transfers: Closing date 5/1.
CONTACT
Marilyn Jaye, Student Financial Services Manager
160 Herrick Road, Newton Centre, MA 02459
(617) 559-8642

Hellenic College/Holy Cross
Brookline, Massachusetts
www.hchc.edu   Federal Code: 002154

4-year private liberal arts and seminary college in large town, affiliated with Eastern Orthodox Church.
Enrollment: 84 undergrads. 24 full-time freshmen.
Selectivity: Admits over 75% of applicants.
BASIC COSTS (2005-2006)
Tuition and fees: $15,775.
Room and board: $9,260.
FINANCIAL AID PICTURE (2004-2005)
Students with need: Out of 24 full-time freshmen who applied for aid, 24 were judged to have need. Of these, 24 received aid. Average financial aid package met 45% of need; average scholarship/grant was $12,000; average loan was $2,625.
Students without need: This college only awards aid to students with need.
Cumulative student debt: 67% of graduating class had student loans; average debt was $19,000.
FINANCIAL AID PROCEDURES
Forms required: FAFSA, institutional form.
Dates and Deadlines: Closing date 4/1. Applicants notified on a rolling basis starting 10/1; must reply within 2 week(s) of notification.
Transfers: No deadline. Applicants notified on a rolling basis; must reply within 2 week(s) of notification.

CONTACT
George Georgenes, Director of Financial Aid
50 Goddard Avenue, Brookline, MA 02445
(617) 850-1297

Holyoke Community College
Holyoke, Massachusetts
www.hcc.mass.edu   Federal Code: 002170

2-year public community college in large town.
Enrollment: 5,580 undergrads, 46% part-time. 1,143 full-time freshmen.
Selectivity: Open admission; but selective for some programs.
BASIC COSTS (2005-2006)
Tuition and fees: $3,188; out-of-state residents $9,368.
Per-credit charge: $24; out-of-state residents $230.
FINANCIAL AID PICTURE (2004-2005)
Students with need: 80% of average financial aid package awarded as scholarships/grants, 20% awarded as loans/jobs. Need-based aid available for part-time students. Work study available nights.
Students without need: No-need awards available for academics, art, leadership, music/drama.
FINANCIAL AID PROCEDURES
Forms required: FAFSA.
Dates and Deadlines: Priority date 5/1; no closing date. Applicants notified on a rolling basis starting 5/1; must reply within 2 week(s) of notification.
CONTACT
Karen Derouin, Director of Financial Aid
303 Homestead Avenue, Holyoke, MA 01040
(413) 552-2248

Laboure College
Boston, Massachusetts
www.laboure.edu   Federal Code: 006324

2-year private health science and junior college in very large city, affiliated with Roman Catholic Church.
Enrollment: 450 undergrads.
Selectivity: Admits less than 50% of applicants.
BASIC COSTS (2005-2006)
Tuition and fees: $12,680.
Per-credit charge: $410.
FINANCIAL AID PICTURE
Students with need: Need-based aid available for full-time and part-time students. Work study available nights.
Students without need: No-need awards available for academics, alumni affiliation, leadership, religious affiliation.
Additional info: Allied Health Scholarship: covers cost of general education courses for students enrolled in electroneurodiagnostic technology, health information technology, and nutrition and food management programs; constitutes significant reduction in tuition. Caritas Christi Scholarship: for students who work 16 hours per week at a Caritas Christi healthcare agency; covers 25% of tuition for nursing and radiation therapy courses; also covers 50% of cost of nursing courses for students with LPN credential. Evening LPN Scholarship: discounts tuition 75% for evening nursing majors with LPN credential.
FINANCIAL AID PROCEDURES
Forms required: FAFSA, institutional form.
Dates and Deadlines: Priority date 4/1; no closing date. Applicants notified on a rolling basis starting 5/15; must reply within 2 week(s) of notification.

Transfers: Priority date 12/1.
CONTACT
Mark Virello, Chief Financial Officer
2120 Dorchester Avenue, Boston, MA 02124-5698
(617) 296-8300 ext. 4066

Lasell College
Newton, Massachusetts
www.lasell.edu   Federal Code: 002158

4-year private business and liberal arts college in small city.
Enrollment: 1,207 undergrads, 1% part-time. 373 full-time freshmen.
Selectivity: Admits 50 to 75% of applicants.

BASIC COSTS (2006-2007)
Tuition and fees: $20,900.
Per-credit charge: $660.
Room and board: $9,200.

FINANCIAL AID PICTURE (2005-2006)
Students with need: Out of 337 full-time freshmen who applied for aid, 295 were judged to have need. Of these, 295 received aid, and 27 had their full need met. Average financial aid package met 68% of need; average scholarship/grant was $12,200; average loan was $2,500. For part-time students, average financial aid package was $7,300.
Students without need: 46 full-time freshmen who did not demonstrate need for aid received scholarships/grants; average award was $14,800. No-need awards available for academics, alumni affiliation, leadership.
Cumulative student debt: 93% of graduating class had student loans; average debt was $20,800.

FINANCIAL AID PROCEDURES
Forms required: FAFSA, institutional form.
Dates and Deadlines: Priority date 3/1; no closing date. Applicants notified on a rolling basis starting 2/15; must reply by 5/1 or within 2 week(s) of notification.

CONTACT
Michele Kosboth, Director of Student Financial Planning
1844 Commonwealth Avenue, Newton, MA 02466
(617) 243-2227

Lesley University
Cambridge, Massachusetts
www.lesley.edu/lc   Federal Code: 002160

4-year private liberal arts and teachers college in very large city.
Enrollment: 1,079 undergrads, 12% part-time. 249 full-time freshmen.
Selectivity: Admits 50 to 75% of applicants.

BASIC COSTS (2006-2007)
Tuition and fees: $24,450.
Per-credit charge: $1,020.
Room and board: $10,500.

FINANCIAL AID PICTURE (2005-2006)
Students with need: Out of 234 full-time freshmen who applied for aid, 189 were judged to have need. Of these, 189 received aid, and 18 had their full need met. Average financial aid package met 70% of need; average scholarship/grant was $12,741; average loan was $3,507. For part-time students, average financial aid package was $9,860.
Students without need: 40 full-time freshmen who did not demonstrate need for aid received scholarships/grants; average award was $5,938. No-need awards available for academics, alumni affiliation, art, leadership, minority status, state/district residency.

Scholarships offered: Freshmen scholarships; $5,000 to full tuition; for students with strong academic backgrounds who have shown a commitment to community service and making a difference in the lives of others.
Cumulative student debt: 90% of graduating class had student loans; average debt was $13,650.

FINANCIAL AID PROCEDURES
Forms required: FAFSA, institutional form.
Dates and Deadlines: Priority date 3/1; no closing date. Applicants notified on a rolling basis starting 3/15.
Transfers: Priority date 3/15.

CONTACT
Scott Jewell, Director of Financial Aid
29 Everett Street, Cambridge, MA 02138-2790
(617) 349-8667

Marian Court College
Swampscott, Massachusetts
www.mariancourt.edu   Federal Code: 006873

2-year private junior college in large town, affiliated with Roman Catholic Church.
Enrollment: 220 full-time undergrads.

BASIC COSTS (2005-2006)
Tuition and fees: $12,000.
Additional info: Evening program: $675 for 3 credit course. Tuition/fee waivers available for adults.

FINANCIAL AID PICTURE
Students with need: Need-based aid available for full-time and part-time students.
Students without need: No-need awards available for academics.

FINANCIAL AID PROCEDURES
Forms required: FAFSA, institutional form.
Dates and Deadlines: Priority date 4/1; no closing date. Applicants notified on a rolling basis starting 4/15.

CONTACT
Melissa Faye, Director of Financial Aid
35 Little's Point Road, Swampscott, MA 01907-2896
(781) 595-6768

Massachusetts Bay Community College
Wellesley Hills, Massachusetts
www.massbay.edu   Federal Code: 002171

2-year public community college in large town.
Enrollment: 4,512 undergrads, 54% part-time. 814 full-time freshmen.
Selectivity: Open admission; but selective for some programs.

BASIC COSTS (2005-2006)
Tuition and fees: $3,570; out-of-state residents $9,750.
Per-credit charge: $24; out-of-state residents $230.
Additional info: Tuition/fee waivers available for unemployed or children of unemployed.

FINANCIAL AID PICTURE (2004-2005)
Students with need: 72% of average financial aid package awarded as scholarships/grants, 28% awarded as loans/jobs. Need-based aid available for part-time students.

FINANCIAL AID PROCEDURES
Forms required: FAFSA, institutional form.
Dates and Deadlines: Priority date 8/30; no closing date. Applicants notified on a rolling basis starting 4/1.

Massachusetts — Massachusetts Bay Community College

CONTACT
Paula Ogden, Director of Financial Aid/Assistant Dean of Students
50 Oakland Street, Wellesley Hills, MA 02481
(781) 239-2600

Massachusetts College of Art
Boston, Massachusetts
www.massart.edu Federal Code: 002180

4-year public visual arts college in very large city.
Enrollment: 1,549 undergrads, 12% part-time. 265 full-time freshmen.
Selectivity: Admits 50 to 75% of applicants.

BASIC COSTS (2005-2006)
Tuition and fees: $6,850; out-of-state residents $16,060.
Room and board: $9,800.
Additional info: Out-of-state students pay required fees of $8960. Tuition/fee waivers available for unemployed or children of unemployed.

FINANCIAL AID PICTURE (2005-2006)
Students with need: Out of 216 full-time freshmen who applied for aid, 161 were judged to have need. Of these, 161 received aid. For part-time students, average financial aid package was $5,958.
Students without need: No-need awards available for academics, art, leadership, minority status.
Additional info: Tuition waiver available to Vietnam veterans.

FINANCIAL AID PROCEDURES
Forms required: FAFSA.
Dates and Deadlines: Priority date 3/15; no closing date. Applicants notified on a rolling basis starting 3/15; must reply within 3 week(s) of notification.
Transfers: Priority date 5/1. Financial aid transcripts required.

CONTACT
Kenneth Berryhill, Director of Financial Aid
621 Huntington Avenue, Boston, MA 02115-5882
(617) 879-7846

Massachusetts College of Liberal Arts
North Adams, Massachusetts
www.mcla.mass.edu Federal Code: 002187

4-year public liberal arts college in large town.
Enrollment: 1,430 undergrads.
Selectivity: Admits 50 to 75% of applicants.

BASIC COSTS (2005-2006)
Tuition and fees: $5,617; out-of-state residents $14,562.
Room and board: $6,681.
Additional info: Tuition/fee waivers available for unemployed or children of unemployed.

FINANCIAL AID PICTURE
Students with need: Need-based aid available for full-time and part-time students.
Students without need: No-need awards available for academics, alumni affiliation, art, leadership, minority status, music/drama.

FINANCIAL AID PROCEDURES
Forms required: FAFSA, institutional form.
Dates and Deadlines: Priority date 4/1; no closing date. Applicants notified on a rolling basis starting 4/1; must reply within 2 week(s) of notification.

CONTACT
Elizabeth Petri, Director of Financial Aid
375 Church Street, North Adams, MA 01247
(413) 662-5000

Massachusetts College of Pharmacy and Health Sciences
Boston, Massachusetts
www.mcphs.edu Federal Code: 002165

4-year private health science and pharmacy college in very large city.
Enrollment: 1,854 undergrads, 5% part-time. 395 full-time freshmen.
Selectivity: Admits over 75% of applicants.

BASIC COSTS (2005-2006)
Tuition and fees: $21,050.
Per-credit charge: $750.
Room and board: $11,220.

FINANCIAL AID PICTURE (2005-2006)
Students with need: Out of 377 full-time freshmen who applied for aid, 336 were judged to have need. Of these, 334 received aid, and 27 had their full need met. Average financial aid package met 48% of need; average scholarship/grant was $8,227; average loan was $4,666. For part-time students, average financial aid package was $7,435.
Students without need: 56 full-time freshmen who did not demonstrate need for aid received scholarships/grants; average award was $10,288. No-need awards available for academics.
Cumulative student debt: 90% of graduating class had student loans; average debt was $40,000.

FINANCIAL AID PROCEDURES
Forms required: FAFSA.
Dates and Deadlines: Priority date 3/15; no closing date. Applicants notified on a rolling basis.
Transfers: Massachusetts State Grant deadline May 1.

CONTACT
Carrie Glass, Director of Student Financial Services
179 Longwood Avenue, Boston, MA 02115-5896
(617) 732-2864

Massachusetts Institute of Technology
Cambridge, Massachusetts Federal Code: 002178
web.mit.edu CSS Code: 3514

4-year private university in small city.
Enrollment: 4,053 undergrads, 1% part-time. 1,083 full-time freshmen.
Selectivity: Admits less than 50% of applicants.

BASIC COSTS (2006-2007)
Tuition and fees: $33,600.
Room and board: $9,950.

FINANCIAL AID PICTURE (2004-2005)
Students with need: Out of 872 full-time freshmen who applied for aid, 712 were judged to have need. Of these, 712 received aid, and 712 had their full need met. Average financial aid package met 100% of need; average scholarship/grant was $25,666; average loan was $3,321. For part-time students, average financial aid package was $15,234.
Students without need: This college only awards aid to students with need.
Cumulative student debt: 50% of graduating class had student loans; average debt was $19,748.

FINANCIAL AID PROCEDURES
Forms required: FAFSA, CSS PROFILE.
Dates and Deadlines: Closing date 2/1. Applicants notified by 4/1; must reply by 5/1.
Transfers: Access to MIT funds may be limited to fewer than 8 terms.

CONTACT
Elizabeth Hicks, Executive Director of Student Financial Services
77 Massachusetts Avenue, Rm 3-108, Cambridge, MA 02139-4307
(617) 253-4971

Massachusetts Maritime Academy
Buzzards Bay, Massachusetts
www.maritime.edu   Federal Code: 002181

4-year public military and maritime college in large town.
Enrollment: 951 undergrads, 3% part-time. 271 full-time freshmen.
Selectivity: Admits 50 to 75% of applicants.

BASIC COSTS (2005-2006)
Tuition and fees: $5,107; out-of-state residents $15,912.
Room and board: $6,464.
Additional info: Semester at Sea cost $2,929.

FINANCIAL AID PICTURE (2004-2005)
Students with need: Out of 245 full-time freshmen who applied for aid, 161 were judged to have need. Of these, 161 received aid, and 82 had their full need met. Average financial aid package met 45% of need; average scholarship/grant was $1,030; average loan was $2,625. Need-based aid available for part-time students.
Students without need: 77 full-time freshmen who did not demonstrate need for aid received scholarships/grants; average award was $1,030. No-need awards available for academics, leadership.

FINANCIAL AID PROCEDURES
Forms required: FAFSA, institutional form.
Dates and Deadlines: Priority date 4/30; no closing date. Applicants notified on a rolling basis starting 3/1.

CONTACT
Elizabeth Benway, Financial Aid Director
101 Academy Drive, Buzzards Bay, MA 02532-1803
(508) 830-5086

Massasoit Community College
Brockton, Massachusetts
www.massasoit.mass.edu   Federal Code: 002177

2-year public community college in small city.
Enrollment: 4,960 undergrads, 41% part-time. 1,057 full-time freshmen.
Selectivity: Open admission; but selective for some programs.

BASIC COSTS (2005-2006)
Tuition and fees: $3,330; out-of-state residents $9,510.
Per-credit charge: $24; out-of-state residents $230.
Additional info: Tuition/fee waivers available for adults, unemployed or children of unemployed.

FINANCIAL AID PICTURE
Students with need: Need-based aid available for full-time students.
Students without need: This college only awards aid to students with need.

FINANCIAL AID PROCEDURES
Forms required: FAFSA.
Dates and Deadlines: Priority date 4/15; no closing date. Applicants notified on a rolling basis starting 6/1.

CONTACT
Mary Courtright, Director of Financial Aid
One Massasoit Boulevard, Brockton, MA 02302-3996
(508) 588-9100

Merrimack College
North Andover, Massachusetts
www.merrimack.edu   Federal Code: 002120

4-year private business and liberal arts college in large town, affiliated with Roman Catholic Church.
Enrollment: 2,113 undergrads, 8% part-time. 544 full-time freshmen.
Selectivity: Admits 50 to 75% of applicants.

BASIC COSTS (2006-2007)
Tuition and fees: $27,070.
Per-credit charge: $985.
Room and board: $10,705.

FINANCIAL AID PICTURE (2005-2006)
Students with need: Out of 440 full-time freshmen who applied for aid, 405 were judged to have need. Of these, 405 received aid, and 340 had their full need met. Average financial aid package met 70% of need; average scholarship/grant was $13,000; average loan was $3,625. Need-based aid available for part-time students.
Students without need: 40 full-time freshmen who did not demonstrate need for aid received scholarships/grants; average award was $10,000. No-need awards available for academics, athletics, leadership, minority status, music/drama, religious affiliation.
Scholarships offered: 35 full-time freshmen received athletic scholarships; average amount $20,000.
Cumulative student debt: 70% of graduating class had student loans; average debt was $17,125.
Additional info: Accept the Challenge program provides tuition for students from Lawrence who meet program criteria.

FINANCIAL AID PROCEDURES
Forms required: FAFSA.
Dates and Deadlines: Closing date 2/1. Applicants notified by 3/15; must reply by 5/1 or within 2 week(s) of notification.
Transfers: Priority date 3/1; closing date 4/30.

CONTACT
Christine Mordach, Director of Financial Aid
315 Turnpike Street, North Andover, MA 01845
(978) 837-5186

Middlesex Community College
Bedford, Massachusetts
www.middlesex.mass.edu   Federal Code: 009936

2-year public community college in small city.
Enrollment: 3,400 full-time undergrads.
Selectivity: Open admission; but selective for some programs.

BASIC COSTS (2005-2006)
Tuition and fees: $3,600; out-of-state residents $9,780.
Per-credit charge: $24; out-of-state residents $230.
Additional info: New England resident tuition $123 per-credit-hour. Tuition/fee waivers available for adults.

FINANCIAL AID PICTURE
Students with need: Need-based aid available for full-time and part-time students. Work study available nights, weekends, and for part-time students.
Additional info: Application priority date 5/1 for Massachusetts state funds.

FINANCIAL AID PROCEDURES
Forms required: FAFSA, institutional form.
Dates and Deadlines: No deadline. Applicants notified on a rolling basis starting 6/1; must reply within 2 week(s) of notification.

CONTACT
Beverly Guerin, Financial Aid Director
33 Kearney Square, Lowell, MA 01852-1987
(978) 656-3242

Montserrat College of Art
Beverly, Massachusetts
www.montserrat.edu   Federal Code: 013774

4-year private visual arts college in small city.
Enrollment: 299 undergrads, 7% part-time. 75 full-time freshmen.
Selectivity: Admits over 75% of applicants.

BASIC COSTS (2006-2007)
Tuition and fees: $21,300.
Per-credit charge: $854.
Room and board: $5,500.

FINANCIAL AID PICTURE (2005-2006)
Students with need: Out of 74 full-time freshmen who applied for aid, 55 were judged to have need. Of these, 55 received aid. Average financial aid package met 26% of need; average scholarship/grant was $4,717; average loan was $2,928. For part-time students, average financial aid package was $5,077.
Students without need: No-need awards available for academics, art.
Scholarships offered: Talent Awards; $1,000-$8,000 a year; based on artisitic and academic ability.

FINANCIAL AID PROCEDURES
Forms required: FAFSA, institutional form.
Dates and Deadlines: Closing date 3/1. Applicants notified on a rolling basis starting 12/20; must reply within 2 week(s) of notification.
Transfers: Priority date 3/1; no deadline.

CONTACT
Creda Camacho, Director of Financial Aid
23 Essex Street, Beverly, MA 01915
(978) 922-8222

Mount Holyoke College
South Hadley, Massachusetts   Federal Code: 002192
www.mtholyoke.edu   CSS Code: 3529

4-year private liberal arts college for women in large town.
Enrollment: 2,064 undergrads, 2% part-time. 497 full-time freshmen.
Selectivity: Admits 50 to 75% of applicants.

BASIC COSTS (2006-2007)
Tuition and fees: $34,256.
Per-credit charge: $1,065.
Room and board: $10,040.

FINANCIAL AID PICTURE (2005-2006)
Students with need: Out of 370 full-time freshmen who applied for aid, 285 were judged to have need. Of these, 285 received aid, and 285 had their full need met. Average financial aid package met 100% of need; average scholarship/grant was $24,079; average loan was $2,659. For part-time students, average financial aid package was $22,981.
Students without need: 46 full-time freshmen who did not demonstrate need for aid received scholarships/grants; average award was $13,422. No-need awards available for academics, leadership.
Scholarships offered: Mount Holyoke College Leadership Awards; limited number; based on high school scholarship and extracurricular achievement; conditional annual renewal.
Cumulative student debt: 69% of graduating class had student loans; average debt was $19,877.

Additional info: Parent loan plans include MASSPLAN, Achievers and PLUS. 10-month payment plan offered.

FINANCIAL AID PROCEDURES
Forms required: FAFSA, CSS PROFILE.
Dates and Deadlines: Priority date 1/15; closing date 2/1. Applicants notified by 3/25; must reply by 5/1.
Transfers: Priority date 2/1; closing date 5/31. Applicants notified on a rolling basis; must reply within 4 week(s) of notification. Financial aid transcripts from all schools previously attended required.

CONTACT
Kathy Blaisdell, Director of Student Financial Services
50 College Street, South Hadley, MA 01075-1488
(413) 538-2291

Mount Ida College
Newton, Massachusetts
www.mountida.edu   Federal Code: 002193

4-year private liberal arts college in small city.
Enrollment: 1,290 undergrads.
Selectivity: Admits over 75% of applicants.

BASIC COSTS (2006-2007)
Tuition and fees: $20,450.
Room and board: $10,225.

FINANCIAL AID PICTURE (2005-2006)
Students with need: 34% of average financial aid package awarded as scholarships/grants, 66% awarded as loans/jobs. Need-based aid available for part-time students.

FINANCIAL AID PROCEDURES
Forms required: FAFSA, institutional form.
Dates and Deadlines: Priority date 5/1; no closing date. Applicants notified on a rolling basis starting 3/1; must reply within 3 week(s) of notification.

CONTACT
Linda Mularczyk, Director of Financial Aid
777 Dedham Street, Newton, MA 02459
(617) 928-4785

Mount Wachusett Community College
Gardner, Massachusetts
www.mwcc.mass.edu   Federal Code: 002172

2-year public community college in large town.
Enrollment: 3,696 undergrads, 48% part-time. 758 full-time freshmen.
Selectivity: Open admission; but selective for some programs.

BASIC COSTS (2005-2006)
Tuition and fees: $4,080; out-of-state residents $10,230.
Per-credit charge: $25; out-of-state residents $230.
Additional info: New England resident tuition is $1,150.

FINANCIAL AID PICTURE (2005-2006)
Students with need: 74% of average financial aid package awarded as scholarships/grants, 26% awarded as loans/jobs. Need-based aid available for part-time students. Work study available nights.
Students without need: This college only awards aid to students with need.

FINANCIAL AID PROCEDURES
Forms required: FAFSA, institutional form.
Dates and Deadlines: Priority date 4/15; no closing date. Applicants notified on a rolling basis starting 5/1.

CONTACT
JoEllen Soucier, Director of Financial Aid
444 Green Street, Gardner, MA 01440-1000
(978) 632-6600 ext. 524

New England Conservatory of Music
Boston, Massachusetts
www.newenglandconservatory.edu Federal Code: 002194

4-year private music college in very large city.
Enrollment: 404 undergrads.
Selectivity: Admits less than 50% of applicants.

BASIC COSTS (2006-2007)
Tuition and fees: $29,300.
Room and board: $16,239.
Additional info: On-campus residents pay $335 health fee.

FINANCIAL AID PICTURE (2004-2005)
Students with need: 59% of average financial aid package awarded as scholarships/grants, 41% awarded as loans/jobs. Need-based aid available for part-time students. Work study available nights, weekends, and for part-time students.
Students without need: No-need awards available for music/drama.

FINANCIAL AID PROCEDURES
Forms required: FAFSA, institutional form.
Dates and Deadlines: Priority date 12/1; closing date 2/1. Applicants notified on a rolling basis starting 4/1; must reply by 5/1 or within 2 week(s) of notification.

CONTACT
Lauren Urbanek, Director of Financial Aid
290 Huntington Avenue, Boston, MA 02115
(617) 585-1110

New England Institute of Art
Brookline, Massachusetts
www.neia.aii.edu Federal Code: 007486

4-year for-profit visual arts and technical college in very large city.
Enrollment: 965 full-time undergrads.
Selectivity: Admits less than 50% of applicants.

BASIC COSTS (2005-2006)
Tuition and fees: $18,300.
Per-credit charge: $595.
Additional info: Tuition at time of enrollment locked for 4 years.

FINANCIAL AID PICTURE
Students with need: Need-based aid available for full-time and part-time students. Work study available nights, weekends, and for part-time students.
Students without need: No-need awards available for academics.

FINANCIAL AID PROCEDURES
Forms required: FAFSA, institutional form.
Dates and Deadlines: Priority date 5/1; no closing date. Applicants notified on a rolling basis starting 3/1.

CONTACT
Anna Kelly, Director of Student Financial Services
10 Brookline Place West, Brookline, MA 02445-7295
(617) 739-1700

Newbury College
Brookline, Massachusetts
www.newbury.edu Federal Code: 007484

4-year private business and liberal arts college in large city.
Enrollment: 1,250 undergrads.

BASIC COSTS (2006-2007)
Tuition and fees: $18,200.
Per-credit charge: $570.
Room and board: $8,975.

FINANCIAL AID PICTURE (2005-2006)
Students with need: 51% of average financial aid package awarded as scholarships/grants, 49% awarded as loans/jobs. Need-based aid available for part-time students. Work study available nights.
Students without need: This college only awards aid to students with need.

FINANCIAL AID PROCEDURES
Forms required: FAFSA.
Dates and Deadlines: Closing date 5/1. Applicants notified on a rolling basis starting 4/1; must reply within 2 week(s) of notification.
Transfers: No deadline.

CONTACT
Jeannie Gonzales, Director of Financial Assistance
129 Fisher Avenue, Brookline, MA 02445
(617) 730-7196

Nichols College
Dudley, Massachusetts
www.nichols.edu Federal Code: 002197

4-year private business and liberal arts college in small town.
Enrollment: 1,193 undergrads, 25% part-time. 312 full-time freshmen.
Selectivity: Admits over 75% of applicants.

BASIC COSTS (2005-2006)
Tuition and fees: $22,250.
Per-credit charge: $733.
Room and board: $8,290.

FINANCIAL AID PICTURE (2004-2005)
Students with need: Out of 287 full-time freshmen who applied for aid, 259 were judged to have need. Of these, 252 received aid, and 61 had their full need met. Average financial aid package met 69% of need; average scholarship/grant was $10,686; average loan was $5,270. For part-time students, average financial aid package was $4,184.
Students without need: 47 full-time freshmen who did not demonstrate need for aid received scholarships/grants; average award was $10,272. No-need awards available for academics, ROTC.
Cumulative student debt: 87% of graduating class had student loans; average debt was $31,842.

FINANCIAL AID PROCEDURES
Forms required: FAFSA.
Dates and Deadlines: Closing date 3/1. Applicants notified on a rolling basis starting 3/15; must reply within 2 week(s) of notification.

CONTACT
Diane Gillespie, Director of Admissions & Financial Aid
Office of Admissions, Dudley, MA 01571-5000
(508) 213-2276

North Shore Community College
Danvers, Massachusetts
www.northshore.edu   Federal Code: 002173

2-year public community college in small city.
Enrollment: 5,800 undergrads, 54% part-time. 977 full-time freshmen.
Selectivity: Open admission; but selective for some programs.

BASIC COSTS (2005-2006)
Tuition and fees: $3,480; out-of-state residents $10,440.
Per-credit charge: $25; out-of-state residents $257.
Additional info: New England Regional tuition: $125.50 per-credit-hour.

FINANCIAL AID PICTURE (2004-2005)
Students with need: Out of 618 full-time freshmen who applied for aid, 553 were judged to have need. Of these, 486 received aid. Average financial aid package met 18% of need; average scholarship/grant was $1,869; average loan was $1,542. For part-time students, average financial aid package was $1,271.
Students without need: This college only awards aid to students with need.

FINANCIAL AID PROCEDURES
Forms required: FAFSA.
Dates and Deadlines: Priority date 5/1; no closing date. Applicants notified on a rolling basis starting 6/1; must reply within 2 week(s) of notification.

CONTACT
Delbert Brown, Director of Student Financial Services
One Ferncroft Road, Danvers, MA 01923-0840
(978) 762-4000

Northeastern University
Boston, Massachusetts   Federal Code: 002199
www.northeastern.edu   CSS Code: 3667

5-year private university in very large city.
Enrollment: 14,730 undergrads. 2,831 full-time freshmen.
Selectivity: Admits less than 50% of applicants.

BASIC COSTS (2006-2007)
Tuition and fees: $30,309.
Room and board: $10,950.

FINANCIAL AID PICTURE (2005-2006)
Students with need: Out of 2,244 full-time freshmen who applied for aid, 1,770 were judged to have need. Of these, 1,763 received aid, and 293 had their full need met. Average financial aid package met 64% of need; average scholarship/grant was $13,524; average loan was $3,460.
Students without need: 805 full-time freshmen who did not demonstrate need for aid received scholarships/grants; average award was $13,352. No-need awards available for academics, athletics, minority status.
Scholarships offered: 43 full-time freshmen received athletic scholarships; average amount $20,628.

FINANCIAL AID PROCEDURES
Forms required: FAFSA, CSS PROFILE.
Dates and Deadlines: Closing date 2/15. Applicants notified on a rolling basis starting 2/15; must reply by 5/1.
Transfers: Institutional application and financial aid transcript from all previously attended colleges required.

CONTACT
M. Seamus Harreys, Dean and Director of Student Financial Services
360 Huntington Avenue, 150 Richards Hall, Boston, MA 02115-9959
(617) 373-3190

Northern Essex Community College
Haverhill, Massachusetts
www.necc.mass.edu   Federal Code: 002174

2-year public community college in small city.
Enrollment: 5,509 undergrads, 60% part-time. 905 full-time freshmen.
Selectivity: Open admission; but selective for some programs.

BASIC COSTS (2005-2006)
Tuition and fees: $3,150; out-of-state residents $10,380.
Per-credit charge: $25; out-of-state residents $266.
Additional info: New England residents pay $122 per-credit-hour.

FINANCIAL AID PICTURE
Students with need: Need-based aid available for full-time and part-time students.
Students without need: No-need awards available for academics.

FINANCIAL AID PROCEDURES
Forms required: FAFSA.
Dates and Deadlines: Priority date 5/1; no closing date. Applicants notified on a rolling basis starting 3/1; must reply within 2 week(s) of notification.

CONTACT
Nancy Sabin, Assistant Dean for Financial Aid
100 Elliott Street, Haverhill, MA 01830-2399
(978) 556-3737

Pine Manor College
Chestnut Hill, Massachusetts
www.pmc.edu   Federal Code: 002201

4-year private liberal arts college for women in very large city.
Enrollment: 455 undergrads, 2% part-time. 166 full-time freshmen.
Selectivity: Admits over 75% of applicants.

BASIC COSTS (2005-2006)
Tuition and fees: $15,538.
Room and board: $9,500.

FINANCIAL AID PICTURE (2004-2005)
Students with need: Out of 161 full-time freshmen who applied for aid, 158 were judged to have need. Of these, 157 received aid, and 18 had their full need met. Average financial aid package met 75% of need; average scholarship/grant was $11,413; average loan was $4,189. For part-time students, average financial aid package was $4,021.
Students without need: 8 full-time freshmen who did not demonstrate need for aid received scholarships/grants; average award was $7,531. No-need awards available for academics, alumni affiliation, leadership.
Scholarships offered: Distinguished Scholar Award; $5,000; 3.5 GPA from accredited secondary school, no grade below C, 1100 combined SAT or a composite score of 24 on the ACT. Presidential Scholar Award; $3,500; 3.2 GPA from accredited secondary school, no grade below C, 1000 combined SAT or a composite score of 21 on the ACT. Faculty Scholar Award; $2,000; 3.0 GPA from accredited secondary school, no grade below C, 900 combined SAT or a composite score of 19 on the ACT. All SAT scores exclusive of Writing. Elkins Leadership Award; $3,000; demonstrated leadership roles, 2.5 GPA at accredited high school or college, no grade lower than D. Phi Theta Kappa Scholarship; $3,000; for transfers. Collegiate Articulation Transfer Award; $2,000; successful completion of AA with 2.0 GPA from community college within articulation agreement.

FINANCIAL AID PROCEDURES
Forms required: FAFSA.
Dates and Deadlines: Priority date 5/1; no closing date. Applicants notified on a rolling basis starting 3/1; must reply by 5/1 or within 2 week(s) of notification.

CONTACT
Robin Engel, Dean of Admissions and Financial Aid
400 Heath Street, Chestnut Hill, MA 02467
(617) 731-7104

Quinsigamond Community College
Worcester, Massachusetts
www.qcc.mass.edu   Federal Code: 002175

2-year public community college in small city.
Enrollment: 4,772 undergrads, 47% part-time. 952 full-time freshmen.
Selectivity: Open admission; but selective for some programs.

BASIC COSTS (2005-2006)
Tuition and fees: $3,820; out-of-state residents $10,000.
Per-credit charge: $24; out-of-state residents $230.

FINANCIAL AID PICTURE (2005-2006)
Students with need: 83% of average financial aid package awarded as scholarships/grants, 17% awarded as loans/jobs. Need-based aid available for part-time students. Work study available nights, weekends, and for part-time students.
Students without need: This college only awards aid to students with need.

FINANCIAL AID PROCEDURES
Forms required: FAFSA.
Dates and Deadlines: Priority date 4/1; no closing date. Applicants notified on a rolling basis starting 4/1.

CONTACT
Iris Godes, Dean of Enrollment Management
670 West Boylston Street, Worcester, MA 01606
(508) 854-4261

Regis College
Weston, Massachusetts
www.regiscollege.edu   Federal Code: 002206

4-year private liberal arts college for women in large town, affiliated with Roman Catholic Church.
Enrollment: 843 undergrads, 26% part-time. 161 full-time freshmen.
Selectivity: Admits over 75% of applicants.

BASIC COSTS (2006-2007)
Tuition and fees: $23,680.
Room and board: $10,560.

FINANCIAL AID PICTURE (2005-2006)
Students with need: Out of 150 full-time freshmen who applied for aid, 139 were judged to have need. Of these, 131 received aid, and 12 had their full need met. Average financial aid package met 66% of need; average scholarship/grant was $11,396; average loan was $4,351. For part-time students, average financial aid package was $5,470.
Students without need: 13 full-time freshmen who did not demonstrate need for aid received scholarships/grants; average award was $8,769. No-need awards available for academics, alumni affiliation, leadership, minority status, religious affiliation, state/district residency.
Scholarships offered: Family tuition discount scholarship; offered during any semester in which 2 or more unmarried, dependent siblings attend on a full-time basis.
Cumulative student debt: 77% of graduating class had student loans; average debt was $24,094.

FINANCIAL AID PROCEDURES
Forms required: FAFSA, institutional form.
Dates and Deadlines: Priority date 2/15; no closing date. Applicants notified on a rolling basis starting 3/15; must reply by 5/1.

CONTACT
Dolores Ludwick, Director of Financial Aid
235 Wellesley Street, Weston, MA 02493-1571
(781) 768-7180

Roxbury Community College
Roxbury Crossing, Massachusetts
www.rcc.mass.edu   Federal Code: 011930

2-year public community college in very large city.
Enrollment: 2,015 undergrads, 57% part-time. 391 full-time freshmen.
Selectivity: Open admission; but selective for some programs.

BASIC COSTS (2005-2006)
Tuition and fees: $3,510; out-of-state residents $10,140.
Per-credit charge: $26; out-of-state residents $247.
Additional info: New England Regional per-credit-hour charge is $105.

FINANCIAL AID PICTURE
Students with need: Need-based aid available for full-time and part-time students.
Students without need: This college only awards aid to students with need.

FINANCIAL AID PROCEDURES
Forms required: FAFSA, institutional form.
Dates and Deadlines: Priority date 5/1; no closing date. Applicants notified on a rolling basis starting 6/15; must reply within 2 week(s) of notification.

CONTACT
Ray O'Rourke, Director of Financial Aid
1234 Columbus Avenue, Roxbury Crossing, MA 02120-3400
(617) 541-5322

St. John's Seminary College
Brighton, Massachusetts
www.sjs.edu   Federal Code: 002214

4-year private liberal arts and seminary college for men in very large city, affiliated with Roman Catholic Church.

BASIC COSTS (2005-2006)
Tuition and fees: $11,250.
Room and board: $6,250.
Additional info: Tuition/fee waivers available for minority students.

FINANCIAL AID PICTURE
Students with need: Need-based aid available for full-time students.
Students without need: No-need awards available for state/district residency.

FINANCIAL AID PROCEDURES
Forms required: FAFSA.
Dates and Deadlines: No deadline. Applicants notified on a rolling basis; must reply within 3 week(s) of notification.

CONTACT
John Lynch, Business Manager, Financial Aid Officer
127 Lake Street, Brighton, MA 02135
(617) 254-2610

Salem State College
Salem, Massachusetts
www.salemstate.edu   Federal Code: 002188

4-year public university in large town.
Enrollment: 6,687 undergrads, 20% part-time. 1,208 full-time freshmen.
Selectivity: Admits over 75% of applicants.

BASIC COSTS (2005-2006)
Tuition and fees: $5,594; out-of-state residents $11,734.
Room and board: $6,678.
Additional info: New England Regional tuition and fees per year: $6049. Tuition/fee waivers available for unemployed or children of unemployed.

FINANCIAL AID PICTURE
Students with need: Need-based aid available for full-time and part-time students. Work study available nights, weekends, and for part-time students.
Students without need: No-need awards available for academics, alumni affiliation, art, leadership, music/drama, state/district residency.
Additional info: Tuition waivers for qualified veterans and National Guard members. Grant assistance available for eligible adult students.

FINANCIAL AID PROCEDURES
Forms required: FAFSA.
Dates and Deadlines: Priority date 4/1; no closing date. Applicants notified on a rolling basis starting 4/1; must reply within 2 week(s) of notification.

CONTACT
Mary Benda, Director of Financial Aid
352 Lafayette Street, Salem, MA 01970-5353
(978) 542-6112

School of the Museum of Fine Arts
Boston, Massachusetts
www.smfa.edu   Federal Code: 004667

4-year private visual arts college in very large city.
Enrollment: 677 undergrads, 10% part-time. 158 full-time freshmen.
Selectivity: Admits over 75% of applicants.

BASIC COSTS (2005-2006)
Tuition and fees: $24,760.
Per-credit charge: $1,000.
Room only: $11,600.

FINANCIAL AID PICTURE (2005-2006)
Students with need: Out of 124 full-time freshmen who applied for aid, 118 were judged to have need. Of these, 118 received aid, and 8 had their full need met. Average financial aid package met 43% of need; average scholarship/grant was $10,521; average loan was $2,553. For part-time students, average financial aid package was $4,930.
Students without need: 3 full-time freshmen who did not demonstrate need for aid received scholarships/grants; average award was $3,667. No-need awards available for art.
Scholarships offered: Awarded on strength of portfolio and potential for growth as an artist; no separate application needed.

FINANCIAL AID PROCEDURES
Forms required: FAFSA, institutional form.
Dates and Deadlines: Priority date 3/15; no closing date. Applicants notified on a rolling basis starting 4/15; must reply by 5/1 or within 2 week(s) of notification.

CONTACT
Elizabeth Goreham, Director of Financial Aid
230 The Fenway, Boston, MA 02115
(800) 776-0135

Simmons College
Boston, Massachusetts
www.simmons.edu   Federal Code: 002208

4-year private liberal arts college for women in large city.
Enrollment: 1,846 undergrads, 9% part-time. 403 full-time freshmen.
Selectivity: Admits 50 to 75% of applicants.

BASIC COSTS (2006-2007)
Tuition and fees: $26,702.
Per-credit charge: $809.
Room and board: $10,710.

FINANCIAL AID PICTURE (2005-2006)
Students with need: Out of 340 full-time freshmen who applied for aid, 301 were judged to have need. Of these, 299 received aid, and 18 had their full need met. Average financial aid package met 60% of need; average scholarship/grant was $11,751; average loan was $3,018. For part-time students, average financial aid package was $10,698.
Students without need: 16 full-time freshmen who did not demonstrate need for aid received scholarships/grants; average award was $10,667. No-need awards available for academics, alumni affiliation, leadership, minority status.
Cumulative student debt: 90% of graduating class had student loans; average debt was $26,300.

FINANCIAL AID PROCEDURES
Forms required: FAFSA.
Dates and Deadlines: Priority date 2/15; closing date 3/1. Applicants notified on a rolling basis starting 3/15; must reply by 5/1 or within 4 week(s) of notification.
Transfers: Priority date 3/1; closing date 4/1. Applicants notified on a rolling basis starting 3/15; must reply by 5/1 or within 4 week(s) of notification. Combination of grants, loans, employment opportunities available.

CONTACT
Diane Hallisey, Director of Student Financial Services
300 The Fenway, Boston, MA 02115-5898
(617) 521-2004

Simon's Rock College of Bard
Great Barrington, Massachusetts   Federal Code: 009645
www.simons-rock.edu   CSS Code: 3795

4-year private liberal arts college in small town.
Enrollment: 380 undergrads.
Selectivity: Admits 50 to 75% of applicants.

BASIC COSTS (2006-2007)
Tuition and fees: $35,384.
Per-credit charge: $1,360.
Room and board: $9,260.

FINANCIAL AID PICTURE (2004-2005)
Students with need: 88% of average financial aid package awarded as scholarships/grants, 12% awarded as loans/jobs. Need-based aid available for part-time students. Work study available nights, weekends, and for part-time students.
Students without need: No-need awards available for academics, alumni affiliation, leadership, state/district residency.
Scholarships offered: Acceleration to Excellence Program (AEP); 2 years full tuition; based on excellent grades, community service, maturity; 20-25 awarded. Special application process.

FINANCIAL AID PROCEDURES
Forms required: FAFSA, CSS PROFILE.

Dates and Deadlines: Priority date 4/15; no closing date. Applicants notified on a rolling basis starting 4/15; must reply within 2 week(s) of notification.

CONTACT
Ann Murtaugh, Director of Financial Aid
84 Alford Road, Great Barrington, MA 01230-1990
(413) 528-7297

Smith College
Northampton, Massachusetts
www.smith.edu
Federal Code: 002209
CSS Code: 3762

4-year private liberal arts college for women in large town.
Enrollment: 2,635 undergrads, 1% part-time. 615 full-time freshmen.
Selectivity: Admits less than 50% of applicants.

BASIC COSTS (2006-2007)
Tuition and fees: $32,558.
Per-credit charge: $1,010.
Room and board: $10,880.

FINANCIAL AID PICTURE (2005-2006)
Students with need: Out of 466 full-time freshmen who applied for aid, 366 were judged to have need. Of these, 366 received aid, and 366 had their full need met. Average financial aid package met 100% of need; average scholarship/grant was $25,169; average loan was $2,058. For part-time students, average financial aid package was $27,033.
Students without need: 62 full-time freshmen who did not demonstrate need for aid received scholarships/grants; average award was $3,465. No-need awards available for academics, state/district residency.
Scholarships offered: Zollman Scholarships: half-tuition; for academic excellence; 5 to 10 awarded. STRIDE scholarship: $5,000 per year for academic excellence; about 35 awarded. Springfield Partnership: full tuition; for academic excellence in Springfield public high school; up to 3 awarded. Picker Engineering scholarships: $10,000 per year. Mary Maples Dunn scholarships: $3,000 per year.
Cumulative student debt: 69% of graduating class had student loans; average debt was $25,023.
Additional info: Financial aid policy guarantees to meet full financial need, as calculated by college, of all admitted students. Evaluation and ratings based strictly on academic and personal qualities of each applicant, with no consideration of financial need. Full aid packages offered to most qualified students until aid budget exhausted. College need-blind for 95% to 99% of applicants.

FINANCIAL AID PROCEDURES
Forms required: FAFSA, CSS PROFILE.
Dates and Deadlines: Closing date 2/1. Applicants notified by 4/1; must reply by 5/1.
Transfers: Priority date 2/15; closing date 5/15. Applicants who apply after admission decision is made cannot receive college aid until they complete at least 32 credits at Smith.

CONTACT
Deborah Luekens, Director of Student Financial Services
7 College Lane, Northampton, MA 01063
(413) 585-2530

Springfield College
Springfield, Massachusetts
www.spfldcol.edu
Federal Code: 002211
CSS Code: 3763

4-year private health science and liberal arts college in small city.
Enrollment: 2,188 undergrads, 1% part-time. 574 full-time freshmen.
Selectivity: Admits 50 to 75% of applicants.

BASIC COSTS (2006-2007)
Tuition and fees: $22,715.
Per-credit charge: $679.
Room and board: $8,760.

FINANCIAL AID PICTURE (2005-2006)
Students with need: 62% of average financial aid package awarded as scholarships/grants, 38% awarded as loans/jobs.
Additional info: Co-operative education program available to students after freshman year.

FINANCIAL AID PROCEDURES
Forms required: FAFSA, CSS PROFILE.
Dates and Deadlines: Priority date 3/15; no closing date. Applicants notified on a rolling basis starting 3/15; must reply by 5/1 or within 2 week(s) of notification.
Transfers: Priority date 4/15.

CONTACT
Edward Ciosek, Director of Financial Aid
263 Alden Street, Springfield, MA 01109
(413) 748-3000

Springfield Technical Community College
Springfield, Massachusetts
www.stcc.edu
Federal Code: 005549

2-year public community and technical college in small city.
Enrollment: 4,751 undergrads, 47% part-time. 829 full-time freshmen.
Selectivity: Open admission; but selective for some programs.

BASIC COSTS (2005-2006)
Tuition and fees: $3,354; out-of-state residents $9,864.
Per-credit charge: $25; out-of-state residents $242.
Additional info: New England reciprocal rate is $220 per credit-hour, including fees.

FINANCIAL AID PICTURE (2004-2005)
Students with need: 80% of average financial aid package awarded as scholarships/grants, 20% awarded as loans/jobs. Need-based aid available for part-time students.
Students without need: This college only awards aid to students with need.

FINANCIAL AID PROCEDURES
Forms required: FAFSA, institutional form.
Dates and Deadlines: Priority date 4/1; no closing date. Applicants notified on a rolling basis starting 7/1.

CONTACT
Mary Forni, Coordinator of Financial Aid Services
One Armory Square, Springfield, MA 01102-9000
(413) 755-4214

Stonehill College
Easton, Massachusetts
www.stonehill.edu
Federal Code: 002217
CSS Code: 3770

4-year private liberal arts college in large town, affiliated with Roman Catholic Church.
Enrollment: 2,366 undergrads, 5% part-time. 618 full-time freshmen.
Selectivity: Admits 50 to 75% of applicants.

BASIC COSTS (2006-2007)
Tuition and fees: $27,080.
Room and board: $11,040.
Additional info: Tuition/fee waivers available for minority students.

FINANCIAL AID PICTURE (2005-2006)
Students with need: Out of 519 full-time freshmen who applied for aid, 398 were judged to have need. Of these, 398 received aid, and 113 had their full need met. Average financial aid package met 82% of need; average scholarship/grant was $13,594; average loan was $4,798. For part-time students, average financial aid package was $15,744.
Students without need: 174 full-time freshmen who did not demonstrate need for aid received scholarships/grants; average award was $11,272. No-need awards available for academics, athletics, leadership, minority status, music/drama, ROTC.
Scholarships offered: 14 full-time freshmen received athletic scholarships; average amount $12,175.
Cumulative student debt: 75% of graduating class had student loans; average debt was $19,712.

FINANCIAL AID PROCEDURES
Forms required: FAFSA, CSS PROFILE.
Dates and Deadlines: Closing date 2/1. Applicants notified by 4/1; must reply by 5/1.
Transfers: Closing date 4/1.

CONTACT
Eileen O'Leary, Director of Student Aid and Finance
320 Washington Street, Easton, MA 02357-0100
(508) 565-1088

Suffolk University
Boston, Massachusetts
www.suffolk.edu
Federal Code: 002218

4-year private university in very large city.
Enrollment: 4,595 undergrads, 12% part-time. 1,121 full-time freshmen.
Selectivity: Admits over 75% of applicants.

BASIC COSTS (2006-2007)
Tuition and fees: $22,690.
Per-credit charge: $593.
Room and board: $12,996.

FINANCIAL AID PICTURE (2005-2006)
Students with need: Out of 862 full-time freshmen who applied for aid, 642 were judged to have need. Of these, 641 received aid, and 95 had their full need met. Average financial aid package met 63% of need; average scholarship/grant was $6,685; average loan was $3,768. For part-time students, average financial aid package was $9,977.
Students without need: 101 full-time freshmen who did not demonstrate need for aid received scholarships/grants; average award was $6,978. No-need awards available for academics, alumni affiliation.
Scholarships offered: Amounts vary; based on academic achievement, talent, and contribution to applicant's school and community.
Cumulative student debt: 61% of graduating class had student loans; average debt was $19,012.
Additional info: Foreign students may apply for institutional employment awards.

FINANCIAL AID PROCEDURES
Forms required: FAFSA, institutional form.
Dates and Deadlines: Closing date 4/1. Applicants notified on a rolling basis starting 3/1; must reply within 2 week(s) of notification.

CONTACT
Christine Perry, Director of Financial Aid
8 Ashburton Place, Boston, MA 02108
(617) 720-3579

Tufts University
Medford, Massachusetts
www.tufts.edu
Federal Code: 002219
CSS Code: 3901

4-year private university in small city.
Enrollment: 5,048 undergrads, 2% part-time. 1,365 full-time freshmen.
Selectivity: Admits less than 50% of applicants.

BASIC COSTS (2005-2006)
Tuition and fees: $32,621.
Room and board: $9,397.

FINANCIAL AID PICTURE (2005-2006)
Students with need: Out of 753 full-time freshmen who applied for aid, 534 were judged to have need. Of these, 534 received aid, and 534 had their full need met. Average financial aid package met 100% of need; average scholarship/grant was $23,271; average loan was $3,025.
Students without need: This college only awards aid to students with need.
Scholarships offered: National Merit Scholarships; $500 for non-need; $2,000 for need.
Cumulative student debt: 40% of graduating class had student loans; average debt was $14,400.

FINANCIAL AID PROCEDURES
Forms required: FAFSA, CSS PROFILE.
Dates and Deadlines: Priority date 2/1; closing date 2/15. Applicants notified by 4/5; must reply by 5/1.
Transfers: Closing date 3/1.

CONTACT
Patricia Reilly, Director of Financial Aid
Bendetson Hall, Medford, MA 02155-5555
(617) 627-2000

University of Massachusetts Amherst
Amherst, Massachusetts
www.umass.edu
Federal Code: 002221

4-year public university in large town.
Enrollment: 18,812 undergrads, 5% part-time. 4,306 full-time freshmen.
Selectivity: Admits over 75% of applicants.

BASIC COSTS (2005-2006)
Tuition and fees: $9,278; out-of-state residents $18,397.
Room and board: $6,517.

FINANCIAL AID PICTURE (2004-2005)
Students with need: Out of 2,581 full-time freshmen who applied for aid, 1,785 were judged to have need. Of these, 1,681 received aid, and 219 had their full need met. Average financial aid package met 81% of need; average scholarship/grant was $6,366; average loan was $1,281. For part-time students, average financial aid package was $8,470.
Students without need: 10 full-time freshmen who did not demonstrate need for aid received scholarships/grants; average award was $4,829. No-need awards available for academics, art, athletics, music/drama, ROTC, state/district residency.
Scholarships offered: Merit: All applicants automatically reviewed for merit scholarships. **Athletic:** 34 full-time freshmen received athletic scholarships; average amount $9,560.
Cumulative student debt: 61% of graduating class had student loans; average debt was $14,672.

FINANCIAL AID PROCEDURES
Forms required: FAFSA.
Dates and Deadlines: Priority date 3/1; no closing date. Applicants notified on a rolling basis starting 4/1.

Transfers: Financial aid transcripts required.

CONTACT
Kenneth Burnham, Director of Financial Aid
University Admissions Center, Amherst, MA 01003-9291
(413) 545-0801

University of Massachusetts Boston
Boston, Massachusetts
www.umb.edu   Federal Code: 002222

4-year public university in very large city.
Enrollment: 7,621 undergrads, 28% part-time. 567 full-time freshmen.
Selectivity: Admits 50 to 75% of applicants.

BASIC COSTS (2005-2006)
Tuition and fees: $8,265; out-of-state residents $19,320.
Additional info: Tuition/fee waivers available for minority students.

FINANCIAL AID PICTURE (2004-2005)
Students with need: Out of 445 full-time freshmen who applied for aid, 379 were judged to have need. Of these, 370 received aid, and 149 had their full need met. Average financial aid package met 86% of need; average scholarship/grant was $6,046; average loan was $2,009. For part-time students, average financial aid package was $8,054.
Students without need: 57 full-time freshmen who did not demonstrate need for aid received scholarships/grants; average award was $3,638. No-need awards available for academics, leadership, ROTC.
Additional info: Some Massachusetts state employees and Massachusetts Vietnam veterans eligible for tuition waiver. Some waivers available based on talent and academic excellence.

FINANCIAL AID PROCEDURES
Forms required: FAFSA.
Dates and Deadlines: Priority date 3/1; no closing date. Applicants notified on a rolling basis starting 4/1; must reply within 4 week(s) of notification.
Transfers: Priority date 6/1.

CONTACT
Judy Keyes, Director of Financial Aid Services
100 Morrissey Boulevard, Boston, MA 02125-3393
(617) 287-6300

University of Massachusetts Dartmouth
North Dartmouth, Massachusetts
www.umassd.edu   Federal Code: 002210

4-year public university in large town.
Enrollment: 7,173 undergrads, 11% part-time. 1,729 full-time freshmen.
Selectivity: Admits 50 to 75% of applicants.

BASIC COSTS (2005-2006)
Tuition and fees: $8,036; out-of-state residents $17,638.
Room and board: $8,268.
Additional info: Out-of-state students pay required fees of $9,539.

FINANCIAL AID PICTURE
Students with need: Need-based aid available for full-time and part-time students. Work study available nights, weekends, and for part-time students.
Students without need: No-need awards available for academics, minority status, ROTC, state/district residency.
Scholarships offered: Chancellor's Merit Scholarship; approximately $2,000; for Massachusetts high school seniors with combined SAT 1250 (exclusive of Writing) and above and in top 25% of class, 50 awarded. Solveig E.J. Balestracci Scholarship; $1,000; for academic achievement in marine-related area for residents of New Bedford, Dartmouth, Acushnet, Westport, Mattapoisett, Marion, Rochester or Lakeville; 1 awarded. Donald E. & Anne L. Walker Merit Scholarship; $750-$1,000 (renewable); based on superior SAT score and high school rank, essay and interview; 2-4 awarded. Boivon Scholarship; $1,000; based on academic involvement in French language and culture. Wal-Mart Scholarship; $5,000 per year (renewable); for certain engineering and science majors; 2 awarded.

FINANCIAL AID PROCEDURES
Forms required: FAFSA.
Dates and Deadlines: Priority date 3/1; no closing date. Applicants notified on a rolling basis starting 3/25; must reply within 3 week(s) of notification.

CONTACT
Bruce Palmer, Director of Financial Aid
285 Old Westport Road, North Dartmouth, MA 02747-2300
(508) 999-8632

University of Massachusetts Lowell
Lowell, Massachusetts
www.uml.edu   Federal Code: 002161

4-year public university in small city.
Enrollment: 5,695 full-time undergrads. 996 full-time freshmen.
Selectivity: Admits 50 to 75% of applicants.

BASIC COSTS (2005-2006)
Tuition and fees: $8,166; out-of-state residents $19,066.
Per-credit charge: $61; out-of-state residents $357.
Room and board: $6,311.

FINANCIAL AID PICTURE (2004-2005)
Students with need: Out of 745 full-time freshmen who applied for aid, 486 were judged to have need. Of these, 473 received aid, and 349 had their full need met. Average financial aid package met 94% of need; average scholarship/grant was $3,720; average loan was $2,545. For part-time students, average financial aid package was $6,071.
Students without need: 33 full-time freshmen who did not demonstrate need for aid received scholarships/grants; average award was $3,298. No-need awards available for academics, art, athletics, ROTC.
Scholarships offered: 36 full-time freshmen received athletic scholarships; average amount $5,376.

FINANCIAL AID PROCEDURES
Forms required: FAFSA.
Dates and Deadlines: Priority date 3/1; no closing date. Applicants notified on a rolling basis starting 3/25.

CONTACT
Richard Barrett, Director of Financial Aid
883 Broadway Street, Room 110, Lowell, MA 01854-5104
(978) 934-4220

Urban College of Boston
Boston, Massachusetts
www.urbancollege.edu   Federal Code: 031305

2-year private community college in very large city.
Enrollment: 521 undergrads, 97% part-time. 4 full-time freshmen.
Selectivity: Open admission.

BASIC COSTS (2006-2007)
Tuition and fees: $3,780.
Per-credit charge: $125.

FINANCIAL AID PICTURE (2004-2005)
Students with need: Need-based aid available for part-time students.

Students without need: This college only awards aid to students with need.

FINANCIAL AID PROCEDURES
Forms required: FAFSA.
Dates and Deadlines: No deadline. Applicants notified on a rolling basis starting 4/15.

CONTACT
Patricia Harden, Director of Financial Aid
178 Tremont Street, Seventh Floor, Boston, MA 02111
(617) 292-4723 ext. 6220

Wellesley College
Wellesley, Massachusetts
www.wellesley.edu
Federal Code: 002224
CSS Code: 3957

4-year private liberal arts college for women in large town.
Enrollment: 2,224 undergrads, 1% part-time. 605 full-time freshmen.
Selectivity: Admits less than 50% of applicants.

BASIC COSTS (2006-2007)
Tuition and fees: $33,072.
Room and board: $10,216.

FINANCIAL AID PICTURE (2005-2006)
Students with need: Out of 454 full-time freshmen who applied for aid, 364 were judged to have need. Of these, 364 received aid, and 364 had their full need met. Average financial aid package met 100% of need; average scholarship/grant was $26,239; average loan was $2,463. Need-based aid available for part-time students.
Students without need: This college only awards aid to students with need.
Cumulative student debt: 51% of graduating class had student loans; average debt was $11,821.

FINANCIAL AID PROCEDURES
Forms required: FAFSA, CSS PROFILE, institutional form.
Dates and Deadlines: Closing date 1/15. Applicants notified by 4/1; must reply by 5/1.
Transfers: Closing date 2/10.

CONTACT
Kathryn Osmond, Director of Student Financial Services
106 Central Street, Wellesley, MA 02481-8203
(781) 283-2360

Wentworth Institute of Technology
Boston, Massachusetts
www.wit.edu
Federal Code: 002225

4-year private engineering and technical college in very large city.
Enrollment: 3,579 undergrads, 12% part-time. 852 full-time freshmen.
Selectivity: Admits 50 to 75% of applicants.

BASIC COSTS (2006-2007)
Tuition and fees: $19,300.
Per-credit charge: $605.
Room and board: $9,300.
Additional info: Tuition includes cost of laptop computer.

FINANCIAL AID PICTURE (2004-2005)
Students with need: Out of 852 full-time freshmen who applied for aid, 568 were judged to have need. Of these, 568 received aid, and 24 had their full need met. Average financial aid package met 40% of need; average scholarship/grant was $2,163; average loan was $3,076. For part-time students, average financial aid package was $5,720.
Students without need: 161 full-time freshmen who did not demonstrate need for aid received scholarships/grants; average award was $3,657. No-need awards available for academics, leadership, ROTC.
Scholarships offered: Applicants for admission automatically considered for merit scholarships.
Cumulative student debt: 80% of graduating class had student loans; average debt was $20,928.

FINANCIAL AID PROCEDURES
Forms required: FAFSA.
Dates and Deadlines: Priority date 3/1; no closing date. Applicants notified on a rolling basis starting 3/15; must reply within 2 week(s) of notification.
Transfers: Review of NSLDS history within 30 days of beginning of enrollment required.

CONTACT
Rachelle Shahan-Riehl, Director of Financial Aid
550 Huntington Avenue, Boston, MA 02115
(617) 989-4020

Western New England College
Springfield, Massachusetts
www.wnec.edu
Federal Code: 002226

4-year private business college in small city.
Enrollment: 2,828 undergrads, 17% part-time. 663 full-time freshmen.
Selectivity: Admits 50 to 75% of applicants.

BASIC COSTS (2005-2006)
Tuition and fees: $23,164.
Per-credit charge: $452.
Room and board: $8,890.

FINANCIAL AID PICTURE (2005-2006)
Students with need: Out of 618 full-time freshmen who applied for aid, 493 were judged to have need. Of these, 490 received aid, and 43 had their full need met. Average financial aid package met 70% of need; average scholarship/grant was $9,868; average loan was $3,321. For part-time students, average financial aid package was $5,426.
Students without need: 68 full-time freshmen who did not demonstrate need for aid received scholarships/grants; average award was $7,538. No-need awards available for academics, ROTC.

FINANCIAL AID PROCEDURES
Forms required: FAFSA.
Dates and Deadlines: Priority date 4/1; no closing date. Applicants notified on a rolling basis starting 3/15; must reply by 5/1 or within 2 week(s) of notification.

CONTACT
Kathy Chambers, Associate Director of Financial Aid
1215 Wilbraham Road, Springfield, MA 01119-2684
(800) 325-1122 ext. 2080

Westfield State College
Westfield, Massachusetts
www.wsc.ma.edu
Federal Code: 002189

4-year public liberal arts and teachers college in large town.
Enrollment: 4,488 undergrads, 9% part-time. 1,180 full-time freshmen.
Selectivity: Admits 50 to 75% of applicants.

BASIC COSTS (2005-2006)
Tuition and fees: $5,657; out-of-state residents $11,737.
Room and board: $5,580.
Additional info: New England Regional tuition and fees per year: $6142.

FINANCIAL AID PICTURE (2004-2005)
Students with need: 48% of average financial aid package awarded as scholarships/grants, 52% awarded as loans/jobs. Need-based aid available for part-time students.
Students without need: No-need awards available for academics.

FINANCIAL AID PROCEDURES
Forms required: FAFSA.
Dates and Deadlines: Priority date 3/1; no closing date. Applicants notified by 4/15.

CONTACT
Catherine Ryan, Director of Student Administrative Services/Financial Aid
577 Western Avenue, Westfield, MA 01086-1630
(413) 572-5218

Wheaton College
Norton, Massachusetts
www.wheatoncollege.edu
Federal Code: 002227
CSS Code: 3963

4-year private liberal arts college in large town.
Enrollment: 1,559 undergrads. 466 full-time freshmen.
Selectivity: Admits less than 50% of applicants.

BASIC COSTS (2006-2007)
Tuition and fees: $34,610.
Room and board: $8,150.
Additional info: Freshmen pay one-time $50 general fee (non-refundable); all residents pay annual $120 technology fee.

FINANCIAL AID PICTURE (2005-2006)
Students with need: Out of 270 full-time freshmen who applied for aid, 227 were judged to have need. Of these, 227 received aid, and 94 had their full need met. Average financial aid package met 94% of need; average scholarship/grant was $19,030; average loan was $3,566. For part-time students, average financial aid package was $4,800.
Students without need: 67 full-time freshmen who did not demonstrate need for aid received scholarships/grants; average award was $12,523. No-need awards available for academics.
Scholarships offered: Balfour Scholarship; $12,500 annually plus $4,000 total in research/internship/community service stipends. Trustee Scholarship; $10,000 annually plus $4,000 total in research/internship/community service stipends. Community Scholarship; $7,500 annually plus $3,000 total in research/internship/community service stipends. All selected from top 15% of applicant pool.
Cumulative student debt: 61% of graduating class had student loans; average debt was $22,380.

FINANCIAL AID PROCEDURES
Forms required: FAFSA, CSS PROFILE.
Dates and Deadlines: Closing date 2/1. Applicants notified by 4/1; must reply by 5/1.
Transfers: Closing date 4/15. Applicants notified by 5/15; must reply by 6/1. Very limited institutional grant funds available for late transfer applicants.

CONTACT
Robin Randall, Assistant Vice President for Enrollment and Student Financial Services
26 East Main Street, Norton, MA 02766
(508) 286-8232

Wheelock College
Boston, Massachusetts
www.wheelock.edu
Federal Code: 002228

4-year private liberal arts and teachers college in very large city.
Enrollment: 675 undergrads, 6% part-time.
Selectivity: Admits over 75% of applicants.

BASIC COSTS (2005-2006)
Tuition and fees: $23,625.
Room and board: $9,450.

FINANCIAL AID PICTURE
Students with need: Need-based aid available for full-time and part-time students. Work study available nights, weekends, and for part-time students.
Students without need: No-need awards available for academics, job skills, leadership, minority status.
Scholarships offered: Wheelock College Grants; awarded based SAT score of 1000 (exclusive of Writing) plus 3.0 GPA; renewable if 3.0 GPA maintained.

FINANCIAL AID PROCEDURES
Forms required: FAFSA, institutional form.
Dates and Deadlines: Closing date 3/1. Applicants notified on a rolling basis starting 3/1; must reply by 5/1.
Transfers: Priority date 2/15; closing date 4/15. Applicants notified by 3/15.

CONTACT
Melissa Holster, Director of Financial Aid
200 The Riverway, Boston, MA 02215-4176
(617) 879-2206

Williams College
Williamstown, Massachusetts
www.williams.edu
Federal Code: 002229
CSS Code: 3965

4-year private liberal arts college in small town.
Enrollment: 1,970 undergrads. 536 full-time freshmen.
Selectivity: Admits less than 50% of applicants.

BASIC COSTS (2006-2007)
Tuition and fees: $33,700.
Room and board: $8,950.

FINANCIAL AID PICTURE (2005-2006)
Students with need: Out of 319 full-time freshmen who applied for aid, 264 were judged to have need. Of these, 264 received aid, and 264 had their full need met. Average financial aid package met 100% of need; average scholarship/grant was $29,507; average loan was $2,128. For part-time students, average financial aid package was $39,684.
Students without need: This college only awards aid to students with need.
Cumulative student debt: 39% of graduating class had student loans; average debt was $10,900.

FINANCIAL AID PROCEDURES
Forms required: FAFSA, CSS PROFILE.
Dates and Deadlines: Closing date 2/15. Applicants notified by 4/1; must reply by 5/1.
Transfers: Closing date 3/1.

CONTACT
Paul Boyer, Director of Financial Aid
33 Stetson Court, Williamstown, MA 01267
(413) 597-3131

Worcester Polytechnic Institute
Worcester, Massachusetts
www.wpi.edu
Federal Code: 002233
CSS Code: 3969

4-year private university in small city.
Enrollment: 2,838 undergrads, 1% part-time. 747 full-time freshmen.
Selectivity: Admits over 75% of applicants.

BASIC COSTS (2006-2007)
Tuition and fees: $33,318.
Room and board: $9,960.

FINANCIAL AID PICTURE (2004-2005)
Students with need: Out of 695 full-time freshmen who applied for aid, 559 were judged to have need. Of these, 555 received aid, and 234 had their full need met. Average financial aid package met 76% of need; average scholarship/grant was $17,390; average loan was $4,558. For part-time students, average financial aid package was $4,657.
Students without need: 114 full-time freshmen who did not demonstrate need for aid received scholarships/grants; average award was $18,461. No-need awards available for academics, minority status, ROTC.
Scholarships offered: Merit scholarships; vary in amounts, but typically range between $12,500 and $25,000; renewable for 4 years.
Cumulative student debt: 94% of graduating class had student loans; average debt was $27,384.

FINANCIAL AID PROCEDURES
Forms required: FAFSA. Parents' and student's prior-year federal tax returns and W-2 statements required.
Dates and Deadlines: Closing date 2/1. Applicants notified by 4/1; must reply by 5/1.
Transfers: Closing date 3/1. Applicants notified by 4/15; must reply within 2 week(s) of notification.

CONTACT
Monica Blondin, Director, Financial Aid
100 Institute Road, Worcester, MA 01609-2280
(508) 831-5469

Worcester State College
Worcester, Massachusetts
www.worcester.edu
Federal Code: 002190

4-year public liberal arts and teachers college in small city.
Enrollment: 3,964 undergrads, 19% part-time. 623 full-time freshmen.
Selectivity: Admits 50 to 75% of applicants.

BASIC COSTS (2005-2006)
Tuition and fees: $5,079; out-of-state residents $11,159.
Per-credit charge: $40; out-of-state residents $294.
Room and board: $7,420.

FINANCIAL AID PICTURE (2004-2005)
Students with need: Out of 477 full-time freshmen who applied for aid, 317 were judged to have need. Of these, 305 received aid, and 137 had their full need met. Average financial aid package met 75% of need; average scholarship/grant was $1,717; average loan was $1,022. For part-time students, average financial aid package was $5,116.
Students without need: 19 full-time freshmen who did not demonstrate need for aid received scholarships/grants; average award was $2,199. No-need awards available for academics, alumni affiliation.
Scholarships offered: Presidential Scholarships; full in-state tuition and fees; 3.5 GPA and 1150 SAT; 15 awarded. Tsongas Scholarships; full in-state tuition and fees to Massachusetts residents; 3.7 GPA and 1200 SAT; 5 awarded. Access Scholarships; $1000 per year; opportunity for underserved groups; 2.5 GPA and 900 SAT; 15 awarded. Teacher Education Scholarship; full in-state tuition and fees; 3.5 GPA and 1150 SAT; for future teachers; 15 awarded. Honors Scholarship; $1,500 per year; 3.2 GPA and 1100 SAT; 25 awarded. All SAT scores exclusive of Writing. Transfer Scholarship; $1,000; requires associate's degree and 3.2 GPA; 25 awarded to Massachusetts residents.
Cumulative student debt: 43% of graduating class had student loans; average debt was $11,843.
Additional info: Veterans, Native Americans and those certified by Massachusetts Rehabilitation Commission and Massachusetts Commission for the Blind considered for tuition waivers while funds available. Tuition also waived for needy Massachusetts residents and in-state National Guard members.

FINANCIAL AID PROCEDURES
Forms required: FAFSA, institutional form.
Dates and Deadlines: Priority date 3/1; no closing date. Applicants notified on a rolling basis starting 3/1; must reply within 2 week(s) of notification.
Transfers: Many scholarships not available to transfer students; some available only to transfer students.

CONTACT
Jayne McGinn, Director of Financial Aid
486 Chandler Street, Worcester, MA 01602-2597
(508) 929-8056

Michigan

Adrian College
Adrian, Michigan
www.adrian.edu
Federal Code: 002234

4-year private liberal arts college in large town, affiliated with United Methodist Church.
Enrollment: 971 undergrads, 4% part-time. 293 full-time freshmen.
Selectivity: Admits over 75% of applicants.

BASIC COSTS (2005-2006)
Tuition and fees: $18,630.
Per-credit charge: $585.
Room and board: $6,170.

FINANCIAL AID PICTURE (2005-2006)
Students with need: Out of 291 full-time freshmen who applied for aid, 242 were judged to have need. Of these, 242 received aid, and 224 had their full need met. Average financial aid package met 99% of need; average scholarship/grant was $10,709; average loan was $3,845. For part-time students, average financial aid package was $9,058.
Students without need: 46 full-time freshmen who did not demonstrate need for aid received scholarships/grants; average award was $7,639. No-need awards available for academics, alumni affiliation, art, music/drama, religious affiliation.
Scholarships offered: Academic scholarships; based on ACT score of 20 and GPA of 3.0.

FINANCIAL AID PROCEDURES
Forms required: FAFSA.
Dates and Deadlines: Closing date 3/15. Applicants notified on a rolling basis starting 3/15; must reply by 5/1 or within 2 week(s) of notification.
Transfers: Closing date 3/1.

CONTACT
Mike Hague, Associate Vice President for Financial Services
110 South Madison Street, Adrian, MI 49221-2575
(517) 265-5161 ext. 4306

Albion College
Albion, Michigan
www.albion.edu   Federal Code: 002235

4-year private liberal arts college in large town, affiliated with United Methodist Church.
Enrollment: 1,953 undergrads, 1% part-time. 559 full-time freshmen.
Selectivity: Admits over 75% of applicants.

BASIC COSTS (2006-2007)
Tuition and fees: $26,122.
Per-credit charge: $1,090.
Room and board: $7,408.

FINANCIAL AID PICTURE (2005-2006)
Students with need: Out of 442 full-time freshmen who applied for aid, 355 were judged to have need. Of these, 355 received aid, and 258 had their full need met. Average financial aid package met 97% of need; average scholarship/grant was $16,890; average loan was $3,297.
Students without need: 190 full-time freshmen who did not demonstrate need for aid received scholarships/grants; average award was $11,474. No-need awards available for academics, alumni affiliation, art, leadership, minority status, music/drama, religious affiliation, state/district residency.
Scholarships offered: Distinguished Albion Scholarships; full tuition for 4 years; awarded to students who present original research during on-campus competition; up to 10 awarded. Trustee Scholarships; $13,000; based on GPA and SAT or ACT. Presidential Scholarships; $11,500; based on GPA and SAT or ACT. Performing Arts Scholarships; up to $3,000. Speech Communication Scholarships; up to $8,000. Fine Arts Scholarships; up to $3,000. Diversity Awards; $4,000 renewable annually; awarded to students involved with promoting and enhancing multicultural on-campus relations.

FINANCIAL AID PROCEDURES
Forms required: FAFSA.
Dates and Deadlines: Priority date 2/15; no closing date. Applicants notified on a rolling basis starting 3/15; must reply by 5/1 or within 2 week(s) of notification.
Transfers: Closing date 2/15.

CONTACT
Kristi Maze, Associate Vice President for Enrollment and Financial Aid
611 East Porter Street, Albion, MI 49224-1831
(517) 629-0440

Alma College
Alma, Michigan
www.alma.edu   Federal Code: 002236

4-year private liberal arts college in small town, affiliated with Presbyterian Church (USA).
Enrollment: 1,242 undergrads, 1% part-time. 336 full-time freshmen.
Selectivity: Admits over 75% of applicants.

BASIC COSTS (2006-2007)
Tuition and fees: $22,380.
Per-credit charge: $860.
Room and board: $7,774.

FINANCIAL AID PICTURE (2005-2006)
Students with need: Out of 336 full-time freshmen who applied for aid, 257 were judged to have need. Of these, 257 received aid, and 78 had their full need met. Average financial aid package met 86% of need; average scholarship/grant was $15,322; average loan was $4,613. For part-time students, average financial aid package was $15,870.
Students without need: 75 full-time freshmen who did not demonstrate need for aid received scholarships/grants; average award was $16,112. No-need awards available for academics, alumni affiliation, art, music/drama.
Scholarships offered: Distinguished Scholar Award; up to full tuition; awarded to designated National Merit Scholarship Finalist. Trustee Honors Scholarship; $12,000; awarded on basis of superior academic achievement, national test scores. Presidential Scholarships; $11,000; awarded on basis of outstanding scholarship and high national test scores. Dean's Scholarship; $10,000; awarded on basis on academic achievement and high national test scores. Tartan Scholars Award; $7,000; based on academic achievement or high national test scores. Performance Scholarships; up to $1,000; awarded to students with a demonstrated high level of accomplishment in the fine or performing arts.
Cumulative student debt: 87% of graduating class had student loans; average debt was $18,947.
Additional info: Auditions required for music, drama, dance scholarship candidates. Portfolios required for art scholarship candidates.

FINANCIAL AID PROCEDURES
Forms required: FAFSA.
Dates and Deadlines: No deadline. Applicants notified on a rolling basis starting 3/1; must reply within 3 week(s) of notification.
Transfers: Priority date 3/1; no deadline. Applicants notified on a rolling basis starting 3/1; must reply within 3 week(s) of notification.

CONTACT
Christopher Brown, Director of Student Financial Assistance
614 West Superior Street, Alma, MI 48801-1599
(989) 463-7347

Alpena Community College
Alpena, Michigan
www.alpenacc.edu   Federal Code: 002237

2-year public community college in large town.
Enrollment: 1,853 undergrads.
Selectivity: Open admission; but selective for some programs.

BASIC COSTS (2005-2006)
Tuition and fees: $2,660; out-of-district residents $3,740; out-of-state residents $4,820.
Per-credit charge: $72; out-of-district residents $108; out-of-state residents $144.

FINANCIAL AID PICTURE (2005-2006)
Students with need: 66% of average financial aid package awarded as scholarships/grants, 34% awarded as loans/jobs. Need-based aid available for part-time students.
Students without need: No-need awards available for academics, art, athletics, job skills, leadership, music/drama.

FINANCIAL AID PROCEDURES
Forms required: FAFSA.
Dates and Deadlines: Priority date 8/1; no closing date. Applicants notified on a rolling basis starting 5/15; must reply within 3 week(s) of notification.

CONTACT
Max Lindsay, Dean of Students
666 Johnson Street, Alpena, MI 49707
(989) 358-7205

Andrews University
Berrien Springs, Michigan
www.andrews.edu   Federal Code: 002238

4-year private university in small town, affiliated with Seventh-day Adventists.
Enrollment: 1,571 undergrads, 7% part-time. 325 full-time freshmen.
Selectivity: Admits less than 50% of applicants.

BASIC COSTS (2006-2007)
Tuition and fees: $17,664.
Per-credit charge: $717.
Room and board: $6,460.

FINANCIAL AID PICTURE (2004-2005)
Students with need: Out of 323 full-time freshmen who applied for aid, 214 were judged to have need. Of these, 214 received aid, and 99 had their full need met. Average financial aid package met 99% of need; average scholarship/grant was $6,291; average loan was $2,553. For part-time students, average financial aid package was $19,437.
Students without need: 107 full-time freshmen who did not demonstrate need for aid received scholarships/grants; average award was $4,973. No-need awards available for academics, alumni affiliation, leadership, music/drama, religious affiliation.

FINANCIAL AID PROCEDURES
Forms required: FAFSA, institutional form.
Dates and Deadlines: Priority date 3/31; no closing date. Applicants notified on a rolling basis starting 3/15.

CONTACT
Jerri Gifford, Director of Student Financial Services Berrien Springs, MI 49104
(269) 471-7771

Aquinas College
Grand Rapids, Michigan
www.aquinas.edu   Federal Code: 002239

4-year private liberal arts college in small city, affiliated with Roman Catholic Church.
Enrollment: 1,782 undergrads, 18% part-time. 366 full-time freshmen.
Selectivity: Admits over 75% of applicants. GED not accepted.

BASIC COSTS (2006-2007)
Tuition and fees: $19,000.
Per-credit charge: $594.
Room and board: $6,174.
Additional info: Tuition/fee waivers available for adults.

FINANCIAL AID PICTURE (2005-2006)
Students with need: Out of 334 full-time freshmen who applied for aid, 279 were judged to have need. Of these, 279 received aid, and 125 had their full need met. Average financial aid package met 89% of need; average scholarship/grant was $12,518; average loan was $1,928. For part-time students, average financial aid package was $5,203.
Students without need: 26 full-time freshmen who did not demonstrate need for aid received scholarships/grants; average award was $8,785. No-need awards available for academics, alumni affiliation, art, athletics, leadership, religious affiliation.
Scholarships offered: *Merit:* Spectrum Scholarship; awarded to students who have excelled in academics, leadership or community service. Renewable scholarships; $3,000 to full tuition. *Athletic:* 17 full-time freshmen received athletic scholarships; average amount $2,335.
Cumulative student debt: 65% of graduating class had student loans; average debt was $14,645.

FINANCIAL AID PROCEDURES
Forms required: FAFSA.
Dates and Deadlines: Priority date 2/15; no closing date. Applicants notified on a rolling basis starting 4/1; must reply within 2 week(s) of notification.
Transfers: Priority date 4/15; closing date 7/1.

CONTACT
David Steffee, Director of Financial Aid
1607 Robinson Road Southeast, Grand Rapids, MI 49506-1799
(616) 632-2893

Baker College of Auburn Hills
Auburn Hills, Michigan
www.baker.edu   Federal Code: E00466

4-year private business and technical college in small city.
Enrollment: 3,517 undergrads.
Selectivity: Open admission.

BASIC COSTS (2006-2007)
Tuition and fees: $8,100.
Per-credit charge: $180.

FINANCIAL AID PICTURE
Students with need: Work study available nights, weekends, and for part-time students.
Students without need: No-need awards available for academics, alumni affiliation.

FINANCIAL AID PROCEDURES
Forms required: FAFSA, institutional form.
Dates and Deadlines: Priority date 2/21; closing date 9/1. Applicants notified on a rolling basis starting 4/1.
Transfers: Must have been deemed financial aid-eligible at previous school.

CONTACT
Greg Little, Financial Aid Director
1500 University Drive, Auburn Hills, MI 48326
(248) 340-0600

Baker College of Cadillac
Cadillac, Michigan
www.baker.edu   Federal Code: E00461

4-year private business and health science college in large town.
Enrollment: 1,559 undergrads.
Selectivity: Open admission.

BASIC COSTS (2005-2006)
Tuition and fees: $7,875.
Per-credit charge: $175.

FINANCIAL AID PICTURE
Students with need: Need-based aid available for full-time and part-time students. Work study available nights, weekends, and for part-time students.
Students without need: No-need awards available for academics.
Scholarships offered: Baker College Career Scholarships; $400 per term for 4 years; based on 2.5 GPA after junior year of high school. Board of Regents Scholarships; half tuition for 4 years; based on 3.5 GPA through grade 11.

FINANCIAL AID PROCEDURES
Forms required: FAFSA, institutional form.
Dates and Deadlines: Priority date 2/21; no closing date. Applicants notified on a rolling basis starting 5/1.
Transfers: Priority date 3/20; closing date 9/1.

CONTACT
Kristin Bonney, Financial Aid Officer
9600 East 13th Street, Cadillac, MI 49601
(231) 876-3118

Baker College of Clinton Township
Clinton Township, Michigan
www.baker.edu   Federal Code: E00462

4-year private business and technical college in very large city.
Enrollment: 5,103 undergrads.
Selectivity: Open admission; but selective for some programs.

BASIC COSTS (2006-2007)
Tuition and fees: $8,100.
Per-credit charge: $180.

FINANCIAL AID PICTURE
Students with need: Need-based aid available for full-time and part-time students. Work study available nights, weekends, and for part-time students.
Students without need: No-need awards available for academics, minority status.

FINANCIAL AID PROCEDURES
Forms required: FAFSA, institutional form.
Dates and Deadlines: Priority date 2/21; closing date 9/1. Applicants notified on a rolling basis starting 4/1.

CONTACT
Lisa Harvener, Vice President of Student Services
34401 Gratiot Avenue, Clinton Township, MI 48035
(586) 790-9589

Baker College of Muskegon
Muskegon, Michigan
www.baker.edu   Federal Code: E00463

4-year private business and technical college in small city.
Enrollment: 4,744 undergrads.
Selectivity: Open admission; but selective for some programs.

BASIC COSTS (2006-2007)
Tuition and fees: $8,100.
Per-credit charge: $180.
Room only: $2,500.

FINANCIAL AID PICTURE
Students with need: Need-based aid available for full-time and part-time students. Work study available nights, weekends, and for part-time students.
Students without need: No-need awards available for academics, minority status.
Scholarships offered: Career Scholarship; $4,800 over 4 years; based on high school GPA over 3.0. Board Regents Scholarship; one-half tuition for 4 years; based on GPA over 3.5. Alternative Scholarship; one-half tuition for 2 years; based on academic success in alternative high school education program.

FINANCIAL AID PROCEDURES
Forms required: FAFSA, institutional form.
Dates and Deadlines: Priority date 2/21; no closing date. Applicants notified on a rolling basis starting 4/1.
Transfers: Priority date 3/21.

CONTACT
Director of Financial Aid
1903 Marquette Avenue, Muskegon, MI 49442
(231) 777-5231

Baker College of Owosso
Owosso, Michigan
www.baker.edu   Federal Code: E00464

4-year private business and technical college in large town.
Enrollment: 2,823 undergrads.
Selectivity: Open admission.

BASIC COSTS (2006-2007)
Tuition and fees: $8,100.
Per-credit charge: $180.
Room only: $2,500.

FINANCIAL AID PICTURE
Students with need: Need-based aid available for full-time and part-time students. Work study available nights, weekends, and for part-time students.
Students without need: No-need awards available for academics, minority status.

FINANCIAL AID PROCEDURES
Forms required: FAFSA, institutional form.
Dates and Deadlines: Priority date 2/21; closing date 9/1. Applicants notified on a rolling basis starting 4/1.
Transfers: Priority date 3/21.

CONTACT
David Lewis, Financial Aid Director
1020 South Washington Street, Owosso, MI 48867
(989) 720-3430

Baker College of Port Huron
Port Huron, Michigan
www.baker.edu   Federal Code: E00465

4-year private business and technical college in large town.
Enrollment: 1,578 undergrads.
Selectivity: Open admission; but selective for some programs.

BASIC COSTS (2006-2007)
Tuition and fees: $8,100.
Per-credit charge: $180.

FINANCIAL AID PICTURE
Students with need: Need-based aid available for full-time and part-time students. Work study available nights.
Students without need: This college only awards aid to students with need.

FINANCIAL AID PROCEDURES
Forms required: FAFSA, institutional form.
Dates and Deadlines: Priority date 2/21; no closing date. Applicants notified on a rolling basis starting 4/1.
Transfers: Priority date 3/21; closing date 9/1.

CONTACT
Financial Aid Director
3403 Lapeer Road, Port Huron, MI 48060-2597
(810) 985-7000

Bay de Noc Community College
Escanaba, Michigan
www.baycollege.edu   Federal Code: 002240

2-year public community college in large town.
Enrollment: 2,033 undergrads, 39% part-time. 425 full-time freshmen.
Selectivity: Open admission.

458 **Michigan** Bay de Noc Community College

BASIC COSTS (2005-2006)
Tuition and fees: $2,120; out-of-district residents $3,035; out-of-state residents $4,655.
Per-credit charge: $65; out-of-district residents $95; out-of-state residents $149.
Room and board: $3,840.
Additional info: Tuition and instructional fees charged on per contact hour basis.

FINANCIAL AID PICTURE
Students with need: Need-based aid available for full-time and part-time students. Work study available nights, weekends, and for part-time students.
Students without need: No-need awards available for academics.

FINANCIAL AID PROCEDURES
Forms required: FAFSA.
Dates and Deadlines: Priority date 4/1; no closing date. Applicants notified on a rolling basis starting 2/1; must reply within 2 week(s) of notification.

CONTACT
Sue Hebert, Financial Aid Director
2001 North Lincoln Road, Escanaba, MI 49829-2511
(906) 786-5802 ext. 1215

Bay Mills Community College
Brimley, Michigan
www.bmcc.edu   Federal Code: 030666

2-year public community college in rural community.
Enrollment: 175 full-time undergrads.
Selectivity: Open admission.

BASIC COSTS (2005-2006)
Tuition and fees: $2,910.
Per-credit charge: $85.

FINANCIAL AID PICTURE
Students with need: Work study available nights.

FINANCIAL AID PROCEDURES
Forms required: FAFSA, institutional form.

CONTACT
Tina Miller, Financial Aid Director
12214 West Lakeshore Drive, Brimley, MI 49715
(906) 248-3354 ext. 4224

Calvin College
Grand Rapids, Michigan
www.calvin.edu   Federal Code: 002241

4-year private liberal arts college in large city, affiliated with Christian Reformed Church.
Enrollment: 4,040 undergrads, 2% part-time. 1,007 full-time freshmen.
Selectivity: Admits over 75% of applicants.

BASIC COSTS (2006-2007)
Tuition and fees: $20,470.
Per-credit charge: $480.
Room and board: $7,040.

FINANCIAL AID PICTURE (2005-2006)
Students with need: Out of 831 full-time freshmen who applied for aid, 628 were judged to have need. Of these, 628 received aid, and 162 had their full need met. Average financial aid package met 83% of need; average scholarship/grant was $9,200; average loan was $4,000. For part-time students, average financial aid package was $9,700.
Students without need: 320 full-time freshmen who did not demonstrate need for aid received scholarships/grants; average award was $4,200. No-need awards available for academics, alumni affiliation, art, leadership, minority status, music/drama, religious affiliation, state/district residency.
Cumulative student debt: 67% of graduating class had student loans; average debt was $19,400.

FINANCIAL AID PROCEDURES
Forms required: FAFSA, institutional form.
Dates and Deadlines: Priority date 2/15; no closing date. Applicants notified on a rolling basis starting 3/15.
Transfers: Priority date 3/15; closing date 8/15. Applicants notified on a rolling basis starting 3/15.

CONTACT
Edward Kerestly, Director of Scholarships and Financial Aid
3201 Burton Street SE, Grand Rapids, MI 49546
(616) 526-6134

Central Michigan University
Mount Pleasant, Michigan
www.cmich.edu   Federal Code: 002243

4-year public university in large town.
Enrollment: 19,715 undergrads, 11% part-time. 3,714 full-time freshmen.
Selectivity: Admits over 75% of applicants.

BASIC COSTS (2005-2006)
Tuition and fees: $6,390; out-of-state residents $14,850.
Per-credit charge: $213; out-of-state residents $495.
Room and board: $6,376.
Additional info: Tuition at time of enrollment locked for 4 years.

FINANCIAL AID PICTURE (2005-2006)
Students with need: Out of 2,900 full-time freshmen who applied for aid, 1,961 were judged to have need. Of these, 1,947 received aid, and 1,533 had their full need met. Average financial aid package met 99% of need; average scholarship/grant was $4,784; average loan was $3,605. For part-time students, average financial aid package was $8,383.
Students without need: 606 full-time freshmen who did not demonstrate need for aid received scholarships/grants; average award was $3,357. No-need awards available for academics, alumni affiliation, art, athletics, leadership, minority status, music/drama, ROTC, state/district residency.
Scholarships offered: Merit: President's Award; for out-of-state students; based on high school GPA of 3.0 or higher; awarded differential between in and out-of-state tuition. **Athletic:** 47 full-time freshmen received athletic scholarships; average amount $11,889.
Cumulative student debt: 64% of graduating class had student loans; average debt was $16,537.
Additional info: Tuition waiver for Native American students qualifying under state program criteria.

FINANCIAL AID PROCEDURES
Forms required: FAFSA.
Dates and Deadlines: Priority date 3/21; no closing date. Applicants notified on a rolling basis starting 4/1.

CONTACT
Michael Owens, Director, Scholarships and Financial Aid
Admissions Office, Mount Pleasant, MI 48859
(989) 774-3674

Cleary University
Howell, Michigan
www.cleary.edu   Federal Code: 002246

4-year private university and business college in small city.
Enrollment: 490 undergrads, 19% part-time. 43 full-time freshmen.

BASIC COSTS (2006-2007)
Tuition and fees: $12,825.
Per-credit charge: $285.
Additional info: Tuition prices guaranteed if student enrolled continuously. Tuition includes all books and fees. Tuition at time of enrollment locked for 4 years.

FINANCIAL AID PICTURE (2004-2005)
Students with need: Average financial aid package met 41% of need; average scholarship/grant was $1,234; average loan was $1,130. For part-time students, average financial aid package was $8,798.
Students without need: No-need awards available for academics.
Scholarships offered: Gil Bursley Scholarship; $500; full-time senior enrolled in bachelor's degree program with a 3.0 cumulative GPA; at least one awarded annually. Owen J. Cleary Endowed Scholarship; $500; students entering senior year with minmimum of 2.5 GPA, must demonstrate academic success and leadership in the community and university; 2 awarded annually. Oren Beutler Endowed Scholarship; $750, new or continuing full-time student maintaining minimum of 3.0 GPA, demonstrated leadership and service to community; one awarded annually, renewable for 4 years.
Additional info: Filing electronically preferred; paper applications available. Tuition guarantee based on continuous enrollment. Essay and recommendations required for scholarship consideration.

FINANCIAL AID PROCEDURES
Forms required: FAFSA.
Dates and Deadlines: Priority date 3/15; closing date 8/15. Applicants notified on a rolling basis; must reply within 2 week(s) of notification.

CONTACT
Vesta Smith-Campbell, Director of Financial Aid
3750 Cleary Drive, Howell, MI 48843
(517) 548-3670

College for Creative Studies
Detroit, Michigan
www.ccscad.edu   Federal Code: 006771

4-year private visual arts college in very large city.
Enrollment: 1,270 undergrads.
Selectivity: Admits 50 to 75% of applicants.

BASIC COSTS (2006-2007)
Tuition and fees: $24,635.
Per-credit charge: $783.
Room only: $3,900.

FINANCIAL AID PICTURE (2004-2005)
Students with need: 26% of average financial aid package awarded as scholarships/grants, 74% awarded as loans/jobs. Need-based aid available for part-time students. Work study available nights, weekends, and for part-time students.
Students without need: No-need awards available for academics, art.

FINANCIAL AID PROCEDURES
Forms required: FAFSA.
Dates and Deadlines: Priority date 2/21; no closing date. Applicants notified on a rolling basis starting 3/15; must reply within 3 week(s) of notification.
Transfers: Priority date 3/21.

CONTACT
Kristin Moskovitz, Director of Financial Aid
201 East Kirby, Detroit, MI 48202-4034
(313) 664-7495

Concordia University
Ann Arbor, Michigan
www.cuaa.edu   Federal Code: 002247

4-year private liberal arts and teachers college in small city, affiliated with Lutheran Church - Missouri Synod.
Enrollment: 535 undergrads, 7% part-time. 115 full-time freshmen.
Selectivity: Admits over 75% of applicants.

BASIC COSTS (2006-2007)
Tuition and fees: $19,010.
Per-credit charge: $620.
Room and board: $7,350.
Additional info: Additional one-time fees for all undergraduates include: $125 pre-enrollment deposit, $100 matriculation fee.

FINANCIAL AID PICTURE (2005-2006)
Students with need: Out of 108 full-time freshmen who applied for aid, 93 were judged to have need. Of these, 93 received aid, and 21 had their full need met. Average financial aid package met 86% of need; average scholarship/grant was $12,076; average loan was $4,427. For part-time students, average financial aid package was $6,675.
Students without need: 20 full-time freshmen who did not demonstrate need for aid received scholarships/grants; average award was $4,226. No-need awards available for academics, alumni affiliation, art, athletics, leadership, music/drama, religious affiliation.
Scholarships offered: 18 full-time freshmen received athletic scholarships; average amount $8,179.
Cumulative student debt: 83% of graduating class had student loans; average debt was $28,280.

FINANCIAL AID PROCEDURES
Forms required: FAFSA, institutional form.
Dates and Deadlines: Closing date 3/1. Applicants notified on a rolling basis starting 3/1; must reply within 3 week(s) of notification.
Transfers: Priority date 5/1. Applicants notified on a rolling basis; must reply within 3 week(s) of notification.

CONTACT
Sandy Tarbox, Director of Student Financial Aid
4090 Geddes Road, Ann Arbor, MI 48105
(734) 995-7408

Cornerstone University
Grand Rapids, Michigan
www.cornerstone.edu   Federal Code: 002266

4-year private university and liberal arts college in large city, affiliated with Baptist faith.
Enrollment: 2,105 undergrads, 17% part-time. 272 full-time freshmen.
Selectivity: Admits over 75% of applicants.

BASIC COSTS (2006-2007)
Tuition and fees: $17,080.
Per-credit charge: $642.
Room and board: $5,860.
Additional info: Tuition includes laptop computer.

Michigan Cornerstone University

FINANCIAL AID PICTURE (2004-2005)
Students with need: Out of 269 full-time freshmen who applied for aid, 223 were judged to have need. Of these, 223 received aid, and 54 had their full need met. Average financial aid package met 88% of need; average scholarship/grant was $7,852; average loan was $3,160. For part-time students, average financial aid package was $8,618.
Students without need: 43 full-time freshmen who did not demonstrate need for aid received scholarships/grants; average award was $4,756. No-need awards available for academics, athletics, leadership, music/drama, state/district residency.
Scholarships offered: *Merit:* Academic scholarships; based on high school GPA and ACT scores. *Athletic:* 29 full-time freshmen received athletic scholarships; average amount $5,450.
Cumulative student debt: 79% of graduating class had student loans; average debt was $23,710.
Additional info: Audition required for music scholarship applicants.

FINANCIAL AID PROCEDURES
Forms required: FAFSA.
Dates and Deadlines: Priority date 3/1; no closing date. Applicants notified on a rolling basis starting 3/15; must reply within 2 week(s) of notification.
Transfers: No deadline.

CONTACT
Geoff Marsh, Director of Student Financial Services
1001 East Beltline NE, Grand Rapids, MI 49525
(616) 222-1424

Davenport University
Grand Rapids, Michigan
www.davenport.edu
Federal Code: 015260

4-year private business and health science college in small city.
Enrollment: 11,733 undergrads, 74% part-time. 538 full-time freshmen.
Selectivity: Open admission.

BASIC COSTS (2006-2007)
Tuition and fees: $11,700.
Per-credit charge: $385.

FINANCIAL AID PICTURE (2004-2005)
Students with need: Out of 509 full-time freshmen who applied for aid, 481 were judged to have need. Of these, 463 received aid, and 34 had their full need met. Average financial aid package met 50% of need; average scholarship/grant was $3,781; average loan was $2,486. For part-time students, average financial aid package was $8,284.
Students without need: 28 full-time freshmen who did not demonstrate need for aid received scholarships/grants; average award was $5,419. No-need awards available for academics, alumni affiliation, athletics, leadership.
Scholarships offered: 12 full-time freshmen received athletic scholarships; average amount $3,101.
Cumulative student debt: 75% of graduating class had student loans; average debt was $8,439.

FINANCIAL AID PROCEDURES
Forms required: FAFSA.
Dates and Deadlines: Priority date 3/15; no closing date. Applicants notified on a rolling basis starting 3/1; must reply within 2 week(s) of notification.

CONTACT
Susan Crkovski, Executive Director of Financial Aid
6191 Kraft Avenue, Grand Rapids, MI 49512
(800) 632-9569

Delta College
University Center, Michigan
www.delta.edu
Federal Code: 002251

2-year public community and junior college in small city.
Enrollment: 10,184 undergrads, 62% part-time.
Selectivity: Open admission.

BASIC COSTS (2005-2006)
Tuition and fees: $2,400; out-of-district residents $3,345; out-of-state residents $4,680.
Per-credit charge: $73; out-of-district residents $104; out-of-state residents $149.

FINANCIAL AID PICTURE
Students with need: Need-based aid available for full-time and part-time students. Work study available nights.
Students without need: No-need awards available for academics, athletics.

FINANCIAL AID PROCEDURES
Forms required: FAFSA.
Dates and Deadlines: Priority date 8/1; no closing date. Applicants notified on a rolling basis; must reply within 2 week(s) of notification.
Transfers: No deadline. Applicants notified on a rolling basis.

CONTACT
Kim Donat, Financial Aid Director
1961 Delta Road, University Center, MI 48710
(989) 686-9080

Eastern Michigan University
Ypsilanti, Michigan
www.emich.edu
Federal Code: 002259

4-year public university in small city.
Enrollment: 18,165 undergrads, 29% part-time. 2,281 full-time freshmen.
Selectivity: Admits over 75% of applicants.

BASIC COSTS (2005-2006)
Tuition and fees: $6,508; out-of-state residents $17,863.
Per-credit charge: $182; out-of-state residents $561.
Room and board: $6,356.

FINANCIAL AID PICTURE (2004-2005)
Students with need: Out of 1,791 full-time freshmen who applied for aid, 1,305 were judged to have need. Of these, 1,254 received aid, and 61 had their full need met. Average financial aid package met 62% of need; average scholarship/grant was $3,471; average loan was $3,088. For part-time students, average financial aid package was $4,690.
Students without need: 326 full-time freshmen who did not demonstrate need for aid received scholarships/grants; average award was $2,041. No-need awards available for academics, alumni affiliation, art, athletics, leadership, music/drama, ROTC, state/district residency.
Scholarships offered: 90 full-time freshmen received athletic scholarships; average amount $10,607.
Cumulative student debt: 58% of graduating class had student loans; average debt was $21,397.

FINANCIAL AID PROCEDURES
Forms required: FAFSA.
Dates and Deadlines: Priority date 3/15; no closing date. Applicants notified on a rolling basis starting 3/15.

CONTACT
Bernice Lindke, Director of Financial Aid
400 Pierce Hall, Ypsilanti, MI 48197
(734) 487-0455

Ferris State University
Big Rapids, Michigan
www.ferris.edu   Federal Code: 002260

4-year public university in large town.
Enrollment: 11,051 undergrads, 20% part-time. 1,922 full-time freshmen.
Selectivity: Admits less than 50% of applicants.

BASIC COSTS (2005-2006)
Tuition and fees: $6,856; out-of-state residents $13,596.
Per-credit charge: $265; out-of-state residents $530.
Room and board: $6,816.
Additional info: Midwest Compact states of Illinois, Indiana, Kansas, Minnesota, Missouri, Nebraska, Ohio, and Wisconsin pay discounted tuition.

FINANCIAL AID PICTURE (2004-2005)
Students with need: Out of 1,780 full-time freshmen who applied for aid, 1,561 were judged to have need. Of these, 1,235 received aid, and 124 had their full need met. Average financial aid package met 75% of need; average scholarship/grant was $3,000; average loan was $1,800. Need-based aid available for part-time students.
Students without need: 111 full-time freshmen who did not demonstrate need for aid received scholarships/grants; average award was $2,000. No-need awards available for academics, alumni affiliation, art, athletics, leadership, minority status, music/drama, religious affiliation, ROTC.
Scholarships offered: 43 full-time freshmen received athletic scholarships; average amount $4,000.
Cumulative student debt: 85% of graduating class had student loans; average debt was $14,750.

FINANCIAL AID PROCEDURES
Forms required: FAFSA.
Dates and Deadlines: Priority date 3/1; no closing date. Applicants notified on a rolling basis starting 3/1; must reply within 2 week(s) of notification.

CONTACT
Carla Erlewine, Associate Director of Financial Aid
1201 S. State Street, CSS 201, Big Rapids, MI 49307-2714
(231) 591-2110

Finlandia University
Hancock, Michigan
www.finlandia.edu   Federal Code: 002322

4-year private university and liberal arts college in small town, affiliated with Evangelical Lutheran Church in America.
Enrollment: 548 undergrads, 14% part-time. 109 full-time freshmen.
Selectivity: Admits over 75% of applicants.

BASIC COSTS (2006-2007)
Tuition and fees: $16,300.
Per-credit charge: $540.
Room and board: $5,524.

FINANCIAL AID PICTURE (2004-2005)
Students with need: Out of 92 full-time freshmen who applied for aid, 84 were judged to have need. Of these, 84 received aid. For part-time students, average financial aid package was $6,000.
Students without need: No-need awards available for academics, leadership.
Additional info: Work/study program; up to $2,800 per year.

FINANCIAL AID PROCEDURES
Forms required: FAFSA, institutional form.
Dates and Deadlines: Priority date 3/1; closing date 8/1. Applicants notified on a rolling basis starting 3/1.

Transfers: Applicants notified on a rolling basis starting 2/1; must reply within 2 week(s) of notification.

CONTACT
Sandra Turnquist, Director of Financial Aid
601 Quincy Street, Hancock, MI 49930-1882
(906) 487-7261

Glen Oaks Community College
Centreville, Michigan
www.glenoaks.cc.mi.us   Federal Code: 002263

2-year public community college in rural community.
Enrollment: 950 undergrads.
Selectivity: Open admission; but selective for some programs.

BASIC COSTS (2006-2007)
Tuition and fees: $2,281; out-of-district residents $3,211; out-of-state residents $4,111.
Per-credit charge: $64; out-of-district residents $95; out-of-state residents $125.

FINANCIAL AID PICTURE (2004-2005)
Students with need: 99% of average financial aid package awarded as scholarships/grants, 1% awarded as loans/jobs. Need-based aid available for part-time students. Work study available nights.
Students without need: No-need awards available for academics, art, athletics, leadership, minority status, music/drama.

FINANCIAL AID PROCEDURES
Forms required: FAFSA, institutional form.
Dates and Deadlines: No deadline. Applicants notified on a rolling basis.

CONTACT
Matthew Soucy, Director of Financial Aid and Scholarship
62249 Shimmel Road, Centreville, MI 49032-9719
(269) 467-9945 ext. 250

Gogebic Community College
Ironwood, Michigan
www.gogebic.edu   Federal Code: 002264

2-year public community college in small town.
Enrollment: 525 full-time undergrads.
Selectivity: Open admission; but selective for some programs.

BASIC COSTS (2005-2006)
Tuition and fees: $2,568; out-of-district residents $3,168; out-of-state residents $3,948.
Per-credit charge: $74; out-of-district residents $94; out-of-state residents $120.
Additional info: Reciprocity tuition is the same as in-state, out-of-district tuition, $94 per-credit-hour.

FINANCIAL AID PICTURE
Students with need: Need-based aid available for full-time and part-time students. Work study available nights, weekends, and for part-time students.
Students without need: No-need awards available for academics, art, athletics, job skills, leadership, music/drama, state/district residency.

FINANCIAL AID PROCEDURES
Forms required: FAFSA.
Dates and Deadlines: Priority date 5/1; no closing date. Applicants notified on a rolling basis starting 3/15; must reply within 2 week(s) of notification.

CONTACT
Sue Forbes, Director of Financial Aid
E4946 Jackson Road, Ironwood, MI 49938
(906) 932-4231 ext. 206

Grace Bible College
Grand Rapids, Michigan
www.gbcol.edu   Federal Code: 002265

4-year private Bible and liberal arts college in small city, affiliated with Grace Gospel Fellowship.
Enrollment: 160 undergrads, 6% part-time. 30 full-time freshmen.
Selectivity: Admits 50 to 75% of applicants.

BASIC COSTS (2005-2006)
Tuition and fees: $10,950.
Per-credit charge: $450.
Room and board: $6,860.

FINANCIAL AID PICTURE (2004-2005)
Students with need: 46% of average financial aid package awarded as scholarships/grants, 54% awarded as loans/jobs. Need-based aid available for part-time students.
Students without need: No-need awards available for academics, music/drama, religious affiliation.

FINANCIAL AID PROCEDURES
Forms required: FAFSA.
Dates and Deadlines: Priority date 3/1; no closing date. Applicants notified on a rolling basis starting 5/15; must reply within 2 week(s) of notification.

CONTACT
Marlene DeVries, Financial Aid Director
PO Box 910, Grand Rapids, MI 49509
(616) 261-8557

Grand Rapids Community College
Grand Rapids, Michigan
www.grcc.edu   Federal Code: 002267

2-year public community college in small city.
Enrollment: 13,193 undergrads, 52% part-time. 2,225 full-time freshmen.
Selectivity: Open admission; but selective for some programs.

BASIC COSTS (2005-2006)
Tuition and fees: $2,185; out-of-district residents $3,750; out-of-state residents $5,350.
Per-credit charge: $70; out-of-district residents $125; out-of-state residents $175.
Additional info: Tuition charged per contact hour.

FINANCIAL AID PICTURE (2005-2006)
Students with need: Out of 1,839 full-time freshmen who applied for aid, 1,406 were judged to have need. Of these, 1,309 received aid, and 262 had their full need met. For part-time students, average financial aid package was $2,256.
Students without need: 226 full-time freshmen who did not demonstrate need for aid received scholarships/grants; average award was $1,485. No-need awards available for academics, alumni affiliation, art, athletics, leadership, minority status, music/drama, state/district residency.
Scholarships offered: *Merit:* Michigan Merit Award; $2,500; based on Michigan Educational Assessment Program scores. *Athletic:* 21 full-time freshmen received athletic scholarships; average amount $1,248.
Additional info: Tuition reimbursement and/or child-care services for single parents and displaced homemakers who meet Perkins guidelines.

FINANCIAL AID PROCEDURES
Forms required: FAFSA.
Dates and Deadlines: Priority date 4/1; no closing date. Applicants notified on a rolling basis starting 5/1; must reply within 3 week(s) of notification.

CONTACT
Jill Nutt, Executive Director of Student Financial Services
143 Bostwick Northeast, Grand Rapids, MI 49503-3295
(616) 234-4030

Grand Valley State University
Allendale, Michigan
www.gvsu.edu   Federal Code: 002268

4-year public university in small town.
Enrollment: 18,715 undergrads, 12% part-time. 3,401 full-time freshmen.
Selectivity: Admits 50 to 75% of applicants.

BASIC COSTS (2005-2006)
Tuition and fees: $6,220; out-of-state residents $12,510.
Per-credit charge: $271; out-of-state residents $532.
Room and board: $6,360.
Additional info: Junior and senior in-state students pay $6448 per year or $281 per credit hour. Junior and senior out-of-state students pay $12,932 per year or $550 per credit hour. Tuition/fee waivers available for minority students.

FINANCIAL AID PICTURE (2005-2006)
Students with need: Out of 3,092 full-time freshmen who applied for aid, 2,009 were judged to have need. Of these, 2,009 received aid, and 2,009 had their full need met. Average financial aid package met 100% of need; average scholarship/grant was $4,190; average loan was $2,638. For part-time students, average financial aid package was $2,690.
Students without need: 1,252 full-time freshmen who did not demonstrate need for aid received scholarships/grants; average award was $2,340. No-need awards available for academics, alumni affiliation, art, athletics, minority status, music/drama, state/district residency.
Scholarships offered: 85 full-time freshmen received athletic scholarships; average amount $5,500.
Cumulative student debt: 73% of graduating class had student loans; average debt was $16,606.
Additional info: College traditionally funds 100% of each student's demonstrated need.

FINANCIAL AID PROCEDURES
Forms required: FAFSA.
Dates and Deadlines: Priority date 2/15; no closing date. Applicants notified on a rolling basis starting 4/15; must reply within 3 week(s) of notification.

CONTACT
Ken Fridsma, Director of Financial Aid
One Campus Drive, Allendale, MI 49401-9403
(616) 331-3234

Great Lakes Christian College
Lansing, Michigan
www.glcc.edu   Federal Code: 002269

4-year private Bible college in small city, affiliated with Church of Christ (Christian).
Enrollment: 160 full-time undergrads. 25 full-time freshmen.
Selectivity: Admits over 75% of applicants.

BASIC COSTS (2005-2006)
Tuition and fees: $8,448.
Per-credit charge: $264.

Room and board: $5,200.
FINANCIAL AID PICTURE (2004-2005)
Students with need: Out of 25 full-time freshmen who applied for aid, 17 were judged to have need. Of these, 17 received aid. Average financial aid package met 55% of need; average scholarship/grant was $5,961; average loan was $2,072. For part-time students, average financial aid package was $4,863.
Students without need: 8 full-time freshmen who did not demonstrate need for aid received scholarships/grants; average award was $3,427. No-need awards available for academics, alumni affiliation, music/drama.
Cumulative student debt: 89% of graduating class had student loans; average debt was $17,673.
FINANCIAL AID PROCEDURES
Forms required: FAFSA, state aid form, institutional form.
Dates and Deadlines: Priority date 8/1; no closing date. Applicants notified on a rolling basis starting 5/1; must reply within 3 week(s) of notification.
Transfers: Priority date 3/31; closing date 8/31. Applicants notified on a rolling basis; must reply within 3 week(s) of notification. FAFSA due by 06/30.
CONTACT
Tedd Kees, Director of Financial Aid
6211 West Willow Highway, Lansing, MI 48917-1231
(517) 321-0242 ext. 227

Henry Ford Community College
Dearborn, Michigan
www.hfcc.edu   Federal Code: 002270

2-year public community college in small city.
Enrollment: 5,250 full-time undergrads.
Selectivity: Open admission; but selective for some programs.
BASIC COSTS (2005-2006)
Tuition and fees: $2,112; out-of-district residents $3,762; out-of-state residents $4,002.
Per-credit charge: $57; out-of-district residents $112; out-of-state residents $120.
FINANCIAL AID PICTURE
Students with need: Work study available nights, weekends, and for part-time students.
FINANCIAL AID PROCEDURES
Forms required: FAFSA.
Dates and Deadlines: Priority date 4/1; no closing date. Applicants notified on a rolling basis starting 3/1.
CONTACT
David Cunningham, Director of Financial Services
5101 Evergreen Road, Dearborn, MI 48128
(313) 845-9616

Hillsdale College
Hillsdale, Michigan
www.hillsdale.edu   Federal Code: 002272

4-year private liberal arts college in large town.
Enrollment: 1,304 undergrads, 3% part-time. 335 full-time freshmen.
Selectivity: Admits over 75% of applicants.
BASIC COSTS (2006-2007)
Tuition and fees: $18,260.
Per-credit charge: $700.
Room and board: $7,030.

FINANCIAL AID PICTURE (2004-2005)
Students with need: Out of 315 full-time freshmen who applied for aid, 300 were judged to have need. Of these, 300 received aid, and 140 had their full need met. Average financial aid package met 75% of need; average scholarship/grant was $8,500; average loan was $2,500.
Students without need: 85 full-time freshmen who did not demonstrate need for aid received scholarships/grants; average award was $7,600. No-need awards available for academics, alumni affiliation, art, athletics, leadership, music/drama, state/district residency.
Scholarships offered: *Merit:* Distinct Honor Scholarship; full tuition; 3 awarded. Presidential Scholarship; half tuition; 30 awarded. Trustee Scholarship; up to $8,000; 40 awarded. *Athletic:* 65 full-time freshmen received athletic scholarships; average amount $10,600.
Cumulative student debt: 64% of graduating class had student loans; average debt was $15,500.
Additional info: Campus employment available.
FINANCIAL AID PROCEDURES
Forms required: FAFSA, institutional form. Required for returning students only.
Dates and Deadlines: Priority date 3/1; no closing date. Applicants notified on a rolling basis starting 2/1; must reply by 5/1 or within 3 week(s) of notification.
CONTACT
Richard Moeggenberg, Director of Financial Aid
33 East College Street, Hillsdale, MI 49242
(517) 607-2350

Hope College
Holland, Michigan
www.hope.edu   Federal Code: 002273

4-year private liberal arts college in small city, affiliated with Reformed Church in America.
Enrollment: 3,070 undergrads, 2% part-time. 775 full-time freshmen.
Selectivity: Admits over 75% of applicants.
BASIC COSTS (2006-2007)
Tuition and fees: $22,570.
Room and board: $6,982.
FINANCIAL AID PICTURE (2004-2005)
Students with need: Out of 630 full-time freshmen who applied for aid, 471 were judged to have need. Of these, 471 received aid, and 168 had their full need met. Average financial aid package met 86% of need; average scholarship/grant was $14,114; average loan was $3,367. For part-time students, average financial aid package was $6,576.
Students without need: This college only awards aid to students with need.
Scholarships offered: Merit Scholarships range from $3,000 - $17,000 per year; 1474 awarded last year. Talent Awards; $2,500; for music, art, theater, and creative writing.
Cumulative student debt: 62% of graduating class had student loans; average debt was $20,783.
FINANCIAL AID PROCEDURES
Forms required: FAFSA, institutional form.
Dates and Deadlines: Priority date 3/1; no closing date. Applicants notified on a rolling basis starting 3/20; must reply by 5/1 or within 2 week(s) of notification.
Transfers: Priority date 5/1.
CONTACT
Phyllis Hooyman, Director of Financial Aid
69 East 10th Street, Holland, MI 49422-9000
(888) 439-8907

Jackson Community College
Jackson, Michigan
www.jccmi.edu   Federal Code: 002274

2-year public community college in small city.
Enrollment: 5,151 undergrads, 60% part-time. 102 full-time freshmen.
Selectivity: Open admission; but selective for some programs.

BASIC COSTS (2005-2006)
Tuition and fees: $2,691; out-of-district residents $3,591; out-of-state residents $4,461.
Per-credit charge: $74; out-of-district residents $104; out-of-state residents $133.

FINANCIAL AID PICTURE
Students with need: Need-based aid available for full-time and part-time students. Work study available nights, weekends, and for part-time students.
Students without need: No-need awards available for academics, art, leadership, music/drama, state/district residency.

FINANCIAL AID PROCEDURES
Forms required: FAFSA, institutional form.
Dates and Deadlines: Priority date 4/1; no closing date. Applicants notified on a rolling basis starting 3/1.

CONTACT
Thomas Vainner, Vice President for Administration
2111 Emmons Road, Jackson, MI 49201-8399
(517) 796-8436

Kalamazoo College
Kalamazoo, Michigan
www.kzoo.edu   Federal Code: 002275

4-year private liberal arts college in small city.
Enrollment: 1,226 undergrads. 310 full-time freshmen.
Selectivity: Admits 50 to 75% of applicants.

BASIC COSTS (2006-2007)
Tuition and fees: $27,149.
Room and board: $6,915.

FINANCIAL AID PICTURE (2005-2006)
Students with need: Out of 237 full-time freshmen who applied for aid, 179 were judged to have need. Of these, 179 received aid, and 148 had their full need met.
Students without need: 129 full-time freshmen who did not demonstrate need for aid received scholarships/grants; average award was $9,095. No-need awards available for academics, alumni affiliation.
Scholarships offered: Honors Scholarship; $2,000-$11,000; based on academic and co-curricular record and accomplishments; varied number awarded. Competitive Scholarships; $2,000-$3,000; based on written exam in a subject area or a fine arts audition.
Additional info: Paid career development internship and senior project experiences available on campus.

FINANCIAL AID PROCEDURES
Forms required: FAFSA, institutional form.
Dates and Deadlines: Priority date 2/15; no closing date. Applicants notified on a rolling basis starting 3/21; must reply by 5/1.
Transfers: Priority date 3/15.

CONTACT
Marian Conrad, Director of Financial Aid
1200 Academy Street, Kalamazoo, MI 49006-3295
(269) 337-7192

Kalamazoo Valley Community College
Kalamazoo, Michigan
www.kvcc.edu   Federal Code: 006949

2-year public community college in small city.
Enrollment: 9,210 undergrads, 58% part-time. 1,094 full-time freshmen.
Selectivity: Open admission.

BASIC COSTS (2005-2006)
Tuition and fees: $1,650; out-of-district residents $2,820; out-of-state residents $3,840.
Per-credit charge: $55; out-of-district residents $94; out-of-state residents $128.

FINANCIAL AID PICTURE
Students with need: Need-based aid available for full-time and part-time students. Work study available nights, weekends, and for part-time students.
Students without need: No-need awards available for academics, athletics.

FINANCIAL AID PROCEDURES
Forms required: FAFSA, institutional form.
Dates and Deadlines: Priority date 6/1; no closing date. Applicants notified on a rolling basis starting 5/1; must reply within 2 week(s) of notification.

CONTACT
Roger Miller, Director of Financial Aid
6767 West O Avenue, P.O. Box 4070, Kalamazoo, MI 49003-4070
(269) 488-4340

Kellogg Community College
Battle Creek, Michigan
www.kellogg.edu   Federal Code: 002276

2-year public community college in small city.
Enrollment: 4,357 undergrads, 62% part-time. 476 full-time freshmen.
Selectivity: Open admission; but selective for some programs.

BASIC COSTS (2005-2006)
Tuition and fees: $2,010; out-of-district residents $3,180; out-of-state residents $4,710.
Per-credit charge: $62; out-of-district residents $101; out-of-state residents $152.

FINANCIAL AID PICTURE (2004-2005)
Students with need: 83% of average financial aid package awarded as scholarships/grants, 17% awarded as loans/jobs. Need-based aid available for part-time students. Work study available nights.
Students without need: No-need awards available for academics, alumni affiliation, athletics.

FINANCIAL AID PROCEDURES
Forms required: FAFSA, institutional form.
Dates and Deadlines: Priority date 4/1; no closing date. Applicants notified on a rolling basis starting 4/1.

CONTACT
450 North Avenue, Battle Creek, MI 49017-3397
(269) 965-4123

Kendall College of Art and Design of Ferris State University
Grand Rapids, Michigan
www.kcad.edu   Federal Code: 002260

4-year public visual arts college in large city.
Enrollment: 758 undergrads.

Selectivity: Admits over 75% of applicants.

BASIC COSTS (2005-2006)
Tuition and fees: $11,925; out-of-state residents $17,910.
Per-credit charge: $265; out-of-state residents $398.
Additional info: Studio art courses: $460 per-credit-hour in-state and $690 out-of-state. General education courses: $265 per-credit-hour in-state and $398 out-of-state.

FINANCIAL AID PICTURE (2005-2006)
Students with need: Need-based aid available for full-time and part-time students. Work study available nights, weekends, and for part-time students.
Students without need: This college only awards aid to students with need.

FINANCIAL AID PROCEDURES
Forms required: FAFSA.
Dates and Deadlines: Closing date 2/15. Applicants notified on a rolling basis starting 4/15; must reply within 4 week(s) of notification.

CONTACT
Lori Deforest, Financial Aid Officer
17 Fountain Street NW, Grand Rapids, MI 49503-3002
(616) 451-2787

Kettering University
Flint, Michigan
www.kettering.edu   Federal Code: 002262

5-year private university and engineering college in small city.
Enrollment: 2,411 undergrads. 495 full-time freshmen.
Selectivity: Admits 50 to 75% of applicants. GED not accepted.

BASIC COSTS (2006-2007)
Tuition and fees: $24,908.
Per-credit charge: $766.
Room and board: $5,608.
Additional info: Tuition/fee waivers available for minority students.

FINANCIAL AID PICTURE (2005-2006)
Students with need: Out of 493 full-time freshmen who applied for aid, 442 were judged to have need. Of these, 442 received aid, and 56 had their full need met. Average financial aid package met 48% of need; average scholarship/grant was $4,376; average loan was $2,594. Need-based aid available for part-time students.
Students without need: 84 full-time freshmen who did not demonstrate need for aid received scholarships/grants; average award was $8,156. No-need awards available for academics, alumni affiliation, leadership, minority status, state/district residency.
Scholarships offered: Various scholarships; $20,000-$40,000 for 4 years; based on merit. Special renewable scholarships, including Society of Women's Engineers (SWE), US FIRST Robotics, Society of Automotive Engineers (SAE), DECA, Science Olympiad; $250-$5,000 per year. Other endowed scholarships/awards based on merit and/or need or special factors such as single-parent household.
Cumulative student debt: 59% of graduating class had student loans; average debt was $40,617.
Additional info: All undergraduate students participate in paid professional co-op work experience in industry that typically begins in freshman year. Total student earnings over 4.5-year program typically range from $40,000 to $65,000.

FINANCIAL AID PROCEDURES
Forms required: FAFSA, institutional form.
Dates and Deadlines: Priority date 2/14; no closing date. Applicants notified on a rolling basis starting 2/6; must reply within 2 week(s) of notification.

Transfers: No deadline. Applicants notified on a rolling basis starting 2/6; must reply within 2 week(s) of notification. In addition to all forms of need-based aid, transfer students are eligible for merit scholarships.

CONTACT
Diane Bice, Director of Financial Aid
1700 West Third Avenue, Flint, MI 48504-4898
(810) 762-7859

Kirtland Community College
Roscommon, Michigan
www.kirtland.edu   Federal Code: 007171

2-year public community college in rural community.
Enrollment: 1,386 undergrads, 57% part-time. 154 full-time freshmen.
Selectivity: Open admission; but selective for some programs.

BASIC COSTS (2005-2006)
Tuition and fees: $2,276; out-of-district residents $4,100; out-of-state residents $4,815.
Per-credit charge: $67; out-of-district residents $128; out-of-state residents $152.

FINANCIAL AID PICTURE
Students with need: Need-based aid available for full-time and part-time students.
Additional info: Federal Work Study available.

FINANCIAL AID PROCEDURES
Forms required: FAFSA.
Dates and Deadlines: Priority date 5/15; no closing date. Applicants notified on a rolling basis.

CONTACT
Christin Horndt, Director of Financial Aid
10775 North St. Helen Road, Roscommon, MI 48653
(989) 275-5121

Kuyper College
Grand Rapids, Michigan
www.reformed.edu   Federal Code: 002311

4-year private Bible college in large city, affiliated with Reformed Presbyterian tradition.
Enrollment: 262 undergrads, 16% part-time. 46 full-time freshmen.
Selectivity: Admits 50 to 75% of applicants.

BASIC COSTS (2006-2007)
Tuition and fees: $11,865.
Room and board: $6,000.

FINANCIAL AID PICTURE (2004-2005)
Students with need: Out of 42 full-time freshmen who applied for aid, 38 were judged to have need. Of these, 37 received aid, and 8 had their full need met. Average financial aid package met 64% of need; average scholarship/grant was $5,921; average loan was $2,588. For part-time students, average financial aid package was $5,918.
Students without need: 6 full-time freshmen who did not demonstrate need for aid received scholarships/grants; average award was $1,850. No-need awards available for academics, leadership, minority status.
Scholarships offered: Christian Leadership Scholarship; $1,500 renewable annually; based on Christian service activities, 3.2 cumulative GPA; 2 awarded. Presidential Scholarship; $5,000 renewable annually; based on essay and 3.8 cumulative GPA; 2 awarded.
Cumulative student debt: 48% of graduating class had student loans; average debt was $12,900.

Michigan Kuyper College

FINANCIAL AID PROCEDURES
Forms required: FAFSA, institutional form.
Dates and Deadlines: Priority date 3/1; no closing date. Applicants notified on a rolling basis starting 3/20; must reply within 2 week(s) of notification.

CONTACT
Agnes Russell, Financial Aid Administrator
3333 East Beltline NE, Grand Rapids, MI 49525-9749
(616) 988-3656

Lake Michigan College
Benton Harbor, Michigan
www.lakemichigancollege.edu   Federal Code: 002277

2-year public community college in large town.
Enrollment: 4,041 undergrads.
Selectivity: Open admission; but selective for some programs.

BASIC COSTS (2005-2006)
Tuition and fees: $2,330; out-of-district residents $2,696; out-of-state residents $3,480.
Per-credit charge: $67; out-of-district residents $79; out-of-state residents $105.
Additional info: Tuition/fee waivers available for adults.

FINANCIAL AID PICTURE (2004-2005)
Students with need: 94% of average financial aid package awarded as scholarships/grants, 6% awarded as loans/jobs.

FINANCIAL AID PROCEDURES
Forms required: FAFSA.
Dates and Deadlines: Priority date 3/1; no closing date. Applicants notified on a rolling basis; must reply within 2 week(s) of notification.

CONTACT
Anne Tews, Director of Financial Aid
2755 East Napier Avenue, Benton Harbor, MI 49022-1899
(269) 927-3507 ext. 5200

Lake Superior State University
Sault Ste. Marie, Michigan
www.lssu.edu   Federal Code: 002293

4-year public university in small city.
Enrollment: 2,753 undergrads, 16% part-time. 569 full-time freshmen.
Selectivity: Admits over 75% of applicants.

BASIC COSTS (2005-2006)
Tuition and fees: $6,308; out-of-state residents $12,296.
Room and board: $6,536.
Additional info: Residents of Ontario, Canada pay in-state rates. Residents of Kansas, Minnesota, Missouri, Nebraska and North Dakota are eligible for the Midwest Consortium agreement rate.

FINANCIAL AID PICTURE (2004-2005)
Students with need: Average financial aid package met 78% of need; average scholarship/grant was $3,338; average loan was $3,164. For part-time students, average financial aid package was $6,032.
Students without need: 65 full-time freshmen who did not demonstrate need for aid received scholarships/grants; average award was $2,359. No-need awards available for academics, alumni affiliation, athletics.
Scholarships offered: *Merit:* Board of Trustees Michigan Valedictorian Scholarship; up to $1,200 per year. Board of Trustees Academic Achievement Scholarship; up to $1,500 per year; 3.0 GPA and 19 ACT score. Board of Trustees Academic Honors Scholarship; up to $2,000 per year; 3.5 GPA and 24 ACT score. Board of Trustees Academic Excellence Scholarship; up to $4,000 per year; 3.7 GPA and 25 ACT score. Board of Trustees Distinguished Scholarship; up to $6,000 per year; 3.8 GPA and 27 ACT score. *Athletic:* 31 full-time freshmen received athletic scholarships; average amount $4,264.
Cumulative student debt: 63% of graduating class had student loans; average debt was $17,458.

FINANCIAL AID PROCEDURES
Forms required: FAFSA.
Dates and Deadlines: Priority date 2/21; no closing date. Applicants notified on a rolling basis starting 11/1; must reply within 3 week(s) of notification.
Transfers: Closing date 3/1. Applicants notified on a rolling basis starting 4/1.

CONTACT
Deborah Rynberg, Director of Financial Aid
650 West Easterday Avenue, Sault Ste. Marie, MI 49783-1699
(906) 635-2678

Lansing Community College
Lansing, Michigan
www.lansing.cc.mi.us   Federal Code: 002278

2-year public community college in small city.
Enrollment: 9,730 undergrads, 68% part-time. 621 full-time freshmen.
Selectivity: Open admission; but selective for some programs.

BASIC COSTS (2006-2007)
Tuition and fees: $2,000; out-of-district residents $3,200; out-of-state residents $4,400.
Per-credit charge: $65; out-of-district residents $105; out-of-state residents $145.

FINANCIAL AID PICTURE
Students with need: Need-based aid available for full-time and part-time students. Work study available nights, weekends, and for part-time students.
Students without need: No-need awards available for academics, athletics.

FINANCIAL AID PROCEDURES
Forms required: FAFSA.
Dates and Deadlines: Priority date 7/5; no closing date. Applicants notified on a rolling basis starting 4/3.
Transfers: Priority date 7/15.

CONTACT
Barbara Larson, Vice President, Administrative Services (CFO)
422 North Washington Square, Lansing, MI 48901
(517) 483-1296

Lawrence Technological University
Southfield, Michigan
www.ltu.edu   Federal Code: 002279

4-year private university in small city.
Enrollment: 2,482 undergrads, 36% part-time. 308 full-time freshmen.
Selectivity: Admits over 75% of applicants.

BASIC COSTS (2006-2007)
Tuition and fees: $19,306.
Per-credit charge: $635.
Room and board: $7,537.

FINANCIAL AID PICTURE (2004-2005)
Students with need: Out of 269 full-time freshmen who applied for aid, 189 were judged to have need. Of these, 189 received aid, and 13 had their full need met. Average financial aid package met 78% of need; average scholarship/grant was $7,317; average loan was $2,696. For part-time students, average financial aid package was $1,627.

Students without need: 54 full-time freshmen who did not demonstrate need for aid received scholarships/grants; average award was $5,359. No-need awards available for academics, alumni affiliation, job skills, minority status, ROTC, state/district residency.
Cumulative student debt: 50% of graduating class had student loans; average debt was $24,250.
Additional info: State deadline for Michigan Competitive Scholarship and Michigan Tuition Grant 3/1.

FINANCIAL AID PROCEDURES
Forms required: FAFSA.
Dates and Deadlines: Priority date 4/1; no closing date. Applicants notified on a rolling basis starting 3/1; must reply within 2 week(s) of notification.

CONTACT
Mark Martin, Director of Student Financial Aid
21000 West Ten Mile Road, Southfield, MI 48075-1058
(248) 204-2120

Macomb Community College
Warren, Michigan
www.macomb.edu   Federal Code: 008906

2-year public community college in small city.
Enrollment: 11,815 undergrads, 64% part-time. 1,227 full-time freshmen.
Selectivity: Open admission; but selective for some programs.

BASIC COSTS (2006-2007)
Tuition and fees: $2,055; out-of-district residents $3,109; out-of-state residents $4,039.
Per-credit charge: $65; out-of-district residents $99; out-of-state residents $129.

FINANCIAL AID PICTURE (2005-2006)
Students with need: Need-based aid available for part-time students. Work study available nights, weekends, and for part-time students.
Students without need: No-need awards available for academics, athletics, leadership, music/drama, state/district residency.

FINANCIAL AID PROCEDURES
Forms required: FAFSA, institutional form.
Dates and Deadlines: Priority date 4/15; no closing date. Applicants notified on a rolling basis starting 5/15; must reply within 2 week(s) of notification.
Transfers: Must submit financial aid transcripts from all institutions attended.

CONTACT
Judy Florian, Director of Financial Aid
14500 East Twelve Mile Road, Warren, MI 48088-3896
(586) 445-7228

Madonna University
Livonia, Michigan
www.madonna.edu   Federal Code: 002282

4-year private university and liberal arts college in small city, affiliated with Roman Catholic Church.
Enrollment: 3,073 undergrads, 46% part-time. 181 full-time freshmen.
Selectivity: Admits over 75% of applicants.

BASIC COSTS (2006-2007)
Tuition and fees: $10,960.
Per-credit charge: $362.
Room and board: $5,946.
Additional info: Nursing students pay $410 per credit hour. Non-resident aliens pay $2,500 deposit.

FINANCIAL AID PICTURE (2004-2005)
Students with need: Out of 110 full-time freshmen who applied for aid, 85 were judged to have need. Of these, 85 received aid, and 16 had their full need met. Average financial aid package met 52% of need; average scholarship/grant was $3,945; average loan was $1,883. For part-time students, average financial aid package was $5,528.
Students without need: 87 full-time freshmen who did not demonstrate need for aid received scholarships/grants; average award was $3,308. No-need awards available for academics, alumni affiliation, art, athletics, minority status, music/drama, religious affiliation, state/district residency.
Scholarships offered: 22 full-time freshmen received athletic scholarships; average amount $1,866.
Cumulative student debt: 40% of graduating class had student loans; average debt was $19,252.

FINANCIAL AID PROCEDURES
Forms required: FAFSA.
Dates and Deadlines: Priority date 2/21; no closing date. Applicants notified on a rolling basis starting 4/1; must reply by 9/1 or within 2 week(s) of notification.
Transfers: Deadline for state aid is July 1.

CONTACT
Chris Ziegler, Director of Financial Aid
36600 Schoolcraft Road, Livonia, MI 48150
(734) 432-5664

Marygrove College
Detroit, Michigan
www.marygrove.edu   Federal Code: 002284

4-year private liberal arts college in very large city, affiliated with Roman Catholic Church.
Enrollment: 677 undergrads, 42% part-time. 73 full-time freshmen.
Selectivity: Admits less than 50% of applicants.

BASIC COSTS (2006-2007)
Tuition and fees: $13,880.
Per-credit charge: $488.
Room and board: $6,400.

FINANCIAL AID PICTURE (2005-2006)
Students with need: 38% of average financial aid package awarded as scholarships/grants, 62% awarded as loans/jobs. Need-based aid available for part-time students.
Students without need: This college only awards aid to students with need.

FINANCIAL AID PROCEDURES
Forms required: FAFSA, institutional form.
Dates and Deadlines: Priority date 3/15; no closing date. Applicants notified on a rolling basis starting 5/15; must reply within 2 week(s) of notification.

CONTACT
Patricia Chaplin, Director of Financial Aid
8425 West McNichols Road, Detroit, MI 48221
(313) 927-1245

Michigan State University
East Lansing, Michigan
www.msu.edu   Federal Code: 002290

4-year public university in small city.
Enrollment: 35,330 undergrads, 9% part-time. 7,306 full-time freshmen.
Selectivity: Admits over 75% of applicants.

BASIC COSTS (2005-2006)
Tuition and fees: $7,880; out-of-state residents $19,632.
Per-credit charge: $233; out-of-state residents $625.
Room and board: $6,228.

FINANCIAL AID PICTURE (2005-2006)
Students with need: Out of 4,934 full-time freshmen who applied for aid, 3,090 were judged to have need. Of these, 3,088 received aid, and 976 had their full need met. Average financial aid package met 78% of need; average scholarship/grant was $4,322; average loan was $2,748. For part-time students, average financial aid package was $7,041.
Students without need: This college only awards aid to students with need.
Scholarships offered: 58 full-time freshmen received athletic scholarships; average amount $12,921.
Cumulative student debt: 52% of graduating class had student loans; average debt was $21,037.

FINANCIAL AID PROCEDURES
Forms required: FAFSA.
Dates and Deadlines: Priority date 3/1; no closing date. Applicants notified on a rolling basis starting 3/15; must reply within 4 week(s) of notification.

CONTACT
Richard Shipman, Director of Financial Aid
250 Administration Building, East Lansing, MI 48824-1046
(517) 353-5940

Michigan Technological University
Houghton, Michigan
www.mtu.edu   Federal Code: 002292

4-year public university in small town.
Enrollment: 5,516 undergrads, 7% part-time. 1,324 full-time freshmen.
Selectivity: Admits over 75% of applicants.

BASIC COSTS (2005-2006)
Tuition and fees: $8,194; out-of-state residents $19,384.
Per-credit charge: $252; out-of-state residents $625.
Room and board: $6,375.

FINANCIAL AID PICTURE (2005-2006)
Students with need: Out of 1,104 full-time freshmen who applied for aid, 700 were judged to have need. Of these, 699 received aid, and 218 had their full need met. Average financial aid package met 82% of need; average scholarship/grant was $5,829; average loan was $3,712. Need-based aid available for part-time students.
Students without need: 238 full-time freshmen who did not demonstrate need for aid received scholarships/grants; average award was $2,973. No-need awards available for academics, alumni affiliation, athletics, leadership, minority status, ROTC, state/district residency.
Scholarships offered: Merit: Michigan Technological University Scholar Awards; full tuition, room and board, allowance for books; based on merit, Michigan residency, recommendation by high school teacher by mid-October of senior year. Presidential Scholars Program; $1,000 to full tuition; based on merit, Michigan residency, high school class rank. Michigan Technological University Merit Scholarships; $1,000-$2,000; based on merit and need, U.S. citizenship, high school class rank, finalist status in National Merit Scholarship Qualifying Test. National Scholars Program; $6,000-$12,000; merit-based for non-Michigan resident of U.S. or Canada. Alumni Legacy Award; equal to difference of resident and nonresident tuition; for non-Michigan residents who are children or grandchildren of alumni. Michigan Tech Alumni Legacy Award; $250 per year for maximum of 4 years; for Michigan residents who are children or grandchildren of alumni. **Athletic:** 33 full-time freshmen received athletic scholarships; average amount $9,391.
Cumulative student debt: 53% of graduating class had student loans; average debt was $13,587.

FINANCIAL AID PROCEDURES
Forms required: FAFSA.
Dates and Deadlines: Priority date 2/18; no closing date. Applicants notified on a rolling basis starting 3/1; must reply within 4 week(s) of notification.
Transfers: Closing date 3/1. Applicants notified by 4/15; must reply by 5/1.

CONTACT
Timothy Malette, Director of Financial Aid
1400 Townsend Drive, Houghton, MI 49931-1295
(906) 987-2622

Mid Michigan Community College
Harrison, Michigan
www.midmich.edu   Federal Code: 006768

2-year public community college in small town.
Enrollment: 3,276 undergrads, 54% part-time. 533 full-time freshmen.
Selectivity: Open admission; but selective for some programs.

BASIC COSTS (2006-2007)
Tuition and fees: $2,023; out-of-district residents $3,620; out-of-state residents $6,410.
Additional info: Tuition/fee waivers available for adults.

FINANCIAL AID PICTURE
Students with need: Need-based aid available for full-time and part-time students.
Students without need: No-need awards available for academics.
Scholarships offered: Scholastic Incentive Scholarships; $350 per semester; for any student who completes full-time semester, is enrolled full-time for next regular semester, maintains GPA of 3.5 through 3.89; $500 per semester for students meeting above criteria, maintaining a cumulative GPA of 3.9 through 4.0.

FINANCIAL AID PROCEDURES
Forms required: FAFSA, institutional form.
Dates and Deadlines: Priority date 5/1; no closing date. Applicants notified on a rolling basis starting 4/1; must reply within 2 week(s) of notification.

CONTACT
Gale Crandell, Financial Aid Director
1375 South Clare Avenue, Harrison, MI 48625
(989) 386-6622

Monroe County Community College
Monroe, Michigan
www.monroeccc.edu   Federal Code: 002294

2-year public community college in large town.
Enrollment: 4,180 undergrads.
Selectivity: Open admission; but selective for some programs.

BASIC COSTS (2005-2006)
Tuition and fees: $2,030; out-of-district residents $3,230; out-of-state residents $3,530.
Per-credit charge: $62; out-of-district residents $102; out-of-state residents $112.
Additional info: Tuition/fee waivers available for minority students.

FINANCIAL AID PICTURE
Students with need: Need-based aid available for full-time and part-time students. Work study available nights, weekends, and for part-time students.
Students without need: No-need awards available for academics, alumni affiliation, art, leadership, music/drama, state/district residency.

FINANCIAL AID PROCEDURES
Forms required: FAFSA, institutional form.

Dates and Deadlines: Priority date 4/1; no closing date. Applicants notified on a rolling basis starting 4/1; must reply within 2 week(s) of notification.

CONTACT
Tracy Vogt, Director of Financial Aid/Placement
1555 South Raisinville Road, Monroe, MI 48161
(734) 384-4135

Montcalm Community College
Sidney, Michigan
www.montcalm.edu   Federal Code: 002295

2-year public community and liberal arts college in rural community.
Enrollment: 1,796 undergrads, 61% part-time. 150 full-time freshmen.
Selectivity: Open admission; but selective for some programs.

BASIC COSTS (2005-2006)
Tuition and fees: $2,085; out-of-district residents $3,105; out-of-state residents $3,975.
Per-credit charge: $64; out-of-district residents $98; out-of-state residents $127.

FINANCIAL AID PICTURE
Students with need: Need-based aid available for full-time and part-time students.
Students without need: No-need awards available for academics, state/district residency.

FINANCIAL AID PROCEDURES
Forms required: FAFSA, institutional form.
Dates and Deadlines: Priority date 2/15; no closing date. Applicants notified on a rolling basis starting 6/15; must reply within 2 week(s) of notification.
Transfers: Priority date 4/1.

CONTACT
Rebecca Powell, Director of Financial Aid
2800 College Drive, Sidney, MI 48885
(989) 328-1228

Mott Community College
Flint, Michigan
www.mcc.edu   Federal Code: 002261

2-year public community college in large city.
Enrollment: 7,337 undergrads, 67% part-time. 551 full-time freshmen.
Selectivity: Open admission; but selective for some programs.

BASIC COSTS (2006-2007)
Tuition and fees: $2,508; out-of-district residents $3,638; out-of-state residents $4,776.
Per-credit charge: $76; out-of-district residents $113; out-of-state residents $151.

FINANCIAL AID PICTURE (2004-2005)
Students with need: 75% of average financial aid package awarded as scholarships/grants, 25% awarded as loans/jobs. Need-based aid available for part-time students. Work study available nights, weekends, and for part-time students.
Students without need: No-need awards available for academics, alumni affiliation, art, athletics, leadership, minority status, music/drama, state/district residency.

FINANCIAL AID PROCEDURES
Forms required: FAFSA.
Dates and Deadlines: No deadline. Applicants notified on a rolling basis starting 5/1.
Transfers: Pell Grants adjusted for amount used at another institution.

CONTACT
Carlos Cisneros, Director of Financial Aid
1401 East Court Street, Flint, MI 48503-2089
(810) 762-0144

North Central Michigan College
Petoskey, Michigan
www.ncmc.cc.mi.us   Federal Code: 002299

2-year public community college in small town.
Enrollment: 1,935 undergrads.
Selectivity: Open admission; but selective for some programs.

BASIC COSTS (2005-2006)
Tuition and fees: $2,175; out-of-district residents $3,294; out-of-state residents $4,037.
Per-credit charge: $64; out-of-district residents $101; out-of-state residents $126.
Room only: $2,300.

FINANCIAL AID PICTURE
Students with need: Need-based aid available for full-time and part-time students. Work study available nights, weekends, and for part-time students.

FINANCIAL AID PROCEDURES
Forms required: FAFSA, institutional form.
Dates and Deadlines: Priority date 4/15; no closing date. Applicants notified on a rolling basis starting 4/30.

CONTACT
Virginia Panoff, Director of Financial Aid
1515 Howard Street, Petoskey, MI 49770
(231) 348-6627

Northern Michigan University
Marquette, Michigan
www.nmu.edu   Federal Code: 002301

4-year public university in large town.
Enrollment: 8,500 undergrads, 8% part-time. 1,470 full-time freshmen.
Selectivity: Admits over 75% of applicants.

BASIC COSTS (2005-2006)
Tuition and fees: $5,958; out-of-state residents $9,702.
Per-credit charge: $222; out-of-state residents $378.
Room and board: $6,013.
Additional info: Includes one-time athletic fee. All full-time students provided with IBM ThinkPad or Apple iBook with software as part of tuition and fees. Tuition/fee waivers available for minority students.

FINANCIAL AID PICTURE (2004-2005)
Students with need: Out of 1,467 full-time freshmen who applied for aid, 887 were judged to have need. Of these, 879 received aid, and 110 had their full need met. Average financial aid package met 80% of need; average scholarship/grant was $3,856; average loan was $2,941. For part-time students, average financial aid package was $4,289.
Students without need: No-need awards available for academics, alumni affiliation, art, athletics, leadership, minority status, music/drama, religious affiliation, ROTC, state/district residency.
Scholarships offered: *Merit:* Talent recognition awards available in art and design, music, and theatre. Freshman Fellowship: $1,000 in student employment; based on minimum high school 3.5 GPA and ACT 24. Dr. Edgar L. Harden Scholarship: based on minimum 3.5 GPA and ACT 24. National Academics Award: $2,000 per year to an unlimited number of non-Michigan residents; minimum 3.0 GPA and ACT 19. NMU Merit Excellence Award: awards $2,750 per year or $3,500 on campus; based on minimum 3.0 GPA and ACT

Michigan Northern Michigan University

33. NMU Merit Award: $2,250 or $3,000 on campus; minimum 3.0 GPA and ACT 30-32. NMU Scholars Award: $1,250 or $2,000 on campus; minimum 3.0 GPA and ACT 27-29. NMU Outstanding Achievement: $750 or $1,500; minimum 3.0 GPA and ACT 25-26. **Athletic:** 12 full-time freshmen received athletic scholarships; average amount $5,991.
Cumulative student debt: 67% of graduating class had student loans; average debt was $16,842.
Additional info: Audition or portfolio required for music, drama, and art scholarship applicants. Alumni Dependent Tuition Program gives resident tuition rates to nonresident dependents of NMU alumni who received master's, baccalaureate, or associate degree; renewable.

FINANCIAL AID PROCEDURES
Forms required: FAFSA.
Dates and Deadlines: Priority date 3/1; no closing date. Applicants notified on a rolling basis starting 4/1; must reply within 2 week(s) of notification.

CONTACT
1401 Presque Isle Avenue, Marquette, MI 49855
(906) 227-2327

Northwestern Michigan College
Traverse City, Michigan
www.nmc.edu   Federal Code: 002302

2-year public community college in small city.
Enrollment: 3,949 undergrads, 52% part-time. 646 full-time freshmen.
Selectivity: Open admission; but selective for some programs.

BASIC COSTS (2005-2006)
Tuition and fees: $2,564; out-of-district residents $4,200; out-of-state residents $5,151.
Per-credit charge: $79; out-of-district residents $130; out-of-state residents $160.
Room and board: $6,285.
Additional info: Tuition/fee waivers available for adults, minority students, unemployed or children of unemployed.

FINANCIAL AID PICTURE (2004-2005)
Students with need: 53% of average financial aid package awarded as scholarships/grants, 47% awarded as loans/jobs. Need-based aid available for part-time students. Work study available nights, weekends, and for part-time students.
Students without need: No-need awards available for academics, art, job skills, leadership, minority status, music/drama, ROTC, state/district residency.

FINANCIAL AID PROCEDURES
Forms required: FAFSA.
Dates and Deadlines: Priority date 4/1; no closing date. Applicants notified on a rolling basis starting 5/1; must reply within 2 week(s) of notification.

CONTACT
Deb Faas, Coordinator of Financial Aid
1701 East Front Street, Traverse City, MI 49686
(231) 995-1035

Northwood University
Midland, Michigan
www.northwood.edu   Federal Code: 004072

4-year private university and business college in large town.
Enrollment: 1,924 undergrads, 2% part-time. 490 full-time freshmen.
Selectivity: Admits over 75% of applicants.

BASIC COSTS (2006-2007)
Tuition and fees: $15,801.
Per-credit charge: $317.
Room and board: $6,942.

FINANCIAL AID PICTURE (2005-2006)
Students with need: Out of 398 full-time freshmen who applied for aid, 327 were judged to have need. Of these, 327 received aid, and 90 had their full need met. Average financial aid package met 99% of need; average scholarship/grant was $5,948; average loan was $2,452. For part-time students, average financial aid package was $7,902.
Students without need: 57 full-time freshmen who did not demonstrate need for aid received scholarships/grants; average award was $6,602. No-need awards available for academics, alumni affiliation, athletics, minority status.
Scholarships offered: *Merit:* Scholarships; $4,000-$9,000; based on test scores and GPA; unlimited number awarded. *Athletic:* 23 full-time freshmen received athletic scholarships; average amount $10,006.
Cumulative student debt: 57% of graduating class had student loans; average debt was $18,389.

FINANCIAL AID PROCEDURES
Forms required: FAFSA.
Dates and Deadlines: No deadline. Applicants notified on a rolling basis starting 3/1.

CONTACT
Theresa Mieler, Financial Aid Director
4000 Whiting Drive, Midland, MI 48640
(989) 837-4230

Oakland Community College
Bloomfield Hills, Michigan
www.oaklandcc.edu   Federal Code: 002303

2-year public community college in large city.
Enrollment: 13,047 undergrads, 69% part-time. 907 full-time freshmen.
Selectivity: Open admission.

BASIC COSTS (2005-2006)
Tuition and fees: $1,725; out-of-district residents $2,871; out-of-state residents $3,997.
Per-credit charge: $55; out-of-district residents $93; out-of-state residents $131.

FINANCIAL AID PICTURE (2005-2006)
Students with need: 64% of average financial aid package awarded as scholarships/grants, 36% awarded as loans/jobs. Need-based aid available for part-time students.
Students without need: No-need awards available for academics, athletics.

FINANCIAL AID PROCEDURES
Forms required: FAFSA.
Dates and Deadlines: Priority date 4/15; no closing date. Applicants notified on a rolling basis starting 4/15.
Transfers: Closing date 6/30. Michigan residency required for aid to transfer students.

CONTACT
Wilma Porter, Director of Financial Assistance and Scholarships
2480 Opdyke Road, Bloomfield Hills, MI 48304-2266
(248) 341-2000

Oakland University
Rochester, Michigan
www.oakland.edu   Federal Code: 002307

4-year public university in small city.
Enrollment: 12,945 undergrads, 25% part-time. 2,016 full-time freshmen.
Selectivity: Admits over 75% of applicants.

BASIC COSTS (2005-2006)
Tuition and fees: $5,856; out-of-state residents $13,056.
Room and board: $6,080.

FINANCIAL AID PICTURE (2004-2005)
Students with need: Out of 1,059 full-time freshmen who applied for aid, 688 were judged to have need. Of these, 654 received aid, and 248 had their full need met. Average financial aid package met 87.7% of need; average scholarship/grant was $3,451; average loan was $2,224. For part-time students, average financial aid package was $4,594.
Students without need: 283 full-time freshmen who did not demonstrate need for aid received scholarships/grants; average award was $2,091. No-need awards available for academics, art, athletics, leadership, music/drama, state/district residency.
Scholarships offered: *Merit:* Wide range of scholarships awarded on the basis of accomplishment. *Athletic:* 36 full-time freshmen received athletic scholarships; average amount $7,056.

FINANCIAL AID PROCEDURES
Forms required: FAFSA.
Dates and Deadlines: Priority date 2/15; no closing date. Applicants notified on a rolling basis starting 3/15.
Transfers: Closing date 4/1.

CONTACT
Cindy Hermsen, Director of Financial Aid
101 North Foundation Hall, Rochester, MI 48309-4401
(248) 370-2550

Olivet College
Olivet, Michigan
www.olivetcollege.edu   Federal Code: 002308

4-year private liberal arts college in rural community, affiliated with Congregational Christian Churches and United Church of Christ.
Enrollment: 1,020 undergrads.

BASIC COSTS (2006-2007)
Tuition and fees: $17,584.
Room and board: $6,060.

FINANCIAL AID PICTURE (2005-2006)
Students with need: Need-based aid available for full-time and part-time students.
Students without need: This college only awards aid to students with need.
Scholarships offered: Scholarships up to $2,000 for students who demonstrate history of community service and civic responsibility during high school or college. Academic merit scholarships up to full tuition per year. All scholarships renewable for 4 years.

FINANCIAL AID PROCEDURES
Forms required: FAFSA.
Dates and Deadlines: No deadline. Applicants notified on a rolling basis starting 2/1; must reply within 3 week(s) of notification.

CONTACT
Chris Snow, Chief Financial Officer
320 South Main Street, Olivet, MI 49076

Rochester College
Rochester Hills, Michigan
www.rc.edu   Federal Code: 002288

4-year private liberal arts college in small city, affiliated with Church of Christ.
Enrollment: 1,100 undergrads.

BASIC COSTS (2005-2006)
Tuition and fees: $12,356.
Per-credit charge: $360.
Room and board: $6,560.
Additional info: Tuition at time of enrollment locked for 4 years; tuition/fee waivers available for minority students.

FINANCIAL AID PICTURE
Students with need: Need-based aid available for full-time and part-time students. Work study available nights, weekends, and for part-time students.
Students without need: No-need awards available for academics, alumni affiliation, athletics, leadership, music/drama, state/district residency.

FINANCIAL AID PROCEDURES
Forms required: FAFSA.
Dates and Deadlines: Priority date 8/1; no closing date. Applicants notified on a rolling basis starting 6/1; must reply within 2 week(s) of notification.

CONTACT
Holly Johnson, Director of Financial Aid
800 West Avon Road, Rochester Hills, MI 48307
(248) 218-2038

Saginaw Valley State University
University Center, Michigan
www.svsu.edu   Federal Code: 002314

4-year public university in small city.
Enrollment: 7,714 undergrads, 22% part-time. 1,208 full-time freshmen.
Selectivity: Admits over 75% of applicants.

BASIC COSTS (2005-2006)
Tuition and fees: $5,282; out-of-state residents $11,891.
Per-credit charge: $163; out-of-state residents $383.
Room and board: $6,150.

FINANCIAL AID PICTURE (2004-2005)
Students with need: Out of 1,162 full-time freshmen who applied for aid, 726 were judged to have need. Of these, 713 received aid, and 219 had their full need met. Average financial aid package met 70% of need; average scholarship/grant was $2,885; average loan was $2,236. For part-time students, average financial aid package was $4,601.
Students without need: 363 full-time freshmen who did not demonstrate need for aid received scholarships/grants; average award was $3,229. No-need awards available for academics, art, athletics, leadership, minority status, music/drama.
Scholarships offered: *Merit:* Presidential Scholarships; full tuition/fees and books; 1st or 2nd in high school class. Award for Excellence; full tuition and fees; 3.7 GPA, 28 ACT. University Scholarship; full tuition and fees; 3.5 GPA. University Foundation; tuition and fees; 3.5 GPA, 24 ACT. Various private scholarships also available. *Athletic:* 59 full-time freshmen received athletic scholarships; average amount $2,997.
Cumulative student debt: 52% of graduating class had student loans; average debt was $19,333.

FINANCIAL AID PROCEDURES
Forms required: FAFSA.
Dates and Deadlines: Priority date 2/14; no closing date. Applicants notified on a rolling basis starting 3/20; must reply within 10 week(s) of notification.

Transfers: No deadline. Applicants notified on a rolling basis; must reply within 10 week(s) of notification. Community college scholarship, private scholarships, and Transfer Dean's scholarships available.

CONTACT
Robert Lemuel, Director of Scholarships and Financial Aid
7400 Bay Road, University Center, MI 48710
(989) 964-4103

Schoolcraft College
Livonia, Michigan
www.schoolcraft.cc.mi.us   Federal Code: 002315

2-year public community college in small city.
Enrollment: 3,380 full-time undergrads.
Selectivity: Open admission.

BASIC COSTS (2005-2006)
Tuition and fees: $2,080; out-of-district residents $3,040; out-of-state residents $4,420.
Per-credit charge: $65; out-of-district residents $97; out-of-state residents $143.

FINANCIAL AID PICTURE (2004-2005)
Students with need: 74% of average financial aid package awarded as scholarships/grants, 26% awarded as loans/jobs. Work study available nights, weekends, and for part-time students.
Students without need: No-need awards available for academics, athletics, leadership, music/drama, state/district residency.
Scholarships offered: Trustee Scholarships; $1,000-$1,200; renewable for 2nd year; based on essay, placement test, trustee application, graduation from local high school; 80 awarded.

FINANCIAL AID PROCEDURES
Forms required: FAFSA.
Dates and Deadlines: No deadline. Applicants notified on a rolling basis starting 6/1.

CONTACT
Julieanne Tobin, Director Enrollment Management
18600 Haggerty Road, Livonia, MI 48152-2696
(734) 462-4433

Southwestern Michigan College
Dowagiac, Michigan
www.swmich.edu   Federal Code: 002317

2-year public community college in small town.
Enrollment: 2,016 undergrads, 52% part-time. 321 full-time freshmen.
Selectivity: Open admission; but selective for some programs.

BASIC COSTS (2006-2007)
Tuition and fees: $2,860; out-of-district residents $3,451; out-of-state residents $3,676.
Per-credit charge: $75; out-of-district residents $94; out-of-state residents $101.

FINANCIAL AID PICTURE
Students with need: Need-based aid available for full-time and part-time students. Work study available nights, weekends, and for part-time students.
Students without need: No-need awards available for academics, art, leadership, music/drama.

FINANCIAL AID PROCEDURES
Forms required: FAFSA, institutional form.
Dates and Deadlines: Priority date 8/1; no closing date. Applicants notified on a rolling basis starting 4/1; must reply within 4 week(s) of notification.

CONTACT
Rob Wirt, Director of Financial Aid
58900 Cherry Grove Road, Dowagiac, MI 49047-9793
(269) 782-1313

Spring Arbor University
Spring Arbor, Michigan
www.arbor.edu   Federal Code: 002318

4-year private university and liberal arts college in rural community, affiliated with Free Methodist Church of North America.
Enrollment: 2,447 undergrads, 23% part-time. 329 full-time freshmen.
Selectivity: Admits over 75% of applicants.

BASIC COSTS (2006-2007)
Tuition and fees: $17,386.
Room and board: $6,070.
Additional info: Per-credit-hour charges: 1-7 and 15 or more hours, $400; 8-11 hours, $450.

FINANCIAL AID PICTURE (2004-2005)
Students with need: Out of 306 full-time freshmen who applied for aid, 267 were judged to have need. Of these, 267 received aid, and 129 had their full need met. Average financial aid package met 93% of need; average scholarship/grant was $9,661; average loan was $3,462. For part-time students, average financial aid package was $7,460.
Students without need: 12 full-time freshmen who did not demonstrate need for aid received scholarships/grants; average award was $1,949. No-need awards available for academics, art, athletics.
Scholarships offered: 31 full-time freshmen received athletic scholarships; average amount $3,006.
Cumulative student debt: 84% of graduating class had student loans; average debt was $11,989.

FINANCIAL AID PROCEDURES
Forms required: FAFSA.
Dates and Deadlines: Priority date 3/1; no closing date. Applicants notified on a rolling basis starting 4/1; must reply within 2 week(s) of notification.
Transfers: No deadline. Financial aid transcript required from each college previously attended.

CONTACT
Lois Hardy, Director of Financial Aid
106 East Main Street, Spring Arbor, MI 49283-9799
(517) 750-1200

University of Detroit Mercy
Detroit, Michigan
www.udmercy.edu   Federal Code: 002323

4-year private university in very large city, affiliated with Roman Catholic Church.
Enrollment: 2,892 undergrads, 33% part-time. 498 full-time freshmen.
Selectivity: Admits 50 to 75% of applicants.

BASIC COSTS (2005-2006)
Tuition and fees: $22,470.
Per-credit charge: $535.
Room and board: $7,328.
Additional info: Engineering and architecture students pay slightly higher tuition.

FINANCIAL AID PICTURE (2005-2006)
Students with need: Average financial aid package met 89% of need; average scholarship/grant was $18,531; average loan was $3,579. For part-time students, average financial aid package was $2,809.

Students without need: No-need awards available for academics, alumni affiliation, athletics, leadership, minority status, music/drama, religious affiliation.

FINANCIAL AID PROCEDURES
Forms required: FAFSA.
Dates and Deadlines: Priority date 3/1; no closing date. Applicants notified on a rolling basis starting 3/1; must reply within 3 week(s) of notification.

CONTACT
Sandra Ross, Director of Scholarship and Financial Aid
4001 West McNichols Road, Detroit, MI 48221-3038
(313) 993-3350

University of Michigan
Ann Arbor, Michigan   Federal Code: 002325
www.umich.edu   CSS Code: 1839

4-year public university in small city.
Enrollment: 25,282 undergrads, 4% part-time. 5,961 full-time freshmen.
Selectivity: Admits 50 to 75% of applicants.

BASIC COSTS (2005-2006)
Tuition and fees: $9,213; out-of-state residents $27,601.
Per-credit charge: $349; out-of-state residents $1,115.
Room and board: $7,374.

FINANCIAL AID PICTURE (2004-2005)
Students with need: Out of 3,320 full-time freshmen who applied for aid, 2,932 were judged to have need. Of these, 2,932 received aid, and 2,639 had their full need met. Average financial aid package met 90% of need; average scholarship/grant was $6,886; average loan was $4,305. Need-based aid available for part-time students.
Students without need: 1,985 full-time freshmen who did not demonstrate need for aid received scholarships/grants; average award was $4,475. No-need awards available for academics, alumni affiliation, art, athletics, leadership, minority status, music/drama, religious affiliation, ROTC, state/district residency.
Scholarships offered: 112 full-time freshmen received athletic scholarships; average amount $21,851.
Cumulative student debt: 42% of graduating class had student loans; average debt was $22,312.

FINANCIAL AID PROCEDURES
Forms required: FAFSA, CSS PROFILE.
Dates and Deadlines: Priority date 2/15; closing date 4/30. Applicants notified on a rolling basis starting 3/15; must reply within 2 week(s) of notification.
Transfers: Community College Scholarship available for qualified students.

CONTACT
Pamela Fowler, Director for Office of Financial Aid
1220 Student Activities Building, Ann Arbor, MI 48109-1316
(734) 763-6600

University of Michigan: Dearborn
Dearborn, Michigan
www.umd.umich.edu   Federal Code: 002326

4-year public university in small city.
Enrollment: 5,942 undergrads, 35% part-time. 656 full-time freshmen.
Selectivity: Admits 50 to 75% of applicants.

BASIC COSTS (2005-2006)
Tuition and fees: $7,116; out-of-state residents $15,008.
Per-credit charge: $256; out-of-state residents $582.

FINANCIAL AID PICTURE (2004-2005)
Students with need: Out of 451 full-time freshmen who applied for aid, 317 were judged to have need. Of these, 311 received aid, and 90 had their full need met. Average financial aid package met 31% of need; average scholarship/grant was $3,919; average loan was $1,554.
Students without need: 79 full-time freshmen who did not demonstrate need for aid received scholarships/grants; average award was $8,099. No-need awards available for academics, alumni affiliation, athletics, job skills, leadership, minority status, ROTC.
Scholarships offered: 11 full-time freshmen received athletic scholarships; average amount $1,036.
Cumulative student debt: 23% of graduating class had student loans; average debt was $13,150.

FINANCIAL AID PROCEDURES
Forms required: FAFSA.
Dates and Deadlines: Priority date 2/14; no closing date. Applicants notified on a rolling basis starting 3/1; must reply within 3 week(s) of notification.

CONTACT
John Mason, Director of Financial Aid
4901 Evergreen Road, 1145 UC, Dearborn, MI 48128-1491
(313) 593-5000

University of Michigan: Flint
Flint, Michigan
www.umflint.edu   Federal Code: 002327

4-year public university and branch campus college in small city.
Enrollment: 5,481 undergrads, 38% part-time. 474 full-time freshmen.
Selectivity: Admits over 75% of applicants.

BASIC COSTS (2005-2006)
Tuition and fees: $6,398; out-of-state residents $12,150.
Per-credit charge: $240; out-of-state residents $480.

FINANCIAL AID PICTURE (2004-2005)
Students with need: Out of 342 full-time freshmen who applied for aid, 236 were judged to have need. Of these, 231 received aid, and 7 had their full need met. For part-time students, average financial aid package was $5,244.
Students without need: 18 full-time freshmen who did not demonstrate need for aid received scholarships/grants; average award was $2,772. No-need awards available for academics, art, leadership, minority status, music/drama.
Cumulative student debt: 66% of graduating class had student loans; average debt was $21,888.
Additional info: SAT/ACT scores must be submitted for scholarship consideration.

FINANCIAL AID PROCEDURES
Forms required: FAFSA.
Dates and Deadlines: Priority date 3/1; no closing date. Applicants notified on a rolling basis starting 3/15.
Transfers: Must not be in default or owe refunds for Title IV aid.

CONTACT
Lori Vedder, Director of Financial Aid
303 East Kearsley Street, Flint, MI 48502-1950
(810) 762-3444

Walsh College of Accountancy and Business Administration
Troy, Michigan
www.walshcollege.edu   Federal Code: 004071

Upper-division private business college in large city.
Enrollment: 939 undergrads, 81% part-time.
Selectivity: Open admission.

BASIC COSTS (2006-2007)
Tuition and fees: $7,730.
Per-credit charge: $250.

FINANCIAL AID PICTURE (2004-2005)
Students with need: Average financial aid package for all full-time undergraduates was $7,619; for part-time $9,693. 24% awarded as scholarships/grants, 76% awarded as loans/jobs.
Students without need: No-need awards available for academics.

FINANCIAL AID PROCEDURES
Forms required: FAFSA.
Dates and Deadlines: Priority date 3/23; no closing date. Applicants notified on a rolling basis.

CONTACT
Howard Thomas, Director, Financial Aid
PO Box 7006, Troy, MI 48007-7006
(248) 823-1285

Wayne County Community College
Detroit, Michigan
www.wcccd.edu   Federal Code: 009230

2-year public community college in very large city.
Enrollment: 14,258 undergrads, 78% part-time. 1,119 full-time freshmen.
Selectivity: Open admission; but selective for some programs.

BASIC COSTS (2006-2007)
Tuition and fees: $2,055; out-of-district residents $2,543; out-of-state residents $3,120.
Per-credit charge: $56; out-of-district residents $72; out-of-state residents $91.

FINANCIAL AID PICTURE (2004-2005)
Students with need: 87% of average financial aid package awarded as scholarships/grants, 13% awarded as loans/jobs. Need-based aid available for part-time students. Work study available nights, weekends, and for part-time students.
Additional info: High school diploma, GED, or passing grade on ABT required for financial aid.

FINANCIAL AID PROCEDURES
Forms required: FAFSA.
Dates and Deadlines: Priority date 6/1; no closing date. Applicants notified on a rolling basis starting 5/1.

CONTACT
Tawi Moore, Associate Vice Chancellor of Financial Aid & Alumni Relations
801 West Fort Street, Detroit, MI 48226
(313) 496-2595

Wayne State University
Detroit, Michigan
www.wayne.edu   Federal Code: 002329

4-year public university in very large city.
Enrollment: 19,505 undergrads, 40% part-time. 2,425 full-time freshmen.
Selectivity: Admits 50 to 75% of applicants.

BASIC COSTS (2005-2006)
Tuition and fees: $6,389; out-of-state residents $13,721.
Per-credit charge: $189; out-of-state residents $434.
Room and board: $6,775.

FINANCIAL AID PICTURE (2004-2005)
Students with need: Average financial aid package met 43% of need; average scholarship/grant was $3,085; average loan was $2,457. For part-time students, average financial aid package was $4,558.
Students without need: No-need awards available for academics, art, athletics, leadership, music/drama.
Cumulative student debt: 50% of graduating class had student loans; average debt was $20,746.

FINANCIAL AID PROCEDURES
Forms required: FAFSA.
Dates and Deadlines: Priority date 3/1; no closing date. Applicants notified on a rolling basis starting 4/15; must reply within 2 week(s) of notification.

CONTACT
Catherine Kay, Director of Scholarships and Financial Aid
42 West Warren, Detroit, MI 48202
(313) 577-3378

West Shore Community College
Scottville, Michigan
www.westshore.edu   Federal Code: 007950

2-year public community college in rural community.
Enrollment: 1,097 undergrads.
Selectivity: Open admission; but selective for some programs.

BASIC COSTS (2005-2006)
Tuition and fees: $2,103; out-of-district residents $3,333; out-of-state residents $4,383.
Per-credit charge: $65; out-of-district residents $106; out-of-state residents $141.

FINANCIAL AID PICTURE (2005-2006)
Students with need: 77% of average financial aid package awarded as scholarships/grants, 23% awarded as loans/jobs. Need-based aid available for part-time students. Work study available nights, weekends, and for part-time students.

FINANCIAL AID PROCEDURES
Forms required: FAFSA.
Dates and Deadlines: Priority date 3/15; no closing date. Applicants notified on a rolling basis starting 5/15; must reply within 2 week(s) of notification.

CONTACT
Victoria Oddo, Director of Student Services
3000 North Stiles Road, Scottville, MI 49454-0277
(231) 845-6211

Western Michigan University
Kalamazoo, Michigan
www.wmich.edu Federal Code: 002330

4-year public university in small city.
Enrollment: 21,287 undergrads, 12% part-time. 3,500 full-time freshmen.
Selectivity: Admits over 75% of applicants.

BASIC COSTS (2005-2006)
Tuition and fees: $6,478; out-of-state residents $15,856.
Per-credit charge: $194; out-of-state residents $506.
Room and board: $6,651.

FINANCIAL AID PICTURE (2004-2005)
Students with need: Out of 2,950 full-time freshmen who applied for aid, 2,100 were judged to have need. Of these, 2,100 received aid, and 1,400 had their full need met. Average financial aid package met 68% of need; average scholarship/grant was $4,200; average loan was $2,500. Need-based aid available for part-time students.
Students without need: 260 full-time freshmen who did not demonstrate need for aid received scholarships/grants; average award was $2,300. No-need awards available for academics, art, athletics, minority status, music/drama, ROTC, state/district residency.
Scholarships offered: *Merit:* Medallion Scholarship Program; $1,200-$8,000 annually; based on academic performance in high school (3.8 GPA, minimum 25 ACT or 1130 SAT, exclusive of Writing); renewable for students maintaining full-time enrollment and 3.25 minimum GPA. *Athletic:* 80 full-time freshmen received athletic scholarships; average amount $4,600.
Cumulative student debt: 47% of graduating class had student loans; average debt was $15,300.

FINANCIAL AID PROCEDURES
Forms required: FAFSA.
Dates and Deadlines: Priority date 3/15; no closing date. Applicants notified on a rolling basis starting 3/15.

CONTACT
Mark Delorey, Director of Financial Aid
1903 West Michigan Avenue, Kalamazoo, MI 49008-5211
(269) 387-6000

Minnesota

Academy College
Bloomington, Minnesota
www.academycollege.edu Federal Code: 013505

2-year for-profit junior and technical college in large city.
Enrollment: 290 undergrads, 28% part-time. 30 full-time freshmen.
Selectivity: Open admission.

BASIC COSTS (2005-2006)
Additional info: Tuition ranges from $215 to $369 per-credit-hour depending on program.

FINANCIAL AID PICTURE
Students with need: Need-based aid available for full-time and part-time students. Work study available nights.

FINANCIAL AID PROCEDURES
Forms required: FAFSA, institutional form.

CONTACT
Mary Erickson, Director of Administration
1101 East 78th Street, Bloomington, MN 55420
(952) 851-0066

Alexandria Technical College
Alexandria, Minnesota
www.alextech.edu Federal Code: 005544

2-year public technical college in large town.
Enrollment: 1,725 undergrads.
Selectivity: Open admission; but selective for some programs.

BASIC COSTS (2005-2006)
Tuition and fees: $3,857; out-of-state residents $7,419.
Per-credit charge: $119; out-of-state residents $238.

FINANCIAL AID PICTURE
Students with need: Need-based aid available for full-time and part-time students.
Students without need: This college only awards aid to students with need.

FINANCIAL AID PROCEDURES
Forms required: FAFSA, institutional form.
Dates and Deadlines: Priority date 5/1; no closing date. Applicants notified on a rolling basis starting 6/30; must reply within 2 week(s) of notification.

CONTACT
Gary McFarland, Financial Aid Coordinator
1601 Jefferson Street, Alexandria, MN 56308-3799
(320) 762-4540

Anoka Technical College
Anoka, Minnesota
www.anokatech.edu Federal Code: 007350

2-year public technical college in large town.
Enrollment: 2,020 undergrads.
Selectivity: Open admission.

BASIC COSTS (2005-2006)
Tuition and fees: $4,309; out-of-state residents $8,195.
Per-credit charge: $130; out-of-state residents $259.
Additional info: Various reciprocity agreements with some neighboring states provide tuition reduction to out-of-state students.

FINANCIAL AID PICTURE
Students with need: Need-based aid available for full-time and part-time students.
Students without need: This college only awards aid to students with need.

FINANCIAL AID PROCEDURES
Forms required: FAFSA, institutional form.
Dates and Deadlines: No deadline. Applicants notified on a rolling basis starting 5/1.

CONTACT
Nancy Maki, Director of Financial Aid
1355 West Highway 10, Anoka, MN 55303
(763) 576-4760

Anoka-Ramsey Community College
Coon Rapids, Minnesota
www.anokaramsey.edu Federal Code: 002332

2-year public community college in small city.
Enrollment: 7,230 undergrads.
Selectivity: Open admission; but selective for some programs and for out-of-state students.

Minnesota — Anoka-Ramsey Community College

BASIC COSTS (2005-2006)
Tuition and fees: $3,582; out-of-state residents $6,780.
Per-credit charge: $107; out-of-state residents $213.
Additional info: Various reciprocity agreements with some neighboring states provide tuition reduction to out-of-state students.

FINANCIAL AID PICTURE
Students with need: Work study available nights, weekends, and for part-time students.
Students without need: This college only awards aid to students with need.

FINANCIAL AID PROCEDURES
Forms required: FAFSA, institutional form.
Dates and Deadlines: Priority date 6/1; no closing date. Applicants notified on a rolling basis; must reply within 2 week(s) of notification.

CONTACT
Karla Seymour, Financial Aid Officer
11200 Mississippi Boulevard NW, Coon Rapids, MN 55433
(763) 427-2600

Art Institutes International Minnesota
Minneapolis, Minnesota
www.aim.artinstitutes.edu   Federal Code: 010248

4-year for-profit culinary school and visual arts college in very large city.
Enrollment: 1,594 undergrads, 44% part-time.
Selectivity: Open admission.

BASIC COSTS (2006-2007)
Tuition and fees: $17,190.
Per-credit charge: $382.
Additional info: Typical full-time credit load 16 credits/quarter. Starter kits for most programs $550-850. Tuition at time of enrollment locked for 4 years.

FINANCIAL AID PICTURE
Students with need: Need-based aid available for full-time students.

FINANCIAL AID PROCEDURES
Forms required: FAFSA.

CONTACT
Matt Van Hove, Director of Administrative and Financial Services
15 South Ninth Street, Minneapolis, MN 55402
(612) 332-3361

Augsburg College
Minneapolis, Minnesota
www.augsburg.edu   Federal Code: 002334

4-year private liberal arts college in large city, affiliated with Evangelical Lutheran Church in America.
Enrollment: 2,668 undergrads, 18% part-time. 389 full-time freshmen.
Selectivity: Admits over 75% of applicants.

BASIC COSTS (2006-2007)
Tuition and fees: $23,422.
Room and board: $6,604.

FINANCIAL AID PICTURE (2004-2005)
Students with need: Out of 248 full-time freshmen who applied for aid, 201 were judged to have need. Of these, 199 received aid, and 39 had their full need met. Average financial aid package met 74% of need; average scholarship/grant was $11,877; average loan was $3,212. For part-time students, average financial aid package was $12,220.

Students without need: 82 full-time freshmen who did not demonstrate need for aid received scholarships/grants; average award was $17,302. No-need awards available for academics, alumni affiliation, leadership, minority status, music/drama, religious affiliation.
Scholarships offered: President's Scholarships; up to full tuition annually; 3.7 GPA and ACT/SAT score 27 or higher; number awarded determined annually. Regents Scholarships; $3,000-$9,000; top 30% of class rank or test scores. Must apply before 5/1 for both scholarships.

FINANCIAL AID PROCEDURES
Forms required: FAFSA.
Dates and Deadlines: Priority date 4/15; closing date 8/1. Applicants notified on a rolling basis starting 3/1; must reply within 3 week(s) of notification.

CONTACT
Paul Terrio, Director of Enrollment Services
2211 Riverside Avenue, Minneapolis, MN 55454
(612) 330-1046

Bemidji State University
Bemidji, Minnesota
www.bemidjistate.edu   Federal Code: 002336

4-year public university in large town.
Enrollment: 4,396 undergrads, 27% part-time. 592 full-time freshmen.
Selectivity: Admits 50 to 75% of applicants.

BASIC COSTS (2005-2006)
Tuition and fees: $6,016; out-of-state residents $6,016.
Per-credit charge: $191; out-of-state residents $191.
Room and board: $5,166.
Additional info: Tuition/fee waivers available for minority students.

FINANCIAL AID PICTURE (2005-2006)
Students with need: Out of 465 full-time freshmen who applied for aid, 316 were judged to have need. Of these, 315 received aid, and 99 had their full need met. Average financial aid package met 75% of need; average scholarship/grant was $4,677; average loan was $2,666. For part-time students, average financial aid package was $6,194.
Students without need: 144 full-time freshmen who did not demonstrate need for aid received scholarships/grants; average award was $6,135. No-need awards available for academics, alumni affiliation, art, music/drama.
Scholarships offered: 72 full-time freshmen received athletic scholarships; average amount $3,054.
Cumulative student debt: 66% of graduating class had student loans; average debt was $16,121.

FINANCIAL AID PROCEDURES
Forms required: FAFSA, institutional form.
Dates and Deadlines: Priority date 5/15; no closing date. Applicants notified on a rolling basis starting 5/15.

CONTACT
Paul Lindseth, Director of Financial Aid
1500 Birchmont Drive Northeast, D-102, Bemidji, MN 56601
(218) 755-2034

Bethany Lutheran College
Mankato, Minnesota
www.blc.edu   Federal Code: 002337

4-year private liberal arts college in large town, affiliated with Evangelical Lutheran Synod.
Enrollment: 565 undergrads, 7% part-time. 165 full-time freshmen.
Selectivity: Admits over 75% of applicants.

BASIC COSTS (2006-2007)
Tuition and fees: $16,508.
Per-credit charge: $690.
Room and board: $5,278.

FINANCIAL AID PICTURE (2004-2005)
Students with need: Out of 148 full-time freshmen who applied for aid, 135 were judged to have need. Of these, 135 received aid, and 44 had their full need met. Average financial aid package met 86.19% of need; average scholarship/grant was $9,512; average loan was $3,384. For part-time students, average financial aid package was $8,203.
Students without need: 23 full-time freshmen who did not demonstrate need for aid received scholarships/grants; average award was $7,219. No-need awards available for academics, art, athletics, music/drama.
Cumulative student debt: 75% of graduating class had student loans; average debt was $18,654.

FINANCIAL AID PROCEDURES
Forms required: FAFSA, institutional form.
Dates and Deadlines: Priority date 4/15; no closing date. Applicants notified on a rolling basis starting 3/1; must reply within 2 week(s) of notification.

CONTACT
Jeffrey Younge, Financial Aid Director
700 Luther Drive, Mankato, MN 56001-4490
(507) 344-7328

Bethel University
Saint Paul, Minnesota
www.bethel.edu   Federal Code: 002338

4-year private liberal arts college in large city, affiliated with Baptist General Conference.
Enrollment: 3,172 undergrads, 10% part-time. 719 full-time freshmen.
Selectivity: Admits over 75% of applicants.

BASIC COSTS (2006-2007)
Tuition and fees: $22,700.
Per-credit charge: $865.
Room and board: $7,140.

FINANCIAL AID PICTURE (2005-2006)
Students with need: Out of 568 full-time freshmen who applied for aid, 462 were judged to have need. Of these, 462 received aid, and 104 had their full need met. Average financial aid package met 79% of need; average scholarship/grant was $9,817; average loan was $3,979. For part-time students, average financial aid package was $8,783.
Students without need: 180 full-time freshmen who did not demonstrate need for aid received scholarships/grants; average award was $4,580. No-need awards available for academics, alumni affiliation, art, job skills, leadership, music/drama, religious affiliation.
Cumulative student debt: 75% of graduating class had student loans; average debt was $25,325.

FINANCIAL AID PROCEDURES
Forms required: FAFSA, institutional form.
Dates and Deadlines: Priority date 4/15; no closing date. Applicants notified on a rolling basis starting 3/1; must reply by 5/1 or within 3 week(s) of notification.

CONTACT
Jeff Olson, Director of Financial Aid
3900 Bethel Drive, Saint Paul, MN 55112-6999
(651) 638-6241

Capella University
Minneapolis, Minnesota
www.capellauniversity.edu   Federal Code: 032673

4-year for-profit virtual university in very large city.
Enrollment: 2,358 undergrads.

BASIC COSTS (2005-2006)
Tuition and fees: $13,050.
Per-credit charge: $290.
Additional info: Costs vary by program.

FINANCIAL AID PICTURE
Students with need: Need-based aid available for full-time and part-time students.

CONTACT
Tim Lehman, Director of Financial Aid
222 South Sixth Street, 9th Floor, Minneapolis, MN 55402
(888) 227-3552

Carleton College
Northfield, Minnesota
www.carleton.edu   Federal Code: 002340
                                 CSS Code: 6081

4-year private liberal arts college in large town.
Enrollment: 1,936 undergrads. 541 full-time freshmen.
Selectivity: Admits less than 50% of applicants.

BASIC COSTS (2006-2007)
Tuition and fees: $34,272.
Room and board: $8,592.

FINANCIAL AID PICTURE (2004-2005)
Students with need: Out of 414 full-time freshmen who applied for aid, 368 were judged to have need. Of these, 368 received aid, and 368 had their full need met. Average financial aid package met 100% of need; average scholarship/grant was $21,611; average loan was $2,730.
Students without need: 34 full-time freshmen who did not demonstrate need for aid received scholarships/grants; average award was $3,803. No-need awards available for academics.
Scholarships offered: National Merit, National Achievement, National Hispanic Scholars Awards; $2,000 per year; based on outstanding academic achievement and promise.
Cumulative student debt: 60% of graduating class had student loans; average debt was $17,842.
Additional info: Full financial need of all admitted applicants met through combination of work, loans, grants.

FINANCIAL AID PROCEDURES
Forms required: FAFSA, CSS PROFILE.
Dates and Deadlines: Closing date 2/15. Applicants notified by 4/1; must reply by 5/1 or within 2 week(s) of notification.
Transfers: Closing date 3/15. Applicants notified by 5/15; must reply by 6/1 or within 2 week(s) of notification.

CONTACT
Rodney Oto, Director of Student Financial Services
100 South College Street, Northfield, MN 55057
(507) 646-4138

Central Lakes College
Brainerd, Minnesota
www.clcmn.edu　　　　　　　　　　Federal Code: 002339

2-year public community and technical college in large town.
Enrollment: 2,768 undergrads.
Selectivity: Open admission; but selective for some programs.

BASIC COSTS (2005-2006)
Tuition and fees: $3,940.
Per-credit charge: $116.

FINANCIAL AID PICTURE (2005-2006)
Students with need: 43% of average financial aid package awarded as scholarships/grants, 57% awarded as loans/jobs. Need-based aid available for part-time students.

FINANCIAL AID PROCEDURES
Forms required: FAFSA, institutional form.
Dates and Deadlines: Priority date 6/1; no closing date. Applicants notified on a rolling basis starting 6/10; must reply within 2 week(s) of notification.

CONTACT
Mike Barnaby, Director of Financial Aid
501 West College Drive, Brainerd, MN 56401
(218) 855-8025

Century Community and Technical College
White Bear Lake, Minnesota
www.century.edu　　　　　　　　　　Federal Code: 010546

2-year public community and technical college in large town.
Enrollment: 7,527 undergrads, 52% part-time. 957 full-time freshmen.
Selectivity: Open admission; but selective for some programs.

BASIC COSTS (2005-2006)
Tuition and fees: $3,858; out-of-state residents $7,338.
Per-credit charge: $116; out-of-state residents $232.
Additional info: Various reciprocity agreements with some neighboring states provide tuition reduction to out-of-state students.

FINANCIAL AID PICTURE (2005-2006)
Students with need: 39% of average financial aid package awarded as scholarships/grants, 61% awarded as loans/jobs. Need-based aid available for part-time students.
Students without need: This college only awards aid to students with need.
Additional info: Minnesota resident out of high school or not enrolled in college for 7 years without bachelor's or other higher degree offered cost of tuition and books for 1 course in 1 semester up to maximum of 5 credits.

FINANCIAL AID PROCEDURES
Forms required: FAFSA, institutional form.
Dates and Deadlines: No deadline. Applicants notified on a rolling basis starting 5/15.

CONTACT
Lois Larson, Financial Aid Director
3300 Century Avenue North, White Bear Lake, MN 55110
(651) 779-3305

College of St. Benedict
St. Joseph, Minnesota
www.csbsju.edu　　　　　　　　　　Federal Code: 002341

4-year private liberal arts college for women in small town, affiliated with Roman Catholic Church.
Enrollment: 1,992 undergrads. 576 full-time freshmen.
Selectivity: Admits over 75% of applicants.

BASIC COSTS (2006-2007)
Tuition and fees: $24,924.
Per-credit charge: $1,020.
Room and board: $6,898.

FINANCIAL AID PICTURE (2005-2006)
Students with need: Out of 474 full-time freshmen who applied for aid, 393 were judged to have need. Of these, 393 received aid, and 228 had their full need met. Average financial aid package met 94% of need; average scholarship/grant was $14,435; average loan was $5,107. Need-based aid available for part-time students.
Students without need: 164 full-time freshmen who did not demonstrate need for aid received scholarships/grants; average award was $9,605. No-need awards available for academics, art, leadership, minority status, music/drama, ROTC.
Scholarships offered: Regents/Trustees Scholarships; $12,500; minimum 3.6 GPA, ACT 30, SAT 1320 (exclusive of Writing), demonstrated leadership and service, faculty interview. President's Scholarships; $7,000-$10,500; GPA, high school rank, ACT/SAT scores, leadership and service. Dean's Scholarships; $3,000-$6,500; GPA, high school rank, ACT/SAT scores, leadership and service. Art, Music and Theater Scholarships; up to $2,000; excellence in these subjects in high school, portfolio, tape, audition. Diversity Leadership Scholarships; up to $5,000; demonstrated diversity leadership and service in the area of cultural and ethnic diversity, personal statement on topic. Army ROTC and ROTC Nursing Scholarships; $20,000; demonstrated leadership potential, high school GPA, class standing, ACT/SAT scores, high achievement with broad interests and willingness to take on challenges. Phi Theta Kappa Scholarship; $1,000; member of Phi Theta Kappa(transfer students only).
Cumulative student debt: 72% of graduating class had student loans; average debt was $24,764.

FINANCIAL AID PROCEDURES
Forms required: FAFSA, institutional form.
Dates and Deadlines: Priority date 3/15; no closing date. Applicants notified on a rolling basis starting 3/15.

CONTACT
Jane Haugen, Executive Director of Financial Aid
PO Box 7155, Collegeville, MN 56321-7155
(320) 363-5388

College of St. Catherine
St. Paul, Minnesota
www.stkate.edu　　　　　　　　　　Federal Code: 002342

4-year private liberal arts college for women in large city, affiliated with Roman Catholic Church.
Enrollment: 3,511 undergrads, 33% part-time. 385 full-time freshmen.
Selectivity: Admits over 75% of applicants.

BASIC COSTS (2006-2007)
Tuition and fees: $22,750.
Per-credit charge: $754.
Room and board: $6,432.

FINANCIAL AID PICTURE (2005-2006)
Students with need: Average financial aid package met 78% of need; average scholarship/grant was $7,991; average loan was $3,710. For part-time students, average financial aid package was $14,849.
Students without need: No-need awards available for academics, leadership.
Scholarships offered: St. Catherine of Alexandria Merit Scholarships; $2,000-$6,000; high school seniors in top 15% of class, evidence of academic preparation, outstanding leadership abilities, involvement in extracurricular activities and community service; renewable for 3 years.
Cumulative student debt: 78% of graduating class had student loans; average debt was $27,519.
Additional info: Audition required for music scholarships.

FINANCIAL AID PROCEDURES
Forms required: FAFSA, institutional form.
Dates and Deadlines: Priority date 4/15; no closing date. Applicants notified on a rolling basis starting 3/30; must reply within 2 week(s) of notification.

CONTACT
Pam Johnson, Director of Financial Aid
2004 Randolph Avenue, St. Paul, MN 55105
(651) 690-6540

College of St. Scholastica
Duluth, Minnesota
www.css.edu
Federal Code: 002343

4-year private liberal arts college in small city, affiliated with Roman Catholic Church.
Enrollment: 1,986 undergrads, 5% part-time. 491 full-time freshmen.
Selectivity: Admits over 75% of applicants.

BASIC COSTS (2006-2007)
Tuition and fees: $23,574.
Per-credit charge: $688.
Room and board: $6,514.
Additional info: Tuition/fee waivers available for minority students.

FINANCIAL AID PICTURE (2005-2006)
Students with need: Out of 429 full-time freshmen who applied for aid, 376 were judged to have need. Of these, 374 received aid, and 301 had their full need met. Average financial aid package met 80% of need; average scholarship/grant was $4,877; average loan was $3,368. For part-time students, average financial aid package was $6,924.
Students without need: 88 full-time freshmen who did not demonstrate need for aid received scholarships/grants; average award was $9,381. No-need awards available for academics, alumni affiliation, religious affiliation, ROTC.
Scholarships offered: Benedictine Scholarship; $5,000-$12,000 per year for up to 4 years. Opportunity Grants; $4,000-$6,000. Both based on GPA, SAT/ACT score; unlimited number awarded. Divisional Merit Awards; $2,000-$4,000; available to transfer students; based on major.
Cumulative student debt: 84% of graduating class had student loans; average debt was $29,942.

FINANCIAL AID PROCEDURES
Forms required: FAFSA, institutional form.
Dates and Deadlines: Priority date 3/15; no closing date. Applicants notified on a rolling basis starting 3/1; must reply by 5/1 or within 2 week(s) of notification.

CONTACT
Jon Erickson, Director of Financial Aid
1200 Kenwood Avenue, Duluth, MN 55811-4199
(218) 723-6047

College of Visual Arts
St. Paul, Minnesota
www.cva.edu
Federal Code: 007462

4-year private visual arts college in large city.
Enrollment: 190 undergrads, 8% part-time. 38 full-time freshmen.

BASIC COSTS (2006-2007)
Tuition and fees: $19,936.

FINANCIAL AID PICTURE (2005-2006)
Students with need: Average financial aid package met 36% of need; average scholarship/grant was $4,766; average loan was $2,113. For part-time students, average financial aid package was $5,280.
Students without need: No-need awards available for academics, art.

FINANCIAL AID PROCEDURES
Forms required: FAFSA, institutional form.
Dates and Deadlines: Priority date 4/15; closing date 6/1. Applicants notified on a rolling basis starting 1/1; must reply within 2 week(s) of notification.
Transfers: Priority date 4/1.

CONTACT
Bonnie Burgoyne, Director of Financial Aid
344 Summit Avenue, St. Paul, MN 55102-2199
(651) 224-3416

Concordia College: Moorhead
Moorhead, Minnesota
www.concordiacollege.edu
Federal Code: 002346

4-year private liberal arts college in small city, affiliated with Evangelical Lutheran Church in America.
Enrollment: 2,686 undergrads, 1% part-time. 769 full-time freshmen.
Selectivity: Admits over 75% of applicants.

BASIC COSTS (2006-2007)
Tuition and fees: $20,980.
Per-credit charge: $818.
Room and board: $5,090.

FINANCIAL AID PICTURE (2004-2005)
Students with need: Out of 668 full-time freshmen who applied for aid, 547 were judged to have need. Of these, 547 received aid, and 129 had their full need met. Average financial aid package met 93% of need; average scholarship/grant was $9,972; average loan was $4,794. Need-based aid available for part-time students.
Students without need: This college only awards aid to students with need.
Scholarships offered: Concordia National Merit Scholarship; $10,000 per year for 4 years; for National Merit Scholarship finalists listing Concordia as their first choice. Soli Deo Gloria Scholarship; $12,000 per year for 4 years; based on test scores, class rank or GPA, essay and interview. Faculty Scholarships; $8,000 per year for 4 years; based on test scores, class rank or GPA, essay, and faculty interview. Excellence Scholarships; $5,000-$7,000 per year for 4 years; based on test scores, class rank or GPA, essay, and faculty interview. Performing Arts Scholarships; $1,500-$3,500 per year for 4 years; available in music drama, forensics.
Cumulative student debt: 74% of graduating class had student loans; average debt was $21,532.
Additional info: Students in ACCORD program (age 25 and older) may apply for tuition reductions for first 4 courses.

FINANCIAL AID PROCEDURES
Forms required: FAFSA, institutional form.
Dates and Deadlines: Priority date 4/15; no closing date. Applicants notified on a rolling basis starting 2/15.

CONTACT
Jane Williams, Director of Financial Aid
901 Eighth Street South, Moorhead, MN 56562-9981
(218) 299-3010

Concordia University: St. Paul
St. Paul, Minnesota
www.csp.edu   Federal Code: 002347

4-year private university in large city, affiliated with Lutheran Church - Missouri Synod.
Enrollment: 1,594 undergrads, 9% part-time. 164 full-time freshmen.
Selectivity: Admits 50 to 75% of applicants.

BASIC COSTS (2006-2007)
Tuition and fees: $22,378.
Per-credit charge: $466.
Room and board: $6,596.

FINANCIAL AID PICTURE (2005-2006)
Students with need: Out of 163 full-time freshmen who applied for aid, 140 were judged to have need. Of these, 140 received aid, and 35 had their full need met. Average financial aid package met 78% of need; average scholarship/grant was $13,391; average loan was $2,748. For part-time students, average financial aid package was $7,151.
Students without need: 19 full-time freshmen who did not demonstrate need for aid received scholarships/grants; average award was $6,035. No-need awards available for academics, art, athletics, minority status, music/drama, religious affiliation.
Scholarships offered: *Merit:* Academic scholarships for freshmen; $2,000-$8,000. Academic scholarships for transfers into traditional programs; up to $6,000. *Athletic:* 12 full-time freshmen received athletic scholarships; average amount $3,600.
Cumulative student debt: 68% of graduating class had student loans; average debt was $20,715.
Additional info: Church districts and local congregations are major sources of aid for church-vocation students.

FINANCIAL AID PROCEDURES
Forms required: FAFSA, institutional form.
Dates and Deadlines: Priority date 5/1; no closing date. Applicants notified on a rolling basis starting 3/1; must reply within 3 week(s) of notification.

CONTACT
Brian Heinemann, Financial Aid Director
275 Syndicate Street North, St. Paul, MN 55104-5494
(651) 603-6300

Crossroads College
Rochester, Minnesota
www.crossroadscollege.edu   Federal Code: 002366

4-year private Bible college in small city, affiliated with Christian Church.
Enrollment: 165 undergrads.

BASIC COSTS (2006-2007)
Tuition and fees: $11,270.
Per-credit charge: $330.
Room only: $3,500.

FINANCIAL AID PICTURE (2004-2005)
Students with need: 57% of average financial aid package awarded as scholarships/grants, 43% awarded as loans/jobs. Need-based aid available for part-time students. Work study available nights.
Students without need: No-need awards available for academics, leadership, music/drama, religious affiliation.
Scholarships offered: Home-Educated Grant; $500 per semester if home-schooled for two years during high school. Travel Grant; $500 per semester for student who resides in states other than Minnesota, Iowa, Wisconsin. Crossroads Matching Grant; church funds matched up to $500 per semester; awarded to first year students.

FINANCIAL AID PROCEDURES
Forms required: FAFSA, institutional form.
Dates and Deadlines: Priority date 4/1; no closing date. Applicants notified on a rolling basis starting 2/1; must reply within 4 week(s) of notification.
Transfers: Mid-year transfer students will have financial aid calculated with the prior school term award in mind.

CONTACT
Polly Kellogg-Bradley, Director of Financial Aid
920 Mayowood Road SW, Rochester, MN 55902
(507) 535-3308

Crown College
St. Bonifacius, Minnesota
www.crown.edu   Federal Code: 002383

4-year private Bible and liberal arts college in small town, affiliated with Christian and Missionary Alliance.
Enrollment: 1,054 undergrads, 24% part-time. 169 full-time freshmen.
Selectivity: Admits 50 to 75% of applicants.

BASIC COSTS (2006-2007)
Tuition and fees: $17,054.
Per-credit charge: $713.
Room and board: $6,654.
Additional info: Tuition/fee waivers available for minority students.

FINANCIAL AID PICTURE (2005-2006)
Students with need: Out of 151 full-time freshmen who applied for aid, 137 were judged to have need. Of these, 137 received aid, and 13 had their full need met. Average financial aid package met 57% of need; average scholarship/grant was $4,036; average loan was $3,193. For part-time students, average financial aid package was $6,070.
Students without need: 13 full-time freshmen who did not demonstrate need for aid received scholarships/grants; average award was $2,500. No-need awards available for academics, alumni affiliation, leadership, minority status, music/drama, religious affiliation.
Cumulative student debt: 84% of graduating class had student loans; average debt was $22,672.

FINANCIAL AID PROCEDURES
Forms required: FAFSA, institutional form.
Dates and Deadlines: Priority date 4/1; closing date 8/1. Applicants notified on a rolling basis starting 4/1; must reply within 4 week(s) of notification.
Transfers: No deadline. Applicants notified on a rolling basis. Cannot have attended more than 4 years of college to receive state grant.

CONTACT
Cheryl Fernandez, Director of Financial Aid
8700 College View Drive, St. Bonifacius, MN 55375-9001
(952) 446-4177

Dakota County Technical College
Rosemount, Minnesota
www.dctc.edu   Federal Code: 010402

2-year public technical college in large town.
Enrollment: 2,281 undergrads, 38% part-time. 767 full-time freshmen.
Selectivity: Open admission; but selective for some programs.

BASIC COSTS (2006-2007)
Tuition and fees: $4,586; out-of-state residents $8,668.
Per-credit charge: $136; out-of-state residents $272.
Additional info: Various reciprocity agreements with neighboring states provides tuition reduction to some out-of-state students.

FINANCIAL AID PICTURE (2004-2005)
Students with need: 33% of average financial aid package awarded as scholarships/grants, 67% awarded as loans/jobs. Need-based aid available for part-time students. Work study available nights, weekends, and for part-time students.
Students without need: No-need awards available for academics, leadership.
Scholarships offered: Dakota County Techical College scholarship.

FINANCIAL AID PROCEDURES
Forms required: FAFSA.
Dates and Deadlines: No deadline. Applicants notified on a rolling basis starting 3/15.
Transfers: No deadline. FAFSA must be processed within 14 days of the first day of the semester to be considered for Minnesota State Grant for the semester.

CONTACT
Scott Roelke, Director of Scholarships and Financial Aid
1300 145th Street East, Rosemount, MN 55068
(651) 423-8299

Dunwoody College of Technology
Minneapolis, Minnesota
www.dunwoody.edu   Federal Code: 004641

2-year private technical college in very large city.
Enrollment: 1,292 undergrads, 7% part-time. 261 full-time freshmen.
Selectivity: Admits 50 to 75% of applicants.

BASIC COSTS (2006-2007)
Tuition and fees: $14,685.

FINANCIAL AID PICTURE (2005-2006)
Students with need: Average financial aid package met 38% of need; average scholarship/grant was $4,518; average loan was $3,409. For part-time students, average financial aid package was $6,715.
Students without need: No-need awards available for academics.

FINANCIAL AID PROCEDURES
Forms required: FAFSA, institutional form.
Dates and Deadlines: Priority date 6/1; no closing date. Applicants notified on a rolling basis starting 6/15.

CONTACT
Barb Charboneau, Financial Aid Director
818 Dunwoody Boulevard, Minneapolis, MN 55403-1192
(612) 374-5800 ext. 2027

Fond du Lac Tribal and Community College
Cloquet, Minnesota
www.fdltcc.edu   Federal Code: E00482

2-year public community college in large town.
Enrollment: 1,950 undergrads.
Selectivity: Open admission.

BASIC COSTS (2005-2006)
Tuition and fees: $3,976; out-of-state residents $7,499.
Per-credit charge: $117; out-of-state residents $235.
Additional info: Cost for double room is $10.18 per day.

FINANCIAL AID PICTURE
Students with need: Need-based aid available for full-time and part-time students.
Students without need: No-need awards available for academics.

FINANCIAL AID PROCEDURES
Forms required: FAFSA, institutional form.
Dates and Deadlines: Priority date 3/15; no closing date. Applicants notified on a rolling basis starting 4/15.

CONTACT
David Sutherland, Director of Financial Aid
2101 14th Street, Cloquet, MN 55720
(218) 879-0816

Globe College
Oakdale, Minnesota
www.globecollege.com   Federal Code: 004642

4-year for-profit business and health science college in large town.
Enrollment: 848 undergrads.
Selectivity: Open admission.

BASIC COSTS (2005-2006)
Tuition and fees: $14,850.
Per-credit charge: $330.

FINANCIAL AID PICTURE
Students with need: Need-based aid available for full-time and part-time students.

FINANCIAL AID PROCEDURES
Forms required: FAFSA, institutional form.
Dates and Deadlines: No deadline. Applicants notified on a rolling basis starting 5/1.

CONTACT
Jay White, Financial Aid Director
7166 10th Street North, Oakdale, MN 55128-5939
(651) 730-5100

Gustavus Adolphus College
St. Peter, Minnesota
www.gustavus.edu   Federal Code: 002353

4-year private liberal arts college in small town, affiliated with Evangelical Lutheran Church in America.
Enrollment: 2,545 undergrads. 705 full-time freshmen.
Selectivity: Admits over 75% of applicants.

BASIC COSTS (2006-2007)
Tuition and fees: $26,700.
Room and board: $6,400.

FINANCIAL AID PICTURE
Students with need: Need-based aid available for full-time students. Work study available nights, weekends, and for part-time students.
Students without need: No-need awards available for academics, alumni affiliation, music/drama, ROTC.
Scholarships offered: Partners in Scholarship; $9,000; academic; 35 awarded. Presidential Scholarship; $12,500; National Merit finalist; 25 awarded. Trustee Scholarship; $1,000-$6,500; academic. Alumni Scholarship; $1,500; academic for children of alumni. Jussi Bjorling Scholarship; $3,000; music; 40 awarded. Anderson Theatre and Dance Scholarship; $2,000; theatre and dance; 15 awarded. Norelius Service Award; $500-1,500; volunteer

leadership. Gustavus State Scholarship; $12,000; academic; 1 awarded. Dean's Scholarship; $7,500; 35 awarded.

FINANCIAL AID PROCEDURES
Forms required: FAFSA, institutional form. CSS PROFILE required of students desiring a financial aid award before March 1 of their applicant year.
Dates and Deadlines: Priority date 2/15; closing date 4/15. Applicants notified on a rolling basis starting 3/1; must reply by 5/1 or within 2 week(s) of notification.

CONTACT
Robert Helgeson, Director of Student Financial Assistance
800 West College Avenue, St. Peter, MN 56082
(507) 933-7527

Hamline University
St. Paul, Minnesota
www.hamline.edu   Federal Code: 002354

4-year private university and liberal arts college in very large city, affiliated with United Methodist Church.
Enrollment: 1,944 undergrads, 2% part-time. 460 full-time freshmen.
Selectivity: Admits over 75% of applicants.

BASIC COSTS (2006-2007)
Tuition and fees: $24,076.
Per-credit charge: $747.
Room and board: $7,280.

FINANCIAL AID PICTURE (2005-2006)
Students with need: Out of 443 full-time freshmen who applied for aid, 354 were judged to have need. Of these, 354 received aid, and 102 had their full need met. Average financial aid package met 77% of need; average scholarship/grant was $7,413; average loan was $517. For part-time students, average financial aid package was $14,968.
Students without need: 86 full-time freshmen who did not demonstrate need for aid received scholarships/grants; average award was $13,382. No-need awards available for academics, alumni affiliation, art, job skills, leadership, minority status, music/drama, religious affiliation, state/district residency.
Scholarships offered: Presidential Scholarship; $6,000 to full tuition; for students with excellent academic ability, strong sense of motivation. Hamline Honors Scholarship; $4,000-$8,000; for students with successful academic record, involvement in school and community activities. Hamline Trustee Scholarship; $3,000-$6,500; for new first-year students who have excelled academically. Departmental scholarships in Biology, Chemistry, Communication Studies, French, German, Music, Physics, Theatre, Creative Writing; $3,000-$4,000 depending on department. Diversity scholarships; $3,000. Eagle Scout or Gold Award scholarships; amount varies. All scholarships renewable for a total of four years.
Cumulative student debt: 81% of graduating class had student loans; average debt was $23,197.

FINANCIAL AID PROCEDURES
Forms required: FAFSA, state aid form, institutional form.
Dates and Deadlines: Priority date 3/1; no closing date. Applicants notified on a rolling basis starting 3/1; must reply within 2 week(s) of notification.
Transfers: Priority date 4/1; no deadline. Applicants notified on a rolling basis; must reply within 2 week(s) of notification. Students who qualify for a Minnesota State Grant must carry 15 semester credits to qualify for the full grant each semester. If less credit is carried the grant is pro-rated.

CONTACT
Lynette Wahl, Director of Financial Aid
1536 Hewitt Avenue, St. Paul, MN 55104-1284
(651) 523-3000

Inver Hills Community College
Inver Grove Heights, Minnesota
www.inverhills.edu   Federal Code: 006935

2-year public community college in large town.
Enrollment: 4,166 undergrads, 59% part-time. 727 full-time freshmen.
Selectivity: Open admission; but selective for some programs.

BASIC COSTS (2005-2006)
Tuition and fees: $4,179; out-of-state residents $7,953.
Per-credit charge: $126; out-of-state residents $252.
Additional info: Reciprocity agreements for in-state tuition rates with some neighboring states.

FINANCIAL AID PICTURE (2005-2006)
Students with need: Average financial aid package met 67% of need; average scholarship/grant was $1,500; average loan was $2,625. For part-time students, average financial aid package was $9,000.
Students without need: This college only awards aid to students with need.
Cumulative student debt: 49% of graduating class had student loans; average debt was $4,713.

FINANCIAL AID PROCEDURES
Forms required: FAFSA.
Dates and Deadlines: No deadline. Applicants notified on a rolling basis starting 6/1.
Transfers: No deadline. Applicants notified on a rolling basis.

CONTACT
John Pogue, Financial Aid Officer
2500 East 80th Street, Inver Grove Heights, MN 55076-3224
(651) 450-8518

Itasca Community College
Grand Rapids, Minnesota
www.itascacc.edu   Federal Code: 002356

2-year public community college in large town.
Enrollment: 1,137 undergrads.
Selectivity: Open admission; but selective for some programs.

BASIC COSTS (2005-2006)
Tuition and fees: $4,148; out-of-state residents $5,072.
Per-credit charge: $123; out-of-state residents $154.
Additional info: Different reciprocity agreements for Wisconsin, North Dakota, and South Dakota.

FINANCIAL AID PICTURE (2004-2005)
Students with need: 48% of average financial aid package awarded as scholarships/grants, 52% awarded as loans/jobs. Need-based aid available for part-time students. Work study available nights.
Students without need: No-need awards available for academics, leadership.

FINANCIAL AID PROCEDURES
Forms required: FAFSA.
Dates and Deadlines: Priority date 5/1; no closing date. Applicants notified on a rolling basis starting 4/1.

CONTACT
Patty Holycross, Director of Financial Aid
1851 Highway 169 East, Grand Rapids, MN 55744
(218) 327-4467

Lake Superior College
Duluth, Minnesota
www.lsc.edu Federal Code: 005757

2-year public community and technical college in small city.
Enrollment: 3,511 undergrads, 38% part-time. 462 full-time freshmen.
Selectivity: Open admission; but selective for some programs.

BASIC COSTS (2006-2007)
Tuition and fees: $3,927; out-of-state residents $7,377.
Per-credit charge: $115; out-of-state residents $230.
Additional info: Various reciprocity plans for residents of neighboring states may reduce tuition for out-of-state students.

FINANCIAL AID PICTURE (2004-2005)
Students with need: 36% of average financial aid package awarded as scholarships/grants, 64% awarded as loans/jobs. Need-based aid available for part-time students. Work study available nights, weekends, and for part-time students.
Students without need: No-need awards available for academics, leadership.

FINANCIAL AID PROCEDURES
Forms required: FAFSA.
Dates and Deadlines: Priority date 5/1; no closing date. Applicants notified on a rolling basis starting 5/1.
Transfers: No deadline.

CONTACT
Sandra Olin, Director of Financial Aid
2101 Trinity Road, Duluth, MN 55811
(218) 733-7601

Lakeland Academy Division of Herzing College
Crystal, Minnesota
www.herzing.edu Federal Code: 007590

2-year for-profit health science college in large city.
Enrollment: 341 undergrads.
Selectivity: Admits over 75% of applicants.

BASIC COSTS (2006-2007)
Additional info: Cost of full programs ranges from $13,360 to $43,585, including fees and books.

FINANCIAL AID PICTURE (2004-2005)
Students with need: 38% of average financial aid package awarded as scholarships/grants, 62% awarded as loans/jobs.

FINANCIAL AID PROCEDURES
Forms required: FAFSA.

CONTACT
Jill Riverso, Director of Financial Aid
5700 West Broadway, Crystal, MN 55428
(763) 535-3000

Leech Lake Tribal College
Cass Lake, Minnesota
www.lltc.org Federal Code: 030964

2-year private community college in small town.
Enrollment: 170 undergrads.

BASIC COSTS (2005-2006)
Tuition and fees: $3,330.
Per-credit charge: $100.

FINANCIAL AID PICTURE
Students with need: Need-based aid available for full-time and part-time students.
Students without need: This college only awards aid to students with need.

FINANCIAL AID PROCEDURES
Forms required: FAFSA.

CONTACT
Vicki Radke, Controller
PO Box 180, Cass Lake, MN 56633
(218) 335-4200

Macalester College
St. Paul, Minnesota
www.macalester.edu Federal Code: 002358
 CSS Code: 6390

4-year private liberal arts college in large city, affiliated with Presbyterian Church (USA).
Enrollment: 1,843 undergrads, 1% part-time. 491 full-time freshmen.
Selectivity: Admits less than 50% of applicants.

BASIC COSTS (2006-2007)
Tuition and fees: $31,038.
Per-credit charge: $965.
Room and board: $7,982.

FINANCIAL AID PICTURE (2005-2006)
Students with need: Out of 377 full-time freshmen who applied for aid, 348 were judged to have need. Of these, 348 received aid, and 348 had their full need met. Average financial aid package met 100% of need; average scholarship/grant was $20,455; average loan was $2,896. For part-time students, average financial aid package was $13,291.
Students without need: 30 full-time freshmen who did not demonstrate need for aid received scholarships/grants; average award was $3,806. No-need awards available for academics, minority status.
Scholarships offered: National Merit Scholarships; $5,000; to National Merit Finalists whose first choice college is Macalester and who are offered admission. DeWitt Wallace Distinguished Scholarships; minimum $3,000; open to National Merit semifinalists, commended students, and finalists not awarded National Merit Scholarship. DeWitt Wallace Scholarships; minimum $3,000; to selected middle-income students who need assistance to attend Macalester and whose academic records have shown them to be worthy of recognition. Catherine Lealtad Scholarships; minimum $3,000; to African American, Latino, and Native American students with strong high school records. Students who are National Achievement or National Hispanic Scholarship finalists and who have achieved a strong high school record will receive a minimum annual award of $5,000.
Cumulative student debt: 75% of graduating class had student loans; average debt was $14,889.
Additional info: College meets full need for all admitted students. Minnesota Self Loan available to qualified students.

FINANCIAL AID PROCEDURES
Forms required: FAFSA, CSS PROFILE.
Dates and Deadlines: Priority date 2/8; no closing date. Applicants notified by 4/1; must reply by 5/1 or within 1 week(s) of notification.
Transfers: Applicants notified by 5/15; must reply within 2 week(s) of notification.

484 Minnesota Macalester College

CONTACT
Brian Lindeman, Director of Financial Aid
1600 Grand Avenue, St. Paul, MN 55105-1899
(651) 696-6214

Martin Luther College
New Ulm, Minnesota
www.mlc-wels.edu   Federal Code: 002361

4-year private college of theology and education in large town, affiliated with Wisconsin Evangelical Lutheran Synod.
Enrollment: 815 undergrads, 2% part-time. 185 full-time freshmen.
Selectivity: Admits over 75% of applicants.

BASIC COSTS (2005-2006)
Tuition and fees: $8,925.
Per-credit charge: $175.
Room and board: $3,475.

FINANCIAL AID PICTURE (2004-2005)
Students with need: Out of 177 full-time freshmen who applied for aid, 144 were judged to have need. Of these, 144 received aid, and 55 had their full need met. Average financial aid package met 52% of need; average scholarship/grant was $3,900; average loan was $3,400. Need-based aid available for part-time students.
Students without need: 110 full-time freshmen who did not demonstrate need for aid received scholarships/grants; average award was $800. No-need awards available for academics, alumni affiliation, leadership, music/drama, religious affiliation.
Scholarships offered: Academic scholarship: $500, 3.75 GPA after 6 semesters of high school or 27 ACT. Presidential scholarship: $1,000, to student selected as high school valedictorian or ranked first in class after 7 semesters.
Cumulative student debt: 60% of graduating class had student loans; average debt was $12,357.

FINANCIAL AID PROCEDURES
Forms required: FAFSA, institutional form.
Dates and Deadlines: Closing date 4/15. Applicants notified by 4/1; must reply by 8/15.

CONTACT
Gene Slettedahl, Director of Financial Aid
1995 Luther Court, New Ulm, MN 56073-3965
(507) 354-8221

Mesabi Range Community and Technical College
Virginia, Minnesota
www.mr.mnscu.edu   Federal Code: 004009

2-year public community and technical college in large town.
Enrollment: 1,374 undergrads.
Selectivity: Open admission.

BASIC COSTS (2005-2006)
Tuition and fees: $4,028; out-of-state residents $4,928.
Per-credit charge: $120; out-of-state residents $150.
Room only: $2,750.

FINANCIAL AID PICTURE
Students with need: Need-based aid available for full-time and part-time students. Work study available nights, weekends, and for part-time students.
Students without need: No-need awards available for state/district residency.

FINANCIAL AID PROCEDURES
Forms required: FAFSA, institutional form.
Dates and Deadlines: Priority date 4/22; no closing date. Applicants notified on a rolling basis starting 5/1; must reply within 2 week(s) of notification.

CONTACT
George Walters, Director of Financial Aid
1001 Chestnut Street West, Virginia, MN 55792-3448
(218) 741-3095

Metropolitan State University
St. Paul, Minnesota
www.metrostate.edu   Federal Code: 010374

4-year public university in very large city.
Enrollment: 5,452 undergrads, 64% part-time. 58 full-time freshmen.
Selectivity: Admits over 75% of applicants.

BASIC COSTS (2005-2006)
Tuition and fees: $4,682; out-of-state residents $9,111.
Per-credit charge: $148; out-of-state residents $295.

FINANCIAL AID PICTURE (2004-2005)
Students with need: Out of 49 full-time freshmen who applied for aid, 46 were judged to have need. Of these, 44 received aid, and 1 had their full need met. Average financial aid package met 36% of need; average scholarship/grant was $2,013; average loan was $2,564. For part-time students, average financial aid package was $5,278.
Students without need: No-need awards available for academics, leadership, minority status, state/district residency.

FINANCIAL AID PROCEDURES
Forms required: FAFSA.
Dates and Deadlines: Priority date 5/1; no closing date. Applicants notified on a rolling basis starting 5/1; must reply within 2 week(s) of notification.

CONTACT
Robert Bode, Director of Financial Aid
700 East Seventh Street, St. Paul, MN 55106-5000
(651) 793-1414

Minneapolis College of Art and Design
Minneapolis, Minnesota
www.mcad.edu   Federal Code: 002365

4-year private visual arts college in very large city.
Enrollment: 656 undergrads, 5% part-time. 124 full-time freshmen.
Selectivity: Admits over 75% of applicants.

BASIC COSTS (2005-2006)
Tuition and fees: $25,040.
Per-credit charge: $827.
Room and board: $4,290.

FINANCIAL AID PICTURE (2004-2005)
Students with need: Out of 108 full-time freshmen who applied for aid, 92 were judged to have need. Of these, 91 received aid, and 9 had their full need met. Average financial aid package met 49% of need; average scholarship/grant was $7,922; average loan was $2,674. For part-time students, average financial aid package was $12,704.
Students without need: 17 full-time freshmen who did not demonstrate need for aid received scholarships/grants; average award was $12,913. No-need awards available for academics, alumni affiliation, art.
Scholarships offered: Admissions Merit Scholarships; $6,000-$12,000; based on admissions file. Students admitted to the college by February 15 automatically entered into scholarship competition.

Cumulative student debt: 91% of graduating class had student loans; average debt was $37,196.

FINANCIAL AID PROCEDURES
Forms required: FAFSA.
Dates and Deadlines: Priority date 3/15; no closing date. Applicants notified on a rolling basis starting 4/1; must reply by 5/1 or within 2 week(s) of notification.

CONTACT
Laura Link, Director, Financial Aid Office
2501 Stevens Avenue South, Minneapolis, MN 55404
(612) 874-8782

Minneapolis Community and Technical College
Minneapolis, Minnesota
www.minneapolis.edu   Federal Code: 002362

2-year public community and technical college in large city.
Enrollment: 7,546 undergrads.
Selectivity: Open admission; but selective for some programs.

BASIC COSTS (2005-2006)
Tuition and fees: $4,028; out-of-state residents $7,694.
Per-credit charge: $122; out-of-state residents $244.

FINANCIAL AID PICTURE (2004-2005)
Students with need: 38% of average financial aid package awarded as scholarships/grants, 62% awarded as loans/jobs. Need-based aid available for part-time students. Work study available nights, weekends, and for part-time students.
Students without need: This college only awards aid to students with need.

FINANCIAL AID PROCEDURES
Forms required: FAFSA.
Dates and Deadlines: Priority date 6/1; no closing date. Applicants notified on a rolling basis starting 7/15; must reply within 2 week(s) of notification.

CONTACT
Angela Christiansen, Director of Financial Aid
1501 Hennepin Avenue, Minneapolis, MN 55403-1779
(612) 659-6240

Minnesota School of Business
Richfield, Minnesota
www.msbcollege.edu   Federal Code: 017145

4-year for-profit business and technical college in very large city.
Enrollment: 941 undergrads, 54% part-time. 51 full-time freshmen.

BASIC COSTS (2006-2007)
Tuition and fees: $15,800.
Per-credit charge: $350.

FINANCIAL AID PICTURE (2004-2005)
Students with need: Out of 31 full-time freshmen who applied for aid, 28 were judged to have need. Of these, 22 received aid. Average financial aid package met 5% of need; average scholarship/grant was $395; average loan was $721. For part-time students, average financial aid package was $3,047.

FINANCIAL AID PROCEDURES
Forms required: FAFSA, state aid form, institutional form.
Dates and Deadlines: No deadline. Applicants notified on a rolling basis starting 7/1; must reply within 2 week(s) of notification.

CONTACT
Tim Jacobson, Financial Aid Director
1401 West 76 Street, Suite 500, Richfield, MN 55423
(612) 861-2000

Minnesota School of Business: Brooklyn Center
Brooklyn Center, Minnesota
www.msbcollege.edu   Federal Code: 004646

2-year for-profit business college in large town.
Enrollment: 600 undergrads.

BASIC COSTS (2005-2006)
Tuition and fees: $14,900.
Per-credit charge: $330.

FINANCIAL AID PICTURE
Students with need: Need-based aid available for full-time and part-time students.
Students without need: This college only awards aid to students with need.

FINANCIAL AID PROCEDURES
Forms required: FAFSA.

CONTACT
Thomas Hensch, Director, Financial Aid
5910 Shingle Creek Parkway, Brooklyn Center, MN 55430
(763) 566-7777

Minnesota State College - Southeast Technical
Winona, Minnesota
www.southeastmn.edu   Federal Code: 002393

2-year public technical college in large town.
Enrollment: 1,702 undergrads, 34% part-time. 418 full-time freshmen.
Selectivity: Open admission.

BASIC COSTS (2005-2006)
Tuition and fees: $4,055; out-of-state residents $7,753.
Per-credit charge: $123; out-of-state residents $247.
Additional info: Various reciprocity agreements with neighboring states provide tuition reduction to some out-of-state students.

FINANCIAL AID PICTURE (2005-2006)
Students with need: Average financial aid package met 60% of need; average scholarship/grant was $4,050; average loan was $2,625. Need-based aid available for part-time students.
Students without need: No-need awards available for academics, state/district residency.
Scholarships offered: Rose Tandeski Memorial Scholarship; $2,500; based on submission of autobiography; number awarded varies annually.
Cumulative student debt: 90% of graduating class had student loans; average debt was $6,625.

FINANCIAL AID PROCEDURES
Forms required: FAFSA, state aid form, institutional form.
Dates and Deadlines: No deadline. Applicants notified on a rolling basis; must reply within 3 week(s) of notification.
Transfers: Priority date 5/15; closing date 6/30. Applicants notified on a rolling basis. Mid-year transfer application forms must be accompanied by financial aid transcript.

CONTACT
Anne Dahlen, Director of Financial Aid
1250 Homer Road, Winona, MN 55987-0409
(507) 453-2710

Minnesota State Community and Technical College - Fergus Falls
Fergus Falls, Minnesota
www.minnesota.edu   Federal Code: 002352

2-year public community and technical college in large town.
Enrollment: 4,734 undergrads, 26% part-time. 1,587 full-time freshmen.
Selectivity: Open admission.

BASIC COSTS (2005-2006)
Tuition and fees: $4,364; out-of-state residents $8,201.
Per-credit charge: $128; out-of-state residents $256.
Room and board: $2,750.
Additional info: Various reciprocity agreements provide tuition reduction to some out-of-state students. Tuition/fee waivers available for adults.

FINANCIAL AID PICTURE
Students with need: Need-based aid available for full-time and part-time students. Work study available nights, weekends, and for part-time students.
Scholarships offered: Academic and leadership scholarships; $400-$1,000 each; available to 1st and 2nd year students; over 150 awarded annually.

FINANCIAL AID PROCEDURES
Forms required: FAFSA, institutional form.
Dates and Deadlines: Priority date 6/1; no closing date. Applicants notified on a rolling basis starting 7/1.
Transfers: No deadline. Applicants notified on a rolling basis.

CONTACT
Tom Whelihan, Director of Financial Aid
1414 College Way, Fergus Falls, MN 56537-1000
(218) 736-1534

Minnesota State University: Mankato
Mankato, Minnesota
www.mnsu.edu   Federal Code: 002360

4-year public university in large town.
Enrollment: 12,241 undergrads, 8% part-time. 2,232 full-time freshmen.
Selectivity: Admits over 75% of applicants.

BASIC COSTS (2005-2006)
Tuition and fees: $5,402; out-of-state residents $10,750.
Per-credit charge: $187; out-of-state residents $400.
Room and board: $4,770.

FINANCIAL AID PICTURE (2005-2006)
Students with need: Out of 1,831 full-time freshmen who applied for aid, 1,117 were judged to have need. Of these, 1,098 received aid, and 495 had their full need met. Average financial aid package met 77% of need; average scholarship/grant was $3,750; average loan was $3,280. For part-time students, average financial aid package was $5,046.
Students without need: This college only awards aid to students with need.
Scholarships offered: 73 full-time freshmen received athletic scholarships; average amount $4,773.
Cumulative student debt: 75% of graduating class had student loans; average debt was $16,500.

FINANCIAL AID PROCEDURES
Forms required: FAFSA.
Dates and Deadlines: Priority date 3/15; no closing date. Applicants notified on a rolling basis starting 3/30; must reply within 2 week(s) of notification.

CONTACT
Sandra Loerts, Director of Financial Aid
122 Taylor Center, Mankato, MN 56001
(507) 389-1185

Minnesota State University: Moorhead
Moorhead, Minnesota
www.mnstate.edu   Federal Code: 002367

4-year public university in small city.
Enrollment: 6,881 undergrads, 11% part-time. 1,112 full-time freshmen.

BASIC COSTS (2005-2006)
Tuition and fees: $5,225.
Per-credit charge: $149.
Room and board: $4,974.
Additional info: Out-of-state students pay same rate as in-state.

FINANCIAL AID PICTURE
Students with need: Need-based aid available for full-time and part-time students.
Students without need: No-need awards available for academics, athletics, state/district residency.

FINANCIAL AID PROCEDURES
Forms required: FAFSA, institutional form.
Dates and Deadlines: Priority date 3/1; no closing date. Applicants notified on a rolling basis starting 5/1; must reply within 2 week(s) of notification.

CONTACT
Carolyn Zehren, Director of Financial Aid and Scholarships
Owens Hall, Moorhead, MN 56563
(218) 236-2251

Minnesota West Community and Technical College: Worthington Campus
Worthington, Minnesota
www.mnwest.mnscu.edu   Federal Code: 005263

2-year public community and technical college in large town.
Enrollment: 2,180 full-time undergrads.
Selectivity: Open admission.

BASIC COSTS (2005-2006)
Tuition and fees: $4,174; out-of-state residents $8,001.
Per-credit charge: $128; out-of-state residents $255.
Additional info: Tuition is the same for in-state and out-of-state students.

FINANCIAL AID PICTURE
Students with need: Need-based aid available for full-time and part-time students.

FINANCIAL AID PROCEDURES
Forms required: FAFSA.
Dates and Deadlines: Priority date 6/1; no closing date. Applicants notified on a rolling basis starting 7/1; must reply within 2 week(s) of notification.

CONTACT
Faith Drent, Financial Aid Officer
1450 Collegeway, Worthington, MN 56187
(507) 372-2107

National American University: St. Paul
Bloomington, Minnesota
www.national.edu Federal Code: E00640

4-year for-profit branch campus and business college in very large city.
Enrollment: 270 undergrads.
Selectivity: Open admission.

BASIC COSTS (2005-2006)
Tuition and fees: $13,365.
Per-credit charge: $290.
Additional info: Online courses: $225 per-credit-hour.

FINANCIAL AID PICTURE
Students with need: Need-based aid available for full-time and part-time students. Work study available nights, weekends, and for part-time students.
Students without need: No-need awards available for academics.

FINANCIAL AID PROCEDURES
Forms required: FAFSA.
Dates and Deadlines: Priority date 8/21; no closing date. Applicants notified on a rolling basis.

CONTACT
Financial Aid Coordinator
Mall of America West 112 West Market, Bloomington, MN 55425
(952) 883-0439

Normandale Community College
Bloomington, Minnesota
www.normandale.edu Federal Code: 007954

2-year public community college in very large city.
Enrollment: 8,304 undergrads, 50% part-time.
Selectivity: Open admission; but selective for some programs.

BASIC COSTS (2005-2006)
Tuition and fees: $3,976; out-of-state residents $7,589.
Per-credit charge: $120; out-of-state residents $241.
Additional info: Various reciprocity agreements with some neighboring states provide tuition reduction to out-of-state students.

FINANCIAL AID PICTURE (2004-2005)
Students with need: 57% of average financial aid package awarded as scholarships/grants, 43% awarded as loans/jobs. Need-based aid available for part-time students. Work study available nights, weekends, and for part-time students.

FINANCIAL AID PROCEDURES
Forms required: FAFSA.
Dates and Deadlines: Priority date 4/1; no closing date. Applicants notified on a rolling basis starting 4/15.

CONTACT
Catherine Breuer, Associate Dean for Financial Aid and Scholarships
9700 France Avenue South, Bloomington, MN 55431
(952) 487-8202

North Central University
Minneapolis, Minnesota
www.northcentral.edu Federal Code: 002369

4-year private university and Bible college in large city, affiliated with Assemblies of God.
Enrollment: 1,217 undergrads, 7% part-time. 236 full-time freshmen.
Selectivity: Admits over 75% of applicants.

BASIC COSTS (2005-2006)
Tuition and fees: $12,166.
Per-credit charge: $376.
Room and board: $4,480.

FINANCIAL AID PICTURE (2004-2005)
Students with need: 62% of average financial aid package awarded as scholarships/grants, 38% awarded as loans/jobs. Need-based aid available for part-time students.
Students without need: No-need awards available for academics, music/drama.
Scholarships offered: Christian leadership scholarship; $6,000 per year; renewable up to 4 years; GPA 2.5 or above, ministry and community involvement.
Cumulative student debt: 84% of graduating class had student loans; average debt was $22,597.

FINANCIAL AID PROCEDURES
Forms required: FAFSA, institutional form.
Dates and Deadlines: Priority date 4/1; closing date 5/1. Applicants notified on a rolling basis starting 3/15; must reply within 2 week(s) of notification.
Transfers: No deadline.

CONTACT
Donna Jager, Director of Financial Aid
910 Elliot Avenue, Minneapolis, MN 55404
(800) 289-4488 ext. 289

Northland Community & Technical College
Thief River Falls, Minnesota
www.northlandcollege.edu Federal Code: 002385

2-year public community and technical college in small town.
Enrollment: 2,017 undergrads.
Selectivity: Open admission.

BASIC COSTS (2005-2006)
Tuition and fees: $4,209.
Per-credit charge: $128.
Additional info: Tuition is the same for both in-state and out-of-state students.

FINANCIAL AID PICTURE (2005-2006)
Students with need: 43% of average financial aid package awarded as scholarships/grants, 57% awarded as loans/jobs. Need-based aid available for part-time students. Work study available nights.
Students without need: No-need awards available for academics.

FINANCIAL AID PROCEDURES
Forms required: FAFSA.
Dates and Deadlines: Priority date 5/1; no closing date. Applicants notified on a rolling basis starting 5/15.

CONTACT
Donna Quam, Financial Aid Director
1101 Highway 1 East, Thief River Falls, MN 56701
(218) 347-6239

Northwest Technical College
Bemidji, Minnesota
www.ntcmn.edu Federal Code: 005759

2-year public technical college in large town.
Enrollment: 833 undergrads, 30% part-time. 197 full-time freshmen.
Selectivity: Open admission.

BASIC COSTS (2005-2006)
Tuition and fees: $4,125; out-of-state residents $4,125.
Per-credit charge: $129; out-of-state residents $129.
Additional info: Residence halls available at Bemidji State University.

FINANCIAL AID PICTURE (2005-2006)
Students with need: 46% of average financial aid package awarded as scholarships/grants, 54% awarded as loans/jobs. Need-based aid available for part-time students. Work study available nights.
Students without need: This college only awards aid to students with need.

FINANCIAL AID PROCEDURES
Forms required: FAFSA, institutional form.
Dates and Deadlines: Priority date 7/1; no closing date. Applicants notified on a rolling basis.
Transfers: Closing date 8/24.

CONTACT
Paul Lindseth, Director of Financial Aid
905 Grant Avenue Southeast, Bemidji, MN 56601-4907
(218) 333-6648

Northwest Technical Institute
Eden Prairie, Minnesota
www.nti.edu   Federal Code: 008267

2-year for-profit technical college in small city.
Enrollment: 85 undergrads.

BASIC COSTS (2005-2006)
Tuition and fees: $14,185.
Per-credit charge: $443.
Additional info: Tuition at time of enrollment locked for 2 years.

FINANCIAL AID PICTURE
Students with need: Need-based aid available for full-time and part-time students.

FINANCIAL AID PROCEDURES
Forms required: FAFSA, institutional form.
Dates and Deadlines: No deadline. Applicants notified on a rolling basis; must reply within 2 week(s) of notification.

CONTACT
Michael Kotchevar, President
11995 Singletree Lane, Eden Prairie, MN 55344-5351
(952) 944-0080 ext. 101

Northwestern College
Saint Paul, Minnesota
www.nwc.edu   Federal Code: 002371

4-year private Bible and liberal arts college in large city, affiliated with nondenominational tradition.
Enrollment: 1,760 undergrads, 2% part-time. 407 full-time freshmen.
Selectivity: Admits over 75% of applicants.

BASIC COSTS (2006-2007)
Tuition and fees: $19,990.
Per-credit charge: $850.
Room and board: $6,460.
Additional info: Tuition/fee waivers available for minority students.

FINANCIAL AID PICTURE (2004-2005)
Students with need: Out of 403 full-time freshmen who applied for aid, 341 were judged to have need. Of these, 338 received aid, and 32 had their full need met. Average financial aid package met 68% of need; average scholarship/grant was $10,539; average loan was $3,569. For part-time students, average financial aid package was $9,159.
Students without need: 57 full-time freshmen who did not demonstrate need for aid received scholarships/grants; average award was $4,067. No-need awards available for academics, alumni affiliation, leadership, music/drama.
Scholarships offered: Eagle Scholars Program; $11,500 per year; ACT score of 30 or SAT score of 1320 (exclusive of writing); up to 20 awarded yearly.
Cumulative student debt: 62% of graduating class had student loans; average debt was $16,656.

FINANCIAL AID PROCEDURES
Forms required: FAFSA, state aid form, institutional form.
Dates and Deadlines: Priority date 3/1; closing date 6/1. Applicants notified on a rolling basis starting 3/1; must reply within 2 week(s) of notification.

CONTACT
Richard Blatchley, Director of Financial Aid
3003 Snelling Avenue North, Saint Paul, MN 55113
(651) 631-5212

Oak Hills Christian College
Bemidji, Minnesota
www.oakhills.edu   Federal Code: 016116

4-year private Bible college in large town, affiliated with interdenominational tradition.
Enrollment: 165 undergrads, 8% part-time. 41 full-time freshmen.
Selectivity: Admits 50 to 75% of applicants.

BASIC COSTS (2006-2007)
Tuition and fees: $11,940.
Room and board: $4,450.

FINANCIAL AID PICTURE (2004-2005)
Students with need: Out of 41 full-time freshmen who applied for aid, 39 were judged to have need. Of these, 39 received aid. Average financial aid package met 59% of need; average scholarship/grant was $6,080; average loan was $2,436. For part-time students, average financial aid package was $4,910.
Students without need: 2 full-time freshmen who did not demonstrate need for aid received scholarships/grants; average award was $3,208. No-need awards available for academics, alumni affiliation.
Cumulative student debt: 100% of graduating class had student loans; average debt was $28,455.

FINANCIAL AID PROCEDURES
Forms required: FAFSA, institutional form.
Dates and Deadlines: No deadline. Applicants notified on a rolling basis starting 3/1.

CONTACT
Dan Hovestol, Financial Aid Director
1600 Oak Hills Road, SW, Bemidji, MN 56601
(218) 751-8671 ext. 1220

Pine Technical College
Pine City, Minnesota
www.pinetech.edu   Federal Code: 005535

2-year public technical college in small town.
Enrollment: 456 undergrads, 53% part-time. 46 full-time freshmen.

Selectivity: Open admission; but selective for some programs.

BASIC COSTS (2005-2006)
Tuition and fees: $3,726; out-of-state residents $7,026.
Per-credit charge: $110; out-of-state residents $220.
Additional info: Various reciprocity agreements with some neighboring states provide tuition reduction to out-of-state students.

FINANCIAL AID PICTURE (2004-2005)
Students with need: 63% of average financial aid package awarded as scholarships/grants, 37% awarded as loans/jobs. Need-based aid available for part-time students.
Students without need: No-need awards available for academics, state/district residency.

FINANCIAL AID PROCEDURES
Forms required: FAFSA, institutional form.
Dates and Deadlines: Priority date 5/5; no closing date. Applicants notified on a rolling basis starting 6/5.

CONTACT
Susan Pixley, Financial Aid Director
900 Fourth Street SE, Pine City, MN 55063
(320) 629-5100 ext. 161

Rainy River Community College
International Falls, Minnesota
www.rrcc.mnscu.edu   Federal Code: 006775

2-year public community and technical college in small town.
Enrollment: 390 undergrads.
Selectivity: Open admission.

BASIC COSTS (2005-2006)
Tuition and fees: $4,178; out-of-state residents $5,096.
Per-credit charge: $122; out-of-state residents $153.
Additional info: Tuition/fee waivers available for unemployed or children of unemployed.

FINANCIAL AID PICTURE
Students with need: Need-based aid available for full-time and part-time students. Work study available nights, weekends, and for part-time students.
Students without need: No-need awards available for academics, alumni affiliation, minority status, state/district residency.
Additional info: Many scholarship and employment opportunities for applicants showing little or no need.

FINANCIAL AID PROCEDURES
Forms required: FAFSA, institutional form.
Dates and Deadlines: Priority date 6/1; no closing date. Applicants notified on a rolling basis starting 5/1; must reply within 3 week(s) of notification.

CONTACT
Scott Riley, Director of Financial Aid
1501 Highway 71, International Falls, MN 56649
(218) 285-7722

Rasmussen College-Eagan
Eagan, Minnesota
www.rasmussen.edu   Federal Code: 004648

2-year for-profit business college in small city.
Enrollment: 475 undergrads.
Selectivity: Open admission.

BASIC COSTS (2005-2006)
Additional info: Regular courses: $275/credit; networking classes: $370/credit; child care classes: $175/credit.

FINANCIAL AID PICTURE
Students with need: Need-based aid available for full-time and part-time students.
Students without need: This college only awards aid to students with need.

FINANCIAL AID PROCEDURES
Forms required: FAFSA, institutional form.
Dates and Deadlines: No deadline. Applicants notified on a rolling basis.

CONTACT
Brian Arndt, Financial Aid Director
3500 Federal Drive, Eagan, MN 55122
(651) 687-9009

Rasmussen College-Minnetonka
Minnetonka, Minnesota
www.rasmussen.edu   Federal Code: 011686

2-year for-profit business and junior college in very large city.
Enrollment: 336 undergrads.
Selectivity: Open admission.

BASIC COSTS (2005-2006)
Additional info: Regular courses: $275/credit; networking classes: $370/credit; child care classes: $175/credit. Tuition at time of enrollment locked for 2 years.

FINANCIAL AID PICTURE
Students with need: Need-based aid available for full-time and part-time students.

FINANCIAL AID PROCEDURES
Forms required: FAFSA, state aid form, institutional form.
Dates and Deadlines: No deadline. Applicants notified on a rolling basis.

CONTACT
Daniel Vega, Financial Aid Director
12450 Wayzata Boulevard, Minnetonka, MN 55305-9845
(952) 545-2000

Rasmussen College-St. Cloud
St. Cloud, Minnesota
www.rasmussen.edu   Federal Code: 008694

2-year for-profit community and junior college in small city.
Enrollment: 456 undergrads.
Selectivity: Open admission.

BASIC COSTS (2005-2006)
Additional info: Regular courses: $275/credit; networking classes: $370/credit; child care classes: $175/credit.

FINANCIAL AID PICTURE (2005-2006)
Students with need: 34% of average financial aid package awarded as scholarships/grants, 66% awarded as loans/jobs. Need-based aid available for part-time students. Work study available nights, weekends, and for part-time students.
Students without need: No-need awards available for academics.

FINANCIAL AID PROCEDURES
Forms required: FAFSA, institutional form.
Dates and Deadlines: No deadline. Applicants notified on a rolling basis starting 1/4.

CONTACT
Carol Dockendorf, Financial Aid Officer
226 Park Avenue South, St. Cloud, MN 56301-3713
(320) 251-5600

Ridgewater College
Willmar, Minnesota
www.ridgewater.edu   Federal Code: 005252

2-year public community and technical college in large town.
Enrollment: 3,617 undergrads. 1,054 full-time freshmen.
Selectivity: Open admission; but selective for some programs.

BASIC COSTS (2005-2006)
Tuition and fees: $4,134; out-of-state residents $4,134.
Per-credit charge: $123; out-of-state residents $123.
Additional info: Some courses may carry higher per credit hour charge. Reciprocity agreements for in-state tuition rates with some neighboring states. Tuition/fee waivers available for adults.

FINANCIAL AID PICTURE (2005-2006)
Students with need: 54% of average financial aid package awarded as scholarships/grants, 46% awarded as loans/jobs. Need-based aid available for part-time students.
Additional info: Special funds are available for adult transfer students returning or continuing education after a 7-year absence from academic training. ALLISS grants provide reimbursement for one class, up to five credits for one semester.

FINANCIAL AID PROCEDURES
Forms required: FAFSA, institutional form.
Dates and Deadlines: No deadline. Applicants notified on a rolling basis.

CONTACT
Jim Rice, Director of Financial Aid
2101 15th Avenue NW, Willmar, MN 56201
(320) 231-2921

Riverland Community College
Austin, Minnesota
www.riverland.cc.mn.us   Federal Code: 002335

2-year public community and technical college in large town.
Enrollment: 3,563 undergrads, 58% part-time. 700 full-time freshmen.
Selectivity: Open admission; but selective for some programs.

BASIC COSTS (2005-2006)
Tuition and fees: $4,109; out-of-state residents $7,968.
Per-credit charge: $121; out-of-state residents $121.
Additional info: Some courses carry a higher per-credit-hour charge. Various reciprocity agreements with some neighboring states provide tuition reduction to out-of-state students.

FINANCIAL AID PICTURE (2004-2005)
Students with need: For part-time students, average financial aid package was $2,643.
Students without need: This college only awards aid to students with need.
Cumulative student debt: 37% of graduating class had student loans; average debt was $2,300.
Additional info: One class tuition-free for Minnesota residents over 25 who have not attended college for at least 7 years.

FINANCIAL AID PROCEDURES
Forms required: FAFSA.
Dates and Deadlines: Priority date 5/15; no closing date. Applicants notified on a rolling basis; must reply within 5 week(s) of notification.

CONTACT
Judy Robeck, Financial Aid Director
1900 Eighth Avenue Northwest, Austin, MN 55912-1407
(507) 433-0511

St. Cloud State University
St. Cloud, Minnesota
www.stcloudstate.edu   Federal Code: 002377

4-year public university in small city.
Enrollment: 13,120 undergrads, 13% part-time. 2,115 full-time freshmen.
Selectivity: Admits over 75% of applicants.

BASIC COSTS (2005-2006)
Tuition and fees: $5,322; out-of-state residents $10,894.
Per-credit charge: $159; out-of-state residents $344.
Room and board: $4,688.

FINANCIAL AID PICTURE (2005-2006)
Students with need: Out of 1,545 full-time freshmen who applied for aid, 1,046 were judged to have need. Of these, 1,046 received aid, and 744 had their full need met. Average financial aid package met 94% of need; average scholarship/grant was $3,971; average loan was $3,874. For part-time students, average financial aid package was $8,102.
Students without need: 218 full-time freshmen who did not demonstrate need for aid received scholarships/grants; average award was $1,639. No-need awards available for academics, art, athletics, leadership, music/drama.
Scholarships offered: 43 full-time freshmen received athletic scholarships; average amount $3,339.
Cumulative student debt: 52% of graduating class had student loans; average debt was $20,431.

FINANCIAL AID PROCEDURES
Forms required: FAFSA, institutional form.
Dates and Deadlines: Closing date 6/30. Applicants notified on a rolling basis starting 6/3.

CONTACT
Frank Loncorich, Financial Aid Director
720 Fourth Avenue South, St. Cloud, MN 56301-4498
(320) 308-2244

St. Cloud Technical College
St. Cloud, Minnesota
www.sctc.edu   Federal Code: 005534

2-year public technical college in small city.
Enrollment: 3,017 undergrads, 29% part-time. 716 full-time freshmen.
Selectivity: Open admission; but selective for some programs.

BASIC COSTS (2005-2006)
Tuition and fees: $3,968; out-of-state residents $7,646.
Per-credit charge: $123; out-of-state residents $245.
Additional info: Higher per-credit-hour charges may apply to some programs. Various reciprocity agreements with some neighboring states provide tuition reduction to out-of-state students.

FINANCIAL AID PICTURE (2004-2005)
Students with need: 45% of average financial aid package awarded as scholarships/grants, 55% awarded as loans/jobs. Need-based aid available for part-time students. Work study available nights, weekends, and for part-time students.

Students without need: No-need awards available for academics, leadership.

FINANCIAL AID PROCEDURES
Forms required: FAFSA, institutional form.
Dates and Deadlines: Priority date 5/15; no closing date. Applicants notified on a rolling basis starting 6/1.

CONTACT
Anita Baugh, Financial Aid Director
1540 Northway Drive, St. Cloud, MN 56303
(320) 308-5961

St. John's University
Collegeville, Minnesota
www.csbsju.edu   Federal Code: 002379

4-year private university and liberal arts college for men in rural community, affiliated with Roman Catholic Church.
Enrollment: 1,842 undergrads. 447 full-time freshmen.
Selectivity: Admits over 75% of applicants.

BASIC COSTS (2006-2007)
Tuition and fees: $24,924.
Per-credit charge: $1,020.
Room and board: $6,496.

FINANCIAL AID PICTURE (2005-2006)
Students with need: Out of 339 full-time freshmen who applied for aid, 271 were judged to have need. Of these, 271 received aid, and 135 had their full need met. Average financial aid package met 92% of need; average scholarship/grant was $14,142; average loan was $3,875. Need-based aid available for part-time students.
Students without need: 160 full-time freshmen who did not demonstrate need for aid received scholarships/grants; average award was $8,584. No-need awards available for academics, art, leadership, minority status, music/drama, ROTC.
Scholarships offered: Regents/Trustees Scholarship; $12,500; minimum GPA of 3.6 and minimum ACT of 30 or minimum SAT of 1320 (exclusive of writing); demonstrated leadership and service; faculty interview. President's Scholarships; $7,000-$10,500; GPA, high school rank, ACT/SAT scores, leadership and service. Dean's Scholarships; $3,000-$6,500; GPA, high school rank, ACT/SAT scores, leadership and service. Art; up to $2,000; portfolio review. Music; up to $2,000; portfolio review and audition. Theater; up to $2,000; interview. All based on excellence in subject area. Diversity Leadership Scholarship; up to $5,000; demonstrated leadership and service in the area of cultural and ethnic diversity, essay on specified topic required.
Cumulative student debt: 63% of graduating class had student loans; average debt was $24,663.

FINANCIAL AID PROCEDURES
Forms required: FAFSA, institutional form.
Dates and Deadlines: Priority date 3/15; no closing date. Applicants notified on a rolling basis starting 3/15; must reply by 5/1 or within 3 week(s) of notification.

CONTACT
Jane Haugen, Executive Director of Financial Aid
PO Box 7155, Collegeville, MN 56321-7155
(320) 363-3664

St. Mary's University of Minnesota
Winona, Minnesota
www.smumn.edu   Federal Code: 002380

4-year private university in large town, affiliated with Roman Catholic Church.
Enrollment: 1,635 undergrads, 22% part-time. 311 full-time freshmen.
Selectivity: Admits over 75% of applicants.

BASIC COSTS (2005-2006)
Tuition and fees: $19,149.
Per-credit charge: $620.
Room and board: $5,720.

FINANCIAL AID PICTURE (2005-2006)
Students with need: Out of 250 full-time freshmen who applied for aid, 213 were judged to have need. Of these, 213 received aid, and 130 had their full need met. Average financial aid package met 94% of need; average scholarship/grant was $8,350; average loan was $4,375. Need-based aid available for part-time students.
Students without need: No-need awards available for academics, art, leadership, music/drama.
Cumulative student debt: 73% of graduating class had student loans; average debt was $26,633.

FINANCIAL AID PROCEDURES
Forms required: FAFSA.
Dates and Deadlines: Priority date 3/15; no closing date. Applicants notified on a rolling basis starting 3/5; must reply within 3 week(s) of notification.

CONTACT
Jayne Wobig, Director of Financial Aid
700 Terrace Heights, #2, Winona, MN 55987-1399
(507) 457-1437

St. Olaf College
Northfield, Minnesota
www.stolaf.edu   Federal Code: 002382
                        CSS Code: 6638

4-year private liberal arts college in large town, affiliated with Evangelical Lutheran Church in America.
Enrollment: 3,007 undergrads. 764 full-time freshmen.
Selectivity: Admits 50 to 75% of applicants.

BASIC COSTS (2006-2007)
Tuition and fees: $28,200.
Per-credit charge: $880.
Room and board: $7,400.
Additional info: Tuition/fee waivers available for adults.

FINANCIAL AID PICTURE (2005-2006)
Students with need: Out of 577 full-time freshmen who applied for aid, 475 were judged to have need. Of these, 475 received aid, and 475 had their full need met. Average financial aid package met 100% of need; average scholarship/grant was $15,103; average loan was $4,343.
Students without need: 129 full-time freshmen who did not demonstrate need for aid received scholarships/grants; average award was $7,801. No-need awards available for academics, leadership, music/drama.
Scholarships offered: Regents Academic Awards; $10,000. Presidential Academic Scholarship; $6,000. National Merit Scholarships; $7,500. National Hispanic Scholar/National Achievement Scholarships; $7,500. TRiO Scholarship; $2,000 - $6,000. Leadership in Community and Church award; $4,000. Music scholarships; $1,500 - $6,000. National Merit Commended; $1,500.00. All 4-year renewable; number awarded varies yearly.
Cumulative student debt: 65% of graduating class had student loans; average debt was $19,410.

Additional info: Limited number of music lesson fee waivers available for music majors, awarded on audition basis only.

FINANCIAL AID PROCEDURES
Forms required: FAFSA, CSS PROFILE.
Dates and Deadlines: Priority date 12/1; closing date 2/1. Applicants notified on a rolling basis starting 3/1; must reply by 5/1 or within 2 week(s) of notification.
Transfers: Applicants notified by 3/1; must reply by 5/1 or within 2 week(s) of notification.

CONTACT
Katharine Ruby, Director of Financial Aid
1520 St. Olaf Avenue, Northfield, MN 55057
(507) 646-3019

St. Paul College
Saint Paul, Minnesota
www.saintpaul.edu   Federal Code: 005533

2-year public community and technical college in large city.
Enrollment: 3,431 undergrads, 56% part-time. 1,277 full-time freshmen.
Selectivity: Open admission.

BASIC COSTS (2005-2006)
Tuition and fees: $3,791; out-of-state residents $7,283.
Per-credit charge: $116; out-of-state residents $233.
Additional info: Various reciprocity agreements with some neighboring states provide tuition reduction to out-of-state students.

FINANCIAL AID PICTURE (2004-2005)
Students with need: 60% of average financial aid package awarded as scholarships/grants, 40% awarded as loans/jobs. Need-based aid available for part-time students. Work study available nights.
Students without need: No-need awards available for leadership.

FINANCIAL AID PROCEDURES
Forms required: FAFSA.
Dates and Deadlines: No deadline. Applicants notified on a rolling basis starting 6/1.

CONTACT
Susan Prater, Financial Aid Director
235 Marshall Avenue, St. Paul, MN 55102-1800
(651) 846-1386

South Central College
North Mankato, Minnesota
www.southcentral.edu   Federal Code: 009891

2-year public technical college in large town.
Enrollment: 5,000 undergrads.
Selectivity: Open admission.

BASIC COSTS (2005-2006)
Tuition and fees: $3,818.
Per-credit charge: $114.
Additional info: Out-of-state students pay same rate as in-state students.

FINANCIAL AID PICTURE
Students with need: Need-based aid available for full-time and part-time students.

FINANCIAL AID PROCEDURES
Forms required: FAFSA, institutional form.
Dates and Deadlines: No deadline. Applicants notified on a rolling basis.

CONTACT
Jayne Dinse, Financial Aid Director
1920 Lee Boulevard, North Mankato, MN 56003
(507) 389-7200

Southwest Minnesota State University
Marshall, Minnesota
www.southwest.msus.edu   Federal Code: 002375

4-year public liberal arts and technical college in large town.
Enrollment: 2,640 undergrads, 13% part-time. 544 full-time freshmen.
Selectivity: Admits over 75% of applicants.

BASIC COSTS (2005-2006)
Tuition and fees: $5,855.
Per-credit charge: $162.
Room and board: $5,120.
Additional info: Participates in pilot project allowing one tuition rate for in-state and out-of-state.

FINANCIAL AID PICTURE (2005-2006)
Students with need: 62% of average financial aid package awarded as scholarships/grants, 38% awarded as loans/jobs. Need-based aid available for part-time students.
Students without need: No-need awards available for academics, art, athletics, leadership, minority status, music/drama, state/district residency.

FINANCIAL AID PROCEDURES
Forms required: FAFSA, institutional form.
Dates and Deadlines: Priority date 4/1; no closing date. Applicants notified on a rolling basis starting 5/15.

CONTACT
David Vikander, Director of Financial Aid
1501 State Street, Marshall, MN 56258-1598
(507) 537-7021

University of Minnesota: Crookston
Crookston, Minnesota
www.UMCrookston.edu   Federal Code: 004069

4-year public branch campus college in small town.
Enrollment: 1,053 undergrads, 19% part-time. 206 full-time freshmen.
Selectivity: Admits over 75% of applicants.

BASIC COSTS (2005-2006)
Tuition and fees: $8,119; out-of-state residents $8,119.
Per-credit charge: $195; out-of-state residents $195.
Room and board: $5,038.
Additional info: Laptop computer included in fees. Tuition/fee waivers available for minority students.

FINANCIAL AID PICTURE (2004-2005)
Students with need: Out of 179 full-time freshmen who applied for aid, 152 were judged to have need. Of these, 151 received aid, and 63 had their full need met. Average financial aid package met 80% of need; average scholarship/grant was $4,802; average loan was $5,917. For part-time students, average financial aid package was $5,306.
Students without need: 30 full-time freshmen who did not demonstrate need for aid received scholarships/grants; average award was $3,052. No-need awards available for academics, athletics, leadership, minority status, ROTC, state/district residency.
Cumulative student debt: 60% of graduating class had student loans; average debt was $14,521.
Additional info: Tuition guarantee plan available to all students who apply for it.

FINANCIAL AID PROCEDURES
Forms required: FAFSA.
Dates and Deadlines: Priority date 3/1; no closing date. Applicants notified on a rolling basis starting 3/15; must reply within 3 week(s) of notification.

CONTACT
Keith Knapp, Director of Financial Aid
2900 University Avenue, Crookston, MN 56716-5001
(218) 281-8569

University of Minnesota: Duluth
Duluth, Minnesota
www.d.umn.edu   Federal Code: 002388

4-year public university in small city.
Enrollment: 8,995 undergrads, 12% part-time. 2,136 full-time freshmen.
Selectivity: Admits over 75% of applicants.

BASIC COSTS (2005-2006)
Tuition and fees: $8,512; out-of-state residents $19,619.
Per-credit charge: $239; out-of-state residents $609.
Room and board: $5,544.

FINANCIAL AID PICTURE (2005-2006)
Students with need: Out of 1,722 full-time freshmen who applied for aid, 1,093 were judged to have need. Of these, 1,081 received aid, and 600 had their full need met. Average financial aid package met 60% of need; average scholarship/grant was $5,438; average loan was $2,811. For part-time students, average financial aid package was $5,973.
Students without need: 431 full-time freshmen who did not demonstrate need for aid received scholarships/grants; average award was $1,300. No-need awards available for academics, athletics, ROTC.
Scholarships offered: 38 full-time freshmen received athletic scholarships; average amount $4,793.
Cumulative student debt: 71% of graduating class had student loans; average debt was $20,205.

FINANCIAL AID PROCEDURES
Forms required: FAFSA.
Dates and Deadlines: Priority date 3/31; no closing date. Applicants notified on a rolling basis starting 3/1; must reply within 2 week(s) of notification.

CONTACT
Brenda Herzig, Director of Financial Aid
1117 University Drive, Duluth, MN 55812-3000
(218) 726-8000

University of Minnesota: Morris
Morris, Minnesota
www.morris.umn.edu   Federal Code: 002389

4-year public university and liberal arts college in small town.
Enrollment: 1,530 undergrads, 3% part-time. 355 full-time freshmen.
Selectivity: Admits over 75% of applicants.

BASIC COSTS (2005-2006)
Tuition and fees: $9,722; out-of-state residents $9,722.
Per-credit charge: $273.
Room and board: $5,750.
Additional info: Tuition is the same for all students, both in-state and out-of-state, except for Wisconsin students who pay a lower rate due to reciprocity agreement.

FINANCIAL AID PICTURE (2005-2006)
Students with need: Average financial aid package met 83% of [need]; average scholarship/grant was $6,613; average loan was $6,423. Need-b[ased aid] available for part-time students.
Students without need: No-need awards available for academics, alumni affiliation, leadership, minority status, music/drama.
Scholarships offered: Chancellor's Scholarship; $2,000/year for 4 years; top 5%. Dean's Scholarship; $1,500/year for 4 years; top 10%. Founder's Scholarship; $500/year for 4 years; top 20%. National Merit Scholarship; $4,000 scholarship over four years; 2.5 GPA. Presidential Scholarship; $3,000/year for 4 years; 60 awarded/ year. President's Outstanding Multi-Ethnic Scholarship; $1,000 to $3,000/year for four years.
Cumulative student debt: 75% of graduating class had student loans; average debt was $15,490.
Additional info: Land-grant program waiving tuition for Native Americans.

FINANCIAL AID PROCEDURES
Forms required: FAFSA.
Dates and Deadlines: Priority date 3/1; no closing date. Applicants notified on a rolling basis starting 3/1; must reply within 3 week(s) of notification.

CONTACT
Pam Engebretson, Director of Financial Aid
600 East 4th Street, Morris, MN 56267
(800) 992-8863

University of Minnesota: Twin Cities
Minneapolis, Minnesota
www.umn.edu/tc   Federal Code: 003969

4-year public university in very large city.
Enrollment: 28,957 undergrads, 10% part-time. 5,276 full-time freshmen.
Selectivity: Admits 50 to 75% of applicants.

BASIC COSTS (2005-2006)
Tuition and fees: $8,622; out-of-state residents $20,252.
Per-credit charge: $275; out-of-state residents $722.
Room and board: $6,722.

FINANCIAL AID PICTURE (2005-2006)
Students with need: Out of 4,095 full-time freshmen who applied for aid, 2,598 were judged to have need. Of these, 2,518 received aid, and 1,276 had their full need met. Average financial aid package met 85% of need; average scholarship/grant was $6,842; average loan was $6,058. For part-time students, average financial aid package was $7,351.
Students without need: 877 full-time freshmen who did not demonstrate need for aid received scholarships/grants; average award was $3,981. No-need awards available for academics, art, athletics, job skills, leadership, minority status, music/drama, ROTC, state/district residency.

FINANCIAL AID PROCEDURES
Forms required: FAFSA.
Dates and Deadlines: Priority date 1/15; no closing date. Applicants notified on a rolling basis starting 2/15.

CONTACT
Kris Wright, Director of Financial Aid
240 Williamson Hall, 231 Pillsbury Drive Southeast, Minneapolis, MN 55455-0115
(612) 624-1111

Minnesota University of St. Thomas

University of St. Thomas
St. Paul, Minnesota
www.stthomas.edu Federal Code: 002345

4-year private university and liberal arts college in very large city, affiliated with Roman Catholic Church.
Enrollment: 5,442 undergrads, 6% part-time. 1,323 full-time freshmen.
Selectivity: Admits over 75% of applicants.

BASIC COSTS (2006-2007)
Tuition and fees: $24,808.
Per-credit charge: $762.
Room and board: $6,932.

FINANCIAL AID PICTURE (2005-2006)
Students with need: Out of 891 full-time freshmen who applied for aid, 632 were judged to have need. Of these, 632 received aid, and 312 had their full need met. Average financial aid package met 78% of need; average scholarship/grant was $10,124; average loan was $2,763. For part-time students, average financial aid package was $15,011.
Students without need: 250 full-time freshmen who did not demonstrate need for aid received scholarships/grants; average award was $9,511. No-need awards available for academics, music/drama, ROTC.
Cumulative student debt: 66% of graduating class had student loans; average debt was $26,621.

FINANCIAL AID PROCEDURES
Forms required: FAFSA.
Dates and Deadlines: Priority date 4/1; no closing date. Applicants notified on a rolling basis starting 3/1; must reply within 3 week(s) of notification.
Transfers: Recognition scholarship available for Minnesota community college transfer students.

CONTACT
Kris Getting, Director of Admissions and Financial Aid
2115 Summit Avenue, 32F, St. Paul, MN 55455-0115
(651) 962-6550

Vermilion Community College
Ely, Minnesota
www.vcc.edu Federal Code: 002350

2-year public community and technical college in small town.
Enrollment: 800 undergrads.
Selectivity: Open admission.

BASIC COSTS (2005-2006)
Tuition and fees: $4,188; out-of-state residents $5,117.
Per-credit charge: $124; out-of-state residents $155.
Room and board: $4,630.
Additional info: Various reciprocity agreements with some neighboring states provide tuition reduction to out-of-state students.

FINANCIAL AID PICTURE
Students with need: Need-based aid available for full-time and part-time students. Work study available nights, weekends, and for part-time students.
Students without need: No-need awards available for academics.

FINANCIAL AID PROCEDURES
Forms required: FAFSA, institutional form.
Dates and Deadlines: No deadline. Applicants notified on a rolling basis starting 4/1.

CONTACT
Gina Faver, Financial Aid Director
1900 East Camp Street, Ely, MN 55731-9989
(218) 365-7200

Winona State University
Winona, Minnesota
www.winona.edu Federal Code: 002394

4-year public university in large town.
Enrollment: 7,447 undergrads.
Selectivity: Admits over 75% of applicants.

BASIC COSTS (2005-2006)
Tuition and fees: $5,661; out-of-state residents $9,607.
Per-credit charge: $163; out-of-state residents $296.
Room and board: $5,470.
Additional info: Fees include mandatory laptop lease for full-time students.

FINANCIAL AID PICTURE (2004-2005)
Students with need: 34% of average financial aid package awarded as scholarships/grants, 66% awarded as loans/jobs. Need-based aid available for part-time students. Work study available nights, weekends, and for part-time students.
Students without need: No-need awards available for academics, alumni affiliation, art, athletics, leadership, minority status, music/drama.
Scholarships offered: Outstanding Academics Honors Award: $2,500, renewable, top 5% of class, ACT 32 or above. WSU Foundation Board Scholarship: $2,000 renewable, top 15% of class, ACT 28-31, essay/interview. Presidential Honor Scholarships; $1,500 renewable; top 15% of class, ACT 28-31; $1,000, renewable, top 10% of class, ACT 27; $750, renewable, top 15% of class, ACT 26. Resident Tuition Scholarships: $3,400, renewable, to out-of-state students, top 15% of class or ACT 25.

FINANCIAL AID PROCEDURES
Forms required: FAFSA.
Dates and Deadlines: Priority date 3/1; no closing date. Applicants notified on a rolling basis starting 3/1; must reply within 2 week(s) of notification.

CONTACT
Greg Peterson, Director of Financial Aid
Office of Admissions, Winona, MN 55987
(800) 342-5978

Mississippi

Alcorn State University
Alcorn State, Mississippi
www.alcorn.edu Federal Code: 002396

4-year public university and agricultural college in rural community.
Enrollment: 2,962 undergrads, 10% part-time. 552 full-time freshmen.
Selectivity: Admits 50 to 75% of applicants.

BASIC COSTS (2005-2006)
Tuition and fees: $3,919; out-of-state residents $8,887.
Per-credit charge: $163; out-of-state residents $370.
Room and board: $4,272.

FINANCIAL AID PICTURE (2004-2005)
Students with need: Out of 552 full-time freshmen who applied for aid, 448 were judged to have need. Of these, 386 received aid, and 315 had their full need met. Average financial aid package met 70% of need; average scholarship/grant was $5,250; average loan was $2,625. For part-time students, average financial aid package was $7,432.
Students without need: 134 full-time freshmen who did not demonstrate need for aid received scholarships/grants; average award was $5,485. No-need awards available for academics, athletics, ROTC.
Scholarships offered: 55 full-time freshmen received athletic scholarships; average amount $6,726.

Cumulative student debt: 73% of graduating class had student loans; average debt was $17,000.

FINANCIAL AID PROCEDURES
Forms required: FAFSA, institutional form.
Dates and Deadlines: Priority date 4/1; no closing date. Applicants notified on a rolling basis starting 4/1; must reply within 4 week(s) of notification.

CONTACT
Juanita Russell, Director of Financial Aid
1000 ASU Drive #300, Alcorn State, MS 39096-7500
(601) 877-6190

Belhaven College
Jackson, Mississippi
www.belhaven.edu   Federal Code: 002397

4-year private liberal arts college in large city, affiliated with Presbyterian Church (USA).
Enrollment: 2,228 undergrads, 3% part-time. 202 full-time freshmen.
Selectivity: Admits 50 to 75% of applicants.

BASIC COSTS (2006-2007)
Tuition and fees: $14,774.
Per-credit charge: $470.
Room and board: $5,704.

FINANCIAL AID PICTURE (2005-2006)
Students with need: 27% of average financial aid package awarded as scholarships/grants, 73% awarded as loans/jobs. Need-based aid available for part-time students. Work study available nights, weekends, and for part-time students.
Students without need: No-need awards available for academics, art, athletics, leadership, minority status, music/drama, state/district residency.

FINANCIAL AID PROCEDURES
Forms required: FAFSA, state aid form.
Dates and Deadlines: Priority date 3/1; no closing date. Applicants notified on a rolling basis starting 2/1; must reply within 4 week(s) of notification.

CONTACT
Linda Phillips, Director of Financial Aid
1500 Peachtree Street, Jackson, MS 39202
(601) 968-5933

Blue Mountain College
Blue Mountain, Mississippi
www.bmc.edu   Federal Code: 002398

4-year private liberal arts college in rural community, affiliated with Southern Baptist Convention.
Enrollment: 344 undergrads, 18% part-time. 42 full-time freshmen.
Selectivity: Admits 50 to 75% of applicants.

BASIC COSTS (2006-2007)
Tuition and fees: $7,490.
Per-credit charge: $230.
Room and board: $3,766.

FINANCIAL AID PICTURE (2005-2006)
Students with need: Out of 36 full-time freshmen who applied for aid, 28 were judged to have need. Of these, 28 received aid, and 23 had their full need met. Average financial aid package met 82% of need; average scholarship/grant was $2,225; average loan was $2,673. For part-time students, average financial aid package was $6,733.
Students without need: 7 full-time freshmen who did not demonstrate need for aid received scholarships/grants; average award was $3,525. No-need awards available for academics, alumni affiliation, athletics, religious affiliation, state/district residency.
Scholarships offered: 4 full-time freshmen received athletic scholarships; average amount $10,070.
Cumulative student debt: 83% of graduating class had student loans; average debt was $11,484.

FINANCIAL AID PROCEDURES
Forms required: FAFSA, institutional form.
Dates and Deadlines: Priority date 6/1; closing date 8/1. Applicants notified on a rolling basis starting 5/1; must reply within 2 week(s) of notification.
Transfers: No deadline.

CONTACT
Angie Gossett, Director of Financial Aid
PO Box 160, Blue Mountain, MS 38610-0160
(662) 685-4771 ext. 141

Coahoma Community College
Clarksdale, Mississippi
www.coahomacc.edu   Federal Code: 002401

2-year public community college in rural community.
Enrollment: 1,946 undergrads.
Selectivity: Open admission; but selective for some programs.

BASIC COSTS (2005-2006)
Tuition and fees: $1,800; out-of-state residents $3,100.
Per-credit charge: $90.
Room and board: $2,914.

FINANCIAL AID PICTURE
Students with need: Need-based aid available for full-time and part-time students.
Students without need: This college only awards aid to students with need.

FINANCIAL AID PROCEDURES
Forms required: FAFSA, institutional form.
Dates and Deadlines: Priority date 4/1; no closing date. Applicants notified on a rolling basis starting 7/1.
Transfers: Priority date 3/1.

CONTACT
Patricia Brooks, Director of Financial Aid
3240 Friars Point Road, Clarksdale, MS 38614-9799
(662) 627-2571

Copiah-Lincoln Community College
Wesson, Mississippi
www.colin.edu   Federal Code: 002402

2-year public community college in small town.
Enrollment: 3,010 undergrads.
Selectivity: Open admission; but selective for some programs.

BASIC COSTS (2006-2007)
Tuition and fees: $1,800; out-of-state residents $3,600.
Per-credit charge: $105; out-of-state residents $180.
Room and board: $3,050.
Additional info: Parking Fee: 20.00.

FINANCIAL AID PICTURE
Students with need: Need-based aid available for full-time and part-time students. Work study available nights, weekends, and for part-time students.
Students without need: No-need awards available for academics, art, athletics, job skills, leadership, music/drama, state/district residency.

FINANCIAL AID PROCEDURES
Forms required: FAFSA.
Dates and Deadlines: Priority date 4/1; no closing date. Applicants notified on a rolling basis starting 4/1; must reply within 2 week(s) of notification.
CONTACT
Leslie Smith, Director of Financial Aid
Box 649, Wesson, MS 39191
(601) 643-8340

Delta State University
Cleveland, Mississippi
www.deltastate.edu   Federal Code: 002403

4-year public university in large town.
Enrollment: 3,258 undergrads, 15% part-time. 393 full-time freshmen.
Selectivity: Admits over 75% of applicants.
BASIC COSTS (2005-2006)
Tuition and fees: $3,761; out-of-state residents $8,947.
Per-credit charge: $157; out-of-state residents $373.
Room and board: $4,248.
FINANCIAL AID PICTURE (2004-2005)
Students with need: 34% of average financial aid package awarded as scholarships/grants, 66% awarded as loans/jobs. Need-based aid available for part-time students. Work study available nights, weekends, and for part-time students.
Students without need: No-need awards available for academics, alumni affiliation, art, athletics, leadership, music/drama, religious affiliation, ROTC, state/district residency.
FINANCIAL AID PROCEDURES
Forms required: FAFSA, institutional form.
Dates and Deadlines: Priority date 3/1; no closing date. Applicants notified on a rolling basis starting 4/1; must reply within 2 week(s) of notification.
CONTACT
Ann Mullins, Director of Student Financial Assistance
Kent Wyatt Hall Rm 117, Cleveland, MS 38733
(662) 846-4670

Hinds Community College
Raymond, Mississippi
www.hindscc.edu   Federal Code: 002407

2-year public branch campus and community college in small town.
Enrollment: 10,552 undergrads.
Selectivity: Open admission; but selective for some programs.
BASIC COSTS (2005-2006)
Tuition and fees: $1,740; out-of-state residents $3,946.
Per-credit charge: $85; out-of-state residents $170.
Room and board: $2,240.
FINANCIAL AID PICTURE
Students with need: Need-based aid available for full-time and part-time students.
Students without need: No-need awards available for academics, art, athletics, job skills, leadership, minority status, music/drama, state/district residency.
FINANCIAL AID PROCEDURES
Forms required: FAFSA.
Dates and Deadlines: Priority date 4/1; no closing date. Applicants notified on a rolling basis starting 5/15; must reply within 2 week(s) of notification.

Transfers: Financial aid transcripts from all previous colleges must be on file prior to award letter being released.
CONTACT
Thurman Mitchell, Director of Financial Aid, Raymond Campus
505 East Main Street, Raymond, MS 39154-1100
(601) 857-3450

Itawamba Community College
Fulton, Mississippi
www.iccms.edu   Federal Code: 002409

2-year public community college in small town.
Enrollment: 6,000 undergrads.
Selectivity: Open admission; but selective for some programs.
BASIC COSTS (2005-2006)
Tuition and fees: $1,480; out-of-state residents $3,230.
Per-credit charge: $75.
Room and board: $2,554.
FINANCIAL AID PICTURE
Students with need: Need-based aid available for full-time and part-time students.
Students without need: No-need awards available for academics, art, athletics, leadership, music/drama, state/district residency.
FINANCIAL AID PROCEDURES
Forms required: FAFSA, institutional form.
Dates and Deadlines: Priority date 4/30; no closing date. Applicants notified on a rolling basis starting 4/15.
CONTACT
Bobby Walker, Director of Financial Aid
602 West Hill Street, Fulton, MS 38843
(662) 862-8222

Jackson State University
Jackson, Mississippi
www.jsums.edu   Federal Code: 002410

4-year public university in small city.
Enrollment: 6,637 undergrads, 14% part-time. 1,131 full-time freshmen.
Selectivity: Admits less than 50% of applicants.
BASIC COSTS (2005-2006)
Tuition and fees: $3,964; out-of-state residents $8,872.
Per-credit charge: $165; out-of-state residents $369.
Room and board: $4,994.
FINANCIAL AID PICTURE (2004-2005)
Students with need: 46% of average financial aid package awarded as scholarships/grants, 54% awarded as loans/jobs. Need-based aid available for part-time students.
Students without need: This college only awards aid to students with need.
FINANCIAL AID PROCEDURES
Forms required: FAFSA.
Dates and Deadlines: Priority date 4/1; closing date 5/1. Applicants notified on a rolling basis starting 5/1.
CONTACT
Betty Moncure, Director, Admissions and Financial Aid
1400 JR Lynch Street, Jackson, MS 39217
(601) 979-2227

Jones County Junior College
Ellisville, Mississippi
www.jcjc.cc.ms.us   Federal Code: 002411

2-year public junior college in small town.
Enrollment: 4,791 undergrads.
Selectivity: Open admission; but selective for some programs.

BASIC COSTS (2005-2006)
Tuition and fees: $1,720; out-of-state residents $3,620.
Per-credit charge: $75; out-of-state residents $160.
Room and board: $2,712.

FINANCIAL AID PICTURE (2004-2005)
Students with need: 98% of average financial aid package awarded as scholarships/grants, 2% awarded as loans/jobs. Need-based aid available for part-time students. Work study available nights, weekends, and for part-time students.
Students without need: No-need awards available for academics, athletics, state/district residency.

FINANCIAL AID PROCEDURES
Forms required: FAFSA, state aid form, institutional form.
Dates and Deadlines: Priority date 5/1; no closing date. Applicants notified on a rolling basis starting 6/1; must reply within 2 week(s) of notification.

CONTACT
Tina Flanagan, Director of Student Financial Aid
900 South Court Street, Ellisville, MS 39437
(601) 477-4040

Magnolia Bible College
Kosciusko, Mississippi
www.magnolia.edu   Federal Code: 016788

4-year private Bible college in small town, affiliated with Church of Christ.
Enrollment: 24 undergrads, 17% part-time. 1 full-time freshmen.
Selectivity: Open admission.

BASIC COSTS (2006-2007)
Tuition and fees: $6,090.
Per-credit charge: $200.
Room only: $1,500.
Additional info: Reduced tuition for Attala County residents: $1,950 full-time, $65 per credit hour, $90 required fees.

FINANCIAL AID PICTURE (2004-2005)
Students with need: Out of 1 full-time freshmen who applied for aid, 1 were judged to have need. Of these, 1 received aid. Need-based aid available for part-time students.
Students without need: No-need awards available for academics, leadership, religious affiliation.

FINANCIAL AID PROCEDURES
Forms required: FAFSA, institutional form.
Dates and Deadlines: Priority date 8/1; no closing date. Applicants notified on a rolling basis starting 4/15; must reply within 4 week(s) of notification.

CONTACT
A. Coker, Financial Aid Coordinator
PO Box 1109, Kosciusko, MS 39090
(662) 289-2896 ext. 106

Meridian Community College
Meridian, Mississippi
www.meridiancc.edu   Federal Code: 002413

2-year public community college in large town.
Enrollment: 3,435 undergrads, 27% part-time. 1,227 full-time freshmen.
Selectivity: Open admission; but selective for some programs.

BASIC COSTS (2005-2006)
Tuition and fees: $1,630; out-of-state residents $2,920.
Per-credit charge: $80; out-of-state residents $137.
Room and board: $3,350.

FINANCIAL AID PICTURE (2004-2005)
Students with need: 77% of average financial aid package awarded as scholarships/grants, 23% awarded as loans/jobs. Need-based aid available for part-time students.
Students without need: No-need awards available for academics, art, athletics, leadership, music/drama, state/district residency.

FINANCIAL AID PROCEDURES
Forms required: FAFSA, institutional form.
Dates and Deadlines: Priority date 6/1; no closing date. Applicants notified on a rolling basis starting 5/15; must reply within 2 week(s) of notification.

CONTACT
Soraya Bazyari-Welden, Director of Financial Aid
910 Highway 19, North, Meridian, MS 39307-5890
(601) 484-8628

Millsaps College
Jackson, Mississippi
www.millsaps.edu   Federal Code: 002414

4-year private business and liberal arts college in large city, affiliated with United Methodist Church.
Enrollment: 1,065 undergrads, 3% part-time. 258 full-time freshmen.
Selectivity: Admits over 75% of applicants.

BASIC COSTS (2006-2007)
Tuition and fees: $22,032.
Per-credit charge: $640.
Room and board: $7,956.

FINANCIAL AID PICTURE (2005-2006)
Students with need: Out of 207 full-time freshmen who applied for aid, 156 were judged to have need. Of these, 156 received aid, and 50 had their full need met. Average financial aid package met 85% of need; average scholarship/grant was $14,618; average loan was $3,544. For part-time students, average financial aid package was $5,620.
Students without need: 95 full-time freshmen who did not demonstrate need for aid received scholarships/grants; average award was $15,061. No-need awards available for academics, art, leadership, music/drama, religious affiliation.
Cumulative student debt: 63% of graduating class had student loans; average debt was $22,285.

FINANCIAL AID PROCEDURES
Forms required: FAFSA, institutional form.
Dates and Deadlines: Priority date 3/1; no closing date. Applicants notified on a rolling basis starting 3/15; must reply by 5/1 or within 2 week(s) of notification.
Transfers: No deadline. Applicants notified on a rolling basis starting 3/15; must reply by 5/1 or within 2 week(s) of notification.

Mississippi Millsaps College

CONTACT
Patrick James, Director of Financial Aid
1701 North State Street, Jackson, MS 39210-0001
(601) 974-1220

Mississippi College
Clinton, Mississippi
www.mc.edu   Federal Code: 002415

4-year private university in large city, affiliated with Southern Baptist Convention.
Enrollment: 2,543 undergrads, 13% part-time. 379 full-time freshmen.
Selectivity: Admits 50 to 75% of applicants.

BASIC COSTS (2006-2007)
Tuition and fees: $12,288.
Per-credit charge: $365.
Room and board: $5,894.

FINANCIAL AID PICTURE (2005-2006)
Students with need: Out of 309 full-time freshmen who applied for aid, 163 were judged to have need. Of these, 163 received aid, and 72 had their full need met. Average financial aid package met 80% of need; average scholarship/grant was $10,652; average loan was $3,681. For part-time students, average financial aid package was $11,665.
Students without need: 145 full-time freshmen who did not demonstrate need for aid received scholarships/grants; average award was $9,536. No-need awards available for academics, alumni affiliation, art, leadership, music/drama, religious affiliation.
Scholarships offered: Merit Scholarships; up to $10,000; based on various criteria including leadership, academics, church and community involvement; extensive number awarded including some specifically for transfers.
Additional info: Student reply date for institutional scholarships: May 1.

FINANCIAL AID PROCEDURES
Forms required: FAFSA, state aid form.
Dates and Deadlines: Priority date 3/1; no closing date. Applicants notified on a rolling basis starting 3/1; must reply by 5/1.

CONTACT
Mary Givhan, Director of Financial Aid
PO Box 4026, Clinton, MS 39058
(601) 925-3800

Mississippi Delta Community College
Moorhead, Mississippi
www.msdelta.edu   Federal Code: 002416

2-year public community college in rural community.
Enrollment: 925 undergrads.
Selectivity: Open admission; but selective for some programs.

BASIC COSTS (2005-2006)
Tuition and fees: $1,850; out-of-state residents $3,458.
Room and board: $2,130.

FINANCIAL AID PICTURE
Students with need: Need-based aid available for full-time students.
Students without need: No-need awards available for academics, athletics, state/district residency.

FINANCIAL AID PROCEDURES
Forms required: FAFSA, institutional form.
Dates and Deadlines: Priority date 8/1; no closing date. Applicants notified on a rolling basis; must reply within 2 week(s) of notification.

CONTACT
Angie Sherrer, Director of Financial Aid
Box 668, Moorhead, MS 38761
(662) 246-6263

Mississippi Gulf Coast Community College: Jefferson Davis Campus
Perkinston, Mississippi
www.mgccc.edu   Federal Code: 002419

2-year public community college in large city.
Enrollment: 10,315 undergrads, 37% part-time. 1,858 full-time freshmen.
Selectivity: Open admission; but selective for some programs.

BASIC COSTS (2005-2006)
Tuition and fees: $1,602; out-of-state residents $3,448.
Per-credit charge: $75; out-of-state residents $152.
Additional info: $15 rental fee required per book.

FINANCIAL AID PICTURE
Students with need: Need-based aid available for full-time students.
Students without need: This college only awards aid to students with need.

FINANCIAL AID PROCEDURES
Forms required: institutional form.
Dates and Deadlines: Priority date 6/1; no closing date. Applicants notified on a rolling basis starting 7/1.

CONTACT
Sheree Bond, Financial Aid
PO Box 548, Perkinston, MS 39573
(601) 928-6350

Mississippi State University
Mississippi State, Mississippi
www.msstate.edu   Federal Code: 002423

4-year public university in large town.
Enrollment: 12,261 undergrads, 10% part-time. 1,787 full-time freshmen.
Selectivity: Admits 50 to 75% of applicants.

BASIC COSTS (2005-2006)
Tuition and fees: $4,312; out-of-state residents $9,769.
Per-credit charge: $180; out-of-state residents $407.
Room and board: $5,859.

FINANCIAL AID PICTURE (2004-2005)
Students with need: Out of 1,240 full-time freshmen who applied for aid, 1,054 were judged to have need. Of these, 1,017 received aid, and 297 had their full need met. Average financial aid package met 63% of need; average scholarship/grant was $3,665; average loan was $2,651. Need-based aid available for part-time students.
Students without need: This college only awards aid to students with need.
Scholarships offered: *Merit:* Entering Freshman Awards; ranging from $250-$3,750 per semester. Community College Transfer Awards; ranging from $500-$700 per semester. *Athletic:* 74 full-time freshmen received athletic scholarships; average amount $8,708.
Cumulative student debt: 49% of graduating class had student loans; average debt was $18,230.
Additional info: No institutional closing date for FAFSA.

FINANCIAL AID PROCEDURES
Forms required: FAFSA.

Dates and Deadlines: Priority date 4/1; no closing date. Applicants notified on a rolling basis starting 12/1; must reply by 5/1.

CONTACT
Bruce Crain
Box 6305, Mississippi State, MS 39762
(662) 325-2450

Pearl River Community College
Poplarville, Mississippi
www.prcc.edu   Federal Code: 002430

2-year public community college in small town.
Enrollment: 3,679 undergrads.
Selectivity: Open admission; but selective for some programs.

BASIC COSTS (2005-2006)
Tuition and fees: $1,726; out-of-state residents $4,124.
Per-credit charge: $86; out-of-state residents $186.
Room and board: $2,718.

FINANCIAL AID PICTURE (2004-2005)
Students with need: 98% of average financial aid package awarded as scholarships/grants, 2% awarded as loans/jobs. Need-based aid available for part-time students.
Students without need: No-need awards available for academics, alumni affiliation, athletics, leadership, music/drama, state/district residency.

FINANCIAL AID PROCEDURES
Forms required: FAFSA, institutional form.
Dates and Deadlines: Priority date 4/17; no closing date. Applicants notified on a rolling basis.

CONTACT
Peggy Shoemake, Director of Financial Aid
101 Highway 11 North, Poplarville, MS 39470
(601) 403-1000

Rust College
Holly Springs, Mississippi
www.rustcollege.edu   Federal Code: 002433

4-year private liberal arts college in small town, affiliated with United Methodist Church.
Enrollment: 935 undergrads, 13% part-time. 288 full-time freshmen.
Selectivity: Admits less than 50% of applicants.

BASIC COSTS (2005-2006)
Tuition and fees: $6,200.
Per-credit charge: $267.
Room and board: $2,750.
Additional info: Tuition/fee waivers available for adults.

FINANCIAL AID PICTURE (2005-2006)
Students with need: Out of 255 full-time freshmen who applied for aid, 255 were judged to have need. Of these, 255 received aid, and 150 had their full need met. Average financial aid package met 59% of need; average scholarship/grant was $6,139; average loan was $1,793. Need-based aid available for part-time students.
Students without need: 33 full-time freshmen who did not demonstrate need for aid received scholarships/grants; average award was $3,898. No-need awards available for academics, leadership, music/drama, religious affiliation, state/district residency.
Scholarships offered: Honor Track; full tuition; based on top 10% of high school graduating class, GPA 3.5 and above, ACT 22 or above, SAT 1030 or above, 3 letters of recommendation, essay; 17 awarded. Presidential Scholarship; $2,000; for top 10% of high school graduating class, GPA 3.25 and above, ACT 19 and above, SAT 910 and above; 17 awarded. Academic Dean's Scholarship; for top 10% of high school graduating class, GPA 3.0 or above, ACT 17 and above, SAT 830 and above; 17 awarded. SAT scores exclusive of Writing.

FINANCIAL AID PROCEDURES
Forms required: FAFSA, state aid form, institutional form.
Dates and Deadlines: Closing date 5/1. Applicants notified on a rolling basis starting 5/1; must reply within 2 week(s) of notification.
Transfers: No deadline. Financial aid transcripts from previous schools required.

CONTACT
Helen Street, Director of Financial Aid
150 Rust Avenue, Holly Springs, MS 38635-2328
(662) 252-8000 ext. 4062

Southwest Mississippi Community College
Summit, Mississippi
www.smcc.edu   Federal Code: 002436

2-year public community college in rural community.
Enrollment: 1,865 undergrads, 22% part-time. 561 full-time freshmen.
Selectivity: Open admission.

BASIC COSTS (2005-2006)
Tuition and fees: $1,800; out-of-state residents $3,600.
Per-credit charge: $75; out-of-state residents $165.
Room and board: $2,180.

FINANCIAL AID PICTURE
Students with need: Need-based aid available for full-time and part-time students.

FINANCIAL AID PROCEDURES
Dates and Deadlines: No deadline. Applicants notified on a rolling basis.

CONTACT
Stacey Hodges, Director of Financial Aid
1156 College Drive, Summit, MS 39666
(601) 276-3707

Tougaloo College
Tougaloo, Mississippi
www.tougaloo.edu   Federal Code: 002439

4-year private liberal arts college in large city, affiliated with United Christian Mission Society and United Church of Christ.
Enrollment: 934 undergrads, 4% part-time. 208 full-time freshmen.
Selectivity: Admits over 75% of applicants.

BASIC COSTS (2005-2006)
Tuition and fees: $9,035.
Per-credit charge: $367.
Room and board: $6,220.
Additional info: Tuition/fee waivers available for adults.

FINANCIAL AID PICTURE (2005-2006)
Students with need: Average financial aid package met 90% of need; average scholarship/grant was $2,025. Need-based aid available for part-time students.
Students without need: No-need awards available for academics, athletics, ROTC.
Cumulative student debt: 80% of graduating class had student loans; average debt was $40,000.

Mississippi — Tougaloo College

FINANCIAL AID PROCEDURES
Forms required: FAFSA, state aid form, institutional form.
Dates and Deadlines: Priority date 4/15; no closing date. Applicants notified on a rolling basis starting 5/1; must reply within 2 week(s) of notification.

CONTACT
Inez Morris, Director of Financial Aid
500 West County Line Road, Tougaloo, MS 39174
(601) 977-7766

University of Mississippi
University, Mississippi
www.olemiss.edu   Federal Code: 002440

4-year public university in large town.
Enrollment: 12,117 undergrads, 8% part-time. 2,136 full-time freshmen.
Selectivity: Admits 50 to 75% of applicants.

BASIC COSTS (2005-2006)
Tuition and fees: $4,320; out-of-state residents $9,744.
Per-credit charge: $180; out-of-state residents $406.
Room and board: $4,698.
Additional info: Tuition/fee waivers available for minority students.

FINANCIAL AID PICTURE (2004-2005)
Students with need: Out of 1,325 full-time freshmen who applied for aid, 809 were judged to have need. Of these, 792 received aid, and 149 had their full need met. Average financial aid package met 53% of need; average scholarship/grant was $3,875; average loan was $2,448. For part-time students, average financial aid package was $5,311.
Students without need: 785 full-time freshmen who did not demonstrate need for aid received scholarships/grants; average award was $4,157. No-need awards available for academics, alumni affiliation, art, athletics, leadership, minority status, music/drama, ROTC, state/district residency.
Scholarships offered: 74 full-time freshmen received athletic scholarships; average amount $10,259.

FINANCIAL AID PROCEDURES
Forms required: FAFSA.
Dates and Deadlines: Priority date 3/15; no closing date. Applicants notified on a rolling basis starting 4/1; must reply within 3 week(s) of notification.
Transfers: Priority date 2/1.

CONTACT
Laura Diven-Brown, Director
145 Martindale, University, MS 38677-1848
(800) 891-4596

University of Mississippi Medical Center
Jackson, Mississippi
www.umc.edu   Federal Code: 004688

Upper-division public university and health science college in large city.
Enrollment: 557 undergrads.
Selectivity: Open admission; but selective for some programs. GED not accepted.

BASIC COSTS (2005-2006)
Tuition and fees: $3,531; out-of-state residents $7,391.
Per-credit charge: $147; out-of-state residents $308.
Room only: $2,412.
Additional info: Tuition and fees quoted are for nursing program. Required fees vary per program.

FINANCIAL AID PICTURE
Students with need: Need-based aid available for full-time and part-time students.
Students without need: This college only awards aid to students with need.

FINANCIAL AID PROCEDURES
Forms required: FAFSA, state aid form, institutional form.
Dates and Deadlines: Closing date 4/1. Applicants notified by 7/15; must reply within 2 week(s) of notification.

CONTACT
Stacey Carter, Director of Student Financial Aid
2500 North State Street, Jackson, MS 39216
(601) 984-1117

University of Southern Mississippi
Hattiesburg, Mississippi
www.usm.edu   Federal Code: 002441

4-year public university in small city.
Enrollment: 12,468 undergrads, 14% part-time. 1,559 full-time freshmen.
Selectivity: Admits 50 to 75% of applicants.

BASIC COSTS (2005-2006)
Tuition and fees: $4,310; out-of-state residents $9,740.
Per-credit charge: $180; out-of-state residents $406.
Room and board: $4,818.

FINANCIAL AID PICTURE (2004-2005)
Students with need: Out of 1,227 full-time freshmen who applied for aid, 982 were judged to have need. Of these, 965 received aid, and 191 had their full need met. Average financial aid package met 77% of need; average scholarship/grant was $3,296; average loan was $2,851. For part-time students, average financial aid package was $5,239.
Students without need: 187 full-time freshmen who did not demonstrate need for aid received scholarships/grants; average award was $2,910.
Scholarships offered: 86 full-time freshmen received athletic scholarships; average amount $5,296.
Cumulative student debt: 65% of graduating class had student loans; average debt was $15,776.

FINANCIAL AID PROCEDURES
Forms required: FAFSA, institutional form.
Dates and Deadlines: Priority date 3/15; no closing date. Applicants notified on a rolling basis starting 4/1; must reply within 4 week(s) of notification.
Transfers: Merit scholarships available to community college transfer students based on college GPA.

CONTACT
Kristi Motter, Director of Financial Aid
118 College Drive #5166, Hattiesburg, MS 39406-0001
(601) 266-4111

Wesley College
Florence, Mississippi
www.wesleycollege.edu   Federal Code: 011461

4-year private Bible college in small town, affiliated with Congregational Methodist Church.
Enrollment: 86 undergrads, 26% part-time. 16 full-time freshmen.
Selectivity: Admits 50 to 75% of applicants.

BASIC COSTS (2005-2006)
Tuition and fees: $6,620.
Per-credit charge: $200.

Room and board: $2,960.

FINANCIAL AID PICTURE (2004-2005)
Students with need: Out of 16 full-time freshmen who applied for aid, 15 were judged to have need. Of these, 15 received aid, and 1 had their full need met. Average financial aid package met 65% of need; average scholarship/grant was $3,165; average loan was $2,625. For part-time students, average financial aid package was $5,134.
Students without need: 3 full-time freshmen who did not demonstrate need for aid received scholarships/grants; average award was $1,683. No-need awards available for academics, alumni affiliation, leadership, religious affiliation.
Cumulative student debt: 73% of graduating class had student loans; average debt was $13,587.

FINANCIAL AID PROCEDURES
Forms required: FAFSA.
Dates and Deadlines: Closing date 5/14. Applicants notified on a rolling basis starting 7/1; must reply within 2 week(s) of notification.

CONTACT
William Devore, Director of Financial Aid
PO Box 1070, Florence, MS 39073-0070
(601) 845-2265

William Carey College
Hattiesburg, Mississippi
www.wmcarey.edu   Federal Code: 002447

4-year private liberal arts college in small city, affiliated with Baptist faith.
Enrollment: 1,840 undergrads.
Selectivity: Open admission; but selective for some programs.

BASIC COSTS (2005-2006)
Tuition and fees: $8,415.
Per-credit charge: $270.
Room and board: $3,465.

FINANCIAL AID PICTURE (2004-2005)
Students with need: Average financial aid package for all full-time undergraduates was $11,500. 16% awarded as scholarships/grants, 84% awarded as loans/jobs. Need-based aid available for part-time students. Work study available nights, weekends, and for part-time students.
Students without need: No-need awards available for academics, alumni affiliation, art, athletics, music/drama, religious affiliation.
Cumulative student debt: 85% of graduating class had student loans; average debt was $16,000.

FINANCIAL AID PROCEDURES
Forms required: FAFSA.
Dates and Deadlines: Priority date 4/1; closing date 9/1. Applicants notified on a rolling basis starting 6/1; must reply within 2 week(s) of notification.

CONTACT
William Curry, Director of Admissions/Financial Aid
498 Tuscan Avenue, Hattiesburg, MS 39401-5499
(601) 318-6153

Missouri

Avila University
Kansas City, Missouri
www.avila.edu   Federal Code: 002449

4-year private university and liberal arts college in very large city, affiliated with Roman Catholic Church.
Enrollment: 1,118 undergrads, 22% part-time. 154 full-time freshmen.
Selectivity: Admits 50 to 75% of applicants.

BASIC COSTS (2006-2007)
Tuition and fees: $17,750.
Per-credit charge: $455.
Room and board: $5,500.

FINANCIAL AID PICTURE (2005-2006)
Students with need: Average financial aid package met 19% of need; average scholarship/grant was $5,598; average loan was $3,712. For part-time students, average financial aid package was $5,741.
Students without need: No-need awards available for academics, alumni affiliation, art, athletics, music/drama, religious affiliation.
Cumulative student debt: 100% of graduating class had student loans; average debt was $17,804.
Additional info: Financial aid adjusted for increases in tuition based on need.

FINANCIAL AID PROCEDURES
Forms required: FAFSA, institutional form.
Dates and Deadlines: Priority date 4/1; no closing date. Applicants notified on a rolling basis starting 2/1; must reply within 3 week(s) of notification.
Transfers: No deadline. Applicants notified on a rolling basis; must reply within 2 week(s) of notification. Non-need-based academic scholarship available for transfer students.

CONTACT
Kimberly Warren, Director of Financial Aid
11901 Wornall Road, Kansas City, MO 64145-1698
(816) 501-3600

Baptist Bible College
Springfield, Missouri
www.baptist.edu   Federal Code: 013208

4-year private Bible and seminary college in small city, affiliated with Baptist Bible Fellowship.
Enrollment: 616 undergrads, 12% part-time. 165 full-time freshmen.
Selectivity: Open admission.

BASIC COSTS (2006-2007)
Tuition and fees: $13,460.
Room and board: $5,400.

FINANCIAL AID PICTURE (2004-2005)
Students with need: 42% of average financial aid package awarded as scholarships/grants, 58% awarded as loans/jobs. Need-based aid available for part-time students.
Scholarships offered: Founder's Scholarship; $5,500-$9,500. Bible Scholarships; $800 per year.

FINANCIAL AID PROCEDURES
Forms required: FAFSA, institutional form.
Dates and Deadlines: Closing date 5/1. Applicants notified on a rolling basis; must reply within 2 week(s) of notification.

502 **Missouri** Baptist Bible College

CONTACT
Bob Kotulski, Financial Aid Director
628 East Kearney Street, Springfield, MO 65803
(417) 268-6036

Blue River Community College
Independence, Missouri
www.mcckc.edu   Federal Code: 009140

2-year public community college in small city.
Enrollment: 1,811 undergrads, 50% part-time. 228 full-time freshmen.
Selectivity: Open admission.

BASIC COSTS (2006-2007)
Tuition and fees: $2,190; out-of-district residents $3,990; out-of-state residents $5,400.
Per-credit charge: $73; out-of-district residents $133; out-of-state residents $180.

FINANCIAL AID PICTURE (2004-2005)
Students with need: Out of 181 full-time freshmen who applied for aid, 126 were judged to have need. Of these, 106 received aid, and 5 had their full need met. For part-time students, average financial aid package was $2,008.
Students without need: 4 full-time freshmen who did not demonstrate need for aid received scholarships/grants; average award was $1,574. No-need awards available for academics, athletics, leadership.

FINANCIAL AID PROCEDURES
Forms required: FAFSA, institutional form.
Dates and Deadlines: Priority date 5/30; closing date 8/20. Applicants notified on a rolling basis starting 4/8.
Transfers: No deadline.

CONTACT
Cindy Butler, District Director, Student Financial Aid
3200 Broadway, Kansas City, MO 64111-2429
(816) 759-1527

Calvary Bible College and Theological Seminary
Kansas City, Missouri
www.calvary.edu   Federal Code: 002450

4-year private Bible and seminary college in large city, affiliated with nondenominational tradition.
Enrollment: 281 undergrads, 20% part-time. 36 full-time freshmen.
Selectivity: Open admission.

BASIC COSTS (2005-2006)
Tuition and fees: $6,936.
Per-credit charge: $240.
Room and board: $3,900.
Additional info: Tuition/fee waivers available for minority students.

FINANCIAL AID PICTURE (2004-2005)
Students with need: 87% of average financial aid package awarded as scholarships/grants, 13% awarded as loans/jobs. Need-based aid available for part-time students.
Students without need: No-need awards available for academics, alumni affiliation, religious affiliation.

FINANCIAL AID PROCEDURES
Forms required: FAFSA, institutional form.
Dates and Deadlines: Priority date 3/1; closing date 4/1. Applicants notified on a rolling basis starting 4/1.

CONTACT
Rachel Russiaky, Financial Aid Counselor
15800 Calvary Road, Kansas City, MO 64147
(816) 322-5152 ext. 1313

Central Christian College of the Bible
Moberly, Missouri
www.cccb.edu   Federal Code: TG5165

4-year private Bible college in large town, affiliated with Christian Church.
Enrollment: 517 undergrads.

BASIC COSTS (2005-2006)
Additional info: Full-time students receive full scholarship. Room and board $5,000. Required fees $750.

FINANCIAL AID PICTURE
Students with need: Need-based aid available for full-time and part-time students.

FINANCIAL AID PROCEDURES
Forms required: FAFSA.
Dates and Deadlines: Priority date 3/15; closing date 4/1. Applicants notified by 5/15; must reply within 2 week(s) of notification.

CONTACT
Rhonda Dunham, Financial Aid Director
911 East Urbandale Drive, Moberly, MO 65270-1997
(888) 263-3900

Central Methodist University
Fayette, Missouri
www.centralmethodist.edu   Federal Code: E00605

4-year private liberal arts college in small town, affiliated with United Methodist Church.
Enrollment: 818 undergrads. 193 full-time freshmen.

BASIC COSTS (2005-2006)
Tuition and fees: $15,200.
Per-credit charge: $140.
Room and board: $5,360.

FINANCIAL AID PICTURE (2005-2006)
Students with need: Out of 171 full-time freshmen who applied for aid, 146 were judged to have need. Of these, 146 received aid, and 4 had their full need met. Average financial aid package met 72% of need; average scholarship/grant was $4,662; average loan was $2,625. For part-time students, average financial aid package was $3,423.
Students without need: 5 full-time freshmen who did not demonstrate need for aid received scholarships/grants; average award was $6,600. No-need awards available for academics, alumni affiliation, athletics, music/drama, religious affiliation.

FINANCIAL AID PROCEDURES
Forms required: FAFSA.
Dates and Deadlines: Priority date 3/15; no closing date. Applicants notified on a rolling basis starting 1/30; must reply within 2 week(s) of notification.
Transfers: Institutional financial assistance based on merit is determined by college transfer GPA.

CONTACT
Linda Mackey, Director of Financial Aid
411 Central Methodist Square, Fayette, MO 65248-1198
(660) 248-6245

Central Missouri State University
Warrensburg, Missouri
www.cmsu.edu   Federal Code: 02454

4-year public university in large town.
Enrollment: 8,254 undergrads, 14% part-time. 1,440 full-time freshmen.
Selectivity: Admits over 75% of applicants.

BASIC COSTS (2006-2007)
Tuition and fees: $5,835; out-of-state residents $11,250.
Room and board: $5,412.

FINANCIAL AID PICTURE (2004-2005)
Students with need: Out of 1,172 full-time freshmen who applied for aid, 812 were judged to have need. Of these, 790 received aid, and 132 had their full need met. Average financial aid package met 77% of need; average scholarship/grant was $1,631; average loan was $1,258. For part-time students, average financial aid package was $3,155.
Students without need: 557 full-time freshmen who did not demonstrate need for aid received scholarships/grants; average award was $2,690. No-need awards available for academics, alumni affiliation, art, athletics, leadership, minority status, music/drama, ROTC, state/district residency.
Scholarships offered: 71 full-time freshmen received athletic scholarships; average amount $3,733.
Cumulative student debt: 63% of graduating class had student loans; average debt was $9,632.

FINANCIAL AID PROCEDURES
Forms required: FAFSA.
Dates and Deadlines: Priority date 3/1; no closing date. Applicants notified on a rolling basis starting 3/1; must reply within 2 week(s) of notification.

CONTACT
Phil Shreves, Director, Student Financial Assistance
WDE 1401, Warrensburg, MO 64093
(660) 543-8080

College of the Ozarks
Point Lookout, Missouri
www.cofo.edu   Federal Code: 002500

4-year private liberal arts college in small town, affiliated with Presbyterian Church (USA).
Enrollment: 1,332 undergrads, 2% part-time. 240 full-time freshmen.
Selectivity: Admits less than 50% of applicants.

BASIC COSTS (2006-2007)
Per-credit charge: $295.
Room and board: $4,100.
Additional info: Cost of full-time tuition met through a combination of institutional work program and federal, state, and institutional funding. Required fees: $280. Full-time students participating in the work program work 15 hours per week for 16 weeks and one 40-hour work week per semester. Part-time students (commuters only) and full-time students not participating in the work program pay $295 per credit hour for tuition and an additional $280 per year as required fees.

FINANCIAL AID PICTURE (2005-2006)
Students with need: Average financial aid package met 84% of need; average scholarship/grant was $12,527. For part-time students, average financial aid package was $5,376.
Students without need: No-need awards available for academics, art, athletics, leadership, music/drama, ROTC, state/district residency.
Cumulative student debt: 5% of graduating class had student loans; average debt was $4,648.

FINANCIAL AID PROCEDURES
Forms required: FAFSA.
Dates and Deadlines: Priority date 2/15; no closing date. Applicants notified by 7/1.
Transfers: No deadline. Applicants notified on a rolling basis starting 2/15.

CONTACT
Kyla McCarty, Financial Aid Director
PO Box 17, Point Lookout, MO 65726-0017
(417) 334-6411 ext. 4290

Columbia College
Columbia, Missouri
www.ccis.edu   Federal Code: 002456

4-year private liberal arts college in small city, affiliated with Christian Church (Disciples of Christ).
Enrollment: 943 undergrads, 20% part-time. 151 full-time freshmen.
Selectivity: Admits 50 to 75% of applicants.

BASIC COSTS (2006-2007)
Tuition and fees: $12,414.
Per-credit charge: $266.
Room and board: $5,164.

FINANCIAL AID PICTURE (2005-2006)
Students with need: Out of 145 full-time freshmen who applied for aid, 90 were judged to have need. Of these, 87 received aid, and 13 had their full need met. Average financial aid package met 72% of need; average scholarship/grant was $6,092; average loan was $2,839. For part-time students, average financial aid package was $9,542.
Students without need: 33 full-time freshmen who did not demonstrate need for aid received scholarships/grants; average award was $4,094. No-need awards available for academics, alumni affiliation, art, athletics, leadership, music/drama, religious affiliation, ROTC, state/district residency.
Scholarships offered: *Merit:* Columbia College Scholarships, full tuition and room, minimum 3.5 high school GPA required. Awarded on competitive basis; selection process includes campus visit, interview, essay. Renewable with minimum 3.5 GPA. Half-tuition scholarships, minimum 3.4 high school GPA and ACT score of 24 required, renewable for 3 years with minimum 3.4 GPA. *Athletic:* 10 full-time freshmen received athletic scholarships; average amount $12,350.
Cumulative student debt: 65% of graduating class had student loans; average debt was $14,879.

FINANCIAL AID PROCEDURES
Forms required: FAFSA, institutional form.
Dates and Deadlines: Priority date 3/15; no closing date. Applicants notified on a rolling basis starting 3/1; must reply within 2 week(s) of notification.
Transfers: No deadline. Applicants notified on a rolling basis starting 3/15; must reply within 2 week(s) of notification.

CONTACT
Sharon Abernathy, Director of Financial Aid
1001 Rogers Street, Columbia, MO 65216
(573) 875-7360

Conception Seminary College
Conception, Missouri
www.conceptionabbey.org   Federal Code: 002467

4-year private seminary college for men in rural community, affiliated with Roman Catholic Church.
Enrollment: 112 undergrads.

Missouri — Conception Seminary College

BASIC COSTS (2005-2006)
Tuition and fees: $12,298.
Per-credit charge: $200.
Room and board: $7,200.

FINANCIAL AID PICTURE
Students with need: Need-based aid available for full-time and part-time students. Work study available nights, weekends, and for part-time students.
Students without need: No-need awards available for academics.

FINANCIAL AID PROCEDURES
Forms required: FAFSA.
Dates and Deadlines: No deadline. Applicants notified on a rolling basis starting 8/1; must reply by 8/20.

CONTACT
Justin Hernandez, Financial Aid Officer
Box 502, Conception, MO 64433-0502
(660) 944-2851

Cottey College
Nevada, Missouri
www.cottey.edu   Federal Code: 002458

2-year private junior and liberal arts college for women in small town.
Enrollment: 290 undergrads.

BASIC COSTS (2005-2006)
Tuition and fees: $12,310.
Room and board: $5,200.

FINANCIAL AID PICTURE
Students with need: Need-based aid available for full-time and part-time students.
Students without need: No-need awards available for academics, alumni affiliation, art, athletics, music/drama.

FINANCIAL AID PROCEDURES
Forms required: FAFSA.
Dates and Deadlines: Priority date 3/30; no closing date. Applicants notified on a rolling basis starting 3/15; must reply by 5/1.

CONTACT
Sherry Pennington, Coordinator of Financial Aid
1000 West Austin Boulevard, Nevada, MO 64772
(417) 667-8181 ext. 2190

Crowder College
Neosho, Missouri
www.crowder.edu   Federal Code: 002459

2-year public community and liberal arts college in small town.
Enrollment: 2,290 undergrads, 43% part-time. 446 full-time freshmen.
Selectivity: Open admission; but selective for some programs.

BASIC COSTS (2005-2006)
Tuition and fees: $2,220; out-of-district residents $3,000; out-of-state residents $3,810.
Per-credit charge: $62; out-of-district residents $88; out-of-state residents $115.
Room and board: $3,870.

FINANCIAL AID PICTURE
Students with need: Need-based aid available for full-time and part-time students. Work study available nights, weekends, and for part-time students.
Students without need: This college only awards aid to students with need.

FINANCIAL AID PROCEDURES
Forms required: FAFSA, institutional form.
Dates and Deadlines: Priority date 7/1; no closing date. Applicants notified on a rolling basis starting 5/15.

CONTACT
Michelle Paul, Director of Financial Aid
601 LaClede Avenue, Neosho, MO 64850
(417) 451-3223 ext. 5566

Culver-Stockton College
Canton, Missouri
www.culver.edu   Federal Code: 002460

4-year private liberal arts college in small town, affiliated with Christian Church (Disciples of Christ).
Enrollment: 840 undergrads, 9% part-time. 153 full-time freshmen.
Selectivity: Admits over 75% of applicants.

BASIC COSTS (2006-2007)
Tuition and fees: $15,450.
Per-credit charge: $420.
Room and board: $6,550.

FINANCIAL AID PICTURE (2005-2006)
Students with need: Out of 153 full-time freshmen who applied for aid, 141 were judged to have need. Of these, 141 received aid, and 29 had their full need met. Average financial aid package met 74% of need; average scholarship/grant was $9,537; average loan was $2,899. For part-time students, average financial aid package was $4,857.
Students without need: 12 full-time freshmen who did not demonstrate need for aid received scholarships/grants; average award was $14,200. No-need awards available for academics, alumni affiliation, art, athletics, job skills, leadership, music/drama, religious affiliation, state/district residency.
Scholarships offered: 17 full-time freshmen received athletic scholarships; average amount $2,580.
Cumulative student debt: 96% of graduating class had student loans; average debt was $18,429.
Additional info: Interview required for scholarships, audition required for music students, portfolio required for art students.

FINANCIAL AID PROCEDURES
Forms required: FAFSA.
Dates and Deadlines: Priority date 4/1; closing date 6/15. Applicants notified on a rolling basis starting 2/15; must reply within 2 week(s) of notification.
Transfers: Must reply within 2 week(s) of notification.

CONTACT
Tina Wiseman, Director of Financial Aid
One College Hill, Canton, MO 63435-1299
(573) 288-6306

Deaconess College of Nursing
St. Louis, Missouri
www.deaconess.edu   Federal Code: 006385

4-year for-profit nursing college in very large city, affiliated with United Church of Christ.
Enrollment: 580 undergrads.
Selectivity: Admits less than 50% of applicants.

BASIC COSTS (2005-2006)
Tuition and fees: $13,900.
Per-credit charge: $455.
Room and board: $4,800.

Additional info: Students enrolled in web-based program pay $465 per credit-hour.

FINANCIAL AID PICTURE
Students with need: Need-based aid available for full-time and part-time students.
Students without need: No-need awards available for academics.
Scholarships offered: Tenet Nurse Citizen Award, full tuition, based on application, essay, interview, renewable with 3.25 GPA, 1 awarded; Chancellor's Award, half tuition, for students with 24 ACT, 3.5 GPA, number awarded subject to fund availability; Merit Scholarships, up to $3,000, based on academic achievement, number awarded subject to fund availability.

FINANCIAL AID PROCEDURES
Forms required: FAFSA, institutional form.
Dates and Deadlines: No deadline. Applicants notified on a rolling basis starting 4/1; must reply within 2 week(s) of notification.
Transfers: No deadline.

CONTACT
Michelle Mohn, Financial Counselor
6150 Oakland Avenue, St. Louis, MO 63139
(314) 768-5604

DeVry University: Kansas City
Kansas City, Missouri
www.kc.devry.edu   Federal Code: 002455

4-year for-profit university in large city.
Enrollment: 1,097 undergrads, 26% part-time. 338 full-time freshmen.

BASIC COSTS (2005-2006)
Tuition and fees: $12,140.
Per-credit charge: $440.

FINANCIAL AID PICTURE (2004-2005)
Students with need: Out of 222 full-time freshmen who applied for aid, 210 were judged to have need. Of these, 207 received aid, and 13 had their full need met. Average financial aid package met 43% of need; average scholarship/grant was $4,763; average loan was $6,080. For part-time students, average financial aid package was $6,714.
Students without need: This college only awards aid to students with need.

FINANCIAL AID PROCEDURES
Forms required: FAFSA.
Dates and Deadlines: No deadline. Applicants notified on a rolling basis.

CONTACT
Maureen Kelly, Senior Associate Director of Financial Aid
11224 Holmes Street, Kansas City, MO 64131-3626
(816) 941-0439

Drury University
Springfield, Missouri
www.drury.edu   Federal Code: 002461

4-year private university and liberal arts college in large city, affiliated with United Church of Christ and Christian Church (Disciples of Christ).
Enrollment: 1,577 undergrads, 2% part-time. 367 full-time freshmen.
Selectivity: Admits over 75% of applicants.

BASIC COSTS (2006-2007)
Tuition and fees: $15,387.
Per-credit charge: $500.
Room and board: $5,790.

FINANCIAL AID PICTURE (2004-2005)
Students with need: Out of 354 full-time freshmen who applied for aid, 339 were judged to have need. Of these, 339 received aid, and 296 had their full need met. Average financial aid package met 84% of need; average scholarship/grant was $6,102; average loan was $3,962. For part-time students, average financial aid package was $2,750.
Students without need: 71 full-time freshmen who did not demonstrate need for aid received scholarships/grants; average award was $2,917. No-need awards available for academics, alumni affiliation, art, athletics, job skills, leadership, minority status, music/drama, religious affiliation.
Scholarships offered: *Merit:* Trustee Scholarship; 10 awarded; tuition, room and board. Presidential Scholarship; 10 awarded; $10,000 a year. Academic Honor Scholarship; $500 to $5,000 a year. Peter Hudson Ethnic Diversity Scholarship; 2 awarded; $8,000 a year. Samuel Drury Award; $8,000 a year. Leadership Award; $1,000 a year. Dean Award; top 2% of high school class awarded; $1,000 a year. International Baccalaureate Award; $1,000 a year. *Athletic:* 21 full-time freshmen received athletic scholarships; average amount $6,287.
Cumulative student debt: 44% of graduating class had student loans; average debt was $15,450.

FINANCIAL AID PROCEDURES
Forms required: FAFSA, institutional form.
Dates and Deadlines: Closing date 3/15. Applicants notified on a rolling basis starting 3/30; must reply within 2 week(s) of notification.
Transfers: No deadline.

CONTACT
Annette Avery, Director of Financial Aid
900 North Benton Avenue, Springfield, MO 65802
(417) 873-7312

East Central College
Union, Missouri
www.eastcentral.edu   Federal Code: 008862

2-year public community college in small town.
Enrollment: 2,709 undergrads, 51% part-time. 492 full-time freshmen.
Selectivity: Open admission; but selective for some programs.

BASIC COSTS (2006-2007)
Tuition and fees: $2,130; out-of-district residents $2,910; out-of-state residents $4,230.
Per-credit charge: $61; out-of-district residents $87; out-of-state residents $131.

FINANCIAL AID PICTURE (2004-2005)
Students with need: Average financial aid package for all full-time undergraduates was $2,603. 72% awarded as scholarships/grants, 28% awarded as loans/jobs. Need-based aid available for part-time students. Work study available nights, weekends, and for part-time students.
Students without need: No-need awards available for academics, alumni affiliation, art, athletics, music/drama, state/district residency.

FINANCIAL AID PROCEDURES
Forms required: FAFSA.
Dates and Deadlines: Priority date 3/30; no closing date. Applicants notified on a rolling basis starting 3/15.

CONTACT
Todd Martin, Director of Financial Aid
1964 Prairie Dell Road, Union, MO 63084-0529
(636) 583-5195 ext. 2211

Evangel University
Springfield, Missouri
www.evangel.edu Federal Code: 002463

4-year private liberal arts college in small city, affiliated with Assemblies of God.
Enrollment: 1,941 undergrads.
Selectivity: Admits over 75% of applicants.

BASIC COSTS (2006-2007)
Tuition and fees: $13,784.
Per-credit charge: $498.
Room and board: $4,850.

FINANCIAL AID PICTURE (2004-2005)
Students with need: 38% of average financial aid package awarded as scholarships/grants, 62% awarded as loans/jobs. Need-based aid available for part-time students. Work study available nights, weekends, and for part-time students.
Students without need: This college only awards aid to students with need.

FINANCIAL AID PROCEDURES
Forms required: FAFSA.
Dates and Deadlines: Priority date 3/1; closing date 6/1. Applicants notified on a rolling basis starting 4/1; must reply within 3 week(s) of notification.

CONTACT
Kathy White, Director of Financial Aid
1111 North Glenstone, Springfield, MO 65802
(417) 865-2811

Everest College: Springfield
Springfield, Missouri
www.springfield-college.com Federal Code: 022506

2-year for-profit junior college in small city.
Enrollment: 550 undergrads.

BASIC COSTS (2005-2006)
Tuition and fees: $12,425.
Per-credit charge: $265.
Additional info: Tuition at time of enrollment locked for 2 years.

FINANCIAL AID PICTURE
Students with need: Need-based aid available for full-time and part-time students.
Students without need: This college only awards aid to students with need.

FINANCIAL AID PROCEDURES
Forms required: FAFSA.
Dates and Deadlines: No deadline. Applicants notified on a rolling basis.

CONTACT
Brenda Groover, Financial Aid Director
1010 West Sunshine, Springfield, MO 65807
(417) 864-7220

Fontbonne University
St. Louis, Missouri
www.fontbonne.edu Federal Code: 002464

4-year private liberal arts college in very large city, affiliated with Roman Catholic Church.
Enrollment: 2,005 undergrads, 23% part-time. 187 full-time freshmen.
Selectivity: Admits 50 to 75% of applicants.

BASIC COSTS (2006-2007)
Tuition and fees: $17,440.
Per-credit charge: $465.
Room and board: $6,739.

FINANCIAL AID PICTURE (2005-2006)
Students with need: 38% of average financial aid package awarded as scholarships/grants, 62% awarded as loans/jobs. Need-based aid available for part-time students. Work study available nights, weekends, and for part-time students.
Students without need: No-need awards available for academics, alumni affiliation, art, leadership, minority status, music/drama, religious affiliation, state/district residency.
Scholarships offered: Dean's Scholarship; $6,000-$8,000; GPA, ACT, rank criteria. Alumni Scholarship; $1,000-$6,000; GPA, ACT and class rank criteria. Presidential Scholarship; up to full tuition. Campus Service Scholarship;$500-$3,000; activities, leadership. Art, theater, English, writing and computer science scholarships also available.

FINANCIAL AID PROCEDURES
Forms required: FAFSA, institutional form.
Dates and Deadlines: Priority date 4/1; no closing date. Applicants notified on a rolling basis starting 2/1; must reply within 2 week(s) of notification.

CONTACT
Nicole Moore, Director of Financial Aid
6800 Wydown Boulevard, St. Louis, MO 63105
(314) 889-1414

Hannibal-LaGrange College
Hannibal, Missouri
www.hlg.edu Federal Code: 009089

4-year private liberal arts college in large town, affiliated with Southern Baptist Convention.
Enrollment: 952 undergrads, 8% part-time. 112 full-time freshmen.

BASIC COSTS (2006-2007)
Tuition and fees: $12,680.
Per-credit charge: $407.
Room and board: $4,930.

FINANCIAL AID PICTURE (2005-2006)
Students with need: Need-based aid available for part-time students.
Students without need: No-need awards available for academics, art, athletics, music/drama, religious affiliation.
Additional info: Work-study opportunities vary according to on- and off-campus needs.

FINANCIAL AID PROCEDURES
Forms required: FAFSA, institutional form.
Dates and Deadlines: Closing date 7/1. Applicants notified on a rolling basis; must reply by 8/31.

CONTACT
Amy Blackwell, Associate Dean of Financial Aid
2800 Palmyra Road, Hannibal, MO 63401
(573) 221-3675 ext. 279

Harris-Stowe State University
St. Louis, Missouri
www.hssu.edu Federal Code: 002466

4-year public business and teachers college in large city.
Enrollment: 1,496 undergrads.

BASIC COSTS (2005-2006)
Tuition and fees: $4,650; out-of-state residents $8,869.
Per-credit charge: $145; out-of-state residents $285.

FINANCIAL AID PICTURE (2005-2006)
Students with need: 53% of average financial aid package awarded as scholarships/grants, 47% awarded as loans/jobs. Need-based aid available for part-time students. Work study available nights, weekends, and for part-time students.
Students without need: No-need awards available for academics, athletics, music/drama, state/district residency.

FINANCIAL AID PROCEDURES
Forms required: FAFSA, institutional form.
Dates and Deadlines: Priority date 4/1; no closing date. Must reply within 3 week(s) of notification.

CONTACT
Regina Blackshear, Director of Financial Aid
3026 Laclede Avenue, St. Louis, MO 63103-2199
(314) 340-3500

Hickey College
St. Louis, Missouri
www.hickeycollege.edu
Federal Code: 014209

4-year for-profit business and technical college in very large city.
Enrollment: 500 undergrads.
Selectivity: Open admission; but selective for some programs.

BASIC COSTS (2005-2006)
Tuition and fees: $11,120.
Room and board: $5,320.

FINANCIAL AID PICTURE
Students with need: Need-based aid available for full-time students.

FINANCIAL AID PROCEDURES
Forms required: FAFSA.
Dates and Deadlines: No deadline. Applicants notified on a rolling basis.

CONTACT
Deana Pecoroni, Director, Student Services
940 West Port Plaza, St. Louis, MO 63146
(314) 434-2212 ext. 128

Jefferson College
Hillsboro, Missouri
www.jeffco.edu
Federal Code: 002468

2-year public community and technical college in rural community.
Enrollment: 3,900 undergrads, 43% part-time. 839 full-time freshmen.
Selectivity: Open admission; but selective for some programs.

BASIC COSTS (2006-2007)
Tuition and fees: $1,980; out-of-district residents $2,790; out-of-state residents $3,570.
Per-credit charge: $53; out-of-district residents $80; out-of-state residents $106.
Room and board: $5,794.

FINANCIAL AID PICTURE (2004-2005)
Students with need: Out of 655 full-time freshmen who applied for aid, 454 were judged to have need. Of these, 411 received aid, and 12 had their full need met. Average financial aid package met 40% of need; average scholarship/grant was $1,817; average loan was $1,920. For part-time students, average financial aid package was $2,163.
Students without need: 21 full-time freshmen who did not demonstrate need for aid received scholarships/grants; average award was $1,026. No-need awards available for academics, art, athletics, leadership, music/drama, state/district residency.
Scholarships offered: 64 full-time freshmen received athletic scholarships; average amount $4,673.
Cumulative student debt: 25% of graduating class had student loans; average debt was $7,476.

FINANCIAL AID PROCEDURES
Forms required: FAFSA.
Dates and Deadlines: Priority date 4/1; no closing date. Applicants notified on a rolling basis starting 4/15.

CONTACT
Julie Pierce, Director of Admissions and Financial Aid
1000 Viking Drive, Hillsboro, MO 63050-2441
(636) 797-3000 ext. 212

Kansas City Art Institute
Kansas City, Missouri
www.kcai.edu
Federal Code: 002473

4-year private visual arts college in large city.
Enrollment: 582 undergrads, 1% part-time. 86 full-time freshmen.
Selectivity: Admits 50 to 75% of applicants.

BASIC COSTS (2005-2006)
Tuition and fees: $22,392.
Per-credit charge: $900.
Room and board: $7,150.

FINANCIAL AID PICTURE (2005-2006)
Students with need: Average financial aid package met 65% of need; average scholarship/grant was $12,432; average loan was $4,250. For part-time students, average financial aid package was $6,000.
Students without need: No-need awards available for academics, art.
Cumulative student debt: 87% of graduating class had student loans; average debt was $21,125.
Additional info: February 15 and March 15 priority application dates for merit scholarships; deadline July 1.

FINANCIAL AID PROCEDURES
Forms required: FAFSA.
Dates and Deadlines: Priority date 3/15; no closing date. Applicants notified on a rolling basis starting 4/1; must reply within 2 week(s) of notification.
Transfers: Must reply within 2 week(s) of notification.

CONTACT
Christal Williams, Director of Financial Aid
4415 Warwick Boulevard, Kansas City, MO 64111-1762
(816) 802-3337

Kansas City College of Legal Studies
Kansas City, Missouri
www.metropolitancollege.edu
Federal Code: 030993

4-year private branch campus and technical college in very large city.
Enrollment: 108 undergrads.

BASIC COSTS (2005-2006)
Tuition and fees: $6,534.
Additional info: Quoted tuition is for bachelor's degree in court reporting. Estimated cost of books $260. Tuition for associate paralegal program $6,593 per academic year; estimated cost of books $1,050. Tuition at time of enrollment locked for 4 years.

FINANCIAL AID PICTURE (2005-2006)
Students with need: Need-based aid available for part-time students.
Students without need: This college only awards aid to students with need.

FINANCIAL AID PROCEDURES
Forms required: FAFSA, institutional form.
Dates and Deadlines: No deadline.

CONTACT
Cori Deaton, Financial Aid Director
800 East 101st Terrace, Suite 100, Kansas City, MO 64131
(816) 444-2232

Lincoln University
Jefferson City, Missouri
www.lincolnu.edu   Federal Code: 002479

4-year public university and liberal arts college in small city.
Enrollment: 2,543 undergrads, 21% part-time. 600 full-time freshmen.
Selectivity: Open admission; but selective for some programs and for out-of-state students.

BASIC COSTS (2005-2006)
Tuition and fees: $4,602; out-of-state residents $8,249.
Per-credit charge: $143; out-of-state residents $325.
Room and board: $3,790.

FINANCIAL AID PICTURE
Students with need: Need-based aid available for full-time and part-time students.
Students without need: No-need awards available for academics, athletics, ROTC, state/district residency.

FINANCIAL AID PROCEDURES
Forms required: FAFSA.
Dates and Deadlines: Priority date 3/1; no closing date. Applicants notified on a rolling basis starting 2/1; must reply within 2 week(s) of notification.

CONTACT
Alfred Robinson, Director of Financial Aid and Student Employment
820 Chestnut Street/B-7 Young Hall, Jefferson City, MO 65102
(573) 681-5363

Lindenwood University
St. Charles, Missouri
www.lindenwood.edu   Federal Code: 002480

4-year private university and liberal arts college in very large city, affiliated with Presbyterian Church (USA).
Enrollment: 5,258 undergrads, 4% part-time. 820 full-time freshmen.
Selectivity: Admits less than 50% of applicants.

BASIC COSTS (2006-2007)
Tuition and fees: $12,240.
Per-credit charge: $340.
Room and board: $6,000.

FINANCIAL AID PICTURE (2005-2006)
Students with need: 61% of average financial aid package awarded as scholarships/grants, 39% awarded as loans/jobs. Need-based aid available for part-time students. Work study available nights, weekends, and for part-time students.
Students without need: No-need awards available for academics, alumni affiliation, art, athletics, job skills, leadership, music/drama, ROTC.

FINANCIAL AID PROCEDURES
Forms required: FAFSA.
Dates and Deadlines: Priority date 4/1; no closing date. Applicants notified on a rolling basis; must reply within 2 week(s) of notification.

CONTACT
Lori Bode, Director of Financial Aid and Management
209 South Kingshighway, St. Charles, MO 63301-1695
(636) 949-4923

Longview Community College
Lee's Summit, Missouri
www.mcckc.edu   Federal Code: 009140

2-year public community college in small city.
Enrollment: 3,651 undergrads, 48% part-time. 449 full-time freshmen.
Selectivity: Open admission; but selective for some programs.

BASIC COSTS (2005-2006)
Tuition and fees: $2,280; out-of-district residents $4,170; out-of-state residents $5,550.
Per-credit charge: $76; out-of-district residents $134; out-of-state residents $180.

FINANCIAL AID PICTURE (2004-2005)
Students with need: Out of 358 full-time freshmen who applied for aid, 247 were judged to have need. Of these, 210 received aid, and 28 had their full need met. For part-time students, average financial aid package was $1,913.
Students without need: 20 full-time freshmen who did not demonstrate need for aid received scholarships/grants; average award was $1,337. No-need awards available for academics, athletics, leadership.
Scholarships offered: 9 full-time freshmen received athletic scholarships; average amount $974.

FINANCIAL AID PROCEDURES
Forms required: FAFSA, institutional form.
Dates and Deadlines: Priority date 5/30; closing date 8/20. Applicants notified on a rolling basis starting 4/8.
Transfers: No deadline.

CONTACT
Cindy Butler, District Director, Student Financial Aid
500 Longview Road, Lee's Summit, MO 64081-2105
(816) 759-1527

Maple Woods Community College
Kansas City, Missouri
www.mcckc.edu   Federal Code: 004432

2-year public community college in large city.
Enrollment: 2,913 undergrads, 47% part-time. 600 full-time freshmen.
Selectivity: Open admission; but selective for some programs.

BASIC COSTS (2006-2007)
Tuition and fees: $2,340; out-of-district residents $4,140; out-of-state residents $5,550.
Per-credit charge: $73; out-of-district residents $133; out-of-state residents $180.

FINANCIAL AID PICTURE (2004-2005)
Students with need: Out of 343 full-time freshmen who applied for aid, 211 were judged to have need. Of these, 181 received aid, and 16 had their full need met. For part-time students, average financial aid package was $2,354.
Students without need: 6 full-time freshmen who did not demonstrate need for aid received scholarships/grants; average award was $1,248. No-need awards available for academics, athletics, leadership.

Scholarships offered: 6 full-time freshmen received athletic scholarships; average amount $1,819.

FINANCIAL AID PROCEDURES
Forms required: FAFSA, institutional form.
Dates and Deadlines: Priority date 5/30; no closing date. Applicants notified on a rolling basis.

CONTACT
Cindy Butler, District Director, Student Financial Aid
2601 NE Barry Road, Kansas City, MO 64156-1299
(816) 759-1527

Maryville University of Saint Louis
St. Louis, Missouri
www.maryville.edu   Federal Code: 002482

4-year private university in very large city.
Enrollment: 2,532 undergrads, 36% part-time. 322 full-time freshmen.
Selectivity: Admits 50 to 75% of applicants.

BASIC COSTS (2006-2007)
Tuition and fees: $18,120.
Per-credit charge: $540.
Room and board: $7,720.

FINANCIAL AID PICTURE (2005-2006)
Students with need: 58% of average financial aid package awarded as scholarships/grants, 42% awarded as loans/jobs. Need-based aid available for part-time students. Work study available weekends and for part-time students.
Students without need: No-need awards available for academics, art, leadership, minority status, religious affiliation, state/district residency.
Scholarships offered: University Scholars Program: full-time freshmen with composite ACT score of 28 or SAT 1170 (exclusive of Writing); high school GPA 3.5-4.0. Special application and interview required.

FINANCIAL AID PROCEDURES
Forms required: FAFSA, institutional form.
Dates and Deadlines: Priority date 3/1; no closing date. Applicants notified on a rolling basis starting 2/1; must reply by 5/1 or within 2 week(s) of notification.
Transfers: Outstanding Transfer Student Awards.

CONTACT
Martha Harbaugh, Director of Financial Aid
13550 Conway Road, St. Louis, MO 63141-7299
(314) 529-9360

Metro Business College: Jefferson City
Jefferson City, Missouri
www.metrobusinesscollege.edu   Federal Code: 014710

2-year for-profit business and health science college in large town.
Enrollment: 157 undergrads, 9% part-time. 32 full-time freshmen.
Selectivity: Open admission; but selective for some programs.

BASIC COSTS (2005-2006)
Additional info: $2,695 per quarter; book rental included. Required fee $100.

FINANCIAL AID PICTURE
Students with need: Need-based aid available for full-time and part-time students.

FINANCIAL AID PROCEDURES
Forms required: FAFSA, institutional form.
Dates and Deadlines: No deadline. Applicants notified on a rolling basis.

CONTACT
Debbie Jenkins, Financial Aid Coordinator
1407 Southwest Boulevard, Jefferson City, MO 65109
(573) 635-6600

Mineral Area College
Park Hills, Missouri
www.mineralarea.edu   Federal Code: 002486

2-year public community college in small town.
Enrollment: 2,342 undergrads.
Selectivity: Open admission; but selective for some programs.

BASIC COSTS (2005-2006)
Tuition and fees: $2,160; out-of-district residents $2,880; out-of-state residents $3,540.
Per-credit charge: $72; out-of-district residents $96; out-of-state residents $118.
Room and board: $2,475.

FINANCIAL AID PICTURE
Students with need: Need-based aid available for full-time and part-time students.
Students without need: No-need awards available for academics, alumni affiliation, art, athletics, leadership, music/drama, state/district residency.

FINANCIAL AID PROCEDURES
Forms required: FAFSA.
Dates and Deadlines: Priority date 4/1; no closing date. Applicants notified on a rolling basis starting 2/15; must reply within 4 week(s) of notification.

CONTACT
Denise Sebastian, Financial Aid Director
PO Box 1000, Park Hills, MO 63601-1000
(573) 518-2133

Missouri Baptist University
St. Louis, Missouri
www.mobap.edu   Federal Code: 007540

4-year private university and liberal arts college in very large city, affiliated with Southern Baptist Convention.
Enrollment: 1,425 undergrads, 19% part-time. 204 full-time freshmen.
Selectivity: Admits 50 to 75% of applicants.

BASIC COSTS (2005-2006)
Tuition and fees: $13,830.
Per-credit charge: $460.
Room and board: $6,000.

FINANCIAL AID PICTURE
Students with need: Need-based aid available for full-time and part-time students.
Students without need: No-need awards available for academics, alumni affiliation, athletics, leadership, music/drama, religious affiliation.

FINANCIAL AID PROCEDURES
Forms required: FAFSA, institutional form.
Dates and Deadlines: Priority date 4/1; no closing date. Applicants notified on a rolling basis starting 4/15; must reply within 2 week(s) of notification.
Transfers: Institutional academic scholarships available.

CONTACT
Laurie Wallace, Director of Financial Services
One College Park Drive, St. Louis, MO 63141-8698
(314) 392-2366

Missouri College
St. Louis, Missouri
www.missouricollege.com Federal Code: 009795

2-year for-profit technical college in very large city.
Enrollment: 750 undergrads.

FINANCIAL AID PICTURE
Students with need: Need-based aid available for full-time and part-time students. Work study available nights.

FINANCIAL AID PROCEDURES
Forms required: FAFSA.
Dates and Deadlines: No deadline.

CONTACT
Leslie Harmon, Director of Financial Aid
10121 Manchester Road, St. Louis, MO 63122-1583
(314) 821-7700

Missouri Southern State University
Joplin, Missouri
www.mssu.edu Federal Code: 002488

4-year public university and liberal arts college in large town.
Enrollment: 4,842 undergrads, 22% part-time. 839 full-time freshmen.
Selectivity: Admits over 75% of applicants.

BASIC COSTS (2005-2006)
Tuition and fees: $3,916; out-of-state residents $7,666.
Per-credit charge: $125; out-of-state residents $250.
Room and board: $4,770.

FINANCIAL AID PICTURE (2005-2006)
Students with need: 11% of average financial aid package awarded as scholarships/grants, 89% awarded as loans/jobs. Need-based aid available for part-time students.
Students without need: No-need awards available for academics, alumni affiliation, art, athletics, job skills, leadership, minority status, music/drama, state/district residency.

FINANCIAL AID PROCEDURES
Forms required: FAFSA.
Dates and Deadlines: Priority date 2/15; no closing date. Applicants notified on a rolling basis starting 2/15; must reply within 3 week(s) of notification.

CONTACT
James Gilbert, Director of Student Financial Aid
3950 East Newman Road, Joplin, MO 64801-1595
(417) 625-9325

Missouri State University
Springfield, Missouri
www.smsu.edu Federal Code: 002503

4-year public university in small city.
Enrollment: 14,463 undergrads, 13% part-time. 2,579 full-time freshmen.
Selectivity: Admits over 75% of applicants.

BASIC COSTS (2005-2006)
Tuition and fees: $5,454; out-of-state residents $10,374.
Per-credit charge: $164; out-of-state residents $328.
Room and board: $4,980.

FINANCIAL AID PICTURE (2005-2006)
Students with need: Average financial aid package met 62% of need; average scholarship/grant was $4,595; average loan was $2,708. For part-time students, average financial aid package was $4,765.
Students without need: No-need awards available for academics, alumni affiliation, art, athletics, job skills, leadership, minority status, music/drama, ROTC, state/district residency.
Scholarships offered: Presidential Scholarships; full tuition, room, and board; based on ACT score 30 or higher and rank in top 10% of class; 40 awarded, application deadline January 15. Board of Governors Scholarships; cover basic fees for 32 credit hours per year (plus two thirds of out of state fees for non-residents); based on ACT score of 28 and either top 10% class rank or GPA of 3.85; unlimited number of awards. Freshman Academic Scholarships; $2,000 per year (plus two thirds of out of state fees for non-residents); based on ACT score of 26 and either top 20% class rank or GPA of 3.7; unlimited number of awards. Freshman Recognition Scholarships; $1,000 per year (plus two thirds of out of state fees for non-residents); based on ACT score of 24 and either top 10% class rank or GPA of 3.85; unlimited number of awards. Multicultural Leadership Scholarships; cover required student fees (in-state); for students in top half of class who have demonstrated leadership in the minority community; 50 awarded; February 1 deadline. Applications must be received by March 1 to be considered for scholarships, unless otherwise noted.
Cumulative student debt: 54% of graduating class had student loans; average debt was $12,997.
Additional info: Extensive scholarship program offered to freshmen and transfer students. Out-of-state fee stipends available. Student employment service available to assist students in securing employment on campus and in community.

FINANCIAL AID PROCEDURES
Forms required: FAFSA.
Dates and Deadlines: Priority date 3/30; no closing date. Applicants notified on a rolling basis starting 4/15.
Transfers: Priority date 3/31.

CONTACT
Billie Jo Hamilton, Director of Financial Aid
901 South National Avenue, Springfield, MO 65804-0094
(417) 836-5262

Missouri State University: West Plains
West Plains, Missouri
www.wp.missouristate.edu Federal Code: 031060

2-year public university and branch campus college in small town.
Enrollment: 1,264 undergrads, 31% part-time. 350 full-time freshmen.
Selectivity: Open admission; but selective for some programs.

BASIC COSTS (2005-2006)
Tuition and fees: $3,124; out-of-state residents $6,034.
Per-credit charge: $97; out-of-state residents $194.
Room and board: $4,558.

FINANCIAL AID PICTURE
Students with need: Work study available nights, weekends, and for part-time students.

FINANCIAL AID PROCEDURES
Dates and Deadlines: Priority date 3/31; no closing date.

CONTACT
Donna Bassham, Coordinator of Financial Aid
128 Garfield, West Plains, MO 65775
(417) 255-7243

Missouri Technical School
St. Louis, Missouri
www.motech.edu   Federal Code: 016272

4-year for-profit engineering and technical college in very large city.
Enrollment: 201 undergrads.

BASIC COSTS (2005-2006)
Per-credit charge: $450.
Additional info: Costs for calendar year: lab fees $95 per term, apartment assistance housing $4800.

FINANCIAL AID PICTURE
Students with need: Need-based aid available for full-time and part-time students.
Students without need: This college only awards aid to students with need.

FINANCIAL AID PROCEDURES
Forms required: FAFSA, institutional form.
Dates and Deadlines: No deadline. Applicants notified on a rolling basis.

CONTACT
Cindy Ann Sinnott, Financial Aid Director
1167 Corporate Lake Drive, St. Louis, MO 63132-1716
(314) 569-3600 ext. 316

Missouri Valley College
Marshall, Missouri
www.moval.edu   Federal Code: 002489

4-year private liberal arts college in large town, affiliated with Presbyterian Church (USA).
Enrollment: 1,405 undergrads.

BASIC COSTS (2006-2007)
Tuition and fees: $15,250.
Room and board: $5,650.

FINANCIAL AID PICTURE
Students with need: Need-based aid available for full-time and part-time students. Work study available nights, weekends, and for part-time students.
Students without need: No-need awards available for academics, state/district residency.
Scholarships offered: Talent scholarships, 100 awards ranging from $1,000 to $13,000 (average $5,000) for general achievement (academic, athletic, artistic, other).

FINANCIAL AID PROCEDURES
Forms required: FAFSA, state aid form.
Dates and Deadlines: Priority date 3/1; no closing date. Applicants notified on a rolling basis starting 2/1; must reply within 6 week(s) of notification.
Transfers: Closing date 3/1.

CONTACT
Jennifer Malotte, Director of Financial Aid
500 East College Street, Marshall, MO 65340
(660) 831-4176

Missouri Western State University
St. Joseph, Missouri
www.missouriwestern.edu   Federal Code: 002490

4-year public business and liberal arts college in small city.
Enrollment: 4,769 undergrads.
Selectivity: Open admission; but selective for some programs.

BASIC COSTS (2005-2006)
Tuition and fees: $4,778; out-of-state residents $8,408.
Per-credit charge: $146; out-of-state residents $267.
Room and board: $4,400.

FINANCIAL AID PICTURE (2005-2006)
Students with need: 46% of average financial aid package awarded as scholarships/grants, 54% awarded as loans/jobs. Need-based aid available for part-time students.
Students without need: No-need awards available for academics, alumni affiliation, art, athletics, job skills, leadership, minority status, music/drama, state/district residency.

FINANCIAL AID PROCEDURES
Forms required: FAFSA, institutional form.
Dates and Deadlines: Closing date 3/1. Applicants notified on a rolling basis starting 4/5; must reply within 3 week(s) of notification.

CONTACT
Angela Beam, Director of Student Financial Aid
4525 Downs Drive, St. Joseph, MO 64507
(816) 271-4361

Moberly Area Community College
Moberly, Missouri
www.macc.edu   Federal Code: 002491

2-year public community college in large town.
Enrollment: 2,776 undergrads, 38% part-time. 740 full-time freshmen.
Selectivity: Open admission; but selective for some programs.

BASIC COSTS (2005-2006)
Tuition and fees: $1,890; out-of-district residents $2,670; out-of-state residents $4,080.
Per-credit charge: $55; out-of-district residents $81; out-of-state residents $128.
Room only: $1,800.

FINANCIAL AID PICTURE (2004-2005)
Students with need: Out of 518 full-time freshmen who applied for aid, 376 were judged to have need. Of these, 376 received aid, and 94 had their full need met. Average financial aid package met 50% of need; average scholarship/grant was $2,277; average loan was $2,634. For part-time students, average financial aid package was $4,850.
Students without need: 18 full-time freshmen who did not demonstrate need for aid received scholarships/grants; average award was $797. No-need awards available for academics, alumni affiliation, art, athletics, leadership, music/drama.
Scholarships offered: 11 full-time freshmen received athletic scholarships; average amount $6,010.

FINANCIAL AID PROCEDURES
Forms required: FAFSA.
Dates and Deadlines: Priority date 4/1; no closing date. Applicants notified on a rolling basis starting 4/1; must reply by 7/15 or within 2 week(s) of notification.

CONTACT
Amy Hager, Director of Financial Aid
101 College Avenue, Moberly, MO 65270-1304
(660) 263-4110 ext. 301

National American University: Kansas City
Independence, Missouri
www.national.edu

4-year for-profit university in large city.
Enrollment: 330 undergrads.
Selectivity: Open admission.

BASIC COSTS (2005-2006)
Additional info: Technology fees vary by program.

FINANCIAL AID PICTURE
Students with need: Need-based aid available for full-time and part-time students. Work study available nights, weekends, and for part-time students.
Students without need: This college only awards aid to students with need.

FINANCIAL AID PROCEDURES
Forms required: FAFSA, institutional form.
Dates and Deadlines: No deadline. Applicants notified on a rolling basis starting 6/4.

CONTACT
David Turner, Financial Aid Officer
3620 Arrowhead Avenue, Independence, MO 64057
(816) 412-7736

North Central Missouri College
Trenton, Missouri
www.ncmissouri.edu   Federal Code: 002514

2-year public community college in small town.
Enrollment: 946 undergrads, 27% part-time. 230 full-time freshmen.
Selectivity: Open admission; but selective for some programs.

BASIC COSTS (2005-2006)
Tuition and fees: $2,130; out-of-district residents $3,000; out-of-state residents $4,020.
Per-credit charge: $56; out-of-district residents $85; out-of-state residents $119.
Room and board: $4,404.
Additional info: Tuition/fee waivers available for adults, minority students.

FINANCIAL AID PICTURE
Students with need: Need-based aid available for full-time and part-time students. Work study available nights, weekends, and for part-time students.
Students without need: No-need awards available for academics, athletics, minority status, music/drama.

FINANCIAL AID PROCEDURES
Forms required: FAFSA, institutional form.
Dates and Deadlines: Priority date 3/15; no closing date. Applicants notified on a rolling basis starting 3/15.
Transfers: Transfer students may not receive same awards after transferring since some funds campus-based.

CONTACT
John Brandt, Financial Aid Officer
1301 Main Street, Trenton, MO 64683
(660) 359-3948 ext. 402

Northwest Missouri State University
Maryville, Missouri
www.nwmissouri.edu   Federal Code: 002496

4-year public university in large town.
Enrollment: 5,269 undergrads, 11% part-time. 1,268 full-time freshmen.
Selectivity: Admits less than 50% of applicants.

BASIC COSTS (2006-2007)
Tuition and fees: $5,910; out-of-state residents $9,960.
Per-credit charge: $184; out-of-state residents $318.
Room and board: $5,792.
Additional info: New student fee of $75. Primary textbooks included in tuition. Tuition/fee waivers available for minority students.

FINANCIAL AID PICTURE (2004-2005)
Students with need: 35% of average financial aid package awarded as scholarships/grants, 65% awarded as loans/jobs. Need-based aid available for part-time students. Work study available nights, weekends, and for part-time students.
Students without need: No-need awards available for academics, alumni affiliation, art, athletics, job skills, leadership, minority status, music/drama, state/district residency.

FINANCIAL AID PROCEDURES
Forms required: FAFSA.
Dates and Deadlines: Priority date 4/1; no closing date. Applicants notified on a rolling basis starting 3/15; must reply within 2 week(s) of notification.
Transfers: No deadline. Applicants notified on a rolling basis starting 5/10. Transfer scholarship based on academic record.

CONTACT
Del Morley, Director of Financial Assistance
800 University Drive, Maryville, MO 64468-6001
(660) 562-1363

Ozark Christian College
Joplin, Missouri
www.occ.edu   Federal Code: 015569

4-year private Bible college in large town, affiliated with nondenominational tradition.
Enrollment: 827 undergrads, 12% part-time. 209 full-time freshmen.

BASIC COSTS (2006-2007)
Tuition and fees: $7,830.
Per-credit charge: $245.
Room and board: $4,050.

FINANCIAL AID PICTURE (2005-2006)
Students with need: 47% of average financial aid package awarded as scholarships/grants, 53% awarded as loans/jobs. Need-based aid available for part-time students.
Students without need: No-need awards available for academics, leadership.
Cumulative student debt: 43% of graduating class had student loans; average debt was $14,587.

FINANCIAL AID PROCEDURES
Forms required: FAFSA.
Dates and Deadlines: Priority date 4/1; no closing date. Applicants notified on a rolling basis starting 6/1; must reply within 4 week(s) of notification.
Transfers: Academic transcripts required. ACT scores may qualify student for grants or scholarships.

CONTACT
Kim Balentine, Director of Financial Aid
1111 North Main Street, Joplin, MO 64801
(417) 624-2518

Ozarks Technical Community College
Springfield, Missouri
www.otc.edu   Federal Code: 030830

2-year public community and technical college in small city.
Enrollment: 7,999 undergrads, 43% part-time. 1,656 full-time freshmen.
Selectivity: Open admission; but selective for some programs.

BASIC COSTS (2005-2006)
Tuition and fees: $2,700; out-of-district residents $3,300; out-of-state residents $4,200.
Per-credit charge: $78; out-of-district residents $98; out-of-state residents $128.

FINANCIAL AID PICTURE
Students with need: Need-based aid available for full-time and part-time students.
Students without need: This college only awards aid to students with need.

FINANCIAL AID PROCEDURES
Forms required: FAFSA, institutional form.
Dates and Deadlines: Priority date 5/1; closing date 7/1. Applicants notified on a rolling basis starting 5/16.

CONTACT
Jeff Ford, Director of Financial Aid
1001 East Chestnut Expressway, Springfield, MO 65802
(417) 895-7142

Park University
Parkville, Missouri
www.park.edu   Federal Code: 002498

4-year private university in small town.
Enrollment: 11,857 undergrads, 92% part-time. 166 full-time freshmen.
Selectivity: Admits 50 to 75% of applicants.

BASIC COSTS (2006-2007)
Tuition and fees: $7,260.
Per-credit charge: $242.
Room and board: $5,180.
Additional info: Tuition varies by program and hours taken.

FINANCIAL AID PICTURE (2004-2005)
Students with need: Out of 134 full-time freshmen who applied for aid, 124 were judged to have need. Of these, 124 received aid, and 36 had their full need met. Average financial aid package met 76% of need; average scholarship/grant was $1,910; average loan was $2,590. For part-time students, average financial aid package was $5,380.
Students without need: No-need awards available for academics, alumni affiliation, art, athletics, job skills, leadership, minority status, music/drama, religious affiliation, ROTC.

FINANCIAL AID PROCEDURES
Forms required: FAFSA, institutional form.
Dates and Deadlines: Priority date 4/1; closing date 8/1. Applicants notified on a rolling basis starting 4/1.

CONTACT
Cathy Colapietro, Director of Admissions and Student Financial Services
8700 River Park Drive, Parkville, MO 64152
(816) 741-2000 ext. 6290

Patricia Stevens College
St. Louis, Missouri
www.patriciastevenscollege.edu   Federal Code: 008552

2-year for-profit business and junior college in very large city.
Enrollment: 177 undergrads, 27% part-time. 130 full-time freshmen.
Selectivity: Open admission.

BASIC COSTS (2006-2007)
Tuition and fees: $10,150.
Per-credit charge: $195.
Additional info: Books included in tuition. Tuition at time of enrollment locked for 2 years.

FINANCIAL AID PICTURE
Students with need: Need-based aid available for full-time and part-time students.
Students without need: This college only awards aid to students with need.

FINANCIAL AID PROCEDURES
Forms required: FAFSA.
Dates and Deadlines: No deadline. Applicants notified on a rolling basis.

CONTACT
Greg Elsenrath, Financial Aid Director
330 North Fourth Street, Suite 306, St. Louis, MO 63102
(314) 421-0949 ext. 17

Penn Valley Community College
Kansas City, Missouri
www.mcckc.edu   Federal Code: 002484

2-year public community college in large city.
Enrollment: 3,550 undergrads, 64% part-time. 261 full-time freshmen.
Selectivity: Open admission; but selective for some programs.

BASIC COSTS (2006-2007)
Tuition and fees: $2,190; out-of-district residents $3,990; out-of-state residents $5,400.
Per-credit charge: $73; out-of-district residents $133; out-of-state residents $180.

FINANCIAL AID PICTURE (2004-2005)
Students with need: Out of 261 full-time freshmen who applied for aid, 243 were judged to have need. Of these, 226 received aid, and 5 had their full need met. For part-time students, average financial aid package was $2,142.
Students without need: 4 full-time freshmen who did not demonstrate need for aid received scholarships/grants; average award was $1,184. No-need awards available for academics, athletics, leadership.
Scholarships offered: 5 full-time freshmen received athletic scholarships; average amount $1,880.

FINANCIAL AID PROCEDURES
Forms required: FAFSA, institutional form.
Dates and Deadlines: Priority date 5/30; no closing date. Applicants notified on a rolling basis starting 4/8.

CONTACT
Cindy Butler, District Director, Student Financial Aid
3201 Southwest Trafficway, Kansas City, MO 64111-2429
(816) 759-1527

Ranken Technical College
St. Louis, Missouri
www.ranken.edu   Federal Code: 012500

4-year private technical college in very large city.
Enrollment: 1,617 undergrads, 35% part-time. 477 full-time freshmen.
Selectivity: Open admission.

BASIC COSTS (2006-2007)
Tuition and fees: $10,670.
Additional info: Book and tool costs vary by program.

FINANCIAL AID PICTURE
Students with need: Need-based aid available for full-time and part-time students. Work study available nights.

FINANCIAL AID PROCEDURES
Forms required: FAFSA.
Dates and Deadlines: No deadline. Applicants notified on a rolling basis starting 4/1.

CONTACT
Michelle Williams, Director, Financial Aid
4431 Finney Avenue, St. Louis, MO 63113
(314) 286-4866

Research College of Nursing
Kansas City, Missouri
www.researchcollege.edu   Federal Code: 006392

4-year for-profit nursing college in very large city, affiliated with Roman Catholic Church.
Enrollment: 246 undergrads, 1% part-time. 50 full-time freshmen.
Selectivity: Admits 50 to 75% of applicants.

BASIC COSTS (2005-2006)
Tuition and fees: $19,600.
Per-credit charge: $630.
Room and board: $6,100.

FINANCIAL AID PICTURE (2005-2006)
Students with need: 42% of average financial aid package awarded as scholarships/grants, 58% awarded as loans/jobs. Need-based aid available for part-time students.
Additional info: Financial aid handled by Rockhurst University for freshmen and sophomores.

FINANCIAL AID PROCEDURES
Forms required: FAFSA, institutional form.
Dates and Deadlines: Priority date 3/15; no closing date. Applicants notified on a rolling basis starting 3/15.

CONTACT
Stacie Withers, Director of Financial Aid
2525 East Meyer Boulevard, Kansas City, MO 64132-1199
(816) 995-2814

Rockhurst University
Kansas City, Missouri
www.rockhurst.edu   Federal Code: 002499

4-year private business and liberal arts college in very large city, affiliated with Roman Catholic Church.
Enrollment: 1,385 undergrads, 12% part-time. 305 full-time freshmen.
Selectivity: Admits 50 to 75% of applicants.

BASIC COSTS (2006-2007)
Tuition and fees: $20,840.
Per-credit charge: $675.
Room and board: $6,000.

FINANCIAL AID PICTURE (2004-2005)
Students with need: Out of 303 full-time freshmen who applied for aid, 272 were judged to have need. Of these, 272 received aid, and 10 had their full need met. Average financial aid package met 100% of need; average scholarship/grant was $5,850; average loan was $2,319. For part-time students, average financial aid package was $9,606.
Students without need: 21 full-time freshmen who did not demonstrate need for aid received scholarships/grants; average award was $8,473. No-need awards available for academics, alumni affiliation, art, athletics, leadership, music/drama, ROTC.
Scholarships offered: 32 full-time freshmen received athletic scholarships; average amount $9,837.
Cumulative student debt: 79% of graduating class had student loans; average debt was $25,823.
Additional info: Auditions, portfolios required for some scholarships.

FINANCIAL AID PROCEDURES
Forms required: FAFSA.
Dates and Deadlines: Priority date 3/1; closing date 6/1. Applicants notified on a rolling basis starting 1/30; must reply within 4 week(s) of notification.
Transfers: Must reply within 2 week(s) of notification. Scholarships awarded to qualified first-time transfers.

CONTACT
Carla Boren, Director of Financial Aid
1100 Rockhurst Road, Kansas City, MO 64110-2561
(816) 501-4100

St. Charles Community College
Cottleville, Missouri
www.stchas.edu   Federal Code: 025306

2-year public community college in small city.
Enrollment: 5,746 undergrads, 46% part-time. 1,080 full-time freshmen.
Selectivity: Open admission; but selective for some programs.

BASIC COSTS (2006-2007)
Tuition and fees: $2,280; out-of-district residents $3,360; out-of-state residents $4,980.
Per-credit charge: $76; out-of-district residents $112; out-of-state residents $166.

FINANCIAL AID PICTURE (2004-2005)
Students with need: 68% of average financial aid package awarded as scholarships/grants, 32% awarded as loans/jobs. Need-based aid available for part-time students.
Students without need: No-need awards available for academics, art, athletics, leadership, music/drama.

FINANCIAL AID PROCEDURES
Forms required: FAFSA, institutional form.
Dates and Deadlines: Priority date 6/1; no closing date. Applicants notified on a rolling basis starting 3/1; must reply within 3 week(s) of notification.

CONTACT
Kathy Brockgreitens-Gober, Director of Admissions/Registrar/Financial Assistance
4601 Mid Rivers Mall Drive, Cottleville, MO 63376
(636) 922-8270

St. Louis Christian College
Florissant, Missouri
www.slcconline.edu   Federal Code: 012580

4-year private Bible college in small city, affiliated with Christian Church.
Enrollment: 261 undergrads, 19% part-time. 44 full-time freshmen.

BASIC COSTS (2005-2006)
Room and board: $5,000.
Additional info: Full-time residential students receive full scholarships for tuition; required fees are $900 annually. Full-time commuter students pay $125 per-credit-hour; required fees, $900.

FINANCIAL AID PICTURE (2005-2006)
Students with need: 50% of average financial aid package awarded as scholarships/grants, 50% awarded as loans/jobs. Need-based aid available for part-time students.
Students without need: No-need awards available for academics, alumni affiliation, leadership, music/drama, religious affiliation.
Scholarships offered: President's Scholarship; full tuition; ACT score 30 or higher; 1 available. Chancellor's Scholarships; two-thirds tuition; ACT 28 or higher; 2 available. Dean's Scholarships; half tuition; ACT 28 or higher; unlimited number available.

FINANCIAL AID PROCEDURES
Forms required: FAFSA, institutional form.
Dates and Deadlines: Closing date 8/1. Applicants notified on a rolling basis starting 7/20; must reply within 2 week(s) of notification.

CONTACT
Cathi Wilhoit, Financial Aid Director
1360 Grandview Drive, Florissant, MO 63033
(314) 837-6777 ext. 1101

St. Louis Community College at Meramec
St. Louis, Missouri
www.stlcc.edu   Federal Code: 002471

2-year public community college in large city.
Enrollment: 12,130 undergrads.
Selectivity: Open admission; but selective for some programs.

BASIC COSTS (2005-2006)
Tuition and fees: $2,340; out-of-district residents $3,090; out-of-state residents $4,140.
Per-credit charge: $78; out-of-district residents $103; out-of-state residents $138.

FINANCIAL AID PICTURE
Students with need: Need-based aid available for full-time and part-time students.

FINANCIAL AID PROCEDURES
Forms required: FAFSA, institutional form.
Dates and Deadlines: Closing date 6/30. Applicants notified on a rolling basis starting 2/1.

CONTACT
Helen Nauman, Manager of Student Aid
11333 Big Bend Boulevard, Kirkwood, MO 63122-5799
(314) 984-7500

St. Louis University
St. Louis, Missouri
www.slu.edu   Federal Code: 002506

4-year private university in very large city, affiliated with Roman Catholic Church.
Enrollment: 7,081 undergrads, 8% part-time. 1,669 full-time freshmen.
Selectivity: Admits over 75% of applicants.

BASIC COSTS (2006-2007)
Tuition and fees: $26,375.
Per-credit charge: $915.
Room and board: $8,410.
Additional info: Tuition/fee waivers available for adults.

FINANCIAL AID PICTURE (2005-2006)
Students with need: Average financial aid package met 64% of need; average scholarship/grant was $13,434; average loan was $3,450. For part-time students, average financial aid package was $6,697.
Students without need: No-need awards available for academics, art, athletics, leadership, music/drama, religious affiliation, ROTC.
Cumulative student debt: 67% of graduating class had student loans; average debt was $24,552.
Additional info: Physical therapy scholarship candidates must apply by December 1.

FINANCIAL AID PROCEDURES
Forms required: FAFSA.
Dates and Deadlines: Priority date 3/1; no closing date. Applicants notified on a rolling basis starting 3/1; must reply by 5/1 or within 4 week(s) of notification.
Transfers: Priority date 2/1; no deadline. Applicants notified on a rolling basis starting 3/1. Students should file FAFSA by March 1 for Missouri state funds.

CONTACT
Cari Wickliffe, Financial Aid Director
221 North Grand Boulevard, St. Louis, MO 63103-2097
(314) 977-2350

St. Luke's College
Kansas City, Missouri
www.saintlukescollege.edu   Federal Code: 009782

Upper-division private nursing college in large city, affiliated with Episcopal Church.
Enrollment: 113 undergrads, 10% part-time.

BASIC COSTS (2005-2006)
Tuition and fees: $9,520.
Per-credit charge: $295.

FINANCIAL AID PICTURE
Students with need: Need-based aid available for full-time and part-time students.

FINANCIAL AID PROCEDURES
Forms required: FAFSA, institutional form.
Dates and Deadlines: No deadline. Applicants notified by 5/1.

CONTACT
Jeff Gannon, Director of Financial Aid
8320 Ward Parkway, Suite 300, Kansas City, MO 64114
(816) 932-2194

Southeast Missouri State University
Cape Girardeau, Missouri
www.semo.edu   Federal Code: 002501

4-year public university in large town.
Enrollment: 8,380 undergrads, 19% part-time. 1,391 full-time freshmen.
Selectivity: Admits over 75% of applicants.

BASIC COSTS (2005-2006)
Tuition and fees: $5,145; out-of-state residents $9,000.
Per-credit charge: $159; out-of-state residents $287.
Room and board: $5,321.

FINANCIAL AID PICTURE (2004-2005)
Students with need: Out of 1,058 full-time freshmen who applied for aid, 755 were judged to have need. Of these, 753 received aid, and 145 had their full need met. Average financial aid package met 66% of need; average scholarship/grant was $3,986; average loan was $2,690. For part-time students, average financial aid package was $4,021.
Students without need: 284 full-time freshmen who did not demonstrate need for aid received scholarships/grants; average award was $3,383. No-need awards available for academics, alumni affiliation, art, athletics, job skills, leadership, minority status, music/drama, ROTC, state/district residency.
Scholarships offered: 30 full-time freshmen received athletic scholarships; average amount $9,526.
Cumulative student debt: 63% of graduating class had student loans; average debt was $16,006.

FINANCIAL AID PROCEDURES
Forms required: FAFSA.
Dates and Deadlines: Priority date 3/1; no closing date. Applicants notified on a rolling basis starting 4/1; must reply by 4/1 or within 3 week(s) of notification.
Transfers: Applicants notified on a rolling basis starting 4/1; must reply by 8/15 or within 3 week(s) of notification.

CONTACT
Karen Walker, Director of Financial Aid Services
One University Plaza, Cape Girardeau, MO 63701
(573) 651-2253

Southwest Baptist University
Bolivar, Missouri
www.sbuniv.edu   Federal Code: 002502

4-year private university in small town, affiliated with Southern Baptist Convention.
Enrollment: 2,358 undergrads, 25% part-time. 369 full-time freshmen.
Selectivity: Admits over 75% of applicants.

BASIC COSTS (2006-2007)
Tuition and fees: $14,100.
Room and board: $4,200.

FINANCIAL AID PICTURE (2005-2006)
Students with need: Out of 334 full-time freshmen who applied for aid, 262 were judged to have need. Of these, 261 received aid, and 66 had their full need met. Average financial aid package met 72% of need; average scholarship/grant was $3,866; average loan was $3,641. For part-time students, average financial aid package was $4,321.
Students without need: 94 full-time freshmen who did not demonstrate need for aid received scholarships/grants; average award was $5,192. No-need awards available for academics, art, athletics, minority status, music/drama, state/district residency.
Scholarships offered: 63 full-time freshmen received athletic scholarships; average amount $7,661.
Cumulative student debt: 73% of graduating class had student loans; average debt was $11,268.

FINANCIAL AID PROCEDURES
Forms required: FAFSA, institutional form.
Dates and Deadlines: Priority date 3/15; no closing date. Applicants notified on a rolling basis starting 3/1; must reply within 2 week(s) of notification.

CONTACT
Brad Gamble, Director of Financial Aid
1600 University Avenue, Bolivar, MO 65613-2597
(417) 328-1822

State Fair Community College
Sedalia, Missouri
www.sfccmo.edu   Federal Code: 007628

2-year public community college in large town.
Enrollment: 2,652 undergrads, 41% part-time. 573 full-time freshmen.
Selectivity: Open admission; but selective for some programs.

BASIC COSTS (2005-2006)
Tuition and fees: $2,100; out-of-district residents $2,910; out-of-state residents $4,500.
Per-credit charge: $60; out-of-district residents $87; out-of-state residents $140.

FINANCIAL AID PICTURE (2004-2005)
Students with need: 47% of average financial aid package awarded as scholarships/grants, 53% awarded as loans/jobs. Need-based aid available for part-time students. Work study available nights, weekends, and for part-time students.
Students without need: This college only awards aid to students with need.

FINANCIAL AID PROCEDURES
Forms required: FAFSA.
Dates and Deadlines: Priority date 7/1; no closing date. Applicants notified on a rolling basis starting 7/15; must reply within 3 week(s) of notification.

CONTACT
John Matthews, Director of Financial Aid
3201 West 16th Street, Sedalia, MO 65301-2199
(660) 530-5800 ext. 295

Stephens College
Columbia, Missouri
www.stephens.edu   Federal Code: 002512

4-year private liberal arts college for women in small city.
Enrollment: 734 undergrads, 22% part-time. 157 full-time freshmen.
Selectivity: Admits over 75% of applicants.

BASIC COSTS (2006-2007)
Tuition and fees: $20,500.
Room and board: $7,635.

FINANCIAL AID PICTURE (2005-2006)
Students with need: Out of 139 full-time freshmen who applied for aid, 119 were judged to have need. Of these, 119 received aid, and 35 had their full need met. Average financial aid package met 74% of need; average scholarship/grant was $6,604; average loan was $3,452. For part-time students, average financial aid package was $8,125.
Students without need: No-need awards available for academics, alumni affiliation, athletics, leadership.

Scholarships offered: 15 full-time freshmen received athletic scholarships; average amount $3,007.

FINANCIAL AID PROCEDURES
Forms required: FAFSA.
Dates and Deadlines: Priority date 3/15; no closing date. Applicants notified on a rolling basis starting 3/1; must reply within 2 week(s) of notification.
Transfers: Phi Theta Kappa students transferring from 2-year institutions eligible for Phi Theta Kappa scholarship.

CONTACT
Rachel Touchatt, Director of Financial Aid
1200 East Broadway, Box 2121, Columbia, MO 65215
(800) 876-7207

Three Rivers Community College
Poplar Bluff, Missouri
www.trcc.edu   Federal Code: 004713

2-year public community college in large town.
Enrollment: 2,597 undergrads, 39% part-time. 1,083 full-time freshmen.
Selectivity: Open admission; but selective for some programs.

BASIC COSTS (2005-2006)
Tuition and fees: $2,080; out-of-district residents $3,190; out-of-state residents $3,910.
Per-credit charge: $61; out-of-district residents $98; out-of-state residents $122.
Additional info: Book rental $12 per book. Refundable book deposit fee $25 per semester. Lab fees vary per course.

FINANCIAL AID PICTURE
Students with need: Need-based aid available for full-time and part-time students.
Students without need: No-need awards available for academics, athletics, state/district residency.

FINANCIAL AID PROCEDURES
Forms required: FAFSA, institutional form.
Dates and Deadlines: Priority date 5/1; no closing date. Applicants notified on a rolling basis starting 6/1; must reply within 2 week(s) of notification.

CONTACT
George Jarboe, Vice President for Finance
2080 Three Rivers Boulevard, Poplar Bluff, MO 63901-1308
(573) 840-9662

Truman State University
Kirksville, Missouri
www.admissions.truman.edu   Federal Code: 002495

4-year public university and liberal arts college in large town.
Enrollment: 5,474 undergrads, 2% part-time. 1,480 full-time freshmen.
Selectivity: Admits over 75% of applicants.

BASIC COSTS (2005-2006)
Tuition and fees: $5,862; out-of-state residents $10,042.
Per-credit charge: $239; out-of-state residents $413.
Room and board: $5,380.

FINANCIAL AID PICTURE (2005-2006)
Students with need: Out of 891 full-time freshmen who applied for aid, 534 were judged to have need. Of these, 534 received aid, and 321 had their full need met. Average financial aid package met 81% of need; average scholarship/grant was $2,906; average loan was $3,110. Need-based aid available for part-time students.
Students without need: 918 full-time freshmen who did not demonstrate need for aid received scholarships/grants; average award was $4,006. No-need awards available for academics, alumni affiliation, art, athletics, leadership, music/drama, ROTC, state/district residency.
Scholarships offered: *Merit:* Pershing Scholarship: awards 12 full scholarships for tuition, room and board to outstanding scholars and leaders; provides up to $4,000 for a Study-Abroad experience. Truman Leadership Award: provides amounts up to full tuition, room & board for Missouri residents; awarded to high school seniors who demonstrate energetic leadership in the classroom, school, and community as well as academic acheivement. *Athletic:* 83 full-time freshmen received athletic scholarships; average amount $2,773.
Cumulative student debt: 43% of graduating class had student loans; average debt was $16,546.
Additional info: Out-of-state students whose parents work in Missouri may deduct $1 for every dollar paid in Missouri income taxes from out-of-state tuition.

FINANCIAL AID PROCEDURES
Forms required: FAFSA.
Dates and Deadlines: Priority date 4/1; no closing date. Applicants notified on a rolling basis starting 3/1; must reply within 4 week(s) of notification.
Transfers: Applicants notified on a rolling basis starting 3/1. Limited number of automatic and competitive awards offered to transfer students.

CONTACT
Melinda Wood, Financial Aid Director
McClain Hall 205, Kirksville, MO 63501-9980
(660) 785-4130

University of Missouri: Columbia
Columbia, Missouri
www.missouri.edu   Federal Code: 002516

4-year public university in small city.
Enrollment: 21,046 undergrads, 5% part-time. 4,663 full-time freshmen.
Selectivity: Admits over 75% of applicants.

BASIC COSTS (2005-2006)
Tuition and fees: $7,745; out-of-state residents $17,522.
Per-credit charge: $217; out-of-state residents $542.
Room and board: $6,245.

FINANCIAL AID PICTURE (2005-2006)
Students with need: Out of 3,303 full-time freshmen who applied for aid, 2,072 were judged to have need. Of these, 2,058 received aid, and 520 had their full need met. Average financial aid package met 89% of need; average scholarship/grant was $6,005; average loan was $3,609. For part-time students, average financial aid package was $8,896.
Students without need: 1,322 full-time freshmen who did not demonstrate need for aid received scholarships/grants; average award was $4,181. No-need awards available for academics, alumni affiliation, art, athletics, leadership, minority status, music/drama, ROTC, state/district residency.
Scholarships offered: *Merit:* Varies by division, college, and program. *Athletic:* 192 full-time freshmen received athletic scholarships; average amount $8,968.
Cumulative student debt: 50% of graduating class had student loans; average debt was $17,907.
Additional info: Scholarship available for international students based on success during 1st semester.

FINANCIAL AID PROCEDURES
Forms required: FAFSA.
Dates and Deadlines: Priority date 3/1; no closing date. Applicants notified on a rolling basis starting 4/1; must reply within 4 week(s) of notification.
Transfers: No deadline. Applicants notified on a rolling basis starting 4/1; must reply within 4 week(s) of notification.

Missouri University of Missouri: Columbia

CONTACT
Joe Camille, Director of Student Financial Aid
230 Jesse Hall, Columbia, MO 65211
(573) 882-7506

University of Missouri: Kansas City
Kansas City, Missouri
www.umkc.edu
Federal Code: 002518

4-year public university in large city.
Enrollment: 7,070 undergrads, 20% part-time. 1,008 full-time freshmen.
Selectivity: Admits 50 to 75% of applicants.

BASIC COSTS (2005-2006)
Tuition and fees: $7,394; out-of-state residents $17,171.
Per-credit charge: $217; out-of-state residents $542.
Room and board: $6,670.

FINANCIAL AID PICTURE (2005-2006)
Students with need: Out of 950 full-time freshmen who applied for aid, 642 were judged to have need. Of these, 642 received aid, and 385 had their full need met. Average financial aid package met 56% of need; average scholarship/grant was $6,941; average loan was $3,666. For part-time students, average financial aid package was $5,999.
Students without need: 216 full-time freshmen who did not demonstrate need for aid received scholarships/grants; average award was $3,997. No-need awards available for academics, alumni affiliation, art, athletics, leadership, minority status, music/drama, state/district residency.
Scholarships offered: 21 full-time freshmen received athletic scholarships; average amount $13,089.
Cumulative student debt: 87% of graduating class had student loans; average debt was $16,387.

FINANCIAL AID PROCEDURES
Forms required: FAFSA.
Dates and Deadlines: Priority date 3/1; no closing date. Applicants notified on a rolling basis starting 4/1; must reply within 2 week(s) of notification.

CONTACT
Jan Brandow, Director of Student Financial Aid
5100 Rockhill Road, AC120, Kansas City, MO 64110-2499
(816) 235-1154

University of Missouri: Rolla
Rolla, Missouri
www.umr.edu
Federal Code: 002517

4-year public university and engineering college in large town.
Enrollment: 4,220 undergrads, 8% part-time. 870 full-time freshmen.

BASIC COSTS (2005-2006)
Tuition and fees: $7,536; out-of-state residents $17,313.
Per-credit charge: $217; out-of-state residents $542.
Room and board: $5,840.
Additional info: Tuition/fee waivers available for minority students.

FINANCIAL AID PICTURE (2004-2005)
Students with need: Out of 720 full-time freshmen who applied for aid, 510 were judged to have need. Of these, 500 received aid, and 120 had their full need met. Average financial aid package met 87% of need; average scholarship/grant was $6,700; average loan was $2,970. For part-time students, average financial aid package was $9,410.
Students without need: 300 full-time freshmen who did not demonstrate need for aid received scholarships/grants; average award was $6,820. No-need awards available for academics, alumni affiliation, athletics, job skills, leadership, minority status, music/drama, religious affiliation, ROTC, state/district residency.

FINANCIAL AID PROCEDURES
Forms required: FAFSA.
Dates and Deadlines: Priority date 3/1; no closing date. Applicants notified on a rolling basis; must reply within 3 week(s) of notification.
Transfers: Special scholarships available to transfer students.

CONTACT
Robert Whites, Director of Financial Assistance
106 Parker Hall, Rolla, MO 65409
(573) 341-4282

University of Missouri: St. Louis
St. Louis, Missouri
www.umsl.edu
Federal Code: 002519

4-year public university in very large city.
Enrollment: 9,150 undergrads, 37% part-time. 498 full-time freshmen.
Selectivity: Admits 50 to 75% of applicants.

BASIC COSTS (2005-2006)
Tuition and fees: $7,618; out-of-state residents $17,395.
Per-credit charge: $217; out-of-state residents $542.
Room and board: $6,428.

FINANCIAL AID PICTURE (2005-2006)
Students with need: Out of 340 full-time freshmen who applied for aid, 263 were judged to have need. Of these, 259 received aid, and 39 had their full need met. Average financial aid package met 64% of need; average scholarship/grant was $5,836; average loan was $2,595. For part-time students, average financial aid package was $8,801.
Students without need: 88 full-time freshmen who did not demonstrate need for aid received scholarships/grants; average award was $4,261. No-need awards available for academics, alumni affiliation, art, athletics, music/drama, ROTC, state/district residency.
Scholarships offered: Merit: Curator's Scholarships for Missouri freshmen with high test scores and class rank; unlimited awarded; $3,500 renewable annually. Chancellor's Scholarships for freshmen with strong test scores and class rank; unlimited awarded; $2,500 annually. Pierre Laclede Honors College Scholarships for freshmen and transfer students; varying amounts. Mark Twain Scholarships for freshmen with strong test scores and class rank; $1,000 annually. National Access Scholarships for freshmen and transfer students with strong test scores and grade point average; amount varies. Scholarship to be applied to nonresident fee. **Athletic:** 12 full-time freshmen received athletic scholarships; average amount $9,969.
Cumulative student debt: 47% of graduating class had student loans; average debt was $19,435.

FINANCIAL AID PROCEDURES
Forms required: FAFSA.
Dates and Deadlines: Priority date 4/1; no closing date. Applicants notified on a rolling basis starting 4/1; must reply within 2 week(s) of notification.

CONTACT
Tony Georges, Director of Student Financial Aid
One University Boulevard, St. Louis, MO 63121-4400
(314) 516-5526

Vatterott College: St. Joseph
St. Joseph, Missouri
www.vatterott-college.edu
Federal Code: 026092

2-year for-profit branch campus and technical college in small city.
Enrollment: 240 undergrads.

Selectivity: Open admission.

FINANCIAL AID PICTURE
Students with need: Need-based aid available for full-time and part-time students.
Scholarships offered: Make the Grade Scholarship; up to $1,000, total based on high school grades; for first 12 months after high school graduation.

FINANCIAL AID PROCEDURES
Forms required: FAFSA.
Dates and Deadlines: No deadline.

CONTACT
Marcia Hurley, Financial Aid Administrator
3131 Frederick Avenue, St. Joseph, MO 64506
(816) 364-5399

Washington University in St. Louis
St. Louis, Missouri
www.wustl.edu
Federal Code: 002520
CSS Code: 6929

4-year private university in large city.
Enrollment: 6,495 undergrads, 6% part-time. 1,376 full-time freshmen.
Selectivity: Admits less than 50% of applicants.

BASIC COSTS (2006-2007)
Tuition and fees: $33,788.
Room and board: $10,452.

FINANCIAL AID PICTURE (2005-2006)
Students with need: Out of 915 full-time freshmen who applied for aid, 547 were judged to have need. Of these, 534 received aid, and 534 had their full need met. Average financial aid package met 100% of need; average scholarship/grant was $21,653; average loan was $4,461. Need-based aid available for part-time students.
Students without need: 243 full-time freshmen who did not demonstrate need for aid received scholarships/grants; average award was $9,186. No-need awards available for academics, ROTC.
Scholarships offered: Numerous scholarships available; ranging up to full tuition plus stipend, renewable for 4 years; based on exceptional academic promise.

FINANCIAL AID PROCEDURES
Forms required: FAFSA, CSS PROFILE.
Dates and Deadlines: Closing date 2/15. Applicants notified by 4/1; must reply by 5/1.

CONTACT
William Witbrodt, Director of Student Financial Services
Campus Box 1089, One Brookings Drive, St. Louis, MO 63130-4899
(314) 935-5900

Webster University
St. Louis, Missouri
www.webster.edu
Federal Code: 002521

4-year private university in large city.
Enrollment: 3,407 undergrads, 26% part-time. 453 full-time freshmen.
Selectivity: Admits 50 to 75% of applicants.

BASIC COSTS (2006-2007)
Tuition and fees: $18,240.
Per-credit charge: $465.
Room and board: $7,403.
Additional info: Tuition $20,390 for theater conservatory students.

FINANCIAL AID PICTURE (2004-2005)
Students with need: Out of 408 full-time freshmen who applied for aid, 332 were judged to have need. Of these, 332 received aid. For part-time students, average financial aid package was $9,798.
Students without need: 124 full-time freshmen who did not demonstrate need for aid received scholarships/grants; average award was $9,576. No-need awards available for academics, art, music/drama.
Scholarships offered: Daniel Webster Scholarships for students with 3.8 GPA, top 10% class rank, 29 ACT and interview; 5 awarded; full tuition. Webster Academic Scholarships for students with minimum 3.0 GPA and 23 ACT; unlimited awarded; ranging from $2,000-$10,000. Leadership Scholarships based on minimum 3.3 GPA and 24 ACT, resume of activities; 15 awarded; $1,500.

FINANCIAL AID PROCEDURES
Forms required: FAFSA, institutional form.
Dates and Deadlines: Priority date 4/1; no closing date. Applicants notified on a rolling basis starting 2/9; must reply within 2 week(s) of notification.

CONTACT
Jonathan Gruett, Director of Financial Aid
470 East Lockwood Avenue, St. Louis, MO 63119-3194
(314) 968-6992

Westminster College
Fulton, Missouri
www.westminster-mo.edu
Federal Code: 002523

4-year private liberal arts college in large town, affiliated with Presbyterian Church (USA).
Enrollment: 891 undergrads. 270 full-time freshmen.
Selectivity: Admits over 75% of applicants.

BASIC COSTS (2006-2007)
Tuition and fees: $15,030.
Per-credit charge: $750.
Room and board: $6,140.
Additional info: Tuition/fee waivers available for minority students.

FINANCIAL AID PICTURE (2005-2006)
Students with need: Out of 235 full-time freshmen who applied for aid, 183 were judged to have need. Of these, 183 received aid, and 66 had their full need met. Average financial aid package met 87% of need; average scholarship/grant was $10,896; average loan was $3,358. For part-time students, average financial aid package was $5,403.
Students without need: 132 full-time freshmen who did not demonstrate need for aid received scholarships/grants; average award was $10,319. No-need awards available for academics, alumni affiliation, leadership, minority status, music/drama, state/district residency.
Cumulative student debt: 66% of graduating class had student loans; average debt was $17,534.

FINANCIAL AID PROCEDURES
Forms required: FAFSA.
Dates and Deadlines: Priority date 2/15; no closing date. Applicants notified on a rolling basis starting 2/28; must reply within 3 week(s) of notification.
Transfers: Priority date 2/28.

CONTACT
Aimee Bristow, Director of Financial Aid
501 Westminster Avenue, Fulton, MO 65251-1299
(573) 592-5365

William Jewell College
Liberty, Missouri
www.jewell.edu
Federal Code: 002524

4-year private liberal arts college in large town, affiliated with Baptist faith.
Enrollment: 1,331 undergrads, 3% part-time. 302 full-time freshmen.
Selectivity: Admits 50 to 75% of applicants.

BASIC COSTS (2005-2006)
Tuition and fees: $18,500.
Per-credit charge: $625.
Room and board: $5,350.
Additional info: Tuition/fee waivers available for minority students.

FINANCIAL AID PICTURE (2005-2006)
Students with need: Out of 249 full-time freshmen who applied for aid, 170 were judged to have need. Of these, 170 received aid. For part-time students, average financial aid package was $5,730.
Students without need: No-need awards available for academics, alumni affiliation, art, athletics, job skills, music/drama, religious affiliation.
Scholarships offered: Merit: Distinguished Scholar Award, full tuition, competitive academic scholarship offered annually by invitation only to qualified high school seniors, 4 awarded annually; Oxbridge Scholar Award, $9,000, for students accepted into Oxbridge Honors Program. **Athletic:** 58 full-time freshmen received athletic scholarships; average amount $4,012.
Cumulative student debt: 71% of graduating class had student loans; average debt was $17,133.

FINANCIAL AID PROCEDURES
Forms required: FAFSA.
Dates and Deadlines: Priority date 3/1; no closing date. Applicants notified on a rolling basis starting 1/31.

CONTACT
Susan Armstrong, Director of Student Financial Planning
500 College Hill, Liberty, MO 64068
(816) 415-5977

William Woods University
Fulton, Missouri
www.williamwoods.edu
Federal Code: 002525

4-year private university and liberal arts college in large town, affiliated with Christian Church (Disciples of Christ).
Enrollment: 1,118 undergrads, 28% part-time. 254 full-time freshmen.
Selectivity: Admits 50 to 75% of applicants.

BASIC COSTS (2006-2007)
Tuition and fees: $15,570.
Per-credit charge: $505.
Room and board: $6,100.
Additional info: Commuter students pay additional $50 fee per year.

FINANCIAL AID PICTURE (2005-2006)
Students with need: Out of 194 full-time freshmen who applied for aid, 142 were judged to have need. Of these, 142 received aid, and 43 had their full need met. Average financial aid package met 77% of need; average scholarship/grant was $9,626; average loan was $3,035. For part-time students, average financial aid package was $5,051.
Students without need: 84 full-time freshmen who did not demonstrate need for aid received scholarships/grants; average award was $9,449. No-need awards available for academics, alumni affiliation, art, athletics, leadership, music/drama, religious affiliation.
Scholarships offered: Merit: LEAD (Leading, Educating, Achieving and Developing) Award; $5,000 for campus residents, $2,500 for commuters; based on commitment to campus and community involvement; renewable each year if commitment has been met in previous year. **Athletic:** 5 full-time freshmen received athletic scholarships; average amount $4,592.
Cumulative student debt: 85% of graduating class had student loans; average debt was $13,865.

FINANCIAL AID PROCEDURES
Forms required: FAFSA, institutional form.
Dates and Deadlines: Priority date 3/1; no closing date. Applicants notified on a rolling basis starting 3/15; must reply within 2 week(s) of notification.

CONTACT
Liz Bennett, Director of Financial Aid
One University Avenue, Fulton, MO 65251-2388
(573) 592-4232

Montana

Blackfeet Community College
Browning, Montana
www.bfcc.org
Federal Code: 014902

2-year public community college in small town.
Enrollment: 490 undergrads, 14% part-time. 94 full-time freshmen.
Selectivity: Open admission.

BASIC COSTS (2005-2006)
Tuition and fees: $2,000.
Per-credit charge: $69.

FINANCIAL AID PICTURE
Students with need: Need-based aid available for full-time and part-time students.

FINANCIAL AID PROCEDURES
Forms required: FAFSA, institutional form.
Dates and Deadlines: No deadline.

CONTACT
Margaret Bird, Director of Financial Aid
Highway 2 & 89, PO Box 819, Browning, MT 59417
(406) 338-5421 ext. 245

Carroll College
Helena, Montana
www.carroll.edu
Federal Code: 002526

4-year private liberal arts college in large town, affiliated with Roman Catholic Church.
Enrollment: 1,317 undergrads, 7% part-time. 302 full-time freshmen.
Selectivity: Admits over 75% of applicants.

BASIC COSTS (2006-2007)
Tuition and fees: $18,403.
Per-credit charge: $604.
Room and board: $6,350.

FINANCIAL AID PICTURE (2005-2006)
Students with need: Out of 300 full-time freshmen who applied for aid, 203 were judged to have need. Of these, 203 received aid, and 37 had their full need met. Average financial aid package met 81% of need; average scholarship/grant was $9,394; average loan was $4,617. For part-time students, average financial aid package was $11,616.
Students without need: 96 full-time freshmen who did not demonstrate need for aid received scholarships/grants; average award was $6,681. No-

need awards available for academics, athletics, leadership, music/drama, religious affiliation, ROTC.
Scholarships offered: 18 full-time freshmen received athletic scholarships; average amount $6,828.
Cumulative student debt: 75% of graduating class had student loans; average debt was $25,659.

FINANCIAL AID PROCEDURES
Forms required: FAFSA.
Dates and Deadlines: Priority date 3/1; no closing date. Applicants notified on a rolling basis starting 3/1; must reply within 4 week(s) of notification.

CONTACT
Janet Riis, Director of Financial Aid
1601 North Benton Avenue, Helena, MT 59625
(406) 447-5425

Chief Dull Knife College
Lame Deer, Montana
www.cdkc.edu   Federal Code: 014878

2-year public junior college in rural community.
Enrollment: 110 full-time undergrads.
Selectivity: Open admission.

BASIC COSTS (2005-2006)
Tuition and fees: $2,610.
Per-credit charge: $90.

FINANCIAL AID PICTURE
Students with need: Need-based aid available for full-time and part-time students. Work study available nights.

FINANCIAL AID PROCEDURES
Forms required: FAFSA, institutional form.
Dates and Deadlines: No deadline. Applicants notified on a rolling basis; must reply within 2 week(s) of notification.

CONTACT
Donna Small, Financial Aid Director
Box 98, Lame Deer, MT 59043
(406) 477-6215

Dawson Community College
Glendive, Montana
www.dawson.edu   Federal Code: 002529

2-year public community college in small town.
Enrollment: 436 undergrads, 14% part-time. 120 full-time freshmen.
Selectivity: Open admission.

BASIC COSTS (2005-2006)
Tuition and fees: $2,324; out-of-district residents $3,195; out-of-state residents $6,854.
Per-credit charge: $44; out-of-district residents $75; out-of-state residents $205.
Additional info: Western Undergraduate Exchange tuition: $112 per credit hour, $3,155 full-time.

FINANCIAL AID PICTURE
Students with need: Work study available nights, weekends, and for part-time students.
Students without need: No-need awards available for academics, art, athletics, music/drama.

FINANCIAL AID PROCEDURES
Forms required: FAFSA.

Dates and Deadlines: Priority date 3/1; no closing date. Applicants notified on a rolling basis starting 5/15; must reply within 2 week(s) of notification.

CONTACT
Jolene Myers, Director of Admissions
300 College Drive, Glendive, MT 59330
(406) 377-9410

Flathead Valley Community College
Kalispell, Montana
www.fvcc.edu   Federal Code: 006777

2-year public community college in large town.
Enrollment: 1,337 undergrads. 215 full-time freshmen.
Selectivity: Open admission.

BASIC COSTS (2005-2006)
Tuition and fees: $2,349; out-of-district residents $3,466; out-of-state residents $7,755.
Per-credit charge: $82; out-of-district residents $130; out-of-state residents $283.

FINANCIAL AID PICTURE (2004-2005)
Students with need: Average financial aid package for all full-time undergraduates was $3,215. 76% awarded as scholarships/grants, 24% awarded as loans/jobs. Need-based aid available for part-time students.
Students without need: No-need awards available for academics, athletics.
Cumulative student debt: 19% of graduating class had student loans; average debt was $5,222.

FINANCIAL AID PROCEDURES
Forms required: FAFSA.
Dates and Deadlines: Priority date 3/1; no closing date. Applicants notified by 4/15; must reply within 2 week(s) of notification.

CONTACT
Bonnie Whitehouse, Financial Aid Director
777 Grandview Drive, Kalispell, MT 59901
(406) 756-3849

Fort Peck Community College
Poplar, Montana
www.fpcc.edu   Federal Code: 016616

2-year public community college in small town.
Enrollment: 416 undergrads.
Selectivity: Open admission.

BASIC COSTS (2005-2006)
Tuition and fees: $1,840.
Per-credit charge: $60.
Additional info: Tuition/fee waivers available for adults, minority students.

FINANCIAL AID PICTURE
Students with need: Need-based aid available for full-time and part-time students. Work study available nights.

FINANCIAL AID PROCEDURES
Forms required: FAFSA, institutional form.
Dates and Deadlines: No deadline. Applicants notified on a rolling basis; must reply within 2 week(s) of notification.

CONTACT
Haven Gourneau, Financial Aid Director
Box 398 605 Indian, Poplar, MT 59255-0398
(406) 768-5553

Helena College of Technology of the University of Montana
Helena, Montana
www.hct.umontana.edu   Federal Code: 007570

2-year public technical college in large town.
Enrollment: 525 full-time undergrads.
Selectivity: Open admission.

BASIC COSTS (2005-2006)
Tuition and fees: $2,874; out-of-state residents $7,506.
Additional info: Tuition/fee waivers available for minority students.

FINANCIAL AID PICTURE
Students with need: Need-based aid available for full-time and part-time students.

FINANCIAL AID PROCEDURES
Forms required: FAFSA, institutional form.
Dates and Deadlines: Priority date 4/1; no closing date. Applicants notified on a rolling basis starting 5/1.

CONTACT
Victoria Glass, Director of Financial Aid
1115 North Roberts Street, Helena, MT 59601-3098
(406) 444-6879

Little Big Horn College
Crow Agency, Montana
www.lbhc.cc.mt.us   Federal Code: 016135

2-year private community college in rural community.
Enrollment: 225 full-time undergrads.
Selectivity: Open admission.

BASIC COSTS (2005-2006)
Tuition and fees: $2,700.
Per-credit charge: $75.
Additional info: Tuition/fee waivers available for minority students.

FINANCIAL AID PICTURE
Students with need: Need-based aid available for full-time and part-time students.

FINANCIAL AID PROCEDURES
Dates and Deadlines: No deadline. Applicants notified on a rolling basis.

CONTACT
Rachel Pretty on Top, Financial Aid Officer
Box 370, Crow Agency, MT 59022
(406) 638-3140

Miles Community College
Miles City, Montana
www.milescc.edu   Federal Code: 002528

2-year public community college in small town.
Enrollment: 460 undergrads, 22% part-time. 127 full-time freshmen.
Selectivity: Open admission; but selective for some programs.

BASIC COSTS (2006-2007)
Tuition and fees: $2,835; out-of-district residents $3,705; out-of-state residents $5,895.
Per-credit charge: $56; out-of-district residents $85; out-of-state residents $158.
Room and board: $4,250.

FINANCIAL AID PICTURE
Students with need: Need-based aid available for full-time and part-time students. Work study available nights, weekends, and for part-time students.
Students without need: No-need awards available for academics, athletics, leadership.
Scholarships offered: Montana residents may apply for tuition waivers and scholarships. Students must maintain 3.0 GPA and carry 15 credits. Deadline for application 03/15.

FINANCIAL AID PROCEDURES
Forms required: FAFSA.
Dates and Deadlines: Priority date 3/1; no closing date. Applicants notified on a rolling basis starting 4/15; must reply within 4 week(s) of notification.

CONTACT
Jessie Dufner, Financial Aid Officer
2715 Dickinson Street, Miles City, MT 59301
(406) 874-6171

Montana State University College of Technology-Great Falls
Great Falls, Montana
www.msugf.edu   Federal Code: 009314

2-year public community and technical college in small city.
Enrollment: 1,268 undergrads.
Selectivity: Open admission; but selective for some programs.

BASIC COSTS (2005-2006)
Tuition and fees: $2,877; out-of-state residents $8,181.
Additional info: Tuition/fee waivers available for adults, minority students, unemployed or children of unemployed.

FINANCIAL AID PICTURE (2004-2005)
Students with need: 55% of average financial aid package awarded as scholarships/grants, 45% awarded as loans/jobs. Need-based aid available for part-time students. Work study available nights, weekends, and for part-time students.

FINANCIAL AID PROCEDURES
Forms required: FAFSA, institutional form.
Dates and Deadlines: Priority date 3/1; no closing date. Applicants notified on a rolling basis starting 4/1; must reply within 3 week(s) of notification.

CONTACT
Leah Habel, Financial Aid Director
2100 16th Avenue South, Great Falls, MT 59405
(406) 771-4334

Montana State University: Billings
Billings, Montana
www.msubillings.edu   Federal Code: 002530

4-year public university and technical college in small city.
Enrollment: 4,337 undergrads, 27% part-time. 704 full-time freshmen.
Selectivity: Admits over 75% of applicants.

BASIC COSTS (2005-2006)
Tuition and fees: $4,856; out-of-state residents $13,000.
Room and board: $3,920.

FINANCIAL AID PICTURE (2004-2005)
Students with need: Out of 617 full-time freshmen who applied for aid, 493 were judged to have need. Of these, 468 received aid, and 65 had their full need met. Average financial aid package met 54% of need; average scholarship/grant was $4,086; average loan was $2,414. For part-time students, average financial aid package was $4,924.

Students without need: 27 full-time freshmen who did not demonstrate need for aid received scholarships/grants; average award was $5,550. No-need awards available for academics, alumni affiliation, art, athletics, job skills, leadership, minority status, music/drama, state/district residency.
Scholarships offered: 59 full-time freshmen received athletic scholarships; average amount $7,192.
Cumulative student debt: 67% of graduating class had student loans; average debt was $15,719.
Additional info: Veterans and honors fee waivers offered.

FINANCIAL AID PROCEDURES
Forms required: FAFSA.
Dates and Deadlines: Priority date 3/1; no closing date. Applicants notified on a rolling basis starting 5/1; must reply within 3 week(s) of notification.

CONTACT
Melina Hawkins, Director of Financial Aid
1500 University Drive, Billings, MT 59101-0298
(406) 657-2188

Montana State University: Bozeman
Bozeman, Montana
www.montana.edu   Federal Code: 002532

4-year public university in large town.
Enrollment: 10,771 undergrads, 14% part-time. 2,004 full-time freshmen.
Selectivity: Admits 50 to 75% of applicants.

BASIC COSTS (2005-2006)
Tuition and fees: $5,220; out-of-state residents $14,859.
Room and board: $6,156.
Additional info: Additional $1,338 annually in health insurance required of uninsured students. Tuition/fee waivers available for minority students.

FINANCIAL AID PICTURE (2004-2005)
Students with need: Out of 1,774 full-time freshmen who applied for aid, 1,092 were judged to have need. Of these, 1,057 received aid, and 128 had their full need met. Average financial aid package met 54% of need; average scholarship/grant was $3,939; average loan was $3,302. For part-time students, average financial aid package was $5,618.
Students without need: 190 full-time freshmen who did not demonstrate need for aid received scholarships/grants; average award was $2,536. No-need awards available for academics, alumni affiliation, art, athletics, job skills, leadership, minority status, music/drama, ROTC, state/district residency.
Scholarships offered: 18 full-time freshmen received athletic scholarships; average amount $5,224.
Cumulative student debt: 66% of graduating class had student loans; average debt was $18,081.

FINANCIAL AID PROCEDURES
Forms required: FAFSA.
Dates and Deadlines: Priority date 3/1; no closing date. Applicants notified on a rolling basis starting 4/1; must reply within 3 week(s) of notification.

CONTACT
Brandi Payne, Director of Financial Aid Services
PO Box 172190, Bozeman, MT 59717-2190
(406) 994-2845

Montana Tech of the University of Montana
Butte, Montana
www.mtech.edu   Federal Code: 002531

4-year public engineering and technical college in large town.
Enrollment: 1,894 undergrads, 10% part-time. 300 full-time freshmen.
Selectivity: Admits over 75% of applicants.

BASIC COSTS (2005-2006)
Tuition and fees: $5,123; out-of-state residents $14,114.
Room and board: $5,356.
Additional info: Tuition/fee waivers available for adults, minority students.

FINANCIAL AID PICTURE (2004-2005)
Students with need: Out of 250 full-time freshmen who applied for aid, 225 were judged to have need. Of these, 200 received aid, and 175 had their full need met. Average financial aid package met 75% of need; average scholarship/grant was $2,000; average loan was $2,500. For part-time students, average financial aid package was $35,000.
Students without need: This college only awards aid to students with need.
Scholarships offered: 100 full-time freshmen received athletic scholarships; average amount $2,500.
Cumulative student debt: 80% of graduating class had student loans; average debt was $18,000.

FINANCIAL AID PROCEDURES
Forms required: FAFSA, institutional form.
Dates and Deadlines: Priority date 3/1; no closing date. Applicants notified on a rolling basis starting 4/1; must reply within 2 week(s) of notification.

CONTACT
Mike Richardson, Director of Financial Aid
1300 West Park Street, Butte, MT 59701-8997
(406) 496-4212

Rocky Mountain College
Billings, Montana
www.rocky.edu   Federal Code: 002534

4-year private liberal arts college in small city, affiliated with United Church of Christ, United Methodist Church, and United Presbyterian Church.
Enrollment: 924 undergrads, 4% part-time. 217 full-time freshmen.
Selectivity: Admits over 75% of applicants.

BASIC COSTS (2005-2006)
Tuition and fees: $15,325.
Per-credit charge: $630.
Room and board: $5,480.

FINANCIAL AID PICTURE (2005-2006)
Students with need: Out of 196 full-time freshmen who applied for aid, 149 were judged to have need. Of these, 149 received aid, and 41 had their full need met. Average financial aid package met 73% of need; average scholarship/grant was $9,195; average loan was $1,701. For part-time students, average financial aid package was $9,758.
Students without need: 37 full-time freshmen who did not demonstrate need for aid received scholarships/grants; average award was $8,806. No-need awards available for academics, alumni affiliation, art, athletics, leadership, minority status, music/drama, religious affiliation, state/district residency.
Scholarships offered: 5 full-time freshmen received athletic scholarships; average amount $11,299.
Cumulative student debt: 75% of graduating class had student loans; average debt was $18,653.

Rocky Mountain College (continued)

FINANCIAL AID PROCEDURES
Forms required: FAFSA, institutional form.
Dates and Deadlines: Priority date 3/1; no closing date. Applicants notified on a rolling basis starting 2/1; must reply within 4 week(s) of notification.
CONTACT
Lisa Browning, Director of Financial Aid
1511 Poly Drive, Billings, MT 59102-1796
(406) 657-1031

Salish Kootenai College
Pablo, Montana
www.skc.edu
Federal Code: 015023

4-year private liberal arts college in rural community.
Enrollment: 1,148 undergrads. 409 full-time freshmen.
Selectivity: Open admission; but selective for some programs.

BASIC COSTS (2006-2007)
Tuition and fees: $789; out-of-state residents $23,170.
Additional info: Tuition/fee waivers available for minority students.

FINANCIAL AID PICTURE (2004-2005)
Students with need: Out of 344 full-time freshmen who applied for aid, 178 were judged to have need. Of these, 166 received aid, and 5 had their full need met. Average financial aid package met 54% of need; average scholarship/grant was $4,817; average loan was $2,126. For part-time students, average financial aid package was $2,560.
Students without need: 7 full-time freshmen who did not demonstrate need for aid received scholarships/grants; average award was $1,227.

FINANCIAL AID PROCEDURES
Forms required: FAFSA.
Dates and Deadlines: Priority date 3/31; no closing date. Applicants notified on a rolling basis starting 7/15; must reply within 6 week(s) of notification.
CONTACT
Jeannie Burland, Financial Aid Director
Box 70, Pablo, MT 59855
(406) 275-4855

Stone Child College
Box Elder, Montana
www.montana.edu/wwwscc/
Federal Code: 026109

2-year public community and junior college in rural community.
Enrollment: 200 full-time undergrads.
Selectivity: Open admission.

FINANCIAL AID PICTURE
Students with need: Need-based aid available for full-time and part-time students.
Students without need: No-need awards available for academics.
Additional info: Scholarships available to high school and GED graduates who apply for college admission during the first term after graduation.

FINANCIAL AID PROCEDURES
Forms required: FAFSA, institutional form.
Dates and Deadlines: Priority date 3/1; closing date 6/30. Applicants notified on a rolling basis.
CONTACT
Joseph LaFromboise, Financial Aid Director
RR1 Box 1082, Box Elder, MT 59521-9796
(406) 395-4313

University of Great Falls
Great Falls, Montana
www.ugf.edu
Federal Code: 002527

4-year private university and liberal arts college in small city, affiliated with Roman Catholic Church.
Enrollment: 656 undergrads, 26% part-time. 105 full-time freshmen.
Selectivity: Admits over 75% of applicants.

BASIC COSTS (2006-2007)
Tuition and fees: $15,250.
Per-credit charge: $460.
Room and board: $5,500.

FINANCIAL AID PICTURE (2005-2006)
Students with need: Average financial aid package met 46% of need; average scholarship/grant was $3,410; average loan was $2,704. For part-time students, average financial aid package was $6,366.
Students without need: No-need awards available for academics, art, athletics, job skills, leadership, minority status, music/drama, religious affiliation, state/district residency.
Scholarships offered: Freshmen scholarships; $1,000-$6,000; based on high school GPA; renewable.

FINANCIAL AID PROCEDURES
Forms required: FAFSA.
Dates and Deadlines: Priority date 5/1; no closing date. Applicants notified on a rolling basis starting 2/1; must reply within 2 week(s) of notification.
Transfers: Transfer student scholarships; $2,500-$4,000; based on college GPA; renewable.
CONTACT
Chris Steckmann, Director of Financial Aid
1301 20th Street South, Great Falls, MT 59405
(406) 791-5235

University of Montana: Missoula
Missoula, Montana
www.umt.edu
Federal Code: 002536
CSS Code: 4489

4-year public university and liberal arts college in small city.
Enrollment: 10,125 undergrads.
Selectivity: Admits over 75% of applicants.

BASIC COSTS (2005-2006)
Tuition and fees: $4,703; out-of-state residents $13,419.
Room and board: $5,646.
Additional info: Tuition/fee waivers available for minority students.

FINANCIAL AID PICTURE (2005-2006)
Students with need: 29% of average financial aid package awarded as scholarships/grants, 71% awarded as loans/jobs. Need-based aid available for part-time students. Work study available nights, weekends, and for part-time students.
Students without need: No-need awards available for academics, art, athletics, leadership, music/drama, ROTC, state/district residency.

FINANCIAL AID PROCEDURES
Forms required: FAFSA, CSS PROFILE, institutional form.
Dates and Deadlines: Priority date 3/1; no closing date. Applicants notified on a rolling basis starting 4/1; must reply by 8/1 or within 4 week(s) of notification.
CONTACT
Myron Hanson, Director of Financial Aid
Lommasson Center 103, Missoula, MT 59812
(406) 243-5373

University of Montana: Western
Dillon, Montana
www.umwestern.edu   Federal Code: 002537

4-year public liberal arts and teachers college in small town.
Enrollment: 1,346 undergrads, 18% part-time. 230 full-time freshmen.

BASIC COSTS (2005-2006)
Tuition and fees: $3,939; out-of-state residents $11,915.
Room and board: $4,740.
Additional info: Tuition/fee waivers available for minority students.

FINANCIAL AID PICTURE (2005-2006)
Students with need: Average financial aid package met 16% of need; average scholarship/grant was $2,210; average loan was $2,394. Need-based aid available for part-time students.
Students without need: No-need awards available for academics, alumni affiliation, art, athletics, job skills, leadership, minority status, music/drama, state/district residency.
Additional info: Tuition and/or fee waiver for veterans and Native Americans.

FINANCIAL AID PROCEDURES
Forms required: FAFSA.
Dates and Deadlines: Priority date 3/1; no closing date. Applicants notified on a rolling basis starting 3/1; must reply within 2 week(s) of notification.

CONTACT
Arlene Williams, Director of Financial Aid
710 South Atlantic Street, Dillon, MT 59725
(406) 683-7511

Nebraska

Bellevue University
Bellevue, Nebraska
www.bellevue.edu   Federal Code: 002538

4-year private university and business college in large city.
Enrollment: 4,125 undergrads, 32% part-time. 84 full-time freshmen.
Selectivity: Open admission; but selective for some programs.

BASIC COSTS (2006-2007)
Tuition and fees: $5,345.
Per-credit charge: $175.

FINANCIAL AID PICTURE (2004-2005)
Students with need: Out of 77 full-time freshmen who applied for aid, 77 were judged to have need. Of these, 77 received aid, and 67 had their full need met. For part-time students, average financial aid package was $4,095.
Students without need: No-need awards available for academics, athletics.

FINANCIAL AID PROCEDURES
Forms required: FAFSA, institutional form.
Dates and Deadlines: Priority date 4/15; no closing date. Applicants notified on a rolling basis starting 4/15; must reply within 2 week(s) of notification.
Transfers: No deadline.

CONTACT
Jon Dotterer, Director of Financial Aid
1000 Galvin Road South, Bellevue, NE 68005-3098
(402) 293-3762

Central Community College
Grand Island, Nebraska
www.cccneb.edu   Federal Code: 014468

2-year public community and technical college in large town.
Enrollment: 3,263 undergrads, 49% part-time. 355 full-time freshmen.
Selectivity: Open admission; but selective for some programs and for out-of-state students.

BASIC COSTS (2006-2007)
Tuition and fees: $1,980; out-of-state residents $2,910.
Per-credit charge: $62; out-of-state residents $93.
Room and board: $4,160.

FINANCIAL AID PICTURE (2005-2006)
Students with need: 76% of average financial aid package awarded as scholarships/grants, 24% awarded as loans/jobs. Need-based aid available for part-time students. Work study available nights.
Students without need: No-need awards available for academics, art, athletics, job skills, leadership, music/drama.

FINANCIAL AID PROCEDURES
Forms required: FAFSA, institutional form.
Dates and Deadlines: Priority date 6/1; no closing date. Applicants notified on a rolling basis starting 3/1; must reply within 1 week(s) of notification.

CONTACT
Steve Millnitz, Financial Aid Officer
3134 West Highway 34, Grand Island, NE 68802-4903
(308) 398-7407

Chadron State College
Chadron, Nebraska
www.csc.edu   Federal Code: 002539

4-year public business and liberal arts and teachers college in small town.
Enrollment: 1,994 undergrads, 16% part-time. 298 full-time freshmen.
Selectivity: Open admission; but selective for some programs.

BASIC COSTS (2005-2006)
Tuition and fees: $3,672; out-of-state residents $6,604.
Per-credit charge: $98; out-of-state residents $196.
Room and board: $4,074.

FINANCIAL AID PICTURE
Students with need: Need-based aid available for full-time and part-time students. Work study available nights, weekends, and for part-time students.
Students without need: No-need awards available for academics, alumni affiliation, art, athletics, leadership, minority status, music/drama, state/district residency.

FINANCIAL AID PROCEDURES
Forms required: FAFSA, institutional form.
Dates and Deadlines: Priority date 6/1; no closing date. Applicants notified on a rolling basis starting 4/1; must reply within 2 week(s) of notification.

CONTACT
Sherry Douglas, Director of Financial Aid
1000 Main Street, Chadron, NE 69337
(308) 432-6230

Clarkson College
Omaha, Nebraska
www.clarksoncollege.edu   Federal Code: 009862

4-year private health science college in large city, affiliated with Episcopal Church.
Enrollment: 640 undergrads.
Selectivity: Open admission; but selective for some programs.

BASIC COSTS (2005-2006)
Tuition and fees: $10,932.
Per-credit charge: $345.
Room only: $4,200.
Additional info: Distance learning fee: $33 per credit-hour.

FINANCIAL AID PICTURE
Students with need: Need-based aid available for full-time and part-time students. Work study available nights, weekends, and for part-time students.
Students without need: No-need awards available for academics, alumni affiliation, minority status, religious affiliation.

FINANCIAL AID PROCEDURES
Forms required: FAFSA, institutional form.
Dates and Deadlines: Priority date 4/1; no closing date. Applicants notified on a rolling basis starting 4/13; must reply within 3 week(s) of notification.

CONTACT
Margie Harris, Director of Student Financial Services
101 South 42nd Street, Omaha, NE 68131-2739
(402) 552-2749

College of Saint Mary
Omaha, Nebraska
www.csm.edu   Federal Code: 002540

4-year private nursing and liberal arts college for women in very large city, affiliated with Roman Catholic Church.
Enrollment: 917 undergrads, 30% part-time. 81 full-time freshmen.
Selectivity: Admits 50 to 75% of applicants.

BASIC COSTS (2006-2007)
Tuition and fees: $19,120.
Per-credit charge: $620.
Room and board: $6,070.

FINANCIAL AID PICTURE (2005-2006)
Students with need: Average financial aid package met 51% of need; average scholarship/grant was $8,717; average loan was $3,488. For part-time students, average financial aid package was $4,749.
Students without need: No-need awards available for academics, athletics, music/drama.
Cumulative student debt: 86% of graduating class had student loans; average debt was $13,500.

FINANCIAL AID PROCEDURES
Forms required: FAFSA.
Dates and Deadlines: Priority date 3/1; no closing date. Applicants notified on a rolling basis starting 3/1; must reply within 2 week(s) of notification.
Transfers: Must reply within 2 week(s) of notification. Scholarships available for transfer students.

CONTACT
Caprice Calamaio, Director of Express Center
7000 Mercy Road, Omaha, NE 68106
(402) 399-2362

Concordia University
Seward, Nebraska
www.cune.edu   Federal Code: 002541

4-year private university and teachers college in small town, affiliated with Lutheran Church - Missouri Synod.
Enrollment: 1,123 undergrads, 3% part-time. 289 full-time freshmen.
Selectivity: Admits over 75% of applicants.

BASIC COSTS (2006-2007)
Tuition and fees: $18,750.
Room and board: $4,940.
Additional info: Tuition/fee waivers available for adults.

FINANCIAL AID PICTURE (2005-2006)
Students with need: Average financial aid package met 93% of need; average scholarship/grant was $3,893; average loan was $2,503. For part-time students, average financial aid package was $7,121.
Students without need: No-need awards available for academics, athletics, religious affiliation.
Cumulative student debt: 67% of graduating class had student loans; average debt was $14,034.

FINANCIAL AID PROCEDURES
Forms required: FAFSA, institutional form.
Dates and Deadlines: Priority date 3/1; closing date 5/1. Applicants notified on a rolling basis starting 3/1; must reply within 4 week(s) of notification.

CONTACT
Gloria Hennig, Director of Financial Aid
800 North Columbia Avenue, Seward, NE 68434-9989
(402) 643-7270

Creative Center
Omaha, Nebraska
www.creativecenter.edu   Federal Code: 031643

2-year for-profit visual arts and technical college in large city.
Enrollment: 81 undergrads. 28 full-time freshmen.

BASIC COSTS (2005-2006)
Tuition and fees: $16,900.

FINANCIAL AID PICTURE
Students with need: Need-based aid available for full-time and part-time students.
Students without need: No-need awards available for academics, art.
Scholarships offered: President's Award; $500. Founder's Award; $1,000. Both awards based on quality of portfolio.

FINANCIAL AID PROCEDURES
Dates and Deadlines: No deadline. Applicants notified on a rolling basis starting 1/1.

CONTACT
Michelle Webster, Director of Financial Aid
10850 Emmet Street, Omaha, NE 68164
(402) 898-1000 ext. 203

Creighton University
Omaha, Nebraska
www.creighton.edu   Federal Code: 002542

4-year private university in large city, affiliated with Roman Catholic Church.
Enrollment: 3,904 undergrads, 7% part-time. 972 full-time freshmen.
Selectivity: Admits over 75% of applicants.

BASIC COSTS (2006-2007)
Tuition and fees: $25,126.
Per-credit charge: $756.
Room and board: $7,842.

FINANCIAL AID PICTURE (2005-2006)
Students with need: Out of 766 full-time freshmen who applied for aid, 598 were judged to have need. Of these, 578 received aid, and 280 had their full need met. Average financial aid package met 91% of need; average scholarship/grant was $15,096; average loan was $5,188. Need-based aid available for part-time students.
Students without need: 351 full-time freshmen who did not demonstrate need for aid received scholarships/grants; average award was $8,752. No-need awards available for academics, alumni affiliation, art, athletics, leadership, minority status, music/drama, ROTC.
Scholarships offered: *Merit:* Scott Scholarship; full tuition; for top students admitted to School of Business; 4 awarded. Presidential Scholarship; 75% of tuition; for valedictorian of high school class with 30 or better ACT score; 20 awarded. Creighton scholarship; 3,000-$8,500; for students with 3.75 GPA and 25 or better ACT score. *Athletic:* 24 full-time freshmen received athletic scholarships; average amount $18,577.
Cumulative student debt: 74% of graduating class had student loans; average debt was $26,013.
Additional info: For academic scholarship consideration, student must be admitted by January 1 of fall matriculation.

FINANCIAL AID PROCEDURES
Forms required: FAFSA, institutional form.
Dates and Deadlines: Priority date 4/1; no closing date. Applicants notified on a rolling basis starting 3/15; must reply by 5/1 or within 4 week(s) of notification.
Transfers: If transferring 24 or more hours of credit, student not eligible for academic (non-need) scholarships.

CONTACT
Robert Walker, Director of Financial Aid
2500 California Plaza, Omaha, NE 68178-0001
(402) 280-2731

Dana College
Blair, Nebraska
www.dana.edu
Federal Code: 002543

4-year private liberal arts college in small town, affiliated with Evangelical Lutheran Church in America.
Enrollment: 667 undergrads, 2% part-time. 208 full-time freshmen.
Selectivity: Admits over 75% of applicants.

BASIC COSTS (2005-2006)
Tuition and fees: $17,450.
Per-credit charge: $510.
Room and board: $5,320.

FINANCIAL AID PICTURE (2005-2006)
Students with need: Out of 202 full-time freshmen who applied for aid, 174 were judged to have need. Of these, 174 received aid, and 57 had their full need met. Average financial aid package met 89% of need; average scholarship/grant was $4,678; average loan was $3,412. For part-time students, average financial aid package was $5,427.
Students without need: 28 full-time freshmen who did not demonstrate need for aid received scholarships/grants; average award was $4,412. No-need awards available for academics, alumni affiliation, art, athletics, leadership, music/drama, religious affiliation, ROTC, state/district residency.
Scholarships offered: *Merit:* Leadership Scholarships; $2,000; 20 awards. Departmental scholarships in Biology, Social Work, Communication, Mathematics, Computer Science, English, German, International Studies, History, and Psychology. *Athletic:* 140 full-time freshmen received athletic scholarships; average amount $7,138.
Cumulative student debt: 89% of graduating class had student loans; average debt was $17,774.
Additional info: Auditions recommended for music and drama scholarship applicants. Portfolios recommended for art, graphic design, and cheerleading/dance scholarship applicants.

FINANCIAL AID PROCEDURES
Forms required: FAFSA, institutional form.
Dates and Deadlines: Priority date 3/15; no closing date. Applicants notified on a rolling basis starting 3/1; must reply within 3 week(s) of notification.
Transfers: Must reply within 3 week(s) of notification. Academic scholarships awarded on basis of high school GPA, rank, and test scores for students with 1 year or less as full time college student. Awards for transfers with 27 credits or more will be based on college GPA.

CONTACT
Rita McManigal, Director of Financial Aid
2848 College Drive, Blair, NE 68008-1099
(402) 426-7226

Doane College
Crete, Nebraska
www.doane.edu
Federal Code: 002544

4-year private liberal arts college in small town, affiliated with United Church of Christ.
Enrollment: 1,590 undergrads, 15% part-time. 305 full-time freshmen.
Selectivity: Admits over 75% of applicants.

BASIC COSTS (2006-2007)
Tuition and fees: $18,770.
Room and board: $5,150.

FINANCIAL AID PICTURE (2005-2006)
Students with need: Out of 295 full-time freshmen who applied for aid, 253 were judged to have need. Of these, 253 received aid, and 226 had their full need met. Average financial aid package met 97% of need; average scholarship/grant was $10,211; average loan was $3,000. Need-based aid available for part-time students.
Students without need: No-need awards available for academics, art, athletics, leadership, music/drama, religious affiliation.

FINANCIAL AID PROCEDURES
Forms required: FAFSA, institutional form.
Dates and Deadlines: Priority date 3/1; no closing date. Applicants notified on a rolling basis starting 2/1; must reply within 2 week(s) of notification.

CONTACT
Janet Dodson, Director of Financial Aid
1014 Boswell Avenue, Crete, NE 68333
(402) 826-8260

Grace University
Omaha, Nebraska
www.graceu.edu
Federal Code: 002547

4-year private university and Bible college in very large city, affiliated with interdenominational tradition.
Enrollment: 360 undergrads, 30% part-time. 76 full-time freshmen.
Selectivity: Admits over 75% of applicants.

BASIC COSTS (2006-2007)
Tuition and fees: $13,980.
Per-credit charge: $390.

Room and board: $5,350.
Additional info: Tuition at time of enrollment locked for 4 years.

FINANCIAL AID PICTURE
Students with need: Need-based aid available for full-time and part-time students. Work study available nights.
Students without need: No-need awards available for academics, alumni affiliation, music/drama, religious affiliation.

FINANCIAL AID PROCEDURES
Forms required: FAFSA, institutional form.
Dates and Deadlines: Priority date 2/1; no closing date. Applicants notified on a rolling basis starting 4/15; must reply within 2 week(s) of notification.

CONTACT
Dale Brown, Financial Aid Officer
1311 South Ninth Street, Omaha, NE 68108
(402) 449-2810

Hamilton College: Lincoln
Lincoln, Nebraska
www.hamiltonlincoln.edu   Federal Code: 004721

2-year for-profit business and junior college in large city.
Enrollment: 629 undergrads.
Selectivity: Open admission; but selective for some programs.

BASIC COSTS (2005-2006)
Tuition and fees: $11,575.
Room only: $2,100.
Additional info: Tuition at time of enrollment locked for 2 years.

FINANCIAL AID PICTURE
Students with need: Need-based aid available for full-time and part-time students.
Students without need: This college only awards aid to students with need.

FINANCIAL AID PROCEDURES
Forms required: FAFSA, institutional form.
Dates and Deadlines: No deadline. Applicants notified on a rolling basis.

CONTACT
Jami Frazier, Director of Financial Services
1821 K Street, Lincoln, NE 68508
(402) 474-5315

Hastings College
Hastings, Nebraska
www.hastings.edu   Federal Code: 002548

4-year private liberal arts college in large town, affiliated with Presbyterian Church (USA).
Enrollment: 1,114 undergrads, 1% part-time. 311 full-time freshmen.
Selectivity: Admits over 75% of applicants.

BASIC COSTS (2006-2007)
Tuition and fees: $18,302.
Per-credit charge: $728.
Room and board: $5,148.
Additional info: Tuition/fee waivers available for adults.

FINANCIAL AID PICTURE (2005-2006)
Students with need: Out of 284 full-time freshmen who applied for aid, 239 were judged to have need. Of these, 238 received aid, and 84 had their full need met. Average financial aid package met 76% of need; average scholarship/grant was $9,643; average loan was $3,695. For part-time students, average financial aid package was $5,178.
Students without need: 65 full-time freshmen who did not demonstrate need for aid received scholarships/grants; average award was $7,351. No-need awards available for academics, art, athletics, leadership, music/drama.
Scholarships offered: *Merit:* Walter Scott Scholarship Competition, full-tuition scholarships, for freshmen, 3 awarded, and approximately $12,000 for 20 other students. Trustees Scholarships, $10,000 per year. President's Scholarships, approximately $8,000 per year. Kessler Scholarship, full tuition, for Christian Ministry students, 3 awarded. Christian Ministry scholarships, $3,000 per year, 3 awarded. *Athletic:* 60 full-time freshmen received athletic scholarships; average amount $4,957.
Cumulative student debt: 79% of graduating class had student loans; average debt was $14,598.

FINANCIAL AID PROCEDURES
Forms required: FAFSA, institutional form.
Dates and Deadlines: No deadline. Applicants notified on a rolling basis starting 2/15; must reply within 2 week(s) of notification.
Transfers: No deadline. Stafford loans based on number of transferable credits.

CONTACT
Ian Roberts, Associate Vice President for Administration
710 N Turner Avenue, Hastings, NE 68901-7621
(402) 461-7391

Little Priest Tribal College
Winnebago, Nebraska
www.lptc.bia.edu   Federal Code: 033233

2-year private community college in rural community.
Enrollment: 150 undergrads.
Selectivity: Open admission.

BASIC COSTS (2005-2006)
Tuition and fees: $2,985.
Per-credit charge: $80.

FINANCIAL AID PICTURE
Students with need: Need-based aid available for full-time and part-time students.

FINANCIAL AID PROCEDURES
Forms required: FAFSA, institutional form.
Dates and Deadlines: No deadline.

CONTACT
Darla Wingett, Financial Aid Director
PO Box 270, Winnebago, NE 68071
(402) 878-2380 ext. 104

Metropolitan Community College
Omaha, Nebraska
www.mccneb.edu   Federal Code: 004432

2-year public community and technical college in large city.
Enrollment: 6,244 undergrads, 55% part-time. 905 full-time freshmen.
Selectivity: Open admission; but selective for some programs.

BASIC COSTS (2006-2007)
Tuition and fees: $1,992; out-of-state residents $3,072.
Per-credit charge: $41; out-of-state residents $63.

FINANCIAL AID PICTURE (2005-2006)
Students with need: 87% of average financial aid package awarded as scholarships/grants, 13% awarded as loans/jobs. Need-based aid available for part-time students.
Students without need: No-need awards available for academics.

FINANCIAL AID PROCEDURES
Forms required: FAFSA, institutional form.
Dates and Deadlines: Priority date 3/15; no closing date. Applicants notified on a rolling basis starting 4/15.

CONTACT
Susan Hardy, Director of Financial Aid/Veterans Services
Box 3777, Omaha, NE 68103-0777
(402) 457-2330

Mid-Plains Community College Area
North Platte, Nebraska
www.mpcc.edu   Federal Code: 002557

2-year public community and technical college in large town.
Enrollment: 1,209 undergrads, 30% part-time. 298 full-time freshmen.
Selectivity: Open admission; but selective for some programs.

BASIC COSTS (2006-2007)
Tuition and fees: $2,070; out-of-state residents $2,610.
Per-credit charge: $59; out-of-state residents $77.
Room and board: $4,300.

FINANCIAL AID PICTURE (2004-2005)
Students with need: 63% of average financial aid package awarded as scholarships/grants, 37% awarded as loans/jobs. Need-based aid available for part-time students. Work study available nights.
Students without need: No-need awards available for academics, art, athletics, music/drama.

FINANCIAL AID PROCEDURES
Forms required: FAFSA, institutional form.
Dates and Deadlines: Priority date 5/1; no closing date. Applicants notified on a rolling basis starting 5/1; must reply within 3 week(s) of notification.

CONTACT
Ted Fellers, Director of Financial Aid
1101 Halligan Drive, North Platte, NE 69101
(800) 658-4348

Midland Lutheran College
Fremont, Nebraska
www.mlc.edu   Federal Code: 002553

4-year private liberal arts college in large town, affiliated with Evangelical Lutheran Church in America.
Enrollment: 909 undergrads, 2% part-time. 254 full-time freshmen.
Selectivity: Admits over 75% of applicants.

BASIC COSTS (2006-2007)
Tuition and fees: $19,510.
Room and board: $4,950.
Additional info: Tuition/fee waivers available for minority students.

FINANCIAL AID PICTURE (2004-2005)
Students with need: Out of 246 full-time freshmen who applied for aid, 222 were judged to have need. Of these, 222 received aid, and 71 had their full need met. Average financial aid package met 89% of need; average scholarship/grant was $9,746; average loan was $4,991. For part-time students, average financial aid package was $12,734.
Students without need: 11 full-time freshmen who did not demonstrate need for aid received scholarships/grants; average award was $8,550. No-need awards available for academics, alumni affiliation, art, athletics, leadership, minority status, music/drama, religious affiliation.
Scholarships offered: 17 full-time freshmen received athletic scholarships; average amount $8,550.
Cumulative student debt: 87% of graduating class had student loans; average debt was $19,698.

FINANCIAL AID PROCEDURES
Forms required: FAFSA.
Dates and Deadlines: Priority date 5/1; no closing date. Applicants notified on a rolling basis starting 3/1; must reply within 4 week(s) of notification.

CONTACT
Dean Obenhauer, Director of Financial Aid
900 North Clarkson, Fremont, NE 68025
(402) 721-5480

Nebraska Christian College
Norfolk, Nebraska
www.nechristian.edu   Federal Code: 012976

4-year private Bible college in large town, affiliated with Christian Church/Churches of Christ.
Enrollment: 146 undergrads, 8% part-time. 44 full-time freshmen.

BASIC COSTS (2005-2006)
Tuition and fees: $6,700.
Per-credit charge: $202.
Room and board: $3,900.

FINANCIAL AID PICTURE
Students with need: Need-based aid available for full-time and part-time students.
Students without need: No-need awards available for academics, leadership.

FINANCIAL AID PROCEDURES
Forms required: FAFSA, institutional form.
Dates and Deadlines: Priority date 6/1; no closing date. Applicants notified on a rolling basis starting 5/5.

CONTACT
Linda Bigbee, Financial Aid Officer
1800 Syracuse Avenue, Norfolk, NE 68701
(402) 379-5017

Nebraska College of Technical Agriculture
Curtis, Nebraska
www.ncta.unl.edu   Federal Code: 007358

2-year public agricultural college in rural community.
Enrollment: 244 undergrads. 136 full-time freshmen.
Selectivity: Open admission.

BASIC COSTS (2005-2006)
Tuition and fees: $2,926; out-of-state residents $5,431.
Per-credit charge: $84; out-of-state residents $167.

Nebraska Nebraska College of Technical Agriculture

Room and board: $4,150.

FINANCIAL AID PICTURE (2004-2005)
Students with need: 50% of average financial aid package awarded as scholarships/grants, 50% awarded as loans/jobs. Need-based aid available for part-time students.
Students without need: This college only awards aid to students with need.

FINANCIAL AID PROCEDURES
Forms required: FAFSA.
Dates and Deadlines: Priority date 4/1; no closing date. Applicants notified on a rolling basis starting 5/1; must reply within 2 week(s) of notification.

CONTACT
Mary Ann Mercer, Director of Financial Aid
Route 3, Box 23A, Curtis, NE 69025-0069
(308) 367-4124 ext. 207

Nebraska Indian Community College
Macy, Nebraska
www.thenicc.edu   Federal Code: 015339

2-year public community college in rural community.
Enrollment: 90 undergrads.
Selectivity: Open admission.

BASIC COSTS (2006-2007)
Tuition and fees: $3,200.
Per-credit charge: $80.

FINANCIAL AID PICTURE
Students with need: Need-based aid available for full-time and part-time students.
Students without need: This college only awards aid to students with need.

FINANCIAL AID PROCEDURES
Forms required: FAFSA, state aid form, institutional form.
Dates and Deadlines: Priority date 7/15; no closing date. Applicants notified on a rolling basis starting 8/30; must reply within 2 week(s) of notification.

CONTACT
Colleen Clifford, Director of Financial Aid
2451 St. Mary's Avenue, Omaha, NE 68105
(402) 837-5078 ext. 120

Nebraska Methodist College of Nursing and Allied Health
Omaha, Nebraska
www.methodistcollege.edu   Federal Code: 009937

4-year private health science and nursing college in large city, affiliated with United Methodist Church.
Enrollment: 454 undergrads, 27% part-time. 15 full-time freshmen.
Selectivity: Admits 50 to 75% of applicants.

BASIC COSTS (2006-2007)
Tuition and fees: $11,940.
Per-credit charge: $378.
Room and board: $4,540.

FINANCIAL AID PICTURE (2004-2005)
Students with need: Out of 11 full-time freshmen who applied for aid, 9 were judged to have need. Of these, 9 received aid, and 2 had their full need met. Average financial aid package met 47% of need; average scholarship/grant was $3,243; average loan was $2,844. For part-time students, average financial aid package was $7,510.
Students without need: 3 full-time freshmen who did not demonstrate need for aid received scholarships/grants; average award was $7,500. No-need awards available for academics, leadership, religious affiliation, ROTC.
Scholarships offered: President's Leadership Scholarship; $5,000 per year for 4 years; 3 awarded. Excellence in Allied Health Scholarship; $5,000 per year for 2 years; 3 awarded. Horizon Scholarship; $2,500 per year; based on academic and personal merit; 45 awarded.
Cumulative student debt: 94% of graduating class had student loans; average debt was $30,078.

FINANCIAL AID PROCEDURES
Forms required: FAFSA, institutional form.
Dates and Deadlines: Priority date 5/1; no closing date. Applicants notified on a rolling basis starting 3/1; must reply by 5/1 or within 4 week(s) of notification.

CONTACT
Brenda Boyd, Director of Financial Aid
The Josie Harper Campus, Omaha, NE 68114
(402) 354-4874

Nebraska Wesleyan University
Lincoln, Nebraska
www.nebrwesleyan.edu   Federal Code: 002555

4-year private liberal arts college in small city, affiliated with United Methodist Church.
Enrollment: 1,801 undergrads, 12% part-time. 409 full-time freshmen.
Selectivity: Admits over 75% of applicants.

BASIC COSTS (2006-2007)
Tuition and fees: $19,302.
Per-credit charge: $715.
Room and board: $5,170.
Additional info: Tuition/fee waivers available for adults.

FINANCIAL AID PICTURE (2005-2006)
Students with need: Out of 350 full-time freshmen who applied for aid, 286 were judged to have need. Of these, 286 received aid, and 43 had their full need met. Average financial aid package met 71% of need; average scholarship/grant was $9,836; average loan was $3,709. For part-time students, average financial aid package was $2,103.
Students without need: 111 full-time freshmen who did not demonstrate need for aid received scholarships/grants; average award was $6,250. No-need awards available for academics, art, music/drama, religious affiliation.
Cumulative student debt: 70% of graduating class had student loans; average debt was $17,100.

FINANCIAL AID PROCEDURES
Forms required: FAFSA.
Dates and Deadlines: No deadline. Applicants notified on a rolling basis starting 3/15; must reply within 4 week(s) of notification.

CONTACT
Thomas Ochsner, Director of Scholarships and Financial Aid
5000 St. Paul Avenue, Lincoln, NE 68504
(402) 465-2212

Northeast Community College
Norfolk, Nebraska
www.northeastcollege.com   Federal Code: 002556

2-year public community college in large town.
Enrollment: 2,542 undergrads, 18% part-time. 762 full-time freshmen.
Selectivity: Open admission; but selective for some programs.

BASIC COSTS (2006-2007)
Tuition and fees: $2,085; out-of-state residents $2,528.
Per-credit charge: $59; out-of-state residents $74.
Room and board: $3,984.

FINANCIAL AID PICTURE (2004-2005)
Students with need: Out of 584 full-time freshmen who applied for aid, 476 were judged to have need. Of these, 473 received aid, and 68 had their full need met. Average financial aid package met 51% of need; average scholarship/grant was $2,865; average loan was $2,019. For part-time students, average financial aid package was $2,669.
Students without need: 33 full-time freshmen who did not demonstrate need for aid received scholarships/grants; average award was $677. No-need awards available for academics, athletics, music/drama.
Scholarships offered: 9 full-time freshmen received athletic scholarships.
Cumulative student debt: 58% of graduating class had student loans; average debt was $7,248.

FINANCIAL AID PROCEDURES
Forms required: FAFSA, institutional form.
Dates and Deadlines: No deadline. Applicants notified on a rolling basis; must reply within 2 week(s) of notification.

CONTACT
Joan Zanders, Director of Financial Aid
801 East Benjamin Avenue, Norfolk, NE 68702-0469
(402) 844-7285

Peru State College
Peru, Nebraska
www.peru.edu   Federal Code: 002559

4-year public liberal arts and teachers college in rural community.
Enrollment: 1,600 undergrads.
Selectivity: Open admission; but selective for out-of-state students.

BASIC COSTS (2005-2006)
Tuition and fees: $3,639; out-of-state residents $6,571.
Per-credit charge: $98; out-of-state residents $196.
Room and board: $4,296.

FINANCIAL AID PICTURE
Students with need: Need-based aid available for full-time and part-time students.
Students without need: This college only awards aid to students with need.

FINANCIAL AID PROCEDURES
Forms required: FAFSA, institutional form.
Dates and Deadlines: Priority date 3/1; no closing date. Applicants notified on a rolling basis starting 3/1; must reply within 2 week(s) of notification.
Transfers: Must have financial aid transcripts from all previous schools sent to college.

CONTACT
Diana Lind, Director of Financial Aid
Box 10, Peru, NE 68421-0010
(402) 872-2228

Southeast Community College: Lincoln Campus
Lincoln, Nebraska
www.southeast.edu   Federal Code: 007591

2-year public community college in small city.
Enrollment: 10,500 undergrads.
Selectivity: Open admission.

BASIC COSTS (2005-2006)
Tuition and fees: $1,800; out-of-state residents $2,183.
Per-credit charge: $39; out-of-state residents $48.

FINANCIAL AID PICTURE
Students with need: Need-based aid available for full-time and part-time students. Work study available nights, weekends, and for part-time students.
Students without need: No-need awards available for academics.

FINANCIAL AID PROCEDURES
Forms required: FAFSA, institutional form.
Dates and Deadlines: No deadline. Applicants notified on a rolling basis; must reply within 2 week(s) of notification.

CONTACT
Donna Bargen, Director of Financial Aid
8800 O Street, Lincoln, NE 68520
(402) 437-2610

Union College
Lincoln, Nebraska
www.ucollege.edu   Federal Code: 002563

4-year private liberal arts college in small city, affiliated with Seventh-day Adventists.
Enrollment: 845 undergrads, 11% part-time. 168 full-time freshmen.
Selectivity: Admits less than 50% of applicants.

BASIC COSTS (2006-2007)
Tuition and fees: $15,230.
Per-credit charge: $625.
Room and board: $4,948.

FINANCIAL AID PICTURE (2004-2005)
Students with need: Average financial aid package met 84% of need; average scholarship/grant was $7,838; average loan was $3,788. For part-time students, average financial aid package was $8,360.
Students without need: No-need awards available for academics.
Additional info: Special institutional grants offered to all freshmen and sophomores demonstrating exceptional financial need.

FINANCIAL AID PROCEDURES
Forms required: FAFSA.
Dates and Deadlines: Priority date 5/1; no closing date. Applicants notified on a rolling basis starting 4/15; must reply by 5/2 or within 3 week(s) of notification.

CONTACT
Jack Burdick, Director of Financial Aid
3800 South 48th Street, Lincoln, NE 68506-4300
(402) 486-2505

University of Nebraska - Kearney
Kearney, Nebraska
www.unk.edu   Federal Code: 002551

4-year public university in large town.
Enrollment: 5,346 undergrads, 9% part-time. 1,025 full-time freshmen.
Selectivity: Admits over 75% of applicants.

BASIC COSTS (2005-2006)
Tuition and fees: $4,393; out-of-state residents $8,233.
Room and board: $5,460.

FINANCIAL AID PICTURE (2004-2005)
Students with need: Out of 924 full-time freshmen who applied for aid, 690 were judged to have need. Of these, 683 received aid, and 384 had their full need met. Average financial aid package met 78% of need; average scholarship/grant was $4,668; average loan was $2,472. For part-time students, average financial aid package was $5,160.
Students without need: 159 full-time freshmen who did not demonstrate need for aid received scholarships/grants; average award was $2,990. No-need awards available for academics, athletics, state/district residency.
Scholarships offered: 40 full-time freshmen received athletic scholarships; average amount $1,683.
Cumulative student debt: 72% of graduating class had student loans; average debt was $16,808.

FINANCIAL AID PROCEDURES
Forms required: FAFSA, institutional form.
Dates and Deadlines: Priority date 4/1; no closing date. Applicants notified on a rolling basis starting 3/15; must reply within 3 week(s) of notification.

CONTACT
Mary Sommers, Director of Financial Aid
905 West 25th, Kearney, NE 68849
(308) 865-8520

University of Nebraska - Lincoln
Lincoln, Nebraska
www.unl.edu   Federal Code: 002565

4-year public university in small city.
Enrollment: 17,037 undergrads, 7% part-time. 3,538 full-time freshmen.
Selectivity: Admits over 75% of applicants.

BASIC COSTS (2005-2006)
Tuition and fees: $5,540; out-of-state residents $14,450.
Per-credit charge: $151; out-of-state residents $448.
Room and board: $5,861.
Additional info: Reciprocity agreement for selected programs with University of Missouri-Columbia, Kansas State University, University of South Dakota.

FINANCIAL AID PICTURE (2004-2005)
Students with need: Out of 2,222 full-time freshmen who applied for aid, 1,531 were judged to have need. Of these, 1,505 received aid, and 428 had their full need met. Average financial aid package met 88% of need; average scholarship/grant was $5,512; average loan was $3,066. For part-time students, average financial aid package was $5,996.
Students without need: 436 full-time freshmen who did not demonstrate need for aid received scholarships/grants; average award was $5,030. No-need awards available for academics, alumni affiliation, art, athletics, leadership, minority status, music/drama, state/district residency.
Scholarships offered: 58 full-time freshmen received athletic scholarships; average amount $5,338.
Cumulative student debt: 61% of graduating class had student loans; average debt was $16,909.

FINANCIAL AID PROCEDURES
Forms required: FAFSA.
Dates and Deadlines: Priority date 4/15; no closing date. Applicants notified on a rolling basis starting 4/15.
Transfers: Priority application date of April 1 for scholarship consideration.

CONTACT
Craig Munier, Director of Scholarships and Financial Aid
313 N 13th, Van Brunt Visitors Center, Lincoln, NE 68588-0256
(402) 472-2030

University of Nebraska - Omaha
Omaha, Nebraska
www.unomaha.edu   Federal Code: 002554

4-year public university in large city.
Enrollment: 11,039 undergrads, 23% part-time. 1,696 full-time freshmen.
Selectivity: Admits over 75% of applicants.

BASIC COSTS (2005-2006)
Tuition and fees: $4,825; out-of-state residents $12,872.
Room and board: $4,340.

FINANCIAL AID PICTURE (2005-2006)
Students with need: 41% of average financial aid package awarded as scholarships/grants, 59% awarded as loans/jobs. Need-based aid available for part-time students. Work study available nights, weekends, and for part-time students.
Students without need: No-need awards available for academics, alumni affiliation, art, athletics, leadership, minority status, music/drama, ROTC, state/district residency.
Cumulative student debt: 48% of graduating class had student loans; average debt was $16,900.

FINANCIAL AID PROCEDURES
Forms required: FAFSA.
Dates and Deadlines: Priority date 3/1; no closing date. Applicants notified on a rolling basis starting 4/15; must reply within 2 week(s) of notification.

CONTACT
Randall Sell, Director of Financial Aid
6001 Dodge Street, Omaha, NE 68182-0005
(402) 554-2327

University of Nebraska Medical Center
Omaha, Nebraska
www.unmc.edu   Federal Code: 006895

Upper-division public health science college in very large city.
Enrollment: 846 undergrads, 8% part-time.

BASIC COSTS (2005-2006)
Tuition and fees: $4,895; out-of-state residents $13,805.
Per-credit charge: $151; out-of-state residents $448.
Additional info: Nursing program is $191 per-credit-hour for in-state and $559 per-credit-hour for out-of-state.

FINANCIAL AID PICTURE (2004-2005)
Students with need: 30% of average financial aid package awarded as scholarships/grants, 70% awarded as loans/jobs. Need-based aid available for part-time students.
Cumulative student debt: 77% of graduating class had student loans; average debt was $24,660.
Additional info: Parental data collected from applicants for certain types of aid.

FINANCIAL AID PROCEDURES
Forms required: FAFSA, institutional form.
Dates and Deadlines: No deadline.
Transfers: Priority date 4/1.

CONTACT
Judith Walker, Director of Financial Aid
984230 Nebraska Medical Center, Omaha, NE 68198-4230
(402) 559-4199

Wayne State College
Wayne, Nebraska
www.wsc.edu   Federal Code: 002566

4-year public liberal arts and teachers college in small town.
Enrollment: 2,706 undergrads, 8% part-time. 587 full-time freshmen.
Selectivity: Open admission.

BASIC COSTS (2005-2006)
Tuition and fees: $3,803; out-of-state residents $6,735.
Per-credit charge: $98; out-of-state residents $196.
Room and board: $4,230.

FINANCIAL AID PICTURE (2005-2006)
Students with need: Out of 500 full-time freshmen who applied for aid, 351 were judged to have need. Of these, 346 received aid, and 89 had their full need met. Average financial aid package met 32% of need; average scholarship/grant was $1,479; average loan was $1,516. For part-time students, average financial aid package was $2,397.
Students without need: No-need awards available for academics, alumni affiliation, art, athletics, leadership, minority status, music/drama, religious affiliation, state/district residency.

FINANCIAL AID PROCEDURES
Forms required: FAFSA.
Dates and Deadlines: Priority date 5/1; no closing date. Applicants notified on a rolling basis starting 3/15; must reply within 3 week(s) of notification.

CONTACT
Kyle Rose, Director of Financial Aid
1111 Main Street, Wayne, NE 68787
(402) 375-7230

Western Nebraska Community College
Scottsbluff, Nebraska
www.wncc.net   Federal Code: 002560

2-year public community college in large town.
Enrollment: 1,488 undergrads, 42% part-time. 306 full-time freshmen.
Selectivity: Open admission; but selective for some programs.

BASIC COSTS (2006-2007)
Tuition and fees: $1,980; out-of-state residents $2,310.
Per-credit charge: $54; out-of-state residents $65.
Room and board: $4,000.

FINANCIAL AID PICTURE (2005-2006)
Students with need: Out of 203 full-time freshmen who applied for aid, 170 were judged to have need. Of these, 163 received aid. Average financial aid package met 80% of need; average scholarship/grant was $3,383; average loan was $2,164. For part-time students, average financial aid package was $4,492.
Students without need: 27 full-time freshmen who did not demonstrate need for aid received scholarships/grants; average award was $780. No-need awards available for academics, art, athletics, leadership, music/drama, state/district residency.

Scholarships offered: 46 full-time freshmen received athletic scholarships; average amount $5,830.
Cumulative student debt: 22% of graduating class had student loans; average debt was $3,712.

FINANCIAL AID PROCEDURES
Forms required: FAFSA.
Dates and Deadlines: Priority date 3/1; no closing date. Applicants notified on a rolling basis starting 4/1.
Transfers: State of Nebraska limits the amount of Nebraska State Grant funds a student receives in any one year.

CONTACT
Judy Curry, Director of Financial Aid
1601 East 27th Street, Scottsbluff, NE 69361
(308) 635-6011

York College
York, Nebraska
www.york.edu   Federal Code: 002567

4-year private liberal arts and teachers college in small town, affiliated with Church of Christ.
Enrollment: 443 undergrads, 7% part-time. 138 full-time freshmen.
Selectivity: Admits over 75% of applicants.

BASIC COSTS (2006-2007)
Tuition and fees: $13,500.
Per-credit charge: $422.
Room and board: $4,300.

FINANCIAL AID PICTURE (2004-2005)
Students with need: Out of 117 full-time freshmen who applied for aid, 106 were judged to have need. Of these, 106 received aid, and 49 had their full need met. Average financial aid package met 61% of need; average scholarship/grant was $6,215; average loan was $5,917. For part-time students, average financial aid package was $4,413.
Students without need: 9 full-time freshmen who did not demonstrate need for aid received scholarships/grants; average award was $4,867. No-need awards available for academics, alumni affiliation, athletics, leadership, music/drama.
Scholarships offered: 68 full-time freshmen received athletic scholarships; average amount $3,219.

FINANCIAL AID PROCEDURES
Forms required: FAFSA.
Dates and Deadlines: Priority date 4/30; no closing date. Applicants notified on a rolling basis starting 3/1; must reply within 4 week(s) of notification.

CONTACT
Kimball Matkins, Director of Financial Aid
1125 East 8th Street, York, NE 68467
(402) 363-5624

Nevada

Art Institute of Las Vegas
Henderson, Nevada
www.ailv.artinstitutes.edu   Federal Code: 030846

4-year for-profit culinary school and visual arts college in very large city.
Enrollment: 1,041 undergrads.
Selectivity: Open admission.

BASIC COSTS (2005-2006)
Additional info: Tuition at time of enrollment locked for 4 years.

FINANCIAL AID PICTURE
Students with need: Need-based aid available for full-time and part-time students. Work study available nights, weekends, and for part-time students.
Students without need: No-need awards available for academics, state/district residency.

FINANCIAL AID PROCEDURES
Dates and Deadlines: No deadline. Applicants notified on a rolling basis.
Transfers: No deadline. Applicants notified on a rolling basis.

CONTACT
Dana Sirolli, Director of Student Financial Services
2350 Corporate Circle, Henderson, NV 89074
(702) 369-9944

Career College of Northern Nevada
Reno, Nevada
www.ccnn.edu   Federal Code: 026215

2-year for-profit business and technical college in large city.
Enrollment: 303 undergrads. 303 full-time freshmen.
Selectivity: Open admission.

BASIC COSTS (2005-2006)
Tuition and fees: $7,964.
Per-credit charge: $175.
Additional info: Tuition for associate programs ranges from $14,830 to $18,813; diploma programs $9,887 to $11,085. Fees and books range from $120 to $624.

FINANCIAL AID PICTURE
Students with need: Need-based aid available for full-time students.
Students without need: This college only awards aid to students with need.

FINANCIAL AID PROCEDURES
Forms required: FAFSA.
Dates and Deadlines: Closing date 5/30. Applicants notified on a rolling basis.

CONTACT
L. Nathan Clark, President
1195 A Corporate Boulevard, Reno, NV 89502-2331
(775) 856-2266

Community College of Southern Nevada
Las Vegas, Nevada
www.ccsn.nevada.edu   Federal Code: 010362

2-year public community college in very large city.
Enrollment: 21,188 undergrads. 1,828 full-time freshmen.
Selectivity: Open admission; but selective for some programs.

BASIC COSTS (2005-2006)
Tuition and fees: $1,643; out-of-state residents $6,557.
Per-credit charge: $51; out-of-state residents $215.
Additional info: Reduced tuition for non-residents who are within 50 miles of Nevada border.

FINANCIAL AID PICTURE (2004-2005)
Students with need: 72% of average financial aid package awarded as scholarships/grants, 28% awarded as loans/jobs. Work study available nights, weekends, and for part-time students.
Students without need: No-need awards available for state/district residency.

FINANCIAL AID PROCEDURES
Forms required: FAFSA.
Dates and Deadlines: Priority date 5/1; closing date 6/30. Applicants notified on a rolling basis starting 7/15; must reply within 2 week(s) of notification.

CONTACT
Bernadette Lopez-Garrett, Financial Aid Director
6375 West Charleston Boulevard, Las Vegas, NV 89146-1164
(702) 651-4047

Great Basin College
Elko, Nevada
www.gbcnv.edu   Federal Code: 006977

4-year public community and teachers college in large town.
Enrollment: 1,695 undergrads.
Selectivity: Open admission; but selective for some programs.

BASIC COSTS (2005-2006)
Tuition and fees: $1,643; out-of-state residents $6,558.
Per-credit charge: $51; out-of-state residents $215.
Additional info: Tuition shown is for lower-division classes. Reduced tuition for non-residents who are within 50 miles of Nevada border. Out-of-state residents pay additional fees which are included in tuition.

FINANCIAL AID PICTURE
Students with need: Need-based aid available for full-time and part-time students. Work study available nights, weekends, and for part-time students.

FINANCIAL AID PROCEDURES
Forms required: FAFSA.
Dates and Deadlines: Priority date 6/1; no closing date. Applicants notified on a rolling basis starting 7/1.
Transfers: Priority date 4/1.

CONTACT
Scott Neilsen, Director of Financial Aid
1500 College Parkway, Elko, NV 89801
(775) 753-2267

Heritage College
Las Vegas, Nevada
www.heritagecollege.com   Federal Code: 030432

2-year for-profit business and health science college in large city.
Enrollment: 165 undergrads.
Selectivity: Open admission.

BASIC COSTS (2005-2006)
Additional info: Cost of full programs: associate degree programs $20,404, diploma programs $10,204, including fees and books.

FINANCIAL AID PICTURE
Students with need: Need-based aid available for full-time students.

FINANCIAL AID PROCEDURES
Forms required: FAFSA, institutional form.
Dates and Deadlines: No deadline.

CONTACT
Melissa Hughes, Financial Aid Director
3315 Spring Mountain Road, Las Vegas, NV 89102
(702) 368-2338

Las Vegas College
Las Vegas, Nevada
lasvegas-college.com Federal Code: 015804

2-year for-profit business and health science college in very large city.
Enrollment: 680 undergrads.
Selectivity: Open admission.

FINANCIAL AID PICTURE
Students with need: Need-based aid available for full-time and part-time students. Work study available nights, weekends, and for part-time students.
Students without need: This college only awards aid to students with need.

FINANCIAL AID PROCEDURES
Forms required: FAFSA.
Dates and Deadlines: Applicants notified on a rolling basis; must reply within 2 week(s) of notification.

CONTACT
Terry Farris, Director of Financial Aid
4100 West Flamingo Road, Las Vegas, NV 89103

Morrison University
Reno, Nevada
www.morrison.neumont.edu Federal Code: 009948

4-year for-profit university and business college in small city.
Enrollment: 65 undergrads, 9% part-time. 19 full-time freshmen.
Selectivity: Open admission.

BASIC COSTS (2005-2006)
Additional info: Tuition at time of enrollment locked for 4 years.

FINANCIAL AID PICTURE
Students with need: Need-based aid available for full-time students. Work study available nights.

FINANCIAL AID PROCEDURES
Forms required: FAFSA.
Dates and Deadlines: No deadline. Applicants notified on a rolling basis starting 7/1.

CONTACT
Jim Hadwick, Financial Aid Administrator
10315 Professional Circle, #201, Reno, NV 89521
(775) 850-0700 ext. 110

Sierra Nevada College
Incline Village, Nevada
www.sierranevada.edu Federal Code: 009192

4-year private liberal arts college in small town.
Enrollment: 329 undergrads, 13% part-time. 62 full-time freshmen.
Selectivity: Admits 50 to 75% of applicants.

BASIC COSTS (2005-2006)
Tuition and fees: $19,650.
Room and board: $7,450.

FINANCIAL AID PICTURE (2005-2006)
Students with need: Average financial aid package met 75% of need; average scholarship/grant was $6,050. Need-based aid available for part-time students.
Students without need: No-need awards available for academics, art, athletics.

Scholarships offered: Academic scholarships; range from $2,000-$13,000 per year; renewable.
Cumulative student debt: 80% of graduating class had student loans; average debt was $16,000.

FINANCIAL AID PROCEDURES
Forms required: FAFSA, institutional form.
Dates and Deadlines: Closing date 4/1. Applicants notified on a rolling basis starting 8/15; must reply by 5/1 or within 4 week(s) of notification.
Transfers: Priority date 3/15; no deadline.

CONTACT
Julie Beckman, Director of Financial Aid
999 Tahoe Boulevard, Incline Village, NV 89451-4269
(775) 831-1314 ext. 7440

Truckee Meadows Community College
Reno, Nevada
www.tmcc.edu Federal Code: 010363

2-year public community and technical college in large city.
Enrollment: 8,400 undergrads.
Selectivity: Open admission; but selective for some programs.

BASIC COSTS (2005-2006)
Tuition and fees: $1,643; out-of-state residents $6,558.
Per-credit charge: $51; out-of-state residents $215.
Additional info: Good Neighbor tuition: $30 per-credit-hour in addition to registration costs.

FINANCIAL AID PICTURE
Students with need: Work study available nights, weekends, and for part-time students.
Students without need: No-need awards available for academics, art, leadership, minority status, music/drama, state/district residency.
Additional info: Institutional grants to state residents, short-term emergency loans available. Work-study applications must reply within 10 days of notification.

FINANCIAL AID PROCEDURES
Forms required: FAFSA, institutional form.
Dates and Deadlines: No deadline. Applicants notified by 5/15.
Transfers: Must provide academic transcript from previous institution.

CONTACT
Mona Buckheart, Director of Student Financial Aid
7000 Dandini Boulevard, Reno, NV 89512
(775) 673-7072

University of Nevada: Las Vegas
Las Vegas, Nevada
www.unlv.edu Federal Code: 002569

4-year public university in very large city.
Enrollment: 21,004 undergrads, 26% part-time. 2,928 full-time freshmen.
Selectivity: Admits over 75% of applicants. GED not accepted.

BASIC COSTS (2005-2006)
Tuition and fees: $3,060; out-of-state residents $12,527.
Per-credit charge: $98; out-of-state residents $414.
Room and board: $8,373.
Additional info: Reduced tuition rate for out-of-state students who live within 50 miles of Nevada border and for those who reside in Western Undergraduate Exchange states.

536 Nevada University of Nevada: Las Vegas

FINANCIAL AID PICTURE (2005-2006)

Students with need: Out of 2,505 full-time freshmen who applied for aid, 1,448 were judged to have need. Of these, 1,428 received aid, and 713 had their full need met. Average financial aid package met 65% of need; average scholarship/grant was $2,909; average loan was $2,619. For part-time students, average financial aid package was $4,370.

Students without need: 1,279 full-time freshmen who did not demonstrate need for aid received scholarships/grants; average award was $1,120. No-need awards available for academics, alumni affiliation, art, athletics, job skills, leadership, minority status, music/drama, state/district residency.

Scholarships offered: 130 full-time freshmen received athletic scholarships; average amount $8,405.

Cumulative student debt: 40% of graduating class had student loans; average debt was $17,394.

Additional info: Tuition reduction for state residents through consortium programs and for out-of-state students graduating from high schools in designated counties bordering Nevada, for military dependents residing in-state, and for dependents of children of alumni not residing in-state.

FINANCIAL AID PROCEDURES

Forms required: FAFSA, institutional form.

Dates and Deadlines: Priority date 2/1; no closing date. Applicants notified on a rolling basis starting 4/1; must reply within 2 week(s) of notification.

CONTACT

Stephanie Brown, Executive Director of Enrollment Management
4505 Maryland Parkway Box 451021, Las Vegas, NV 89154-1021
(702) 895-3424

University of Nevada: Reno
Reno, Nevada
www.unr.edu   Federal Code: 002568

4-year public university in small city.

Enrollment: 12,404 undergrads, 17% part-time. 3,132 full-time freshmen.

Selectivity: Admits over 75% of applicants. GED not accepted.

BASIC COSTS (2005-2006)

Tuition and fees: $3,270; out-of-state residents $12,737.
Per-credit charge: $98; out-of-state residents $414.
Room and board: $7,785.
Additional info: Reduced tuition rate for out-of-state students who live within 50 miles of Nevada border.

FINANCIAL AID PICTURE (2004-2005)

Students with need: Out of 1,018 full-time freshmen who applied for aid, 669 were judged to have need. Of these, 654 received aid, and 92 had their full need met. Average financial aid package met 47% of need; average scholarship/grant was $4,238; average loan was $2,465. For part-time students, average financial aid package was $4,865.

Students without need: This college only awards aid to students with need.

Scholarships offered: *Merit:* Presidential scholarship awards; Nevada residents $4,000/year for 4 years; 3.5 unweighted high school GPA and 1380 SAT (exclusive of writing) or 31 ACT scores; must be admitted by 02/01 of year prior to enrollment; only incoming freshman from high school eligible. *Athletic:* 70 full-time freshmen received athletic scholarships; average amount $11,247.

Cumulative student debt: 42% of graduating class had student loans; average debt was $15,696.

Additional info: Reduced out-of-state tuition available for children of alumni and for non-residents from some neighboring counties in California.

FINANCIAL AID PROCEDURES

Dates and Deadlines: Priority date 2/1; no closing date. Applicants notified on a rolling basis starting 4/1; must reply within 2 week(s) of notification.

Transfers: Must reply within 2 week(s) of notification. Transfer GPA must be 2.0 or higher to be eligible for aid.

CONTACT

Nancee Langley, Director, Student Financial Services
Mail Stop 120, Reno, NV 89557
(775) 784-4666

Western Nevada Community College
Carson City, Nevada
www.wncc.edu   Federal Code: 013896

2-year public community college in small city.

Enrollment: 3,244 undergrads, 74% part-time. 273 full-time freshmen.

Selectivity: Open admission; but selective for some programs.

BASIC COSTS (2005-2006)

Tuition and fees: $1,643; out-of-state residents $6,558.
Per-credit charge: $51; out-of-state residents $215.
Additional info: Good Neighbor tuition: $81 per-credit-hour for student living within 50 miles of the Nevada border for one year or more or, graduates of specifically designated high schools or community colleges from neighboring states.

FINANCIAL AID PICTURE

Students with need: Need-based aid available for full-time and part-time students. Work study available nights, weekends, and for part-time students.
Students without need: No-need awards available for academics, state/district residency.

FINANCIAL AID PROCEDURES

Forms required: FAFSA.
Dates and Deadlines: Priority date 4/15; no closing date. Applicants notified on a rolling basis.
Transfers: Maximum loan debt of $14,125 allowed. Loans received at other schools counted toward limit.

CONTACT

Lori Tiede, Director of Financial Aid
2201 West College Parkway, Carson City, NV 89703-7399
(775) 445-3264

New Hampshire

Chester College of New England
Chester, New Hampshire
www.chestercollege.edu   Federal Code: 004733

4-year private visual arts college in rural community.

Enrollment: 218 undergrads, 14% part-time. 55 full-time freshmen.

Selectivity: Admits less than 50% of applicants.

BASIC COSTS (2006-2007)

Tuition and fees: $15,230.
Per-credit charge: $465.
Room and board: $7,600.
Additional info: Lab fees vary per student; average cost $600.

FINANCIAL AID PICTURE (2004-2005)

Students with need: 10% of average financial aid package awarded as scholarships/grants, 90% awarded as loans/jobs. Need-based aid available for part-time students. Work study available nights, weekends, and for part-time students.

Students without need: No-need awards available for academics, art, state/district residency.

FINANCIAL AID PROCEDURES
Forms required: FAFSA, state aid form.
Dates and Deadlines: Priority date 3/15; no closing date. Applicants notified on a rolling basis starting 12/1; must reply within 2 week(s) of notification.

CONTACT
Jason Graves, Director of Financial Aid
40 Chester Street, Chester, NH 03036
(603) 887-7404

Colby-Sawyer College
New London, New Hampshire
www.colby-sawyer.edu   Federal Code: 002572

4-year private liberal arts college in small town.
Enrollment: 964 undergrads, 1% part-time. 304 full-time freshmen.
Selectivity: Admits over 75% of applicants.

BASIC COSTS (2006-2007)
Tuition and fees: $26,350.
Per-credit charge: $880.
Room and board: $9,900.

FINANCIAL AID PICTURE (2004-2005)
Students with need: Out of 231 full-time freshmen who applied for aid, 176 were judged to have need. Of these, 176 received aid, and 7 had their full need met. Average financial aid package met 88% of need; average scholarship/grant was $8,500; average loan was $2,500. For part-time students, average financial aid package was $6,700.
Students without need: 24 full-time freshmen who did not demonstrate need for aid received scholarships/grants; average award was $3,200. No-need awards available for academics, alumni affiliation, art, leadership, music/drama.

FINANCIAL AID PROCEDURES
Forms required: FAFSA, institutional form.
Dates and Deadlines: Priority date 2/15; no closing date. Applicants notified on a rolling basis starting 3/1; must reply by 5/1 or within 2 week(s) of notification.

CONTACT
Richard Ellis, Acting Director of Financial Aid
541 Main Street, New London, NH 03257-7835
(603) 526-3717

Daniel Webster College
Nashua, New Hampshire
www.dwc.edu   Federal Code: 004731

4-year private business and technical college in small city.
Enrollment: 540 undergrads.

BASIC COSTS (2006-2007)
Tuition and fees: $24,135.
Per-credit charge: $978.
Room and board: $8,750.

FINANCIAL AID PICTURE
Students with need: Need-based aid available for full-time and part-time students. Work study available nights, weekends, and for part-time students.
Students without need: No-need awards available for academics, leadership.
Scholarships offered: Scholarships based on GPA and test scores, leadership, guidance counselor recommendation, awarded in amounts ranging from $500 to $7,500. Alumni and other scholarships range from $500 to full tuition.

FINANCIAL AID PROCEDURES
Forms required: FAFSA, institutional form.
Dates and Deadlines: Priority date 3/1; no closing date. Applicants notified on a rolling basis starting 3/15; must reply within 2 week(s) of notification.

CONTACT
Anne-Marie Caruso, Director of Financial Assistance
20 University Drive, Nashua, NH 03063
(603) 577-6590

Dartmouth College
Hanover, New Hampshire   Federal Code: 002573
www.dartmouth.edu   CSS Code: 3351

4-year private university and liberal arts college in large town.
Enrollment: 3,991 undergrads. 1,077 full-time freshmen.
Selectivity: Admits less than 50% of applicants.

BASIC COSTS (2006-2007)
Tuition and fees: $33,612.
Room and board: $9,976.

FINANCIAL AID PICTURE (2004-2005)
Students with need: Out of 656 full-time freshmen who applied for aid, 520 were judged to have need. Of these, 520 received aid, and 520 had their full need met. Average financial aid package met 100% of need; average scholarship/grant was $26,838; average loan was $3,138. Need-based aid available for part-time students.
Students without need: This college only awards aid to students with need.
Cumulative student debt: 48% of graduating class had student loans; average debt was $19,305.

FINANCIAL AID PROCEDURES
Forms required: FAFSA, CSS PROFILE.
Dates and Deadlines: Closing date 2/1. Applicants notified by 4/2; must reply by 5/1.
Transfers: Closing date 3/15. Grant budget for transfer students is limited. Some admitted transfer students may not have their full needs met.

CONTACT
Virginia Hazen, Director of Financial Aid
6016 McNutt Hall, Hanover, NH 03755
(603) 646-2451

Franklin Pierce College
Rindge, New Hampshire
www.fpc.edu   Federal Code: 002575

4-year private liberal arts college in small town.
Enrollment: 1,615 undergrads, 1% part-time. 507 full-time freshmen.
Selectivity: Admits 50 to 75% of applicants.

BASIC COSTS (2006-2007)
Tuition and fees: $25,100.
Per-credit charge: $810.
Room and board: $8,200.

FINANCIAL AID PICTURE (2005-2006)
Students with need: Out of 398 full-time freshmen who applied for aid, 345 were judged to have need. Of these, 345 received aid, and 37 had their full need met. Average financial aid package met 64% of need; average scholarship/grant was $12,044; average loan was $2,875. For part-time students, average financial aid package was $19,930.
Students without need: 97 full-time freshmen who did not demonstrate need for aid received scholarships/grants; average award was $10,786. No-

need awards available for academics, alumni affiliation, athletics, leadership, minority status, music/drama.
Scholarships offered: *Merit:* Marlin Fitzwater Mass Communication: 6 awarded; $2,000. Robert Alvin Performing Arts-Theater, Music, Dance: 2 awarded in each category; $2,000. *Athletic:* 15 full-time freshmen received athletic scholarships; average amount $12,839.
Cumulative student debt: 80% of graduating class had student loans; average debt was $28,036.

FINANCIAL AID PROCEDURES
Forms required: FAFSA.
Dates and Deadlines: Priority date 3/1; no closing date. Applicants notified on a rolling basis starting 4/1; must reply within 2 week(s) of notification.

CONTACT
Ken Ferera, Director of Financial Aid
20 College Road, Rindge, NH 03461-0060
(603) 899-4180

Granite State College
Concord, New Hampshire
www.granite.edu   Federal Code: 031013

4-year public liberal arts college in large town.
Enrollment: 1,105 undergrads, 59% part-time.

BASIC COSTS (2005-2006)
Tuition and fees: $6,045; out-of-state residents $6,645.
Per-credit charge: $195; out-of-state residents $215.

FINANCIAL AID PICTURE (2004-2005)
Students with need: 31% of average financial aid package awarded as scholarships/grants, 69% awarded as loans/jobs.

FINANCIAL AID PROCEDURES
Dates and Deadlines: No deadline. Applicants notified on a rolling basis.

CONTACT
Kimberly Dowd, Director of Financial Aid
8 Old Suncook Road, Concord, NH 03301-7317
(603) 228-3000 ext. 322

Keene State College
Keene, New Hampshire
www.keene.edu   Federal Code: 002590

4-year public liberal arts and teachers college in large town.
Enrollment: 4,370 undergrads, 5% part-time. 1,101 full-time freshmen.
Selectivity: Admits over 75% of applicants.

BASIC COSTS (2005-2006)
Tuition and fees: $7,352; out-of-state residents $14,192.
Per-credit charge: $226; out-of-state residents $510.
Room and board: $6,484.
Additional info: New England Regional tuition is 150% of in-state public institution tuition.

FINANCIAL AID PICTURE (2004-2005)
Students with need: Out of 906 full-time freshmen who applied for aid, 639 were judged to have need. Of these, 620 received aid, and 120 had their full need met. Average financial aid package met 70% of need; average scholarship/grant was $4,458; average loan was $2,934. For part-time students, average financial aid package was $4,420.
Students without need: 83 full-time freshmen who did not demonstrate need for aid received scholarships/grants; average award was $2,187. No-need awards available for academics, alumni affiliation, art, music/drama.

Cumulative student debt: 74% of graduating class had student loans; average debt was $20,065.

FINANCIAL AID PROCEDURES
Forms required: FAFSA.
Dates and Deadlines: Closing date 3/1. Applicants notified on a rolling basis; must reply within 4 week(s) of notification.
Transfers: Applicants notified on a rolling basis; must reply within 4 week(s) of notification.

CONTACT
Patricia Blodgett, Director of Financial Aid
229 Main Street, Keene, NH 03435-2604
(603) 358-2280

Magdalen College
Warner, New Hampshire
www.magdalen.edu

4-year private liberal arts college in small town, affiliated with Roman Catholic Church.
Enrollment: 71 undergrads, 1% part-time. 28 full-time freshmen.
Selectivity: Admits over 75% of applicants.

BASIC COSTS (2006-2007)
Tuition and fees: $10,750.
Room and board: $6,500.

FINANCIAL AID PICTURE
Students with need: Need-based aid available for full-time and part-time students.
Students without need: This college only awards aid to students with need.

FINANCIAL AID PROCEDURES
Forms required: institutional form.
Dates and Deadlines: Closing date 6/30. Applicants notified by 7/1; must reply by 7/1 or within 4 week(s) of notification.

CONTACT
Donald Regan, Vice President
511 Kearsarge Mountain Road, Warner, NH 03278
(603) 456-2656

McIntosh College
Dover, New Hampshire
www.mcintoshcollege.edu   Federal Code: 004730

2-year for-profit community college in large town.
Enrollment: 1,402 undergrads.
Selectivity: Open admission.

BASIC COSTS (2006-2007)
Additional info: Cost of full associate programs vary from $26,500 to $39,500. Cost of room and board for length of program: $13,200. Tuition at time of enrollment locked for 2 years.

FINANCIAL AID PICTURE
Students with need: Need-based aid available for full-time and part-time students. Work study available nights, weekends, and for part-time students.
Students without need: This college only awards aid to students with need.

FINANCIAL AID PROCEDURES
Forms required: FAFSA.
Dates and Deadlines: No deadline. Applicants notified on a rolling basis; must reply within 4 week(s) of notification.

New England College
Henniker, New Hampshire
www.nec.edu   Federal Code: 002579

4-year private liberal arts and teachers college in small town.
Enrollment: 1,008 undergrads, 6% part-time. 350 full-time freshmen.
Selectivity: Admits over 75% of applicants.

BASIC COSTS (2006-2007)
Tuition and fees: $24,136.
Per-credit charge: $1,140.
Room and board: $8,456.
Additional info: Tuition/fee waivers available for adults.

FINANCIAL AID PICTURE (2005-2006)
Students with need: Out of 281 full-time freshmen who applied for aid, 251 were judged to have need. Of these, 249 received aid, and 153 had their full need met. Average financial aid package met 83% of need; average scholarship/grant was $11,375; average loan was $6,810. For part-time students, average financial aid package was $10,833.
Students without need: 39 full-time freshmen who did not demonstrate need for aid received scholarships/grants; average award was $7,099. No-need awards available for academics, alumni affiliation, art, job skills, leadership, music/drama.
Cumulative student debt: 74% of graduating class had student loans; average debt was $31,753.

FINANCIAL AID PROCEDURES
Forms required: FAFSA, institutional form.
Dates and Deadlines: Priority date 4/1; no closing date. Applicants notified on a rolling basis starting 1/12; must reply within 2 week(s) of notification.
Transfers: No deadline. May 1 deadline for state grant consideration.

CONTACT
Lauren Hughes, Director of Student Financial Services
26 Bridge Street, Henniker, NH 03242
(603) 428-2226

New Hampshire Community Technical College: Berlin
Berlin, New Hampshire
www.berlin.nhctc.edu   Federal Code: 005291

2-year public community and technical college in large town.
Enrollment: 587 undergrads.

BASIC COSTS (2005-2006)
Tuition and fees: $5,040; out-of-state residents $11,400.
Per-credit charge: $164; out-of-state residents $376.
Additional info: New England Regional Plan $246 per credit hour.

FINANCIAL AID PICTURE
Students with need: Need-based aid available for full-time and part-time students.
Students without need: This college only awards aid to students with need.

FINANCIAL AID PROCEDURES
Forms required: FAFSA, institutional form.
Dates and Deadlines: Priority date 5/1; no closing date. Applicants notified on a rolling basis starting 5/1; must reply within 2 week(s) of notification.

CONTACT
Toni Baptiste, Director of Financial Aid
23 Cataract Avenue, Dover, NH 03820-3990
(888) 262-1111

CONTACT
Jacqueline Catello, Financial Aid Officer
2020 Riverside Drive, Berlin, NH 03570
(603) 752-1113

New Hampshire Community Technical College: Claremont
Claremont, New Hampshire
www.ncctc.edu   Federal Code: 007560

2-year public technical college in large town.
Enrollment: 1,200 undergrads.
Selectivity: Open admission; but selective for some programs.

BASIC COSTS (2005-2006)
Tuition and fees: $5,010; out-of-state residents $11,370.
Per-credit charge: $164; out-of-state residents $376.
Additional info: New England Regional tuition: $246 per credit hour.

FINANCIAL AID PICTURE
Students with need: Need-based aid available for full-time and part-time students.
Students without need: This college only awards aid to students with need.

FINANCIAL AID PROCEDURES
Forms required: FAFSA.
Dates and Deadlines: Priority date 5/1; no closing date. Applicants notified on a rolling basis; must reply within 2 week(s) of notification.

CONTACT
Julia Dower, Director of Financial Aid
One College Drive, Claremont, NH 03743-9707
(603) 542-7744

New Hampshire Community Technical College: Manchester
Manchester, New Hampshire
www.manchester.nhctc.edu   Federal Code: 002582

2-year public community and technical college in small city.
Enrollment: 3,000 undergrads.
Selectivity: Open admission; but selective for some programs.

BASIC COSTS (2005-2006)
Tuition and fees: $5,070; out-of-state residents $11,430.
Per-credit charge: $164; out-of-state residents $376.
Additional info: New England Regional tuition: $246 per credit hour.

FINANCIAL AID PICTURE
Students with need: Work study available nights, weekends, and for part-time students.
Students without need: This college only awards aid to students with need.
Additional info: 100% of direct educational expenses met for all financial aid applicants.

FINANCIAL AID PROCEDURES
Forms required: FAFSA, institutional form.
Dates and Deadlines: Priority date 5/1; no closing date. Applicants notified on a rolling basis starting 4/15; must reply within 2 week(s) of notification.

CONTACT
Pat Lamontagne, Financial Aid Officer
1066 Front Street, Manchester, NH 03102-8518
(603) 668-6706 ext. 273

New Hampshire Community Technical College: Nashua
Nashua, New Hampshire
www.nashua.nhctc.edu
Federal Code: 009236

2-year public community and technical college in small city.
Enrollment: 1,386 undergrads.
Selectivity: Open admission; but selective for some programs.

BASIC COSTS (2005-2006)
Tuition and fees: $5,023; out-of-state residents $11,383.
Per-credit charge: $164; out-of-state residents $376.
Additional info: New England Regional tuition: $246 per credit hour.

FINANCIAL AID PICTURE (2004-2005)
Students with need: 51% of average financial aid package awarded as scholarships/grants, 49% awarded as loans/jobs. Need-based aid available for part-time students. Work study available nights.
Students without need: This college only awards aid to students with need.

FINANCIAL AID PROCEDURES
Forms required: FAFSA.
Dates and Deadlines: Priority date 5/1; no closing date. Applicants notified on a rolling basis starting 3/1; must reply within 2 week(s) of notification.

CONTACT
Shirley Silva-Paige, Director of Financial Aid
505 Amherst Street, Nashua, NH 03063
(603) 882-6923

New Hampshire Technical Institute
Concord, New Hampshire
www.nhti.edu
Federal Code: 002581

2-year public community and technical college in large town.
Enrollment: 2,729 undergrads.
Selectivity: Admits over 75% of applicants.

BASIC COSTS (2005-2006)
Tuition and fees: $5,400; out-of-state residents $11,760.
Per-credit charge: $164; out-of-state residents $376.
Room and board: $6,110.
Additional info: New England Regional tuition: $246 per credit hour.

FINANCIAL AID PICTURE (2005-2006)
Students with need: Need-based aid available for part-time students. Work study available nights, weekends, and for part-time students.
Students without need: This college only awards aid to students with need.
Cumulative student debt: 60% of graduating class had student loans; average debt was $15,000.
Additional info: 60% of students who apply receive some form of financial aid. State school; all financial aid need-based, primarily from federal sources. No scholarships awarded.

FINANCIAL AID PROCEDURES
Forms required: FAFSA, institutional form.
Dates and Deadlines: Priority date 5/1; no closing date. Applicants notified on a rolling basis starting 6/1; must reply within 2 week(s) of notification.
Transfers: No deadline. Applicants notified on a rolling basis.

CONTACT
Sheri Gonthier, Financial Aid Director
31 College Drive, Concord, NH 03301
(603) 271-7136

Plymouth State University
Plymouth, New Hampshire
www.plymouth.edu
Federal Code: 002591

4-year public university and teachers college in small town.
Enrollment: 4,081 undergrads, 3% part-time. 1,052 full-time freshmen.
Selectivity: Admits over 75% of applicants.

BASIC COSTS (2005-2006)
Tuition and fees: $7,028; out-of-state residents $13,868.
Per-credit charge: $226; out-of-state residents $510.
Room and board: $6,780.
Additional info: New England Regional tuition is 150% of in-state public institution tuition.

FINANCIAL AID PICTURE (2004-2005)
Students with need: Out of 904 full-time freshmen who applied for aid, 638 were judged to have need. Of these, 623 received aid, and 23 had their full need met. Average financial aid package met 57% of need; average scholarship/grant was $4,274; average loan was $2,554. For part-time students, average financial aid package was $4,680.
Students without need: 46 full-time freshmen who did not demonstrate need for aid received scholarships/grants; average award was $2,136. No-need awards available for academics, minority status, music/drama.
Scholarships offered: Presidential Scholars; $3,000 based on outstanding academic performance and overall achievement; 15 awarded. PSU Scholars; $2,000; based on overall merit and past achievement; 48 awarded. New Hampshire Top Scholars; $2,500; New Hampshire residents in top 15%; 44 awarded. Music/theatre talent grants; $2,500; based on talent and audition; 10 awarded. ALANA; $2,000; minority students based on student's admission application.
Cumulative student debt: 73% of graduating class had student loans; average debt was $23,088.

FINANCIAL AID PROCEDURES
Forms required: FAFSA.
Dates and Deadlines: Priority date 3/1; no closing date. Applicants notified on a rolling basis starting 3/1; must reply by 5/1.

CONTACT
June Schlabach, Director of Financial Aid
17 High Street MSC 52, Plymouth, NH 03264-1595
(603) 535-2338

Rivier College
Nashua, New Hampshire
www.rivier.edu
Federal Code: 002586

4-year private liberal arts college in small city, affiliated with Roman Catholic Church.
Enrollment: 1,380 undergrads, 39% part-time. 202 full-time freshmen.
Selectivity: Admits 50 to 75% of applicants.

BASIC COSTS (2006-2007)
Tuition and fees: $21,370.
Per-credit charge: $699.
Room and board: $7,942.

FINANCIAL AID PICTURE (2004-2005)
Students with need: Out of 202 full-time freshmen who applied for aid, 186 were judged to have need. Of these, 186 received aid, and 58 had their full need met. Average financial aid package met 74% of need; average scholarship/grant was $9,479; average loan was $5,313. For part-time students, average financial aid package was $8,064.

Students without need: 16 full-time freshmen who did not demonstrate need for aid received scholarships/grants; average award was $10,910. No-need awards available for academics, alumni affiliation, minority status.

Scholarships offered: Dean's Scholarship for high school seniors with minimum 1000 SAT (exclusive of writing) and 3.0 GPA; renewable annually with minimum 2.67 cumulative GPA; $6,000 for residents, $5,000 for commuters. Presidential Scholarship for high school seniors with minimum 1150 SAT (exclusive of writing) and 3.4 GPA; renewable annually with minimum 3.0 cumulative GPA; $7,000 for residents, $6,000 for commuters. Catholic High School Grant for students graduating from Catholic high school, renewable annually with 2.5 cumulative GPA; $4,000 for residents, $3,000 for commuters. Honors Scholarship for honors program participants; $10,000 for residents, $2,000 for commuters. Alumni Scholarship for children of Rivier alumni, renewable annually with minimum 2.0 cumulative GPA; $2,000. Trustee Scholarship for high school seniors with minimum 1200 SAT (exclusive of writing) and 3.4 GPA, renewable annually with minimum 3.0 cumulative GPA; $8,000 for residents, $7,000 for commuters. Founders Scholarship for National Merit Finalists; full tuition, renewable with minimum 3.0 cumulative GPA.

Cumulative student debt: 85% of graduating class had student loans; average debt was $28,052.

FINANCIAL AID PROCEDURES

Forms required: FAFSA.

Dates and Deadlines: Priority date 2/1; no closing date. Applicants notified on a rolling basis starting 3/1; must reply by 5/1 or within 2 week(s) of notification.

Transfers: Priority date 3/1. Scholarship for transfer students with minimum 3.0 GPA and 15 transferable credits.

CONTACT

Valerie Patnaude, Director of Financial Aid
420 Main Street, Nashua, NH 03060-5086
(603) 897-8510

St. Anselm College
Manchester, New Hampshire Federal Code: 002587
www.anselm.edu CSS Code: 3748

4-year private nursing and liberal arts college in small city, affiliated with Roman Catholic Church.

Enrollment: 1,952 undergrads, 1% part-time. 519 full-time freshmen.
Selectivity: Admits 50 to 75% of applicants.

BASIC COSTS (2006-2007)
Tuition and fees: $26,100.
Room and board: $9,620.
Additional info: Tuition/fee waivers available for minority students.

FINANCIAL AID PICTURE (2005-2006)
Students with need: 64% of average financial aid package awarded as scholarships/grants, 36% awarded as loans/jobs. Need-based aid available for part-time students. Work study available nights, weekends, and for part-time students.

Students without need: No-need awards available for academics, athletics, state/district residency.

Scholarships offered: Presidential Scholarships; 350 awarded; based on academic performance (grades, class rank, SAT results) and extracurricular experience; $6,000 to $11,500.

FINANCIAL AID PROCEDURES
Forms required: FAFSA, CSS PROFILE.
Dates and Deadlines: Priority date 3/1; no closing date. Applicants notified on a rolling basis starting 3/10; must reply by 5/1.
Transfers: Merit scholarships are not available for transfer students.

CONTACT
Elizabeth Keuffel, Director of Financial Aid
100 Saint Anselm Drive, Manchester, NH 03102-1310
(603) 641-7110

Southern New Hampshire University
Manchester, New Hampshire
www.snhu.edu Federal Code: 002580

4-year private university in small city.
Enrollment: 1,706 undergrads, 3% part-time. 426 full-time freshmen.
Selectivity: Admits 50 to 75% of applicants.

BASIC COSTS (2006-2007)
Tuition and fees: $21,714.
Room and board: $8,480.

FINANCIAL AID PICTURE (2005-2006)
Students with need: Out of 368 full-time freshmen who applied for aid, 315 were judged to have need. Of these, 315 received aid, and 36 had their full need met. Average financial aid package met 70% of need; average scholarship/grant was $9,740; average loan was $2,572. For part-time students, average financial aid package was $14,841.

Students without need: 63 full-time freshmen who did not demonstrate need for aid received scholarships/grants; average award was $4,038. No-need awards available for academics, alumni affiliation, athletics, leadership, state/district residency.

Scholarships offered: 19 full-time freshmen received athletic scholarships; average amount $11,948.

FINANCIAL AID PROCEDURES
Forms required: FAFSA.
Dates and Deadlines: Priority date 3/15; no closing date. Applicants notified on a rolling basis starting 3/1; must reply within 3 week(s) of notification.
Transfers: Priority date 6/15.

CONTACT
Timothy Dreyer, Director of Financial Aid
2500 North River Road, Manchester, NH 03106-1045
(603) 668-2211

Thomas More College of Liberal Arts
Merrimack, New Hampshire
www.thomasmorecollege.edu Federal Code: 030431

4-year private liberal arts college in large town, affiliated with Roman Catholic Church.

Enrollment: 86 undergrads, 1% part-time. 19 full-time freshmen.
Selectivity: Admits over 75% of applicants.

BASIC COSTS (2005-2006)
Tuition and fees: $10,650.
Per-credit charge: $175.
Room and board: $8,000.

FINANCIAL AID PICTURE (2005-2006)
Students with need: Out of 18 full-time freshmen who applied for aid, 9 were judged to have need. Of these, 9 received aid. Average financial aid package met 70% of need; average scholarship/grant was $4,564; average loan was $2,438. Need-based aid available for part-time students.

Students without need: 9 full-time freshmen who did not demonstrate need for aid received scholarships/grants; average award was $5,433. No-need awards available for academics.

Scholarships offered: Thomas More Scholarship; several awarded; based on superior academic achievement, exceptional promise or potential; full and/or partial tuition. Commuter Grants; offered to full-time students within com-

muting distance of the college; 25% of tuition. Faith and Reason Essay Contest; 4 awarded; based on essay; half tuition for four years. Summer Program Scholarship; for students who have attended the Thomas More College Summer Program for high school students; $1,000 per year.
Cumulative student debt: 80% of graduating class had student loans; average debt was $17,878.

FINANCIAL AID PROCEDURES
Forms required: FAFSA.
Dates and Deadlines: Priority date 5/1; no closing date. Applicants notified on a rolling basis starting 5/15; must reply within 2 week(s) of notification.

CONTACT
Pamela Bernstein, Business Manager
Six Manchester Street, Merrimack, NH 03054-4818
(603) 324-1494

University of New Hampshire
Durham, New Hampshire
www.unh.edu
Federal Code: 002589

4-year public university in small town.
Enrollment: 11,063 undergrads, 2% part-time. 2,410 full-time freshmen.
Selectivity: Admits 50 to 75% of applicants.

BASIC COSTS (2005-2006)
Tuition and fees: $9,778; out-of-state residents $21,498.
Per-credit charge: $321; out-of-state residents $810.
Room and board: $7,032.
Additional info: New England Regional Student Program tuition 175% of in-state public institution tuition. Students in following majors pay differential per academic year: engineering, computer science, business-economics-hospitality management (Whittemore School). Tuition/fee waivers available for minority students.

FINANCIAL AID PICTURE (2004-2005)
Students with need: Out of 1,961 full-time freshmen who applied for aid, 1,487 were judged to have need. Of these, 1,459 received aid, and 359 had their full need met. Average financial aid package met 82% of need; average scholarship/grant was $2,708; average loan was $2,345. For part-time students, average financial aid package was $9,987.
Students without need: 521 full-time freshmen who did not demonstrate need for aid received scholarships/grants; average award was $5,274. No-need awards available for academics, art, athletics, leadership, music/drama, ROTC.
Scholarships offered: *Merit:* Presidential Scholarship: half tuition. Various other awards recognizing outstanding high school achievement determined during freshmen candidate application review process, no additional application materials required. *Athletic:* 54 full-time freshmen received athletic scholarships; average amount $19,478.
Cumulative student debt: 68% of graduating class had student loans; average debt was $21,459.

FINANCIAL AID PROCEDURES
Forms required: FAFSA.
Dates and Deadlines: Priority date 3/1; no closing date. Applicants notified on a rolling basis starting 3/1.

CONTACT
Susan Allen, Director of Financial Aid
Grant House, 4 Garrison Avenue, Durham, NH 03824
(603) 862-3600

University of New Hampshire at Manchester
Manchester, New Hampshire
www.unhm.unh.edu
Federal Code: 002589

4-year public university and liberal arts college in small city.
Enrollment: 779 undergrads, 29% part-time. 119 full-time freshmen.

BASIC COSTS (2005-2006)
Tuition and fees: $7,103; out-of-state residents $17,753.
Per-credit charge: $235; out-of-state residents $734.
Additional info: New England Regional Student tuition is 150% of in-state public institution tuition.

FINANCIAL AID PICTURE
Students with need: Work study available nights, weekends, and for part-time students.
Students without need: No-need awards available for academics, state/district residency.

FINANCIAL AID PROCEDURES
Forms required: FAFSA.
Dates and Deadlines: Closing date 5/1. Applicants notified on a rolling basis starting 4/1; must reply within 2 week(s) of notification.

CONTACT
Jodi Abad, Director of Financial Aid
400 Commercial Street, Manchester, NH 03101-1113
(603) 641-4189

New Jersey

Atlantic Cape Community College
Mays Landing, New Jersey
www.atlantic.edu
Federal Code: 002596

2-year public community college in small town.
Enrollment: 6,845 undergrads.
Selectivity: Open admission; but selective for some programs.

BASIC COSTS (2005-2006)
Tuition and fees: $2,610; out-of-district residents $4,800; out-of-state residents $8,100.
Per-credit charge: $73; out-of-district residents $146; out-of-state residents $256.
Additional info: Tuition/fee waivers available for unemployed or children of unemployed.

FINANCIAL AID PICTURE
Students with need: Need-based aid available for full-time and part-time students.
Scholarships offered: Howard Persina Scholarship for hospitality management students. Barbara Rimm Memorial Scholarship for nursing majors. William R. Cohn Memorial Scholarship for accounting students. Atlantic City Restaurant Association Scholarship for culinary arts students. Math and Science Scholarship.
Additional info: Installment plan available for culinary arts majors. Employees of Atlantic City casinos may attend ACCC at in-county rates regardless of where they live.

FINANCIAL AID PROCEDURES
Forms required: FAFSA, institutional form.
Dates and Deadlines: Priority date 5/1; no closing date. Applicants notified on a rolling basis starting 5/1.

CONTACT
Fred Mason, Director of Financial Aid
5100 Black Horse Pike, Mays Landing, NJ 08330
(609) 343-5082

Berkeley College
West Paterson, New Jersey
www.berkeleycollege.edu   Federal Code: 007502

4-year for-profit business college in large town.
Enrollment: 2,406 undergrads, 15% part-time. 743 full-time freshmen.
Selectivity: Admits over 75% of applicants.

BASIC COSTS (2006-2007)
Tuition and fees: $17,700.
Per-credit charge: $415.
Room and board: $9,000.
Additional info: Tuition at time of enrollment locked for 4 years.

FINANCIAL AID PICTURE
Students with need: Need-based aid available for full-time students.
Students without need: No-need awards available for academics, alumni affiliation.
Additional info: Alumni scholarship examination given in November and December. Full and partial scholarships awarded.

FINANCIAL AID PROCEDURES
Forms required: FAFSA.
Dates and Deadlines: No deadline. Applicants notified on a rolling basis starting 3/1; must reply within 6 week(s) of notification.

CONTACT
Joan Kinni, Director, Student Finance
44 Rifle Camp Road, West Paterson, NJ 07424-0440
(973) 278-5400 ext. 1350

Bloomfield College
Bloomfield, New Jersey
www.bloomfield.edu   Federal Code: 002597

4-year private liberal arts college in large town, affiliated with Presbyterian Church (USA).
Enrollment: 2,181 undergrads, 21% part-time. 403 full-time freshmen.
Selectivity: Admits less than 50% of applicants.

BASIC COSTS (2006-2007)
Tuition and fees: $16,400.
Per-credit charge: $1,650.
Room and board: $8,100.

FINANCIAL AID PICTURE (2005-2006)
Students with need: Out of 398 full-time freshmen who applied for aid, 357 were judged to have need. Of these, 353 received aid, and 199 had their full need met. Average financial aid package met 70% of need; average scholarship/grant was $12,071; average loan was $2,838. For part-time students, average financial aid package was $8,142.
Students without need: 22 full-time freshmen who did not demonstrate need for aid received scholarships/grants; average award was $5,523. No-need awards available for academics, alumni affiliation, athletics, leadership, religious affiliation.
Scholarships offered: *Merit:* Trustee Scholar Award: $6,000 to $8,000, high school GPA of 3.2 or higher, top 25% of graduating class, competitive SAT scores; Presidential Scholarship: $4,000 to $6,000, high school GPA of 3.0 or higher, top 33% of graduating class, competitive SAT scores; Transfer Scholarship: $3,000, transfer students from 2-year colleges with GPA of 3.0 or higher; Community Service Scholarships: awards of up to half-tuition to high school seniors with a commitment to community service; Phi Theta Kappa Transfer Scholarships: $3,500 for transfer students from 2-year colleges with GPA of 3.5 or higher who are members of Phi Theta Kappa. *Athletic:* 10 full-time freshmen received athletic scholarships; average amount $7,830.

FINANCIAL AID PROCEDURES
Forms required: FAFSA.
Dates and Deadlines: Priority date 3/15; closing date 6/1. Applicants notified on a rolling basis starting 3/27; must reply within 2 week(s) of notification.
Transfers: Closing date 6/1. Applicants notified on a rolling basis starting 3/15; must reply by 3/15 or within 2 week(s) of notification.

CONTACT
Luis Gonzales, Director of Financial Aid
One Park Place, Bloomfield, NJ 07003-9981
(973) 748-9000 ext. 212

Brookdale Community College
Lincroft, New Jersey
www.brookdalecc.edu   Federal Code: 008404

2-year public community college in small city.
Enrollment: 11,438 undergrads.
Selectivity: Open admission; but selective for some programs.

BASIC COSTS (2005-2006)
Tuition and fees: $3,331; out-of-district residents $6,083; out-of-state residents $7,328.
Per-credit charge: $92; out-of-district residents $184; out-of-state residents $225.
Additional info: Tuition/fee waivers available for unemployed or children of unemployed.

FINANCIAL AID PICTURE
Students with need: Need-based aid available for full-time and part-time students.
Students without need: No-need awards available for athletics.

FINANCIAL AID PROCEDURES
Forms required: FAFSA, institutional form.
Dates and Deadlines: Priority date 5/1; no closing date. Applicants notified on a rolling basis starting 5/1; must reply within 2 week(s) of notification.

CONTACT
Michael Bennett, Director of Financial Aid
765 Newman Springs Road, Lincroft, NJ 07738
(732) 224-2361

Burlington County College
Pemberton, New Jersey
www.bcc.edu   Federal Code: 007730

2-year public community college in small town.
Enrollment: 6,534 undergrads, 46% part-time. 1,499 full-time freshmen.
Selectivity: Open admission; but selective for some programs.

BASIC COSTS (2005-2006)
Tuition and fees: $2,116; out-of-district residents $2,950; out-of-state residents $4,900.
Per-credit charge: $66; out-of-district residents $85; out-of-state residents $150.
Additional info: Tuition/fee waivers available for unemployed or children of unemployed.

New Jersey Burlington County College

FINANCIAL AID PICTURE
Students with need: Need-based aid available for full-time and part-time students.
Students without need: This college only awards aid to students with need.

FINANCIAL AID PROCEDURES
Forms required: FAFSA, institutional form.
Dates and Deadlines: No deadline. Applicants notified on a rolling basis starting 7/1; must reply within 3 week(s) of notification.

CONTACT
Maurice Thomas, Assistant Director of Financial Aid
601 Pemberton-Browns Mills Road, Pemberton, NJ 08068-1599
(609) 894-9311 ext. 1575

Caldwell College
Caldwell, New Jersey
www.caldwell.edu   Federal Code: 002598

4-year private liberal arts college in large town, affiliated with Roman Catholic Church.
Enrollment: 1,550 undergrads, 32% part-time. 316 full-time freshmen.
Selectivity: Admits over 75% of applicants.

BASIC COSTS (2006-2007)
Tuition and fees: $20,200.
Per-credit charge: $490.
Room and board: $7,995.

FINANCIAL AID PICTURE (2005-2006)
Students with need: Out of 275 full-time freshmen who applied for aid, 270 were judged to have need. Of these, 270 received aid, and 212 had their full need met. Average financial aid package met 75% of need; average scholarship/grant was $7,300; average loan was $3,800. For part-time students, average financial aid package was $2,000.
Students without need: 90 full-time freshmen who did not demonstrate need for aid received scholarships/grants; average award was $3,500. No-need awards available for academics, alumni affiliation, art, athletics, leadership, music/drama, religious affiliation.
Scholarships offered: 32 full-time freshmen received athletic scholarships; average amount $6,000.
Cumulative student debt: 74% of graduating class had student loans; average debt was $20,500.

FINANCIAL AID PROCEDURES
Forms required: FAFSA, state aid form, institutional form.
Dates and Deadlines: Priority date 4/15; no closing date. Applicants notified on a rolling basis starting 3/1; must reply within 4 week(s) of notification.
Transfers: No deadline. Students who have filed for aid through the state previously must file FAFSA by June 1 for succeeding year.

CONTACT
Lissa Anderson, Financial Aid Executive Director
9 Ryerson Avenue, Caldwell, NJ 07006-6195
(973) 618-3222

Camden County College
Blackwood, New Jersey
www.camdencc.edu   Federal Code: 006865

2-year public community college in large town.
Enrollment: 7,249 full-time undergrads.
Selectivity: Open admission; but selective for some programs.

BASIC COSTS (2005-2006)
Tuition and fees: $2,580; out-of-state residents $2,700.
Per-credit charge: $73; out-of-state residents $77.
Additional info: Tuition/fee waivers available for unemployed or children of unemployed.

FINANCIAL AID PICTURE
Students with need: Need-based aid available for full-time and part-time students.

FINANCIAL AID PROCEDURES
Forms required: FAFSA, institutional form.
Dates and Deadlines: Closing date 7/1. Applicants notified on a rolling basis starting 7/1.
Transfers: Must submit financial aid transcripts from all previously attended institutions.

CONTACT
Aquila Galgon, Director of Financial Aid
Box 200, Blackwood, NJ 08012
(856) 227-7200

Centenary College
Hackettstown, New Jersey
www.centenarycollege.edu   Federal Code: 002599

4-year private liberal arts college in large town, affiliated with United Methodist Church.
Enrollment: 1,887 undergrads, 14% part-time. 243 full-time freshmen.
Selectivity: Admits over 75% of applicants.

BASIC COSTS (2006-2007)
Tuition and fees: $22,030.
Per-credit charge: $420.
Room and board: $8,400.
Additional info: Additional fees required for equine majors and for comprehensive learning support program.

FINANCIAL AID PICTURE (2005-2006)
Students with need: Out of 243 full-time freshmen who applied for aid, 214 were judged to have need. Of these, 211 received aid, and 38 had their full need met. Average financial aid package met 70% of need; average scholarship/grant was $12,945; average loan was $3,414. For part-time students, average financial aid package was $9,224.
Students without need: 34 full-time freshmen who did not demonstrate need for aid received scholarships/grants; average award was $16,213. No-need awards available for academics, alumni affiliation, art, leadership, state/district residency.
Scholarships offered: Academic awards based on minimum GPA of 2.5, SAT 800 (exclusive of Writing) or ACT 16. Leadership awards available based on demonstrated leadership ability and potential. Equine Award, Centenary Resident Grant, Out-of-State Centenary Grant, Skylands Centenary Grant, Centenary United Methodist Scholarship also available.
Cumulative student debt: 98% of graduating class had student loans; average debt was $20,383.

FINANCIAL AID PROCEDURES
Forms required: FAFSA.
Dates and Deadlines: Priority date 4/15; no closing date. Applicants notified on a rolling basis starting 3/1.
Transfers: Students from New Jersey colleges who have received tuition aid grants (TAG) must apply by state deadline. Students must submit financial aid transcripts from all previous institutions attended.

CONTACT
Mike Corso, Director of Financial Aid
400 Jefferson Street, Hackettstown, NJ 07840-9989
(908) 852-1400 ext. 2350

The College of New Jersey
Ewing, New Jersey
www.tcnj.edu
Federal Code: 002642

4-year public liberal arts college in large town.
Enrollment: 5,836 undergrads, 2% part-time. 1,241 full-time freshmen.
Selectivity: Admits less than 50% of applicants.

BASIC COSTS (2005-2006)
Tuition and fees: $9,707; out-of-state residents $14,970.
Per-credit charge: $250; out-of-state residents $436.
Room and board: $8,458.
Additional info: Tuition/fee waivers available for unemployed or children of unemployed.

FINANCIAL AID PICTURE (2005-2006)
Students with need: Out of 428 full-time freshmen who applied for aid, 428 were judged to have need. Of these, 404 received aid, and 50 had their full need met. Average financial aid package met 51% of need; average scholarship/grant was $12,033; average loan was $5,337. For part-time students, average financial aid package was $5,324.
Students without need: 584 full-time freshmen who did not demonstrate need for aid received scholarships/grants; average award was $3,684. No-need awards available for academics, art, minority status, music/drama, ROTC, state/district residency.
Cumulative student debt: 51% of graduating class had student loans; average debt was $17,673.
Additional info: Merit scholarships available to New Jersey high school graduates based on academic distinction. Limited number of scholarships available to out-of-state students who demonstrate exceptional academic achievement in high school and on SAT.

FINANCIAL AID PROCEDURES
Forms required: FAFSA.
Dates and Deadlines: Priority date 3/1; closing date 10/1. Applicants notified on a rolling basis starting 7/15; must reply within 2 week(s) of notification.
Transfers: No deadline.

CONTACT
Jamie Hightower, Director of Student Financial Services
Box 7718, Ewing, NJ 08628
(609) 771-2211

College of St. Elizabeth
Morristown, New Jersey
www.cse.edu
Federal Code: 002600

4-year private liberal arts college for women in large town, affiliated with Roman Catholic Church.
Enrollment: 1,073 undergrads, 38% part-time. 206 full-time freshmen.
Selectivity: Admits over 75% of applicants.

BASIC COSTS (2005-2006)
Tuition and fees: $19,440.
Per-credit charge: $587.
Room and board: $8,975.
Additional info: Tuition/fee waivers available for adults.

FINANCIAL AID PICTURE (2004-2005)
Students with need: Out of 161 full-time freshmen who applied for aid, 135 were judged to have need. Of these, 133 received aid, and 28 had their full need met. Average financial aid package met 79% of need; average scholarship/grant was $15,112; average loan was $2,512. For part-time students, average financial aid package was $5,595.
Students without need: 57 full-time freshmen who did not demonstrate need for aid received scholarships/grants; average award was $11,749. No-need awards available for academics, alumni affiliation, art, leadership, state/district residency.
Scholarships offered: Presidential Scholarship for campus residents; full tuition. Elizabethan Scholarship; $8,000-$10,000. Seton Scholarship; $3,000-$7,000. Awards guaranteed to eligible students who apply by March 1 and enroll by May 1 for fall semester. Spring semester awards dependent upon availability of funds. International scholarships awarded annually for fall semester only to first year students enrolled in Women's College; covers tuition, room and board; very competitive, based on academic record, SAT scores (if submitted) and TOEFL score.
Cumulative student debt: 67% of graduating class had student loans; average debt was $18,915.

FINANCIAL AID PROCEDURES
Forms required: FAFSA.
Dates and Deadlines: Priority date 3/1; no closing date. Applicants notified on a rolling basis starting 11/15; must reply by 5/1 or within 2 week(s) of notification.
Transfers: Priority date 4/15; closing date 8/20. Scholarships available for full-time students who enroll immediately following full-time enrollment at another college. Applicants must have completed minimum 32 credits and have minimum 3.0 GPA. Awards range from $3,500 to half tuition. Minimum of 5 awarded annually. Preference given to applications received by June 1 for fall semester and by December 1 for spring semester. Limited number of partial scholarships awarded to international students.

CONTACT
Vincent Tunstall, Director of Financial Aid
2 Convent Road, Morristown, NJ 07960-6989
(973) 290-4445

County College of Morris
Randolph, New Jersey
www.ccm.edu
Federal Code: 007106

2-year public community college in large town.
Enrollment: 6,288 undergrads.
Selectivity: Open admission; but selective for some programs.

BASIC COSTS (2005-2006)
Tuition and fees: $3,045; out-of-district residents $5,685; out-of-state residents $7,815.
Per-credit charge: $88; out-of-district residents $176; out-of-state residents $247.
Additional info: Tuition reciprocity agreements with neighboring counties allow some out-of-county residents to pay in-county rates. Tuition/fee waivers available for unemployed or children of unemployed.

FINANCIAL AID PICTURE
Students with need: Need-based aid available for full-time and part-time students.
Students without need: No-need awards available for athletics.

FINANCIAL AID PROCEDURES
Forms required: FAFSA.
Dates and Deadlines: Priority date 3/1; no closing date. Applicants notified on a rolling basis starting 5/1.

CONTACT
Harvey Willis, Director, Financial Aid
214 Center Grove Road, Randolph, NJ 07869-2086
(973) 328-5230

Cumberland County College
Vineland, New Jersey
www.cccnj.net   Federal Code: 002601

2-year public community college in small city.
Enrollment: 3,256 undergrads.
Selectivity: Open admission; but selective for some programs.

BASIC COSTS (2006-2007)
Tuition and fees: $2,940; out-of-district residents $5,340; out-of-state residents $10,140.
Additional info: $9 per-credit-hour technology fee in addition to the comprehensive fee included above. Tuition data are based on 30 credits for a full academic year. Tuition/fee waivers available for unemployed or children of unemployed.

FINANCIAL AID PICTURE (2004-2005)
Students with need: 66% of average financial aid package awarded as scholarships/grants, 34% awarded as loans/jobs. Need-based aid available for part-time students.
Students without need: No-need awards available for academics.

FINANCIAL AID PROCEDURES
Forms required: FAFSA.
Dates and Deadlines: No deadline. Applicants notified on a rolling basis; must reply within 3 week(s) of notification.

CONTACT
Kimberly Mitchell, Director, Financial Aid
PO Box 1500, Vineland, NJ 08362-9912
(609) 691-8600

DeVry University: North Brunswick
North Brunswick, New Jersey
www.nj.devry.edu   Federal Code: 009228

4-year for-profit university in small city.
Enrollment: 1,491 undergrads, 23% part-time. 248 full-time freshmen.

BASIC COSTS (2005-2006)
Tuition and fees: $12,240.
Per-credit charge: $505.

FINANCIAL AID PICTURE
Students with need: Need-based aid available for full-time and part-time students.
Students without need: This college only awards aid to students with need.

FINANCIAL AID PROCEDURES
Forms required: FAFSA.
Dates and Deadlines: No deadline. Applicants notified on a rolling basis.

CONTACT
Albert Cama, Director of Financial Aid
630 US Highway One, North Brunswick, NJ 08902-3362
(800) 333-3879

Drew University
Madison, New Jersey
www.drew.edu   Federal Code: 002603
                   CSS Code: 2193

4-year private university and liberal arts college in large town, affiliated with United Methodist Church.
Enrollment: 1,561 undergrads, 2% part-time. 418 full-time freshmen.
Selectivity: Admits over 75% of applicants.

BASIC COSTS (2006-2007)
Tuition and fees: $33,054.
Per-credit charge: $1,355.
Room and board: $9,001.

FINANCIAL AID PICTURE (2004-2005)
Students with need: Out of 302 full-time freshmen who applied for aid, 225 were judged to have need. Of these, 223 received aid, and 82 had their full need met. Average financial aid package met 83% of need; average scholarship/grant was $17,024; average loan was $3,536. Need-based aid available for part-time students.
Students without need: 128 full-time freshmen who did not demonstrate need for aid received scholarships/grants; average award was $12,259. No-need awards available for academics, art, minority status, music/drama.
Cumulative student debt: 60% of graduating class had student loans; average debt was $17,586.

FINANCIAL AID PROCEDURES
Forms required: FAFSA, CSS PROFILE.
Dates and Deadlines: Closing date 2/15. Applicants notified by 3/31; must reply by 5/1.
Transfers: No deadline.

CONTACT
Mary Beth Carey, Dean of College Admissions and Financial Assistance
36 Madison Avenue, Madison, NJ 07940-1493
(973) 408-3112

Essex County College
Newark, New Jersey
www.essex.edu   Federal Code: 007107

2-year public community college in large city.
Enrollment: 9,359 undergrads, 42% part-time. 1,956 full-time freshmen.
Selectivity: Open admission; but selective for some programs.

BASIC COSTS (2006-2007)
Tuition and fees: $3,345; out-of-district residents $5,775; out-of-state residents $5,775.
Per-credit charge: $81; out-of-district residents $162; out-of-state residents $162.
Additional info: Tuition/fee waivers available for unemployed or children of unemployed.

FINANCIAL AID PICTURE
Students with need: Need-based aid available for full-time and part-time students.

FINANCIAL AID PROCEDURES
Forms required: FAFSA, institutional form.
Dates and Deadlines: Priority date 6/30; no closing date. Applicants notified on a rolling basis starting 6/15; must reply within 3 week(s) of notification.

CONTACT
Mildred Cofer, Director of Financial Aid
303 University Avenue, Newark, NJ 07102
(973) 877-3000

Fairleigh Dickinson University: College at Florham
Madison, New Jersey
www.fdu.edu

4-year private business and liberal arts college in large town.
Enrollment: 2,495 undergrads, 8% part-time. 480 full-time freshmen.
Selectivity: Admits 50 to 75% of applicants.

BASIC COSTS (2005-2006)
Tuition and fees: $24,904.
Per-credit charge: $725.
Room and board: $9,008.

FINANCIAL AID PICTURE (2004-2005)
Students with need: Out of 480 full-time freshmen who applied for aid, 420 were judged to have need. Of these, 420 received aid. For part-time students, average financial aid package was $6,193.
Students without need: 153 full-time freshmen who did not demonstrate need for aid received scholarships/grants; average award was $7,449. No-need awards available for academics, alumni affiliation, leadership.

FINANCIAL AID PROCEDURES
Forms required: FAFSA.
Dates and Deadlines: Priority date 2/15; no closing date. Applicants notified on a rolling basis starting 4/1; must reply by 5/1 or within 2 week(s) of notification.

CONTACT
Margaret McGrail, University Director
285 Madison Avenue, Madison, NJ 07940
(973) 443-8700

Fairleigh Dickinson University: Metropolitan Campus
Teaneck, New Jersey
www.fdu.edu   Federal Code: 002604

4-year private university in large town.
Enrollment: 3,284 undergrads, 36% part-time. 350 full-time freshmen.
Selectivity: Admits 50 to 75% of applicants.

BASIC COSTS (2005-2006)
Tuition and fees: $23,144.
Per-credit charge: $725.
Room and board: $9,482.

FINANCIAL AID PICTURE (2004-2005)
Students with need: Out of 350 full-time freshmen who applied for aid, 332 were judged to have need. Of these, 332 received aid. For part-time students, average financial aid package was $2,715.
Students without need: 37 full-time freshmen who did not demonstrate need for aid received scholarships/grants; average award was $4,572. No-need awards available for academics, alumni affiliation, art, athletics, leadership, state/district residency.
Scholarships offered: 39 full-time freshmen received athletic scholarships; average amount $14,533.

FINANCIAL AID PROCEDURES
Forms required: FAFSA.
Dates and Deadlines: Priority date 2/15; no closing date. Applicants notified on a rolling basis starting 4/1; must reply by 5/1 or within 2 week(s) of notification.

CONTACT
Margaret McGrail, University Director of Financial Aid
1000 River Road, H-DH3-10, Teaneck, NJ 07666-1996
(201) 692-2363

Felician College
Lodi, New Jersey
www.felician.edu   Federal Code: 002610

4-year private liberal arts college in large city, affiliated with Roman Catholic Church.
Enrollment: 1,464 undergrads, 22% part-time. 245 full-time freshmen.
Selectivity: Admits over 75% of applicants.

BASIC COSTS (2005-2006)
Tuition and fees: $18,600.
Per-credit charge: $570.
Room and board: $7,950.
Additional info: Tuition/fee waivers available for adults.

FINANCIAL AID PICTURE (2004-2005)
Students with need: Out of 213 full-time freshmen who applied for aid, 119 were judged to have need. Of these, 119 received aid, and 24 had their full need met. Average financial aid package met 85% of need; average scholarship/grant was $6,000; average loan was $3,500. For part-time students, average financial aid package was $4,000.
Students without need: 33 full-time freshmen who did not demonstrate need for aid received scholarships/grants; average award was $9,962. No-need awards available for academics, alumni affiliation, athletics, religious affiliation.
Scholarships offered: 75 full-time freshmen received athletic scholarships; average amount $5,550.

FINANCIAL AID PROCEDURES
Forms required: FAFSA, institutional form.
Dates and Deadlines: Priority date 6/1; no closing date. Applicants notified on a rolling basis starting 4/1; must reply within 2 week(s) of notification.

CONTACT
Marc Chalfin, Executive Vice President for Business and Finance
262 South Main Street, Lodi, NJ 07644-2198
(201) 559-6000 ext. 6010

Georgian Court University
Lakewood, New Jersey
www.georgian.edu   Federal Code: 002608

4-year private university and liberal arts college for women in large town, affiliated with Roman Catholic Church.
Enrollment: 1,740 undergrads, 24% part-time. 186 full-time freshmen.
Selectivity: Admits 50 to 75% of applicants.

BASIC COSTS (2006-2007)
Tuition and fees: $20,632.
Per-credit charge: $528.
Room and board: $7,800.

FINANCIAL AID PICTURE (2004-2005)
Students with need: Average financial aid package met 56% of need; average scholarship/grant was $10,036; average loan was $2,920. For part-time students, average financial aid package was $7,835.
Students without need: 71 full-time freshmen who did not demonstrate need for aid received scholarships/grants; average award was $5,583. No-need awards available for academics, alumni affiliation, art, athletics, leadership, minority status, music/drama, religious affiliation.

FINANCIAL AID PROCEDURES
Forms required: FAFSA, institutional form.
Dates and Deadlines: Priority date 3/1; no closing date. Applicants notified on a rolling basis starting 2/1; must reply within 2 week(s) of notification.

Transfers: Transfer students who have outstanding financial obligations to previous college or who are in default are not admitted before being cleared by previous college or following federal guidelines concerning defaults.

CONTACT
Carol Strauss, Director of Financial Aid
900 Lakewood Avenue, Lakewood, NJ 08701-2697
(732) 364-2200 ext. 2258

Gloucester County College
Sewell, New Jersey
www.gccnj.edu   Federal Code: 006901

2-year public community college in large town.
Enrollment: 3,205 full-time undergrads.
Selectivity: Open admission; but selective for some programs.

BASIC COSTS (2005-2006)
Tuition and fees: $2,760; out-of-district residents $2,790; out-of-state residents $4,980.
Per-credit charge: $74; out-of-district residents $75; out-of-state residents $148.
Additional info: On-line courses per-credit-hour charge: $90.

FINANCIAL AID PICTURE
Students with need: Need-based aid available for full-time and part-time students. Work study available nights.
Students without need: This college only awards aid to students with need.

FINANCIAL AID PROCEDURES
Forms required: FAFSA, institutional form.
Dates and Deadlines: Priority date 5/1; no closing date. Applicants notified on a rolling basis starting 3/20.

CONTACT
Jeffrey Williams, Financial Aid Director
1400 Tanyard Road, Sewell, NJ 08080
(856) 415-2210

Hudson County Community College
Jersey City, New Jersey
www.hccc.edu   Federal Code: 012954

2-year public community college in large city.
Enrollment: 6,336 undergrads, 41% part-time. 1,432 full-time freshmen.
Selectivity: Open admission.

BASIC COSTS (2005-2006)
Tuition and fees: $3,213; out-of-district residents $5,553; out-of-state residents $7,893.
Per-credit charge: $78; out-of-district residents $156; out-of-state residents $234.

FINANCIAL AID PICTURE
Students with need: Need-based aid available for full-time and part-time students.
Students without need: This college only awards aid to students with need.

FINANCIAL AID PROCEDURES
Forms required: FAFSA.
Dates and Deadlines: Priority date 7/15; no closing date. Applicants notified on a rolling basis starting 6/1; must reply within 1 week(s) of notification.
Transfers: No deadline.

CONTACT
Pamela Norris-Littles, Director of Financial Aid
70 Sip Avenue, Jersey City, NJ 07306
(201) 714-2145

Kean University
Union, New Jersey
www.kean.edu   Federal Code: 002622

4-year public university and liberal arts college in small city.
Enrollment: 9,612 undergrads, 22% part-time. 1,391 full-time freshmen.
Selectivity: Admits 50 to 75% of applicants.

BASIC COSTS (2005-2006)
Tuition and fees: $7,507; out-of-state residents $10,139.
Per-credit charge: $251; out-of-state residents $339.
Room and board: $8,374.

FINANCIAL AID PICTURE (2005-2006)
Students with need: Out of 1,167 full-time freshmen who applied for aid, 841 were judged to have need. Of these, 806 received aid, and 69 had their full need met. Average financial aid package met 54% of need; average scholarship/grant was $6,091; average loan was $2,688. For part-time students, average financial aid package was $5,179.
Students without need: 59 full-time freshmen who did not demonstrate need for aid received scholarships/grants; average award was $2,564. No-need awards available for academics, alumni affiliation, art, leadership, music/drama.
Cumulative student debt: 40% of graduating class had student loans; average debt was $13,128.

FINANCIAL AID PROCEDURES
Forms required: FAFSA.
Dates and Deadlines: Priority date 3/15; no closing date. Applicants notified on a rolling basis starting 3/15; must reply by 5/1.

CONTACT
Sandra Bembry, Director of Financial Aid
1000 Morris Avenue, Union, NJ 07083-0411
(908) 737-3190

Mercer County Community College
Trenton, New Jersey
www.mccc.edu   Federal Code: 002641

2-year public community college in small city.
Enrollment: 7,805 undergrads, 59% part-time. 1,296 full-time freshmen.
Selectivity: Open admission.

BASIC COSTS (2006-2007)
Tuition and fees: $2,940; out-of-district residents $3,945; out-of-state residents $6,045.
Per-credit charge: $98; out-of-district residents $132; out-of-state residents $202.
Additional info: Tuition/fee waivers available for unemployed or children of unemployed.

FINANCIAL AID PICTURE (2004-2005)
Students with need: 72% of average financial aid package awarded as scholarships/grants, 28% awarded as loans/jobs. Need-based aid available for part-time students. Work study available nights.
Students without need: No-need awards available for academics, athletics, state/district residency.
Scholarships offered: MCCC Foundation Scholarship: $2,500; top 25% of high school class; 15 total awards. NJ STARS program: for top 20% of HS class.

FINANCIAL AID PROCEDURES
Forms required: FAFSA.
Dates and Deadlines: No deadline. Applicants notified on a rolling basis.

CONTACT
Reginald Page, Director of Financial Aid
Box B, Trenton, NJ 08690-1099
(609) 586-4800 ext. 3210

Middlesex County College
Edison, New Jersey
www.middlesexcc.edu   Federal Code: 002615

2-year public community college in small city.
Enrollment: 9,943 undergrads.
Selectivity: Open admission; but selective for some programs.

BASIC COSTS (2005-2006)
Tuition and fees: $3,180; out-of-district residents $5,557; out-of-state residents $5,557.
Per-credit charge: $79; out-of-district residents $158; out-of-state residents $158.
Additional info: Out-of-county and out-of-state students pay additional $675 in required fees.

FINANCIAL AID PICTURE
Students with need: Need-based aid available for full-time and part-time students.

FINANCIAL AID PROCEDURES
Forms required: FAFSA, institutional form.
Dates and Deadlines: Priority date 4/1; no closing date. Applicants notified on a rolling basis starting 5/4.

CONTACT
Gail Scott Bey, Director of Financial Aid
2600 Woodbridge Avenue, Edison, NJ 08818-3050
(732) 906-2520

Monmouth University
West Long Branch, New Jersey
www.monmouth.edu   Federal Code: 002616

4-year private university in small town.
Enrollment: 4,513 undergrads, 9% part-time. 873 full-time freshmen.
Selectivity: Admits 50 to 75% of applicants.

BASIC COSTS (2006-2007)
Tuition and fees: $21,868.
Per-credit charge: $615.
Room and board: $8,588.

FINANCIAL AID PICTURE (2004-2005)
Students with need: Out of 764 full-time freshmen who applied for aid, 763 were judged to have need. Of these, 763 received aid, and 104 had their full need met. Average financial aid package met 78% of need; average scholarship/grant was $9,050; average loan was $3,012. For part-time students, average financial aid package was $9,170.
Students without need: 314 full-time freshmen who did not demonstrate need for aid received scholarships/grants; average award was $5,832. No-need awards available for academics, alumni affiliation, art, athletics, leadership.
Scholarships offered: *Merit:* Academic Excellence Awards: from $2,000-$15,000; based on SAT scores and high school GPA; renewable annually as long as required GPA is maintained. *Athletic:* 12 full-time freshmen received athletic scholarships; average amount $8,135.

Cumulative student debt: 72% of graduating class had student loans; average debt was $27,800.

FINANCIAL AID PROCEDURES
Forms required: FAFSA.
Dates and Deadlines: No deadline. Applicants notified on a rolling basis starting 2/1; must reply within 2 week(s) of notification.
Transfers: Priority date 3/1; closing date 6/30. Applicants notified on a rolling basis; must reply within 2 week(s) of notification.

CONTACT
Claire Alasio, Associate Vice President for Enrollment Management
400 Cedar Avenue, West Long Branch, NJ 07764-1898
(732) 571-3400

Montclair State University
Upper Montclair, New Jersey
www.montclair.edu   Federal Code: 002617

4-year public university in large town.
Enrollment: 12,007 undergrads, 18% part-time. 1,907 full-time freshmen.
Selectivity: Admits 50 to 75% of applicants.

BASIC COSTS (2005-2006)
Tuition and fees: $7,570; out-of-state residents $12,018.
Per-credit charge: $186; out-of-state residents $334.
Room and board: $8,618.
Additional info: Tuition/fee waivers available for unemployed or children of unemployed.

FINANCIAL AID PICTURE (2005-2006)
Students with need: Out of 1,152 full-time freshmen who applied for aid, 939 were judged to have need. Of these, 804 received aid, and 236 had their full need met. Average financial aid package met 53% of need; average scholarship/grant was $5,603; average loan was $2,760. For part-time students, average financial aid package was $4,667.
Students without need: 51 full-time freshmen who did not demonstrate need for aid received scholarships/grants; average award was $4,438. No-need awards available for academics, alumni affiliation, art, leadership, minority status, music/drama, religious affiliation, ROTC, state/district residency.
Cumulative student debt: 53% of graduating class had student loans; average debt was $16,654.

FINANCIAL AID PROCEDURES
Forms required: FAFSA.
Dates and Deadlines: Priority date 3/1; no closing date. Applicants notified on a rolling basis starting 4/1; must reply within 2 week(s) of notification.
Transfers: Students will be eligible for financial aid beginning fall semester of the academic year for which they are admitted.

CONTACT
Bryan Terry, Director of Financial Aid
One Normal Avenue, Upper Montclair, NJ 07043-1624
(973) 655-4461

New Jersey City University
Jersey City, New Jersey
www.njcu.edu   Federal Code: 002613

4-year public liberal arts college in small city.
Enrollment: 5,949 undergrads, 30% part-time. 659 full-time freshmen.
Selectivity: Admits 50 to 75% of applicants.

BASIC COSTS (2005-2006)
Tuition and fees: $7,040; out-of-state residents $12,080.
Per-credit charge: $173; out-of-state residents $341.

Room and board: $7,306.

FINANCIAL AID PICTURE (2004-2005)
Students with need: Out of 570 full-time freshmen who applied for aid, 503 were judged to have need. Of these, 479 received aid, and 443 had their full need met. Average financial aid package met 68% of need; average scholarship/grant was $6,020; average loan was $2,412. For part-time students, average financial aid package was $4,599.
Students without need: This college only awards aid to students with need.

FINANCIAL AID PROCEDURES
Forms required: FAFSA.
Dates and Deadlines: Applicants notified by 5/4.

CONTACT
Carmen Panlilio, Director of Financial Aid
2039 Kennedy Boulevard, Jersey City, NJ 07305-1597
(201) 200-3173

New Jersey Institute of Technology
Newark, New Jersey
www.njit.edu   Federal Code: 002621

4-year public university in very large city.
Enrollment: 4,909 undergrads, 18% part-time. 668 full-time freshmen.
Selectivity: Admits 50 to 75% of applicants.

BASIC COSTS (2005-2006)
Tuition and fees: $9,822; out-of-state residents $16,026.
Per-credit charge: $321; out-of-state residents $628.
Room and board: $8,958.

FINANCIAL AID PICTURE (2004-2005)
Students with need: Out of 666 full-time freshmen who applied for aid, 398 were judged to have need. Of these, 398 received aid, and 76 had their full need met. Average financial aid package met 87% of need; average scholarship/grant was $4,678; average loan was $2,929. For part-time students, average financial aid package was $7,707.
Students without need: 366 full-time freshmen who did not demonstrate need for aid received scholarships/grants; average award was $3,818. No-need awards available for academics, alumni affiliation, art, leadership, minority status, music/drama, ROTC, state/district residency.
Scholarships offered: 38 full-time freshmen received athletic scholarships; average amount $5,431.
Cumulative student debt: 45% of graduating class had student loans; average debt was $15,000.
Additional info: Extensive co-op program for all majors.

FINANCIAL AID PROCEDURES
Forms required: FAFSA.
Dates and Deadlines: Priority date 3/15; closing date 5/15. Applicants notified on a rolling basis starting 3/1; must reply within 2 week(s) of notification.
Transfers: Priority date 5/15.

CONTACT
Kathy Bialk, Director of Financial Aid
University Heights, Newark, NJ 07102
(973) 596-3478

Ocean County College
Toms River, New Jersey
www.ocean.edu   Federal Code: 002624

2-year public community college in small city.
Enrollment: 6,635 undergrads, 42% part-time. 1,339 full-time freshmen.
Selectivity: Open admission; but selective for some programs.

BASIC COSTS (2006-2007)
Tuition and fees: $3,390; out-of-district residents $4,350; out-of-state residents $6,600.
Per-credit charge: $86; out-of-district residents $118; out-of-state residents $193.
Additional info: Tuition/fee waivers available for unemployed or children of unemployed.

FINANCIAL AID PICTURE
Students with need: Need-based aid available for full-time and part-time students.
Students without need: This college only awards aid to students with need.

FINANCIAL AID PROCEDURES
Forms required: FAFSA.
Dates and Deadlines: Priority date 5/31; no closing date. Applicants notified on a rolling basis starting 7/15; must reply within 1 week(s) of notification.

CONTACT
Director of Financial Aid
College Drive, Toms River, NJ 08754-2001
(732) 255-0400 ext. 2020

Passaic County Community College
Paterson, New Jersey   Federal Code: 009994
www.pccc.cc.nj.us   CSS Code: 2694

2-year public community college in small city.
Enrollment: 7,000 undergrads.
Selectivity: Open admission; but selective for some programs.

BASIC COSTS (2005-2006)
Tuition and fees: $2,748; out-of-state residents $4,938.
Per-credit charge: $73; out-of-state residents $146.
Additional info: Additional course fees up to maximum of $600 per year. Tuition/fee waivers available for unemployed or children of unemployed.

FINANCIAL AID PICTURE
Students with need: Need-based aid available for full-time and part-time students.
Students without need: No-need awards available for academics.
Additional info: Limited scholarship funds available for low income students eligible for federal or state aid.

FINANCIAL AID PROCEDURES
Forms required: FAFSA, CSS PROFILE.
Dates and Deadlines: Priority date 8/1; no closing date. Applicants notified on a rolling basis starting 8/1; must reply within 2 week(s) of notification.
Transfers: Priority date 5/15; closing date 6/30.

CONTACT
Sheila Attias, Director of Financial Aid
One College Boulevard, Paterson, NJ 07505-1179
(973) 684-6800

Princeton University
Princeton, New Jersey
www.princeton.edu   Federal Code: 002627

4-year private university in large town.
Enrollment: 4,710 undergrads. 1,179 full-time freshmen.
Selectivity: Admits less than 50% of applicants. GED not accepted.

BASIC COSTS (2006-2007)
Tuition and fees: $33,000.
Room and board: $9,200.

FINANCIAL AID PICTURE (2004-2005)
Students with need: Out of 715 full-time freshmen who applied for aid, 608 were judged to have need. Of these, 608 received aid, and 608 had their full need met. Average financial aid package met 100% of need; average scholarship/grant was $26,121.
Students without need: This college only awards aid to students with need.
Cumulative student debt: 27% of graduating class had student loans; average debt was $4,350.
Additional info: All aid is need based; all aid is grant money (no loans); meets full demonstrated need.

FINANCIAL AID PROCEDURES
Forms required: FAFSA, institutional form.
Dates and Deadlines: Priority date 2/1; no closing date. Applicants notified by 4/1; must reply by 5/1.

CONTACT
Don Betterton, Director of Financial Aid
Box 430, Princeton, NJ 08544-0430
(609) 258-3330

Ramapo College of New Jersey
Mahwah, New Jersey
www.ramapo.edu   Federal Code: 009344

4-year public liberal arts college in large town.
Enrollment: 4,860 undergrads, 14% part-time. 755 full-time freshmen.
Selectivity: Admits less than 50% of applicants.

BASIC COSTS (2005-2006)
Tuition and fees: $8,791; out-of-state residents $13,708.
Per-credit charge: $190; out-of-state residents $344.
Room and board: $9,464.
Additional info: Tuition/fee waivers available for minority students, unemployed or children of unemployed.

FINANCIAL AID PICTURE (2004-2005)
Students with need: Out of 574 full-time freshmen who applied for aid, 391 were judged to have need. Of these, 367 received aid, and 45 had their full need met. Average financial aid package met 86% of need; average scholarship/grant was $8,904; average loan was $2,579. For part-time students, average financial aid package was $4,338.
Students without need: 129 full-time freshmen who did not demonstrate need for aid received scholarships/grants; average award was $8,991. No-need awards available for academics, state/district residency.
Cumulative student debt: 36% of graduating class had student loans; average debt was $15,871.

FINANCIAL AID PROCEDURES
Forms required: FAFSA.
Dates and Deadlines: Priority date 3/1; no closing date. Applicants notified on a rolling basis starting 4/1; must reply by 5/1 or within 2 week(s) of notification.

CONTACT
Mark Singer, Director of Financial Aid
505 Ramapo Valley Road, Mahwah, NJ 07430-1680
(201) 684-7549

Raritan Valley Community College
Somerville, New Jersey
www.raritanval.edu   Federal Code: 007731

2-year public community college in large town.
Enrollment: 4,945 undergrads, 50% part-time. 799 full-time freshmen.
Selectivity: Open admission; but selective for some programs.

BASIC COSTS (2006-2007)
Tuition and fees: $3,295.
Per-credit charge: $81.
Additional info: Tuition/fee waivers available for unemployed or children of unemployed.

FINANCIAL AID PICTURE (2004-2005)
Students with need: Out of 319 full-time freshmen who applied for aid, 209 were judged to have need. Of these, 196 received aid, and 10 had their full need met. Average financial aid package met 65% of need; average scholarship/grant was $1,723; average loan was $1,482. For part-time students, average financial aid package was $2,194.
Students without need: 29 full-time freshmen who did not demonstrate need for aid received scholarships/grants; average award was $860. No-need awards available for academics.
Cumulative student debt: 13% of graduating class had student loans; average debt was $4,267.

FINANCIAL AID PROCEDURES
Forms required: FAFSA.
Dates and Deadlines: No deadline. Applicants notified on a rolling basis starting 7/1.

CONTACT
John Trojan, Vice President of Finance and Facilities
PO Box 3300, Somerville, NJ 08876-1265
(908) 526-1200 ext. 8268

Richard Stockton College of New Jersey
Pomona, New Jersey
www.stockton.edu   Federal Code: 009345

4-year public liberal arts college in large town.
Enrollment: 6,371 undergrads, 12% part-time. 796 full-time freshmen.
Selectivity: Admits 50 to 75% of applicants.

BASIC COSTS (2005-2006)
Tuition and fees: $7,870; out-of-state residents $11,055.
Per-credit charge: $172; out-of-state residents $278.
Room and board: $8,109.
Additional info: Tuition/fee waivers available for unemployed or children of unemployed.

FINANCIAL AID PICTURE (2005-2006)
Students with need: Out of 645 full-time freshmen who applied for aid, 461 were judged to have need. Of these, 445 received aid, and 262 had their full need met. Average financial aid package met 62% of need; average scholarship/grant was $6,512; average loan was $3,042. For part-time students, average financial aid package was $8,088.
Students without need: 69 full-time freshmen who did not demonstrate need for aid received scholarships/grants; average award was $2,798. No-need awards available for academics, art, leadership, minority status, music/drama, state/district residency.
Scholarships offered: Freshman Scholarship Program; awarded to incoming freshmen with high school class rank in the top 15% or higher and 1150 SAT (exclusive of writing) or better; awards range up to full tuition, fees, and housing for all four years. RSCNJ Foundation scholarships; awarded to incoming freshman, transfer students and those who are already enrolled at

the college based on their academic merit and/or financial need; some scholarships have stipulations, such as enrollment in a particular study program.
Cumulative student debt: 64% of graduating class had student loans; average debt was $15,875.

FINANCIAL AID PROCEDURES
Forms required: FAFSA.
Dates and Deadlines: Priority date 3/1; no closing date. Applicants notified on a rolling basis starting 4/1; must reply within 2 week(s) of notification.

CONTACT
Jeanne Lewis, Director of Financial Aid
Jim Leeds Road, Pomona, NJ 08240-0195
(609) 652-4201

Rider University
Lawrenceville, New Jersey
www.rider.edu   Federal Code: 002628

4-year private university in large town.
Enrollment: 4,139 undergrads, 13% part-time. 941 full-time freshmen.
Selectivity: Admits over 75% of applicants.

BASIC COSTS (2006-2007)
Tuition and fees: $24,790.
Per-credit charge: $800.
Room and board: $9,280.

FINANCIAL AID PICTURE (2004-2005)
Students with need: Out of 808 full-time freshmen who applied for aid, 666 were judged to have need. Of these, 666 received aid, and 131 had their full need met. Average financial aid package met 70% of need; average scholarship/grant was $12,707; average loan was $3,214. For part-time students, average financial aid package was $7,064.
Students without need: 144 full-time freshmen who did not demonstrate need for aid received scholarships/grants; average award was $9,221. No-need awards available for academics, alumni affiliation, art, athletics, minority status, music/drama, state/district residency.
Scholarships offered: 74 full-time freshmen received athletic scholarships; average amount $11,929.
Cumulative student debt: 72% of graduating class had student loans; average debt was $28,636.

FINANCIAL AID PROCEDURES
Forms required: FAFSA.
Dates and Deadlines: Priority date 3/1; closing date 6/1. Applicants notified on a rolling basis starting 4/15.
Transfers: No deadline.

CONTACT
John Williams, Director of Student Financial Services
2083 Lawrenceville Road, Lawrenceville, NJ 08648-3099
(609) 896-5360

Rowan University
Glassboro, New Jersey
www.rowan.edu   Federal Code: 002609

4-year public university and liberal arts college in large town.
Enrollment: 8,065 undergrads, 11% part-time. 1,254 full-time freshmen.
Selectivity: Admits less than 50% of applicants.

BASIC COSTS (2005-2006)
Tuition and fees: $8,606; out-of-state residents $14,900.
Per-credit charge: $262; out-of-state residents $524.
Room and board: $8,242.

FINANCIAL AID PICTURE (2004-2005)
Students with need: Out of 1,143 full-time freshmen who applied for aid, 1,098 were judged to have need. Of these, 1,022 received aid, and 360 had their full need met. Average financial aid package met 66% of need; average scholarship/grant was $5,722; average loan was $3,252. For part-time students, average financial aid package was $4,148.
Students without need: No-need awards available for academics, alumni affiliation, leadership, minority status, music/drama, ROTC.
Cumulative student debt: 97% of graduating class had student loans; average debt was $9,575.

FINANCIAL AID PROCEDURES
Forms required: FAFSA.
Dates and Deadlines: Closing date 3/15. Applicants notified on a rolling basis starting 5/1; must reply within 2 week(s) of notification.

CONTACT
Louis Tavarez, Director of Financial Aid
Savitz Hall, 201 Mullica Hill Road, Glassboro, NJ 08028
(856) 256-4250

Rutgers, The State University of New Jersey: Camden Regional Campus
Camden, New Jersey
www.rutgers.edu   Federal Code: 002629

4-year public university in small city.
Enrollment: 3,774 undergrads, 22% part-time. 353 full-time freshmen.
Selectivity: Admits 50 to 75% of applicants.

BASIC COSTS (2005-2006)
Tuition and fees: $9,028; out-of-state residents $16,626.
Per-credit charge: $237; out-of-state residents $484.
Room and board: $8,078.
Additional info: Tuition/fee waivers available for unemployed or children of unemployed.

FINANCIAL AID PICTURE (2005-2006)
Students with need: Out of 295 full-time freshmen who applied for aid, 207 were judged to have need. Of these, 206 received aid, and 76 had their full need met. Average financial aid package met 74% of need; average scholarship/grant was $7,404; average loan was $2,773. For part-time students, average financial aid package was $4,913.
Students without need: 42 full-time freshmen who did not demonstrate need for aid received scholarships/grants; average award was $4,869. No-need awards available for academics, alumni affiliation, art, athletics, minority status, music/drama, religious affiliation, ROTC, state/district residency.
Scholarships offered: *Merit:* Outstanding Scholarship Recruitment Program: $2,500-$7,500, for selected in-state resident applicants based on SAT scores and class rank, 2,500 awarded; Carr Scholarship: $10,000, for selected minority applicants, 150 awarded; Class of 1941 Scholarship: $1,941, descendent of 1941 alumni preferred, 1 awarded; National Merit Scholarship for National Merit finalists: $1,000-$2,000, 15 or more awarded; National Achievement Scholarship for National Achievement finalists: $1,000-$2,000, 2 awarded; Rockland County-Herman T. Hopper Scholarship: out-of-state tuition, for Rockland County, New York resident, 1 awarded; Rutgers University Academic Achievement Award: $1,000, for in- and out-of-state minority students, 20 awarded; Rutgers University Alumni Federation Scholarship: $1,000, for children of Rutgers University alumni, 20 awarded; Rutgers University National Scholarship: $5,000, for out-of-state students, about 100 awards university-wide. *Athletic:* 42 full-time freshmen received athletic scholarships; average amount $4,869.
Cumulative student debt: 69% of graduating class had student loans; average debt was $17,378.

FINANCIAL AID PROCEDURES
Forms required: FAFSA.
Dates and Deadlines: Priority date 3/15; no closing date. Applicants notified on a rolling basis starting 2/1; must reply within 2 week(s) of notification.

CONTACT
John Brugel, University Director of Financial Aid
406 Penn Street, Camden, NJ 08102
(856) 225-6039

Rutgers, The State University of New Jersey: New Brunswick/Piscataway Campus
Piscataway, New Jersey
www.rutgers.edu   Federal Code: 002629

4-year public university in large town.
Enrollment: 26,172 undergrads, 7% part-time. 5,230 full-time freshmen.
Selectivity: Admits 50 to 75% of applicants.

BASIC COSTS (2005-2006)
Tuition and fees: $9,108; out-of-state residents $16,706.
Per-credit charge: $237; out-of-state residents $484.
Room and board: $8,578.
Additional info: Tuition and fees may vary by program. Tuition/fee waivers available for unemployed or children of unemployed.

FINANCIAL AID PICTURE (2005-2006)
Students with need: Out of 4,016 full-time freshmen who applied for aid, 2,751 were judged to have need. Of these, 2,691 received aid, and 1,093 had their full need met. Average financial aid package met 69% of need; average scholarship/grant was $8,579; average loan was $3,010. For part-time students, average financial aid package was $5,024.
Students without need: 568 full-time freshmen who did not demonstrate need for aid received scholarships/grants; average award was $5,641. No-need awards available for academics, alumni affiliation, art, athletics, leadership, minority status, music/drama, religious affiliation, state/district residency.
Scholarships offered: *Merit:* Outstanding Scholarship Recruitment Program: $2,500-$7,500, for selected in-state resident applicants based on SAT scores and class rank, 2,500 awarded; Carr Scholarship: $10,000, for selected minority applicants, 150 awarded; Class of 1941 Scholarship: $1,941, descendent of Class of 1941 alumni preferred, 1 awarded; National Merit Scholarship for National Merit finalists: $1,000-$2,000, 15 or more awarded; National Achievement Scholarship for National Achievement finalists: $1,000-$2,000, 2 awarded; Rockland County-Herman T. Hopper Scholarship: out-of-state tuition, for Rockland County, New York resident, 1 awarded; Rutgers University Academic Achievement Award for in- and out-of-state minority students: $1,000, 20 awarded; Rutgers University Alumni Federation Scholarship, $1,000, for children of Rutgers University alumni, 20 awarded; Rutgers University National Scholarship for out-of-state students: $5,000, about 100 awards university-wide. *Athletic:* 623 full-time freshmen received athletic scholarships; average amount $6,365.
Cumulative student debt: 63% of graduating class had student loans; average debt was $15,362.

FINANCIAL AID PROCEDURES
Forms required: FAFSA.
Dates and Deadlines: Priority date 3/15; no closing date. Applicants notified on a rolling basis starting 2/1; must reply within 2 week(s) of notification.

CONTACT
John Brugel, University Director of Financial Aid
65 Davidson Road, Room 202, Piscataway, NJ 08854-8097
(732) 932-1766

Rutgers, The State University of New Jersey: Newark Regional Campus
Newark, New Jersey
www.rutgers.edu   Federal Code: 002629

4-year public university in large city.
Enrollment: 5,963 undergrads, 18% part-time. 702 full-time freshmen.
Selectivity: Admits less than 50% of applicants.

BASIC COSTS (2005-2006)
Tuition and fees: $8,812; out-of-state residents $16,411.
Per-credit charge: $237; out-of-state residents $484.
Room and board: $9,110.
Additional info: Tuition/fee waivers available for unemployed or children of unemployed.

FINANCIAL AID PICTURE (2005-2006)
Students with need: Out of 549 full-time freshmen who applied for aid, 439 were judged to have need. Of these, 426 received aid, and 112 had their full need met. Average financial aid package met 81% of need; average scholarship/grant was $8,210; average loan was $2,927. For part-time students, average financial aid package was $4,941.
Students without need: 38 full-time freshmen who did not demonstrate need for aid received scholarships/grants; average award was $6,922. No-need awards available for academics, alumni affiliation, art, athletics, leadership, minority status, music/drama, religious affiliation, state/district residency.
Scholarships offered: *Merit:* Outstanding Scholarship Recruitment Program: $2,500-$7,500, for selected in-state resident applicants based on SAT scores and class rank, 2,500 awarded; Carr Scholarship: $10,000, for selected minority applicants, 150 awarded; Class of 1941 Scholarship: $1,941, descendent of Class of 1941 alumni preferred, 1 awarded; National Merit Scholarship for National Merit finalists: $1,000-$2,000, 15 or more awarded; National Achievement Scholarship for National Achievement finalists: 1,000-$2,000, 2 awarded; Rockland County-Herman T. Hopper Scholarship: out-of-state tuition, for Rockland County, New York resident, 1 awarded; Rutgers University Academic Achievement Award: $1,000, for in- and out-of-state minority students, 20 awarded; Rutgers University Alumni Federation Scholarship: $1,000, for children of Rutgers University alumni, 20 awarded; James Bryan Scholarship: $400, for selected in-state freshmen, 3 awarded; Rutgers University National Scholarship: $5,000, for out-of-state students, about 100 awards university-wide. *Athletic:* 39 full-time freshmen received athletic scholarships; average amount $6,975.
Cumulative student debt: 85% of graduating class had student loans; average debt was $16,553.

FINANCIAL AID PROCEDURES
Forms required: FAFSA.
Dates and Deadlines: Priority date 3/15; no closing date. Applicants notified on a rolling basis starting 2/1; must reply within 2 week(s) of notification.

CONTACT
John Brugel, University Director of Financial Aid
249 University Avenue, Newark, NJ 07102-1896
(973) 353-1766

St. Peter's College
Jersey City, New Jersey
www.spc.edu   Federal Code: 002638

4-year private liberal arts college in small city, affiliated with Roman Catholic Church.
Enrollment: 2,095 undergrads, 14% part-time. 491 full-time freshmen.
Selectivity: Admits 50 to 75% of applicants.

BASIC COSTS (2006-2007)
Tuition and fees: $21,650.
Per-credit charge: $730.
Room and board: $9,260.

FINANCIAL AID PICTURE (2004-2005)
Students with need: 79% of average financial aid package awarded as scholarships/grants, 21% awarded as loans/jobs.
Students without need: No-need awards available for academics, athletics.
Scholarships offered: Academic Awards based on minimum SAT of 1100 (exclusive of Writing), minimum GPA of 3.0, and in top 20% of class; 50 awarded; full tuition. Incentive Awards for selected applicants with some qualities necessary for academic awards but who are otherwise ineligible; ranging from $500-$4,000 annually. Residential Grants based on academics and extracurricular activities; $500-$2,500 toward housing.
Additional info: Cooperative education internships available in all majors, with average salaries exceeding $5,200.

FINANCIAL AID PROCEDURES
Forms required: FAFSA.
Dates and Deadlines: Priority date 3/15; no closing date. Applicants notified on a rolling basis starting 2/15; must reply by 5/1 or within 2 week(s) of notification.
Transfers: Student and parents (if dependent students) must be New Jersey residents for at least 1 year prior to start date. Students must complete the renewal application before June 1.

CONTACT
Debra Wulff, Director of Financial Aid
2641 Kennedy Boulevard, Jersey City, NJ 07306
(201) 915-9308

Salem Community College
Carneys Point, New Jersey
www.salemcc.edu   Federal Code: 005461

2-year public community college in small town.
Enrollment: 990 undergrads, 44% part-time. 183 full-time freshmen.
Selectivity: Open admission; but selective for some programs.

BASIC COSTS (2005-2006)
Tuition and fees: $3,305; out-of-state residents $3,605.
Per-credit charge: $80; out-of-state residents $90.
Additional info: Tuition/fee waivers available for unemployed or children of unemployed.

FINANCIAL AID PICTURE (2004-2005)
Students with need: 83% of average financial aid package awarded as scholarships/grants, 17% awarded as loans/jobs. Need-based aid available for part-time students.
Students without need: This college only awards aid to students with need.

FINANCIAL AID PROCEDURES
Forms required: FAFSA, institutional form.
Dates and Deadlines: Priority date 6/1; no closing date. Applicants notified on a rolling basis starting 4/1; must reply within 2 week(s) of notification.

CONTACT
Suzanne Campo, Coordinator of Financial Aid
460 Hollywood Avenue, Carneys Point, NJ 08069-2799
(856) 351-2699

Seton Hall University
South Orange, New Jersey
www.shu.edu   Federal Code: 002632

4-year private university in large town, affiliated with Roman Catholic Church.
Enrollment: 5,093 undergrads, 6% part-time. 1,235 full-time freshmen.
Selectivity: Admits over 75% of applicants.

BASIC COSTS (2006-2007)
Tuition and fees: $24,720.
Per-credit charge: $759.
Room and board: $10,466.
Additional info: Required fees include lease of laptop computer.

FINANCIAL AID PICTURE (2004-2005)
Students with need: Out of 1,080 full-time freshmen who applied for aid, 930 were judged to have need. Of these, 906 received aid, and 177 had their full need met. Average financial aid package met 74% of need; average scholarship/grant was $5,179; average loan was $2,533. For part-time students, average financial aid package was $5,661.
Students without need: 170 full-time freshmen who did not demonstrate need for aid received scholarships/grants; average award was $11,366. No-need awards available for academics, alumni affiliation, athletics, leadership, minority status, ROTC, state/district residency.
Scholarships offered: 44 full-time freshmen received athletic scholarships; average amount $20,115.
Cumulative student debt: 68% of graduating class had student loans; average debt was $29,108.

FINANCIAL AID PROCEDURES
Forms required: FAFSA.
Dates and Deadlines: Priority date 2/15; no closing date. Applicants notified on a rolling basis starting 3/1; must reply by 5/1 or within 4 week(s) of notification.
Transfers: Transfer academic scholarships available.

CONTACT
Elizabeth Rollins, Director of Financial Aid
400 South Orange Avenue, South Orange, NJ 07079-2680
(973) 761-9350

Somerset Christian College
Zarephath, New Jersey
www.somerset.edu   Federal Code: 036663

2-year private Bible college in small town, affiliated with Pillar of Fire International.
Enrollment: 126 undergrads, 80% part-time. 3 full-time freshmen.

BASIC COSTS (2005-2006)
Tuition and fees: $5,750.
Per-credit charge: $185.

FINANCIAL AID PICTURE
Students with need: Need-based aid available for full-time and part-time students.
Students without need: This college only awards aid to students with need.

FINANCIAL AID PROCEDURES
Forms required: FAFSA, state aid form.
Dates and Deadlines: No deadline. Applicants notified on a rolling basis starting 1/31.

CONTACT
Ellen Johnson, Financial Aid Counselor
10 Liberty Square, Zarephath, NJ 08890
(800) 234-9305

Stevens Institute of Technology
Hoboken, New Jersey
www.stevens.edu   Federal Code: 002639

4-year private university and engineering college in small city.
Enrollment: 1,786 undergrads. 484 full-time freshmen.
Selectivity: Admits less than 50% of applicants. GED not accepted.

BASIC COSTS (2005-2006)
Tuition and fees: $31,835.
Per-credit charge: $956.
Room and board: $9,500.

FINANCIAL AID PICTURE (2005-2006)
Students with need: Out of 430 full-time freshmen who applied for aid, 350 were judged to have need. Of these, 350 received aid, and 95 had their full need met. Average financial aid package met 86% of need; average scholarship/grant was $14,530; average loan was $3,546. Need-based aid available for part-time students.
Students without need: 40 full-time freshmen who did not demonstrate need for aid received scholarships/grants; average award was $10,106. No-need awards available for academics, leadership, music/drama, ROTC.
Scholarships offered: Neupauer Scholarship: full tuition; for top candidates in freshman class. Edwin A. Stevens Scholarship: $3,000-$16,000; for top candidates in freshman class. Becton Dickinson Scholarship: full tuition; for top student pursuing engineering degree. DeBaun performing arts scholarship: $3,000-$5,000.
Cumulative student debt: 68% of graduating class had student loans; average debt was $14,700.

FINANCIAL AID PROCEDURES
Forms required: FAFSA.
Dates and Deadlines: Priority date 2/15; no closing date. Applicants notified on a rolling basis starting 3/30; must reply by 5/1.
Transfers: Transfer merit scholarships, Phi Theta Kappa awards.

CONTACT
David Sheridan, Dean of Enrollment Services
Castle Point on Hudson, Hoboken, NJ 07030
(201) 216-5555

Sussex County Community College
Newton, New Jersey
www.sussex.edu   Federal Code: 025688

2-year public community college in small town.
Enrollment: 2,573 undergrads, 41% part-time. 511 full-time freshmen.
Selectivity: Open admission; but selective for some programs.

BASIC COSTS (2006-2007)
Tuition and fees: $2,820; out-of-state residents $5,130.
Per-credit charge: $77; out-of-district residents $154; out-of-state residents $154.
Additional info: Residents of Wayne, Monroe and Pike County (PA): $114 per credit hour. Tuition/fee waivers available for unemployed or children of unemployed.

FINANCIAL AID PICTURE
Students with need: Need-based aid available for full-time and part-time students.
Students without need: This college only awards aid to students with need.

FINANCIAL AID PROCEDURES
Forms required: FAFSA, institutional form.
Dates and Deadlines: Closing date 6/1. Applicants notified on a rolling basis; must reply within 2 week(s) of notification.

CONTACT
James Pegg, Director, Financial Aid
One College Hill, Newton, NJ 07860
(973) 300-2225

Thomas Edison State College
Trenton, New Jersey
www.tesc.edu   Federal Code: 011648

4-year public liberal arts college in small city.
Enrollment: 10,904 undergrads, 100% part-time.
Selectivity: Open admission; but selective for some programs.

BASIC COSTS (2005-2006)
Tuition and fees: $3,780; out-of-state residents $5,400.
Per-credit charge: $110; out-of-state residents $145.

FINANCIAL AID PICTURE (2005-2006)
Students with need: 22% of average financial aid package awarded as scholarships/grants, 78% awarded as loans/jobs.
Additional info: Financial aid applications should be received two months before each new term begins.

FINANCIAL AID PROCEDURES
Forms required: FAFSA, institutional form.
Dates and Deadlines: No deadline. Applicants notified on a rolling basis.
Transfers: No deadline. Applicants notified on a rolling basis; must reply within 4 week(s) of notification.

CONTACT
James Owens, Director of Financial Aid
101 West State Street, Trenton, NJ 08608-1176
(609) 633-9658

Union County College
Cranford, New Jersey
www.ucc.edu   Federal Code: 002643

2-year public community college in large town.
Enrollment: 8,998 undergrads, 46% part-time. 896 full-time freshmen.
Selectivity: Open admission; but selective for some programs.

BASIC COSTS (2006-2007)
Tuition and fees: $3,240; out-of-district residents $5,700; out-of-state residents $5,700.
Per-credit charge: $82; out-of-district residents $164; out-of-state residents $164.
Additional info: Tuition/fee waivers available for unemployed or children of unemployed.

FINANCIAL AID PICTURE (2004-2005)
Students with need: 81% of average financial aid package awarded as scholarships/grants, 19% awarded as loans/jobs. Need-based aid available for part-time students.
Students without need: This college only awards aid to students with need.
Scholarships offered: Over 100 scholarships available to UCC students, including Freeholder Scholars Program for students with record of academic

success in high school with a 3.0 average, full-time college enrollment, Union County resident, and annual family income less than $75,000.

FINANCIAL AID PROCEDURES
Forms required: FAFSA, institutional form.
Dates and Deadlines: Priority date 5/1; no closing date. Must reply within 2 week(s) of notification.

CONTACT
Elizabeth Riquez, Director of Financial Aid
1033 Springfield Avenue, Cranford, NJ 07016-1599
(908) 709-7018

University of Medicine and Dentistry of New Jersey: School of Health Related Professions
Newark, New Jersey
www.shrp.umdj.edu

Upper-division public health science college in large city.
Enrollment: 600 undergrads.

BASIC COSTS (2005-2006)
Tuition and fees: $7,160; out-of-state residents $10,490.
Per-credit charge: $222; out-of-state residents $333.
Additional info: Fees are 50% higher for out-of-state students.

FINANCIAL AID PICTURE
Students with need: Need-based aid available for full-time and part-time students.

FINANCIAL AID PROCEDURES
Forms required: FAFSA, institutional form.
Transfers: Priority date 5/4. Notification of awards on rolling basis; students must reply within 3 weeks of notification.

CONTACT
Cheryl White, Senior Financial Aid Analyst
65 Bergen Street, Newark, NJ 07107-3001
(973) 972-4376

University of Medicine and Dentistry of New Jersey: School of Nursing
Newark, New Jersey

4-year public nursing college in large city.
Enrollment: 530 undergrads.

BASIC COSTS (2006-2007)
Tuition and fees: $11,288; out-of-state residents $15,736.
Per-credit charge: $222; out-of-state residents $333.
Additional info: Certain undergraduate degree programs are joint degree programs: associate degree with Middlesex County College, bachelor's degrees with Ramapo College and Rowan University. Tuition is determined for general education courses by joint degree partner. Tuition for nursing courses is determined by the School of Nursing.

FINANCIAL AID PICTURE
Students with need: Need-based aid available for full-time and part-time students.

FINANCIAL AID PROCEDURES
Dates and Deadlines: Priority date 3/1; no closing date. Applicants notified on a rolling basis.

CONTACT
Michael Katz, University Director of Financial Aid
65 Bergen Street, Room 1126, Newark, NJ 07101
(973) 972-4376

Warren County Community College
Washington, New Jersey
www.warren.edu   Federal Code: 016857

2-year public community college in small town.
Enrollment: 1,732 undergrads.
Selectivity: Open admission; but selective for some programs.

BASIC COSTS (2005-2006)
Tuition and fees: $2,925; out-of-district residents $3,225; out-of-state residents $3,825.
Per-credit charge: $75; out-of-district residents $85; out-of-state residents $105.
Additional info: Tuition/fee waivers available for unemployed or children of unemployed.

FINANCIAL AID PICTURE
Students with need: Work study available nights, weekends, and for part-time students.
Students without need: No-need awards available for academics, state/district residency.

FINANCIAL AID PROCEDURES
Forms required: FAFSA, institutional form.
Dates and Deadlines: Closing date 7/1. Applicants notified on a rolling basis starting 4/1; must reply within 2 week(s) of notification.
Transfers: No deadline.

CONTACT
Jay Alexander, Director of Financial Aid
Route 57 West, Washington, NJ 07882-4343
(908) 835-2329

Westminster Choir College of Rider University
Princeton, New Jersey
www.rider.edu/284.htm

4-year private music college in small town.
Enrollment: 324 undergrads.

BASIC COSTS (2006-2007)
Tuition and fees: $24,630.
Per-credit charge: $800.
Room and board: $9,640.

FINANCIAL AID PICTURE
Students with need: Need-based aid available for full-time students.
Additional info: Approximately 130 churches employ students for weekend positions as organists, directors, and soloists. Average earnings are $2,000 to $3,000 per year.

FINANCIAL AID PROCEDURES
Forms required: FAFSA.
Dates and Deadlines: Priority date 3/1; no closing date. Applicants notified on a rolling basis starting 4/1; must reply within 2 week(s) of notification.

CONTACT
Elizabeth Guzikowski, Assistant Director of Student Financial Services
101 Walnut Lane, Princeton, NJ 08540-3899
(609) 896-5360

William Paterson University of New Jersey
Wayne, New Jersey
www.wpunj.edu Federal Code: 002625

4-year public university and liberal arts college in large town.
Enrollment: 9,037 undergrads, 18% part-time. 1,296 full-time freshmen.
Selectivity: Admits 50 to 75% of applicants.

BASIC COSTS (2005-2006)
Tuition and fees: $8,740; out-of-state residents $13,856.
Per-credit charge: $281; out-of-state residents $448.
Room and board: $9,060.
Additional info: Tuition/fee waivers available for unemployed or children of unemployed.

FINANCIAL AID PICTURE (2005-2006)
Students with need: Out of 1,015 full-time freshmen who applied for aid, 746 were judged to have need. Of these, 710 received aid, and 199 had their full need met. Average financial aid package met 82% of need; average scholarship/grant was $6,412; average loan was $2,584. For part-time students, average financial aid package was $5,965.
Students without need: 60 full-time freshmen who did not demonstrate need for aid received scholarships/grants; average award was $5,790. No-need awards available for academics, alumni affiliation, minority status, music/drama.
Scholarships offered: Trustee Scholarship, full tuition for freshmen; Residential Scholarships, full tuition for freshmen and transfers; Distinguished, Academic Excellence, and African American and Hispanic Students scholarships, $1,000 annually for 4 years.
Cumulative student debt: 50% of graduating class had student loans; average debt was $11,483.

FINANCIAL AID PROCEDURES
Forms required: FAFSA.
Dates and Deadlines: Closing date 4/1. Applicants notified on a rolling basis starting 3/1; must reply within 2 week(s) of notification.

CONTACT
Robert Baumel, Director of Financial Aid
300 Pompton Road, Wayne, NJ 07470
(973) 720-2202

New Mexico

Albuquerque Technical-Vocational Institute
Albuquerque, New Mexico
www.tvi.edu Federal Code: 004742

2-year public community and technical college in very large city.
Enrollment: 18,557 undergrads, 64% part-time. 1,605 full-time freshmen.
Selectivity: Open admission.

BASIC COSTS (2005-2006)
Tuition and fees: $1,045; out-of-district residents $1,224; out-of-state residents $5,223.
Per-credit charge: $40; out-of-district residents $48; out-of-state residents $214.
Additional info: In-district students do not pay tuition for technical courses, only arts and sciences courses.

FINANCIAL AID PICTURE (2004-2005)
Students with need: 44% of average financial aid package awarded as scholarships/grants, 56% awarded as loans/jobs. Need-based aid available for part-time students.
Students without need: No-need awards available for academics, state/district residency.

FINANCIAL AID PROCEDURES
Forms required: FAFSA.
Dates and Deadlines: Priority date 3/1; no closing date. Applicants notified by 5/1.

CONTACT
Lee Carillo, Director of Financial Aid
525 Buena Vista Southeast, Albuquerque, NM 87106
(505) 224-3090

Clovis Community College
Clovis, New Mexico
www.clovis.edu Federal Code: 004743

2-year public community and junior college in large town.
Enrollment: 2,048 undergrads, 68% part-time. 129 full-time freshmen.
Selectivity: Open admission; but selective for some programs.

BASIC COSTS (2006-2007)
Tuition and fees: $784; out-of-district residents $832; out-of-state residents $1,504.

FINANCIAL AID PICTURE (2005-2006)
Students with need: 94% of average financial aid package awarded as scholarships/grants, 6% awarded as loans/jobs. Need-based aid available for part-time students. Work study available nights, weekends, and for part-time students.
Students without need: No-need awards available for academics, state/district residency.

FINANCIAL AID PROCEDURES
Forms required: FAFSA.
Dates and Deadlines: Priority date 9/1; no closing date. Applicants notified on a rolling basis starting 4/15.

CONTACT
April Chavez, Director of Financial Aid
417 Schepps Boulevard, Clovis, NM 88101-8381
(505) 769-4060

College of Santa Fe
Santa Fe, New Mexico
www.csf.edu Federal Code: 002649

4-year private liberal arts college in small city.
Enrollment: 1,225 undergrads, 49% part-time. 116 full-time freshmen.
Selectivity: Admits 50 to 75% of applicants.

BASIC COSTS (2005-2006)
Tuition and fees: $22,276.
Per-credit charge: $720.
Room and board: $6,702.

FINANCIAL AID PICTURE (2005-2006)
Students with need: Average financial aid package met 77% of need; average scholarship/grant was $7,782; average loan was $3,661. For part-time students, average financial aid package was $7,238.
Students without need: No-need awards available for academics, alumni affiliation, art, athletics, leadership, minority status, music/drama.

558 New Mexico College of Santa Fe

Cumulative student debt: 63% of graduating class had student loans; average debt was $17,540.

FINANCIAL AID PROCEDURES
Forms required: FAFSA.
Dates and Deadlines: Priority date 3/15; no closing date. Applicants notified on a rolling basis starting 3/1; must reply by 5/1 or within 2 week(s) of notification.
Transfers: No deadline. Applicants notified on a rolling basis starting 3/1; must reply by 5/1 or within 2 week(s) of notification. No financial aid credited to student accounts until all financial aid transcripts received.

CONTACT
Jill Robertson, Director, Student Financial Services
1600 Saint Michael's Drive, Santa Fe, NM 87505-7634
(505) 473-6454

College of the Southwest
Hobbs, New Mexico
www.csw.edu   Federal Code: 013935

4-year private liberal arts and teachers college in large town.
Enrollment: 504 undergrads, 22% part-time. 74 full-time freshmen.
Selectivity: Admits less than 50% of applicants.

BASIC COSTS (2006-2007)
Tuition and fees: $10,500.
Per-credit charge: $350.
Room and board: $5,400.

FINANCIAL AID PICTURE (2005-2006)
Students with need: Out of 72 full-time freshmen who applied for aid, 60 were judged to have need. Of these, 60 received aid, and 25 had their full need met. Average financial aid package met 76% of need; average scholarship/grant was $5,166; average loan was $2,465. Need-based aid available for part-time students.
Students without need: 10 full-time freshmen who did not demonstrate need for aid received scholarships/grants; average award was $4,695. No-need awards available for academics, alumni affiliation, athletics, leadership, music/drama, religious affiliation, state/district residency.
Scholarships offered: 20 full-time freshmen received athletic scholarships; average amount $4,643.
Cumulative student debt: 63% of graduating class had student loans; average debt was $12,420.

FINANCIAL AID PROCEDURES
Forms required: FAFSA, institutional form.
Dates and Deadlines: Priority date 4/1; closing date 6/1. Applicants notified on a rolling basis starting 4/1; must reply within 2 week(s) of notification.
Transfers: Priority date 3/1; closing date 6/15.

CONTACT
Kerrie Mitchell, Financial Aid Officer
6610 Lovington Highway, Hobbs, NM 88240
(505) 392-6563

Dona Ana Branch Community College of New Mexico State University
Las Cruces, New Mexico
www.nmsu.edu   Federal Code: 002657

2-year public branch campus and community college in small city.
Enrollment: 2,224 full-time undergrads.
Selectivity: Open admission; but selective for some programs.

BASIC COSTS (2005-2006)
Tuition and fees: $1,080; out-of-district residents $1,320; out-of-state residents $3,024.
Per-credit charge: $45; out-of-district residents $55; out-of-state residents $126.
Room and board: $5,332.

FINANCIAL AID PICTURE (2004-2005)
Students with need: Need-based aid available for full-time and part-time students.

FINANCIAL AID PROCEDURES
Forms required: FAFSA.
Dates and Deadlines: Priority date 3/1; no closing date. Applicants notified on a rolling basis starting 5/1.

CONTACT
Gladys Chairez, Financial Aid Advisor
MSC-3DA, Las Cruces, NM 88003-8001
(505) 527-696

Eastern New Mexico University
Portales, New Mexico
www.enmu.edu   Federal Code: 002651

4-year public university in large town.
Enrollment: 3,043 undergrads, 18% part-time. 563 full-time freshmen.
Selectivity: Admits 50 to 75% of applicants.

BASIC COSTS (2005-2006)
Tuition and fees: $2,784; out-of-state residents $8,340.
Per-credit charge: $116; out-of-state residents $348.
Room and board: $4,480.

FINANCIAL AID PICTURE (2005-2006)
Students with need: Out of 361 full-time freshmen who applied for aid, 359 were judged to have need. Of these, 359 received aid, and 289 had their full need met. Average financial aid package met 36% of need; average scholarship/grant was $3,034; average loan was $2,753. For part-time students, average financial aid package was $6,582.
Students without need: 55 full-time freshmen who did not demonstrate need for aid received scholarships/grants; average award was $3,236. No-need awards available for academics, alumni affiliation, art, athletics, leadership, music/drama, state/district residency.
Scholarships offered: 53 full-time freshmen received athletic scholarships; average amount $2,208.
Cumulative student debt: 1% of graduating class had student loans; average debt was $10,772.
Additional info: Not all merit scholarships are need-based.

FINANCIAL AID PROCEDURES
Forms required: FAFSA.
Dates and Deadlines: Priority date 3/1; no closing date. Applicants notified by 4/1; must reply within 3 week(s) of notification.
Transfers: Child care grants and non-need-based college work study limited to New Mexico residents.

CONTACT
Joyce Eldridge, Director of Financial Aid
Station Seven, Portales, NM 88130
(505) 562-2194

Eastern New Mexico University: Roswell Campus
Roswell, New Mexico
www.roswell.enmu.edu   Federal Code: 002651

2-year public branch campus and community college in large town.
Enrollment: 2,501 undergrads, 56% part-time. 350 full-time freshmen.
Selectivity: Open admission; but selective for some programs.

BASIC COSTS (2006-2007)
Tuition and fees: $1,128; out-of-district residents $1,164; out-of-state residents $4,394.
Per-credit charge: $41; out-of-district residents $43; out-of-state residents $177.
Room and board: $4,439.

FINANCIAL AID PICTURE (2004-2005)
Students with need: Out of 288 full-time freshmen who applied for aid, 260 were judged to have need. Of these, 255 received aid, and 43 had their full need met. Average financial aid package met 15% of need; average scholarship/grant was $2,141; average loan was $614. For part-time students, average financial aid package was $1,859.
Students without need: 1 full-time freshmen who did not demonstrate need for aid received scholarships/grants; average award was $250.
Scholarships offered: New Mexico Lottery Scholarship: tuition for New Mexico residents; must attend school full-time the semester following high school graduation or GED and maintain 12 credit hours and 2.5 GPA.

FINANCIAL AID PROCEDURES
Forms required: FAFSA.
Dates and Deadlines: Priority date 4/1; no closing date. Applicants notified on a rolling basis starting 7/1; must reply within 3 week(s) of notification.
Transfers: All students receiving state aid must be New Mexico residents and enrolled in at least 6 credit hours.

CONTACT
Jessie Hall, Director of Financial Aid
Box 6000, Roswell, NM 88202-6000
(505) 624-7152

Institute of American Indian Arts
Santa Fe, New Mexico
www.iaiancad.org   Federal Code: 014152

4-year public visual arts and junior college in small city.
Enrollment: 203 undergrads, 19% part-time. 12 full-time freshmen.
Selectivity: Admits less than 50% of applicants.

BASIC COSTS (2005-2006)
Tuition and fees: $2,490.
Per-credit charge: $100; out-of-state residents $100.
Room and board: $4,536.

FINANCIAL AID PICTURE
Students with need: Need-based aid available for full-time and part-time students. Work study available nights.
Scholarships offered: IAIA merit scholarships: available to all students with GPA 3.0, $1,000; GPA 3.5, $1,500; and GPA 4.0, $2,000.
Additional info: For American Indian and Alaskan natives, financial aid available through Tribe or Native Corporation in which student is enrolled.

FINANCIAL AID PROCEDURES
Forms required: FAFSA, institutional form.
Dates and Deadlines: Priority date 3/15; no closing date. Applicants notified on a rolling basis starting 5/1.

CONTACT
Dorothy Espinoza, Financial Aid Manager
83 Avan Nu Po Road, Santa Fe, NM 87508-1300
(505) 424-2330

Mesalands Community College
Tucumcari, New Mexico
www.mesalands.edu   Federal Code: 032063

2-year public community and technical college in small town.
Enrollment: 312 undergrads, 31% part-time. 32 full-time freshmen.
Selectivity: Open admission.

BASIC COSTS (2005-2006)
Tuition and fees: $1,394; out-of-state residents $2,264.
Per-credit charge: $37; out-of-state residents $66.

FINANCIAL AID PICTURE (2004-2005)
Students with need: Out of 32 full-time freshmen who applied for aid, 32 were judged to have need. Of these, 32 received aid. Average financial aid package met 21% of need; average scholarship/grant was $1,713. For part-time students, average financial aid package was $480.
Students without need: No-need awards available for academics, athletics, leadership, minority status, music/drama, state/district residency.
Scholarships offered: 8 full-time freshmen received athletic scholarships; average amount $600.

FINANCIAL AID PROCEDURES
Forms required: FAFSA.
Dates and Deadlines: Priority date 4/1; no closing date. Applicants notified on a rolling basis starting 4/1; must reply within 3 week(s) of notification.

CONTACT
Theresa Beres, Director of Financial Aid
911 South Tenth Street, Tucumcari, NM 88401
(505) 461-4413

New Mexico Highlands University
Las Vegas, New Mexico
www.nmhu.edu   Federal Code: 002653

4-year public university in large town.
Enrollment: 1,784 undergrads, 31% part-time. 257 full-time freshmen.
Selectivity: Open admission.

BASIC COSTS (2005-2006)
Tuition and fees: $2,300; out-of-state residents $3,440.
Room and board: $4,298.

FINANCIAL AID PICTURE (2005-2006)
Students with need: Out of 238 full-time freshmen who applied for aid, 211 were judged to have need. Of these, 209 received aid, and 51 had their full need met. Average financial aid package met 68% of need; average scholarship/grant was $4,766; average loan was $1,339. For part-time students, average financial aid package was $7,315.
Students without need: 26 full-time freshmen who did not demonstrate need for aid received scholarships/grants; average award was $2,158. No-need awards available for academics, athletics, leadership, minority status, music/drama, state/district residency.
Scholarships offered: 28 full-time freshmen received athletic scholarships; average amount $1,945.
Additional info: Work study funds available on no-need basis to state residents.

FINANCIAL AID PROCEDURES
Forms required: FAFSA.

Dates and Deadlines: Closing date 3/1. Applicants notified on a rolling basis starting 5/15; must reply within 2 week(s) of notification.
Transfers: Priority date 3/1; closing date 6/30.

CONTACT
Eileen Sedillo, Director of Financial Aid
Box 9000, Las Vegas, NM 87701
(505) 454-3318

New Mexico Institute of Mining and Technology
Socorro, New Mexico
www.nmt.edu   Federal Code: 002654

4-year public engineering and liberal arts college in small town.
Enrollment: 1,184 undergrads, 5% part-time. 279 full-time freshmen.
Selectivity: Admits over 75% of applicants.

BASIC COSTS (2005-2006)
Tuition and fees: $3,643; out-of-state residents $10,463.
Per-credit charge: $131; out-of-state residents $415.
Room and board: $4,836.

FINANCIAL AID PICTURE (2005-2006)
Students with need: Average financial aid package met 94% of need; average scholarship/grant was $4,444; average loan was $3,470. For part-time students, average financial aid package was $7,422.
Students without need: No-need awards available for academics, alumni affiliation, minority status, state/district residency.
Scholarships offered: Up to $3,500 annually; for transfer students with college GPA of 3.5 and 30 degree credit hours.
Additional info: Campus research projects offer student employment based on merit.

FINANCIAL AID PROCEDURES
Forms required: FAFSA, institutional form.
Dates and Deadlines: Priority date 6/1; no closing date. Applicants notified on a rolling basis starting 6/1; must reply within 2 week(s) of notification.
Transfers: Priority date 3/1. Financial aid transcripts required from all colleges attended.

CONTACT
Annette Kaus, Director of Financial Aid
801 Leroy Place, Socorro, NM 87801
(505) 835-5333

New Mexico Junior College
Hobbs, New Mexico
www.nmjc.cc.nm.us   Federal Code: 002655

2-year public community and technical college in large town.
Enrollment: 2,600 undergrads.
Selectivity: Open admission; but selective for some programs.

BASIC COSTS (2005-2006)
Tuition and fees: $730; out-of-district residents $1,138; out-of-state residents $1,258.
Per-credit charge: $22; out-of-district residents $39; out-of-state residents $44.
Room and board: $3,200.

FINANCIAL AID PICTURE
Students with need: Need-based aid available for full-time and part-time students.

FINANCIAL AID PROCEDURES
Forms required: FAFSA.

Dates and Deadlines: Priority date 6/1; no closing date. Applicants notified on a rolling basis; must reply within 2 week(s) of notification.

CONTACT
Laura Marquez, Assistant Director of Financial Aid
1 Thunderbird Circle, Hobbs, NM 88240
(505) 392-4510

New Mexico Military Institute Junior College
Roswell, New Mexico
www.nmmi.edu   Federal Code: 002656

2-year public junior and military college in large town.
Enrollment: 450 undergrads.

BASIC COSTS (2005-2006)
Tuition and fees: $7,670; out-of-state residents $10,166.
Additional info: Tuition costs include room and board, uniform, supplies, and fees.

FINANCIAL AID PICTURE
Students with need: Need-based aid available for full-time students.
Students without need: No-need awards available for academics, athletics, ROTC, state/district residency.

FINANCIAL AID PROCEDURES
Forms required: FAFSA.
Dates and Deadlines: Priority date 4/1; no closing date. Applicants notified on a rolling basis starting 5/1; must reply within 3 week(s) of notification.
Transfers: New Mexico Scholars Program, New Mexico Success Scholarship.

CONTACT
Sonya Rodriguez, Financial Aid Director
101 West College Boulevard, Roswell, NM 88201-5173
(505) 622-6250

New Mexico State University
Las Cruces, New Mexico
www.nmsu.edu   Federal Code: 002657

4-year public university in small city.
Enrollment: 11,929 undergrads, 15% part-time. 1,990 full-time freshmen.
Selectivity: Admits over 75% of applicants.

BASIC COSTS (2005-2006)
Tuition and fees: $3,918; out-of-state residents $13,206.
Per-credit charge: $163; out-of-state residents $550.
Room and board: $5,332.

FINANCIAL AID PICTURE (2005-2006)
Students with need: Out of 1,471 full-time freshmen who applied for aid, 1,198 were judged to have need. Of these, 1,160 received aid, and 173 had their full need met. Average financial aid package met 61% of need; average scholarship/grant was $6,203; average loan was $2,698. For part-time students, average financial aid package was $5,197.
Students without need: 547 full-time freshmen who did not demonstrate need for aid received scholarships/grants; average award was $3,161. No-need awards available for academics, alumni affiliation, athletics, leadership, minority status, state/district residency.
Scholarships offered: 23 full-time freshmen received athletic scholarships; average amount $11,752.

FINANCIAL AID PROCEDURES
Forms required: FAFSA, institutional form.

Dates and Deadlines: Priority date 3/1; no closing date. Applicants notified on a rolling basis starting 4/1; must reply within 4 week(s) of notification.

CONTACT
Tyler Pruett, Director of Financial Aid
Box 30001, MSC 3A, Las Cruces, NM 88003-8001
(505) 646-4105

New Mexico State University at Alamogordo
Alamogordo, New Mexico
www.alamo.nmsu.edu Federal Code: 002658

2-year public branch campus college in large town.
Enrollment: 1,445 undergrads.
Selectivity: Open admission; but selective for some programs.

BASIC COSTS (2005-2006)
Tuition and fees: $1,260; out-of-district residents $1,404; out-of-state residents $4,020.
Per-credit charge: $50; out-of-district residents $56; out-of-state residents $165.

FINANCIAL AID PICTURE
Students with need: Need-based aid available for full-time and part-time students.
Students without need: No-need awards available for academics, state/district residency.

FINANCIAL AID PROCEDURES
Forms required: FAFSA, institutional form.
Dates and Deadlines: Applicants notified by 6/1.

CONTACT
Sharon Fischer, Financial Aid Coordinator
2400 North Scenic Drive, Alamogordo, NM 88310
(505) 439-3600

New Mexico State University at Carlsbad
Carlsbad, New Mexico
cavern.nmsu.edu Federal Code: 002657

2-year public branch campus and community college in large town.
Enrollment: 1,600 undergrads.
Selectivity: Open admission; but selective for some programs.

BASIC COSTS (2005-2006)
Tuition and fees: $1,128; out-of-district residents $1,248; out-of-state residents $2,544.
Per-credit charge: $45; out-of-district residents $50; out-of-state residents $104.

FINANCIAL AID PICTURE
Students with need: Need-based aid available for full-time and part-time students.
Students without need: No-need awards available for academics, state/district residency.

FINANCIAL AID PROCEDURES
Forms required: FAFSA.
Dates and Deadlines: Priority date 3/1; no closing date. Applicants notified on a rolling basis starting 5/3; must reply within 4 week(s) of notification.

CONTACT
Judi Sears, Financial Aid Coordinator
1500 University Drive, Carlsbad, NM 88220
(505) 234-9226

New Mexico State University at Grants
Grants, New Mexico
www.grants.nmsu.edu Federal Code: 008854

2-year public branch campus and community college in small town.
Enrollment: 700 undergrads.
Selectivity: Open admission.

BASIC COSTS (2005-2006)
Tuition and fees: $1,152; out-of-district residents $1,272; out-of-state residents $2,664.
Per-credit charge: $47; out-of-district residents $52; out-of-state residents $110.

FINANCIAL AID PICTURE
Students with need: Need-based aid available for full-time and part-time students. Work study available nights, weekends, and for part-time students.

FINANCIAL AID PROCEDURES
Forms required: FAFSA, institutional form.
Dates and Deadlines: Priority date 3/5; no closing date. Applicants notified on a rolling basis starting 6/15; must reply by 8/28.

CONTACT
Ida Chavez, Campus Financial Officer
1500 North Third Street, Grants, NM 87020
(505) 287-7981

Northern New Mexico College
Espanola, New Mexico
www.nnmcc.edu Federal Code: 005286

4-year public community and teachers college in small town.
Enrollment: 2,200 undergrads.
Selectivity: Open admission; but selective for some programs and for out-of-state students.

BASIC COSTS (2005-2006)
Tuition and fees: $958; out-of-state residents $2,374.
Per-credit charge: $33; out-of-state residents $92.
Room and board: $3,528.
Additional info: Upper division courses are $90 per-credit-hour for in-state students and $367 per-credit-hour for out-of-state students.

FINANCIAL AID PICTURE
Students with need: Need-based aid available for full-time students.
Students without need: This college only awards aid to students with need.

FINANCIAL AID PROCEDURES
Forms required: FAFSA.
Dates and Deadlines: Priority date 3/1; no closing date. Applicants notified on a rolling basis starting 6/1; must reply within 2 week(s) of notification.

CONTACT
Alfredo Montoya, Director of Financial Aid
921 Paseo de Onate, Espanola, NM 87532
(505) 747-2128 ext. 128

St. John's College
Santa Fe, New Mexico
www.stjohnscollege.edu Federal Code: 002093
 CSS Code: 4737

4-year private liberal arts college in small city.
Enrollment: 435 undergrads, 1% part-time. 119 full-time freshmen.
Selectivity: Admits over 75% of applicants.

New Mexico St. John's College

BASIC COSTS (2006-2007)
Tuition and fees: $34,506.
Room and board: $8,270.

FINANCIAL AID PICTURE (2005-2006)
Students with need: Out of 86 full-time freshmen who applied for aid, 81 were judged to have need. Of these, 81 received aid, and 79 had their full need met. Average financial aid package met 95% of need; average scholarship/grant was $18,063; average loan was $3,187. For part-time students, average financial aid package was $14,430.
Students without need: No-need awards available for state/district residency.
Additional info: 100% of need met for most of those qualified to receive aid. Families receive individual attention in determining need fairly. Independent students must submit parental data. Financial aid information also required of noncustodial parent in cases of separation or divorce. Aid awarded first-come, first-served until institutional money exhausted. Apply early by February 15; after April 1 aid difficult to obtain.

FINANCIAL AID PROCEDURES
Forms required: FAFSA, CSS PROFILE.
Dates and Deadlines: Priority date 2/15; no closing date. Applicants notified on a rolling basis starting 12/1; must reply by 5/1 or within 2 week(s) of notification.

CONTACT
Michael Rodriguez, Director of Financial Aid
1160 Camino Cruz Blanca, Santa Fe, NM 87505-4599
(505) 984-6058

San Juan College
Farmington, New Mexico
www.sanjuancollege.edu   Federal Code: 002660

2-year public community college in large town.
Enrollment: 4,345 undergrads, 42% part-time. 694 full-time freshmen.
Selectivity: Open admission.

BASIC COSTS (2006-2007)
Tuition and fees: $600; out-of-state residents $840.
Per-credit charge: $25; out-of-state residents $35.

FINANCIAL AID PICTURE (2004-2005)
Students with need: 54% of average financial aid package awarded as scholarships/grants, 46% awarded as loans/jobs. Need-based aid available for part-time students. Work study available nights, weekends, and for part-time students.
Students without need: No-need awards available for academics, state/district residency.

FINANCIAL AID PROCEDURES
Forms required: FAFSA.
Dates and Deadlines: No deadline. Applicants notified on a rolling basis starting 7/1; must reply within 2 week(s) of notification.

CONTACT
Roger Evans, Director of Financial Aid
4601 College Boulevard, Farmington, NM 87402-4699
(505) 326-3311

Santa Fe Community College
Santa Fe, New Mexico
www.sfccnm.edu   Federal Code: 016065

2-year public community college in small city.
Enrollment: 1,729 undergrads.
Selectivity: Open admission.

BASIC COSTS (2005-2006)
Tuition and fees: $1,050; out-of-district residents $1,364; out-of-state residents $2,368.
Per-credit charge: $31; out-of-district residents $42; out-of-state residents $75.

FINANCIAL AID PICTURE (2004-2005)
Students with need: 14% of average financial aid package awarded as scholarships/grants, 86% awarded as loans/jobs. Need-based aid available for part-time students. Work study available nights, weekends, and for part-time students.

FINANCIAL AID PROCEDURES
Forms required: FAFSA, institutional form.
Dates and Deadlines: Priority date 3/1; no closing date. Applicants notified on a rolling basis starting 7/15; must reply within 4 week(s) of notification.

CONTACT
Willie Bachicha, Financial Aid Director
6401 Richards Avenue, Santa Fe, NM 87508-4887
(505) 428-1268

Southwestern Indian Polytechnic Institute
Albuquerque, New Mexico
www.sipi.bia.edu   Federal Code: 011185

2-year public community and technical college in large city.
Enrollment: 614 undergrads, 24% part-time. 231 full-time freshmen.
Selectivity: Open admission.

BASIC COSTS (2006-2007)
Additional info: Students with valid membership in U.S. federally recognized Indian tribe attend tuition-free. Required fees: full-time Lodge student $280.00, full-time commuter $225.00, part-time $150.00. Tuition/fee waivers available for minority students.

FINANCIAL AID PICTURE (2004-2005)
Students with need: Out of 231 full-time freshmen who applied for aid, 231 were judged to have need. Of these, 231 received aid. Need-based aid available for part-time students.
Students without need: 69 full-time freshmen who did not demonstrate need for aid received scholarships/grants; average award was $500. No-need awards available for academics, leadership, minority status.

FINANCIAL AID PROCEDURES
Forms required: FAFSA.
Dates and Deadlines: Closing date 3/1. Applicants notified on a rolling basis starting 9/30.
Transfers: No deadline.

CONTACT
Marilyn Pargas, Financial Aid Specialist
9169 Coors Road Northwest, Albuquerque, NM 87184
(505) 346-2344

University of New Mexico
Albuquerque, New Mexico
www.unm.edu   Federal Code: 002663

4-year public university in very large city.
Enrollment: 18,330 undergrads, 20% part-time. 3,016 full-time freshmen.
Selectivity: Admits 50 to 75% of applicants.

BASIC COSTS (2005-2006)
Tuition and fees: $4,109; out-of-state residents $13,438.
Per-credit charge: $171; out-of-state residents $560.
Room and board: $6,518.

FINANCIAL AID PICTURE
Students with need: Need-based aid available for full-time and part-time students. Work study available nights, weekends, and for part-time students.
Students without need: No-need awards available for academics, alumni affiliation, art, athletics, job skills, leadership, minority status, music/drama, religious affiliation, ROTC, state/district residency.
Scholarships offered: Bridge to Success Scholarship: $1,000 for first semester only while awaiting other scholarship aid; requires New Mexico residency, full-time status in degree-granting program, and acceptable GED test score and/or requisite high school GPA per sponsor.
Additional info: Regent scholarship program has priority date of December 1. UNM scholars program has deadline of February 1.

FINANCIAL AID PROCEDURES
Forms required: FAFSA.
Dates and Deadlines: Priority date 3/1; no closing date. Applicants notified on a rolling basis starting 4/15.
Transfers: Closing date 5/30.

CONTACT
Kathleen O'Keefe, Director of Financial Aid
Office of Admissions, Albuquerque, NM 87196-4895
(505) 277-2041

Western New Mexico University
Silver City, New Mexico
www.wnmu.edu
Federal Code: 002664

4-year public university in large town.
Enrollment: 1,857 undergrads, 24% part-time. 332 full-time freshmen.
Selectivity: Open admission.

BASIC COSTS (2005-2006)
Tuition and fees: $2,863; out-of-state residents $9,565.
Room and board: $4,460.

FINANCIAL AID PICTURE (2004-2005)
Students with need: Out of 243 full-time freshmen who applied for aid, 243 were judged to have need. Of these, 243 received aid, and 23 had their full need met. Average financial aid package met 64% of need; average scholarship/grant was $3,221; average loan was $2,526. For part-time students, average financial aid package was $6,353.
Students without need: 31 full-time freshmen who did not demonstrate need for aid received scholarships/grants; average award was $2,601. No-need awards available for academics, athletics, state/district residency.
Scholarships offered: 35 full-time freshmen received athletic scholarships; average amount $2,546.
Cumulative student debt: 35% of graduating class had student loans; average debt was $5,782.

FINANCIAL AID PROCEDURES
Forms required: FAFSA, institutional form.
Dates and Deadlines: Closing date 4/1. Applicants notified on a rolling basis starting 4/1; must reply within 2 week(s) of notification.

CONTACT
Charles Kelly, Director of Financial Aid
Castorena 106, Silver City, NM 88062
(505) 538-6173

New York

Adelphi University
Garden City, New York
www.adelphi.edu
Federal Code: 002666

4-year private university in large town.
Enrollment: 4,718 undergrads, 16% part-time. 769 full-time freshmen.
Selectivity: Admits 50 to 75% of applicants.

BASIC COSTS (2006-2007)
Tuition and fees: $20,900.
Room and board: $9,500.
Additional info: Tuition, fees, and per-credit-hour charges for upper-division nursing, social work, and education programs are slightly higher.

FINANCIAL AID PICTURE (2004-2005)
Students with need: Out of 693 full-time freshmen who applied for aid, 590 were judged to have need. Of these, 590 received aid. Average financial aid package met 29.3% of need; average scholarship/grant was $4,958; average loan was $3,240. Need-based aid available for part-time students.
Students without need: 181 full-time freshmen who did not demonstrate need for aid received scholarships/grants; average award was $8,901. No-need awards available for academics, alumni affiliation, art, athletics, job skills, leadership, minority status, music/drama, religious affiliation.
Scholarships offered: *Merit:* Trustee Scholarship: up to full tuition, top 10% of high school class, 1350 SAT, 3.7 GPA required; 12 available. Presidential Scholarship: $12,500 to $14,500, top 10% of high school class, 1350 SAT, 3.5 GPA required; 25 available. Provost Scholarship: $10,000 to $12,000, top 15% of high school class, 1250 SAT, 3.3 GPA required; 55 available. Dean's Scholarship: $4,000 to $9,500, top 25% of high school class, 1000 SAT, 3.0 GPA required; 252 available. SAT scores listed exclusive of Writing.
Athletic: 16 full-time freshmen received athletic scholarships; average amount $7,113.
Cumulative student debt: 81% of graduating class had student loans; average debt was $22,000.

FINANCIAL AID PROCEDURES
Forms required: FAFSA, state aid form.
Dates and Deadlines: Priority date 3/1; no closing date. Applicants notified on a rolling basis starting 3/1.

CONTACT
Sheryl Mihopulos, Director of Financial Aid
One South Avenue, Levermore 110, Garden City, NY 11530-0701
(516) 877-3080

Adirondack Community College
Queensbury, New York
www.sunyacc.edu
Federal Code: 002860

2-year public community college in large town.
Enrollment: 2,903 undergrads, 32% part-time. 701 full-time freshmen.
Selectivity: Open admission; but selective for some programs.

BASIC COSTS (2005-2006)
Tuition and fees: $3,062; out-of-state residents $5,932.
Per-credit charge: $120; out-of-state residents $240.

FINANCIAL AID PICTURE
Students with need: Need-based aid available for full-time and part-time students.
Students without need: This college only awards aid to students with need.

Scholarships offered: Academic Excellence Scholarship for local high school graduate, 1st or 2nd in class, top 10%, GPA 3.5; $750 per semester for up to 4 semesters. Hill Scholarship for Fort Edward high school graduate; $500 per semester for 4 semesters.

FINANCIAL AID PROCEDURES
Forms required: FAFSA, state aid form, institutional form.
Dates and Deadlines: Priority date 4/15; no closing date. Applicants notified on a rolling basis starting 5/1.

CONTACT
Maureen Reilly, Director of Financial Aid
640 Bay Road, Queensbury, NY 12804
(518) 743-2223

Albany College of Pharmacy
Albany, New York
www.acp.edu

6-year private health science and pharmacy college in small city.
Enrollment: 855 undergrads. 280 full-time freshmen.
Selectivity: Admits 50 to 75% of applicants.

BASIC COSTS (2005-2006)
Tuition and fees: $20,370.
Per-credit charge: $610.
Room and board: $6,100.
Additional info: Fees include mandatory laptop purchase.

FINANCIAL AID PICTURE (2005-2006)
Students with need: Out of 212 full-time freshmen who applied for aid, 168 were judged to have need. Of these, 166 received aid, and 12 had their full need met. Average financial aid package met 52% of need; average scholarship/grant was $5,875; average loan was $3,423.
Students without need: No-need awards available for academics.

FINANCIAL AID PROCEDURES
Forms required: FAFSA.
Dates and Deadlines: Priority date 2/1; no closing date.

CONTACT
Tiffany Guitierrez, Director of Financial Aid
106 New Scotland Avenue, Albany, NY 12208
(518) 694-7258

Alfred University
Alfred, New York
www.alfred.edu   Federal Code: 002668

4-year private university in rural community.
Enrollment: 1,905 undergrads, 2% part-time. 506 full-time freshmen.
Selectivity: Admits over 75% of applicants.

BASIC COSTS (2006-2007)
Tuition and fees: $22,100.
Per-credit charge: $690.
Room and board: $10,040.
Additional info: Reported cost information for programs with private source of institutional control (nonprofit). Cost of public programs, such as those offered by the New York State College of Ceramics (SUNY), may vary by program.

FINANCIAL AID PICTURE (2004-2005)
Students with need: Out of 452 full-time freshmen who applied for aid, 406 were judged to have need. Of these, 406 received aid, and 346 had their full need met. Average financial aid package met 94% of need; average scholarship/grant was $14,574; average loan was $4,146.

Students without need: 86 full-time freshmen who did not demonstrate need for aid received scholarships/grants; average award was $7,136. No-need awards available for academics, art, leadership, music/drama.
Cumulative student debt: 90% of graduating class had student loans; average debt was $19,125.

FINANCIAL AID PROCEDURES
Forms required: FAFSA, state aid form, institutional form.
Dates and Deadlines: Priority date 2/1; no closing date. Applicants notified on a rolling basis starting 2/15; must reply by 5/1 or within 2 week(s) of notification.
Transfers: No deadline. Applicants notified on a rolling basis starting 2/15; must reply by 5/1 or within 2 week(s) of notification.

CONTACT
Earl Pierce, Director of Student Financial Aid
Alumni Hall, Alfred, NY 14802-1205
(607) 871-2159

American Academy McAllister Institute of Funeral Service
New York, New York
www.funeraleducation.org   Federal Code: 010813

2-year private school of mortuary science in very large city.
Enrollment: 105 undergrads.
Selectivity: Open admission.

BASIC COSTS (2006-2007)
Tuition and fees: $9,975.
Additional info: Tuition at time of enrollment locked for 2 years.

FINANCIAL AID PICTURE
Students with need: Need-based aid available for full-time students.
Students without need: This college only awards aid to students with need.

FINANCIAL AID PROCEDURES
Forms required: FAFSA, state aid form.
Dates and Deadlines: Applicants notified on a rolling basis starting 7/1; must reply by 9/1 or within 3 week(s) of notification.
Transfers: Priority date 6/1.

CONTACT
Jaway Tso, Financial Aid Administrator
619 West 54th Street, New York, NY 10019-3602
(212) 220-4275

American Academy of Dramatic Arts
New York, New York
www.aada.org   Federal Code: 007465

2-year private junior and performing arts college in very large city.
Enrollment: 220 undergrads. 56 full-time freshmen.
Selectivity: Admits 50 to 75% of applicants.

BASIC COSTS (2006-2007)
Tuition and fees: $17,400.

FINANCIAL AID PICTURE (2005-2006)
Students with need: Average financial aid package met 57% of need; average scholarship/grant was $5,400; average loan was $2,800.
Students without need: This college only awards aid to students with need.
Additional info: Need-based incentive grants of $200-$500 for first-year students available. Merit awards of $500-$1,500. Scholarships of $500-$3,000

available for second year. Scholarships of $500-$5,000 available for post-degree third year.

FINANCIAL AID PROCEDURES
Forms required: FAFSA, institutional form.
Dates and Deadlines: No deadline. Applicants notified on a rolling basis.

CONTACT
Roberto Lopez, Financial Aid Director
120 Madison Avenue, New York, NY 10016
(212) 686-9244 ext. 342

ASA Institute of Business and Computer Technology
Brooklyn, New York
www.asa.edu   Federal Code: 030955

2-year for-profit business and junior college in very large city.
Enrollment: 2,961 undergrads, 2% part-time. 926 full-time freshmen.
Selectivity: Admits over 75% of applicants.

BASIC COSTS (2005-2006)
Tuition and fees: $9,430.
Additional info: Tuition at time of enrollment locked for 2 years.

FINANCIAL AID PICTURE (2005-2006)
Students with need: Out of 926 full-time freshmen who applied for aid, 833 were judged to have need. Of these, 833 received aid, and 490 had their full need met. Average financial aid package met 90% of need; average scholarship/grant was $6,575; average loan was $2,625. Need-based aid available for part-time students.
Students without need: 76 full-time freshmen who did not demonstrate need for aid received scholarships/grants; average award was $2,400. No-need awards available for academics, alumni affiliation, state/district residency.
Cumulative student debt: 67% of graduating class had student loans; average debt was $4,288.
Additional info: Tuition at time of enrollment guaranteed to all students until graduation, provided no break in enrollment.

FINANCIAL AID PROCEDURES
Forms required: FAFSA, state aid form.
Dates and Deadlines: No deadline. Applicants notified on a rolling basis starting 7/5; must reply by 10/5.

CONTACT
Victoria Shtamler, Assistant Vice President of Financial Aid
151 Lawrence Street, Brooklyn, NY 11201-9805
(718) 532-1431

Bard College
Annandale-on-Hudson, New York   Federal Code: 002671
www.bard.edu   CSS Code: 2037

4-year private liberal arts college in small town, affiliated with Episcopal Church.
Enrollment: 1,555 undergrads, 3% part-time. 515 full-time freshmen.
Selectivity: Admits less than 50% of applicants.

BASIC COSTS (2006-2007)
Tuition and fees: $34,782.
Room and board: $9,850.

FINANCIAL AID PICTURE (2005-2006)
Students with need: Out of 359 full-time freshmen who applied for aid, 289 were judged to have need. Of these, 289 received aid, and 169 had their full need met. Average financial aid package met 87% of need; average scholarship/grant was $24,046; average loan was $1,614. For part-time students, average financial aid package was $7,047.
Students without need: 33 full-time freshmen who did not demonstrate need for aid received scholarships/grants; average award was $9,708. No-need awards available for academics.
Scholarships offered: Distinguished Scientist Scholarship: full tuition; for students intending to major in math or sciences; 10-20 awarded annually.
Cumulative student debt: 71% of graduating class had student loans; average debt was $18,345.
Additional info: Excellence and Equal Cost Program for students who graduate in top 10 of public high school class lowers fees to levels equivalent to those at home state university or college.

FINANCIAL AID PROCEDURES
Forms required: FAFSA, CSS PROFILE, state aid form.
Dates and Deadlines: Priority date 2/1; closing date 2/15. Applicants notified by 4/1; must reply by 5/1.

CONTACT
Denise Ackerman, Director of Financial Aid
30 Campus Road, Annandale-on-Hudson, NY 12504-5000
(845) 758-7526

Barnard College
New York, New York   Federal Code: 002708
www.barnard.edu   CSS Code: 2038

4-year private liberal arts college for women in very large city.
Enrollment: 2,356 undergrads, 3% part-time. 571 full-time freshmen.
Selectivity: Admits less than 50% of applicants.

BASIC COSTS (2006-2007)
Tuition and fees: $33,078.
Per-credit charge: $1,060.
Room and board: $11,392.

FINANCIAL AID PICTURE (2005-2006)
Students with need: Out of 329 full-time freshmen who applied for aid, 241 were judged to have need. Of these, 241 received aid, and 241 had their full need met. Average financial aid package met 100% of need; average scholarship/grant was $25,413; average loan was $2,376. Need-based aid available for part-time students.
Students without need: This college only awards aid to students with need.
Cumulative student debt: 45% of graduating class had student loans; average debt was $19,496.

FINANCIAL AID PROCEDURES
Forms required: FAFSA, CSS PROFILE, state aid form, institutional form.
Dates and Deadlines: Closing date 2/1. Applicants notified by 4/1; must reply by 5/1.
Transfers: Closing date 4/1. Transfers admitted in the spring are not eligible for institutional grant aid.

CONTACT
Alison Rabil, Director of Financial Aid
3009 Broadway, New York, NY 10027-6598
(212) 854-2154

Berkeley College
White Plains, New York
www.berkeleycollege.edu   Federal Code: 007421

4-year for-profit business college in small city.
Enrollment: 608 undergrads, 7% part-time. 154 full-time freshmen.

BASIC COSTS (2006-2007)
Tuition and fees: $17,700.
Per-credit charge: $415.
Room and board: $9,000.
Additional info: Part-time students pay $75 administrative fee per quarter. Tuition at time of enrollment locked for 4 years.

FINANCIAL AID PICTURE
Students with need: Need-based aid available for full-time students.
Students without need: No-need awards available for academics, alumni affiliation.
Additional info: Alumni scholarship examination given in November and December. Full and partial scholarships awarded.

FINANCIAL AID PROCEDURES
Forms required: FAFSA, state aid form.
Dates and Deadlines: No deadline. Applicants notified on a rolling basis starting 3/1; must reply within 6 week(s) of notification.

CONTACT
Yessennia Arocho-Bannerman, Director, Financial Aid
99 Church Street, White Plains, NY 10601
(914) 694-1122

Berkeley College of New York City
New York, New York
www.berkeleycollege.edu   Federal Code: 008556

4-year for-profit business college in very large city.
Enrollment: 2,307 undergrads, 8% part-time. 648 full-time freshmen.
Selectivity: Admits 50 to 75% of applicants.

BASIC COSTS (2006-2007)
Tuition and fees: $17,700.
Per-credit charge: $415.
Additional info: Part-time students pay $75 administrative fee per quarter. Tuition at time of enrollment locked for 4 years.

FINANCIAL AID PICTURE
Students with need: Need-based aid available for full-time students.
Students without need: No-need awards available for academics, alumni affiliation.
Additional info: Alumni scholarship examination given in November and December. Full and partial scholarships awarded.

FINANCIAL AID PROCEDURES
Forms required: FAFSA.
Dates and Deadlines: No deadline. Applicants notified on a rolling basis starting 3/1; must reply within 6 week(s) of notification.
Transfers: New York State TAP Grant eligibility may be affected.

CONTACT
Andrea John, Director, Financial Aid
3 East 43rd Street, New York, NY 10017
(212) 986-4343

Broome Community College
Binghamton, New York
www.sunybroome.edu   Federal Code: 002862

2-year public community college in small city.
Enrollment: 5,008 undergrads.
Selectivity: Open admission.

BASIC COSTS (2005-2006)
Tuition and fees: $3,046; out-of-state residents $5,860.
Per-credit charge: $118; out-of-state residents $236.

FINANCIAL AID PICTURE (2004-2005)
Students with need: 74% of average financial aid package awarded as scholarships/grants, 26% awarded as loans/jobs. Need-based aid available for part-time students.
Students without need: This college only awards aid to students with need.

FINANCIAL AID PROCEDURES
Forms required: FAFSA.
Dates and Deadlines: Priority date 3/1; no closing date. Applicants notified on a rolling basis starting 3/15; must reply within 2 week(s) of notification.

CONTACT
Douglas Lusasik, Director of Financial Aid
Box 1017, Binghamton, NY 13902
(607) 778-5028

Bryant & Stratton College: Albany
Albany, New York
www.bryantstratton.edu   Federal Code: 004749

2-year for-profit business college in small city.
Enrollment: 469 undergrads, 25% part-time. 105 full-time freshmen.

BASIC COSTS (2006-2007)
Tuition and fees: $12,450.

FINANCIAL AID PICTURE (2004-2005)
Students with need: 57% of average financial aid package awarded as scholarships/grants, 43% awarded as loans/jobs. Need-based aid available for part-time students. Work study available nights, weekends, and for part-time students.
Students without need: This college only awards aid to students with need.

FINANCIAL AID PROCEDURES
Forms required: FAFSA, state aid form.
Dates and Deadlines: No deadline. Applicants notified on a rolling basis.

CONTACT
Judy Harris, Business Office Director
1259 Central Avenue, Albany, NY 12205
(518) 437-1802

Bryant & Stratton College: Syracuse
Syracuse, New York
www.bryantstratton.edu   Federal Code: 008276

2-year for-profit business college in small city.
Enrollment: 633 undergrads.

BASIC COSTS (2006-2007)
Tuition and fees: $12,450.
Per-credit charge: $415.

FINANCIAL AID PICTURE
Students with need: Work study available nights, weekends, and for part-time students.
Students without need: This college only awards aid to students with need.

FINANCIAL AID PROCEDURES
Forms required: FAFSA.
Dates and Deadlines: No deadline. Applicants notified on a rolling basis starting 10/1.
Transfers: Priority date 5/1.

CONTACT
Tami Eiklor, Financial Aid Supervisor
953 James Street, Syracuse, NY 13203
(315) 472-6603

Canisius College
Buffalo, New York
www.canisius.edu   Federal Code: 002681

4-year private liberal arts and teachers college in large city, affiliated with Roman Catholic Church.
Enrollment: 3,395 undergrads, 3% part-time. 774 full-time freshmen.
Selectivity: Admits 50 to 75% of applicants. GED not accepted.

BASIC COSTS (2006-2007)
Tuition and fees: $24,857.
Per-credit charge: $683.
Room and board: $9,480.
Additional info: Tuition/fee waivers available for minority students.

FINANCIAL AID PICTURE (2005-2006)
Students with need: Out of 696 full-time freshmen who applied for aid, 621 were judged to have need. Of these, 619 received aid, and 194 had their full need met. Average financial aid package met 84% of need; average scholarship/grant was $14,812; average loan was $2,996. Need-based aid available for part-time students.
Students without need: 127 full-time freshmen who did not demonstrate need for aid received scholarships/grants; average award was $10,298. No-need awards available for academics, alumni affiliation, art, athletics, job skills, music/drama, religious affiliation, ROTC.
Scholarships offered: *Merit:* Presidential Scholarships: $20,000 per year for four years. Ignatian Scholarships: $15,000 per year for four years; applicants who apply for admission by November 15 given priority consideration. Trustee's Scholarship: $12,000 per year for on-campus student, $10,000 per year for off-campus student; based on high school GPA, test scores. Dean's Scholarship: $10,000 per year for on-campus student, $8,000 per year for off-campus student; based on high school GPA, test scores. Benefactor's Scholarship: $7,000 per year for on-campus student, $5,000 per year for off-campus student; based on high school GPA, test scores. Transfer Scholarships: students accepted for transfer admission automatically evaluated for academic merit scholarship based on college GPA. International Scholarships: international students, including Canadian students, may be eligible for academic scholarships based on academic records. *Athletic:* 22 full-time freshmen received athletic scholarships; average amount $12,246.
Cumulative student debt: 72% of graduating class had student loans; average debt was $21,801.

FINANCIAL AID PROCEDURES
Forms required: FAFSA, state aid form, institutional form.
Dates and Deadlines: Priority date 2/15; no closing date. Applicants notified on a rolling basis starting 3/1; must reply within 2 week(s) of notification.

CONTACT
Curtis Gaume, Director of Student Financial Aid
2001 Main Street, Buffalo, NY 14208-1098
(800) 541-6348

Cayuga County Community College
Auburn, New York
www.cayuga-cc.edu   Federal Code: 002861

2-year public community college in large town.
Enrollment: 2,825 undergrads.
Selectivity: Open admission; but selective for some programs.

BASIC COSTS (2005-2006)
Tuition and fees: $3,327; out-of-state residents $6,227.
Per-credit charge: $105; out-of-state residents $210.

FINANCIAL AID PICTURE
Students with need: Need-based aid available for full-time and part-time students. Work study available nights, weekends, and for part-time students.
Students without need: This college only awards aid to students with need.

FINANCIAL AID PROCEDURES
Forms required: FAFSA, state aid form.
Dates and Deadlines: Closing date 5/1. Applicants notified on a rolling basis starting 6/1.

CONTACT
Judi Miladin, Director of Financial Aid
197 Franklin Street, Auburn, NY 13021-3099
(315) 255-1743 ext. 2470

Cazenovia College
Cazenovia, New York
www.cazenovia.edu   Federal Code: 002685

4-year private liberal arts college in small town.
Enrollment: 919 undergrads, 12% part-time. 285 full-time freshmen.
Selectivity: Admits over 75% of applicants.

BASIC COSTS (2006-2007)
Tuition and fees: $20,180.
Room and board: $8,445.

FINANCIAL AID PICTURE (2005-2006)
Students with need: Out of 265 full-time freshmen who applied for aid, 234 were judged to have need. Of these, 234 received aid, and 43 had their full need met. Average financial aid package met 70% of need; average scholarship/grant was $8,500; average loan was $2,626. Need-based aid available for part-time students.
Students without need: 25 full-time freshmen who did not demonstrate need for aid received scholarships/grants; average award was $5,788. No-need awards available for academics.
Cumulative student debt: 85% of graduating class had student loans; average debt was $27,321.

FINANCIAL AID PROCEDURES
Forms required: FAFSA, state aid form.
Dates and Deadlines: Priority date 3/15; no closing date. Applicants notified on a rolling basis starting 11/1; must reply by 5/1 or within 2 week(s) of notification.
Transfers: No deadline. Applicants notified on a rolling basis starting 11/1; must reply by 5/1 or within 2 week(s) of notification.

CONTACT
Christine Mandel, Director of Financial Aid
3 Sullivan Street, Cazenovia, NY 13035
(315) 655-7887

City University of New York: Baruch College
New York, New York
www.baruch.cuny.edu   Federal Code: 007273

4-year public business and liberal arts college in very large city.
Enrollment: 12,617 undergrads, 23% part-time. 1,625 full-time freshmen.
Selectivity: Admits less than 50% of applicants.

BASIC COSTS (2005-2006)
Tuition and fees: $4,318; out-of-state residents $11,118.
Per-credit charge: $170; out-of-state residents $360.

FINANCIAL AID PICTURE (2005-2006)
Students with need: Out of 1,471 full-time freshmen who applied for aid, 1,240 were judged to have need. Of these, 1,211 received aid, and 310 had their full need met. Average financial aid package met 67% of need; average scholarship/grant was $4,800; average loan was $2,300. For part-time students, average financial aid package was $2,700.
Students without need: 105 full-time freshmen who did not demonstrate need for aid received scholarships/grants; average award was $1,600. No-need awards available for academics, alumni affiliation, state/district residency.
Scholarships offered: *Merit:* Honors college scholarships based on SAT scores and high school GPA. *Athletic:* 240 full-time freshmen received athletic scholarships; average amount $3,000.

FINANCIAL AID PROCEDURES
Forms required: FAFSA, state aid form.
Dates and Deadlines: Priority date 3/15; closing date 4/30. Applicants notified on a rolling basis starting 4/1; must reply by 6/1 or within 6 week(s) of notification.

CONTACT
James Murphy, Vice President, Enrollment and Director of Undergraduate Administration and Financial Aid
One Bernard Baruch Way, Box H-0720, New York, NY 10010-5585
(646) 312-1360

City University of New York: Borough of Manhattan Community College
New York, New York
www.bmcc.cuny.edu   Federal Code: 002691

2-year public community college in very large city.
Enrollment: 17,998 undergrads.
Selectivity: Open admission; but selective for some programs.

BASIC COSTS (2005-2006)
Tuition and fees: $3,066; out-of-state residents $5,966.
Per-credit charge: $120; out-of-state residents $190.

FINANCIAL AID PICTURE (2004-2005)
Students with need: 89% of average financial aid package awarded as scholarships/grants, 11% awarded as loans/jobs. Need-based aid available for part-time students.
Students without need: This college only awards aid to students with need.

FINANCIAL AID PROCEDURES
Forms required: FAFSA, institutional form.
Dates and Deadlines: Priority date 4/15; closing date 5/1. Applicants notified on a rolling basis starting 8/1; must reply within 2 week(s) of notification.

CONTACT
Howard Entin, Director of Financial Aid
199 Chambers Street, New York, NY 10007-1097
(212) 220-1430

City University of New York: Bronx Community College
Bronx, New York
www.bcc.cuny.edu   Federal Code: 002692

2-year public community college in very large city.
Enrollment: 8,186 undergrads, 38% part-time. 1,245 full-time freshmen.

BASIC COSTS (2005-2006)
Tuition and fees: $3,102; out-of-state residents $6,002.
Per-credit charge: $120; out-of-state residents $190.

FINANCIAL AID PICTURE
Students with need: Need-based aid available for full-time students.

FINANCIAL AID PROCEDURES
Forms required: FAFSA.
Dates and Deadlines: Closing date 7/15. Applicants notified on a rolling basis starting 8/1.

CONTACT
Orlando Lopez, Financial Aid Officer
West 181st Street and University Avenue, Bronx, NY 10453
(718) 289-5700

City University of New York: Brooklyn College
Brooklyn, New York
www.brooklyn.cuny.edu   Federal Code: 002687

4-year public liberal arts college in very large city.
Enrollment: 11,068 undergrads, 27% part-time. 1,372 full-time freshmen.
Selectivity: Admits less than 50% of applicants.

BASIC COSTS (2005-2006)
Tuition and fees: $4,375; out-of-state residents $11,175.
Per-credit charge: $170; out-of-state residents $360.

FINANCIAL AID PICTURE (2005-2006)
Students with need: Out of 1,196 full-time freshmen who applied for aid, 1,065 were judged to have need. Of these, 1,065 received aid, and 1,019 had their full need met. Average financial aid package met 99% of need; average scholarship/grant was $3,300; average loan was $2,050. For part-time students, average financial aid package was $2,675.
Students without need: No-need awards available for academics, art, leadership, music/drama, state/district residency.
Scholarships offered: Presidential Scholarship Program: for 25 freshman students for 8 tuition payments totalling $13,000. Brooklyn College Freshman Scholarships: $1,000 per year of study at Brooklyn College. Many scholarships for freshman students based on degree of study, academic merit, and community service.

FINANCIAL AID PROCEDURES
Forms required: FAFSA, state aid form.
Dates and Deadlines: Priority date 4/1; no closing date. Applicants notified on a rolling basis starting 5/1.

CONTACT
Sherwood Johnson, Director of Financial Aid
2900 Bedford Avenue, Brooklyn, NY 11210
(718) 951-5051

City University of New York: City College
New York, New York
www.ccny.cuny.edu   Federal Code: 002688

4-year public university in very large city.
Enrollment: 9,264 undergrads.
Selectivity: Admits over 75% of applicants.

BASIC COSTS (2005-2006)
Tuition and fees: $4,277; out-of-state residents $11,077.
Per-credit charge: $170; out-of-state residents $360.

FINANCIAL AID PICTURE (2005-2006)
Students with need: 62% of average financial aid package awarded as scholarships/grants, 38% awarded as loans/jobs.
Students without need: This college only awards aid to students with need.

FINANCIAL AID PROCEDURES
Forms required: FAFSA.
Dates and Deadlines: Priority date 4/1; no closing date. Applicants notified on a rolling basis starting 4/15.

CONTACT
Thelma Mason, Director of Financial Aid
160 Convent Avenue, New York, NY 10031
(212) 650-7000

City University of New York: College of Staten Island
Staten Island, New York
www.csi.cuny.edu   Federal Code: 002698

4-year public liberal arts college in very large city.
Enrollment: 10,598 undergrads, 31% part-time. 1,887 full-time freshmen.
Selectivity: Admits over 75% of applicants.

BASIC COSTS (2005-2006)
Tuition and fees: $4,326; out-of-state residents $11,126.
Per-credit charge: $170; out-of-state residents $360.

FINANCIAL AID PICTURE (2005-2006)
Students with need: Out of 1,490 full-time freshmen who applied for aid, 1,053 were judged to have need. Of these, 1,017 received aid, and 92 had their full need met. Average financial aid package met 59% of need; average scholarship/grant was $5,087; average loan was $2,526. For part-time students, average financial aid package was $3,946.
Students without need: 177 full-time freshmen who did not demonstrate need for aid received scholarships/grants; average award was $1,929. No-need awards available for academics, art, athletics, job skills, leadership, minority status, music/drama, state/district residency.

FINANCIAL AID PROCEDURES
Forms required: FAFSA, state aid form.
Dates and Deadlines: Closing date 3/31. Applicants notified on a rolling basis starting 6/30.
Transfers: No deadline.

CONTACT
Sherman Whipkey, Director of Financial Aid
2800 Victory Boulevard 2A-104, Staten Island, NY 10314
(718) 982-2030

City University of New York: Hostos Community College
Bronx, New York
www.hostos.cuny.edu   Federal Code: 008611

2-year public community college in very large city.
Enrollment: 4,059 undergrads, 32% part-time. 644 full-time freshmen.
Selectivity: Open admission; but selective for some programs.

BASIC COSTS (2005-2006)
Tuition and fees: $3,104; out-of-state residents $6,004.
Per-credit charge: $120; out-of-state residents $190.

FINANCIAL AID PICTURE (2005-2006)
Students with need: Need-based aid available for full-time and part-time students.

FINANCIAL AID PROCEDURES
Forms required: FAFSA, state aid form, institutional form.
Dates and Deadlines: Priority date 7/1; no closing date. Applicants notified on a rolling basis; must reply within 3 week(s) of notification.

CONTACT
Joseph Alicea, Director of Financial Aid
120 East 149th Street, Room D210, Bronx, NY 10451
(718) 518-6555

City University of New York: Hunter College
New York, New York
www.hunter.cuny.edu   Federal Code: 002689

4-year public liberal arts college in very large city.
Enrollment: 14,357 undergrads, 28% part-time. 1,820 full-time freshmen.
Selectivity: Admits less than 50% of applicants.

BASIC COSTS (2005-2006)
Tuition and fees: $4,347; out-of-state residents $11,147.
Per-credit charge: $170; out-of-state residents $360.
Room only: $3,129.
Additional info: Dormitory availability very limited.

FINANCIAL AID PICTURE (2004-2005)
Students with need: Out of 1,476 full-time freshmen who applied for aid, 1,213 were judged to have need. Of these, 1,180 received aid, and 1,077 had their full need met. Average financial aid package met 68% of need; average scholarship/grant was $5,921; average loan was $2,322. For part-time students, average financial aid package was $4,005.
Students without need: 4 full-time freshmen who did not demonstrate need for aid received scholarships/grants. No-need awards available for academics.

FINANCIAL AID PROCEDURES
Forms required: FAFSA, state aid form.
Dates and Deadlines: Priority date 5/1; no closing date. Applicants notified on a rolling basis starting 5/15.

CONTACT
Aristalia Rodriguez, Director of Financial Aid
695 Park Avenue, New York, NY 10021
(212) 772-4820

City University of New York: John Jay College of Criminal Justice
New York, New York
www.jjay.cuny.edu   Federal Code: 002693

4-year public college of criminal justice and public safety in very large city.
Enrollment: 12,278 undergrads, 24% part-time. 2,659 full-time freshmen.
Selectivity: Admits over 75% of applicants.

BASIC COSTS (2005-2006)
Tuition and fees: $4,278; out-of-state residents $11,078.
Per-credit charge: $170; out-of-state residents $360.

FINANCIAL AID PICTURE (2004-2005)
Students with need: Out of 2,400 full-time freshmen who applied for aid, 2,400 were judged to have need. Of these, 2,226 received aid. Average financial aid package met 85% of need; average scholarship/grant was $2,770. For part-time students, average financial aid package was $6,375.
Students without need: No-need awards available for academics, state/district residency.
Cumulative student debt: 45% of graduating class had student loans; average debt was $13,240.

FINANCIAL AID PROCEDURES
Forms required: FAFSA.
Dates and Deadlines: No deadline. Applicants notified on a rolling basis starting 7/15; must reply within 2 week(s) of notification.

CONTACT
Arnold Osansky, Director of Financial Aid
445 West 59th Street, New York, NY 10019
(212) 237-8151

City University of New York: Kingsborough Community College
Brooklyn, New York
www.kbcc.cuny.edu   Federal Code: 002694

2-year public community college in very large city.
Enrollment: 10,751 undergrads.
Selectivity: Open admission.

BASIC COSTS (2005-2006)
Tuition and fees: $3,098; out-of-state residents $5,998.
Per-credit charge: $120; out-of-state residents $190.

FINANCIAL AID PICTURE
Students with need: Need-based aid available for full-time and part-time students.
Students without need: This college only awards aid to students with need.

FINANCIAL AID PROCEDURES
Forms required: FAFSA.
Dates and Deadlines: Closing date 4/30. Applicants notified on a rolling basis; must reply within 2 week(s) of notification.

CONTACT
Wayne Harewood, Director of Financial Aid
2001 Oriental Boulevard, Brooklyn, NY 11235
(718) 368-4644

City University of New York: LaGuardia Community College
Long Island City, New York
www.lagcc.cuny.edu   Federal Code: 010051

2-year public community college in very large city.
Enrollment: 11,285 undergrads, 40% part-time. 1,774 full-time freshmen.
Selectivity: Open admission.

BASIC COSTS (2005-2006)
Tuition and fees: $3,090; out-of-state residents $5,990.
Per-credit charge: $120; out-of-state residents $190.

FINANCIAL AID PICTURE (2005-2006)
Students with need: 83% of average financial aid package awarded as scholarships/grants, 17% awarded as loans/jobs. Need-based aid available for part-time students. Work study available nights, weekends, and for part-time students.
Students without need: This college only awards aid to students with need.
Cumulative student debt: 4% of graduating class had student loans; average debt was $6,498.

FINANCIAL AID PROCEDURES
Forms required: FAFSA, state aid form.
Dates and Deadlines: No deadline. Applicants notified on a rolling basis starting 8/1; must reply within 4 week(s) of notification.

CONTACT
Gail Baksh-Jarrett, Director of Financial Aid
31-10 Thomson Avenue, Long Island City, NY 11101
(718) 482-7200

City University of New York: Lehman College
Bronx, New York
www.lehman.cuny.edu   Federal Code: 007022

4-year public liberal arts college in very large city.
Enrollment: 7,805 undergrads, 35% part-time. 851 full-time freshmen.
Selectivity: Admits less than 50% of applicants.

BASIC COSTS (2005-2006)
Tuition and fees: $4,288; out-of-state residents $11,088.
Per-credit charge: $170; out-of-state residents $360.

FINANCIAL AID PICTURE (2004-2005)
Students with need: Out of 777 full-time freshmen who applied for aid, 775 were judged to have need. Of these, 773 received aid, and 12 had their full need met. Average financial aid package met 72% of need; average scholarship/grant was $1,609; average loan was $1,202. For part-time students, average financial aid package was $1,696.
Students without need: This college only awards aid to students with need.

FINANCIAL AID PROCEDURES
Forms required: FAFSA, state aid form.
Dates and Deadlines: No deadline. Applicants notified on a rolling basis starting 3/1.
Transfers: Applicants notified on a rolling basis starting 3/1.

CONTACT
David Martinez, Director of Financial Aid
250 Bedford Park Boulevard West, Bronx, NY 10468
(718) 960-8545

City University of New York: Medgar Evers College
Brooklyn, New York
www.mec.cuny.edu
Federal Code: 010097

4-year public liberal arts college in very large city.
Enrollment: 4,841 undergrads, 35% part-time. 696 full-time freshmen.
Selectivity: Open admission; but selective for some programs.

BASIC COSTS (2005-2006)
Tuition and fees: $4,250; out-of-state residents $11,050.
Per-credit charge: $170; out-of-state residents $360.

FINANCIAL AID PICTURE (2005-2006)
Students with need: 89% of average financial aid package awarded as scholarships/grants, 11% awarded as loans/jobs. Need-based aid available for part-time students. Work study available weekends and for part-time students.

FINANCIAL AID PROCEDURES
Forms required: FAFSA, state aid form.
Dates and Deadlines: No deadline. Applicants notified on a rolling basis; must reply by 3/5 or within 2 week(s) of notification.
Transfers: Priority date 3/6.

CONTACT
Conley James, Director of Financial Aid
1665 Bedford Avenue, Brooklyn, NY 11225-2201
(718) 270-6139

City University of New York: New York City College of Technology
Brooklyn, New York
www.citytech.cuny.edu
Federal Code: 002696

4-year public technical college in very large city.
Enrollment: 11,795 undergrads, 40% part-time. 2,171 full-time freshmen.
Selectivity: Open admission; but selective for some programs.

BASIC COSTS (2005-2006)
Tuition and fees: $4,287; out-of-state residents $11,087.
Per-credit charge: $170; out-of-state residents $360.

FINANCIAL AID PICTURE (2005-2006)
Students with need: 74% of average financial aid package awarded as scholarships/grants, 26% awarded as loans/jobs. Need-based aid available for part-time students.
Students without need: No-need awards available for state/district residency.
Additional info: Foreign students applying for aid must have resided in New York for at least a year.

FINANCIAL AID PROCEDURES
Forms required: FAFSA.
Dates and Deadlines: Priority date 5/15; no closing date.

CONTACT
Sandra Higgins, Director of Financial Aid
300 Jay Street Namm G17, Brooklyn, NY 11201
(718) 260-5700

City University of New York: Queens College
Flushing, New York
www.qc.cuny.edu
Federal Code: 002690

4-year public liberal arts college in very large city.
Enrollment: 12,320 undergrads, 28% part-time. 1,470 full-time freshmen.
Selectivity: Admits less than 50% of applicants.

BASIC COSTS (2005-2006)
Tuition and fees: $4,375; out-of-state residents $11,175.
Per-credit charge: $170; out-of-state residents $360.

FINANCIAL AID PICTURE (2005-2006)
Students with need: Average financial aid package met 77% of need; average scholarship/grant was $1,250; average loan was $2,625. For part-time students, average financial aid package was $5,400.
Students without need: No-need awards available for academics, athletics, music/drama, state/district residency.
Scholarships offered: CUNY Honors College: full tuition. Regents Award for Deceased or Disabled Veterans: $450 per year. Vietnam Veteran Tuition Aid Program: cost of tuition per semester. Regents Award for children of deceased police officers, firefighters, or corrections officers: $450 per year. Paul Douglas Teacher Scholarship Program: up to $5,000 per year. State Aid to Native Americans: $1,100 per year. SEEK Presidential Scholarship; Beinstock Memorial Scholarship for students with disabilities; CMP Publications Scholarship in Journalism or English; Daly Scholarship in the Physical Sciences; Foster Scholarship for women and minorities; Kupferberg Memorial Scholarship; Linakis Scholarship; Mitsui USA Scholarships; Nagdimon Scholarship; Queens College Scholarships; Weprin Memorial Scholarship in the Public Interest.
Cumulative student debt: 40% of graduating class had student loans; average debt was $12,000.

FINANCIAL AID PROCEDURES
Forms required: FAFSA, state aid form, institutional form.
Dates and Deadlines: Priority date 2/1; no closing date. Applicants notified on a rolling basis starting 3/1; must reply within 3 week(s) of notification.
Transfers: Priority date 5/1; no deadline. Applicants notified on a rolling basis.

CONTACT
Rena Smith-Kiawu, Director of Financial Aid
65-30 Kissena Boulevard, Jefferson 117, Flushing, NY 11367-1597
(718) 997-5123

City University of New York: Queensborough Community College
Bayside, New York
www.qcc.cuny.edu
Federal Code: 002697

2-year public community college in very large city.
Enrollment: 10,695 undergrads, 42% part-time. 2,072 full-time freshmen.
Selectivity: Open admission.

BASIC COSTS (2005-2006)
Tuition and fees: $3,084; out-of-state residents $5,984.
Per-credit charge: $120; out-of-state residents $190.

FINANCIAL AID PICTURE (2004-2005)
Students with need: Need-based aid available for full-time students.

FINANCIAL AID PROCEDURES
Forms required: FAFSA, institutional form.
Dates and Deadlines: No deadline. Applicants notified on a rolling basis starting 7/15.

CONTACT
Veronica Lukas, Director of Financial Aid
Springfield Boulevard & 56th Avenue, Bayside, NY 11364-1497
(718) 631-6262

City University of New York: York College
Jamaica, New York
www.york.cuny.edu   Federal Code: 004759

4-year public liberal arts college in very large city.
Enrollment: 5,753 undergrads, 33% part-time. 747 full-time freshmen.

BASIC COSTS (2005-2006)
Tuition and fees: $4,260; out-of-state residents $11,060.
Per-credit charge: $170; out-of-state residents $360.

FINANCIAL AID PICTURE (2004-2005)
Students with need: Out of 619 full-time freshmen who applied for aid, 552 were judged to have need. Of these, 538 received aid, and 1 had their full need met. Average financial aid package met 32% of need; average scholarship/grant was $3,017; average loan was $1,791. For part-time students, average financial aid package was $1,773.

FINANCIAL AID PROCEDURES
Forms required: FAFSA, state aid form.
Dates and Deadlines: Priority date 5/1; no closing date. Applicants notified on a rolling basis starting 3/1.
Transfers: No deadline. Applicants notified on a rolling basis starting 3/1.

CONTACT
Cathy Tsiapanos, Director of Financial Aid
94-20 Guy R. Brewer Boulevard, Jamaica, NY 11451-9989
(718) 262-2000 ext. 2230

Clarkson University
Potsdam, New York
www.clarkson.edu   Federal Code: 002699

4-year private university in large town.
Enrollment: 2,624 undergrads. 630 full-time freshmen.
Selectivity: Admits over 75% of applicants.

BASIC COSTS (2006-2007)
Tuition and fees: $27,090.
Per-credit charge: $889.
Room and board: $9,648.
Additional info: Tuition/fee waivers available for minority students.

FINANCIAL AID PICTURE (2005-2006)
Students with need: Average financial aid package met 87% of need; average scholarship/grant was $13,588; average loan was $2,926. Need-based aid available for part-time students.
Students without need: No-need awards available for academics, alumni affiliation, leadership, minority status, ROTC.
Cumulative student debt: 81% of graduating class had student loans; average debt was $19,942.

FINANCIAL AID PROCEDURES
Forms required: FAFSA, state aid form, institutional form.
Dates and Deadlines: Priority date 3/1; no closing date. Applicants notified on a rolling basis starting 3/23; must reply by 5/1 or within 2 week(s) of notification.
Transfers: Closing date 4/15. Applicants notified on a rolling basis. Presidential Scholarships, Phi Theta Kappa scholarships and Alpha Beta Gamma Awards available, in addition to state and federal programs.

CONTACT
April Grant, Assoc. Director of Financial Assistance
Holcroft House, Potsdam, NY 13699-5605
(315) 268-6400

Clinton Community College
Plattsburgh, New York
www.clinton.edu   Federal Code: 006787

2-year public community college in large town.
Enrollment: 1,494 full-time undergrads.
Selectivity: Open admission; but selective for some programs.

BASIC COSTS (2005-2006)
Tuition and fees: $3,236; out-of-state residents $7,766.
Per-credit charge: $125; out-of-state residents $312.

FINANCIAL AID PICTURE (2005-2006)
Students with need: 65% of average financial aid package awarded as scholarships/grants, 35% awarded as loans/jobs. Need-based aid available for part-time students.
Students without need: This college only awards aid to students with need.

FINANCIAL AID PROCEDURES
Forms required: FAFSA, state aid form.
Dates and Deadlines: Priority date 6/2; no closing date. Applicants notified on a rolling basis starting 5/1; must reply within 2 week(s) of notification.

CONTACT
Karen Burnam, Director of Financial Aid
136 Clinton Point Drive, Plattsburgh, NY 12901-4297
(518) 562-4125

Cochran School of Nursing-St. John's Riverside Hospital
Yonkers, New York
www.riversidehealth.org   Federal Code: 006443

2-year private nursing college in small city.
Enrollment: 309 undergrads, 52% part-time.

BASIC COSTS (2006-2007)
Additional info: Tuition and fees for full 2-year AAS program $20,149.

FINANCIAL AID PICTURE (2005-2006)
Students with need: 27% of average financial aid package awarded as scholarships/grants, 73% awarded as loans/jobs. Need-based aid available for part-time students.
Students without need: This college only awards aid to students with need.

FINANCIAL AID PROCEDURES
Forms required: FAFSA.
Dates and Deadlines: No deadline. Applicants notified on a rolling basis.

CONTACT
Geraldine Owens, Financial Aid Officer
967 North Broadway, Yonkers, NY 10701
(914) 964-4265

Colgate University
Hamilton, New York
www.colgate.edu
Federal Code: 002701
CSS Code: 2086

4-year private liberal arts college in small town.
Enrollment: 2,743 undergrads. 729 full-time freshmen.
Selectivity: Admits less than 50% of applicants.

BASIC COSTS (2006-2007)
Tuition and fees: $35,030.
Room and board: $8,530.

FINANCIAL AID PICTURE (2005-2006)
Students with need: Out of 272 full-time freshmen who applied for aid, 219 were judged to have need. Of these, 219 received aid, and 219 had their full need met. Average financial aid package met 100% of need; average scholarship/grant was $27,326; average loan was $2,571.
Students without need: No-need awards available for athletics.
Scholarships offered: 37 full-time freshmen received athletic scholarships; average amount $29,825.
Cumulative student debt: 38% of graduating class had student loans; average debt was $13,452.

FINANCIAL AID PROCEDURES
Forms required: FAFSA, CSS PROFILE.
Dates and Deadlines: Closing date 1/15. Applicants notified by 4/1; must reply by 5/1 or within 2 week(s) of notification.
Transfers: Closing date 3/15. Applicants notified by 4/30; must reply by 5/15 or within 2 week(s) of notification. Financial aid for transfer students extremely limited.

CONTACT
Marcelle Tyburski, Director of Financial Aid
13 Oak Drive, Hamilton, NY 13346-1383
(315) 228-7431

College of Mount St. Vincent
Riverdale, New York
www.mountsaintvincent.edu
Federal Code: 002703

4-year private liberal arts college in very large city, affiliated with Roman Catholic Church.
Enrollment: 1,423 undergrads, 12% part-time. 353 full-time freshmen.
Selectivity: Admits 50 to 75% of applicants.

BASIC COSTS (2006-2007)
Tuition and fees: $21,550.
Per-credit charge: $660.
Room and board: $8,500.

FINANCIAL AID PICTURE (2005-2006)
Students with need: Out of 333 full-time freshmen who applied for aid, 288 were judged to have need. Of these, 288 received aid. Average financial aid package met 74% of need; average scholarship/grant was $8,553; average loan was $2,500. Need-based aid available for part-time students.
Students without need: This college only awards aid to students with need.
Cumulative student debt: 80% of graduating class had student loans; average debt was $17,000.

FINANCIAL AID PROCEDURES
Forms required: FAFSA, state aid form.
Dates and Deadlines: Priority date 3/1; no closing date. Applicants notified on a rolling basis starting 3/1; must reply by 5/1 or within 3 week(s) of notification.
Transfers: Priority date 5/15. Applicants notified on a rolling basis starting 3/1; must reply by 5/1 or within 3 week(s) of notification.

CONTACT
Monica Simotas, Director of Financial Aid
6301 Riverdale Avenue, Riverdale, NY 10471-1093
(718) 405-3289

College of New Rochelle
New Rochelle, New York
www.cnr.edu
Federal Code: 002704

4-year private nursing and liberal arts college for women in small city, affiliated with Roman Catholic Church.
Enrollment: 1,041 undergrads, 32% part-time. 138 full-time freshmen.
Selectivity: Admits less than 50% of applicants.

BASIC COSTS (2006-2007)
Tuition and fees: $21,910.
Per-credit charge: $722.
Room and board: $8,200.
Additional info: Tuition for incoming students includes required laptop for each student.

FINANCIAL AID PICTURE (2004-2005)
Students with need: Out of 136 full-time freshmen who applied for aid, 122 were judged to have need. Of these, 122 received aid, and 122 had their full need met. Average financial aid package met 100% of need; average scholarship/grant was $11,882; average loan was $8,626. For part-time students, average financial aid package was $6,598.
Students without need: 13 full-time freshmen who did not demonstrate need for aid received scholarships/grants; average award was $10,969. No-need awards available for academics, art, leadership.

FINANCIAL AID PROCEDURES
Forms required: FAFSA, institutional form.
Dates and Deadlines: Priority date 3/1; no closing date. Applicants notified on a rolling basis starting 1/1; must reply within 2 week(s) of notification.

CONTACT
Ann Pelak, Director of Financial Aid
29 Castle Place, New Rochelle, NY 10805-2339
(914) 654-5225

College of Saint Rose
Albany, New York
www.strose.edu
Federal Code: 002705

4-year private liberal arts and teachers college in small city, affiliated with Roman Catholic Church.
Enrollment: 3,005 undergrads, 7% part-time. 535 full-time freshmen.
Selectivity: Admits 50 to 75% of applicants.

BASIC COSTS (2006-2007)
Tuition and fees: $19,268.
Room and board: $8,116.

FINANCIAL AID PICTURE (2004-2005)
Students with need: Out of 510 full-time freshmen who applied for aid, 441 were judged to have need. Of these, 440 received aid, and 18 had their full need met. Average financial aid package met 59% of need; average scholarship/grant was $3,520; average loan was $1,278. For part-time students, average financial aid package was $4,079.
Students without need: 59 full-time freshmen who did not demonstrate need for aid received scholarships/grants; average award was $1,878. No-need awards available for academics, alumni affiliation, art, athletics, minority status, music/drama.
Scholarships offered: *Merit:* Rooney Gibbons Scholarship; award amounts range from $2,000 to full tuition; freshmen applicants admitted by February 1

automatically considered. **Athletic:** 5 full-time freshmen received athletic scholarships; average amount $3,250.

FINANCIAL AID PROCEDURES
Forms required: FAFSA.
Dates and Deadlines: Priority date 3/1; closing date 10/1. Applicants notified on a rolling basis starting 3/15; must reply by 5/1 or within 2 week(s) of notification.

CONTACT
James Vallee, Director of Financial Aid
432 Western Avenue, Albany, NY 12203
(518) 458-5424

College of Westchester
White Plains, New York
www.cw.edu   Federal Code: 005208

2-year for-profit business college in large town.
Enrollment: 1,034 undergrads, 20% part-time. 197 full-time freshmen.

BASIC COSTS (2006-2007)
Tuition and fees: $19,125.
Per-credit charge: $420.
Additional info: Tuition/fee waivers available for unemployed or children of unemployed.

FINANCIAL AID PICTURE
Students with need: Need-based aid available for full-time and part-time students. Work study available nights, weekends, and for part-time students.
Students without need: No-need awards available for academics, alumni affiliation.

FINANCIAL AID PROCEDURES
Forms required: FAFSA, state aid form, institutional form.
Dates and Deadlines: No deadline. Applicants notified on a rolling basis starting 1/6; must reply within 2 week(s) of notification.

CONTACT
Dianne Pepitone, Director, Student Financial Services
325 Central Park Avenue, White Plains, NY 10602
(914) 948-4442 ext. 473

Columbia University: Columbia College
New York, New York   Federal Code: E00485
www.college.columbia.edu   CSS Code: 2116

4-year private university and liberal arts college in very large city.
Enrollment: 4,225 undergrads. 1,024 full-time freshmen.
Selectivity: Admits less than 50% of applicants.

BASIC COSTS (2005-2006)
Tuition and fees: $33,246.
Room and board: $9,338.

FINANCIAL AID PICTURE (2005-2006)
Students with need: Out of 622 full-time freshmen who applied for aid, 546 were judged to have need. Of these, 546 received aid, and 546 had their full need met. Average financial aid package met 100% of need; average scholarship/grant was $25,440; average loan was $3,257.
Students without need: This college only awards aid to students with need.
Cumulative student debt: 37% of graduating class had student loans; average debt was $13,870.

FINANCIAL AID PROCEDURES
Forms required: FAFSA, CSS PROFILE, institutional form.
Dates and Deadlines: Closing date 2/10. Applicants notified by 4/1; must reply by 5/1.
Transfers: Closing date 4/1. Institutional financial aid for transfer candidates limited at this time.

CONTACT
David Charlow, Director of Student Affairs/Financial Aid
1130 Amsterdam Avenue MC2807, New York, NY 10027
(212) 854-3711

Columbia University: Fu Foundation School of Engineering and Applied Science
New York, New York   Federal Code: E00486
www.engineering.columbia.edu   CSS Code: 2111

4-year private engineering college in very large city.
Enrollment: 1,430 undergrads. 315 full-time freshmen.
Selectivity: Admits less than 50% of applicants.

BASIC COSTS (2005-2006)
Tuition and fees: $33,246.
Room and board: $9,338.

FINANCIAL AID PICTURE (2005-2006)
Students with need: Out of 208 full-time freshmen who applied for aid, 187 were judged to have need. Of these, 187 received aid, and 187 had their full need met. Average financial aid package met 100% of need; average scholarship/grant was $24,180; average loan was $3,375.
Students without need: This college only awards aid to students with need.
Cumulative student debt: 41% of graduating class had student loans; average debt was $14,227.

FINANCIAL AID PROCEDURES
Forms required: FAFSA, CSS PROFILE, institutional form.
Dates and Deadlines: Closing date 2/10. Applicants notified by 4/1; must reply by 5/1.
Transfers: Closing date 4/1. Institutional financial aid very limited for transfer applicants.

CONTACT
David Charlow, Dean, Student Affairs/Director, Financial Aid
1130 Amsterdam Avenue, MC2807, New York, NY 10027
(212) 854-3711

Columbia University: School of General Studies
New York, New York
www.gs.columbia.edu   Federal Code: E00487

4-year private university and liberal arts college in very large city.
Enrollment: 1,146 undergrads, 44% part-time. 20 full-time freshmen.
Selectivity: Admits less than 50% of applicants.

BASIC COSTS (2005-2006)
Tuition and fees: $31,765.
Per-credit charge: $1,030.
Additional info: Institutionally managed double-occupancy apartments available starting at $600/month.

FINANCIAL AID PICTURE (2004-2005)
Students with need: 48% of average financial aid package awarded as scholarships/grants, 52% awarded as loans/jobs. Need-based aid available for part-time students.

Students without need: This college only awards aid to students with need.
Scholarships offered: All applicants should submit General Studies Application for Financial Aid.

FINANCIAL AID PROCEDURES
Forms required: FAFSA, institutional form.
Dates and Deadlines: Priority date 4/15; closing date 6/1. Applicants notified on a rolling basis; must reply within 2 week(s) of notification.
Transfers: Applicants notified on a rolling basis starting 4/1; must reply within 2 week(s) of notification.

CONTACT
William Bailey, Director of Educational Financing
408 Lewisohn Hall, Mail Code 4101, 2970 Broadway, New York, NY 10027
(212) 854-5410

Columbia University: School of Nursing
New York, New York
www.nursing.hs.columbia.edu   Federal Code: E00124

Upper-division private university and nursing college in very large city.
Enrollment: 2 undergrads.

BASIC COSTS (2006-2007)
Tuition and fees: $30,853.
Room only: $4,600.
Additional info: Tuition at time of enrollment locked for 2 years.

FINANCIAL AID PICTURE
Students with need: Need-based aid available for full-time and part-time students.

FINANCIAL AID PROCEDURES
Forms required: FAFSA.
Dates and Deadlines: No deadline. Applicants notified on a rolling basis starting 1/1; must reply within 2 week(s) of notification.

CONTACT
Oscar Vasquez, Director of Financial Aid
630 West 168th Street, New York, NY 10032
(212) 305-5756

Columbia-Greene Community College
Hudson, New York
www.sunycgcc.edu   Federal Code: 006789

2-year public community college in small town.
Enrollment: 963 full-time undergrads.
Selectivity: Open admission; but selective for some programs.

BASIC COSTS (2005-2006)
Tuition and fees: $3,042; out-of-state residents $5,874.
Per-credit charge: $118; out-of-state residents $236.

FINANCIAL AID PICTURE
Students with need: Need-based aid available for full-time and part-time students. Work study available nights, weekends, and for part-time students.
Students without need: No-need awards available for academics, state/district residency.

FINANCIAL AID PROCEDURES
Forms required: FAFSA, institutional form.
Dates and Deadlines: Priority date 5/1; no closing date. Applicants notified on a rolling basis starting 7/1; must reply within 2 week(s) of notification.

CONTACT
Earl Tretheway, Director of Financial Aid
4400 Route 23, Hudson, NY 12534

Concordia College
Bronxville, New York
www.concordia-ny.edu   Federal Code: 002709

4-year private liberal arts college in small town, affiliated with Lutheran Church - Missouri Synod.
Enrollment: 533 undergrads, 2% part-time. 189 full-time freshmen.
Selectivity: Admits 50 to 75% of applicants.

BASIC COSTS (2006-2007)
Tuition and fees: $20,700.
Room and board: $8,230.

FINANCIAL AID PICTURE
Students with need: Need-based aid available for full-time and part-time students. Work study available nights, weekends, and for part-time students.
Students without need: No-need awards available for academics, athletics, leadership, music/drama.
Scholarships offered: Fellows Scholarship at $8,000 a year for 1200 SAT (exclusive of writing) and 95 average. Merit scholarships ranging between $4,000-6,000 for 80 average and above. Athletic, leadership, academic, and music scholarships and Lutheran students grants available.

FINANCIAL AID PROCEDURES
Forms required: FAFSA, state aid form.
Dates and Deadlines: Priority date 4/1; no closing date. Applicants notified on a rolling basis starting 4/1; must reply by 5/1 or within 3 week(s) of notification.

CONTACT
Kenneth Fick, Director of Financial Aid
171 White Plains Road, Bronxville, NY 10708
(914) 337-9300

Cooper Union for the Advancement of Science and Art
New York, New York
www.cooper.edu   Federal Code: 002710
                       CSS Code: 2097

4-year private visual arts and engineering college in very large city.
Enrollment: 929 undergrads. 216 full-time freshmen.
Selectivity: Admits less than 50% of applicants.

BASIC COSTS (2006-2007)
Tuition and fees: $31,500.
Room only: $9,360.
Additional info: Every student admitted receives full tuition scholarship, covering tuition only, for duration of enrollment.

FINANCIAL AID PICTURE (2004-2005)
Students with need: Average financial aid package met 90% of need; average scholarship/grant was $3,323; average loan was $1,848.
Students without need: No-need awards available for academics.
Cumulative student debt: 32% of graduating class had student loans; average debt was $11,617.
Additional info: All students receive full-tuition scholarships. Students able to document need receive financial aid package that may include combination of grants, loans, work-study, internships.

FINANCIAL AID PROCEDURES
Forms required: FAFSA, CSS PROFILE.

Dates and Deadlines: Priority date 4/15; closing date 6/1. Applicants notified by 6/1; must reply by 6/30 or within 2 week(s) of notification.

CONTACT
Mary Ruokonen, Director of Financial Aid
30 Cooper Square, Suite 300, New York, NY 10003-7183
(212) 353-4130

Cornell University
Ithaca, New York
www.cornell.edu
Federal Code: 002711
CSS Code: 2098

4-year private university in large town.
Enrollment: 13,474 undergrads. 3,076 full-time freshmen.
Selectivity: Admits less than 50% of applicants.

BASIC COSTS (2006-2007)
Tuition and fees: $32,981.
Room and board: $10,726.
Additional info: Tuition amounts listed are for Endowed/Private colleges only: Architecture, Art & Planning; Arts & Sciences; Engineering; Hotel Administration. Contract/State college amounts differ and vary by program.

FINANCIAL AID PICTURE (2005-2006)
Students with need: Out of 1,967 full-time freshmen who applied for aid, 1,499 were judged to have need. Of these, 1,499 received aid, and 1,499 had their full need met. Average financial aid package met 100% of need; average scholarship/grant was $21,000; average loan was $6,300.
Students without need: This college only awards aid to students with need.
Cumulative student debt: 54% of graduating class had student loans; average debt was $23,450.

FINANCIAL AID PROCEDURES
Forms required: FAFSA, CSS PROFILE, institutional form.
Dates and Deadlines: Closing date 2/11. Applicants notified by 4/1; must reply by 5/1 or within 2 week(s) of notification.
Transfers: Submit Cornell aid application forms in addition to regular required forms.

CONTACT
Thomas Keane, Director, Financial Aid and Student Employment
410 Thurston Avenue, Ithaca, NY 14853-2488
(607) 255-2000

Corning Community College
Corning, New York
www.corning-cc.edu
Federal Code: 002863

2-year public community college in large town.
Enrollment: 3,500 undergrads.
Selectivity: Open admission; but selective for some programs.

BASIC COSTS (2005-2006)
Tuition and fees: $3,448; out-of-state residents $6,548.
Per-credit charge: $129; out-of-state residents $258.

FINANCIAL AID PICTURE
Students with need: Need-based aid available for full-time and part-time students. Work study available weekends and for part-time students.
Students without need: This college only awards aid to students with need.

FINANCIAL AID PROCEDURES
Forms required: FAFSA.
Dates and Deadlines: Priority date 4/1; no closing date. Applicants notified on a rolling basis starting 4/15; must reply within 2 week(s) of notification.

CONTACT
Barbara Snow, Director of Financial Aid
One Academic Drive, Corning, NY 14830
(607) 962-9011

Culinary Institute of America
Hyde Park, New York
www.ciachef.edu
Federal Code: 007304

4-year private culinary school in large town.
Enrollment: 2,713 undergrads.
Selectivity: Admits 50 to 75% of applicants.

BASIC COSTS (2005-2006)
Tuition and fees: $20,775.
Room and board: $6,820.

FINANCIAL AID PICTURE (2004-2005)
Students with need: Average financial aid package for all full-time undergraduates was $10,663. 31% awarded as scholarships/grants, 69% awarded as loans/jobs. Work study available nights, weekends, and for part-time students.
Students without need: No-need awards available for academics, alumni affiliation, job skills, leadership, minority status.
Scholarships offered: Cream of the Crop Scholarship; up to $20,000; 10 per year; for prospective students with outstanding academic and leadership skills.

FINANCIAL AID PROCEDURES
Forms required: FAFSA.
Dates and Deadlines: Closing date 2/15. Applicants notified by 4/1; must reply by 5/1 or within 4 week(s) of notification.

CONTACT
Patricia Arcuri, Director of Financial Aid
1946 Campus Drive, Hyde Park, NY 12538-1499
(845) 451-1243

Daemen College
Amherst, New York
www.daemen.edu
Federal Code: 002808

4-year private liberal arts college in small city.
Enrollment: 1,440 undergrads, 12% part-time. 264 full-time freshmen.
Selectivity: Admits over 75% of applicants.

BASIC COSTS (2005-2006)
Tuition and fees: $16,800.
Per-credit charge: $545.
Room and board: $7,780.

FINANCIAL AID PICTURE (2004-2005)
Students with need: Out of 223 full-time freshmen who applied for aid, 211 were judged to have need. Of these, 211 received aid, and 45 had their full need met. Average financial aid package met 88% of need; average scholarship/grant was $7,484; average loan was $3,231. For part-time students, average financial aid package was $6,233.
Students without need: 10 full-time freshmen who did not demonstrate need for aid received scholarships/grants; average award was $5,035. No-need awards available for academics, alumni affiliation, art, athletics.
Scholarships offered: *Merit:* President's Scholarship, Dean's Scholarship, and Alumni Grant; $3,000-$10,000; based on high school GPA, SAT scores, and resident status. Daemen College Trustee Scholarship; two $15,000 awards; four $12,000 awards. Visual Arts Scholarship; two $5,000 awards.
Athletic: 9 full-time freshmen received athletic scholarships; average amount $3,389.

Cumulative student debt: 74% of graduating class had student loans; average debt was $13,323.

FINANCIAL AID PROCEDURES
Forms required: FAFSA, state aid form.
Dates and Deadlines: Priority date 2/15; no closing date. Applicants notified on a rolling basis starting 2/1; must reply within 2 week(s) of notification.

CONTACT
Jeffrey Pagano, Director of Financial Aid
4380 Main Street, Amherst, NY 14226-3592
(716) 839-8254

DeVry Institute of Technology: New York
Long Island City, New York
http://www.ny.devry.edu/   Federal Code: 003099

4-year for-profit business and technical college in very large city.
Enrollment: 1,264 undergrads, 26% part-time. 257 full-time freshmen.

BASIC COSTS (2005-2006)
Tuition and fees: $13,410.
Per-credit charge: $475.

FINANCIAL AID PICTURE
Students with need: Need-based aid available for full-time and part-time students.
Students without need: This college only awards aid to students with need.

FINANCIAL AID PROCEDURES
Forms required: FAFSA.
Dates and Deadlines: No deadline. Applicants notified on a rolling basis.

CONTACT
Elvira Senese, Director, Student Finance
3020 Thomson Avenue, Long Island City, NY 11101-3051
(718) 472-2728

Dominican College of Blauvelt
Orangeburg, New York
www.dc.edu   Federal Code: 002713

4-year private health science and liberal arts college in small town, affiliated with Roman Catholic Church.
Enrollment: 1,386 undergrads, 23% part-time. 289 full-time freshmen.
Selectivity: Admits over 75% of applicants.

BASIC COSTS (2005-2006)
Tuition and fees: $17,910.
Per-credit charge: $515.
Room and board: $8,720.

FINANCIAL AID PICTURE (2005-2006)
Students with need: Average financial aid package met 76% of need; average scholarship/grant was $10,584; average loan was $2,766. For part-time students, average financial aid package was $5,637.
Students without need: No-need awards available for academics, athletics.
Scholarships offered: All applicants will be considered for non-need based scholarships or grants based on high school GPA and SAT/ACT scores.
Additional info: Individual financial aid counseling available.

FINANCIAL AID PROCEDURES
Forms required: FAFSA, state aid form, institutional form.
Dates and Deadlines: Priority date 2/15; no closing date. Applicants notified on a rolling basis starting 2/1.

CONTACT
Eileen Felske, Director of Financial Aid
470 Western Highway, Orangeburg, NY 10962-1210
(845) 359-7800 ext. 226

Dowling College
Oakdale, New York
www.dowling.edu   Federal Code: 002667

4-year private liberal arts college in large town.
Enrollment: 3,627 undergrads, 37% part-time. 441 full-time freshmen.
Selectivity: Admits over 75% of applicants.

BASIC COSTS (2005-2006)
Tuition and fees: $17,040.
Per-credit charge: $540.
Room only: $5,800.

FINANCIAL AID PICTURE (2005-2006)
Students with need: Out of 373 full-time freshmen who applied for aid, 309 were judged to have need. Of these, 306 received aid, and 16 had their full need met. Average financial aid package met 87% of need; average scholarship/grant was $2,742; average loan was $2,469. For part-time students, average financial aid package was $8,550.
Students without need: 106 full-time freshmen who did not demonstrate need for aid received scholarships/grants; average award was $4,111. No-need awards available for academics, alumni affiliation, athletics.
Scholarships offered: 10 full-time freshmen received athletic scholarships; average amount $13,212.
Cumulative student debt: 81% of graduating class had student loans; average debt was $5,091.

FINANCIAL AID PROCEDURES
Forms required: FAFSA, state aid form.
Dates and Deadlines: Priority date 4/30; no closing date. Applicants notified on a rolling basis starting 3/1.
Transfers: No deadline. Applicants notified on a rolling basis. Academic scholarships available for transfers with associate degrees.

CONTACT
Diane Beltrani, Director of Enrollment Services and Financial Aid
150 Idle Hour Boulevard, Oakdale, NY 11769-1999
(631) 244-3030

Dutchess Community College
Poughkeepsie, New York
www.sunydutchess.edu   Federal Code: 002864

2-year public community college in large town.
Enrollment: 6,807 undergrads.
Selectivity: Open admission; but selective for some programs.

BASIC COSTS (2005-2006)
Tuition and fees: $2,986; out-of-state residents $5,586.
Per-credit charge: $105; out-of-state residents $210.

FINANCIAL AID PICTURE
Students with need: Need-based aid available for full-time and part-time students.

FINANCIAL AID PROCEDURES
Forms required: FAFSA, state aid form, institutional form.
Dates and Deadlines: Priority date 5/1; no closing date. Applicants notified on a rolling basis starting 5/15; must reply within 2 week(s) of notification.

CONTACT
Susan Mead, Director of Financial Aid
53 Pendell Road, Poughkeepsie, NY 12601-1595
(845) 431-8030

D'Youville College
Buffalo, New York
www.dyc.edu
Federal Code: 002712

4-year private health science and teachers college in large city.
Enrollment: 1,330 undergrads, 12% part-time. 167 full-time freshmen.
Selectivity: Admits 50 to 75% of applicants.

BASIC COSTS (2006-2007)
Tuition and fees: $16,800.
Room and board: $8,300.
Additional info: Substantial tuition reduction depending on SAT scores.

FINANCIAL AID PICTURE (2004-2005)
Students with need: Out of 159 full-time freshmen who applied for aid, 144 were judged to have need. Of these, 143 received aid, and 24 had their full need met. Average financial aid package met 79% of need; average scholarship/grant was $9,620; average loan was $3,418. For part-time students, average financial aid package was $12,791.
Students without need: 22 full-time freshmen who did not demonstrate need for aid received scholarships/grants; average award was $9,590. No-need awards available for academics, leadership, ROTC.

FINANCIAL AID PROCEDURES
Forms required: FAFSA, state aid form.
Dates and Deadlines: Priority date 3/1; no closing date. Applicants notified on a rolling basis starting 4/1; must reply within 3 week(s) of notification.
Transfers: .

CONTACT
Lorraine Metz, Director of Financial Aid
320 Porter Avenue, Buffalo, NY 14201-1084
(716) 829-7500

Eastman School of Music of the University of Rochester
Rochester, New York
www.rochester.edu/eastman
Federal Code: 008124
CSS Code: 2224

4-year private music college in large city.
Enrollment: 503 undergrads.
Selectivity: Admits less than 50% of applicants.

BASIC COSTS (2006-2007)
Tuition and fees: $29,172.
Per-credit charge: $945.
Room and board: $10,552.

FINANCIAL AID PICTURE (2005-2006)
Students with need: 50% of average financial aid package awarded as scholarships/grants, 50% awarded as loans/jobs. Need-based aid available for part-time students.
Students without need: No-need awards available for academics, alumni affiliation, music/drama.
Scholarships offered: All merit scholarships awarded based on admission criteria, and do not require separate application, audition, or interview.

FINANCIAL AID PROCEDURES
Forms required: FAFSA, CSS PROFILE, institutional form.

Dates and Deadlines: Priority date 2/1; no closing date. Applicants notified on a rolling basis starting 3/15; must reply by 5/1 or within 2 week(s) of notification.

CONTACT
Mary Ellen Nugent, Director of Financial Aid
26 Gibbs Street, Rochester, NY 14604-2599
(585) 274-1070

Elmira Business Institute
Elmira, New York
www.ebi-college.com
Federal Code: 009043

2-year for-profit business and technical college in large town.
Enrollment: 265 undergrads, 16% part-time. 77 full-time freshmen.
Selectivity: Open admission.

BASIC COSTS (2005-2006)
Additional info: Program cost for 16 month associate degree in office technology (medical or legal) $19,520. Includes tuition, fees, books, graduation costs. Costs of other programs vary. Tuition at time of enrollment locked for 2 years.

FINANCIAL AID PICTURE
Students with need: Need-based aid available for full-time and part-time students.
Students without need: This college only awards aid to students with need.

FINANCIAL AID PROCEDURES
Forms required: FAFSA, state aid form, institutional form.
Dates and Deadlines: Closing date 5/1.

CONTACT
Kathy Hamilton, Vice President
303 North Main Street, Elmira, NY 14901
(607) 733-7177

Elmira College
Elmira, New York
www.elmira.edu
Federal Code: 002718

4-year private liberal arts college in large town.
Enrollment: 1,382 undergrads, 15% part-time. 305 full-time freshmen.
Selectivity: Admits 50 to 75% of applicants.

BASIC COSTS (2006-2007)
Tuition and fees: $30,050.
Room and board: $9,100.

FINANCIAL AID PICTURE (2005-2006)
Students with need: Out of 272 full-time freshmen who applied for aid, 250 were judged to have need. Of these, 250 received aid, and 39 had their full need met. Average financial aid package met 80% of need; average scholarship/grant was $17,500; average loan was $4,631. Need-based aid available for part-time students.
Students without need: 51 full-time freshmen who did not demonstrate need for aid received scholarships/grants; average award was $15,861. No-need awards available for academics, leadership, ROTC.
Scholarships offered: Scholarships for valedictorian and salutatorian: 20 awarded; full and 75% tuition respectively, renewable. Scholarships based on GPA, test scores, and class rank: $15,000, $12,000, $10,000 or $7,000 renewable awards.
Cumulative student debt: 69% of graduating class had student loans; average debt was $25,347.

Additional info: Sibling Scholarship program provides 50% discounts on second family member's room and board, regardless of need.

FINANCIAL AID PROCEDURES
Forms required: FAFSA, state aid form.
Dates and Deadlines: Priority date 2/1; closing date 6/30. Applicants notified on a rolling basis starting 2/1; must reply by 5/1 or within 2 week(s) of notification.
Transfers: Priority date 3/1; no deadline. Applicants notified on a rolling basis starting 2/1; must reply by 5/1.

CONTACT
Kathleen Cohen, Dean of Financial Aid
One Park Place, Elmira, NY 14901
(607) 735-1728

Erie Community College: City Campus
Buffalo, New York
www.ecc.edu   Federal Code: 010684

2-year public community college in large city.
Enrollment: 2,685 undergrads, 21% part-time. 556 full-time freshmen.
Selectivity: Open admission; but selective for some programs.

BASIC COSTS (2005-2006)
Tuition and fees: $3,235; out-of-district residents $6,135; out-of-state residents $6,135.
Per-credit charge: $121; out-of-state residents $242.
Additional info: Tuition discounts available for off-site and off-times courses.

FINANCIAL AID PICTURE (2004-2005)
Students with need: 72% of average financial aid package awarded as scholarships/grants, 28% awarded as loans/jobs. Need-based aid available for part-time students. Work study available weekends and for part-time students.
Students without need: This college only awards aid to students with need.

FINANCIAL AID PROCEDURES
Forms required: FAFSA, state aid form.
Dates and Deadlines: Priority date 6/1; no closing date. Applicants notified on a rolling basis starting 4/1; must reply within 2 week(s) of notification.

CONTACT
Bernice Anson, Director of Financial Aid
121 Ellicott Street, Buffalo, NY 14203-2698
(716) 851-1182

Erie Community College: North Campus
Williamsville, New York
www.ecc.edu   Federal Code: 010684

2-year public community college in large town.
Enrollment: 5,101 undergrads, 26% part-time. 991 full-time freshmen.
Selectivity: Open admission; but selective for some programs.

BASIC COSTS (2005-2006)
Tuition and fees: $3,235; out-of-district residents $6,135; out-of-state residents $6,135.
Per-credit charge: $121; out-of-state residents $242.
Additional info: Tuition discounts available for off-site and off-times courses.

FINANCIAL AID PICTURE (2004-2005)
Students with need: 72% of average financial aid package awarded as scholarships/grants, 28% awarded as loans/jobs. Need-based aid available for part-time students. Work study available weekends and for part-time students.
Students without need: This college only awards aid to students with need.

FINANCIAL AID PROCEDURES
Forms required: FAFSA, state aid form.
Dates and Deadlines: Priority date 6/1; no closing date. Applicants notified on a rolling basis starting 4/1; must reply within 2 week(s) of notification.

CONTACT
Bernice Anson, Director of Financial Aid
6205 Main Street, Williamsville, NY 14221-7095
(716) 851-1477

Erie Community College: South Campus
Orchard Park, New York
www.ecc.edu   Federal Code: 010684

2-year public community college in large town.
Enrollment: 3,253 undergrads, 23% part-time. 792 full-time freshmen.
Selectivity: Open admission; but selective for some programs.

BASIC COSTS (2005-2006)
Tuition and fees: $3,235; out-of-district residents $6,135; out-of-state residents $6,135.
Per-credit charge: $121; out-of-state residents $242.
Additional info: Tuition discounts available for off-site and off-times courses.

FINANCIAL AID PICTURE (2004-2005)
Students with need: 72% of average financial aid package awarded as scholarships/grants, 28% awarded as loans/jobs. Need-based aid available for part-time students. Work study available weekends and for part-time students.
Students without need: This college only awards aid to students with need.

FINANCIAL AID PROCEDURES
Forms required: FAFSA, state aid form.
Dates and Deadlines: Priority date 6/1; no closing date. Applicants notified on a rolling basis starting 4/1; must reply within 2 week(s) of notification.

CONTACT
Bernice Anson, Director of Financial Aid
4041 Southwestern Boulevard, Orchard Park, NY 14127-2199
(716) 851-1677

Eugene Lang College The New School for Liberal Arts
New York, New York
www.lang.edu   Federal Code: 002780

4-year private liberal arts college in very large city.
Enrollment: 985 undergrads, 5% part-time. 231 full-time freshmen.
Selectivity: Admits 50 to 75% of applicants.

BASIC COSTS (2006-2007)
Tuition and fees: $29,210.
Per-credit charge: $976.
Room and board: $11,750.

FINANCIAL AID PICTURE (2005-2006)
Students with need: Out of 157 full-time freshmen who applied for aid, 128 were judged to have need. Of these, 128 received aid, and 11 had their full need met. Average financial aid package met 88% of need; average scholarship/grant was $13,312; average loan was $3,339.
Students without need: 10 full-time freshmen who did not demonstrate need for aid received scholarships/grants; average award was $1,672. No-need awards available for academics.

Cumulative student debt: 67% of graduating class had student loans; average debt was $16,400.

FINANCIAL AID PROCEDURES
Forms required: FAFSA, state aid form.
Dates and Deadlines: Priority date 3/1; no closing date. Applicants notified on a rolling basis starting 3/1; must reply within 4 week(s) of notification.
Transfers: Must reply within 4 week(s) of notification.

CONTACT
Eileen Doyle, Assistant Vice President for Financial Aid
65 West 11th Street (3rd floor), New York, NY 10011-8693
(212) 229-8930

Excelsior College
Albany, New York
www.excelsior.edu
Federal Code: 014251

4-year private virtual liberal arts college in small city.
Enrollment: 26,277 undergrads, 100% part-time.
Selectivity: Open admission; but selective for some programs.

BASIC COSTS (2005-2006)
Additional info: Students are charged a $995 enrollment fee and $250 per credit hour. Because of the nontraditional pricing, the school does not charge a set tuition based on 15 credit hours per semester.

FINANCIAL AID PICTURE (2004-2005)
Students with need: 3% of average financial aid package awarded as scholarships/grants, 97% awarded as loans/jobs. Need-based aid available for part-time students.
Students without need: This college only awards aid to students with need.
Additional info: College approved for all veterans' educational benefit programs.

FINANCIAL AID PROCEDURES
Forms required: institutional form.
Dates and Deadlines: Priority date 7/1; no closing date. Applicants notified on a rolling basis starting 8/1; must reply within 2 week(s) of notification.

CONTACT
Donna Cooper, Director of Financial Aid
7 Columbia Circle, Albany, NY 12203-5159
(518) 464-8500

Fashion Institute of Technology
New York, New York
www.fitnyc.edu
Federal Code: 002866

4-year public visual arts and business college in very large city.
Enrollment: 7,540 undergrads, 14% part-time. 1,021 full-time freshmen.
Selectivity: Admits less than 50% of applicants.

BASIC COSTS (2005-2006)
Tuition and fees: $3,444; out-of-state residents $9,592.
Per-credit charge: $128; out-of-state residents $384.
Room and board: $7,066.
Additional info: Bachelor's degree full-time tuition $4350 for state residents, $10,610 for nonresidents.

FINANCIAL AID PICTURE (2005-2006)
Students with need: Out of 762 full-time freshmen who applied for aid, 467 were judged to have need. Of these, 463 received aid, and 112 had their full need met. Average financial aid package met 76% of need; average scholarship/grant was $3,726; average loan was $2,668. For part-time students, average financial aid package was $4,269.

Students without need: This college only awards aid to students with need.

FINANCIAL AID PROCEDURES
Forms required: FAFSA, state aid form, institutional form.
Dates and Deadlines: Priority date 2/15; no closing date. Applicants notified on a rolling basis starting 4/15; must reply within 2 week(s) of notification.

CONTACT
Mina Friedmann, Director of Financial Aid
Seventh Avenue at 27 Street, New York, NY 10001-5992
(212) 217-7999

Finger Lakes Community College
Canandaigua, New York
www.flcc.edu
Federal Code: 007532

2-year public community college in small town.
Enrollment: 3,368 undergrads, 23% part-time. 910 full-time freshmen.
Selectivity: Open admission; but selective for some programs.

BASIC COSTS (2005-2006)
Tuition and fees: $3,150; out-of-state residents $6,050.
Per-credit charge: $117; out-of-state residents $241.

FINANCIAL AID PICTURE (2004-2005)
Students with need: 66% of average financial aid package awarded as scholarships/grants, 34% awarded as loans/jobs. Need-based aid available for part-time students. Work study available nights, weekends, and for part-time students.
Students without need: This college only awards aid to students with need.

FINANCIAL AID PROCEDURES
Forms required: FAFSA, state aid form, institutional form.
Dates and Deadlines: Priority date 4/1; no closing date. Applicants notified on a rolling basis starting 3/1.

CONTACT
Nancy Van Zetta, Director, Financial Aid
4355 Lake Shore Drive, Canandaigua, NY 14424-8395
(585) 394-3500 ext. 7275

Five Towns College
Dix Hills, New York
www.fivetowns.edu
Federal Code: 012561

4-year for-profit music and liberal arts college in large town.
Enrollment: 1,088 undergrads, 4% part-time. 266 full-time freshmen.
Selectivity: Admits over 75% of applicants.

BASIC COSTS (2005-2006)
Tuition and fees: $14,350.
Per-credit charge: $585.
Room and board: $10,250.

FINANCIAL AID PICTURE (2005-2006)
Students with need: Average financial aid package met 45% of need; average scholarship/grant was $4,000; average loan was $2,500. For part-time students, average financial aid package was $4,000.
Students without need: No-need awards available for academics, music/drama.
Cumulative student debt: 77% of graduating class had student loans; average debt was $13,000.

FINANCIAL AID PROCEDURES
Forms required: FAFSA, state aid form, institutional form.

Dates and Deadlines: Priority date 3/31; no closing date. Applicants notified on a rolling basis; must reply within 4 week(s) of notification.

CONTACT
Mary Venezia, Financial Aid Administrator
305 North Service Road, Dix Hills, NY 11746-6055
(631) 424-7000 ext. 2113

Fordham University
Bronx, New York
www.fordham.edu
Federal Code: 002722
CSS Code: 2259

4-year private university in very large city, affiliated with Roman Catholic Church.
Enrollment: 7,281 undergrads, 7% part-time. 1,677 full-time freshmen.
Selectivity: Admits less than 50% of applicants.

BASIC COSTS (2005-2006)
Tuition and fees: $27,775.
Per-credit charge: $925.
Room and board: $10,895.

FINANCIAL AID PICTURE (2004-2005)
Students with need: Out of 1,332 full-time freshmen who applied for aid, 1,162 were judged to have need. Of these, 1,147 received aid, and 233 had their full need met. Average financial aid package met 82% of need; average scholarship/grant was $17,493; average loan was $3,267. For part-time students, average financial aid package was $9,237.
Students without need: 132 full-time freshmen who did not demonstrate need for aid received scholarships/grants; average award was $7,444. No-need awards available for academics, athletics, ROTC.
Scholarships offered: 33 full-time freshmen received athletic scholarships; average amount $16,741.

FINANCIAL AID PROCEDURES
Forms required: FAFSA, CSS PROFILE.
Dates and Deadlines: Closing date 2/1. Applicants notified on a rolling basis starting 4/1; must reply by 5/1 or within 2 week(s) of notification.
Transfers: Priority date 2/1; closing date 5/1.

CONTACT
Angela Van Dekker, Director of Financial Aid
East 441 Fordham Road, Bronx, NY 10458
(718) 817-5069

Fulton-Montgomery Community College
Johnstown, New York
www.fmcc.suny.edu
Federal Code: 002867

2-year public community college in large town.
Enrollment: 1,749 undergrads.
Selectivity: Open admission; but selective for some programs.

BASIC COSTS (2005-2006)
Tuition and fees: $3,215; out-of-state residents $6,140.
Per-credit charge: $122; out-of-state residents $244.

FINANCIAL AID PICTURE (2004-2005)
Students with need: 64% of average financial aid package awarded as scholarships/grants, 36% awarded as loans/jobs. Need-based aid available for part-time students. Work study available nights, weekends, and for part-time students.
Students without need: No-need awards available for academics.
Scholarships offered: Academic Excellence Scholarship: $1,000 a year with limit of 2 years for residents of Fulton, Montgomery, or Hamilton or Galway Central School District. Applicants must have 3.5 cumulative GPA, submit an essay and list of extracurricular activities, and be enrolled full-time at college. Must maintain 3.3 cumulative GPA. CTW Scholarship: $1,000 a year with limit of 2 years, for Montgomery residents or applicants who attend high school in Montgomery County. Applicants must have B average. Must maintain 3.3 cumulative GPA at end of first year.

FINANCIAL AID PROCEDURES
Forms required: FAFSA, state aid form.
Dates and Deadlines: Priority date 6/1; no closing date. Applicants notified on a rolling basis starting 6/15; must reply within 2 week(s) of notification.

CONTACT
Rebecca Cozzocrea, Coordinator of Financial Aid
2805 State Highway 67, Johnstown, NY 12095
(518) 762-4651 ext. 8201

Genesee Community College
Batavia, New York
www.genesee.edu
Federal Code: 006782

2-year public community college in large town.
Enrollment: 3,951 undergrads, 25% part-time. 1,032 full-time freshmen.
Selectivity: Open admission; but selective for some programs.

BASIC COSTS (2005-2006)
Tuition and fees: $3,390; out-of-state residents $3,790.
Per-credit charge: $120; out-of-state residents $130.

FINANCIAL AID PICTURE
Students with need: Need-based aid available for full-time and part-time students. Work study available nights, weekends, and for part-time students.
Students without need: No-need awards available for athletics, music/drama.

FINANCIAL AID PROCEDURES
Forms required: FAFSA, state aid form.
Dates and Deadlines: Priority date 3/1; closing date 5/1. Applicants notified on a rolling basis starting 4/15; must reply within 2 week(s) of notification.
Transfers: No deadline.

CONTACT
Joseph Bailey, Director of Financial Aid
One College Road, Batavia, NY 14020-9704
(585) 345-6900

Globe Institute of Technology
New York, New York
www.globe.edu
Federal Code: 025408

4-year for-profit business and technical college in very large city.
Enrollment: 1,712 undergrads.
Selectivity: Open admission; but selective for some programs.

BASIC COSTS (2006-2007)
Tuition and fees: $9,086.
Per-credit charge: $370.
Room and board: $4,500.
Additional info: Tuition at time of enrollment locked for 4 years; tuition/fee waivers available for adults, minority students, unemployed or children of unemployed.

FINANCIAL AID PICTURE (2005-2006)
Students with need: Need-based aid available for full-time and part-time students. Work study available nights, weekends, and for part-time students.

FINANCIAL AID PROCEDURES
Forms required: FAFSA, state aid form, institutional form.
Dates and Deadlines: No deadline. Applicants notified on a rolling basis.

Transfers: No deadline. Applicants notified on a rolling basis.

CONTACT
Marcus Browne, Director of Financial Aid
291 Broadway, New York, NY 10007
(212) 349-4330

Hamilton College
Clinton, New York
www.hamilton.edu
Federal Code: 002728
CSS Code: 2286

4-year private liberal arts college in small town.
Enrollment: 1,798 undergrads. 498 full-time freshmen.
Selectivity: Admits less than 50% of applicants.

BASIC COSTS (2006-2007)
Tuition and fees: $34,980.
Room and board: $8,910.

FINANCIAL AID PICTURE (2005-2006)
Students with need: Out of 347 full-time freshmen who applied for aid, 269 were judged to have need. Of these, 269 received aid, and 269 had their full need met. Average financial aid package met 100% of need; average scholarship/grant was $22,175; average loan was $2,878.
Students without need: 22 full-time freshmen who did not demonstrate need for aid received scholarships/grants; average award was $10,799. No-need awards available for academics, leadership, state/district residency.
Scholarships offered: $10,000 and $3,000 summer research grants; 10 awards to top applicants in entering class.
Additional info: Will meet demonstrated need of all aided applicants.

FINANCIAL AID PROCEDURES
Forms required: FAFSA, CSS PROFILE, state aid form, institutional form.
Dates and Deadlines: Closing date 1/1. Applicants notified by 4/1; must reply by 5/1.

CONTACT
Matt Malatesta, Director of Financial Aid
198 College Hill Road, Clinton, NY 13323-1293
(315) 859-4434

Hartwick College
Oneonta, New York
www.hartwick.edu
Federal Code: 002729

4-year private liberal arts college in large town.
Enrollment: 1,444 undergrads, 3% part-time. 411 full-time freshmen.
Selectivity: Admits over 75% of applicants.

BASIC COSTS (2006-2007)
Tuition and fees: $29,605.
Per-credit charge: $915.
Room and board: $7,910.
Additional info: New students (freshmen and transfers) must purchase laptop from the college; cost of computer ($1,575) is included in required fees for 2006/2007: $2,155.

FINANCIAL AID PICTURE (2005-2006)
Students with need: Out of 350 full-time freshmen who applied for aid, 310 were judged to have need. Of these, 310 received aid, and 55 had their full need met. Average financial aid package met 82% of need; average scholarship/grant was $9,065; average loan was $3,861. Need-based aid available for part-time students.
Students without need: 81 full-time freshmen who did not demonstrate need for aid received scholarships/grants; average award was $7,346. No-need awards available for academics, alumni affiliation, athletics, leadership, state/district residency.
Scholarships offered: 5 full-time freshmen received athletic scholarships; average amount $17,789.

FINANCIAL AID PROCEDURES
Forms required: FAFSA, institutional form.
Dates and Deadlines: Priority date 2/15; no closing date. Applicants notified on a rolling basis starting 2/16; must reply by 5/1 or within 2 week(s) of notification.
Transfers: Priority date 3/1; closing date 5/1.

CONTACT
Melissa Allen, Senior Associate Director of Financial Aid
Box 4022, Oneonta, NY 13820-4022
(607) 431-4130

Helene Fuld College of Nursing
New York, New York
www.helenefuld.edu
Federal Code: 015395

2-year private nursing and junior college in very large city.
Enrollment: 350 undergrads.

BASIC COSTS (2006-2007)
Tuition and fees: $13,337.
Per-credit charge: $238.

FINANCIAL AID PICTURE
Students with need: Need-based aid available for full-time and part-time students.
Students without need: This college only awards aid to students with need.

FINANCIAL AID PROCEDURES
Forms required: FAFSA, state aid form.
Dates and Deadlines: No deadline. Applicants notified on a rolling basis.

CONTACT
Andrine Thomas, Financial Aid Counselor and Loan Coordinator
1879 Madison Avenue, New York, NY 10035
(212) 423-2771

Herkimer County Community College
Herkimer, New York
www.hccc.ntcnet.com
Federal Code: 004788

2-year public community college in small town.
Enrollment: 3,531 undergrads.
Selectivity: Open admission; but selective for some programs.

BASIC COSTS (2005-2006)
Tuition and fees: $3,130; out-of-state residents $5,330.
Per-credit charge: $117; out-of-state residents $208.
Additional info: Tuition/fee waivers available for unemployed or children of unemployed.

FINANCIAL AID PICTURE
Students with need: Need-based aid available for full-time and part-time students. Work study available nights, weekends, and for part-time students.

FINANCIAL AID PROCEDURES
Forms required: FAFSA, state aid form.
Dates and Deadlines: Priority date 5/1; no closing date. Applicants notified on a rolling basis starting 4/1; must reply within 2 week(s) of notification.

CONTACT
Susan Tripp, Director of Financial Aid
100 Reservoir Road, Herkimer, NY 13350
(315) 866-0300 ext. 8282

Hilbert College
Hamburg, New York
www.hilbert.edu
Federal Code: 002735

4-year private liberal arts college in large town, affiliated with Roman Catholic Church.
Enrollment: 1,059 undergrads, 22% part-time. 158 full-time freshmen.
Selectivity: Admits over 75% of applicants.

BASIC COSTS (2006-2007)
Tuition and fees: $15,700.
Per-credit charge: $350.
Room and board: $5,900.
Additional info: Tuition/fee waivers available for minority students.

FINANCIAL AID PICTURE (2005-2006)
Students with need: Average financial aid package met 73% of need; average scholarship/grant was $8,466; average loan was $3,560. For part-time students, average financial aid package was $4,743.
Students without need: No-need awards available for academics, leadership, minority status, state/district residency.
Cumulative student debt: 91% of graduating class had student loans; average debt was $21,496.

FINANCIAL AID PROCEDURES
Forms required: FAFSA, state aid form.
Dates and Deadlines: Priority date 3/1; no closing date. Applicants notified on a rolling basis starting 3/15; must reply within 2 week(s) of notification.

CONTACT
Beverly Chudy, Director of Student Financial Aid
5200 South Park Avenue, Hamburg, NY 14075-1597
(716) 649-7900

Hobart and William Smith Colleges
Geneva, New York
www.hws.edu
Federal Code: 002731
CSS Code: 2294

4-year private liberal arts college in large town.
Enrollment: 1,855 undergrads. 545 full-time freshmen.
Selectivity: Admits 50 to 75% of applicants.

BASIC COSTS (2006-2007)
Tuition and fees: $34,688.
Room and board: $8,828.

FINANCIAL AID PICTURE (2005-2006)
Students with need: Average financial aid package met 90% of need; average scholarship/grant was $22,193; average loan was $2,394.
Students without need: No-need awards available for academics, art, leadership, music/drama.
Scholarships offered: Cornelius and Muriel P. Wood Scholarship and Richard Hersh Scholarship: each provide full tuition for 4 years. Trustee Scholarship for Academic Excellence: $19,000 annually, for 4 years; based on GPA, test scores, class standing; 50 awarded. Faculty Scholarships: ranging from $3,000-$12,000; 25-50 awarded. Phi Theta Kappa Trustee Scholarship: $2,500-$19,000 annually; for academically qualified transfer students with 2-year degree from junior or community college. Presidential Leaders Scholarship: $3,000-$14,000; based on academic excellence, leadership, personal qualities; 25-50 awarded. Arts Scholarships: $3,000-$14,000; for special talent in visual and performing arts; 15 awarded. Blackwell Medical Scholarships: full tuition for four years; MCAT waived, guaranteed seat at Upstate Medical Center at Syracuse University.
Cumulative student debt: 65% of graduating class had student loans; average debt was $21,454.

FINANCIAL AID PROCEDURES
Forms required: FAFSA, CSS PROFILE, state aid form.
Dates and Deadlines: Closing date 2/1. Applicants notified by 4/1; must reply by 5/1 or within 2 week(s) of notification.
Transfers: No deadline. Applicants notified on a rolling basis; must reply within 2 week(s) of notification.

CONTACT
Don Emmons, Vice-President for Enrollment, Dean of Admissions and Financial Aid
629 South Main Street, Geneva, NY 14456
(315) 781-3315

Hofstra University
Hempstead, New York
www.hofstra.edu
Federal Code: 002732

4-year private university in large city.
Enrollment: 8,701 undergrads, 9% part-time. 1,764 full-time freshmen.
Selectivity: Admits 50 to 75% of applicants.

BASIC COSTS (2005-2006)
Tuition and fees: $23,130.
Per-credit charge: $670.
Room and board: $9,500.

FINANCIAL AID PICTURE (2005-2006)
Students with need: Out of 1,400 full-time freshmen who applied for aid, 1,110 were judged to have need. Of these, 1,090 received aid, and 210 had their full need met. Average financial aid package met 55% of need; average scholarship/grant was $10,100; average loan was $3,025. For part-time students, average financial aid package was $7,250.
Students without need: 350 full-time freshmen who did not demonstrate need for aid received scholarships/grants; average award was $9,800. No-need awards available for academics, art, athletics, leadership, music/drama, ROTC, state/district residency.
Scholarships offered: Merit: Hofstra's Distinguished Academic Scholar Program: number awarded varies; full tuition; for students with outstanding academic achievement. Hofstra Honors College Scholarships: varying amounts; awarded to students in Honors College. **Athletic:** 30 full-time freshmen received athletic scholarships; average amount $24,525.
Cumulative student debt: 61% of graduating class had student loans; average debt was $20,500.
Additional info: Special financial aid funds may be available for applicants with special talents, those with superior academic ability, minority applicants, and low/middle income applicants.

FINANCIAL AID PROCEDURES
Forms required: FAFSA, state aid form.
Dates and Deadlines: Priority date 2/15; no closing date. Applicants notified on a rolling basis starting 3/15; must reply within 2 week(s) of notification.
Transfers: Awarded on basis of state residency, full-time status, remaining semester eligibility, and income level.

CONTACT
Janice Contino, Director of Financial Aid
Admissions Center, 100 Hofstra University, Hempstead, NY 11549
(516) 463-6680

Houghton College
Houghton, New York
www.houghton.edu   Federal Code: 002734

4-year private liberal arts college in rural community, affiliated with Wesleyan Church.
Enrollment: 1,368 undergrads, 3% part-time. 324 full-time freshmen.
Selectivity: Admits over 75% of applicants.

BASIC COSTS (2006-2007)
Tuition and fees: $20,400.
Room and board: $6,680.
Additional info: Tuition includes laptop computer, printer, fees. Tuition/fee waivers available for minority students.

FINANCIAL AID PICTURE (2004-2005)
Students with need: Out of 319 full-time freshmen who applied for aid, 299 were judged to have need. Of these, 299 received aid, and 48 had their full need met. Average financial aid package met 75% of need; average scholarship/grant was $11,337; average loan was $3,306. For part-time students, average financial aid package was $13,268.
Students without need: 25 full-time freshmen who did not demonstrate need for aid received scholarships/grants; average award was $4,869. No-need awards available for academics, alumni affiliation, art, athletics, music/drama, religious affiliation, ROTC, state/district residency.
Scholarships offered: Academic Excellence Scholarships: ranging from $1,250-$12,500; based on academic record, co-curricular involvement, recommendations. Wesleyan Grant: awards $1,000 to members of Wesley Church. Willard J. Houghton Ministerial Scholarship: awards renewable $5,000 to student preparing for Wesleyan pastorate; based on recommendation of local District Board of Ministerial Development.
Cumulative student debt: 71% of graduating class had student loans; average debt was $16,028.

FINANCIAL AID PROCEDURES
Forms required: FAFSA.
Dates and Deadlines: Priority date 3/1; no closing date. Applicants notified on a rolling basis starting 3/15; must reply by 5/1 or within 4 week(s) of notification.

CONTACT
Troy Martin, Director of Student Financial Services
One Willard Avenue/Box 128, Houghton, NY 14744-0128
(585) 567-9328

Hudson Valley Community College
Troy, New York
www.hvcc.edu   Federal Code: 002868

2-year public community college in small city.
Enrollment: 8,879 undergrads.
Selectivity: Open admission; but selective for some programs.

BASIC COSTS (2005-2006)
Tuition and fees: $3,355; out-of-state residents $8,755.
Per-credit charge: $112; out-of-state residents $336.

FINANCIAL AID PICTURE (2005-2006)
Students with need: 66% of average financial aid package awarded as scholarships/grants, 34% awarded as loans/jobs.

FINANCIAL AID PROCEDURES
Forms required: FAFSA.
Dates and Deadlines: Priority date 5/30; no closing date. Applicants notified on a rolling basis starting 5/1; must reply within 2 week(s) of notification.

CONTACT
Lisa Van Wie, Director of Financial Aid
80 Vandenburgh Avenue, Troy, NY 12180
(518) 629-4822

Iona College
New Rochelle, New York
www.iona.edu   Federal Code: 002737

4-year private business and liberal arts college in small city, affiliated with Roman Catholic Church.
Enrollment: 3,327 undergrads, 6% part-time. 779 full-time freshmen.
Selectivity: Admits 50 to 75% of applicants.

BASIC COSTS (2006-2007)
Tuition and fees: $23,218.
Per-credit charge: $714.
Room and board: $9,998.
Additional info: Tuition/fee waivers available for minority students.

FINANCIAL AID PICTURE (2005-2006)
Students with need: Out of 763 full-time freshmen who applied for aid, 613 were judged to have need. Of these, 608 received aid, and 124 had their full need met. Average financial aid package met 19% of need; average scholarship/grant was $3,788; average loan was $2,367. For part-time students, average financial aid package was $3,214.
Students without need: 141 full-time freshmen who did not demonstrate need for aid received scholarships/grants; average award was $9,635. No-need awards available for academics, alumni affiliation, athletics, ROTC.
Scholarships offered: 50 full-time freshmen received athletic scholarships; average amount $9,231.
Cumulative student debt: 70% of graduating class had student loans; average debt was $21,495.

FINANCIAL AID PROCEDURES
Forms required: FAFSA, state aid form, institutional form.
Dates and Deadlines: Closing date 4/15. Must reply by 5/1 or within 2 week(s) of notification.

CONTACT
Mary Grant, Associate Director of Student Financial Services
715 North Avenue, New Rochelle, NY 10801-1890
(914) 633-2497

Island Drafting and Technical Institute
Amityville, New York
www.idti.edu   Federal Code: 007375

2-year for-profit technical college in large town.
Enrollment: 185 undergrads.
Selectivity: Open admission.

BASIC COSTS (2005-2006)
Tuition and fees: $12,200.
Per-credit charge: $395.
Additional info: Tuition at time of enrollment locked for 2 years.

FINANCIAL AID PICTURE
Students with need: Need-based aid available for full-time students.
Students without need: This college only awards aid to students with need.

FINANCIAL AID PROCEDURES
Dates and Deadlines: No deadline. Applicants notified on a rolling basis.

CONTACT
James DiLiberto, Dean
128 Broadway, Amityville, NY 11701-2704
(631) 264-0465

Ithaca College
Ithaca, New York
www.ithaca.edu
Federal Code: 002739

4-year private health science and liberal arts college in large town.
Enrollment: 5,997 undergrads, 1% part-time. 1,680 full-time freshmen.
Selectivity: Admits over 75% of applicants.

BASIC COSTS (2006-2007)
Tuition and fees: $26,832.
Per-credit charge: $894.
Room and board: $10,314.

FINANCIAL AID PICTURE (2005-2006)
Students with need: Out of 1,358 full-time freshmen who applied for aid, 1,250 were judged to have need. Of these, 1,248 received aid, and 648 had their full need met. Average financial aid package met 89% of need; average scholarship/grant was $8,133; average loan was $6,768. For part-time students, average financial aid package was $8,403.
Students without need: 139 full-time freshmen who did not demonstrate need for aid received scholarships/grants; average award was $8,411. No-need awards available for academics, alumni affiliation, leadership, music/drama, ROTC.
Scholarships offered: President's Scholarship: awarded for academic achievement to approximately 10% of applicants; $12,000-$15,000. Dean's Scholarship: awarded for academic ability to approximately top 11% to 30% of applicants; $4,000-$8,000. ALANA Scholarship: awarded for academic achievement to 25% of applicants who are representatives of minority groups; $3,000-$12,000 in addition to President's or Dean's Scholarship. MLK Scholarships: awarded to approximately 15 students annually who demonstrate academic excellence and community service involvement; $17,000 each. Ithaca Leadership Scholarship: awarded for demonstrated record of leadership and above average academic performance; 30 new awards available per year; $7,000 each. Ithaca Premier Talent Scholarship: for selected applicants majoring in music and theater; approximately 10 available; maximum award of $15,000. Ithaca Sibling Grant: awarded to students who have concurrently enrolled sibling attending Ithaca College; $1,000. Park Scholar Achievement: awarded for outstanding achievement in communications; covers full cost of attendance; approximately 20 new scholarships available per year. Ithaca College Merit Scholarship and Ithaca College National Merit Recognition Award: for students who designate Ithaca their first-choice institution to National Merit Scholarship Corporation; $2,000 scholarship plus Ithaca College President's Scholarship of $15,000.

FINANCIAL AID PROCEDURES
Forms required: FAFSA. CSS PROFILE required of early decision applicants; deadline November 1.
Dates and Deadlines: Priority date 2/1; no closing date. Applicants notified on a rolling basis starting 2/15.
Transfers: No deadline. Applicants notified on a rolling basis. All need-based and merit awards available for freshmen also available for transfers.

CONTACT
Larry Chambers, Director of Financial Aid
100 Job Hall, Ithaca, NY 14850-7020
(800) 429-4275

Jamestown Business College
Jamestown, New York
www.jbcny.org
Federal Code: 008495

2-year for-profit business and junior college in large town.
Enrollment: 299 undergrads, 4% part-time. 84 full-time freshmen.
Selectivity: Admits over 75% of applicants.

BASIC COSTS (2006-2007)
Tuition and fees: $9,300.

FINANCIAL AID PICTURE (2004-2005)
Students with need: 70% of average financial aid package awarded as scholarships/grants, 30% awarded as loans/jobs. Need-based aid available for part-time students.
Students without need: No-need awards available for academics.

FINANCIAL AID PROCEDURES
Forms required: FAFSA, state aid form.
Dates and Deadlines: No deadline. Applicants notified on a rolling basis starting 2/15.

CONTACT
Diane Sturzenbecker, Financial Aid Officer
7 Fairmount Avenue, Jamestown, NY 14702-0429
(716) 664-5100

Jamestown Community College
Jamestown, New York
www.sunyjcc.edu
Federal Code: 002869

2-year public community college in large town.
Enrollment: 3,592 undergrads, 32% part-time. 921 full-time freshmen.
Selectivity: Open admission; but selective for some programs.

BASIC COSTS (2005-2006)
Tuition and fees: $3,676; out-of-state residents $6,826.
Per-credit charge: $132; out-of-state residents $238.

FINANCIAL AID PICTURE
Students with need: Need-based aid available for full-time and part-time students. Work study available nights, weekends, and for part-time students.
Students without need: No-need awards available for academics, alumni affiliation, athletics, music/drama, state/district residency.
Additional info: 100% resident tuition scholarship (less federal and state grants) for students in top 20% of high school graduating class with Regents diploma if residents of Chautauqua, Cattaraugus, or Allegany counties. Guaranteed in-state tuition rate for students in Warren, Potter, McKean and Forest counties in Pennsylvania, in top 20% of graduating class with an academic diploma.

FINANCIAL AID PROCEDURES
Forms required: FAFSA, state aid form.
Dates and Deadlines: Priority date 3/1; no closing date. Applicants notified on a rolling basis starting 4/15.

CONTACT
Laurie Vorp, Director of Financial Aid
525 Falconer Street, Jamestown, NY 14702-0020
(716) 665-5220

Jefferson Community College
Watertown, New York
www.sunyjefferson.edu   Federal Code: 002870

2-year public community college in large town.
Enrollment: 3,590 undergrads.
Selectivity: Open admission; but selective for some programs.

BASIC COSTS (2005-2006)
Tuition and fees: $3,280; out-of-state residents $4,710.
Per-credit charge: $122; out-of-state residents $182.

FINANCIAL AID PICTURE (2005-2006)
Students with need: Need-based aid available for part-time students.
Students without need: This college only awards aid to students with need.

FINANCIAL AID PROCEDURES
Forms required: FAFSA, state aid form, institutional form.
Dates and Deadlines: Priority date 4/1; closing date 8/15. Applicants notified on a rolling basis starting 4/15; must reply within 2 week(s) of notification.
Transfers: No deadline.

CONTACT
Betsy Penrose, Director of Financial Aid
1220 Coffeen Street, Watertown, NY 13601
(315) 786-2355

Juilliard School
New York, New York
www.juilliard.edu   Federal Code: 002742

4-year private music and performing arts college in very large city.
Enrollment: 478 undergrads. 96 full-time freshmen.
Selectivity: Admits less than 50% of applicants.

BASIC COSTS (2006-2007)
Tuition and fees: $25,610.
Room and board: $10,095.

FINANCIAL AID PICTURE (2005-2006)
Students with need: Out of 91 full-time freshmen who applied for aid, 72 were judged to have need. Of these, 72 received aid, and 19 had their full need met. Average financial aid package met 85% of need; average scholarship/grant was $17,493; average loan was $4,429. Need-based aid available for part-time students.
Students without need: 1 full-time freshmen who did not demonstrate need for aid received scholarships/grants; average award was $5,000. No-need awards available for music/drama.
Cumulative student debt: 66% of graduating class had student loans; average debt was $23,831.

FINANCIAL AID PROCEDURES
Forms required: FAFSA, institutional form.
Dates and Deadlines: Closing date 3/1. Applicants notified on a rolling basis starting 4/1; must reply by 5/1 or within 2 week(s) of notification.

CONTACT
Joan Warren, Dean for Financial Aid
60 Lincoln Center Plaza, New York, NY 10023-6588
(212) 799-5000

Katharine Gibbs School: New York
New York, New York
www.gibbsny.com   Federal Code: 007398

2-year for-profit business college in very large city.
Enrollment: 2,047 undergrads.

BASIC COSTS (2005-2006)
Additional info: Tuition for associate degree programs ranges from $22,050 to $24,850. Fees $30 per term, $180 for 18-month program.

FINANCIAL AID PICTURE
Students with need: Need-based aid available for full-time and part-time students.

FINANCIAL AID PROCEDURES
Dates and Deadlines: No deadline. Applicants notified on a rolling basis; must reply within 3 week(s) of notification.

CONTACT
Lillian Hawkins, Director of Financial Aid
50 West 40th Street, 1st Floor, New York, NY 10138
(212) 867-9309

Keuka College
Keuka Park, New York
www.keuka.edu   Federal Code: 002744

4-year private liberal arts college in rural community, affiliated with American Baptist Churches in the USA.
Enrollment: 939 undergrads, 1% part-time. 268 full-time freshmen.
Selectivity: Admits over 75% of applicants.

BASIC COSTS (2005-2006)
Tuition and fees: $18,360.
Per-credit charge: $595.
Room and board: $7,980.

FINANCIAL AID PICTURE (2005-2006)
Students with need: Out of 267 full-time freshmen who applied for aid, 245 were judged to have need. Of these, 245 received aid, and 81 had their full need met. Average financial aid package met 84% of need; average scholarship/grant was $12,809; average loan was $5,345. For part-time students, average financial aid package was $6,018.
Students without need: 27 full-time freshmen who did not demonstrate need for aid received scholarships/grants; average award was $16,936. No-need awards available for academics, alumni affiliation, leadership, minority status, religious affiliation.
Scholarships offered: Goals Scholarship: 1/2 tuition; 82 average and 1000 SAT or 22 ACT required. Dean's Scholarship: 1/2-full tuition; 82 average and 1000 SAT or 22 ACT required. Presidential Scholarship: full tuition; based on GPA, SAT scores, class rank. SAT scores listed are exclusive of Writing portion.
Cumulative student debt: 86% of graduating class had student loans; average debt was $13,041.

FINANCIAL AID PROCEDURES
Forms required: FAFSA.
Dates and Deadlines: Priority date 3/15; no closing date. Applicants notified on a rolling basis starting 3/1; must reply by 5/1 or within 2 week(s) of notification.

CONTACT
Jennifer Bates, Director of Financial Aid
Wagner House, Keuka Park, NY 14478-0098
(315) 279-5232

King's College
New York, New York
www.tkc.edu
CSS Code: 2871

4-year private liberal arts college in very large city, affiliated with nondenominational tradition.
Enrollment: 213 undergrads, 9% part-time. 80 full-time freshmen.
Selectivity: Admits 50 to 75% of applicants.

BASIC COSTS (2006-2007)
Tuition and fees: $18,940.
Per-credit charge: $775.
Room only: $7,980.

FINANCIAL AID PICTURE (2005-2006)
Students with need: Out of 74 full-time freshmen who applied for aid, 59 were judged to have need. Of these, 59 received aid, and 7 had their full need met. Average financial aid package met 73% of need; average scholarship/grant was $12,916. For part-time students, average financial aid package was $6,364.
Students without need: 21 full-time freshmen who did not demonstrate need for aid received scholarships/grants; average award was $7,949. No-need awards available for academics, leadership.
Scholarships offered: Presidential Scholarships: unlimited number; based on SAT/ACTs and National Merit; award ranges from $1,500 to $8,000. Founders Scholarships: 4 awards given; $10,000 each; based on essay and presentation. Competition held in February.
Additional info: School does not participate in Title IV federal financial aid; students must file PROFILE and/or TAP application for institutional aid consideration.

FINANCIAL AID PROCEDURES
Forms required: CSS PROFILE, state aid form.
Dates and Deadlines: Priority date 12/15; closing date 3/1. Applicants notified by 3/15; must reply by 5/1.

CONTACT
Jody Bell, Director of Financial Aid
350 5th Avenue, 15th Floor, New York, NY 10118
(212) 659-3608

Laboratory Institute of Merchandising
New York, New York
www.limcollege.edu
Federal Code: 007466

4-year for-profit college of fashion business in very large city.
Enrollment: 792 undergrads, 2% part-time. 197 full-time freshmen.
Selectivity: Admits 50 to 75% of applicants.

BASIC COSTS (2005-2006)
Tuition and fees: $17,050.
Per-credit charge: $525.
Room only: $10,000.

FINANCIAL AID PICTURE (2004-2005)
Students with need: 55% of average financial aid package awarded as scholarships/grants, 45% awarded as loans/jobs. Need-based aid available for part-time students.
Students without need: This college only awards aid to students with need.
Cumulative student debt: 60% of graduating class had student loans; average debt was $16,491.

FINANCIAL AID PROCEDURES
Forms required: FAFSA, state aid form, institutional form.
Dates and Deadlines: Priority date 4/15; no closing date. Applicants notified on a rolling basis; must reply within 2 week(s) of notification.

CONTACT
Christopher Barto, Director of Student Financial Services
12 East 53rd Street, New York, NY 10022
(212) 752-1530

Le Moyne College
Syracuse, New York
www.lemoyne.edu
Federal Code: 002748

4-year private liberal arts college in small city, affiliated with Roman Catholic Church.
Enrollment: 2,436 undergrads, 6% part-time. 473 full-time freshmen.
Selectivity: Admits 50 to 75% of applicants.

BASIC COSTS (2006-2007)
Tuition and fees: $22,580.
Per-credit charge: $464.
Room and board: $8,620.

FINANCIAL AID PICTURE (2004-2005)
Students with need: Out of 389 full-time freshmen who applied for aid, 389 were judged to have need. Of these, 389 received aid, and 119 had their full need met. Average financial aid package met 88% of need; average scholarship/grant was $14,765; average loan was $3,286. For part-time students, average financial aid package was $6,095.
Students without need: 46 full-time freshmen who did not demonstrate need for aid received scholarships/grants; average award was $9,133. No-need awards available for academics, alumni affiliation, athletics, leadership, minority status, ROTC.
Scholarships offered: *Merit:* Presidential Scholarships: $17,500; Dean Scholarships: $13,000; Leadership Scholarships: $5,500; all based on academic criteria (GPA, rank, test scores). Loyola Scholarships: $13,000; for students of color, based on academic criteria. *Athletic:* 45 full-time freshmen received athletic scholarships; average amount $7,159.
Cumulative student debt: 87% of graduating class had student loans; average debt was $19,137.
Additional info: Parent loan program at low interest, monthly payment plans and alternative loans for students.

FINANCIAL AID PROCEDURES
Forms required: FAFSA, state aid form, institutional form.
Dates and Deadlines: Priority date 2/1; no closing date. Applicants notified by 3/15; must reply by 5/1 or within 2 week(s) of notification.
Transfers: Priority date 6/1; no deadline. Must reply by 5/1 or within 2 week(s) of notification.

CONTACT
William Cheetham, Director of Financial Aid
1419 Salt Springs Road, Syracuse, NY 13214-1301
(315) 445-4400

Long Island Business Institute
Commack, New York
www.libi.edu
Federal Code: 014514

2-year for-profit business college in large town.
Enrollment: 888 undergrads, 24% part-time. 298 full-time freshmen.
Selectivity: Open admission; but selective for some programs.

BASIC COSTS (2006-2007)
Tuition and fees: $10,125.
Per-credit charge: $325.
Additional info: Tuition varies by program.

New York Long Island Business Institute

FINANCIAL AID PICTURE (2005-2006)
Students with need: Out of 290 full-time freshmen who applied for aid, 290 were judged to have need. Of these, 290 received aid. Average financial aid package met 80% of need; average scholarship/grant was $3,000; average loan was $2,600. For part-time students, average financial aid package was $1,000.
Students without need: No-need awards available for academics.

FINANCIAL AID PROCEDURES
Forms required: FAFSA, state aid form.
Dates and Deadlines: No deadline. Must reply within 2 week(s) of notification.

CONTACT
Nazaret Kiregian, Director of Financial Aid
6500 Jericho Turnpike, Commack, NY 11725
(631) 499-7100 ext. 11

Long Island University: Brooklyn Campus
Brooklyn, New York
www.liu.edu
Federal Code: 004779

4-year private university and branch campus college in very large city.
Enrollment: 5,297 undergrads, 17% part-time. 978 full-time freshmen.
Selectivity: Admits 50 to 75% of applicants.

BASIC COSTS (2005-2006)
Tuition and fees: $23,230.
Per-credit charge: $689.
Room and board: $7,860.

FINANCIAL AID PICTURE
Students with need: Need-based aid available for full-time and part-time students.

FINANCIAL AID PROCEDURES
Forms required: FAFSA.
Dates and Deadlines: No deadline. Applicants notified on a rolling basis.

CONTACT
Rose Iannicelli, Dean of Student Financial Services
1 University Plaza, Brooklyn, NY 11201
(718) 488-1037

Long Island University: C. W. Post Campus
Brookville, New York
www.liu.edu
Federal Code: 002751
CSS Code: 2070

4-year private university and branch campus college in small town.
Enrollment: 5,149 undergrads, 13% part-time. 949 full-time freshmen.
Selectivity: Admits over 75% of applicants.

BASIC COSTS (2005-2006)
Tuition and fees: $23,230.
Per-credit charge: $689.
Room and board: $9,020.

FINANCIAL AID PICTURE
Students with need: Need-based aid available for full-time and part-time students. Work study available nights, weekends, and for part-time students.

FINANCIAL AID PROCEDURES
Forms required: FAFSA, CSS PROFILE, state aid form.
Dates and Deadlines: Priority date 3/1; no closing date. Applicants notified on a rolling basis starting 3/1; must reply by 5/1.
Transfers: Applicants notified on a rolling basis starting 3/1; must reply by 5/1.

CONTACT
Edward Boss, Director of Student Financial Services
720 Northern Boulevard, Brookville, NY 11548-1300
(516) 299-2338

Manhattan College
Riverdale, New York
www.manhattan.edu
Federal Code: 002758

4-year private engineering and liberal arts college in very large city, affiliated with Roman Catholic Church.
Enrollment: 3,026 undergrads, 5% part-time. 721 full-time freshmen.
Selectivity: Admits 50 to 75% of applicants.

BASIC COSTS (2006-2007)
Tuition and fees: $21,550.
Room and board: $8,800.
Additional info: Program fees range from $1,000 to $1,900 depending on program.

FINANCIAL AID PICTURE
Students with need: Need-based aid available for full-time students. Work study available nights, weekends, and for part-time students.
Students without need: This college only awards aid to students with need.

FINANCIAL AID PROCEDURES
Forms required: FAFSA.
Dates and Deadlines: Priority date 2/15; closing date 4/15. Applicants notified on a rolling basis starting 1/1; must reply by 5/1.
Transfers: Priority date 4/15; no deadline.

CONTACT
Ed Keough, Director of Student Financial Services
4513 Manhattan College Parkway, Riverdale, NY 10471
(718) 862-7300

Manhattan School of Music
New York, New York
www.msmnyc.edu
Federal Code: 002759
CSS Code: 2396

4-year private music college in very large city.
Enrollment: 416 undergrads, 2% part-time. 98 full-time freshmen.
Selectivity: Admits less than 50% of applicants.

BASIC COSTS (2006-2007)
Tuition and fees: $27,860.
Per-credit charge: $1,200.
Room and board: $12,800.
Additional info: Health fee of $2,100 required unless already insured.

FINANCIAL AID PICTURE (2004-2005)
Students with need: 56% of average financial aid package awarded as scholarships/grants, 44% awarded as loans/jobs. Need-based aid available for part-time students. Work study available nights, weekends, and for part-time students.
Students without need: No-need awards available for academics, alumni affiliation, leadership, music/drama.

FINANCIAL AID PROCEDURES
Forms required: FAFSA, CSS PROFILE, institutional form.
Dates and Deadlines: Closing date 3/1. Applicants notified by 4/1; must reply by 5/1 or within 2 week(s) of notification.

CONTACT
Amy Anderson, Director of Admission and Financial Aid
120 Claremont Avenue, New York, NY 10027-4698
(212) 749-2802 ext. 4463

Manhattanville College
Purchase, New York
www.manhattanville.edu   Federal Code: 002760

4-year private liberal arts and teachers college in small town.
Enrollment: 1,713 undergrads, 4% part-time. 501 full-time freshmen.
Selectivity: Admits 50 to 75% of applicants.

BASIC COSTS (2006-2007)
Tuition and fees: $28,000.
Per-credit charge: $620.
Room and board: $11,550.

FINANCIAL AID PICTURE (2004-2005)
Students with need: Out of 391 full-time freshmen who applied for aid, 340 were judged to have need. Of these, 338 received aid, and 59 had their full need met. Average financial aid package met 81% of need; average scholarship/grant was $11,137; average loan was $3,132. For part-time students, average financial aid package was $9,673.
Students without need: 122 full-time freshmen who did not demonstrate need for aid received scholarships/grants; average award was $9,038. No-need awards available for academics, art, music/drama.
Additional info: Upper level students may earn additional money and academic credit through internship program.

FINANCIAL AID PROCEDURES
Forms required: FAFSA, state aid form.
Dates and Deadlines: Closing date 3/1. Applicants notified on a rolling basis starting 2/1; must reply by 5/1 or within 2 week(s) of notification.
Transfers: No deadline.

CONTACT
Maria Barlaam, Director of Financial Aid
2900 Purchase Street, Purchase, NY 10577
(914) 323-5357

Mannes College The New School for Music
New York, New York
www.mannes.edu   Federal Code: 002780

4-year private music college in very large city.
Enrollment: 208 undergrads, 10% part-time. 36 full-time freshmen.
Selectivity: Admits less than 50% of applicants.

BASIC COSTS (2006-2007)
Tuition and fees: $28,210.
Per-credit charge: $912.
Room and board: $11,750.
Additional info: Tuition/fee waivers available for unemployed or children of unemployed.

FINANCIAL AID PICTURE (2005-2006)
Students with need: Average financial aid package met 57% of need; average scholarship/grant was $3,116; average loan was $2,625.
Students without need: No-need awards available for academics, music/drama.
Cumulative student debt: 60% of graduating class had student loans; average debt was $18,025.
Additional info: Closing date for scholarship applications 2 weeks prior to audition date.

FINANCIAL AID PROCEDURES
Forms required: FAFSA, state aid form.
Dates and Deadlines: Priority date 3/1; no closing date. Applicants notified on a rolling basis starting 3/1; must reply within 4 week(s) of notification.

CONTACT
Eileen Doyle, Executive Director of Undergraduate Financial Aid
150 West 85th Street, New York, NY 10024
(212) 580-0210

Maria College
Albany, New York
www.mariacollege.edu   Federal Code: 002763

2-year private junior college in small city.
Enrollment: 719 undergrads, 70% part-time. 68 full-time freshmen.
Selectivity: Admits 50 to 75% of applicants.

BASIC COSTS (2005-2006)
Tuition and fees: $7,600.
Per-credit charge: $270.

FINANCIAL AID PICTURE (2005-2006)
Students with need: Out of 59 full-time freshmen who applied for aid, 56 were judged to have need. Of these, 56 received aid, and 49 had their full need met. Average financial aid package met 87% of need; average scholarship/grant was $4,064; average loan was $2,128. For part-time students, average financial aid package was $3,819.
Students without need: This college only awards aid to students with need.
Cumulative student debt: 75% of graduating class had student loans; average debt was $7,688.

FINANCIAL AID PROCEDURES
Forms required: FAFSA, state aid form.
Dates and Deadlines: No deadline. Applicants notified on a rolling basis starting 2/1; must reply within 2 week(s) of notification.

CONTACT
Kenneth Clough, Director of Student Records
700 New Scotland Avenue, Albany, NY 12208
(518) 438-3111 ext. 229

Marist College
Poughkeepsie, New York
www.marist.edu   Federal Code: 002765

4-year private liberal arts college in small city.
Enrollment: 4,851 undergrads, 9% part-time. 1,017 full-time freshmen.
Selectivity: Admits less than 50% of applicants.

BASIC COSTS (2005-2006)
Tuition and fees: $21,202.
Per-credit charge: $475.
Room and board: $9,364.
Additional info: Tuition/fee waivers available for minority students.

FINANCIAL AID PICTURE (2005-2006)
Students with need: Out of 858 full-time freshmen who applied for aid, 625 were judged to have need. Of these, 624 received aid, and 151 had their full need met. Average financial aid package met 78% of need; average scholarship/grant was $10,971; average loan was $3,565. For part-time students, average financial aid package was $5,055.
Students without need: 270 full-time freshmen who did not demonstrate need for aid received scholarships/grants; average award was $6,314. No-

need awards available for academics, athletics, music/drama, state/district residency.
Scholarships offered: *Merit:* Awards vary, as much as $12,000 per recipient. *Athletic:* 70 full-time freshmen received athletic scholarships; average amount $7,880.
Cumulative student debt: 54% of graduating class had student loans; average debt was $20,419.

FINANCIAL AID PROCEDURES
Forms required: FAFSA, institutional form.
Dates and Deadlines: Priority date 2/15; closing date 5/1. Applicants notified on a rolling basis starting 3/15; must reply by 5/1 or within 2 week(s) of notification.
Transfers: No deadline. FAFSA should be filed as soon as possible after January 1.

CONTACT
Joe Weglarz, Director of Financial Aid
3399 North Road, Poughkeepsie, NY 12601-1387
(845) 575-3230

Marymount Manhattan College
New York, New York
www.mmm.edu   Federal Code: 002769

4-year private liberal arts college in very large city.
Enrollment: 1,908 undergrads, 17% part-time. 431 full-time freshmen.
Selectivity: Admits over 75% of applicants.

BASIC COSTS (2006-2007)
Tuition and fees: $19,638.
Per-credit charge: $598.
Room and board: $12,090.

FINANCIAL AID PICTURE (2005-2006)
Students with need: Average financial aid package met 46% of need; average scholarship/grant was $3,469; average loan was $2,594. For part-time students, average financial aid package was $4,922.
Students without need: No-need awards available for academics, art, leadership, music/drama.
Cumulative student debt: 57% of graduating class had student loans; average debt was $29,706.
Additional info: Limited international scholarships for top applicants.

FINANCIAL AID PROCEDURES
Forms required: FAFSA.
Dates and Deadlines: Priority date 3/15; no closing date. Applicants notified on a rolling basis starting 3/15; must reply by 5/1 or within 2 week(s) of notification.
Transfers: Applicants notified by 3/1. Must submit academic and financial transcripts from previous institutions.

CONTACT
Maria DeInnocentiis, Director of Financial Aid
221 East 71st Street, New York, NY 10021-4597
(212) 517-0500

Medaille College
Buffalo, New York
www.medaille.edu   Federal Code: 002777

4-year private liberal arts college in large city.
Enrollment: 1,718 undergrads, 8% part-time. 305 full-time freshmen.
Selectivity: Admits 50 to 75% of applicants.

BASIC COSTS (2006-2007)
Tuition and fees: $15,780.
Per-credit charge: $560.
Room and board: $8,024.
Additional info: Tuition/fee waivers available for adults.

FINANCIAL AID PICTURE (2004-2005)
Students with need: Out of 296 full-time freshmen who applied for aid, 296 were judged to have need. Of these, 296 received aid, and 27 had their full need met. Average financial aid package met 70% of need; average scholarship/grant was $4,000; average loan was $3,200. For part-time students, average financial aid package was $6,400.
Students without need: 55 full-time freshmen who did not demonstrate need for aid received scholarships/grants; average award was $1,500. No-need awards available for academics, state/district residency.
Scholarships offered: Trustee Scholarships; for a 92 average or higher; $5,000 per year. Presidential Scholarships; for a 90-91 average; $2,000 per year. Dean Scholarships; for an 88-89 average; $1,500 per year. Merit Scholarships; for an 85-87 average; $1,000 per year.
Cumulative student debt: 65% of graduating class had student loans; average debt was $20,000.

FINANCIAL AID PROCEDURES
Forms required: FAFSA, state aid form, institutional form.
Dates and Deadlines: Priority date 4/15; no closing date. Applicants notified on a rolling basis starting 5/1; must reply within 2 week(s) of notification.

CONTACT
Catherine Buzanski, Director of Financial Aid
18 Agassiz Circle, Buffalo, NY 14214
(716) 880-2256

Mercy College
Dobbs Ferry, New York
www.mercy.edu   Federal Code: 002772

4-year private liberal arts college in small town.
Enrollment: 5,204 undergrads. 576 full-time freshmen.
Selectivity: Admits less than 50% of applicants.

BASIC COSTS (2006-2007)
Tuition and fees: $12,570.
Per-credit charge: $520.
Room and board: $8,678.

FINANCIAL AID PICTURE
Students with need: Need-based aid available for full-time and part-time students. Work study available nights, weekends, and for part-time students.
Students without need: No-need awards available for athletics.

FINANCIAL AID PROCEDURES
Forms required: FAFSA, state aid form.
Dates and Deadlines: Priority date 6/1; no closing date. Applicants notified on a rolling basis starting 3/1; must reply within 4 week(s) of notification.

CONTACT
Janice Spikereit, Director of Processing Financial Aid
555 Broadway, Dobbs Ferry, NY 10522
(800) 637-2969

Metropolitan College of New York
New York, New York
www.metropolitan.edu   Federal Code: 009769

4-year private business and liberal arts college in very large city.
Enrollment: 1,072 undergrads.

Selectivity: Admits over 75% of applicants.

BASIC COSTS (2005-2006)
Tuition and fees: $14,540.
Per-credit charge: $445.
Additional info: Tuition at time of enrollment locked for 4 years.

FINANCIAL AID PICTURE
Students with need: Need-based aid available for full-time and part-time students.
Students without need: No-need awards available for academics.
Scholarships offered: Presidential scholarships; up to $1,300 per semester; based on academic merit; given to top 10% of accepted students each semester.
Additional info: Limited merit scholarships.

FINANCIAL AID PROCEDURES
Forms required: FAFSA, state aid form.
Dates and Deadlines: Priority date 8/15; no closing date. Applicants notified on a rolling basis.

CONTACT
Rica Feng, Director of Financial Aid
75 Varick Street, New York, NY 10013-1919
(212) 343-1234 ext. 5004

Mildred Elley
Latham, New York
www.mildred-elley.edu   Federal Code: 022195

2-year for-profit business college in very large city.
Enrollment: 400 undergrads.
Selectivity: Open admission.

BASIC COSTS (2006-2007)
Tuition and fees: $9,750.
Per-credit charge: $325.
Additional info: Tuition at time of enrollment locked for 2 years.

FINANCIAL AID PICTURE
Students with need: Need-based aid available for full-time and part-time students. Work study available nights.
Students without need: This college only awards aid to students with need.

FINANCIAL AID PROCEDURES
Forms required: FAFSA, state aid form.

CONTACT
Sandy Christiansen, Director of Financial Aid
800 New Loudon Road, Suite 5120, Latham, NY 12110
(518) 786-0855 ext. 228

Mohawk Valley Community College
Utica, New York
www.mvcc.edu   Federal Code: 002871

2-year public community college in small city.
Enrollment: 4,642 undergrads, 20% part-time. 1,351 full-time freshmen.
Selectivity: Open admission; but selective for some programs.

BASIC COSTS (2005-2006)
Tuition and fees: $3,294; out-of-state residents $6,244.
Per-credit charge: $115; out-of-state residents $230.
Room and board: $6,670.

FINANCIAL AID PICTURE (2005-2006)
Students with need: Out of 1,183 full-time freshmen who applied for aid, 757 were judged to have need. Of these, 688 received aid, and 488 had their full need met. Average financial aid package met 92% of need; average scholarship/grant was $2,610; average loan was $1,940. For part-time students, average financial aid package was $1,996.

FINANCIAL AID PROCEDURES
Forms required: FAFSA, institutional form.
Dates and Deadlines: Priority date 4/15; no closing date. Applicants notified on a rolling basis starting 3/1; must reply within 2 week(s) of notification.
Transfers: Applicants notified on a rolling basis.

CONTACT
Annette Broski, Director, Student Financial Aid
1101 Sherman Drive, Utica, NY 13501-5394
(315) 792-5415

Molloy College
Rockville Centre, New York
www.molloy.edu   Federal Code: 002775

4-year private liberal arts college in large town, affiliated with Roman Catholic Church.
Enrollment: 2,589 undergrads, 28% part-time. 290 full-time freshmen.
Selectivity: Admits 50 to 75% of applicants.

BASIC COSTS (2005-2006)
Tuition and fees: $16,810.
Per-credit charge: $525.
Additional info: Tuition/fee waivers available for unemployed or children of unemployed.

FINANCIAL AID PICTURE (2004-2005)
Students with need: Out of 290 full-time freshmen who applied for aid, 238 were judged to have need. Of these, 238 received aid, and 54 had their full need met. Average financial aid package met 65% of need; average scholarship/grant was $7,518; average loan was $3,583. For part-time students, average financial aid package was $7,475.
Students without need: 50 full-time freshmen who did not demonstrate need for aid received scholarships/grants; average award was $13,935. No-need awards available for academics, art, athletics, leadership, music/drama.
Scholarships offered: *Merit:* Molloy Scholar Scholarship: full tuition for minimum 95 high school average and minimum 1250 SAT or 28 ACT; 10 awarded annually; renewable for 3.5 cumulative GPA. Dominican Academic Scholarship: $1,000 through $8,500 for minimum 88 high school average and minimum 1000 SAT (exclusive of Writing); 50 awarded annually, renewable with 3.0 cumulative GPA. Community Service Awards: $1,000 to $3,000, renewable for 2.5 cumulative GPA, awarded to incoming freshmen demonstrating commitment to community and school; 10 awarded annually. *Athletic:* 18 full-time freshmen received athletic scholarships; average amount $5,689.
Cumulative student debt: 86% of graduating class had student loans; average debt was $23,000.

FINANCIAL AID PROCEDURES
Forms required: FAFSA, state aid form.
Dates and Deadlines: Priority date 4/15; closing date 5/1. Applicants notified by 3/1.
Transfers: All transfer applicants with a minimum of 30 credits and 3.0 GPA automatically considered for transfer scholarships ranging from $1,500-$3,000.

CONTACT
Ana Lockward, Director of Financial Aid
PO Box 5002, Rockville Centre, NY 11570
(516) 678-5000 ext. 6249

Monroe College
Bronx, New York
www.monroecollege.edu Federal Code: 004799

4-year for-profit business college in very large city.
Enrollment: 5,866 undergrads, 10% part-time. 1,258 full-time freshmen.
Selectivity: Admits 50 to 75% of applicants.

BASIC COSTS (2005-2006)
Tuition and fees: $9,760.
Room and board: $6,900.

FINANCIAL AID PICTURE (2004-2005)
Students with need: Average financial aid package met 86% of need; average scholarship/grant was $7,300; average loan was $3,434. For part-time students, average financial aid package was $4,200.
Students without need: This college only awards aid to students with need.

FINANCIAL AID PROCEDURES
Forms required: FAFSA.
Dates and Deadlines: Closing date 3/31. Applicants notified on a rolling basis starting 7/1.

CONTACT
Howard Leslie, Dean of Student Financial Services
Monroe College Way, Bronx, NY 10468
(718) 933-6700

Monroe Community College
Rochester, New York
www.monroecc.edu Federal Code: 002872

2-year public community college in large city.
Enrollment: 15,652 undergrads.
Selectivity: Open admission; but selective for some programs.

BASIC COSTS (2005-2006)
Tuition and fees: $2,855; out-of-state residents $5,455.
Per-credit charge: $109; out-of-state residents $218.

FINANCIAL AID PICTURE (2004-2005)
Students with need: 71% of average financial aid package awarded as scholarships/grants, 29% awarded as loans/jobs. Need-based aid available for part-time students. Work study available nights.
Students without need: This college only awards aid to students with need.

FINANCIAL AID PROCEDURES
Forms required: FAFSA.
Dates and Deadlines: Priority date 5/1; no closing date. Applicants notified on a rolling basis; must reply within 2 week(s) of notification.

CONTACT
Jerome St. Croix, Director of Financial Aid
Office of Admissions-Monroe Community College, Rochester, NY 14692-8908
(585) 292-2050

Mount St. Mary College
Newburgh, New York
www.msmc.edu Federal Code: 002778

4-year private liberal arts college in large town.
Enrollment: 2,002 undergrads, 19% part-time. 356 full-time freshmen.
Selectivity: Admits over 75% of applicants.

BASIC COSTS (2005-2006)
Tuition and fees: $16,930.
Per-credit charge: $547.
Room and board: $8,320.

FINANCIAL AID PICTURE (2005-2006)
Students with need: Out of 270 full-time freshmen who applied for aid, 209 were judged to have need. Of these, 208 received aid, and 44 had their full need met. For part-time students, average financial aid package was $7,457.
Students without need: This college only awards aid to students with need.
Scholarships offered: Presidential Scholarship: approximately 65% of tuition; renewable each year with a 3.0 GPA. Merit Grants: range from $3,000-$8,000; renewable each year with a 2.5 GPA. Both based upon acceptance into full-time, traditional program, SAT/ACT test scores, high school GPA, and high school class rank.
Cumulative student debt: 70% of graduating class had student loans; average debt was $20,000.

FINANCIAL AID PROCEDURES
Forms required: FAFSA, institutional form.
Dates and Deadlines: Closing date 2/15. Applicants notified on a rolling basis starting 4/1; must reply within 2 week(s) of notification.
Transfers: Closing date 3/15. Must reply within 2 week(s) of notification.

CONTACT
Susan Twomey, Director of Financial Aid
330 Powell Avenue, Newburgh, NY 12550
(845) 569-3194

Nassau Community College
Garden City, New York
www.ncc.edu Federal Code: 002873

2-year public community college in very large city.
Enrollment: 19,316 undergrads, 32% part-time. 4,462 full-time freshmen.
Selectivity: Open admission; but selective for some programs.

BASIC COSTS (2005-2006)
Tuition and fees: $3,364; out-of-state residents $6,504.
Per-credit charge: $131; out-of-state residents $262.

FINANCIAL AID PICTURE (2005-2006)
Students with need: Out of 3,747 full-time freshmen who applied for aid, 2,598 were judged to have need. Of these, 2,295 received aid, and 49 had their full need met. Average financial aid package met 80% of need; average scholarship/grant was $950; average loan was $1,843. For part-time students, average financial aid package was $3,526.
Students without need: 12 full-time freshmen who did not demonstrate need for aid received scholarships/grants. No-need awards available for academics.
Cumulative student debt: 8% of graduating class had student loans; average debt was $3,062.

FINANCIAL AID PROCEDURES
Forms required: FAFSA, state aid form.
Dates and Deadlines: Priority date 6/1; no closing date. Applicants notified on a rolling basis; must reply within 1 week(s) of notification.

CONTACT
Evangeline Manjares, Assistant Dean, Financial Aid
Office of Admissions, Garden City, NY 11530
(516) 572-7396

Nazareth College of Rochester
Rochester, New York
www.naz.edu   Federal Code: 002779

4-year private liberal arts college in large city.
Enrollment: 2,013 undergrads, 8% part-time. 451 full-time freshmen.
Selectivity: Admits over 75% of applicants.

BASIC COSTS (2006-2007)
Tuition and fees: $21,616.
Per-credit charge: $493.
Room and board: $8,920.

FINANCIAL AID PICTURE (2005-2006)
Students with need: Out of 421 full-time freshmen who applied for aid, 346 were judged to have need. Of these, 346 received aid, and 98 had their full need met. Average financial aid package met 83% of need; average scholarship/grant was $11,818; average loan was $3,031. For part-time students, average financial aid package was $6,100.
Students without need: 102 full-time freshmen who did not demonstrate need for aid received scholarships/grants; average award was $9,287. No-need awards available for academics, alumni affiliation, art, minority status, music/drama, ROTC, state/district residency.
Scholarships offered: Presidential Scholarship; $12,500 to full tuition. Dean's Scholarship; $10,000-12,000. Founders Scholarship; $7,500-9,500. Trustee Scholarship; $5,000-7,000. All awarded based on grades, test scores, class rank, and course load. Campus diversity, regional, art, music, and theater scholarships also available.
Cumulative student debt: 82% of graduating class had student loans; average debt was $19,785.

FINANCIAL AID PROCEDURES
Forms required: FAFSA. CSS PROFILE required of early decision applicants only.
Dates and Deadlines: Priority date 12/15; closing date 5/1. Applicants notified on a rolling basis starting 2/20; must reply by 5/1 or within 2 week(s) of notification.
Transfers: No deadline.

CONTACT
Bruce Woolley, Director of Financial Aid
4245 East Avenue, Rochester, NY 14618-3790
(585) 389-2310

New York Institute of Technology
Old Westbury, New York
www.nyit.edu   Federal Code: 002782

4-year private university and health science college in large town.
Enrollment: 6,155 undergrads, 35% part-time. 843 full-time freshmen.
Selectivity: Admits over 75% of applicants.

BASIC COSTS (2005-2006)
Tuition and fees: $19,236.
Per-credit charge: $630.
Room only: $10,804.
Additional info: Room only charges apply to Manhattan campus; board charges vary on other campuses. Tuition/fee costs reported for nontechnology majors, vary for other programs. Tuition/fee waivers available for unemployed or children of unemployed.

FINANCIAL AID PICTURE (2004-2005)
Students with need: 56% of average financial aid package awarded as scholarships/grants, 44% awarded as loans/jobs. Need-based aid available for part-time students.
Students without need: No-need awards available for academics, athletics.

FINANCIAL AID PROCEDURES
Forms required: FAFSA.
Dates and Deadlines: Priority date 3/1; no closing date. Applicants notified on a rolling basis starting 3/15; must reply by 5/1 or within 2 week(s) of notification.

CONTACT
Clair Jacobi, Director of Financial Aid
Box 8000, Old Westbury, NY 11568
(516) 686-3835

New York School of Interior Design
New York, New York
www.nysid.edu   Federal Code: 013606

4-year private college of interior design in very large city.
Enrollment: 630 undergrads, 73% part-time. 48 full-time freshmen.
Selectivity: Admits less than 50% of applicants.

BASIC COSTS (2006-2007)
Tuition and fees: $18,820.
Per-credit charge: $620.

FINANCIAL AID PICTURE (2004-2005)
Students with need: Out of 28 full-time freshmen who applied for aid, 28 were judged to have need. Of these, 28 received aid. Average financial aid package met 50% of need; average scholarship/grant was $5,000; average loan was $2,625. Need-based aid available for part-time students.
Students without need: This college only awards aid to students with need.
Cumulative student debt: 15% of graduating class had student loans; average debt was $30,000.

FINANCIAL AID PROCEDURES
Forms required: FAFSA, state aid form, institutional form.
Dates and Deadlines: Priority date 5/1; no closing date. Applicants notified on a rolling basis starting 2/1; must reply within 2 week(s) of notification.
Transfers: Applicants notified on a rolling basis.

CONTACT
Nina Bunchuk, Financial Aid Administrator
170 East 70th Street, New York, NY 10021-5110
(212) 472-1500 ext. 212

New York University
New York, New York
www.nyu.edu   Federal Code: 002785

4-year private university in very large city.
Enrollment: 20,150 undergrads, 7% part-time. 4,642 full-time freshmen.
Selectivity: Admits less than 50% of applicants.

BASIC COSTS (2005-2006)
Tuition and fees: $31,690.
Per-credit charge: $881.
Room and board: $11,480.

FINANCIAL AID PICTURE (2005-2006)
Students with need: Out of 3,168 full-time freshmen who applied for aid, 2,490 were judged to have need. Of these, 2,477 received aid. Average financial aid package met 68% of need; average scholarship/grant was $13,275; average loan was $4,377. For part-time students, average financial aid package was $7,833.
Students without need: 456 full-time freshmen who did not demonstrate need for aid received scholarships/grants; average award was $7,020. No-need awards available for academics.

Cumulative student debt: 61% of graduating class had student loans; average debt was $29,480.
Additional info: Both need-based and merit scholarships available to first-time students. Range from $1,000 to $25,000.

FINANCIAL AID PROCEDURES
Forms required: FAFSA, state aid form.
Dates and Deadlines: Closing date 2/15. Applicants notified on a rolling basis starting 4/1; must reply by 5/1.
Transfers: Priority date 3/1; no deadline.

CONTACT
Barbara Hall, Associate Provost for Admissions and Financial Aid
22 Washington Square North, New York, NY 10011-9108
(212) 998-4444

Niagara County Community College
Sanborn, New York
www.niagaracc.suny.edu   Federal Code: 002874

2-year public community college in rural community.
Enrollment: 4,062 undergrads, 22% part-time. 1,058 full-time freshmen.
Selectivity: Open admission; but selective for some programs.

BASIC COSTS (2005-2006)
Tuition and fees: $3,396; out-of-state residents $4,944.
Per-credit charge: $129; out-of-state residents $194.

FINANCIAL AID PICTURE (2004-2005)
Students with need: 58% of average financial aid package awarded as scholarships/grants, 42% awarded as loans/jobs. Need-based aid available for part-time students. Work study available nights.
Students without need: This college only awards aid to students with need.
Additional info: Assistance offered placing students in part-time employment. Students can charge books, food coupons, or $100 advance against anticipated financial aid.

FINANCIAL AID PROCEDURES
Forms required: FAFSA, state aid form.
Dates and Deadlines: Priority date 4/1; no closing date. Applicants notified on a rolling basis starting 5/1; must reply within 2 week(s) of notification.
Transfers: Must file appropriate state and federal change forms at least 4 weeks before registration date.

CONTACT
James Trimboli, Director of Financial Aid
3111 Saunders Settlement Road, Sanborn, NY 14132-9460
(716) 614-6266

Niagara University
Niagara University, New York
www.niagara.edu   Federal Code: 002788

4-year private university in small city, affiliated with Roman Catholic Church.
Enrollment: 2,912 undergrads, 4% part-time. 732 full-time freshmen.
Selectivity: Admits over 75% of applicants.

BASIC COSTS (2005-2006)
Tuition and fees: $19,925.
Per-credit charge: $635.
Room and board: $8,450.
Additional info: Tuition at time of enrollment locked for 4 years.

FINANCIAL AID PICTURE (2005-2006)
Students with need: Out of 657 full-time freshmen who applied for aid, 532 were judged to have need. Of these, 520 received aid, and 136 had their full need met. Average financial aid package met 86% of need; average scholarship/grant was $10,446; average loan was $3,660. For part-time students, average financial aid package was $11,044.
Students without need: 136 full-time freshmen who did not demonstrate need for aid received scholarships/grants; average award was $8,600. No-need awards available for academics, athletics, music/drama, ROTC.
Scholarships offered: 26 full-time freshmen received athletic scholarships; average amount $14,750.
Cumulative student debt: 75% of graduating class had student loans; average debt was $19,753.
Additional info: Opportunity program available for academically and economically disadvantaged students.

FINANCIAL AID PROCEDURES
Forms required: FAFSA, state aid form.
Dates and Deadlines: Priority date 2/15; no closing date. Applicants notified on a rolling basis starting 3/1; must reply within 3 week(s) of notification.
Transfers: Academic scholarship available: $5,800-$6,700 per year based on minimum 3.0 GPA from transfer institution; $3,700 per year based on 2.5-2.99 GPA.

CONTACT
Maureen Salfi, Director of Financial Aid Niagara University, NY 14109
(716) 286-8686

North Country Community College
Saranac Lake, New York
www.nccc.edu   Federal Code: 007111

2-year public community college in small town.
Enrollment: 1,181 undergrads, 17% part-time. 346 full-time freshmen.
Selectivity: Open admission; but selective for some programs.

BASIC COSTS (2005-2006)
Tuition and fees: $3,640; out-of-state residents $8,590.
Per-credit charge: $130; out-of-state residents $340.

FINANCIAL AID PICTURE (2004-2005)
Students with need: Out of 336 full-time freshmen who applied for aid, 277 were judged to have need. Of these, 277 received aid, and 103 had their full need met. Average financial aid package met 54% of need; average scholarship/grant was $3,785; average loan was $1,344. For part-time students, average financial aid package was $600.
Students without need: This college only awards aid to students with need.

FINANCIAL AID PROCEDURES
Forms required: FAFSA, state aid form.
Dates and Deadlines: Priority date 4/1; no closing date. Applicants notified on a rolling basis starting 4/1; must reply within 3 week(s) of notification.

CONTACT
Edwin Trathen, Assistant to the President for Enrollment Management
23 Santanoni Avenue, Saranac Lake, NY 12983
(518) 891-2915 ext. 229

Nyack College
Nyack, New York
www.nyack.edu   Federal Code: 002790

4-year private liberal arts college in large town, affiliated with Christian and Missionary Alliance.
Enrollment: 1,976 undergrads.

BASIC COSTS (2006-2007)
Tuition and fees: $16,300.
Per-credit charge: $640.
Room and board: $7,600.

FINANCIAL AID PICTURE (2004-2005)
Students with need: 54% of average financial aid package awarded as scholarships/grants, 46% awarded as loans/jobs.
Students without need: No-need awards available for academics, alumni affiliation, art, athletics, leadership, minority status, music/drama, religious affiliation, state/district residency.

FINANCIAL AID PROCEDURES
Forms required: FAFSA, state aid form.
Dates and Deadlines: Priority date 3/1; no closing date. Applicants notified on a rolling basis starting 3/1; must reply by 4/1 or within 4 week(s) of notification.

CONTACT
Andres Valenzuela, Director of Student Financial Services
1 South Boulevard, Nyack, NY 10960-3698
(845) 358-1710 ext. 791

Onondaga Community College
Syracuse, New York
www.sunyocc.edu   Federal Code: 002875

2-year public community college in small city.
Enrollment: 8,263 undergrads.
Selectivity: Open admission; but selective for some programs.

BASIC COSTS (2005-2006)
Tuition and fees: $3,490; out-of-district residents $6,670; out-of-state residents $9,850.
Per-credit charge: $125; out-of-district residents $250; out-of-state residents $375.

FINANCIAL AID PICTURE (2004-2005)
Students with need: Need-based aid available for part-time students.
Students without need: This college only awards aid to students with need.

FINANCIAL AID PROCEDURES
Forms required: FAFSA, state aid form.
Dates and Deadlines: Priority date 2/15; no closing date. Applicants notified on a rolling basis starting 4/15; must reply within 4 week(s) of notification.

CONTACT
Lorna Roberts, Director of Financial Aid
4941 Onondaga Road, Syracuse, NY 13215
(315) 469-2291

Orange County Community College
Middletown, New York
orange.cc.ny.us   Federal Code: 002876

2-year public community college in large town.
Enrollment: 6,441 undergrads, 48% part-time. 1,185 full-time freshmen.
Selectivity: Open admission; but selective for some programs.

BASIC COSTS (2005-2006)
Tuition and fees: $3,218; out-of-state residents $6,118.
Per-credit charge: $120; out-of-state residents $240.
Additional info: Tuition/fee waivers available for unemployed or children of unemployed.

FINANCIAL AID PICTURE
Students with need: Need-based aid available for full-time and part-time students.

FINANCIAL AID PROCEDURES
Forms required: FAFSA, state aid form, institutional form.
Dates and Deadlines: Priority date 5/1; no closing date. Applicants notified on a rolling basis starting 5/1; must reply within 4 week(s) of notification.

CONTACT
Sue Sheehan, Assistant Vice President of Student Affairs
115 South Street, Middletown, NY 10940-0115
(845) 341-4190

Pace University
New York, New York
www.pace.edu   Federal Code: 002791

4-year private university in very large city.
Enrollment: 5,021 undergrads, 13% part-time. 966 full-time freshmen.
Selectivity: Admits over 75% of applicants.

BASIC COSTS (2005-2006)
Tuition and fees: $25,384.
Per-credit charge: $710.
Room and board: $8,940.
Additional info: Tuition at time of enrollment locked for 4 years.

FINANCIAL AID PICTURE (2005-2006)
Students with need: Average financial aid package met 53% of need; average scholarship/grant was $13,153; average loan was $3,054. For part-time students, average financial aid package was $5,517.
Students without need: No-need awards available for academics, athletics.
Cumulative student debt: 67% of graduating class had student loans; average debt was $29,060.

FINANCIAL AID PROCEDURES
Forms required: FAFSA, state aid form.
Dates and Deadlines: Priority date 2/15; no closing date. Applicants notified on a rolling basis starting 2/28; must reply by 5/1 or within 2 week(s) of notification.

CONTACT
Christine Falzerano, Acting University Director, Financial Aid
1 Pace Plaza, New York, NY 10038
(212) 346-1300

Parsons The New School for Design
New York, New York
www.parsons.edu   Federal Code: 002780

4-year private visual arts college in very large city.
Enrollment: 3,072 undergrads, 7% part-time. 481 full-time freshmen.
Selectivity: Admits less than 50% of applicants.

BASIC COSTS (2006-2007)
Tuition and fees: $30,930.
Per-credit charge: $1,032.
Room and board: $11,750.

FINANCIAL AID PICTURE (2005-2006)
Students with need: Out of 291 full-time freshmen who applied for aid, 209 were judged to have need. Of these, 206 received aid, and 36 had their full need met. Average financial aid package met 58% of need; average scholarship/grant was $8,812; average loan was $2,287. Need-based aid available for part-time students.

Students without need: 107 full-time freshmen who did not demonstrate need for aid received scholarships/grants; average award was $2,553. No-need awards available for academics, music/drama.
Cumulative student debt: 66% of graduating class had student loans; average debt was $22,623.

FINANCIAL AID PROCEDURES
Forms required: FAFSA, state aid form.
Dates and Deadlines: Priority date 3/1; no closing date. Applicants notified on a rolling basis starting 3/1; must reply within 4 week(s) of notification.

CONTACT
Eileen Doyle, Assistant Provost for University Financial Aid and Enrollment Management
66 Fifth Avenue, New York, NY 10011
(212) 229-8930

Paul Smith's College
Paul Smiths, New York
www.paulsmiths.edu   Federal Code: 002795

4-year private liberal arts college in rural community.
Enrollment: 841 undergrads, 2% part-time. 308 full-time freshmen.
Selectivity: Admits over 75% of applicants.

BASIC COSTS (2006-2007)
Tuition and fees: $17,490.
Room and board: $7,420.
Additional info: Program fees range from $550 to $1,790 depending on program.

FINANCIAL AID PICTURE (2005-2006)
Students with need: Out of 301 full-time freshmen who applied for aid, 280 were judged to have need. Of these, 280 received aid, and 44 had their full need met. Average financial aid package met 69% of need; average scholarship/grant was $7,316; average loan was $3,227.
Students without need: 21 full-time freshmen who did not demonstrate need for aid received scholarships/grants; average award was $5,695. No-need awards available for academics.
Cumulative student debt: 90% of graduating class had student loans; average debt was $6,625.
Additional info: Merit aid only for international students; no financial aid application required.

FINANCIAL AID PROCEDURES
Forms required: FAFSA.
Dates and Deadlines: Priority date 3/31; no closing date. Applicants notified on a rolling basis starting 3/5; must reply within 4 week(s) of notification.
Transfers: No deadline. Applicants notified by 2/5; must reply within 4 week(s) of notification.

CONTACT
Mary Ellen Chamberlain, Director of Financial Aid
PO Box 265, Routes 30 & 86, Paul Smiths, NY 12970-0265
(518) 327-6220

Phillips Beth Israel School of Nursing
New York, New York
www.futurenursebi.org   Federal Code: 006438

2-year private nursing college in very large city.
Enrollment: 195 undergrads, 80% part-time. 3 full-time freshmen.
Selectivity: Admits less than 50% of applicants.

BASIC COSTS (2006-2007)
Tuition and fees: $16,560.
Per-credit charge: $300.

FINANCIAL AID PICTURE (2005-2006)
Students with need: Average financial aid package met 34% of need; average scholarship/grant was $4,600; average loan was $5,125. For part-time students, average financial aid package was $5,980.
Students without need: No-need awards available for academics.
Scholarships offered: Hillman Scholarship Program; variable number awarded each year; based on academic achievement; full tuition, books, and uniforms. Karpas Scholarship Program; 15 awarded each year; based on academic achievement; $3,000 a year.

FINANCIAL AID PROCEDURES
Forms required: FAFSA, state aid form, institutional form.
Dates and Deadlines: Closing date 6/1. Applicants notified by 7/1; must reply within 2 week(s) of notification.

CONTACT
Eli Moinester, Financial Aid Officer
776 Sixth Avenue, Fourth Floor, New York, NY 10001
(212) 614-6104

Polytechnic University
Brooklyn, New York   Federal Code: 002796
www.poly.edu   CSS Code: 2668

4-year private university in very large city.
Enrollment: 1,494 undergrads, 4% part-time. 328 full-time freshmen.
Selectivity: Admits 50 to 75% of applicants.

BASIC COSTS (2006-2007)
Tuition and fees: $29,789.
Per-credit charge: $915.
Room and board: $8,500.

FINANCIAL AID PICTURE (2004-2005)
Students with need: Out of 324 full-time freshmen who applied for aid, 274 were judged to have need. Of these, 274 received aid, and 210 had their full need met. Average financial aid package met 91% of need; average scholarship/grant was $7,346; average loan was $5,275. For part-time students, average financial aid package was $6,648.
Students without need: 50 full-time freshmen who did not demonstrate need for aid received scholarships/grants; average award was $16,077. No-need awards available for academics.
Scholarships offered: Board of Trustees Scholarships; amounts equal to full tuition, less any outside aid for which students are eligible; awarded to academically superior freshmen. Geiger/Fialkov Scholarships; amounts equal to full tuition less any outside aid for which students are eligible; awarded to superior freshmen majoring in engineering or computer science. High School Principal's Scholarship; high school principals in New York metropolitan region nominate outstanding graduates for a scholarship of $10,000 per year; Scholarship Committee selects recipients. Students must file FAFSA to be eligible for merit scholarships.
Cumulative student debt: 78% of graduating class had student loans; average debt was $22,332.

FINANCIAL AID PROCEDURES
Forms required: FAFSA, CSS PROFILE, state aid form, institutional form.
Dates and Deadlines: Priority date 3/1; no closing date. Applicants notified on a rolling basis starting 3/15; must reply within 2 week(s) of notification.
Transfers: Priority date 5/5.

CONTACT
Nicholas Simos, Director of Financial Aid
6 Metrotech Center, Brooklyn, NY 11201-2999
(718) 260-3600

Pratt Institute
Brooklyn, New York
www.pratt.edu   Federal Code: 002798

4-year private university and visual arts college in very large city.
Enrollment: 3,070 undergrads, 5% part-time. 607 full-time freshmen.
Selectivity: Admits 50 to 75% of applicants.

BASIC COSTS (2006-2007)
Tuition and fees: $29,230.
Per-credit charge: $910.
Room and board: $8,752.

FINANCIAL AID PICTURE (2005-2006)
Students with need: Out of 517 full-time freshmen who applied for aid, 442 were judged to have need. Of these, 442 received aid. Average financial aid package met 65% of need; average scholarship/grant was $8,115; average loan was $4,661. Need-based aid available for part-time students.
Students without need: 53 full-time freshmen who did not demonstrate need for aid received scholarships/grants; average award was $9,150. No-need awards available for academics, art.

FINANCIAL AID PROCEDURES
Forms required: FAFSA, institutional form.
Dates and Deadlines: Closing date 2/1. Applicants notified on a rolling basis starting 4/15.
Transfers: Must reply by 5/1 or within 2 week(s) of notification.

CONTACT
Karen Price Scott, Director of Financial Aid
200 Willoughby Avenue, Brooklyn, NY 11205
(718) 636-3519

Rensselaer Polytechnic Institute
Troy, New York
www.rpi.edu   Federal Code: 002803

4-year private university in small city.
Enrollment: 4,921 undergrads. 1,240 full-time freshmen.
Selectivity: Admits over 75% of applicants.

BASIC COSTS (2006-2007)
Tuition and fees: $33,496.
Per-credit charge: $1,019.
Room and board: $9,915.

FINANCIAL AID PICTURE (2005-2006)
Students with need: Out of 1,079 full-time freshmen who applied for aid, 926 were judged to have need. Of these, 926 received aid, and 530 had their full need met. Average financial aid package met 93% of need; average scholarship/grant was $22,133; average loan was $6,000.
Students without need: 249 full-time freshmen who did not demonstrate need for aid received scholarships/grants; average award was $14,906. No-need awards available for academics, alumni affiliation, art, athletics, leadership, minority status, music/drama, ROTC.
Scholarships offered: *Merit:* Rensselaer Medals: $15,000; awarded by participating high schools for excellence in science and mathematics. Emily Roebling Award: $7,500; to top ranking female admitted students. *Athletic:* 10 full-time freshmen received athletic scholarships; average amount $42,360.
Cumulative student debt: 75% of graduating class had student loans; average debt was $27,235.

FINANCIAL AID PROCEDURES
Forms required: FAFSA, state aid form.
Dates and Deadlines: Closing date 2/15. Applicants notified by 3/25.
Transfers: No deadline. Applicants notified on a rolling basis starting 3/31.

CONTACT
James Stevenson, Director of Financial Aid
110 Eighth Street, Troy, NY 12180-3590
(518) 276-6813

Roberts Wesleyan College
Rochester, New York
www.roberts.edu   Federal Code: 002805

4-year private liberal arts college in large city, affiliated with Free Methodist Church of North America.
Enrollment: 1,408 undergrads, 10% part-time. 243 full-time freshmen.
Selectivity: Admits over 75% of applicants.

BASIC COSTS (2006-2007)
Tuition and fees: $20,002.
Per-credit charge: $802.
Room and board: $7,448.

FINANCIAL AID PICTURE (2004-2005)
Students with need: Out of 227 full-time freshmen who applied for aid, 210 were judged to have need. Of these, 210 received aid, and 27 had their full need met. Average financial aid package met 24% of need; average scholarship/grant was $11,153; average loan was $4,020. For part-time students, average financial aid package was $9,099.
Students without need: 33 full-time freshmen who did not demonstrate need for aid received scholarships/grants; average award was $8,560. No-need awards available for academics, alumni affiliation, art, athletics, music/drama, religious affiliation, ROTC, state/district residency.
Scholarships offered: 7 full-time freshmen received athletic scholarships; average amount $7,383.
Additional info: Dollars for Scholars offer matching grants of up to $750.

FINANCIAL AID PROCEDURES
Forms required: FAFSA, state aid form.
Dates and Deadlines: Priority date 3/15; no closing date. Applicants notified on a rolling basis starting 3/15; must reply by 5/1 or within 2 week(s) of notification.

CONTACT
Stephen Field, Director of Student Financial Services
2301 Westside Drive, Rochester, NY 14624-1997
(585) 594-6150

Rochester Business Institute
Rochester, New York
www.rochester-institute.com   Federal Code: 004811

2-year for-profit business college in large city.
Enrollment: 1,103 undergrads.
Selectivity: Admits over 75% of applicants.

BASIC COSTS (2005-2006)
Tuition and fees: $11,750.
Per-credit charge: $250.

FINANCIAL AID PICTURE
Students with need: Need-based aid available for full-time and part-time students. Work study available nights, weekends, and for part-time students.
Students without need: This college only awards aid to students with need.
Cumulative student debt: 92% of graduating class had student loans; average debt was $7,500.

FINANCIAL AID PROCEDURES
Forms required: FAFSA, state aid form, institutional form.

Dates and Deadlines: No deadline. Applicants notified on a rolling basis starting 3/15; must reply within 4 week(s) of notification.

CONTACT
Kandace Reid, Financial Aid Director
1630 Portland Avenue, Rochester, NY 14621-3007
(585) 266-0430

Rochester Institute of Technology
Rochester, New York
www.rit.edu   Federal Code: 002806

4-year private university in large city.
Enrollment: 12,423 undergrads, 8% part-time. 2,250 full-time freshmen.
Selectivity: Admits 50 to 75% of applicants.

BASIC COSTS (2006-2007)
Tuition and fees: $24,651.
Room and board: $8,748.
Additional info: Tuition/fee waivers available for unemployed or children of unemployed.

FINANCIAL AID PICTURE (2004-2005)
Students with need: Out of 1,975 full-time freshmen who applied for aid, 1,690 were judged to have need. Of these, 1,690 received aid, and 1,400 had their full need met. Average financial aid package met 90% of need; average scholarship/grant was $10,600; average loan was $4,500. For part-time students, average financial aid package was $5,800.
Students without need: 230 full-time freshmen who did not demonstrate need for aid received scholarships/grants; average award was $6,500. No-need awards available for academics, art, leadership, ROTC.
Scholarships offered: Presidential Scholarships: up to $10,000 per year; top 10% of high school class with minimum SAT combined score of 1220 (or ACT 27) or top 20% of high school class with minimum SAT score of 1270 (or ACT 28); more than 600 awarded each year. SAT scores exclusive of Writing portion.
Additional info: Most juniors and seniors participate in a cooperative education program, earning an average $5,000 per year through paid employment in jobs related to major.

FINANCIAL AID PROCEDURES
Forms required: FAFSA, state aid form.
Dates and Deadlines: Priority date 3/1; no closing date. Applicants notified on a rolling basis starting 3/15; must reply by 5/1 or within 2 week(s) of notification.
Transfers: Priority date 3/15. Applicants notified on a rolling basis. Applicant must provide financial aid transcripts from any college attended previously. Special merit scholarship programs available specifically for transfers with high GPA.

CONTACT
Verna Hazen, Director of Financial Aid
60 Lomb Memorial Drive, Rochester, NY 14623-5604
(585) 475-2186

Rockland Community College
Suffern, New York
www.sunyrockland.edu   Federal Code: 002877

2-year public community college in large town.
Enrollment: 6,325 undergrads.
Selectivity: Open admission.

BASIC COSTS (2005-2006)
Tuition and fees: $3,065; out-of-state residents $5,865.
Per-credit charge: $116; out-of-state residents $232.

FINANCIAL AID PICTURE (2005-2006)
Students with need: 100% of average financial aid package awarded as scholarships/grants, 0% awarded as loans/jobs. Need-based aid available for part-time students. Work study available nights, weekends, and for part-time students.
Scholarships offered: SUNY Empire State Honors Minority Scholarships available to African American, Latino, and Native American students; 8 awarded; $1,000 per semester for 4 semesters. Jack Watson Scholarships based on minimum 3.5 high school GPA or 94 average in Regents; 5 awarded; $1,162.50 per semester, renewable for 2nd year. Alumni Scholarships for children of alumni with 75 average; varying amounts.

FINANCIAL AID PROCEDURES
Forms required: FAFSA, institutional form.
Dates and Deadlines: Priority date 6/15; no closing date. Applicants notified on a rolling basis starting 6/1; must reply within 3 week(s) of notification.

CONTACT
Marvin Oppenheim, Director of Financial Aid
145 College Road, Suffern, NY 10901
(845) 574-4000

Russell Sage College
Troy, New York
www.sage.edu/rsc   Federal Code: 002810

4-year private comprehensive college for women in small city.
Enrollment: 801 undergrads, 5% part-time. 117 full-time freshmen.
Selectivity: Admits over 75% of applicants.

BASIC COSTS (2006-2007)
Tuition and fees: $24,720.
Per-credit charge: $795.
Room and board: $8,370.

FINANCIAL AID PICTURE (2005-2006)
Students with need: Out of 116 full-time freshmen who applied for aid, 110 were judged to have need. Of these, 110 received aid. For part-time students, average financial aid package was $13,378.
Students without need: 6 full-time freshmen who did not demonstrate need for aid received scholarships/grants; average award was $9,266. No-need awards available for academics, alumni affiliation.
Scholarships offered: Multiple awards to qualified students: presidential and dean's scholarship, Girl Scout scholarship, first-generation scholarship, valedictorian-salutatorian scholarship, student Sage scholarship, endowed scholarships for minority students and specific majors.
Cumulative student debt: 90% of graduating class had student loans; average debt was $20,600.

FINANCIAL AID PROCEDURES
Forms required: FAFSA, state aid form.
Dates and Deadlines: Priority date 3/1; no closing date. Applicants notified on a rolling basis starting 3/15; must reply by 5/1 or within 2 week(s) of notification.
Transfers: Phi Theta Kappa Transfer Scholarship available.

CONTACT
James Dease, Associate Vice President for Student Services
45 Ferry Street, Troy, NY 12180-4115
(518) 244-4525

Sage College of Albany
Albany, New York
www.sage.edu Federal Code: 002811

4-year private college of applied and professional studies in small city.
Enrollment: 941 undergrads, 34% part-time. 86 full-time freshmen.
Selectivity: Admits less than 50% of applicants.

BASIC COSTS (2006-2007)
Tuition and fees: $17,520.
Per-credit charge: $795.
Room and board: $8,520.

FINANCIAL AID PICTURE (2005-2006)
Students with need: Out of 84 full-time freshmen who applied for aid, 80 were judged to have need. Of these, 80 received aid. For part-time students, average financial aid package was $7,091.
Students without need: 4 full-time freshmen who did not demonstrate need for aid received scholarships/grants; average award was $5,250. No-need awards available for academics, art, leadership.
Scholarships offered: Multiple awards to qualified students: presidential and dean's scholarships, first-generation scholarship, art scholarship, valedictorian-salutatorian scholarship, diversity leadership scholarship. Endowed scholarships available for minority students and specific majors.

FINANCIAL AID PROCEDURES
Forms required: FAFSA, state aid form.
Dates and Deadlines: Priority date 3/1; no closing date. Applicants notified on a rolling basis starting 3/15; must reply within 2 week(s) of notification.
Transfers: Phi Theta Kappa transfer scholarship available.

CONTACT
James Dease, Associate Vice President for Student Services
140 New Scotland Avenue, Albany, NY 12208
(518) 292-1783

St. Bonaventure University
St. Bonaventure, New York
www.sbu.edu Federal Code: 002817

4-year private university in large town, affiliated with Roman Catholic Church.
Enrollment: 2,072 undergrads, 2% part-time. 476 full-time freshmen.
Selectivity: Admits over 75% of applicants.

BASIC COSTS (2006-2007)
Tuition and fees: $22,515.
Per-credit charge: $650.
Room and board: $7,760.
Additional info: Tuition/fee waivers available for minority students.

FINANCIAL AID PICTURE
Students with need: Need-based aid available for full-time and part-time students. Work study available nights, weekends, and for part-time students.
Students without need: No-need awards available for academics, art, athletics, leadership, minority status, music/drama, religious affiliation, ROTC, state/district residency.

FINANCIAL AID PROCEDURES
Forms required: FAFSA, state aid form, institutional form.
Dates and Deadlines: Priority date 2/1; no closing date. Applicants notified on a rolling basis starting 4/1; must reply by 5/1 or within 3 week(s) of notification.
Transfers: Closing date 5/1.

CONTACT
Elisabeth Rankin, Director of Financial Aid
Route 417, St. Bonaventure, NY 14778-2284
(716) 375-2400

St. Elizabeth College of Nursing
Utica, New York
www.secon.edu Federal Code: 006461

2-year private nursing college in small city, affiliated with Roman Catholic Church.
Enrollment: 210 undergrads, 34% part-time. 27 full-time freshmen.
Selectivity: Admits 50 to 75% of applicants.

BASIC COSTS (2006-2007)
Tuition and fees: $11,286.
Per-credit charge: $230.

FINANCIAL AID PICTURE (2005-2006)
Students with need: 55% of average financial aid package awarded as scholarships/grants, 45% awarded as loans/jobs. Need-based aid available for part-time students.

FINANCIAL AID PROCEDURES
Forms required: FAFSA, state aid form.
Dates and Deadlines: No deadline. Applicants notified on a rolling basis starting 1/1; must reply within 2 week(s) of notification.

CONTACT
Sherry Wojnas, Director, Financial Aid
2215 Genesee Street, Utica, NY 13501
(315) 798-8206

St. Francis College
Brooklyn Heights, New York
www.stfranciscollege.edu Federal Code: 002820

4-year private liberal arts college in very large city, affiliated with Roman Catholic Church.
Enrollment: 2,299 undergrads, 12% part-time. 497 full-time freshmen.
Selectivity: Admits over 75% of applicants.

BASIC COSTS (2005-2006)
Tuition and fees: $12,890.
Per-credit charge: $440.
Additional info: Tuition/fee waivers available for unemployed or children of unemployed.

FINANCIAL AID PICTURE (2005-2006)
Students with need: Out of 467 full-time freshmen who applied for aid, 388 were judged to have need. Of these, 388 received aid. For part-time students, average financial aid package was $3,052.
Students without need: No-need awards available for academics, athletics.
Scholarships offered: Presidential Scholarship: full tuition; minimum high school GPA 90, minimum SAT 1150. St. Francis Scholarship: $7,500; minimum high school GPA 85, minimum 1100 SAT. St. Clare Scholarship: $6,500; minimum 1100 SAT. St. Clare Scholarship: $6,500; minimum 85 high school GPA, minimum 1000 SAT. Dean's Scholarship: $3,500; minimum 1000 SAT. All scholarships renewable annually for 4-year period, provided student maintains full-time status and cumulative GPA of at least 3.0. SAT scores listed exclusive of Writing portion.

FINANCIAL AID PROCEDURES
Forms required: FAFSA, state aid form.
Dates and Deadlines: Priority date 2/15; no closing date. Applicants notified on a rolling basis starting 3/15; must reply within 2 week(s) of notification.

CONTACT
Joseph Cummings, Director, Student Financial Services
180 Remsen Street, Brooklyn Heights, NY 11201-9902
(718) 489-5255

St. John Fisher College
Rochester, New York
www.sjfc.edu   Federal Code: 002821

4-year private liberal arts college in large town, affiliated with Roman Catholic Church.
Enrollment: 2,631 undergrads, 7% part-time. 530 full-time freshmen.
Selectivity: Admits 50 to 75% of applicants.

BASIC COSTS (2006-2007)
Tuition and fees: $20,710.
Per-credit charge: $555.
Room and board: $8,880.

FINANCIAL AID PICTURE (2004-2005)
Students with need: Out of 502 full-time freshmen who applied for aid, 443 were judged to have need. Of these, 443 received aid, and 42 had their full need met. Average financial aid package met 84% of need; average scholarship/grant was $11,728; average loan was $4,433.
Students without need: 71 full-time freshmen who did not demonstrate need for aid received scholarships/grants; average award was $5,449. No-need awards available for academics.
Scholarships offered: Founders Award: $7,500. Presidential Scholarship: $9,000. Trustees Scholarship: $10,000. Fisher Service Scholars Program: one-third of cost of education; must be nominated. First Generation Scholars Program: $5,000 to one-third of cost of education; must be nominated. Honors and Science Scholars: $2,500 per year ($2,000 in scholarship and $500 in the form of book voucher); Science Scholars also receive laptop computer to use throughout 4 years of enrollment.
Cumulative student debt: 85% of graduating class had student loans; average debt was $31,174.

FINANCIAL AID PROCEDURES
Forms required: FAFSA, state aid form.
Dates and Deadlines: Priority date 2/15; no closing date. Applicants notified on a rolling basis starting 3/21; must reply by 5/1 or within 3 week(s) of notification.
Transfers: Closing date 2/15. Applicants notified on a rolling basis; must reply within 3 week(s) of notification.

CONTACT
Angela Monnat, Director of Financial Aid
3690 East Avenue, Rochester, NY 14618-3597
(585) 385-8042

St. John's University
Queens, New York
www.stjohns.edu   Federal Code: 002823

4-year private university in very large city, affiliated with Roman Catholic Church.
Enrollment: 12,340 undergrads, 5% part-time. 2,996 full-time freshmen.
Selectivity: Admits 50 to 75% of applicants.

BASIC COSTS (2005-2006)
Tuition and fees: $23,370.
Per-credit charge: $760.
Room and board: $11,000.
Additional info: Tuition may vary by program and class year. Tuition at time of enrollment locked for 4 years.

FINANCIAL AID PICTURE (2004-2005)
Students with need: Out of 2,723 full-time freshmen who applied for aid, 2,506 were judged to have need. Of these, 2,506 received aid, and 294 had their full need met. Average financial aid package met 71% of need; average scholarship/grant was $8,753; average loan was $3,290. For part-time students, average financial aid package was $9,356.
Students without need: 145 full-time freshmen who did not demonstrate need for aid received scholarships/grants; average award was $7,813. No-need awards available for academics, alumni affiliation, art, athletics, leadership, music/drama, religious affiliation, ROTC.
Scholarships offered: 48 full-time freshmen received athletic scholarships; average amount $22,272.
Cumulative student debt: 69% of graduating class had student loans; average debt was $21,122.

FINANCIAL AID PROCEDURES
Forms required: FAFSA.
Dates and Deadlines: Priority date 2/1; no closing date. Applicants notified on a rolling basis starting 3/15; must reply within 2 week(s) of notification.
Transfers: No deadline. Must reply within 2 week(s) of notification. Scholarships available if 24 credits college study completed with a minimum GPA of 3.0.

CONTACT
Jorge Rodriguez, Assistant Vice President/Executive Director of Financial Aid
8000 Utopia Parkway, Queens, NY 11439
(718) 990-2000

St. Joseph's College
Brooklyn, New York
www.sjcny.edu   Federal Code: 002825

4-year private liberal arts and teachers college in very large city.
Enrollment: 3,760 undergrads, 22% part-time. 141 full-time freshmen.
Selectivity: Admits over 75% of applicants.

BASIC COSTS (2005-2006)
Tuition and fees: $12,386.
Per-credit charge: $382.

FINANCIAL AID PICTURE (2005-2006)
Students with need: Out of 128 full-time freshmen who applied for aid, 85 were judged to have need. Of these, 85 received aid, and 60 had their full need met. Average financial aid package met 85% of need; average scholarship/grant was $10,000; average loan was $2,500. Need-based aid available for part-time students.
Students without need: 35 full-time freshmen who did not demonstrate need for aid received scholarships/grants; average award was $4,500. No-need awards available for academics, alumni affiliation, leadership.

FINANCIAL AID PROCEDURES
Forms required: FAFSA, state aid form, institutional form.
Dates and Deadlines: Priority date 2/25; no closing date. Applicants notified on a rolling basis starting 4/1; must reply by 5/1 or within 2 week(s) of notification.
Transfers: Priority date 3/15; no deadline.

CONTACT
Carol Sullivan, Director of Financial Aid
245 Clinton Avenue, Brooklyn, NY 11205-3688
(718) 636-6808

St. Joseph's College of Nursing
Syracuse, New York
www.sjhsyr.org/nursing   Federal Code: 006467

2-year private nursing college in small city, affiliated with Roman Catholic Church.
Enrollment: 271 undergrads. 23 full-time freshmen.
Selectivity: Admits less than 50% of applicants.

BASIC COSTS (2005-2006)
Tuition and fees: $8,516.
Per-credit charge: $275.
Room only: $3,200.

FINANCIAL AID PICTURE
Students with need: Need-based aid available for full-time and part-time students.
Students without need: This college only awards aid to students with need.

FINANCIAL AID PROCEDURES
Forms required: FAFSA, state aid form.
Dates and Deadlines: Priority date 4/15; no closing date. Applicants notified on a rolling basis starting 6/15.
Transfers: Priority date 5/30.

CONTACT
Theresa Moser, Director of Financial Aid
206 Prospect Avenue, Syracuse, NY 13203
(315) 448-5040

St. Joseph's College: Suffolk Campus
Patchogue, New York
www.sjcny.edu   Federal Code: E00505

4-year private branch campus and liberal arts college in large town.
Enrollment: 3,760 undergrads, 22% part-time. 467 full-time freshmen.
Selectivity: Admits over 75% of applicants.

BASIC COSTS (2005-2006)
Tuition and fees: $12,956.
Per-credit charge: $402.

FINANCIAL AID PICTURE (2005-2006)
Students with need: Out of 419 full-time freshmen who applied for aid, 388 were judged to have need. Of these, 388 received aid, and 286 had their full need met. Average financial aid package met 32% of need; average scholarship/grant was $5,630; average loan was $2,584. Need-based aid available for part-time students.
Students without need: 132 full-time freshmen who did not demonstrate need for aid received scholarships/grants; average award was $6,399. No-need awards available for academics.
Scholarships offered: Board of Trustees Scholarship: full tuition less outside aid for the normal length of matriculation; entering freshmen with a 92 high school academic average and 1200 total on SAT. Alumni Scholarship: variable award on a yearly basis to children of alumni. Scholastic Achievement Award: up to $5,000 a year for the normal length of matriculation; entering freshmen with a 86 high school academic average and 1020 total on SAT. Academic Achievement Scholarship: automatically awards up to $3,000 for 3.6 GPA or better and $1,500 for 3.3 GPA or better to entering transfer students with 3.3 or better and an associate degree. SAT scores listed exclusive of writing portion.

FINANCIAL AID PROCEDURES
Forms required: FAFSA, state aid form, institutional form.
Dates and Deadlines: Priority date 2/25; no closing date. Must reply within 2 week(s) of notification.
Transfers: Priority date 3/15.

CONTACT
Carol Sullivan, Director of Financial Aid
155 West Roe Boulevard, Patchogue, NY 11772-2603
(631) 447-3214

St. Lawrence University
Canton, New York
www.stlawu.edu   Federal Code: 002829

4-year private liberal arts college in small town.
Enrollment: 2,104 undergrads. 537 full-time freshmen.
Selectivity: Admits 50 to 75% of applicants.

BASIC COSTS (2006-2007)
Tuition and fees: $33,910.
Room and board: $8,630.

FINANCIAL AID PICTURE (2005-2006)
Students with need: Out of 415 full-time freshmen who applied for aid, 372 were judged to have need. Of these, 372 received aid, and 203 had their full need met. Average financial aid package met 95% of need; average scholarship/grant was $19,303; average loan was $2,878.
Students without need: 62 full-time freshmen who did not demonstrate need for aid received scholarships/grants; average award was $13,104. No-need awards available for academics, alumni affiliation, athletics, minority status.
Scholarships offered: *Merit:* Community Service Award: $15,000. *Athletic:* 7 full-time freshmen received athletic scholarships; average amount $39,759.

FINANCIAL AID PROCEDURES
Forms required: FAFSA, institutional form.
Dates and Deadlines: Closing date 2/15. Applicants notified by 3/31; must reply by 5/1 or within 2 week(s) of notification.
Transfers: Closing date 3/15. Applicants notified on a rolling basis starting 3/30; must reply within 2 week(s) of notification.

CONTACT
Patricia Farmer, Director of Financial Aid
Payson Hall, Canton, NY 13617
(315) 229-5265

St. Thomas Aquinas College
Sparkill, New York
www.stac.edu   Federal Code: 002832

4-year private liberal arts college in large town.
Enrollment: 1,409 undergrads, 7% part-time. 327 full-time freshmen.
Selectivity: Admits over 75% of applicants.

BASIC COSTS (2006-2007)
Tuition and fees: $17,600.
Per-credit charge: $575.
Room and board: $9,120.

FINANCIAL AID PICTURE (2004-2005)
Students with need: 55% of average financial aid package awarded as scholarships/grants, 45% awarded as loans/jobs. Need-based aid available for part-time students.
Students without need: No-need awards available for academics, athletics.

FINANCIAL AID PROCEDURES
Forms required: FAFSA, state aid form.
Dates and Deadlines: Priority date 2/15; no closing date. Applicants notified on a rolling basis starting 3/1; must reply by 5/1 or within 2 week(s) of notification.
Transfers: Closing date 5/1.

CONTACT
Anna Chrissotimos, Director of Financial Aid
125 Route 340, Sparkill, NY 10976
(845) 398-4097

Sarah Lawrence College
Bronxville, New York
www.sarahlawrence.edu
Federal Code: 002813
CSS Code: 2810

4-year private liberal arts college in small city.
Enrollment: 1,264 undergrads, 5% part-time. 376 full-time freshmen.
Selectivity: Admits less than 50% of applicants.

BASIC COSTS (2006-2007)
Tuition and fees: $36,088.
Per-credit charge: $1,176.
Room and board: $12,152.

FINANCIAL AID PICTURE (2005-2006)
Students with need: Out of 229 full-time freshmen who applied for aid, 187 were judged to have need. Of these, 187 received aid, and 168 had their full need met. Average financial aid package met 92% of need; average scholarship/grant was $22,392; average loan was $2,258. For part-time students, average financial aid package was $22,623.
Students without need: This college only awards aid to students with need.
Cumulative student debt: 63% of graduating class had student loans; average debt was $13,607.

FINANCIAL AID PROCEDURES
Forms required: FAFSA, CSS PROFILE.
Dates and Deadlines: Closing date 2/1. Applicants notified by 4/1; must reply by 5/1.
Transfers: Closing date 3/15. Maximum institutional grant to transfer students is $27,000 a year. Loans and work study available above and beyond this grant.

CONTACT
Heather McDonnell, Director of Financial Aid
One Mead Way, Bronxville, NY 10708-5999
(914) 395-2570

Schenectady County Community College
Schenectady, New York
www.sunysccc.edu
Federal Code: 006785

2-year public community college in small city.
Enrollment: 3,046 undergrads.
Selectivity: Open admission; but selective for some programs.

BASIC COSTS (2005-2006)
Tuition and fees: $2,868; out-of-state residents $5,618.
Per-credit charge: $108; out-of-state residents $216.

FINANCIAL AID PICTURE (2004-2005)
Students with need: 56% of average financial aid package awarded as scholarships/grants, 44% awarded as loans/jobs. Need-based aid available for part-time students.
Students without need: This college only awards aid to students with need.

FINANCIAL AID PROCEDURES
Forms required: FAFSA.
Dates and Deadlines: Priority date 5/1; no closing date. Applicants notified on a rolling basis starting 4/15; must reply by 8/31.

CONTACT
Brian McGarvey, Director of Financial Aid
78 Washington Avenue, Schenectady, NY 12305
(518) 381-1352

School of Visual Arts
New York, New York
www.schoolofvisualarts.edu
Federal Code: 007468

4-year for-profit visual arts college in very large city.
Enrollment: 3,003 undergrads, 4% part-time. 585 full-time freshmen.
Selectivity: Admits 50 to 75% of applicants.

BASIC COSTS (2006-2007)
Tuition and fees: $22,080.
Per-credit charge: $740.
Room only: $9,800.
Additional info: Additional departmental fees vary by department.

FINANCIAL AID PICTURE (2005-2006)
Students with need: Out of 454 full-time freshmen who applied for aid, 382 were judged to have need. Of these, 377 received aid, and 5 had their full need met. Average financial aid package met 41% of need; average scholarship/grant was $6,219; average loan was $2,872. Need-based aid available for part-time students.
Students without need: 15 full-time freshmen who did not demonstrate need for aid received scholarships/grants; average award was $8,024. No-need awards available for art.
Cumulative student debt: 63% of graduating class had student loans; average debt was $36,869.

FINANCIAL AID PROCEDURES
Forms required: FAFSA, state aid form.
Dates and Deadlines: Priority date 2/1; closing date 3/1. Applicants notified on a rolling basis starting 2/15; must reply within 4 week(s) of notification.
Transfers: No deadline.

CONTACT
Javier Vega, Director of Financial Aid
209 East 23rd Street, New York, NY 10010-3994
(212) 592-2039

Siena College
Loudonville, New York
www.siena.edu
Federal Code: 002816

4-year private liberal arts college in large town, affiliated with Roman Catholic Church.
Enrollment: 3,240 undergrads, 6% part-time. 715 full-time freshmen.
Selectivity: Admits 50 to 75% of applicants.

BASIC COSTS (2006-2007)
Tuition and fees: $21,525.
Per-credit charge: $410.
Room and board: $8,475.

FINANCIAL AID PICTURE (2004-2005)
Students with need: Out of 641 full-time freshmen who applied for aid, 519 were judged to have need. Of these, 518 received aid, and 75 had their full need met. Average financial aid package met 76% of need; average scholarship/grant was $11,185; average loan was $2,815. For part-time students, average financial aid package was $8,316.
Students without need: 102 full-time freshmen who did not demonstrate need for aid received scholarships/grants; average award was $5,655. No-need awards available for academics, art, athletics, leadership, minority status, ROTC, state/district residency.

Scholarships offered: 65 full-time freshmen received athletic scholarships; average amount $12,374.
Cumulative student debt: 73% of graduating class had student loans; average debt was $17,415.

FINANCIAL AID PROCEDURES
Forms required: FAFSA, state aid form.
Dates and Deadlines: Closing date 2/15. Applicants notified by 4/1; must reply by 5/1.
Transfers: Priority date 3/1.

CONTACT
Mary Lawyer, Assistant Vice President for Financial Aid
515 Loudon Road, Loudonville, NY 12211-1462
(518) 783-2427

Skidmore College
Saratoga Springs, New York
www.skidmore.edu
Federal Code: 002814
CSS Code: 2815

4-year private liberal arts college in large town.
Enrollment: 2,727 undergrads, 8% part-time. 695 full-time freshmen.
Selectivity: Admits less than 50% of applicants.

BASIC COSTS (2006-2007)
Tuition and fees: $34,694.
Per-credit charge: $1,140.
Room and board: $9,556.

FINANCIAL AID PICTURE (2005-2006)
Students with need: Out of 352 full-time freshmen who applied for aid, 281 were judged to have need. Of these, 281 received aid, and 237 had their full need met. Average financial aid package met 98% of need; average scholarship/grant was $23,209; average loan was $2,404.
Students without need: 4 full-time freshmen who did not demonstrate need for aid received scholarships/grants; average award was $10,000. No-need awards available for music/drama.
Scholarships offered: Porter Presidential Scholarships in Science and Mathematics: $10,000 annually for 4 years; based on outstanding ability and achievement in mathematics, science, or computer science. Filene Undergraduate Music Scholarships: $10,000 annually for 4 years; based on music ability.
Cumulative student debt: 48% of graduating class had student loans; average debt was $15,857.

FINANCIAL AID PROCEDURES
Forms required: FAFSA, CSS PROFILE.
Dates and Deadlines: Closing date 1/15. Applicants notified by 4/1; must reply by 5/1.
Transfers: Some transfer students eligible for need-based grant assistance. Other transfer students eligible for grant assistance after 1 full year of enrollment or at beginning of junior year, whichever comes first.

CONTACT
Robert Shorb, Director of Student Aid and Family Finance
815 North Broadway, Saratoga Springs, NY 12866
(518) 580-5750

State University of New York at Albany
Albany, New York
www.albany.edu
Federal Code: 002835

4-year public university in small city.
Enrollment: 11,680 undergrads, 5% part-time. 2,546 full-time freshmen.
Selectivity: Admits 50 to 75% of applicants.

BASIC COSTS (2005-2006)
Tuition and fees: $5,810; out-of-state residents $12,070.
Per-credit charge: $181; out-of-state residents $442.
Room and board: $8,050.

FINANCIAL AID PICTURE (2005-2006)
Students with need: Out of 2,082 full-time freshmen who applied for aid, 1,387 were judged to have need. Of these, 1,371 received aid, and 182 had their full need met. Average financial aid package met 72% of need; average scholarship/grant was $4,728; average loan was $3,390. For part-time students, average financial aid package was $5,335.
Students without need: 278 full-time freshmen who did not demonstrate need for aid received scholarships/grants; average award was $2,023. No-need awards available for academics, athletics, state/district residency.
Scholarships offered: *Merit:* Presidential Scholars Program: NY residents can receive up to $3,500 per year and out-of-state students can qualify for up to $6,000 per year in renewable scholarship funding; requires high school average of at least 90 and combined SAT score (exclusive of Writing) in upper 1200s or higher. *Athletic:* 31 full-time freshmen received athletic scholarships; average amount $12,862.
Cumulative student debt: 74% of graduating class had student loans; average debt was $14,392.

FINANCIAL AID PROCEDURES
Forms required: FAFSA, state aid form.
Dates and Deadlines: Closing date 4/15. Applicants notified on a rolling basis starting 3/15; must reply by 5/1 or within 2 week(s) of notification.
Transfers: Students from other institutions transferring mid-year need to have financial aid transcript sent from their institution to school financial aid office.

CONTACT
Brenda Wright, Associate Director of Financial Aid
Office of Undergraduate Admissions, University Administration Building 101, Albany, NY 12222
(518) 442-5757

State University of New York at Binghamton
Binghamton, New York
www.binghamton.edu
Federal Code: 002836

4-year public university in small city.
Enrollment: 11,065 undergrads, 3% part-time. 2,079 full-time freshmen.
Selectivity: Admits less than 50% of applicants.

BASIC COSTS (2005-2006)
Tuition and fees: $5,826; out-of-state residents $12,086.
Per-credit charge: $181; out-of-state residents $442.
Room and board: $8,152.

FINANCIAL AID PICTURE (2005-2006)
Students with need: Out of 1,604 full-time freshmen who applied for aid, 891 were judged to have need. Of these, 881 received aid, and 790 had their full need met. Average financial aid package met 77% of need; average scholarship/grant was $4,874; average loan was $2,957. For part-time students, average financial aid package was $8,797.
Students without need: 73 full-time freshmen who did not demonstrate need for aid received scholarships/grants; average award was $1,305. No-need awards available for academics, art, athletics, leadership, minority status, music/drama, state/district residency.
Scholarships offered: 56 full-time freshmen received athletic scholarships; average amount $8,208.
Cumulative student debt: 60% of graduating class had student loans; average debt was $14,734.

New York State University of New York at Binghamton

FINANCIAL AID PROCEDURES
Forms required: FAFSA, state aid form. CSS PROFILE required of early decision applicants only.
Dates and Deadlines: Priority date 3/1; no closing date. Applicants notified on a rolling basis starting 3/15; must reply within 2 week(s) of notification.
CONTACT
Dennis Chavez, Director of Financial Aid and Employment
Box 6001, Binghamton, NY 13902-6001
(607) 777-2428

State University of New York at Buffalo
Buffalo, New York
www.buffalo.edu   Federal Code: 002837

4-year public university in large city.
Enrollment: 17,830 undergrads, 6% part-time. 3,220 full-time freshmen.
Selectivity: Admits 50 to 75% of applicants.

BASIC COSTS (2005-2006)
Tuition and fees: $6,059; out-of-state residents $12,319.
Per-credit charge: $181; out-of-state residents $442.
Room and board: $8,486.
Additional info: Tuition/fee waivers available for minority students.

FINANCIAL AID PICTURE (2005-2006)
Students with need: Out of 2,432 full-time freshmen who applied for aid, 1,691 were judged to have need. Of these, 1,594 received aid, and 765 had their full need met. Average financial aid package met 80% of need; average scholarship/grant was $3,310; average loan was $2,253. For part-time students, average financial aid package was $6,875.
Students without need: 604 full-time freshmen who did not demonstrate need for aid received scholarships/grants; average award was $2,772. No-need awards available for academics, athletics, minority status, music/drama, state/district residency.
Scholarships offered: *Merit:* Honors program includes scholarships for high academic achievement, high SAT scores. *Athletic:* 25 full-time freshmen received athletic scholarships; average amount $7,385.
Cumulative student debt: 70% of graduating class had student loans; average debt was $17,833.

FINANCIAL AID PROCEDURES
Forms required: FAFSA.
Dates and Deadlines: Priority date 3/1; no closing date. Applicants notified on a rolling basis starting 2/1.
CONTACT
Terri Mangione, Senior Associate Vice Provost & Director of Student Academic Records & Financial Services
12 Capen Hall, Buffalo, NY 14260
(716) 645-2450

State University of New York at Farmingdale
Farmingdale, New York
www.farmingdale.edu   Federal Code: 002858

4-year public technical college in large town.
Enrollment: 5,280 undergrads, 27% part-time. 995 full-time freshmen.
Selectivity: Admits 50 to 75% of applicants.

BASIC COSTS (2005-2006)
Tuition and fees: $5,267; out-of-state residents $11,527.
Per-credit charge: $181; out-of-state residents $442.
Room and board: $10,244.

FINANCIAL AID PICTURE
Students with need: Need-based aid available for full-time and part-time students.
Students without need: No-need awards available for academics.
FINANCIAL AID PROCEDURES
Forms required: FAFSA, state aid form, institutional form.
Dates and Deadlines: Priority date 4/1; no closing date. Applicants notified on a rolling basis starting 4/1.
CONTACT
Catherine Malnichuck, Director of Financial Services
2350 Broad Hollow Road, Farmingdale, NY 11735-1021
(631) 420-2578

State University of New York at New Paltz
New Paltz, New York
www.newpaltz.edu   Federal Code: 002846

4-year public liberal arts college in large town.
Enrollment: 6,169 undergrads, 8% part-time. 807 full-time freshmen.
Selectivity: Admits less than 50% of applicants.

BASIC COSTS (2005-2006)
Tuition and fees: $5,260; out-of-state residents $11,520.
Per-credit charge: $181; out-of-state residents $442.
Room and board: $7,220.

FINANCIAL AID PICTURE (2004-2005)
Students with need: Out of 690 full-time freshmen who applied for aid, 448 were judged to have need. Of these, 445 received aid, and 98 had their full need met. Average financial aid package met 71% of need; average scholarship/grant was $2,324; average loan was $1,918. For part-time students, average financial aid package was $2,344.
Students without need: 34 full-time freshmen who did not demonstrate need for aid received scholarships/grants; average award was $1,999. No-need awards available for academics, art, minority status, music/drama.
Cumulative student debt: 75% of graduating class had student loans; average debt was $18,900.

FINANCIAL AID PROCEDURES
Forms required: FAFSA, state aid form.
Dates and Deadlines: Priority date 3/15; no closing date. Applicants notified on a rolling basis starting 4/1; must reply within 4 week(s) of notification.
Transfers: No deadline.
CONTACT
Daniel Sistarenik, Director of Financial Aid
75 South Manheim Boulevard, Suite 1, New Paltz, NY 12561-2499
(845) 257-3250

State University of New York at Oswego
Oswego, New York
www.oswego.edu   Federal Code: 002848

4-year public university and liberal arts college in large town.
Enrollment: 7,000 undergrads, 6% part-time. 1,363 full-time freshmen.
Selectivity: Admits 50 to 75% of applicants.

BASIC COSTS (2005-2006)
Tuition and fees: $5,315; out-of-state residents $11,575.
Per-credit charge: $181; out-of-state residents $442.
Room and board: $8,340.

FINANCIAL AID PICTURE (2004-2005)

Students with need: Out of 1,228 full-time freshmen who applied for aid, 923 were judged to have need. Of these, 899 received aid, and 243 had their full need met. Average financial aid package met 75% of need; average scholarship/grant was $4,503; average loan was $3,243. For part-time students, average financial aid package was $7,093.

Students without need: 256 full-time freshmen who did not demonstrate need for aid received scholarships/grants; average award was $3,696. No-need awards available for academics, state/district residency.

Scholarships offered: Scholarships based on top 15% of class rank for freshmen $4,400 annually for 4 years, $1,250 annually for 4 years, $500 annually for 4 years. Additional residential scholarships for out-of-state freshmen and transfers: $4,490 annually, $17,960 for 4 years (requires on-campus housing). Transfers entering in the fall with 60 credits and a 3.3 GPA are eligible for a one time scholarship of $1,000.

Cumulative student debt: 80% of graduating class had student loans; average debt was $18,917.

FINANCIAL AID PROCEDURES

Forms required: FAFSA.
Dates and Deadlines: Priority date 4/1; no closing date. Applicants notified on a rolling basis starting 3/1; must reply by 5/1 or within 3 week(s) of notification.
Transfers: Transfer students entering in January need to supply financial aid transcipts from prior colleges.

CONTACT

Mark Humbert, Director of Financial Aid
229 Sheldon Hall, Oswego, NY 13126-3599
(315) 312-2248

State University of New York at Purchase
Purchase, New York
www.purchase.edu   Federal Code: 006791

4-year public college of liberal arts and visual and performing arts in large town.
Enrollment: 3,396 undergrads, 7% part-time. 717 full-time freshmen.
Selectivity: Admits less than 50% of applicants.

BASIC COSTS (2005-2006)

Tuition and fees: $5,504; out-of-state residents $11,764.
Per-credit charge: $181; out-of-state residents $442.
Room and board: $8,446.

FINANCIAL AID PICTURE (2004-2005)

Students with need: Out of 501 full-time freshmen who applied for aid, 329 were judged to have need. Of these, 329 received aid, and 33 had their full need met. Average financial aid package met 62.05% of need; average scholarship/grant was $5,286; average loan was $3,320. For part-time students, average financial aid package was $9,169.

Students without need: 170 full-time freshmen who did not demonstrate need for aid received scholarships/grants; average award was $16,162. No-need awards available for academics, art, minority status, music/drama.

Cumulative student debt: 72% of graduating class had student loans; average debt was $17,504.

Additional info: All applicants automatically considered for scholarship upon review of applications, essays, auditions, and/or portfolio.

FINANCIAL AID PROCEDURES

Forms required: FAFSA, state aid form.
Dates and Deadlines: Priority date 3/1; no closing date. Applicants notified on a rolling basis starting 3/1; must reply within 2 week(s) of notification.
Transfers: Financial aid transcripts required from all previously attended institutions.

CONTACT

Emilie Devine, Director of Financial Aid
735 Anderson Hill Road, Purchase, NY 10577-1400
(914) 251-6350

State University of New York at Stony Brook
Stony Brook, New York
www.stonybrook.edu   Federal Code: 002838

4-year public university in large town.
Enrollment: 14,095 undergrads, 7% part-time. 2,105 full-time freshmen.
Selectivity: Admits 50 to 75% of applicants.

BASIC COSTS (2005-2006)

Tuition and fees: $5,575; out-of-state residents $11,835.
Per-credit charge: $181; out-of-state residents $442.
Room and board: $8,050.

FINANCIAL AID PICTURE (2004-2005)

Students with need: Out of 1,702 full-time freshmen who applied for aid, 1,232 were judged to have need. Of these, 1,210 received aid, and 115 had their full need met. Average financial aid package met 67% of need; average scholarship/grant was $5,977; average loan was $2,763. For part-time students, average financial aid package was $4,338.

Students without need: 376 full-time freshmen who did not demonstrate need for aid received scholarships/grants; average award was $2,487. No-need awards available for academics, athletics.

Scholarships offered: 54 full-time freshmen received athletic scholarships; average amount $8,398.

FINANCIAL AID PROCEDURES

Forms required: FAFSA.
Dates and Deadlines: Priority date 3/1; no closing date. Applicants notified on a rolling basis starting 3/1; must reply by 5/1 or within 2 week(s) of notification.

CONTACT

Jacqueline Pascariello, Director Financial Aid Stony Brook, NY 11794-1901
(631) 689-6000

State University of New York College at Brockport
Brockport, New York
www.brockport.edu   Federal Code: 002841

4-year public liberal arts college in small town.
Enrollment: 6,852 undergrads, 11% part-time. 981 full-time freshmen.
Selectivity: Admits less than 50% of applicants.

BASIC COSTS (2005-2006)

Tuition and fees: $5,293; out-of-state residents $11,553.
Per-credit charge: $181; out-of-state residents $442.
Room and board: $8,062.

FINANCIAL AID PICTURE (2004-2005)

Students with need: Out of 906 full-time freshmen who applied for aid, 693 were judged to have need. Of these, 689 received aid, and 184 had their full need met. Average financial aid package met 83% of need; average scholarship/grant was $3,759; average loan was $4,216. For part-time students, average financial aid package was $4,774.

Students without need: 49 full-time freshmen who did not demonstrate need for aid received scholarships/grants; average award was $4,034. No-need awards available for academics, alumni affiliation, leadership, minority status, ROTC, state/district residency.

Scholarships offered: Extraordinary Academic Scholarships: ranging from $1,000 to $12,573 per year; minimum qualifications include SAT scores of 1100 (24 ACT), rank in top 25% of class, and GPA 90 or higher. SAT score listed exclusive of Writing portion.
Cumulative student debt: 81% of graduating class had student loans; average debt was $19,083.

FINANCIAL AID PROCEDURES
Forms required: FAFSA, state aid form.
Dates and Deadlines: Priority date 2/15; no closing date. Applicants notified on a rolling basis starting 2/15; must reply within 4 week(s) of notification.
Transfers: Academic scholarships available to transfer students with minimum 3.75 GPA and junior status (at least 54 completed credits); $1,000 per year for up to two years.

CONTACT
Scott Atkinson, Associate Vice President for Enrollment Management and Student Affairs
350 New Campus Drive, Brockport, NY 14420-2915
(585) 395-2501

State University of New York College at Buffalo
Buffalo, New York
www.buffalostate.edu   Federal Code: 002842

4-year public liberal arts and teachers college in large city.
Enrollment: 8,722 undergrads, 11% part-time. 1,314 full-time freshmen.
Selectivity: Admits less than 50% of applicants.

BASIC COSTS (2005-2006)
Tuition and fees: $5,231; out-of-state residents $11,491.
Per-credit charge: $181; out-of-state residents $442.
Room and board: $6,672.
Additional info: Tuition/fee waivers available for minority students.

FINANCIAL AID PICTURE (2004-2005)
Students with need: Out of 1,242 full-time freshmen who applied for aid, 1,072 were judged to have need. Of these, 759 received aid, and 486 had their full need met. Average financial aid package met 72% of need; average scholarship/grant was $3,262; average loan was $3,368. For part-time students, average financial aid package was $6,208.
Students without need: This college only awards aid to students with need.
Scholarships offered: Empire Minority Scholarships: $1,000 annually for 4 years. Honors Program: $2,000 for 2 years and $1,000 for remaining 2 years.

FINANCIAL AID PROCEDURES
Forms required: FAFSA.
Dates and Deadlines: Priority date 3/15; closing date 5/1. Applicants notified on a rolling basis starting 5/1; must reply within 4 week(s) of notification.
Transfers: No deadline.

CONTACT
Kent McGowan, Director of Financial Aid
1300 Elmwood Avenue, Moot Hall, Buffalo, NY 14222-1095
(716) 878-4000

State University of New York College at Cortland
Cortland, New York
www.cortland.edu   Federal Code: 002843

4-year public university and liberal arts and teachers college in large town.
Enrollment: 5,871 undergrads, 2% part-time. 1,093 full-time freshmen.
Selectivity: Admits less than 50% of applicants.

BASIC COSTS (2005-2006)
Tuition and fees: $5,341; out-of-state residents $11,601.
Per-credit charge: $181; out-of-state residents $442.
Room and board: $7,650.

FINANCIAL AID PICTURE (2004-2005)
Students with need: Out of 977 full-time freshmen who applied for aid, 687 were judged to have need. Of these, 671 received aid, and 100 had their full need met. Average financial aid package met 73% of need; average scholarship/grant was $3,384; average loan was $2,624. Need-based aid available for part-time students.
Students without need: 194 full-time freshmen who did not demonstrate need for aid received scholarships/grants; average award was $6,819. No-need awards available for academics, leadership.

FINANCIAL AID PROCEDURES
Forms required: FAFSA.
Dates and Deadlines: Closing date 4/1. Applicants notified on a rolling basis starting 3/1; must reply by 5/1 or within 2 week(s) of notification.
Transfers: Federal regulations require financial aid transcript from each postsecondary school attended even if student did not receive aid.

CONTACT
David Canaski, Director of Financial Aid
PO Box 2000, Cortland, NY 13045-0900
(607) 753-4717

State University of New York College at Fredonia
Fredonia, New York
www.fredonia.edu   Federal Code: 002844

4-year public liberal arts college in large town.
Enrollment: 5,026 undergrads, 4% part-time. 1,019 full-time freshmen.
Selectivity: Admits 50 to 75% of applicants.

BASIC COSTS (2005-2006)
Tuition and fees: $5,441; out-of-state residents $11,701.
Per-credit charge: $181; out-of-state residents $442.
Room and board: $7,570.

FINANCIAL AID PICTURE (2005-2006)
Students with need: Out of 927 full-time freshmen who applied for aid, 604 were judged to have need. Of these, 595 received aid, and 127 had their full need met. Average financial aid package met 68% of need; average scholarship/grant was $3,541; average loan was $2,888. For part-time students, average financial aid package was $5,936.
Students without need: 117 full-time freshmen who did not demonstrate need for aid received scholarships/grants; average award was $1,661. No-need awards available for academics, alumni affiliation, art, leadership, minority status, music/drama.
Scholarships offered: Foundation Freshman Award: 30 awarded; minimum 91 high school average, 1250 SAT or 28 ACT; $3,000. Fredonia Achievement Award: 60 awarded; minimum 87 high school average, 1100 SAT or 25 ACT, minimum 3.0 GPA for transfer students; $1,000. Fredonia Award for Excellence: high school valedictorians and salutatorians; $2,500 renewable for 4 years. Out-of-State Student Scholarships: 90 high school average, 1250 SAT or 28 ACT, 3.25 GPA for transfer students. SAT scores listed are exclusive of Writing portion. Foundation Academic Scholarship: awarded to Group 1 & 2 students in the natural and social sciences.
Cumulative student debt: 81% of graduating class had student loans; average debt was $12,500.

FINANCIAL AID PROCEDURES
Forms required: FAFSA, state aid form.

Dates and Deadlines: Priority date 1/31; closing date 5/15. Applicants notified on a rolling basis starting 3/10; must reply within 4 week(s) of notification.
Transfers: Applicants notified on a rolling basis starting 10/15. Financial aid transcripts required from prior institutions attended.

CONTACT
Daniel Tramuta, Director of Financial Aid
178 Central Avenue, Fredonia, NY 14063-1136
(716) 673-3253

State University of New York College at Geneseo
Geneseo, New York
www.geneseo.edu   Federal Code: 002845

4-year public liberal arts college in small town.
Enrollment: 5,292 undergrads, 2% part-time. 1,025 full-time freshmen.
Selectivity: Admits less than 50% of applicants.

BASIC COSTS (2005-2006)
Tuition and fees: $5,520; out-of-state residents $11,780.
Per-credit charge: $181; out-of-state residents $442.
Room and board: $7,750.

FINANCIAL AID PICTURE (2005-2006)
Students with need: Out of 856 full-time freshmen who applied for aid, 434 were judged to have need. Of these, 434 received aid, and 325 had their full need met. Average financial aid package met 75% of need; average scholarship/grant was $2,450; average loan was $3,495. Need-based aid available for part-time students.
Students without need: 45 full-time freshmen who did not demonstrate need for aid received scholarships/grants; average award was $2,146. No-need awards available for academics, art, leadership, minority status, music/drama, religious affiliation, ROTC, state/district residency.
Cumulative student debt: 75% of graduating class had student loans; average debt was $16,000.

FINANCIAL AID PROCEDURES
Forms required: FAFSA, state aid form.
Dates and Deadlines: Closing date 2/15. Applicants notified on a rolling basis starting 3/15; must reply by 5/1.

CONTACT
Archie Cureton, Director of Financial Aid
1 College Circle, Geneseo, NY 14454-1471
(585) 245-5731

State University of New York College at Old Westbury
Old Westbury, New York
www.oldwestbury.edu   Federal Code: 007109

4-year public university and liberal arts college in small city.
Enrollment: 3,215 undergrads, 16% part-time. 407 full-time freshmen.
Selectivity: Admits 50 to 75% of applicants.

BASIC COSTS (2005-2006)
Tuition and fees: $5,071; out-of-state residents $11,331.
Per-credit charge: $181; out-of-state residents $442.
Room and board: $8,082.

FINANCIAL AID PICTURE (2005-2006)
Students with need: Out of 334 full-time freshmen who applied for aid, 332 were judged to have need. Of these, 296 received aid, and 332 had their full need met. Average financial aid package met 45.05% of need; average scholarship/grant was $5,645; average loan was $1,661. For part-time students, average financial aid package was $3,097.
Students without need: No-need awards available for academics.
Cumulative student debt: 51% of graduating class had student loans; average debt was $13,733.

FINANCIAL AID PROCEDURES
Forms required: FAFSA, state aid form, institutional form.
Dates and Deadlines: Closing date 4/13. Applicants notified on a rolling basis starting 4/24; must reply within 2 week(s) of notification.
Transfers: Must reply within 2 week(s) of notification. Financial aid transcript required.

CONTACT
Delores James, Director of Financial Aid
Box 307, Old Westbury, NY 11568-0307
(516) 876-3222

State University of New York College at Oneonta
Oneonta, New York
www.oneonta.edu   Federal Code: 002847

4-year public liberal arts college in large town.
Enrollment: 5,589 undergrads, 2% part-time. 1,143 full-time freshmen.
Selectivity: Admits less than 50% of applicants.

BASIC COSTS (2005-2006)
Tuition and fees: $5,362; out-of-state residents $11,622.
Per-credit charge: $181; out-of-state residents $442.
Room and board: $7,400.

FINANCIAL AID PICTURE (2005-2006)
Students with need: Out of 974 full-time freshmen who applied for aid, 659 were judged to have need. Of these, 638 received aid, and 93 had their full need met. Average financial aid package met 58% of need; average scholarship/grant was $3,697; average loan was $3,434. For part-time students, average financial aid package was $5,498.
Students without need: 286 full-time freshmen who did not demonstrate need for aid received scholarships/grants; average award was $3,835. No-need awards available for academics, athletics.
Scholarships offered: Presidential Scholarships: $3,500; awarded to more than 60 applicants for academics, service, and extracurricular activities. Organization of Ancillary Services: $1,000; awarded to 64 applicants for academics, service, and extracurricular activities. OAS Minority Student Merit Scholarships: $3,500; awarded to 6 applicants for academics, service, and extracurricular activities. Mildred Haight Memorial Scholarships: $500; awarded to 22 applicants for academics. Edward Griesmer Transfer Scholarships: $2,500; awarded to 2 applicants for academics and residence.
Cumulative student debt: 76% of graduating class had student loans; average debt was $8,308.

FINANCIAL AID PROCEDURES
Forms required: FAFSA, state aid form.
Dates and Deadlines: Priority date 2/15; no closing date. Applicants notified on a rolling basis starting 3/1; must reply within 4 week(s) of notification.
Transfers: No deadline. Applicants notified on a rolling basis starting 3/1.

CONTACT
C. Goodhue, Director of Student Financial Aid
Admissions, Alumni Hall, Oneonta, NY 13820-4016
(607) 436-2532

State University of New York College at Plattsburgh
Plattsburgh, New York
www.plattsburgh.edu
Federal Code: 002849

4-year public liberal arts and teachers college in large town.
Enrollment: 5,304 undergrads, 5% part-time. 1,028 full-time freshmen.
Selectivity: Admits 50 to 75% of applicants.

BASIC COSTS (2005-2006)
Tuition and fees: $5,297; out-of-state residents $11,557.
Per-credit charge: $181; out-of-state residents $442.
Room and board: $7,206.

FINANCIAL AID PICTURE (2005-2006)
Students with need: Out of 846 full-time freshmen who applied for aid, 618 were judged to have need. Of these, 606 received aid, and 178 had their full need met. Average financial aid package met 85% of need; average scholarship/grant was $5,102; average loan was $4,023. For part-time students, average financial aid package was $6,632.
Students without need: 309 full-time freshmen who did not demonstrate need for aid received scholarships/grants; average award was $4,144. No-need awards available for academics, alumni affiliation, art, leadership, music/drama, state/district residency.
Cumulative student debt: 73% of graduating class had student loans; average debt was $17,865.

FINANCIAL AID PROCEDURES
Forms required: FAFSA, state aid form.
Dates and Deadlines: Priority date 3/1; no closing date. Applicants notified on a rolling basis starting 3/31; must reply within 6 week(s) of notification.
Transfers: Closing date 3/1. Applicants notified by 3/31.

CONTACT
Todd Moravec, Director of Financial Aid
Kehoe Administration Building, Plattsburgh, NY 12901
(518) 564-4076

State University of New York College at Potsdam
Potsdam, New York
www.potsdam.edu
Federal Code: 002850

4-year public liberal arts and teachers college in large town.
Enrollment: 3,570 undergrads, 3% part-time. 734 full-time freshmen.
Selectivity: Admits 50 to 75% of applicants.

BASIC COSTS (2005-2006)
Tuition and fees: $5,289; out-of-state residents $11,549.
Per-credit charge: $181; out-of-state residents $442.
Room and board: $7,670.
Additional info: Music Fee $300 (annual); Concert Fee $230 (annual) for the 2005-2006 academic year.

FINANCIAL AID PICTURE (2005-2006)
Students with need: Out of 660 full-time freshmen who applied for aid, 489 were judged to have need. Of these, 487 received aid, and 390 had their full need met. Average financial aid package met 80% of need; average scholarship/grant was $5,992; average loan was $3,314. For part-time students, average financial aid package was $8,940.
Students without need: 135 full-time freshmen who did not demonstrate need for aid received scholarships/grants; average award was $2,730. No-need awards available for academics, art, leadership, minority status, music/drama, ROTC.
Scholarships offered: Adirondack Scholars Program: based upon high school GPA and standardized test scores. Mt. Emmons Scholarship: covers balance of in-state tuition and mandatory fees after TAP awards, $500 book stipend, residence hall fee waiver and board; renewable with minimum 3.25 GPA; 5 awarded. Navigator Scholarship: range from $1,000-$2,000; awarded to students who show academic promise and the potential for leadership; must have 1100 or greater SAT (exclusive of Writing) or ACT composite of 23 or minimum 90 high school average and history of participation and leadership in extracurricular activities and community service.
Cumulative student debt: 82% of graduating class had student loans; average debt was $16,117.
Additional info: Apply early to access limited, need-based awards.

FINANCIAL AID PROCEDURES
Forms required: FAFSA, state aid form.
Dates and Deadlines: Priority date 3/1; no closing date. Applicants notified on a rolling basis starting 2/1; must reply within 4 week(s) of notification.
Transfers: Adirondack Scholars Program: for incoming transfer students based upon outstanding academic achievement as measured by previous college GPA. Pacesetter Scholarship: $1,000 residence hall waiver to students with minimum cumulative GPA of 3.25 and higher. Renewable for 1 additional year with a cumulative 3.25 GPA. Capstone Scholarship: 6 $2,000 awards for students with minimum cumulative GPA of 3.50 and 13 $1,000 awards for students with minimum cumulative GPA of 3.25-3.49. Renewable for 1 additional year with a cumulative 3.25 GPA. Applies to fall applicants only.

CONTACT
Susan Aldrich, Director of Financial Aid
44 Pierrepont Avenue, Potsdam, NY 13676
(315) 267-2162

State University of New York College of Agriculture and Technology at Cobleskill
Cobleskill, New York
www.cobleskill.edu
Federal Code: 002856
CSS Code: 2524

2-year public agricultural and technical college in small town.
Enrollment: 2,511 undergrads, 3% part-time. 1,107 full-time freshmen.
Selectivity: Admits 50 to 75% of applicants.

BASIC COSTS (2005-2006)
Tuition and fees: $5,370; out-of-state residents $11,630.
Per-credit charge: $181; out-of-state residents $442.
Room and board: $7,670.

FINANCIAL AID PICTURE (2004-2005)
Students with need: Out of 914 full-time freshmen who applied for aid, 734 were judged to have need. Of these, 723 received aid, and 30 had their full need met. Average financial aid package met 59% of need; average scholarship/grant was $4,515; average loan was $2,794. For part-time students, average financial aid package was $3,938.
Students without need: No-need awards available for academics, alumni affiliation, leadership, state/district residency.
Scholarships offered: Application deadline for scholarships March 15. Separate application required, which is available through the admissions office.

FINANCIAL AID PROCEDURES
Forms required: FAFSA, CSS PROFILE.
Dates and Deadlines: Closing date 3/15. Applicants notified by 4/15; must reply within 2 week(s) of notification.
Transfers: No deadline. Applicants notified on a rolling basis.

CONTACT
Richard Young, Director of Financial Aid Cobleskill, NY 12043
(800) 295-8998

State University of New York College of Agriculture and Technology at Morrisville
Morrisville, New York
www.morrisville.edu   Federal Code: 002859

2-year public junior and technical college in small town.
Enrollment: 3,009 undergrads, 13% part-time. 1,056 full-time freshmen.
Selectivity: Admits 50 to 75% of applicants.

BASIC COSTS (2005-2006)
Tuition and fees: $5,215; out-of-state residents $11,475.
Per-credit charge: $181; out-of-state residents $442.
Room and board: $7,070.
Additional info: Out-of-state associate degree students pay $7,210 tuition.

FINANCIAL AID PICTURE (2005-2006)
Students with need: Out of 989 full-time freshmen who applied for aid, 872 were judged to have need. Of these, 867 received aid, and 16 had their full need met. Average financial aid package met 15% of need; average scholarship/grant was $4,439; average loan was $2,510. For part-time students, average financial aid package was $4,009.
Students without need: 23 full-time freshmen who did not demonstrate need for aid received scholarships/grants; average award was $1,994. No-need awards available for academics.
Cumulative student debt: 78% of graduating class had student loans; average debt was $9,742.

FINANCIAL AID PROCEDURES
Forms required: FAFSA, state aid form.
Dates and Deadlines: Priority date 2/1; no closing date. Applicants notified on a rolling basis starting 3/1.

CONTACT
Tom David, Director of Financial Aid
PO Box 901, Morrisville, NY 13408-0901
(800) 626-5844

State University of New York College of Environmental Science and Forestry
Syracuse, New York
www.esf.edu   Federal Code: 002851

4-year public university in small city.
Enrollment: 1,372 undergrads, 3% part-time. 260 full-time freshmen.
Selectivity: Admits 50 to 75% of applicants.

BASIC COSTS (2005-2006)
Tuition and fees: $5,032; out-of-state residents $11,292.
Per-credit charge: $181; out-of-state residents $442.
Additional info: Room and board available through Syracuse University.

FINANCIAL AID PICTURE (2005-2006)
Students with need: Average financial aid package met 100% of need; average scholarship/grant was $4,500; average loan was $4,625. For part-time students, average financial aid package was $6,250.
Students without need: No-need awards available for academics.

FINANCIAL AID PROCEDURES
Forms required: FAFSA, state aid form.
Dates and Deadlines: Priority date 3/1; no closing date. Applicants notified on a rolling basis starting 3/15; must reply within 2 week(s) of notification.

CONTACT
John View, Director of Financial Aid
106 Bray Hall, Syracuse, NY 13210
(315) 470-6670

State University of New York College of Technology at Alfred
Alfred, New York
www.alfredstate.edu   Federal Code: 002854

2-year public agricultural and liberal arts and technical college in rural community.
Enrollment: 3,184 undergrads, 5% part-time. 1,106 full-time freshmen.
Selectivity: Admits 50 to 75% of applicants.

BASIC COSTS (2005-2006)
Tuition and fees: $5,343; out-of-state residents $8,203.
Per-credit charge: $181; out-of-state residents $300.
Room and board: $7,230.
Additional info: Tuition for bachelor's degree: full-time out-of-state tuition $10,610; per-credit-hour $442 out-of-state.

FINANCIAL AID PICTURE (2004-2005)
Students with need: 59% of average financial aid package awarded as scholarships/grants, 41% awarded as loans/jobs. Need-based aid available for part-time students. Work study available nights, weekends, and for part-time students.
Students without need: No-need awards available for academics, alumni affiliation, job skills, minority status.

FINANCIAL AID PROCEDURES
Forms required: FAFSA, state aid form.
Dates and Deadlines: Priority date 3/1; no closing date. Applicants notified on a rolling basis starting 3/1; must reply within 3 week(s) of notification.

CONTACT
Laura Giglio, Director of Financial Aid
Huntington Administration Building, Alfred, NY 14802-1196
(607) 587-4215

State University of New York College of Technology at Canton
Canton, New York
www.canton.edu   Federal Code: 002855

2-year public technical college in small town.
Enrollment: 2,246 undergrads, 7% part-time. 799 full-time freshmen.
Selectivity: Admits over 75% of applicants.

BASIC COSTS (2005-2006)
Tuition and fees: $5,370; out-of-state residents $8,230.
Per-credit charge: $181; out-of-state residents $300.
Room and board: $7,760.
Additional info: Out-of-state tuition for bachelor's degree program: $10,610; $442 per-credit-hour. Tuition/fee waivers available for unemployed or children of unemployed.

FINANCIAL AID PICTURE
Students with need: Need-based aid available for full-time and part-time students.

FINANCIAL AID PROCEDURES
Forms required: FAFSA, state aid form.
Dates and Deadlines: Priority date 3/15; no closing date. Applicants notified on a rolling basis starting 2/1; must reply within 4 week(s) of notification.
Transfers: Financial aid transcripts required from all previously attended schools for mid-year transfers.

CONTACT
Kerrie Cooper, Director of Financial Aid
34 Cornell Drive, Canton, NY 13617-1098
(315) 386-7123

State University of New York College of Technology at Delhi
Delhi, New York
www.delhi.edu
Federal Code: 002857

2-year public technical college in small town.
Enrollment: 2,483 undergrads, 12% part-time. 930 full-time freshmen.
Selectivity: Open admission; but selective for some programs.

BASIC COSTS (2005-2006)
Tuition and fees: $5,319; out-of-state residents $8,179.
Per-credit charge: $181; out-of-state residents $300.
Room and board: $7,380.
Additional info: Out-of-state tuition for bachelor's program: $10,610; per-credit-hour $442.

FINANCIAL AID PICTURE (2004-2005)
Students with need: 64% of average financial aid package awarded as scholarships/grants, 36% awarded as loans/jobs. Need-based aid available for part-time students.

FINANCIAL AID PROCEDURES
Forms required: FAFSA, state aid form.
Dates and Deadlines: Priority date 2/15; no closing date. Applicants notified on a rolling basis starting 3/1; must reply within 2 week(s) of notification.

CONTACT
Nancy Hughes, Financial Aid Director
2 Main Street, Delhi, NY 13753-1190
(607) 746-4000

State University of New York Downstate Medical Center
Brooklyn, New York
www.downstate.edu
Federal Code: 002839

Upper-division public health science and nursing college in very large city.
Enrollment: 345 undergrads.

BASIC COSTS (2005-2006)
Tuition and fees: $4,710; out-of-state residents $10,970.
Per-credit charge: $181; out-of-state residents $442.
Room and board: $11,774.

FINANCIAL AID PICTURE
Students with need: Need-based aid available for full-time and part-time students.

FINANCIAL AID PROCEDURES
Forms required: FAFSA.
Dates and Deadlines: Priority date 3/1; no closing date. Applicants notified on a rolling basis.

CONTACT
Julia Clayton, Director of Financial Aid
450 Clarkson Avenue, Box 60, Brooklyn, NY 11203-2098
(718) 270-2488

State University of New York Empire State College
Saratoga Springs, New York
www.esc.edu
Federal Code: 010286

4-year public liberal arts college in large town.
Enrollment: 8,485 undergrads, 63% part-time. 230 full-time freshmen.
Selectivity: Admits over 75% of applicants.

BASIC COSTS (2005-2006)
Tuition and fees: $4,575; out-of-state residents $10,835.
Per-credit charge: $181; out-of-state residents $442.

FINANCIAL AID PICTURE (2004-2005)
Students with need: 30% of average financial aid package awarded as scholarships/grants, 70% awarded as loans/jobs.

FINANCIAL AID PROCEDURES
Forms required: FAFSA, state aid form.
Dates and Deadlines: No deadline. Applicants notified on a rolling basis; must reply within 3 week(s) of notification.

CONTACT
Eileen Corrigan, Director of Financial Services
111 West Avenue, Saratoga Springs, NY 12866
(518) 587-2100 ext. 2712

State University of New York Institute of Technology at Utica/Rome
Utica, New York
www.sunyit.edu
Federal Code: 011678

4-year public school of information systems & engineering technologies in small city.
Enrollment: 1,727 undergrads, 29% part-time. 81 full-time freshmen.
Selectivity: Admits less than 50% of applicants. GED not accepted.

BASIC COSTS (2005-2006)
Tuition and fees: $5,285; out-of-state residents $11,545.
Per-credit charge: $181; out-of-state residents $442.
Room and board: $7,290.

FINANCIAL AID PICTURE (2004-2005)
Students with need: Out of 77 full-time freshmen who applied for aid, 62 were judged to have need. Of these, 61 received aid, and 18 had their full need met. Average financial aid package met 83% of need; average scholarship/grant was $2,236; average loan was $2,196. For part-time students, average financial aid package was $3,042.
Students without need: 10 full-time freshmen who did not demonstrate need for aid received scholarships/grants; average award was $3,263. No-need awards available for academics.
Cumulative student debt: 55% of graduating class had student loans; average debt was $15,900.

FINANCIAL AID PROCEDURES
Forms required: FAFSA, state aid form.
Dates and Deadlines: No deadline. Applicants notified on a rolling basis starting 3/17; must reply within 2 week(s) of notification.
Transfers: No deadline. Applicants notified on a rolling basis starting 3/17; must reply within 2 week(s) of notification.

CONTACT
Stewart Richard, Director of Financial Aid
Box 3050, Utica, NY 13504-3050
(315) 792-7210

State University of New York Maritime College
Throggs Neck, New York
www.sunymaritime.edu
Federal Code: 002853

4-year public maritime college in very large city.
Enrollment: 1,150 undergrads.

Selectivity: Admits 50 to 75% of applicants.

BASIC COSTS (2005-2006)
Tuition and fees: $6,380; out-of-state residents $12,640.
Per-credit charge: $181; out-of-state residents $442.
Room and board: $8,200.
Additional info: Additional required uniform charges.

FINANCIAL AID PICTURE (2005-2006)
Students with need: Work study available nights, weekends, and for part-time students.
Students without need: No-need awards available for academics, ROTC, state/district residency.
Scholarships offered: Admiral's Scholarships; full-tuition. NROTC/AFROTC Scholarships; full room and board for 4 years.
Additional info: All cadets who are United States citizens, physically qualified for Merchant Marine license, and not yet 25 at time of enrollment are eligible to apply for Student Incentive Payment (SIP) of $3,000 per year from Maritime Administration of the Department of Transportation. Out-of-state students who elect to participate in SIP pay in-state tuition fees.

FINANCIAL AID PROCEDURES
Forms required: FAFSA, institutional form.
Dates and Deadlines: Priority date 2/15; no closing date. Applicants notified on a rolling basis starting 3/1; must reply by 3/15 or within 4 week(s) of notification.

CONTACT
Paul Bamonte, Director of Financial Aid
6 Pennyfield Avenue, Throggs Neck, NY 10465-4198
(718) 409-7267

State University of New York Upstate Medical University
Syracuse, New York
www.upstate.edu   Federal Code: 002840

Upper-division public health science and nursing college in small city.
Enrollment: 230 undergrads, 35% part-time.

BASIC COSTS (2005-2006)
Tuition and fees: $4,751; out-of-state residents $11,011.
Per-credit charge: $181; out-of-state residents $442.
Room only: $3,743.

FINANCIAL AID PICTURE
Students with need: Need-based aid available for full-time and part-time students.
Students without need: This college only awards aid to students with need.

FINANCIAL AID PROCEDURES
Forms required: FAFSA.
Dates and Deadlines: Priority date 3/1; no closing date. Applicants notified on a rolling basis starting 6/1; must reply within 2 week(s) of notification.

CONTACT
Irvin Bodofsky, Director of Financial Aid
766 Irving Avenue, Syracuse, NY 13210
(315) 464-4329

Suffolk County Community College
Selden, New York
www.sunysuffolk.edu   Federal Code: 002878

2-year public community college in large town.
Enrollment: 21,180 undergrads.
Selectivity: Open admission; but selective for some programs.

BASIC COSTS (2005-2006)
Tuition and fees: $3,326; out-of-state residents $6,416.
Per-credit charge: $129; out-of-state residents $258.

FINANCIAL AID PICTURE (2004-2005)
Students with need: 83% of average financial aid package awarded as scholarships/grants, 17% awarded as loans/jobs. Need-based aid available for part-time students.
Students without need: No-need awards available for academics, minority status, state/district residency.

FINANCIAL AID PROCEDURES
Forms required: FAFSA.
Dates and Deadlines: Priority date 4/15; closing date 6/1. Applicants notified on a rolling basis starting 5/15; must reply within 2 week(s) of notification.

CONTACT
Nancy Dunnagan, Director of Financial Aid
533 College Road, Selden, NY 11784
(631) 451-4110

Sullivan County Community College
Loch Sheldrake, New York
www.sullivan.suny.edu   Federal Code: 002879

2-year public community college in small town.
Enrollment: 1,428 undergrads, 26% part-time. 462 full-time freshmen.
Selectivity: Open admission; but selective for some programs.

BASIC COSTS (2005-2006)
Tuition and fees: $3,276; out-of-state residents $6,276.
Per-credit charge: $112; out-of-state residents $149.

FINANCIAL AID PICTURE
Students with need: Need-based aid available for full-time and part-time students.
Additional info: 60% of students hold part-time jobs locally.

FINANCIAL AID PROCEDURES
Forms required: FAFSA.
Dates and Deadlines: Priority date 4/15; no closing date. Applicants notified on a rolling basis starting 5/15; must reply within 2 week(s) of notification.

CONTACT
James Winderl, Director of Financial Aid
112 College Road, Loch Sheldrake, NY 12759-5151
(845) 434-5750 ext. 4231

Swedish Institute
New York, New York
www.swedishinstitute.com   Federal Code: 021700

2-year for-profit health science college in very large city.
Enrollment: 400 undergrads.

BASIC COSTS (2005-2006)
Tuition and fees: $8,388.
Per-credit charge: $275.

FINANCIAL AID PICTURE
Students with need: Need-based aid available for full-time and part-time students.
Students without need: This college only awards aid to students with need.

FINANCIAL AID PROCEDURES
Forms required: FAFSA, institutional form.
Dates and Deadlines: No deadline.

CONTACT
John Tonkinson, CFO
226 West 26th Street, 5th Floor, New York, NY 10001-6700
(212) 924-5900 ext. 124

Syracuse University
Syracuse, New York
www.syracuse.edu
Federal Code: 002882
CSS Code: 2823

4-year private university in small city.
Enrollment: 11,441 undergrads, 1% part-time. 3,248 full-time freshmen.
Selectivity: Admits 50 to 75% of applicants.

BASIC COSTS (2006-2007)
Tuition and fees: $29,965.
Room and board: $10,980.

FINANCIAL AID PICTURE (2005-2006)
Students with need: Out of 2,377 full-time freshmen who applied for aid, 1,929 were judged to have need. Of these, 1,929 received aid, and 1,254 had their full need met. Average financial aid package met 84% of need; average scholarship/grant was $16,600; average loan was $3,800. Need-based aid available for part-time students.
Students without need: 446 full-time freshmen who did not demonstrate need for aid received scholarships/grants; average award was $8,600. No-need awards available for academics, art, athletics, music/drama, ROTC.
Scholarships offered: 78 full-time freshmen received athletic scholarships; average amount $30,520.
Cumulative student debt: 70% of graduating class had student loans; average debt was $19,200.

FINANCIAL AID PROCEDURES
Forms required: FAFSA, CSS PROFILE.
Dates and Deadlines: Closing date 2/1. Applicants notified by 4/1; must reply by 5/1.

CONTACT
Christopher Walsh, Dean of Financial Aid Services
100 Crouse-Hinds Hall, Syracuse, NY 13244
(315) 443-1513

Tompkins-Cortland Community College
Dryden, New York
www.tc3.edu
Federal Code: 006788

2-year public community college in small town.
Enrollment: 2,812 undergrads, 25% part-time. 695 full-time freshmen.
Selectivity: Open admission; but selective for some programs.

BASIC COSTS (2005-2006)
Tuition and fees: $3,653; out-of-state residents $7,053.
Per-credit charge: $120; out-of-state residents $250.

FINANCIAL AID PICTURE (2004-2005)
Students with need: 45% of average financial aid package awarded as scholarships/grants, 55% awarded as loans/jobs. Need-based aid available for part-time students. Work study available nights, weekends, and for part-time students.
Students without need: No-need awards available for academics.

FINANCIAL AID PROCEDURES
Forms required: FAFSA, state aid form, institutional form.
Dates and Deadlines: Priority date 4/15; no closing date. Applicants notified on a rolling basis starting 3/15; must reply within 4 week(s) of notification.

CONTACT
Michael McGraw, Director of Financial Aid
170 North Street, Dryden, NY 13053-0139
(607) 844-8211

Trocaire College
Buffalo, New York
www.trocaire.edu
Federal Code: 002812

2-year private junior college in large city, affiliated with Roman Catholic Church.
Enrollment: 1,109 undergrads.
Selectivity: Open admission; but selective for some programs.

BASIC COSTS (2006-2007)
Tuition and fees: $10,771.
Per-credit charge: $410.

FINANCIAL AID PICTURE
Students with need: Need-based aid available for full-time and part-time students.
Students without need: No-need awards available for academics, alumni affiliation.

FINANCIAL AID PROCEDURES
Forms required: FAFSA, state aid form.
Dates and Deadlines: Priority date 3/31; no closing date. Applicants notified on a rolling basis starting 3/1; must reply within 2 week(s) of notification.

CONTACT
Janet McGrath, Director of Financial Aid
360 Choate Avenue, Buffalo, NY 14220
(716) 826-1200

Ulster County Community College
Stone Ridge, New York
www.sunyulster.edu
Federal Code: 002880

2-year public community college in small town.
Enrollment: 2,238 undergrads.
Selectivity: Open admission; but selective for some programs.

BASIC COSTS (2005-2006)
Tuition and fees: $3,596; out-of-state residents $6,796.
Per-credit charge: $107; out-of-state residents $214.

FINANCIAL AID PICTURE (2005-2006)
Students with need: Need-based aid available for part-time students.

FINANCIAL AID PROCEDURES
Forms required: FAFSA.
Dates and Deadlines: Priority date 6/1; no closing date. Applicants notified on a rolling basis starting 6/1; must reply within 2 week(s) of notification.

CONTACT
Mildred Brown, Director of Financial Aid
Cottekill Road, Stone Ridge, NY 12484
(845) 687-5000

Union College
Schenectady, New York
www.union.edu
Federal Code: 002889
CSS Code: 2920

4-year private engineering and liberal arts college in small city.
Enrollment: 2,190 undergrads. 552 full-time freshmen.
Selectivity: Admits less than 50% of applicants. GED not accepted.

BASIC COSTS (2006-2007)
Comprehensive fee: $44,043.
Additional info: Rebates offered to students living off-campus and/or not using a meal plan.

FINANCIAL AID PICTURE (2004-2005)
Students with need: Out of 330 full-time freshmen who applied for aid, 254 were judged to have need. Of these, 254 received aid, and 254 had their full need met. Average financial aid package met 100% of need; average scholarship/grant was $23,287; average loan was $2,967. Need-based aid available for part-time students.
Students without need: 71 full-time freshmen who did not demonstrate need for aid received scholarships/grants; average award was $11,576. No-need awards available for academics, ROTC.
Cumulative student debt: 53% of graduating class had student loans; average debt was $15,132.
Additional info: Cancellable loans given to eligible students who engage in public service work after graduation. Loans cancellable at rate of 20% for each year of service.

FINANCIAL AID PROCEDURES
Forms required: FAFSA, CSS PROFILE, state aid form.
Dates and Deadlines: Closing date 2/1. Applicants notified by 4/1; must reply by 5/1.
Transfers: Closing date 3/1. Financial aid applicants must submit the CSS PROFILE form and FAFSA to their respective processing agencies at least two months prior to application deadline.

CONTACT
Beth Post, Director of Financial Aid and Family Financing
Grant Hall, Schenectady, NY 12308-2311
(518) 388-6123

United States Merchant Marine Academy
Kings Point, New York
www.usmma.edu
Federal Code: G02892

4-year public engineering and military college in large town.
Enrollment: 1,021 undergrads. 284 full-time freshmen.
Selectivity: Admits less than 50% of applicants. GED not accepted.

BASIC COSTS (2005-2006)
Additional info: All midshipmen receive full tuition, room and board, and medical and dental expenses from the federal government. Total required fees $6,253 including purchase of laptop computer, color printer, and PDA for $2,960. International students pay required fees plus $8,092 (international student fee).

FINANCIAL AID PICTURE (2004-2005)
Students with need: Out of 141 full-time freshmen who applied for aid, 73 were judged to have need. Of these, 73 received aid. Average financial aid package met 100% of need; average scholarship/grant was $2,711; average loan was $2,414.
Additional info: Students paid by steamship companies while at sea.

FINANCIAL AID PROCEDURES
Forms required: FAFSA, institutional form.
Dates and Deadlines: Closing date 5/1. Applicants notified on a rolling basis starting 1/31.

CONTACT
James Skinner, Director of Financial Aid
300 Steamboat Road, Kings Point, NY 11024-1699
(516) 773-5295

United States Military Academy
West Point, New York
www.usma.edu
Federal Code: 002893

4-year public engineering and military college in small town.
Enrollment: 4,231 undergrads. 1,194 full-time freshmen.
Selectivity: Admits less than 50% of applicants.

BASIC COSTS (2006-2007)
Additional info: All cadets members of U.S. Army and receive annual salary of $10,140. Tuition, room and board, medical, and dental care provided at no cost to cadets. Deposit of $2,900 required for initial uniforms, books, supplies, personal computer, and fees. First-year cadets who cannot pay deposit receive no-interest loan; payments deducted from cadet salary.

CONTACT
Stephanie Martin, Treasurer
646 Swift Road, West Point, NY 10996-1905
(845) 938-5516

University of Rochester
Rochester, New York
www.rochester.edu
Federal Code: 002894
CSS Code: 2928

4-year private university in large city.
Enrollment: 4,532 undergrads, 2% part-time. 1,107 full-time freshmen.
Selectivity: Admits less than 50% of applicants.

BASIC COSTS (2006-2007)
Tuition and fees: $33,426.
Room and board: $10,552.
Additional info: Tuition/fee waivers available for minority students.

FINANCIAL AID PICTURE (2005-2006)
Students with need: Average financial aid package met 100% of need; average scholarship/grant was $21,544; average loan was $4,023. For part-time students, average financial aid package was $9,247.
Students without need: No-need awards available for academics, alumni affiliation, leadership, music/drama, ROTC, state/district residency.
Cumulative student debt: 56% of graduating class had student loans; average debt was $26,100.
Additional info: Alternative loans and financing information available.

FINANCIAL AID PROCEDURES
Forms required: FAFSA, CSS PROFILE, state aid form.
Dates and Deadlines: Closing date 2/1. Applicants notified by 4/1; must reply by 5/1.
Transfers: Priority date 2/1; no deadline.

CONTACT
Charles Puls, Director of Financial Aid
100 Wallis Hall, Rochester, NY 14627-0251
(585) 275-3226

Utica College
Utica, New York
www.utica.edu
Federal Code: 002883

4-year private liberal arts college in small city.
Enrollment: 2,334 undergrads, 13% part-time. 430 full-time freshmen.

Selectivity: Admits over 75% of applicants.

BASIC COSTS (2006-2007)
Tuition and fees: $23,440.
Per-credit charge: $780.
Room and board: $9,510.

FINANCIAL AID PICTURE (2005-2006)
Students with need: Out of 415 full-time freshmen who applied for aid, 387 were judged to have need. Of these, 387 received aid, and 36 had their full need met. Average financial aid package met 78% of need; average scholarship/grant was $9,859. For part-time students, average financial aid package was $10,829.
Students without need: 30 full-time freshmen who did not demonstrate need for aid received scholarships/grants; average award was $5,945. No-need awards available for academics.
Cumulative student debt: 89% of graduating class had student loans; average debt was $25,565.

FINANCIAL AID PROCEDURES
Forms required: FAFSA, state aid form.
Dates and Deadlines: Priority date 2/15; no closing date. Applicants notified on a rolling basis starting 2/1; must reply by 5/1 or within 4 week(s) of notification.

CONTACT
Elizabeth Wilson, Director of Financial Aid
1600 Burrstone Road, Utica, NY 13502-4892
(315) 792-3179

Vassar College
Poughkeepsie, New York
www.vassar.edu
Federal Code: 002895
CSS Code: 2956

4-year private liberal arts college in small city.
Enrollment: 2,331 undergrads, 1% part-time. 647 full-time freshmen.
Selectivity: Admits less than 50% of applicants.

BASIC COSTS (2006-2007)
Tuition and fees: $36,030.
Room and board: $8,130.

FINANCIAL AID PICTURE (2005-2006)
Students with need: Out of 422 full-time freshmen who applied for aid, 302 were judged to have need. Of these, 302 received aid, and 302 had their full need met. Average financial aid package met 100% of need; average scholarship/grant was $23,920; average loan was $2,283.
Students without need: This college only awards aid to students with need.
Cumulative student debt: 56% of graduating class had student loans; average debt was $19,038.

FINANCIAL AID PROCEDURES
Forms required: FAFSA, CSS PROFILE, state aid form, institutional form.
Dates and Deadlines: Closing date 2/1. Applicants notified by 3/30; must reply by 5/1.
Transfers: Closing date 4/1. Limited number of need-based award packages offered to transfers.

CONTACT
Michael Fraher, Director of Financial Aid
Box 10, 124 Raymond Avenue, Poughkeepsie, NY 12604-0077
(845) 437-5320

Vaughn College of Aeronautics and Technology
Flushing, New York
www.vaughn.edu
Federal Code: 002665

4-year private engineering and technical college in very large city.
Enrollment: 1,119 undergrads, 25% part-time. 197 full-time freshmen.
Selectivity: Admits over 75% of applicants.

BASIC COSTS (2005-2006)
Tuition and fees: $13,680.
Per-credit charge: $450.

FINANCIAL AID PICTURE (2005-2006)
Students with need: Out of 187 full-time freshmen who applied for aid, 173 were judged to have need. Of these, 173 received aid, and 20 had their full need met. Average financial aid package met 80% of need; average scholarship/grant was $1,000; average loan was $1,313. For part-time students, average financial aid package was $1,500.
Students without need: This college only awards aid to students with need.
Cumulative student debt: 72% of graduating class had student loans; average debt was $17,125.

FINANCIAL AID PROCEDURES
Forms required: FAFSA, state aid form.
Dates and Deadlines: Priority date 3/1; no closing date. Applicants notified on a rolling basis.
Transfers: No deadline. Applicants notified on a rolling basis.

CONTACT
Sinu Jacob, Director of Financial Aid
86-01 23rd Avenue, Flushing, NY 11369
(718) 429-6600

Villa Maria College of Buffalo
Buffalo, New York
www.villa.edu
Federal Code: 002896

2-year private liberal arts college in large city, affiliated with Roman Catholic Church.
Enrollment: 489 undergrads, 19% part-time. 141 full-time freshmen.
Selectivity: Open admission; but selective for some programs.

BASIC COSTS (2006-2007)
Tuition and fees: $11,705.
Per-credit charge: $380.
Additional info: Costs quoted for 2-year programs. Bachelor's degree program costs as of Fall 2006: $13,300 tuition, $495 required fees, $445/credit hour. Tuition/fee waivers available for unemployed or children of unemployed.

FINANCIAL AID PICTURE (2004-2005)
Students with need: Out of 133 full-time freshmen who applied for aid, 109 were judged to have need. Of these, 109 received aid, and 100 had their full need met. Average financial aid package met 1% of need; average scholarship/grant was $1; average loan was $1. For part-time students, average financial aid package was $2.
Students without need: 2 full-time freshmen who did not demonstrate need for aid received scholarships/grants; average award was $1,000. No-need awards available for academics, alumni affiliation, art, leadership, minority status, music/drama, religious affiliation, state/district residency.
Cumulative student debt: 71% of graduating class had student loans; average debt was $4,623.

FINANCIAL AID PROCEDURES
Forms required: FAFSA.

Dates and Deadlines: Priority date 4/1; no closing date. Applicants notified by 5/1; must reply within 3 week(s) of notification.

CONTACT
Diane Kasprzak, Director of Financial Aid and Veterans' Affairs
240 Pine Ridge Road, Buffalo, NY 14225
(716) 896-0700 ext. 1850

Wagner College
Staten Island, New York
www.wagner.edu   Federal Code: 002899

4-year private liberal arts college in very large city, affiliated with Lutheran Church in America.
Enrollment: 1,962 undergrads, 4% part-time. 579 full-time freshmen.
Selectivity: Admits 50 to 75% of applicants.

BASIC COSTS (2006-2007)
Tuition and fees: $27,300.
Room and board: $8,400.
Additional info: Tuition/fee waivers available for unemployed or children of unemployed.

FINANCIAL AID PICTURE (2005-2006)
Students with need: Out of 465 full-time freshmen who applied for aid, 359 were judged to have need. Of these, 359 received aid, and 87 had their full need met. Average financial aid package met 72% of need; average scholarship/grant was $12,357; average loan was $3,432.
Students without need: 158 full-time freshmen who did not demonstrate need for aid received scholarships/grants; average award was $8,143. No-need awards available for academics, athletics, leadership, music/drama.
Scholarships offered: 22 full-time freshmen received athletic scholarships; average amount $16,603.
Cumulative student debt: 81% of graduating class had student loans; average debt was $13,026.

FINANCIAL AID PROCEDURES
Forms required: FAFSA, state aid form, institutional form.
Dates and Deadlines: Priority date 2/15; no closing date. Applicants notified on a rolling basis starting 3/1; must reply within 3 week(s) of notification.
Transfers: No deadline. Applicants notified on a rolling basis starting 3/1; must reply within 3 week(s) of notification.

CONTACT
Theresa Weimer, Director of Financial Aid
One Campus Road, Staten Island, NY 10301-4495
(718) 390-3183

Webb Institute
Glen Cove, New York
www.webb-institute.edu   Federal Code: 002900

4-year private maritime college in large town.
Enrollment: 80 undergrads. 20 full-time freshmen.
Selectivity: Admits less than 50% of applicants. GED not accepted.

BASIC COSTS (2006-2007)
Room and board: $8,340.
Additional info: All students receive 4-year, full-tuition scholarships.

FINANCIAL AID PICTURE (2005-2006)
Students with need: Out of 7 full-time freshmen who applied for aid, 6 were judged to have need. Of these, 6 received aid, and 2 had their full need met. Average financial aid package met 81% of need; average scholarship/grant was $4,050; average loan was $2,389.
Students without need: This college only awards aid to students with need.
Cumulative student debt: 17% of graduating class had student loans; average debt was $11,612.

FINANCIAL AID PROCEDURES
Forms required: FAFSA.
Dates and Deadlines: Closing date 7/1. Applicants notified by 8/1; must reply within 2 week(s) of notification.

CONTACT
Stephen Ostendorff, Director of Financial Aid
298 Crescent Beach Road, Glen Cove, NY 11542-1398
(516) 671-2213 ext. 104

Wells College
Aurora, New York
www.wells.edu   Federal Code: 002901

4-year private liberal arts college in rural community.
Enrollment: 407 undergrads, 1% part-time. 130 full-time freshmen.
Selectivity: Admits 50 to 75% of applicants.

BASIC COSTS (2006-2007)
Tuition and fees: $16,680.
Per-credit charge: $600.
Room and board: $7,500.

FINANCIAL AID PICTURE (2005-2006)
Students with need: Out of 122 full-time freshmen who applied for aid, 99 were judged to have need. Of these, 99 received aid, and 29 had their full need met. Average financial aid package met 92% of need; average scholarship/grant was $12,620; average loan was $3,407. Need-based aid available for part-time students.
Students without need: This college only awards aid to students with need.
Scholarships offered: Henry Wells Scholarship: guaranteed first-year internship or related experience and paid $3,000 internship or experiential learning program in student's upper-class years; must have minimum combined score of 1150 on the critical reading and math sections of SAT, or a 28 on ACT, as well as GPA of at least 3.5. 21st Century Leadership Award: $20,000 over 4 years; must have GPA of at least 3.5, required to submit leadership transcript. Applicants for both scholarships must be nominated by guidance counselor.
Cumulative student debt: 91% of graduating class had student loans; average debt was $17,125.

FINANCIAL AID PROCEDURES
Forms required: FAFSA. CSS PROFILE required of Early Decision candidates only.
Dates and Deadlines: Priority date 2/15; no closing date. Applicants notified on a rolling basis starting 3/1; must reply by 5/1 or within 4 week(s) of notification.
Transfers: Priority date 3/1; no deadline. Applicants notified on a rolling basis starting 3/1; must reply by 8/1.

CONTACT
Cathleen Patella, Director of Financial Aid
170 Main Street, Aurora, NY 13026
(315) 364-3289

Westchester Community College
Valhalla, New York
www.sunywcc.edu   Federal Code: 002881

2-year public community college in large town.
Enrollment: 9,470 undergrads. 1,631 full-time freshmen.
Selectivity: Open admission; but selective for some programs.

BASIC COSTS (2005-2006)
Tuition and fees: $3,493; out-of-state residents $8,219.
Per-credit charge: $132; out-of-state residents $330.

FINANCIAL AID PICTURE (2004-2005)
Students with need: 91% of average financial aid package awarded as scholarships/grants, 9% awarded as loans/jobs. Need-based aid available for part-time students. Work study available nights, weekends, and for part-time students.
Students without need: No-need awards available for academics.
Cumulative student debt: 11% of graduating class had student loans; average debt was $5,574.

FINANCIAL AID PROCEDURES
Forms required: FAFSA, state aid form, institutional form.
Dates and Deadlines: No deadline. Applicants notified on a rolling basis; must reply within 4 week(s) of notification.
Transfers: No deadline.

CONTACT
Eleanor Hackett, Director of Financial Aid
75 Grasslands Road, Valhalla, NY 10595
(914) 606-6773

Yeshiva Mikdash Melech
Brooklyn, New York   Federal Code: 014615

4-year private rabbinical college for men in very large city, affiliated with Jewish faith.
Enrollment: 89 undergrads, 15% part-time. 56 full-time freshmen.
Selectivity: Admits over 75% of applicants.

BASIC COSTS (2006-2007)
Tuition and fees: $6,500.
Room and board: $3,800.
Additional info: Tuition/fee waivers available for adults.

FINANCIAL AID PICTURE (2004-2005)
Students with need: 98% of average financial aid package awarded as scholarships/grants, 2% awarded as loans/jobs. Need-based aid available for part-time students. Work study available nights.
Students without need: No-need awards available for academics, leadership, religious affiliation.

FINANCIAL AID PROCEDURES
Forms required: FAFSA.
Dates and Deadlines: No deadline. Applicants notified on a rolling basis starting 5/1.
Transfers: No deadline. Applicants notified on a rolling basis starting 5/1.

CONTACT
Samuel Ani, Financial Aid Administrator
1326 Ocean Parkway, Brooklyn, NY 11230
(718) 339-1090

North Carolina

Alamance Community College
Graham, North Carolina
www.alamancecc.edu   Federal Code: 005463

2-year public community college in large town.
Enrollment: 3,428 undergrads, 53% part-time. 399 full-time freshmen.
Selectivity: Open admission; but selective for some programs.

BASIC COSTS (2005-2006)
Tuition and fees: $1,215; out-of-state residents $6,615.
Per-credit charge: $40; out-of-state residents $220.

FINANCIAL AID PICTURE (2004-2005)
Students with need: Out of 263 full-time freshmen who applied for aid, 260 were judged to have need. Of these, 250 received aid. Average financial aid package met 40% of need; average scholarship/grant was $3,000. For part-time students, average financial aid package was $1,500.
Students without need: 50 full-time freshmen who did not demonstrate need for aid received scholarships/grants; average award was $500. No-need awards available for academics, state/district residency.

FINANCIAL AID PROCEDURES
Forms required: FAFSA.
Dates and Deadlines: Priority date 5/15; no closing date. Applicants notified on a rolling basis starting 3/15; must reply within 2 week(s) of notification.
Transfers: Supplemental educational opportunity grants limited.

CONTACT
Steve Reinhartsen, Coordinator of Placement and Financial Aid
Box 8000, Graham, NC 27253
(336) 506-4109

Appalachian State University
Boone, North Carolina
www.appstate.edu   Federal Code: 002906

4-year public university in large town.
Enrollment: 12,619 undergrads, 5% part-time. 2,543 full-time freshmen.
Selectivity: Admits 50 to 75% of applicants.

BASIC COSTS (2005-2006)
Tuition and fees: $3,436; out-of-state residents $13,178.
Room and board: $5,410.

FINANCIAL AID PICTURE (2005-2006)
Students with need: Out of 1,666 full-time freshmen who applied for aid, 822 were judged to have need. Of these, 785 received aid, and 277 had their full need met. Average financial aid package met 74% of need; average scholarship/grant was $4,450; average loan was $2,526. For part-time students, average financial aid package was $5,844.
Students without need: 257 full-time freshmen who did not demonstrate need for aid received scholarships/grants; average award was $20,165. No-need awards available for academics, alumni affiliation, art, athletics, job skills, leadership, minority status, music/drama, religious affiliation, ROTC, state/district residency.
Scholarships offered: 42 full-time freshmen received athletic scholarships; average amount $6,228.
Cumulative student debt: 50% of graduating class had student loans; average debt was $15,433.

FINANCIAL AID PROCEDURES
Forms required: FAFSA.

Dates and Deadlines: Priority date 3/15; no closing date. Applicants notified on a rolling basis starting 4/1; must reply within 3 week(s) of notification.

CONTACT
Esther Captain, Director of Financial Aid
ASU Box 32004, Boone, NC 28608
(828) 262-2190

Barton College
Wilson, North Carolina
www.barton.edu   Federal Code: 002908

4-year private liberal arts college in large town, affiliated with Christian Church (Disciples of Christ).
Enrollment: 1,189 undergrads, 23% part-time. 247 full-time freshmen.
Selectivity: Admits 50 to 75% of applicants.

BASIC COSTS (2006-2007)
Tuition and fees: $17,484.
Per-credit charge: $696.
Room and board: $6,264.
Additional info: Tuition/fee waivers available for adults.

FINANCIAL AID PICTURE (2004-2005)
Students with need: Out of 215 full-time freshmen who applied for aid, 192 were judged to have need. Of these, 192 received aid, and 32 had their full need met. Average financial aid package met 75% of need; average scholarship/grant was $4,790; average loan was $2,858. For part-time students, average financial aid package was $5,429.
Students without need: 38 full-time freshmen who did not demonstrate need for aid received scholarships/grants; average award was $2,289. No-need awards available for academics, alumni affiliation, athletics, leadership, religious affiliation, state/district residency.
Scholarships offered: *Merit:* Presidential Scholarship; $6,000. High Honors Scholarship; $4,500. *Athletic:* 12 full-time freshmen received athletic scholarships; average amount $7,009.
Cumulative student debt: 71% of graduating class had student loans; average debt was $17,272.

FINANCIAL AID PROCEDURES
Forms required: FAFSA.
Dates and Deadlines: Priority date 4/1; no closing date. Applicants notified on a rolling basis starting 2/1; must reply within 2 week(s) of notification.

CONTACT
Bettie Westbrook, Director of Financial Aid
Box 5000, Wilson, NC 27893
(252) 399-6323

Beaufort County Community College
Washington, North Carolina
www.beaufortccc.edu   Federal Code: 008558

2-year public community college in small town.
Enrollment: 733 undergrads.
Selectivity: Open admission; but selective for some programs.

BASIC COSTS (2005-2006)
Tuition and fees: $1,245; out-of-state residents $6,645.
Per-credit charge: $40; out-of-state residents $220.

FINANCIAL AID PICTURE
Students with need: Need-based aid available for full-time and part-time students.
Students without need: No-need awards available for academics, leadership.

FINANCIAL AID PROCEDURES
Forms required: FAFSA.
Dates and Deadlines: Priority date 6/1; no closing date. Applicants notified on a rolling basis starting 5/1; must reply within 2 week(s) of notification.

CONTACT
Harold Smith, Director of Financial Aid
Box 1069, Washington, NC 27889
(252) 940-6222

Belmont Abbey College
Belmont, North Carolina
www.belmontabbeycollege.edu   Federal Code: 002910

4-year private liberal arts college in small town, affiliated with Roman Catholic Church.
Enrollment: 857 undergrads, 7% part-time. 224 full-time freshmen.
Selectivity: Admits over 75% of applicants.

BASIC COSTS (2005-2006)
Tuition and fees: $17,510.
Per-credit charge: $499.
Room and board: $8,588.

FINANCIAL AID PICTURE (2005-2006)
Students with need: Average financial aid package met 64% of need; average scholarship/grant was $10,797; average loan was $2,232. For part-time students, average financial aid package was $5,262.
Students without need: No-need awards available for academics, athletics, leadership, religious affiliation, state/district residency.
Scholarships offered: Many merit scholarships offered; ranging from $500 to $20,000; based solely on academic achievement.
Cumulative student debt: 68% of graduating class had student loans; average debt was $14,618.

FINANCIAL AID PROCEDURES
Forms required: FAFSA.
Dates and Deadlines: Priority date 4/1; no closing date. Applicants notified on a rolling basis starting 3/1; must reply within 2 week(s) of notification.

CONTACT
Anne Stevens, Director of Enrollment Management
100 Belmont - Mt. Holly Road, Belmont, NC 28012-2795
(704) 825-6718

Bennett College
Greensboro, North Carolina
www.bennett.edu   Federal Code: 002911

4-year private liberal arts college for women in small city, affiliated with United Methodist Church.
Enrollment: 572 undergrads, 1% part-time. 205 full-time freshmen.
Selectivity: Admits 50 to 75% of applicants.

BASIC COSTS (2006-2007)
Tuition and fees: $14,150.
Per-credit charge: $513.
Room and board: $6,258.

FINANCIAL AID PICTURE (2005-2006)
Students with need: Out of 169 full-time freshmen who applied for aid, 152 were judged to have need. Of these, 150 received aid, and 7 had their full need met. Average financial aid package met 38% of need; average scholarship/grant was $6,788; average loan was $2,485. For part-time students, average financial aid package was $7,198.

Students without need: 25 full-time freshmen who did not demonstrate need for aid received scholarships/grants; average award was $13,495. No-need awards available for state/district residency.
Cumulative student debt: 75% of graduating class had student loans; average debt was $16,983.

FINANCIAL AID PROCEDURES
Forms required: FAFSA, institutional form.
Dates and Deadlines: Closing date 4/15. Applicants notified by 7/15.

CONTACT
Monty Hickman, Financial Aid Officer
900 East Washington Street, Greensboro, NC 27401-3239
(336) 517-2204

Bladen Community College
Dublin, North Carolina
www.bladen.cc.nc.us   Federal Code: 007987

2-year public community college in rural community.
Enrollment: 1,340 undergrads.
Selectivity: Open admission; but selective for some programs.

BASIC COSTS (2005-2006)
Tuition and fees: $1,245; out-of-state residents $6,645.
Per-credit charge: $40; out-of-state residents $220.

FINANCIAL AID PICTURE
Students with need: Need-based aid available for full-time and part-time students. Work study available nights.

FINANCIAL AID PROCEDURES
Forms required: FAFSA.
Dates and Deadlines: Priority date 6/1; no closing date. Applicants notified on a rolling basis starting 8/1; must reply within 2 week(s) of notification.

CONTACT
Marva Dinkins, Financial Aid Director
Box 266, Dublin, NC 28332
(910) 879-5562

Blue Ridge Community College
Flat Rock, North Carolina
www.blueridge.edu   Federal Code: 009684

2-year public community college in small town.
Enrollment: 2,075 undergrads.
Selectivity: Open admission; but selective for some programs.

BASIC COSTS (2005-2006)
Tuition and fees: $1,255; out-of-state residents $6,655.
Per-credit charge: $40; out-of-state residents $220.

FINANCIAL AID PICTURE (2004-2005)
Students with need: 98% of average financial aid package awarded as scholarships/grants, 2% awarded as loans/jobs. Need-based aid available for part-time students. Work study available nights.
Students without need: No-need awards available for academics, athletics, leadership, minority status, state/district residency.

FINANCIAL AID PROCEDURES
Forms required: FAFSA, institutional form.
Dates and Deadlines: Priority date 6/30; no closing date. Applicants notified on a rolling basis starting 2/1; must reply within 4 week(s) of notification.

CONTACT
Rita Blythe, Financial Aid Officer
180 West Campus Drive, Flat Rock, NC 28731-9624
(828) 694-1815

Brevard College
Brevard, North Carolina
www.brevard.edu   Federal Code: 002912

4-year private liberal arts college in small town, affiliated with United Methodist Church.
Enrollment: 582 undergrads, 3% part-time. 147 full-time freshmen.
Selectivity: Admits 50 to 75% of applicants.

BASIC COSTS (2006-2007)
Tuition and fees: $17,220.
Room and board: $6,150.
Additional info: Telecommunications fee $600 for on-campus residents.

FINANCIAL AID PICTURE (2005-2006)
Students with need: Out of 113 full-time freshmen who applied for aid, 99 were judged to have need. Of these, 99 received aid, and 25 had their full need met. Average financial aid package met 78% of need; average scholarship/grant was $10,264; average loan was $2,984. For part-time students, average financial aid package was $7,228.
Students without need: 36 full-time freshmen who did not demonstrate need for aid received scholarships/grants; average award was $7,215. No-need awards available for academics, art, athletics, job skills, leadership, music/drama, religious affiliation, state/district residency.
Scholarships offered: 29 full-time freshmen received athletic scholarships; average amount $5,400.
Cumulative student debt: 63% of graduating class had student loans; average debt was $19,293.

FINANCIAL AID PROCEDURES
Forms required: FAFSA, state aid form.
Dates and Deadlines: Priority date 4/15; no closing date. Applicants notified on a rolling basis starting 2/1; must reply within 4 week(s) of notification.

CONTACT
Lisanne Masterson, Associate Dean of Financial Aid
400 North Broad Street, Brevard, NC 28712
(828) 884-8287

Brunswick Community College
Supply, North Carolina
www.brunswickcc.edu   Federal Code: 015285

2-year public community college in small town.
Enrollment: 993 undergrads, 49% part-time. 125 full-time freshmen.
Selectivity: Open admission; but selective for some programs.

BASIC COSTS (2005-2006)
Tuition and fees: $1,258; out-of-state residents $6,658.
Per-credit charge: $40; out-of-state residents $220.

FINANCIAL AID PICTURE
Students with need: Need-based aid available for full-time and part-time students.
Students without need: No-need awards available for academics, state/district residency.
Scholarships offered: La Dane Williamson Scholarship; must be a resident of Brunswick County for 5 years prior to application, must be a high school graduate of Brunswick County or complete GED or adult high school diploma program at Brunswick Community College; recipient must not be eligible for Pell; $1,200 per year for 2 years. Brunswick Family Scholarship for Brunswick

County residents of 3 years prior to application; GED or high school graduate; recipient must not be eligible for Pell; may cover total amount of tuition and fees.
Additional info: Attendance required at financial aid orientation session for those receiving federal student aid.

FINANCIAL AID PROCEDURES
Forms required: FAFSA, institutional form.
Dates and Deadlines: Priority date 6/1; closing date 6/15. Applicants notified on a rolling basis starting 3/1; must reply by 6/30 or within 2 week(s) of notification.
Transfers: Priority date 6/30; no deadline.

CONTACT
Paula Almond, Coordinator of Financial Aid and Veterans Affairs
Box 30, Supply, NC 28462
(910) 755-7422

Cabarrus College of Health Sciences
Concord, North Carolina
www.cabarruscollege.edu   Federal Code: 015358

4-year private health science and nursing college in small city.
Enrollment: 301 undergrads, 31% part-time. 21 full-time freshmen.
Selectivity: Admits 50 to 75% of applicants.

BASIC COSTS (2005-2006)
Tuition and fees: $7,400.
Per-credit charge: $230.

FINANCIAL AID PICTURE (2004-2005)
Students with need: 60% of average financial aid package awarded as scholarships/grants, 40% awarded as loans/jobs.

CONTACT
Valerie Richard, Director of Financial Aid
401 Medical Park Drive, Concord, NC 28025-2405
(704) 783-2445

Caldwell Community College and Technical Institute
Hudson, North Carolina
www.cccti.edu   Federal Code: 004835

2-year public community and technical college in small town.
Enrollment: 3,108 undergrads, 60% part-time. 415 full-time freshmen.
Selectivity: Open admission; but selective for some programs.

BASIC COSTS (2005-2006)
Tuition and fees: $1,225; out-of-state residents $6,625.
Per-credit charge: $40; out-of-state residents $220.

FINANCIAL AID PICTURE
Students with need: Need-based aid available for full-time and part-time students.
Students without need: This college only awards aid to students with need.

FINANCIAL AID PROCEDURES
Forms required: FAFSA.
Dates and Deadlines: Priority date 4/1; no closing date. Applicants notified on a rolling basis starting 6/30.

CONTACT
Dianne Henderson, Director of Financial Aid
2855 Hickory Boulevard, Hudson, NC 28638-2672
(828) 726-2714

Campbell University
Buies Creek, North Carolina
www.campbell.edu   Federal Code: 002913

4-year private university and liberal arts college in small town, affiliated with Southern Baptist Convention.
Enrollment: 2,679 undergrads, 5% part-time. 717 full-time freshmen.
Selectivity: Admits 50 to 75% of applicants.

BASIC COSTS (2006-2007)
Tuition and fees: $17,156.
Per-credit charge: $275.
Room and board: $5,740.

FINANCIAL AID PICTURE (2005-2006)
Students with need: Out of 653 full-time freshmen who applied for aid, 538 were judged to have need. Of these, 538 received aid, and 145 had their full need met. Average financial aid package met 100% of need; average scholarship/grant was $3,851; average loan was $2,809. For part-time students, average financial aid package was $6,423.
Students without need: 136 full-time freshmen who did not demonstrate need for aid received scholarships/grants; average award was $7,452. No-need awards available for academics, athletics, music/drama, religious affiliation, ROTC, state/district residency.
Scholarships offered: *Merit:* Presidential Scholarships; $9,000-$12,000; SAT 1150 or ACT 25 and GPA 3.4. Campbell Scholarship; $5,000-8,000; SAT 1000 or ACT 21 and GPA 3.0. (SAT scores exclusive of Writing). *Athletic:* 21 full-time freshmen received athletic scholarships; average amount $9,132.
Cumulative student debt: 65% of graduating class had student loans; average debt was $14,200.

FINANCIAL AID PROCEDURES
Forms required: FAFSA.
Dates and Deadlines: Priority date 3/15; no closing date. Applicants notified on a rolling basis starting 4/15; must reply within 2 week(s) of notification.

CONTACT
Nancy Beasley, Director of Financial Aid
PO Box 546, Buies Creek, NC 27506
(800) 334-4111 ext. 1310

Cape Fear Community College
Wilmington, North Carolina
www.cfcc.edu   Federal Code: 005320

2-year public community college in small city.
Enrollment: 6,156 undergrads.
Selectivity: Open admission; but selective for some programs.

BASIC COSTS (2005-2006)
Tuition and fees: $1,253; out-of-state residents $6,653.
Per-credit charge: $40; out-of-state residents $220.

FINANCIAL AID PICTURE (2004-2005)
Students with need: Need-based aid available for part-time students. Work study available nights.
Students without need: No-need awards available for academics, job skills.

FINANCIAL AID PROCEDURES
Forms required: FAFSA.
Dates and Deadlines: Priority date 6/1; no closing date. Applicants notified on a rolling basis starting 4/1; must reply within 2 week(s) of notification.

North Carolina Cape Fear Community College

CONTACT
Linda Smiley, Director of Financial Aid
411 North Front Street, Wilmington, NC 28401-3910
(910) 362-7055

Carolinas College of Health Sciences
Charlotte, North Carolina
www.carolinascollege.edu   Federal Code: 031042

2-year public health science and junior college in very large city.
Enrollment: 401 undergrads.

BASIC COSTS (2006-2007)
Tuition and fees: $5,750.
Per-credit charge: $185.
Additional info: Tuition varies by program.

FINANCIAL AID PICTURE (2004-2005)
Students with need: 37% of average financial aid package awarded as scholarships/grants, 63% awarded as loans/jobs. Need-based aid available for part-time students.
Students without need: No-need awards available for academics.

FINANCIAL AID PROCEDURES
Forms required: FAFSA, institutional form.
Dates and Deadlines: Priority date 5/1; no closing date. Applicants notified on a rolling basis starting 5/1.

CONTACT
Jill Powell, Financial Aid Officer
PO Box 32861, Charlotte, NC 28232
(704) 355-8894

Carteret Community College
Morehead City, North Carolina
www.carteret.cc.nc.us   Federal Code: 008081

2-year public community college in small town.
Enrollment: 1,700 undergrads, 55% part-time. 183 full-time freshmen.
Selectivity: Open admission; but selective for some programs.

BASIC COSTS (2005-2006)
Tuition and fees: $1,236; out-of-state residents $6,636.
Per-credit charge: $40; out-of-state residents $220.

FINANCIAL AID PICTURE
Students with need: Need-based aid available for full-time and part-time students.
Students without need: No-need awards available for academics, leadership, minority status, state/district residency.
Additional info: Institutional student loan program administered by college. Student may charge up to $600 for books, supplies and tuition per quarter. Repayment due by 11th week of semester.

FINANCIAL AID PROCEDURES
Forms required: FAFSA, institutional form.
Dates and Deadlines: No deadline. Applicants notified on a rolling basis; must reply within 2 week(s) of notification.

CONTACT
Brenda Long, Financial Aid Officer
3505 Arendell Street, Morehead City, NC 28557-2989
(252) 222-6147

Catawba College
Salisbury, North Carolina
www.catawba.edu   Federal Code: 002914

4-year private liberal arts college in large town, affiliated with United Church of Christ.
Enrollment: 1,256 undergrads, 3% part-time. 260 full-time freshmen.
Selectivity: Admits 50 to 75% of applicants.

BASIC COSTS (2006-2007)
Tuition and fees: $19,690.
Per-credit charge: $525.
Room and board: $6,570.

FINANCIAL AID PICTURE (2004-2005)
Students with need: Out of 234 full-time freshmen who applied for aid, 190 were judged to have need. Of these, 190 received aid, and 63 had their full need met. Average financial aid package met 80% of need; average scholarship/grant was $3,958; average loan was $4,329. For part-time students, average financial aid package was $5,720.
Students without need: No-need awards available for academics, athletics, leadership, music/drama, state/district residency.

FINANCIAL AID PROCEDURES
Forms required: FAFSA, state aid form.
Dates and Deadlines: Priority date 3/1; no closing date. Applicants notified on a rolling basis starting 2/15; must reply within 2 week(s) of notification.

CONTACT
Melanie McCulloh, Director of Scholarships and Financial Assistance
2300 West Innes Street, Salisbury, NC 28144
(704) 637-4416

Catawba Valley Community College
Hickory, North Carolina
www.cvcc.edu   Federal Code: 005318

2-year public community college in large town.
Enrollment: 4,200 undergrads, 50% part-time. 632 full-time freshmen.
Selectivity: Open admission; but selective for some programs.

BASIC COSTS (2005-2006)
Tuition and fees: $1,209; out-of-state residents $6,609.
Per-credit charge: $40; out-of-state residents $220.

FINANCIAL AID PICTURE (2004-2005)
Students with need: Out of 507 full-time freshmen who applied for aid, 285 were judged to have need. Of these, 239 received aid, and 6 had their full need met. Need-based aid available for part-time students.
Students without need: No-need awards available for academics, athletics, leadership, music/drama.

FINANCIAL AID PROCEDURES
Forms required: FAFSA.
Dates and Deadlines: Closing date 3/15. Applicants notified on a rolling basis starting 5/15.

CONTACT
Debbie Barger, Director of Scholarships and Financial Aid
2550 Highway 70 Southeast, Hickory, NC 28602
(828) 327-7000 ext. 4214

Central Carolina Community College
Sanford, North Carolina
www.cccc.edu   Federal Code: 005449

2-year public community college in large town.
Enrollment: 3,366 undergrads.
Selectivity: Open admission; but selective for some programs.

BASIC COSTS (2005-2006)
Tuition and fees: $1,223; out-of-state residents $6,623.
Per-credit charge: $40; out-of-state residents $220.

FINANCIAL AID PICTURE
Students with need: Need-based aid available for full-time and part-time students. Work study available nights.
Students without need: No-need awards available for academics.

FINANCIAL AID PROCEDURES
Forms required: FAFSA, institutional form.
Dates and Deadlines: Priority date 3/15; closing date 5/1. Applicants notified on a rolling basis starting 7/1; must reply within 2 week(s) of notification.
Transfers: No deadline.

CONTACT
Jackie Thomas, Director of Financial Aid
1105 Kelly Drive, Sanford, NC 27330
(919) 718-7205

Central Piedmont Community College
Charlotte, North Carolina
www.cpcc.edu   Federal Code: 002915

2-year public community college in very large city.
Enrollment: 10,535 undergrads, 57% part-time. 967 full-time freshmen.
Selectivity: Open admission; but selective for some programs.

BASIC COSTS (2005-2006)
Tuition and fees: $1,255; out-of-state residents $6,655.
Per-credit charge: $40; out-of-state residents $220.

FINANCIAL AID PICTURE
Students with need: Need-based aid available for full-time and part-time students.
Students without need: No-need awards available for academics, minority status.

FINANCIAL AID PROCEDURES
Forms required: FAFSA.
Dates and Deadlines: Priority date 4/3; closing date 6/3. Applicants notified on a rolling basis.

CONTACT
Debbie Brooks, Director, Student Financial Aid
Box 35009, Charlotte, NC 28235-5009
(704) 330-6942

Chowan College
Murfreesboro, North Carolina
www.chowan.edu   Federal Code: 002916

4-year private liberal arts college in rural community, affiliated with Southern Baptist Convention.
Enrollment: 797 undergrads, 5% part-time. 208 full-time freshmen.
Selectivity: Admits 50 to 75% of applicants.

BASIC COSTS (2006-2007)
Tuition and fees: $15,950.
Per-credit charge: $305.
Room and board: $6,800.
Additional info: $90 Communications fee for residents only.

FINANCIAL AID PICTURE (2004-2005)
Students with need: Out of 191 full-time freshmen who applied for aid, 175 were judged to have need. Of these, 175 received aid, and 17 had their full need met. Average financial aid package met 58% of need; average scholarship/grant was $7,520; average loan was $2,461. For part-time students, average financial aid package was $11,148.
Students without need: 29 full-time freshmen who did not demonstrate need for aid received scholarships/grants; average award was $9,719. No-need awards available for academics, athletics, leadership, music/drama, religious affiliation, state/district residency.
Scholarships offered: Scholarship program for students serving as student body president who qualify for admission; full tuition.
Cumulative student debt: 80% of graduating class had student loans; average debt was $17,725.

FINANCIAL AID PROCEDURES
Forms required: FAFSA.
Dates and Deadlines: Priority date 3/1; no closing date. Applicants notified on a rolling basis starting 3/1; must reply within 2 week(s) of notification.

CONTACT
Stephanie Harrell, Director of Financial Aid
200 Jones Drive, Murfreesboro, NC 27855-9901
(252) 398-1229

Cleveland Community College
Shelby, North Carolina
www.clevelandcommunitycollege.edu Federal Code: 008082

2-year public community college in large town.
Enrollment: 1,749 undergrads, 53% part-time. 173 full-time freshmen.
Selectivity: Open admission; but selective for some programs.

BASIC COSTS (2005-2006)
Tuition and fees: $1,223; out-of-state residents $6,623.
Per-credit charge: $40; out-of-state residents $220.

FINANCIAL AID PICTURE (2004-2005)
Students with need: Average financial aid package for all full-time undergraduates was $2,300. 98% awarded as scholarships/grants, 2% awarded as loans/jobs. Need-based aid available for part-time students.

FINANCIAL AID PROCEDURES
Forms required: FAFSA.
Dates and Deadlines: Priority date 7/1; no closing date. Applicants notified on a rolling basis.

CONTACT
Andy Gardner, Director of Financial Aid
137 South Post Road, Shelby, NC 28152
(704) 484-4096

Coastal Carolina Community College
Jacksonville, North Carolina
www.coastal.cc.nc.us   Federal Code: 005316

2-year public community college in large town.
Enrollment: 3,801 undergrads, 49% part-time. 518 full-time freshmen.
Selectivity: Open admission; but selective for some programs.

BASIC COSTS (2005-2006)
Tuition and fees: $1,215; out-of-state residents $6,615.
Per-credit charge: $40; out-of-state residents $220.

FINANCIAL AID PICTURE
Students with need: Need-based aid available for full-time and part-time students. Work study available nights, weekends, and for part-time students.
Students without need: No-need awards available for academics, state/district residency.

FINANCIAL AID PROCEDURES
Forms required: FAFSA, institutional form.
Dates and Deadlines: Priority date 5/15; no closing date. Applicants notified on a rolling basis starting 5/15; must reply within 2 week(s) of notification.

CONTACT
John Kopka, Director of Financial Aid & Veterans Programs
444 Western Boulevard, Jacksonville, NC 28546-6877
(910) 938-6247

College of the Albemarle
Elizabeth City, North Carolina
www.albemarle.cc.nc.us   Federal Code: 002917

2-year public branch campus and community college in large town.
Enrollment: 1,200 undergrads.
Selectivity: Open admission; but selective for some programs.

BASIC COSTS (2005-2006)
Tuition and fees: $1,255; out-of-state residents $6,655.
Per-credit charge: $40; out-of-state residents $220.

FINANCIAL AID PICTURE
Students with need: Need-based aid available for full-time and part-time students.
Students without need: No-need awards available for academics, art, leadership, minority status, music/drama, state/district residency.
Additional info: Separate application must be submitted for COA Private Scholarships.

FINANCIAL AID PROCEDURES
Forms required: FAFSA.
Dates and Deadlines: Priority date 3/15; no closing date. Applicants notified on a rolling basis starting 5/1; must reply within 2 week(s) of notification.

CONTACT
Angie Dawson, Director of Scholarships and Student Aid
1208 North Road Street, Elizabeth City, NC 27906-2327
(252) 335-0821 ext. 2355

Craven Community College
New Bern, North Carolina
www.cravencc.edu   Federal Code: 008086

2-year public community college in large town.
Enrollment: 2,988 undergrads.
Selectivity: Open admission; but selective for some programs.

BASIC COSTS (2005-2006)
Tuition and fees: $1,255; out-of-state residents $6,655.
Per-credit charge: $40; out-of-state residents $220.

FINANCIAL AID PICTURE (2004-2005)
Students with need: 86% of average financial aid package awarded as scholarships/grants, 14% awarded as loans/jobs.
Students without need: This college only awards aid to students with need.

FINANCIAL AID PROCEDURES
Forms required: FAFSA.
Dates and Deadlines: Priority date 3/31; no closing date. Applicants notified on a rolling basis starting 6/1.

CONTACT
Kathy Banks, Director of Financial Aid
800 College Court, New Bern, NC 28562
(252) 638-7216

Davidson College
Davidson, North Carolina   Federal Code: 002918
www.davidson.edu   CSS Code: 5150

4-year private liberal arts college in small town, affiliated with Presbyterian Church (USA).
Enrollment: 1,678 undergrads. 462 full-time freshmen.
Selectivity: Admits less than 50% of applicants. GED not accepted.

BASIC COSTS (2006-2007)
Tuition and fees: $30,194.
Room and board: $8,590.

FINANCIAL AID PICTURE (2004-2005)
Students with need: Out of 262 full-time freshmen who applied for aid, 165 were judged to have need. Of these, 165 received aid, and 165 had their full need met. Average financial aid package met 100% of need. Need-based aid available for part-time students.
Students without need: No-need awards available for academics, art, athletics, leadership, minority status, music/drama, ROTC.
Scholarships offered: Thompson S./Sarah S. Baker Scholarships; comprehensive fees; for first-time students with highest achievements; 3 awarded. John Montgomery Belk Scholarship; comprehensive fees; for Southeast applicants with highest achievements; 6 awarded. Amos Norris Scholarship; full cost; for first-time student athlete; 1 awarded. William Holt Terry Scholarships; full tuition; for first-year students with leadership skills and personal qualities, 2 awarded. John I. Smith Scholars Programs; full tuition; for first-year students with leadership, academic excellence, and commitment to community service; 2 awarded.
Cumulative student debt: 30% of graduating class had student loans; average debt was $22,976.

FINANCIAL AID PROCEDURES
Forms required: FAFSA, CSS PROFILE.
Dates and Deadlines: Closing date 2/15. Applicants notified by 4/1; must reply by 5/1.
Transfers: Priority date 2/15; closing date 3/15.

CONTACT
Kathleen Stevenson, Senior Associate Dean of Admission and Financial Aid
Box 7156, Davidson, NC 28035-7156
(704) 894-2232

Davidson County Community College
Lexington, North Carolina
www.davidson.cc.nc.us   Federal Code: 002919

2-year public community college in large town.
Enrollment: 2,685 undergrads.
Selectivity: Open admission; but selective for some programs.

BASIC COSTS (2005-2006)
Tuition and fees: $1,255; out-of-state residents $6,655.
Per-credit charge: $40; out-of-state residents $220.

FINANCIAL AID PICTURE (2004-2005)
Students with need: 98% of average financial aid package awarded as scholarships/grants, 2% awarded as loans/jobs. Need-based aid available for part-time students.
Students without need: No-need awards available for academics, leadership.

FINANCIAL AID PROCEDURES
Forms required: FAFSA, institutional form.
Dates and Deadlines: Priority date 7/1; no closing date. Applicants notified on a rolling basis starting 7/1; must reply within 2 week(s) of notification.

CONTACT
Anita Pennix, Coordinator, Financial Aid
PO Box 1287, Lexington, NC 27293-1287
(336) 249-8186 ext. 237

Duke University
Durham, North Carolina
www.duke.edu
Federal Code: 002920
CSS Code: 5156

4-year private university in small city, affiliated with United Methodist Church.
Enrollment: 6,259 undergrads. 1,724 full-time freshmen.
Selectivity: Admits less than 50% of applicants. GED not accepted.

BASIC COSTS (2005-2006)
Tuition and fees: $32,409.
Per-credit charge: $930.
Room and board: $8,830.

FINANCIAL AID PICTURE (2005-2006)
Students with need: 79% of average financial aid package awarded as scholarships/grants, 21% awarded as loans/jobs.
Students without need: No-need awards available for academics, alumni affiliation, art, athletics, leadership, minority status, religious affiliation, ROTC, state/district residency.

FINANCIAL AID PROCEDURES
Forms required: FAFSA, CSS PROFILE.
Dates and Deadlines: Closing date 2/1. Applicants notified by 4/1; must reply by 5/1 or within 4 week(s) of notification.

CONTACT
Nerissa Rivera, Coordinator Financial Aid
2138 Campus Drive, Durham, NC 27708
(919) 684-6225

Durham Technical Community College
Durham, North Carolina
www.durhamtech.edu
Federal Code: 005448

2-year public community and technical college in small city.
Enrollment: 5,698 undergrads.
Selectivity: Open admission; but selective for some programs.

BASIC COSTS (2005-2006)
Tuition and fees: $1,230; out-of-state residents $6,630.
Per-credit charge: $40; out-of-state residents $220.

FINANCIAL AID PICTURE
Students with need: Need-based aid available for full-time and part-time students. Work study available nights.
Students without need: No-need awards available for academics, state/district residency.
Additional info: Special funds available to single parents or displaced homemakers for tuition, fees, books, supplies and child care expenses.

FINANCIAL AID PROCEDURES
Forms required: FAFSA.
Dates and Deadlines: Applicants notified on a rolling basis; must reply within 3 week(s) of notification.

CONTACT
Kay Jedlica, Financial Aid Officer
1637 Lawson Street, Durham, NC 27703
(919) 686-3661

East Carolina University
Greenville, North Carolina
www.ecu.edu
Federal Code: 002923

4-year public university in small city.
Enrollment: 17,593 undergrads, 10% part-time. 3,223 full-time freshmen.
Selectivity: Admits 50 to 75% of applicants.

BASIC COSTS (2005-2006)
Tuition and fees: $3,627; out-of-state residents $14,141.
Room and board: $6,840.

FINANCIAL AID PICTURE (2005-2006)
Students with need: Out of 2,485 full-time freshmen who applied for aid, 1,401 were judged to have need. Of these, 1,401 received aid, and 1,362 had their full need met. Average financial aid package met 23% of need; average scholarship/grant was $8,843; average loan was $5,391. For part-time students, average financial aid package was $7,044.
Students without need: 136 full-time freshmen who did not demonstrate need for aid received scholarships/grants; average award was $7,582. No-need awards available for academics, alumni affiliation, art, athletics, minority status, ROTC.
Scholarships offered: 70 full-time freshmen received athletic scholarships; average amount $12,470.
Cumulative student debt: 28% of graduating class had student loans; average debt was $19,614.

FINANCIAL AID PROCEDURES
Forms required: FAFSA.
Dates and Deadlines: Priority date 4/15; no closing date. Applicants notified on a rolling basis starting 3/15; must reply within 3 week(s) of notification.

CONTACT
Rose Stelma, Director of Student Financial Aid
Office of Undergraduate Admissions, Greenville, NC 27858-4353
(252) 328-6610

Edgecombe Community College
Tarboro, North Carolina
www.edgecombe.edu
Federal Code: 008855

2-year public community college in large town.
Enrollment: 1,727 undergrads, 56% part-time. 128 full-time freshmen.
Selectivity: Open admission; but selective for some programs.

BASIC COSTS (2005-2006)
Tuition and fees: $1,209; out-of-state residents $6,609.
Per-credit charge: $40; out-of-state residents $220.

FINANCIAL AID PICTURE (2004-2005)
Students with need: Out of 102 full-time freshmen who applied for aid, 91 were judged to have need. Of these, 91 received aid, and 69 had their full need met. Average financial aid package met 90% of need; average scholarship/grant was $2,050; average loan was $3,600. For part-time students, average financial aid package was $475.

Students without need: This college only awards aid to students with need.
Cumulative student debt: 5% of graduating class had student loans; average debt was $4,850.

FINANCIAL AID PROCEDURES
Forms required: FAFSA, institutional form.
Dates and Deadlines: Closing date 6/30. Applicants notified on a rolling basis starting 8/15; must reply within 3 week(s) of notification.
Transfers: No deadline.

CONTACT
LaShawn Cooper, Director of Financial Aid
2009 West Wilson Street, Tarboro, NC 27886
(252) 823-5166 ext. 257

Elizabeth City State University
Elizabeth City, North Carolina
www.ecsu.edu
Federal Code: 002926

4-year public liberal arts college in large town.
Enrollment: 2,414 undergrads, 6% part-time. 560 full-time freshmen.
Selectivity: Admits over 75% of applicants.

BASIC COSTS (2005-2006)
Tuition and fees: $2,493; out-of-state residents $10,832.
Room and board: $4,710.

FINANCIAL AID PICTURE
Students with need: Need-based aid available for full-time students. Work study available nights, weekends, and for part-time students.
Students without need: No-need awards available for academics, athletics, minority status, ROTC, state/district residency.

FINANCIAL AID PROCEDURES
Forms required: FAFSA.
Dates and Deadlines: Priority date 3/1; closing date 8/15. Applicants notified on a rolling basis starting 6/1; must reply within 3 week(s) of notification.
Transfers: Closing date 8/1. Applicants notified on a rolling basis starting 6/1; must reply within 3 week(s) of notification.

CONTACT
Dawn Brumsey, Associate Director of Financial Aid
1704 Weeksville Road, Campus Box 901, Elizabeth City, NC 27909
(252) 335-3283

Elon University
Elon, North Carolina
www.elon.edu
Federal Code: 002927
CSS Code: 5183

4-year private university and liberal arts college in large town, affiliated with United Church of Christ.
Enrollment: 4,702 undergrads, 2% part-time. 1,237 full-time freshmen.
Selectivity: Admits less than 50% of applicants.

BASIC COSTS (2006-2007)
Tuition and fees: $20,441.
Per-credit charge: $634.
Room and board: $6,850.

FINANCIAL AID PICTURE (2005-2006)
Students with need: Out of 734 full-time freshmen who applied for aid, 441 were judged to have need. Of these, 438 received aid. Average financial aid package met 68% of need; average scholarship/grant was $7,332; average loan was $2,768. Need-based aid available for part-time students.
Students without need: 266 full-time freshmen who did not demonstrate need for aid received scholarships/grants; average award was $4,544. No-need awards available for academics, art, athletics, leadership, music/drama, ROTC, state/district residency.
Scholarships offered: *Merit:* Presidential Scholarships; ranging from $1,000-$3,750 annually; based on academic credentials. Fellows Programs (Communications, Science, Jefferson-Pilot Business, Honors, Isabella Cannon Leadership); $1,000-$6,000 annually; based on merit. North Carolina Teaching Fellows; $13,000 annually. Engineering Scholarships; $3,000 annually. *Athletic:* 66 full-time freshmen received athletic scholarships; average amount $13,751.
Cumulative student debt: 45% of graduating class had student loans; average debt was $21,687.

FINANCIAL AID PROCEDURES
Forms required: FAFSA, CSS PROFILE, institutional form.
Dates and Deadlines: Priority date 2/15; no closing date. Applicants notified on a rolling basis starting 3/30.

CONTACT
Pat Murphy, Director of Financial Planning
2700 Campus Box, Elon, NC 27244-2010
(336) 278-7640

Fayetteville State University
Fayetteville, North Carolina
www.uncfsu.edu
Federal Code: 002928

4-year public university in small city.
Enrollment: 4,935 undergrads. 684 full-time freshmen.
Selectivity: Admits over 75% of applicants.

BASIC COSTS (2005-2006)
Tuition and fees: $2,521; out-of-state residents $12,257.
Room and board: $4,120.

FINANCIAL AID PICTURE (2004-2005)
Students with need: Out of 684 full-time freshmen who applied for aid, 582 were judged to have need. Of these, 495 received aid, and 50 had their full need met. Average financial aid package met 78% of need; average scholarship/grant was $1,500; average loan was $2,200. Need-based aid available for part-time students.
Students without need: 73 full-time freshmen who did not demonstrate need for aid received scholarships/grants; average award was $4,373. No-need awards available for academics, alumni affiliation, athletics, music/drama, ROTC, state/district residency.
Scholarships offered: 29 full-time freshmen received athletic scholarships; average amount $3,600.

FINANCIAL AID PROCEDURES
Forms required: FAFSA.
Dates and Deadlines: Priority date 3/1; closing date 4/1. Applicants notified on a rolling basis starting 4/15; must reply within 2 week(s) of notification.

CONTACT
Lois McKoy, Director of Financial Aid
1200 Murchison Road, Fayetteville, NC 28301-4298
(910) 672-1325

Fayetteville Technical Community College
Fayetteville, North Carolina
www.faytechcc.edu
Federal Code: 007640

2-year public community and technical college in large city.
Enrollment: 9,403 undergrads, 55% part-time. 1,061 full-time freshmen.
Selectivity: Open admission; but selective for some programs.

BASIC COSTS (2005-2006)
Tuition and fees: $1,245; out-of-state residents $6,645.
Per-credit charge: $40; out-of-state residents $220.

FINANCIAL AID PICTURE (2004-2005)
Students with need: 72% of average financial aid package awarded as scholarships/grants, 28% awarded as loans/jobs. Need-based aid available for part-time students.

FINANCIAL AID PROCEDURES
Forms required: FAFSA.
Dates and Deadlines: Priority date 6/1; closing date 7/15. Applicants notified on a rolling basis starting 5/1; must reply by 8/8 or within 2 week(s) of notification.
Transfers: No deadline.

CONTACT
Pat Stephenson, Financial Aid Director
PO Box 35236, Fayetteville, NC 28303-0236
(910) 678-8448

Forsyth Technical Community College
Winston-Salem, North Carolina
www.forsyth.tec.nc.us   Federal Code: 005317

2-year public community and technical college in small city.
Enrollment: 6,996 undergrads.
Selectivity: Open admission; but selective for some programs.

BASIC COSTS (2005-2006)
Tuition and fees: $1,235; out-of-state residents $6,635.
Per-credit charge: $40; out-of-state residents $220.

FINANCIAL AID PICTURE (2004-2005)
Students with need: 99% of average financial aid package awarded as scholarships/grants, 1% awarded as loans/jobs. Need-based aid available for part-time students. Work study available nights.
Students without need: This college only awards aid to students with need.
Additional info: Apply for aid as close to January 1 as possible for best consideration.

FINANCIAL AID PROCEDURES
Forms required: FAFSA, institutional form.
Dates and Deadlines: Priority date 6/1; no closing date. Applicants notified on a rolling basis starting 7/1; must reply within 2 week(s) of notification.
Transfers: Priority date 6/1; no deadline. Mid-year transfer students must submit a financial aid transcript from previous college in order for financial aid office to award any Federal Pell Grant funds to eligible students.

CONTACT
Ricky Hodges, Director of Student Financial Services
2100 Silas Creek Parkway, Winston-Salem, NC 27103

Gardner-Webb University
Boiling Springs, North Carolina
www.gardner-webb.edu   Federal Code: 002929

4-year private university and liberal arts college in small town, affiliated with Southern Baptist Convention.
Enrollment: 2,629 undergrads, 15% part-time. 441 full-time freshmen.
Selectivity: Admits 50 to 75% of applicants.

BASIC COSTS (2006-2007)
Tuition and fees: $17,240.
Per-credit charge: $305.
Room and board: $5,740.

Additional info: $170 communication fee and $30 residence hall activity fee for resident students.

FINANCIAL AID PICTURE (2005-2006)
Students with need: Out of 387 full-time freshmen who applied for aid, 312 were judged to have need. Of these, 312 received aid, and 95 had their full need met. Average financial aid package met 62% of need; average scholarship/grant was $2,430; average loan was $2,211. For part-time students, average financial aid package was $2,089.
Students without need: 78 full-time freshmen who did not demonstrate need for aid received scholarships/grants; average award was $5,395. No-need awards available for academics, athletics, leadership, minority status, music/drama, state/district residency.
Scholarships offered: 55 full-time freshmen received athletic scholarships; average amount $8,146.
Cumulative student debt: 52% of graduating class had student loans; average debt was $6,921.

FINANCIAL AID PROCEDURES
Forms required: FAFSA.
Dates and Deadlines: No deadline. Applicants notified on a rolling basis starting 3/1; must reply within 2 week(s) of notification.

CONTACT
Debra Hintz, Director of Financial Planning
Box 817, Boiling Springs, NC 28017
(704) 406-4243

Gaston College
Dallas, North Carolina
www.gaston.cc.nc.us   Federal Code: 002973

2-year public community college in small town.
Enrollment: 2,000 full-time undergrads.
Selectivity: Open admission; but selective for some programs.

BASIC COSTS (2005-2006)
Tuition and fees: $1,211; out-of-state residents $6,611.
Per-credit charge: $40; out-of-state residents $220.

FINANCIAL AID PICTURE (2004-2005)
Students with need: 90% of average financial aid package awarded as scholarships/grants, 10% awarded as loans/jobs.
Students without need: No-need awards available for academics, state/district residency.
Scholarships offered: Academic Scholarship: over 30 available, $1,100, GPA of 3.0 or better. Careers Scholarship: 10 available, $1,100 each, must pursue career in specified engineering technologies or industrial technologies major and have GPA of 3.0 or better.
Additional info: Grants/scholarships available for women pursuing nontraditional roles.

FINANCIAL AID PROCEDURES
Forms required: FAFSA, institutional form.
Dates and Deadlines: Priority date 3/15; no closing date. Applicants notified on a rolling basis.

CONTACT
Peggy Oates, Director of Financial Aid and Veterans Affairs
201 Highway 321 South, Dallas, NC 28034-1499
(704) 922-6227

Greensboro College
Greensboro, North Carolina
www.gborocollege.edu   Federal Code: 002930

4-year private liberal arts college in small city, affiliated with United Methodist Church.
Enrollment: 850 undergrads.
Selectivity: Admits 50 to 75% of applicants.

BASIC COSTS (2005-2006)
Tuition and fees: $18,120.
Per-credit charge: $480.
Room and board: $6,920.

FINANCIAL AID PICTURE
Students with need: Need-based aid available for full-time and part-time students. Work study available nights, weekends, and for part-time students.
Students without need: No-need awards available for academics, alumni affiliation, art, leadership, music/drama, religious affiliation, state/district residency.
Scholarships offered: Presidential Scholarships; full tuition, fees, room, and board; number of awards vary. Additional merit-based or talent-based scholarships awarded; number and dollar amounts vary.

FINANCIAL AID PROCEDURES
Forms required: FAFSA, state aid form, institutional form.
Dates and Deadlines: Priority date 4/15; no closing date. Applicants notified on a rolling basis starting 2/1; must reply within 2 week(s) of notification.

CONTACT
Ron Elmore, Director of Financial Aid
815 West Market Street, Greensboro, NC 27401-1875
(336) 272-7102

Guilford College
Greensboro, North Carolina
www.guilford.edu   Federal Code: 002931

4-year private liberal arts college in small city, affiliated with Society of Friends (Quaker).
Enrollment: 2,682 undergrads, 16% part-time. 438 full-time freshmen.
Selectivity: Admits 50 to 75% of applicants.

BASIC COSTS (2006-2007)
Tuition and fees: $23,020.
Per-credit charge: $698.
Room and board: $6,690.
Additional info: Tuition/fee waivers available for adults.

FINANCIAL AID PICTURE (2004-2005)
Students with need: Out of 339 full-time freshmen who applied for aid, 263 were judged to have need. Of these, 263 received aid, and 54 had their full need met. Average financial aid package met 95% of need; average scholarship/grant was $14,250; average loan was $5,096. For part-time students, average financial aid package was $4,421.
Students without need: 161 full-time freshmen who did not demonstrate need for aid received scholarships/grants; average award was $7,703. No-need awards available for academics, art, job skills, leadership, minority status, music/drama, religious affiliation, state/district residency.
Scholarships offered: Honors Scholarship; $7,500 to full tuition. Presidential Scholarship; $5,000. Incentive grants; $3,000; based on participation or leadership in school or community activities. Quaker Leadership Scholarships; $3,000; candidates must be active members of the Religious Society of Friends.

FINANCIAL AID PROCEDURES
Forms required: FAFSA.
Dates and Deadlines: Priority date 3/1; no closing date. Applicants notified on a rolling basis starting 2/15; must reply by 5/1 or within 4 week(s) of notification.

CONTACT
Dianne Harrison, Director of Financial Aid
Admissions, New Garden Hall, Greensboro, NC 27410-4108
(336) 316-2354

Guilford Technical Community College
Jamestown, North Carolina
www.gtcc.edu   Federal Code: 004838

2-year public community college in large city.
Enrollment: 9,448 undergrads.
Selectivity: Open admission; but selective for some programs.

BASIC COSTS (2005-2006)
Tuition and fees: $1,260; out-of-state residents $6,660.
Per-credit charge: $40; out-of-state residents $220.

FINANCIAL AID PICTURE
Students with need: Need-based aid available for full-time and part-time students.

FINANCIAL AID PROCEDURES
Forms required: FAFSA.
Dates and Deadlines: Priority date 3/15; no closing date. Applicants notified on a rolling basis starting 7/1; must reply within 2 week(s) of notification.

CONTACT
Lisa Koretoff, Director of Financial Aid
PO Box 309, Jamestown, NC 27282
(336) 334-4822 ext. 5352

Halifax Community College
Weldon, North Carolina
www.halfaxcc.edu   Federal Code: 007986

2-year public community college in small town.
Enrollment: 1,500 undergrads.
Selectivity: Open admission; but selective for some programs.

BASIC COSTS (2005-2006)
Tuition and fees: $1,245; out-of-state residents $6,645.
Per-credit charge: $40; out-of-state residents $220.

FINANCIAL AID PICTURE
Students with need: Need-based aid available for full-time students.

FINANCIAL AID PROCEDURES
Dates and Deadlines: Priority date 7/1; no closing date. Applicants notified on a rolling basis starting 8/1; must reply within 2 week(s) of notification.

CONTACT
Tara Keeter, Director, Financial Aid
Drawer 809, Weldon, NC 27890
(252) 536-7223

Haywood Community College
Clyde, North Carolina
www.haywood.edu   Federal Code: 008083

2-year public community and technical college in rural community.
Enrollment: 1,411 undergrads.
Selectivity: Open admission; but selective for some programs.

BASIC COSTS (2005-2006)
Tuition and fees: $1,234; out-of-state residents $6,634.
Per-credit charge: $40; out-of-state residents $220.

FINANCIAL AID PICTURE (2004-2005)
Students with need: Need-based aid available for part-time students.
Students without need: No-need awards available for academics.
Additional info: Complete FAFSA by priority filing date for consideration for institutional scholarships.

FINANCIAL AID PROCEDURES
Forms required: FAFSA, institutional form.
Dates and Deadlines: Priority date 4/1; no closing date. Applicants notified on a rolling basis starting 4/15; must reply within 2 week(s) of notification.

CONTACT
Kathy Lovedahl, Coordinator Financial Aid
185 Freelander Drive, Clyde, NC 28721-9454
(828) 627-4506

High Point University
High Point, North Carolina
www.highpoint.edu   Federal Code: 002933

4-year private university in small city, affiliated with United Methodist Church.
Enrollment: 2,507 undergrads, 7% part-time. 412 full-time freshmen.
Selectivity: Admits 50 to 75% of applicants.

BASIC COSTS (2006-2007)
Tuition and fees: $18,130.
Per-credit charge: $281.
Room and board: $7,390.

FINANCIAL AID PICTURE (2004-2005)
Students with need: Out of 351 full-time freshmen who applied for aid, 339 were judged to have need. Of these, 339 received aid, and 15 had their full need met. Average financial aid package met 78% of need; average scholarship/grant was $4,000; average loan was $2,626. Need-based aid available for part-time students.
Students without need: 73 full-time freshmen who did not demonstrate need for aid received scholarships/grants; average award was $9,120. No-need awards available for academics, alumni affiliation, art, athletics, music/drama, religious affiliation, state/district residency.
Scholarships offered: *Merit:* At least 3 full tuition scholarships, at least 50 $7,000 scholarships, and at least 50 $5,000 scholarships awarded annually to entering freshmen based on academic merit. Application and interview required. *Athletic:* 36 full-time freshmen received athletic scholarships; average amount $9,700.
Cumulative student debt: 83% of graduating class had student loans; average debt was $20,125.

FINANCIAL AID PROCEDURES
Forms required: FAFSA.
Dates and Deadlines: Priority date 3/1; no closing date. Applicants notified on a rolling basis starting 4/1; must reply within 3 week(s) of notification.

CONTACT
Dana Kelly, Director of Financial Aid
833 Montlieu Avenue, High Point, NC 27262-3598
(336) 841-9128

Isothermal Community College
Spindale, North Carolina
www.isothermal.edu   Federal Code: 002934

2-year public community college in small town.
Enrollment: 1,743 undergrads.
Selectivity: Open admission.

BASIC COSTS (2005-2006)
Tuition and fees: $1,213; out-of-state residents $6,613.
Per-credit charge: $40; out-of-state residents $220.

FINANCIAL AID PICTURE
Students with need: Need-based aid available for full-time and part-time students. Work study available nights.
Students without need: No-need awards available for academics, job skills, leadership, minority status, music/drama, state/district residency.

FINANCIAL AID PROCEDURES
Forms required: FAFSA, institutional form.
Dates and Deadlines: Priority date 5/31; no closing date. Applicants notified on a rolling basis starting 4/30; must reply within 4 week(s) of notification.

CONTACT
Jeffery Boyle, Director of Financial Aid
PO Box 804, Spindale, NC 28160
(828) 286-3636 ext. 242

James Sprunt Community College
Kenansville, North Carolina
www.sprunt.com   Federal Code: 007687

2-year public community college in rural community.
Enrollment: 936 undergrads, 40% part-time. 69 full-time freshmen.
Selectivity: Open admission; but selective for some programs.

BASIC COSTS (2005-2006)
Tuition and fees: $1,255; out-of-state residents $6,655.
Per-credit charge: $40; out-of-state residents $220.

FINANCIAL AID PICTURE (2004-2005)
Students with need: Out of 46 full-time freshmen who applied for aid, 46 were judged to have need. Of these, 46 received aid. Average financial aid package met 60% of need; average scholarship/grant was $600; average loan was $2,500. Need-based aid available for part-time students.
Students without need: This college only awards aid to students with need.
Cumulative student debt: 10% of graduating class had student loans; average debt was $6,125.

FINANCIAL AID PROCEDURES
Forms required: FAFSA, state aid form, institutional form.
Dates and Deadlines: Priority date 6/1; no closing date. Applicants notified on a rolling basis starting 7/15; must reply within 2 week(s) of notification.

CONTACT
Connie Taylor, Financial Aid Officer
Box 398, Kenansville, NC 28349-0398
(910) 296-2503

John Wesley College
High Point, North Carolina
www.johnwesley.edu
Federal Code: 013819

4-year private Bible college in small city, affiliated with interdenominational tradition.
Enrollment: 140 undergrads, 36% part-time. 12 full-time freshmen.
Selectivity: Admits 50 to 75% of applicants.

BASIC COSTS (2005-2006)
Tuition and fees: $9,226.
Room only: $1,990.

FINANCIAL AID PICTURE (2004-2005)
Students with need: Out of 12 full-time freshmen who applied for aid, 12 were judged to have need. Of these, 12 received aid. Average financial aid package met 50% of need; average scholarship/grant was $500; average loan was $2,625. Need-based aid available for part-time students.
Scholarships offered: Early Acceptance; $100. Academic Honor; 10% of tuition.
Cumulative student debt: 65% of graduating class had student loans; average debt was $17,125.
Additional info: Early Acceptance Scholarships, Academic Honor Scholarships, Married Student Credit and Minister/Missionary Dependent Scholarship available.

FINANCIAL AID PROCEDURES
Forms required: FAFSA.
Dates and Deadlines: Priority date 3/15; no closing date. Applicants notified on a rolling basis starting 6/1; must reply within 3 week(s) of notification.
Transfers: Closing date 3/15.

CONTACT
Shirley Carter, Director of Financial Aid
2314 North Centennial, High Point, NC 27265-3197
(336) 889-2262 ext. 129

Johnson & Wales University
Charlotte, North Carolina
www.jwu.edu/charlotte/

4-year private university in very large city.
Enrollment: 2,156 undergrads. 789 full-time freshmen.
Selectivity: Admits 50 to 75% of applicants.

BASIC COSTS (2006-2007)
Tuition and fees: $20,826.
Per-credit charge: $368.
Room and board: $8,300.

FINANCIAL AID PICTURE (2005-2006)
Students with need: Out of 726 full-time freshmen who applied for aid, 655 were judged to have need. Of these, 654 received aid, and 9 had their full need met. Average financial aid package met 63% of need; average scholarship/grant was $5,513; average loan was $6,361. For part-time students, average financial aid package was $5,892.
Students without need: 95 full-time freshmen who did not demonstrate need for aid received scholarships/grants; average award was $4,429.

FINANCIAL AID PROCEDURES
Dates and Deadlines: No deadline. Applicants notified by 3/1.

CONTACT
Director of Financial Aid
801 West Trade Street, Charlotte, NC 28202
(866) 598-2427

Johnson C. Smith University
Charlotte, North Carolina
www.jcsu.edu
Federal Code: 002936

4-year private university and liberal arts college in very large city.
Enrollment: 1,404 undergrads, 5% part-time. 444 full-time freshmen.
Selectivity: Admits less than 50% of applicants.

BASIC COSTS (2005-2006)
Tuition and fees: $14,399.
Per-credit charge: $254.
Room and board: $5,563.

FINANCIAL AID PICTURE (2005-2006)
Students with need: Out of 399 full-time freshmen who applied for aid, 342 were judged to have need. Of these, 342 received aid, and 15 had their full need met. Average financial aid package met 40% of need; average scholarship/grant was $3,000; average loan was $2,625. Need-based aid available for part-time students.
Students without need: No-need awards available for academics, athletics, ROTC, state/district residency.
Cumulative student debt: 90% of graduating class had student loans; average debt was $25,000.

FINANCIAL AID PROCEDURES
Forms required: FAFSA.
Dates and Deadlines: Priority date 3/1; no closing date. Applicants notified on a rolling basis starting 3/1; must reply within 2 week(s) of notification.

CONTACT
Cynthia Anderson, Director of Financial Aid
100 Beatties Ford Road, Charlotte, NC 28216-5398
(704) 378-1035

Johnston Community College
Smithfield, North Carolina
www.johnston.cc.nc.us
Federal Code: 009336

2-year public community and technical college in large town.
Enrollment: 4,088 undergrads, 60% part-time. 447 full-time freshmen.
Selectivity: Open admission; but selective for some programs.

BASIC COSTS (2005-2006)
Tuition and fees: $1,253; out-of-state residents $6,653.
Per-credit charge: $40; out-of-state residents $220.

FINANCIAL AID PICTURE (2004-2005)
Students with need: 85% of average financial aid package awarded as scholarships/grants, 15% awarded as loans/jobs. Need-based aid available for part-time students.
Students without need: This college only awards aid to students with need.

FINANCIAL AID PROCEDURES
Forms required: FAFSA, institutional form.
Dates and Deadlines: Priority date 5/31; no closing date. Applicants notified on a rolling basis starting 6/1; must reply within 2 week(s) of notification.

CONTACT
Betty Woodall, Financial Aid Officer
Box 2350, Smithfield, NC 27577
(919) 209-2028

King's College
Charlotte, North Carolina
www.kingscollegecharlotte.edu

2-year for-profit community and technical college in large city.
Enrollment: 537 undergrads.

BASIC COSTS (2006-2007)
Tuition and fees: $11,960.
Room and board: $5,960.

FINANCIAL AID PICTURE
Students with need: Need-based aid available for full-time students.
Students without need: This college only awards aid to students with need.

FINANCIAL AID PROCEDURES
Forms required: FAFSA.
Dates and Deadlines: Applicants notified on a rolling basis.

CONTACT
Eunice Torifa, Director of Student Services
322 Lamar Avenue, Charlotte, NC 28204
(704) 688-3616

Lees-McRae College
Banner Elk, North Carolina
www.lmc.edu   Federal Code: 002923

4-year private liberal arts college in rural community, affiliated with Presbyterian Church (USA).
Enrollment: 874 undergrads.
Selectivity: Admits 50 to 75% of applicants.

BASIC COSTS (2006-2007)
Tuition and fees: $18,000.
Per-credit charge: $480.
Room and board: $6,000.

FINANCIAL AID PICTURE (2005-2006)
Students with need: 60% of average financial aid package awarded as scholarships/grants, 40% awarded as loans/jobs. Need-based aid available for part-time students. Work study available nights, weekends, and for part-time students.
Students without need: No-need awards available for academics, alumni affiliation, athletics, leadership, minority status, music/drama, religious affiliation, state/district residency.

FINANCIAL AID PROCEDURES
Forms required: FAFSA.
Dates and Deadlines: Priority date 3/15; no closing date. Applicants notified on a rolling basis starting 3/1; must reply within 2 week(s) of notification.

CONTACT
Brenda Duvall, Director of Financial Aid
Box 128, Banner Elk, NC 28604
(828) 898-8793

Lenoir Community College
Kinston, North Carolina
www.lenoir.cc.nc.us   Federal Code: 002940

2-year public community college in large town.
Enrollment: 2,016 undergrads, 40% part-time. 319 full-time freshmen.
Selectivity: Open admission; but selective for some programs.

BASIC COSTS (2005-2006)
Tuition and fees: $1,260; out-of-state residents $6,660.
Per-credit charge: $40; out-of-state residents $220.

FINANCIAL AID PICTURE
Students with need: Need-based aid available for full-time and part-time students. Work study available nights.
Students without need: No-need awards available for academics, athletics, leadership, state/district residency.

FINANCIAL AID PROCEDURES
Forms required: institutional form.
Dates and Deadlines: Priority date 6/1; closing date 7/15. Applicants notified on a rolling basis starting 7/1; must reply within 2 week(s) of notification.

CONTACT
Mary Anne Dawson, Director of Student Financial Aid
Box 188, Kinston, NC 28502-0188
(252) 527-6223

Lenoir-Rhyne College
Hickory, North Carolina
www.lrc.edu   Federal Code: 002941

4-year private liberal arts college in large town, affiliated with Evangelical Lutheran Church in America.
Enrollment: 1,374 undergrads.
Selectivity: Admits over 75% of applicants.

BASIC COSTS (2006-2007)
Tuition and fees: $20,180.
Room and board: $7,130.
Additional info: Tuition/fee waivers available for minority students.

FINANCIAL AID PICTURE (2004-2005)
Students with need: 70% of average financial aid package awarded as scholarships/grants, 30% awarded as loans/jobs. Need-based aid available for part-time students. Work study available nights, weekends, and for part-time students.
Students without need: No-need awards available for academics, alumni affiliation, athletics, leadership, minority status, music/drama, religious affiliation, ROTC, state/district residency.

FINANCIAL AID PROCEDURES
Forms required: FAFSA, institutional form.
Dates and Deadlines: Priority date 3/15; closing date 8/15. Applicants notified on a rolling basis starting 3/15; must reply within 4 week(s) of notification.

CONTACT
Eva Harmon, Director of Admissions and Financial Aid
PO Box 7227, Hickory, NC 28603
(828) 328-7304

Livingstone College
Salisbury, North Carolina
www.livingstone.edu   Federal Code: 002942

4-year private liberal arts college in large town, affiliated with African Methodist Episcopal Zion Church.
Enrollment: 895 undergrads, 4% part-time. 187 full-time freshmen.
Selectivity: Admits over 75% of applicants.

BASIC COSTS (2005-2006)
Tuition and fees: $12,174.
Room and board: $5,641.

630 North Carolina Livingstone College

FINANCIAL AID PICTURE (2004-2005)
Students with need: 50% of average financial aid package awarded as scholarships/grants, 50% awarded as loans/jobs. Need-based aid available for part-time students. Work study available nights, weekends, and for part-time students.
Students without need: No-need awards available for academics, alumni affiliation, athletics, leadership, music/drama, religious affiliation, ROTC, state/district residency.

FINANCIAL AID PROCEDURES
Forms required: FAFSA, state aid form.
Dates and Deadlines: Closing date 5/1. Applicants notified by 5/1; must reply within 4 week(s) of notification.

CONTACT
Terry Jeffries, Director of Financial Aid
701 West Monroe Street, Salisbury, NC 28144-5213
(704) 216-6069

Louisburg College
Louisburg, North Carolina
www.louisburg.edu   Federal Code: 002943

2-year private junior college in small town, affiliated with United Methodist Church.
Enrollment: 771 undergrads.
Selectivity: Admits over 75% of applicants.

BASIC COSTS (2006-2007)
Tuition and fees: $11,690.
Room and board: $6,890.

FINANCIAL AID PICTURE (2005-2006)
Students with need: Need-based aid available for full-time students. Work study available nights, weekends, and for part-time students.
Additional info: Job location and development program helps students obtain work in the community.

FINANCIAL AID PROCEDURES
Forms required: FAFSA, institutional form.
Dates and Deadlines: Priority date 3/15; no closing date. Applicants notified on a rolling basis starting 3/15.

CONTACT
Sean Van Pallandt, Director of Financial Aid
501 North Main Street, Louisburg, NC 27549
(919) 497-3203

Mars Hill College
Mars Hill, North Carolina
www.mhc.edu   Federal Code: 002944

4-year private liberal arts college in small town, affiliated with Baptist faith.
Enrollment: 1,308 undergrads.

BASIC COSTS (2006-2007)
Tuition and fees: $17,950.
Room and board: $6,248.

FINANCIAL AID PICTURE
Students with need: Need-based aid available for full-time and part-time students. Work study available nights.
Students without need: No-need awards available for academics, art, athletics, religious affiliation, state/district residency.
Scholarships offered: Awards based on merit, SAT/ACT scores, and GPA. Money available for four years, requiring minimum GPA.

FINANCIAL AID PROCEDURES
Forms required: FAFSA, state aid form, institutional form.
Dates and Deadlines: No deadline. Applicants notified on a rolling basis; must reply within 2 week(s) of notification.

CONTACT
Donna Banks, Director of Financial Aid
Blackwell Hall, Box 370, Mars Hill, NC 28754
(828) 689-1123

Martin Community College
Williamston, North Carolina
www.martincc.edu   Federal Code: 007988

2-year public community and technical college in small town.
Enrollment: 658 undergrads, 36% part-time. 84 full-time freshmen.
Selectivity: Open admission; but selective for some programs.

BASIC COSTS (2005-2006)
Tuition and fees: $1,223; out-of-state residents $6,623.
Per-credit charge: $40; out-of-state residents $220.

FINANCIAL AID PICTURE (2004-2005)
Students with need: 68% of average financial aid package awarded as scholarships/grants, 32% awarded as loans/jobs. Need-based aid available for part-time students. Work study available nights.
Students without need: No-need awards available for academics.

FINANCIAL AID PROCEDURES
Forms required: FAFSA.
Dates and Deadlines: Priority date 5/1; no closing date. Applicants notified on a rolling basis starting 5/1.

CONTACT
Elvis Jones, Financial Aid Officer
1161 Kehukee Park Road, Williamston, NC 27892-9988
(252) 792-1521 ext. 244

Mayland Community College
Spruce Pine, North Carolina
www.mayland.edu   Federal Code: 011197

2-year public community college in small town.
Enrollment: 1,500 undergrads.
Selectivity: Open admission; but selective for some programs.

BASIC COSTS (2005-2006)
Tuition and fees: $1,245; out-of-state residents $6,645.
Per-credit charge: $40; out-of-state residents $220.

FINANCIAL AID PICTURE
Students with need: Need-based aid available for full-time and part-time students.

FINANCIAL AID PROCEDURES
Forms required: FAFSA, institutional form.
Dates and Deadlines: Priority date 3/15; no closing date. Applicants notified on a rolling basis starting 6/15.

CONTACT
Pamela Ellis, Financial Aid Coordinator
Box 547, Spruce Pine, NC 28777
(828) 765-7351

McDowell Technical Community College
Marion, North Carolina
www.mcdowelltech.cc.nc.us   Federal Code: 008085

2-year public community and technical college in small town.
Enrollment: 755 undergrads.
Selectivity: Open admission; but selective for some programs.

BASIC COSTS (2005-2006)
Tuition and fees: $1,203; out-of-state residents $6,603.
Per-credit charge: $40; out-of-state residents $220.

FINANCIAL AID PICTURE (2004-2005)
Students with need: 99% of average financial aid package awarded as scholarships/grants, 1% awarded as loans/jobs. Work study available nights.
Students without need: This college only awards aid to students with need.

FINANCIAL AID PROCEDURES
Forms required: FAFSA, institutional form.
Dates and Deadlines: Priority date 3/15; no closing date. Applicants notified on a rolling basis starting 7/1.

CONTACT
Kim Shuford, Financial Aid Officer
54 College Drive, Marion, NC 28752
(828) 652-0602

Meredith College
Raleigh, North Carolina
www.meredith.edu   Federal Code: 002945

4-year private liberal arts college for women in large city.
Enrollment: 1,837 undergrads, 12% part-time. 451 full-time freshmen.
Selectivity: Admits over 75% of applicants. GED not accepted.

BASIC COSTS (2006-2007)
Tuition and fees: $21,200.
Per-credit charge: $555.
Room and board: $5,940.
Additional info: Tuition includes laptop computer.

FINANCIAL AID PICTURE (2005-2006)
Students with need: Out of 376 full-time freshmen who applied for aid, 310 were judged to have need. Of these, 310 received aid, and 49 had their full need met. Average financial aid package met 70% of need; average scholarship/grant was $11,719; average loan was $2,773. For part-time students, average financial aid package was $6,528.
Students without need: 88 full-time freshmen who did not demonstrate need for aid received scholarships/grants; average award was $5,189. No-need awards available for academics, art, leadership, minority status, music/drama, religious affiliation, state/district residency.
Scholarships offered: Presidential Scholarships; tuition plus stipend for study abroad; based on academic achievement; 3-5 awarded annually.
Cumulative student debt: 79% of graduating class had student loans; average debt was $21,266.

FINANCIAL AID PROCEDURES
Forms required: FAFSA.
Dates and Deadlines: Priority date 2/15; no closing date. Applicants notified on a rolling basis starting 3/15; must reply by 5/1 or within 2 week(s) of notification.

CONTACT
Kevin Michaelsen, Director, Financial Assistance
3800 Hillsborough Street, Raleigh, NC 27607-5298
(919) 760-8565

Methodist College
Fayetteville, North Carolina
www.methodist.edu   Federal Code: 002946

4-year private liberal arts college in small city, affiliated with United Methodist Church.
Enrollment: 1,944 undergrads.
Selectivity: Admits over 75% of applicants.

BASIC COSTS (2006-2007)
Tuition and fees: $19,080.
Per-credit charge: $605.
Room and board: $7,170.
Additional info: Professional golf management, professional tennis management, and music students have additional fees.

FINANCIAL AID PICTURE (2004-2005)
Students with need: 66% of average financial aid package awarded as scholarships/grants, 34% awarded as loans/jobs. Need-based aid available for part-time students. Work study available nights, weekends, and for part-time students.
Students without need: No-need awards available for academics, alumni affiliation, leadership, music/drama, religious affiliation, ROTC, state/district residency.
Scholarships offered: Presidential Scholarship: $3,500-10,000/yr, 3.1+ GPA, 1000+ SAT or 22+ ACT. Merit scholarship: $3,250-4,250, residential freshmen, 2.9+ GPA, 900+ SAT or 19+ ACT, leadership. SAT scores exclusive of Writing.

FINANCIAL AID PROCEDURES
Forms required: FAFSA.
Dates and Deadlines: Priority date 5/1; closing date 7/1. Applicants notified on a rolling basis starting 3/1; must reply within 2 week(s) of notification.

CONTACT
Bonnie Adamson, Director of Financial Aid
5400 Ramsey Street, Fayetteville, NC 28311-1498
(910) 630-7192

Miller-Motte Technical College
Wilmington, North Carolina
www.miller-motte.com   Federal Code: E00896

4-year for-profit technical college in small city.
Enrollment: 775 undergrads, 6% part-time. 14 full-time freshmen.
Selectivity: Open admission; but selective for some programs.

BASIC COSTS (2006-2007)
Tuition and fees: $12,800.
Per-credit charge: $200.
Additional info: Tuition at time of enrollment locked for 4 years.

FINANCIAL AID PICTURE
Students with need: Need-based aid available for full-time and part-time students. Work study available nights, weekends, and for part-time students.
Students without need: This college only awards aid to students with need.

FINANCIAL AID PROCEDURES
Forms required: FAFSA, institutional form.
Dates and Deadlines: No deadline.

CONTACT
Michele Carroll, Financial Aid Officer
5000 Market Street, Wilmington, NC 28405
(910) 392-4660

Mitchell Community College
Statesville, North Carolina
www.mitchell.cc.nc.us   Federal Code: 002947

2-year public community college in large town.
Enrollment: 986 full-time undergrads.
Selectivity: Open admission; but selective for some programs.

BASIC COSTS (2005-2006)
Tuition and fees: $1,245; out-of-state residents $6,645.
Per-credit charge: $40; out-of-state residents $220.

FINANCIAL AID PICTURE
Students with need: Need-based aid available for full-time and part-time students.

FINANCIAL AID PROCEDURES
Forms required: FAFSA, institutional form.
Dates and Deadlines: No deadline. Applicants notified on a rolling basis starting 3/1; must reply within 2 week(s) of notification.
Transfers: Students are monitored through NSLDS's Transfer Monitoring List.

CONTACT
Candace Cooper, Financial Aid Officer
500 West Broad Street, Statesville, NC 28677
(704) 878-3256

Montgomery Community College
Troy, North Carolina
www.montgomery.edu   Federal Code: 008087

2-year public community college in small town.
Enrollment: 631 undergrads, 49% part-time. 78 full-time freshmen.
Selectivity: Open admission; but selective for some programs.

BASIC COSTS (2005-2006)
Tuition and fees: $1,245; out-of-state residents $6,645.
Per-credit charge: $40; out-of-state residents $220.

FINANCIAL AID PICTURE
Students with need: Need-based aid available for full-time and part-time students. Work study available nights.
Students without need: No-need awards available for academics, minority status, state/district residency.

FINANCIAL AID PROCEDURES
Forms required: FAFSA, institutional form.
Dates and Deadlines: Priority date 7/15; no closing date. Applicants notified on a rolling basis starting 6/1.

CONTACT
Matthew Woodard, Financial Aid Officer
1011 Page Street, Troy, NC 27371-0787
(910) 576-6222 ext. 226

Montreat College
Montreat, North Carolina
www.montreat.edu   Federal Code: 002948

4-year private liberal arts college in small town, affiliated with Presbyterian Church (USA).
Enrollment: 984 undergrads, 2% part-time. 138 full-time freshmen.

BASIC COSTS (2006-2007)
Tuition and fees: $16,182.
Room and board: $5,258.

FINANCIAL AID PICTURE (2005-2006)
Students with need: 44% of average financial aid package awarded as scholarships/grants, 56% awarded as loans/jobs. Need-based aid available for part-time students. Work study available nights, weekends, and for part-time students.
Students without need: No-need awards available for academics, alumni affiliation, art, athletics, job skills, leadership, music/drama, religious affiliation, state/district residency.
Cumulative student debt: 89% of graduating class had student loans; average debt was $21,486.

FINANCIAL AID PROCEDURES
Forms required: FAFSA, state aid form, institutional form.
Dates and Deadlines: Priority date 3/15; no closing date. Applicants notified on a rolling basis starting 1/15; must reply within 2 week(s) of notification.
Transfers: No deadline. Applicants notified on a rolling basis starting 1/6; must reply within 2 week(s) of notification.

CONTACT
Lisa Lankford, Dean of Admissions and Financial Aid
Box 1267, Montreat, NC 28757-1267
(800) 545-4656

Mount Olive College
Mount Olive, North Carolina
www.mountolivecollege.edu   Federal Code: 002949

4-year private liberal arts college in small town, affiliated with Free Will Baptists.
Enrollment: 2,474 undergrads, 27% part-time. 550 full-time freshmen.
Selectivity: Admits 50 to 75% of applicants.

BASIC COSTS (2006-2007)
Tuition and fees: $12,620.
Per-credit charge: $215.
Room and board: $4,952.

FINANCIAL AID PICTURE (2004-2005)
Students with need: Out of 360 full-time freshmen who applied for aid, 198 were judged to have need. Of these, 189 received aid, and 38 had their full need met. Average financial aid package met 69% of need; average scholarship/grant was $5,669; average loan was $1,755. For part-time students, average financial aid package was $5,394.
Students without need: 85 full-time freshmen who did not demonstrate need for aid received scholarships/grants; average award was $2,601. No-need awards available for academics, art, athletics, leadership, music/drama, religious affiliation, state/district residency.
Scholarships offered: 26 full-time freshmen received athletic scholarships; average amount $3,222.
Cumulative student debt: 57% of graduating class had student loans; average debt was $8,901.

FINANCIAL AID PROCEDURES
Forms required: FAFSA, state aid form.
Dates and Deadlines: Priority date 3/1; no closing date. Applicants notified on a rolling basis starting 2/14; must reply within 2 week(s) of notification.
Transfers: Special scholarship program available for transfers from North Carolina community colleges.

CONTACT
Karen Statler, Director of Financial Aid
634 Henderson Street, Mount Olive, NC 28365
(919) 658-7164

Nash Community College
Rocky Mount, North Carolina
www.nash.cc.nc.us Federal Code: 008557

2-year public community college in small city.
Enrollment: 1,948 undergrads.
Selectivity: Open admission; but selective for some programs.

BASIC COSTS (2005-2006)
Tuition and fees: $1,245; out-of-state residents $6,645.
Per-credit charge: $40; out-of-state residents $220.

FINANCIAL AID PICTURE
Students with need: Need-based aid available for full-time and part-time students.
Students without need: No-need awards available for academics.

FINANCIAL AID PROCEDURES
Forms required: FAFSA, institutional form.
Dates and Deadlines: Priority date 6/30; no closing date. Applicants notified on a rolling basis starting 7/15.

CONTACT
Tammy Lester, Financial Aid Officer
Box 7488, Rocky Mount, NC 27804-0488
(252) 451-8371

North Carolina Agricultural and Technical State University
Greensboro, North Carolina
www.ncat.edu Federal Code: 002905

4-year public agricultural and technical college in small city.
Enrollment: 9,649 undergrads, 9% part-time. 2,239 full-time freshmen.
Selectivity: Admits over 75% of applicants.

BASIC COSTS (2005-2006)
Tuition and fees: $3,114; out-of-state residents $12,556.
Room and board: $5,254.

FINANCIAL AID PICTURE (2005-2006)
Students with need: Average financial aid package met 50% of need; average scholarship/grant was $4,181; average loan was $4,457. Need-based aid available for part-time students.
Students without need: No-need awards available for academics, athletics, music/drama, ROTC.
Cumulative student debt: 75% of graduating class had student loans; average debt was $20,052.

FINANCIAL AID PROCEDURES
Forms required: FAFSA.
Dates and Deadlines: Priority date 3/15; no closing date. Applicants notified on a rolling basis starting 4/1; must reply within 2 week(s) of notification.

CONTACT
Sherri Avent, Director of Student Financial Aid
1601 East Market Street - Webb Hall, Greensboro, NC 27411
(800) 443-0835

North Carolina Central University
Durham, North Carolina
www.nccu.edu Federal Code: 002950

4-year public university in small city.
Enrollment: 5,827 undergrads, 15% part-time. 1,195 full-time freshmen.
Selectivity: Admits over 75% of applicants.

BASIC COSTS (2005-2006)
Tuition and fees: $3,146; out-of-state residents $12,890.
Room and board: $4,528.

FINANCIAL AID PICTURE
Students with need: Need-based aid available for full-time and part-time students.
Students without need: No-need awards available for academics, alumni affiliation, athletics, minority status, music/drama, state/district residency.
Additional info: Departmental grants based on need plus other available criteria.

FINANCIAL AID PROCEDURES
Forms required: FAFSA.
Dates and Deadlines: Priority date 4/1; no closing date. Applicants notified by 5/1; must reply within 2 week(s) of notification.

CONTACT
Sharon Oliver, Director of Student Financial Aid
PO Box 19717, Durham, NC 27707
(919) 530-6180

North Carolina School of the Arts
Winston-Salem, North Carolina
www.ncarts.edu Federal Code: 003981

4-year public conservatory and college of visual and performing arts in small city.
Enrollment: 720 undergrads. 152 full-time freshmen.
Selectivity: Admits less than 50% of applicants.

BASIC COSTS (2005-2006)
Tuition and fees: $4,335; out-of-state residents $15,615.
Room and board: $5,956.
Additional info: Required fees may vary by program.

FINANCIAL AID PICTURE (2004-2005)
Students with need: Out of 101 full-time freshmen who applied for aid, 75 were judged to have need. Of these, 75 received aid, and 1 had their full need met. Average financial aid package met 78% of need; average scholarship/grant was $5,452; average loan was $2,372. Need-based aid available for part-time students.
Students without need: 14 full-time freshmen who did not demonstrate need for aid received scholarships/grants; average award was $1,769. No-need awards available for academics, art, leadership, minority status, music/drama, state/district residency.
Cumulative student debt: 69% of graduating class had student loans; average debt was $19,196.

FINANCIAL AID PROCEDURES
Forms required: FAFSA.
Dates and Deadlines: Priority date 3/1; no closing date. Applicants notified on a rolling basis starting 4/1; must reply within 2 week(s) of notification.

CONTACT
Jane Kamiab, Director of Financial Aid
1533 South Main Street, Winston-Salem, NC 27127-2188
(336) 770-3297

North Carolina State University
Raleigh, North Carolina
www.ncsu.edu Federal Code: 002972

4-year public university in large city.
Enrollment: 20,546 undergrads, 7% part-time. 4,365 full-time freshmen.

Selectivity: Admits 50 to 75% of applicants. GED not accepted.

BASIC COSTS (2005-2006)
Tuition and fees: $4,338; out-of-state residents $16,536.
Room and board: $6,851.

FINANCIAL AID PICTURE (2005-2006)
Students with need: Out of 2,911 full-time freshmen who applied for aid, 1,733 were judged to have need. Of these, 1,703 received aid, and 638 had their full need met. Average financial aid package met 83% of need; average scholarship/grant was $6,216; average loan was $2,208. For part-time students, average financial aid package was $5,907.
Students without need: 2,208 full-time freshmen who did not demonstrate need for aid received scholarships/grants; average award was $6,597. No-need awards available for academics, alumni affiliation, athletics, leadership, ROTC, state/district residency.
Scholarships offered: 48 full-time freshmen received athletic scholarships; average amount $13,708.
Cumulative student debt: 52% of graduating class had student loans; average debt was $14,505.
Additional info: Freshman Merit Scholarships; students submitting complete admissions application by the November 1 Early Action deadline automatically considered, additional information may be required after initial review.

FINANCIAL AID PROCEDURES
Forms required: FAFSA, institutional form. CSS PROFILE recommended for early scholarship consideration.
Dates and Deadlines: Priority date 3/1; no closing date. Applicants notified on a rolling basis starting 3/1.

CONTACT
Julia Mallette, Associate Vice Provost and Director of Scholarships and Financial Aid
112 Peele Hall, Box 7103, Raleigh, NC 27695-7103
(919) 515-2421

North Carolina Wesleyan College
Rocky Mount, North Carolina
www.ncwc.edu   Federal Code: 002951

4-year private liberal arts college in small city, affiliated with United Methodist Church.
Enrollment: 1,752 undergrads, 36% part-time. 321 full-time freshmen.
Selectivity: Admits over 75% of applicants.

BASIC COSTS (2005-2006)
Tuition and fees: $16,000.
Room and board: $6,670.

FINANCIAL AID PICTURE (2004-2005)
Students with need: Out of 300 full-time freshmen who applied for aid, 270 were judged to have need. Of these, 270 received aid. Average financial aid package met 88% of need; average scholarship/grant was $14,650; average loan was $2,580. For part-time students, average financial aid package was $6,860.
Students without need: 21 full-time freshmen who did not demonstrate need for aid received scholarships/grants; average award was $7,252. No-need awards available for academics, music/drama, religious affiliation.
Cumulative student debt: 88% of graduating class had student loans; average debt was $17,125.
Additional info: Scholarships based on GPA. Various scholarship and leadership awards available.

FINANCIAL AID PROCEDURES
Forms required: FAFSA.
Dates and Deadlines: Priority date 3/1; no closing date. Applicants notified on a rolling basis starting 1/1; must reply within 2 week(s) of notification.

CONTACT
Brenda Mercer, Director of Financial Aid
3400 North Wesleyan Boulevard, Rocky Mount, NC 27804
(252) 985-5295

Pamlico Community College
Grantsboro, North Carolina
www.pamlico.cc.nc.us   Federal Code: 007031

2-year public community college in rural community.
Enrollment: 400 undergrads.
Selectivity: Open admission.

BASIC COSTS (2005-2006)
Tuition and fees: $1,200; out-of-state residents $6,600.
Per-credit charge: $40; out-of-state residents $220.

FINANCIAL AID PICTURE (2005-2006)
Students with need: 93% of average financial aid package awarded as scholarships/grants, 7% awarded as loans/jobs.
Additional info: Jobs Training Partner Act and Displaced Homemaker Programs cover tuition, books, fees.

FINANCIAL AID PROCEDURES
Forms required: FAFSA.
Dates and Deadlines: No deadline. Applicants notified on a rolling basis.

CONTACT
Jamie Gibbs
PO Box 185, Grantsboro, NC 28529
(252) 249-1851 ext. 3021

Peace College
Raleigh, North Carolina
www.peace.edu   Federal Code: 002953

4-year private liberal arts college for women in large city, affiliated with Presbyterian Church (USA).
Enrollment: 662 undergrads, 2% part-time. 256 full-time freshmen.
Selectivity: Admits over 75% of applicants.

BASIC COSTS (2005-2006)
Tuition and fees: $19,265.
Per-credit charge: $400.
Room and board: $6,918.

FINANCIAL AID PICTURE (2004-2005)
Students with need: Out of 208 full-time freshmen who applied for aid, 174 were judged to have need. Of these, 174 received aid, and 32 had their full need met. Average financial aid package met 75% of need; average scholarship/grant was $10,450; average loan was $2,240.
Students without need: 82 full-time freshmen who did not demonstrate need for aid received scholarships/grants; average award was $8,287. No-need awards available for academics.

FINANCIAL AID PROCEDURES
Forms required: FAFSA.
Dates and Deadlines: Priority date 3/15; no closing date. Applicants notified on a rolling basis starting 3/1; must reply by 5/1 or within 2 week(s) of notification.
Transfers: Priority date 3/1. Transfer merit scholarships available.

CONTACT
Craig Barfield, Director of Financial Aid
15 East Peace Street, Raleigh, NC 27604
(919) 508-2249

Pfeiffer University
Misenheimer, North Carolina
www.pfeiffer.edu Federal Code: 002955

4-year private university and liberal arts college in rural community, affiliated with United Methodist Church.
Enrollment: 1,174 undergrads, 11% part-time. 195 full-time freshmen.
Selectivity: Admits over 75% of applicants.

BASIC COSTS (2005-2006)
Tuition and fees: $15,590.
Per-credit charge: $355.
Room and board: $6,310.

FINANCIAL AID PICTURE (2004-2005)
Students with need: Out of 195 full-time freshmen who applied for aid, 195 were judged to have need. Of these, 158 received aid, and 48 had their full need met. Average financial aid package met 81% of need; average scholarship/grant was $9,140; average loan was $2,895. For part-time students, average financial aid package was $4,480.
Students without need: 75 full-time freshmen who did not demonstrate need for aid received scholarships/grants; average award was $5,932. No-need awards available for academics, alumni affiliation, athletics, leadership, music/drama, religious affiliation, state/district residency.
Scholarships offered: *Merit:* Honor, Presidential, University, and Legacy Scholarships - from $3,500 to full tuition per year. *Athletic:* 23 full-time freshmen received athletic scholarships; average amount $5,605.

FINANCIAL AID PROCEDURES
Forms required: FAFSA, state aid form.
Dates and Deadlines: Priority date 5/1; no closing date. Applicants notified on a rolling basis starting 3/1; must reply within 2 week(s) of notification.
Transfers: Priority date 3/15.

CONTACT
Amy Brown, Director of Financial Aid
Box 960, Misenheimer, NC 28109
(704) 463-1360 ext. 2070

Piedmont Baptist College
Winston-Salem, North Carolina
www.pbc.edu Federal Code: 002956

5-year private Bible and seminary college in small city, affiliated with Baptist faith.
Enrollment: 239 undergrads.

BASIC COSTS (2006-2007)
Tuition and fees: $10,600.
Per-credit charge: $385.
Room and board: $5,050.

FINANCIAL AID PICTURE
Students with need: Need-based aid available for full-time and part-time students. Work study available nights, weekends, and for part-time students.

FINANCIAL AID PROCEDURES
Forms required: institutional form.
Dates and Deadlines: No deadline. Applicants notified on a rolling basis starting 3/1.

CONTACT
Polly Trachian, Financial Aid Officer
716 Franklin Street, Winston-Salem, NC 27101-5133
(336) 725-8344 ext. 2322

Pitt Community College
Greenville, North Carolina
www.pitt.cc.nc.us Federal Code: 004062

2-year public community and technical college in small city.
Enrollment: 5,100 undergrads.
Selectivity: Open admission; but selective for some programs.

BASIC COSTS (2005-2006)
Tuition and fees: $1,255; out-of-state residents $6,655.
Per-credit charge: $40; out-of-state residents $220.

FINANCIAL AID PICTURE
Students with need: Need-based aid available for full-time and part-time students. Work study available nights.
Students without need: No-need awards available for academics, athletics, ROTC.

FINANCIAL AID PROCEDURES
Forms required: FAFSA.
Dates and Deadlines: Priority date 3/15; no closing date. Applicants notified on a rolling basis starting 2/1.

CONTACT
Lisa Reichstein, Financial Aid Director
PO Drawer 7007, Greenville, NC 27835-7007
(252) 321-4339

Queens University of Charlotte
Charlotte, North Carolina
www.queens.edu/admissions Federal Code: 002957

4-year private university in large city, affiliated with Presbyterian Church (USA).
Enrollment: 1,567 undergrads, 35% part-time. 242 full-time freshmen.
Selectivity: Admits 50 to 75% of applicants.

BASIC COSTS (2006-2007)
Tuition and fees: $19,450.
Per-credit charge: $290.
Room and board: $6,980.

FINANCIAL AID PICTURE (2005-2006)
Students with need: Out of 144 full-time freshmen who applied for aid, 144 were judged to have need. Of these, 144 received aid, and 33 had their full need met. Average financial aid package met 77% of need; average scholarship/grant was $12,484; average loan was $2,325. For part-time students, average financial aid package was $6,192.
Students without need: No-need awards available for academics, art, athletics, leadership, minority status, music/drama, religious affiliation, state/district residency.
Scholarships offered: Presidential Scholarships; full tuition; based on special application/recommendations; deadline 12/15; 10 awarded.
Cumulative student debt: 86% of graduating class had student loans; average debt was $16,270.

FINANCIAL AID PROCEDURES
Forms required: FAFSA, state aid form.
Dates and Deadlines: Priority date 3/1; no closing date. Applicants notified on a rolling basis starting 3/1; must reply by 5/1 or within 3 week(s) of notification.
Transfers: No deadline. Applicants notified on a rolling basis starting 3/1; must reply by 5/1 or within 3 week(s) of notification.

CONTACT
Eileen Dills, Associate Vice President of Student Financial Services
1900 Selwyn Avenue, Charlotte, NC 28274
(704) 337-2225

Randolph Community College
Asheboro, North Carolina
www.randolph.edu   Federal Code: 005447

2-year public community and technical college in large town.
Enrollment: 2,291 undergrads.
Selectivity: Open admission; but selective for some programs.

BASIC COSTS (2005-2006)
Tuition and fees: $1,245; out-of-state residents $6,645.
Per-credit charge: $40; out-of-state residents $220.

FINANCIAL AID PICTURE
Students with need: Work study available nights.
Students without need: No-need awards available for academics, leadership, minority status, state/district residency.

FINANCIAL AID PROCEDURES
Forms required: FAFSA.
Dates and Deadlines: Priority date 5/1; no closing date. Applicants notified on a rolling basis; must reply within 4 week(s) of notification.
Transfers: No deadline.

CONTACT
Director of Financial Aid
PO Box 1009, Asheboro, NC 27204-1009
(336) 633-0222

Richmond Community College
Hamlet, North Carolina
www.richmondcc.edu   Federal Code: 005464

2-year public community college in small town.
Enrollment: 1,500 undergrads.
Selectivity: Open admission; but selective for some programs.

BASIC COSTS (2005-2006)
Tuition and fees: $1,223; out-of-state residents $6,623.
Per-credit charge: $40; out-of-state residents $220.

FINANCIAL AID PICTURE
Students with need: Need-based aid available for full-time and part-time students. Work study available nights.
Students without need: No-need awards available for academics, leadership.

FINANCIAL AID PROCEDURES
Forms required: FAFSA, institutional form.
Dates and Deadlines: Priority date 5/1; no closing date. Applicants notified on a rolling basis starting 6/1; must reply within 2 week(s) of notification.

CONTACT
Beth McQueen, Director of Financial Aid
Box 1189, Hamlet, NC 28345
(910) 582-7108

Roanoke Bible College
Elizabeth City, North Carolina
www.roanokebible.edu   Federal Code: 014101

4-year private Bible college in large town, affiliated with Church of Christ.
Enrollment: 177 undergrads, 11% part-time. 31 full-time freshmen.
Selectivity: Admits less than 50% of applicants.

BASIC COSTS (2005-2006)
Tuition and fees: $8,225.
Per-credit charge: $230.
Room and board: $4,760.

FINANCIAL AID PICTURE (2004-2005)
Students with need: Out of 30 full-time freshmen who applied for aid, 25 were judged to have need. Of these, 25 received aid, and 4 had their full need met. Average financial aid package met 70% of need; average scholarship/grant was $4,496; average loan was $2,276. For part-time students, average financial aid package was $4,038.
Students without need: 5 full-time freshmen who did not demonstrate need for aid received scholarships/grants; average award was $2,349. No-need awards available for academics, alumni affiliation, leadership, music/drama, religious affiliation.
Scholarships offered: Full tuition and half tuition available, based on demonstration of exceptional academic ability.
Cumulative student debt: 72% of graduating class had student loans; average debt was $16,063.

FINANCIAL AID PROCEDURES
Forms required: FAFSA, institutional form.
Dates and Deadlines: Priority date 3/15; closing date 5/1. Applicants notified on a rolling basis starting 4/1; must reply within 2 week(s) of notification.

CONTACT
Julie Fields, Director of Financial Aid
715 North Poindexter Street, Elizabeth City, NC 27909
(252) 334-2020

Roanoke-Chowan Community College
Ahoskie, North Carolina
www.roanokechowan.edu   Federal Code: 008613

2-year public community college in small town.
Enrollment: 950 undergrads.
Selectivity: Open admission; but selective for some programs.

BASIC COSTS (2005-2006)
Tuition and fees: $1,255; out-of-state residents $6,655.
Per-credit charge: $40; out-of-state residents $220.

FINANCIAL AID PICTURE
Students with need: Need-based aid available for full-time and part-time students.
Students without need: No-need awards available for academics.

FINANCIAL AID PROCEDURES
Forms required: FAFSA.
Dates and Deadlines: No deadline. Applicants notified on a rolling basis starting 7/1.

CONTACT
Ethelene Custis, Fianacial Aid Director
109 Community College Road, Ahoskie, NC 27910-9522
(252) 862-1224

Robeson Community College
Lumberton, North Carolina
www.robeson.cc.nc.us   Federal Code: 008612

2-year public community and technical college in large town.
Enrollment: 2,365 undergrads.
Selectivity: Open admission; but selective for some programs.

BASIC COSTS (2005-2006)
Tuition and fees: $1,245; out-of-state residents $6,645.
Per-credit charge: $40; out-of-state residents $220.

FINANCIAL AID PICTURE
Students with need: Need-based aid available for full-time and part-time students.

FINANCIAL AID PROCEDURES
Forms required: FAFSA.
Dates and Deadlines: Priority date 5/15; no closing date. Applicants notified on a rolling basis starting 7/31.

CONTACT
Vanessa Cogdell, Director of Financial Aid
PO Box 1420, Lumberton, NC 28359
(910) 272-3352

Rockingham Community College
Wentworth, North Carolina
www.rcc.cc.nc.us   Federal Code: 002958

2-year public community college in rural community.
Enrollment: 1,762 undergrads.
Selectivity: Open admission; but selective for some programs.

BASIC COSTS (2005-2006)
Tuition and fees: $1,259; out-of-state residents $6,659.
Per-credit charge: $40; out-of-state residents $220.

FINANCIAL AID PICTURE (2004-2005)
Students with need: 57% of average financial aid package awarded as scholarships/grants, 43% awarded as loans/jobs. Need-based aid available for part-time students.
Students without need: No-need awards available for academics, art, job skills, leadership, minority status, state/district residency.

FINANCIAL AID PROCEDURES
Forms required: FAFSA, institutional form.
Dates and Deadlines: Priority date 3/15; no closing date. Applicants notified on a rolling basis starting 5/30; must reply within 2 week(s) of notification.

CONTACT
Coe Greene, Director of Financial Aid
Box 38, Wentworth, NC 27375-0038
(336) 342-4261 ext. 2204

Rowan-Cabarrus Community College
Salisbury, North Carolina
www.rccc.cc.nc.us   Federal Code: 005754

2-year public community and technical college in large town.
Enrollment: 5,431 undergrads.
Selectivity: Open admission; but selective for some programs.

BASIC COSTS (2005-2006)
Tuition and fees: $1,249; out-of-state residents $6,649.
Per-credit charge: $40; out-of-state residents $220.

FINANCIAL AID PICTURE
Students with need: Need-based aid available for full-time and part-time students. Work study available nights.
Students without need: No-need awards available for academics, job skills, state/district residency.

FINANCIAL AID PROCEDURES
Forms required: FAFSA.
Dates and Deadlines: Priority date 3/15; closing date 5/1. Applicants notified on a rolling basis starting 5/1; must reply within 3 week(s) of notification.
Transfers: No deadline.

CONTACT
Lisa Ledbetter, Director, Financial Aid
Box 1595, Salisbury, NC 28145
(704) 637-0760 ext. 273

St. Andrews Presbyterian College
Laurinburg, North Carolina
www.sapc.edu   Federal Code: 002967

4-year private liberal arts college in large town, affiliated with Presbyterian Church (USA).
Enrollment: 741 undergrads, 6% part-time. 227 full-time freshmen.
Selectivity: Admits over 75% of applicants.

BASIC COSTS (2006-2007)
Tuition and fees: $18,062.
Per-credit charge: $410.
Room and board: $6,640.

FINANCIAL AID PICTURE (2004-2005)
Students with need: Out of 172 full-time freshmen who applied for aid, 144 were judged to have need. Of these, 144 received aid, and 28 had their full need met. Average financial aid package met 73% of need; average scholarship/grant was $9,601; average loan was $2,259. For part-time students, average financial aid package was $5,884.
Students without need: 79 full-time freshmen who did not demonstrate need for aid received scholarships/grants; average award was $9,094. No-need awards available for academics, alumni affiliation, athletics, leadership, music/drama, religious affiliation.
Scholarships offered: 31 full-time freshmen received athletic scholarships; average amount $3,624.
Cumulative student debt: 70% of graduating class had student loans; average debt was $12,325.

FINANCIAL AID PROCEDURES
Forms required: FAFSA.
Dates and Deadlines: Priority date 5/1; no closing date. Applicants notified on a rolling basis starting 10/1; must reply within 2 week(s) of notification.

CONTACT
Kim Driggers, Director, Student Planning
1700 Dogwood Mile, Laurinburg, NC 28352
(910) 277-5560

St. Augustine's College
Raleigh, North Carolina
www.st-aug.edu   Federal Code: 002968

4-year private liberal arts college in large city, affiliated with Episcopal Church.
Enrollment: 1,143 undergrads.
Selectivity: Admits less than 50% of applicants.

BASIC COSTS (2005-2006)
Tuition and fees: $11,428.
Per-credit charge: $375.
Room and board: $5,844.

FINANCIAL AID PICTURE (2004-2005)
Students with need: Need-based aid available for part-time students.
Students without need: No-need awards available for academics, art, athletics, leadership, minority status, music/drama, religious affiliation; ROTC, state/district residency.

Scholarships offered: Institutional Merit Scholarships based on high school record, evidence of leadership, and SAT score.

FINANCIAL AID PROCEDURES
Forms required: FAFSA, institutional form.
Dates and Deadlines: Closing date 3/15. Applicants notified on a rolling basis starting 5/1; must reply within 2 week(s) of notification.
Transfers: All transfer students must submit a financial aid transcript.

CONTACT
Rochelle King, Director of Financial Aid
1315 Oakwood Avenue, Raleigh, NC 27610-2298
(919) 516-4131

Salem College
Winston-Salem, North Carolina
www.salem.edu   Federal Code: 002960

4-year private liberal arts college for women in small city, affiliated with Moravian Church in America.
Enrollment: 834 undergrads, 16% part-time. 151 full-time freshmen.
Selectivity: Admits 50 to 75% of applicants.

BASIC COSTS (2006-2007)
Tuition and fees: $18,164.
Per-credit charge: $920.
Room and board: $9,551.
Additional info: Tuition/fee waivers available for adults.

FINANCIAL AID PICTURE (2004-2005)
Students with need: Out of 140 full-time freshmen who applied for aid, 111 were judged to have need. Of these, 111 received aid, and 111 had their full need met. Average financial aid package met 100% of need; average scholarship/grant was $11,077; average loan was $2,625. For part-time students, average financial aid package was $7,304.
Students without need: 40 full-time freshmen who did not demonstrate need for aid received scholarships/grants; average award was $10,577. No-need awards available for academics, alumni affiliation, art, job skills, leadership, minority status, music/drama, religious affiliation, state/district residency.

FINANCIAL AID PROCEDURES
Forms required: FAFSA.
Dates and Deadlines: Priority date 3/15; no closing date. Applicants notified on a rolling basis starting 3/1; must reply by 5/1 or within 2 week(s) of notification.

CONTACT
Ronnette King, Director of Financial Aid
PO Box 10548, Winston-Salem, NC 27108
(336) 721-2808

Sampson Community College
Clinton, North Carolina
www.sampson.cc.nc.us   Federal Code: 007892

2-year public community college in small town.
Enrollment: 1,467 undergrads.
Selectivity: Open admission; but selective for some programs.

BASIC COSTS (2005-2006)
Tuition and fees: $1,241; out-of-state residents $6,641.
Per-credit charge: $40; out-of-state residents $220.

FINANCIAL AID PICTURE
Students with need: Need-based aid available for full-time and part-time students.
Students without need: No-need awards available for academics, state/district residency.
Additional info: Short-term loans available to students waiting for federal aid to be approved. Covers tuition, fees and books only.

FINANCIAL AID PROCEDURES
Forms required: FAFSA.
Dates and Deadlines: Priority date 7/1; no closing date. Applicants notified on a rolling basis starting 7/15; must reply within 2 week(s) of notification.

CONTACT
Judy Tart, Director of Financial Aid
PO Box 318, Clinton, NC 28329
(910) 592-8084 ext. 2024

Sandhills Community College
Pinehurst, North Carolina
www.sandhills.edu   Federal Code: 002961

2-year public community college in small town.
Enrollment: 1,300 undergrads.
Selectivity: Open admission; but selective for some programs.

BASIC COSTS (2005-2006)
Tuition and fees: $1,255; out-of-state residents $6,655.
Per-credit charge: $40; out-of-state residents $220.

FINANCIAL AID PICTURE
Students with need: Need-based aid available for full-time and part-time students.
Students without need: No-need awards available for academics.
Scholarships offered: Sandhills Scholars; upper 15% of graduating class; 11 awarded.
Additional info: Scholarships available, limited loan capability.

FINANCIAL AID PROCEDURES
Forms required: FAFSA.
Dates and Deadlines: Priority date 6/1; no closing date. Applicants notified on a rolling basis starting 2/1; must reply by 8/1 or within 4 week(s) of notification.

CONTACT
John Frye, Director of Financial Aid
3395 Airport Road, Pinehurst, NC 28374
(910) 695-3743

Shaw University
Raleigh, North Carolina
www.shawuniversity.edu   Federal Code: 002962

4-year private university and liberal arts college in large city, affiliated with Baptist faith.
Enrollment: 2,536 undergrads.
Selectivity: Admits 50 to 75% of applicants.

BASIC COSTS (2006-2007)
Tuition and fees: $10,020.
Per-credit charge: $345.
Room and board: $6,410.

FINANCIAL AID PICTURE (2004-2005)
Students with need: 53% of average financial aid package awarded as scholarships/grants, 47% awarded as loans/jobs. Need-based aid available for part-time students. Work study available nights, weekends, and for part-time students.
Students without need: No-need awards available for academics, athletics, ROTC.

Scholarships offered: Presidential Scholarship, based on GPA and SAT.
FINANCIAL AID PROCEDURES
Forms required: FAFSA.
Dates and Deadlines: Closing date 3/1. Applicants notified on a rolling basis starting 4/30.
CONTACT
Kamesia Ewing, Director of Financial Aid
118 East South Street, Raleigh, NC 27601
(919) 546-8240

South College
Asheville, North Carolina   Federal Code: 010264

2-year for-profit health science and technical college in small city.
Enrollment: 120 undergrads.
Selectivity: Open admission; but selective for some programs.
FINANCIAL AID PICTURE
Students with need: Need-based aid available for full-time and part-time students.
FINANCIAL AID PROCEDURES
Forms required: FAFSA.
Dates and Deadlines: No deadline. Applicants notified on a rolling basis.
CONTACT
Jason Fair, Financial Aid Director
29 Turtle Creek Drive, Asheville, NC 28803
(828) 277-5521

South Piedmont Community College
Polkton, North Carolina
www.spcc.edu   Federal Code: 007985

2-year public community college in small city.
Enrollment: 1,928 undergrads. 667 full-time freshmen.
Selectivity: Open admission; but selective for some programs.
BASIC COSTS (2005-2006)
Tuition and fees: $1,263; out-of-state residents $6,663.
Per-credit charge: $40; out-of-state residents $220.
FINANCIAL AID PICTURE
Students with need: Need-based aid available for full-time and part-time students. Work study available nights, weekends, and for part-time students.
Additional info: Small amount of nonfederal scholarship aid available.
FINANCIAL AID PROCEDURES
Forms required: FAFSA.
Dates and Deadlines: No deadline. Applicants notified on a rolling basis.
CONTACT
Vickie Cameron, Director of Financial Aid
PO Box 126, Polkton, NC 28135
(704) 272-5325

Southeastern Community College
Whiteville, North Carolina
www.sccnc.edu   Federal Code: 002964

2-year public community college in small town.
Enrollment: 1,593 undergrads, 42% part-time. 165 full-time freshmen.
Selectivity: Open admission; but selective for some programs.
BASIC COSTS (2005-2006)
Tuition and fees: $1,246; out-of-state residents $6,646.
Per-credit charge: $40; out-of-state residents $220.
FINANCIAL AID PICTURE (2005-2006)
Students with need: 93% of average financial aid package awarded as scholarships/grants, 7% awarded as loans/jobs. Need-based aid available for part-time students.
Students without need: No-need awards available for academics, athletics, leadership, music/drama, state/district residency.
FINANCIAL AID PROCEDURES
Forms required: FAFSA.
Dates and Deadlines: Priority date 4/1; no closing date. Applicants notified on a rolling basis starting 6/1; must reply within 2 week(s) of notification.
CONTACT
Glenn Hanson, Director of Financial Aid
4564 Chadbourn Highway, Whiteville, NC 28472-0151
(910) 642-7141 ext. 214

Southwestern Community College
Sylva, North Carolina
www.southwest.cc.nc.us   Federal Code: 008466

2-year public community college in rural community.
Enrollment: 1,540 undergrads.
Selectivity: Open admission; but selective for some programs.
BASIC COSTS (2005-2006)
Tuition and fees: $1,247; out-of-state residents $6,647.
Per-credit charge: $40; out-of-state residents $220.
FINANCIAL AID PICTURE (2004-2005)
Students with need: 91% of average financial aid package awarded as scholarships/grants, 9% awarded as loans/jobs. Need-based aid available for part-time students.
FINANCIAL AID PROCEDURES
Forms required: FAFSA.
Dates and Deadlines: Priority date 4/30; no closing date. Applicants notified on a rolling basis starting 5/1; must reply within 2 week(s) of notification.
CONTACT
Melody Lawrence, Director of Financial Aid
447 College Drive, Sylva, NC 28779
(828) 586-4091 ext. 224

Stanly Community College
Albemarle, North Carolina
www.stanly.edu   Federal Code: 011194

2-year public community college in large town.
Enrollment: 1,500 undergrads.
Selectivity: Open admission; but selective for some programs.
BASIC COSTS (2005-2006)
Tuition and fees: $1,255; out-of-state residents $6,655.
Per-credit charge: $40; out-of-state residents $220.
FINANCIAL AID PICTURE
Students with need: Need-based aid available for full-time and part-time students.
Students without need: This college only awards aid to students with need.
FINANCIAL AID PROCEDURES
Forms required: FAFSA, institutional form.

Dates and Deadlines: Priority date 4/15; no closing date. Applicants notified on a rolling basis starting 6/5; must reply within 2 week(s) of notification.

CONTACT
Petra Fields, Director of Financial Aid
141 College Drive, Albemarle, NC 28001
(704) 991-0231

Surry Community College
Dobson, North Carolina
www.surry.edu   Federal Code: 002970

2-year public community college in rural community.
Enrollment: 3,273 undergrads.
Selectivity: Open admission; but selective for some programs.

BASIC COSTS (2005-2006)
Tuition and fees: $1,243; out-of-state residents $6,643.
Per-credit charge: $40; out-of-state residents $220.

FINANCIAL AID PICTURE (2004-2005)
Students with need: 96% of average financial aid package awarded as scholarships/grants, 4% awarded as loans/jobs. Need-based aid available for part-time students. Work study available nights.
Students without need: No-need awards available for academics.

FINANCIAL AID PROCEDURES
Forms required: FAFSA, institutional form.
Dates and Deadlines: Priority date 5/1; no closing date. Applicants notified on a rolling basis starting 6/1; must reply within 2 week(s) of notification.
Transfers: Priority date 6/1.

CONTACT
Jamie Childress, Financial Aid Officer
630 South Main Street, Dobson, NC 27017
(336) 386-3245

Tri-County Community College
Murphy, North Carolina
www.tricountycc.edu   Federal Code: 009430

2-year public community college in rural community.
Enrollment: 741 undergrads.
Selectivity: Open admission.

BASIC COSTS (2005-2006)
Tuition and fees: $1,241; out-of-state residents $6,641.
Per-credit charge: $40; out-of-state residents $220.

FINANCIAL AID PICTURE (2004-2005)
Students with need: 98% of average financial aid package awarded as scholarships/grants, 2% awarded as loans/jobs. Need-based aid available for part-time students.
Students without need: This college only awards aid to students with need.

FINANCIAL AID PROCEDURES
Forms required: FAFSA.
Dates and Deadlines: Priority date 6/30; no closing date. Applicants notified on a rolling basis starting 6/1; must reply within 4 week(s) of notification.

CONTACT
Diane Owl, Financial Aid Officer
4600 Highway 64 East, Murphy, NC 28906
(828) 837-6810

University of North Carolina at Asheville
Asheville, North Carolina
www.unca.edu   Federal Code: 002907

4-year public university and liberal arts college in small city.
Enrollment: 3,124 undergrads, 12% part-time. 698 full-time freshmen.
Selectivity: Admits 50 to 75% of applicants. GED not accepted.

BASIC COSTS (2005-2006)
Tuition and fees: $3,526; out-of-state residents $13,326.
Room and board: $5,712.

FINANCIAL AID PICTURE (2004-2005)
Students with need: Out of 503 full-time freshmen who applied for aid, 289 were judged to have need. Of these, 284 received aid, and 83 had their full need met. Average financial aid package met 73% of need; average scholarship/grant was $2,825; average loan was $2,338. For part-time students, average financial aid package was $6,259.
Students without need: 97 full-time freshmen who did not demonstrate need for aid received scholarships/grants; average award was $2,365. No-need awards available for academics, alumni affiliation, art, athletics, job skills, leadership, minority status, music/drama, state/district residency.
Scholarships offered: *Merit:* North Carolina Teaching Fellows program; $6,500 per year; for outstanding North Carolina high school students with desire and talent to become teachers. University Laurels Program; $500 to full in-state tuition and fees; essay, list of co-curricular activities and participation in Laurels Interview Day. Western North Carolina Leadership Scholarship; $1,000, renewable; solid academic record and leadership ability. Recipients must be from one of 24 Western North Carolina counties. *Athletic:* 22 full-time freshmen received athletic scholarships; average amount $4,142.
Cumulative student debt: 51% of graduating class had student loans; average debt was $15,309.

FINANCIAL AID PROCEDURES
Forms required: FAFSA.
Dates and Deadlines: Priority date 3/1; no closing date. Applicants notified on a rolling basis starting 3/15.

CONTACT
Scot Schaeffer, Director of Admissions and Financial Aid
CPO#1320, UNCA, Asheville, NC 28804-8510
(828) 251-6535

University of North Carolina at Chapel Hill
Chapel Hill, North Carolina   Federal Code: 002974
www.unc.edu   CSS Code: 5816

4-year public university in large town.
Enrollment: 16,278 undergrads, 2% part-time. 3,511 full-time freshmen.
Selectivity: Admits less than 50% of applicants. GED not accepted.

BASIC COSTS (2005-2006)
Tuition and fees: $4,515; out-of-state residents $18,313.
Room and board: $6,590.

FINANCIAL AID PICTURE (2004-2005)
Students with need: Out of 2,611 full-time freshmen who applied for aid, 1,174 were judged to have need. Of these, 1,139 received aid, and 885 had their full need met. Average financial aid package met 95% of need; average scholarship/grant was $7,091; average loan was $2,752. For part-time students, average financial aid package was $6,762.
Students without need: 722 full-time freshmen who did not demonstrate need for aid received scholarships/grants; average award was $4,206. No-need awards available for academics, alumni affiliation, art, athletics, leadership, music/drama, religious affiliation, state/district residency.

Scholarships offered: Merit: Morehead Scholarships; full tuition and expenses; 55 awarded; academic merit, leadership, athletics, moral character. Robertson Scholarships; full cost of tuition and expenses; 15 awarded; academic merit, leadership, community service, multi-cultural interests. Carolina Scholars; $7,500 - $15,000; 40 awarded; academic merit, leadership, residency specifications. Pogue Scholarships; $7,500; 22 awarded; academic merit, leadership, ethnicity (African American/Native American), North Carolina residency. College Fellows Awards; $2,500; 15 awarded; academic merit, leadership, North Carolina residency. Davie Scholarships; $6,500-$12,000; 20 awarded; academic merit, leadership. Jackson Scholarships; $2,500; 5 awards; academic merit, leadership, North Carolina residency. Other academic scholarships; $2,500, full cost; 5 awarded; academic merit, leadership, residency specifications. **Athletic:** 83 full-time freshmen received athletic scholarships; average amount $10,611.

FINANCIAL AID PROCEDURES
Forms required: FAFSA, CSS PROFILE.
Dates and Deadlines: Priority date 3/1; no closing date. Applicants notified on a rolling basis starting 3/15; must reply by 5/1.

CONTACT
Shirley Ort, Director for Office of Student Aid/Associate Provost
Jackson Hall CB #2200, Chapel Hill, NC 27599-2200
(919) 962-8396

University of North Carolina at Charlotte
Charlotte, North Carolina
www.uncc.edu   Federal Code: 002975

4-year public university in very large city.
Enrollment: 16,225 undergrads, 16% part-time. 2,998 full-time freshmen.
Selectivity: Admits over 75% of applicants.

BASIC COSTS (2005-2006)
Tuition and fees: $3,551; out-of-state residents $13,963.
Room and board: $5,730.

FINANCIAL AID PICTURE (2005-2006)
Students with need: Out of 2,019 full-time freshmen who applied for aid, 1,391 were judged to have need. Of these, 1,309 received aid, and 341 had their full need met. Average financial aid package met 60% of need; average scholarship/grant was $4,191; average loan was $2,574. For part-time students, average financial aid package was $7,786.
Students without need: 561 full-time freshmen who did not demonstrate need for aid received scholarships/grants; average award was $6,447. No-need awards available for academics, athletics, leadership, music/drama.
Scholarships offered: 33 full-time freshmen received athletic scholarships; average amount $4,452.
Cumulative student debt: 56% of graduating class had student loans; average debt was $18,402.

FINANCIAL AID PROCEDURES
Forms required: FAFSA.
Dates and Deadlines: Priority date 4/1; no closing date. Applicants notified on a rolling basis starting 4/1; must reply within 3 week(s) of notification.

CONTACT
Anthony Carter, Director of Student Financial Aid
9201 University City Boulevard, Charlotte, NC 28223-0001
(704) 687-2461

University of North Carolina at Greensboro
Greensboro, North Carolina
www.uncg.edu   Federal Code: 002976

4-year public university in small city.
Enrollment: 12,172 undergrads, 13% part-time. 2,400 full-time freshmen.
Selectivity: Admits 50 to 75% of applicants. GED not accepted.

BASIC COSTS (2005-2006)
Tuition and fees: $3,467; out-of-state residents $14,735.
Room and board: $5,614.

FINANCIAL AID PICTURE (2005-2006)
Students with need: Out of 1,806 full-time freshmen who applied for aid, 1,640 were judged to have need. Of these, 1,583 received aid, and 358 had their full need met. Average financial aid package met 53% of need; average scholarship/grant was $3,558; average loan was $2,446. For part-time students, average financial aid package was $5,658.
Students without need: 138 full-time freshmen who did not demonstrate need for aid received scholarships/grants; average award was $3,650. No-need awards available for academics, alumni affiliation, art, athletics, leadership, music/drama, state/district residency.
Scholarships offered: 40 full-time freshmen received athletic scholarships; average amount $8,595.
Cumulative student debt: 60% of graduating class had student loans; average debt was $13,661.

FINANCIAL AID PROCEDURES
Forms required: FAFSA.
Dates and Deadlines: Priority date 3/1; no closing date. Applicants notified on a rolling basis starting 3/15; must reply within 3 week(s) of notification.

CONTACT
Deborah Tollefson, Director of Financial Aid
123 Mossman Building, Greensboro, NC 27402-6166
(336) 334-5702

University of North Carolina at Pembroke
Pembroke, North Carolina
www.uncp.edu   Federal Code: 002954

4-year public university and liberal arts college in small town.
Enrollment: 4,454 undergrads, 18% part-time. 957 full-time freshmen.
Selectivity: Admits over 75% of applicants.

BASIC COSTS (2005-2006)
Tuition and fees: $2,980; out-of-state residents $12,420.
Room and board: $4,960.

FINANCIAL AID PICTURE (2005-2006)
Students with need: Out of 839 full-time freshmen who applied for aid, 690 were judged to have need. Of these, 666 received aid, and 64 had their full need met. Average financial aid package met 56% of need; average scholarship/grant was $4,144; average loan was $2,552. For part-time students, average financial aid package was $4,752.
Students without need: 48 full-time freshmen who did not demonstrate need for aid received scholarships/grants; average award was $1,241. No-need awards available for alumni affiliation.
Cumulative student debt: 57% of graduating class had student loans; average debt was $14,423.

FINANCIAL AID PROCEDURES
Forms required: FAFSA.
Dates and Deadlines: Closing date 3/15. Applicants notified on a rolling basis starting 4/15; must reply within 2 week(s) of notification.

North Carolina University of North Carolina at Pembroke

CONTACT
Bruce Blackmon, Director of Financial Aid
Box 1510, Pembroke, NC 28372
(910) 521-6255

University of North Carolina at Wilmington
Wilmington, North Carolina
www.uncw.edu
Federal Code: 002984

4-year public university in small city.
Enrollment: 10,249 undergrads, 7% part-time. 1,936 full-time freshmen.
Selectivity: Admits 50 to 75% of applicants.

BASIC COSTS (2005-2006)
Tuition and fees: $3,695; out-of-state residents $13,630.
Room and board: $6,412.

FINANCIAL AID PICTURE (2005-2006)
Students with need: Out of 1,047 full-time freshmen who applied for aid, 578 were judged to have need. Of these, 578 received aid, and 407 had their full need met. Average financial aid package met 89% of need; average scholarship/grant was $3,761; average loan was $2,836. For part-time students, average financial aid package was $6,088.
Students without need: 24 full-time freshmen who did not demonstrate need for aid received scholarships/grants; average award was $1,602. No-need awards available for academics, alumni affiliation, art, athletics, leadership, music/drama, state/district residency.
Scholarships offered: 38 full-time freshmen received athletic scholarships; average amount $5,488.
Cumulative student debt: 52% of graduating class had student loans; average debt was $15,620.

FINANCIAL AID PROCEDURES
Forms required: FAFSA, institutional form.
Dates and Deadlines: Priority date 3/15; no closing date. Applicants notified on a rolling basis starting 4/1; must reply within 3 week(s) of notification.

CONTACT
Emily Bliss, Director of Financial Aid & Veteran Services
601 South College Road, Wilmington, NC 28403-5904
(910) 962-3177

Vance-Granville Community College
Henderson, North Carolina
www.vgcc.edu
Federal Code: 009903

2-year public community college in large town.
Enrollment: 3,500 undergrads.
Selectivity: Open admission; but selective for some programs.

BASIC COSTS (2005-2006)
Tuition and fees: $1,223; out-of-state residents $6,623.
Per-credit charge: $40; out-of-state residents $220.

FINANCIAL AID PICTURE (2005-2006)
Students with need: 2% of average financial aid package awarded as scholarships/grants, 98% awarded as loans/jobs. Need-based aid available for part-time students.
Students without need: No-need awards available for academics.

FINANCIAL AID PROCEDURES
Forms required: FAFSA.
Dates and Deadlines: Priority date 7/15; no closing date. Applicants notified on a rolling basis starting 5/1; must reply within 2 week(s) of notification.

CONTACT
Frank Clark, Financial Aid Officer
Box 917, Henderson, NC 27536
(252) 492-2061

Wake Forest University
Winston-Salem, North Carolina
www.wfu.edu
Federal Code: 002978
CSS Code: 5885

4-year private university in small city.
Enrollment: 4,231 undergrads, 3% part-time. 1,114 full-time freshmen.
Selectivity: Admits less than 50% of applicants.

BASIC COSTS (2006-2007)
Tuition and fees: $32,140.
Per-credit charge: $1,250.
Room and board: $8,800.
Additional info: Tuition covers cost of an IBM Thinkpad computer and inkjet printer for freshmen.

FINANCIAL AID PICTURE (2005-2006)
Students with need: Out of 585 full-time freshmen who applied for aid, 421 were judged to have need. Of these, 418 received aid, and 165 had their full need met. Average financial aid package met 90% of need; average scholarship/grant was $17,826; average loan was $5,404. For part-time students, average financial aid package was $15,580.
Students without need: 340 full-time freshmen who did not demonstrate need for aid received scholarships/grants; average award was $8,621. No-need awards available for academics, alumni affiliation, art, athletics, leadership, music/drama, religious affiliation, ROTC, state/district residency.
Scholarships offered: *Merit:* Reynolds Scholarship; full tuition, room and board, books, fees for 4 years, also provides for summer study; 6 awarded. Joseph G. Gordon Scholarship for underrepresented students with exceptional promise and leadership; full tuition for 4 years; 7 awarded. Carswell Scholarship; based on intellect and leadership; between 3/4 and full tuition for 4 years, including summer grant for travel and study projects; 10-12 awarded. Presidential Scholarship for students gifted in areas such as writing, studio art, music theater, debate, leadership, dance, entrepreneurship, and community service; $11,200 annually for 4 years, 20 awarded. Poteat Scholarship for North Carolina residents who are active members of a Baptist Church in North Carolina, must make an active contribution to church and society; $11,200 annually for 4 years; 18 awarded. *Athletic:* 68 full-time freshmen received athletic scholarships; average amount $25,426.
Cumulative student debt: 39% of graduating class had student loans; average debt was $22,831.

FINANCIAL AID PROCEDURES
Forms required: FAFSA, CSS PROFILE, state aid form.
Dates and Deadlines: Priority date 2/1; closing date 3/1. Applicants notified by 4/1; must reply by 5/1 or within 4 week(s) of notification.
Transfers: Priority date 2/1.

CONTACT
William Wells, Director of Financial Aid
PO Box 7305 Reynolda Station, Winston-Salem, NC 27109
(336) 758-5154

Wake Technical Community College
Raleigh, North Carolina
www.wake.tec.nc.us
Federal Code: 004844

2-year public community and technical college in small city.
Enrollment: 10,500 undergrads.
Selectivity: Open admission; but selective for some programs.

BASIC COSTS (2005-2006)
Tuition and fees: $1,235; out-of-state residents $6,635.
Per-credit charge: $40; out-of-state residents $220.

FINANCIAL AID PICTURE
Students with need: Need-based aid available for full-time and part-time students.
Students without need: No-need awards available for academics, job skills, leadership, state/district residency.

FINANCIAL AID PROCEDURES
Forms required: FAFSA, institutional form.
Dates and Deadlines: Priority date 3/15; no closing date. Applicants notified on a rolling basis starting 4/1; must reply within 2 week(s) of notification.
Transfers: Child care grant and NCCCS Grant and Loan Program available.

CONTACT
Regina Huggins, Financial Aid Director
9101 Fayetteville Road, Raleigh, NC 27603
(919) 662-3254

Warren Wilson College
Asheville, North Carolina
www.warren-wilson.edu   Federal Code: 002979

4-year private liberal arts college in small city, affiliated with Presbyterian Church (USA).
Enrollment: 823 undergrads, 1% part-time. 244 full-time freshmen.
Selectivity: Admits over 75% of applicants.

BASIC COSTS (2006-2007)
Tuition and fees: $20,126.
Room and board: $6,000.
Additional info: All resident students required to work 15 hours per week in college's work program. $2,472 earnings credited toward tuition costs.

FINANCIAL AID PICTURE (2005-2006)
Students with need: Average financial aid package met 69% of need; average scholarship/grant was $8,805; average loan was $2,581. Need-based aid available for part-time students.
Students without need: No-need awards available for academics, art, job skills, leadership, religious affiliation, state/district residency.
Scholarships offered: Wilson Honor; 1 awarded; $5,000 annually. Warner Honor; 2 awarded; $4,000 annually. Transfer Honor; 2 awarded; $2,000 annually. Sutton Honor; 20 awarded; $1,000 annually. Work Scholarship; 2 awarded; $1,500 annually. Service Scholarship; 2 awarded; $1,500 annually. National Merit; unlimited numbers awarded; $4,000 annually. Valedictorian/Salutatorian Scholarship; 10 awarded; $2,000 annually. North Carolina Presidential Scholarship; 30 awarded; $1,000 annually. All renewable with 3.0 cumulative GPA and successful completion of a minimum of 12 credit hours each semester.
Cumulative student debt: 59% of graduating class had student loans; average debt was $16,211.

FINANCIAL AID PROCEDURES
Forms required: FAFSA, state aid form, institutional form.
Dates and Deadlines: Priority date 4/1; no closing date. Applicants notified on a rolling basis starting 3/1; must reply within 3 week(s) of notification.
Transfers: No deadline. Applicants notified on a rolling basis starting 3/1; must reply within 3 week(s) of notification.

CONTACT
Kathy Pack, Director of Financial Aid
Office of Admission, Asheville, NC 28815-9000
(828) 771-2082

Wayne Community College
Goldsboro, North Carolina
www.wayne.cc.nc.us   Federal Code: 008216

2-year public community college in large town.
Enrollment: 2,919 undergrads.
Selectivity: Open admission; but selective for some programs.

BASIC COSTS (2005-2006)
Tuition and fees: $1,217; out-of-state residents $6,617.
Per-credit charge: $40; out-of-state residents $220.

FINANCIAL AID PICTURE
Students with need: Need-based aid available for full-time and part-time students. Work study available nights.
Students without need: No-need awards available for academics, job skills.

FINANCIAL AID PROCEDURES
Forms required: FAFSA, institutional form.
Dates and Deadlines: Priority date 3/15; no closing date. Applicants notified on a rolling basis starting 6/1; must reply within 2 week(s) of notification.

CONTACT
Yvonne Goodman, Financial Aid Director
PO Box 8002, Goldsboro, NC 27533-8002
(919) 735-5151

Western Carolina University
Cullowhee, North Carolina
www.wcu.edu   Federal Code: 002981

4-year public university in small town.
Enrollment: 6,889 undergrads, 13% part-time. 1,494 full-time freshmen.
Selectivity: Admits 50 to 75% of applicants.

BASIC COSTS (2005-2006)
Tuition and fees: $3,624; out-of-state residents $13,060.
Room and board: $4,900.

FINANCIAL AID PICTURE (2004-2005)
Students with need: Out of 1,066 full-time freshmen who applied for aid, 702 were judged to have need. Of these, 696 received aid, and 425 had their full need met. Average financial aid package met 78% of need; average scholarship/grant was $3,523; average loan was $2,603. For part-time students, average financial aid package was $6,498.
Students without need: 199 full-time freshmen who did not demonstrate need for aid received scholarships/grants; average award was $2,097. No-need awards available for academics, art, athletics, leadership, music/drama, state/district residency.
Scholarships offered: 21 full-time freshmen received athletic scholarships; average amount $7,456.

FINANCIAL AID PROCEDURES
Forms required: FAFSA, institutional form.
Dates and Deadlines: Priority date 3/31; no closing date. Applicants notified on a rolling basis starting 4/1.

CONTACT
Nancy Dillard, Director of Student Financial Aid
242 HFR Administration Bldg, Cullowhee, NC 28723
(828) 227-7290

Western Piedmont Community College
Morganton, North Carolina
www.wpcc.edu   Federal Code: 002982

2-year public community college in large town.
Enrollment: 2,223 undergrads.
Selectivity: Open admission; but selective for some programs.

BASIC COSTS (2005-2006)
Tuition and fees: $1,212; out-of-state residents $6,612.
Per-credit charge: $40; out-of-state residents $220.

FINANCIAL AID PICTURE (2005-2006)
Students with need: 93% of average financial aid package awarded as scholarships/grants, 7% awarded as loans/jobs. Need-based aid available for part-time students.
Students without need: No-need awards available for academics.

FINANCIAL AID PROCEDURES
Forms required: FAFSA.
Dates and Deadlines: Priority date 6/1; no closing date. Applicants notified on a rolling basis starting 6/15; must reply within 2 week(s) of notification.

CONTACT
Keith Conley, Director of Financial Aid
1001 Burkemont Avenue, Morganton, NC 28655-4511
(828) 438-6042

Wilson Technical Community College
Wilson, North Carolina
www.wilsontech.edu   Federal Code: 004845

2-year public community and technical college in large town.
Enrollment: 1,686 undergrads, 49% part-time. 97 full-time freshmen.
Selectivity: Open admission; but selective for some programs.

BASIC COSTS (2005-2006)
Tuition and fees: $1,302; out-of-state residents $7,062.
Per-credit charge: $40; out-of-state residents $220.

FINANCIAL AID PICTURE (2004-2005)
Students with need: Average financial aid package met 65% of need; average scholarship/grant was $3,900. For part-time students, average financial aid package was $3,900.
Students without need: No-need awards available for academics.

FINANCIAL AID PROCEDURES
Forms required: FAFSA, institutional form.
Dates and Deadlines: Priority date 3/15; no closing date. Applicants notified on a rolling basis.

CONTACT
S Bissette, Director of Financial Aid and Veterans Affairs
Box 4305, Wilson, NC 27893-0305
(252) 246-1274

Wilkes Community College
Wilkesboro, North Carolina
www.wilkescc.edu   Federal Code: 002983

2-year public community college in small town.
Enrollment: 2,414 undergrads, 47% part-time. 318 full-time freshmen.
Selectivity: Open admission; but selective for some programs.

BASIC COSTS (2005-2006)
Tuition and fees: $1,248; out-of-state residents $6,648.
Per-credit charge: $40; out-of-state residents $220.

FINANCIAL AID PICTURE (2004-2005)
Students with need: Out of 198 full-time freshmen who applied for aid, 164 were judged to have need. Of these, 126 received aid, and 90 had their full need met. Average financial aid package met 63% of need; average scholarship/grant was $400; average loan was $1,800. For part-time students, average financial aid package was $1,200.
Students without need: 55 full-time freshmen who did not demonstrate need for aid received scholarships/grants; average award was $400. No-need awards available for academics, art, job skills, leadership, minority status, music/drama, state/district residency.

FINANCIAL AID PROCEDURES
Forms required: FAFSA.
Dates and Deadlines: Priority date 5/1; closing date 6/1. Applicants notified on a rolling basis starting 4/1; must reply by 8/1.
Transfers: No deadline.

CONTACT
Vickie Call, Director of Financial Aid
1328 South Collegiate Drive, Wilkesboro, NC 28697-0120
(336) 838-6146

Wingate University
Wingate, North Carolina
www.wingate.edu   Federal Code: 002985

4-year private liberal arts college in small town, affiliated with Baptist faith.
Enrollment: 1,332 undergrads, 2% part-time. 370 full-time freshmen.
Selectivity: Admits over 75% of applicants.

BASIC COSTS (2006-2007)
Tuition and fees: $17,650.
Per-credit charge: $550.
Room and board: $6,750.

FINANCIAL AID PICTURE (2004-2005)
Students with need: Average financial aid package met 77% of need; average scholarship/grant was $3,021; average loan was $2,538. For part-time students, average financial aid package was $3,704.
Students without need: No-need awards available for academics, alumni affiliation, art, athletics, leadership, music/drama, religious affiliation, state/district residency.
Cumulative student debt: 70% of graduating class had student loans; average debt was $18,759.
Additional info: Tuition payment plans available with no interest charges for $50 per year enrollment fee. Institutional aid may not be available after June 1.

FINANCIAL AID PROCEDURES
Forms required: FAFSA.
Dates and Deadlines: Priority date 5/1; no closing date. Applicants notified on a rolling basis starting 3/1; must reply within 2 week(s) of notification.
Transfers: Priority date 3/1. Must submit financial aid transcripts from previous colleges attended.

CONTACT
Teresa Williams, Director of Financial Planning
Campus Box 3059, Wingate, NC 28174-0157
(704) 233-8209

Winston-Salem State University
Winston-Salem, North Carolina
www.wssu.edu Federal Code: 002986

4-year public university and health science college in small city.
Enrollment: 5,128 undergrads, 10% part-time. 891 full-time freshmen.
Selectivity: Admits over 75% of applicants.

BASIC COSTS (2005-2006)
Tuition and fees: $2,804; out-of-state residents $11,444.
Room and board: $5,278.

FINANCIAL AID PICTURE (2004-2005)
Students with need: Out of 761 full-time freshmen who applied for aid, 744 were judged to have need. Of these, 699 received aid. Average financial aid package met 71% of need; average scholarship/grant was $2,878; average loan was $2,499. For part-time students, average financial aid package was $2,472.
Students without need: 13 full-time freshmen who did not demonstrate need for aid received scholarships/grants; average award was $3,089. No-need awards available for academics, athletics, ROTC, state/district residency.
Scholarships offered: 35 full-time freshmen received athletic scholarships; average amount $3,386.

FINANCIAL AID PROCEDURES
Forms required: FAFSA.
Dates and Deadlines: Priority date 4/1; closing date 5/1. Applicants notified by 5/15; must reply within 2 week(s) of notification.
Transfers: Closing date 3/15. Applicants notified on a rolling basis.

CONTACT
Theodore Hindsman, Director of Financial Aid
601 Martin Luther King Jr Drive, Winston-Salem, NC 27110
(336) 750-3280

North Dakota

Aakers College: Fargo
Fargo, North Dakota
www.aakers.edu Federal Code: 004846

2-year for-profit business college in small city.
Enrollment: 577 undergrads, 37% part-time. 176 full-time freshmen.
Selectivity: Open admission.

BASIC COSTS (2006-2007)
Tuition and fees: $10,048.
Additional info: Per course tuition is $785 for general courses and $1000 for network support courses.

FINANCIAL AID PICTURE (2004-2005)
Students with need: Average financial aid package for all full-time undergraduates was $4,950. 16% awarded as scholarships/grants, 84% awarded as loans/jobs. Need-based aid available for part-time students. Work study available nights.
Students without need: This college only awards aid to students with need.

FINANCIAL AID PROCEDURES
Forms required: FAFSA, institutional form.
Dates and Deadlines: No deadline. Applicants notified on a rolling basis starting 1/1.

CONTACT
Darwin Olson, Financial Aid Director
4012 19th Avenue Southwest, Fargo, ND 58103
(701) 277-3889

Bismarck State College
Bismarck, North Dakota
www.bismarckstate.edu Federal Code: 002988

2-year public community college in small city.
Enrollment: 3,370 undergrads.
Selectivity: Open admission; but selective for some programs.

BASIC COSTS (2005-2006)
Tuition and fees: $3,369; out-of-state residents $8,022.
Per-credit charge: $93; out-of-state residents $248.
Room and board: $3,628.
Additional info: Full-time annual tuition for residents of Minnesota: $3,600. Full-time annual tuition for residents of South Dakota, Montana, Manitoba, Saskatchewan: $3,483. Full-time annual tuition for residents of Alaska, Arizona, California, Colorado, Hawaii, Idaho, New Mexico, Nevada, Oregon, Utah, Washington, and Wyoming: $3,944. Tuition for Internet courses $140 per credit hour. Tuition/fee waivers available for minority students.

FINANCIAL AID PICTURE
Students with need: Need-based aid available for full-time and part-time students. Work study available nights, weekends, and for part-time students.
Students without need: This college only awards aid to students with need.
Scholarships offered: Academic Scholarship; $900; for students enrolled in 15 credit hours who maintain 3.0 GPA; 79 awarded.

FINANCIAL AID PROCEDURES
Forms required: FAFSA.
Dates and Deadlines: Priority date 3/15; no closing date. Applicants notified on a rolling basis starting 6/1; must reply within 3 week(s) of notification.
Transfers: Financial aid based on funds available.

CONTACT
Jeffrey Jacobs, Director of Financial Aid
PO Box 5587, Bismarck, ND 58506-5587
(701) 224-5494

Cankdeska Cikana Community College
Fort Totten, North Dakota
www.littlehoop.edu Federal Code: 015793

2-year public community college in rural community.
Enrollment: 167 undergrads.
Selectivity: Open admission.

BASIC COSTS (2006-2007)
Tuition and fees: $2,190.
Per-credit charge: $85.

FINANCIAL AID PICTURE (2004-2005)
Students with need: 78% of average financial aid package awarded as scholarships/grants, 22% awarded as loans/jobs. Need-based aid available for part-time students.
Students without need: This college only awards aid to students with need.

FINANCIAL AID PROCEDURES
Forms required: FAFSA, institutional form.
Dates and Deadlines: Closing date 8/20. Applicants notified on a rolling basis.

CONTACT
Kristi Black, Director of Financial Aid
Box 269, Fort Totten, ND 58335
(701) 766-1341

Dickinson State University
Dickinson, North Dakota
www.dsu.nodak.edu
Federal Code: 002989

4-year public university in large town.
Enrollment: 2,516 undergrads, 30% part-time. 359 full-time freshmen.
Selectivity: Open admission; but selective for some programs.

BASIC COSTS (2005-2006)
Tuition and fees: $4,154; out-of-state residents $9,713.
Per-credit charge: $139; out-of-state residents $370.
Room and board: $3,694.
Additional info: Tuition for Minnesota residents: $3,630. Tuition for South Dakota, Montana, Manitoba, Saskatchewan residents: $4,160. Tuition/fee waivers available for minority students.

FINANCIAL AID PICTURE (2005-2006)
Students with need: 25% of average financial aid package awarded as scholarships/grants, 75% awarded as loans/jobs. Need-based aid available for part-time students. Work study available nights, weekends, and for part-time students.
Students without need: No-need awards available for academics, alumni affiliation, art, athletics, job skills, leadership, minority status, music/drama, religious affiliation, state/district residency.
Additional info: Scholarships available to new students, priority deadline December 1.

FINANCIAL AID PROCEDURES
Forms required: FAFSA.
Dates and Deadlines: Priority date 3/15; no closing date. Must reply within 2 week(s) of notification.

CONTACT
Sandy Klein, Director of Financial Aid
291 Campus Drive, Dickinson, ND 58601-4896
(701) 483-2371

Jamestown College
Jamestown, North Dakota
www.jc.edu
Federal Code: 002990

4-year private liberal arts college in large town, affiliated with Presbyterian Church (USA).
Enrollment: 1,019 undergrads, 6% part-time. 282 full-time freshmen.
Selectivity: Admits over 75% of applicants.

BASIC COSTS (2006-2007)
Tuition and fees: $10,550.
Room and board: $4,340.

FINANCIAL AID PICTURE (2005-2006)
Students with need: Out of 280 full-time freshmen who applied for aid, 222 were judged to have need. Of these, 222 received aid, and 43 had their full need met. Average financial aid package met 67% of need; average scholarship/grant was $6,165; average loan was $3,193. For part-time students, average financial aid package was $4,614.
Students without need: 58 full-time freshmen who did not demonstrate need for aid received scholarships/grants; average award was $7,400. No-need awards available for academics, alumni affiliation, art, athletics, leadership, music/drama, religious affiliation.

Scholarships offered: *Merit:* Wilson Scholarships; full tuition; for academic merit and leadership. Presidential Scholarships; $8,000 annually; for academic merit and leadership. Honor Scholarships; $6,000 annually; for academic merit and leadership. Arnold Chemistry Scholarships; $6,500 annually; for chemistry majors. Music Major scholarships; $6,500 annually. Trustee scholarships; $5,000 annually. *Athletic:* 46 full-time freshmen received athletic scholarships; average amount $1,559.
Cumulative student debt: 96% of graduating class had student loans; average debt was $19,732.
Additional info: FAFSA must be received by March 15th for North Dakota residents to be considered for North Dakota state grants.

FINANCIAL AID PROCEDURES
Forms required: FAFSA.
Dates and Deadlines: Priority date 6/1; no closing date. Applicants notified on a rolling basis starting 4/1; must reply within 6 week(s) of notification.
Transfers: No deadline. Applicants notified on a rolling basis starting 4/1; must reply within 6 week(s) of notification.

CONTACT
Margery Michael, Director of Financial Aid
6081 College Lane, Jamestown, ND 58405
(701) 252-3467 ext. 2556

Lake Region State College
Devils Lake, North Dakota
www.lrsc.nodak.edu
Federal Code: 002991

2-year public community college in small town.
Enrollment: 640 undergrads, 42% part-time. 135 full-time freshmen.
Selectivity: Open admission; but selective for some programs.

BASIC COSTS (2005-2006)
Tuition and fees: $3,339; out-of-state residents $3,339.
Per-credit charge: $106; out-of-state residents $106.
Room and board: $3,790.
Additional info: Tuition for Minnesota residents must follow reciprocity procedures, but tuition will be waived to the ND rate. Tuition/fee waivers available for minority students.

FINANCIAL AID PICTURE (2005-2006)
Students with need: 42% of average financial aid package awarded as scholarships/grants, 58% awarded as loans/jobs. Need-based aid available for part-time students. Work study available nights, weekends, and for part-time students.
Students without need: No-need awards available for academics, athletics, leadership, music/drama, state/district residency.
Cumulative student debt: 70% of graduating class had student loans; average debt was $4,000.

FINANCIAL AID PROCEDURES
Forms required: FAFSA.
Dates and Deadlines: Priority date 3/15; no closing date. Applicants notified on a rolling basis starting 5/15; must reply within 2 week(s) of notification.
Transfers: No deadline. Must reply within 4 week(s) of notification.

CONTACT
Katie Nettell, Director of Financial Aid
1801 North College Drive, Devils Lake, ND 58301-1598
(701) 662-1516

Mayville State University
Mayville, North Dakota
www.mayvillestate.edu
Federal Code: 002993

4-year public business and teachers college in small town.
Enrollment: 912 undergrads, 31% part-time. 161 full-time freshmen.
Selectivity: Open admission; but selective for some programs.

BASIC COSTS (2005-2006)
Tuition and fees: $4,943; out-of-state residents $10,454.
Per-credit charge: $138; out-of-state residents $367.
Room and board: $3,724.
Additional info: Full-time tuition for South Dakota, Montana, Manitoba, and Saskatchewan residents: $4,125. Full-time tuition for Western Undergraduate Exchange states: $4,950. Tuition/fee waivers available for minority students.

FINANCIAL AID PICTURE (2004-2005)
Students with need: Out of 126 full-time freshmen who applied for aid, 98 were judged to have need. Of these, 93 received aid, and 38 had their full need met. Average financial aid package met 76% of need; average scholarship/grant was $2,752; average loan was $2,848. For part-time students, average financial aid package was $3,452.
Students without need: 9 full-time freshmen who did not demonstrate need for aid received scholarships/grants; average award was $849. No-need awards available for academics, athletics, leadership, minority status, music/drama, state/district residency.
Scholarships offered: *Merit:* Non-resident academic Scholarship; $1,650 to $5,500 per year; based on academic criteria of freshmen from select states. *Athletic:* 14 full-time freshmen received athletic scholarships; average amount $739.
Cumulative student debt: 77% of graduating class had student loans; average debt was $18,190.

FINANCIAL AID PROCEDURES
Forms required: FAFSA.
Dates and Deadlines: Priority date 4/15; no closing date. Applicants notified on a rolling basis starting 5/1; must reply within 2 week(s) of notification.

CONTACT
Shirley Hanson, Director of Financial Aid
330 Third Street, NE, Mayville, ND 58257-1299
(701) 788-4893

Medcenter One College of Nursing
Bismarck, North Dakota
www.medcenterone.com/college/nursing.htm
Federal Code: 009354

Upper-division private nursing college in small city.
Enrollment: 92 undergrads, 4% part-time.

BASIC COSTS (2005-2006)
Tuition and fees: $9,151.
Per-credit charge: $350.
Room only: $1,800.

FINANCIAL AID PICTURE (2004-2005)
Students with need: Average financial aid package for all full-time undergraduates was $12,708; for part-time $12,000. 52% awarded as scholarships/grants, 48% awarded as loans/jobs. Work study available weekends and for part-time students.
Cumulative student debt: 100% of graduating class had student loans; average debt was $19,002.

FINANCIAL AID PROCEDURES
Forms required: FAFSA, institutional form.
Dates and Deadlines: Priority date 3/15; no closing date. Applicants notified on a rolling basis starting 6/15; must reply within 2 week(s) of notification.
Transfers: Priority date 3/1; no deadline. Applicants notified on a rolling basis starting 6/1; must reply within 2 week(s) of notification.

CONTACT
Janell Thomas, Director/Registrar
512 North 7th Street, Bismarck, ND 58501-4494
(701) 323-6270

Minot State University
Minot, North Dakota
www.minotstateu.edu
Federal Code: 002994

4-year public university and liberal arts college in large town.
Enrollment: 3,547 undergrads, 30% part-time. 138 full-time freshmen.
Selectivity: Admits over 75% of applicants.

BASIC COSTS (2005-2006)
Tuition and fees: $4,092; out-of-state residents $9,870.
Per-credit charge: $144; out-of-state residents $385.
Room and board: $3,590.
Additional info: Full-time tuition for Minnesota residents: $3,772. Full-time tuition for South Dakota, Montana, Manitoba, Saskatchewan residents: $4,325. Tuition/fee waivers available for minority students.

FINANCIAL AID PICTURE (2004-2005)
Students with need: Out of 138 full-time freshmen who applied for aid, 122 were judged to have need. Of these, 108 received aid. Average financial aid package met 59% of need; average scholarship/grant was $1,199; average loan was $1,764. For part-time students, average financial aid package was $4,147.
Students without need: 20 full-time freshmen who did not demonstrate need for aid received scholarships/grants; average award was $3,654. No-need awards available for academics, alumni affiliation, art, athletics, minority status, music/drama, state/district residency.
Additional info: Scholarship application deadline is February 15.

FINANCIAL AID PROCEDURES
Forms required: FAFSA.
Dates and Deadlines: Priority date 3/15; no closing date. Applicants notified on a rolling basis starting 5/1; must reply within 2 week(s) of notification.

CONTACT
Dale Gehring, Director of Financial Aid
500 University Avenue West, Minot, ND 58707-5002
(701) 858-3375

Minot State University: Bottineau Campus
Bottineau, North Dakota
www.misu-b.nodak.edu
Federal Code: 002995

2-year public branch campus and junior college in small town.
Enrollment: 300 full-time undergrads.
Selectivity: Open admission.

BASIC COSTS (2005-2006)
Tuition and fees: $3,202; out-of-state residents $7,502.
Per-credit charge: $107; out-of-state residents $286.
Room and board: $3,511.
Additional info: Tuition for Minnesota residents: $3,600. Tuition for South Dakota, Montana residents: $3,219. Tuition for Canadian provinces: $2,575. Tuition/fee waivers available for minority students.

FINANCIAL AID PICTURE
Students with need: Need-based aid available for full-time and part-time students. Work study available nights, weekends, and for part-time students.
Students without need: No-need awards available for academics, alumni affiliation, athletics, music/drama.

FINANCIAL AID PROCEDURES
Forms required: FAFSA.
Dates and Deadlines: Priority date 4/15; no closing date. Applicants notified on a rolling basis starting 6/1; must reply within 2 week(s) of notification.

CONTACT
Diane Christenson, Financial Aid Officer
105 Simrall Boulevard, Bottineau, ND 58318-1198
(701) 228-5437

North Dakota State College of Science
Wahpeton, North Dakota
www.ndscs.nodak.edu   Federal Code: 002996

2-year public junior and technical college in small town.
Enrollment: 2,457 undergrads.
Selectivity: Open admission; but selective for some programs.

BASIC COSTS (2005-2006)
Tuition and fees: $3,268; out-of-state residents $7,990.
Per-credit charge: $94; out-of-state residents $252.
Room and board: $3,898.
Additional info: Full-time tuition for Minnesota residents $3,600. Full-time tuition for South Dakota, Montana, Saskatchewan, Manitoba residents $3,533. Tuition/fee waivers available for minority students.

FINANCIAL AID PICTURE
Students with need: Need-based aid available for full-time and part-time students. Work study available nights, weekends, and for part-time students.
Students without need: No-need awards available for academics, athletics, job skills, music/drama, state/district residency.

FINANCIAL AID PROCEDURES
Forms required: FAFSA, institutional form.
Dates and Deadlines: Priority date 4/15; no closing date. Applicants notified on a rolling basis starting 6/1; must reply within 2 week(s) of notification.

CONTACT
Karen Reilly, Director of Financial Aid
800 North 6th Street, Wahpeton, ND 58076
(701) 671-2207

North Dakota State University
Fargo, North Dakota
www.ndsu.edu   Federal Code: 002997

4-year public university in small city.
Enrollment: 10,496 undergrads, 10% part-time.
Selectivity: Admits over 75% of applicants.

BASIC COSTS (2005-2006)
Tuition and fees: $5,264; out-of-state residents $12,545.
Per-credit charge: $182; out-of-state residents $485.
Room and board: $5,130.
Additional info: Tuition for Minnesota residents: $4,756. Tuition for South Dakota, Montana, Manitoba, Saskatchewan residents: $6,540. Tuition/fee waivers available for minority students.

FINANCIAL AID PICTURE (2004-2005)
Students with need: Average financial aid package met 75% of need; average scholarship/grant was $3,154; average loan was $2,958. For part-time students, average financial aid package was $4,121.
Students without need: No-need awards available for academics, alumni affiliation, art, athletics, leadership, minority status, music/drama, ROTC, state/district residency.
Scholarships offered: New Student Scholarships; vary in amount awarded; based on a composite ACT of at least 25 or an SAT of at least 1200 (exclusive of writing), and a cumulative GPA of at least 3.5.
Cumulative student debt: 70% of graduating class had student loans; average debt was $23,197.

FINANCIAL AID PROCEDURES
Forms required: FAFSA.
Dates and Deadlines: Closing date 3/15. Applicants notified on a rolling basis starting 3/15.

CONTACT
James Kennedy, Director of Student Financial Services
Ceres Hall 124, Fargo, ND 58105-5454
(701) 231-7533

Sitting Bull College
Fort Yates, North Dakota
www.sittingbull.edu   Federal Code: 014993

2-year public community college in small town.
Enrollment: 289 undergrads.
Selectivity: Open admission.

BASIC COSTS (2006-2007)
Tuition and fees: $3,140.
Per-credit charge: $100.

FINANCIAL AID PICTURE
Students with need: Need-based aid available for full-time and part-time students.

FINANCIAL AID PROCEDURES
Forms required: FAFSA, institutional form.
Dates and Deadlines: Priority date 5/1; no closing date. Applicants notified on a rolling basis starting 7/15; must reply within 6 week(s) of notification.

CONTACT
Donna Seaboy, Director of Financial Aid
1341 92nd Street, Fort Yates, ND 58538
(701) 854-3864

Trinity Bible College
Ellendale, North Dakota
www.trinitybiblecollege.edu   Federal Code: 012059

4-year private Bible college in rural community, affiliated with Assemblies of God.
Enrollment: 290 undergrads, 10% part-time. 64 full-time freshmen.
Selectivity: Admits less than 50% of applicants.

BASIC COSTS (2006-2007)
Tuition and fees: $11,868.
Per-credit charge: $350.
Room and board: $4,520.

FINANCIAL AID PICTURE (2005-2006)
Students with need: For part-time students, average financial aid package was $6,144.

Students without need: No-need awards available for academics, alumni affiliation, art, leadership, music/drama, religious affiliation.

FINANCIAL AID PROCEDURES
Forms required: FAFSA.
Dates and Deadlines: Priority date 3/1; closing date 9/1. Applicants notified on a rolling basis starting 3/1; must reply within 3 week(s) of notification.

CONTACT
Don Flaherty, Financial Aid Director
50 South Sixth Avenue, Ellendale, ND 58436-7150
(888) 822-2329

University of Mary
Bismarck, North Dakota
www.umary.edu   Federal Code: 002992

4-year private university in small city, affiliated with Roman Catholic Church.
Enrollment: 2,102 undergrads, 7% part-time. 352 full-time freshmen.
Selectivity: Admits over 75% of applicants.

BASIC COSTS (2006-2007)
Tuition and fees: $11,374.
Per-credit charge: $350.
Room and board: $4,310.

FINANCIAL AID PICTURE (2004-2005)
Students with need: 50% of average financial aid package awarded as scholarships/grants, 50% awarded as loans/jobs. Need-based aid available for part-time students. Work study available nights, weekends, and for part-time students.
Students without need: No-need awards available for academics, athletics, leadership, state/district residency.
Scholarships offered: Presidential Merit Awards; large number awarded; ranging from $1,000-$7,000 annually, guaranteed for 4 years. Athletic and music scholarships; limited number awarded; varying amounts. Music scholarships require audition. Drama/Forensics; limited number; varying amounts.

FINANCIAL AID PROCEDURES
Forms required: FAFSA.
Dates and Deadlines: Priority date 3/15; no closing date. Applicants notified on a rolling basis starting 4/1; must reply within 2 week(s) of notification.
Transfers: Priority date 5/1; no deadline. Applicants notified on a rolling basis starting 5/1; must reply within 2 week(s) of notification.

CONTACT
Dave Hanson, Director of Student Financial Aid
7500 University Drive, Bismarck, ND 58504-9652
(701) 355-8079 ext. 283

University of North Dakota
Grand Forks, North Dakota
www.und.edu   Federal Code: 003005

4-year public university in small city.
Enrollment: 10,498 undergrads, 11% part-time. 1,856 full-time freshmen.
Selectivity: Admits 50 to 75% of applicants.

BASIC COSTS (2005-2006)
Tuition and fees: $5,327; out-of-state residents $12,659.
Per-credit charge: $183; out-of-state residents $488.
Room and board: $4,787.
Additional info: Tuition for South Dakota, Montana, Saskatchewan, Manitoba residents: $7521. Tuition/fee waivers available for minority students.

FINANCIAL AID PICTURE (2005-2006)
Students with need: Average financial aid package met 83% of need; average scholarship/grant was $2,967; average loan was $3,309. For part-time students, average financial aid package was $9,920.
Students without need: No-need awards available for academics, alumni affiliation, art, athletics, job skills, leadership, minority status, music/drama, ROTC, state/district residency.
Scholarships offered: 15 freshmen will receive $2,500 a year for 4 years; they are either National Merit Finalists listing UND as first choice and in top 10% of graduating class, or in top 10% and have minimum composite of 32 on the ACT. 55 scholarships of $2,000/yr for 4 years provided to students in top 10% of graduating class who are National Merit Semifinalists or have ACT composite of 29-31. 40 students with ACT of 27-28 and in upper 10% of graduating class will receive $1,000 for their freshman year.

FINANCIAL AID PROCEDURES
Forms required: FAFSA.
Dates and Deadlines: Priority date 3/15; no closing date. Applicants notified on a rolling basis starting 5/15; must reply within 4 week(s) of notification.

CONTACT
Robin Holden, Director of Student Financial Aid
PO Box 8357, Grand Forks, ND 58202
(701) 777-3121

Valley City State University
Valley City, North Dakota
www.vcsu.edu   Federal Code: 003008

4-year public liberal arts and teachers college in small town.
Enrollment: 1,011 undergrads, 23% part-time. 173 full-time freshmen.
Selectivity: Admits over 75% of applicants.

BASIC COSTS (2005-2006)
Tuition and fees: $4,932; out-of-state residents $10,656.
Per-credit charge: $114; out-of-state residents $305.
Room and board: $3,535.

FINANCIAL AID PICTURE (2004-2005)
Students with need: Average financial aid package met 74% of need; average scholarship/grant was $2,933; average loan was $2,924. For part-time students, average financial aid package was $5,735.
Students without need: No-need awards available for academics, alumni affiliation, athletics, leadership, minority status, music/drama.
Cumulative student debt: 36% of graduating class had student loans; average debt was $18,209.

FINANCIAL AID PROCEDURES
Forms required: FAFSA.
Dates and Deadlines: Priority date 3/15; no closing date. Applicants notified on a rolling basis starting 1/15; must reply within 2 week(s) of notification.
Transfers: Priority date 4/15.

CONTACT
Betty Schumacher, Director of Financial Aid
101 College Street Southwest, Valley City, ND 58072-4098
(701) 845-7412

Williston State College
Williston, North Dakota
www.wsc.nodak.edu   Federal Code: 003007

2-year public community college in large town.
Enrollment: 947 undergrads, 41% part-time. 170 full-time freshmen.
Selectivity: Open admission; but selective for some programs.

BASIC COSTS (2005-2006)
Tuition and fees: $2,850; out-of-state residents $3,950.
Per-credit charge: $85; out-of-state residents $127.
Room and board: $2,800.
Additional info: Tuition for Minnesota residents: $3,600. Tuition/fee waivers available for minority students.

FINANCIAL AID PICTURE
Students with need: Need-based aid available for full-time and part-time students. Work study available nights, weekends, and for part-time students.
Students without need: No-need awards available for academics, athletics.

FINANCIAL AID PROCEDURES
Forms required: FAFSA.
Dates and Deadlines: Priority date 3/15; no closing date. Applicants notified on a rolling basis starting 5/15.

CONTACT
Lynn Hagen-Aaberg, Financial Aid Director
1410 University Avenue, Williston, ND 58802-1326
(701) 774-4244

Ohio

Antioch College
Yellow Springs, Ohio
www.antioch-college.edu   Federal Code: 003010

4-year private liberal arts college in small town.
Enrollment: 380 undergrads. 46 full-time freshmen.
Selectivity: Admits 50 to 75% of applicants.

BASIC COSTS (2006-2007)
Tuition and fees: $27,212.
Per-credit charge: $435.
Room and board: $7,004.
Additional info: Tuition/fee waivers available for unemployed or children of unemployed.

FINANCIAL AID PICTURE (2005-2006)
Students with need: Average financial aid package met 100% of need; average scholarship/grant was $11,898; average loan was $2,852. Need-based aid available for part-time students.
Students without need: No-need awards available for academics, art, leadership, music/drama.
Cumulative student debt: 97% of graduating class had student loans; average debt was $17,125.
Additional info: Middle Income Assistance Program provides interest-free loans to students who qualify for little or no financial aid. If student maintains constant enrollment and graduates within normal time frame, loan forgiven at commencement.

FINANCIAL AID PROCEDURES
Forms required: FAFSA, institutional form.
Dates and Deadlines: Priority date 2/1; no closing date. Applicants notified on a rolling basis starting 3/1; must reply by 5/1.

CONTACT
Robin Heise, Director of Financial Aid Services
795 Livermore Street, Yellow Springs, OH 45387
(937) 769-1000

Antioch University McGregor
Yellow Springs, Ohio
www.mcgregor.edu   Federal Code: E00553

4-year private branch campus and liberal arts college in small town.
Enrollment: 152 undergrads.

BASIC COSTS (2005-2006)
Tuition and fees: $9,666.
Per-credit charge: $256.

FINANCIAL AID PICTURE (2004-2005)
Students with need: 41% of average financial aid package awarded as scholarships/grants, 59% awarded as loans/jobs. Need-based aid available for part-time students.

FINANCIAL AID PROCEDURES
Dates and Deadlines: No deadline. Applicants notified on a rolling basis.

CONTACT
Kathy John, Director of Financial Aid
800 Livermore Street, Yellow Springs, OH 45387
(937) 769-1840

Art Academy of Cincinnati
Cincinnati, Ohio
www.artacademy.edu   Federal Code: 003011

4-year private visual arts college in large city.
Enrollment: 176 undergrads.
Selectivity: Admits less than 50% of applicants.

BASIC COSTS (2006-2007)
Tuition and fees: $19,600.
Per-credit charge: $810.
Room and board: $6,800.

FINANCIAL AID PICTURE
Students with need: Need-based aid available for full-time and part-time students.
Students without need: No-need awards available for academics, alumni affiliation, art.
Additional info: 40 annual scholarships awarded to entering and transfer students and 50 to continuing students based on spring portfolio competition.

FINANCIAL AID PROCEDURES
Forms required: FAFSA.
Dates and Deadlines: Priority date 4/1; no closing date. Applicants notified on a rolling basis starting 3/1.

CONTACT
Karen Geiger, Financial Aid Director
1125 St. Gregory Street, Cincinnati, OH 45202-1700
(513) 562-8751

Ashland University
Ashland, Ohio
www.ashland.edu   Federal Code: 003012

4-year private university and liberal arts college in large town, affiliated with Brethren Church.
Enrollment: 2,741 undergrads, 8% part-time. 541 full-time freshmen.
Selectivity: Admits over 75% of applicants.

BASIC COSTS (2006-2007)
Tuition and fees: $21,430.
Per-credit charge: $635.
Room and board: $7,790.

FINANCIAL AID PICTURE (2005-2006)
Students with need: Out of 534 full-time freshmen who applied for aid, 430 were judged to have need. Of these, 430 received aid. Average financial aid package met 90% of need; average scholarship/grant was $11,729; average loan was $3,192. For part-time students, average financial aid package was $8,523.
Students without need: 92 full-time freshmen who did not demonstrate need for aid received scholarships/grants; average award was $7,170. No-need awards available for academics, alumni affiliation, art, athletics, job skills, leadership, minority status, music/drama, religious affiliation.
Scholarships offered: *Merit:* Presidential Scholarships for selected applicants with a GPA of 3.75-4.0 and an ACT score from 29-36 or SAT score from 1270-1600, $6,000; GPA of 3.5-3.74 and ACT score from 26-28 or SAT score from 1160-1260, $5,000; GPA of 3.25-3.49 and ACT score from 23-25 or SAT score from 1060-1150, $4,000. Achievement Scholarships for selected applicants with a GPA of 3.0-3.24 and ACT score from 21-22 or SAT score from 970-1050; $2,000. SAT scores exclusive of Writing. **Athletic:** 12 full-time freshmen received athletic scholarships; average amount $13,312.
Cumulative student debt: 75% of graduating class had student loans; average debt was $18,250.

FINANCIAL AID PROCEDURES
Forms required: FAFSA, institutional form.
Dates and Deadlines: Priority date 3/15; no closing date. Applicants notified on a rolling basis starting 3/15; must reply within 3 week(s) of notification.

CONTACT
Stephen Howell, Director of Financial Aid
401 College Avenue, Ashland, OH 44805-9981
(419) 289-5002

Baldwin-Wallace College
Berea, Ohio
www.bw.edu
Federal Code: 003014

4-year private liberal arts college in large town, affiliated with United Methodist Church.
Enrollment: 3,493 undergrads, 15% part-time. 598 full-time freshmen.
Selectivity: Admits over 75% of applicants.

BASIC COSTS (2006-2007)
Tuition and fees: $21,236.
Per-credit charge: $674.
Room and board: $6,974.
Additional info: Conservatory tuition is higher. Tuition/fee waivers available for minority students.

FINANCIAL AID PICTURE (2005-2006)
Students with need: Out of 576 full-time freshmen who applied for aid, 473 were judged to have need. Of these, 473 received aid, and 260 had their full need met. Average financial aid package met 88% of need; average scholarship/grant was $11,837; average loan was $2,875. For part-time students, average financial aid package was $6,733.
Students without need: 107 full-time freshmen who did not demonstrate need for aid received scholarships/grants; average award was $7,860. No-need awards available for academics, alumni affiliation, art, leadership, minority status, music/drama, religious affiliation, state/district residency.
Scholarships offered: Presidential Scholarship; $11,000; minimum ACT of 26 or SAT of 1180 and either 3.9 GPA or top 5% high school rank. Trustees Scholarship; $8,500; minimum ACT of 24 or SAT of 1100 and either 3.6 GPA or top 15% high school rank. Dean's Scholarship; $6,000; minimum ACT of 22 or SAT of 1030 and either a 3.3 GPA or top 25% high school rank. Griffiths Scholarship; up to $4,000; for conservatory students who demonstrate outstanding musicianship and talent. Heritage Award; $4,000; for students who will enrich the College's cultural diversity; must have a minimum GPA of 3.3 and be in the top 25% of their high school class. Conservatory Merit Award; for talented conservatory students with financial need. Alumni Award; up to $2,000; automatically awarded to children and grandchildren of alumni. Sibling Award; $1,000 for each full-time sibling enrolled. Ministerial Award; up to half tuition; for dependent students of ordained United Methodist ministers. Achievement Award; $1,000 to $4,000; awarded to admitted students with outstanding leadership, participation, extracurricular involvement and community services. Scholars Award; $6,000; awarded to admitted students with excellent academic achievement who have not received an automatic academic scholarship. (SAT scores are exclusive of Writing).
Cumulative student debt: 95% of graduating class had student loans; average debt was $16,250.

FINANCIAL AID PROCEDURES
Forms required: FAFSA.
Dates and Deadlines: Priority date 5/1; closing date 9/1. Applicants notified on a rolling basis starting 2/14.
Transfers: Priority date 7/1; closing date 9/15.

CONTACT
George Rolleston, Director of Financial Aid
275 Eastland Road, Berea, OH 44017-2088
(440) 826-2108

Belmont Technical College
St. Clairsville, Ohio
www.btc.edu
Federal Code: 009941

2-year public community and technical college in small town.
Enrollment: 1,630 undergrads.
Selectivity: Open admission; but selective for some programs.

BASIC COSTS (2005-2006)
Tuition and fees: $3,555; out-of-state residents $6,255.
Per-credit charge: $79; out-of-state residents $139.
Additional info: Tuition/fee waivers available for unemployed or children of unemployed.

FINANCIAL AID PICTURE
Students with need: Need-based aid available for full-time and part-time students.
Students without need: No-need awards available for state/district residency.

FINANCIAL AID PROCEDURES
Forms required: FAFSA.
Dates and Deadlines: No deadline. Applicants notified on a rolling basis starting 6/1; must reply within 2 week(s) of notification.

CONTACT
Susan Galavich, Director of Financial Aid
120 Fox Shannon Place, St. Clairsville, OH 43950
(740) 695-9500

Bluffton University
Bluffton, Ohio
www.bluffton.edu
Federal Code: 003016

4-year private liberal arts college in small town, affiliated with Mennonite Church.
Enrollment: 1,046 undergrads, 5% part-time. 230 full-time freshmen.
Selectivity: Admits 50 to 75% of applicants.

Bluffton University (continued)

BASIC COSTS (2006-2007)
Tuition and fees: $20,570.
Per-credit charge: $840.
Room and board: $7,082.
Additional info: Tuition/fee waivers available for minority students.

FINANCIAL AID PICTURE (2005-2006)
Students with need: Out of 220 full-time freshmen who applied for aid, 207 were judged to have need. Of these, 207 received aid, and 145 had their full need met. Average financial aid package met 95.9% of need; average scholarship/grant was $13,712; average loan was $3,820. For part-time students, average financial aid package was $11,366.
Students without need: 23 full-time freshmen who did not demonstrate need for aid received scholarships/grants; average award was $8,110. No-need awards available for academics, art, job skills, leadership, minority status, music/drama, state/district residency.
Scholarships offered: Academic distinction scholarship; tuition equalization scholarship plus $1,000; minimum 3.5 GPA, 25 ACT or 1140 SAT. Academic honors scholarship; tuition equalization scholarship plus $2,000; minimum 27 ACT or 1220 SAT. SAT scores exclusive of Writing. Tuition equalization is the difference between tuition and fees at Bluffton and the average tuition and fees at selected four-year public institutions in Ohio during the previous year.
Cumulative student debt: 77% of graduating class had student loans; average debt was $27,441.
Additional info: Tuition Equalization Scholarship Program guarantees qualified students nonrepayable financial aid that is at a minimum the difference between Bluffton University tuition and the average tuition at the 3 Ohio public universities with highest tuition. Requirements: minimum 23 ACT or 1050 SAT and rank in top 25% of high school class or 3.0 GPA.

FINANCIAL AID PROCEDURES
Forms required: FAFSA.
Dates and Deadlines: Priority date 5/1; closing date 10/1. Applicants notified on a rolling basis starting 3/1; must reply within 3 week(s) of notification.
Transfers: Institutional non-need-based aid for transfer students awarded based on test scores in combination with work at previous institutions and high school academic performance.

CONTACT
Lawrence Matthews, Director of Financial Aid
1 University Drive, Bluffton, OH 45817-2104
(419) 358-3266

Bowling Green State University
Bowling Green, Ohio
www.bgsu.edu
Federal Code: 003018

4-year public university in large town.
Enrollment: 15,846 undergrads, 6% part-time. 3,869 full-time freshmen.
Selectivity: Admits over 75% of applicants.

BASIC COSTS (2005-2006)
Tuition and fees: $8,560; out-of-state residents $15,868.
Per-credit charge: $419; out-of-state residents $768.
Room and board: $6,434.

FINANCIAL AID PICTURE (2004-2005)
Students with need: Out of 3,145 full-time freshmen who applied for aid, 2,441 were judged to have need. Of these, 2,431 received aid, and 359 had their full need met. Average financial aid package met 50% of need; average scholarship/grant was $3,571; average loan was $2,751. For part-time students, average financial aid package was $5,739.
Students without need: 337 full-time freshmen who did not demonstrate need for aid received scholarships/grants; average award was $5,077. No-need awards available for academics, alumni affiliation, art, athletics, leadership, minority status, music/drama, ROTC, state/district residency.
Scholarships offered: 72 full-time freshmen received athletic scholarships; average amount $11,880.
Cumulative student debt: 72% of graduating class had student loans; average debt was $21,594.

FINANCIAL AID PROCEDURES
Forms required: FAFSA.
Dates and Deadlines: No deadline. Applicants notified on a rolling basis starting 4/15; must reply within 3 week(s) of notification.

CONTACT
Craig Cornell, Director
110 McFall Center, Bowling Green, OH 43403-0085
(419) 372-2651

Bowling Green State University: Firelands College
Huron, Ohio
www.firelands.bgsu.edu
Federal Code: 003018

2-year public branch campus college in small town.
Enrollment: 2,055 undergrads.
Selectivity: Open admission.

BASIC COSTS (2005-2006)
Tuition and fees: $4,098; out-of-state residents $11,406.
Per-credit charge: $201; out-of-state residents $550.

FINANCIAL AID PICTURE (2005-2006)
Students with need: 28% of average financial aid package awarded as scholarships/grants, 72% awarded as loans/jobs. Need-based aid available for part-time students.
Students without need: This college only awards aid to students with need.
Scholarships offered: FOCUS Scholarship (Firelands Opportunities in College for Under-represented Students); full tuition scholarships in all Firelands majors for historically under-represented students; 4-6 awards annually.
Additional info: Scholarship application deadline May 1. Technology computer loan program available. Based on need, students may receive computer on semester by semester loan basis.

FINANCIAL AID PROCEDURES
Forms required: FAFSA.
Dates and Deadlines: Priority date 3/1; no closing date. Applicants notified on a rolling basis starting 4/15; must reply within 2 week(s) of notification.

CONTACT
Debralee Divers, Director of Admissions and Financial Aid
One University Drive, Huron, OH 44839
(419) 433-5560

Bradford School
Columbus, Ohio
www.bradfordschoolcolumbus.edu
Federal Code: 016474

2-year for-profit business and technical college in very large city.
Enrollment: 429 undergrads. 429 full-time freshmen.
Selectivity: Admits over 75% of applicants.

BASIC COSTS (2006-2007)
Tuition and fees: $12,180.
Room only: $5,600.
Additional info: Tuition at time of enrollment locked for 2 years.

FINANCIAL AID PICTURE
Students with need: Need-based aid available for full-time students.

Students without need: This college only awards aid to students with need.
Scholarships offered: Two $1,000 and 8 $500 scholarships awarded to top 10 entering freshmen.

FINANCIAL AID PROCEDURES
Forms required: FAFSA.
Dates and Deadlines: No deadline. Applicants notified on a rolling basis.

CONTACT
Christina Stolar, Director of Financial Aid
2469 Stelzer Road, Columbus, OH 43219
(614) 416-6200

Bryant & Stratton College: Cleveland
Cleveland, Ohio
www.bryantstratton.edu   Federal Code: 022744

2-year for-profit technical college in very large city.
Enrollment: 254 undergrads.

BASIC COSTS (2006-2007)
Tuition and fees: $12,450.
Per-credit charge: $415.

FINANCIAL AID PICTURE (2004-2005)
Students with need: 65% of average financial aid package awarded as scholarships/grants, 35% awarded as loans/jobs. Need-based aid available for part-time students. Work study available nights.
Students without need: No-need awards available for academics.

FINANCIAL AID PROCEDURES
Forms required: FAFSA, institutional form.
Dates and Deadlines: Priority date 9/1; closing date 10/31. Applicants notified on a rolling basis starting 5/1; must reply within 2 week(s) of notification.
Transfers: No deadline. By state regulation, Ohio Institutional Grant can be awarded only 3 times a fiscal year.

CONTACT
Donna McCullough, Director of Financial Services
1700 East 13th Street, Cleveland, OH 44114-3203
(216) 771-1700

Bryant & Stratton College: Parma
Parma, Ohio
www.bryantstratton.edu   Federal Code: 015298

2-year for-profit business and junior college in small city.
Enrollment: 329 undergrads, 44% part-time. 98 full-time freshmen.
Selectivity: Admits over 75% of applicants.

BASIC COSTS (2006-2007)
Tuition and fees: $11,820.
Per-credit charge: $394.

FINANCIAL AID PICTURE (2005-2006)
Students with need: 35% of average financial aid package awarded as scholarships/grants, 65% awarded as loans/jobs. Need-based aid available for part-time students. Work study available nights.
Students without need: This college only awards aid to students with need.
Additional info: Competitive and matching scholarships offered to high school seniors.

FINANCIAL AID PROCEDURES
Forms required: FAFSA.
Dates and Deadlines: No deadline. Applicants notified on a rolling basis starting 6/1.
Transfers: Transfer form must be completed for state grant.

CONTACT
Colleen Garlbotti, Director of Financial Aid
12955 Snow Road, Parma, OH 44130-1013
(216) 771-1700

Bryant & Stratton College: Willoughby Hills
Willoughby Hills, Ohio
www.bryantstratton.edu   Federal Code: 022744

2-year for-profit business college in small town.
Enrollment: 271 undergrads.
Selectivity: Open admission.

BASIC COSTS (2005-2006)
Tuition and fees: $11,820.
Per-credit charge: $394.

FINANCIAL AID PICTURE (2004-2005)
Students with need: Need-based aid available for part-time students.
Students without need: No-need awards available for academics.

FINANCIAL AID PROCEDURES
Forms required: FAFSA.
Dates and Deadlines: No deadline. Applicants notified on a rolling basis.

CONTACT
Roxann Moten, Financial Aid Advisor
27557 Chardon Road, Willoughby Hills, OH 44092
(440) 944-6800

Capital University
Columbus, Ohio
www.capital.edu   Federal Code: 003023

4-year private university in very large city, affiliated with Evangelical Lutheran Church in America.
Enrollment: 2,751 undergrads, 19% part-time. 602 full-time freshmen.
Selectivity: Admits over 75% of applicants.

BASIC COSTS (2006-2007)
Tuition and fees: $25,100.
Per-credit charge: $786.
Room and board: $6,552.

FINANCIAL AID PICTURE (2004-2005)
Students with need: Out of 573 full-time freshmen who applied for aid, 515 were judged to have need. Of these, 515 received aid, and 92 had their full need met. Average financial aid package met 81% of need; average scholarship/grant was $15,032; average loan was $3,514. For part-time students, average financial aid package was $5,713.
Students without need: 82 full-time freshmen who did not demonstrate need for aid received scholarships/grants; average award was $10,367. No-need awards available for academics, alumni affiliation, art, minority status, music/drama, religious affiliation, ROTC, state/district residency.
Scholarships offered: Scholarships and grants from $1,000 to full tuition available. Transfer students also eligible for scholarships.
Cumulative student debt: 80% of graduating class had student loans; average debt was $24,092.

FINANCIAL AID PROCEDURES
Forms required: FAFSA.

Dates and Deadlines: Priority date 2/28; no closing date. Applicants notified on a rolling basis starting 3/1; must reply by 5/1.
Transfers: Priority date 7/15.

CONTACT
Jerry Wade, Director of Financial Aid
One College and Main, Columbus, OH 43209-2394
(614) 236-6511

Case Western Reserve University
Cleveland, Ohio
www.case.edu   Federal Code: E00077

4-year private university in very large city.
Enrollment: 3,824 undergrads, 4% part-time. 1,162 full-time freshmen.
Selectivity: Admits 50 to 75% of applicants.

BASIC COSTS (2006-2007)
Tuition and fees: $31,738.
Per-credit charge: $1,296.
Room and board: $9,280.
Additional info: Tuition varies for first-year and continuing students. $400 technology fee for resident students only.

FINANCIAL AID PICTURE (2005-2006)
Students with need: Out of 991 full-time freshmen who applied for aid, 812 were judged to have need. Of these, 809 received aid, and 667 had their full need met. Average financial aid package met 96% of need; average scholarship/grant was $20,783; average loan was $4,836. Need-based aid available for part-time students.
Students without need: 283 full-time freshmen who did not demonstrate need for aid received scholarships/grants; average award was $15,206. No-need awards available for academics, art, leadership, music/drama.

FINANCIAL AID PROCEDURES
Forms required: FAFSA, institutional form.
Dates and Deadlines: Priority date 2/1; no closing date. Applicants notified on a rolling basis starting 2/15; must reply by 5/1 or within 2 week(s) of notification.
Transfers: Priority date 5/15. Transfers not eligible for merit-based scholarships.

CONTACT
Donald Chenelle, Director of University Financial Aid
Tomlinson Hall, Cleveland, OH 44106-7055
(216) 368-4530

Cedarville University
Cedarville, Ohio
www.cedarville.edu   Federal Code: 003025

4-year private university and liberal arts college in small town, affiliated with Baptist faith.
Enrollment: 3,028 undergrads, 3% part-time. 761 full-time freshmen.
Selectivity: Admits over 75% of applicants.

BASIC COSTS (2006-2007)
Tuition and fees: $17,120.
Per-credit charge: $535.
Room and board: $5,010.

FINANCIAL AID PICTURE (2005-2006)
Students with need: Average financial aid package met 24% of need; average scholarship/grant was $1,422; average loan was $2,723. For part-time students, average financial aid package was $9,938.
Students without need: No-need awards available for academics, alumni affiliation, athletics, leadership, minority status, music/drama, ROTC, state/district residency.
Cumulative student debt: 67% of graduating class had student loans; average debt was $19,258.

FINANCIAL AID PROCEDURES
Forms required: FAFSA.
Dates and Deadlines: Priority date 3/1; no closing date. Applicants notified on a rolling basis starting 3/1; must reply within 4 week(s) of notification.
Transfers: No deadline. Applicants notified on a rolling basis starting 2/1.

CONTACT
Fred Merritt, Director of Financial Aid
251 North Main Street, Cedarville, OH 45314
(937) 766-7866

Central Ohio Technical College
Newark, Ohio
www.cotc.edu   Federal Code: 011046

2-year public technical college in large town.
Enrollment: 2,884 undergrads, 52% part-time. 284 full-time freshmen.
Selectivity: Open admission; but selective for some programs.

BASIC COSTS (2005-2006)
Tuition and fees: $3,384; out-of-state residents $5,634.
Per-credit charge: $94; out-of-state residents $169.

FINANCIAL AID PICTURE (2004-2005)
Students with need: 41% of average financial aid package awarded as scholarships/grants, 59% awarded as loans/jobs. Need-based aid available for part-time students.
Students without need: No-need awards available for academics.
Scholarships offered: Presidential Achievement Award based on minimum high school GPA of 3.0; 5 awarded; $1,800 annually. Minority Achievement Award based on minimum high school GPA of 2.5; 2 awarded; $850 annually.
Cumulative student debt: 57% of graduating class had student loans; average debt was $10,405.

FINANCIAL AID PROCEDURES
Forms required: FAFSA.
Dates and Deadlines: Priority date 3/1; no closing date. Applicants notified on a rolling basis starting 5/1; must reply within 3 week(s) of notification.

CONTACT
Faith Phillips, Director of Financial Aid
1179 University Drive, Newark, OH 43055
(740) 366-9435

Central State University
Wilberforce, Ohio
www.centralstate.edu   Federal Code: 003026

4-year public university and liberal arts college in rural community.
Enrollment: 1,589 undergrads, 9% part-time. 341 full-time freshmen.
Selectivity: Admits less than 50% of applicants.

BASIC COSTS (2005-2006)
Tuition and fees: $4,994; out-of-state residents $10,814.
Room and board: $6,982.

FINANCIAL AID PICTURE (2004-2005)
Students with need: 51% of average financial aid package awarded as scholarships/grants, 49% awarded as loans/jobs. Need-based aid available for part-time students. Work study available nights, weekends, and for part-time students.

Students without need: No-need awards available for academics, alumni affiliation, art, athletics, leadership, music/drama, religious affiliation, ROTC.

FINANCIAL AID PROCEDURES
Forms required: FAFSA, institutional form.
Dates and Deadlines: Priority date 2/15; no closing date. Applicants notified on a rolling basis starting 5/1.
Transfers: No deadline.

CONTACT
Veronica Leech, Director of Financial Aid
PO Box 1004, Wilberforce, OH 45384-1004
(937) 376-6579

Chatfield College
St. Martin, Ohio
www.chatfield.edu
Federal Code: 010880

2-year private community and liberal arts college in rural community, affiliated with Roman Catholic Church.
Enrollment: 280 undergrads.
Selectivity: Open admission.

BASIC COSTS (2005-2006)
Tuition and fees: $8,740.
Per-credit charge: $280.

FINANCIAL AID PICTURE
Students with need: Need-based aid available for full-time and part-time students.
Students without need: No-need awards available for academics, leadership.
Additional info: Institutional grants/scholarships given primarily to first-year students to reduce debt load during initial year.

FINANCIAL AID PROCEDURES
Forms required: FAFSA, institutional form.
Dates and Deadlines: Priority date 4/25; closing date 8/7. Applicants notified on a rolling basis starting 4/1; must reply within 2 week(s) of notification.

CONTACT
Rebecca Cluxton, Director of Financial Aid
20918 State Route 251, St. Martin, OH 45118
(513) 875-3344

Cincinnati Christian University
Cincinnati, Ohio
www.ccuniversity.edu
Federal Code: 003029

4-year private university in very large city, affiliated with Church of Christ/Christian Church.
Enrollment: 765 undergrads, 12% part-time. 147 full-time freshmen.
Selectivity: Admits over 75% of applicants.

BASIC COSTS (2006-2007)
Tuition and fees: $10,000.
Per-credit charge: $310.
Room and board: $5,960.

FINANCIAL AID PICTURE (2005-2006)
Students with need: Out of 138 full-time freshmen who applied for aid, 132 were judged to have need. Of these, 110 received aid. Average financial aid package met 78% of need; average scholarship/grant was $1,220; average loan was $2,625. Need-based aid available for part-time students.
Students without need: 32 full-time freshmen who did not demonstrate need for aid received scholarships/grants; average award was $2,749.

Cumulative student debt: 62% of graduating class had student loans; average debt was $18,100.

FINANCIAL AID PROCEDURES
Forms required: FAFSA.
Dates and Deadlines: Priority date 3/1; closing date 7/15. Applicants notified by 4/5; must reply by 6/5 or within 2 week(s) of notification.
Transfers: No deadline.

CONTACT
Robbin Moore, Director of Financial Aid
2700 Glenway Avenue, Cincinnati, OH 45204-3200
(513) 244-8100 ext. 8450

Cincinnati College of Mortuary Science
Cincinnati, Ohio
www.ccms.edu
Federal Code: 010906

4-year private school of mortuary science in large city.
Enrollment: 140 undergrads. 11 full-time freshmen.
Selectivity: Open admission.

BASIC COSTS (2006-2007)
Tuition and fees: $13,500.

FINANCIAL AID PICTURE
Students with need: Need-based aid available for full-time and part-time students.
Students without need: This college only awards aid to students with need.

FINANCIAL AID PROCEDURES
Forms required: FAFSA.
Dates and Deadlines: Priority date 7/1; no closing date. Applicants notified on a rolling basis starting 3/1; must reply within 2 week(s) of notification.

CONTACT
Patsy Leon, Financial Aid/Admissions Officer
645 West North Bend Road, Cincinnati, OH 45224-1428
(513) 761-2020

Cincinnati State Technical and Community College
Cincinnati, Ohio
www.cincinnatistate.edu
Federal Code: 010345

2-year public community and technical college in large city.
Enrollment: 7,489 undergrads, 55% part-time. 1,340 full-time freshmen.
Selectivity: Open admission; but selective for some programs.

BASIC COSTS (2005-2006)
Tuition and fees: $3,507; out-of-state residents $6,912.
Per-credit charge: $76; out-of-state residents $151.

FINANCIAL AID PICTURE
Students with need: Need-based aid available for full-time and part-time students. Work study available nights, weekends, and for part-time students.
Students without need: No-need awards available for academics, athletics, state/district residency.

FINANCIAL AID PROCEDURES
Forms required: FAFSA.
Dates and Deadlines: Priority date 2/15; no closing date. Applicants notified on a rolling basis starting 3/15; must reply within 4 week(s) of notification.

CONTACT
Dawnia Smith, Director of Student Financial Aid/Scholarships
3520 Central Parkway, Cincinnati, OH 45223-2690
(513) 569-1530

Cleveland Institute of Art
Cleveland, Ohio
www.cia.edu   Federal Code: 003982

4-year private visual arts college in very large city.
Enrollment: 536 undergrads, 5% part-time. 100 full-time freshmen.
Selectivity: Admits 50 to 75% of applicants.

BASIC COSTS (2006-2007)
Tuition and fees: $28,891.
Per-credit charge: $1,120.
Room and board: $9,444.

FINANCIAL AID PICTURE (2004-2005)
Students with need: Out of 84 full-time freshmen who applied for aid, 79 were judged to have need. Of these, 77 received aid, and 4 had their full need met. Average financial aid package met 51% of need; average scholarship/grant was $9,338; average loan was $3,704. For part-time students, average financial aid package was $7,368.
Students without need: 20 full-time freshmen who did not demonstrate need for aid received scholarships/grants; average award was $9,135. No-need awards available for academics, art.
Cumulative student debt: 85% of graduating class had student loans; average debt was $31,300.

FINANCIAL AID PROCEDURES
Forms required: FAFSA, institutional form.
Dates and Deadlines: Priority date 3/15; no closing date. Applicants notified on a rolling basis starting 3/16; must reply within 4 week(s) of notification.

CONTACT
Michael Warinner, Director Financial Aid
11141 East Boulevard, Cleveland, OH 44106
(216) 421-7425

Cleveland Institute of Music
Cleveland, Ohio
www.cim.edu   Federal Code: 003031

4-year private music college in very large city.
Enrollment: 207 undergrads. 63 full-time freshmen.
Selectivity: Admits less than 50% of applicants.

BASIC COSTS (2006-2007)
Tuition and fees: $29,127.
Room and board: $9,334.

FINANCIAL AID PICTURE
Students with need: Need-based aid available for full-time and part-time students.

FINANCIAL AID PROCEDURES
Forms required: FAFSA, institutional form.
Dates and Deadlines: Priority date 2/15; no closing date. Applicants notified on a rolling basis starting 4/1; must reply by 5/1 or within 2 week(s) of notification.

CONTACT
Kristie Gripp, Director of Financial Aid
11021 East Boulevard, Cleveland, OH 44106
(216) 791-5002 ext. 262

Cleveland State University
Cleveland, Ohio
www.csuohio.edu   Federal Code: 003032

4-year public university in very large city.
Enrollment: 9,155 undergrads, 28% part-time. 1,026 full-time freshmen.
Selectivity: Open admission; but selective for some programs and for out-of-state students.

BASIC COSTS (2005-2006)
Tuition and fees: $7,344; out-of-state residents $13,056.
Per-credit charge: $306; out-of-state residents $544.
Room and board: $6,809.

FINANCIAL AID PICTURE (2005-2006)
Students with need: Out of 829 full-time freshmen who applied for aid, 736 were judged to have need. Of these, 715 received aid, and 36 had their full need met. Average financial aid package met 43% of need; average scholarship/grant was $5,200; average loan was $2,699. For part-time students, average financial aid package was $5,788.
Students without need: 108 full-time freshmen who did not demonstrate need for aid received scholarships/grants; average award was $8,887. No-need awards available for academics, alumni affiliation, art, athletics, leadership, minority status, music/drama, religious affiliation, ROTC, state/district residency.
Scholarships offered: 35 full-time freshmen received athletic scholarships; average amount $9,523.

FINANCIAL AID PROCEDURES
Forms required: FAFSA.
Dates and Deadlines: Priority date 2/15; no closing date. Applicants notified on a rolling basis starting 3/15; must reply within 4 week(s) of notification.

CONTACT
Judy Richards, Director of Financial Aid
1806 East 22th Street, Cleveland, OH 44115-2403
(888) 278-6446

College of Art Advertising
Cincinnati, Ohio   Federal Code: 015963

2-year for-profit visual arts college in large city.
Enrollment: 20 undergrads. 2 full-time freshmen.
Selectivity: Open admission.

BASIC COSTS (2005-2006)
Tuition and fees: $8,265.

FINANCIAL AID PICTURE
Students with need: Need-based aid available for full-time and part-time students.

FINANCIAL AID PROCEDURES
Forms required: FAFSA.
Dates and Deadlines: No deadline.

CONTACT
Laura Speed, Director of Financial Aid
4343 Bridgetown Road, Cincinnati, OH 45211-4427
(513) 574-1010

College of Mount St. Joseph
Cincinnati, Ohio
www.msj.edu   Federal Code: 003033

4-year private liberal arts college in very large city, affiliated with Roman Catholic Church.
Enrollment: 1,881 undergrads, 29% part-time. 307 full-time freshmen.
Selectivity: Admits 50 to 75% of applicants.

BASIC COSTS (2006-2007)
Tuition and fees: $20,080.
Per-credit charge: $440.
Room and board: $6,300.

FINANCIAL AID PICTURE (2005-2006)
Students with need: Out of 274 full-time freshmen who applied for aid, 250 were judged to have need. Of these, 250 received aid, and 158 had their full need met. Average financial aid package met 90% of need; average scholarship/grant was $8,787; average loan was $3,730. For part-time students, average financial aid package was $12,267.
Students without need: 34 full-time freshmen who did not demonstrate need for aid received scholarships/grants; average award was $7,264. No-need awards available for academics, art, leadership, music/drama, ROTC, state/district residency.
Scholarships offered: Presidential Scholarship; $10,000; 26-36 ACT or 1170 SAT. Trustee Scholarship; $9,000; 24-25 ACT or 1090 SAT. Dean's Scholarship; $7,000; 22-23 ACT or 1020 SAT. Merit Award; $4,000; 20-21 ACT or 940 SAT. Challenge Award; $2,000 per semester; 18-19 ACT or 860 SAT. Transfer Scholarship; 3.00 college GPA with at least 24 hours earned. SAT scores exclusive of Writing.
Cumulative student debt: 80% of graduating class had student loans; average debt was $134.
Additional info: College offers financial aid to full and part-time students. Unlimited, renewable merit-based scholarships are offered.

FINANCIAL AID PROCEDURES
Forms required: FAFSA.
Dates and Deadlines: Priority date 3/1; no closing date. Applicants notified on a rolling basis starting 2/15; must reply by 5/1 or within 4 week(s) of notification.
Transfers: Applicants notified on a rolling basis starting 2/15; must reply within 4 week(s) of notification.

CONTACT
Kathryn Kelly, Director of Student Administrative Services
5701 Delhi Road, Cincinnati, OH 45233-1670
(513) 244-4418

College of Wooster
Wooster, Ohio   Federal Code: 003037
www.wooster.edu   CSS Code: 1134

4-year private liberal arts college in large town.
Enrollment: 1,810 undergrads. 535 full-time freshmen.
Selectivity: Admits 50 to 75% of applicants.

BASIC COSTS (2006-2007)
Tuition and fees: $30,060.
Room and board: $7,520.

FINANCIAL AID PICTURE (2005-2006)
Students with need: Out of 406 full-time freshmen who applied for aid, 313 were judged to have need. Of these, 313 received aid, and 284 had their full need met. Average financial aid package met 92% of need; average scholarship/grant was $17,281; average loan was $5,564. Need-based aid available for part-time students.
Students without need: 197 full-time freshmen who did not demonstrate need for aid received scholarships/grants; average award was $12,591. No-need awards available for academics, minority status, music/drama, religious affiliation, state/district residency.
Cumulative student debt: 55% of graduating class had student loans; average debt was $19,989.

FINANCIAL AID PROCEDURES
Forms required: FAFSA, CSS PROFILE, institutional form.
Dates and Deadlines: Priority date 2/15; no closing date. Applicants notified by 3/15; must reply by 5/1 or within 4 week(s) of notification.

CONTACT
David Miller, Director of Financial Aid
847 College Avenue, Wooster, OH 44691-2363
(330) 263-2317

Columbus College of Art and Design
Columbus, Ohio
www.ccad.edu   Federal Code: 003039

4-year private visual arts college in very large city.
Enrollment: 1,308 undergrads, 4% part-time. 206 full-time freshmen.
Selectivity: Admits 50 to 75% of applicants.

BASIC COSTS (2006-2007)
Tuition and fees: $21,296.
Per-credit charge: $864.
Room and board: $6,600.

FINANCIAL AID PICTURE (2004-2005)
Students with need: Out of 179 full-time freshmen who applied for aid, 135 were judged to have need. Of these, 133 received aid, and 41 had their full need met. Average financial aid package met 62% of need; average scholarship/grant was $9,998; average loan was $3,361. For part-time students, average financial aid package was $12,276.
Students without need: 31 full-time freshmen who did not demonstrate need for aid received scholarships/grants; average award was $10,873. No-need awards available for academics, art, ROTC, state/district residency.
Cumulative student debt: 99% of graduating class had student loans; average debt was $31,078.

FINANCIAL AID PROCEDURES
Forms required: FAFSA.
Dates and Deadlines: Priority date 3/2; closing date 6/3. Applicants notified on a rolling basis starting 3/15; must reply within 2 week(s) of notification.

CONTACT
Anna Marie Schofield, Director of Financial Aid
107 North Ninth Street, Columbus, OH 43215-3875
(614) 222-3274

Columbus State Community College
Columbus, Ohio
www.cscc.edu   Federal Code: 006867

2-year public community and technical college in very large city.
Enrollment: 15,268 undergrads.
Selectivity: Open admission; but selective for some programs.

BASIC COSTS (2005-2006)
Tuition and fees: $3,420; out-of-state residents $7,560.
Per-credit charge: $76; out-of-state residents $168.

FINANCIAL AID PICTURE (2004-2005)
Students with need: 62% of average financial aid package awarded as scholarships/grants, 38% awarded as loans/jobs. Need-based aid available for part-time students. Work study available nights, weekends, and for part-time students.
Students without need: No-need awards available for athletics, state/district residency.

FINANCIAL AID PROCEDURES
Forms required: FAFSA.
Dates and Deadlines: Priority date 7/24; no closing date. Applicants notified on a rolling basis starting 4/1.

CONTACT
Martin Maliwesky, Director of Financial Aid
550 East Spring Street, Columbus, OH 43216-1609
(614) 287-2648

Cuyahoga Community College: Metropolitan Campus
Cleveland, Ohio
www.tri-c.edu   Federal Code: 003040

2-year public community college in very large city.
Enrollment: 11,416 undergrads, 52% part-time. 1,598 full-time freshmen.
Selectivity: Open admission; but selective for some programs.

BASIC COSTS (2005-2006)
Tuition and fees: $2,300; out-of-district residents $3,044; out-of-state residents $6,230.
Per-credit charge: $77; out-of-district residents $101; out-of-state residents $208.

FINANCIAL AID PICTURE (2005-2006)
Students with need: Average financial aid package met 100% of need; average scholarship/grant was $4,683; average loan was $2,697. For part-time students, average financial aid package was $4,401.
Students without need: No-need awards available for academics, art, athletics, leadership, minority status, music/drama.
Cumulative student debt: 24% of graduating class had student loans; average debt was $7,122.

FINANCIAL AID PROCEDURES
Forms required: FAFSA, institutional form.
Dates and Deadlines: No deadline. Applicants notified on a rolling basis starting 5/6.

CONTACT
Angela Johnson, Campus Director
2900 Community College Avenue, Cleveland, OH 44115-2878
(216) 987-4100

Davis College
Toledo, Ohio
www.daviscollege.edu   Federal Code: 004855

2-year for-profit junior college in large city.
Enrollment: 440 undergrads, 51% part-time. 88 full-time freshmen.
Selectivity: Admits over 75% of applicants.

BASIC COSTS (2006-2007)
Tuition and fees: $8,580.
Per-credit charge: $225.

FINANCIAL AID PICTURE (2004-2005)
Students with need: Out of 88 full-time freshmen who applied for aid, 88 were judged to have need. Of these, 88 received aid, and 10 had their full need met. Average financial aid package met 12% of need; average scholarship/grant was $6,461; average loan was $2,203. For part-time students, average financial aid package was $4,066.
Students without need: This college only awards aid to students with need.

FINANCIAL AID PROCEDURES
Forms required: FAFSA.
Dates and Deadlines: No deadline. Applicants notified on a rolling basis.

CONTACT
Carole Lulfs, Director of Financial Aid
4747 Monroe Street, Toledo, OH 43623
(419) 473-2700

Defiance College
Defiance, Ohio
www.defiance.edu   Federal Code: 003041

4-year private liberal arts college in large town, affiliated with United Church of Christ.
Enrollment: 827 undergrads.
Selectivity: Admits 50 to 75% of applicants.

BASIC COSTS (2006-2007)
Tuition and fees: $19,815.
Per-credit charge: $325.
Room and board: $6,170.
Additional info: Tuition/fee waivers available for adults.

FINANCIAL AID PICTURE
Students with need: Need-based aid available for full-time and part-time students. Work study available nights, weekends, and for part-time students.
Students without need: No-need awards available for academics, leadership.
Scholarships offered: Defiance Scholarship; full tuition; based on minimum high school GPA of 3.8, ACT score of 28 or SAT of 1860, essay, 2 letters of recommendation, interview; up to 3 awarded annually. Pilgrim Scholarship; up to $11,000; 3.4 GPA, 24 ACT, 1650 SAT, essay, 2 letters of recommendation, interview. Bonner Leader Award; extensive community service background, interview; up to 10 awarded annually. Citizen Leader; $1,000 award; five hours of community service per week, campus visit and essay required. Lillian Rae Dunlap Award; $1,000; minimum 2.25 GPA, recognizes the achievements of under-represented students.

FINANCIAL AID PROCEDURES
Forms required: FAFSA.
Dates and Deadlines: Priority date 3/1; no closing date. Applicants notified on a rolling basis starting 3/15; must reply within 3 week(s) of notification.

CONTACT
Amy Francis, Director of Financial Aid
701 North Clinton Street, Defiance, OH 43512-1695
(419) 784-4010

Denison University
Granville, Ohio
www.denison.edu   Federal Code: 003042

4-year private liberal arts college in small town.
Enrollment: 2,296 undergrads. 622 full-time freshmen.
Selectivity: Admits less than 50% of applicants.

BASIC COSTS (2006-2007)
Tuition and fees: $30,660.
Per-credit charge: $930.
Room and board: $8,560.
Additional info: Tuition/fee waivers available for adults.

FINANCIAL AID PICTURE (2005-2006)
Students with need: Out of 374 full-time freshmen who applied for aid, 286 were judged to have need. Of these, 286 received aid, and 114 had their full need met. Average financial aid package met 93% of need; average scholarship/grant was $24,545; average loan was $4,182. Need-based aid available for part-time students.
Students without need: 289 full-time freshmen who did not demonstrate need for aid received scholarships/grants; average award was $12,213. No-need awards available for academics, leadership, music/drama, state/district residency.
Scholarships offered: Denison Faculty Scholarship for Achievement for valedictorians and salutatorians; 35 awarded; 75% or full tuition. Tyree Scholarship for highly qualified African-American students; 30 awarded; half tuition. Parajon Scholarship for highly qualified students of Asian, Hispanic, and/or Native American heritage; 60 awarded; half tuition. Alumni Awards for students who have excellent academic record, special talents in the arts, or demonstrated leadership and service to school or community; ranging from 20% to 67% tuition annually. Trustee Scholarship for Achievement for valedictorians and salutatorians; 43 awarded; 75% tuition. Heritage Scholarships (half tuition) for academic achievement. Carr Scholarship; 35 awarded; 75% or full tuition. University Scholarship; 15 awarded; 75% tuition, awarded to highly qualified candidates who are invited into the honors program. Provost awards; 122 awarded; up to 40% tuition.
Cumulative student debt: 49% of graduating class had student loans; average debt was $14,657.

FINANCIAL AID PROCEDURES
Forms required: FAFSA.
Dates and Deadlines: Priority date 2/15; no closing date. Applicants notified by 3/30; must reply by 5/1 or within 2 week(s) of notification.

CONTACT
Nancy Hoover, Director of Financial Aid and Student Employment
Box H, Granville, OH 43023
(740) 587-6279

DeVry University: Columbus
Columbus, Ohio
www.devrycols.edu   Federal Code: 003099

4-year for-profit university in very large city.
Enrollment: 2,418 undergrads, 32% part-time. 816 full-time freshmen.

BASIC COSTS (2005-2006)
Tuition and fees: $12,140.
Per-credit charge: $440.

FINANCIAL AID PICTURE (2004-2005)
Students with need: Out of 567 full-time freshmen who applied for aid, 530 were judged to have need. Of these, 530 received aid, and 24 had their full need met. Average financial aid package met 44% of need; average scholarship/grant was $4,775; average loan was $5,251. For part-time students, average financial aid package was $7,031.
Students without need: This college only awards aid to students with need.

FINANCIAL AID PROCEDURES
Forms required: FAFSA.
Dates and Deadlines: No deadline. Applicants notified on a rolling basis.

CONTACT
Cynthia Price, Director of Financial Aid
1350 Alum Creek Drive, Columbus, OH 43209-2705
(614) 253-7291

Edison State Community College
Piqua, Ohio
www.edisonohio.edu   Federal Code: 012750

2-year public community college in large town.
Enrollment: 3,095 undergrads, 64% part-time. 200 full-time freshmen.
Selectivity: Open admission; but selective for some programs.

BASIC COSTS (2005-2006)
Tuition and fees: $3,270; out-of-state residents $6,060.
Per-credit charge: $93; out-of-state residents $186.

FINANCIAL AID PICTURE
Students with need: Need-based aid available for full-time and part-time students. Work study available nights, weekends, and for part-time students.
Students without need: No-need awards available for academics, athletics.

FINANCIAL AID PROCEDURES
Forms required: FAFSA, institutional form.
Dates and Deadlines: Priority date 5/2; no closing date. Applicants notified on a rolling basis starting 5/15.

CONTACT
Kathi Richards, Director of Student Financial Aid
1973 Edison Drive, Piqua, OH 45356-9253
(937) 778-7910

ETI Technical College of Niles
Niles, Ohio
www.eticollege.edu   Federal Code: 030790

2-year for-profit technical college in large city.
Enrollment: 323 undergrads.
Selectivity: Open admission; but selective for some programs.

BASIC COSTS (2006-2007)
Additional info: Full-time tuition varies by program: $5950-$6400.

FINANCIAL AID PICTURE (2005-2006)
Students with need: 69% of average financial aid package awarded as scholarships/grants, 31% awarded as loans/jobs.

CONTACT
Kay Madigan, Financial Aid Director
2076 Youngstown Warren Road, Niles, OH 44446-4398
(330) 652-9919

Franciscan University of Steubenville
Steubenville, Ohio
www.franciscan.edu   Federal Code: 003036

4-year private university in large town, affiliated with Roman Catholic Church.
Enrollment: 1,902 undergrads, 5% part-time. 400 full-time freshmen.
Selectivity: Admits over 75% of applicants.

BASIC COSTS (2006-2007)
Tuition and fees: $17,350.
Per-credit charge: $565.
Room and board: $5,950.

FINANCIAL AID PICTURE (2005-2006)
Students with need: 58% of average financial aid package awarded as scholarships/grants, 42% awarded as loans/jobs. Need-based aid available for part-time students. Work study available nights, weekends, and for part-time students.
Students without need: No-need awards available for academics, leadership, religious affiliation.
FINANCIAL AID PROCEDURES
Forms required: FAFSA.
Dates and Deadlines: No deadline. Applicants notified on a rolling basis starting 3/15; must reply within 3 week(s) of notification.
Transfers: Closing date 8/1.
CONTACT
John Herrmann, Director of Student Financial Services
1235 University Boulevard, Steubenville, OH 43952-1763
(740) 283-6211

Franklin University
Columbus, Ohio
www.franklin.edu   Federal Code: 003046

4-year private university and business college in very large city.
Enrollment: 6,027 undergrads, 66% part-time. 68 full-time freshmen.
Selectivity: Open admission.

BASIC COSTS (2005-2006)
Tuition and fees: $7,320.
Per-credit charge: $244.

FINANCIAL AID PICTURE (2005-2006)
Students with need: Out of 48 full-time freshmen who applied for aid, 45 were judged to have need. Of these, 44 received aid. Need-based aid available for part-time students.
Students without need: 2 full-time freshmen who did not demonstrate need for aid received scholarships/grants; average award was $900. No-need awards available for academics, leadership, minority status.
FINANCIAL AID PROCEDURES
Forms required: FAFSA.
Dates and Deadlines: Priority date 6/15; no closing date. Applicants notified on a rolling basis; must reply within 2 week(s) of notification.
Transfers: One scholarship specifically for transfer students: Transfer Achievement.
CONTACT
Goldie Langley, Director of Financial Aid
201 South Grant Avenue, Columbus, OH 43215-5399
(614) 797-4700

Gallipolis Career College
Gallipolis, Ohio
www.gallipoliscareercollege.com   Federal Code: 030079

2-year for-profit business and technical college in small town.
Enrollment: 157 undergrads, 5% part-time. 26 full-time freshmen.
Selectivity: Open admission.

BASIC COSTS (2005-2006)
Tuition and fees: $8,100.
Per-credit charge: $180.
Additional info: One-time registration fee $50; fee for one hour lab $60 per quarter; fee for two hour lab $70 per quarter.

FINANCIAL AID PICTURE
Students with need: Need-based aid available for full-time and part-time students.
Students without need: This college only awards aid to students with need.
FINANCIAL AID PROCEDURES
Forms required: FAFSA, institutional form.
Dates and Deadlines: No deadline.
CONTACT
Jeanette Shirey, Financial Aid Administrator
1176 Jackson Pike, Suite 312, Gallipolis, OH 45631
(740) 446-4367

God's Bible School and College
Cincinnati, Ohio
www.gbs.edu   Federal Code: 015691

4-year private Bible college in large city, affiliated with interdenominational tradition.
Enrollment: 271 undergrads. 53 full-time freshmen.
Selectivity: Admits over 75% of applicants.

BASIC COSTS (2006-2007)
Tuition and fees: $4,860.
Per-credit charge: $162.
Room and board: $3,300.

FINANCIAL AID PICTURE (2004-2005)
Students with need: Need-based aid available for part-time students.
Students without need: No-need awards available for academics, leadership, music/drama, religious affiliation.
Additional info: Institutional work scholarships available.
FINANCIAL AID PROCEDURES
Forms required: FAFSA.
Dates and Deadlines: Priority date 4/30; closing date 8/1. Applicants notified on a rolling basis.
CONTACT
Lisa Profitt, Director of Admissions and Financial Aid
1810 Young Street, Cincinnati, OH 45202
(513) 721-7944 ext. 205

Heidelberg College
Tiffin, Ohio
www.heidelberg.edu   Federal Code: 003048

4-year private liberal arts college in large town, affiliated with United Church of Christ.
Enrollment: 1,101 undergrads, 3% part-time. 326 full-time freshmen.
Selectivity: Admits 50 to 75% of applicants.

BASIC COSTS (2006-2007)
Tuition and fees: $17,400.
Per-credit charge: $530.
Room and board: $7,530.

FINANCIAL AID PICTURE (2005-2006)
Students with need: Out of 290 full-time freshmen who applied for aid, 266 were judged to have need. Of these, 266 received aid, and 30 had their full need met. Average financial aid package met 83% of need; average scholarship/grant was $10,739; average loan was $3,564. Need-based aid available for part-time students.
Students without need: 26 full-time freshmen who did not demonstrate need for aid received scholarships/grants; average award was $7,696. No-

need awards available for academics, music/drama, religious affiliation, state/district residency.
Cumulative student debt: 87% of graduating class had student loans; average debt was $26,125.

FINANCIAL AID PROCEDURES
Forms required: FAFSA.
Dates and Deadlines: Priority date 3/1; no closing date. Applicants notified on a rolling basis starting 3/15; must reply within 2 week(s) of notification.

CONTACT
Juli Weininger, Director of Financial Aid
310 East Market Street, Tiffin, OH 44883-2462
(419) 448-2293

Hiram College
Hiram, Ohio
www.hiram.edu   Federal Code: 003049

4-year private liberal arts college in rural community, affiliated with Christian Church (Disciples of Christ).
Enrollment: 1,086 undergrads, 19% part-time. 215 full-time freshmen.
Selectivity: Admits over 75% of applicants.

BASIC COSTS (2005-2006)
Tuition and fees: $24,180.
Room and board: $7,610.
Additional info: Tuition at time of enrollment locked for 4 years.

FINANCIAL AID PICTURE
Students with need: Need-based aid available for full-time and part-time students. Work study available nights, weekends, and for part-time students.
Students without need: No-need awards available for academics, alumni affiliation, art, leadership, minority status, music/drama, religious affiliation, state/district residency.

FINANCIAL AID PROCEDURES
Forms required: FAFSA.
Dates and Deadlines: Priority date 3/1; no closing date. Applicants notified on a rolling basis starting 2/15; must reply by 5/1 or within 2 week(s) of notification.
Transfers: Transfer merit scholarships available. Phi Theta Kappa scholarships available.

CONTACT
Ann Marie Gruber, Director of Student Financial Aid
Teachout Price Hall, Hiram, OH 44234
(330) 569-5107

Hocking College
Nelsonville, Ohio
www.hocking.edu   Federal Code: 007598

2-year public technical college in small town.
Enrollment: 3,362 undergrads, 25% part-time. 1,202 full-time freshmen.
Selectivity: Open admission; but selective for some programs.

BASIC COSTS (2005-2006)
Tuition and fees: $3,348; out-of-state residents $6,696.
Per-credit charge: $93; out-of-state residents $186.

FINANCIAL AID PICTURE (2004-2005)
Students with need: Out of 955 full-time freshmen who applied for aid, 754 were judged to have need. Of these, 754 received aid. Need-based aid available for part-time students.
Students without need: 182 full-time freshmen who did not demonstrate need for aid received scholarships/grants. No-need awards available for academics, minority status, state/district residency.

FINANCIAL AID PROCEDURES
Forms required: FAFSA, institutional form.
Dates and Deadlines: Priority date 2/28; no closing date. Applicants notified on a rolling basis starting 4/15.
Transfers: Non-entitlement aid awarded on first-come, first-serve basis.

CONTACT
Roger Springer, Financial Services Director
3301 Hocking Parkway, Nelsonville, OH 45764-9704
(740) 753-7080

International College of Broadcasting
Dayton, Ohio
www.icbcollege.com   Federal Code: 013132

2-year for-profit technical college in small city.
Enrollment: 120 undergrads.

BASIC COSTS (2006-2007)
Tuition and fees: $8,235.
Per-credit charge: $268.

FINANCIAL AID PICTURE
Students with need: Need-based aid available for full-time and part-time students.

FINANCIAL AID PROCEDURES
Forms required: FAFSA.
Dates and Deadlines: No deadline. Applicants notified on a rolling basis starting 11/1.

CONTACT
Zena Williams, Financial Aid Director
6 South Smithville Road, Dayton, OH 45431
(937) 258-8251 ext. 203

James A. Rhodes State College
Lima, Ohio
www.rhodesstate.edu   Federal Code: 010027

2-year public technical college in large town.
Enrollment: 2,558 undergrads.
Selectivity: Open admission; but selective for some programs.

BASIC COSTS (2005-2006)
Tuition and fees: $3,951; out-of-state residents $7,902.
Per-credit charge: $88; out-of-state residents $176.

FINANCIAL AID PICTURE
Students with need: Need-based aid available for full-time and part-time students. Work study available nights, weekends, and for part-time students.
Students without need: No-need awards available for academics.

FINANCIAL AID PROCEDURES
Forms required: FAFSA.
Dates and Deadlines: Priority date 4/1; no closing date. Applicants notified on a rolling basis starting 5/1; must reply within 2 week(s) of notification.

CONTACT
Cathy Kohli, Director of Financial Aid
4240 Campus Drive, Lima, OH 45804-3597
(419) 995-8800

Jefferson Community College
Steubenville, Ohio
www.jcc.edu
Federal Code: 007275

2-year public community and technical college in large town.
Enrollment: 1,697 undergrads, 46% part-time. 353 full-time freshmen.
Selectivity: Open admission; but selective for some programs.

BASIC COSTS (2005-2006)
Tuition and fees: $2,550; out-of-district residents $2,730; out-of-state residents $3,450.
Per-credit charge: $85; out-of-district residents $91; out-of-state residents $115.
Additional info: Residents of 5 neighboring West Virginia counties eligible for in-state, out-of-district tuition rates.

FINANCIAL AID PICTURE (2004-2005)
Students with need: Out of 292 full-time freshmen who applied for aid, 188 were judged to have need. Of these, 186 received aid, and 152 had their full need met. Average financial aid package met 75% of need; average scholarship/grant was $3,576. For part-time students, average financial aid package was $2,024.
Students without need: This college only awards aid to students with need.
Scholarships offered: Horizon Grant; two-year tuition scholarship; awarded to all students graduating from a Jefferson County high school with a 2.5 or above grade point average; student must enroll full-time for the fall semester immediately following high school graduation.

FINANCIAL AID PROCEDURES
Forms required: FAFSA, institutional form.
Dates and Deadlines: Priority date 7/1; no closing date. Applicants notified on a rolling basis starting 6/15.

CONTACT
Beth Sikole, Director of Student Information and Financial Aid
4000 Sunset Boulevard, Steubenville, OH 43952
(740) 264-5591 ext. 135

John Carroll University
University Heights, Ohio
www.jcu.edu
Federal Code: 003050

4-year private university in large town, affiliated with Roman Catholic Church.
Enrollment: 3,242 undergrads, 2% part-time. 786 full-time freshmen.
Selectivity: Admits over 75% of applicants.

BASIC COSTS (2006-2007)
Tuition and fees: $25,072.
Per-credit charge: $750.
Room and board: $7,790.

FINANCIAL AID PICTURE (2005-2006)
Students with need: Out of 687 full-time freshmen who applied for aid, 562 were judged to have need. Of these, 562 received aid, and 164 had their full need met. Average financial aid package met 86% of need; average scholarship/grant was $13,404; average loan was $3,896. For part-time students, average financial aid package was $11,501.
Students without need: 62 full-time freshmen who did not demonstrate need for aid received scholarships/grants; average award was $8,831. No-need awards available for academics, ROTC, state/district residency.
Scholarships offered: The full tuition Castellano Scholarship is awarded each year to a student who will study Latin or Greek; the Mastin Scholarship is offered to 3 students each year who will study natural sciences or math; the Ignatian Mission Scholarship is offered each year to graduates of Jesuit high schools.

Additional info: Institutional form for need analysis required from upperclassmen and transfer students only.

FINANCIAL AID PROCEDURES
Forms required: FAFSA.
Dates and Deadlines: Priority date 3/1; no closing date. Applicants notified on a rolling basis starting 3/1; must reply by 5/1 or within 4 week(s) of notification.
Transfers: Renewable scholarships for students transferring from local community colleges.

CONTACT
Patrick Prosser, Director of Financial Aid
20700 North Park Boulevard, University Heights, OH 44118-4581
(216) 397-4248

Kent State University
Kent, Ohio
www.kent.edu
Federal Code: 003051

4-year public university in large town.
Enrollment: 18,365 undergrads, 15% part-time. 3,746 full-time freshmen.
Selectivity: Admits over 75% of applicants.

BASIC COSTS (2005-2006)
Tuition and fees: $7,954; out-of-state residents $15,386.
Per-credit charge: $363; out-of-state residents $701.
Room and board: $6,640.

FINANCIAL AID PICTURE (2005-2006)
Students with need: Out of 3,002 full-time freshmen who applied for aid, 2,368 were judged to have need. Of these, 2,368 received aid, and 296 had their full need met. Average financial aid package met 55% of need; average scholarship/grant was $4,868; average loan was $3,233. For part-time students, average financial aid package was $5,603.
Students without need: 360 full-time freshmen who did not demonstrate need for aid received scholarships/grants; average award was $4,178. No-need awards available for academics, alumni affiliation, art, athletics, leadership, minority status, music/drama, ROTC, state/district residency.
Scholarships offered: *Merit:* Trustee Scholarship; $1,000-$2,500 annually; based on minimum GPA 3.25, ACT scores, leadership activities; 500 available. *Athletic:* 42 full-time freshmen received athletic scholarships; average amount $13,904.
Cumulative student debt: 69% of graduating class had student loans; average debt was $21,066.
Additional info: Participant in U.S. Department of Education's Quality Assurance Program and Experimental Sites Program.

FINANCIAL AID PROCEDURES
Forms required: FAFSA.
Dates and Deadlines: Priority date 3/1; no closing date. Applicants notified on a rolling basis starting 3/15; must reply within 2 week(s) of notification.

CONTACT
Mark Evans, Director of Student Financial Aid
PO Box 5190, Kent, OH 44242-0001
(330) 672-2972

Kent State University: Ashtabula Regional Campus
Ashtabula, Ohio
www.ashtabula.kent.edu
Federal Code: 003051

2-year public branch campus college in large town.
Enrollment: 1,313 undergrads, 49% part-time. 204 full-time freshmen.
Selectivity: Open admission; but selective for some programs.

BASIC COSTS (2005-2006)
Tuition and fees: $4,586; out-of-state residents $12,018.
Per-credit charge: $209; out-of-state residents $547.
Additional info: Per-credit-hour charges for upper division classes are $227 in-state and $547 out-of-state.

FINANCIAL AID PICTURE (2005-2006)
Students with need: Average financial aid package met 55% of need; average scholarship/grant was $4,365; average loan was $2,632. For part-time students, average financial aid package was $4,821.
Students without need: No-need awards available for academics, alumni affiliation, art, athletics, job skills, leadership, minority status, music/drama, ROTC, state/district residency.
Cumulative student debt: 64% of graduating class had student loans; average debt was $16,059.

FINANCIAL AID PROCEDURES
Forms required: FAFSA.
Dates and Deadlines: Priority date 3/1; no closing date. Applicants notified on a rolling basis starting 3/15; must reply within 2 week(s) of notification.

CONTACT
Kelly Sanford, Admissions Counselor
3325 West l3th Street, Ashtabula, OH 44004
(440) 964-3322

Kent State University: East Liverpool Regional Campus
East Liverpool, Ohio
www.kenteliv.kent.edu   Federal Code: 003051

2-year public branch campus college in large town.
Enrollment: 765 undergrads, 56% part-time. 97 full-time freshmen.
Selectivity: Open admission; but selective for some programs.

BASIC COSTS (2005-2006)
Tuition and fees: $4,586; out-of-state residents $12,018.
Per-credit charge: $209; out-of-state residents $547.

FINANCIAL AID PICTURE (2005-2006)
Students with need: Average financial aid package met 52% of need; average scholarship/grant was $4,173; average loan was $2,632. For part-time students, average financial aid package was $4,814.
Students without need: No-need awards available for academics, alumni affiliation, art, athletics, leadership, minority status, music/drama, ROTC, state/district residency.
Cumulative student debt: 84% of graduating class had student loans; average debt was $17,450.

FINANCIAL AID PROCEDURES
Forms required: FAFSA.
Dates and Deadlines: Priority date 3/1; no closing date. Applicants notified on a rolling basis starting 3/15; must reply within 2 week(s) of notification.

CONTACT
Judy Olabisi, Fianacial Aid Coordinator
400 East Fourth Street, East Liverpool, OH 43920
(330) 385-3805

Kent State University: Salem Regional Campus
Salem, Ohio
www.salem.kent.edu   Federal Code: 003061

2-year public branch campus college in large town.
Enrollment: 1,174 undergrads, 47% part-time. 175 full-time freshmen.

Selectivity: Open admission; but selective for some programs.

BASIC COSTS (2005-2006)
Tuition and fees: $4,586; out-of-state residents $12,018.
Per-credit charge: $209; out-of-state residents $547.

FINANCIAL AID PICTURE (2005-2006)
Students with need: Average financial aid package met 52% of need; average scholarship/grant was $3,285; average loan was $2,557. For part-time students, average financial aid package was $4,822.
Students without need: No-need awards available for academics, alumni affiliation, art, athletics, leadership, minority status, music/drama, ROTC.
Cumulative student debt: 66% of graduating class had student loans; average debt was $17,227.

FINANCIAL AID PROCEDURES
Forms required: FAFSA.
Dates and Deadlines: Priority date 3/1; no closing date. Applicants notified on a rolling basis starting 3/15; must reply within 2 week(s) of notification.
Transfers: Priority date 2/15.

CONTACT
Donna Holcomb, Financial Aid Advisor
2491 State Route 45 South, Salem, OH 44460
(440) 834-3737

Kent State University: Stark Campus
Canton, Ohio
www.stark.kent.edu   Federal Code: 003054

2-year public branch campus college in small city.
Enrollment: 3,418 undergrads, 39% part-time. 608 full-time freshmen.
Selectivity: Open admission; but selective for some programs.

BASIC COSTS (2005-2006)
Tuition and fees: $4,586; out-of-state residents $12,018.
Per-credit charge: $209; out-of-state residents $547.

FINANCIAL AID PICTURE (2005-2006)
Students with need: Out of 458 full-time freshmen who applied for aid, 379 were judged to have need. Of these, 379 received aid, and 37 had their full need met. Average financial aid package met 52% of need; average scholarship/grant was $3,076; average loan was $2,668. For part-time students, average financial aid package was $4,845.
Students without need: 13 full-time freshmen who did not demonstrate need for aid received scholarships/grants; average award was $2,841. No-need awards available for academics, alumni affiliation, art, athletics, leadership, minority status, music/drama, ROTC, state/district residency.
Cumulative student debt: 74% of graduating class had student loans; average debt was $21,024.

FINANCIAL AID PROCEDURES
Forms required: FAFSA.
Dates and Deadlines: Priority date 3/1; no closing date. Applicants notified on a rolling basis starting 3/15; must reply within 2 week(s) of notification.

CONTACT
Nina Antram, Financial Aid Officer
6000 Frank Avenue NW, Canton, OH 44720-7599
(330) 499-9600

Kent State University: Trumbull Campus
Warren, Ohio
www.trumbull.kent.edu   Federal Code: 003051

2-year public branch campus college in small city.
Enrollment: 1,897 undergrads, 54% part-time. 247 full-time freshmen.

Selectivity: Open admission.

BASIC COSTS (2005-2006)
Tuition and fees: $4,586; out-of-state residents $12,018.
Per-credit charge: $209; out-of-state residents $547.

FINANCIAL AID PICTURE (2005-2006)
Students with need: Out of 198 full-time freshmen who applied for aid, 166 were judged to have need. Of these, 166 received aid, and 11 had their full need met. Average financial aid package met 52% of need; average scholarship/grant was $3,876; average loan was $2,669. For part-time students, average financial aid package was $4,546.
Students without need: 6 full-time freshmen who did not demonstrate need for aid received scholarships/grants; average award was $2,470. No-need awards available for academics, alumni affiliation, art, athletics, leadership, minority status, music/drama, ROTC, state/district residency.
Cumulative student debt: 54% of graduating class had student loans; average debt was $20,129.

FINANCIAL AID PROCEDURES
Forms required: FAFSA.
Dates and Deadlines: Priority date 3/1; no closing date. Applicants notified on a rolling basis starting 3/15; must reply within 2 week(s) of notification.

CONTACT
Nina Antram, Financial Aid Coordinator
4314 Mahoning Avenue, NW, Warren, OH 44483-1998
(330) 847-0571

Kent State University: Tuscarawas Campus
New Philadelphia, Ohio
www.tusc.kent.edu
Federal Code: 003051

2-year public branch campus college in large town.
Enrollment: 1,682 undergrads, 49% part-time. 265 full-time freshmen.
Selectivity: Open admission; but selective for some programs and for out-of-state students.

BASIC COSTS (2005-2006)
Tuition and fees: $4,586; out-of-state residents $12,018.
Per-credit charge: $209; out-of-state residents $547.

FINANCIAL AID PICTURE (2005-2006)
Students with need: Average financial aid package met 53% of need; average scholarship/grant was $3,588; average loan was $2,683. For part-time students, average financial aid package was $4,437.
Students without need: No-need awards available for academics, alumni affiliation, art, athletics, leadership, minority status, music/drama, ROTC.
Cumulative student debt: 62% of graduating class had student loans; average debt was $14,831.

FINANCIAL AID PROCEDURES
Forms required: FAFSA.
Dates and Deadlines: Closing date 3/1. Applicants notified on a rolling basis starting 3/15; must reply within 2 week(s) of notification.
Transfers: Financial aid transcripts from all previous institutions required.

CONTACT
Linda Argento, Financial Aid Officer
330 University Drive Northeast, New Philadelphia, OH 44663-9403
(330) 339-3391

Kenyon College
Gambier, Ohio
www.kenyon.edu
Federal Code: 003065
CSS Code: 1370

4-year private liberal arts college in rural community.
Enrollment: 1,629 undergrads. 440 full-time freshmen.
Selectivity: Admits less than 50% of applicants.

BASIC COSTS (2006-2007)
Tuition and fees: $36,050.
Room and board: $5,900.

FINANCIAL AID PICTURE (2005-2006)
Students with need: Out of 227 full-time freshmen who applied for aid, 205 were judged to have need. Of these, 205 received aid, and 121 had their full need met. Average financial aid package met 98% of need; average scholarship/grant was $22,525; average loan was $2,140.
Students without need: 108 full-time freshmen who did not demonstrate need for aid received scholarships/grants; average award was $13,085. No-need awards available for academics, leadership, minority status.
Scholarships offered: Honor Scholarships, Science Scholarships, African-American Scholarships, Latino Scholarships, and Asian-American Scholarships competitively based on excellence in academic achievement, extracurricular leadership, and community involvement, and range from $11,000-$26,000 annually. Distinguished Academic Scholarships based on academic accomplishment, standardized test results, and extracurricular achievement; $4,000-$12,000. Scholarships for National Merit finalists available.
Cumulative student debt: 60% of graduating class had student loans; average debt was $19,190.

FINANCIAL AID PROCEDURES
Forms required: FAFSA, CSS PROFILE.
Dates and Deadlines: Closing date 2/15. Applicants notified by 4/1; must reply by 5/1.
Transfers: Priority date 4/15. Applicants notified by 5/15; must reply by 6/1.

CONTACT
Craig Daugherty, Director of Financial Aid
Ransom Hall, Gambier, OH 43022
(740) 427-5430

Kettering College of Medical Arts
Kettering, Ohio
www.kcma.edu
Federal Code: 007035

2-year private health science and nursing college in small city, affiliated with Seventh-day Adventists.
Enrollment: 738 undergrads, 42% part-time. 54 full-time freshmen.
Selectivity: Admits less than 50% of applicants.

BASIC COSTS (2005-2006)
Tuition and fees: $8,020.
Per-credit charge: $260.
Additional info: Tuition and fees may vary by program.

FINANCIAL AID PICTURE
Students with need: Need-based aid available for full-time and part-time students.
Students without need: No-need awards available for academics.

FINANCIAL AID PROCEDURES
Forms required: FAFSA, institutional form.
Dates and Deadlines: Priority date 3/31; no closing date. Applicants notified on a rolling basis starting 5/15; must reply within 3 week(s) of notification.

CONTACT
Kim Snell, Director of Student Finance
3737 Southern Boulevard, Kettering, OH 45429-1299
(937) 296-7210

Lake Erie College
Painesville, Ohio
www.lec.edu   Federal Code: 003066

4-year private liberal arts college in large town.
Enrollment: 654 undergrads, 14% part-time. 116 full-time freshmen.
Selectivity: Admits over 75% of applicants.

BASIC COSTS (2006-2007)
Tuition and fees: $22,890.
Per-credit charge: $545.
Room and board: $7,010.
Additional info: Equestrian fee $880 per course.

FINANCIAL AID PICTURE (2004-2005)
Students with need: 52% of average financial aid package awarded as scholarships/grants, 48% awarded as loans/jobs. Need-based aid available for part-time students. Work study available nights, weekends, and for part-time students.
Students without need: No-need awards available for academics, art, leadership, music/drama, state/district residency.
Additional info: Twins' scholarship, sibling discount.

FINANCIAL AID PROCEDURES
Forms required: FAFSA.
Dates and Deadlines: Priority date 5/1; no closing date. Applicants notified on a rolling basis; must reply within 2 week(s) of notification.
Transfers: No deadline.

CONTACT
Tricia Canfield, Director of Financial Aid
391 West Washington Street, Painesville, OH 44077-3389
(440) 375-7100

Lakeland Community College
Kirtland, Ohio
www.lakelandcc.edu   Federal Code: 006804

2-year public community college in large town.
Enrollment: 8,600 undergrads.
Selectivity: Open admission; but selective for some programs.

BASIC COSTS (2005-2006)
Tuition and fees: $2,546; out-of-district residents $3,119; out-of-state residents $6,670.
Per-credit charge: $74; out-of-district residents $94; out-of-state residents $212.

FINANCIAL AID PICTURE
Students with need: Need-based aid available for full-time and part-time students. Work study available nights, weekends, and for part-time students.
Students without need: No-need awards available for academics, art, athletics, job skills, leadership, minority status, music/drama, state/district residency.
Additional info: Loans available for tuition and books.

FINANCIAL AID PROCEDURES
Forms required: FAFSA, institutional form.
Dates and Deadlines: Priority date 3/1; no closing date. Applicants notified on a rolling basis starting 5/1.
Transfers: Ohio Instructional Grant Transfer Form.

CONTACT
Melissa Amspaugh, Director of Financial Aid
7700 Clocktower Drive, Kirtland, OH 44094
(440) 953-7070

Laura and Alvin Siegal College of Judaic Studies
Beachwood, Ohio
www.siegalcollege.edu   Federal Code: 012838

4-year private liberal arts and teachers college in large town, affiliated with Jewish faith.
Enrollment: 12 undergrads.

BASIC COSTS (2006-2007)
Tuition and fees: $15,775.
Per-credit charge: $525.
Additional info: Tuition/fee waivers available for adults.

FINANCIAL AID PICTURE (2005-2006)
Students with need: Need-based aid available for part-time students.

FINANCIAL AID PROCEDURES
Forms required: institutional form.
Dates and Deadlines: No deadline. Applicants notified on a rolling basis.

CONTACT
Ruth Kronick, Director of Student Services
26500 Shaker Boulevard, Beachwood, OH 44122
(216) 464-4050 ext. 101

Lourdes College
Sylvania, Ohio
www.lourdes.edu   Federal Code: 003069

4-year private liberal arts college in large town, affiliated with Roman Catholic Church.
Enrollment: 1,526 undergrads, 45% part-time. 73 full-time freshmen.
Selectivity: Admits less than 50% of applicants.

BASIC COSTS (2006-2007)
Tuition and fees: $13,200.
Per-credit charge: $390.

FINANCIAL AID PICTURE (2004-2005)
Students with need: Out of 58 full-time freshmen who applied for aid, 52 were judged to have need. Of these, 52 received aid. For part-time students, average financial aid package was $5,140.
Students without need: No-need awards available for academics, art, minority status, music/drama, state/district residency.

FINANCIAL AID PROCEDURES
Forms required: FAFSA.
Dates and Deadlines: Priority date 3/1; no closing date. Applicants notified on a rolling basis starting 3/1; must reply within 4 week(s) of notification.

CONTACT
Greg Guzman, Director of Financial Aid
6832 Convent Boulevard, Sylvania, OH 43560-2898
(419) 824-3732

Malone College
Canton, Ohio
www.malone.edu   Federal Code: 003072

4-year private liberal arts college in small city, affiliated with Evangelical Friends Church-Eastern Region.
Enrollment: 1,842 undergrads, 9% part-time. 357 full-time freshmen.
Selectivity: Admits over 75% of applicants.

BASIC COSTS (2006-2007)
Tuition and fees: $17,790.
Per-credit charge: $330.
Room and board: $6,400.

FINANCIAL AID PICTURE (2005-2006)
Students with need: Out of 334 full-time freshmen who applied for aid, 293 were judged to have need. Of these, 293 received aid, and 48 had their full need met. Average financial aid package met 70% of need; average scholarship/grant was $9,703; average loan was $3,167. For part-time students, average financial aid package was $5,246.
Students without need: 42 full-time freshmen who did not demonstrate need for aid received scholarships/grants; average award was $4,726. No-need awards available for academics, alumni affiliation, athletics, leadership, music/drama, religious affiliation.
Scholarships offered: 18 full-time freshmen received athletic scholarships; average amount $7,756.
Cumulative student debt: 72% of graduating class had student loans; average debt was $18,482.
Additional info: Prepayment discounts and deferred payments are available for students in the adult degree-completion programs.

FINANCIAL AID PROCEDURES
Forms required: FAFSA.
Dates and Deadlines: Priority date 3/1; closing date 7/31. Applicants notified on a rolling basis starting 3/1; must reply within 2 week(s) of notification.

CONTACT
Michael Bole, Director of Financial Aid
515 25th Street Northwest, Canton, OH 44709-3897
(330) 471-8100 ext. 8159

Marietta College
Marietta, Ohio
www.marietta.edu   Federal Code: 003073

4-year private liberal arts college in large town.
Enrollment: 1,344 undergrads, 5% part-time. 387 full-time freshmen.
Selectivity: Admits over 75% of applicants.

BASIC COSTS (2005-2006)
Tuition and fees: $22,655.
Room and board: $6,445.
Additional info: Tuition/fee waivers available for minority students.

FINANCIAL AID PICTURE (2005-2006)
Students with need: Average financial aid package met 90% of need; average scholarship/grant was $13,852; average loan was $3,219. For part-time students, average financial aid package was $6,775.
Students without need: 48 full-time freshmen who did not demonstrate need for aid received scholarships/grants; average award was $7,589. No-need awards available for academics, alumni affiliation, art, leadership, minority status, music/drama, state/district residency.
Scholarships offered: Dean's Scholarship; $4,000-$6,000; minimum 3.25 GPA and 25 ACT or 1150 SAT. President's Scholarships; $6,000-$9,000; minimum 3.50 GPA and 27 ACT or 1200 SAT. Trustees Scholarships; $9,000-13,000; minimum 3.75 GPA and 30 ACT or 1350 SAT. Academic Accomplishment Scholarships; $5,000; for selected minority students. Fine Arts Competition and Music Scholarships; $3,500; based on auditions or portfolios. Hugh O'Brien Youth Leadership Scholarships; $3,000. English Honors Scholarships; $2,500; based on essay submission. Rickey Physics Scholarships; full tuition; for students demonstrating high academic potential in physics. Forensic Scholarships; $1,500; for students demonstrating high aptitude in public speaking. (All SAT scores are exclusive of the Writing portion.).
Additional info: Auditions for music and theater required for competitive scholarships.

FINANCIAL AID PROCEDURES
Forms required: FAFSA, institutional form.
Dates and Deadlines: Priority date 3/1; closing date 4/15. Applicants notified on a rolling basis starting 3/1; must reply by 5/1 or within 2 week(s) of notification.
Transfers: Priority date 4/15; closing date 6/15. Applicants notified on a rolling basis starting 3/1; must reply within 2 week(s) of notification.

CONTACT
Kevin Lamb, Director of Student Financial Services
215 Fifth Street, Marietta, OH 45750-4005
(740) 376-4712

Marion Technical College
Marion, Ohio
www.mtc.edu   Federal Code: 010736

2-year public technical college in large town.
Enrollment: 1,425 undergrads.
Selectivity: Open admission; but selective for some programs.

BASIC COSTS (2005-2006)
Tuition and fees: $3,456; out-of-state residents $5,364.
Per-credit charge: $96; out-of-state residents $149.

FINANCIAL AID PICTURE (2005-2006)
Students with need: 97% of average financial aid package awarded as scholarships/grants, 3% awarded as loans/jobs. Need-based aid available for part-time students.
Students without need: No-need awards available for academics, leadership, minority status.
Scholarships offered: Foundation Scholarship; first year full tuition; for applicants in top 5% of class. President's Scholarship; $1,200; for applicants in top 50% of class. Tech Prep Scholarship; $1,200; for graduates of Tech Prep program. All scholarships require 2.5 GPA and successful completion of proficiency exams.

FINANCIAL AID PROCEDURES
Forms required: FAFSA, institutional form.
Dates and Deadlines: Closing date 6/1. Applicants notified on a rolling basis.
Transfers: No deadline. Applicants notified on a rolling basis.

CONTACT
R Andrew Harper, Vice President of Student Services
1467 Mount Vernon Avenue, Marion, OH 43302-5694
(740) 389-4636 ext. 221

MedCentral College of Nursing
Mansfield, Ohio
www.medcentral.edu   Federal Code: 035864

4-year private nursing college in small city.
Enrollment: 360 undergrads, 18% part-time. 86 full-time freshmen.

BASIC COSTS (2006-2007)
Tuition and fees: $9,750.
Per-credit charge: $275.
Room only: $4,800.

FINANCIAL AID PICTURE
Students with need: Need-based aid available for full-time and part-time students. Work study available nights, weekends, and for part-time students.
Students without need: No-need awards available for academics, leadership.

FINANCIAL AID PROCEDURES
Forms required: FAFSA, institutional form.
Dates and Deadlines: Priority date 4/2; closing date 9/15. Applicants notified on a rolling basis starting 9/1; must reply by 5/1.

CONTACT
Allen Wright, Director of Financial Aid
335 Glessner Avenue, Mansfield, OH 44903-2265
(419) 520-2600

Mercy College of Northwest Ohio
Toledo, Ohio
www.mercycollege.edu   Federal Code: 030970

4-year private health science and nursing college in large city, affiliated with Roman Catholic Church.
Enrollment: 741 undergrads, 47% part-time. 75 full-time freshmen.
Selectivity: Admits 50 to 75% of applicants.

BASIC COSTS (2006-2007)
Tuition and fees: $9,290.
Additional info: Actual cost is based on credit hours taken - 12 or more credits $270/ credit hour, less than 12 credit hours $299/credit hour.

FINANCIAL AID PICTURE (2005-2006)
Students with need: 30% of average financial aid package awarded as scholarships/grants, 70% awarded as loans/jobs. Need-based aid available for part-time students. Work study available weekends and for part-time students.
Students without need: This college only awards aid to students with need.

FINANCIAL AID PROCEDURES
Forms required: FAFSA.
Dates and Deadlines: No deadline. Applicants notified on a rolling basis starting 4/15; must reply within 4 week(s) of notification.

CONTACT
Charlotte Frary, Acting Financial Aid Officer
2221 Madison Avenue, Toledo, OH 43624
(419) 251-1598

Miami University: Hamilton Campus
Hamilton, Ohio
www.ham.muohio.edu   Federal Code: 003077

2-year public branch campus college in small city.
Enrollment: 3,223 undergrads.
Selectivity: Open admission; but selective for some programs.

BASIC COSTS (2005-2006)
Tuition and fees: $4,068; out-of-state residents $15,600.
Per-credit charge: $170; out-of-state residents $650.

FINANCIAL AID PICTURE
Students with need: Need-based aid available for full-time and part-time students. Work study available nights, weekends, and for part-time students.
Students without need: No-need awards available for academics, athletics, leadership, minority status, state/district residency.
Additional info: Special gift funds for needy, multicultural students who enter with appropriate academic record. Separate application required for scholarships; closing date January 31.

FINANCIAL AID PROCEDURES
Forms required: FAFSA.
Dates and Deadlines: Priority date 2/15; no closing date. Applicants notified on a rolling basis starting 4/1.
Transfers: Transfer students must complete one semester at Miami University to be considered for scholarships.

CONTACT
Ann Alfers, Financial Aid Coordinator
1601 University Boulevard, Hamilton, OH 45011-3399
(513) 785-3123

Miami University: Oxford Campus
Oxford, Ohio
www.muohio.edu   Federal Code: 003077

4-year public university in small town.
Enrollment: 14,582 undergrads, 2% part-time. 3,159 full-time freshmen.

BASIC COSTS (2005-2006)
Tuition and fees: $21,487; out-of-state residents $21,507.
Per-credit charge: $896; out-of-state residents $906.
Room and board: $7,610.
Additional info: All full-time, in-state students receive scholarships between $10,000 and $11,200 for the academic year, resulting in net tuition of $9,877 to $8,677.

FINANCIAL AID PICTURE (2005-2006)
Students with need: Out of 2,178 full-time freshmen who applied for aid, 1,466 were judged to have need. Of these, 1,455 received aid, and 518 had their full need met. Average financial aid package met 78% of need; average scholarship/grant was $3,056; average loan was $2,790. For part-time students, average financial aid package was $15,105.
Students without need: 1,140 full-time freshmen who did not demonstrate need for aid received scholarships/grants; average award was $10,901. No-need awards available for academics, art, athletics, leadership, minority status, music/drama, state/district residency.
Scholarships offered: *Merit:* Ohio Resident Scholarship and Ohio Leader Scholarship; added together, amounts range from $10,000 to $11,250 depending on need; all full-time students who are Ohio residents are eligible.
Athletic: 76 full-time freshmen received athletic scholarships; average amount $15,567.
Cumulative student debt: 48% of graduating class had student loans; average debt was $21,522.

FINANCIAL AID PROCEDURES
Forms required: FAFSA.
Dates and Deadlines: Priority date 2/15; no closing date. Applicants notified on a rolling basis starting 3/31; must reply by 5/1 or within 3 week(s) of notification.
Transfers: Institutional merit scholarships not available to transfer students during first year of enrollment.

CONTACT
Chuck Knepfle, Director of Student Financial Aid
301 South Campus Avenue, Oxford, OH 45056-3434
(513) 529-8734

Mount Carmel College of Nursing
Columbus, Ohio
www.mccn.edu   Federal Code: 030719

4-year private nursing college in very large city.
Enrollment: 582 undergrads, 18% part-time. 58 full-time freshmen.
Selectivity: Admits 50 to 75% of applicants.

BASIC COSTS (2005-2006)
Tuition and fees: $6,052.
Per-credit charge: $278.

FINANCIAL AID PICTURE (2005-2006)
Students with need: 35% of average financial aid package awarded as scholarships/grants, 65% awarded as loans/jobs.

FINANCIAL AID PROCEDURES
Forms required: FAFSA, institutional form.
Dates and Deadlines: Priority date 4/1; no closing date. Applicants notified on a rolling basis.

CONTACT
Carol Graham, Financial Aid Director
127 South Davis Avenue, Columbus, OH 43222-1589
(614) 234-5800

Mount Union College
Alliance, Ohio
www.muc.edu   Federal Code: 003083

4-year private liberal arts college in large town, affiliated with United Methodist Church.
Enrollment: 2,005 undergrads, 1% part-time. 554 full-time freshmen.
Selectivity: Admits over 75% of applicants.

BASIC COSTS (2005-2006)
Tuition and fees: $19,850.
Per-credit charge: $820.
Room and board: $5,990.
Additional info: Tuition/fee waivers available for minority students.

FINANCIAL AID PICTURE (2004-2005)
Students with need: Out of 496 full-time freshmen who applied for aid, 451 were judged to have need. Of these, 451 received aid, and 100 had their full need met. Average financial aid package met 78% of need; average scholarship/grant was $11,041; average loan was $4,104. For part-time students, average financial aid package was $16,076.
Students without need: 95 full-time freshmen who did not demonstrate need for aid received scholarships/grants; average award was $8,405. No-need awards available for academics, alumni affiliation, art, job skills, leadership, music/drama, religious affiliation, ROTC, state/district residency.
Cumulative student debt: 88% of graduating class had student loans; average debt was $17,582.

FINANCIAL AID PROCEDURES
Forms required: FAFSA, institutional form.
Dates and Deadlines: Priority date 4/1; no closing date. Applicants notified on a rolling basis starting 3/15; must reply within 4 week(s) of notification.

CONTACT
Sandra Pittenger, Director of Student Financial Services
1972 Clark Avenue, Alliance, OH 44601-3993
(330) 823-2674

Mount Vernon Nazarene University
Mount Vernon, Ohio
www.mvnu.edu   Federal Code: 007085

4-year private university in large town, affiliated with Church of the Nazarene.
Enrollment: 2,037 undergrads, 6% part-time. 380 full-time freshmen.
Selectivity: Admits over 75% of applicants.

BASIC COSTS (2006-2007)
Tuition and fees: $16,876.
Per-credit charge: $579.
Room and board: $5,090.

FINANCIAL AID PICTURE (2005-2006)
Students with need: Out of 380 full-time freshmen who applied for aid, 319 were judged to have need. Of these, 319 received aid, and 55 had their full need met. Average financial aid package met 78% of need; average scholarship/grant was $7,600; average loan was $3,228. For part-time students, average financial aid package was $4,303.
Students without need: 40 full-time freshmen who did not demonstrate need for aid received scholarships/grants; average award was $3,136. No-need awards available for academics, athletics, leadership, minority status, music/drama, religious affiliation, state/district residency.
Scholarships offered: *Merit:* Hugh C. Benner Excellence Scholarship; $4,000 per year. Hugh C. Benner Memorial Scholarship; $3,250 per year. Hugh C. Benner Scholarship; $2,500 per year. Distinction Scholarship; $2,000 per year. Honor Scholarship; $1,500 per year. All based on ACT or SAT scores and require a minimum GPA to be maintained. Rank Scholarship; $1,250 per year; based on ACT or SAT scores and high school GPA or class rank, require maintenance of minimum GPA. Valedictorian/Salutatorian Scholarship; $500 per year; require maintenance of minimum GPA. Top Ten Scholarship; $1,000 per year; must rank in top ten of class at MVNU. *Athletic:* 13 full-time freshmen received athletic scholarships; average amount $2,140.
Cumulative student debt: 79% of graduating class had student loans; average debt was $20,293.

FINANCIAL AID PROCEDURES
Forms required: FAFSA, institutional form.
Dates and Deadlines: Priority date 3/15; no closing date. Applicants notified on a rolling basis starting 2/15; must reply within 2 week(s) of notification.
Transfers: No deadline. Applicants notified on a rolling basis starting 9/1. Filing deadline for Ohio financial aid is October 1st.

CONTACT
Steve Tracht, Director of Student Financial Planning
800 Martinsburg Road, Mount Vernon, OH 43050
(740) 392-6868 ext. 4520

Muskingum College
New Concord, Ohio
www.muskingum.edu   Federal Code: 003084

4-year private liberal arts college in small town, affiliated with Presbyterian Church (USA).
Enrollment: 1,639 undergrads, 4% part-time. 434 full-time freshmen.
Selectivity: Admits over 75% of applicants.

BASIC COSTS (2006-2007)
Tuition and fees: $17,195.
Per-credit charge: $345.
Room and board: $6,740.
Additional info: Tuition/fee waivers available for minority students.

FINANCIAL AID PICTURE (2005-2006)
Students with need: 73% of average financial aid package awarded as scholarships/grants, 27% awarded as loans/jobs. Need-based aid available for part-time students.
Students without need: No-need awards available for academics, alumni affiliation, art, minority status, music/drama, religious affiliation, state/district residency.
Additional info: Scholarship priority date 02/01.

FINANCIAL AID PROCEDURES
Forms required: FAFSA, institutional form.
Dates and Deadlines: Priority date 3/15; closing date 8/1. Applicants notified on a rolling basis starting 3/1; must reply by 5/1 or within 2 week(s) of notification.

CONTACT
Jeff Zellers, Director of Student Financial Services
163 Stormont Street, New Concord, OH 43762-1160
(740) 826-8139

Oberlin College
Oberlin, Ohio
www.oberlin.edu
Federal Code: 003086
CSS Code: 1587

4-year private music and liberal arts college in small town.
Enrollment: 2,845 undergrads, 3% part-time. 741 full-time freshmen.
Selectivity: Admits less than 50% of applicants.

BASIC COSTS (2006-2007)
Tuition and fees: $34,426.
Per-credit charge: $1,360.
Room and board: $8,720.

FINANCIAL AID PICTURE (2005-2006)
Students with need: Out of 491 full-time freshmen who applied for aid, 411 were judged to have need. Of these, 411 received aid, and 411 had their full need met. Average financial aid package met 100% of need; average scholarship/grant was $17,202; average loan was $3,890. For part-time students, average financial aid package was $23,147.
Students without need: 104 full-time freshmen who did not demonstrate need for aid received scholarships/grants; average award was $12,461. No-need awards available for academics, leadership, music/drama, state/district residency.
Scholarships offered: Bonner Scholarship; based on community service. John Frederick Oberlin Scholarship; based on academic merit. Stern Scholarship; based on excellence in sciences. Mary Elizabeth Johnston Scholarship; based on academic merit; available to Ohio residents only. Dean's Scholarship; available to Conservatory of Music students.
Cumulative student debt: 60% of graduating class had student loans; average debt was $16,900.

FINANCIAL AID PROCEDURES
Forms required: FAFSA, CSS PROFILE, institutional form.
Dates and Deadlines: Closing date 1/15. Applicants notified by 4/1; must reply by 5/1 or within 2 week(s) of notification.
Transfers: Closing date 3/1. Limited scholarship funding available for transfer students.

CONTACT
Robert Reddy, Director of Financial Aid
Carnegie Building, 101 North Professor Street, Oberlin, OH 44074
(440) 775-8142

Ohio Business College: Sandusky
Sandusky, Ohio
www.ohiobusinesscollege.edu
Federal Code: 021585

2-year for-profit business college in small city.
Enrollment: 260 undergrads.
Selectivity: Open admission.

BASIC COSTS (2005-2006)
Tuition and fees: $8,685.
Per-credit charge: $183.

FINANCIAL AID PICTURE
Students with need: Need-based aid available for full-time and part-time students.

FINANCIAL AID PROCEDURES
Forms required: FAFSA.
Dates and Deadlines: No deadline.

CONTACT
Gerilyn Lehmann, Financial Aid Administrator
4020 Milan Road, Sandusky, OH 44870
(419) 627-8345 ext. 14

Ohio Dominican University
Columbus, Ohio
www.ohiodominican.edu
Federal Code: 003035

4-year private university and liberal arts college in very large city, affiliated with Roman Catholic Church.
Enrollment: 2,185 undergrads, 26% part-time. 372 full-time freshmen.
Selectivity: Admits 50 to 75% of applicants.

BASIC COSTS (2006-2007)
Tuition and fees: $20,570.
Per-credit charge: $425.
Room and board: $6,800.

FINANCIAL AID PICTURE
Students with need: Need-based aid available for full-time and part-time students. Work study available nights, weekends, and for part-time students.
Students without need: No-need awards available for academics, athletics, state/district residency.

FINANCIAL AID PROCEDURES
Forms required: FAFSA.
Dates and Deadlines: Priority date 4/1; no closing date. Applicants notified on a rolling basis starting 3/1; must reply within 2 week(s) of notification.

CONTACT
Cindy Hahn, Director of Financial Aid
1216 Sunbury Road, Columbus, OH 43219
(614) 251-4640

Ohio Institute of Photography and Technology
Dayton, Ohio
www.oipt.com
Federal Code: 013562

2-year for-profit technical college in small city.
Enrollment: 658 undergrads. 138 full-time freshmen.
Selectivity: Open admission; but selective for some programs.

Ohio Institute of Photography and Technology

BASIC COSTS (2006-2007)
Tuition and fees: $18,889.
Per-credit charge: $333.
Additional info: Tuition listed reflects the Photographic Techonology program. Tuition varies by program.

FINANCIAL AID PICTURE
Students with need: Need-based aid available for full-time and part-time students.

FINANCIAL AID PROCEDURES
Forms required: FAFSA, institutional form.
Dates and Deadlines: No deadline. Applicants notified on a rolling basis starting 3/1.

CONTACT
Director of Financial Aid
2029 Edgefield Road, Dayton, OH 45439
(937) 294-6155

Ohio Northern University
Ada, Ohio
www.onu.edu   Federal Code: 003089

4-year private university in small town, affiliated with United Methodist Church.
Enrollment: 2,541 undergrads, 1% part-time. 809 full-time freshmen.
Selectivity: Admits over 75% of applicants.

BASIC COSTS (2005-2006)
Tuition and fees: $27,045.
Per-credit charge: $745.
Room and board: $6,720.
Additional info: Tuition and fees for engineering $28,680; pharmacy $30,180. Tuition/fee waivers available for minority students.

FINANCIAL AID PICTURE (2005-2006)
Students with need: Average financial aid package met 96% of need; average scholarship/grant was $13,681; average loan was $3,991. Need-based aid available for part-time students.
Students without need: No-need awards available for academics, alumni affiliation, art, leadership, music/drama, ROTC, state/district residency.
Scholarships offered: Presidential Scholarship; up to $25,000; minimum 3.5 GPA, 30 ACT or 1320 SAT, and on-campus competition. Trustees Scholarship; up to $22,000; minimum 3.5 GPA, 28 ACT or 1240 SAT, and on-campus competition. Academic Honors Scholarship; up to $20,000; minimum 3.3 GPA, 26 ACT or 1170 SAT, and on-campus competition. Distinguished Achievement Scholarship; up to $16,000; minimum 3.2 GPA, 24 ACT or 1090 SAT, on-campus competition, and leadership activities. Deans Scholarship; $6,000 to $12,000; minimum 3.3 GPA and 25 ACT or 1130 SAT. Criteria listed is for the Colleges of Arts & Sciences, Business Administration and Engineering. The College of Pharmacy has slightly higher credentials. SAT scores exclusive of Writing.
Cumulative student debt: 79% of graduating class had student loans; average debt was $20,740.

FINANCIAL AID PROCEDURES
Forms required: FAFSA, institutional form.
Dates and Deadlines: Priority date 4/15; closing date 6/1. Applicants notified on a rolling basis starting 2/15; must reply within 2 week(s) of notification.

CONTACT
Craig Sneider, Director of Financial Aid
525 South Main Street, Ada, OH 45810-1599
(419) 772-2272

Ohio State University Agricultural Technical Institute
Wooster, Ohio
www.ati.osu.edu   Federal Code: 003090

2-year public agricultural college in large town.
Enrollment: 821 undergrads, 12% part-time. 356 full-time freshmen.
Selectivity: Open admission; but selective for out-of-state students.

BASIC COSTS (2005-2006)
Tuition and fees: $5,478; out-of-state residents $16,701.
Additional info: $900 optional meal plan.

FINANCIAL AID PICTURE (2005-2006)
Students with need: Out of 317 full-time freshmen who applied for aid, 266 were judged to have need. Of these, 227 received aid, and 19 had their full need met. Average financial aid package met 55% of need; average scholarship/grant was $1,884. Need-based aid available for part-time students.
Students without need: This college only awards aid to students with need.

FINANCIAL AID PROCEDURES
Forms required: FAFSA.
Dates and Deadlines: Priority date 3/1; no closing date. Applicants notified on a rolling basis starting 5/1; must reply within 4 week(s) of notification.
Transfers: Priority date 1/1; closing date 3/1.

CONTACT
Barbara LaMoreaux, Coordinator, Financial Aid
1328 Dover Road, Wooster, OH 44691

Ohio State University: Columbus Campus
Columbus, Ohio
www.osu.edu   Federal Code: 003090

4-year public university in very large city.
Enrollment: 36,029 undergrads, 7% part-time. 5,940 full-time freshmen.
Selectivity: Admits 50 to 75% of applicants.

BASIC COSTS (2005-2006)
Tuition and fees: $8,082; out-of-state residents $19,305.
Room and board: $7,770.

FINANCIAL AID PICTURE (2004-2005)
Students with need: Out of 4,783 full-time freshmen who applied for aid, 3,264 were judged to have need. Of these, 3,262 received aid, and 976 had their full need met. Average financial aid package met 71.6% of need; average scholarship/grant was $7,095; average loan was $2,761. For part-time students, average financial aid package was $7,933.
Students without need: 1,744 full-time freshmen who did not demonstrate need for aid received scholarships/grants; average award was $3,645. No-need awards available for academics, alumni affiliation, art, athletics, job skills, leadership, minority status, music/drama, ROTC, state/district residency.
Scholarships offered: 70 full-time freshmen received athletic scholarships; average amount $17,549.
Cumulative student debt: 58% of graduating class had student loans; average debt was $17,821.

FINANCIAL AID PROCEDURES
Forms required: FAFSA.
Dates and Deadlines: Priority date 3/1; no closing date. Applicants notified by 4/5; must reply by 5/1 or within 4 week(s) of notification.

CONTACT
Natala Hart, Director of Office of Student Financial Aid
110 Enarson Hall, Columbus, OH 43210
(614) 292-0300

Ohio State University: Lima Campus
Lima, Ohio
www.lima.ohio-state.edu   Federal Code: 003090

4-year public branch campus college in large town.
Enrollment: 965 undergrads, 13% part-time. 269 full-time freshmen.
Selectivity: Open admission; but selective for out-of-state students.

BASIC COSTS (2005-2006)
Tuition and fees: $5,310; out-of-state residents $16,533.

FINANCIAL AID PICTURE (2005-2006)
Students with need: Out of 222 full-time freshmen who applied for aid, 165 were judged to have need. Of these, 165 received aid, and 16 had their full need met. Average financial aid package met 52% of need; average scholarship/grant was $3,156; average loan was $2,700. For part-time students, average financial aid package was $7,136.
Students without need: 19 full-time freshmen who did not demonstrate need for aid received scholarships/grants; average award was $978. No-need awards available for academics.

FINANCIAL AID PROCEDURES
Forms required: FAFSA.
Dates and Deadlines: Priority date 3/1; no closing date. Applicants notified on a rolling basis starting 5/1; must reply within 4 week(s) of notification.

CONTACT
Diane Douglass, Director for Financial Aid
4240 Campus Drive, Lima, OH 45804-3596
(419) 995-8299

Ohio State University: Mansfield Campus
Mansfield, Ohio
www.mansfield.ohio-state.edu   Federal Code: 003090

4-year public branch campus college in small city.
Enrollment: 1,209 undergrads, 20% part-time. 419 full-time freshmen.
Selectivity: Open admission; but selective for out-of-state students.

BASIC COSTS (2005-2006)
Tuition and fees: $5,310; out-of-state residents $16,533.

FINANCIAL AID PICTURE (2005-2006)
Students with need: Out of 325 full-time freshmen who applied for aid, 254 were judged to have need. Of these, 253 received aid, and 30 had their full need met. Average financial aid package met 54% of need; average scholarship/grant was $3,891; average loan was $2,725. For part-time students, average financial aid package was $7,734.
Students without need: 45 full-time freshmen who did not demonstrate need for aid received scholarships/grants; average award was $1,871. No-need awards available for academics.

FINANCIAL AID PROCEDURES
Forms required: FAFSA.
Dates and Deadlines: Priority date 3/1; no closing date. Applicants notified on a rolling basis starting 5/1; must reply within 4 week(s) of notification.

CONTACT
Eva Eichinger, Coordinator of Admissions and Financial Aid
1680 University Drive, Mansfield, OH 44906
(419) 755-4011

Ohio State University: Marion Campus
Marion, Ohio
www.marion.ohio-state.edu   Federal Code: 003090

4-year public branch campus college in large town.
Enrollment: 1,299 undergrads, 14% part-time. 396 full-time freshmen.
Selectivity: Open admission; but selective for out-of-state students.

BASIC COSTS (2005-2006)
Tuition and fees: $5,310; out-of-state residents $16,533.

FINANCIAL AID PICTURE (2005-2006)
Students with need: Out of 308 full-time freshmen who applied for aid, 251 were judged to have need. Of these, 250 received aid, and 38 had their full need met. Average financial aid package met 59% of need; average scholarship/grant was $3,583; average loan was $2,963. For part-time students, average financial aid package was $7,651.
Students without need: 43 full-time freshmen who did not demonstrate need for aid received scholarships/grants; average award was $2,057. No-need awards available for academics.

FINANCIAL AID PROCEDURES
Forms required: FAFSA.
Dates and Deadlines: Priority date 3/1; no closing date. Applicants notified on a rolling basis starting 5/1; must reply within 4 week(s) of notification.

CONTACT
Michael Short, Coordinator of Financial Aid
1465 Mount Vernon Avenue, Marion, OH 43302
(740) 389-6786 ext. 6273

Ohio State University: Newark Campus
Newark, Ohio
www.newark.osu.edu   Federal Code: 003095

4-year public branch campus college in large town.
Enrollment: 1,952 undergrads, 13% part-time. 747 full-time freshmen.
Selectivity: Open admission; but selective for out-of-state students.

BASIC COSTS (2005-2006)
Tuition and fees: $5,310; out-of-state residents $16,533.

FINANCIAL AID PICTURE (2005-2006)
Students with need: Out of 596 full-time freshmen who applied for aid, 429 were judged to have need. Of these, 428 received aid, and 40 had their full need met. Average financial aid package met 50% of need; average scholarship/grant was $3,650; average loan was $2,766. For part-time students, average financial aid package was $5,953.
Students without need: 11 full-time freshmen who did not demonstrate need for aid received scholarships/grants; average award was $2,895. No-need awards available for academics.

FINANCIAL AID PROCEDURES
Forms required: FAFSA.
Dates and Deadlines: Priority date 3/1; no closing date. Applicants notified on a rolling basis starting 5/1; must reply within 4 week(s) of notification.

CONTACT
Faith Phillips, Director of Financial Aid
1179 University Drive, Newark, OH 43055
(740) 366-9435

Ohio University
Athens, Ohio
www.ohio.edu   Federal Code: 003100

4-year public university in large town.
Enrollment: 17,042 undergrads, 6% part-time. 4,140 full-time freshmen.
Selectivity: Admits over 75% of applicants.

BASIC COSTS (2005-2006)
Tuition and fees: $8,235; out-of-state residents $17,199.
Per-credit charge: $213; out-of-state residents $508.
Room and board: $8,745.

FINANCIAL AID PICTURE (2005-2006)
Students with need: Out of 3,589 full-time freshmen who applied for aid, 2,187 were judged to have need. Of these, 2,141 received aid, and 356 had their full need met. Average financial aid package met 48% of need; average scholarship/grant was $4,046; average loan was $2,658. For part-time students, average financial aid package was $6,583.
Students without need: 779 full-time freshmen who did not demonstrate need for aid received scholarships/grants; average award was $3,007. No-need awards available for academics, art, athletics, minority status, music/drama, religious affiliation, ROTC.
Scholarships offered: 86 full-time freshmen received athletic scholarships; average amount $13,074.
Cumulative student debt: 62% of graduating class had student loans; average debt was $18,101.

FINANCIAL AID PROCEDURES
Forms required: FAFSA.
Dates and Deadlines: Priority date 3/15; closing date 4/1. Applicants notified on a rolling basis starting 4/1; must reply within 3 week(s) of notification.

CONTACT
Sondra Williams, Director, Student Financial Aid and Scholarships
120 Chubb Hall, Athens, OH 45701-2979
(740) 593-4141

Ohio University: Chillicothe Campus
Chillicothe, Ohio
http://oucweb.chillicothe.ohiou.edu   Federal Code: 003102

4-year public branch campus college in large town.
Enrollment: 1,692 undergrads.
Selectivity: Open admission; but selective for some programs.

BASIC COSTS (2005-2006)
Tuition and fees: $4,323; out-of-state residents $8,646.
Per-credit charge: $115; out-of-state residents $246.

FINANCIAL AID PICTURE
Students with need: Need-based aid available for full-time and part-time students.

FINANCIAL AID PROCEDURES
Forms required: FAFSA.
Dates and Deadlines: No deadline. Applicants notified on a rolling basis.

CONTACT
Dennis Bothel, Coordinator of Academic Advising
101 University Drive, PO Box 629, Chillicothe, OH 45601
(740) 774-7228

Ohio University: Eastern Campus
St. Clairsville, Ohio
www.eastern.ohiou.edu   Federal Code: 003101

4-year public branch campus college in small town.
Enrollment: 777 undergrads.
Selectivity: Open admission; but selective for some programs.

BASIC COSTS (2005-2006)
Tuition and fees: $4,323; out-of-state residents $8,646.
Per-credit charge: $115; out-of-state residents $246.

FINANCIAL AID PICTURE (2004-2005)
Students with need: 46% of average financial aid package awarded as scholarships/grants, 54% awarded as loans/jobs. Need-based aid available for part-time students.
Students without need: No-need awards available for academics, alumni affiliation, minority status.

FINANCIAL AID PROCEDURES
Forms required: FAFSA.
Dates and Deadlines: Priority date 3/15; no closing date. Applicants notified by 5/15.
Transfers: Priority date 3/1; closing date 5/1.

CONTACT
Kevin Chenoweth, Student Services Manager
45425 National Road West, St. Clairsville, OH 43950
(740) 695-1720 ext. 209

Ohio University: Lancaster Campus
Lancaster, Ohio
www.lancaster.ohiou.edu   Federal Code: 003104

4-year public branch campus college in large town.
Enrollment: 1,705 undergrads.
Selectivity: Open admission; but selective for some programs.

BASIC COSTS (2005-2006)
Tuition and fees: $4,323; out-of-state residents $8,646.
Per-credit charge: $115; out-of-state residents $246.

FINANCIAL AID PICTURE
Students with need: Need-based aid available for full-time and part-time students.
Additional info: Scholarship application deadline April 1.

FINANCIAL AID PROCEDURES
Forms required: FAFSA.
Dates and Deadlines: Priority date 2/15; no closing date. Applicants notified on a rolling basis; must reply within 2 week(s) of notification.

CONTACT
Pat Fox, Coordinator, Financial Aid
1570 Granville Pike, Lancaster, OH 43130
(740) 654-6711 ext. 209

Ohio University: Southern Campus at Ironton
Ironton, Ohio
www.southern.ohiou.edu   Federal Code: 003100

4-year public branch campus college in large town.
Enrollment: 2,000 undergrads.
Selectivity: Open admission.

BASIC COSTS (2005-2006)
Tuition and fees: $4,146; out-of-state residents $5,868.
Per-credit charge: $114; out-of-state residents $165.

FINANCIAL AID PICTURE
Students with need: Need-based aid available for full-time and part-time students.

FINANCIAL AID PROCEDURES
Forms required: FAFSA.
Dates and Deadlines: No deadline. Applicants notified on a rolling basis.

CONTACT
Jackie Lundy, Chief Financial Aid Officer
1804 Liberty Avenue, Ironton, OH 45638
(740) 533-4600

Ohio Valley College of Technology
East Liverpool, Ohio
www.ovct.edu   Federal Code: 016261

2-year for-profit business and technical college in large town.
Enrollment: 174 undergrads.

BASIC COSTS (2006-2007)
Tuition and fees: $7,490.

FINANCIAL AID PICTURE
Students with need: Need-based aid available for full-time and part-time students.
Students without need: This college only awards aid to students with need.

FINANCIAL AID PROCEDURES
Forms required: FAFSA.
Dates and Deadlines: No deadline. Applicants notified on a rolling basis; must reply within 6 week(s) of notification.

CONTACT
Virginia Hutchison, Financial Aid Officer
16808 St. Clair Avenue, PO Box 7000, East Liverpool, OH 43920

Ohio Wesleyan University
Delaware, Ohio
http://web.owu.edu   Federal Code: 003109

4-year private liberal arts college in large town, affiliated with United Methodist Church.
Enrollment: 1,956 undergrads, 1% part-time. 597 full-time freshmen.
Selectivity: Admits 50 to 75% of applicants.

BASIC COSTS (2006-2007)
Tuition and fees: $30,290.
Room and board: $7,790.

FINANCIAL AID PICTURE (2005-2006)
Students with need: Out of 420 full-time freshmen who applied for aid, 351 were judged to have need. Of these, 351 received aid, and 105 had their full need met. Average financial aid package met 85% of need; average scholarship/grant was $15,595; average loan was $3,245. For part-time students, average financial aid package was $3,142.
Students without need: 238 full-time freshmen who did not demonstrate need for aid received scholarships/grants; average award was $11,747. No-need awards available for academics, alumni affiliation, art, leadership, minority status, music/drama, religious affiliation, state/district residency.
Scholarships offered: Presidential scholarships; full tuition; 25 awarded. Trustee scholarships; 75% of tuition; 40 awarded. Faculty scholarships; 50% of tuition; 140 awarded.
Cumulative student debt: 60% of graduating class had student loans; average debt was $22,619.

FINANCIAL AID PROCEDURES
Forms required: FAFSA, institutional form.
Dates and Deadlines: Priority date 3/1; closing date 5/1. Applicants notified on a rolling basis starting 2/15; must reply by 5/1 or within 2 week(s) of notification.
Transfers: Must reply within 2 week(s) of notification.

CONTACT
Greg Matthews, Assistant Vice President of Admission and Financial Aid
75 South Sandusky Street, Delaware, OH 43015-2398
(740) 368-3050

Otterbein College
Westerville, Ohio
www.otterbein.edu   Federal Code: 003110
                           CSS Code: 1597

4-year private liberal arts college in large town, affiliated with United Methodist Church.
Enrollment: 2,724 undergrads, 17% part-time. 630 full-time freshmen.
Selectivity: Admits less than 50% of applicants.

BASIC COSTS (2006-2007)
Tuition and fees: $23,871.
Per-credit charge: $285.
Room and board: $6,789.
Additional info: Tuition/fee waivers available for adults, minority students.

FINANCIAL AID PICTURE
Students with need: Work study available nights, weekends, and for part-time students.
Students without need: No-need awards available for academics, alumni affiliation, art, leadership, minority status, music/drama, state/district residency.

FINANCIAL AID PROCEDURES
Forms required: FAFSA, CSS PROFILE.
Dates and Deadlines: Priority date 4/1; no closing date. Applicants notified on a rolling basis starting 2/15; must reply by 5/1.
Transfers: Transfer students must complete appropriate state grant transfer paperwork.

CONTACT
Thomas Yarnell, Director of Financial Aid
One Otterbein College, Westerville, OH 43081
(614) 823-1502

Owens Community College: Toledo
Toledo, Ohio
www.owens.edu   Federal Code: 005753

2-year public community college in large city.
Enrollment: 8,485 undergrads, 51% part-time. 1,394 full-time freshmen.
Selectivity: Open admission; but selective for some programs.

BASIC COSTS (2005-2006)
Tuition and fees: $2,784; out-of-state residents $5,208.
Per-credit charge: $116; out-of-state residents $217.

FINANCIAL AID PICTURE (2004-2005)
Students with need: Out of 1,361 full-time freshmen who applied for aid, 1,058 were judged to have need. Of these, 1,049 received aid, and 28 had their full need met. Average financial aid package met 51% of need; average scholarship/grant was $1,869; average loan was $2,218. For part-time students, average financial aid package was $4,417.
Students without need: 5 full-time freshmen who did not demonstrate need for aid received scholarships/grants; average award was $900. No-need awards available for academics, alumni affiliation, athletics, leadership, state/district residency.
Scholarships offered: 15 full-time freshmen received athletic scholarships; average amount $3,258.
Cumulative student debt: 48% of graduating class had student loans; average debt was $10,788.
Additional info: Other types of financial aid available: federal family education loan program, private foundation loan (SCHELL).

FINANCIAL AID PROCEDURES
Forms required: FAFSA.
Dates and Deadlines: Priority date 3/31; no closing date. Applicants notified by 2/7.

CONTACT
Betsy Johnson, Director of Financial Aid
PO Box 10000, Toledo, OH 43699-1947
(567) 661-7343

Pontifical College Josephinum
Columbus, Ohio
www.pcj.edu   Federal Code: 003113

4-year private liberal arts and seminary college for men in very large city, affiliated with Roman Catholic Church.
Enrollment: 76 undergrads. 11 full-time freshmen.
Selectivity: Admits over 75% of applicants.

BASIC COSTS (2005-2006)
Tuition and fees: $14,635.
Per-credit charge: $635.
Room and board: $7,000.

FINANCIAL AID PICTURE (2004-2005)
Students with need: Out of 9 full-time freshmen who applied for aid, 4 were judged to have need. Of these, 4 received aid. Average financial aid package met 82% of need; average scholarship/grant was $1,000; average loan was $2,625. Need-based aid available for part-time students.
Students without need: This college only awards aid to students with need.
Cumulative student debt: 10% of graduating class had student loans; average debt was $15,417.

FINANCIAL AID PROCEDURES
Forms required: FAFSA, institutional form.
Dates and Deadlines: Priority date 9/2; no closing date. Applicants notified on a rolling basis starting 8/15; must reply within 2 week(s) of notification.

CONTACT
Marky Leichtnam, Director of Financial Aid
7625 North High Street, Columbus, OH 43235-1499
(614) 985-2212

Remington College: Cleveland
Cleveland, Ohio
www.remingtoncollege.edu   Federal Code: 007777

2-year for-profit technical college in very large city.
Enrollment: 682 undergrads.

BASIC COSTS (2006-2007)
Additional info: Costs for full 24-month Associate Degree program $31,490; includes tuition, fees, books and supplies, laptop computer. Cost of 8-month Diploma program $11,730.

FINANCIAL AID PICTURE
Students with need: Need-based aid available for full-time students. Work study available nights.
Students without need: This college only awards aid to students with need.

FINANCIAL AID PROCEDURES
Forms required: FAFSA.
Dates and Deadlines: No deadline.

CONTACT
Christine Todd, Director of Financial Services
14445 Broadway Avenue, Cleveland, OH 44125
(216) 475-7520

Shawnee State University
Portsmouth, Ohio
www.shawnee.edu   Federal Code: 009942

4-year public university in large town.
Enrollment: 3,017 undergrads, 14% part-time. 498 full-time freshmen.
Selectivity: Open admission; but selective for some programs.

BASIC COSTS (2005-2006)
Tuition and fees: $5,508; out-of-state residents $9,396.
Per-credit charge: $153; out-of-state residents $261.
Room and board: $6,729.

FINANCIAL AID PICTURE
Students with need: Need-based aid available for full-time and part-time students.
Students without need: No-need awards available for academics.
Additional info: ACT recommended for scholarship applicants.

FINANCIAL AID PROCEDURES
Forms required: FAFSA, institutional form.
Dates and Deadlines: Priority date 6/15; no closing date. Applicants notified on a rolling basis starting 5/1; must reply within 4 week(s) of notification.

CONTACT
Barbara Bradbury, Financial Aid Director
940 Second Street, Portsmouth, OH 45662
(740) 351-4243

Sinclair Community College
Dayton, Ohio
www.sinclair.edu   Federal Code: 003119

2-year public community college in small city.
Enrollment: 15,215 undergrads, 55% part-time. 1,435 full-time freshmen.
Selectivity: Open admission; but selective for some programs.

BASIC COSTS (2005-2006)
Tuition and fees: $1,910; out-of-district residents $3,121; out-of-state residents $5,940.
Per-credit charge: $42; out-of-district residents $69; out-of-state residents $132.

FINANCIAL AID PICTURE (2005-2006)
Students with need: Need-based aid available for part-time students.
Students without need: No-need awards available for academics, athletics, state/district residency.

FINANCIAL AID PROCEDURES
Forms required: FAFSA, institutional form.
Dates and Deadlines: Priority date 5/1; closing date 8/1. Applicants notified on a rolling basis.
Transfers: No deadline.

CONTACT
Kathy Wiesenauer, Director of Financial Aid and Scholarships
444 West Third Street, Dayton, OH 45402-1460
(937) 512-3000

Southeastern Business College
Chillicothe, Ohio
www.careersohio.com   Federal Code: 020568

2-year for-profit business college in large town.
Enrollment: 96 undergrads, 25% part-time. 17 full-time freshmen.
Selectivity: Open admission.

BASIC COSTS (2005-2006)
Per-credit charge: $185.
Additional info: Per-credit-hour cost is $185, plus $300 annual technology fee.

FINANCIAL AID PICTURE
Students with need: Need-based aid available for full-time and part-time students.
Students without need: This college only awards aid to students with need.
Scholarships offered: Ohio Legislative Scholarship, administered by the Ohio Council of Private Colleges and Schools, for Ohio-resident high school seniors nominated by their state representative who reviews applications; 2-year tuition for associate degree valued at $11,500.

FINANCIAL AID PROCEDURES
Forms required: FAFSA, institutional form.
Transfers: No deadline.

CONTACT
Connie Pruitt, Financial Aid Coordinator
1855 Western Avenue, Chillicothe, OH 45601-1038
(740) 774-2063

Southeastern Business College: Jackson
Jackson, Ohio
www.southeasternbusinesscollege.com

2-year for-profit business college in large town.
Enrollment: 72 undergrads, 24% part-time. 46 full-time freshmen.
Selectivity: Open admission.

BASIC COSTS (2006-2007)
Tuition and fees: $8,625.
Per-credit charge: $185.
Additional info: Per-credit-hour cost is $185 plus $300 annual technology fee.

FINANCIAL AID PICTURE
Students with need: Need-based aid available for full-time and part-time students. Work study available nights.
Students without need: This college only awards aid to students with need.

FINANCIAL AID PROCEDURES
Forms required: FAFSA, institutional form.
Dates and Deadlines: No deadline. Applicants notified on a rolling basis.

CONTACT
Financial Aid Officer
504 McCarty Lane, Jackson, OH 45640
(740) 286-1554

Southeastern Business College: Lancaster
Lancaster, Ohio
www.careersohio.com   Federal Code: 020568

2-year for-profit business and technical college in large town.
Enrollment: 71 undergrads.
Selectivity: Open admission.

BASIC COSTS (2006-2007)
Tuition and fees: $9,380.
Per-credit charge: $185.

FINANCIAL AID PICTURE
Students with need: Need-based aid available for full-time and part-time students. Work study available nights.
Students without need: This college only awards aid to students with need.

FINANCIAL AID PROCEDURES
Forms required: FAFSA, institutional form.
Dates and Deadlines: Closing date 4/30. Applicants notified by 6/1; must reply within 2 week(s) of notification.

CONTACT
Ronda Valentine, Financial Aid Representative
1522 Sheridan Drive, Lancaster, OH 43130-1303
(740) 687-6126

Southeastern Business College: New Boston
New Boston, Ohio
www.southeasternbusinesscollege.com

2-year for-profit branch campus and business college in rural community.
Enrollment: 80 undergrads, 15% part-time. 14 full-time freshmen.
Selectivity: Open admission.

FINANCIAL AID PICTURE
Students with need: Need-based aid available for full-time and part-time students.

FINANCIAL AID PROCEDURES
Forms required: FAFSA.
Dates and Deadlines: No deadline.

CONTACT
Angie Gammon, Financial Aid Officer
3879 Rhodes Avenue, New Boston, OH 45662
(740) 456-4124

Southern State Community College
Hillsboro, Ohio
www.sscc.edu   Federal Code: 012870

2-year public community college in small town.
Enrollment: 2,311 undergrads, 44% part-time. 394 full-time freshmen.
Selectivity: Open admission; but selective for some programs.

BASIC COSTS (2005-2006)
Tuition and fees: $3,213; out-of-state residents $6,189.
Per-credit charge: $82; out-of-state residents $159.

FINANCIAL AID PICTURE (2004-2005)
Students with need: 59% of average financial aid package awarded as scholarships/grants, 41% awarded as loans/jobs. Need-based aid available for part-time students.
Students without need: No-need awards available for academics, art, athletics, music/drama.

FINANCIAL AID PROCEDURES
Forms required: FAFSA, institutional form.
Dates and Deadlines: Priority date 7/1; closing date 9/1. Applicants notified by 4/15; must reply within 2 week(s) of notification.
Transfers: No deadline.

CONTACT
Janeen Deatley, Financial Aid Director
100 Hobart Drive, Hillsboro, OH 45133
(937) 393-3431 ext. 2610

Southwestern College: Tri-County
Cincinnati, Ohio
www.swcollege.net   Federal Code: 012128

2-year for-profit business and nursing college in small city.
Enrollment: 220 undergrads.
Selectivity: Open admission.

BASIC COSTS (2005-2006)
Tuition and fees: $8,670.
Additional info: One time $100 registration fee for the first quarter.

FINANCIAL AID PICTURE
Students with need: Need-based aid available for full-time students.
Students without need: This college only awards aid to students with need.

FINANCIAL AID PROCEDURES
Forms required: FAFSA, state aid form.

CONTACT
Johnnye Powers, Financial Aid Director
149 Northland Boulevard, Cincinnati, OH 45246
(513) 874-0432

Stark State College of Technology
North Canton, Ohio
www.starkstate.edu   Federal Code: 011141

2-year public technical college in small city.
Enrollment: 4,235 undergrads, 64% part-time. 596 full-time freshmen.
Selectivity: Open admission; but selective for some programs.

BASIC COSTS (2005-2006)
Tuition and fees: $3,600; out-of-state residents $5,100.
Per-credit charge: $100; out-of-state residents $150.

FINANCIAL AID PICTURE (2005-2006)
Students with need: Out of 569 full-time freshmen who applied for aid, 480 were judged to have need. Of these, 457 received aid, and 296 had their full need met. Average financial aid package met 65% of need; average scholarship/grant was $1,055; average loan was $1,151. For part-time students, average financial aid package was $1,968.
Students without need: This college only awards aid to students with need.

FINANCIAL AID PROCEDURES
Forms required: FAFSA, institutional form.
Dates and Deadlines: Priority date 5/1; no closing date. Applicants notified on a rolling basis starting 4/1; must reply within 4 week(s) of notification.

CONTACT
Amy Baker, Director of Financial Aid
6200 Frank Avenue NW, North Canton, OH 44720
(334) 494-6170

Stautzenberger College
Toledo, Ohio
www.sctoday.edu   Federal Code: 004866

2-year for-profit business and technical college in large city.
Enrollment: 750 undergrads.
Selectivity: Open admission.

BASIC COSTS (2006-2007)
Tuition and fees: $4,795.
Per-credit charge: $155.
Additional info: Tuition ranges from $155 to $330 per-credit-hour depending on program.

FINANCIAL AID PICTURE
Students with need: Need-based aid available for full-time and part-time students.
Students without need: This college only awards aid to students with need.

FINANCIAL AID PROCEDURES
Forms required: FAFSA.
Dates and Deadlines: No deadline. Applicants notified on a rolling basis.

CONTACT
Mari Huffman, Financial Aid Officer
5355 Southwyck Boulevard, Toledo, OH 43614
(419) 866-0261

Technology Education College
Columbus, Ohio
www.teceducation.com   Federal Code: 011005

2-year for-profit technical college in very large city.
Enrollment: 500 undergrads.
Selectivity: Open admission.

BASIC COSTS (2005-2006)
Additional info: Tuition varies per program, but averages $9,300 per academic year.

FINANCIAL AID PICTURE
Students with need: Need-based aid available for full-time and part-time students.
Students without need: This college only awards aid to students with need.

FINANCIAL AID PROCEDURES
Forms required: FAFSA.
Dates and Deadlines: No deadline. Applicants notified on a rolling basis.
CONTACT
David Barron, Director of Financial Aid
2745 Winchester Pike, Columbus, OH 43232
(614) 759-7700

Tiffin University
Tiffin, Ohio
www.tiffin.edu   Federal Code: 003121

4-year private university and business college in large town.
Enrollment: 1,180 undergrads, 7% part-time. 282 full-time freshmen.
Selectivity: Admits 50 to 75% of applicants.
BASIC COSTS (2006-2007)
Tuition and fees: $15,870.
Per-credit charge: $529.
Room and board: $6,775.
FINANCIAL AID PICTURE (2005-2006)
Students with need: Out of 269 full-time freshmen who applied for aid, 242 were judged to have need. Of these, 242 received aid, and 46 had their full need met. Average financial aid package met 11% of need; average scholarship/grant was $4,397; average loan was $2,467. For part-time students, average financial aid package was $8,273.
Students without need: 26 full-time freshmen who did not demonstrate need for aid received scholarships/grants; average award was $7,199. No-need awards available for academics, alumni affiliation, athletics, leadership, music/drama, state/district residency.
Scholarships offered: 13 full-time freshmen received athletic scholarships; average amount $4,423.
Cumulative student debt: 82% of graduating class had student loans; average debt was $19,994.
FINANCIAL AID PROCEDURES
Forms required: FAFSA.
Dates and Deadlines: Priority date 1/1; no closing date. Applicants notified on a rolling basis starting 2/15; must reply within 2 week(s) of notification.
CONTACT
Tera Van Doran, Director of Financial Aid
155 Miami Street, Tiffin, OH 44883
(800) 968-6446 ext. 3279

Trumbull Business College
Warren, Ohio
www.tbc-trumbullbusiness.com   Federal Code: 013585

2-year for-profit business college in small town.
Enrollment: 415 undergrads.
Selectivity: Open admission.
BASIC COSTS (2005-2006)
Tuition and fees: $9,525.
Per-credit charge: $210.
FINANCIAL AID PICTURE
Students with need: Need-based aid available for full-time and part-time students.
FINANCIAL AID PROCEDURES
Forms required: FAFSA.

CONTACT
Florence Henning, Director of Financial Assistance
3200 Ridge Road, Warren, OH 44484
(330) 369-3200 ext. 12

Union Institute & University
Cincinnati, Ohio
www.tui.edu   Federal Code: 010923

4-year private university and liberal arts college in very large city.
Enrollment: 1,122 undergrads, 40% part-time. 30 full-time freshmen.
BASIC COSTS (2005-2006)
Tuition and fees: $11,120.
Per-credit charge: $368.
FINANCIAL AID PICTURE (2004-2005)
Students with need: 36% of average financial aid package awarded as scholarships/grants, 64% awarded as loans/jobs. Need-based aid available for part-time students.
Students without need: No-need awards available for academics, state/district residency.
FINANCIAL AID PROCEDURES
Forms required: FAFSA, institutional form.
Dates and Deadlines: No deadline. Must reply within 4 week(s) of notification.
CONTACT
Victoria Walker, Director of Financial Aid
440 East McMillan Street, Cincinnati, OH 45206-1925
(800) 486-3116

University of Akron
Akron, Ohio
www.uakron.edu   Federal Code: 003123

4-year public university in small city.
Enrollment: 16,288 undergrads, 24% part-time. 2,918 full-time freshmen.
Selectivity: Admits over 75% of applicants.
BASIC COSTS (2005-2006)
Tuition and fees: $7,958; out-of-state residents $16,682.
Room and board: $7,208.
FINANCIAL AID PICTURE (2005-2006)
Students with need: Out of 2,300 full-time freshmen who applied for aid, 1,847 were judged to have need. Of these, 1,847 received aid, and 98 had their full need met. Average financial aid package met 47% of need; average scholarship/grant was $4,513; average loan was $2,519. For part-time students, average financial aid package was $5,228.
Students without need: 216 full-time freshmen who did not demonstrate need for aid received scholarships/grants; average award was $3,238. No-need awards available for academics, art, athletics, leadership, minority status, music/drama, ROTC, state/district residency.
Scholarships offered: *Merit:* Scholarships for Excellence; $9,000 per year; 3.5 GPA, class rank top 10%, 27 ACT, 1210 SAT (exclusive of Writing); deadline February 1. Presidential Scholarships; $3,000 per year; criteria same as for Scholarship for Excellence. Honors Scholarships; $1,500-$3,000 per year; top 10% of class, GPA 3.5, deadline December 31. Jim and Vanita Oeschlager Leadership Award; $1,000-$17,000 per year; based on leadership and service. National Merit Scholarship; tuition, fees, room and board first year, full tuition second through fourth years; based on selection as National Merit Finalist. Academic Scholarship; $500-$1,500 per year; upper 20% of high school class, 21 ACT, 3.25 GPA. Akron Advantage Award; non-resident surcharge reduction of $5,584 per year for students with at least a 3.0 GPA

or 21 ACT from Delaware, Illinois, Indiana, Kentucky, Maryland, Michigan, New Jersey, New York, Pennsylvania, Virginia, or West Virginia. **Athletic:** 65 full-time freshmen received athletic scholarships; average amount $9,783.

FINANCIAL AID PROCEDURES
Forms required: FAFSA, institutional form.
Dates and Deadlines: Priority date 2/1; no closing date. Applicants notified on a rolling basis starting 4/15; must reply within 2 week(s) of notification.
Transfers: Priority date 4/1; no deadline. Applicants notified on a rolling basis starting 6/15; must reply within 2 week(s) of notification.

CONTACT
Douglas McNutt, Director, Student Financial Aid
277 East Buchtel Common, Akron, OH 44325-2001
(330) 972-7032

University of Akron: Wayne College
Orrville, Ohio
www.wayne.uakron.edu   Federal Code: 003123

2-year public branch campus and junior college in small town.
Enrollment: 1,540 undergrads, 41% part-time. 206 full-time freshmen.
Selectivity: Open admission.

BASIC COSTS (2005-2006)
Tuition and fees: $5,029; out-of-state residents $12,837.

FINANCIAL AID PICTURE
Students with need: Need-based aid available for full-time and part-time students. Work study available nights, weekends, and for part-time students.
Students without need: No-need awards available for academics, art, athletics, leadership, minority status, music/drama, state/district residency.
Additional info: All financial aid processed through University of Akron.

FINANCIAL AID PROCEDURES
Forms required: FAFSA, institutional form.
Dates and Deadlines: Closing date 3/15. Applicants notified on a rolling basis starting 4/15.

CONTACT
Barb Caillet, Financial Aid Counselor
1901 Smucker Road, Orrville, OH 44667-9758
(330) 684-8900

University of Cincinnati
Cincinnati, Ohio
www.uc.edu   Federal Code: 003125

4-year public university in large city.
Enrollment: 18,860 undergrads, 15% part-time. 3,863 full-time freshmen.
Selectivity: Admits over 75% of applicants.

BASIC COSTS (2005-2006)
Tuition and fees: $8,883; out-of-state residents $22,635.
Per-credit charge: $247; out-of-state residents $629.
Room and board: $7,485.

FINANCIAL AID PICTURE (2005-2006)
Students with need: Out of 2,921 full-time freshmen who applied for aid, 2,322 were judged to have need. Of these, 2,273 received aid, and 128 had their full need met. Average financial aid package met 63% of need; average scholarship/grant was $5,393; average loan was $3,408. For part-time students, average financial aid package was $6,195.
Students without need: 611 full-time freshmen who did not demonstrate need for aid received scholarships/grants; average award was $4,734. No-need awards available for academics, alumni affiliation, art, athletics, leadership, minority status, music/drama, ROTC, state/district residency.

Scholarships offered: 48 full-time freshmen received athletic scholarships; average amount $17,281.
Cumulative student debt: 66% of graduating class had student loans; average debt was $16,794.

FINANCIAL AID PROCEDURES
Forms required: FAFSA.
Dates and Deadlines: No deadline. Applicants notified on a rolling basis starting 3/10; must reply within 2 week(s) of notification.

CONTACT
Connie Williams, Director, Financial Aid
PO Box 210091, Cincinnati, OH 45221-0091
(513) 556-6982

University of Cincinnati: Clermont College
Batavia, Ohio
www.ucclermont.edu   Federal Code: 003125

2-year public branch campus college in small town.
Enrollment: 2,452 undergrads, 36% part-time. 513 full-time freshmen.
Selectivity: Open admission; but selective for some programs.

BASIC COSTS (2005-2006)
Tuition and fees: $4,299; out-of-state residents $10,785.
Per-credit charge: $120; out-of-state residents $300.

FINANCIAL AID PICTURE (2005-2006)
Students with need: Out of 21 full-time freshmen who applied for aid, 19 were judged to have need. Of these, 17 received aid, and 1 had their full need met. Average financial aid package met 37% of need; average scholarship/grant was $1,135; average loan was $1,759. For part-time students, average financial aid package was $5,208.
Students without need: 1 full-time freshmen who did not demonstrate need for aid received scholarships/grants; average award was $120. No-need awards available for academics, state/district residency.
Additional info: All financial aid applications and awards administered through Uptown campus except in-house loans and scholarships.

FINANCIAL AID PROCEDURES
Forms required: FAFSA.
Dates and Deadlines: No deadline. Applicants notified on a rolling basis.

CONTACT
Shirley Quinn, Financial Aid Officer
4200 Clermont College Drive, Batavia, OH 45103
(513) 732-5284

University of Cincinnati: Raymond Walters College
Cincinnati, Ohio
www.rwc.uc.edu   Federal Code: 003125

2-year public branch campus college in large city.
Enrollment: 3,942 undergrads.
Selectivity: Open admission; but selective for some programs.

BASIC COSTS (2005-2006)
Tuition and fees: $4,938; out-of-state residents $12,801.
Per-credit charge: $138; out-of-state residents $356.

FINANCIAL AID PICTURE
Students with need: Need-based aid available for full-time and part-time students.

Students without need: This college only awards aid to students with need.
Scholarships offered: Dean's scholarships; $1,500 based on GPA (2.5 required), tech prep program participation, 2-page essay; 10 available. Cincinnatus Scholarship Competition; $1,500 to full tuition, room, board and books; must have 26 ACT or be in top 5% of high school class to qualify to compete.
Additional info: All financial aid applications and awards administered through main campus.

FINANCIAL AID PROCEDURES
Forms required: FAFSA.
Dates and Deadlines: Priority date 3/15; no closing date. Applicants notified on a rolling basis starting 3/15; must reply within 2 week(s) of notification.

CONTACT
Chris Powers, Director of Enrollment Management
9555 Plainfield Road, Cincinnati, OH 45236-1096
(513) 745-5740

University of Dayton
Dayton, Ohio
www.udayton.edu   Federal Code: 003127

4-year private university in small city, affiliated with Roman Catholic Church.
Enrollment: 7,270 undergrads, 5% part-time. 1,816 full-time freshmen.
Selectivity: Admits over 75% of applicants.

BASIC COSTS (2006-2007)
Tuition and fees: $23,970.
Per-credit charge: $767.
Room and board: $7,190.
Additional info: All incoming students required to purchase a computer from the university. International students pay additional $75 per month for health and accident insurance. Engineering majors required to pay additional $750 per semester in fees. Tuition/fee waivers available for adults.

FINANCIAL AID PICTURE (2004-2005)
Students with need: Out of 1,442 full-time freshmen who applied for aid, 1,094 were judged to have need. Of these, 1,092 received aid, and 550 had their full need met. Average financial aid package met 94% of need; average scholarship/grant was $9,185; average loan was $3,145. For part-time students, average financial aid package was $4,188.
Students without need: 651 full-time freshmen who did not demonstrate need for aid received scholarships/grants; average award was $5,320. No-need awards available for academics, alumni affiliation, art, athletics, leadership, music/drama, ROTC, state/district residency.
Scholarships offered: *Merit:* Berry Scholarships; full tuition; based on GPA, ACT/SAT scores, service and leadership. Marianist Heritage Awards; $1,000 to full tuition; available to all graduates of Marianist high schools who meet academic criteria. Music talent awards; $1,000 to $5,000; based on auditions. President's Scholarship; $1,000 to $10,000; based on GPA, ACT/SAT scores, service and leadership. Visual arts awards; amounts vary; based on student portfolios. Chaminade Scholarships; $2,500; for students accepted to the Chaminade Scholars Program. National Merit Scholarships; $1,000 to $2,000; available to all students who are selected by the National Merit Scholarship Corporation and select UD as their first choice. Army ROTC awards; supplements U.S. Army ROTC awards with scholarship incentives. *Athletic:* 31 full-time freshmen received athletic scholarships; average amount $15,512.
Cumulative student debt: 67% of graduating class had student loans; average debt was $20,151.

FINANCIAL AID PROCEDURES
Forms required: FAFSA.
Dates and Deadlines: Priority date 3/31; no closing date. Applicants notified on a rolling basis starting 2/25.

Transfers: Applicants notified on a rolling basis starting 2/25. Students must submit FAFSA prior to October 1 each year for consideration for state funds.

CONTACT
Jeff Daniels, Director of Financial Aid
300 College Park, Dayton, OH 45469-1300
(937) 229-4311

University of Findlay
Findlay, Ohio
www.findlay.edu   Federal Code: 003045

4-year private university and liberal arts college in large town, affiliated with Church of God.
Enrollment: 3,034 undergrads, 13% part-time. 586 full-time freshmen.
Selectivity: Admits 50 to 75% of applicants.

BASIC COSTS (2006-2007)
Tuition and fees: $22,796.
Per-credit charge: $481.
Room and board: $7,792.
Additional info: Pre-veterinary and equestrian students pay higher tuition in years one and two; pharmacy students pay higher tuition throughout the program.

FINANCIAL AID PICTURE (2004-2005)
Students with need: Out of 412 full-time freshmen who applied for aid, 410 were judged to have need. Of these, 410 received aid, and 35 had their full need met. Average financial aid package met 75% of need; average scholarship/grant was $9,828; average loan was $2,600.
Students without need: 84 full-time freshmen who did not demonstrate need for aid received scholarships/grants; average award was $9,368. No-need awards available for academics, alumni affiliation, athletics, music/drama, state/district residency.
Scholarships offered: *Merit:* Full tuition available to select valedictorian/salutatorians. Automatic academic awards available based on GPA, test scores. *Athletic:* 54 full-time freshmen received athletic scholarships; average amount $9,398.

FINANCIAL AID PROCEDURES
Forms required: FAFSA.
Dates and Deadlines: Priority date 3/1; closing date 8/1. Applicants notified on a rolling basis starting 3/1; must reply within 2 week(s) of notification.
Transfers: Priority date 8/1; closing date 9/1.

CONTACT
Arman Habegger, Director of Financial Aid
1000 North Main Street, Findlay, OH 45840-3695
(419) 434-4791

University of Northwestern Ohio
Lima, Ohio
www.unoh.edu   Federal Code: 004861

2-year private business and technical college in large town.
Enrollment: 2,087 undergrads, 11% part-time. 600 full-time freshmen.
Selectivity: Admits over 75% of applicants.

BASIC COSTS (2005-2006)
Tuition and fees: $8,730.
Per-credit charge: $190.
Room and board: $6,020.
Additional info: $235 per credit hour charge for virtual classes. Tuition/fee waivers available for minority students.

Ohio University of Northwestern Ohio

FINANCIAL AID PICTURE (2004-2005)
Students with need: Out of 588 full-time freshmen who applied for aid, 242 were judged to have need. Of these, 242 received aid, and 11 had their full need met. Average financial aid package met 83% of need; average scholarship/grant was $4,211. For part-time students, average financial aid package was $3,011.
Students without need: 89 full-time freshmen who did not demonstrate need for aid received scholarships/grants; average award was $3,044. No-need awards available for academics, job skills, minority status.

FINANCIAL AID PROCEDURES
Forms required: FAFSA.
Dates and Deadlines: Priority date 4/1; no closing date. Applicants notified on a rolling basis starting 4/30; must reply within 2 week(s) of notification.
Transfers: No deadline. Applicants notified on a rolling basis.

CONTACT
Wendell Shick, Director of Financial Aid
1441 North Cable Road, Lima, OH 45805
(419) 227-3141

University of Rio Grande
Rio Grande, Ohio
www.rio.edu   Federal Code: 003116

4-year private community and liberal arts college in rural community.
Enrollment: 1,811 undergrads, 19% part-time. 360 full-time freshmen.
Selectivity: Open admission; but selective for some programs.

BASIC COSTS (2005-2006)
Tuition and fees: $572; out-of-district residents $13,322; out-of-state residents $14,402.
Room and board: $6,404.
Additional info: West Virginia residents pay $9,120 per year for the first two years only.

FINANCIAL AID PICTURE (2004-2005)
Students with need: 50% of average financial aid package awarded as scholarships/grants, 50% awarded as loans/jobs.
Students without need: No-need awards available for academics, alumni affiliation, athletics, leadership, music/drama, state/district residency.

FINANCIAL AID PROCEDURES
Forms required: FAFSA, institutional form.
Dates and Deadlines: Priority date 3/15; no closing date. Applicants notified on a rolling basis starting 1/15; must reply within 3 week(s) of notification.

CONTACT
Jenny Dyer, Financial Aid Director
218 North College Avenue, Rio Grande, OH 45674
(740) 245-7218

University of Toledo
Toledo, Ohio
www.utoledo.edu   Federal Code: 003131

4-year public university in large city.
Enrollment: 15,288 undergrads, 16% part-time. 3,061 full-time freshmen.
Selectivity: Open admission; but selective for some programs and for out-of-state students.

BASIC COSTS (2005-2006)
Tuition and fees: $7,521; out-of-state residents $16,333.
Per-credit charge: $268; out-of-state residents $635.
Room and board: $8,312.

FINANCIAL AID PICTURE (2005-2006)
Students with need: Out of 2,300 full-time freshmen who applied for aid, 1,728 were judged to have need. Of these, 1,703 received aid, and 189 had their full need met. Average financial aid package met 51% of need; average scholarship/grant was $5,043; average loan was $2,890. For part-time students, average financial aid package was $6,136.
Students without need: 313 full-time freshmen who did not demonstrate need for aid received scholarships/grants; average award was $2,900. No-need awards available for academics, art, athletics, leadership, minority status, music/drama, ROTC, state/district residency.
Scholarships offered: *Merit:* Freshman merit scholarships; $100 to $4,500; 400 awarded. *Athletic:* 12 full-time freshmen received athletic scholarships; average amount $9,829.
Cumulative student debt: 66% of graduating class had student loans; average debt was $21,531.
Additional info: March priority date for federal aid. Students encouraged to apply as early as December for priority consideration for institutional aid.

FINANCIAL AID PROCEDURES
Forms required: FAFSA.
Dates and Deadlines: Priority date 4/1; no closing date. Applicants notified on a rolling basis starting 3/31; must reply within 4 week(s) of notification.

CONTACT
Carolyn Baumgartner, Director of Financial Aid
2801 West Bancroft Street, Toledo, OH 43606-3398
(419) 530-2800

Urbana University
Urbana, Ohio
www.urbana.edu   Federal Code: 003133

4-year private liberal arts college in large town.
Enrollment: 1,443 undergrads.

BASIC COSTS (2006-2007)
Tuition and fees: $16,349.
Per-credit charge: $337.
Room and board: $6,832.

FINANCIAL AID PICTURE (2005-2006)
Students with need: Average financial aid package met 35% of need; average scholarship/grant was $1,809; average loan was $2,625. Need-based aid available for part-time students.
Students without need: No-need awards available for academics, alumni affiliation, athletics, music/drama.
Scholarships offered: All regularly accepted students receive cash scholarship for academics, music, or athletics.

FINANCIAL AID PROCEDURES
Forms required: FAFSA.
Dates and Deadlines: Closing date 4/1. Applicants notified on a rolling basis starting 3/1; must reply within 4 week(s) of notification.
Transfers: No deadline.

CONTACT
Amy Barnhart, Director of Financial Aid
579 College Way, Urbana, OH 43078
(937) 484-1359

Ursuline College
Pepper Pike, Ohio
www.ursuline.edu   Federal Code: 003134

4-year private liberal arts college for women in small town, affiliated with Roman Catholic Church.
Enrollment: 1,118 undergrads, 33% part-time. 138 full-time freshmen.
Selectivity: Admits 50 to 75% of applicants.

BASIC COSTS (2006-2007)
Tuition and fees: $20,090.
Per-credit charge: $662.
Room and board: $8,794.

FINANCIAL AID PICTURE (2004-2005)
Students with need: Out of 130 full-time freshmen who applied for aid, 122 were judged to have need. Of these, 122 received aid, and 40 had their full need met. Average financial aid package met 86% of need; average scholarship/grant was $8,412; average loan was $3,171. For part-time students, average financial aid package was $9,184.
Students without need: 11 full-time freshmen who did not demonstrate need for aid received scholarships/grants; average award was $6,591. No-need awards available for academics, art, athletics, leadership, religious affiliation, ROTC.
Scholarships offered: *Merit:* Ursuline Scholarship; $5-7,000 renewable. Ursuline Award; $1,500 - 3,500 renewable. Presidential Scholarship; $11,000 renewable. Dean's Scholarship; $9,000 renewable. Unlimited number available for each. *Athletic:* 48 full-time freshmen received athletic scholarships; average amount $4,293.
Cumulative student debt: 67% of graduating class had student loans; average debt was $23,000.

FINANCIAL AID PROCEDURES
Forms required: FAFSA, institutional form.
Dates and Deadlines: Priority date 3/15; no closing date. Applicants notified on a rolling basis starting 3/1; must reply within 2 week(s) of notification.

CONTACT
Mary Lynn Perri, Director of Financial Aid
2550 Lander Road, Pepper Pike, OH 44124-4398
(440) 646-8309

Walsh University
North Canton, Ohio
www.walsh.edu   Federal Code: 003135

4-year private university and liberal arts college in small city, affiliated with Roman Catholic Church.
Enrollment: 1,859 undergrads, 24% part-time. 447 full-time freshmen.
Selectivity: Admits over 75% of applicants.

BASIC COSTS (2006-2007)
Tuition and fees: $17,720.
Per-credit charge: $560.
Room and board: $7,130.
Additional info: Tuition/fee waivers available for minority students.

FINANCIAL AID PICTURE (2005-2006)
Students with need: Average financial aid package met 81% of need; average scholarship/grant was $6,722; average loan was $2,117. For part-time students, average financial aid package was $7,442.
Students without need: No-need awards available for academics, alumni affiliation, athletics, music/drama, religious affiliation, state/district residency.
Scholarships offered: $1,000 for incoming freshmen who have graduated from Catholic high school.

Cumulative student debt: 79% of graduating class had student loans; average debt was $18,775.

FINANCIAL AID PROCEDURES
Forms required: FAFSA, institutional form.
Dates and Deadlines: Priority date 3/15; no closing date. Applicants notified on a rolling basis starting 3/15; must reply within 4 week(s) of notification.
Transfers: No deadline. Applicants notified on a rolling basis starting 3/15.

CONTACT
Holly Van Gilder, Financial Aid Director
2020 East Maple Street, North Canton, OH 44720-3396
(330) 490-7146

Wilmington College
Wilmington, Ohio
www.wilmington.edu   Federal Code: 003142

4-year private liberal arts college in large town, affiliated with Society of Friends (Quaker).
Enrollment: 1,723 undergrads, 20% part-time. 366 full-time freshmen.
Selectivity: Admits over 75% of applicants.

BASIC COSTS (2006-2007)
Tuition and fees: $20,656.
Per-credit charge: $395.
Room and board: $7,406.

FINANCIAL AID PICTURE
Students with need: Need-based aid available for full-time and part-time students.
Students without need: No-need awards available for academics, alumni affiliation, religious affiliation, state/district residency.

FINANCIAL AID PROCEDURES
Forms required: FAFSA.
Dates and Deadlines: Priority date 3/31; closing date 6/1. Applicants notified on a rolling basis starting 3/1; must reply by 5/1 or within 2 week(s) of notification.

CONTACT
Cheryl Louallen, Director of Financial Aid
Box 1325 Pyle Center, Wilmington, OH 45177
(937) 382-6661 ext. 249

Wittenberg University
Springfield, Ohio
www.wittenberg.edu   Federal Code: 003143

4-year private liberal arts college in small city, affiliated with Evangelical Lutheran Church in America.
Enrollment: 1,880 undergrads, 1% part-time. 496 full-time freshmen.
Selectivity: Admits over 75% of applicants. GED not accepted.

BASIC COSTS (2006-2007)
Tuition and fees: $29,280.
Per-credit charge: $969.
Room and board: $7,498.

FINANCIAL AID PICTURE (2005-2006)
Students with need: Out of 427 full-time freshmen who applied for aid, 357 were judged to have need. Of these, 356 received aid, and 162 had their full need met. Average financial aid package met 92% of need; average scholarship/grant was $18,312; average loan was $3,046. For part-time students, average financial aid package was $7,226.
Students without need: This college only awards aid to students with need.

Scholarships offered: Smith Family Scholar Award; full tuition; renewable; based on academic achievement and other qualities. University Scholar Award; half tuition; renewable; based on academic achievement and other qualities. Broadwell Chinn Scholarship; half tuition; renewable; based on minority status, academic achievement, and other qualitites.
Cumulative student debt: 69% of graduating class had student loans; average debt was $21,615.
Additional info: Auditions required from applicants for music, theater, and dance scholarships. Portfolio required of applicants for art scholarships.

FINANCIAL AID PROCEDURES
Forms required: FAFSA.
Dates and Deadlines: Priority date 3/15; no closing date. Applicants notified on a rolling basis starting 2/15; must reply by 5/1 or within 2 week(s) of notification.
Transfers: Priority date 5/15.

CONTACT
Jonathan Green, Director of Financial Aid
Ward Street and North Wittenberg, Springfield, OH 45501-0720
(937) 327-7321

Wright State University
Dayton, Ohio
www.wright.edu   Federal Code: 003078

4-year public university in small city.
Enrollment: 11,785 undergrads, 12% part-time. 2,302 full-time freshmen.
Selectivity: Open admission; but selective for some programs.

BASIC COSTS (2005-2006)
Tuition and fees: $6,864; out-of-state residents $13,239.
Per-credit charge: $209; out-of-state residents $404.
Room and board: $6,750.

FINANCIAL AID PICTURE (2004-2005)
Students with need: Out of 2,208 full-time freshmen who applied for aid, 1,736 were judged to have need. Of these, 1,736 received aid, and 815 had their full need met. Average financial aid package met 60% of need; average scholarship/grant was $3,982; average loan was $2,301. Need-based aid available for part-time students.
Students without need: 384 full-time freshmen who did not demonstrate need for aid received scholarships/grants; average award was $3,055. No-need awards available for academics, alumni affiliation, art, athletics, job skills, leadership, minority status, music/drama, ROTC.
Scholarships offered: 58 full-time freshmen received athletic scholarships; average amount $10,907.
Additional info: Academic scholarship applications must be submitted by February 1.

FINANCIAL AID PROCEDURES
Forms required: FAFSA.
Dates and Deadlines: Priority date 3/1; no closing date. Applicants notified on a rolling basis starting 2/15; must reply within 2 week(s) of notification.

CONTACT
David Darr, Director of Financial Aid
3640 Colonel Glenn Highway, Dayton, OH 45435
(937) 775-5727

Wright State University: Lake Campus
Celina, Ohio
www.wright.edu/lake   Federal Code: 003078

2-year public branch campus college in small town.
Enrollment: 665 undergrads, 21% part-time. 141 full-time freshmen.
Selectivity: Open admission; but selective for some programs.

BASIC COSTS (2005-2006)
Tuition and fees: $4,617; out-of-state residents $10,992.
Per-credit charge: $142; out-of-state residents $337.
Additional info: Tuition at time of enrollment locked for 2 years.

FINANCIAL AID PICTURE
Students with need: Need-based aid available for full-time and part-time students.
Students without need: No-need awards available for academics, athletics, state/district residency.
Additional info: Academic scholarship application deadline February 1. All financial aid applications and awards administered by Dayton campus.

FINANCIAL AID PROCEDURES
Forms required: FAFSA, institutional form.
Dates and Deadlines: Priority date 2/15; no closing date. Applicants notified on a rolling basis; must reply within 2 week(s) of notification.

CONTACT
B.J. Hobler, Registrar
7600 State Route 703, Celina, OH 45822-2952
(419) 586-0336

Xavier University
Cincinnati, Ohio
www.xavier.edu   Federal Code: 003144

4-year private university in large city, affiliated with Roman Catholic Church.
Enrollment: 3,729 undergrads, 11% part-time. 765 full-time freshmen.
Selectivity: Admits 50 to 75% of applicants.

BASIC COSTS (2006-2007)
Tuition and fees: $23,880.
Room and board: $8,640.
Additional info: Tuition/fee waivers available for adults, minority students.

FINANCIAL AID PICTURE (2005-2006)
Students with need: Out of 612 full-time freshmen who applied for aid, 440 were judged to have need. Of these, 440 received aid, and 129 had their full need met. Average financial aid package met 79% of need; average scholarship/grant was $10,809; average loan was $3,447. For part-time students, average financial aid package was $5,675.
Students without need: 227 full-time freshmen who did not demonstrate need for aid received scholarships/grants; average award was $9,385. No-need awards available for academics, alumni affiliation, art, athletics, job skills, minority status, music/drama, ROTC.
Scholarships offered: *Merit:* Xavier Service Fellowships; full room and board; four year scholarships to students demonstrating high academic achievement, outstanding service and leadership; 5 awarded annually. St. Francis Xavier Scholarships; full tuition; based on leadership, talent and highest academic achievement; renewable for 8 semesters; number awarded varies. Pedro Arrupe Scholarship; full tuition; awarded to African-American student in recognition of high academic achievement and community involvement; 1 awarded every four years. Weninger Scholarship; partial to full tuition; awarded to African-Americans for high academic achievement; renewable for 8 semesters; number awarded varies. Miguel Pro Scholarship, partial to full tuition, awarded to Hispanic/Latino students for high academic achievement, renewable for 8 semesters, number awarded varies. Chancellor Scholarship, valued at minimally $12,000, based on leadership, talent & highest academic achievement, 15 awarded annually. Trustee, Schawe, Presidential & Honor Scholarships, values range from $5,000 to $11,000; based on academic achievement; number awarded varies. *Athletic:* 33 full-time freshmen received athletic scholarships; average amount $9,737.
Cumulative student debt: 58% of graduating class had student loans; average debt was $19,300.

FINANCIAL AID PROCEDURES
Forms required: FAFSA.
Dates and Deadlines: Priority date 2/15; no closing date. Applicants notified on a rolling basis starting 3/1; must reply by 5/1.

CONTACT
Paul Calme, Director of Financial Aid
3800 Victory Parkway, Cincinnati, OH 45207-5311
(513) 745-3142

Youngstown State University
Youngstown, Ohio
www.ysu.edu   Federal Code: 003145

4-year public university in small city.
Enrollment: 11,501 undergrads, 20% part-time. 1,997 full-time freshmen.
Selectivity: Open admission; but selective for some programs and for out-of-state students.

BASIC COSTS (2005-2006)
Tuition and fees: $6,333; out-of-state residents $11,541.
Per-credit charge: $264; out-of-state residents $481.
Room and board: $6,280.
Additional info: Residents of any out-of-state area within 100 miles of campus are charged $8,804.88 yearly tuition. Per credit hour charge is $366.87.

FINANCIAL AID PICTURE (2004-2005)
Students with need: 29% of average financial aid package awarded as scholarships/grants, 71% awarded as loans/jobs. Need-based aid available for part-time students.
Students without need: No-need awards available for academics, alumni affiliation, athletics, ROTC, state/district residency.

FINANCIAL AID PROCEDURES
Forms required: FAFSA, institutional form.
Dates and Deadlines: Priority date 2/15; no closing date. Applicants notified on a rolling basis starting 5/30.

CONTACT
Elaine Ruse, Director of Scholarships and Financial Aid
One University Plaza, Youngstown, OH 44555-0001
(330) 941-3505

Zane State College
Zanesville, Ohio
www.zanestate.edu   Federal Code: 008133

2-year public technical college in large town.
Enrollment: 1,537 undergrads, 33% part-time. 293 full-time freshmen.
Selectivity: Open admission; but selective for some programs.

BASIC COSTS (2005-2006)
Tuition and fees: $3,623; out-of-state residents $7,245.
Per-credit charge: $81; out-of-state residents $161.

FINANCIAL AID PICTURE
Students with need: Need-based aid available for full-time and part-time students.

FINANCIAL AID PROCEDURES
Forms required: FAFSA.
Dates and Deadlines: Priority date 5/1; closing date 7/15. Must reply by 9/1.

CONTACT
Jennifer Clipner, Financial Aid Director
1555 Newark Road, Zanesville, OH 43701-2626
(740) 454-2501 ext. 1275

Oklahoma

Bacone College
Muskogee, Oklahoma
www.bacone.edu   Federal Code: 003147

4-year private liberal arts college in large town, affiliated with American Baptist Churches in the USA.
Enrollment: 790 undergrads, 22% part-time. 147 full-time freshmen.
Selectivity: Admits 50 to 75% of applicants.

BASIC COSTS (2005-2006)
Tuition and fees: $9,220.
Per-credit charge: $350.
Room and board: $5,700.

FINANCIAL AID PICTURE (2005-2006)
Students with need: Average financial aid package met 89% of need; average scholarship/grant was $5,300; average loan was $2,625. For part-time students, average financial aid package was $5,338.
Students without need: This college only awards aid to students with need.
Cumulative student debt: 92% of graduating class had student loans; average debt was $10,000.

FINANCIAL AID PROCEDURES
Forms required: FAFSA.
Dates and Deadlines: Priority date 3/31; no closing date. Applicants notified on a rolling basis starting 4/1; must reply within 2 week(s) of notification.
Transfers: No deadline. Applicants notified on a rolling basis.

CONTACT
Cassie Doupe, Director of Financial Aid
2299 Old Bacone Road, Muskogee, OK 74403

Cameron University
Lawton, Oklahoma
www.cameron.edu   Federal Code: 003150

4-year public university and liberal arts college in small city.
Enrollment: 5,076 undergrads, 38% part-time. 1,382 full-time freshmen.
Selectivity: Open admission; but selective for some programs.

BASIC COSTS (2005-2006)
Tuition and fees: $3,240; out-of-state residents $7,830.
Per-credit charge: $74; out-of-state residents $227.
Room and board: $3,292.

FINANCIAL AID PICTURE (2004-2005)
Students with need: Out of 612 full-time freshmen who applied for aid, 529 were judged to have need. Of these, 510 received aid, and 325 had their full need met. Average financial aid package met 95% of need; average scholarship/grant was $6,050; average loan was $2,000. For part-time students, average financial aid package was $5,400.
Students without need: 39 full-time freshmen who did not demonstrate need for aid received scholarships/grants; average award was $569. No-need awards available for academics, alumni affiliation, art, athletics, leadership, music/drama, ROTC.
Scholarships offered: 6 full-time freshmen received athletic scholarships; average amount $2,120.
Cumulative student debt: 30% of graduating class had student loans; average debt was $7,500.

FINANCIAL AID PROCEDURES
Forms required: FAFSA.

Dates and Deadlines: Priority date 6/15; no closing date. Applicants notified on a rolling basis starting 4/1; must reply within 2 week(s) of notification.
Transfers: Priority date 6/1. Academic and financial aid transcripts required.

CONTACT
Caryn Pacheco, Director of Financial Assistance
2800 West Gore Boulevard, Lawton, OK 73505-6377
(580) 581-2293

Carl Albert State College
Poteau, Oklahoma
www.carlalbert.edu   Federal Code: 003176

2-year public community and junior college in large town.
Enrollment: 2,535 undergrads, 36% part-time. 411 full-time freshmen.
Selectivity: Open admission; but selective for some programs.

BASIC COSTS (2005-2006)
Tuition and fees: $2,042; out-of-state residents $5,012.
Per-credit charge: $45; out-of-state residents $144.
Room and board: $2,924.
Additional info: Tuition/fee waivers available for minority students.

FINANCIAL AID PICTURE
Students with need: Need-based aid available for full-time and part-time students. Work study available nights.
Students without need: This college only awards aid to students with need.

FINANCIAL AID PROCEDURES
Forms required: FAFSA, institutional form.
Dates and Deadlines: No deadline. Applicants notified on a rolling basis.

CONTACT
Robin Benson, Director of Financial Aid
1507 South McKenna, Poteau, OK 74953-5208
(918) 647-1343

Connors State College
Warner, Oklahoma
www.connorsstate.edu   Federal Code: 003153

2-year public community and junior college in rural community.
Enrollment: 1,984 undergrads, 34% part-time. 482 full-time freshmen.
Selectivity: Open admission; but selective for some programs.

BASIC COSTS (2005-2006)
Tuition and fees: $2,190; out-of-state residents $5,245.
Per-credit charge: $56; out-of-state residents $158.
Room and board: $5,804.

FINANCIAL AID PICTURE (2005-2006)
Students with need: 74% of average financial aid package awarded as scholarships/grants, 26% awarded as loans/jobs. Need-based aid available for part-time students.
Students without need: No-need awards available for academics, alumni affiliation, athletics, leadership, state/district residency.

FINANCIAL AID PROCEDURES
Forms required: FAFSA, institutional form.
Dates and Deadlines: Priority date 2/28; closing date 5/1. Applicants notified on a rolling basis starting 4/1; must reply within 2 week(s) of notification.

CONTACT
Wanda Fuller, Director of Financial Aid
RR 1, Box 1000, Warner, OK 74469-9700
(918) 463-6220

East Central University
Ada, Oklahoma
www.ecok.edu   Federal Code: 003154

4-year public university in large town.
Enrollment: 4,065 undergrads.

BASIC COSTS (2005-2006)
Tuition and fees: $3,256; out-of-state residents $7,889.
Per-credit charge: $75; out-of-state residents $229.
Room and board: $3,000.

FINANCIAL AID PICTURE (2005-2006)
Students with need: Need-based aid available for full-time and part-time students.
Students without need: No-need awards available for academics, athletics.

FINANCIAL AID PROCEDURES
Forms required: FAFSA, institutional form.
Dates and Deadlines: Closing date 3/1. Applicants notified on a rolling basis starting 4/15; must reply within 2 week(s) of notification.

CONTACT
Marcia Carter, Director of Student Financial Aid
PMBJ8, 1100 East 14th Street, Ada, OK 74820
(580) 332-8000

Eastern Oklahoma State College
Wilburton, Oklahoma
www.eosc.edu   Federal Code: 003155

2-year public community college in small town.
Enrollment: 2,976 undergrads.
Selectivity: Open admission; but selective for some programs.

BASIC COSTS (2005-2006)
Tuition and fees: $2,278; out-of-state residents $5,559.
Per-credit charge: $62; out-of-state residents $171.
Room and board: $3,494.
Additional info: Tuition/fee waivers available for minority students, unemployed or children of unemployed.

FINANCIAL AID PICTURE
Students with need: Need-based aid available for full-time and part-time students.
Students without need: This college only awards aid to students with need.

FINANCIAL AID PROCEDURES
Forms required: FAFSA, institutional form.
Dates and Deadlines: Priority date 3/1; no closing date. Applicants notified on a rolling basis starting 5/1; must reply within 2 week(s) of notification.
Transfers: Priority date 4/30.

CONTACT
Leah Miller, Director, Financial Aid
1301 West Main Street, Wilburton, OK 74578-4999
(918) 465-2361 ext. 207

Metropolitan College
Tulsa, Oklahoma
www.metropolitancollege.edu   Federal Code: 030813

4-year private college of legal studies in very large city.
Enrollment: 81 undergrads.
Selectivity: Open admission.

FINANCIAL AID PICTURE
Students with need: Need-based aid available for full-time and part-time students.
Students without need: This college only awards aid to students with need.

FINANCIAL AID PROCEDURES
Forms required: FAFSA.
Dates and Deadlines: No deadline. Applicants notified on a rolling basis.

CONTACT
Marsais Broadway, Director of Financial Aid
10820 E. 45th St., Ste. #B-101, Tulsa, OK 74146
(918) 627-9300

Mid-America Christian University
Oklahoma City, Oklahoma
www.macu.edu   Federal Code: 006942

4-year private university and liberal arts college in very large city, affiliated with Church of God.
Enrollment: 710 undergrads.

BASIC COSTS (2006-2007)
Tuition and fees: $11,100.
Per-credit charge: $440.
Room and board: $4,550.

FINANCIAL AID PICTURE
Students with need: Need-based aid available for full-time and part-time students.
Students without need: No-need awards available for academics, leadership, minority status, music/drama.

FINANCIAL AID PROCEDURES
Forms required: FAFSA.
Dates and Deadlines: Priority date 5/1; no closing date. Applicants notified on a rolling basis starting 5/1.

CONTACT
James Menefee, Director of Student Financial Services
3500 SW 119th Street, Oklahoma City, OK 73170
(405) 692-3182

National Education Center: Spartan School of Aeronautics
Tulsa, Oklahoma
www.spartan.edu   Federal Code: 007678

4-year for-profit technical college in large city.
Enrollment: 595 undergrads.

BASIC COSTS (2006-2007)
Additional info: Tech program tuition is $12,000 per academic year; flight program tuition is approximately $14,000 per academic year; bachelor's program tuition is $8,910 per academic year. Books/Tools and supplies will vary by program. Tuition at time of enrollment locked for 4 years.

FINANCIAL AID PICTURE
Students with need: Need-based aid available for full-time and part-time students. Work study available nights, weekends, and for part-time students.

FINANCIAL AID PROCEDURES
Forms required: FAFSA, institutional form.
Dates and Deadlines: No deadline. Applicants notified on a rolling basis starting 2/1; must reply within 2 week(s) of notification.
Transfers: No deadline. Applicants notified on a rolling basis; must reply within 2 week(s) of notification.

CONTACT
Rick Cox, Director of Financial Aid
Box 582833, Tulsa, OK 74158
(918) 836-6886

Northeastern Oklahoma Agricultural and Mechanical College
Miami, Oklahoma
www.neoam.edu   Federal Code: 316000

2-year public community and junior college in large town.
Enrollment: 1,812 undergrads, 21% part-time. 653 full-time freshmen.
Selectivity: Open admission.

BASIC COSTS (2005-2006)
Tuition and fees: $2,067; out-of-state residents $5,190.
Per-credit charge: $47; out-of-state residents $151.
Room and board: $3,628.

FINANCIAL AID PICTURE (2004-2005)
Students with need: Out of 578 full-time freshmen who applied for aid, 430 were judged to have need. Of these, 430 received aid, and 79 had their full need met. Average financial aid package met 74% of need; average scholarship/grant was $3,884; average loan was $1,613. For part-time students, average financial aid package was $2,138.
Students without need: 82 full-time freshmen who did not demonstrate need for aid received scholarships/grants; average award was $1,900. No-need awards available for academics, art, athletics, leadership, music/drama, state/district residency.
Scholarships offered: 93 full-time freshmen received athletic scholarships; average amount $1,849.

FINANCIAL AID PROCEDURES
Forms required: FAFSA, institutional form.
Dates and Deadlines: Priority date 4/1; no closing date. Applicants notified on a rolling basis starting 4/1; must reply by 8/30 or within 2 week(s) of notification.
Transfers: Priority date 4/30.

CONTACT
Tammy Higgins, Director of Financial Aid
200 I Street NE, Miami, OK 74354-6497
(918) 540-6235

Northeastern State University
Tahlequah, Oklahoma
www.nsuok.edu   Federal Code: 003161

4-year public university in large town.
Enrollment: 8,613 undergrads, 24% part-time. 1,070 full-time freshmen.
Selectivity: Admits over 75% of applicants.

BASIC COSTS (2005-2006)
Tuition and fees: $3,300; out-of-state residents $8,100.
Per-credit charge: $77; out-of-state residents $235.
Room and board: $3,100.
Additional info: Tuition/fee waivers available for adults, minority students.

FINANCIAL AID PICTURE (2005-2006)
Students with need: Average financial aid package met 63% of need; average scholarship/grant was $1,845; average loan was $1,107. For part-time students, average financial aid package was $2,597.

Students without need: No-need awards available for academics, alumni affiliation, art, athletics, leadership, minority status, music/drama, state/district residency.
Scholarships offered: Honors Program: $2,600 per year (minimum 28 ACT required), or up to $6,850 per year (minimum 30 ACT required); determined primarily by ACT and 3.8 high school GPA.
Cumulative student debt: 69% of graduating class had student loans; average debt was $17,824.
Additional info: Participates in off-campus job location & development program to assist students with off-campus employers to earn money for college expenses.

FINANCIAL AID PROCEDURES
Forms required: FAFSA, institutional form.
Dates and Deadlines: Priority date 4/15; no closing date. Applicants notified on a rolling basis starting 3/15; must reply within 3 week(s) of notification.
Transfers: Priority date 1/15. State grant deadline is April 30.

CONTACT
Teri Cochran, Director of Student Financial Services
600 North Grand Avenue, Tahlequah, OK 74464
(918) 456-5511 ext. 3456

Northwestern Oklahoma State University
Alva, Oklahoma
www.nwalva.edu   Federal Code: 003163

4-year public university and teachers college in small town.
Enrollment: 1,775 undergrads.
Selectivity: Admits over 75% of applicants.

BASIC COSTS (2005-2006)
Tuition and fees: $3,270; out-of-state residents $8,100.
Per-credit charge: $84; out-of-state residents $245.
Room and board: $2,980.

FINANCIAL AID PICTURE
Students with need: Need-based aid available for full-time and part-time students. Work study available nights, weekends, and for part-time students.
Students without need: No-need awards available for academics, alumni affiliation, art, athletics, leadership, music/drama.

FINANCIAL AID PROCEDURES
Forms required: FAFSA, institutional form.
Dates and Deadlines: No deadline. Applicants notified on a rolling basis starting 5/1.

CONTACT
Irala Magee, Director of Financial Aid
709 Oklahoma Boulevard, Alva, OK 73717-2799
(580) 327-8542

Oklahoma Baptist University
Shawnee, Oklahoma
www.okbu.edu   Federal Code: 003164

4-year private university and liberal arts college in large town, affiliated with Southern Baptist Convention.
Enrollment: 1,441 undergrads, 3% part-time. 370 full-time freshmen.
Selectivity: Admits 50 to 75% of applicants.

BASIC COSTS (2005-2006)
Tuition and fees: $13,846.
Room and board: $4,340.

FINANCIAL AID PICTURE (2004-2005)
Students with need: Out of 353 full-time freshmen who applied for aid, 238 were judged to have need. Of these, 238 received aid, and 164 had their full need met. Average financial aid package met 65% of need; average scholarship/grant was $3,446; average loan was $3,151. Need-based aid available for part-time students.
Students without need: 115 full-time freshmen who did not demonstrate need for aid received scholarships/grants; average award was $5,101. No-need awards available for academics, athletics, ROTC.
Scholarships offered: *Merit:* Prichard Church Vocation Scholarship; $1,600; offered to all students preparing for vocational ministry associated with Southern Baptist Convention. *Athletic:* 89 full-time freshmen received athletic scholarships; average amount $3,923.
Cumulative student debt: 57% of graduating class had student loans; average debt was $16,500.

FINANCIAL AID PROCEDURES
Forms required: FAFSA.
Dates and Deadlines: Priority date 3/1; no closing date. Applicants notified on a rolling basis starting 4/1; must reply by 5/1 or within 2 week(s) of notification.
Transfers: Priority date 6/1. Students on financial aid suspension from previous institution must complete at least 12 hours with 2.0 GPA to be eligible for aid.

CONTACT
Bob Womack, Director of Student Financial Services
500 West University, Shawnee, OK 74804
(405) 878-2016

Oklahoma Christian University
Oklahoma City, Oklahoma
www.oc.edu   Federal Code: 003165

4-year private liberal arts college in large city, affiliated with Church of Christ.
Enrollment: 1,835 undergrads. 533 full-time freshmen.
Selectivity: Open admission.

BASIC COSTS (2006-2007)
Tuition and fees: $14,976.
Per-credit charge: $560.
Room and board: $5,510.
Additional info: Tuition/fee waivers available for minority students.

FINANCIAL AID PICTURE (2005-2006)
Students with need: Out of 533 full-time freshmen who applied for aid, 397 were judged to have need. Of these, 397 received aid, and 103 had their full need met. Average financial aid package met 42% of need; average scholarship/grant was $1,430; average loan was $2,435. For part-time students, average financial aid package was $7,550.
Students without need: 124 full-time freshmen who did not demonstrate need for aid received scholarships/grants; average award was $2,753. No-need awards available for academics, alumni affiliation, art, athletics, job skills, leadership, music/drama, religious affiliation, ROTC.
Scholarships offered: 109 full-time freshmen received athletic scholarships; average amount $4,521.
Cumulative student debt: 74% of graduating class had student loans; average debt was $22,365.

FINANCIAL AID PROCEDURES
Forms required: FAFSA, institutional form.
Dates and Deadlines: Priority date 3/15; closing date 8/31. Applicants notified on a rolling basis starting 3/1; must reply within 4 week(s) of notification.

CONTACT
Clint LaRue, Director, Financial Services
Box 11000, Oklahoma City, OK 73136-1100
(405) 425-5190

Oklahoma City Community College
Oklahoma City, Oklahoma
www.okccc.edu   Federal Code: 010391

2-year public community college in large city.
Enrollment: 12,589 undergrads.
Selectivity: Open admission; but selective for some programs.

BASIC COSTS (2005-2006)
Tuition and fees: $2,071; out-of-state residents $5,413.
Per-credit charge: $48; out-of-state residents $160.

FINANCIAL AID PICTURE
Students with need: Need-based aid available for full-time and part-time students. Work study available nights, weekends, and for part-time students.
Students without need: No-need awards available for academics, state/district residency.

FINANCIAL AID PROCEDURES
Forms required: FAFSA, institutional form.
Dates and Deadlines: Priority date 7/1; no closing date. Applicants notified on a rolling basis starting 5/1.

CONTACT
Harold Case, Director of Financial Aid
7777 South May Avenue, Oklahoma City, OK 73159
(405) 682-7524

Oklahoma City University
Oklahoma City, Oklahoma
www.okcu.edu   Federal Code: 003166

4-year private university and liberal arts college in very large city, affiliated with United Methodist Church.
Enrollment: 1,911 undergrads, 23% part-time. 287 full-time freshmen.
Selectivity: Admits over 75% of applicants.

BASIC COSTS (2006-2007)
Tuition and fees: $19,200.
Per-credit charge: $610.
Room and board: $6,560.

FINANCIAL AID PICTURE (2004-2005)
Students with need: Out of 243 full-time freshmen who applied for aid, 177 were judged to have need. Of these, 177 received aid, and 33 had their full need met. Average financial aid package met 68% of need; average scholarship/grant was $11,090; average loan was $2,256. For part-time students, average financial aid package was $7,521.
Students without need: 48 full-time freshmen who did not demonstrate need for aid received scholarships/grants; average award was $7,570. No-need awards available for academics, art, athletics, job skills, leadership, music/drama, religious affiliation.
Scholarships offered: 48 full-time freshmen received athletic scholarships; average amount $6,855.
Cumulative student debt: 46% of graduating class had student loans; average debt was $24,054.

FINANCIAL AID PROCEDURES
Forms required: FAFSA, institutional form.
Dates and Deadlines: Priority date 3/1; closing date 6/30. Applicants notified on a rolling basis starting 2/24; must reply within 2 week(s) of notification.
Transfers: Applicants notified on a rolling basis starting 2/24; must reply within 2 week(s) of notification. Financial aid transcripts required from all previously attended institutions whether having received financial aid or not.

CONTACT
Denise Flis, Director of Financial Aid
2501 North Blackwelder Avenue, Oklahoma City, OK 73106
(405) 208-5211

Oklahoma Panhandle State University
Goodwell, Oklahoma
www.opsu.edu   Federal Code: 003174

4-year public agricultural and liberal arts college in rural community.
Enrollment: 1,046 undergrads, 12% part-time. 198 full-time freshmen.
Selectivity: Open admission.

BASIC COSTS (2005-2006)
Tuition and fees: $3,372; out-of-state residents $5,618.
Per-credit charge: $76; out-of-state residents $226.
Room and board: $4,270.

FINANCIAL AID PICTURE (2004-2005)
Students with need: 54% of average financial aid package awarded as scholarships/grants, 46% awarded as loans/jobs. Need-based aid available for part-time students.
Students without need: This college only awards aid to students with need.

FINANCIAL AID PROCEDURES
Forms required: FAFSA, institutional form.
Dates and Deadlines: Priority date 8/25; no closing date. Applicants notified on a rolling basis starting 6/15.
Transfers: No deadline. Applicants notified on a rolling basis.

CONTACT
Mel Riley, Director of Financial Aid
OPSU Admissions, Goodwell, OK 73939-0430
(580) 349-1582

Oklahoma State University
Stillwater, Oklahoma
www.okstate.edu   Federal Code: 003170

4-year public university in large town.
Enrollment: 18,773 undergrads, 11% part-time. 3,116 full-time freshmen.
Selectivity: Admits over 75% of applicants.

BASIC COSTS (2005-2006)
Tuition and fees: $4,365; out-of-state residents $12,388.
Per-credit charge: $103; out-of-state residents $371.
Room and board: $5,848.

FINANCIAL AID PICTURE (2004-2005)
Students with need: Out of 2,074 full-time freshmen who applied for aid, 1,449 were judged to have need. Of these, 1,418 received aid, and 240 had their full need met. Average financial aid package met 75% of need; average scholarship/grant was $3,869; average loan was $2,722. For part-time students, average financial aid package was $5,911.
Students without need: 732 full-time freshmen who did not demonstrate need for aid received scholarships/grants; average award was $2,474. No-need awards available for academics, alumni affiliation, art, athletics, job skills, leadership, music/drama, ROTC.
Scholarships offered: 32 full-time freshmen received athletic scholarships; average amount $8,470.

Cumulative student debt: 56% of graduating class had student loans; average debt was $17,719.

FINANCIAL AID PROCEDURES

Forms required: FAFSA.

Dates and Deadlines: No deadline. Applicants notified on a rolling basis starting 3/15; must reply within 2 week(s) of notification.

CONTACT

Charles Bruce, Director of Financial Aid
324 Student Union, Stillwater, OK 74078
(405) 744-6604

Oklahoma State University: Oklahoma City

Oklahoma City, Oklahoma
www.osuokc.edu   Federal Code: 009647

2-year public community and technical college in very large city.

Enrollment: 5,879 undergrads.

Selectivity: Open admission; but selective for some programs.

BASIC COSTS (2005-2006)

Tuition and fees: $2,450; out-of-state residents $6,290.

Per-credit charge: $63; out-of-state residents $191.

Additional info: Tuition/fee waivers available for adults, minority students.

FINANCIAL AID PICTURE

Students with need: Need-based aid available for full-time students.

Students without need: This college only awards aid to students with need.

FINANCIAL AID PROCEDURES

Forms required: FAFSA.

Dates and Deadlines: Priority date 7/15; no closing date. Applicants notified on a rolling basis starting 8/1; must reply within 2 week(s) of notification.

CONTACT

Bessie Carter, Director of Financial Aid
900 North Portland, Oklahoma City, OK 73107-6195
(405) 945-8646

Oklahoma State University: Okmulgee

Okmulgee, Oklahoma
www.osu-okmulgee.edu   Federal Code: 003172

2-year public branch campus and technical college in large town.

Enrollment: 2,240 undergrads.

Selectivity: Open admission; but selective for some programs.

BASIC COSTS (2005-2006)

Tuition and fees: $3,150; out-of-state residents $7,500.

Per-credit charge: $75; out-of-state residents $220.

Room and board: $4,851.

FINANCIAL AID PICTURE

Students with need: Need-based aid available for full-time and part-time students. Work study available nights, weekends, and for part-time students.

FINANCIAL AID PROCEDURES

Forms required: FAFSA, institutional form.

Dates and Deadlines: Priority date 4/1; no closing date. Applicants notified on a rolling basis.

Transfers: Requirement of financial aid transcript from any institution(s) attended during transferring academic year.

CONTACT

Barrett Bell, Director of Enrollment Services
1801 East Fourth Street, Okmulgee, OK 74447-3901
(918) 293-5290

Oklahoma Wesleyan University

Bartlesville, Oklahoma
www.okwu.edu   Federal Code: 003151

4-year private liberal arts college in large town, affiliated with Wesleyan Church.

Enrollment: 966 undergrads.

BASIC COSTS (2006-2007)

Tuition and fees: $14,550.

Room and board: $5,350.

FINANCIAL AID PICTURE (2005-2006)

Students with need: 19% of average financial aid package awarded as scholarships/grants, 81% awarded as loans/jobs. Need-based aid available for part-time students.

FINANCIAL AID PROCEDURES

Forms required: FAFSA, institutional form.

Dates and Deadlines: Priority date 4/1; no closing date. Applicants notified on a rolling basis starting 4/1; must reply by 5/1 or within 2 week(s) of notification.

CONTACT

Lee Kanakis, Director of Financial Aid
2201 Silver Lake Road, Bartlesville, OK 74006
(918) 335-6237

Oral Roberts University

Tulsa, Oklahoma
www.oru.edu   Federal Code: 003985

4-year private university and liberal arts college in large city, affiliated with non-denominational tradition.

Enrollment: 3,265 undergrads.

Selectivity: Admits 50 to 75% of applicants.

BASIC COSTS (2006-2007)

Tuition and fees: $16,670.

Per-credit charge: $674.

Room and board: $7,060.

FINANCIAL AID PICTURE (2005-2006)

Students with need: Average financial aid package met 86% of need; average scholarship/grant was $8,414; average loan was $6,716. For part-time students, average financial aid package was $6,665.

Students without need: No-need awards available for academics, art, athletics, job skills, leadership, music/drama.

FINANCIAL AID PROCEDURES

Forms required: FAFSA.

Dates and Deadlines: Priority date 3/15; no closing date. Applicants notified on a rolling basis starting 2/15; must reply by 7/15.

Transfers: Transfer applicants eligible for some scholarships.

CONTACT

Scott Carr, Director of Financial Aid
7777 South Lewis Avenue, Tulsa, OK 74171
(918) 495-6510

Platt College: Tulsa
Tulsa, Oklahoma
www.plattcollege.org

1-year for-profit health science college.
Enrollment: 52 undergrads.
Selectivity: Open admission.

BASIC COSTS (2005-2006)
Additional info: Tuition varies by program.

FINANCIAL AID PICTURE
Students with need: Need-based aid available for full-time and part-time students.
Students without need: This college only awards aid to students with need.

FINANCIAL AID PROCEDURES
Forms required: FAFSA.
Dates and Deadlines: No deadline.

CONTACT
Ronda Kay, Director of Financial Aid
3801 South Sheridan, Tulsa, OK 74145-1132
(918) 663-9000

Redlands Community College
El Reno, Oklahoma
www.redlandscc.edu
Federal Code: 003156

2-year public community college in large town.
Enrollment: 1,986 undergrads, 56% part-time. 236 full-time freshmen.
Selectivity: Open admission; but selective for some programs.

BASIC COSTS (2005-2006)
Tuition and fees: $2,310; out-of-state residents $4,560.
Per-credit charge: $46; out-of-state residents $121.
Additional info: Tuition/fee waivers available for adults.

FINANCIAL AID PICTURE (2004-2005)
Students with need: 82% of average financial aid package awarded as scholarships/grants, 18% awarded as loans/jobs. Need-based aid available for part-time students. Work study available nights, weekends, and for part-time students.
Students without need: No-need awards available for academics, athletics, leadership.

FINANCIAL AID PROCEDURES
Forms required: FAFSA.
Dates and Deadlines: Priority date 3/30; no closing date. Applicants notified on a rolling basis starting 6/1; must reply within 2 week(s) of notification.

CONTACT
Jenny White, Coordinator of Financial Aid
1300 South Country Club Road, El Reno, OK 73036
(866) 415-6367 ext. 1442

Rogers State University
Claremore, Oklahoma
www.rsu.edu
Federal Code: 003168

4-year public university in large town.
Enrollment: 3,636 undergrads, 50% part-time. 683 full-time freshmen.
Selectivity: Open admission; but selective for some programs.

BASIC COSTS (2005-2006)
Tuition and fees: $3,300; out-of-state residents $7,860.
Per-credit charge: $76; out-of-state residents $228.

FINANCIAL AID PICTURE (2005-2006)
Students with need: Out of 653 full-time freshmen who applied for aid, 561 were judged to have need. Of these, 544 received aid, and 55 had their full need met. Average financial aid package met 14% of need; average scholarship/grant was $1,850; average loan was $1,200. For part-time students, average financial aid package was $2,000.
Students without need: 17 full-time freshmen who did not demonstrate need for aid received scholarships/grants; average award was $400. No-need awards available for academics.

FINANCIAL AID PROCEDURES
Forms required: FAFSA, institutional form.
Dates and Deadlines: Priority date 3/1; no closing date. Applicants notified on a rolling basis starting 4/1; must reply within 3 week(s) of notification.
Transfers: No deadline. Applicants notified on a rolling basis starting 4/7; must reply within 3 week(s) of notification.

CONTACT
Jennifer Watkins, Director, Financial Aid
1701 West Will Rogers Boulevard, Claremore, OK 74017
(918) 343-7555

Rose State College
Midwest City, Oklahoma
www.rose.edu
Federal Code: 009185

2-year public community college in small city.
Enrollment: 8,125 undergrads, 63% part-time. 713 full-time freshmen.
Selectivity: Open admission; but selective for some programs.

BASIC COSTS (2005-2006)
Tuition and fees: $1,963; out-of-state residents $5,252.
Per-credit charge: $47; out-of-state residents $157.

FINANCIAL AID PICTURE (2004-2005)
Students with need: 48% of average financial aid package awarded as scholarships/grants, 52% awarded as loans/jobs. Need-based aid available for part-time students. Work study available nights, weekends, and for part-time students.
Students without need: No-need awards available for academics, athletics.

FINANCIAL AID PROCEDURES
Forms required: FAFSA.
Dates and Deadlines: Priority date 6/1; no closing date. Applicants notified on a rolling basis starting 3/1; must reply within 4 week(s) of notification.

CONTACT
Steve Daffer, Director of Financial Aid
6420 Southeast 15th Street, Midwest City, OK 73110
(405) 733-7424

St. Gregory's University
Shawnee, Oklahoma
www.stgregorys.edu
Federal Code: 003813

4-year private university and liberal arts college in large town, affiliated with Roman Catholic Church.
Enrollment: 775 undergrads, 38% part-time. 94 full-time freshmen.
Selectivity: Admits over 75% of applicants.

BASIC COSTS (2005-2006)
Tuition and fees: $12,636.
Per-credit charge: $395.

Room and board: $5,320.
Additional info: Tuition/fee waivers available for adults.

FINANCIAL AID PICTURE (2004-2005)
Students with need: Out of 92 full-time freshmen who applied for aid, 92 were judged to have need. Of these, 92 received aid, and 14 had their full need met. Average financial aid package met 69% of need; average scholarship/grant was $6,236; average loan was $2,027. Need-based aid available for part-time students.
Students without need: 16 full-time freshmen who did not demonstrate need for aid received scholarships/grants; average award was $2,206. No-need awards available for academics, alumni affiliation, art, athletics, job skills, leadership, music/drama, religious affiliation.
Scholarships offered: *Merit:* Leadership Scholarship: $500 - $2,000. Academic Scholarship: $500 - $5,100. *Athletic:* 29 full-time freshmen received athletic scholarships; average amount $3,738.
Cumulative student debt: 39% of graduating class had student loans; average debt was $9,845.

FINANCIAL AID PROCEDURES
Forms required: FAFSA, institutional form.
Dates and Deadlines: Priority date 4/1; no closing date. Applicants notified on a rolling basis starting 2/15; must reply within 2 week(s) of notification.

CONTACT
Jonna Raney, Director of Financial Aid
1900 West MacArthur Drive, Shawnee, OK 74804
(405) 878-5412

Seminole State College
Seminole, Oklahoma
www.ssc.cc.ok.us   Federal Code: 003178

2-year public community college in small town.
Enrollment: 1,806 undergrads.
Selectivity: Open admission; but selective for some programs.

BASIC COSTS (2005-2006)
Tuition and fees: $2,293; out-of-state residents $5,384.
Per-credit charge: $46; out-of-state residents $150.
Room and board: $4,464.

FINANCIAL AID PICTURE (2004-2005)
Students with need: 75% of average financial aid package awarded as scholarships/grants, 25% awarded as loans/jobs.
Students without need: No-need awards available for academics, athletics, state/district residency.

FINANCIAL AID PROCEDURES
Forms required: FAFSA, institutional form.
Dates and Deadlines: Priority date 7/15; no closing date. Applicants notified on a rolling basis starting 3/1; must reply within 4 week(s) of notification.

CONTACT
Chris Lindley, Director of Enrollment Management
2701 Boren Boulevard, Seminole, OK 74868
(405) 382-9247

Southeastern Oklahoma State University
Durant, Oklahoma
www.sosu.edu   Federal Code: 003179

4-year public liberal arts and teachers college in large town.
Enrollment: 3,602 undergrads, 17% part-time. 312 full-time freshmen.
Selectivity: Admits 50 to 75% of applicants.

BASIC COSTS (2005-2006)
Tuition and fees: $3,254; out-of-state residents $8,075.
Per-credit charge: $73; out-of-state residents $234.
Room and board: $3,250.
Additional info: Tuition/fee waivers available for minority students.

FINANCIAL AID PICTURE (2004-2005)
Students with need: Out of 245 full-time freshmen who applied for aid, 210 were judged to have need. Of these, 209 received aid, and 92 had their full need met. Average financial aid package met 60% of need; average scholarship/grant was $1,170; average loan was $1,183. For part-time students, average financial aid package was $1,117.
Students without need: 13 full-time freshmen who did not demonstrate need for aid received scholarships/grants; average award was $1,446. No-need awards available for academics, alumni affiliation, art, athletics, job skills, leadership, minority status, music/drama, religious affiliation, state/district residency.
Scholarships offered: 17 full-time freshmen received athletic scholarships; average amount $1,156.
Cumulative student debt: 30% of graduating class had student loans; average debt was $6,124.

FINANCIAL AID PROCEDURES
Forms required: FAFSA, institutional form.
Dates and Deadlines: Priority date 3/1; no closing date. Applicants notified on a rolling basis starting 4/15; must reply within 2 week(s) of notification.

CONTACT
Sherry Foster, Director of Student Financial Aid
1405 North Fourth Avenue, PMB 4225, Durant, OK 74701-0607
(580) 745-2186

Southwestern Christian University
Bethany, Oklahoma
www.swcu.edu   Federal Code: 003180

4-year private Bible college in large town, affiliated with Pentecostal Holiness Church.
Enrollment: 188 undergrads, 12% part-time. 45 full-time freshmen.
Selectivity: Admits 50 to 75% of applicants.

BASIC COSTS (2005-2006)
Tuition and fees: $8,250.
Per-credit charge: $275.
Room and board: $4,400.
Additional info: Adult Education Program is $295 per-credit-hour.

FINANCIAL AID PICTURE (2005-2006)
Students with need: Out of 44 full-time freshmen who applied for aid, 41 were judged to have need. Of these, 40 received aid, and 30 had their full need met. Average financial aid package met 81% of need; average scholarship/grant was $1,500; average loan was $4,000. For part-time students, average financial aid package was $5,000.
Students without need: 1 full-time freshmen who did not demonstrate need for aid received scholarships/grants; average award was $1,000. No-need awards available for academics, alumni affiliation, leadership, music/drama, religious affiliation.
Cumulative student debt: 78% of graduating class had student loans; average debt was $14,000.

FINANCIAL AID PROCEDURES
Forms required: FAFSA.
Dates and Deadlines: Priority date 8/1; no closing date. Applicants notified on a rolling basis starting 5/1; must reply within 2 week(s) of notification.

CONTACT
Mark Arthur, Director of Financial Aid
Box 340, Bethany, OK 73008
(405) 789-7661 ext. 3456

Southwestern Oklahoma State University
Weatherford, Oklahoma
www.swosu.edu   Federal Code: 003181

4-year public university in large town.
Enrollment: 4,338 undergrads.
Selectivity: Admits over 75% of applicants.

BASIC COSTS (2005-2006)
Tuition and fees: $3,240; out-of-state residents $7,740.
Per-credit charge: $83; out-of-state residents $233.
Room and board: $3,339.

FINANCIAL AID PICTURE
Students with need: Need-based aid available for full-time and part-time students.
Students without need: No-need awards available for academics, alumni affiliation, art, athletics, music/drama, state/district residency.

FINANCIAL AID PROCEDURES
Forms required: FAFSA, institutional form.
Dates and Deadlines: Closing date 3/1. Applicants notified by 3/20; must reply by 4/6.
Transfers: Priority date 3/1.

CONTACT
Larry Hollingsworth, Director of Student Financial Services
100 Campus Drive, Weatherford, OK 73096
(508) 774-3786

Tulsa Community College
Tulsa, Oklahoma
www.tulsacc.edu   Federal Code: 009763

2-year public community college in large city.
Enrollment: 13,274 undergrads.
Selectivity: Open admission; but selective for some programs.

BASIC COSTS (2005-2006)
Tuition and fees: $2,276; out-of-state residents $6,008.
Per-credit charge: $48; out-of-state residents $172.
Additional info: Tuition/fee waivers available for minority students.

FINANCIAL AID PICTURE
Students with need: Need-based aid available for full-time and part-time students. Work study available nights, weekends, and for part-time students.
Students without need: No-need awards available for academics, art, leadership, music/drama, state/district residency.

FINANCIAL AID PROCEDURES
Forms required: FAFSA, institutional form.
Dates and Deadlines: Priority date 8/1; no closing date. Applicants notified on a rolling basis starting 4/1; must reply within 2 week(s) of notification.

CONTACT
Debra MacIntyre, Director of Student Financial Services
6111 East Skelly Drive, Tulsa, OK 74135
(918) 595-7155

Tulsa Welding School
Tulsa, Oklahoma
www.weldingschool.com   Federal Code: 015733

2-year for-profit technical college in very large city.
Enrollment: 515 undergrads.
Selectivity: Open admission.

BASIC COSTS (2005-2006)
Additional info: Tuition and fees vary by program from $7,110 to $12,490.

FINANCIAL AID PICTURE
Students with need: Need-based aid available for full-time students.
Students without need: This college only awards aid to students with need.

FINANCIAL AID PROCEDURES
Forms required: FAFSA.

CONTACT
Ava Edens, Financial Aid Director
2545 East 11th Street, Tulsa, OK 74104-3909
(918) 587-6789

University of Central Oklahoma
Edmond, Oklahoma
www.ucok.edu   Federal Code: 003152

4-year public university in small city.
Enrollment: 14,625 undergrads, 28% part-time. 1,897 full-time freshmen.

BASIC COSTS (2005-2006)
Tuition and fees: $3,292; out-of-state residents $8,302.
Per-credit charge: $94; out-of-state residents $261.
Room and board: $4,476.
Additional info: Tuition/fee waivers available for minority students.

FINANCIAL AID PICTURE
Students with need: Need-based aid available for full-time students.
Students without need: No-need awards available for academics, alumni affiliation, art, athletics, leadership, minority status, music/drama, ROTC, state/district residency.

FINANCIAL AID PROCEDURES
Forms required: FAFSA, institutional form.
Dates and Deadlines: Priority date 5/15; no closing date. Applicants notified on a rolling basis starting 4/15; must reply within 3 week(s) of notification.

CONTACT
Sheila Fugett, Director of Financial Aid
100 North University Drive, Edmond, OK 73034-0151
(405) 974-3334

University of Oklahoma
Norman, Oklahoma
www.ou.edu   Federal Code: 003184

4-year public university in small city.
Enrollment: 20,967 undergrads, 13% part-time. 3,564 full-time freshmen.
Selectivity: Admits over 75% of applicants.

BASIC COSTS (2005-2006)
Tuition and fees: $4,408; out-of-state residents $12,301.
Per-credit charge: $95; out-of-state residents $359.
Room and board: $6,361.
Additional info: Tuition/fee waivers available for minority students.

Oklahoma — University of Oklahoma

FINANCIAL AID PICTURE (2004-2005)
Students with need: Out of 2,054 full-time freshmen who applied for aid, 1,758 were judged to have need. Of these, 1,758 received aid, and 820 had their full need met. Average financial aid package met 85% of need; average scholarship/grant was $3,984; average loan was $3,110. For part-time students, average financial aid package was $6,826.
Students without need: 310 full-time freshmen who did not demonstrate need for aid received scholarships/grants; average award was $1,008. No-need awards available for academics, alumni affiliation, art, athletics, leadership, music/drama, religious affiliation, ROTC.
Scholarships offered: *Merit:* President's Leadership Class for leadership: $1,000; 85 awarded. Scholar's Program for academic merit: amounts ranging from $1,000-$1,500; number awarded varies. University Achievement Class for leadership and academics: $1,000; number awarded varies. *Athletic:* 70 full-time freshmen received athletic scholarships; average amount $11,137.
Cumulative student debt: 45% of graduating class had student loans; average debt was $18,537.
Additional info: Institutional loans are available for early applicants who do not qualify for federal or state need-based aid.

FINANCIAL AID PROCEDURES
Forms required: FAFSA.
Dates and Deadlines: Priority date 3/1; no closing date. Applicants notified on a rolling basis starting 3/15; must reply within 6 week(s) of notification.
Transfers: Transfer leadership resident tuition waiver, transfer academic excellence tuition waiver.

CONTACT
Brad Burnett, Director of Financial Aid
1000 Asp Avenue, Norman, OK 73019-4076
(405) 325-5505

University of Science and Arts of Oklahoma
Chickasha, Oklahoma
www.usao.edu
Federal Code: 003167

4-year public university and liberal arts college in large town.
Enrollment: 1,222 undergrads, 13% part-time. 267 full-time freshmen.
Selectivity: Admits over 75% of applicants.

BASIC COSTS (2005-2006)
Tuition and fees: $3,480; out-of-state residents $8,220.
Per-credit charge: $83; out-of-state residents $241.
Room and board: $4,170.

FINANCIAL AID PICTURE (2005-2006)
Students with need: Out of 224 full-time freshmen who applied for aid, 173 were judged to have need. Of these, 170 received aid, and 37 had their full need met. Average financial aid package met 67% of need; average scholarship/grant was $4,948; average loan was $2,227. For part-time students, average financial aid package was $4,751.
Students without need: 56 full-time freshmen who did not demonstrate need for aid received scholarships/grants; average award was $3,957. No-need awards available for academics, art, athletics, leadership, music/drama, state/district residency.
Scholarships offered: 12 full-time freshmen received athletic scholarships; average amount $6,969.
Cumulative student debt: 67% of graduating class had student loans; average debt was $11,378.

FINANCIAL AID PROCEDURES
Forms required: FAFSA, institutional form.
Dates and Deadlines: Priority date 3/15; no closing date. Applicants notified on a rolling basis starting 3/15; must reply within 4 week(s) of notification.
Transfers: No deadline. Applicants notified on a rolling basis; must reply within 6 week(s) of notification.

CONTACT
Nancy Moats, Director of Financial Aid
1727 West Alabama, Chickasha, OK 73018-5322
(405) 574-1240

University of Tulsa
Tulsa, Oklahoma
www.utulsa.edu
Federal Code: 003185

4-year private university in large city, affiliated with Presbyterian Church (USA).
Enrollment: 2,749 undergrads, 5% part-time. 677 full-time freshmen.
Selectivity: Admits over 75% of applicants.

BASIC COSTS (2006-2007)
Tuition and fees: $20,738.
Per-credit charge: $741.
Room and board: $7,052.
Additional info: A one-time $375 fee is charged first-time students for orientation, life-time transcripts, course drop/add transactions, and graduation/commencement.

FINANCIAL AID PICTURE (2004-2005)
Students with need: Out of 631 full-time freshmen who applied for aid, 358 were judged to have need. Of these, 358 received aid, and 115 had their full need met. Average financial aid package met 83% of need; average scholarship/grant was $4,736; average loan was $4,457. For part-time students, average financial aid package was $6,713.
Students without need: 237 full-time freshmen who did not demonstrate need for aid received scholarships/grants; average award was $9,243. No-need awards available for academics, alumni affiliation, art, athletics, leadership, minority status, music/drama, religious affiliation.
Scholarships offered: 80 full-time freshmen received athletic scholarships; average amount $14,947.
Cumulative student debt: 65% of graduating class had student loans; average debt was $22,330.

FINANCIAL AID PROCEDURES
Forms required: FAFSA, institutional form.
Dates and Deadlines: Priority date 4/1; no closing date. Applicants notified on a rolling basis starting 3/1; must reply by 5/1 or within 2 week(s) of notification.
Transfers: Priority date 5/1. Applicants notified on a rolling basis starting 3/1; must reply by 5/1 or within 2 week(s) of notification.

CONTACT
Vicki Hendrickson, Director of Student Financial Services
600 South College Avenue, Tulsa, OK 74104-3189
(918) 631-2526

Vatterott College
Oklahoma City, Oklahoma
www.vatterott-college.com
Federal Code: 020693

1-year for-profit branch campus and technical college in very large city.
Enrollment: 375 undergrads.
Selectivity: Open admission.

BASIC COSTS (2005-2006)
Additional info: Diploma programs $20,000. Associate programs $30,000. Bachelor's program in heating, air conditioning, refrigeration, and ventilation is $52,000. Cost includes tuition, fees, books, supplies, and labs.

FINANCIAL AID PICTURE
Students with need: Need-based aid available for full-time students.
Students without need: This college only awards aid to students with need.

FINANCIAL AID PROCEDURES
Forms required: FAFSA.
Dates and Deadlines: No deadline.

CONTACT
Kelly Harjo, Financial Aid Director
4629 Northwest 23rd Street, Oklahoma City, OK 73127
(405) 945-0088

Western College of Southern California
Oklahoma City, Oklahoma
www.platt.org   Federal Code: 023068

1-year for-profit branch campus and health science college in small city.
Enrollment: 220 undergrads.
Selectivity: Open admission; but selective for some programs.

BASIC COSTS (2005-2006)
Additional info: Tuition varies by program. Full-time tuition ranges from $7,295 to $13,345. Required fees $100.

FINANCIAL AID PICTURE
Students with need: Need-based aid available for full-time students.

FINANCIAL AID PROCEDURES
Forms required: FAFSA.

CONTACT
Amy Hocker, Financial Aid Director (OK City campus)
309 South Ann Arbor, Oklahoma City, OK 73128
(405) 946-7799

Western Oklahoma State College
Altus, Oklahoma
www.wosc.edu   Federal Code: 003146

2-year public community college in large town.
Enrollment: 1,919 undergrads.
Selectivity: Open admission.

BASIC COSTS (2005-2006)
Tuition and fees: $2,230; out-of-state residents $5,365.
Per-credit charge: $47; out-of-state residents $151.
Room and board: $3,600.

FINANCIAL AID PICTURE (2004-2005)
Students with need: 69% of average financial aid package awarded as scholarships/grants, 31% awarded as loans/jobs. Need-based aid available for part-time students. Work study available nights, weekends, and for part-time students.
Students without need: No-need awards available for academics, alumni affiliation, art, athletics, leadership, music/drama, state/district residency.

FINANCIAL AID PROCEDURES
Forms required: FAFSA, institutional form.
Dates and Deadlines: Priority date 3/1; no closing date. Applicants notified on a rolling basis; must reply within 3 week(s) of notification.

CONTACT
Myrna Cross, Director of Financial Aid
2801 North Main Street, Altus, OK 73521
(580) 477-7709

Oregon

Art Institute of Portland
Portland, Oregon
www.aipd.artinstitutes.edu   Federal Code: 007819

4-year for-profit visual arts and liberal arts college in large city.
Enrollment: 1,580 undergrads, 32% part-time. 224 full-time freshmen.

BASIC COSTS (2006-2007)
Tuition and fees: $17,460.
Per-credit charge: $388.
Room and board: $5,625.
Additional info: Tuition at time of enrollment locked for 4 years.

FINANCIAL AID PICTURE (2004-2005)
Students with need: Out of 204 full-time freshmen who applied for aid, 202 were judged to have need. Of these, 201 received aid, and 2 had their full need met. Average financial aid package met 1% of need; average scholarship/grant was $1,370; average loan was $2,625. For part-time students, average financial aid package was $5,157.
Students without need: 14 full-time freshmen who did not demonstrate need for aid received scholarships/grants; average award was $1,088. No-need awards available for art.
Cumulative student debt: 73% of graduating class had student loans; average debt was $25,154.
Additional info: Applicants encouraged to apply early for financial aid. Scholarship deadlines range from January 1 to March 1.

FINANCIAL AID PROCEDURES
Forms required: FAFSA.
Dates and Deadlines: Priority date 3/1; no closing date. Applicants notified on a rolling basis starting 1/1; must reply within 5 week(s) of notification.
Transfers: No deadline. Applicants notified on a rolling basis starting 1/1.

CONTACT
Mickey Jacobson, Director of Student Financial Services
1122 Northwest Davis Street, Portland, OR 97209-2911
(503) 382-4784

Blue Mountain Community College
Pendleton, Oregon
www.bluecc.edu   Federal Code: 003186

2-year public community college in large town.
Enrollment: 1,252 undergrads, 58% part-time. 236 full-time freshmen.
Selectivity: Open admission; but selective for some programs.

BASIC COSTS (2006-2007)
Tuition and fees: $2,796; out-of-state residents $5,496.
Per-credit charge: $60; out-of-state residents $120.
Additional info: Washington, Idaho, Nevada, and California state residents pay in-state tuition.

FINANCIAL AID PICTURE
Students with need: Need-based aid available for full-time and part-time students. Work study available nights, weekends, and for part-time students.
Students without need: No-need awards available for athletics, music/drama.

FINANCIAL AID PROCEDURES
Forms required: FAFSA.
Dates and Deadlines: Priority date 3/30; no closing date. Applicants notified on a rolling basis starting 4/1; must reply within 2 week(s) of notification.

CONTACT
Theresa Bosworth, Director of Financial Aid
PO Box 100, Pendleton, OR 97801
(541) 278-5790

Central Oregon Community College
Bend, Oregon
www.cocc.edu   Federal Code: 003188

2-year public community college in small city.
Enrollment: 3,233 undergrads, 55% part-time. 408 full-time freshmen.
Selectivity: Open admission; but selective for some programs.

BASIC COSTS (2005-2006)
Tuition and fees: $2,903; out-of-district residents $3,893; out-of-state residents $7,898.
Per-credit charge: $61; out-of-district residents $83.
Room and board: $6,380.

FINANCIAL AID PICTURE
Students with need: Need-based aid available for full-time and part-time students.
Students without need: No-need awards available for academics, leadership.
Additional info: Institution-sponsored short-term loans. Extensive part-time student employment.

FINANCIAL AID PROCEDURES
Forms required: FAFSA, institutional form.
Dates and Deadlines: Priority date 3/31; no closing date. Applicants notified on a rolling basis starting 5/1; must reply within 4 week(s) of notification.

CONTACT
Kevin Multop, Director of Financial Aid
2600 Northwest College Way, Bend, OR 97701-5998
(541) 383-7260

Chemeketa Community College
Salem, Oregon
www.chemeketa.edu   Federal Code: 003218

2-year public community and junior college in small city.
Enrollment: 9,838 undergrads.
Selectivity: Open admission; but selective for some programs.

BASIC COSTS (2005-2006)
Tuition and fees: $2,790; out-of-state residents $9,135.
Per-credit charge: $58; out-of-state residents $199.
Additional info: Domestic out-of-state students pay in-state rate after first quarter; international students have additional required fees.

FINANCIAL AID PICTURE (2004-2005)
Students with need: 51% of average financial aid package awarded as scholarships/grants, 49% awarded as loans/jobs. Need-based aid available for part-time students. Work study available nights, weekends, and for part-time students.
Students without need: This college only awards aid to students with need.
Cumulative student debt: 18% of graduating class had student loans; average debt was $7,214.

FINANCIAL AID PROCEDURES
Forms required: FAFSA.
Dates and Deadlines: Priority date 4/1; no closing date. Applicants notified on a rolling basis starting 6/30; must reply within 2 week(s) of notification.

Transfers: Priority date 6/30; no deadline. Applicants notified on a rolling basis; must reply within 4 week(s) of notification.

CONTACT
Kathy Campbell, Financial Aid Director
Attention: Admissions, Salem, OR 97309-7070
(503) 399-5018

Clackamas Community College
Oregon City, Oregon
www.clackamas.cc.or.us   Federal Code: 004878

2-year public community college in small city.
Enrollment: 7,727 undergrads.
Selectivity: Open admission; but selective for some programs.

BASIC COSTS (2005-2006)
Tuition and fees: $2,700; out-of-state residents $8,910.
Per-credit charge: $56; out-of-state residents $194.
Additional info: In-state tuition applies to residents of Oregon, Washington, Idaho, Nevada and California. Tuition at time of enrollment locked for 2 years.

FINANCIAL AID PICTURE
Students with need: Need-based aid available for full-time and part-time students. Work study available nights, weekends, and for part-time students.
Students without need: No-need awards available for academics, art, athletics, leadership, music/drama.
Additional info: Institutional tuition rebate guarantee. Frozen tuition rates for new fall students who graduate within 3 years. Any tuition increase levied by college during those 3 years will be refunded to student upon graduation.

FINANCIAL AID PROCEDURES
Forms required: FAFSA.
Dates and Deadlines: Priority date 4/10; no closing date. Applicants notified on a rolling basis starting 3/15; must reply within 3 week(s) of notification.

CONTACT
Mary Jo Jackson, Director, Student Financial Services
19600 South Molalla Avenue, Oregon City, OR 97045
(503) 657-6958 ext. 2422

Clatsop Community College
Astoria, Oregon
www.clatsop.cc.or.us   Federal Code: 003189

2-year public community college in large town.
Enrollment: 1,610 undergrads.
Selectivity: Open admission; but selective for some programs.

BASIC COSTS (2005-2006)
Tuition and fees: $2,835; out-of-state residents $5,400.
Per-credit charge: $57; out-of-state residents $114.

FINANCIAL AID PICTURE
Students with need: Need-based aid available for full-time and part-time students.
Students without need: No-need awards available for academics.
Scholarships offered: Rochester scholarships awarded to mathematics or science majors; 3.0 GPA minimum; 3 reference letters required; between $3,000 and $5,000; number of awards varies yearly.

FINANCIAL AID PROCEDURES
Forms required: FAFSA, institutional form.
Dates and Deadlines: Priority date 5/1; no closing date. Applicants notified on a rolling basis starting 2/1.

Transfers: Students who apply after July 1 may only be eligible for Pell Grants and loans depending on availability of funds. Reply deadline 1 week before start of classes.

CONTACT
Sharon Boring, Director of Financial Aid
1653 Jerome Avenue, Astoria, OR 97103
(503) 338-2322

Concordia University
Portland, Oregon
www.cu-portland.edu   Federal Code: 003191

4-year private university and liberal arts college in very large city, affiliated with Lutheran Church - Missouri Synod.
Enrollment: 912 undergrads, 13% part-time. 124 full-time freshmen.
Selectivity: Admits 50 to 75% of applicants.

BASIC COSTS (2006-2007)
Tuition and fees: $19,090.
Per-credit charge: $615.
Room and board: $3,305.
Additional info: Per-credit-hour charge for less than 6 credits in a given term: $314. Tuition/fee waivers available for adults.

FINANCIAL AID PICTURE (2004-2005)
Students with need: Out of 114 full-time freshmen who applied for aid, 105 were judged to have need. Of these, 105 received aid, and 68 had their full need met. Average financial aid package met 85% of need; average scholarship/grant was $10,000; average loan was $3,000. For part-time students, average financial aid package was $8,000.
Students without need: 9 full-time freshmen who did not demonstrate need for aid received scholarships/grants; average award was $6,000. No-need awards available for academics, athletics, leadership, music/drama, religious affiliation.
Scholarships offered: *Merit:* President's Scholarship: based on Academic Index; $8,000. Regent's Scholarship: calculated from high school GPA and ACT/SAT score; $6,000. University Award: calculated from high school GPA and ACT/SAT score; $4,500. Dean's Award: based on academic index; $5,000. Honors Scholarship: 50% tuition. *Athletic:* 54 full-time freshmen received athletic scholarships; average amount $3,000.
Cumulative student debt: 85% of graduating class had student loans; average debt was $15,000.

FINANCIAL AID PROCEDURES
Forms required: FAFSA.
Dates and Deadlines: No deadline. Applicants notified on a rolling basis starting 3/15; must reply by 5/1 or within 3 week(s) of notification.
Transfers: No deadline. Applicants notified on a rolling basis.

CONTACT
James Cullen, Financial Aid Director
2811 Northeast Holman Street, Portland, OR 97211
(503) 280-8514

Corban College
Salem, Oregon
www.corban.edu   Federal Code: 001339

4-year private liberal arts college in small city, affiliated with Baptist faith.
Enrollment: 771 undergrads, 15% part-time. 167 full-time freshmen.
Selectivity: Admits over 75% of applicants.

BASIC COSTS (2006-2007)
Tuition and fees: $19,294.
Per-credit charge: $795.
Room and board: $7,084.

FINANCIAL AID PICTURE (2005-2006)
Students with need: Out of 155 full-time freshmen who applied for aid, 142 were judged to have need. Of these, 141 received aid, and 34 had their full need met. Average financial aid package met 71% of need; average scholarship/grant was $8,981; average loan was $5,659. For part-time students, average financial aid package was $8,667.
Students without need: 21 full-time freshmen who did not demonstrate need for aid received scholarships/grants; average award was $7,789. No-need awards available for academics, alumni affiliation, athletics, leadership, music/drama.
Scholarships offered: 7 full-time freshmen received athletic scholarships; average amount $3,697.

FINANCIAL AID PROCEDURES
Forms required: FAFSA.
Dates and Deadlines: Priority date 2/15; no closing date. Applicants notified by 3/1; must reply within 4 week(s) of notification.

CONTACT
Nathan Warthan, Director of Financial Aid
5000 Deer Park Drive SE, Salem, OR 97301-9392
(503) 375-7006

Eastern Oregon University
LaGrande, Oregon
www.eou.edu   Federal Code: 003193

4-year public university and liberal arts college in large town.
Enrollment: 2,956 undergrads, 31% part-time. 354 full-time freshmen.
Selectivity: Admits 50 to 75% of applicants.

BASIC COSTS (2005-2006)
Tuition and fees: $5,840; out-of-state residents $5,840.
Per-credit charge: $101.
Room and board: $7,300.

FINANCIAL AID PICTURE (2005-2006)
Students with need: Out of 308 full-time freshmen who applied for aid, 234 were judged to have need. Of these, 232 received aid, and 114 had their full need met. Average financial aid package met 44% of need; average scholarship/grant was $3,610; average loan was $1,947. For part-time students, average financial aid package was $6,741.
Students without need: 3 full-time freshmen who did not demonstrate need for aid received scholarships/grants; average award was $1,657. No-need awards available for academics, art, athletics, leadership, minority status, music/drama, state/district residency.
Scholarships offered: *Merit:* University Scholars Scholarships: 65 awards, tuition (renewable). Based on personal essay, recommendations, GPA, activities and awards. Minorities encouraged to apply. *Athletic:* 27 full-time freshmen received athletic scholarships; average amount $905.
Cumulative student debt: 75% of graduating class had student loans; average debt was $16,171.

FINANCIAL AID PROCEDURES
Forms required: FAFSA.
Dates and Deadlines: Priority date 3/1; no closing date. Applicants notified on a rolling basis starting 4/1; must reply within 4 week(s) of notification.
Transfers: No deadline. Applicants notified on a rolling basis.

CONTACT
Eric Bucks, Director of Financial Aid
One University Boulevard, LaGrande, OR 97850
(541) 962-3550

Eugene Bible College
Eugene, Oregon
www.ebc.edu
Federal Code: 015167

4-year private Bible college in small city, affiliated with Open Bible Standard Churches.
Enrollment: 180 undergrads, 11% part-time. 60 full-time freshmen.
Selectivity: Admits less than 50% of applicants.

BASIC COSTS (2005-2006)
Tuition and fees: $8,301.
Per-credit charge: $220.
Room and board: $4,575.

FINANCIAL AID PICTURE (2005-2006)
Students with need: Average financial aid package met 55% of need; average scholarship/grant was $2,000; average loan was $2,625. For part-time students, average financial aid package was $1,100.
Students without need: No-need awards available for academics, athletics, leadership, music/drama.
Scholarships offered: Honors award: $300 to all who qualify, based on high school GPA of 3.7 or higher.
Cumulative student debt: 90% of graduating class had student loans; average debt was $25,000.
Additional info: Some early acceptance awards possible for those admitted by May 15. Distance awards to those coming from over 1000 miles away. Some awards for husbands and wives enrolled at same time.

FINANCIAL AID PROCEDURES
Forms required: FAFSA.
Dates and Deadlines: Priority date 5/1; closing date 9/1. Applicants notified on a rolling basis starting 7/15; must reply within 4 week(s) of notification.
Transfers: No deadline.

CONTACT
Rulena Mellor, Director of Financial Aid
2155 Bailey Hill Road, Eugene, OR 97405
(800) 322-2638

George Fox University
Newberg, Oregon
www.georgefox.edu
Federal Code: 003194

4-year private university and seminary college in large town, affiliated with Society of Friends (Quaker).
Enrollment: 1,831 undergrads, 16% part-time. 459 full-time freshmen.
Selectivity: Admits over 75% of applicants.

BASIC COSTS (2006-2007)
Tuition and fees: $22,570.
Per-credit charge: $690.
Room and board: $7,210.
Additional info: Tuition/fee waivers available for minority students.

FINANCIAL AID PICTURE (2005-2006)
Students with need: 69% of average financial aid package awarded as scholarships/grants, 31% awarded as loans/jobs. Need-based aid available for part-time students.
Students without need: No-need awards available for academics, alumni affiliation, art, minority status, music/drama, religious affiliation, state/district residency.
Scholarships offered: Academic merit awards are based on GPA, SAT/ACT scores and rigor of high school curriculum. Awards range from $2,500-$10,000 per year, renewable based on academic performance.
Additional info: Audition required for music and drama scholarships.

FINANCIAL AID PROCEDURES
Forms required: FAFSA, state aid form.
Dates and Deadlines: Priority date 2/1; no closing date. Applicants notified on a rolling basis starting 3/1; must reply within 6 week(s) of notification.

CONTACT
Rob Clark, Director of Financial Aid
414 North Meridian Street, Newberg, OR 97132-2697
(503) 554-2230

Lane Community College
Eugene, Oregon
www.lanecc.edu
Federal Code: 003196

2-year public community college in small city.
Enrollment: 5,266 undergrads.
Selectivity: Open admission; but selective for some programs.

BASIC COSTS (2005-2006)
Tuition and fees: $3,323; out-of-state residents $10,838.
Per-credit charge: $67; out-of-state residents $234.

FINANCIAL AID PICTURE (2004-2005)
Students with need: 52% of average financial aid package awarded as scholarships/grants, 48% awarded as loans/jobs. Need-based aid available for part-time students. Work study available nights, weekends, and for part-time students.
Students without need: No-need awards available for art, athletics, minority status, music/drama.

FINANCIAL AID PROCEDURES
Forms required: FAFSA.
Dates and Deadlines: Priority date 2/15; no closing date. Applicants notified on a rolling basis starting 6/1; must reply within 2 week(s) of notification.

CONTACT
Burt Logan, Director of Financial Aid
4000 East 30th Avenue, Eugene, OR 97405
(541) 463-3100

Lewis & Clark College
Portland, Oregon
www.lclark.edu
Federal Code: 003197

4-year private liberal arts college in very large city.
Enrollment: 1,909 undergrads, 1% part-time. 489 full-time freshmen.
Selectivity: Admits 50 to 75% of applicants.

BASIC COSTS (2006-2007)
Tuition and fees: $29,772.
Per-credit charge: $1,489.
Room and board: $8,048.

FINANCIAL AID PICTURE (2005-2006)
Students with need: Out of 395 full-time freshmen who applied for aid, 294 were judged to have need. Of these, 294 received aid, and 119 had their full need met. Average financial aid package met 90% of need; average scholarship/grant was $20,519; average loan was $4,050. For part-time students, average financial aid package was $18,815.
Students without need: 75 full-time freshmen who did not demonstrate need for aid received scholarships/grants; average award was $6,753. No-need awards available for academics, leadership, music/drama.
Scholarships offered: Neely Scholarship, up to 10 awards, full tuition. Trustee Scholarship, up to 15 awards, half tuition. Deans Scholarships, $4,000-$8,000. Music scholarships, $1,000-$6,000, by audition. Forensic

scholarships, $1,000-$5,000, separate application required. Leadership and service awards of $5,000.
Cumulative student debt: 57% of graduating class had student loans; average debt was $19,156.

FINANCIAL AID PROCEDURES
Forms required: FAFSA.
Dates and Deadlines: Priority date 3/1; no closing date. Applicants notified on a rolling basis starting 3/1; must reply by 5/1.
Transfers: Transfers eligible for merit-based Dean's scholarships of up to $10,000, not eligible for Neely or Trustee scholarships. Financial aid transcript form from previous institutions required.

CONTACT
Glendi Gaddis, Director of Student Financial Services
0615 SW Palatine Hill Road, Portland, OR 97219-7899
(503) 768-7090

Linfield College
McMinnville, Oregon
www.linfield.edu   Federal Code: 003198

4-year private business and liberal arts college in large town, affiliated with American Baptist Churches in the USA.
Enrollment: 1,693 undergrads, 1% part-time. 488 full-time freshmen.
Selectivity: Admits 50 to 75% of applicants.

BASIC COSTS (2006-2007)
Tuition and fees: $24,174.
Per-credit charge: $745.
Room and board: $7,080.

FINANCIAL AID PICTURE (2005-2006)
Students with need: Out of 317 full-time freshmen who applied for aid, 317 were judged to have need. Of these, 317 received aid, and 125 had their full need met. Average financial aid package met 85% of need; average scholarship/grant was $7,730; average loan was $3,304. For part-time students, average financial aid package was $7,721.
Students without need: 122 full-time freshmen who did not demonstrate need for aid received scholarships/grants; average award was $9,390. No-need awards available for academics, music/drama.
Scholarships offered: Linfield Merit Award: range from half to full tuition; for National Merit Scholarship Finalists who list Linfield as first choice. Linfield Trustee Scholarships: range from $10,300 to $15,000; based on academic record; must have 3.75 GPA. Linfield Faculty Scholarships: $5,800 to $10,600; based on academic record; must have 3.4 GPA. Transfer Scholarships: $5,300 to $10,600; for students who have attended 2- or 4-year accredited colleges full-time and have earned at least 3.25 GPA. Phi Theta Kappa Scholarships: $2,000; up to 10 awarded each year to members of Phi Theta Kappa; must have a 3.25 GPA in transferable courses. Linfield Competitive Scholarships: range from $10,000-$16,000; competitive scholarship application must be submitted along with an application for admission; competitions held on McMinnville Campus by invitation only. Music Achievement Awards: $1,500-$2,500; audition or recorded performance required, must intend to major or minor in music. Leadership/Service Scholarship: up to $3,000; up to 5 awards each year to students who have demonstrated high levels of leadership, initiative, and service to others through student government, school activities, community organizations, and church or social service agencies; invitations to apply extended by April 1 each year; candidates must complete separate application. Academic All-Star Scholarships: supplement other academic scholarships with $2,500 for first place and $1,500 for 2nd or 3rd place.
Cumulative student debt: 75% of graduating class had student loans; average debt was $24,594.

FINANCIAL AID PROCEDURES
Forms required: FAFSA.
Dates and Deadlines: Priority date 2/1; no closing date. Applicants notified by 4/1; must reply by 5/1.
Transfers: Priority date 2/15. Merit scholarships available for qualified transfer students.

CONTACT
Dan Preston, Director of Financial Aid and Dean of Enrollment Services
900 SE Baker Street, McMinnville, OR 97218-6894
(503) 883-2225

Linn-Benton Community College
Albany, Oregon
www.linnbenton.edu   Federal Code: 006938

2-year public community college in large town.
Enrollment: 5,049 undergrads, 46% part-time. 922 full-time freshmen.
Selectivity: Open admission; but selective for some programs.

BASIC COSTS (2006-2007)
Tuition and fees: $3,109; out-of-state residents $7,654.
Per-credit charge: $65; out-of-state residents $166.
Additional info: Tuition/fee waivers available for unemployed or children of unemployed.

FINANCIAL AID PICTURE (2004-2005)
Students with need: 64% of average financial aid package awarded as scholarships/grants, 36% awarded as loans/jobs. Need-based aid available for part-time students. Work study available nights, weekends, and for part-time students.
Students without need: No-need awards available for academics, art, job skills, leadership, music/drama, state/district residency.

FINANCIAL AID PROCEDURES
Forms required: FAFSA.
Dates and Deadlines: Priority date 4/1; no closing date. Applicants notified on a rolling basis starting 4/15; must reply within 2 week(s) of notification.

CONTACT
John Snyder, Director of Financial Aid
6500 Southwest Pacific Boulevard, Albany, OR 97321-3779
(541) 917-4850

Marylhurst University
Marylhurst, Oregon
www.marylhurst.edu   Federal Code: 003199

4-year private university and liberal arts college in large town, affiliated with Roman Catholic Church.
Enrollment: 730 undergrads.
Selectivity: Open admission; but selective for some programs.

BASIC COSTS (2005-2006)
Tuition and fees: $14,220.
Per-credit charge: $308.

FINANCIAL AID PICTURE
Students with need: Need-based aid available for full-time and part-time students. Work study available weekends and for part-time students.
Students without need: No-need awards available for academics.

FINANCIAL AID PROCEDURES
Forms required: FAFSA, institutional form.
Dates and Deadlines: Priority date 6/1; no closing date. Applicants notified on a rolling basis starting 5/1.

698 Oregon Marylhurst University

CONTACT
Marlena McKee-Flores, Director of Financial Aid
PO Box 261, Marylhurst, OR 97036-0261
(503) 699-6253

Multnomah Bible College
Portland, Oregon
www.multnomah.edu   Federal Code: 003206

4-year private Bible and seminary college in large city, affiliated with interdenominational tradition.
Enrollment: 590 undergrads, 10% part-time. 79 full-time freshmen.
Selectivity: Admits over 75% of applicants.

BASIC COSTS (2005-2006)
Tuition and fees: $11,750.
Per-credit charge: $486.
Room and board: $5,060.

FINANCIAL AID PICTURE (2004-2005)
Students with need: Out of 75 full-time freshmen who applied for aid, 60 were judged to have need. Of these, 60 received aid, and 7 had their full need met. Average financial aid package met 50% of need; average scholarship/grant was $4,089; average loan was $2,420. For part-time students, average financial aid package was $4,680.
Students without need: 18 full-time freshmen who did not demonstrate need for aid received scholarships/grants; average award was $9,905. No-need awards available for academics.

FINANCIAL AID PROCEDURES
Forms required: FAFSA, institutional form.
Dates and Deadlines: Priority date 3/1; closing date 8/1. Applicants notified on a rolling basis starting 4/1; must reply within 3 week(s) of notification.

CONTACT
David Allen, Financial Aid Officer
8435 Northeast Glisan Street, Portland, OR 97220-5898
(503) 251-5337

Northwest Christian College
Eugene, Oregon
www.nwcc.edu   Federal Code: 003208

4-year private liberal arts college in small city, affiliated with Christian Church (Disciples of Christ).
Enrollment: 391 undergrads, 4% part-time. 48 full-time freshmen.
Selectivity: Admits 50 to 75% of applicants.

BASIC COSTS (2005-2006)
Tuition and fees: $18,380.
Per-credit charge: $607.
Room and board: $5,918.

FINANCIAL AID PICTURE (2005-2006)
Students with need: Out of 46 full-time freshmen who applied for aid, 42 were judged to have need. Of these, 42 received aid, and 8 had their full need met. Average financial aid package met 74% of need; average scholarship/grant was $11,997; average loan was $2,019. For part-time students, average financial aid package was $7,293.
Students without need: 6 full-time freshmen who did not demonstrate need for aid received scholarships/grants; average award was $5,892. No-need awards available for academics, athletics, leadership, music/drama, religious affiliation.
Scholarships offered: *Merit:* Presidential Scholarship; $5,000 per year, superior leadership and achievement and 2 of the following: 3.75 GPA, 1200 SAT, top 15% class rank. Dean's Scholarship; $4,000 per year, superior leadership and achievement and 2 of the following: 3.5 GPA, 1100 SAT, top 33% class rank. Achievement/Leadership Award; $3,000 per year, record of leadership/achievement and 2 of the following: 3.0 GPA, 1000 SAT, top 60% class rank. Valedictorian/Salutatorian Scholarship; $6,000 per year, meet criteria for Presidential Scholarship and graduate as valedictorian or salutatorian. SAT scores are exclusive of the writing portion. *Athletic:* 3 full-time freshmen received athletic scholarships; average amount $2,969.
Cumulative student debt: 75% of graduating class had student loans; average debt was $17,585.

FINANCIAL AID PROCEDURES
Forms required: FAFSA.
Dates and Deadlines: Priority date 3/1; no closing date. Applicants notified on a rolling basis starting 4/1.
Transfers: No deadline. Applicants notified on a rolling basis.

CONTACT
Jocelyn Hubbs, Associate Director of Financial Aid
828 East 11th Avenue, Eugene, OR 97401-3745
(541) 684-7291

Oregon Health & Science University
Portland, Oregon
www.ohsu.edu   Federal Code: 004883

Upper-division public university in large city.
Enrollment: 649 undergrads, 27% part-time.

BASIC COSTS (2005-2006)
Room only: $3,560.
Additional info: Tuition shown is for nursing program; costs for other programs vary. Tuition/fee waivers available for minority students.

FINANCIAL AID PICTURE
Students with need: Need-based aid available for full-time and part-time students.

FINANCIAL AID PROCEDURES
Forms required: FAFSA.
Dates and Deadlines: Priority date 3/1; no closing date. Applicants notified on a rolling basis starting 5/31.

CONTACT
Cherie Honnell, Director of Financial Aid/Registrar
3181 SW Sam Jackson Park Road, Portland, OR 97239
(503) 494-7800

Oregon Institute of Technology
Klamath Falls, Oregon
www.oit.edu   Federal Code: 003211

4-year public engineering and health science college in large town.
Enrollment: 2,578 undergrads, 27% part-time. 248 full-time freshmen.
Selectivity: Admits over 75% of applicants.

BASIC COSTS (2005-2006)
Tuition and fees: $5,457; out-of-state residents $15,573.
Per-credit charge: $104; out-of-state residents $318.
Room and board: $6,037.
Additional info: Tuition/fee waivers available for minority students.

FINANCIAL AID PICTURE (2004-2005)
Students with need: 37% of average financial aid package awarded as scholarships/grants, 63% awarded as loans/jobs. Need-based aid available for part-time students. Work study available weekends and for part-time students.

Students without need: No-need awards available for academics, athletics, leadership, minority status.

FINANCIAL AID PROCEDURES
Forms required: FAFSA.
Dates and Deadlines: Priority date 3/1; no closing date. Applicants notified on a rolling basis starting 4/1; must reply within 3 week(s) of notification.

CONTACT
Tracey Lehmann, Director of Financial Aid
3201 Campus Drive, Klamath Falls, OR 97601
(541) 885-1280

Oregon State University
Corvallis, Oregon
www.oregonstate.edu   Federal Code: 003210

4-year public university in small city.
Enrollment: 13,862 undergrads. 2,798 full-time freshmen.
Selectivity: Admits over 75% of applicants.

BASIC COSTS (2005-2006)
Tuition and fees: $5,442; out-of-state residents $17,502.
Per-credit charge: $116; out-of-state residents $451.
Room and board: $7,659.

FINANCIAL AID PICTURE (2005-2006)
Students with need: Out of 2,124 full-time freshmen who applied for aid, 1,508 were judged to have need. Of these, 1,458 received aid, and 361 had their full need met. Average financial aid package met 69% of need; average scholarship/grant was $2,344; average loan was $2,153. For part-time students, average financial aid package was $7,141.
Students without need: No-need awards available for academics, athletics, job skills, leadership, minority status, ROTC, state/district residency.
Scholarships offered: 85 full-time freshmen received athletic scholarships; average amount $12,259.

FINANCIAL AID PROCEDURES
Forms required: FAFSA.
Dates and Deadlines: Priority date 2/1; closing date 5/1. Applicants notified on a rolling basis starting 4/1; must reply within 4 week(s) of notification.
Transfers: Priority date 3/1; no deadline.

CONTACT
Kate Peterson, Director of Financial Aid
104 Kerr Administration Building, Corvallis, OR 97331-2130
(541) 731-2241

Pacific Northwest College of Art
Portland, Oregon
www.pnca.edu   Federal Code: 003207

4-year private visual arts college in large city.
Enrollment: 288 undergrads, 12% part-time. 33 full-time freshmen.
Selectivity: Admits 50 to 75% of applicants.

BASIC COSTS (2005-2006)
Tuition and fees: $17,296.
Per-credit charge: $710.

FINANCIAL AID PICTURE (2005-2006)
Students with need: Out of 25 full-time freshmen who applied for aid, 22 were judged to have need. Of these, 22 received aid, and 4 had their full need met. Average financial aid package met 72% of need; average scholarship/grant was $3,369; average loan was $2,596. For part-time students, average financial aid package was $12,904.
Students without need: No-need awards available for academics, art.

Scholarships offered: Leta Kennedy Student Scholarships; $10,000; based on artistic merit; number of awards undetermined. Dorothy Lemelson Scholarship; cost of attendance; based on artistic and academic merit; renewable up to 4 years; 1 award. Other renewable scholarships are available. All highly competitive; deadline March 1.

FINANCIAL AID PROCEDURES
Forms required: FAFSA.
Dates and Deadlines: Priority date 3/1; closing date 8/1. Applicants notified on a rolling basis starting 4/1; must reply by 5/1 or within 4 week(s) of notification.
Transfers: No deadline.

CONTACT
Peggy Burgus, Director of Financial Aid
1241 NW Johnson Street, Portland, OR 97209
(503) 821-8972

Pacific University
Forest Grove, Oregon
www.pacificu.edu   Federal Code: 003212

4-year private university in large town, affiliated with United Church of Christ.
Enrollment: 1,210 undergrads, 3% part-time. 324 full-time freshmen.
Selectivity: Admits over 75% of applicants.

BASIC COSTS (2006-2007)
Tuition and fees: $22,534.
Per-credit charge: $916.
Room and board: $6,468.

FINANCIAL AID PICTURE (2005-2006)
Students with need: Out of 304 full-time freshmen who applied for aid, 252 were judged to have need. Of these, 252 received aid, and 98 had their full need met. Average financial aid package met 89% of need; average scholarship/grant was $12,626; average loan was $5,349. For part-time students, average financial aid package was $12,100.
Students without need: 63 full-time freshmen who did not demonstrate need for aid received scholarships/grants; average award was $9,553. No-need awards available for academics, art, music/drama, religious affiliation.
Scholarships offered: Honors Scholarship: $9,000. Presidential Scholarship: $8,000. Trustee Scholarship: $7,500. University Scholarship: $6,500. Pacesetters Scholarship: $1,000 to $3,000. Number of awards varies.
Cumulative student debt: 84% of graduating class had student loans; average debt was $25,581.

FINANCIAL AID PROCEDURES
Forms required: FAFSA.
Dates and Deadlines: Priority date 2/15; no closing date. Applicants notified on a rolling basis starting 3/1; must reply within 2 week(s) of notification.

CONTACT
Dala Ramsey, Director of Financial Aid
2043 College Way, Forest Grove, OR 97116-1797
(503) 352-2222

Pioneer Pacific College
Wilsonville, Oregon
www.pioneerpacific.edu   Federal Code: 016520

4-year for-profit technical college in large town.
Enrollment: 370 undergrads. 84 full-time freshmen.
Selectivity: Open admission; but selective for some programs.

BASIC COSTS (2006-2007)
Tuition and fees: $9,560.

Additional info: Costs vary by program from $9,358 to $22,053. Quoted annual tuition is for criminal justice. Certain programs have additional lab fees. Tuition at time of enrollment locked for 4 years.

FINANCIAL AID PICTURE
Students with need: Need-based aid available for full-time and part-time students.
Students without need: This college only awards aid to students with need.
Scholarships offered: High school scholarship program and community scholarship program available.

FINANCIAL AID PROCEDURES
Forms required: FAFSA.
Dates and Deadlines: No deadline. Applicants notified on a rolling basis starting 3/15.

CONTACT
Stacey Maurer, Executive Director of Financial Aid
27501 Southwest Parkway Avenue, Wilsonville, OR 97070
(503) 682-3903

Portland Community College
Portland, Oregon
www.pcc.edu   Federal Code: 003213

2-year public community college in very large city.
Enrollment: 22,142 undergrads.
Selectivity: Open admission; but selective for some programs.

BASIC COSTS (2005-2006)
Tuition and fees: $2,970; out-of-state residents $8,730.
Per-credit charge: $62; out-of-state residents $190.

FINANCIAL AID PICTURE
Students with need: Need-based aid available for full-time and part-time students. Work study available nights, weekends, and for part-time students.
Students without need: This college only awards aid to students with need.

FINANCIAL AID PROCEDURES
Forms required: FAFSA.
Dates and Deadlines: Priority date 3/1; no closing date. Applicants notified on a rolling basis starting 6/1; must reply within 3 week(s) of notification.

CONTACT
Corbett Gottfried, Director of Financial Aid
Box 19000, Portland, OR 97280-0990
(503) 977-4934

Portland State University
Portland, Oregon
www.pdx.edu   Federal Code: 003216

4-year public university in very large city.
Enrollment: 15,797 undergrads, 32% part-time. 1,227 full-time freshmen.
Selectivity: Admits over 75% of applicants.

BASIC COSTS (2005-2006)
Tuition and fees: $5,202; out-of-state residents $17,127.
Per-credit charge: $95; out-of-state residents $355.
Room and board: $6,992.
Additional info: Tuition/fee waivers available for minority students.

FINANCIAL AID PICTURE (2005-2006)
Students with need: Out of 804 full-time freshmen who applied for aid, 577 were judged to have need. Of these, 561 received aid, and 54 had their full need met. Average financial aid package met 46% of need; average scholarship/grant was $3,983; average loan was $2,748. For part-time students, average financial aid package was $6,154.
Students without need: 74 full-time freshmen who did not demonstrate need for aid received scholarships/grants; average award was $2,143. No-need awards available for academics, art, athletics, music/drama, state/district residency.
Scholarships offered: 22 full-time freshmen received athletic scholarships; average amount $7,454.
Cumulative student debt: 70% of graduating class had student loans; average debt was $18,085.

FINANCIAL AID PROCEDURES
Forms required: FAFSA.
Dates and Deadlines: No deadline. Applicants notified on a rolling basis; must reply within 4 week(s) of notification.

CONTACT
Gary Garoffolo, Associate Director of Financial Aid
PO Box 751-ADM, Portland, OR 97207-0751
(800) 547-8887

Reed College
Portland, Oregon
www.reed.edu   Federal Code: 003217
                        CSS Code: 4654

4-year private liberal arts college in very large city.
Enrollment: 1,283 undergrads, 1% part-time. 354 full-time freshmen.
Selectivity: Admits less than 50% of applicants.

BASIC COSTS (2006-2007)
Tuition and fees: $34,530.
Per-credit charge: $1,450.
Room and board: $9,000.

FINANCIAL AID PICTURE (2005-2006)
Students with need: Out of 224 full-time freshmen who applied for aid, 177 were judged to have need. Of these, 165 received aid, and 158 had their full need met. Average financial aid package met 100% of need; average scholarship/grant was $27,387; average loan was $2,684.
Students without need: This college only awards aid to students with need.
Cumulative student debt: 61% of graduating class had student loans; average debt was $17,175.
Additional info: College meets demonstrated need of continuing students who have attended Reed minimum of 2 semesters, who file financial aid applications on time, and who maintain satisfactory academic progress. Institutional aid consideration is for a total of 8 semesters.

FINANCIAL AID PROCEDURES
Forms required: FAFSA, CSS PROFILE, institutional form.
Dates and Deadlines: Closing date 1/15. Applicants notified by 4/1; must reply by 5/1 or within 2 week(s) of notification.
Transfers: Priority date 2/1; closing date 3/1.

CONTACT
Leslie Limper, Director of Financial Aid
3203 Southeast Woodstock Boulevard, Portland, OR 97202-8199
(800) 547-4750

Rogue Community College
Grants Pass, Oregon
www.roguecc.edu
Federal Code: 010071

2-year public community college in large town.
Enrollment: 3,349 undergrads, 58% part-time. 323 full-time freshmen.
Selectivity: Open admission; but selective for some programs.

BASIC COSTS (2005-2006)
Tuition and fees: $2,985; out-of-state residents $3,525.
Per-credit charge: $59; out-of-state residents $71.
Additional info: Washington, Idaho, Nevada and California residents pay in-state tuition. Tuition/fee waivers available for unemployed or children of unemployed.

FINANCIAL AID PICTURE
Students with need: Need-based aid available for full-time and part-time students.

FINANCIAL AID PROCEDURES
Forms required: FAFSA, institutional form.
Dates and Deadlines: Priority date 5/1; no closing date. Applicants notified on a rolling basis; must reply within 2 week(s) of notification.

CONTACT
Anna Manley, Director of Financial Aid
3345 Redwood Highway, Grants Pass, OR 97527
(541) 956-7501

Southern Oregon University
Ashland, Oregon
www.sou.edu
Federal Code: 003219

4-year public university and liberal arts college in large town.
Enrollment: 4,238 undergrads, 18% part-time. 725 full-time freshmen.
Selectivity: Admits over 75% of applicants.

BASIC COSTS (2005-2006)
Tuition and fees: $5,085; out-of-state residents $16,059.
Per-credit charge: $105; out-of-state residents $372.
Room and board: $6,843.
Additional info: Tuition/fee waivers available for minority students.

FINANCIAL AID PICTURE (2005-2006)
Students with need: 54% of average financial aid package awarded as scholarships/grants, 46% awarded as loans/jobs. Need-based aid available for part-time students. Work study available nights, weekends, and for part-time students.
Students without need: No-need awards available for academics, alumni affiliation, art, athletics, leadership, minority status, music/drama, religious affiliation, state/district residency.

FINANCIAL AID PROCEDURES
Forms required: FAFSA.
Dates and Deadlines: No deadline. Applicants notified on a rolling basis starting 3/1; must reply within 2 week(s) of notification.

CONTACT
Debbie Beck, Associate Director of Financial Aid
1250 Siskiyou Boulevard, Ashland, OR 97520-5032
(541) 552-6161

Southwestern Oregon Community College
Coos Bay, Oregon
www.socc.edu
Federal Code: 003220

2-year public culinary school and community college in large town.
Enrollment: 1,923 undergrads, 49% part-time. 430 full-time freshmen.
Selectivity: Open admission; but selective for some programs.

BASIC COSTS (2005-2006)
Tuition and fees: $3,105.
Per-credit charge: $60.
Room and board: $5,155.
Additional info: Tuition/fee waivers available for adults, unemployed or children of unemployed.

FINANCIAL AID PICTURE (2004-2005)
Students with need: Need-based aid available for part-time students.

FINANCIAL AID PROCEDURES
Forms required: FAFSA.
Dates and Deadlines: Priority date 2/28; closing date 6/30. Applicants notified on a rolling basis starting 5/1; must reply within 3 week(s) of notification.

CONTACT
Robin Bunnell, Associate Dean of Enrollment/Student Services
1988 Newmark Avenue, Coos Bay, OR 97420-2956
(541) 888-7339

Treasure Valley Community College
Ontario, Oregon
www.tvcc.cc
Federal Code: 003221

2-year public community college in small town.
Enrollment: 1,762 undergrads, 41% part-time. 408 full-time freshmen.
Selectivity: Open admission.

BASIC COSTS (2006-2007)
Tuition and fees: $3,420; out-of-state residents $3,870.
Per-credit charge: $67; out-of-state residents $77.
Room and board: $4,845.

FINANCIAL AID PICTURE (2005-2006)
Students with need: Average financial aid package met 33% of need; average scholarship/grant was $3,364; average loan was $2,109. For part-time students, average financial aid package was $3,910.
Students without need: No-need awards available for academics, athletics, leadership, music/drama, state/district residency.
Cumulative student debt: 52% of graduating class had student loans; average debt was $10,042.

FINANCIAL AID PROCEDURES
Forms required: FAFSA.
Dates and Deadlines: Priority date 4/1; no closing date. Applicants notified on a rolling basis starting 5/1.

CONTACT
Kevin Jensen, Director of Financial Aid
650 College Boulevard, Ontario, OR 97914
(541) 881-8822 ext. 286

Umpqua Community College
Roseburg, Oregon
www.umpqua.edu   Federal Code: 003222

2-year public community college in large town.
Enrollment: 2,133 undergrads.
Selectivity: Open admission.

BASIC COSTS (2005-2006)
Tuition and fees: $2,880; out-of-state residents $8,100.
Per-credit charge: $59; out-of-state residents $175.

FINANCIAL AID PICTURE
Students with need: Need-based aid available for full-time and part-time students.
Students without need: This college only awards aid to students with need.

FINANCIAL AID PROCEDURES
Forms required: FAFSA.
Dates and Deadlines: Priority date 3/1; no closing date. Applicants notified on a rolling basis starting 5/1; must reply within 2 week(s) of notification.

CONTACT
Laurie Spangenberg, Director of Financial Aid
1140 College Road, Roseburg, OR 97470-0226
(541) 440-4602

University of Oregon
Eugene, Oregon
www.uoregon.edu   Federal Code: 003223

4-year public university in small city.
Enrollment: 16,164 undergrads, 8% part-time. 3,141 full-time freshmen.
Selectivity: Admits over 75% of applicants.

BASIC COSTS (2005-2006)
Tuition and fees: $5,613; out-of-state residents $17,445.
Per-credit charge: $104; out-of-state residents $407.
Room and board: $7,496.

FINANCIAL AID PICTURE (2005-2006)
Students with need: Out of 2,008 full-time freshmen who applied for aid, 1,174 were judged to have need. Of these, 1,106 received aid, and 198 had their full need met. Average financial aid package met 55% of need; average scholarship/grant was $4,005; average loan was $3,669. For part-time students, average financial aid package was $6,945.
Students without need: 389 full-time freshmen who did not demonstrate need for aid received scholarships/grants; average award was $1,579. No-need awards available for academics, athletics, leadership, minority status, music/drama, ROTC, state/district residency.
Scholarships offered: Presidential Scholarship; up to $6,000 per year for up to four years. National Merit Scholarship; $2,000 for up to 4 years. Laurel Award; amounts vary, apply annually. General University Scholarship; up to $2,700, apply annually. Dean's Scholarship; up to $5,000 per year for up to 12 terms. Diversity-Building Scholarship; for ethnic minority or first generation and/or non-traditional UO students. ROTC Scholarships.
Cumulative student debt: 60% of graduating class had student loans; average debt was $18,029.

FINANCIAL AID PROCEDURES
Forms required: FAFSA.
Dates and Deadlines: Priority date 3/1; closing date 6/30. Applicants notified on a rolling basis starting 4/15; must reply within 4 week(s) of notification.

CONTACT
Elizabeth Bickford, Director, Financial Aid
1217 University of Oregon, Eugene, OR 97403-1217
(541) 346-3221

University of Portland
Portland, Oregon
www.up.edu   Federal Code: 003224

4-year private university in large city, affiliated with Roman Catholic Church.
Enrollment: 2,860 undergrads, 1% part-time. 748 full-time freshmen.
Selectivity: Admits over 75% of applicants.

BASIC COSTS (2006-2007)
Tuition and fees: $26,390.
Per-credit charge: $822.
Room and board: $7,850.

FINANCIAL AID PICTURE (2005-2006)
Students with need: Out of 632 full-time freshmen who applied for aid, 482 were judged to have need. Of these, 480 received aid, and 148 had their full need met. Average financial aid package met 86% of need; average scholarship/grant was $13,807; average loan was $2,944. Need-based aid available for part-time students.
Students without need: 243 full-time freshmen who did not demonstrate need for aid received scholarships/grants; average award was $12,041. No-need awards available for academics, athletics, music/drama, ROTC.
Scholarships offered: President's Scholarship; up to $10,000. Holy Cross Scholarship; up to $6,000. Both based on academic excellence, other factors including school and community involvement. Arthur A. Schulte Scholarship; up to $6,000. In all cases, number of awards not limited.

FINANCIAL AID PROCEDURES
Forms required: FAFSA, institutional form.
Dates and Deadlines: Priority date 3/1; no closing date. Applicants notified by 3/15; must reply within 3 week(s) of notification.

CONTACT
Tracy Reisinger, Director of Financial Aid
5000 North Willamette Boulevard, Portland, OR 97203-5798
(503) 943-7311

Warner Pacific College
Portland, Oregon
www.warnerpacific.edu   Federal Code: 003225

4-year private liberal arts college in very large city, affiliated with Church of God.
Enrollment: 556 undergrads, 2% part-time. 66 full-time freshmen.
Selectivity: Open admission; but selective for some programs.

BASIC COSTS (2005-2006)
Tuition and fees: $19,150.
Room and board: $5,360.
Additional info: Per-credit-hour charges vary: part-time 1-5 credits $410; half-time 6-11 credits $800.

FINANCIAL AID PICTURE
Students with need: Need-based aid available for full-time and part-time students.
Students without need: No-need awards available for academics, athletics, leadership, minority status, music/drama, religious affiliation.

FINANCIAL AID PROCEDURES
Forms required: FAFSA.

Dates and Deadlines: Priority date 6/1; closing date 8/15. Applicants notified on a rolling basis starting 4/1; must reply within 4 week(s) of notification.
Transfers: Closing date 8/1.

CONTACT
Cindy Pollard, Director of Student Financial Assistance
2219 SE 68th Avenue, Portland, OR 97215-4026
(503) 517-1020

Western Oregon University
Monmouth, Oregon
www.wou.edu
Federal Code: 003209

4-year public liberal arts and teachers college in small town.
Enrollment: 4,136 undergrads, 9% part-time. 706 full-time freshmen.
Selectivity: Admits 50 to 75% of applicants.

BASIC COSTS (2005-2006)
Tuition and fees: $4,478; out-of-state residents $13,709.
Room and board: $6,654.
Additional info: Tuition/fee waivers available for minority students.

FINANCIAL AID PICTURE (2004-2005)
Students with need: Out of 642 full-time freshmen who applied for aid, 473 were judged to have need. Of these, 427 received aid, and 58 had their full need met. Average financial aid package met 65% of need; average scholarship/grant was $4,530; average loan was $3,732. For part-time students, average financial aid package was $5,708.
Students without need: 164 full-time freshmen who did not demonstrate need for aid received scholarships/grants; average award was $7,341. No-need awards available for academics, art, athletics, leadership, minority status, music/drama, ROTC, state/district residency.
Scholarships offered: 24 full-time freshmen received athletic scholarships; average amount $1,247.
Cumulative student debt: 48% of graduating class had student loans; average debt was $14,300.

FINANCIAL AID PROCEDURES
Forms required: FAFSA.
Dates and Deadlines: Priority date 3/1; no closing date. Applicants notified on a rolling basis starting 4/1; must reply within 2 week(s) of notification.

CONTACT
Donna Fossum, Director of Financial Aid
345 North Monmouth Avenue, Monmouth, OR 97361
(503) 838-8475

Willamette University
Salem, Oregon
www.willamette.edu
Federal Code: 003227
CSS Code: 4954

4-year private university and liberal arts college in small city, affiliated with United Methodist Church.
Enrollment: 1,813 undergrads, 1% part-time. 444 full-time freshmen.
Selectivity: Admits 50 to 75% of applicants.

BASIC COSTS (2006-2007)
Tuition and fees: $30,018.
Room and board: $7,250.
Additional info: $440 optional health insurance.

FINANCIAL AID PICTURE (2005-2006)
Students with need: Out of 353 full-time freshmen who applied for aid, 297 were judged to have need. Of these, 297 received aid, and 117 had their full need met. Average financial aid package met 92% of need; average scholarship/grant was $18,666; average loan was $3,797. For part-time students, average financial aid package was $18,246.
Students without need: 126 full-time freshmen who did not demonstrate need for aid received scholarships/grants; average award was $8,340. No-need awards available for academics, leadership, minority status, music/drama.
Scholarships offered: Presidential Scholarship: $15,000 to full tuition; based on 3.8 GPA, 1350 SAT or 30 ACT; 25 awards. Elmer and Grace Goudy Scholarship: $12,000; based on 3.7 GPA, 1300 SAT or 29 ACT; 40 awards. National Merit, National Hispanic and National Achievement Scholars: $15,000 to full tuition; based on PSAT. Multicultural Achievement Scholarships: $5,000-$10,000; based on academic achievement and extracurricular contributions. Willamette Honor Scholarships: $5,000-$10,000; based on superior academic and cocurricular experience. Music, forensics, theater scholarships: based on talent. Mark O. Hatfield Scholarship: full tuition; based on excellent academic record and demonstrated commitment to service leadership. Trustee's Scholarship: $15,000; based on 3.85 GPA, 1400 SAT or 32 ACT. All SAT scores exclusive of Writing.
Cumulative student debt: 79% of graduating class had student loans; average debt was $18,756.

FINANCIAL AID PROCEDURES
Forms required: FAFSA. CSS PROFILE required of early action applicants.
Dates and Deadlines: Closing date 2/1. Applicants notified by 4/1; must reply by 5/1 or within 2 week(s) of notification.

CONTACT
Patricia Hoban, Director of Financial Aid
900 State Street, Salem, OR 97301-3922
(503) 370-6273

Pennsylvania

Academy of Medical Arts and Business
Harrisburg, Pennsylvania
www.acadcampus.com
Federal Code: 022342

2-year for-profit business and health science college in small city.
Enrollment: 230 undergrads.

BASIC COSTS (2005-2006)
Tuition and fees: $10,440.

FINANCIAL AID PICTURE
Students with need: Need-based aid available for full-time and part-time students. Work study available nights.
Students without need: This college only awards aid to students with need.
Scholarships offered: 9 half-tuition scholarships available to degree-seeking students.

FINANCIAL AID PROCEDURES
Forms required: FAFSA, state aid form.
Dates and Deadlines: No deadline. Applicants notified on a rolling basis.
Transfers: State grant deadline for first-time recipients August 1. Renewal application deadline May 1.

CONTACT
Tracy Stewart, Financial Aid Coordinator
2301 Academy Drive, Harrisburg, PA 17112-1012
(717) 545-4747

Albright College
Reading, Pennsylvania
www.albright.edu
Federal Code: 003229

4-year private liberal arts college in small city, affiliated with United Methodist Church.
Enrollment: 2,074 undergrads. 451 full-time freshmen.
Selectivity: Admits 50 to 75% of applicants.

BASIC COSTS (2006-2007)
Tuition and fees: $27,420.
Per-credit charge: $1,389.
Room and board: $8,158.
Additional info: Tuition/fee waivers available for minority students.

FINANCIAL AID PICTURE (2005-2006)
Students with need: Out of 406 full-time freshmen who applied for aid, 365 were judged to have need. Of these, 364 received aid, and 67 had their full need met. Average financial aid package met 78% of need; average scholarship/grant was $16,255; average loan was $3,948. For part-time students, average financial aid package was $3,760.
Students without need: 66 full-time freshmen who did not demonstrate need for aid received scholarships/grants; average award was $14,327. No-need awards available for academics, alumni affiliation, art, leadership, minority status, music/drama, religious affiliation.
Cumulative student debt: 88% of graduating class had student loans; average debt was $24,671.

FINANCIAL AID PROCEDURES
Forms required: FAFSA.
Dates and Deadlines: Priority date 3/1; no closing date. Applicants notified on a rolling basis starting 2/15; must reply by 5/1 or within 2 week(s) of notification.
Transfers: Priority date 6/1.

CONTACT
Paul Gazzerro, V P for Administration & Finance
13th & Bern Streets, Reading, PA 19612-5234
(610) 921-7515

Allegheny College
Meadville, Pennsylvania
www.allegheny.edu
Federal Code: 003230

4-year private liberal arts college in large town, affiliated with United Methodist Church.
Enrollment: 2,016 undergrads. 561 full-time freshmen.
Selectivity: Admits 50 to 75% of applicants.

BASIC COSTS (2006-2007)
Tuition and fees: $28,300.
Per-credit charge: $1,167.
Room and board: $7,000.

FINANCIAL AID PICTURE (2005-2006)
Students with need: Out of 478 full-time freshmen who applied for aid, 395 were judged to have need. Of these, 395 received aid, and 205 had their full need met. Average financial aid package met 94% of need; average scholarship/grant was $15,625; average loan was $4,360. For part-time students, average financial aid package was $4,950.
Students without need: 156 full-time freshmen who did not demonstrate need for aid received scholarships/grants; average award was $10,835. No-need awards available for academics, leadership, minority status, state/district residency.
Scholarships offered: Trustee Scholarships; up to $15,000 per year.
Cumulative student debt: 78% of graduating class had student loans; average debt was $24,825.

FINANCIAL AID PROCEDURES
Forms required: FAFSA.
Dates and Deadlines: Priority date 2/15; no closing date. Applicants notified on a rolling basis starting 3/1; must reply by 5/1 or within 4 week(s) of notification.
Transfers: Closing date 6/7. Applicants notified on a rolling basis; must reply within 3 week(s) of notification. Trustee Scholarships, up to $12,500, available for entering transfer students with high school rank in top 25% of class and high academic achievement in college.

CONTACT
Sheryle Proper, Director of Financial Aid
520 North Main Street, Meadville, PA 16335
(800) 835-7780

Alvernia College
Reading, Pennsylvania
www.alvernia.edu
Federal Code: 003233

4-year private liberal arts college in small city, affiliated with Roman Catholic Church.
Enrollment: 1,881 undergrads, 20% part-time. 285 full-time freshmen.
Selectivity: Admits over 75% of applicants.

BASIC COSTS (2006-2007)
Tuition and fees: $20,422.
Per-credit charge: $570.
Room and board: $8,193.

FINANCIAL AID PICTURE (2005-2006)
Students with need: Out of 269 full-time freshmen who applied for aid, 240 were judged to have need. Of these, 240 received aid, and 87 had their full need met. Average financial aid package met 84% of need; average scholarship/grant was $6,784; average loan was $3,496.
Students without need: 29 full-time freshmen who did not demonstrate need for aid received scholarships/grants; average award was $7,800. No-need awards available for academics, alumni affiliation.
Cumulative student debt: 91% of graduating class had student loans; average debt was $6,985.

FINANCIAL AID PROCEDURES
Forms required: FAFSA, state aid form.
Dates and Deadlines: No deadline. Applicants notified on a rolling basis starting 2/1; must reply within 2 week(s) of notification.

CONTACT
Lora Myers, Financial Aid Director
400 St. Bernardine Street, Reading, PA 19607-1799
(610) 796-8356

Antonelli Institute of Art and Photography
Erdenheim, Pennsylvania
www.antonelli.edu
Federal Code: 007430

2-year for-profit visual arts and junior college in large town.
Enrollment: 187 undergrads, 2% part-time. 117 full-time freshmen.
Selectivity: Admits 50 to 75% of applicants.

BASIC COSTS (2006-2007)
Additional info: Annual Tuition for graphic design/commercial art students is $15,450; for photography students $17,150. Required fees $125.

FINANCIAL AID PICTURE (2005-2006)
Students with need: Average financial aid package met 35% of need. Need-based aid available for part-time students.
Students without need: This college only awards aid to students with need.
Cumulative student debt: 71% of graduating class had student loans; average debt was $16,000.

FINANCIAL AID PROCEDURES
Forms required: FAFSA.
Dates and Deadlines: No deadline. Applicants notified on a rolling basis; must reply within 2 week(s) of notification.
Transfers: Priority date 3/15; closing date 8/1.

CONTACT
Eugene Awot, Director of Financial Aid
300 Montgomery Avenue, Erdenheim, PA 19038-8242
(215) 836-2222

Arcadia University
Glenside, Pennsylvania
www.arcadia.edu   Federal Code: 003235

4-year private university in large town, affiliated with Presbyterian Church (USA).
Enrollment: 1,955 undergrads, 11% part-time. 440 full-time freshmen.
Selectivity: Admits over 75% of applicants.

BASIC COSTS (2006-2007)
Tuition and fees: $25,900.
Per-credit charge: $442.
Room and board: $9,660.

FINANCIAL AID PICTURE (2005-2006)
Students with need: Average financial aid package met 82.49% of need; average scholarship/grant was $15,216; average loan was $4,840. For part-time students, average financial aid package was $10,778.
Students without need: No-need awards available for academics, alumni affiliation, art, leadership.
Scholarships offered: Distinguished Scholarships: range from $1,000 to full tuition for full-time freshmen. Arcadia University Achievement Awards: range from $1,000-$6,000 for full-time undergraduates who have demonstrated outstanding leadership, exceptional community and/or volunteer service or special talents.
Additional info: Early Financial Aid Estimate Service offered September through January. Students may use this service before applying for admission.

FINANCIAL AID PROCEDURES
Forms required: FAFSA, institutional form.
Dates and Deadlines: Priority date 3/1; no closing date. Applicants notified on a rolling basis starting 2/15; must reply by 5/1.

CONTACT
Elizabeth Rihl Lewinsky, Assistant VP of Enrollment Management
450 South Easton Road, Glenside, PA 19038-3295
(215) 572-2980

Art Institute of Philadelphia
Philadelphia, Pennsylvania
www.aiph.aii.edu   Federal Code: 008350

4-year for-profit visual arts college in very large city.
Enrollment: 3,374 undergrads, 28% part-time. 600 full-time freshmen.
Selectivity: Open admission.

BASIC COSTS (2006-2007)
Tuition and fees: $18,195.
Per-credit charge: $401.
Room only: $7,002.
Additional info: One-time activities fee of $50 for bachelor's, $35 for associate. Additionally, several programs have quarterly supplies fees that vary. Tuition at time of enrollment locked for 4 years.

FINANCIAL AID PICTURE (2005-2006)
Students with need: 12% of average financial aid package awarded as scholarships/grants, 88% awarded as loans/jobs. Need-based aid available for part-time students. Work study available nights, weekends, and for part-time students.
Additional info: Institute-sponsored scholarships available.

FINANCIAL AID PROCEDURES
Forms required: FAFSA, institutional form.
Dates and Deadlines: Closing date 5/1. Applicants notified on a rolling basis starting 3/1; must reply within 2 week(s) of notification.
Transfers: No deadline. Transfer students applying for financial aid must meet standards for satisfactory academic progress as defined by State Grant Program.

CONTACT
Felicia Bryant, Director of Student Financial Services
1622 Chestnut Street, Philadelphia, PA 19103-5198
(215) 567-7080 ext. 6392

Baptist Bible College of Pennsylvania
Clarks Summit, Pennsylvania
www.bbc.edu   Federal Code: 002670

4-year private Bible and seminary college in small city, affiliated with Baptist faith.
Enrollment: 697 undergrads, 4% part-time. 144 full-time freshmen.
Selectivity: Admits over 75% of applicants.

BASIC COSTS (2006-2007)
Tuition and fees: $13,980.
Per-credit charge: $432.
Room and board: $5,600.

FINANCIAL AID PICTURE (2005-2006)
Students with need: Need-based aid available for part-time students. Work study available nights, weekends, and for part-time students.
Students without need: No-need awards available for academics, leadership, music/drama, religious affiliation.

FINANCIAL AID PROCEDURES
Forms required: FAFSA, institutional form.
Dates and Deadlines: Closing date 5/1. Applicants notified on a rolling basis starting 4/1.

CONTACT
Tom Pollock, Director of Student Financial Services
538 Venard Road, Clarks Summit, PA 18411-1297
(570) 586-2400

Berks Technical Institute
Wyomissing, Pennsylvania
www.berks.edu   Federal Code: 017149

2-year for-profit business and technical college in small city.
Enrollment: 585 undergrads.
Selectivity: Open admission.

BASIC COSTS (2005-2006)
Additional info: Tuition for diploma program ranges from $9,600 to $17,000; tuition for degree program ranges from $21,000 to $30,000.

FINANCIAL AID PICTURE
Students with need: Need-based aid available for full-time and part-time students.
Students without need: This college only awards aid to students with need.

FINANCIAL AID PROCEDURES
Forms required: FAFSA, state aid form.
Dates and Deadlines: No deadline. Applicants notified on a rolling basis; must reply within 2 week(s) of notification.
Transfers: Deadline for first-time financial aid applicants is August 1. Deadline for renewal applicants is May 1.

CONTACT
Valerie Westmere, Financial Aid Director
2205 Ridgewood Road, Wyomissing, PA 19610
(610) 372-1722

Bidwell Training Center
Pittsburgh, Pennsylvania
www.bidwell-training.org   Federal Code: 031015

1-year for-profit business and health science college in large city.
Enrollment: 130 undergrads.

BASIC COSTS (2005-2006)
Additional info: Tuition per year ranges from $6,000 to $10,000, includes all fees. Programs offered at no cost to Pennsylvania residents.

FINANCIAL AID PICTURE
Students with need: Need-based aid available for full-time students.
Students without need: This college only awards aid to students with need.

FINANCIAL AID PROCEDURES
Forms required: FAFSA.
Dates and Deadlines: No deadline. Applicants notified on a rolling basis.

CONTACT
Ken Huselton, Director of Student Services
1815 Metropolitan Street, Pittsburgh, PA 15233
(412) 323-4000

Bloomsburg University of Pennsylvania
Bloomsburg, Pennsylvania
www.bloomu.edu   Federal Code: 003315

4-year public university and liberal arts college in large town.
Enrollment: 7,575 undergrads, 5% part-time. 1,693 full-time freshmen.
Selectivity: Admits 50 to 75% of applicants.

BASIC COSTS (2005-2006)
Tuition and fees: $6,226; out-of-state residents $13,586.
Per-credit charge: $204; out-of-state residents $511.
Room and board: $5,476.
Additional info: Tuition/fee waivers available for minority students.

FINANCIAL AID PICTURE (2005-2006)
Students with need: Out of 1,490 full-time freshmen who applied for aid, 1,416 were judged to have need. Of these, 1,373 received aid, and 1,236 had their full need met. Average financial aid package met 65% of need; average scholarship/grant was $4,491; average loan was $2,479. For part-time students, average financial aid package was $6,374.

Students without need: 35 full-time freshmen who did not demonstrate need for aid received scholarships/grants; average award was $1,476. No-need awards available for academics, art, athletics, job skills, leadership, minority status, music/drama, ROTC, state/district residency.
Scholarships offered: 57 full-time freshmen received athletic scholarships; average amount $2,111.
Cumulative student debt: 68% of graduating class had student loans; average debt was $16,442.

FINANCIAL AID PROCEDURES
Forms required: FAFSA.
Dates and Deadlines: Priority date 3/15; no closing date. Applicants notified on a rolling basis starting 4/1.
Transfers: Evaluation of transfer credits must be completed before financial aid can be finalized.

CONTACT
Thomas Lyons, Director of Financial Aid
104 Student Service Center, Bloomsburg, PA 17815
(570) 389-4297

Bryn Athyn College of the New Church
Bryn Athyn, Pennsylvania
www.brynathyn.edu   Federal Code: 003228

4-year private liberal arts college in small town, affiliated with General Church of the New Jerusalem (Swedenborgian).
Enrollment: 138 undergrads, 4% part-time. 45 full-time freshmen.
Selectivity: Admits over 75% of applicants.

BASIC COSTS (2006-2007)
Tuition and fees: $10,114.
Room and board: $5,574.

FINANCIAL AID PICTURE (2005-2006)
Students with need: Out of 30 full-time freshmen who applied for aid, 24 were judged to have need. Of these, 24 received aid, and 9 had their full need met. Average financial aid package met 74% of need; average scholarship/grant was $6,162; average loan was $877. For part-time students, average financial aid package was $5,500.
Students without need: 3 full-time freshmen who did not demonstrate need for aid received scholarships/grants; average award was $1,000. No-need awards available for academics, leadership, religious affiliation.
Cumulative student debt: 37% of graduating class had student loans; average debt was $5,062.

FINANCIAL AID PROCEDURES
Forms required: FAFSA, institutional form.
Dates and Deadlines: Closing date 6/1. Applicants notified on a rolling basis starting 4/30; must reply by 9/30.
Transfers: No deadline. Applicants notified on a rolling basis starting 7/1; must reply within 6 week(s) of notification.

CONTACT
William Alden, Director of Business Administration
P.O. Box 717, Bryn Athyn, PA 19009-0717
(267) 502-2630

Bryn Mawr College
Bryn Mawr, Pennsylvania
www.brynmawr.edu   Federal Code: 003237
                          CSS Code: 2049

4-year private liberal arts college for women in very large city.
Enrollment: 1,323 undergrads, 1% part-time. 354 full-time freshmen.
Selectivity: Admits less than 50% of applicants.

BASIC COSTS (2006-2007)
Tuition and fees: $33,010.
Room and board: $10,550.

FINANCIAL AID PICTURE (2005-2006)
Students with need: Out of 252 full-time freshmen who applied for aid, 202 were judged to have need. Of these, 202 received aid, and 198 had their full need met. Average financial aid package met 98% of need; average scholarship/grant was $24,396; average loan was $3,525. For part-time students, average financial aid package was $11,500.
Students without need: This college only awards aid to students with need.
Cumulative student debt: 57% of graduating class had student loans; average debt was $17,018.

FINANCIAL AID PROCEDURES
Forms required: FAFSA, CSS PROFILE.
Dates and Deadlines: Closing date 2/4. Applicants notified by 3/23; must reply by 5/1.
Transfers: Closing date 3/15. Must reply by 5/1.

CONTACT
Ethel Desmarais, Director of Financial Aid
101 North Merion Avenue, Bryn Mawr, PA 19010-2899
(610) 526-5245

Bucknell University
Lewisburg, Pennsylvania
www.bucknell.edu
Federal Code: 003238
CSS Code: 2050

4-year private university in small town.
Enrollment: 3,460 undergrads. 920 full-time freshmen.
Selectivity: Admits less than 50% of applicants.

BASIC COSTS (2006-2007)
Tuition and fees: $36,002.
Room and board: $7,366.

FINANCIAL AID PICTURE (2005-2006)
Students with need: Out of 541 full-time freshmen who applied for aid, 418 were judged to have need. Of these, 418 received aid, and 418 had their full need met. Average financial aid package met 100% of need; average scholarship/grant was $18,400; average loan was $4,000.
Students without need: 14 full-time freshmen who did not demonstrate need for aid received scholarships/grants; average award was $14,540. No-need awards available for academics, art, athletics, leadership, music/drama, ROTC.
Scholarships offered: Merit: Scholarships available to a limited number of students who have demonstrated exceptional achievements in academics, art and performing arts, music, and athletics (limited to basketball). **Athletic:** 6 full-time freshmen received athletic scholarships; average amount $10,000.
Cumulative student debt: 62% of graduating class had student loans; average debt was $17,400.

FINANCIAL AID PROCEDURES
Forms required: FAFSA, CSS PROFILE.
Dates and Deadlines: Closing date 1/1. Applicants notified by 4/1; must reply by 5/1.
Transfers: Closing date 3/15. Applicants notified by 5/1; must reply by 6/1. Aid restricted to 2-year college graduates.

CONTACT
Andrea Leithner, Director of Financial Aid
Freas Hall, Lewisburg, PA 17837-9988
(570) 577-1331

Bucks County Community College
Newtown, Pennsylvania
www.bucks.edu
Federal Code: 003239

2-year public community college in large town.
Enrollment: 9,596 undergrads, 58% part-time. 1,687 full-time freshmen.
Selectivity: Open admission; but selective for some programs.

BASIC COSTS (2005-2006)
Tuition and fees: $3,157; out-of-district residents $5,827; out-of-state residents $8,497.
Per-credit charge: $89; out-of-district residents $178; out-of-state residents $267.
Additional info: In-state out-of-district required fees $787; out-of-state required fees $1087.

FINANCIAL AID PICTURE (2004-2005)
Students with need: 66% of average financial aid package awarded as scholarships/grants, 34% awarded as loans/jobs. Need-based aid available for part-time students. Work study available nights, weekends, and for part-time students.
Students without need: No-need awards available for academics.

FINANCIAL AID PROCEDURES
Forms required: FAFSA, institutional form.
Dates and Deadlines: Priority date 5/1; no closing date. Applicants notified on a rolling basis starting 6/1; must reply within 2 week(s) of notification.
Transfers: No deadline. Applicants notified by 6/1; must reply within 2 week(s) of notification.

CONTACT
Fran McKeown, Director of Financial Aid
275 Swamp Road, Newtown, PA 18940
(215) 968-8200

Business Institute of Pennsylvania: Meadville
Meadville, Pennsylvania
www.biop.edu
Federal Code: E00693

2-year for-profit business college in large town.
Enrollment: 69 undergrads. 44 full-time freshmen.
Selectivity: Admits over 75% of applicants.

BASIC COSTS (2006-2007)
Tuition and fees: $8,050.
Per-credit charge: $250.

FINANCIAL AID PICTURE
Students with need: Need-based aid available for full-time and part-time students.
Students without need: No-need awards available for academics.

FINANCIAL AID PROCEDURES
Forms required: FAFSA.
Transfers: Closing date 5/1. Applicants notified on a rolling basis.

CONTACT
Dorothy Gagliardi, Director of Financial Aid
628 Arch Street, Suite B105, Meadville, PA 16335
(724) 983-0700

Butler County Community College
Butler, Pennsylvania
www.bc3.edu
Federal Code: 003240

2-year public community college in large town.
Enrollment: 3,809 undergrads, 48% part-time. 509 full-time freshmen.
Selectivity: Open admission; but selective for some programs.

BASIC COSTS (2005-2006)
Tuition and fees: $2,640; out-of-district residents $4,770; out-of-state residents $6,900.
Per-credit charge: $71; out-of-district residents $142; out-of-state residents $213.

FINANCIAL AID PICTURE (2004-2005)
Students with need: 51% of average financial aid package awarded as scholarships/grants, 49% awarded as loans/jobs. Need-based aid available for part-time students.
Students without need: No-need awards available for academics, state/district residency.

FINANCIAL AID PROCEDURES
Forms required: FAFSA.
Dates and Deadlines: Priority date 4/15; no closing date. Applicants notified on a rolling basis starting 5/1; must reply within 2 week(s) of notification.

CONTACT
Jean Walker, Director of Financial Aid
PO Box 1203, Butler, PA 16003-1203
(724) 287-8711 ext. 8329

Cabrini College
Radnor, Pennsylvania
www.cabrini.edu
Federal Code: 003241

4-year private liberal arts college in large town, affiliated with Roman Catholic Church.
Enrollment: 1,715 undergrads, 10% part-time. 526 full-time freshmen.
Selectivity: Admits 50 to 75% of applicants.

BASIC COSTS (2006-2007)
Tuition and fees: $25,950.
Room and board: $9,800.

FINANCIAL AID PICTURE (2005-2006)
Students with need: Out of 482 full-time freshmen who applied for aid, 416 were judged to have need. Of these, 416 received aid, and 74 had their full need met. Average financial aid package met 88% of need; average scholarship/grant was $5,065; average loan was $2,932. For part-time students, average financial aid package was $6,723.
Students without need: 69 full-time freshmen who did not demonstrate need for aid received scholarships/grants; average award was $8,670. No-need awards available for academics, alumni affiliation.
Cumulative student debt: 84% of graduating class had student loans; average debt was $17,400.

FINANCIAL AID PROCEDURES
Forms required: FAFSA.
Dates and Deadlines: Closing date 4/1. Applicants notified on a rolling basis starting 3/1.
Transfers: Achievement scholarships available.

CONTACT
Michael Colahan, Financial Aid Director
610 King of Prussia Road, Radnor, PA 19087-3698
(610) 902-8420

California University of Pennsylvania
California, Pennsylvania
www.cup.edu
Federal Code: 003316

4-year public university in small town.
Enrollment: 5,827 undergrads, 10% part-time. 982 full-time freshmen.
Selectivity: Admits over 75% of applicants.

BASIC COSTS (2005-2006)
Tuition and fees: $6,491; out-of-state residents $8,945.
Per-credit charge: $204; out-of-state residents $511.
Room and board: $7,908.
Additional info: Tuition/fee waivers available for adults, minority students.

FINANCIAL AID PICTURE (2004-2005)
Students with need: Out of 953 full-time freshmen who applied for aid, 773 were judged to have need. Of these, 751 received aid, and 29 had their full need met. For part-time students, average financial aid package was $5,292.
Students without need: 27 full-time freshmen who did not demonstrate need for aid received scholarships/grants; average award was $1,795. No-need awards available for academics, athletics, minority status.
Scholarships offered: 9 full-time freshmen received athletic scholarships; average amount $3,176.

FINANCIAL AID PROCEDURES
Forms required: FAFSA, state aid form.
Dates and Deadlines: Priority date 5/1; no closing date. Applicants notified on a rolling basis starting 4/1; must reply within 3 week(s) of notification.

CONTACT
Robert Thorn, Director of Financial Aid
250 University Avenue, California, PA 15419-1394
(724) 938-4415

Cambria-Rowe Business College
Johnstown, Pennsylvania
www.crbc.net
Federal Code: 004889

2-year for-profit business college in small city.
Enrollment: 232 undergrads.

BASIC COSTS (2005-2006)
Tuition and fees: $8,325.
Additional info: Depending on choice of laptop, fees could be as much as $990.

FINANCIAL AID PICTURE
Students with need: Need-based aid available for full-time and part-time students.
Students without need: No-need awards available for academics, leadership.
Scholarships offered: Presidential Grant; 3 awarded; 50% tuition; FBLA Scholarship; 2 awarded; $3,000.

FINANCIAL AID PROCEDURES
Forms required: FAFSA, state aid form.
Dates and Deadlines: Closing date 8/1. Applicants notified on a rolling basis.
Transfers: Closing date 5/1.

CONTACT
Judy Miller, Financial Aid Adviser
221 Central Avenue, Johnstown, PA 15902
(814) 536-5168

Cambria-Rowe Business College: Indiana
Indiana, Pennsylvania
www.crbc.net   Federal Code: 004889

2-year for-profit business and technical college in large town.
Enrollment: 130 undergrads.
Selectivity: Open admission.

BASIC COSTS (2005-2006)
Tuition and fees: $8,325.
Additional info: Depending on choice of laptop, fees could be as much as $990.

FINANCIAL AID PICTURE
Students with need: Need-based aid available for full-time and part-time students.

FINANCIAL AID PROCEDURES
Forms required: FAFSA.
Dates and Deadlines: No deadline. Applicants notified on a rolling basis.

CONTACT
Judy Miller
422 South 13th Street, Indiana, PA 15701
(814) 536-5168

Career Training Academy
New Kensington, Pennsylvania
www.careerta.com   Federal Code: 026095

2-year for-profit career school in small town.
Enrollment: 191 undergrads.
Selectivity: Open admission; but selective for some programs.

BASIC COSTS (2005-2006)
Additional info: Total cost of 15-month associate degree program in massage therapy: $18,366 (includes tuition, books, portable massage table, uniforms, lab fees, insurance, graduation fees). Total cost of 15-month associate degree program in medical assistance: $14,572 (includes tuition, books, uniforms, lab fees, insurance, graduation fees). Other diploma programs will vary in cost and required length of study. Tuition at time of enrollment locked for 2 years.

FINANCIAL AID PICTURE
Students with need: Need-based aid available for full-time students.
Students without need: This college only awards aid to students with need.
Additional info: Work study available after class day.

FINANCIAL AID PROCEDURES
Forms required: FAFSA, institutional form.
Dates and Deadlines: No deadline.

CONTACT
Karen Schonbachler, Financial Services Coordinator
950 Fifth Avenue, New Kensington, PA 15068

Career Training Academy: Monroeville
Monroeville, Pennsylvania
www.careerta.edu   Federal Code: 026095

2-year for-profit branch campus college in small city.
Enrollment: 86 undergrads. 13 full-time freshmen.
Selectivity: Open admission.

BASIC COSTS (2005-2006)
Additional info: Tuition ranges from $3,300 to $16,500 depending on program; required fees range from $180 to $1,100 depending on program.

FINANCIAL AID PICTURE
Students with need: Need-based aid available for full-time and part-time students.
Students without need: This college only awards aid to students with need.

FINANCIAL AID PROCEDURES
Forms required: FAFSA, state aid form, institutional form.

CONTACT
Karen Schonbachler, Financial Aid Supervisor
4314 Old William Penn Highway #103, Monroeville, PA 15146
(724) 337-1000

Carlow University
Pittsburgh, Pennsylvania
www.carlow.edu   Federal Code: 003303

4-year private liberal arts college for women in large city, affiliated with Roman Catholic Church.
Enrollment: 1,602 undergrads, 27% part-time. 273 full-time freshmen.
Selectivity: Admits 50 to 75% of applicants.

BASIC COSTS (2005-2006)
Tuition and fees: $17,450.
Per-credit charge: $550.
Room and board: $6,870.
Additional info: Tuition/fee waivers available for unemployed or children of unemployed.

FINANCIAL AID PICTURE (2005-2006)
Students with need: Need-based aid available for part-time students.
Students without need: No-need awards available for academics, athletics, leadership, religious affiliation.
Scholarships offered: Full tuition: 3.75 GPA, 1300 SAT. Half tuition: 3.5 GPA, 1200 SAT. Presidential: $5,000; 3.25 GPA, 1100 SAT. Valedictorian: $5,000. McAuley: $4,000, 3.25 GPA, 950 SAT, one per Catholic high school in diocese of Pittsburgh, Johnston/Altoona and Greensburg. Messer: $4,000 to math/engineering majors in 3/2 program with Carnegie-Mellon, reviewed individually. Legacy: to daughters or granddaughters of alumnae, requires 3.25 GPA and 900 SAT. Dean's Recognition: 3.25 GPA and 900 SAT. Sister Maurice Whalen: to those who submit projects to Pittsburgh Regional Science and Engineering Fair, also requires 3.25 GPA and 1000 SAT. Rose Marie Beard Women of Spirit Honors Scholarship: GPA 3.5 or higher, 1100 SAT or better, ranked in top 15% of high school class, evidence of significant leadership, awards $4,000 for first year for 6 students and is added to any other Carlow-awarded scholarships. All SAT scores exclusive of Writing.
Cumulative student debt: 79% of graduating class had student loans; average debt was $23,395.

FINANCIAL AID PROCEDURES
Forms required: FAFSA.
Dates and Deadlines: Priority date 4/1; no closing date. Applicants notified on a rolling basis starting 3/1; must reply within 2 week(s) of notification.
Transfers: Applicants notified by 3/1; must reply within 2 week(s) of notification. May 1 deadline for Pennsylvania State Aid Grant.

CONTACT
Natalie Wilson, Director of Financial Aid
3333 Fifth Avenue, Pittsburgh, PA 15213-3165
(412) 578-6058

Carnegie Mellon University
Pittsburgh, Pennsylvania
www.cmu.edu
Federal Code: 003242

4-year private university in large city.
Enrollment: 5,494 undergrads, 2% part-time. 1,407 full-time freshmen.
Selectivity: Admits less than 50% of applicants.

BASIC COSTS (2006-2007)
Tuition and fees: $34,578.
Per-credit charge: $475.
Room and board: $9,280.

FINANCIAL AID PICTURE (2005-2006)
Students with need: Out of 969 full-time freshmen who applied for aid, 755 were judged to have need. Of these, 752 received aid, and 270 had their full need met. Average financial aid package met 80% of need; average scholarship/grant was $17,288; average loan was $3,470. For part-time students, average financial aid package was $15,712.
Students without need: 107 full-time freshmen who did not demonstrate need for aid received scholarships/grants; average award was $11,533. No-need awards available for academics, art, leadership, minority status, music/drama, state/district residency.
Cumulative student debt: 48% of graduating class had student loans; average debt was $26,500.
Additional info: Early need analysis offered; merit awards available. Students notified within week to 10 days of receipt of financial aid application.

FINANCIAL AID PROCEDURES
Forms required: FAFSA, institutional form.
Dates and Deadlines: Priority date 2/15; closing date 5/1. Applicants notified by 3/15.
Transfers: Students applying for Spring transfer must file FAFSA by November 1. College of Fine Arts applicants applying for Fall transfer must file FAFSA by February 15. All other applicants for Fall transfer must submit FAFSA by May 1.

CONTACT
Linda Anderson, Director of Enrollment Services
5000 Forbes Avenue, Pittsburgh, PA 15213-3890
(412) 268-8186

Cedar Crest College
Allentown, Pennsylvania
www.cedarcrest.edu
Federal Code: 003243

4-year private liberal arts college for women in small city.
Enrollment: 1,820 undergrads, 48% part-time. 201 full-time freshmen.
Selectivity: Admits 50 to 75% of applicants.

BASIC COSTS (2006-2007)
Tuition and fees: $23,848.
Room and board: $8,256.
Additional info: Fee of $300 required of resident students.

FINANCIAL AID PICTURE (2005-2006)
Students with need: Out of 197 full-time freshmen who applied for aid, 171 were judged to have need. Of these, 171 received aid, and 29 had their full need met. Average financial aid package met 76% of need; average scholarship/grant was $13,349; average loan was $3,391. For part-time students, average financial aid package was $5,520.
Students without need: 27 full-time freshmen who did not demonstrate need for aid received scholarships/grants; average award was $10,132. No-need awards available for academics, alumni affiliation, art, leadership, music/drama.
Scholarships offered: Presidential Scholarship: up to half tuition; for all incoming freshmen with SAT scores over 1150 and in top 10% of class (renewable for four years with GPA of 3.0). High School Achievement Award: $5,000 per year (renewable for four years with GPA of 3.0); for incoming freshmen with SAT of 1150 and in top 20% of class. Girl Scout Gold Awards: $1,000 per year; for recipients of the Girl Scout Gold Award. Art, Dance, and Performing Arts Scholarships: $1,500 per year; based on portfolio review, audition, and commitment to the creative process. Governor's School of Excellence Award: $1,000 per year; for graduates of Governor's Schools of Excellence. Hugh O'Brian Youth (HOBY) Awards: $1,000 per year; for freshmen who are HOBY alumnae. SAT scores exclusive of Writing portion.
Cumulative student debt: 97% of graduating class had student loans; average debt was $22,820.

FINANCIAL AID PROCEDURES
Forms required: FAFSA, institutional form.
Dates and Deadlines: No deadline. Applicants notified on a rolling basis starting 11/1; must reply by 5/1 or within 3 week(s) of notification.
Transfers: Certain academic scholarships are available for transfers only, such as the Phi Theta Kappa Scholarship.

CONTACT
Lori Williams, Director of Financial Aid
100 College Drive, Allentown, PA 18104-6196
(610) 740-3785

Central Pennsylvania College
Summerdale, Pennsylvania
www.centralpenn.edu
Federal Code: 004890

4-year for-profit business and technical college in rural community.
Enrollment: 981 undergrads, 29% part-time. 159 full-time freshmen.
Selectivity: Open admission; but selective for some programs.

BASIC COSTS (2005-2006)
Tuition and fees: $11,610.
Per-credit charge: $305.
Room and board: $6,360.

FINANCIAL AID PICTURE
Students with need: Need-based aid available for full-time and part-time students.
Students without need: No-need awards available for academics, alumni affiliation, job skills, leadership, minority status, state/district residency.

FINANCIAL AID PROCEDURES
Forms required: FAFSA, state aid form, institutional form.
Dates and Deadlines: Priority date 3/15; no closing date. Applicants notified on a rolling basis starting 2/1; must reply within 2 week(s) of notification.

CONTACT
Kathy Shepard, Financial Aid Director
College Hill & Valley Roads, Summerdale, PA 17093-0309
(717) 728-2261

Chatham College
Pittsburgh, Pennsylvania
www.chatham.edu
Federal Code: 003244

4-year private liberal arts college for women in large city.
Enrollment: 470 undergrads, 9% part-time. 117 full-time freshmen.
Selectivity: Admits 50 to 75% of applicants.

BASIC COSTS (2005-2006)
Tuition and fees: $23,170.
Per-credit charge: $555.

Room and board: $7,410.

FINANCIAL AID PICTURE (2005-2006)
Students with need: Out of 112 full-time freshmen who applied for aid, 88 were judged to have need. Of these, 88 received aid. Average financial aid package met 70% of need; average scholarship/grant was $9,339; average loan was $4,625. For part-time students, average financial aid package was $2,852.
Students without need: 13 full-time freshmen who did not demonstrate need for aid received scholarships/grants; average award was $6,915. No-need awards available for academics, alumni affiliation, leadership, music/drama.
Scholarships offered: Based on academic excellence, students may qualify for Presidential, Trustee or Founders' Scholarship. Presidential: up to $12,000; Trustee: up to $9,000; Founders': up to $7,000. Renewable annually based on GPA of 2.8 or higher.
Cumulative student debt: 97% of graduating class had student loans; average debt was $18,655.

FINANCIAL AID PROCEDURES
Forms required: FAFSA.
Dates and Deadlines: Priority date 5/1; no closing date. Applicants notified on a rolling basis starting 2/15; must reply by 5/1 or within 2 week(s) of notification.
Transfers: Special scholarships are available for transfer students.

CONTACT
Jennifer Burns, Director of Financial Aid
Woodland Road, Pittsburgh, PA 15232
(412) 365-1777

Chestnut Hill College
Philadelphia, Pennsylvania
www.chc.edu   Federal Code: 003245

4-year private liberal arts college in very large city, affiliated with Roman Catholic Church.
Enrollment: 1,000 undergrads, 20% part-time. 216 full-time freshmen.
Selectivity: Admits 50 to 75% of applicants.

BASIC COSTS (2006-2007)
Tuition and fees: $22,750.
Room and board: $7,950.

FINANCIAL AID PICTURE (2004-2005)
Students with need: Out of 208 full-time freshmen who applied for aid, 167 were judged to have need. Of these, 167 received aid, and 2 had their full need met. Average financial aid package met 48% of need; average scholarship/grant was $6,000; average loan was $2,625.
Students without need: 15 full-time freshmen who did not demonstrate need for aid received scholarships/grants; average award was $5,000. No-need awards available for academics, alumni affiliation, leadership, religious affiliation.
Scholarships offered: 4-year, full-tuition and partial-tuition awards based on academic merit offered. Application priority date is January 15 for merit-based scholarships.
Cumulative student debt: 67% of graduating class had student loans; average debt was $26,250.

FINANCIAL AID PROCEDURES
Forms required: FAFSA.
Dates and Deadlines: Closing date 4/15. Applicants notified on a rolling basis starting 1/31; must reply by 5/1 or within 3 week(s) of notification.

CONTACT
Crystal Filer-Ogden, Director of Financial Aid
9601 Germantown Avenue, Philadelphia, PA 19118-2693
(215) 248-7100

Cheyney University of Pennsylvania
Cheyney, Pennsylvania
www.cheyney.edu   Federal Code: 003317

4-year public university in small town.
Enrollment: 1,351 undergrads, 4% part-time. 396 full-time freshmen.
Selectivity: Admits 50 to 75% of applicants.

BASIC COSTS (2005-2006)
Tuition and fees: $5,818; out-of-state residents $13,178.
Per-credit charge: $204; out-of-state residents $511.
Room and board: $5,679.
Additional info: Tuition for MD, NY, NJ and Delaware is $9,814. Required fees for all out of state students is $975. Tuition/fee waivers available for minority students.

FINANCIAL AID PICTURE
Students with need: Need-based aid available for full-time and part-time students.
Students without need: No-need awards available for academics, athletics.

FINANCIAL AID PROCEDURES
Forms required: FAFSA.
Dates and Deadlines: Priority date 5/1; no closing date. Applicants notified on a rolling basis starting 4/1; must reply within 2 week(s) of notification.

CONTACT
James Brown, Director of Financial Aid
1837 University Circle/PO Box 200, Cheyney, PA 19319-0019
(610) 399-2302

CHI Institute: Broomall
Broomall, Pennsylvania
www.chitraining.com   Federal Code: 007781

2-year for-profit technical college in large town.
Enrollment: 865 undergrads.

BASIC COSTS (2005-2006)
Additional info: Tuition ranges from $9,000 - $21,000 per 18-month program. Required fees $400.

FINANCIAL AID PICTURE
Students with need: Need-based aid available for full-time and part-time students.

FINANCIAL AID PROCEDURES
Forms required: FAFSA.
Dates and Deadlines: No deadline. Applicants notified on a rolling basis.

CONTACT
Chrissy Kapusinak, Director of Financial Aid
1991 Sproul Road, Suite 42, Broomall, PA 19008
(610) 353-7630

Clarion University of Pennsylvania
Clarion, Pennsylvania
www.clarion.edu   Federal Code: 003318

4-year public university in small town.
Enrollment: 5,938 undergrads, 11% part-time. 1,183 full-time freshmen.
Selectivity: Admits over 75% of applicants.

BASIC COSTS (2005-2006)
Tuition and fees: $6,437; out-of-state residents $11,345.
Per-credit charge: $211; out-of-state residents $409.

Room and board: $5,604.
Additional info: Tuition/fee waivers available for minority students.

FINANCIAL AID PICTURE (2005-2006)
Students with need: Out of 1,089 full-time freshmen who applied for aid, 882 were judged to have need. Of these, 846 received aid, and 117 had their full need met. Average financial aid package met 63% of need; average scholarship/grant was $4,698; average loan was $2,473. For part-time students, average financial aid package was $3,755.
Students without need: 56 full-time freshmen who did not demonstrate need for aid received scholarships/grants; average award was $2,550. No-need awards available for academics, art, athletics, leadership, minority status, music/drama, state/district residency.
Scholarships offered: 58 full-time freshmen received athletic scholarships; average amount $2,899.
Cumulative student debt: 83% of graduating class had student loans; average debt was $14,791.
Additional info: Application closing date for academic scholarships March 15.

FINANCIAL AID PROCEDURES
Forms required: FAFSA.
Dates and Deadlines: Priority date 4/15; no closing date. Applicants notified on a rolling basis starting 3/1.

CONTACT
Kenneth Grugel, Director of Financial Aid
840 Wood Street, Clarion, PA 16214
(814) 226-2315

College Misericordia
Dallas, Pennsylvania
www.misericordia.edu
Federal Code: 003247

4-year private liberal arts college in small city, affiliated with Roman Catholic Church.
Enrollment: 1,966 undergrads, 27% part-time. 324 full-time freshmen.
Selectivity: Admits over 75% of applicants.

BASIC COSTS (2006-2007)
Tuition and fees: $20,860.
Per-credit charge: $425.
Room and board: $8,640.
Additional info: Tuition/fee waivers available for adults.

FINANCIAL AID PICTURE (2005-2006)
Students with need: Out of 302 full-time freshmen who applied for aid, 260 were judged to have need. Of these, 260 received aid, and 48 had their full need met. Average financial aid package met 72% of need; average scholarship/grant was $9,934; average loan was $5,176. For part-time students, average financial aid package was $4,655.
Students without need: 42 full-time freshmen who did not demonstrate need for aid received scholarships/grants; average award was $6,835. No-need awards available for academics, alumni affiliation, leadership, minority status, state/district residency.
Scholarships offered: McAuley Award: range from $1,000-$5,000 per year; based on out-of-classroom activities. Partnership Scholarships: $2,500 per year; to encourage students interested in specific careers. Academic Scholarships: range from $2,000-$12,000 per year; based on academic abilities.
Cumulative student debt: 87% of graduating class had student loans; average debt was $18,013.

FINANCIAL AID PROCEDURES
Forms required: FAFSA, institutional form.
Dates and Deadlines: Priority date 3/1; closing date 5/1. Applicants notified on a rolling basis starting 3/15; must reply by 5/1.
Transfers: No deadline. Applicants notified on a rolling basis starting 3/15.

CONTACT
Margaret Charnick, Director of Financial Aid
301 Lake Street, Dallas, PA 18612-1098
(570) 674-6280

Commonwealth Technical Institute
Johnstown, Pennsylvania
www.hgac.org

2-year private technical college in small city.
Enrollment: 101 undergrads. 101 full-time freshmen.
Selectivity: Open admission.

BASIC COSTS (2005-2006)
Tuition and fees: $11,224.
Room and board: $9,516.

FINANCIAL AID PICTURE
Students with need: Work study available nights, weekends, and for part-time students.

FINANCIAL AID PROCEDURES
Forms required: FAFSA.
Dates and Deadlines: Closing date 5/1. Applicants notified on a rolling basis.

CONTACT
Financial Aid Administrator
727 Goucher Street, Johnstown, PA 15905-3902
(814) 255-8351

Community College of Allegheny County
Pittsburgh, Pennsylvania
www.ccac.edu

2-year public community college in very large city.
Enrollment: 9,918 undergrads.
Selectivity: Open admission; but selective for some programs.

BASIC COSTS (2005-2006)
Tuition and fees: $2,669; out-of-district residents $5,069; out-of-state residents $7,469.
Per-credit charge: $80; out-of-district residents $160; out-of-state residents $240.
Additional info: Required fees vary for out-of-district and out-of-state students; out-of-district tuition varies based on county. If county has own community college, tuition is $4800 per year (fees $374). If county does not have community college, tuition is $2820 per year (fees $374). Nursing and allied health courses subject to $16 per-credit fee.

FINANCIAL AID PICTURE (2004-2005)
Students with need: 74% of average financial aid package awarded as scholarships/grants, 26% awarded as loans/jobs. Need-based aid available for part-time students. Work study available nights, weekends, and for part-time students.
Students without need: No-need awards available for academics, athletics, minority status.

FINANCIAL AID PROCEDURES
Forms required: FAFSA.
Dates and Deadlines: Priority date 5/1; no closing date. Applicants notified by 5/20.

CONTACT
Director of Financial Aid
800 Allegheny Avenue, Pittsburgh, PA 15233
(412) 323-2323

Community College of Beaver County
Monaca, Pennsylvania
www.ccbc.edu   Federal Code: 006807

2-year public community college in small town.
Enrollment: 2,535 undergrads.
Selectivity: Open admission; but selective for some programs.

BASIC COSTS (2005-2006)
Tuition and fees: $2,925; out-of-district residents $6,825; out-of-state residents $10,200.
Per-credit charge: $80; out-of-district residents $195; out-of-state residents $293.
Additional info: Out-of-district students pay additional $450 fee; out-of-state students pay additional $900 fee.

FINANCIAL AID PICTURE (2004-2005)
Students with need: 67% of average financial aid package awarded as scholarships/grants, 33% awarded as loans/jobs. Need-based aid available for part-time students. Work study available nights, weekends, and for part-time students.
Students without need: No-need awards available for academics, athletics, state/district residency.
Scholarships offered: Academic Excellence Scholarship: full tuition.

FINANCIAL AID PROCEDURES
Forms required: FAFSA, state aid form, institutional form.
Dates and Deadlines: Priority date 5/1; closing date 7/1. Applicants notified on a rolling basis starting 8/5; must reply within 2 week(s) of notification.
Transfers: Priority date 5/5.

CONTACT
Doug Mahler, Director of Financial Aid
One Campus Drive, Monaca, PA 15061-2588
(724) 775-8561 ext. 260

Community College of Philadelphia
Philadelphia, Pennsylvania
www.ccp.edu   Federal Code: 003249

2-year public community college in very large city.
Enrollment: 16,670 undergrads, 71% part-time. 1,777 full-time freshmen.
Selectivity: Open admission; but selective for some programs.

BASIC COSTS (2005-2006)
Tuition and fees: $3,900; out-of-district residents $7,200; out-of-state residents $10,140.
Per-credit charge: $104; out-of-district residents $208; out-of-state residents $312.
Additional info: Non-Philadelphia residents pay additional fee of $10 per credit hour; out-of-state residents pay additional $20 per credit hour.

FINANCIAL AID PICTURE
Students with need: Need-based aid available for full-time and part-time students. Work study available nights, weekends, and for part-time students.
Students without need: This college only awards aid to students with need.

FINANCIAL AID PROCEDURES
Forms required: FAFSA, institutional form.
Dates and Deadlines: Closing date 5/1. Applicants notified on a rolling basis.
Transfers: No deadline.

CONTACT
Gim Lim, Director of Financial Aid
1700 Spring Garden Street, Philadelphia, PA 19130-3991
(215) 751-8270

Consolidated School of Business: Lancaster
Lancaster, Pennsylvania
www.csb.edu   Federal Code: 030299

2-year for-profit business college in small city.
Enrollment: 143 undergrads.
Selectivity: Open admission.

BASIC COSTS (2005-2006)
Additional info: Pre-evaluation placement testing fee $50. Tuition at time of enrollment locked for 2 years.

FINANCIAL AID PICTURE
Students with need: Need-based aid available for full-time and part-time students.

FINANCIAL AID PROCEDURES
Forms required: FAFSA, state aid form.
Dates and Deadlines: No deadline. Applicants notified on a rolling basis.

CONTACT
William Hoyt, Director of Financial Aid
2124 Ambassador Circle, Lancaster, PA 17603
(717) 394-6211

Consolidated School of Business: York
York, Pennsylvania
www.csb.edu   Federal Code: 022896

2-year for-profit business college in small city.
Enrollment: 160 undergrads.
Selectivity: Open admission.

BASIC COSTS (2005-2006)
Additional info: Pre-evaluation/placement testing fee $50. Tuition at time of enrollment locked for 2 years.

FINANCIAL AID PICTURE
Students with need: Need-based aid available for full-time and part-time students.

FINANCIAL AID PROCEDURES
Forms required: FAFSA, state aid form.
Dates and Deadlines: No deadline. Applicants notified on a rolling basis.

CONTACT
William Hoyt, Director of Financial Aid
York City Business and Industry Park, York, PA 17404
(717) 764-9550

Curtis Institute of Music
Philadelphia, Pennsylvania   Federal Code: 003251
www.curtis.edu   CSS Code: 2100

4-year private music college in very large city.
Enrollment: 147 undergrads. 10 full-time freshmen.
Selectivity: Admits less than 50% of applicants.

BASIC COSTS (2006-2007)
Additional info: All students given full-tuition scholarship. Required fees $1,910; for bachelor of music students $2,010; additional expenses per annum $14,275 (includes books, supplies, living expenses and miscellaneous).

FINANCIAL AID PICTURE (2005-2006)
Students with need: Out of 10 full-time freshmen who applied for aid, 10 were judged to have need. Of these, 10 received aid, and 2 had their full need met. Average financial aid package met 79% of need; average scholarship/grant was $5,745; average loan was $2,756.
Students without need: This college only awards aid to students with need.
Cumulative student debt: 55% of graduating class had student loans; average debt was $15,353.
Additional info: All students accepted on full-tuition scholarship basis.

FINANCIAL AID PROCEDURES
Forms required: FAFSA, CSS PROFILE, institutional form.
Dates and Deadlines: Closing date 3/1. Applicants notified by 4/1; must reply by 5/1.

CONTACT
Janice Miller, Director, Student Financial Assistance
1726 Locust Street, Philadelphia, PA 19103-6187
(215) 893-5252

Dean Institute of Technology
Pittsburgh, Pennsylvania
www.deantech.edu
Federal Code: 009186

2-year for-profit technical college in large city.
Enrollment: 221 undergrads, 39% part-time. 33 full-time freshmen.
Selectivity: Open admission.

BASIC COSTS (2005-2006)
Additional info: Air-conditioning/refrigeration: 15-month day course $16,400, night course $7,800. 7-month courses in welding or building maintenance $6,600. Electrical technician: 15-month day course or 30-month night course, $16,400. Tools/materials fees not included in tuition.

FINANCIAL AID PICTURE
Students with need: Need-based aid available for full-time and part-time students.

FINANCIAL AID PROCEDURES
Forms required: FAFSA.
Dates and Deadlines: Closing date 8/1. Applicants notified on a rolling basis; must reply within 8 week(s) of notification.

CONTACT
Nancy Grom, Director of Financial Aid
1501 West Liberty Avenue, Pittsburgh, PA 15226
(412) 531-4433 ext. 121

Delaware County Community College
Media, Pennsylvania
www.dccc.edu
Federal Code: 007110

2-year public community college in large town.
Enrollment: 10,627 undergrads, 58% part-time. 1,533 full-time freshmen.
Selectivity: Open admission; but selective for some programs.

BASIC COSTS (2005-2006)
Tuition and fees: $2,560; out-of-district residents $5,020; out-of-state residents $7,480.
Per-credit charge: $82; out-of-district residents $164; out-of-state residents $246.
Additional info: Additional instructional support fee of $570-$870 based on courses taken.

FINANCIAL AID PICTURE (2005-2006)
Students with need: 68% of average financial aid package awarded as scholarships/grants, 32% awarded as loans/jobs. Need-based aid available for part-time students. Work study available nights, weekends, and for part-time students.
Additional info: COPE grants offered to educationally and economically disadvantaged students.

FINANCIAL AID PROCEDURES
Forms required: FAFSA.
Dates and Deadlines: Priority date 5/1; no closing date. Applicants notified on a rolling basis starting 5/30; must reply within 4 week(s) of notification.

CONTACT
Ray Toole, Director of Financial Aid
901 South Media Line Road, Media, PA 19063
(610) 359-5330

Delaware Valley College
Doylestown, Pennsylvania
www.devalcol.edu
Federal Code: 003252

4-year private liberal arts college in large town.
Enrollment: 1,843 undergrads, 13% part-time. 454 full-time freshmen.
Selectivity: Admits over 75% of applicants.

BASIC COSTS (2005-2006)
Tuition and fees: $21,794.
Per-credit charge: $560.
Room and board: $8,130.
Additional info: $400 additional technology fee for resident students. Tuition/fee waivers available for adults.

FINANCIAL AID PICTURE (2005-2006)
Students with need: Out of 392 full-time freshmen who applied for aid, 353 were judged to have need. Of these, 353 received aid, and 250 had their full need met. Average financial aid package met 79% of need; average scholarship/grant was $13,410; average loan was $2,275. For part-time students, average financial aid package was $3,984.
Students without need: 90 full-time freshmen who did not demonstrate need for aid received scholarships/grants; average award was $9,754. No-need awards available for academics, alumni affiliation, music/drama.
Cumulative student debt: 68% of graduating class had student loans; average debt was $17,482.

FINANCIAL AID PROCEDURES
Forms required: FAFSA.
Dates and Deadlines: Priority date 4/1; no closing date. Applicants notified on a rolling basis starting 2/1; must reply by 5/1.

CONTACT
Robert Sauer, Director of Financial Aid
700 East Butler Avenue, Doylestown, PA 18901-2697
(215) 489-2272

DeSales University
Center Valley, Pennsylvania
www.desales.edu
Federal Code: 003986

4-year private university in small town, affiliated with Roman Catholic Church.
Enrollment: 2,489 undergrads, 29% part-time. 434 full-time freshmen.
Selectivity: Admits over 75% of applicants.

BASIC COSTS (2006-2007)
Tuition and fees: $22,100.
Room and board: $8,250.

FINANCIAL AID PICTURE (2004-2005)
Students with need: 56% of average financial aid package awarded as scholarships/grants, 44% awarded as loans/jobs. Need-based aid available for part-time students.
Students without need: No-need awards available for academics, leadership, music/drama.
Scholarships offered: Presidential Scholarships; full tuition; for students ranking in top 5% of class and 1300 SAT. Trustee Scholarships; ranging from $6,000; for students within top 15% of class, minimum 1200 SAT. DeSales Scholarships; $4,000; for students within top 25% of class, minimum 1100 SAT. (All SAT scores are exclusive of writing).

FINANCIAL AID PROCEDURES
Forms required: FAFSA, state aid form, institutional form.
Dates and Deadlines: Priority date 2/1; closing date 5/1. Applicants notified on a rolling basis starting 2/15; must reply by 5/1 or within 2 week(s) of notification.
Transfers: No deadline. Transfer scholarships require 3.0 GPA, 8 completed courses. Transfer Opportunity Program (TOP), a grant equal to tuition at participating community college, requires an associate degree to qualify.

CONTACT
Chanel Greene, Director of Financial Aid
2755 Station Avenue, Center Valley, PA 18034-9568
(610) 282-1100 ext. 1287

DeVry University: Ft. Washington
Fort Washington, Pennsylvania
www.devry.edu

4-year for-profit university in large town.
Enrollment: 710 undergrads, 29% part-time. 125 full-time freshmen.

BASIC COSTS (2005-2006)
Tuition and fees: $13,410.
Per-credit charge: $475.

FINANCIAL AID PICTURE
Students with need: Need-based aid available for full-time and part-time students.
Students without need: This college only awards aid to students with need.

FINANCIAL AID PROCEDURES
Forms required: FAFSA.
Dates and Deadlines: No deadline. Applicants notified on a rolling basis.

CONTACT
Citristal Claiborne, Director of Financial Aid
1140 Virginia Drive, Fort Washington, PA 19034-3204
(215) 591-5724

Dickinson College
Carlisle, Pennsylvania
www.dickinson.edu
Federal Code: 003253
CSS Code: 2186

4-year private liberal arts college in large town.
Enrollment: 2,301 undergrads. 648 full-time freshmen.
Selectivity: Admits less than 50% of applicants.

BASIC COSTS (2006-2007)
Tuition and fees: $33,829.
Per-credit charge: $1,046.
Room and board: $8,480.

FINANCIAL AID PICTURE (2005-2006)
Students with need: Out of 422 full-time freshmen who applied for aid, 330 were judged to have need. Of these, 322 received aid, and 267 had their full need met. Average financial aid package met 99% of need; average scholarship/grant was $22,575; average loan was $3,628.
Students without need: 63 full-time freshmen who did not demonstrate need for aid received scholarships/grants; average award was $10,973. No-need awards available for academics, ROTC.
Scholarships offered: John Dickinson and Benjamin Rush Scholarships: awarded to most academically competitive students; additional Engage the World Fellowship for selected John Dickinson Scholarship winners. Stafford Scholarships: for life sciences, fund research support. John Montgomery Scholarship: awarded to first-year students who possess strong credentials, talent in the arts, or competency in 2 foreign languages in addition to English. Scholars must also demonstrate strong leadership in high school and community.
Cumulative student debt: 71% of graduating class had student loans; average debt was $20,982.

FINANCIAL AID PROCEDURES
Forms required: FAFSA, CSS PROFILE, state aid form.
Dates and Deadlines: Closing date 2/1. Applicants notified by 3/20; must reply by 5/1 or within 2 week(s) of notification.
Transfers: Closing date 4/1. Must reply within 2 week(s) of notification.

CONTACT
Judith Carter, Director of Financial Aid
PO Box 1773, Carlisle, PA 17013-2896
(717) 245-1308

Douglas Education Center
Monessen, Pennsylvania
www.douglas-school.com
Federal Code: 013957

2-year for-profit visual arts and business college in small town.
Enrollment: 233 undergrads.

FINANCIAL AID PICTURE
Students with need: Need-based aid available for full-time and part-time students. Work study available nights, weekends, and for part-time students.
Students without need: This college only awards aid to students with need.

FINANCIAL AID PROCEDURES
Dates and Deadlines: No deadline. Applicants notified on a rolling basis.

CONTACT
Alison Pfender, Director of Financial Aid
130 Seventh Street, Monessen, PA 15062
(724) 684-3684 ext. 101

Drexel University
Philadelphia, Pennsylvania
www.drexel.edu
Federal Code: 003256

5-year private university in very large city.
Enrollment: 11,936 undergrads, 15% part-time. 2,457 full-time freshmen.
Selectivity: Admits over 75% of applicants.

BASIC COSTS (2006-2007)
Tuition and fees: $25,450.
Room and board: $12,015.
Additional info: Tuition listed is for 5-year program.

FINANCIAL AID PICTURE (2005-2006)
Students with need: Out of 2,257 full-time freshmen who applied for aid, 1,679 were judged to have need. Of these, 1,671 received aid, and 229 had their full need met. Average financial aid package met 64% of need; average scholarship/grant was $4,388; average loan was $3,002.
Students without need: 530 full-time freshmen who did not demonstrate need for aid received scholarships/grants; average award was $9,890. No-need awards available for academics, alumni affiliation, art, athletics, leadership, music/drama, ROTC.
Scholarships offered: 62 full-time freshmen received athletic scholarships; average amount $20,127.
Cumulative student debt: 85% of graduating class had student loans; average debt was $25,347.

FINANCIAL AID PROCEDURES
Forms required: FAFSA.
Dates and Deadlines: Closing date 3/1. Applicants notified on a rolling basis starting 3/15.
Transfers: Priority date 3/2. Scholarships available in amounts up to $8,000. 3.2 cumulative GPA, minimum 30 hours completed at time of application required for eligibility.

CONTACT
Douglas Boucher, Director of Financial Aid
3141 Chestnut Street, Philadelphia, PA 19104-2875
(215) 895-1626

DuBois Business College
DuBois, Pennsylvania
www.dbcollege.com   Federal Code: 004893

2-year for-profit business and technical college in large town.
Enrollment: 250 undergrads.
Selectivity: Open admission.

FINANCIAL AID PICTURE
Students with need: Need-based aid available for full-time students.

FINANCIAL AID PROCEDURES
Forms required: FAFSA.
Dates and Deadlines: Closing date 8/1. Applicants notified on a rolling basis.

CONTACT
Karen Alderton, Financial Aid Director
One Beaver Drive, DuBois, PA 15801
(814) 371-06920

Duquesne University
Pittsburgh, Pennsylvania
www.duq.edu   Federal Code: 003258

4-year private university in large city, affiliated with Roman Catholic Church.
Enrollment: 5,606 undergrads, 5% part-time. 1,208 full-time freshmen.
Selectivity: Admits over 75% of applicants.

BASIC COSTS (2005-2006)
Tuition and fees: $21,480.
Room and board: $8,054.

FINANCIAL AID PICTURE (2004-2005)
Students with need: Out of 1,037 full-time freshmen who applied for aid, 864 were judged to have need. Of these, 861 received aid, and 473 had their full need met. Average financial aid package met 82% of need; average scholarship/grant was $11,689; average loan was $3,571. For part-time students, average financial aid package was $5,938.
Students without need: 281 full-time freshmen who did not demonstrate need for aid received scholarships/grants; average award was $6,733. No-need awards available for academics, athletics, music/drama, ROTC.
Scholarships offered: *Merit:* Competitive scholarships available for academically and/or artistically talented students. *Athletic:* 70 full-time freshmen received athletic scholarships; average amount $12,728.
Cumulative student debt: 77% of graduating class had student loans; average debt was $23,205.

FINANCIAL AID PROCEDURES
Forms required: FAFSA, institutional form.
Dates and Deadlines: Closing date 5/1. Applicants notified on a rolling basis starting 3/1; must reply by 5/1 or within 3 week(s) of notification.
Transfers: No deadline. Must reply within 3 week(s) of notification.

CONTACT
Richard Esposito, Director of Financial Aid
600 Forbes Avenue, Administration Building, Pittsburgh, PA 15282-0201
(412) 396-6607

East Stroudsburg University of Pennsylvania
East Stroudsburg, Pennsylvania
www3.esu.edu   Federal Code: 003320

4-year public university in large town.
Enrollment: 5,441 undergrads, 8% part-time. 1,076 full-time freshmen.
Selectivity: Admits 50 to 75% of applicants.

BASIC COSTS (2005-2006)
Tuition and fees: $6,399; out-of-state residents $13,719.
Per-credit charge: $204; out-of-state residents $511.
Room and board: $4,794.

FINANCIAL AID PICTURE (2004-2005)
Students with need: Out of 925 full-time freshmen who applied for aid, 643 were judged to have need. Of these, 619 received aid, and 427 had their full need met. Average financial aid package met 80% of need; average scholarship/grant was $3,180; average loan was $2,422. For part-time students, average financial aid package was $3,356.
Students without need: 217 full-time freshmen who did not demonstrate need for aid received scholarships/grants; average award was $6,903. No-need awards available for academics, alumni affiliation, art, athletics, leadership, minority status, music/drama, religious affiliation.
Scholarships offered: 29 full-time freshmen received athletic scholarships; average amount $1,493.

FINANCIAL AID PROCEDURES
Forms required: FAFSA.
Dates and Deadlines: Closing date 3/1. Applicants notified by 4/1; must reply by 5/1.

CONTACT
Phyllis Swinson, Associate Director of Financial Aid
200 Prospect Street, East Stroudsburg, PA 18301-2999
(570) 422-2800

Edinboro University of Pennsylvania
Edinboro, Pennsylvania
www.edinboro.edu   Federal Code: 003321

4-year public university in small town.
Enrollment: 6,312 undergrads, 11% part-time. 1,241 full-time freshmen.
Selectivity: Admits over 75% of applicants.

BASIC COSTS (2005-2006)
Tuition and fees: $6,289; out-of-state residents $11,197.
Per-credit charge: $204; out-of-state residents $409.
Room and board: $5,783.

FINANCIAL AID PICTURE (2004-2005)
Students with need: Out of 1,195 full-time freshmen who applied for aid, 1,027 were judged to have need. Of these, 999 received aid, and 56 had their full need met. Average financial aid package met 78% of need; average scholarship/grant was $2,832; average loan was $2,107. For part-time students, average financial aid package was $3,940.
Students without need: 102 full-time freshmen who did not demonstrate need for aid received scholarships/grants; average award was $2,444. No-need awards available for academics, alumni affiliation, art, athletics, job skills, leadership, minority status, music/drama, religious affiliation, ROTC, state/district residency.
Scholarships offered: 25 full-time freshmen received athletic scholarships; average amount $1,808.
Cumulative student debt: 67% of graduating class had student loans; average debt was $17,034.

FINANCIAL AID PROCEDURES
Forms required: FAFSA.
Dates and Deadlines: Priority date 3/15; closing date 5/1. Applicants notified on a rolling basis starting 3/31; must reply within 2 week(s) of notification.

CONTACT
Dorothy Body, Assistant Vice President for Student Financial Support and Services
148 Meadville Street, Edinboro, PA 16444
(888) 611-2680

Elizabethtown College
Elizabethtown, Pennsylvania
www.etown.edu
Federal Code: 003262

4-year private liberal arts college in large town, affiliated with Church of the Brethren.
Enrollment: 2,082 undergrads, 11% part-time. 508 full-time freshmen.
Selectivity: Admits 50 to 75% of applicants.

BASIC COSTS (2006-2007)
Tuition and fees: $26,950.
Per-credit charge: $660.
Room and board: $7,300.

FINANCIAL AID PICTURE (2005-2006)
Students with need: Out of 451 full-time freshmen who applied for aid, 366 were judged to have need. Of these, 366 received aid, and 116 had their full need met. Average financial aid package met 83% of need; average scholarship/grant was $15,210; average loan was $2,927. Need-based aid available for part-time students.
Students without need: 73 full-time freshmen who did not demonstrate need for aid received scholarships/grants; average award was $14,816. No-need awards available for academics, art, music/drama, religious affiliation.
Scholarships offered: Presidential Scholarships; $13,500 annually; top 2% of class and minimum 1300 SAT score. Provost Scholarships; from $10,000-$12,000 annually; top 10% of class with minimum 1150 SAT; unlimited number awarded. Dean's Scholarships; $4,000-$9,500 annually; for students with very strong academic achievement who do not qualify for other merit awards; unlimited number awarded. Music scholarships; from $1,000-4,000; by audition. SAT scores are exclusive of the writing portion.

FINANCIAL AID PROCEDURES
Forms required: FAFSA, institutional form.
Dates and Deadlines: Priority date 3/15; no closing date. Applicants notified on a rolling basis starting 3/1; must reply by 5/1 or within 2 week(s) of notification.

CONTACT
Elizabeth McCloud, Director of Financial Aid
One Alpha Drive, Elizabethtown, PA 17022-2298
(717) 361-1404

Erie Business Center
Erie, Pennsylvania
www.eriebc.edu
Federal Code: 004894

2-year for-profit business college in small city.
Enrollment: 455 undergrads.
Selectivity: Open admission.

BASIC COSTS (2005-2006)
Tuition and fees: $7,870.
Per-credit charge: $234.
Room only: $2,560.

FINANCIAL AID PICTURE
Students with need: Need-based aid available for full-time and part-time students.

FINANCIAL AID PROCEDURES
Forms required: FAFSA.
Dates and Deadlines: No deadline.
Transfers: Applicants notified on a rolling basis.

CONTACT
Barbara Heller, Financial Aid Administrator
246 West Ninth Street, Erie, PA 16501
(814) 456-7504 ext. 23

Franklin & Marshall College
Lancaster, Pennsylvania
www.fandm.edu
Federal Code: 003265
CSS Code: 2261

4-year private liberal arts college in small city.
Enrollment: 1,981 undergrads, 1% part-time. 582 full-time freshmen.
Selectivity: Admits less than 50% of applicants.

BASIC COSTS (2006-2007)
Tuition and fees: $34,450.
Per-credit charge: $1,075.
Room and board: $8,540.

FINANCIAL AID PICTURE (2005-2006)
Students with need: Out of 475 full-time freshmen who applied for aid, 367 were judged to have need. Of these, 365 received aid, and 365 had their full need met. Average financial aid package met 100% of need; average scholarship/grant was $20,967; average loan was $3,507. For part-time students, average financial aid package was $16,063.
Students without need: 141 full-time freshmen who did not demonstrate need for aid received scholarships/grants; average award was $8,209. No-need awards available for academics, art, leadership, music/drama.
Scholarships offered: John Marshall Scholarships; $12,500 awarded annually; independent initiative in intellectual or service areas considered. National Merit Recognition; $18,000 renewable annually. Presidential Scholarships; $7,500 annually. All based on academic performance, class rank. Klein Scholarship; $5,000; awarded based on academic and community achievement. Gray Scholarship; awarded to outstanding applicants of African-, Latino-, and Asian-American descent; minimizes loans.

Pennsylvania Franklin & Marshall College

Cumulative student debt: 61% of graduating class had student loans; average debt was $19,391.

FINANCIAL AID PROCEDURES
Forms required: FAFSA, CSS PROFILE, institutional form.
Dates and Deadlines: Priority date 2/1; closing date 3/1. Applicants notified by 3/15; must reply by 5/1.
Transfers: Closing date 2/1.

CONTACT
Chris Hanlon, Director of Student Aid
Box 3003, Lancaster, PA 17604-3003
(717) 291-3991

Gannon University
Erie, Pennsylvania
www.gannon.edu
Federal Code: 003266

4-year private university in small city, affiliated with Roman Catholic Church.
Enrollment: 2,394 undergrads, 9% part-time. 622 full-time freshmen.
Selectivity: Admits over 75% of applicants.

BASIC COSTS (2006-2007)
Tuition and fees: $19,996.
Per-credit charge: $605.
Room and board: $7,880.
Additional info: Engineering and health sciences tuition $20,680. Tuition/fee waivers available for adults, unemployed or children of unemployed.

FINANCIAL AID PICTURE (2005-2006)
Students with need: Out of 597 full-time freshmen who applied for aid, 537 were judged to have need. Of these, 537 received aid, and 102 had their full need met. Average financial aid package met 75% of need; average scholarship/grant was $12,687; average loan was $2,182. For part-time students, average financial aid package was $3,432.
Students without need: 63 full-time freshmen who did not demonstrate need for aid received scholarships/grants; average award was $6,764. No-need awards available for academics, athletics, leadership, music/drama, religious affiliation, ROTC.
Scholarships offered: *Merit:* Academic Awards: ranging from $1,000-$17,000 annually based on high school rank, GPA, and test scores. Research Scholarships by application: $1,000 annually. University Scholar Awards: $3,500 annually based on high school rank, GPA, and test scores. Leadership Awards: $1,000-$3,500 annually, based on leadership and activities. Diocesan Scholarship: $1,000 to full tuition annually for student(s) who attended high school in Diocese of Erie. Athletic scholarships range from $1,000 to full tuition, room and board. *Athletic:* 16 full-time freshmen received athletic scholarships; average amount $16,666.
Cumulative student debt: 75% of graduating class had student loans; average debt was $24,148.

FINANCIAL AID PROCEDURES
Forms required: FAFSA, institutional form.
Dates and Deadlines: Priority date 3/15; no closing date. Applicants notified on a rolling basis starting 11/15; must reply by 5/1 or within 4 week(s) of notification.

CONTACT
Sharon Krahe, Director of Financial Aid
109 University Square, Erie, PA 16541-0001
(814) 871-7337

Geneva College
Beaver Falls, Pennsylvania
www.geneva.edu
Federal Code: 003267

4-year private liberal arts college in large town, affiliated with Reformed Presbyterian Church of North America.
Enrollment: 1,762 undergrads. 349 full-time freshmen.
Selectivity: Admits 50 to 75% of applicants.

BASIC COSTS (2006-2007)
Tuition and fees: $18,460.
Per-credit charge: $615.
Room and board: $6,960.
Additional info: Tuition/fee waivers available for minority students.

FINANCIAL AID PICTURE (2005-2006)
Students with need: Average financial aid package met 75% of need; average scholarship/grant was $9,987; average loan was $3,187. For part-time students, average financial aid package was $9,598.
Students without need: No-need awards available for academics, athletics, music/drama, religious affiliation.
Scholarships offered: Academic scholarships, scholarships for National Merit finalists and semifinalists, grants for members of controlling church and other denominations identified by the college.

FINANCIAL AID PROCEDURES
Forms required: FAFSA.
Dates and Deadlines: Priority date 3/15; no closing date. Applicants notified on a rolling basis starting 3/1; must reply by 5/1 or within 4 week(s) of notification.

CONTACT
Steven Bell, Director of Financial Aid
3200 College Avenue, Beaver Falls, PA 15010
(724) 847-6530

Gettysburg College
Gettysburg, Pennsylvania
www.gettysburg.edu
Federal Code: 003268
CSS Code: 2275

4-year private liberal arts college in large town.
Enrollment: 2,463 undergrads. 697 full-time freshmen.
Selectivity: Admits less than 50% of applicants.

BASIC COSTS (2006-2007)
Tuition and fees: $34,050.
Room and board: $8,260.

FINANCIAL AID PICTURE (2005-2006)
Students with need: Out of 479 full-time freshmen who applied for aid, 384 were judged to have need. Of these, 384 received aid, and 384 had their full need met. Average financial aid package met 100% of need; average scholarship/grant was $20,095; average loan was $3,466.
Students without need: 99 full-time freshmen who did not demonstrate need for aid received scholarships/grants; average award was $9,060. No-need awards available for academics, music/drama.
Scholarships offered: Presidential and Dean's Scholarships: high school class rank and standardized test scores; number awarded varies. Wagnild Scholarship and Sunderman Scholarships for music talent: audition required.
Cumulative student debt: 59% of graduating class had student loans; average debt was $21,810.

FINANCIAL AID PROCEDURES
Forms required: FAFSA, CSS PROFILE.
Dates and Deadlines: Closing date 2/15. Applicants notified by 3/27; must reply by 5/1.
Transfers: Priority date 4/15. Must reply within 2 week(s) of notification.

CONTACT
Timothy Opgenorth, Director of Financial Aid
300 North Washington Street, Gettysburg, PA 17325-1484
(717) 337-6611

Grove City College
Grove City, Pennsylvania
www.gcc.edu   Federal Code: G03269

4-year private liberal arts college in small town, affiliated with Presbyterian Church (USA).
Enrollment: 2,310 undergrads. 580 full-time freshmen.
Selectivity: Admits less than 50% of applicants.

BASIC COSTS (2006-2007)
Tuition and fees: $10,962.
Per-credit charge: $350.
Room and board: $5,766.
Additional info: Tuition includes cost of tablet PC and printer.

FINANCIAL AID PICTURE (2005-2006)
Students with need: Out of 352 full-time freshmen who applied for aid, 241 were judged to have need. Of these, 241 received aid, and 36 had their full need met. Average financial aid package met 56% of need; average scholarship/grant was $5,104.
Students without need: 180 full-time freshmen who did not demonstrate need for aid received scholarships/grants; average award was $4,919. No-need awards available for academics, leadership, minority status.
Scholarships offered: Trustee Scholarships: $5,000; issued to a select group of accepted students who meet academic requirements; 24 awarded. Presidential Scholarships: $500; for all valedictorians in class of 30 or more, salutatorians in class of 100 or more, and National Merit Finalists. Engineering Scholarships: $2,500; 4 awarded.
Cumulative student debt: 53% of graduating class had student loans; average debt was $23,409.
Additional info: Institutional aid applications required for institutional scholarships, loans, and student employment.

FINANCIAL AID PROCEDURES
Forms required: state aid form, institutional form.
Dates and Deadlines: Closing date 4/15. Applicants notified on a rolling basis starting 3/15; must reply by 5/1.
Transfers: Closing date 12/15. Applicants notified on a rolling basis; must reply within 2 week(s) of notification. Financial aid form must be submitted with transfer enrollment application.

CONTACT
Patty Peterson, Director of Financial Aid
100 Campus Drive, Grove City, PA 16127-2104
(724) 458-3300

Gwynedd-Mercy College
Gwynedd Valley, Pennsylvania
www.gmc.edu   Federal Code: 003270

4-year private health science and liberal arts college in large town, affiliated with Roman Catholic Church.
Enrollment: 2,031 undergrads, 39% part-time. 279 full-time freshmen.
Selectivity: Admits 50 to 75% of applicants.

BASIC COSTS (2005-2006)
Tuition and fees: $17,980.
Per-credit charge: $380.
Room and board: $8,290.
Additional info: Tuition and fees for nursing and allied health programs $18,580; $430 per-credit-hour charge.

FINANCIAL AID PICTURE (2004-2005)
Students with need: Out of 251 full-time freshmen who applied for aid, 213 were judged to have need. Of these, 213 received aid, and 50 had their full need met. Average financial aid package met 85% of need; average scholarship/grant was $10,686; average loan was $3,082. Need-based aid available for part-time students.
Students without need: 79 full-time freshmen who did not demonstrate need for aid received scholarships/grants; average award was $9,712. No-need awards available for academics, leadership.
Scholarships offered: Presidential scholarship, $10,000: must have SAT scores of 1200 or above and be in top 30% of class, essay required, Feb. 15 deadline. Connelly Scholarship, $6,000 - $7,000, must have SAT scores of 1100 or above and be in top 50% of class. Mother Mary Bernard Scholarship, $4,500 - $5,000, must have SAT scores of 1000 or above, be in top 50% of class, and have documented leadership experience. Yearly scholarship for Catholic school graduates, $2,000 (tuition incentive grant). All SAT scores are exclusive of Writing.
Cumulative student debt: 85% of graduating class had student loans; average debt was $18,708.

FINANCIAL AID PROCEDURES
Forms required: FAFSA, institutional form.
Dates and Deadlines: Priority date 3/1; closing date 7/15. Applicants notified on a rolling basis starting 3/1; must reply by 5/1 or within 2 week(s) of notification.
Transfers: Priority date 3/15.

CONTACT
Barbara Kaufmann, Director of Student Financial Aid
1325 Sumneytown Pike, Gwynedd Valley, PA 19437-0901
(215) 646-7300 ext. 483

Harcum College
Bryn Mawr, Pennsylvania
www.harcum.edu   Federal Code: 003272

2-year private junior college in large town.
Enrollment: 734 undergrads, 31% part-time. 127 full-time freshmen.
Selectivity: Admits 50 to 75% of applicants.

BASIC COSTS (2005-2006)
Tuition and fees: $14,522.
Per-credit charge: $478.
Room and board: $6,900.

FINANCIAL AID PICTURE
Students with need: Need-based aid available for full-time and part-time students. Work study available nights, weekends, and for part-time students.
Students without need: No-need awards available for academics, leadership.
Scholarships offered: Scholarships available based on academic achievement.

FINANCIAL AID PROCEDURES
Forms required: FAFSA, institutional form.
Dates and Deadlines: Priority date 4/15; no closing date. Applicants notified on a rolling basis starting 3/1; must reply within 3 week(s) of notification.
Transfers: Priority date 3/15.

CONTACT
Mindy Henken, Financial Aid Director
750 Montgomery Avenue, Bryn Mawr, PA 19010-3476
(610) 526-6098

Harrisburg Area Community College
Harrisburg, Pennsylvania
www.hacc.edu   Federal Code: 003273

2-year public community college in small city.
Enrollment: 9,507 undergrads, 67% part-time. 974 full-time freshmen.
Selectivity: Open admission; but selective for some programs.

BASIC COSTS (2005-2006)
Tuition and fees: $3,360; out-of-district residents $5,760; out-of-state residents $8,160.
Per-credit charge: $95; out-of-district residents $175; out-of-state residents $255.
Additional info: Out-of-district students pay $570 in yearly fees; out-of-state, $630.

FINANCIAL AID PICTURE (2004-2005)
Students with need: 31% of average financial aid package awarded as scholarships/grants, 69% awarded as loans/jobs. Need-based aid available for part-time students.
Students without need: No-need awards available for academics.
Additional info: Federal work study community service positions available.

FINANCIAL AID PROCEDURES
Forms required: FAFSA, institutional form.
Dates and Deadlines: Priority date 4/1; no closing date. Applicants notified on a rolling basis starting 6/1.
Transfers: PHEAA state grants require separate academic progress review by financial aid staff.

CONTACT
Robert Ritz, Director of Financial Aid
One HACC Drive, Cooper 206, Harrisburg, PA 17110-2999
(717) 780-2330

Haverford College
Haverford, Pennsylvania   Federal Code: 003274
www.haverford.edu   CSS Code: 2289

4-year private liberal arts college in large town.
Enrollment: 1,155 undergrads. 316 full-time freshmen.
Selectivity: Admits less than 50% of applicants.

BASIC COSTS (2006-2007)
Tuition and fees: $33,710.
Room and board: $10,390.
Additional info: Freshmen subject to one-time fee of $170.

FINANCIAL AID PICTURE (2005-2006)
Students with need: Out of 180 full-time freshmen who applied for aid, 132 were judged to have need. Of these, 132 received aid, and 132 had their full need met. Average financial aid package met 100% of need; average scholarship/grant was $25,462; average loan was $2,727.
Students without need: This college only awards aid to students with need.
Cumulative student debt: 36% of graduating class had student loans; average debt was $16,330.

FINANCIAL AID PROCEDURES
Forms required: FAFSA, state aid form. Required for all students wishing to be considered for institutional funds.
Dates and Deadlines: Closing date 1/31. Applicants notified by 4/8; must reply by 5/1.
Transfers: Closing date 3/1.

CONTACT
David Hoy, Director of Financial Aid
370 West Lancaster Avenue, Haverford, PA 19041-1392
(610) 893-1350

Holy Family University
Philadelphia, Pennsylvania
www.holyfamily.edu   Federal Code: 003275

4-year private liberal arts college in very large city, affiliated with Roman Catholic Church.
Enrollment: 2,335 undergrads.
Selectivity: Admits 50 to 75% of applicants.

BASIC COSTS (2005-2006)
Tuition and fees: $17,740.
Per-credit charge: $380.

FINANCIAL AID PICTURE
Students with need: Need-based aid available for full-time students. Work study available nights, weekends, and for part-time students.
Students without need: No-need awards available for academics, alumni affiliation, athletics.

FINANCIAL AID PROCEDURES
Forms required: FAFSA, institutional form.
Dates and Deadlines: Priority date 3/1; no closing date. Applicants notified on a rolling basis starting 4/1; must reply within 2 week(s) of notification.

CONTACT
Janice Hetrick, Director of Financial Aid
9801 Frankford Avenue, Philadelphia, PA 19114-2009
(215) 637-5538

Hussian School of Art
Philadelphia, Pennsylvania
www.hussianart.edu   Federal Code: 007469

2-year for-profit visual arts and technical college in very large city.
Enrollment: 155 undergrads. 43 full-time freshmen.
Selectivity: Admits over 75% of applicants.

BASIC COSTS (2006-2007)
Tuition and fees: $10,465.
Per-credit charge: $300.

FINANCIAL AID PICTURE (2004-2005)
Students with need: 39% of average financial aid package awarded as scholarships/grants, 61% awarded as loans/jobs. Need-based aid available for part-time students.
Students without need: This college only awards aid to students with need.
Cumulative student debt: 85% of graduating class had student loans; average debt was $16,334.

FINANCIAL AID PROCEDURES
Forms required: FAFSA, institutional form.
Dates and Deadlines: No deadline. Applicants notified on a rolling basis starting 2/15; must reply within 3 week(s) of notification.
Transfers: Priority date 3/15; no deadline. Applicants notified on a rolling basis starting 4/1.

CONTACT
Susan Cohen, Financial Aid Director
1118 Market Street, Philadelphia, PA 19107
(215) 981-0900

ICM School of Business & Medical Careers
Pittsburgh, Pennsylvania
www.icmschool.com   Federal Code: 007436

2-year for-profit business and health science college in large city.
Enrollment: 1,189 undergrads, 5% part-time. 302 full-time freshmen.
BASIC COSTS (2005-2006)
Tuition and fees: $14,848.
Additional info: Tuition costs include books and supplies.
FINANCIAL AID PICTURE (2004-2005)
Students with need: 74% of average financial aid package awarded as scholarships/grants, 26% awarded as loans/jobs.
FINANCIAL AID PROCEDURES
Dates and Deadlines: Closing date 4/30.
CONTACT
Christopher Fox, Director of Financial Aid
10 Wood Street, Pittsburgh, PA 15222
(412) 261-2647 ext. 265

Immaculata University
Immaculata, Pennsylvania
www.immaculata.edu   Federal Code: 003276

4-year private university and liberal arts college in large town, affiliated with Roman Catholic Church.
Enrollment: 691 undergrads. 160 full-time freshmen.
Selectivity: Admits over 75% of applicants.
BASIC COSTS (2006-2007)
Tuition and fees: $20,575.
Room and board: $9,335.
Additional info: Tuition and fees for entering freshmen guaranteed to not increase for the 4 years they are enrolled. Tuition at time of enrollment locked for 4 years.
FINANCIAL AID PICTURE (2004-2005)
Students with need: Out of 149 full-time freshmen who applied for aid, 130 were judged to have need. Of these, 129 received aid, and 14 had their full need met. Average financial aid package met 63% of need; average scholarship/grant was $11,335; average loan was $2,474. For part-time students, average financial aid package was $3,800.
Students without need: 28 full-time freshmen who did not demonstrate need for aid received scholarships/grants; average award was $10,189. No-need awards available for academics, alumni affiliation, leadership, minority status, music/drama, religious affiliation, state/district residency.
Cumulative student debt: 80% of graduating class had student loans; average debt was $1,360.
FINANCIAL AID PROCEDURES
Forms required: FAFSA.
Dates and Deadlines: Priority date 2/15; closing date 4/15. Applicants notified on a rolling basis starting 1/1; must reply within 2 week(s) of notification.
Transfers: No deadline. Applicants notified on a rolling basis starting 1/1; must reply within 2 week(s) of notification.
CONTACT
Peter Lysionek, Director of Financial Aid
PO Box 642, Immaculata, PA 19345-0642
(610) 647-4400 ext. 3026

Indiana University of Pennsylvania
Indiana, Pennsylvania
www.iup.edu   Federal Code: 003277

4-year public university in large town.
Enrollment: 11,788 undergrads, 5% part-time. 2,467 full-time freshmen.
Selectivity: Admits 50 to 75% of applicants.
BASIC COSTS (2005-2006)
Tuition and fees: $6,221; out-of-state residents $13,581.
Per-credit charge: $204; out-of-state residents $511.
Room and board: $4,988.
FINANCIAL AID PICTURE (2005-2006)
Students with need: Average financial aid package met 79% of need; average scholarship/grant was $4,052; average loan was $3,036. For part-time students, average financial aid package was $5,932.
Students without need: No-need awards available for academics, alumni affiliation, art, athletics, job skills, leadership, music/drama, ROTC, state/district residency.
Cumulative student debt: 80% of graduating class had student loans; average debt was $17,550.
FINANCIAL AID PROCEDURES
Forms required: FAFSA, state aid form.
Dates and Deadlines: Closing date 4/15. Applicants notified on a rolling basis starting 3/15.
Transfers: Must reply within 2 week(s) of notification.
CONTACT
Patricia McCarthy, Director of Financial Aid
117 John Sutton Hall, 1011 South Drive, Indiana, PA 15705-1088
(724) 357-2218

JNA Institute of Culinary Arts
Philadelphia, Pennsylvania
www.culinaryarts.com   Federal Code: 031033

2-year for-profit technical college in very large city.
Enrollment: 64 undergrads.
Selectivity: Open admission.
BASIC COSTS (2006-2007)
Additional info: Tuition for 15-month associate program, $14,000; 6-month professional cooking diploma program, $7,000. Required fees $75 for both programs. Books and supplies are $225 for the diploma program and $1,065 for the associate program. Tuition at time of enrollment locked for 2 years.
FINANCIAL AID PICTURE
Students with need: Need-based aid available for full-time students.
FINANCIAL AID PROCEDURES
Forms required: FAFSA.
CONTACT
Gerald Connor, Financial Aid Director
1212 South Broad Street, Philadelphia, PA 19146
(215) 468-8800

Johnson College
Scranton, Pennsylvania
www.johnson.edu   Federal Code: 014734

2-year private technical college in small city.
Enrollment: 376 undergrads.
Selectivity: Open admission; but selective for some programs.

Pennsylvania Johnson College

BASIC COSTS (2005-2006)
Tuition and fees: $12,763.
Per-credit charge: $300.
Room only: $2,975.

FINANCIAL AID PICTURE (2005-2006)
Students with need: Need-based aid available for part-time students. Work study available nights, weekends, and for part-time students.
Students without need: No-need awards available for academics.

FINANCIAL AID PROCEDURES
Forms required: FAFSA, institutional form.
Dates and Deadlines: Priority date 4/28; no closing date. Applicants notified on a rolling basis starting 4/15; must reply within 2 week(s) of notification.
Transfers: Priority date 5/1.

CONTACT
Jo-Ann Orcutt, Director of Financial Aid
3427 North Main Avenue, Scranton, PA 18508
(570) 342-6404 ext. 126

Juniata College
Huntingdon, Pennsylvania
www.juniata.edu   Federal Code: 003279

4-year private liberal arts college in small town, affiliated with Church of the Brethren.
Enrollment: 1,379 undergrads, 1% part-time. 388 full-time freshmen.
Selectivity: Admits 50 to 75% of applicants.

BASIC COSTS (2006-2007)
Tuition and fees: $27,550.
Per-credit charge: $1,120.
Room and board: $7,680.
Additional info: Tuition/fee waivers available for adults.

FINANCIAL AID PICTURE (2005-2006)
Students with need: Out of 347 full-time freshmen who applied for aid, 310 were judged to have need. Of these, 310 received aid, and 56 had their full need met. Average financial aid package met 78.6% of need; average scholarship/grant was $15,668; average loan was $3,448. Need-based aid available for part-time students.
Students without need: 72 full-time freshmen who did not demonstrate need for aid received scholarships/grants; average award was $12,358. No-need awards available for academics, art, leadership, minority status, music/drama, state/district residency.
Scholarships offered: Arts scholarships, environmental responsibility scholarships, leadership scholarships, service and peacemaking scholarships: each awarding 1 full tuition, room and board, 2 full tuition; nominated by alumni. Friendship scholarships: $2,000 awarded to international student. Calvert Ellis scholarships: $10,000-12,000 for high high school GPA or SAT scores; Juniata Presidential scholarships: $7,500-9,500 for high high school GPA or SAT scores. Juniata transfer scholarships: $8,500 for transfer student member of Phi Theta Kappa from 2-year college; $5,000-7,000 for 2-year college transfers with high GPA. Juniata PAR (program for area residents) scholarships: half tuition for area residents (nontraditional and others). North American Indian scholarship: (need-based) up to $10,000 for Native American. Ray Day scholarship: up to $5,000 for a minority student. John & Irene Dale scholarship: $3,000 for information technology student. Robert Steele Memorial scholarship: (need-based) up to $4,000 for medical/science student. Metz scholarship: up to $5,000 for intended major in business/economics; Anna Groninger Smith Memorial scholarship: (need-based) up to $4,000 for woman in business studies. W & M Donham scholarships: up to $2,000 for New England residents majoring in business/economics. Alumni scholarships: up to $5,000 for children of alumni. Church of the Brethren scholarships: up to $5,000 for Church of the Brethren members in various majors. Dorothy Baker Johnson Memorial scholarship: up to $4,000 for women aiming for careers that require advanced degree. Charles & Floretta Gibson scholarships: (need-based) for excellent character. Sam Hayes Jr. scholarship: (need-based) up to $1,500 for Pennsylvania FFA or 4H member.
Cumulative student debt: 77% of graduating class had student loans; average debt was $22,131.

FINANCIAL AID PROCEDURES
Forms required: FAFSA.
Dates and Deadlines: Closing date 3/1. Applicants notified on a rolling basis starting 3/1; must reply by 5/1 or within 2 week(s) of notification.
Transfers: Juniata Transfer Scholarships; Juniata PhiTheta Kappa Transfer Scholarship.

CONTACT
Randall Rennell, Director of Student Financial Planning
18th and Moore Streets, Huntingdon, PA 16652
(814) 641-3142

Keystone College
La Plume, Pennsylvania
www.keystone.edu   Federal Code: 003280

4-year private junior and liberal arts college in small town.
Enrollment: 1,568 undergrads, 22% part-time. 365 full-time freshmen.
Selectivity: Admits over 75% of applicants.

BASIC COSTS (2005-2006)
Tuition and fees: $15,020.
Per-credit charge: $325.
Room and board: $7,790.
Additional info: Tuition/fee waivers available for adults.

FINANCIAL AID PICTURE (2004-2005)
Students with need: Average financial aid package met 97% of need; average scholarship/grant was $6,450; average loan was $2,625. For part-time students, average financial aid package was $1,662.
Students without need: 42 full-time freshmen who did not demonstrate need for aid received scholarships/grants; average award was $6,000. No-need awards available for academics, art, job skills, leadership, ROTC.
Scholarships offered: Academic Excellence Scholarship; one-half tuition up to full tuition; for all full-time, first-time students in the top 5% of their class with SAT scores of 1100 or above (exclusive of Writing). Presidential Scholarship; up to $6,500 each year; based on class rank and SAT/ACT scores. Trustee Scholarship; up to $6,000 each year; based on class rank and SAT/ACT scores. Leadership Award; up to $5,000 each year; students demonstrating non-athletic leadership skills in high school.

FINANCIAL AID PROCEDURES
Forms required: FAFSA, state aid form.
Dates and Deadlines: Priority date 5/1; no closing date. Applicants notified on a rolling basis starting 11/1; must reply by 5/1 or within 3 week(s) of notification.
Transfers: Closing date 8/1.

CONTACT
Ginger Kline, Director of Financial Aid
One College Green, La Plume, PA 18440-1099
(570) 945-8967

King's College
Wilkes-Barre, Pennsylvania
www.kings.edu   Federal Code: 003282

4-year private business and liberal arts college in small city, affiliated with Roman Catholic Church.
Enrollment: 1,955 undergrads, 6% part-time. 479 full-time freshmen.

Selectivity: Admits over 75% of applicants.

BASIC COSTS (2006-2007)
Tuition and fees: $22,280.
Per-credit charge: $445.
Room and board: $8,590.

FINANCIAL AID PICTURE (2005-2006)
Students with need: Out of 449 full-time freshmen who applied for aid, 399 were judged to have need. Of these, 399 received aid, and 70 had their full need met. Average financial aid package met 76% of need; average scholarship/grant was $5,699; average loan was $3,674. For part-time students, average financial aid package was $5,550.
Students without need: 77 full-time freshmen who did not demonstrate need for aid received scholarships/grants; average award was $7,964. No-need awards available for academics, leadership, ROTC.
Cumulative student debt: 88% of graduating class had student loans; average debt was $17,263.
Additional info: Most minority students receive some aid in the form of a diversity scholarship.

FINANCIAL AID PROCEDURES
Forms required: FAFSA, institutional form.
Dates and Deadlines: Priority date 2/15; no closing date. Applicants notified on a rolling basis starting 3/1; must reply within 2 week(s) of notification.

CONTACT
Ellen McGuire, Director of Financial Aid
133 North River Street, Wilkes-Barre, PA 18711
(570) 208-5868

Kutztown University of Pennsylvania
Kutztown, Pennsylvania
www.kutztown.edu   Federal Code: 003322

4-year public university in small town.
Enrollment: 8,267 undergrads, 6% part-time. 2,090 full-time freshmen.
Selectivity: Admits over 75% of applicants.

BASIC COSTS (2005-2006)
Tuition and fees: $6,426; out-of-state residents $13,786.
Per-credit charge: $204; out-of-state residents $511.
Room and board: $5,508.

FINANCIAL AID PICTURE (2004-2005)
Students with need: Out of 1,836 full-time freshmen who applied for aid, 1,348 were judged to have need. Of these, 1,348 received aid, and 582 had their full need met. Average financial aid package met 52% of need; average scholarship/grant was $4,304; average loan was $2,587. For part-time students, average financial aid package was $4,597.
Students without need: 85 full-time freshmen who did not demonstrate need for aid received scholarships/grants; average award was $1,887. No-need awards available for academics, alumni affiliation, art, athletics, leadership, minority status, music/drama, state/district residency.
Scholarships offered: 27 full-time freshmen received athletic scholarships; average amount $1,915.
Cumulative student debt: 78% of graduating class had student loans; average debt was $14,479.

FINANCIAL AID PROCEDURES
Forms required: FAFSA.
Dates and Deadlines: Priority date 2/15; no closing date. Applicants notified on a rolling basis starting 3/30.

CONTACT
Anita Faust, Director of Financial Aid
Admissions Center, Kutztown, PA 19530-0730
(610) 683-4077

La Roche College
Pittsburgh, Pennsylvania
www.laroche.edu   Federal Code: 003987

4-year private liberal arts college in large city, affiliated with Roman Catholic Church.
Enrollment: 1,421 undergrads, 15% part-time. 304 full-time freshmen.
Selectivity: Admits 50 to 75% of applicants.

BASIC COSTS (2006-2007)
Tuition and fees: $18,220.
Per-credit charge: $528.
Room and board: $7,564.

FINANCIAL AID PICTURE (2005-2006)
Students with need: Out of 218 full-time freshmen who applied for aid, 185 were judged to have need. Of these, 185 received aid, and 57 had their full need met. Average financial aid package met 89% of need; average scholarship/grant was $3,030; average loan was $2,783. For part-time students, average financial aid package was $5,125.
Students without need: 113 full-time freshmen who did not demonstrate need for aid received scholarships/grants; average award was $7,732. No-need awards available for academics.
Cumulative student debt: 80% of graduating class had student loans; average debt was $18,000.

FINANCIAL AID PROCEDURES
Forms required: FAFSA.
Dates and Deadlines: Priority date 4/15; closing date 5/1. Applicants notified on a rolling basis starting 2/15; must reply within 2 week(s) of notification.

CONTACT
John Matsko, Director of Financial Aid
9000 Babcock Boulevard, Pittsburgh, PA 15237
(412) 536-1120

La Salle University
Philadelphia, Pennsylvania
www.lasalle.edu   Federal Code: 003287

4-year private university and liberal arts college in very large city, affiliated with Roman Catholic Church.
Enrollment: 4,238 undergrads, 21% part-time. 804 full-time freshmen.
Selectivity: Admits 50 to 75% of applicants.

BASIC COSTS (2006-2007)
Tuition and fees: $27,810.
Room and board: $10,300.

FINANCIAL AID PICTURE (2004-2005)
Students with need: Out of 716 full-time freshmen who applied for aid, 641 were judged to have need. Of these, 641 received aid, and 118 had their full need met. Average financial aid package met 74% of need; average scholarship/grant was $13,822; average loan was $3,059. For part-time students, average financial aid package was $6,181.
Students without need: 109 full-time freshmen who did not demonstrate need for aid received scholarships/grants; average award was $9,866. No-need awards available for academics, athletics, ROTC.
Scholarships offered: *Merit:* Christian Brothers Scholarship; full tuition; based on academics and extracurricular leadership. Community Service Scholarship; half tuition; based on involvement in community service and academics. Mission Grant; $4,000; for graduate of Catholic high school, 2.75 GPA or ranked in top 50% of class. *Athletic:* 36 full-time freshmen received athletic scholarships; average amount $9,312.
Cumulative student debt: 78% of graduating class had student loans; average debt was $30,611.

FINANCIAL AID PROCEDURES
Forms required: FAFSA.
Dates and Deadlines: Priority date 2/15; no closing date. Applicants notified on a rolling basis starting 3/15; must reply by 5/1 or within 2 week(s) of notification.

CONTACT
Michael Wisnieski, Director of Financial Aid
1900 West Olney Avenue, Philadelphia, PA 19141-1199
(215) 951-1070

Lackawanna College
Scranton, Pennsylvania
www.lackawanna.edu   Federal Code: 003283

2-year private junior college in small city.
Enrollment: 1,195 undergrads, 33% part-time. 329 full-time freshmen.
Selectivity: Open admission.

BASIC COSTS (2005-2006)
Tuition and fees: $9,470.
Per-credit charge: $310.
Room and board: $6,300.

FINANCIAL AID PICTURE (2004-2005)
Students with need: Out of 288 full-time freshmen who applied for aid, 267 were judged to have need. Of these, 262 received aid, and 17 had their full need met. Average financial aid package met 65% of need; average scholarship/grant was $6,450; average loan was $2,625. For part-time students, average financial aid package was $5,850.
Students without need: 7 full-time freshmen who did not demonstrate need for aid received scholarships/grants; average award was $1,200. No-need awards available for academics, athletics, leadership.
Scholarships offered: 14 full-time freshmen received athletic scholarships; average amount $3,000.
Cumulative student debt: 88% of graduating class had student loans; average debt was $11,185.
Additional info: To receive institutional funds, all students, including athletes, must apply for financial aid.

FINANCIAL AID PROCEDURES
Forms required: FAFSA, state aid form, institutional form.
Dates and Deadlines: Priority date 5/1; no closing date. Applicants notified on a rolling basis starting 5/1.
Transfers: No deadline. Applicants notified on a rolling basis.

CONTACT
Babara Hapeman, Director of Financial Aid
501 Vine Street, Scranton, PA 18509
(570) 961-7859

Lafayette College
Easton, Pennsylvania
www.lafayette.edu   Federal Code: 003284
                       CSS Code: 2361

4-year private engineering and liberal arts college in large town, affiliated with Presbyterian Church (USA).
Enrollment: 2,310 undergrads, 2% part-time. 597 full-time freshmen.
Selectivity: Admits less than 50% of applicants.

BASIC COSTS (2006-2007)
Tuition and fees: $31,669.
Room and board: $9,864.

FINANCIAL AID PICTURE (2005-2006)
Students with need: Out of 397 full-time freshmen who applied for aid, 322 were judged to have need. Of these, 322 received aid, and 322 had their full need met. Average financial aid package met 100% of need; average scholarship/grant was $24,266; average loan was $3,250. For part-time students, average financial aid package was $3,975.
Students without need: 38 full-time freshmen who did not demonstrate need for aid received scholarships/grants; average award was $13,421. No-need awards available for academics, leadership, ROTC.
Scholarships offered: Marquis Scholarships, $16,000 annually, based on academic merit. Trustee Scholarship, $8,000 annually, based on academic merit, awarded to 15% of each entering class.
Cumulative student debt: 51% of graduating class had student loans; average debt was $19,373.
Additional info: Parent loans, of up to $7,500 annually, are available with college absorbing interest while student is enrolled. Family has 8 years after graduation to repay. Not limited to those demonstrating need.

FINANCIAL AID PROCEDURES
Forms required: FAFSA, CSS PROFILE.
Dates and Deadlines: Closing date 2/15. Applicants notified on a rolling basis starting 3/15; must reply by 5/1.
Transfers: Closing date 5/1.

CONTACT
Arlina DeNardo, Director of Student Financial Aid
118 Markle Hall, Easton, PA 18042-1770
(610) 330-5055

Lancaster Bible College
Lancaster, Pennsylvania
www.lbc.edu   Federal Code: 003285

4-year private Bible college in small city, affiliated with nondenominational tradition.
Enrollment: 679 undergrads, 13% part-time. 189 full-time freshmen.
Selectivity: Admits 50 to 75% of applicants.

BASIC COSTS (2005-2006)
Tuition and fees: $12,795.
Room and board: $5,700.

FINANCIAL AID PICTURE (2004-2005)
Students with need: 68% of average financial aid package awarded as scholarships/grants, 32% awarded as loans/jobs. Need-based aid available for part-time students. Work study available nights, weekends, and for part-time students.
Students without need: No-need awards available for academics, alumni affiliation, leadership, music/drama, state/district residency.
Scholarships offered: Child of Full-time Christian Worker Scholarship: available to dependent students where major wage earner or head of household is in full-time Christian work. Scholarship is 50 percent reduction in tuition, room and board. The reduction includes federal and state aid and other institutional scholarships. Remainder of reduction paid by school.

FINANCIAL AID PROCEDURES
Forms required: FAFSA, state aid form.
Dates and Deadlines: Priority date 5/1; no closing date. Applicants notified on a rolling basis starting 3/15; must reply within 3 week(s) of notification.

CONTACT
Karen Fox, Director of Financial Aid
901 Eden Road, Lancaster, PA 17608-3403
(717) 560-8254

Laurel Business Institute
Uniontown, Pennsylvania
www.laurelbusiness.edu Federal Code: 017118

2-year for-profit business and technical college in large town.
Enrollment: 300 undergrads.

FINANCIAL AID PICTURE
Students with need: Work study available nights, weekends, and for part-time students.
Students without need: This college only awards aid to students with need.
Scholarships offered: One full tuition, several half tuition (including GED scholarships), based on high school transcripts or GED scores, letters of reference, and personal interview.

FINANCIAL AID PROCEDURES
Forms required: FAFSA, institutional form.
Dates and Deadlines: Closing date 8/1. Applicants notified on a rolling basis; must reply within 4 week(s) of notification.
Transfers: No deadline.

CONTACT
Stephanie Migyanko, Director of Financial Aid
11 North Penn Street, Uniontown, PA 15401
(724) 439-4900

Lebanon Valley College
Annville, Pennsylvania
www.lvc.edu Federal Code: 003288

4-year private liberal arts college in small town, affiliated with United Methodist Church.
Enrollment: 1,702 undergrads, 6% part-time. 454 full-time freshmen.
Selectivity: Admits over 75% of applicants.

BASIC COSTS (2006-2007)
Tuition and fees: $26,385.
Per-credit charge: $455.
Room and board: $7,115.
Additional info: Tuition/fee waivers available for minority students.

FINANCIAL AID PICTURE (2005-2006)
Students with need: Out of 426 full-time freshmen who applied for aid, 366 were judged to have need. Of these, 365 received aid, and 137 had their full need met. Average financial aid package met 88% of need; average scholarship/grant was $15,235; average loan was $3,622. For part-time students, average financial aid package was $3,151.
Students without need: 77 full-time freshmen who did not demonstrate need for aid received scholarships/grants; average award was $10,125. No-need awards available for academics, alumni affiliation, music/drama, ROTC.
Scholarships offered: Vickroy scholarship; half tuition; automatic for admitted applicants in top 10% of graduating class. Leadership scholarship; one-third tuition; automatic for admitted applicants in top 20% of graduating class. Achievement scholarship; one-quarter tuition; automatic for admitted applicants in top 30% of graduating class.
Cumulative student debt: 73% of graduating class had student loans; average debt was $24,236.

FINANCIAL AID PROCEDURES
Forms required: FAFSA, institutional form.
Dates and Deadlines: Priority date 3/1; no closing date. Applicants notified on a rolling basis starting 3/1; must reply by 5/1 or within 2 week(s) of notification.
Transfers: Students transferring 15 or fewer credits are considered for scholarships on the same basis as high school seniors. Students transferring 16 or more credits are considered for scholarships based on their college academic performance and program.

CONTACT
Kendra Feigert, Director of Financial Aid
101 North College Avenue, Annville, PA 17003
(717) 867-6181

Lehigh Carbon Community College
Schnecksville, Pennsylvania
www.lccc.edu Federal Code: 006810

2-year public community college in small town.
Enrollment: 6,564 undergrads, 61% part-time. 959 full-time freshmen.
Selectivity: Open admission; but selective for some programs.

BASIC COSTS (2006-2007)
Tuition and fees: $2,715; out-of-district residents $5,010; out-of-state residents $7,305.
Per-credit charge: $77; out-of-district residents $154; out-of-state residents $231.
Additional info: Out-of-district students pay $690 in fees; out-of-state students pay $960 in fees.

FINANCIAL AID PICTURE (2004-2005)
Students with need: Out of 502 full-time freshmen who applied for aid, 361 were judged to have need. Of these, 345 received aid, and 297 had their full need met. Average financial aid package met 60% of need; average scholarship/grant was $3,093; average loan was $2,309. For part-time students, average financial aid package was $3,834.
Students without need: 10 full-time freshmen who did not demonstrate need for aid received scholarships/grants; average award was $1,589. No-need awards available for academics, state/district residency.
Cumulative student debt: 22% of graduating class had student loans; average debt was $2,220.

FINANCIAL AID PROCEDURES
Forms required: FAFSA.
Dates and Deadlines: No deadline. Applicants notified on a rolling basis starting 5/5; must reply within 2 week(s) of notification.
Transfers: No deadline. Applicants notified on a rolling basis.

CONTACT
Marian Snyder, Director of Financial Aid
4525 Education Park Drive, Schnecksville, PA 18078
(610) 799-1133

Lehigh University
Bethlehem, Pennsylvania
www.lehigh.edu Federal Code: 003289
  CSS Code: 2365

4-year private university in small city.
Enrollment: 4,656 undergrads, 1% part-time. 1,223 full-time freshmen.
Selectivity: Admits less than 50% of applicants.

BASIC COSTS (2006-2007)
Tuition and fees: $33,770.
Per-credit charge: $1,395.
Room and board: $8,920.

FINANCIAL AID PICTURE (2005-2006)
Students with need: Out of 754 full-time freshmen who applied for aid, 573 were judged to have need. Of these, 568 received aid, and 242 had their full need met. Average financial aid package met 97% of need; average scholarship/grant was $19,990; average loan was $3,215. For part-time students, average financial aid package was $7,732.

Students without need: 95 full-time freshmen who did not demonstrate need for aid received scholarships/grants; average award was $10,759. No-need awards available for academics, art, athletics, leadership, music/drama, ROTC.
Scholarships offered: *Merit:* Asa Packer Scholarships: $15,000; for students with exceptional academic and leadership skills. Dean's Scholarships: $10,000; for students who excel academically and demonstrate leadership skills. Baker Scholarship: $2,500; for students who demonstrate excellence in music or theater and have a superior academic record. Choral Arts Scholarships: $2,500; for students with singing talent. President's Scholarships: full tuition; for fifth year of study for seniors with 3.5 GPA and minimum 90 credits completed at institution. *Athletic:* 9 full-time freshmen received athletic scholarships; average amount $38,068.
Cumulative student debt: 52% of graduating class had student loans; average debt was $23,418.

FINANCIAL AID PROCEDURES
Forms required: FAFSA, CSS PROFILE.
Dates and Deadlines: Closing date 2/15. Applicants notified by 3/30; must reply by 5/1 or within 3 week(s) of notification.
Transfers: Closing date 4/15.

CONTACT
Linda Bell, Director of Financial Aid
27 Memorial Drive West, Bethlehem, PA 18015-3094
(610) 758-3181

Lehigh Valley College
Center Valley, Pennsylvania
www.lehighvalley.edu   Federal Code: 008889

2-year for-profit business and technical college in small city.
Enrollment: 1,236 undergrads.
Selectivity: Open admission.

BASIC COSTS (2005-2006)
Additional info: Tuition varies from $26,280 to $29,520 depending on program. Fees vary by program. Tuition at time of enrollment locked for 2 years.

FINANCIAL AID PICTURE
Students with need: Need-based aid available for full-time and part-time students. Work study available nights, weekends, and for part-time students.
Cumulative student debt: 95% of graduating class had student loans; average debt was $15,000.

FINANCIAL AID PROCEDURES
Forms required: FAFSA, state aid form, institutional form.
Dates and Deadlines: No deadline. Applicants notified on a rolling basis.

CONTACT
Tarek Richan, Director of Student Financial
2809 East Saucon Valley Road, Center Valley, PA 18034
(610) 791-5100

Lincoln University
Lincoln University, Pennsylvania
www.lincoln.edu   Federal Code: 003290

4-year public university and liberal arts college in rural community.
Enrollment: 1,700 undergrads, 3% part-time. 630 full-time freshmen.
Selectivity: Admits less than 50% of applicants.

BASIC COSTS (2005-2006)
Tuition and fees: $7,028; out-of-state residents $10,704.
Per-credit charge: $218; out-of-state residents $371.
Room and board: $6,898.

Additional info: Out of state students pay an additional $564 in fees.

FINANCIAL AID PICTURE (2005-2006)
Students with need: Out of 599 full-time freshmen who applied for aid, 553 were judged to have need. Of these, 547 received aid, and 36 had their full need met. Average financial aid package met 45% of need; average scholarship/grant was $5,142; average loan was $2,673. For part-time students, average financial aid package was $6,875.
Students without need: 22 full-time freshmen who did not demonstrate need for aid received scholarships/grants; average award was $8,096. No-need awards available for academics, alumni affiliation, leadership, music/drama.
Cumulative student debt: 78% of graduating class had student loans; average debt was $17,000.

FINANCIAL AID PROCEDURES
Forms required: FAFSA.
Dates and Deadlines: Closing date 5/1. Applicants notified on a rolling basis starting 4/1; must reply within 3 week(s) of notification.

CONTACT
Thelma Ross, Director of Financial Aid
PO BOX 179, Lincoln University, PA 19352-0999
(800) 561-2606

Lock Haven University of Pennsylvania
Lock Haven, Pennsylvania
www.lhup.edu   Federal Code: 003323

4-year public university and liberal arts and teachers college in small town.
Enrollment: 4,794 undergrads, 6% part-time. 1,162 full-time freshmen.
Selectivity: Admits over 75% of applicants.

BASIC COSTS (2005-2006)
Tuition and fees: $6,258; out-of-state residents $11,618.
Per-credit charge: $204; out-of-state residents $428.
Room and board: $5,840.
Additional info: Tuition/fee waivers available for minority students.

FINANCIAL AID PICTURE (2005-2006)
Students with need: Out of 1,104 full-time freshmen who applied for aid, 861 were judged to have need. Of these, 861 received aid, and 474 had their full need met. Average financial aid package met 73% of need; average scholarship/grant was $4,283; average loan was $2,500. For part-time students, average financial aid package was $2,200.
Students without need: 37 full-time freshmen who did not demonstrate need for aid received scholarships/grants; average award was $1,200. No-need awards available for academics, art, athletics, leadership, minority status, music/drama, ROTC, state/district residency.
Scholarships offered: 56 full-time freshmen received athletic scholarships; average amount $2,155.
Cumulative student debt: 75% of graduating class had student loans; average debt was $19,500.

FINANCIAL AID PROCEDURES
Forms required: FAFSA, institutional form.
Dates and Deadlines: Priority date 3/15; no closing date. Applicants notified on a rolling basis starting 3/1; must reply by 5/1 or within 2 week(s) of notification.
Transfers: Priority date 4/1.

CONTACT
James Theeuwes, Director of Student Financial Services
Akeley Hall, Lock Haven, PA 17745
(877) 405-3057

Luzerne County Community College
Nanticoke, Pennsylvania
www.luzerne.edu   Federal Code: 006811

2-year public community college in large town.
Enrollment: 6,144 undergrads.
Selectivity: Open admission; but selective for some programs.

BASIC COSTS (2005-2006)
Tuition and fees: $2,760; out-of-district residents $5,340; out-of-state residents $7,920.
Per-credit charge: $76; out-of-district residents $152; out-of-state residents $228.

FINANCIAL AID PICTURE
Students with need: Need-based aid available for full-time and part-time students.

FINANCIAL AID PROCEDURES
Forms required: FAFSA, institutional form.
Dates and Deadlines: Priority date 4/15; no closing date. Applicants notified on a rolling basis starting 7/1.

CONTACT
Mary Kosin, Director of Financial Aid
1333 South Prospect Street, Nanticoke, PA 18634-9804
(570) 740-0395

Lycoming College
Williamsport, Pennsylvania
www.lycoming.edu   Federal Code: 003293

4-year private liberal arts college in large town, affiliated with United Methodist Church.
Enrollment: 1,450 undergrads, 1% part-time. 357 full-time freshmen.
Selectivity: Admits over 75% of applicants.

BASIC COSTS (2006-2007)
Tuition and fees: $25,770.
Per-credit charge: $785.
Room and board: $6,826.
Additional info: Tuition/fee waivers available for minority students.

FINANCIAL AID PICTURE (2005-2006)
Students with need: Out of 330 full-time freshmen who applied for aid, 293 were judged to have need. Of these, 293 received aid, and 50 had their full need met. Average financial aid package met 76% of need; average scholarship/grant was $14,694; average loan was $3,489. For part-time students, average financial aid package was $7,507.
Students without need: 48 full-time freshmen who did not demonstrate need for aid received scholarships/grants; average award was $9,504. No-need awards available for academics, art, leadership, music/drama.
Cumulative student debt: 87% of graduating class had student loans; average debt was $23,343.

FINANCIAL AID PROCEDURES
Forms required: FAFSA, institutional form.
Dates and Deadlines: Priority date 3/1; no closing date. Applicants notified on a rolling basis starting 3/1; must reply by 5/1.
Transfers: No deadline.

CONTACT
Jamie Lowthert, Director of Financial Aid
700 College Place, Williamsport, PA 17701
(570) 321-4041

Manor College
Jenkintown, Pennsylvania
www.manor.edu   Federal Code: 003294

2-year private junior college in small town, affiliated with Ukrainian Catholic Church.
Enrollment: 738 undergrads, 39% part-time. 148 full-time freshmen.

BASIC COSTS (2005-2006)
Tuition and fees: $10,900.
Per-credit charge: $229.
Room and board: $5,096.
Additional info: Tuition for allied health program $10,960 per year, $325 per credit hour.

FINANCIAL AID PICTURE (2005-2006)
Students with need: Out of 145 full-time freshmen who applied for aid, 121 were judged to have need. Of these, 121 received aid, and 8 had their full need met. Average financial aid package met 40% of need; average scholarship/grant was $4,751; average loan was $2,625. For part-time students, average financial aid package was $4,541.
Students without need: This college only awards aid to students with need.
Scholarships offered: Basilian Scholarship: for every freshman with A or B high school average and minimum SAT score of 900 (exclusive of Writing).
Cumulative student debt: 97% of graduating class had student loans; average debt was $6,800.

FINANCIAL AID PROCEDURES
Forms required: FAFSA, institutional form.
Dates and Deadlines: Priority date 5/1; no closing date. Applicants notified on a rolling basis starting 3/1; must reply within 2 week(s) of notification.
Transfers: Priority date 4/1; closing date 5/1. Applicants notified on a rolling basis; must reply within 2 week(s) of notification. Require academic transcript prior to packaging financial aid.

CONTACT
Dan Campbell, Director of Financial Aid
700 Fox Chase Road, Jenkintown, PA 19046-3319
(215) 885-2360

Mansfield University of Pennsylvania
Mansfield, Pennsylvania
www.mnsfld.edu   Federal Code: 003324

4-year public university and liberal arts college in small town.
Enrollment: 2,886 undergrads, 7% part-time. 707 full-time freshmen.
Selectivity: Admits 50 to 75% of applicants.

BASIC COSTS (2005-2006)
Tuition and fees: $6,408; out-of-state residents $13,768.
Per-credit charge: $204; out-of-state residents $511.
Room and board: $6,120.

FINANCIAL AID PICTURE (2004-2005)
Students with need: Out of 656 full-time freshmen who applied for aid, 528 were judged to have need. Of these, 528 received aid, and 226 had their full need met. Average financial aid package met 52% of need; average scholarship/grant was $4,051; average loan was $2,600. For part-time students, average financial aid package was $7,606.
Students without need: 34 full-time freshmen who did not demonstrate need for aid received scholarships/grants; average award was $1,534. No-need awards available for academics, art, athletics, leadership, music/drama, state/district residency.
Scholarships offered: 38 full-time freshmen received athletic scholarships; average amount $1,630.

Cumulative student debt: 77% of graduating class had student loans; average debt was $22,821.

FINANCIAL AID PROCEDURES
Forms required: FAFSA, institutional form.
Dates and Deadlines: Priority date 3/15; no closing date. Applicants notified on a rolling basis starting 3/15; must reply within 2 week(s) of notification.

CONTACT
Barbara Schmitt, Director of Financial Aid
Alumni Hall, Mansfield, PA 16933
(570) 662-4129

Marywood University
Scranton, Pennsylvania
www.marywood.edu   Federal Code: 003296

4-year private university in small city, affiliated with Roman Catholic Church.
Enrollment: 1,807 undergrads, 8% part-time. 302 full-time freshmen.
Selectivity: Admits over 75% of applicants.

BASIC COSTS (2006-2007)
Tuition and fees: $22,670.
Room and board: $9,100.

FINANCIAL AID PICTURE
Students with need: Need-based aid available for full-time and part-time students. Work study available nights, weekends, and for part-time students.
Students without need: No-need awards available for academics, alumni affiliation, art, leadership, minority status, music/drama, ROTC.
Scholarships offered: Presidential Scholarships: full tuition, for students with SAT scores of at least 1300 and rank in upper tenth of graduating class. IHM Scholarships: for students with SAT scores of 1150 or more and rank in the upper fifth of high school class. (SAT scores exclusive of Writing.) Marywood Grants: for students with demonstrated academic ability. Talent awards for students who demonstrate proficiency in music, art or theater and major in 1 of those areas. Other non-need-based merit scholarships available.

FINANCIAL AID PROCEDURES
Forms required: FAFSA, institutional form.
Dates and Deadlines: Priority date 2/15; no closing date. Applicants notified on a rolling basis starting 3/1; must reply by 5/1 or within 3 week(s) of notification.

CONTACT
Stanley Skrutski, Director of Financial Aid
2300 Adams Avenue, Scranton, PA 18509-1598
(570) 348-6225

Mercyhurst College
Erie, Pennsylvania
www.mercyhurst.edu   Federal Code: 003297

4-year private liberal arts college in small city, affiliated with Roman Catholic Church.
Enrollment: 3,800 undergrads, 11% part-time. 693 full-time freshmen.
Selectivity: Admits over 75% of applicants.

BASIC COSTS (2006-2007)
Tuition and fees: $20,364.
Per-credit charge: $631.
Room and board: $7,458.
Additional info: Tuition/fee waivers available for adults, minority students, unemployed or children of unemployed.

FINANCIAL AID PICTURE (2005-2006)
Students with need: Out of 691 full-time freshmen who applied for aid, 508 were judged to have need. Of these, 508 received aid, and 401 had their full need met. Average financial aid package met 87% of need; average scholarship/grant was $9,322; average loan was $2,515. Need-based aid available for part-time students.
Students without need: 143 full-time freshmen who did not demonstrate need for aid received scholarships/grants; average award was $8,673. No-need awards available for academics, alumni affiliation, art, athletics, leadership, minority status, music/drama, religious affiliation, ROTC.
Scholarships offered: 38 full-time freshmen received athletic scholarships; average amount $13,486.
Cumulative student debt: 93% of graduating class had student loans; average debt was $21,000.

FINANCIAL AID PROCEDURES
Forms required: FAFSA, institutional form.
Dates and Deadlines: Priority date 3/1; no closing date. Applicants notified on a rolling basis starting 2/15; must reply by 5/1 or within 2 week(s) of notification.
Transfers: No deadline. Applicants notified on a rolling basis; must reply within 2 week(s) of notification.

CONTACT
Daniel Shumate, Director of Financial Aid
501 East 38th Street, Erie, PA 16546-0001
(814) 824-2471

Messiah College
Grantham, Pennsylvania
www.messiah.edu   Federal Code: 003298

4-year private liberal arts college in small town, affiliated with interdenominational tradition.
Enrollment: 2,888 undergrads, 1% part-time. 707 full-time freshmen.
Selectivity: Admits 50 to 75% of applicants.

BASIC COSTS (2006-2007)
Tuition and fees: $23,290.
Per-credit charge: $945.
Room and board: $7,060.
Additional info: Tuition/fee waivers available for adults.

FINANCIAL AID PICTURE (2005-2006)
Students with need: Out of 605 full-time freshmen who applied for aid, 484 were judged to have need. Of these, 484 received aid, and 128 had their full need met. Average financial aid package met 63% of need; average scholarship/grant was $4,742; average loan was $2,069. For part-time students, average financial aid package was $5,987.
Students without need: 128 full-time freshmen who did not demonstrate need for aid received scholarships/grants; average award was $8,095. No-need awards available for academics, alumni affiliation, art, leadership, music/drama, religious affiliation.
Cumulative student debt: 70% of graduating class had student loans; average debt was $27,322.

FINANCIAL AID PROCEDURES
Forms required: FAFSA.
Dates and Deadlines: Priority date 4/1; no closing date. Applicants notified on a rolling basis starting 3/15; must reply by 5/1 or within 4 week(s) of notification.

CONTACT
Greg Gearhart, Director of Financial Aid
PO Box 3005, Grantham, PA 17027-0800
(717) 691-6007

Metropolitan Career Center
Philadelphia, Pennsylvania
www.mccweb-gt.org   Federal Code: 031091

2-year private technical college in very large city.
Enrollment: 135 undergrads.
Selectivity: Open admission.

BASIC COSTS (2005-2006)
Tuition and fees: $8,494.
Per-credit charge: $274.
Additional info: Books and supplies included in cost of tuition.

FINANCIAL AID PICTURE
Students with need: Need-based aid available for full-time and part-time students.

FINANCIAL AID PROCEDURES
Forms required: FAFSA.

CONTACT
Director of Financial Aid
100 South Broad Street, Suite 830, Philadelphia, PA 19110
(215) 568-9215 ext. 314

Millersville University of Pennsylvania
Millersville, Pennsylvania
www.millersville.edu   Federal Code: 003325

4-year public university and liberal arts college in small town.
Enrollment: 6,847 undergrads, 8% part-time. 1,396 full-time freshmen.
Selectivity: Admits 50 to 75% of applicants.

BASIC COSTS (2005-2006)
Tuition and fees: $6,235; out-of-state residents $13,595.
Per-credit charge: $204; out-of-state residents $511.
Room and board: $5,878.

FINANCIAL AID PICTURE (2004-2005)
Students with need: Out of 1,206 full-time freshmen who applied for aid, 819 were judged to have need. Of these, 795 received aid, and 96 had their full need met. Average financial aid package met 72% of need; average scholarship/grant was $4,380; average loan was $2,615. For part-time students, average financial aid package was $4,817.
Students without need: 29 full-time freshmen who did not demonstrate need for aid received scholarships/grants; average award was $2,301. No-need awards available for academics, athletics, minority status.
Scholarships offered: 17 full-time freshmen received athletic scholarships; average amount $1,468.
Cumulative student debt: 62% of graduating class had student loans; average debt was $16,103.

FINANCIAL AID PROCEDURES
Forms required: FAFSA.
Dates and Deadlines: Closing date 3/15. Applicants notified on a rolling basis starting 3/19; must reply within 2 week(s) of notification.
Transfers: No deadline.

CONTACT
Dwight Horsey, Director of Financial Aid
PO Box 1002, Millersville, PA 17551-0302
(717) 872-3026

Montgomery County Community College
Blue Bell, Pennsylvania
www.mc3.edu   Federal Code: 004452

2-year public community college in large town.
Enrollment: 10,874 undergrads, 56% part-time. 1,947 full-time freshmen.
Selectivity: Open admission; but selective for some programs.

BASIC COSTS (2006-2007)
Tuition and fees: $2,910; out-of-district residents $5,430; out-of-state residents $7,950.
Per-credit charge: $84; out-of-district residents $168; out-of-state residents $252.
Additional info: Required fees for out-of-county students $690; for out-of-state $990.

FINANCIAL AID PICTURE (2004-2005)
Students with need: Out of 837 full-time freshmen who applied for aid, 551 were judged to have need. Of these, 431 received aid, and 33 had their full need met. Average financial aid package met 18% of need; average scholarship/grant was $1,747; average loan was $1,257. For part-time students, average financial aid package was $1,701.
Students without need: 141 full-time freshmen who did not demonstrate need for aid received scholarships/grants; average award was $1,350. No-need awards available for academics.

FINANCIAL AID PROCEDURES
Forms required: FAFSA.
Dates and Deadlines: Closing date 5/1. Applicants notified on a rolling basis starting 2/1.
Transfers: Priority date 5/1; no deadline.

CONTACT
Cindy Haney, Director of Financial Aid
340 DeKalb Pike, Blue Bell, PA 19422
(215) 641-6566

Moore College of Art and Design
Philadelphia, Pennsylvania
www.moore.edu   Federal Code: 003300

4-year private visual arts college for women in very large city.
Enrollment: 493 undergrads, 14% part-time. 90 full-time freshmen.
Selectivity: Admits over 75% of applicants.

BASIC COSTS (2005-2006)
Tuition and fees: $22,846.
Per-credit charge: $920.
Room and board: $8,654.

FINANCIAL AID PICTURE (2005-2006)
Students with need: 45% of average financial aid package awarded as scholarships/grants, 55% awarded as loans/jobs. Need-based aid available for part-time students.
Students without need: No-need awards available for academics.
Cumulative student debt: 97% of graduating class had student loans; average debt was $8,324.

FINANCIAL AID PROCEDURES
Forms required: FAFSA.
Dates and Deadlines: Priority date 3/1; closing date 5/1. Applicants notified on a rolling basis starting 2/15; must reply within 2 week(s) of notification.
Transfers: Priority date 5/1; no deadline.

Moravian College
Bethlehem, Pennsylvania
www.moravian.edu
Federal Code: 003301
CSS Code: 2418

4-year private liberal arts college in small city, affiliated with Moravian Church in America.
Enrollment: 1,636 undergrads, 7% part-time. 382 full-time freshmen.
Selectivity: Admits 50 to 75% of applicants.

BASIC COSTS (2006-2007)
Tuition and fees: $26,775.
Room and board: $7,760.

FINANCIAL AID PICTURE (2005-2006)
Students with need: Out of 343 full-time freshmen who applied for aid, 277 were judged to have need. Of these, 277 received aid, and 50 had their full need met. Average financial aid package met 76% of need; average scholarship/grant was $12,492; average loan was $3,307. For part-time students, average financial aid package was $7,856.
Students without need: 88 full-time freshmen who did not demonstrate need for aid received scholarships/grants; average award was $13,559. No-need awards available for academics, alumni affiliation, leadership, music/drama, religious affiliation, ROTC.
Scholarships offered: Comenius Scholarship: from $10,000 to full tuition. Founders Scholarship: $4,000-$8,000; for top 25%, 1150 SAT (exclusive of Writing). Trustee Scholarship; $6,000-10,000; must be National Honor Society member, in top 20% of class, and have at least 500 each on Math and Critical Reading sections of SAT. Other scholarships available based on leadership and interest in promoting diversity and/or challenging circumstances in attending college.

FINANCIAL AID PROCEDURES
Forms required: FAFSA, CSS PROFILE.
Dates and Deadlines: Priority date 2/14; closing date 3/15. Applicants notified on a rolling basis starting 4/1; must reply by 5/1 or within 2 week(s) of notification.
Transfers: Priority date 4/1; no deadline.

CONTACT
Stephen Cassel, Director of Financial Aid
1200 Main Street, Bethlehem, PA 18018
(610) 861-1330

Mount Aloysius College
Cresson, Pennsylvania
www.mtaloy.edu
Federal Code: 003302

4-year private liberal arts college in small town, affiliated with Roman Catholic Church.
Enrollment: 1,424 undergrads, 19% part-time. 277 full-time freshmen.
Selectivity: Admits over 75% of applicants.

BASIC COSTS (2005-2006)
Tuition and fees: $14,530.
Per-credit charge: $450.
Room and board: $6,190.
Additional info: Tuition/fee waivers available for unemployed or children of unemployed.

FINANCIAL AID PICTURE (2004-2005)
Students with need: Out of 277 full-time freshmen who applied for aid, 238 were judged to have need. Of these, 238 received aid. Average financial aid package met 23% of need; average scholarship/grant was $2,800; average loan was $2,600. For part-time students, average financial aid package was $3,800.
Students without need: 39 full-time freshmen who did not demonstrate need for aid received scholarships/grants; average award was $2,100. No-need awards available for academics, art, leadership, music/drama, religious affiliation.
Cumulative student debt: 79% of graduating class had student loans; average debt was $20,970.

FINANCIAL AID PROCEDURES
Forms required: FAFSA.
Dates and Deadlines: Priority date 2/15; no closing date. Applicants notified on a rolling basis starting 3/15; must reply within 4 week(s) of notification.
Transfers: No deadline.

CONTACT
Stacy Schenk, Financial Aid Director
7373 Admiral Peary Highway, Cresson, PA 16630
(814) 886-6357

Muhlenberg College
Allentown, Pennsylvania
www.muhlenberg.edu
Federal Code: 003304
CSS Code: 2424

4-year private liberal arts college in small city, affiliated with Evangelical Lutheran Church in America.
Enrollment: 2,396 undergrads, 6% part-time. 576 full-time freshmen.
Selectivity: Admits less than 50% of applicants.

BASIC COSTS (2006-2007)
Tuition and fees: $30,715.
Room and board: $7,525.

FINANCIAL AID PICTURE (2005-2006)
Students with need: Out of 377 full-time freshmen who applied for aid, 274 were judged to have need. Of these, 269 received aid, and 252 had their full need met. Average financial aid package met 94% of need; average scholarship/grant was $16,155; average loan was $2,829. For part-time students, average financial aid package was $4,423.
Students without need: 184 full-time freshmen who did not demonstrate need for aid received scholarships/grants; average award was $11,331. No-need awards available for academics, art, leadership, music/drama.
Cumulative student debt: 84% of graduating class had student loans; average debt was $15,292.

FINANCIAL AID PROCEDURES
Forms required: FAFSA, CSS PROFILE, institutional form.
Dates and Deadlines: Closing date 2/15. Applicants notified by 4/1; must reply by 5/1.
Transfers: Closing date 4/15. Transfers awarded aid on a funds-available basis after returning students and freshmen have been served.

CONTACT
Gregory Mitton, Director of Financial Aid
2400 Chew Street, Allentown, PA 18104
(484) 664-3175

Neumann College
Aston, Pennsylvania
www.neumann.edu   Federal Code: 003988

4-year private liberal arts college in large town, affiliated with Roman Catholic Church.
Enrollment: 2,313 undergrads, 21% part-time. 522 full-time freshmen.
Selectivity: Admits over 75% of applicants.

BASIC COSTS (2006-2007)
Tuition and fees: $18,632.
Per-credit charge: $411.
Room and board: $8,576.

FINANCIAL AID PICTURE (2005-2006)
Students with need: Out of 470 full-time freshmen who applied for aid, 450 were judged to have need. Of these, 450 received aid, and 250 had their full need met. Average financial aid package met 65% of need; average scholarship/grant was $17,000; average loan was $6,625.
Students without need: This college only awards aid to students with need.
Cumulative student debt: 70% of graduating class had student loans; average debt was $20,000.

FINANCIAL AID PROCEDURES
Forms required: FAFSA.
Dates and Deadlines: No deadline. Applicants notified on a rolling basis; must reply within 2 week(s) of notification.

CONTACT
Dennis Murphy, Director of Financial Aid
One Neumann Drive, Aston, PA 19014-1298
(610) 558-5520

New Castle School of Trades
Pulaski, Pennsylvania
www.ncstrades.com   Federal Code: 007780

2-year for-profit technical college in rural community.
Enrollment: 364 undergrads.

BASIC COSTS (2006-2007)
Tuition and fees: $14,280.
Additional info: Figure given, which is an average cost of all programs, is for school's entire 15-month course of study.

FINANCIAL AID PICTURE (2004-2005)
Students with need: 43% of average financial aid package awarded as scholarships/grants, 57% awarded as loans/jobs. Need-based aid available for part-time students.

CONTACT
Trudy Sotter, Financial Aid
4164 US 422, Pulaski, PA 16143-9721
(724) 964-8811

Newport Business Institute
Lower Burrell, Pennsylvania
www.newportbusiness.com   Federal Code: 004901

2-year private business college in small town.
Enrollment: 90 undergrads.
Selectivity: Open admission.

BASIC COSTS (2005-2006)
Tuition and fees: $8,700.

FINANCIAL AID PICTURE
Students with need: Need-based aid available for full-time and part-time students.
Students without need: No-need awards available for academics, leadership.

FINANCIAL AID PROCEDURES
Forms required: FAFSA, state aid form.
Dates and Deadlines: Closing date 5/1. Applicants notified on a rolling basis starting 5/1.

CONTACT
Rosemary Leipertz, Director of Financial Aid
945 Greensburg Road, Lower Burrell, PA 15068
(724) 339-7542

Northampton County Area Community College
Bethlehem, Pennsylvania
www.northampton.edu   Federal Code: 007191

2-year public community college in small city.
Enrollment: 8,563 undergrads, 57% part-time. 1,406 full-time freshmen.
Selectivity: Open admission; but selective for some programs.

BASIC COSTS (2005-2006)
Tuition and fees: $2,820; out-of-district residents $4,920; out-of-state residents $7,020.
Per-credit charge: $70; out-of-district residents $140; out-of-state residents $210.
Room and board: $5,944.
Additional info: Out-of-district students pay $60 fee per credit hour; out-of-state students pay $87 fee per credit hour.

FINANCIAL AID PICTURE (2005-2006)
Students with need: Average financial aid package for all full-time undergraduates was $2,100; for part-time $1,050. 69% awarded as scholarships/grants, 31% awarded as loans/jobs. Work study available nights, weekends, and for part-time students.
Students without need: No-need awards available for academics, alumni affiliation, art, leadership, minority status, music/drama.

FINANCIAL AID PROCEDURES
Forms required: FAFSA, institutional form.
Dates and Deadlines: Closing date 3/31. Applicants notified on a rolling basis starting 6/1; must reply within 2 week(s) of notification.

CONTACT
Cindy King, Director of Financial Aid
3835 Green Pond Road, Bethlehem, PA 18020
(610) 861-5510

Oakbridge Academy of Arts
Lower Burrell, Pennsylvania
www.oakbridgeacademy.com   Federal Code: 015063

2-year private visual arts college in large town.
Enrollment: 90 undergrads.

BASIC COSTS (2005-2006)
Tuition and fees: $9,150.

FINANCIAL AID PICTURE
Students with need: Need-based aid available for full-time and part-time students.
Students without need: This college only awards aid to students with need.

Scholarships offered: Jeanne H. Mullen art scholarship; half tuition; based on portfolio; 2 awarded per year.

FINANCIAL AID PROCEDURES
Forms required: FAFSA, state aid form.
Dates and Deadlines: Closing date 5/1. Applicants notified on a rolling basis.

CONTACT
Rosemary Leipertz, Financial Aid Director
1250 Greensburg Road, Lower Burrell, PA 15068
(724) 335-5336

Orleans Technical Institute - Center City Campus
Philadelphia, Pennsylvania
www.orleanstech.org

2-year private technical college in very large city.
Enrollment: 135 undergrads.

BASIC COSTS (2005-2006)
Tuition and fees: $7,575.
Additional info: Tuition for full associate program (28 months) $25,750.

FINANCIAL AID PICTURE
Students with need: Need-based aid available for full-time and part-time students.

FINANCIAL AID PROCEDURES
Forms required: FAFSA, institutional form.
Dates and Deadlines: No deadline. Applicants notified on a rolling basis.

CONTACT
Latanya Byrd, Financial Aid Director
1845 Walnut Street, 7th Floor, Philadelphia, PA 19103-4707
(215) 854-1822

Peirce College
Philadelphia, Pennsylvania
www.peirce.edu   Federal Code: 003309

4-year private business and technical college in very large city.
Enrollment: 1,971 undergrads, 58% part-time. 54 full-time freshmen.
Selectivity: Open admission.

BASIC COSTS (2005-2006)
Tuition and fees: $12,760.
Per-credit charge: $392.

FINANCIAL AID PICTURE (2004-2005)
Students with need: Out of 34 full-time freshmen who applied for aid, 34 were judged to have need. Of these, 34 received aid, and 30 had their full need met. For part-time students, average financial aid package was $5,724.
Students without need: 6 full-time freshmen who did not demonstrate need for aid received scholarships/grants; average award was $1,859. No-need awards available for academics, leadership.
Scholarships offered: Academic Achievement Scholarships for new freshmen: $2,000-4,000; top 15 percent of graduating class, above average standardized test scores, 2 letters of recommendation; Transfer Students Scholarship: $2,000-4,000; 2 letters of recommendation; must transfer minimum of 24 credits. Out of State Scholarships: to non-Pennsylvania students. Dual Admission Scholarships with: Delaware County Community College, Harrisburg Area Community College, Mercer Community College, Bucks Community College, Burlington Community College, Community College of Philadelphia, and Northampton Community College for students with 3.0 GPA or higher.

Cumulative student debt: 80% of graduating class had student loans; average debt was $14,000.
Additional info: Tuition discounts available for U.S. students serving in U.S. military and in protect-and-serve fields.

FINANCIAL AID PROCEDURES
Forms required: FAFSA.
Dates and Deadlines: Priority date 6/1; no closing date. Applicants notified on a rolling basis; must reply within 3 week(s) of notification.

CONTACT
Lisa Gargiulo, Manager, Student Financial Services
1420 Pine Street, Philadelphia, PA 19102-4699
(888) 467-3472 ext. 9370

Penn State Abington
Abington, Pennsylvania
www.abington.psu.edu   Federal Code: 003329

4-year public branch campus college in small city.
Enrollment: 2,593 undergrads, 12% part-time. 689 full-time freshmen.
Selectivity: Admits over 75% of applicants.

BASIC COSTS (2005-2006)
Tuition and fees: $10,190; out-of-state residents $15,322.
Per-credit charge: $393; out-of-state residents $619.
Additional info: Tuition/fee waivers available for minority students.

FINANCIAL AID PICTURE (2004-2005)
Students with need: Out of 575 full-time freshmen who applied for aid, 443 were judged to have need. Of these, 433 received aid, and 22 had their full need met. Average financial aid package met 68% of need; average scholarship/grant was $5,291; average loan was $2,521. For part-time students, average financial aid package was $8,579.
Students without need: 48 full-time freshmen who did not demonstrate need for aid received scholarships/grants; average award was $2,537. No-need awards available for academics, athletics, minority status, ROTC.
Cumulative student debt: 65% of graduating class had student loans; average debt was $22,400.

FINANCIAL AID PROCEDURES
Forms required: FAFSA.
Dates and Deadlines: Priority date 2/15; no closing date. Applicants notified on a rolling basis starting 2/15.
Transfers: Closing date 5/1. Schools required to obtain student aid information through National Student Loan Data System (NSLDS).

CONTACT
Anna Griswold, Assistant Vice Provost for Student Aid
106 Sutherland Building, Abington, PA 19001
(814) 865-6301

Penn State Altoona
Altoona, Pennsylvania
www.aa.psu.edu   Federal Code: 003329

4-year public branch campus college in small city.
Enrollment: 3,499 undergrads, 7% part-time. 1,255 full-time freshmen.
Selectivity: Admits over 75% of applicants.

BASIC COSTS (2005-2006)
Tuition and fees: $10,626; out-of-state residents $16,024.
Per-credit charge: $423; out-of-state residents $648.
Room and board: $7,060.
Additional info: Tuition/fee waivers available for minority students.

FINANCIAL AID PICTURE (2004-2005)

Students with need: Out of 1,041 full-time freshmen who applied for aid, 830 were judged to have need. Of these, 812 received aid, and 45 had their full need met. Average financial aid package met 63% of need; average scholarship/grant was $4,250; average loan was $2,694. For part-time students, average financial aid package was $8,896.

Students without need: 43 full-time freshmen who did not demonstrate need for aid received scholarships/grants; average award was $2,210. No-need awards available for academics, athletics, minority status, ROTC.

Cumulative student debt: 65% of graduating class had student loans; average debt was $22,400.

FINANCIAL AID PROCEDURES

Forms required: FAFSA.
Dates and Deadlines: Priority date 2/15; no closing date. Applicants notified on a rolling basis starting 2/15.
Transfers: Closing date 5/1. Schools required to obtain student aid information through National Student Loan Data System (NSLDS).

CONTACT

Anna Griswold, Assistant Vice Provost for Student Aid
E108 E. Raymond Smith Building, Altoona, PA 16601-3760
(814) 865-6301

Penn State Beaver
Monaca, Pennsylvania
www.br.psu.edu   Federal Code: 003329

2-year public branch campus college in small town.
Enrollment: 574 undergrads, 10% part-time. 193 full-time freshmen.
Selectivity: Admits over 75% of applicants.

BASIC COSTS (2005-2006)

Tuition and fees: $10,200; out-of-state residents $15,332.
Per-credit charge: $393; out-of-state residents $619.
Room and board: $7,060.
Additional info: Tuition/fee waivers available for minority students.

FINANCIAL AID PICTURE (2004-2005)

Students with need: Out of 180 full-time freshmen who applied for aid, 149 were judged to have need. Of these, 148 received aid, and 6 had their full need met. Average financial aid package met 64% of need; average scholarship/grant was $4,526; average loan was $2,587. For part-time students, average financial aid package was $10,021.

Students without need: 6 full-time freshmen who did not demonstrate need for aid received scholarships/grants; average award was $1,120. No-need awards available for academics, athletics, minority status, ROTC.

Cumulative student debt: 65% of graduating class had student loans; average debt was $22,400.

FINANCIAL AID PROCEDURES

Forms required: FAFSA.
Dates and Deadlines: Priority date 2/15; no closing date. Applicants notified on a rolling basis starting 2/15.
Transfers: Closing date 5/1. Schools required to obtain student aid information through National Student Loan Data System (NSLDS).

CONTACT

Anna Griswold, Assistant Vice Provost for Student Aid
100 University Drive, Monaca, PA 15061-2799
(814) 865-6301

Penn State Berks
Reading, Pennsylvania
www.bk.psu.edu   Federal Code: 003329

4-year public branch campus college in small city.
Enrollment: 2,303 undergrads, 8% part-time. 788 full-time freshmen.
Selectivity: Admits over 75% of applicants.

BASIC COSTS (2005-2006)

Tuition and fees: $10,626; out-of-state residents $16,024.
Per-credit charge: $423; out-of-state residents $648.
Room and board: $7,670.
Additional info: Tuition/fee waivers available for minority students.

FINANCIAL AID PICTURE (2004-2005)

Students with need: Out of 637 full-time freshmen who applied for aid, 450 were judged to have need. Of these, 444 received aid, and 14 had their full need met. Average financial aid package met 61% of need; average scholarship/grant was $4,530; average loan was $2,612. For part-time students, average financial aid package was $9,558.

Students without need: 40 full-time freshmen who did not demonstrate need for aid received scholarships/grants; average award was $1,719. No-need awards available for academics, athletics, minority status, ROTC.

Cumulative student debt: 65% of graduating class had student loans; average debt was $22,400.

FINANCIAL AID PROCEDURES

Forms required: FAFSA.
Dates and Deadlines: Priority date 2/15; no closing date. Applicants notified on a rolling basis starting 2/15.
Transfers: Closing date 5/1. Schools required to obtain student aid information through National Student Loan Data System (NSLDS).

CONTACT

Anna Griswold, Assistant Vice Provost for Student Aid
Tulpehocken Road, PO Box 7009, Reading, PA 19610-6009
(814) 865-6301

Penn State Delaware County
Media, Pennsylvania
www.de.psu.edu   Federal Code: 006922

2-year public branch campus college in small town.
Enrollment: 1,388 undergrads, 11% part-time. 429 full-time freshmen.
Selectivity: Admits over 75% of applicants.

BASIC COSTS (2005-2006)

Tuition and fees: $10,200; out-of-state residents $15,332.
Per-credit charge: $393; out-of-state residents $619.
Additional info: Tuition/fee waivers available for minority students.

FINANCIAL AID PICTURE (2004-2005)

Students with need: Out of 322 full-time freshmen who applied for aid, 232 were judged to have need. Of these, 229 received aid, and 13 had their full need met. Average financial aid package met 62% of need; average scholarship/grant was $4,950; average loan was $2,382. For part-time students, average financial aid package was $7,292.

Students without need: 27 full-time freshmen who did not demonstrate need for aid received scholarships/grants; average award was $3,258. No-need awards available for academics, athletics, minority status, ROTC.

Cumulative student debt: 65% of graduating class had student loans; average debt was $22,400.

FINANCIAL AID PROCEDURES

Forms required: FAFSA.
Dates and Deadlines: Priority date 2/15; no closing date. Applicants notified on a rolling basis starting 2/15.

Transfers: Closing date 5/1. Schools required to obtain student aid information through National Student Loan Data System (NSLDS).

CONTACT
Anna Griswold, Assistant Vice Provost for Student Aid
25 Yearsley Mill Road, Media, PA 19063-5596
(814) 865-6301

Penn State Dubois
DuBois, Pennsylvania
www.ds.psu.edu   Federal Code: 003335

2-year public branch campus college in small town.
Enrollment: 658 undergrads, 17% part-time. 208 full-time freshmen.
Selectivity: Admits over 75% of applicants.

BASIC COSTS (2005-2006)
Tuition and fees: $10,190; out-of-state residents $15,322.
Per-credit charge: $393; out-of-state residents $619.
Additional info: Tuition/fee waivers available for minority students.

FINANCIAL AID PICTURE (2004-2005)
Students with need: Out of 200 full-time freshmen who applied for aid, 178 were judged to have need. Of these, 178 received aid, and 14 had their full need met. Average financial aid package met 72% of need; average scholarship/grant was $4,480; average loan was $2,609. For part-time students, average financial aid package was $9,300.
Students without need: 5 full-time freshmen who did not demonstrate need for aid received scholarships/grants; average award was $4,420. No-need awards available for academics, athletics, minority status, ROTC.
Cumulative student debt: 65% of graduating class had student loans; average debt was $22,400.

FINANCIAL AID PROCEDURES
Forms required: FAFSA.
Dates and Deadlines: No deadline. Applicants notified on a rolling basis starting 2/15.
Transfers: Closing date 5/1. Schools required to obtain student aid information through National Student Loan Data System (NSLDS).

CONTACT
Anna Griswold, Assistant Vice Provost for Student Aid
101 Hiller, DuBois, PA 15801
(814) 865-6301

Penn State Erie, The Behrend College
Erie, Pennsylvania
www.pennstatebehrend.psu.edu   Federal Code: 003329

4-year public branch campus college in small city.
Enrollment: 3,231 undergrads, 5% part-time. 849 full-time freshmen.
Selectivity: Admits over 75% of applicants.

BASIC COSTS (2005-2006)
Tuition and fees: $10,626; out-of-state residents $16,024.
Per-credit charge: $423; out-of-state residents $648.
Room and board: $7,060.
Additional info: Tuition/fee waivers available for minority students.

FINANCIAL AID PICTURE (2004-2005)
Students with need: Out of 750 full-time freshmen who applied for aid, 602 were judged to have need. Of these, 592 received aid, and 46 had their full need met. Average financial aid package met 68% of need; average scholarship/grant was $4,511; average loan was $2,848. For part-time students, average financial aid package was $8,344.
Students without need: 47 full-time freshmen who did not demonstrate need for aid received scholarships/grants; average award was $2,412. No-need awards available for academics, athletics, minority status, ROTC.
Cumulative student debt: 65% of graduating class had student loans; average debt was $22,400.

FINANCIAL AID PROCEDURES
Forms required: FAFSA.
Dates and Deadlines: Priority date 2/15; no closing date. Applicants notified on a rolling basis starting 2/15.
Transfers: Closing date 5/1. Schools required to obtain student aid information through National Student Loan Data System (NSLDS).

CONTACT
Anna Griswold, Assistant Vice Provost for Student Aid
5091 Station Road, Erie, PA 16563-0105
(814) 865-6301

Penn State Fayette
Uniontown, Pennsylvania
www.fe.psu.edu   Federal Code: 003329

2-year public branch campus college in large town.
Enrollment: 839 undergrads, 22% part-time. 148 full-time freshmen.
Selectivity: Admits over 75% of applicants.

BASIC COSTS (2005-2006)
Tuition and fees: $10,190; out-of-state residents $15,322.
Per-credit charge: $393; out-of-state residents $619.
Additional info: Tuition/fee waivers available for minority students.

FINANCIAL AID PICTURE (2004-2005)
Students with need: Out of 137 full-time freshmen who applied for aid, 125 were judged to have need. Of these, 124 received aid, and 12 had their full need met. Average financial aid package met 68% of need; average scholarship/grant was $4,556; average loan was $2,667. For part-time students, average financial aid package was $8,909.
Students without need: 6 full-time freshmen who did not demonstrate need for aid received scholarships/grants; average award was $1,071. No-need awards available for academics, athletics, minority status, ROTC.
Cumulative student debt: 65% of graduating class had student loans; average debt was $22,400.

FINANCIAL AID PROCEDURES
Forms required: FAFSA.
Dates and Deadlines: Priority date 2/15; no closing date. Applicants notified on a rolling basis starting 2/15.
Transfers: Closing date 5/1. Schools required to obtain student aid information through National Student Loan Data System (NSLDS).

CONTACT
Anna Griswold, Assistant Vice Provost for Student Aid
108 Williams Building, Uniontown, PA 15401-0519
(814) 865-6301

Penn State Harrisburg
Middletown, Pennsylvania
www.hbg.psu.edu   Federal Code: 003329

4-year public branch campus college in small town.
Enrollment: 1,955 undergrads, 20% part-time. 160 full-time freshmen.
Selectivity: Admits 50 to 75% of applicants.

BASIC COSTS (2005-2006)
Tuition and fees: $10,616; out-of-state residents $16,014.
Per-credit charge: $423; out-of-state residents $648.

Room and board: $8,560.
Additional info: Tuition/fee waivers available for minority students.

FINANCIAL AID PICTURE (2004-2005)
Students with need: Out of 135 full-time freshmen who applied for aid, 94 were judged to have need. Of these, 92 received aid, and 13 had their full need met. Average financial aid package met 69% of need; average scholarship/grant was $5,368; average loan was $2,781. For part-time students, average financial aid package was $10,036.
Students without need: 9 full-time freshmen who did not demonstrate need for aid received scholarships/grants; average award was $4,155. No-need awards available for academics, athletics, minority status, ROTC.
Cumulative student debt: 65% of graduating class had student loans; average debt was $22,400.

FINANCIAL AID PROCEDURES
Forms required: FAFSA.
Dates and Deadlines: Priority date 2/15; no closing date. Applicants notified on a rolling basis starting 2/15.
Transfers: Closing date 5/1. Schools required to obtain student aid information through National Student Loan Data System (NSLDS).

CONTACT
Anna Griswold, Assistant Vice Provost for Student Aid
Swatapa Building, 777 West Harrisburg Pike, Middletown, PA 17057-4898
(814) 865-6301

Penn State Hazleton
Hazleton, Pennsylvania
www.hn.psu.edu   Federal Code: 003338

2-year public branch campus college in large town.
Enrollment: 1,015 undergrads, 3% part-time. 474 full-time freshmen.
Selectivity: Admits over 75% of applicants.

BASIC COSTS (2005-2006)
Tuition and fees: $10,190; out-of-state residents $15,322.
Per-credit charge: $393; out-of-state residents $619.
Room and board: $7,060.
Additional info: Tuition/fee waivers available for minority students.

FINANCIAL AID PICTURE (2004-2005)
Students with need: Out of 403 full-time freshmen who applied for aid, 318 were judged to have need. Of these, 313 received aid, and 21 had their full need met. Average financial aid package met 65% of need; average scholarship/grant was $4,479; average loan was $2,625. For part-time students, average financial aid package was $6,934.
Students without need: 14 full-time freshmen who did not demonstrate need for aid received scholarships/grants; average award was $2,389. No-need awards available for academics, athletics, minority status, ROTC.
Cumulative student debt: 65% of graduating class had student loans; average debt was $22,400.

FINANCIAL AID PROCEDURES
Forms required: FAFSA.
Dates and Deadlines: Priority date 2/15; no closing date. Applicants notified on a rolling basis starting 2/15.
Transfers: Closing date 5/1. Schools required to obtain student aid information through National Student Loan Data System (NSLDS).

CONTACT
Anna Griswold, Assistant Vice Provost for Student Aid
110 Admin. Building, 76 University Drive, Hazleton, PA 18202
(814) 865-6301

Penn State Lehigh Valley
Fogelsville, Pennsylvania
www.lv.psu.edu   Federal Code: 003329

4-year public branch campus college in rural community.
Enrollment: 592 undergrads, 18% part-time. 163 full-time freshmen.
Selectivity: Admits 50 to 75% of applicants.

BASIC COSTS (2005-2006)
Tuition and fees: $10,200; out-of-state residents $15,332.
Per-credit charge: $393; out-of-state residents $619.
Additional info: Tuition/fee waivers available for minority students.

FINANCIAL AID PICTURE (2004-2005)
Students with need: Out of 134 full-time freshmen who applied for aid, 96 were judged to have need. Of these, 93 received aid, and 4 had their full need met. Average financial aid package met 68% of need; average scholarship/grant was $4,533; average loan was $2,712. For part-time students, average financial aid package was $9,353.
Students without need: 8 full-time freshmen who did not demonstrate need for aid received scholarships/grants; average award was $1,526. No-need awards available for academics, athletics, minority status, ROTC.
Cumulative student debt: 65% of graduating class had student loans; average debt was $22,400.

FINANCIAL AID PROCEDURES
Forms required: FAFSA.
Dates and Deadlines: Priority date 2/15; no closing date. Applicants notified on a rolling basis starting 2/15.
Transfers: Closing date 5/1. Schools required to obtain student aid information through National Student Loan Data System (NSLDS).

CONTACT
Anna Griswold, Assistant Vice Provost for Student Aid
8380 Mohr Lane, Academic Building, Fogelsville, PA 18051-9999
(814) 865-6301

Penn State McKeesport
McKeesport, Pennsylvania
www.mk.psu.edu   Federal Code: 003329

2-year public branch campus college in large town.
Enrollment: 611 undergrads, 9% part-time. 224 full-time freshmen.
Selectivity: Admits over 75% of applicants.

BASIC COSTS (2005-2006)
Tuition and fees: $10,180; out-of-state residents $15,312.
Per-credit charge: $393; out-of-state residents $619.
Room and board: $7,060.
Additional info: Tuition/fee waivers available for minority students.

FINANCIAL AID PICTURE (2004-2005)
Students with need: Out of 202 full-time freshmen who applied for aid, 172 were judged to have need. Of these, 168 received aid, and 6 had their full need met. Average financial aid package met 68% of need; average scholarship/grant was $4,393; average loan was $2,609. For part-time students, average financial aid package was $8,479.
Students without need: 11 full-time freshmen who did not demonstrate need for aid received scholarships/grants; average award was $973. No-need awards available for academics, athletics, minority status, ROTC.
Cumulative student debt: 65% of graduating class had student loans; average debt was $22,400.

FINANCIAL AID PROCEDURES
Forms required: FAFSA.
Dates and Deadlines: Priority date 2/15; no closing date. Applicants notified on a rolling basis starting 2/15.

Transfers: Closing date 5/1. Schools required to obtain student aid information through National Student Loan Data System (NSLDS).

CONTACT
Anna Griswold, Assistant Vice Provost for Student Aid
101 Frable Building, 4000 University Drive, McKeesport, PA 15132
(814) 865-6301

Penn State Mont Alto
Mont Alto, Pennsylvania
www.ma.psu.edu   Federal Code: 003340

2-year public branch campus college in rural community.
Enrollment: 847 undergrads, 24% part-time. 262 full-time freshmen.
Selectivity: Admits over 75% of applicants.

BASIC COSTS (2005-2006)
Tuition and fees: $10,200; out-of-state residents $15,332.
Per-credit charge: $393; out-of-state residents $619.
Room and board: $7,060.
Additional info: Tuition/fee waivers available for minority students.

FINANCIAL AID PICTURE (2004-2005)
Students with need: Out of 229 full-time freshmen who applied for aid, 189 were judged to have need. Of these, 187 received aid, and 13 had their full need met. Average financial aid package met 69% of need; average scholarship/grant was $4,827; average loan was $2,824. For part-time students, average financial aid package was $10,571.
Students without need: 14 full-time freshmen who did not demonstrate need for aid received scholarships/grants; average award was $3,038. No-need awards available for academics, athletics, minority status, ROTC.
Cumulative student debt: 65% of graduating class had student loans; average debt was $22,400.

FINANCIAL AID PROCEDURES
Forms required: FAFSA.
Dates and Deadlines: Priority date 2/15; no closing date. Applicants notified on a rolling basis starting 2/15.
Transfers: Closing date 5/1. Schools required to obtain student aid information through National Student Loan Data System (NSLDS).

CONTACT
Anna Griswold, Assistant Vice Provost for Student Aid
1 Campus Drive, Mont Alto, PA 17237-9703
(814) 865-6301

Penn State New Kensington
New Kensington, Pennsylvania
www.nk.psu.edu   Federal Code: 003329

2-year public branch campus college in large town.
Enrollment: 733 undergrads, 20% part-time. 179 full-time freshmen.
Selectivity: Admits over 75% of applicants.

BASIC COSTS (2005-2006)
Tuition and fees: $10,200; out-of-state residents $15,332.
Per-credit charge: $393; out-of-state residents $619.
Additional info: Tuition/fee waivers available for minority students.

FINANCIAL AID PICTURE (2004-2005)
Students with need: Out of 155 full-time freshmen who applied for aid, 123 were judged to have need. Of these, 122 received aid, and 10 had their full need met. Average financial aid package met 63% of need; average scholarship/grant was $3,694; average loan was $2,576. For part-time students, average financial aid package was $8,731.
Students without need: 9 full-time freshmen who did not demonstrate need for aid received scholarships/grants; average award was $1,472. No-need awards available for academics, athletics, minority status, ROTC.
Cumulative student debt: 65% of graduating class had student loans; average debt was $22,400.

FINANCIAL AID PROCEDURES
Forms required: FAFSA.
Dates and Deadlines: Priority date 2/15; no closing date. Applicants notified on a rolling basis starting 2/15.
Transfers: Closing date 5/1. Schools required to obtain student aid information through National Student Loan Data System (NSLDS).

CONTACT
Anna Griswold, Assistant Vice Provost for Student Aid
3550 Seventh Street Road, Route 780, New Kensington, PA 15068-1765
(814) 865-6301

Penn State Schuylkill - Capital College
Schuylkill Haven, Pennsylvania
www.sl.psu.edu   Federal Code: 003343

4-year public branch campus college in small town.
Enrollment: 778 undergrads, 12% part-time. 272 full-time freshmen.
Selectivity: Admits over 75% of applicants.

BASIC COSTS (2005-2006)
Tuition and fees: $10,180; out-of-state residents $15,312.
Per-credit charge: $393; out-of-state residents $619.
Room only: $3,630.
Additional info: Tuition/fee waivers available for minority students.

FINANCIAL AID PICTURE (2004-2005)
Students with need: Out of 246 full-time freshmen who applied for aid, 217 were judged to have need. Of these, 215 received aid, and 5 had their full need met. Average financial aid package met 61% of need; average scholarship/grant was $5,009; average loan was $2,621. For part-time students, average financial aid package was $8,346.
Students without need: 7 full-time freshmen who did not demonstrate need for aid received scholarships/grants; average award was $766. No-need awards available for academics, athletics, minority status, ROTC.
Cumulative student debt: 65% of graduating class had student loans; average debt was $22,400.

FINANCIAL AID PROCEDURES
Forms required: FAFSA.
Dates and Deadlines: Priority date 2/15; no closing date. Applicants notified on a rolling basis starting 2/15.
Transfers: Closing date 5/1. Schools required to obtain student aid information through National Student Loan Data System (NSLDS).

CONTACT
Anna Griswold, Assistant Vice Provost for Student Aid
200 University Drive, A102 Administration Building, Schuylkill Haven, PA 17972-2208
(814) 865-6301

Penn State Shenango
Sharon, Pennsylvania
www.shenango.psu.edu   Federal Code: 003329

2-year public branch campus college in large town.
Enrollment: 665 undergrads, 34% part-time. 139 full-time freshmen.
Selectivity: Admits over 75% of applicants.

BASIC COSTS (2005-2006)
Tuition and fees: $10,200; out-of-state residents $15,332.
Per-credit charge: $393; out-of-state residents $619.
Additional info: Tuition/fee waivers available for minority students.

FINANCIAL AID PICTURE (2004-2005)
Students with need: Out of 129 full-time freshmen who applied for aid, 107 were judged to have need. Of these, 106 received aid, and 5 had their full need met. Average financial aid package met 66% of need; average scholarship/grant was $4,908; average loan was $2,705. For part-time students, average financial aid package was $8,917.
Students without need: 12 full-time freshmen who did not demonstrate need for aid received scholarships/grants; average award was $742. No-need awards available for academics, athletics, minority status, ROTC.
Cumulative student debt: 65% of graduating class had student loans; average debt was $22,400.

FINANCIAL AID PROCEDURES
Forms required: FAFSA.
Dates and Deadlines: Priority date 2/15; no closing date. Applicants notified on a rolling basis starting 2/15.
Transfers: Closing date 5/1. Schools required to obtain student aid information through National Student Loan Data System (NSLDS).

CONTACT
Anna Griswold, Assistant Vice Provost for Student Aid
147 Shenango Avenue, Room 206, Sharon Hall, Sharon, PA 16146-1597
(814) 865-6301

Penn State University Park
University Park, Pennsylvania
www.psu.edu   Federal Code: 003329

4-year public university in large town.
Enrollment: 33,672 undergrads, 3% part-time. 5,900 full-time freshmen.
Selectivity: Admits 50 to 75% of applicants.

BASIC COSTS (2005-2006)
Tuition and fees: $11,508; out-of-state residents $21,744.
Per-credit charge: $459; out-of-state residents $886.
Room and board: $7,060.
Additional info: Tuition/fee waivers available for minority students.

FINANCIAL AID PICTURE (2004-2005)
Students with need: Out of 4,424 full-time freshmen who applied for aid, 2,909 were judged to have need. Of these, 2,808 received aid, and 304 had their full need met. Average financial aid package met 68% of need; average scholarship/grant was $5,033; average loan was $2,756. For part-time students, average financial aid package was $9,852.
Students without need: 738 full-time freshmen who did not demonstrate need for aid received scholarships/grants; average award was $3,880. No-need awards available for academics, athletics, minority status, ROTC.
Scholarships offered: 102 full-time freshmen received athletic scholarships; average amount $20,232.
Cumulative student debt: 65% of graduating class had student loans; average debt was $22,400.

FINANCIAL AID PROCEDURES
Forms required: FAFSA.
Dates and Deadlines: Priority date 2/15; no closing date. Applicants notified on a rolling basis starting 2/15.
Transfers: Closing date 5/1. Schools required to obtain student aid information through National Student Loan Data System (NSLDS).

CONTACT
Anna Griswold, Assistant Vice Provost for Student Aid
201 Shields Building, University Park, PA 16804-3000
(814) 865-6301

Penn State Wilkes-Barre
Lehman, Pennsylvania
www.wb.psu.edu   Federal Code: 003329

4-year public branch campus college in small city.
Enrollment: 565 undergrads, 9% part-time. 170 full-time freshmen.
Selectivity: Admits over 75% of applicants.

BASIC COSTS (2005-2006)
Tuition and fees: $10,200; out-of-state residents $15,332.
Per-credit charge: $393; out-of-state residents $619.
Additional info: Tuition/fee waivers available for minority students.

FINANCIAL AID PICTURE (2004-2005)
Students with need: Out of 149 full-time freshmen who applied for aid, 106 were judged to have need. Of these, 104 received aid, and 5 had their full need met. Average financial aid package met 64% of need; average scholarship/grant was $4,096; average loan was $2,440. For part-time students, average financial aid package was $9,624.
Students without need: 12 full-time freshmen who did not demonstrate need for aid received scholarships/grants; average award was $2,721. No-need awards available for academics, athletics, minority status, ROTC.
Cumulative student debt: 65% of graduating class had student loans; average debt was $22,400.

FINANCIAL AID PROCEDURES
Forms required: FAFSA.
Dates and Deadlines: Priority date 2/15; no closing date. Applicants notified on a rolling basis starting 2/15.
Transfers: Closing date 5/1. Schools required to obtain student aid information through National Student Loan Data System (NSLDS).

CONTACT
Anna Griswold, Assistant Vice Provost for Student Aid
Box PSU, Lehman, PA 18627-0217
(814) 865-6301

Penn State Worthington Scranton
Dunmore, Pennsylvania
www.sn.psu.edu   Federal Code: 003344

2-year public branch campus college in large town.
Enrollment: 1,077 undergrads, 21% part-time. 243 full-time freshmen.
Selectivity: Admits over 75% of applicants.

BASIC COSTS (2005-2006)
Tuition and fees: $10,180; out-of-state residents $15,312.
Per-credit charge: $393; out-of-state residents $619.
Additional info: Tuition/fee waivers available for minority students.

FINANCIAL AID PICTURE (2004-2005)
Students with need: Out of 219 full-time freshmen who applied for aid, 184 were judged to have need. Of these, 181 received aid, and 7 had their full need met. Average financial aid package met 62% of need; average scholarship/grant was $3,987; average loan was $2,517. For part-time students, average financial aid package was $8,570.
Students without need: 14 full-time freshmen who did not demonstrate need for aid received scholarships/grants; average award was $1,465. No-need awards available for academics, athletics, minority status, ROTC.
Cumulative student debt: 65% of graduating class had student loans; average debt was $22,400.

FINANCIAL AID PROCEDURES
Forms required: FAFSA.
Dates and Deadlines: Priority date 2/15; no closing date. Applicants notified on a rolling basis starting 2/15.

Transfers: Closing date 5/1. Schools required to obtain student aid information through National Student Loan Data System (NSLDS).

CONTACT

Anna Griswold, Assistant Vice Provost for Student Aid
120 Ridge View Drive, Dunmore, PA 18512-1602
(814) 865-6301

Penn State York

York, Pennsylvania
www.yk.psu.edu Federal Code: 003347

2-year public branch campus college in large town.
Enrollment: 1,053 undergrads, 29% part-time. 274 full-time freshmen.
Selectivity: Admits over 75% of applicants.

BASIC COSTS (2005-2006)

Tuition and fees: $10,180; out-of-state residents $15,312.
Per-credit charge: $393; out-of-state residents $619.
Additional info: Tuition/fee waivers available for minority students.

FINANCIAL AID PICTURE (2004-2005)

Students with need: Out of 227 full-time freshmen who applied for aid, 170 were judged to have need. Of these, 169 received aid, and 20 had their full need met. Average financial aid package met 64% of need; average scholarship/grant was $3,285; average loan was $2,337. For part-time students, average financial aid package was $7,876.
Students without need: 18 full-time freshmen who did not demonstrate need for aid received scholarships/grants; average award was $3,053. No-need awards available for academics, athletics, minority status, ROTC.
Cumulative student debt: 65% of graduating class had student loans; average debt was $22,400.

FINANCIAL AID PROCEDURES

Forms required: FAFSA.
Dates and Deadlines: Priority date 2/15; no closing date. Applicants notified on a rolling basis starting 2/15.
Transfers: Closing date 5/1. Schools required to obtain student aid information through National Student Loan Data System (NSLDS).

CONTACT

Anna Griswold, Assistant Vice Provost for Student Aid
1031 Edgecomb Avenue, York, PA 17403-3398
(814) 865-6301

Pennsylvania College of Technology

Williamsport, Pennsylvania
www.pct.edu Federal Code: 003395

4-year public technical college in small city.
Enrollment: 6,440 undergrads, 14% part-time. 1,631 full-time freshmen.
Selectivity: Open admission; but selective for some programs.

BASIC COSTS (2005-2006)

Tuition and fees: $10,080; out-of-state residents $12,660.
Per-credit charge: $286; out-of-state residents $372.
Room and board: $6,900.

FINANCIAL AID PICTURE

Students with need: Need-based aid available for full-time and part-time students. Work study available nights, weekends, and for part-time students.
Students without need: No-need awards available for academics, alumni affiliation.

FINANCIAL AID PROCEDURES

Forms required: FAFSA, institutional form.
Dates and Deadlines: Priority date 4/1; no closing date. Applicants notified on a rolling basis starting 6/1; must reply by 7/1 or within 4 week(s) of notification.

CONTACT

Dennis Correll, Director of Financial Aid
One College Avenue, Williamsport, PA 17701
(570) 327-4766

Pennsylvania Highlands Community College

Johnstown, Pennsylvania
www.pennhighlands.edu Federal Code: 031804

2-year public community college in large town.
Enrollment: 1,300 undergrads.
Selectivity: Open admission.

BASIC COSTS (2005-2006)

Tuition and fees: $2,610; out-of-district residents $4,710; out-of-state residents $6,810.
Per-credit charge: $70; out-of-district residents $140; out-of-state residents $210.

FINANCIAL AID PICTURE

Students with need: Need-based aid available for full-time and part-time students. Work study available nights.
Students without need: No-need awards available for academics, state/district residency.

FINANCIAL AID PROCEDURES

Forms required: FAFSA.
Dates and Deadlines: Closing date 5/1. Applicants notified on a rolling basis starting 1/1; must reply within 1 week(s) of notification.

CONTACT

Brenda Coughenour, Director of Financial Aid
PO Box 68, Johnstown, PA 15907-0068
(814) 532-5315

Pennsylvania Institute of Technology

Media, Pennsylvania
www.pit.edu Federal Code: 010998

2-year private technical college in small town.
Enrollment: 257 undergrads.
Selectivity: Open admission.

BASIC COSTS (2005-2006)

Tuition and fees: $9,000.
Per-credit charge: $300.
Additional info: Part time students pay a technology fee of $11 per credit hour.

FINANCIAL AID PICTURE (2005-2006)

Students with need: 31% of average financial aid package awarded as scholarships/grants, 69% awarded as loans/jobs. Need-based aid available for part-time students. Work study available nights, weekends, and for part-time students.
Students without need: No-need awards available for academics, leadership.
Scholarships offered: Presidential Scholarship: half tuition scholarship for current high school graduates. SAT scores required.

FINANCIAL AID PROCEDURES

Forms required: FAFSA, institutional form.

Dates and Deadlines: Closing date 8/1. Applicants notified on a rolling basis starting 7/1.
Transfers: No deadline.

CONTACT
Susan Hood, Director of Financial Aid
800 Manchester Avenue, Media, PA 19063-4098
(610) 892-1520

Pennsylvania School of Business
Allentown, Pennsylvania
www.pennschoolofbusiness.edu Federal Code: 022552

2-year for-profit technical college in small city.
Enrollment: 200 undergrads.
Selectivity: Open admission.

BASIC COSTS (2005-2006)
Additional info: Tuition for associate-degree program (15 months): $16,202.

FINANCIAL AID PICTURE
Students with need: Need-based aid available for full-time and part-time students.

FINANCIAL AID PROCEDURES
Forms required: FAFSA.
Dates and Deadlines: No deadline. Applicants notified on a rolling basis.

CONTACT
Bill Barber, Director
2201 Hangar Place, Allentown, PA 18103
(610) 264-8029

Philadelphia Biblical University
Langhorne, Pennsylvania
www.pbu.edu Federal Code: 003351

4-year private university and Bible college in small town, affiliated with Protestant Evangelical tradition.
Enrollment: 1,063 undergrads, 8% part-time. 230 full-time freshmen.
Selectivity: Admits over 75% of applicants.

BASIC COSTS (2006-2007)
Tuition and fees: $15,875.
Per-credit charge: $649.
Room and board: $6,550.

FINANCIAL AID PICTURE (2005-2006)
Students with need: Out of 197 full-time freshmen who applied for aid, 174 were judged to have need. Of these, 174 received aid, and 58 had their full need met. Average financial aid package met 78.6% of need; average scholarship/grant was $10,075; average loan was $3,201. For part-time students, average financial aid package was $4,090.
Students without need: 44 full-time freshmen who did not demonstrate need for aid received scholarships/grants; average award was $7,670. No-need awards available for academics, leadership, music/drama.
Cumulative student debt: 70% of graduating class had student loans; average debt was $15,000.

FINANCIAL AID PROCEDURES
Forms required: FAFSA.
Dates and Deadlines: Priority date 5/1; no closing date. Applicants notified on a rolling basis starting 3/15.

CONTACT
William Kellaris, Director of Financial Aid
200 Manor Avenue, Langhorne, PA 19047-2990
(215) 702-4246

Philadelphia University
Philadelphia, Pennsylvania
www.philau.edu Federal Code: 003354

4-year private university in very large city.
Enrollment: 2,707 undergrads, 10% part-time. 683 full-time freshmen.
Selectivity: Admits 50 to 75% of applicants.

BASIC COSTS (2006-2007)
Tuition and fees: $23,818.
Per-credit charge: $767.
Room and board: $8,212.

FINANCIAL AID PICTURE (2005-2006)
Students with need: Out of 591 full-time freshmen who applied for aid, 510 were judged to have need. Of these, 510 received aid, and 75 had their full need met. Average financial aid package met 79% of need; average scholarship/grant was $11,323; average loan was $3,113. For part-time students, average financial aid package was $7,293.
Students without need: 164 full-time freshmen who did not demonstrate need for aid received scholarships/grants; average award was $4,660. No-need awards available for academics, athletics, leadership.
Scholarships offered: 10 full-time freshmen received athletic scholarships; average amount $9,260.
Cumulative student debt: 74% of graduating class had student loans; average debt was $22,917.

FINANCIAL AID PROCEDURES
Forms required: FAFSA.
Dates and Deadlines: Priority date 4/15; no closing date. Applicants notified on a rolling basis starting 2/10; must reply by 5/1 or within 3 week(s) of notification.

CONTACT
Lisa Cooper, Director of Financial Aid
School House Lane and Henry Avenue, Philadelphia, PA 19144-5497
(215) 951-2940

Pittsburgh Institute of Aeronautics
Pittsburgh, Pennsylvania
www.pia.edu Federal Code: 005310

2-year private technical college in large city.
Enrollment: 200 undergrads.

BASIC COSTS (2005-2006)
Tuition and fees: $10,335.

FINANCIAL AID PICTURE
Students with need: Need-based aid available for full-time students.

FINANCIAL AID PROCEDURES
Forms required: FAFSA.
Dates and Deadlines: Priority date 5/1; no closing date. Applicants notified on a rolling basis.

CONTACT
Darla Mroski, Assistant Director of Finance
Box 10897, Pittsburgh, PA 15236-0897
(412) 462-9011

Pittsburgh Institute of Mortuary Science
Pittsburgh, Pennsylvania
www.p-i-m-s.com   Federal Code: 010814

2-year private technical college in large city.
Enrollment: 150 undergrads.
Selectivity: Open admission.

BASIC COSTS (2005-2006)
Tuition and fees: $12,800.
Per-credit charge: $240.

FINANCIAL AID PICTURE
Students with need: Need-based aid available for full-time and part-time students.

FINANCIAL AID PROCEDURES
Forms required: FAFSA.
Dates and Deadlines: No deadline. Applicants notified on a rolling basis.

CONTACT
Karen Rocco, Financial Aid Officer
5808 Baum Boulevard, Pittsburgh, PA 15206-3706
(412) 362-8500

Pittsburgh Technical Institute
Oakdale, Pennsylvania
www.pti.edu   Federal Code: 007437

2-year for-profit technical college in large town.
Enrollment: 1,860 undergrads. 1,041 full-time freshmen.
Selectivity: Open admission; but selective for some programs.

BASIC COSTS (2005-2006)
Additional info: Tuition and supply costs vary by program and student use. Tuition at time of enrollment locked for 2 years.

FINANCIAL AID PICTURE (2004-2005)
Students with need: 57% of average financial aid package awarded as scholarships/grants, 43% awarded as loans/jobs. Need-based aid available for part-time students.

FINANCIAL AID PROCEDURES
Forms required: FAFSA, state aid form, institutional form.
Dates and Deadlines: Priority date 3/15; no closing date. Applicants notified on a rolling basis.
Transfers: Closing date 5/1. Applicants notified on a rolling basis.

CONTACT
Alison Seagle
1111 McKee Road, Oakdale, PA 15071-3205
(412) 809-5140

PJA School
Upper Darby, Pennsylvania
www.pjaschool.com   Federal Code: 023013

2-year for-profit business and junior college in very large city.
Enrollment: 245 undergrads.

BASIC COSTS (2005-2006)
Tuition and fees: $9,930.
Additional info: Books and materials included in cost of tuition. Tuition at time of enrollment locked for 2 years.

FINANCIAL AID PICTURE
Students with need: Need-based aid available for full-time and part-time students.
Students without need: This college only awards aid to students with need.
Additional info: PJA works with various funding agencies, including the Office of Vocational Rehabilitation, Delaware County Office of Employment and Training, Chester County Office of Employment and Training, Philadelphia Workforce Development Corporation, and Veteran's Administration. PJA also offers an interest-free payment plan.

FINANCIAL AID PROCEDURES
Forms required: FAFSA, institutional form.
Dates and Deadlines: No deadline. Applicants notified on a rolling basis.

CONTACT
Tina Bastian, Director of Financial Aid
7900 West Chester Pike, Upper Darby, PA 19082
(610) 789-6700

Point Park University
Pittsburgh, Pennsylvania
www.pointpark.edu   Federal Code: 003357

4-year private university in large city.
Enrollment: 2,932 undergrads, 23% part-time. 458 full-time freshmen.
Selectivity: Admits over 75% of applicants.

BASIC COSTS (2006-2007)
Tuition and fees: $17,770.
Per-credit charge: $489.
Room and board: $7,880.
Additional info: Cost of tuition in bachelor of arts and bachelor of fine arts programs within conservatory of performing arts: $19120 or $558 per credit hour. Tuition/fee waivers available for adults, minority students, unemployed or children of unemployed.

FINANCIAL AID PICTURE (2005-2006)
Students with need: Average financial aid package met 70% of need; average scholarship/grant was $7,716; average loan was $4,530. For part-time students, average financial aid package was $8,474.
Students without need: No-need awards available for academics, alumni affiliation, art, athletics, job skills, leadership, music/drama.
Cumulative student debt: 95% of graduating class had student loans; average debt was $25,289.

FINANCIAL AID PROCEDURES
Forms required: FAFSA.
Dates and Deadlines: Priority date 5/1; no closing date. Applicants notified on a rolling basis starting 2/15; must reply within 3 week(s) of notification.

CONTACT
Sandra Cronin, Director of Financial Aid
201 Wood Street, Pittsburgh, PA 15222-1984
(412) 392-3935

Robert Morris University
Moon Township, Pennsylvania
www.rmu.edu   Federal Code: 001746

4-year private university in large town.
Enrollment: 3,877 undergrads, 20% part-time. 685 full-time freshmen.
Selectivity: Admits over 75% of applicants.

BASIC COSTS (2006-2007)
Tuition and fees: $16,590.
Per-credit charge: $545.
Room and board: $8,410.

FINANCIAL AID PICTURE (2005-2006)
Students with need: Out of 636 full-time freshmen who applied for aid, 533 were judged to have need. Of these, 533 received aid, and 154 had their full need met. Average financial aid package met 75% of need; average scholarship/grant was $7,960; average loan was $4,528. For part-time students, average financial aid package was $6,027.
Students without need: 140 full-time freshmen who did not demonstrate need for aid received scholarships/grants; average award was $8,979. No-need awards available for academics, alumni affiliation, athletics, job skills, leadership, minority status, music/drama, religious affiliation, state/district residency.
Scholarships offered: 27 full-time freshmen received athletic scholarships; average amount $7,151.

FINANCIAL AID PROCEDURES
Forms required: FAFSA.
Dates and Deadlines: No deadline. Applicants notified on a rolling basis starting 3/15; must reply within 2 week(s) of notification.

CONTACT
Shari Payne, Director of Financial Aid
6001 University Boulevard, Moon Township, PA 15108-1189
(412) 299-2450

Rosedale Technical Institute
Pittsburgh, Pennsylvania
www.rosedaletech.org   Federal Code: 012050

2-year private technical college in large city.
Enrollment: 240 undergrads.
Selectivity: Open admission.

BASIC COSTS (2005-2006)
Tuition and fees: $9,060.

FINANCIAL AID PICTURE
Students with need: Need-based aid available for full-time students.

FINANCIAL AID PROCEDURES
Forms required: FAFSA.
Dates and Deadlines: Closing date 8/1.

CONTACT
Kathleen Stein, Director of Financial Aid
4634 Browns Hill Road, Pittsburgh, PA 15217
(412) 521-6200

Rosemont College
Rosemont, Pennsylvania
www.rosemont.edu   Federal Code: 003360

4-year private liberal arts college for women in small town, affiliated with Roman Catholic Church.
Enrollment: 644 undergrads, 34% part-time. 109 full-time freshmen.
Selectivity: Admits 50 to 75% of applicants.

BASIC COSTS (2005-2006)
Tuition and fees: $20,560.
Per-credit charge: $750.
Room and board: $8,800.
Additional info: Tuition/fee waivers available for adults.

FINANCIAL AID PICTURE (2005-2006)
Students with need: Out of 106 full-time freshmen who applied for aid, 98 were judged to have need. Of these, 98 received aid, and 27 had their full need met. Average financial aid package met 77% of need; average scholarship/grant was $16,507; average loan was $3,108. Need-based aid available for part-time students.
Students without need: 13 full-time freshmen who did not demonstrate need for aid received scholarships/grants; average award was $10,327. No-need awards available for academics, alumni affiliation, art, job skills, religious affiliation.

FINANCIAL AID PROCEDURES
Forms required: FAFSA.
Dates and Deadlines: Priority date 2/15; no closing date. Applicants notified on a rolling basis starting 2/15; must reply by 5/1 or within 4 week(s) of notification.

CONTACT
Melissa Walsh, Director of Financial Aid
1400 Montgomery Avenue, Rosemont, PA 19010
(610) 527-0200 ext. 2220

St. Francis University
Loretto, Pennsylvania
www.francis.edu   Federal Code: 003366

4-year private university and liberal arts college in rural community, affiliated with Roman Catholic Church.
Enrollment: 1,360 undergrads, 8% part-time. 364 full-time freshmen.
Selectivity: Admits over 75% of applicants.

BASIC COSTS (2006-2007)
Tuition and fees: $22,224.
Per-credit charge: $668.
Room and board: $7,640.
Additional info: Tuition/fee waivers available for adults.

FINANCIAL AID PICTURE (2005-2006)
Students with need: 66% of average financial aid package awarded as scholarships/grants, 34% awarded as loans/jobs. Need-based aid available for part-time students. Work study available nights, weekends, and for part-time students.
Students without need: No-need awards available for academics, alumni affiliation, athletics, music/drama, religious affiliation.
Cumulative student debt: 95% of graduating class had student loans; average debt was $19,690.

FINANCIAL AID PROCEDURES
Forms required: FAFSA.
Dates and Deadlines: Priority date 5/1; no closing date. Applicants notified on a rolling basis starting 3/1.
Transfers: Associate degree transfer scholarship based on academic achievement. Returning adult student scholarships available to qualifying transfers after one semester.

CONTACT
Vincent Frank, Director of Financial Aid
Box 600, Loretto, PA 15940

St. Joseph's University
Philadelphia, Pennsylvania
www.sju.edu   Federal Code: 003367

4-year private university in very large city, affiliated with Roman Catholic Church.
Enrollment: 4,979 undergrads, 15% part-time. 1,128 full-time freshmen.
Selectivity: Admits less than 50% of applicants. GED not accepted.

BASIC COSTS (2006-2007)
Tuition and fees: $29,095.
Per-credit charge: $419.
Room and board: $10,170.
Additional info: $950 per credit hour for credits over 5 courses. $200 freshman orientation fee.

FINANCIAL AID PICTURE (2005-2006)
Students with need: Out of 793 full-time freshmen who applied for aid, 593 were judged to have need. Of these, 593 received aid, and 135 had their full need met. Average financial aid package met 79% of need; average scholarship/grant was $8,729; average loan was $4,125. Need-based aid available for part-time students.
Students without need: 237 full-time freshmen who did not demonstrate need for aid received scholarships/grants; average award was $8,321. No-need awards available for academics, art, athletics, minority status, music/drama, ROTC.
Scholarships offered: 80 full-time freshmen received athletic scholarships; average amount $12,874.
Cumulative student debt: 71% of graduating class had student loans; average debt was $16,120.

FINANCIAL AID PROCEDURES
Forms required: FAFSA.
Dates and Deadlines: Priority date 2/15; closing date 5/1. Applicants notified on a rolling basis starting 2/15; must reply by 5/1.
Transfers: Financial aid for transfers subject to availability of funds.

CONTACT
Eileen Tucker, Director of Financial Aid
5600 City Avenue, Philadelphia, PA 19131
(610) 660-1556

St. Vincent College
Latrobe, Pennsylvania
www.stvincent.edu   Federal Code: 003368

4-year private liberal arts college in large town, affiliated with Roman Catholic Church.
Enrollment: 1,483 undergrads, 2% part-time. 485 full-time freshmen.
Selectivity: Admits 50 to 75% of applicants.

BASIC COSTS (2005-2006)
Tuition and fees: $21,679.
Per-credit charge: $660.
Room and board: $7,348.

FINANCIAL AID PICTURE (2005-2006)
Students with need: Out of 480 full-time freshmen who applied for aid, 392 were judged to have need. Of these, 392 received aid, and 97 had their full need met. Average financial aid package met 93% of need; average scholarship/grant was $12,849; average loan was $1,905. For part-time students, average financial aid package was $10,375.
Students without need: 82 full-time freshmen who did not demonstrate need for aid received scholarships/grants; average award was $10,956. No-need awards available for academics, leadership, minority status, music/drama.
Scholarships offered: *Merit:* Academic Merit Scholarship: $1,000 to $11,000; based on high school GPA, class rank, and SAT scores. Wimmer Scholarship: open to students in top 10 percent of their high school class; based on exam; top scorer awarded full tuition, next 4 scorers awarded between $12,000 and full scholarship. Leadership Merit Grant: $500 to $3,000, based on extracurricular activities and recommendations. *Athletic:* 108 full-time freshmen received athletic scholarships; average amount $4,578.

FINANCIAL AID PROCEDURES
Forms required: FAFSA, state aid form.
Dates and Deadlines: Priority date 3/1; closing date 5/1. Applicants notified on a rolling basis starting 3/1; must reply within 2 week(s) of notification.

CONTACT
David Collins, Assistant Vice President, Admission and Financial Aid
300 Fraser Purchase Road, Latrobe, PA 15650-2690
(800) 782-5549

Schuylkill Institute of Business & Technology
Pottsville, Pennsylvania
www.sibt.edu   Federal Code: 014984

2-year for-profit technical college in small town.
Enrollment: 135 undergrads. 36 full-time freshmen.
Selectivity: Open admission.

BASIC COSTS (2005-2006)
Tuition and fees: $10,500.
Per-credit charge: $271.
Additional info: Programs cost between $7,100 and $25,000 and last between 9 and 24 months. Tuition at time of enrollment locked for 2 years.

FINANCIAL AID PICTURE (2005-2006)
Students with need: Need-based aid available for part-time students.
Students without need: This college only awards aid to students with need.

FINANCIAL AID PROCEDURES
Forms required: FAFSA.
Dates and Deadlines: Priority date 4/25; closing date 5/1. Applicants notified by 10/1; must reply by 10/15.
Transfers: No deadline.

CONTACT
Nancy Davis, Financial Aid Director
118 South Centre Street, Pottsville, PA 17901
(570) 622-4835

Seton Hill University
Greensburg, Pennsylvania
www.setonhill.edu   Federal Code: 003362

4-year private university and liberal arts college in large town, affiliated with Roman Catholic Church.
Enrollment: 1,427 undergrads, 14% part-time. 336 full-time freshmen.
Selectivity: Admits 50 to 75% of applicants.

BASIC COSTS (2005-2006)
Tuition and fees: $23,180.
Room and board: $7,450.
Additional info: Tuition/fee waivers available for adults.

FINANCIAL AID PICTURE (2005-2006)
Students with need: Out of 334 full-time freshmen who applied for aid, 328 were judged to have need. Of these, 328 received aid, and 46 had their full need met. Average financial aid package met 83% of need; average scholarship/grant was $13,200; average loan was $3,291. For part-time students, average financial aid package was $6,208.
Students without need: 3 full-time freshmen who did not demonstrate need for aid received scholarships/grants; average award was $11,214. No-need awards available for academics, alumni affiliation, art, athletics, job skills, music/drama, religious affiliation.
Scholarships offered: *Merit:* Presidential scholarships available. Awards range up to one-half of tuition per year. Scholarships for valedictorians, Girl Scout Gold awardees, Hugh O'Brien Youth, Governor's School of Excellence

participants, and Maureen O'Brien Leadership award. **Athletic:** 12 full-time freshmen received athletic scholarships; average amount $15,110.
Cumulative student debt: 74% of graduating class had student loans; average debt was $26,281.
Additional info: Up to half tuition reduction for students in top 10% of high school class. Up to one-third tuition reduction for students in top 20% of high school class. Up to 25% tuition reduction for students in top 30% of class.

FINANCIAL AID PROCEDURES
Forms required: FAFSA, state aid form, institutional form.
Dates and Deadlines: Priority date 6/1; no closing date. Applicants notified on a rolling basis starting 11/1; must reply within 2 week(s) of notification.
Transfers: No deadline. Applicants notified on a rolling basis starting 1/1; must reply within 2 week(s) of notification. Scholarship available for full-time transfer students with cumulative 3.5 GPA.

CONTACT
Maryann Dudas, Director of Financial Aid
Seton Hill Drive, Greensburg, PA 15601
(724) 838-4293

Shippensburg University of Pennsylvania
Shippensburg, Pennsylvania
www.ship.edu   Federal Code: 003326

4-year public university in small town.
Enrollment: 6,395 undergrads, 4% part-time. 1,499 full-time freshmen.
Selectivity: Admits 50 to 75% of applicants.

BASIC COSTS (2005-2006)
Tuition and fees: $6,175; out-of-state residents $13,598.
Per-credit charge: $204; out-of-state residents $511.
Room and board: $5,710.

FINANCIAL AID PICTURE (2005-2006)
Students with need: Out of 1,243 full-time freshmen who applied for aid, 804 were judged to have need. Of these, 766 received aid, and 101 had their full need met. Average financial aid package met 64% of need; average scholarship/grant was $4,115; average loan was $2,755. For part-time students, average financial aid package was $5,636.
Students without need: 147 full-time freshmen who did not demonstrate need for aid received scholarships/grants; average award was $2,245. No-need awards available for academics, athletics.
Scholarships offered: 76 full-time freshmen received athletic scholarships; average amount $2,142.
Cumulative student debt: 67% of graduating class had student loans; average debt was $17,976.

FINANCIAL AID PROCEDURES
Forms required: FAFSA.
Dates and Deadlines: Priority date 3/15; no closing date. Applicants notified on a rolling basis; must reply within 2 week(s) of notification.

CONTACT
Peter D'Annibale, Director of Financial Aid
1871 Old Main Drive, Shippensburg, PA 17257-2299
(717) 477-1131

Slippery Rock University of Pennsylvania
Slippery Rock, Pennsylvania
www.sru.edu   Federal Code: 003327

4-year public university in rural community.
Enrollment: 7,336 undergrads, 6% part-time. 1,452 full-time freshmen.
Selectivity: Admits less than 50% of applicants.

BASIC COSTS (2005-2006)
Tuition and fees: $6,211; out-of-state residents $13,571.
Per-credit charge: $204; out-of-state residents $511.
Room and board: $4,980.

FINANCIAL AID PICTURE (2005-2006)
Students with need: Out of 1,355 full-time freshmen who applied for aid, 928 were judged to have need. Of these, 915 received aid, and 575 had their full need met. Average financial aid package met 77% of need; average scholarship/grant was $3,300; average loan was $2,352. For part-time students, average financial aid package was $5,345.
Students without need: 381 full-time freshmen who did not demonstrate need for aid received scholarships/grants; average award was $3,849. No-need awards available for academics, alumni affiliation, art, athletics, job skills, leadership, minority status, music/drama, ROTC, state/district residency.
Scholarships offered: 61 full-time freshmen received athletic scholarships; average amount $2,929.
Cumulative student debt: 76% of graduating class had student loans; average debt was $20,054.
Additional info: May 1 closing date for Pennsylvania state grants.

FINANCIAL AID PROCEDURES
Forms required: FAFSA.
Dates and Deadlines: Priority date 5/1; no closing date. Applicants notified on a rolling basis starting 3/15; must reply within 4 week(s) of notification.

CONTACT
Patricia Hladio, Director of Financial Aid
1 Morrow Way, Slippery Rock, PA 16057-1383
(724) 738-2044

South Hills School of Business & Technology
State College, Pennsylvania
www.southhills.edu   Federal Code: 013263

2-year for-profit business and technical college in large town.
Enrollment: 646 undergrads, 6% part-time. 366 full-time freshmen.
Selectivity: Open admission; but selective for some programs.

BASIC COSTS (2006-2007)
Tuition and fees: $11,737.
Per-credit charge: $323.

FINANCIAL AID PICTURE (2004-2005)
Students with need: Out of 366 full-time freshmen who applied for aid, 366 were judged to have need. Of these, 366 received aid. Average financial aid package met 73% of need; average scholarship/grant was $73; average loan was $2,625. Need-based aid available for part-time students.
Students without need: This college only awards aid to students with need.

FINANCIAL AID PROCEDURES
Forms required: FAFSA.
Dates and Deadlines: Closing date 6/30. Applicants notified on a rolling basis starting 7/5.
Transfers: No deadline.

CONTACT
Harriet Arndt, Financial Aid Director
480 Waupelani Drive, State College, PA 16801-4516
(814) 234-7755

Susquehanna University
Selinsgrove, Pennsylvania
www.susqu.edu
Federal Code: 003369
CSS Code: 2820

4-year private university and liberal arts college in small town, affiliated with Evangelical Lutheran Church in America.
Enrollment: 1,898 undergrads, 1% part-time. 512 full-time freshmen.
Selectivity: Admits over 75% of applicants.

BASIC COSTS (2006-2007)
Tuition and fees: $27,620.
Per-credit charge: $825.
Room and board: $7,600.

FINANCIAL AID PICTURE (2005-2006)
Students with need: Out of 418 full-time freshmen who applied for aid, 338 were judged to have need. Of these, 336 received aid, and 74 had their full need met. Average financial aid package met 79% of need; average scholarship/grant was $14,709; average loan was $3,238. For part-time students, average financial aid package was $21,590.
Students without need: 143 full-time freshmen who did not demonstrate need for aid received scholarships/grants; average award was $8,437. No-need awards available for academics, alumni affiliation, leadership, minority status, music/drama, ROTC.
Scholarships offered: Scholarships range from $1,000 to $16,000 renewable annually. Recognize outstanding academic achievement, personal accomplishment, and/or musical talent.
Additional info: Graduated pay scale for federal work-study program.

FINANCIAL AID PROCEDURES
Forms required: FAFSA, CSS PROFILE.
Dates and Deadlines: Priority date 3/1; closing date 5/1. Applicants notified on a rolling basis starting 2/15; must reply by 5/1.
Transfers: Priority date 5/1; closing date 7/1. Transfer students eligible for financial aid and scholarship consideration.

CONTACT
Helen Nunn, Director of Financial Aid
514 University Avenue, Selinsgrove, PA 17870-1040
(570) 372-4450

Swarthmore College
Swarthmore, Pennsylvania
www.swarthmore.edu
Federal Code: 003370
CSS Code: 2821

4-year private liberal arts college in small town.
Enrollment: 1,461 undergrads. 389 full-time freshmen.
Selectivity: Admits less than 50% of applicants.

BASIC COSTS (2006-2007)
Tuition and fees: $33,232.
Room and board: $10,300.

FINANCIAL AID PICTURE (2005-2006)
Students with need: Out of 257 full-time freshmen who applied for aid, 200 were judged to have need. Of these, 200 received aid, and 200 had their full need met. Average financial aid package met 100% of need; average scholarship/grant was $26,824; average loan was $2,199.
Students without need: 3 full-time freshmen who did not demonstrate need for aid received scholarships/grants; average award was $31,196. No-need awards available for academics, leadership, state/district residency.
Cumulative student debt: 36% of graduating class had student loans; average debt was $12,413.
Additional info: Swarthmore meets 100% of demonstrated financial need for all admitted students.

FINANCIAL AID PROCEDURES
Forms required: FAFSA, CSS PROFILE, state aid form, institutional form.
Dates and Deadlines: Closing date 2/15. Applicants notified by 4/1; must reply by 5/1.
Transfers: Closing date 4/1. Applicants notified by 5/15. No aid consideration possible for foreign national transfer applicants.

CONTACT
Laura Talbot, Director of Financial Aid
500 College Avenue, Swarthmore, PA 19081
(610) 328-8358

Temple University
Philadelphia, Pennsylvania
www.temple.edu
Federal Code: 003371

4-year public university in very large city.
Enrollment: 23,450 undergrads, 11% part-time. 3,593 full-time freshmen.
Selectivity: Admits 50 to 75% of applicants.

BASIC COSTS (2005-2006)
Tuition and fees: $9,640; out-of-state residents $17,236.
Per-credit charge: $354; out-of-state residents $596.
Room and board: $8,188.

FINANCIAL AID PICTURE (2004-2005)
Students with need: Out of 3,380 full-time freshmen who applied for aid, 2,692 were judged to have need. Of these, 2,636 received aid, and 825 had their full need met. Average financial aid package met 87% of need; average scholarship/grant was $5,116; average loan was $2,881. For part-time students, average financial aid package was $7,966.
Students without need: 917 full-time freshmen who did not demonstrate need for aid received scholarships/grants; average award was $4,066. No-need awards available for academics, art, athletics, music/drama, ROTC.
Scholarships offered: 29 full-time freshmen received athletic scholarships; average amount $13,235.
Cumulative student debt: 72% of graduating class had student loans; average debt was $23,772.

FINANCIAL AID PROCEDURES
Forms required: FAFSA.
Dates and Deadlines: Closing date 3/1. Applicants notified on a rolling basis starting 2/15; must reply by 5/1 or within 3 week(s) of notification.
Transfers: Priority date 3/1; no deadline. Must reply within 2 week(s) of notification.

CONTACT
John Morris, Director, Student Financial Services
1st Floor Conwell Hall, Philadelphia, PA 19122-6096
(215) 204-2244

Thiel College
Greenville, Pennsylvania
www.thiel.edu
Federal Code: 003376

4-year private liberal arts college in small town, affiliated with Evangelical Lutheran Church in America.
Enrollment: 1,295 undergrads, 3% part-time. 427 full-time freshmen.
Selectivity: Admits over 75% of applicants.

BASIC COSTS (2006-2007)
Tuition and fees: $18,720.
Per-credit charge: $725.
Room and board: $7,544.

FINANCIAL AID PICTURE (2005-2006)
Students with need: Out of 415 full-time freshmen who applied for aid, 353 were judged to have need. Of these, 353 received aid, and 71 had their full need met. Average financial aid package met 78% of need; average scholarship/grant was $11,135; average loan was $3,662. For part-time students, average financial aid package was $5,620.
Students without need: 74 full-time freshmen who did not demonstrate need for aid received scholarships/grants; average award was $6,293. No-need awards available for academics, alumni affiliation, leadership, religious affiliation, state/district residency.
Cumulative student debt: 87% of graduating class had student loans; average debt was $20,000.

FINANCIAL AID PROCEDURES
Forms required: FAFSA, state aid form.
Dates and Deadlines: Priority date 3/15; no closing date. Applicants notified on a rolling basis starting 2/15; must reply within 2 week(s) of notification.
Transfers: Priority date 6/1.

CONTACT
Cynthia Farrell, Director of Financial Aid
75 College Avenue, Greenville, PA 16125-2181
(724) 589-2250

Thomas Jefferson University: College of Health Professions
Philadelphia, Pennsylvania
www.jefferson.edu/jchp   Federal Code: 012393

Upper-division private health science and nursing college in very large city.
Enrollment: 802 undergrads, 16% part-time. 98 full-time freshmen.

BASIC COSTS (2005-2006)
Tuition and fees: $21,975.
Per-credit charge: $726.

FINANCIAL AID PICTURE (2004-2005)
Students with need: 46% of average financial aid package awarded as scholarships/grants, 54% awarded as loans/jobs.
Students without need: No-need awards available for academics, leadership, state/district residency.
Scholarships offered: Range of merit-based scholarships exist for selected applicants.

FINANCIAL AID PROCEDURES
Forms required: FAFSA, institutional form.
Dates and Deadlines: Closing date 5/1. Applicants notified on a rolling basis starting 4/1; must reply within 2 week(s) of notification.
Transfers: Applicants notified on a rolling basis starting 11/15; must reply within 2 week(s) of notification.

CONTACT
Susan Batchelor, University Director of Financial Aid
130 South Ninth Street, Edison Building, Suite 100, Philadelphia, PA 19107
(215) 955-2867

Triangle Tech: DuBois
DuBois, Pennsylvania
www.triangle-tech.edu   Federal Code: 021744

2-year for-profit technical college in small city.
Enrollment: 243 undergrads. 139 full-time freshmen.
Selectivity: Open admission.

BASIC COSTS (2006-2007)
Tuition and fees: $11,866.

FINANCIAL AID PICTURE (2004-2005)
Students with need: Average financial aid package for all full-time undergraduates was $8,863. 47% awarded as scholarships/grants, 53% awarded as loans/jobs. Need-based aid available for part-time students.
Students without need: This college only awards aid to students with need.

FINANCIAL AID PROCEDURES
Forms required: FAFSA, state aid form, institutional form.
Dates and Deadlines: No deadline. Applicants notified on a rolling basis.

CONTACT
Catherine Waxter, Corporate Director of Financial Aid
PO Box 551, DuBois, PA 15801-0551
(724) 832-1050

Triangle Tech: Erie
Erie, Pennsylvania
www.triangle-tech.edu   Federal Code: 014417

2-year for-profit technical college in small city.
Enrollment: 137 undergrads. 53 full-time freshmen.
Selectivity: Open admission.

FINANCIAL AID PICTURE (2004-2005)
Students with need: 39% of average financial aid package awarded as scholarships/grants, 61% awarded as loans/jobs. Need-based aid available for part-time students.

FINANCIAL AID PROCEDURES
Forms required: FAFSA.
Dates and Deadlines: Applicants notified on a rolling basis.

CONTACT
Cathy Waxter, Corporate Director of Financial Aid
2000 Liberty Street, Erie, PA 16502-2594
(724) 832-1050

Triangle Tech: Greensburg
Greensburg, Pennsylvania
www.triangle-tech.edu   Federal Code: 014895

2-year for-profit technical college in large town.
Enrollment: 243 undergrads. 104 full-time freshmen.
Selectivity: Open admission.

BASIC COSTS (2005-2006)
Tuition and fees: $11,712.
Per-credit charge: $317.
Additional info: Tuition at time of enrollment locked for 2 years.

FINANCIAL AID PICTURE (2004-2005)
Students with need: Average financial aid package for all full-time undergraduates was $8,685. 46% awarded as scholarships/grants, 54% awarded as loans/jobs. Need-based aid available for part-time students.

FINANCIAL AID PROCEDURES
Forms required: FAFSA.
Dates and Deadlines: No deadline. Applicants notified on a rolling basis.

CONTACT
Catherine Waxter, Director of Financial Aid
222 East Pittsburgh Street, Suite A, Greensburg, PA 15601-3304
(724) 832-1050

Triangle Tech: Pittsburgh
Pittsburgh, Pennsylvania
www.triangle-tech.edu   Federal Code: 007839

2-year for-profit technical college in very large city.
Enrollment: 309 undergrads. 95 full-time freshmen.
Selectivity: Open admission.

BASIC COSTS (2005-2006)
Tuition and fees: $11,712.
Per-credit charge: $317.

FINANCIAL AID PICTURE (2004-2005)
Students with need: Average financial aid package for all full-time undergraduates was $950. Work study available nights.
Students without need: This college only awards aid to students with need.

FINANCIAL AID PROCEDURES
Forms required: institutional form.
Dates and Deadlines: No deadline. Applicants notified on a rolling basis.

CONTACT
Cathy Waxter, Corporate Director of Financial Aid
1940 Perrysville Avenue, Pittsburgh, PA 15214-3897
(412) 359-1000

University of Pennsylvania
Philadelphia, Pennsylvania
www.upenn.edu   Federal Code: 003378
                                         CSS Code: 2926

4-year private university in very large city.
Enrollment: 9,841 undergrads, 3% part-time. 2,543 full-time freshmen.
Selectivity: Admits less than 50% of applicants.

BASIC COSTS (2006-2007)
Tuition and fees: $34,156.
Room and board: $9,804.

FINANCIAL AID PICTURE (2004-2005)
Students with need: Out of 1,285 full-time freshmen who applied for aid, 1,004 were judged to have need. Of these, 1,004 received aid, and 1,004 had their full need met. Average financial aid package met 100% of need; average scholarship/grant was $22,651; average loan was $3,028. Need-based aid available for part-time students.
Students without need: This college only awards aid to students with need.
Cumulative student debt: 41% of graduating class had student loans; average debt was $21,133.

FINANCIAL AID PROCEDURES
Forms required: FAFSA, CSS PROFILE, state aid form, institutional form.
Dates and Deadlines: Priority date 2/15; no closing date. Applicants notified on a rolling basis starting 4/1; must reply by 5/1.
Transfers: Closing date 3/15. Must reply by 5/1.

CONTACT
William Schilling, Director of Financial Aid
1 College Hall, Philadelphia, PA 19104
(215) 898-1988

University of Pittsburgh
Pittsburgh, Pennsylvania
www.pitt.edu   Federal Code: 008815

4-year public university in large city.
Enrollment: 16,585 undergrads, 9% part-time. 2,991 full-time freshmen.
Selectivity: Admits 50 to 75% of applicants. GED not accepted.

BASIC COSTS (2005-2006)
Tuition and fees: $11,436; out-of-state residents $20,784.
Per-credit charge: $412; out-of-state residents $772.
Room and board: $8,830.

FINANCIAL AID PICTURE (2005-2006)
Students with need: Out of 2,617 full-time freshmen who applied for aid, 1,981 were judged to have need. Of these, 1,964 received aid, and 887 had their full need met. Average financial aid package met 89% of need; average scholarship/grant was $5,053; average loan was $4,007. Need-based aid available for part-time students.
Students without need: 169 full-time freshmen who did not demonstrate need for aid received scholarships/grants; average award was $7,716. No-need awards available for academics, athletics.
Scholarships offered: *Merit:* Academic Scholarships available with a range of awards from $1,000 to full tuition, room and board. These scholarships can be renewed for up to 4 years with a 3.0 GPA. *Athletic:* 17 full-time freshmen received athletic scholarships; average amount $9,616.

FINANCIAL AID PROCEDURES
Forms required: FAFSA, institutional form.
Dates and Deadlines: Priority date 3/1; closing date 6/1. Applicants notified on a rolling basis starting 3/1; must reply by 5/1 or within 2 week(s) of notification.
Transfers: Priority date 5/1; no deadline. Transfer students not eligible for freshman scholarships.

CONTACT
Betsy Porter, Director, Office of Admissions and Financial Aid
4227 Fifth Avenue, 1st Floor, Alumni Hall, Pittsburgh, PA 15260
(412) 624-7488

University of Pittsburgh at Bradford
Bradford, Pennsylvania
www.upb.pitt.edu   Federal Code: 003380

4-year public university and liberal arts college in large town.
Enrollment: 1,142 undergrads, 18% part-time. 239 full-time freshmen.
Selectivity: Admits over 75% of applicants.

BASIC COSTS (2005-2006)
Tuition and fees: $10,538; out-of-state residents $20,426.
Per-credit charge: $380; out-of-state residents $760.
Room and board: $6,470.

FINANCIAL AID PICTURE (2005-2006)
Students with need: 46% of average financial aid package awarded as scholarships/grants, 54% awarded as loans/jobs. Need-based aid available for part-time students. Work study available nights, weekends, and for part-time students.
Students without need: No-need awards available for academics, alumni affiliation, ROTC, state/district residency.
Cumulative student debt: 85% of graduating class had student loans; average debt was $19,313.

FINANCIAL AID PROCEDURES
Forms required: FAFSA.
Dates and Deadlines: Priority date 3/1; no closing date. Applicants notified on a rolling basis starting 4/1; must reply within 2 week(s) of notification.

Transfers: Transfers must meet academic policy guidelines.

CONTACT
Melissa Ibanez, Director of Financial Aid
300 Campus Drive, Bradford, PA 16701
(814) 362-7550

University of Pittsburgh at Greensburg
Greensburg, Pennsylvania
www.upg.pitt.edu   Federal Code: 003381

4-year public branch campus and liberal arts college in large town.
Enrollment: 1,795 undergrads, 9% part-time. 463 full-time freshmen.

BASIC COSTS (2005-2006)
Tuition and fees: $10,562; out-of-state residents $20,450.
Per-credit charge: $380; out-of-state residents $760.
Room and board: $6,960.

FINANCIAL AID PICTURE (2004-2005)
Students with need: Out of 406 full-time freshmen who applied for aid, 322 were judged to have need. Of these, 315 received aid. Average financial aid package met 59% of need; average scholarship/grant was $4,007; average loan was $2,852. For part-time students, average financial aid package was $5,358.
Students without need: 20 full-time freshmen who did not demonstrate need for aid received scholarships/grants; average award was $3,100. No-need awards available for academics, leadership, minority status.

FINANCIAL AID PROCEDURES
Forms required: FAFSA, state aid form, institutional form.
Dates and Deadlines: Priority date 3/1; closing date 5/1. Applicants notified on a rolling basis starting 4/15; must reply within 3 week(s) of notification.
Transfers: No deadline.

CONTACT
Brandi Darr, Director of Admissions and Financial Aid
1150 Mount Pleasant Road, Greensburg, PA 15601
(724) 836-9880

University of Pittsburgh at Johnstown
Johnstown, Pennsylvania
www.upj.pitt.edu   Federal Code: 008815

4-year public engineering and liberal arts college in small city.
Enrollment: 3,113 undergrads, 6% part-time. 861 full-time freshmen.
Selectivity: Admits over 75% of applicants.

BASIC COSTS (2005-2006)
Tuition and fees: $10,540; out-of-state residents $20,428.
Per-credit charge: $380; out-of-state residents $760.
Room and board: $6,300.

FINANCIAL AID PICTURE (2004-2005)
Students with need: Out of 775 full-time freshmen who applied for aid, 667 were judged to have need. Of these, 621 received aid, and 60 had their full need met. Average financial aid package met 44% of need; average scholarship/grant was $4,061; average loan was $2,355. For part-time students, average financial aid package was $4,959.
Students without need: 39 full-time freshmen who did not demonstrate need for aid received scholarships/grants; average award was $2,438. No-need awards available for academics, athletics, leadership, minority status.
Scholarships offered: *Merit:* President's Scholarships and Leadership Scholarships: $1,500 to full tuition yearly; renewable; 1220 SAT (exclusive of Writing), 3.8 GPA, and top 10% of graduating class. Students are selected on rolling basis, although priority is given to those who apply by 12/01. Information found on application for admission and all submitted admission materials used in selection criteria. *Athletic:* 26 full-time freshmen received athletic scholarships; average amount $4,573.
Cumulative student debt: 83% of graduating class had student loans; average debt was $18,962.

FINANCIAL AID PROCEDURES
Forms required: FAFSA.
Dates and Deadlines: Priority date 4/1; no closing date. Applicants notified on a rolling basis starting 3/15; must reply within 2 week(s) of notification.

CONTACT
Jeanine Lawn, Director of Financial Aid
450 Schoolhouse Road, 157 Blackington Hall, Johnstown, PA 15904-1200
(800) 881-5544

University of Pittsburgh at Titusville
Titusville, Pennsylvania
www.upt.pitt.edu   Federal Code: 003383

2-year public branch campus and liberal arts college in small town.
Enrollment: 523 undergrads, 22% part-time. 159 full-time freshmen.
Selectivity: Admits over 75% of applicants.

BASIC COSTS (2005-2006)
Tuition and fees: $9,400; out-of-state residents $18,300.
Per-credit charge: $335; out-of-state residents $677.
Room and board: $7,334.
Additional info: Tuition/fee waivers available for adults.

FINANCIAL AID PICTURE (2005-2006)
Students with need: Average financial aid package met 85% of need; average scholarship/grant was $7,443; average loan was $2,625. For part-time students, average financial aid package was $6,375.
Students without need: No-need awards available for academics, athletics, state/district residency.
Scholarships offered: $2,000 merit scholarships; up to 5 for the top 5 students with science as a major, renewable with a 3.0 GPA and continued science major. Presidential scholarships; $2,000; awarded based on high school academic record; 6 awarded. Other scholarships available.
Cumulative student debt: 98% of graduating class had student loans; average debt was $10,125.

FINANCIAL AID PROCEDURES
Forms required: FAFSA, institutional form.
Dates and Deadlines: No deadline. Applicants notified on a rolling basis; must reply within 2 week(s) of notification.
Transfers: Priority date 3/1; no deadline. PA residents by May 1 for PHEAA. Transfer students must have completed 24 credits to renew.

CONTACT
Nicole Neely, Director of Student Financial Services
UPT Admissions Office, Titusville, PA 16354
(814) 827-4495

University of Scranton
Scranton, Pennsylvania
www.scranton.edu   Federal Code: 003384

4-year private university and liberal arts college in small city, affiliated with Roman Catholic Church.
Enrollment: 4,014 undergrads, 4% part-time. 943 full-time freshmen.
Selectivity: Admits over 75% of applicants.

BASIC COSTS (2006-2007)
Tuition and fees: $25,938.
Per-credit charge: $712.
Room and board: $10,224.

FINANCIAL AID PICTURE (2005-2006)
Students with need: Out of 799 full-time freshmen who applied for aid, 632 were judged to have need. Of these, 629 received aid, and 72 had their full need met. Average financial aid package met 73% of need; average scholarship/grant was $11,571; average loan was $3,422. For part-time students, average financial aid package was $6,654.
Students without need: This college only awards aid to students with need.
Cumulative student debt: 70% of graduating class had student loans; average debt was $23,222.

FINANCIAL AID PROCEDURES
Forms required: FAFSA.
Dates and Deadlines: Priority date 2/15; no closing date. Applicants notified on a rolling basis starting 3/1; must reply by 5/1 or within 2 week(s) of notification.
Transfers: Institutional grants available based on financial need.

CONTACT
William Burke, Director of Financial Aid
800 Linden Street, Scranton, PA 18510-4699
(570) 941-7700

University of the Arts
Philadelphia, Pennsylvania
www.uarts.edu   Federal Code: 003350

4-year private visual arts and performing arts college in very large city.
Enrollment: 2,057 undergrads, 1% part-time. 510 full-time freshmen.
Selectivity: Admits less than 50% of applicants.

BASIC COSTS (2005-2006)
Tuition and fees: $24,330.
Per-credit charge: $1,010.
Room only: $5,900.

FINANCIAL AID PICTURE
Students with need: Need-based aid available for full-time and part-time students. Work study available nights, weekends, and for part-time students.
Students without need: No-need awards available for academics, art, music/drama.
Scholarships offered: Merit awards available to students who demonstrate exceptional talent and academic abilities.

FINANCIAL AID PROCEDURES
Forms required: FAFSA.
Dates and Deadlines: Priority date 2/15; no closing date. Applicants notified on a rolling basis starting 3/15; must reply within 2 week(s) of notification.
Transfers: Undergraduate transfers not eligible for federal, state, or university aid, if four-year degree previously conferred.

CONTACT
Director of Financial Aid
320 South Broad Street, Philadelphia, PA 19102
(215) 717-6170

University of the Sciences in Philadelphia
Philadelphia, Pennsylvania
www.usip.edu   Federal Code: 003353

4-year private health science and pharmacy college in very large city.
Enrollment: 1,962 undergrads, 1% part-time. 521 full-time freshmen.
Selectivity: Admits 50 to 75% of applicants.

BASIC COSTS (2005-2006)
Tuition and fees: $23,982.
Room and board: $9,380.
Additional info: Tiered cost structure applies to students enrolled in 5- and 6-year programs that lead to professional degrees.

FINANCIAL AID PICTURE
Students with need: Need-based aid available for full-time and part-time students.
Students without need: No-need awards available for academics, athletics.

FINANCIAL AID PROCEDURES
Forms required: FAFSA.
Dates and Deadlines: Closing date 3/15. Applicants notified on a rolling basis starting 1/15; must reply by 5/1 or within 2 week(s) of notification.

CONTACT
Nick Flocco, Director of Financial Aid
600 South 43rd Street, Philadelphia, PA 19104-4495
(215) 596-8894

Ursinus College
Collegeville, Pennsylvania   Federal Code: 003385
www.ursinus.edu   CSS Code: 2931

4-year private liberal arts college in small town.
Enrollment: 1,555 undergrads. 419 full-time freshmen.
Selectivity: Admits 50 to 75% of applicants.

BASIC COSTS (2006-2007)
Tuition and fees: $33,200.
Room and board: $7,600.

FINANCIAL AID PICTURE (2005-2006)
Students with need: Out of 411 full-time freshmen who applied for aid, 326 were judged to have need. Of these, 326 received aid, and 245 had their full need met. Average financial aid package met 85% of need; average scholarship/grant was $20,243; average loan was $3,649.
Students without need: 85 full-time freshmen who did not demonstrate need for aid received scholarships/grants; average award was $10,000. No-need awards available for alumni affiliation.
Cumulative student debt: 81% of graduating class had student loans; average debt was $21,500.

FINANCIAL AID PROCEDURES
Forms required: FAFSA, CSS PROFILE, institutional form.
Dates and Deadlines: Closing date 2/15. Applicants notified by 4/1; must reply by 5/1.
Transfers: Closing date 8/1.

CONTACT
Suzanne Sparrow, Director of Student Financial Services
P.O. Box 1000, Collegeville, PA 19426-1000
(610) 409-3600

Valley Forge Christian College
Phoenixville, Pennsylvania
www.vfcc.edu   Federal Code: 003306

4-year private liberal arts college in large town, affiliated with Assemblies of God.
Enrollment: 878 undergrads, 4% part-time. 211 full-time freshmen.
Selectivity: Admits 50 to 75% of applicants.

BASIC COSTS (2006-2007)
Tuition and fees: $11,755.
Room and board: $5,850.

FINANCIAL AID PICTURE (2005-2006)
Students with need: Average financial aid package met 47% of need; average scholarship/grant was $4,812; average loan was $2,568. For part-time students, average financial aid package was $5,815.
Students without need: No-need awards available for academics, leadership, music/drama, religious affiliation, state/district residency.
Scholarships offered: Trustee's Scholarship, President's Scholarship, Dean's Scholarship, Professor's Scholarship ranging from full tuition/minimum 3.56 GPA, 1300 SAT or 29 ACT, and upper 10% class rank, to $1,000-$2,000 for minimum 3.5 GPA and minimum 1030 SAT or 22 ACT, application required, renewable with maintenance of 3.5 GPA. SAT scores exclusive of Writing.
Cumulative student debt: 94% of graduating class had student loans; average debt was $2,670.

FINANCIAL AID PROCEDURES
Forms required: FAFSA.
Dates and Deadlines: Priority date 5/1; no closing date. Applicants notified on a rolling basis starting 3/15; must reply within 3 week(s) of notification.

CONTACT
Evie Meyer, Director of Financial Aid
1401 Charlestown Road, Phoenixville, PA 19460
(610) 917-1498

Valley Forge Military College
Wayne, Pennsylvania
www.vfmac.edu   Federal Code: 003386

2-year private junior and military college in small city.
Enrollment: 188 undergrads.

BASIC COSTS (2005-2006)
Tuition and fees: $22,070.
Room and board: $6,480.

FINANCIAL AID PICTURE
Students with need: Need-based aid available for full-time students.
Students without need: No-need awards available for academics, alumni affiliation, athletics, music/drama, ROTC, state/district residency.
Additional info: Students enrolled in advanced military science program can receive up to $5,000 from the Army. In addition, competitively awarded ROTC scholarships pay average of another $14,100 per school year for direct educational expenses.

FINANCIAL AID PROCEDURES
Forms required: FAFSA, institutional form.
Dates and Deadlines: Closing date 5/1. Applicants notified on a rolling basis starting 5/15; must reply within 2 week(s) of notification.
Transfers: Must submit financial aid transcripts from all previously attended colleges, even if aid was not received.

CONTACT
Greg Potts, Financial Aid Director
1001 Eagle Road, Wayne, PA 19087
(610) 989-1300

Vet Tech Institute
Pittsburgh, Pennsylvania
www.vettechinstitute.com   Federal Code: 008568

2-year for-profit health science and technical college in large city.
Enrollment: 296 undergrads.

BASIC COSTS (2005-2006)
Tuition and fees: $23,700.
Additional info: Tuition at time of enrollment locked for 2 years.

FINANCIAL AID PICTURE
Students with need: Work study available nights.
Students without need: No-need awards available for academics.
Scholarships offered: $1,000 scholarships: 5 offered to commuters. $2,000 scholarships: 2 offered to students not living at home. Awarded based on results of examination given at school in November and March.

FINANCIAL AID PROCEDURES
Forms required: FAFSA, state aid form.
Dates and Deadlines: No deadline. Applicants notified on a rolling basis.

CONTACT
Donna Durr, Financial Aid Coordinator
125 Seventh Street, Pittsburgh, PA 15222-3400
(800) 570-0693

Villanova University
Villanova, Pennsylvania
www.villanova.edu   Federal Code: 003388

4-year private university in small town, affiliated with Roman Catholic Church.
Enrollment: 6,802 undergrads, 5% part-time. 1,625 full-time freshmen.
Selectivity: Admits 50 to 75% of applicants.

BASIC COSTS (2006-2007)
Tuition and fees: $33,300.
Room and board: $9,560.
Additional info: Tuition costs include laptop for all freshmen.

FINANCIAL AID PICTURE (2005-2006)
Students with need: Out of 1,054 full-time freshmen who applied for aid, 741 were judged to have need. Of these, 733 received aid, and 172 had their full need met. Average financial aid package met 85% of need; average scholarship/grant was $18,878; average loan was $3,110. For part-time students, average financial aid package was $10,192.
Students without need: 105 full-time freshmen who did not demonstrate need for aid received scholarships/grants; average award was $11,028. No-need awards available for academics, alumni affiliation, athletics, leadership, minority status, religious affiliation, ROTC.
Scholarships offered: 40 full-time freshmen received athletic scholarships; average amount $295,612.
Cumulative student debt: 56% of graduating class had student loans; average debt was $28,549.

FINANCIAL AID PROCEDURES
Forms required: FAFSA, institutional form.
Dates and Deadlines: Closing date 2/7. Applicants notified by 3/24; must reply by 5/1.

Transfers: Closing date 7/15. Applicants notified on a rolling basis starting 5/1; must reply within 2 week(s) of notification. FAFSA application and institution's own form must be submitted by February 7.

CONTACT
Bonnie Lee Behm, Director of Financial Assistance
800 Lancaster Avenue, Villanova, PA 19085-1672
(610) 519-4010

Washington and Jefferson College
Washington, Pennsylvania
www.washjeff.edu   Federal Code: 003389

4-year private liberal arts college in large town.
Enrollment: 1,399 undergrads. 388 full-time freshmen.
Selectivity: Admits less than 50% of applicants.

BASIC COSTS (2006-2007)
Tuition and fees: $28,080.
Room and board: $7,602.

FINANCIAL AID PICTURE (2005-2006)
Students with need: Out of 353 full-time freshmen who applied for aid, 301 were judged to have need. Of these, 301 received aid, and 65 had their full need met. Average financial aid package met 80% of need; average scholarship/grant was $14,800; average loan was $2,696. For part-time students, average financial aid package was $506.
Students without need: 74 full-time freshmen who did not demonstrate need for aid received scholarships/grants; average award was $9,519. No-need awards available for academics, alumni affiliation.
Scholarships offered: Howard J. Burnett Presidential Scholarship: for selected incoming freshman students with outstanding academic performance, achievement, and citizenship; GPA of 3.10 required for renewal each year. W&J Scholars Award: for selected incoming freshman students who exhibit meritorious academic and extracurricular abilities; GPA of 2.80 required for renewal each year. Dean's Award: for selected incoming freshman students with commendable academic performance, achievement, and citizenship; GPA of 2.50 required for renewal each year. Alumni Scholarship: for incoming freshman students who are sons or daughters of alumni; GPA of 2.50 required for renewal each year. Joseph Hardy Sr. Scholarship: for selected freshman students in the Entrepreneurial studies program; awards vary according to financial need and are renewed annually subject to a review of academic performance, financial need, and continued study in the Entrepreneurial Studies Program. W&J Challenge Grant: for selected students showing academic promise; a GPA of 2.50 required for annual renewal.
Cumulative student debt: 75% of graduating class had student loans; average debt was $17,000.

FINANCIAL AID PROCEDURES
Forms required: FAFSA.
Dates and Deadlines: Priority date 2/15; no closing date. Applicants notified on a rolling basis starting 3/1; must reply by 5/1.
Transfers: No deadline. Applicants notified on a rolling basis starting 3/1.

CONTACT
Michelle Vettorel, Director of Financial Aid
60 South Lincoln Street, Washington, PA 15301
(724) 223-6019

Waynesburg College
Waynesburg, Pennsylvania
www.waynesburg.edu   Federal Code: 003391

4-year private liberal arts college in small town, affiliated with Presbyterian Church (USA).
Enrollment: 1,440 undergrads, 10% part-time. 341 full-time freshmen.
Selectivity: Admits 50 to 75% of applicants.

BASIC COSTS (2006-2007)
Tuition and fees: $15,780.
Per-credit charge: $650.
Room and board: $6,370.

FINANCIAL AID PICTURE (2005-2006)
Students with need: Average financial aid package met 81% of need; average scholarship/grant was $10,159; average loan was $2,833. For part-time students, average financial aid package was $5,820.
Students without need: No-need awards available for academics, alumni affiliation, job skills, leadership, religious affiliation, state/district residency.
Scholarships offered: Presidential Honor Scholarship: $4,500 annually. Honor Scholarship: $3,000 annually. College Leadership Program: $1,000-$1,600 annually. All for outstanding students. A.B. Miller Scholarship: $6,000-$8,000 annually.
Cumulative student debt: 80% of graduating class had student loans; average debt was $17,125.

FINANCIAL AID PROCEDURES
Forms required: FAFSA, state aid form.
Dates and Deadlines: Priority date 3/15; no closing date. Applicants notified on a rolling basis starting 2/15; must reply within 2 week(s) of notification.

CONTACT
Matthew Stokan, Director of Financial Aid
51 West College Street, Waynesburg, PA 15370
(724) 852-3208

West Chester University of Pennsylvania
West Chester, Pennsylvania
www.wcupa.edu   Federal Code: 003328

4-year public university in large town.
Enrollment: 10,395 undergrads, 7% part-time. 1,901 full-time freshmen.
Selectivity: Admits less than 50% of applicants.

BASIC COSTS (2005-2006)
Tuition and fees: $6,147; out-of-state residents $13,507.
Per-credit charge: $204; out-of-state residents $511.
Room and board: $6,208.
Additional info: Tuition/fee waivers available for minority students.

FINANCIAL AID PICTURE (2004-2005)
Students with need: Need-based aid available for part-time students. Work study available nights, weekends, and for part-time students.

FINANCIAL AID PROCEDURES
Forms required: FAFSA.
Dates and Deadlines: Priority date 3/1; no closing date. Applicants notified on a rolling basis starting 4/15; must reply within 3 week(s) of notification.

CONTACT
Dana Parker, Director of Financial Aid
Messikomer Hall, West Chester, PA 19383
(610) 436-2627

Western School of Health and Business Careers
Pittsburgh, Pennsylvania
www.westernschoolpitt.com   Federal Code: 022023

2-year for-profit technical college in very large city.
Enrollment: 550 undergrads.
Selectivity: Open admission; but selective for some programs.

BASIC COSTS (2005-2006)
Additional info: Depending on program, cost ranges from $8,000 to $28,800, includes lab fees, books, and registration fee.

FINANCIAL AID PICTURE
Students with need: Need-based aid available for full-time students.

FINANCIAL AID PROCEDURES
Forms required: FAFSA.
Dates and Deadlines: No deadline. Applicants notified on a rolling basis.

CONTACT
Eileen Randolph, Director of Financial Aid
421 Seventh Avenue, Pittsburgh, PA 15219
(412) 281-2600

Western School of Health and Business Careers: Monroeville
Monroeville, Pennsylvania
www.wshb-monroeville.com   Federal Code: 022023

2-year for-profit business and health science college in large town.
Enrollment: 525 undergrads.

BASIC COSTS (2005-2006)
Additional info: Tuition ranges from $8,825 for dental assistant diploma program to $17,925 for 15-month associate degree surgical technician program. Tuition includes books, registration and lab fees.

FINANCIAL AID PICTURE
Students with need: Need-based aid available for full-time and part-time students.

FINANCIAL AID PROCEDURES
Dates and Deadlines: No deadline. Applicants notified on a rolling basis.

CONTACT
Dana Stoudt, Director of Financial Aid
One Monroeville Center, Suite 125, Monroeville, PA 15146
(412) 373-6400 ext. 12

Westminster College
New Wilmington, Pennsylvania   Federal Code: 003392
www.westminster.edu   CSS Code: 2975

4-year private liberal arts college in small town, affiliated with Presbyterian Church (USA).
Enrollment: 1,387 undergrads, 1% part-time. 359 full-time freshmen.
Selectivity: Admits over 75% of applicants.

BASIC COSTS (2005-2006)
Tuition and fees: $22,680.
Per-credit charge: $680.
Room and board: $6,600.
Additional info: Tuition/fee waivers available for adults.

FINANCIAL AID PICTURE (2004-2005)
Students with need: 70% of average financial aid package awarded as scholarships/grants, 30% awarded as loans/jobs. Need-based aid available for part-time students.
Students without need: No-need awards available for academics, athletics.

FINANCIAL AID PROCEDURES
Forms required: FAFSA, CSS PROFILE, institutional form.
Dates and Deadlines: Closing date 5/1. Applicants notified on a rolling basis starting 3/1.

CONTACT
Robert Latta, Director of Financial Aid
Admissions, Westminster College, New Wilmington, PA 16172-0001
(724) 946-7102

Westmoreland County Community College
Youngwood, Pennsylvania
www.wccc-pa.edu   Federal Code: 010176

2-year public community college in small town.
Enrollment: 5,146 undergrads, 52% part-time. 675 full-time freshmen.
Selectivity: Open admission; but selective for some programs.

BASIC COSTS (2005-2006)
Tuition and fees: $2,100; out-of-district residents $4,050; out-of-state residents $6,000.
Per-credit charge: $65; out-of-district residents $130; out-of-state residents $195.
Additional info: Out of district and out of state students pay an addition $150 in fees.

FINANCIAL AID PICTURE
Students with need: Need-based aid available for full-time and part-time students. Work study available nights.
Students without need: No-need awards available for academics.

FINANCIAL AID PROCEDURES
Forms required: FAFSA, institutional form.
Dates and Deadlines: No deadline. Applicants notified on a rolling basis starting 5/1.

CONTACT
Gary Means, Director of Financial Aid
400 Armbrust Road, Youngwood, PA 15697-1895
(724) 925-4063

Widener University
Chester, Pennsylvania
www.widener.edu   Federal Code: 003313

4-year private university in large town.
Enrollment: 2,493 undergrads, 5% part-time. 645 full-time freshmen.
Selectivity: Admits over 75% of applicants.

BASIC COSTS (2006-2007)
Tuition and fees: $26,750.
Per-credit charge: $878.
Room and board: $9,640.
Additional info: $900 additional fee for engineering students.

FINANCIAL AID PICTURE (2005-2006)
Students with need: Out of 597 full-time freshmen who applied for aid, 541 were judged to have need. Of these, 539 received aid, and 104 had their full need met. Average financial aid package met 79% of need; average scholarship/grant was $12,330; average loan was $3,763. For part-time students, average financial aid package was $6,927.
Students without need: 75 full-time freshmen who did not demonstrate need for aid received scholarships/grants; average award was $8,812. No-need awards available for academics, leadership, music/drama, ROTC.
Scholarships offered: Academic scholarships: range from $4,000 to full tuition, based on high school SAT and GPA; all levels renewable. Transfer scholarships: ranging from $2,500 to $10,000, based on GPA and minimum of 24 transferable credits. Music, leadership and community service scholarships: based on performance evaluations.
Cumulative student debt: 79% of graduating class had student loans; average debt was $26,348.

FINANCIAL AID PROCEDURES
Forms required: FAFSA.
Dates and Deadlines: Priority date 2/15; no closing date. Applicants notified on a rolling basis starting 3/15; must reply within 4 week(s) of notification.

CONTACT
Thomas Malloy, Director of Financial Aid
One University Place, Chester, PA 19013
(610) 499-4174

Wilkes University
Wilkes-Barre, Pennsylvania
www.wilkes.edu   Federal Code: 003394

4-year private university in small city.
Enrollment: 2,147 undergrads, 8% part-time. 551 full-time freshmen.
Selectivity: Admits over 75% of applicants.

BASIC COSTS (2006-2007)
Tuition and fees: $22,990.
Per-credit charge: $605.
Room and board: $9,190.

FINANCIAL AID PICTURE (2004-2005)
Students with need: Out of 539 full-time freshmen who applied for aid, 474 were judged to have need. Of these, 472 received aid, and 78 had their full need met. Average financial aid package met 83% of need; average scholarship/grant was $13,264; average loan was $2,116. For part-time students, average financial aid package was $7,304.
Students without need: 75 full-time freshmen who did not demonstrate need for aid received scholarships/grants; average award was $9,163. No-need awards available for academics, leadership, minority status, music/drama.
Cumulative student debt: 82% of graduating class had student loans; average debt was $20,711.

FINANCIAL AID PROCEDURES
Forms required: FAFSA, institutional form.
Dates and Deadlines: Priority date 3/1; no closing date. Applicants notified on a rolling basis starting 2/21.

CONTACT
Rachael Lohman, Director of Financial Aid
Chase Hall/184 South River Street, Wilkes-Barre, PA 18766
(570) 408-4346

Wilson College
Chambersburg, Pennsylvania
www.wilson.edu   Federal Code: 003396

4-year private liberal arts college for women in large town, affiliated with Presbyterian Church (USA).
Enrollment: 516 undergrads, 37% part-time. 75 full-time freshmen.
Selectivity: Admits 50 to 75% of applicants.

BASIC COSTS (2005-2006)
Tuition and fees: $20,050.
Room and board: $7,610.

FINANCIAL AID PICTURE (2005-2006)
Students with need: Out of 68 full-time freshmen who applied for aid, 59 were judged to have need. Of these, 58 received aid, and 11 had their full need met. Average financial aid package met 74% of need; average scholarship/grant was $12,411; average loan was $3,345. For part-time students, average financial aid package was $5,269.
Students without need: 14 full-time freshmen who did not demonstrate need for aid received scholarships/grants; average award was $18,845. No-need awards available for academics, alumni affiliation, religious affiliation, state/district residency.
Scholarships offered: Scholarships for full-time students who are members of Presbyterian Church, USA. Curran Scholarships; awarded to incoming students with significant community service. Phoenix Merit Scholarships; $10,000; for full-time freshmen with 3.0 GPA and 1100 SAT or 24 ACT, or $5,000 for 3.0 GPA with 900 SAT or 19 ACT. SAT scores exclusive of Writing.
Cumulative student debt: 91% of graduating class had student loans; average debt was $25,534.

FINANCIAL AID PROCEDURES
Forms required: FAFSA, state aid form, institutional form.
Dates and Deadlines: Priority date 4/1; no closing date. Applicants notified on a rolling basis starting 2/15.
Transfers: Tuition scholarships available to transfer articulation students who hold associate degrees from Harrisburg Area Community College, Hagerstown Community College, Central Penn College, Luzerne County Community College, Lehigh Carbon Community College, Harcum College, Frederick Community College, and Howard Community College. Transfer Merit Scholarships for students with 3.0 GPA.

CONTACT
Linda Brittain, Associate Dean of Enrollment and Director of Financial Aid
1015 Philadelphia Avenue, Chambersburg, PA 17201-1285
(717) 262-2016

York College of Pennsylvania
York, Pennsylvania
www.ycp.edu   Federal Code: 003399

4-year private liberal arts college in small city.
Enrollment: 5,170 undergrads, 14% part-time. 1,079 full-time freshmen.
Selectivity: Admits 50 to 75% of applicants.

BASIC COSTS (2006-2007)
Tuition and fees: $11,160.
Per-credit charge: $318.
Room and board: $6,950.

FINANCIAL AID PICTURE (2005-2006)
Students with need: Out of 933 full-time freshmen who applied for aid, 558 were judged to have need. Of these, 550 received aid, and 109 had their full need met. Average financial aid package met 71% of need; average scholarship/grant was $4,225; average loan was $2,512. For part-time students, average financial aid package was $5,012.

Students without need: 148 full-time freshmen who did not demonstrate need for aid received scholarships/grants; average award was $3,134. No-need awards available for academics, art, music/drama.
Scholarships offered: Trustee Scholarships: full tuition, for students with top 20% class rank and SATs over 1210, 10 awarded. Valedictorian and Salutatorian Scholarships: half tuition, unlimited number awarded. Dean's Academic Scholarship: one-third tuition, to students with top 40% class rank, SATs over 1150, 175 awarded. SAT scores exclusive of the writing portion.
Cumulative student debt: 68% of graduating class had student loans; average debt was $18,198.

FINANCIAL AID PROCEDURES
Forms required: FAFSA.
Dates and Deadlines: Priority date 3/1; no closing date. Applicants notified on a rolling basis starting 2/15; must reply within 4 week(s) of notification.

CONTACT
Calvin Williams, Director of Financial Aid
441 Country Club Road, York, PA 17403-3651
(717) 849-1682

Yorktowne Business Institute
York, Pennsylvania
www.ybi.edu   Federal Code: 014766

2-year for-profit business and health science college in small city.
Enrollment: 315 undergrads.
Selectivity: Open admission; but selective for some programs.

BASIC COSTS (2005-2006)
Additional info: Tuition $17,625 for business and medical programs with $55 student fee, $27,225 for culinary program with $130 student fee. Tuition at time of enrollment locked for 2 years.

FINANCIAL AID PICTURE
Students with need: Need-based aid available for full-time and part-time students.

FINANCIAL AID PROCEDURES
Forms required: FAFSA, state aid form.
Dates and Deadlines: Priority date 5/1; no closing date.

CONTACT
Deborah Bostick, Financial Aid Director
West 7th Avenue, York, PA 17404-2034
(717) 846-5000

Puerto Rico

Atlantic College
Guaynabo, Puerto Rico
www.atlanticcollege-pr.com   Federal Code: 016871

4-year private visual arts and business college in small city.
Enrollment: 725 undergrads, 14% part-time. 133 full-time freshmen.
Selectivity: Open admission.

BASIC COSTS (2005-2006)
Tuition and fees: $4,230.
Per-credit charge: $105.
Additional info: Tuition at time of enrollment locked for 4 years.

FINANCIAL AID PICTURE
Students with need: Need-based aid available for full-time and part-time students. Work study available nights.
Students without need: This college only awards aid to students with need.

FINANCIAL AID PROCEDURES
Forms required: FAFSA, institutional form.
Dates and Deadlines: Closing date 6/30. Applicants notified on a rolling basis starting 4/1; must reply within 2 week(s) of notification.
Transfers: Priority date 1/7; closing date 6/7.

CONTACT
Velma Aponte, Coordinator
PO Box 3918, Guaynabo, PR 00970
(787) 789-4251

Bayamon Central University
Bayamon, Puerto Rico
www.ucb.edu.pr   Federal Code: 010015

4-year private university in large city, affiliated with Roman Catholic Church.
Enrollment: 2,465 undergrads, 19% part-time. 266 full-time freshmen.
Selectivity: Open admission; but selective for some programs and for out-of-state students.

BASIC COSTS (2005-2006)
Tuition and fees: $4,280.
Per-credit charge: $145.

FINANCIAL AID PICTURE
Students with need: Need-based aid available for full-time and part-time students. Work study available nights.
Students without need: This college only awards aid to students with need.

FINANCIAL AID PROCEDURES
Forms required: FAFSA, institutional form.
Dates and Deadlines: No deadline.
Transfers: Priority date 5/30.

CONTACT
Velma Aponte, Director of Financial Aid Office
PO Box 1725, Bayamon, PR 00960-1725
(787) 786-3030 ext. 2116

Columbia College
Caguas, Puerto Rico
www.columbiaco.edu

4-year for-profit business and technical college in small city.
Enrollment: 810 undergrads, 38% part-time. 235 full-time freshmen.
Selectivity: Open admission; but selective for some programs.

BASIC COSTS (2005-2006)
Tuition and fees: $4,030.

FINANCIAL AID PICTURE (2004-2005)
Students with need: Out of 212 full-time freshmen who applied for aid, 212 were judged to have need. Of these, 212 received aid. For part-time students, average financial aid package was $4,550.
Students without need: This college only awards aid to students with need.

CONTACT
Virginia Guang, Financial Aid Administrator
PO Box 8517, Caguas, PR 00726
(787) 743-4041 ext. 223

Conservatory of Music of Puerto Rico
San Juan, Puerto Rico
www.cmpr.edu
Federal Code: 010819

4-year public music college in large city.
Enrollment: 304 undergrads, 28% part-time. 77 full-time freshmen.
Selectivity: Admits 50 to 75% of applicants.

FINANCIAL AID PICTURE (2004-2005)
Students with need: Out of 39 full-time freshmen who applied for aid, 39 were judged to have need. Of these, 39 received aid. Average financial aid package met 40% of need; average scholarship/grant was $927. Need-based aid available for part-time students.
Students without need: This college only awards aid to students with need.
Cumulative student debt: 6% of graduating class had student loans; average debt was $15,000.

FINANCIAL AID PROCEDURES
Forms required: FAFSA, institutional form.
Dates and Deadlines: Priority date 6/30; no closing date. Applicants notified on a rolling basis starting 8/30.
Transfers: Closing date 4/15.

CONTACT
Jorge Medina, Financial Aid Officer
Rafael Lamar # 350 Esq. Roosevelt, San Juan, PR 00918-2199
(787) 751-0160 ext. 231

Humacao Community College
Humacao, Puerto Rico
www.humacaocommunitycollege.com
Federal Code: 014952

2-year private business and community college in large city.
Enrollment: 501 undergrads, 30% part-time. 127 full-time freshmen.
Selectivity: Open admission.

BASIC COSTS (2005-2006)
Tuition and fees: $4,275.
Per-credit charge: $100.

FINANCIAL AID PICTURE
Students with need: Need-based aid available for full-time and part-time students. Work study available nights.
Students without need: This college only awards aid to students with need.

FINANCIAL AID PROCEDURES
Forms required: FAFSA, state aid form, institutional form.
Dates and Deadlines: Priority date 1/1; closing date 6/30. Applicants notified on a rolling basis starting 3/4.
Transfers: No deadline.

CONTACT
Carmen Delgado, Financial Aid Director
PO Box 9139, Humacao, PR 00792
(787) 852-1430 ext. 28

Inter American University of Puerto Rico: Aguadilla Campus
Aguadilla, Puerto Rico
www.aguadilla.inter.edu
Federal Code: 003939

4-year private university and liberal arts college in small city.
Enrollment: 4,059 undergrads, 15% part-time. 843 full-time freshmen.

BASIC COSTS (2005-2006)
Tuition and fees: $4,564.
Per-credit charge: $140.
Additional info: Tuition at time of enrollment locked for 4 years.

FINANCIAL AID PICTURE
Students with need: Need-based aid available for full-time and part-time students. Work study available nights, weekends, and for part-time students.
Students without need: No-need awards available for academics.

FINANCIAL AID PROCEDURES
Forms required: FAFSA.
Dates and Deadlines: Closing date 4/30. Applicants notified by 6/15; must reply by 8/8.
Transfers: No deadline.

CONTACT
Juan Gonzalez, Director of Financial Aid
Box 20000, Aguadilla, PR 00605
(787) 891-0925 ext. 2110

Inter American University of Puerto Rico: Barranquitas Campus
Barranquitas, Puerto Rico
www.br.inter.edu
Federal Code: 005027

4-year private university and branch campus college in large town.
Enrollment: 2,297 undergrads, 18% part-time. 380 full-time freshmen.
Selectivity: Admits less than 50% of applicants.

BASIC COSTS (2005-2006)
Tuition and fees: $4,564.
Per-credit charge: $140.
Additional info: Tuition at time of enrollment locked for 4 years; tuition/fee waivers available for adults, minority students.

FINANCIAL AID PICTURE (2005-2006)
Students with need: Average financial aid package met 1% of need; average scholarship/grant was $87; average loan was $172. For part-time students, average financial aid package was $148.
Students without need: This college only awards aid to students with need.
Cumulative student debt: 12% of graduating class had student loans; average debt was $6,000.

FINANCIAL AID PROCEDURES
Forms required: FAFSA.
Dates and Deadlines: Closing date 4/30. Applicants notified on a rolling basis; must reply within 2 week(s) of notification.

CONTACT
Eduardo Fontanez, Director of Financial Aid
PO Box 517, Barranquitas, PR 00794
(787) 857-3600 ext. 2050

Inter American University of Puerto Rico: Bayamon Campus
Bayamon, Puerto Rico
www.bc.inter.edu
Federal Code: 003938

4-year private university and engineering college in small city.
Enrollment: 5,184 undergrads, 17% part-time. 1,249 full-time freshmen.
Selectivity: Admits less than 50% of applicants.

BASIC COSTS (2005-2006)
Tuition and fees: $4,612.
Per-credit charge: $140.

FINANCIAL AID PICTURE (2004-2005)
Students with need: Out of 1,209 full-time freshmen who applied for aid, 1,179 were judged to have need. Of these, 861 received aid, and 7 had their full need met. Average financial aid package met 3% of need; average scholarship/grant was $270; average loan was $291. For part-time students, average financial aid package was $178.
Students without need: This college only awards aid to students with need.
Scholarships offered: 8 full-time freshmen received athletic scholarships; average amount $183.

FINANCIAL AID PROCEDURES
Forms required: FAFSA.
Dates and Deadlines: Priority date 6/30; no closing date. Applicants notified on a rolling basis starting 5/10.

CONTACT
Hector Vargas, Interim Director of Financial Aid
500 Dr. John Will Harris Road, Bayamon, PR 00957
(787) 279-1912 ext. 2025

Inter American University of Puerto Rico: Fajardo Campus
Fajardo, Puerto Rico
fajardo.inter.edu   Federal Code: 010763

4-year private university and branch campus college in large town, affiliated with nondenominational tradition.
Enrollment: 2,206 undergrads. 481 full-time freshmen.
Selectivity: Admits less than 50% of applicants.

BASIC COSTS (2005-2006)
Tuition and fees: $4,200.
Per-credit charge: $140.

FINANCIAL AID PICTURE (2004-2005)
Students with need: Out of 467 full-time freshmen who applied for aid, 460 were judged to have need. Of these, 406 received aid, and 1 had their full need met. Average financial aid package met 2% of need; average scholarship/grant was $129; average loan was $278. For part-time students, average financial aid package was $200.
Scholarships offered: 2 full-time freshmen received athletic scholarships; average amount $301.

FINANCIAL AID PROCEDURES
Forms required: FAFSA, institutional form.
Dates and Deadlines: Closing date 4/30. Applicants notified on a rolling basis.

CONTACT
Lydia Santiago, Dean of Administration
PO Box 70003, Fajardo, PR 00738-7003
(787) 863-2390 ext. 2241

Inter American University of Puerto Rico: Guayama Campus
Guayama, Puerto Rico
www.inter.edu   Federal Code: 010764

4-year private university in large town.
Enrollment: 2,155 undergrads, 19% part-time. 441 full-time freshmen.
Selectivity: Admits over 75% of applicants.

BASIC COSTS (2005-2006)
Tuition and fees: $4,564.
Per-credit charge: $140.

FINANCIAL AID PICTURE (2004-2005)
Students with need: Out of 437 full-time freshmen who applied for aid, 427 were judged to have need. Of these, 298 received aid. Average financial aid package met 3% of need; average scholarship/grant was $128; average loan was $298. For part-time students, average financial aid package was $278.
Students without need: This college only awards aid to students with need.
Scholarships offered: 4 full-time freshmen received athletic scholarships; average amount $506.

FINANCIAL AID PROCEDURES
Forms required: FAFSA, institutional form.
Dates and Deadlines: Closing date 4/29. Applicants notified by 6/15; must reply by 7/30.
Transfers: No deadline.

CONTACT
Jose Vechini Rodriguez, Director of Financial Aid
PO Box 10004, Guayama, PR 00785
(787) 864-2222 ext. 2206

Inter American University of Puerto Rico: Ponce Campus
Mercedita, Puerto Rico
ponce.inter.edu   Federal Code: 005029

4-year private university in large town.
Enrollment: 5,146 undergrads, 17% part-time. 1,249 full-time freshmen.
Selectivity: Admits 50 to 75% of applicants.

BASIC COSTS (2005-2006)
Tuition and fees: $4,576.
Per-credit charge: $140.

FINANCIAL AID PICTURE (2004-2005)
Students with need: Out of 894 full-time freshmen who applied for aid, 846 were judged to have need. Of these, 600 received aid, and 1 had their full need met. Average financial aid package met 2% of need; average scholarship/grant was $127; average loan was $270.
Students without need: This college only awards aid to students with need.
Scholarships offered: Scholarship program for first-time freshmen with a high school academic index of 3.0 or higher.

FINANCIAL AID PROCEDURES
Forms required: FAFSA.
Dates and Deadlines: No deadline.

CONTACT
Juan Portalatin, Director of Financial Aid
104 Turpo Industrial Park Road #1, Mercedita, PR 00715-1602
(787) 841-0102

Inter American University of Puerto Rico: San German Campus
San German, Puerto Rico
www.sg.inter.edu   Federal Code: 00714

4-year private university in large town.
Enrollment: 4,872 undergrads, 13% part-time. 194 full-time freshmen.

BASIC COSTS (2005-2006)
Tuition and fees: $4,616.
Per-credit charge: $140.
Room and board: $2,400.
Additional info: Tuition at time of enrollment locked for 4 years.

FINANCIAL AID PICTURE (2004-2005)
Students with need: Out of 172 full-time freshmen who applied for aid, 142 were judged to have need. Of these, 78 received aid, and 4 had their full need met. Average financial aid package met 1% of need; average scholarship/grant was $14; average loan was $30. For part-time students, average financial aid package was $296.
Students without need: No-need awards available for academics, athletics.
Scholarships offered: 6 full-time freshmen received athletic scholarships; average amount $137.

FINANCIAL AID PROCEDURES
Forms required: FAFSA, institutional form.
Dates and Deadlines: Closing date 5/14. Applicants notified on a rolling basis; must reply by 8/1.

CONTACT
Maria Lugo, Director of Financial Aid
Box 5100, San German, PR 00683-9801
(787) 264-1912

National College of Business & Technology: Arecibo
Arecibo, Puerto Rico
www.nationalcollegepr.edu   Federal Code: 015953

2-year for-profit business college in small city.
Enrollment: 1,439 undergrads.

FINANCIAL AID PICTURE
Students with need: Need-based aid available for full-time and part-time students. Work study available nights, weekends, and for part-time students.

FINANCIAL AID PROCEDURES
Dates and Deadlines: Priority date 12/31; closing date 4/29. Applicants notified on a rolling basis starting 5/2; must reply by 5/15 or within 2 week(s) of notification.

CONTACT
Desi Lopez-Padilla, Vice President of Development and Financial Aid
Arecibo Centro Plaza, Arecibo, PR 00614
(787) 780-5134 ext. 4110

National College of Business & Technology: Bayamon
Bayamon, Puerto Rico
www.nationalcollegepr.edu   Federal Code: 015953

2-year for-profit business and technical college in small city.
Enrollment: 2,102 undergrads. 690 full-time freshmen.
Selectivity: Open admission; but selective for some programs.

BASIC COSTS (2005-2006)
Per-credit charge: $120.

FINANCIAL AID PICTURE (2004-2005)
Students with need: Out of 662 full-time freshmen who applied for aid, 649 were judged to have need. Of these, 649 received aid. Average financial aid package met 60% of need; average scholarship/grant was $4,650; average loan was $2,000. For part-time students, average financial aid package was $2,325.
Students without need: This college only awards aid to students with need.

FINANCIAL AID PROCEDURES
Forms required: FAFSA.
Dates and Deadlines: Priority date 12/31; closing date 4/29. Applicants notified on a rolling basis starting 5/2; must reply by 5/15 or within 2 week(s) of notification.
Transfers: No deadline.

CONTACT
Desi Lopez, Vice President of Financial Aid and Compliance
PO Box 2036, Highway 2, Bayamon, PR 00960
(787) 780-5134 ext. 4403

Pontifical Catholic University of Puerto Rico
Ponce, Puerto Rico
www.pucpr.edu   Federal Code: 003936

4-year private university in small city, affiliated with Roman Catholic Church.
Enrollment: 7,273 undergrads.
Selectivity: Admits 50 to 75% of applicants.

FINANCIAL AID PICTURE (2005-2006)
Students with need: Average financial aid package met 71% of need; average scholarship/grant was $4,300; average loan was $1,000. Need-based aid available for part-time students.
Students without need: No-need awards available for academics, athletics.
Cumulative student debt: 70% of graduating class had student loans; average debt was $3,500.

FINANCIAL AID PROCEDURES
Forms required: FAFSA, institutional form.
Dates and Deadlines: Priority date 5/1; no closing date. Applicants notified by 6/15; must reply within 4 week(s) of notification.
Transfers: Priority date 5/8. Distribution of awards based on availability of funds when application received.

CONTACT
Rosalia Martinez, Director of Financial Aid
2250 Las Americas Avenue, Suite 284, Ponce, PR 00717-9777
(787) 841-2000 ext. 1054

Universidad Adventista de las Antillas
Mayaguez, Puerto Rico
www.uaa.edu   Federal Code: 005019

4-year private university and liberal arts college in small city, affiliated with Seventh-day Adventists.
Enrollment: 760 undergrads, 7% part-time. 152 full-time freshmen.
Selectivity: Open admission; but selective for some programs.

BASIC COSTS (2006-2007)
Tuition and fees: $6,060.
Per-credit charge: $130.
Room and board: $1,300.
Additional info: Tuition for nonresident aliens is the sum of private tuition ($3680) and the Form I-20 deposit ($4000); after the first year, these students receive credit refund at registration ($500 per semester).

FINANCIAL AID PICTURE
Students with need: Need-based aid available for full-time and part-time students.

FINANCIAL AID PROCEDURES
Forms required: FAFSA, institutional form.

Dates and Deadlines: No deadline. Applicants notified on a rolling basis starting 8/15; must reply within 3 week(s) of notification.

CONTACT
Heriberto Juarbe, Director of Financial Aid
PO Box 118, Mayaguez, PR 00681-0118
(787) 834-9595

Universidad del Este
Carolina, Puerto Rico
www.suagm.edu   Federal Code: 011718

4-year private business and liberal arts college in small city.
Enrollment: 10,136 undergrads, 27% part-time. 1,865 full-time freshmen.
Selectivity: Open admission; but selective for some programs.

FINANCIAL AID PICTURE (2004-2005)
Students with need: 88% of average financial aid package awarded as scholarships/grants, 12% awarded as loans/jobs. Need-based aid available for part-time students.
Students without need: No-need awards available for academics, athletics.

FINANCIAL AID PROCEDURES
Forms required: FAFSA, state aid form, institutional form.
Dates and Deadlines: Priority date 5/30; no closing date. Applicants notified by 7/30.

CONTACT
Clotilde Santiago, Admissions and Financial Aid Director
PO Box 2010, Carolina, PR 00981-2010
(787) 257-7373 ext. 3401

Universidad Metropolitana
Rio Piedras, Puerto Rico
www.suagm.edu/umet   Federal Code: 025875

4-year private university and liberal arts college in large city.
Enrollment: 9,046 undergrads, 21% part-time. 1,792 full-time freshmen.

BASIC COSTS (2005-2006)
Tuition and fees: $3,872.

FINANCIAL AID PICTURE (2004-2005)
Students with need: Need-based aid available for part-time students. Work study available nights.
Students without need: This college only awards aid to students with need.

FINANCIAL AID PROCEDURES
Forms required: FAFSA.
Dates and Deadlines: Priority date 5/30; no closing date. Applicants notified by 7/30.

CONTACT
Evelyn Robledo, Admissions and Financial Aid Director
Apartado 21150, Rio Piedras, PR 00928
(787) 766-1717 ext. 6587

Universidad Politecnica de Puerto Rico
Hato Rey, Puerto Rico
www.pupr.edu   Federal Code: 014055

5-year private university and engineering college in large city.
Enrollment: 5,070 undergrads, 50% part-time. 863 full-time freshmen.
Selectivity: Admits over 75% of applicants.

BASIC COSTS (2005-2006)
Tuition and fees: $5,922.

FINANCIAL AID PICTURE
Students with need: Need-based aid available for full-time and part-time students.
Students without need: No-need awards available for academics, music/drama.

FINANCIAL AID PROCEDURES
Forms required: FAFSA, institutional form.
Dates and Deadlines: Closing date 6/30. Applicants notified by 7/15.

CONTACT
Lydia Cruz, Director of Financial Aid
PO Box 192017, San Juan, PR 00918-2017
(787) 622-8000 ext. 249

University College of San Juan
San Juan, Puerto Rico
www.cunisanjuan.edu   Federal Code: 010567

2-year public community and technical college in very large city.
Enrollment: 961 undergrads, 16% part-time. 216 full-time freshmen.
Selectivity: Admits over 75% of applicants.

BASIC COSTS (2006-2007)
Tuition and fees: $2,380.
Per-credit charge: $85.
Additional info: Tuition at time of enrollment locked for 2 years.

FINANCIAL AID PICTURE
Students with need: Need-based aid available for full-time and part-time students.
Students without need: This college only awards aid to students with need.

FINANCIAL AID PROCEDURES
Forms required: FAFSA, institutional form.
Dates and Deadlines: Closing date 9/30. Applicants notified by 10/30.
Transfers: Financial aid transcripts.

CONTACT
Maria de los A. Quinones, Director of Financial Aid
180 Jose R. Oliver Avenue, San Juan, PR 00918
(787) 250-7111 ext. 2286

University of Puerto Rico: Aguadilla
Aguadilla, Puerto Rico
www.uprag.edu   Federal Code: 012123

4-year public liberal arts and technical college in small city.
Enrollment: 2,969 undergrads, 12% part-time. 761 full-time freshmen.
Selectivity: Admits less than 50% of applicants.

BASIC COSTS (2005-2006)
Tuition and fees: $1,344; out-of-state residents $3,192.
Per-credit charge: $40.

FINANCIAL AID PICTURE (2004-2005)
Students with need: 83% of average financial aid package awarded as scholarships/grants, 17% awarded as loans/jobs. Need-based aid available for part-time students.
Students without need: This college only awards aid to students with need.

FINANCIAL AID PROCEDURES
Forms required: FAFSA, institutional form.

Dates and Deadlines: Closing date 5/6. Applicants notified on a rolling basis starting 4/1; must reply within 1 week(s) of notification.
Transfers: No deadline.

CONTACT
Doris Roman, Financial Aid Director
Box 250160, Aguadilla, PR 00604
(787) 890-0109

University of Puerto Rico: Arecibo
Arecibo, Puerto Rico
www.upra.edu   Federal Code: 007228

4-year public university in small city.
Enrollment: 3,931 undergrads, 12% part-time. 938 full-time freshmen.
Selectivity: Admits less than 50% of applicants.

BASIC COSTS (2005-2006)
Tuition and fees: $1,691; out-of-state residents $3,539.
Per-credit charge: $40.

FINANCIAL AID PICTURE (2004-2005)
Students with need: Out of 938 full-time freshmen who applied for aid, 740 were judged to have need. Of these, 740 received aid. Need-based aid available for part-time students.
Students without need: This college only awards aid to students with need.

FINANCIAL AID PROCEDURES
Forms required: FAFSA, institutional form.
Dates and Deadlines: Closing date 4/27.
Transfers: Closing date 5/27.

CONTACT
Luis Rodriguez, Financial Aid Officer
PO Box 4010, Arecibo, PR 00614-4010
(787) 815-0000 ext. 4501

University of Puerto Rico: Carolina Regional College
Carolina, Puerto Rico
www.uprc.edu   Federal Code: 003942

4-year public university in small city.
Enrollment: 3,879 undergrads, 30% part-time. 677 full-time freshmen.

BASIC COSTS (2005-2006)
Tuition and fees: $2,256; out-of-state residents $3,192.
Per-credit charge: $40.

FINANCIAL AID PICTURE
Students with need: Out of 677 full-time freshmen who applied for aid, 677 were judged to have need. Of these, 677 received aid. Average financial aid package met 42% of need; average scholarship/grant was $697.
Students without need: This college only awards aid to students with need.

FINANCIAL AID PROCEDURES
Forms required: FAFSA, institutional form.
Dates and Deadlines: Closing date 5/15. Applicants notified on a rolling basis starting 6/10.

CONTACT
Santa Castro, Financial Aid Officer/Director
PO Box 4800, Carolina, PR 00984-4800
(787) 769-0188

University of Puerto Rico: Cayey University College
Cayey, Puerto Rico
www.cayey.upr.edu   Federal Code: 007206

4-year public liberal arts college in large town.
Enrollment: 3,668 undergrads, 13% part-time. 633 full-time freshmen.
Selectivity: Admits 50 to 75% of applicants.

BASIC COSTS (2005-2006)
Tuition and fees: $1,344; out-of-state residents $3,192.
Per-credit charge: $40.
Additional info: Tuition at time of enrollment locked for 4 years.

FINANCIAL AID PICTURE (2005-2006)
Students with need: Out of 568 full-time freshmen who applied for aid, 505 were judged to have need. Of these, 505 received aid. Need-based aid available for part-time students.
Students without need: This college only awards aid to students with need.

FINANCIAL AID PROCEDURES
Forms required: FAFSA.
Dates and Deadlines: Closing date 6/30. Applicants notified by 7/30.
Transfers: Priority date 1/30; closing date 2/28.

CONTACT
Maribel Cardin, Director of Financial Aid
Oficina de Admisiones UPR- Cayey, Cayey, PR 00736
(787) 738-2161 ext. 2061

University of Puerto Rico: Humacao
Humacao, Puerto Rico
www.uprh.edu   Federal Code: 003942

4-year public university and liberal arts college in small city.
Enrollment: 3,976 undergrads, 12% part-time. 856 full-time freshmen.
Selectivity: Admits less than 50% of applicants.

BASIC COSTS (2005-2006)
Tuition and fees: $1,344; out-of-state residents $3,336.
Per-credit charge: $40.

FINANCIAL AID PICTURE (2004-2005)
Students with need: 90% of average financial aid package awarded as scholarships/grants, 10% awarded as loans/jobs. Need-based aid available for part-time students.
Students without need: No-need awards available for academics, athletics, music/drama.

FINANCIAL AID PROCEDURES
Forms required: FAFSA, institutional form.
Dates and Deadlines: Closing date 7/31. Applicants notified by 9/30.

CONTACT
Mariolga Rotger, Director of Financial Aid
100 Road 908 CUH Station, Humacao, PR 00791
(787) 850-0000 ext. 9342

University of Puerto Rico: Ponce
Ponce, Puerto Rico
upr-ponce.upr.edu   Federal Code: 009652

4-year public university and branch campus college in small city.
Enrollment: 3,158 undergrads, 9% part-time. 749 full-time freshmen.

Selectivity: Admits less than 50% of applicants.

BASIC COSTS (2005-2006)
Tuition and fees: $1,344; out-of-state residents $3,336.
Per-credit charge: $40.

FINANCIAL AID PICTURE (2005-2006)
Students with need: 87% of average financial aid package awarded as scholarships/grants, 13% awarded as loans/jobs.
Students without need: This college only awards aid to students with need.

FINANCIAL AID PROCEDURES
Forms required: FAFSA, institutional form.
Dates and Deadlines: Closing date 5/30. Applicants notified by 10/15.

CONTACT
Carmelo Vega, Financial Aid Officer
Box 7186, Ponce, PR 00732
(787) 844-8181 ext. 2555

University of Puerto Rico: Rio Piedras
San Juan, Puerto Rico
www.rrp.upr.edu   Federal Code: 007108

4-year public university in large city.
Enrollment: 16,407 undergrads, 18% part-time. 2,363 full-time freshmen.
Selectivity: Admits less than 50% of applicants.

BASIC COSTS (2005-2006)
Tuition and fees: $1,344; out-of-state residents $3,336.
Per-credit charge: $40.
Room and board: $6,620.
Additional info: Tuition is based on per-credit-hour charge. For 2005-06 undergraduate credit cost is $40. First-time, first-year students take 12 to 15 credits per semester. Per-term required fees are: construction $47, technologies $25. Annual required fees ($216) represent 3 terms (first and second semester and one summer session).

FINANCIAL AID PICTURE (2005-2006)
Students with need: Need-based aid available for part-time students.
Students without need: This college only awards aid to students with need.
Additional info: Tuition waived for honor students, athletes, members of chorus, and others with special talents.

FINANCIAL AID PROCEDURES
Forms required: FAFSA.

CONTACT
Luz Santiago, Director of Financial Aid
Box 23344, San Juan, PR 00931-3344

University of Puerto Rico: Utuado
Utuado, Puerto Rico
http://upr-utuado.upr.clu.edu/   Federal Code: 010922

4-year public agricultural college in large town.
Enrollment: 1,395 undergrads, 11% part-time. 474 full-time freshmen.
Selectivity: Admits less than 50% of applicants. GED not accepted.

BASIC COSTS (2005-2006)
Tuition and fees: $1,344; out-of-state residents $3,336.
Per-credit charge: $40.

FINANCIAL AID PICTURE
Students with need: Need-based aid available for full-time and part-time students. Work study available nights.
Students without need: This college only awards aid to students with need.

FINANCIAL AID PROCEDURES
Forms required: FAFSA.
Dates and Deadlines: Priority date 5/31; no closing date. Applicants notified on a rolling basis starting 9/30; must reply within 4 week(s) of notification.
Transfers: Priority date 5/30; closing date 6/15. Closing date for Pell grant applicants is March 31.

CONTACT
Edgar Salva, Financial Assistance Officer
PO Box 2500, Utuado, PR 00641
(787) 894-2828 ext. 2603

University of the Sacred Heart
Santurce, Puerto Rico
www.sagrado.edu   Federal Code: 003937

4-year private university and liberal arts college in large city, affiliated with Roman Catholic Church.
Enrollment: 4,324 undergrads, 20% part-time. 993 full-time freshmen.

BASIC COSTS (2005-2006)
Tuition and fees: $5,210.
Per-credit charge: $150.
Room only: $1,900.

FINANCIAL AID PICTURE
Students with need: Need-based aid available for full-time and part-time students.
Students without need: No-need awards available for academics, athletics.

FINANCIAL AID PROCEDURES
Forms required: FAFSA, institutional form.
Dates and Deadlines: Closing date 5/30. Applicants notified on a rolling basis starting 6/15; must reply by 8/30.
Transfers: No deadline.

CONTACT
Luis Aquiles, Director, Financial Aid
Universidad del Sagrado Corazon Oficina de Nuevo Ingreso, San Juan, PR 00914-0383

Rhode Island

Brown University
Providence, Rhode Island   Federal Code: 003401
www.brown.edu   CSS Code: 3094

4-year private university and liberal arts college in small city.
Enrollment: 5,927 undergrads, 1% part-time. 1,440 full-time freshmen.
Selectivity: Admits less than 50% of applicants. GED not accepted.

BASIC COSTS (2006-2007)
Tuition and fees: $35,352.
Room and board: $9,134.

FINANCIAL AID PICTURE
Students with need: Need-based aid available for full-time and part-time students.
Students without need: This college only awards aid to students with need.

FINANCIAL AID PROCEDURES
Forms required: FAFSA, CSS PROFILE.

Dates and Deadlines: Closing date 2/1. Applicants notified by 4/1; must reply by 5/1.
Transfers: Closing date 4/15.

CONTACT
Michael Bartini, Director of Financial Aid
45 Prospect Street, Providence, RI 02912
(401) 863-2721

Bryant University
Smithfield, Rhode Island
www.bryant.edu   Federal Code: 003402

4-year private business and liberal arts college in large town.
Enrollment: 3,177 undergrads, 5% part-time. 761 full-time freshmen.
Selectivity: Admits 50 to 75% of applicants.

BASIC COSTS (2006-2007)
Tuition and fees: $26,099.
Per-credit charge: $313.
Room and board: $10,293.
Additional info: Tuition includes cost of laptop computer. $500 non-refundable enrollment commitment deposit is required of both residents and commuters.

FINANCIAL AID PICTURE (2005-2006)
Students with need: Out of 531 full-time freshmen who applied for aid, 460 were judged to have need. Of these, 460 received aid, and 67 had their full need met. Average financial aid package met 77% of need; average scholarship/grant was $10,040; average loan was $4,390. For part-time students, average financial aid package was $5,347.
Students without need: 63 full-time freshmen who did not demonstrate need for aid received scholarships/grants; average award was $8,500. No-need awards available for athletics, minority status, ROTC.
Scholarships offered: 14 full-time freshmen received athletic scholarships; average amount $11,519.

FINANCIAL AID PROCEDURES
Forms required: FAFSA.
Dates and Deadlines: Closing date 2/15. Applicants notified by 3/24; must reply by 5/1.
Transfers: Closing date 4/1.

CONTACT
John Canning, Director of Financial Aid
1150 Douglas Pike, Smithfield, RI 02917
(401) 232-6020

Community College of Rhode Island
Warwick, Rhode Island
www.ccri.edu   Federal Code: 004916

2-year public community college in small city.
Enrollment: 13,086 undergrads, 60% part-time. 1,918 full-time freshmen.
Selectivity: Open admission; but selective for some programs.

BASIC COSTS (2005-2006)
Tuition and fees: $2,470; out-of-state residents $6,700.
Per-credit charge: $102; out-of-state residents $307.
Additional info: Tuition/fee waivers available for unemployed or children of unemployed.

FINANCIAL AID PICTURE
Students with need: Need-based aid available for full-time and part-time students. Work study available nights, weekends, and for part-time students.
Students without need: No-need awards available for athletics.

FINANCIAL AID PROCEDURES
Forms required: FAFSA, institutional form.
Dates and Deadlines: Priority date 3/1; no closing date. Applicants notified on a rolling basis starting 5/1; must reply within 2 week(s) of notification.

CONTACT
Christine Jenkins, Associate Dean of Enrollment Services
400 East Avenue, Warwick, RI 02886-1807
(401) 455-6006

Johnson & Wales University
Providence, Rhode Island
www.jwu.edu   Federal Code: 003404

4-year private university in small city.
Enrollment: 9,335 undergrads, 10% part-time. 2,429 full-time freshmen.
Selectivity: Admits over 75% of applicants.

BASIC COSTS (2006-2007)
Tuition and fees: $20,826.
Per-credit charge: $368.
Room and board: $9,300.
Additional info: Tuition at time of enrollment locked for 4 years.

FINANCIAL AID PICTURE (2005-2006)
Students with need: Out of 2,069 full-time freshmen who applied for aid, 1,793 were judged to have need. Of these, 1,784 received aid, and 44 had their full need met. Average financial aid package met 63% of need; average scholarship/grant was $5,175; average loan was $6,203. For part-time students, average financial aid package was $5,107.
Students without need: 291 full-time freshmen who did not demonstrate need for aid received scholarships/grants; average award was $4,090. No-need awards available for academics, leadership.
Cumulative student debt: 68% of graduating class had student loans; average debt was $17,704.

FINANCIAL AID PROCEDURES
Forms required: FAFSA.
Dates and Deadlines: No deadline. Applicants notified on a rolling basis starting 3/1; must reply within 2 week(s) of notification.
Transfers: Transfer scholarships available.

CONTACT
Lynn Robinson, Director of Financial Aid
8 Abbott Park Place, Providence, RI 02903-3703
(800) 342-5598 ext. 4648

New England Institute of Technology
Warwick, Rhode Island
www.neit.edu   Federal Code: 007845

4-year private technical college in small city.
Enrollment: 3,066 undergrads.
Selectivity: Open admission.

BASIC COSTS (2006-2007)
Tuition and fees: $15,765.
Per-credit charge: $375.
Additional info: Fees vary from $1,365 to $2,415 according to program. Tuition at time of enrollment locked for 4 years.

FINANCIAL AID PICTURE
Students with need: Need-based aid available for full-time and part-time students.
Students without need: No-need awards available for academics.

Additional info: Tuition at time of first enrollment guaranteed all students for 2 years.

FINANCIAL AID PROCEDURES
Forms required: FAFSA, institutional form.
Dates and Deadlines: Priority date 6/1; no closing date. Applicants notified on a rolling basis starting 6/15.

CONTACT
Larry Blair, Director of Financial Aid
2500 Post Road, Warwick, RI 02886-2286
(401) 467-7744

Providence College
Providence, Rhode Island
www.providence.edu
Federal Code: 003406
CSS Code: 3693

4-year private liberal arts college in small city, affiliated with Roman Catholic Church.
Enrollment: 3,889 undergrads. 1,067 full-time freshmen.
Selectivity: Admits 50 to 75% of applicants. GED not accepted.

BASIC COSTS (2006-2007)
Tuition and fees: $27,345.
Per-credit charge: $893.
Room and board: $9,765.
Additional info: Tuition/fee waivers available for minority students.

FINANCIAL AID PICTURE (2005-2006)
Students with need: Out of 785 full-time freshmen who applied for aid, 579 were judged to have need. Of these, 579 received aid, and 122 had their full need met. Average financial aid package met 88% of need; average scholarship/grant was $12,796; average loan was $3,625. Need-based aid available for part-time students.
Students without need: 128 full-time freshmen who did not demonstrate need for aid received scholarships/grants; average award was $7,500. No-need awards available for academics, athletics, minority status, ROTC.
Scholarships offered: 54 full-time freshmen received athletic scholarships; average amount $13,766.
Cumulative student debt: 65% of graduating class had student loans; average debt was $23,000.

FINANCIAL AID PROCEDURES
Forms required: FAFSA, CSS PROFILE.
Dates and Deadlines: Closing date 2/1. Applicants notified by 4/1; must reply by 5/1.
Transfers: Closing date 4/15. Applicants notified by 6/30.

CONTACT
Sandra Olivira, Executive Director, Financial Aid
Harkins Hall 222, 549 River Avenue, Providence, RI 02918-0001
(401) 865-2286

Rhode Island College
Providence, Rhode Island
www.ric.edu
Federal Code: 003407

4-year public liberal arts college in small city.
Enrollment: 7,097 undergrads, 27% part-time. 1,073 full-time freshmen.
Selectivity: Admits 50 to 75% of applicants.

BASIC COSTS (2005-2006)
Tuition and fees: $4,796; out-of-state residents $12,108.
Per-credit charge: $168; out-of-state residents $466.
Room and board: $6,750.

Additional info: Tuition/fee waivers available for unemployed or children of unemployed.

FINANCIAL AID PICTURE
Students with need: Need-based aid available for full-time and part-time students. Work study available nights, weekends, and for part-time students.
Students without need: No-need awards available for academics, alumni affiliation, art, music/drama.
Scholarships offered: Presidential Scholarships; $2,000 per year; for entering freshmen in the top 30% of class with minimum combined SAT score of 1100 (exclusive of Writing) who apply for admission by Dec 15; approximately 100 awards available to each entering class.

FINANCIAL AID PROCEDURES
Forms required: FAFSA, institutional form.
Dates and Deadlines: Priority date 3/1; no closing date. Applicants notified on a rolling basis starting 3/15; must reply within 3 week(s) of notification.
Transfers: Priority date 5/15.

CONTACT
James Hanbury, Director of Financial Aid
600 Mount Pleasant Avenue, Providence, RI 02908
(401) 456-8033

Rhode Island School of Design
Providence, Rhode Island
www.risd.edu
Federal Code: 003409
CSS Code: 3726

4-year private visual arts college in small city.
Enrollment: 1,878 undergrads. 405 full-time freshmen.
Selectivity: Admits less than 50% of applicants.

BASIC COSTS (2006-2007)
Tuition and fees: $31,430.
Per-credit charge: $1,035.
Room and board: $9,360.

FINANCIAL AID PICTURE (2004-2005)
Students with need: Out of 231 full-time freshmen who applied for aid, 184 were judged to have need. Of these, 175 received aid, and 21 had their full need met. Average financial aid package met 66% of need; average scholarship/grant was $12,340; average loan was $3,100.
Students without need: 2 full-time freshmen who did not demonstrate need for aid received scholarships/grants; average award was $10,000.

FINANCIAL AID PROCEDURES
Forms required: FAFSA, CSS PROFILE.
Dates and Deadlines: Closing date 2/15. Applicants notified by 4/1; must reply by 5/1.
Transfers: Closing date 3/7. Transfer students with previous undergraduate degree not eligible for scholarship aid.

CONTACT
Peter Riefler, Director of Financial Aid
Two College Street, Providence, RI 02903-2791
(401) 454-6636

Roger Williams University
Bristol, Rhode Island
www.rwu.edu
Federal Code: 003410
CSS Code: 3729

4-year private university and liberal arts college in large town.
Enrollment: 4,358 undergrads, 14% part-time. 1,205 full-time freshmen.
Selectivity: Admits over 75% of applicants.

Roger Williams University (continued)

BASIC COSTS (2006-2007)
Tuition and fees: $24,550.
Per-credit charge: $960.
Room and board: $10,792.
Additional info: Tuition differential for architecture program.

FINANCIAL AID PICTURE (2005-2006)
Students with need: Out of 935 full-time freshmen who applied for aid, 746 were judged to have need. Of these, 734 received aid, and 389 had their full need met. Average financial aid package met 78% of need; average scholarship/grant was $8,734; average loan was $3,091. For part-time students, average financial aid package was $10,378.
Students without need: 176 full-time freshmen who did not demonstrate need for aid received scholarships/grants; average award was $5,840. No-need awards available for academics, ROTC.
Scholarships offered: Deadline 2/1. Admissions application acts as scholarship application. No separate forms required.
Cumulative student debt: 80% of graduating class had student loans; average debt was $28,147.

FINANCIAL AID PROCEDURES
Forms required: FAFSA, CSS PROFILE.
Dates and Deadlines: Closing date 2/1. Applicants notified on a rolling basis starting 3/20; must reply by 5/1 or within 2 week(s) of notification.

CONTACT
Tracy DaCosta, Associate Dean of Enrollment Management
One Old Ferry Road, Bristol, RI 02809
(401) 254-3100

Salve Regina University
Newport, Rhode Island
www.salve.edu
Federal Code: 003411
CSS Code: 3759

4-year private university and liberal arts college in small city, affiliated with Roman Catholic Church.
Enrollment: 2,068 undergrads, 4% part-time. 568 full-time freshmen.
Selectivity: Admits 50 to 75% of applicants.

BASIC COSTS (2006-2007)
Tuition and fees: $25,175.
Per-credit charge: $833.
Room and board: $9,800.

FINANCIAL AID PICTURE (2005-2006)
Students with need: Out of 474 full-time freshmen who applied for aid, 381 were judged to have need. Of these, 375 received aid, and 46 had their full need met. Average financial aid package met 72% of need; average scholarship/grant was $13,425; average loan was $2,710. For part-time students, average financial aid package was $11,169.
Students without need: 109 full-time freshmen who did not demonstrate need for aid received scholarships/grants; average award was $6,651. No-need awards available for academics, music/drama, ROTC.
Cumulative student debt: 81% of graduating class had student loans; average debt was $21,925.

FINANCIAL AID PROCEDURES
Forms required: FAFSA, CSS PROFILE.
Dates and Deadlines: Priority date 3/1; no closing date. Applicants notified on a rolling basis starting 3/1; must reply by 5/1 or within 2 week(s) of notification.
Transfers: No deadline. Applicants notified on a rolling basis; must reply by 5/1 or within 2 week(s) of notification. Must provide financial aid transcripts from previous institutions attended.

CONTACT
Aida Mirante, Director of Financial Aid
100 Ochre Point Avenue, Newport, RI 02840-4192
(401) 341-2901

University of Rhode Island
Kingston, Rhode Island
www.uri.edu
Federal Code: 003414

4-year public university in small town.
Enrollment: 11,162 undergrads, 13% part-time. 2,323 full-time freshmen.
Selectivity: Admits over 75% of applicants.

BASIC COSTS (2005-2006)
Tuition and fees: $7,284; out-of-state residents $19,926.
Per-credit charge: $219; out-of-state residents $746.
Room and board: $8,560.
Additional info: Tuition/fee waivers available for unemployed or children of unemployed.

FINANCIAL AID PICTURE (2005-2006)
Students with need: Out of 2,134 full-time freshmen who applied for aid, 1,656 were judged to have need. Of these, 1,333 received aid, and 1,106 had their full need met. Average financial aid package met 67% of need; average scholarship/grant was $6,353; average loan was $6,184. For part-time students, average financial aid package was $7,156.
Students without need: 186 full-time freshmen who did not demonstrate need for aid received scholarships/grants; average award was $4,711. No-need awards available for academics, alumni affiliation, art, athletics, leadership, minority status, music/drama, ROTC.
Scholarships offered: *Merit:* Centennial Scholarship, up to full tuition for full-time students with 3.0 GPA or better, 1120 SAT score, 1150 for engineering and pharmacy in top third of class, 525 awarded per year. SAT scores exclusive of Writing. *Athletic:* 10 full-time freshmen received athletic scholarships; average amount $1,179.
Cumulative student debt: 56% of graduating class had student loans; average debt was $16,200.

FINANCIAL AID PROCEDURES
Forms required: FAFSA.
Dates and Deadlines: Priority date 3/1; no closing date. Applicants notified on a rolling basis starting 3/21; must reply by 5/1 or within 2 week(s) of notification.

CONTACT
Harry Amaral, Director of Enrollment Services
14 Upper College Road, Kingston, RI 02881-1391
(401) 874-9500

South Carolina

Aiken Technical College
Graniteville, South Carolina
www.atc.edu
Federal Code: 010056

2-year public community and technical college in small city.
Enrollment: 2,432 undergrads, 43% part-time. 370 full-time freshmen.
Selectivity: Open admission; but selective for some programs.

BASIC COSTS (2005-2006)
Tuition and fees: $3,036; out-of-district residents $3,396; out-of-state residents $8,330.
Additional info: Out of state students pay an additional $188 in fees.

FINANCIAL AID PICTURE (2004-2005)
Students with need: For part-time students, average financial aid package was $944.
Students without need: No-need awards available for academics, athletics, leadership, minority status, state/district residency.
Scholarships offered: Vernon Ford Scholarships; $1,000 annually; for candidates with minimum GPA of 3.0; 8 awarded annually. N. Augusta 2000; $2,000 annually; 2 awarded. Wachenhut Criminal Justice Scholarship; $1,000; 1 awarded. Presidential; $10,000 annually; 10 awarded.

FINANCIAL AID PROCEDURES
Forms required: FAFSA.
Dates and Deadlines: Priority date 5/1; closing date 6/30. Applicants notified on a rolling basis starting 4/1; must reply within 2 week(s) of notification.
Transfers: Applicants notified on a rolling basis; must reply within 2 week(s) of notification.

CONTACT
Amanda Chittum, Director of Financial Aid
PO Box 400, Graniteville, SC 29829
(803) 593-9954 ext. 1261

Allen University
Columbia, South Carolina
www.allenuniversity.edu   Federal Code: 003417

4-year private university and liberal arts college in large city, affiliated with African Methodist Episcopal Church.
Enrollment: 624 undergrads, 4% part-time. 211 full-time freshmen.
Selectivity: Open admission.

BASIC COSTS (2005-2006)
Tuition and fees: $7,764.
Room and board: $4,210.

FINANCIAL AID PICTURE
Students with need: Need-based aid available for full-time and part-time students.
Students without need: No-need awards available for academics, athletics, music/drama, ROTC.

FINANCIAL AID PROCEDURES
Forms required: FAFSA.
Dates and Deadlines: Priority date 4/15; closing date 7/20. Applicants notified on a rolling basis starting 4/1; must reply within 2 week(s) of notification.
Transfers: No deadline.

CONTACT
Donna Foster, Director of Financial Aid
1530 Harden Street, Columbia, SC 29204
(803) 376-5740

Anderson University
Anderson, South Carolina
www.ac.edu   Federal Code: 003418

4-year private liberal arts college in large town, affiliated with Southern Baptist Convention.
Enrollment: 1,418 undergrads, 10% part-time. 367 full-time freshmen.
Selectivity: Admits over 75% of applicants.

BASIC COSTS (2006-2007)
Tuition and fees: $16,550.
Per-credit charge: $410.
Room and board: $6,400.
Additional info: Tuition/fee waivers available for adults.

FINANCIAL AID PICTURE (2004-2005)
Students with need: Out of 362 full-time freshmen who applied for aid, 323 were judged to have need. Of these, 323 received aid, and 97 had their full need met. Average financial aid package met 64% of need; average scholarship/grant was $8,098; average loan was $3,608. For part-time students, average financial aid package was $12,826.
Students without need: 38 full-time freshmen who did not demonstrate need for aid received scholarships/grants; average award was $5,772. No-need awards available for academics, alumni affiliation, art, athletics, leadership, minority status, music/drama, religious affiliation, state/district residency.
Scholarships offered: 59 full-time freshmen received athletic scholarships; average amount $4,359.
Cumulative student debt: 76% of graduating class had student loans; average debt was $15,125.

FINANCIAL AID PROCEDURES
Forms required: FAFSA.
Dates and Deadlines: Priority date 3/1; closing date 7/30. Applicants notified on a rolling basis starting 3/15; must reply within 2 week(s) of notification.

CONTACT
Jeff Holliday, Director of Financial Aid
316 Boulevard, Anderson, SC 29621
(864) 231-2070

Benedict College
Columbia, South Carolina
www.benedict.edu   Federal Code: 003420

4-year private liberal arts college in very large city, affiliated with American Baptist Churches in the USA.
Enrollment: 2,552 undergrads, 2% part-time. 536 full-time freshmen.
Selectivity: Open admission.

BASIC COSTS (2005-2006)
Tuition and fees: $12,954.
Per-credit charge: $388.
Room and board: $5,958.

FINANCIAL AID PICTURE
Students with need: Need-based aid available for full-time and part-time students.

FINANCIAL AID PROCEDURES
Forms required: FAFSA.
Dates and Deadlines: Priority date 4/15; no closing date. Applicants notified on a rolling basis starting 4/15.

CONTACT
Sul Black, Director of Financial Aid
1600 Harden Street, Columbia, SC 29204
(803) 253-5105

Central Carolina Technical College
Sumter, South Carolina
www.cctech.edu   Federal Code: 003995

2-year public community and technical college in large town.
Enrollment: 3,244 undergrads, 71% part-time. 307 full-time freshmen.
Selectivity: Open admission; but selective for some programs.

BASIC COSTS (2005-2006)
Tuition and fees: $2,700; out-of-district residents $3,168; out-of-state residents $4,800.

FINANCIAL AID PICTURE

Students with need: Need-based aid available for full-time and part-time students. Work study available nights.
Students without need: This college only awards aid to students with need.

FINANCIAL AID PROCEDURES

Forms required: FAFSA, state aid form.
Dates and Deadlines: Priority date 6/15; no closing date. Applicants notified on a rolling basis; must reply within 2 week(s) of notification.

CONTACT

William Whitlock, Director of Financial Aid
506 North Guignard Drive, Sumter, SC 29150
(803) 778-7831

Charleston Southern University
Charleston, South Carolina
www.csuniv.edu   Federal Code: 003419

4-year private university and liberal arts college in large city, affiliated with Southern Baptist Convention.
Enrollment: 2,586 undergrads, 15% part-time. 521 full-time freshmen.
Selectivity: Admits 50 to 75% of applicants.

BASIC COSTS (2006-2007)
Tuition and fees: $16,780.
Per-credit charge: $271.
Room and board: $6,450.

FINANCIAL AID PICTURE (2004-2005)
Students with need: Out of 472 full-time freshmen who applied for aid, 432 were judged to have need. Of these, 432 received aid, and 102 had their full need met. Average financial aid package met 73% of need; average scholarship/grant was $10,161; average loan was $3,432. For part-time students, average financial aid package was $8,590.
Students without need: 61 full-time freshmen who did not demonstrate need for aid received scholarships/grants; average award was $7,295. No-need awards available for academics, athletics, religious affiliation, ROTC.
Scholarships offered: 34 full-time freshmen received athletic scholarships; average amount $9,387.
Cumulative student debt: 90% of graduating class had student loans; average debt was $24,251.

FINANCIAL AID PROCEDURES
Forms required: FAFSA, state aid form.
Dates and Deadlines: Priority date 4/15; no closing date. Applicants notified on a rolling basis starting 3/1; must reply within 2 week(s) of notification.

CONTACT
Cheryl Burton, Director of Financial Aid
9200 University Boulevard, Charleston, SC 29423-8087
(843) 863-7050

The Citadel
Charleston, South Carolina
www.citadel.edu   Federal Code: 003423

4-year public military college in large city.
Enrollment: 2,176 undergrads, 3% part-time. 585 full-time freshmen.
Selectivity: Admits over 75% of applicants.

BASIC COSTS (2005-2006)
Tuition and fees: $6,522; out-of-state residents $15,918.
Per-credit charge: $198; out-of-state residents $397.
Room and board: $4,840.

Additional info: Students in Corps of Cadets required to pay $998 in fees which include laundry and dry cleaning charges and infirmary fees. Freshmen also pay $5,200 deposit and upperclassmen pay $1,630 deposit for uniforms, books, and supplies.

FINANCIAL AID PICTURE (2005-2006)
Students with need: Out of 456 full-time freshmen who applied for aid, 319 were judged to have need. Of these, 305 received aid, and 62 had their full need met. Average financial aid package met 56% of need; average scholarship/grant was $9,231; average loan was $3,154. For part-time students, average financial aid package was $1,676.
Students without need: 106 full-time freshmen who did not demonstrate need for aid received scholarships/grants; average award was $8,756. No-need awards available for academics, athletics, leadership, music/drama, religious affiliation, ROTC, state/district residency.
Scholarships offered: 54 full-time freshmen received athletic scholarships; average amount $15,611.
Cumulative student debt: 44% of graduating class had student loans; average debt was $9,300.

FINANCIAL AID PROCEDURES
Forms required: FAFSA.
Dates and Deadlines: Closing date 3/1. Applicants notified on a rolling basis starting 4/1; must reply within 2 week(s) of notification.
Transfers: No deadline.

CONTACT
Henry Fuller, Director of Financial Aid
171 Moultrie Street, Charleston, SC 29409
(843) 953-5187

Claflin University
Orangeburg, South Carolina
www.claflin.edu   Federal Code: 003424

4-year private liberal arts college in large town, affiliated with United Methodist Church.
Enrollment: 1,624 undergrads, 2% part-time. 385 full-time freshmen.
Selectivity: Admits less than 50% of applicants.

BASIC COSTS (2005-2006)
Tuition and fees: $10,890.
Room and board: $5,908.

FINANCIAL AID PICTURE (2005-2006)
Students with need: Average financial aid package met 69% of need; average scholarship/grant was $2,141; average loan was $1,625.
Cumulative student debt: 87% of graduating class had student loans; average debt was $16,560.

FINANCIAL AID PROCEDURES
Forms required: FAFSA, institutional form.
Dates and Deadlines: Priority date 4/15; no closing date. Applicants notified on a rolling basis starting 5/15; must reply within 2 week(s) of notification.

CONTACT
Yolanda Frazier, Interim Director of Financial Aid
400 Magnolia Street, Orangeburg, SC 29115
(803) 535-5334

Clemson University
Clemson, South Carolina
www.clemson.edu   Federal Code: 003425

4-year public university in small town.
Enrollment: 13,959 undergrads, 5% part-time. 2,893 full-time freshmen.

College of Charleston **South Carolina** 765

Selectivity: Admits 50 to 75% of applicants.

BASIC COSTS (2005-2006)
Tuition and fees: $9,016; out-of-state residents $18,640.
Room and board: $5,780.
Additional info: Laptop computer now required of all entering new students. This cost has been estimated at $1600.

FINANCIAL AID PICTURE (2004-2005)
Students with need: 37% of average financial aid package awarded as scholarships/grants, 63% awarded as loans/jobs. Need-based aid available for part-time students. Work study available nights, weekends, and for part-time students.
Students without need: No-need awards available for academics, art, athletics, leadership, minority status, music/drama, ROTC, state/district residency.

FINANCIAL AID PROCEDURES
Forms required: FAFSA.
Dates and Deadlines: Priority date 4/1; no closing date. Applicants notified on a rolling basis starting 4/1; must reply within 3 week(s) of notification.
Transfers: Transfer students must earn 12 semester hours before being considered for institutional scholarship.

CONTACT
Marvin Carmichael, Director of Student Financial Aid
105 Sikes Hall, Clemson, SC 29634-5124
(864) 656-2280

Coastal Carolina University
Conway, South Carolina
www.coastal.edu   Federal Code: 003451

4-year public university in small city.
Enrollment: 6,115 undergrads, 6% part-time. 1,322 full-time freshmen.
Selectivity: Admits 50 to 75% of applicants.

BASIC COSTS (2005-2006)
Tuition and fees: $6,940; out-of-state residents $15,180.
Per-credit charge: $290; out-of-state residents $630.
Room and board: $6,280.

FINANCIAL AID PICTURE (2004-2005)
Students with need: Out of 1,021 full-time freshmen who applied for aid, 839 were judged to have need. Of these, 838 received aid, and 287 had their full need met. Average financial aid package met 58% of need; average scholarship/grant was $3,347; average loan was $6,088. For part-time students, average financial aid package was $5,077.
Students without need: 333 full-time freshmen who did not demonstrate need for aid received scholarships/grants; average award was $7,125. No-need awards available for academics, art, athletics, leadership, music/drama, state/district residency.
Scholarships offered: 66 full-time freshmen received athletic scholarships; average amount $5,645.
Cumulative student debt: 62% of graduating class had student loans; average debt was $20,923.

FINANCIAL AID PROCEDURES
Forms required: FAFSA.
Dates and Deadlines: Priority date 3/1; no closing date. Applicants notified on a rolling basis starting 3/1.

CONTACT
Glenn Hanson, Director of Financial Aid
PO Box 261954, Conway, SC 29528-6054
(843) 349-2313

Coker College
Hartsville, South Carolina
www.coker.edu   Federal Code: 003427

4-year private liberal arts college in large town.
Enrollment: 548 undergrads.

BASIC COSTS (2005-2006)
Tuition and fees: $17,288.
Per-credit charge: $707.
Room and board: $5,660.
Additional info: Tuition/fee waivers available for adults.

FINANCIAL AID PICTURE (2005-2006)
Students with need: 50% of average financial aid package awarded as scholarships/grants, 50% awarded as loans/jobs. Need-based aid available for part-time students. Work study available nights, weekends, and for part-time students.
Students without need: No-need awards available for academics, art, athletics, music/drama.
Scholarships offered: Scholarships for Excellence; awarded on a competitive basis to students showing potential for continued high performance and leadership; up to $17,000 per year; candidates may be invited to campus for interviews. President's Scholarships; based upon SAT or ACT score and high school GPA; up to $7,500 per year. Dean's Scholarships; based upon SAT or ACT score and high school GPA; up to $7,000 per year. Departmental Scholarships; Art, Dance, Music, Theater, Biology, and Chemistry scholarships to talented students; Language and Literature/ creative writing scholarship; range from $500 to $4,000 per year; Art, Dance, Music, and Theater scholarships require an audition or portfolio; some departments require an interview. Intercollegiate athletics scholarships available in all 12 sponsored sports, including baseball, basketball, cross-country, golf, soccer, and tennis for men and basketball, cross-country, soccer, softball, tennis, and volleyball for women; work-awards are available to qualified student-trainers. Valedictorian Scholarships; $500 per year to students ranked number one in their class at the end of their junior year or first semester of their senior year.
Additional info: Endowed scholarship program for qualified applicants. June 1 deadline for filing South Carolina Tuition Grant forms.

FINANCIAL AID PROCEDURES
Forms required: FAFSA.
Dates and Deadlines: Priority date 4/1; closing date 6/1. Applicants notified on a rolling basis starting 12/1; must reply by 5/1 or within 3 week(s) of notification.
Transfers: No deadline.

CONTACT
Betty Williams, Director of Financial Aid
300 East College Avenue, Hartsville, SC 29550
(843) 383-8005

College of Charleston
Charleston, South Carolina
www.cofc.edu   Federal Code: 003428

4-year public liberal arts college in large city.
Enrollment: 9,501 undergrads, 6% part-time. 1,988 full-time freshmen.
Selectivity: Admits 50 to 75% of applicants.

BASIC COSTS (2005-2006)
Tuition and fees: $6,668; out-of-state residents $15,342.
Per-credit charge: $278; out-of-state residents $639.
Room and board: $6,948.

South Carolina   College of Charleston

FINANCIAL AID PICTURE
Students with need: Need-based aid available for full-time and part-time students.
Students without need: No-need awards available for academics, alumni affiliation, art, athletics, music/drama.
Scholarships offered: Foundation Scholarships: from $1,000-$4,000 annually for up to 4 years; based on high school performance, test scores, and leadership qualities, no additional application required.

FINANCIAL AID PROCEDURES
Forms required: FAFSA.
Dates and Deadlines: Priority date 3/15; no closing date. Applicants notified on a rolling basis starting 4/10; must reply within 8 week(s) of notification.
Transfers: No aid available to transfer students who enroll for first time in summer school.

CONTACT
Donald Griggs, Director of Financial Assistance and Veterans Affairs
66 George Street, Charleston, SC 29424-0001
(843) 953-5540

Columbia College
Columbia, South Carolina
www.columbiacollegesc.edu   Federal Code: 003430

4-year private liberal arts college for women in large city, affiliated with United Methodist Church.
Enrollment: 1,093 undergrads, 21% part-time. 261 full-time freshmen.
Selectivity: Admits over 75% of applicants.

BASIC COSTS (2006-2007)
Tuition and fees: $20,302.
Per-credit charge: $534.
Room and board: $6,022.

FINANCIAL AID PICTURE (2004-2005)
Students with need: Out of 240 full-time freshmen who applied for aid, 199 were judged to have need. Of these, 199 received aid, and 142 had their full need met. Average financial aid package met 82% of need; average scholarship/grant was $8,309; average loan was $3,444. For part-time students, average financial aid package was $8,790.
Students without need: 52 full-time freshmen who did not demonstrate need for aid received scholarships/grants; average award was $9,656. No-need awards available for academics, alumni affiliation, art, athletics, leadership, music/drama.
Scholarships offered: *Merit:* Founders Scholarship; full tuition. Presidential Scholarships; $10,000 annually. Trustees Scholarships; $8,000 annually. *Athletic:* 3 full-time freshmen received athletic scholarships; average amount $3,333.
Cumulative student debt: 83% of graduating class had student loans; average debt was $27,617.

FINANCIAL AID PROCEDURES
Forms required: FAFSA.
Dates and Deadlines: Priority date 4/1; no closing date. Applicants notified on a rolling basis starting 3/15; must reply within 2 week(s) of notification.
Transfers: Priority date 4/15. Must meet institutional standards of satisfactory academic progress.

CONTACT
Anita Kaminer Elliott, Director of Financial Aid
1301 Columbia College Drive, Columbia, SC 29203
(803) 786-3612

Columbia International University
Columbia, South Carolina
www.ciu.edu   Federal Code: 003429

4-year private university and Bible college in small city, affiliated with multidenominational/evangelical churches.
Enrollment: 540 undergrads, 8% part-time. 90 full-time freshmen.
Selectivity: Admits 50 to 75% of applicants.

BASIC COSTS (2006-2007)
Tuition and fees: $14,825.
Per-credit charge: $600.
Room and board: $5,712.
Additional info: Tuition/fee waivers available for minority students.

FINANCIAL AID PICTURE
Students with need: Need-based aid available for full-time and part-time students. Work study available nights, weekends, and for part-time students.
Students without need: No-need awards available for academics, state/district residency.
Additional info: Spouse scholarship program; special short quarter scholarships for missionaries on furlough.

FINANCIAL AID PROCEDURES
Forms required: FAFSA, institutional form.
Dates and Deadlines: Closing date 3/15. Applicants notified on a rolling basis starting 4/1; must reply within 4 week(s) of notification.
Transfers: FAFSA must be processed by June 30th for state need-based aid. State aid requires one-year residency prior to award in most cases. Non-need-based state aid requires graduation from a state high school.

CONTACT
Mary Bisesi, Director of Financial Aid
PO Box 3122, Columbia, SC 29230-3122
(803) 754-4100 ext. 3036

Converse College
Spartanburg, South Carolina
www.converse.edu   Federal Code: 003431

4-year private music and liberal arts college for women in small city.
Enrollment: 769 undergrads, 16% part-time. 189 full-time freshmen.
Selectivity: Admits over 75% of applicants.

BASIC COSTS (2006-2007)
Tuition and fees: $22,234.
Per-credit charge: $740.
Room and board: $6,848.

FINANCIAL AID PICTURE (2005-2006)
Students with need: Out of 139 full-time freshmen who applied for aid, 118 were judged to have need. Of these, 118 received aid, and 47 had their full need met. Average financial aid package met 89% of need; average scholarship/grant was $16,115; average loan was $3,440. For part-time students, average financial aid package was $6,970.
Students without need: 61 full-time freshmen who did not demonstrate need for aid received scholarships/grants; average award was $15,966. No-need awards available for academics, alumni affiliation, art, athletics, leadership, music/drama, ROTC, state/district residency.
Scholarships offered: 11 full-time freshmen received athletic scholarships; average amount $5,202.
Cumulative student debt: 58% of graduating class had student loans; average debt was $16,641.

FINANCIAL AID PROCEDURES
Forms required: FAFSA.

Dates and Deadlines: Priority date 3/15; no closing date. Applicants notified on a rolling basis starting 3/15; must reply by 5/1 or within 2 week(s) of notification.

CONTACT
Margaret Collins, Director of Scholarships and Financial Assistance
580 East Main Street, Spartanburg, SC 29302-0006
(864) 596-9019

Denmark Technical College
Denmark, South Carolina
www.denmarktech.edu   Federal Code: 005363

2-year public technical college in small town.
Enrollment: 1,232 undergrads.
Selectivity: Open admission.

BASIC COSTS (2005-2006)
Tuition and fees: $2,278; out-of-state residents $4,366.
Room and board: $3,096.

FINANCIAL AID PICTURE
Students with need: Need-based aid available for full-time and part-time students.

FINANCIAL AID PROCEDURES
Forms required: FAFSA.
Dates and Deadlines: No deadline. Applicants notified on a rolling basis starting 6/1; must reply within 2 week(s) of notification.

CONTACT
Clara Moses, Director of Financial Aid
Solomon Blatt Boulevard, Denmark, SC 29042
(803) 793-5161

Erskine College
Due West, South Carolina
www.erskine.edu   Federal Code: 003432

4-year private liberal arts and seminary college in rural community, affiliated with Associate Reformed Presbyterian Church.
Enrollment: 589 undergrads, 1% part-time. 177 full-time freshmen.
Selectivity: Admits 50 to 75% of applicants.

BASIC COSTS (2006-2007)
Tuition and fees: $20,275.
Per-credit charge: $698.
Room and board: $6,951.

FINANCIAL AID PICTURE (2004-2005)
Students with need: Out of 170 full-time freshmen who applied for aid, 143 were judged to have need. Of these, 143 received aid, and 46 had their full need met. Average financial aid package met 84% of need; average scholarship/grant was $8,501; average loan was $2,150. For part-time students, average financial aid package was $3,000.
Students without need: 43 full-time freshmen who did not demonstrate need for aid received scholarships/grants; average award was $9,126. No-need awards available for academics, alumni affiliation, art, athletics, leadership, minority status, music/drama, religious affiliation, state/district residency.
Scholarships offered: 38 full-time freshmen received athletic scholarships; average amount $3,621.
Additional info: Filing deadline 5/1 for institutional form, 6/30 for state form.

FINANCIAL AID PROCEDURES
Forms required: FAFSA, institutional form.
Dates and Deadlines: Priority date 4/1; no closing date. Applicants notified on a rolling basis starting 12/15; must reply within 2 week(s) of notification.
Transfers: Closing date 5/1. South Carolina residents must have earned 24 hours in previous year to receive SC tuition grant and 30 hours plus 3.0 GPA to receive the Life Scholarship.

CONTACT
Becky Pressley, Director of Financial Aid
PO Box 338, Due West, SC 29639-0176
(864) 379-8832

Florence-Darlington Technical College
Florence, South Carolina
www.fdtc.edu   Federal Code: 003990

2-year public community and technical college in small city.
Enrollment: 3,994 undergrads, 45% part-time. 701 full-time freshmen.
Selectivity: Open admission; but selective for some programs.

BASIC COSTS (2005-2006)
Tuition and fees: $2,986; out-of-district residents $3,248; out-of-state residents $5,082.

FINANCIAL AID PICTURE
Students with need: Need-based aid available for full-time and part-time students.
Students without need: No-need awards available for academics.

FINANCIAL AID PROCEDURES
Forms required: FAFSA.
Dates and Deadlines: Priority date 5/1; no closing date. Applicants notified on a rolling basis starting 7/1; must reply within 2 week(s) of notification.

CONTACT
Joseph Durant, Director of Financial Assistance
PO Box 100548, Florence, SC 29501-0548
(843) 661-8085

Forrest Junior College
Anderson, South Carolina
www.forrestcollege.edu   Federal Code: 004924

2-year for-profit community and junior college in large town.
Enrollment: 126 undergrads, 10% part-time. 3 full-time freshmen.
Selectivity: Open admission; but selective for some programs.

BASIC COSTS (2006-2007)
Tuition and fees: $5,350.
Per-credit charge: $110.

FINANCIAL AID PICTURE
Students with need: Need-based aid available for full-time and part-time students. Work study available nights, weekends, and for part-time students.
Students without need: This college only awards aid to students with need.

FINANCIAL AID PROCEDURES
Forms required: FAFSA.
Dates and Deadlines: No deadline. Applicants notified on a rolling basis starting 4/30; must reply by 5/31 or within 4 week(s) of notification.

CONTACT
Kathy Montgomery, Director of Financial Aid
601 East River Street, Anderson, SC 29624
(864) 225-7653

Francis Marion University
Florence, South Carolina
www.fmarion.edu Federal Code: 009226

4-year public university and liberal arts college in small city.
Enrollment: 3,182 undergrads, 5% part-time. 801 full-time freshmen.
Selectivity: Admits 50 to 75% of applicants.

BASIC COSTS (2005-2006)
Tuition and fees: $5,984; out-of-state residents $11,833.
Per-credit charge: $292; out-of-state residents $585.
Room and board: $5,130.

FINANCIAL AID PICTURE (2004-2005)
Students with need: Out of 611 full-time freshmen who applied for aid, 519 were judged to have need. Of these, 458 received aid. Need-based aid available for part-time students.
Students without need: No-need awards available for academics, music/drama.

FINANCIAL AID PROCEDURES
Forms required: FAFSA, institutional form.
Dates and Deadlines: Priority date 3/1; no closing date. Applicants notified on a rolling basis starting 4/15.
Transfers: Institutional scholarships available after 1 semester completed in residence.

CONTACT
Kim Ellisor, Director of Financial Assistance
PO Box 100547, Florence, SC 29501-0547
(843) 661-1190

Furman University
Greenville, South Carolina
www.furman.edu Federal Code: 003434

4-year private liberal arts college in small city.
Enrollment: 2,774 undergrads, 3% part-time. 688 full-time freshmen.
Selectivity: Admits 50 to 75% of applicants.

BASIC COSTS (2006-2007)
Tuition and fees: $28,840.
Per-credit charge: $886.
Room and board: $7,552.

FINANCIAL AID PICTURE (2005-2006)
Students with need: Out of 406 full-time freshmen who applied for aid, 289 were judged to have need. Of these, 289 received aid, and 130 had their full need met. Average financial aid package met 91% of need; average scholarship/grant was $21,735; average loan was $1,705. For part-time students, average financial aid package was $5,027.
Students without need: 226 full-time freshmen who did not demonstrate need for aid received scholarships/grants; average award was $10,830. No-need awards available for academics, alumni affiliation, art, athletics, leadership, minority status, music/drama, religious affiliation, ROTC, state/district residency.
Scholarships offered: Merit: Over 100 renewable merit scholarships offered to entering freshmen, including 4 Herman W. Lay Scholarships for room, board and tuition, 10 Duke Scholarships for full tuition, 30 Founders (half-tuition) Scholarships and 35 Bell Tower Scholarships (quarter-tuition). **Athletic:** 48 full-time freshmen received athletic scholarships; average amount $20,783.
Cumulative student debt: 38% of graduating class had student loans; average debt was $21,860.
Additional info: 5-point comprehensive education financing plan includes financial aid packaging, money management counseling, debt management counseling, outside scholarship coordination, and summer job-match program.

FINANCIAL AID PROCEDURES
Forms required: FAFSA, state aid form, institutional form.
Dates and Deadlines: Closing date 1/15. Applicants notified by 3/15; must reply by 5/1.
Transfers: Closing date 6/1. For South Carolina Tuition Grant, must have earned 24 credits in previous year. For Life Scholarship, must have earned 3.0 cumulative GPA and 30 credits earned.

CONTACT
Martin Carney, Director of Financial Aid
3300 Poinsett Highway, Greenville, SC 29613
(864) 294-2204

Greenville Technical College
Greenville, South Carolina
www.greenvilletech.com Federal Code: 003991

2-year public community and technical college in large city.
Enrollment: 11,619 undergrads, 54% part-time. 1,616 full-time freshmen.
Selectivity: Open admission; but selective for some programs.

BASIC COSTS (2005-2006)
Tuition and fees: $3,000; out-of-district residents $3,250; out-of-state residents $6,110.
Additional info: Tuition/fee waivers available for unemployed or children of unemployed.

FINANCIAL AID PICTURE (2004-2005)
Students with need: 53% of average financial aid package awarded as scholarships/grants, 47% awarded as loans/jobs. Need-based aid available for part-time students. Work study available nights.
Students without need: No-need awards available for academics, state/district residency.

FINANCIAL AID PROCEDURES
Forms required: FAFSA.
Dates and Deadlines: Priority date 5/1; no closing date. Applicants notified on a rolling basis starting 6/15; must reply within 2 week(s) of notification.

CONTACT
Janie Reid, Financial Aid Director
P. O. Box 5616, Greenville, SC 29606-5616
(864) 250-8128

Horry-Georgetown Technical College
Conway, South Carolina
www.hgtc.edu Federal Code: 004925

2-year public community and technical college in large town.
Enrollment: 5,348 undergrads.
Selectivity: Open admission; but selective for some programs.

BASIC COSTS (2005-2006)
Tuition and fees: $2,864; out-of-district residents $3,448; out-of-state residents $4,472.

FINANCIAL AID PICTURE (2005-2006)
Students with need: 91% of average financial aid package awarded as scholarships/grants, 9% awarded as loans/jobs. Need-based aid available for part-time students.
Additional info: Participates in South Carolina lottery tuition assistance program. Full-time technical college students who are state residents receive assistance for tuition not covered by federal or need-based grants.

FINANCIAL AID PROCEDURES
Forms required: FAFSA.
Dates and Deadlines: Priority date 4/1; closing date 6/30. Applicants notified on a rolling basis starting 4/1.

CONTACT
Susan Thompson, Director of Financial Aid
PO Box 261966, Conway, SC 29528
(843) 349-5251

Lander University
Greenwood, South Carolina
www.lander.edu   Federal Code: 003435

4-year public liberal arts and teachers college in large town.
Enrollment: 2,552 undergrads, 7% part-time. 655 full-time freshmen.
Selectivity: Open admission; but selective for some programs.

BASIC COSTS (2005-2006)
Tuition and fees: $7,188; out-of-state residents $13,528.
Per-credit charge: $275; out-of-state residents $564.
Room and board: $5,332.

FINANCIAL AID PICTURE (2004-2005)
Students with need: Out of 536 full-time freshmen who applied for aid, 423 were judged to have need. Of these, 421 received aid, and 105 had their full need met. Average financial aid package met 77% of need; average scholarship/grant was $2,000; average loan was $2,000. Need-based aid available for part-time students.
Students without need: 24 full-time freshmen who did not demonstrate need for aid received scholarships/grants; average award was $2,396. No-need awards available for academics, art, athletics, leadership, music/drama.
Scholarships offered: 2 full-time freshmen received athletic scholarships; average amount $3,950.
Cumulative student debt: 54% of graduating class had student loans; average debt was $16,500.

FINANCIAL AID PROCEDURES
Forms required: FAFSA.
Dates and Deadlines: Priority date 4/15; no closing date. Applicants notified on a rolling basis starting 4/15; must reply within 4 week(s) of notification.

CONTACT
Fred Hardin, Director of Financial Aid
Stanley Avenue, Greenwood, SC 29649-2099
(864) 388-8340

Limestone College
Gaffney, South Carolina
www.limestone.edu   Federal Code: 003436

4-year private liberal arts college in large town.
Enrollment: 676 undergrads, 2% part-time. 251 full-time freshmen.
Selectivity: Admits 50 to 75% of applicants.

BASIC COSTS (2006-2007)
Tuition and fees: $15,000.
Per-credit charge: $625.
Room and board: $6,000.

FINANCIAL AID PICTURE (2004-2005)
Students with need: Out of 180 full-time freshmen who applied for aid, 151 were judged to have need. Of these, 151 received aid, and 31 had their full need met. Average financial aid package met 66% of need; average scholarship/grant was $7,644; average loan was $2,372. For part-time students, average financial aid package was $8,173.
Students without need: 45 full-time freshmen who did not demonstrate need for aid received scholarships/grants; average award was $7,565. No-need awards available for academics, alumni affiliation, art, athletics, job skills, leadership, music/drama, religious affiliation, ROTC, state/district residency.
Scholarships offered: *Merit:* Presidential Scholarship; full tuition; SAT above 1300, GPA 3.5 or above; 1 available. Academic Dean Scholarships; partial tuition; based on academic achievement (GPA 3.0 or above). Founders Scholarships; partial tuition; GPA 2.75 or above. R.S. Campbell Scholarship; SAT above 1100, GPA 3.25 or above; 1 available. Leadership Scholarship; partial tuition; based on evidence of student leadership. Drada Hoover Scholarship; SAT 1200 or higher; GPA 3.5; top 10% of graduating class. SAT scores exclusive of Writing. *Athletic:* 30 full-time freshmen received athletic scholarships; average amount $3,987.
Cumulative student debt: 66% of graduating class had student loans; average debt was $17,110.

FINANCIAL AID PROCEDURES
Forms required: FAFSA.
Dates and Deadlines: Priority date 2/1; no closing date. Applicants notified on a rolling basis starting 1/15; must reply within 3 week(s) of notification.
Transfers: Priority date 5/1; no deadline. Applicants notified on a rolling basis; must reply within 3 week(s) of notification.

CONTACT
Lauren Mack, Director of Financial Aid
1115 College Drive, Gaffney, SC 29340-3799
(800) 795-7151 ext. 4598

Medical University of South Carolina
Charleston, South Carolina
www.musc.edu   Federal Code: 003438

Upper-division public health science and nursing college in large city.
Enrollment: 288 undergrads, 29% part-time.

BASIC COSTS (2005-2006)
Tuition and fees: $8,568; out-of-state residents $23,344.
Additional info: Undergraduate costs vary by program, by year, and by college. Tuition/fee waivers available for minority students.

FINANCIAL AID PICTURE (2004-2005)
Students with need: Average financial aid package for all full-time undergraduates was $10,050; for part-time $7,517. 15% awarded as scholarships/grants, 85% awarded as loans/jobs.
Students without need: No-need awards available for academics, alumni affiliation, minority status, state/district residency.

FINANCIAL AID PROCEDURES
Forms required: FAFSA, institutional form.
Dates and Deadlines: Priority date 3/10; no closing date. Applicants notified on a rolling basis starting 4/21.

CONTACT
Pearl Givens, Director, Student Financial Aid
41 Bee Street, Charleston, SC 29425
(843) 792-25536

Midlands Technical College
Columbia, South Carolina
www.midlandstech.edu   Federal Code: 003993

2-year public technical college in small city.
Enrollment: 10,243 undergrads, 54% part-time.
Selectivity: Open admission; but selective for some programs.

South Carolina — Midlands Technical College

BASIC COSTS (2005-2006)
Tuition and fees: $3,004; out-of-district residents $3,876; out-of-state residents $8,812.

FINANCIAL AID PICTURE
Students with need: Need-based aid available for full-time and part-time students.

FINANCIAL AID PROCEDURES
Forms required: FAFSA.
Dates and Deadlines: Priority date 4/15; no closing date. Applicants notified on a rolling basis; must reply within 2 week(s) of notification.

CONTACT
Michele Bowles, Director of Student Aid
PO Box 2408, Columbia, SC 29202
(803) 738-7691

Morris College
Sumter, South Carolina
www.morris.edu   Federal Code: 218399

4-year private liberal arts college in large town, affiliated with Baptist faith.
Enrollment: 863 undergrads, 2% part-time. 209 full-time freshmen.
Selectivity: Admits over 75% of applicants.

BASIC COSTS (2006-2007)
Tuition and fees: $8,812.
Per-credit charge: $357.
Room and board: $3,982.

FINANCIAL AID PICTURE (2005-2006)
Students with need: Out of 209 full-time freshmen who applied for aid, 203 were judged to have need. Of these, 203 received aid, and 5 had their full need met. Average financial aid package met 86% of need; average scholarship/grant was $8,150; average loan was $2,625. For part-time students, average financial aid package was $6,087.
Students without need: This college only awards aid to students with need.
Scholarships offered: *Merit:* Luns C. Richardson Endowed Scholarship, Morris College Presidential Scholarship. *Athletic:* 15 full-time freshmen received athletic scholarships; average amount $1,200.
Cumulative student debt: 97% of graduating class had student loans; average debt was $19,000.
Additional info: Students are encouraged to complete FAFSA on the web.

FINANCIAL AID PROCEDURES
Forms required: FAFSA, state aid form, institutional form.
Dates and Deadlines: Priority date 3/30; no closing date. Applicants notified on a rolling basis starting 6/1; must reply within 2 week(s) of notification.

CONTACT
Sandra Gibson, Financial Aid Officer
100 West College Street, Sumter, SC 29150-3599
(803) 934-3238

Newberry College
Newberry, South Carolina
www.newberry.edu   Federal Code: 003440

4-year private liberal arts college in small city, affiliated with Evangelical Lutheran Church in America.
Enrollment: 841 undergrads. 276 full-time freshmen.
Selectivity: Admits 50 to 75% of applicants.

BASIC COSTS (2006-2007)
Tuition and fees: $19,631.
Per-credit charge: $350.
Room and board: $6,880.

FINANCIAL AID PICTURE (2005-2006)
Students with need: Out of 264 full-time freshmen who applied for aid, 194 were judged to have need. Of these, 194 received aid, and 115 had their full need met. Average financial aid package met 70% of need. Need-based aid available for part-time students.
Students without need: No-need awards available for academics, alumni affiliation, athletics, music/drama, religious affiliation, ROTC, state/district residency.

FINANCIAL AID PROCEDURES
Forms required: FAFSA, institutional form.
Dates and Deadlines: Priority date 3/15; no closing date. Applicants notified on a rolling basis starting 3/1; must reply by 5/1 or within 2 week(s) of notification.
Transfers: Available for scholarship excellence.

CONTACT
Susanne Nelson, Director of Financial Aid
2100 College Street, Newberry, SC 29108
(803) 321-5128

North Greenville College
Tigerville, South Carolina
www.ngc.edu   Federal Code: 003441

4-year private liberal arts college in rural community, affiliated with Southern Baptist Convention.
Enrollment: 1,724 undergrads, 5% part-time. 437 full-time freshmen.
Selectivity: Admits over 75% of applicants.

BASIC COSTS (2006-2007)
Tuition and fees: $10,760.
Per-credit charge: $200.
Room and board: $6,190.

FINANCIAL AID PICTURE (2005-2006)
Students with need: Average financial aid package met 70% of need; average scholarship/grant was $1,000; average loan was $2,625. For part-time students, average financial aid package was $700.
Students without need: This college only awards aid to students with need.

FINANCIAL AID PROCEDURES
Forms required: FAFSA.
Dates and Deadlines: Priority date 6/1; closing date 6/30. Applicants notified on a rolling basis starting 8/1; must reply within 2 week(s) of notification.
Transfers: No deadline.

CONTACT
Mike Jordan, Director of Financial Aid
PO Box 1892, Tigerville, SC 29688-1892
(864) 977-7050

Northeastern Technical College
Cheraw, South Carolina
www.netc.edu   Federal Code: 007602

2-year public community and technical college in small town.
Enrollment: 999 undergrads, 47% part-time. 198 full-time freshmen.
Selectivity: Open admission; but selective for some programs.

BASIC COSTS (2005-2006)
Tuition and fees: $2,526; out-of-district residents $2,718; out-of-state residents $4,110.

FINANCIAL AID PICTURE (2005-2006)
Students with need: 97% of average financial aid package awarded as scholarships/grants, 3% awarded as loans/jobs.

FINANCIAL AID PROCEDURES
Forms required: FAFSA.
Dates and Deadlines: No deadline. Applicants notified on a rolling basis; must reply within 8 week(s) of notification.

CONTACT
Sheryl Marshall, Coordinator of Student Financial Assistance
Drawer 1007, Cheraw, SC 29520
(843) 921-6939

Orangeburg-Calhoun Technical College
Orangeburg, South Carolina
www.octech.edu   Federal Code: 006815

2-year public community and technical college in large town.
Enrollment: 2,453 undergrads.
Selectivity: Open admission; but selective for some programs.

BASIC COSTS (2005-2006)
Tuition and fees: $2,640; out-of-district residents $3,288; out-of-state residents $4,734.

FINANCIAL AID PICTURE
Students with need: Need-based aid available for full-time and part-time students.
Students without need: This college only awards aid to students with need.
Scholarships offered: College Foundation Scholarship; full academic tuition; for high school valedictorians and salutatorians.

FINANCIAL AID PROCEDURES
Forms required: FAFSA, institutional form.
Dates and Deadlines: Priority date 6/4; no closing date. Applicants notified on a rolling basis starting 5/1; must reply within 2 week(s) of notification.
Transfers: Priority date 6/1. Financial aid transcripts required of mid-year transfers prior to disbursement of aid.

CONTACT
Caroline Wagasky, Director of Institutional Research
3250 St. Matthews Road, Orangeburg, SC 29118-8222
(803) 535-1249

Piedmont Technical College
Greenwood, South Carolina
www.ptc.edu   Federal Code: 003992

2-year public community and technical college in small city.
Enrollment: 4,680 undergrads.
Selectivity: Open admission; but selective for some programs.

BASIC COSTS (2005-2006)
Tuition and fees: $2,740; out-of-district residents $3,172; out-of-state residents $4,372.
Additional info: The full-time in-district rates for two semesters are $2496 or $2784, determined by county of residence. The per-credit-hour in-district rates are $104 or $116.

FINANCIAL AID PICTURE
Students with need: Need-based aid available for full-time and part-time students. Work study available nights, weekends, and for part-time students.
Students without need: This college only awards aid to students with need.

FINANCIAL AID PROCEDURES
Forms required: FAFSA.
Dates and Deadlines: Priority date 5/1; no closing date. Applicants notified on a rolling basis starting 6/1; must reply within 2 week(s) of notification.

CONTACT
Director of Financial Aid
Box 1467, Greenwood, SC 29648
(864) 941-8365

Presbyterian College
Clinton, South Carolina
www.presby.edu   Federal Code: 003445

4-year private liberal arts college in small town, affiliated with Presbyterian Church (USA).
Enrollment: 1,149 undergrads, 1% part-time. 313 full-time freshmen.
Selectivity: Admits over 75% of applicants.

BASIC COSTS (2006-2007)
Tuition and fees: $24,626.
Per-credit charge: $940.
Room and board: $7,756.

FINANCIAL AID PICTURE (2005-2006)
Students with need: Out of 249 full-time freshmen who applied for aid, 193 were judged to have need. Of these, 193 received aid, and 23 had their full need met. Average financial aid package met 92% of need; average scholarship/grant was $21,813; average loan was $3,881. For part-time students, average financial aid package was $6,500.
Students without need: 104 full-time freshmen who did not demonstrate need for aid received scholarships/grants; average award was $13,488. No-need awards available for academics, alumni affiliation, athletics, job skills, leadership, minority status, music/drama, religious affiliation, ROTC.
Scholarships offered: *Merit:* Academic and leadership scholarships, applications by December 5; number and amounts awarded vary; music awards based on audition. *Athletic:* 82 full-time freshmen received athletic scholarships; average amount $6,319.
Cumulative student debt: 55% of graduating class had student loans; average debt was $21,517.

FINANCIAL AID PROCEDURES
Forms required: FAFSA, institutional form.
Dates and Deadlines: Priority date 3/1; no closing date. Applicants notified on a rolling basis starting 4/1; must reply by 5/1.

CONTACT
Judi Gillespie, Director of Financial Aid
503 South Broad Street, Clinton, SC 29325-9989
(864) 833-8290

South Carolina State University
Orangeburg, South Carolina
www.scsu.edu   Federal Code: 003446

4-year public university in large town.
Enrollment: 3,839 undergrads, 7% part-time. 1,002 full-time freshmen.
Selectivity: Admits over 75% of applicants.

BASIC COSTS (2005-2006)
Tuition and fees: $6,480; out-of-state residents $13,288.
Per-credit charge: $270; out-of-state residents $554.
Room and board: $4,920.

FINANCIAL AID PICTURE
Students with need: Need-based aid available for full-time students.
Students without need: No-need awards available for academics, athletics, ROTC.

FINANCIAL AID PROCEDURES
Forms required: FAFSA.
Dates and Deadlines: Closing date 5/1. Applicants notified on a rolling basis starting 6/15; must reply by 8/1 or within 4 week(s) of notification.
Transfers: Must provide documentation on amount of state aid received, and which semesters it was received, prior to transfer.

CONTACT
Sandra Davis, Director of Financial Aid
300 College Street NE, Orangeburg, SC 29117
(803) 536-7185

South University
Columbia, South Carolina
www.southuniversity.com   Federal Code: 004922

4-year for-profit university and business and health science college in small city.
Enrollment: 425 undergrads, 32% part-time. 26 full-time freshmen.
Selectivity: Open admission; but selective for some programs.

FINANCIAL AID PICTURE
Students with need: Need-based aid available for full-time and part-time students.
Students without need: This college only awards aid to students with need.

FINANCIAL AID PROCEDURES
Forms required: FAFSA.
Dates and Deadlines: Priority date 5/30; no closing date. Applicants notified on a rolling basis starting 5/30.

CONTACT
Walter Haversat, Financial Aid Director
3810 Main Street, Columbia, SC 29203
(803) 799-9082

Southern Wesleyan University
Central, South Carolina
www.swu.edu   Federal Code: 003422

4-year private university and liberal arts college in small town, affiliated with Wesleyan Church.
Enrollment: 1,995 undergrads, 4% part-time. 154 full-time freshmen.
Selectivity: Admits 50 to 75% of applicants.

BASIC COSTS (2006-2007)
Tuition and fees: $16,150.
Per-credit charge: $480.
Room and board: $5,800.

FINANCIAL AID PICTURE (2005-2006)
Students with need: Average financial aid package met 65% of need; average scholarship/grant was $9,191; average loan was $1,990. For part-time students, average financial aid package was $6,639.
Students without need: No-need awards available for academics, alumni affiliation, athletics, job skills, leadership, minority status, music/drama, religious affiliation, ROTC.
Cumulative student debt: 99% of graduating class had student loans; average debt was $24,032.

FINANCIAL AID PROCEDURES
Forms required: FAFSA, institutional form.
Dates and Deadlines: Priority date 3/31; closing date 6/30. Applicants notified on a rolling basis starting 2/1; must reply within 3 week(s) of notification.

CONTACT
Jeff Dennis, Financial Aid Director
PO Box 1020, Central, SC 29630-1020
(800) 289-1292

Spartanburg Methodist College
Spartanburg, South Carolina
www.smcsc.edu   Federal Code: 003447

2-year private junior and liberal arts college in small city, affiliated with United Methodist Church.
Enrollment: 716 undergrads, 3% part-time. 405 full-time freshmen.
Selectivity: Admits over 75% of applicants.

BASIC COSTS (2006-2007)
Tuition and fees: $10,400.
Per-credit charge: $272.
Room and board: $5,962.
Additional info: $150 enrollment fee for first-time enrollees. Tuition/fee waivers available for adults, unemployed or children of unemployed.

FINANCIAL AID PICTURE (2005-2006)
Students with need: Out of 400 full-time freshmen who applied for aid, 393 were judged to have need. Of these, 393 received aid, and 37 had their full need met. Average financial aid package met 80% of need; average scholarship/grant was $2,500; average loan was $2,400. For part-time students, average financial aid package was $3,500.
Students without need: 10 full-time freshmen who did not demonstrate need for aid received scholarships/grants; average award was $3,258. No-need awards available for academics, athletics, job skills, leadership, music/drama, religious affiliation, state/district residency.
Scholarships offered: *Merit:* Milliken Scholars; $4,100. Camak Scholars; $3,500. Trustee Scholars; $3,000. Presidential Scholars; $2,400. *Athletic:* 98 full-time freshmen received athletic scholarships; average amount $1,793.
Additional info: College strives to meet 100% of established financial need of all students.

FINANCIAL AID PROCEDURES
Forms required: FAFSA.
Dates and Deadlines: Priority date 6/30; closing date 8/22. Applicants notified on a rolling basis starting 3/1; must reply within 2 week(s) of notification.
Transfers: No deadline. Applicants notified on a rolling basis starting 3/1; must reply within 2 week(s) of notification. To be eligible for financial aid, full time students must pass the equivalent of 12 hours.

CONTACT
Carolyn Sparks, Assistant Dean of Financial Aid
1000 Powell Mill Road, Spartanburg, SC 29301-5899
(864) 587-4298

Spartanburg Technical College
Spartanburg, South Carolina
www.stcsc.edu   Federal Code: 003994

2-year public community and technical college in large town.
Enrollment: 4,409 undergrads.
Selectivity: Open admission; but selective for some programs.

BASIC COSTS (2005-2006)
Tuition and fees: $2,902; out-of-district residents $3,618; out-of-state residents $5,490.

FINANCIAL AID PICTURE (2004-2005)
Students with need: 97% of average financial aid package awarded as scholarships/grants, 3% awarded as loans/jobs. Need-based aid available for part-time students.
Additional info: Participates in South Carolina lottery tuition assistance program. Full-time technical college students who are state residents receive assistance for tuition not covered by federal or need-based grants.

FINANCIAL AID PROCEDURES
Forms required: FAFSA.
Dates and Deadlines: Priority date 2/28; closing date 5/1. Applicants notified on a rolling basis starting 5/1.
Transfers: No deadline.

CONTACT
Nancy Garmroth, Dean of Admissions and Financial Aid
Box 4386, Spartanburg, SC 29305
(864) 592-4810

Technical College of the Lowcountry
Beaufort, South Carolina
www.tcl.edu   Federal Code: 009910

2-year public community and technical college in small town.
Enrollment: 1,689 undergrads.
Selectivity: Open admission; but selective for some programs.

BASIC COSTS (2005-2006)
Tuition and fees: $3,050; out-of-state residents $5,932.

FINANCIAL AID PICTURE
Students with need: Need-based aid available for full-time and part-time students.
Students without need: This college only awards aid to students with need.
Additional info: State lottery aid may be available to South Carolina residents who take 6 credit hours or more.

FINANCIAL AID PROCEDURES
Forms required: FAFSA.
Dates and Deadlines: No deadline. Applicants notified on a rolling basis starting 7/1.

CONTACT
Cleo Martin, Coordinator of Financial Aid
921 South Ribaut Road, Beaufort, SC 29901-1288
(843) 525-8337

Tri-County Technical College
Pendleton, South Carolina
www.tctc.edu   Federal Code: 004926

2-year public technical college in small town.
Enrollment: 3,800 undergrads.
Selectivity: Open admission; but selective for some programs.

BASIC COSTS (2005-2006)
Tuition and fees: $2,738; out-of-district residents $3,024; out-of-state residents $6,084.

FINANCIAL AID PICTURE
Students with need: Need-based aid available for full-time and part-time students. Work study available nights.
Students without need: No-need awards available for academics, state/district residency.
Scholarships offered: General and departmental scholarships; more than 125 awarded. Some with special qualification criteria, such as student's career field or place of residency.
Additional info: Deadline for application to institutional scholarships April 2.

FINANCIAL AID PROCEDURES
Forms required: FAFSA.
Dates and Deadlines: Priority date 6/30; no closing date. Applicants notified on a rolling basis starting 6/15; must reply within 2 week(s) of notification.
Transfers: Priority date 5/1; no deadline. Applicants notified on a rolling basis starting 6/1.

CONTACT
Stuart Spires, Director of Financial Aid
Box 587, Pendleton, SC 29670
(864) 646-8361

Trident Technical College
Charleston, South Carolina
www.tridenttech.edu   Federal Code: 004920

2-year public community and technical college in large city.
Enrollment: 10,128 undergrads.
Selectivity: Open admission; but selective for some programs.

BASIC COSTS (2005-2006)
Tuition and fees: $2,950; out-of-district residents $3,276; out-of-state residents $5,586.

FINANCIAL AID PICTURE
Students with need: Need-based aid available for full-time and part-time students.
Scholarships offered: Numerous scholarship opportunities are available through the Trident Technical College Foundation.

FINANCIAL AID PROCEDURES
Forms required: FAFSA.
Dates and Deadlines: No deadline. Applicants notified on a rolling basis; must reply within 6 week(s) of notification.

CONTACT
Ellen Green, Director of Financial Aid
Box 118067, AM-M, Charleston, SC 29423-8067
(843) 574-6147

University of South Carolina
Columbia, South Carolina
www.sc.edu   Federal Code: 003448

4-year public university in small city.
Enrollment: 17,781 undergrads, 8% part-time. 3,308 full-time freshmen.
Selectivity: Admits 50 to 75% of applicants.

BASIC COSTS (2005-2006)
Tuition and fees: $7,314; out-of-state residents $18,956.
Per-credit charge: $324; out-of-state residents $844.

Room and board: $6,083.
Additional info: Health professions (pharmacy, health, nursing), law and medical professions have higher undergraduate and graduate fees.

FINANCIAL AID PICTURE (2004-2005)
Students with need: Out of 2,293 full-time freshmen who applied for aid, 1,573 were judged to have need. Of these, 1,564 received aid, and 473 had their full need met. Average financial aid package met 74% of need; average scholarship/grant was $3,529; average loan was $1,860. For part-time students, average financial aid package was $6,662.
Students without need: 1,397 full-time freshmen who did not demonstrate need for aid received scholarships/grants; average award was $5,654. No-need awards available for academics, alumni affiliation, art, athletics, job skills, leadership, minority status, music/drama, religious affiliation, ROTC, state/district residency.
Scholarships offered: 165 full-time freshmen received athletic scholarships; average amount $7,801.

FINANCIAL AID PROCEDURES
Forms required: FAFSA.
Dates and Deadlines: Priority date 4/1; no closing date. Applicants notified on a rolling basis starting 4/1.

CONTACT
Edgar Miller, Director of Financial Aid and Scholarships
Office of Undergraduate Admissions, Columbia, SC 29208
(803) 777-8134

University of South Carolina at Aiken
Aiken, South Carolina
www.usca.edu   Federal Code: 003449

4-year public university and liberal arts college in large town.
Enrollment: 2,851 undergrads, 20% part-time. 562 full-time freshmen.
Selectivity: Admits less than 50% of applicants.

BASIC COSTS (2005-2006)
Tuition and fees: $6,158; out-of-state residents $12,300.
Per-credit charge: $258; out-of-state residents $520.
Room and board: $5,560.

FINANCIAL AID PICTURE
Students with need: Need-based aid available for full-time and part-time students.

FINANCIAL AID PROCEDURES
Forms required: FAFSA.
Dates and Deadlines: Priority date 3/15; no closing date. Applicants notified on a rolling basis starting 5/20; must reply within 2 week(s) of notification.
Transfers: Financial aid transcripts from previous institutions required.

CONTACT
Glenn Shumpert, Director of Financial Aid
471 University Parkway, Aiken, SC 29801
(803) 641-3476

University of South Carolina at Beaufort
Beaufort, South Carolina
www.uscb.edu   Federal Code: 003450

4-year public liberal arts college in large town.
Enrollment: 1,227 undergrads, 45% part-time. 195 full-time freshmen.

BASIC COSTS (2005-2006)
Tuition and fees: $5,284; out-of-state residents $12,200.
Per-credit charge: $207; out-of-state residents $495.

FINANCIAL AID PICTURE
Students with need: Need-based aid available for full-time and part-time students. Work study available nights, weekends, and for part-time students.
Students without need: This college only awards aid to students with need.

FINANCIAL AID PROCEDURES
Forms required: FAFSA.
Dates and Deadlines: Priority date 4/15; no closing date. Applicants notified on a rolling basis starting 5/31; must reply within 2 week(s) of notification.

CONTACT
Patricia Greene, Director and VA Coordinator of Financial Aid
801 Carteret Street, Beaufort, SC 29902
(843) 521-4117

University of South Carolina at Sumter
Sumter, South Carolina
www.uscsumter.edu   Federal Code: 003426

2-year public branch campus college in small city.
Enrollment: 823 undergrads, 31% part-time. 194 full-time freshmen.
Selectivity: Admits 50 to 75% of applicants.

BASIC COSTS (2005-2006)
Tuition and fees: $4,344; out-of-state residents $10,404.
Per-credit charge: $169; out-of-state residents $422.

FINANCIAL AID PICTURE (2005-2006)
Students with need: 68% of average financial aid package awarded as scholarships/grants, 32% awarded as loans/jobs. Need-based aid available for part-time students. Work study available nights, weekends, and for part-time students.
Students without need: This college only awards aid to students with need.

FINANCIAL AID PROCEDURES
Forms required: FAFSA.
Dates and Deadlines: Priority date 4/15; no closing date. Applicants notified on a rolling basis starting 4/16; must reply within 2 week(s) of notification.

CONTACT
Sue Sims, Financial Aid Director
200 Miller Road, Sumter, SC 29150-2498
(803) 938-3766

University of South Carolina at Union
Union, South Carolina
http://uscunion.sc.edu   Federal Code: 004927

2-year public branch campus college in small town.
Enrollment: 300 undergrads.

BASIC COSTS (2005-2006)
Tuition and fees: $4,344; out-of-state residents $10,404.
Per-credit charge: $169; out-of-state residents $422.

FINANCIAL AID PICTURE
Students with need: Work study available nights, weekends, and for part-time students.
Students without need: This college only awards aid to students with need.

FINANCIAL AID PROCEDURES
Forms required: FAFSA.
Dates and Deadlines: Priority date 4/15; no closing date. Applicants notified on a rolling basis starting 7/15; must reply within 2 week(s) of notification.

CONTACT
Bobby Holcombe, Financial Aid Director
PO Drawer 729, Union, SC 29379
(864) 429-8728

University of South Carolina Upstate
Spartanburg, South Carolina
www.uscupstate.edu   Federal Code: 006951

4-year public university in small city.
Enrollment: 4,334 undergrads, 1% part-time. 627 full-time freshmen.
Selectivity: Admits 50 to 75% of applicants.

BASIC COSTS (2005-2006)
Tuition and fees: $6,762; out-of-state residents $13,600.
Per-credit charge: $282; out-of-state residents $583.
Room and board: $5,860.

FINANCIAL AID PICTURE (2004-2005)
Students with need: Out of 489 full-time freshmen who applied for aid, 407 were judged to have need. Of these, 403 received aid, and 101 had their full need met. Average financial aid package met 36% of need; average scholarship/grant was $3,356; average loan was $2,340. For part-time students, average financial aid package was $6,639.
Students without need: 17 full-time freshmen who did not demonstrate need for aid received scholarships/grants; average award was $2,074. No-need awards available for academics, athletics, minority status, ROTC, state/district residency.
Scholarships offered: 88 full-time freshmen received athletic scholarships; average amount $2,218.
Cumulative student debt: 63% of graduating class had student loans; average debt was $17,354.
Additional info: Out-of-state students who are recipients of financial aid may qualify for out-of-state fee waiver. Educational benefits available to veterans and children of deceased/disabled veterans.

FINANCIAL AID PROCEDURES
Forms required: FAFSA, institutional form.
Dates and Deadlines: Priority date 3/1; closing date 7/15. Applicants notified on a rolling basis starting 5/1; must reply within 2 week(s) of notification.
Transfers: Students eligible for financial assistance for total of 5 years or 10 full-time semesters at all post-secondary institutions attended for the bachelor's degree, and 5 full-time semesters of enrollment for associate's degree in nursing.

CONTACT
Kim Jenerette, Director of Financial Aid and Scholarships
800 University Way, Spartanburg, SC 29303
(864) 503-5340

University of South Carolina: Salkehatchie Regional Campus
Allendale, South Carolina
www.uscsalkehatchie.sc.edu   Federal Code: 003454

2-year public branch campus college in small town.
Enrollment: 547 undergrads.

BASIC COSTS (2005-2006)
Tuition and fees: $4,344; out-of-state residents $10,404.
Per-credit charge: $169; out-of-state residents $422.

FINANCIAL AID PICTURE (2004-2005)
Students with need: 0% of average financial aid package awarded as scholarships/grants, 100% awarded as loans/jobs. Need-based aid available for part-time students. Work study available nights, weekends, and for part-time students.
Students without need: No-need awards available for academics.

FINANCIAL AID PROCEDURES
Forms required: FAFSA.
Dates and Deadlines: Priority date 4/30; no closing date. Applicants notified on a rolling basis starting 6/1.

CONTACT
Julie Hadwin, Director of Financial Aid
PO Box 617, Allendale, SC 29810
(803) 584-3446

Voorhees College
Denmark, South Carolina
www.voorhees.edu   Federal Code: 003455

4-year private liberal arts college in small town, affiliated with Episcopal Church.
Enrollment: 708 undergrads. 240 full-time freshmen.
Selectivity: Admits less than 50% of applicants.

BASIC COSTS (2005-2006)
Tuition and fees: $7,726.
Room and board: $4,572.

FINANCIAL AID PICTURE (2005-2006)
Students with need: Out of 201 full-time freshmen who applied for aid, 194 were judged to have need. Of these, 194 received aid, and 13 had their full need met. Average financial aid package met 52% of need; average scholarship/grant was $5,341; average loan was $1,981. Need-based aid available for part-time students.
Students without need: 46 full-time freshmen who did not demonstrate need for aid received scholarships/grants; average award was $9,844.

FINANCIAL AID PROCEDURES
Forms required: FAFSA, institutional form.
Dates and Deadlines: Priority date 4/15; no closing date. Applicants notified on a rolling basis starting 3/1; must reply within 2 week(s) of notification.

CONTACT
Augusta Kitchen, Director of Student Financial Aid
213 Wiggins Road, Denmark, SC 29042
(803) 703-7109

Williamsburg Technical College
Kingstree, South Carolina
www.wiltech.edu   Federal Code: 009322

2-year public community and technical college in small town.
Enrollment: 300 undergrads.
Selectivity: Open admission.

BASIC COSTS (2005-2006)
Tuition and fees: $2,692; out-of-state residents $4,990.

FINANCIAL AID PICTURE
Students with need: Need-based aid available for full-time and part-time students. Work study available nights, weekends, and for part-time students.
Students without need: No-need awards available for academics, leadership, minority status, state/district residency.
Additional info: Tuition waivers for children of war veterans.

FINANCIAL AID PROCEDURES
Forms required: FAFSA.
Dates and Deadlines: Priority date 4/15; no closing date. Applicants notified on a rolling basis starting 7/1; must reply within 4 week(s) of notification.

CONTACT
Michael Scott, Director of Financial Aid
601 Martin Luther King Jr. Avenue, Kingstree, SC 29556-4197
(843) 355-4166

Winthrop University
Rock Hill, South Carolina
www.winthrop.edu
Federal Code: 003456

4-year public university in small city.
Enrollment: 5,000 undergrads.

BASIC COSTS (2005-2006)
Tuition and fees: $8,756; out-of-state residents $16,150.
Room and board: $5,352.

FINANCIAL AID PICTURE
Students with need: Need-based aid available for full-time and part-time students.
Students without need: No-need awards available for academics, art, athletics, music/drama, state/district residency.
Scholarships offered: Music scholarships and athletic grants, amounts vary. International Baccalaureate Scholarship for students who graduate with IB diploma; full tuition.
Additional info: Academic scholarships from $1,500 to full tuition and board awarded to approximately one-third of entering freshman class each year.

FINANCIAL AID PROCEDURES
Forms required: FAFSA.
Dates and Deadlines: Priority date 3/1; no closing date. Applicants notified on a rolling basis starting 4/1; must reply within 2 week(s) of notification.
Transfers: Transfer students are not eligible for academic scholarship their first year.

CONTACT
Betty Whalen, Director, Financial Resource Center
701 Oakland Avenue, Rock Hill, SC 29733
(803) 323-2189

Wofford College
Spartanburg, South Carolina
www.wofford.edu
Federal Code: 003457

4-year private liberal arts college in small city, affiliated with United Methodist Church.
Enrollment: 1,163 undergrads, 1% part-time. 321 full-time freshmen.
Selectivity: Admits 50 to 75% of applicants.

BASIC COSTS (2006-2007)
Tuition and fees: $26,110.
Per-credit charge: $940.
Room and board: $7,260.

FINANCIAL AID PICTURE (2005-2006)
Students with need: Out of 224 full-time freshmen who applied for aid, 162 were judged to have need. Of these, 162 received aid, and 87 had their full need met. Average financial aid package met 85% of need; average scholarship/grant was $16,532; average loan was $2,942. For part-time students, average financial aid package was $6,185.
Students without need: 83 full-time freshmen who did not demonstrate need for aid received scholarships/grants; average award was $10,466. No-need awards available for academics, athletics, leadership, music/drama, religious affiliation, ROTC, state/district residency.
Scholarships offered: 20 full-time freshmen received athletic scholarships; average amount $18,324.
Cumulative student debt: 49% of graduating class had student loans; average debt was $10,242.

FINANCIAL AID PROCEDURES
Forms required: FAFSA.
Dates and Deadlines: Priority date 3/15; no closing date. Applicants notified on a rolling basis starting 3/31; must reply by 5/1.

CONTACT
Donna Hawkins, Director of Financial Aid
429 North Church Street, Spartanburg, SC 29303-3663
(864) 597-4149

York Technical College
Rock Hill, South Carolina
www.yorktech.com
Federal Code: 003996

2-year public technical college in large town.
Enrollment: 3,583 undergrads, 43% part-time. 626 full-time freshmen.
Selectivity: Open admission; but selective for some programs.

BASIC COSTS (2005-2006)
Tuition and fees: $3,036; out-of-district residents $3,400; out-of-state residents $6,664.

FINANCIAL AID PICTURE (2005-2006)
Students with need: For part-time students, average financial aid package was $1,500.

FINANCIAL AID PROCEDURES
Forms required: FAFSA.
Dates and Deadlines: Priority date 6/1; no closing date. Applicants notified on a rolling basis starting 7/1.

CONTACT
Regina Venson, Financial Aid Department Manager
452 South Anderson Road, Rock Hill, SC 29730
(803) 327-8005

South Dakota

Augustana College
Sioux Falls, South Dakota
www.augie.edu
Federal Code: 003458

4-year private liberal arts college in small city, affiliated with Evangelical Lutheran Church in America.
Enrollment: 1,621 undergrads. 391 full-time freshmen.
Selectivity: Admits over 75% of applicants.

BASIC COSTS (2006-2007)
Tuition and fees: $19,986.
Per-credit charge: $290.
Room and board: $5,664.
Additional info: Tuition/fee waivers available for minority students.

FINANCIAL AID PICTURE (2005-2006)
Students with need: 62% of average financial aid package awarded as scholarships/grants, 38% awarded as loans/jobs. Need-based aid available for part-time students. Work study available nights, weekends, and for part-time students.

Students without need: No-need awards available for academics, alumni affiliation, art, athletics, leadership, minority status, music/drama, religious affiliation.

FINANCIAL AID PROCEDURES
Forms required: FAFSA.
Dates and Deadlines: Priority date 3/1; no closing date. Applicants notified on a rolling basis starting 3/15; must reply by 5/1 or within 3 week(s) of notification.

CONTACT
Brenda Murtha, Director of Financial Aid
2001 South Summit Avenue, Sioux Falls, SD 57197-9990
(605) 274-5216

Black Hills State University
Spearfish, South Dakota
www.bhsu.edu   Federal Code: 003459

4-year public liberal arts and teachers college in small town.
Enrollment: 3,166 undergrads.
Selectivity: Admits over 75% of applicants.

BASIC COSTS (2005-2006)
Tuition and fees: $4,754; out-of-state residents $9,741.
Per-credit charge: $76; out-of-state residents $243.
Room and board: $3,960.
Additional info: Reciprocity agreements reduce tuition for some out-of-state students.

FINANCIAL AID PICTURE
Students with need: Need-based aid available for full-time and part-time students.
Students without need: This college only awards aid to students with need.

FINANCIAL AID PROCEDURES
Forms required: FAFSA.
Dates and Deadlines: Closing date 2/15. Applicants notified on a rolling basis starting 5/15; must reply within 3 week(s) of notification.

CONTACT
Deb Henriksen, Director of Financial Aid
University Street Box 9502, Spearfish, SD 57799-9502
(605) 642-6581

Dakota State University
Madison, South Dakota
www.dsu.edu   Federal Code: 003463

4-year public university in small town.
Enrollment: 1,457 undergrads, 20% part-time. 296 full-time freshmen.
Selectivity: Admits over 75% of applicants.

BASIC COSTS (2005-2006)
Tuition and fees: $4,832; out-of-state residents $9,819.
Per-credit charge: $76; out-of-state residents $243.
Room and board: $3,665.
Additional info: Reciprocity agreements reduce tuition for some out-of-state students. Tuition/fee waivers available for adults.

FINANCIAL AID PICTURE (2004-2005)
Students with need: Out of 276 full-time freshmen who applied for aid, 220 were judged to have need. Of these, 216 received aid, and 63 had their full need met. Average financial aid package met 78% of need; average scholarship/grant was $2,764; average loan was $2,953. For part-time students, average financial aid package was $4,863.

Students without need: 48 full-time freshmen who did not demonstrate need for aid received scholarships/grants; average award was $3,663. No-need awards available for academics, alumni affiliation, art, athletics, leadership, minority status, music/drama, state/district residency.
Scholarships offered: 33 full-time freshmen received athletic scholarships; average amount $1,163.
Additional info: Application deadline for grants and scholarships March 1. No deadline for loan and job applications.

FINANCIAL AID PROCEDURES
Forms required: FAFSA.
Dates and Deadlines: Priority date 3/1; no closing date. Applicants notified on a rolling basis starting 4/15; must reply within 2 week(s) of notification.

CONTACT
Rosie Jamison, Financial Aid Director
820 North Washington Avenue, Madison, SD 57042
(605) 256-5152

Dakota Wesleyan University
Mitchell, South Dakota
www.dwu.edu   Federal Code: 003461

4-year private university and liberal arts college in large town, affiliated with United Methodist Church.
Enrollment: 755 undergrads, 3% part-time. 136 full-time freshmen.

BASIC COSTS (2005-2006)
Tuition and fees: $15,700.
Per-credit charge: $330.
Room and board: $4,800.

FINANCIAL AID PICTURE (2005-2006)
Students with need: Out of 136 full-time freshmen who applied for aid, 115 were judged to have need. Of these, 115 received aid, and 6 had their full need met. Average financial aid package met 76% of need; average scholarship/grant was $5,324; average loan was $3,126. For part-time students, average financial aid package was $2,550.
Students without need: 5 full-time freshmen who did not demonstrate need for aid received scholarships/grants; average award was $11,696. No-need awards available for academics, alumni affiliation, art, athletics, leadership, minority status, music/drama, religious affiliation.
Scholarships offered: *Merit:* Academic scholarships awarded based on combination of ACT scores and GPA. Awarded for 4 years. *Athletic:* 88 full-time freshmen received athletic scholarships; average amount $3,369.

FINANCIAL AID PROCEDURES
Forms required: FAFSA.
Dates and Deadlines: Priority date 4/1; no closing date. Applicants notified on a rolling basis starting 3/1; must reply within 2 week(s) of notification.

CONTACT
Nicole Popp, Financial Aid Counselor
1200 West University Avenue, Mitchell, SD 57301-4398
(605) 995-2659

Kilian Community College
Sioux Falls, South Dakota
www.kilian.edu   Federal Code: 015000

2-year private community college in small city.
Enrollment: 506 undergrads, 80% part-time. 27 full-time freshmen.
Selectivity: Open admission.

South Dakota — Kilian Community College

BASIC COSTS (2005-2006)
Tuition and fees: $5,950.
Per-credit charge: $195.

FINANCIAL AID PICTURE (2004-2005)
Students with need: Out of 24 full-time freshmen who applied for aid, 24 were judged to have need. Of these, 24 received aid, and 4 had their full need met. Average financial aid package met 60% of need; average scholarship/grant was $2,000; average loan was $2,625. Need-based aid available for part-time students.
Students without need: 2 full-time freshmen who did not demonstrate need for aid received scholarships/grants; average award was $200. No-need awards available for academics, leadership.
Cumulative student debt: 85% of graduating class had student loans; average debt was $14,125.

FINANCIAL AID PROCEDURES
Forms required: FAFSA, institutional form.
Dates and Deadlines: No deadline. Applicants notified on a rolling basis starting 7/1; must reply within 2 week(s) of notification.
Transfers: No deadline. Applicants notified on a rolling basis starting 7/1; must reply within 2 week(s) of notification.

CONTACT
Glen Poppinga, Director of Financial Aid
300 East 6th Street, Sioux Falls, SD 57103-7020
(605) 221-3100

Lake Area Technical Institute
Watertown, South Dakota
www.lati.tec.sd.us   Federal Code: 005309

2-year public technical college in large town.
Enrollment: 1,170 undergrads.

BASIC COSTS (2005-2006)
Tuition and fees: $3,350.
Per-credit charge: $64.

FINANCIAL AID PICTURE
Students with need: Need-based aid available for full-time and part-time students.
Students without need: This college only awards aid to students with need.

FINANCIAL AID PROCEDURES
Forms required: FAFSA.
Dates and Deadlines: Priority date 4/15; no closing date. Applicants notified on a rolling basis starting 5/1.

CONTACT
Richard Coplan, Financial Aid Coordinator
PO Box 730, Watertown, SD 57201
(605) 882-5284

Mitchell Technical Institute
Mitchell, South Dakota
www.mitchelltech.com   Federal Code: 008284

2-year public culinary school and technical college in large town.
Enrollment: 807 undergrads, 16% part-time. 445 full-time freshmen.
Selectivity: Open admission.

BASIC COSTS (2005-2006)
Tuition and fees: $2,820.
Per-credit charge: $64.

FINANCIAL AID PICTURE (2005-2006)
Students with need: Average financial aid package met 62% of need; average scholarship/grant was $2,951; average loan was $2,550. Need-based aid available for part-time students.

FINANCIAL AID PROCEDURES
Forms required: FAFSA.
Dates and Deadlines: No deadline. Applicants notified on a rolling basis; must reply within 3 week(s) of notification.

CONTACT
Grant Uecker, Financial Aid Coordinator
821 North Capital, Mitchell, SD 57301
(605) 995-3025 ext. 2316

Mount Marty College
Yankton, South Dakota
www.mtmc.edu   Federal Code: 003465

4-year private liberal arts college in large town, affiliated with Roman Catholic Church.
Enrollment: 907 undergrads, 22% part-time. 139 full-time freshmen.
Selectivity: Admits over 75% of applicants.

BASIC COSTS (2006-2007)
Tuition and fees: $16,582.
Per-credit charge: $562.
Room and board: $4,958.

FINANCIAL AID PICTURE (2005-2006)
Students with need: Average financial aid package met 78% of need; average scholarship/grant was $10,431; average loan was $3,284. For part-time students, average financial aid package was $5,836.
Students without need: No-need awards available for academics, art, athletics, leadership, music/drama, religious affiliation.
Cumulative student debt: 85% of graduating class had student loans; average debt was $26,304.
Additional info: Prestige scholarships application deadline 2/1.

FINANCIAL AID PROCEDURES
Forms required: FAFSA, institutional form.
Dates and Deadlines: Priority date 3/1; no closing date. Applicants notified on a rolling basis starting 3/15; must reply within 2 week(s) of notification.

CONTACT
Kenneth Kocer, Director of Financial Assistance
1105 West Eighth Street, Yankton, SD 57078
(605) 668-1589

Northern State University
Aberdeen, South Dakota
www.northern.edu   Federal Code: 003466

4-year public university and liberal arts college in large town.
Enrollment: 1,872 undergrads, 15% part-time. 370 full-time freshmen.
Selectivity: Admits over 75% of applicants.

BASIC COSTS (2005-2006)
Tuition and fees: $4,700; out-of-state residents $9,687.
Per-credit charge: $76; out-of-state residents $243.
Room and board: $3,821.
Additional info: Reciprocity agreements reduce tuition for some out-of-state students.

FINANCIAL AID PICTURE
Students with need: Need-based aid available for full-time and part-time students.

Students without need: No-need awards available for academics, athletics, state/district residency.

FINANCIAL AID PROCEDURES
Forms required: FAFSA.
Dates and Deadlines: Priority date 3/1; no closing date. Applicants notified on a rolling basis starting 5/1; must reply within 2 week(s) of notification.
Transfers: Financial aid transcript(s) required from all schools previously attended.

CONTACT
Sharon Kienow, Director of Student Financial Assistance
1200 South Jay Street, Aberdeen, SD 57401-7198
(605) 626-2640

Presentation College
Aberdeen, South Dakota
www.presentation.edu   Federal Code: 003467

4-year private business and health science college in large town, affiliated with Roman Catholic Church.
Enrollment: 668 undergrads.
Selectivity: Admits over 75% of applicants.

BASIC COSTS (2006-2007)
Tuition and fees: $12,300.
Per-credit charge: $450.
Room and board: $4,775.

FINANCIAL AID PICTURE
Students with need: Need-based aid available for full-time and part-time students. Work study available nights, weekends, and for part-time students.

FINANCIAL AID PROCEDURES
Forms required: FAFSA.
Dates and Deadlines: Priority date 4/1; no closing date. Applicants notified on a rolling basis starting 5/1; must reply within 2 week(s) of notification.

CONTACT
Val Weisser, Financial Aid Director
1500 North Main Street, Aberdeen, SD 57401
(605) 229-8429

South Dakota School of Mines and Technology
Rapid City, South Dakota
www.sdsmt.edu   Federal Code: 003470

4-year public university and engineering college in small city.
Enrollment: 1,724 undergrads, 11% part-time. 352 full-time freshmen.
Selectivity: Admits over 75% of applicants.

BASIC COSTS (2005-2006)
Tuition and fees: $4,757; out-of-state residents $9,744.
Per-credit charge: $76; out-of-state residents $243.
Room and board: $3,904.
Additional info: Reciprocity agreements reduce tuition for some out-of-state students. Tuition/fee waivers available for adults.

FINANCIAL AID PICTURE (2004-2005)
Students with need: Out of 321 full-time freshmen who applied for aid, 181 were judged to have need. Of these, 180 received aid, and 80 had their full need met. Average financial aid package met 81% of need; average scholarship/grant was $3,520; average loan was $2,731. For part-time students, average financial aid package was $5,861.

Students without need: 72 full-time freshmen who did not demonstrate need for aid received scholarships/grants; average award was $2,465. No-need awards available for academics, athletics, leadership, ROTC.
Scholarships offered: *Merit:* Presidential Scholarship: $100 to $5,000; 5 awarded. Surbeck Scholars: $7,000; 2 awarded. All based on ACT/SAT scores, high school GPA, and class rank. Number of awards may vary from year to year depending on availability of funding. *Athletic:* 17 full-time freshmen received athletic scholarships; average amount $2,515.
Cumulative student debt: 21% of graduating class had student loans; average debt was $1,623.
Additional info: Closing date for scholarship applications February 1.

FINANCIAL AID PROCEDURES
Forms required: FAFSA.
Dates and Deadlines: Priority date 3/15; no closing date. Applicants notified on a rolling basis starting 5/1; must reply within 3 week(s) of notification.

CONTACT
David Martin, Director of Financial Aid
501 East St. Joseph Street, Rapid City, SD 57701
(605) 394-2274

South Dakota State University
Brookings, South Dakota
www.sdstate.edu   Federal Code: 003471

4-year public university in large town.
Enrollment: 8,752 undergrads, 12% part-time. 1,788 full-time freshmen.
Selectivity: Admits over 75% of applicants.

BASIC COSTS (2005-2006)
Tuition and fees: $4,732; out-of-state residents $9,719.
Per-credit charge: $76; out-of-state residents $243.
Room and board: $4,770.
Additional info: Reduced out-of-state tuition for Minnesota students.

FINANCIAL AID PICTURE (2005-2006)
Students with need: Out of 1,559 full-time freshmen who applied for aid, 1,418 were judged to have need. Of these, 1,414 received aid, and 972 had their full need met. Average financial aid package met 86% of need; average scholarship/grant was $3,148; average loan was $1,804. Need-based aid available for part-time students.
Students without need: 491 full-time freshmen who did not demonstrate need for aid received scholarships/grants; average award was $1,042. No-need awards available for academics, art, athletics, leadership, minority status, music/drama, ROTC, state/district residency.
Scholarships offered: *Merit:* Academic scholarships for first-year freshmen: $500-$6,500; based on academic performance in high school; 1010 awarded. Minimum academic scholarship for new first-year students: $1,000; based on minimum score of 24 or higher on ACT; renewable. *Athletic:* 74 full-time freshmen received athletic scholarships; average amount $4,331.
Cumulative student debt: 81% of graduating class had student loans; average debt was $19,520.
Additional info: Financial aid awarded to approximately 87 percent of all undergraduates.

FINANCIAL AID PROCEDURES
Forms required: FAFSA.
Dates and Deadlines: Priority date 3/15; no closing date. Applicants notified on a rolling basis starting 4/1; must reply within 3 week(s) of notification.
Transfers: Must reply within 3 week(s) of notification.

CONTACT
Jay Larsen, Director of Financial Aid
Box 2201 ADM 200, Brookings, SD 57007-0649
(605) 688-4695

Southeast Technical Institute
Sioux Falls, South Dakota
www.southeasttech.com   Federal Code: 008285

2-year public technical college in small city.
Enrollment: 2,320 undergrads, 18% part-time. 583 full-time freshmen.
Selectivity: Open admission; but selective for some programs.

BASIC COSTS (2006-2007)
Tuition and fees: $3,340.
Per-credit charge: $69.
Additional info: $450 per semester laptop fee required for some students. Students able to keep laptop after paying for 4 semesters of the lease.

FINANCIAL AID PICTURE
Students with need: Need-based aid available for full-time and part-time students.
Students without need: This college only awards aid to students with need.

FINANCIAL AID PROCEDURES
Forms required: FAFSA.
Dates and Deadlines: Priority date 5/1; no closing date. Applicants notified on a rolling basis starting 5/1; must reply within 3 week(s) of notification.

CONTACT
Carol Bogaard, Financial Aid Officer
2320 North Career Avenue, Sioux Falls, SD 57107
(605) 367-4465

University of Sioux Falls
Sioux Falls, South Dakota
www.usiouxfalls.edu   Federal Code: 003469

4-year private liberal arts college in small city, affiliated with American Baptist Churches in the USA.
Enrollment: 1,262 undergrads.
Selectivity: Admits over 75% of applicants.

BASIC COSTS (2006-2007)
Tuition and fees: $16,720.
Per-credit charge: $270.
Room and board: $5,100.

FINANCIAL AID PICTURE
Students with need: Need-based aid available for full-time and part-time students.
Students without need: No-need awards available for academics, alumni affiliation, art, athletics, job skills, leadership, minority status, music/drama, religious affiliation, state/district residency.

FINANCIAL AID PROCEDURES
Forms required: FAFSA.
Dates and Deadlines: Priority date 3/1; no closing date. Applicants notified on a rolling basis starting 3/1; must reply within 2 week(s) of notification.

CONTACT
Laura Olson, Director of Financial Aid
1101 West 22nd Street, Sioux Falls, SD 57105-1699
(605) 331-6623

University of South Dakota
Vermillion, South Dakota
www.usd.edu   Federal Code: 003474

4-year public university in small town.
Enrollment: 5,728 undergrads, 26% part-time. 945 full-time freshmen.
Selectivity: Admits over 75% of applicants.

BASIC COSTS (2005-2006)
Tuition and fees: $4,829; out-of-state residents $9,816.
Per-credit charge: $76; out-of-state residents $76.
Room and board: $4,240.
Additional info: Reciprocity agreement in place for Minnesota residents. Reduced tuition for Iowa residents.

FINANCIAL AID PICTURE (2004-2005)
Students with need: Out of 786 full-time freshmen who applied for aid, 547 were judged to have need. Of these, 488 received aid, and 413 had their full need met. Average financial aid package met 75% of need; average scholarship/grant was $2,996; average loan was $2,694. For part-time students, average financial aid package was $4,782.
Students without need: 257 full-time freshmen who did not demonstrate need for aid received scholarships/grants; average award was $2,983. No-need awards available for academics, art, athletics, leadership, minority status, music/drama, ROTC.
Scholarships offered: 74 full-time freshmen received athletic scholarships; average amount $2,714.
Cumulative student debt: 80% of graduating class had student loans; average debt was $19,535.

FINANCIAL AID PROCEDURES
Forms required: FAFSA.
Dates and Deadlines: Priority date 3/15; no closing date. Applicants notified on a rolling basis starting 5/5.

CONTACT
Julie Pier, Director of Student Financial Aid
414 East Clark Street, Vermillion, SD 57069-2390
(605) 677-5446

Western Dakota Technical Institute
Rapid City, South Dakota
www.westerndakotatech.org   Federal Code: 010170

2-year public technical college in small city.
Enrollment: 817 full-time undergrads.
Selectivity: Open admission; but selective for some programs.

BASIC COSTS (2005-2006)
Tuition and fees: $3,453.
Per-credit charge: $64.
Additional info: Total program cost ranges from $4,500- $12,700 depending on course of study.

FINANCIAL AID PICTURE
Students with need: Need-based aid available for full-time and part-time students. Work study available nights, weekends, and for part-time students.

FINANCIAL AID PROCEDURES
Forms required: FAFSA.
Dates and Deadlines: Priority date 4/20; no closing date. Applicants notified on a rolling basis starting 6/30; must reply within 2 week(s) of notification.

CONTACT
Starla Russell, Financial Aid Coordinator
800 Mickelson Drive, Rapid City, SD 57703
(605) 394-4034

Tennessee

American Baptist College of ABT Seminary
Nashville, Tennessee
www.abcnash.edu   Federal Code: 010460

4-year private Bible college in very large city, affiliated with Baptist faith.
Enrollment: 105 undergrads.

BASIC COSTS (2005-2006)
Tuition and fees: $5,160.
Per-credit charge: $168.
Room only: $1,600.

FINANCIAL AID PICTURE
Students with need: Need-based aid available for full-time students.

FINANCIAL AID PROCEDURES
Forms required: FAFSA.
Dates and Deadlines: No deadline. Applicants notified on a rolling basis; must reply within 2 week(s) of notification.

CONTACT
Marcella Lockhart, Director of Enrollment Management
1800 Baptist World Center Drive, Nashville, TN 37207
(615) 687-6896 ext. 2227

Aquinas College
Nashville, Tennessee
www.aquinas-tn.edu   Federal Code: 003477

4-year private nursing and liberal arts college in very large city, affiliated with Roman Catholic Church.
Enrollment: 918 undergrads, 64% part-time. 38 full-time freshmen.

BASIC COSTS (2006-2007)
Tuition and fees: $14,045.
Per-credit charge: $454.
Additional info: Additional $40 per-credit hour for nursing classes. Additional required fees for nursing and teacher education programs.

FINANCIAL AID PICTURE (2005-2006)
Students with need: 41% of average financial aid package awarded as scholarships/grants, 59% awarded as loans/jobs. Need-based aid available for part-time students. Work study available nights.
Students without need: No-need awards available for academics, alumni affiliation, leadership, religious affiliation.
Cumulative student debt: 82% of graduating class had student loans; average debt was $24,000.

FINANCIAL AID PROCEDURES
Forms required: FAFSA.
Dates and Deadlines: Priority date 3/1; no closing date. Applicants notified on a rolling basis starting 3/1; must reply within 2 week(s) of notification.
Transfers: No deadline. Applicants notified on a rolling basis; must reply within 2 week(s) of notification.

CONTACT
Zelena O'Sullivan, Director of Financial Aid
4210 Harding Road, Nashville, TN 37205-2086
(615) 297-7545 ext. 442

Austin Peay State University
Clarksville, Tennessee
www.apsu.edu   Federal Code: 003478

4-year public university and liberal arts college in small city.
Enrollment: 7,964 undergrads, 27% part-time. 1,196 full-time freshmen.
Selectivity: Admits over 75% of applicants.

BASIC COSTS (2005-2006)
Tuition and fees: $4,635; out-of-state residents $13,947.
Per-credit charge: $161; out-of-state residents $565.
Room and board: $4,800.

FINANCIAL AID PICTURE (2004-2005)
Students with need: 47% of average financial aid package awarded as scholarships/grants, 53% awarded as loans/jobs. Need-based aid available for part-time students.
Students without need: No-need awards available for academics, art, athletics, leadership, minority status, music/drama, ROTC, state/district residency.

FINANCIAL AID PROCEDURES
Forms required: FAFSA.
Dates and Deadlines: Priority date 4/1; no closing date. Applicants notified on a rolling basis starting 5/1; must reply within 2 week(s) of notification.

CONTACT
Donna Price, Director of Financial Aid
PO Box 4548, Clarksville, TN 37044
(931) 221-7907

Belmont University
Nashville, Tennessee
www.belmont.edu   Federal Code: 003479

4-year private university in very large city, affiliated with Baptist faith.
Enrollment: 3,570 undergrads, 9% part-time. 727 full-time freshmen.
Selectivity: Admits 50 to 75% of applicants.

BASIC COSTS (2006-2007)
Tuition and fees: $18,420.
Per-credit charge: $670.
Room and board: $7,076.

FINANCIAL AID PICTURE (2004-2005)
Students with need: Out of 657 full-time freshmen who applied for aid, 384 were judged to have need. Of these, 368 received aid, and 115 had their full need met. Average financial aid package met 45% of need; average scholarship/grant was $4,797; average loan was $2,586. For part-time students, average financial aid package was $5,212.
Students without need: 160 full-time freshmen who did not demonstrate need for aid received scholarships/grants; average award was $4,344. No-need awards available for academics, art, athletics, leadership, music/drama, religious affiliation, state/district residency.
Scholarships offered: 58 full-time freshmen received athletic scholarships; average amount $9,556.
Cumulative student debt: 56% of graduating class had student loans; average debt was $18,007.

FINANCIAL AID PROCEDURES
Forms required: FAFSA.
Dates and Deadlines: Priority date 3/1; no closing date. Applicants notified on a rolling basis starting 3/15; must reply by 5/1 or within 2 week(s) of notification.
Transfers: Applicants notified on a rolling basis starting 3/1; must reply by 5/1 or within 2 week(s) of notification. Scholarships available.

CONTACT
Paula Gill, Director of Student Financial Services
1900 Belmont Boulevard, Nashville, TN 37212-3757
(615) 460-6403

Bethel College
McKenzie, Tennessee
www.bethel-college.edu   Federal Code: 003480

4-year private liberal arts college in small town, affiliated with Presbyterian Church (USA).
Enrollment: 1,187 undergrads, 19% part-time. 234 full-time freshmen.
Selectivity: Admits 50 to 75% of applicants.

BASIC COSTS (2005-2006)
Tuition and fees: $10,016.
Per-credit charge: $310.
Room and board: $5,760.

FINANCIAL AID PICTURE (2005-2006)
Students with need: Need-based aid available for part-time students. Work study available nights, weekends, and for part-time students.
Students without need: No-need awards available for academics, athletics, music/drama, religious affiliation, state/district residency.

FINANCIAL AID PROCEDURES
Forms required: FAFSA, institutional form.
Dates and Deadlines: Priority date 3/3; closing date 6/30. Applicants notified on a rolling basis starting 3/1.
Transfers: Financial aid transcripts from previously attended institutions required.

CONTACT
Laura Bateman, Director of Financial Aid
325 Cherry Avenue, McKenzie, TN 38201
(610) 799-1133

Bryan College
Dayton, Tennessee
www.bryan.edu   Federal Code: 003536

4-year private liberal arts college in small town, affiliated with interdenominational tradition.
Enrollment: 765 undergrads, 1% part-time. 184 full-time freshmen.

BASIC COSTS (2006-2007)
Tuition and fees: $15,450.
Per-credit charge: $625.
Room and board: $4,540.
Additional info: Tuition/fee waivers available for adults.

FINANCIAL AID PICTURE (2004-2005)
Students with need: 42% of average financial aid package awarded as scholarships/grants, 58% awarded as loans/jobs. Need-based aid available for part-time students.
Students without need: No-need awards available for academics, alumni affiliation, art, athletics, job skills, leadership, music/drama.

FINANCIAL AID PROCEDURES
Forms required: FAFSA, institutional form.
Dates and Deadlines: Priority date 3/1; no closing date. Applicants notified on a rolling basis starting 1/1; must reply within 2 week(s) of notification.

CONTACT
Michael Sapienza, Director of Admissions & Financial Aid
PO Box 7000, Dayton, TN 37321-7000
(423) 775-7339

Carson-Newman College
Jefferson City, Tennessee
www.cn.edu   Federal Code: 003481

4-year private liberal arts college in small town, affiliated with Southern Baptist Convention.
Enrollment: 1,834 undergrads, 5% part-time. 449 full-time freshmen.
Selectivity: Admits over 75% of applicants.

BASIC COSTS (2006-2007)
Tuition and fees: $16,060.
Per-credit charge: $635.
Room and board: $5,200.
Additional info: Tuition/fee waivers available for adults, minority students.

FINANCIAL AID PICTURE (2005-2006)
Students with need: Out of 422 full-time freshmen who applied for aid, 339 were judged to have need. Of these, 339 received aid, and 102 had their full need met. Average financial aid package met 83% of need; average scholarship/grant was $10,414; average loan was $2,714. For part-time students, average financial aid package was $5,892.
Students without need: 101 full-time freshmen who did not demonstrate need for aid received scholarships/grants; average award was $9,649. No-need awards available for academics, art, athletics, leadership, minority status, music/drama, religious affiliation, ROTC.
Scholarships offered: 17 full-time freshmen received athletic scholarships; average amount $4,322.
Cumulative student debt: 71% of graduating class had student loans; average debt was $16,512.

FINANCIAL AID PROCEDURES
Forms required: FAFSA, institutional form.
Dates and Deadlines: Priority date 4/1; no closing date. Applicants notified on a rolling basis starting 2/1; must reply within 2 week(s) of notification.

CONTACT
Danette Seale, Special Assist to Provost for Enroll Services
1646 Russell Avenue, Jefferson City, TN 37760
(865) 471-3247

Chattanooga State Technical Community College
Chattanooga, Tennessee
www.chattanoogastate.edu   Federal Code: 003998

2-year public community and technical college in small city.
Enrollment: 6,542 undergrads, 50% part-time. 1,030 full-time freshmen.
Selectivity: Open admission; but selective for some programs.

BASIC COSTS (2005-2006)
Tuition and fees: $2,413; out-of-state residents $8,827.
Per-credit charge: $91; out-of-state residents $369.

FINANCIAL AID PICTURE (2005-2006)
Students with need: Out of 845 full-time freshmen who applied for aid, 659 were judged to have need. Of these, 642 received aid, and 195 had their full need met. Average financial aid package met 73% of need; average scholarship/grant was $3,230; average loan was $1,975. For part-time students, average financial aid package was $3,538.
Students without need: 106 full-time freshmen who did not demonstrate need for aid received scholarships/grants; average award was $1,767. No-need awards available for state/district residency.
Scholarships offered: 10 full-time freshmen received athletic scholarships; average amount $4,308.

FINANCIAL AID PROCEDURES
Forms required: FAFSA.
Dates and Deadlines: Priority date 4/1; no closing date. Applicants notified on a rolling basis starting 4/1; must reply within 2 week(s) of notification.

CONTACT
Tara Mathis, Executive Officer Financial Aid
4501 Amnicola Highway, Chattanooga, TN 37406
(423) 697-4402

Christian Brothers University
Memphis, Tennessee
www.cbu.edu   Federal Code: 003482

4-year private university in very large city, affiliated with Roman Catholic Church.
Enrollment: 1,466 undergrads, 22% part-time. 258 full-time freshmen.
Selectivity: Admits 50 to 75% of applicants.

BASIC COSTS (2006-2007)
Tuition and fees: $20,080.
Per-credit charge: $615.
Room and board: $5,650.
Additional info: Tuition/fee waivers available for adults.

FINANCIAL AID PICTURE (2004-2005)
Students with need: Out of 244 full-time freshmen who applied for aid, 202 were judged to have need. Of these, 202 received aid, and 56 had their full need met. Average financial aid package met 99% of need; average scholarship/grant was $5,622; average loan was $3,338. For part-time students, average financial aid package was $6,299.
Students without need: 52 full-time freshmen who did not demonstrate need for aid received scholarships/grants; average award was $10,358. No-need awards available for academics, athletics, state/district residency.
Scholarships offered: 30 full-time freshmen received athletic scholarships; average amount $5,438.
Additional info: ROTC scholarships available to qualified applicants.

FINANCIAL AID PROCEDURES
Forms required: FAFSA.
Dates and Deadlines: Priority date 3/1; no closing date. Applicants notified on a rolling basis starting 3/1; must reply within 2 week(s) of notification.

CONTACT
Jim Shannon, Director of Student Financial Resources
650 East Parkway South, Memphis, TN 38104-5519
(901) 321-3305

Cleveland State Community College
Cleveland, Tennessee
www.clevelandstatecc.edu   Federal Code: 003999

2-year public community college in small city.
Enrollment: 2,367 undergrads, 39% part-time. 503 full-time freshmen.
Selectivity: Open admission; but selective for some programs.

BASIC COSTS (2005-2006)
Tuition and fees: $2,385; out-of-state residents $8,799.
Per-credit charge: $91; out-of-state residents $369.

FINANCIAL AID PICTURE (2005-2006)
Students with need: Average financial aid package met 73% of need; average scholarship/grant was $4,034; average loan was $2,314. For part-time students, average financial aid package was $2,893.
Students without need: No-need awards available for athletics, minority status.

FINANCIAL AID PROCEDURES
Forms required: FAFSA, institutional form.
Dates and Deadlines: Priority date 6/15; no closing date. Applicants notified on a rolling basis starting 7/1; must reply within 2 week(s) of notification.

CONTACT
Geraldine Parks, Director of Financial Aid
3535 Adkisson Drive, Cleveland, TN 37320-3570
(423) 478-6215

Columbia State Community College
Columbia, Tennessee
www.columbiastate.edu   Federal Code: 003483

2-year public community college in large town.
Enrollment: 4,056 undergrads, 46% part-time. 687 full-time freshmen.
Selectivity: Open admission; but selective for some programs.

BASIC COSTS (2005-2006)
Tuition and fees: $2,373; out-of-state residents $8,787.
Per-credit charge: $91; out-of-state residents $369.

FINANCIAL AID PICTURE
Students with need: Need-based aid available for full-time and part-time students.
Students without need: No-need awards available for academics, athletics, state/district residency.

FINANCIAL AID PROCEDURES
Forms required: FAFSA, institutional form.
Dates and Deadlines: Closing date 3/15. Applicants notified on a rolling basis starting 5/15; must reply within 2 week(s) of notification.

CONTACT
David Ogden, Director, Financial Assistance
1665 Hampshire Pike, Columbia, TN 38401
(931) 540-2583

Crichton College
Memphis, Tennessee
www.crichton.edu   Federal Code: 009982

4-year private liberal arts college in very large city, affiliated with nondenominational tradition.
Enrollment: 972 undergrads, 48% part-time. 119 full-time freshmen.

BASIC COSTS (2006-2007)
Tuition and fees: $10,176.
Per-credit charge: $415.
Room only: $3,750.

FINANCIAL AID PICTURE (2005-2006)
Students with need: Average financial aid package met 57% of need; average scholarship/grant was $4,943; average loan was $2,938. For part-time students, average financial aid package was $4,682.
Students without need: No-need awards available for academics, alumni affiliation, athletics, leadership, music/drama, religious affiliation.

FINANCIAL AID PROCEDURES
Forms required: FAFSA, institutional form.
Dates and Deadlines: Priority date 3/15; no closing date. Applicants notified on a rolling basis starting 3/1; must reply within 2 week(s) of notification.

CONTACT
Jim Avery, CFO
255 North Highland, Memphis, TN 38111
(901) 320-9760

Cumberland University
Lebanon, Tennessee
www.cumberland.edu   Federal Code: 003485

4-year private university and liberal arts college in large town.
Enrollment: 1,031 undergrads, 9% part-time. 196 full-time freshmen.
Selectivity: Admits 50 to 75% of applicants.

BASIC COSTS (2006-2007)
Tuition and fees: $14,810.
Per-credit charge: $585.
Room and board: $4,960.

FINANCIAL AID PICTURE (2004-2005)
Students with need: Out of 186 full-time freshmen who applied for aid, 163 were judged to have need. Of these, 163 received aid, and 35 had their full need met. Average financial aid package met 59% of need; average scholarship/grant was $4,959; average loan was $2,185. For part-time students, average financial aid package was $8,548.
Students without need: 26 full-time freshmen who did not demonstrate need for aid received scholarships/grants; average award was $6,129. No-need awards available for academics, art, athletics, music/drama.
Scholarships offered: 21 full-time freshmen received athletic scholarships; average amount $7,640.
Cumulative student debt: 59% of graduating class had student loans; average debt was $19,279.

FINANCIAL AID PROCEDURES
Forms required: FAFSA, institutional form.
Dates and Deadlines: Priority date 2/1; no closing date. Applicants notified on a rolling basis starting 5/1; must reply within 2 week(s) of notification.
Transfers: Priority date 2/15. Applicants notified on a rolling basis starting 5/1.

CONTACT
Judy Jordan, VP of Fiscal Affairs
One Cumberland Square, Lebanon, TN 37087
(615) 444-2562 ext. 1222

Dyersburg State Community College
Dyersburg, Tennessee
www.dscc.edu   Federal Code: 006835

2-year public community college in large town.
Enrollment: 2,213 undergrads. 495 full-time freshmen.
Selectivity: Open admission; but selective for some programs.

BASIC COSTS (2005-2006)
Tuition and fees: $2,393; out-of-state residents $8,807.
Per-credit charge: $91; out-of-state residents $369.

FINANCIAL AID PICTURE (2004-2005)
Students with need: Out of 458 full-time freshmen who applied for aid, 363 were judged to have need. Of these, 336 received aid, and 23 had their full need met. Average financial aid package met 37% of need; average scholarship/grant was $2,868; average loan was $2,325. For part-time students, average financial aid package was $2,353.
Students without need: 17 full-time freshmen who did not demonstrate need for aid received scholarships/grants; average award was $922. No-need awards available for academics, alumni affiliation, athletics, job skills, leadership, minority status, music/drama, state/district residency.
Scholarships offered: 25 full-time freshmen received athletic scholarships; average amount $852.

FINANCIAL AID PROCEDURES
Forms required: FAFSA.
Dates and Deadlines: Priority date 3/1; no closing date. Applicants notified on a rolling basis starting 3/1; must reply within 2 week(s) of notification.

CONTACT
Sandra Rockett, Director of Financial Aid
1510 Lake Road, Dyersburg, TN 38024
(731) 286-3238

East Tennessee State University
Johnson City, Tennessee
www.etsu.edu   Federal Code: 003487

4-year public university in small city.
Enrollment: 9,486 undergrads, 14% part-time. 1,569 full-time freshmen.
Selectivity: Admits over 75% of applicants.

BASIC COSTS (2005-2006)
Tuition and fees: $4,487; out-of-state residents $13,799.
Per-credit charge: $161; out-of-state residents $565.
Room and board: $5,428.

FINANCIAL AID PICTURE (2005-2006)
Students with need: Out of 1,477 full-time freshmen who applied for aid, 1,039 were judged to have need. Of these, 1,025 received aid, and 384 had their full need met. Average financial aid package met 84% of need; average scholarship/grant was $24,350; average loan was $780. For part-time students, average financial aid package was $3,429.
Students without need: 191 full-time freshmen who did not demonstrate need for aid received scholarships/grants; average award was $3,593. No-need awards available for academics, alumni affiliation, art, athletics, job skills, leadership, minority status, music/drama, religious affiliation, state/district residency.
Scholarships offered: 36 full-time freshmen received athletic scholarships; average amount $8,509.
Cumulative student debt: 28% of graduating class had student loans; average debt was $18,956.
Additional info: Housing costs payable by installment.

FINANCIAL AID PROCEDURES
Forms required: FAFSA.
Dates and Deadlines: Priority date 3/1; no closing date. Applicants notified on a rolling basis starting 5/15; must reply within 3 week(s) of notification.

CONTACT
Margaret Miller, Director of Financial Aid
ETSU Box 70731, Johnson City, TN 37614-0731
(423) 439-4300

Fisk University
Nashville, Tennessee
www.fisk.edu   Federal Code: 003490

4-year private liberal arts college in very large city, affiliated with United Church of Christ.
Enrollment: 813 undergrads, 5% part-time. 178 full-time freshmen.
Selectivity: Admits over 75% of applicants.

BASIC COSTS (2006-2007)
Tuition and fees: $13,969.
Per-credit charge: $551.
Room and board: $7,012.

FINANCIAL AID PICTURE (2004-2005)
Students with need: Out of 158 full-time freshmen who applied for aid, 151 were judged to have need. Of these, 149 received aid, and 4 had their full need met. Average financial aid package met 51% of need; average scholarship/grant was $4,974; average loan was $3,483. For part-time students, average financial aid package was $7,911.
Students without need: This college only awards aid to students with need.
Cumulative student debt: 75% of graduating class had student loans; average debt was $12,740.

FINANCIAL AID PROCEDURES
Forms required: FAFSA.
Dates and Deadlines: Priority date 3/1; closing date 7/1. Applicants notified on a rolling basis starting 4/1; must reply within 2 week(s) of notification.

CONTACT
Damien Jackson, Director of Financial Aid
1000 17th Avenue North, Nashville, TN 37208-3051
(615) 329-8585

Free Will Baptist Bible College
Nashville, Tennessee
www.fwbbc.edu   Federal Code: 030018

4-year private Bible college in very large city, affiliated with Free Will Baptists.
Enrollment: 357 undergrads, 14% part-time. 65 full-time freshmen.
Selectivity: Open admission.

BASIC COSTS (2005-2006)
Tuition and fees: $10,238.
Per-credit charge: $320.
Room and board: $4,588.

FINANCIAL AID PICTURE
Students with need: Need-based aid available for full-time and part-time students. Work study available nights, weekends, and for part-time students.
Students without need: No-need awards available for academics, art, music/drama.
Scholarships offered: Presidential Honors Scholarship; $1,000 per semester, renewable for 8 semesters; 3.25 GPA and at least 3.5 high school GPA and ACT score of 29 or above; awarded to four students yearly.

FINANCIAL AID PROCEDURES
Forms required: FAFSA, institutional form.
Dates and Deadlines: Priority date 4/15; no closing date. Applicants notified on a rolling basis starting 7/1; must reply within 2 week(s) of notification.

CONTACT
Jeff Caudill, Director of Student Financial Aid
3606 West End Avenue, Nashville, TN 37205-0117
(615) 844-5250

Freed-Hardeman University
Henderson, Tennessee
www.fhu.edu   Federal Code: 003492

4-year private university and liberal arts college in small town, affiliated with Church of Christ.
Enrollment: 1,459 undergrads. 371 full-time freshmen.
Selectivity: Admits over 75% of applicants.

BASIC COSTS (2006-2007)
Tuition and fees: $13,192.
Per-credit charge: $370.
Room and board: $6,550.

FINANCIAL AID PICTURE (2005-2006)
Students with need: Out of 335 full-time freshmen who applied for aid, 292 were judged to have need. Of these, 292 received aid, and 60 had their full need met. Average financial aid package met 70% of need; average scholarship/grant was $7,545; average loan was $3,722. For part-time students, average financial aid package was $11,316.
Students without need: 64 full-time freshmen who did not demonstrate need for aid received scholarships/grants; average award was $11,802. No-need awards available for academics, art, athletics, leadership, minority status, music/drama, state/district residency.

FINANCIAL AID PROCEDURES
Forms required: FAFSA.
Dates and Deadlines: Priority date 3/1; no closing date. Applicants notified on a rolling basis starting 3/1; must reply within 4 week(s) of notification.

CONTACT
Larry Cyr, Director of Financial Aid
158 East Main Street, Henderson, TN 38340
(731) 989-6662

Hiwassee College
Madisonville, Tennessee
www.hiwassee.edu   Federal Code: 003494

2-year private junior and liberal arts college in small town, affiliated with United Methodist Church.
Enrollment: 381 undergrads, 29% part-time. 137 full-time freshmen.
Selectivity: Admits 50 to 75% of applicants.

BASIC COSTS (2006-2007)
Tuition and fees: $10,140.
Per-credit charge: $410.
Room and board: $5,920.
Additional info: Tuition/fee waivers available for adults.

FINANCIAL AID PICTURE (2004-2005)
Students with need: 75% of average financial aid package awarded as scholarships/grants, 25% awarded as loans/jobs. Need-based aid available for part-time students. Work study available nights, weekends, and for part-time students.
Students without need: No-need awards available for academics, alumni affiliation, athletics, job skills, leadership, music/drama, religious affiliation, state/district residency.

FINANCIAL AID PROCEDURES
Forms required: FAFSA, institutional form.
Dates and Deadlines: Priority date 5/1; no closing date. Applicants notified on a rolling basis starting 4/1; must reply within 2 week(s) of notification.
Transfers: No deadline. Applicants notified on a rolling basis starting 5/1; must reply within 2 week(s) of notification.

CONTACT
James Hemphill, Director of Financial Aid
225 Hiwassee College Drive, Madisonville, TN 37354-6099
(423) 420-1239

Jackson State Community College
Jackson, Tennessee
www.jscc.edu   Federal Code: 004937

2-year public community college in small city.
Enrollment: 3,859 undergrads, 47% part-time. 685 full-time freshmen.
Selectivity: Open admission; but selective for some programs.

786   Tennessee Jackson State Community College

BASIC COSTS (2005-2006)
Tuition and fees: $2,395; out-of-state residents $8,809.
Per-credit charge: $91; out-of-state residents $369.
Additional info: Tuition/fee waivers available for adults, minority students.

FINANCIAL AID PICTURE (2004-2005)
Students with need: Out of 446 full-time freshmen who applied for aid, 346 were judged to have need. Of these, 331 received aid, and 30 had their full need met. Average financial aid package met 81% of need; average scholarship/grant was $3,008; average loan was $6,873. For part-time students, average financial aid package was $2,109.
Students without need: 80 full-time freshmen who did not demonstrate need for aid received scholarships/grants; average award was $1,748. No-need awards available for academics, art, athletics, job skills, leadership, minority status, music/drama.
Scholarships offered: 18 full-time freshmen received athletic scholarships; average amount $1,732.
Cumulative student debt: 2% of graduating class had student loans; average debt was $2,525.

FINANCIAL AID PROCEDURES
Forms required: FAFSA, institutional form.
Dates and Deadlines: Priority date 4/1; no closing date. Applicants notified on a rolling basis starting 6/1; must reply within 2 week(s) of notification.

CONTACT
Dewana Latimer, Director of Financial Aid
2046 North Parkway, Jackson, TN 38301-3797
(731) 425-2605

John A. Gupton College
Nashville, Tennessee
www.guptoncollege.com   Federal Code: 008859

2-year private school of mortuary science in large city.
Enrollment: 98 undergrads, 11% part-time. 46 full-time freshmen.
Selectivity: Open admission.

BASIC COSTS (2005-2006)
Tuition and fees: $6,880.
Per-credit charge: $215.
Room only: $3,600.

FINANCIAL AID PICTURE (2004-2005)
Students with need: 64% of average financial aid package awarded as scholarships/grants, 36% awarded as loans/jobs. Need-based aid available for part-time students.
Students without need: This college only awards aid to students with need.

FINANCIAL AID PROCEDURES
Forms required: FAFSA.
Dates and Deadlines: No deadline. Applicants notified on a rolling basis.

CONTACT
B. Steven Spann, President/CFO
1616 Church Street, Nashville, TN 37203-2920
(615) 327-3927

Johnson Bible College
Knoxville, Tennessee
www.jbc.edu   Federal Code: 003495

4-year private Bible college in small city, affiliated with Christian Church.
Enrollment: 776 undergrads, 1% part-time. 184 full-time freshmen.
Selectivity: Admits over 75% of applicants.

BASIC COSTS (2006-2007)
Tuition and fees: $6,830.
Per-credit charge: $254.
Room and board: $4,910.
Additional info: Part-time students pay mandatory fee of $30.42 per credit hour. Tuition/fee waivers available for minority students.

FINANCIAL AID PICTURE (2005-2006)
Students with need: Out of 183 full-time freshmen who applied for aid, 154 were judged to have need. Of these, 154 received aid. Average financial aid package met 42% of need; average scholarship/grant was $1,620; average loan was $1,150. For part-time students, average financial aid package was $1,240.
Students without need: No-need awards available for academics, leadership, minority status, music/drama, religious affiliation, state/district residency.
Cumulative student debt: 54% of graduating class had student loans; average debt was $15,200.

FINANCIAL AID PROCEDURES
Forms required: FAFSA, institutional form.
Dates and Deadlines: Priority date 5/1; closing date 8/1. Applicants notified by 4/30; must reply within 2 week(s) of notification.
Transfers: No deadline.

CONTACT
Janette Overton, Financial Aid Director
7900 Johnson Drive, Knoxville, TN 37998-0001
(865) 251-2303

King College
Bristol, Tennessee
www.king.edu   Federal Code: 003496

4-year private Bible and liberal arts college in large town, affiliated with Presbyterian Church (USA).
Enrollment: 807 undergrads, 2% part-time. 208 full-time freshmen.
Selectivity: Admits over 75% of applicants.

BASIC COSTS (2006-2007)
Tuition and fees: $18,345.
Per-credit charge: $575.
Room and board: $6,200.

FINANCIAL AID PICTURE (2005-2006)
Students with need: Out of 197 full-time freshmen who applied for aid, 160 were judged to have need. Of these, 160 received aid, and 43 had their full need met. Average financial aid package met 77% of need; average scholarship/grant was $13,391; average loan was $2,618. For part-time students, average financial aid package was $9,888.
Students without need: 35 full-time freshmen who did not demonstrate need for aid received scholarships/grants; average award was $12,027. No-need awards available for academics, art, athletics, job skills, leadership, music/drama.
Scholarships offered: 48 full-time freshmen received athletic scholarships; average amount $5,894.
Cumulative student debt: 99% of graduating class had student loans; average debt was $16,635.

FINANCIAL AID PROCEDURES
Forms required: FAFSA.
Dates and Deadlines: Priority date 3/1; no closing date. Applicants notified on a rolling basis starting 3/15; must reply within 2 week(s) of notification.

CONTACT
Brenda Clark, Financial Aid Director
1350 King College Road, Bristol, TN 37620-2699
(423) 652-4725

Lambuth University
Jackson, Tennessee
www.lambuth.edu   Federal Code: 003498

4-year private university and liberal arts college in small city, affiliated with United Methodist Church.
Enrollment: 786 undergrads, 3% part-time. 234 full-time freshmen.
Selectivity: Admits 50 to 75% of applicants.

BASIC COSTS (2006-2007)
Tuition and fees: $16,380.
Per-credit charge: $634.
Room and board: $6,710.
Additional info: Tuition/fee waivers available for adults.

FINANCIAL AID PICTURE (2005-2006)
Students with need: Out of 217 full-time freshmen who applied for aid, 180 were judged to have need. Of these, 180 received aid, and 152 had their full need met. Average financial aid package met 83% of need; average scholarship/grant was $12,871; average loan was $1,346. Need-based aid available for part-time students.
Students without need: 33 full-time freshmen who did not demonstrate need for aid received scholarships/grants; average award was $10,459. No-need awards available for academics, alumni affiliation, art, athletics, job skills, leadership, minority status, music/drama, religious affiliation.
Scholarships offered: *Merit:* Hyde Scholarships; require admission acceptance deadline of 2/1; ACT 30+, GPA 3.5+; 2 full scholarships; highly competitive. Tennessee Hope Lottery Scholarships matched by Lambuth; up to $3,300. *Athletic:* 15 full-time freshmen received athletic scholarships; average amount $6,713.
Cumulative student debt: 80% of graduating class had student loans; average debt was $17,000.
Additional info: Part-time students eligible for federal and state aid, but not institutional aid.

FINANCIAL AID PROCEDURES
Forms required: FAFSA.
Dates and Deadlines: Priority date 2/15; no closing date. Applicants notified on a rolling basis starting 3/1; must reply by 5/1 or within 2 week(s) of notification.

CONTACT
Lisa Warmath, Director of Financial Aid
705 Lambuth Boulevard, Jackson, TN 38301-5296
(731) 425-3332

Lee University
Cleveland, Tennessee
www.leeuniversity.edu   Federal Code: 003500

4-year private university and liberal arts college in large town, affiliated with Church of God.
Enrollment: 3,573 undergrads, 7% part-time. 755 full-time freshmen.
Selectivity: Open admission; but selective for some programs.

BASIC COSTS (2006-2007)
Tuition and fees: $10,258.
Per-credit charge: $412.
Room and board: $5,024.

FINANCIAL AID PICTURE (2005-2006)
Students with need: Average financial aid package met 62% of need; average scholarship/grant was $7,000; average loan was $2,819. For part-time students, average financial aid package was $5,617.
Students without need: No-need awards available for academics, alumni affiliation, athletics, leadership, minority status, music/drama, religious affiliation, state/district residency.
Cumulative student debt: 71% of graduating class had student loans; average debt was $26,203.

FINANCIAL AID PROCEDURES
Forms required: FAFSA.
Dates and Deadlines: Priority date 3/15; no closing date. Applicants notified on a rolling basis starting 2/1; must reply within 3 week(s) of notification.

CONTACT
Michael Ellis, Director of Student Financial Aid
1120 North Ocoee Street, Cleveland, TN 37320-3450
(423) 614-8304

LeMoyne-Owen College
Memphis, Tennessee
www.loc.edu   Federal Code: 003501

4-year private liberal arts college in very large city, affiliated with United Church of Christ and Tennessee Baptist Convention.
Enrollment: 809 undergrads, 15% part-time. 105 full-time freshmen.

BASIC COSTS (2005-2006)
Tuition and fees: $9,618.
Per-credit charge: $401.
Room and board: $4,620.

FINANCIAL AID PICTURE
Students with need: Need-based aid available for full-time and part-time students.

FINANCIAL AID PROCEDURES
Forms required: FAFSA.
Dates and Deadlines: Priority date 4/15; no closing date. Applicants notified on a rolling basis starting 4/1.

CONTACT
Phyllis Wilson, Director of Student Financial Services
807 Walker Avenue, Memphis, TN 38126
(901) 435-1555

Lincoln Memorial University
Harrogate, Tennessee
www.lmunet.edu   Federal Code: 003502

4-year private university and liberal arts college in small town.
Enrollment: 1,225 undergrads, 17% part-time. 173 full-time freshmen.
Selectivity: Admits less than 50% of applicants.

BASIC COSTS (2005-2006)
Tuition and fees: $13,104.
Per-credit charge: $546.
Room and board: $5,040.

FINANCIAL AID PICTURE
Students with need: Need-based aid available for full-time and part-time students.
Students without need: No-need awards available for academics, athletics, music/drama, state/district residency.

FINANCIAL AID PROCEDURES
Forms required: FAFSA.
Dates and Deadlines: Priority date 4/1; no closing date. Applicants notified on a rolling basis starting 4/15; must reply within 3 week(s) of notification.

CONTACT
Christy Graham, Dean of Financial Aid
6965 Cumberland Gap Parkway, Harrogate, TN 37752
(423) 869-6336

Lipscomb University
Nashville, Tennessee
www.lipscomb.edu   Federal Code: 003486

4-year private Bible and liberal arts college in very large city, affiliated with Church of Christ.
Enrollment: 2,278 undergrads, 9% part-time. 475 full-time freshmen.
Selectivity: Admits over 75% of applicants.

BASIC COSTS (2006-2007)
Tuition and fees: $15,566.
Per-credit charge: $575.
Room and board: $6,730.

FINANCIAL AID PICTURE (2004-2005)
Students with need: Out of 430 full-time freshmen who applied for aid, 309 were judged to have need. Of these, 288 received aid, and 288 had their full need met. Average financial aid package met 84% of need; average scholarship/grant was $2,789; average loan was $2,479. Need-based aid available for part-time students.
Students without need: 158 full-time freshmen who did not demonstrate need for aid received scholarships/grants; average award was $5,878. No-need awards available for academics, alumni affiliation, art, athletics, music/drama, religious affiliation, ROTC.
Scholarships offered: 47 full-time freshmen received athletic scholarships; average amount $28,625.
Cumulative student debt: 70% of graduating class had student loans; average debt was $18,000.

FINANCIAL AID PROCEDURES
Forms required: FAFSA.
Dates and Deadlines: Priority date 3/1; no closing date. Applicants notified on a rolling basis starting 3/15.

CONTACT
Karita Waters, Director of Financial Aid
3901 Granny White Pike, Nashville, TN 37204-3951
(615) 269-1791

Martin Methodist College
Pulaski, Tennessee
www.martinmethodist.edu   Federal Code: 003504

4-year private liberal arts college in small town, affiliated with United Methodist Church.
Enrollment: 728 undergrads, 20% part-time. 192 full-time freshmen.
Selectivity: Open admission; but selective for some programs.

BASIC COSTS (2006-2007)
Tuition and fees: $15,391.
Per-credit charge: $629.
Room and board: $5,600.

FINANCIAL AID PICTURE (2004-2005)
Students with need: 74% of average financial aid package awarded as scholarships/grants, 26% awarded as loans/jobs. Need-based aid available for part-time students. Work study available nights, weekends, and for part-time students.
Students without need: No-need awards available for academics, art, athletics, leadership, music/drama, religious affiliation, state/district residency.
Scholarships offered: Two full academic scholarships per year awarded through interview and essay competition.

FINANCIAL AID PROCEDURES
Forms required: FAFSA, institutional form.
Dates and Deadlines: No deadline. Applicants notified on a rolling basis starting 3/1; must reply within 2 week(s) of notification.
Transfers: Closing date 9/13.

CONTACT
D. Ann Neville, Dean of Students and Director of Financial Aid
433 West Madison, Pulaski, TN 38478-2799
(931) 363-9869

Maryville College
Maryville, Tennessee
www.maryvillecollege.edu   Federal Code: 003505

4-year private liberal arts college in small city, affiliated with Presbyterian Church (USA).
Enrollment: 1,120 undergrads, 2% part-time. 333 full-time freshmen.
Selectivity: Admits over 75% of applicants.

BASIC COSTS (2006-2007)
Tuition and fees: $23,800.
Per-credit charge: $964.
Room and board: $7,400.

FINANCIAL AID PICTURE (2005-2006)
Students with need: Out of 333 full-time freshmen who applied for aid, 270 were judged to have need. Of these, 270 received aid, and 92 had their full need met. Average financial aid package met 91% of need; average scholarship/grant was $13,991; average loan was $1,575. For part-time students, average financial aid package was $17,431.
Students without need: 63 full-time freshmen who did not demonstrate need for aid received scholarships/grants; average award was $2,285. No-need awards available for academics, art, leadership, minority status, music/drama, religious affiliation, state/district residency.
Scholarships offered: Presidential Scholarship, full tuition, awarded for leadership and academic ability. Dean's Scholarship, consisting of a large portion of tuition awarded to selected entering freshman with 3.5 GPA.

FINANCIAL AID PROCEDURES
Forms required: FAFSA.
Dates and Deadlines: Priority date 3/1; no closing date. Applicants notified on a rolling basis starting 3/15; must reply within 4 week(s) of notification.

CONTACT
Richard Brand, Director of Financial Aid
502 East Lamar Alexander Parkway, Maryville, TN 37804-5907
(865) 981-8100

Memphis College of Art
Memphis, Tennessee
www.mca.edu   Federal Code: 003507

4-year private visual arts college in very large city.
Enrollment: 314 undergrads, 14% part-time. 55 full-time freshmen.
Selectivity: Admits less than 50% of applicants.

BASIC COSTS (2006-2007)
Tuition and fees: $19,760.
Per-credit charge: $835.
Room and board: $7,600.

FINANCIAL AID PICTURE (2005-2006)
Students with need: Out of 55 full-time freshmen who applied for aid, 49 were judged to have need. Of these, 49 received aid, and 34 had their full need met. Average financial aid package met 90% of need; average scholarship/grant was $3,000; average loan was $3,500. For part-time students, average financial aid package was $4,000.
Students without need: 9 full-time freshmen who did not demonstrate need for aid received scholarships/grants; average award was $3,500. No-need awards available for academics, art.
Scholarships offered: Full tuition award; merit; 1 available. Half tuition award; merit; 6 available. All renewable.
Cumulative student debt: 90% of graduating class had student loans; average debt was $20,000.
Additional info: Students considered for institutional resources through admissions application process.

FINANCIAL AID PROCEDURES
Forms required: FAFSA.
Dates and Deadlines: Priority date 3/1; no closing date. Applicants notified on a rolling basis; must reply within 3 week(s) of notification.
Transfers: Priority date 8/1. Applicants notified on a rolling basis; must reply within 3 week(s) of notification. Grants of $1,000 awarded to students who attended accredited junior or community college earning at least 60 credit hours.

CONTACT
Kara Ziegemeier, Director of Financial Aid
Overton Park, 1930 Poplar Avenue, Memphis, TN 38104-2764
(901) 272-5136

Middle Tennessee State University
Murfreesboro, Tennessee
www.mtsu.edu   Federal Code: 003510

4-year public university in small city.
Enrollment: 20,279 undergrads, 15% part-time. 3,130 full-time freshmen.
Selectivity: Admits over 75% of applicants.

BASIC COSTS (2005-2006)
Tuition and fees: $4,600; out-of-state residents $13,912.
Per-credit charge: $161; out-of-state residents $565.
Room and board: $5,626.

FINANCIAL AID PICTURE (2004-2005)
Students with need: Average financial aid package met 84% of need; average scholarship/grant was $2,295; average loan was $1,553. For part-time students, average financial aid package was $5,113.
Students without need: No-need awards available for academics, alumni affiliation, art, athletics, job skills, leadership, minority status, music/drama, religious affiliation, ROTC, state/district residency.
Cumulative student debt: 11% of graduating class had student loans; average debt was $19,800.
Additional info: Application filing deadline for scholarships February 15.

FINANCIAL AID PROCEDURES
Forms required: FAFSA.
Dates and Deadlines: Priority date 5/1; no closing date. Applicants notified on a rolling basis starting 4/15; must reply within 2 week(s) of notification.

CONTACT
David Hutton, Director of Student Financial Aid
1301 East Main Street, Murfreesboro, TN 37132
(615) 898-2830

Miller-Motte Technical College
Clarksville, Tennessee
www.miller-motte.com/clarksvillemain.html
                Federal Code: 026142

2-year for-profit business and health science college in small city.
Enrollment: 356 undergrads.
Selectivity: Open admission; but selective for some programs.

BASIC COSTS (2005-2006)
Additional info: Tuition at time of enrollment locked for 2 years.

FINANCIAL AID PICTURE
Students with need: Need-based aid available for full-time and part-time students. Work study available nights, weekends, and for part-time students.
Students without need: This college only awards aid to students with need.

FINANCIAL AID PROCEDURES
Forms required: FAFSA, institutional form.
Dates and Deadlines: No deadline. Applicants notified on a rolling basis.
Transfers: No deadline.

CONTACT
Donna Green, Financial Aid Director
1820 Business Park Drive, Clarksville, TN 37040
(931) 553-0071

Milligan College
Milligan College, Tennessee
www.milligan.edu   Federal Code: 003511

4-year private liberal arts college in small city, affiliated with independent Christian churches.
Enrollment: 744 undergrads, 2% part-time. 192 full-time freshmen.
Selectivity: Admits over 75% of applicants.

BASIC COSTS (2006-2007)
Tuition and fees: $18,320.
Per-credit charge: $490.
Room and board: $5,030.

FINANCIAL AID PICTURE (2004-2005)
Students with need: Out of 174 full-time freshmen who applied for aid, 143 were judged to have need. Of these, 143 received aid, and 69 had their full need met. Average financial aid package met 66% of need; average scholarship/grant was $4,738; average loan was $2,611. For part-time students, average financial aid package was $5,671.
Students without need: 33 full-time freshmen who did not demonstrate need for aid received scholarships/grants; average award was $5,104. No-need awards available for academics, alumni affiliation, art, athletics, job skills, minority status, music/drama, religious affiliation, state/district residency.
Scholarships offered: 66 full-time freshmen received athletic scholarships; average amount $6,077.
Cumulative student debt: 70% of graduating class had student loans; average debt was $23,794.

FINANCIAL AID PROCEDURES
Forms required: FAFSA.
Dates and Deadlines: Priority date 3/1; no closing date. Applicants notified on a rolling basis starting 3/15; must reply within 2 week(s) of notification.

CONTACT
Becky Brewster, Director of Student Financial Services
Box 210, Milligan College, TN 37682
(423) 461-8967

Motlow State Community College
Lynchburg, Tennessee
www.mscc.cc.tn.us   Federal Code: 006836

2-year public community college in rural community.
Enrollment: 3,030 undergrads, 34% part-time. 804 full-time freshmen.
Selectivity: Open admission.

BASIC COSTS (2005-2006)
Tuition and fees: $2,389; out-of-state residents $8,803.
Per-credit charge: $91; out-of-state residents $369.

FINANCIAL AID PICTURE
Students with need: Need-based aid available for full-time and part-time students.
Students without need: No-need awards available for academics, alumni affiliation, art, athletics, leadership, state/district residency.

FINANCIAL AID PROCEDURES
Forms required: FAFSA.
Dates and Deadlines: No deadline. Applicants notified on a rolling basis starting 3/15.

CONTACT
Joe Myers, Director of Financial Aid and Scholarships
Box 8500, Lynchburg, TN 37352
(931) 393-1553

Nashville State Community College
Nashville, Tennessee
www.nscc.edu   Federal Code: 007534

2-year public community and technical college in large city.
Enrollment: 7,198 undergrads.
Selectivity: Open admission; but selective for some programs.

BASIC COSTS (2005-2006)
Tuition and fees: $2,377; out-of-state residents $8,791.
Per-credit charge: $91; out-of-state residents $369.

FINANCIAL AID PICTURE (2005-2006)
Students with need: 61% of average financial aid package awarded as scholarships/grants, 39% awarded as loans/jobs. Need-based aid available for part-time students. Work study available nights, weekends, and for part-time students.
Students without need: No-need awards available for academics, minority status.

FINANCIAL AID PROCEDURES
Forms required: FAFSA, institutional form.
Dates and Deadlines: Priority date 3/1; no closing date. Applicants notified on a rolling basis starting 6/1; must reply within 2 week(s) of notification.

CONTACT
Stephen White, Director of Financial Aid
120 White Bridge Road, Nashville, TN 37209-4515
(615) 353-3250

National College of Business & Technology: Tennessee
Nashville, Tennessee
www.ncbt.edu   Federal Code: 003726

2-year for-profit business and technical college in large city.
Enrollment: 382 undergrads.
Selectivity: Open admission.

BASIC COSTS (2006-2007)
Tuition and fees: $8,976.
Per-credit charge: $187.

FINANCIAL AID PICTURE
Students with need: Need-based aid available for full-time and part-time students.
Students without need: This college only awards aid to students with need.

FINANCIAL AID PROCEDURES
Forms required: FAFSA.
Dates and Deadlines: No deadline.

CONTACT
Pamela Cotton, Director of Financial Aid and Compliance Officer
PO Box 6400, Roanoke, VA 24017
(615) 333-3344

Northeast State Technical Community College
Blountville, Tennessee
www.NortheastState.edu   Federal Code: 005378

2-year public community and technical college in small city.
Enrollment: 4,860 undergrads, 46% part-time. 775 full-time freshmen.
Selectivity: Open admission; but selective for some programs.

BASIC COSTS (2005-2006)
Tuition and fees: $2,393; out-of-state residents $8,807.
Per-credit charge: $91; out-of-state residents $369.

FINANCIAL AID PICTURE (2005-2006)
Students with need: 75% of average financial aid package awarded as scholarships/grants, 25% awarded as loans/jobs. Need-based aid available for part-time students. Work study available nights.
Students without need: No-need awards available for academics, alumni affiliation, art, job skills, leadership, minority status, music/drama, religious affiliation.

FINANCIAL AID PROCEDURES
Forms required: FAFSA.
Dates and Deadlines: Priority date 3/31; no closing date. Applicants notified on a rolling basis starting 3/1; must reply within 3 week(s) of notification.

CONTACT
Cruzita Lucero, Director of Financial Aid
Box 246, Blountville, TN 37617-0246
(423) 323-0252

Nossi College of Art
Goodlettsville, Tennessee
www.nossi.com   Federal Code: 017347

2-year private visual arts and technical college in large town.
Enrollment: 330 undergrads.

BASIC COSTS (2006-2007)
Additional info: Tuition for first year (3 semesters) $9,840; required fees $240.

FINANCIAL AID PICTURE
Students with need: Need-based aid available for full-time and part-time students.

CONTACT
Mary Kidd, Financial Aid Director
907 Rivergate Parkway, Building E-6, Goodlettsville, TN 37072
(615) 851-1088

O'More College of Design
Franklin, Tennessee
www.omorecollege.edu　　　　　Federal Code: 014663

4-year private visual arts college in large town.
Enrollment: 70 undergrads.
Selectivity: Admits less than 50% of applicants.

BASIC COSTS (2005-2006)
Tuition and fees: $12,880.
Per-credit charge: $510.

FINANCIAL AID PICTURE (2005-2006)
Students with need: Average financial aid package met 20% of need; average scholarship/grant was $2,000; average loan was $1,500. Need-based aid available for part-time students.
Students without need: This college only awards aid to students with need.
Scholarships offered: Academic scholarships available.

FINANCIAL AID PROCEDURES
Forms required: FAFSA.
Dates and Deadlines: Priority date 4/1; closing date 7/30. Applicants notified on a rolling basis starting 8/1; must reply by 7/30.
Transfers: Priority date 5/5; no deadline.

CONTACT
Amy Shelton, Financial Aid Director
423 South Margin Street, Franklin, TN 37064-0908
(615) 794-4254 ext. 227

Pellissippi State Technical Community College
Knoxville, Tennessee
www.pstcc.edu　　　　　Federal Code: 012693

2-year public community and technical college in small city.
Enrollment: 6,430 undergrads, 42% part-time. 1,067 full-time freshmen.
Selectivity: Open admission.

BASIC COSTS (2005-2006)
Tuition and fees: $2,414; out-of-state residents $8,828.
Per-credit charge: $91; out-of-state residents $369.

FINANCIAL AID PICTURE (2005-2006)
Students with need: 73% of average financial aid package awarded as scholarships/grants, 27% awarded as loans/jobs. Need-based aid available for part-time students. Work study available nights, weekends, and for part-time students.
Students without need: No-need awards available for academics, art, minority status, music/drama.

FINANCIAL AID PROCEDURES
Forms required: FAFSA.
Dates and Deadlines: Priority date 5/1; no closing date. Applicants notified on a rolling basis starting 7/15; must reply within 2 week(s) of notification.

CONTACT
Pat Peace, Director of Financial Aid and Veterans Affairs
Box 22990, Knoxville, TN 37933-0990
(423) 694-6565

Rhodes College
Memphis, Tennessee
www.rhodes.edu　　　　　Federal Code: 003519
　　　　　　　　　　　　　　　CSS Code: 1730

4-year private liberal arts college in very large city, affiliated with Presbyterian Church (USA).
Enrollment: 1,655 undergrads, 5% part-time. 429 full-time freshmen.
Selectivity: Admits less than 50% of applicants.

BASIC COSTS (2006-2007)
Tuition and fees: $29,112.
Per-credit charge: $1,010.
Room and board: $7,180.

FINANCIAL AID PICTURE (2005-2006)
Students with need: Out of 267 full-time freshmen who applied for aid, 152 were judged to have need. Of these, 151 received aid, and 107 had their full need met. Average financial aid package met 94% of need; average scholarship/grant was $15,983; average loan was $4,076. For part-time students, average financial aid package was $19,306.
Students without need: 197 full-time freshmen who did not demonstrate need for aid received scholarships/grants; average award was $10,266. No-need awards available for academics, art, minority status, music/drama, religious affiliation.
Cumulative student debt: 47% of graduating class had student loans; average debt was $45,151.
Additional info: Auditions required for theater and music achievement awards and art achievement awards. Interviews recommended for merit scholarships.

FINANCIAL AID PROCEDURES
Forms required: FAFSA, CSS PROFILE.
Dates and Deadlines: Closing date 1/15. Applicants notified by 4/1; must reply by 5/1.

CONTACT
Forrest Stuart, Director of Financial Aid
2000 North Parkway, Memphis, TN 38112
(901) 843-3810

Roane State Community College
Harriman, Tennessee
www.roanestate.edu　　　　　Federal Code: 009914

2-year public community and junior college in small town.
Enrollment: 4,352 undergrads, 39% part-time. 850 full-time freshmen.
Selectivity: Open admission; but selective for some programs.

BASIC COSTS (2005-2006)
Tuition and fees: $2,387; out-of-state residents $8,801.
Per-credit charge: $91; out-of-state residents $369.

FINANCIAL AID PICTURE
Students with need: Need-based aid available for full-time and part-time students. Work study available nights, weekends, and for part-time students.
Students without need: No-need awards available for academics, art, athletics, leadership, music/drama, state/district residency.

FINANCIAL AID PROCEDURES
Forms required: FAFSA, institutional form.
Dates and Deadlines: Priority date 4/1; no closing date. Applicants notified on a rolling basis starting 5/1.

CONTACT
Joy Goldberg, Director of Scholarships and Financial Aid
276 Patton Lane, Harriman, TN 37748
(865) 882-4545

South College
Knoxville, Tennessee
www.southcollegetn.edu   Federal Code: 004938

4-year for-profit liberal arts college in small city.
Enrollment: 502 undergrads, 26% part-time.

BASIC COSTS (2005-2006)
Additional info: Tuition $17,200 for physical therapy assistance, radiography, health science, post-baccalaureate education certificate, and nursing pre-professional programs.

FINANCIAL AID PICTURE
Students with need: Need-based aid available for full-time and part-time students.
Students without need: This college only awards aid to students with need.

FINANCIAL AID PROCEDURES
Forms required: FAFSA, institutional form.
Dates and Deadlines: No deadline. Applicants notified on a rolling basis.

CONTACT
Larry Broadwater, Financial Aid Director
200 Hayfield Road, Knoxville, TN 37922
(865) 251-1800

Southern Adventist University
Collegedale, Tennessee
www.southern.edu   Federal Code: 003518

4-year private university and liberal arts college in small town, affiliated with Seventh-day Adventists.
Enrollment: 2,390 undergrads. 500 full-time freshmen.
Selectivity: Admits 50 to 75% of applicants.

BASIC COSTS (2006-2007)
Tuition and fees: $14,784.
Per-credit charge: $604.
Room and board: $4,604.

FINANCIAL AID PICTURE (2005-2006)
Students with need: Average financial aid package met 60% of need; average scholarship/grant was $4,500; average loan was $3,700. For part-time students, average financial aid package was $9,500.
Students without need: No-need awards available for academics, alumni affiliation, art, leadership, music/drama.
Scholarships offered: Freshman scholarship based on combination of high school GPA, ACT/SAT scores, leadership positions held.

FINANCIAL AID PROCEDURES
Forms required: FAFSA, state aid form.
Dates and Deadlines: Priority date 3/1; no closing date. Applicants notified on a rolling basis starting 2/15; must reply within 2 week(s) of notification.

CONTACT
Marc Grundy, Director of Student Finance
Box 370, Collegedale, TN 37315-0370
(423) 236-2844

Southwest Tennessee Community College
Memphis, Tennessee
www.southwest.tn.edu   Federal Code: 010439

2-year public community and technical college in very large city.
Enrollment: 9,518 undergrads.
Selectivity: Open admission; but selective for some programs.

BASIC COSTS (2005-2006)
Tuition and fees: $2,377; out-of-state residents $8,791.
Per-credit charge: $91; out-of-state residents $369.
Additional info: Tuition/fee waivers available for minority students.

FINANCIAL AID PICTURE
Students with need: Need-based aid available for full-time and part-time students.
Students without need: This college only awards aid to students with need.
Scholarships offered: President's Academic Scholarship for excellence; $1,200 annually; for students in top 20% of graduating class with an 18 or better ACT, must work 150 hours, recipients usually recruited from Shelby and Fayette counties; 15 awarded.
Additional info: State grants available to eligible students who apply by 4/1.

FINANCIAL AID PROCEDURES
Forms required: FAFSA.
Dates and Deadlines: Priority date 3/15; no closing date. Applicants notified on a rolling basis starting 6/1; must reply within 4 week(s) of notification.
Transfers: Priority date 4/15.

CONTACT
Daniel Miller, Director of Financial Aid
PO Box 780, Memphis, TN 38101-0780
(901) 333-5960

Tennessee State University
Nashville, Tennessee
www.tnstate.edu   Federal Code: 003522

4-year public university in large city.
Enrollment: 6,423 undergrads, 16% part-time. 996 full-time freshmen.
Selectivity: Admits less than 50% of applicants.

BASIC COSTS (2005-2006)
Tuition and fees: $4,334; out-of-state residents $13,646.
Per-credit charge: $161; out-of-state residents $565.
Room and board: $4,620.
Additional info: Tuition/fee waivers available for minority students.

FINANCIAL AID PICTURE (2005-2006)
Students with need: 36% of average financial aid package awarded as scholarships/grants, 64% awarded as loans/jobs.
Students without need: No-need awards available for academics.

FINANCIAL AID PROCEDURES
Forms required: FAFSA.
Dates and Deadlines: Priority date 4/1; no closing date. Applicants notified on a rolling basis starting 7/10; must reply within 2 week(s) of notification.

CONTACT
Mary Chambliss, Director of Financial Aid
3500 John A. Merritt Boulevard, Nashville, TN 37209-1561
(615) 963-5701

Tennessee Technological University
Cookeville, Tennessee
www.tntech.edu   Federal Code: 003523

4-year public university in large town.
Enrollment: 7,167 undergrads, 10% part-time. 1,410 full-time freshmen.
Selectivity: Admits over 75% of applicants.

BASIC COSTS (2005-2006)
Tuition and fees: $4,424; out-of-state residents $13,736.
Per-credit charge: $161; out-of-state residents $565.
Room and board: $5,820.
Additional info: Tuition/fee waivers available for minority students.

FINANCIAL AID PICTURE (2004-2005)
Students with need: Out of 1,381 full-time freshmen who applied for aid, 819 were judged to have need. Of these, 804 received aid, and 239 had their full need met. Average financial aid package met 84% of need; average scholarship/grant was $3,476; average loan was $1,477. For part-time students, average financial aid package was $4,795.
Students without need: 466 full-time freshmen who did not demonstrate need for aid received scholarships/grants; average award was $5,092. No-need awards available for academics, alumni affiliation, art, athletics, leadership, minority status, music/drama, ROTC, state/district residency.
Scholarships offered: *Merit:* Presidential Scholarship; $5,000 renewable annually. National Merit Finalist Scholarship; 9 awarded. *Athletic:* 57 full-time freshmen received athletic scholarships; average amount $9,814.
Additional info: Tuition and/or fee waivers available for children of Tennessee public school teachers.

FINANCIAL AID PROCEDURES
Forms required: FAFSA.
Dates and Deadlines: Priority date 3/15; no closing date. Applicants notified on a rolling basis starting 3/15; must reply within 2 week(s) of notification.

CONTACT
Lester McKenzie, Director of Student Financial Aid
Office of Admissions, Cookeville, TN 38505-0001
(931) 372-3073

Tennessee Temple University
Chattanooga, Tennessee
www.tntemple.edu   Federal Code: 003524

4-year private university and Bible college in small city, affiliated with Baptist faith.
Enrollment: 423 undergrads.

BASIC COSTS (2006-2007)
Tuition and fees: $8,870.
Per-credit charge: $300.
Room and board: $5,930.

FINANCIAL AID PICTURE (2005-2006)
Students with need: 46% of average financial aid package awarded as scholarships/grants, 54% awarded as loans/jobs. Need-based aid available for part-time students. Work study available nights, weekends, and for part-time students.
Students without need: No-need awards available for academics, alumni affiliation, athletics, leadership, music/drama, state/district residency.

FINANCIAL AID PROCEDURES
Forms required: FAFSA.
Dates and Deadlines: Priority date 3/31; no closing date. Applicants notified on a rolling basis starting 2/15; must reply within 2 week(s) of notification.

CONTACT
Ricky Taphorn, Director of Financial Aid
1815 Union Avenue, Chattanooga, TN 37404
(423) 493-4207

Tennessee Wesleyan College
Athens, Tennessee
www.twcnet.edu   Federal Code: 003525

4-year private nursing and liberal arts and teachers college in large town, affiliated with United Methodist Church.
Enrollment: 847 undergrads, 14% part-time. 167 full-time freshmen.
Selectivity: Admits over 75% of applicants.

BASIC COSTS (2005-2006)
Tuition and fees: $13,550.
Per-credit charge: $375.
Room and board: $5,100.
Additional info: Tuition/fee waivers available for minority students.

FINANCIAL AID PICTURE (2005-2006)
Students with need: Average financial aid package met 73% of need; average scholarship/grant was $8,552; average loan was $1,881. For part-time students, average financial aid package was $7,721.
Students without need: No-need awards available for academics, alumni affiliation, athletics, job skills, minority status, music/drama, religious affiliation.
Cumulative student debt: 81% of graduating class had student loans; average debt was $15,042.

FINANCIAL AID PROCEDURES
Forms required: FAFSA, institutional form.
Dates and Deadlines: No deadline. Applicants notified on a rolling basis starting 2/15; must reply within 2 week(s) of notification.

CONTACT
Robert Perry, Director of Financial Aid
204 East College Street, Athens, TN 37371-0040
(423) 746-5215

Trevecca Nazarene University
Nashville, Tennessee
www.trevecca.edu   Federal Code: 003526

4-year private university and liberal arts college in very large city, affiliated with Church of the Nazarene.
Enrollment: 1,172 undergrads, 20% part-time. 237 full-time freshmen.
Selectivity: Admits 50 to 75% of applicants.

BASIC COSTS (2006-2007)
Tuition and fees: $14,774.
Room and board: $6,470.

FINANCIAL AID PICTURE (2004-2005)
Students with need: Out of 180 full-time freshmen who applied for aid, 154 were judged to have need. Of these, 101 received aid, and 26 had their full need met. Average financial aid package met 47% of need; average scholarship/grant was $8,176; average loan was $3,820. For part-time students, average financial aid package was $8,457.
Students without need: 123 full-time freshmen who did not demonstrate need for aid received scholarships/grants; average award was $8,486. No-need awards available for academics, alumni affiliation, athletics, leadership, music/drama, religious affiliation.
Scholarships offered: 6 full-time freshmen received athletic scholarships; average amount $14,724.
Cumulative student debt: 73% of graduating class had student loans; average debt was $24,000.

FINANCIAL AID PROCEDURES
Forms required: FAFSA.
Dates and Deadlines: Priority date 3/1; no closing date. Applicants notified on a rolling basis starting 3/15.

CONTACT
Eddie White, Assistant Director of Financial Aid
333 Murfreesboro Road, Nashville, TN 37210
(615) 248-1242

Tusculum College
Greeneville, Tennessee
www.tusculum.edu   Federal Code: 003527

4-year private liberal arts college in large town, affiliated with Presbyterian Church (USA).
Enrollment: 2,289 undergrads, 2% part-time. 306 full-time freshmen.
Selectivity: Admits 50 to 75% of applicants.

BASIC COSTS (2006-2007)
Tuition and fees: $16,170.
Room and board: $6,480.

FINANCIAL AID PICTURE
Students with need: Need-based aid available for full-time and part-time students. Work study available nights, weekends, and for part-time students.
Students without need: No-need awards available for academics, athletics, leadership, religious affiliation, state/district residency.

FINANCIAL AID PROCEDURES
Forms required: FAFSA.
Dates and Deadlines: Closing date 2/15. Applicants notified on a rolling basis starting 3/1; must reply within 3 week(s) of notification.

CONTACT
Pat Shannon, Director of Financial Aid
60 Shiloh Road, Greeneville, TN 37743
(423) 636-7300 ext. 5373

Union University
Jackson, Tennessee
www.uu.edu   Federal Code: 003528

4-year private university and liberal arts college in small city, affiliated with Southern Baptist Convention.
Enrollment: 2,038 undergrads, 21% part-time. 373 full-time freshmen.
Selectivity: Admits over 75% of applicants.

BASIC COSTS (2006-2007)
Tuition and fees: $17,590.
Per-credit charge: $585.
Room and board: $6,200.
Additional info: Tuition/fee waivers available for minority students.

FINANCIAL AID PICTURE (2005-2006)
Students with need: Out of 352 full-time freshmen who applied for aid, 287 were judged to have need. Of these, 287 received aid. For part-time students, average financial aid package was $3,900.
Students without need: 81 full-time freshmen who did not demonstrate need for aid received scholarships/grants; average award was $11,210. No-need awards available for academics, alumni affiliation, art, athletics, leadership, minority status, music/drama, religious affiliation.
Cumulative student debt: 52% of graduating class had student loans; average debt was $17,645.

FINANCIAL AID PROCEDURES
Forms required: FAFSA, institutional form.
Dates and Deadlines: Priority date 2/1; closing date 3/1. Applicants notified on a rolling basis starting 2/15; must reply by 5/1 or within 2 week(s) of notification.

CONTACT
John Brandt, Director of Financial Aid
1050 Union University Drive, Jackson, TN 38305-3697
(731) 661-5015

University of Memphis
Memphis, Tennessee
www.memphis.edu   Federal Code: 003509

4-year public university in very large city.
Enrollment: 15,228 undergrads, 25% part-time. 2,004 full-time freshmen.
Selectivity: Admits 50 to 75% of applicants.

BASIC COSTS (2005-2006)
Tuition and fees: $5,084; out-of-state residents $14,898.
Per-credit charge: $178; out-of-state residents $588.
Room and board: $6,069.

FINANCIAL AID PICTURE (2004-2005)
Students with need: Out of 1,412 full-time freshmen who applied for aid, 1,063 were judged to have need. Of these, 1,043 received aid, and 124 had their full need met. Average financial aid package met 82% of need; average scholarship/grant was $3,299; average loan was $1,665. For part-time students, average financial aid package was $4,862.
Students without need: This college only awards aid to students with need.
Scholarships offered: 15 full-time freshmen received athletic scholarships; average amount $3,240.
Cumulative student debt: 28% of graduating class had student loans; average debt was $21,493.

FINANCIAL AID PROCEDURES
Forms required: FAFSA.
Dates and Deadlines: Priority date 3/1; closing date 6/30. Applicants notified on a rolling basis starting 3/1; must reply within 2 week(s) of notification.

CONTACT
Richard Ritzman, Director of Student Financial Aid
101 Wilder Tower, Memphis, TN 38152
(901) 678-4825

University of Tennessee: Chattanooga
Chattanooga, Tennessee
www.utc.edu   Federal Code: 003529

4-year public university in large city.
Enrollment: 7,115 undergrads, 13% part-time. 1,454 full-time freshmen.
Selectivity: Admits over 75% of applicants.

BASIC COSTS (2005-2006)
Tuition and fees: $4,500; out-of-state residents $14,424.
Per-credit charge: $150; out-of-state residents $527.
Room and board: $6,474.

FINANCIAL AID PICTURE (2005-2006)
Students with need: Out of 1,296 full-time freshmen who applied for aid, 787 were judged to have need. Of these, 729 received aid, and 281 had their full need met. Average financial aid package met 83% of need; average scholarship/grant was $3,865; average loan was $2,560. Need-based aid available for part-time students.
Students without need: 278 full-time freshmen who did not demonstrate need for aid received scholarships/grants; average award was $2,461. No-need awards available for academics, alumni affiliation, art, athletics, job skills, leadership, minority status, music/drama, religious affiliation, state/district residency.

Scholarships offered: 94 full-time freshmen received athletic scholarships; average amount $11,057.
Cumulative student debt: 48% of graduating class had student loans; average debt was $15,348.

FINANCIAL AID PROCEDURES
Forms required: FAFSA, institutional form.
Dates and Deadlines: Priority date 4/1; no closing date. Applicants notified on a rolling basis starting 3/15.
Transfers: No deadline. Applicants notified on a rolling basis starting 3/15.

CONTACT
Rexann Bumpus, Director of Financial Aid
615 McCallie Avenue, Chattanooga, TN 37403
(423) 425-4677

University of Tennessee: Knoxville
Knoxville, Tennessee
www.tennessee.edu   Federal Code: 003530

4-year public university in large city.
Enrollment: 19,878 undergrads, 6% part-time. 3,511 full-time freshmen.
Selectivity: Admits 50 to 75% of applicants.

BASIC COSTS (2005-2006)
Tuition and fees: $5,290; out-of-state residents $16,060.
Per-credit charge: $193; out-of-state residents $642.
Room and board: $5,210.
Additional info: Out-of-state students pay additional required fees.

FINANCIAL AID PICTURE (2004-2005)
Students with need: Out of 2,161 full-time freshmen who applied for aid, 1,403 were judged to have need. Of these, 1,314 received aid, and 222 had their full need met. Average financial aid package met 66% of need; average scholarship/grant was $6,225; average loan was $2,582. For part-time students, average financial aid package was $4,952.
Students without need: This college only awards aid to students with need.
Scholarships offered: *Merit:* Academic College Scholarship Application part of financial aid forms, must be completed by all students. *Athletic:* 24 full-time freshmen received athletic scholarships; average amount $21,337.
Additional info: Application priority date for scholarships 2/1.

FINANCIAL AID PROCEDURES
Forms required: FAFSA.
Dates and Deadlines: Priority date 3/1; no closing date. Applicants notified on a rolling basis starting 3/15; must reply within 3 week(s) of notification.
Transfers: Transfer students must provide financial aid transcripts from all colleges previously attended regardless of whether any aid was received.

CONTACT
Jeff Gerkin, Director of Financial Aid
320 Student Services Building, Knoxville, TN 37996-0230
(865) 974-3131

University of Tennessee: Martin
Martin, Tennessee
www.utm.edu   Federal Code: 003531

4-year public university in small town.
Enrollment: 5,489 undergrads, 9% part-time. 1,232 full-time freshmen.
Selectivity: Admits over 75% of applicants.

BASIC COSTS (2005-2006)
Tuition and fees: $4,493; out-of-state residents $13,547.
Per-credit charge: $156; out-of-state residents $534.
Room and board: $4,220.

FINANCIAL AID PICTURE (2005-2006)
Students with need: Average financial aid package met 75% of need; average scholarship/grant was $4,493; average loan was $2,680. For part-time students, average financial aid package was $7,762.
Students without need: This college only awards aid to students with need.
Cumulative student debt: 57% of graduating class had student loans; average debt was $16,749.

FINANCIAL AID PROCEDURES
Forms required: FAFSA.
Dates and Deadlines: Priority date 3/1; no closing date. Applicants notified on a rolling basis starting 4/1.

CONTACT
Sandy Neel, Director of Student Financial Assistance
200 Hall Moody Administration Building, Martin, TN 38238
(731) 881-7040

University of the South
Sewanee, Tennessee
www.sewanee.edu   Federal Code: 003534

4-year private university in small town, affiliated with Episcopal Church.
Enrollment: 1,402 undergrads. 421 full-time freshmen.
Selectivity: Admits 50 to 75% of applicants. GED not accepted.

BASIC COSTS (2006-2007)
Tuition and fees: $28,750.
Per-credit charge: $1,035.
Room and board: $8,160.

FINANCIAL AID PICTURE (2005-2006)
Students with need: Out of 248 full-time freshmen who applied for aid, 168 were judged to have need. Of these, 168 received aid, and 131 had their full need met. Average financial aid package met 94% of need; average scholarship/grant was $17,663; average loan was $3,182.
Students without need: 76 full-time freshmen who did not demonstrate need for aid received scholarships/grants; average award was $11,712. No-need awards available for academics, minority status, religious affiliation.
Scholarships offered: Benedict Scholars Program for exceptional freshmen; 3 full cost scholarships. Wilkins Scholarships for outstanding incoming freshmen; half tuition, 25 awarded.
Cumulative student debt: 36% of graduating class had student loans; average debt was $14,926.

FINANCIAL AID PROCEDURES
Forms required: FAFSA, institutional form.
Dates and Deadlines: Priority date 3/1; no closing date. Applicants notified by 4/1; must reply within 4 week(s) of notification.

CONTACT
David Gelinas, Director of Financial Aid
735 University Avenue, Sewanee, TN 37383
(931) 598-1312

Vanderbilt University
Nashville, Tennessee
www.vanderbilt.edu   Federal Code: 003535
                           CSS Code: 1871

4-year private university in very large city.
Enrollment: 6,286 undergrads, 1% part-time. 1,622 full-time freshmen.
Selectivity: Admits less than 50% of applicants.

796 Tennessee Vanderbilt University

BASIC COSTS (2005-2006)
Tuition and fees: $31,730.
Room and board: $10,286.

FINANCIAL AID PICTURE (2005-2006)
Students with need: Out of 864 full-time freshmen who applied for aid, 753 were judged to have need. Of these, 751 received aid, and 743 had their full need met. Average financial aid package met 100% of need; average scholarship/grant was $25,749; average loan was $3,096.
Students without need: 231 full-time freshmen who did not demonstrate need for aid received scholarships/grants; average award was $13,216. No-need awards available for academics, minority status, music/drama, state/district residency.
Scholarships offered: 52 full-time freshmen received athletic scholarships; average amount $26,741.
Cumulative student debt: 31% of graduating class had student loans; average debt was $19,585.
Additional info: Various payment plans available.

FINANCIAL AID PROCEDURES
Forms required: FAFSA, CSS PROFILE.
Dates and Deadlines: Priority date 2/1; no closing date. Applicants notified on a rolling basis starting 4/1; must reply by 5/1.
Transfers: Priority date 4/15.

CONTACT
David Mohning, Director, Student Financial Aid
2305 West End Avenue, Nashville, TN 37203-1727
(615) 322-3591

Volunteer State Community College
Gallatin, Tennessee
www.volstate.edu   Federal Code: 009912

2-year public community and junior college in small city.
Enrollment: 5,643 undergrads, 43% part-time. 1,019 full-time freshmen.
Selectivity: Open admission; but selective for some programs.

BASIC COSTS (2005-2006)
Tuition and fees: $2,383; out-of-state residents $8,797.
Per-credit charge: $91; out-of-state residents $369.
Additional info: Tuition/fee waivers available for minority students.

FINANCIAL AID PICTURE (2004-2005)
Students with need: 66% of average financial aid package awarded as scholarships/grants, 34% awarded as loans/jobs. Need-based aid available for part-time students.
Students without need: No-need awards available for academics, art, athletics, leadership, minority status, music/drama, religious affiliation, state/district residency.

FINANCIAL AID PROCEDURES
Forms required: FAFSA, institutional form.
Dates and Deadlines: Priority date 4/15; no closing date. Applicants notified on a rolling basis; must reply within 2 week(s) of notification.
Transfers: No deadline.

CONTACT
Sue Pedigo, Director of Financial Aid
1480 Nashville Pike, Gallatin, TN 37066
(615) 452-8600 ext. 3456

Walters State Community College
Morristown, Tennessee
www.ws.edu   Federal Code: 008863

2-year public community college in small city.
Enrollment: 4,325 undergrads, 35% part-time. 938 full-time freshmen.
Selectivity: Open admission; but selective for some programs.

BASIC COSTS (2005-2006)
Tuition and fees: $2,381; out-of-state residents $8,795.
Per-credit charge: $91; out-of-state residents $369.
Additional info: Tuition/fee waivers available for minority students.

FINANCIAL AID PICTURE (2004-2005)
Students with need: Out of 649 full-time freshmen who applied for aid, 449 were judged to have need. Of these, 427 received aid, and 51 had their full need met. Average financial aid package met 59% of need; average scholarship/grant was $2,802; average loan was $1,621. For part-time students, average financial aid package was $2,698.
Students without need: 113 full-time freshmen who did not demonstrate need for aid received scholarships/grants; average award was $1,720. No-need awards available for academics, athletics, music/drama, state/district residency.
Scholarships offered: 10 full-time freshmen received athletic scholarships; average amount $1,483.
Cumulative student debt: 60% of graduating class had student loans; average debt was $5,406.

FINANCIAL AID PROCEDURES
Forms required: FAFSA.
Dates and Deadlines: No deadline. Applicants notified on a rolling basis.

CONTACT
Linda Mason, Director of Financial Aid
500 South Davy Crockett Parkway, Morristown, TN 37813-6899
(423) 585-6811

Texas

Abilene Christian University
Abilene, Texas
www.acu.edu   Federal Code: 003537

4-year private university in small city, affiliated with Church of Christ.
Enrollment: 4,079 undergrads, 4% part-time. 949 full-time freshmen.
Selectivity: Admits 50 to 75% of applicants.

BASIC COSTS (2006-2007)
Tuition and fees: $16,330.
Per-credit charge: $521.
Room and board: $6,129.

FINANCIAL AID PICTURE (2004-2005)
Students with need: Out of 941 full-time freshmen who applied for aid, 572 were judged to have need. Of these, 570 received aid, and 263 had their full need met. Average financial aid package met 73% of need; average scholarship/grant was $8,057; average loan was $2,830. For part-time students, average financial aid package was $6,308.
Students without need: 295 full-time freshmen who did not demonstrate need for aid received scholarships/grants; average award was $5,010. No-need awards available for academics, art, athletics, leadership, minority status, music/drama, religious affiliation, state/district residency.
Scholarships offered: *Merit:* Presidential Scholarship; half or full tuition; based on interview, ACT or SAT scores. Heritage Award; $1,000 per year; based on Church of Christ, ACT or SAT scores. Transfer Scholarship; $1,000-

$2,000; based on GPA. **Athletic:** 41 full-time freshmen received athletic scholarships; average amount $6,985.
Additional info: Early estimate service available.

FINANCIAL AID PROCEDURES
Forms required: FAFSA, institutional form.
Dates and Deadlines: Priority date 3/1; no closing date. Applicants notified on a rolling basis starting 4/1.

CONTACT
Gary West, Director of Student Financial Services
ACU Box 29000, Abilene, TX 79699
(325) 674-2643

Alvin Community College
Alvin, Texas
www.alvincollege.edu   Federal Code: 003539

2-year public community and liberal arts college in large town.
Enrollment: 2,819 undergrads.
Selectivity: Open admission; but selective for some programs.

BASIC COSTS (2006-2007)
Tuition and fees: $1,190; out-of-district residents $1,970; out-of-state residents $3,650.
Per-credit charge: $28; out-of-district residents $54; out-of-state residents $110.

FINANCIAL AID PICTURE
Students with need: Need-based aid available for full-time and part-time students. Work study available nights, weekends, and for part-time students.
Students without need: This college only awards aid to students with need.

FINANCIAL AID PROCEDURES
Forms required: FAFSA.
Dates and Deadlines: Priority date 6/30; no closing date. Applicants notified on a rolling basis; must reply within 2 week(s) of notification.

CONTACT
Dora Sims, Director of Student Financial Aid and Placement
3110 Mustang Road, Alvin, TX 77511-4898
(281) 756-3524

Angelina College
Lufkin, Texas
www.angelina.edu   Federal Code: 006661

2-year public community college in large town.
Enrollment: 4,778 undergrads, 52% part-time. 907 full-time freshmen.
Selectivity: Open admission; but selective for some programs.

BASIC COSTS (2005-2006)
Tuition and fees: $1,050; out-of-district residents $1,560; out-of-state residents $2,160.
Per-credit charge: $28; out-of-district residents $45; out-of-state residents $65.
Room and board: $4,250.
Additional info: Students taking 1-3 credits pay higher per-credit-hour charge.

FINANCIAL AID PICTURE (2004-2005)
Students with need: Out of 749 full-time freshmen who applied for aid, 703 were judged to have need. Of these, 681 received aid. Need-based aid available for part-time students.
Students without need: This college only awards aid to students with need.

FINANCIAL AID PROCEDURES
Forms required: FAFSA, institutional form.
Dates and Deadlines: Priority date 7/15; no closing date. Applicants notified on a rolling basis starting 7/15.

CONTACT
Rebecca Innerarity, Director of Financial Aid
PO Box 1768, Lufkin, TX 75902-1768
(936) 633-5291

Angelo State University
San Angelo, Texas
www.angelo.edu   Federal Code: 003541

4-year public university in small city.
Enrollment: 5,658 undergrads, 15% part-time. 1,271 full-time freshmen.
Selectivity: Admits over 75% of applicants.

BASIC COSTS (2005-2006)
Tuition and fees: $4,290; out-of-state residents $12,570.
Per-credit charge: $106; out-of-state residents $382.
Room and board: $5,314.

FINANCIAL AID PICTURE (2004-2005)
Students with need: Out of 917 full-time freshmen who applied for aid, 569 were judged to have need. Of these, 569 received aid, and 425 had their full need met. Average financial aid package met 75% of need; average scholarship/grant was $2,495; average loan was $1,960. For part-time students, average financial aid package was $4,239.
Students without need: 68 full-time freshmen who did not demonstrate need for aid received scholarships/grants; average award was $2,134. No-need awards available for academics, athletics, leadership, music/drama, ROTC.
Scholarships offered: Merit: Carr Academic Scholarship program; average award $2,200 per semester; 1 of every 6 students receives. Special Academic Scholarships available for undergraduates planning on majoring in chemistry/biochemistry, mathematics, physics, French, or German. **Athletic:** 4 full-time freshmen received athletic scholarships; average amount $2,098.

FINANCIAL AID PROCEDURES
Forms required: FAFSA, institutional form.
Dates and Deadlines: Priority date 5/1; no closing date. Applicants notified on a rolling basis starting 4/1.
Transfers: No deadline. Applicants notified on a rolling basis.

CONTACT
Lyn Wheeler, Director of Financial Aid
ASU Station #11014, San Angelo, TX 76909-1014
(800) 946-8627

Arlington Baptist College
Arlington, Texas
www.abconline.edu   Federal Code: 014305

4-year private Bible college in very large city, affiliated with Baptist faith.
Enrollment: 181 undergrads, 21% part-time. 32 full-time freshmen.
Selectivity: Open admission.

BASIC COSTS (2005-2006)
Tuition and fees: $5,490.
Per-credit charge: $165.
Room and board: $3,800.

FINANCIAL AID PICTURE (2005-2006)
Students with need: Out of 32 full-time freshmen who applied for aid, 30 were judged to have need. Of these, 30 received aid, and 30 had their full need met. For part-time students, average financial aid package was $1,601.
Students without need: This college only awards aid to students with need.
Cumulative student debt: 70% of graduating class had student loans; average debt was $8,900.

FINANCIAL AID PROCEDURES
Forms required: FAFSA.
Dates and Deadlines: Priority date 8/15; no closing date. Applicants notified on a rolling basis.

CONTACT
David Clogston, Business Manager
3001 West Division, Arlington, TX 76012
(817) 431-8741

Art Institute of Dallas
Dallas, Texas
www.aid.edu   Federal Code: 017360

4-year for-profit visual arts college in very large city.
Enrollment: 1,010 full-time undergrads.
Selectivity: Open admission; but selective for some programs.

BASIC COSTS (2005-2006)
Additional info: Tuition for full bachelor's degree programs (180 credits): $64,800.00; for full associate degree programs (105 credits) $37,800. Per credit hour cost $360.

FINANCIAL AID PICTURE
Students with need: Need-based aid available for full-time students.

FINANCIAL AID PROCEDURES
Forms required: FAFSA.
Dates and Deadlines: Applicants notified on a rolling basis.

CONTACT
Two North Park, 8080 Park Lane, Dallas, TX 75231
(214) 692-8080

ATI Career Training Center
Dallas, Texas
http://ati.edu-search.com/   Federal Code: 025966

2-year for-profit technical college in very large city.
Enrollment: 820 full-time undergrads.

BASIC COSTS (2005-2006)
Additional info: One-time comprehensive rate per program ranging from $3,715 for 12-month massage therapy program to $31,243 for 2-year respiratory therapy technician program.

FINANCIAL AID PICTURE
Students with need: Need-based aid available for full-time students.
Students without need: This college only awards aid to students with need.
Additional info: Limited work-study positions available during school hours.

FINANCIAL AID PROCEDURES
Forms required: FAFSA, institutional form.

CONTACT
Karen Eilert, Director of Financial Aid
10003 Technology Boulevard, West, Dallas, TX 75220
(214) 902-8191

Austin College
Sherman, Texas
www.austincollege.edu   Federal Code: 003543

4-year private liberal arts and teachers college in small city, affiliated with Presbyterian Church (USA).
Enrollment: 1,291 undergrads. 348 full-time freshmen.
Selectivity: Admits 50 to 75% of applicants.

BASIC COSTS (2006-2007)
Tuition and fees: $23,355.
Per-credit charge: $846.
Room and board: $7,741.

FINANCIAL AID PICTURE (2005-2006)
Students with need: Out of 273 full-time freshmen who applied for aid, 194 were judged to have need. Of these, 194 received aid, and 192 had their full need met. Average financial aid package met 100% of need; average scholarship/grant was $14,574; average loan was $5,724. Need-based aid available for part-time students.
Students without need: 139 full-time freshmen who did not demonstrate need for aid received scholarships/grants; average award was $9,328. No-need awards available for academics, alumni affiliation, art, leadership, music/drama, religious affiliation, state/district residency.
Scholarships offered: Presidential Scholarships; full tuition; up to 10 awarded. Leadership Institute Merit-Based Scholarships; 4-year value of $40,000; up to 15 awarded. Sara Bernice Moseley Scholarship for Outstanding Presbyterian Students; $2,000-$10,000 per year. Distinguished Alumni Scholarship; $10,000 per year.
Cumulative student debt: 82% of graduating class had student loans; average debt was $26,164.

FINANCIAL AID PROCEDURES
Forms required: FAFSA, institutional form.
Dates and Deadlines: Priority date 4/1; no closing date. Applicants notified on a rolling basis starting 3/1; must reply by 5/1.

CONTACT
Laurie Coulter, Executive Director of Financial Aid
900 North Grand, Suite 6N, Sherman, TX 75090-4400
(903) 813-2900

Austin Community College
Austin, Texas
www.austincc.edu   Federal Code: 012015

2-year public community college in very large city.
Enrollment: 31,908 undergrads, 72% part-time. 1,540 full-time freshmen.
Selectivity: Open admission; but selective for some programs.

BASIC COSTS (2005-2006)
Tuition and fees: $1,590; out-of-district residents $3,480; out-of-state residents $6,090.
Per-credit charge: $39; out-of-district residents $102; out-of-state residents $189.

FINANCIAL AID PICTURE (2004-2005)
Students with need: Out of 627 full-time freshmen who applied for aid, 462 were judged to have need. Of these, 392 received aid. Need-based aid available for part-time students.

FINANCIAL AID PROCEDURES
Forms required: FAFSA, institutional form.
Dates and Deadlines: Closing date 4/1. Applicants notified on a rolling basis starting 6/1; must reply within 2 week(s) of notification.

CONTACT
Terry Bazan, Director, Financial Assistance
5930 Middle Fiskville Road, Austin, TX 78752-4390
(512) 223-7550

Austin Graduate School of Theology
Austin, Texas
www.austingrad.edu   Federal Code: 017322

Upper-division private Bible and seminary college in large city, affiliated with Church of Christ.
Enrollment: 27 undergrads, 89% part-time.

BASIC COSTS (2005-2006)
Tuition and fees: $5,700.
Per-credit charge: $190.

FINANCIAL AID PICTURE (2004-2005)
Students with need: 54% of average financial aid package awarded as scholarships/grants, 46% awarded as loans/jobs. Need-based aid available for part-time students. Work study available nights.
Students without need: No-need awards available for academics, leadership.
Additional info: Generous scholarships for students taking at least 12 hours. Federal work study program available. Institutional work study program (need-based) available.

FINANCIAL AID PROCEDURES
Forms required: FAFSA, institutional form.
Dates and Deadlines: Priority date 7/1; closing date 8/1.
Transfers: No deadline.

CONTACT
Dave Arthur, Vice President
1909 University Avenue, Austin, TX 78705
(512) 476-2772

Baylor University
Waco, Texas
www.baylor.edu   Federal Code: 003545

4-year private university in small city, affiliated with Baptist faith.
Enrollment: 11,751 undergrads, 3% part-time. 3,161 full-time freshmen.
Selectivity: Admits 50 to 75% of applicants.

BASIC COSTS (2006-2007)
Tuition and fees: $22,814.
Per-credit charge: $857.
Room and board: $7,125.
Additional info: Tuition at time of enrollment locked for 4 years.

FINANCIAL AID PICTURE (2005-2006)
Students with need: Out of 2,282 full-time freshmen who applied for aid, 1,739 were judged to have need. Of these, 1,739 received aid, and 278 had their full need met. Average financial aid package met 70% of need; average scholarship/grant was $12,114; average loan was $2,015. For part-time students, average financial aid package was $7,260.
Students without need: 1,101 full-time freshmen who did not demonstrate need for aid received scholarships/grants; average award was $6,880. No-need awards available for academics, art, athletics, job skills, leadership, music/drama, ROTC.
Scholarships offered: *Merit:* Regent's scholarship; full tuition; limited to National Merit finalists who list Baylor as first choice; unlimited number. President's Scholarship; $32,000 divided over 4 years. Provost's Baylor Scholarship; $26,000 divided over 4 years. Dean's Scholarship; $14,000 divided over 4 years. Founder's Scholarship; $6,000 divided over 4 years. Unlimited number of all awarded based on high school rank and SAT/ACT scores. Achievement Scholarship (awarded in addition to the above); ranging from $4,000 to $12,000; based on SAT/ACT scores. *Athletic:* 70 full-time freshmen received athletic scholarships; average amount $19,899.

FINANCIAL AID PROCEDURES
Forms required: FAFSA.
Dates and Deadlines: Priority date 3/1; no closing date. Applicants notified on a rolling basis starting 3/10; must reply by 5/1 or within 2 week(s) of notification.
Transfers: No deadline. Applicants notified on a rolling basis starting 3/10; must reply by 5/1 or within 2 week(s) of notification.

CONTACT
Cliff Neel, Assistant Vice President and Director of Academic Scholarships and Financial Aid
One Bear Place #97056, Waco, TX 76798-7056
(800) 229-5678

Blinn College
Brenham, Texas
www.blinn.edu   Federal Code: 003549

2-year public junior college in large town.
Enrollment: 7,085 full-time undergrads.
Selectivity: Open admission; but selective for some programs.

BASIC COSTS (2005-2006)
Tuition and fees: $1,680; out-of-district residents $2,460; out-of-state residents $4,890.
Per-credit charge: $28; out-of-district residents $54; out-of-state residents $135.
Room and board: $3,800.

FINANCIAL AID PICTURE
Students with need: Need-based aid available for full-time and part-time students.

FINANCIAL AID PROCEDURES
Forms required: FAFSA, institutional form.
Dates and Deadlines: Priority date 6/1; no closing date. Applicants notified on a rolling basis starting 7/1.

CONTACT
Scot Mertz, Director of Financial Aid
902 College Avenue, Brenham, TX 77833
(979) 830-4144

Brazosport College
Lake Jackson, Texas
www.brazosport.edu   Federal Code: 007287

2-year public community college in large town.
Enrollment: 3,607 undergrads.
Selectivity: Open admission; but selective for some programs.

BASIC COSTS (2005-2006)
Tuition and fees: $1,140; out-of-district residents $1,770; out-of-state residents $3,180.
Per-credit charge: $28; out-of-district residents $49; out-of-state residents $96.

FINANCIAL AID PICTURE (2004-2005)
Students with need: 95% of average financial aid package awarded as scholarships/grants, 5% awarded as loans/jobs. Need-based aid available for part-time students.

Students without need: No-need awards available for academics, art, job skills, leadership, music/drama, state/district residency.

FINANCIAL AID PROCEDURES
Forms required: FAFSA, institutional form.
Dates and Deadlines: Priority date 7/1; no closing date. Applicants notified on a rolling basis starting 5/1.

CONTACT
Kay Wright, Director of Financial Aid
500 College Drive, Lake Jackson, TX 77566
(979) 230-3377

Cedar Valley College
Lancaster, Texas
www.cedarvalleycollege.edu   Federal Code: 014035

2-year public community college in large town.
Enrollment: 3,331 undergrads, 65% part-time. 330 full-time freshmen.
Selectivity: Open admission.

BASIC COSTS (2005-2006)
Tuition and fees: $990; out-of-district residents $1,800; out-of-state residents $2,880.
Per-credit charge: $33; out-of-district residents $60; out-of-state residents $96.

FINANCIAL AID PICTURE
Students with need: Need-based aid available for full-time students.

FINANCIAL AID PROCEDURES
Forms required: FAFSA.
Dates and Deadlines: Priority date 5/1; no closing date. Applicants notified on a rolling basis.

CONTACT
Frank Ellis, Director of Financial Aid
3030 North Dallas Avenue, Lancaster, TX 75134
(972) 860-8280

Central Texas College
Killeen, Texas
www.ctcd.edu   Federal Code: 004003

2-year public community and technical college in small city.
Enrollment: 12,781 undergrads, 88% part-time. 631 full-time freshmen.
Selectivity: Open admission; but selective for some programs.

BASIC COSTS (2005-2006)
Tuition and fees: $1,200; out-of-district residents $1,410; out-of-state residents $4,140.
Per-credit charge: $32; out-of-district residents $39; out-of-state residents $130.
Room and board: $3,140.

FINANCIAL AID PICTURE (2004-2005)
Students with need: 86% of average financial aid package awarded as scholarships/grants, 14% awarded as loans/jobs. Need-based aid available for part-time students. Work study available nights, weekends, and for part-time students.
Students without need: This college only awards aid to students with need.

FINANCIAL AID PROCEDURES
Forms required: FAFSA, institutional form.
Dates and Deadlines: Closing date 7/1. Applicants notified on a rolling basis starting 3/1; must reply within 4 week(s) of notification.

CONTACT
Annabelle Smith, Director of Student Financial Aid
Box 1800, Killeen, TX 76540
(254) 526-1508

Clarendon College
Clarendon, Texas
www.clarendoncollege.edu   Federal Code: 003554

2-year public community college in rural community.
Enrollment: 1,051 undergrads, 51% part-time. 350 full-time freshmen.
Selectivity: Open admission; but selective for some programs.

BASIC COSTS (2006-2007)
Tuition and fees: $2,070; out-of-district residents $2,580; out-of-state residents $3,030.
Per-credit charge: $38; out-of-district residents $70; out-of-state residents $55.
Room and board: $3,100.

FINANCIAL AID PICTURE (2004-2005)
Students with need: Out of 150 full-time freshmen who applied for aid, 150 were judged to have need. Of these, 150 received aid, and 40 had their full need met. Average financial aid package met 60% of need; average scholarship/grant was $3,500; average loan was $1,750. For part-time students, average financial aid package was $2,500.
Students without need: No-need awards available for academics, art, athletics, leadership, music/drama, state/district residency.

FINANCIAL AID PROCEDURES
Forms required: FAFSA, institutional form.
Dates and Deadlines: Priority date 7/1; closing date 9/1. Applicants notified on a rolling basis starting 8/1; must reply by 8/15 or within 2 week(s) of notification.
Transfers: No deadline.

CONTACT
Tami Brown, Director of Student Financial Aid
PO Box 968, Clarendon, TX 79226
(806) 874-3571 ext. 112

Coastal Bend College
Beeville, Texas
www.coastalbend.edu   Federal Code: 003546

2-year public community college in large town.
Enrollment: 3,366 undergrads.
Selectivity: Open admission; but selective for some programs.

BASIC COSTS (2005-2006)
Tuition and fees: $1,730; out-of-district residents $3,500; out-of-state residents $3,950.
Room only: $1,560.
Additional info: Meal ticket (a la carte) food service available.

FINANCIAL AID PICTURE (2004-2005)
Students with need: 79% of average financial aid package awarded as scholarships/grants, 21% awarded as loans/jobs. Need-based aid available for part-time students.
Students without need: No-need awards available for academics, leadership.

FINANCIAL AID PROCEDURES
Forms required: FAFSA, institutional form.
Dates and Deadlines: Priority date 4/1; no closing date. Applicants notified on a rolling basis starting 5/1; must reply within 2 week(s) of notification.

CONTACT
Patsy Freman, Director of Financial Aid
3800 Charco Road, Beeville, TX 78102
(361) 354-2238

College of Saint Thomas More
Fort Worth, Texas
www.cstm.edu   Federal Code: 031894

4-year private liberal arts college in very large city, affiliated with Roman Catholic Church.
Enrollment: 37 undergrads, 43% part-time. 4 full-time freshmen.

BASIC COSTS (2005-2006)
Tuition and fees: $12,000.
Per-credit charge: $400.

FINANCIAL AID PICTURE
Students with need: Need-based aid available for full-time and part-time students. Work study available nights.

CONTACT
Corky Swanson, Financial Aid Department
3020 Lubbock Avenue, Fort Worth, TX 76109
(817) 923-8459

College of the Mainland
Texas City, Texas
www.com.edu   Federal Code: 007096

2-year public community and technical college in large town.
Enrollment: 4,019 undergrads.
Selectivity: Open admission; but selective for some programs.

BASIC COSTS (2005-2006)
Tuition and fees: $956; out-of-district residents $1,946; out-of-state residents $2,846.
Per-credit charge: $26; out-of-district residents $59; out-of-state residents $89.

FINANCIAL AID PICTURE
Students with need: Need-based aid available for full-time and part-time students. Work study available nights, weekends, and for part-time students.
Students without need: This college only awards aid to students with need.

FINANCIAL AID PROCEDURES
Forms required: FAFSA, institutional form.
Dates and Deadlines: No deadline. Applicants notified on a rolling basis.
Transfers: Priority date 8/1.

CONTACT
Rebecca Miles, Director of Financial Aid
1200 Amburn Road, Texas City, TX 77591
(409) 938-1211 ext. 274

Collin County Community College District
Plano, Texas
www.ccccd.edu   Federal Code: 016792

2-year public community college in large city.
Enrollment: 18,039 undergrads, 60% part-time. 2,439 full-time freshmen.
Selectivity: Open admission; but selective for some programs.

BASIC COSTS (2006-2007)
Tuition and fees: $1,144; out-of-district residents $1,384; out-of-state residents $2,914.
Per-credit charge: $37; out-of-district residents $43; out-of-state residents $90.

FINANCIAL AID PICTURE (2005-2006)
Students with need: Out of 899 full-time freshmen who applied for aid, 676 were judged to have need. Of these, 585 received aid, and 128 had their full need met. Average financial aid package met 34% of need; average scholarship/grant was $3,444; average loan was $2,243. For part-time students, average financial aid package was $2,948.
Students without need: 35 full-time freshmen who did not demonstrate need for aid received scholarships/grants; average award was $726. No-need awards available for academics, art, athletics, music/drama.
Scholarships offered: 18 full-time freshmen received athletic scholarships; average amount $3,094.
Cumulative student debt: 25% of graduating class had student loans; average debt was $6,542.

FINANCIAL AID PROCEDURES
Forms required: FAFSA, institutional form.
Dates and Deadlines: Priority date 6/1; closing date 6/30. Applicants notified on a rolling basis starting 5/1; must reply within 2 week(s) of notification.
Transfers: Applicants must have cumulative GPA of 2.0 and less than 90 transferable credit hours.

CONTACT
Debra Wilkison, Director of Financial Aid
2800 East Spring Creek Parkway, Plano, TX 75074
(972) 881-5760

Commonwealth Institute of Funeral Service
Houston, Texas
www.commonwealthinst.org   Federal Code: 003556

2-year private school of mortuary science in very large city.
Enrollment: 136 undergrads, 7% part-time. 33 full-time freshmen.

BASIC COSTS (2005-2006)
Additional info: Full five-quarter program costs $9,500, which includes application and graduation fee.

FINANCIAL AID PICTURE
Students with need: Need-based aid available for full-time and part-time students.
Students without need: This college only awards aid to students with need.
Scholarships offered: Scholarship awards; $250-$500 based on funds available; recipients selected on academic achievement, leadership and professional promise, as well as any stipulations by the donor, by a committee of Commonwealth Institute graduate employers, alumni, and benefactors.

FINANCIAL AID PROCEDURES
Forms required: FAFSA.
Dates and Deadlines: Priority date 7/10; no closing date. Applicants notified on a rolling basis starting 7/12.

CONTACT
Dennis Christie, Director of Financial Aid
415 Barren Springs Drive, Houston, TX 77090-5913
(281) 873-0262

Concordia University at Austin
Austin, Texas
www.concordia.edu   Federal Code: 003557

4-year private university and liberal arts college in very large city, affiliated with Lutheran Church - Missouri Synod.
Enrollment: 1,021 undergrads, 26% part-time. 194 full-time freshmen.
Selectivity: Admits 50 to 75% of applicants.

BASIC COSTS (2005-2006)
Tuition and fees: $16,850.
Per-credit charge: $558.
Room and board: $6,900.
Additional info: Tuition/fee waivers available for adults.

FINANCIAL AID PICTURE
Students with need: Need-based aid available for full-time and part-time students.
Students without need: No-need awards available for academics, leadership, music/drama, religious affiliation.

FINANCIAL AID PROCEDURES
Forms required: FAFSA, institutional form.
Dates and Deadlines: Priority date 4/15; closing date 7/1. Applicants notified on a rolling basis starting 3/1; must reply within 2 week(s) of notification.
Transfers: Financial aid transcripts from all previously attended trade/technical schools and colleges/universities required.

CONTACT
Kathy Shryer, Director of Financial Assistance
3400 Interstate 35 North, Austin, TX 78705-2799
(512) 486-2000

Dallas Baptist University
Dallas, Texas
www.dbu.edu   Federal Code: 003560

4-year private university in very large city, affiliated with Baptist faith.
Enrollment: 3,567 undergrads, 41% part-time. 358 full-time freshmen.
Selectivity: Admits 50 to 75% of applicants.

BASIC COSTS (2006-2007)
Tuition and fees: $13,050.
Per-credit charge: $435.
Room and board: $4,959.

FINANCIAL AID PICTURE (2005-2006)
Students with need: Out of 330 full-time freshmen who applied for aid, 202 were judged to have need. Of these, 197 received aid, and 113 had their full need met. Average financial aid package met 70% of need; average scholarship/grant was $2,742; average loan was $2,438. For part-time students, average financial aid package was $4,639.
Students without need: 71 full-time freshmen who did not demonstrate need for aid received scholarships/grants; average award was $9,403. No-need awards available for academics, alumni affiliation, athletics, job skills, leadership, music/drama, religious affiliation.
Scholarships offered: 16 full-time freshmen received athletic scholarships; average amount $6,089.
Cumulative student debt: 55% of graduating class had student loans; average debt was $18,763.

FINANCIAL AID PROCEDURES
Forms required: FAFSA, institutional form.
Dates and Deadlines: Priority date 3/15; closing date 5/1. Applicants notified on a rolling basis.
Transfers: No deadline.

CONTACT
Donald Zackary, Director of Financial Aid
3000 Mountain Creek Parkway, Dallas, TX 75211-9299
(214) 333-5363

Dallas Christian College
Dallas, Texas
www.dallas.edu   Federal Code: 006941

4-year private Bible college in very large city, affiliated with nondenominational tradition.
Enrollment: 260 full-time undergrads.
Selectivity: Admits less than 50% of applicants.

BASIC COSTS (2005-2006)
Tuition and fees: $8,185.
Per-credit charge: $249.
Room and board: $5,000.

FINANCIAL AID PICTURE
Students with need: Need-based aid available for full-time and part-time students.

FINANCIAL AID PROCEDURES
Forms required: FAFSA, institutional form.
Dates and Deadlines: Closing date 4/15. Applicants notified on a rolling basis; must reply within 2 week(s) of notification.

CONTACT
Robin Walker, Financial Aid Officer
2700 Christian Parkway, Dallas, TX 75234-7299
(972) 241-3371

Del Mar College
Corpus Christi, Texas
www.delmar.edu   Federal Code: 003563

2-year public community college in large city.
Enrollment: 12,006 undergrads, 69% part-time. 590 full-time freshmen.
Selectivity: Open admission; but selective for some programs.

BASIC COSTS (2006-2007)
Tuition and fees: $1,910; out-of-district residents $4,160; out-of-state residents $5,210.
Per-credit charge: $35; out-of-district residents $110; out-of-state residents $145.

FINANCIAL AID PICTURE (2004-2005)
Students with need: 73% of average financial aid package awarded as scholarships/grants, 27% awarded as loans/jobs. Need-based aid available for part-time students. Work study available nights, weekends, and for part-time students.
Students without need: This college only awards aid to students with need.

FINANCIAL AID PROCEDURES
Forms required: FAFSA.
Dates and Deadlines: Priority date 5/1; no closing date. Applicants notified on a rolling basis starting 7/1; must reply within 2 week(s) of notification.

CONTACT
Enrique Garcia, Assistant Dean of Financial Aid
101 Baldwin Boulevard, Corpus Christi, TX 78404-3897
(361) 698-1293

DeVry University: Irving
Dallas, Texas
www.devry.edu   Federal Code: 010139

4-year for-profit university in small city.
Enrollment: 1,596 undergrads, 31% part-time. 337 full-time freshmen.

BASIC COSTS (2005-2006)
Tuition and fees: $12,140.
Per-credit charge: $440.

FINANCIAL AID PICTURE (2004-2005)
Students with need: Out of 192 full-time freshmen who applied for aid, 180 were judged to have need. Of these, 177 received aid, and 14 had their full need met. Average financial aid package met 42% of need; average scholarship/grant was $4,383; average loan was $5,422. For part-time students, average financial aid package was $6,937.
Students without need: This college only awards aid to students with need.

FINANCIAL AID PROCEDURES
Forms required: FAFSA.
Dates and Deadlines: No deadline. Applicants notified on a rolling basis starting 7/1.

CONTACT
Nga Phan, Director, Financial Aid
4800 Regent Boulevard, Dallas, TX 75063-2439
(972) 929-9740

East Texas Baptist University
Marshall, Texas
www.etbu.edu   Federal Code: 003564

4-year private university and liberal arts college in large town, affiliated with Baptist faith.
Enrollment: 1,241 undergrads, 5% part-time. 301 full-time freshmen.
Selectivity: Admits over 75% of applicants.

BASIC COSTS (2006-2007)
Tuition and fees: $13,700.
Per-credit charge: $475.
Room and board: $4,190.
Additional info: Tuition at time of enrollment locked for 4 years.

FINANCIAL AID PICTURE (2005-2006)
Students with need: Out of 294 full-time freshmen who applied for aid, 242 were judged to have need. Of these, 242 received aid, and 61 had their full need met. Average financial aid package met 89% of need; average scholarship/grant was $5,284; average loan was $2,605. For part-time students, average financial aid package was $6,269.
Students without need: 52 full-time freshmen who did not demonstrate need for aid received scholarships/grants; average award was $4,858. No-need awards available for academics, alumni affiliation, leadership, music/drama, religious affiliation.
Cumulative student debt: 81% of graduating class had student loans; average debt was $16,777.

FINANCIAL AID PROCEDURES
Forms required: FAFSA, institutional form.
Dates and Deadlines: Closing date 6/1. Applicants notified on a rolling basis starting 1/15; must reply within 3 week(s) of notification.
Transfers: Applicants notified on a rolling basis starting 1/15. Transfers may be ineligible for scholarships based on ACT/SAT tests.

CONTACT
Katherine Evans, Director of Financial Aid
1209 North Grove, Marshall, TX 75670-1498
(903) 923-2138

Eastfield College
Mesquite, Texas
www.efc.dcccd.edu   Federal Code: 008510

2-year public community and liberal arts college in small city.
Enrollment: 3,275 full-time undergrads.
Selectivity: Open admission.

BASIC COSTS (2005-2006)
Tuition and fees: $990; out-of-district residents $1,800; out-of-state residents $2,880.
Per-credit charge: $33; out-of-district residents $60; out-of-state residents $96.

FINANCIAL AID PICTURE
Students with need: Need-based aid available for full-time and part-time students. Work study available nights, weekends, and for part-time students.
Scholarships offered: Lecroy Scholars Program; $2,400 ($600 per semester); based on demonstrated church, community or academic leadership and GPA 3.0; requires enrollment in 12 hours for awarding semester and participation in Lecroy Scholars events; 5-10 awarded. Erin Tierney Kramp Encouragement Program; $2,400 ($600 per semester); based on demonstrated courage in the face of adversity, moral character, leadership, and high academic standards; requires enrollment in 8 hours for awarding semester, and maintenance of high academic standards; 2 awarded.

FINANCIAL AID PROCEDURES
Forms required: FAFSA, institutional form.
Dates and Deadlines: Priority date 5/1; no closing date. Applicants notified on a rolling basis starting 4/15.

CONTACT
Reva Rattan, Dean of Financial Aid
3737 Motley Drive, Mesquite, TX 75150
(972) 860-7188

El Centro College
Dallas, Texas
www.elcentrocollege.edu   Federal Code: 004453

2-year public community college in very large city.
Enrollment: 4,686 undergrads, 74% part-time. 237 full-time freshmen.
Selectivity: Open admission; but selective for some programs.

BASIC COSTS (2005-2006)
Tuition and fees: $990; out-of-district residents $1,800; out-of-state residents $2,880.
Per-credit charge: $33; out-of-district residents $60; out-of-state residents $96.
Additional info: Tuition/fee waivers available for minority students, unemployed or children of unemployed.

FINANCIAL AID PICTURE
Students with need: Need-based aid available for full-time and part-time students.
Additional info: Interview required for financial aid applicants.

FINANCIAL AID PROCEDURES
Forms required: FAFSA.
Dates and Deadlines: Priority date 5/1; no closing date. Applicants notified on a rolling basis; must reply within 2 week(s) of notification.

Transfers: Financial aid transcript may be required from previous institutions attended.

CONTACT
John Wells, Director of Financial Aid
801 Main Street, Dallas, TX 75202
(214) 860-2099

El Paso Community College
El Paso, Texas
www.epcc.edu   Federal Code: 010387

2-year public community college in very large city.
Enrollment: 26,000 undergrads.
Selectivity: Open admission; but selective for some programs.

BASIC COSTS (2005-2006)
Tuition and fees: $1,212; out-of-state residents $1,686.
Per-credit charge: $44; out-of-state residents $73.
Additional info: Per-credit-hour costs listed are for each additional credit-hour beyond one credit-hour for in-state students, and beyond six credit-hours for out-of-state students.

FINANCIAL AID PICTURE
Students with need: Work study available nights, weekends, and for part-time students.
Students without need: No-need awards available for academics, athletics.

FINANCIAL AID PROCEDURES
Forms required: FAFSA, institutional form.
Dates and Deadlines: Priority date 5/1; no closing date. Applicants notified on a rolling basis starting 7/1; must reply within 2 week(s) of notification.

CONTACT
Linda Gonzalez-Hensge, Director of Student Financial Services
Box 20500, El Paso, TX 79998
(915) 831-2566

Frank Phillips College
Borger, Texas
www.fpctx.edu   Federal Code: 003568

2-year public community and junior college in large town.
Enrollment: 803 undergrads, 27% part-time. 93 full-time freshmen.
Selectivity: Open admission.

BASIC COSTS (2005-2006)
Tuition and fees: $1,710; out-of-district residents $2,280; out-of-state residents $2,490.
Per-credit charge: $57; out-of-district residents $76; out-of-state residents $83.
Room and board: $3,100.

FINANCIAL AID PICTURE
Students with need: Need-based aid available for full-time and part-time students. Work study available nights, weekends, and for part-time students.
Students without need: No-need awards available for academics, athletics, music/drama, state/district residency.
Scholarships offered: Various scholarships available including BEDC, Presidential, Dean's, Access, Opportunity, and Re-entering Adult Learner.
Additional info: Some Texas fire department and police department personnel, active duty military personnel, children of military missing in action may qualify for reduced or waived tuition. Out-of-state tuition waived for students living in Oklahoma counties adjacent to Texas.

FINANCIAL AID PROCEDURES
Forms required: FAFSA, institutional form.

Dates and Deadlines: Applicants notified on a rolling basis; must reply within 2 week(s) of notification.

CONTACT
Randy Braidfoot, Director Financial Aid
Box 5118, Borger, TX 79008-5118
(806) 457-4200 ext. 718

Galveston College
Galveston, Texas
www.gc.edu   Federal Code: 004972

2-year public community college in small city.
Enrollment: 2,230 undergrads, 62% part-time. 190 full-time freshmen.
Selectivity: Open admission; but selective for some programs.

BASIC COSTS (2005-2006)
Tuition and fees: $1,414; out-of-state residents $2,744.
Per-credit charge: $30; out-of-state residents $60.

FINANCIAL AID PICTURE
Students with need: Need-based aid available for full-time and part-time students.
Students without need: This college only awards aid to students with need.

FINANCIAL AID PROCEDURES
Forms required: FAFSA.
Dates and Deadlines: Priority date 6/9; no closing date. Applicants notified on a rolling basis starting 6/1.

CONTACT
Ron Crumedy, Financial Aid Manager
4015 Avenue Q, Galveston, TX 77550
(409) 944-1235

Grayson County College
Denison, Texas
www.grayson.edu   Federal Code: 003570

2-year public community and technical college in large town.
Enrollment: 2,000 full-time undergrads.
Selectivity: Open admission; but selective for some programs.

BASIC COSTS (2005-2006)
Tuition and fees: $1,260; out-of-district residents $1,470; out-of-state residents $2,940.
Per-credit charge: $42; out-of-district residents $49; out-of-state residents $98.
Room and board: $3,284.

FINANCIAL AID PICTURE
Students with need: Need-based aid available for full-time and part-time students.
Additional info: Short term loans available.

FINANCIAL AID PROCEDURES
Forms required: FAFSA.
Dates and Deadlines: No deadline. Applicants notified on a rolling basis; must reply within 5 week(s) of notification.

CONTACT
Dana Akins, Director of Financial Aid
6101 Grayson Drive, Denison, TX 75020
(903) 463-8642

Hallmark Institute of Aeronautics
San Antonio, Texas
www.hallmarkinstitute.com   Federal Code: 010509

2-year for-profit technical college in very large city.
Enrollment: 233 undergrads. 67 full-time freshmen.
Selectivity: Admits 50 to 75% of applicants.

BASIC COSTS (2005-2006)
Additional info: Tuition for combined associate program in airframe technology or powerplant technology: $21,915. Tuition for diploma programs ranges from $12,181 to $17,384. Costs include books, equipment and supplies. Required fees: $200. Registration fee: $100. Course fees vary. International students pay additional 8%. Tuition at time of enrollment locked for 2 years.

FINANCIAL AID PICTURE
Students with need: Need-based aid available for full-time students.

FINANCIAL AID PROCEDURES
Forms required: FAFSA.
Dates and Deadlines: No deadline. Applicants notified on a rolling basis.

CONTACT
Grace Calixto, Director of Financial Planning
8901 Wetmore Road, San Antonio, TX 78230
(210) 690-9000

Hallmark Institute of Technology
San Antonio, Texas
www.hallmarkinstitute.com   Federal Code: 010509

2-year for-profit business and technical college in very large city.
Enrollment: 538 undergrads. 117 full-time freshmen.
Selectivity: Admits less than 50% of applicants.

BASIC COSTS (2006-2007)
Additional info: Costs for associate programs range from $15,050 to $24,210; additional registration fee $100 for all programs. Tuition at time of enrollment locked for 2 years.

FINANCIAL AID PICTURE
Students with need: Need-based aid available for full-time students.

FINANCIAL AID PROCEDURES
Forms required: FAFSA.
Dates and Deadlines: No deadline. Applicants notified on a rolling basis.

CONTACT
Grace Calixto, Director of Financial Planning
10401 IH 10 West, San Antonio, TX 78230-1737
(210) 690-9000

Hardin-Simmons University
Abilene, Texas
www.hsutx.edu   Federal Code: 003571

4-year private university in small city, affiliated with Baptist faith.
Enrollment: 1,987 undergrads, 10% part-time. 435 full-time freshmen.
Selectivity: Admits 50 to 75% of applicants.

BASIC COSTS (2006-2007)
Tuition and fees: $15,626.
Per-credit charge: $495.
Room and board: $4,580.
Additional info: Tuition at time of enrollment locked for 4 years.

FINANCIAL AID PICTURE (2005-2006)
Students with need: Out of 434 full-time freshmen who applied for aid, 306 were judged to have need. Of these, 306 received aid, and 83 had their full need met. Average financial aid package met 67% of need; average scholarship/grant was $4,431; average loan was $2,394. For part-time students, average financial aid package was $7,956.
Students without need: 77 full-time freshmen who did not demonstrate need for aid received scholarships/grants; average award was $4,548. No-need awards available for academics, art, job skills, leadership, music/drama, religious affiliation.
Cumulative student debt: 72% of graduating class had student loans; average debt was $26,144.

FINANCIAL AID PROCEDURES
Forms required: FAFSA.
Dates and Deadlines: Priority date 3/15; no closing date. Applicants notified on a rolling basis starting 1/1.

CONTACT
Shane Davidson, Associate Vice President of Enrollment Services
PO Box 16050, Abilene, TX 79698-0001
(325) 670-1206

Hill College
Hillsboro, Texas
www.hillcollege.edu   Federal Code: 003573

2-year public community and junior college in small town.
Enrollment: 3,016 undergrads, 55% part-time. 497 full-time freshmen.
Selectivity: Open admission; but selective for some programs.

BASIC COSTS (2005-2006)
Tuition and fees: $1,310; out-of-district residents $1,550; out-of-state residents $1,950.
Per-credit charge: $43; out-of-district residents $51; out-of-state residents $51.
Room and board: $3,190.

FINANCIAL AID PICTURE (2004-2005)
Students with need: 97% of average financial aid package awarded as scholarships/grants, 3% awarded as loans/jobs. Need-based aid available for part-time students.
Students without need: No-need awards available for academics, athletics, music/drama.

FINANCIAL AID PROCEDURES
Forms required: FAFSA, institutional form.
Dates and Deadlines: Priority date 8/1; no closing date. Applicants notified on a rolling basis.

CONTACT
Susan Russell, Director of Student Financial Aid
Box 619, Hillsboro, TX 76645

Houston Baptist University
Houston, Texas
www.hbu.edu   Federal Code: 003576

4-year private university and liberal arts college in very large city, affiliated with Baptist General Convention of Texas.
Enrollment: 1,873 undergrads, 14% part-time. 309 full-time freshmen.
Selectivity: Admits 50 to 75% of applicants.

BASIC COSTS (2006-2007)
Tuition and fees: $16,500.
Per-credit charge: $505.

Room and board: $5,055.
Additional info: Tuition at time of enrollment locked for 4 years.

FINANCIAL AID PICTURE (2005-2006)
Students with need: Average financial aid package met 59% of need; average scholarship/grant was $7,021; average loan was $2,162. For part-time students, average financial aid package was $11,038.
Students without need: No-need awards available for academics, alumni affiliation, art, athletics, leadership, music/drama, religious affiliation.
Scholarships offered: Endowed Academic Scholarship; full or three quarters tuition for four years; limited number available; for new freshmen with 1300 SAT or 30 ACT. Founders Academic Scholarship; $6,000 per year; minimum 1250 SAT or 28 ACT required for freshmen, 3.75 GPA on 30 or more semester hours required for transfers. Presidential Academic Scholarship; $4,300 per year, renewable; 1175 SAT or 26 ACT required for freshmen, 3.5 GPA required for transfers. Legacy Grant; $2,700 per year; renewable; 1100 SAT or 24 ACT required for freshman, 3.25 GPA required for transfers. All SAT scores are exclusive of Writing. Valedictorian Scholarship; $1,500 per year; renewable; for valedictorians from Texas high schools. Ministerial Dependents Grant; $4,300 per year; for dependent children of ordained/licensed Southern Baptist ministers and missionaries. Grants-In-Aid; awards vary; for students who contribute special abilities or services to the University; awarded in music, art, athletics and nursing. Church Matching Award; awards vary.
Cumulative student debt: 80% of graduating class had student loans; average debt was $16,932.

FINANCIAL AID PROCEDURES
Forms required: FAFSA.
Dates and Deadlines: Priority date 3/1; closing date 4/15. Applicants notified on a rolling basis starting 3/10.

CONTACT
Sherry Byrd, Director of Financial Aid
7502 Fondren Road, Houston, TX 77074-3298
(281) 649-3471

Houston Community College System
Houston, Texas
www.hccs.edu   Federal Code: 010422

2-year public community college in very large city.
Enrollment: 39,516 undergrads.
Selectivity: Open admission; but selective for some programs.

BASIC COSTS (2005-2006)
Tuition and fees: $1,470; out-of-district residents $3,090; out-of-state residents $3,690.
Per-credit charge: $49; out-of-district residents $103; out-of-state residents $123.

FINANCIAL AID PICTURE
Students with need: Need-based aid available for full-time and part-time students. Work study available nights, weekends, and for part-time students.

FINANCIAL AID PROCEDURES
Forms required: FAFSA.
Dates and Deadlines: Priority date 8/15; no closing date. Applicants notified on a rolling basis starting 6/1; must reply within 2 week(s) of notification.

CONTACT
Alex Prince, Chief Financial Aid Officer
3100 Main, Houston, TX 77266-7517
(713) 718-8550

Howard College
Big Spring, Texas
www.howardcollege.edu   Federal Code: 003574

2-year public community college in large town.
Enrollment: 2,663 undergrads, 68% part-time. 161 full-time freshmen.
Selectivity: Open admission; but selective for some programs.

BASIC COSTS (2005-2006)
Tuition and fees: $1,312; out-of-district residents $1,672; out-of-state residents $2,312.
Room and board: $3,140.

FINANCIAL AID PICTURE
Students with need: Need-based aid available for full-time and part-time students.
Students without need: No-need awards available for academics, athletics, leadership, music/drama.

FINANCIAL AID PROCEDURES
Forms required: FAFSA, institutional form.
Dates and Deadlines: Priority date 4/1; no closing date. Applicants notified on a rolling basis starting 7/15; must reply within 2 week(s) of notification.

CONTACT
Ann Duncan, Director of Financial Aid
1001 Birdwell Lane, Big Spring, TX 79720
(432) 264-5083

Howard Payne University
Brownwood, Texas
www.hputx.edu   Federal Code: 003575

4-year private liberal arts and teachers college in large town, affiliated with Baptist faith.
Enrollment: 1,364 undergrads.
Selectivity: Admits 50 to 75% of applicants.

BASIC COSTS (2006-2007)
Tuition and fees: $14,470.
Per-credit charge: $485.
Room and board: $4,794.

FINANCIAL AID PICTURE
Students with need: Need-based aid available for full-time and part-time students.
Students without need: No-need awards available for academics, alumni affiliation, art, job skills, music/drama.

FINANCIAL AID PROCEDURES
Forms required: FAFSA, institutional form.
Dates and Deadlines: Priority date 3/1; no closing date. Applicants notified on a rolling basis starting 3/30; must reply within 3 week(s) of notification.

CONTACT
Glenda Huff, Director of Student Financial Aid
1000 Fisk Avenue, Brownwood, TX 76801
(325) 649-8015

Huston-Tillotson College
Austin, Texas
www.htu.edu   Federal Code: 003577

4-year private liberal arts college in very large city, affiliated with United Church of Christ and United Methodist Church.
Enrollment: 630 undergrads, 7% part-time. 176 full-time freshmen.

BASIC COSTS (2006-2007)
Tuition and fees: $8,850.
Per-credit charge: $258.
Room and board: $5,892.

FINANCIAL AID PICTURE (2004-2005)
Students with need: Out of 161 full-time freshmen who applied for aid, 161 were judged to have need. Of these, 149 received aid, and 135 had their full need met. Average financial aid package met 77% of need; average scholarship/grant was $1,263; average loan was $2,325. For part-time students, average financial aid package was $3,185.
Students without need: 5 full-time freshmen who did not demonstrate need for aid received scholarships/grants; average award was $6,540. No-need awards available for academics, alumni affiliation, art, athletics, job skills, leadership, minority status, music/drama, religious affiliation, ROTC, state/district residency.
Scholarships offered: 14 full-time freshmen received athletic scholarships; average amount $5,402.
Cumulative student debt: 91% of graduating class had student loans; average debt was $17,000.

FINANCIAL AID PROCEDURES
Forms required: FAFSA, institutional form.
Dates and Deadlines: Priority date 3/15; closing date 4/1. Applicants notified on a rolling basis starting 4/1; must reply within 4 week(s) of notification.
Transfers: No deadline.

CONTACT
Antonio Holloway, Director of Financial Aid
900 Chicon Street, Austin, TX 78702-2795
(512) 505-3031

Jacksonville College
Jacksonville, Texas
www.jacksonville-college.edu   Federal Code: 003579

2-year private junior and liberal arts college in large town, affiliated with Baptist faith.
Enrollment: 216 undergrads.
Selectivity: Open admission.

BASIC COSTS (2006-2007)
Tuition and fees: $5,846.
Per-credit charge: $175.
Room and board: $2,628.

FINANCIAL AID PICTURE (2004-2005)
Students with need: 97% of average financial aid package awarded as scholarships/grants, 3% awarded as loans/jobs.
Students without need: No-need awards available for academics, athletics, music/drama, religious affiliation, state/district residency.

FINANCIAL AID PROCEDURES
Forms required: FAFSA.
Dates and Deadlines: Priority date 8/1; no closing date. Applicants notified on a rolling basis.

CONTACT
Don Compton, Financial Aid Officer
105 B.J. Albritton Drive, Jacksonville, TX 75766-4759
(903) 586-2518

Jarvis Christian College
Hawkins, Texas
www.jarvis.edu   Federal Code: 003637

4-year private liberal arts and teachers college in rural community, affiliated with Christian Church (Disciples of Christ).
Enrollment: 561 undergrads. 98 full-time freshmen.
Selectivity: Admits 50 to 75% of applicants.

BASIC COSTS (2006-2007)
Tuition and fees: $6,980.
Room and board: $4,156.

FINANCIAL AID PICTURE (2004-2005)
Students with need: Out of 98 full-time freshmen who applied for aid, 81 were judged to have need. Of these, 81 received aid, and 67 had their full need met. Average financial aid package met 79% of need; average scholarship/grant was $3,400; average loan was $1,313. For part-time students, average financial aid package was $2,750.
Students without need: 17 full-time freshmen who did not demonstrate need for aid received scholarships/grants; average award was $4,770. No-need awards available for academics, athletics, religious affiliation.
Scholarships offered: 4 full-time freshmen received athletic scholarships; average amount $2,411.
Additional info: High school transcript required for scholarship consideration.

FINANCIAL AID PROCEDURES
Forms required: FAFSA.
Dates and Deadlines: Priority date 6/30; no closing date. Applicants notified on a rolling basis starting 5/1; must reply within 2 week(s) of notification.
Transfers: Priority date 4/15.

CONTACT
Eric King, Director of Admission and Financial Aid
PO Box 1470, Hawkins, TX 75765-1470
(903) 769-5741

Kilgore College
Kilgore, Texas
www.kilgore.edu   Federal Code: 003580

2-year public community college in large town.
Enrollment: 4,752 undergrads.
Selectivity: Open admission; but selective for some programs.

BASIC COSTS (2005-2006)
Tuition and fees: $1,050; out-of-district residents $2,190; out-of-state residents $3,030.
Per-credit charge: $35; out-of-district residents $73; out-of-state residents $101.
Room and board: $3,630.
Additional info: Tuition/fee waivers available for unemployed or children of unemployed.

FINANCIAL AID PICTURE (2004-2005)
Students with need: 95% of average financial aid package awarded as scholarships/grants, 5% awarded as loans/jobs. Need-based aid available for part-time students.
Students without need: No-need awards available for academics, alumni affiliation, art, athletics, job skills, leadership, music/drama, state/district residency.
Scholarships offered: Presidential Scholarships; tuition, fees and books for 4 semesters; ACT 25 or top 10% of senior class; 20 available; renewable at 2.5 GPA.
Additional info: State of Texas grants and loans available for honor graduates with unmet needs and for non-traditional students.

FINANCIAL AID PROCEDURES
Forms required: FAFSA, state aid form, institutional form.
Dates and Deadlines: Priority date 6/1; closing date 7/15. Applicants notified on a rolling basis starting 3/1; must reply within 2 week(s) of notification.
Transfers: No deadline. Transfer students must submit financial aid transcript from previous school plus all appropriate internal aid forms and show proof of high school graduation or GED.

CONTACT
Annette Morgan, Director of Financial Aid
1100 Broadway, Kilgore, TX 75662-3299
(903) 983-8183

Lamar State College at Orange
Orange, Texas
www.lsco.edu   Federal Code: 016748

2-year public junior and liberal arts college in small city.
Enrollment: 1,000 full-time undergrads.
Selectivity: Open admission; but selective for some programs.

BASIC COSTS (2005-2006)
Tuition and fees: $3,070; out-of-state residents $11,350.
Per-credit charge: $76; out-of-state residents $352.

FINANCIAL AID PICTURE (2004-2005)
Students with need: 98% of average financial aid package awarded as scholarships/grants, 2% awarded as loans/jobs. Need-based aid available for part-time students.
Students without need: This college only awards aid to students with need.

FINANCIAL AID PROCEDURES
Forms required: FAFSA, institutional form.
Dates and Deadlines: Priority date 4/1; no closing date. Applicants notified on a rolling basis starting 5/15; must reply within 2 week(s) of notification.

CONTACT
Kerry Olson, Director of Financial Aid
410 West Front Street, Orange, TX 77630
(409) 882-3317

Lamar State College at Port Arthur
Port Arthur, Texas
www.lamarpa.edu   Federal Code: 016666

2-year public community and technical college in small city.
Enrollment: 1,150 full-time undergrads.
Selectivity: Open admission; but selective for some programs.

BASIC COSTS (2005-2006)
Tuition and fees: $3,100; out-of-state residents $11,380.
Per-credit charge: $76; out-of-state residents $352.

FINANCIAL AID PICTURE
Students with need: Need-based aid available for full-time and part-time students. Work study available nights, weekends, and for part-time students.
Students without need: This college only awards aid to students with need.

FINANCIAL AID PROCEDURES
Forms required: FAFSA, institutional form.
Dates and Deadlines: Priority date 4/1; no closing date. Applicants notified on a rolling basis starting 4/15; must reply within 2 week(s) of notification.

CONTACT
Diane Hargett, Director of Financial Aid
Box 310, Port Arthur, TX 77641-0310
(409) 984-6203

Lamar University
Beaumont, Texas
www.lamar.edu   Federal Code: 003581

4-year public university in small city.
Enrollment: 9,682 undergrads, 31% part-time. 1,585 full-time freshmen.
Selectivity: Admits 50 to 75% of applicants.

BASIC COSTS (2006-2007)
Tuition and fees: $4,722; out-of-state residents $12,972.
Per-credit charge: $120; out-of-state residents $396.
Room and board: $5,888.

FINANCIAL AID PICTURE (2005-2006)
Students with need: Out of 1,109 full-time freshmen who applied for aid, 713 were judged to have need. Of these, 600 received aid, and 114 had their full need met. Average financial aid package met 65% of need. For part-time students, average financial aid package was $1,217.
Students without need: 600 full-time freshmen who did not demonstrate need for aid received scholarships/grants; average award was $900.
Cumulative student debt: 65% of graduating class had student loans; average debt was $856.

FINANCIAL AID PROCEDURES
Forms required: FAFSA, institutional form.
Dates and Deadlines: Priority date 4/1; no closing date. Applicants notified on a rolling basis starting 4/1; must reply within 2 week(s) of notification.

CONTACT
Jill Rowley, Director of Financial Aid
Box 10009, Beaumont, TX 77705
(409) 880-8450

Laredo Community College
Laredo, Texas
www.laredo.edu   Federal Code: 003582

2-year public community college in large city.
Enrollment: 8,147 undergrads, 61% part-time. 801 full-time freshmen.
Selectivity: Open admission; but selective for some programs.

BASIC COSTS (2005-2006)
Tuition and fees: $1,626; out-of-district residents $2,586; out-of-state residents $3,546.
Per-credit charge: $32; out-of-district residents $64; out-of-state residents $96.
Room only: $2,200.

FINANCIAL AID PICTURE (2005-2006)
Students with need: 91% of average financial aid package awarded as scholarships/grants, 9% awarded as loans/jobs.

FINANCIAL AID PROCEDURES
Forms required: FAFSA, state aid form, institutional form.
Dates and Deadlines: Priority date 5/1; no closing date. Applicants notified on a rolling basis.

CONTACT
Adriana Marin, Director of Financial Aid
West End Washington Street, Laredo, TX 78040-4395
(956) 721-5360

Lee College
Baytown, Texas
www.lee.edu   Federal Code: 003583

2-year public community college in small city.
Enrollment: 2,394 undergrads, 59% part-time. 172 full-time freshmen.
Selectivity: Open admission; but selective for some programs.

BASIC COSTS (2005-2006)
Tuition and fees: $1,294; out-of-district residents $2,044; out-of-state residents $3,094.
Per-credit charge: $25; out-of-district residents $50; out-of-state residents $85.

FINANCIAL AID PICTURE
Students with need: Need-based aid available for full-time and part-time students.
Students without need: No-need awards available for academics, art, athletics, job skills, music/drama.

FINANCIAL AID PROCEDURES
Forms required: FAFSA.
Dates and Deadlines: Priority date 4/1; no closing date. Applicants notified on a rolling basis starting 6/1.

CONTACT
Sharon Mullins, Financial Aid Officer
Box 818, Baytown, TX 77522
(281) 425-6362

LeTourneau University
Longview, Texas
www.letu.edu   Federal Code: 003584

4-year private university in small city, affiliated with nondenominational tradition.
Enrollment: 3,565 undergrads, 61% part-time. 328 full-time freshmen.
Selectivity: Admits over 75% of applicants.

BASIC COSTS (2006-2007)
Tuition and fees: $16,920.
Room and board: $6,590.
Additional info: Tuition for 1-6 hours is $304 per credit, for 7-11 hours is $668 per credit.

FINANCIAL AID PICTURE (2004-2005)
Students with need: Out of 286 full-time freshmen who applied for aid, 232 were judged to have need. Of these, 232 received aid, and 37 had their full need met. Average financial aid package met 73% of need; average scholarship/grant was $9,049; average loan was $2,819. For part-time students, average financial aid package was $4,940.
Students without need: 70 full-time freshmen who did not demonstrate need for aid received scholarships/grants; average award was $1,650. No-need awards available for academics, leadership.
Scholarships offered: Honor scholarship; up to $3,000 per year; GPA 3.0-3.29, ACT minimum score 25 or SAT minimum score 1150. Dean's Scholarship; up to $4,500 per year; GPA 3.3-3.59, ACT minimum 27 or SAT minimum 1200. Presidential Scholarship; up to $6,000 per year; GPA 3.60 and up, ACT minimum score 29 or SAT minimum score 1300. All SAT scores exclusive of writing.
Cumulative student debt: 87% of graduating class had student loans; average debt was $28,426.

FINANCIAL AID PROCEDURES
Forms required: FAFSA.
Dates and Deadlines: Priority date 2/15; no closing date. Applicants notified on a rolling basis starting 3/1; must reply within 3 week(s) of notification.

CONTACT
Denise Welch, Director of Financial Aid
PO Box 7001, Longview, TX 75607
(903) 233-3430

Lon Morris College
Jacksonville, Texas
www.lonmorris.edu   Federal Code: 003585

2-year private junior and liberal arts college in large town, affiliated with United Methodist Church.
Enrollment: 396 undergrads.

BASIC COSTS (2005-2006)
Tuition and fees: $9,400.
Room and board: $5,600.
Additional info: Tuition/fee waivers available for minority students.

FINANCIAL AID PICTURE (2005-2006)
Students with need: 71% of average financial aid package awarded as scholarships/grants, 29% awarded as loans/jobs. Need-based aid available for part-time students.
Students without need: No-need awards available for academics, athletics.

FINANCIAL AID PROCEDURES
Forms required: FAFSA, state aid form, institutional form.
Dates and Deadlines: Priority date 5/1; no closing date. Applicants notified on a rolling basis starting 4/1; must reply within 3 week(s) of notification.
Transfers: Closing date 8/1.

CONTACT
Kris Marquis, Financial Aid Director
800 College Avenue, Jacksonville, TX 75766
(903) 589-4061

Lubbock Christian University
Lubbock, Texas
www.lcu.edu   Federal Code: 003586

4-year private university and liberal arts college in small city, affiliated with Church of Christ.
Enrollment: 1,764 undergrads, 22% part-time. 311 full-time freshmen.
Selectivity: Admits 50 to 75% of applicants.

BASIC COSTS (2006-2007)
Tuition and fees: $13,644.
Room and board: $4,600.

FINANCIAL AID PICTURE (2005-2006)
Students with need: Out of 240 full-time freshmen who applied for aid, 201 were judged to have need. Of these, 199 received aid, and 27 had their full need met. Average financial aid package met 70% of need; average scholarship/grant was $6,796; average loan was $3,254. For part-time students, average financial aid package was $5,883.
Students without need: 59 full-time freshmen who did not demonstrate need for aid received scholarships/grants; average award was $10,685. No-need awards available for academics, art, athletics, leadership, music/drama.
Scholarships offered: 16 full-time freshmen received athletic scholarships; average amount $5,705.
Cumulative student debt: 81% of graduating class had student loans; average debt was $22,192.

FINANCIAL AID PROCEDURES
Forms required: FAFSA, institutional form.
Dates and Deadlines: Priority date 6/1; closing date 8/1. Applicants notified on a rolling basis starting 3/1; must reply within 2 week(s) of notification.

Transfers: No deadline.
CONTACT
Amy Hardesty, Director of Financial Aid
5601 19th Street, Lubbock, TX 79407
(806) 720-7178

McMurry University
Abilene, Texas
www.mcm.edu   Federal Code: 003591

4-year private university and liberal arts college in small city, affiliated with United Methodist Church.
Enrollment: 1,396 undergrads, 15% part-time. 290 full-time freshmen.
Selectivity: Admits over 75% of applicants.

BASIC COSTS (2006-2007)
Tuition and fees: $15,170.
Per-credit charge: $475.
Room and board: $5,918.

FINANCIAL AID PICTURE (2005-2006)
Students with need: Out of 276 full-time freshmen who applied for aid, 240 were judged to have need. Of these, 240 received aid, and 39 had their full need met. Average financial aid package met 88% of need; average scholarship/grant was $9,181; average loan was $2,764. For part-time students, average financial aid package was $7,586.
Students without need: 23 full-time freshmen who did not demonstrate need for aid received scholarships/grants; average award was $4,421. No-need awards available for academics, art, music/drama, religious affiliation, ROTC.
Cumulative student debt: 82% of graduating class had student loans; average debt was $20,055.

FINANCIAL AID PROCEDURES
Forms required: FAFSA.
Dates and Deadlines: Priority date 3/15; no closing date. Applicants notified on a rolling basis starting 2/1; must reply within 3 week(s) of notification.
Transfers: No deadline.

CONTACT
Rachel Atkins, Director of Financial Aid
South 14th and Sayles Boulevard, Abilene, TX 79697-0001
(325) 793-4709

Midland College
Midland, Texas
www.midland.edu   Federal Code: 009797

2-year public community college in small city.
Enrollment: 4,585 undergrads.
Selectivity: Open admission; but selective for some programs.

BASIC COSTS (2005-2006)
Tuition and fees: $1,350; out-of-district residents $1,710; out-of-state residents $2,580.
Per-credit charge: $37; out-of-district residents $49; out-of-state residents $78.
Room and board: $3,520.
Additional info: Additional $48 charge per credit hour for baccalaureate program.

FINANCIAL AID PICTURE (2005-2006)
Students with need: 12% of average financial aid package awarded as scholarships/grants, 88% awarded as loans/jobs. Need-based aid available for part-time students.
Students without need: No-need awards available for academics, athletics, minority status, music/drama, state/district residency.
Scholarships offered: Abell-Hangar Foundations Scholarships; varying amounts; renewable; available for full-time or part-time study to any Midland High, Midland Lee, or Greenwood High School graduate.

FINANCIAL AID PROCEDURES
Forms required: FAFSA.
Dates and Deadlines: Closing date 6/1. Applicants notified on a rolling basis starting 5/15; must reply within 2 week(s) of notification.
Transfers: No deadline.

CONTACT
Laticia Williams, Director of Financial Aid
3600 North Garfield, Midland, TX 79705
(432) 685-4733

Midwestern State University
Wichita Falls, Texas
www.mwsu.edu   Federal Code: 003592

4-year public university and liberal arts college in small city.
Enrollment: 5,537 undergrads, 28% part-time. 845 full-time freshmen.
Selectivity: Admits over 75% of applicants.

BASIC COSTS (2006-2007)
Tuition and fees: $4,566; out-of-state residents $12,816.
Room and board: $5,220.

FINANCIAL AID PICTURE (2005-2006)
Students with need: Average financial aid package met 71% of need; average scholarship/grant was $4,414; average loan was $2,526. For part-time students, average financial aid package was $4,388.
Students without need: 205 full-time freshmen who did not demonstrate need for aid received scholarships/grants; average award was $1,489. No-need awards available for academics, alumni affiliation, art, athletics, leadership, minority status, music/drama.
Additional info: Employees offered educational incentive plan in which tuition reimbursed provided employee meets stated criteria. Additionally, dependents and children of faculty and staff may receive scholarship to defer local tuition and fees.

FINANCIAL AID PROCEDURES
Forms required: FAFSA, institutional form.
Dates and Deadlines: Priority date 5/1; no closing date. Applicants notified on a rolling basis starting 3/15; must reply within 2 week(s) of notification.

CONTACT
Kathy Pennartz, Director of Financial Aid
3410 Taft Boulevard, Wichita Falls, TX 76308-2099
(940) 397-4214

Mountain View College
Dallas, Texas
www.mvc.dcccd.edu   Federal Code: 008503

2-year public community college in very large city.
Enrollment: 3,976 undergrads.
Selectivity: Open admission.

BASIC COSTS (2005-2006)
Tuition and fees: $990; out-of-district residents $1,800; out-of-state residents $2,880.
Per-credit charge: $33; out-of-district residents $60; out-of-state residents $96.
Additional info: Tuition/fee waivers available for adults.

FINANCIAL AID PICTURE (2005-2006)
Students with need: 98% of average financial aid package awarded as scholarships/grants, 2% awarded as loans/jobs. Need-based aid available for part-time students. Work study available nights, weekends, and for part-time students.
Students without need: No-need awards available for academics.

FINANCIAL AID PROCEDURES
Forms required: FAFSA, institutional form.
Dates and Deadlines: Priority date 5/1; no closing date. Applicants notified on a rolling basis starting 6/1.

CONTACT
Dana Mingo, Director of Financial Aid
4849 West Illinois Avenue, Dallas, TX 75211-6599
(214) 860-8688

Navarro College
Corsicana, Texas
www.nav.cc.tx.us
Federal Code: 003593

2-year public community college in large town.
Enrollment: 6,512 undergrads.
Selectivity: Open admission; but selective for some programs.

BASIC COSTS (2005-2006)
Tuition and fees: $1,210; out-of-district residents $1,840; out-of-state residents $2,450.
Per-credit charge: $115; out-of-district residents $136; out-of-state residents $729.
Room and board: $3,854.

FINANCIAL AID PICTURE (2004-2005)
Students with need: 61% of average financial aid package awarded as scholarships/grants, 39% awarded as loans/jobs.

FINANCIAL AID PROCEDURES
Forms required: FAFSA.
Dates and Deadlines: Priority date 6/1; no closing date. Applicants notified on a rolling basis starting 7/1; must reply within 2 week(s) of notification.

CONTACT
Ed Ephlin, Director of Financial Aid
3200 West Seventh Avenue, Corsicana, TX 75110
(903) 875-7361

North Central Texas College
Gainesville, Texas
www.nctc.edu
Federal Code: 003558

2-year public community college in large town.
Enrollment: 7,009 undergrads.
Selectivity: Open admission; but selective for some programs.

BASIC COSTS (2005-2006)
Tuition and fees: $1,260; out-of-district residents $2,040; out-of-state residents $3,000.
Per-credit charge: $33; out-of-district residents $59; out-of-state residents $91.
Room and board: $3,350.

FINANCIAL AID PICTURE
Students with need: Need-based aid available for full-time and part-time students. Work study available nights.
Students without need: This college only awards aid to students with need.

FINANCIAL AID PROCEDURES
Forms required: FAFSA.
Dates and Deadlines: Priority date 5/1; no closing date. Applicants notified on a rolling basis starting 6/1; must reply within 4 week(s) of notification.

CONTACT
Janet Dragoo, Director of Financial Aid
1525 West California, Gainesville, TX 76240

North Harris Montgomery Community College District
The Woodlands, Texas
www.nhmccd.edu
Federal Code: 011145

2-year public community college in large city.
Enrollment: 35,921 undergrads, 73% part-time. 2,169 full-time freshmen.
Selectivity: Open admission; but selective for some programs.

BASIC COSTS (2006-2007)
Tuition and fees: $1,224; out-of-district residents $2,424; out-of-state residents $2,874.
Per-credit charge: $52; out-of-district residents $92; out-of-state residents $220.

FINANCIAL AID PICTURE (2004-2005)
Students with need: 82% of average financial aid package awarded as scholarships/grants, 18% awarded as loans/jobs. Need-based aid available for part-time students. Work study available nights, weekends, and for part-time students.
Students without need: No-need awards available for academics.

FINANCIAL AID PROCEDURES
Forms required: FAFSA, institutional form.
Dates and Deadlines: Priority date 4/1; no closing date. Applicants notified on a rolling basis starting 7/1.

CONTACT
Ken Lynn, Deputy Vice Chancellor, Finance
5000 Research Forest Drive, The Woodlands, TX 77381-4356
(832) 813-6545

North Lake College
Irving, Texas
www.northlakecollege.edu
Federal Code: 014036

2-year public community college in small city.
Enrollment: 7,000 undergrads.
Selectivity: Open admission.

BASIC COSTS (2005-2006)
Tuition and fees: $990; out-of-district residents $1,800; out-of-state residents $2,880.
Per-credit charge: $33; out-of-district residents $60; out-of-state residents $96.

FINANCIAL AID PICTURE
Students with need: Need-based aid available for full-time and part-time students.

FINANCIAL AID PROCEDURES
Forms required: FAFSA.
Dates and Deadlines: Priority date 5/1; no closing date. Applicants notified on a rolling basis.

CONTACT
Paul Felix, Director of Financial Aid
5001 North MacArthur Boulevard, Irving, TX 75038-3899
(972) 273-3321

Northeast Texas Community College
Mount Pleasant, Texas
www.ntcc.edu   Federal Code: 016396

2-year public community college in large town.
Enrollment: 1,275 full-time undergrads.
Selectivity: Open admission; but selective for some programs.

BASIC COSTS (2005-2006)
Tuition and fees: $1,740; out-of-district residents $2,520; out-of-state residents $3,780.
Per-credit charge: $27; out-of-district residents $53; out-of-state residents $95.
Room and board: $3,260.

FINANCIAL AID PICTURE
Students with need: Need-based aid available for full-time and part-time students.
Students without need: No-need awards available for academics, art, athletics, job skills, music/drama, state/district residency.

FINANCIAL AID PROCEDURES
Forms required: FAFSA, institutional form.
Dates and Deadlines: Priority date 6/1; no closing date. Applicants notified on a rolling basis starting 6/1.

CONTACT
Patricia Durst, Director of Financial Aid
Box 1307, Mount Pleasant, TX 75456-1307
(903) 572-1911 ext. 207

Northwest Vista College
San Antonio, Texas
www.accd.edu/nvc   Federal Code: 033723

2-year public community college in very large city.
Enrollment: 9,162 undergrads, 63% part-time. 759 full-time freshmen.
Selectivity: Open admission.

BASIC COSTS (2006-2007)
Tuition and fees: $1,472; out-of-district residents $2,672; out-of-state residents $5,072.

FINANCIAL AID PICTURE
Students with need: Need-based aid available for full-time and part-time students. Work study available nights, weekends, and for part-time students.
Students without need: No-need awards available for academics, leadership.

FINANCIAL AID PROCEDURES
Forms required: FAFSA.
Dates and Deadlines: Priority date 4/1; no closing date. Applicants notified on a rolling basis starting 5/15; must reply within 2 week(s) of notification.

CONTACT
Noe Ortiz, Financial Aid Director
3535 North Ellison Drive, San Antonio, TX 78251-4217
(210) 348-2100

Northwood University: Texas Campus
Cedar Hill, Texas
www.northwood.edu   Federal Code: 013040

4-year private university and business college in large town.
Enrollment: 578 undergrads, 3% part-time. 127 full-time freshmen.
Selectivity: Admits 50 to 75% of applicants.

BASIC COSTS (2006-2007)
Tuition and fees: $15,801.
Per-credit charge: $317.
Room and board: $6,889.

FINANCIAL AID PICTURE (2005-2006)
Students with need: Out of 117 full-time freshmen who applied for aid, 101 were judged to have need. Of these, 101 received aid, and 17 had their full need met. Average financial aid package met 61% of need; average scholarship/grant was $5,709; average loan was $2,441. For part-time students, average financial aid package was $11,236.
Students without need: 6 full-time freshmen who did not demonstrate need for aid received scholarships/grants; average award was $6,875. No-need awards available for academics, alumni affiliation, athletics, leadership, minority status, state/district residency.
Scholarships offered: *Merit:* Merit Scholarships; $4,000-$9,000; based on test scores and GPA; unlimited number awarded. *Athletic:* 15 full-time freshmen received athletic scholarships; average amount $5,786.
Cumulative student debt: 71% of graduating class had student loans; average debt was $16,346.

FINANCIAL AID PROCEDURES
Forms required: FAFSA.
Dates and Deadlines: No deadline. Applicants notified on a rolling basis starting 3/1.

CONTACT
Michael Rhodes, Director of Financial Aid
1114 West FM 1382, Cedar Hill, TX 75104
(972) 293-5430

Odessa College
Odessa, Texas
www.odessa.edu   Federal Code: 003596

2-year public community college in small city.
Enrollment: 4,790 undergrads, 61% part-time. 482 full-time freshmen.
Selectivity: Open admission; but selective for some programs.

BASIC COSTS (2006-2007)
Tuition and fees: $1,440; out-of-district residents $1,740; out-of-state residents $2,190.
Room and board: $4,770.

FINANCIAL AID PICTURE (2004-2005)
Students with need: 88% of average financial aid package awarded as scholarships/grants, 12% awarded as loans/jobs. Need-based aid available for part-time students. Work study available nights.
Students without need: No-need awards available for academics, athletics, music/drama.

FINANCIAL AID PROCEDURES
Forms required: FAFSA.
Dates and Deadlines: Priority date 5/1; no closing date. Applicants notified on a rolling basis starting 6/15.

CONTACT
Dee Nesmith, Director of Financial Aid
201 West University, Odessa, TX 79764-7127
(432) 335-6429

Our Lady of the Lake University of San Antonio
San Antonio, Texas
www.ollusa.edu   Federal Code: 003598

4-year private university in very large city, affiliated with Roman Catholic Church.
Enrollment: 1,792 undergrads, 31% part-time. 269 full-time freshmen.
Selectivity: Admits 50 to 75% of applicants.

BASIC COSTS (2006-2007)
Tuition and fees: $17,900.
Per-credit charge: $581.
Room and board: $5,678.

FINANCIAL AID PICTURE (2004-2005)
Students with need: 42% of average financial aid package awarded as scholarships/grants, 58% awarded as loans/jobs. Need-based aid available for part-time students. Work study available nights, weekends, and for part-time students.
Students without need: No-need awards available for academics, alumni affiliation, art, music/drama.
Scholarships offered: General academic scholarship; $1,205 awarded yearly (renewable). Art/fine arts and music; 4 awarded yearly (renewable). Children of faculty/staff; 60 awarded yearly (renewable). All based on GPA scores and high school record.
Cumulative student debt: 83% of graduating class had student loans; average debt was $26,000.

FINANCIAL AID PROCEDURES
Forms required: FAFSA.
Dates and Deadlines: Priority date 4/1; no closing date. Applicants notified on a rolling basis starting 4/1; must reply within 2 week(s) of notification.

CONTACT
Diana Perez, Director of Financial Aid
411 Southwest 24th Street, San Antonio, TX 78207-4689
(210) 434-6711 ext. 2299

Palo Alto College
San Antonio, Texas
www.accd.edu   Federal Code: 016615

2-year public community college in very large city.
Enrollment: 8,199 undergrads.
Selectivity: Open admission.

BASIC COSTS (2005-2006)
Tuition and fees: $1,472; out-of-district residents $2,672; out-of-state residents $5,072.

FINANCIAL AID PICTURE (2004-2005)
Students with need: Need-based aid available for part-time students.
Students without need: This college only awards aid to students with need.
Scholarships offered: Alamo Community College District Scholarship; $1,000; 50 awarded.

FINANCIAL AID PROCEDURES
Forms required: FAFSA, state aid form.
Dates and Deadlines: Priority date 3/31; closing date 6/1. Applicants notified on a rolling basis starting 5/31.

CONTACT
Lamar Duarte, Director of Financial Aid
1400 West Villaret, San Antonio, TX 78224
(210) 921-5316

Panola College
Carthage, Texas
www.panola.edu   Federal Code: 003600

2-year public community and junior college in small town.
Enrollment: 1,906 undergrads, 51% part-time. 307 full-time freshmen.
Selectivity: Open admission; but selective for some programs.

BASIC COSTS (2005-2006)
Tuition and fees: $1,350; out-of-district residents $2,040; out-of-state residents $2,430.
Room and board: $3,300.

FINANCIAL AID PICTURE (2004-2005)
Students with need: Average financial aid package met 85% of need; average scholarship/grant was $1,000. For part-time students, average financial aid package was $1,000.
Students without need: No-need awards available for academics, alumni affiliation, art, athletics, leadership, music/drama.
Scholarships offered: Several departmental and organization sponsored scholarships. Presidential scholarship. Dean's scholarship.

FINANCIAL AID PROCEDURES
Forms required: FAFSA, institutional form.
Dates and Deadlines: Priority date 6/5; no closing date. Applicants notified on a rolling basis starting 6/1.
Transfers: No deadline. Applicants notified on a rolling basis.

CONTACT
Tommy Young, Director of Financial Aid
1109 West Panola Street, Carthage, TX 75633
(903) 693-2039

Paris Junior College
Paris, Texas
www.paris.cc.tx.us   Federal Code: 003601

2-year public community and junior college in large town.
Enrollment: 4,071 undergrads, 56% part-time. 522 full-time freshmen.
Selectivity: Open admission; but selective for some programs.

BASIC COSTS (2006-2007)
Tuition and fees: $1,320; out-of-district residents $2,025; out-of-state residents $3,200.
Room and board: $3,500.

FINANCIAL AID PICTURE
Students with need: Need-based aid available for full-time and part-time students.
Students without need: No-need awards available for athletics, music/drama.

FINANCIAL AID PROCEDURES
Forms required: FAFSA.
Dates and Deadlines: Priority date 6/1; no closing date. Applicants notified on a rolling basis starting 6/1.

CONTACT
Linda Slawson, Director of Financial Aid
2400 Clarksville Street, Paris, TX 75460
(903) 782-0256

Prairie View A&M University
Prairie View, Texas
www.pvamu.edu   Federal Code: 003630

4-year public university in small town.
Enrollment: 5,402 undergrads, 10% part-time. 1,094 full-time freshmen.
Selectivity: Admits 50 to 75% of applicants.

BASIC COSTS (2006-2007)
Tuition and fees: $5,461; out-of-state residents $13,741.
Per-credit charge: $50; out-of-state residents $325.
Room and board: $6,474.

FINANCIAL AID PICTURE (2005-2006)
Students with need: Average financial aid package met 76% of need; average scholarship/grant was $2,765; average loan was $3,875. Need-based aid available for part-time students.
Students without need: No-need awards available for academics, athletics, ROTC.
Cumulative student debt: 77% of graduating class had student loans; average debt was $20,000.

FINANCIAL AID PROCEDURES
Forms required: FAFSA, institutional form.
Dates and Deadlines: Closing date 3/1. Applicants notified by 6/1; must reply by 8/1.
Transfers: Minimum 2.0 GPA from all colleges attended required to be considered for financial aid.

CONTACT
Tracie Matthews, Director of Financial Aid
PO Box 3089, Prairie View, TX 77446
(936) 857-2422

Remington College: Houston
Houston, Texas
www.remingtoncollege.edu   Federal Code: E00672

2-year for-profit technical college in very large city.
Enrollment: 507 undergrads.
Selectivity: Open admission.

BASIC COSTS (2005-2006)
Additional info: Cost of tuition, books, tools and lab fees for all full associate programs (24 months): $30,480. Allied Health diploma program (8 months): $11,280. Registration fee $50. Tuition at time of enrollment locked for 2 years.

FINANCIAL AID PICTURE
Students with need: Need-based aid available for full-time and part-time students. Work study available nights.
Students without need: No-need awards available for state/district residency.

FINANCIAL AID PROCEDURES
Forms required: FAFSA, institutional form.
Dates and Deadlines: No deadline. Applicants notified on a rolling basis.

CONTACT
Jill Brown, Director, Financial Services
3110 Hayes Road Suite 380, Houston, TX 77082
(281) 899-1240

Rice University
Houston, Texas   Federal Code: 003604
www.rice.edu   CSS Code: 6609

4-year private university in very large city.
Enrollment: 2,988 undergrads, 1% part-time. 722 full-time freshmen.
Selectivity: Admits less than 50% of applicants.

BASIC COSTS (2005-2006)
Tuition and fees: $23,746.
Per-credit charge: $972.
Room and board: $9,122.

FINANCIAL AID PICTURE (2005-2006)
Students with need: Out of 533 full-time freshmen who applied for aid, 287 were judged to have need. Of these, 287 received aid, and 287 had their full need met. Average financial aid package met 100% of need; average scholarship/grant was $21,157; average loan was $1,276. Need-based aid available for part-time students.
Students without need: 123 full-time freshmen who did not demonstrate need for aid received scholarships/grants; average award was $7,052. No-need awards available for academics, alumni affiliation, art, athletics, leadership, minority status, music/drama, ROTC, state/district residency.
Scholarships offered: 58 full-time freshmen received athletic scholarships; average amount $26,088.
Cumulative student debt: 28% of graduating class had student loans; average debt was $14,166.

FINANCIAL AID PROCEDURES
Forms required: FAFSA, CSS PROFILE.
Dates and Deadlines: Priority date 3/1; no closing date. Applicants notified by 4/15; must reply by 5/1.
Transfers: Priority date 4/1.

CONTACT
Julia Benz, Director of Student Financial Services
6100 Main Street, MS17, Houston, TX 77251-1892
(713) 348-4958

Richland College
Dallas, Texas
www.rlc.dcccd.edu   Federal Code: 008504

2-year public community college in very large city.
Enrollment: 4,650 full-time undergrads.
Selectivity: Open admission.

BASIC COSTS (2005-2006)
Tuition and fees: $990; out-of-district residents $1,800; out-of-state residents $2,880.
Per-credit charge: $33; out-of-district residents $60; out-of-state residents $96.

FINANCIAL AID PICTURE
Students with need: Need-based aid available for full-time and part-time students. Work study available nights.
Students without need: No-need awards available for art, leadership, music/drama.

FINANCIAL AID PROCEDURES
Forms required: FAFSA.
Dates and Deadlines: Priority date 5/2; no closing date. Applicants notified on a rolling basis starting 6/1; must reply within 2 week(s) of notification.

CONTACT
David Ximenez, Director of Financial Aid
12800 Abrams Road, Dallas, TX 75243-2199
(972) 238-6188

St. Edward's University
Austin, Texas
www.stedwards.edu   Federal Code: 003621

4-year private university and liberal arts college in very large city, affiliated with Roman Catholic Church.
Enrollment: 3,930 undergrads, 24% part-time. 649 full-time freshmen.
Selectivity: Admits 50 to 75% of applicants.

BASIC COSTS (2006-2007)
Tuition and fees: $18,800.
Per-credit charge: $628.
Room and board: $6,900.

FINANCIAL AID PICTURE (2005-2006)
Students with need: Out of 530 full-time freshmen who applied for aid, 402 were judged to have need. Of these, 401 received aid, and 191 had their full need met. Average financial aid package met 80% of need; average scholarship/grant was $12,129; average loan was $3,563. For part-time students, average financial aid package was $5,838.
Students without need: 88 full-time freshmen who did not demonstrate need for aid received scholarships/grants; average award was $6,216. No-need awards available for academics, art, athletics, leadership, music/drama, ROTC.
Scholarships offered: *Merit:* Freshmen scholarship; $1,000 to full tuition for up to four years; requirements range from talent (theater) to top 10% of high school class and minimum 1250 SAT (exclusive of writing). Full-time students can apply for university scholarships after completion of one fall semester. Academic scholarships require 3.0 GPA; service scholarships require 2.75 GPA, significant community service involvement. *Athletic:* 35 full-time freshmen received athletic scholarships; average amount $8,107.
Cumulative student debt: 62% of graduating class had student loans; average debt was $24,280.

FINANCIAL AID PROCEDURES
Forms required: FAFSA.
Dates and Deadlines: Priority date 3/1; no closing date. Applicants notified on a rolling basis starting 2/15; must reply by 5/1 or within 2 week(s) of notification.

CONTACT
Doris Constantine, Director of Student Financial Services
3001 South Congress Avenue, Austin, TX 78704
(512) 448-8520

St. Mary's University
San Antonio, Texas
www.stmarytx.edu   Federal Code: 003623

4-year private university in very large city, affiliated with Roman Catholic Church.
Enrollment: 2,374 undergrads, 8% part-time. 464 full-time freshmen.
Selectivity: Admits 50 to 75% of applicants.

BASIC COSTS (2006-2007)
Tuition and fees: $20,534.
Per-credit charge: $580.
Room and board: $6,780.

FINANCIAL AID PICTURE (2004-2005)
Students with need: Out of 395 full-time freshmen who applied for aid, 363 were judged to have need. Of these, 363 received aid, and 109 had their full need met. Average financial aid package met 74% of need; average scholarship/grant was $12,236; average loan was $4,224. For part-time students, average financial aid package was $9,545.
Students without need: 91 full-time freshmen who did not demonstrate need for aid received scholarships/grants; average award was $10,424. No-need awards available for academics, alumni affiliation, athletics, leadership, music/drama, ROTC.
Scholarships offered: 37 full-time freshmen received athletic scholarships; average amount $11,746.
Cumulative student debt: 77% of graduating class had student loans; average debt was $23,447.

FINANCIAL AID PROCEDURES
Forms required: FAFSA.
Dates and Deadlines: Priority date 2/15; no closing date. Applicants notified on a rolling basis starting 5/1; must reply within 2 week(s) of notification.

CONTACT
David Krause, Director of Financial Assistance
One Camino Santa Maria, San Antonio, TX 78228
(210) 436-3141

St. Philip's College
San Antonio, Texas
www.accd.edu/spc   Federal Code: 003608

2-year public community college in very large city.
Enrollment: 9,792 undergrads, 57% part-time. 951 full-time freshmen.
Selectivity: Open admission.

BASIC COSTS (2005-2006)
Tuition and fees: $1,472; out-of-district residents $2,672; out-of-state residents $5,072.

FINANCIAL AID PICTURE (2004-2005)
Students with need: 68% of average financial aid package awarded as scholarships/grants, 32% awarded as loans/jobs. Need-based aid available for part-time students. Work study available nights, weekends, and for part-time students.
Students without need: This college only awards aid to students with need.

FINANCIAL AID PROCEDURES
Forms required: FAFSA.
Dates and Deadlines: Priority date 3/1; no closing date. Applicants notified on a rolling basis starting 7/15.

CONTACT
Diego Bernal, Director of Financial Aid
1801 Martin Luther King Drive, San Antonio, TX 78203
(210) 531-3272

Sam Houston State University
Huntsville, Texas
www.shsu.edu   Federal Code: 003606

4-year public university in large town.
Enrollment: 13,200 undergrads, 15% part-time. 2,165 full-time freshmen.
Selectivity: Admits 50 to 75% of applicants.

BASIC COSTS (2006-2007)
Tuition and fees: $4,928; out-of-state residents $13,178.
Per-credit charge: $120; out-of-state residents $395.

Room and board: $5,598.

FINANCIAL AID PICTURE (2005-2006)
Students with need: Out of 1,531 full-time freshmen who applied for aid, 1,062 were judged to have need. Of these, 1,062 received aid. For part-time students, average financial aid package was $4,599.
Students without need: 286 full-time freshmen who did not demonstrate need for aid received scholarships/grants; average award was $2,013. No-need awards available for academics, athletics, ROTC.
Scholarships offered: 61 full-time freshmen received athletic scholarships; average amount $6,091.

FINANCIAL AID PROCEDURES
Forms required: FAFSA, institutional form.
Dates and Deadlines: Priority date 3/31; closing date 5/31. Applicants notified on a rolling basis starting 5/1; must reply within 4 week(s) of notification.

CONTACT
Patty Mabry, Director of Financial Aid
Box 2418, Huntsville, TX 77341-2418
(936) 294-1724

San Antonio College
San Antonio, Texas
www.accd.edu/sac
Federal Code: 009163

2-year public community college in very large city.
Enrollment: 20,565 undergrads.
Selectivity: Open admission; but selective for some programs.

BASIC COSTS (2006-2007)
Tuition and fees: $1,472; out-of-district residents $2,672; out-of-state residents $5,072.
Per-credit charge: $40; out-of-district residents $80; out-of-state residents $160.

FINANCIAL AID PICTURE
Students with need: Work study available nights, weekends, and for part-time students.
Additional info: Leveraging Educational Assistance Partnership (LEAP), public student incentive grant, towards excellence access and success grants (Texas and Texas II grants) available.

FINANCIAL AID PROCEDURES
Dates and Deadlines: Priority date 3/1; no closing date. Applicants notified by 7/1.

CONTACT
Tom Campos, Director of Student Financial Services
1300 San Pedro Avenue, San Antonio, TX 78212-4299
(210) 733-2150

San Jacinto College: North
Houston, Texas
www.sjcd.edu
Federal Code: E00718

2-year public community and technical college in very large city.
Enrollment: 5,536 undergrads.
Selectivity: Open admission; but selective for some programs.

BASIC COSTS (2006-2007)
Tuition and fees: $1,480; out-of-district residents $2,280; out-of-state residents $2,920.

FINANCIAL AID PICTURE (2005-2006)
Students with need: 67% of average financial aid package awarded as scholarships/grants, 33% awarded as loans/jobs. Need-based aid available for part-time students. Work study available nights, weekends, and for part-time students.
Students without need: This college only awards aid to students with need.

FINANCIAL AID PROCEDURES
Forms required: FAFSA, institutional form.
Dates and Deadlines: Priority date 6/1; no closing date. Applicants notified on a rolling basis starting 8/1; must reply within 2 week(s) of notification.

CONTACT
Mike Ramsey, Counselor of Financial Aid
5800 Uvalde Road, Houston, TX 77049
(281) 998-6150

Schreiner University
Kerrville, Texas
www.schreiner.edu
Federal Code: 003610

4-year private liberal arts college in large town, affiliated with Presbyterian Church (USA).
Enrollment: 765 undergrads, 10% part-time. 207 full-time freshmen.
Selectivity: Admits 50 to 75% of applicants.

BASIC COSTS (2006-2007)
Tuition and fees: $15,880.
Per-credit charge: $660.
Room and board: $7,810.

FINANCIAL AID PICTURE (2004-2005)
Students with need: Out of 184 full-time freshmen who applied for aid, 162 were judged to have need. Of these, 161 received aid, and 18 had their full need met. Average financial aid package met 65% of need; average scholarship/grant was $8,566; average loan was $2,084. For part-time students, average financial aid package was $7,727.
Students without need: 45 full-time freshmen who did not demonstrate need for aid received scholarships/grants; average award was $12,497. No-need awards available for academics, alumni affiliation, art, job skills, leadership, music/drama, religious affiliation.
Scholarships offered: Awards for students with exceptional academic achievement and leadership abilities; partial and full tuition; 3.5 GPA and 1100 SAT (exclusive of writing) or 24 ACT; 66 awarded after participation in the Schreiner Scholars program.
Cumulative student debt: 83% of graduating class had student loans; average debt was $21,455.

FINANCIAL AID PROCEDURES
Forms required: institutional form.
Dates and Deadlines: Priority date 4/1; closing date 8/1. Applicants notified on a rolling basis starting 2/21; must reply within 2 week(s) of notification.
Transfers: Priority date 4/15; no deadline.

CONTACT
Toni Bryant, Director of Financial Aid
2100 Memorial Boulevard, Kerrville, TX 78028-5697
(800) 343-4919

South Plains College
Levelland, Texas
www.southplainscollege.edu
Federal Code: 003611

2-year public community and junior college in large town.
Enrollment: 9,069 undergrads, 61% part-time. 1,198 full-time freshmen.

Selectivity: Open admission; but selective for some programs.

BASIC COSTS (2005-2006)
Tuition and fees: $1,712; out-of-district residents $2,372; out-of-state residents $2,852.
Room and board: $3,100.

FINANCIAL AID PICTURE
Students with need: Need-based aid available for full-time and part-time students.
Students without need: No-need awards available for academics, athletics.

FINANCIAL AID PROCEDURES
Forms required: FAFSA.
Dates and Deadlines: Priority date 6/1; no closing date. Applicants notified on a rolling basis starting 6/30; must reply within 2 week(s) of notification.

CONTACT
Jim Ann Batenhorst, Director of Financial Aid
1401 College Avenue, Levelland, TX 79336
(806) 894-9611

South Texas College
McAllen, Texas
www.southtexascollege.edu   Federal Code: 031034

2-year public community and technical college in small city.
Enrollment: 17,138 undergrads.
Selectivity: Open admission; but selective for some programs.

BASIC COSTS (2005-2006)
Tuition and fees: $1,940; out-of-district residents $2,453; out-of-state residents $6,230.

FINANCIAL AID PICTURE (2005-2006)
Students with need: 98% of average financial aid package awarded as scholarships/grants, 2% awarded as loans/jobs. Need-based aid available for part-time students. Work study available nights, weekends, and for part-time students.
Students without need: This college only awards aid to students with need.

FINANCIAL AID PROCEDURES
Forms required: FAFSA.
Dates and Deadlines: Priority date 3/1; no closing date. Applicants notified on a rolling basis starting 4/15.

CONTACT
Miguel Carranza, Director
3201 West Pecan Boulevard, McAllen, TX 78502
(956) 872-8375

Southern Methodist University
Dallas, Texas   Federal Code: 003613
www.smu.edu   CSS Code: 6660

4-year private university in large town, affiliated with United Methodist Church.
Enrollment: 6,196 undergrads, 4% part-time. 1,402 full-time freshmen.
Selectivity: Admits 50 to 75% of applicants. GED not accepted.

BASIC COSTS (2006-2007)
Tuition and fees: $28,630.
Per-credit charge: $1,058.
Room and board: $10,115.

FINANCIAL AID PICTURE (2005-2006)
Students with need: Out of 644 full-time freshmen who applied for aid, 471 were judged to have need. Of these, 468 received aid, and 270 had their full need met. Average financial aid package met 91% of need; average scholarship/grant was $11,918; average loan was $2,555. For part-time students, average financial aid package was $12,614.
Students without need: 604 full-time freshmen who did not demonstrate need for aid received scholarships/grants; average award was $5,188. No-need awards available for academics, art, athletics, leadership, music/drama, religious affiliation, ROTC, state/district residency.
Scholarships offered: 61 full-time freshmen received athletic scholarships; average amount $30,274.
Cumulative student debt: 43% of graduating class had student loans; average debt was $18,571.

FINANCIAL AID PROCEDURES
Forms required: FAFSA, CSS PROFILE.
Dates and Deadlines: Priority date 2/15; no closing date. Applicants notified on a rolling basis starting 3/15.
Transfers: Priority date 4/1. Merit scholarships available for community college and senior institution honor transfers. Students entering without scholarship aid will receive need-based aid up to cost of tuition.

CONTACT
Mark Peterson, Executive Director of Enrollment Services
PO Box 750181, Dallas, TX 75275-0181
(214) 768-2068

Southwest Texas Junior College
Uvalde, Texas
www.swtjc.cc.tx.us   Federal Code: 003614

2-year public community and junior college in large town.
Enrollment: 2,250 full-time undergrads.
Selectivity: Open admission.

BASIC COSTS (2005-2006)
Tuition and fees: $1,439; out-of-district residents $2,092; out-of-state residents $2,369.
Per-credit charge: $29; out-of-district residents $51; out-of-state residents $60.
Room and board: $2,320.
Additional info: Additional fees for off-campus classes may apply.

FINANCIAL AID PICTURE
Students with need: Need-based aid available for full-time and part-time students.

FINANCIAL AID PROCEDURES
Forms required: FAFSA.
Dates and Deadlines: Priority date 6/15; no closing date. Applicants notified on a rolling basis starting 5/1; must reply within 2 week(s) of notification.

CONTACT
Ismael Talavera, Director of Financial Aid
Garner Field Road, Uvalde, TX 78801
(830) 278-4401

Southwestern Adventist University
Keene, Texas
www.swau.edu   Federal Code: 003619

4-year private university and liberal arts college in small town, affiliated with Seventh-day Adventists.
Enrollment: 870 undergrads.

Texas Southwestern Adventist University

BASIC COSTS (2006-2007)
Tuition and fees: $13,636.
Per-credit charge: $554.
Room and board: $6,124.

FINANCIAL AID PICTURE
Students with need: Need-based aid available for full-time and part-time students.
Students without need: No-need awards available for academics, athletics, leadership, music/drama.

FINANCIAL AID PROCEDURES
Forms required: FAFSA, institutional form.
Dates and Deadlines: Priority date 3/15; no closing date. Applicants notified on a rolling basis starting 4/15.

CONTACT
Patty Norwood, Financial Aid Director
Box 567, Keene, TX 76059
(817) 645-3921 ext. 262

Southwestern Assemblies of God University
Waxahachie, Texas
www.sagu.edu
Federal Code: 003616

4-year private university and Bible college in large town, affiliated with Assemblies of God.
Enrollment: 1,300 full-time undergrads.
Selectivity: Admits 50 to 75% of applicants.

BASIC COSTS (2005-2006)
Tuition and fees: $10,110.
Per-credit charge: $315.
Room and board: $4,715.

FINANCIAL AID PICTURE
Students with need: Need-based aid available for full-time and part-time students.

FINANCIAL AID PROCEDURES
Forms required: FAFSA.
Dates and Deadlines: Priority date 3/1; closing date 6/1. Applicants notified on a rolling basis starting 6/1; must reply within 2 week(s) of notification.

CONTACT
Matt Dufrene, Director of Financial Aid
1200 Sycamore Street, Waxahachie, TX 75165
(972) 937-4010

Southwestern University
Georgetown, Texas
www.southwestern.edu
Federal Code: 003620

4-year private liberal arts college in large town, affiliated with United Methodist Church.
Enrollment: 1,296 undergrads, 1% part-time. 324 full-time freshmen.
Selectivity: Admits 50 to 75% of applicants.

BASIC COSTS (2006-2007)
Tuition and fees: $23,650.
Per-credit charge: $985.
Room and board: $7,590.

FINANCIAL AID PICTURE (2005-2006)
Students with need: Out of 231 full-time freshmen who applied for aid, 175 were judged to have need. Of these, 175 received aid, and 112 had their full need met. Average financial aid package met 98% of need; average scholarship/grant was $16,275; average loan was $2,760. For part-time students, average financial aid package was $19,795.
Students without need: 98 full-time freshmen who did not demonstrate need for aid received scholarships/grants; average award was $8,042. No-need awards available for academics, art, music/drama.
Scholarships offered: University Scholar; $3,000 per year. Southwestern Scholar; $5,000 per year. Students who meet criteria are guaranteed award if they apply by deadline. Competitive awards; range from $7,500 per year to full tuition, room, and board.
Cumulative student debt: 52% of graduating class had student loans; average debt was $18,446.
Additional info: Family loan program (PATH): borrow up to $22,500 annually with a fixed, monthly payment plan; students who ranked in top 10% of high school class or received an academic merit scholarship may be subsidized.

FINANCIAL AID PROCEDURES
Forms required: FAFSA.
Dates and Deadlines: Closing date 3/1. Applicants notified on a rolling basis starting 3/21; must reply by 5/1 or within 2 week(s) of notification.
Transfers: Priority date 3/1; closing date 5/15.

CONTACT
James Gaeta, Director of Financial Aid
1001 East University Avenue, Georgetown, TX 78626
(512) 863-1259

Stephen F. Austin State University
Nacogdoches, Texas
www.sfasu.edu
Federal Code: 003624

4-year public university in large town.
Enrollment: 9,806 undergrads, 13% part-time. 1,536 full-time freshmen.
Selectivity: Admits 50 to 75% of applicants.

BASIC COSTS (2005-2006)
Tuition and fees: $4,718; out-of-state residents $12,998.
Per-credit charge: $187; out-of-state residents $463.
Room and board: $5,459.

FINANCIAL AID PICTURE (2004-2005)
Students with need: Out of 1,208 full-time freshmen who applied for aid, 803 were judged to have need. Of these, 789 received aid, and 216 had their full need met. Average financial aid package met 75% of need; average scholarship/grant was $2,425; average loan was $1,262. For part-time students, average financial aid package was $3,874.
Students without need: 166 full-time freshmen who did not demonstrate need for aid received scholarships/grants; average award was $3,120. No-need awards available for academics, alumni affiliation, art, athletics, leadership, music/drama, ROTC, state/district residency.
Scholarships offered: Merit: Academic Excellence Scholarship Program; $2,000 per year; rank in top 10% of high school class or top quartile class with 1100 SAT (exclusive of writing) or 24 ACT; renewable with 3.5 GPA. Dugas full support scholarships; $4,000 per semester; active member of School of Honors; 3 awarded. University Scholars Program awards; $1,000 per semester; minimum 1220 SAT, 27 ACT, 3.0 GPA maintenance; up to 11 awarded. Student Foundation Association Leadership Scholarship; amounts vary; demonstrated leadership capabilities and academic achievement throughout high school career; 1 awarded. **Athletic:** 51 full-time freshmen received athletic scholarships; average amount $5,423.
Cumulative student debt: 62% of graduating class had student loans; average debt was $17,243.

FINANCIAL AID PROCEDURES
Forms required: FAFSA.
Dates and Deadlines: Priority date 4/1; closing date 5/15. Applicants notified on a rolling basis starting 4/10; must reply within 3 week(s) of notification.

CONTACT
Mike O'Rear, Director of Financial Aid
Box 13051, SFA Station, Nacogdoches, TX 75962-3051
(936) 468-2403

Sul Ross State University
Alpine, Texas
www.sulross.edu   Federal Code: 003625

4-year public university in small town.
Enrollment: 1,500 full-time undergrads.

BASIC COSTS (2006-2007)
Tuition and fees: $4,336; out-of-state residents $12,586.
Per-credit charge: $100; out-of-state residents $375.
Room and board: $6,300.

FINANCIAL AID PICTURE
Students with need: Need-based aid available for full-time and part-time students.
Students without need: No-need awards available for academics, alumni affiliation, leadership.

FINANCIAL AID PROCEDURES
Forms required: FAFSA, institutional form.
Dates and Deadlines: Priority date 5/1; no closing date. Applicants notified on a rolling basis starting 5/1; must reply within 2 week(s) of notification.

CONTACT
Rowena Gallego, Director Student Financial Assistance
Box C-2, Alpine, TX 79832
(432) 837-8055

Tarleton State University
Stephenville, Texas
www.tarleton.edu   Federal Code: 003631

4-year public university in large town.
Enrollment: 7,595 undergrads, 20% part-time. 1,267 full-time freshmen.
Selectivity: Admits over 75% of applicants.

BASIC COSTS (2006-2007)
Tuition and fees: $4,627; out-of-state residents $12,877.
Per-credit charge: $120; out-of-state residents $395.
Room and board: $5,930.
Additional info: Distance learning fee additional $40 per credit hour.

FINANCIAL AID PICTURE (2004-2005)
Students with need: Out of 967 full-time freshmen who applied for aid, 900 were judged to have need. Of these, 817 received aid, and 430 had their full need met. Average financial aid package met 71% of need; average scholarship/grant was $4,100; average loan was $2,116. For part-time students, average financial aid package was $5,569.
Students without need: 192 full-time freshmen who did not demonstrate need for aid received scholarships/grants; average award was $4,130. No-need awards available for academics, alumni affiliation, art, athletics, leadership, ROTC.
Scholarships offered: 29 full-time freshmen received athletic scholarships; average amount $2,857.
Cumulative student debt: 57% of graduating class had student loans; average debt was $16,379.

FINANCIAL AID PROCEDURES
Forms required: FAFSA.
Dates and Deadlines: Priority date 4/1; closing date 10/15. Applicants notified on a rolling basis starting 2/1; must reply within 2 week(s) of notification.
Transfers: No deadline.

CONTACT
Betty Murray, Director, Student Financial Aid
Box T-0030, Stephenville, TX 76402
(254) 968-9070

Tarrant County College
Fort Worth, Texas
www.tccd.edu   Federal Code: 003626

2-year public community college in very large city.
Enrollment: 11,800 full-time undergrads.
Selectivity: Open admission; but selective for some programs.

BASIC COSTS (2006-2007)
Tuition and fees: $1,500; out-of-district residents $1,890; out-of-state residents $4,500.
Per-credit charge: $50; out-of-district residents $63; out-of-state residents $150.

FINANCIAL AID PICTURE (2004-2005)
Students with need: 78% of average financial aid package awarded as scholarships/grants, 22% awarded as loans/jobs.
Students without need: No-need awards available for academics.

FINANCIAL AID PROCEDURES
Forms required: FAFSA, institutional form.
Dates and Deadlines: Priority date 4/15; no closing date. Applicants notified on a rolling basis starting 3/1; must reply within 2 week(s) of notification.

CONTACT
David Ximenez, Director of Financial Aid
1500 Houston Street, Fort Worth, TX 76102
(817) 515-5353

Temple College
Temple, Texas
www.templejc.edu   Federal Code: 003627

2-year public community college in small city.
Enrollment: 3,720 undergrads, 64% part-time. 401 full-time freshmen.
Selectivity: Open admission; but selective for some programs.

BASIC COSTS (2006-2007)
Tuition and fees: $1,860; out-of-district residents $2,850; out-of-state residents $4,500.
Per-credit charge: $62; out-of-district residents $95; out-of-state residents $150.

FINANCIAL AID PICTURE
Students with need: Need-based aid available for full-time and part-time students. Work study available nights.
Students without need: This college only awards aid to students with need.

FINANCIAL AID PROCEDURES
Forms required: FAFSA.
Dates and Deadlines: Priority date 6/1; no closing date. Applicants notified on a rolling basis starting 5/1; must reply within 4 week(s) of notification.

CONTACT
Lanette Wigginton, Director of Financial Aid
2600 South First Street, Temple, TX 76504-7435
(254) 298-8321

Texarkana College
Texarkana, Texas
www.texarkanacollege.edu   Federal Code: 003628

2-year public community college in small city.
Enrollment: 4,122 undergrads.
Selectivity: Open admission.

BASIC COSTS (2005-2006)
Tuition and fees: $960; out-of-district residents $1,470; out-of-state residents $1,970.
Per-credit charge: $29; out-of-district residents $46; out-of-state residents $63.
Additional info: Arkansas and Oklahoma residents pay out-of-district rates.

FINANCIAL AID PICTURE
Students with need: Need-based aid available for full-time and part-time students. Work study available nights, weekends, and for part-time students.
Students without need: No-need awards available for academics, athletics.

FINANCIAL AID PROCEDURES
Forms required: FAFSA, institutional form.
Dates and Deadlines: Priority date 6/1; no closing date. Applicants notified on a rolling basis starting 3/1.

CONTACT
Dawna Vise, Director of Financial Aid
2500 North Robison Road, Texarkana, TX 75599
(903) 838-4541

Texas A&M University
College Station, Texas
www.tamu.edu   Federal Code: 003632

4-year public university in small city.
Enrollment: 36,227 undergrads, 9% part-time. 6,774 full-time freshmen.
Selectivity: Admits 50 to 75% of applicants.

BASIC COSTS (2006-2007)
Tuition and fees: $6,966; out-of-state residents $15,216.
Per-credit charge: $146; out-of-state residents $421.
Room and board: $7,052.

FINANCIAL AID PICTURE (2005-2006)
Students with need: Average financial aid package met 71% of need; average scholarship/grant was $7,103; average loan was $3,153. For part-time students, average financial aid package was $4,487.
Students without need: No-need awards available for academics, alumni affiliation, art, athletics, job skills, leadership, music/drama, ROTC, state/district residency.
Cumulative student debt: 36% of graduating class had student loans; average debt was $15,927.
Additional info: Short-term loans available. Out-of-state students awarded academic scholarships of $1,000 or more are eligible for waiver of out-of-state tuition.

FINANCIAL AID PROCEDURES
Forms required: FAFSA, institutional form.
Dates and Deadlines: No deadline. Applicants notified on a rolling basis starting 4/1; must reply within 4 week(s) of notification.
Transfers: Must provide previous financial aid transcript.

CONTACT
Joseph Pettibon, Director of Student Financial Aid
PO Box 30014, College Station, TX 77842-3014
(979) 845-3236

Texas A&M University-Baylor College of Dentistry
Dallas, Texas
www.bcd.tamhsc.edu   Federal Code: 004948

Upper-division public health science college in very large city.
Enrollment: 59 undergrads, 2% part-time.

BASIC COSTS (2005-2006)
Tuition and fees: $4,117; out-of-state residents $12,397.
Per-credit charge: $104; out-of-state residents $380.

FINANCIAL AID PICTURE (2005-2006)
Students with need: 26% of average financial aid package awarded as scholarships/grants, 74% awarded as loans/jobs. Need-based aid available for part-time students.
Students without need: No-need awards available for academics.
Cumulative student debt: 67% of graduating class had student loans; average debt was $27,236.

FINANCIAL AID PROCEDURES
Forms required: FAFSA, institutional form.
Dates and Deadlines: Priority date 3/15; no closing date. Applicants notified on a rolling basis starting 6/1; must reply within 2 week(s) of notification.

CONTACT
Kay Egbert, Director of Student Aid
PO Box 660677, Dallas, TX 75266-0677

Texas A&M University-Commerce
Commerce, Texas
www.tamu-commerce.edu   Federal Code: 003565

4-year public university in small town.
Enrollment: 6,234 undergrads.
Selectivity: Admits 50 to 75% of applicants.

BASIC COSTS (2005-2006)
Tuition and fees: $4,136; out-of-state residents $12,416.
Room and board: $6,060.

FINANCIAL AID PICTURE (2005-2006)
Students with need: Average financial aid package met 80% of need; average scholarship/grant was $5,875; average loan was $1,545. For part-time students, average financial aid package was $4,846.
Additional info: Work-study also available for full-time students.

FINANCIAL AID PROCEDURES
Forms required: FAFSA, institutional form.
Dates and Deadlines: Priority date 4/1; no closing date. Applicants notified on a rolling basis starting 4/1; must reply within 2 week(s) of notification.

CONTACT
Smithenia Harris, Director of Financial Aid
Box 3011, Commerce, TX 75429-3011
(903) 886-5095

Texas A&M University-Galveston
Galveston, Texas
www.tamug.edu   Federal Code: 003632

4-year public university and branch campus college in small city.
Enrollment: 1,636 undergrads, 9% part-time. 461 full-time freshmen.
Selectivity: Admits over 75% of applicants.

BASIC COSTS (2005-2006)
Tuition and fees: $5,118; out-of-state residents $13,398.
Per-credit charge: $137; out-of-state residents $413.
Room and board: $4,870.

FINANCIAL AID PICTURE (2004-2005)
Students with need: Average financial aid package met 13% of need; average scholarship/grant was $3,987; average loan was $1,912. For part-time students, average financial aid package was $8,074.
Students without need: No-need awards available for academics, state/district residency.
Cumulative student debt: 70% of graduating class had student loans; average debt was $10,857.

FINANCIAL AID PROCEDURES
Forms required: FAFSA.
Dates and Deadlines: Priority date 4/1; no closing date. Applicants notified on a rolling basis starting 3/15; must reply within 3 week(s) of notification.

CONTACT
Dennis Carlton, Director of Financial Aid
PO Box 1675, Galveston, TX 77553-1675
(409) 740-4500

Texas A&M University-Kingsville
Kingsville, Texas
www.tamuk.edu   Federal Code: 003639

4-year public university in large town.
Enrollment: 4,665 full-time undergrads.
Selectivity: Admits over 75% of applicants.

BASIC COSTS (2005-2006)
Tuition and fees: $4,326; out-of-state residents $12,606.
Per-credit charge: $102; out-of-state residents $378.
Room and board: $4,654.

FINANCIAL AID PICTURE
Students with need: Need-based aid available for full-time students.
Students without need: No-need awards available for academics, leadership.

FINANCIAL AID PROCEDURES
Forms required: FAFSA.
Dates and Deadlines: Applicants notified on a rolling basis.

CONTACT
Raul Villarreal, Director of Financial Aid Programs
MSC 105, Kingsville, TX 78363-8201
(361) 593-3911

Texas A&M University-Texarkana
Texarkana, Texas
www.tamut.edu   Federal Code: 031703

Upper-division public university in small city.
Enrollment: 1,000 undergrads, 62% part-time.

BASIC COSTS (2005-2006)
Tuition and fees: $3,185; out-of-state residents $11,465.

FINANCIAL AID PICTURE (2005-2006)
Students with need: 52% of average financial aid package awarded as scholarships/grants, 48% awarded as loans/jobs. Need-based aid available for part-time students.
Students without need: This college only awards aid to students with need.

FINANCIAL AID PROCEDURES
Forms required: FAFSA, institutional form.
Dates and Deadlines: Priority date 5/1; closing date 11/1. Applicants notified on a rolling basis; must reply within 6 week(s) of notification.
Transfers: No deadline. Must have completed minimum of 54 semester hours of transferable college credit to apply for financial aid. Notified applicants must reply within 45 days from date of award letter. Exceptions made on individual basis. March 1 financial aid deadline for scholarships.

CONTACT
Marilyn Raney, Director of Financial Aid
2600 North Robinson Road, Texarkana, TX 75505
(903) 233-3060

Texas Christian University
Fort Worth, Texas
www.tcu.edu   Federal Code: 003636

4-year private university in large city, affiliated with Christian Church (Disciples of Christ).
Enrollment: 7,056 undergrads, 5% part-time. 1,610 full-time freshmen.
Selectivity: Admits 50 to 75% of applicants. GED not accepted.

BASIC COSTS (2006-2007)
Tuition and fees: $23,028.
Per-credit charge: $800.
Room and board: $7,520.

FINANCIAL AID PICTURE (2005-2006)
Students with need: Out of 875 full-time freshmen who applied for aid, 613 were judged to have need. Of these, 610 received aid, and 289 had their full need met. Average financial aid package met 71% of need; average scholarship/grant was $10,246; average loan was $4,809. For part-time students, average financial aid package was $9,928.
Students without need: 400 full-time freshmen who did not demonstrate need for aid received scholarships/grants; average award was $8,117. No-need awards available for academics, alumni affiliation, art, athletics, leadership, minority status, music/drama, religious affiliation, ROTC, state/district residency.
Scholarships offered: 57 full-time freshmen received athletic scholarships; average amount $13,835.

FINANCIAL AID PROCEDURES
Forms required: FAFSA, institutional form.
Dates and Deadlines: Closing date 5/1. Applicants notified on a rolling basis starting 3/1; must reply by 5/1 or within 2 week(s) of notification.
Transfers: Priority date 6/1.

CONTACT
Michael Scott, Director of Scholarships and Student Financial Aid
TCU Box 297013, Fort Worth, TX 76129
(817) 257-7858

Texas College
Tyler, Texas
www.texascollege.edu   Federal Code: 003638

4-year private liberal arts college in small city, affiliated with Christian Methodist Episcopal Church.
Enrollment: 794 undergrads.
Selectivity: Open admission.

BASIC COSTS (2006-2007)
Tuition and fees: $7,910.
Per-credit charge: $330.
Room and board: $5,600.
Additional info: Tuition/fee waivers available for adults.

FINANCIAL AID PICTURE (2004-2005)
Students with need: 68% of average financial aid package awarded as scholarships/grants, 32% awarded as loans/jobs. Work study available nights.
Students without need: This college only awards aid to students with need.

FINANCIAL AID PROCEDURES
Forms required: FAFSA, institutional form.
Dates and Deadlines: Priority date 6/1; no closing date. Applicants notified on a rolling basis starting 4/15; must reply within 2 week(s) of notification.

CONTACT
Reggie Brazzle, Director of Financial Aid
2404 North Grand Avenue, Tyler, TX 75712-4500
(903) 593-8311 ext. 2278

Texas Lutheran University
Seguin, Texas
www.tlu.edu   Federal Code: 003641

4-year private university and liberal arts college in large town, affiliated with Evangelical Lutheran Church in America.
Enrollment: 1,360 undergrads, 3% part-time. 385 full-time freshmen.
Selectivity: Admits 50 to 75% of applicants.

BASIC COSTS (2006-2007)
Tuition and fees: $18,840.
Per-credit charge: $630.
Room and board: $6,450.

FINANCIAL AID PICTURE (2004-2005)
Students with need: Out of 356 full-time freshmen who applied for aid, 284 were judged to have need. Of these, 284 received aid, and 71 had their full need met. Average financial aid package met 72% of need; average scholarship/grant was $5,700; average loan was $3,148. For part-time students, average financial aid package was $5,682.
Students without need: 99 full-time freshmen who did not demonstrate need for aid received scholarships/grants; average award was $6,183. No-need awards available for academics, alumni affiliation, art, job skills, leadership, music/drama, religious affiliation.
Scholarships offered: Pacesetter Award for College Excellence; up to $14,000 per year; 3.5 GPA and SAT/ACT 1250/28 or rank in top 10% of class with minimum 1100/24 SAT/ACT score; must be accepted by specific date and be invited to participate in on-campus Pacesetter event. Academic Excellence Award; up to $7,000 per year; minimum articulated high school GPA of 3.25 and either SAT/ACT 1150/25 or rank in top 15% of class; awarded automatically upon acceptance to TLU. All SAT scores exclusive of Writing.
Cumulative student debt: 63% of graduating class had student loans; average debt was $27,139.

FINANCIAL AID PROCEDURES
Forms required: FAFSA.
Dates and Deadlines: Priority date 4/1; no closing date. Applicants notified on a rolling basis starting 3/1; must reply within 2 week(s) of notification.

CONTACT
Norm Jones, Vice President for Enrollment Services
1000 West Court Street, Seguin, TX 78155-5999
(830) 372-8075

Texas Southern University
Houston, Texas
www.tsu.edu   Federal Code: 003642

4-year public university in very large city.
Enrollment: 9,760 undergrads, 21% part-time. 1,803 full-time freshmen.
Selectivity: Open admission; but selective for some programs.

BASIC COSTS (2005-2006)
Tuition and fees: $4,468; out-of-state residents $12,748.
Per-credit charge: $50; out-of-state residents $326.
Room and board: $6,296.
Additional info: Tuition/fee waivers available for minority students.

FINANCIAL AID PICTURE
Students with need: Need-based aid available for full-time and part-time students. Work study available nights, weekends, and for part-time students.
Students without need: This college only awards aid to students with need.

FINANCIAL AID PROCEDURES
Forms required: FAFSA.
Dates and Deadlines: Priority date 5/1; no closing date. Applicants notified on a rolling basis starting 6/1.
Transfers: Priority date 4/1; closing date 8/30.

CONTACT
Albert Tezno, Director of Financial Aid
3100 Cleburne Street, Houston, TX 77004
(713) 313-7802

Texas State Technical College: Harlingen
Harlingen, Texas
www.harlingen.tstc.edu   Federal Code: 009225

2-year public technical college in small city.
Enrollment: 1,600 undergrads.
Selectivity: Open admission; but selective for some programs.

BASIC COSTS (2005-2006)
Tuition and fees: $2,330; out-of-state residents $5,450.
Per-credit charge: $58; out-of-state residents $162.
Room and board: $2,538.

FINANCIAL AID PICTURE (2005-2006)
Students with need: 83% of average financial aid package awarded as scholarships/grants, 17% awarded as loans/jobs. Need-based aid available for part-time students.

FINANCIAL AID PROCEDURES
Forms required: FAFSA, institutional form.
Dates and Deadlines: Closing date 4/13. Applicants notified on a rolling basis starting 6/30; must reply within 2 week(s) of notification.

CONTACT
Mary Adams, Director of Financial Aid
1902 North Loop 499, Harlingen, TX 78550-3697
(956) 364-4332

Texas State Technical College: Waco
Waco, Texas
www.waco.tstc.edu   Federal Code: 003634

2-year public technical college in small city.
Enrollment: 4,431 undergrads, 30% part-time. 1,549 full-time freshmen.
Selectivity: Open admission.

BASIC COSTS (2005-2006)
Tuition and fees: $2,333; out-of-state residents $5,453.
Per-credit charge: $58; out-of-state residents $162.
Room and board: $3,990.

FINANCIAL AID PICTURE (2005-2006)
Students with need: 57% of average financial aid package awarded as scholarships/grants, 43% awarded as loans/jobs. Need-based aid available for part-time students.
Students without need: This college only awards aid to students with need.

FINANCIAL AID PROCEDURES
Forms required: FAFSA.
Dates and Deadlines: Priority date 6/1; no closing date. Applicants notified on a rolling basis starting 5/15.

CONTACT
Jackie Adler, Director, Financial Aid
3801 Campus Drive, Waco, TX 76705
(254) 867-4814

Texas State Technical College: West Texas
Sweetwater, Texas
www.westtexas.tstc.edu   Federal Code: 009932

2-year public technical college in large town.
Enrollment: 1,385 undergrads, 39% part-time. 260 full-time freshmen.
Selectivity: Open admission; but selective for some programs.

BASIC COSTS (2005-2006)
Tuition and fees: $2,330; out-of-state residents $5,450.
Per-credit charge: $58; out-of-state residents $162.
Room and board: $3,450.

FINANCIAL AID PICTURE (2004-2005)
Students with need: 42% of average financial aid package awarded as scholarships/grants, 58% awarded as loans/jobs. Need-based aid available for part-time students. Work study available nights, weekends, and for part-time students.
Students without need: No-need awards available for academics, leadership.
Cumulative student debt: 82% of graduating class had student loans; average debt was $3,830.

FINANCIAL AID PROCEDURES
Forms required: FAFSA, institutional form.
Dates and Deadlines: Priority date 5/1; no closing date. Applicants notified on a rolling basis starting 7/1.
Transfers: No deadline. Applicants notified on a rolling basis starting 7/1; must reply by 8/20.

CONTACT
MaryLou Bledsoe, Director of Financial Aid
300 College Drive, Sweetwater, TX 79556
(325) 235-7378

Texas State University: San Marcos
San Marcos, Texas
www.txstate.edu   Federal Code: 003615

4-year public university in large town.
Enrollment: 22,986 undergrads, 20% part-time. 2,993 full-time freshmen.
Selectivity: Admits over 75% of applicants.

BASIC COSTS (2005-2006)
Tuition and fees: $5,252; out-of-state residents $13,532.
Room and board: $5,610.

FINANCIAL AID PICTURE (2005-2006)
Students with need: Out of 1,996 full-time freshmen who applied for aid, 1,389 were judged to have need. Of these, 1,292 received aid, and 165 had their full need met. Average financial aid package met 73% of need; average scholarship/grant was $4,550; average loan was $2,395. For part-time students, average financial aid package was $8,328.
Students without need: 222 full-time freshmen who did not demonstrate need for aid received scholarships/grants; average award was $4,897. No-need awards available for academics, art, athletics, leadership, music/drama, ROTC, state/district residency.
Scholarships offered: *Merit:* Roy and Joan C. Mitte Foundation Scholarships; $5,050; 25 awarded; based on National Merit Competition finalist/semi-finalist status or valedictorian/salutatorian of high school class, or in top 5% of graduating class. President's Endowed Scholarships; $1,000; 9 awarded; based on minimum ACT score of 24 or SAT score of 1000 (exclusive of writing), rank in upper 25% of high school class. Freshmen Program Scholarships; $200-$700; 10 awarded; based on ACT/SAT scores, high school grades, high school leadership activities. *Athletic:* 69 full-time freshmen received athletic scholarships; average amount $7,501.
Cumulative student debt: 59% of graduating class had student loans; average debt was $16,838.

FINANCIAL AID PROCEDURES
Forms required: FAFSA.
Dates and Deadlines: Priority date 4/1; no closing date. Applicants notified on a rolling basis starting 5/1; must reply within 3 week(s) of notification.

CONTACT
Mariko Gomez, Director of Financial Aid
429 North Guadalupe Street, San Marcos, TX 78666-5709
(512) 245-2315

Texas Tech University
Lubbock, Texas
www.ttu.edu   Federal Code: 003644

4-year public university in small city.
Enrollment: 22,967 undergrads, 9% part-time. 3,866 full-time freshmen.
Selectivity: Admits 50 to 75% of applicants.

BASIC COSTS (2005-2006)
Tuition and fees: $6,152; out-of-state residents $14,432.
Per-credit charge: $129; out-of-state residents $405.
Room and board: $6,506.
Additional info: Students from adjacent counties in New Mexico and Oklahoma pay in-state tuition rates; students from all other counties in New Mexico and Oklahoma pay reduced out-of-state tuition rates.

FINANCIAL AID PICTURE (2004-2005)
Students with need: Out of 3,048 full-time freshmen who applied for aid, 1,739 were judged to have need. Of these, 1,669 received aid. For part-time students, average financial aid package was $4,888.
Students without need: 1,717 full-time freshmen who did not demonstrate need for aid received scholarships/grants; average award was $2,337. No-

need awards available for academics, art, athletics, job skills, leadership, music/drama, ROTC.

Scholarships offered: *Merit:* Presidential Plus Scholarship; $12,700 per year for up to 5 years; awarded to National Merit Finalists who select Texas Tech as school of choice. Texas Tech Select Scholarship; $1,000 per year for up to 5 years (may be combined with other merit scholarship offers); awarded to National Merit Semi-Finalists. Presidential Endowed Scholarship; $4,000 per year for up to 5 years; awarded to students in top 10% of high school graduating class with SAT 1400 or ACT 31. Honors Endowed Scholarship; $2,500 per year up to 5 years; awarded to students in top 10% of high school graduating class with SAT 1300 or ACT 29. University Scholars Scholarship: $1,500 per year up to 4 years; awarded to students in top 10% of high school graduating class with SAT 1250 or ACT 28. Superior Scholastic Achievement Scholarship; $1,000 per year up to four years; awarded to students in top 10% of high school graduating class with SAT 1200 or ACT 26. All SAT scores exclusive of Writing. *Athletic:* 64 full-time freshmen received athletic scholarships; average amount $9,208.

FINANCIAL AID PROCEDURES
Forms required: FAFSA.
Dates and Deadlines: Priority date 5/1; no closing date. Applicants notified on a rolling basis; must reply within 2 week(s) of notification.

CONTACT
Becky Wilson, Director of Financial Aid
Box 45005, Lubbock, TX 79409-5005
(806) 742-3681

Texas Wesleyan University
Fort Worth, Texas
www.txwesleyan.edu   Federal Code: 003645

4-year private university in large city, affiliated with United Methodist Church.
Enrollment: 1,335 undergrads, 27% part-time. 174 full-time freshmen.
Selectivity: Admits less than 50% of applicants.

BASIC COSTS (2005-2006)
Tuition and fees: $14,000.
Per-credit charge: $435.
Room and board: $4,760.

FINANCIAL AID PICTURE
Students with need: Need-based aid available for full-time and part-time students. Work study available nights, weekends, and for part-time students.
Students without need: This college only awards aid to students with need.

FINANCIAL AID PROCEDURES
Forms required: FAFSA, institutional form.
Dates and Deadlines: Priority date 4/15; no closing date. Applicants notified on a rolling basis starting 4/15; must reply within 2 week(s) of notification.

CONTACT
Dean Carpenter, Director of Financial Aid
1201 Wesleyan Street, Fort Worth, TX 76105-1536
(817) 531-4420

Texas Woman's University
Denton, Texas
www.twu.edu   Federal Code: 003646

4-year public university in small city.
Enrollment: 6,226 undergrads, 27% part-time. 696 full-time freshmen.
Selectivity: Admits 50 to 75% of applicants.

BASIC COSTS (2006-2007)
Tuition and fees: $5,010; out-of-state residents $13,290.
Per-credit charge: $123; out-of-state residents $399.
Room and board: $5,598.

FINANCIAL AID PICTURE (2005-2006)
Students with need: Out of 538 full-time freshmen who applied for aid, 402 were judged to have need. Of these, 394 received aid, and 343 had their full need met. Average financial aid package met 98% of need; average scholarship/grant was $4,206; average loan was $2,230. For part-time students, average financial aid package was $9,865.
Students without need: 75 full-time freshmen who did not demonstrate need for aid received scholarships/grants; average award was $3,339.
Scholarships offered: *Merit:* Chancellor's Endowed Scholarship; full tuition and fees, room and board; based on high school valedictorian status, extracurricular activities, SAT score; 2 awarded. Presidential Scholarship; full tuition and fees; awarded to valedictorian or salutatorian. Honors Scholarship; $1,500 annually up to 4 years; based on admission to honors program and SAT score. New Freshman Scholarship; $1,500 annually up to 4 years; based on SAT/ACT score, class rank and GPA. Transfer Student Scholarship; $1,500 annually up to 4 years; based on GPA, must have completed at least 12 credit hours. New Student Scholarship; $1,800 annually up to four years; based on high school rank, ACT/SAT score; 150 awarded. *Athletic:* 21 full-time freshmen received athletic scholarships; average amount $3,689.
Cumulative student debt: 54% of graduating class had student loans; average debt was $18,125.

FINANCIAL AID PROCEDURES
Forms required: FAFSA, institutional form.
Dates and Deadlines: Priority date 4/1; no closing date. Applicants notified on a rolling basis starting 3/1; must reply within 2 week(s) of notification.

CONTACT
Governor Jackson, Director of Financial Aid
Box 425589, Denton, TX 76204-5589
(940) 898-3050

Trinity University
San Antonio, Texas
www.trinity.edu   Federal Code: 003647

4-year private liberal arts college in very large city, affiliated with Presbyterian Church (USA).
Enrollment: 2,523 undergrads, 2% part-time. 651 full-time freshmen.
Selectivity: Admits 50 to 75% of applicants.

BASIC COSTS (2006-2007)
Tuition and fees: $23,286.
Per-credit charge: $964.
Room and board: $8,198.

FINANCIAL AID PICTURE
Students with need: Need-based aid available for full-time students.
Students without need: No-need awards available for academics, leadership, music/drama.

FINANCIAL AID PROCEDURES
Forms required: FAFSA.
Dates and Deadlines: Priority date 2/1; closing date 4/1. Applicants notified on a rolling basis starting 4/1; must reply by 5/1 or within 4 week(s) of notification.
Transfers: Priority date 5/1; no deadline.

CONTACT
Patricia Jost, Director of Financial Aid
One Trinity Place, San Antonio, TX 78212
(210) 999-8315

Trinity Valley Community College
Athens, Texas
www.tvcc.edu   Federal Code: 003572

2-year public community college in large town.
Enrollment: 5,825 undergrads.
Selectivity: Open admission; but selective for some programs.

BASIC COSTS (2005-2006)
Tuition and fees: $1,050; out-of-district residents $1,650; out-of-state residents $2,400.
Per-credit charge: $20; out-of-district residents $40; out-of-state residents $65.
Room and board: $3,400.
Additional info: Tuition/fee waivers available for adults.

FINANCIAL AID PICTURE
Students with need: Need-based aid available for full-time and part-time students. Work study available nights, weekends, and for part-time students.
Students without need: No-need awards available for academics, athletics.

FINANCIAL AID PROCEDURES
Forms required: FAFSA, institutional form.
Dates and Deadlines: Priority date 7/1; no closing date. Applicants notified on a rolling basis starting 7/1; must reply within 2 week(s) of notification.
Transfers: Students on suspension at previous institution ineligible to receive aid.

CONTACT
Julie Lively, Director of Financial Aid
100 Cardinal Drive, Athens, TX 75751
(903) 675-6233

Tyler Junior College
Tyler, Texas
www.tjc.edu   Federal Code: 003648

2-year public junior college in small city.
Enrollment: 8,500 full-time undergrads.
Selectivity: Open admission; but selective for some programs.

BASIC COSTS (2005-2006)
Tuition and fees: $1,520; out-of-district residents $2,480; out-of-state residents $2,780.
Per-credit charge: $20; out-of-district residents $52; out-of-state residents $62.
Room and board: $4,000.

FINANCIAL AID PICTURE
Students with need: Need-based aid available for full-time and part-time students.
Students without need: No-need awards available for academics, alumni affiliation, art, athletics, leadership, music/drama.

FINANCIAL AID PROCEDURES
Forms required: FAFSA, institutional form.
Dates and Deadlines: Priority date 6/1; no closing date. Applicants notified on a rolling basis starting 3/1; must reply within 2 week(s) of notification.
Transfers: Financial aid transcript required if student enrolled same year elsewhere.

CONTACT
Devon Wiggins, Director of Student Financial Aid and Scholarship
Box 9020, Tyler, TX 75711-9020
(903) 510-2646

University of Dallas
Irving, Texas
www.udallas.edu   Federal Code: 003651

4-year private university and liberal arts college in small city, affiliated with Roman Catholic Church.
Enrollment: 1,058 undergrads, 1% part-time. 243 full-time freshmen.
Selectivity: Admits over 75% of applicants.

BASIC COSTS (2006-2007)
Tuition and fees: $21,805.
Per-credit charge: $900.
Room and board: $7,332.

FINANCIAL AID PICTURE (2004-2005)
Students with need: Out of 203 full-time freshmen who applied for aid, 161 were judged to have need. Of these, 161 received aid, and 34 had their full need met. Average financial aid package met 78% of need; average scholarship/grant was $11,388; average loan was $2,638. For part-time students, average financial aid package was $6,816.
Students without need: 74 full-time freshmen who did not demonstrate need for aid received scholarships/grants; average award was $7,971. No-need awards available for academics, art, leadership, music/drama.
Cumulative student debt: 70% of graduating class had student loans; average debt was $21,700.

FINANCIAL AID PROCEDURES
Forms required: FAFSA.
Dates and Deadlines: Priority date 3/1; closing date 7/1. Applicants notified on a rolling basis starting 3/1; must reply by 5/1 or within 2 week(s) of notification.
Transfers: Priority date 4/1; closing date 7/15. Must reply by 5/1 or within 2 week(s) of notification.

CONTACT
Curt Eley, Dean of Enrollment Management
1845 East Northgate Drive, Irving, TX 75062-4736
(972) 721-5266

University of Houston
Houston, Texas
www.uh.edu   Federal Code: 003652

4-year public university in very large city.
Enrollment: 26,959 undergrads, 27% part-time. 3,210 full-time freshmen.
Selectivity: Admits over 75% of applicants.

BASIC COSTS (2005-2006)
Tuition and fees: $5,163; out-of-state residents $13,443.
Per-credit charge: $50; out-of-state residents $326.
Room and board: $6,030.

FINANCIAL AID PICTURE (2005-2006)
Students with need: Out of 1,393 full-time freshmen who applied for aid, 1,245 were judged to have need. Of these, 1,153 received aid, and 37 had their full need met. Average financial aid package met 53% of need; average scholarship/grant was $5,847; average loan was $2,736. For part-time students, average financial aid package was $5,921.
Students without need: This college only awards aid to students with need.
Scholarships offered: 50 full-time freshmen received athletic scholarships; average amount $10,322.
Additional info: 45-day and 90-day institutional loans available.

FINANCIAL AID PROCEDURES
Forms required: FAFSA.

Dates and Deadlines: No deadline. Applicants notified on a rolling basis starting 5/1; must reply within 4 week(s) of notification.

CONTACT
Robert Sheridan, Executive Director of Scholarships and Financial Aid
122 East Cullen Building, Houston, TX 77204-2023
(713) 743-1010

University of Houston: Clear Lake
Houston, Texas
www.uhcl.edu   Federal Code: 011711

Upper-division public university in very large city.
Enrollment: 3,913 undergrads, 47% part-time.

BASIC COSTS (2006-2007)
Tuition and fees: $4,653; out-of-state residents $13,595.
Per-credit charge: $117; out-of-state residents $393.
Room only: $6,456.

FINANCIAL AID PICTURE (2004-2005)
Students with need: Average financial aid package for all full-time undergraduates was $7,394; for part-time $6,746. 24% awarded as scholarships/grants, 76% awarded as loans/jobs. Work study available nights, weekends, and for part-time students.
Students without need: No-need awards available for academics, state/district residency.
Cumulative student debt: 79% of graduating class had student loans; average debt was $15,967.

FINANCIAL AID PROCEDURES
Forms required: FAFSA, institutional form.
Dates and Deadlines: No deadline. Applicants notified on a rolling basis starting 6/4; must reply within 4 week(s) of notification.
Transfers: Priority date 4/1; no deadline. Applicants notified by 5/15; must reply within 4 week(s) of notification.

CONTACT
Lynda McKendree, Director, Financial Aid/Veterans Affairs
2700 Bay Area Boulevard, Houston, TX 77058-1098
(281) 283-2481

University of Houston: Downtown
Houston, Texas
www.uhd.edu   Federal Code: 003612

4-year public university in very large city.
Enrollment: 11,359 undergrads, 48% part-time. 792 full-time freshmen.
Selectivity: Open admission.

BASIC COSTS (2006-2007)
Tuition and fees: $4,456; out-of-state residents $12,666.

FINANCIAL AID PICTURE (2004-2005)
Students with need: Out of 693 full-time freshmen who applied for aid, 656 were judged to have need. Of these, 569 received aid, and 5 had their full need met. Average financial aid package met 28% of need; average scholarship/grant was $3,591; average loan was $2,155. For part-time students, average financial aid package was $4,592.
Students without need: 210 full-time freshmen who did not demonstrate need for aid received scholarships/grants; average award was $2,244. No-need awards available for academics, leadership.
Cumulative student debt: 77% of graduating class had student loans; average debt was $13,196.

FINANCIAL AID PROCEDURES
Forms required: FAFSA, institutional form.

Dates and Deadlines: Closing date 4/1. Applicants notified on a rolling basis starting 6/1; must reply within 4 week(s) of notification.

CONTACT
LaTasha Goudeau, Director of Financial Aid
One Main Street, 350-South, Houston, TX 77002
(713) 221-8041

University of Houston: Victoria
Victoria, Texas
www.uhv.edu   Federal Code: 013231

Upper-division public university in small city.
Enrollment: 1,188 undergrads, 62% part-time.

BASIC COSTS (2005-2006)
Tuition and fees: $4,350; out-of-state residents $12,630.
Per-credit charge: $108; out-of-state residents $384.

FINANCIAL AID PICTURE (2004-2005)
Students with need: Average financial aid package for all full-time undergraduates was $6,669; for part-time $5,500. 43% awarded as scholarships/grants, 57% awarded as loans/jobs. Work study available nights, weekends, and for part-time students.
Students without need: No-need awards available for academics, leadership, state/district residency.
Cumulative student debt: 54% of graduating class had student loans; average debt was $18,114.
Additional info: Short-term loans available at registration.

FINANCIAL AID PROCEDURES
Forms required: FAFSA, institutional form.
Dates and Deadlines: Priority date 4/15; no closing date. Applicants notified on a rolling basis starting 5/20; must reply within 3 week(s) of notification.

CONTACT
Carolyn Mallory, Financial Aid Coordinator
3007 North Ben Wilson, Victoria, TX 77901-4450
(361) 570-4131

University of Mary Hardin-Baylor
Belton, Texas
www.umhb.edu   Federal Code: 003588

4-year private university in large town, affiliated with Baptist faith.
Enrollment: 2,532 undergrads, 11% part-time. 498 full-time freshmen.
Selectivity: Admits 50 to 75% of applicants.

BASIC COSTS (2006-2007)
Tuition and fees: $15,660.
Per-credit charge: $475.
Room and board: $4,500.
Additional info: Tuition/fee waivers available for minority students.

FINANCIAL AID PICTURE (2005-2006)
Students with need: Out of 472 full-time freshmen who applied for aid, 360 were judged to have need. Of these, 353 received aid, and 84 had their full need met. Average financial aid package met 64% of need; average scholarship/grant was $5,334; average loan was $2,514. For part-time students, average financial aid package was $8,525.
Students without need: 125 full-time freshmen who did not demonstrate need for aid received scholarships/grants; average award was $3,314. No-need awards available for academics, art, leadership, music/drama, religious affiliation.
Cumulative student debt: 80% of graduating class had student loans; average debt was $15,819.

FINANCIAL AID PROCEDURES
Forms required: FAFSA, institutional form.
Dates and Deadlines: Priority date 3/1; no closing date. Applicants notified on a rolling basis starting 2/1; must reply within 2 week(s) of notification.

CONTACT
Ron Brown, Director of Financial Aid
900 College Street, Belton, TX 76513
(254) 295-4517

University of North Texas
Denton, Texas
www.unt.edu   Federal Code: 003594

4-year public university and liberal arts college in small city.
Enrollment: 25,308 undergrads, 22% part-time. 3,564 full-time freshmen.
Selectivity: Admits 50 to 75% of applicants.

BASIC COSTS (2006-2007)
Tuition and fees: $6,112; out-of-state residents $14,362.
Per-credit charge: $141; out-of-state residents $416.
Room and board: $5,625.

FINANCIAL AID PICTURE (2005-2006)
Students with need: Out of 2,442 full-time freshmen who applied for aid, 1,567 were judged to have need. Of these, 1,541 received aid, and 405 had their full need met. Average financial aid package met 73% of need; average scholarship/grant was $4,034; average loan was $2,534. For part-time students, average financial aid package was $6,536.
Students without need: 382 full-time freshmen who did not demonstrate need for aid received scholarships/grants; average award was $3,180. No-need awards available for academics.
Scholarships offered: 62 full-time freshmen received athletic scholarships; average amount $9,665.
Cumulative student debt: 38% of graduating class had student loans; average debt was $18,092.

FINANCIAL AID PROCEDURES
Forms required: FAFSA.
Dates and Deadlines: Priority date 6/1; no closing date. Applicants notified on a rolling basis starting 4/1.

CONTACT
Carolyn Cunningham, Director of Financial Aid
1401 West Prairie, Suite 309, Denton, TX 76203
(940) 565-2016

University of St. Thomas
Houston, Texas
www.stthom.edu   Federal Code: 003654

4-year private university and liberal arts college in very large city, affiliated with Roman Catholic Church.
Enrollment: 1,776 undergrads, 24% part-time. 290 full-time freshmen.
Selectivity: Admits over 75% of applicants.

BASIC COSTS (2006-2007)
Tuition and fees: $17,860.
Per-credit charge: $590.
Room and board: $7,500.

FINANCIAL AID PICTURE (2005-2006)
Students with need: Out of 203 full-time freshmen who applied for aid, 173 were judged to have need. Of these, 171 received aid, and 21 had their full need met. Average financial aid package met 68% of need; average scholarship/grant was $9,958; average loan was $2,815. For part-time students, average financial aid package was $7,316.
Students without need: 9 full-time freshmen who did not demonstrate need for aid received scholarships/grants; average award was $8,829. No-need awards available for academics, leadership, music/drama, religious affiliation, state/district residency.
Cumulative student debt: 63% of graduating class had student loans; average debt was $21,626.

FINANCIAL AID PROCEDURES
Forms required: FAFSA.
Dates and Deadlines: Priority date 3/1; no closing date. Applicants notified on a rolling basis starting 3/1; must reply within 4 week(s) of notification.

CONTACT
Scott Moore, Dean of Scholarships and Financial Aid
3800 Montrose Boulevard, Houston, TX 77006-4696
(713) 942-3465

University of Texas at Arlington
Arlington, Texas
www.uta.edu   Federal Code: 003656

4-year public university in large city.
Enrollment: 19,222 undergrads, 29% part-time. 1,782 full-time freshmen.
Selectivity: Admits 50 to 75% of applicants. GED not accepted.

BASIC COSTS (2005-2006)
Tuition and fees: $5,561; out-of-state residents $13,843.
Per-credit charge: $130; out-of-state residents $406.
Room and board: $6,628.

FINANCIAL AID PICTURE (2005-2006)
Students with need: Out of 1,180 full-time freshmen who applied for aid, 1,035 were judged to have need. Of these, 1,035 received aid, and 169 had their full need met. Average financial aid package met 71% of need; average scholarship/grant was $3,998; average loan was $4,096. For part-time students, average financial aid package was $6,737.
Students without need: 431 full-time freshmen who did not demonstrate need for aid received scholarships/grants; average award was $2,032. No-need awards available for academics, art, athletics, leadership, music/drama, ROTC.
Scholarships offered: Merit: Academic Scholarships; $1,000-$4,000 per year, renewable; based on minimum SAT 1050 (exclusive of writing) or ACT 22, top 25% of high school class. **Athletic:** 45 full-time freshmen received athletic scholarships; average amount $6,179.
Cumulative student debt: 42% of graduating class had student loans; average debt was $16,780.

FINANCIAL AID PROCEDURES
Forms required: FAFSA.
Dates and Deadlines: Priority date 5/15; no closing date. Applicants notified on a rolling basis starting 4/1; must reply within 3 week(s) of notification.
Transfers: Must reply within 3 week(s) of notification. To receive Texas grant or Texas B on Time loan, student must have either received Texas grant at prior school or completed associates degree at prior school.

CONTACT
Karen Krause, Director
Box 19111, Arlington, TX 76019
(817) 272-3561

University of Texas at Austin
Austin, Texas
www.utexas.edu   Federal Code: 003658

4-year public university in very large city.
Enrollment: 35,734 undergrads, 7% part-time. 6,791 full-time freshmen.
Selectivity: Admits 50 to 75% of applicants.

BASIC COSTS (2005-2006)
Tuition and fees: $6,972; out-of-state residents $16,310.
Room and board: $6,360.

FINANCIAL AID PICTURE (2005-2006)
Students with need: Out of 4,550 full-time freshmen who applied for aid, 4,000 were judged to have need. Of these, 3,950 received aid, and 3,630 had their full need met. Average financial aid package met 90% of need; average scholarship/grant was $6,750; average loan was $3,650. Need-based aid available for part-time students.
Students without need: 1,140 full-time freshmen who did not demonstrate need for aid received scholarships/grants; average award was $3,500. No-need awards available for academics, art, athletics, leadership, music/drama, ROTC, state/district residency.
Cumulative student debt: 39% of graduating class had student loans; average debt was $16,850.

FINANCIAL AID PROCEDURES
Forms required: FAFSA.
Dates and Deadlines: Priority date 4/1; no closing date. Applicants notified on a rolling basis starting 3/15; must reply within 4 week(s) of notification.

CONTACT
Lawrence Burt, Associate Vice President and Director of Student Financial Services
PO Box 8058, Austin, TX 78713-8058
(512) 475-6282

University of Texas at Brownsville
Brownsville, Texas
www.utb.edu   Federal Code: 030646

4-year public university and community college in small city.
Enrollment: 10,690 undergrads.
Selectivity: Open admission; but selective for some programs.

BASIC COSTS (2005-2006)
Tuition and fees: $3,895; out-of-state residents $12,175.
Per-credit charge: $94; out-of-state residents $370.

FINANCIAL AID PICTURE
Students with need: Need-based aid available for full-time and part-time students.

FINANCIAL AID PROCEDURES
Forms required: FAFSA.
Dates and Deadlines: Priority date 4/1; closing date 8/15. Applicants notified on a rolling basis; must reply within 4 week(s) of notification.

CONTACT
Mari Chapa, Director of Financial Aid
80 Fort Brown, Brownsville, TX 78520
(956) 544-8277

University of Texas at Dallas
Richardson, Texas
www.utdallas.edu   Federal Code: 009741

4-year public university in very large city.
Enrollment: 9,243 undergrads, 29% part-time. 1,071 full-time freshmen.
Selectivity: Admits 50 to 75% of applicants.

BASIC COSTS (2005-2006)
Tuition and fees: $6,831; out-of-state residents $15,111.
Per-credit charge: $198; out-of-state residents $474.
Room and board: $6,244.

FINANCIAL AID PICTURE (2004-2005)
Students with need: Out of 651 full-time freshmen who applied for aid, 446 were judged to have need. Of these, 446 received aid, and 189 had their full need met. Average financial aid package met 64% of need; average scholarship/grant was $3,996; average loan was $4,506. For part-time students, average financial aid package was $11,617.
Students without need: 95 full-time freshmen who did not demonstrate need for aid received scholarships/grants; average award was $7,374. No-need awards available for academics.
Scholarships offered: Eugene McDermott Scholars Program Awards; full tuition and fees plus domestic and international travel costs for enhancement of scholar's education; based on being in top 10% of high school class, high scores on entrance exams, evidence of leadership abilities; 20 awarded.

FINANCIAL AID PROCEDURES
Forms required: FAFSA.
Dates and Deadlines: Priority date 3/1; closing date 4/12. Applicants notified by 4/15; must reply within 3 week(s) of notification.
Transfers: Priority date 4/1.

CONTACT
Maria Ramos, Director of Financial Aid
Office of Admissions, Richardson, TX 75083-0688
(972) 883-2941

University of Texas at El Paso
El Paso, Texas
www.utep.edu   Federal Code: 003661

4-year public university in very large city.
Enrollment: 15,806 undergrads, 31% part-time. 2,361 full-time freshmen.
Selectivity: Admits over 75% of applicants.

BASIC COSTS (2005-2006)
Tuition and fees: $4,888; out-of-state residents $13,218.
Per-credit charge: $131; out-of-state residents $407.
Additional info: Mexican citizens who show need may qualify for in-state tuition.

FINANCIAL AID PICTURE (2004-2005)
Students with need: Out of 1,950 full-time freshmen who applied for aid, 1,536 were judged to have need. Of these, 1,519 received aid, and 209 had their full need met. Average financial aid package met 71% of need; average scholarship/grant was $5,068; average loan was $2,773. For part-time students, average financial aid package was $8,432.
Students without need: 179 full-time freshmen who did not demonstrate need for aid received scholarships/grants; average award was $1,208. No-need awards available for academics, alumni affiliation, art, athletics, job skills, leadership, minority status, music/drama, religious affiliation, ROTC, state/district residency.
Scholarships offered: 39 full-time freshmen received athletic scholarships; average amount $7,676.

Cumulative student debt: 47% of graduating class had student loans; average debt was $6,538.
Additional info: Emergency loans available.

FINANCIAL AID PROCEDURES
Forms required: FAFSA, institutional form.
Dates and Deadlines: Closing date 3/15. Applicants notified by 6/30; must reply within 2 week(s) of notification.
Transfers: No deadline.

CONTACT
Raul Lerma, Interim Director of Financial Aid
500 West University Avenue, El Paso, TX 79968-0510
(915) 747-5204

University of Texas at San Antonio
San Antonio, Texas
www.utsa.edu   Federal Code: 010115

4-year public university in very large city.
Enrollment: 23,282 undergrads, 25% part-time. 4,367 full-time freshmen.
Selectivity: Admits over 75% of applicants.

BASIC COSTS (2006-2007)
Tuition and fees: $6,296; out-of-state residents $14,546.
Per-credit charge: $142; out-of-state residents $417.
Room and board: $7,452.

FINANCIAL AID PICTURE (2004-2005)
Students with need: Out of 3,518 full-time freshmen who applied for aid, 2,619 were judged to have need. Of these, 2,490 received aid, and 208 had their full need met. Average financial aid package met 56% of need; average scholarship/grant was $4,195; average loan was $2,356. For part-time students, average financial aid package was $4,667.
Students without need: 237 full-time freshmen who did not demonstrate need for aid received scholarships/grants; average award was $1,308. No-need awards available for academics, alumni affiliation, art, athletics, job skills, leadership, music/drama, ROTC, state/district residency.
Scholarships offered: 41 full-time freshmen received athletic scholarships; average amount $6,281.
Cumulative student debt: 63% of graduating class had student loans; average debt was $18,000.

FINANCIAL AID PROCEDURES
Forms required: FAFSA, institutional form.
Dates and Deadlines: Priority date 3/31; no closing date. Applicants notified on a rolling basis starting 4/1; must reply within 4 week(s) of notification.
Transfers: No deadline. Applicants notified on a rolling basis starting 4/1; must reply within 4 week(s) of notification.

CONTACT
Lisa Blazer, Director of Student Financial Aid
6900 North Loop 1604 West, San Antonio, TX 78249-0617
(210) 458-8000

University of Texas at Tyler
Tyler, Texas
www.uttyler.edu   Federal Code: 011163

4-year public university in small city.
Enrollment: 4,618 undergrads, 23% part-time. 545 full-time freshmen.
Selectivity: Admits over 75% of applicants.

BASIC COSTS (2006-2007)
Tuition and fees: $4,942; out-of-state residents $13,192.
Per-credit charge: $50; out-of-state residents $325.

FINANCIAL AID PICTURE
Students with need: Need-based aid available for full-time and part-time students.
Students without need: No-need awards available for academics, art, leadership, music/drama.
Additional info: Apply early for all programs.

FINANCIAL AID PROCEDURES
Forms required: FAFSA.
Dates and Deadlines: Priority date 4/1; no closing date. Applicants notified on a rolling basis starting 4/15; must reply within 3 week(s) of notification.

CONTACT
Candice Garner, Director of Financial Aid
3900 University Boulevard, Tyler, TX 75799
(903) 566-7180

University of Texas Health Science Center at Houston
Houston, Texas
www.uth.tmc.edu   Federal Code: 013956

Upper-division public university and health science college in very large city.
Enrollment: 380 undergrads.

BASIC COSTS (2005-2006)
Tuition and fees: $5,602; out-of-state residents $17,268.
Per-credit charge: $109; out-of-state residents $368.
Room and board: $6,060.
Additional info: Nursing program students must attend for full calendar year (fall, spring, summer semesters).

FINANCIAL AID PICTURE
Students with need: Need-based aid available for full-time and part-time students.
Students without need: This college only awards aid to students with need.

FINANCIAL AID PROCEDURES
Forms required: FAFSA, institutional form.
Dates and Deadlines: No deadline. Applicants notified on a rolling basis starting 6/1.

CONTACT
Carl Gordon, Director of Student Financial Aid
Box 20036, Houston, TX 77225
(713) 500-3860

University of Texas Health Science Center at San Antonio
San Antonio, Texas
www.uthscsa.edu   Federal Code: 003659

Upper-division public university and health science college in very large city.
Enrollment: 676 undergrads.

BASIC COSTS (2005-2006)
Tuition and fees: $3,260; out-of-state residents $11,540.
Additional info: Tuition and fees vary by program.

FINANCIAL AID PICTURE (2004-2005)
Students with need: 19% of average financial aid package awarded as scholarships/grants, 81% awarded as loans/jobs.
Additional info: Students strongly advised to provide parental information on need analysis form regardless of dependency status.

FINANCIAL AID PROCEDURES
Forms required: FAFSA, institutional form.
Dates and Deadlines: Priority date 3/15; no closing date. Applicants notified on a rolling basis.

CONTACT
Robert Lawson, Director of Student Financial Aid
7703 Floyd Curl Drive, San Antonio, TX 78229
(210) 567-2635

University of Texas Medical Branch at Galveston
Galveston, Texas
www.utmb.edu   Federal Code: 013976

Upper-division public health science and nursing college in small city.
Enrollment: 500 undergrads, 46% part-time.

BASIC COSTS (2005-2006)
Tuition and fees: $3,401; out-of-state residents $11,681.
Per-credit charge: $90; out-of-state residents $366.
Additional info: Required fees and tuition vary by program.

FINANCIAL AID PICTURE (2004-2005)
Students with need: 7% of average financial aid package awarded as scholarships/grants, 93% awarded as loans/jobs. Need-based aid available for part-time students. Work study available nights, weekends, and for part-time students.
Students without need: No-need awards available for academics, minority status, state/district residency.

FINANCIAL AID PROCEDURES
Forms required: FAFSA.
Dates and Deadlines: No deadline. Applicants notified on a rolling basis; must reply within 4 week(s) of notification.

CONTACT
Carl Gordon, Associate Director of Enrollment Services and University Financial Aid Officer
301 University Boulevard, Galveston, TX 77555-1305
(409) 772-1215

University of Texas of the Permian Basin
Odessa, Texas
www.utpb.edu   Federal Code: 009930

4-year public university in small city.
Enrollment: 2,621 undergrads.
Selectivity: Admits over 75% of applicants.

BASIC COSTS (2005-2006)
Tuition and fees: $4,147; out-of-state residents $12,427.
Per-credit charge: $109; out-of-state residents $385.
Room and board: $4,058.
Additional info: New Mexico residents pay $4,170 for full-year tuition or $139 per-credit-hour.

FINANCIAL AID PICTURE
Students with need: Need-based aid available for full-time and part-time students. Work study available nights, weekends, and for part-time students.
Students without need: No-need awards available for academics.

FINANCIAL AID PROCEDURES
Forms required: FAFSA, institutional form.
Dates and Deadlines: Priority date 5/1; no closing date. Applicants notified on a rolling basis starting 6/1; must reply within 2 week(s) of notification.

CONTACT
Robert Vasquez, Director of Financial Aid and Placement
4901 East University Boulevard, Odessa, TX 79762
(432) 552-2620

University of Texas Southwestern Medical Center at Dallas
Dallas, Texas
www.utsouthwestern.edu   Federal Code: 010019

Upper-division public university and health science college in very large city.
Enrollment: 116 undergrads, 16% part-time.

BASIC COSTS (2006-2007)
Tuition and fees: $3,810; out-of-state residents $12,150.
Per-credit charge: $100; out-of-state residents $378.

FINANCIAL AID PICTURE (2005-2006)
Students with need: Average financial aid package for all full-time undergraduates was $15,200; for part-time $12,700. 17% awarded as scholarships/grants, 83% awarded as loans/jobs. Work study available nights, weekends, and for part-time students.
Cumulative student debt: 71% of graduating class had student loans; average debt was $27,000.

FINANCIAL AID PROCEDURES
Dates and Deadlines: No deadline. Must reply within 2 week(s) of notification.

CONTACT
Charles Kettlewell, Registrar and Director of Financial Aid
5323 Harry Hines Boulevard, Dallas, TX 75390-9162
(214) 648-3611

University of Texas: Pan American
Edinburg, Texas
www.utpa.edu   Federal Code: 003599

4-year public university in small city.
Enrollment: 14,129 undergrads, 25% part-time. 1,602 full-time freshmen.

BASIC COSTS (2006-2007)
Tuition and fees: $4,160; out-of-state residents $12,410.
Room and board: $5,095.
Additional info: Mexican citizens may be eligible for in-state tuition rates.

FINANCIAL AID PICTURE (2004-2005)
Students with need: Out of 1,463 full-time freshmen who applied for aid, 1,390 were judged to have need. Of these, 1,377 received aid, and 55 had their full need met. Average financial aid package met 73% of need; average scholarship/grant was $6,958; average loan was $1,449. For part-time students, average financial aid package was $5,474.
Students without need: 96 full-time freshmen who did not demonstrate need for aid received scholarships/grants; average award was $4,602. No-need awards available for academics, alumni affiliation, art, athletics, leadership, music/drama, ROTC, state/district residency.
Cumulative student debt: 84% of graduating class had student loans; average debt was $12,453.

FINANCIAL AID PROCEDURES
Forms required: FAFSA.
Dates and Deadlines: Closing date 3/1. Applicants notified on a rolling basis starting 3/15; must reply within 2 week(s) of notification.

CONTACT
Michelle Alvarado, Director of Financial Services
1201 West University Drive, Edinburg, TX 78541-2999
(956) 381-2392

University of the Incarnate Word
San Antonio, Texas
www.uiw.edu   Federal Code: 003578

4-year private university and liberal arts college in very large city, affiliated with Roman Catholic Church.
Enrollment: 4,278 undergrads, 40% part-time. 573 full-time freshmen.
Selectivity: Admits over 75% of applicants.

BASIC COSTS (2006-2007)
Tuition and fees: $18,272.
Per-credit charge: $555.
Room and board: $6,475.
Additional info: Pharmacy annual tuition $25,500 and fees $500.

FINANCIAL AID PICTURE (2005-2006)
Students with need: Out of 542 full-time freshmen who applied for aid, 425 were judged to have need. Of these, 425 received aid, and 272 had their full need met. Average financial aid package met 68% of need; average scholarship/grant was $8,274; average loan was $2,838. For part-time students, average financial aid package was $9,850.
Students without need: 115 full-time freshmen who did not demonstrate need for aid received scholarships/grants; average award was $5,869. No-need awards available for academics, alumni affiliation, art, athletics, leadership, music/drama, religious affiliation, ROTC.
Scholarships offered: 19 full-time freshmen received athletic scholarships; average amount $12,533.
Cumulative student debt: 80% of graduating class had student loans; average debt was $23,383.
Additional info: Students encouraged to pursue outside scholarship programs.

FINANCIAL AID PROCEDURES
Forms required: FAFSA.
Dates and Deadlines: Priority date 1/1; no closing date. Applicants notified on a rolling basis starting 2/15; must reply within 2 week(s) of notification.

CONTACT
Amy Carcanagues, Director of Financial Assistance
4301 Broadway, San Antonio, TX 78209-6397
(210) 829-6008

Vernon College
Vernon, Texas
www.vernoncollege.edu   Federal Code: 010060

2-year public community and junior college in large town.
Enrollment: 2,803 undergrads.
Selectivity: Open admission; but selective for some programs.

BASIC COSTS (2005-2006)
Tuition and fees: $1,380; out-of-district residents $1,995; out-of-state residents $3,120.
Per-credit charge: $46; out-of-district residents $67; out-of-state residents $104.
Room and board: $3,036.

FINANCIAL AID PICTURE (2004-2005)
Students with need: 82% of average financial aid package awarded as scholarships/grants, 18% awarded as loans/jobs. Need-based aid available for part-time students. Work study available nights, weekends, and for part-time students.
Students without need: This college only awards aid to students with need.

FINANCIAL AID PROCEDURES
Forms required: FAFSA.
Dates and Deadlines: Priority date 7/1; no closing date. Applicants notified on a rolling basis starting 4/1.
Transfers: No deadline. Applicants notified on a rolling basis.

CONTACT
Melissa Elliot, Director of Financial Aid
4400 College Drive, Vernon, TX 76384
(940) 552-6291 ext. 2206

Wade College
Dallas, Texas
www.wadecollege.com   Federal Code: 010130

2-year for-profit junior college in very large city.
Enrollment: 230 undergrads.
Selectivity: Open admission.

BASIC COSTS (2005-2006)
Tuition and fees: $10,410.
Room only: $3,360.
Additional info: Tuition at time of enrollment locked for 2 years.

FINANCIAL AID PICTURE
Students with need: Need-based aid available for full-time and part-time students. Work study available nights, weekends, and for part-time students.
Students without need: This college only awards aid to students with need.

FINANCIAL AID PROCEDURES
Forms required: FAFSA.
Dates and Deadlines: No deadline. Applicants notified on a rolling basis; must reply within 4 week(s) of notification.

CONTACT
Lisa Hoover, Director of Financial Aid
Box 586343, Dallas, TX 75258
(214) 637-3530

Wayland Baptist University
Plainview, Texas
www.wbu.edu   Federal Code: 003663

4-year private university and liberal arts college in large town, affiliated with Southern Baptist Convention.
Enrollment: 937 undergrads, 10% part-time. 222 full-time freshmen.
Selectivity: Admits 50 to 75% of applicants.

BASIC COSTS (2006-2007)
Tuition and fees: $10,800.
Per-credit charge: $340.
Room and board: $3,584.

Texas Wayland Baptist University

FINANCIAL AID PICTURE (2005-2006)
Students with need: Out of 175 full-time freshmen who applied for aid, 146 were judged to have need. Of these, 146 received aid, and 30 had their full need met. Average financial aid package met 77% of need; average scholarship/grant was $7,632; average loan was $2,037. For part-time students, average financial aid package was $2,422.
Students without need: 48 full-time freshmen who did not demonstrate need for aid received scholarships/grants; average award was $8,192. No-need awards available for academics, alumni affiliation, art, athletics, job skills, leadership, minority status, music/drama, religious affiliation, state/district residency.
Scholarships offered: 9 full-time freshmen received athletic scholarships; average amount $7,855.
Cumulative student debt: 78% of graduating class had student loans; average debt was $13,972.

FINANCIAL AID PROCEDURES
Forms required: FAFSA, institutional form.
Dates and Deadlines: Priority date 5/1; no closing date. Applicants notified on a rolling basis starting 2/15; must reply within 4 week(s) of notification.

CONTACT
Karen LaQuey, Director of Financial Aid
1900 West Seventh Street, CMB #712, Plainview, TX 79072
(806) 291-3520

Weatherford College
Weatherford, Texas
www.wc.edu
Federal Code: 003664

2-year public community college in large town.
Enrollment: 4,552 undergrads.
Selectivity: Open admission; but selective for some programs.

BASIC COSTS (2005-2006)
Tuition and fees: $1,440; out-of-district residents $1,950; out-of-state residents $3,150.
Per-credit charge: $48; out-of-district residents $65; out-of-state residents $105.
Room and board: $6,715.

FINANCIAL AID PICTURE
Students with need: Work study available nights, weekends, and for part-time students.
Students without need: This college only awards aid to students with need.

FINANCIAL AID PROCEDURES
Forms required: FAFSA.
Dates and Deadlines: Priority date 7/3; no closing date. Applicants notified on a rolling basis; must reply within 2 week(s) of notification.

CONTACT
Kathy Bassham, Director of Student Financial Aid
225 College Park Drive, Weatherford, TX 76086
(817) 598-6295

West Texas A&M University
Canyon, Texas
www.wtamu.edu
Federal Code: 003665

4-year public university in large town.
Enrollment: 5,730 undergrads; 22% part-time. 813 full-time freshmen.
Selectivity: Admits 50 to 75% of applicants.

BASIC COSTS (2006-2007)
Tuition and fees: $4,314; out-of-state residents $12,564.
Per-credit charge: $120; out-of-state residents $382.
Room and board: $5,110.
Additional info: Out-of-district students from border counties pay in-state tuition. Tuition reduction plan available to students from border states.

FINANCIAL AID PICTURE (2004-2005)
Students with need: Out of 621 full-time freshmen who applied for aid, 458 were judged to have need. Of these, 447 received aid, and 445 had their full need met. Average financial aid package met 77% of need; average scholarship/grant was $4,562; average loan was $2,123. For part-time students, average financial aid package was $5,913.
Students without need: 146 full-time freshmen who did not demonstrate need for aid received scholarships/grants; average award was $3,236. No-need awards available for academics, art, athletics, leadership, music/drama, state/district residency.
Scholarships offered: 41 full-time freshmen received athletic scholarships; average amount $2,950.
Additional info: Scholarship deadline February 1.

FINANCIAL AID PROCEDURES
Forms required: FAFSA.
Dates and Deadlines: Priority date 4/15; no closing date. Applicants notified on a rolling basis starting 3/1; must reply within 2 week(s) of notification.
Transfers: No deadline. Applicants notified on a rolling basis; must reply within 2 week(s) of notification. Must provide financial aid transcripts through last semester of attendance. All academic transcripts must be on file.

CONTACT
Jim Reed, Director of Financial Aid
2501 Fourth Avenue, WTAMU Box 60907, Canyon, TX 79016-0001
(806) 651-2055

Western Technical College
El Paso, Texas
www.wtc-ep.edu
Federal Code: 014535

2-year for-profit technical college in very large city.
Enrollment: 435 undergrads.
Selectivity: Open admission; but selective for some programs.

BASIC COSTS (2005-2006)
Additional info: Tuition varies by program. Automotive: $18,150; refrigeration: $18,150; welding: $10,257; computer: $22,230; electronics: $18,525; medical assisting: $8,640; massage therapy: $3,600; health information: $11,115. Registration fee $100.

FINANCIAL AID PICTURE
Students with need: Need-based aid available for full-time and part-time students.
Students without need: This college only awards aid to students with need.

FINANCIAL AID PROCEDURES
Forms required: FAFSA.
Dates and Deadlines: No deadline. Applicants notified on a rolling basis.

CONTACT
Jennifer Phillips, Financial Aid Director
1000 Texas Avenue, El Paso, TX 79901
(915) 532-3737 ext. 105

Western Texas College
Snyder, Texas
www.wtc.edu Federal Code: 009549

2-year public community and junior college in large town.
Enrollment: 462 full-time undergrads.
Selectivity: Open admission; but selective for some programs.

BASIC COSTS (2006-2007)
Tuition and fees: $1,530; out-of-district residents $1,680; out-of-state residents $1,830.
Per-credit charge: $36; out-of-district residents $41; out-of-state residents $46.
Room and board: $3,900.

FINANCIAL AID PICTURE (2004-2005)
Students with need: Average financial aid package met 53% of need; average scholarship/grant was $2,000. Need-based aid available for part-time students.
Students without need: No-need awards available for academics, art, athletics, leadership, music/drama, state/district residency.

FINANCIAL AID PROCEDURES
Forms required: FAFSA, institutional form.
Dates and Deadlines: Priority date 7/1; no closing date. Applicants notified on a rolling basis starting 5/1; must reply within 2 week(s) of notification.

CONTACT
Kathy Hall, Director of Student Financial Aid
6200 College Avenue, Snyder, TX 79549
(325) 573-8511 ext. 309

Wharton County Junior College
Wharton, Texas
www.wcjc.edu Federal Code: 003668

2-year public junior college in small town.
Enrollment: 6,029 undergrads, 56% part-time. 1,031 full-time freshmen.
Selectivity: Open admission; but selective for some programs.

BASIC COSTS (2006-2007)
Tuition and fees: $1,620; out-of-district residents $2,700; out-of-state residents $3,660.
Per-credit charge: $32; out-of-state residents $64.
Room and board: $2,600.

FINANCIAL AID PICTURE
Students with need: Need-based aid available for full-time and part-time students.
Students without need: No-need awards available for academics, athletics.

FINANCIAL AID PROCEDURES
Forms required: FAFSA.
Dates and Deadlines: Closing date 6/1. Applicants notified on a rolling basis starting 8/1; must reply by 8/15.
Transfers: Closing date 7/1.

CONTACT
Richard Hyde, Director of Financial Aid
911 Boling Highway, Wharton, TX 77488-0080
(979) 532-4560 ext. 6345

Wiley College
Marshall, Texas
www.wileyc.edu Federal Code: 003669

4-year private liberal arts college in large town, affiliated with United Methodist Church.
Enrollment: 792 undergrads, 9% part-time. 155 full-time freshmen.
Selectivity: Open admission; but selective for some programs.

BASIC COSTS (2005-2006)
Tuition and fees: $7,334.
Room and board: $4,510.

FINANCIAL AID PICTURE (2004-2005)
Students with need: Out of 119 full-time freshmen who applied for aid, 117 were judged to have need. Of these, 117 received aid, and 56 had their full need met. Average financial aid package met 45% of need; average scholarship/grant was $4,652; average loan was $1,986. Need-based aid available for part-time students.
Students without need: This college only awards aid to students with need.

FINANCIAL AID PROCEDURES
Forms required: FAFSA, institutional form.
Dates and Deadlines: No deadline. Applicants notified on a rolling basis.

CONTACT
Cecila Jones, Assistant Director of Financial Aid
711 Wiley Avenue, Marshall, TX 75670
(903) 927-3353

Utah

Brigham Young University
Provo, Utah
www.byu.edu Federal Code: 003670

4-year private university in small city, affiliated with Church of Jesus Christ of Latter-day Saints.
Enrollment: 30,798 undergrads, 11% part-time. 5,809 full-time freshmen.
Selectivity: Admits over 75% of applicants.

BASIC COSTS (2006-2007)
Tuition and fees: $3,620.
Per-credit charge: $185.
Room and board: $5,640.
Additional info: Undergraduate 2-semester tuition $7240 for nonmembers of The Church of Jesus Christ of Latter-day Saints. Undergraduate per-credit-hour charge $371 for nonmembers.

FINANCIAL AID PICTURE (2004-2005)
Students with need: Out of 5,793 full-time freshmen who applied for aid, 1,353 were judged to have need. Of these, 1,178 received aid. Average financial aid package met 30% of need; average scholarship/grant was $1,756; average loan was $837. For part-time students, average financial aid package was $4,126.
Students without need: 2,073 full-time freshmen who did not demonstrate need for aid received scholarships/grants; average award was $2,762. No-need awards available for academics, art, athletics, leadership, minority status, music/drama, religious affiliation, ROTC, state/district residency.
Scholarships offered: 66 full-time freshmen received athletic scholarships; average amount $5,801.
Cumulative student debt: 35% of graduating class had student loans; average debt was $12,955.

FINANCIAL AID PROCEDURES
Forms required: FAFSA.
Dates and Deadlines: Closing date 6/30. Applicants notified on a rolling basis starting 4/1.
Transfers: Must provide financial aid transcript.

CONTACT
Paul Conrad, Director of Financial Aid
A-153 ASB, BYU, Provo, UT 84602
(801) 422-4104

College of Eastern Utah
Price, Utah
www.ceu.edu   Federal Code: 003676

2-year public community college in small town.
Enrollment: 1,811 undergrads.
Selectivity: Open admission; but selective for some programs.

BASIC COSTS (2005-2006)
Tuition and fees: $1,980; out-of-state residents $7,121.
Room and board: $3,268.

FINANCIAL AID PICTURE
Students with need: Need-based aid available for full-time and part-time students. Work study available nights, weekends, and for part-time students.
Students without need: No-need awards available for academics, art, athletics, leadership, minority status, music/drama, religious affiliation, state/district residency.

FINANCIAL AID PROCEDURES
Forms required: FAFSA, institutional form.
Dates and Deadlines: Priority date 2/1; no closing date. Applicants notified on a rolling basis starting 3/15; must reply within 2 week(s) of notification.

CONTACT
Bill Osborn, Financial Aid Director
451 East 400 North, Price, UT 84501
(435) 613-5207

Dixie State College of Utah
St. George, Utah
www.dixie.edu   Federal Code: 003671

2-year public community and technical college in small city.
Enrollment: 5,082 undergrads, 34% part-time. 1,175 full-time freshmen.
Selectivity: Open admission; but selective for some programs.

BASIC COSTS (2005-2006)
Tuition and fees: $1,984; out-of-state residents $7,390.
Room and board: $2,780.

FINANCIAL AID PICTURE (2005-2006)
Students with need: 55% of average financial aid package awarded as scholarships/grants, 45% awarded as loans/jobs. Work study available nights, weekends, and for part-time students.
Students without need: No-need awards available for academics, alumni affiliation, art, athletics, leadership, minority status, music/drama.

FINANCIAL AID PROCEDURES
Forms required: FAFSA.
Dates and Deadlines: Priority date 4/1; no closing date. Applicants notified on a rolling basis starting 5/1; must reply within 2 week(s) of notification.

CONTACT
Peggy Leavitt, Director of Financial Aid
225 South 700 East, St. George, UT 84770-3876
(435) 652-7575

Everest College: Salt Lake City
West Valley City, Utah
www.cci.edu   Federal Code: 022985

2-year for-profit business and junior college in small city.
Enrollment: 700 undergrads.

BASIC COSTS (2005-2006)
Tuition and fees: $12,675.
Per-credit charge: $280.

FINANCIAL AID PICTURE
Students with need: Need-based aid available for full-time and part-time students. Work study available nights.
Students without need: No-need awards available for academics.

FINANCIAL AID PROCEDURES
Forms required: FAFSA, institutional form.
Dates and Deadlines: No deadline. Applicants notified on a rolling basis.

CONTACT
Rachelle Rowan, Director of Financial Aid
3280 W 3500 S, West Valley City, UT 84119-2668
(801) 485-0221

LDS Business College
Salt Lake City, Utah
www.ldsbc.edu   Federal Code: 003672

2-year private business and junior college in small city, affiliated with Church of Jesus Christ of Latter-day Saints.
Enrollment: 1,252 undergrads.
Selectivity: Open admission.

BASIC COSTS (2006-2007)
Tuition and fees: $2,540.
Per-credit charge: $105.
Room only: $2,236.
Additional info: Students who are not members of The Church of Jesus Christ of Latter-day Saints pay tuition of $3,720 per academic year, $155 per-credit-hour.

FINANCIAL AID PICTURE (2004-2005)
Students with need: 2% of average financial aid package awarded as scholarships/grants, 98% awarded as loans/jobs. Need-based aid available for part-time students.
Students without need: No-need awards available for academics, leadership.
Scholarships offered: Service scholarships for The Church of Jesus Christ of Latter-day Saints missionaries who have returned from mission within past year. Covers half tuition for one semester.

FINANCIAL AID PROCEDURES
Forms required: FAFSA.
Dates and Deadlines: Priority date 7/1; no closing date. Applicants notified on a rolling basis starting 3/1; must reply within 3 week(s) of notification.

CONTACT
Doug Horne, Financial Aid Administrator
411 East South Temple, Salt Lake City, UT 84111-1392
(801) 524-8110

Salt Lake Community College
Salt Lake City, Utah
www.slcc.edu   Federal Code: 005220

2-year public community and technical college in very large city.
Enrollment: 22,527 undergrads, 65% part-time. 1,632 full-time freshmen.
Selectivity: Open admission; but selective for some programs.

BASIC COSTS (2005-2006)
Tuition and fees: $2,312; out-of-state residents $7,232.
Additional info: Tuition/fee waivers available for adults, minority students.

FINANCIAL AID PICTURE (2004-2005)
Students with need: 60% of average financial aid package awarded as scholarships/grants, 40% awarded as loans/jobs. Need-based aid available for part-time students. Work study available nights, weekends, and for part-time students.
Students without need: No-need awards available for academics, alumni affiliation, art, athletics, leadership, minority status, music/drama.

FINANCIAL AID PROCEDURES
Forms required: FAFSA, institutional form.
Dates and Deadlines: Priority date 5/1; no closing date. Applicants notified on a rolling basis starting 5/1; must reply within 4 week(s) of notification.

CONTACT
Cristi Easton, Director of Financial Aid
4600 South Redwood Road, Salt Lake City, UT 84130-0808
(801) 957-4410

Snow College
Ephraim, Utah
www.snow.edu   Federal Code: 003679

2-year public community and junior college in small town.
Enrollment: 3,333 undergrads.
Selectivity: Open admission.

BASIC COSTS (2005-2006)
Tuition and fees: $1,996; out-of-state residents $7,204.
Room and board: $3,000.

FINANCIAL AID PICTURE
Students with need: Need-based aid available for full-time students.
Students without need: No-need awards available for academics, athletics, state/district residency.

FINANCIAL AID PROCEDURES
Forms required: FAFSA, institutional form.
Dates and Deadlines: Priority date 3/1; closing date 7/15. Applicants notified on a rolling basis starting 8/1; must reply within 1 week(s) of notification.
Transfers: Priority date 3/15; closing date 6/15. F.A.T. required for midyear transfers.

CONTACT
Jack Dalene, Director of Financial Aid
150 East College Avenue, Ephraim, UT 84627
(435) 283-7132

Southern Utah University
Cedar City, Utah
www.suu.edu   Federal Code: 003678

4-year public university in large town.
Enrollment: 4,999 undergrads. 1,015 full-time freshmen.
Selectivity: Admits over 75% of applicants.

BASIC COSTS (2005-2006)
Tuition and fees: $3,358; out-of-state residents $9,878.
Room and board: $4,154.

FINANCIAL AID PICTURE (2004-2005)
Students with need: Average financial aid package met 70% of need; average scholarship/grant was $2,530; average loan was $2,966. For part-time students, average financial aid package was $1,688.
Students without need: 260 full-time freshmen who did not demonstrate need for aid received scholarships/grants; average award was $3,941. No-need awards available for academics, art, athletics, job skills, leadership, music/drama, state/district residency.
Scholarships offered: 27 full-time freshmen received athletic scholarships; average amount $3,852.
Cumulative student debt: 64% of graduating class had student loans; average debt was $11,239.

FINANCIAL AID PROCEDURES
Forms required: FAFSA, institutional form.
Dates and Deadlines: No deadline. Applicants notified on a rolling basis starting 2/1.

CONTACT
Paul Morris, Director of Financial Aid
351 West Center Street, Cedar City, UT 84720
(435) 586-7735

Stevens-Henager College: Murray
Salt Lake City, Utah
www.stevenshenager.edu

2-year for-profit business college in large town.
Enrollment: 400 undergrads.
Selectivity: Admits over 75% of applicants.

FINANCIAL AID PICTURE (2005-2006)
Students with need: 99% of average financial aid package awarded as scholarships/grants, 1% awarded as loans/jobs.
Additional info: Financial aid application must be completed prior to enrollment.

CONTACT
Rebecca Brown
838 West Vine Street, Salt Lake City, UT 84123
(800) 622-2640

University of Utah
Salt Lake City, Utah
www.utah.edu   Federal Code: 003675

4-year public university in large city.
Enrollment: 21,695 undergrads, 29% part-time. 2,427 full-time freshmen.
Selectivity: Admits over 75% of applicants.

BASIC COSTS (2005-2006)
Tuition and fees: $4,299; out-of-state residents $13,372.
Room and board: $5,678.

FINANCIAL AID PICTURE (2005-2006)
Students with need: Out of 1,301 full-time freshmen who applied for aid, 715 were judged to have need. Of these, 705 received aid, and 115 had their full need met. Average financial aid package met 47% of need; average scholarship/grant was $4,414; average loan was $2,903. For part-time students, average financial aid package was $6,395.
Students without need: 247 full-time freshmen who did not demonstrate need for aid received scholarships/grants; average award was $2,819. No-

need awards available for academics, art, athletics, leadership, minority status, music/drama, ROTC, state/district residency.
Scholarships offered: 4 full-time freshmen received athletic scholarships; average amount $13,735.
Cumulative student debt: 45% of graduating class had student loans; average debt was $12,806.

FINANCIAL AID PROCEDURES
Forms required: FAFSA, institutional form.
Dates and Deadlines: Priority date 3/15; no closing date. Applicants notified on a rolling basis starting 4/15; must reply within 6 week(s) of notification.

CONTACT
Karen Henriquez, Associate Director of Financial Aid
201 South 1460 East Room 250S, Salt Lake City, UT 84112-9057
(801) 581-6211

Utah Career College
West Jordan, Utah
www.utahcollege.edu   Federal Code: 011166

2-year for-profit technical college in small city.
Enrollment: 505 undergrads, 74% part-time. 25 full-time freshmen.
Selectivity: Open admission.

BASIC COSTS (2005-2006)
Additional info: Books and fees range from $300 to $400 per quarter.

FINANCIAL AID PICTURE (2004-2005)
Students with need: 30% of average financial aid package awarded as scholarships/grants, 70% awarded as loans/jobs. Need-based aid available for part-time students.
Students without need: This college only awards aid to students with need.

FINANCIAL AID PROCEDURES
Forms required: FAFSA, institutional form.
Dates and Deadlines: No deadline. Applicants notified on a rolling basis starting 7/1; must reply within 2 week(s) of notification.

CONTACT
Elisha Goaddard, Director of Financial Aid
1902 West 7800 South, West Jordan, UT 84088
(801) 304-4224

Utah State University
Logan, Utah
www.usu.edu   Federal Code: 003677

4-year public university in small city.
Enrollment: 12,530 undergrads, 16% part-time. 1,906 full-time freshmen.

BASIC COSTS (2005-2006)
Tuition and fees: $3,672; out-of-state residents $10,616.
Room and board: $4,330.

FINANCIAL AID PICTURE
Students with need: Need-based aid available for full-time and part-time students. Work study available nights, weekends, and for part-time students.
Students without need: This college only awards aid to students with need.

FINANCIAL AID PROCEDURES
Forms required: FAFSA, institutional form.
Dates and Deadlines: No deadline. Applicants notified on a rolling basis starting 4/1; must reply within 4 week(s) of notification.

CONTACT
Judy Lecheminant, Director of Financial Aid
0160 Old Main Hill, Logan, UT 84322-0160
(435) 797-0173

Utah Valley State College
Orem, Utah
www.uvsc.edu   Federal Code: 004027

4-year public university and technical college in small city.
Enrollment: 19,331 undergrads, 43% part-time. 2,328 full-time freshmen.
Selectivity: Open admission.

BASIC COSTS (2005-2006)
Tuition and fees: $3,022; out-of-state residents $9,472.

FINANCIAL AID PICTURE (2005-2006)
Students with need: Average financial aid package met 54% of need; average scholarship/grant was $2,889; average loan was $2,123. For part-time students, average financial aid package was $4,474.
Students without need: No-need awards available for academics, alumni affiliation, art, athletics, leadership, minority status, music/drama.
Cumulative student debt: 28% of graduating class had student loans; average debt was $6,273.

FINANCIAL AID PROCEDURES
Forms required: FAFSA, institutional form.
Dates and Deadlines: Priority date 5/1; no closing date. Applicants notified on a rolling basis starting 1/1; must reply within 2 week(s) of notification.

CONTACT
Michael Francis, Assistant Vice President for Business Services
800 West University Parkway, Orem, UT 84058-5999
(801) 863-8442

Weber State University
Ogden, Utah
www.weber.edu   Federal Code: 003680

4-year public university in small city.
Enrollment: 17,688 undergrads, 42% part-time. 2,233 full-time freshmen.
Selectivity: Open admission; but selective for some programs.

BASIC COSTS (2005-2006)
Tuition and fees: $3,138; out-of-state residents $9,599.
Room and board: $6,400.

FINANCIAL AID PICTURE (2004-2005)
Students with need: Out of 1,041 full-time freshmen who applied for aid, 863 were judged to have need. Of these, 477 received aid, and 50 had their full need met. Average financial aid package met 54% of need; average scholarship/grant was $2,865; average loan was $1,841. For part-time students, average financial aid package was $3,711.
Students without need: This college only awards aid to students with need.

FINANCIAL AID PROCEDURES
Forms required: FAFSA, institutional form.
Dates and Deadlines: Priority date 3/1; no closing date. Applicants notified on a rolling basis starting 3/15; must reply within 2 week(s) of notification.

CONTACT
Tula Paras, Associate Director of Financial Aid
1137 University Circle, Ogden, UT 84408-1137
(801) 626-7569

Westminster College
Salt Lake City, Utah
www.westminstercollege.edu   Federal Code: 003681

4-year private liberal arts college in large city.
Enrollment: 1,842 undergrads, 11% part-time. 341 full-time freshmen.
Selectivity: Admits over 75% of applicants.

BASIC COSTS (2006-2007)
Tuition and fees: $21,030.
Per-credit charge: $860.
Room and board: $6,140.

FINANCIAL AID PICTURE (2005-2006)
Students with need: Out of 271 full-time freshmen who applied for aid, 221 were judged to have need. Of these, 221 received aid, and 113 had their full need met. Average financial aid package met 91% of need; average scholarship/grant was $11,241; average loan was $3,397. For part-time students, average financial aid package was $11,250.
Students without need: 113 full-time freshmen who did not demonstrate need for aid received scholarships/grants; average award was $8,946. No-need awards available for academics, alumni affiliation, art, athletics, leadership, minority status, music/drama, religious affiliation.
Scholarships offered: 4 full-time freshmen received athletic scholarships; average amount $4,250.
Cumulative student debt: 64% of graduating class had student loans; average debt was $16,450.

FINANCIAL AID PROCEDURES
Forms required: FAFSA.
Dates and Deadlines: Priority date 4/15; no closing date. Applicants notified on a rolling basis starting 3/15; must reply within 3 week(s) of notification.

CONTACT
Ruth Henneman, Director of Financial Aid
1840 South 1300 East, Salt Lake City, UT 84105
(801) 832-2500

Vermont

Bennington College
Bennington, Vermont
www.bennington.edu   Federal Code: 003682
                      CSS Code: 3080

4-year private liberal arts college in large town.
Enrollment: 571 undergrads, 1% part-time. 137 full-time freshmen.
Selectivity: Admits 50 to 75% of applicants.

BASIC COSTS (2006-2007)
Tuition and fees: $35,250.
Room and board: $8,730.

FINANCIAL AID PICTURE (2005-2006)
Students with need: Out of 98 full-time freshmen who applied for aid, 91 were judged to have need. Of these, 91 received aid, and 4 had their full need met. Average financial aid package met 75% of need; average scholarship/grant was $21,211; average loan was $2,281. For part-time students, average financial aid package was $11,678.
Students without need: 3 full-time freshmen who did not demonstrate need for aid received scholarships/grants; average award was $7,325. No-need awards available for academics.
Cumulative student debt: 72% of graduating class had student loans; average debt was $20,340.
Additional info: All applicants for undergraduate admission will be considered for scholarships based on the quality of their overall application.

FINANCIAL AID PROCEDURES
Forms required: FAFSA, institutional form. CSS profile required of early decision applicants only.
Dates and Deadlines: Priority date 3/1; no closing date. Applicants notified by 3/30; must reply by 5/1 or within 2 week(s) of notification.
Transfers: Priority date 3/15; closing date 8/1. Applicants notified on a rolling basis starting 5/1; must reply by 6/1 or within 2 week(s) of notification.

CONTACT
Ken Himmelman, Dean of Admissions and Financial Aid
One College Drive, Bennington, VT 05201-6003
(802) 440-4325

Burlington College
Burlington, Vermont
www.burlingtoncollege.edu   Federal Code: 012183

4-year private liberal arts college in small city.
Enrollment: 188 undergrads.

BASIC COSTS (2006-2007)
Tuition and fees: $15,600.
Per-credit charge: $515.
Room only: $5,500.

FINANCIAL AID PICTURE
Students with need: Need-based aid available for full-time and part-time students. Work study available nights, weekends, and for part-time students.
Students without need: This college only awards aid to students with need.

FINANCIAL AID PROCEDURES
Forms required: FAFSA.
Dates and Deadlines: Priority date 6/1; closing date 8/1. Applicants notified on a rolling basis starting 4/1.
Transfers: No deadline.

CONTACT
Karan Lapan, Financial Aid Adviser
95 North Avenue, Burlington, VT 05401
(802) 862-9610

Castleton State College
Castleton, Vermont
www.castleton.edu   Federal Code: 003683

4-year public liberal arts college in small town.
Enrollment: 1,840 undergrads, 9% part-time. 460 full-time freshmen.
Selectivity: Admits over 75% of applicants.

BASIC COSTS (2005-2006)
Tuition and fees: $6,484; out-of-state residents $13,804.
Per-credit charge: $263; out-of-state residents $568.
Room and board: $6,674.
Additional info: New England Board of Higher Education rate for students from other New England states: 150% of Vermont resident tuition.

FINANCIAL AID PICTURE
Students with need: Need-based aid available for full-time and part-time students.
Students without need: No-need awards available for academics, alumni affiliation, art, leadership, music/drama, state/district residency.

FINANCIAL AID PROCEDURES
Forms required: FAFSA.

Vermont — Castleton State College

Dates and Deadlines: Priority date 2/15; no closing date. Applicants notified on a rolling basis starting 1/1; must reply by 5/1 or within 2 week(s) of notification.

CONTACT
Kathy O'Meara, Financial Aid Director
Seminary Street, Castleton, VT 05735
(802) 468-1286

Champlain College
Burlington, Vermont
www.champlain.edu   Federal Code: 003684

4-year private business and liberal arts college in small city.
Enrollment: 2,296 undergrads, 23% part-time. 392 full-time freshmen.
Selectivity: Admits 50 to 75% of applicants.

BASIC COSTS (2006-2007)
Tuition and fees: $16,250.
Per-credit charge: $440.
Room and board: $10,125.

FINANCIAL AID PICTURE (2004-2005)
Students with need: Out of 361 full-time freshmen who applied for aid, 268 were judged to have need. Of these, 257 received aid, and 49 had their full need met. Average financial aid package met 58% of need; average scholarship/grant was $4,869; average loan was $4,886. For part-time students, average financial aid package was $6,683.
Students without need: 90 full-time freshmen who did not demonstrate need for aid received scholarships/grants; average award was $10,544. No-need awards available for academics, leadership.
Scholarships offered: Competitive, non-need-based academic/community service scholarships; application deadline is Jan. 15.

FINANCIAL AID PROCEDURES
Forms required: FAFSA, state aid form, institutional form.
Dates and Deadlines: Closing date 5/1. Applicants notified on a rolling basis starting 3/1; must reply within 2 week(s) of notification.

CONTACT
David Myette, Director of Financial Aid
163 South Willard Street, Burlington, VT 05402-0670
(802) 860-2730

College of St. Joseph in Vermont
Rutland, Vermont
www.csj.edu   Federal Code: 003685

4-year private liberal arts and teachers college in large town, affiliated with Roman Catholic Church.
Enrollment: 236 undergrads, 26% part-time. 43 full-time freshmen.
Selectivity: Admits 50 to 75% of applicants.

BASIC COSTS (2006-2007)
Tuition and fees: $14,900.
Room and board: $7,150.

FINANCIAL AID PICTURE (2005-2006)
Students with need: Out of 42 full-time freshmen who applied for aid, 36 were judged to have need. Of these, 36 received aid, and 11 had their full need met. Average financial aid package met 84% of need; average scholarship/grant was $10,748; average loan was $3,920. For part-time students, average financial aid package was $5,211.
Students without need: 5 full-time freshmen who did not demonstrate need for aid received scholarships/grants; average award was $12,995. No-need awards available for academics, athletics.
Cumulative student debt: 80% of graduating class had student loans; average debt was $24,633.
Additional info: Instructors at local Catholic schools are granted a tuition reduction.

FINANCIAL AID PROCEDURES
Forms required: FAFSA, institutional form.
Dates and Deadlines: Priority date 3/1; no closing date. Applicants notified on a rolling basis starting 3/15.

CONTACT
Yvonne Payrits, Financial Aid Director
71 Clement Road, Rutland, VT 05701-3899
(802) 773-5900 ext. 3218

Community College of Vermont
Waterbury, Vermont
www.ccv.edu   Federal Code: 011167

2-year public community college in small town.
Enrollment: 3,909 undergrads.
Selectivity: Open admission.

BASIC COSTS (2005-2006)
Tuition and fees: $4,990; out-of-state residents $9,880.
Per-credit charge: $163; out-of-state residents $326.
Additional info: New England Board of Higher Education rate for students from other New England states: 150% of Vermont resident tuition. Available to degree candidates in academic areas not offered by educational institutions in their home states.

FINANCIAL AID PICTURE
Students with need: Need-based aid available for full-time and part-time students. Work study available nights.
Students without need: This college only awards aid to students with need.

FINANCIAL AID PROCEDURES
Forms required: FAFSA, state aid form, institutional form.
Dates and Deadlines: No deadline. Applicants notified on a rolling basis starting 9/1; must reply within 3 week(s) of notification.

CONTACT
Pam Chisholm, Director for Financial Aid
103 South Main Street, Waterbury, VT 05676-0120
(802) 241-3535

Goddard College
Plainfield, Vermont
www.goddard.edu   Federal Code: 003686

4-year private liberal arts college in rural community.
Enrollment: 159 undergrads. 7 full-time freshmen.
Selectivity: Open admission; but selective for some programs.

FINANCIAL AID PICTURE (2005-2006)
Students with need: Average financial aid package met 37% of need; average scholarship/grant was $5,400; average loan was $2,177. For part-time students, average financial aid package was $5,751.
Students without need: No-need awards available for academics, art, job skills, leadership, music/drama, state/district residency.
Cumulative student debt: 84% of graduating class had student loans; average debt was $21,591.

FINANCIAL AID PROCEDURES
Forms required: FAFSA.

Dates and Deadlines: Applicants notified on a rolling basis starting 4/15; must reply within 4 week(s) of notification.

CONTACT
Beverly Jene, Director of Financial Aid
123 Pitkin Road, Plainfield, VT 05667
(802) 454-8311

Green Mountain College
Poultney, Vermont
www.greenmtn.edu
Federal Code: 003687
CSS Code: 3418

4-year private liberal arts college in small town, affiliated with United Methodist Church.
Enrollment: 684 undergrads, 4% part-time. 253 full-time freshmen.
Selectivity: Admits over 75% of applicants.

BASIC COSTS (2006-2007)
Tuition and fees: $23,322.
Per-credit charge: $756.
Room and board: $8,426.

FINANCIAL AID PICTURE (2005-2006)
Students with need: Average financial aid package met 80% of need; average scholarship/grant was $14,444; average loan was $4,492. For part-time students, average financial aid package was $9,545.
Students without need: No-need awards available for academics, art, leadership, music/drama, religious affiliation.
Scholarships offered: Scholarships for art, performing arts, environmental service, leadership, service; ranging from $500-$5,000, renewable annually.
Cumulative student debt: 95% of graduating class had student loans; average debt was $23,894.
Additional info: Service/recognition awards available to all students.

FINANCIAL AID PROCEDURES
Forms required: FAFSA. CSS Profile is recommended and is optional to receive an earlier financial aid package.
Dates and Deadlines: Priority date 3/1; no closing date. Applicants notified on a rolling basis starting 1/1; must reply by 5/1 or within 4 week(s) of notification.
Transfers: Applicants notified on a rolling basis; must reply by 5/1 or within 4 week(s) of notification.

CONTACT
Wendy Ellis, Director of Financial Aid
One College Circle, Poultney, VT 05764
(802) 287-8210

Johnson State College
Johnson, Vermont
www.jsc.vsc.edu
Federal Code: 003688

4-year public liberal arts college in small town.
Enrollment: 1,452 undergrads, 30% part-time. 241 full-time freshmen.
Selectivity: Admits over 75% of applicants.

BASIC COSTS (2005-2006)
Tuition and fees: $6,484; out-of-state residents $13,804.
Per-credit charge: $263; out-of-state residents $568.
Room and board: $6,674.
Additional info: New England Board of Higher Education rate for students from other New England states: 150% of Vermont resident tuition. Available to degree candidates in academic areas not offered by educational institutions in their home states.

FINANCIAL AID PICTURE (2004-2005)
Students with need: 10% of average financial aid package awarded as scholarships/grants, 90% awarded as loans/jobs. Need-based aid available for part-time students.
Students without need: No-need awards available for academics.

FINANCIAL AID PROCEDURES
Forms required: FAFSA, state aid form.
Dates and Deadlines: Priority date 3/1; no closing date. Applicants notified on a rolling basis starting 4/1; must reply within 3 week(s) of notification.
Transfers: Financial aid transcripts from previously attended colleges required.

CONTACT
Penny Howrigan, Associate Dean of Enrollment Services
337 College Hill, Johnson, VT 05656
(800) 635-2356

Landmark College
Putney, Vermont
www.landmark.edu
Federal Code: 017157

2-year private liberal arts college in small town.
Enrollment: 371 undergrads, 37% part-time. 61 full-time freshmen.
Selectivity: Admits 50 to 75% of applicants.

BASIC COSTS (2006-2007)
Tuition and fees: $39,270.
Room and board: $7,200.
Additional info: Notebook computer and software required. Cost through school $1,850.

FINANCIAL AID PICTURE (2005-2006)
Students with need: Average financial aid package for all full-time undergraduates was $16,400. 61% awarded as scholarships/grants, 39% awarded as loans/jobs. Need-based aid available for part-time students. Work study available nights, weekends, and for part-time students.
Students without need: This college only awards aid to students with need.
Cumulative student debt: 35% of graduating class had student loans; average debt was $10,200.
Additional info: Students encouraged to apply to their state departments of vocational rehabilitation for additional financial assistance.

FINANCIAL AID PROCEDURES
Forms required: FAFSA, institutional form.
Dates and Deadlines: Priority date 3/30; no closing date. Applicants notified on a rolling basis starting 4/30; must reply within 2 week(s) of notification.

CONTACT
Cathy Mullins, Director of Financial Aid
River Road South, Putney, VT 05346
(802) 387-6736

Lyndon State College
Lyndonville, Vermont
www.lyndonstate.edu
Federal Code: 003689

4-year public liberal arts and teachers college in small town.
Enrollment: 1,273 undergrads, 10% part-time. 326 full-time freshmen.
Selectivity: Admits over 75% of applicants.

BASIC COSTS (2005-2006)
Tuition and fees: $6,484; out-of-state residents $13,804.
Per-credit charge: $263; out-of-state residents $568.
Room and board: $6,674.

Additional info: New England Board of Higher Education rate for students from other New England states: 150% of Vermont resident tuition. Available to degree candidates in academic areas not offered by educational institutions in their home states.

FINANCIAL AID PICTURE
Students with need: Need-based aid available for full-time and part-time students. Work study available nights, weekends, and for part-time students.
Students without need: No-need awards available for academics, leadership.

FINANCIAL AID PROCEDURES
Forms required: FAFSA.
Dates and Deadlines: Priority date 2/1; no closing date. Applicants notified on a rolling basis starting 4/1; must reply within 2 week(s) of notification.

CONTACT
Tanya Bradley, Director of Financial Aid
1001 College Road, Lyndonville, VT 05851
(802) 626-6218

Marlboro College
Marlboro, Vermont
www.marlboro.edu   Federal Code: 003690

4-year private liberal arts college in rural community.
Enrollment: 340 undergrads, 4% part-time. 79 full-time freshmen.
Selectivity: Admits 50 to 75% of applicants.

BASIC COSTS (2006-2007)
Tuition and fees: $29,240.
Per-credit charge: $945.
Room and board: $8,600.

FINANCIAL AID PICTURE (2005-2006)
Students with need: Out of 63 full-time freshmen who applied for aid, 50 were judged to have need. Of these, 50 received aid. Average financial aid package met 80% of need; average scholarship/grant was $9,940; average loan was $3,542. Need-based aid available for part-time students.
Students without need: 5 full-time freshmen who did not demonstrate need for aid received scholarships/grants; average award was $10,000. No-need awards available for academics, art, leadership, music/drama.
Scholarships offered: 50th Anniversary and Presidential Scholarships: based upon academic record, writing skills, demonstrated leadership ability, interviews and standardized test scores.
Cumulative student debt: 80% of graduating class had student loans; average debt was $18,404.

FINANCIAL AID PROCEDURES
Forms required: FAFSA.
Dates and Deadlines: Priority date 3/1; no closing date. Applicants notified on a rolling basis starting 2/15; must reply by 5/1 or within 2 week(s) of notification.

CONTACT
Alan Young, Dean of Enrollment and Financial Aid
PO Box A, Marlboro, VT 05344-0300
(802) 258-9237

Middlebury College
Middlebury, Vermont
www.middlebury.edu   Federal Code: 003691
                      CSS Code: 3526

4-year private liberal arts college in small town.
Enrollment: 2,415 undergrads, 1% part-time. 553 full-time freshmen.
Selectivity: Admits less than 50% of applicants.

BASIC COSTS (2006-2007)
Comprehensive fee: $44,330.

FINANCIAL AID PICTURE (2004-2005)
Students with need: Out of 318 full-time freshmen who applied for aid, 257 were judged to have need. Of these, 257 received aid, and 257 had their full need met. Average financial aid package met 100% of need; average scholarship/grant was $24,002; average loan was $3,411. Need-based aid available for part-time students.
Students without need: This college only awards aid to students with need.
Additional info: College maintains need-blind admissions policy and meets full demonstrated financial need of students who qualify for admission, to degree resources permit.

FINANCIAL AID PROCEDURES
Forms required: FAFSA, CSS PROFILE, institutional form.
Dates and Deadlines: Priority date 11/15; closing date 1/1. Applicants notified by 4/1; must reply by 5/1.
Transfers: Closing date 3/1. Applicants notified by 4/15.

CONTACT
Kim Downs, Director of Student Financial Services
The Emma Willard House, Middlebury, VT 05753-6002
(802) 443-5158

New England Culinary Institute
Montpelier, Vermont
www.neci.edu   Federal Code: 022540

2-year for-profit culinary school in large town.
Enrollment: 525 undergrads.

BASIC COSTS (2005-2006)
Tuition and fees: $24,050.
Room and board: $6,415.
Additional info: Costs will vary with program.

FINANCIAL AID PICTURE
Students with need: Need-based aid available for full-time students. Work study available nights, weekends, and for part-time students.
Scholarships offered: Second Generation Scholarship: $1,000 awarded to students recommended by alumni. James Beard Foundation: $1,000 - $2,000 awarded. Massachusetts Restaurant Association: up to $2,500 awarded. National Restaurant Association: up to $2,000 awarded.

FINANCIAL AID PROCEDURES
Forms required: FAFSA.
Dates and Deadlines: No deadline. Applicants notified on a rolling basis.

CONTACT
Richard Goodwin, Chief Financial Officer
250 Main Street, Montpelier, VT 05602
(802) 223-6324

Norwich University
Northfield, Vermont
www.norwich.edu   Federal Code: 003692
                   CSS Code: 3669

4-year private university and military college in small town.
Enrollment: 1,900 undergrads.
Selectivity: Admits 50 to 75% of applicants.

BASIC COSTS (2006-2007)
Tuition and fees: $21,831.
Per-credit charge: $500.
Room and board: $7,964.

Additional info: Military students pay an additional $1,380 per year for cadet uniform for first and second years.

FINANCIAL AID PICTURE
Students with need: Need-based aid available for full-time and part-time students.
Students without need: No-need awards available for academics, leadership, music/drama, ROTC.
Additional info: Winners of ROTC scholarships receive full room and board; must maintain 2.75 GPA. Renewable up to 4 years.

FINANCIAL AID PROCEDURES
Forms required: FAFSA, CSS PROFILE, institutional form.
Dates and Deadlines: Priority date 3/1; no closing date. Applicants notified on a rolling basis starting 12/15.

CONTACT
Karen McGrath, Dean of Enrollment Management
158 Harmon Drive, Northfield, VT 05663
(802) 485-2015

St. Michael's College
Colchester, Vermont
www.smcvt.edu   Federal Code: 003694

4-year private liberal arts college in large town, affiliated with Roman Catholic Church.
Enrollment: 1,950 undergrads, 1% part-time. 592 full-time freshmen.
Selectivity: Admits 50 to 75% of applicants.

BASIC COSTS (2006-2007)
Tuition and fees: $28,515.
Per-credit charge: $945.
Room and board: $6,990.

FINANCIAL AID PICTURE (2005-2006)
Students with need: Out of 494 full-time freshmen who applied for aid, 411 were judged to have need. Of these, 411 received aid, and 157 had their full need met. Average financial aid package met 88% of need; average scholarship/grant was $14,611; average loan was $3,809. Need-based aid available for part-time students.
Students without need: 88 full-time freshmen who did not demonstrate need for aid received scholarships/grants; average award was $8,952. No-need awards available for academics, athletics, ROTC.
Scholarships offered: *Merit:* Dean's Scholarship; $12,500, renewable annually for four years; based on combined SAT score of 1200 (exclusive of writing,) 3.5 GPA in a college prep program, other factors such as leadership and community service considered. Presidential Scholarships; up to $25,000 renewable annualy for four years; requires Vermont residency; 4 awarded. Book awards based on community service; up to $25,000 renewable annualy for four years; essay required. *Athletic:* 3 full-time freshmen received athletic scholarships; average amount $22,220.
Cumulative student debt: 72% of graduating class had student loans; average debt was $20,706.

FINANCIAL AID PROCEDURES
Forms required: FAFSA. CSS Profile should be submitted by students who apply for early action and wish early estimate on aid.
Dates and Deadlines: Closing date 3/15. Applicants notified on a rolling basis starting 4/1; must reply by 5/1 or within 2 week(s) of notification.

CONTACT
Nelberta Lunde, Director of Financial Aid
One Winooski Park, Colchester, VT 05439
(802) 654-3243

Southern Vermont College
Bennington, Vermont
www.svc.edu   Federal Code: 003693

4-year private liberal arts college in large town.
Enrollment: 387 undergrads, 17% part-time. 71 full-time freshmen.
Selectivity: Admits 50 to 75% of applicants.

BASIC COSTS (2006-2007)
Tuition and fees: $15,100.
Per-credit charge: $420.
Room and board: $7,350.
Additional info: Health insurance, if applicable, $450/semester.

FINANCIAL AID PICTURE (2004-2005)
Students with need: 31% of average financial aid package awarded as scholarships/grants, 69% awarded as loans/jobs. Need-based aid available for part-time students. Work study available nights, weekends, and for part-time students.
Students without need: No-need awards available for academics, leadership.
Scholarships offered: Everett Scholarship; based on academic merit; from $1,000-$5,000; deadline March 1, renewable. Leadership Scholarships and Presidential Scholarships; awarded to 5 first-time freshmen; $2,000; renewable annually.
Additional info: Financial aid provided through Vermont Student Assistance Corporation (VSAC).

FINANCIAL AID PROCEDURES
Forms required: FAFSA, state aid form, institutional form.
Dates and Deadlines: Priority date 5/1; no closing date. Applicants notified on a rolling basis starting 3/1; must reply by 5/1 or within 2 week(s) of notification.
Transfers: $1,000 need-based transfer scholarship available for each transfer.

CONTACT
Yvonne Whitaker, Director of Financial Aid Services
982 Mansion Drive, Bennington, VT 05201
(877) 563-6076

Sterling College
Craftsbury Common, Vermont
www.sterlingcollege.edu   Federal Code: 014991

4-year private agricultural and liberal arts college in rural community.
Enrollment: 97 undergrads, 7% part-time. 18 full-time freshmen.
Selectivity: Admits 50 to 75% of applicants.

BASIC COSTS (2006-2007)
Tuition and fees: $17,780.
Per-credit charge: $545.
Room and board: $6,520.
Additional info: Students receive $1,400 tuition and book credit in exchange for work done on campus.

FINANCIAL AID PICTURE (2004-2005)
Students with need: Out of 17 full-time freshmen who applied for aid, 14 were judged to have need. Of these, 14 received aid. Average financial aid package met 77% of need; average scholarship/grant was $9,255; average loan was $2,625. For part-time students, average financial aid package was $6,721.
Students without need: 2 full-time freshmen who did not demonstrate need for aid received scholarships/grants; average award was $1,000. No-need awards available for academics, leadership, state/district residency.
Scholarships offered: Achievement Scholarships: $700-$1,200; demonstration of a significant life achievement. Vermont Scholarship: $1,000-$2,000;

applicants who live in the state of Vermont. Bounder Scholarship: $30-$500; applicants who live west of the Mississippi or in the Deep South. Presidential Scholarship: $500-$5,000; applicants who have performed well academically, pursued some degree of activity in environmental, outdoor leadership, or resource management. SCA Award: $1,000; alumni of Student Conservation Association. Transfer Award: $1,000; transfer students for transfer costs. Environmental Steward Scholarship: full-tuition; awarded to a student who has displayed an exceptional commitment to the environment. Vermont Youth Conservation Corps Award: $1,000; awarded to alumni of the VYCC.
Cumulative student debt: 57% of graduating class had student loans; average debt was $28,251.

FINANCIAL AID PROCEDURES
Forms required: FAFSA, state aid form, institutional form.
Dates and Deadlines: Priority date 3/15; no closing date. Applicants notified on a rolling basis starting 2/1; must reply by 5/1 or within 2 week(s) of notification.

CONTACT
Edward Houston, Director of Financial Aid
PO Box 72, Craftsbury Common, VT 05827-0072
(800) 648-3591

University of Vermont
Burlington, Vermont
www.uvm.edu
Federal Code: 003696

4-year public university in large town.
Enrollment: 8,784 undergrads, 4% part-time. 1,953 full-time freshmen.
Selectivity: Admits over 75% of applicants.

BASIC COSTS (2005-2006)
Tuition and fees: $10,748; out-of-state residents $24,934.
Per-credit charge: $394; out-of-state residents $985.
Room and board: $7,321.
Additional info: Additional $24 fee for on-campus students.

FINANCIAL AID PICTURE (2004-2005)
Students with need: Out of 1,395 full-time freshmen who applied for aid, 1,102 were judged to have need. Of these, 1,094 received aid, and 1,074 had their full need met. Average financial aid package met 87% of need; average scholarship/grant was $12,913; average loan was $5,455. For part-time students, average financial aid package was $8,410.
Students without need: 302 full-time freshmen who did not demonstrate need for aid received scholarships/grants; average award was $2,684. No-need awards available for academics, art, athletics, ROTC.
Scholarships offered: 30 full-time freshmen received athletic scholarships; average amount $15,990.
Cumulative student debt: 66% of graduating class had student loans; average debt was $21,723.

FINANCIAL AID PROCEDURES
Forms required: FAFSA.
Dates and Deadlines: Priority date 2/10; no closing date. Applicants notified on a rolling basis starting 3/15; must reply within 4 week(s) of notification.

CONTACT
Cecilia Dry, Assistant Controller
194 South Prospect Street, Burlington, VT 05401-3596
(802) 656-5700

Vermont Technical College
Randolph Center, Vermont
www.vtc.edu
Federal Code: 003698

4-year public agricultural and engineering college in small town.
Enrollment: 1,216 undergrads, 15% part-time. 239 full-time freshmen.
Selectivity: Admits 50 to 75% of applicants.

BASIC COSTS (2005-2006)
Tuition and fees: $7,852; out-of-state residents $14,812.
Per-credit charge: $320; out-of-state residents $610.
Room and board: $6,674.
Additional info: New England Board of Higher Education rate for students from other New England states: 150% of Vermont resident tuition. Available to degree candidates in academic areas not offered by educational institutions in their home states. Dental Hygiene program: $9624/$24,096 in-state/out-of-state per year. LPN program: $10,560/$20,130 in-state/out-of-state per year.

FINANCIAL AID PICTURE (2004-2005)
Students with need: Out of 212 full-time freshmen who applied for aid, 180 were judged to have need. Of these, 179 received aid, and 24 had their full need met. Average financial aid package met 68% of need; average scholarship/grant was $4,104; average loan was $2,856. For part-time students, average financial aid package was $7,340.
Students without need: 4 full-time freshmen who did not demonstrate need for aid received scholarships/grants; average award was $7,186. No-need awards available for academics.
Scholarships offered: Presidential Scholarship: $5,000; awarded to 5 non-residents. Scholars program: full tuition for 2 years (excluding room and board); awarded to 4 Vermont students.
Cumulative student debt: 80% of graduating class had student loans; average debt was $12,600.

FINANCIAL AID PROCEDURES
Forms required: FAFSA.
Dates and Deadlines: Priority date 3/1; no closing date. Applicants notified on a rolling basis starting 3/15; must reply within 2 week(s) of notification.

CONTACT
Cathy McCullough, Director of Financial Aid
PO Box 500, Randolph Center, VT 05061-0500
(800) 965-8790

Woodbury College
Montpelier, Vermont
www.woodbury-college.edu
Federal Code: 014348

4-year private technical college in small town.
Enrollment: 131 undergrads, 29% part-time. 10 full-time freshmen.
Selectivity: Open admission; but selective for some programs.

BASIC COSTS (2005-2006)
Tuition and fees: $15,150.
Per-credit charge: $625.

FINANCIAL AID PICTURE
Students with need: Need-based aid available for full-time and part-time students. Work study available nights, weekends, and for part-time students.

FINANCIAL AID PROCEDURES
Forms required: FAFSA, state aid form.

CONTACT
Marcy Spaulding, Director of Financial Aid
660 Elm Street, Montpelier, VT 05602
(802) 229-0516 ext. 245

Virginia

Art Institute of Washington
Arlington, Virginia
www.aiw.artinstitutes.edu   Federal Code: 009270

4-year for-profit culinary school and visual arts college in small city.
Enrollment: 1,100 undergrads.
Selectivity: Admits 50 to 75% of applicants.

BASIC COSTS (2006-2007)
Tuition and fees: $18,960.
Per-credit charge: $395.
Room only: $7,125.

FINANCIAL AID PICTURE
Students with need: Need-based aid available for part-time students.

FINANCIAL AID PROCEDURES
Forms required: FAFSA, institutional form.

CONTACT
Andrea Kemp, Director of Student Financial Services
1820 North Fort Myer Drive, Arlington, VA 22209-1802
(703) 358-9550

Averett University
Danville, Virginia
www.averett.edu   Federal Code: 003702

4-year private university and liberal arts college in small city.
Enrollment: 824 undergrads, 4% part-time. 245 full-time freshmen.
Selectivity: Admits over 75% of applicants.

BASIC COSTS (2006-2007)
Tuition and fees: $19,762.
Room and board: $6,448.

FINANCIAL AID PICTURE (2005-2006)
Students with need: Out of 220 full-time freshmen who applied for aid, 186 were judged to have need. Of these, 186 received aid, and 31 had their full need met. Average financial aid package met 73% of need; average scholarship/grant was $11,097; average loan was $3,968. For part-time students, average financial aid package was $5,329.
Students without need: 59 full-time freshmen who did not demonstrate need for aid received scholarships/grants; average award was $13,635. No-need awards available for academics, alumni affiliation, art, leadership, minority status, music/drama, religious affiliation, state/district residency.
Cumulative student debt: 70% of graduating class had student loans; average debt was $16,398.

FINANCIAL AID PROCEDURES
Forms required: FAFSA, state aid form.
Dates and Deadlines: Priority date 4/1; no closing date. Applicants notified on a rolling basis starting 2/15; must reply within 2 week(s) of notification.
Transfers: Closing date 4/1. Applicants notified on a rolling basis starting 2/15; must reply within 2 week(s) of notification.

CONTACT
Carl Bradsher, Dean of Financial Assistance
420 West Main Street, Danville, VA 24541
(434) 791-5890

Blue Ridge Community College
Weyers Cave, Virginia
www.brcc.edu   Federal Code: 006819

2-year public community college in rural community.
Enrollment: 3,527 undergrads, 60% part-time. 376 full-time freshmen.
Selectivity: Open admission; but selective for some programs.

BASIC COSTS (2005-2006)
Tuition and fees: $2,185; out-of-state residents $6,565.
Per-credit charge: $68; out-of-state residents $214.

FINANCIAL AID PICTURE
Students with need: Need-based aid available for full-time and part-time students.
Students without need: No-need awards available for academics, job skills, leadership, minority status.

FINANCIAL AID PROCEDURES
Forms required: FAFSA, institutional form.
Dates and Deadlines: Priority date 5/1; no closing date. Applicants notified on a rolling basis starting 5/30; must reply within 2 week(s) of notification.

CONTACT
Robert Clemmer, Financial Aid Officer
Box 80, Weyers Cave, VA 24486-9989
(540) 234-9261 ext. 2223

Bluefield College
Bluefield, Virginia
www.bluefield.edu   Federal Code: 003703

4-year private liberal arts college in large town, affiliated with Southern Baptist Convention.
Enrollment: 776 undergrads, 11% part-time. 103 full-time freshmen.

BASIC COSTS (2006-2007)
Tuition and fees: $12,305.
Per-credit charge: $382.
Room and board: $6,032.
Additional info: Tuition/fee waivers available for adults.

FINANCIAL AID PICTURE
Students with need: Need-based aid available for full-time and part-time students. Work study available nights, weekends, and for part-time students.
Students without need: No-need awards available for academics, art, athletics, leadership, music/drama, religious affiliation.

FINANCIAL AID PROCEDURES
Forms required: FAFSA, state aid form, institutional form.
Dates and Deadlines: Priority date 3/1; no closing date. Applicants notified on a rolling basis; must reply within 3 week(s) of notification.
Transfers: Scholarships of up to $2,000 per year available.

CONTACT
Debbie Checchio, Director of Financial Aid
3000 College Drive, Bluefield, VA 24605
(276) 326-4215

Bridgewater College
Bridgewater, Virginia
www.bridgewater.edu   Federal Code: 003704

4-year private liberal arts college in small town, affiliated with Church of the Brethren.
Enrollment: 1,493 undergrads. 394 full-time freshmen.

Selectivity: Admits over 75% of applicants.

BASIC COSTS (2006-2007)
Tuition and fees: $20,190.
Per-credit charge: $650.
Room and board: $9,060.
Additional info: Tuition/fee waivers available for minority students.

FINANCIAL AID PICTURE (2005-2006)
Students with need: Out of 348 full-time freshmen who applied for aid, 275 were judged to have need. Of these, 275 received aid, and 88 had their full need met. Average financial aid package met 85% of need; average scholarship/grant was $14,547; average loan was $2,570. For part-time students, average financial aid package was $6,227.
Students without need: 113 full-time freshmen who did not demonstrate need for aid received scholarships/grants; average award was $9,016. No-need awards available for academics, minority status, music/drama, religious affiliation, state/district residency.
Scholarships offered: President's Merit Plus Award; full tuition; minimum 3.8 high school GPA, 1350 SAT, 30 ACT; maximum 10 recipients. President's Merit Award; $12,000; minimum 3.8 high school GPA, 1200 SAT, 27 ACT. McKinney ACE Scholarships; $6,000 to $10,000; based on high school GPA (3.0 or higher) and SAT score (1100 or higher). All SAT scores exclusive of Writing.
Cumulative student debt: 69% of graduating class had student loans; average debt was $25,780.
Additional info: GED required of home-schooled students applying for Title IV federal aid.

FINANCIAL AID PROCEDURES
Forms required: FAFSA, state aid form.
Dates and Deadlines: Priority date 3/1; no closing date. Applicants notified on a rolling basis starting 3/15; must reply within 2 week(s) of notification.
Transfers: McKinney ACE merit scholarships available to students with 12 or more transferable credits; $4,000 to $10,000 based on GPA and test scores.

CONTACT
J Fairchilds, Director of Financial Aid
402 East College Street, Bridgewater, VA 22812-1599
(540) 828-5377

Bryant & Stratton College: Virginia Beach
Virginia Beach, Virginia
www.bryantstratton.edu   Federal Code: 010061

2-year for-profit business and junior college in large city.
Enrollment: 435 undergrads, 48% part-time. 116 full-time freshmen.
Selectivity: Open admission.

BASIC COSTS (2006-2007)
Tuition and fees: $11,820.
Per-credit charge: $394.
Additional info: Technology fee $100 per semester.

FINANCIAL AID PICTURE
Students with need: Need-based aid available for full-time and part-time students. Work study available nights.

FINANCIAL AID PROCEDURES
Forms required: FAFSA.
Dates and Deadlines: No deadline. Applicants notified on a rolling basis.

CONTACT
Anita Wyche, Director of Financial Aid
301 Centre Pointe Drive, Virginia Beach, VA 23462-4417
(757) 499-7900

Christendom College
Front Royal, Virginia
www.christendom.edu

4-year private liberal arts college in large town, affiliated with Roman Catholic Church.
Enrollment: 379 undergrads, 2% part-time. 105 full-time freshmen.
Selectivity: Admits over 75% of applicants.

BASIC COSTS (2006-2007)
Tuition and fees: $16,740.
Room and board: $6,066.

FINANCIAL AID PICTURE (2005-2006)
Students with need: Average financial aid package met 90% of need; average scholarship/grant was $8,500; average loan was $4,705.
Students without need: No-need awards available for academics, alumni affiliation.
Cumulative student debt: 55% of graduating class had student loans; average debt was $11,080.
Additional info: Christendom accepts no direct federal aid, nor does it participate in indirect programs of federal aid.

FINANCIAL AID PROCEDURES
Forms required: institutional form.
Dates and Deadlines: Priority date 4/1; closing date 6/1. Applicants notified on a rolling basis starting 2/1; must reply within 4 week(s) of notification.

CONTACT
Alisa Polk, Financial Aid Officer
134 Christendom Drive, Front Royal, VA 22630
(800) 877-5456

Christopher Newport University
Newport News, Virginia
www.cnu.edu   Federal Code: 003706

4-year public university and liberal arts college in small city.
Enrollment: 4,496 undergrads, 7% part-time. 1,175 full-time freshmen.

BASIC COSTS (2006-2007)
Tuition and fees: $6,460; out-of-state residents $13,532.
Per-credit charge: $270; out-of-state residents $565.
Room and board: $8,100.

FINANCIAL AID PICTURE (2005-2006)
Students with need: Out of 916 full-time freshmen who applied for aid, 517 were judged to have need. Of these, 512 received aid, and 101 had their full need met. Average financial aid package met 72% of need; average scholarship/grant was $3,461; average loan was $1,983. Need-based aid available for part-time students.
Students without need: 104 full-time freshmen who did not demonstrate need for aid received scholarships/grants; average award was $1,242. No-need awards available for academics, leadership, music/drama, ROTC, state/district residency.
Scholarships offered: University Scholarship and Leadership Scholarship awards for incoming freshmen are renewable for all 4 years.

FINANCIAL AID PROCEDURES
Forms required: FAFSA.
Dates and Deadlines: Priority date 3/1; no closing date. Applicants notified on a rolling basis starting 2/21; must reply within 2 week(s) of notification.

CONTACT
Mary Wigginton, Director of Financial Aid
1 University Place, Newport News, VA 23606
(757) 594-7170

College of William and Mary
Williamsburg, Virginia
www.wm.edu
Federal Code: 003705
CSS Code: 5115

4-year public university in large town.
Enrollment: 5,540 undergrads, 1% part-time. 1,340 full-time freshmen.
Selectivity: Admits less than 50% of applicants.

BASIC COSTS (2006-2007)
Tuition and fees: $8,205; out-of-state residents $24,625.
Per-credit charge: $196; out-of-state residents $750.
Room and board: $6,932.
Additional info: Out-of-State students pay an additional $138 in required fees.

FINANCIAL AID PICTURE (2004-2005)
Students with need: 62% of average financial aid package awarded as scholarships/grants, 38% awarded as loans/jobs.
Students without need: No-need awards available for academics, athletics, leadership.

FINANCIAL AID PROCEDURES
Forms required: FAFSA. CSS PROFILE required of early decision applicants only.
Dates and Deadlines: Priority date 2/15; closing date 3/15. Applicants notified on a rolling basis starting 3/10; must reply by 5/1.

CONTACT
Edward Irish, Director of Student Financial Aid
PO Box 8795, Williamsburg, VA 23187-8795
(757) 221-2420

Dabney S. Lancaster Community College
Clifton Forge, Virginia
www.dslcc.edu
Federal Code: 004996

2-year public community college in small town.
Enrollment: 1,311 undergrads.
Selectivity: Open admission; but selective for some programs.

BASIC COSTS (2005-2006)
Tuition and fees: $2,157; out-of-state residents $6,537.
Per-credit charge: $68; out-of-state residents $214.

FINANCIAL AID PICTURE
Students with need: Need-based aid available for full-time and part-time students.

FINANCIAL AID PROCEDURES
Forms required: FAFSA, institutional form.
Dates and Deadlines: Priority date 3/15; no closing date. Applicants notified on a rolling basis starting 4/15; must reply within 2 week(s) of notification.

CONTACT
Sandra Haverlack, Financial Aid Officer
Box 1000, Clifton Forge, VA 24422
(540) 863-2822

Danville Community College
Danville, Virginia
www.dcc.vccs.edu
Federal Code: 003758

2-year public community college in small city.
Enrollment: 2,355 undergrads.
Selectivity: Open admission; but selective for some programs.

BASIC COSTS (2005-2006)
Tuition and fees: $2,185; out-of-state residents $6,565.
Per-credit charge: $68; out-of-state residents $214.

FINANCIAL AID PICTURE (2004-2005)
Students with need: Need-based aid available for part-time students.
Students without need: This college only awards aid to students with need.
Scholarships offered: Educational Foundation Scholarship; $250 to $1,500; based on separate application; deadline mid-March prior to award year.

FINANCIAL AID PROCEDURES
Forms required: FAFSA.
Dates and Deadlines: Priority date 6/1; no closing date. Applicants notified on a rolling basis starting 5/1; must reply within 2 week(s) of notification.
Transfers: Limited aid available to transfer students admitted in spring semester.

CONTACT
Mary Gore, Assistant Coordinator of Financial Aid
1008 South Main Street, Danville, VA 24541
(434) 797-8439

DeVry University: Arlington
Arlington, Virginia
www.crys.devry.edu

4-year for-profit university in very large city.
Enrollment: 459 undergrads, 33% part-time. 196 full-time freshmen.

BASIC COSTS (2005-2006)
Tuition and fees: $13,410.
Per-credit charge: $475.

FINANCIAL AID PICTURE (2004-2005)
Students with need: Out of 97 full-time freshmen who applied for aid, 92 were judged to have need. Of these, 92 received aid, and 5 had their full need met. Average financial aid package met 35% of need; average scholarship/grant was $3,770; average loan was $5,877. For part-time students, average financial aid package was $5,545.
Students without need: This college only awards aid to students with need.

FINANCIAL AID PROCEDURES
Forms required: FAFSA.
Dates and Deadlines: No deadline. Applicants notified on a rolling basis starting 7/1.

CONTACT
Roberta McDevitt, Director of Student Finance
2450 Crystal Drive, Arlington, VA 22202
(703) 414-4000

Eastern Mennonite University
Harrisonburg, Virginia
www.emu.edu
Federal Code: 003708

4-year private university and liberal arts college in large town, affiliated with Mennonite Church.
Enrollment: 998 undergrads, 3% part-time. 202 full-time freshmen.
Selectivity: Admits over 75% of applicants.

BASIC COSTS (2006-2007)
Tuition and fees: $20,670.
Room and board: $6,550.

FINANCIAL AID PICTURE (2005-2006)
Students with need: Out of 184 full-time freshmen who applied for aid, 169 were judged to have need. Of these, 169 received aid, and 56 had their full need met. Average financial aid package met 88% of need; average scholarship/grant was $7,010; average loan was $4,600. For part-time students, average financial aid package was $6,100.
Students without need: 25 full-time freshmen who did not demonstrate need for aid received scholarships/grants; average award was $8,790. No-need awards available for academics, alumni affiliation, music/drama, religious affiliation, state/district residency.
Scholarships offered: President's Scholarship for GPA of 3.9 or higher; Academic Achievement Scholarship for minimum 3.2 GPA; University Grant for minimum 2.5 GPA; minimum SAT score of 920 (exclusive of Writing) or ACT score of 20 required for all scholarships. Amounts based on GPA and test scores; no limit on number of awards. Full-tuition scholarships available for 2 honors program applicants with highest test scores and GPA; half tuition scholarships available for next 10 candidates.
Cumulative student debt: 94% of graduating class had student loans; average debt was $17,680.

FINANCIAL AID PROCEDURES
Forms required: FAFSA, state aid form.
Dates and Deadlines: Priority date 4/15; no closing date. Applicants notified on a rolling basis starting 2/1; must reply within 4 week(s) of notification.

CONTACT
Michele Hensley, Director of Financial Assistance
1200 Park Road, Harrisonburg, VA 22802-2462
(540) 432-4137

Eastern Shore Community College
Melfa, Virginia
www.es.vccs.edu   Federal Code: 003748

2-year public community college in rural community.
Enrollment: 576 undergrads.
Selectivity: Open admission.

BASIC COSTS (2005-2006)
Tuition and fees: $2,166; out-of-state residents $6,546.
Per-credit charge: $68; out-of-state residents $214.

FINANCIAL AID PICTURE
Students with need: Need-based aid available for full-time and part-time students.

FINANCIAL AID PROCEDURES
Forms required: FAFSA.
Dates and Deadlines: Priority date 5/1; no closing date. Applicants notified on a rolling basis starting 6/1; must reply within 2 week(s) of notification.

CONTACT
P Bryan Smith, Financial Aid Officer
29300 Lankford Highway, Melfa, VA 23410-9755
(757) 789-1732

ECPI College of Technology
Virginia Beach, Virginia
www.ecpi.edu   Federal Code: 010198

4-year for-profit health science and technical college in large city.
Enrollment: 4,853 undergrads, 4% part-time. 792 full-time freshmen.

BASIC COSTS (2005-2006)
Additional info: Required fee is for books.

FINANCIAL AID PICTURE
Students with need: Need-based aid available for full-time and part-time students. Work study available nights.
Students without need: No-need awards available for academics.

FINANCIAL AID PROCEDURES
Forms required: institutional form.
Dates and Deadlines: No deadline. Applicants notified on a rolling basis.

CONTACT
Jeff Arthur, Vice President of Financial Aid
5555 Greenwich Road, Suite 300, Virginia Beach, VA 23462-6542
(757) 671-7171

Emory & Henry College
Emory, Virginia
www.ehc.edu   Federal Code: 003709

4-year private liberal arts college in rural community, affiliated with United Methodist Church.
Enrollment: 1,027 undergrads, 3% part-time. 338 full-time freshmen.
Selectivity: Admits over 75% of applicants.

BASIC COSTS (2006-2007)
Tuition and fees: $20,860.
Per-credit charge: $870.
Room and board: $7,360.

FINANCIAL AID PICTURE (2005-2006)
Students with need: Out of 317 full-time freshmen who applied for aid, 276 were judged to have need. Of these, 276 received aid, and 80 had their full need met. Average financial aid package met 74% of need; average scholarship/grant was $11,711; average loan was $2,543. For part-time students, average financial aid package was $14,502.
Students without need: This college only awards aid to students with need.
Cumulative student debt: 76% of graduating class had student loans; average debt was $15,465.
Additional info: Virginia residents eligible for additional in-state tuition grants.

FINANCIAL AID PROCEDURES
Forms required: FAFSA, state aid form.
Dates and Deadlines: Priority date 4/1; closing date 8/1. Applicants notified on a rolling basis starting 2/1; must reply within 4 week(s) of notification.

CONTACT
Scarlett Cortner, Coordinator, Financial Aid
Box 10, Emory, VA 24327
(276) 944-6115

Ferrum College
Ferrum, Virginia
www.ferrum.edu   Federal Code: 003711

4-year private liberal arts college in rural community, affiliated with United Methodist Church.
Enrollment: 991 undergrads, 3% part-time. 334 full-time freshmen.
Selectivity: Admits 50 to 75% of applicants.

BASIC COSTS (2006-2007)
Tuition and fees: $19,520.
Per-credit charge: $465.
Room and board: $6,300.

FINANCIAL AID PICTURE

Students with need: Need-based aid available for full-time and part-time students. Work study available nights, weekends, and for part-time students.
Students without need: No-need awards available for academics, job skills, leadership, religious affiliation, state/district residency.
Scholarships offered: Ferrum Scholarship, $7,000-10,000, high school GPA must be 3.0 or higher and NEW SAT score must be 1500 or higher; Ferrum Merit Grant, $1,000-8,000, high school GPA must be 2.0 or higher and NEW SAT score must be in the range of 1050 to 1490.

FINANCIAL AID PROCEDURES

Forms required: FAFSA, state aid form.
Dates and Deadlines: Priority date 4/1; no closing date. Applicants notified on a rolling basis starting 3/1.

CONTACT

Doug Clark, Vice President for Enrollment
Spilman-Daniel House, Ferrum, VA 24088
(540) 365-4282

George Mason University
Fairfax, Virginia
www.gmu.edu   Federal Code: 003749

4-year public university in large town.
Enrollment: 17,529 undergrads, 23% part-time. 2,215 full-time freshmen.
Selectivity: Admits 50 to 75% of applicants.

BASIC COSTS (2005-2006)

Tuition and fees: $5,922; out-of-state residents $17,202.
Per-credit charge: $245; out-of-state residents $715.
Room and board: $6,480.

FINANCIAL AID PICTURE (2004-2005)

Students with need: Out of 1,380 full-time freshmen who applied for aid, 918 were judged to have need. Of these, 866 received aid, and 89 had their full need met. Average financial aid package met 64% of need; average scholarship/grant was $4,708; average loan was $2,787. For part-time students, average financial aid package was $5,174.
Students without need: 207 full-time freshmen who did not demonstrate need for aid received scholarships/grants; average award was $3,964. No-need awards available for academics, athletics, minority status, music/drama, ROTC, state/district residency.
Scholarships offered: 49 full-time freshmen received athletic scholarships; average amount $11,369.
Cumulative student debt: 37% of graduating class had student loans; average debt was $13,607.

FINANCIAL AID PROCEDURES

Forms required: FAFSA.
Dates and Deadlines: Priority date 3/1; no closing date. Applicants notified on a rolling basis starting 4/1; must reply within 3 week(s) of notification.

CONTACT

Jevita de Freitas, Director, Student Financial Planning
4400 University Drive, MSN 3A4, Fairfax, VA 22030

Germanna Community College
Locust Grove, Virginia
www.gcc.vccs.edu   Federal Code: 008660

2-year public community college in rural community.
Enrollment: 5,019 undergrads.
Selectivity: Open admission; but selective for some programs.

BASIC COSTS (2005-2006)

Tuition and fees: $2,173; out-of-state residents $6,567.
Per-credit charge: $68; out-of-state residents $214.

FINANCIAL AID PICTURE (2004-2005)

Students with need: 91% of average financial aid package awarded as scholarships/grants, 9% awarded as loans/jobs. Need-based aid available for part-time students.
Students without need: No-need awards available for academics.

FINANCIAL AID PROCEDURES

Forms required: FAFSA.
Dates and Deadlines: Priority date 4/1; no closing date. Applicants notified on a rolling basis starting 5/15; must reply within 2 week(s) of notification.

CONTACT

Jim Brunner, Financial Aid Coordinator
2130 Germanna Highway, Locust Grove, VA 22508-2102
(540) 727-3033

Hampden-Sydney College
Hampden-Sydney, Virginia
www.hsc.edu   Federal Code: 003713
                     CSS Code: 5291

4-year private liberal arts college for men in rural community, affiliated with Presbyterian Church (USA).
Enrollment: 1,060 undergrads. 322 full-time freshmen.
Selectivity: Admits 50 to 75% of applicants.

BASIC COSTS (2006-2007)

Tuition and fees: $26,344.
Room and board: $8,125.

FINANCIAL AID PICTURE (2005-2006)

Students with need: Out of 240 full-time freshmen who applied for aid, 159 were judged to have need. Of these, 159 received aid, and 65 had their full need met. Average financial aid package met 88.5% of need; average scholarship/grant was $15,444; average loan was $2,974.
Students without need: 160 full-time freshmen who did not demonstrate need for aid received scholarships/grants; average award was $21,697. No-need awards available for academics, leadership, religious affiliation, ROTC, state/district residency.
Scholarships offered: Allan Scholarship; $16,000 annually. Venable Scholarship; $12,000 annually. Patrick Henry Scholarship; $8,000 annually. Achievement Awards; $5,000 annually. All based on academic ability.
Cumulative student debt: 54% of graduating class had student loans; average debt was $19,818.

FINANCIAL AID PROCEDURES

Forms required: FAFSA, CSS PROFILE, state aid form.
Dates and Deadlines: Priority date 3/1; no closing date. Applicants notified on a rolling basis starting 3/1; must reply by 5/1 or within 2 week(s) of notification.
Transfers: No deadline. Applicants notified on a rolling basis; must reply within 2 week(s) of notification.

CONTACT

Keith Wellings, Director of Financial Aid
Box 667, Hampden-Sydney, VA 23943
(434) 223-6119

Hampton University
Hampton, Virginia
www.hamptonu.edu   Federal Code: 003714

4-year private university in small city.
Enrollment: 5,225 undergrads, 6% part-time. 1,165 full-time freshmen.
Selectivity: Admits 50 to 75% of applicants.

BASIC COSTS (2006-2007)
Tuition and fees: $14,818.
Room and board: $6,746.

FINANCIAL AID PICTURE (2005-2006)
Students with need: 36% of average financial aid package awarded as scholarships/grants, 64% awarded as loans/jobs. Need-based aid available for part-time students. Work study available nights, weekends, and for part-time students.
Students without need: No-need awards available for academics, athletics, leadership, music/drama, ROTC.

FINANCIAL AID PROCEDURES
Forms required: FAFSA.
Dates and Deadlines: Priority date 3/1; no closing date. Applicants notified on a rolling basis starting 4/15; must reply within 2 week(s) of notification.

CONTACT
Marcia Boyd, Financial Aid Director
Office of Admissions, Hampton, VA 23668
(757) 727-5332

Hollins University
Roanoke, Virginia
www.hollins.edu   Federal Code: 003715

4-year private university and liberal arts college for women in small city.
Enrollment: 818 undergrads, 6% part-time. 184 full-time freshmen.
Selectivity: Admits over 75% of applicants.

BASIC COSTS (2006-2007)
Tuition and fees: $24,325.
Per-credit charge: $744.
Room and board: $8,650.

FINANCIAL AID PICTURE (2005-2006)
Students with need: Out of 165 full-time freshmen who applied for aid, 130 were judged to have need. Of these, 130 received aid, and 33 had their full need met. Average financial aid package met 81% of need; average scholarship/grant was $13,042; average loan was $3,287. For part-time students, average financial aid package was $11,323.
Students without need: 54 full-time freshmen who did not demonstrate need for aid received scholarships/grants; average award was $8,414. No-need awards available for academics, alumni affiliation, art, leadership, minority status, music/drama, state/district residency.
Scholarships offered: Scholar Awards; $5,000 full tuition; academic merit. Founder's Awards; $1,500-$7,000; organizational involvement. Creative Talent Awards; $1,500-$7,000; distinguished achievement or outstanding involvement in art, photography/film, creative writing, music, dance or theatre.
Cumulative student debt: 64% of graduating class had student loans; average debt was $19,592.

FINANCIAL AID PROCEDURES
Forms required: FAFSA, state aid form.
Dates and Deadlines: Priority date 2/15; no closing date. Applicants notified on a rolling basis starting 3/15.
Transfers: Priority date 7/1; closing date 7/15.

CONTACT
Amy Moore, Director of Scholarships and Financial Assistance
P.O. Box 9707, Roanoke, VA 24020-1707
(540) 362-6332

J. Sargeant Reynolds Community College
Richmond, Virginia
www.reynolds.edu   Federal Code: 003759

2-year public community college in very large city.
Enrollment: 7,621 undergrads.
Selectivity: Open admission; but selective for some programs.

BASIC COSTS (2005-2006)
Tuition and fees: $2,269; out-of-state residents $6,649.
Per-credit charge: $68; out-of-state residents $214.

FINANCIAL AID PICTURE
Students with need: Need-based aid available for full-time and part-time students. Work study available nights, weekends, and for part-time students.
Students without need: No-need awards available for academics.
Scholarships offered: Local Board Scholarship for high school students with minimum 3.0 GPA; 23 awarded; full tuition. Eric and Jeanette Lipman Endowed Scholarship based on academic excellence; number and amount awarded varies. Central Fidelity Bank Scholarship for first-year students; minimum 2.5 cumulative GPA; 2 awarded; $1,500.

FINANCIAL AID PROCEDURES
Forms required: FAFSA.
Dates and Deadlines: Priority date 6/30; no closing date. Applicants notified on a rolling basis starting 7/15; must reply within 2 week(s) of notification.

CONTACT
Diane Branch Thompson, Assistant Director of Financial Aid
Admissions and Records, Richmond, VA 23285-5622
(804) 523-5137

James Madison University
Harrisonburg, Virginia
www.jmu.edu   Federal Code: 003721

4-year public university in large town.
Enrollment: 15,287 undergrads, 3% part-time. 3,796 full-time freshmen.
Selectivity: Admits 50 to 75% of applicants.

BASIC COSTS (2006-2007)
Tuition and fees: $6,290; out-of-state residents $16,232.
Room and board: $5,756.

FINANCIAL AID PICTURE (2005-2006)
Students with need: Out of 2,769 full-time freshmen who applied for aid, 1,403 were judged to have need. Of these, 1,205 received aid, and 1,128 had their full need met. Average financial aid package met 62% of need; average scholarship/grant was $5,827; average loan was $2,904. For part-time students, average financial aid package was $5,838.
Students without need: 118 full-time freshmen who did not demonstrate need for aid received scholarships/grants; average award was $2,246. No-need awards available for academics, alumni affiliation, art, athletics, leadership, minority status, music/drama, state/district residency.
Scholarships offered: 87 full-time freshmen received athletic scholarships; average amount $13,055.
Cumulative student debt: 53% of graduating class had student loans; average debt was $12,591.

FINANCIAL AID PROCEDURES
Forms required: FAFSA.

Dates and Deadlines: Priority date 3/1; no closing date. Applicants notified on a rolling basis starting 4/1; must reply within 4 week(s) of notification.

CONTACT
Lisa Turner, Director of Financial Aid and Scholarships
Sonner Hall MSC 0101, Harrisonburg, VA 22807
(540) 568-7820

Jefferson College of Health Sciences
Roanoke, Virginia
www.jchs.edu   Federal Code: 009893

4-year private health science and nursing college in small city.
Enrollment: 873 undergrads.

BASIC COSTS (2006-2007)
Tuition and fees: $13,860.
Per-credit charge: $400.
Additional info: Tuition for physician assistant program: $48,860 for full 2-year program.

FINANCIAL AID PICTURE
Students with need: Need-based aid available for full-time and part-time students.
Students without need: No-need awards available for academics.
Scholarships offered: Commonwealth Award for all full-time Virginia students; $2,400. Merit Awards available to full-time out-of-state students based on SAT/GPA; amounts vary.

FINANCIAL AID PROCEDURES
Forms required: FAFSA, institutional form.
Dates and Deadlines: No deadline. Applicants notified on a rolling basis; must reply within 2 week(s) of notification.

CONTACT
Deborah Johnson, Financial Aid Officer
Box 13186, Roanoke, VA 24031-3186
(540) 985-8483

John Tyler Community College
Chester, Virginia
www.jtcc.edu   Federal Code: 004004

2-year public community college in small city.
Enrollment: 3,681 undergrads.
Selectivity: Open admission; but selective for some programs.

BASIC COSTS (2005-2006)
Tuition and fees: $2,171; out-of-state residents $6,551.
Per-credit charge: $68; out-of-state residents $214.

FINANCIAL AID PICTURE (2004-2005)
Students with need: 76% of average financial aid package awarded as scholarships/grants, 24% awarded as loans/jobs. Need-based aid available for part-time students. Work study available nights, weekends, and for part-time students.
Students without need: No-need awards available for academics, state/district residency.

FINANCIAL AID PROCEDURES
Forms required: FAFSA.
Dates and Deadlines: Priority date 5/15; closing date 7/15. Applicants notified on a rolling basis starting 6/20.

CONTACT
Laurie Schiavone, Coordinator of Financial Aid
13101 Jefferson Davis Highway, Chester, VA 23831-5316
(804) 706-5235

Liberty University
Lynchburg, Virginia
www.liberty.edu   Federal Code: 010392

4-year private university and seminary college in small city, affiliated with Baptist faith.
Enrollment: 9,879 undergrads, 15% part-time. 1,922 full-time freshmen.
Selectivity: Admits 50 to 75% of applicants.

BASIC COSTS (2006-2007)
Tuition and fees: $15,350.
Per-credit charge: $480.
Room and board: $5,400.

FINANCIAL AID PICTURE (2005-2006)
Students with need: Out of 1,800 full-time freshmen who applied for aid, 1,458 were judged to have need. Of these, 1,451 received aid, and 211 had their full need met. Average financial aid package met 57% of need; average scholarship/grant was $2,895; average loan was $2,445. For part-time students, average financial aid package was $4,463.
Students without need: 429 full-time freshmen who did not demonstrate need for aid received scholarships/grants; average award was $4,864. No-need awards available for academics, alumni affiliation, athletics, leadership, music/drama, religious affiliation, ROTC, state/district residency.
Scholarships offered: *Merit:* Liberty Academic Achievement Scholarship: based on combination of high school grades and standardized test scores. Students may qualify for up to $6,000. Additional $3,500 could be applied if student is also accepted into the Honors Program. *Athletic:* 64 full-time freshmen received athletic scholarships; average amount $11,297.
Cumulative student debt: 42% of graduating class had student loans; average debt was $11,885.

FINANCIAL AID PROCEDURES
Forms required: FAFSA, state aid form.
Dates and Deadlines: Closing date 3/1. Applicants notified on a rolling basis starting 3/15; must reply within 3 week(s) of notification.
Transfers: Applicants notified on a rolling basis starting 3/15; must reply within 3 week(s) of notification.

CONTACT
Rhonda Allbeck, Director of Student Financial Aid
1971 University Boulevard, Lynchburg, VA 24502
(434) 582-2270

Longwood University
Farmville, Virginia
www.whylongwood.com   Federal Code: 003719

4-year public university in small town.
Enrollment: 3,674 undergrads, 2% part-time. 921 full-time freshmen.
Selectivity: Admits over 75% of applicants.

BASIC COSTS (2006-2007)
Tuition and fees: $7,589; out-of-state residents $15,209.
Room and board: $6,522.
Additional info: Required laptop computer for first year students $1,600.

Virginia Longwood University

FINANCIAL AID PICTURE (2004-2005)
Students with need: Out of 648 full-time freshmen who applied for aid, 411 were judged to have need. Of these, 411 received aid, and 95 had their full need met. Average financial aid package met 76% of need; average scholarship/grant was $4,673; average loan was $3,230. Need-based aid available for part-time students.
Students without need: 243 full-time freshmen who did not demonstrate need for aid received scholarships/grants; average award was $4,205. No-need awards available for academics, alumni affiliation, art, athletics, leadership, music/drama, ROTC, state/district residency.
Scholarships offered: Merit: Longwood Scholars; $2,200. Presidential Merit Scholarships; $500. Hull Education; full tuition (in-state rates) and fees. Citizen Scholars; $6,500. All awards based on grades and test scores. **Athletic:** 40 full-time freshmen received athletic scholarships; average amount $7,576.
Cumulative student debt: 80% of graduating class had student loans; average debt was $16,302.

FINANCIAL AID PROCEDURES
Forms required: FAFSA.
Dates and Deadlines: Priority date 3/1; no closing date. Applicants notified on a rolling basis starting 4/1; must reply within 2 week(s) of notification.

CONTACT
Michael Barree, Director of Financial Aid
201 High Street, Farmville, VA 23909-1898
(434) 395-2077

Lord Fairfax Community College
Middletown, Virginia
www.lfcc.edu   Federal Code: 008659

2-year public community college in rural community.
Enrollment: 5,490 undergrads.
Selectivity: Open admission.

BASIC COSTS (2005-2006)
Tuition and fees: $2,171; out-of-state residents $6,551.
Per-credit charge: $68; out-of-state residents $214.

FINANCIAL AID PICTURE
Students with need: Need-based aid available for full-time and part-time students.
Students without need: This college only awards aid to students with need.

FINANCIAL AID PROCEDURES
Forms required: FAFSA.
Dates and Deadlines: Priority date 5/1; no closing date. Applicants notified on a rolling basis starting 6/1.

CONTACT
Karen Bucher, Coordinator of Financial Aid
173 Skirmisher Lane, Middletown, VA 22645
(540) 868-7131

Lynchburg College
Lynchburg, Virginia
www.lynchburg.edu   Federal Code: 003720

4-year private liberal arts college in small city, affiliated with Christian Church (Disciples of Christ).
Enrollment: 1,998 undergrads, 4% part-time. 554 full-time freshmen.
Selectivity: Admits 50 to 75% of applicants.

BASIC COSTS (2006-2007)
Tuition and fees: $25,565.
Per-credit charge: $350.
Room and board: $6,800.
Additional info: Tuition/fee waivers available for adults.

FINANCIAL AID PICTURE (2005-2006)
Students with need: Out of 457 full-time freshmen who applied for aid, 352 were judged to have need. Of these, 352 received aid, and 107 had their full need met. Average financial aid package met 95% of need; average scholarship/grant was $15,060; average loan was $3,076. For part-time students, average financial aid package was $8,134.
Students without need: 202 full-time freshmen who did not demonstrate need for aid received scholarships/grants; average award was $8,379. No-need awards available for academics, art, leadership, music/drama, state/district residency.
Cumulative student debt: 85% of graduating class had student loans; average debt was $18,517.

FINANCIAL AID PROCEDURES
Forms required: FAFSA, state aid form.
Dates and Deadlines: Priority date 3/1; no closing date. Applicants notified on a rolling basis starting 3/5; must reply by 5/1 or within 2 week(s) of notification.
Transfers: Priority date 7/1.

CONTACT
Michelle Davis, Director of Financial Aid
1501 Lakeside Drive, Lynchburg, VA 24501
(434) 544-8228

Mary Baldwin College
Staunton, Virginia
www.mbc.edu   Federal Code: 003723

4-year private liberal arts college for women in large town, affiliated with Presbyterian Church (USA).
Enrollment: 1,339 undergrads, 29% part-time. 262 full-time freshmen.
Selectivity: Admits over 75% of applicants.

BASIC COSTS (2006-2007)
Tuition and fees: $21,450.
Per-credit charge: $355.
Room and board: $6,100.

FINANCIAL AID PICTURE (2004-2005)
Students with need: Out of 244 full-time freshmen who applied for aid, 217 were judged to have need. Of these, 215 received aid, and 96 had their full need met. Average financial aid package met 88% of need; average scholarship/grant was $12,133; average loan was $1,852. For part-time students, average financial aid package was $7,703.
Students without need: 40 full-time freshmen who did not demonstrate need for aid received scholarships/grants; average award was $12,831. No-need awards available for academics, leadership, state/district residency.
Cumulative student debt: 81% of graduating class had student loans; average debt was $21,240.

FINANCIAL AID PROCEDURES
Forms required: FAFSA, state aid form.
Dates and Deadlines: Priority date 5/15; no closing date. Applicants notified on a rolling basis starting 2/1.

CONTACT
Lisa Branson, Dean of Admissions and Financial Aid
Office of Admissions, Staunton, VA 24401
(540) 887-7022

Marymount University
Arlington, Virginia
www.marymount.edu   Federal Code: 003724

4-year private university in small city, affiliated with Roman Catholic Church.
Enrollment: 2,268 undergrads, 18% part-time. 422 full-time freshmen.
Selectivity: Admits over 75% of applicants.

BASIC COSTS (2006-2007)
Tuition and fees: $19,199.
Per-credit charge: $620.
Room and board: $8,212.

FINANCIAL AID PICTURE (2005-2006)
Students with need: Out of 325 full-time freshmen who applied for aid, 246 were judged to have need. Of these, 241 received aid, and 52 had their full need met. Average financial aid package met 78% of need; average scholarship/grant was $7,253; average loan was $2,629. For part-time students, average financial aid package was $5,080.
Students without need: 95 full-time freshmen who did not demonstrate need for aid received scholarships/grants; average award was $8,147. No-need awards available for academics, alumni affiliation, leadership, state/district residency.
Scholarships offered: Freshman Academic Scholarship: requires GPA of 3.0 or better and combined SAT (exclusive of writing) score of 1100 or higher.
Cumulative student debt: 71% of graduating class had student loans; average debt was $24,950.

FINANCIAL AID PROCEDURES
Forms required: FAFSA, state aid form.
Dates and Deadlines: Priority date 6/1; no closing date. Applicants notified on a rolling basis; must reply within 2 week(s) of notification.
Transfers: No deadline. Applicants notified on a rolling basis; must reply within 2 week(s) of notification. Academic scholarships available; apply by May 1.

CONTACT
Debbie Raines, Director of Financial Aid
2807 North Glebe Road, Arlington, VA 22207-4299
(703) 284-1530

Miller-Motte Technical College: Lynchburg
Lynchburg, Virginia
www.miller-motte.com

2-year for-profit technical college in small city.
Enrollment: 215 undergrads.
Selectivity: Open admission.

FINANCIAL AID PICTURE
Students with need: Need-based aid available for full-time and part-time students. Work study available nights.
Students without need: This college only awards aid to students with need.

FINANCIAL AID PROCEDURES
Forms required: FAFSA.
Dates and Deadlines: No deadline. Applicants notified on a rolling basis.

CONTACT
1011 Creekside Lane, Lynchburg, VA 24502
(434) 239-5222

Mountain Empire Community College
Big Stone Gap, Virginia
www.me.vccs.edu   Federal Code: 009629

2-year public community college in small town.
Enrollment: 1,743 undergrads, 42% part-time. 480 full-time freshmen.
Selectivity: Open admission; but selective for some programs.

BASIC COSTS (2005-2006)
Tuition and fees: $2,211; out-of-state residents $6,591.
Per-credit charge: $68; out-of-state residents $214.

FINANCIAL AID PICTURE (2004-2005)
Students with need: Average financial aid package for all full-time undergraduates was $5,100. 98% awarded as scholarships/grants, 2% awarded as loans/jobs. Need-based aid available for part-time students.
Students without need: No-need awards available for academics, state/district residency.
Scholarships offered: Presidential Honor Scholarship: full tuition; for valedictorian or salutatorian. Dean's Academic Honor Award: $500-$1,000; for top 10 in graduating class.
Additional info: The college does not participate in loan programs. All financial aid is in form of grants, scholarships, or work study.

FINANCIAL AID PROCEDURES
Forms required: FAFSA.
Dates and Deadlines: Priority date 5/1; no closing date. Applicants notified on a rolling basis starting 1/1.

CONTACT
Perry Carroll, Director of Enrollment Services
3441 Mountain Empire Road, Big Stone Gap, VA 24219
(276) 523-2400 ext. 470

National College of Business & Technology: Bluefield
Bluefield, Virginia
www.ncbt.edu   Federal Code: 003726

2-year for-profit business college in small city.
Enrollment: 170 undergrads.
Selectivity: Open admission.

BASIC COSTS (2006-2007)
Tuition and fees: $8,976.
Per-credit charge: $187.

FINANCIAL AID PICTURE
Students with need: Need-based aid available for full-time and part-time students.
Students without need: This college only awards aid to students with need.

FINANCIAL AID PROCEDURES
Forms required: FAFSA.
Dates and Deadlines: No deadline. Applicants notified on a rolling basis starting 9/1.

CONTACT
Pamela Cotton, National College of Business & Technology: Bluefield
100 Logan Street, Bluefield, VA 24605
(540) 986-1800

National College of Business & Technology: Charlottesville
Charlottesville, Virginia
www.ncbt.edu
Federal Code: 003726

2-year for-profit business college in small city.
Enrollment: 126 undergrads.
Selectivity: Open admission.

BASIC COSTS (2006-2007)
Tuition and fees: $8,976.

FINANCIAL AID PICTURE
Students with need: Need-based aid available for full-time and part-time students.
Students without need: This college only awards aid to students with need.

FINANCIAL AID PROCEDURES
Forms required: FAFSA.
Dates and Deadlines: No deadline. Applicants notified on a rolling basis.

CONTACT
Pamela Cotton, Director of Financial Aid and Compliance Officer
1819 Emmet Street, Charlottesville, VA 22901
(540) 986-1800

National College of Business & Technology: Danville
Danville, Virginia
www.ncbt.edu
Federal Code: 003726

2-year for-profit branch campus and business college in small city.
Enrollment: 262 undergrads.
Selectivity: Open admission.

BASIC COSTS (2006-2007)
Tuition and fees: $8,976.
Per-credit charge: $187.

FINANCIAL AID PICTURE
Students with need: Need-based aid available for full-time and part-time students.
Students without need: This college only awards aid to students with need.

FINANCIAL AID PROCEDURES
Forms required: FAFSA.
Dates and Deadlines: No deadline. Applicants notified on a rolling basis starting 9/1.

CONTACT
Pamela Cotton, Director of Financial Aid and Compliance Officer
PO Box 6400, Roanoke, VA 24017
(540) 986-1800

National College of Business & Technology: Harrisonburg
Harrisonburg, Virginia
www.ncbt.edu
Federal Code: 003726

2-year for-profit business college in large town.
Enrollment: 234 undergrads.
Selectivity: Open admission.

BASIC COSTS (2006-2007)
Tuition and fees: $8,976.
Per-credit charge: $187.

FINANCIAL AID PICTURE
Students with need: Need-based aid available for full-time and part-time students.
Students without need: This college only awards aid to students with need.

FINANCIAL AID PROCEDURES
Forms required: FAFSA.
Dates and Deadlines: No deadline. Applicants notified on a rolling basis starting 9/1.

CONTACT
Pamela Cotton, Director of Financial Aid and Compliance Officer
PO Box 6400, Roanoke, VA 24017
(540) 986-1800

National College of Business & Technology: Lynchburg
Lynchburg, Virginia
www.ncbt.edu
Federal Code: 010489

2-year for-profit business college in small city.
Enrollment: 283 undergrads.
Selectivity: Open admission.

BASIC COSTS (2006-2007)
Tuition and fees: $8,976.
Per-credit charge: $187.

FINANCIAL AID PICTURE
Students with need: Need-based aid available for full-time and part-time students.
Students without need: This college only awards aid to students with need.

FINANCIAL AID PROCEDURES
Forms required: FAFSA.
Dates and Deadlines: No deadline. Applicants notified on a rolling basis starting 9/1.

CONTACT
Pamela Cotton, Director of Financial Aid and Compliance Officer
PO Box 6400, Roanoke, VA 24017
(540) 986-1000

National College of Business & Technology: Martinsville
Martinsville, Virginia
www.ncbt.edu
Federal Code: 003726

2-year private business and junior college in small city.
Enrollment: 277 undergrads.
Selectivity: Open admission.

BASIC COSTS (2006-2007)
Tuition and fees: $8,976.
Per-credit charge: $187.

FINANCIAL AID PICTURE
Students with need: Need-based aid available for full-time and part-time students.
Students without need: This college only awards aid to students with need.

FINANCIAL AID PROCEDURES
Forms required: FAFSA.
Dates and Deadlines: No deadline. Applicants notified on a rolling basis.

CONTACT
Pamela Cotton, Director of Financial Aid and Compliance Officer
PO Box 6400, Roanoke, VA 24017
(540) 986-1800

National College of Business & Technology: Salem
Roanoke, Virginia
www.ncbt.edu   Federal Code: 003726

4-year for-profit business college in large city.
Enrollment: 639 undergrads.
Selectivity: Open admission.

BASIC COSTS (2006-2007)
Tuition and fees: $8,976.

FINANCIAL AID PICTURE
Students with need: Need-based aid available for full-time and part-time students.
Students without need: This college only awards aid to students with need.

FINANCIAL AID PROCEDURES
Forms required: FAFSA.
Dates and Deadlines: No deadline. Applicants notified on a rolling basis.

CONTACT
Pamela Cotton, Director of Financial Aid
PO Box 6400, Roanoke, VA 24017-0400
(540) 986-1800

New River Community College
Dublin, Virginia
www.nr.edu   Federal Code: 005223

2-year public community college in rural community.
Enrollment: 2,105 undergrads.
Selectivity: Open admission.

BASIC COSTS (2005-2006)
Tuition and fees: $2,170; out-of-state residents $6,550.
Per-credit charge: $68; out-of-state residents $214.

FINANCIAL AID PICTURE (2004-2005)
Students with need: 69% of average financial aid package awarded as scholarships/grants, 31% awarded as loans/jobs. Need-based aid available for part-time students.

FINANCIAL AID PROCEDURES
Forms required: FAFSA, institutional form.
Dates and Deadlines: Priority date 4/15; no closing date. Applicants notified on a rolling basis starting 6/1.

CONTACT
Joseph Sheffey, Coordinator of Financial Aid
Drawer 1127, Dublin, VA 24084
(540) 674-3615

Norfolk State University
Norfolk, Virginia
www.nsu.edu   Federal Code: 003765

4-year public university in small city.
Enrollment: 5,246 undergrads, 16% part-time. 970 full-time freshmen.
Selectivity: Admits 50 to 75% of applicants.

BASIC COSTS (2006-2007)
Tuition and fees: $5,056; out-of-state residents $15,376.
Per-credit charge: $223; out-of-state residents $567.
Room and board: $6,667.

FINANCIAL AID PICTURE (2004-2005)
Students with need: Out of 897 full-time freshmen who applied for aid, 782 were judged to have need. Of these, 772 received aid, and 26 had their full need met. Average financial aid package met 83% of need; average scholarship/grant was $5,521; average loan was $2,918. For part-time students, average financial aid package was $5,548.
Students without need: 171 full-time freshmen who did not demonstrate need for aid received scholarships/grants; average award was $4,580. No-need awards available for academics, alumni affiliation, athletics, leadership, music/drama, ROTC, state/district residency.
Scholarships offered: 41 full-time freshmen received athletic scholarships; average amount $3,936.
Cumulative student debt: 76% of graduating class had student loans; average debt was $16,175.

FINANCIAL AID PROCEDURES
Forms required: FAFSA.
Dates and Deadlines: Priority date 5/31; no closing date. Applicants notified on a rolling basis starting 4/1; must reply within 2 week(s) of notification.

CONTACT
Estherine Harding, Director of Student Financial Services
700 Park Avenue, Norfolk, VA 23504
(757) 823-8381

Old Dominion University
Norfolk, Virginia
www.odu.edu   Federal Code: 003728

4-year public university in small city.
Enrollment: 14,605 undergrads, 27% part-time. 2,055 full-time freshmen.
Selectivity: Admits 50 to 75% of applicants.

BASIC COSTS (2006-2007)
Tuition and fees: $6,098; out-of-state residents $16,658.
Per-credit charge: $197; out-of-state residents $549.
Room and board: $6,640.

FINANCIAL AID PICTURE (2005-2006)
Students with need: Out of 1,550 full-time freshmen who applied for aid, 1,421 were judged to have need. Of these, 1,224 received aid, and 722 had their full need met. Average financial aid package met 68% of need; average scholarship/grant was $3,954; average loan was $2,678. For part-time students, average financial aid package was $4,618.
Students without need: 98 full-time freshmen who did not demonstrate need for aid received scholarships/grants; average award was $2,893. No-need awards available for academics, alumni affiliation, art, athletics, leadership, music/drama, ROTC, state/district residency.
Scholarships offered: 57 full-time freshmen received athletic scholarships; average amount $8,780.
Cumulative student debt: 80% of graduating class had student loans; average debt was $16,775.

Virginia Old Dominion University

FINANCIAL AID PROCEDURES
Forms required: FAFSA.
Dates and Deadlines: Priority date 2/15; closing date 3/15. Applicants notified on a rolling basis starting 2/1; must reply within 2 week(s) of notification.
Transfers: Applicants notified on a rolling basis starting 2/1; must reply within 2 week(s) of notification.

CONTACT
Veronica Finch, Acting Director of Financial Aid
108 Rollins Hall, 5115 Hampton Boulevard, Norfolk, VA 23529
(757) 683-3633

Patrick Henry Community College
Martinsville, Virginia
www.ph.vccs.edu   Federal Code: 003751

2-year public community college in large town.
Enrollment: 3,229 undergrads.
Selectivity: Open admission.

BASIC COSTS (2005-2006)
Tuition and fees: $2,151; out-of-state residents $6,531.
Per-credit charge: $68; out-of-state residents $214.

FINANCIAL AID PICTURE
Students with need: Need-based aid available for full-time and part-time students.

FINANCIAL AID PROCEDURES
Forms required: FAFSA.
Dates and Deadlines: Priority date 6/1; no closing date. Applicants notified on a rolling basis starting 6/15.

CONTACT
Bill Wingfield, Financial Aid
Box 5311, Martinsville, VA 24115-5311
(276) 656-0317

Paul D. Camp Community College
Franklin, Virginia
www.pc.vccs.edu   Federal Code: 009159

2-year public community college in small town.
Enrollment: 793 undergrads.
Selectivity: Open admission; but selective for some programs.

BASIC COSTS (2005-2006)
Tuition and fees: $2,121; out-of-state residents $6,501.
Per-credit charge: $68; out-of-state residents $214.

FINANCIAL AID PICTURE
Students with need: Need-based aid available for full-time and part-time students. Work study available nights.

FINANCIAL AID PROCEDURES
Forms required: FAFSA.
Dates and Deadlines: Priority date 6/1; no closing date. Applicants notified on a rolling basis starting 8/1; must reply within 2 week(s) of notification.

CONTACT
Teresa King, Financial Aid Coordinator
100 North College Drive, Franklin, VA 23851-0737
(757) 925-6307

Piedmont Virginia Community College
Charlottesville, Virginia
www.pvcc.edu   Federal Code: 009928

2-year public community college in large town.
Enrollment: 2,806 undergrads, 66% part-time. 353 full-time freshmen.
Selectivity: Open admission; but selective for some programs.

BASIC COSTS (2005-2006)
Tuition and fees: $2,199; out-of-state residents $6,579.
Per-credit charge: $68; out-of-state residents $214.

FINANCIAL AID PICTURE (2004-2005)
Students with need: 96% of average financial aid package awarded as scholarships/grants, 4% awarded as loans/jobs. Need-based aid available for part-time students. Work study available nights.
Students without need: This college only awards aid to students with need.

FINANCIAL AID PROCEDURES
Forms required: FAFSA, institutional form.
Dates and Deadlines: Priority date 3/31; no closing date. Applicants notified on a rolling basis starting 5/1.
Transfers: No deadline. Must meet Satisfactory Academic Progress standards.

CONTACT
Carol Larson, Director of Financial Aid
501 College Drive, Charlottesville, VA 22902-7589
(434) 961-5405

Radford University
Radford, Virginia
www.radford.edu   Federal Code: 003732

4-year public university in large town.
Enrollment: 8,419 undergrads, 5% part-time. 1,828 full-time freshmen.
Selectivity: Admits over 75% of applicants.

BASIC COSTS (2005-2006)
Tuition and fees: $5,130; out-of-state residents $12,368.
Per-credit charge: $214; out-of-state residents $515.
Room and board: $6,120.

FINANCIAL AID PICTURE (2004-2005)
Students with need: Out of 1,148 full-time freshmen who applied for aid, 731 were judged to have need. Of these, 701 received aid. Average financial aid package met 70% of need; average scholarship/grant was $5,241; average loan was $2,492. For part-time students, average financial aid package was $6,458.
Students without need: 85 full-time freshmen who did not demonstrate need for aid received scholarships/grants; average award was $3,454. No-need awards available for academics, athletics, ROTC.
Scholarships offered: 38 full-time freshmen received athletic scholarships; average amount $3,778.
Cumulative student debt: 63% of graduating class had student loans; average debt was $14,702.
Additional info: Student's need and grades considered. Top consideration given to those with greatest need and who apply by deadline.

FINANCIAL AID PROCEDURES
Forms required: FAFSA.
Dates and Deadlines: Priority date 3/1; no closing date. Applicants notified on a rolling basis starting 4/15.

CONTACT
Barbara Porter, Director of Financial Aid
Radford University Admissions, 209 Martin Hall, Radford, VA 24142
(540) 831-5408

Randolph-Macon College
Ashland, Virginia
www.rmc.edu   Federal Code: 003733

4-year private liberal arts college in small town, affiliated with United Methodist Church.
Enrollment: 1,097 undergrads, 1% part-time. 305 full-time freshmen.
Selectivity: Admits over 75% of applicants.

BASIC COSTS (2006-2007)
Tuition and fees: $25,345.
Per-credit charge: $915.
Room and board: $7,695.

FINANCIAL AID PICTURE (2005-2006)
Students with need: Out of 239 full-time freshmen who applied for aid, 189 were judged to have need. Of these, 189 received aid, and 48 had their full need met. Average financial aid package met 86% of need; average scholarship/grant was $14,629; average loan was $4,645. Need-based aid available for part-time students.
Students without need: 111 full-time freshmen who did not demonstrate need for aid received scholarships/grants; average award was $12,714. No-need awards available for academics, alumni affiliation, minority status, religious affiliation, state/district residency.
Scholarships offered: Presidential Scholarships: awarded to outstanding entering applicants based on school record and ACT or SAT scores. Grants range from up to $20,000 per year.
Cumulative student debt: 70% of graduating class had student loans; average debt was $15,130.

FINANCIAL AID PROCEDURES
Forms required: FAFSA, state aid form.
Dates and Deadlines: Priority date 2/1; closing date 3/1. Applicants notified by 3/15; must reply by 5/1 or within 2 week(s) of notification.
Transfers: Closing date 3/1. Applicants notified by 3/15; must reply by 5/1.

CONTACT
Mary Neal, Director of Financial Aid
PO Box 5005, Ashland, VA 23005-5505
(804) 752-7529

Randolph-Macon Woman's College
Lynchburg, Virginia
www.rmwc.edu   Federal Code: 003734

4-year private liberal arts college for women in small city, affiliated with United Methodist Church.
Enrollment: 681 undergrads, 2% part-time. 184 full-time freshmen.
Selectivity: Admits over 75% of applicants.

BASIC COSTS (2006-2007)
Tuition and fees: $24,410.
Per-credit charge: $996.
Room and board: $8,800.
Additional info: Room and board charges include free use of laundry facilities. Tuition/fee waivers available for adults.

FINANCIAL AID PICTURE (2005-2006)
Students with need: Out of 138 full-time freshmen who applied for aid, 112 were judged to have need. Of these, 112 received aid, and 57 had their full need met. Average financial aid package met 92% of need; average scholarship/grant was $17,465; average loan was $2,526. For part-time students, average financial aid package was $10,625.
Students without need: 72 full-time freshmen who did not demonstrate need for aid received scholarships/grants; average award was $16,310. No-need awards available for academics, alumni affiliation, art, leadership, minority status, music/drama, religious affiliation, state/district residency.
Scholarships offered: Gottwald Scholarship: full tuition plus travel stipend; based on academic profile; 12 awarded.
Cumulative student debt: 70% of graduating class had student loans; average debt was $25,500.
Additional info: College offers approximately $2 million annually to incoming first-year students. Grants range up to full tuition. Student must reapply each year.

FINANCIAL AID PROCEDURES
Forms required: FAFSA, state aid form.
Dates and Deadlines: Priority date 3/1; no closing date. Applicants notified on a rolling basis starting 3/1; must reply by 5/1 or within 2 week(s) of notification.
Transfers: Priority date 2/1.

CONTACT
Katherine Cooper, Director of Financial Planning and Analysis
2500 Rivermont Avenue, Lynchburg, VA 24503-1526
(434) 947-8128

Rappahannock Community College
Glenns, Virginia
www.rcc.vccs.edu   Federal Code: 009160

2-year public community college in rural community.
Enrollment: 2,870 undergrads.
Selectivity: Open admission.

BASIC COSTS (2005-2006)
Tuition and fees: $2,151; out-of-state residents $6,531.
Per-credit charge: $68; out-of-state residents $214.

FINANCIAL AID PICTURE
Students with need: Need-based aid available for full-time and part-time students.

FINANCIAL AID PROCEDURES
Forms required: FAFSA, institutional form.
Dates and Deadlines: Priority date 5/15; no closing date. Applicants notified on a rolling basis starting 6/30.

CONTACT
Carolyn Ward, Director of Financial Aid
12745 College Drive, Glenns, VA 23149
(804) 758-6737

Richard Bland College
Petersburg, Virginia
www.rbc.edu   Federal Code: 003707

2-year public junior and liberal arts college in small city.
Enrollment: 1,105 undergrads, 28% part-time. 46 full-time freshmen.
Selectivity: Admits over 75% of applicants.

BASIC COSTS (2006-2007)

Tuition and fees: $2,520; out-of-state residents $10,240.
Per-credit charge: $98; out-of-state residents $427.
Additional info: Out of State students pay an additional required capitol fee of $46 per year.

FINANCIAL AID PICTURE (2004-2005)

Students with need: Out of 44 full-time freshmen who applied for aid, 38 were judged to have need. Of these, 38 received aid, and 4 had their full need met. Average financial aid package met 50% of need; average scholarship/grant was $728. For part-time students, average financial aid package was $2,350.
Students without need: 8 full-time freshmen who did not demonstrate need for aid received scholarships/grants; average award was $1,000. No-need awards available for academics, state/district residency.
Scholarships offered: Presidential Scholarships: average $1,000; for full-time first-time Virginia residents; based on minimum 3.5 high school GPA.

FINANCIAL AID PROCEDURES

Forms required: FAFSA, institutional form.
Dates and Deadlines: Priority date 5/1; no closing date. Applicants notified by 6/1; must reply within 2 week(s) of notification.

CONTACT

Tony Jones, Director of Financial Aid
11301 Johnson Road, Petersburg, VA 23805
(804) 862-6223

Roanoke College
Salem, Virginia
www.roanoke.edu   Federal Code: 003736

4-year private liberal arts college in large town, affiliated with Evangelical Lutheran Church in America.
Enrollment: 1,877 undergrads, 3% part-time. 534 full-time freshmen.
Selectivity: Admits 50 to 75% of applicants.

BASIC COSTS (2006-2007)

Tuition and fees: $24,653.
Per-credit charge: $1,145.
Room and board: $8,152.
Additional info: Tuition/fee waivers available for adults.

FINANCIAL AID PICTURE (2005-2006)

Students with need: Out of 398 full-time freshmen who applied for aid, 396 were judged to have need. Of these, 396 received aid, and 91 had their full need met. Average financial aid package met 93% of need; average scholarship/grant was $16,416; average loan was $3,230. For part-time students, average financial aid package was $4,627.
Students without need: 111 full-time freshmen who did not demonstrate need for aid received scholarships/grants; average award was $9,150. No-need awards available for academics, minority status, music/drama, religious affiliation.
Scholarships offered: William Beard Scholarship; 2 awarded; full tuition, room and board. Bittle Scholarship; full tuition; 6 awarded. Baughman Scholarship; half tuition; 25 awarded. Roanoke College Scholarship;$3,000-$6,000; variable number awarded. All based on superior academics and leadership ability.
Cumulative student debt: 72% of graduating class had student loans; average debt was $18,543.

FINANCIAL AID PROCEDURES

Forms required: FAFSA, state aid form.
Dates and Deadlines: Priority date 3/1; no closing date. Applicants notified on a rolling basis starting 11/1; must reply within 2 week(s) of notification.

CONTACT

Thomas Blair, Director of Financial Aid
221 College Lane, Salem, VA 24153-3794
(540) 375-2235

St. Paul's College
Lawrenceville, Virginia
www.saintpauls.edu   Federal Code: 003739

4-year private liberal arts college in small town, affiliated with Episcopal Church.
Enrollment: 690 full-time undergrads.
Selectivity: Admits 50 to 75% of applicants.

BASIC COSTS (2006-2007)

Tuition and fees: $11,500.
Per-credit charge: $450.
Room and board: $5,890.
Additional info: Tuition/fee waivers available for minority students.

FINANCIAL AID PICTURE (2004-2005)

Students with need: 51% of average financial aid package awarded as scholarships/grants, 49% awarded as loans/jobs.
Students without need: No-need awards available for academics, athletics, leadership.

FINANCIAL AID PROCEDURES

Forms required: FAFSA, state aid form.
Dates and Deadlines: No deadline. Applicants notified on a rolling basis starting 1/15; must reply by 7/1 or within 4 week(s) of notification.

CONTACT

Hester Austin-Walker, Director of Financial Aid
115 College Drive, Lawrenceville, VA 23868
(434) 848-6497

Shenandoah University
Winchester, Virginia
www.su.edu   Federal Code: 003737

4-year private university in small city, affiliated with United Methodist Church.
Enrollment: 1,562 undergrads, 3% part-time. 329 full-time freshmen.
Selectivity: Admits 50 to 75% of applicants.

BASIC COSTS (2006-2007)

Tuition and fees: $21,290.
Room and board: $7,650.

FINANCIAL AID PICTURE (2004-2005)

Students with need: Out of 245 full-time freshmen who applied for aid, 245 were judged to have need. Of these, 245 received aid, and 49 had their full need met. Average financial aid package met 84% of need; average scholarship/grant was $4,897; average loan was $3,677. For part-time students, average financial aid package was $3,972.
Students without need: 45 full-time freshmen who did not demonstrate need for aid received scholarships/grants; average award was $4,232. No-need awards available for academics, job skills, music/drama, religious affiliation, state/district residency.

FINANCIAL AID PROCEDURES

Forms required: FAFSA, state aid form.
Dates and Deadlines: Priority date 2/15; no closing date. Applicants notified on a rolling basis starting 3/15; must reply within 2 week(s) of notification.
Transfers: Priority date 3/1.

CONTACT
Nancy Bragg, Director of Financial Aid
1460 University Drive, Winchester, VA 22601-5195
(540) 665-4538

Southside Virginia Community College
Alberta, Virginia
www.sv.vccs.edu Federal Code: 008661

2-year public community college in rural community.
Enrollment: 2,390 undergrads, 55% part-time. 228 full-time freshmen.
Selectivity: Open admission; but selective for some programs.

BASIC COSTS (2005-2006)
Tuition and fees: $2,181; out-of-state residents $6,561.
Per-credit charge: $68; out-of-state residents $214.

FINANCIAL AID PICTURE (2005-2006)
Students with need: 97% of average financial aid package awarded as scholarships/grants, 3% awarded as loans/jobs. Need-based aid available for part-time students. Work study available nights.
Students without need: No-need awards available for academics.
Scholarships offered: Guaranteed Academic Merit Award, $1,500, for high school graduates within college's service area with 3.0 GPA who do not receive at least $1,500 in need-based aid.

FINANCIAL AID PROCEDURES
Forms required: FAFSA.
Dates and Deadlines: Priority date 6/1; closing date 8/1. Applicants notified on a rolling basis starting 6/15.
Transfers: State aid limited to in-state residents.

CONTACT
Brent Richey, Director of Financial Aid
109 Campus Drive, Alberta, VA 23821
(434) 736-2026

Sweet Briar College
Sweet Briar, Virginia
www.sbc.edu Federal Code: 003742

4-year private liberal arts college for women in rural community.
Enrollment: 556 undergrads, 2% part-time. 180 full-time freshmen.
Selectivity: Admits over 75% of applicants.

BASIC COSTS (2006-2007)
Tuition and fees: $23,540.
Per-credit charge: $775.
Room and board: $9,480.
Additional info: Tuition/fee waivers available for adults.

FINANCIAL AID PICTURE (2005-2006)
Students with need: Out of 123 full-time freshmen who applied for aid, 123 were judged to have need. Of these, 122 received aid, and 116 had their full need met. Average financial aid package met 36% of need; average scholarship/grant was $14,320; average loan was $3,848. For part-time students, average financial aid package was $7,860.
Students without need: 85 full-time freshmen who did not demonstrate need for aid received scholarships/grants; average award was $10,826. No-need awards available for academics, art, leadership, music/drama, state/district residency.
Scholarships offered: Founders and Prothro Scholarships: up to $15,000. Commonwealth Scholarships: up to $13,000. International Scholarships: up to $12,500; for international students of traditional college age who intend to study at Sweet Briar for 4 years and live in residence halls. Betty Bean Black Scholarships: up to $12,000. Sweet Briar Scholarships: up to $9,000; for students with special talents in specific area. All awards based on academic qualifications; renewable annually with specified GPA.
Cumulative student debt: 56% of graduating class had student loans; average debt was $17,808.

FINANCIAL AID PROCEDURES
Forms required: FAFSA.
Dates and Deadlines: Priority date 3/1; no closing date. Applicants notified on a rolling basis starting 3/1; must reply by 5/1 or within 2 week(s) of notification.
Transfers: Closing date 7/15.

CONTACT
Bobbi Carpenter, Director of Financial Aid
PO Box B, Sweet Briar, VA 24595

Thomas Nelson Community College
Hampton, Virginia
www.tncc.edu Federal Code: 006871

2-year public community college in small city.
Enrollment: 6,498 undergrads, 62% part-time. 674 full-time freshmen.
Selectivity: Open admission; but selective for some programs.

BASIC COSTS (2005-2006)
Tuition and fees: $2,142; out-of-state residents $6,522.
Per-credit charge: $68; out-of-state residents $214.

FINANCIAL AID PICTURE
Students with need: Need-based aid available for full-time and part-time students. Work study available nights.

FINANCIAL AID PROCEDURES
Forms required: FAFSA.
Dates and Deadlines: Priority date 5/1; no closing date. Applicants notified on a rolling basis starting 6/1; must reply within 2 week(s) of notification.

CONTACT
Lisa Smith, Interim Director of Financial Aid, Veterans Affairs, and Scholarships
Box 9407, Hampton, VA 23670
(757) 825-2848

Tidewater Community College
Norfolk, Virginia
www.tcc.vccs.edu Federal Code: 003712

2-year public community college in large city.
Enrollment: 12,196 undergrads.
Selectivity: Open admission; but selective for some programs.

BASIC COSTS (2005-2006)
Tuition and fees: $2,281; out-of-state residents $6,661.
Per-credit charge: $68; out-of-state residents $214.

FINANCIAL AID PICTURE
Students with need: Need-based aid available for full-time and part-time students.
Students without need: This college only awards aid to students with need.

FINANCIAL AID PROCEDURES
Forms required: FAFSA.
Dates and Deadlines: Priority date 4/1; no closing date. Applicants notified on a rolling basis starting 4/1.

CONTACT
Norma Ferki, Director of Financial Aid
7000 College Drive/Portsmouth Campus, Portsmouth, VA 23703
(757) 822-1360

University of Mary Washington
Fredericksburg, Virginia
www.umw.edu   Federal Code: 003746

4-year public liberal arts college in small city.
Enrollment: 3,951 undergrads, 11% part-time. 869 full-time freshmen.
Selectivity: Admits 50 to 75% of applicants.

BASIC COSTS (2005-2006)
Tuition and fees: $5,634; out-of-state residents $14,776.
Per-credit charge: $199; out-of-state residents $579.
Room and board: $7,134.

FINANCIAL AID PICTURE (2005-2006)
Students with need: Out of 610 full-time freshmen who applied for aid, 392 were judged to have need. Of these, 392 received aid, and 36 had their full need met. Average financial aid package met 60% of need; average scholarship/grant was $2,825; average loan was $2,515. For part-time students, average financial aid package was $4,200.
Students without need: 135 full-time freshmen who did not demonstrate need for aid received scholarships/grants; average award was $1,080. No-need awards available for academics, art, leadership, minority status, music/drama, state/district residency.
Scholarships offered: Scholastic Excellence Award: from $500 to $3,400; honors admissions are automatically considered. Two Virginia residents will receive tuition, fees, room and board up to $10,000. All scholarships are renewable.
Cumulative student debt: 72% of graduating class had student loans; average debt was $12,665.

FINANCIAL AID PROCEDURES
Forms required: FAFSA.
Dates and Deadlines: Priority date 3/1; no closing date. Applicants notified by 4/15; must reply by 5/1 or within 2 week(s) of notification.

CONTACT
Deborah Harber, Senior Associate Dean for Financial Aid
1301 College Avenue, Fredericksburg, VA 22401-5358
(540) 654-2468

University of Richmond
University of Richmond, Virginia
www.richmond.edu   Federal Code: 003744

4-year private university and liberal arts college in very large city.
Enrollment: 2,853 undergrads, 1% part-time. 775 full-time freshmen.
Selectivity: Admits less than 50% of applicants.

BASIC COSTS (2006-2007)
Tuition and fees: $36,550.
Per-credit charge: $1,460.
Room and board: $6,060.

FINANCIAL AID PICTURE (2005-2006)
Students with need: Average financial aid package met 100% of need; average scholarship/grant was $23,594; average loan was $2,829. For part-time students, average financial aid package was $34,279.
Students without need: No-need awards available for academics, art, athletics, leadership, minority status, music/drama, ROTC, state/district residency.
Scholarships offered: Over 50 merit-based scholarships available, ranging from one-half to full tuition.
Cumulative student debt: 41% of graduating class had student loans; average debt was $18,500.
Additional info: Interview required for University, Oldham, Ethyl, and CIGNA. Undergraduate research grants available.

FINANCIAL AID PROCEDURES
Forms required: FAFSA, institutional form.
Dates and Deadlines: Closing date 2/25. Applicants notified by 4/1; must reply by 5/1 or within 4 week(s) of notification.

CONTACT
Cindy Deffenbaugh, Director of Student Financial Aid
28 Westhampton Way, University of Richmond, VA 23173
(804) 289-8438

University of Virginia
Charlottesville, Virginia
www.virginia.edu   Federal Code: 003745

4-year public university in small city.
Enrollment: 13,387 undergrads, 2% part-time. 3,105 full-time freshmen.
Selectivity: Admits less than 50% of applicants.

BASIC COSTS (2006-2007)
Tuition and fees: $7,845; out-of-state residents $25,769.
Room and board: $6,909.
Additional info: Out of state students pay an additional $176.

FINANCIAL AID PICTURE (2005-2006)
Students with need: Out of 1,652 full-time freshmen who applied for aid, 737 were judged to have need. Of these, 737 received aid, and 737 had their full need met. Average financial aid package met 100% of need; average scholarship/grant was $11,886; average loan was $3,828. For part-time students, average financial aid package was $13,269.
Students without need: 432 full-time freshmen who did not demonstrate need for aid received scholarships/grants; average award was $7,106. No-need awards available for academics, athletics, leadership, minority status, state/district residency.
Scholarships offered: 114 full-time freshmen received athletic scholarships; average amount $17,612.
Cumulative student debt: 30% of graduating class had student loans; average debt was $15,176.

FINANCIAL AID PROCEDURES
Forms required: FAFSA, institutional form.
Dates and Deadlines: Priority date 3/1; no closing date. Applicants notified by 4/5.

CONTACT
Yvonne Hubbard, Director Student Financial Services
Office of Admission, Charlottesville, VA 22904-4160
(434) 982-6000

University of Virginia's College at Wise
Wise, Virginia
www.uvawise.edu   Federal Code: 003747

4-year public liberal arts college in small town.
Enrollment: 1,623 undergrads, 11% part-time. 373 full-time freshmen.
Selectivity: Admits over 75% of applicants.

BASIC COSTS (2005-2006)
Tuition and fees: $5,081; out-of-state residents $15,159.
Per-credit charge: $123; out-of-state residents $539.

Room and board: $5,995.
Additional info: Capital fee of $50 for out of state students.

FINANCIAL AID PICTURE (2004-2005)
Students with need: Out of 340 full-time freshmen who applied for aid, 262 were judged to have need. Of these, 262 received aid, and 249 had their full need met. Average financial aid package met 95% of need; average scholarship/grant was $4,163; average loan was $2,125. For part-time students, average financial aid package was $3,911.
Students without need: 67 full-time freshmen who did not demonstrate need for aid received scholarships/grants; average award was $1,900. No-need awards available for academics, alumni affiliation, art, athletics, job skills, leadership, music/drama, religious affiliation, state/district residency.
Scholarships offered: 27 full-time freshmen received athletic scholarships; average amount $1,502.
Cumulative student debt: 70% of graduating class had student loans; average debt was $9,157.

FINANCIAL AID PROCEDURES
Forms required: FAFSA.
Dates and Deadlines: Priority date 4/1; no closing date. Applicants notified on a rolling basis starting 2/15; must reply within 4 week(s) of notification.

CONTACT
Bill Wendle, Director of Financial Aid
One College Avenue, Wise, VA 24293-4412
(276) 328-0139

Virginia Commonwealth University
Richmond, Virginia
www.vcu.edu   Federal Code: 003735

4-year public university in small city.
Enrollment: 18,691 undergrads, 14% part-time. 3,477 full-time freshmen.
Selectivity: Admits 50 to 75% of applicants.

BASIC COSTS (2006-2007)
Tuition and fees: $5,819; out-of-state residents $17,496.
Per-credit charge: $176; out-of-state residents $663.
Room and board: $7,536.
Additional info: Capital Outlay Fee of $60 additional for out-of-state students.

FINANCIAL AID PICTURE (2004-2005)
Students with need: Out of 2,445 full-time freshmen who applied for aid, 1,766 were judged to have need. Of these, 1,699 received aid, and 84 had their full need met. Average financial aid package met 42% of need; average scholarship/grant was $3,959; average loan was $2,857. For part-time students, average financial aid package was $4,818.
Students without need: 211 full-time freshmen who did not demonstrate need for aid received scholarships/grants; average award was $4,105. No-need awards available for academics, art, athletics, leadership, music/drama.
Scholarships offered: *Merit:* Presidential; covers in-state tuition, fees, room and board; based on high school academic achievement, strength of curriculum, GPA and SAT or ACT scores; 25 awarded. Provost; covers in-state tuition and fees; primarily based on high school academic achievement, including strength of curriculum, GPA and SAT or ACT scores; 100 per year. Deans; covers one-half in-state tuition and fees; primarily based on high school academic achievement, including strength of curriculum, GPA and SAT or ACT scores; 125 per year. In addition to the above, endowed merit based awards that are school specific offered for varying amounts. *Athletic:* 53 full-time freshmen received athletic scholarships; average amount $9,091.
Cumulative student debt: 66% of graduating class had student loans; average debt was $20,069.

FINANCIAL AID PROCEDURES
Forms required: FAFSA.
Dates and Deadlines: Priority date 3/1; no closing date. Applicants notified by 3/15; must reply by 5/1 or within 2 week(s) of notification.
Transfers: Applicants notified by 6/6; must reply within 2 week(s) of notification.

CONTACT
Susan Kadir, Director of Financial Aid
Box 842526, Richmond, VA 23284-2526
(804) 828-6669

Virginia Highlands Community College
Abingdon, Virginia
www.vhcc.edu   Federal Code: 007099

2-year public community college in small town.
Enrollment: 1,667 undergrads.
Selectivity: Open admission; but selective for some programs.

BASIC COSTS (2005-2006)
Tuition and fees: $2,143; out-of-state residents $6,523.
Per-credit charge: $68; out-of-state residents $214.

FINANCIAL AID PICTURE (2004-2005)
Students with need: 89% of average financial aid package awarded as scholarships/grants, 11% awarded as loans/jobs.

FINANCIAL AID PROCEDURES
Forms required: FAFSA, institutional form.
Dates and Deadlines: No deadline. Applicants notified on a rolling basis starting 5/1.

CONTACT
David Matlock, Director of Admissions, Records and Financial Aid
PO Box 828, Abingdon, VA 24212-0828
(276) 739-2412

Virginia Intermont College
Bristol, Virginia
www.vic.edu   Federal Code: 003752

4-year private liberal arts college in large town, affiliated with Baptist faith.
Enrollment: 1,126 undergrads, 13% part-time. 166 full-time freshmen.
Selectivity: Admits 50 to 75% of applicants.

BASIC COSTS (2006-2007)
Tuition and fees: $17,845.
Per-credit charge: $220.
Room and board: $6,095.

FINANCIAL AID PICTURE (2004-2005)
Students with need: Out of 133 full-time freshmen who applied for aid, 111 were judged to have need. Of these, 111 received aid, and 8 had their full need met. Average financial aid package met 58% of need; average scholarship/grant was $10,186; average loan was $2,516. For part-time students, average financial aid package was $3,796.
Students without need: 39 full-time freshmen who did not demonstrate need for aid received scholarships/grants; average award was $9,360. No-need awards available for academics, alumni affiliation, art, athletics, minority status, music/drama, religious affiliation, state/district residency.
Scholarships offered: 22 full-time freshmen received athletic scholarships; average amount $12,037.
Cumulative student debt: 83% of graduating class had student loans; average debt was $18,700.

FINANCIAL AID PROCEDURES
Forms required: FAFSA, state aid form.

Dates and Deadlines: Closing date 3/1. Applicants notified on a rolling basis starting 2/15; must reply within 3 week(s) of notification.
Transfers: No deadline. Limited to a certain number of units of state aid.
CONTACT
Denise Posey, Financial Aid Director
1013 Moore Street, Bristol, VA 24201
(276) 466-7871

Virginia Military Institute
Lexington, Virginia
www.vmi.edu
Federal Code: 003753

4-year public liberal arts and military college in small town.
Enrollment: 1,369 undergrads. 363 full-time freshmen.
Selectivity: Admits 50 to 75% of applicants. GED not accepted.

BASIC COSTS (2006-2007)
Tuition and fees: $9,329; out-of-state residents $24,225.
Room and board: $5,988.

FINANCIAL AID PICTURE (2004-2005)
Students with need: Out of 243 full-time freshmen who applied for aid, 194 were judged to have need. Of these, 193 received aid, and 121 had their full need met. Average financial aid package met 93% of need; average scholarship/grant was $7,459; average loan was $3,400.
Students without need: 58 full-time freshmen who did not demonstrate need for aid received scholarships/grants; average award was $6,755. No-need awards available for academics, alumni affiliation, athletics, leadership, music/drama, ROTC, state/district residency.
Scholarships offered: *Merit:* Institute Scholarship; up to $19,830; 10-12 awarded; for superior academic performance, demonstrated character and leadership, extracurricular activities, 3.7 high school GPA, minimum 1250 SAT (exclusive of Writing) or 27 ACT, rank in top 5% of class. *Athletic:* 38 full-time freshmen received athletic scholarships; average amount $11,182.

FINANCIAL AID PROCEDURES
Forms required: FAFSA, institutional form.
Dates and Deadlines: Closing date 3/1. Applicants notified on a rolling basis starting 3/1.
CONTACT
Timothy Golden, Director of Financial Aid
Office of Admissions, Lexington, VA 24450-9967
(540) 464-7208

Virginia Polytechnic Institute and State University
Blacksburg, Virginia
www.vt.edu
Federal Code: 003754

4-year public university in large town.
Enrollment: 21,534 undergrads, 2% part-time. 4,928 full-time freshmen.
Selectivity: Admits 50 to 75% of applicants.

BASIC COSTS (2005-2006)
Tuition and fees: $6,378; out-of-state residents $17,717.
Per-credit charge: $207; out-of-state residents $679.
Room and board: $4,760.

FINANCIAL AID PICTURE (2004-2005)
Students with need: Out of 3,426 full-time freshmen who applied for aid, 2,292 were judged to have need. Of these, 1,832 received aid, and 54 had their full need met. Average financial aid package met 71% of need; average scholarship/grant was $5,199; average loan was $3,240. Need-based aid available for part-time students.
Students without need: 416 full-time freshmen who did not demonstrate need for aid received scholarships/grants; average award was $1,773. No-need awards available for art, athletics, ROTC.
Scholarships offered: 95 full-time freshmen received athletic scholarships; average amount $9,405.
Cumulative student debt: 54% of graduating class had student loans; average debt was $18,385.

FINANCIAL AID PROCEDURES
Forms required: FAFSA.
Dates and Deadlines: Priority date 3/11; no closing date. Applicants notified on a rolling basis starting 3/30; must reply by 5/1 or within 4 week(s) of notification.
Transfers: Priority date 2/1; closing date 3/11. Based on family EFC per FAFSA and available resources.
CONTACT
Barry Simmons, Director of Financial Aid
201 Burruss Hall, Blacksburg, VA 24061-0202
(540) 231-9555

Virginia State University
Petersburg, Virginia
www.vsu.edu
Federal Code: 003764

4-year public university in large town.
Enrollment: 4,278 undergrads, 5% part-time. 1,106 full-time freshmen.
Selectivity: Admits over 75% of applicants.

BASIC COSTS (2005-2006)
Tuition and fees: $4,834; out-of-state residents $9,852.
Per-credit charge: $161; out-of-state residents $402.
Room and board: $6,484.
Additional info: Out-of-state residents pay an addition $58 state capital outlay fee.

FINANCIAL AID PICTURE (2004-2005)
Students with need: 37% of average financial aid package awarded as scholarships/grants, 63% awarded as loans/jobs. Need-based aid available for part-time students. Work study available nights, weekends, and for part-time students.
Students without need: No-need awards available for academics, alumni affiliation, art, athletics, job skills, leadership, music/drama, religious affiliation, ROTC.
Scholarships offered: Presidential Scholarships: 3.2 GPA, SAT 1100 or ACT 24; $7,000. Provost's Scholarships: 3.0 GPA, SAT 1000 or ACT 21; $3,500. SAT exclusive of Writing. Fine and Performing Arts Scholarships: outstanding talent in music or fine arts, audition or portfolio may be required, recommendation required; $1,500. Math, Science, and Technology Scholarships: 3.0 GPA, above average ability in math, science, or technology, recommendation and essay required; $1,500.
Additional info: Strongly recommend that students apply for scholarship assistance through federal, state, local and private agencies.

FINANCIAL AID PROCEDURES
Forms required: FAFSA, institutional form.
Dates and Deadlines: Priority date 3/31; closing date 5/1. Applicants notified on a rolling basis starting 5/1; must reply within 2 week(s) of notification.
Transfers: Priority date 3/1.
CONTACT
Henry Debose, Director of Financial Aid
One Hayden Street, Petersburg, VA 23806
(804) 524-5990

Virginia Union University
Richmond, Virginia
www.vuu.edu   Federal Code: 003766

4-year private university and liberal arts college in small city, affiliated with Baptist faith.
Enrollment: 1,344 undergrads, 3% part-time. 337 full-time freshmen.
Selectivity: Admits 50 to 75% of applicants.

BASIC COSTS (2006-2007)
Tuition and fees: $13,154.
Per-credit charge: $497.
Room and board: $5,880.

FINANCIAL AID PICTURE (2005-2006)
Students with need: Out of 329 full-time freshmen who applied for aid, 299 were judged to have need. Of these, 297 received aid, and 94 had their full need met. Average financial aid package met 81% of need; average scholarship/grant was $3,959; average loan was $3,642. For part-time students, average financial aid package was $7,590.
Students without need: 2 full-time freshmen who did not demonstrate need for aid received scholarships/grants; average award was $2,415. No-need awards available for academics, athletics, ROTC, state/district residency.
Scholarships offered: 18 full-time freshmen received athletic scholarships; average amount $9,468.
Cumulative student debt: 98% of graduating class had student loans; average debt was $17,560.

FINANCIAL AID PROCEDURES
Forms required: FAFSA.
Dates and Deadlines: Priority date 4/27; no closing date. Applicants notified on a rolling basis starting 5/1; must reply within 2 week(s) of notification.
Transfers: Student must submit a financial aid transcript from all prior schools attended before receiving aid.

CONTACT
Phenie Golatt, Director of Financial Aid
1500 North Lombardy Street, Richmond, VA 23220
(804) 257-5882

Virginia Wesleyan College
Norfolk, Virginia
www.vwc.edu   Federal Code: 003767

4-year private liberal arts college in large city, affiliated with United Methodist Church.
Enrollment: 1,313 undergrads, 15% part-time. 352 full-time freshmen.
Selectivity: Admits over 75% of applicants.

BASIC COSTS (2006-2007)
Tuition and fees: $23,136.
Per-credit charge: $957.
Room and board: $6,850.
Additional info: Damage deposit of $75 for residents. Tuition/fee waivers available for adults.

FINANCIAL AID PICTURE (2004-2005)
Students with need: Out of 344 full-time freshmen who applied for aid, 305 were judged to have need. Of these, 271 received aid, and 41 had their full need met. Average financial aid package met 71% of need; average scholarship/grant was $4,061; average loan was $3,214. For part-time students, average financial aid package was $3,274.
Students without need: 65 full-time freshmen who did not demonstrate need for aid received scholarships/grants; average award was $5,297. No-need awards available for academics, art, leadership, music/drama, religious affiliation, state/district residency.

FINANCIAL AID PROCEDURES
Forms required: FAFSA, state aid form.
Dates and Deadlines: Priority date 3/1; no closing date. Applicants notified on a rolling basis starting 2/15; must reply by 5/1 or within 2 week(s) of notification.
Transfers: 4 semester maximum of special aid available for students who graduated with a 3.0 GPA and earned an associate degree from a local community college. Must enroll full time and maintain 2.5 GPA minimum.

CONTACT
Eugenia Hickman, Director of Financial Aid
1584 Wesleyan Drive, Norfolk, VA 23502-5599
(757) 455-3345

Virginia Western Community College
Roanoke, Virginia
www.virginiawestern.edu   Federal Code: 003760

2-year public community college in small city.
Enrollment: 8,244 undergrads.
Selectivity: Open admission; but selective for some programs.

BASIC COSTS (2005-2006)
Tuition and fees: $2,168; out-of-state residents $6,548.
Per-credit charge: $68; out-of-state residents $214.

FINANCIAL AID PICTURE
Students with need: Need-based aid available for full-time and part-time students.
Students without need: No-need awards available for academics, state/district residency.

FINANCIAL AID PROCEDURES
Forms required: FAFSA.
Dates and Deadlines: No deadline. Applicants notified on a rolling basis starting 4/1.
Transfers: No deadline. Applicants notified on a rolling basis.

CONTACT
Larry Ewing, Financial Aid Officer
Box 14007, Roanoke, VA 24038
(540) 857-7331

Washington and Lee University
Lexington, Virginia   Federal Code: 003768
www.wlu.edu   CSS Code: 5887

4-year private university and liberal arts college in small town.
Enrollment: 1,745 undergrads. 460 full-time freshmen.
Selectivity: Admits less than 50% of applicants.

BASIC COSTS (2006-2007)
Tuition and fees: $31,850.
Room and board: $7,942.

FINANCIAL AID PICTURE (2004-2005)
Students with need: Out of 232 full-time freshmen who applied for aid, 172 were judged to have need. Of these, 167 received aid, and 142 had their full need met. Average financial aid package met 99% of need; average scholarship/grant was $19,728; average loan was $3,273. Need-based aid available for part-time students.
Students without need: 34 full-time freshmen who did not demonstrate need for aid received scholarships/grants; average award was $12,091. No-need awards available for academics.

862 **Virginia** Washington and Lee University

Cumulative student debt: 35% of graduating class had student loans; average debt was $17,374.
Additional info: Various memorial and endowed scholarships are available. Interested students should refer to the W&L Financial Assistance brochure available from Financial Aid.

FINANCIAL AID PROCEDURES
Forms required: FAFSA, CSS PROFILE.
Dates and Deadlines: Closing date 2/1. Applicants notified by 4/1; must reply by 5/1.
Transfers: Transfer students are awarded institutional funds only after commitments to enrolled students are met. Notification usually in late summer.

CONTACT
John DeCourcy, Director of Student Financial Aid
204 West Washington Street, Lexington, VA 24450-2116
(540) 458-8715

Wytheville Community College
Wytheville, Virginia
www.wcc.vccs.edu   Federal Code: 003761

2-year public community college in small town.
Enrollment: 723 undergrads.
Selectivity: Open admission; but selective for some programs.

BASIC COSTS (2005-2006)
Tuition and fees: $2,151; out-of-state residents $6,531.
Per-credit charge: $68; out-of-state residents $214.

FINANCIAL AID PICTURE
Students with need: Need-based aid available for full-time and part-time students.
Students without need: This college only awards aid to students with need.

FINANCIAL AID PROCEDURES
Forms required: FAFSA, institutional form.
Dates and Deadlines: Priority date 4/1; no closing date. Applicants notified on a rolling basis starting 5/1; must reply within 4 week(s) of notification.

CONTACT
Gail Carlton, Financial Aid Coordinator
1000 East Main Street, Wytheville, VA 24382
(540) 223-4703

Washington

Antioch University Seattle
Seattle, Washington
www.antiochsea.edu   Federal Code: 003010

Upper-division private university and liberal arts college in very large city.
Enrollment: 260 undergrads.

BASIC COSTS (2005-2006)
Tuition and fees: $18,135.
Per-credit charge: $400.

FINANCIAL AID PICTURE (2005-2006)
Students with need: 44% of average financial aid package awarded as scholarships/grants, 56% awarded as loans/jobs. Need-based aid available for part-time students. Work study available nights, weekends, and for part-time students.

FINANCIAL AID PROCEDURES
Forms required: FAFSA, institutional form.
Dates and Deadlines: Priority date 4/15; no closing date. Applicants notified on a rolling basis starting 5/1; must reply within 2 week(s) of notification.

CONTACT
Katy Gilroy, Financial Aid Officer
2326 Sixth Avenue, Seattle, WA 98121-1814
(206) 441-5352 ext. 5010

Art Institute of Seattle
Seattle, Washington
www.ais.edu   Federal Code: 016210

4-year for-profit visual arts and technical college in very large city.
Enrollment: 3,020 undergrads.

BASIC COSTS (2005-2006)
Tuition and fees: $17,100.
Per-credit charge: $380.
Room and board: $9,045.
Additional info: Tuition at time of enrollment locked for 4 years.

FINANCIAL AID PICTURE
Students with need: Need-based aid available for full-time and part-time students. Work study available nights, weekends, and for part-time students.
Students without need: No-need awards available for academics, art.

FINANCIAL AID PROCEDURES
Forms required: FAFSA, state aid form.
Dates and Deadlines: Priority date 4/15; no closing date. Applicants notified on a rolling basis; must reply within 4 week(s) of notification.

CONTACT
Rod Bigelow, Director of Administrative and Financial Services
2323 Elliott Avenue, Seattle, WA 98121
(206) 239-2261

Bastyr University
Kenmore, Washington
www.bastyr.edu   Federal Code: 016059

Upper-division private university and health science college in small city.
Enrollment: 239 undergrads, 11% part-time.

BASIC COSTS (2005-2006)
Tuition and fees: $15,381.
Per-credit charge: $304.

FINANCIAL AID PICTURE
Students with need: Need-based aid available for full-time and part-time students. Work study available nights, weekends, and for part-time students.
Students without need: This college only awards aid to students with need.

FINANCIAL AID PROCEDURES
Forms required: FAFSA, institutional form.
Dates and Deadlines: Priority date 6/1; no closing date. Applicants notified on a rolling basis starting 5/15; must reply within 2 week(s) of notification.

CONTACT
Richard Dent, Director of Student Enrollment
14500 Juanita Drive NE, Kenmore, WA 98028
(425) 602-3074

Bellevue Community College
Bellevue, Washington
www.bcc.ctc.edu   Federal Code: 003769

2-year public community college in small city.
Enrollment: 4,631 undergrads, 52% part-time. 89 full-time freshmen.
Selectivity: Open admission; but selective for some programs.

BASIC COSTS (2005-2006)
Tuition and fees: $2,655; out-of-state residents $7,863.
Per-credit charge: $79; out-of-state residents $251.

FINANCIAL AID PICTURE (2004-2005)
Students with need: Average financial aid package for all full-time undergraduates was $2,999. 76% awarded as scholarships/grants, 24% awarded as loans/jobs. Need-based aid available for part-time students. Work study available nights, weekends, and for part-time students.
Students without need: No-need awards available for academics, athletics.

FINANCIAL AID PROCEDURES
Forms required: FAFSA, institutional form.
Dates and Deadlines: Priority date 4/15; no closing date. Applicants notified on a rolling basis starting 8/1.

CONTACT
Sherri Ballantyne, Director of Financial Aid
3000 Landerholm Circle SE, Bellevue, WA 98007-6484
(425) 564-2227

Bellingham Technical College
Bellingham, Washington
www.btc.ctc.edu   Federal Code: 016227

2-year public technical college in small city.
Enrollment: 1,829 full-time undergrads.
Selectivity: Open admission.

BASIC COSTS (2005-2006)
Tuition and fees: $2,835.

FINANCIAL AID PICTURE
Students with need: Need-based aid available for full-time and part-time students.
Students without need: This college only awards aid to students with need.

FINANCIAL AID PROCEDURES
Forms required: FAFSA.
Dates and Deadlines: Priority date 4/30; no closing date. Applicants notified on a rolling basis starting 7/1; must reply within 2 week(s) of notification.

CONTACT
Lester Ishimoto, Director of Financial Aid
3028 Lindbergh Avenue, Bellingham, WA 98225
(360) 715-8351

Big Bend Community College
Moses Lake, Washington
www.bigbend.edu   Federal Code: 003770

2-year public community college in large town.
Enrollment: 1,170 undergrads.
Selectivity: Open admission; but selective for some programs.

BASIC COSTS (2005-2006)
Tuition and fees: $2,871; out-of-state residents $3,351.
Per-credit charge: $75; out-of-state residents $89.
Room and board: $5,160.
Additional info: Tuition/fee waivers available for unemployed or children of unemployed.

FINANCIAL AID PICTURE (2004-2005)
Students with need: 72% of average financial aid package awarded as scholarships/grants, 28% awarded as loans/jobs. Need-based aid available for part-time students. Work study available nights, weekends, and for part-time students.
Students without need: This college only awards aid to students with need.

FINANCIAL AID PROCEDURES
Forms required: FAFSA, institutional form.
Dates and Deadlines: Priority date 4/15; no closing date. Applicants notified on a rolling basis starting 5/15; must reply within 2 week(s) of notification.

CONTACT
Sherry Keeler, Director of Financial Aid
7662 Chanute Street, Moses Lake, WA 98837-3299
(509) 793-2034

Central Washington University
Ellensburg, Washington
www.cwu.edu   Federal Code: 003771

4-year public university in large town.
Enrollment: 9,148 undergrads.
Selectivity: Admits over 75% of applicants.

BASIC COSTS (2005-2006)
Tuition and fees: $4,766; out-of-state residents $13,100.
Per-credit charge: $138; out-of-state residents $416.
Room and board: $6,924.

FINANCIAL AID PICTURE (2004-2005)
Students with need: 43% of average financial aid package awarded as scholarships/grants, 57% awarded as loans/jobs. Need-based aid available for part-time students.
Students without need: No-need awards available for academics, alumni affiliation, art, athletics, job skills, leadership, minority status, music/drama, religious affiliation, ROTC, state/district residency.

FINANCIAL AID PROCEDURES
Forms required: FAFSA.
Dates and Deadlines: Priority date 3/1; no closing date. Applicants notified on a rolling basis starting 4/15; must reply within 4 week(s) of notification.
Transfers: Equal Opportunity Grant available for junior-level transfers from selected Washington counties. May receive up to $2,500/year for three years.

CONTACT
Agnes Canedo, Director of Financial Aid
400 East University Way, Ellensburg, WA 98926-7463
(509) 963-1611

Centralia College
Centralia, Washington
www.centralia.edu   Federal Code: 003772

2-year public community college in large town.
Enrollment: 3,278 undergrads, 65% part-time.
Selectivity: Open admission; but selective for some programs.

BASIC COSTS (2005-2006)
Tuition and fees: $2,702; out-of-state residents $3,167.
Per-credit charge: $72; out-of-state residents $244.
Additional info: Tuition/fee waivers available for unemployed or children of unemployed.

FINANCIAL AID PICTURE (2004-2005)
Students with need: 92% of average financial aid package awarded as scholarships/grants, 8% awarded as loans/jobs. Need-based aid available for part-time students.
Students without need: No-need awards available for academics, alumni affiliation, art, leadership, minority status, music/drama.

FINANCIAL AID PROCEDURES
Forms required: FAFSA, institutional form.
Dates and Deadlines: Priority date 5/1; no closing date. Applicants notified on a rolling basis starting 7/10; must reply within 2 week(s) of notification.

CONTACT
Tracy Smothers, Director of Financial Aid
600 West Locust, Centralia, WA 98531
(360) 736-9391 ext. 234

City University
Bellevue, Washington
www.cityu.edu   Federal Code: 013022

4-year private university in very large city.
Enrollment: 1,131 full-time undergrads.
Selectivity: Open admission.

BASIC COSTS (2006-2007)
Tuition and fees: $12,435.
Per-credit charge: $254.

FINANCIAL AID PICTURE
Students with need: Need-based aid available for full-time and part-time students.
Students without need: No-need awards available for academics.
Additional info: All degree programs approved for veteran's administration educational benefits.

FINANCIAL AID PROCEDURES
Forms required: FAFSA, institutional form.
Dates and Deadlines: No deadline. Applicants notified on a rolling basis.

CONTACT
Jean Roberts, Director of Financial Aid
11900 NE 1st Street, Bellevue, WA 98005
(800) 426-5596

Clark College
Vancouver, Washington
www.clark.edu   Federal Code: 003773

2-year public community college in small city.
Enrollment: 5,750 undergrads, 45% part-time. 731 full-time freshmen.
Selectivity: Open admission; but selective for some programs.

BASIC COSTS (2005-2006)
Tuition and fees: $2,704; out-of-state residents $7,912.
Per-credit charge: $72; out-of-state residents $244.
Additional info: Tuition/fee waivers available for unemployed or children of unemployed.

FINANCIAL AID PICTURE (2004-2005)
Students with need: 70% of average financial aid package awarded as scholarships/grants, 30% awarded as loans/jobs. Need-based aid available for part-time students. Work study available nights, weekends, and for part-time students.
Students without need: No-need awards available for academics, alumni affiliation, art, athletics, job skills, leadership, minority status, music/drama, religious affiliation, ROTC, state/district residency.
Scholarships offered: Clark College Foundation Scholarships; range from $500 to full tuition; recipients selected from those completing Clark's Foundation Standard Scholarship application form.

FINANCIAL AID PROCEDURES
Forms required: FAFSA, institutional form.
Dates and Deadlines: Priority date 5/1; no closing date. Applicants notified on a rolling basis starting 5/1; must reply within 2 week(s) of notification.

CONTACT
Alex Montoya, Director of Financial Aid
1800 East McLoughlin Boulevard, Vancouver, WA 98663-3598
(360) 992-2153

Clover Park Technical College
Lakewood, Washington
www.cptc.edu   Federal Code: 015984

2-year public technical college in small city.
Enrollment: 1,685 undergrads.
Selectivity: Open admission; but selective for some programs.

BASIC COSTS (2005-2006)
Tuition and fees: $3,108; out-of-state residents $3,108.
Additional info: Tuition Costs and fees vary by program; From $3,022 to $3,455 per academic year.

FINANCIAL AID PICTURE (2004-2005)
Students with need: 72% of average financial aid package awarded as scholarships/grants, 28% awarded as loans/jobs. Need-based aid available for part-time students. Work study available nights, weekends, and for part-time students.
Students without need: This college only awards aid to students with need.

FINANCIAL AID PROCEDURES
Forms required: FAFSA, institutional form.
Dates and Deadlines: Priority date 6/15; closing date 8/25. Applicants notified on a rolling basis.

CONTACT
Karen Specht, Financial Aid Director
4500 Steilacoom Boulevard SW, Lakewood, WA 98499-4098
(253) 589-5660

Columbia Basin College
Pasco, Washington
www.columbiabasin.edu   Federal Code: 003774

2-year public community college in small city.
Enrollment: 6,438 undergrads.
Selectivity: Open admission; but selective for some programs.

BASIC COSTS (2005-2006)
Tuition and fees: $2,614; out-of-state residents $3,195.
Per-credit charge: $93; out-of-state residents $126.
Additional info: Tuition/fee waivers available for unemployed or children of unemployed.

FINANCIAL AID PICTURE (2004-2005)
Students with need: 78% of average financial aid package awarded as scholarships/grants, 22% awarded as loans/jobs. Need-based aid available for part-time students. Work study available nights, weekends, and for part-time students.
Students without need: No-need awards available for academics, athletics, state/district residency.

FINANCIAL AID PROCEDURES
Forms required: FAFSA, institutional form.
Dates and Deadlines: Priority date 4/1; no closing date. Applicants notified on a rolling basis starting 6/15; must reply within 2 week(s) of notification.

CONTACT
Ceci Ratliff, Director of Student Financial Services
2600 North 20th Avenue, Pasco, WA 99301
(509) 547-0511 ext. 2304

Cornish College of the Arts
Seattle, Washington
www.cornish.edu   Federal Code: 012315

4-year private visual arts and music college in very large city.
Enrollment: 663 undergrads.
Selectivity: Admits 50 to 75% of applicants.

BASIC COSTS (2006-2007)
Tuition and fees: $22,400.
Additional info: Design Major required to have a laptop computer and Adobe software, estimated cost = $3000.00.

FINANCIAL AID PICTURE
Students with need: Need-based aid available for full-time and part-time students. Work study available nights, weekends, and for part-time students.
Students without need: No-need awards available for academics.

FINANCIAL AID PROCEDURES
Forms required: FAFSA, institutional form.
Dates and Deadlines: Priority date 2/15; no closing date. Applicants notified on a rolling basis starting 4/15; must reply by 5/1 or within 2 week(s) of notification.
Transfers: No deadline. Applicants notified on a rolling basis; must reply by 2/15.

CONTACT
Monique Theriault, Director for Financial Aid
1000 Lenora Street, Seattle, WA 98121
(206) 726-5014

Crown College
Tacoma, Washington
www.crowncollege.edu   Federal Code: 014843

4-year for-profit business college in large city.
Enrollment: 293 undergrads.
Selectivity: Open admission; but selective for some programs.

BASIC COSTS (2006-2007)
Tuition and fees: $7,500.
Per-credit charge: $250.

FINANCIAL AID PICTURE
Students with need: Need-based aid available for full-time students.
Students without need: This college only awards aid to students with need.

FINANCIAL AID PROCEDURES
Forms required: FAFSA.

CONTACT
Misty Lee, Director of Financial Aid
8739 South Hosmer Street, Tacoma, WA 98444-1836
(253) 531-3123

DeVry University: Federal Way
Federal Way, Washington
www.sea.devry.edu

4-year for-profit university in large city.
Enrollment: 773 undergrads, 29% part-time. 72 full-time freshmen.

BASIC COSTS (2005-2006)
Tuition and fees: $13,410.
Per-credit charge: $475.

FINANCIAL AID PICTURE
Students with need: Need-based aid available for full-time and part-time students.
Students without need: This college only awards aid to students with need.

FINANCIAL AID PROCEDURES
Forms required: FAFSA.
Dates and Deadlines: No deadline. Applicants notified on a rolling basis.

CONTACT
Scott Sand, Director of Financial Aid
3600 South 344th Way, Federal Way, WA 98001-9558
(253) 943-3060

DigiPen Institute of Technology
Redmond, Washington
www.digipen.edu   Federal Code: 037243

4-year for-profit visual arts and engineering college in large town.
Enrollment: 618 undergrads. 177 full-time freshmen.
Selectivity: Admits less than 50% of applicants.

BASIC COSTS (2005-2006)
Per-credit charge: $345.

FINANCIAL AID PICTURE
Students with need: Need-based aid available for full-time and part-time students.
Students without need: This college only awards aid to students with need.
Scholarships offered: WASL scholarship, 50 percent of tuition costs for entire program, WASL test scores must be a level 4 on Math and a level 3 for all other components, and a Yes for both the writing and listening components, maximum of 30 awarded every year. Careers that work scholarship, $1,000 divided into four semesters, applications available from high school counselors.

FINANCIAL AID PROCEDURES
Forms required: FAFSA, institutional form.
Dates and Deadlines: No deadline. Applicants notified on a rolling basis starting 1/1; must reply within 4 week(s) of notification.

CONTACT
Kim King, Director of Financial Aid
5001-150th Avenue NE., Redmond, WA 98052
(425) 895-4446

Eastern Washington University
Cheney, Washington
www.ewu.edu　　　　　　　　　Federal Code: 003775

4-year public university in large town.
Enrollment: 9,356 undergrads, 14% part-time. 1,783 full-time freshmen.
Selectivity: Admits over 75% of applicants.

BASIC COSTS (2005-2006)
Tuition and fees: $4,301; out-of-state residents $13,574.
Room and board: $5,933.

FINANCIAL AID PICTURE (2004-2005)
Students with need: Out of 1,374 full-time freshmen who applied for aid, 1,032 were judged to have need. Of these, 999 received aid, and 246 had their full need met. Average financial aid package met 43% of need; average scholarship/grant was $4,468; average loan was $2,335. For part-time students, average financial aid package was $6,147.
Students without need: 37 full-time freshmen who did not demonstrate need for aid received scholarships/grants; average award was $3,050. No-need awards available for academics, alumni affiliation, athletics, ROTC.
Scholarships offered: *Merit:* Killin Scholarship; $3,500; three awards; for academic excellence, must have 3.7 GPA and 1100 SAT score (exclustive of writing.) Honors Scholarship; $2,500; 38 awards; for academic excellence. Presidential Scholarship; $2,000; 75 awards; based on GPA, SAT, early admission. *Athletic:* 22 full-time freshmen received athletic scholarships; average amount $6,848.
Additional info: Prepaid tuition plan available to Washington state residents.

FINANCIAL AID PROCEDURES
Forms required: FAFSA.
Dates and Deadlines: Priority date 4/1; no closing date. Applicants notified on a rolling basis starting 4/1; must reply within 4 week(s) of notification.
Transfers: Educational Opportunity Grant(EOG); financially needy, placebound students with AA or junior status, $2500 renewable, rolling priority, first-come, first-served at end of each month beginning April 1, ending September 30.

CONTACT
Bruce Defrates, Director of Financial Aid
101 Sutton Hall, Cheney, WA 99004-2447
(509) 359-2314

Edmonds Community College
Lynnwood, Washington
www.edcc.edu　　　　　　　　　Federal Code: 005001

2-year public community college in small city.
Enrollment: 7,600 undergrads.
Selectivity: Open admission.

BASIC COSTS (2005-2006)
Tuition and fees: $2,652; out-of-state residents $7,860.
Per-credit charge: $72; out-of-state residents $244.

FINANCIAL AID PICTURE
Students with need: Need-based aid available for full-time and part-time students. Work study available nights.
Students without need: No-need awards available for athletics.

FINANCIAL AID PROCEDURES
Forms required: FAFSA, institutional form.
Dates and Deadlines: Priority date 5/1; no closing date. Applicants notified on a rolling basis starting 6/1; must reply within 4 week(s) of notification.

CONTACT
Rae-Ellen Berthelsen, Associate Dean Financial Aid
20000 68th Avenue West, Lynnwood, WA 98036-5912
(425) 640-1457

Everett Community College
Everett, Washington
www.everettcc.edu　　　　　　　Federal Code: 003776

2-year public community college in small city.
Enrollment: 2,746 undergrads, 45% part-time. 256 full-time freshmen.
Selectivity: Open admission; but selective for some programs.

BASIC COSTS (2005-2006)
Tuition and fees: $2,550; out-of-state residents $7,758.
Per-credit charge: $72; out-of-state residents $244.
Additional info: Tuition at time of enrollment locked for 2 years.

FINANCIAL AID PICTURE (2004-2005)
Students with need: Out of 71 full-time freshmen who applied for aid, 59 were judged to have need. Of these, 59 received aid. Average financial aid package met 19% of need; average scholarship/grant was $2,026; average loan was $1,103. For part-time students, average financial aid package was $2,223.
Students without need: This college only awards aid to students with need.
Scholarships offered: 6 full-time freshmen received athletic scholarships; average amount $200.
Cumulative student debt: 7% of graduating class had student loans; average debt was $6,000.

FINANCIAL AID PROCEDURES
Forms required: FAFSA, institutional form.
Dates and Deadlines: Priority date 5/2; no closing date. Applicants notified on a rolling basis starting 6/15; must reply within 4 week(s) of notification.
Transfers: No deadline. Applicants notified on a rolling basis starting 6/15; must reply within 4 week(s) of notification.

CONTACT
Laurie Franklin, Director of Student Financial Services
2000 Tower Street, Everett, WA 98201-1352
(425) 388-9280

Evergreen State College
Olympia, Washington
www.evergreen.edu　　　　　　　Federal Code: 008155

4-year public liberal arts college in small city.
Enrollment: 3,962 undergrads, 8% part-time. 480 full-time freshmen.
Selectivity: Admits over 75% of applicants.

BASIC COSTS (2005-2006)
Tuition and fees: $4,337; out-of-state residents $14,747.
Room and board: $6,924.

FINANCIAL AID PICTURE (2004-2005)
Students with need: Out of 415 full-time freshmen who applied for aid, 229 were judged to have need. Of these, 218 received aid, and 101 had their full need met. Average financial aid package met 77% of need; average scholarship/grant was $4,815; average loan was $2,862. For part-time students, average financial aid package was $6,852.
Students without need: 9 full-time freshmen who did not demonstrate need for aid received scholarships/grants; average award was $3,900. No-need awards available for academics, athletics, state/district residency.
Scholarships offered: 5 full-time freshmen received athletic scholarships; average amount $1,561.

Cumulative student debt: 59% of graduating class had student loans; average debt was $13,818.
Additional info: Application deadline for merit and cultural diversity scholarships February 1. Minority students may apply for tuition and fee waiver scholarships; amount of award equal to in-state tuition and fees. Discount waiver for employees. To meet priority deadline for required financial aid forms, official results of FAFSA must be received by March 15.

FINANCIAL AID PROCEDURES
Forms required: FAFSA, institutional form.
Dates and Deadlines: Priority date 3/15; no closing date. Applicants notified on a rolling basis starting 4/15; must reply within 4 week(s) of notification.

CONTACT
Brian Shirley, Director of Financial Aid
2700 Evergreen Parkway NW, Olympia, WA 98505
(360) 867-6205

Gonzaga University
Spokane, Washington
www.gonzaga.edu Federal Code: 003778

4-year private university and liberal arts college in large city, affiliated with Roman Catholic Church.
Enrollment: 4,060 undergrads, 3% part-time. 970 full-time freshmen.
Selectivity: Admits 50 to 75% of applicants. GED not accepted.

BASIC COSTS (2006-2007)
Tuition and fees: $25,012.
Per-credit charge: $715.
Room and board: $7,220.
Additional info: Tuition/fee waivers available for adults.

FINANCIAL AID PICTURE (2004-2005)
Students with need: Out of 824 full-time freshmen who applied for aid, 610 were judged to have need. Of these, 608 received aid, and 119 had their full need met. Average financial aid package met 83% of need; average scholarship/grant was $12,554; average loan was $4,097. For part-time students, average financial aid package was $3,893.
Students without need: 311 full-time freshmen who did not demonstrate need for aid received scholarships/grants; average award was $5,638. No-need awards available for academics, alumni affiliation, athletics, leadership, minority status, music/drama, ROTC.
Scholarships offered: 41 full-time freshmen received athletic scholarships; average amount $15,323.
Cumulative student debt: 68% of graduating class had student loans; average debt was $23,113.

FINANCIAL AID PROCEDURES
Forms required: FAFSA.
Dates and Deadlines: Priority date 2/1; closing date 6/30. Applicants notified on a rolling basis starting 3/1; must reply by 5/1 or within 3 week(s) of notification.

CONTACT
Thayne McCulloh, Dean of Student Financial Services
502 East Boone Avenue, Spokane, WA 99258-0001
(509) 323-6582

Grays Harbor College
Aberdeen, Washington
www.ghc.edu Federal Code: 003779

2-year public community college in large town.
Enrollment: 858 undergrads, 33% part-time. 85 full-time freshmen.
Selectivity: Open admission; but selective for some programs.

BASIC COSTS (2005-2006)
Tuition and fees: $2,622; out-of-state residents $7,830.
Per-credit charge: $72; out-of-state residents $244.
Additional info: Tuition/fee waivers available for adults, unemployed or children of unemployed.

FINANCIAL AID PICTURE (2004-2005)
Students with need: 81% of average financial aid package awarded as scholarships/grants, 19% awarded as loans/jobs. Need-based aid available for part-time students. Work study available nights.
Students without need: No-need awards available for academics, art, athletics, music/drama.

FINANCIAL AID PROCEDURES
Forms required: FAFSA, institutional form.
Dates and Deadlines: Priority date 5/1; no closing date. Applicants notified on a rolling basis starting 5/15.

CONTACT
Nadine Hibbs, Director of Financial Aid
1620 Edward P Smith Drive, Aberdeen, WA 98520
(360) 538-4081

Green River Community College
Auburn, Washington
www.greenriver.edu Federal Code: 003780

2-year public community college in large town.
Enrollment: 4,220 undergrads.
Selectivity: Open admission; but selective for some programs.

BASIC COSTS (2005-2006)
Tuition and fees: $2,743; out-of-state residents $3,139.
Per-credit charge: $72; out-of-state residents $85.

FINANCIAL AID PICTURE
Students with need: Need-based aid available for full-time and part-time students.
Students without need: This college only awards aid to students with need.

FINANCIAL AID PROCEDURES
Forms required: FAFSA, institutional form.
Dates and Deadlines: Priority date 4/15; no closing date. Applicants notified on a rolling basis starting 6/30; must reply within 2 week(s) of notification.

CONTACT
Mary Edington, Director of Financial Aid
12401 South East 320th Street, Auburn, WA 98092
(253) 833-9111 ext. 2440

Henry Cogswell College
Everett, Washington
www.henrycogswell.edu Federal Code: 016175

4-year private engineering and liberal arts college in small city.
Enrollment: 200 undergrads, 41% part-time. 36 full-time freshmen.
Selectivity: Admits over 75% of applicants.

BASIC COSTS (2005-2006)
Tuition and fees: $16,680.
Per-credit charge: $695.

FINANCIAL AID PICTURE (2005-2006)
Students with need: Out of 31 full-time freshmen who applied for aid, 28 were judged to have need. Of these, 28 received aid, and 2 had their full need met. Average financial aid package met 29% of need; average scholarship/grant was $1,606; average loan was $1,666. For part-time students, average financial aid package was $4,901.
Students without need: This college only awards aid to students with need.
Additional info: Many students qualify for tuition reimbursement from industry employers.

FINANCIAL AID PROCEDURES
Forms required: FAFSA, institutional form.
Dates and Deadlines: Priority date 3/1; no closing date. Applicants notified by 4/1; must reply within 4 week(s) of notification.
Transfers: No deadline. Applicants notified on a rolling basis starting 4/1; must reply within 4 week(s) of notification.

CONTACT
tbd, Financial Aid Director
3002 Colby Avenue, Everett, WA 98201
(425) 258-3351

Heritage University
Toppenish, Washington
www.heritage.edu   Federal Code: 003777

4-year private liberal arts and teachers college in small town, affiliated with interdenominational tradition.
Enrollment: 756 undergrads, 28% part-time. 94 full-time freshmen.
Selectivity: Admits 50 to 75% of applicants.

BASIC COSTS (2006-2007)
Tuition and fees: $9,645.
Per-credit charge: $320.

FINANCIAL AID PICTURE (2004-2005)
Students with need: Out of 94 full-time freshmen who applied for aid, 91 were judged to have need. Of these, 82 received aid, and 2 had their full need met. Average financial aid package met 57% of need; average scholarship/grant was $7,033; average loan was $1,960. For part-time students, average financial aid package was $9,116.
Students without need: No-need awards available for academics, leadership, minority status.

FINANCIAL AID PROCEDURES
Forms required: FAFSA, institutional form.
Dates and Deadlines: Priority date 2/10; no closing date. Applicants notified on a rolling basis; must reply within 2 week(s) of notification.

CONTACT
Fernanez Diane, Director, Financial Aid Office
3240 Fort Road, Toppenish, WA 98948-9599
(509) 865-8502

Highline Community College
Des Moines, Washington
www.highline.ctc.edu   Federal Code: 003781

2-year public community college in large town.
Enrollment: 5,610 undergrads.
Selectivity: Open admission; but selective for some programs.

BASIC COSTS (2005-2006)
Tuition and fees: $2,520; out-of-state residents $7,728.
Per-credit charge: $72; out-of-state residents $244.

FINANCIAL AID PICTURE
Students with need: Need-based aid available for full-time and part-time students.

FINANCIAL AID PROCEDURES
Forms required: FAFSA.
Dates and Deadlines: Priority date 4/4; no closing date. Applicants notified on a rolling basis starting 6/1.

CONTACT
Steve Seeman, Director of Financial Aid
2400 South 240th Street, Des Moines, WA 98198-9800
(206) 878-3710

Lake Washington Technical College
Kirkland, Washington
www.lwtc.ctc.edu   Federal Code: 005373

2-year public technical college in large town.
Enrollment: 3,600 undergrads.
Selectivity: Open admission; but selective for some programs.

BASIC COSTS (2005-2006)
Additional info: Tuition fees vary by program.

FINANCIAL AID PICTURE
Students with need: Need-based aid available for full-time and part-time students.

FINANCIAL AID PROCEDURES
Forms required: FAFSA, institutional form.
Dates and Deadlines: Priority date 4/15; no closing date. Applicants notified on a rolling basis.

CONTACT
Jennifer Bacon, Director of Financial Aid
11605 132nd Avenue, NE, Kirkland, WA 98034

Lower Columbia College
Longview, Washington   Federal Code: 003782
www.lcc.ctc.edu   CSS Code: 4402

2-year public community college in small city.
Enrollment: 1,592 undergrads, 30% part-time. 272 full-time freshmen.
Selectivity: Open admission; but selective for some programs.

BASIC COSTS (2005-2006)
Tuition and fees: $2,645; out-of-state residents $3,226.
Per-credit charge: $78; out-of-state residents $100.
Additional info: Tuition/fee waivers available for adults, unemployed or children of unemployed.

FINANCIAL AID PICTURE (2004-2005)
Students with need: 74% of average financial aid package awarded as scholarships/grants, 26% awarded as loans/jobs.
Students without need: This college only awards aid to students with need.

FINANCIAL AID PROCEDURES
Forms required: CSS PROFILE, institutional form.
Dates and Deadlines: Priority date 5/1; no closing date. Applicants notified on a rolling basis starting 4/21; must reply within 2 week(s) of notification.
Transfers: State need grant awards transfer with student, if previously awarded at another WA institution, SEOG usually not available to transfer students. Student employment, loans, Pell Grant available.

CONTACT
James Gorman, Financial Aid Officer
1600 Maple Street, Longview, WA 98632-0310
(360) 442-2311

North Seattle Community College
Seattle, Washington
www.northseattle.edu   Federal Code: 009704

2-year public community college in very large city.
Enrollment: 2,993 undergrads, 36% part-time. 659 full-time freshmen.
Selectivity: Open admission.

BASIC COSTS (2005-2006)
Tuition and fees: $2,552; out-of-state residents $7,760.
Per-credit charge: $72; out-of-state residents $244.
Additional info: Tuition/fee waivers available for unemployed or children of unemployed.

FINANCIAL AID PICTURE (2004-2005)
Students with need: 89% of average financial aid package awarded as scholarships/grants, 11% awarded as loans/jobs. Need-based aid available for part-time students. Work study available nights, weekends, and for part-time students.

FINANCIAL AID PROCEDURES
Forms required: FAFSA, institutional form.
Dates and Deadlines: Priority date 4/30; closing date 8/31. Applicants notified on a rolling basis starting 8/1; must reply within 2 week(s) of notification.

CONTACT
Suzanne Scheldt, Director of Financial Aid
9600 College Way North, Seattle, WA 98103
(206) 528-4700

Northwest College of Art
Poulsbo, Washington
www.nca.edu   Federal Code: 026021

4-year for-profit visual arts college in small town.
Enrollment: 140 undergrads.

BASIC COSTS (2006-2007)
Tuition and fees: $14,400.
Per-credit charge: $625.

FINANCIAL AID PICTURE
Students with need: Need-based aid available for full-time and part-time students.
Students without need: No-need awards available for academics, art.

FINANCIAL AID PROCEDURES
Forms required: FAFSA.
Dates and Deadlines: Priority date 3/1; closing date 6/1. Applicants notified on a rolling basis.

CONTACT
Heidi Townsend, Financial Aid Officer
16301 Creative Drive NE, Poulsbo, WA 98370
(360) 779-9993

Northwest University
Kirkland, Washington
www.northwestu.edu   Federal Code: 003783

4-year private university and liberal arts college in small city, affiliated with Assemblies of God.
Enrollment: 1,089 undergrads, 5% part-time. 187 full-time freshmen.
Selectivity: Admits over 75% of applicants.

BASIC COSTS (2006-2007)
Tuition and fees: $18,144.
Per-credit charge: $750.
Room and board: $6,450.

FINANCIAL AID PICTURE (2005-2006)
Students with need: Out of 163 full-time freshmen who applied for aid, 138 were judged to have need. Of these, 135 received aid, and 36 had their full need met. Average financial aid package met 70% of need; average scholarship/grant was $8,644; average loan was $2,931. For part-time students, average financial aid package was $9,462.
Students without need: 40 full-time freshmen who did not demonstrate need for aid received scholarships/grants; average award was $6,243. No-need awards available for academics, art, athletics, leadership, music/drama, religious affiliation.
Scholarships offered: 5 full-time freshmen received athletic scholarships; average amount $10,157.
Cumulative student debt: 88% of graduating class had student loans; average debt was $19,171.

FINANCIAL AID PROCEDURES
Forms required: FAFSA, institutional form.
Dates and Deadlines: Priority date 3/1; no closing date. Applicants notified on a rolling basis starting 3/3; must reply within 4 week(s) of notification.

CONTACT
Lana Walter, Director of Financial Aid
5520 108th Avenue NE, Kirkland, WA 98083-0579
(425) 889-5210

Olympic College
Bremerton, Washington
www.olympic.edu   Federal Code: 003784

2-year public community and liberal arts college in large town.
Enrollment: 3,371 undergrads, 46% part-time. 393 full-time freshmen.
Selectivity: Open admission; but selective for some programs.

BASIC COSTS (2005-2006)
Tuition and fees: $2,625; out-of-state residents $4,034.
Per-credit charge: $72; out-of-state residents $116.

FINANCIAL AID PICTURE (2005-2006)
Students with need: 67% of average financial aid package awarded as scholarships/grants, 33% awarded as loans/jobs. Need-based aid available for part-time students. Work study available nights.
Students without need: No-need awards available for academics, state/district residency.

FINANCIAL AID PROCEDURES
Forms required: FAFSA, institutional form.
Dates and Deadlines: Priority date 3/1; no closing date. Applicants notified on a rolling basis starting 6/1; must reply within 2 week(s) of notification.

CONTACT
Robert Parker, Associate Dean, Student Financial Services
1600 Chester Avenue, Bremerton, WA 98337-1699
(360) 475-7160

Pacific Lutheran University
Tacoma, Washington
www.plu.edu　　　　　　　　　　　　Federal Code: 003785

4-year private university in large city, affiliated with Evangelical Lutheran Church in America.
Enrollment: 3,331 undergrads, 5% part-time. 722 full-time freshmen.
Selectivity: Admits over 75% of applicants.

BASIC COSTS (2006-2007)
Tuition and fees: $23,450.
Per-credit charge: $731.
Room and board: $7,135.

FINANCIAL AID PICTURE (2004-2005)
Students with need: Out of 640 full-time freshmen who applied for aid, 508 were judged to have need. Of these, 506 received aid, and 195 had their full need met. Average financial aid package met 93% of need; average scholarship/grant was $8,538; average loan was $4,329. For part-time students, average financial aid package was $11,301.
Students without need: 127 full-time freshmen who did not demonstrate need for aid received scholarships/grants; average award was $6,071. No-need awards available for academics, alumni affiliation, art, leadership, music/drama, ROTC.
Cumulative student debt: 60% of graduating class had student loans; average debt was $24,244.

FINANCIAL AID PROCEDURES
Forms required: FAFSA.
Dates and Deadlines: Priority date 1/31; no closing date. Applicants notified on a rolling basis starting 3/1; must reply by 5/1 or within 4 week(s) of notification.

CONTACT
Kay Soltis, Director of Financial Aid
Office of Admissions, Tacoma, WA 98447-0003
(253) 535-7134

Peninsula College
Port Angeles, Washington
www.pc.ctc.edu　　　　　　　　　　Federal Code: 003786

2-year public community college in large town.
Enrollment: 1,070 undergrads, 33% part-time. 136 full-time freshmen.
Selectivity: Open admission; but selective for some programs.

BASIC COSTS (2005-2006)
Tuition and fees: $2,532; out-of-state residents $3,008.
Per-credit charge: $75; out-of-state residents $88.
Additional info: Tuition/fee waivers available for unemployed or children of unemployed.

FINANCIAL AID PICTURE
Students with need: Need-based aid available for full-time and part-time students.
Students without need: No-need awards available for academics, athletics, job skills.

FINANCIAL AID PROCEDURES
Forms required: FAFSA, institutional form.
Dates and Deadlines: Priority date 4/1; no closing date. Applicants notified on a rolling basis starting 6/1; must reply within 2 week(s) of notification.

CONTACT
Cheryl Reid, Director of Financial Aid
1502 East Lauridsen Boulevard, Port Angeles, WA 98362
(360) 417-6394

Pierce College
Lakewood, Washington
www.pierce.ctc.edu　　　　　　　　Federal Code: 005000

2-year public community college in small city.
Enrollment: 4,639 undergrads, 47% part-time. 674 full-time freshmen.
Selectivity: Open admission; but selective for some programs.

BASIC COSTS (2005-2006)
Tuition and fees: $2,454; out-of-state residents $2,907.
Per-credit charge: $72; out-of-state residents $86.
Additional info: Tuition/fee waivers available for unemployed or children of unemployed.

FINANCIAL AID PICTURE
Students with need: Need-based aid available for full-time and part-time students.
Students without need: No-need awards available for academics, athletics, music/drama.

FINANCIAL AID PROCEDURES
Forms required: FAFSA, institutional form.
Dates and Deadlines: Priority date 4/15; no closing date. Applicants notified on a rolling basis starting 4/15.

CONTACT
Robert Walker, Director of Financial Aid
9401 Farwest Drive SW, Lakewood, WA 98498-1999
(253) 964-6544

Puget Sound Christian College
Everett, Washington
www.pscc.edu　　　　　　　　　　　Federal Code: 013681

4-year private Bible college in large town, affiliated with nondenominational tradition.
Enrollment: 140 undergrads.

BASIC COSTS (2005-2006)
Tuition and fees: $10,120.
Per-credit charge: $415.
Room and board: $5,770.

FINANCIAL AID PICTURE
Students with need: Need-based aid available for full-time and part-time students. Work study available nights, weekends, and for part-time students.
Students without need: No-need awards available for academics, alumni affiliation, music/drama, religious affiliation.
Scholarships offered: Elite President's Scholarships, $4,000, minimum 3.5 GPA, 6 awarded. Honors President's Scholarship, $2,500, 3.0 GPA or 900 SAT combined score (exclusive of Writing), 24 awarded. Essays and minister recommendation required with scholarship applications.

FINANCIAL AID PROCEDURES
Forms required: FAFSA, institutional form.
Dates and Deadlines: Priority date 5/1; closing date 8/15. Applicants notified on a rolling basis starting 4/15; must reply within 3 week(s) of notification.
Transfers: No deadline.

CONTACT
Radine Herrick, Financial Aid Director
2610 Wetmore Avenue, Everett, WA 98206
(425) 257-3090 ext. 572

Renton Technical College
Renton, Washington
www.RTC.edu   Federal Code: 014001

2-year public technical college in large town.
Enrollment: 1,290 undergrads.
Selectivity: Open admission.

BASIC COSTS (2005-2006)
Tuition and fees: $2,866; out-of-state residents $2,866.

FINANCIAL AID PICTURE
Students with need: Need-based aid available for full-time and part-time students.
Students without need: This college only awards aid to students with need.

FINANCIAL AID PROCEDURES
Forms required: FAFSA, institutional form.
Dates and Deadlines: No deadline. Applicants notified on a rolling basis.

CONTACT
Debbie Solomon, Director of Financial Aid
3000 Northeast Fourth Street, Renton, WA 98056-4195
(425) 235-5841

Saint Martin's University
Lacey, Washington
www.stmartin.edu   Federal Code: 003794

4-year private liberal arts college in large town, affiliated with Roman Catholic Church.
Enrollment: 936 full-time undergrads.
Selectivity: Admits 50 to 75% of applicants.

BASIC COSTS (2006-2007)
Tuition and fees: $21,155.
Per-credit charge: $689.
Room and board: $6,400.

FINANCIAL AID PICTURE (2005-2006)
Students with need: 56% of average financial aid package awarded as scholarships/grants, 44% awarded as loans/jobs. Need-based aid available for part-time students. Work study available nights, weekends, and for part-time students.
Students without need: No-need awards available for academics, alumni affiliation, athletics, music/drama, state/district residency.
Scholarships offered: Valedictorian Scholarships; awarded after competitive interviews of high school valedictorians; 2 available; full scholarships.

FINANCIAL AID PROCEDURES
Forms required: FAFSA.
Dates and Deadlines: Priority date 3/1; no closing date. Applicants notified on a rolling basis starting 3/15; must reply within 3 week(s) of notification.

CONTACT
Rebecca Wonderly, Director of Financial Aid
5300 Pacific Avenue Southeast, Lacey, WA 98503
(360) 438-4397

Seattle Central Community College
Seattle, Washington
www.seattlecentral.org   Federal Code: 003787

2-year public community college in very large city.
Enrollment: 5,830 undergrads.
Selectivity: Open admission; but selective for some programs.

BASIC COSTS (2005-2006)
Tuition and fees: $2,666; out-of-state residents $7,874.
Per-credit charge: $71; out-of-state residents $243.
Additional info: Tuition at time of enrollment locked for 2 years; tuition/fee waivers available for unemployed or children of unemployed.

FINANCIAL AID PICTURE (2004-2005)
Students with need: Need-based aid available for part-time students. Work study available nights, weekends, and for part-time students.
Students without need: This college only awards aid to students with need.
Additional info: Currently enrolled international students can apply for institutional scholarship in second year of study.

FINANCIAL AID PROCEDURES
Forms required: FAFSA, institutional form.
Dates and Deadlines: Priority date 4/30; closing date 8/6. Applicants notified on a rolling basis; must reply within 2 week(s) of notification.

CONTACT
Joan Ray, Assistant Dean, Financial Student Services
1701 Broadway, Seattle, WA 98122
(206) 587-3844

Seattle Pacific University
Seattle, Washington
www.spu.edu   Federal Code: 003788

4-year private university in very large city, affiliated with Free Methodist Church of North America.
Enrollment: 2,978 undergrads, 4% part-time. 710 full-time freshmen.
Selectivity: Admits over 75% of applicants.

BASIC COSTS (2006-2007)
Tuition and fees: $23,391.
Per-credit charge: $641.
Room and board: $7,818.

FINANCIAL AID PICTURE (2005-2006)
Students with need: Out of 578 full-time freshmen who applied for aid, 467 were judged to have need. Of these, 467 received aid, and 104 had their full need met. Average financial aid package met 81% of need; average scholarship/grant was $15,431; average loan was $4,778. For part-time students, average financial aid package was $16,494.
Students without need: 195 full-time freshmen who did not demonstrate need for aid received scholarships/grants; average award was $11,096. No-need awards available for academics, alumni affiliation, art, athletics, leadership, minority status, music/drama, religious affiliation, ROTC.
Scholarships offered: 8 full-time freshmen received athletic scholarships; average amount $11,317.
Cumulative student debt: 68% of graduating class had student loans; average debt was $22,569.

FINANCIAL AID PROCEDURES
Forms required: FAFSA.
Dates and Deadlines: Priority date 1/31; no closing date. Applicants notified on a rolling basis starting 3/15; must reply by 5/1 or within 4 week(s) of notification.

CONTACT
Jordan Grant, Director of Financial Aid
3307 Third Avenue West, Seattle, WA 98119-1997
(206) 281-2061

Seattle University
Seattle, Washington
www.seattleu.edu   Federal Code: 003790

4-year private university in very large city, affiliated with Roman Catholic Church.
Enrollment: 4,110 undergrads, 7% part-time. 761 full-time freshmen.
Selectivity: Admits 50 to 75% of applicants.

BASIC COSTS (2006-2007)
Tuition and fees: $24,615.
Per-credit charge: $547.
Room and board: $8,703.
Additional info: $200 admission fee, $90 matriculation fee required. $90 per-credit-hour charge for credit by examination. $90 per-credit-hour charge for validation of field experience. $65 removal fee for incompletes.

FINANCIAL AID PICTURE (2005-2006)
Students with need: Out of 674 full-time freshmen who applied for aid, 514 were judged to have need. Of these, 509 received aid, and 226 had their full need met. Average financial aid package met 86% of need; average scholarship/grant was $19,528; average loan was $3,464. For part-time students, average financial aid package was $14,578.
Students without need: 10 full-time freshmen who did not demonstrate need for aid received scholarships/grants; average award was $6,510. No-need awards available for academics, alumni affiliation, athletics, leadership, minority status, music/drama, ROTC, state/district residency.
Scholarships offered: *Merit:* Sullivan Leadership Award: full tuition, room and board for 4 years, for entering freshmen of Oregon, Washington, or Idaho residency; service, leadership, strong academics (3.5 GPA) important, 6 awarded. Presidential Scholarship: $11,000 annually for 4 years. Trustee Scholarship: $8,000 annually for 4 years. Campion Scholarship: $5,000 annually for 4 years; for first-time freshmen of U.S. citizenship or permanent resident status, strong academic and extracurricular records important. *Athletic:* 12 full-time freshmen received athletic scholarships; average amount $4,625.
Cumulative student debt: 68% of graduating class had student loans; average debt was $25,311.

FINANCIAL AID PROCEDURES
Forms required: FAFSA.
Dates and Deadlines: Priority date 2/1; no closing date. Applicants notified on a rolling basis starting 3/21; must reply by 5/1 or within 2 week(s) of notification.
Transfers: Closing date 3/1.

CONTACT
Jim White, Director of Financial Aid
901 12th Avenue, Seattle, WA 98122-4340
(206) 296-2000

Shoreline Community College
Shoreline, Washington
www.shoreline.edu   Federal Code: 003791

2-year public community college in small city.
Enrollment: 3,299 undergrads.
Selectivity: Open admission; but selective for some programs.

BASIC COSTS (2005-2006)
Tuition and fees: $2,364; out-of-state residents $4,482.
Per-credit charge: $72; out-of-state residents $141.

FINANCIAL AID PICTURE
Students with need: Work study available nights, weekends, and for part-time students.
Additional info: Tuition and/or fee waiver for students with need on space-available basis.

FINANCIAL AID PROCEDURES
Forms required: FAFSA, institutional form.
Dates and Deadlines: Priority date 4/1; no closing date. Applicants notified on a rolling basis starting 8/1; must reply within 3 week(s) of notification.

CONTACT
Gayle Holm, Interim Director of Financial Services
16101 Greenwood Avenue North, Seattle, WA 98133
(206) 546-4762

Skagit Valley College
Mount Vernon, Washington
www.skagit.edu   Federal Code: 003792

2-year public community college in large town.
Enrollment: 2,400 full-time undergrads.
Selectivity: Open admission.

BASIC COSTS (2005-2006)
Tuition and fees: $2,580; out-of-state residents $2,991.
Per-credit charge: $75; out-of-state residents $92.
Additional info: Tuition/fee waivers available for unemployed or children of unemployed.

FINANCIAL AID PICTURE
Students with need: Need-based aid available for full-time and part-time students. Work study available nights, weekends, and for part-time students.
Students without need: This college only awards aid to students with need.

FINANCIAL AID PROCEDURES
Forms required: FAFSA, institutional form.
Dates and Deadlines: Priority date 3/1; no closing date. Applicants notified on a rolling basis starting 7/1; must reply within 2 week(s) of notification.

CONTACT
Steve Epperson, Financial Aid Director
2405 East College Way, Mount Vernon, WA 98273
(360) 416-7666

South Puget Sound Community College
Olympia, Washington
www.spscc.ctc.edu   Federal Code: 005372

2-year public community and junior college in small city.
Enrollment: 5,044 undergrads.
Selectivity: Open admission; but selective for some programs.

BASIC COSTS (2005-2006)
Tuition and fees: $2,435; out-of-state residents $2,824.
Per-credit charge: $72; out-of-state residents $85.

FINANCIAL AID PICTURE
Students with need: Need-based aid available for full-time and part-time students.
Students without need: No-need awards available for academics, athletics.

FINANCIAL AID PROCEDURES
Forms required: FAFSA, institutional form.
Dates and Deadlines: Priority date 5/1; no closing date. Applicants notified on a rolling basis starting 7/10; must reply within 2 week(s) of notification.

CONTACT
Carla Idohl-Corwin, Dean of Student Financial Services
2011 Mottman Road Southwest, Olympia, WA 98512-6218
(360) 754-7711

South Seattle Community College
Seattle, Washington
www.southseattle.edu   Federal Code: 009706

2-year public community college in very large city.
Enrollment: 1,829 undergrads, 56% part-time.
Selectivity: Open admission.

BASIC COSTS (2005-2006)
Tuition and fees: $2,552; out-of-state residents $7,760.
Per-credit charge: $72; out-of-state residents $244.
Additional info: Tuition/fee waivers available for unemployed or children of unemployed.

FINANCIAL AID PICTURE (2005-2006)
Students with need: 92% of average financial aid package awarded as scholarships/grants, 8% awarded as loans/jobs. Need-based aid available for part-time students.
Students without need: No-need awards available for academics, state/district residency.

FINANCIAL AID PROCEDURES
Forms required: FAFSA, institutional form.
Dates and Deadlines: No deadline. Applicants notified on a rolling basis starting 7/1.

CONTACT
Lorraine Odom, Financial Aid Director
6000 16th Avenue Southwest, Seattle, WA 98106-1499
(206) 764-5317

Spokane Community College
Spokane, Washington
www.scc.spokane.edu   Federal Code: 003793

2-year public community college in small city.
Enrollment: 6,152 undergrads, 15% part-time. 1,756 full-time freshmen.
Selectivity: Open admission; but selective for some programs.

BASIC COSTS (2005-2006)
Tuition and fees: $2,546; out-of-state residents $7,754.
Per-credit charge: $72; out-of-state residents $244.
Additional info: Tuition/fee waivers available for unemployed or children of unemployed.

FINANCIAL AID PICTURE (2004-2005)
Students with need: 97% of average financial aid package awarded as scholarships/grants, 3% awarded as loans/jobs.
Students without need: No-need awards available for athletics.

FINANCIAL AID PROCEDURES
Forms required: FAFSA, institutional form.
Dates and Deadlines: No deadline. Applicants notified on a rolling basis; must reply within 2 week(s) of notification.

CONTACT
Sue Jarvis, Director for Financial Aid
1810 North Greene Street, Spokane, WA 99217-5399
(509) 533-7017

Spokane Falls Community College
Spokane, Washington
www.spokanefalls.edu   Federal Code: 009544

2-year public community college in small city.
Enrollment: 5,528 undergrads, 28% part-time. 1,384 full-time freshmen.
Selectivity: Open admission; but selective for some programs.

BASIC COSTS (2005-2006)
Tuition and fees: $2,576; out-of-state residents $7,784.
Per-credit charge: $72; out-of-state residents $244.
Additional info: Tuition/fee waivers available for unemployed or children of unemployed.

FINANCIAL AID PICTURE
Students with need: Need-based aid available for full-time and part-time students.
Students without need: This college only awards aid to students with need.

FINANCIAL AID PROCEDURES
Forms required: FAFSA, institutional form.
Dates and Deadlines: Priority date 4/1; no closing date. Applicants notified on a rolling basis starting 5/15; must reply within 2 week(s) of notification.

CONTACT
Karen Driscoll, Assistant Dean of Student Services for Financial Aid
3410 West Fort George Wright Drive, Spokane, WA 99224
(509) 533-3550

Tacoma Community College
Tacoma, Washington
www.tacoma.ctc.edu   Federal Code: 003796

2-year public community college in small city.
Enrollment: 6,480 undergrads.
Selectivity: Open admission.

BASIC COSTS (2005-2006)
Tuition and fees: $2,610; out-of-state residents $2,999.
Per-credit charge: $75; out-of-state residents $88.
Additional info: Tuition/fee waivers available for unemployed or children of unemployed.

FINANCIAL AID PICTURE
Students with need: Need-based aid available for full-time and part-time students. Work study available nights, weekends, and for part-time students.
Students without need: This college only awards aid to students with need.

FINANCIAL AID PROCEDURES
Forms required: FAFSA, institutional form.
Dates and Deadlines: Priority date 3/26; no closing date. Applicants notified on a rolling basis starting 7/20; must reply within 4 week(s) of notification.

CONTACT
April Retherford, Dean of Enrollment and Financial Aid Services
6501 South 19th Street, Tacoma, WA 98466-9971

Trinity Lutheran College
Issaquah, Washington
www.tlc.edu   Federal Code: 013525

4-year private Bible and liberal arts college in large town, affiliated with Lutheran Church.
Enrollment: 107 undergrads, 15% part-time.
Selectivity: Admits 50 to 75% of applicants.

BASIC COSTS (2005-2006)
Tuition and fees: $12,000.
Per-credit charge: $290.
Room and board: $5,900.

FINANCIAL AID PICTURE

Students with need: Need-based aid available for full-time and part-time students. Work study available nights, weekends, and for part-time students.
Students without need: No-need awards available for academics, alumni affiliation, art, leadership, music/drama.

FINANCIAL AID PROCEDURES

Forms required: FAFSA, institutional form.
Dates and Deadlines: Priority date 3/1; no closing date. Applicants notified on a rolling basis starting 3/15; must reply within 2 week(s) of notification.
Transfers: No deadline. Applicants notified on a rolling basis starting 3/15; must reply within 2 week(s) of notification.

CONTACT

Susan Dalgleish, Director of Financial Aid
4221 228th Avenue Southeast, Issaquah, WA 98029
(425) 961-5514

University of Puget Sound
Tacoma, Washington
www.ups.edu   Federal Code: 003797

4-year private university and liberal arts college in small city.
Enrollment: 2,589 undergrads, 1% part-time. 670 full-time freshmen.
Selectivity: Admits 50 to 75% of applicants.

BASIC COSTS (2006-2007)
Tuition and fees: $30,060.
Per-credit charge: $942.
Room and board: $8,000.

FINANCIAL AID PICTURE (2005-2006)

Students with need: Out of 491 full-time freshmen who applied for aid, 393 were judged to have need. Of these, 393 received aid, and 105 had their full need met. Average financial aid package met 82% of need; average scholarship/grant was $16,270; average loan was $3,699. Need-based aid available for part-time students.
Students without need: 162 full-time freshmen who did not demonstrate need for aid received scholarships/grants; average award was $6,943. No-need awards available for academics, alumni affiliation, art, leadership, music/drama, religious affiliation.
Scholarships offered: Wyatt Trustee Scholarship, $9,000 annually; Trustee Scholarships, $8,000 annually; President's Scholarships, $6,000 annually; Dean's Scholarships, $3,000 annually; all admitted freshmen; renewable for 3 additional years.
Cumulative student debt: 60% of graduating class had student loans; average debt was $25,842.
Additional info: Cooperative education allows qualified upperclassmen to alternate semesters of full-time study and full-time work.

FINANCIAL AID PROCEDURES
Forms required: FAFSA.
Dates and Deadlines: Priority date 2/1; no closing date. Applicants notified on a rolling basis starting 3/15; must reply by 5/1 or within 2 week(s) of notification.
Transfers: Priority date 3/1; no deadline. Applicants notified on a rolling basis.

CONTACT
Maggie Mittuch, Director of Student Financial Services
1500 North Warner Street, Tacoma, WA 98416-1062
(253) 879-3214

University of Washington
Seattle, Washington
www.washington.edu   Federal Code: 003798

4-year public university in very large city.
Enrollment: 25,469 undergrads, 9% part-time. 4,857 full-time freshmen.
Selectivity: Admits 50 to 75% of applicants.

BASIC COSTS (2005-2006)
Tuition and fees: $5,620; out-of-state residents $19,917.
Room and board: $7,164.

FINANCIAL AID PICTURE (2005-2006)
Students with need: Average financial aid package met 87% of need; average scholarship/grant was $5,000; average loan was $4,200.
Students without need: No-need awards available for academics, alumni affiliation, art, athletics, leadership, music/drama, ROTC.
Cumulative student debt: 50% of graduating class had student loans; average debt was $15,700.
Additional info: Tuition not due until third week of term.

FINANCIAL AID PROCEDURES
Forms required: FAFSA.
Dates and Deadlines: Priority date 2/28; no closing date. Applicants notified on a rolling basis starting 4/1; must reply within 3 week(s) of notification.

CONTACT
Kay Lewis, Director, Financial Aid
1410 Northeast Campus Parkway, Box 355852, Seattle, WA 98195-5852
(206) 543-6101

Walla Walla College
College Place, Washington
www.wwc.edu   Federal Code: 003799

4-year private university and liberal arts college in large town, affiliated with Seventh-day Adventists.
Enrollment: 1,596 undergrads, 5% part-time. 346 full-time freshmen.
Selectivity: Admits over 75% of applicants.

BASIC COSTS (2006-2007)
Tuition and fees: $19,917.
Per-credit charge: $516.
Room and board: $3,993.

FINANCIAL AID PICTURE (2004-2005)
Students with need: Out of 336 full-time freshmen who applied for aid, 230 were judged to have need. Of these, 229 received aid, and 54 had their full need met. Average financial aid package met 88% of need; average scholarship/grant was $5,632; average loan was $5,219. For part-time students, average financial aid package was $14,789.
Students without need: 99 full-time freshmen who did not demonstrate need for aid received scholarships/grants; average award was $4,036. No-need awards available for academics, leadership, music/drama.
Cumulative student debt: 72% of graduating class had student loans; average debt was $23,688.

FINANCIAL AID PROCEDURES
Forms required: FAFSA, institutional form.
Dates and Deadlines: No deadline. Applicants notified on a rolling basis starting 3/15.

CONTACT
Cassie Ragenovich, Director of Student Financial Services
204 South College Avenue, College Place, WA 99324-3000
(509) 527-2815

Walla Walla Community College
Walla Walla, Washington
www.wwcc.edu   Federal Code: 005006

2-year public community and technical college in large town.
Enrollment: 2,255 undergrads, 32% part-time. 417 full-time freshmen.
Selectivity: Open admission; but selective for some programs.

BASIC COSTS (2005-2006)
Tuition and fees: $2,595; out-of-state residents $3,176.
Per-credit charge: $79.
Additional info: Tuition/fee waivers available for unemployed or children of unemployed.

FINANCIAL AID PICTURE (2004-2005)
Students with need: 69% of average financial aid package awarded as scholarships/grants, 31% awarded as loans/jobs. Need-based aid available for part-time students. Work study available nights.
Students without need: No-need awards available for academics, athletics, music/drama.

FINANCIAL AID PROCEDURES
Forms required: FAFSA, institutional form.
Dates and Deadlines: Priority date 3/1; no closing date. Applicants notified on a rolling basis starting 6/1; must reply within 2 week(s) of notification.

CONTACT
Terri Johnson, Director of Financial Aid
500 Tausick Way, Walla Walla, WA 99362-9270
(509) 527-4301

Washington State University
Pullman, Washington
www.wsu.edu   Federal Code: 003800

4-year public university in large town.
Enrollment: 19,077 undergrads, 13% part-time. 3,089 full-time freshmen.
Selectivity: Admits 50 to 75% of applicants.

BASIC COSTS (2005-2006)
Tuition and fees: $6,010; out-of-state residents $15,018.
Room and board: $6,746.

FINANCIAL AID PICTURE (2004-2005)
Students with need: Out of 2,191 full-time freshmen who applied for aid, 1,395 were judged to have need. Of these, 1,389 received aid, and 426 had their full need met. Average financial aid package met 95% of need; average scholarship/grant was $4,771; average loan was $3,042. For part-time students, average financial aid package was $7,868.
Students without need: 380 full-time freshmen who did not demonstrate need for aid received scholarships/grants; average award was $4,064. No-need awards available for academics, alumni affiliation, art, athletics, job skills, leadership, minority status, music/drama, religious affiliation, ROTC, state/district residency.
Scholarships offered: 83 full-time freshmen received athletic scholarships; average amount $11,630.
Cumulative student debt: 49% of graduating class had student loans; average debt was $20,494.

FINANCIAL AID PROCEDURES
Forms required: FAFSA.
Dates and Deadlines: Priority date 3/1; no closing date. Applicants notified on a rolling basis starting 4/15.
Transfers: No deadline. Applicants notified on a rolling basis starting 4/15. President's Scholarship available for transfer students with minimum 3.9 GPA.

CONTACT
Wayne Sparks, Director of Student Financial Aid
370 Lighty Student Services Bldg, Pullman, WA 99164-1067
(509) 335-9711

Wenatchee Valley College
Wenatchee, Washington
www.wvc.edu   Federal Code: 003801

2-year public community college in small city.
Enrollment: 2,670 undergrads.
Selectivity: Open admission; but selective for some programs.

BASIC COSTS (2005-2006)
Tuition and fees: $2,571; out-of-state residents $2,960.
Per-credit charge: $72; out-of-state residents $85.
Additional info: Tuition/fee waivers available for adults, unemployed or children of unemployed.

FINANCIAL AID PICTURE (2004-2005)
Students with need: 60% of average financial aid package awarded as scholarships/grants, 40% awarded as loans/jobs. Need-based aid available for part-time students.
Students without need: No-need awards available for academics, athletics, leadership.

FINANCIAL AID PROCEDURES
Forms required: FAFSA.
Dates and Deadlines: Closing date 3/1. Applicants notified by 7/2; must reply within 3 week(s) of notification.

CONTACT
Kevin Berg, Financial Aid Director
1300 Fifth Street, Wenatchee, WA 98801-1799
(509) 682-6845

Western Washington University
Bellingham, Washington
www.wwu.edu   Federal Code: 003802

4-year public university in small city.
Enrollment: 12,816 undergrads, 7% part-time. 2,366 full-time freshmen.
Selectivity: Admits 50 to 75% of applicants.

BASIC COSTS (2005-2006)
Tuition and fees: $4,737; out-of-state residents $14,688.
Per-credit charge: $137; out-of-state residents $469.
Room and board: $6,524.
Additional info: Tuition/fee waivers available for adults, minority students.

FINANCIAL AID PICTURE (2005-2006)
Students with need: Out of 1,651 full-time freshmen who applied for aid, 844 were judged to have need. Of these, 819 received aid, and 199 had their full need met. Average financial aid package met 87% of need; average scholarship/grant was $5,608; average loan was $2,895. For part-time students, average financial aid package was $7,801.
Students without need: 48 full-time freshmen who did not demonstrate need for aid received scholarships/grants; average award was $1,566. No-need awards available for academics, alumni affiliation, art, athletics, leadership, minority status, music/drama, state/district residency.
Scholarships offered: 13 full-time freshmen received athletic scholarships; average amount $4,273.
Cumulative student debt: 58% of graduating class had student loans; average debt was $15,784.
Additional info: Short-term student loans ranging from $100 to $1,000 available on a quarterly basis.

FINANCIAL AID PROCEDURES
Forms required: FAFSA.
Dates and Deadlines: Priority date 2/15; no closing date. Applicants notified on a rolling basis starting 3/20; must reply within 3 week(s) of notification.
Transfers: No deadline. Applicants notified on a rolling basis starting 3/20; must reply within 3 week(s) of notification. Some state aid not available for out-of-state transfer students.

CONTACT
Clara Capron, Director of Financial Aid
516 High Street, Bellingham, WA 98225-9009
(360) 650-3470

Whatcom Community College
Bellingham, Washington
www.whatcom.ctc.edu   Federal Code: 010364

2-year public community college in small city.
Enrollment: 2,959 undergrads.
Selectivity: Open admission.

BASIC COSTS (2005-2006)
Tuition and fees: $2,484; out-of-state residents $7,692.
Per-credit charge: $73; out-of-state residents $245.

FINANCIAL AID PICTURE (2004-2005)
Students with need: 71% of average financial aid package awarded as scholarships/grants, 29% awarded as loans/jobs. Need-based aid available for part-time students. Work study available nights.
Students without need: No-need awards available for academics, athletics, state/district residency.

FINANCIAL AID PROCEDURES
Forms required: FAFSA, institutional form.
Dates and Deadlines: No deadline. Applicants notified on a rolling basis starting 7/1; must reply within 3 week(s) of notification.

CONTACT
Mary Easley, Director, Financial Aid and Veterans Programs
237 West Kellogg Road, Bellingham, WA 98226
(360) 647-3260

Whitman College
Walla Walla, Washington   Federal Code: 003803
www.whitman.edu   CSS Code: 4951

4-year private liberal arts college in large town.
Enrollment: 1,488 undergrads, 1% part-time. 361 full-time freshmen.
Selectivity: Admits less than 50% of applicants.

BASIC COSTS (2006-2007)
Tuition and fees: $30,806.
Per-credit charge: $1,280.
Room and board: $7,840.

FINANCIAL AID PICTURE (2005-2006)
Students with need: Average financial aid package met 98% of need; average scholarship/grant was $17,400; average loan was $3,450. For part-time students, average financial aid package was $14,250.
Students without need: No-need awards available for academics, art, minority status, music/drama.
Cumulative student debt: 45% of graduating class had student loans; average debt was $16,200.

FINANCIAL AID PROCEDURES
Forms required: FAFSA, CSS PROFILE.
Dates and Deadlines: Priority date 1/15; closing date 2/1. Applicants notified on a rolling basis starting 12/20; must reply within 2 week(s) of notification.

CONTACT
Varga Fox, Director of Financial Aid Services
345 Boyer Avenue, Walla Walla, WA 99362-2046
(509) 527-5178

Whitworth College
Spokane, Washington
www.whitworth.edu   Federal Code: 003804

4-year private liberal arts college in large city, affiliated with Presbyterian Church (USA).
Enrollment: 2,156 undergrads, 5% part-time. 451 full-time freshmen.
Selectivity: Admits 50 to 75% of applicants.

BASIC COSTS (2006-2007)
Tuition and fees: $24,154.
Per-credit charge: $994.
Room and board: $7,030.

FINANCIAL AID PICTURE (2005-2006)
Students with need: Out of 399 full-time freshmen who applied for aid, 317 were judged to have need. Of these, 316 received aid, and 72 had their full need met. Average financial aid package met 83% of need; average scholarship/grant was $12,851; average loan was $3,757. For part-time students, average financial aid package was $12,050.
Students without need: 112 full-time freshmen who did not demonstrate need for aid received scholarships/grants; average award was $8,604. No-need awards available for academics, alumni affiliation, art, music/drama, religious affiliation, ROTC.
Scholarships offered: Merit scholarships: $4,000 to 8,500; based on GPA, SAT/ACT scores and class rank.
Cumulative student debt: 73% of graduating class had student loans; average debt was $18,246.

FINANCIAL AID PROCEDURES
Forms required: FAFSA.
Dates and Deadlines: Priority date 3/1; no closing date. Applicants notified on a rolling basis starting 3/1; must reply by 5/1 or within 4 week(s) of notification.
Transfers: Priority date 4/1.

CONTACT
Wendy Olson, Director of Financial Aid
300 West Hawthorne Road, Spokane, WA 99251-0002
(509) 777-3215

Yakima Valley Community College
Yakima, Washington
www.yvcc.edu   Federal Code: 003805

2-year public community college in small city.
Enrollment: 6,225 undergrads. 3,755 full-time freshmen.
Selectivity: Open admission; but selective for some programs.

BASIC COSTS (2005-2006)
Tuition and fees: $2,550; out-of-state residents $2,939.
Per-credit charge: $72; out-of-state residents $85.
Additional info: Tuition/fee waivers available for unemployed or children of unemployed.

FINANCIAL AID PICTURE (2004-2005)
Students with need: 74% of average financial aid package awarded as scholarships/grants, 26% awarded as loans/jobs. Need-based aid available for part-time students.
Students without need: No-need awards available for academics, athletics, music/drama.

FINANCIAL AID PROCEDURES
Forms required: FAFSA, institutional form.
Dates and Deadlines: Priority date 5/1; no closing date. Applicants notified on a rolling basis starting 8/1; must reply within 2 week(s) of notification.
Transfers: No deadline. Applicants notified on a rolling basis starting 8/1; must reply within 2 week(s) of notification.

CONTACT
Leslie Blackaby, Director of Financial Aid
PO Box 22520, Yakima, WA 98907-2520
(509) 574-6855

West Virginia

Alderson-Broaddus College
Philippi, West Virginia
www.ab.edu   Federal Code: 003806

4-year private liberal arts college in small town, affiliated with American Baptist Churches in the USA.
Enrollment: 623 undergrads, 8% part-time. 150 full-time freshmen.
Selectivity: Admits over 75% of applicants.

BASIC COSTS (2006-2007)
Tuition and fees: $19,090.
Per-credit charge: $630.
Room and board: $6,150.

FINANCIAL AID PICTURE (2004-2005)
Students with need: Out of 150 full-time freshmen who applied for aid, 145 were judged to have need. Of these, 145 received aid, and 5 had their full need met. Average financial aid package met 91% of need; average scholarship/grant was $9,735; average loan was $3,594. For part-time students, average financial aid package was $9,400.
Students without need: 2 full-time freshmen who did not demonstrate need for aid received scholarships/grants; average award was $8,500. No-need awards available for academics, athletics, music/drama.
Scholarships offered: 1 full-time freshmen received athletic scholarships; average amount $5,000.
Cumulative student debt: 86% of graduating class had student loans; average debt was $26,313.

FINANCIAL AID PROCEDURES
Forms required: FAFSA, state aid form.
Dates and Deadlines: Priority date 3/1; no closing date. Applicants notified on a rolling basis starting 2/15; must reply within 2 week(s) of notification.

CONTACT
Brian Weingart, Director of Financial Aid
College Hill, Philippi, WV 26416
(304) 457-6354

Appalachian Bible College
Bradley, West Virginia
www.abc.edu   Federal Code: 007544

4-year private Bible college in rural community, affiliated with nondenominational tradition.
Enrollment: 230 undergrads, 7% part-time. 46 full-time freshmen.
Selectivity: Admits 50 to 75% of applicants.

BASIC COSTS (2006-2007)
Tuition and fees: $8,820.
Per-credit charge: $313.
Room and board: $4,680.

FINANCIAL AID PICTURE (2004-2005)
Students with need: 64% of average financial aid package awarded as scholarships/grants, 36% awarded as loans/jobs. Need-based aid available for part-time students.
Scholarships offered: Scholastic Achievement Scholarship; $1,000 per year; minimum 26 ACT or 1180 SAT (exclusive of Writing).

FINANCIAL AID PROCEDURES
Forms required: FAFSA, state aid form, institutional form.
Dates and Deadlines: Closing date 6/15. Applicants notified on a rolling basis starting 6/15; must reply by 8/1 or within 4 week(s) of notification.

CONTACT
Shirley Carfrey, Director of Financial Aid
PO Box ABC, Bradley, WV 25818-1353
(304) 877-6428 ext. 3247

Bethany College
Bethany, West Virginia
www.bethanywv.edu   Federal Code: 003808

4-year private liberal arts college in rural community, affiliated with Christian Church (Disciples of Christ).
Enrollment: 888 undergrads. 238 full-time freshmen.
Selectivity: Admits over 75% of applicants.

BASIC COSTS (2006-2007)
Tuition and fees: $15,940.
Room and board: $7,625.

FINANCIAL AID PICTURE (2005-2006)
Students with need: Out of 233 full-time freshmen who applied for aid, 233 were judged to have need. Of these, 233 received aid.
Students without need: No-need awards available for academics, alumni affiliation, art, leadership, music/drama, religious affiliation.
Cumulative student debt: 91% of graduating class had student loans; average debt was $17,071.
Additional info: Scholarships available for travel program.

FINANCIAL AID PROCEDURES
Forms required: FAFSA.
Dates and Deadlines: Priority date 3/1; closing date 5/1. Applicants notified on a rolling basis starting 2/1; must reply within 3 week(s) of notification.
Transfers: No deadline.

CONTACT
Sandra Neel, Assoc. V.P. Student Services
Office of Admission, Bethany, WV 26032-0428
(304) 829-7141

Bluefield State College
Bluefield, West Virginia
www.bluefieldstate.edu
Federal Code: 003809

4-year public community and technical college in large town.
Enrollment: 1,790 undergrads. 567 full-time freshmen.

BASIC COSTS (2005-2006)
Tuition and fees: $3,410; out-of-state residents $7,014.
Per-credit charge: $142; out-of-state residents $292.

FINANCIAL AID PICTURE (2004-2005)
Students with need: Out of 450 full-time freshmen who applied for aid, 375 were judged to have need. Of these, 375 received aid, and 90 had their full need met. Average financial aid package met 70% of need; average scholarship/grant was $3,010; average loan was $3,000. For part-time students, average financial aid package was $2,700.
Students without need: 75 full-time freshmen who did not demonstrate need for aid received scholarships/grants; average award was $1,400. No-need awards available for academics, alumni affiliation, athletics, leadership, minority status, state/district residency.
Scholarships offered: 30 full-time freshmen received athletic scholarships; average amount $1,900.

FINANCIAL AID PROCEDURES
Forms required: FAFSA, state aid form, institutional form.
Dates and Deadlines: Closing date 3/1. Applicants notified on a rolling basis starting 6/1.
Transfers: No deadline.

CONTACT
Tom Ilse, Director of Financial Aid
219 Rock Street, Bluefield, WV 24701
(304) 327-4020

Concord University
Athens, West Virginia
www.concord.edu
Federal Code: 003810

4-year public university in small town.
Enrollment: 3,015 undergrads.

BASIC COSTS (2005-2006)
Tuition and fees: $3,912; out-of-state residents $8,686.
Per-credit charge: $163; out-of-state residents $362.
Room and board: $5,796.

FINANCIAL AID PICTURE
Students with need: Need-based aid available for full-time and part-time students.
Students without need: No-need awards available for academics, alumni affiliation, art, athletics, job skills, leadership, minority status, music/drama, state/district residency.
Additional info: Room and board may be paid in 2 installments each semester: 60% at registration, 40% six weeks later. March 1 is priority deadline for state forms. April 15 is priority deadline for FAFSA.

FINANCIAL AID PROCEDURES
Forms required: FAFSA, state aid form, institutional form.
Dates and Deadlines: Applicants notified on a rolling basis starting 3/1; must reply within 2 week(s) of notification.

CONTACT
Patricia Harmon, Director of Financial Aid
PO Box 1000, Athens, WV 24712-1000
(304) 384-6069

Corinthian Schools: National Institute of Technology
Cross Lanes, West Virginia
www.cci.edu
Federal Code: 010356

2-year for-profit technical college in large town.
Enrollment: 400 undergrads.
Selectivity: Open admission; but selective for some programs.

BASIC COSTS (2005-2006)
Additional info: Electronics program $24,150. Medical Assistant $11,130. Massage Therapy program $11,663. Homeland Security Specialist program $10,920. Pharmacy Technician program $11,506.

FINANCIAL AID PICTURE
Students with need: Need-based aid available for full-time students.
Students without need: No-need awards available for academics, art.

FINANCIAL AID PROCEDURES
Forms required: FAFSA.
Dates and Deadlines: No deadline. Applicants notified on a rolling basis.

CONTACT
Matt Lane, Finance Director
5514 Big Tyler Road, Cross Lanes, WV 25313
(304) 776-6290

Davis and Elkins College
Elkins, West Virginia
www.davisandelkins.edu
Federal Code: 003811

4-year private liberal arts college in small town, affiliated with Presbyterian Church (USA).
Enrollment: 543 undergrads, 10% part-time. 124 full-time freshmen.
Selectivity: Admits less than 50% of applicants.

BASIC COSTS (2006-2007)
Tuition and fees: $17,730.
Per-credit charge: $605.
Room and board: $6,300.

FINANCIAL AID PICTURE (2004-2005)
Students with need: Out of 124 full-time freshmen who applied for aid, 89 were judged to have need. Of these, 89 received aid, and 41 had their full need met. Average financial aid package met 86% of need; average scholarship/grant was $2,115; average loan was $2,219. For part-time students, average financial aid package was $5,701.
Students without need: This college only awards aid to students with need.
Scholarships offered: 54 full-time freshmen received athletic scholarships; average amount $4,135.
Cumulative student debt: 76% of graduating class had student loans; average debt was $13,380.

FINANCIAL AID PROCEDURES
Forms required: FAFSA.
Dates and Deadlines: Priority date 3/1; no closing date. Applicants notified on a rolling basis starting 5/1; must reply within 2 week(s) of notification.
Transfers: No deadline. Applicants notified on a rolling basis starting 5/1; must reply within 2 week(s) of notification.

CONTACT
Susan George, Director of Financial Aid
100 Campus Drive, Elkins, WV 26241
(304) 637-1373

Eastern West Virginia Community and Technical College
Moorefield, West Virginia
www.eastern.wvnet.edu

2-year public community and technical college in rural community.
Enrollment: 255 undergrads, 71% part-time. 15 full-time freshmen.
Selectivity: Open admission.

BASIC COSTS (2005-2006)
Tuition and fees: $1,634; out-of-state residents $6,824.
Per-credit charge: $68; out-of-state residents $284.

FINANCIAL AID PICTURE (2005-2006)
Students with need: 88% of average financial aid package awarded as scholarships/grants, 12% awarded as loans/jobs. Need-based aid available for part-time students.

FINANCIAL AID PROCEDURES
Forms required: FAFSA, institutional form.
Dates and Deadlines: Priority date 6/1; no closing date. Applicants notified on a rolling basis; must reply within 2 week(s) of notification.

CONTACT
Robert Eagle, Director of Financial Aid
1929 State Road 55, Moorefield, WV 26836
(304) 434-8000

Glenville State College
Glenville, West Virginia
www.glenville.edu   Federal Code: 003813

4-year public liberal arts and teachers college in rural community.
Enrollment: 1,305 undergrads, 9% part-time. 301 full-time freshmen.
Selectivity: Admits over 75% of applicants.

BASIC COSTS (2005-2006)
Tuition and fees: $3,628; out-of-state residents $8,640.
Per-credit charge: $151; out-of-state residents $360.
Room and board: $5,300.

FINANCIAL AID PICTURE (2004-2005)
Students with need: Out of 282 full-time freshmen who applied for aid, 243 were judged to have need. Of these, 231 received aid, and 58 had their full need met. Average financial aid package met 79% of need; average scholarship/grant was $4,484; average loan was $3,029. Need-based aid available for part-time students.
Students without need: 27 full-time freshmen who did not demonstrate need for aid received scholarships/grants; average award was $27. No-need awards available for academics, art, athletics, music/drama.
Scholarships offered: 9 full-time freshmen received athletic scholarships; average amount $3,605.
Cumulative student debt: 71% of graduating class had student loans; average debt was $16,079.

FINANCIAL AID PROCEDURES
Forms required: FAFSA.
Dates and Deadlines: Priority date 3/1; no closing date. Applicants notified on a rolling basis starting 4/1; must reply within 2 week(s) of notification.

CONTACT
Karen Lay, Financial Aid Officer
200 High Street, Glenville, WV 26351-1292
(304) 462-4103

Marshall University
Huntington, West Virginia
www.marshall.edu   Federal Code: 003815

4-year public university in small city.
Enrollment: 9,161 undergrads, 11% part-time. 1,683 full-time freshmen.
Selectivity: Open admission; but selective for some programs and for out-of-state students.

BASIC COSTS (2005-2006)
Tuition and fees: $3,932; out-of-state residents $10,634.
Per-credit charge: $164; out-of-state residents $443.
Room and board: $6,262.

FINANCIAL AID PICTURE (2005-2006)
Students with need: Out of 1,060 full-time freshmen who applied for aid, 733 were judged to have need. Of these, 724 received aid, and 285 had their full need met. Average financial aid package met 52% of need; average scholarship/grant was $4,015; average loan was $3,578. For part-time students, average financial aid package was $5,186.
Students without need: 312 full-time freshmen who did not demonstrate need for aid received scholarships/grants; average award was $5,326. No-need awards available for academics, art, athletics, minority status, music/drama, ROTC, state/district residency.
Scholarships offered: *Merit:* Michael Perry Scholarship: $500 to incoming freshman with 3.2 GPA and 20 ACT score; $750 to incoming freshman with 3.5 GPA and 23 ACT, or 3.2 GPA and 25 ACT; all one year only. Presidential Scholarship: $1,250; 3.5 GPA and 25 ACT; renewable with 3.5 cumulative GPA. John Marshall Scholarship: tuition waiver plus $1,250 stipend; 3.5 GPA and 30 ACT; renewable yearly with 3.5 cumulative college GPA. Yeager scholarship: full tuition and fees, full room and board, book allowance, stipend, personal computer for use during program, and $4,000 toward study abroad; ACT 28/ SAT 1260 (exclusive of writing). *Athletic:* 47 full-time freshmen received athletic scholarships; average amount $8,269.
Cumulative student debt: 60% of graduating class had student loans; average debt was $17,053.

FINANCIAL AID PROCEDURES
Forms required: FAFSA, state aid form.
Dates and Deadlines: Priority date 3/1; no closing date. Applicants notified on a rolling basis starting 5/1; must reply within 2 week(s) of notification.
Transfers: Priority date 1/1.

CONTACT
Jack Toney, Director of Financial Aid
One John Marshall Drive, Huntington, WV 25755
(304) 696-3162

Mountain State University
Beckley, West Virginia
www.mountainstate.edu   Federal Code: 003807

4-year private university and health science college in large town.
Enrollment: 3,837 undergrads. 288 full-time freshmen.
Selectivity: Open admission; but selective for some programs.

BASIC COSTS (2006-2007)
Tuition and fees: $7,800.
Room and board: $5,636.

FINANCIAL AID PICTURE (2004-2005)
Students with need: Out of 288 full-time freshmen who applied for aid, 221 were judged to have need. Of these, 221 received aid. Average financial aid package met 37% of need; average scholarship/grant was $3,319; average loan was $2,533. For part-time students, average financial aid package was $5,365.

Students without need: 4 full-time freshmen who did not demonstrate need for aid received scholarships/grants; average award was $4,047. No-need awards available for academics, alumni affiliation, athletics, leadership, minority status.
Scholarships offered: 6 full-time freshmen received athletic scholarships; average amount $6,527.
Cumulative student debt: 69% of graduating class had student loans; average debt was $23,570.

FINANCIAL AID PROCEDURES
Forms required: FAFSA.
Dates and Deadlines: No deadline. Applicants notified on a rolling basis starting 4/1.

CONTACT
Sue Pack, Director of Financial Aid
609 South Kanawha Street, Beckley, WV 25802-9003
(304) 253-7351 ext. 1443

Ohio Valley University
Vienna, West Virginia
www.ovc.edu   Federal Code: 003819

4-year private university and liberal arts college in small city, affiliated with Church of Christ.
Enrollment: 516 undergrads, 3% part-time. 86 full-time freshmen.

BASIC COSTS (2005-2006)
Tuition and fees: $13,092.
Per-credit charge: $366.
Room and board: $5,660.

FINANCIAL AID PICTURE (2005-2006)
Students with need: Out of 86 full-time freshmen who applied for aid, 65 were judged to have need. Of these, 65 received aid, and 16 had their full need met. Average financial aid package met 63% of need; average scholarship/grant was $7,219; average loan was $2,971. For part-time students, average financial aid package was $4,259.
Students without need: 35 full-time freshmen who did not demonstrate need for aid received scholarships/grants; average award was $7,732. No-need awards available for academics, athletics, job skills, leadership, music/drama.
Scholarships offered: 22 full-time freshmen received athletic scholarships; average amount $5,442.
Cumulative student debt: 80% of graduating class had student loans; average debt was $9,035.

FINANCIAL AID PROCEDURES
Forms required: FAFSA.
Dates and Deadlines: Priority date 2/15; no closing date. Applicants notified on a rolling basis starting 3/15; must reply within 4 week(s) of notification.

CONTACT
Marjorie Lyons, Director of Student Financial Services
One Campus View Drive, Vienna, WV 26105
(304) 865-6077

Potomac State College of West Virginia University
Keyser, West Virginia
www.potomacstatecollege.edu   Federal Code: 003829

2-year public branch campus and junior college in small town.
Enrollment: 1,279 undergrads.
Selectivity: Open admission.

BASIC COSTS (2005-2006)
Tuition and fees: $2,328; out-of-state residents $7,872.
Per-credit charge: $98; out-of-state residents $329.
Room and board: $4,914.
Additional info: Tuition/fee waivers available for adults.

FINANCIAL AID PICTURE (2004-2005)
Students with need: 96% of average financial aid package awarded as scholarships/grants, 4% awarded as loans/jobs. Need-based aid available for part-time students. Work study available nights, weekends, and for part-time students.
Students without need: No-need awards available for academics, athletics, leadership.

FINANCIAL AID PROCEDURES
Forms required: FAFSA.
Dates and Deadlines: Priority date 3/1; no closing date. Applicants notified on a rolling basis starting 4/1; must reply within 2 week(s) of notification.

CONTACT
Beth Little, Director of Enrollment Services
One Grand Central Park, Suite 2090, Keyser, WV 26726
(304) 788-6820

Salem International University
Salem, West Virginia
www.salemiu.edu   Federal Code: 003820

4-year for-profit university and liberal arts college in small town.
Enrollment: 489 undergrads, 18% part-time. 118 full-time freshmen.

BASIC COSTS (2005-2006)
Tuition and fees: $11,040.
Per-credit charge: $265.
Room and board: $4,790.
Additional info: First year students tuition is $10,100. All returning students tuition is $15,295.

FINANCIAL AID PICTURE
Students with need: Need-based aid available for full-time and part-time students. Work study available nights, weekends, and for part-time students.
Students without need: No-need awards available for academics.
Scholarships offered: Scholarships based on high school GPA, standardized test scores; extensive amount awarded. Breed-related awards for students in the equine career and industry management program. Awards for academically excellent GED diploma recipients.

FINANCIAL AID PROCEDURES
Forms required: FAFSA.
Dates and Deadlines: Priority date 4/15; no closing date. Applicants notified on a rolling basis starting 2/15; must reply within 4 week(s) of notification.

CONTACT
Charlotte Lake, Director of Financial Aid
223 West Main Street, Salem, WV 26426
(304) 326-0205

Shepherd University
Shepherdstown, West Virginia
www.shepherd.edu   Federal Code: 003822

4-year public university in small town.
Enrollment: 3,436 undergrads, 15% part-time. 657 full-time freshmen.
Selectivity: Admits over 75% of applicants.

BASIC COSTS (2005-2006)
Tuition and fees: $4,046; out-of-state residents $10,618.
Per-credit charge: $169; out-of-state residents $442.
Room and board: $6,020.
Additional info: Tuition/fee waivers available for minority students.

FINANCIAL AID PICTURE (2005-2006)
Students with need: Out of 571 full-time freshmen who applied for aid, 333 were judged to have need. Of these, 319 received aid, and 67 had their full need met. Average financial aid package met 70% of need; average scholarship/grant was $3,627; average loan was $2,368. For part-time students, average financial aid package was $7,511.
Students without need: 145 full-time freshmen who did not demonstrate need for aid received scholarships/grants; average award was $6,842. No-need awards available for academics, art, athletics, job skills, leadership, minority status, music/drama, state/district residency.
Scholarships offered: Merit: Rubye Clyde and Burkhart Scholarship; $5,000; renewable; based on GPA of 3.5 and 30 ACT or 1270 SAT, exclusive of writing; 4 awarded. Alumni Honors Scholarship; ; minimum 3.5 GPA and 30 ACT or 1270 SAT, exclusive of writing; 2 awarded each year to incoming students.
Athletic: 41 full-time freshmen received athletic scholarships; average amount $4,465.
Cumulative student debt: 68% of graduating class had student loans; average debt was $14,887.

FINANCIAL AID PROCEDURES
Forms required: FAFSA, state aid form.
Dates and Deadlines: Priority date 3/1; no closing date. Applicants notified on a rolling basis starting 3/15; must reply within 3 week(s) of notification.
Transfers: No deadline. Applicants notified on a rolling basis starting 11/1; must reply within 3 week(s) of notification.

CONTACT
Elizabeth Sturm, Director of Financial Aid
PO Box 3210, Shepherdstown, WV 25443-3210
(304) 876-5470

Southern West Virginia Community and Technical College
Mount Gay, West Virginia
www.southern.wvnet.edu   Federal Code: 003816

2-year public community college in small town.
Enrollment: 1,379 undergrads.
Selectivity: Open admission; but selective for some programs.

BASIC COSTS (2005-2006)
Tuition and fees: $1,634; out-of-state residents $6,824.
Per-credit charge: $68; out-of-state residents $284.

FINANCIAL AID PICTURE
Students with need: Need-based aid available for full-time and part-time students.

FINANCIAL AID PROCEDURES
Forms required: FAFSA.
Dates and Deadlines: No deadline. Applicants notified on a rolling basis.

CONTACT
James Owens, Financial Aid Director
PO Box 2900, Mount Gay, WV 25637
(304) 792-7098 ext. 256

University of Charleston
Charleston, West Virginia
www.ucwv.edu   Federal Code: 003818

4-year private university and liberal arts college in small city.
Enrollment: 900 undergrads, 5% part-time. 274 full-time freshmen.
Selectivity: Admits over 75% of applicants.

BASIC COSTS (2006-2007)
Tuition and fees: $21,000.
Per-credit charge: $400.
Room and board: $7,600.
Additional info: Tuition for pharmacy students: $23,200.

FINANCIAL AID PICTURE (2005-2006)
Students with need: Average financial aid package met 88% of need; average scholarship/grant was $5,800; average loan was $6,500. For part-time students, average financial aid package was $4,200.
Students without need: No-need awards available for academics, alumni affiliation, art, athletics, leadership, music/drama, ROTC.

FINANCIAL AID PROCEDURES
Forms required: FAFSA.
Dates and Deadlines: Closing date 3/1. Applicants notified on a rolling basis starting 4/1; must reply by 5/1 or within 4 week(s) of notification.
Transfers: Priority date 3/1.

CONTACT
Janet Ruge, Director of Financial Aid
2300 MacCorkle Avenue, SE, Charleston, WV 25304
(304) 257-4759

Valley College of Technology
Martinsburg, West Virginia
www.vct.edu   Federal Code: G26094

2-year for-profit business and technical college in small city.
Enrollment: 17 undergrads. 14 full-time freshmen.

BASIC COSTS (2006-2007)
Tuition and fees: $7,300.
Per-credit charge: $225.
Additional info: Tuition varies according to program.

FINANCIAL AID PICTURE (2004-2005)
Students with need: 55% of average financial aid package awarded as scholarships/grants, 45% awarded as loans/jobs. Need-based aid available for part-time students.

FINANCIAL AID PROCEDURES
Forms required: FAFSA, institutional form.
Dates and Deadlines: No deadline. Applicants notified on a rolling basis.
Transfers: No deadline. Applicants notified on a rolling basis.

CONTACT
Tangene Umstead, Director of Financial Aid
287 Aikens Center, Martinsburg, WV 25401
(304) 263-0979

West Liberty State College
West Liberty, West Virginia
www.wlsc.edu   Federal Code: 003823

4-year public liberal arts college in rural community.
Enrollment: 2,160 undergrads, 9% part-time. 446 full-time freshmen.
Selectivity: Admits over 75% of applicants.

BASIC COSTS (2005-2006)
Tuition and fees: $3,686; out-of-state residents $9,054.
Per-credit charge: $150; out-of-state residents $374.
Room and board: $5,456.

FINANCIAL AID PICTURE (2005-2006)
Students with need: Out of 430 full-time freshmen who applied for aid, 261 were judged to have need. Of these, 249 received aid, and 147 had their full need met. Average financial aid package met 76% of need; average scholarship/grant was $3,807; average loan was $2,582. For part-time students, average financial aid package was $4,747.
Students without need: 34 full-time freshmen who did not demonstrate need for aid received scholarships/grants; average award was $2,684. No-need awards available for academics, alumni affiliation, art, athletics, leadership, music/drama.
Additional info: Non-need based student employment available at food service, college union, bookstore, and tutoring office. Resident assistant and campus security jobs also available.

FINANCIAL AID PROCEDURES
Forms required: FAFSA.
Dates and Deadlines: Priority date 3/1; no closing date. Applicants notified on a rolling basis starting 2/15; must reply within 2 week(s) of notification.
Transfers: Financial aid transcript required from all previous colleges attended regardless of whether aid was received.

CONTACT
Scott Cook, Financial Aid Director
Box 295, West Liberty, WV 26074-0295
(304) 336-8016

West Virginia Northern Community College
Wheeling, West Virginia
www.northern.wvnet.edu   Federal Code: 010920

2-year public community college in large town.
Enrollment: 2,148 undergrads, 36% part-time. 333 full-time freshmen.
Selectivity: Open admission; but selective for some programs.

BASIC COSTS (2005-2006)
Tuition and fees: $1,752; out-of-state residents $5,592.
Per-credit charge: $73; out-of-state residents $233.
Additional info: Tuition/fee waivers available for adults.

FINANCIAL AID PICTURE
Students with need: Need-based aid available for full-time and part-time students.

FINANCIAL AID PROCEDURES
Forms required: FAFSA, institutional form.
Dates and Deadlines: Priority date 3/15; no closing date. Applicants notified on a rolling basis starting 3/10.

CONTACT
Janet Fike, Director, Financial Aid
1704 Market Street, Wheeling, WV 26003
(304) 233-5900 ext. 4363

West Virginia State University
Institute, West Virginia
www.wvstateu.edu   Federal Code: 003826

4-year public liberal arts and teachers college in small town.
Enrollment: 3,455 undergrads, 31% part-time. 351 full-time freshmen.
Selectivity: Admits less than 50% of applicants.

BASIC COSTS (2005-2006)
Tuition and fees: $3,548; out-of-state residents $8,124.
Per-credit charge: $147; out-of-state residents $338.
Room and board: $4,850.

FINANCIAL AID PICTURE
Students with need: Need-based aid available for full-time and part-time students. Work study available nights, weekends, and for part-time students.
Students without need: No-need awards available for academics, athletics, ROTC, state/district residency.

FINANCIAL AID PROCEDURES
Forms required: FAFSA.
Dates and Deadlines: Priority date 3/1; closing date 6/15. Applicants notified on a rolling basis starting 2/15; must reply within 2 week(s) of notification.

CONTACT
Mary Blizzard, Director of Financial Aid
Campus Box 197, Institute, WV 25112-1000
(304) 766-3131

West Virginia University
Morgantown, West Virginia
www.wvu.edu   Federal Code: 003827

4-year public university in small city.
Enrollment: 19,510 undergrads, 5% part-time. 4,539 full-time freshmen.
Selectivity: Admits over 75% of applicants.

BASIC COSTS (2005-2006)
Tuition and fees: $4,164; out-of-state residents $12,874.
Per-credit charge: $176; out-of-state residents $538.
Room and board: $6,342.
Additional info: Tuition/fee waivers available for minority students.

FINANCIAL AID PICTURE (2005-2006)
Students with need: Out of 2,525 full-time freshmen who applied for aid, 2,014 were judged to have need. Of these, 1,917 received aid, and 863 had their full need met. Average financial aid package met 87% of need; average scholarship/grant was $3,149; average loan was $3,493. For part-time students, average financial aid package was $5,742.
Students without need: 1,226 full-time freshmen who did not demonstrate need for aid received scholarships/grants; average award was $5,096. No-need awards available for academics, alumni affiliation, art, athletics, job skills, leadership, minority status, music/drama, state/district residency.
Scholarships offered: 70 full-time freshmen received athletic scholarships; average amount $12,670.
Cumulative student debt: 62% of graduating class had student loans; average debt was $13,798.
Additional info: February 1 closing date for freshman scholarships.

FINANCIAL AID PROCEDURES
Forms required: FAFSA, state aid form.
Dates and Deadlines: Closing date 3/1. Applicants notified on a rolling basis starting 3/15; must reply within 4 week(s) of notification.

CONTACT
Kaye Widney, Director of Financial Aid
Admissions and Records Office, Morgantown, WV 26506-6009
(800) 344-9881

West Virginia University at Parkersburg
Parkersburg, West Virginia
www.wvup.edu   Federal Code: 003828

4-year public community college in large town.
Enrollment: 3,114 undergrads, 30% part-time. 546 full-time freshmen.
Selectivity: Open admission; but selective for some programs.

BASIC COSTS (2005-2006)
Tuition and fees: $1,668; out-of-state residents $5,892.
Per-credit charge: $70; out-of-state residents $246.
Additional info: Bachelor degree program: $2,280 annually or $95 per credit hour for residents; $6,024 annually or $251 per credit hour for nonresidents.

FINANCIAL AID PICTURE (2005-2006)
Students with need: Average financial aid package met 78% of need; average scholarship/grant was $5,200; average loan was $2,800. For part-time students, average financial aid package was $3,850.
Students without need: No-need awards available for academics, state/district residency.
Cumulative student debt: 82% of graduating class had student loans; average debt was $11,500.

FINANCIAL AID PROCEDURES
Forms required: FAFSA.
Dates and Deadlines: Priority date 3/1; no closing date. Applicants notified on a rolling basis; must reply within 2 week(s) of notification.

CONTACT
August Kafer, Director of Financial Aid
300 Campus Drive, Parkersburg, WV 26104-8647
(304) 424-8210

West Virginia University Institute of Technology
Montgomery, West Virginia
www.wvutech.edu   Federal Code: 003825

4-year public engineering and technical college in small town.
Enrollment: 1,959 undergrads.
Selectivity: Admits 50 to 75% of applicants.

BASIC COSTS (2005-2006)
Tuition and fees: $4,078; out-of-state residents $10,416.
Per-credit charge: $170; out-of-state residents $434.
Room and board: $4,810.

FINANCIAL AID PICTURE
Students with need: Need-based aid available for full-time students. Work study available nights, weekends, and for part-time students.
Additional info: Room and board may be deferred for up to 60 days. First 50% due in 30 days.

FINANCIAL AID PROCEDURES
Forms required: FAFSA, institutional form.
Dates and Deadlines: Priority date 2/1; closing date 4/1. Applicants notified on a rolling basis; must reply within 3 week(s) of notification.

CONTACT
Nina Morton, Director of Financial Aid
405 Fayette Pike, Montgomery, WV 25136-2436
(304) 442-3228

West Virginia Wesleyan College
Buckhannon, West Virginia
www.wvwc.edu   Federal Code: 003830

4-year private liberal arts college in small town, affiliated with United Methodist Church.
Enrollment: 1,366 undergrads, 2% part-time. 348 full-time freshmen.
Selectivity: Admits over 75% of applicants.

BASIC COSTS (2006-2007)
Tuition and fees: $21,330.
Room and board: $5,550.

FINANCIAL AID PICTURE (2005-2006)
Students with need: Out of 314 full-time freshmen who applied for aid, 278 were judged to have need. Of these, 278 received aid, and 92 had their full need met. Average financial aid package met 89% of need; average scholarship/grant was $16,861; average loan was $3,098.
Students without need: 70 full-time freshmen who did not demonstrate need for aid received scholarships/grants; average award was $11,475. No-need awards available for academics, alumni affiliation, art, athletics, leadership, music/drama, religious affiliation.
Scholarships offered: 88 full-time freshmen received athletic scholarships; average amount $4,000.

FINANCIAL AID PROCEDURES
Forms required: FAFSA.
Dates and Deadlines: Priority date 2/15; no closing date. Applicants notified on a rolling basis starting 3/15; must reply within 4 week(s) of notification.
Transfers: Priority date 3/15. Financial aid transcripts required from all institutions previously attended.

CONTACT
Tammy Crites, Admission and Financial Planning
59 College Avenue, Buckhannon, WV 26201-2998
(304) 473-8080

Wheeling Jesuit University
Wheeling, West Virginia
www.wju.edu   Federal Code: 003831

4-year private university and liberal arts college in small city, affiliated with Roman Catholic Church.
Enrollment: 1,188 undergrads, 12% part-time. 285 full-time freshmen.
Selectivity: Admits over 75% of applicants.

BASIC COSTS (2006-2007)
Tuition and fees: $22,186.
Per-credit charge: $556.
Room and board: $6,808.

FINANCIAL AID PICTURE (2005-2006)
Students with need: Out of 267 full-time freshmen who applied for aid, 237 were judged to have need. Of these, 237 received aid, and 95 had their full need met. Average financial aid package met 95% of need; average scholarship/grant was $7,200; average loan was $2,380. For part-time students, average financial aid package was $4,900.
Students without need: 30 full-time freshmen who did not demonstrate need for aid received scholarships/grants; average award was $9,419. No-need awards available for academics, alumni affiliation, athletics, leadership, music/drama.
Scholarships offered: 9 full-time freshmen received athletic scholarships; average amount $2,222.
Cumulative student debt: 72% of graduating class had student loans; average debt was $20,052.

FINANCIAL AID PROCEDURES

Forms required: FAFSA.
Dates and Deadlines: Priority date 2/15; no closing date. Applicants notified on a rolling basis starting 3/15; must reply within 2 week(s) of notification.
Transfers: Must reply within 2 week(s) of notification. Academic scholarships available to qualified transfer students.

CONTACT

Christie Tomczyk, Director of Financial Aid
316 Washington Avenue, Wheeling, WV 26003-6295
(800) 624-6992 ext. 2304

Wisconsin

Alverno College
Milwaukee, Wisconsin
www.alverno.edu   Federal Code: 003832

4-year private liberal arts college for women in very large city, affiliated with Roman Catholic Church.
Enrollment: 2,047 undergrads, 26% part-time. 262 full-time freshmen.
Selectivity: Admits 50 to 75% of applicants.

BASIC COSTS (2006-2007)
Tuition and fees: $16,334.
Per-credit charge: $666.
Room and board: $5,954.
Additional info: Slightly higher per credit charge for nursing majors.

FINANCIAL AID PICTURE (2004-2005)
Students with need: 61% of average financial aid package awarded as scholarships/grants, 39% awarded as loans/jobs. Need-based aid available for part-time students. Work study available nights, weekends, and for part-time students.
Students without need: No-need awards available for academics, alumni affiliation, leadership, minority status, music/drama.

FINANCIAL AID PROCEDURES
Forms required: FAFSA, institutional form.
Dates and Deadlines: Priority date 4/15; no closing date. Applicants notified on a rolling basis starting 4/15; must reply within 2 week(s) of notification.
Transfers: No deadline. Scholarships ranging from $2,400 to $3,600 available based on minimum 2.5 college GPA for students with at least 12 college credits.

CONTACT
Mark Levine, Director, Student Financial Planning/Resources
3400 South 43rd Street, Milwaukee, WI 53234-3922
(414) 382-6046

Bellin College of Nursing
Green Bay, Wisconsin
www.bcon.edu   Federal Code: 006639

4-year private nursing college in small city.
Enrollment: 247 undergrads, 14% part-time. 23 full-time freshmen.
Selectivity: Admits less than 50% of applicants.

BASIC COSTS (2005-2006)
Tuition and fees: $14,791.

FINANCIAL AID PICTURE (2004-2005)
Students with need: Average financial aid package for all full-time undergraduates was $12,285; for part-time $10,277. 42% awarded as scholarships/grants, 58% awarded as loans/jobs. Work study available nights, weekends, and for part-time students.
Students without need: No-need awards available for academics.
Scholarships offered: Merit Scholarship; $1,000-$2,500 renewable conditionally; based on academics (high school GPA, ACT scores); no application form required; number awarded varies. Dr. Fergus Scholarship; approximately $2,500 renewable annually; awarded to Merit Scholarship recipient; 1 awarded.
Cumulative student debt: 93% of graduating class had student loans; average debt was $25,305.
Additional info: Freshmen and sophomores receive aid through University of Wisconsin-Green Bay. Juniors and seniors receive aid through Bellin College of Nursing.

FINANCIAL AID PROCEDURES
Forms required: FAFSA.
Dates and Deadlines: Priority date 3/1; no closing date. Applicants notified on a rolling basis starting 4/1; must reply within 2 week(s) of notification.
Transfers: No deadline. Applicants notified on a rolling basis starting 4/1; must reply within 2 week(s) of notification. Students with 4-year degrees ineligible for all federal and state grant programs.

CONTACT
Lena Goodman, Director of Financial Aid
PO Box 23400, Green Bay, WI 54305-3400
(920) 433-5801

Beloit College
Beloit, Wisconsin
www.beloit.edu   Federal Code: 003835

4-year private liberal arts college in large town.
Enrollment: 1,328 undergrads, 1% part-time. 326 full-time freshmen.
Selectivity: Admits 50 to 75% of applicants.

BASIC COSTS (2006-2007)
Tuition and fees: $28,350.
Room and board: $6,162.
Additional info: Tuition/fee waivers available for adults.

FINANCIAL AID PICTURE (2005-2006)
Students with need: Out of 309 full-time freshmen who applied for aid, 262 were judged to have need. Of these, 262 received aid, and 262 had their full need met. Average financial aid package met 100% of need; average scholarship/grant was $15,676; average loan was $4,420.
Students without need: 40 full-time freshmen who did not demonstrate need for aid received scholarships/grants; average award was $14,025. No-need awards available for academics, leadership, minority status, music/drama.
Scholarships offered: Presidential Scholarship; $54,000 divided over 8 semesters; based on application and mandatory interviews.
Cumulative student debt: 59% of graduating class had student loans; average debt was $20,339.

FINANCIAL AID PROCEDURES
Forms required: FAFSA, state aid form, institutional form.
Dates and Deadlines: Priority date 1/15; closing date 3/1. Applicants notified on a rolling basis starting 3/15; must reply by 5/1 or within 2 week(s) of notification.
Transfers: No deadline. Applicants notified on a rolling basis starting 3/15.

CONTACT
Jane Hessian, Director of Financial Aid
700 College Street, Beloit, WI 53511-5595
(608) 363-2663

Blackhawk Technical College
Janesville, Wisconsin
www.blackhawk.edu   Federal Code: 005390

2-year public technical college in small city.
Enrollment: 2,476 undergrads.
Selectivity: Open admission; but selective for some programs.

BASIC COSTS (2006-2007)
Tuition and fees: $2,741; out-of-state residents $16,220.
Per-credit charge: $87; out-of-state residents $536.
Additional info: Material fees vary by program; minimum $4 per credit. Tuition/fee waivers available for adults, minority students, unemployed or children of unemployed.

FINANCIAL AID PICTURE (2004-2005)
Students with need: 61% of average financial aid package awarded as scholarships/grants, 39% awarded as loans/jobs. Need-based aid available for part-time students.

FINANCIAL AID PROCEDURES
Dates and Deadlines: Priority date 4/1; closing date 6/15. Applicants notified on a rolling basis starting 4/15; must reply within 2 week(s) of notification.

CONTACT
Barbara Erlandson, Financial Aid Officer
Box 5009, Janesville, WI 53547
(608) 757-7664

Bryant & Stratton College: Milwaukee
Milwaukee, Wisconsin
www.bryantstratton.edu   Federal Code: 005009

2-year for-profit business and junior college in very large city.
Enrollment: 870 undergrads, 25% part-time. 655 full-time freshmen.

FINANCIAL AID PICTURE
Students with need: Work study available nights.
Students without need: This college only awards aid to students with need.

FINANCIAL AID PROCEDURES
Forms required: FAFSA.
Dates and Deadlines: No deadline. Applicants notified on a rolling basis; must reply within 2 week(s) of notification.

CONTACT
Greg Bradner, Business Director
310 West Wisconsin Avenue, Suite 500, Milwaukee, WI 53203
(414) 276-5200

Cardinal Stritch University
Milwaukee, Wisconsin
www.stritch.edu   Federal Code: 003837

4-year private liberal arts college in very large city, affiliated with Roman Catholic Church.
Enrollment: 3,100 undergrads.
Selectivity: Admits over 75% of applicants.

BASIC COSTS (2006-2007)
Tuition and fees: $16,830.
Per-credit charge: $515.
Room and board: $5,430.
Additional info: Additional $55 per credit for the nursing program.

FINANCIAL AID PICTURE
Students with need: Need-based aid available for full-time and part-time students.
Students without need: No-need awards available for academics, art, athletics, music/drama.

FINANCIAL AID PROCEDURES
Forms required: FAFSA, institutional form.
Dates and Deadlines: Priority date 4/15; no closing date. Applicants notified on a rolling basis starting 3/1; must reply within 3 week(s) of notification.

CONTACT
Amy Hoss, Director of Financial Aid
6801 North Yates Road, Box 516, Milwaukee, WI 53217-7516
(414) 410-4048

Carroll College
Waukesha, Wisconsin
www.cc.edu   Federal Code: 003838

4-year private liberal arts college in small city, affiliated with Presbyterian Church (USA).
Enrollment: 2,663 undergrads, 15% part-time. 598 full-time freshmen.
Selectivity: Admits over 75% of applicants.

BASIC COSTS (2006-2007)
Tuition and fees: $19,910.
Per-credit charge: $235.
Room and board: $6,070.

FINANCIAL AID PICTURE (2005-2006)
Students with need: Out of 557 full-time freshmen who applied for aid, 451 were judged to have need. Of these, 451 received aid, and 252 had their full need met. Average financial aid package met 94% of need; average scholarship/grant was $10,512; average loan was $2,531. Need-based aid available for part-time students.
Students without need: 142 full-time freshmen who did not demonstrate need for aid received scholarships/grants; average award was $7,902. No-need awards available for academics, alumni affiliation, art, leadership, minority status, music/drama, religious affiliation, ROTC, state/district residency.
Scholarships offered: Trustee Scholarship; $10,000 per year. Voorhees Scholarship; $9,000 per year. Charles Carroll Scholarship; $8,000 per year.
Cumulative student debt: 57% of graduating class had student loans; average debt was $18,404.

FINANCIAL AID PROCEDURES
Forms required: FAFSA.
Dates and Deadlines: Priority date 4/15; no closing date. Applicants notified on a rolling basis starting 2/15; must reply by 5/1 or within 2 week(s) of notification.

CONTACT
Dawn Scott, Director of Student Financial Services
100 North East Avenue, Waukesha, WI 53186-9988
(262) 524-7296

Carthage College
Kenosha, Wisconsin
www.carthage.edu
Federal Code: 003839

4-year private liberal arts college in small city, affiliated with Evangelical Lutheran Church in America.
Enrollment: 2,432 undergrads, 12% part-time. 578 full-time freshmen.
Selectivity: Admits over 75% of applicants.

BASIC COSTS (2006-2007)
Tuition and fees: $23,650.
Per-credit charge: $345.
Room and board: $6,800.

FINANCIAL AID PICTURE (2005-2006)
Students with need: Out of 519 full-time freshmen who applied for aid, 428 were judged to have need. Of these, 427 received aid, and 120 had their full need met. Average financial aid package met 69% of need; average scholarship/grant was $10,520; average loan was $4,554. For part-time students, average financial aid package was $7,235.
Students without need: 136 full-time freshmen who did not demonstrate need for aid received scholarships/grants; average award was $11,011. No-need awards available for academics, alumni affiliation, art, leadership, minority status, music/drama, religious affiliation.

FINANCIAL AID PROCEDURES
Forms required: FAFSA.
Dates and Deadlines: Priority date 2/15; no closing date. Applicants notified on a rolling basis starting 3/1.
Transfers: Priority date 3/1.

CONTACT
Director of Financial Aid
2001 Alford Park Drive, Kenosha, WI 53140-1994
(262) 551-6001

Chippewa Valley Technical College
Eau Claire, Wisconsin
www.cvtc.edu
Federal Code: 005304

2-year public technical college in small city.
Enrollment: 5,627 undergrads.
Selectivity: Open admission; but selective for some programs.

BASIC COSTS (2005-2006)
Tuition and fees: $2,560; out-of-state residents $15,454.
Per-credit charge: $81; out-of-state residents $510.
Additional info: Additional $4 fee per lecture course.

FINANCIAL AID PICTURE
Students with need: Need-based aid available for full-time and part-time students. Work study available nights, weekends, and for part-time students.
Scholarships offered: TOP Grant; $250 per semester, up to $1,000 total; must be enrolled full-time in Wisconsin technical college within 3 years of graduating from a Wisconsin high school, maintain minimum semester 2.0 GPA, and enroll in occupational associate degree or one-two year technical diploma program.

FINANCIAL AID PROCEDURES
Forms required: FAFSA.
Dates and Deadlines: Priority date 3/15; no closing date. Applicants notified on a rolling basis starting 6/1; must reply within 2 week(s) of notification.

CONTACT
Mary Gorud, Financial Aid Officer
620 West Clairemont Avenue, Eau Claire, WI 54701-6162
(715) 833-6250

College of Menominee Nation
Keshena, Wisconsin
www.menominee.edu
Federal Code: 031251

2-year private tribal college in rural community.
Enrollment: 472 undergrads.
Selectivity: Open admission.

BASIC COSTS (2005-2006)
Tuition and fees: $5,220.
Per-credit charge: $172.

FINANCIAL AID PICTURE
Students with need: Need-based aid available for full-time and part-time students. Work study available nights.
Students without need: This college only awards aid to students with need.

FINANCIAL AID PROCEDURES
Forms required: FAFSA.
Dates and Deadlines: Applicants notified on a rolling basis.

CONTACT
Kathleen Klaus, Financial Aid Director
N172 STH 47/55, Keshena, WI 54135
(715) 799-5600 ext. 3039

Columbia College of Nursing
Milwaukee, Wisconsin
www.ccon.edu
Federal Code: 003838

4-year private nursing college in very large city.
Enrollment: 259 undergrads.

BASIC COSTS (2006-2007)
Tuition and fees: $17,925.
Per-credit charge: $466.
Room and board: $5,000.

FINANCIAL AID PICTURE (2005-2006)
Students with need: Need-based aid available for part-time students. Work study available nights, weekends, and for part-time students.
Students without need: No-need awards available for academics, minority status.
Additional info: Students must apply to and meet financial aid requirements of Carroll College.

FINANCIAL AID PROCEDURES
Forms required: FAFSA.
Dates and Deadlines: No deadline. Applicants notified on a rolling basis starting 2/15; must reply by 5/1 or within 2 week(s) of notification.

CONTACT
Debra Duff, Financial Aid Officer
Mount Mary College Enrollment Office; 2900 North Menominee River Parkway, Milwaukee, WI 53222-4597

Concordia University Wisconsin
Mequon, Wisconsin
www.cuw.edu
Federal Code: 003842

4-year private university and liberal arts college in large town, affiliated with Lutheran Church - Missouri Synod.
Enrollment: 3,650 undergrads, 46% part-time. 382 full-time freshmen.
Selectivity: Admits over 75% of applicants.

BASIC COSTS (2005-2006)
Tuition and fees: $17,280.
Per-credit charge: $717.
Room and board: $6,540.

FINANCIAL AID PICTURE (2005-2006)
Students with need: Out of 373 full-time freshmen who applied for aid, 300 were judged to have need. Of these, 300 received aid, and 111 had their full need met. Average financial aid package met 78% of need; average scholarship/grant was $10,099; average loan was $4,860. For part-time students, average financial aid package was $8,618.
Students without need: 75 full-time freshmen who did not demonstrate need for aid received scholarships/grants; average award was $7,529. No-need awards available for academics, alumni affiliation, music/drama, religious affiliation.
Cumulative student debt: 68% of graduating class had student loans; average debt was $17,270.

FINANCIAL AID PROCEDURES
Forms required: FAFSA, institutional form.
Dates and Deadlines: Priority date 5/1; no closing date. Applicants notified on a rolling basis starting 1/15; must reply within 3 week(s) of notification.

CONTACT
Steve Taylor, Director of Financial Aid
12800 North Lake Shore Drive, Mequon, WI 53097
(262) 243-4392

Edgewood College
Madison, Wisconsin
www.edgewood.edu   Federal Code: 003848

4-year private liberal arts college in small city, affiliated with Roman Catholic Church.
Enrollment: 1,826 undergrads, 21% part-time. 281 full-time freshmen.
Selectivity: Admits over 75% of applicants.

BASIC COSTS (2006-2007)
Tuition and fees: $18,000.
Per-credit charge: $567.
Room and board: $6,056.

FINANCIAL AID PICTURE (2004-2005)
Students with need: 47% of average financial aid package awarded as scholarships/grants, 53% awarded as loans/jobs. Need-based aid available for part-time students. Work study available nights, weekends, and for part-time students.
Students without need: No-need awards available for academics, alumni affiliation, art, leadership, minority status, music/drama, religious affiliation.
Additional info: Auditions required for music scholarships, portfolios required for fine arts scholarships, essays required for a number of institutional scholarships, including AHANA Student Advancement Award, Alumni Association Scholarship, O'Connor Memorial Scholarship.

FINANCIAL AID PROCEDURES
Forms required: FAFSA, institutional form.
Dates and Deadlines: Priority date 3/15; no closing date. Applicants notified on a rolling basis starting 3/30; must reply within 2 week(s) of notification.

CONTACT
Kari Gribble, Director of Financial Aid
1000 Edgewood College Drive, Madison, WI 53711-1997
(608) 663-2206

Gateway Technical College
Kenosha, Wisconsin
www.gtc.edu   Federal Code: 005389

2-year public technical college in small city.
Enrollment: 5,704 undergrads, 78% part-time. 378 full-time freshmen.
Selectivity: Open admission; but selective for some programs.

BASIC COSTS (2006-2007)
Tuition and fees: $2,912; out-of-state residents $16,391.
Per-credit charge: $87; out-of-state residents $536.
Additional info: Materials fees vary by program; minimum $4 per credit.

FINANCIAL AID PICTURE
Students with need: Need-based aid available for full-time and part-time students.
Students without need: No-need awards available for state/district residency.

FINANCIAL AID PROCEDURES
Forms required: FAFSA, institutional form.
Dates and Deadlines: Priority date 7/1; no closing date. Applicants notified on a rolling basis starting 5/1; must reply within 2 week(s) of notification.

CONTACT
Janice Riutta, Director of Student Financial Aid
3520 30th Avenue, Kenosha, WI 53144
(262) 564-3072

Herzing College
Madison, Wisconsin
www.herzing.edu   Federal Code: 009621

3-year for-profit business and technical college in small city.
Enrollment: 652 undergrads.
Selectivity: Open admission.

BASIC COSTS (2006-2007)
Additional info: For associate degrees: $11,475 for computer, electronics and telecommunications program, $11,385 for CAD drafting program, $12,445 for computer information systems program, $12,530 for computer network technology program. For bachelor's degrees: $10,875 for technology management program, $12,445 for computer information systems program.

FINANCIAL AID PICTURE
Students with need: Need-based aid available for full-time and part-time students.

FINANCIAL AID PROCEDURES
Forms required: FAFSA, institutional form.
Dates and Deadlines: No deadline. Applicants notified on a rolling basis.

CONTACT
Beverly Faga, Director of Student Services
5218 East Terrace Drive, Madison, WI 53718
(608) 249-6611

Lakeland College
Sheboygan, Wisconsin
www.lakeland.edu   Federal Code: 003854

4-year private liberal arts college in small city, affiliated with United Church of Christ.
Enrollment: 3,373 undergrads.
Selectivity: Admits 50 to 75% of applicants.

BASIC COSTS (2006-2007)
Tuition and fees: $16,796.
Per-credit charge: $560.
Room and board: $6,195.
Additional info: Tuition at time of enrollment locked for 4 years.

FINANCIAL AID PICTURE (2005-2006)
Students with need: 46% of average financial aid package awarded as scholarships/grants, 54% awarded as loans/jobs. Need-based aid available for part-time students. Work study available nights, weekends, and for part-time students.
Students without need: No-need awards available for academics.

FINANCIAL AID PROCEDURES
Forms required: FAFSA, institutional form.
Dates and Deadlines: Priority date 5/1; closing date 7/1. Applicants notified on a rolling basis starting 2/1; must reply within 2 week(s) of notification.

CONTACT
Patty Taylor, Director of Financial Aid
Box 359, Sheboygan, WI 53082-0359
(920) 565-1297

Lakeshore Technical College
Cleveland, Wisconsin
www.gotoltc.edu   Federal Code: 009194

2-year public technical college in rural community.
Enrollment: 2,309 undergrads.
Selectivity: Open admission.

BASIC COSTS (2005-2006)
Tuition and fees: $2,548; out-of-state residents $15,442.
Per-credit charge: $81; out-of-state residents $510.
Additional info: Materials fees vary by program; minimum $4 per course.

FINANCIAL AID PICTURE
Students with need: Need-based aid available for full-time and part-time students. Work study available nights.
Students without need: This college only awards aid to students with need.

FINANCIAL AID PROCEDURES
Forms required: FAFSA, institutional form.
Dates and Deadlines: Priority date 6/1; no closing date. Applicants notified on a rolling basis starting 6/1; must reply within 3 week(s) of notification.

CONTACT
Corey Givens-Novak, Financial Aid Manager
1290 North Avenue, Cleveland, WI 53015-9761
(920) 693-1118

Lawrence University
Appleton, Wisconsin
www.lawrence.edu   Federal Code: 003856

4-year private music and liberal arts college in small city.
Enrollment: 1,405 undergrads, 3% part-time. 401 full-time freshmen.
Selectivity: Admits 50 to 75% of applicants. GED not accepted.

BASIC COSTS (2006-2007)
Tuition and fees: $29,598.
Room and board: $6,382.

FINANCIAL AID PICTURE (2005-2006)
Students with need: Out of 318 full-time freshmen who applied for aid, 250 were judged to have need. Of these, 250 received aid, and 250 had their full need met. Average financial aid package met 100% of need; average scholarship/grant was $17,080; average loan was $4,510. Need-based aid available for part-time students.
Students without need: 125 full-time freshmen who did not demonstrate need for aid received scholarships/grants; average award was $9,251. No-need awards available for academics, alumni affiliation, minority status, music/drama, state/district residency.
Scholarships offered: Trustee Scholarships; $10,000 per year. Presidential Scholarships; $7,500 per year. Alumni Scholarships; $5,000 per year. Conservatory Scholarships; $2,000-$10,000 per year.
Cumulative student debt: 66% of graduating class had student loans; average debt was $19,294.
Additional info: The first $1,000 (aggregate) of independently-sponsored scholarships received by a needy student will reduce student's loan or work-study commitment. Half of scholarships in excess of $1,000 will offset loan or work-study and the other half will reduce institutional grant funding.

FINANCIAL AID PROCEDURES
Forms required: FAFSA, institutional form.
Dates and Deadlines: Priority date 3/15; no closing date. Applicants notified on a rolling basis starting 3/15; must reply by 5/1 or within 2 week(s) of notification.
Transfers: Priority date 5/15. Applicants notified on a rolling basis starting 6/1.

CONTACT
Steven Syverson, Dean of Admissions and Financial Aid
Box 599, Appleton, WI 54912-0599
(920) 832-6583

Madison Area Technical College
Madison, Wisconsin
www.madison.tec.wi.us   Federal Code: 004007

2-year public community and technical college in small city.
Enrollment: 14,233 undergrads.
Selectivity: Open admission; but selective for some programs.

BASIC COSTS (2005-2006)
Tuition and fees: $2,642; out-of-state residents $15,536.
Per-credit charge: $81; out-of-state residents $510.
Additional info: Additional fee of $4 per lecture course.

FINANCIAL AID PICTURE (2004-2005)
Students with need: 55% of average financial aid package awarded as scholarships/grants, 45% awarded as loans/jobs.

FINANCIAL AID PROCEDURES
Forms required: FAFSA.
Dates and Deadlines: Priority date 4/15; no closing date. Applicants notified on a rolling basis starting 4/15.

CONTACT
Timothy Jacobson, Financial Aid Supervisor
3350 Anderson Street, Madison, WI 53704-2599

Maranatha Baptist Bible College
Watertown, Wisconsin
www.mbbc.edu   Federal Code: 016394

4-year private Bible college in large town, affiliated with Baptist faith.
Enrollment: 786 undergrads, 5% part-time. 222 full-time freshmen.
Selectivity: Admits 50 to 75% of applicants.

BASIC COSTS (2006-2007)
Tuition and fees: $9,110.
Per-credit charge: $255.
Room and board: $5,200.

FINANCIAL AID PICTURE
Students with need: Need-based aid available for full-time and part-time students.
Students without need: No-need awards available for academics.

FINANCIAL AID PROCEDURES
Forms required: FAFSA.
Dates and Deadlines: Priority date 3/1; no closing date. Applicants notified on a rolling basis starting 2/1; must reply within 2 week(s) of notification.
Transfers: Financial aid transcript or equivalent required.

CONTACT
Randy Hibbs, Associate Financial Aid Director
745 West Main Street, Watertown, WI 53094
(920) 206-2318

Marian College of Fond du Lac
Fond du Lac, Wisconsin
www.mariancollege.edu   Federal Code: 003861

4-year private liberal arts college in large town, affiliated with Roman Catholic Church.
Enrollment: 1,872 undergrads, 29% part-time. 262 full-time freshmen.
Selectivity: Admits over 75% of applicants.

BASIC COSTS (2006-2007)
Tuition and fees: $17,625.
Per-credit charge: $280.
Room and board: $5,200.

FINANCIAL AID PICTURE (2005-2006)
Students with need: Out of 261 full-time freshmen who applied for aid, 221 were judged to have need. Of these, 221 received aid, and 96 had their full need met. Average financial aid package met 90% of need; average scholarship/grant was $9,521; average loan was $3,488. For part-time students, average financial aid package was $8,732.
Students without need: 37 full-time freshmen who did not demonstrate need for aid received scholarships/grants; average award was $4,964. No-need awards available for academics, ROTC, state/district residency.
Scholarships offered: Academic Achievement Award; $7,500; based on 3.5 GPA or higher, 25 ACT, top 15 percent of class; 7 awarded. Presidential Scholarship; $5,000; based on 3.1 GPA or higher, top 20 percent of class. Naber Leadership Scholarship; $3,000; based on 2.5 GPA or higher, top 50 percent of class.
Cumulative student debt: 92% of graduating class had student loans; average debt was $20,850.

FINANCIAL AID PROCEDURES
Forms required: FAFSA, institutional form.
Dates and Deadlines: Priority date 3/1; no closing date. Applicants notified on a rolling basis starting 3/1; must reply within 4 week(s) of notification.

CONTACT
Debra McKinney, Director of Financial Aid
45 South National Avenue, Fond du Lac, WI 54935-4699
(920) 923-7614

Marquette University
Milwaukee, Wisconsin
www.marquette.edu   Federal Code: 003863

4-year private university in very large city, affiliated with Roman Catholic Church.
Enrollment: 7,718 undergrads, 4% part-time. 1,780 full-time freshmen.
Selectivity: Admits 50 to 75% of applicants.

BASIC COSTS (2006-2007)
Tuition and fees: $25,074.
Per-credit charge: $465.
Room and board: $8,120.

FINANCIAL AID PICTURE (2005-2006)
Students with need: Out of 1,421 full-time freshmen who applied for aid, 1,093 were judged to have need. Of these, 1,091 received aid, and 372 had their full need met. Average financial aid package met 78% of need; average scholarship/grant was $14,044; average loan was $3,696. For part-time students, average financial aid package was $6,687.
Students without need: 195 full-time freshmen who did not demonstrate need for aid received scholarships/grants; average award was $8,828. No-need awards available for academics, athletics, leadership, music/drama, ROTC.
Scholarships offered: *Merit:* Ignatius Scholarships; $6,000-$11,000. College Scholarships; $5,000. Raynor Scholarships; full tuition; 3 awarded. National Merit Scholarships; $2,000. *Athletic:* 27 full-time freshmen received athletic scholarships; average amount $19,129.
Cumulative student debt: 52% of graduating class had student loans; average debt was $26,345.

FINANCIAL AID PROCEDURES
Forms required: FAFSA.
Dates and Deadlines: Priority date 2/1; no closing date. Applicants notified on a rolling basis starting 4/1; must reply by 5/1 or within 3 week(s) of notification.
Transfers: Transfer scholarships available.

CONTACT
Daniel Goyette, Director of Student Financial Aid
PO Box 1881, Milwaukee, WI 53201-1881
(414) 288-0200

Mid-State Technical College
Wisconsin Rapids, Wisconsin
www.mstc.edu   Federal Code: 005380

2-year public technical college in large town.
Enrollment: 7,900 undergrads.
Selectivity: Open admission; but selective for some programs.

BASIC COSTS (2005-2006)
Tuition and fees: $2,536; out-of-state residents $15,430.
Per-credit charge: $81; out-of-state residents $510.

FINANCIAL AID PICTURE (2004-2005)
Students with need: 59% of average financial aid package awarded as scholarships/grants, 41% awarded as loans/jobs. Need-based aid available for part-time students. Work study available nights, weekends, and for part-time students.
Students without need: No-need awards available for academics, leadership.

FINANCIAL AID PROCEDURES
Forms required: FAFSA.
Dates and Deadlines: No deadline. Applicants notified on a rolling basis starting 5/30; must reply within 2 week(s) of notification.

CONTACT
MaryJo Green, Financial Aid Supervisor
500 32nd Street North, Wisconsin Rapids, WI 54494
(715) 422-5501

Milwaukee Area Technical College
Milwaukee, Wisconsin
www.matc.edu   Federal Code: 003866

2-year public junior and technical college in very large city.
Enrollment: 14,817 undergrads, 63% part-time. 1,105 full-time freshmen.
Selectivity: Open admission; but selective for some programs and for out-of-state students.

BASIC COSTS (2005-2006)
Tuition and fees: $2,677; out-of-state residents $15,571.
Per-credit charge: $81; out-of-state residents $510.
Additional info: Material fees vary by program. Tuition/fee waivers available for minority students.

FINANCIAL AID PICTURE (2004-2005)
Students with need: Out of 716 full-time freshmen who applied for aid, 582 were judged to have need. Of these, 523 received aid. Average financial aid package met 50% of need; average scholarship/grant was $3,377; average loan was $2,153. For part-time students, average financial aid package was $3,327.
Students without need: 3 full-time freshmen who did not demonstrate need for aid received scholarships/grants; average award was $1,333. No-need awards available for academics.
Cumulative student debt: 25% of graduating class had student loans; average debt was $12,865.

FINANCIAL AID PROCEDURES
Forms required: FAFSA.
Dates and Deadlines: Priority date 3/15; no closing date. Applicants notified on a rolling basis starting 4/15.
Transfers: No deadline. Applicants notified on a rolling basis starting 4/15.

CONTACT
Al Pinckney, Director of Financial Aid
700 West State Street, Milwaukee, WI 53233-1443
(414) 297-6279

Milwaukee School of Engineering
Milwaukee, Wisconsin
www.msoe.edu   Federal Code: 003868

4-year private university in very large city.
Enrollment: 2,092 undergrads, 13% part-time. 452 full-time freshmen.
Selectivity: Admits 50 to 75% of applicants.

BASIC COSTS (2006-2007)
Tuition and fees: $24,960.
Per-credit charge: $432.
Room and board: $6,189.
Additional info: $1,140 technology package required for all full-time first-year students.

FINANCIAL AID PICTURE (2004-2005)
Students with need: Out of 412 full-time freshmen who applied for aid, 369 were judged to have need. Of these, 368 received aid, and 50 had their full need met. Average financial aid package met 72% of need; average scholarship/grant was $13,919; average loan was $2,702. For part-time students, average financial aid package was $8,943.
Students without need: 77 full-time freshmen who did not demonstrate need for aid received scholarships/grants; average award was $11,449. No-need awards available for academics, ROTC.
Scholarships offered: President Scholarship; full tuition; awarded to students with high academic standing; 6 awarded.
Cumulative student debt: 85% of graduating class had student loans; average debt was $31,808.
Additional info: More than 90 percent of full-time students receive financial assistance. More than 60 percent receive academic scholarships.

FINANCIAL AID PROCEDURES
Forms required: FAFSA.
Dates and Deadlines: Priority date 3/15; no closing date. Applicants notified on a rolling basis starting 3/1; must reply within 2 week(s) of notification.

CONTACT
Benjamin Dobner, Director of Student Financial Services
1025 North Broadway, Milwaukee, WI 53202-3109
(414) 277-7223

Moraine Park Technical College
Fond du Lac, Wisconsin
www.morainepark.edu   Federal Code: 005303

2-year public technical college in large town.
Enrollment: 4,200 undergrads.
Selectivity: Open admission; but selective for some programs.

BASIC COSTS (2005-2006)
Tuition and fees: $2,536; out-of-state residents $15,430.
Per-credit charge: $81; out-of-state residents $510.
Additional info: Additional fee of $4 per lecture course.

FINANCIAL AID PICTURE (2004-2005)
Students with need: 61% of average financial aid package awarded as scholarships/grants, 39% awarded as loans/jobs. Need-based aid available for part-time students. Work study available nights, weekends, and for part-time students.
Students without need: No-need awards available for academics, job skills, leadership, minority status, state/district residency.

FINANCIAL AID PROCEDURES
Forms required: FAFSA, institutional form.
Dates and Deadlines: Priority date 5/1; no closing date. Applicants notified on a rolling basis starting 6/15; must reply within 2 week(s) of notification.

CONTACT
Karen Zuehlke, Financial Aid Specialist
235 North National Avenue, Fond du Lac, WI 54935-1940
(920) 929-2123

Mount Mary College
Milwaukee, Wisconsin
www.mtmary.edu   Federal Code: 003869

4-year private liberal arts college for women in very large city, affiliated with Roman Catholic Church.
Enrollment: 1,346 undergrads, 32% part-time. 160 full-time freshmen.
Selectivity: Admits 50 to 75% of applicants.

BASIC COSTS (2006-2007)
Tuition and fees: $18,128.
Per-credit charge: $485.
Room and board: $5,990.

FINANCIAL AID PICTURE (2005-2006)
Students with need: Out of 125 full-time freshmen who applied for aid, 115 were judged to have need. Of these, 115 received aid, and 15 had their full need met. Average financial aid package met 72% of need; average scholarship/grant was $9,679; average loan was $3,113. For part-time students, average financial aid package was $12,887.
Students without need: 41 full-time freshmen who did not demonstrate need for aid received scholarships/grants; average award was $5,660. No-need awards available for academics, alumni affiliation, art, leadership, music/drama.
Cumulative student debt: 77% of graduating class had student loans; average debt was $9,040.

FINANCIAL AID PROCEDURES
Forms required: FAFSA.
Dates and Deadlines: Priority date 3/1; no closing date. Applicants notified on a rolling basis starting 1/1; must reply within 2 week(s) of notification.

CONTACT
Debra Duff, Director of Financial Aid
2900 North Menomonee River Parkway, Milwaukee, WI 53222
(414) 256-1258

Nicolet Area Technical College
Rhinelander, Wisconsin
www.nicoletcollege.edu   Federal Code: 008919

2-year public community and technical college in small town.
Enrollment: 988 undergrads.

BASIC COSTS (2005-2006)
Tuition and fees: $2,513; out-of-state residents $15,407.
Per-credit charge: $81; out-of-state residents $510.
Additional info: Material fees vary by program; minimum $4 per course.

FINANCIAL AID PICTURE (2004-2005)
Students with need: 78% of average financial aid package awarded as scholarships/grants, 22% awarded as loans/jobs.

FINANCIAL AID PROCEDURES
Forms required: FAFSA, institutional form.
Dates and Deadlines: Priority date 4/15; no closing date. Applicants notified on a rolling basis starting 6/1; must reply within 2 week(s) of notification.

CONTACT
William Peshel, Director of Financial Aid
Box 518, Rhinelander, WI 54501
(715) 365-4423

Northcentral Technical College
Wausau, Wisconsin
www.ntc.edu   Federal Code: 005387

2-year public community and technical college in small city.
Enrollment: 4,955 undergrads.
Selectivity: Open admission; but selective for some programs.

BASIC COSTS (2006-2007)
Tuition and fees: $2,730; out-of-state residents $16,209.
Per-credit charge: $87; out-of-state residents $536.
Additional info: Materials fees vary by program; minimum $4 per course.

FINANCIAL AID PICTURE (2004-2005)
Students with need: Average financial aid package for all full-time undergraduates was $5,600. 61% awarded as scholarships/grants, 39% awarded as loans/jobs. Need-based aid available for part-time students.

FINANCIAL AID PROCEDURES
Forms required: FAFSA.
Dates and Deadlines: Priority date 4/1; no closing date. Applicants notified on a rolling basis starting 6/15; must reply within 2 week(s) of notification.
Transfers: No deadline.

CONTACT
Sue Berens, Financial Aid Specialist
1000 West Campus Drive, Wausau, WI 54401
(715) 675-3331 ext. 4028

Northeast Wisconsin Technical College
Green Bay, Wisconsin
www.nwtc.edu   Federal Code: 005301

2-year public community and technical college in small city.
Enrollment: 5,450 undergrads, 53% part-time.
Selectivity: Open admission; but selective for some programs.

BASIC COSTS (2005-2006)
Tuition and fees: $2,538; out-of-state residents $15,432.
Per-credit charge: $81; out-of-state residents $510.
Additional info: Additional fee of $4 per lecture course.

FINANCIAL AID PICTURE (2004-2005)
Students with need: 59% of average financial aid package awarded as scholarships/grants, 41% awarded as loans/jobs. Need-based aid available for part-time students. Work study available nights.

FINANCIAL AID PROCEDURES
Forms required: FAFSA.
Dates and Deadlines: Priority date 4/1; no closing date. Applicants notified on a rolling basis starting 5/1; must reply within 2 week(s) of notification.

CONTACT
Heather Hill, Financial Aid Director
2740 West Mason Street, Green Bay, WI 54307-9042
(920) 498-5444

Northland College
Ashland, Wisconsin
www.northland.edu   Federal Code: 003875

4-year private liberal arts college in small town, affiliated with United Church of Christ.
Enrollment: 691 undergrads, 7% part-time. 127 full-time freshmen.
Selectivity: Admits over 75% of applicants.

BASIC COSTS (2006-2007)
Tuition and fees: $20,789.
Per-credit charge: $390.
Room and board: $5,891.

FINANCIAL AID PICTURE (2004-2005)
Students with need: Out of 122 full-time freshmen who applied for aid, 108 were judged to have need. Of these, 108 received aid, and 16 had their full need met. Average financial aid package met 83% of need; average scholarship/grant was $11,340; average loan was $3,464. Need-based aid available for part-time students.
Students without need: 4 full-time freshmen who did not demonstrate need for aid received scholarships/grants; average award was $9,567. No-need awards available for academics, alumni affiliation, leadership, minority status, music/drama.
Cumulative student debt: 84% of graduating class had student loans; average debt was $20,164.

FINANCIAL AID PROCEDURES
Forms required: FAFSA.
Dates and Deadlines: Priority date 4/15; no closing date. Applicants notified on a rolling basis starting 3/1; must reply by 5/1 or within 4 week(s) of notification.

CONTACT
Tracey Roseth, Director of Financial Aid
1411 Ellis Avenue, Ashland, WI 54806
(715) 682-1255

Ripon College
Ripon, Wisconsin
www.ripon.edu
Federal Code: 003884

4-year private liberal arts college in small town, affiliated with United Church of Christ.
Enrollment: 945 undergrads, 1% part-time. 259 full-time freshmen.
Selectivity: Admits over 75% of applicants.

BASIC COSTS (2006-2007)
Tuition and fees: $22,437.
Per-credit charge: $890.
Room and board: $6,060.

FINANCIAL AID PICTURE (2004-2005)
Students with need: Out of 253 full-time freshmen who applied for aid, 204 were judged to have need. Of these, 204 received aid, and 88 had their full need met. Average financial aid package met 95% of need; average scholarship/grant was $14,360; average loan was $4,156. Need-based aid available for part-time students.
Students without need: 54 full-time freshmen who did not demonstrate need for aid received scholarships/grants; average award was $14,471. No-need awards available for academics, alumni affiliation, art, leadership, minority status, music/drama, religious affiliation, ROTC, state/district residency.
Scholarships offered: Pickard Scholarships; one full-tuition awarded and ten $60,000 awarded; both types by invitation only. Presidential Scholarships; $48,000; minimum 3.8 GPA, top 5% of class, ACT 30, SAT 1340; by invitation only. Knop Scholars Program; $50,000; science major, 3.8 GPA, top 5% of class, interview, by invitation only, one awarded. Faculty Scholarships; $40,000; 3.76 GPA, ACT 29, SAT 1300. Dean's Scholarships; $34,000; 3.51 GPA, ACT 27, SAT 1220. Founder's Scholarships; $28,000; 3.36 GPA, ACT 25, SAT 1140. Honor Scholarships; $24,000; 3.2 GPA, ACT 24, SAT 1110. US Army ROTC Scholarships; $80,000+. Diversity Scholarships; $60,000; application required. Forensics Academic Scholarships; $40,000; 3.5 GPA, ACT 27, SAT 1220, interview. All SAT scores exclusive of Writing. Valedictorian Scholarships; $24,000. Art Scholarships; $20,000 maximum award; portfolio. Theatre Scholarships; $20,000 maximum; interview. Music Scholarships; $20,000; audition. Service Awards; $20,000; not available to academic scholarship recipients. Boy/Girl State Scholarships; $16,000 maximum award. Legacy Awards; $8,000. United Church of Christ Scholarships; $8,000; application required. National Latin Exam; $8,000.
Cumulative student debt: 90% of graduating class had student loans; average debt was $16,492.
Additional info: Institution strives to meet 100 percent of students' demonstrated financial need for all four years.

FINANCIAL AID PROCEDURES
Forms required: FAFSA.
Dates and Deadlines: Priority date 3/1; no closing date. Applicants notified on a rolling basis starting 3/1; must reply within 2 week(s) of notification.

CONTACT
Steven Schuetz, Director of Financial Aid
300 Seward Street, Ripon, WI 54971-0248
(920) 748-8101

St. Norbert College
De Pere, Wisconsin
www.snc.edu
Federal Code: 003892

4-year private liberal arts college in large town, affiliated with Roman Catholic Church.
Enrollment: 1,942 undergrads, 1% part-time. 525 full-time freshmen.
Selectivity: Admits over 75% of applicants.

BASIC COSTS (2006-2007)
Tuition and fees: $23,497.
Per-credit charge: $722.
Room and board: $6,319.

FINANCIAL AID PICTURE (2004-2005)
Students with need: Out of 416 full-time freshmen who applied for aid, 344 were judged to have need. Of these, 344 received aid, and 123 had their full need met. Average financial aid package met 88% of need; average scholarship/grant was $12,740; average loan was $3,881. For part-time students, average financial aid package was $12,256.
Students without need: 151 full-time freshmen who did not demonstrate need for aid received scholarships/grants; average award was $10,414. No-need awards available for academics, art, leadership, minority status, music/drama, ROTC, state/district residency.

FINANCIAL AID PROCEDURES
Forms required: FAFSA.
Dates and Deadlines: Priority date 3/1; no closing date. Applicants notified on a rolling basis starting 3/15; must reply within 2 week(s) of notification.

CONTACT
Jeff Zahn, Director of Financial Aid
100 Grant Street, De Pere, WI 54115-2099
(920) 403-3071

Silver Lake College
Manitowoc, Wisconsin
www.sl.edu
Federal Code: 003850

4-year private liberal arts college in large town, affiliated with Roman Catholic Church.
Enrollment: 413 undergrads, 53% part-time. 33 full-time freshmen.
Selectivity: Admits over 75% of applicants.

BASIC COSTS (2006-2007)
Tuition and fees: $17,108.
Per-credit charge: $525.
Room only: $4,400.

FINANCIAL AID PICTURE (2005-2006)
Students with need: Out of 31 full-time freshmen who applied for aid, 27 were judged to have need. Of these, 27 received aid, and 3 had their full need met. Average financial aid package met 84% of need; average scholarship/grant was $12,279; average loan was $2,572. For part-time students, average financial aid package was $7,059.
Students without need: 5 full-time freshmen who did not demonstrate need for aid received scholarships/grants; average award was $3,300. No-need awards available for academics, art, athletics, leadership, music/drama, religious affiliation, state/district residency.
Scholarships offered: 1 full-time freshmen received athletic scholarships; average amount $2,000.
Cumulative student debt: 70% of graduating class had student loans; average debt was $18,934.

FINANCIAL AID PROCEDURES
Forms required: FAFSA.

Dates and Deadlines: Priority date 3/15; no closing date. Applicants notified on a rolling basis starting 3/15; must reply within 2 week(s) of notification.
Transfers: Transfer Merit Scholarships and Phi Theta Kappa Scholarships are available, as well as other institutional scholarship and grant assistance.

CONTACT
Michelle Krajnik, Director of Student Financial Aid
2406 South Alverno Road, Manitowoc, WI 54220
(920) 686-6122

Southwest Wisconsin Technical College
Fennimore, Wisconsin
www.swtc.edu   Federal Code: 007699

2-year public technical college in rural community.
Enrollment: 1,450 undergrads.
Selectivity: Open admission.

BASIC COSTS (2005-2006)
Tuition and fees: $2,487; out-of-state residents $15,381.
Per-credit charge: $81; out-of-state residents $510.
Additional info: Materials fees vary by program; minimum $4.00 per course.

FINANCIAL AID PICTURE
Students with need: Work study available nights.

FINANCIAL AID PROCEDURES
Forms required: FAFSA, institutional form.
Dates and Deadlines: Priority date 4/15; no closing date. Applicants notified on a rolling basis starting 5/15; must reply within 4 week(s) of notification.

CONTACT
Joy Kite, Director of Financial Aid
1800 Bronson Boulevard, Fennimore, WI 53809
(608) 822-3262 ext. 2319

University of Wisconsin-Baraboo/Sauk County
Baraboo, Wisconsin
www.baraboo.uwc.edu   Federal Code: 003897

2-year public branch campus and liberal arts college in large town.
Enrollment: 485 undergrads.

BASIC COSTS (2005-2006)
Tuition and fees: $4,292; out-of-state residents $12,992.
Per-credit charge: $166; out-of-state residents $528.
Additional info: Minnesota reciprocity tuition: $3,576 full-time, $149 per-credit-hour.

FINANCIAL AID PICTURE
Students with need: Need-based aid available for full-time and part-time students. Work study available nights.
Students without need: This college only awards aid to students with need.
Scholarships offered: Campus scholarship program offering non-need based awards ranging from $250 to full tuition.

FINANCIAL AID PROCEDURES
Forms required: FAFSA, institutional form.
Dates and Deadlines: Priority date 4/15; no closing date. Applicants notified on a rolling basis starting 4/15; must reply within 3 week(s) of notification.

CONTACT
Marilyn Krump, Director of Financial Aid
1006 Connie Road, Baraboo, WI 53913-1098
(608) 263-7727

University of Wisconsin-Eau Claire
Eau Claire, Wisconsin
www.uwec.edu   Federal Code: 003917

4-year public university in small city.
Enrollment: 9,929 undergrads, 6% part-time. 2,026 full-time freshmen.
Selectivity: Admits 50 to 75% of applicants.

BASIC COSTS (2005-2006)
Tuition and fees: $5,179; out-of-state residents $15,225.
Per-credit charge: $184; out-of-state residents $603.
Room and board: $4,737.

FINANCIAL AID PICTURE (2004-2005)
Students with need: Out of 1,524 full-time freshmen who applied for aid, 844 were judged to have need. Of these, 836 received aid, and 574 had their full need met. Average financial aid package met 95% of need; average scholarship/grant was $3,643; average loan was $3,516. For part-time students, average financial aid package was $5,902.
Students without need: 329 full-time freshmen who did not demonstrate need for aid received scholarships/grants; average award was $1,525. No-need awards available for academics, art, leadership, minority status, music/drama, state/district residency.
Scholarships offered: Chancellor's Award: full in-state tuition for 1 year, 6 awards. Dean's Awards: $1,000, 20 awards. Wisconsin Academic Excellence Scholars for selected high school valedictorians: $2,250, renewable. National Merit Scholarship finalists: full, in-state fees, for top 25% of high school class with ACT composite of 25 or more, though some require ACT of 28 or 30.
Cumulative student debt: 65% of graduating class had student loans; average debt was $16,953.

FINANCIAL AID PROCEDURES
Forms required: FAFSA.
Dates and Deadlines: Priority date 4/15; no closing date. Applicants notified on a rolling basis starting 4/15.

CONTACT
Kathleen Sahlhoff, Director of Financial Aid
112 Schofield Hall, Eau Claire, WI 54701
(715) 836-3373

University of Wisconsin-Fond du Lac
Fond du Lac, Wisconsin
www.fdl.uwc.edu

2-year public branch campus college in large town.
Enrollment: 765 undergrads.

BASIC COSTS (2005-2006)
Tuition and fees: $4,230; out-of-state residents $12,930.
Per-credit charge: $166; out-of-state residents $528.
Additional info: Minnesota reciprocity tuition: $3,576 full-time, $149 per-credit-hour.

FINANCIAL AID PICTURE
Students with need: Need-based aid available for full-time and part-time students.

FINANCIAL AID PROCEDURES
Forms required: FAFSA, institutional form.
Dates and Deadlines: Priority date 4/15; no closing date. Applicants notified on a rolling basis starting 6/1; must reply within 2 week(s) of notification.
Transfers: Priority date 4/1.

894   Wisconsin University of Wisconsin-Fond du Lac

CONTACT
Marilyn Krump, Director of Financial Aid
400 University Drive, Fond du Lac, WI 54935-2998
(920) 929-3600

University of Wisconsin-Green Bay
Green Bay, Wisconsin
www.uwgb.edu   Federal Code: 003899

4-year public university and liberal arts college in small city.
Enrollment: 5,321 undergrads, 16% part-time. 895 full-time freshmen.
Selectivity: Admits 50 to 75% of applicants.

BASIC COSTS (2005-2006)
Tuition and fees: $5,425; out-of-state residents $15,471.
Per-credit charge: $178; out-of-state residents $597.
Room and board: $4,775.

FINANCIAL AID PICTURE (2005-2006)
Students with need: Out of 773 full-time freshmen who applied for aid, 498 were judged to have need. Of these, 463 received aid, and 157 had their full need met. Average financial aid package met 74% of need; average scholarship/grant was $4,125; average loan was $3,030. For part-time students, average financial aid package was $7,654.
Students without need: 34 full-time freshmen who did not demonstrate need for aid received scholarships/grants; average award was $2,399. No-need awards available for academics, art, athletics, leadership, minority status, music/drama.
Scholarships offered: *Merit:* Tuition is waived per state mandate for children of Wisconsin soldiers and policemen who are slain in the line of duty. *Athletic:* 21 full-time freshmen received athletic scholarships; average amount $5,928.
Cumulative student debt: 61% of graduating class had student loans; average debt was $12,222.
Additional info: Auditions required for music and theater scholarships.

FINANCIAL AID PROCEDURES
Forms required: FAFSA.
Dates and Deadlines: Priority date 4/15; no closing date. Applicants notified on a rolling basis starting 11/1; must reply within 3 week(s) of notification.

CONTACT
Ron Ronnenberg, Director of Financial Aid and Student Employment
2420 Nicolet Drive, Green Bay, WI 54311-7001
(920) 465-2075

University of Wisconsin-La Crosse
La Crosse, Wisconsin
www.uwlax.edu   Federal Code: 003919

4-year public university in small city.
Enrollment: 7,908 undergrads, 4% part-time. 1,522 full-time freshmen.
Selectivity: Admits 50 to 75% of applicants.

BASIC COSTS (2005-2006)
Tuition and fees: $5,074; out-of-state residents $15,120.
Per-credit charge: $180; out-of-state residents $599.
Room and board: $4,820.
Additional info: Minnesota Reciprocity Tuition: $4,780; $199 per credit hour.

FINANCIAL AID PICTURE (2004-2005)
Students with need: Out of 1,122 full-time freshmen who applied for aid, 886 were judged to have need. Of these, 851 received aid, and 740 had their full need met. Average financial aid package met 80% of need; average scholarship/grant was $1,609; average loan was $3,265. For part-time students, average financial aid package was $3,539.
Students without need: 54 full-time freshmen who did not demonstrate need for aid received scholarships/grants; average award was $447. No-need awards available for academics, alumni affiliation, art, leadership, minority status, music/drama, ROTC.
Scholarships offered: Chancellor's Scholar Awards; up to $3,000; available to nonresidents; 50 available. Design for Diversity nonresident tuition waivers; $10,000 per year; for ethnic minoirities; 30 available.
Cumulative student debt: 70% of graduating class had student loans; average debt was $13,948.
Additional info: "Return to Wisconsin" program provides 25 percent waiver of nonresident portion of tuition to children and grandchildren of alumni who are residents of states other than Wisconsin and Minnesota.

FINANCIAL AID PROCEDURES
Forms required: FAFSA, institutional form.
Dates and Deadlines: Priority date 3/15; no closing date. Applicants notified on a rolling basis starting 3/10; must reply by 5/10 or within 3 week(s) of notification.

CONTACT
Louise Jahnke, Associate Director of Financial Aid
1725 State Street, Room 115 Main Hall, La Crosse, WI 54601
(608) 785-8604

University of Wisconsin-Madison
Madison, Wisconsin
www.wisc.edu   Federal Code: 003895

4-year public university in small city.
Enrollment: 28,458 undergrads, 5% part-time. 5,617 full-time freshmen.
Selectivity: Admits 50 to 75% of applicants.

BASIC COSTS (2005-2006)
Tuition and fees: $6,280; out-of-state residents $20,280.
Per-credit charge: $234; out-of-state residents $817.
Room and board: $6,500.
Additional info: Minnesota Reciprocity Tuition: $7,806.

FINANCIAL AID PICTURE (2004-2005)
Students with need: Out of 3,777 full-time freshmen who applied for aid, 1,885 were judged to have need. Of these, 1,753 received aid, and 594 had their full need met. For part-time students, average financial aid package was $10,665.
Students without need: 1,170 full-time freshmen who did not demonstrate need for aid received scholarships/grants; average award was $2,716. No-need awards available for academics, alumni affiliation, athletics, minority status, music/drama, ROTC.
Scholarships offered: 80 full-time freshmen received athletic scholarships; average amount $14,324.

FINANCIAL AID PROCEDURES
Forms required: FAFSA, institutional form.
Dates and Deadlines: No deadline. Applicants notified on a rolling basis starting 4/1; must reply within 3 week(s) of notification.

CONTACT
Susan Fischer, Director Student Financial Services
Armory & Gymnasium, Madison, WI 53706-1481
(608) 262-3060

University of Wisconsin-Marathon County
Wausau, Wisconsin
www.uwmc.uwc.edu

2-year public branch campus college in large town.
Enrollment: 1,200 full-time undergrads.

BASIC COSTS (2005-2006)
Tuition and fees: $4,197; out-of-state residents $12,897.
Per-credit charge: $166; out-of-state residents $528.
Additional info: Minnesota reciprocity tuition: $3,576 full-time, $149 per-credit-hour.

FINANCIAL AID PICTURE
Students with need: Need-based aid available for full-time and part-time students. Work study available nights.
Students without need: This college only awards aid to students with need.

FINANCIAL AID PROCEDURES
Forms required: FAFSA, institutional form.
Dates and Deadlines: Priority date 4/15; no closing date. Applicants notified on a rolling basis starting 6/1; must reply within 3 week(s) of notification.

CONTACT
Nolan Beck, Director of Student Services
518 South Seventh Avenue, Wausau, WI 54401-5396
(715) 261-6235

University of Wisconsin-Marinette
Marinette, Wisconsin
www.marinette.uwc.edu   Federal Code: 003897

2-year public branch campus and liberal arts college in large town.
Enrollment: 364 undergrads, 24% part-time. 218 full-time freshmen.
Selectivity: Admits over 75% of applicants.

BASIC COSTS (2005-2006)
Tuition and fees: $4,177; out-of-state residents $12,877.
Per-credit charge: $166; out-of-state residents $528.
Additional info: Minnesota reciprocity tuition: $3,576 full-time, $149 per-credit-hour.

FINANCIAL AID PICTURE
Students with need: Need-based aid available for full-time and part-time students. Work study available nights.
Students without need: This college only awards aid to students with need.

FINANCIAL AID PROCEDURES
Forms required: FAFSA.
Dates and Deadlines: Priority date 4/1; no closing date. Applicants notified on a rolling basis.

CONTACT
Cynthia Bailey, Assistant Dean for Student Services
750 West Bay Shore Street, Marinette, WI 54143
(715) 735-4301

University of Wisconsin-Marshfield/Wood County
Marshfield, Wisconsin
www.marshfield.uwc.edu   Federal Code: 003897

2-year public branch campus college in large town.
Enrollment: 650 undergrads.

BASIC COSTS (2005-2006)
Tuition and fees: $4,207; out-of-state residents $12,907.
Per-credit charge: $166; out-of-state residents $528.
Additional info: Minnesota reciprocity tuition: $3,576 full-time, $149 per-credit-hour.

FINANCIAL AID PICTURE
Students with need: Need-based aid available for full-time and part-time students. Work study available nights, weekends, and for part-time students.
Students without need: This college only awards aid to students with need.
Scholarships offered: Special Entering Scholarships; $1,000; based on academic excellence; 2 awarded. Ken and Ardyce Helting Scholarship; $1,000; priority given to physically challenged or learning disabled; 1 awarded. Valedictorian, Salutatorian and National Merit Finalist and Semi-Finalists; $1,000, ACT of 25 or better. Greenhouse Scholarship; priority to students in Environmental Studies; 1 awarded. Patrice Ptacek Memorial Scholarship; 2 letters of recommendation; 1 awarded. Woman of the Future Scholarship; $1,000; must be full-time female freshman entering sophomore year, well-defined career goals other than nursing; 1 awarded.

FINANCIAL AID PROCEDURES
Forms required: FAFSA.
Dates and Deadlines: Priority date 4/15; no closing date. Applicants notified on a rolling basis starting 5/15; must reply within 3 week(s) of notification.

CONTACT
Jeff Meece, Director of Student Services
2000 West Fifth Street, Marshfield, WI 54449
(715) 389-6500

University of Wisconsin-Milwaukee
Milwaukee, Wisconsin
www.uwm.edu   Federal Code: 003896

4-year public university in very large city.
Enrollment: 21,662 undergrads, 14% part-time. 3,770 full-time freshmen.
Selectivity: Admits over 75% of applicants.

BASIC COSTS (2005-2006)
Tuition and fees: $6,220; out-of-state residents $18,972.
Per-credit charge: $229; out-of-state residents $760.
Room and board: $6,078.

FINANCIAL AID PICTURE (2004-2005)
Students with need: Out of 2,714 full-time freshmen who applied for aid, 1,930 were judged to have need. Of these, 1,803 received aid, and 491 had their full need met. Average financial aid package met 58% of need; average scholarship/grant was $4,243; average loan was $2,755. For part-time students, average financial aid package was $5,220.
Students without need: 126 full-time freshmen who did not demonstrate need for aid received scholarships/grants; average award was $1,774.

FINANCIAL AID PROCEDURES
Forms required: FAFSA.
Dates and Deadlines: Priority date 3/1; no closing date. Applicants notified on a rolling basis starting 3/1.

Wisconsin — University of Wisconsin-Milwaukee

CONTACT
Mary Roggeman, Director of Financial Aid
Box 749, Milwaukee, WI 53201
(414) 229-6300

University of Wisconsin-Oshkosh
Oshkosh, Wisconsin
www.uwosh.edu
Federal Code: 003920

4-year public university in small city.
Enrollment: 9,592 undergrads, 11% part-time. 1,632 full-time freshmen.
Selectivity: Admits over 75% of applicants.

BASIC COSTS (2005-2006)
Tuition and fees: $4,977; out-of-state residents $15,023.
Per-credit charge: $183; out-of-state residents $601.
Room and board: $4,784.

FINANCIAL AID PICTURE (2004-2005)
Students with need: Out of 1,305 full-time freshmen who applied for aid, 914 were judged to have need. Of these, 914 received aid, and 457 had their full need met. Average financial aid package met 50% of need; average scholarship/grant was $1,800; average loan was $2,500. For part-time students, average financial aid package was $1,575.
Students without need: 22 full-time freshmen who did not demonstrate need for aid received scholarships/grants; average award was $88,000. No-need awards available for academics, alumni affiliation, art, leadership, minority status, music/drama, state/district residency.

FINANCIAL AID PROCEDURES
Forms required: FAFSA.
Dates and Deadlines: Priority date 3/15; no closing date. Applicants notified on a rolling basis starting 5/1; must reply within 2 week(s) of notification.
Transfers: Must send financial aid transcript to university.

CONTACT
Beatrice Contreras, Director of Financial Aid
800 Algoma Boulevard, Oshkosh, WI 54901-8602
(920) 424-3377

University of Wisconsin-Parkside
Kenosha, Wisconsin
www.uwp.edu
Federal Code: 005015

4-year public university in small city.
Enrollment: 4,590 undergrads, 23% part-time. 888 full-time freshmen.
Selectivity: Admits over 75% of applicants.

BASIC COSTS (2005-2006)
Tuition and fees: $5,001; out-of-state residents $15,767.
Per-credit charge: $178; out-of-state residents $597.
Room and board: $5,550.

FINANCIAL AID PICTURE (2004-2005)
Students with need: Out of 621 full-time freshmen who applied for aid, 586 were judged to have need. Of these, 503 received aid, and 383 had their full need met. Average financial aid package met 87% of need; average scholarship/grant was $3,108; average loan was $2,666. For part-time students, average financial aid package was $4,727.
Students without need: No-need awards available for academics, art, athletics, minority status, music/drama, state/district residency.
Cumulative student debt: 56% of graduating class had student loans; average debt was $17,158.

FINANCIAL AID PROCEDURES
Forms required: FAFSA.
Dates and Deadlines: Priority date 3/15; no closing date. Applicants notified on a rolling basis starting 4/1; must reply within 2 week(s) of notification.

CONTACT
Randall McCready, Director of Financial Aid
PO Box 2000, Kenosha, WI 53141-2000
(262) 595-2574

University of Wisconsin-Platteville
Platteville, Wisconsin
www.uwplatt.edu
Federal Code: 003921

4-year public university in large town.
Enrollment: 5,631 undergrads, 8% part-time. 1,214 full-time freshmen.
Selectivity: Admits over 75% of applicants.

BASIC COSTS (2005-2006)
Tuition and fees: $4,981; out-of-state residents $15,027.
Per-credit charge: $178; out-of-state residents $597.
Room and board: $4,658.
Additional info: Minnesota reciprocity tuition: $4,780 full-time, $199 per credit hour.

FINANCIAL AID PICTURE
Students with need: Need-based aid available for full-time and part-time students. Work study available nights, weekends, and for part-time students.
Students without need: This college only awards aid to students with need.

FINANCIAL AID PROCEDURES
Forms required: FAFSA.
Dates and Deadlines: Priority date 3/15; no closing date. Applicants notified on a rolling basis starting 6/1; must reply within 2 week(s) of notification.

CONTACT
Liz Tucker, Director of Financial Aid
One University Plaza, Platteville, WI 53818
(608) 342-1836

University of Wisconsin-Richland
Richland Center, Wisconsin
www.richland.uwc.edu
Federal Code: 003897

2-year public liberal arts college in small town.
Enrollment: 464 undergrads.

BASIC COSTS (2005-2006)
Tuition and fees: $4,249; out-of-state residents $12,949.
Per-credit charge: $166; out-of-state residents $528.
Additional info: Minnesota Reciprocity tuition: $3,576 full-time, $149 per-credit-hour.

FINANCIAL AID PICTURE
Students with need: Need-based aid available for full-time and part-time students. Work study available nights, weekends, and for part-time students.
Students without need: This college only awards aid to students with need.
Scholarships offered: Richland Campus Foundation Scholarships available for new, continuing and transfer students.

FINANCIAL AID PROCEDURES
Forms required: FAFSA.
Dates and Deadlines: Priority date 4/15; no closing date. Applicants notified on a rolling basis starting 5/15; must reply within 3 week(s) of notification.

CONTACT
John Poole, Director of Student Services
1200 Highway 14 West, Richland Center, WI 53581
(608) 647-6186 ext. 3

University of Wisconsin-River Falls
River Falls, Wisconsin
www.uwrf.edu   Federal Code: 003923

4-year public university in large town.
Enrollment: 5,504 undergrads, 5% part-time. 1,192 full-time freshmen.
Selectivity: Admits over 75% of applicants.

BASIC COSTS (2005-2006)
Tuition and fees: $4,962; out-of-state residents $15,008.
Per-credit charge: $178; out-of-state residents $597.
Room and board: $4,400.
Additional info: Minnesota reciprocity tuition: $4,780 full-time, $199 per-credit-hour.

FINANCIAL AID PICTURE (2004-2005)
Students with need: 34% of average financial aid package awarded as scholarships/grants, 66% awarded as loans/jobs. Need-based aid available for part-time students. Work study available nights, weekends, and for part-time students.
Students without need: This college only awards aid to students with need.

FINANCIAL AID PROCEDURES
Forms required: FAFSA.
Dates and Deadlines: Priority date 3/15; no closing date. Applicants notified on a rolling basis starting 4/1; must reply within 3 week(s) of notification.
Transfers: No deadline. Applicants notified on a rolling basis starting 4/1.

CONTACT
Beth Boisen, Assistant Director of Financial Aid
410 South Third Street, River Falls, WI 54022-5001
(715) 425-3141

University of Wisconsin-Rock County
Janesville, Wisconsin
www.rock.uwc.edu   Federal Code: 003897

2-year public branch campus and liberal arts college in small city.
Enrollment: 616 undergrads. 274 full-time freshmen.

BASIC COSTS (2005-2006)
Tuition and fees: $4,228; out-of-state residents $12,928.
Per-credit charge: $166; out-of-state residents $528.
Additional info: Minnesota reciprocity tuition: $3,576 full-time, $149 per-credit-hour.

FINANCIAL AID PICTURE
Students with need: Need-based aid available for full-time and part-time students. Work study available nights, weekends, and for part-time students.
Students without need: This college only awards aid to students with need.

FINANCIAL AID PROCEDURES
Forms required: FAFSA, institutional form.
Dates and Deadlines: Priority date 4/15; no closing date. Applicants notified on a rolling basis starting 6/1; must reply within 3 week(s) of notification.

CONTACT
Linda Osborn, Director of Financial Aid
2909 Kellogg Avenue, Janesville, WI 53546-5699
(608) 758-6523

University of Wisconsin-Stevens Point
Stevens Point, Wisconsin
www.uwsp.edu   Federal Code: 003924

4-year public university in large town.
Enrollment: 8,328 undergrads, 7% part-time. 1,527 full-time freshmen.
Selectivity: Admits over 75% of applicants.

BASIC COSTS (2005-2006)
Tuition and fees: $4,928; out-of-state residents $14,974.
Per-credit charge: $178; out-of-state residents $597.
Room and board: $4,322.
Additional info: Minnesota Reciprocity tuition $4,780 full-year or $199 per-credit-hour.

FINANCIAL AID PICTURE (2004-2005)
Students with need: Out of 1,284 full-time freshmen who applied for aid, 752 were judged to have need. Of these, 714 received aid, and 461 had their full need met. Average financial aid package met 93% of need; average scholarship/grant was $4,078; average loan was $3,206. For part-time students, average financial aid package was $5,186.
Students without need: 84 full-time freshmen who did not demonstrate need for aid received scholarships/grants; average award was $2,072. No-need awards available for academics, ROTC.
Cumulative student debt: 67% of graduating class had student loans; average debt was $14,975.

FINANCIAL AID PROCEDURES
Forms required: FAFSA.
Dates and Deadlines: Priority date 3/15; closing date 6/15. Applicants notified on a rolling basis starting 5/1; must reply within 4 week(s) of notification.
Transfers: No deadline.

CONTACT
Paul Watson, Director of Financial Aid
Student Services Center, Stevens Point, WI 54481
(715) 346-4771

University of Wisconsin-Stout
Menomonie, Wisconsin
www.uwstout.edu   Federal Code: 003915

4-year public university in large town.
Enrollment: 7,248 undergrads, 9% part-time. 1,685 full-time freshmen.

BASIC COSTS (2005-2006)
Tuition and fees: $6,452; out-of-state residents $16,785.
Per-credit charge: $187; out-of-state residents $627.
Room and board: $4,572.

FINANCIAL AID PICTURE (2005-2006)
Students with need: Out of 1,305 full-time freshmen who applied for aid, 816 were judged to have need. Of these, 816 received aid, and 370 had their full need met. Average financial aid package met 83% of need; average scholarship/grant was $3,811; average loan was $3,170. For part-time students, average financial aid package was $7,660.
Students without need: 201 full-time freshmen who did not demonstrate need for aid received scholarships/grants; average award was $1,370. No-need awards available for academics.
Scholarships offered: Wisconsin Academic Excellence Scholarship; $2,250; selected by high school. National Merit Finalist Scholarship; $2,000; automatically awarded to NMSQT finalist. National Merit Semifinalist Scholarship; $1,000; automatically awarded to NMSQT semifinalist. Chancellor's Academic Honor Scholarship; $1,000; automatically awarded to top 5% of high school class with ACT of 25 who enroll by July 15th.

Cumulative student debt: 73% of graduating class had student loans; average debt was $18,496.

FINANCIAL AID PROCEDURES
Forms required: FAFSA.
Dates and Deadlines: Priority date 3/15; no closing date. Applicants notified on a rolling basis starting 4/1; must reply within 4 week(s) of notification.

CONTACT
Beth Resech, Director of Financial Aid
1 Clocktower Plaza, Menomonie, WI 54751
(715) 232-1363

University of Wisconsin-Superior
Superior, Wisconsin
www.uwsuper.edu
Federal Code: 003925

4-year public university and liberal arts college in large town.
Enrollment: 2,507 undergrads, 15% part-time. 336 full-time freshmen.
Selectivity: Admits 50 to 75% of applicants.

BASIC COSTS (2005-2006)
Tuition and fees: $5,182; out-of-state residents $15,228.
Per-credit charge: $184; out-of-state residents $603.
Room and board: $4,422.
Additional info: Minnesota reciprocity tuition: $4,780 full-time, $199 per-credit-hour. Tuition/fee waivers available for minority students.

FINANCIAL AID PICTURE (2005-2006)
Students with need: For part-time students, average financial aid package was $6,260.
Students without need: No-need awards available for academics, art, leadership, minority status, music/drama.
Additional info: Tuition Assistance Program (TAP) available to non-resident students on limited basis.

FINANCIAL AID PROCEDURES
Forms required: FAFSA.
Dates and Deadlines: Priority date 4/15; no closing date. Applicants notified on a rolling basis starting 3/15.
Transfers: No deadline. Applicants notified on a rolling basis starting 3/15.

CONTACT
Anne Podgorak, Director of Financial Aid
Belknap and Catlin, PO Box 2000, Superior, WI 54880
(715) 394-8200

University of Wisconsin-Waukesha
Waukesha, Wisconsin
www.waukesha.uwc.edu
Federal Code: 003897

2-year public branch campus and junior college in small city.
Enrollment: 2,064 undergrads.

BASIC COSTS (2005-2006)
Tuition and fees: $4,206; out-of-state residents $12,906.
Per-credit charge: $166; out-of-state residents $528.
Additional info: Minnesota reciprocity tuition: $3,576 full-time, $149 per-credit-hour.

FINANCIAL AID PICTURE (2004-2005)
Students with need: 58% of average financial aid package awarded as scholarships/grants, 42% awarded as loans/jobs. Need-based aid available for part-time students. Work study available nights, weekends, and for part-time students.
Students without need: No-need awards available for academics, leadership, minority status, music/drama.

Scholarships offered: University of Wisconsin-Waukesha Scholarship Program; numerous scholarships; amounts vary.

FINANCIAL AID PROCEDURES
Forms required: FAFSA.
Dates and Deadlines: Priority date 4/15; no closing date. Applicants notified on a rolling basis starting 5/15; must reply within 3 week(s) of notification.

CONTACT
Judy Becker, Coordinator of Financial Aid
1500 University Drive, Waukesha, WI 53188
(262) 521-5210

University of Wisconsin-Whitewater
Whitewater, Wisconsin
www.uww.edu
Federal Code: 003926

4-year public university in large town.
Enrollment: 9,123 undergrads, 7% part-time. 1,701 full-time freshmen.
Selectivity: Admits 50 to 75% of applicants.

BASIC COSTS (2005-2006)
Tuition and fees: $5,305; out-of-state residents $15,703.
Per-credit charge: $184; out-of-state residents $618.
Room and board: $4,070.
Additional info: Minnesota reciprocity tuition: $4,780 full-time, $199 per-credit-hour.

FINANCIAL AID PICTURE (2005-2006)
Students with need: Out of 1,427 full-time freshmen who applied for aid, 949 were judged to have need. Of these, 887 received aid, and 390 had their full need met. Average financial aid package met 70% of need; average scholarship/grant was $4,860; average loan was $3,014. Need-based aid available for part-time students.
Students without need: 195 full-time freshmen who did not demonstrate need for aid received scholarships/grants; average award was $2,264. No-need awards available for academics, alumni affiliation, art, leadership, minority status, music/drama, ROTC, state/district residency.
Cumulative student debt: 63% of graduating class had student loans; average debt was $17,394.

FINANCIAL AID PROCEDURES
Forms required: FAFSA.
Dates and Deadlines: Priority date 3/15; no closing date. Applicants notified on a rolling basis starting 4/1; must reply within 2 week(s) of notification.
Transfers: No deadline. Applicants notified on a rolling basis starting 4/1; must reply within 2 week(s) of notification.

CONTACT
Carol Miller, Director of Financial Aid
800 West Main Street, Whitewater, WI 53190-1790
(262) 472-1130

Viterbo University
La Crosse, Wisconsin
www.viterbo.edu
Federal Code: 003911

4-year private university and liberal arts college in small city, affiliated with Roman Catholic Church.
Enrollment: 1,778 undergrads.
Selectivity: Admits over 75% of applicants.

BASIC COSTS (2006-2007)
Tuition and fees: $17,640.
Per-credit charge: $505.
Room and board: $5,640.

Additional info: Additional fees for some art, dietetics, science courses, and nursing clinicals. Tuition/fee waivers available for minority students.

FINANCIAL AID PICTURE
Students with need: Need-based aid available for full-time and part-time students. Work study available nights, weekends, and for part-time students.
Students without need: No-need awards available for academics, alumni affiliation, art, athletics, leadership, minority status, music/drama, ROTC.
Scholarships offered: Fine Arts Scholarships; up to $10,000 per year; for incoming full-time freshmen and transfer students talented in areas of art, music or theatre. Dr. Scholl Scholarship; full, four-year tuition; must enroll full-time and maintain a 3.5 GPA, 1 awarded. Viterbo University Scholarship; $1,000-$8,000 per year; based on academic history; incoming freshmen and transfers automatically considered; renewable.
Additional info: Approximately 97 percent of traditional undergraduate students receive financial aid. Average financial aid package $15,270.

FINANCIAL AID PROCEDURES
Forms required: FAFSA, institutional form.
Dates and Deadlines: Priority date 3/15; no closing date. Applicants notified on a rolling basis starting 4/1; must reply within 3 week(s) of notification.

CONTACT
Terry Norman, Director of Financial Aid
900 Viterbo Drive, La Crosse, WI 54601-8804
(608) 796-3900

Waukesha County Technical College
Pewaukee, Wisconsin
www.wctc.edu Federal Code: 005294

2-year public technical college in large town.
Enrollment: 6,393 undergrads.
Selectivity: Open admission; but selective for some programs.

BASIC COSTS (2006-2007)
Tuition and fees: $2,887; out-of-state residents $16,366.
Per-credit charge: $87; out-of-state residents $536.
Additional info: Fees may vary by program; minimum $4 materials fee per course. $10 per credit fee for online courses.

FINANCIAL AID PICTURE
Students with need: Need-based aid available for full-time students. Work study available nights.
Students without need: No-need awards available for academics.

FINANCIAL AID PROCEDURES
Forms required: FAFSA, institutional form.
Dates and Deadlines: Priority date 3/31; no closing date. Applicants notified on a rolling basis.

CONTACT
Tom Rabe, Director of Financial Aid
800 Main Street, Pewaukee, WI 53072
(262) 691-5436

Western Wisconsin Technical College
La Crosse, Wisconsin
www.wwtc.edu Federal Code: 003840

2-year public community and technical college in small city.
Enrollment: 4,069 undergrads, 56% part-time. 419 full-time freshmen.
Selectivity: Open admission; but selective for some programs.

BASIC COSTS (2006-2007)
Tuition and fees: $2,861; out-of-state residents $16,340.
Per-credit charge: $87; out-of-state residents $536.
Room and board: $3,810.
Additional info: Fees vary by program; minimum $4 materials fee per course. Tuition/fee waivers available for unemployed or children of unemployed.

FINANCIAL AID PICTURE (2004-2005)
Students with need: 53% of average financial aid package awarded as scholarships/grants, 47% awarded as loans/jobs. Need-based aid available for part-time students. Work study available nights, weekends, and for part-time students.

FINANCIAL AID PROCEDURES
Forms required: FAFSA, institutional form.
Dates and Deadlines: Priority date 3/1; no closing date. Applicants notified on a rolling basis starting 4/1.

CONTACT
Judith Erickson, Student Financial Services Manager
PO Box 908, La Crosse, WI 54602-0908
(608) 785-9302

Wisconsin Indianhead Technical College
Shell Lake, Wisconsin
www.witc.edu Federal Code: 011824

2-year public technical college in rural community.
Enrollment: 2,969 undergrads, 48% part-time. 573 full-time freshmen.

BASIC COSTS (2005-2006)
Tuition and fees: $2,573; out-of-state residents $15,467.
Per-credit charge: $81; out-of-state residents $510.
Additional info: Materials fees vary by program; minimum $4 per course. Additional fees vary by campus among college's four campuses.

FINANCIAL AID PICTURE (2004-2005)
Students with need: 52% of average financial aid package awarded as scholarships/grants, 48% awarded as loans/jobs. Need-based aid available for part-time students. Work study available nights, weekends, and for part-time students.
Students without need: No-need awards available for state/district residency.

FINANCIAL AID PROCEDURES
Forms required: FAFSA.
Dates and Deadlines: Applicants notified on a rolling basis.

CONTACT
Shane Evenson, Director, Financial Aid
505 Pine Ridge Drive, Shell Lake, WI 54871
(715) 468-2815 ext. 2246

Wisconsin Lutheran College
Milwaukee, Wisconsin
www.wlc.edu Federal Code: 014658

4-year private liberal arts college in very large city, affiliated with Wisconsin Evangelical Lutheran Synod.
Enrollment: 691 undergrads.

BASIC COSTS (2005-2006)
Tuition and fees: $17,470.
Per-credit charge: $530.
Room and board: $6,080.

FINANCIAL AID PICTURE
Students with need: Need-based aid available for full-time and part-time students. Work study available nights, weekends, and for part-time students.

Students without need: No-need awards available for academics, art, leadership, minority status, music/drama, state/district residency.
Scholarships offered: Presidential Scholarship; $8,000 ($9,000 if ACT is 30 or greater); based on ACT score of 27 or higher plus top 10% of HS class or 3.7 GPA; no limit on number of awards. Academic Scholarship; $7,500; ACT score of 24 or higher and top 25% of high school class or 3.4 GPA. To qualify, students must be admitted in good standing by May 1.

FINANCIAL AID PROCEDURES
Forms required: FAFSA, institutional form.
Dates and Deadlines: Priority date 3/1; no closing date. Applicants notified on a rolling basis starting 3/15; must reply within 2 week(s) of notification.
Transfers: Transfer scholarship and transfer grant available for qualifying students.

CONTACT
Linda Loeffel, Director of Financial Aid
8800 West Bluemound Road, Milwaukee, WI 53226-4699
(414) 443-8856

Wyoming

Casper College
Casper, Wyoming
www.caspercollege.edu   Federal Code: 003928

2-year public community college in small city.
Enrollment: 2,792 undergrads, 34% part-time. 574 full-time freshmen.
Selectivity: Open admission; but selective for some programs and for out-of-state students.

BASIC COSTS (2005-2006)
Tuition and fees: $1,536; out-of-state residents $4,296.
Per-credit charge: $57; out-of-state residents $172.
Room and board: $3,460.
Additional info: Western Undergraduate Exchange students pay $96 per credit-hour and $2136 per year for full-time students.

FINANCIAL AID PICTURE
Students with need: Need-based aid available for full-time and part-time students. Work study available nights, weekends, and for part-time students.
Students without need: No-need awards available for academics, art, athletics, leadership, music/drama, state/district residency.

FINANCIAL AID PROCEDURES
Forms required: FAFSA.
Dates and Deadlines: Priority date 3/15; no closing date. Applicants notified on a rolling basis starting 4/1.
Transfers: No deadline. Applicants notified on a rolling basis starting 4/1.

CONTACT
Darry Voigt, Director of Financial Aid
125 College Drive, Casper, WY 82601
(307) 268-2510

Central Wyoming College
Riverton, Wyoming
www.cwc.edu   Federal Code: 005018

2-year public community college in large town.
Enrollment: 1,027 undergrads, 37% part-time. 197 full-time freshmen.
Selectivity: Open admission; but selective for some programs.

BASIC COSTS (2005-2006)
Tuition and fees: $1,872; out-of-state residents $4,632.
Per-credit charge: $57; out-of-state residents $172.
Room and board: $2,880.
Additional info: Students from Western Undergraduate Exchange states pay $2,136 in tuition per year.

FINANCIAL AID PICTURE (2004-2005)
Students with need: Out of 179 full-time freshmen who applied for aid, 83 were judged to have need. Of these, 83 received aid. Need-based aid available for part-time students.
Students without need: No-need awards available for academics, alumni affiliation, art, athletics, leadership, minority status, music/drama, state/district residency.
Scholarships offered: Honors Scholarships; in-state tuition and general fees plus $300 book stipend; for graduating high school seniors with minimum 3.5 cumulative GPA or minimum ACT composite 25. Seniors Scholarships; in-state tuition; for graduating high school seniors with 3.0-3.49 cumulative GPA or minimum ACT composite 22. Full academic scholarships; in-state tuition, general fees, room and board, books and supplies; for Wyoming National Merit finalists.
Cumulative student debt: 30% of graduating class had student loans; average debt was $6,625.

FINANCIAL AID PROCEDURES
Forms required: FAFSA, institutional form.
Dates and Deadlines: Priority date 4/15; no closing date. Applicants notified on a rolling basis starting 5/1; must reply within 2 week(s) of notification.

CONTACT
Jacque Burns, Financial Aid Officer
2660 Peck Avenue, Riverton, WY 82501
(307) 855-2150

Eastern Wyoming College
Torrington, Wyoming
www.ewc.wy.edu   Federal Code: 003929

2-year public community college in small town.
Enrollment: 608 undergrads, 30% part-time. 137 full-time freshmen.
Selectivity: Open admission.

BASIC COSTS (2005-2006)
Tuition and fees: $1,848; out-of-state residents $4,608.
Per-credit charge: $57; out-of-state residents $172.
Room and board: $3,204.
Additional info: Students from Western Undergraduate Exchange pay $2,136 tuition plus fees per year; $89 per-credit-hour.

FINANCIAL AID PICTURE
Students with need: Need-based aid available for full-time and part-time students. Work study available nights, weekends, and for part-time students.
Students without need: No-need awards available for academics, art, athletics, leadership, music/drama.
Additional info: Installment payment plan on room and board contracts offered.

FINANCIAL AID PROCEDURES
Forms required: FAFSA, institutional form.
Dates and Deadlines: Priority date 3/15; no closing date. Applicants notified on a rolling basis starting 1/1.

CONTACT
Pam Palermo, Financial Aid Director
3200 West C Street, Torrington, WY 82240
(800) 658-3195 ext. 8325

Laramie County Community College
Cheyenne, Wyoming
www.lccc.wy.edu   Federal Code: 009259

2-year public community college in small city.
Enrollment: 2,884 undergrads.
Selectivity: Open admission; but selective for some programs.

BASIC COSTS (2005-2006)
Tuition and fees: $1,884; out-of-state residents $4,644.
Per-credit charge: $57; out-of-state residents $172.
Room and board: $4,872.
Additional info: Students from Western Undergraduate Exchange schools and Nebraska residents pay $2064 in tuition and fees per year; $86 per credit hour.

FINANCIAL AID PICTURE (2004-2005)
Students with need: Need-based aid available for part-time students.

FINANCIAL AID PROCEDURES
Forms required: FAFSA, institutional form.
Dates and Deadlines: Priority date 4/1; no closing date. Applicants notified on a rolling basis starting 6/1; must reply within 2 week(s) of notification.

CONTACT
Dennis Schroeder, Director of Financial Aid
1400 East College Drive, Cheyenne, WY 82007
(307) 778-1215

Northwest College
Powell, Wyoming
www.northwestcollege.edu   Federal Code: 003931

2-year public community college in small town.
Enrollment: 1,513 undergrads, 26% part-time. 402 full-time freshmen.
Selectivity: Open admission; but selective for some programs and for out-of-state students.

BASIC COSTS (2005-2006)
Tuition and fees: $1,880; out-of-state residents $4,640.
Per-credit charge: $57; out-of-state residents $172.
Room and board: $3,376.
Additional info: Students from Western Undergraduate Exchange schools pay $2,064 tuition; $86 per-credit-hour; $512 required fees.

FINANCIAL AID PICTURE
Students with need: Work study available nights.
Students without need: No-need awards available for academics, athletics.
Additional info: Interview, essay recommended for scholarships.

FINANCIAL AID PROCEDURES
Forms required: FAFSA, institutional form.
Dates and Deadlines: Priority date 5/1; no closing date. Applicants notified on a rolling basis starting 5/1; must reply within 2 week(s) of notification.

CONTACT
Beverly Bell, Director of Financial Aid
231 West 6th Street, Powell, WY 82435
(307) 754-6104

Sheridan College
Sheridan, Wyoming
www.sheridan.edu   Federal Code: 003930

2-year public community college in large town.
Enrollment: 1,556 undergrads, 36% part-time. 277 full-time freshmen.
Selectivity: Open admission; but selective for some programs.

BASIC COSTS (2005-2006)
Tuition and fees: $1,891; out-of-state residents $4,651.
Per-credit charge: $57; out-of-state residents $172.
Room and board: $3,840.

FINANCIAL AID PICTURE (2004-2005)
Students with need: 67% of average financial aid package awarded as scholarships/grants, 33% awarded as loans/jobs. Need-based aid available for part-time students. Work study available nights, weekends, and for part-time students.
Students without need: No-need awards available for academics, athletics.
Scholarships offered: Merit scholarships; in-state tuition and fees; must have minimum composite ACT score of 25 or minimum SAT of 1120 (exclusive of Writing); renewable.
Cumulative student debt: 34% of graduating class had student loans; average debt was $5,837.

FINANCIAL AID PROCEDURES
Forms required: FAFSA, institutional form.
Dates and Deadlines: Priority date 3/1; no closing date. Applicants notified on a rolling basis; must reply within 3 week(s) of notification.

CONTACT
Randy Thompson, Director
PO Box 1500, Sheridan, WY 82801-1500
(307) 674-6446 ext. 2100

University of Wyoming
Laramie, Wyoming
www.uwyo.edu   Federal Code: 003932

4-year public university in large town.
Enrollment: 8,984 undergrads, 15% part-time. 1,397 full-time freshmen.
Selectivity: Admits over 75% of applicants.

BASIC COSTS (2006-2007)
Tuition and fees: $3,515; out-of-state residents $10,055.
Per-credit charge: $94; out-of-state residents $312.
Room and board: $6,861.
Additional info: International students must pay an additional $35 fee per semester.

FINANCIAL AID PICTURE (2004-2005)
Students with need: Out of 1,257 full-time freshmen who applied for aid, 843 were judged to have need. Of these, 826 received aid, and 455 had their full need met. Average financial aid package met 75% of need; average scholarship/grant was $1,849; average loan was $2,010. Need-based aid available for part-time students.
Students without need: 219 full-time freshmen who did not demonstrate need for aid received scholarships/grants; average award was $1,436. No-need awards available for academics, alumni affiliation, art, athletics, leadership, minority status, music/drama, religious affiliation, ROTC, state/district residency.
Scholarships offered: *Merit:* Western Heritage Scholarship; number awarded and packages vary. President's High School Honor Scholarship; covers undergraduate fees and tuition; number awarded varies. *Athletic:* 220 full-time freshmen received athletic scholarships; average amount $3,947.

FINANCIAL AID PROCEDURES
Forms required: FAFSA.
Dates and Deadlines: Priority date 2/1; no closing date. Applicants notified on a rolling basis starting 3/1; must reply within 3 week(s) of notification.

Wyoming University of Wyoming

CONTACT
David Gruen, Director of Student Financial Aid
Department 3314/1000 East University Avenue, Laramie, WY 82071
(307) 766-2116

Western Wyoming Community College
Rock Springs, Wyoming
www.wwcc.wy.edu   Federal Code: 003933

2-year public community college in large town.
Enrollment: 1,789 undergrads, 42% part-time. 300 full-time freshmen.
Selectivity: Open admission; but selective for some programs.

BASIC COSTS (2005-2006)
Tuition and fees: $1,658; out-of-state residents $4,418.
Per-credit charge: $57; out-of-state residents $172.
Room and board: $3,517.

FINANCIAL AID PICTURE (2004-2005)
Students with need: Out of 220 full-time freshmen who applied for aid, 186 were judged to have need. Of these, 186 received aid. Need-based aid available for part-time students.
Students without need: No-need awards available for academics, art, athletics, music/drama, state/district residency.
Scholarships offered: 33 full-time freshmen received athletic scholarships.

FINANCIAL AID PROCEDURES
Forms required: FAFSA.
Dates and Deadlines: Priority date 4/1; no closing date. Applicants notified on a rolling basis starting 3/15; must reply within 2 week(s) of notification.

CONTACT
Stacee Hanson, Financial Aid Director
Box 428, Rock Springs, WY 82902-0428
(307) 382-1643

Part IV

Scholarship Lists

Academic scholarships

Alabama
Alabama State University
Athens State University
Auburn University at Montgomery
Birmingham-Southern College
Bishop State Community College
Calhoun Community College
Central Alabama Community College
Chattahoochee Valley Community College
Enterprise-Ozark Community College
Faulkner University
Gadsden State Community College
George C. Wallace State Community College
    George C. Wallace Community College at
        Dothan
        Selma
Huntingdon College
J. F. Drake State Technical College
Jacksonville State University
Jefferson Davis Community College
Jefferson State Community College
Judson College
Lurleen B. Wallace Community College
Marion Military Institute
Northeast Alabama Community College
Northwest-Shoals Community College
Oakwood College
Samford University
Snead State Community College
Southeastern Bible College
Southern Christian University
Spring Hill College
Stillman College
Talladega College
Trenholm State Technical College
Troy University
Tuskegee University
University of Alabama
University of Alabama
    Birmingham
    Huntsville
University of Mobile
University of Montevallo
University of North Alabama
University of South Alabama
University of West Alabama
Wallace State Community College at Hanceville

Alaska
Alaska Pacific University
University of Alaska
    Anchorage
    Fairbanks
    Southeast

Arizona
Arizona State University
Arizona State University West
Arizona Western College
DeVry University
    Phoenix
Eastern Arizona College
Embry-Riddle Aeronautical University: Prescott Campus
Grand Canyon University
Mesa Community College
Northern Arizona University
Northland Pioneer College
Pima Community College
Prescott College
Scottsdale Community College
South Mountain Community College
Southwestern College
University of Arizona
Yavapai College

Arkansas
Arkansas Northeastern College
Arkansas State University
Arkansas State University
    Beebe
    Mountain Home
Arkansas Tech University
Central Baptist College
Crowley's Ridge College
Ecclesia College
Harding University
Henderson State University
Hendrix College
John Brown University
Lyon College
Mid-South Community College
National Park Community College
North Arkansas College
Northwest Arkansas Community College
Ouachita Baptist University
Philander Smith College
Phillips Community College of the University of Arkansas
Rich Mountain Community College
Southeast Arkansas College
Southern Arkansas University
Southern Arkansas University Tech
University of Arkansas
University of Arkansas
    Community College at Batesville
    Community College at Hope
    Fort Smith
    Monticello
    Pine Bluff
University of Central Arkansas
University of the Ozarks
Williams Baptist College

California
Academy of Art University
Alliant International University
American Academy of Dramatic Arts: West
Art Institute
    of California: Los Angeles
    of California: Orange County
Azusa Pacific University
Bethany University
Bethesda Christian University
Biola University
Brooks College
California Baptist University
California College of the Arts
California Institute of Technology
California Institute of the Arts
California Lutheran University
California Maritime Academy
California Polytechnic State University: San Luis Obispo
California State Polytechnic University: Pomona
California State University
    Chico
    Dominguez Hills
    Fresno
    Fullerton
    Long Beach
    Monterey Bay
    Northridge
    Stanislaus
Chaffey College
Chapman University
Claremont McKenna College
College of the Canyons
College of the Siskiyous
Columbia College
Concordia University
Deep Springs College
    Fremont
    Long Beach
    Pomona
    West Hills
Dominican University of California
East Los Angeles College
El Camino College
Empire College
Fashion Institute of Design and Merchandising
Fashion Institute of Design and Merchandising
    San Diego
    San Francisco
Fresno Pacific University
Glendale Community College
Golden Gate University
Golden West College
Harvey Mudd College
Holy Names University
Hope International University
Humboldt State University
Humphreys College
King's College and Seminary
La Sierra University
LIFE Pacific College
Loyola Marymount University
Marymount College
Master's College
Menlo College
Merced College
Mills College
Mount St. Mary's College
Mount San Jacinto College
National Hispanic University
NewSchool of Architecture & Design
Notre Dame de Namur University
Occidental College
Ohlone College
Orange Coast College
Otis College of Art and Design
Patten University
Pepperdine University
Pitzer College
Point Loma Nazarene University
Riverside Community College
St. Mary's College of California
Samuel Merritt College
San Diego Christian College
San Diego State University
San Francisco State University
San Joaquin Delta College
Santa Clara University
Santa Rosa Junior College
Scripps College
Simpson University
Sonoma State University
Taft College
University of California
    Berkeley
    Irvine
    Los Angeles
    Riverside
    San Diego
    Santa Cruz
University of California: Merced
University of Judaism
University of La Verne
University of Redlands
University of San Diego
University of San Francisco
University of Southern California
University of the Pacific
Vanguard University of Southern California
Westmont College
Westwood College of Technology
    Inland Empire
Whittier College
William Jessup University
Woodbury University
Yuba Community College District

Colorado
Adams State College
Arapahoe Community College
Boulder College of Massage Therapy
Colorado Christian University
Colorado College
Colorado Mountain College
    Alpine Campus
    Spring Valley Campus
    Timberline Campus
Colorado Northwestern Community College
Colorado School of Mines
Colorado State University
Colorado State University
    Pueblo
Colorado Technical University
Fort Lewis College
Front Range Community College
Johnson & Wales University
Mesa State College
Metropolitan State College of Denver
Morgan Community College
Northeastern Junior College
Otero Junior College
Pueblo Community College
Regis University
Remington College
    Colorado Springs
Rocky Mountain College of Art & Design
Trinidad State Junior College
University of Colorado
    Boulder
    Colorado Springs
    Denver and Health Sciences Center
University of Denver
University of Northern Colorado
Western State College of Colorado
Westwood College of Technology

Connecticut
Albertus Magnus College
Briarwood College
Central Connecticut State University
Eastern Connecticut State University
Fairfield University
Housatonic Community College
International College of Hospitality Management
Lyme Academy College of Fine Arts
Mitchell College
Northwestern Connecticut Community College
Norwalk Community College
Quinnipiac University
Sacred Heart University
St. Joseph College
Southern Connecticut State University
Trinity College
Tunxis Community College
University of Bridgeport
University of Connecticut
University of Hartford
University of New Haven
Western Connecticut State University

Delaware
Delaware State University
Delaware Technical and Community College
    Owens Campus
    Stanton/Wilmington Campus
University of Delaware
Wesley College
Wilmington College

District of Columbia
American University
Catholic University of America
Corcoran College of Art and Design
Gallaudet University
George Washington University

Howard University
Southeastern University
Trinity University

Florida
Art Institute of Fort Lauderdale
Baptist College of Florida
Barry University
Beacon College
Bethune-Cookman College
Brevard Community College
Broward Community College
Carlos Albizu University
Central Florida Community College
Chipola College
Clearwater Christian College
Eckerd College
Edward Waters College
Embry-Riddle Aeronautical University
Embry-Riddle Aeronautical University: Extended Campus
Flagler College
Florida Agricultural and Mechanical University
Florida Atlantic University
Florida Christian College
Florida College
Florida Community College at Jacksonville
Florida Gulf Coast University
Florida Institute of Technology
Florida International University
Florida Keys Community College
Florida Metropolitan University
    Melbourne Campus
Florida Southern College
Florida State University
Gulf Coast Community College
Hobe Sound Bible College
Indian River Community College
International Academy of Design and Technology: Tampa
International College
Jacksonville University
Johnson & Wales University
Jones College
Lake City Community College
Lake-Sumter Community College
Lynn University
Manatee Community College
Miami Dade College
New College of Florida
North Florida Community College
Northwood University
    Florida Campus
Nova Southeastern University
Okaloosa-Walton College
Palm Beach Atlantic University
Palm Beach Community College
Pasco-Hernando Community College
Pensacola Junior College
Polk Community College
Rollins College
St. Leo University
St. Petersburg College
St. Thomas University
Santa Fe Community College
Schiller International University
Seminole Community College
South Florida Community College
South University: West Palm Beach Campus
Southeastern College of the Assemblies of God
Stetson University
Tallahassee Community College
University of Central Florida
University of Florida
University of Miami
University of North Florida
University of South Florida
University of Tampa
University of West Florida
Warner Southern College
Webber International University

Georgia
Agnes Scott College
Albany State University
Albany Technical College
Andrew College
Armstrong Atlantic State University
Athens Technical College
Augusta State University
Berry College
Brenau University
Brewton-Parker College
Clark Atlanta University
Clayton State University
Coastal Georgia Community College
Columbus State University
Covenant College
Dalton State College
Darton College
    Alpharetta
    Decatur
East Georgia College
Emmanuel College
Emory University
Fort Valley State University
Gainesville State College
Georgia College and State University
Georgia Highlands College
Georgia Institute of Technology
Georgia Southern University
Georgia Southwestern State University
Georgia State University
Gordon College
Kennesaw State University
LaGrange College
Life University
Macon State College
Medical College of Georgia
Mercer University
Middle Georgia College
Morehouse College
North Georgia College & State University
Oglethorpe University
Oxford College of Emory University
Paine College
Piedmont College
Reinhardt College
Savannah College of Art and Design
Savannah State University
Savannah Technical College
Shorter College
South Georgia College
Southern Polytechnic State University
Spelman College
Thomas University
Toccoa Falls College
Truett-McConnell College
University of Georgia
University of West Georgia
Valdosta State University
Waycross College
Wesleyan College
Young Harris College

Hawaii
Brigham Young University-Hawaii
Chaminade University of Honolulu
Hawaii Pacific University
University of Hawaii
    Honolulu Community College
    Manoa
    West Oahu

Idaho
Albertson College of Idaho
Boise Bible College
Boise State University
Brigham Young University-Idaho
Eastern Idaho Technical College
Idaho State University
Lewis-Clark State College
North Idaho College
Northwest Nazarene University
University of Idaho

Illinois
Augustana College
Aurora University
Benedictine University
Black Hawk College
Blackburn College
Bradley University
Carl Sandburg College
Chicago State University
City Colleges of Chicago
    Kennedy-King College
    Malcolm X College
College of DuPage
College of Lake County
Columbia College Chicago
Concordia University
Danville Area Community College
DePaul University
    Addison
    Chicago
    Tinley Park
Dominican University
East-West University
Eastern Illinois University
Elgin Community College
Elmhurst College
Eureka College
Governors State University
Greenville College
Harrington College of Design
Highland Community College
Illinois College
Illinois Eastern Community Colleges
    Frontier Community College
    Lincoln Trail College
    Olney Central College
    Wabash Valley College
Illinois Institute of Technology
Illinois State University
Illinois Wesleyan University
Joliet Junior College
Judson College
Kaskaskia College
Kendall College
Kishwaukee College
Knox College
Lake Forest College
Lake Land College
Lewis University
Lexington College
Lincoln Land Community College
Loyola University of Chicago
MacCormac College
MacMurray College
McHenry County College
McKendree College
Millikin University
Monmouth College
Moody Bible Institute
Moraine Valley Community College
Morrison Institute of Technology
National-Louis University
North Central College
North Park University
Northeastern Illinois University
Northern Illinois University
Northwestern Business College
Oakton Community College
Olivet Nazarene University
Parkland College
Principia College
Quincy University
Rend Lake College
Richland Community College
Robert Morris College: Chicago
Rock Valley College
Rockford College
Roosevelt University
Saint Anthony College of Nursing
St. Francis Medical Center College of Nursing
St. Xavier University
Sauk Valley Community College
School of the Art Institute of Chicago
Shimer College
South Suburban College of Cook County
Southeastern Illinois College
Southern Illinois University Carbondale
Southern Illinois University Edwardsville
Southwestern Illinois College
Spoon River College
Springfield College in Illinois
Trinity Christian College
Trinity International University
Triton College
University of Chicago
University of Illinois
    Chicago
    Springfield
    Urbana-Champaign
University of St. Francis
VanderCook College of Music
Waubonsee Community College
Western Illinois University
Wheaton College
William Rainey Harper College

Indiana
Ancilla College
Anderson University
Ball State University
Bethel College
Butler University
Calumet College of St. Joseph
DePauw University
Earlham College
Franklin College
Goshen College
Grace College
Hanover College
Holy Cross College
Huntington University
Indiana Institute of Technology
Indiana State University
Indiana University
    Bloomington
    East
    Kokomo
    Northwest
    South Bend
    Southeast
Indiana University-Purdue University Fort Wayne
Indiana University-Purdue University Indianapolis
Indiana Wesleyan University
Manchester College
Marian College
Oakland City University
Purdue University
Purdue University
    Calumet
    North Central Campus
Rose-Hulman Institute of Technology
St. Joseph's College
St. Mary-of-the-Woods College
Saint Mary's College
Taylor University
Taylor University: Fort Wayne
Tri-State University
University of Evansville
University of Indianapolis
University of St. Francis
University of Southern Indiana
Valparaiso University
Vincennes University
Wabash College

Iowa
AIB College of Business
Allen College
Ashford University
Briar Cliff University

Buena Vista University
Central College
Clarke College
Coe College
Cornell College
Des Moines Area Community College
Dordt College
Drake University
Ellsworth Community College
Emmaus Bible College
Faith Baptist Bible College and Theological Seminary
Graceland University
Grand View College
Grinnell College
Hamilton College
    Cedar Rapids
Hawkeye Community College
Iowa State University
Iowa Wesleyan College
Kaplan University
Loras College
Luther College
Maharishi University of Management
Mercy College of Health Sciences
Morningside College
Mount Mercy College
North Iowa Area Community College
Northeast Iowa Community College
Northwestern College
St. Ambrose University
St. Luke's College
Simpson College
Southeastern Community College
    North Campus
Southwestern Community College
University of Dubuque
University of Iowa
University of Northern Iowa
Upper Iowa University
Vatterott College
Waldorf College
Wartburg College
Western Iowa Tech Community College
William Penn University

Kansas
Allen County Community College
Baker University
Barclay College
Barton County Community College
Benedictine College
Bethany College
Bethel College
Butler County Community College
Central Christian College of Kansas
Coffeyville Community College
Colby Community College
Cowley County Community College
Dodge City Community College
Donnelly College
Emporia State University
Garden City Community College
Hesston College
Highland Community College
Hutchinson Community College
Johnson County Community College
Kansas City Kansas Community College
Kansas State University
Kansas Wesleyan University
Labette Community College
Manhattan Area Technical College
Manhattan Christian College
McPherson College
MidAmerica Nazarene University
Neosho County Community College
Newman University
North Central Kansas Technical College
Ottawa University
Pittsburg State University
Pratt Community College
Seward County Community College

Southwestern College
Sterling College
Tabor College
University of Kansas
University of Kansas Medical Center
University of St. Mary
Washburn University of Topeka
Wichita State University

Kentucky
Asbury College
Ashland Community and Technical College
Beckfield College
Bellarmine University
Big Sandy Community and Technical College
Bluegrass Community and Technical College
Brescia University
Centre College
Clear Creek Baptist Bible College
Daymar College
Eastern Kentucky University
Georgetown College
Hopkinsville Community College
Jefferson Community College
Kentucky Christian University
Kentucky Mountain Bible College
Kentucky State University
Kentucky Wesleyan College
Louisville Technical Institute
Maysville Community College
Mid-Continent University
Midway College
Morehead State University
Murray State University
National College of Business & Technology
    Danville
    Florence
    Lexington
    Louisville
    Pikeville
    Richmond
Northern Kentucky University
Owensboro Community College
Pikeville College
St. Catharine College
Somerset Community College
Southeast Kentucky Community and Technical College
Spalding University
Spencerian College: Lexington
Thomas More College
Transylvania University
Union College
University of Kentucky
University of Louisville
University of the Cumberlands
Western Kentucky University

Louisiana
Bossier Parish Community College
Centenary College of Louisiana
Delgado Community College
Dillard University
Grambling State University
Louisiana State University
    Alexandria
Louisiana State University and Agricultural and Mechanical College
Louisiana State University Health Sciences Center
Louisiana Tech University
Loyola University New Orleans
New Orleans School of Urban Missions
Nicholls State University
Northwestern State University
Our Lady of Holy Cross College
St. Joseph Seminary College
Southeastern Louisiana University
Southern University and Agricultural and Mechanical College
Tulane University
University of Louisiana at Lafayette

University of Louisiana at Monroe
University of New Orleans
Xavier University of Louisiana

Maine
Bowdoin College
College of the Atlantic
Eastern Maine Community College
Husson College
Maine College of Art
Maine Maritime Academy
New England School of Communications
St. Joseph's College
Southern Maine Community College
Thomas College
Unity College
University of Maine
University of Maine
    Augusta
    Farmington
    Fort Kent
    Machias
    Presque Isle
University of New England
University of Southern Maine
Washington County Community College
York County Community College

Maryland
Allegany College of Maryland
Baltimore Hebrew University
Baltimore International College
Bowie State University
Capitol College
Carroll Community College
Cecil Community College
Chesapeake College
College of Notre Dame of Maryland
College of Southern Maryland
Columbia Union College
Coppin State University
Frederick Community College
Frostburg State University
Garrett College
Goucher College
Hood College
Johns Hopkins University
Johns Hopkins University: Peabody Conservatory of Music
Loyola College in Maryland
Maryland Institute College of Art
McDaniel College
Montgomery College
Mount St. Mary's University
Prince George's Community College
St. Mary's College of Maryland
Salisbury University
Towson University
University of Maryland
    Baltimore County
    College Park
    Eastern Shore
    University College
Villa Julie College
Washington Bible College
Washington College
Wor-Wic Community College

Massachusetts
American International College
Anna Maria College
Art Institute of Boston at Lesley University
Assumption College
Atlantic Union College
Babson College
Bay Path College
Becker College
Benjamin Franklin Institute of Technology
Bentley College
Berklee College of Music
Boston Architectural Center
Boston College

Boston University
Brandeis University
Bridgewater State College
Bristol Community College
Bunker Hill Community College
Cape Cod Community College
Clark University
College of the Holy Cross
Curry College
Dean College
Eastern Nazarene College
Elms College
Emerson College
Emmanuel College
Endicott College
Fisher College
Fitchburg State College
Framingham State College
Franklin W. Olin College of Engineering
Gordon College
Hampshire College
Hebrew College
Hellenic College/Holy Cross
Holyoke Community College
Laboure College
Lasell College
Lesley University
Marian Court College
Massachusetts College of Art
Massachusetts College of Liberal Arts
Massachusetts College of Pharmacy and Health Sciences
Massachusetts Maritime Academy
Merrimack College
Montserrat College of Art
Mount Holyoke College
New England Institute of Art
Newbury College
Nichols College
North Shore Community College
Northeastern University
Northern Essex Community College
Pine Manor College
Quinsigamond Community College
Regis College
Salem State College
Simmons College
Simon's Rock College of Bard
Smith College
Stonehill College
Suffolk University
Tufts University
University of Massachusetts
    Amherst
    Boston
    Dartmouth
    Lowell
Wentworth Institute of Technology
Western New England College
Westfield State College
Wheaton College
Wheelock College
Worcester Polytechnic Institute
Worcester State College

Michigan
Adrian College
Albion College
Alma College
Alpena Community College
Andrews University
Aquinas College
Baker College
    of Auburn Hills
    of Cadillac
    of Clinton Township
    of Flint
    of Jackson
    of Muskegon
    of Owosso
    of Port Huron
Bay de Noc Community College

Calvin College
Central Michigan University
Cleary University
College for Creative Studies
Concordia University
Cornerstone University
Davenport University
Delta College
Eastern Michigan University
Ferris State University
Finlandia University
Glen Oaks Community College
Gogebic Community College
Grace Bible College
Grand Rapids Community College
Grand Valley State University
Great Lakes Christian College
Hillsdale College
Hope College
Jackson Community College
Kalamazoo College
Kalamazoo Valley Community College
Kellogg Community College
Kendall College of Art and Design of Ferris State University
Kettering University
Kuyper College
Lake Superior State University
Lansing Community College
Lawrence Technological University
Macomb Community College
Madonna University
Marygrove College
Michigan State University
Michigan Technological University
Mid Michigan Community College
Monroe County Community College
Montcalm Community College
Mott Community College
Northern Michigan University
Northwestern Michigan College
Northwood University
Oakland Community College
Oakland University
Olivet College
Rochester College
Saginaw Valley State University
Schoolcraft College
Siena Heights University
Southwestern Michigan College
Spring Arbor University
University of Detroit Mercy
University of Michigan
University of Michigan
   Dearborn
   Flint
Walsh College of Accountancy and Business Administration
Washtenaw Community College
Wayne State University
Western Michigan University

Minnesota
Augsburg College
Bemidji State University
Bethany Lutheran College
Bethel University
Brown College
Carleton College
College of St. Benedict
College of St. Catherine
College of St. Scholastica
College of Visual Arts
Concordia College: Moorhead
Concordia University: St. Paul
Crossroads College
Crown College
Dakota County Technical College
Dunwoody College of Technology
Fond du Lac Tribal and Community College
Gustavus Adolphus College
Hamline University
Inver Hills Community College
Itasca Community College
Lake Superior College
Macalester College
Martin Luther College
Metropolitan State University
Minneapolis College of Art and Design
Minnesota State College - Southeast Technical
Minnesota State University
   Mankato
   Moorhead
National American University
   St. Paul
North Central University
North Hennepin Community College
Northland Community & Technical College
Northwestern College
Oak Hills Christian College
Pine Technical College
Rainy River Community College
Rasmussen College
   Mankato
   St. Cloud
St. Cloud State University
St. Cloud Technical College
St. John's University
St. Mary's University of Minnesota
St. Olaf College
Southwest Minnesota State University
University of Minnesota
   Crookston
   Duluth
   Morris
   Twin Cities
University of St. Thomas
Vermilion Community College
Winona State University

Mississippi
Alcorn State University
Belhaven College
Blue Mountain College
Coahoma Community College
Copiah-Lincoln Community College
Delta State University
East Central Community College
Hinds Community College
Holmes Community College
Itawamba Community College
Jackson State University
Jones County Junior College
Magnolia Bible College
Meridian Community College
Millsaps College
Mississippi College
Mississippi Delta Community College
Mississippi Gulf Coast Community College
   Jefferson Davis Campus
Mississippi State University
Mississippi Valley State University
Pearl River Community College
Rust College
Tougaloo College
University of Mississippi
University of Mississippi Medical Center
Wesley College
William Carey College

Missouri
Avila University
Blue River Community College
Calvary Bible College and Theological Seminary
Central Methodist University
Central Missouri State University
College of the Ozarks
Columbia College
Conception Seminary College
Cottey College
Crowder College
Culver-Stockton College
Deaconess College of Nursing
Drury University
East Central College
Evangel University
Fontbonne University
Hannibal-LaGrange College
Harris-Stowe State University
Jefferson College
Kansas City Art Institute
Lincoln University
Lindenwood University
Longview Community College
Maple Woods Community College
Maryville University of Saint Louis
Mineral Area College
Missouri Baptist University
Missouri Southern State University
Missouri State University
Missouri Technical School
Missouri Valley College
Missouri Western State University
Moberly Area Community College
North Central Missouri College
Northwest Missouri State University
Ozark Christian College
Park University
Penn Valley Community College
Rockhurst University
St. Charles Community College
St. Louis Christian College
St. Louis University
Southeast Missouri State University
Southwest Baptist University
State Fair Community College
Stephens College
Three Rivers Community College
Truman State University
University of Missouri
   Columbia
   Kansas City
   Rolla
   St. Louis
Washington University in St. Louis
Webster University
Westminster College
William Jewell College
William Woods University

Montana
Carroll College
Dawson Community College
Flathead Valley Community College
Miles Community College
Montana State University
   Billings
   Bozeman
Montana Tech of the University of Montana
Rocky Mountain College
Stone Child College
University of Great Falls
University of Montana: Missoula
University of Montana: Western

Nebraska
Bellevue University
Central Community College
Chadron State College
Clarkson College
College of Saint Mary
Concordia University
Creative Center
Creighton University
Dana College
Doane College
Grace University
Hastings College
Metropolitan Community College
Mid-Plains Community College Area
Midland Lutheran College
Nebraska Christian College
Nebraska Methodist College of Nursing and Allied Health
Nebraska Wesleyan University
Northeast Community College
Peru State College
Southeast Community College
   Lincoln Campus
Union College
University of Nebraska
   Kearney
   Lincoln
   Omaha
Wayne State College
Western Nebraska Community College
York College

Nevada
   of Las Vegas
DeVry University: Las Vegas
Sierra Nevada College
Truckee Meadows Community College
University of Nevada
   Las Vegas
Western Nevada Community College

New Hampshire
Chester College of New England
Colby-Sawyer College
Daniel Webster College
Franklin Pierce College
Keene State College
McIntosh College
New England College
Plymouth State University
Rivier College
St. Anselm College
Southern New Hampshire University
Thomas More College of Liberal Arts
University of New Hampshire
University of New Hampshire at Manchester

New Jersey
Berkeley College
Bloomfield College
Burlington County College
Caldwell College
Centenary College
The College of New Jersey
College of St. Elizabeth
Cumberland County College
Drew University
Fairleigh Dickinson University
   College at Florham
   Metropolitan Campus
Felician College
Georgian Court University
Kean University
Mercer County Community College
Monmouth University
Montclair State University
New Jersey Institute of Technology
Ocean County College
Passaic County Community College
Ramapo College of New Jersey
Raritan Valley Community College
Richard Stockton College of New Jersey
Rider University
Rowan University
Rutgers, The State University of New Jersey
   Camden Regional Campus
   New Brunswick/Piscataway Campus
   Newark Regional Campus
St. Peter's College
Salem Community College
Seton Hall University
Somerset Christian College
Stevens Institute of Technology
Union County College
Warren County Community College
William Paterson University of New Jersey

New Mexico
Albuquerque Technical-Vocational Institute
Clovis Community College
College of Santa Fe
College of the Southwest
Eastern New Mexico University

Academic scholarships

Mesalands Community College
New Mexico Highlands University
New Mexico Institute of Mining and Technology
New Mexico Military Institute Junior College
New Mexico State University
New Mexico State University
    Alamogordo
    Carlsbad
Northern New Mexico College
San Juan College
Southwestern Indian Polytechnic Institute
University of New Mexico
Western New Mexico University

New York
Adelphi University
Adirondack Community College
Albany College of Pharmacy
Alfred University
ASA Institute of Business and Computer Technology
Bard College
Berkeley College
Berkeley College of New York City
Briarcliffe College
Bryant & Stratton Business Institute
    Bryant & Stratton College: Albany
    Bryant & Stratton College: Syracuse
Canisius College
Cayuga County Community College
Cazenovia College
City University of New York
    Baruch College
    Brooklyn College
    City College
    College of Staten Island
    Hunter College
    John Jay College of Criminal Justice
    Lehman College
    Queens College
Clarkson University
College of Mount St. Vincent
College of New Rochelle
College of Saint Rose
College of Westchester
Columbia University
    School of General Studies
Columbia-Greene Community College
Concordia College
Cooper Union for the Advancement of Science and Art
Culinary Institute of America
Daemen College
DeVry Institute of Technology
    New York
Dominican College of Blauvelt
Dowling College
D'Youville College
Eastman School of Music of the University of Rochester
Elmira College
Eugene Lang College The New School for Liberal Arts
Finger Lakes Community College
Five Towns College
Fordham University
Fulton-Montgomery Community College
Hamilton College
Hartwick College
Hilbert College
Hobart and William Smith Colleges
Hofstra University
Houghton College
Iona College
Ithaca College
Jamestown Business College
Jamestown Community College
Jefferson Community College
Keuka College
King's College
Laboratory Institute of Merchandising
Le Moyne College

Long Island Business Institute
Manhattan College
Manhattan School of Music
Manhattanville College
Mannes College The New School for Music
Marist College
Marymount Manhattan College
Medaille College
Metropolitan College of New York
Molloy College
Monroe College
Mount St. Mary College
Nassau Community College
Nazareth College of Rochester
New York Institute of Technology
New York University
Niagara County Community College
Niagara University
Nyack College
Onondaga Community College
Pace University
Parsons The New School for Design
Paul Smith's College
Phillips Beth Israel School of Nursing
Polytechnic University
Pratt Institute
Rensselaer Polytechnic Institute
Roberts Wesleyan College
Rochester Institute of Technology
Russell Sage College
Sage College of Albany
St. Bonaventure University
St. Francis College
St. John Fisher College
St. John's University
St. Joseph's College
St. Joseph's College: Suffolk Campus
St. Lawrence University
St. Thomas Aquinas College
Schenectady County Community College
Siena College
State University of New York
    Albany
    Binghamton
    Buffalo
    College at Brockport
    College at Buffalo
    College at Cortland
    College at Fredonia
    College at Geneseo
    College at Old Westbury
    College at Oneonta
    College at Plattsburgh
    College at Potsdam
    College of Agriculture and Technology at Cobleskill
    College of Agriculture and Technology at Morrisville
    College of Environmental Science and Forestry
    College of Technology at Alfred
    Farmingdale
    Institute of Technology at Utica/Rome
    Maritime College
    New Paltz
    Oswego
    Purchase
    Stony Brook
Suffolk County Community College
Syracuse University
Tompkins-Cortland Community College
Trocaire College
Union College
University of Rochester
Utica College
Vaughn College of Aeronautics and Technology
Villa Maria College of Buffalo
Wagner College
Webb Institute
Wells College
Westchester Community College
Yeshiva Mikdash Melech

North Carolina
Alamance Community College
Appalachian State University
Asheville-Buncombe Technical Community College
Barton College
Beaufort County Community College
Belmont Abbey College
Blue Ridge Community College
Brevard College
Brunswick Community College
Campbell University
Cape Fear Community College
Carolinas College of Health Sciences
Carteret Community College
Catawba College
Catawba Valley Community College
Central Carolina Community College
Central Piedmont Community College
Chowan College
Coastal Carolina Community College
College of the Albemarle
Davidson College
Davidson County Community College
Duke University
Durham Technical Community College
East Carolina University
Elizabeth City State University
Elon University
Fayetteville State University
Forsyth Technical Community College
Gardner-Webb University
Gaston College
Greensboro College
Guilford College
Haywood Community College
High Point University
Isothermal Community College
James Sprunt Community College
Johnson C. Smith University
Johnston Community College
Lees-McRae College
Lenoir Community College
Lenoir-Rhyne College
Livingstone College
Mars Hill College
Martin Community College
McDowell Technical Community College
Meredith College
Methodist College
Montgomery Community College
Montreat College
Mount Olive College
Nash Community College
North Carolina Agricultural and Technical State University
North Carolina Central University
North Carolina School of the Arts
North Carolina State University
North Carolina Wesleyan College
Peace College
Pfeiffer University
Pitt Community College
Queens University of Charlotte
Randolph Community College
Richmond Community College
Roanoke Bible College
Roanoke-Chowan Community College
Rockingham Community College
Rowan-Cabarrus Community College
St. Andrews Presbyterian College
St. Augustine's College
Salem College
Sampson Community College
Sandhills Community College
Shaw University
Southeastern Community College
Stanly Community College
Surry Community College
University of North Carolina
    Asheville
    Chapel Hill
    Charlotte
    Greensboro
    Wilmington
Vance-Granville Community College
Wake Forest University
Wake Technical Community College
Warren Wilson College
Wayne Community College
Western Carolina University
Western Piedmont Community College
Wilkes Community College
Wilson Technical Community College
Wingate University
Winston-Salem State University

North Dakota
Aakers College: Fargo
Bismarck State College
Dickinson State University
Jamestown College
Lake Region State College
Mayville State University
Minot State University
Minot State University: Bottineau Campus
North Dakota State College of Science
North Dakota State University
Trinity Bible College
University of Mary
University of North Dakota
Valley City State University
Williston State College

Ohio
Antioch College
Art Academy of Cincinnati
Art Institute of Cincinnati
Ashland University
Baldwin-Wallace College
Bluffton University
Bowling Green State University
Bowling Green State University: Firelands College
Bryant & Stratton College
    Willoughby Hills
Bryant & Stratton College: Cleveland
Capital University
Case Western Reserve University
Cedarville University
Central Ohio Technical College
Central State University
Chatfield College
Cincinnati State Technical and Community College
Circleville Bible College
Cleveland Institute of Art
Cleveland State University
College of Mount St. Joseph
College of Wooster
Columbus College of Art and Design
Cuyahoga Community College
    Metropolitan Campus
David N. Myers University
Defiance College
Denison University
    Columbus
Edison State Community College
Franciscan University of Steubenville
Franklin University
God's Bible School and College
Heidelberg College
Hiram College
Hocking College
James A. Rhodes State College
Jefferson Community College
John Carroll University
Kent State University
Kent State University
    Ashtabula Regional Campus
    East Liverpool Regional Campus
    Salem Regional Campus
    Stark Campus
    Trumbull Campus

Academic scholarships

Tuscarawas Campus
Kenyon College
Kettering College of Medical Arts
Lake Erie College
Lakeland Community College
Lourdes College
Malone College
Marietta College
Marion Technical College
MedCentral College of Nursing
Mercy College of Northwest Ohio
Miami University
    Hamilton Campus
    Oxford Campus
Mount Union College
Mount Vernon Nazarene University
Muskingum College
Oberlin College
Ohio Dominican University
Ohio Northern University
Ohio State University
    Agricultural Technical Institute
    Columbus Campus
    Lima Campus
    Mansfield Campus
    Marion Campus
    Newark Campus
Ohio University
Ohio University
    Eastern Campus
Ohio Wesleyan University
Otterbein College
Owens Community College
    Toledo
Pontifical College Josephinum
Shawnee State University
Sinclair Community College
Southern State Community College
Stark State College of Technology
Tiffin University
Union Institute & University
University of Akron
University of Akron: Wayne College
University of Cincinnati
University of Cincinnati
    Clermont College
    Raymond Walters College
University of Dayton
University of Findlay
University of Northwestern Ohio
University of Rio Grande
University of Toledo
Urbana University
Ursuline College
Walsh University
Wilmington College
Wittenberg University
Wright State University
Wright State University: Lake Campus
Xavier University
Youngstown State University

Oklahoma
Cameron University
Carl Albert State College
Connors State College
East Central University
Mid-America Christian University
Northeastern Oklahoma Agricultural and Mechanical College
Northeastern State University
Northwestern Oklahoma State University
Oklahoma Baptist University
Oklahoma Christian University
Oklahoma City Community College
Oklahoma City University
Oklahoma Panhandle State University
Oklahoma State University
Oklahoma State University
    Oklahoma City
Oral Roberts University
Redlands Community College
Rogers State University
Rose State College
St. Gregory's University
Seminole State College
Southeastern Oklahoma State University
Southern Nazarene University
Southwestern Christian University
Southwestern Oklahoma State University
Tulsa Community College
University of Central Oklahoma
University of Oklahoma
University of Science and Arts of Oklahoma
University of Tulsa
Western Oklahoma State College

Oregon
Central Oregon Community College
Chemeketa Community College
Clackamas Community College
Clatsop Community College
Concordia University
Corban College
DeVry University: Portland
Eastern Oregon University
Eugene Bible College
George Fox University
Lewis & Clark College
Linfield College
Linn-Benton Community College
Marylhurst University
Mount Hood Community College
Multnomah Bible College
Northwest Christian College
Oregon Institute of Technology
Oregon State University
Pacific Northwest College of Art
Pacific University
Portland State University
Southern Oregon University
Treasure Valley Community College
Umpqua Community College
University of Oregon
University of Portland
Warner Pacific College
Western Oregon University
Willamette University

Pennsylvania
Albright College
Allegheny College
Alvernia College
Arcadia University
Baptist Bible College of Pennsylvania
Berks Technical Institute
Bloomsburg University of Pennsylvania
Bryn Athyn College of the New Church
Bryn Mawr College
Bucknell University
Bucks County Community College
Business Institute of Pennsylvania
Business Institute of Pennsylvania
    Meadville
Butler County Community College
Cabrini College
California University of Pennsylvania
Cambria-Rowe Business College
Carlow University
Carnegie Mellon University
Cedar Crest College
Central Pennsylvania College
Chatham College
Chestnut Hill College
Cheyney University of Pennsylvania
Clarion University of Pennsylvania
College Misericordia
Community College of Allegheny County
Community College of Beaver County
Delaware Valley College
DeSales University
    Ft. Washington
Dickinson College
Drexel University
Duquesne University
East Stroudsburg University of Pennsylvania
Edinboro University of Pennsylvania
Elizabethtown College
Franklin & Marshall College
Gannon University
Geneva College
Gettysburg College
Grove City College
Gwynedd-Mercy College
Harcum College
Harrisburg Area Community College
Holy Family University
Immaculata University
Indiana University of Pennsylvania
Johnson College
Juniata College
Keystone College
King's College
Kutztown University of Pennsylvania
La Roche College
La Salle University
Lackawanna College
Lafayette College
Lancaster Bible College
Lebanon Valley College
Lehigh Carbon Community College
Lehigh University
Lincoln University
Lock Haven University of Pennsylvania
Lycoming College
Manor College
Mansfield University of Pennsylvania
Marywood University
Mercyhurst College
Messiah College
Millersville University of Pennsylvania
Montgomery County Community College
Moore College of Art and Design
Moravian College
Mount Aloysius College
Muhlenberg College
Newport Business Institute
Northampton County Area Community College
Peirce College
Penn State
    Abington
    Altoona
    Beaver
    Berks
    Delaware County
    Dubois
    Erie, The Behrend College
    Fayette
    Harrisburg
    Hazleton
    Lehigh Valley
    McKeesport
    Mont Alto
    New Kensington
    Schuylkill - Capital College
    Shenango
    University Park
    Wilkes-Barre
    Worthington Scranton
    York
Pennsylvania College of Technology
Pennsylvania Highlands Community College
Pennsylvania Institute of Technology
Philadelphia Biblical University
Philadelphia University
Point Park University
Robert Morris University
Rosemont College
St. Francis University
St. Joseph's University
St. Vincent College
Seton Hill University
Shippensburg University of Pennsylvania
Slippery Rock University of Pennsylvania
Susquehanna University
Swarthmore College
Temple University
Thiel College
Thomas Jefferson University: College of Health Professions
Triangle Tech
    DuBois
    Pittsburgh
University of Pittsburgh
University of Pittsburgh
    Bradford
    Greensburg
    Johnstown
    Titusville
University of Scranton
University of the Arts
University of the Sciences in Philadelphia
Valley Forge Christian College
Valley Forge Military College
Vet Tech Institute
Villanova University
Washington and Jefferson College
Waynesburg College
Westminster College
Westmoreland County Community College
Widener University
Wilkes University
Wilson College
York College of Pennsylvania

Puerto Rico
Inter American University of Puerto Rico
    Aguadilla Campus
    Bayamon Campus
    San German Campus
Pontifical Catholic University of Puerto Rico
Turabo University
Universidad del Este
Universidad Metropolitana
Universidad Politecnica de Puerto Rico
University of Puerto Rico
    Bayamon University College
    Carolina Regional College
    Cayey University College
    Humacao
    Mayaguez
    Utuado
University of the Sacred Heart

Rhode Island
Johnson & Wales University
New England Institute of Technology
Providence College
Rhode Island College
Roger Williams University
Salve Regina University
University of Rhode Island

South Carolina
Aiken Technical College
Allen University
Anderson University
Charleston Southern University
The Citadel
Clemson University
Coastal Carolina University
Coker College
College of Charleston
Columbia College
Columbia International University
Converse College
Erskine College
Florence-Darlington Technical College
Francis Marion University
Furman University
Greenville Technical College
Lander University
Limestone College
Medical University of South Carolina
Morris College
Newberry College
North Greenville College
Piedmont Technical College

Presbyterian College
South Carolina State University
Southern Wesleyan University
Spartanburg Methodist College
Tri-County Technical College
University of South Carolina
University of South Carolina
    Beaufort
    Salkehatchie Regional Campus
    Sumter
    Union
    Upstate
Williamsburg Technical College
Winthrop University
Wofford College

South Dakota
Augustana College
Black Hills State University
Dakota State University
Dakota Wesleyan University
Kilian Community College
Mount Marty College
Northern State University
South Dakota School of Mines and Technology
South Dakota State University
Southeast Technical Institute
University of Sioux Falls
University of South Dakota

Tennessee
Aquinas College
Austin Peay State University
Belmont University
Bethel College
Bryan College
Carson-Newman College
Christian Brothers University
Columbia State Community College
Crichton College
Cumberland University
Dyersburg State Community College
East Tennessee State University
Fisk University
Free Will Baptist Bible College
Freed-Hardeman University
Hiwassee College
Jackson State Community College
Johnson Bible College
King College
Lambuth University
Lee University
Lincoln Memorial University
Lipscomb University
Martin Methodist College
Maryville College
Memphis College of Art
Middle Tennessee State University
Milligan College
Motlow State Community College
Nashville State Community College
    Tennessee
Northeast State Technical Community College
O'More College of Design
Pellissippi State Technical Community College
Rhodes College
Roane State Community College
Southern Adventist University
Southwest Tennessee Community College
Tennessee State University
Tennessee Technological University
Tennessee Temple University
Tennessee Wesleyan College
Trevecca Nazarene University
Tusculum College
Union University
University of Memphis
University of Tennessee
    Chattanooga
    Knoxville
    Martin
University of the South

Vanderbilt University
Volunteer State Community College
Walters State Community College

Texas
Abilene Christian University
Alvin Community College
Amarillo College
Angelina College
Angelo State University
Austin College
Austin Graduate School of Theology
Baylor University
Brazosport College
Central Texas College
Clarendon College
Coastal Bend College
College of the Mainland
Collin County Community College District
Commonwealth Institute of Funeral Service
Concordia University at Austin
Dallas Baptist University
    Irving
DeVry University: Houston
East Texas Baptist University
El Paso Community College
Frank Phillips College
Galveston College
Hardin-Simmons University
Hill College
Houston Baptist University
Howard College
Howard Payne University
Huston-Tillotson College
Jacksonville College
Jarvis Christian College
Kilgore College
Lee College
LeTourneau University
Lon Morris College
Lubbock Christian University
McMurry University
Midland College
Midwestern State University
Mountain View College
North Central Texas College
North Harris Montgomery Community College District
Northeast Texas Community College
Northwest Vista College
Northwood University: Texas Campus
Odessa College
Our Lady of the Lake University of San Antonio
Palo Alto College
Panola College
Paul Quinn College
Prairie View A&M University
Rice University
St. Edward's University
St. Mary's University
Sam Houston State University
San Jacinto College
    North
Schreiner University
South Plains College
South Texas College
Southern Methodist University
Southwestern Adventist University
Southwestern University
Stephen F. Austin State University
Sul Ross State University
Tarleton State University
Tarrant County College
Texarkana College
Texas A&M University
Texas A&M University
    Baylor College of Dentistry
    Galveston
    Kingsville
    Texarkana
Texas Christian University
Texas Lutheran University

Texas Southern University
Texas State Technical College
    Waco
    West Texas
Texas State University: San Marcos
Texas Tech University
Texas Wesleyan University
Trinity University
Trinity Valley Community College
Tyler Junior College
University of Dallas
University of Houston
University of Houston
    Clear Lake
    Downtown
    Victoria
University of Mary Hardin-Baylor
University of North Texas
University of St. Thomas
University of Texas
    Arlington
    Austin
    Dallas
    El Paso
    Medical Branch at Galveston
    Pan American
    of the Permian Basin
    San Antonio
    Tyler
University of the Incarnate Word
Vernon College
Victoria College
Wayland Baptist University
West Texas A&M University
Western Technical College
Western Texas College
Wharton County Junior College

Utah
Brigham Young University
College of Eastern Utah
Dixie State College of Utah
Everest College: Salt Lake City
LDS Business College
Salt Lake Community College
Snow College
Southern Utah University
University of Utah
Utah State University
Utah Valley State College
Weber State University
Westminster College

Vermont
Bennington College
Castleton State College
Champlain College
College of St. Joseph in Vermont
Goddard College
Green Mountain College
Johnson State College
Lyndon State College
Marlboro College
Norwich University
St. Michael's College
Southern Vermont College
Sterling College
University of Vermont
Vermont Technical College

Virginia
Averett University
Blue Ridge Community College
Bluefield College
Bridgewater College
Central Virginia Community College
Christendom College
Christopher Newport University
College of William and Mary
    Arlington
Eastern Mennonite University
ECPI College of Technology

Emory & Henry College
Ferrum College
George Mason University
Germanna Community College
Hampden-Sydney College
Hampton University
Hollins University
J. Sargeant Reynolds Community College
James Madison University
Jefferson College of Health Sciences
John Tyler Community College
Liberty University
Longwood University
Lynchburg College
Mary Baldwin College
Marymount University
Mountain Empire Community College
    Bluefield
    Charlottesville
    Danville
    Harrisonburg
    Lynchburg
    Martinsville
Norfolk State University
Northern Virginia Community College
Old Dominion University
Piedmont Virginia Community College
Radford University
Randolph-Macon College
Randolph-Macon Woman's College
Richard Bland College
Roanoke College
St. Paul's College
Shenandoah University
Southside Virginia Community College
Southwest Virginia Community College
Sweet Briar College
University of Mary Washington
University of Richmond
University of Virginia
University of Virginia's College at Wise
Virginia Commonwealth University
Virginia Intermont College
Virginia Military Institute
Virginia State University
Virginia Union University
Virginia Wesleyan College
Virginia Western Community College
Washington and Lee University
Wytheville Community College

Washington
Art Institute of Seattle
Bellevue Community College
Big Bend Community College
Central Washington University
Centralia College
City University
Clark College
Columbia Basin College
Cornish College of the Arts
Eastern Washington University
Everett Community College
Evergreen State College
Gonzaga University
Grays Harbor College
Heritage University
Northwest College of Art
Northwest University
Olympic College
Pacific Lutheran University
Peninsula College
Pierce College
Puget Sound Christian College
Saint Martin's University
Seattle Pacific University
Seattle University
Skagit Valley College
South Puget Sound Community College
South Seattle Community College
Tacoma Community College
Trinity Lutheran College

Academic scholarships

University of Puget Sound
University of Washington
Walla Walla College
Walla Walla Community College
Washington State University
Wenatchee Valley College
Western Washington University
Whatcom Community College
Whitman College
Whitworth College
Yakima Valley Community College

West Virginia
Alderson-Broaddus College
Bethany College
Bluefield State College
Concord University
Corinthian Schools: National Institute of Technology
Davis and Elkins College
Glenville State College
Marshall University
Mountain State University
Ohio Valley University
Potomac State College of West Virginia University
Salem International University
Shepherd University
University of Charleston
West Liberty State College
West Virginia State University
West Virginia University
West Virginia University at Parkersburg
West Virginia Wesleyan College
Wheeling Jesuit University

Wisconsin
Alverno College
Bellin College of Nursing
Beloit College
Cardinal Stritch University
Carroll College
Carthage College
College of Menominee Nation
Columbia College of Nursing
Concordia University Wisconsin
Edgewood College
Lakeland College
Lakeshore Technical College
Lawrence University
Maranatha Baptist Bible College
Marian College of Fond du Lac
Marquette University
Mid-State Technical College
Milwaukee Area Technical College
Milwaukee School of Engineering
Moraine Park Technical College
Mount Mary College
Northland College
Ripon College
St. Norbert College
Silver Lake College
University of Wisconsin
    Baraboo/Sauk County
    Eau Claire
    Green Bay
    La Crosse
    Madison
    Marshfield/Wood County
    Oshkosh
    Parkside
    Richland
    River Falls
    Rock County
    Stevens Point
    Stout
    Superior
    Waukesha
    Whitewater
Viterbo University
Waukesha County Technical College
Wisconsin Lutheran College

Wyoming
Casper College
Central Wyoming College
Eastern Wyoming College
Northwest College
Sheridan College
University of Wyoming
Western Wyoming Community College

Art scholarships

Alabama
Alabama State University
Athens State University
Auburn University at Montgomery
Birmingham-Southern College
Chattahoochee Valley Community College
Enterprise-Ozark Community College
Faulkner University
Huntingdon College
Jacksonville State University
Jefferson State Community College
Judson College
Lurleen B. Wallace Community College
Northeast Alabama Community College
Northwest-Shoals Community College
Snead State Community College
Talladega College
University of Alabama
University of Alabama
    Birmingham
    Huntsville
University of Mobile
University of Montevallo
University of North Alabama
University of South Alabama

Alaska
University of Alaska
    Fairbanks

Arizona
Arizona State University
Eastern Arizona College
Grand Canyon University
Northern Arizona University
Northland Pioneer College
Pima Community College
University of Arizona

Arkansas
Arkansas State University
Arkansas Tech University
Harding University
Henderson State University
Hendrix College
John Brown University
Lyon College
Southern Arkansas University
University of Arkansas
University of Arkansas
    Pine Bluff
University of the Ozarks
Williams Baptist College

California
Academy of Art University
Art Institute
    of California: Orange County
Biola University
California Baptist University
California College of the Arts
California Institute of the Arts
California Lutheran University
California Polytechnic State University: San Luis Obispo
California State Polytechnic University: Pomona
California State University
    Chico
    Long Beach
    Stanislaus
Chapman University
College of the Canyons
College of the Siskiyous
Concordia University
El Camino College
Irvine Valley College
Master's College
Mount St. Mary's College
Otis College of Art and Design
Pepperdine University
Point Loma Nazarene University
Riverside Community College
San Diego State University
San Francisco Art Institute
Santa Rosa Junior College
Sonoma State University
University of California
    Riverside
    San Diego
    Santa Cruz
University of La Verne
University of Redlands
University of Southern California
Westmont College
Whittier College

Colorado
Adams State College
Colorado State University
Colorado State University
    Pueblo
Fort Lewis College
Mesa State College
Metropolitan State College of Denver
Rocky Mountain College of Art & Design
University of Colorado
    Boulder
    Denver and Health Sciences Center
University of Denver
Western State College of Colorado

Connecticut
Albertus Magnus College
Fairfield University
Lyme Academy College of Fine Arts
Northwestern Connecticut Community College
Sacred Heart University
University of Connecticut
University of Hartford

Delaware
University of Delaware

District of Columbia
Corcoran College of Art and Design
George Washington University
Howard University

Florida
Barry University
Chipola College
Eckerd College
Edison College
Flagler College
Florida Agricultural and Mechanical University
Florida Community College at Jacksonville
Florida International University
Florida Keys Community College
Florida Southern College
Jacksonville University
Lake-Sumter Community College
Lynn University
Manatee Community College
Miami Dade College
North Florida Community College
Okaloosa-Walton College
Rollins College
St. Petersburg College
Santa Fe Community College
Seminole Community College
Stetson University
Tallahassee Community College
University of Florida
University of South Florida
University of Tampa
University of West Florida
Warner Southern College

Georgia
Andrew College
Augusta State University
Berry College
Brenau University
Brewton-Parker College
Clark Atlanta University
Columbus State University
Covenant College
Darton College
Emmanuel College
Emory University
Gainesville State College
Georgia College and State University
Georgia Highlands College
Georgia Southern University
Georgia State University
Kennesaw State University
LaGrange College
Mercer University
Middle Georgia College
Morehouse College
North Georgia College & State University
Oglethorpe University
Piedmont College
Reinhardt College
Savannah College of Art and Design
Shorter College
University of West Georgia
Valdosta State University
Wesleyan College
Young Harris College

Hawaii
Brigham Young University-Hawaii
Chaminade University of Honolulu
University of Hawaii
    Manoa

Idaho
Albertson College of Idaho
Idaho State University
Lewis-Clark State College
North Idaho College
Northwest Nazarene University

Illinois
American Academy of Art
Augustana College
Aurora University
Black Hawk College
Bradley University
Carl Sandburg College
College of DuPage
College of Lake County
Columbia College Chicago
DePaul University
Eastern Illinois University
Elgin Community College
Elmhurst College
Eureka College
Greenville College
Illinois College
Illinois Institute of Art-Schaumburg
Illinois State University
Illinois Wesleyan University
Knox College
Lake Forest College
Lewis University
MacMurray College
McKendree College
Millikin University
Monmouth College
North Central College
North Park University
Northeastern Illinois University
Oakton Community College
Olivet Nazarene University
Parkland College
Quincy University
Rend Lake College
Robert Morris College: Chicago
School of the Art Institute of Chicago
South Suburban College of Cook County
Southeastern Illinois College
Southern Illinois University Carbondale
Southern Illinois University Edwardsville
Springfield College in Illinois
Trinity Christian College
University of Illinois
    Chicago
    Springfield
    Urbana-Champaign
University of St. Francis
Waubonsee Community College
Western Illinois University
Wheaton College
William Rainey Harper College

Indiana
Bethel College
Grace College
Huntington University
Indiana State University
Indiana University
    Bloomington
    Southeast
Indiana Wesleyan University
Manchester College
Marian College
Oakland City University
St. Mary-of-the-Woods College
Taylor University
University of Evansville
University of Indianapolis
University of St. Francis
University of Southern Indiana
Valparaiso University
Vincennes University
Wabash College

Iowa
Ashford University
Briar Cliff University
Buena Vista University
Central College
Clarke College
Coe College
Cornell College
Dordt College
Drake University
Ellsworth Community College
Graceland University
Grand View College
Iowa State University
Iowa Wesleyan College
Kirkwood Community College
Luther College
Morningside College
Mount Mercy College
North Iowa Area Community College
Northwestern College
St. Ambrose University
Simpson College
University of Northern Iowa

Kansas
Allen County Community College
Baker University
Benedictine College
Bethany College
Bethel College
Coffeyville Community College
Emporia State University

Garden City Community College
Highland Community College
Kansas City Kansas Community College
Kansas State University
Kansas Wesleyan University
McPherson College
MidAmerica Nazarene University
Neosho County Community College
Pittsburg State University
Pratt Community College
Sterling College
Tabor College
University of Kansas
University of St. Mary
Washburn University of Topeka
Wichita State University

Kentucky
Bellarmine University
Brescia University
Eastern Kentucky University
Georgetown College
Jefferson Community College
Kentucky Wesleyan College
Louisville Technical Institute
Midway College
Morehead State University
Murray State University
Northern Kentucky University
Thomas More College
Transylvania University
University of Kentucky
University of Louisville
University of the Cumberlands
Western Kentucky University

Louisiana
Centenary College of Louisiana
Dillard University
Louisiana State University and Agricultural and Mechanical College
Louisiana Tech University
Loyola University New Orleans
Northwestern State University
University of Louisiana at Monroe
Xavier University of Louisiana

Maine
Maine College of Art
University of Maine
University of Maine
 Machias
 Presque Isle
York County Community College

Maryland
Bowie State University
Chesapeake College
College of Notre Dame of Maryland
Goucher College
Maryland Institute College of Art
Montgomery College
St. Mary's College of Maryland
Salisbury University
Towson University
University of Maryland
 Baltimore County
 College Park
 Eastern Shore
Villa Julie College

Massachusetts
Art Institute of Boston at Lesley University
Boston Architectural Center
Boston University
Bristol Community College
Cape Cod Community College
Emmanuel College
Endicott College
Holyoke Community College
Lesley University
Massachusetts College of Art
Massachusetts College of Liberal Arts
Montserrat College of Art
Salem State College
School of the Museum of Fine Arts
University of Massachusetts
 Amherst
 Lowell

Michigan
Adrian College
Albion College
Alma College
Alpena Community College
Aquinas College
Calvin College
Central Michigan University
College for Creative Studies
Concordia University
Eastern Michigan University
Ferris State University
Glen Oaks Community College
Gogebic Community College
Grand Rapids Community College
Grand Valley State University
Hillsdale College
Hope College
Jackson Community College
Kendall College of Art and Design of Ferris State University
Madonna University
Marygrove College
Michigan State University
Monroe County Community College
Mott Community College
Northern Michigan University
Northwestern Michigan College
Oakland University
Olivet College
Saginaw Valley State University
Siena Heights University
Southwestern Michigan College
Spring Arbor University
University of Michigan
University of Michigan
 Flint
Wayne State University
Western Michigan University

Minnesota
Bemidji State University
Bethany Lutheran College
Bethel University
College of St. Benedict
College of Visual Arts
Concordia University: St. Paul
Hamline University
Minneapolis College of Art and Design
Minnesota State University
 Mankato
Riverland Community College
St. Cloud State University
St. John's University
St. Mary's University of Minnesota
Southwest Minnesota State University
University of Minnesota
 Twin Cities
Winona State University

Mississippi
Belhaven College
Copiah-Lincoln Community College
Delta State University
Hinds Community College
Itawamba Community College
Meridian Community College
Millsaps College
Mississippi College
Mississippi State University
University of Mississippi
William Carey College

Missouri
Avila University
Central Missouri State University
College of the Ozarks
Columbia College
Cottey College
Crowder College
Culver-Stockton College
Drury University
East Central College
Evangel University
Fontbonne University
Hannibal-LaGrange College
Jefferson College
Kansas City Art Institute
Lindenwood University
Maryville University of Saint Louis
Mineral Area College
Missouri Southern State University
Missouri State University
Missouri Western State University
Moberly Area Community College
Northwest Missouri State University
Park University
Rockhurst University
St. Charles Community College
St. Louis University
Southeast Missouri State University
Southwest Baptist University
State Fair Community College
Truman State University
University of Missouri
 Columbia
 Kansas City
 St. Louis
Webster University
William Jewell College
William Woods University

Montana
Dawson Community College
Montana State University
 Billings
 Bozeman
Rocky Mountain College
University of Great Falls
University of Montana: Missoula
University of Montana: Western

Nebraska
Central Community College
Chadron State College
Creative Center
Creighton University
Dana College
Doane College
Hastings College
Mid-Plains Community College Area
Midland Lutheran College
Nebraska Wesleyan University
Peru State College
University of Nebraska
 Lincoln
 Omaha
Wayne State College
Western Nebraska Community College

Nevada
Sierra Nevada College
Truckee Meadows Community College
University of Nevada
 Las Vegas

New Hampshire
Chester College of New England
Colby-Sawyer College
Keene State College
New England College
University of New Hampshire

New Jersey
Caldwell College
Centenary College
The College of New Jersey
College of St. Elizabeth
Drew University
Fairleigh Dickinson University
 Metropolitan Campus
Georgian Court University
Kean University
Monmouth University
Montclair State University
New Jersey Institute of Technology
Richard Stockton College of New Jersey
Rider University
Rutgers, The State University of New Jersey
 Camden Regional Campus
 New Brunswick/Piscataway Campus
 Newark Regional Campus
Union County College

New Mexico
College of Santa Fe
Eastern New Mexico University
University of New Mexico

New York
Adelphi University
Alfred University
Canisius College
City University of New York
 Brooklyn College
 College of Staten Island
College of New Rochelle
College of Saint Rose
Daemen College
Hobart and William Smith Colleges
Hofstra University
Houghton College
Manhattanville College
Marymount Manhattan College
Molloy College
Nazareth College of Rochester
Nyack College
Pratt Institute
Rensselaer Polytechnic Institute
Roberts Wesleyan College
Rochester Institute of Technology
Sage College of Albany
St. Bonaventure University
St. John's University
School of Visual Arts
Siena College
State University of New York
 Binghamton
 College at Fredonia
 College at Geneseo
 College at Plattsburgh
 College at Potsdam
 New Paltz
 Purchase
Syracuse University
Villa Maria College of Buffalo

North Carolina
Appalachian State University
Brevard College
College of the Albemarle
Davidson College
Duke University
East Carolina University
Elon University
Greensboro College
Guilford College
High Point University
Mars Hill College
Meredith College
Montreat College
Mount Olive College
North Carolina School of the Arts
Queens University of Charlotte
Rockingham Community College
St. Augustine's College
Salem College
University of North Carolina
 Asheville
 Chapel Hill
 Greensboro

Wilmington
Wake Forest University
Warren Wilson College
Western Carolina University
Wilkes Community College
Wingate University

North Dakota
Dickinson State University
Jamestown College
Minot State University
North Dakota State University
Trinity Bible College
University of North Dakota

Ohio
Antioch College
Art Academy of Cincinnati
Art Institute of Cincinnati
Ashland University
Baldwin-Wallace College
Bluffton University
Bowling Green State University
Bowling Green State University: Firelands College
Capital University
Case Western Reserve University
Central State University
Cleveland Institute of Art
Cleveland State University
College of Mount St. Joseph
Columbus College of Art and Design
Cuyahoga Community College
   Metropolitan Campus
Hiram College
Kent State University
Kent State University
   Ashtabula Regional Campus
   East Liverpool Regional Campus
   Salem Regional Campus
   Stark Campus
   Trumbull Campus
   Tuscarawas Campus
Lake Erie College
Lakeland Community College
Lourdes College
Marietta College
Miami University
   Oxford Campus
Mount Union College
Muskingum College
Ohio Northern University
Ohio State University
   Columbus Campus
Ohio University
Ohio Wesleyan University
Otterbein College
Pontifical College Josephinum
School of Advertising Art
Southern State Community College
University of Akron
University of Akron: Wayne College
University of Cincinnati
University of Dayton
University of Toledo
Ursuline College
Wittenberg University
Wright State University
Xavier University

Oklahoma
Cameron University
Carl Albert State College
Northeastern Oklahoma Agricultural and Mechanical College
Northeastern State University
Northwestern Oklahoma State University
Oklahoma Christian University
Oklahoma City University
Oklahoma Panhandle State University
Oklahoma State University
Oral Roberts University
St. Gregory's University
Southeastern Oklahoma State University
Southwestern Oklahoma State University
Tulsa Community College
University of Central Oklahoma
University of Oklahoma
University of Science and Arts of Oklahoma
University of Tulsa
Western Oklahoma State College

Oregon
Art Institute of Portland
Clackamas Community College
Eastern Oregon University
George Fox University
Lane Community College
Linn-Benton Community College
Pacific Northwest College of Art
Pacific University
Portland State University
Southern Oregon University
Western Oregon University

Pennsylvania
Albright College
Arcadia University
Berks Technical Institute
Bloomsburg University of Pennsylvania
Bucknell University
Carnegie Mellon University
Cedar Crest College
Clarion University of Pennsylvania
Drexel University
East Stroudsburg University of Pennsylvania
Edinboro University of Pennsylvania
Elizabethtown College
Franklin & Marshall College
Indiana University of Pennsylvania
Juniata College
Keystone College
Kutztown University of Pennsylvania
Lehigh University
Lock Haven University of Pennsylvania
Lycoming College
Mansfield University of Pennsylvania
Marywood University
Mercyhurst College
Messiah College
Mount Aloysius College
Muhlenberg College
Northampton County Area Community College
Oakbridge Academy of Arts
Point Park University
Rosemont College
St. Joseph's University
Seton Hill University
Slippery Rock University of Pennsylvania
Temple University
University of the Arts
York College of Pennsylvania

Puerto Rico
Humacao Community College

Rhode Island
Rhode Island College
University of Rhode Island

South Carolina
Anderson University
Clemson University
Coastal Carolina University
Coker College
College of Charleston
Columbia College
Converse College
Erskine College
Furman University
Lander University
Limestone College
University of South Carolina
Winthrop University

South Dakota
Augustana College
Dakota State University
Dakota Wesleyan University
Mount Marty College
South Dakota State University
University of Sioux Falls
University of South Dakota

Tennessee
Austin Peay State University
Belmont University
Bryan College
Carson-Newman College
Cumberland University
East Tennessee State University
Free Will Baptist Bible College
Freed-Hardeman University
Jackson State Community College
King College
Lambuth University
Lipscomb University
Martin Methodist College
Maryville College
Memphis College of Art
Middle Tennessee State University
Milligan College
Motlow State Community College
Northeast State Technical Community College
Pellissippi State Technical Community College
Rhodes College
Roane State Community College
Southern Adventist University
Tennessee Technological University
Union University
University of Memphis
University of Tennessee
   Chattanooga
   Knoxville
   Martin
Volunteer State Community College

Texas
Abilene Christian University
Angelina College
Austin College
Baylor University
Brazosport College
Clarendon College
College of the Mainland
Collin County Community College District
Galveston College
Hardin-Simmons University
Houston Baptist University
Howard Payne University
Huston-Tillotson College
Kilgore College
Lee College
Lubbock Christian University
McMurry University
Midwestern State University
Northeast Texas Community College
Our Lady of the Lake University of San Antonio
Panola College
Rice University
Richland College
St. Edward's University
San Jacinto College
   North
Schreiner University
Southern Methodist University
Southwestern University
Stephen F. Austin State University
Tarleton State University
Texas A&M University
Texas Christian University
Texas Lutheran University
Texas State University: San Marcos
Texas Tech University
Tyler Junior College
University of Dallas
University of Houston
University of Mary Hardin-Baylor
University of Texas
   Arlington
   Austin
   El Paso
   Pan American
   San Antonio
   Tyler
University of the Incarnate Word
Victoria College
Wayland Baptist University
West Texas A&M University
Western Technical College
Western Texas College

Utah
Brigham Young University
College of Eastern Utah
Dixie State College of Utah
Salt Lake Community College
Southern Utah University
University of Utah
Utah State University
Utah Valley State College
Weber State University
Westminster College

Vermont
Castleton State College
Goddard College
Green Mountain College
Marlboro College
University of Vermont

Virginia
Averett University
Bluefield College
Emory & Henry College
Hollins University
James Madison University
Longwood University
Lynchburg College
Old Dominion University
Randolph-Macon Woman's College
Sweet Briar College
University of Mary Washington
University of Richmond
University of Virginia's College at Wise
Virginia Commonwealth University
Virginia Intermont College
Virginia Polytechnic Institute and State University
Virginia State University
Virginia Wesleyan College

Washington
Art Institute of Seattle
Big Bend Community College
Central Washington University
Centralia College
Clark College
Everett Community College
Grays Harbor College
Northwest College of Art
Northwest University
Pacific Lutheran University
Seattle Pacific University
Trinity Lutheran College
University of Puget Sound
University of Washington
Washington State University
Western Washington University
Whitman College
Whitworth College

West Virginia
Bethany College
Concord University
Corinthian Schools: National Institute of Technology
Davis and Elkins College
Glenville State College
Marshall University

Shepherd University
University of Charleston
West Liberty State College
West Virginia University
West Virginia Wesleyan College

Wisconsin
Cardinal Stritch University
Carroll College
Carthage College
Edgewood College
Mount Mary College
Ripon College
St. Norbert College
Silver Lake College
University of Wisconsin
    Baraboo/Sauk County
    Eau Claire
    Green Bay
    La Crosse
    Oshkosh
    Parkside
    Richland
    River Falls
    Superior
    Whitewater
Viterbo University
Wisconsin Lutheran College

Wyoming
Casper College
Central Wyoming College
Eastern Wyoming College
University of Wyoming
Western Wyoming Community College

Athletic scholarships

Archery

Arizona
Dine College M,W

California
College of the Redwoods M

Texas
Texas A&M University W

Badminton

California
Fresno City College M,W

New Jersey
New Jersey Institute of Technology M

Texas
Texas Southmost College M,W

Wisconsin
Milwaukee Area Technical College M

Baseball

Alabama
Alabama Agricultural and Mechanical University M
Alabama State University M
Auburn University M
Auburn University at Montgomery M
Bevill State Community College M
Birmingham-Southern College M
Central Alabama Community College M
Chattahoochee Valley Community College M
Concordia College M
Enterprise-Ozark Community College M
Faulkner State Community College M
Gadsden State Community College M
George C. Wallace State Community College
    George C. Wallace Community College at Dothan M
    Selma M
Jacksonville State University M
Jefferson Davis Community College M
Jefferson State Community College M
Lawson State Community College M
Lurleen B. Wallace Community College M
Miles College M
Northwest-Shoals Community College M
Samford University M
Shelton State Community College M
Snead State Community College M
Southern Union State Community College M
Spring Hill College M
Troy University M
Tuskegee University M
University of Alabama M
University of Alabama
    Birmingham M
    Huntsville M
University of Mobile M
University of Montevallo M
University of North Alabama M
University of South Alabama M
University of West Alabama M
Wallace State Community College at Hanceville M

Arizona
Arizona State University M
Arizona Western College M
Central Arizona College M
Cochise College M
Eastern Arizona College M
Gateway Community College M
Glendale Community College M
Grand Canyon University M
Pima Community College M
Scottsdale Community College M
South Mountain Community College M
University of Arizona M
Yavapai College M

Arkansas
Arkansas State University M
Arkansas Tech University M
Harding University M
Henderson State University M
Lyon College M
Ouachita Baptist University M
Southern Arkansas University M
University of Arkansas M
University of Arkansas
    Fort Smith M
    Little Rock M
University of Central Arkansas M
Williams Baptist College M

California
Azusa Pacific University M
Biola University M
California Baptist University M
California Polytechnic State University: San Luis Obispo M
California State Polytechnic University: Pomona M
California State University
    Chico M
    Fresno M
    Fullerton M
    Long Beach M
    Los Angeles M
    Northridge M
    Sacramento M
    San Bernardino M
    Stanislaus M
Concordia University M
Fresno City College M
Fresno Pacific University M
Grossmont Community College M
Loyola Marymount University M
Master's College M
Patten University M
Pepperdine University M
Point Loma Nazarene University M
St. Mary's College of California M
San Diego State University M
San Jose State University M
Santa Clara University M
Sonoma State University M
Stanford University M
University of California
    Berkeley M
    Davis M
    Irvine M
    Los Angeles M
    Riverside M
    Santa Barbara M
University of San Diego M
University of San Francisco M
University of Southern California M
University of the Pacific M
Vanguard University of Southern California M
Westmont College M
Yuba Community College District M

Colorado
Arapahoe Community College M
Colorado Christian University M
Colorado Northwestern Community College M
Colorado School of Mines M
Mesa State College M
Metropolitan State College of Denver M
Northeastern Junior College M
Otero Junior College M
Regis University M
Trinidad State Junior College M
University of Denver M
University of Northern Colorado M

Connecticut
Central Connecticut State University M
Fairfield University M
Post University M
Quinnipiac University M
University of Bridgeport M
University of Connecticut M
University of Hartford M
University of New Haven M

Delaware
Delaware State University M
Delaware Technical and Community College
    Owens Campus M
    Stanton/Wilmington Campus M
University of Delaware M
Wilmington College M

District of Columbia
George Washington University M
Georgetown University M
Howard University M

Florida
Barry University M
Bethune-Cookman College M
Brevard Community College M
Broward Community College M
Central Florida Community College M
Chipola College M
Daytona Beach Community College M
Eckerd College M
Edward Waters College M
Embry-Riddle Aeronautical University M
Flagler College M
Florida Atlantic University M
Florida College M
Florida Community College at Jacksonville M
Florida Gulf Coast University M
Florida Institute of Technology M
Florida International University M
Florida Memorial University M
Florida Southern College M
Florida State University M
Gulf Coast Community College M
Hillsborough Community College M
Indian River Community College M
Jacksonville University M
Lake City Community College M
Lake-Sumter Community College M
Lynn University M
Manatee Community College M
Miami Dade College M
North Florida Community College M
Northwood University
    Florida Campus M
Nova Southeastern University M
Okaloosa-Walton College M
Palm Beach Community College M
Pasco-Hernando Community College M
Pensacola Junior College M
Polk Community College M
Rollins College M
St. Johns River Community College M
St. Leo University M
St. Petersburg College M
St. Thomas University M
Santa Fe Community College M
Stetson University M
Tallahassee Community College M
University of Central Florida M
University of Florida M
University of Miami M
University of North Florida M
University of South Florida M
University of Tampa M
University of West Florida M
Warner Southern College M
Webber International University M

Georgia
Abraham Baldwin Agricultural College M
Albany State University M
Andrew College M
Armstrong Atlantic State University M
Augusta State University M
Berry College M
Brewton-Parker College M
Columbus State University M
Darton College M
Emmanuel College M
Georgia College and State University M
Georgia Institute of Technology M
Georgia Perimeter College M
Georgia Southern University M
Georgia Southwestern State University M
Georgia State University M
Gordon College M
Kennesaw State University M
Mercer University M
Middle Georgia College M
Paine College M
Reinhardt College M
Savannah State University M
Shorter College M
Southern Polytechnic State University M
Thomas University M
University of Georgia M
University of West Georgia M
Valdosta State University M
Young Harris College M

Hawaii
Hawaii Pacific University M
University of Hawaii
    Manoa M

Idaho
Albertson College of Idaho M
College of Southern Idaho M
Lewis-Clark State College M
Northwest Nazarene University M

Illinois
Black Hawk College M
Bradley University M
Carl Sandburg College M
Chicago State University M
College of Lake County M
Danville Area Community College M
Elgin Community College M
Highland Community College M
Illinois Central College M
Illinois Eastern Community Colleges
    Lincoln Trail College M
    Olney Central College M
    Wabash Valley College M
Illinois Institute of Technology M
Illinois State University M
John A. Logan College M
Judson College M
Kankakee Community College M
Kaskaskia College M
Kishwaukee College M

Lake Land College M
Lewis and Clark Community College M
Lewis University M
McHenry County College M
McKendree College M
Moraine Valley Community College M
Morton College M
Northwestern University M
Olivet Nazarene University M
Parkland College M
Quincy University M
Rend Lake College M
Robert Morris College: Chicago M
St. Xavier University M
Sauk Valley Community College M
South Suburban College of Cook County M
Southeastern Illinois College M
Southern Illinois University Carbondale M
Southern Illinois University Edwardsville M
Southwestern Illinois College M
Springfield College in Illinois M
Trinity Christian College M
Trinity International University M
University of Illinois
    Chicago M
    Urbana-Champaign M
University of St. Francis M
Western Illinois University M

Indiana
Ancilla College M
Ball State University M
Bethel College M
Butler University M
Calumet College of St. Joseph M
Goshen College M
Grace College M
Huntington University M
Indiana Institute of Technology M
Indiana State University M
Indiana University
    Bloomington M
    Southeast M
Indiana University-Purdue University Fort Wayne M
Indiana Wesleyan University M
Marian College M
Oakland City University M
Purdue University M
St. Joseph's College M
Taylor University M
University of Evansville M
University of Indianapolis M
University of Notre Dame M
University of St. Francis M
University of Southern Indiana M
Valparaiso University M
Vincennes University M

Iowa
Ashford University M
Briar Cliff University M
Clinton Community College M
Des Moines Area Community College M
Dordt College M
Ellsworth Community College M
Graceland University M
Grand View College M
Indian Hills Community College M
Iowa Central Community College M
Iowa Lakes Community College M
Iowa Wesleyan College M
Iowa Western Community College M
Kirkwood Community College M
Morningside College M
Muscatine Community College M
North Iowa Area Community College M
Northwestern College M
St. Ambrose University M
Scott Community College M
Southwestern Community College M
University of Iowa M

University of Northern Iowa M
Waldorf College M
William Penn University M

Kansas
Allen County Community College M
Baker University M
Barton County Community College M
Benedictine College M
Bethany College M
Brown Mackie College M
Butler County Community College M
Central Christian College of Kansas M
Cloud County Community College M
Coffeyville Community College M
Colby Community College M
Cowley County Community College M
Dodge City Community College M
Emporia State University M
Fort Scott Community College M
Friends University M
Garden City Community College M
Hesston College M
Highland Community College M
Hutchinson Community College M
Johnson County Community College M
Kansas City Kansas Community College M
Kansas State University M
Kansas Wesleyan University M
Labette Community College M
MidAmerica Nazarene University M
Neosho County Community College M
Newman University M
Ottawa University M
Pittsburg State University M
Pratt Community College M
Seward County Community College M
Sterling College M
Tabor College M
University of Kansas M
University of St. Mary M
Washburn University of Topeka M
Wichita State University M

Kentucky
Alice Lloyd College M
Bellarmine University M
Brescia University M
Campbellsville University M
Eastern Kentucky University M
Georgetown College M
Kentucky State University M
Kentucky Wesleyan College M
Lindsey Wilson College M
Mid-Continent University M
Morehead State University M
Murray State University M
Northern Kentucky University M
Pikeville College M
St. Catharine College M
Spalding University M
Union College M
University of Kentucky M
University of Louisville M
University of the Cumberlands M
Western Kentucky University M

Louisiana
Bossier Parish Community College M
Centenary College of Louisiana M
Delgado Community College M
Grambling State University M
Louisiana State University
    Shreveport M
Louisiana State University and Agricultural and Mechanical College M
Louisiana Tech University M
Nicholls State University M
Northwestern State University M
Southeastern Louisiana University M
Southern University and Agricultural and Mechanical College M

University of Louisiana at Lafayette M
University of Louisiana at Monroe M
University of New Orleans M

Maine
University of Maine M

Maryland
Anne Arundel Community College M
Chesapeake College M
College of Southern Maryland M
Columbia Union College M
Community College of Baltimore County M
Coppin State University M
Garrett College M
Hagerstown Community College M
Mount St. Mary's University M
Prince George's Community College M
Towson University M
University of Maryland
    Baltimore County M
    College Park M
    Eastern Shore M

Massachusetts
American International College M
Dean College M
Northeastern University M
Stonehill College M
University of Massachusetts
    Amherst M

Michigan
Aquinas College M
Central Michigan University M
Concordia University M
Eastern Michigan University M
Glen Oaks Community College M
Grand Rapids Community College M
Grand Valley State University M
Henry Ford Community College M
Hillsdale College M
Kalamazoo Valley Community College M
Kellogg Community College M
Lake Michigan College M
Macomb Community College M
Madonna University M
Michigan State University M
Northwood University M
Oakland University M
Rochester College M
Saginaw Valley State University M
Siena Heights University M
Spring Arbor University M
University of Michigan M

Minnesota
Concordia University: St. Paul M
Minnesota State University
    Mankato M
St. Cloud State University M
Southwest Minnesota State University M
University of Minnesota
    Crookston M
    Duluth M
    Twin Cities M
Winona State University M

Mississippi
Alcorn State University M
Belhaven College M
Copiah-Lincoln Community College M
Delta State University M
Hinds Community College M
Holmes Community College M
Itawamba Community College M
Jackson State University M
Jones County Junior College M
Meridian Community College M
Mississippi Gulf Coast Community College
    Jefferson Davis Campus M
Mississippi State University M
Mississippi Valley State University M

Southwest Mississippi Community College M
University of Mississippi M
University of Southern Mississippi M
William Carey College M

Missouri
Avila University M
Central Methodist University M
Central Missouri State University M
College of the Ozarks M
Crowder College M
Culver-Stockton College M
Drury University M
Evangel University M
Hannibal-LaGrange College M
Harris-Stowe State University M
Jefferson College M
Lincoln University M
Longview Community College M
Maple Woods Community College M
Mineral Area College M
Missouri Baptist University M
Missouri Southern State University M
Missouri State University M
Missouri Valley College M
Missouri Western State University M
North Central Missouri College M
Park University M
Research College of Nursing M
Rockhurst University M
St. Charles Community College M
St. Louis University M
Southeast Missouri State University M
Southwest Baptist University M
Three Rivers Community College M
Truman State University M
University of Missouri
    Columbia M
    Rolla M
    St. Louis M
William Jewell College M
William Woods University M

Montana
Miles Community College M

Nebraska
Bellevue University M
Concordia University M
Creighton University M
Dana College M
Doane College M
Hastings College M
Mid-Plains Community College Area M
Midland Lutheran College M
Peru State College M
University of Nebraska
    Kearney M
    Lincoln M
    Omaha M
Wayne State College M
Western Nebraska Community College M
York College M

Nevada
Community College of Southern Nevada M
University of Nevada
    Las Vegas M
    Reno M

New Hampshire
Franklin Pierce College M
Southern New Hampshire University M

New Jersey
Bloomfield College M
Brookdale Community College M
Caldwell College M
Fairleigh Dickinson University
    Metropolitan Campus M
Mercer County Community College M
Monmouth University M
New Jersey Institute of Technology M

Rider University M
Rutgers, The State University of New Jersey
    New Brunswick/Piscataway Campus M
St. Peter's College M
Salem Community College M
Seton Hall University M
Sussex County Community College M

New Mexico
College of the Southwest M
Eastern New Mexico University M
New Mexico Highlands University M
New Mexico Junior College M
New Mexico Military Institute Junior College M
New Mexico State University M
University of New Mexico M

New York
Adelphi University M
Canisius College M
City University of New York
    Queens College M
College of Saint Rose M
Concordia College M
Dominican College of Blauvelt M
Dowling College M
Fordham University M
Globe Institute of Technology M
Hofstra University M
Iona College M
Le Moyne College M
Manhattan College M
Marist College M
Mercy College M
Molloy College M
Monroe Community College M
New York Institute of Technology M
Niagara University M
Nyack College M
Pace University M
St. Bonaventure University M
St. Francis College M
St. John's University M
St. Thomas Aquinas College M
Siena College M
State University of New York
    Albany M
    Binghamton M
    Buffalo M
    Stony Brook M
Wagner College M

North Carolina
Appalachian State University M
Barton College M
Belmont Abbey College M
Brevard College M
Campbell University M
Catawba College M
Davidson College M
Duke University M
East Carolina University M
Elon University M
Gardner-Webb University M
High Point University M
Lenoir Community College M
Lenoir-Rhyne College M
Louisburg College M
Mars Hill College M
Montreat College M
Mount Olive College M
North Carolina Agricultural and Technical State
    University M
North Carolina State University M
Pfeiffer University M
Pitt Community College M
St. Andrews Presbyterian College M
St. Augustine's College M
Shaw University M
Southeastern Community College M
University of North Carolina
    Asheville M
    Chapel Hill M
    Charlotte M
    Greensboro M
    Pembroke M
    Wilmington M
Wake Forest University M
Western Carolina University M
Wingate University M

North Dakota
Dickinson State University M
Jamestown College M
Mayville State University M
Minot State University M
Minot State University: Bottineau Campus M
North Dakota State University M
University of Mary M
University of North Dakota M
Valley City State University M
Williston State College M

Ohio
Ashland University M
Bowling Green State University M
Cedarville University M
Clark State Community College M
Cleveland State University M
Kent State University M
Lakeland Community College M
Malone College M
Miami University
    Oxford Campus M
Mount Vernon Nazarene University M
Ohio Dominican University M
Ohio State University
    Columbus Campus M
Ohio University M
Shawnee State University M
Sinclair Community College M
University of Akron M
University of Cincinnati M
University of Dayton M
University of Findlay M
University of Rio Grande M
University of Toledo M
Urbana University M
Walsh University M
Wright State University M
Xavier University M
Youngstown State University M

Oklahoma
Bacone College M
Cameron University M
Carl Albert State College M
Connors State College M
East Central University M
Eastern Oklahoma State College M
Northeastern Oklahoma Agricultural and
    Mechanical College M
Northeastern State University M
Northwestern Oklahoma State University M
Oklahoma Baptist University M
Oklahoma City University M
Oklahoma State University M
Oklahoma Wesleyan University M
Oral Roberts University M
Redlands Community College M
Rose State College M
St. Gregory's University M
Seminole State College M
Southeastern Oklahoma State University M
Southern Nazarene University M
Southwestern Oklahoma State University M
University of Central Oklahoma M
University of Oklahoma M
University of Science and Arts of Oklahoma M
Western Oklahoma State College M

Oregon
Blue Mountain Community College M
Chemeketa Community College M
Clackamas Community College M
Concordia University M
Corban University M
Eastern Oregon University M
Lane Community College M
Linn-Benton Community College M
Mount Hood Community College M
Oregon Institute of Technology M
Oregon State University M
Portland State University M
Southwestern Oregon Community College M
Treasure Valley Community College M
University of Portland M

Pennsylvania
Bloomsburg University of Pennsylvania M
California University of Pennsylvania M
Drexel University M
Duquesne University M
East Stroudsburg University of Pennsylvania M
Gannon University M
Geneva College M
Indiana University of Pennsylvania M
Kutztown University of Pennsylvania M
La Salle University M
Lackawanna College M
Lehigh University M
Lock Haven University of Pennsylvania M
Mansfield University of Pennsylvania M
Mercyhurst College M
Millersville University of Pennsylvania M
Penn State
    University Park M
Philadelphia University M
Point Park University M
St. Joseph's University M
Seton Hill University M
Shippensburg University of Pennsylvania M
Slippery Rock University of Pennsylvania M
Temple University M
University of Pittsburgh M
University of the Sciences in Philadelphia M
Villanova University M
West Chester University of Pennsylvania M

Puerto Rico
Inter American University of Puerto Rico
    Aguadilla Campus M
    Bayamon Campus M
    Ponce Campus M,W
    San German Campus M
Turabo University M
Universidad Metropolitana M,W
Universidad Politecnica de Puerto Rico M
University of Puerto Rico
    Carolina Regional College M
    Cayey University College M
    Humacao M
    Mayaguez M
    Utuado M

Rhode Island
Bryant University M
Community College of Rhode Island M
University of Rhode Island M

South Carolina
Anderson University M
Charleston Southern University M
The Citadel M
Claflin University M
Clemson University M
Coastal Carolina University M
Coker College M
College of Charleston M
Erskine College M
Francis Marion University M
Furman University M
Lander University M
Limestone College M
Morris College M
Newberry College M
North Greenville College M
Presbyterian College M
Southern Wesleyan University M
Spartanburg Methodist College M
University of South Carolina M
University of South Carolina
    Aiken M
    Upstate M
Voorhees College M
Winthrop University M
Wofford College M

South Dakota
Augustana College M
Dakota State University M
Dakota Wesleyan University M
Mount Marty College M
South Dakota State University M
University of Sioux Falls M
University of South Dakota M

Tennessee
Austin Peay State University M
Belmont University M
Bethel College M
Bryan College M
Carson-Newman College M
Chattanooga State Technical Community
    College M
Christian Brothers University M
Cleveland State Community College M
Columbia State Community College M
Crichton College M
Cumberland University M
Dyersburg State Community College M
East Tennessee State University M
Freed-Hardeman University M
Hiwassee College M
Jackson State Community College M
King College M
Lambuth University M
Lee University M
LeMoyne-Owen College M
Lincoln Memorial University M
Lipscomb University M
Middle Tennessee State University M
Milligan College M
Motlow State Community College M
Roane State Community College M
Southwest Tennessee Community College M
Tennessee Technological University M
Tennessee Temple University M
Tennessee Wesleyan College M
Trevecca Nazarene University M
Tusculum College M
Union University M
University of Memphis M
University of Tennessee
    Knoxville M
    Martin M
Vanderbilt University M
Volunteer State Community College M
Walters State Community College M

Texas
Abilene Christian University M
Alvin Community College M
Angelina College M
Angelo State University M
Baylor University M
Blinn College M
Clarendon College M
Dallas Baptist University M
El Paso Community College M
Frank Phillips College M
Galveston College M
Grayson County College M
Hill College M
Houston Baptist University M
Howard College M
Jarvis Christian College M
Lamar University M
Laredo Community College M
Lon Morris College M

Lubbock Christian University M
McLennan Community College M
North Central Texas College M
Northwood University: Texas Campus M
Odessa College M
Paris Junior College M
Prairie View A&M University M
Ranger College M
Rice University M
St. Edward's University M
St. Mary's University M
Sam Houston State University M
San Jacinto College
    North M
Tarleton State University M
Texas A&M University M
Texas A&M University
    Kingsville M
Texas Christian University M
Texas Southern University M
Texas Southmost College M
Texas State University: San Marcos M
Texas Tech University M
University of Houston M
University of Texas
    Arlington M
    Austin M
    Pan American M
    San Antonio M
University of the Incarnate Word M
Vernon College M
Wayland Baptist University M
West Texas A&M University M
Western Texas College M
Wharton County Junior College M
Wiley College M

Utah
Brigham Young University M
College of Eastern Utah M
Dixie State College of Utah M
Salt Lake Community College M
Snow College M
Southern Utah University M
University of Utah M
Utah Valley State College M

Vermont
University of Vermont M

Virginia
Bluefield College M
College of William and Mary M
George Mason University M
James Madison University M
Liberty University M
Longwood University M
Norfolk State University M
Old Dominion University M
Radford University M
St. Paul's College M
University of Richmond M
University of Virginia M
University of Virginia's College at Wise M
Virginia Commonwealth University M
Virginia Intermont College M
Virginia Military Institute M
Virginia Polytechnic Institute and State University M
Virginia State University M

Washington
Big Bend Community College M
Central Washington University M
Centralia College M
Edmonds Community College M
Everett Community College M
Gonzaga University M
Grays Harbor College M
Green River Community College M
Lower Columbia College M
Olympic College M
Pierce College M

Saint Martin's University M
Shoreline Community College M
Skagit Valley College M
Spokane Community College M
Tacoma Community College M
University of Washington M
Walla Walla Community College M
Washington State University M
Wenatchee Valley College M
Yakima Valley Community College M

West Virginia
Alderson-Broaddus College M
Bluefield State College M
Concord University M
Davis and Elkins College M
Marshall University M
Ohio Valley University M
Potomac State College of West Virginia University M
Salem International University M
Shepherd University M
University of Charleston M
West Liberty State College M
West Virginia State University M
West Virginia University M
West Virginia University Institute of Technology M
West Virginia Wesleyan College M

Wisconsin
Cardinal Stritch University M
Milwaukee Area Technical College M,W
University of Wisconsin
    Milwaukee M
    Parkside M
Viterbo University M

Basketball

Alabama
Alabama Agricultural and Mechanical University M,W
Alabama State University M,W
Auburn University M,W
Auburn University at Montgomery M,W
Bevill State Community College M,W
Birmingham-Southern College M,W
Concordia College M,W
Enterprise-Ozark Community College M,W
Faulkner State Community College M,W
Faulkner University M
Gadsden State Community College M,W
George C. Wallace State Community College Selma M,W
Jacksonville State University M,W
Jefferson Davis Community College M
Judson College W
Lawson State Community College M,W
Lurleen B. Wallace Community College M,W
Marion Military Institute M
Miles College M
Northwest-Shoals Community College M,W
Samford University M,W
Shelton State Community College M,W
Snead State Community College M,W
Southern Union State Community College M,W
Spring Hill College M,W
Troy University M,W
Tuskegee University M,W
University of Alabama M,W
University of Alabama
    Birmingham M,W
    Huntsville M,W
University of Mobile M,W
University of Montevallo M,W
University of North Alabama M,W
University of South Alabama M,W
University of West Alabama M,W
Wallace State Community College at Hanceville M,W

Alaska
University of Alaska
    Anchorage M,W
    Fairbanks M,W

Arizona
Arizona State University M,W
Arizona Western College M
Central Arizona College M,W
Cochise College M,W
Eastern Arizona College M,W
Glendale Community College M,W
Grand Canyon University M,W
Mesa Community College M,W
Northern Arizona University M,W
Northland Pioneer College M,W
Pima Community College M,W
Scottsdale Community College M,W
South Mountain Community College M,W
University of Arizona M,W
Yavapai College M,W

Arkansas
Arkansas State University M,W
Arkansas Tech University M,W
Ecclesia College M,W
Harding University M,W
Henderson State University M,W
John Brown University M,W
Lyon College M,W
North Arkansas College M,W
Ouachita Baptist University M,W
Philander Smith College M,W
Southern Arkansas University M,W
University of Arkansas M,W
University of Arkansas
    Fort Smith M,W
    Little Rock M
    Monticello M,W
    Pine Bluff M,W
University of Central Arkansas M,W
Williams Baptist College M,W

California
Azusa Pacific University M,W
Bethany University M,W
Biola University M,W
California Baptist University M,W
California Polytechnic State University: San Luis Obispo M,W
California State Polytechnic University: Pomona M,W
California State University
    Bakersfield M
    Chico M,W
    Fresno M,W
    Fullerton M,W
    Long Beach M,W
    Los Angeles M,W
    Northridge M,W
    Sacramento M,W
    San Bernardino M,W
    Stanislaus M,W
Concordia University M,W
Dominican University of California M,W
Fresno City College M,W
Fresno Pacific University M,W
Grossmont Community College M,W
Holy Names University M,W
Hope International University M,W
Humboldt State University M,W
Loyola Marymount University M,W
Master's College M,W
Notre Dame de Namur University M,W
Patten University M,W
Pepperdine University M,W
Point Loma Nazarene University M,W
St. Mary's College of California M,W
San Diego Christian College M,W
San Diego State University M,W
San Jose State University M,W
Santa Clara University M,W

Sonoma State University M,W
Stanford University M,W
University of California
    Berkeley M,W
    Davis M,W
    Irvine M,W
    Los Angeles M,W
    Riverside M,W
    Santa Barbara M,W
University of San Diego M,W
University of San Francisco M,W
University of Southern California M,W
University of the Pacific M,W
Vanguard University of Southern California M,W
Westmont College M,W
William Jessup University M,W
Yuba Community College District M,W

Colorado
Adams State College M,W
Colorado Christian University M,W
Colorado Northwestern Community College M,W
Colorado School of Mines M,W
Colorado State University M,W
Colorado State University
    Pueblo M,W
Fort Lewis College M,W
Mesa State College M,W
Metropolitan State College of Denver M,W
Northeastern Junior College M,W
Otero Junior College M,W
Regis University M,W
Trinidad State Junior College M
University of Colorado
    Boulder M,W
    Colorado Springs M,W
University of Denver M,W
University of Northern Colorado M,W
Western State College of Colorado M,W

Connecticut
Central Connecticut State University M,W
Fairfield University M,W
Post University M,W
Quinnipiac University M,W
Sacred Heart University M,W
Southern Connecticut State University M,W
University of Bridgeport M,W
University of Connecticut M,W
University of Hartford M,W
University of New Haven M,W

Delaware
Delaware State University M,W
Delaware Technical and Community College Stanton/Wilmington Campus M,W
Goldey-Beacom College M,W
University of Delaware M,W
Wilmington College M,W

District of Columbia
American University M,W
George Washington University M,W
Georgetown University M,W
Howard University M,W
University of the District of Columbia M,W

Florida
Barry University M,W
Bethune-Cookman College M,W
Brevard Community College M,W
Broward Community College M,W
Central Florida Community College M,W
Chipola College M,W
Daytona Beach Community College M,W
Eckerd College M,W
Edward Waters College M,W
Embry-Riddle Aeronautical University M
Flagler College M
Florida Agricultural and Mechanical University M

Florida Atlantic University M,W
Florida College M
Florida Community College at Jacksonville M,W
Florida Gulf Coast University M,W
Florida Institute of Technology M,W
Florida International University M,W
Florida Memorial University M,W
Florida Southern College M,W
Florida State University M,W
Gulf Coast Community College M,W
Hillsborough Community College M,W
Indian River Community College M,W
Jacksonville University M,W
Lynn University M,W
Manatee Community College M
Miami Dade College M,W
North Florida Community College W
Nova Southeastern University M,W
Okaloosa-Walton College M,W
Palm Beach Community College M,W
Pasco-Hernando Community College M
Pensacola Junior College M,W
Polk Community College M
Rollins College M,W
St. Johns River Community College M
St. Leo University M,W
St. Petersburg College M,W
Santa Fe Community College M,W
Stetson University M,W
Tallahassee Community College M,W
University of Central Florida M,W
University of Florida M,W
University of Miami M,W
University of North Florida M,W
University of South Florida M,W
University of Tampa M,W
University of West Florida M,W
Warner Southern College M,W
Webber International University M,W

Georgia
Abraham Baldwin Agricultural College M
Albany State University M,W
Armstrong Atlantic State University M,W
Atlanta Metropolitan College M,W
Augusta State University M,W
Berry College M,W
Brenau University W
Brewton-Parker College M,W
Clark Atlanta University M,W
Clayton State University M,W
Columbus State University M,W
Covenant College M,W
Darton College W
Emmanuel College M,W
Fort Valley State University M,W
Georgia College and State University M,W
Georgia Institute of Technology M,W
Georgia Perimeter College M,W
Georgia Southern University M,W
Georgia Southwestern State University M,W
Georgia State University M,W
Kennesaw State University M,W
Mercer University M,W
Middle Georgia College M,W
Morehouse College M
North Georgia College & State University M,W
Paine College M,W
Reinhardt College M,W
Savannah State University M,W
Shorter College M,W
Southern Polytechnic State University M,W
Truett-McConnell College M,W
University of Georgia M,W
University of West Georgia M,W
Valdosta State University M,W

Hawaii
Brigham Young University-Hawaii M
Chaminade University of Honolulu M
Hawaii Pacific University M
University of Hawaii
 Hilo M
 Manoa M,W

Idaho
Albertson College of Idaho M,W
Boise State University M,W
College of Southern Idaho M,W
Idaho State University M,W
Lewis-Clark State College M,W
North Idaho College M,W
Northwest Nazarene University M,W
University of Idaho M,W

Illinois
Black Hawk College M,W
Black Hawk College
 East Campus M,W
Bradley University M,W
Carl Sandburg College M,W
Chicago State University M,W
City Colleges of Chicago
 Kennedy-King College M,W
 Malcolm X College M,W
 Wright College M,W
College of Lake County M,W
Danville Area Community College M,W
DePaul University M,W
Eastern Illinois University M,W
Elgin Community College M,W
Highland Community College M,W
Illinois Central College M,W
Illinois Eastern Community Colleges
 Lincoln Trail College M,W
 Olney Central College M,W
 Wabash Valley College M,W
Illinois Institute of Technology M,W
Illinois State University M,W
John A. Logan College M,W
Judson College M,W
Kankakee Community College M,W
Kaskaskia College M,W
Kishwaukee College M,W
Lake Land College M,W
Lewis and Clark Community College M,W
Lewis University M,W
Lincoln Land Community College M,W
Loyola University of Chicago M,W
McHenry County College M,W
McKendree College M,W
Moraine Valley Community College M,W
Morton College M,W
Northwestern University M,W
Olivet Nazarene University M,W
Parkland College M,W
Quincy University M,W
Rend Lake College M,W
Robert Morris College: Chicago M,W
St. Xavier University M
Sauk Valley Community College M,W
South Suburban College of Cook County M,W
Southeastern Illinois College M,W
Southern Illinois University Carbondale M,W
Southern Illinois University Edwardsville M,W
Southwestern Illinois College M,W
Trinity Christian College M,W
Trinity International University M,W
University of Illinois
 Chicago M,W
 Springfield M,W
 Urbana-Champaign M,W
University of St. Francis M,W
Waubonsee Community College M,W
Western Illinois University M,W

Indiana
Ancilla College M,W
Ball State University M,W
Bethel College M,W
Butler University M,W
Calumet College of St. Joseph M,W
Goshen College M,W
Grace College M,W
Huntington University M,W
Indiana Institute of Technology M,W
Indiana State University M,W
Indiana University
 Bloomington M,W
 South Bend M,W
 Southeast M,W
Indiana University-Purdue University Fort Wayne M,W
Indiana University-Purdue University Indianapolis M,W
Indiana Wesleyan University M,W
Marian College M,W
Oakland City University M,W
Purdue University M,W
Purdue University
 Calumet M,W
St. Joseph's College M,W
St. Mary-of-the-Woods College W
Taylor University M,W
Taylor University: Fort Wayne M,W
University of Evansville M,W
University of Indianapolis M,W
University of Notre Dame M,W
University of St. Francis M,W
University of Southern Indiana M,W
Valparaiso University M,W
Vincennes University M,W

Iowa
Ashford University M,W
Briar Cliff University M,W
Clinton Community College M
Des Moines Area Community College M,W
Dordt College M,W
Drake University M,W
Ellsworth Community College M,W
Graceland University M,W
Grand View College M,W
Indian Hills Community College M
Iowa Central Community College M,W
Iowa Lakes Community College M,W
Iowa State University M,W
Iowa Wesleyan College M,W
Iowa Western Community College M,W
Kirkwood Community College M,W
Marshalltown Community College M,W
Morningside College M,W
Muscatine Community College M
North Iowa Area Community College M,W
Northwestern College M,W
St. Ambrose University M,W
Scott Community College M
Southwestern Community College M,W
University of Iowa M,W
University of Northern Iowa M,W
Waldorf College M,W
William Penn University M,W

Kansas
Allen County Community College M,W
Baker University M,W
Barton County Community College M,W
Benedictine College M,W
Bethany College M,W
Bethel College M,W
Brown Mackie College M,W
Butler County Community College M,W
Central Christian College of Kansas M,W
Cloud County Community College M,W
Coffeyville Community College M,W
Colby Community College M,W
Cowley County Community College M,W
Dodge City Community College M,W
Emporia State University M,W
Fort Hays State University M,W
Fort Scott Community College M,W
Friends University M,W
Garden City Community College M,W
Hesston College M,W
Highland Community College M,W
Hutchinson Community College M,W
Johnson County Community College M,W
Kansas City Kansas Community College M,W
Kansas State University M,W
Kansas Wesleyan University M,W
Labette Community College M,W
McPherson College M,W
MidAmerica Nazarene University M,W
Neosho County Community College M,W
Newman University M,W
Ottawa University M,W
Pittsburg State University M,W
Pratt Community College M,W
Seward County Community College M,W
Southwestern College M,W
Sterling College M,W
Tabor College M,W
University of Kansas M,W
University of St. Mary M,W
Washburn University of Topeka M,W
Wichita State University M,W

Kentucky
Alice Lloyd College M,W
Asbury College M,W
Bellarmine University M,W
Brescia University M,W
Campbellsville University M,W
Eastern Kentucky University M,W
Georgetown College M,W
Kentucky State University M,W
Kentucky Wesleyan College M,W
Lindsey Wilson College M,W
Midway College W
Morehead State University M,W
Murray State University M,W
Northern Kentucky University M,W
Pikeville College M,W
St. Catharine College M,W
Spalding University M,W
Union College M,W
University of Kentucky M,W
University of Louisville M,W
University of the Cumberlands M,W
Western Kentucky University M,W

Louisiana
Bossier Parish Community College M
Centenary College of Louisiana M,W
Delgado Community College M
Dillard University M,W
Grambling State University M,W
Louisiana State University and Agricultural and Mechanical College M,W
Louisiana Tech University M,W
Loyola University New Orleans M,W
Nicholls State University M,W
Northwestern State University M,W
Southeastern Louisiana University M,W
Southern University
 New Orleans M,W
Southern University and Agricultural and Mechanical College M,W
University of Louisiana at Lafayette M,W
University of Louisiana at Monroe M,W
University of New Orleans M,W
Xavier University of Louisiana M,W

Maine
Unity College M
University of Maine M,W
University of Maine
 Augusta M,W

Maryland
Allegany College of Maryland M,W
Anne Arundel Community College M,W
Bowie State University M,W
Chesapeake College M,W
College of Southern Maryland M
Columbia Union College M,W
Community College of Baltimore County M,W
Coppin State University M,W
Garrett College M,W

Hagerstown Community College M,W
Howard Community College M,W
Loyola College in Maryland M,W
Morgan State University M,W
Mount St. Mary's University M,W
Prince George's Community College M,W
Towson University M,W
University of Maryland
    Baltimore County M,W
    College Park M,W
    Eastern Shore M,W

Massachusetts
American International College M,W
Assumption College M,W
Bentley College M,W
Boston College M,W
Boston University M,W
College of the Holy Cross M,W
Dean College M,W
Massasoit Community College M
Merrimack College M,W
Mount Ida College M
Northeastern University M,W
Roxbury Community College M
Stonehill College M,W
University of Massachusetts
    Amherst M,W
    Lowell M,W

Michigan
Alpena Community College M,W
Aquinas College M,W
Central Michigan University M,W
Concordia University M,W
Cornerstone University M,W
Delta College M,W
Eastern Michigan University M,W
Ferris State University M,W
Glen Oaks Community College M,W
Gogebic Community College M,W
Grand Rapids Community College M,W
Grand Valley State University M,W
Henry Ford Community College M,W
Hillsdale College M,W
Kalamazoo Valley Community College M,W
Kellogg Community College M,W
Lake Michigan College M,W
Lake Superior State University M,W
Lansing Community College M,W
Macomb Community College M,W
Madonna University M,W
Michigan State University M,W
Michigan Technological University M,W
Mott Community College M,W
Northern Michigan University M,W
Northwood University M,W
Oakland Community College M,W
Oakland University M,W
Rochester College M,W
Saginaw Valley State University M,W
Schoolcraft College M,W
Siena Heights University M,W
Spring Arbor University M,W
University of Detroit Mercy M,W
University of Michigan M,W
University of Michigan
    Dearborn M,W
Wayne State University M,W
Western Michigan University M,W

Minnesota
Bemidji State University M,W
Concordia University: St. Paul M,W
Minnesota State University
    Mankato M,W
    Moorhead M,W
St. Cloud State University M,W
Southwest Minnesota State University M,W
University of Minnesota
    Crookston M,W
    Duluth M,W

Twin Cities M,W
Winona State University M,W

Mississippi
Alcorn State University M,W
Belhaven College M,W
Coahoma Community College M,W
Copiah-Lincoln Community College M,W
Delta State University M,W
East Central Community College M,W
Hinds Community College M,W
Holmes Community College M,W
Itawamba Community College M,W
Jackson State University M,W
Jones County Junior College M,W
Meridian Community College M,W
Mississippi Gulf Coast Community College
    Jefferson Davis Campus M,W
Mississippi State University M,W
Mississippi Valley State University M,W
Southwest Mississippi Community College M,W
Tougaloo College M,W
University of Mississippi M,W
University of Southern Mississippi M,W
William Carey College M,W

Missouri
Avila University M,W
Central Methodist University M,W
Central Missouri State University M,W
College of the Ozarks M,W
Columbia College M,W
Cottey College W
Crowder College W
Culver-Stockton College M,W
Drury University M,W
Evangel University M,W
Hannibal-LaGrange College M,W
Harris-Stowe State University M,W
Jefferson College W
Lincoln University M,W
Mineral Area College M,W
Missouri Baptist University M,W
Missouri Southern State University M,W
Missouri State University M,W
Missouri Valley College M,W
Missouri Western State University M,W
Moberly Area Community College M,W
North Central Missouri College M,W
Park University M,W
Penn Valley Community College M
Research College of Nursing M,W
Rockhurst University M,W
St. Louis University M,W
Southeast Missouri State University M,W
Southwest Baptist University M,W
St. Louis Community College
    Meramec M,W
State Fair Community College M,W
Stephens College W
Three Rivers Community College M,W
Truman State University M,W
University of Missouri
    Columbia M,W
    Kansas City M,W
    Rolla M,W
    St. Louis M,W
William Jewell College M,W
William Woods University W

Montana
Carroll College M,W
Dawson Community College M,W
Miles Community College M,W
Montana State University
    Billings M,W
    Bozeman M,W
Montana Tech of the University of Montana M,W
Rocky Mountain College M,W
University of Great Falls M,W

University of Montana: Missoula M,W
University of Montana: Western M,W

Nebraska
Bellevue University M
Central Community College M
Chadron State College M,W
College of Saint Mary W
Concordia University M,W
Creighton University M,W
Dana College M,W
Doane College M,W
Hastings College M,W
Mid-Plains Community College Area M,W
Midland Lutheran College M,W
Nebraska College of Technical Agriculture M,W
Northeast Community College M,W
Peru State College M,W
University of Nebraska
    Kearney M,W
    Lincoln M,W
    Omaha M,W
Wayne State College M,W
Western Nebraska Community College M,W
York College M,W

Nevada
University of Nevada
    Las Vegas M,W
    Reno M,W

New Hampshire
Franklin Pierce College M,W
St. Anselm College M,W
Southern New Hampshire University M,W
University of New Hampshire M,W

New Jersey
Bloomfield College M,W
Brookdale Community College M,W
Caldwell College M,W
Essex County College M,W
Fairleigh Dickinson University
    Metropolitan Campus M,W
Felician College M,W
Georgian Court University W
Mercer County Community College M,W
Monmouth University M,W
New Jersey Institute of Technology M,W
Ocean County College M
Rider University M,W
Rutgers, The State University of New Jersey
    New Brunswick/Piscataway Campus M,W
St. Peter's College M,W
Salem Community College W
Seton Hall University M,W
Union County College W

New Mexico
Eastern New Mexico University M,W
New Mexico Highlands University M,W
New Mexico Junior College M,W
New Mexico Military Institute Junior College M
New Mexico State University M,W
University of New Mexico M,W
Western New Mexico University M,W

New York
Adelphi University M,W
Canisius College M,W
City University of New York
    Queens College M,W
Colgate University M,W
College of Saint Rose M,W
Concordia College M,W
Daemen College M,W
Dominican College of Blauvelt M,W
Dowling College M,W
Fordham University M,W
Genesee Community College M,W
Globe Institute of Technology M,W
Hofstra University M,W
Houghton College M,W

Iona College M,W
Le Moyne College M,W
Manhattan College M,W
Marist College M,W
Mercy College M,W
Molloy College M,W
Monroe College M
Monroe Community College M
New York Institute of Technology M
Niagara County Community College M,W
Niagara University M,W
Nyack College M,W
Pace University M,W
Roberts Wesleyan College M,W
St. Bonaventure University M,W
St. Francis College M,W
St. John's University M,W
St. Thomas Aquinas College M,W
Siena College M,W
State University of New York
    Albany M,W
    Binghamton M,W
    Buffalo M,W
    College of Technology at Alfred M,W
    Stony Brook M,W
Syracuse University M,W
Wagner College M,W

North Carolina
Appalachian State University M,W
Barton College M,W
Belmont Abbey College M,W
Brevard College M,W
Campbell University M,W
Catawba College M,W
Davidson College M,W
Duke University M,W
East Carolina University M,W
Elizabeth City State University M,W
Elon University M,W
Fayetteville State University M,W
Gardner-Webb University M,W
High Point University M,W
Johnson C. Smith University M,W
Lees-McRae College M,W
Lenoir Community College M
Lenoir-Rhyne College M,W
Livingstone College M,W
Louisburg College M,W
Mars Hill College M,W
Montreat College M,W
Mount Olive College M,W
North Carolina Agricultural and Technical State University M,W
North Carolina Central University M,W
North Carolina State University M,W
Pfeiffer University M,W
Queens University of Charlotte M,W
St. Andrews Presbyterian College M,W
St. Augustine's College M,W
Shaw University M,W
University of North Carolina
    Asheville M,W
    Chapel Hill M,W
    Charlotte M,W
    Greensboro M,W
    Pembroke M,W
    Wilmington M,W
Wake Forest University M,W
Western Carolina University M,W
Wingate University M,W
Winston-Salem State University M,W

North Dakota
Bismarck State College M,W
Dickinson State University M,W
Jamestown College M,W
Lake Region State College M,W
Mayville State University M,W
Minot State University M,W
Minot State University: Bottineau Campus M,W
North Dakota State College of Science M,W

North Dakota State University M,W
University of Mary M,W
University of North Dakota M,W
Valley City State University M,W
Williston State College M,W

Ohio
Ashland University M,W
Bowling Green State University M,W
Cedarville University M,W
Central State University M,W
Cincinnati State Technical and Community College M,W
Clark State Community College M,W
Cleveland State University M,W
Columbus State Community College M,W
Edison State Community College M,W
Kent State University M,W
Lakeland Community College M,W
Malone College M,W
Miami University
    Oxford Campus M,W
Mount Vernon Nazarene University M,W
Ohio Dominican University M,W
Ohio State University
    Columbus Campus M,W
Ohio University M,W
Owens Community College
    Toledo M,W
Shawnee State University M,W
Sinclair Community College M,W
Southern State Community College M,W
University of Akron M,W
University of Cincinnati M,W
University of Dayton M,W
University of Findlay M,W
University of Rio Grande M,W
University of Toledo M,W
Urbana University M,W
Ursuline College W
Walsh University M,W
Wright State University M,W
Xavier University M,W
Youngstown State University M,W

Oklahoma
Bacone College M,W
Cameron University M,W
Carl Albert State College M,W
Connors State College M,W
East Central University M,W
Eastern Oklahoma State College M,W
Northeastern Oklahoma Agricultural and Mechanical College M,W
Northeastern State University M,W
Northwestern Oklahoma State University M,W
Oklahoma Baptist University M,W
Oklahoma Christian University M,W
Oklahoma City University M,W
Oklahoma Panhandle State University M,W
Oklahoma State University M,W
Oklahoma Wesleyan University M,W
Oral Roberts University M,W
Redlands Community College M,W
Rose State College M,W
St. Gregory's University M,W
Seminole State College M,W
Southeastern Oklahoma State University M,W
Southern Nazarene University M,W
Southwestern Oklahoma State University M,W
University of Central Oklahoma M,W
University of Oklahoma M,W
University of Science and Arts of Oklahoma M,W
University of Tulsa M,W
Western Oklahoma State College M,W

Oregon
Blue Mountain Community College M,W
Chemeketa Community College M,W
Clackamas Community College M,W
Concordia University M,W
Corban College M,W
Eastern Oregon University M,W
Lane Community College M,W
Linn-Benton Community College M,W
Mount Hood Community College M,W
Northwest Christian College M,W
Oregon Institute of Technology M,W
Oregon State University M,W
Portland Community College M,W
Portland State University M,W
Southern Oregon University M,W
Southwestern Oregon Community College M,W
Treasure Valley Community College M,W
University of Oregon M,W
University of Portland M,W
Warner Pacific College M,W

Pennsylvania
Bloomsburg University of Pennsylvania M,W
Bucknell University M,W
California University of Pennsylvania M,W
Carlow University W
Cheyney University of Pennsylvania M,W
Community College of Beaver County M
Drexel University M,W
Duquesne University M,W
East Stroudsburg University of Pennsylvania M,W
Edinboro University of Pennsylvania M,W
Gannon University M,W
Geneva College M,W
Harcum College M,W
Holy Family University M,W
Indiana University of Pennsylvania M,W
Kutztown University of Pennsylvania M,W
La Salle University M,W
Lackawanna College M,W
Lehigh University M,W
Lock Haven University of Pennsylvania M,W
Mansfield University of Pennsylvania M,W
Mercyhurst College M,W
Millersville University of Pennsylvania M,W
Penn State
    University Park M,W
Philadelphia University M,W
Point Park University M,W
Robert Morris University M,W
St. Francis University M,W
St. Joseph's University M,W
Seton Hill University M,W
Shippensburg University of Pennsylvania M,W
Slippery Rock University of Pennsylvania M,W
Temple University M,W
University of Pittsburgh M,W
University of Pittsburgh
    Johnstown M,W
    Titusville M,W
University of the Sciences in Philadelphia M,W
Valley Forge Military College M
Villanova University M,W
West Chester University of Pennsylvania M,W
Westminster College M,W

Puerto Rico
Bayamon Central University M,W
Inter American University of Puerto Rico
    Aguadilla Campus M,W
    Bayamon Campus M,W
    Fajardo Campus M
    Guayama Campus M,W
    Ponce Campus M,W
    San German Campus M,W
Turabo University M,W
Universidad del Este M,W
Universidad Metropolitana M,W
University of Puerto Rico
    Bayamon University College M,W
    Carolina Regional College M,W
    Cayey University College M,W
    Humacao M,W
    Mayaguez M,W
    Ponce M,W
    Utuado M,W
University of the Sacred Heart M

Rhode Island
Bryant University M,W
Community College of Rhode Island M,W
Providence College M,W
University of Rhode Island M,W

South Carolina
Aiken Technical College M
Allen University M
Anderson University M,W
Charleston Southern University M,W
The Citadel M
Claflin University M,W
Clemson University M,W
Coastal Carolina University M,W
Coker College M,W
College of Charleston M,W
Columbia College W
Converse College W
Erskine College M,W
Francis Marion University M,W
Furman University M,W
Lander University M,W
Limestone College M,W
Morris College M,W
Newberry College M,W
North Greenville College M,W
Presbyterian College M,W
South Carolina State University M,W
Southern Wesleyan University M,W
Spartanburg Methodist College M,W
University of South Carolina M,W
University of South Carolina
    Aiken M,W
    Upstate M,W
Voorhees College M,W
Winthrop University M,W
Wofford College M,W

South Dakota
Augustana College M,W
Black Hills State University M,W
Dakota State University M,W
Dakota Wesleyan University M,W
Mount Marty College M,W
Northern State University M,W
South Dakota School of Mines and Technology M,W
South Dakota State University M,W
University of Sioux Falls M,W
University of South Dakota M,W

Tennessee
Austin Peay State University M,W
Belmont University M,W
Bethel College M,W
Bryan College M,W
Carson-Newman College M,W
Chattanooga State Technical Community College M,W
Christian Brothers University M,W
Cleveland State Community College M,W
Columbia State Community College M,W
Crichton College M
Cumberland University M,W
Dyersburg State Community College M,W
East Tennessee State University M,W
Freed-Hardeman University M,W
Hiwassee College M,W
Jackson State Community College M,W
King College M,W
Lambuth University M,W
Lee University M,W
LeMoyne-Owen College M,W
Lincoln Memorial University M,W
Lipscomb University M,W
Martin Methodist College M,W
Middle Tennessee State University M,W
Milligan College M,W
Motlow State Community College M,W
Roane State Community College M,W
Southwest Tennessee Community College M,W
Tennessee State University M,W
Tennessee Technological University M,W
Tennessee Temple University M,W
Tennessee Wesleyan College M,W
Trevecca Nazarene University M,W
Tusculum College M,W
Union University M,W
University of Memphis M,W
University of Tennessee
    Chattanooga M,W
    Knoxville M,W
    Martin M,W
Vanderbilt University M,W
Volunteer State Community College M,W
Walters State Community College M,W

Texas
Abilene Christian University M,W
Angelina College M,W
Angelo State University M,W
Baylor University M,W
Blinn College M,W
Clarendon College M,W
Collin County Community College District M,W
Frank Phillips College M,W
Grayson County College M,W
Hill College M,W
Houston Baptist University M,W
Howard College M,W
Jacksonville College M,W
Jarvis Christian College M,W
Kilgore College M,W
Lamar University M,W
Lee College M
Lon Morris College M,W
Lubbock Christian University M,W
McLennan Community College M,W
Midland College M,W
Midwestern State University M,W
Odessa College M,W
Panola College M,W
Paris Junior College M,W
Prairie View A&M University M,W
Ranger College M,W
Rice University M,W
St. Edward's University M,W
St. Mary's University M,W
Sam Houston State University M,W
San Jacinto College
    North W
South Plains College M,W
Southern Methodist University M,W
Southwestern Assemblies of God University M,W
Stephen F. Austin State University M,W
Tarleton State University M,W
Temple College M,W
Texas A&M University M,W
Texas A&M University
    Commerce M,W
    Kingsville M,W
Texas Christian University M,W
Texas Southern University M,W
Texas State University: San Marcos M,W
Texas Tech University M,W
Texas Woman's University W
Trinity Valley Community College M,W
Tyler Junior College M,W
University of Houston M,W
University of North Texas M,W
University of Texas
    Arlington M,W
    Austin M,W
    Pan American M,W
    San Antonio M,W
University of the Incarnate Word M,W
Wayland Baptist University M,W
Weatherford College M,W
West Texas A&M University M,W
Wiley College M,W

Utah
Brigham Young University M,W
College of Eastern Utah M,W
Dixie State College of Utah M,W
Salt Lake Community College M,W
Snow College M,W
Southern Utah University M,W
University of Utah M,W
Utah State University M,W
Utah Valley State College M,W
Weber State University M,W

Vermont
St. Michael's College M,W
University of Vermont M,W

Virginia
Bluefield College M,W
College of William and Mary M,W
George Mason University M,W
Hampton University M,W
James Madison University M,W
Liberty University M,W
Longwood University M,W
Norfolk State University M,W
Old Dominion University M,W
Radford University M,W
St. Paul's College M,W
University of Richmond M,W
University of Virginia M,W
University of Virginia's College at Wise M,W
Virginia Commonwealth University M,W
Virginia Intermont College M,W
Virginia Military Institute M
Virginia Polytechnic Institute and State University M,W
Virginia State University M,W
Virginia Union University M,W

Washington
Big Bend Community College M,W
Central Washington University M,W
Centralia College M,W
Clark College M,W
Eastern Washington University M,W
Edmonds Community College M,W
Everett Community College M,W
Evergreen State College M,W
Gonzaga University M,W
Grays Harbor College M,W
Green River Community College M,W
Highline Community College M,W
Lower Columbia College M,W
North Seattle Community College M,W
Northwest University M,W
Olympic College M,W
Peninsula College M,W
Pierce College M,W
Saint Martin's University M,W
Seattle Pacific University M,W
Seattle University M,W
Shoreline Community College M,W
Skagit Valley College M,W
Spokane Community College M,W
Tacoma Community College M,W
University of Washington M,W
Walla Walla Community College M,W
Washington State University M,W
Wenatchee Valley College M,W
Western Washington University M,W
Whatcom Community College M,W
Yakima Valley Community College M,W

West Virginia
Alderson-Broaddus College M,W
Bluefield State College M,W
Concord University M,W
Davis and Elkins College M,W
Glenville State College M,W
Marshall University M,W
Mountain State University M
Ohio Valley University M,W
Potomac State College of West Virginia University M,W
Salem International University M,W
Shepherd University M,W
University of Charleston M,W
West Liberty State College M,W
West Virginia State University M,W
West Virginia University M,W
West Virginia University Institute of Technology M,W
West Virginia Wesleyan College M,W
Wheeling Jesuit University M,W

Wisconsin
Cardinal Stritch University M,W
Marquette University M,W
Silver Lake College W
University of Wisconsin
   Green Bay M,W
   Milwaukee M,W
   Parkside M,W
Viterbo University M,W

Wyoming
Casper College M,W
Eastern Wyoming College M
Laramie County Community College M
Northwest College M,W
Sheridan College M,W
University of Wyoming M,W
Western Wyoming Community College M,W

Bowling

Arkansas
Arkansas State University W
University of Arkansas
   Pine Bluff W

Delaware
Delaware State University W

Florida
Bethune-Cookman College W

Illinois
McKendree College M,W
Robert Morris College: Chicago W

Indiana
Vincennes University M,W

Kansas
Newman University M,W
Wichita State University M,W

Kentucky
Pikeville College M,W

Louisiana
Southern University and Agricultural and Mechanical College W

Maryland
Coppin State University W
Morgan State University W
Prince George's Community College M,W

Michigan
Aquinas College M,W
Saginaw Valley State University M

Mississippi
Alcorn State University W
Jackson State University M,W
Mississippi Valley State University M,W

Missouri
Missouri Baptist University M,W

Nebraska
University of Nebraska
   Lincoln W

New Jersey
Fairleigh Dickinson University
   Metropolitan Campus W

New York
Globe Institute of Technology M,W

North Carolina
Blue Ridge Community College M
Livingstone College M,W
North Carolina Central University M,W
St. Augustine's College W
Shaw University W

Pennsylvania
Cheyney University of Pennsylvania W

Tennessee
King College M,W

Texas
Prairie View A&M University W
Texas Southern University W

Virginia
Norfolk State University W

Boxing

Connecticut
Southern Connecticut State University M

Puerto Rico
Universidad Metropolitana M,W

Cheerleading

Alabama
Faulkner State Community College M,W
Gadsden State Community College W
Northwest-Shoals Community College M,W
Shelton State Community College M,W
Southern Union State Community College M,W
Troy University M,W
University of Alabama M,W
University of Alabama
   Huntsville M,W

Arizona
Glendale Community College M,W

Arkansas
University of Arkansas
   Fort Smith M,W
   Monticello M,W
University of Central Arkansas M,W
Williams Baptist College M,W

Delaware
University of Delaware M,W

Florida
Florida College W
Pensacola Junior College M,W
University of Central Florida M,W
Warner Southern College M,W
Webber International University M,W

Georgia
Mercer University M,W
Reinhardt College M,W
University of West Georgia M,W

Hawaii
University of Hawaii
   Manoa M,W

Idaho
Boise State University M,W
North Idaho College M,W

Illinois
Kaskaskia College M,W
McKendree College M,W
Northwestern University M,W
Olivet Nazarene University M,W
Rend Lake College W
Southern Illinois University Carbondale M,W

Indiana
Ancilla College W
Grace College M,W
Indiana Institute of Technology M,W
Indiana Wesleyan University M,W
Marian College M,W
Oakland City University W
University of St. Francis M,W

Iowa
Drake University M,W
Iowa Western Community College M,W
St. Ambrose University M,W
Waldorf College W
William Penn University W

Kansas
Allen County Community College M,W
Baker University M,W
Barton County Community College M,W
Benedictine College M,W
Central Christian College of Kansas M,W
Coffeyville Community College M,W
Dodge City Community College M,W
Emporia State University M,W
Fort Scott Community College W
Garden City Community College M,W
Labette Community College M,W
McPherson College M,W
MidAmerica Nazarene University M,W
Neosho County Community College M,W
Newman University M,W
Ottawa University M,W
Pittsburg State University M,W
Pratt Community College M,W
Seward County Community College M,W
Southwestern College M,W
Tabor College M,W
Washburn University of Topeka M,W
Wichita State University M,W

Kentucky
Bellarmine University M,W
Murray State University M,W
Northern Kentucky University M,W
Union College M,W
University of Louisville M,W
University of the Cumberlands M,W

Louisiana
Bossier Parish Community College M,W
Delgado Community College W
Southeastern Louisiana University M,W
University of Louisiana at Lafayette M,W
University of Louisiana at Monroe M,W

Maryland
Morgan State University W
University of Maryland
   College Park W

Michigan
Madonna University W
Northwood University M,W
University of Detroit Mercy M,W

Mississippi
Itawamba Community College M,W
Mississippi Gulf Coast Community College
   Jefferson Davis Campus M,W
University of Mississippi M,W

Athletic scholarships 925

William Carey College M,W

Missouri
Avila University W
Culver-Stockton College M,W
Drury University M,W
Evangel University M,W
Hannibal-LaGrange College M,W
Harris-Stowe State University W
Missouri Baptist University M,W
Missouri Southern State University M,W
Missouri Valley College M,W
Moberly Area Community College M,W
Northwest Missouri State University M,W
Southeast Missouri State University M,W
William Jewell College M,W

Nebraska
Dana College M,W
Hastings College W

Nevada
University of Nevada
    Las Vegas M,W

New York
Hofstra University M,W
Nyack College M,W

North Carolina
Brevard College M,W
Campbell University W
Elon University M,W
Gardner-Webb University M,W
Lees-McRae College M,W
Lenoir-Rhyne College M,W
Mars Hill College M,W
Methodist College M,W
University of North Carolina
    Wilmington M,W

Ohio
Kent State University M,W
University of Rio Grande M,W
Urbana University W

Oklahoma
Cameron University M,W
Carl Albert State College W
Eastern Oklahoma State College M,W
Northeastern Oklahoma Agricultural and
    Mechanical College M,W
Oklahoma Christian University M,W
Oklahoma City University M,W
Oklahoma Panhandle State University M,W
Rose State College M,W
Southeastern Oklahoma State University W
Southwestern Oklahoma State University M,W
University of Tulsa M,W
Western Oklahoma State College M,W

Oregon
Southwestern Oregon Community College M,W
University of Oregon M,W

Pennsylvania
Kutztown University of Pennsylvania W
Lackawanna College W
Penn State
    University Park M,W
St. Francis University M,W
Seton Hill University M,W
Temple University M,W

Puerto Rico
University of Puerto Rico
    Humacao M,W

South Carolina
Anderson University W
Clemson University M,W
Limestone College M,W
Morris College M,W

Newberry College W
North Greenville College M,W
Southern Wesleyan University M,W
Spartanburg Methodist College M,W

South Dakota
Dakota Wesleyan University M,W

Tennessee
Bethel College M,W
Crichton College W
Cumberland University M,W
Freed-Hardeman University W
Hiwassee College M,W
King College M,W
Lambuth University M,W
Tennessee Technological University M,W
Tennessee Wesleyan College M,W
Tusculum College W
University of Memphis M,W
University of Tennessee
    Martin M,W

Texas
Clarendon College M,W
East Texas Baptist University M,W
Houston Baptist University M,W
Howard College M,W
Lubbock Christian University M,W
St. Edward's University M,W
South Plains College M,W
Southwestern Assemblies of God University W
Tarleton State University M,W
Tyler Junior College M,W
Western Texas College W

Utah
Brigham Young University M,W

Virginia
Liberty University M,W
Old Dominion University M,W
Virginia Intermont College W

Washington
Walla Walla Community College W

West Virginia
Mountain State University M,W
University of Charleston M,W

Wyoming
University of Wyoming M,W
Western Wyoming Community College W

Cricket

California
College of the Redwoods M

Cross-country

Alabama
Alabama Agricultural and Mechanical
    University M,W
Alabama State University M,W
Auburn University M,W
Birmingham-Southern College M,W
Jacksonville State University M,W
Lurleen B. Wallace Community College M,W
Miles College M,W
Northwest-Shoals Community College M
Samford University M,W
Southern Union State Community College M,W
Spring Hill College M,W
Troy University M,W
University of Alabama M,W
University of Alabama
    Birmingham W
    Huntsville M,W

University of Mobile M,W
University of North Alabama M,W
University of South Alabama M,W
University of West Alabama M,W
Wallace State Community College at Hanceville
    M,W

Alaska
University of Alaska
    Anchorage M,W
    Fairbanks M,W

Arizona
Arizona State University M,W
Central Arizona College M,W
Dine College M,W
Gateway Community College M,W
Glendale Community College M,W
Mesa Community College M,W
Northern Arizona University M,W
Pima Community College M,W
Scottsdale Community College M,W
University of Arizona M,W
Yavapai College W

Arkansas
Arkansas State University M,W
Arkansas Tech University W
Harding University M,W
Henderson State University W
Lyon College M,W
Ouachita Baptist University W
Southern Arkansas University W
University of Arkansas M,W
University of Arkansas
    Little Rock M,W
    Monticello W
    Pine Bluff M,W

California
Alliant International University M,W
Azusa Pacific University M,W
Biola University M,W
California Polytechnic State University: San Luis
    Obispo M
California State Polytechnic University: Pomona
    M,W
California State University
    Chico M,W
    Fresno M,W
    Fullerton M,W
    Long Beach M,W
    Los Angeles M,W
    Northridge M,W
    Sacramento M,W
    Stanislaus M,W
Concordia University M,W
Fresno City College M,W
Fresno Pacific University M,W
Holy Names University M,W
Humboldt State University M,W
Loyola Marymount University M,W
Master's College M,W
Pepperdine University M,W
Point Loma Nazarene University M,W
St. Mary's College of California M,W
San Diego State University M,W
San Jose State University M,W
Santa Clara University M,W
Santiago Canyon College M,W
Sonoma State University W
Stanford University M,W
University of California
    Berkeley M,W
    Davis M,W
    Irvine M,W
    Los Angeles M,W
    Riverside M,W
    Santa Barbara M,W
University of San Diego M,W
University of San Francisco M,W
University of Southern California M,W
University of the Pacific W

Vanguard University of Southern California
    M,W
Westmont College M,W
William Jessup University M,W
Yuba Community College District M,W

Colorado
Adams State College M,W
Colorado Christian University M,W
Colorado Northwestern Community College
    M,W
Colorado School of Mines M,W
Colorado State University M,W
Fort Lewis College M,W
Mesa State College W
Regis University M,W
University of Colorado
    Boulder M,W
    Colorado Springs M,W
University of Northern Colorado W
Western State College of Colorado M,W

Connecticut
Central Connecticut State University M,W
Post University M
Quinnipiac University M,W
Sacred Heart University M,W
University of Connecticut M,W
University of Hartford M,W
University of New Haven M,W

Delaware
Goldey-Beacom College M
Wilmington College M,W

District of Columbia
American University M,W
George Washington University M,W
Georgetown University M,W
Howard University M,W

Florida
Bethune-Cookman College M,W
Embry-Riddle Aeronautical University M,W
Flagler College M,W
Florida Atlantic University M,W
Florida Institute of Technology M,W
Florida Southern College M,W
Florida State University M,W
Jacksonville University W
Nova Southeastern University W
St. Leo University M,W
St. Thomas University M,W
Stetson University M,W
University of Central Florida M,W
University of Florida M,W
University of Miami M,W
University of North Florida M,W
University of South Florida M,W
University of Tampa M,W
University of West Florida M,W
Warner Southern College M,W
Webber International University M,W

Georgia
Albany State University M,W
Andrew College M,W
Augusta State University M,W
Berry College M,W
Brenau University W
Clark Atlanta University M,W
Clayton State University M,W
Columbus State University M,W
Covenant College M,W
Georgia College and State University M,W
Georgia Institute of Technology M,W
Georgia Southern University W
Georgia State University M,W
Kennesaw State University M,W
Mercer University M,W
Middle Georgia College M,W
Morehouse College M
Paine College M,W

Reinhardt College M,W
Savannah State University W
Shorter College M,W
Truett-McConnell College M,W
University of Georgia M,W
University of West Georgia M,W
Young Harris College M,W

Hawaii
Brigham Young University-Hawaii M,W
Chaminade University of Honolulu M,W
Hawaii Pacific University M,W
University of Hawaii
    Hilo M,W
    Manoa W

Idaho
Albertson College of Idaho M,W
Boise State University M,W
College of Southern Idaho M,W
Idaho State University M,W
Lewis-Clark State College M,W
Northwest Nazarene University M,W
University of Idaho M,W

Illinois
Bradley University M,W
Chicago State University M,W
College of Lake County M,W
Danville Area Community College M,W
DePaul University M,W
Eastern Illinois University M,W
Illinois Institute of Technology M,W
Illinois State University M,W
Judson College M,W
Lewis University M,W
Loyola University of Chicago M,W
McKendree College M,W
Moraine Valley Community College M,W
Morton College M,W
Northwestern University W
Olivet Nazarene University M,W
Rend Lake College M
Robert Morris College: Chicago M,W
St. Xavier University M,W
Sauk Valley Community College M,W
Southern Illinois University Carbondale M,W
Southern Illinois University Edwardsville M,W
Trinity Christian College M,W
University of Illinois
    Chicago M,W
    Urbana-Champaign M,W
University of St. Francis W
Waubonsee Community College M,W
Western Illinois University M,W

Indiana
Ball State University M,W
Bethel College M,W
Butler University M,W
Calumet College of St. Joseph M,W
Goshen College M,W
Grace College M,W
Huntington University M,W
Indiana State University M,W
Indiana University
    Bloomington M,W
Indiana University-Purdue University Fort
    Wayne M,W
Indiana University-Purdue University
    Indianapolis M,W
Indiana Wesleyan University M,W
Marian College M,W
Oakland City University M,W
Purdue University M,W
St. Joseph's College M,W
Taylor University M,W
University of Evansville M,W
University of Indianapolis M,W
University of Notre Dame M,W
University of St. Francis M,W
University of Southern Indiana M,W
Valparaiso University M,W

Vincennes University M,W

Iowa
Ashford University M,W
Briar Cliff University M,W
Dordt College M,W
Drake University M,W
Ellsworth Community College M,W
Graceland University M,W
Grand View College M,W
Iowa State University M,W
Morningside College M,W
North Iowa Area Community College M,W
Northwestern College M,W
St. Ambrose University M,W
University of Iowa M,W
University of Northern Iowa M,W
William Penn University M,W

Kansas
Allen County Community College M,W
Baker University M,W
Barton County Community College M,W
Benedictine College M,W
Bethany College M,W
Butler County Community College M,W
Central Christian College of Kansas M,W
Cloud County Community College M,W
Coffeyville Community College M,W
Colby Community College M,W
Emporia State University M,W
Fort Hays State University M,W
Fort Scott Community College M,W
Garden City Community College M,W
Highland Community College M,W
Hutchinson Community College M,W
Johnson County Community College M,W
Kansas City Kansas Community College M,W
Kansas State University M,W
Kansas Wesleyan University M,W
McPherson College M,W
MidAmerica Nazarene University M,W
Neosho County Community College M,W
Newman University M,W
Ottawa University M,W
Pittsburg State University M,W
Pratt Community College M,W
Southwestern College M,W
Sterling College M,W
Tabor College M,W
University of Kansas M,W
Wichita State University M,W

Kentucky
Asbury College M,W
Bellarmine University M,W
Campbellsville University M,W
Eastern Kentucky University M,W
Georgetown College M,W
Kentucky State University M,W
Lindsey Wilson College M,W
Morehead State University M,W
Murray State University M,W
Northern Kentucky University M,W
Pikeville College M,W
Union College M,W
University of Kentucky M,W
University of Louisville M,W
University of the Cumberlands M,W
Western Kentucky University M,W

Louisiana
Centenary College of Louisiana M,W
Dillard University M,W
Louisiana State University and Agricultural and
    Mechanical College M,W
Louisiana Tech University M,W
Nicholls State University M,W
Northwestern State University M,W
Southeastern Louisiana University M,W
Southern University and Agricultural and
    Mechanical College M,W
University of Louisiana at Lafayette M,W

University of Louisiana at Monroe M,W
University of New Orleans M,W
Xavier University of Louisiana M,W

Maine
Unity College M,W
University of Maine M,W

Maryland
Anne Arundel Community College M,W
Bowie State University M,W
Columbia Union College M,W
Coppin State University M,W
Hagerstown Community College M,W
Loyola College in Maryland M,W
Morgan State University M,W
Mount St. Mary's University M,W
Towson University M,W
University of Maryland
    Baltimore County M,W
    Eastern Shore M,W

Massachusetts
Boston College W
Boston University M,W
Merrimack College W
Northeastern University M,W
Stonehill College M,W
University of Massachusetts
    Amherst M,W
    Lowell M,W

Michigan
Aquinas College M,W
Central Michigan University M,W
Concordia University M,W
Cornerstone University M,W
Delta College M
Eastern Michigan University M,W
Ferris State University M,W
Grand Rapids Community College M,W
Grand Valley State University M,W
Hillsdale College M,W
Lake Superior State University M,W
Lansing Community College M,W
Macomb Community College M,W
Madonna University M,W
Michigan State University M,W
Michigan Technological University W
Mott Community College M,W
Northern Michigan University W
Northwood University M,W
Oakland Community College M,W
Oakland University M,W
Saginaw Valley State University M,W
Schoolcraft College W
Siena Heights University M,W
Spring Arbor University M,W
University of Detroit Mercy M,W
University of Michigan M,W
Wayne State University M,W
Western Michigan University M,W

Minnesota
Concordia University: St. Paul M,W
Minnesota State University
    Mankato M,W
    Moorhead M,W
St. Cloud State University M,W
University of Minnesota
    Duluth W
    Twin Cities M,W
Winona State University W

Mississippi
Alcorn State University M,W
Belhaven College M,W
Delta State University W
Jackson State University M,W
Mississippi State University M,W
Mississippi Valley State University M,W
Tougaloo College M,W
University of Mississippi M,W

University of Southern Mississippi M,W

Missouri
Central Methodist University M,W
Central Missouri State University M,W
Drury University M,W
Evangel University M,W
Hannibal-LaGrange College M,W
Lincoln University W
Missouri Baptist University M,W
Missouri Southern State University M,W
Missouri State University M,W
Missouri Valley College M,W
Northwest Missouri State University M,W
Park University M,W
Research College of Nursing M,W
St. Louis University M,W
Southeast Missouri State University M,W
Southwest Baptist University M,W
Truman State University M,W
University of Missouri
    Columbia M,W
    Kansas City M,W
    Rolla M,W
William Jewell College M,W
William Woods University M,W

Montana
Flathead Valley Community College M,W
Montana State University
    Billings M,W
    Bozeman M,W
University of Great Falls M,W
University of Montana: Missoula M,W

Nebraska
College of Saint Mary W
Concordia University M,W
Creighton University M,W
Dana College M,W
Doane College M,W
Hastings College M,W
Midland Lutheran College M,W
University of Nebraska
    Kearney M,W
    Lincoln M,W
    Omaha W
Wayne State College M,W
York College M,W

Nevada
University of Nevada
    Las Vegas W
    Reno W

New Hampshire
Southern New Hampshire University M,W
University of New Hampshire M,W

New Jersey
Bloomfield College M
Caldwell College W
Fairleigh Dickinson University
    Metropolitan Campus M,W
Felician College M,W
Georgian Court University W
Monmouth University M,W
Rider University M,W
Rutgers, The State University of New Jersey
    New Brunswick/Piscataway Campus M,W
St. Peter's College M,W
Seton Hall University M,W

New Mexico
College of the Southwest M,W
Eastern New Mexico University M,W
New Mexico Highlands University M,W
New Mexico State University M,W
University of New Mexico M,W

New York
Adelphi University M,W
Canisius College M,W

College of Saint Rose M,W
Daemen College M,W
Fordham University M,W
Globe Institute of Technology M,W
Hofstra University M,W
Houghton College M,W
Iona College M,W
Le Moyne College M,W
Manhattan College M,W
Marist College M,W
Mercy College M,W
Molloy College M,W
New York Institute of Technology M,W
Niagara University M,W
Nyack College M,W
Pace University M,W
Roberts Wesleyan College M,W
St. Francis College M,W
St. John's University W
St. Thomas Aquinas College M,W
Siena College M,W
State University of New York
    Albany M,W
    Binghamton M,W
    Buffalo M,W
    College of Technology at Alfred M,W
    Stony Brook M,W
Syracuse University M,W
Wagner College M,W

North Carolina
Appalachian State University M,W
Barton College M,W
Belmont Abbey College M,W
Brevard College M,W
Campbell University M,W
Catawba College M,W
Davidson College M,W
East Carolina University M,W
Elon University M,W
Fayetteville State University M,W
Gardner-Webb University M,W
High Point University M,W
Johnson C. Smith University M,W
Lees-McRae College M,W
Lenoir-Rhyne College M,W
Livingstone College M,W
Mars Hill College M,W
Montreat College M,W
Mount Olive College M,W
North Carolina Agricultural and Technical State
    University M,W
North Carolina Central University M,W
North Carolina State University M,W
Pfeiffer University M,W
Queens University of Charlotte M,W
St. Andrews Presbyterian College M,W
St. Augustine's College M,W
Shaw University M,W
University of North Carolina
    Asheville M,W
    Chapel Hill M,W
    Charlotte M,W
    Greensboro M,W
    Pembroke M,W
    Wilmington M,W
Wake Forest University M,W
Western Carolina University M,W
Wingate University M,W
Winston-Salem State University M,W

North Dakota
Dickinson State University M,W
Jamestown College M,W
Minot State
North Dakota State University M,W
University of Mary M,W
University of North Dakota M,W

Ohio
Ashland University M,W
Bowling Green State University M,W
Cedarville University M,W
Central State University M,W
Cleveland State University W
Kent State University M,W
Malone College M,W
Miami University
    Oxford Campus M,W
Mount Vernon Nazarene University M,W
Ohio State University
    Columbus Campus M,W
Ohio University M,W
Shawnee State University M,W
University of Akron M,W
University of Dayton M,W
University of Findlay M,W
University of Rio Grande M,W
University of Toledo M,W
Ursuline College W
Walsh University M,W
Wright State University M,W
Xavier University M,W
Youngstown State University M,W

Oklahoma
Cameron University M
East Central University M,W
Oklahoma Baptist University M,W
Oklahoma Christian University M,W
Oklahoma Panhandle State University M,W
Oklahoma State University M,W
Oral Roberts University M,W
St. Gregory's University M,W
Southeastern Oklahoma State University W
Southern Nazarene University M,W
Southwestern Oklahoma State University W
University of Central Oklahoma M,W
University of Oklahoma M,W
University of Tulsa M,W

Oregon
Clackamas Community College M,W
Concordia University M,W
Corban College M,W
Eastern Oregon University M,W
Lane Community College M,W
Mount Hood Community College M,W
Oregon Institute of Technology M,W
Portland State University M,W
Southern Oregon University M,W
Southwestern Oregon Community College M,W
University of Oregon M,W
University of Portland M,W
Warner Pacific College M,W

Pennsylvania
Bloomsburg University of Pennsylvania M,W
California University of Pennsylvania M,W
Cheyney University of Pennsylvania M,W
Duquesne University M,W
East Stroudsburg University of Pennsylvania
    M,W
Edinboro University of Pennsylvania M,W
Gannon University M,W
Geneva College M,W
Holy Family University W
Indiana University of Pennsylvania M,W
Kutztown University of Pennsylvania M,W
La Salle University M,W
Lackawanna College M,W
Lehigh University M,W
Lock Haven University of Pennsylvania M,W
Mansfield University of Pennsylvania W
Mercyhurst College M,W
Millersville University of Pennsylvania M,W
Penn State
    University Park M,W
Philadelphia University M,W
Point Park University M,W
Robert Morris University M,W
St. Francis University M,W
St. Joseph's University M,W
Seton Hill University M,W
Shippensburg University of Pennsylvania M,W
Slippery Rock University of Pennsylvania M,W
University of Pittsburgh M,W
University of the Sciences in Philadelphia M,W
Villanova University M,W
West Chester University of Pennsylvania M,W
Westminster College W

Puerto Rico
Bayamon Central University M,W
Inter American University of Puerto Rico
    Aguadilla Campus M,W
    Bayamon Campus M,W
    Guayama Campus M,W
    San German Campus M,W
Turabo University M,W
Universidad del Este M,W
Universidad Politecnica de Puerto Rico M
University of Puerto Rico
    Carolina Regional College M,W
    Cayey University College M,W
    Humacao M,W
    Mayaguez M,W
    Ponce M,W
    Utuado M,W
University of the Sacred Heart M,W

Rhode Island
Bryant University M,W
Providence College M,W
University of Rhode Island M,W

South Carolina
Anderson University M,W
Charleston Southern University M,W
The Citadel M,W
Claflin University M,W
Clemson University M,W
Coastal Carolina University M,W
Coker College M,W
College of Charleston M,W
Converse College W
Erskine College M,W
Francis Marion University M,W
Furman University M,W
Lander University W
Limestone College M,W
Morris College M,W
Newberry College M,W
North Greenville College M,W
Presbyterian College M,W
South Carolina State University M,W
Southern Wesleyan University M,W
Spartanburg Methodist College M,W
University of South Carolina W
University of South Carolina
    Aiken W
    Upstate M,W
Voorhees College M,W
Winthrop University M,W
Wofford College M,W

South Dakota
Augustana College M,W
Black Hills State University M,W
Dakota Wesleyan University M,W
Mount Marty College M,W
South Dakota School of Mines and Technology
    M,W
South Dakota State University M,W
University of Sioux Falls M,W
University of South Dakota M,W

Tennessee
Austin Peay State University M,W
Belmont University M,W
Bethel College M,W
Bryan College M,W
Carson-Newman College M,W
Christian Brothers University M,W
Crichton College M,W
Cumberland University M,W
East Tennessee State University M,W
Hiwassee College M,W
Lambuth University M,W
Lee University M,W
LeMoyne-Owen College M
Lincoln Memorial University M,W
Lipscomb University M,W
Middle Tennessee State University M,W
Milligan College M,W
Tennessee Technological University M,W
Tennessee Wesleyan College M,W
Tusculum College M,W
Union University M,W
University of Memphis M,W
University of Tennessee
    Chattanooga M,W
    Knoxville M,W
    Martin M,W
Vanderbilt University W

Texas
Abilene Christian University M,W
Angelo State University M,W
Baylor University M,W
Dallas Baptist University W
Lamar University M,W
Midwestern State University W
Northwood University: Texas Campus M,W
Prairie View A&M University M,W
Rice University M,W
Sam Houston State University M,W
South Plains College M,W
Southern Methodist University M,W
Stephen F. Austin State University M,W
Tarleton State University M,W
Texas A&M University M,W
Texas A&M University
    Commerce M,W
Texas Christian University M,W
Texas Southern University M,W
Texas State University: San Marcos M,W
Texas Tech University M,W
University of Houston M,W
University of Texas
    Arlington M,W
    Austin M,W
    Pan American M,W
    San Antonio M,W
University of the Incarnate Word M,W
Wayland Baptist University M,W
West Texas A&M University M,W
Western Texas College M,W

Utah
Brigham Young University M,W
University of Utah W
Utah State University M,W
Utah Valley State College M,W
Weber State University M,W

Vermont
University of Vermont M,W

Virginia
College of William and Mary M,W
George Mason University M,W
Hampton University M,W
James Madison University M,W
Liberty University M,W
Longwood University M,W
Norfolk State University M,W
Radford University M,W
St. Paul's College M,W
University of Richmond W
University of Virginia M,W
University of Virginia's College at Wise M,W
Virginia Commonwealth University M,W
Virginia Intermont College M,W
Virginia Military Institute M,W
Virginia Polytechnic Institute and State
    University M,W
Virginia State University M,W

Washington
Central Washington University M,W
Clark College M,W
Eastern Washington University M,W
Everett Community College M,W
Evergreen State College M,W
Gonzaga University M,W
Highline Community College M,W
Northwest University M,W
Saint Martin's University M,W
Seattle Pacific University M,W
Seattle University M,W
Spokane Community College M,W
University of Washington M,W
Washington State University M,W
Western Washington University M,W

West Virginia
Alderson-Broaddus College M,W
Bluefield State College M,W
Concord University M,W
Davis and Elkins College M,W
Glenville State College M,W
Marshall University M,W
Ohio Valley University M,W
University of Charleston M,W
West Liberty State College M,W
West Virginia University W
West Virginia Wesleyan College M,W
Wheeling Jesuit University M,W

Wisconsin
Marquette University M,W
Milwaukee Area Technical College M,W
Silver Lake College M,W
University of Wisconsin
 Green Bay M,W
 Milwaukee M,W
 Parkside M,W

Wyoming
University of Wyoming M,W

Diving

Alabama
Auburn University M,W
University of Alabama M,W

Arizona
Arizona State University M,W
Northern Arizona University W
University of Arizona M,W

Arkansas
Ouachita Baptist University M,W
University of Arkansas W

California
California Baptist University M,W
California State University
 Northridge M,W
College of the Redwoods M
Pepperdine University W
San Diego State University W
San Jose State University W
Stanford University M,W
University of California
 Berkeley M,W
 Davis M,W
 Irvine M,W
University of San Diego W
University of Southern California M,W

Colorado
Colorado State University W
University of Denver M,W

Connecticut
Central Connecticut State University W
Fairfield University M,W

Southern Connecticut State University M
University of Connecticut M,W

District of Columbia
George Washington University M,W
Howard University M,W

Florida
Florida State University M,W
Indian River Community College M,W
University of Florida M,W
University of Miami M,W

Georgia
Georgia Institute of Technology M,W
Georgia Southern University W
University of Georgia M,W

Hawaii
University of Hawaii
 Manoa M,W

Illinois
Eastern Illinois University M,W
Illinois Institute of Technology M,W
Illinois State University W
Northwestern University M,W
Southern Illinois University Carbondale M,W
University of Illinois
 Chicago M,W
 Urbana-Champaign W
Western Illinois University M,W

Indiana
Ball State University M,W
Indiana University
 Bloomington M,W
Indiana University-Purdue University
 Indianapolis M,W
Purdue University M,W
University of Evansville M,W
University of Notre Dame M,W
Valparaiso University M,W

Iowa
University of Iowa M,W

Kentucky
Asbury College M,W
University of Kentucky M,W
University of Louisville M,W
Western Kentucky University M

Maine
University of Maine M,W

Maryland
Loyola College in Maryland M,W
Towson University M,W
University of Maryland
 Baltimore County M,W

Massachusetts
Boston College W
Boston University M,W
Northeastern University W
University of Massachusetts
 Amherst M,W

Michigan
Eastern Michigan University M,W
Grand Rapids Community College M,W
Grand Valley State University M,W
Hillsdale College W
Michigan State University M,W
Oakland University M,W
University of Michigan M,W
Wayne State University M,W

Minnesota
Minnesota State University
 Mankato M,W
 Moorhead M
St. Cloud State University M,W

University of Minnesota
 Twin Cities M,W

Mississippi
Delta State University M,W

Missouri
Drury University M,W
St. Louis University M,W
University of Missouri
 Columbia M,W

Nebraska
University of Nebraska
 Kearney W
 Lincoln W

Nevada
University of Nevada
 Las Vegas M
 Reno W

New Hampshire
University of New Hampshire W

New Jersey
Rider University M,W
Rutgers, The State University of New Jersey
 New Brunswick/Piscataway Campus M,W
St. Peter's College M,W

New Mexico
University of New Mexico W

New York
Fordham University M,W
Iona College M,W
Marist College M,W
Niagara University M,W
St. Bonaventure University M,W
St. Francis College M,W
Siena College W
State University of New York
 Binghamton M,W
 Stony Brook M,W
Syracuse University M,W

North Carolina
Davidson College M,W
East Carolina University M,W
University of North Carolina
 Chapel Hill W
 Wilmington M,W

North Dakota
University of North Dakota M,W

Ohio
Ashland University M,W
Bowling Green State University M,W
Cleveland State University M,W
Miami University
 Oxford Campus M,W
Ohio State University
 Columbus Campus M,W
Ohio University M,W
University of Akron W
University of Findlay M,W
University of Toledo W
Wright State University M,W

Pennsylvania
Gannon University M,W
Indiana University of Pennsylvania M,W
La Salle University M,W
Lehigh University M,W
Penn State
 University Park M,W
St. Francis University W
Slippery Rock University of Pennsylvania M,W
University of Pittsburgh M,W
Villanova University W
West Chester University of Pennsylvania M,W

Rhode Island
University of Rhode Island M,W

South Carolina
Clemson University M,W
College of Charleston M,W
University of South Carolina M,W

South Dakota
University of South Dakota M,W

Tennessee
University of Tennessee
 Knoxville M,W

Texas
Southern Methodist University M,W
Texas A&M University M,W
Texas Christian University M,W
University of Houston W
University of North Texas W
University of Texas
 Austin M,W

Utah
Brigham Young University M,W
University of Utah M,W

Vermont
University of Vermont W

Virginia
George Mason University M,W
Old Dominion University M,W
University of Richmond W
University of Virginia M,W
Virginia Military Institute M
Virginia Polytechnic Institute and State
 University M,W

Washington
University of Washington M,W

West Virginia
West Virginia University M,W

Wisconsin
University of Wisconsin
 Green Bay M,W
 Milwaukee M,W

Wyoming
University of Wyoming M,W

Equestrian

California
California State University
 Fresno W

Georgia
University of Georgia W

Indiana
St. Mary-of-the-Woods College W

Kansas
Kansas State University W

Kentucky
Midway College W
Murray State University M,W

Massachusetts
Mount Ida College W
Stonehill College W

Nebraska
Nebraska College of Technical Agriculture M,W

New York
Dowling College W
Molloy College M,W
Vassar College M,W

North Carolina
St. Andrews Presbyterian College M,W

Oklahoma
Oklahoma State University W

Oregon
Linn-Benton Community College M,W

Pennsylvania
Seton Hill University M,W

South Carolina
University of South Carolina W

Texas
Baylor University W
Southern Methodist University W
Texas A&M University W
West Texas A&M University W

Virginia
Virginia Intermont College M,W

Fencing

California
California State University
   Fullerton M,W
Stanford University M,W

Illinois
Northwestern University W

Indiana
University of Notre Dame M,W

Michigan
University of Detroit Mercy M,W
Wayne State University M,W

New Jersey
Fairleigh Dickinson University
   Metropolitan Campus W
New Jersey Institute of Technology M,W
Rutgers, The State University of New Jersey
   New Brunswick/Piscataway Campus M,W

New York
City University of New York
   Queens College W
St. John's University M,W

Ohio
Cleveland State University M,W
Ohio State University
   Columbus Campus M,W

Pennsylvania
Penn State
   University Park M,W
Temple University W

Field Hockey

California
Stanford University W
University of California
   Berkeley W
University of the Pacific W

Connecticut
Fairfield University W
Quinnipiac University W
University of Connecticut W

Delaware
University of Delaware W

District of Columbia
American University W
Georgetown University W

Illinois
Northwestern University W

Indiana
Ball State University W

Iowa
University of Iowa W

Kentucky
Bellarmine University W
University of Louisville W

Maine
University of Maine W

Maryland
Towson University W
University of Maryland
   College Park W

Massachusetts
American International College W
Boston College W
Boston University W
Northeastern University W
Stonehill College W
University of Massachusetts
   Amherst W

Michigan
Central Michigan University W
Michigan State University W
University of Michigan W

Missouri
Missouri State University W
St. Louis University W

New Hampshire
Franklin Pierce College W
University of New Hampshire W

New Jersey
Monmouth University W
Rider University W
Rutgers, The State University of New Jersey
   New Brunswick/Piscataway Campus W

New York
Colgate University W
Hofstra University W
Houghton College W
Siena College W
State University of New York
   Albany W
Syracuse University W

North Carolina
Appalachian State University W
Catawba College W
Davidson College W
Duke University W
University of North Carolina
   Chapel Hill W
Wake Forest University W

Ohio
Kent State University W
Miami University
   Oxford Campus W
Ohio State University
   Columbus Campus W
Ohio University W

Pennsylvania
Bloomsburg University of Pennsylvania W
Drexel University W
East Stroudsburg University of Pennsylvania W
Indiana University of Pennsylvania W
Kutztown University of Pennsylvania W
La Salle University W
Lehigh University W
Lock Haven University of Pennsylvania W
Mansfield University of Pennsylvania W
Mercyhurst College W
Millersville University of Pennsylvania W
Penn State
   University Park W
Philadelphia University W
Robert Morris University W
St. Francis University W
St. Joseph's University W
Seton Hill University W
Shippensburg University of Pennsylvania W
Slippery Rock University of Pennsylvania W
Temple University W
Villanova University W
West Chester University of Pennsylvania W

Rhode Island
Bryant University W
Providence College W
University of Rhode Island W

Vermont
University of Vermont W

Virginia
College of William and Mary W
James Madison University W
Longwood University W
Old Dominion University W
Radford University W
University of Richmond W
University of Virginia W
Virginia Commonwealth University W

Football (non-tackle)

Illinois
Olivet Nazarene University M

Louisiana
Southern University and Agricultural and
   Mechanical College M

Football (tackle)

Alabama
Alabama Agricultural and Mechanical
   University M
Alabama State University M
Auburn University M
Jacksonville State University M
Miles College M
Samford University M
Troy University M
Tuskegee University M
University of Alabama M
University of Alabama
   Birmingham M
University of North Alabama M
University of West Alabama M

Arizona
Arizona State University M
Arizona Western College M
Eastern Arizona College M
Glendale Community College M
Mesa Community College M
Northern Arizona University M
Pima Community College M
Scottsdale Community College M
University of Arizona M

Arkansas
Arkansas State University M
Arkansas Tech University M
Harding University M
Henderson State University M
Ouachita Baptist University M
Southern Arkansas University M
University of Arkansas M
University of Arkansas
   Monticello M
   Pine Bluff M
University of Central Arkansas M

California
Azusa Pacific University M
California Polytechnic State University: San Luis
   Obispo M
California State University
   Fresno M
   Sacramento M
Fresno City College M
Grossmont Community College M
Humboldt State University M
San Diego State University M
San Jose State University M
Stanford University M
University of California
   Berkeley M
   Davis M
   Los Angeles M
University of Southern California M
Yuba Community College District M

Colorado
Adams State College M
Colorado School of Mines M
Colorado State University M
Fort Lewis College M
Mesa State College M
University of Colorado
   Boulder M
University of Northern Colorado M
Western State College of Colorado M

Connecticut
Sacred Heart University M
Southern Connecticut State University M
University of Connecticut M

Delaware
Delaware State University M
University of Delaware M

District of Columbia
Georgetown University M
Howard University M

Florida
Bethune-Cookman College M
Florida Agricultural and Mechanical University M
Florida Atlantic University M
Florida State University M
University of Central Florida M
University of Florida M
University of Miami M
University of South Florida M
Webber International University M

Georgia
Albany State University M
Clark Atlanta University M
Fort Valley State University M
Georgia Institute of Technology M
Georgia Military College M
Georgia Southern University M
Morehouse College M
Savannah State University M
Shorter College M

University of Georgia M
University of West Georgia M
Valdosta State University M

Hawaii
University of Hawaii
    Manoa M

Idaho
Boise State University M
Idaho State University M
University of Idaho M

Illinois
Eastern Illinois University M
Illinois State University M
McKendree College M
Northwestern University M
Olivet Nazarene University M
Quincy University M
St. Xavier University M
Southern Illinois University Carbondale M
Trinity International University M
University of Illinois
    Urbana-Champaign M
University of St. Francis M
Western Illinois University M

Indiana
Ball State University M
Indiana State University M
Indiana University
    Bloomington M
Purdue University M
St. Joseph's College M
Taylor University M
University of Indianapolis M
University of Notre Dame M
University of St. Francis M

Iowa
Briar Cliff University M
Dordt College M
Ellsworth Community College M
Graceland University M
Iowa Central Community College M
Iowa State University M
Iowa Wesleyan College M
Morningside College M
North Iowa Area Community College M
Northwestern College M
St. Ambrose University M
University of Iowa M
University of Northern Iowa M
Waldorf College M
William Penn University M

Kansas
Baker University M
Benedictine College M
Bethany College M
Bethel College M
Butler County Community College M
Coffeyville Community College M
Dodge City Community College M
Emporia State University M
Fort Hays State University M
Fort Scott Community College M
Friends University M
Garden City Community College M
Highland Community College M
Hutchinson Community College M
Kansas State University M
Kansas Wesleyan University M
McPherson College M
MidAmerica Nazarene University M
Ottawa University M
Pittsburg State University M
Southwestern College M
Sterling College M
Tabor College M
University of Kansas M
University of St. Mary M

Washburn University of Topeka M

Kentucky
Campbellsville University M
Eastern Kentucky University M
Georgetown College M
Kentucky State University M
Kentucky Wesleyan College M
Murray State University M
Pikeville College M
Union College M
University of Kentucky M
University of Louisville M
University of the Cumberlands M
Western Kentucky University M

Louisiana
Grambling State University M
Louisiana State University and Agricultural and
    Mechanical College M
Louisiana Tech University M
Nicholls State University M
Northwestern State University M
Southeastern Louisiana University M
Southern University and Agricultural and
    Mechanical College M
University of Louisiana at Lafayette M
University of Louisiana at Monroe M

Maine
University of Maine M

Maryland
Bowie State University M
Morgan State University M
Towson University M
University of Maryland
    College Park M

Massachusetts
American International College M
Boston College M
Dean College M
Northeastern University M
Stonehill College M
University of Massachusetts
    Amherst M

Michigan
Central Michigan University M
Eastern Michigan University M
Ferris State University M
Grand Rapids Community College M
Grand Valley State University M
Hillsdale College M
Michigan State University M
Michigan Technological University M
Northern Michigan University M
Northwood University M
Saginaw Valley State University M
University of Michigan M
Western Michigan University M

Minnesota
Bemidji State University M
Concordia University: St. Paul M
Minnesota State University
    Mankato M
    Moorhead M
St. Cloud State University M
Southwest Minnesota State University M
University of Minnesota
    Crookston M
    Duluth M
    Twin Cities M
Winona State University M

Mississippi
Alcorn State University M
Belhaven College M
Coahoma Community College M
Copiah-Lincoln Community College M
Delta State University M

East Central Community College M
Hinds Community College M
Holmes Community College M
Itawamba Community College M
Jackson State University M
Jones County Junior College M
Mississippi Gulf Coast Community College
    Jefferson Davis Campus M
Mississippi State University M
Mississippi Valley State University M
Southwest Mississippi Community College M
University of Mississippi M
University of Southern Mississippi M

Missouri
Avila University M
Central Methodist University M
Central Missouri State University M
Culver-Stockton College M
Evangel University M
Lincoln University M
Missouri Southern State University M
Missouri State University M
Missouri Valley College M
Missouri Western State University M
Northwest Missouri State University M
Southeast Missouri State University M
Southwest Baptist University M
Truman State University M
University of Missouri
    Columbia M
    Rolla M
William Jewell College M

Montana
Carroll College M
Montana State University
    Bozeman M
Montana Tech of the University of Montana M
Rocky Mountain College M
University of Montana: Missoula M
University of Montana: Western M

Nebraska
Chadron State College M
Concordia University M
Dana College M
Doane College M
Hastings College M
Midland Lutheran College M
Peru State College M
University of Nebraska
    Kearney M
    Lincoln M
    Omaha M
Wayne State College M

Nevada
University of Nevada
    Las Vegas M
    Reno M

New Hampshire
University of New Hampshire M

New Jersey
Monmouth University M
Rutgers, The State University of New Jersey
    New Brunswick/Piscataway Campus M

New Mexico
Eastern New Mexico University M
New Mexico Highlands University M
New Mexico Military Institute Junior College M
New Mexico State University M
University of New Mexico M
Western New Mexico University M

New York
Hofstra University M
State University of New York
    Albany M
    Buffalo M

    College of Technology at Alfred M
    Stony Brook M
Syracuse University M

North Carolina
Appalachian State University M
Brevard College M
Catawba College M
Duke University M
East Carolina University M
Elizabeth City State University M
Elon University M
Fayetteville State University M
Gardner-Webb University M
Johnson C. Smith University M
Lenoir-Rhyne College M
Livingstone College M
Mars Hill College M
North Carolina Agricultural and Technical State
    University M
North Carolina Central University M
North Carolina State University M
St. Augustine's College M
Shaw University M
University of North Carolina
    Chapel Hill M
Wake Forest University M
Western Carolina University M
Wingate University M
Winston-Salem State University M

North Dakota
Dickinson State University M
Jamestown College M
Mayville State University M
Minot State University M
North Dakota State College of Science M
North Dakota State University M
University of Mary M
University of North Dakota M
Valley City State University M

Ohio
Ashland University M
Bowling Green State University M
Kent State University M
Malone College M
Miami University
    Oxford Campus M
Ohio Dominican University M
Ohio State University
    Columbus Campus M
Ohio University M
University of Akron M
University of Cincinnati M
University of Findlay M
University of Toledo M
Urbana University M
Walsh University M
Youngstown State University M

Oklahoma
East Central University M
Northeastern Oklahoma Agricultural and
    Mechanical College M
Northeastern State University M
Northwestern Oklahoma State University M
Oklahoma Panhandle State University M
Oklahoma State University M
Southeastern Oklahoma State University M
Southwestern Oklahoma State University M
University of Central Oklahoma M
University of Oklahoma M
University of Tulsa M

Oregon
Eastern Oregon University M
Oregon State University M
Portland State University M
Southern Oregon University M
University of Oregon M

Athletic scholarships

Pennsylvania
Bloomsburg University of Pennsylvania M
California University of Pennsylvania M
Cheyney University of Pennsylvania M
East Stroudsburg University of Pennsylvania M
Edinboro University of Pennsylvania M
Gannon University M
Geneva College M
Indiana University of Pennsylvania M
Kutztown University of Pennsylvania M
Lackawanna College M
Lehigh University M
Lock Haven University of Pennsylvania M
Mansfield University of Pennsylvania M
Mercyhurst College M
Millersville University of Pennsylvania M
Penn State
    University Park M
Robert Morris University M
St. Francis University M
Seton Hill University M
Shippensburg University of Pennsylvania M
Slippery Rock University of Pennsylvania M
Temple University M
University of Pittsburgh M
Valley Forge Military College M
Villanova University M
West Chester University of Pennsylvania M
Westminster College M

Rhode Island
University of Rhode Island M

South Carolina
Charleston Southern University M
The Citadel M
Clemson University M
Coastal Carolina University M
Furman University M
Newberry College M
North Greenville College M
Presbyterian College M
South Carolina State University M
University of South Carolina M
Wofford College M

South Dakota
Augustana College M
Black Hills State University M
Dakota State University M
Dakota Wesleyan University M
Northern State University M
South Dakota School of Mines and Technology M
South Dakota State University M
University of Sioux Falls M
University of South Dakota M

Tennessee
Bethel College M
Carson-Newman College M
Cumberland University M
Lambuth University M
Middle Tennessee State University M
Tennessee State University M
Tennessee Technological University M
Tusculum College M
University of Memphis M
University of Tennessee
    Chattanooga M
    Knoxville M
    Martin M
Vanderbilt University M

Texas
Abilene Christian University M
Angelo State University M
Baylor University M
Blinn College M
Kilgore College M
Midwestern State University M
Prairie View A&M University M
Ranger College M
Rice University M
Sam Houston State University M
Southern Methodist University M
Southwestern Assemblies of God University M
Stephen F. Austin State University M
Tarleton State University M
Texas A&M University M
Texas A&M University
    Commerce M
    Kingsville M
Texas Christian University M
Texas Southern University M
Texas State University: San Marcos M
Texas Tech University M
Trinity Valley Community College M
Tyler Junior College M
University of Houston M
University of North Texas M
University of Texas
    Austin M
West Texas A&M University M

Utah
Brigham Young University M
Dixie State College of Utah M
Snow College M
Southern Utah University M
University of Utah M
Utah State University M
Weber State University M

Virginia
College of William and Mary M
Hampton University M
James Madison University M
Liberty University M
Norfolk State University M
University of Richmond M
University of Virginia M
University of Virginia's College at Wise M
Virginia Military Institute M
Virginia Polytechnic Institute and State University M
Virginia State University M
Virginia Union University M

Washington
Central Washington University M
Eastern Washington University M
University of Washington M
Washington State University M
Western Washington University M

West Virginia
Concord University M
Glenville State College M
Marshall University M
Shepherd University M
University of Charleston M
West Liberty State College M
West Virginia State University M
West Virginia University M
West Virginia University Institute of Technology M
West Virginia Wesleyan College M

Wyoming
University of Wyoming M

Golf

Alabama
Alabama State University M,W
Auburn University M,W
Birmingham-Southern College M,W
Central Alabama Community College M
Faulkner State Community College M,W
Gadsden State Community College M
Jacksonville State University M,W
Northwest-Shoals Community College M
Samford University M,W
Spring Hill College M,W
Troy University M,W
University of Alabama M,W
University of Alabama
    Birmingham M,W
University of Mobile M,W
University of Montevallo M,W
University of North Alabama M
University of South Alabama M
Wallace State Community College at Hanceville M

Arizona
Arizona State University M,W
Eastern Arizona College M
Gateway Community College M,W
Glendale Community College M
Grand Canyon University M
Mesa Community College M
Northern Arizona University W
Northland Pioneer College M,W
Pima Community College M,W
Scottsdale Community College M
University of Arizona M,W

Arkansas
Arkansas State University M,W
Arkansas Tech University M
Harding University M,W
Henderson State University M,W
Lyon College M,W
Ouachita Baptist University M
University of Arkansas M,W
University of Arkansas
    Fort Smith M,W
    Little Rock M,W
    Monticello M,W
    Pine Bluff M,W

California
Bethany University M
California Baptist University W
California State University
    Bakersfield M
    Chico M,W
    Fresno M,W
    Long Beach M,W
    Northridge M
    Sacramento M
    San Bernardino M
    Stanislaus M
Concordia University M,W
Fresno City College M,W
Holy Names University M
Loyola Marymount University M
Master's College M
Pepperdine University M,W
Point Loma Nazarene University M
St. Mary's College of California M,W
San Diego State University M,W
San Jose State University M,W
Santa Clara University M,W
Santiago Canyon College M,W
Sonoma State University M
Stanford University M,W
University of California
    Berkeley M,W
    Davis M,W
    Irvine M,W
    Los Angeles M,W
    Santa Barbara M
University of San Diego M
University of San Francisco M,W
University of Southern California M,W
University of the Pacific M

Colorado
Adams State College M,W
Colorado Christian University M,W
Colorado School of Mines M,W
Colorado State University M,W
Colorado State University
    Pueblo M
Fort Lewis College M
Mesa State College W
Regis University M,W
Trinidad State Junior College M,W
University of Colorado
    Boulder M,W
    Colorado Springs M
University of Denver W
University of Northern Colorado M,W

Connecticut
Central Connecticut State University M
Quinnipiac University M
Sacred Heart University M,W
University of Connecticut M
University of Hartford M,W
University of New Haven M

Delaware
Goldey-Beacom College M,W
Wilmington College M

District of Columbia
George Washington University M
Georgetown University M,W

Florida
Barry University M,W
Bethune-Cookman College M,W
Brevard Community College M,W
Daytona Beach Community College W
Eckerd College W
Embry-Riddle Aeronautical University M,W
Flagler College M,W
Florida Atlantic University M,W
Florida Gulf Coast University M,W
Florida Institute of Technology M,W
Florida International University W
Florida Southern College M,W
Florida State University M,W
Jacksonville University M,W
Lake City Community College W
Lynn University M,W
Northwood University
    Florida Campus M,W
Nova Southeastern University M,W
Rollins College M,W
St. Leo University M,W
St. Petersburg College W
St. Thomas University M
Stetson University M,W
University of Central Florida M,W
University of Florida M,W
University of Miami W
University of North Florida M
University of South Florida M,W
University of Tampa M
University of West Florida M,W
Warner Southern College M,W
Webber International University M,W

Georgia
Abraham Baldwin Agricultural College M
Andrew College M,W
Armstrong Atlantic State University M
Augusta State University M,W
Berry College M,W
Clayton State University M
Columbus State University M
Covenant College M
Darton College M,W
Georgia College and State University M
Georgia Institute of Technology M
Georgia Southern University M
Georgia Southwestern State University M,W
Georgia State University M,W
Kennesaw State University M
Mercer University M,W
Reinhardt College M
Shorter College W
Thomas University M,W
Truett-McConnell College M

University of Georgia M,W
Valdosta State University M
Young Harris College M,W

Hawaii
Chaminade University of Honolulu M,W
Hawaii Pacific University M,W
University of Hawaii
    Hilo M
    Manoa M,W

Idaho
Albertson College of Idaho M,W
Boise State University M,W
Idaho State University M,W
Lewis-Clark State College M,W
Northwest Nazarene University M
University of Idaho M,W

Illinois
Black Hawk College M
Bradley University M,W
Chicago State University M,W
College of Lake County M,W
Danville Area Community College M,W
DePaul University M
Eastern Illinois University M,W
Elgin Community College M
Highland Community College M
Illinois State University M,W
John A. Logan College M,W
Kaskaskia College M,W
Kishwaukee College M,W
Lewis and Clark Community College M
Lewis University M,W
Loyola University of Chicago M,W
McKendree College M,W
Moraine Valley Community College M
Northwestern University M,W
Olivet Nazarene University M
Parkland College M
Quincy University M,W
Rend Lake College M,W
Robert Morris College: Chicago M,W
Sauk Valley Community College M
Southern Illinois University Carbondale M,W
Southern Illinois University Edwardsville M,W
Springfield College in Illinois M
University of Illinois
    Urbana-Champaign M,W
University of St. Francis M,W
Waubonsee Community College M
Western Illinois University M,W

Indiana
Ancilla College M
Ball State University M
Bethel College M
Butler University M,W
Calumet College of St. Joseph M,W
Goshen College M
Grace College M
Huntington University M
Indiana State University M
Indiana University
    Bloomington M,W
Indiana University-Purdue University Fort Wayne M,W
Indiana University-Purdue University Indianapolis M,W
Indiana Wesleyan University M
Marian College M,W
Oakland City University M,W
Purdue University M,W
St. Joseph's College M,W
Taylor University M
University of Evansville M,W
University of Indianapolis M,W
University of Notre Dame M,W
University of St. Francis M,W
University of Southern Indiana M,W
Vincennes University M

Iowa
Ashford University M
Briar Cliff University M,W
Clinton Community College M,W
Dordt College M
Drake University M,W
Ellsworth Community College M,W
Graceland University M,W
Grand View College M,W
Indian Hills Community College M
Iowa Central Community College M,W
Iowa Lakes Community College M,W
Iowa State University M,W
Iowa Wesleyan College M,W
Kirkwood Community College M
Marshalltown Community College M,W
Morningside College M,W
Muscatine Community College M,W
North Iowa Area Community College M,W
Northwestern College M,W
St. Ambrose University M,W
Scott Community College M,W
Southwestern Community College M
University of Iowa M,W
University of Northern Iowa M,W
Waldorf College M,W
William Penn University M

Kansas
Allen County Community College M,W
Baker University M,W
Barton County Community College M,W
Benedictine College M,W
Bethany College M
Bethel College M,W
Central Christian College of Kansas M,W
Coffeyville Community College M
Colby Community College M,W
Cowley County Community College M
Dodge City Community College M,W
Friends University M
Hutchinson Community College M
Johnson County Community College M
Kansas City Kansas Community College M
Kansas State University M,W
Kansas Wesleyan University M,W
Newman University M,W
Ottawa University M
Pittsburg State University M
Pratt Community College M,W
Southwestern College M,W
University of Kansas M,W
Washburn University of Topeka M
Wichita State University M,W

Kentucky
Bellarmine University M,W
Brescia University M,W
Campbellsville University M,W
Eastern Kentucky University M,W
Georgetown College M,W
Kentucky State University M
Kentucky Wesleyan College M,W
Lindsey Wilson College M,W
Morehead State University M
Murray State University M,W
Northern Kentucky University M,W
Pikeville College M,W
St. Catharine College M,W
Union College M,W
University of Kentucky M,W
University of Louisville M
University of the Cumberlands M,W
Western Kentucky University M,W

Louisiana
Centenary College of Louisiana M,W
Grambling State University M
Louisiana State University and Agricultural and Mechanical College M,W
Louisiana Tech University M
Nicholls State University M,W
Southeastern Louisiana University M
Southern University and Agricultural and Mechanical College M,W
University of Louisiana at Lafayette M
University of Louisiana at Monroe M
University of New Orleans M,W

Maryland
College of Southern Maryland M,W
Coppin State University W
Loyola College in Maryland M
Mount St. Mary's University M,W
Towson University M
University of Maryland
    College Park M,W

Michigan
Aquinas College M,W
Concordia University M
Cornerstone University M
Delta College M,W
Eastern Michigan University M,W
Ferris State University M,W
Grand Rapids Community College M
Grand Valley State University M,W
Kalamazoo Valley Community College M
Lake Michigan College M
Lansing Community College M
Madonna University M,W
Michigan State University M,W
Mott Community College M
Northern Michigan University M
Northwood University M,W
Oakland Community College M
Oakland University M,W
Saginaw Valley State University M
Siena Heights University M
Spring Arbor University M
University of Detroit Mercy M
University of Michigan M,W
Western Michigan University W

Minnesota
Concordia University: St. Paul M,W
Minnesota State University
    Mankato M,W
    Moorhead W
St. Cloud State University M,W
Southwest Minnesota State University W
University of Minnesota
    Twin Cities M,W
Winona State University M,W

Mississippi
Alcorn State University M,W
Belhaven College M,W
Delta State University M
Itawamba Community College M
Jackson State University M,W
Meridian Community College M
Mississippi Gulf Coast Community College
    Jefferson Davis Campus M
Mississippi State University M,W
Mississippi Valley State University M,W
Southwest Mississippi Community College M
University of Mississippi M,W
University of Southern Mississippi M,W
William Carey College M,W

Missouri
Avila University W
Central Methodist University M,W
Central Missouri State University M
Culver-Stockton College M,W
Drury University M,W
Evangel University M,W
Hannibal-LaGrange College M
Lincoln University M
Missouri Baptist University M,W
Missouri Southern State University M
Missouri State University M,W
Missouri Valley College M,W
Missouri Western State University M
Park University W
Penn Valley Community College M
Research College of Nursing M,W
Rockhurst University M,W
St. Louis University M
Southwest Baptist University M
Truman State University M,W
University of Missouri
    Columbia M,W
    Kansas City M,W
    St. Louis M,W
William Jewell College M,W
William Woods University M,W

Montana
Carroll College W
Miles Community College M,W
Montana State University
    Billings M,W
    Bozeman W
Montana Tech of the University of Montana M,W
Rocky Mountain College W
University of Great Falls M,W
University of Montana: Missoula W
University of Montana: Western M,W

Nebraska
Chadron State College W
Concordia University M,W
Creighton University M,W
Dana College W
Doane College M,W
Hastings College M,W
Mid-Plains Community College Area M
Midland Lutheran College M,W
Nebraska College of Technical Agriculture M,W
University of Nebraska
    Kearney M,W
    Lincoln M,W
Wayne State College M,W
York College M,W

Nevada
University of Nevada
    Las Vegas M
    Reno M,W

New Jersey
Brookdale Community College M
Caldwell College M
Fairleigh Dickinson University
    Metropolitan Campus M
Monmouth University M,W
Rider University M
Rutgers, The State University of New Jersey
    New Brunswick/Piscataway Campus M,W
St. Peter's College M
Seton Hall University M

New Mexico
College of the Southwest M,W
New Mexico Junior College M
New Mexico Military Institute Junior College M
New Mexico State University M,W
University of New Mexico M,W
Western New Mexico University M,W

New York
Adelphi University M
Canisius College M
City University of New York
    Queens College M
College of Saint Rose M
Daemen College M
Dominican College of Blauvelt M
Dowling College M
Hofstra University M,W
Iona College M
Le Moyne College M
Manhattan College M
Mercy College M
Niagara University M

Nyack College M
Pace University M,W
St. Bonaventure University M
St. John's University M,W
St. Thomas Aquinas College M,W
Siena College M,W
State University of New York
　　Albany W
　　Binghamton M
Wagner College M,W

North Carolina
Appalachian State University M,W
Barton College M
Belmont Abbey College M
Brevard College M
Campbell University M,W
Catawba College M,W
Davidson College M
Duke University M,W
East Carolina University M,W
Elon University M,W
Fayetteville State University M
Gardner-Webb University M,W
High Point University M,W
Johnson C. Smith University M,W
Lees-McRae College M
Lenoir-Rhyne College M
Louisburg College M,W
Mars Hill College M
Montreat College M
Mount Olive College M
North Carolina Central University M,W
North Carolina State University M,W
Pfeiffer University M,W
Pitt Community College M
Queens University of Charlotte M,W
St. Andrews Presbyterian College M
St. Augustine's College M,W
University of North Carolina
　　Chapel Hill M,W
　　Charlotte M
　　Greensboro M,W
　　Pembroke M
　　Wilmington M,W
Wake Forest University M,W
Western Carolina University M,W
Wingate University M,W

North Dakota
Dickinson State University M,W
Jamestown College M,W
Minot State University M,W
North Dakota State University W
University of North Dakota M,W

Ohio
Ashland University M,W
Bowling Green State University M,W
Cedarville University M
Central State University M,W
Cleveland State University M,W
Kent State University M,W
Lakeland Community College M,W
Malone College M,W
Miami University
　　Oxford Campus M
Mount Vernon Nazarene University M
Ohio Dominican University M,W
Ohio State University
　　Columbus Campus M,W
Ohio University M
Shawnee State University M
Sinclair Community College M
University of Akron M
University of Dayton M,W
University of Findlay M,W
University of Toledo M,W
Urbana University M
Ursuline College W
Walsh University M,W
Wright State University M

Xavier University M,W
Youngstown State University M,W

Oklahoma
Cameron University M,W
East Central University M
Northeastern State University M,W
Oklahoma Baptist University M,W
Oklahoma Christian University M
Oklahoma City University M
Oklahoma Panhandle State University M,W
Oklahoma State University M,W
Oklahoma Wesleyan University M
Oral Roberts University M,W
Redlands Community College W
St. Gregory's University M,W
Seminole State College M,W
Southern Nazarene University M,W
Southwestern Oklahoma State University M,W
University of Central Oklahoma M,W
University of Oklahoma M,W
University of Tulsa M,W

Oregon
Concordia University M,W
Corban College M
Oregon State University M,W
Portland State University M,W
Southwestern Oregon Community College M,W
University of Oregon M,W
University of Portland M,W

Pennsylvania
California University of Pennsylvania M,W
Duquesne University M
Gannon University M,W
Holy Family University M
Indiana University of Pennsylvania M
Kutztown University of Pennsylvania W
La Salle University M,W
Lackawanna College M,W
Lehigh University M,W
Mercyhurst College M,W
Millersville University of Pennsylvania M
Penn State
　　University Park M,W
Philadelphia University M
Robert Morris University M,W
St. Francis University M,W
St. Joseph's University M
Seton Hill University M,W
Slippery Rock University of Pennsylvania M,W
Temple University M
University of Pittsburgh
　　Titusville M
University of the Sciences in Philadelphia M,W
West Chester University of Pennsylvania M,W

Rhode Island
Bryant University M
University of Rhode Island M

South Carolina
Anderson University M,W
Charleston Southern University M,W
The Citadel M,W
Clemson University M
Coastal Carolina University M,W
Coker College M
College of Charleston M,W
Francis Marion University M
Furman University M,W
Lander University M
Limestone College M,W
Morris College M
Newberry College M,W
North Greenville College M
Presbyterian College M
South Carolina State University M
Southern Wesleyan University M
Spartanburg Methodist College M
University of South Carolina M,W
University of South Carolina

　　Aiken M
Winthrop University M,W
Wofford College M,W

South Dakota
Dakota Wesleyan University M,W
Northern State University W
South Dakota State University M,W
University of Sioux Falls M,W

Tennessee
Austin Peay State University M,W
Belmont University M,W
Bethel College M
Carson-Newman College M
Christian Brothers University M,W
Cleveland State Community College M,W
Cumberland University M,W
East Tennessee State University M,W
Hiwassee College M,W
King College M,W
Lambuth University M,W
Lee University M
LeMoyne-Owen College M,W
Lincoln Memorial University M,W
Lipscomb University M,W
Martin Methodist College M
Middle Tennessee State University M,W
Milligan College M,W
Tennessee Technological University M,W
Tennessee Wesleyan College M,W
Trevecca Nazarene University M,W
Tusculum College M,W
Union University M
University of Memphis M,W
University of Tennessee
　　Chattanooga M,W
　　Knoxville M
　　Martin M
Vanderbilt University M,W
Walters State Community College M

Texas
Abilene Christian University M
Baylor University M,W
Hill College M
Lamar University M,W
Lon Morris College M
Lubbock Christian University M,W
McLennan Community College M
Midland College M
Northwood University: Texas Campus M,W
Odessa College M
Paris Junior College M
Prairie View A&M University M,W
Rice University M
St. Edward's University M,W
St. Mary's University M
Sam Houston State University M,W
Southern Methodist University M,W
Stephen F. Austin State University M
Tarleton State University W
Texas A&M University M,W
Texas A&M University
　　Commerce M
Texas Christian University M,W
Texas Southern University M,W
Texas State University: San Marcos M,W
Texas Tech University M,W
Texas Wesleyan University M
Tyler Junior College M,W
University of Houston M
University of North Texas M,W
University of Texas
　　Arlington M
　　Austin M,W
　　Pan American M,W
　　San Antonio M
University of the Incarnate Word M,W
Wayland Baptist University M
West Texas A&M University M,W

Utah
Brigham Young University M,W
Dixie State College of Utah M
Southern Utah University M
University of Utah M
Utah State University M
Utah Valley State College M,W
Weber State University M,W

Virginia
Bluefield College M
George Mason University M
Hampton University M,W
Liberty University M
Longwood University M,W
Old Dominion University M
Radford University M,W
St. Paul's College M
University of Richmond M,W
University of Virginia M,W
Virginia Commonwealth University M
Virginia Intermont College M
Virginia Military Institute M
Virginia Polytechnic Institute and State
　　University M
Virginia State University M,W
Virginia Union University M,W

Washington
Centralia College W
Eastern Washington University W
Edmonds Community College M,W
Gonzaga University M,W
Grays Harbor College M,W
Green River Community College M
Lower Columbia College M
Olympic College M,W
Saint Martin's University M,W
Skagit Valley College M,W
Spokane Community College M,W
Tacoma Community College M,W
University of Washington M,W
Walla Walla Community College M,W
Washington State University M,W
Western Washington University M,W

West Virginia
Alderson-Broaddus College M,W
Bluefield State College M
Concord University M
Davis and Elkins College M
Glenville State College M,W
Marshall University M,W
Ohio Valley University M,W
Salem International University M,W
University of Charleston M
West Liberty State College M,W
West Virginia University Institute of Technology M
West Virginia Wesleyan College M
Wheeling Jesuit University M,W

Wisconsin
Marquette University M
University of Wisconsin
　　Green Bay M
　　Parkside M

Wyoming
Eastern Wyoming College M
University of Wyoming M,W

Gymnastics

Alabama
Auburn University W
University of Alabama W

Alaska
University of Alaska
　　Anchorage W

Arizona
Arizona State University W
University of Arizona W

Arkansas
University of Arkansas W

California
California Polytechnic State University: San Luis
  Obispo W
California State University
  Fullerton W
  Sacramento W
San Jose State University W
Stanford University M,W
University of California
  Berkeley M,W
  Davis W
  Los Angeles W
  Santa Barbara W

Colorado
University of Denver W

Connecticut
Southern Connecticut State University M
University of Bridgeport W

District of Columbia
George Washington University W
Howard University M,W

Florida
University of Florida W

Georgia
University of Georgia W

Idaho
Boise State University W

Illinois
Illinois State University W
University of Illinois
  Chicago M,W
  Urbana-Champaign M,W

Indiana
Ball State University W

Iowa
Iowa State University W
University of Iowa M,W

Kansas
Fort Hays State University M

Kentucky
University of Kentucky W

Louisiana
Centenary College of Louisiana W
Louisiana State University and Agricultural and
  Mechanical College W

Maryland
Columbia Union College M,W
Towson University W
University of Maryland
  College Park W

Michigan
Central Michigan University W
Eastern Michigan University W
Michigan State University W
University of Michigan M,W
Western Michigan University W

Minnesota
University of Minnesota
  Twin Cities M,W
Winona State University W

Missouri
Southeast Missouri State University W
University of Missouri
  Columbia W

Nebraska
University of Nebraska
  Lincoln M,W

New Hampshire
University of New Hampshire W

New Jersey
Rutgers, The State University of New Jersey
  New Brunswick/Piscataway Campus W

North Carolina
North Carolina State University W
University of North Carolina
  Chapel Hill W

Ohio
Bowling Green State University W
Kent State University W
Ohio State University
  Columbus Campus M,W

Oklahoma
University of Oklahoma M,W

Oregon
Oregon State University W

Pennsylvania
Penn State
  University Park M,W
Temple University M,W
University of Pittsburgh W
West Chester University of Pennsylvania W

Rhode Island
University of Rhode Island W

Tennessee
Southern Adventist University M,W

Texas
Texas Woman's University W

Utah
Brigham Young University W
Southern Utah University W
University of Utah W
Utah State University W

Virginia
College of William and Mary M,W

Washington
Seattle Pacific University W

West Virginia
West Virginia University W

Ice hockey

Alabama
University of Alabama
  Huntsville M

Alaska
University of Alaska
  Anchorage M
  Fairbanks M

Colorado
Colorado College M
University of Denver M,W

Connecticut
Quinnipiac University M,W
Sacred Heart University M,W

University of Connecticut M,W

Illinois
McKendree College M,W

Indiana
University of Notre Dame M

Iowa
Dordt College M

Maine
University of Maine M,W

Massachusetts
American International College M
Bentley College M
Boston College M
Boston University W
Merrimack College M
Northeastern University M,W
University of Massachusetts
  Amherst M
  Lowell M

Michigan
Ferris State University M
Lake Superior State University M
Michigan State University M
Michigan Technological University M
Northern Michigan University M
University of Michigan M
University of Michigan
  Dearborn M
Wayne State University M,W
Western Michigan University M

Minnesota
Bemidji State University M
Minnesota State University
  Mankato M,W
St. Cloud State University M,W
University of Minnesota
  Duluth M,W
  Twin Cities M,W

Nebraska
University of Nebraska
  Omaha M

New Hampshire
New England College M,W
University of New Hampshire M,W

New York
Canisius College M
Clarkson University M,W
Colgate University M,W
Monroe Community College M
Niagara University M,W
Rensselaer Polytechnic Institute M,W
St. Lawrence University M,W

North Dakota
Minot State University: Bottineau Campus M
University of North Dakota M,W

Ohio
Bowling Green State University M
Ohio State University
  Columbus Campus M,W

Pennsylvania
Mercyhurst College M,W
Robert Morris University M,W

Rhode Island
Providence College M,W

Vermont
University of Vermont M,W

Judo

Hawaii
Hawaii Tokai International College M,W

Kentucky
University of the Cumberlands M,W

Puerto Rico
Inter American University of Puerto Rico
  Aguadilla Campus M,W
Turabo University W
University of Puerto Rico
  Cayey University College W
  Humacao M,W

Lacrosse

California
Stanford University W
University of California
  Davis W

Colorado
University of Denver M,W

Connecticut
Central Connecticut State University W
Fairfield University M,W
Quinnipiac University M,W
Sacred Heart University M,W
University of Hartford M
University of New Haven W

Delaware
University of Delaware M,W
Wilmington College W

District of Columbia
American University W
Georgetown University M,W

Florida
St. Leo University M

Illinois
Northwestern University W

Indiana
Butler University M
University of Notre Dame M,W

Kentucky
Bellarmine University M

Maryland
Anne Arundel Community College M,W
Community College of Baltimore County M,W
Johns Hopkins University M,W
Loyola College in Maryland M,W
Mount St. Mary's University M,W
Towson University M,W
University of Maryland
  Baltimore County M,W
  College Park M,W

Massachusetts
American International College W
Boston College W
Boston University W
Dean College M,W
Mount Ida College M
Stonehill College W
University of Massachusetts
  Amherst M,W
  Lowell M

New Hampshire
Southern New Hampshire University M,W
University of New Hampshire W

New Jersey
Monmouth University W
Rutgers, The State University of New Jersey
New Brunswick/Piscataway Campus M,W

New York
Adelphi University M,W
Canisius College M,W
Colgate University M,W
Dominican College of Blauvelt M,W
Dowling College M
Globe Institute of Technology M
Hofstra University M,W
Iona College W
Le Moyne College M,W
Manhattan College M,W
Marist College M,W
Molloy College M,W
Monroe Community College M
New York Institute of Technology M
Niagara University W
Pace University M
St. John's University M
St. Thomas Aquinas College W
Siena College M,W
State University of New York
Albany M,W
Binghamton M,W
Stony Brook M,W
Syracuse University M,W
Wagner College M,W

North Carolina
Catawba College M
Davidson College W
Duke University M
Lees-McRae College M
Mars Hill College M
Pfeiffer University M,W
Queens University of Charlotte M,W
St. Andrews Presbyterian College M
University of North Carolina
Chapel Hill M,W
Wingate University M

Ohio
Ohio State University
Columbus Campus M,W

Oregon
University of Oregon W

Pennsylvania
Bloomsburg University of Pennsylvania W
Drexel University M
Duquesne University W
East Stroudsburg University of Pennsylvania W
Gannon University W
Indiana University of Pennsylvania W
La Salle University W
Lehigh University M,W
Lock Haven University of Pennsylvania W
Mercyhurst College M,W
Millersville University of Pennsylvania W
Penn State
University Park M,W
Philadelphia University W
Robert Morris University M,W
St. Francis University M
St. Joseph's University M,W
Seton Hill University M
Shippensburg University of Pennsylvania W
Temple University W
West Chester University of Pennsylvania M,W

Rhode Island
Bryant University M,W

South Carolina
Limestone College M,W
Presbyterian College M,W

Tennessee
Vanderbilt University W

Vermont
University of Vermont M,W

Virginia
College of William and Mary W
James Madison University W
Longwood University W
Old Dominion University W
University of Richmond W
University of Virginia M,W
Virginia Military Institute M
Virginia Polytechnic Institute and State University W

West Virginia
Wheeling Jesuit University M

Rifle

Alabama
Birmingham-Southern College W
Jacksonville State University M,W

Alaska
University of Alaska
Fairbanks M,W

California
University of San Francisco M,W

Colorado
Regis University W

Georgia
Mercer University M,W
North Georgia College & State University M,W

Illinois
DePaul University W

Kentucky
Morehead State University M,W
Murray State University M,W
University of Kentucky M,W

Mississippi
University of Mississippi W

Missouri
University of Missouri
Kansas City M,W

Nebraska
University of Nebraska
Lincoln W

Nevada
University of Nevada
Reno M,W

Ohio
University of Akron W

Tennessee
Austin Peay State University W
Tennessee Technological University M,W
University of Memphis M,W
University of Tennessee
Martin M,W

Virginia
George Mason University M,W
Virginia Military Institute M

West Virginia
West Virginia University M,W

Rodeo

Alabama
Troy University M,W
University of West Alabama M

Arizona
Central Arizona College M
Cochise College M
Dine College M,W
Northland Pioneer College M

Arkansas
Southern Arkansas University M,W
University of Arkansas
Monticello M,W

Colorado
Northeastern Junior College M,W

Idaho
Boise State University M,W
College of Southern Idaho M,W

Kansas
Coffeyville Community College M,W
Colby Community College M
Dodge City Community College M,W
Fort Hays State University M
Fort Scott Community College M,W
Garden City Community College M,W
Pratt Community College M,W

Kentucky
Murray State University M,W

Missouri
Missouri Valley College M,W
Northwest Missouri State University M,W

Montana
Dawson Community College M,W
Miles Community College M,W
Montana State University
Bozeman M,W
University of Montana: Missoula M
University of Montana: Western M,W

Nebraska
Chadron State College M,W
Nebraska College of Technical Agriculture M,W

New Mexico
College of the Southwest M,W
Eastern New Mexico University M,W

North Dakota
Dickinson State University M

Oklahoma
Eastern Oklahoma State College M,W
Northeastern Oklahoma Agricultural and Mechanical College M,W
Northwestern Oklahoma State University M,W
Oklahoma Panhandle State University M,W
Southeastern Oklahoma State University M,W
Southwestern Oklahoma State University M,W

Oregon
Blue Mountain Community College M,W
Eastern Oregon University M,W

Tennessee
University of Tennessee
Martin M,W

Texas
Clarendon College M,W
Howard College M,W
North Central Texas College M
Odessa College M,W
Panola College M,W
Sam Houston State University M,W
South Plains College M,W
Tarleton State University M,W
Vernon College M
Weatherford College M
Western Texas College M,W
Wharton County Junior College M,W

Utah
Southern Utah University M,W

Washington
Walla Walla Community College M,W

Wyoming
Casper College M,W
Central Wyoming College M,W
Eastern Wyoming College M,W
Laramie County Community College M,W
Sheridan College M,W
University of Wyoming M,W

Rowing (crew)

California
California State University
Sacramento W
Humboldt State University W
Loyola Marymount University W
San Diego State University W
University of California
Berkeley M,W
Davis W
Irvine M,W
University of Southern California W

Delaware
University of Delaware W

District of Columbia
George Washington University M,W
Georgetown University M,W

Florida
Barry University W
Florida Institute of Technology W
Jacksonville University M,W
Nova Southeastern University W
University of Central Florida W
University of Miami W
University of Tampa W

Indiana
Indiana University
Bloomington W
University of Notre Dame W

Iowa
University of Iowa W

Kansas
Kansas State University W
University of Kansas W

Kentucky
Murray State University W
University of Louisville W

Massachusetts
Boston University M,W
Northeastern University M,W
University of Massachusetts
Amherst W

Michigan
Eastern Michigan University W
Michigan State University W
University of Michigan W

Nebraska
Creighton University W

New Jersey
Rutgers, The State University of New Jersey
    New Brunswick/Piscataway Campus M,W

New York
Dowling College M,W
Fordham University W
Marist College W
State University of New York
    Buffalo W
Syracuse University M,W

North Carolina
Duke University W
University of North Carolina
    Chapel Hill W

Ohio
Ohio State University
    Columbus Campus W

Oklahoma
University of Tulsa W

Pennsylvania
Drexel University M,W
Duquesne University W
Lehigh University W
Mercyhurst College M,W
Philadelphia University M,W
Robert Morris University W
St. Joseph's University M,W
Temple University M,W

South Carolina
Clemson University W

Tennessee
University of Tennessee
    Knoxville W

Texas
Southern Methodist University W
University of Texas
    Austin W

Virginia
University of Virginia W

Washington
Gonzaga University W
University of Washington M,W
Washington State University W
Western Washington University M,W

West Virginia
University of Charleston M,W
West Virginia University W

Rugby

California
University of California
    Berkeley M

Illinois
Eastern Illinois University W

Skiing

Alaska
University of Alaska
    Anchorage M,W
    Fairbanks M,W

Colorado
Colorado Mountain College
    Alpine Campus M,W
    Spring Valley Campus M,W
    Timberline Campus M,W

University of Colorado
    Boulder M,W
University of Denver M,W
Western State College of Colorado M,W

Idaho
Albertson College of Idaho M,W
Boise State University M

Massachusetts
University of Massachusetts
    Amherst M,W

Michigan
Michigan Technological University W
Northern Michigan University M,W

Minnesota
St. Cloud State University W
University of Minnesota
    Twin Cities M,W

Montana
Montana State University
    Bozeman W
Rocky Mountain College M,W

Nevada
Sierra Nevada College M,W
University of Nevada
    Reno M,W

New Hampshire
University of New Hampshire M,W

New Mexico
University of New Mexico M,W

North Carolina
Lees-McRae College M,W

Tennessee
Carson-Newman College M,W

Utah
University of Utah M,W

Vermont
University of Vermont M,W

West Virginia
Davis and Elkins College M,W

Wisconsin
University of Wisconsin
    Green Bay M,W

Soccer

Alabama
Auburn University W
Auburn University at Montgomery M,W
Birmingham-Southern College M,W
Samford University W
Shelton State Community College W
Spring Hill College M,W
Troy University W
University of Alabama W
University of Alabama
    Birmingham M,W
    Huntsville M,W
University of Mobile M,W
University of Montevallo M,W
University of North Alabama W
University of South Alabama W
Wallace State Community College at Hanceville M

Arizona
Arizona State University W
Arizona Western College M
Cochise College W

Embry-Riddle Aeronautical University: Prescott
    Campus M,W
Glendale Community College M,W
Grand Canyon University M
Mesa Community College M
Northern Arizona University W
Pima Community College M,W
Scottsdale Community College M
South Mountain Community College M
University of Arizona W
Yavapai College M

Arkansas
Arkansas State University W
Harding University M,W
John Brown University M,W
Lyon College M,W
Ouachita Baptist University M,W
University of Arkansas W
University of Arkansas
    Little Rock M,W
Williams Baptist College M

California
Alliant International University M,W
Azusa Pacific University M,W
Biola University M,W
California Baptist University M,W
California Polytechnic State University: San Luis
    Obispo M,W
California State Polytechnic University: Pomona
    M,W
California State University
    Bakersfield M,W
    Chico M,W
    Fresno W
    Fullerton M,W
    Los Angeles M,W
    Northridge M
    Sacramento M,W
    San Bernardino M,W
    Stanislaus M,W
Concordia University M,W
Dominican University of California M,W
Fresno City College M,W
Fresno Pacific University M,W
Grossmont Community College W
Holy Names University M,W
Hope International University M,W
Humboldt State University M,W
Loyola Marymount University M,W
Master's College M,W
Notre Dame de Namur University M,W
Pepperdine University W
Point Loma Nazarene University M
St. Mary's College of California M,W
San Diego Christian College M
San Diego State University M,W
San Jose State University M,W
Santa Clara University M,W
Santiago Canyon College M,W
Sonoma State University M,W
Stanford University M,W
University of California
    Berkeley M,W
    Davis M,W
    Irvine M,W
    Los Angeles M,W
    Santa Barbara M,W
University of San Diego M,W
University of San Francisco M,W
University of Southern California W
University of the Pacific W
Vanguard University of Southern California
    M,W
Westmont College M,W
William Jessup University M,W
Yuba Community College District M,W

Colorado
Adams State College W
Colorado Christian University M,W

Colorado College W
Colorado School of Mines M
Colorado State University
    Pueblo M,W
Fort Lewis College M,W
Mesa State College W
Metropolitan State College of Denver M,W
Regis University W
University of Colorado
    Boulder W
    Colorado Springs M
University of Denver M,W
University of Northern Colorado W

Connecticut
Central Connecticut State University M,W
Fairfield University M,W
Norwalk Community College M,W
Post University M,W
Quinnipiac University M,W
Sacred Heart University M,W
Southern Connecticut State University M,W
University of Bridgeport M,W
University of Connecticut M,W
University of Hartford W
University of New Haven M,W

Delaware
Delaware Technical and Community College
    Stanton/Wilmington Campus M,W
Goldey-Beacom College M,W
University of Delaware M,W
Wilmington College M,W

District of Columbia
American University M,W
George Washington University M,W
Georgetown University M,W
Howard University M

Florida
Barry University M,W
Eckerd College M,W
Embry-Riddle Aeronautical University M,W
Flagler College M,W
Florida Atlantic University M,W
Florida Institute of Technology M,W
Florida International University M,W
Florida Southern College M,W
Florida State University W
Jacksonville University M,W
Lynn University M,W
Northwood University
    Florida Campus M,W
Nova Southeastern University M,W
Polk Community College W
Rollins College M,W
St. Leo University M,W
St. Thomas University M,W
Stetson University M,W
University of Central Florida M,W
University of Florida W
University of Miami W
University of North Florida M,W
University of South Florida M,W
University of Tampa W
University of West Florida M,W
Warner Southern College M,W
Webber International University M,W

Georgia
Andrew College M,W
Berry College M,W
Brenau University W
Brewton-Parker College M,W
Clayton State University M,W
Columbus State University W
Covenant College M,W
Emmanuel College M,W
Georgia College and State University W
Georgia Military College W
Georgia Perimeter College M,W
Georgia Southern University M,W

Georgia Southwestern State University M,W
Georgia State University M,W
Gordon College M,W
Kennesaw State University W
Mercer University M,W
Middle Georgia College M,W
Morehouse College M
North Georgia College & State University M,W
Reinhardt College M,W
Shorter College M,W
Thomas University M,W
Truett-McConnell College M,W
University of Georgia W
Young Harris College M,W

Hawaii
Hawaii Pacific University M,W
University of Hawaii
    Manoa W

Idaho
Albertson College of Idaho M,W
Boise State University W
Idaho State University W
Northwest Nazarene University W
University of Idaho W

Illinois
Bradley University M
College of Lake County M,W
DePaul University M,W
Eastern Illinois University M,W
Elgin Community College M,W
Illinois Institute of Technology M,W
Illinois State University M,W
Judson College M,W
Kankakee Community College M
Kishwaukee College M
Lewis and Clark Community College M
Lewis University M,W
Lincoln Land Community College M
Loyola University of Chicago M,W
McHenry County College M
McKendree College M,W
Moraine Valley Community College M,W
Morton College M
Northwestern University M,W
Olivet Nazarene University M,W
Parkland College M,W
Quincy University M,W
Robert Morris College: Chicago M,W
St. Xavier University M,W
South Suburban College of Cook County M
Southern Illinois University Edwardsville M,W
Southwestern Illinois College M
Springfield College in Illinois M,W
Trinity Christian College M,W
Trinity International University M,W
University of Illinois
    Chicago M
    Springfield M
University of St. Francis M,W
Waubonsee Community College M,W
Western Illinois University M,W

Indiana
Bethel College M
Butler University M,W
Calumet College of St. Joseph M,W
Goshen College M,W
Grace College M,W
Huntington University M,W
Indiana Institute of Technology M,W
Indiana State University W
Indiana University
    Bloomington M,W
Indiana University-Purdue University Fort Wayne M,W
Indiana University-Purdue University Indianapolis M,W
Indiana Wesleyan University M,W
Marian College M,W
Oakland City University M,W
Purdue University W
St. Joseph's College M,W
St. Mary-of-the-Woods College W
Taylor University M,W
Taylor University: Fort Wayne M
University of Evansville M,W
University of Indianapolis M,W
University of Notre Dame M,W
University of St. Francis M,W
University of Southern Indiana M,W
Valparaiso University M,W

Iowa
Ashford University M,W
Briar Cliff University M,W
Clinton Community College M,W
Dordt College M,W
Drake University M,W
Graceland University M,W
Grand View College M,W
Iowa Central Community College M,W
Iowa State University W
Iowa Wesleyan College M,W
Kirkwood Community College M
Morningside College M,W
Muscatine Community College M,W
North Iowa Area Community College M,W
Northwestern College M,W
St. Ambrose University M,W
Scott Community College M,W
University of Iowa W
University of Northern Iowa W
Waldorf College M,W
William Penn University M,W

Kansas
Allen County Community College M,W
Baker University M,W
Barton County Community College M,W
Benedictine College M,W
Bethany College M,W
Bethel College M,W
Central Christian College of Kansas M,W
Cloud County Community College M,W
Coffeyville Community College M,W
Emporia State University W
Friends University M,W
Garden City Community College M,W
Hesston College M
Hutchinson Community College W
Johnson County Community College M
Kansas City Kansas Community College M
Kansas Wesleyan University M,W
MidAmerica Nazarene University M,W
Neosho County Community College M,W
Newman University M,W
Ottawa University M,W
Southwestern College M,W
Sterling College M,W
Tabor College M,W
University of Kansas W
University of St. Mary M,W
Washburn University of Topeka W

Kentucky
Asbury College M,W
Bellarmine University M,W
Brescia University M,W
Campbellsville University M,W
Georgetown College M,W
Kentucky Wesleyan College M,W
Lindsey Wilson College M,W
Mid-Continent University M
Morehead State University W
Murray State University W
Northern Kentucky University M,W
Pikeville College M,W
St. Catharine College M,W
Spalding University M,W
Union College M,W
University of Kentucky M,W
University of Louisville M,W
University of the Cumberlands M,W
Western Kentucky University M

Louisiana
Bossier Parish Community College W
Centenary College of Louisiana M,W
Louisiana State University and Agricultural and Mechanical College W
Nicholls State University W
Northwestern State University W
Southeastern Louisiana University W
Southern University and Agricultural and Mechanical College W
University of Louisiana at Lafayette W
University of Louisiana at Monroe W

Maine
Unity College M
University of Maine M,W
University of Maine
    Augusta W

Maryland
Anne Arundel Community College M,W
Chesapeake College W
College of Southern Maryland M,W
Columbia Union College M,W
Community College of Baltimore County M,W
Hagerstown Community College M,W
Loyola College in Maryland M,W
Mount St. Mary's University M,W
Prince George's Community College W
Towson University M,W
University of Maryland
    Baltimore County M,W
    College Park M,W
    Eastern Shore M

Massachusetts
American International College W
Boston College M,W
Boston University M,W
Dean College M
Massasoit Community College W
Merrimack College W
Mount Ida College M,W
Northeastern University M,W
Stonehill College M,W
University of Massachusetts
    Amherst M,W
    Lowell M,W

Michigan
Aquinas College M,W
Central Michigan University W
Concordia University M,W
Cornerstone University M,W
Delta College M
Eastern Michigan University W
Grand Rapids Community College W
Grand Valley State University W
Madonna University M,W
Michigan State University M,W
Northern Michigan University W
Northwood University M,W
Oakland University M,W
Rochester College M,W
Saginaw Valley State University M,W
Schoolcraft College M,W
Siena Heights University M,W
Spring Arbor University M,W
University of Detroit Mercy M,W
University of Michigan M,W
Western Michigan University M,W

Minnesota
Bemidji State University W
Concordia University: St. Paul W
Minnesota State University
    Mankato W
    Moorhead W
St. Cloud State University W
Southwest Minnesota State University W
University of Minnesota
    Crookston W
    Duluth W
    Twin Cities W
Winona State University W

Mississippi
Alcorn State University W
Belhaven College M,W
Delta State University M,W
Hinds Community College M
Holmes Community College W
Meridian Community College M
Mississippi State University W
University of Mississippi W
University of Southern Mississippi W
William Carey College M,W

Missouri
Avila University M,W
Central Methodist University M,W
Central Missouri State University W
Columbia College M
Culver-Stockton College M,W
Drury University M,W
East Central College M
Hannibal-LaGrange College M,W
Harris-Stowe State University M,W
Jefferson College M
Missouri Baptist University M,W
Missouri Southern State University M,W
Missouri State University M,W
Missouri Valley College M,W
Northwest Missouri State University W
Park University M,W
Research College of Nursing M,W
Rockhurst University M,W
St. Louis University M,W
Southeast Missouri State University W
Southwest Baptist University W
St. Louis Community College
    Meramec M,W
Truman State University M,W
University of Missouri
    Columbia W
    Kansas City M
    Rolla M,W
    St. Louis M,W
William Jewell College M,W
William Woods University M,W

Montana
Carroll College W
Flathead Valley Community College M
Montana State University
    Billings M,W
Rocky Mountain College W
University of Great Falls W
University of Montana: Missoula W

Nebraska
Bellevue University M,W
College of Saint Mary W
Concordia University M,W
Creighton University M,W
Dana College M,W
Doane College M,W
Hastings College M,W
Midland Lutheran College W
Wayne State College W
Western Nebraska Community College M,W
York College M,W

Nevada
University of Nevada
    Las Vegas M,W
    Reno W

New Hampshire
Franklin Pierce College M,W
Southern New Hampshire University M,W
University of New Hampshire M,W

New Jersey
Bloomfield College M,W
Caldwell College M,W
Essex County College M
Fairleigh Dickinson University
    Metropolitan Campus M,W
Felician College M,W
Georgian Court University W
Mercer County Community College M,W
Monmouth University M,W
New Jersey Institute of Technology M,W
Ocean County College M,W
Rider University M,W
Rutgers, The State University of New Jersey
    New Brunswick/Piscataway Campus M,W
St. Peter's College M,W
Seton Hall University M,W
Sussex County Community College W

New Mexico
College of the Southwest M,W
New Mexico Highlands University W
University of New Mexico M,W

New York
Adelphi University M,W
Bryant & Stratton Business Institute
    Bryant & Stratton College: Syracuse M,W
Canisius College M,W
City University of New York
    Queens College W
Colgate University M,W
College of Saint Rose M,W
Concordia College M,W
Daemen College M,W
Dominican College of Blauvelt M,W
Dowling College M
Fordham University M,W
Genesee Community College W
Globe Institute of Technology M,W
Hartwick College M
Hofstra University M,W
Houghton College M,W
Iona College M,W
Jamestown Community College M
Le Moyne College M,W
Manhattan College M,W
Marist College M,W
Mercy College M
Molloy College M,W
Monroe Community College M,W
New York Institute of Technology M,W
Niagara University M,W
Nyack College M,W
Pace University W
Roberts Wesleyan College M,W
St. Bonaventure University M,W
St. Francis College M
St. John's University M,W
St. Thomas Aquinas College M,W
Siena College M,W
State University of New York
    Albany M,W
    Binghamton M,W
    Buffalo M,W
    College at Oneonta M
    Stony Brook M,W
Syracuse University M,W
Wagner College W

North Carolina
Appalachian State University M
Barton College M,W
Belmont Abbey College M,W
Brevard College M,W
Campbell University M,W
Catawba College M,W
Davidson College M,W
Duke University M,W
East Carolina University W
Elon University M,W
Gardner-Webb University M,W
High Point University M,W
Lees-McRae College M,W
Lenoir-Rhyne College M,W
Louisburg College M,W
Mars Hill College M,W
Montreat College M,W
Mount Olive College M,W
North Carolina State University M,W
Pfeiffer University M,W
Queens University of Charlotte M,W
St. Andrews Presbyterian College M,W
University of North Carolina
    Asheville M,W
    Chapel Hill M,W
    Charlotte M,W
    Greensboro M,W
    Pembroke M
    Wilmington M,W
Wake Forest University M,W
Western Carolina University W
Wingate University M,W

North Dakota
Jamestown College W
Mayville State University M,W
North Dakota State University W
University of Mary M,W
University of North Dakota W

Ohio
Ashland University M,W
Bowling Green State University M,W
Bryant & Stratton College
    Willoughby Hills M
Cedarville University M,W
Cincinnati State Technical and Community
    College M,W
Cleveland State University M,W
Kent State University W
Lakeland Community College M
Malone College M,W
Miami University
    Oxford Campus W
Mount Vernon Nazarene University M,W
Ohio Dominican University M,W
Ohio State University
    Columbus Campus M,W
Shawnee State University M,W
Southern State Community College M
University of Akron M,W
University of Dayton M,W
University of Findlay M,W
University of Rio Grande M,W
University of Toledo W
Urbana University M,W
Ursuline College W
Walsh University M,W
Wright State University M
Xavier University M,W
Youngstown State University W

Oklahoma
East Central University W
Northeastern State University M,W
Northwestern Oklahoma State University W
Oklahoma Baptist University M,W
Oklahoma Christian University M,W
Oklahoma City University M,W
Oklahoma State University W
Oklahoma Wesleyan University M,W
Oral Roberts University M,W
St. Gregory's University M,W
Southern Nazarene University M,W
Southwestern Oklahoma State University M,W
University of Central Oklahoma W
University of Oklahoma W
University of Science and Arts of Oklahoma
    M,W
University of Tulsa W

Oregon
Concordia University M,W
Corban College M,W
Eastern Oregon University M,W
Oregon Institute of Technology W
Oregon State University M,W
Portland State University W
Southern Oregon University W
Southwestern Oregon Community College M,W
University of Oregon W
University of Portland M,W
Warner Pacific College M,W

Pennsylvania
Bloomsburg University of Pennsylvania M,W
California University of Pennsylvania M,W
Carlow University W
Drexel University M,W
Duquesne University M,W
East Stroudsburg University of Pennsylvania
    M,W
Edinboro University of Pennsylvania W
Gannon University M,W
Geneva College M,W
Holy Family University M,W
Indiana University of Pennsylvania W
Kutztown University of Pennsylvania M,W
La Salle University M,W
Lehigh University M,W
Lock Haven University of Pennsylvania M,W
Mercyhurst College M,W
Millersville University of Pennsylvania M,W
Penn State
    University Park M,W
Philadelphia University M,W
Point Park University M
Robert Morris University M,W
St. Francis University M,W
St. Joseph's University M,W
Seton Hill University M,W
Shippensburg University of Pennsylvania M,W
Slippery Rock University of Pennsylvania M,W
Temple University M,W
University of Pittsburgh M,W
Villanova University M,W
West Chester University of Pennsylvania M,W

Puerto Rico
Inter American University of Puerto Rico
    Aguadilla Campus M
    Bayamon Campus M
    Guayama Campus M
    San German Campus M
Turabo University M
University of Puerto Rico
    Cayey University College M
    Mayaguez M

Rhode Island
Bryant University M,W
Community College of Rhode Island M,W
Providence College M,W
University of Rhode Island M,W

South Carolina
Anderson University M,W
Charleston Southern University M,W
The Citadel M,W
Clemson University M,W
Coastal Carolina University M,W
Coker College M,W
College of Charleston M,W
Columbia College W
Converse College W
Erskine College M,W
Francis Marion University M,W
Furman University M,W
Lander University M,W
Limestone College M,W
Newberry College M,W
North Greenville College M,W
Presbyterian College M,W
Southern Wesleyan University M,W
Spartanburg Methodist College M,W
University of South Carolina M,W
University of South Carolina
    Aiken M
    Upstate M,W
Winthrop University M,W
Wofford College M,W

South Dakota
Augustana College W
Dakota State University M,W
Dakota Wesleyan University M,W
Mount Marty College M,W
South Dakota State University W
University of Sioux Falls M,W
University of South Dakota W

Tennessee
Belmont University M,W
Bethel College M,W
Bryan College M,W
Carson-Newman College M,W
Christian Brothers University M,W
Crichton College M,W
Cumberland University M,W
East Tennessee State University W
Freed-Hardeman University M,W
Hiwassee College M,W
King College M,W
Lambuth University M,W
Lee University M,W
Lincoln Memorial University M,W
Lipscomb University M,W
Martin Methodist College M,W
Middle Tennessee State University W
Milligan College M,W
Tennessee Technological University W
Tennessee Temple University M
Tennessee Wesleyan College M,W
Trevecca Nazarene University M,W
Tusculum College M,W
Union University M,W
University of Memphis M,W
University of Tennessee
    Chattanooga W
    Knoxville W
    Martin W
Vanderbilt University M,W

Texas
Angelo State University W
Baylor University W
Cedar Valley College W
Dallas Baptist University W
Hill College W
Lon Morris College M
Midwestern State University M,W
Northwood University: Texas Campus M,W
Prairie View A&M University W
Rice University W
St. Edward's University M,W
St. Mary's University M,W
Sam Houston State University W
Southern Methodist University M,W
Stephen F. Austin State University W
Texas A&M University W
Texas A&M University
    Commerce W
Texas Christian University W
Texas State University: San Marcos W
Texas Tech University W
Texas Woman's University W
Tyler Junior College M
University of Houston W
University of North Texas W
University of Texas
    Austin W
    San Antonio W
University of the Incarnate Word M,W
West Texas A&M University M,W

Utah
Brigham Young University W
Dixie State College of Utah W
University of Utah W
Utah State University W

Utah Valley State College W

Vermont
University of Vermont M,W

Virginia
Bluefield College M,W
College of William and Mary M,W
George Mason University M,W
James Madison University M,W
Liberty University M,W
Longwood University M,W
Old Dominion University M,W
Radford University M,W
University of Richmond M,W
University of Virginia M,W
Virginia Commonwealth University M,W
Virginia Intermont College M,W
Virginia Military Institute M
Virginia Polytechnic Institute and State University M,W

Washington
Central Washington University W
Clark College M,W
Eastern Washington University W
Edmonds Community College M,W
Everett Community College M,W
Evergreen State College M,W
Gonzaga University M,W
Green River Community College M
Highline Community College M,W
Lower Columbia College W
Northwest University M,W
Olympic College M,W
Peninsula College M
Pierce College M
Seattle Pacific University M
Seattle University M,W
Shoreline Community College M,W
Skagit Valley College M,W
Spokane Community College W
Tacoma Community College M
University of Washington M,W
Walla Walla Community College M,W
Washington State University W
Wenatchee Valley College M,W
Western Washington University M,W
Whatcom Community College M

West Virginia
Alderson-Broaddus College M
Concord University W
Davis and Elkins College M,W
Marshall University M,W
Ohio Valley University M,W
Salem International University M,W
Shepherd University M,W
University of Charleston M,W
West Virginia University M,W
West Virginia Wesleyan College M,W
Wheeling Jesuit University M,W

Wisconsin
Cardinal Stritch University M,W
Marquette University M,W
Milwaukee Area Technical College M,W
University of Wisconsin
    Green Bay M,W
    Milwaukee M,W
    Parkside M,W
Viterbo University M,W

Wyoming
Laramie County Community College M,W
University of Wyoming W

Softball

Alabama
Alabama State University W
Auburn University W
Bevill State Community College W
Birmingham-Southern College W
Central Alabama Community College W
Chattahoochee Valley Community College W
Concordia College W
Enterprise-Ozark Community College W
Faulkner State Community College W
Faulkner University W
Gadsden State Community College W
George C. Wallace State Community College
    George C. Wallace Community College at Dothan M
    Selma W
Jacksonville State University W
Jefferson Davis Community College W
Jefferson State Community College W
Judson College W
Lurleen B. Wallace Community College W
Miles College W
Northwest-Shoals Community College W
Samford University W
Shelton State Community College W
Snead State Community College W
Southern Union State Community College W
Spring Hill College W
Troy University W
University of Alabama W
University of Alabama
    Birmingham W
    Huntsville W
University of Mobile W
University of North Alabama W
University of West Alabama W
Wallace State Community College at Hanceville W

Arizona
Arizona State University W
Arizona Western College W
Central Arizona College W
Eastern Arizona College W
Gateway Community College W
Glendale Community College W
Mesa Community College W
Pima Community College W
Scottsdale Community College W
South Mountain Community College W
University of Arizona W

Arkansas
Henderson State University W
Ouachita Baptist University W
Southern Arkansas University W
University of Arkansas W
University of Arkansas
    Monticello W
Williams Baptist College W

California
Azusa Pacific University W
Bethany University W
Biola University W
California Baptist University W
California Polytechnic State University: San Luis Obispo W
California State University
    Bakersfield W
    Chico W
    Fresno W
    Fullerton W
    Long Beach W
    Northridge W
    Sacramento W
    San Bernardino W
    Stanislaus W
Concordia University W
Dominican University of California W
Fresno City College W
Grossmont Community College W
Hope International University W
Humboldt State University W
Loyola Marymount University W
Master's College W
Notre Dame de Namur University W
Point Loma Nazarene University W
St. Mary's College of California W
San Diego State University W
San Jose State University W
Santa Clara University W
Sonoma State University W
Stanford University W
University of California
    Berkeley W
    Davis W
    Los Angeles W
    Riverside W
    Santa Barbara W
University of San Diego W
University of the Pacific W
Vanguard University of Southern California W
Yuba Community College District W

Colorado
Adams State College W
Arapahoe Community College W
Colorado Northwestern Community College W
Colorado School of Mines W
Colorado State University W
Fort Lewis College W
Mesa State College W
Northeastern Junior College W
Otero Junior College W
Regis University W
University of Colorado
    Colorado Springs W
University of Northern Colorado W

Connecticut
Central Connecticut State University W
Fairfield University W
Post University W
Quinnipiac University W
Sacred Heart University W
Southern Connecticut State University W
University of Bridgeport W
University of Connecticut W
University of New Haven W

Delaware
Delaware State University W
Delaware Technical and Community College
    Owens Campus W
Goldey-Beacom College W
University of Delaware W
Wilmington College W

Florida
Barry University W
Bethune-Cookman College W
Brevard Community College W
Broward Community College W
Central Florida Community College W
Chipola College W
Daytona Beach Community College W
Eckerd College W
Edward Waters College W
Florida Atlantic University W
Florida Community College at Jacksonville W
Florida Gulf Coast University W
Florida Institute of Technology W
Florida Southern College W
Florida State University W
Gulf Coast Community College W
Hillsborough Community College W
Indian River Community College W
Jacksonville University W
Lake City Community College W
Lake-Sumter Community College W
Lynn University W
Manatee Community College W
Miami Dade College W
North Florida Community College W
Northwood University
    Florida Campus W
Nova Southeastern University W
Okaloosa-Walton College W
Palm Beach Community College W
Pasco-Hernando Community College W
Pensacola Junior College W
Polk Community College W
Rollins College W
St. Johns River Community College W
St. Leo University W
St. Petersburg College W
St. Thomas University W
Santa Fe Community College W
Stetson University W
Tallahassee Community College W
University of Central Florida W
University of Florida W
University of North Florida W
University of South Florida W
University of Tampa W
University of West Florida W
Warner Southern College W
Webber International University W

Georgia
Abraham Baldwin Agricultural College W
Albany State University W
Andrew College W
Armstrong Atlantic State University W
Augusta State University W
Brenau University W
Brewton-Parker College W
Columbus State University W
Darton College W
Emmanuel College W
Georgia College and State University W
Georgia Institute of Technology W
Georgia Perimeter College W
Georgia Southern University W
Georgia Southwestern State University W
Georgia State University W
Gordon College W
Kennesaw State University W
Mercer University W
Middle Georgia College W
North Georgia College & State University W
Paine College W
Reinhardt College W
South Georgia College W
Thomas University W
Truett-McConnell College W
University of Georgia W
University of West Georgia W
Valdosta State University W
Young Harris College W

Hawaii
Brigham Young University-Hawaii W
Chaminade University of Honolulu W
Hawaii Pacific University W
University of Hawaii
    Hilo W
    Manoa W

Idaho
Albertson College of Idaho W
North Idaho College W
Northwest Nazarene University W

Illinois
Black Hawk College W
Bradley University W
Carl Sandburg College W
College of Lake County W
Danville Area Community College W
DePaul University W
Eastern Illinois University W
Elgin Community College W
Highland Community College W

Illinois Central College W
Illinois Eastern Community Colleges
    Lincoln Trail College W
    Olney Central College W
    Wabash Valley College W
Illinois State University W
John A. Logan College W
Judson College W
Kankakee Community College W
Kaskaskia College W
Kishwaukee College W
Lake Land College W
Lewis University W
Lincoln Land Community College W
Loyola University of Chicago W
McHenry County College W
McKendree College W
Moraine Valley Community College W
Morton College W
Northwestern University W
Olivet Nazarene University W
Parkland College W
Quincy University W
Rend Lake College W
Robert Morris College: Chicago W
St. Xavier University W
Sauk Valley Community College W
South Suburban College of Cook County W
Southeastern Illinois College W
Southern Illinois University Carbondale W
Southern Illinois University Edwardsville W
Southwestern Illinois College W
Springfield College in Illinois W
Trinity Christian College W
Trinity International University W
University of Illinois
    Chicago W
    Springfield W
University of St. Francis W
Waubonsee Community College W
Western Illinois University W

Indiana
Ancilla College W
Ball State University W
Bethel College W
Butler University W
Calumet College of St. Joseph W
Goshen College W
Grace College W
Huntington University W
Indiana Institute of Technology W
Indiana State University W
Indiana University
    Bloomington W
Indiana University-Purdue University Fort Wayne W
Indiana University-Purdue University Indianapolis W
Indiana Wesleyan University W
Marian College W
Oakland City University W
Purdue University W
St. Joseph's College W
St. Mary-of-the-Woods College W
Taylor University W
University of Evansville W
University of Indianapolis W
University of Notre Dame W
University of St. Francis W
University of Southern Indiana W
Valparaiso University W

Iowa
Ashford University W
Briar Cliff University W
Clinton Community College W
Dordt College W
Drake University W
Ellsworth Community College W
Graceland University W
Grand View College W

Indian Hills Community College W
Iowa Central Community College W
Iowa Lakes Community College W
Iowa State University W
Iowa Wesleyan College W
Iowa Western Community College W
Kirkwood Community College W
Marshalltown Community College W
Morningside College W
North Iowa Area Community College W
Northwestern College W
St. Ambrose University W
Scott Community College W
Southwestern Community College W
University of Iowa W
University of Northern Iowa W
Waldorf College W
William Penn University W

Kansas
Allen County Community College W
Baker University W
Barton County Community College W
Benedictine College W
Bethany College W
Brown Mackie College W
Butler County Community College W
Central Christian College of Kansas W
Cloud County Community College W
Coffeyville Community College W
Colby Community College W
Cowley County Community College W
Dodge City Community College W
Emporia State University W
Fort Hays State University W
Fort Scott Community College W
Friends University W
Garden City Community College W
Highland Community College W
Hutchinson Community College W
Johnson County Community College W
Kansas City Kansas Community College W
Kansas Wesleyan University W
Labette Community College W
McPherson College W
MidAmerica Nazarene University W
Neosho County Community College W
Newman University W
Ottawa University W
Pittsburg State University W
Pratt Community College W
Seward County Community College W
Southwestern College W
Sterling College W
Tabor College W
University of Kansas W
University of St. Mary W
Washburn University of Topeka W
Wichita State University W

Kentucky
Bellarmine University W
Brescia University W
Campbellsville University W
Eastern Kentucky University W
Georgetown College W
Kentucky State University W
Kentucky Wesleyan College W
Lindsey Wilson College W
Mid-Continent University W
Midway College W
Morehead State University W
Northern Kentucky University W
Pikeville College W
St. Catharine College W
Spalding University W
Union College W
University of Kentucky W
University of the Cumberlands W
Western Kentucky University W

Louisiana
Bossier Parish Community College W
Centenary College of Louisiana W
Louisiana State University and Agricultural and Mechanical College W
Louisiana Tech University W
Nicholls State University W
Northwestern State University W
Southeastern Louisiana University W
Southern University and Agricultural and Mechanical College W
University of Louisiana at Lafayette W
University of Louisiana at Monroe W

Maine
University of Maine W

Maryland
Anne Arundel Community College W
Bowie State University W
Chesapeake College W
College of Southern Maryland W
Columbia Union College W
Community College of Baltimore County W
Coppin State University W
Hagerstown Community College W
Morgan State University W
Mount St. Mary's University W
Prince George's Community College W
Towson University W
University of Maryland
    Baltimore County W
    College Park W
    Eastern Shore W

Massachusetts
American International College W
Boston College W
Boston University W
Dean College W
Massasoit Community College W
Merrimack College W
Mount Ida College W
Stonehill College W
University of Massachusetts
    Amherst W

Michigan
Alpena Community College W
Aquinas College W
Central Michigan University W
Concordia University W
Cornerstone University W
Delta College W
Eastern Michigan University W
Ferris State University W
Glen Oaks Community College W
Grand Valley State University W
Henry Ford Community College W
Hillsdale College W
Kalamazoo Valley Community College W
Kellogg Community College W
Lake Michigan College W
Lake Superior State University W
Madonna University W
Michigan State University W
Northwood University W
Oakland Community College W
Oakland University W
Rochester College W
Saginaw Valley State University W
Siena Heights University W
Spring Arbor University W
University of Detroit Mercy W
University of Michigan W
Western Michigan University W

Minnesota
Bemidji State University W
Concordia University: St. Paul W
Minnesota State University
    Mankato W

    Moorhead W
St. Cloud State University W
Southwest Minnesota State University W
University of Minnesota
    Crookston W
    Duluth W
    Twin Cities W
Winona State University W

Mississippi
Alcorn State University W
Belhaven College W
Delta State University W
East Central Community College W
Hinds Community College W
Holmes Community College W
Itawamba Community College W
Jackson State University W
Jones County Junior College W
Meridian Community College W
Mississippi Gulf Coast Community College
    Jefferson Davis Campus W
Mississippi State University W
Mississippi Valley State University W
Southwest Mississippi Community College W
University of Mississippi W
University of Southern Mississippi W
William Carey College W

Missouri
Avila University W
Central Methodist University W
Central Missouri State University W
Columbia College W
Culver-Stockton College W
East Central College W
Evangel University W
Hannibal-LaGrange College W
Harris-Stowe State University W
Jefferson College W
Lincoln University W
Missouri Baptist University W
Missouri Southern State University W
Missouri State University W
Missouri Valley College W
Missouri Western State University W
North Central Missouri College W
Northwest Missouri State University W
Park University W
Rockhurst University W
St. Charles Community College W
St. Louis University W
Southeast Missouri State University W
Southwest Baptist University W
St. Louis Community College
    Meramec W
Truman State University W
University of Missouri
    Columbia W
    Kansas City W
    Rolla W
    St. Louis W
William Jewell College W
William Woods University W

Montana
Montana State University
    Billings W
University of Great Falls W

Nebraska
Bellevue University W
College of Saint Mary W
Concordia University W
Creighton University W
Dana College W
Doane College W
Hastings College W
Mid-Plains Community College Area W
Midland Lutheran College W
Peru State College W
University of Nebraska
    Kearney W

Athletic scholarships

Lincoln W
Omaha W
Wayne State College W
Western Nebraska Community College W
York College W

Nevada
Community College of Southern Nevada W
University of Nevada
    Las Vegas W
    Reno W

New Hampshire
Franklin Pierce College W
Southern New Hampshire University M,W

New Jersey
Bloomfield College W
Brookdale Community College W
Caldwell College W
Fairleigh Dickinson University
    Metropolitan Campus W
Felician College W
Georgian Court University W
Mercer County Community College W
Monmouth University W
Ocean County College W
Rider University W
Rutgers, The State University of New Jersey
    New Brunswick/Piscataway Campus W
St. Peter's College W
Salem Community College W
Seton Hall University W

New Mexico
College of the Southwest W
Eastern New Mexico University W
New Mexico Highlands University W
New Mexico State University W
University of New Mexico W
Western New Mexico University W

New York
Adelphi University W
Canisius College W
City University of New York
    Queens College W
Colgate University W
College of Saint Rose W
Concordia University W
Dominican College of Blauvelt W
Dowling College W
Fordham University W
Globe Institute of Technology W
Hofstra University W
Iona College W
Le Moyne College W
Manhattan College W
Marist College W
Mercy College W
Molloy College W
New York Institute of Technology W
Niagara University W
Nyack College W
Pace University W
St. Bonaventure University W
St. Francis College W
St. John's University W
St. Thomas Aquinas College W
Siena College W
State University of New York
    Albany W
    Binghamton W
    Buffalo W
    Stony Brook W
Syracuse University W
Wagner College W

North Carolina
Barton College W
Belmont Abbey College W
Brevard College W
Campbell University W

Catawba College W
East Carolina University W
Elizabeth City State University W
Elon University W
Fayetteville State University W
Gardner-Webb University W
Johnson C. Smith University W
Lees-McRae College W
Lenoir-Rhyne College W
Louisburg College W
Mars Hill College W
Montreat College W
Mount Olive College W
North Carolina Central University W
North Carolina State University W
Pfeiffer University W
Pitt Community College W
Queens University of Charlotte W
St. Andrews Presbyterian College W
St. Augustine's College W
Shaw University W
University of North Carolina
    Chapel Hill W
    Charlotte W
    Greensboro W
    Pembroke W
    Wilmington W
Wingate University W
Winston-Salem State University W

North Dakota
Dickinson State University W
Jamestown College W
Mayville State University W
Minot State University W
North Dakota State University W
University of Mary W
University of North Dakota W
Valley City State University W

Ohio
Ashland University W
Bowling Green State University W
Cedarville University W
Cleveland State University W
Kent State University W
Lakeland Community College W
Malone College W
Miami University
    Oxford Campus W
Mount Vernon Nazarene University W
Ohio Dominican University W
Ohio State University
    Columbus Campus W
Ohio University W
Shawnee State University W
Southern State Community College W
University of Akron W
University of Dayton W
University of Findlay W
University of Rio Grande W
University of Toledo W
Urbana University W
Ursuline College W
Walsh University W
Wright State University W
Youngstown State University W

Oklahoma
Bacone College W
Cameron University W
Carl Albert State College W
Connors State College W
East Central University W
Eastern Oklahoma State College W
Northeastern Oklahoma Agricultural and
    Mechanical College W
Northeastern State University W
Oklahoma Baptist University W
Oklahoma Christian University W
Oklahoma City University W
Oklahoma Panhandle State University M,W

Oklahoma State University W
Rose State College W
St. Gregory's University W
Seminole State College W
Southeastern Oklahoma State University W
Southern Nazarene University W
Southwestern Oklahoma State University W
University of Central Oklahoma W
University of Oklahoma W
University of Science and Arts of Oklahoma W
University of Tulsa W
Western Oklahoma State College W

Oregon
Blue Mountain Community College W
Clackamas Community College W
Concordia University W
Corban College W
Eastern Oregon University W
Northwest Christian College W
Oregon Institute of Technology W
Oregon State University W
Portland State University W
Southern Oregon University W
Southwestern Oregon Community College W
University of Oregon W

Pennsylvania
Bloomsburg University of Pennsylvania W
California University of Pennsylvania W
Carlow University W
Community College of Beaver County W
Drexel University W
East Stroudsburg University of Pennsylvania W
Edinboro University of Pennsylvania W
Gannon University W
Geneva College W
Holy Family University W
Indiana University of Pennsylvania W
Kutztown University of Pennsylvania W
La Salle University W
Lackawanna College W
Lehigh University W
Lock Haven University of Pennsylvania W
Mansfield University of Pennsylvania W
Mercyhurst College W
Millersville University of Pennsylvania W
Penn State
    University Park W
Philadelphia University W
Point Park University W
Robert Morris University W
St. Francis University W
St. Joseph's University W
Seton Hill University W
Shippensburg University of Pennsylvania W
Slippery Rock University of Pennsylvania W
Temple University W
University of Pittsburgh W
University of the Sciences in Philadelphia W
Villanova University W
West Chester University of Pennsylvania W
Westminster College W

Puerto Rico
Inter American University of Puerto Rico
    Aguadilla Campus M,W
    Bayamon Campus M,W
    Guayama Campus M,W
    Ponce Campus M,W
Universidad Metropolitana M,W
University of Puerto Rico
    Carolina Regional College W
    Cayey University College M
    Humacao W
    Mayaguez W
    Ponce M,W
    Utuado W

Rhode Island
Bryant University W
Community College of Rhode Island W
Providence College W

University of Rhode Island W

South Carolina
Aiken Technical College W
Anderson University W
Charleston Southern University W
Claflin University W
Coastal Carolina University W
Coker College W
College of Charleston W
Erskine College W
Francis Marion University W
Furman University W
Lander University W
Limestone College W
Morris College W
Newberry College W
North Greenville College W
Presbyterian College W
South Carolina State University W
Southern Wesleyan University W
Spartanburg Methodist College W
University of South Carolina W
University of South Carolina
    Aiken W
    Upstate W
Voorhees College W
Winthrop University W

South Dakota
Augustana College W
Dakota State University W
Dakota Wesleyan University W
Mount Marty College W
Northern State University W
South Dakota State University W
University of Sioux Falls W
University of South Dakota W

Tennessee
Austin Peay State University W
Belmont University W
Bethel College W
Carson-Newman College W
Christian Brothers University W
Cleveland State Community College W
Cumberland University W
Dyersburg State Community College W
East Tennessee State University W
Freed-Hardeman University W
Hiwassee College W
Jackson State Community College W
King College W
Lambuth University W
Lee University W
LeMoyne-Owen College W
Lincoln Memorial University W
Lipscomb University W
Martin Methodist College W
Middle Tennessee State University W
Milligan College W
Motlow State Community College W
Roane State Community College W
Southwest Tennessee Community College W
Tennessee Technological University W
Tennessee Wesleyan College W
Trevecca Nazarene University W
Tusculum College W
Union University W
University of Tennessee
    Chattanooga W
    Knoxville W
    Martin W
Volunteer State Community College W
Walters State Community College W

Texas
Abilene Christian University W
Alvin Community College W
Angelo State University W
Baylor University W
Blinn College M
Clarendon College W

Frank Phillips College W
Galveston College W
Grayson County College W
Hill College W
Houston Baptist University W
Howard College W
Lon Morris College W
Midland College W
Midwestern State University W
Northwood University: Texas Campus W
Odessa College W
Paris Junior College W
Prairie View A&M University W
Ranger College W
St. Edward's University W
Sam Houston State University W
Stephen F. Austin State University W
Tarleton State University W
Temple College W
Texas A&M University W
Texas A&M University
 Kingsville W
Texas State University: San Marcos W
Texas Tech University W
Texas Woman's University W
University of Houston W
University of North Texas W
University of Texas
 Arlington W
 Austin W
 San Antonio W
University of the Incarnate Word W
Vernon College W
Western Texas College W
Wiley College W

Utah
Brigham Young University W
Dixie State College of Utah W
Salt Lake Community College W
Snow College W
Southern Utah University W
University of Utah W
Utah State University W
Utah Valley State College W

Vermont
University of Vermont W

Virginia
Bluefield College W
George Mason University W
Hampton University W
James Madison University W
Liberty University W
Longwood University W
Norfolk State University W
Radford University W
St. Paul's College W
University of Virginia W
University of Virginia's College at Wise W
Virginia Intermont College W
Virginia Polytechnic Institute and State
 University W
Virginia State University W
Virginia Union University W

Washington
Big Bend Community College W
Central Washington University W
Centralia College W
Edmonds Community College W
Everett Community College W
Grays Harbor College W
Green River Community College W
Highline Community College W
Lower Columbia College W
Olympic College W
Peninsula College W
Pierce College W
Saint Martin's University W
Seattle University W
Shoreline Community College W

Skagit Valley College W
Spokane Community College W
University of Washington W
Walla Walla Community College W
Wenatchee Valley College W
Western Washington University W
Yakima Valley Community College W

West Virginia
Alderson-Broaddus College W
Bluefield State College W
Concord University W
Davis and Elkins College W
Glenville State College W
Marshall University W
Mountain State University W
Ohio Valley University W
Potomac State College of West Virginia
 University W
Salem International University W
Shepherd University W
University of Charleston W
West Liberty State College W
West Virginia State University W
West Virginia University Institute of Technology
 W
West Virginia Wesleyan College W
Wheeling Jesuit University W

Wisconsin
Cardinal Stritch University W
University of Wisconsin
 Green Bay W
 Parkside W
Viterbo University W

Squash

Nebraska
University of Nebraska
 Lincoln W

New York
Fordham University M

Swimming

Alabama
Auburn University M,W
Spring Hill College M,W
University of Alabama M,W

Alaska
University of Alaska
 Fairbanks W

Arizona
Arizona State University M,W
Northern Arizona University M,W
University of Arizona M,W

Arkansas
Henderson State University M,W
John Brown University W
Ouachita Baptist University M,W
University of Arkansas W
University of Arkansas
 Little Rock M,W

California
Biola University M,W
California Baptist University M,W
California State University
 Bakersfield M,W
 Northridge M,W
 San Bernardino M,W
Grossmont Community College M,W
Loyola Marymount University W
Pepperdine University W
San Diego State University W

San Jose State University W
Stanford University M,W
University of California
 Berkeley M,W
 Davis M,W
 Irvine M,W
 Los Angeles W
 Santa Barbara M,W
University of San Diego W
University of Southern California M,W
University of the Pacific M,W

Colorado
Colorado School of Mines M,W
Colorado State University M,W
Metropolitan State College of Denver M,W
University of Denver M,W
University of Northern Colorado W

Connecticut
Central Connecticut State University W
Fairfield University M,W
Southern Connecticut State University M
University of Bridgeport W
University of Connecticut M,W

Delaware
University of Delaware W

District of Columbia
George Washington University M,W
Georgetown University M,W
Howard University M,W

Florida
Broward Community College M,W
Florida Atlantic University M,W
Florida Southern College M,W
Florida State University M,W
Indian River Community College M,W
St. Leo University M,W
University of Florida M,W
University of Miami M,W
University of North Florida W
University of Tampa M,W

Georgia
Darton College M,W
Georgia Institute of Technology M,W
Georgia Southern University W
University of Georgia M,W

Hawaii
University of Hawaii
 Manoa M,W

Idaho
Albertson College of Idaho M,W

Illinois
Eastern Illinois University M,W
Illinois Institute of Technology M,W
Illinois State University W
Lewis University M,W
Northwestern University M,W
Southern Illinois University Carbondale M,W
University of Illinois
 Chicago M,W
 Urbana-Champaign W
Western Illinois University M,W

Indiana
Ball State University M,W
Indiana University
 Bloomington M,W
Indiana University-Purdue University
 Indianapolis M,W
Purdue University M,W
University of Evansville M,W
University of Indianapolis M,W
University of Notre Dame M,W
Valparaiso University M,W
Vincennes University M,W

Iowa
Iowa State University W
Morningside College M,W
University of Iowa M,W
University of Northern Iowa W

Kansas
University of Kansas W

Kentucky
Asbury College M,W
University of Kentucky M,W
University of Louisville M,W
University of the Cumberlands M,W
Western Kentucky University M,W

Louisiana
Centenary College of Louisiana M,W
Louisiana State University and Agricultural and
 Mechanical College M,W
Tulane University W
University of Louisiana at Monroe M,W
University of New Orleans M,W

Maine
University of Maine W

Maryland
Loyola College in Maryland M,W
Mount St. Mary's University W
Towson University M,W
University of Maryland
 Baltimore County M,W
 College Park M,W

Massachusetts
Boston College W
Boston University M,W
Northeastern University W
University of Massachusetts
 Amherst M,W
 Lowell M

Michigan
Eastern Michigan University M,W
Grand Rapids Community College M,W
Grand Valley State University M,W
Hillsdale College W
Michigan State University M,W
Northern Michigan University W
Oakland University M,W
University of Michigan M,W
Wayne State University M,W

Minnesota
Minnesota State University
 Mankato M,W
St. Cloud State University M,W
University of Minnesota
 Twin Cities M,W

Mississippi
Delta State University M,W

Missouri
Drury University M,W
Missouri State University M,W
St. Louis University M,W
Stephens College W
Truman State University M,W
University of Missouri
 Columbia M,W
 Rolla M

Nebraska
University of Nebraska
 Kearney W
 Lincoln W

Nevada
University of Nevada
 Las Vegas M,W
 Reno W

New Hampshire
University of New Hampshire W

New Jersey
New Jersey Institute of Technology M,W
Rider University M,W
Rutgers, The State University of New Jersey
　New Brunswick/Piscataway Campus M,W
St. Peter's College M,W
Seton Hall University M,W

New Mexico
New Mexico State University W
University of New Mexico W

New York
Adelphi University M,W
Canisius College W
City University of New York
　Queens College M,W
College of Saint Rose M,W
Fordham University M,W
Iona College M,W
Manhattan College W
Marist College M,W
Monroe Community College M,W
Niagara University M,W
St. Bonaventure University M,W
St. Francis College M,W
Siena College W
State University of New York
　Binghamton M,W
　Buffalo M,W
　Stony Brook M,W
Syracuse University M,W
Wagner College W

North Carolina
Campbell University W
Catawba College W
Davidson College M,W
East Carolina University M,W
Gardner-Webb University W
Mars Hill College W
North Carolina Agricultural and Technical State
　University W
North Carolina State University M,W
Pfeiffer University W
University of North Carolina
　Chapel Hill M,W
　Wilmington M,W
Wingate University M,W

North Dakota
University of North Dakota M,W

Ohio
Ashland University M,W
Bowling Green State University M,W
Cleveland State University M,W
Miami University
　Oxford Campus M,W
Ohio State University
　Columbus Campus M,W
Ohio University M,W
University of Akron W
University of Findlay M,W
University of Toledo W
Wright State University M,W
Xavier University M,W
Youngstown State University W

Oregon
Oregon State University W

Pennsylvania
Bloomsburg University of Pennsylvania M,W
California University of Pennsylvania W
Drexel University M,W
Duquesne University M,W
East Stroudsburg University of Pennsylvania W
Edinboro University of Pennsylvania W
Gannon University M,W

Indiana University of Pennsylvania M,W
Kutztown University of Pennsylvania M,W
La Salle University M,W
Lehigh University M,W
Lock Haven University of Pennsylvania W
Mansfield University of Pennsylvania W
Millersville University of Pennsylvania W
Penn State
　University Park M,W
St. Francis University W
Shippensburg University of Pennsylvania M,W
Slippery Rock University of Pennsylvania M,W
University of Pittsburgh M,W
Villanova University W
West Chester University of Pennsylvania W
Westminster College W

Puerto Rico
Bayamon Central University M,W
Inter American University of Puerto Rico
　Bayamon Campus M,W
Turabo University M,W
University of Puerto Rico
　Humacao M,W
　Mayaguez M,W
University of the Sacred Heart M,W

Rhode Island
Bryant University M,W
University of Rhode Island M,W

South Carolina
Clemson University M,W
College of Charleston M,W
Limestone College M,W
University of South Carolina M,W

South Dakota
South Dakota State University M,W
University of South Dakota M,W

Tennessee
Lambuth University M,W
University of Tennessee
　Knoxville M,W

Texas
Rice University W
Southern Methodist University M,W
Texas A&M University M,W
Texas Christian University M,W
University of Houston W
University of North Texas W
University of Texas
　Austin M,W
University of the Incarnate Word W

Utah
Brigham Young University M,W
University of Utah M,W

Vermont
University of Vermont W

Virginia
George Mason University M,W
Old Dominion University M,W
Radford University W
University of Richmond W
University of Virginia M,W
Virginia Military Institute M
Virginia Polytechnic Institute and State
　University M,W

Washington
Seattle University M,W
University of Washington M,W
Washington State University W

West Virginia
Marshall University W
University of Charleston M,W
West Virginia University M,W

West Virginia Wesleyan College M,W
Wheeling Jesuit University M,W

Wisconsin
University of Wisconsin
　Green Bay M,W
　Milwaukee M,W

Wyoming
University of Wyoming M,W

Synchronized swimming

Alabama
University of Alabama
　Birmingham W

California
Stanford University W

New York
Canisius College W

Ohio
Walsh University W

Rhode Island
University of Rhode Island W

Texas
University of the Incarnate Word W

Table tennis

Arizona
South Mountain Community College M,W

Puerto Rico
Inter American University of Puerto Rico
　Aguadilla Campus M,W
　Bayamon Campus M,W
　Ponce Campus M,W
Universidad del Este M,W
Universidad Metropolitana M,W
University of Puerto Rico
　Carolina Regional College M,W
　Cayey University College M,W
　Mayaguez M,W
　Ponce M,W

Tennis

Alabama
Alabama Agricultural and Mechanical
　University M,W
Alabama State University M,W
Auburn University M,W
Auburn University at Montgomery M,W
Birmingham-Southern College M,W
Central Alabama Community College M,W
Faulkner State Community College M,W
Gadsden State Community College M,W
Jacksonville State University M,W
Judson College W
Miles College M,W
Northwest-Shoals Community College W
Samford University M,W
Snead State Community College W
Spring Hill College M,W
Troy University M,W
University of Alabama M,W
University of Alabama
　Birmingham M,W
　Huntsville M,W
University of Mobile W
University of Montevallo M,W
University of North Alabama M,W

University of South Alabama M,W
Wallace State Community College at Hanceville
　M,W

Arizona
Arizona State University M,W
Eastern Arizona College W
Gateway Community College M,W
Glendale Community College M,W
Grand Canyon University W
Northern Arizona University M,W
Pima Community College M,W
Scottsdale Community College M,W
South Mountain Community College M,W
University of Arizona M,W

Arkansas
Arkansas State University W
Arkansas Tech University W
Harding University M,W
Henderson State University W
John Brown University M,W
Lyon College M,W
Ouachita Baptist University M,W
Southern Arkansas University W
University of Arkansas M,W
University of Arkansas
　Fort Smith M,W
　Little Rock M,W

California
Alliant International University M,W
Azusa Pacific University M
Biola University W
California Baptist University W
California Polytechnic State University: San Luis
　Obispo M,W
California State Polytechnic University: Pomona
　M,W
California State University
　Bakersfield W
　Fresno M,W
　Fullerton W
　Long Beach W
　Los Angeles M,W
　Northridge W
　Sacramento M,W
Concordia University M,W
Dominican University of California M,W
Fresno City College M,W
Fresno Pacific University M,W
Grossmont Community College M,W
Hope International University M,W
Loyola Marymount University M,W
Marymount College M,W
Master's College W
Pepperdine University M,W
Point Loma Nazarene University M,W
St. Mary's College of California M,W
San Diego State University M,W
San Jose State University W
Santa Clara University M,W
Sonoma State University M,W
Stanford University M,W
University of California
　Berkeley M,W
　Irvine M,W
　Los Angeles M,W
　Riverside M,W
　Santa Barbara M,W
University of San Diego M,W
University of San Francisco M,W
University of Southern California M,W
University of the Pacific M,W
Vanguard University of Southern California
　M,W
Westmont College M,W
Yuba Community College District M,W

Colorado
Colorado Christian University M,W
Colorado School of Mines M,W
Colorado State University W

Colorado State University
    Pueblo M,W
Mesa State College M,W
Metropolitan State College of Denver M,W
University of Colorado
    Boulder M,W
    Colorado Springs M,W
University of Denver M,W
University of Northern Colorado M,W

Connecticut
Fairfield University M,W
Quinnipiac University M,W
Sacred Heart University M,W
University of Connecticut M,W
University of Hartford M,W
University of New Haven W

Delaware
Delaware State University M,W
Goldey-Beacom College M

District of Columbia
George Washington University M,W
Georgetown University M,W
Howard University M,W

Florida
Barry University M,W
Bethune-Cookman College M,W
Broward Community College M,W
Central Florida Community College W
Eckerd College M,W
Embry-Riddle Aeronautical University M,W
Flagler College M,W
Florida Atlantic University M,W
Florida Community College at Jacksonville W
Florida Gulf Coast University M,W
Florida Institute of Technology M,W
Florida International University W
Florida Southern College M,W
Florida State University M,W
Hillsborough Community College W
Jacksonville University M,W
Lynn University M,W
Northwood University
    Florida Campus M,W
Nova Southeastern University W
Pasco-Hernando Community College W
Rollins College M,W
St. Leo University M,W
St. Thomas University M,W
Stetson University M,W
University of Central Florida M,W
University of Florida M,W
University of Miami M,W
University of North Florida M,W
University of South Florida M,W
University of Tampa W
University of West Florida M,W
Warner Southern College M,W
Webber International University M,W

Georgia
Abraham Baldwin Agricultural College M,W
Albany State University M
Armstrong Atlantic State University M,W
Augusta State University M,W
Berry College M,W
Brenau University W
Clark Atlanta University M,W
Clayton State University W
Columbus State University M,W
Darton College M,W
Emmanuel College M,W
Fort Valley State University M,W
Georgia College and State University M,W
Georgia Institute of Technology M,W
Georgia Perimeter College M,W
Georgia Southern University M,W
Georgia Southwestern State University M,W
Georgia State University M,W
Gordon College W

Kennesaw State University W
Mercer University M,W
Morehouse College M
North Georgia College & State University M,W
Reinhardt College M,W
Savannah State University W
Shorter College M,W
South Georgia College W
University of Georgia M,W
Young Harris College W

Hawaii
Brigham Young University-Hawaii M,W
Chaminade University of Honolulu M,W
Hawaii Pacific University M,W
University of Hawaii
    Hilo M,W
    Manoa M,W

Idaho
Albertson College of Idaho W
Boise State University M,W
Idaho State University M,W
Lewis-Clark State College M,W
University of Idaho M,W

Illinois
Bradley University M,W
Chicago State University M,W
College of Lake County M,W
DePaul University M,W
Eastern Illinois University M,W
Elgin Community College M,W
Illinois State University M,W
Judson College M,W
Lake Land College M,W
Lewis and Clark Community College M,W
Lewis University M,W
McHenry County College M,W
McKendree College M,W
Moraine Valley Community College M,W
Northwestern University M,W
Olivet Nazarene University M,W
Quincy University M,W
Rend Lake College W
Robert Morris College: Chicago W
Sauk Valley Community College M,W
Southern Illinois University Carbondale M,W
Southern Illinois University Edwardsville M,W
Southwestern Illinois College M,W
University of Illinois
    Chicago M,W
    Springfield M,W
    Urbana-Champaign M,W
University of St. Francis M,W
Waubonsee Community College M,W
Western Illinois University M,W

Indiana
Ball State University M,W
Bethel College M,W
Butler University M,W
Goshen College M,W
Grace College M,W
Huntington University M,W
Indiana State University M,W
Indiana University
    Bloomington M,W
Indiana University-Purdue University Fort Wayne M,W
Indiana University-Purdue University Indianapolis M,W
Indiana Wesleyan University M,W
Marian College M,W
Oakland City University M,W
Purdue University M,W
Taylor University M,W
University of Evansville W
University of Indianapolis M,W
University of Notre Dame M,W
University of St. Francis W
University of Southern Indiana M,W
Valparaiso University M,W

Vincennes University M

Iowa
Dordt College M,W
Drake University M,W
Graceland University M,W
Iowa State University W
Morningside College M,W
Northwestern College M,W
St. Ambrose University M,W
University of Iowa M,W
University of Northern Iowa W

Kansas
Baker University M,W
Barton County Community College M,W
Benedictine College M,W
Bethany College M,W
Bethel College M,W
Butler County Community College M,W
Central Christian College of Kansas M,W
Cowley County Community College M,W
Emporia State University M,W
Fort Hays State University W
Friends University M,W
Hutchinson Community College M,W
Johnson County Community College M,W
Kansas State University W
Kansas Wesleyan University M,W
Labette Community College W
Newman University M,W
Seward County Community College M,W
Southwestern College M,W
Tabor College M,W
University of Kansas W
Washburn University of Topeka M,W
Wichita State University M,W

Kentucky
Asbury College M,W
Bellarmine University M,W
Brescia University W
Campbellsville University M,W
Eastern Kentucky University M,W
Georgetown College M,W
Kentucky State University M,W
Kentucky Wesleyan College W
Lindsey Wilson College M,W
Midway College W
Morehead State University M,W
Murray State University M,W
Northern Kentucky University M,W
Pikeville College M,W
Union College M,W
University of Kentucky M,W
University of Louisville M,W
University of the Cumberlands M,W
Western Kentucky University M,W

Louisiana
Centenary College of Louisiana M,W
Dillard University M,W
Grambling State University M,W
Louisiana State University and Agricultural and Mechanical College M,W
Louisiana Tech University W
Nicholls State University M,W
Northwestern State University W
Southeastern Louisiana University M,W
Southern University and Agricultural and Mechanical College M,W
University of Louisiana at Lafayette M,W
University of New Orleans M,W
Xavier University of Louisiana M,W

Maryland
College of Southern Maryland M,W
Community College of Baltimore County M,W
Coppin State University M,W
Loyola College in Maryland M,W
Morgan State University M,W
Mount St. Mary's University M,W
Towson University M,W

University of Maryland
    Baltimore County M,W
    College Park W
    Eastern Shore M,W

Massachusetts
Boston College W
Boston University W
Merrimack College W
Northeastern University M
Stonehill College M,W
University of Massachusetts
    Amherst W
    Lowell M,W

Michigan
Aquinas College M,W
Eastern Michigan University W
Ferris State University M,W
Glen Oaks Community College W
Grand Rapids Community College W
Grand Valley State University M,W
Henry Ford Community College M,W
Lake Superior State University M,W
Michigan State University M,W
Michigan Technological University W
Northwood University M,W
Oakland Community College W
Oakland University W
Saginaw Valley State University W
Spring Arbor University M,W
University of Detroit Mercy W
University of Michigan M,W
Wayne State University M,W
Western Michigan University M,W

Minnesota
Bemidji State University W
Minnesota State University
    Mankato M,W
    Moorhead W
St. Cloud State University M,W
Southwest Minnesota State University W
University of Minnesota
    Duluth M,W
    Twin Cities M,W
Winona State University M,W

Mississippi
Alcorn State University M,W
Belhaven College M,W
Blue Mountain College W
Delta State University M,W
Hinds Community College M,W
Holmes Community College M,W
Jones County Junior College M,W
Meridian Community College M,W
Mississippi Gulf Coast Community College
    Jefferson Davis Campus M,W
Mississippi State University M,W
Mississippi Valley State University M,W
Southwest Mississippi Community College M,W
Tougaloo College M,W
University of Mississippi M,W
University of Southern Mississippi M,W

Missouri
Drury University M,W
Evangel University M,W
Lincoln University W
Missouri Baptist University W
Missouri Southern State University W
Missouri State University M,W
Missouri Valley College M,W
Missouri Western State University W
Northwest Missouri State University M,W
Research College of Nursing M,W
Rockhurst University M,W
St. Louis University W
Southeast Missouri State University W
Southwest Baptist University M,W
Stephens College W

Athletic scholarships

Truman State University M,W
University of Missouri
   Columbia W
   Kansas City M,W
   St. Louis M,W
William Jewell College M,W

Montana
Montana State University
   Billings M,W
   Bozeman M,W
University of Montana: Missoula M,W

Nebraska
Concordia University M,W
Creighton University M,W
Hastings College M,W
Midland Lutheran College M,W
University of Nebraska
   Kearney M,W
   Lincoln M,W

Nevada
University of Nevada
   Las Vegas M,W
   Reno M,W

New Hampshire
Franklin Pierce College M,W
Southern New Hampshire University M,W
University of New Hampshire W

New Jersey
Caldwell College M
Fairleigh Dickinson University
   Metropolitan Campus M,W
Georgian Court University W
Monmouth University M,W
New Jersey Institute of Technology M,W
Rider University M,W
Rutgers, The State University of New Jersey
   New Brunswick/Piscataway Campus M,W
St. Peter's College M,W
Seton Hall University W

New Mexico
College of Santa Fe M,W
Eastern New Mexico University W
New Mexico Military Institute Junior College M
New Mexico State University M,W
University of New Mexico M,W
Western New Mexico University M,W

New York
Adelphi University M,W
City University of New York
   Queens College M,W
College of Saint Rose W
Concordia College M,W
Dowling College M,W
Fordham University M,W
Hofstra University M,W
Le Moyne College M,W
Manhattan College M,W
Marist College M,W
Mercy College M
Molloy College W
Niagara University M,W
Pace University M,W
St. Bonaventure University M,W
St. Francis College M,W
St. John's University M,W
Siena College M,W
State University of New York
   Albany W
   Binghamton M,W
   Buffalo M,W
   Stony Brook M,W
Syracuse University W
Wagner College M,W

North Carolina
Appalachian State University M,W
Barton College M,W
Belmont Abbey College M,W
Brevard College M,W
Campbell University M,W
Catawba College M,W
Davidson College M,W
Duke University M,W
East Carolina University M,W
Elon University M,W
Fayetteville State University W
Gardner-Webb University M,W
High Point University M,W
Johnson C. Smith University M,W
Lees-McRae College M,W
Lenoir-Rhyne College W
Mars Hill College M,W
Montreat College M,W
Mount Olive College M,W
North Carolina Agricultural and Technical State
   University M,W
North Carolina Central University M,W
North Carolina State University M,W
Pfeiffer University M,W
Queens University of Charlotte M,W
St. Andrews Presbyterian College W
St. Augustine's College M,W
Shaw University M,W
University of North Carolina
   Asheville M,W
   Chapel Hill M,W
   Charlotte M,W
   Greensboro M,W
   Wilmington M,W
Wake Forest University M,W
Western Carolina University W
Wingate University M,W
Winston-Salem State University M,W

North Dakota
University of Mary M,W
University of North Dakota W

Ohio
Bowling Green State University M,W
Cedarville University M,W
Central State University M,W
Cleveland State University M,W
Malone College M,W
Miami University
   Oxford Campus W
Ohio Dominican University M,W
Ohio State University
   Columbus Campus M,W
Shawnee State University W
Sinclair Community College M,W
University of Akron W
University of Dayton M,W
University of Findlay M,W
University of Toledo M,W
Ursuline College W
Walsh University M,W
Wright State University M,W
Xavier University M,W
Youngstown State University M,W

Oklahoma
Cameron University M,W
East Central University M,W
Northeastern State University W
Oklahoma Baptist University M,W
Oklahoma Christian University M,W
Oklahoma State University M,W
Oral Roberts University M,W
Seminole State College M,W
Southeastern Oklahoma State University M,W
Southern Nazarene University M,W
University of Central Oklahoma M,W
University of Oklahoma M,W
University of Tulsa M,W

Oregon
Portland State University W
Southern Oregon University W
University of Oregon M,W
University of Portland M,W

Pennsylvania
Bloomsburg University of Pennsylvania M,W
California University of Pennsylvania W
Carlow University W
Drexel University M
Duquesne University M,W
East Stroudsburg University of Pennsylvania
   M,W
Edinboro University of Pennsylvania M,W
Geneva College W
Indiana University of Pennsylvania W
Kutztown University of Pennsylvania M,W
La Salle University M,W
Lehigh University M,W
Mercyhurst College M,W
Millersville University of Pennsylvania M,W
Penn State
   University Park M,W
Philadelphia University M,W
Robert Morris University M,W
St. Francis University M,W
St. Joseph's University M,W
Seton Hill University M,W
Shippensburg University of Pennsylvania W
Slippery Rock University of Pennsylvania W
Temple University M,W
University of Pittsburgh W
University of the Sciences in Philadelphia M,W
West Chester University of Pennsylvania M,W
Westminster College W

Puerto Rico
Inter American University of Puerto Rico
   Aguadilla Campus M,W
   Bayamon Campus M,W
   San German Campus M,W
Turabo University M,W
Universidad del Este M,W
University of Puerto Rico
   Bayamon University College M,W
   Carolina Regional College M,W
   Cayey University College M
   Humacao W
   Mayaguez M,W
   Ponce M,W
   Utuado M,W
University of the Sacred Heart M

Rhode Island
Bryant University M,W
University of Rhode Island W

South Carolina
Anderson University M,W
Charleston Southern University M,W
The Citadel M
Claflin University M,W
Clemson University M,W
Coastal Carolina University M,W
Coker College M,W
College of Charleston M,W
Columbia College W
Converse College W
Erskine College W
Francis Marion University M,W
Furman University M,W
Lander University M,W
Limestone College M,W
Morris College M,W
Newberry College M,W
North Greenville College M,W
Presbyterian College M,W
South Carolina State University M,W
Spartanburg Methodist College M,W
University of South Carolina M,W
University of South Carolina
   Aiken M
   Upstate M,W
Winthrop University M,W
Wofford College M,W

South Dakota
Dakota State University M,W
Northern State University W
South Dakota State University M,W
University of Sioux Falls M,W

Tennessee
Austin Peay State University M,W
Belmont University M,W
Bethel College M,W
Carson-Newman College M,W
Christian Brothers University M,W
Cumberland University M,W
East Tennessee State University M,W
Freed-Hardeman University M,W
King College M,W
Lambuth University M,W
Lee University M,W
LeMoyne-Owen College M,W
Lincoln Memorial University M,W
Lipscomb University M,W
Martin Methodist College M,W
Middle Tennessee State University M,W
Milligan College M,W
Tennessee Technological University M,W
Tennessee Wesleyan College M,W
Tusculum College M,W
Union University M,W
University of Memphis M,W
University of Tennessee
   Chattanooga M,W
   Knoxville M,W
   Martin M,W
Vanderbilt University M,W

Texas
Abilene Christian University M,W
Baylor University M,W
Collin County Community College District M,W
Dallas Baptist University W
Lamar University M,W
Laredo Community College M,W
Lee College W
McLennan Community College W
Midwestern State University M,W
North Central Texas College W
Prairie View A&M University M,W
Rice University M,W
St. Edward's University M,W
St. Mary's University M,W
Sam Houston State University M,W
Southern Methodist University M,W
Stephen F. Austin State University W
Tarleton State University W
Temple College M,W
Texas A&M University M,W
Texas A&M University
   Kingsville M,W
Texas Christian University M,W
Texas Southern University M,W
Texas State University: San Marcos W
Texas Tech University M,W
Tyler Junior College M,W
University of Houston W
University of North Texas W
University of Texas
   Austin W
   Pan American M,W
   San Antonio M,W
University of the Incarnate Word M,W
Weatherford College W

Utah
Brigham Young University M,W
Southern Utah University W
University of Utah M,W
Utah State University M,W
Weber State University M,W

Virginia
Bluefield College M,W
College of William and Mary M,W
George Mason University M,W
Hampton University M,W
Liberty University M,W
Longwood University M,W
Norfolk State University M,W
Old Dominion University M,W
Radford University M,W
St. Paul's College M,W
University of Richmond M,W
University of Virginia M,W
University of Virginia's College at Wise M,W
Virginia Commonwealth University M,W
Virginia Intermont College M,W
Virginia Military Institute M
Virginia Polytechnic Institute and State University M,W
Virginia State University M,W
Virginia Union University M,W

Washington
Eastern Washington University M,W
Gonzaga University M,W
Green River Community College M,W
Shoreline Community College M,W
Skagit Valley College M,W
Spokane Community College M,W
University of Washington M,W
Washington State University W

West Virginia
Bluefield State College M,W
Concord University M,W
Marshall University W
Salem International University M,W
Shepherd University M,W
University of Charleston M,W
West Liberty State College M,W
West Virginia University W
West Virginia University Institute of Technology M,W
West Virginia Wesleyan College M,W

Wisconsin
Marquette University M,W
University of Wisconsin
   Green Bay M,W
   Milwaukee W

Wyoming
University of Wyoming W

Track and field

Alabama
Alabama Agricultural and Mechanical University M,W
Alabama State University M,W
Auburn University M,W
Lawson State Community College M
Miles College M,W
Samford University M,W
Troy University M,W
University of Alabama M,W
University of Alabama
   Birmingham W
   Huntsville M,W
University of South Alabama M,W
Wallace State Community College at Hanceville M,W

Arizona
Arizona State University M,W
Central Arizona College M,W
Gateway Community College M,W
Glendale Community College M,W
Mesa Community College M,W
Northern Arizona University M,W
Pima Community College M,W
Scottsdale Community College M,W
University of Arizona M,W

Arkansas
Arkansas State University M,W
Harding University M,W
University of Arkansas M,W
University of Arkansas
   Little Rock M,W
   Pine Bluff M,W

California
Alliant International University M,W
Azusa Pacific University M,W
Biola University M,W
California Polytechnic State University: San Luis Obispo M,W
California State Polytechnic University: Pomona M,W
California State University
   Bakersfield M,W
   Chico M,W
   Fresno M,W
   Fullerton M,W
   Long Beach M,W
   Los Angeles M,W
   Northridge M,W
   Sacramento M,W
   Stanislaus M,W
Concordia University M,W
Fresno City College M,W
Fresno Pacific University M,W
Humboldt State University M,W
Point Loma Nazarene University M,W
San Diego State University W
Santiago Canyon College M,W
Sonoma State University W
Stanford University M,W
University of California
   Berkeley M,W
   Irvine M,W
   Los Angeles M,W
   Riverside M,W
   Santa Barbara M,W
University of Southern California M,W
Vanguard University of Southern California M,W
Westmont College M,W
Yuba Community College District M,W

Colorado
Adams State College M,W
Colorado School of Mines M,W
Colorado State University M,W
University of Colorado
   Boulder M,W
   Colorado Springs M,W
University of Northern Colorado M,W
Western State College of Colorado M,W

Connecticut
Central Connecticut State University M,W
Quinnipiac University M,W
Sacred Heart University M,W
Southern Connecticut State University M
University of Connecticut M,W
University of New Haven M,W

Delaware
Delaware State University M,W
University of Delaware W

District of Columbia
American University M,W
Georgetown University M,W
Howard University M,W

Florida
Bethune-Cookman College M,W
Edward Waters College M
Embry-Riddle Aeronautical University M,W
Florida Agricultural and Mechanical University M,W
Florida Atlantic University W
Florida International University M,W
Florida Memorial University M
Florida State University M,W
Jacksonville University W
University of Central Florida W
University of Florida M,W
University of Miami M,W
University of North Florida M,W
University of South Florida M,W
Warner Southern College M,W
Webber International University M,W

Georgia
Albany State University M,W
Berry College M,W
Fort Valley State University M,W
Georgia Institute of Technology M,W
Georgia Southern University W
Georgia State University M,W
Kennesaw State University M,W
Morehouse College M
Paine College M,W
Savannah State University M,W
Shorter College M,W
University of Georgia M,W

Hawaii
University of Hawaii
   Manoa W

Idaho
Albertson College of Idaho M,W
Boise State University M,W
Idaho State University M,W
Northwest Nazarene University M,W
University of Idaho M,W

Illinois
Bradley University W
Chicago State University M,W
Danville Area Community College M,W
DePaul University M,W
Eastern Illinois University M,W
Illinois State University M,W
Lewis University M,W
Loyola University of Chicago M,W
McKendree College M,W
Olivet Nazarene University M,W
Rend Lake College M
Robert Morris College: Chicago W
Southern Illinois University Carbondale M,W
Southern Illinois University Edwardsville M,W
Trinity Christian College M,W
University of Illinois
   Chicago M,W
   Urbana-Champaign M,W
University of St. Francis W
Western Illinois University M,W

Indiana
Ball State University M,W
Goshen College M,W
Grace College M,W
Huntington University M,W
Indiana State University M,W
Indiana University
   Bloomington M,W
Indiana University-Purdue University Fort Wayne W
Indiana Wesleyan University M,W
Marian College M,W
Purdue University M,W
St. Joseph's College M,W
Taylor University M,W
University of Indianapolis M,W
University of Notre Dame M,W
University of St. Francis M,W
Valparaiso University M,W
Vincennes University M,W

Iowa
Ashford University M,W
Briar Cliff University M,W
Dordt College M,W
Drake University M,W
Graceland University M,W
Iowa Lakes Community College M,W
Iowa State University M,W
Iowa Wesleyan College M,W
Morningside College M,W
North Iowa Area Community College M,W
Northwestern College M,W
St. Ambrose University M,W
University of Iowa M,W
University of Northern Iowa M,W
William Penn University M,W

Kansas
Allen County Community College M,W
Baker University M,W
Barton County Community College M,W
Benedictine College M,W
Bethany College M,W
Bethel College M,W
Butler County Community College M,W
Cloud County Community College M,W
Coffeyville Community College M,W
Colby Community College M,W
Emporia State University M,W
Fort Hays State University M,W
Garden City Community College M,W
Highland Community College M,W
Hutchinson Community College M,W
Johnson County Community College M,W
Kansas City Kansas Community College M,W
Kansas State University M,W
Kansas Wesleyan University M,W
McPherson College M,W
MidAmerica Nazarene University M,W
Neosho County Community College M,W
Ottawa University M,W
Pittsburg State University M,W
Pratt Community College M,W
Southwestern College M,W
Sterling College M,W
Tabor College M,W
University of Kansas M,W
Wichita State University M,W

Kentucky
Bellarmine University M,W
Campbellsville University M,W
Eastern Kentucky University M,W
Kentucky State University M,W
Lindsey Wilson College M,W
Morehead State University M,W
Murray State University M,W
University of Kentucky M,W
University of Louisville M,W
University of the Cumberlands M,W
Western Kentucky University M,W

Louisiana
Grambling State University M,W
Louisiana State University and Agricultural and Mechanical College M,W
Louisiana Tech University M,W
Nicholls State University W
Northwestern State University M,W
Southeastern Louisiana University M,W
Southern University and Agricultural and Mechanical College M,W
University of Louisiana at Lafayette M,W
University of Louisiana at Monroe M,W
University of New Orleans M,W

Maine
University of Maine M,W

Maryland
Bowie State University M,W
Columbia Union College M,W

Coppin State University M,W
Hagerstown Community College M,W
Morgan State University M,W
Mount St. Mary's University M,W
Towson University M,W
University of Maryland
    Baltimore County M,W
    College Park M,W
    Eastern Shore M,W

Massachusetts
Boston College M,W
Boston University M,W
Northeastern University M,W
Stonehill College M,W
University of Massachusetts
    Amherst M,W
    Lowell M,W

Michigan
Aquinas College M,W
Central Michigan University M,W
Cornerstone University M,W
Eastern Michigan University M,W
Ferris State University M,W
Grand Rapids Community College M,W
Grand Valley State University M,W
Hillsdale College M,W
Lake Superior State University M,W
Macomb Community College M,W
Michigan State University M,W
Michigan Technological University W
Northern Michigan University W
Northwood University M,W
Saginaw Valley State University M,W
Siena Heights University M,W
University of Detroit Mercy M,W
University of Michigan M,W
Western Michigan University M,W

Minnesota
Bemidji State University M,W
Concordia University: St. Paul M,W
Minnesota State University
    Mankato M,W
    Moorhead M,W
St. Cloud State University M,W
University of Minnesota
    Duluth M,W
    Twin Cities M,W
Winona State University W

Mississippi
Alcorn State University M,W
Hinds Community College M
Holmes Community College M
Jackson State University M,W
Jones County Junior College M
Mississippi State University M,W
Mississippi Valley State University M,W
University of Mississippi M,W
University of Southern Mississippi M,W

Missouri
Central Methodist University M,W
Central Missouri State University M,W
Evangel University M,W
Harris-Stowe State University W
Lincoln University M,W
Missouri Baptist University W
Missouri Southern State University M,W
Missouri State University M,W
Missouri Valley College M,W
Northwest Missouri State University M,W
Park University M,W
Southeast Missouri State University M,W
Southwest Baptist University M,W
Truman State University M,W
University of Missouri
    Columbia M,W
    Kansas City M,W
    Rolla M,W
William Jewell College M,W

Montana
Montana State University
    Bozeman M,W
University of Montana: Missoula M,W

Nebraska
Chadron State College M,W
Concordia University M,W
Dana College M,W
Doane College M,W
Hastings College M,W
Midland Lutheran College M,W
University of Nebraska
    Kearney M,W
    Lincoln M,W
Wayne State College M,W
York College M,W

Nevada
University of Nevada
    Las Vegas W
    Reno W

New Hampshire
University of New Hampshire M,W

New Jersey
Essex County College M,W
Fairleigh Dickinson University
    Metropolitan Campus M,W
Felician College M,W
Monmouth University M,W
Rider University M,W
Rutgers, The State University of New Jersey
    New Brunswick/Piscataway Campus M,W
St. Peter's College M,W
Seton Hall University M,W

New Mexico
College of the Southwest M,W
Eastern New Mexico University M,W
New Mexico Military Institute Junior College M
New Mexico State University W
University of New Mexico M,W

New York
Adelphi University M,W
Fordham University M,W
Globe Institute of Technology M,W
Houghton College M,W
Iona College M,W
Manhattan College M,W
Marist College M,W
Molloy College M,W
New York Institute of Technology M,W
Pace University M,W
Roberts Wesleyan College M,W
St. Francis College M,W
St. John's University W
St. Thomas Aquinas College M,W
State University of New York
    Albany M,W
    Binghamton M,W
    Buffalo M,W
    College of Technology at Alfred M,W
    Stony Brook M,W
Syracuse University M,W
Wagner College M,W

North Carolina
Appalachian State University M,W
Brevard College M,W
Campbell University M,W
Davidson College M,W
East Carolina University M,W
Elon University W
Fayetteville State University W
Gardner-Webb University M,W
High Point University M,W
Johnson C. Smith University M,W
Lees-McRae College M,W
Livingstone College M,W
Mars Hill College M,W
North Carolina Agricultural and Technical State
    University M,W
North Carolina Central University M,W
North Carolina State University M,W
St. Augustine's College M,W
Shaw University M,W
University of North Carolina
    Asheville M,W
    Chapel Hill M,W
    Charlotte M,W
    Pembroke M
    Wilmington M,W
Wake Forest University M,W
Western Carolina University M,W
Winston-Salem State University M,W

North Dakota
Dickinson State University M,W
Jamestown College M,W
Minot State University M,W
North Dakota State University M,W
University of Mary M,W
University of North Dakota M,W

Ohio
Ashland University M,W
Bowling Green State University M,W
Cedarville University M,W
Central State University M,W
Kent State University M,W
Malone College M,W
Miami University
    Oxford Campus M,W
Ohio State University
    Columbus Campus M,W
Ohio University M,W
University of Akron M,W
University of Dayton W
University of Findlay M,W
University of Rio Grande M,W
University of Toledo M,W
Walsh University M,W
Wright State University W
Xavier University M,W
Youngstown State University M,W

Oklahoma
Oklahoma Baptist University M,W
Oklahoma Christian University M,W
Oklahoma State University M,W
Oral Roberts University M,W
Southern Nazarene University M,W
University of Central Oklahoma M,W
University of Oklahoma M,W
University of Tulsa M,W

Oregon
Clackamas Community College M,W
Concordia University M,W
Eastern Oregon University M,W
Lane Community College M,W
Mount Hood Community College M,W
Oregon Institute of Technology M,W
Portland State University M,W
Southern Oregon University M,W
Southwestern Oregon Community College M,W
University of Oregon M,W
University of Portland M,W
Warner Pacific College M,W

Pennsylvania
Bloomsburg University of Pennsylvania M,W
California University of Pennsylvania M,W
Cheyney University of Pennsylvania M,W
Duquesne University M,W
East Stroudsburg University of Pennsylvania
    M,W
Edinboro University of Pennsylvania M,W
Geneva College M,W
Indiana University of Pennsylvania M,W
Kutztown University of Pennsylvania M,W
La Salle University M,W
Lehigh University M,W
Lock Haven University of Pennsylvania M,W
Millersville University of Pennsylvania M,W
Penn State
    University Park M,W
Robert Morris University M,W
St. Francis University M,W
St. Joseph's University M,W
Shippensburg University of Pennsylvania M,W
Slippery Rock University of Pennsylvania M,W
Temple University M,W
University of Pittsburgh M,W
Villanova University M,W
West Chester University of Pennsylvania M,W

Puerto Rico
Bayamon Central University M,W
Inter American University of Puerto Rico
    Aguadilla Campus M,W
    Bayamon Campus M,W
    Fajardo Campus M,W
    Guayama Campus M,W
    Ponce Campus M,W
    San German Campus M,W
Turabo University M,W
Universidad del Este M,W
Universidad Metropolitana M,W
University of Puerto Rico
    Bayamon University College M,W
    Carolina Regional College M,W
    Cayey University College M,W
    Humacao M,W
    Mayaguez M,W
    Ponce M,W
    Utuado M,W
University of the Sacred Heart M,W

Rhode Island
Bryant University M,W
Providence College M,W
University of Rhode Island M,W

South Carolina
Anderson University M,W
Charleston Southern University M,W
The Citadel M,W
Claflin University M,W
Clemson University M,W
Coastal Carolina University M,W
Furman University M,W
Morris College M,W
South Carolina State University M,W
University of South Carolina M,W
Voorhees College M,W
Winthrop University M,W
Wofford College M,W

South Dakota
Augustana College M,W
Black Hills State University M,W
Dakota Wesleyan University M,W
Mount Marty College M,W
Northern State University M,W
South Dakota School of Mines and Technology
    M,W
South Dakota State University M,W
University of Sioux Falls M,W
University of South Dakota M,W

Tennessee
Austin Peay State University W
Belmont University M,W
Bethel College M,W
East Tennessee State University M,W
King College M,W
Lipscomb University M,W
Martin Methodist College M,W
Middle Tennessee State University M,W
Milligan College M,W
Tennessee Technological University W
University of Memphis M,W
University of Tennessee
    Chattanooga M,W
    Knoxville M,W

Vanderbilt University W

Texas
Abilene Christian University M,W
Angelo State University M,W
Baylor University M,W
Dallas Baptist University W
Lamar University M,W
Northwood University: Texas Campus M,W
Prairie View A&M University M,W
Ranger College M,W
Rice University M,W
Sam Houston State University M,W
South Plains College M,W
Southern Methodist University M,W
Stephen F. Austin State University M,W
Tarleton State University M,W
Texas A&M University M,W
Texas A&M University
   Commerce M,W
Texas Christian University M,W
Texas Southern University M,W
Texas State University: San Marcos M,W
Texas Tech University M,W
University of Houston M,W
University of North Texas M,W
University of Texas
   Austin M,W
   Pan American M,W
   San Antonio M,W
Wayland Baptist University M,W
Wiley College M,W

Utah
Brigham Young University M,W
Southern Utah University M,W
University of Utah W
Utah State University M,W
Utah Valley State College M,W
Weber State University M,W

Vermont
University of Vermont M,W

Virginia
College of William and Mary M,W
George Mason University M,W
Hampton University M,W
James Madison University M,W
Liberty University M,W
Norfolk State University M,W
Radford University M,W
St. Paul's College M,W
University of Richmond W
University of Virginia M,W
Virginia Commonwealth University M,W
Virginia Intermont College M,W
Virginia Military Institute M,W
Virginia Polytechnic Institute and State
   University M,W
Virginia State University M,W
Virginia Union University M,W

Washington
Central Washington University M,W
Clark College M,W
Eastern Washington University M,W
Evergreen State College M,W
Highline Community College M,W
Northwest University M,W
Saint Martin's University M,W
Seattle Pacific University M,W
Seattle University M,W
Spokane Community College M,W
University of Washington M,W
Washington State University M,W
Western Washington University M,W

West Virginia
Glenville State College M,W
Marshall University M,W
University of Charleston M,W
West Liberty State College M,W

West Virginia State University M,W
West Virginia University W
West Virginia Wesleyan College M,W
Wheeling Jesuit University M,W

Wisconsin
Marquette University M,W
Milwaukee Area Technical College M,W
University of Wisconsin
   Milwaukee M,W
   Parkside M,W

Wyoming
University of Wyoming M,W

Volleyball

Alabama
Alabama Agricultural and Mechanical
   University W
Alabama State University W
Auburn University W
Bevill State Community College W
Birmingham-Southern College W
Central Alabama Community College W
Faulkner State Community College M,W
Gadsden State Community College W
Jacksonville State University W
Judson College W
Lawson State Community College W
Miles College W
Northwest-Shoals Community College W
Samford University W
Southern Union State Community College W
Spring Hill College W
Troy University W
Tuskegee University W
University of Alabama W
University of Alabama
   Birmingham W
   Huntsville W
University of Montevallo W
University of North Alabama W
University of South Alabama W
University of West Alabama W
Wallace State Community College at Hanceville
   W

Alaska
University of Alaska
   Anchorage W
   Fairbanks W

Arizona
Arizona State University W
Arizona Western College W
Eastern Arizona College W
Embry-Riddle Aeronautical University: Prescott
   Campus W
Glendale Community College W
Grand Canyon University W
Northern Arizona University W
Pima Community College W
Scottsdale Community College W
University of Arizona W
Yavapai College W

Arkansas
Arkansas State University W
Arkansas Tech University W
Harding University W
Henderson State University W
John Brown University W
Lyon College W
Ouachita Baptist University W
Southern Arkansas University W
University of Arkansas W
University of Arkansas
   Fort Smith W
   Little Rock W
   Pine Bluff W

University of Central Arkansas W
Williams Baptist College W

California
Alliant International University W
Azusa Pacific University W
Bethany University M,W
Biola University W
California Baptist University M,W
California Polytechnic State University: San Luis
   Obispo W
California State Polytechnic University: Pomona
   W
California State University
   Bakersfield W
   Chico W
   Fresno W
   Fullerton W
   Long Beach M,W
   Los Angeles W
   Northridge M,W
   Sacramento W
   San Bernardino W
   Stanislaus W
Concordia University W
Dominican University of California W
Fresno City College W
Fresno Pacific University W
Grossmont Community College M,W
Holy Names University M,W
Hope International University M,W
Humboldt State University W
Loyola Marymount University W
Master's College W
Notre Dame de Namur University W
Pepperdine University M,W
Point Loma Nazarene University W
St. Mary's College of California W
San Diego Christian College W
San Diego State University W
San Jose State University W
Santa Clara University W
Sonoma State University W
Stanford University M,W
University of California
   Berkeley W
   Davis M,W
   Irvine M,W
   Los Angeles M,W
   Riverside W
   Santa Barbara M,W
University of San Diego W
University of San Francisco W
University of Southern California M,W
University of the Pacific M,W
Vanguard University of Southern California W
Westmont College W
William Jessup University W
Yuba Community College District W

Colorado
Adams State College W
Colorado Christian University W
Colorado Northwestern Community College W
Colorado School of Mines W
Colorado State University W
Colorado State University
   Pueblo W
Fort Lewis College W
Mesa State College W
Metropolitan State College of Denver W
Northeastern Junior College W
Otero Junior College W
Regis University W
Trinidad State Junior College W
University of Colorado
   Boulder W
   Colorado Springs W
University of Denver W
University of Northern Colorado W
Western State College of Colorado W

Connecticut
Central Connecticut State University W
Fairfield University W
Post University W
Sacred Heart University M,W
University of Bridgeport W
University of Connecticut W
University of Hartford W
University of New Haven M,W

Delaware
Delaware State University W
University of Delaware W
Wilmington College W

District of Columbia
American University W
George Washington University W
Georgetown University W
Howard University W

Florida
Barry University W
Bethune-Cookman College W
Brevard Community College W
Broward Community College W
Eckerd College M,W
Embry-Riddle Aeronautical University W
Flagler College W
Florida Agricultural and Mechanical University
   W
Florida Atlantic University W
Florida College W
Florida Community College at Jacksonville W
Florida Gulf Coast University W
Florida Institute of Technology W
Florida International University W
Florida Memorial University W
Florida Southern College W
Florida State University W
Hillsborough Community College W
Indian River Community College W
Jacksonville University W
Lake-Sumter Community College W
Lynn University W
Manatee Community College W
Miami Dade College W
Northwood University
   Florida Campus W
Nova Southeastern University W
Palm Beach Community College W
Pasco-Hernando Community College W
Pensacola Junior College W
Polk Community College W
Rollins College W
St. Leo University W
St. Petersburg College W
St. Thomas University W
Stetson University W
University of Central Florida W
University of Florida W
University of Miami W
University of North Florida W
University of South Florida W
University of Tampa W
University of West Florida W
Warner Southern College W
Webber International University W

Georgia
Abraham Baldwin Agricultural College W
Albany State University W
Armstrong Atlantic State University W
Augusta State University W
Berry College W
Brenau University W
Brewton-Parker College W
Covenant College W
Fort Valley State University W
Georgia Institute of Technology W
Georgia Southern University W
Georgia State University W

Mercer University W
Paine College W
University of Georgia W
University of West Georgia W

Hawaii
Brigham Young University-Hawaii W
Chaminade University of Honolulu W
Hawaii Pacific University W
University of Hawaii
    Hilo W
    Manoa M,W

Idaho
Albertson College of Idaho W
Boise State University W
College of Southern Idaho W
Idaho State University W
Lewis-Clark State College W
North Idaho College W
Northwest Nazarene University W
University of Idaho W

Illinois
Black Hawk College W
Bradley University W
Carl Sandburg College W
Chicago State University W
College of Lake County W
Danville Area Community College W
DePaul University W
Eastern Illinois University W
Elgin Community College W
Highland Community College W
Illinois Central College W
Illinois Institute of Technology W
Illinois State University W
John A. Logan College W
Judson College W
Kankakee Community College W
Kaskaskia College W
Kishwaukee College W
Lake Land College W
Lewis and Clark Community College W
Lewis University M,W
Loyola University of Chicago M,W
McHenry County College W
McKendree College W
Moraine Valley Community College W
Morton College W
Northwestern University W
Olivet Nazarene University W
Parkland College W
Quincy University M,W
Rend Lake College W
Robert Morris College: Chicago W
St. Xavier University W
Sauk Valley Community College W
South Suburban College of Cook County W
Southern Illinois University Carbondale W
Southern Illinois University Edwardsville W
Southwestern Illinois College W
Springfield College in Illinois W
Trinity Christian College W
Trinity International University W
University of Illinois
    Chicago W
    Springfield W
    Urbana-Champaign W
University of St. Francis W
Waubonsee Community College W
Western Illinois University W

Indiana
Ball State University M,W
Bethel College W
Butler University W
Calumet College of St. Joseph M,W
Goshen College W
Grace College W
Huntington University W
Indiana State University W
Indiana University

Bloomington W
Southeast W
Indiana University-Purdue University Fort Wayne M,W
Indiana University-Purdue University Indianapolis W
Indiana Wesleyan University W
Marian College W
Oakland City University W
Purdue University W
St. Joseph's College W
Taylor University W
Taylor University: Fort Wayne W
University of Evansville W
University of Indianapolis W
University of Notre Dame W
University of St. Francis W
University of Southern Indiana W
Valparaiso University W
Vincennes University W

Iowa
Ashford University W
Briar Cliff University W
Clinton Community College W
Des Moines Area Community College W
Dordt College W
Drake University W
Ellsworth Community College W
Graceland University M,W
Grand View College W
Indian Hills Community College W
Iowa Central Community College W
Iowa Lakes Community College W
Iowa State University W
Iowa Wesleyan College W
Iowa Western Community College W
Kirkwood Community College W
Morningside College W
Muscatine Community College W
North Iowa Area Community College W
Northwestern College W
St. Ambrose University M,W
Scott Community College W
Southwestern Community College W
University of Iowa W
University of Northern Iowa W
Waldorf College W
William Penn University W

Kansas
Allen County Community College W
Baker University W
Barton County Community College W
Benedictine College W
Bethany College W
Bethel College W
Butler County Community College W
Central Christian College of Kansas W
Cloud County Community College W
Coffeyville Community College W
Colby Community College W
Cowley County Community College W
Dodge City Community College W
Emporia State University W
Fort Hays State University W
Fort Scott Community College W
Friends University W
Garden City Community College W
Hesston College W
Highland Community College W
Hutchinson Community College W
Johnson County Community College W
Kansas City Kansas Community College W
Kansas State University W
Kansas Wesleyan University W
Labette Community College W
McPherson College W
MidAmerica Nazarene University W
Neosho County Community College W
Newman University M,W
Ottawa University W

Pittsburg State University W
Pratt Community College W
Seward County Community College W
Southwestern College W
Sterling College W
Tabor College W
University of Kansas W
University of St. Mary W
Washburn University of Topeka W
Wichita State University W

Kentucky
Asbury College W
Bellarmine University W
Brescia University W
Campbellsville University W
Eastern Kentucky University W
Georgetown College W
Kentucky State University W
Kentucky Wesleyan College W
Lindsey Wilson College W
Morehead State University W
Murray State University W
Northern Kentucky University W
Pikeville College W
Spalding University W
Union College W
University of Kentucky W
University of Louisville W
University of the Cumberlands W
Western Kentucky University W

Louisiana
Centenary College of Louisiana W
Dillard University W
Louisiana State University and Agricultural and Mechanical College W
Louisiana Tech University W
Nicholls State University W
Northwestern State University W
Southeastern Louisiana University W
Southern University and Agricultural and Mechanical College W
University of Louisiana at Lafayette W
University of Louisiana at Monroe W
University of New Orleans W
Xavier University of Louisiana W

Maine
Unity College W
University of Maine W

Maryland
Bowie State University W
College of Southern Maryland W
Community College of Baltimore County W
Coppin State University W
Garrett College W
Hagerstown Community College W
Loyola College in Maryland W
Morgan State University W
Prince George's Community College W
Towson University W
University of Maryland
    Baltimore County W
    College Park W
    Eastern Shore W

Massachusetts
American International College W
Boston College W
Dean College W
Merrimack College W
Mount Ida College M
Northeastern University W
Stonehill College W
University of Massachusetts
    Lowell W

Michigan
Alpena Community College W
Aquinas College W
Central Michigan University W

Concordia University W
Cornerstone University W
Delta College W
Eastern Michigan University W
Ferris State University W
Glen Oaks Community College W
Grand Rapids Community College W
Grand Valley State University W
Hillsdale College W
Kalamazoo Valley Community College W
Kellogg Community College W
Lake Michigan College W
Lake Superior State University W
Lansing Community College W
Macomb Community College W
Madonna University W
Michigan State University W
Michigan Technological University W
Mott Community College W
Northern Michigan University W
Northwood University W
Oakland Community College W
Oakland University W
Rochester College W
Saginaw Valley State University W
Schoolcraft College W
Siena Heights University W
Spring Arbor University W
University of Michigan W
University of Michigan
    Dearborn W
Western Michigan University W

Minnesota
Bemidji State University W
Concordia University: St. Paul W
Minnesota State University
    Mankato W
    Moorhead W
St. Cloud State University W
Southwest Minnesota State University W
University of Minnesota
    Crookston W
    Duluth W
    Twin Cities W
Winona State University W

Mississippi
Alcorn State University W
Belhaven College W
Jackson State University W
Mississippi State University W
Mississippi Valley State University W
University of Mississippi W
University of Southern Mississippi W

Missouri
Avila University W
Central Methodist University W
Central Missouri State University W
College of the Ozarks W
Columbia College W
Cottey College W
Culver-Stockton College W
Drury University W
Evangel University W
Hannibal-LaGrange College W
Harris-Stowe State University W
Jefferson College W
Longview Community College W
Mineral Area College W
Missouri Baptist University M,W
Missouri Southern State University W
Missouri State University W
Missouri Valley College M,W
Missouri Western State University W
Northwest Missouri State University W
Park University M,W
Research College of Nursing W
Rockhurst University W
St. Louis University W
Southeast Missouri State University W

Southwest Baptist University W
State Fair Community College W
Stephens College W
Three Rivers Community College W
Truman State University W
University of Missouri
    Columbia W
    Kansas City W
    St. Louis W
William Jewell College W
William Woods University M,W

Montana
Carroll College W
Miles Community College W
Montana State University
    Billings W
    Bozeman W
Montana Tech of the University of Montana W
Rocky Mountain College W
University of Great Falls W
University of Montana: Missoula W
University of Montana: Western W

Nebraska
Bellevue University W
Central Community College W
Chadron State College W
College of Saint Mary W
Concordia University W
Creighton University W
Dana College W
Doane College W
Hastings College W
Mid-Plains Community College Area W
Midland Lutheran College W
Nebraska College of Technical Agriculture M,W
Peru State College W
University of Nebraska
    Kearney W
    Lincoln W
    Omaha W
Wayne State College W
Western Nebraska Community College W
York College W

Nevada
University of Nevada
    Las Vegas W
    Reno W

New Hampshire
Franklin Pierce College W
University of New Hampshire W

New Jersey
Bloomfield College W
Fairleigh Dickinson University
    Metropolitan Campus W
Georgian Court University W
New Jersey Institute of Technology M,W
Rider University W
Rutgers, The State University of New Jersey
    New Brunswick/Piscataway Campus W
    Newark Regional Campus M
St. Peter's College W
Seton Hall University W

New Mexico
College of the Southwest W
Eastern New Mexico University W
New Mexico Highlands University W
New Mexico State University W
University of New Mexico W
Western New Mexico University W

New York
Adelphi University W
Canisius College W
City University of New York
    Queens College M,W
Colgate University W
College of Saint Rose W

Concordia College M,W
Daemen College W
Dominican College of Blauvelt W
Dowling College W
Fordham University W
Genesee Community College W
Globe Institute of Technology W
Hofstra University W
Houghton College W
Iona College W
Le Moyne College W
Manhattan College W
Marist College W
Mercy College W
Molloy College W
New York Institute of Technology W
Niagara University W
Nyack College W
Pace University W
Roberts Wesleyan College M,W
St. Bonaventure University W
St. Francis College W
St. John's University W
Siena College W
State University of New York
    Albany W
    Binghamton W
    Buffalo W
    Stony Brook W
Syracuse University W
Wagner College W

North Carolina
Appalachian State University W
Barton College W
Brevard College W
Campbell University W
Catawba College W
Davidson College W
Duke University W
East Carolina University M,W
Elizabeth City State University W
Elon University W
Fayetteville State University W
Gardner-Webb University W
High Point University W
Johnson C. Smith University W
Lees-McRae College M,W
Lenoir Community College W
Lenoir-Rhyne College W
Livingstone College W
Louisburg College W
Mars Hill College W
Montreat College W
Mount Olive College W
North Carolina Agricultural and Technical State University W
North Carolina Central University W
North Carolina State University W
Pfeiffer University W
Pitt Community College W
Queens University of Charlotte W
St. Andrews Presbyterian College W
St. Augustine's College W
Shaw University W
Southeastern Community College W
University of North Carolina
    Asheville W
    Chapel Hill W
    Charlotte W
    Greensboro W
    Pembroke W
    Wilmington W
Wake Forest University W
Western Carolina University W
Wingate University W
Winston-Salem State University W

North Dakota
Bismarck State College W
Dickinson State University W
Jamestown College W

Mayville State University W
Minot State University W
Minot State University: Bottineau Campus W
North Dakota State College of Science W
North Dakota State University W
University of Mary W
University of North Dakota W
Valley City State University W
Williston State College W

Ohio
Ashland University W
Bowling Green State University W
Cedarville University W
Central State University W
Clark State Community College W
Cleveland State University W
Kent State University W
Lakeland Community College W
Malone College W
Miami University
    Oxford Campus W
Mount Vernon Nazarene University W
Ohio Dominican University W
Ohio State University
    Columbus Campus M,W
Ohio University W
Shawnee State University W
Sinclair Community College W
Southern State Community College W
University of Akron W
University of Dayton W
University of Findlay W
University of Rio Grande W
University of Toledo W
Urbana University W
Ursuline College W
Walsh University W
Wright State University W
Xavier University W
Youngstown State University W

Oklahoma
Cameron University W
Northeastern Oklahoma Agricultural and Mechanical College W
Oklahoma Panhandle State University W
Oklahoma Wesleyan University W
Oral Roberts University W
Redlands Community College W
St. Gregory's University W
Seminole State College M,W
Southeastern Oklahoma State University W
Southern Nazarene University W
University of Central Oklahoma W
University of Oklahoma W
University of Tulsa W

Oregon
Blue Mountain Community College W
Chemeketa Community College W
Clackamas Community College W
Concordia University W
Corban College W
Eastern Oregon University W
Lane Community College W
Linn-Benton Community College W
Mount Hood Community College W
Oregon Institute of Technology W
Oregon State University W
Portland State University W
Southern Oregon University W
Southwestern Oregon Community College W
Treasure Valley Community College W
University of Oregon W
University of Portland W
Warner Pacific College W

Pennsylvania
California University of Pennsylvania W
Carlow University W
Cheyney University of Pennsylvania W
Community College of Beaver County W

Duquesne University W
East Stroudsburg University of Pennsylvania W
Edinboro University of Pennsylvania W
Gannon University W
Geneva College W
Harcum College W
Indiana University of Pennsylvania W
Kutztown University of Pennsylvania W
La Salle University W
Lackawanna College W
Lehigh University W
Lock Haven University of Pennsylvania W
Mercyhurst College M,W
Millersville University of Pennsylvania W
Penn State
    University Park M,W
Philadelphia University W
Point Park University W
Robert Morris University W
St. Francis University M,W
Seton Hill University W
Shippensburg University of Pennsylvania W
Slippery Rock University of Pennsylvania W
Temple University W
University of Pittsburgh W
University of Pittsburgh
    Titusville W
University of the Sciences in Philadelphia W
Villanova University W
West Chester University of Pennsylvania W
Westminster College W

Puerto Rico
Bayamon Central University M,W
Inter American University of Puerto Rico
    Aguadilla Campus M,W
    Bayamon Campus M,W
    Ponce Campus M,W
    San German Campus M,W
Turabo University M,W
Universidad del Este M,W
Universidad Metropolitana M,W
University of Puerto Rico
    Bayamon University College M,W
    Carolina Regional College M,W
    Humacao M,W
    Mayaguez M,W
    Ponce M,W
    Utuado M,W
University of the Sacred Heart M,W

Rhode Island
Bryant University W
Community College of Rhode Island W
University of Rhode Island W

South Carolina
Anderson University W
Charleston Southern University W
The Citadel W
Clemson University W
Coastal Carolina University W
Coker College W
College of Charleston W
Columbia College W
Converse College W
Francis Marion University W
Furman University W
Lander University W
Limestone College W
Morris College W
Newberry College W
North Greenville College W
Presbyterian College W
South Carolina State University W
Southern Wesleyan University W
Spartanburg Methodist College W
University of South Carolina W
University of South Carolina
    Aiken W
    Upstate W
Voorhees College W

Winthrop University W
Wofford College W

South Dakota
Augustana College W
Black Hills State University W
Dakota State University W
Dakota Wesleyan University W
Mount Marty College W
South Dakota School of Mines and Technology W
South Dakota State University W
University of Sioux Falls W
University of South Dakota W

Tennessee
Austin Peay State University W
Belmont University W
Bethel College W
Bryan College W
Carson-Newman College W
Christian Brothers University W
Cumberland University W
East Tennessee State University W
Freed-Hardeman University W
Hiwassee College W
King College W
Lambuth University W
Lee University W
LeMoyne-Owen College W
Lincoln Memorial University W
Lipscomb University W
Martin Methodist College W
Middle Tennessee State University W
Milligan College W
Tennessee Technological University W
Tennessee Temple University W
Tennessee Wesleyan College W
Trevecca Nazarene University W
Tusculum College W
Union University W
University of Memphis W
University of Tennessee
    Chattanooga W
    Knoxville W
    Martin W

Texas
Abilene Christian University W
Alvin Community College W
Angelo State University W
Baylor University W
Blinn College W
Clarendon College W
Dallas Baptist University W
Frank Phillips College W
Galveston College W
Hill College W
Houston Baptist University W
Jacksonville College W
Jarvis Christian College W
Lamar University W
Laredo Community College W
Lee College W
Lon Morris College W
Lubbock Christian University W
Midwestern State University W
North Central Texas College W
Panola College W
Prairie View A&M University W
Rice University W
St. Edward's University W
St. Mary's University W
Sam Houston State University W
Southern Methodist University W
Southwestern Assemblies of God University W
Stephen F. Austin State University W
Tarleton State University W
Temple College W
Texas A&M University W
Texas A&M University
    Commerce W

    Kingsville W
Texas Christian University W
Texas Southern University W
Texas Southmost College W
Texas State University: San Marcos W
Texas Tech University W
Texas Woman's University W
Tyler Junior College W
University of Houston W
University of North Texas W
University of Texas
    Arlington W
    Austin W
    Pan American W
    San Antonio W
University of the Incarnate Word W
Vernon College W
Wayland Baptist University W
West Texas A&M University W
Western Texas College W
Wharton County Junior College W
Wiley College W

Utah
Brigham Young University M,W
College of Eastern Utah W
Dixie State College of Utah W
Salt Lake Community College W
Snow College W
University of Utah W
Utah State University W
Utah Valley State College W
Weber State University W

Virginia
Bluefield College W
College of William and Mary W
George Mason University M,W
Hampton University W
James Madison University W
Liberty University W
Norfolk State University W
Radford University W
St. Paul's College W
University of Virginia W
University of Virginia's College at Wise W
Virginia Commonwealth University W
Virginia Intermont College W
Virginia Polytechnic Institute and State University W
Virginia State University W
Virginia Union University W

Washington
Big Bend Community College W
Central Washington University W
Centralia College W
Clark College W
Eastern Washington University W
Edmonds Community College W
Everett Community College W
Evergreen State College W
Gonzaga University W
Grays Harbor College W
Green River Community College W
Highline Community College W
Lower Columbia College W
Northwest University W
Olympic College W
Pierce College W
Saint Martin's University W
Seattle Pacific University W
Seattle University W
Shoreline Community College W
Skagit Valley College W
Spokane Community College W
Tacoma Community College W
University of Washington W
Walla Walla Community College W
Washington State University W
Western Washington University W
Whatcom Community College W

Yakima Valley Community College W

West Virginia
Alderson-Broaddus College W
Bluefield State College W
Concord University W
Davis and Elkins College W
Glenville State College W
Marshall University W
Mountain State University W
Ohio Valley University W
Salem International University W
Shepherd University W
University of Charleston W
West Liberty State College W
West Virginia University W
West Virginia University Institute of Technology W
West Virginia Wesleyan College W
Wheeling Jesuit University W

Wisconsin
Marquette University W
Milwaukee Area Technical College W
University of Wisconsin
    Green Bay W
    Milwaukee M,W
    Parkside W
Viterbo University W

Wyoming
Casper College W
Eastern Wyoming College W
Laramie County Community College W
Northwest College W
Sheridan College W
University of Wyoming W
Western Wyoming Community College W

Water polo

Arizona
Arizona State University W

California
California Baptist University M,W
California State University
    Bakersfield W
    Long Beach M
Grossmont Community College M,W
Loyola Marymount University M,W
Pepperdine University M
San Diego State University W
San Jose State University W
Santa Clara University M,W
Sonoma State University W
Stanford University M,W
University of California
    Berkeley M,W
    Davis M,W
    Irvine M,W
    Los Angeles M,W
University of Southern California M,W
University of the Pacific M,W

District of Columbia
George Washington University M

Florida
Broward Community College W
Florida Atlantic University W

Hawaii
Brigham Young University-Hawaii M
Chaminade University of Honolulu M
University of Hawaii
    Manoa W

Indiana
Indiana University
    Bloomington W

Michigan
University of Michigan W

New York
City University of New York
    Queens College M,W
Fordham University M
Hartwick College W
Marist College W
St. Francis College M,W
Siena College W
Wagner College W

Pennsylvania
Gannon University M,W
Mercyhurst College M,W
Slippery Rock University of Pennsylvania M,W

Puerto Rico
University of Puerto Rico
    Mayaguez M

West Virginia
Salem International University M

Weight lifting

Connecticut
Norwalk Community College M,W

Puerto Rico
Inter American University of Puerto Rico
    Aguadilla Campus M,W
    Ponce Campus M,W
    San German Campus M,W
Turabo University M,W
Universidad del Este M
Universidad Metropolitana M
University of Puerto Rico
    Carolina Regional College M,W
    Cayey University College M
    Humacao M,W
    Utuado M,W

Washington
Olympic College M,W

Wrestling

Arizona
Arizona State University M
Embry-Riddle Aeronautical University: Prescott Campus M

California
California Polytechnic State University: San Luis Obispo M
California State University
    Bakersfield M
    Fresno M
    Fullerton M
Fresno City College M
Stanford University M
University of California
    Davis M

Colorado
Adams State College M
Colorado School of Mines M
University of Northern Colorado M
Western State College of Colorado M

Connecticut
Sacred Heart University M
Southern Connecticut State University M

Delaware
Delaware State University M

Athletic scholarships

District of Columbia
American University M
Howard University M

Idaho
Boise State University M
North Idaho College M

Illinois
City Colleges of Chicago
    Wright College M,W
Eastern Illinois University M
McKendree College M
Northwestern University M
Southern Illinois University Edwardsville M
Southwestern Illinois College M
University of Illinois
    Urbana-Champaign M
Waubonsee Community College M

Indiana
Indiana University
    Bloomington M
Purdue University M
University of Indianapolis M

Iowa
Briar Cliff University M
Ellsworth Community College M
Iowa Central Community College M
Iowa State University M
Northwestern College M
University of Iowa M
University of Northern Iowa M
Waldorf College M
William Penn University M

Kansas
Colby Community College M
Fort Hays State University M
Labette Community College M
Neosho County Community College M

Kentucky
Campbellsville University M
University of the Cumberlands M,W

Maryland
University of Maryland
    College Park M

Massachusetts
American International College M
Boston University M

Michigan
Central Michigan University M
Eastern Michigan University M
Grand Rapids Community College M
Michigan State University M
University of Michigan M

Minnesota
Minnesota State University
    Mankato M
    Moorhead M
St. Cloud State University M
Southwest Minnesota State University M
University of Minnesota
    Twin Cities M

Missouri
Central Missouri State University M
Missouri Baptist University M
Missouri Valley College M,W
St. Louis Community College
    Meramec M
Truman State University M
University of Missouri
    Columbia M

Montana
University of Great Falls M

Nebraska
Chadron State College M
Dana College M
University of Nebraska
    Kearney M
    Lincoln M
    Omaha M
York College M

New Jersey
Rider University M
Rutgers, The State University of New Jersey
    New Brunswick/Piscataway Campus M

New York
Hofstra University M
Niagara County Community College M
State University of New York
    Binghamton M
    Buffalo M
Wagner College M

North Carolina
Appalachian State University M
Campbell University M
Davidson College M
Duke University M
Gardner-Webb University M
North Carolina Agricultural and Technical State
    University M
North Carolina State University M
University of North Carolina
    Chapel Hill M
    Greensboro M
    Pembroke M

North Dakota
Dickinson State University M
Jamestown College M
North Dakota State University M
University of Mary M

Ohio
Ashland University M
Cleveland State University M
Kent State University M
Ohio State University
    Columbus Campus M
Ohio University M
University of Findlay M

Oklahoma
Oklahoma State University M
University of Central Oklahoma M
University of Oklahoma M

Oregon
Clackamas Community College M
Oregon State University M
Portland State University M
Southern Oregon University M
Southwestern Oregon Community College M
University of Oregon M

Pennsylvania
Bloomsburg University of Pennsylvania M
Drexel University M
Duquesne University M
East Stroudsburg University of Pennsylvania M
Edinboro University of Pennsylvania M
Gannon University M
Kutztown University of Pennsylvania M
Lehigh University M
Lock Haven University of Pennsylvania M
Mansfield University of Pennsylvania M
Mercyhurst College M
Millersville University of Pennsylvania M
Penn State
    University Park M
Shippensburg University of Pennsylvania M
Slippery Rock University of Pennsylvania M
University of Pittsburgh M
University of Pittsburgh
    Johnstown M

Puerto Rico
Inter American University of Puerto Rico
    Bayamon Campus M
University of Puerto Rico
    Bayamon University College M
    Cayey University College M
    Humacao M
    Mayaguez M
University of the Sacred Heart M

South Carolina
Anderson University M
The Citadel M
Limestone College M
Newberry College M
Spartanburg Methodist College M

South Dakota
Augustana College M
Dakota Wesleyan University M
Northern State University M
South Dakota State University M

Tennessee
Carson-Newman College M
Cumberland University M
King College M
University of Tennessee
    Chattanooga M

Utah
Utah Valley State College M

Virginia
George Mason University M
Old Dominion University M
University of Virginia M
Virginia Military Institute M
Virginia Polytechnic Institute and State
    University M

Washington
Highline Community College M
Yakima Valley Community College M

West Virginia
West Liberty State College M
West Virginia University M

Wisconsin
University of Wisconsin
    Parkside M

Wyoming
Northwest College M
University of Wyoming M
Western Wyoming Community College M

Music/drama scholarships

Alabama
Alabama State University
Auburn University at Montgomery
Birmingham-Southern College
Chattahoochee Valley Community College
Enterprise-Ozark Community College
Faulkner University
Huntingdon College
Jacksonville State University
Jefferson State Community College
Judson College
Lurleen B. Wallace Community College
Marion Military Institute
Northeast Alabama Community College
Northwest-Shoals Community College
Samford University
Snead State Community College
Talladega College
University of Alabama
University of Alabama
   Birmingham
   Huntsville
University of Mobile
University of Montevallo
University of North Alabama
University of South Alabama
University of West Alabama
Wallace State Community College at Hanceville

Arizona
Arizona State University
Eastern Arizona College
Grand Canyon University
Northern Arizona University
Northland Pioneer College
Pima Community College
South Mountain Community College
Southwestern College
University of Arizona

Arkansas
Arkansas Northeastern College
Arkansas State University
Arkansas State University
   Beebe
Arkansas Tech University
Crowley's Ridge College
Ecclesia College
Harding University
Henderson State University
Hendrix College
John Brown University
Lyon College
National Park Community College
Northwest Arkansas Community College
Ouachita Baptist University
Phillips Community College of the University of
   Arkansas
Southern Arkansas University
University of Arkansas
University of Arkansas
   Fort Smith
   Monticello
   Pine Bluff
University of Central Arkansas
University of the Ozarks
Williams Baptist College

California
American Academy of Dramatic Arts: West
Azusa Pacific University
Bethany University
Bethesda Christian University
Biola University
California Baptist University
California Institute of the Arts
California Lutheran University
California Polytechnic State University: San Luis
   Obispo
California State Polytechnic University: Pomona
California State University
   Chico
   Fresno
   Long Beach
   Stanislaus
Chapman University
College of the Canyons
College of the Siskiyous
Concordia University
Dominican University of California
El Camino College
Fresno Pacific University
Holy Names University
Hope International University
Irvine Valley College
La Sierra University
Loyola Marymount University
Master's College
Mount St. Mary's College
Mount San Jacinto College
Notre Dame de Namur University
Pepperdine University
Point Loma Nazarene University
Riverside Community College
San Diego Christian College
San Diego State University
San Francisco Conservatory of Music
Santa Clara University
Santa Rosa Junior College
Simpson University
Sonoma State University
University of California
   Riverside
   San Diego
   Santa Cruz
University of La Verne
University of Redlands
University of San Diego
University of Southern California
University of the Pacific
Vanguard University of Southern California
Westmont College
Whittier College
William Jessup University
Yuba Community College District

Colorado
Adams State College
Colorado Christian University
Colorado School of Mines
Colorado State University
Colorado State University
   Pueblo
Fort Lewis College
Mesa State College
Metropolitan State College of Denver
University of Colorado
   Boulder
   Denver and Health Sciences Center
University of Denver
University of Northern Colorado
Western State College of Colorado

Connecticut
Albertus Magnus College
Fairfield University
Sacred Heart University
University of Connecticut
University of Hartford

Delaware
Delaware State University
University of Delaware

District of Columbia
American University
Catholic University of America
George Washington University
Howard University

Florida
Baptist College of Florida
Barry University
Bethune-Cookman College
Central Florida Community College
Chipola College
Clearwater Christian College
Daytona Beach Community College
Eckerd College
Edison College
Flagler College
Florida Christian College
Florida Community College at Jacksonville
Florida Gulf Coast University
Florida International University
Florida Southern College
Gulf Coast Community College
Indian River Community College
Jacksonville University
Lake-Sumter Community College
Lynn University
Manatee Community College
Miami Dade College
North Florida Community College
Okaloosa-Walton College
Palm Beach Atlantic University
Rollins College
St. Leo College
St. Petersburg College
St. Thomas University
Santa Fe Community College
Seminole Community College
South Florida Community College
Southeastern College of the Assemblies of God
Stetson University
Tallahassee Community College
University of Florida
University of Miami
University of North Florida
University of South Florida
University of Tampa
University of West Florida
Warner Southern College

Georgia
Agnes Scott College
Andrew College
Augusta State University
Berry College
Brenau University
Brewton-Parker College
Clark Atlanta University
Columbus State University
Covenant College
Darton College
Emmanuel College
Emory University
Gainesville State College
Georgia College and State University
Georgia Institute of Technology
Georgia Southern University
Georgia State University
Gordon College
Kennesaw State University
LaGrange College
Mercer University
Middle Georgia College
Morehouse College
North Georgia College & State University
Oglethorpe University
Paine College
Piedmont College
Savannah College of Art and Design
Savannah State University
Shorter College
Spelman College
Toccoa Falls College
Truett-McConnell College
University of West Georgia
Valdosta State University
Wesleyan College
Young Harris College

Hawaii
Brigham Young University-Hawaii
Hawaii Pacific University
University of Hawaii
   Manoa

Idaho
Albertson College of Idaho
Boise Bible College
Boise State University
Idaho State University
Lewis-Clark State College
North Idaho College
Northwest Nazarene University
University of Idaho

Illinois
Augustana College
Benedictine University
Black Hawk College
Bradley University
College of DuPage
College of Lake County
Columbia College Chicago
Concordia University
DePaul University
Eastern Illinois University
Elgin Community College
Elmhurst College
Eureka College
Greenville College
Illinois College
Illinois State University
Illinois Wesleyan University
Judson College
Kishwaukee College
Knox College
Lake Forest College
Lewis University
Loyola University of Chicago
MacMurray College
McHenry County College
McKendree College
Millikin University
Monmouth College
Moody Bible Institute
North Central College
North Park University
Northeastern Illinois University
Northwestern University
Oakton Community College
Olivet Nazarene University
Parkland College
Quincy University
Rend Lake College
Roosevelt University
St. Xavier University
South Suburban College of Cook County
Southeastern Illinois College
Southern Illinois University Carbondale
Southern Illinois University Edwardsville
Trinity Christian College
Trinity International University
University of Illinois
   Chicago
   Springfield
   Urbana-Champaign
University of St. Francis

VanderCook College of Music
Waubonsee Community College
Western Illinois University
Wheaton College
William Rainey Harper College

Indiana
American Conservatory of Music
Anderson University
Ball State University
Bethel College
Butler University
DePauw University
Grace College
Hanover College
Huntington University
Indiana Institute of Technology
Indiana State University
Indiana University
    Bloomington
    Southeast
Indiana Wesleyan University
Manchester College
Marian College
Oakland City University
Purdue University
St. Joseph's College
St. Mary-of-the-Woods College
Taylor University
University of Evansville
University of Indianapolis
University of St. Francis
University of Southern Indiana
Valparaiso University
Vincennes University
Wabash College

Iowa
Ashford University
Briar Cliff University
Buena Vista University
Central College
Clarke College
Coe College
Cornell College
Dordt College
Drake University
Ellsworth Community College
Emmaus Bible College
Faith Baptist Bible College and Theological Seminary
Graceland University
Grand View College
Iowa State University
Iowa Wesleyan College
Iowa Western Community College
Kirkwood Community College
Loras College
Luther College
Maharishi University of Management
Morningside College
Mount Mercy College
North Iowa Area Community College
Northwestern College
St. Ambrose University
Simpson College
Southwestern Community College
University of Dubuque
University of Iowa
University of Northern Iowa
Waldorf College
Wartburg College
William Penn University

Kansas
Allen County Community College
Baker University
Barclay College
Benedictine College
Bethany College
Bethel College
Central Christian College of Kansas
Coffeyville Community College
Colby Community College
Emporia State University
Garden City Community College
Hesston College
Highland Community College
Kansas City Kansas Community College
Kansas State University
Kansas Wesleyan University
Manhattan Christian College
MidAmerica Nazarene University
Neosho County Community College
Newman University
Ottawa University
Pittsburg State University
Pratt Community College
Southwestern College
Sterling College
Tabor College
University of Kansas
University of St. Mary
Washburn University of Topeka
Wichita State University

Kentucky
Asbury College
Ashland Community and Technical College
Bellarmine University
Brescia University
Centre College
Eastern Kentucky University
Georgetown College
Kentucky Christian University
Kentucky Mountain Bible College
Kentucky Wesleyan College
Midway College
Morehead State University
Murray State University
Northern Kentucky University
Thomas More College
Transylvania University
Union College
University of Kentucky
University of Louisville
University of the Cumberlands
Western Kentucky University

Louisiana
Bossier Parish Community College
Centenary College of Louisiana
Delgado Community College
Dillard University
Grambling State University
Louisiana State University and Agricultural and Mechanical College
Louisiana Tech University
Northwestern State University
Southeastern Louisiana University
University of Louisiana at Lafayette
University of Louisiana at Monroe
Xavier University of Louisiana

Maine
University of Maine
University of Maine
    Augusta
    Machias
    Presque Isle
University of Southern Maine

Maryland
Bowie State University
College of Notre Dame of Maryland
Columbia Union College
Goucher College
Hood College
Johns Hopkins University: Peabody Conservatory of Music
Montgomery College
Mount St. Mary's University
St. Mary's College of Maryland
Towson University
University of Maryland
Baltimore County
College Park
Eastern Shore
Villa Julie College

Massachusetts
Anna Maria College
Atlantic Union College
Berklee College of Music
Boston Conservatory
Boston University
Bristol Community College
Cape Cod Community College
Dean College
Eastern Nazarene College
Emerson College
Gordon College
Holyoke Community College
Massachusetts College of Liberal Arts
Merrimack College
New England Conservatory of Music
North Shore Community College
Salem State College
Stonehill College
University of Massachusetts Amherst

Michigan
Adrian College
Albion College
Alma College
Alpena Community College
Andrews University
Calvin College
Central Michigan University
Concordia University
Cornerstone University
Eastern Michigan University
Ferris State University
Glen Oaks Community College
Gogebic Community College
Grace Bible College
Grand Rapids Community College
Grand Valley State University
Great Lakes Christian College
Hillsdale College
Hope College
Jackson Community College
Macomb Community College
Madonna University
Marygrove College
Michigan State University
Monroe County Community College
Mott Community College
Northern Michigan University
Northwestern Michigan College
Oakland University
Olivet College
Rochester College
Saginaw Valley State University
Schoolcraft College
Siena Heights University
Southwestern Michigan College
University of Detroit Mercy
University of Michigan
University of Michigan
    Flint
Wayne State University
Western Michigan University

Minnesota
Augsburg College
Bemidji State University
Bethany Lutheran College
Bethel University
College of St. Benedict
Concordia College: Moorhead
Concordia University: St. Paul
Crossroads College
Crown College
Gustavus Adolphus College
Hamline University
Martin Luther College
Minnesota State University
    Mankato
North Central University
Northwestern College
Riverland Community College
St. Cloud State University
St. John's University
St. Mary's University of Minnesota
St. Olaf College
Southwest Minnesota State University
University of Minnesota
    Morris
    Twin Cities
University of St. Thomas
Winona State University

Mississippi
Belhaven College
Copiah-Lincoln Community College
Delta State University
Hinds Community College
Itawamba Community College
Jackson State University
Meridian Community College
Millsaps College
Mississippi College
Mississippi Gulf Coast Community College
    Jefferson Davis Campus
Mississippi State University
Pearl River Community College
Rust College
University of Mississippi
William Carey College

Missouri
Avila University
Central Methodist University
Central Missouri State University
College of the Ozarks
Columbia College
Cottey College
Crowder College
Culver-Stockton College
Drury University
East Central College
Evangel University
Fontbonne University
Hannibal-LaGrange College
Harris-Stowe State University
Jefferson College
Lindenwood University
Mineral Area College
Missouri Baptist University
Missouri Southern State University
Missouri State University
Missouri Western State University
Moberly Area Community College
North Central Missouri College
Northwest Missouri State University
Park University
Rockhurst University
St. Charles Community College
St. Louis Christian College
St. Louis University
Southeast Missouri State University
Southwest Baptist University
State Fair Community College
Truman State University
University of Missouri
    Columbia
    Kansas City
    Rolla
    St. Louis
Webster University
Westminster College
William Jewell College
William Woods University

Montana
Carroll College
Dawson Community College

Montana State University
  Billings
  Bozeman
Rocky Mountain College
University of Great Falls
University of Montana: Missoula
University of Montana: Western

Nebraska
Central Community College
Chadron State College
College of Saint Mary
Creighton University
Dana College
Doane College
Grace University
Hastings College
Mid-Plains Community College Area
Midland Lutheran College
Nebraska Wesleyan University
Northeast Community College
Peru State College
University of Nebraska
  Lincoln
  Omaha
Wayne State College
Western Nebraska Community College
York College

Nevada
Truckee Meadows Community College
University of Nevada
  Las Vegas

New Hampshire
Colby-Sawyer College
Franklin Pierce College
Keene State College
New England College
Plymouth State University
University of New Hampshire

New Jersey
Caldwell College
The College of New Jersey
Drew University
Georgian Court University
Kean University
Montclair State University
New Jersey Institute of Technology
Richard Stockton College of New Jersey
Rider University
Rowan University
Rutgers, The State University of New Jersey
  Camden Regional Campus
  New Brunswick/Piscataway Campus
  Newark Regional Campus
Stevens Institute of Technology
William Paterson University of New Jersey

New Mexico
College of Santa Fe
College of the Southwest
Eastern New Mexico University
Mesalands Community College
New Mexico Highlands University
University of New Mexico

New York
Adelphi University
Alfred University
Canisius College
City University of New York
  Brooklyn College
  College of Staten Island
  Queens College
College of Saint Rose
Concordia College
Eastman School of Music of the University of Rochester
Five Towns College
Genesee Community College
Hobart and William Smith Colleges

Hofstra University
Houghton College
Ithaca College
Jamestown Community College
Juilliard School
Manhattan School of Music
Manhattanville College
Mannes College The New School for Music
Marist College
Marymount Manhattan College
Molloy College
Nazareth College of Rochester
Niagara University
Nyack College
Parsons The New School for Design
Rensselaer Polytechnic Institute
Roberts Wesleyan College
St. Bonaventure University
St. John's University
Skidmore College
State University of New York
  Binghamton
  Buffalo
  College at Fredonia
  College at Geneseo
  College at Plattsburgh
  College at Potsdam
  New Paltz
  Purchase
Syracuse University
University of Rochester
Villa Maria College of Buffalo
Wagner College

North Carolina
Appalachian State University
Brevard College
Campbell University
Catawba College
Catawba Valley Community College
Chowan College
College of the Albemarle
Davidson College
Elon University
Fayetteville State University
Gardner-Webb University
Greensboro College
Guilford College
High Point University
Isothermal Community College
Lees-McRae College
Lenoir-Rhyne College
Livingstone College
Meredith College
Methodist College
Montreat College
Mount Olive College
North Carolina Agricultural and Technical State University
North Carolina Central University
North Carolina School of the Arts
North Carolina Wesleyan College
Pfeiffer University
Queens University of Charlotte
Roanoke Bible College
St. Andrews Presbyterian College
St. Augustine's College
Salem College
Southeastern Community College
University of North Carolina
  Asheville
  Chapel Hill
  Charlotte
  Greensboro
  Wilmington
Wake Forest University
Western Carolina University
Wilkes Community College
Wingate University

North Dakota
Dickinson State University
Jamestown College
Lake Region State College
Mayville State University
Minot State University
Minot State University: Bottineau Campus
North Dakota State College of Science
North Dakota State University
Trinity Bible College
University of North Dakota
Valley City State University

Ohio
Antioch College
Ashland University
Baldwin-Wallace College
Bluffton University
Bowling Green State University
Bowling Green State University: Firelands College
Capital University
Case Western Reserve University
Cedarville University
Central State University
Cleveland State University
College of Mount St. Joseph
College of Wooster
Cuyahoga Community College
  Metropolitan Campus
Denison University
God's Bible School and College
Heidelberg College
Hiram College
Kent State University
Kent State University
  Ashtabula Regional Campus
  East Liverpool Regional Campus
  Salem Regional Campus
  Stark Campus
  Trumbull Campus
  Tuscarawas Campus
Lake Erie College
Lakeland Community College
Lourdes College
Malone College
Marietta College
Miami University
  Oxford Campus
Mount Union College
Mount Vernon Nazarene University
Muskingum College
Oberlin College
Ohio Northern University
Ohio State University
  Columbus Campus
Ohio University
Ohio Wesleyan University
Otterbein College
Pontifical College Josephinum
Southern State Community College
Tiffin University
University of Akron
University of Akron: Wayne College
University of Cincinnati
University of Dayton
University of Findlay
University of Rio Grande
University of Toledo
Urbana University
Walsh University
Wittenberg University
Wright State University
Xavier University

Oklahoma
Cameron University
Carl Albert State College
Mid-America Christian University
Northeastern Oklahoma Agricultural and Mechanical College
Northeastern State University

Northwestern Oklahoma State University
Oklahoma Christian University
Oklahoma City University
Oklahoma State University
Oral Roberts University
St. Gregory's University
Southeastern Oklahoma State University
Southwestern Christian University
Southwestern Oklahoma State University
Tulsa Community College
University of Central Oklahoma
University of Oklahoma
University of Science and Arts of Oklahoma
University of Tulsa
Western Oklahoma State College

Oregon
Blue Mountain Community College
Clackamas Community College
Concordia University
Corban College
Eastern Oregon University
Eugene Bible College
George Fox University
Lane Community College
Lewis & Clark College
Linfield College
Linn-Benton Community College
Northwest Christian College
Pacific University
Portland State University
Southern Oregon University
Treasure Valley Community College
University of Oregon
University of Portland
Warner Pacific College
Western Oregon University
Willamette University

Pennsylvania
Albright College
Baptist Bible College of Pennsylvania
Berks Technical Institute
Bloomsburg University of Pennsylvania
Bucknell University
Carnegie Mellon University
Cedar Crest College
Chatham College
Clarion University of Pennsylvania
Delaware Valley College
DeSales University
Drexel University
Duquesne University
East Stroudsburg University of Pennsylvania
Edinboro University of Pennsylvania
Elizabethtown College
Franklin & Marshall College
Gannon University
Geneva College
Gettysburg College
Immaculata University
Indiana University of Pennsylvania
Juniata College
Kutztown University of Pennsylvania
Lancaster Bible College
Lebanon Valley College
Lehigh University
Lincoln University
Lock Haven University of Pennsylvania
Lycoming College
Mansfield University of Pennsylvania
Marywood University
Mercyhurst College
Messiah College
Moravian College
Mount Aloysius College
Muhlenberg College
Northampton County Area Community College
Philadelphia Biblical University
Point Park University
Robert Morris University
St. Francis University

St. Joseph's University
St. Vincent College
Seton Hill University
Slippery Rock University of Pennsylvania
Susquehanna University
Temple University
University of the Arts
Valley Forge Christian College
Valley Forge Military College
Widener University
Wilkes University
York College of Pennsylvania

Puerto Rico
Humacao Community College
Universidad Politecnica de Puerto Rico
University of Puerto Rico
    Aguadilla
    Arecibo
    Carolina Regional College
    Humacao

Rhode Island
Rhode Island College
Salve Regina University
University of Rhode Island

South Carolina
Allen University
Anderson University
The Citadel
Clemson University
Coastal Carolina University
Coker College
College of Charleston
Columbia College
Converse College
Erskine College
Francis Marion University
Furman University
Lander University
Limestone College
Morris College
Newberry College
Presbyterian College
Southern Wesleyan University
Spartanburg Methodist College
University of South Carolina
Winthrop University
Wofford College

South Dakota
Augustana College
Dakota State University
Dakota Wesleyan University
Mount Marty College
South Dakota State University
University of Sioux Falls
University of South Dakota

Tennessee
Austin Peay State University
Belmont University
Bethel College
Bryan College
Carson-Newman College
Crichton College
Cumberland University
Dyersburg State Community College
East Tennessee State University
Fisk University
Free Will Baptist Bible College
Freed-Hardeman University
Hiwassee College
Jackson State Community College
Johnson Bible College
King College
Lambuth University
Lee University
Lincoln Memorial University
Lipscomb University
Martin Methodist College
Maryville College

Middle Tennessee State University
Milligan College
Northeast State Technical Community College
Pellissippi State Technical Community College
Rhodes College
Roane State Community College
Southern Adventist University
Tennessee Technological University
Tennessee Temple University
Tennessee Wesleyan College
Trevecca Nazarene University
Union University
University of Memphis
University of Tennessee
    Chattanooga
    Knoxville
    Martin
Vanderbilt University
Volunteer State Community College
Walters State Community College

Texas
Abilene Christian University
Angelina College
Angelo State University
Austin College
Baylor University
Brazosport College
Clarendon College
College of the Mainland
Collin County Community College District
Concordia University at Austin
Dallas Baptist University
East Texas Baptist University
Frank Phillips College
Galveston College
Hardin-Simmons University
Hill College
Houston Baptist University
Howard College
Howard Payne University
Huston-Tillotson College
Jacksonville College
Kilgore College
Lee College
Lubbock Christian University
McMurry University
Midland College
Midwestern State University
Northeast Texas Community College
Odessa College
Our Lady of the Lake University of San Antonio
Panola College
Paris Junior College
Paul Quinn College
Rice University
Richland College
St. Edward's University
St. Mary's University
San Jacinto College
    North
Schreiner University
Southern Methodist University
Southwestern Adventist University
Southwestern University
Stephen F. Austin State University
Texas A&M University
Texas Christian University
Texas Lutheran University
Texas State University: San Marcos
Texas Tech University
Trinity University
Tyler Junior College
University of Dallas
University of Houston
University of Mary Hardin-Baylor
University of St. Thomas
University of Texas
    Arlington
    Austin
    El Paso
    Pan American

    San Antonio
    Tyler
University of the Incarnate Word
Vernon College
Victoria College
Wayland Baptist University
West Texas A&M University
Western Technical College
Western Texas College

Utah
Brigham Young University
College of Eastern Utah
Dixie State College of Utah
Salt Lake Community College
Southern Utah University
University of Utah
Utah State University
Utah Valley State College
Weber State University
Westminster College

Vermont
Castleton State College
Goddard College
Green Mountain College
Marlboro College
Norwich University

Virginia
Averett University
Bluefield College
Bridgewater College
Christopher Newport University
Eastern Mennonite University
Emory & Henry College
George Mason University
Hampton University
Hollins University
James Madison University
Liberty University
Longwood University
Lynchburg College
Norfolk State University
Old Dominion University
Randolph-Macon Woman's College
Roanoke College
Shenandoah University
Sweet Briar College
University of Mary Washington
University of Richmond
University of Virginia's College at Wise
Virginia Commonwealth University
Virginia Intermont College
Virginia Military Institute
Virginia State University
Virginia Wesleyan College

Washington
Big Bend Community College
Central Washington University
Centralia College
Clark College
Everett Community College
Gonzaga University
Grays Harbor College
Northwest University
Pacific Lutheran University
Pierce College
Puget Sound Christian College
Saint Martin's University
Seattle Pacific University
Seattle University
Trinity Lutheran College
University of Puget Sound
University of Washington
Walla Walla College
Walla Walla Community College
Washington State University
Western Washington University
Whitman College
Whitworth College
Yakima Valley Community College

West Virginia
Alderson-Broaddus College
Bethany College
Concord University
Davis and Elkins College
Glenville State College
Marshall University
Ohio Valley University
Shepherd University
University of Charleston
West Liberty State College
West Virginia University
West Virginia Wesleyan College
Wheeling Jesuit University

Wisconsin
Alverno College
Beloit College
Cardinal Stritch University
Carroll College
Carthage College
Concordia University Wisconsin
Edgewood College
Lawrence University
Marquette University
Mount Mary College
Northland College
Ripon College
St. Norbert College
Silver Lake College
University of Wisconsin
    Baraboo/Sauk County
    Eau Claire
    Green Bay
    La Crosse
    Madison
    Oshkosh
    Parkside
    Richland
    River Falls
    Rock County
    Superior
    Waukesha
    Whitewater
Viterbo University
Wisconsin Lutheran College

Wyoming
Casper College
Central Wyoming College
Eastern Wyoming College
University of Wyoming
Western Wyoming Community College

ROTC scholarships

Air Force ROTC

Alabama
Alabama State University
Auburn University
Auburn University at Montgomery
Birmingham-Southern College
Bishop State Community College
Enterprise-Ozark Community College
Faulkner University
Huntingdon College
Jefferson State Community College
Marion Military Institute
Miles College
Samford University
Shelton State Community College
Spring Hill College
Stillman College
Troy University
Tuskegee University
University of Alabama
University of Alabama
 Birmingham
University of Mobile
University of Montevallo
University of South Alabama
University of West Alabama

Alaska
University of Alaska
 Anchorage

Arizona
Arizona State University
Chandler-Gilbert Community College
 Williams Campus
Coconino County Community College
DeVry University
 Phoenix
Embry-Riddle Aeronautical University: Prescott Campus
Estrella Mountain Community College
Gateway Community College
Mesa Community College
Northern Arizona University
Phoenix College
Pima Community College
Southwestern College
University of Arizona
Yavapai College

Arkansas
John Brown University
Northwest Arkansas Community College
University of Arkansas
University of Arkansas
 Fort Smith

California
Antelope Valley College
Biola University
California Baptist University
California Institute of Technology
California Lutheran University
California State Polytechnic University: Pomona
California State University
 Dominguez Hills
 Fresno
 Los Angeles
 Northridge
 Sacramento
 San Bernardino
 San Marcos
Chabot College
Chapman University
Claremont McKenna College
College of San Mateo
College of the Sequoias
Cuyamaca College
De Anza College
Foothill College
Fresno City College
Harvey Mudd College
Holy Names University
Irvine Valley College
King's College and Seminary
Los Angeles City College
Los Angeles Mission College
Loyola Marymount University
Mission College
Mount San Antonio College
Mount San Jacinto College
National University
Occidental College
Ohlone College
Pepperdine University
Pitzer College
Point Loma Nazarene University
Riverside Community College
Sacramento City College
St. Mary's College of California
Samuel Merritt College
San Diego Christian College
San Diego City College
San Diego State University
San Francisco State University
San Jose State University
Santa Clara University
Scripps College
Solano Community College
Sonoma State University
Stanford University
University of California
 Berkeley
 Davis
 Irvine
 Los Angeles
 Riverside
 San Diego
 Santa Cruz
University of Redlands
University of San Diego
University of San Francisco
University of Southern California
University of the Pacific
Vanguard University of Southern California
Ventura College
West Valley College
Westmont College
Whittier College

Colorado
Aims Community College
Arapahoe Community College
Colorado Christian University
Colorado School of Mines
Colorado State University
Front Range Community College
Metropolitan State College of Denver
Regis University
University of Colorado
 Boulder
 Denver and Health Sciences Center
University of Denver
University of Northern Colorado

Connecticut
Capital Community College
Central Connecticut State University
Eastern Connecticut State University
Quinnipiac University
Southern Connecticut State University
Tunxis Community College
University of Connecticut
University of Hartford
Wesleyan University
Western Connecticut State University
Yale University

Delaware
Delaware State University
University of Delaware
Wilmington College

District of Columbia
American University
Catholic University of America
George Washington University
Georgetown University
Howard University
University of the District of Columbia

Florida
Barry University
Bethune-Cookman College
Broward Community College
Daytona Beach Community College
Eckerd College
Embry-Riddle Aeronautical University
Florida Agricultural and Mechanical University
Florida Atlantic University
Florida College
Florida International University
Florida Southern College
Florida State University
Hillsborough Community College
Lynn University
Miami Dade College
St. Leo University
Santa Fe Community College
Tallahassee Community College
University of Central Florida
University of Florida
University of Miami
University of South Florida
University of Tampa
University of West Florida

Georgia
Agnes Scott College
Clark Atlanta University
Clayton State University
Emory University
Georgia Institute of Technology
Georgia State University
Kennesaw State University
Morehouse College
Southern Polytechnic State University
Spelman College
University of Georgia
Valdosta State University

Hawaii
Brigham Young University-Hawaii
Chaminade University of Honolulu
Hawaii Pacific University
University of Hawaii
 Honolulu Community College
 Leeward Community College
 Manoa
 West Oahu

Idaho
Lewis-Clark State College
Northwest Nazarene University
University of Idaho

Illinois
Elmhurst College
Governors State University
Illinois Institute of Technology
John A. Logan College
Lewis University
Lincoln Land Community College
McKendree College
North Central College
Northeastern Illinois University
Northwestern University
Parkland College
St. Xavier University
Southern Illinois University Carbondale
Southern Illinois University Edwardsville
Southwestern Illinois College
University of Chicago
University of Illinois
 Chicago
 Urbana-Champaign
Wheaton College

Indiana
Butler University
DePauw University
Holy Cross College
Indiana State University
Indiana University
 Bloomington
 South Bend
 Southeast
Indiana University-Purdue University
 Indianapolis
Purdue University
Rose-Hulman Institute of Technology
St. Mary-of-the-Woods College
Saint Mary's College
University of Notre Dame
Valparaiso University
Vincennes University

Iowa
Coe College
Drake University
Grand View College
Hawkeye Community College
Iowa State University
Iowa Western Community College
University of Iowa

Kansas
Baker University
Haskell Indian Nations University
Kansas State University
Manhattan Christian College
MidAmerica Nazarene University
University of Kansas
University of St. Mary
Washburn University of Topeka

Kentucky
Asbury College
Bellarmine University
Centre College
Eastern Kentucky University
Georgetown College
Kentucky State University
Northern Kentucky University
Spalding University
Sullivan University
Thomas More College
Transylvania University
University of Kentucky
University of Louisville
Western Kentucky University

Louisiana
Delgado Community College
Dillard University
Louisiana State University and Agricultural and Mechanical College
Loyola University New Orleans

Our Lady of Holy Cross College
Our Lady of the Lake College
Southern University
    New Orleans
Southern University and Agricultural and Mechanical College
Tulane University
University of Louisiana at Monroe
University of New Orleans
Xavier University of Louisiana

Maine
University of Maine
    Augusta
University of Southern Maine

Maryland
Bowie State University
Johns Hopkins University
Loyola College in Maryland
Prince George's Community College
Towson University
University of Maryland
    College Park

Massachusetts
American International College
Anna Maria College
Assumption College
Babson College
Bay Path College
Becker College
Boston College
Boston University
Brandeis University
Bridgewater State College
Clark University
College of the Holy Cross
Eastern Nazarene College
Elms College
Endicott College
Fitchburg State College
Gordon College
Harvard College
Holyoke Community College
Massachusetts Institute of Technology
Massachusetts Maritime Academy
Merrimack College
Middlesex Community College
Montserrat College of Art
Mount Holyoke College
Northeastern University
Quinsigamond Community College
Salem State College
Smith College
Springfield College
Tufts University
University of Massachusetts
    Amherst
    Lowell
Wellesley College
Western New England College
Westfield State College
Worcester Polytechnic Institute
Worcester State College

Michigan
Concordia University
Eastern Michigan University
Finlandia University
Lansing Community College
Lawrence Technological University
Michigan State University
Michigan Technological University
Oakland University
University of Michigan
University of Michigan
    Dearborn
Wayne State University

Minnesota
Anoka-Ramsey Community College
Augsburg College

Bethel University
College of St. Catherine
College of St. Scholastica
Concordia College: Moorhead
Concordia University: St. Paul
Hamline University
Inver Hills Community College
Macalester College
Minnesota State University
    Moorhead
Normandale Community College
North Central University
North Hennepin Community College
Northwestern College
University of Minnesota
    Crookston
    Duluth
    Twin Cities
University of St. Thomas

Mississippi
Jones County Junior College
Mississippi State University
University of Mississippi
University of Southern Mississippi
William Carey College

Missouri
Central Methodist University
Central Missouri State University
Columbia College
Harris-Stowe State University
Lincoln University
St. Louis University
Southeast Missouri State University
St. Louis Community College
    Meramec
Stephens College
University of Missouri
    Columbia
    Kansas City
    Rolla
    St. Louis
Washington University in St. Louis
Webster University
Westminster College
William Woods University

Montana
Montana State University
    Bozeman

Nebraska
Bellevue University
Clarkson College
College of Saint Mary
Concordia University
Creighton University
Dana College
Doane College
Nebraska Wesleyan University
University of Nebraska
    Lincoln
    Medical Center
    Omaha
York College

Nevada
University of Nevada
    Las Vegas

New Hampshire
Colby-Sawyer College
Daniel Webster College
Franklin Pierce College
Keene State College
New England College
Plymouth State University
Rivier College
St. Anselm College
Southern New Hampshire University
University of New Hampshire
University of New Hampshire at Manchester

New Jersey
Brookdale Community College
The College of New Jersey
Fairleigh Dickinson University
    College at Florham
    Metropolitan Campus
Kean University
Monmouth University
New Jersey Institute of Technology
Princeton University
Ramapo College of New Jersey
Raritan Valley Community College
Rutgers, The State University of New Jersey
    Camden Regional Campus
    New Brunswick/Piscataway Campus
    Newark Regional Campus
St. Peter's College
Stevens Institute of Technology
Union County College
William Paterson University of New Jersey

New Mexico
Albuquerque Technical-Vocational Institute
College of Santa Fe
Dona Ana Branch Community College of New Mexico State University
National American University
New Mexico State University
New Mexico State University
    Alamogordo
University of New Mexico

New York
Adelphi University
Albany College of Pharmacy
Cazenovia College
Clarkson University
College of Mount St. Vincent
College of Saint Rose
Columbia University
    Columbia College
    Fu Foundation School of Engineering and Applied Science
    School of General Studies
Cornell University
Corning Community College
Dowling College
Elmira College
Fordham University
Globe Institute of Technology
Hamilton College
Hartwick College
Hudson Valley Community College
Iona College
Ithaca College
Le Moyne College
Manhattan College
Maria College
Molloy College
Monroe Community College
Nazareth College of Rochester
New York Institute of Technology
Onondaga Community College
Rensselaer Polytechnic Institute
Roberts Wesleyan College
Rochester Institute of Technology
Russell Sage College
Sage College of Albany
St. Francis College
St. John Fisher College
St. Joseph's College: Suffolk Campus
St. Lawrence University
St. Thomas Aquinas College
Schenectady County Community College
Siena College
Skidmore College
State University of New York
    Albany
    Binghamton
    College at Brockport
    College at Cortland
    College at Geneseo

    College at Old Westbury
    College at Potsdam
    College of Environmental Science and Forestry
    College of Technology at Canton
    Farmingdale
    Maritime College
    Stony Brook
Syracuse University
Union College
University of Rochester
Utica College
Vaughn College of Aeronautics and Technology
Wells College

North Carolina
Belmont Abbey College
Bennett College
Davidson College
Duke University
East Carolina University
Elon University
Fayetteville State University
Greensboro College
Guilford Technical Community College
High Point University
Johnson C. Smith University
Meredith College
Methodist College
North Carolina Agricultural and Technical State University
North Carolina Central University
North Carolina State University
Peace College
Queens University of Charlotte
St. Augustine's College
Shaw University
University of North Carolina
    Chapel Hill
    Charlotte
    Greensboro
    Pembroke
Wingate University

North Dakota
Mayville State University
North Dakota State University
University of North Dakota

Ohio
Ashland University
Baldwin-Wallace College
Bowling Green State University
Capital University
Case Western Reserve University
Cedarville University
Central State University
College of Mount St. Joseph
Columbus State Community College
Cuyahoga Community College
    Metropolitan Campus
Heidelberg College
Hocking College
Kent State University
Kent State University
    Ashtabula Regional Campus
    East Liverpool Regional Campus
    Salem Regional Campus
    Stark Campus
    Trumbull Campus
    Tuscarawas Campus
Lourdes College
Malone College
Miami University
    Hamilton Campus
    Oxford Campus
Mount Union College
Ohio Northern University
Ohio State University
    Columbus Campus
    Lima Campus
    Mansfield Campus

Marion Campus
Newark Campus
Ohio University
Ohio University
Lancaster Campus
Ohio Wesleyan University
Otterbein College
Owens Community College
Toledo
Sinclair Community College
University of Akron
University of Akron: Wayne College
University of Cincinnati
University of Cincinnati
Raymond Walters College
University of Dayton
University of Findlay
University of Toledo
Wittenberg University
Wright State University
Xavier University
Youngstown State University

Oklahoma
Northeastern Oklahoma Agricultural and
 Mechanical College
Oklahoma Baptist University
Oklahoma Christian University
Oklahoma City University
Oklahoma State University
Oklahoma Wesleyan University
Oral Roberts University
Rogers State University
Rose State College
St. Gregory's University
Southern Nazarene University
University of Oklahoma
University of Tulsa

Oregon
Clackamas Community College
Concordia University
Corban College
George Fox University
Linfield College
Linn-Benton Community College
Oregon State University
Pacific University
Portland State University
University of Portland
Warner Pacific College
Western Oregon University
Willamette University

Pennsylvania
Bloomsburg University of Pennsylvania
Bryn Mawr College
Carlow University
Carnegie Mellon University
Chatham College
College Misericordia
Drexel University
Duquesne University
East Stroudsburg University of Pennsylvania
Eastern University
Keystone College
King's College
La Roche College
La Salle University
Lackawanna College
Luzerne County Community College
Marywood University
Penn State
 Abington
 Altoona
 Delaware County
 Hazleton
 University Park
 Wilkes-Barre
 Worthington Scranton
Philadelphia Biblical University
Point Park University

Robert Morris University
Rosemont College
St. Francis University
St. Joseph's University
St. Vincent College
Swarthmore College
Temple University
Thomas Jefferson University: College of Health
 Professions
University of Pennsylvania
University of Pittsburgh
University of Pittsburgh
 Greensburg
University of Scranton
University of the Sciences in Philadelphia
Valley Forge Military College
Villanova University
Washington and Jefferson College
West Chester University of Pennsylvania
Widener University
Wilkes University

Puerto Rico
Bayamon Central University
Inter American University of Puerto Rico
 Bayamon Campus
 Fajardo Campus
 San German Campus
Pontifical Catholic University of Puerto Rico
Universidad Metropolitana
Universidad Politecnica de Puerto Rico
University of Puerto Rico
 Carolina Regional College
 Mayaguez
 Rio Piedras

South Carolina
Anderson University
Benedict College
Charleston Southern University
The Citadel
Clemson University
College of Charleston
Midlands Technical College
South Carolina State University
Southern Wesleyan University
Tri-County Technical College
University of South Carolina
University of South Carolina
 Salkehatchie Regional Campus

South Dakota
Dakota State University
South Dakota State University

Tennessee
Carson-Newman College
Christian Brothers University
Free Will Baptist Bible College
LeMoyne-Owen College
Lipscomb University
Rhodes College
Roane State Community College
Southwest Tennessee Community College
Tennessee State University
Tennessee Technological University
University of Memphis
University of Tennessee
 Knoxville
Vanderbilt University

Texas
Angelo State University
Austin Community College
Baylor University
Concordia University at Austin
Dallas Baptist University
Huston-Tillotson College
Lon Morris College
McLennan Community College
McMurry University
Midwestern State University
Our Lady of the Lake University of San Antonio

Rice University
St. Edward's University
St. Mary's University
San Antonio College
Southern Methodist University
Tarrant County College
Texas A&M University
Texas Christian University
Texas Lutheran University
Texas State University: San Marcos
Texas Tech University
Texas Wesleyan University
Texas Woman's University
Trinity University
University of Dallas
University of Houston
University of Mary Hardin-Baylor
University of North Texas
University of Texas
 Arlington
 Austin
 Dallas
 El Paso
 Pan American
 San Antonio
University of the Incarnate Word
Wayland Baptist University
Weatherford College

Utah
Brigham Young University
Salt Lake Community College
University of Utah
Utah State University
Utah Valley State College
Weber State University
Westminster College

Vermont
Lyndon State College
Norwich University
St. Michael's College

Virginia
George Mason University
James Madison University
Liberty University
Mary Baldwin College
Piedmont Virginia Community College
University of Virginia
Virginia Military Institute
Virginia Polytechnic Institute and State
 University

Washington
Central Washington University
Clark College
Highline Community College
Seattle Pacific University
Seattle University
South Puget Sound Community College
Spokane Community College
University of Washington
Washington State University

West Virginia
Shepherd University
West Virginia University

Wisconsin
Alverno College
Carroll College
Carthage College
Maranatha Baptist Bible College
Marquette University
Milwaukee School of Engineering
University of Wisconsin
 Madison
 Milwaukee
 Superior
 Whitewater
Wisconsin Lutheran College

Wyoming
Laramie County Community College
University of Wyoming

Army ROTC

Alabama
Alabama Agricultural and Mechanical
 University
Alabama State University
Auburn University
Auburn University at Montgomery
Birmingham-Southern College
Bishop State Community College
Chattahoochee Valley Community College
Faulkner University
Gadsden State Community College
Huntingdon College
Jacksonville State University
Jefferson State Community College
Judson College
Marion Military Institute
Miles College
Northwest-Shoals Community College
Samford University
Shelton State Community College
Spring Hill College
Stillman College
Talladega College
Troy University
Tuskegee University
University of Alabama
University of Alabama
 Birmingham
 Huntsville
University of Mobile
University of Montevallo
University of North Alabama
University of South Alabama

Alaska
University of Alaska
 Fairbanks

Arizona
Arizona State University
Central Arizona College
Chandler-Gilbert Community College
 Williams Campus
Coconino County Community College
Embry-Riddle Aeronautical University: Prescott
 Campus
Gateway Community College
Grand Canyon University
Mesa Community College
Northern Arizona University
Paradise Valley Community College
Phoenix College
Pima Community College
University of Arizona
Yavapai College

Arkansas
Arkansas State University
Arkansas Tech University
Central Baptist College
Harding University
Henderson State University
Hendrix College
John Brown University
Northwest Arkansas Community College
Ouachita Baptist University
Ouachita Technical College
Philander Smith College
University of Arkansas
University of Arkansas
 Little Rock
 Monticello
 Pine Bluff
University of Central Arkansas

Williams Baptist College

California
Azusa Pacific University
Biola University
California Baptist University
California Institute of Technology
California Lutheran University
California Polytechnic State University: San Luis Obispo
California State Polytechnic University: Pomona
California State University
    Dominguez Hills
    Fresno
    Fullerton
    Long Beach
    Los Angeles
    Northridge
    Sacramento
    San Bernardino
    San Marcos
Chabot College
Chapman University
Claremont McKenna College
College of San Mateo
Cuyamaca College
De Anza College
Diablo Valley College
El Camino College
Foothill College
Fresno City College
Harvey Mudd College
Holy Names University
King's College and Seminary
Los Angeles City College
Los Angeles Mission College
Loyola Marymount University
Menlo College
Mount San Jacinto College
National Hispanic University
National University
Occidental College
Pepperdine University
Pitzer College
Point Loma Nazarene University
Riverside Community College
Sacramento City College
St. Mary's College of California
Samuel Merritt College
San Diego Christian College
San Diego City College
San Diego State University
San Francisco State University
San Jose State University
Santa Clara University
Scripps College
Sonoma State University
Stanford University
University of California
    Berkeley
    Davis
    Irvine
    Los Angeles
    Riverside
    San Diego
    Santa Barbara
    Santa Cruz
University of La Verne
University of Redlands
University of San Diego
University of San Francisco
University of Southern California
West Valley College
Westmont College
Whittier College

Colorado
Arapahoe Community College
Colorado Christian University
Colorado College
Colorado School of Mines
Colorado State University
Colorado State University
    Pueblo
Colorado Technical University
Community College of Denver
Front Range Community College
Metropolitan State College of Denver
Red Rocks Community College
Regis University
University of Colorado
    Boulder
    Colorado Springs
    Denver and Health Sciences Center
University of Denver
University of Northern Colorado

Connecticut
Capital Community College
Central Connecticut State University
Eastern Connecticut State University
Fairfield University
Post University
Quinnipiac University
Sacred Heart University
Southern Connecticut State University
Trinity College
Tunxis Community College
University of Bridgeport
University of Connecticut
University of Hartford
Western Connecticut State University
Yale University

Delaware
Delaware State University
University of Delaware
Wesley College
Wilmington College

District of Columbia
American University
Catholic University of America
George Washington University
Georgetown University
Howard University
Trinity University
University of the District of Columbia

Florida
Barry University
Bethune-Cookman College
Broward Community College
Clearwater Christian College
Daytona Beach Community College
Eckerd College
Edward Waters College
Embry-Riddle Aeronautical University
Florida Agricultural and Mechanical University
Florida Atlantic University
Florida College
Florida Institute of Technology
Florida International University
Florida Memorial University
Florida Southern College
Florida State University
Hillsborough Community College
Miami Dade College
Okaloosa-Walton College
Pasco-Hernando Community College
Pensacola Junior College
Polk Community College
St. Leo University
Santa Fe Community College
Southeastern College of the Assemblies of God
Stetson University
Tallahassee Community College
University of Central Florida
University of Florida
University of Miami
University of South Florida
University of Tampa
University of West Florida
Valencia Community College

Georgia
Agnes Scott College
Albany State University
Armstrong Atlantic State University
Augusta State University
Clark Atlanta University
Clayton State University
Columbus State University
Darton College
Emory University
Fort Valley State University
Georgia College and State University
Georgia Institute of Technology
Georgia Military College
Georgia Southern University
Georgia State University
Kennesaw State University
Mercer University
Morehouse College
North Georgia College & State University
Paine College
Savannah State University
Southern Polytechnic State University
Spelman College
University of Georgia
University of West Georgia

Hawaii
Brigham Young University-Hawaii
Chaminade University of Honolulu
Hawaii Pacific University
University of Hawaii
    Honolulu Community College
    Leeward Community College
    Manoa
    West Oahu
    Windward Community College

Idaho
Albertson College of Idaho
Boise State University
Brigham Young University-Idaho
Idaho State University
Lewis-Clark State College
Northwest Nazarene University
University of Idaho

Illinois
Aurora University
Benedictine University
Bradley University
Carl Sandburg College
Chicago State University
DePaul University
Eastern Illinois University
Elmhurst College
Governors State University
Illinois Institute of Technology
Illinois State University
Illinois Wesleyan University
John A. Logan College
Kishwaukee College
Lewis and Clark Community College
Lewis University
Lincoln Land Community College
Loyola University of Chicago
McKendree College
Monmouth College
North Central College
Northeastern Illinois University
Northern Illinois University
Northwestern University
Olivet Nazarene University
Parkland College
Robert Morris College: Chicago
Rockford College
Southern Illinois University Carbondale
Southern Illinois University Edwardsville
Spoon River College
University of Chicago
University of Illinois
    Chicago
    Urbana-Champaign
Waubonsee Community College
Western Illinois University
Wheaton College

Indiana
Ball State University
Butler University
DePauw University
Franklin College
Holy Cross College
Indiana State University
Indiana University
    Bloomington
    Northwest
    South Bend
    Southeast
Indiana University-Purdue University
    Indianapolis
Indiana Wesleyan University
Marian College
Purdue University
Purdue University
    Calumet
Rose-Hulman Institute of Technology
St. Mary-of-the-Woods College
Saint Mary's College
University of Indianapolis
University of Notre Dame
University of Southern Indiana
Vincennes University
Wabash College

Iowa
Allen College
Clarke College
Coe College
Drake University
Grand View College
Hawkeye Community College
Iowa State University
Iowa Western Community College
Loras College
University of Dubuque
University of Iowa
University of Northern Iowa

Kansas
Baker University
Benedictine College
Kansas State University
Manhattan Christian College
MidAmerica Nazarene University
Pittsburg State University
University of Kansas
University of St. Mary
Washburn University of Topeka

Kentucky
Asbury College
Bellarmine University
Centre College
Eastern Kentucky University
Georgetown College
Jefferson Community College
Kentucky State University
Midway College
Morehead State University
Murray State University
Northern Kentucky University
Spalding University
Thomas More College
Transylvania University
Union College
University of Kentucky
University of Louisville
University of the Cumberlands
Western Kentucky University

Louisiana
Delgado Community College
Dillard University
Grambling State University

Louisiana State University
　Alexandria
　Shreveport
Louisiana State University and Agricultural and
　Mechanical College
Louisiana Tech University
Loyola University New Orleans
Northwestern State University
Our Lady of Holy Cross College
Southeastern Louisiana University
Southern University
　New Orleans
Southern University and Agricultural and
　Mechanical College
Tulane University
University of Louisiana at Lafayette
University of Louisiana at Monroe
University of New Orleans
Xavier University of Louisiana

Maine
Colby College
Husson College
New England School of Communications
St. Joseph's College
Unity College
University of Maine
University of Maine
　Augusta
University of New England
University of Southern Maine

Maryland
Allegany College of Maryland
Bowie State University
Capitol College
College of Notre Dame of Maryland
Coppin State University
Goucher College
Johns Hopkins University
Loyola College in Maryland
Maryland Institute College of Art
McDaniel College
Morgan State University
Mount St. Mary's University
Prince George's Community College
Salisbury University
Towson University
University of Baltimore
University of Maryland
　Baltimore County
　College Park
Villa Julie College

Massachusetts
American International College
Assumption College
Babson College
Bay Path College
Becker College
Bentley College
Boston College
Boston University
Brandeis University
Bridgewater State College
Clark University
College of the Holy Cross
Curry College
Eastern Nazarene College
Elms College
Emmanuel College
Endicott College
Framingham State College
Gordon College
Hampshire College
Harvard College
Holyoke Community College
Massachusetts Institute of Technology
Massachusetts Maritime Academy
Mount Holyoke College
Nichols College
Northeastern University

Quinsigamond Community College
Regis College
Roxbury Community College
St. John's Seminary College
Simmons College
Smith College
Springfield College
Stonehill College
Suffolk University
Tufts University
University of Massachusetts
　Amherst
　Dartmouth
Wellesley College
Wentworth Institute of Technology
Western New England College
Westfield State College
Wheaton College
Worcester Polytechnic Institute
Worcester State College

Michigan
Alma College
Calvin College
Central Michigan University
Concordia University
Eastern Michigan University
Ferris State University
Finlandia University
Grace Bible College
Hope College
Kalamazoo College
Lansing Community College
Lawrence Technological University
Michigan State University
Michigan Technological University
Northern Michigan University
Spring Arbor University
University of Michigan
University of Michigan
　Dearborn
Washtenaw Community College
Western Michigan University

Minnesota
Anoka-Ramsey Community College
Augsburg College
Bethany Lutheran College
Bethel University
Century Community and Technical College
College of St. Benedict
Concordia College: Moorhead
Concordia University: St. Paul
Gustavus Adolphus College
Lake Superior College
Minnesota State University
　Mankato
　Moorhead
Normandale Community College
North Central University
Northwestern College
St. Cloud State University
St. John's University
St. Mary's University of Minnesota
University of Minnesota
　Twin Cities
University of St. Thomas
Winona State University

Mississippi
Alcorn State University
Hinds Community College
Jackson State University
Millsaps College
Mississippi College
Mississippi State University
Mississippi Valley State University
Tougaloo College
University of Mississippi
University of Southern Mississippi
William Carey College

Missouri
Avila University
Central Methodist University
Central Missouri State University
College of the Ozarks
Columbia College
Drury University
Evangel University
Harris-Stowe State University
Lincoln University
Lindenwood University
Maryville University of Saint Louis
Missouri Baptist University
Missouri State University
Missouri Valley College
Missouri Western State University
Northwest Missouri State University
Park University
Research College of Nursing
Rockhurst University
St. Louis University
Southwest Baptist University
St. Louis Community College
　Florissant Valley
　Meramec
Stephens College
Truman State University
University of Missouri
　Columbia
　Kansas City
　Rolla
　St. Louis
Washington University in St. Louis
Webster University
Westminster College
William Woods University

Montana
Carroll College
Montana State University
　Bozeman
Montana Tech of the University of Montana
University of Montana: Missoula

Nebraska
Bellevue University
Chadron State College
Clarkson College
College of Saint Mary
Concordia University
Creighton University
Dana College
Doane College
Nebraska Methodist College of Nursing and
　Allied Health
Nebraska Wesleyan University
University of Nebraska
　Lincoln
　Medical Center
　Omaha
Wayne State College
York College

Nevada
Community College of Southern Nevada
Sierra Nevada College
Truckee Meadows Community College
University of Nevada
　Las Vegas
　Reno

New Hampshire
Colby-Sawyer College
Daniel Webster College
Dartmouth College
Franklin Pierce College
Granite State College
New England College
Plymouth State University
St. Anselm College
Southern New Hampshire University
University of New Hampshire

University of New Hampshire at Manchester

New Jersey
Bloomfield College
Brookdale Community College
Caldwell College
The College of New Jersey
Fairleigh Dickinson University
　College at Florham
　Metropolitan Campus
Kean University
Middlesex County College
New Jersey Institute of Technology
Princeton University
Raritan Valley Community College
Rider University
Rowan University
Rutgers, The State University of New Jersey
　Camden Regional Campus
　New Brunswick/Piscataway Campus
　Newark Regional Campus
St. Peter's College
Seton Hall University
Stevens Institute of Technology

New Mexico
Albuquerque Technical-Vocational Institute
Dona Ana Branch Community College of New
　Mexico State University
New Mexico Military Institute Junior College
New Mexico State University
University of New Mexico

New York
Adelphi University
Albany College of Pharmacy
Alfred University
Canisius College
Cazenovia College
City University of New York
　Baruch College
　Lehman College
　Queens College
Clarkson University
Colgate University
College of New Rochelle
College of Saint Rose
Columbia University
　Columbia College
　Fu Foundation School of Engineering and
　　Applied Science
　School of General Studies
Cornell University
Corning Community College
Daemen College
D'Youville College
Elmira College
Erie Community College
　City Campus
　North Campus
　South Campus
Finger Lakes Community College
Fordham University
Globe Institute of Technology
Hamilton College
Hartwick College
Herkimer County Community College
Hilbert College
Hofstra University
Houghton College
Hudson Valley Community College
Iona College
Ithaca College
Le Moyne College
Long Island University
　Brooklyn Campus
　C. W. Post Campus
Manhattan College
Maria College
Marist College
Medaille College
Mohawk Valley Community College

Molloy College
Monroe College
Monroe Community College
Nassau Community College
Nazareth College of Rochester
New York Institute of Technology
Niagara County Community College
Niagara University
Onondaga Community College
Orange County Community College
Pace University
Polytechnic University
Rensselaer Polytechnic Institute
Roberts Wesleyan College
Rochester Institute of Technology
Russell Sage College
Sage College of Albany
St. Bonaventure University
St. Francis College
St. John Fisher College
St. John's University
St. Joseph's College: Suffolk Campus
St. Lawrence University
Siena College
Skidmore College
State University of New York
   Albany
   Buffalo
   College at Brockport
   College at Buffalo
   College at Cortland
   College at Geneseo
   College at Old Westbury
   College at Potsdam
   College of Agriculture and Technology at Morrisville
   College of Environmental Science and Forestry
   College of Technology at Alfred
   College of Technology at Canton
   Farmingdale
   Institute of Technology at Utica/Rome
   Maritime College
   Oswego
   Stony Brook
Syracuse University
Union College
University of Rochester
Utica College
Vaughn College of Aeronautics and Technology

North Carolina
Appalachian State University
Belmont Abbey College
Bennett College
Campbell University
Catawba College
College of the Albemarle
Davidson College
Duke University
East Carolina University
Elizabeth City State University
Elon University
Fayetteville State University
Gardner-Webb University
Greensboro College
Guilford Technical Community College
High Point University
Johnson C. Smith University
Lees-McRae College
Lenoir-Rhyne College
Livingstone College
Meredith College
Methodist College
North Carolina Agricultural and Technical State University
North Carolina Central University
North Carolina State University
Peace College
Pfeiffer University
Pitt Community College
Queens University of Charlotte
St. Augustine's College
Shaw University
University of North Carolina
   Chapel Hill
   Charlotte
   Greensboro
   Pembroke
Wake Forest University
Wingate University
Winston-Salem State University

North Dakota
Mayville State University
North Dakota State University
University of North Dakota

Ohio
Bowling Green State University
Capital University
Case Western Reserve University
Cedarville University
Central State University
Cincinnati State Technical and Community College
Cleveland Institute of Art
Cleveland State University
College of Mount St. Joseph
Columbus State Community College
Denison University
DeVry University
   Columbus
Franklin University
Heidelberg College
Hocking College
John Carroll University
Kent State University
Kent State University
   Ashtabula Regional Campus
   East Liverpool Regional Campus
   Salem Regional Campus
   Stark Campus
   Trumbull Campus
   Tuscarawas Campus
Lourdes College
Malone College
Miami University
   Oxford Campus
Mount Union College
Ohio Dominican University
Ohio Northern University
Ohio State University
   Columbus Campus
   Lima Campus
   Mansfield Campus
   Marion Campus
   Newark Campus
Ohio University
Ohio University
   Lancaster Campus
Ohio Wesleyan University
Otterbein College
Owens Community College
   Toledo
Sinclair Community College
Tiffin University
University of Akron
University of Akron: Wayne College
University of Cincinnati
University of Cincinnati
   Clermont College
   Raymond Walters College
University of Dayton
University of Findlay
University of Rio Grande
University of Toledo
Ursuline College
Wittenberg University
Wright State University
Xavier University
Youngstown State University

Oklahoma
Cameron University
Northeastern State University
Oklahoma Christian University
Oklahoma City University
Oklahoma State University
Rose State College
St. Gregory's University
Southern Nazarene University
University of Central Oklahoma
University of Oklahoma

Oregon
Corban College
Linn-Benton Community College
Northwest Christian College
Oregon Institute of Technology
Oregon State University
Pacific University
Portland State University
University of Oregon
University of Portland
Warner Pacific College
Western Oregon University

Pennsylvania
Alvernia College
Arcadia University
Bloomsburg University of Pennsylvania
Bucknell University
Cabrini College
California University of Pennsylvania
Carlow University
Carnegie Mellon University
Cedar Crest College
Chatham College
Cheyney University of Pennsylvania
Clarion University of Pennsylvania
College Misericordia
Community College of Philadelphia
DeSales University
Dickinson College
Drexel University
Duquesne University
East Stroudsburg University of Pennsylvania
Eastern University
Edinboro University of Pennsylvania
Gannon University
Geneva College
Gettysburg College
Grove City College
Harrisburg Area Community College
Immaculata University
Indiana University of Pennsylvania
Keystone College
King's College
Kutztown University of Pennsylvania
La Roche College
La Salle University
Lackawanna College
Lafayette College
Lebanon Valley College
Lehigh Carbon Community College
Lehigh University
Lincoln University
Lock Haven University of Pennsylvania
Lycoming College
Marywood University
Mercyhurst College
Millersville University of Pennsylvania
Moravian College
Muhlenberg College
Neumann College
Penn State
   Abington
   Altoona
   Delaware County
   Erie, The Behrend College
   Harrisburg
   Hazleton
   Lehigh Valley
   Mont Alto
   University Park
   Wilkes-Barre
Pennsylvania College of Technology
Point Park University
Robert Morris University
Rosemont College
St. Francis University
St. Joseph's University
Seton Hill University
Shippensburg University of Pennsylvania
Slippery Rock University of Pennsylvania
Susquehanna University
Swarthmore College
Temple University
University of Pennsylvania
University of Pittsburgh
University of Pittsburgh
   Bradford
   Greensburg
University of Scranton
University of the Sciences in Philadelphia
Valley Forge Military College
Villanova University
Washington and Jefferson College
Waynesburg College
West Chester University of Pennsylvania
Westminster College
Widener University
Wilkes University
Wilson College
York College of Pennsylvania

Puerto Rico
American University of Puerto Rico
Bayamon Central University
Inter American University of Puerto Rico
   Aguadilla Campus
   Bayamon Campus
   Guayama Campus
   San German Campus
Pontifical Catholic University of Puerto Rico
Turabo University
Universidad del Este
Universidad Metropolitana
Universidad Politecnica de Puerto Rico
University of Puerto Rico
   Aguadilla
   Arecibo
   Bayamon University College
   Carolina Regional College
   Cayey University College
   Humacao
   Mayaguez
   Ponce
   Rio Piedras
   Utuado

Rhode Island
Brown University
Bryant University
Community College of Rhode Island
Johnson & Wales University
Providence College
Rhode Island College
Roger Williams University
Salve Regina University
University of Rhode Island

South Carolina
Allen University
Anderson University
Benedict College
The Citadel
Claflin University
Clemson University
Columbia College
Converse College
Denmark Technical College
Furman University
Lander University
Limestone College
Midlands Technical College

Morris College
Newberry College
North Greenville College
Orangeburg-Calhoun Technical College
Presbyterian College
South Carolina State University
Southern Wesleyan University
Spartanburg Methodist College
Tri-County Technical College
University of South Carolina
University of South Carolina
    Lancaster
    Salkehatchie Regional Campus
    Sumter
    Upstate
Voorhees College
Wofford College

South Dakota
Black Hills State University
Dakota State University
Mount Marty College
South Dakota School of Mines and Technology
South Dakota State University
University of South Dakota

Tennessee
Austin Peay State University
Belmont University
Carson-Newman College
Christian Brothers University
Cumberland University
East Tennessee State University
Fisk University
Free Will Baptist Bible College
Jackson State Community College
LeMoyne-Owen College
Lipscomb University
Middle Tennessee State University
Milligan College
Pellissippi State Technical Community College
Rhodes College
Roane State Community College
Southwest Tennessee Community College
Tennessee Technological University
Trevecca Nazarene University
University of Memphis
University of Tennessee
    Knoxville
    Martin
Vanderbilt University
Walters State Community College

Texas
Angelina College
Austin Community College
Cedar Valley College
Central Texas College
Concordia University at Austin
Dallas Baptist University
Del Mar College
El Centro College
El Paso Community College
Houston Baptist University
Houston Community College System
Huston-Tillotson College
Laredo Community College
Lon Morris College
Mountain View College
Our Lady of the Lake University of San Antonio
Prairie View A&M University
Rice University
St. Edward's University
St. Mary's University
St. Philip's College
Sam Houston State University
San Antonio College
San Jacinto College
    North
Southern Methodist University
Southwestern Assemblies of God University
Stephen F. Austin State University
Tarleton State University
Tarrant County College
Texas A&M University
Texas A&M University
    Kingsville
Texas Christian University
Texas Lutheran University
Texas Southern University
Texas State University: San Marcos
Texas Tech University
Texas Wesleyan University
Texas Woman's University
University of Dallas
University of Houston
University of Houston
    Downtown
University of North Texas
University of St. Thomas
University of Texas
    Arlington
    Austin
    Dallas
    El Paso
    Pan American
    San Antonio
University of the Incarnate Word
Wayland Baptist University

Utah
Brigham Young University
Salt Lake Community College
Southern Utah University
University of Utah
Utah State University
Utah Valley State College
Weber State University
Westminster College

Vermont
Castleton State College
Champlain College
Johnson State College
Middlebury College
Norwich University
St. Michael's College
University of Vermont
Vermont Technical College

Virginia
Christopher Newport University
College of William and Mary
George Mason University
Hampden-Sydney College
Hampton University
J. Sargeant Reynolds Community College
James Madison University
John Tyler Community College
Liberty University
Longwood University
Mary Baldwin College
Marymount University
Norfolk State University
Old Dominion University
Piedmont Virginia Community College
Radford University
Randolph-Macon College
Richard Bland College
St. Paul's College
Southside Virginia Community College
Thomas Nelson Community College
University of Richmond
University of Virginia
Virginia Military Institute
Virginia Polytechnic Institute and State University
Virginia State University
Virginia Union University
Virginia Wesleyan College
Virginia Western Community College
Washington and Lee University

Washington
Central Washington University
Clark College
Eastern Washington University
Gonzaga University
Highline Community College
Northwest University
Pacific Lutheran University
Pierce College
Saint Martin's University
Seattle Pacific University
Seattle University
Spokane Community College
Spokane Falls Community College
University of Puget Sound
University of Washington
Washington State University
Whitworth College

West Virginia
Marshall University
University of Charleston
West Virginia State University
West Virginia University
West Virginia University Institute of Technology

Wisconsin
Alverno College
Bellin College of Nursing
Carroll College
Carthage College
Marian College of Fond du Lac
Marquette University
Milwaukee School of Engineering
Ripon College
St. Norbert College
University of Wisconsin
    Green Bay
    La Crosse
    Madison
    Milwaukee
    Oshkosh
    Parkside
    River Falls
    Stevens Point
    Whitewater
Viterbo University
Wisconsin Lutheran College

Wyoming
University of Wyoming

Navy ROTC

Alabama
Alabama Agricultural and Mechanical University
Auburn University
Miles College
Stillman College

Arizona
Gateway Community College
Mesa Community College
Pima Community College
Southwestern College
University of Arizona

California
California Maritime Academy
California State University
    San Marcos
Contra Costa College
Diablo Valley College
Foothill College
Fullerton College
King's College and Seminary
Los Angeles City College
Loyola Marymount University
Mission College
National Hispanic University
National University
Point Loma Nazarene University
Riverside Community College
Sacramento City College
Samuel Merritt College
San Diego State University
San Francisco State University
Sonoma State University
Stanford University
University of California
    Berkeley
    Davis
    Los Angeles
    San Diego
    Santa Cruz
University of Redlands
University of San Diego
University of Southern California
Whittier College

Colorado
Regis University
University of Colorado
    Boulder

Connecticut
Capital Community College
Post University
Tunxis Community College

District of Columbia
Catholic University of America
George Washington University
Georgetown University
University of the District of Columbia

Florida
Embry-Riddle Aeronautical University
Florida Agricultural and Mechanical University
Florida Community College at Jacksonville
Florida State University
Jacksonville University
Pasco-Hernando Community College
Santa Fe Community College
Tallahassee Community College
University of Florida
University of North Florida
University of South Florida
University of Tampa

Georgia
Armstrong Atlantic State University
Clark Atlanta University
Clayton State University
Emory University
Georgia Institute of Technology
Georgia State University
Morehouse College
Savannah State University
Southern Polytechnic State University
Spelman College

Hawaii
University of Hawaii
    Hawaii Community College

Idaho
Lewis-Clark State College
University of Idaho

Illinois
Illinois Institute of Technology
Lincoln Land Community College
Loyola University of Chicago
Northwestern University
Parkland College
University of Illinois
    Chicago
    Urbana-Champaign

Indiana
Indiana University
    South Bend

Indiana University-Purdue University
  Indianapolis
Purdue University
Saint Mary's College
University of Notre Dame

Iowa
Hawkeye Community College
Iowa State University

Kansas
University of Kansas
Washburn University of Topeka

Louisiana
Dillard University
Louisiana State University and Agricultural and
  Mechanical College
Louisiana Tech University
Loyola University New Orleans
Our Lady of Holy Cross College
Southern University
  New Orleans
Southern University and Agricultural and
  Mechanical College
Tulane University
University of New Orleans
Xavier University of Louisiana

Maine
Husson College
Maine Maritime Academy
University of Maine
University of Maine
  Augusta

Maryland
University of Maryland
  College Park

Massachusetts
Babson College
Becker College
Boston College
Boston University
Clark University
College of the Holy Cross
Harvard College
Massachusetts Institute of Technology
Massachusetts Maritime Academy
Northeastern University
Tufts University
Worcester Polytechnic Institute
Worcester State College

Michigan
Eastern Michigan University
Finlandia University
Lawrence Technological University
University of Michigan
University of Michigan
  Dearborn

Minnesota
Anoka-Ramsey Community College
Augsburg College
Concordia University: St. Paul
Lake Superior College
Macalester College
Normandale Community College
University of Minnesota
  Twin Cities
University of St. Thomas

Mississippi
Tougaloo College
University of Mississippi

Missouri
Columbia College
Lincoln University
Stephens College
University of Missouri
  Columbia
  Rolla
Westminster College
William Woods University

Nebraska
University of Nebraska
  Lincoln
York College

New Mexico
Albuquerque Technical-Vocational Institute
National American University
University of New Mexico

New York
Albany College of Pharmacy
City University of New York
  Queens College
College of Saint Rose
Columbia University
  Columbia College
  Fu Foundation School of Engineering and
    Applied Science
Cornell University
Corning Community College
Eastman School of Music of the University of
  Rochester
Fordham University
Globe Institute of Technology
Katharine Gibbs School
  New York
Maria College
Molloy College
Monroe Community College
Rensselaer Polytechnic Institute
Rochester Institute of Technology
Russell Sage College
State University of New York
  College at Brockport
  Maritime College
Union College
University of Rochester

North Carolina
Belmont Abbey College
Duke University
Guilford Technical Community College
North Carolina State University
Peace College
University of North Carolina
  Chapel Hill

Ohio
Cleveland State University
Cuyahoga Community College
  Metropolitan Campus
Miami University
  Hamilton Campus
  Oxford Campus
Ohio State University
  Columbus Campus
  Lima Campus
  Mansfield Campus
  Marion Campus
  Newark Campus
Ohio University
  Lancaster Campus
University of Cincinnati
  Raymond Walters College

Oklahoma
Oklahoma Wesleyan University
University of Oklahoma

Oregon
Oregon State University
Warner Pacific College
Western Oregon University

Pennsylvania
Carlow University
Carnegie Mellon University
Chatham College
Drexel University
Duquesne University
Penn State
  University Park
St. Francis University
St. Joseph's University
Swarthmore College
Temple University
Thomas Jefferson University: College of Health
  Professions
University of Pennsylvania
University of Pittsburgh
Villanova University
Widener University

Puerto Rico
Inter American University of Puerto Rico
  Bayamon Campus
  Ponce Campus
Universidad Metropolitana

South Carolina
The Citadel
Midlands Technical College
University of South Carolina
University of South Carolina
  Salkehatchie Regional Campus

Tennessee
Belmont University
Christian Brothers University
Fisk University
University of Memphis
Vanderbilt University

Texas
Houston Baptist University
Huston-Tillotson College
Lon Morris College
Prairie View A&M University
Rice University
Texas A&M University
Texas A&M University
  Galveston
University of Houston
University of Texas
  Austin

Utah
University of Utah
Weber State University
Westminster College

Vermont
Norwich University

Virginia
Hampton University
Mary Baldwin College
New River Community College
Norfolk State University
Old Dominion University
University of Virginia
Virginia Military Institute
Virginia Polytechnic Institute and State
  University

Washington
Seattle Pacific University
Seattle University
Spokane Community College
University of Washington
Washington State University

West Virginia
Corinthian Schools: National Institute of
  Technology

Wisconsin
Marquette University
Milwaukee School of Engineering
University of Wisconsin
  Madison
Wisconsin Lutheran College

Glossary

Academic Competitiveness Grant. A federal grant program for Pell Grant recipients in their first two years of undergraduate study who completed a "rigorous" high school academic program, as determined by their state or local education agency. The maximum award is $750 for the first year of undergraduate study and $1,300 for the second year, both of which are in addition to the Pell Grant award.

Accelerated program. A college program of study completed in less time than is usually required, most often by attending classes in summer or by taking extra courses during the regular academic terms.

Accreditation. A process that ensures that a college meets acceptable standards in its programs, facilities, and services. Only colleges that are accredited by an agency recognized by the U.S. Department of Education may distribute federal financial aid to their students. Every college described in this book is accredited by such an agency.

ACT assessment. A college entrance examination formerly known as the American College Testing Program, given at test centers in the United States and other countries on specified dates throughout the year. It includes tests in English, mathematics, reading, and science reasoning.

Advanced placement. Admission or assignment of a first-year college student to an advanced course in a certain subject on the basis of evidence that he or she has already completed the equivalent of the college's course in that subject.

Advanced Placement Program® (AP®). A program of the College Board that provides high schools with course descriptions of college subjects and AP® Examinations in those subjects. The AP Program offers 37 exams in 22 subject areas. High schools offer the courses and administer the examinations to interested students. Most colleges and universities in the United States accept qualifying AP Exam grades for credit, advanced placement, or both.

AmeriCorps. A national network of service programs for which people volunteer and from which they earn money that can used to pay for college or pay back student loans.

Appeal. A request that a college reconsider a student's financial aid package.

Articulation agreement. A formal agreement between two higher-education institutions, stating specific policies relating to transfer of credits and recognition of academic achievement in order to facilitate the successful transfer of students without duplication of course work.

Associate degree. A degree granted by a college or university upon completion of a two-year, full-time program of study or its part-time equivalent. In general, the associate of arts (A.A.) or associate of science (A.S.) program is similar to the first two years of a four-year college curriculum. The associate in applied science (A.A.S.) is awarded by many colleges on completion of technological or vocational programs of study.

Award letter. A means of notifying admitted students of the financial aid being offered by the college or university. The award letter provides information on the types and amounts of aid offered, as well as students' responsibilities and the conditions governing the awards. Usually the award letter gives students the opportunity to accept or decline the aid offered, and a deadline by which to respond.

Bachelor's degree. A degree received upon completion of a four- or five-year full-time program of study (or its part-time equivalent) at a college or university. The bachelor of arts (B.A.), bachelor of science (B.S.), and bachelor of fine arts (B.F.A.) are the most common such degrees. College catalogs describe the variety of degrees awarded in each major.

Budget. A plan that shows your total expenses for a given month, semester, or year, and the means by which you'll pay for those expenses. See also *Student expense budget*.

Business college. A college that primarily prepares students to work in an office or entrepreneurial setting. The curriculum may focus on management, clerical positions, or both.

Campus-based programs. Federal financial aid programs that are administered directly by the college's financial aid office, which awards these funds to students using federal guidelines. Includes the Federal Supplemental Educational Opportunity Grant Program, Federal Perkins Loan Program, and the Federal Work-Study Program.

Candidates' reply date. The date by which admitted students must accept or decline an offer of admission and (if any) the college's offer of financial aid. Most colleges and universities follow the College Board-sponsored Candidates' Reply Date Agreement (CRDA), under which they agree to not require a decision from applicants for admission in the fall semester before May 1. The purpose of this agreement is to give applicants time to hear from all the colleges to which they have applied before having to make a commitment to any of them.

Certificate. An award for completing a particular program or course of study, sometimes given by two-year colleges or vocational or technical schools.

CLEP®. See *College-Level Examination Program®*.

CollegeCredit® Education Loans. An array of government and private loans sponsored by the College Board. The Federal Stafford Loan, the Federal Parent Loan for Undergraduate Students (PLUS), and privately sponsored Signature Student Education and Private Parent loans are available.

College-Level Examination Program (CLEP). A series of examinations in undergraduate courses that provides students of any age the opportunity to demonstrate college-level achievement, thereby reducing costs and time to degree completion. The examinations, which are sponsored by the College Board, are administered at colleges year round. All CLEP® exams are delivered on computer, providing test-takers instant score results.

College Scholarship Service® (CSS®). See *CSS/Financial Aid PROFILE®*.

Community/junior college. A college offering two-year programs leading to an associate degree. Community colleges are public institutions, while junior colleges are privately operated on a not-for-profit basis. Most two-year colleges offer both vocational programs (also called "career" or "terminal" programs), as well as the first two years of a four-year program ("academic" or "transfer" programs). Students in the vocational program usually goes directly into a career after graduation, while students in the academic program usually intend to transfer to a four-year institution or an upper-division college.

Consortium. A group of colleges and universities that share a common geographic location. Consortiums of colleges in the same town often allow students at one institution to take classes at neighboring consortium colleges and use facilities such as libraries at the member colleges. Larger consortiums, at the state or regional level, may offer in-state tuition to out-of-state students.

Cooperative education (co-op). A program in which students alternate class attendance and employment in business, industry, or government. Co-op students are typically paid for their work and may receive academic credit for their participation in the program. Under a cooperative plan, five years are normally required for completion of a bachelor's degree, but graduates have the advantage of about a year's practical work experience in addition to their studies.

Core curriculum. A group of courses, usually in the liberal arts, designated by a college as one of the requirements for a degree. Some colleges have both core-curriculum requirements and general-education requirements.

Cost of attendance. A number of expenses, among them tuition and fees (including loan fees), books and supplies, and the student's living expenses while attending school. The cost of attendance is estimated by the school, within guidelines established by federal regulation. The cost of attendance is compared with the student's *expected family contribution* to determine the student's need for financial aid.

Coverdell Education Savings Account (ESA). A federal income-tax provision (formerly referred to as the Education IRA) that enables taxpayers to establish a college savings plan. A maximum of $2,000 may be contributed annually to the account, which earns interest and/or dividends on a tax-free basis.

Credit by examination. Academic credit granted by a college to entering students who have demonstrated proficiency in college-level studies through examinations such as those sponsored by the College Board's Advanced Placement Program and College-Level Examination Program. It is a means of cutting college costs by reducing the number of courses needed to earn a degree.

Credit Hour. The standard unit of measurement for a college course. Each credit hour requires one classroom hour per week. Most college courses are offered in one to five credit-hour increments. For financial aid purposes, students taking at least 12 credit hours of classes in a semester are considered to be attending the college full-time, and students taking at least six credit hours are considered half-time.

CSS code. A four-digit College Board number that students use to designate colleges or scholarship programs to receive their CSS/Financial Aid PROFILE information. If a college requires financial aid applicants to submit the PROFILE, its CSS code will appear in its description in Part III of this book. A complete list of all CSS codes can also be downloaded from the CSS/Financial Aid PROFILE Web site.

CSS/Financial Aid PROFILE®. A Web-based application service offered by the College Board and used by some colleges, universities, and private scholarship programs to award their private financial aid funds. Students complete the online application and supplements, if required. CSS processes and reports the application data to institutions. CSS/Financial Aid PROFILE is not a federal form and may not be used to apply for federal student aid. Students pay a fee to register for PROFILE and to send reports to institutions that use it.

Deferred admission. Postponing enrollment, usually for one year, after being accepted for admission by a college.

Dependent student. For financial aid purposes, students who are under the age of 24, attend an undergraduate program, are not married, do not have children of their own, are not orphans or wards of the court, or veterans of the active-duty armed services.

The term is used to define eligibility for certain financial aid programs, regardless of whether or not the student lives with a parent, receives financial support from a parent, or is claimed on a parent's tax return. If a student is defined as dependent, parental financial information must be supplied on the Free Application for Federal Student Aid, CSS/Financial Aid PROFILE, and institutional aid applications.

Direct Loan Program. See *Federal Direct Loan Program*.

District. See *In-district tuition*.

Dual enrollment. The practice in which a student enrolls in college courses while still in high school, earning both high school and college credit for his or her work.

Early Action. A nonbinding early-decision program in which a student can receive an admission decision from one or more colleges and universities earlier than the standard response date but is not required to accept the admission offer or to make a deposit before May 1. Compare to *Early Decision*, which is a binding program.

Early action single choice. An early-action program in which the student may only apply early action to one college or university.

Early Decision. A binding program where students can receive an admission decision from one college or university before applications are due for regular admission. Participating students commit to enroll at the college if admitted and offered a satisfactory financial aid package.

Elective. A course, not required for one's chosen major or the college's core curriculum, that is selected to fulfill credit hours required for graduation.

Employer tuition assistance. Money that employers offer to employees or their dependents for use in paying education costs. Tuition assistance is considered an outside resource when colleges award financial aid.

Engineering college/institute/school. An institution of higher education that primarily prepares students for careers as licensed professional engineers or engineering technologists.

Expected family contribution (EFC). The total amount students and their families are expected to pay toward college costs from their income and assets for one academic year. The amount is derived from a need analysis of the family's overall financial circumstances. The *Federal Methodology* is used to determine a student's eligibility for federal and state student aid. Colleges and private aid programs may use a different methodology to determine eligibility for nonfederal financial aid. Frequently, these private institutions use the *Institutional Methodology*.

FAFSA. See *Free Application for Federal Student Aid.*

FAFSA on the Web. An electronic option for completing the Free Application for Federal Student Aid (www.fafsa.ed.gov).

Family Educational Rights and Privacy Act (FERPA). A federal law that protects the privacy of student education records. The law applies to all schools that receive funds under an applicable program of the U.S. Department of Education. FERPA gives parents certain rights with respect to their children's education records. These rights transfer to the student when he or she reaches the age of 18 or attends a school beyond the high school level.

Federal code number. A six-digit number that identifies a specific college to which students want their Free Application for Federal Student Aid information submitted. Each college's federal code appears in its profile in Part III of this book. Formerly known as the Title IV code.

Federal Direct Loan Program. A program that allows participating schools to administer subsidized and unsubsidized Stafford and PLUS loans directly to student and parent borrowers. Direct loans have mostly the same terms and conditions as FFELP loans. Funds for these programs are provided by the federal government.

Federal Family Education Loan Program (FFELP). The subsidized and unsubsidized Federal Stafford Loan, PLUS Loan, and Loan Consolidation programs. Funds for these programs are provided by lenders, and the loans are guaranteed by the federal government.

Federal Methodology (FM). A need-analysis formula used by colleges and universities to determine students' financial need for the purpose of awarding federal financial aid. Most colleges also use this methodology to determine need for the purpose of awarding their own institutional funds, but some colleges use the *Institutional Methodology* for that. The Federal Methodology uses information submitted by students on the FAFSA to assess their ability to pay for college and calculate their expected family contribution.

Federal Parents' Loan for Undergraduate Students (PLUS). A program that permits parents of undergraduate students to borrow up to the full cost of education, less any other financial aid the student may have received. The interest rate is variable and is reset each July.

Federal Pell Grant Program. A federally sponsored and administered program that provides need-based grants to undergraduate students. Congress annually sets the dollar range. As of 2006, a Pell Grant cannot exceed $4,050 per year. Eligibility for Pell Grants is based on a student's expected family contribution, the total cost of attendance at the college, and whether the student is attending the college full-time or part-time.

Federal Perkins Loan Program. A federally funded campus-based program that provides low-interest student loans. The maximum amount of loan funds available to an individual for undergraduate and graduate education is $40,000. Repayment need not begin until completion of the student's education, and it may be deferred for limited periods of service in the military, Peace Corps, or approved comparable organizations. The total debt may be forgiven by the federal government if the recipient enters a career of service as a public health nurse, law enforcement officer, public school teacher, or social worker.

Federal Stafford Loan. A program that allows students to borrow money for educational expenses from banks and other lending institutions (and sometimes from the colleges themselves). Subsidized Stafford loans are offered by colleges based on need. The federal government pays the interest on subsidized loans while the borrower is in college, and repayment does not begin until completion of the student's education. Unsubsidized Stafford loans are non-need-based;

anyone may apply for one regardless of their ability to pay for college. The interest on unsubsidized loans begins accumulating immediately. For both programs, the amounts that may be borrowed depend on the student's year in school, and the interest rates are variable.

Federal student aid. A number of programs sponsored by the federal government that award students loans, grants, or work-study jobs for the purpose of meeting their financial need. To receive any federal student aid, a student must demonstrate financial need by filing the Free Application for Federal Student Aid and meet certain other eligibility requirements as described on page 49.

Federal Supplemental Educational Opportunity Grant Program (SEOG). A federal campus-based program that provides need-based grants of up to $4,000 a year for undergraduate study. Each college is given a certain total amount of SEOG money each year to distribute among their financial aid applicants and determines the amount to which the student is entitled.

Federal Work-Study Program. A campus-based financial aid program that allows students to meet some of their financial need by working on- or off-campus while attending school. The wages earned are used to help pay the student's educational costs for the academic year. Job opportunities vary from campus to campus. The time commitment for a work-study job is usually between 10 and 15 hours each week.

Fee waiver. The waiver that significantly reduces the amount a student must pay for an application for admission, application for institutional financial aid, standardized tests, or other college-related expenses. Fee waivers are most commonly awarded to low-income students, but are sometimes also awarded to students who are senior citizens or in the military. See also *Tuition and fee waiver*.

Financial aid. Money awarded to students to help them pay for college. Financial aid comes in the form of gifts (scholarships and grants) and self-help aid (loans and work-study opportunities). Most aid is awarded on the basis of financial need, but some awards are non-need-based. Both need-based and non-need-based aid may or may not be offered on the additional basis of merit.

Financial aid application form. A form that collects information on the student, his or her income and assets, and (for dependent students) his or her parents' income and assets. All students must file the FAFSA to apply for financial aid; some colleges and states also require the CSS/Financial Aid PROFILE or their own institutional or state form.

Financial aid award letter. See *Award letter*.

Financial aid package. The total financial aid offered to a student by a college, including all loans, grants, scholarships, and work-study opportunities.

Financial aid PROFILE. See *CSS/Financial Aid PROFILE*.

Financial need. The difference between the total cost of attending a college and a student's expected family contribution (EFC). Financial aid grants, loans, and work-study will be offered by each college to fill all or a portion of the student's need.

529 Plan. See *Section 529 Plan*.

Fixed interest rate. An interest rate on a loan that is fixed for the lifetime of the loan. Compare to *Variable interest rate*.

For-profit college/university. A higher-education institution not supported by taxes and operated as a for-profit business, either as a publicly traded corporation or as a privately held company. Sometimes referred to as a "proprietary" college.

Free Application for Federal Student Aid (FAFSA). A form completed by all applicants for federal student aid. The FAFSA is also available on the Web, at www.fafsa.ed.gov. In many states, completion of the FAFSA is also sufficient to establish eligibility for state-sponsored aid programs. There is no charge for completing the FAFSA, and you can file it anytime after January 1 of the year for which you are seeking aid (e.g., after January 1, 2007, for the academic year 2007–2008).

Full need. A student's entire financial need at a college. A college that offers a financial aid package covering the complete difference between the cost of attendance and the expected family contribution is "meeting full need." See also *Gapping*.

Full-time status. Enrollment at a college or university for 12 or more credit hours per semester. Students must be enrolled full-time to qualify for the maximum award available to them from federal grant programs.

Gapping. A practice by which a college does not meet the full financial need of an admitted student, leaving a gap that must be filled by the student's own financial resources, in addition to the student's expected family contribution.

General education requirements. Courses that give undergraduates a background in all major academic disciplines: natural sciences, social sciences, mathematics, literature, language, and fine arts. Most colleges have general education requirements that students take in their first and second years, giving students a chance to sample a wide range of courses before selecting a major. At some colleges, general education courses are referred to as the core curriculum; at others, a few courses within the general education requirements are core courses that all students must take.

Gift aid. Financial aid in the form of scholarships or grants that do not have to be repaid.

Grant. A financial aid award given to a student that does not have to be repaid. The terms "grant" and "scholarship" are often used interchangeably to refer to gift aid, but grants tend to be awarded solely on the basis of financial need, while scholarships may require the student to demonstrate merit.

Half-time status. Enrollment at a college or university for at least six credit hours per semester, but fewer than the 12 credit hours required to qualify as full-time. Students must be enrolled at least half-time to qualify for federal student aid loan programs.

Health sciences college. An institution of higher education that primarily prepares students to enter work in a clinic, hospital, or private medical practice. For a complete description of health-related fields of study, see the *College Board Book of Majors*.

HOPE Education Tax Credit. A federal income tax credit of as much as $1,500 per dependent student annually. It is available to eligible taxpayers based on out-of-pocket tuition and fee expenditures for the first two years of undergraduate study, according to income eligibility guidelines. See also *Lifetime Learning Tax Credit*.

Independent student. For financial aid purposes, a student who is either 24 years old or older, married, a veteran, an orphan, or has legal dependents. Independent students do not need to provide parental information to be considered for federal financial aid programs. However, private institutions may require independent students to provide parental information on their institutional forms in order to be considered for nonfederal sources of funding.

In-district tuition. The tuition charged by a community college or state university to residents of the district from which it draws tax support. Districts are usually individual counties or cities, but sometimes are larger.

Individual Retirement Account (IRA). A retirement account that earns income tax-free. Money withdrawn for college expenses is not charged the penalty that normally would be incurred for withdrawing IRA money before age 59½, but is taxed as regular income.

In-state tuition. The tuition that a public institution charges residents of its state. Some community colleges and state universities charge this rate to students who are not residents of their district, but who are residents of their state.

Institutional form. A financial aid application form custom-made by a particular college or university. Some institutional forms are designed to collect additional information on a family's finances beyond what is collected on the FAFSA and are required of all financial aid applicants. Others serve specific purposes and are only required from certain students, for example early-decision applicants or student athletes.

Institutional methodology (IM). A need-analysis formula used by some colleges and universities to determine students' financial need and award their own institutional funds. Compared to the *Federal Methodology*, the IM takes into account a broader and deeper picture of family assets to determine a student's expected family contribution. Most colleges that use the IM collect this additional information through the CSS/Financial Aid PROFILE form, but some collect it using their own customized institutional forms.

International Baccalaureate (IB). A comprehensive and rigorous two-year curriculum (usually taken in the final two years of high school) that is similar to the final year of secondary school in Europe. Some colleges award credit or advanced placement to students who have completed an IB program.

Internship. Any short-term, supervised work, usually related to a student's major, for which academic credit is earned. The work can be full- or part-time, on or off campus, paid or unpaid. Some majors require the student to complete an internship.

Junior college. See *Community/junior college*.

Lender. An organization authorized to make educational loans to students.

Liberal arts. The study of the humanities (literature, the arts, and philosophy), history, foreign languages, social sciences, mathematics, and natural sciences. Liberal arts study guides students in developing general knowledge and reasoning ability rather than specific skills.

Liberal arts college. A college that emphasizes the liberal arts in its core curriculum and academic offerings and does not offer vocation, professional, or pre-professional programs.

Lifetime Learning Tax Credit. A federal income tax credit of as much as $1,000 per household annually; available to eligible taxpayers based on "out-of-pocket" tuition and fee expenditures, according to income eligibility guidelines. Unlike the HOPE Education Tax Credit, it can be used for any year of postsecondary study.

Major. The subject area in which students concentrate during their undergraduate study. At most colleges, students take a third to half of their courses in the major; the rest of their course work is devoted to core requirements and electives. In liberal arts programs, students generally take a third of their courses in their chosen field, which they usually must choose by the beginning of their junior year. In career-related programs, such as nursing or engineering, students may take up to half of their courses in their major.

Maritime college/institute/academy. An institution of higher education that prepares students to operate commercial shipping or fishing vessels. Upon graduation, students of most maritime academies are commissioned as officers in the United States Merchant Marine, and simultaneously commissioned as officers in the U.S. Navy Reserve.

Master Promissory Note (MPN). A special type of promissory note used to obtain a Federal Stafford loan. The MPN is designated for use as both a single-year and a multi-year note (for four-year and graduate/professional schools). Borrowers can sign a MPN once, the time they first borrow, and then receive additional loans during the same year or in subsequent years without signing an additional note.

Matriculation. The process whereby a student is accepted, pays fees, and enrolls in classes, officially becoming a student at the college. This term is only applied to freshmen or to a transfer student's first enrollment.

Merit aid. Financial aid awarded on the basis of academic qualifications, artistic or athletic talent, leadership qualities, or similar qualities. Most merit aid comes in the form of scholarships. Merit aid may be non-need-based, or the merit criteria may be in addition to a requirement that the student demonstrate financial need.

Military college/institute/academy. An institution of higher education that prepares students (who are called "cadets" while enrolled) to become active-duty officers in the armed services. The curriculum usually combines a study of the liberal arts, military science, and engineering. Cadets usually participate in military training assignments during the summer term in addition to attending the college in the fall and spring semesters. The five service academies operated by the United States government do not charge tuition, fees, room, or board, and cadets receive a nominal salary while enrolled.

Minor. Course work that is not as extensive as what is required for a major, but which gives students specialized knowledge of a second field. Students may choose a minor in the department of their major (for example, a major in comparative literature with a minor in German literature), or in a different department (for example, a biology major with a minor in philosophy). College catalogs describe the requirements for minors.

National Science and Mathematics Access to Retain Talent (SMART) Grant. A federal grant program for Pell Grant recipients who are in their third or fourth year of undergraduate study, have declared a major in the sciences, mathematics, engineering, technology, or certain foreign languages, and have maintained a GPA of at least 3.0 in that major. The maximum annual award is $4,000, in addition to the student's Pell Grant.

Need analysis. The process of analyzing the student's household and financial information to calculate an EFC and financial need. See also *Federal Methodology, Institutional Methodology.*

Need-analysis form. See *Financial aid application form.*

Need-based aid. Financial aid (scholarships, grants, loans, or work-study opportunities) given to students who have demonstrated financial need, calculated by subtracting the student's expected family contribution from a college's total cost of attendance. The largest source of need-based aid is the federal government, but colleges, states, and private foundations also award need-based aid to eligible students.

Need-blind admissions. The policy of determining whether a student should be admitted to a college without regard to his or her financial need.

Non-need-based aid. Financial aid awarded without regard to the student's demonstrated ability to pay for college. Unsubsidized loans and scholarships awarded solely on the basis of merit are both non-need-based. Some financial aid sponsors also offer non-need-based grants tied not to merit, but to other qualities, such as state of residence or participation in ROTC.

Nursing college. An institution of higher education that primarily prepares students to become registered nurses (RNs) or licensed practical nurses (LPNs).

Open admission. The college admissions policy of admitting high school graduates and other adults generally without regard to conventional academic qualifications, such as high school subjects, high school grades, and admissions test scores. Virtually all applicants with high school diplomas or their equivalent are accepted, although some programs of study may have additional requirements.

Origination fee. A fee charged to a borrower to cover the costs of processing a loan. The origination fee is usually a percentage of the total amount being borrowed. The origination fee for any loan will be disclosed in the promissory note for that loan.

Out-of-state tuition. The tuition a public college or university charges residents of other states.

Outside resources. Student financial aid granted by a source other than the college that the college must take into account when assembling an aid package. Examples of common outside resources include scholarships from private foundations, employer tuition assistance, and veterans' educational benefits.

Parents' contribution. The amount a student's parents are expected to pay toward college costs from their income and assets. It is derived from need analysis of the parents' overall financial situation. The parents' contribution and the student's contribution together constitute the total expected family contribution (EFC).

Parent's Loan for Undergraduate Students. See *Federal Parents' Loan for Undergraduate Students.*

Part-time status. Enrollment at a college or university for 11 or fewer credit hours per semester.

Pell Grant. See *Federal Pell Grant Program.*

Perkins Loan. See *Federal Perkins Loan Program.*

PLUS loan. See *Federal Parents' Loan for Undergraduate Students.*

Prepaid tuition plan. See *Section 529 Plans.*

Priority date. The date by which applications for financial aid must be received to be given the strongest possible consideration. The college will consider the financial need of applicants who make the priority date before any other applicants. Qualified applicants who do not make the priority date are considered on a first-come, first-served basis, and are only offered financial aid if (and to the extent to which) the college still has sufficient money left over after all the offers it has made. Can also refer to the priority date for admissions applications, where, again, the college will make offers to the priority applicants first, and then consider subsequent applicants on a first-come, first-served basis, making offers only if there is still room in the incoming class.

Private college/university. An educational institution of higher education not supported by public taxes and operated on a not-for-profit basis. May be independent or affiliated with a religious denomination.

PROFILE. See *CSS/Financial Aid PROFILE.*

Promissory note. A binding legal document that a borrower signs to get a loan. By signing this note, a borrower promises to repay the loan, with interest, in specified installments. The promissory note also includes any information about origination fees, grace periods, deferment or cancellation provisions, and the borrower's rights and responsibilities with respect to that loan.

Proprietary college/university. See *For-profit college/university.*

PSAT/NMSQT® (Preliminary SAT/National Merit Scholarship Qualifying Test). A shorter version of the SAT that is administered by high schools to sophomores and juniors each year in October. The PSAT/NMSQT® serves as the qualifying test for scholarships awarded by the National Merit Scholarship Corporation.

Public college/university. An institution of higher education supported by public taxes.

Quarter. An academic calendar period of about 12 weeks. Four quarters make up an academic year, but at colleges using the quarter system, students make normal academic progress by attending three quarters each year. In some colleges, students can accelerate their progress by attending all four quarters in one or more years.

Regular admission. At colleges with early-action or early-decision plans, "regular" admission is the round of admissions conducted in January or February, after the early-admission rounds.

Renewal FAFSA. A simplified reapplication form for federal student aid. The Renewal FAFSA allows continuing students to update the prior year's FAFSA, rather than completing the entire FAFSA for each award year.

Reserve Officers Training Corps (ROTC). Programs conducted by certain colleges in cooperation with the United States Air Force, Army, and Navy reserves. Participating students may receive a merit scholarship while they are in college, and will enter the reserves of their service branch as an officer upon graduation. Naval ROTC includes the Marine Corps. (The Coast Guard and Merchant Marine do not sponsor ROTC programs.) Local recruiting offices of the services themselves can supply detailed information about these programs, as can participating colleges.

Residency requirements. Most colleges and universities require that a student spend a minimum number of terms taking courses on campus (as opposed to independent study, transfer credits from other colleges, or credit-by-examination) to be eligible for graduation. Can also refer to the minimum amount of time a student is required to have lived in a state to be eligible for in-state tuition at a public college or university.

Rolling admission. An admission procedure by which the college considers each student's application as soon as all the required credentials, such as school record and test scores, have been received. The college usually notifies an applicant of its decision within a month. At many colleges, rolling admission allows for early notification and works much like nonbinding early-action programs.

SAR. See *Student Aid Report.*

SAR Acknowledgment. A federal document similar to the SAR that the Department of Education sends to a student who does not provide a valid e-mail address when he or she files the FAFSA through FAFSA on the Web, files through EDExpress at a postsecondary school, or makes changes through Corrections on the Web.

Satisfactory academic progress. Standards set by a college or university to determine whether a student is meeting sufficient academic standards. The student must achieve these standards to continue to receive financial aid.

SAT Reasoning Test™. The College Board's test of developed critical reading, writing, and mathematical reasoning abilities, given on specified dates throughout the year at test centers in the United States and other countries. The SAT® is required by many colleges and sponsors of financial aid programs, and many colleges use scores on the SAT as criteria for the awarding or merit scholarships.

SAT Subject Tests™. College Board tests in specific subjects, given at test centers in the United States and other countries on specified dates throughout the year. Used by colleges not only to help with decisions about admission, but also in course placement.

Scholarship. A type of financial aid that doesn't have to be repaid. Grants are often based on financial need. Scholarships may be based on need, on need combined with merit, or solely on the basis of merit or some other qualification, such as minority status.

School. In this book, used generically to refer interchangeably to colleges, universities, and other institutions of higher education. At some universities, a "school" is a subdivision of the university—for example, the administrative unit that offers nursing courses may be called the "college of nursing" at one institution, and the "school of nursing" at another.

Section 529 College Savings Plan. A state-sponsored plan that allows a student and his or her family to save for college costs in a tax-advantaged savings and investment account. Account earnings from interest, dividends, and capital gains are not taxed as income by the federal government if they are used to pay for higher-education expenses. Depending on the family's state of residence and which state's account they are contributing to, earnings may also be tax free on state income tax, and contributions may also be deductible on state income tax.

Section 529 Plans. State-sponsored college savings programs commonly referred to as "529 Plans" after the section of the Internal Revenue Code that provides the plan's tax breaks. There are two kinds: Section 529 college savings plans and Section 529 prepaid tuition plans.

Section 529 Prepaid Tuition Plan. State-sponsored plans through which parents can pay in advance for tuition at public institutions in their state of residence.

Self-help aid. Student financial aid, such as loans and work-study jobs, that requires repayment or employment.

Semester. A period of about 16 weeks. Colleges on a semester system offer two semesters of instruction a year; there may also be an additional summer session.

SEOG. See *Federal Supplemental Educational Opportunity Grant*.

Simplified needs test. In Federal Methodology need analysis, the simplified needs test excludes assets from the Expected Family Contribution calculation for low- to moderate-income families who file simplified tax returns (1040A, 1040EZ).

SMART Grant. See *National Science and Mathematics Access to Retain Talent Grant*.

Stafford Loan. See *Federal Stafford Loan Program*.

Student Aid Report (SAR). A report produced by the U.S. Department of Education and sent to students in response to their having filed the Free Application for Federal Student Aid (FAFSA). The SAR contains information the student provided on the FAFSA as well as the federally calculated expected family contribution.

Student expense budget. A calculation of the annual cost of attending college that is used to determine your financial need. Student expense budgets usually include tuition and fees, books and supplies, room and board, personal expenses, and transportation. Sometimes additional expenses are included for students with special education needs, students who have a disability, or students who are married or have children.

Student's contribution. The amount you are expected to pay toward college costs from your income and assets. The amount is derived from a need analysis of your resources. Your contribution and your parents' contribution together compose the total expected family contribution.

Subsidized Federal Stafford Loan. See *Federal Stafford Loan Program*.

Subsidized loan. A loan awarded to a student on the basis of financial need. The federal government or the state awarding the loan pays the borrower's interest while they are in college at least half-time, thereby subsidizing the loan.

Supplemental Educational Opportunity Grant. See *Federal Supplemental Educational Opportunity Grant*.

Taxable income. Income earned from wages, salaries, tips, as well as interest income, dividends, alimony, estates or trust income, business or farm profits, and rental or property income. Some scholarship awards must be reported as taxable income.

Teacher's college. A college that specializes in preparing students to teach in elementary or secondary schools. Most teacher's colleges offer a curriculum that combines a study of the liberal arts with the study of pedagogy.

Terminal program. An education program designed to prepare students for immediate employment. These programs usually can be completed in fewer than four years beyond high school and are available in most community colleges and trade schools.

Title IV code. See *Federal code number*.

Transfer program. An academic program in a community or junior college primarily for students who plan to continue their studies in a four-year college or university.

Transfer student. A student who has attended another college for any period, which may be defined by various colleges as any time from a single term up to three years. A transfer student may receive credit for all or some of the courses successfully completed before the transfer.

Trimester. An academic calendar period of about 15 weeks. Three trimesters make up one year. Students normally progress by attending two of the trimesters each year and in some colleges can accelerate their progress by attending all three trimesters in one or more years.

Tuition and fee waiver. Some colleges reduce the tuition and/or fees for some categories of students, such as adults, senior citizens, or children of alumni.

Two-year college. A college that offers only two years of undergraduate study. See *Community/junior college*; see also *Upper-division college*.

Undergraduate. A student in the freshman, sophomore, junior, or senior year of study, as opposed to a graduate student who has earned an undergraduate degree and is pursuing a master's, doctoral, or professional degree.

United Nations semester. A program in which students take courses at a college in the New York City metropolitan area while participating in an internship program at the United Nations.

Unmet need. The difference between a specific student's total available resources and the total cost for the student's attendance at a specific institution.

Unsubsidized Federal Stafford Loan. See *Federal Stafford Loan Program*.

Unsubsidized loan. An education loan that is non-need-based and therefore not subsidized by the federal government; the borrower is responsible for accrued interest throughout the life of the loan.

Upper-division college. A college that offers only the junior and senior years of study. Students must complete their freshman and sophomore years at other institutions before entering the upper-division institution to earn their bachelor's degree.

Variable interest rate. An interest rate that changes on an annual basis to better reflect market rates.

Verification. A procedure whereby a school checks the information the student reported on the FAFSA, usually by requesting a copy of the tax returns filed by the student and, if applicable, the student's spouse and parent(s). Colleges are required by federal regulations to verify a minimum percentage of financial aid applications.

Virtual college/university. A degree-granting, accredited institution wherein all courses are delivered by distance learning, with no physical campus.

Wait list. A list of students who meet the admissions requirements, but will be offered a place in the class only if space becomes available.

William D. Ford Federal Direct Loan Program. See *Federal Direct Loan Program*.

Work-study. An arrangement by which a student combines employment and college study. The employment may be an integral part of the academic program (as in cooperative education and internships) or simply a means of paying for college (as in the need-based *Federal Work-Study Program*).

Alphabetical Index of Colleges

Aakers College
    Fargo (ND), 645
Abilene Christian University (TX), 796
Academy College (MN), 475
Academy of Art University (CA), 180
Academy of Medical Arts and Business (PA), 703
Adams State College (CO), 229
Adelphi University (NY), 563
Adirondack Community College (NY), 563
Adrian College (MI), 454
Agnes Scott College (GA), 282
AIB College of Business (IA), 359
Aiken Technical College (SC), 762
Aims Community College (CO), 229
Alabama Agricultural and Mechanical University (AL), 147
Alabama State University (AL), 147
Alamance Community College (NC), 616
Alaska Bible College (AK), 159
Alaska Pacific University (AK), 159
Albany College of Pharmacy (NY), 564
Albany State University (GA), 282
Albany Technical College (GA), 283
Albertson College of Idaho (ID), 305
Albertus Magnus College (CT), 242
Albion College (MI), 455
Albright College (PA), 704
Albuquerque Technical-Vocational Institute (NM), 557
Alcorn State University (MS), 494
Alderson-Broaddus College (WV), 877
Alexandria Technical College (MN), 475
Alfred University (NY), 564
Alice Lloyd College (KY), 387
Allan Hancock College (CA), 180
Allegany College of Maryland (MD), 416
Allegheny College (PA), 704
Allen College (IA), 359
Allen County Community College (KS), 374
Allen University (SC), 763
Alliant International University (CA), 180
Alma College (MI), 455
Alpena Community College (MI), 455
Alvernia College (PA), 704
Alverno College (WI), 884
Alvin Community College (TX), 797
American Academy McAllister Institute of Funeral Service (NY), 564
American Academy of Art (IL), 308
American Academy of Dramatic Arts (NY), 564
American Academy of Dramatic Arts West (CA), 181
American Baptist College of ABT Seminary (TN), 781
American International College (MA), 428
American River College (CA), 181
American University (DC), 253
Amherst College (MA), 429
Ancilla College (IN), 341
Anderson University (IN), 341
Anderson University (SC), 763
Andrew College (GA), 283
Andrews University (MI), 456
Angelina College (TX), 797
Angelo State University (TX), 797
Anna Maria College (MA), 429
Anne Arundel Community College (MD), 416
Anoka Technical College (MN), 475
Anoka-Ramsey Community College (MN), 475
Antelope Valley College (CA), 181
Antioch College (OH), 650
Antioch University McGregor (OH), 650
Antioch University Santa Barbara (CA), 181
Antioch University Seattle (WA), 862
Antonelli Institute of Art and Photography (PA), 704
Appalachian Bible College (WV), 877
Appalachian State University (NC), 616
Aquinas College (MI), 456
Aquinas College (TN), 781

Arapahoe Community College (CO), 229
Arcadia University (PA), 705
Arizona State University (AZ), 161
Arizona State University West (AZ), 161
Arizona Western College (AZ), 162
Arkansas Baptist College (AR), 169
Arkansas Northeastern College (AR), 169
Arkansas State University (AR), 170
Arkansas State University
    Beebe (AR), 170
    Mountain Home (AR), 170
    Newport (AR), 170
Arkansas Tech University (AR), 170
Arlington Baptist College (TX), 797
Armstrong Atlantic State University (GA), 283
Art Academy of Cincinnati (OH), 650
Art Center College of Design (CA), 181
Art Center Design College (AZ), 162
Art Institute of Boston at Lesley University (MA), 429
Art Institute of California
    Los Angeles (CA), 182
    Orange County (CA), 182
    San Francisco (CA), 182
Art Institute of Colorado (CO), 230
Art Institute of Dallas (TX), 798
Art Institute of Fort Lauderdale (FL), 256
Art Institute of Las Vegas (NV), 533
Art Institute of Philadelphia (PA), 705
Art Institute of Portland (OR), 693
Art Institute of Seattle (WA), 862
Art Institute of Washington (VA), 843
Art Institutes International Minnesota (MN), 476
ASA Institute of Business and Computer Technology (NY), 565
Asbury College (KY), 387
Ashford University (IA), 359
Ashland University (OH), 650
Asnuntuck Community College (CT), 242
Assumption College (MA), 429
Athens State University (AL), 147
Athens Technical College (GA), 283
ATI Career Training Center (TX), 798
Atlanta Christian College (GA), 284
Atlanta Metropolitan College (GA), 284
Atlantic Cape Community College (NJ), 542
Atlantic College (PR), 753
Atlantic Union College (MA), 430
Auburn University (AL), 147
Auburn University at Montgomery (AL), 148
Augsburg College (MN), 476
Augusta State University (GA), 284
Augustana College (IL), 309
Augustana College (SD), 776
Aurora University (IL), 309
Austin College (TX), 798
Austin Community College (TX), 798
Austin Graduate School of Theology (TX), 799
Austin Peay State University (TN), 781
Averett University (VA), 843
Avila University (MO), 501
Azusa Pacific University (CA), 182
Babson College (MA), 430
Bacone College (OK), 683
Bainbridge College (GA), 284
Baker College of Auburn Hills (MI), 456
Baker College of Cadillac (MI), 456
Baker College of Clinton Township (MI), 457
Baker College of Muskegon (MI), 457
Baker College of Owosso (MI), 457
Baker College of Port Huron (MI), 457
Baker University (KS), 375
Baldwin-Wallace College (OH), 651
Ball State University (IN), 341
Baltimore City Community College (MD), 416
Baltimore Hebrew University (MD), 417
Baltimore International College (MD), 417
Baptist Bible College (MO), 501

Baptist Bible College of Pennsylvania (PA), 705
Baptist College of Florida (FL), 257
Barclay College (KS), 375
Bard College (NY), 565
Barnard College (NY), 565
Barry University (FL), 257
Barstow College (CA), 183
Barton College (NC), 617
Barton County Community College (KS), 375
Bastyr University (WA), 862
Bates College (ME), 409
Baton Rouge Community College (LA), 401
Bauder College (GA), 285
Bay de Noc Community College (MI), 457
Bay Mills Community College (MI), 458
Bay Path College (MA), 430
Bay State College (MA), 431
Bayamon Central University (PR), 753
Baylor University (TX), 799
Beacon College (FL), 257
Beaufort County Community College (NC), 617
Becker College (MA), 431
Beckfield College (KY), 388
Belhaven College (MS), 495
Bellarmine University (KY), 388
Bellevue Community College (WA), 863
Bellevue University (NE), 525
Bellin College of Nursing (WI), 884
Bellingham Technical College (WA), 863
Belmont Abbey College (NC), 617
Belmont Technical College (OH), 651
Belmont University (TN), 781
Beloit College (WI), 884
Bel-Rea Institute of Animal Technology (CO), 230
Bemidji State University (MN), 476
Benedict College (SC), 763
Benedictine College (KS), 375
Benedictine University (IL), 309
Benjamin Franklin Institute of Technology (MA), 431
Bennett College (NC), 617
Bennington College (VT), 837
Bentley College (MA), 431
Berea College (KY), 388
Berkeley College (NJ), 543
Berkeley College (NY), 566
Berkeley College of New York City (NY), 566
Berklee College of Music (MA), 432
Berks Technical Institute (PA), 705
Berkshire Community College (MA), 432
Berry College (GA), 285
Bethany College (KS), 376
Bethany College (WV), 877
Bethany Lutheran College (MN), 476
Bethany University (CA), 183
Bethel College (IN), 341
Bethel College (KS), 376
Bethel College (TN), 782
Bethel University (MN), 477
Bethesda Christian University (CA), 183
Bethune-Cookman College (FL), 257
Bidwell Training Center (PA), 706
Big Bend Community College (WA), 863
Big Sandy Community and Technical College (KY), 389
Biola University (CA), 183
Birmingham-Southern College (AL), 148
Bishop State Community College (AL), 148
Bismarck State College (ND), 645
Black Hawk College (IL), 310
Black Hills State University (SD), 777
Blackburn College (IL), 310
Blackfeet Community College (MT), 520
Blackhawk Technical College (WI), 885
Bladen Community College (NC), 618
Blair College (CO), 230
Blessing-Reiman College of Nursing (IL), 310
Blinn College (TX), 799

Bloomfield College (NJ), 543
Bloomsburg University of Pennsylvania (PA), 706
Blue Mountain College (MS), 495
Blue Mountain Community College (OR), 693
Blue Ridge Community College (NC), 618
Blue Ridge Community College (VA), 843
Blue River Community College (MO), 502
Bluefield College (VA), 843
Bluefield State College (WV), 878
Bluegrass Community and Technical College (KY), 389
Bluffton University (OH), 651
Boise Bible College (ID), 306
Boise State University (ID), 306
Bossier Parish Community College (LA), 402
Boston Architectural Center (MA), 432
Boston College (MA), 432
Boston Conservatory (MA), 433
Boston University (MA), 433
Boulder College of Massage Therapy (CO), 230
Bowdoin College (ME), 409
Bowie State University (MD), 417
Bowling Green State University (OH), 652
Bowling Green State University
    Firelands College (OH), 652
Bradford School (OH), 652
Bradley University (IL), 310
Brandeis University (MA), 433
Brazosport College (TX), 799
Brenau University (GA), 285
Brescia University (KY), 389
Brevard College (NC), 618
Brevard Community College (FL), 258
Brewton-Parker College (GA), 285
Briar Cliff University (IA), 360
Briarwood College (CT), 243
Bridgewater College (VA), 843
Bridgewater State College (MA), 434
Brigham Young University (UT), 833
Brigham Young University-Hawaii (HI), 302
Brigham Young University-Idaho (ID), 306
Bristol Community College (MA), 434
Brookdale Community College (NJ), 543
Broome Community College (NY), 566
Broward Community College (FL), 258
Brown Mackie College
    Hopkinsville (KY), 389
Brown University (RI), 759
Brunswick Community College (NC), 618
Bryan College (TN), 782
Bryant & Stratton College
    Albany (NY), 566
    Cleveland (OH), 653
    Milwaukee (WI), 885
    Parma (OH), 653
    Syracuse (NY), 566
    Virginia Beach (VA), 844
    Willoughby Hills (OH), 653
Bryant University (RI), 760
Bryn Athyn College of the New Church (PA), 706
Bryn Mawr College (PA), 706
Bucknell University (PA), 707
Bucks County Community College (PA), 707
Buena Vista University (IA), 360
Bunker Hill Community College (MA), 434
Burlington College (VT), 837
Burlington County College (NJ), 543
Business Institute of Pennsylvania
    Meadville (PA), 707
Butler County Community College (KS), 376
Butler County Community College (PA), 708
Butler University (IN), 342
Cabarrus College of Health Sciences (NC), 619
Cabrini College (PA), 708
Caldwell College (NJ), 544
Caldwell Community College and Technical Institute (NC), 619
California Baptist University (CA), 184
California College of the Arts (CA), 184
California Culinary Academy (CA), 184
California Institute of Technology (CA), 184
California Institute of the Arts (CA), 185
California Lutheran University (CA), 185
California Maritime Academy (CA), 185

California Polytechnic State University
    San Luis Obispo (CA), 186
California School of Culinary Arts (CA), 186
California State Polytechnic University
    Pomona (CA), 186
California State University
    Bakersfield (CA), 186
    Chico (CA), 187
    Dominguez Hills (CA), 187
    East Bay (CA), 187
    Fresno (CA), 187
    Fullerton (CA), 188
    Long Beach (CA), 188
    Los Angeles (CA), 188
    Monterey Bay (CA), 188
    Northridge (CA), 189
    Sacramento (CA), 189
    San Bernardino (CA), 189
    San Marcos (CA), 189
    Stanislaus (CA), 189
California University of Pennsylvania (PA), 708
Calumet College of St. Joseph (IN), 342
Calvary Bible College and Theological Seminary (MO), 502
Calvin College (MI), 458
Cambria-Rowe Business College (PA), 708
Cambria-Rowe Business College: Indiana (PA), 709
Cambridge College (CO), 230
Cambridge College (MA), 434
Camden County College (NJ), 544
Cameron University (OK), 683
Campbell University (NC), 619
Campbellsville University (KY), 390
Canisius College (NY), 567
Cankdeska Cikana Community College (ND), 645
Cape Cod Community College (MA), 434
Cape Fear Community College (NC), 619
Capella University (MN), 477
Capital Community College (CT), 243
Capital University (OH), 653
Cardinal Stritch University (WI), 885
Career College of Northern Nevada (NV), 534
Career Training Academy (PA), 709
Career Training Academy
    Monroeville (PA), 709
Carl Albert State College (OK), 684
Carl Sandburg College (IL), 311
Carleton College (MN), 477
Carlos Albizu University (FL), 258
Carlow University (PA), 709
Carnegie Mellon University (PA), 710
Carolinas College of Health Sciences (NC), 620
Carroll College (MT), 520
Carroll College (WI), 885
Carroll Community College (MD), 417
Carson-Newman College (TN), 782
Carteret Community College (NC), 620
Carthage College (WI), 886
Case Western Reserve University (OH), 654
Casper College (WY), 900
Castleton State College (VT), 837
Catawba College (NC), 620
Catawba Valley Community College (NC), 620
Catholic University of America (DC), 254
Cayuga County Community College (NY), 567
Cazenovia College (NY), 567
Cecil Community College (MD), 418
Cedar Crest College (PA), 710
Cedar Valley College (TX), 800
Cedarville University (OH), 654
Centenary College (NJ), 544
Centenary College of Louisiana (LA), 402
Central Arizona College (AZ), 162
Central Baptist College (AR), 171
Central Carolina Community College (NC), 621
Central Carolina Technical College (SC), 763
Central Christian College of Kansas (KS), 377
Central Christian College of the Bible (MO), 502
Central College (IA), 360
Central Community College (NE), 525
Central Connecticut State University (CT), 243
Central Florida College (FL), 258
Central Florida Community College (FL), 259

Central Georgia Technical College (GA), 286
Central Lakes College (MN), 478
Central Maine Community College (ME), 409
Central Maine Medical Center School of Nursing (ME), 409
Central Methodist University (MO), 502
Central Michigan University (MI), 458
Central Missouri State University (MO), 503
Central Ohio Technical College (OH), 654
Central Oregon Community College (OR), 694
Central Pennsylvania College (PA), 710
Central Piedmont Community College (NC), 621
Central State University (OH), 654
Central Texas College (TX), 800
Central Washington University (WA), 863
Central Wyoming College (WY), 900
Centralia College (WA), 863
Centre College (KY), 390
Century Community and Technical College (MN), 478
Cerro Coso Community College (CA), 190
Chabot College (CA), 190
Chadron State College (NE), 525
Chaffey College (CA), 190
Chaminade University of Honolulu (HI), 302
Champlain College (VT), 838
Chandler-Gilbert Community College: Pecos (AZ), 162
Chapman University (CA), 190
Charleston Southern University (SC), 764
Charter College (AK), 160
Charter Oak State College (CT), 243
Chatfield College (OH), 655
Chatham College (PA), 710
Chattahoochee Technical College (GA), 286
Chattahoochee Valley Community College (AL), 149
Chattanooga State Technical Community College (TN), 782
Chemeketa Community College (OR), 694
Chesapeake College (MD), 418
Chester College of New England (NH), 536
Chestnut Hill College (PA), 711
Cheyney University of Pennsylvania (PA), 711
CHI Institute
    Broomall (PA), 711
Chief Dull Knife College (MT), 521
Chipola College (FL), 259
Chippewa Valley Technical College (WI), 886
Chowan College (NC), 621
Christendom College (VA), 844
Christian Brothers University (TN), 783
Christopher Newport University (VA), 844
Cincinnati Christian University (OH), 655
Cincinnati College of Mortuary Science (OH), 655
Cincinnati State Technical and Community College (OH), 655
The Citadel (SC), 764
Citrus College (CA), 191
City College
    Miami (FL), 259
City College of San Francisco (CA), 191
City Colleges of Chicago
    Harold Washington College (IL), 311
    Harry S. Truman College (IL), 311
    Kennedy-King College (IL), 311
    Malcolm X College (IL), 312
    Olive-Harvey College (IL), 312
    Richard J. Daley College (IL), 312
    Wright College (IL), 312
City University (WA), 864
City University of New York
    Baruch College (NY), 568
    Borough of Manhattan Community College (NY), 568
    Bronx Community College (NY), 568
    Brooklyn College (NY), 568
    City College (NY), 569
    College of Staten Island (NY), 569
    Hostos Community College (NY), 569
    Hunter College (NY), 569
    John Jay College of Criminal Justice (NY), 570
    Kingsborough Community College (NY), 570
    LaGuardia Community College (NY), 570
    Lehman College (NY), 570
    Medgar Evers College (NY), 571
    New York City College of Technology (NY), 571
    Queens College (NY), 571
    Queensborough Community College (NY), 571

York College (NY), 572
Clackamas Community College (OR), 694
Claflin University (SC), 764
Claremont McKenna College (CA), 191
Clarendon College (TX), 800
Clarion University of Pennsylvania (PA), 711
Clark Atlanta University (GA), 286
Clark College (WA), 864
Clark University (MA), 435
Clarke College (IA), 361
Clarkson College (NE), 526
Clarkson University (NY), 572
Clatsop Community College (OR), 694
Clayton State University (GA), 286
Clear Creek Baptist Bible College (KY), 390
Clearwater Christian College (FL), 259
Cleary University (MI), 459
Clemson University (SC), 764
Cleveland Community College (NC), 621
Cleveland Institute of Art (OH), 656
Cleveland Institute of Music (OH), 656
Cleveland State Community College (TN), 783
Cleveland State University (OH), 656
Clinton Community College (NY), 572
Cloud County Community College (KS), 377
Clover Park Technical College (WA), 864
Clovis Community College (NM), 557
Coahoma Community College (MS), 495
Coastal Bend College (TX), 800
Coastal Carolina Community College (NC), 621
Coastal Carolina University (SC), 765
Coastal Georgia Community College (GA), 286
Coastline Community College (CA), 191
Cochise College (AZ), 162
Cochran School of Nursing-St. John's Riverside
    Hospital (NY), 572
Coconino County Community College (AZ), 163
Coe College (IA), 361
Coffeyville Community College (KS), 377
Cogswell Polytechnical College (CA), 192
Coker College (SC), 765
Colby College (ME), 410
Colby Community College (KS), 377
Colby-Sawyer College (NH), 537
Colgate University (NY), 573
College for Creative Studies (MI), 459
College Misericordia (PA), 712
College of Art Advertising (OH), 656
College of Charleston (SC), 765
College of DuPage (IL), 313
College of Eastern Utah (UT), 834
College of Lake County (IL), 313
College of Marin
    Kentfield (CA), 192
College of Menominee Nation (WI), 886
College of Mount St. Joseph (OH), 657
College of Mount St. Vincent (NY), 573
The College of New Jersey (NJ), 545
College of New Rochelle (NY), 573
College of Notre Dame of Maryland (MD), 418
College of Oceaneering (CA), 192
College of Office Technology (IL), 313
College of St. Benedict (MN), 478
College of St. Catherine (MN), 478
College of St. Elizabeth (NJ), 545
College of St. Joseph in Vermont (VT), 838
College of Saint Mary (NE), 526
College of Saint Rose (NY), 573
College of St. Scholastica (MN), 479
College of Saint Thomas More (TX), 801
College of Santa Fe (NM), 557
College of Southern Idaho (ID), 307
College of Southern Maryland (MD), 418
College of the Albemarle (NC), 622
College of the Atlantic (ME), 410
College of the Canyons (CA), 192
College of the Desert (CA), 193
College of the Holy Cross (MA), 435
College of the Mainland (TX), 801
College of the Ozarks (MO), 503
College of the Redwoods (CA), 193
College of the Siskiyous (CA), 193

College of the Southwest (NM), 558
College of Visual Arts (MN), 479
College of Westchester (NY), 574
College of William and Mary (VA), 845
College of Wooster (OH), 657
CollegeAmerica-Denver (CO), 231
Collin County Community College District (TX), 801
Colorado Christian University (CO), 231
Colorado College (CO), 231
Colorado Mountain College
    Alpine Campus (CO), 231
    Spring Valley Campus (CO), 232
    Timberline Campus (CO), 232
Colorado Northwestern Community College (CO), 232
Colorado School of Healing Arts (CO), 232
Colorado School of Mines (CO), 233
Colorado State University (CO), 233
Colorado State University
    Pueblo (CO), 233
Colorado Technical University (CO), 233
Columbia Basin College (WA), 864
Columbia College (CA), 193
Columbia College (MO), 503
Columbia College (PR), 753
Columbia College (SC), 766
Columbia College Chicago (IL), 313
Columbia College of Nursing (WI), 886
Columbia International University (SC), 766
Columbia State Community College (TN), 783
Columbia Union College (MD), 419
Columbia University
    Columbia College (NY), 574
    Fu Foundation School of Engineering and Applied
        Science (NY), 574
    School of General Studies (NY), 574
    School of Nursing (NY), 575
Columbia-Greene Community College (NY), 575
Columbus College of Art and Design (OH), 657
Columbus State Community College (OH), 657
Columbus State University (GA), 287
Columbus Technical College (GA), 287
Commonwealth Institute of Funeral Service (TX), 801
Commonwealth Technical Institute (PA), 712
Community College of Allegheny County (PA), 712
Community College of Aurora (CO), 234
Community College of Baltimore County (MD), 419
Community College of Beaver County (PA), 713
Community College of Denver (CO), 234
Community College of Philadelphia (PA), 713
Community College of Rhode Island (RI), 760
Community College of Southern Nevada (NV), 534
Community College of Vermont (VT), 838
Conception Seminary College (MO), 503
Concord University (WV), 878
Concordia College (AL), 149
Concordia College (NY), 575
Concordia College
    Moorhead (MN), 479
Concordia University (CA), 193
Concordia University (IL), 314
Concordia University (MI), 459
Concordia University (NE), 526
Concordia University (OR), 695
Concordia University at Austin (TX), 802
Concordia University
    St. Paul (MN), 480
Concordia University Wisconsin (WI), 886
Connecticut College (CT), 244
Connors State College (OK), 684
Conservatory of Music of Puerto Rico (PR), 754
Consolidated School of Business
    Lancaster (PA), 713
    York (PA), 713
Converse College (SC), 766
Cooper Union for the Advancement of Science and Art (NY), 575
Copiah-Lincoln Community College (MS), 495
Copper Mountain College (CA), 194
Coppin State University (MD), 419
Corban College (OR), 695
Corcoran College of Art and Design (DC), 254
Corinthian Schools
    National Institute of Technology (WV), 878

Cornell College (IA), 361
Cornell University (NY), 576
Cornerstone University (MI), 459
Corning Community College (NY), 576
Cornish College of the Arts (WA), 865
Cossatot Community College of the University of
    Arkansas (AR), 171
Cottey College (MO), 504
County College of Morris (NJ), 545
Covenant College (GA), 287
Cowley County Community College (KS), 378
Crafton Hills College (CA), 194
Craven Community College (NC), 622
Creative Center (NE), 526
Creighton University (NE), 526
Crichton College (TN), 783
Crossroads College (MN), 480
Crowder College (MO), 504
Crowley's Ridge College (AR), 171
Crown College (MN), 480
Crown College (WA), 865
Culinary Institute of America (NY), 576
Culver-Stockton College (MO), 504
Cumberland County College (NJ), 546
Cumberland University (TN), 784
Curry College (MA), 435
Curtis Institute of Music (PA), 713
Cuyahoga Community College
    Metropolitan Campus (OH), 658
Cuyamaca College (CA), 194
Dabney S. Lancaster Community College (VA), 845
Daemen College (NY), 576
Dakota County Technical College (MN), 480
Dakota State University (SD), 777
Dakota Wesleyan University (SD), 777
Dallas Baptist University (TX), 802
Dallas Christian College (TX), 802
Dalton State College (GA), 287
Dana College (NE), 527
Daniel Webster College (NH), 537
Danville Area Community College (IL), 314
Danville Community College (VA), 845
Dartmouth College (NH), 537
Darton College (GA), 288
Davenport University (MI), 460
Davidson College (NC), 622
Davidson County Community College (NC), 622
Davis and Elkins College (WV), 878
Davis College (OH), 658
Dawson Community College (MT), 521
Daymar College (KY), 391
Daytona Beach Community College (FL), 259
De Anza College (CA), 194
Deaconess College of Nursing (MO), 504
Dean College (MA), 436
Dean Institute of Technology (PA), 714
Deep Springs College (NV), 195
Defiance College (OH), 658
DeKalb Technical College (GA), 288
Del Mar College (TX), 802
Delaware County Community College (PA), 714
Delaware State University (DE), 252
Delaware Technical and Community College
    Stanton/Wilmington Campus (DE), 252
    Terry Campus (DE), 252
Delaware Valley College (PA), 714
Delgado Community College (LA), 402
Delta College (MI), 460
Delta State University (MS), 496
Denison University (OH), 658
Denmark Technical College (SC), 767
DePaul University (IL), 314
DePauw University (IN), 342
Des Moines Area Community College (IA), 362
DeSales University (PA), 714
DeVry Institute of Technology
    New York (NY), 577
DeVry University
    Addison (IL), 314
    Alpharetta (GA), 288
    Arlington (VA), 845
    Chicago (IL), 315

Colorado Springs (CO), 234
Columbus (OH), 659
Decatur (GA), 288
Federal Way (WA), 865
Fremont (CA), 195
Ft. Washington (PA), 715
Irving (TX), 803
Kansas City (MO), 505
Long Beach (CA), 195
Miramar (FL), 260
North Brunswick (NJ), 546
Orlando (FL), 260
Phoenix (AZ), 163
Pomona (CA), 195
Tinley Park (IL), 315
West Hills (CA), 196
Westminster (CO), 234
Diablo Valley College (CA), 196
Dickinson College (PA), 715
Dickinson State University (ND), 646
DigiPen Institute of Technology (WA), 865
Dillard University (LA), 402
Dine College (AZ), 163
Divine Word College (IA), 362
Dixie State College of Utah (UT), 834
Doane College (NE), 527
Dodge City Community College (KS), 378
Dominican College of Blauvelt (NY), 197
Dominican School of Philosophy and Theology (CA), 196
Dominican University (IL), 315
Dominican University of California (CA), 196
Dona Ana Branch Community College of New Mexico State University (NM), 558
Donnelly College (KS), 378
Dordt College (IA), 362
Douglas Education Center (PA), 715
Dowling College (NY), 577
Drake University (IA), 362
Draughons Junior College (KY), 391
Drew University (NJ), 546
Drexel University (PA), 715
Drury University (MO), 505
DuBois Business College (PA), 716
Duke University (NC), 623
Dunwoody College of Technology (MN), 481
Duquesne University (PA), 716
Durham Technical Community College (NC), 623
Dutchess Community College (NY), 577
Dyersburg State Community College (TN), 784
D'Youville College (NY), 578
Earlham College (IN), 342
East Arkansas Community College (AR), 171
East Carolina University (NC), 623
East Central College (MO), 505
East Central University (OK), 684
East Georgia College (GA), 289
East Los Angeles College (CA), 196
East Stroudsburg University of Pennsylvania (PA), 716
East Tennessee State University (TN), 784
East Texas Baptist University (TX), 803
Eastern Arizona College (AZ), 163
Eastern Connecticut State University (CT), 244
Eastern Idaho Technical College (ID), 307
Eastern Illinois University (IL), 316
Eastern Kentucky University (KY), 391
Eastern Maine Community College (ME), 410
Eastern Mennonite University (VA), 845
Eastern Michigan University (MI), 460
Eastern Nazarene College (MA), 436
Eastern New Mexico University (NM), 558
Eastern New Mexico University Roswell Campus (NM), 559
Eastern Oklahoma State College (OK), 684
Eastern Oregon University (OR), 695
Eastern Shore Community College (VA), 846
Eastern Washington University (WA), 866
Eastern West Virginia Community and Technical College (WV), 879
Eastern Wyoming College (WY), 900
Eastfield College (TX), 803
Eastman School of Music of the University of Rochester (NY), 578

East-West University (IL), 315
Ecclesia College (AR), 172
Eckerd College (FL), 260
ECPI College of Technology (VA), 846
Edgecombe Community College (NC), 623
Edgewood College (WI), 887
Edinboro University of Pennsylvania (PA), 716
Edison College (FL), 260
Edison State Community College (OH), 659
Edmonds Community College (WA), 866
Edward Waters College (FL), 261
El Centro College (TX), 803
El Paso Community College (TX), 804
Elgin Community College (IL), 316
Elizabeth City State University (NC), 624
Elizabethtown College (PA), 717
Elizabethtown Community and Technical College (KY), 391
Ellsworth Community College (IA), 363
Elmhurst College (IL), 316
Elmira Business Institute (NY), 578
Elmira College (NY), 578
Elms College (MA), 436
Elon University (NC), 624
Embry-Riddle Aeronautical University (FL), 261
Embry-Riddle Aeronautical University: Extended Campus (FL), 261
Embry-Riddle Aeronautical University: Prescott Campus (AZ), 164
Emerson College (MA), 436
Emmanuel College (GA), 289
Emmanuel College (MA), 437
Emmaus Bible College (IA), 363
Emory & Henry College (VA), 846
Emory University (GA), 289
Empire College (CA), 197
Emporia State University (KS), 378
Endicott College (MA), 437
Erie Business Center (PA), 717
Erie Community College
    City Campus (NY), 579
    North Campus (NY), 579
    South Campus (NY), 579
Erskine College (SC), 767
Essex County College (NJ), 546
Estrella Mountain Community College (AZ), 164
ETI Technical College of Niles (OH), 659
Eugene Bible College (OR), 696
Eugene Lang College The New School for Liberal Arts (NY), 579
Eureka College (IL), 316
Evangel University (MO), 506
Everest College
    Salt Lake City (UT), 834
    Springfield (MO), 506
Everett Community College (WA), 866
Everglades University (FL), 261
Evergreen State College (WA), 866
Excelsior College (NY), 580
Fairfield University (CT), 244
Fairleigh Dickinson University
    College at Florham (NJ), 546
    Metropolitan Campus (NJ), 547
Faith Baptist Bible College and Theological Seminary (IA), 363
Fashion Institute of Technology (NY), 580
Faulkner University (AL), 149
Fayetteville State University (NC), 624
Fayetteville Technical Community College (NC), 624
Feather River College (CA), 197
Felician College (NJ), 547
Ferris State University (MI), 461
Ferrum College (VA), 846
Finger Lakes Community College (NY), 580
Finlandia University (MI), 461
Fisher College (MA), 437
Fisk University (TN), 784
Fitchburg State College (MA), 438
Five Towns College (NY), 580
Flagler College (FL), 262
Flathead Valley Community College (MT), 521
Florence-Darlington Technical College (SC), 767
Florida Agricultural and Mechanical University (FL), 262
Florida Atlantic University (FL), 262
Florida Christian College (FL), 262
Florida College (FL), 263

Florida College of Natural Health (FL), 263
Florida College of Natural Health
    Bradenton (FL), 263
    Maitland (FL), 263
    Miami (FL), 264
Florida Community College at Jacksonville (FL), 264
Florida Gulf Coast University (FL), 264
Florida Hospital College of Health Sciences (FL), 264
Florida Institute of Technology (FL), 264
Florida International University (FL), 265
Florida Keys Community College (FL), 265
Florida Memorial University (FL), 265
Florida Metropolitan University
    Brandon Campus (FL), 266
    Melbourne Campus (FL), 266
    Orlando College North (FL), 266
    Pinellas (FL), 266
    Pompano Beach (FL), 266
    Tampa College (FL), 267
    Tampa College Lakeland (FL), 267
Florida National College (FL), 267
Florida Southern College (FL), 267
Florida State University (FL), 267
Florida Technical College
    Deland (FL), 268
Fond du Lac Tribal and Community College (MN), 481
Fontbonne University (MO), 506
Foothill College (CA), 197
Fordham University (NY), 581
Forrest Junior College (SC), 767
Forsyth Technical Community College (NC), 625
Fort Hays State University (KS), 379
Fort Lewis College (CO), 235
Fort Peck Community College (MT), 521
Fort Valley State University (GA), 289
Framingham State College (MA), 438
Francis Marion University (SC), 768
Franciscan University of Steubenville (OH), 659
Frank Phillips College (TX), 804
Franklin & Marshall College (PA), 717
Franklin College (IN), 343
Franklin Pierce College (NH), 537
Franklin University (OH), 660
Franklin W. Olin College of Engineering (MA), 438
Frederick Community College (MD), 419
Free Will Baptist Bible College (TN), 785
Freed-Hardeman University (TN), 785
Fresno City College (CA), 197
Fresno Pacific University (CA), 198
Friends University (KS), 379
Front Range Community College (CO), 235
Frostburg State University (MD), 420
Full Sail Real World Education (FL), 268
Fulton-Montgomery Community College (NY), 581
Furman University (SC), 768
Gadsden State Community College (AL), 149
Gainesville State College (GA), 290
Gallaudet University (DC), 254
Gallipolis Career College (OH), 660
Galveston College (TX), 804
Gannon University (PA), 718
Garden City Community College (KS), 379
Gardner-Webb University (NC), 625
Garrett College (MD), 420
Gaston College (NC), 625
Gateway Community College (AZ), 164
Gateway Community College (CT), 244
Gateway Technical College (WI), 887
Genesee Community College (NY), 581
Geneva College (PA), 718
George Fox University (OR), 696
George Mason University (VA), 847
George Washington University (DC), 255
Georgetown College (KY), 391
Georgetown University (DC), 255
Georgia College and State University (GA), 290
Georgia Highlands College (GA), 290
Georgia Institute of Technology (GA), 290
Georgia Military College (GA), 291
Georgia Perimeter College (GA), 291
Georgia Southern University (GA), 291
Georgia Southwestern State University (GA), 292

Georgia State University (GA), 292
Georgian Court University (NJ), 547
Germanna Community College (VA), 847
Gettysburg College (PA), 718
Gibbs College (MA), 438
Glen Oaks Community College (MI), 461
Glendale Community College (AZ), 164
Glendale Community College (CA), 198
Glenville State College (WV), 879
Globe College (MN), 481
Globe Institute of Technology (NY), 581
Gloucester County College (NJ), 548
Goddard College (VT), 838
God's Bible School and College (OH), 660
Gogebic Community College (MI), 461
Goldey-Beacom College (DE), 252
Gonzaga University (WA), 867
Gordon College (GA), 292
Gordon College (MA), 439
Goshen College (IN), 343
Goucher College (MD), 420
Governors State University (IL), 317
Grace Bible College (MI), 462
Grace College (IN), 343
Grace University (NE), 527
Graceland University (IA), 364
Grambling State University (LA), 403
Grand Canyon University (AZ), 164
Grand Rapids Community College (MI), 462
Grand Valley State University (MI), 462
Grand View College (IA), 364
Granite State College (NH), 538
Grays Harbor College (WA), 867
Grayson County College (TX), 804
Great Basin College (NV), 534
Great Lakes Christian College (MI), 462
Green Mountain College (VT), 839
Green River Community College (WA), 867
Greenfield Community College (MA), 439
Greensboro College (NC), 626
Greenville College (IL), 317
Greenville Technical College (SC), 768
Grinnell College (IA), 364
Grossmont Community College (CA), 198
Grove City College (PA), 719
Guilford College (NC), 626
Guilford Technical Community College (NC), 626
Gulf Coast Community College (FL), 268
Gupton Jones College of Funeral Service (GA), 292
Gustavus Adolphus College (MN), 481
Gwinnett College (GA), 293
Gwinnett Technical College (GA), 293
Gwynedd-Mercy College (PA), 719
Hagerstown Business College (MD), 421
Hagerstown Community College (MD), 421
Halifax Community College (NC), 626
Hallmark Institute of Aeronautics (TX), 805
Hallmark Institute of Technology (TX), 805
Hamilton College (IA), 364
Hamilton College (NY), 582
Hamilton College
    Cedar Falls (IA), 365
    Cedar Rapids (IA), 365
    Lincoln (NE), 528
Hamline University (MN), 482
Hampden-Sydney College (VA), 847
Hampshire College (MA), 439
Hampton University (VA), 848
Hannibal-LaGrange College (MO), 506
Hanover College (IN), 344
Harcum College (PA), 719
Harding University (AR), 172
Hardin-Simmons University (TX), 805
Harrington College of Design (IL), 317
Harrisburg Area Community College (PA), 720
Harris-Stowe State University (MO), 506
Hartwick College (NY), 582
Harvard College (MA), 439
Harvey Mudd College (CA), 198
Haskell Indian Nations University (KS), 379
Hastings College (NE), 528
Haverford College (PA), 720

Hawaii Business College (HI), 302
Hawaii Pacific University (HI), 302
Hawkeye Community College (IA), 365
Haywood Community College (NC), 626
Hazard Community College (KY), 392
Heald College
    Concord (CA), 199
    Hayward (CA), 199
    Honolulu (HI), 303
    Rancho Cordova (CA), 199
    Roseville (CA), 199
    Salinas (CA), 199
    San Francisco (CA), 200
    San Jose (CA), 200
    Stockton (CA), 200
Heartland Community College (IL), 317
Hebrew College (MA), 440
Heidelberg College (OH), 660
Helena College of Technology of the University of Montana (MT), 522
Helene Fuld College of Nursing (NY), 582
Hellenic College/Holy Cross (MA), 440
Henderson State University (AR), 172
Hendrix College (AR), 172
Henry Cogswell College (WA), 867
Henry Ford Community College (MI), 463
Heritage Christian University (AL), 150
Heritage College (CO), 235
Heritage College (NV), 534
Heritage University (WA), 868
Herkimer County Community College (NY), 582
Herzing College (AL), 150
Herzing College (WI), 887
Hesston College (KS), 380
Hickey College (MO), 507
High Point University (NC), 627
Highland Community College (IL), 318
Highland Community College (KS), 380
Highline Community College (WA), 868
High-Tech Institute (AZ), 165
Hilbert College (NY), 583
Hill College (TX), 805
Hillsborough Community College (FL), 268
Hillsdale College (MI), 463
Hinds Community College (MS), 496
Hiram College (OH), 661
Hiwassee College (TN), 785
Hobart and William Smith Colleges (NY), 583
Hobe Sound Bible College (FL), 269
Hocking College (OH), 661
Hofstra University (NY), 583
Hollins University (VA), 848
Holy Apostles College and Seminary (CT), 245
Holy Cross College (IN), 344
Holy Family University (PA), 720
Holy Names University (CA), 200
Holyoke Community College (MA), 440
Hood College (MD), 421
Hope College (MI), 463
Hope International University (CA), 201
Hopkinsville Community College (KY), 392
Horry-Georgetown Technical College (SC), 768
Houghton College (NY), 584
Housatonic Community College (CT), 245
Houston Baptist University (TX), 805
Houston Community College System (TX), 806
Howard College (TX), 806
Howard Community College (MD), 421
Howard Payne University (TX), 806
Howard University (DC), 255
Hudson County Community College (NJ), 548
Hudson Valley Community College (NY), 584
Humacao Community College (PR), 754
Humboldt State University (CA), 201
Humphreys College (CA), 201
Huntingdon College (AL), 150
Huntington University (IN), 344
Hussian School of Art (PA), 720
Husson College (ME), 411
Huston-Tillotson College (TX), 806
Hutchinson Community College (KS), 380
ICM School of Business & Medical Careers (PA), 721

Idaho State University (ID), 307
Illinois College (IL), 318
Illinois Eastern Community Colleges
    Frontier Community College (IL), 318
    Lincoln Trail College (IL), 319
    Olney Central College (IL), 319
    Wabash Valley College (IL), 319
Illinois Institute of Art-Schaumburg (IL), 319
Illinois Institute of Technology (IL), 320
Illinois State University (IL), 320
Illinois Wesleyan University (IL), 320
Immaculata University (PA), 721
Indian Hills Community College (IA), 365
Indian River Community College (FL), 269
Indiana Business College (IN), 344
Indiana Business College
    Anderson (IN), 345
    Columbus (IN), 345
    Evansville (IN), 345
    Fort Wayne (IN), 345
    Lafayette (IN), 345
    Marion (IN), 345
    Medical (IN), 346
    Muncie (IN), 346
    Terre Haute (IN), 346
Indiana Institute of Technology (IN), 346
Indiana State University (IN), 346
Indiana University Bloomington (IN), 347
Indiana University East (IN), 347
Indiana University Kokomo (IN), 347
Indiana University Northwest (IN), 348
Indiana University of Pennsylvania (PA), 721
Indiana University South Bend (IN), 348
Indiana University Southeast (IN), 348
Indiana University-Purdue University Fort Wayne (IN), 348
Indiana University-Purdue University Indianapolis (IN), 349
Indiana Wesleyan University (IN), 349
Institute of American Indian Arts (NM), 559
IntelliTec College
    Grand Junction (CO), 235
Inter American University of Puerto Rico
    Aguadilla Campus (PR), 754
    Barranquitas Campus (PR), 754
    Bayamon Campus (PR), 754
    Fajardo Campus (PR), 755
    Guayama Campus (PR), 755
    Ponce Campus (PR), 755
    San German Campus (PR), 755
International Academy of Design and Technology
    Chicago (IL), 321
    Orlando (FL), 269
    Tampa (FL), 269
International College (FL), 270
International College of Broadcasting (OH), 661
International College of Hospitality Management (CT), 245
International Institute of the Americas
    Phoenix (AZ), 165
    Tucson (AZ), 165
Inver Hills Community College (MN), 482
Iona College (NY), 584
Iowa Central Community College (IA), 365
Iowa Lakes Community College (IA), 366
Iowa State University (IA), 366
Iowa Wesleyan College (IA), 366
Iowa Western Community College (IA), 367
Irvine Valley College (CA), 201
Island Drafting and Technical Institute (NY), 584
Isothermal Community College (NC), 627
Itasca Community College (MN), 482
Itawamba Community College (MS), 496
Ithaca College (NY), 585
ITI Technical College (LA), 403
Ivy Tech Community College
    Bloomington (IN), 349
    Central Indiana (IN), 350
    Columbus (IN), 350
    East Central (IN), 350
    Kokomo (IN), 350
    Lafayette (IN), 350
    North Central (IN), 351
    Northeast (IN), 351
    Northwest (IN), 351

South Central (IN), 351
Southeast (IN), 351
Southwest (IN), 352
Wabash Valley (IN), 352
Whitewater (IN), 352
J. F. Drake State Technical College (AL), 150
J. Sargeant Reynolds Community College (VA), 848
Jackson Community College (MI), 464
Jackson State Community College (TN), 785
Jackson State University (MS), 496
Jacksonville College (TX), 807
Jacksonville State University (AL), 151
Jacksonville University (FL), 270
James A. Rhodes State College (OH), 661
James Madison University (VA), 848
James Sprunt Community College (NC), 627
Jamestown Business College (NY), 585
Jamestown College (ND), 646
Jamestown Community College (NY), 585
Jarvis Christian College (TX), 807
Jefferson College (MO), 507
Jefferson College of Health Sciences (VA), 849
Jefferson Community College (KY), 392
Jefferson Community College (NY), 586
Jefferson Community College (OH), 662
Jefferson State Community College (AL), 151
JNA Institute of Culinary Arts (PA), 721
John A. Gupton College (TN), 786
John A. Logan College (IL), 321
John Brown University (AR), 173
John Carroll University (OH), 662
John F. Kennedy University (CA), 202
John Tyler Community College (VA), 849
John Wesley College (NC), 628
John Wood Community College (IL), 321
Johns Hopkins University (MD), 422
Johns Hopkins University
    Peabody Conservatory of Music (MD), 422
Johnson & Wales University (CO), 235
Johnson & Wales University (FL), 270
Johnson & Wales University (NC), 628
Johnson & Wales University (RI), 760
Johnson Bible College (TN), 786
Johnson C. Smith University (NC), 628
Johnson College (PA), 721
Johnson County Community College (KS), 381
Johnson State College (VT), 839
Johnston Community College (NC), 628
Joliet Junior College (IL), 321
Jones College (FL), 270
Jones County Junior College (MS), 497
Judson College (AL), 151
Judson College (IL), 321
Juilliard School (NY), 586
Juniata College (PA), 722
Kalamazoo College (MI), 464
Kalamazoo Valley Community College (MI), 464
Kankakee Community College (IL), 322
Kansas City Art Institute (MO), 507
Kansas City College of Legal Studies (MO), 507
Kansas City Kansas Community College (KS), 381
Kansas State University (KS), 381
Kansas Wesleyan University (KS), 381
Kaplan University (IA), 367
Kaskaskia College (IL), 322
Katharine Gibbs School
    New York (NY), 586
Kean University (NJ), 548
Keene State College (NH), 538
Kellogg Community College (MI), 464
Kendall College (IL), 322
Kendall College of Art and Design of Ferris State University (MI), 464
Kennebec Valley Community College (ME), 411
Kennesaw State University (GA), 293
Kent State University (OH), 662
Kent State University
    Ashtabula Regional Campus (OH), 662
    East Liverpool Regional Campus (OH), 663
    Salem Regional Campus (OH), 663
    Stark Campus (OH), 663
    Trumbull Campus (OH), 663

Tuscarawas Campus (OH), 664
Kentucky Christian University (KY), 392
Kentucky Mountain Bible College (KY), 393
Kentucky State University (KY), 393
Kentucky Wesleyan College (KY), 393
Kenyon College (OH), 664
Kettering College of Medical Arts (OH), 664
Kettering University (MI), 465
Keuka College (NY), 586
Key College (FL), 271
Keystone College (PA), 722
Kilgore College (TX), 807
Kilian Community College (SD), 777
King College (TN), 786
King's College (NY), 587
King's College (NC), 629
King's College (PA), 722
King's College and Seminary (CA), 202
Kirkwood Community College (IA), 367
Kirtland Community College (MI), 465
Kishwaukee College (IL), 322
Knox College (IL), 323
Kutztown University of Pennsylvania (PA), 723
Kuyper College (MI), 465
La Roche College (PA), 723
La Salle University (PA), 723
La Sierra University (CA), 202
Labette Community College (KS), 382
Laboratory Institute of Merchandising (NY), 587
Laboure College (MA), 440
Lackawanna College (PA), 724
Lafayette College (PA), 724
LaGrange College (GA), 293
Lake Area Technical Institute (SD), 778
Lake City Community College (FL), 271
Lake Erie College (OH), 665
Lake Forest College (IL), 323
Lake Land College (IL), 323
Lake Michigan College (MI), 466
Lake Region State College (ND), 646
Lake Superior College (MN), 483
Lake Superior State University (MI), 466
Lake Washington Technical College (WA), 868
Lakeland Academy Division of Herzing College (MN), 483
Lakeland College (WI), 887
Lakeland Community College (OH), 665
Lakeshore Technical College (WI), 888
Lake-Sumter Community College (FL), 271
Lakeview College of Nursing (IL), 324
Lamar State College at Orange (TX), 808
Lamar State College at Port Arthur (TX), 808
Lamar University (TX), 808
Lambuth University (TN), 787
Lamson College (AZ), 165
Lancaster Bible College (PA), 724
Lander University (SC), 769
Landmark College (VT), 839
Lane Community College (OR), 696
Lansing Community College (MI), 466
Laramie County Community College (WY), 901
Laredo Community College (TX), 808
Las Positas College (CA), 202
Las Vegas College (NV), 535
Lasell College (MA), 441
Laura and Alvin Siegal College of Judaic Studies (OH), 665
Laurel Business Institute (PA), 725
Lawrence Technological University (MI), 466
Lawrence University (WI), 888
Lawson State Community College (AL), 151
LDS Business College (UT), 834
Le Moyne College (NY), 587
Lebanon Valley College (PA), 725
Lee College (TX), 809
Lee University (TN), 787
Leech Lake Tribal College (MN), 483
Lees-McRae College (NC), 629
Lehigh Carbon Community College (PA), 725
Lehigh University (PA), 725
Lehigh Valley College (PA), 726
LeMoyne-Owen College (TN), 787
Lenoir Community College (NC), 629
Lenoir-Rhyne College (NC), 629

Lesley University (MA), 441
LeTourneau University (TX), 809
Lewis & Clark College (OR), 696
Lewis and Clark Community College (IL), 324
Lewis University (IL), 324
Lewis-Clark State College (ID), 307
Lexington College (IL), 324
Liberty University (VA), 849
LIFE Pacific College (CA), 202
Life University (GA), 294
Limestone College (SC), 769
Lincoln Christian College and Seminary (IL), 325
Lincoln Land Community College (IL), 325
Lincoln Memorial University (TN), 787
Lincoln University (MO), 508
Lincoln University (PA), 726
Lindenwood University (MO), 508
Lindsey Wilson College (KY), 393
Linfield College (OR), 697
Linn-Benton Community College (OR), 697
Lipscomb University (TN), 788
Little Big Horn College (MT), 522
Little Priest Tribal College (NE), 528
Livingstone College (NC), 629
Lock Haven University of Pennsylvania (PA), 726
Loma Linda University (CA), 203
Lon Morris College (TX), 809
Long Beach City College (CA), 203
Long Island Business Institute (NY), 587
Long Island University
    Brooklyn Campus (NY), 588
    C. W. Post Campus (NY), 588
Longview Community College (MO), 508
Longwood University (VA), 849
Loras College (IA), 367
Lord Fairfax Community College (VA), 850
Los Angeles City College (CA), 203
Los Angeles Harbor College (CA), 203
Los Angeles Pierce College (CA), 204
Los Angeles Southwest College (CA), 204
Los Angeles Trade and Technical College (CA), 204
Los Angeles Valley College (CA), 204
Louisburg College (NC), 630
Louisiana State University and Agricultural and Mechanical College (LA), 403
Louisiana State University at Alexandria (LA), 403
Louisiana State University Health Sciences Center (LA), 404
Louisiana State University in Shreveport (LA), 404
Louisiana Tech University (LA), 404
Louisville Technical Institute (KY), 394
Lourdes College (OH), 665
Lower Columbia College (WA), 868
Loyola College in Maryland (MD), 422
Loyola Marymount University (CA), 204
Loyola University New Orleans (LA), 404
Loyola University of Chicago (IL), 325
Lubbock Christian University (TX), 809
Luther College (IA), 367
Luzerne County Community College (PA), 727
Lycoming College (PA), 727
Lyme Academy College of Fine Arts (CT), 245
Lynchburg College (VA), 850
Lyndon State College (VT), 839
Lynn University (FL), 271
Lyon College (AR), 173
Macalester College (MN), 483
MacMurray College (IL), 325
Macomb Community College (MI), 467
Macon State College (GA), 294
Madison Area Technical College (WI), 888
Madisonville Community College (KY), 394
Madonna University (MI), 467
Magdalen College (NH), 538
Magnolia Bible College (MS), 497
Maharishi University of Management (IA), 368
Maine College of Art (ME), 411
Maine Maritime Academy (ME), 411
Malone College (OH), 666
Manatee Community College (FL), 271
Manchester College (IN), 352
Manchester Community College (CT), 246
Manhattan Area Technical College (KS), 382

Manhattan Christian College (KS), 382
Manhattan College (NY), 588
Manhattan School of Music (NY), 588
Manhattanville College (NY), 589
Mannes College The New School for Music (NY), 589
Manor College (PA), 727
Mansfield University of Pennsylvania (PA), 727
Maple Woods Community College (MO), 508
Maranatha Baptist Bible College (WI), 888
Maria College (NY), 589
Marian College (IN), 353
Marian College of Fond du Lac (WI), 889
Marian Court College (MA), 441
Maric College
    Panorama City (CA), 205
Marietta College (OH), 666
Marion Military Institute (AL), 152
Marion Technical College (OH), 666
Marist College (NY), 589
Marlboro College (VT), 840
Marquette University (WI), 889
Mars Hill College (NC), 630
Marshall University (WV), 879
Marshalltown Community College (IA), 368
Martin Community College (NC), 630
Martin Luther College (MN), 484
Martin Methodist College (TN), 788
Mary Baldwin College (VA), 850
Marygrove College (MI), 467
Maryland Institute College of Art (MD), 422
Marylhurst University (OR), 697
Marymount College (CA), 205
Marymount Manhattan College (NY), 590
Marymount University (VA), 851
Maryville College (TN), 788
Maryville University of Saint Louis (MO), 509
Marywood University (PA), 728
Massachusetts Bay Community College (MA), 441
Massachusetts College of Art (MA), 442
Massachusetts College of Liberal Arts (MA), 442
Massachusetts College of Pharmacy and Health
    Sciences (MA), 442
Massachusetts Institute of Technology (MA), 442
Massachusetts Maritime Academy (MA), 443
Massasoit Community College (MA), 443
Master's College (CA), 205
Mayland Community College (NC), 630
Maysville Community College (KY), 394
Mayville State University (ND), 647
McDaniel College (MD), 423
McDowell Technical Community College (NC), 631
McHenry County College (IL), 326
McIntosh College (NH), 538
McKendree College (IL), 326
McMurry University (TX), 810
McPherson College (KS), 382
Medaille College (NY), 590
Medcenter One College of Nursing (ND), 647
MedCentral College of Nursing (OH), 666
Medical College of Georgia (GA), 294
Medical University of South Carolina (SC), 769
Memphis College of Art (TN), 788
Mendocino College (CA), 206
Menlo College (CA), 206
Mercer County Community College (NJ), 548
Mercer University (GA), 294
Mercy College (NY), 590
Mercy College of Health Sciences (IA), 368
Mercy College of Northwest Ohio (OH), 667
Mercyhurst College (PA), 728
Meredith College (NC), 631
Meridian Community College (MS), 497
Merrimack College (MA), 443
Merritt College (CA), 206
Mesa State College (CO), 236
Mesabi Range Community and Technical College (MN), 484
Mesalands Community College (NM), 559
Messiah College (PA), 728
Methodist College (NC), 631
Metro Business College
    Jefferson City (MO), 509
Metropolitan Career Center (PA), 729

Metropolitan College (OK), 684
Metropolitan College of New York (NY), 590
Metropolitan Community College (NE), 528
Metropolitan State College of Denver (CO), 236
Metropolitan State University (MN), 484
Miami Dade College (FL), 272
Miami University
    Hamilton Campus (OH), 667
    Oxford Campus (OH), 667
Michigan State University (MI), 467
Michigan Technological University (MI), 468
Mid Michigan Community College (MI), 468
Mid-America Christian University (OK), 685
MidAmerica Nazarene University (KS), 383
Mid-Continent University (KY), 394
Middle Georgia College (GA), 295
Middle Tennessee State University (TN), 789
Middlebury College (VT), 840
Middlesex Community College (CT), 246
Middlesex Community College (MA), 443
Middlesex County College (NJ), 549
Midland College (TX), 810
Midland Lutheran College (NE), 529
Midlands Technical College (SC), 769
Mid-Plains Community College Area (NE), 529
Mid-South Community College (AR), 173
Mid-State Technical College (WI), 889
Midway College (KY), 395
Midwestern State University (TX), 810
Mildred Elley (NY), 591
Miles College (AL), 152
Miles Community College (MT), 522
Miller-Motte Technical College (NC), 631
Miller-Motte Technical College (TN), 789
Miller-Motte Technical College: Lynchburg (VA), 851
Millersville University of Pennsylvania (PA), 729
Milligan College (TN), 789
Millikin University (IL), 326
Mills College (CA), 206
Millsaps College (MS), 497
Milwaukee Area Technical College (WI), 890
Milwaukee School of Engineering (WI), 890
Mineral Area College (MO), 509
Minneapolis College of Art and Design (MN), 484
Minneapolis Community and Technical College (MN), 485
Minnesota School of Business (MN), 485
Minnesota School of Business
    Brooklyn Center (MN), 485
Minnesota State College
    Southeast Technical (MN), 485
Minnesota State Community and Technical College
    Fergus Falls (MN), 486
Minnesota State University
    Mankato (MN), 486
    Moorhead (MN), 486
Minnesota West Community and Technical College
    Worthington Campus (MN), 486
Minot State University (ND), 647
Minot State University
    Bottineau Campus (ND), 647
MiraCosta College (CA), 207
Mississippi College (MS), 498
Mississippi Delta Community College (MS), 498
Mississippi Gulf Coast Community College
    Jefferson Davis Campus (MS), 498
Mississippi State University (MS), 498
Missouri Baptist University (MO), 509
Missouri College (MO), 510
Missouri Southern State University (MO), 510
Missouri State University (MO), 510
Missouri State University
    West Plains (MO), 510
Missouri Technical School (MO), 511
Missouri Valley College (MO), 511
Missouri Western State University (MO), 511
Mitchell College (CT), 246
Mitchell Community College (NC), 632
Mitchell Technical Institute (SD), 778
Moberly Area Community College (MO), 511
Modesto Junior College (CA), 207
Mohave Community College (AZ), 165
Mohawk Valley Community College (NY), 591

Molloy College (NY), 591
Monmouth College (IL), 327
Monmouth University (NJ), 549
Monroe College (NY), 592
Monroe Community College (NY), 592
Monroe County Community College (MI), 468
Montana State University
    Billings (MT), 522
    Bozeman (MT), 523
Montana State University College of Technology-Great
    Falls (MT), 522
Montana Tech of the University of Montana (MT), 523
Montcalm Community College (MI), 469
Montclair State University (NJ), 549
Monterey Peninsula College (CA), 207
Montgomery College (MD), 423
Montgomery Community College (NC), 632
Montgomery County Community College (PA), 729
Montreat College (NC), 632
Montserrat College of Art (MA), 444
Moody Bible Institute (IL), 327
Moore College of Art and Design (PA), 729
Moraine Park Technical College (WI), 890
Moraine Valley Community College (IL), 327
Moravian College (PA), 730
Morehead State University (KY), 395
Morehouse College (GA), 295
Morgan Community College (CO), 236
Morgan State University (MD), 423
Morningside College (IA), 369
Morris College (SC), 770
Morrison Institute of Technology (IL), 327
Morrison University (NV), 535
Morton College (IL), 327
Motlow State Community College (TN), 790
Mott Community College (MI), 469
Mount Aloysius College (PA), 730
Mount Carmel College of Nursing (OH), 668
Mount Holyoke College (MA), 444
Mount Ida College (MA), 444
Mount Marty College (SD), 778
Mount Mary College (WI), 890
Mount Mercy College (IA), 369
Mount Olive College (NC), 632
Mount St. Mary College (NY), 592
Mount St. Mary's College (CA), 207
Mount St. Mary's University (MD), 423
Mount San Antonio College (CA), 208
Mount San Jacinto College (CA), 208
Mount Union College (OH), 668
Mount Vernon Nazarene University (OH), 668
Mount Wachusett Community College (MA), 444
Mountain Empire Community College (VA), 851
Mountain State University (WV), 879
Mountain View College (TX), 810
MTI College (CA), 208
Muhlenberg College (PA), 730
Multnomah Bible College (OR), 698
Murray State University (KY), 395
Muskingum College (OH), 668
Naropa University (CO), 237
Nash Community College (NC), 633
Nashville State Community College (TN), 790
Nassau Community College (NY), 592
National American University
    Kansas City (MO), 512
    St. Paul (MN), 487
National College of Business & Technology
    Arecibo (PR), 756
    Bayamon (PR), 756
    Bluefield (VA), 851
    Charlottesville (VA), 852
    Danville (KY), 395
    Danville (VA), 852
    Florence (KY), 396
    Harrisonburg (VA), 852
    Lexington (KY), 396
    Louisville (KY), 396
    Lynchburg (VA), 852
    Martinsville (VA), 852
    Pikeville (KY), 396
    Richmond (KY), 397

Salem (VA), 853
Tennessee (TN), 790
National Education Center
    Spartan School of Aeronautics (OK), 685
National Park Community College (AR), 174
National University (CA), 208
Naugatuck Valley Community College (CT), 246
Navarro College (TX), 811
Nazarene Bible College (CO), 237
Nazareth College of Rochester (NY), 593
Nebraska Christian College (NE), 529
Nebraska College of Technical Agriculture (NE), 529
Nebraska Indian Community College (NE), 530
Nebraska Methodist College of Nursing and Allied Health (NE), 530
Nebraska Wesleyan University (NE), 530
Neosho County Community College (KS), 383
Neumann College (PA), 731
New Castle School of Trades (PA), 731
New College of Florida (FL), 272
New England College (NH), 539
New England Conservatory of Music (MA), 445
New England Culinary Institute (VT), 840
New England Institute of Art (MA), 445
New England Institute of Technology (FL), 272
New England Institute of Technology (RI), 760
New England School of Communications (ME), 412
New Hampshire Community Technical College
    Berlin (NH), 539
    Claremont (NH), 539
    Manchester (NH), 539
    Nashua (NH), 540
New Hampshire Technical Institute (NH), 540
New Jersey City University (NJ), 549
New Jersey Institute of Technology (NJ), 550
New Mexico Highlands University (NM), 559
New Mexico Institute of Mining and Technology (NM), 560
New Mexico Junior College (NM), 560
New Mexico Military Institute Junior College (NM), 560
New Mexico State University (NM), 560
New Mexico State University at Alamogordo (NM), 561
New Mexico State University at Carlsbad (NM), 561
New Mexico State University at Grants (NM), 561
New Orleans School of Urban Missions (LA), 405
New River Community College (VA), 853
New York Institute of Technology (NY), 593
New York School of Interior Design (NY), 593
New York University (NY), 593
Newberry College (SC), 770
Newbury College (MA), 445
Newman University (KS), 383
Newport Business Institute (PA), 731
NewSchool of Architecture & Design (CA), 208
Niagara County Community College (NY), 594
Niagara University (NY), 594
Nicholls State University (LA), 405
Nichols College (MA), 445
Nicolet Area Technical College (WI), 891
Norfolk State University (VA), 853
Normandale Community College (MN), 487
North Arkansas College (AR), 174
North Carolina Agricultural and Technical State University (NC), 633
North Carolina Central University (NC), 633
North Carolina School of the Arts (NC), 633
North Carolina State University (NC), 633
North Carolina Wesleyan College (NC), 634
North Central College (IL), 328
North Central Kansas Technical College (KS), 383
North Central Michigan College (MI), 469
North Central Missouri College (MO), 512
North Central Texas College (TX), 811
North Central University (MN), 487
North Country Community College (NY), 594
North Dakota State College of Science (ND), 648
North Dakota State University (ND), 648
North Florida Community College (FL), 272
North Georgia College & State University (GA), 295
North Greenville College (SC), 770
North Harris Montgomery Community College District (TX), 811
North Idaho College (ID), 308
North Iowa Area Community College (IA), 369
North Lake College (TX), 811
North Park University (IL), 328
North Seattle Community College (WA), 869
North Shore Community College (MA), 446
Northampton County Area Community College (PA), 731
Northcentral Technical College (WI), 891
Northcentral University (AZ), 166
Northeast Alabama Community College (AL), 152
Northeast Community College (NE), 531
Northeast Iowa Community College (IA), 369
Northeast State Technical Community College (TN), 790
Northeast Texas Community College (TX), 812
Northeast Wisconsin Technical College (WI), 891
Northeastern Illinois University (IL), 328
Northeastern Junior College (CO), 237
Northeastern Oklahoma Agricultural and Mechanical College (OK), 685
Northeastern State University (OK), 685
Northeastern Technical College (SC), 770
Northeastern University (MA), 446
Northern Arizona University (AZ), 166
Northern Essex Community College (MA), 446
Northern Kentucky University (KY), 397
Northern Maine Community College (ME), 412
Northern Michigan University (MI), 469
Northern New Mexico College (NM), 561
Northern State University (SD), 778
Northland College (WI), 891
Northland Community & Technical College (MN), 487
Northland Pioneer College (AZ), 166
Northwest Arkansas Community College (AR), 174
Northwest Christian College (OR), 698
Northwest College (WY), 901
Northwest College of Art (WA), 869
Northwest Iowa Community College (IA), 370
Northwest Missouri State University (MO), 512
Northwest Nazarene University (ID), 308
Northwest Technical College (MN), 487
Northwest Technical Institute (MN), 488
Northwest University (WA), 869
Northwest Vista College (TX), 812
Northwestern Business College (IL), 329
Northwestern College (IA), 370
Northwestern College (MN), 488
Northwestern Michigan College (MI), 470
Northwestern Oklahoma State University (OK), 686
Northwestern State University (LA), 405
Northwestern Technical College (GA), 295
Northwestern University (IL), 329
Northwest-Shoals Community College (AL), 152
Northwood University (MI), 470
Northwood University
    Florida Campus (FL), 273
    Texas Campus (TX), 812
Norwalk Community College (CT), 247
Norwich University (VT), 840
Nossi College of Art (TN), 790
Notre Dame de Namur University (CA), 209
Nova Southeastern University (FL), 273
Nunez Community College (LA), 405
Nyack College (NY), 594
Oak Hills Christian College (MN), 488
Oakbridge Academy of Arts (PA), 731
Oakland City University (IN), 353
Oakland Community College (MI), 470
Oakland University (MI), 471
Oakton Community College (IL), 329
Oakwood College (AL), 153
Oberlin College (OH), 669
Occidental College (CA), 209
Ocean County College (NJ), 550
Odessa College (TX), 812
Oglethorpe University (GA), 296
Ohio Business College
    Sandusky (OH), 669
Ohio Dominican University (OH), 669
Ohio Institute of Photography and Technology (OH), 669
Ohio Northern University (OH), 670
Ohio State University Agricultural Technical Institute (OH), 670
Ohio State University
    Columbus Campus (OH), 670
    Lima Campus (OH), 671
    Mansfield Campus (OH), 671
    Marion Campus (OH), 671
    Newark Campus (OH), 671
Ohio University (OH), 672
Ohio University
    Chillicothe Campus (OH), 672
    Eastern Campus (OH), 672
    Lancaster Campus (OH), 672
    Southern Campus at Ironton (OH), 672
Ohio Valley College of Technology (OH), 673
Ohio Valley University (WV), 880
Ohio Wesleyan University (OH), 673
Ohlone College (CA), 209
Okaloosa-Walton College (FL), 273
Oklahoma Baptist University (OK), 686
Oklahoma Christian University (OK), 686
Oklahoma City Community College (OK), 687
Oklahoma City University (OK), 687
Oklahoma Panhandle State University (OK), 687
Oklahoma State University (OK), 687
Oklahoma State University
    Oklahoma City (OK), 688
    Okmulgee (OK), 688
Oklahoma Wesleyan University (OK), 688
Old Dominion University (VA), 853
Olivet College (MI), 471
Olivet Nazarene University (IL), 329
Olympic College (WA), 869
O'More College of Design (TN), 791
Onondaga Community College (NY), 595
Oral Roberts University (OK), 688
Orange Coast College (CA), 209
Orange County Community College (NY), 595
Orangeburg-Calhoun Technical College (SC), 771
Oregon Health & Science University (OR), 698
Oregon Institute of Technology (OR), 698
Oregon State University (OR), 699
Orleans Technical Institute
    Center City Campus (PA), 732
Otero Junior College (CO), 237
Otis College of Art and Design (CA), 210
Ottawa University (KS), 384
Otterbein College (OH), 673
Ouachita Baptist University (AR), 174
Ouachita Technical College (AR), 175
Our Lady of Holy Cross College (LA), 406
Our Lady of the Lake College (LA), 406
Our Lady of the Lake University of San Antonio (TX), 813
Owens Community College
    Toledo (OH), 673
Owensboro Community College (KY), 397
Oxford College of Emory University (GA), 296
Ozark Christian College (MO), 512
Ozarka College (AR), 175
Ozarks Technical Community College (MO), 513
Pace University (NY), 595
Pacific Lutheran University (WA), 870
Pacific Northwest College of Art (OR), 699
Pacific Oaks College (CA), 210
Pacific States University (CA), 210
Pacific Union College (CA), 210
Pacific University (OR), 699
Paducah Technical College (KY), 397
Paier College of Art (CT), 247
Paine College (GA), 296
Palm Beach Atlantic University (FL), 273
Palm Beach Community College (FL), 274
Palo Alto College (TX), 813
Palo Verde College (CA), 211
Palomar College (CA), 211
Pamlico Community College (NC), 634
Panola College (TX), 813
Paradise Valley Community College (AZ), 166
Paris Junior College (TX), 813
Park University (MO), 513
Parkland College (IL), 330
Parks College (CO), 238
Parks College
    Aurora (CO), 238
Parsons The New School for Design (NY), 595
Pasco-Hernando Community College (FL), 274
Passaic County Community College (NJ), 550

Patricia Stevens College (MO), 513
Patrick Henry Community College (VA), 854
Patten University (CA), 211
Paul D. Camp Community College (VA), 854
Paul Smith's College (NY), 596
Peace College (NC), 634
Pearl River Community College (MS), 499
Peirce College (PA), 732
Pellissippi State Technical Community College (TN), 791
Peninsula College (WA), 870
Penn State Abington (PA), 732
Penn State Altoona (PA), 732
Penn State Beaver (PA), 733
Penn State Berks (PA), 733
Penn State Delaware County (PA), 733
Penn State Dubois (PA), 734
Penn State Erie, The Behrend College (PA), 734
Penn State Fayette (PA), 734
Penn State Harrisburg (PA), 734
Penn State Hazleton (PA), 735
Penn State Lehigh Valley (PA), 735
Penn State McKeesport (PA), 735
Penn State Mont Alto (PA), 736
Penn State New Kensington (PA), 736
Penn State Schuylkill
    Capital College (PA), 736
Penn State Shenango (PA), 736
Penn State University Park (PA), 737
Penn State Wilkes-Barre (PA), 737
Penn State Worthington Scranton (PA), 737
Penn State York (PA), 738
Penn Valley Community College (MO), 513
Pennsylvania College of Technology (PA), 738
Pennsylvania Highlands Community College (PA), 738
Pennsylvania Institute of Technology (PA), 738
Pennsylvania School of Business (PA), 739
Pepperdine University (CA), 211
Peru State College (NE), 531
Pfeiffer University (NC), 635
Philadelphia Biblical University (PA), 739
Philadelphia University (PA), 739
Philander Smith College (AR), 175
Phillips Beth Israel School of Nursing (NY), 596
Phillips Community College of the University of Arkansas (AR), 175
Phoenix College (AZ), 167
Piedmont Baptist College (NC), 635
Piedmont College (GA), 296
Piedmont Technical College (SC), 771
Piedmont Virginia Community College (VA), 854
Pierce College (WA), 870
Pikes Peak Community College (CO), 238
Pikeville College (KY), 397
Pima Community College (AZ), 167
Pine Manor College (MA), 446
Pine Technical College (MN), 488
Pioneer Pacific College (OR), 699
Pitt Community College (NC), 635
Pittsburg State University (KS), 384
Pittsburgh Institute of Aeronautics (PA), 739
Pittsburgh Institute of Mortuary Science (PA), 740
Pittsburgh Technical Institute (PA), 740
Pitzer College (CA), 212
PJA School (PA), 740
Platt College
    Cerritos (CA), 212
    Los Angeles (CA), 212
    Newport Beach (CA), 212
    Ontario (CA), 212
    San Diego (CA), 213
    Tulsa (OK), 689
Plymouth State University (NH), 540
Point Loma Nazarene University (CA), 213
Point Park University (PA), 740
Polk Community College (FL), 274
Polytechnic University (NY), 596
Pomona College (CA), 213
Pontifical Catholic University of Puerto Rico (PR), 756
Pontifical College Josephinum (OH), 674
Portland Community College (OR), 700
Portland State University (OR), 700
Post University (CT), 247

Potomac College (DC), 255
Potomac State College of West Virginia University (WV), 880
Prairie State College (IL), 330
Prairie View A&M University (TX), 814
Pratt Community College (KS), 384
Pratt Institute (NY), 597
Presbyterian College (SC), 771
Prescott College (AZ), 167
Presentation College (SD), 779
Prince George's Community College (MD), 424
Prince Institute of Professional Studies (AL), 153
Prince William Sound Community College (AK), 160
Princeton University (NJ), 550
Principia College (IL), 330
Professional Careers Institute (IN), 353
Providence College (RI), 761
Pueblo Community College (CO), 238
Puget Sound Christian College (WA), 870
Pulaski Technical College (AR), 176
Purdue University (IN), 353
Purdue University
    Calumet (IN), 354
    North Central Campus (IN), 354
Queens University of Charlotte (NC), 635
Quincy University (IL), 330
Quinebaug Valley Community College (CT), 247
Quinnipiac University (CT), 248
Quinsigamond Community College (MA), 447
Radford University (VA), 854
Rainy River Community College (MN), 489
Ramapo College of New Jersey (NJ), 551
Randolph Community College (NC), 636
Randolph-Macon College (VA), 855
Randolph-Macon Woman's College (VA), 855
Ranken Technical College (MO), 514
Rappahannock Community College (VA), 855
Raritan Valley Community College (NJ), 551
Rasmussen College-Eagan (MN), 489
Rasmussen College-Minnetonka (MN), 489
Rasmussen College-St. Cloud (MN), 489
Red Rocks Community College (CO), 238
Redlands Community College (OK), 689
Reed College (OR), 700
Reedley College (CA), 213
Regis College (MA), 447
Regis University (CO), 239
Reinhardt College (GA), 297
Remington College
    Cleveland (OH), 674
    Colorado Springs (CO), 239
    Honolulu (HI), 303
    Houston (TX), 814
    Jacksonville (FL), 274
    Lafayette (LA), 406
    Mobile (AL), 153
    Tampa (FL), 275
Rend Lake College (IL), 331
Rensselaer Polytechnic Institute (NY), 597
Renton Technical College (WA), 871
Research College of Nursing (MO), 514
Rhode Island College (RI), 761
Rhode Island School of Design (RI), 761
Rhodes College (TN), 791
Rice University (TX), 814
Rich Mountain Community College (AR), 176
Richard Bland College (VA), 855
Richard Stockton College of New Jersey (NJ), 551
Richland College (TX), 814
Richland Community College (IL), 331
Richmond Community College (NC), 636
Rider University (NJ), 552
Ridgewater College (MN), 490
Ringling School of Art and Design (FL), 275
Rio Salado College (AZ), 167
Ripon College (WI), 892
Riverland Community College (MN), 490
Riverside Community College (CA), 214
Rivier College (NH), 540
Roane State Community College (TN), 791
Roanoke Bible College (NC), 636
Roanoke College (VA), 856
Roanoke-Chowan Community College (NC), 636

Robert Morris College
    Chicago (IL), 331
Robert Morris University (PA), 740
Roberts Wesleyan College (NY), 597
Robeson Community College (NC), 636
Rochester Business Institute (NY), 597
Rochester College (MI), 471
Rochester Institute of Technology (NY), 598
Rock Valley College (IL), 331
Rockford Business College (IL), 332
Rockford College (IL), 332
Rockhurst University (MO), 514
Rockingham Community College (NC), 637
Rockland Community College (NY), 598
Rocky Mountain College (MT), 523
Rocky Mountain College of Art & Design (CO), 239
Roger Williams University (RI), 761
Rogers State University (OK), 689
Rogue Community College (OR), 701
Rollins College (FL), 275
Roosevelt University (IL), 332
Rosalind Franklin University of Medicine and Science (IL), 332
Rose State College (OK), 689
Rosedale Technical Institute (PA), 741
Rose-Hulman Institute of Technology (IN), 354
Rosemont College (PA), 741
Rowan University (NJ), 552
Rowan-Cabarrus Community College (NC), 637
Roxbury Community College (MA), 447
Rush University (IL), 333
Russell Sage College (NY), 598
Rust College (MS), 499
Rutgers, The State University of New Jersey
    Camden Regional Campus (NJ), 552
    New Brunswick/Piscataway Campus (NJ), 553
    Newark Regional Campus (NJ), 553
Sacramento City College (CA), 214
Sacred Heart University (CT), 248
Saddleback College (CA), 214
Sage College of Albany (NY), 599
Saginaw Valley State University (MI), 471
St. Ambrose University (IA), 370
St. Andrews Presbyterian College (NC), 637
St. Anselm College (NH), 541
Saint Anthony College of Nursing (IL), 333
St. Augustine's College (NC), 637
St. Bonaventure University (NY), 599
St. Catharine College (KY), 398
St. Charles Community College (MO), 514
St. Cloud State University (MN), 490
St. Cloud Technical College (MN), 490
St. Edward's University (TX), 815
St. Elizabeth College of Nursing (NY), 599
St. Francis College (NY), 599
St. Francis Medical Center College of Nursing (IL), 333
St. Francis University (PA), 741
St. Gregory's University (OK), 689
St. John Fisher College (NY), 600
St. John's College (MD), 424
St. John's College (NM), 561
St. Johns River Community College (FL), 275
St. John's Seminary College (MA), 447
St. John's University (MN), 491
St. John's University (NY), 600
St. Joseph College (CT), 248
St. Joseph Seminary College (LA), 406
St. Joseph's College (IN), 354
St. Joseph's College (ME), 412
St. Joseph's College (NY), 600
St. Joseph's College of Nursing (NY), 601
St. Joseph's College
    Suffolk Campus (NY), 601
St. Joseph's University (PA), 741
St. Lawrence University (NY), 601
St. Leo University (FL), 276
St. Louis Christian College (MO), 515
St. Louis Community College at Meramec (MO), 515
St. Louis University (MO), 515
St. Luke's College (IA), 370
St. Luke's College (MO), 515
Saint Martin's University (WA), 871
St. Mary-of-the-Woods College (IN), 355

Saint Mary's College (IN), 355
St. Mary's College of California (CA), 214
St. Mary's College of Maryland (MD), 424
St. Mary's University (TX), 815
St. Mary's University of Minnesota (MN), 491
St. Michael's College (VT), 841
St. Norbert College (WI), 892
St. Olaf College (MN), 491
St. Paul College (MN), 492
St. Paul's College (VA), 856
St. Peter's College (NJ), 553
St. Petersburg College (FL), 276
St. Philip's College (TX), 815
St. Thomas Aquinas College (NY), 601
St. Thomas University (FL), 276
St. Vincent College (PA), 742
St. Xavier University (IL), 333
Salem College (NC), 638
Salem Community College (NJ), 554
Salem International University (WV), 880
Salem State College (MA), 448
Salisbury University (MD), 425
Salish Kootenai College (MT), 524
Salt Lake Community College (UT), 835
Salve Regina University (RI), 762
Sam Houston State University (TX), 815
Samford University (AL), 153
Sampson Community College (NC), 638
Samuel Merritt College (CA), 215
San Antonio College (TX), 816
San Diego Christian College (CA), 215
San Diego City College (CA), 215
San Diego Miramar College (CA), 215
San Diego State University (CA), 216
San Francisco Art Institute (CA), 216
San Francisco Conservatory of Music (CA), 216
San Francisco State University (CA), 216
San Jacinto College
   North (TX), 816
San Joaquin Delta College (CA), 217
San Joaquin Valley College Inc. (CA), 217
San Jose State University (CA), 217
San Juan College (NM), 562
Sandhills Community College (NC), 638
Santa Barbara City College (CA), 217
Santa Clara University (CA), 218
Santa Fe Community College (FL), 276
Santa Fe Community College (NM), 562
Santa Monica College (CA), 218
Santa Rosa Junior College (CA), 218
Santiago Canyon College (CA), 219
Sarah Lawrence College (NY), 602
Sauk Valley Community College (IL), 334
Savannah College of Art and Design (GA), 297
Savannah Technical College (GA), 297
Sawyer College
   Merrillville (IN), 355
Schenectady County Community College (NY), 602
Schiller International University (FL), 277
School of the Art Institute of Chicago (IL), 334
School of the Museum of Fine Arts (MA), 448
School of Visual Arts (NY), 602
Schoolcraft College (MI), 472
Schreiner University (TX), 816
Schuylkill Institute of Business & Technology (PA), 742
Scottsdale Community College (AZ), 167
Scripps College (CA), 219
Seattle Central Community College (WA), 871
Seattle Pacific University (WA), 871
Seattle University (WA), 872
Seminole Community College (FL), 277
Seminole State College (OK), 690
Seton Hall University (NJ), 554
Seton Hill University (PA), 742
Seward County Community College (KS), 384
Shasta College (CA), 219
Shaw University (NC), 638
Shawnee State University (OH), 674
Sheldon Jackson College (AK), 160
Shelton State Community College (AL), 153
Shenandoah University (VA), 856
Shepherd University (WV), 880

Sheridan College (WY), 901
Shimer College (IL), 334
Shippensburg University of Pennsylvania (PA), 743
Shoreline Community College (WA), 872
Shorter College (GA), 297
Siena College (NY), 602
Sierra College (CA), 219
Sierra Nevada College (NV), 535
Silver Lake College (WI), 892
Simmons College (MA), 448
Simon's Rock College of Bard (MA), 448
Simpson College (IA), 371
Simpson University (CA), 220
Sinclair Community College (OH), 674
Sitting Bull College (ND), 648
Skagit Valley College (WA), 872
Skidmore College (NY), 603
Skyline College (CA), 220
Slippery Rock University of Pennsylvania (PA), 743
Smith College (MA), 449
Snead State Community College (AL), 154
Snow College (UT), 835
Sojourner-Douglass College (MD), 425
Somerset Christian College (NJ), 554
Somerset Community College (KY), 398
Sonoma State University (CA), 220
South Arkansas Community College (AR), 176
South Carolina State University (SC), 771
South Central College (MN), 492
South College (NC), 639
South College (TN), 792
South Dakota School of Mines and Technology (SD), 779
South Dakota State University (SD), 779
South Florida Community College (FL), 277
South Georgia College (GA), 298
South Hills School of Business & Technology (PA), 743
South Mountain Community College (AZ), 168
South Piedmont Community College (NC), 639
South Plains College (TX), 816
South Puget Sound Community College (WA), 872
South Seattle Community College (WA), 873
South Suburban College of Cook County (IL), 335
South Texas College (TX), 817
South University (AL), 154
South University (SC), 772
South University
   West Palm Beach Campus (FL), 277
Southeast Arkansas College (AR), 176
Southeast Community College
   Lincoln Campus (NE), 531
Southeast Kentucky Community and Technical College (KY), 398
Southeast Missouri State University (MO), 516
Southeast Technical Institute (SD), 780
Southeastern Bible College (AL), 154
Southeastern Business College (OH), 675
Southeastern Business College
   Jackson (OH), 675
   Lancaster (OH), 675
   New Boston (OH), 675
Southeastern College of the Assemblies of God (FL), 278
Southeastern Community College (NC), 639
Southeastern Community College
   North Campus (IA), 371
Southeastern Illinois College (IL), 335
Southeastern Louisiana University (LA), 406
Southeastern Oklahoma State University (OK), 690
Southeastern University (DC), 256
Southern Adventist University (TN), 792
Southern Arkansas University (AR), 176
Southern Arkansas University Tech (AR), 177
Southern Christian University (AL), 154
Southern Connecticut State University (CT), 248
Southern Illinois University Carbondale (IL), 335
Southern Illinois University Edwardsville (IL), 335
Southern Maine Community College (ME), 412
Southern Methodist University (TX), 817
Southern New Hampshire University (NH), 541
Southern Oregon University (OR), 701
Southern Polytechnic State University (GA), 298
Southern State Community College (OH), 676
Southern Union State Community College (AL), 155
Southern University and Agricultural and Mechanical

College (LA), 407
Southern University at New Orleans (LA), 407
Southern Utah University (UT), 835
Southern Vermont College (VT), 841
Southern Wesleyan University (SC), 772
Southern West Virginia Community and Technical
   College (WV), 881
Southside Virginia Community College (VA), 857
Southwest Baptist University (MO), 516
Southwest Florida College (FL), 278
Southwest Georgia Technical College (GA), 298
Southwest Minnesota State University (MN), 492
Southwest Mississippi Community College (MS), 499
Southwest Tennessee Community College (TN), 792
Southwest Texas Junior College (TX), 817
Southwest Wisconsin Technical College (WI), 893
Southwestern Adventist University (TX), 817
Southwestern Assemblies of God University (TX), 818
Southwestern Christian University (OK), 690
Southwestern College (AZ), 168
Southwestern College (CA), 220
Southwestern College (KS), 385
Southwestern College
   Tri-County (OH), 676
Southwestern Community College (IA), 371
Southwestern Community College (NC), 639
Southwestern Illinois College (IL), 336
Southwestern Indian Polytechnic Institute (NM), 562
Southwestern Michigan College (MI), 472
Southwestern Oklahoma State University (OK), 691
Southwestern Oregon Community College (OR), 701
Southwestern University (TX), 818
Spalding University (KY), 398
Spartanburg Methodist College (SC), 772
Spartanburg Technical College (SC), 773
Spelman College (GA), 298
Spencerian College
   Lexington (KY), 399
Spokane Community College (WA), 873
Spokane Falls Community College (WA), 873
Spring Arbor University (MI), 472
Spring Hill College (AL), 155
Springfield College (MA), 449
Springfield College in Illinois (IL), 336
Springfield Technical Community College (MA), 449
Stanford University (CA), 221
Stanly Community College (NC), 639
Stark State College of Technology (OH), 676
State Fair Community College (MO), 516
State University of New York at Albany (NY), 603
State University of New York at Binghamton (NY), 603
State University of New York at Buffalo (NY), 604
State University of New York at Farmingdale (NY), 604
State University of New York at New Paltz (NY), 604
State University of New York at Oswego (NY), 604
State University of New York at Purchase (NY), 605
State University of New York at Stony Brook (NY), 605
State University of New York College at Brockport (NY), 605
State University of New York College at Buffalo (NY), 606
State University of New York College at Cortland (NY), 606
State University of New York College at Fredonia (NY), 606
State University of New York College at Geneseo (NY), 607
State University of New York College at Old Westbury (NY), 607
State University of New York College at Oneonta (NY), 607
State University of New York College at Plattsburgh (NY), 608
State University of New York College at Potsdam (NY), 608
State University of New York College of Agriculture and
   Technology at Cobleskill , 608 (NY), 608
State University of New York College of Agriculture and
   Technology at Morrisville , 609 (NY), 609
State University of New York College of Environmental Science
   and Forestry (NY), 609
State University of New York College of Technology at
   Alfred (NY), 609
State University of New York College of Technology at
   Canton (NY), 609
State University of New York College of Technology at
   Delhi (NY), 610
State University of New York Downstate Medical
   Center (NY), 610
State University of New York Empire State College (NY), 610
State University of New York Institute of Technology at

Utica/Rome (NY), 610
State University of New York Maritime College (NY), 610
State University of New York Upstate Medical University (NY), 611
Stautzenberger College (OH), 676
Stephen F. Austin State University (TX), 818
Stephens College (MO), 516
Sterling College (KS), 385
Sterling College (VT), 841
Stetson University (FL), 278
Stevens Institute of Technology (NJ), 555
Stevens-Henager College: Murray (UT), 835
Stillman College (AL), 155
Stone Child College (MT), 524
Stonehill College (MA), 449
Suffolk County Community College (NY), 611
Suffolk University (MA), 450
Sul Ross State University (TX), 819
Sullivan County Community College (NY), 611
Sullivan University (KY), 399
Surry Community College (NC), 640
Susquehanna University (PA), 744
Sussex County Community College (NJ), 555
Swarthmore College (PA), 744
Swedish Institute (NY), 611
Sweet Briar College (VA), 857
Syracuse University (NY), 612
Tabor College (KS), 385
Tacoma Community College (WA), 873
Taft College (CA), 221
Talladega College (AL), 155
Tallahassee Community College (FL), 278
Tarleton State University (TX), 819
Tarrant County College (TX), 819
Taylor Business Institute (IL), 336
Taylor University (IN), 355
Taylor University
    Fort Wayne (IN), 356
Technical College of the Lowcountry (SC), 773
Technology Education College (OH), 676
Teikyo Loretto Heights University (CO), 239
Temple College (TX), 819
Temple University (PA), 744
Tennessee State University (TN), 792
Tennessee Technological University (TN), 792
Tennessee Temple University (TN), 793
Tennessee Wesleyan College (TN), 793
Texarkana College (TX), 820
Texas A&M University (TX), 820
Texas A&M University-Baylor College of Dentistry (TX), 820
Texas A&M University-Commerce (TX), 820
Texas A&M University-Galveston (TX), 821
Texas A&M University-Kingsville (TX), 821
Texas A&M University-Texarkana (TX), 821
Texas Christian University (TX), 821
Texas College (TX), 822
Texas Lutheran University (TX), 822
Texas Southern University (TX), 822
Texas State Technical College
    Harlingen (TX), 822
    Waco (TX), 823
    West Texas (TX), 823
Texas State University
    San Marcos (TX), 823
Texas Tech University (TX), 823
Texas Wesleyan University (TX), 824
Texas Woman's University (TX), 824
Thiel College (PA), 744
Thomas Aquinas College (CA), 221
Thomas College (ME), 413
Thomas Edison State College (NJ), 555
Thomas Jefferson University
    College of Health Professions (PA), 745
Thomas More College (KY), 399
Thomas More College of Liberal Arts (NH), 541
Thomas Nelson Community College (VA), 857
Thomas University (GA), 299
Three Rivers Community College (CT), 249
Three Rivers Community College (MO), 517
Tidewater Community College (VA), 857
Tiffin University (OH), 677
Toccoa Falls College (GA), 299

Tohono O'odham Community College (AZ), 168
Tompkins-Cortland Community College (NY), 612
Tougaloo College (MS), 499
Towson University (MD), 425
Transylvania University (KY), 399
Treasure Valley Community College (OR), 701
Trenholm State Technical College (AL), 156
Trevecca Nazarene University (TN), 793
Triangle Tech
    DuBois (PA), 745
    Erie (PA), 745
    Greensburg (PA), 745
    Pittsburgh (PA), 746
Tri-County Community College (NC), 640
Tri-County Technical College (SC), 773
Trident Technical College (SC), 773
Trinidad State Junior College (CO), 240
Trinity Bible College (ND), 648
Trinity Christian College (IL), 336
Trinity College (CT), 249
Trinity College of Florida (FL), 278
Trinity International University (IL), 337
Trinity Lutheran College (WA), 873
Trinity University (DC), 256
Trinity University (TX), 824
Trinity Valley Community College (TX), 825
Tri-State University (IN), 356
Triton College (IL), 337
Trocaire College (NY), 612
Troy University (AL), 156
Truckee Meadows Community College (NV), 535
Truett-McConnell College (GA), 299
Truman State University (MO), 517
Trumbull Business College (OH), 677
Tufts University (MA), 450
Tulane University (LA), 407
Tulsa Community College (OK), 691
Tulsa Welding School (OK), 691
Tunxis Community College (CT), 249
Tusculum College (TN), 794
Tuskegee University (AL), 156
Tyler Junior College (TX), 825
Ulster County Community College (NY), 612
Umpqua Community College (OR), 702
Union College (KY), 400
Union College (NE), 531
Union College (NY), 613
Union County College (NJ), 555
Union Institute & University (OH), 677
Union University (TN), 794
United States Air Force Academy (CO), 240
United States Coast Guard Academy (CT), 250
United States Merchant Marine Academy (NY), 613
United States Military Academy (NY), 613
United States Naval Academy (MD), 425
Unity College (ME), 413
Universidad Adventista de las Antillas (PR), 756
Universidad del Este (PR), 757
Universidad Metropolitana (PR), 757
Universidad Politecnica de Puerto Rico (PR), 757
University College of San Juan (PR), 757
University of Advancing Technology (AZ), 168
University of Akron (OH), 677
University of Akron
    Wayne College (OH), 678
University of Alabama (AL), 156
University of Alabama at Birmingham (AL), 157
University of Alabama in Huntsville (AL), 157
University of Alaska Anchorage (AK), 160
University of Alaska Fairbanks (AK), 161
University of Alaska Southeast (AK), 161
University of Arizona (AZ), 169
University of Arkansas (AR), 177
University of Arkansas at Fort Smith (AR), 177
University of Arkansas at Little Rock (AR), 178
University of Arkansas at Monticello (AR), 178
University of Arkansas at Pine Bluff (AR), 178
University of Arkansas
    Community College at Batesville (AR), 179
    Community College at Hope (AR), 179
University of Arkansas for Medical Sciences (AR), 178
University of Baltimore (MD), 426

University of Bridgeport (CT), 250
University of California
    Berkeley (CA), 221
    Davis (CA), 222
    Irvine (CA), 222
    Los Angeles (CA), 222
    Merced (CA), 222
    Riverside (CA), 223
    San Diego (CA), 223
    Santa Barbara (CA), 223
    Santa Cruz (CA), 223
University of Central Arkansas (AR), 179
University of Central Florida (FL), 279
University of Central Oklahoma (OK), 691
University of Charleston (WV), 881
University of Chicago (IL), 337
University of Cincinnati (OH), 678
University of Cincinnati
    Clermont College (OH), 678
    Raymond Walters College (OH), 678
University of Colorado at Boulder (CO), 240
University of Colorado at Colorado Springs (CO), 240
University of Colorado at Denver and Health Sciences Center (CO), 241
University of Connecticut (CT), 250
University of Dallas (TX), 825
University of Dayton (OH), 679
University of Delaware (DE), 253
University of Denver (CO), 241
University of Detroit Mercy (MI), 472
University of Dubuque (IA), 371
University of Evansville (IN), 356
University of Findlay (OH), 679
University of Florida (FL), 279
University of Georgia (GA), 300
University of Great Falls (MT), 524
University of Hartford (CT), 250
University of Hawaii at Hilo (HI), 303
University of Hawaii at Manoa (HI), 303
University of Hawaii
    Hawaii Community College (HI), 304
    Honolulu Community College (HI), 304
    Kapiolani Community College (HI), 304
    Kauai Community College (HI), 304
    Leeward Community College (HI), 305
    Maui Community College (HI), 305
    West Oahu (HI), 305
    Windward Community College (HI), 305
University of Houston (TX), 825
University of Houston
    Clear Lake (TX), 826
    Downtown (TX), 826
    Victoria (TX), 826
University of Idaho (ID), 308
University of Illinois at Chicago (IL), 337
University of Illinois at Urbana-Champaign (IL), 338
University of Illinois
    Springfield (IL), 338
University of Indianapolis (IN), 357
University of Iowa (IA), 372
University of Judaism (CA), 224
University of Kansas (KS), 386
University of Kansas Medical Center (KS), 386
University of Kentucky (KY), 400
University of La Verne (CA), 224
University of Louisiana at Lafayette (LA), 408
University of Louisiana at Monroe (LA), 408
University of Louisville (KY), 400
University of Maine (ME), 413
University of Maine at Augusta (ME), 413
University of Maine at Farmington (ME), 414
University of Maine at Fort Kent (ME), 414
University of Maine at Machias (ME), 414
University of Maine at Presque Isle (ME), 415
University of Mary (ND), 649
University of Mary Hardin-Baylor (TX), 826
University of Mary Washington (VA), 858
University of Maryland
    Baltimore (MD), 426
    Baltimore County (MD), 426
    College Park (MD), 426
    Eastern Shore (MD), 427

University College (MD), 427
University of Massachusetts Amherst (MA), 450
University of Massachusetts Boston (MA), 451
University of Massachusetts Dartmouth (MA), 451
University of Massachusetts Lowell (MA), 451
University of Medicine and Dentistry of New Jersey
    School of Health Related Professions (NJ), 556
    School of Nursing (NJ), 556
University of Memphis (TN), 794
University of Miami (FL), 279
University of Michigan (MI), 473
University of Michigan
    Dearborn (MI), 473
    Flint (MI), 473
University of Minnesota
    Crookston (MN), 492
    Duluth (MN), 493
    Morris (MN), 493
    Twin Cities (MN), 493
University of Mississippi (MS), 500
University of Mississippi Medical Center (MS), 500
University of Missouri
    Columbia (MO), 517
    Kansas City (MO), 518
    Rolla (MO), 518
    St. Louis (MO), 518
University of Mobile (AL), 157
University of Montana
    Missoula (MT), 524
    Western (MT), 525
University of Montevallo (AL), 158
University of Nebraska
    Kearney (NE), 532
    Lincoln (NE), 532
    Omaha (NE), 532
University of Nebraska Medical Center (NE), 532
University of Nevada
    Las Vegas (NV), 535
    Reno (NV), 536
University of New England (ME), 415
University of New Hampshire (NH), 542
University of New Hampshire at Manchester (NH), 542
University of New Haven (CT), 251
University of New Mexico (NM), 562
University of New Orleans (LA), 408
University of North Alabama (AL), 158
University of North Carolina at Asheville (NC), 640
University of North Carolina at Chapel Hill (NC), 640
University of North Carolina at Charlotte (NC), 641
University of North Carolina at Greensboro (NC), 641
University of North Carolina at Pembroke (NC), 641
University of North Carolina at Wilmington (NC), 642
University of North Dakota (ND), 649
University of North Florida (FL), 280
University of North Texas (TX), 827
University of Northern Colorado (CO), 241
University of Northern Iowa (IA), 372
University of Northwestern Ohio (OH), 679
University of Notre Dame (IN), 357
University of Oklahoma (OK), 691
University of Oregon (OR), 702
University of Pennsylvania (PA), 746
University of Pittsburgh (PA), 746
University of Pittsburgh at Bradford (PA), 746
University of Pittsburgh at Greensburg (PA), 747
University of Pittsburgh at Johnstown (PA), 747
University of Pittsburgh at Titusville (PA), 747
University of Portland (OR), 702
University of Puerto Rico
    Aguadilla (PR), 757
    Arecibo (PR), 758
    Carolina Regional College (PR), 758
    Cayey University College (PR), 758
    Humacao (PR), 758
    Ponce (PR), 758
    Rio Piedras (PR), 759
    Utuado (PR), 759
University of Puget Sound (WA), 874
University of Redlands (CA), 224
University of Rhode Island (RI), 762
University of Richmond (VA), 858
University of Rio Grande (OH), 680
University of Rochester (NY), 613
University of St. Francis (IL), 338
University of St. Francis (IN), 357
University of St. Mary (KS), 386
University of St. Thomas (MN), 494
University of St. Thomas (TX), 827
University of San Diego (CA), 224
University of San Francisco (CA), 225
University of Science and Arts of Oklahoma (OK), 692
University of Scranton (PA), 747
University of Sioux Falls (SD), 780
University of South Alabama (AL), 158
University of South Carolina (SC), 773
University of South Carolina at Aiken (SC), 774
University of South Carolina at Beaufort (SC), 774
University of South Carolina at Sumter (SC), 774
University of South Carolina at Union (SC), 774
University of South Carolina
    Salkehatchie Regional Campus (SC), 775
University of South Carolina Upstate (SC), 775
University of South Dakota (SD), 780
University of South Florida (FL), 280
University of Southern California (CA), 225
University of Southern Indiana (IN), 358
University of Southern Maine (ME), 415
University of Southern Mississippi (MS), 500
University of Tampa (FL), 280
University of Tennessee
    Chattanooga (TN), 794
    Knoxville (TN), 795
    Martin (TN), 795
University of Texas at Arlington (TX), 827
University of Texas at Austin (TX), 828
University of Texas at Brownsville (TX), 828
University of Texas at Dallas (TX), 828
University of Texas at El Paso (TX), 828
University of Texas at San Antonio (TX), 829
University of Texas at Tyler (TX), 829
University of Texas Health Science Center at Houston (TX), 829
University of Texas Health Science Center at San Antonio (TX), 829
University of Texas Medical Branch at Galveston (TX), 830
University of Texas of the Permian Basin (TX), 830
University of Texas
    Pan American (TX), 830
University of Texas Southwestern Medical Center at Dallas (TX), 830
University of the Arts (PA), 748
University of the Cumberlands (KY), 401
University of the District of Columbia (DC), 256
University of the Incarnate Word (TX), 831
University of the Ozarks (AR), 179
University of the Pacific (CA), 225
University of the Sacred Heart (PR), 759
University of the Sciences in Philadelphia (PA), 748
University of the South (TN), 795
University of Toledo (OH), 680
University of Tulsa (OK), 692
University of Utah (UT), 835
University of Vermont (VT), 842
University of Virginia (VA), 858
University of Virginia's College at Wise (VA), 858
University of Washington (WA), 874
University of West Alabama (AL), 158
University of West Florida (FL), 281
University of West Georgia (GA), 300
University of Wisconsin-Baraboo/Sauk County (WI), 893
University of Wisconsin-Eau Claire (WI), 893
University of Wisconsin-Fond du Lac (WI), 893
University of Wisconsin-Green Bay (WI), 894
University of Wisconsin-La Crosse (WI), 894
University of Wisconsin-Madison (WI), 894
University of Wisconsin-Marathon County (WI), 895
University of Wisconsin-Marinette (WI), 895
University of Wisconsin-Marshfield/Wood County (WI), 895
University of Wisconsin-Milwaukee (WI), 895
University of Wisconsin-Oshkosh (WI), 896
University of Wisconsin-Parkside (WI), 896
University of Wisconsin-Platteville (WI), 896
University of Wisconsin-Richland (WI), 896
University of Wisconsin-River Falls (WI), 897
University of Wisconsin-Rock County (WI), 897
University of Wisconsin-Stevens Point (WI), 897
University of Wisconsin-Stout (WI), 897
University of Wisconsin-Superior (WI), 898
University of Wisconsin-Waukesha (WI), 898
University of Wisconsin-Whitewater (WI), 898
University of Wyoming (WY), 901
Upper Iowa University (IA), 372
Urban College of Boston (MA), 451
Urbana University (OH), 680
Ursinus College (PA), 748
Ursuline College (OH), 681
Utah Career College (UT), 836
Utah State University (UT), 836
Utah Valley State College (UT), 836
Utica College (NY), 613
Valdosta State University (GA), 300
Valencia Community College (FL), 281
Valley City State University (ND), 649
Valley College of Technology (WV), 881
Valley Forge Christian College (PA), 749
Valley Forge Military College (PA), 749
Valparaiso University (IN), 358
Vance-Granville Community College (NC), 642
Vanderbilt University (TN), 795
VanderCook College of Music (IL), 339
Vanguard University of Southern California (CA), 226
Vassar College (NY), 614
Vatterott College (IA), 373
Vatterott College (OK), 692
Vatterott College
    St. Joseph (MO), 518
Vaughn College of Aeronautics and Technology (NY), 614
Vennard College (IA), 373
Vermilion Community College (MN), 494
Vermont Technical College (VT), 842
Vernon College (TX), 831
Vet Tech Institute (PA), 749
Victor Valley College (CA), 226
Villa Julie College (MD), 427
Villa Maria College of Buffalo (NY), 614
Villanova University (PA), 749
Vincennes University (IN), 358
Virginia College at Huntsville (AL), 159
Virginia Commonwealth University (VA), 859
Virginia Highlands Community College (VA), 859
Virginia Intermont College (VA), 859
Virginia Military Institute (VA), 860
Virginia Polytechnic Institute and State University (VA), 860
Virginia State University (VA), 860
Virginia Union University (VA), 861
Virginia Wesleyan College (VA), 861
Virginia Western Community College (VA), 861
Vista Community College (CA), 226
Viterbo University (WI), 898
Volunteer State Community College (TN), 796
Voorhees College (SC), 775
Wabash College (IN), 359
Wade College (TX), 831
Wagner College (NY), 615
Wake Forest University (NC), 642
Wake Technical Community College (NC), 642
Waldorf College (IA), 373
Walla Walla College (WA), 874
Walla Walla Community College (WA), 875
Wallace State Community College at Hanceville (AL), 159
Walsh College of Accountancy and Business Administration (MI), 474
Walsh University (OH), 681
Walters State Community College (TN), 796
Warner Pacific College (OR), 702
Warner Southern College (FL), 281
Warren County Community College (NJ), 556
Warren Wilson College (NC), 643
Wartburg College (IA), 373
Washburn University of Topeka (KS), 386
Washington and Jefferson College (PA), 750
Washington and Lee University (VA), 861
Washington Bible College (MD), 427
Washington College (MD), 428
Washington County Community College (ME), 415
Washington State University (WA), 875
Washington University in St. Louis (MO), 519

Waubonsee Community College (IL), 339
Waukesha County Technical College (WI), 899
Waycross College (GA), 300
Wayland Baptist University (TX), 831
Wayne Community College (NC), 643
Wayne County Community College (MI), 474
Wayne State College (NE), 533
Wayne State University (MI), 474
Waynesburg College (PA), 750
Weatherford College (TX), 832
Webb Institute (NY), 615
Webber International University (FL), 281
Weber State University (UT), 836
Webster College (FL), 282
Webster College
    Holiday (FL), 282
Webster University (MO), 519
Wellesley College (MA), 452
Wells College (NY), 615
Wenatchee Valley College (WA), 875
Wentworth Institute of Technology (MA), 452
Wesley College (DE), 253
Wesley College (MS), 500
Wesleyan College (GA), 301
Wesleyan University (CT), 251
West Chester University of Pennsylvania (PA), 750
West Georgia Technical College (GA), 301
West Hills Community College (CA), 226
West Kentucky Community and Technical College (KY), 401
West Liberty State College (WV), 881
West Los Angeles College (CA), 227
West Shore Community College (MI), 474
West Suburban College of Nursing (IL), 339
West Texas A&M University (TX), 832
West Valley College (CA), 227
West Virginia Northern Community College (WV), 882
West Virginia State University (WV), 882
West Virginia University (WV), 882
West Virginia University at Parkersburg (WV), 883
West Virginia University Institute of Technology (WV), 883
West Virginia Wesleyan College (WV), 883
Westchester Community College (NY), 616
Western Career College
    Emeryville (CA), 227
Western Carolina University (NC), 643
Western College of Southern California (OK), 693
Western Connecticut State University (CT), 251
Western Dakota Technical Institute (SD), 780
Western Illinois University (IL), 339
Western Iowa Tech Community College (IA), 374
Western Kentucky University (KY), 401
Western Michigan University (MI), 475
Western Nebraska Community College (NE), 533
Western Nevada Community College (NV), 536
Western New England College (MA), 452
Western New Mexico University (NM), 563
Western Oklahoma State College (OK), 693
Western Oregon University (OR), 703
Western Piedmont Community College (NC), 644
Western School of Health and Business Careers (PA), 751
Western School of Health and Business Careers
    Monroeville (PA), 751
Western State College of Colorado (CO), 241
Western Technical College (TX), 832
Western Texas College (TX), 833
Western Washington University (WA), 875
Western Wisconsin Technical College (WI), 899
Western Wyoming Community College (WY), 902
Westfield State College (MA), 452
Westminster Choir College of Rider University (NJ), 556
Westminster College (MO), 519
Westminster College (PA), 751
Westminster College (UT), 837
Westmont College (CA), 227
Westmoreland County Community College (PA), 751
Westwood College
    DuPage (IL), 340
Westwood College of Technology (CO), 242
Westwood College of Technology
    Inland Empire (CA), 228
    South (CO), 242
Wharton County Junior College (TX), 833
Whatcom Community College (WA), 876
Wheaton College (IL), 340
Wheaton College (MA), 453
Wheeling Jesuit University (WV), 883
Wheelock College (MA), 453
Whitman College (WA), 876
Whittier College (CA), 228
Whitworth College (WA), 876
Wichita State University (KS), 387
Widener University (PA), 751
Wiley College (TX), 833
Wilkes Community College (NC), 644
Wilkes University (PA), 752
Willamette University (OR), 703
William Carey College (MS), 501
William Jessup University (CA), 228
William Jewell College (MO), 520
William Paterson University of New Jersey (NJ), 557
William Penn University (IA), 374
William Rainey Harper College (IL), 340
William Woods University (MO), 520
Williams Baptist College (AR), 180
Williams College (MA), 453
Williamsburg Technical College (SC), 775
Williston State College (ND), 649
Wilmington College (DE), 253
Wilmington College (OH), 681
Wilson College (PA), 752
Wilson Technical Community College (NC), 644
Wingate University (NC), 644
Winona State University (MN), 494
Winston-Salem State University (NC), 645
Winthrop University (SC), 776
Wisconsin Indianhead Technical College (WI), 899
Wisconsin Lutheran College (WI), 899
Wittenberg University (OH), 681
Wofford College (SC), 776
Woodbury College (VT), 842
Woodbury University (CA), 228
Worcester Polytechnic Institute (MA), 454
Worcester State College (MA), 454
Wor-Wic Community College (MD), 428
Wright State University (OH), 682
Wright State University
    Lake Campus (OH), 682
Wytheville Community College (VA), 862
Xavier University (OH), 682
Xavier University of Louisiana (LA), 408
Yakima Valley Community College (WA), 876
Yale University (CT), 251
Yavapai College (AZ), 169
Yeshiva Mikdash Melech (NY), 616
York College (NE), 533
York College of Pennsylvania (PA), 752
York County Community College (ME), 416
York Technical College (SC), 776
Yorktowne Business Institute (PA), 753
Young Harris College (GA), 301
Youngstown State University (OH), 683
Yuba Community College District (CA), 229
Zane State College (OH), 683

Grant yourself a scholarship.

CLEP® exams offer you the opportunity to earn 3 to 12 college credits for what you already know. This saves tuition dollars and leaves more time for advanced courses and electives. There are 2,900 colleges and universities that grant credit for **CLEP** and 1,300 colleges that administer the 35 computer-based exams. To learn more, visit **CLEP** at **collegeboard.com/clep.**

CollegeBoard
connect to college success™

visit **CLEP**®
collegeboard.com/clep

Get Ready for the SAT® with Help from the Test Maker

The Official SAT Online Course™
- 6 official practice tests
- Interactive instruction
- Answer explanations
- Immediate essay scoring

The Official SAT Study Guide™
- 8 official practice tests
- Test-taking approaches
- Free online score reports
- Sample essays and prompts

#1 BEST SELLER!

The Official SAT Question of the Day™ 2007 Calendar
- 365 practice questions
- Online answer explanations and hints

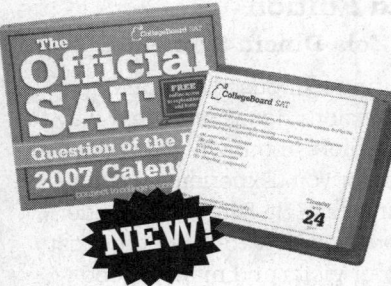

NEW!

Order today at collegeboard.com/srp or at a store near you!

The *Study Guide* and calendar are distributed by Holtzbrinck Publishers, Inc.

CollegeBoard SAT
connect to college success™

Also Available from the College Board

The College Board Scholarship Handbook 2007

This no-nonsense guide speeds you straight to scholarships targeted to who you are, where you live, and what you want to study. Includes detailed profiles of more than 2,100 scholarship, internship, and loan programs.

600 pages, paperbound
ISBN 0-87447-767-0
$27.95

The College Board College Handbook 2007

Get instant access to crucial information on every accredited college in the United States. Completely updated and verified for 2007, this handbook contains detailed descriptions of 3,800 colleges, universities, and technical schools.

2,100 pages, paperbound
ISBN 0-87447-764-6
$28.95

The College Board Book of Majors, 2nd Edition

What's the major for you? Where can you study it? In this book, 180 college professors describe the majors they teach: what you'll study, careers the major can lead to, and how to prepare for the major in high school. Includes listings showing which colleges offer each of 900 majors, and at what degree level.

1,250 pages, paperbound
ISBN 0-87447-765-4
$24.95

The College Application Essay, Revised Edition
by Sarah Myers McGinty

Trying to find a topic for your application essay? Former admissions dean Sarah Myers McGinty shares strategies that will help you stand out from the crowd. Includes critiqued sample essays written by real students, jump starts for writer's block, and a chapter for your parents that explains their role in the process.

160 pages, paperbound
ISBN 0-87447-711-5
$15.95

Campus Visits & College Interviews, 2nd Edition
by Zola Dincin Schneider

Visiting campuses and talking to admissions deans is a great way to learn more about which colleges are right for you. Experienced school counselor Zola Dincin Schneider shows you how to make the most of your visits and make a good impression during interviews. Includes interview tips for the shy.

140 pages, paperbound
ISBN 0-87447-675-5
$12.95

Available wherever books are sold.
Distributed by Holtzbrinck Publishers, Inc.